A 11 AUR

History of the Language Sciences
Geschichte der Sprachwissenschaften
Histoire des sciences du langage

HSK 18.2

Handbücher zur
Sprach- und Kommunikationswissenschaft

Handbooks of Linguistics
and Communication Science

Manuels de linguistique et
des sciences de communication

Mitbegründet von
Gerold Ungeheuer

Herausgegeben von / Edited by / Edités par
Armin Burkhardt
Hugo Steger
Herbert Ernst Wiegand

Band 18.2

Walter de Gruyter · Berlin · New York
2001

History of the Language Sciences
Geschichte der Sprachwissenschaften
Histoire des sciences du langage

An International Handbook on the Evolution of the
Study of Language from the Beginnings to the Present

Ein internationales Handbuch zur Entwicklung der
Sprachforschung von den Anfängen bis zur Gegenwart

Manuel international sur l'évolution de l'étude
du langage des origines à nos jours

Edited by / Herausgegeben von / Edité par
Sylvain Auroux · E. F. K. Koerner
Hans-Josef Niederehe · Kees Versteegh

Volume 2 / 2. Teilband / Tome 2

Walter de Gruyter · Berlin · New York
2001

♾ Printed on acid-free paper which falls within the guidelines of the ANSI to ensure permanence and durability.

Die Deutsche Bibliothek – CIP-Einheitsaufnahme

History of the language sciences : an international handbook on the evolution of the study of language from the beginnings to the present = Geschichte der Sprachwissenschaften / ed. by Sylvain Auroux .... – Berlin ; New York : de Gruyter
   (Handbücher zur Sprach- und Kommunikationswissenschaft ; Bd. 18)

Vol. 2. – (2001)
   ISBN 3-11-016735-2

© Copyright 2001 by Walter de Gruyter GmbH & Co. KG, D-10785 Berlin
All rights reserved, including those of translation into foreign languages. No part of this book may be reproduced in any form or by any means, electronic or mechanical, including photocopy, recording, or any information storage and retrieval system, without permission in writing from the publisher.
Cover design: Rudolf Hübler
Typesetting: Arthur Collignon GmbH, Berlin
Printing: Ott-Druck GmbH
Binding: Lüderitz & Bauer-GmbH, Berlin
Printed in Germany

Contents / Inhalt / Table des matières

Volume 2 / 2. Teilband / Tome 2

XXIII. Studies of the Antecedents to and Connections between National Languages
Vorstellungen von der Entstehung der Nationalsprachen und ihren Beziehungen zueinander
Études des origines et des rapports des langues nationales

145.	Werner Bahner, Frühe dialektologische, etymologische und sprachgeschichtliche Forschungen in Spanien	1095
146.	William Jervis Jones, Early dialectology, etymology and language history in German speaking countries	1105
147.	Jan Noordegraaf, Historical linguistics in the Low Countries: Lambert ten Kate	1115
148.	Even Hovdhaugen, The study of early Germanic languages in Scandinavia: Ihre, Stiernhielm	1124
149.	Robin Smith, Investigating Older Germanic languages in England	1129
150.	Roger Comtet, L'étude des langues slaves en Russie: M. L. Lomonosov	1136
151.	Tiborc Fazekas, Die Entdeckung der Verwandtschaft der finno-ugrischen Sprachen	1144
152.	Rosane Rocher, The knowledge of Sanskrit in Europe until 1800	1156

XXIV. Historical and Comparative Linguistics of the Early 19th Century
Die historische und vergleichende Sprachwissenschaft zu Beginn des 19. Jahrhunderts
La linguistique historique et comparative au début du XIXe siècle

153.	Kurt R. Jankowsky, The renewal of the study of the classical languages within the university system, notably in Germany	1164
154.	Kurt R. Jankowsky, The establishment of Oriental language studies in France, Britain, and Germany	1182
155.	Jean Rousseau, La genèse de la grammaire comparée	1197
156.	N. E. Collinge, The introduction of the historical principle into the study of languages: Grimm	1210

157.	Theodora Bynon, The synthesis of comparative and historical Indo-European studies: August Schleicher	1223

XXV. The Establishment of New Philologies in the 19th Century
Die Herausbildung neuer Philologien im 19. Jahrhundert
Le développement des nouvelles philologies au XIXe siècle

158.	Jürgen Storost, Die 'neuen Philologien', ihre Institutionen und Periodica: Eine Übersicht	1240
159.	Pierre Swiggers, Les débuts et l'évolution de la philologie romane au XIXe siècle, surtout en Allemagne	1272
160.	Uwe Meves, Die Entstehung und frühe Entwicklung der Germanischen Philologie	1286
161.	Karl Gutschmidt, Die Entstehung und frühe Geschichte der Slavischen Philologie	1294
162.	Tiborc Fazekas, Finno-ugrische Philologie und vergleichende Grammatik	1305
163.	Rainer Voigt, Semitische Philologie und vergleichende Grammatik: Geschichte der vergleichenden Semitistik	1311
163a.	Rainer Voigt, Semitohamitische Philologie und vergleichende Grammatik: Geschichte der vergleichenden Semitohamatistik	1318

XXVI. Indo-European Philology and Historical Linguistics and their Legacy
Indo-europäische Philologie, Historische Sprachwissenschaft und ihr Erbe
La philologie indo-européenne et la linguistique historique et leurs legs

164.	Kurt R. Jankowsky, The crisis of historical-comparative linguistics in the 1860s	1326
165.	Eveline Einhauser, Die Entstehung und frühe Entwicklung des junggrammatischen Forschungsprogramms	1338
166.	Kurt R. Jankowsky, The consolidation of the neogrammarian framework	1350
167.	Wilhelm J. G. Möhlig, Die Anwendung der vergleichenden Methode auf afrikanische Sprachen	1367
168.	Robert A. Blust, The comparative method applied to Austronesian languages	1374
169.	John Hewson, The comparative method applied to Amerindian: The reconstruction of Proto-Algonkian	1384
170.	Catherine Bereznak / Lyle Campbell, The comparative method as applied to other Non-Indo-European languages	1391

XXVII.	Language Typology, Language Classification, and the Search for Universals Sprachtypologie, die Klassifizierung der Sprachen und die Suche nach sprachlichen Universalien La typologie linguistique, la classification des langues et la recherche des universaux	
171.	Frans Plank, Typology by the end of the 18th century	1399
172.	Jean Rousseau, La classification des langues au début du XIXe siècle	1414
173.	Manfred Ringmacher, Die Klassifizierung der Sprachen in der Mitte des 19. Jahrhunderts	1427
174.	Manfred Ringmacher, Sprachtypologie und Ethnologie in Europa am Ende des 19. Jahrhunderts	1436
175.	Regna Darnell, Language typology and ethnology in 19th-century North America: Gallatin, Brinton, Powell	1443
176.	George Yonek / Lyle Campbell, Language typology in the 20th century from Sapir to late 20th century approaches	1453
177.	Bernard Comrie, Theories of universal grammar in the late 20th century	1461
XXVIII.	The Analysis of Speech and Unwritten Languages in the 19th Century and its Continuation in the 20th Century Die Erforschung der lautlichen Äußerung und nicht verschrifteter Sprachen im 19. und ihre Fortsetzung im 20. Jahrhundert L'étude de la parole et des langues non-écrites pendant le XIXe siècle et sa continuation au XXe siècle	
178.	J. Alan Kemp, The development of phonetics from the late 18th to the late 19th century	1468
179.	Even Hovdhaugen, Field work and data-elicitation of unwritten languages for descriptive and comparative purposes: Strahlenberg, Sjögren, Castrén, Böthlingk	1480
180.	Enrica Galazzi, Physiologie de la parole et phonétique appliquée au XIXe et au début du XXe siècle	1485
181.	Wolfgang Putschke, Die Dialektologie, ihr Beitrag zur historischen Sprachwissenschaft im 19. Jahrhundert und ihre Kritik am junggrammatischen Programm	1498
182.	Joachim Herrgen, Die Dialektologie des Deutschen	1513
183.	Marinel Gerritsen, The dialectology of Dutch	1536
184.	Graham Shorrocks, The dialectology of English in the British Isles	1553

185.	Tom Priestly, Dialectology in the Slavic countries: An overview from its beginnings to the early 20th century	1563
186.	J. Alan Kemp, The history and development of a universal phonetic alphabet in the 19th century: from the beginnings to the establishment of the IPA	1572
187.	Michael K. C. MacMahon, Modern Language Instruction and Phonetics in the Later 19th century	1585

XXIX. Approaches to Semantics in the 19th and the First Third of the 20th Century
Ansätze zur Semantik im 19. und im ersten Drittel des 20. Jahrhunderts
Les approches à la sémantique au XIXe et au premier tiers du XXe siècle

188.	Brigitte Nerlich, The renewal of semantic questions in the 19th century: The work of Karl Christian Reisig and his successors	1596
189.	Brigitte Nerlich, The development of semasiology in Europe: A survey from the second half of the 19th to the first third of the 20th century	1600
190.	Johannes Kramer, Die frühe Entwicklung des onomasiologischen Ansatzes in der Sprachwissenschaft und Lexikographie des 19. Jahrhunderts	1611
191.	Brigitte Nerlich, The study of meaning change from Reisig to Bréal	1617
192.	Wolfgang Settekorn, Die Forschungsrichtung "Wörter und Sachen"	1628
193.	W. Terrence Gordon, The origin and development of the theory of the semantic field	1650

XXX. Psychology and Physiology in 19th-Century Linguistics
Psychologische und physiologische Ansätze in der Sprachwissenschaft des 19. Jahrhunderts
La psychologie et la physiologie dans la linguistique du XIXe siècle

194.	Clemens Knobloch, Die Beziehungen zwischen Sprache und Denken: Die Ideen Wilhelm von Humboldts und die Anfänge der sprachpsychologischen Forschung	1663
195.	David J. Murray, Language and psychology: 19th-century developments outside Germany: A survey	1679
196.	Gabriel Bergounioux, Le langage et le cerveau: La localisation de la faculté du langage et l'étude des aphasies	1692
197.	Clemens Knobloch, Psychologische Ansätze bei der Erforschung des frühkindlichen Spracherwerbs	1705

XXXI. Structural Linguistics in the 20th Century
Der europäische Strukturalismus im 20. Jahrhundert
Le structuralisme européen au XXe siècle

198.	Manfred Kohrt / Kerstin Kuchaczik, Die Wurzeln des Strukturalismus in der Sprachwissenschaft des 19. Jahrhunderts	1719
199.	René Amacker, La dimension synchronique dans la théorie linguistique de Saussure	1735
200.	René Amacker, Le développement des idées saussuriennes par l'École de Genève	1746
201.	Tsutomu Akamatsu, The development of functionalism from the Prague school to the present	1768
202.	Jørgen Rischl, The Cercle linguistique de Copenhague and glossematics	1790
203.	David G. Butt, Firth, Halliday and the development of systemic-functional theory	1806
204.	Giorgio Graffi, The emphasis on syntax in the early phase of European structuralism: Ries, Jespersen, Mathesius, Guillaume, Tesnière	1838
205.	Heinz J. Weber, Die Entwicklung der Dependenzgrammatik und verwandter Theorien in der 2. Hälfte des 20. Jahrhunderts	1848
206.	Ulrich Püschel, Linguistische Ansätze in der Stilistik des 20. Jahrhunderts	1866
207.	John E. Joseph, The exportation of structuralist ideas from linguistics to other fields: An overview	1880

XXXII. Traditions of Descriptive Linguistics in America
Der amerikanische Deskriptivismus
La linguistique descriptive aux États-Unis

208.	Stephen O. Murray, The ethnolinguistic tradition in 19th-century America: From the earliest beginnings to Boas	1909
209.	Stephen G. Alter, The linguistic legacy of William Dwight Whitney	1923
210.	Stephen O. Murray, Attempts at professionalization of American linguistics: The role of the Linguistic Society of America	1932
211.	Victor Golla, The Sapirian approach to language	1935
212.	John G. Fought, The 'Bloomfield School' and descriptive linguistics	1950
213.	John R. Costello, Tagmemics and the analysis of non-verbal behavior: Pike and his school	1966
214.	John Fought, Distributionalism and immediate constituent analysis	1986
215.	Sheila Embleton, Quantitative methods and lexicostatistics in the 20th Century	1998

Volume 1 / 1. Teilband / Tome 1

Editors' Foreword XXV
Vorwort der Herausgeber..................................... XXXVII
Préface des éditeurs XLIX

I. The Establishment of Linguistic Traditions in the Near East
Die Anfänge sprachwissenschaftlicher Traditionen im Nahen Osten
La constitution des traditions linguistiques au Proche Orient

1. Erica Reiner, The Sumerian and Akkadian linguistic tradition .. 1
2. Joris F. Borghouts, Indigenous Egyptian grammar 5
3. Manfred Dietrich, Die Sprachforschung in Ugarit 14

II. The Establishment of the Chinese Linguistic Tradition
Die Anfänge der Sprachwissenschaft in China
La constitution de la tradition linguistique chinoise

4. Chung-ying Cheng, Classical Chinese philosophies of language: Logic and ontology 19
5. David Branner, The Suí-Táng tradition of *Fǎnqiè* phonology ... 36
6. David Branner, The rime-table system of formal Chinese phonology 46
7. Alain Peyraube, Le rôle du savoir linguistique dans l'éducation et la société chinoise 55
8. Nonna V. Stankevič, La tradition linguistique vietnamienne et ses contacts avec la tradition chinoise 58

III. The Establishment of the Korean Linguistic Tradition
Die Anfänge der koreanischen Sprachforschung
La constitution de la tradition linguistique coréenne

9. Werner Sasse, Die traditionelle Sprachforschung in Korea 63

IV. The Establishment of the Japanese Linguistic Tradition
Die Anfänge der Sprachforschung in Japan
La constitution de la tradition linguistique japonaise

10. Roy Andrew Miller, The Japanese linguistic tradition and the Chinese heritage 72
11. Stefan Kaiser, The first Japanese attempts at describing Chinese and Korean bilingualism 77

12.	Viktoria Eschbach-Szabó, Sprache und Denken in der japanischen Sprachforschung während der *Kokugaku*	85
13.	Viktoria Eschbach-Szabó, Die Frühzeit der neueren japanischen Sprachforschung: Vom *Kokugaku* zum *Kokugogaku*	93
14.	Frits Vos †, The influence of Dutch grammar on Japanese language research	102
15.	Roy Andrew Miller, The role of linguistics in Japanese society and education	104
16.	Roy Andrew Miller, Traditional linguistics and Western linguistics in Japan	108

V. The Establishment of Sanskrit Linguistics
Die Anfänge der Sanskritforschung
La constitution de l'étude du sanskrit

17.	George Cardona, Pāṇini	113
18.	Hartmut Scharfe, Die Entwicklung der Sprachwissenschaft in Indien nach Pāṇini	125
19.	Madhav Deshpande, Indian theories on phonetics	137
20.	Jan Houben, Language and thought in the Sanskrit tradition	146
21.	George Cardona, The organization of grammar in Sanskrit linguistics	157
22.	Johannes Bronkhorst, The relationship between linguistics and other sciences in India	166
23.	Madhav Deshpande, The role of linguistics in Indian society and education	173
24.	Michael C. Shapiro, The Hindi grammatical tradition	178
25.	Vadim B. Kasevic, Indian influence on the linguistic tradition of Burma	182
26.	Bernard Arps, Indian influence on the Old Javanese linguistic tradition	186

VI. The Establishment of Dravidian Linguistics
Die Anfänge der dravidischen Sprachforschung
La constitution de la lingistique dravidienne

27.	Jean-Luc Chevillard, Les débuts de la tradition linguistique tamoule	191
28.	Jean-Luc Chevillard, Le *Tolkāppiyam* et le développement de la tradition linguistique tamoule	194
29.	Jean-Luc Chevillard, Les successeurs du *Tolkāppiyam*: le *Naṉṉūl*, le *Vīracōḻiyam* et les autres écoles	200

VII. The Establishment of Tibetan Linguistics
Die Anfänge der Sprachforschung in Tibet
La constitution de la linguistique tibétaine

30.	Roy Andrew Miller, The early Tibetan grammatical treatises and Thon-mi Sambhoṭa	203
31.	Pieter C. Verhagen, The classical Tibetan grammarians	207
32.	Pieter C. Verhagen, The influence of the Sanskrit tradition on Tibetan indigenous grammar	210

VIII. The Establishment of Hebrew Linguistics
Die Anfänge der hebräischen Sprachforschung
La constitution de la linguistique de l'hébreu

33.	Aaron Dotan, The origins of Hebrew linguistics and the exegetic tradition	215
34.	Irene Zwiep, Die Entwicklung der hebräischen Sprachwissenschaft während des Mittelalters	228
35.	Carlos del Valle, Hebrew linguistics in Arabic	234
36.	Wout Jac. van Bekkum, Hebrew linguistics and comparative Semitic grammar	240

IX. The Establishment of Arabic Linguistics
Die Anfänge der arabischen Sprachforschung
La constitution de la linguistique arabe

37.	Rafael Talmon, The first beginnings of Arabic linguistics: The era of the Old Iraqi School	245
38.	Aryeh Levin, Sībawayhi	252
39.	Michael G. Carter, The development of Arabic linguistics after Sībawayhi: Baṣra, Kūfa and Baghdad	263
40.	Jean-Patrick Guillaume, La nouvelle approche de la grammaire au IVe/Xe siècle: Ibn Ǧinnī (320/932−392/1002)	273
41.	Gérard Troupeau, La période post-classique de la linguistique arabe: d'Ibn Ǧinnī à al-'Astarābāḏī	280
42.	Jonathan Owens, The structure of Arabic grammatical theory	286
43.	Kees Versteegh, Grammar and logic in the Arabic grammatical tradition	300
44.	Jan Peters, Language and revelation in Islamic society	307
45.	Pierre Larcher, Les relations entre la linguistique et les autres sciences dans la société arabo-islamique	312
46.	Mohammed Sawaie, Traditional linguistics and Western linguistics in the Arab world	318
47.	Adel Sidarus, L'influence arabe sur la linguistique copte	321
48.	Robert Ermers, The description of Turkic with the Arabic linguistic model	325
49.	Éva M. Jeremiás, Arabic influence on Persian linguistics	329
50.	Nico Kaptein, Arabic influence on Malay linguistics	333

X. The Establishment of Syriac Linguistics
Die Anfänge der syrischen Sprachforschung
La constitution de la linguistique syriaque

51. Rafael Talmon, Foreign influence in the Syriac grammatical tradition 337
52. Riccardo Contini, The role of linguistics in Syrian society 341

XI. The Establishment of Linguistics in Greece
Die Anfänge der griechischen Sprachforschung
La constitution de la linguistique en Grèce

53. Peter Schmitter, Sprachbezogene Reflexionen im frühen Griechenland 345
54. Hans Arens, Sprache und Denken bei Aristoteles 367
55. Ineke Sluiter, Language and thought in Stoic philosophy 375
56. Frédéric Lambert, La linguistique grecque chez les alexandrins: Aristophane de Byzance et Aristarque 385
57. Vincenzo di Benedetto, Dionysius Thrax and the *Tékhnē* 394
58. David L. Blank, The organization of grammar in ancient Greece 400
59. R. H. Robins †, Greek linguistics in the Byzantine period 417
60. Elmar Siebenhorn, Die Beziehungen der griechischen Sprachforschung zu anderen Disziplinen 424
61. Dirk M. Schenkeveld, The impact of language studies on Greek society and education 430
62. Vít Bubeník, Variety of speech in Greek linguistics: The dialects and the *koinè* 439
63. Mzekala Shanidze, Greek influence in Georgian linguistics 444
64. Jos Weitenberg, Greek influence in Armenian linguistics 447
65. Yannis Kakridis, Greek influence in the grammatical theory of Church Slavonic 450

XII. The Establishment of Linguistics in Rome
Die Anfänge der Sprachforschung in Rom
La constitution de la linguistique à Rome

66. Daniel J. Taylor, Varro and the origin of Roman linguistic theory and practice 455
67. Marc Baratin, À l'origine de la tradition artigraphique latine, entre mythe et réalité 459
68. Françoise Desbordes †, L'*ars grammatica* dans la période post-classique: le *Corpus grammaticorum latinorum* 466
69. Carmen Codoñer, L'organisation de la grammaire dans la tradition latine 474
70. James J. Murphy, Grammar and rhetoric in Roman schools ... 484
71. Arpád Orbán, Augustin und die Sprache 492

XIII. The Cultivation of Latin Grammar in the Early Middle Ages
Die Pflege der lateinischen Grammatik im frühen Mittelalter
La culture de la grammaire latine dans le Haut Moyen-Age

72. Roger Wright, The study of Latin as a foreign language in the Early Middle Ages 501
73. Anneli Luhtala, Linguistics and theology in the Early Medieval West 510
74. Louis Holtz, Alcuin et la redécouverte de Priscien à l'époque carolingienne 525
75. Mark Amsler, The role of linguistics in early medieval education ... 532

XIV. Linguistic Theory in the Late Middle Ages
Sprachtheorien des späten Mittelalters
La théorie linguistique au Bas Moyen-Age

76. Irène Rosier-Catach, La grammaire spéculative du Bas Moyen-Age 541
77. Corneille H. Kneepkens, Linguistic description and analysis in the Late Middle Ages 551
78. Joel Biard, Linguistique et logique durant le Bas Moyen-Age ... 560
79. Louis Kelly, Language study and theology in the Late Middle Ages 572
80. Ludger Kaczmarek, Die Beziehungen der spätmittelalterlichen Sprachforschung zu anderen Gebieten 584

XV. The Cultivation of Latin Grammar in the Late Middle Ages
Die Pflege der lateinischen Grammatik im Spätmittelalter
La culture de la grammaire latine dans le Bas Moyen-Age

81. Anne Grondeux, La *Grammatica positiva* dans le Bas Moyen-Age 598
82. Anders Ahlqvist, The Latin tradition and the Irish language ... 610
83. Ann T. E. Matonis, The Latin tradition and Welsh 614
84. Valeria Micillo, The Latin tradition and Icelandic 617
85. Kees Dekkers, Ælfric and his relation to the Latin tradition ... 625
86. Sylvie Archaimbault, La tradition latine et les langues slaves dans le Bas Moyen-Age 634
87. Hans-J. Niederehe, Sprachstudium und literarische Traditionen: Das Okzitanisch 638

XVI. The Classical Languages in the Age of Humanism
Die klassischen Sprachen im Zeitalter des Humanismus
Les langues classiques à l'époque de l'humanisme

88.	Mirko Tavoni, The traditional study of Latin at the university in the age of Humanism	650
89.	Mirko Tavoni, The rediscovery of the classics in the age of Humanism	657
90.	Bernard Colombat, La réforme du latin à l'époque de l'humanisme	661
91.	Christian Förstel, L'étude du grec à l'époque de l'humanisme	666
92.	Sophie Kessler-Mesguich, L'étude de l'hébreu et des autres langues orientales à l'époque de l'humanisme	673

XVII. The Teaching of Languages in the 15th Through the 18th Centuries in Europe
Der Fremdsprachenunterricht in Europa (15.–16. Jahrhundert)
L'enseignement des langues du XVe au XVIIIe siècle en Europe

93.	Konrad Schröder, Kommerzielle und kulturelle Interessen am Unterricht der Volkssprachen im 15. und 16. Jahrhundert	681
94.	Alda Rossebastiano, La tradition des manuels polyglottes dans l'enseignement des langues	688
95.	Claudio Marazzini, The teaching of Italian in 15th- and 16th-century Europe	699
96.	Otto Ludwig / Claus Ahlzweig, Der Unterricht des Deutschen im 15. und 16. Jahrhundert	705
97.	Barbara Kaltz, Der Unterricht des Französischen im 16. Jahrhundert	711
98.	Manuel Breva-Claramonte, The teaching of Spanish in 16th-century Europe	717
99.	Konrad Schröder, Der Unterricht des Englischen im 16. Jahrhundert	723
100.	Hartmut Bobzin, Der Unterricht des Hebräischen, Arabischen und anderer semitischer Sprachen sowie des Persischen und Türkischen in Europa (bis zum Ende des 18. Jahrhunderts)	728
101.	Konrad Schröder, Die Traditionen des Sprachunterrichts im Europa des 17. und 18. Jahrhunderts	734

XVIII. The Development of Grammatical Traditions for the Literary Vernaculars in Europe
Die neuen Literatursprachen und die Herausbildung ihrer grammatischen Tradition
Le développement des traditions grammaticales concernant les vernaculaires écrits de l'Europe

102.	Claudio Marazzini, Early grammatical descriptions of Italian . . .	742
103.	Miguel Angel Esparza Torres, Frühe grammatische Beschreibungen des Spanischen	749
104.	Maria Leonor Carvalhão Buescu †, Les premières descriptions grammaticales du portugais	756
105.	Andres Max Kristol, Les premières descriptions grammaticales du français	764
106.	Monique Verrac, Les premières descriptions grammaticales de l'anglais	771
107.	Monika Rössig-Hager, Frühe grammatische Beschreibungen des Deutschen	777
108.	Geert Dibbets, Frühe grammatische Beschreibungen des Niederländischen (ca. 1550–ca. 1650)	784
109.	Helmut Schaller, Frühe grammatische Beschreibungen slawischer Sprachen	792
110.	Erich Poppe, Early grammatical descriptions of the Celtic languages	800
111.	Kaisa Häkkinen, Early grammatical descriptions of Finno-Ugric	806

XIX. The Normative Study of the National Languages from the 17th Century Onwards
Das normative Studium der Nationalsprachen ab dem 17. Jahrhundert
L'étude normative des langues nationales à partir du fin du XVIe siècle

112.	Rudolf Engler, Die Accademia della Crusca und die Standardisierung des Italienischen	815
113.	Peter von Polenz, Die Sprachgesellschaften und die Entstehung eines literarischen Standards in Deutschland	827
114.	Jörg Kilian, Entwicklungen in Deutschland im 17. und 18. Jahrhundert außerhalb der Sprachgesellschaften	841
115.	Francine Mazière, La langue et l'État: l'Académie française	852
116.	Ramon Sarmiento, Die Königliche Spanische Akademie und die Pflege der Nationalsprache	863
117.	Maria Leonor Carvalhão Buescu †, L'Académie des Sciences de Lisbonne	870
118.	Ingrid Tieken-Boon van Ostade, Normative studies in England	876
119.	Even Hovdhaugen, Normative studies in the Scandinavian countries	888

120.	Jan Noordegraaf, Normative studies in the Low Countries	893
121.	Sylvie Archaimbault, Les approches normatives en Russie (XVIIIe siècle)	901
122.	Jiří Kraus, Normativ orientierte Sprachforschung zum Tschechischen	907
123.	Jadwiga Puzynina, Normative studies in Poland	912
124.	Tiborc Fazekas, Normativ orientierte Sprachforschung in Ungarn	916
125.	Arnold Cassola, Normative studies in Malta	919

XX. The Study of 'Exotic' Languages by Europeans
Die Europäer und die 'exotischen' Sprachen
La connaissance des langues 'exotiques'

126.	Even Hovdhaugen, The Great Travelers and the studies of 'exotic languages'	925
127.	Edward G. Gray, Missionary linguistics and the description of 'exotic' languages	929
128.	Leonardo Manrique, Das Studium der autochtonen Sprachen Zentralamerikas: Nahuatl	937
129.	Wolfgang Wölck / Utta von Gleich, Das Studium der Eingeborenensprachen Südamerikas: Ketschua	950
130.	Wolf Dietrich, Das Studium der Eingeborenensprachen Südamerikas: Guaraní	960
131.	John Hewson, The study of the native languages of North America: The French tradition	966
132.	Elke Nowak, First descriptive approaches to indigenous languages of British North America	973
133.	Wilhelm J. G. Möhlig, Das Studium der schwarzafrikanischen Sprachen	980
134.	Jean-Luc Chevillard, Das Studium der Eingeborensprachen des indischen Ozeans: Frühe Kontakte mit dem Sanskrit und den dravidischen Sprachen (entfallen)	
135.	Wei Chiao / Magnus Kriegeskorte, Das Studium der Sprachen des Fernen Ostens: Chinesisch	991
136.	Jean-Claude Rivière, La connaissance du malais et des langues de l'Océanie	998

XXI. Theories of Grammar and Language Philosophy in the 17th and 18th Centuries
Grammatiktheorien und Sprachphilosophie im 17. und 18. Jahrhundert
Théories grammaticales et philosophie de langage aux XVIIe et XVIIIe siècles

137.	Claire Lecointre, Les transformations de l'héritage médiéval dans l'Europe du XVIIe siècle	1002

138.	Jean Caravolas, Les origines de la didactique des langues en tant que discipline autonome	1009
139.	Sylvain Auroux, Port-Royal et la tradition française de la grammaire générale	1022
140.	David F. Cram / Jaap Maat, Universal language schemes in the 17th century	1030
141.	Bernd Naumann, Die 'Allgemeine Sprachwissenschaft' um die Wende zum 19. Jahrhundert	1044

XXII. Ideas on the Origin of Language and Languages from the 16th to the 19th Centuries
Vorstellungen vom Sprachursprung und vom Ursprung der Sprachen (16.–18. Jahrhundert)
Conceptions de l'origine des langues et du langage du XVIe au XVIIIe siècle

142.	Daniel Droixhe, Les conceptions du changement et de la parenté des langues européennes aux XVIIe et XVIIIe siècles	1057
143.	Klaus D. Dutz / Ludger Kaczmarek, Vorstellungen über den Ursprung von Sprachen im 16. und 17. Jahrhundert	1071
144.	Harald Haarmann, Die großen Sprachensammlungen vom frühen 18. bis frühen 19. Jahrhundert.	1081

Volume 3 / 3. Teilband / Tome 3
(Preview of Contents / Vorgesehener Inhalt / Table des matières prévus)

XXXIII. Formalization Tendencies and Mathematization in 20th-Century Linguistics, Generative Grammar, and Alternative Approaches
Formalisierungstendenzen und Mathematisierung in der Sprachwissenschaft des 20. Jahrhunderts, die Generative Grammatik und ihre Alternativen
Les tendances vers la formalisation et la mathématisation des théories linguistiques au XXe siècle, la grammaire générative et ses alternatives

The axiomatic method in 20th-century European linguistics

Early tendencies of formalization in 20th-century American linguistics (e. g., Harris, Hockett)

Origin and development of the Chomskyan program: Generative linguistics to 1965

Le développement des grammaires catégorielles et applicatives: Bar-Hillel, Shaumyan

The development of stratificational grammar

The evolution of generative linguistics, 1965–1978

The development of Montague-Grammar

The development of case grammars in the 20th century (Fillmore, Simmons, Grimes, Shank)

Gouvernement et liage; principes et paramètres: la linguistique générative depuis 1978

The development of alternative approaches to generative linguistics: An overview (relational grammar, generalized phrase structure grammar, etc.)

Le développement des grammaires à orientation lexicale

XXXIV. The development of Theories of Semantics, of the Lexicon, and Semantic-Based Theories in the 20th Century
Die Entwicklung von Theorien zur Semantik, zum Lexikon und von semantisch orientierten Grammatiken
Le développement des théories de la sémantique, du lexique et des grammaires sémantiques

Die Zeichentheorie F. de Saussures und die Semantik im 20. Jahrhundert: Ein Überblick

Die Wortfeldtheorie unter dem Einfluß des Strukturalismus

Die Entwicklung der inhaltbezogenen Grammatik in Deutschland: Leo Weisgeber und seine Schule

Die europäische Onomasiologie in der zweiten Hälfte des 20. Jahrhunderts und ihr Verhältnis zur Semasiologie

Die sinnrelationale Semantik als Alternative zur Merkmalsemantik

Research on semantic change after Hermann Paul

The development of sentence-oriented semantic approaches within the generative framework

Semantic theories in 20th-century America: An overview of the different approaches outside of generative grammar: Nida, Goodenough, Lounsbury, Weinreich et al.

Semantic considerations in recent onomastic research: A survey

Semantik und Lexikographie im 20. Jahrhundert

Lexikologie als Theorie des Lexikons einer Grammatik: Eine Übersicht über neuere Entwicklungen

XXXV. Phonology and Morphology in the Later 20th Century
Jüngere Forschungen zur Phonologie und Morphologie
La phonologie et la morphologie au XXe siècle tardif

La phonologie générative jusqu'en 1975

La phonologie générative naturelle et la phonologie naturelle

Autosegmental phonology and underspecification theory

The development of lexical phonology

Le développement de la phonologie prosodique et de la phonologie métrique

Les théories morphologiques dans la linguistique de la fin XXe siècle

Morphologie comme formation des mots au XXe siècle: un survol

Jüngere Entwicklungen in der natürlichen Morphologie

XXXVI. The Study of Language Differenciation in the 20th Century
Die Erforschung der sprachlichen Variation im 20. Jahrhundert
L'étude de la différentiation linguistique au XXe siècle

Homogenität und Heterogenität der Sprache: Die Entwicklung der Diskussion im 20. Jahrhundert

Neuere Entwicklungen in der europäischen Dialektologie

Recent developments in North American dialectology

Die Erforschung der sozialen Variation von Sprachen: Ein Überblick zur Entwicklung in Europa

The analysis of social differenciation of languages: An overview of the development in North America

The development of creolistics and the study of pidgins

Kontaktlinguistik, Sprachkonfliktforschung und Sprachplanung: Überblick über die Tendenzen im 20. Jahrhundert

XXXVII. Historical Linguistics in the Second Half of the 20th Century
Die historische Sprachwissenschaft in der zweiten Hälfte des 20. Jahrhunderts
La linguistique historique dans la deuxième moitié du XXe siècle

The place of historical linguistics in the age of structuralism

Konzepte von der Historizität von Sprachen und von Sprachgeschichte

The investigation of diachronic variety in languages: Traditions and recent developments

Les tendances et les traditions de la lexicographie de la seconde moitié du XXe siècle

The laryngeal and the glottalic theories

Modern theories of linguistic change: An overview

XXXVIII. Critique of Traditional Linguistics and the Development of New Approaches to Language Analysis
Kritik an der traditionellen Sprachwissenschaft und Neuansätze in der Sprachforschung
Critiques et dépassement de la linguistique traditionelle et le développement d'approches neuves au langage

Die Sprachphilosophie Wittgensteins und die Sprachwisssenschaft in der zweiten Hälfte des 20. Jahrhunderts

The interface of linguistics and pragmatics: Its development during the second half of the 20th century

Die Rezeption und Weiterentwicklung der angelsächsischen Sprechakttheorie in der Sprachwissenschaft

Ursprung und Entwicklung der Textlinguistik

Die Rezeption der soziologischen Konversationsanalyse und Ansätze zu einer linguistischen Gesprächsforschung

Le développement des théories énonciatives: Antoine Culioli et son école

XXXIX. 20th-Century Linguistics and Adjacent Fields of Study: Perspectives and Developments
Die Sprachwissenschaft im 20. Jahrhundert und ihre Nachbarwissenschaften: Perspektiven und Entwicklungen
La linguistique et les disciplines voisines au XXe siècle: Perspectives et développements

The ontology and epistemology of linguistics

Linguistics and semiotics I: The impact of Ogden & Richards' *Meaning of Meaning*

Linguistics and semiotics II: C. S. Peirce's influence on 20th-century linguistics

Linguistics and logic I: The influence of Frege and Russell on semantic theory

Sprachwissenschaft und Logik II: Der Einfluß der Quantorenlogik und ihrer Semantik auf die sprachwissenschaftliche Theoriebildung

Sprachwissenschaft und Philosophie I: Der Einfluß der Stereotypentheorie von Hilary Putnam und ihre Rezeption und Weiterentwicklung in der Semantik

Sprachwissenschaft und Philosophie II: Der Einfluß von H. P. Grice auf die Theoriebildung zur sprachlichen Kommunikation

La linguistique et la rhétorique: Un aperçu historique de leurs rapports reciproques au XXe siècle

Sprachwissenschaft und Psychologie I: Ein historischer Überblick über das Verhältnis von Sprache und Denken im 20. Jahrhundert

Linguistique et psychologie II: La théorie des prototypes d'Eleonore Rosch, sa réception critique à l'inténeur de la psychologie et sa réception dans la semantique linguistique

Le langage et les processus cérébraux I: La neurolinguistique du XXe siècle, de l'aphasiologie localiste aux sciences cognitives

Le langage et les processus cérébraux II: Un aperçu du développement de la pathologie du langage au XXe siècle

L'acquisition du langage I: Un aperçu du développement des conceptions de l'apprentissage d'une langue mère au XXe siècle

Language acquisition II: Second language acquisition research in the 20th century

La phonétique au XXe siècle: Un aperçu historique des tendances majeures de son développement

Sprache und Technologie: Die Entstehung neuer Anwendungsfelder sprachwissenschaftlicher Forschung im 20. Jahrhundert

La recherche concernant les langues spéciales et scientifiques: Un aperçu de son développement au XXe siècle

La traduction automatique I: Les premières tentatives jusqu'au rapport ALPAC

La traduction automatique II: Développements récents

Linguistics and artificial intelligence

Language and biology: A survey of problems and principles of biolinguistics

Integrational tendencies in linguistic theory

XL. History of Linguistics — The Field
Die Geschichte der Sprachwissenschaften: Umrisse der Disziplin
Le domaine de l'histoire de la linguistique

Hans-Josef Niederehe, Die Entwicklung der Geschichte der Sprachwissenschaft als Forschungsobjekt

Kees Versteegh, The study of non-Western traditions and its relationship to mainstream linguistic historiography

Sylvain Auroux, Théorie et méthodologie de l'histoire de la linguistique

E. F. K. Koerner, The history of linguistics, its professionalization, and its place within linguistics

XLI. Indexes / Register / Indexes

Index of names / Namenregister / Index des noms
Index of subjects / Sachregister / Index des matières
Index of languages / Sprachenregister / Index des langues

XXIII. Studies of the Antecedents to and Connections between National Languages
Vorstellungen von der Entstehung der Nationalsprachen und ihren Beziehungen zueinander
Études des origines et des rapports des langues nationales

145. Frühe dialektologische, etymologische und sprachgeschichtliche Forschungen in Spanien

1. Historischer Kontext
2. Nebrijas Verstoß
3. Bewertung vorrömischer Substrate
4. Die urkastilische These
5. Verteidigung der lateinischen Herkunft des Kastilischen durch Aldrete
6. Etymologische Untersuchungen und Lexikographie
7. Sprachforschung im 18. Jahrhundert
8. Bibiographie

1. Historischer Kontext

Gegen Ende des 15. Jhs. begannen sich in Spanien die Anfänge einer nationalen Philologie abzuzeichnen. Dies geschah im Gefolge des sich zuerst in Italien artikulierenden klassischen Humanismus und im Rahmen des sich herausbildenden spanischen Nationalstaates. Das Kastilische rückte in stärkerem Maße als übergreifende Landessprache ins Blickfeld. Sie erhielt eine ihr eigene Dignität im Vergleich zu den klassischen Sprachen und zur italienischen Literatursprache zugesprochen. Zugleich gab es vielfältige Bestrebungen, ihre Ausdrucksformen von der Aussprache und Orthographie bis hin zur Syntax zu erfassen und für einen verbindlichen Gebrauch festzulegen. Eng mit solchen Bemühungen waren gelehrte Studien patriotisch gesinnter Humanisten über Geschichte und Charakter des eigenen Volkes verknüpft. In diesem Rahmen nahm die Frage nach der Herkunft und historischen Entwicklung der Landessprache einen besonderen Platz ein, denn schließlich ging es dabei zwischen den zu Interessenverbänden formierten Staaten um nationales Prestige. Rückgriffe auf eine fingierte glorreiche Vergangenheit waren so teilweise vorprogrammiert.

Eine solche Situation führte dazu, daß verschiedene Versuche unternommen wurden, die sprachlichen Gegebenheiten auf der iberischen Halbinsel näher zu betrachten. Eine stärkere Differenzierung zwischen dem Kastilischen und anderen sprachlichen Regionen bzw. Sprachen erschien geboten. Ebenso belebten die Auseinandersetzungen über die erforderlichen orthographischen Normen die etymologischen Untersuchungen. Insbesondere wurde im Zuge der aufkommenden Bildungsbestrebungen der Blick für die Unterschiede zwischen dem Kastilischen und dem Lateinischen geschärft. Zwar fehlte es in den damaligen Diskussionen nicht an phantastischen Etymologien, überspannten Analogien und willkürlich hergestellten Verwandtschaftsbeziehungen zu anderen Sprachen, doch wurden auch sprachhistorische Einsichten gewonnen, die in den folgenden Jahrhunderten weiter ausgebaut und vertieft werden konnten. Es wurde auf die lateinische Herkunft des Spanischen und vielfach auf den genetischen Zusammenhang zwischen den romanischen Sprachen hingewiesen. Auch die einzelnen Substrate, Superstrate und Adstrate bei der Herausbildung des Spanischen gerieten ins Blickfeld.

2. Nebrijas Vorstoß

Der erste spanische Philologe, der solche Probleme aufwarf, war Antonio de Nebrija (1444–1522). Mit seiner *Gramática de la len-*

gua castellana (1492), der ersten gedruckten Grammatik einer romanischen Sprache überhaupt, wollte er zwar ebenso wie mit seinen anderen grammatischen und lexikographischen Werken das Studium des Lateinischen in seinem Lande fördern, doch beschäftigte er sich zu diesem Zweck ebenso intensiv mit dem Kastilischen. Von der Analyse der eigenen Muttersprache ausgehend sollte nämlich ein vertiefter Zugang zum Lateinischen, zur damaligen Sprache der Bildung, ermöglicht werden. Im Kastilischen erblickte er ein eigenständiges Idiom und verglich es mit dem Lateinischen hinsichtlich der Ausdrucksmittel. Er hob hervor, daß das Kastilische gegenüber dem Lateinischen sowohl umfassendere als auch geringere Ausdrucksmöglichkeiten besitze, und zeigte, wie bestimmte spezifisch lateinische Ausdrucksformen und Konstruktionen, vornehmlich beim Verb, im Spanischen adäquat wiedergegeben werden können. Scharfsinnig behandelte er in Abhebung vom Lateinischen typische Aspekte der Namennennungen und Wortbildung im Spanischen. Wie kein Sprachlehrer vor ihm verstand er es in diesem Zusammenhang, Konturen einer konstrastiven Grammatik herauszuarbeiten. Doch auch in historischer Hinsicht gewann er wertvolle Einsichten. Früher als andere italienische oder französische Philologen erkannte er das romanische Futurum und Konditional als *habere*-Kompositionen, "eine Feststellung, die ihm durch die Trennung der beiden Komponenten im Altspanischen und Portugiesischen wohl erleichtert wurde" (Meier 1936: 6).

Nebrijas Vergleich zwischen dem Kastilischen und dem Lateinischen erhielt nicht zuletzt dadurch einen sprachhistorischen Zuschnitt, weil er wie die meisten Philologen des 16. Jhs. seine Muttersprache auf ein verderbtes Latein (*latín corrompido*) zurückführte. Besonders seine Ausführungen über die Orthographie, die er traditionsgemäß als Lehre von den Lauten und ihrer Beziehung verstand, ergaben weitreichende Erkenntnisse. Da seines Erachtens in der Orthographie weitgehende Übereinstimmung zwischen dem Buchstaben (*figura*) und der Lautung (*fuerça*) erreicht werden sollte, prüfte er, ob die im Lateinischen üblichen Buchstaben auch im Spanischen noch eine spezifische Funktion ausübten oder durch die veränderten Lautverhältnisse überflüssig geworden waren. Ebenso betonte er, daß neue Zeichen bzw. Buchstabenkombinationen zur Darstellung moderner Lautungen im Kastilischen erforderlich waren. Deshalb lehnte er eine am Lateinischen orientierte etymologische Schreibweise ab und machte auf solche Fälle aufmerksam, bei denen lateinische Schriftzeichen eine falsche Repräsentierung spanischer Laute ergeben würden.

Bei seinen Überlegungen zur Orthographie stieß Nebrija auf Lautveränderungen, die sich beim Vergleich der lateinischen Ausgangswörter mit ihren spanischen Fortsetzern ablesen ließen. Zugleich griff er hierbei auf Quintilian und die römische grammatische Tradition zurück, wonach sich bestimmte Buchstaben in ihrer Einheit von Graphem und Lautung durch ihre Affinitäten zu anderen Buchstaben leicht verändern.

Nebrija teilte die dann im 16. Jh. vorwaltende Ansicht, daß die in das Römische Reich eindringenden germanischen Völkerschaften in besonderem Maße den Niedergang des Lateinischen beschleunigt und so zur Herausbildung der romanischen Sprachen beigetragen hätten. Eine solche These war zuerst in den Diskussionen italienischer Humanisten um die Mitte des 15. Jhs. aufgetaucht.

3. Bewertung vorrömischer Substrate

Daß die im Laufe der Geschichte erfolgten ethnischen Vermischungen in unterschiedlichem Maße ihre Spuren in den betreffenden Sprachen hinterließen, wurde in den historischen Erörterungen bald zu einem Gemeinplatz. Hierbei gerieten auch die Substrate aus vorrömischer Zeit stärker ins Blickfeld. Mehr als in einem anderen romanischen Land mußten solche Probleme die Gemüter in Spanien bewegen, wo ja im Norden des Landes noch als eine lebende Sprache das zweifellos auf ein vorrömisches Substrat zurückgehende Baskische existierte. Selbstbewußt verkündeten deshalb Gelehrte vornehmlich baskischer Herkunft, daß ihr Idiom einst die vorrömische Sprache Hispaniens schlechthin gewesen sei. In seinem um 1535 verfaßten *Diálogo de la lengua* erwähnte Juan de Valdés, daß diese Ansicht in seiner Zeit häufig vorgebracht werde und wohl früher schon im Umlauf war. Ein historisches und ein sprachliches Argument würden dafür als Stütze dienen. Erstens sei es den römischen Heeren bei ihrer Eroberung der iberischen Halbinsel nach langwierigen Kämpfen kaum gelungen, das gebirgige Baskenland voll in Besitz zu nehmen und dessen Bevölkerung zur Übernahme der lateinischen Sprache zu veranlassen. Und zweitens bestehe zwischen dem Baskischen und jeder anderen, auf der Pyrenäenhalbinsel gesprochenen Sprache keinerlei Übereinstimmung. Dennoch schloß sich Valdés dieser Ansicht nicht an. Seiner Meinung nach sei vielmehr das Griechische der hauptsächlichste Bestandteil der vorrömischen Sprache in Hispanien gewesen.

Die Verfechter der Baskentheorie des 16. und 17. Jhs. verknüpften ihre Darlegungen mit der patristisch-biblischen Lehrmeinung und behaupteten, daß das Baskische als eine der nach der Sprachverwirrung zu Babel entstandenen zweiundsiebzig Ursprachen gelten müsse. Der Anspruch auf ein solches Prädikat forderte ihre Gegner zu einer Gegendarstellung der vorrömischen Sprachverhältnisse auf der Pyrenäenhalbinsel heraus. Es wurde bestritten, daß das Baskische die erste, einst allgemein verbreitete vorrömische Sprache Hispaniens gewesen sei. Die Verfechter der Baskentheorie suchten demgegenüber zu beweisen, daß das Baskische zahlreiche Spuren in der spanischen Toponomastik hinterlassen habe.

4. Die urkastilische These

Um die Wende vom 16. zum 17. Jh. wurde ein Gegenentwurf zur Baskentheorie entwickelt, der damals beträchtliches Aufsehen erregte: die urkastilische Theorie. Ihr Hauptvertreter war Gregorio López Madera (1574—1640), der seine Vorstellungen über das Urkastilische vor allem in seinem Werk *Discursos de la certidumbre de las reliquias descubiertas en Granada desde el año de 1588 hasta el de 1598* (Granada 1601) entwickelte, von dem er nach Binotti (1995: 31) bereits eine frühere Version 1595, ebenfalls in Granada, publiziert hatte. López Madera bezog sich gleichfalls auf die biblisch-pastristische Theorie. Doch seines Erachtens hätten die Ureinwohner, Tubals Geschlecht, nicht baskisch, sondern urkastilisch gesprochen. Diese 'urkastilische' Sprache werde durch das moderne Kastilisch fortgesetzt, trotz der im Laufe der Geschichte erlittenen starken Fremdeinflüsse. Die Basken hingegen seien erst wesentlich später auf die iberische Halbinsel gekommen und nicht über ihre Wohngebiete hinaus gelangt. Außerdem tauge ihr Idiom nicht zur Schriftsprache, so daß es keinesfalls die Sprache in der vorrömischen Zeit sein konnte, in der nach antiker Überlieferung Gesetze und Verse verfaßt worden sind.

Doch López Madera bekämpfte nicht nur die Baskentheorie, sondern in wohl noch stärkerem Maße auch die Korruptionstheorie. Ihn verdroß es, daß seine Muttersprache von einem durch 'Barbaren' verstümmelten Latein herzuleiten sei. Er stellte deshalb die These auf, daß der Bau der urkastilischen Sprache bis zur Gegenwart in seinen wesentlichen Teilen erhalten geblieben sei. Zwar wären im kastilischen Wortschatz zahlreiche fremde Elemente enthalten, die durch Kontakte zu anderen Völkern und vor allem durch Fremdherrschaften aufgenommen wurden, doch auf morpho-syntaktischem Gebiet und in der lexikalischen Idiomatik hätte es keine wesentlichen Veränderungen gegeben: Gerade hier zeige sich, daß die urkastilische Substanz über Jahrtausende hinweg intakt geblieben sei. Immer wieder war López Madera darauf aus, die lateinische Herkunft des Spanischen zu bestreiten. So behauptete er, daß der relativ lange Zeitraum römischer Herrschaft auf der Pyrenäenhalbinsel trotz zahlreicher lexikalischer Entlehnung aus dem Lateinischen die urkastilische Sprache mit ihrem spezifischen Bau nicht zu verdrängen vermochte. Das Lateinische habe in jener Zeit lediglich als Amtssprache gedient. Nur die nach staatlichen Ämtern trachtenden Gesellschaftskreise hätten sich die lateinische Sprache angeeignet, während die breiten Volksschichten an ihrem urkastilischen Idiom festgehalten hätten. Bezeichnenderweise würden sich bei lateinischen Schriftstellern Hispaniens, die ja auch ihre einstige Muttersprache noch beherrschten, dem Urkastilischen nachgebildete Konstruktionen feststellen lassen, argumentierte er.

Die sprachhistorische Konzeption von López Madera fand in Spanien bei bedeutenden humanistischen Sprachgelehrten wie Gonzalo Correas (1570—1644?) oder Jiménez Patón (1569—1640?) nicht zuletzt deshalb eine beachtliche Resonanz, weil damit eine Abwehrhaltung gegen jene italienischen Humanisten bezogen werden konnte, für welche die Tradition des Ciceronianismus das nur ihnen zukommende anspruchsvollste kulturelle Erbe darstellte. Wie in Frankreich mit dem Gallischen das hauptsächlichste vorrömische Substrat zum glorreichen nationalen Fundus hochstilisiert und als eigentlicher Kern der französischen Sprache herausgestellt wurde, so projizierte in Spanien López Madera, unter Rückgriff auf die patristisch-biblische Tradition, die Anfänge des Kastilischen in eine nationale Urzeit zurück. Wesentlich radikaler als in Frankreich wurde hierbei die Bedeutung des Lateins für die eigene Sprachgeschichte auf ein Minimum beschränkt.

5. Verteidigung der lateinischen Herkunft des Kastilischen durch Aldrete

Nur wenige Jahre nach der Publikation des López Madera erschien eine umfassende Auseinandersetzung mit der urkastilischen These. Es handelte sich um das Buch *Del origen, y principio de la lengua castellana ò romance que oi se usa en España* (Rom 1606). Darin suchte Bernardo Aldrete (1560−1641) eingehend die zugunsten der urkastilischen Theorie vorgebrachten Argumente zu entkräften. Indem Aldrete hierbei die Auffassung vom verderbten Latein als Quelle der romanischen Sprachen weiter ausbaute und sie in eine weitgespannte Geschichte der spanischen Sprache einordnete, schuf er eines der bedeutendsten sprachhistorischen Werke seiner Zeit.

Im ersten Teil seines Buches beschäftigte sich Aldrete mit der Romanisierung auf der Pyrenäenhalbinsel. Unter Bezugnahme auf antike und frühmittelalterliche Autoren arbeitete er gegenüber López Madera heraus, daß zwar die lateinische Sprache zunächst nur als Amtssprache diente, doch im Laufe der Zeit die allgemeine Umgangssprache selbst der niederen Volksschichten wurde. Nachdrücklich hob er hervor, daß die Romanisierung in mehreren Etappen erfolgt sei und zuerst in den südlichen Gebieten Hispaniens zum Abschluß kam. Für Aldretes Argumentation war bezeichnend, daß er in seinen Ausführungen über die geschichtlichen Bedingungen der Romanisierung auch auf ähnliche sprachpolitische Gegebenheiten der Neuzeit verwies. Moderne Beispiele besaßen seines Erachtens ebenfalls Beweiskraft, wenn es um die Deutung ähnlicher Vorgänge in zurückliegenden Jahrhunderten ging. So bezog er sich auf die Verbreitung des Spanischen in der Neuen Welt und schloß aus den dabei gewonnenen Ergebnissen auf ähnliche Verhältnisse bei der Romanisierung Hispaniens.

Im zweiten Teil seines Buchs legte er die Herkunft des Kastilischen aus dem Lateinischen in Verbindung mit der Korruptionsthese dar. Aldrete war sich bewußt, daß eine Sprache sich im Laufe der Zeit verändert und sowohl regionale als auch soziale Varietäten aufweist. Die lateinische Sprache in den einzelnen römischen Provinzen habe durch die Kontakte zu den einheimischen Bewohnern, durch unterschiedliche Bildungsverhältnisse und nicht zuletzt durch den bloßen Zeitfaktor manche Veränderungen erfahren. Allerdings hätte dies nicht gereicht, folgerte er, um daraus eine neue Sprache entstehen zu lassen. Hierzu bedurfte es seines Erachtens eines einschneidenden historischen Wandels. Dieser habe in der Zeit der Völkerwanderung eingesetzt, als germanische Völkerschaften in zahlreiche römische Provinzen eindrangen und sich dort als herrschende Schichten etablierten. Sie hätten sich das Latein in einer Weise angeeignet, daß daraus ein neues Idiom entstanden wäre. Dieses barbarische Latein der germanischen Herrscherschicht wäre dann schließlich zur Gemeinsprache schlechthin geworden, weil es die Bewohner der ehemaligen römischen Provinzen aus Willfährigkeit und Angst nachahmten. Aldrete meinte hier seinen sprachpolitischen Grundsatz bestätigt zu sehen, wonach die politische Macht ausschlaggebend dafür sei, welche Sprache gebraucht werde.

Seine These suchte Aldrete anhand sprachlicher Phänomene zu erklären. Hierbei griff er oft zum Sprachvergleich, um durch übergreifende Züge in den romanischen Sprachen die nach López Madera angeblich seit Urzeiten bestehenden Besonderheiten des Kastilischen auf morpho-syntaktischem Gebiet ad absurdum zu führen. Aldrete ging davon aus, daß die germanischen Völkerschaften eine im wesentlichen gleiche Sprache gesprochen hätten und bei ihrer Verhunzung der lateinischen Sprache in den einstigen römischen Provinzen in Italien, Frankreich und Spanien eine ähnliche Grammatik gebrauchten. Was sich daher im grammatischen Bau für das Kastilische feststellen lasse, finde sich mit geringen Unterschieden ebenso im Italienischen und Französischen.

Daß der in der Entwicklung zum Romanischen hin sich vollziehende Wandel vom synthetischen zum analytischen Typus im Lateinischen selbst angelegt war, also einen inneren sprachlichen Entwicklungsprozeß darstellte, blieb bei Aldrete wie bei den meisten Sprachgelehrten seiner Zeit außerhalb des Blickfelds.

Aldrete wies auf ähnliche Züge im Spanischen und anderen romanischen Sprachen hin, zeigte ihre lateinische Grundlage und demonstrierte ihre enge sprachliche Verwandtschaft noch dadurch, daß er das Vaterunser in lateinischer, spanischer, italienischer, katalanischer und portugiesischer Sprache wiedergab. Zugleich suchte er die Unterschiede zwischen diesen Sprachen zu erklären, die er vor allem im Wortschatz, in der Wortbildung und in der lautlichen Entwicklung sah. In den einzelnen Sprachräumen hätte man bei der lexikalischen Fülle der lateinischen Sprache da das eine, dort das andere Wort bevorzugt, unterschiedliche Bedeutungen fortgeführt oder spezielle Übertragungen vorgenommen. Bei den Entlehnungen aus anderen Sprachen spielten jeweils unterschiedliche Kontakte eine Rolle. Auch bei den Neubildungen wurden verschiedene Wege beschritten. Nicht zuletzt ergaben sich spezifische lautliche Veränderungen in den einzelnen Sprachen.

Bei den vokalischen Veränderungen hob Aldrete u. a. den Wandel von lat. *au* > kast. *o* hervor, ebenso den von lat. *e* > kast. *ie* sowie von lat. *o* > kast. *ue*, ohne daß er zwischen kurzem bzw. offenem und langem bzw. geschlossenem *e* bzw. *o* oder zwischen Hauptton und Nebenton unterschied. Bezüglich dieser Veränderungen wies er teilweise auf diesbezügliche Angaben römischer Grammatiker (Varro, Festus, Quintilian) hin. Zugleich belegte er einen solchen Wandel beim Übergang vom Lateinishen zum Spanischen durch eine stattliche Reihe entsprechender Beispiele. Bemerkenswert war auch, wieviele konsonantische Veränderungen Aldrete beim Wandel vom Lateinischen zum Kastilischen herausstellte und diese durch Listen von entsprechenden Beispielen zu dokumentieren suchte. So hob er die Sonorisierung der lateinischen Verschlußlaute *p*, *t*, *c* im Kastilischen hervor und erwähnte bei seiner Aufzählung von Beispielen u. a. Veränderungen wie lat. *apicula* > kast. *abeja*, lat. *acutus* > kast. *agudo*, lat. *amicus* > kast. *amigo*. Unter den zahlreichen lautlichen Veränderungen, die Aldrete anführte und mit Beispielen belegte, finden sich ferner die Palatalisierung der lateinischen Konsonantengruppen *pl* und *cl* zu kast. *ll plaga* > *llaga; plorare* > *llorar* bzw. *clamare* > *llamar; clavis* > *llave*) oder *ct* zu *ch* (*dictus* > *dicho; lacte* > *leche*). Bei den konsonantischen Veränderungen nahm er ebenfalls auf Angaben römischer Grammatiker Bezug und berücksichtigte in seinen Betrachtungen, wie griechische Wörter im Lateinischen lautlich wiedergegeben wurden. In einzelnen Fällen verwies er darauf, wie bestimmte lateinische Konsonanten im Italienischen verändert wurden. Er erwähnte, daß bestimmte lateinische Konsonanten zur gleichen Lautung im Spanischen und Italienischen führten, doch dies durch unterschiedliche Grapheme repräsentiert werde. So entspricht einem spanischen *ñ* ein italienisches *gli*. Hinsichtlich der Veränderung von lat. *m'n* zu kast. *mbre* in Beispielen wie lat. *culmen* > kast. *cumbre* oder lat. *nomen* > kast. *nombre* untermauerte Aldrete die im Spanischen erfolgte Einfügung eines Gleitlautes durch ähnliche Veränderungen im Italienischen (lat. *gremio* > it. *grembo*) oder Französischen (lat. *camera* > frz. *chambre*; lat. *numero* > frz. *nombre*).

Mit den zahlreichen Lautveränderungen, die Aldrete beim Wandel vom Lateinischen zum Spanischen herausstellte, setzte er die entsprechenden Bemühungen Nebrijas auf breiterer Ebene fort und ergänzte sie durch eine vergleichende Sicht. Die meisten dieser von Aldrete hervorgehobenen Lautveränderungen sind später im 19. Jh. von der historisch-vergleichenden Sprachwissenschaft als regelmäßiger Lautwandel herausgearbeitet und von den Junggrammatikern sogar als 'Lautgesetze' betrachtet worden. Verschiedene Gelehrte unserer Zeit vertreten deshalb die Ansicht, daß Aldrete zu den Vätern der romanischen Sprachwissenschaft zu zählen sei. Auch wenn Aldrete zu seiner Zeit die wohl umfassendste Synthese einer Geschichte des Spanischen unter Bezugnahme auf andere romanische Sprachen bot, dürfen wohl seine Erkenntnisse des Lautwandels nicht überbewertet werden. Von einer systematischen Erfassung des Lautwandels konnte bei ihm kaum die Rede sein, trotz der Anwendung von "*la règle des séries*", wie Wagner (1950−51: 122) lobend hervorhebt. Aldrete beachtete überhaupt nicht die Position des einzelnen Lautes. Es spielte für ihn keine Rolle, ob es sich jeweils um betonte oder unbetonte Silben handelte oder ob der betreffende Haupttonvokal in freier oder gedeckter Stellung anzutreffen war. Wie schon Nebrija betrachtete Aldrete die lautlichen Veränderungen unter einem panchronischen und einem historischen Aspekt. Zum anderen machte er im Anschluß an die römische Grammatikertradition auf lautphysiologisch bedingte Affinitäten zwischen einzelnen Lauten aufmerksam. Zum anderen ging es ihm darum, die von ihm als Sprachverderbnis gewerteten Veränderungen vom Lateinischen zum Kastilischen zu zeigen und damit die lateinische Herkunft seiner Muttersprache zu unterstreichen.

Im dritten Teil seines Werkes erörterte Aldrete die nichtlateinischen Elemente im spanischen Wortschatz, die im Laufe der Geschichte durch Kontakte zu anderen Völkern übernommen und eingebürgert worden waren. Relativ ausführlich behandelte er die Wörter griechischer Herkunft, bei denen er zwei Gruppen unterschied. Die eine umfaßte solche Lexeme, die während der römischen Herrschaft ins Lateinische übernommen wurden und dann im Kastilischen erhalten blieben. Die andere bezieht sich auf Bezeichnungen, die er auf das vorrömische griechische Substrat in Teilen der iberischen Halbinsel zurückführte und hierbei auch Toponyme berücksichtigte. Weiterhin erörterte Aldrete die Bezeichnungen hebräischer Herkunft, stellte jedoch eine frühe jüdische Einflußnahme in Abrede. Was sich als hebräisch darbiete, sei meistens auf die Sprache der Phönizier oder Karthager zurückzuführen, die mit dem Hebräischen verwandt seien; besonders treffe das auf Ortsnamen zu.

Ein spezielles Kapitel widmete Aldrete auch den spanischen Wörtern germanischer Herkunft. Dabei hielt er sich vor allem daran, was an diesbezüglichen Angaben in dem Werk von Wolfgang Lazius (1514—1565) zu finden war: *De gentium aliquot migrationibus, sedibus fixis, reliquiis, linguarumque initiis et immutationibus ac dialectis Libri XII* (Basilea 1557) und in dem von Olaus Magnus (1490—1558) *Historia de gentibus septentrionalibus* (Roma 1555). In letzterem wurde vor allem der langobardische Einfluß in Italien erörtert. Aldrete warf diesen Autoren allerdings vor, zuweilen lateinische Wörter als germanische auszugeben. Offensichtlich kannte sich Aldrete auf diesem Gebiet wenig aus. Viele seiner angeführten Etymologien waren unzutreffend. Von den spanischen Gelehrten jener Zeit war der Baske Andrés de Poza (1530—1595) nach Coseriu (1975: 5—16) mit dieser Thematik wesentlich besser vertraut. Da er neun Jahre an der Universität Löwen studiert hatte, beherrschte er das Flämische und kannte wahrscheinlich auch die deutsche Sprache.

Hinsichtlich des arabischen Adstrats in der Geschichte der spanischen Sprache übte Adrete ziemliche Zurückhaltung. Bei seinen Darlegungen über den Wortschatz arabischer Herkunft stützte er sich auf das 1505 in Granada erschienene spanisch-arabische Wörterbuch *Vocabulista arávigo en letra castellana*, das Pedro de Alcalá einst im Auftrag des Erzbischofs von Granada für die unter den Muslims und Neuchristen tätigen Missionare verfaßt hatte. Eine seiner Aufgaben sah er hierbei darin, eine Reihe von arabisch klingenden Wörtern auf ihr eigentlich lateinisches Etymon wieder zurückzuführen wie im Fall von kast. *jabón* auf lat. *sapo, -nis*. Andererseits mußte er eingestehen, daß durch die engen Kontakte von christlich spanischer und muselmanisch arabischer Bevölkerung über viele Jahrhunderte hinweg zahlreiche Entlehnungen aus dem Arabischen erfolgt waren, von denen er aber nur relativ wenige Beispiele bot.

In Aldretes sprachgeschichtlichen Erörterungen nahm die Reconquista eine zentrale Position ein. Ihr Verlauf diente ihm dazu, die in der Gegenwart anzutreffende sprachliche Gliederung der iberischen Halbinsel zu erklären. Hierbei stellte er insbesondere die keilartige Ausbreitung des Kastilischen vom Norden nach dem Süden in Verbindung mit der Rolle der spanischen Monarchie heraus. Nebrija hatte diese Thematik kaum gestreift. Erst Juan de Valdés ging darauf in großen Zügen ein, indem er, von der Reconquista ausgehend, vier vom Lateinischen herzuleitende Sprachen unterschied: das Kastilische, das Valencianische, das Katalanische und das Portugiesische. Die zwischen diesen verwandten Sprachen vorhandenen Unterschiede seien darauf zurückzuführen, daß die jeweiligen Sprachgebiete unter verschiedenen Herrschaften standen und deren Bewohner mit unterschiedlichen Nachbarn enge Kontakte pflegten. In ähnlicher Weise, wenn auch etwas ausführlicher, argumentierte auch Aldrete. Er ging davon aus, daß während der Araberherrschaft die von germanischen Stämmen verstümmelte lateinische Sprache (*romance*) zunächst nur im Norden der Pyrenäenhalbinsel ein Refugium hatte, wohin sich Teile der christlichen Bevölkerung zurückgezogen hatten. In diesen Ausgangsgebieten der dann einsetzenden Reconquista habe sich schließlich dieses '*romance*' je nach Herrschaftsbereich und hierbei existierenden Kontakten zu hilfreichen Nachbarn differenziert. Im Nordosten der Halbinsel bildete sich das dem Provenzalischen recht ähnliche Katalanische heraus, das sich später insbesondere nach der Verbindung der Herrscherhäuser von Aragonien und Katalonien nach dem Südosten ausbreitete. Im Nordwesten der Halbinsel erlangte das '*romance*' mit der Zeit ein Gepräge, das nicht zuletzt durch die Einflußnahme der ersten, aus Frankreich stammenden portugiesischen Herrscher, einschließlich ihres adligen Gefolges, schließlich zum Portugiesischen führte und sich in südwestlicher Richtung ausdehnte. Den wesentlichsten Anteil an der sprachlichen Gliederung der Pyrenäenhalbinsel schrieb Aldrete dem Kastilischen zu, das sich im Zuge der Reconquista keilförmig vom Norden nach dem Süden über den größten Teil der Halbinsel verbreitete. In den zurückeroberten Gebieten sei das Kastilische wieder in der Form eingeführt worden, wie es sich in den gebirgigen Gegenden des Nordens erhalten hatte. Anfangs habe dies kaum Schwierigkeiten gemacht, da die unter maurischer Herrschaft gebliebenen Christen noch ihr 'romance' bewahrt hatten. Doch Jahrhunderte später sei dies schwierig gewesen, da die unter arabischer Herrschaft verbliebene christliche Bevölkerung nur noch arabisch gesprochen hätte. Damit wandte er sich erneut gegen Lopéz Madera, der behauptet hatte, daß die christliche Bevölkerung stets ihre 'urkastilische' Sprache bewahrt habe. Für López Madera hatte die Reconquista in sprachlicher Hinsicht keine entscheidenden Auswirkungen. Er meinte sogar, daß die Mozaraber in Toledo ein reineres und vornehmeres Kastilisch gesprochen hätten als die aus dem rauheren Norden siegreich gegen die Mauren vorrückenden Spanier. Während Aldrete die Unterschiede zwischen dem Kastilischen, Portugiesischen und Katalanischen in Verbindung mit der Reconquista historisch zu begründen suchte, stellten für Lopéz Madera das Portugiesische und Katalanische keine eigenständigen Idiome dar, sondern nur zufällige und verderbte Ausdrucksformen der 'urkastilischen' Substanz. Das Spanische in seiner 'urkastilischen' Substanz habe sich allein unverderbt in Kastilien, im Herzen des Königreichs, erhalten.

Gegenüber der These Maderas von der Konstante idiomatischer Wendungen zeigte Aldrete, daß charakteristische Redeweisen einer Sprache nach Ort und Zeit auf recht unterschiedliche Weise anzutreffen sind und manchmal auch aus anderen Sprachen aufgenommen werden, daher nicht schlechthin als dauerhafte Grundelemente betrachtet werden dürfen. Anhand von Beispielen hob er hervor, daß jede natürliche Sprache bei aller Homogenität diastratische und diatopische Züge sowie idiolektische Besonderheiten auszudrücken vermag, d. h. Partikularitäten im sprachlichen Ausdruck je nach Provinz, Gesellschafts- und Berufsgruppe oder persönlicher Eigenart.

6. Etymologische Untersuchungen und Lexikographie

In den sprachgeschichtlichen Erörterungen des 16. Jhs. war immer wieder auf Entlehnungen aus anderen Sprachen hingewiesen worden. Und Aldrete bemühte sich, mit gewisser Systematik die einzelnen lexikalischen Schichten in einem historischen Längsschnitt herauszustellen. Der Gelehrte jedoch, der sich vorrangig das Ziel stellte, die Etymologien des spanischen Wortschatzes aufzudecken, war Sebastián de Covarrubias (1539—1613). Er war damit erfolgreicher als andere Gelehrte seiner Zeit, die sich auf diesem Gebiet versuchten, so Alejo Venegas (c. 1493—nach 1572) im 8. Kapitel seines 1565 veröffentlichten Werks *Agonía del tránsito de la muerte* oder danach Bartolomé Valverde und Francisco del Rosal, deren etymologische Untersuchungen nur als Manuskripte in den Archiven der Nationalbibliothek in Madrid vorhanden sind (La Viñaza 1893: 1624 ff. bzw. 1631 ff.). Da Covarrubias weitgehend Etymologie im Sinne der diesbezüglichen antiken und mittelalterlichen Tradition verstand, d. h. das ursprüngliche Benennungsmuster beim jeweiligen Wort durch Heranziehung anderer Wörter derselben Sprache aufzudecken suchte, bot sein 1611 erschienener *Tesoro de la Lengua Castellana o Española* allerdings weniger ein etymologisches Wörterbuch im Sinn der neuzeitlichen Sprachwissenschaft, sondern ein umfangreiches einsprachiges Wörterbuch mit enzyklopädischer Tendenz. Es stellt noch heute ein unentbehrliches Hilfsmittel für das Verständnis von Texten der spanischen Literatur des 16. und 17. Jhs. wegen seines außerordentlich großen Reichtums an Wörtern, Wendungen, Sprichwörtern und volkstümlichen Ausdrucksweisen und nicht zuletzt wegen seiner wertvollen Hinweise auf Vorstellungen und Vorfälle jener Epoche dar. Da Covarrubias die Herkunft eines einzelnen Wortes zunächst dadurch aufzuhellen suchte, daß er die einschlägigen Wendungen, häufig anzutreffenden Kollokationen und jeweils verknüpften Phraseologismen heranzog, lotete er die semantische Dimension nach verschiedenen Seiten hin aus. Er verwies auf die stilistischen Aspekte des Wortes, beleuchtete die dazugehörige Wortsippe und erklärte damit im Zusammenhang stehende Wendungen. So vermerkte er, wenn einzelne Wörter als vulgär oder bäurisch galten, in höfischen Kreisen besonders gebraucht wurden, als poetische

Ausdrücke dienten oder jüngste Entlehnungen aus anderen, vor allem romanischen Sprachen, darstellten. Und fachsprachliche Ausdrücke kennzeichnete er als solche. Ebenso führte er zahlreiche Ausdrücke des mittelalterlichen Spanisch an. Zuweilen begnügte sich Covarrubias damit, einfach nur anzugeben, auf welches Wort das angeführte Lexem zurückgeht. Daß der überwiegende Teil des spanischen Wortschatzes in verderbter Form die lateinische Sprache repräsentiere, hob er immer wieder hervor. Meinte er das ursprüngliche Benennungsmotiv für das betreffende Wort in der Ausgangssprache entdeckt zu haben, ging er darauf ein, besonders bei Wörtern hebräischer, griechischer und lateinischer Herkunft. Vielfach setzte er sich hierbei mit anderen etymologischen Deutungen auseinander und brachte zum Schluß seine Interpretation. Charakteristisch für sein Bemühen, das ursprüngliche Benennungsmotiv und damit den 'etymologischen' Kern eines Wortes herauszustellen, war, daß er auch auf die jeweiligen Bezeichnungen in anderen lebenden Sprachen, besonders im Katalanischen, Italienischen und Französischen Bezug nahm.

7. Sprachforschung im 18. Jahrhundert

Bei den im 18. Jh. anzutreffenden sprachgeschichtlichen Betrachtungen über die Herausbildung des Spanischen wurde meistens auf das verwiesen, was Aldrete darüber Anfang des 17. Jhs. vorgebracht hatte. Bezeichnenderweise erfolgt dies auch im Vorwort der *Gramática de la lengua castellana*, die von der Königlich-Spanischen Akademie 1771 herausgegeben wurde. Hier wurde nämlich erneut vermerkt, daß in Hispanien mit dem Niedergang des Römischen Imperiums und der Westgotenherrschaft sowohl seitens der romanischen Bevölkerung als auch seitens der herrschenden germanischen Schichten die lateinische Sprache so verderbt worden sei, daß dies zur Entstehung des '*romance*' und dann schließlich der kastilischen Sprache geführt habe. Bereits 1737 hatte indessen Gregorio Mayáns y Siscar (1699–1781) diese Ansicht in seiner zweibändigen Abhandlung über die Geschichte der spanischen Sprache stillschweigend korrigiert. Dieses Werk trug den Titel *Orígenes de la lengua española, compuestos por varios autores recogidos por Don Gregorio Mayáns i Siscar*. Im ersten Band behandelte Mayáns y Siscar die Herausbildung der spanischen Sprache, und im zweiten Band ließ er linguistische Studien des Siglo de Oro abdrucken, die wichtige Aspekte der spanischen Sprachgeschichte erhellten sollten, darunter erstmals den *Diálogo de la lengua* von Juan de Valdés. Ohne sich direkt mit Aldrete auseinanderzusetzen, dessen Liste der kastilischen Wörter germanischer Herkunft er im zweiten Band seines sprachhistorischen Werks wieder anführte, vermied er es, den Westgoten eine so entscheidende Rolle bei der 'Korruption' des Lateins zuzuschreiben wie Aldrete. Mayáns y Siscar plädierte vielmehr dafür, den Niedergang des Lateins im frühen Mittelalter näher zu untersuchen. Es gelte unbedingt die gegenüber dem klassischen Latein festzustellenden Besonderheiten im Spät- und Mittellatein herauszustellen, um dadurch Licht auf die Anfänge der romanischen Volkssprachen zuwerfen. Und es war wohl symptomatisch, daß er in diesem Zusammenhang auf das 1678 erschienene monumentale *Glossarium mediae et infimae latinitatis* von Charles Du Fresne, sieur du Cange, Bezug nahm. Durch dieses Werk konnte besser begriffen werden, daß sich die lateinische Umgangssprache vom Schriftlatein unterschied und im Verlauf von Jahrhunderten

"so gewaltige Veränderungen durchmachte, daß die romanischen Sprachen sehr wohl daraus hervorgehen mochten, ohne daß man an weitgehende Sprachmischungen zu denken genötigt war." (Ettmayer 1916: 235).

Mayáns y Siscar erwartete auch von einem Studium der ältesten spanischen Texte bessere sprachgeschichtliche Aufschlüsse. Hier werde ersichtlich, wie vornehmlich aus der nach dem Einfall der Araber zunehmenden 'Korruption' des Lateins sich das Spanische herausbildete.

Bei den Darlegungen von Mayáns y Siscar fallen gegenüber Aldretes sprachhistorischen Erläuterungen noch folgende Unterschiede auf: Die Rolle des Keltischen bei den vorrömischen Substraten der iberischen Halbinsel wird wesentlich stärker hervorgehoben. Die sprachhistorische Bedeutung des Baskischen erfährt eine noch stärkere Einschränkung. Die arabischen Elemente im spanischen Wortschatz werden ohne Vorbehalte als wichtige Bestandteile betrachtet. Sie würden den zwanzigsten Teil des kastilischen Vokabulars ausmachen, nicht aber ein Fünftel, wie Joseph Justus Scaliger in *Diatriba de Euro-*

paeorum linguis (1599 bzw. 1610) behauptet hatte.

Wie schon Aldrete maß Mayáns y Siscar der Reconquista maßgebliche Bedeutung für die sprachliche Gliederung der Pyrenäenhalbinsel bei. Er berücksichtigte außer dem Katalanischen, das er mit dem Provenzalischen gleichsetzte, etwas stärker das Portugiesische und bezog sich hierbei auf das ebenfalls 1606 in Lissabon erschienene Werk von Duarte Nunes de Leão *Origem da língua portuguesa*, der zu ähnlichen sprachhistorischen Schlüssen wie Aldrete gelangt war. Das Galicische allerdings ordnete Mayáns y Siscar dem Portugiesischen mit dem Argument unter, daß das Portugiesische schließlich als Schriftsprache diene und offizielle Sprache eines Staatsgebiets sei.

Für die Anerkennung des Galicischen als eigenständiger Sprache setzte sich damals vor allem der Pater Martín Sarmiento (1695–1771) ein. Er gehörte zu den bedeutendsten spanischen Philologen seiner Zeit (Pensado 1960). Vom Studium der altspanischen Sprachdenkmäler erwartete er wertvolle Aufschlüsse über die spanische Sprachgeschichte. Die meisten Schriften von ihm blieben jedoch unveröffentlicht. Lediglich der erste Band seiner *Memorias para la Historia de la Poesia y Poetas españoles* erschien 1775 postum. Erst in den Jahren 1928 bis 1930 wurden mehrere seiner Werke im *Boletín de la Real Academia Española* publiziert. Diese zeigen, daß Sarmiento der spanischen Sprachforschung damals wesentliche Impulse gegeben haben könnte.

Neben dem Studium altspanischer Texte hielt Sarmiento das Studium der Dialekte besonders wichtig für die sprachgeschichtliche Forschung. Seines Erachtens setzten die romanischen Sprachen dialektale Varietäten des im Römischen Imperium gesprochenen Lateins fort, die dann unter den jeweils herrschenden klimatischen und historischen Bedingungen weitere Veränderungen erfuhren. Deshalb würden die älteren Sprachzustände in diesen Sprachen auch mehr Gemeinsamkeiten aufweisen als die modernen. So stehe das Altspanische dem Altfranzösischen der Straßburger Eide viel näher als das Spanische dem Französischen in der Neuzeit.

In der etymologischen Forschung wollte Sarmiento ebenfalls größere Klarheit erreichen. Bestimmte lautliche Veränderungen müßten dann als regelmäßig begriffen werden, wenn sich diese in zehn bis zwölf Fällen belegen ließen. Außerdem gelte es bei den etymologischen Untersuchungen die Gleichheit der Bedeutungen einschließlich der metaphorischen Verwendungen besonders zu beachten. Und nicht zuletzt sollten bezüglich des spanischen Wortschatzes auch das Italienische und das Französische herangezogen werden. Aus der auf der iberischen Halbinsel vor der westgotischen Herrschaft gebrauchten lateinischen Sprache gingen nach Sarmiento in unabhängiger Weise das Kastilische, das Galicische, das Asturische und das Katalanische hervor. Das Portugiesische betrachtete er als einen im Zuge der Reconquista gebildeten galicischen Dialekt, der schließlich als Schriftsprache gebraucht wurde.

Mit besonderer Leidenschaft erforschte Sarmiento das Galicische, sein heimatliches Idiom. Er setzte sich für dessen Dignität gegenüber dem Kastilischen ein, hob die bedeutende Rolle des Galicischen als Literatursprache im spanischen Mittelalter hervor und bemühte sich eifrig, den galicischen Wortschatz allseitig zu erfassen. Der in den Dialekten vorliegenden mündlichen Tradition maß er eine grundlegende Bedeutung für die Sprachgeschichte bei. Hier seien zahlreiche ursprüngliche lexikalische Elemente erhalten geblieben, die in den Schriftsprachen nicht mehr existierten. Deshalb müsse unbedingt der dialektale Wortschatz erfaßt werden. Alles das, was dabei von naturgeschichtlichem Interesse sei, verdiene besonders auch in sprachlicher Hinsicht studiert zu werden. Für das Kastilische sollten seines Erachtens drei verschiedene Glossare angefertigt werden: ein mittellateinisches, eines der altspanischen Literatursprache bis zum Ende des 14. Jhs. und eines für jene volkstümlichen Wörter, die nicht schriftsprachlich belegt und vielfach nur noch in der einen oder anderen spanischen Provinz anzutreffen sind. In ähnlicher Weise sollte dies auch für die Erforschung des Galicischen erfolgen. Immer wieder zeigte es sich, daß Sarmiento sowohl als Philologe als auch als Dialektologe an Probleme der Sprachgeschichte heranging und so neue Blickrichtungen öffnen half.

Für das spanische 18. Jh. war es bezeichnend, daß vorrangig aus nichtkastilischen Gebieten stammende Gelehrte die Geltung und Qualität der spanischen Literatursprache gegenüber dem Lateinischen und vor allem dem Französischen, der damaligen aristokratischen Gesellschaftssprache von universeller Geltung, verteidigten und zugleich das Interesse für die Dialekte und für jene Sprachen Spaniens wecken halfen, die einst als Literatursprachen gepflegt worden waren. Der bedeutende spanische Aufklärer Gaspar Melchor de Jovellanos (1744−1811) gab dem Kastilischen in seinen nationalerzieherischen Programmen einen hohen Stellenwert und beschäftigte sich zugleich mit seinem heimatlichen Dialekt, dem Asturischen (Ángel del Río 1943). Bereits 1724 brachte der Katalane Antonio Bastero in Rom sein Werk *La Crusca provenzale* heraus, in dem er seine Muttersprache mit dem Provenzalischen, der Sprache der Troubadours, gleichsetzte und ihr einen historischen Vorrang vor den anderen romanischen Sprachen zuwies. Und in Katalonien hatten zahlreiche Gelehrte Beziehungen zu Kreisen italienischer Philologen, vor allem zu jenen, welche die Herausbildung der romanischen Sprachen aus dem Lateinischen selbst ohne größere Einwirkung fremder Völkerschaften erklärten. In letzterem Sinn äußerte sich 1756 beispielsweise der Marqués de Llió (Lázaro Carreter 1949: 170), der Präsident der Akademie für die schönen Künste in Barcelona.

8. Bibliographie

Aldrete, Bernardo. 1606. *Del orígen y principio de la lengua castellana ò romance qui oi se usa en España*. Roma: Carlo Vullieto. (Edición facsimilar y estudio de Nieto Jiménez, Lidio 1972−1975, 2 Bde. Madrid: Consejo superior de investigaciones científicas.)

Asensio, Eugenio. 1960. "La lengua compañera del imperio: Historia de una idea de Nebrija en España y Portugal". *RFE* 43. 399−413.

Bahner, Werner. 1956. *Beitrag zum Sprachbewußtsein in der spanischen Literatur des 16. und 17. Jahrhunderts*. Berlin: Rütten & Loening.

−. 1966. *La lingüística española del siglo de Oro: Aportaciones a la conciencia lingüística en la España de los siglos XVI y XVII*. Madrid: Ciencia Nueva.

−. 1984. "Sprachwandel und Etymologie in der spanischen Sprachwissenschaft des Siglo de Oro". *HL* XI. 95−116.

Binotti, Lucia. 1995. *La teoría del 'Castellano Primitivo'. Nacionalismo y reflexión lingüística en el Renacimiento español*. Münster: Nodus.

Braselmann, Petra. 1991. *Humanistische Grammatik und Volkssprache: Zur 'Gramática de la lengua castellana' von Antonio de Nebrija*. Düsseldorf: Droste.

Coseriu, Eugenio. 1975. "Un germanista vizcaíno en el siglo XVI: Andrés de Poza y el elemento germánico del español". *AnL* 13. 5−16.

Covarrubias, Sebastián de. 1611. *Tesoro de la Lengua Castellana o Española*. Madrid: Luis Sanchez. (Edición preparada por Martín de Riquer. Barcelona: S. A. Horta, 1943.)

Droixhe, Daniel. 1978. *La Linguistique et l'appel de l'histoire (1600−1800)*. Genève & Paris: Droz.

Esparza Torres, Miguel Ángel. 1995. *Las ideas lingüísticas de Antonio de Nebrija*. Münster: Nodus.

Ettmayer, Karl Ritter von. 1916. "Vulgärlatein". *Die Erforschung der indogermanischen Sprachen* hg. von Wilhelm Streiberg. I, 231−280. Straßburg: Trübner.

Guitarte, Guillermo. 1984. "La dimension imperial del español en la obra de Aldrete: sobre la aparición del español de América en la lingüística hispánica". *HL* XI. 129−187.

Kukenheim, Louis. 1932. *Contributions à l'histoire de la grammaire italienne, espagnole et française à l'époque de la Renaissance*. Amsterdam: N. V. Noord-Hollandsche Uitgevers-Maatschappij.

Lázaro Carreter, Fernando. 1949. *Las ideas lingüísticas en España durante el siglo XVIII*. Madrid: Consejo superior de investigaciones científicas.

Martínez Alcalde, Mª José. 1992. *Las ideas lingüísticas de Gregorio Mayans*. (= Publicaciones del Ayuntamiento de Oliva, 21.) Valencia: Ayuntamiento de Oliva.

Mayáns y Siscar, Gregorio. 1737. *Orígenes de la lengua española, compuestos por varios autores recogidos por Don Gregorio Mayáns i Siscár*. Madrid: Juan de Zúñiga.

Meier, Harri. 1936. "Spanische Sprachbetrachtung und Geschichtsschreibung am Ende des 15. Jahrhunderts". *RF* 49. 1−20.

−. 1964−65. "Zur Geschichte der romanischen Etymologie". *ASNS* 201. 81−109.

Molina Redondo, José Andrés de. 1968. "Ideas lingüísticas de Bernardo Aldrete". *RFE* 51. 183−207.

Muñoz y Manzano, Cipriano, Conde de la Viñaza. 1893. *Biblioteca histórica de la Filología Castellana*. Madrid: Manuel Tello. (Reimpresión Madrid: Atlas, 1978.)

Nebrija 1492 → Quilis 1984.

Niederehe, Hans-Josef. 1994. *Bibliografía cronológica de la lingüística, la gramática y la lexicografía del español (BICRES). Desde los comienzos hasta el año 1600*. Amsterdam & Philadelphia: Benjamins.

Padley, Arthur. 1988. *Grammatical Theory in Western Europe 1500−1700. Trends in vernacular grammar II*. Cambridge: Cambridge Univ. Press.

Pensado, José. 1960. *Fray Martín Sarmiento: sus ideas lingüísticas*. (= Cuadernos de la cátedra Feijóo, Nr. 8) Oviedo.

−. 1974. *Opúsculos lingüísticos gallegos del siglo XVIII*. Edición y estudio de J. Pensado. Burgos: Editorial Galaxia.

Quilis, Antonio, Hg. Antonio de Nebrija. 1984 [1492]. *Gramática de la lengua Castellana. Estudio y edición crítica*. Madrid: Editora Nacional.

Río, Ángel del. 1943. "Los Estudios de Jovellanos, sobre el dialecto de Asturias". *RFH* 5. 209–243.

Rosal, Francisco del. 1992 [1601]. *Diccionario etimológico: Alfabeto primero de Origen y etimología de todos los vocablos originales de la Lengua Castellana.* Edición facsimilar y estudio de E. Gómez Aguado. Madrid: Consejo Superior de Investigaciones Científicas.

Sarmiento, Ramón, Hg. 1984. *Real Academia Española. Gramática de la Lengua Castellana. 1771.* Madrid: Editora Nacional.

Schlemmer, Gerd. 1983. *Die Rolle des germanischen Substrats in der Geschichte der romanischen Sprachwissenschaft.* Hamburg: Buske.

Valdés, Juan de. 1928 [c. 1535]. *Diálogo de la Lengua.* Edición y notas por José F. Montesinos. Madrid: Espasa-Calpe.

Wagner, Léon. 1950–51. "Contribution à la préhistoire du romanisme". *Conférences de l'Institut de Linguistique de l'Université de Paris* 10. 101–124.

Wunderli, Peter & Petra Braselmann. 1980. "Positions dialectiques chez Bernardo José de Aldrete". *RRL* 25: 4. 437–453.

Zubiaur Bilbao, José Ramon. 1989. *Las ideas lingüísticas vascas en el siglo XVI (Zaldibia, Garibay, Poza).* San Sebastian: Cuadernos Universitarios & Mundaiz.

Werner Bahner, Leipzig (Deutschland)

146. Early dialectology, etymology and language history in German-speaking countries

In memory of Paul Salmon (1921–1997)

1. Introduction
2. The origin of the German language
3. German after Babel
4. Germano-Celtic and its relationship with other languages
5. Relationships within the Germanic family
6. The periodisation of German language history
7. Towards an understanding of German dialects
8. Etymological speculation
9. Conclusion
10. Bibliography

1. Introduction

We focus on a sequence of themes treated by linguists specialising in German, and by specialists in other languages who proved influential in the study of German, mainly within the period 1500–1770. In many of our sources, observations are set within a linguistic framework; but isolated comments elsewhere (e.g. in historical, philosophical and religious works) also prove to be of value.

2. The origin of the German language

"Die ebräische Sprache", remarked Martin Luther, "[...] bettelt nicht, hat ihre eigene Farbe. Die Griechen, Lateinische und Deutsche betteln" (WA, *Tischreden*, vol. I: 1040). Most sources from Theodor Bibliander (1548) onwards saw German as a derivative of Hebrew, itself descended from or identical with the speech of Adam. Exceptionally, the so-called "Upper Rhenish Revolutionary" (ca. 1500: 38b) even claimed Scriptural proof for a German-speaking Adam: "wan Adam ist ein tusch man gewesen. [...] In der arche Noe was nit mer denn Adam sproch, das was Tusch". Others asserted that German had originated with Alexander, Trebeta of Babylon, or the Trojans (Garber 1989). The originality of Hebrew was itself questioned by Philipp Clüver (1616: I, 74) and earlier by the Antwerp doctor Johannes Goropius Becanus, who instead proposed "Scytho-Cimbrian" (Low German/Dutch) for this role (1580: 204), but in general these opinions were cited dismissively, and the orthodox view prevailed, placing German in a derivative, but still dignified, position: Justus Georg Schottelius defined its origin from deep principles, as the union of God and Nature at Babel (1663: 1003).

Later we still find occasional attempts to locate for German a birthplace before Babel, for example in Armenia (Jäger 1686: 10); and Hebrew was increasingly relegated to a post-Paradisal era, making it the sibling of Greek, Latin and German. Daniel Georg Morhof (1682: 4–6) observed, under influence from the Swedish scholar Georg Stiernhielm

(1598−1672), that the primal idiom was probably extinct, but was reflected in surviving languages, among which Hebrew and Scythian-Celtic-German were two sisters (Metcalf 1974, Blume 1978, Brough 1985: 96−98). According to Jakob Friedrich Reimmann (1709: 34, 45), most scholars still regarded Hebrew as the oldest language, but rival claimants were Greek, Ethiopian, Syrian and Cimbrian-Dutch; or possibly the primeval language was extinct. Leibniz implicitly removed Hebrew from her role as universal mother, and placed German cautiously near the origin; he saw an original language splitting into two branches, "Aramaic" (Hebrew-Syrian-Chaldean-Arabic) and Japhetic (or Celto-Scythian) (1717: 283; Schulenburg 1973: 69 ff., 87). Johann Michael Heppius (1697) deduced twelve languages from a Scytho-Celtic matrix. Johann Augustin Egenolff contended that Japheth, who spoke Scythian, Celtic or Gothic, was absent from Babel, and thus the German branch had remained closest to the original (1735/20: I, 79 ff., 115 ff.). In such diverse ways, the origin of German remained a field for uncontrolled speculation, only later giving way to deeper issues of language origin (Herder) and comparativism (Adelung, Grimm).

3. German after Babel

According to Christoph Besold (1619: 47), the confusion of tongues at Babel involved "litterarum radicalium inversionem, transpositionem, literevè radicalis additionem, aut ablationem, vocaliumque immutationem, &c.". Scholars agreed that after Babel all languages became subject to extralinguistic causality (e. g. climate, ethnic mixture, war, political patronage, religion, and the cultivation or neglect of letters). The available diachronic models could accommodate progress and decline, but most German analyses gravitated towards the latter: antiquity implied excellence, and modernity its debasement; lexical admixture was a negation of the language's legitimacy, as founded in Scriptural and Classical authority.

Language history was further contingent upon tribal or national history. From the 16th century, the Germani were seen as descendants of Ascenas/Ashkenaz, son of Gomer, son of Japheth, son of Noah (I Mos. 10) (Metcalf 1953; Gardt 1994: 349−352). After Ashkenaz, non-Biblical legitimation was facilitated by the 15th century re-discovery of Tacitus's *Germania* (Brough 1985: 26 f.), whence the God Tuisto, his son Mannus, and Mannus's three sons, progenitors of the Ingaevones, Herminones, and Istaevones. Long influential in the German tradition was Aventinus (Johannes Turmair), exploiting a spurious text attributed to a Chaldean astrologer-priest Berosus and published by Joannes Annius (Giovanni Nanni) (1512) (Borst 1957−63: 975 ff.). According to Aventinus (1533), Tuitsch (o)/Tuisco (n) was father of the Germans, Danes and Wends; a son or grandson of Noah, his brothers included Gomer (father of Ascanius/Asch/Ashkenast). Wolfgang Lazius made Tuisco Noah's son, conjecturing that the Ascanian dynasty in Saxony was named from this source (1557: 16−19). On Aventinus's authority, the head of the 17th-century Fruchtbringende Gesellschaft, Ludwig von Anhalt-Köthen, was moved to assert a place for German alongside Hebrew, "weill König Deutsch Zu Abrahams Zeiten gelebett" (Krause 1855: 258).

The destruction of such myths by 18th-century historiographers is a study in paradigm shift. Burckhard Gotthelf Struve found the Berosian material incompatible with Scripture and reason (1716: 2−3): for him, the origin of the Germani lay not in Tuisco, Biblical Togarma, Hercules Aegyptius, Troy, Sarmatia, Scandinavia, nor in Gaul; nor (despite Tacitus) were the Germani indigenous, but of Asian, probably Scythian, origin (Metcalf 1974; Gardt 1994: 358−359). Alongside these advances, however, older notions persisted: articles *Teut* and *Teutsch(e)* in Zedler's *Universal-Lexicon* conflate centuries of speculation (1732−52: XLII, 1658 ff.), including fantasies such as the Japhetic descent of the Germani, and the identification of Teut/Tuisco with Adam. From the 1680s, however, other evolutionary models were being applied to German. Languages were recognised as tending to diversify into dialects, and then into mutually unintelligible languages (Harsdörffer 1646: 35 f.). Building on this insight, Jäger (1686: 25) invoked in memorable metaphor the life cycle of language. Defying Scriptural testimony, Hermann von der Hardt claimed (1696) in a letter to Leibniz that as many dialects existed before as after the Flood. The pace of change was variously judged, cataclysmic assumptions ceding to gradual developments (Morhof 1682: 12 ff., citing Stiernhielm). Johann Georg Wachter proposed an interlude after Babel within which differentiation had occurred (Wachter 1727: a4v−a5r).

"Nam natura non facit saltum, neque in locorum intervallis, neque in tempore, neque in ulla alia re: [...]. Itaque ex una & primitiva Lingua [...] suscitatæ sunt primo variæ *dialecti* [...] Dialecti paulatim abierunt in *linguas* [...]. Hunc enim Natura continuo servavit ordinem & quasi Legem in novis Sermonibus producendis [...]".

From the act of God, interest had shifted to a study of natural, quasi-legal processes: "non magis in Etymologiis, quam in Genealogiis admittendi facilè sunt saltus", wrote Leibniz (Schulenburg 1973: 62). Dominant paradigms were changing, with impulses from Scandinavian scholars, data from an increasing range of languages to a greater time-depth, the occasional willingness to question Scripture, and the insights of Leibniz, Ludolf and Hardt.

4. Germano-Celtic and its relationship with other languages

On the idea of an ancient Germano-Celtic unity, Konrad Gesner (1555) reported diversity of opinion, some, like Beatus Rhenanus, denying any relationship between Gallic and Germanic, and others (Aegidius Tschudi, Henricus Glareanus) confident that the Gauls spoke Germanic. The latter hypothesis passed into the mainstream of 17th-century German-language historiography: attaching German to an ancient lineage, it provided a territorially far-flung history, and conveniently undercut the position of French. Schottelius thus grandly traced from Babel via Ascenas an ancestral language 'not unjustly called Celtic", which diversified into dialects, but with its essential continuity unbroken across three millennia (1663: 42, 126, 129, 151−152). Attempts to define the relationship between Germano-Celtic and other languages were often driven by a need to legitimise German, but a fundamental problem was how to differentiate loans, linear inheritance, and descent from a common ancestor; models were also cramped by the inadequate chronology afforded by Scripture.

We find early reference to distant relationships, for example with Scythian, Slavonic, Hungarian and Illyrian (Gesner 1555). Johann Konrad Wack (1713) even derived Bavarian from Syrian, and German (with Saxon, Scythian, Swedish, Gothic and Wendish) from Celtic-Chaldean. With most scholars focusing on primacy rather than cognateness, confused by the many strata of secondary loans, and giving insufficient weight to the evidence of inflectional morphology, key comparative insights continued to be missed, or remained unsystematised. But there were exceptions. Scythian as a hypothetical European proto-language had been advanced by the Dutch scholar Marcus Zuerius Boxhorn (1612−1653). Recognising that German, Latin, Greek and Persian shared 'innumerable words', he posited a common source, using the name of a people documented from Herodotus. The Scythian hypothesis gained a following from the 1680s, for example Stiernhielm, Morhof and Jäger (Brough 1985: 134−140). Though generally cautious in assuming historical descent, and preferring observable comparisons, Leibniz favoured the conjecture, seeing Greek and Teutonic as flowing from a common Scythian source, and the Scythians as originating from near the Black Sea and migrating to Greece, Germany and Gaul (Bonfante 1953, Waterman 1963, Schulenburg 1973, Hoenigswald 1990, Robins 1990). More boldly in an early comparativist insight, Hiob Ludolf observed (1692) that sets such as Greek *kéras*, Latin *cornu* and German *Horn* were "cognati et agnati non descendentes a se invicem, neque pro extraneis, sed pro propinquis ex communi stipite descendentibus habendi" (Schulenburg 1973: 42−43).

Most sensitive were the relations of Germano-Celtic with the three sacred languages Hebrew, Greek and Latin, and with the Romance vernaculars French, Italian and Spanish. Joseph Justus Scaliger gave a welcome lead in promoting Germanic as a major matrix language (alongside Latin, Greek and Slavonic), though he repudiated any genetic links between the four (1610: 117−122). Greek-German and Latin-German correspondences repeatedly attracted attention (Bonfante 1953: 687−689, Metcalf 1974, Gardt 1994: 354−357). In the wayward view of the Revolutionary (ca. 1500), Latin was not descended from Babel, but was an artefact constructed by a certain Greek, Latinus, at the bidding of the Germans, to enable Romance peoples to understand one another (51b). More widely from 1600 the Classical languages ceased to be seen merely as donors, and despite the loans received from them German was sometimes given historical precedence (Zesen 1651b: 9, 168, 210). Founding his entire linguistic opus on the cardinal status of German, Schottelius scorned attempts to prove its derivative nature, as in the language harmonies of Andreas Helvigius (1611) and Georg Cruciger (1616). Indeed, seeing its irreplaceable roots under attack, Schottelius inventorised and glossed nearly 5,000 of them. He was not alone in seeing Latin as the offspring of Germano-Celtic and Greek, or as a dialect of Germano-Celtic, which thus became a universal donor (Schottelius 1663: 37−40, 139−143; Metcalf 1953; Rössing-Hager 1985: 1566; Gardt 1994: 357f.). Notable among other attempts to portray Latin as a recipient was a lexicon by the Swiss linguist Johann Jakob Redinger, "In welchem [...] gewisen wird / wie die Latinishe Sprach us der Tütshen geflossen" (1656). Johann Ludwig Prasch saw Germanic as the mother of Latin (1686: 3−4), whilst for Leibniz Latin probably stemmed from the sisters Greek and Celtic-Germanic (Schulenburg 1973: 76, 94f.).

If Latin was secondary, Romance vernaculars stood even lower in the genealogy, as "illegitimas Latinæ filias" (Schottelius 1663: 24). Germanic material was known to have reached them by borrowing, as well as through supposed genetic inheritance: corruption of Latin by Goths is a familiar theme from Luther, Gesner and Lazius. Wolfgang Hunger, whose etymological acumen was admired by Schottelius and Eckhart, demonstrated (1586) word by word that the non-Latin element in French was mainly of Germanic origin, and that German as a donor merited attention across Europe. A similar motive inspired lists of Romance-German correspondences from Besold (1619) onwards. Treatment of lexical borrowing sheds interesting light on the evolving character of German language historiography: Bibliander had given objective attention to processes of formal change (1548: 160−168), but in 17th-century reactions the transfers from Latin, French and Italian were seen as corroding language, morals and minds, and betraying a language genetically superior to its donors. Later a more scientific approach prevailed, with growing historical awareness and attempts to explore political and social causes, processes of interference, and sociolinguistic mechanisms (Eckhart 1711: 112−122; Leibniz 1717: 268; Egenolff 1735/20: II, 285).

On fundamental genetic questions, hypotheses long flourished. Johann Bödiker (1690) considered that the 72 languages emerging from Babel were not "Hauptsprachen" but dialects; and of "Hauptsprachen" only three existed, Hebrew and its descendants Celtic-German and Slavonic. Leibniz operated with an elastic concept of Japhetic (or Celtic-Scythian) which embraced not only as true relatives Slavonic, Greek, Celtic-Germanic and (from a mixture of the last two) Latin, but also other languages exhibiting similarities, including some from the Baltic, Finno-Ugrian and Turco-Tartaric groups (Schulenburg 1973: 92ff.). Citing supposed correspondences in lexis, morphology and syntax, Georg Leopold Ponat cursorily explored the relationship of German to Persian, Ethiopian, Greek, Latin, Italian, French and English; stressing the pedagogic value of similarities, he called for *Lexica harmonica* in all languages (1713: 91−2, 131).

Further work settled to a more restrained pattern. Revising Bödiker in 1723, Johann Leonhard Frisch interestingly cut the entire section on Babel and language origin, instead itemising as a related set Greek, Latin and the Romance languages, Slavonic and "Teutsch" (including Dutch, Swedish, Danish, Icelandic, English), with some resemblances noted also in Celtic and Baltic languages (Diedrichs 1983: 93ff.). In Johann Christoph Gottsched's synthesis (1762: 189ff.) Latin was a product of Greek and Gaulish; Italian and French had received lexis from Goths, Burgundians, Langobards and Franks; and German had drawn words from Greek, Latin, Italian and French. Citing Simon Pelloutier (*Histoires des Celtes*, 1750) and older authorities, Gottsched concluded that all European languages shared a Celtic-Scythian origin.

5. Relationships within the Germanic family

Exploration of relationships within the Germanic family was better informed, through textual data which was coming to light. Tacitus's tripartite division underlay linguistic thinking but was never easily convertible into precise filiations. Most sensitive was the issue of Germanic unity/diversity, with commentators from Beatus Rhenanus and Lazius emphasizing now one aspect, now the other: Danish, English, Swedish and Scots are all "im Grunde Teutsch" (Schottelius 1663: 33); "alia in ramis, in radice eadem" (Jäger 1686: 25). Whilst recognising emergent national identities, linguists were loth to disregard theorising and discovery in cognate languages: the relics of Gothic (Busbecq, Vulcanius, Junius), antiquarian research and speculation in Scandinavia (Stiernhielm, Rudbeck), runic inscriptions (Worm), Anglo-Saxon scholarship (Junius, Skinner, Hickes) and the boldly Germanocentric historiography of Flemish-Dutch scholars (Goropius, Scrieckius). There was obvious advantage if German, increasingly invested with knowledge of its own linguistic monuments, could stand as major representative of a diasystem, the roots of which stretched much further back than the modern rivals French, Spanish and Italian. For a language in need of restoration, vast lexical resources were there to be tapped, since other Germanic languages preserved material lost to the German branch.

From about 1600 we encounter inventories of Germanic languages, inspired by older lists of tribes and peoples. Hieronymus Megiser's catalogue (1603) (Rössing-Hager 1985: 1587) contains interesting features, including the separation of Danish, Norwegian and Swedish, and the inclusion of Scots alongside English. The "Helvetic" language is seen as closest to ancient Germanic; apart from a mention of Westphalian, "Saxon or Low German" is defined on a Flemish-Dutch-Frisian basis. Schottelius's array (1663: 154) is more overtly hierarchical. He distinguishes between High and Low German dialects (now including "Preusisch" and "Liefländisch"), and these rank higher than the "abstimmige Sprachen" (Icelandic, Norwegian, Danish, Swedish, English, Scottish, Welsh and Gothic). In Schottelius's view, Germano-Celtic unity is still demonstrable from minor parts of speech and lexical roots, but fractured in the "dissonant" branch by changes in pronunciation, other kinds of "mutilation", and an influx of alien words (Gardt 1994: 353 f.). "Niederdeutsch" as a term was often extensible across Holland, Brabant and Flanders, as well as northern Germany, and Schottelius was not alone in pursuing an inclusive policy with regard to Dutch, by 1650 a flourishing national language. Leibniz too valued its proximity to High German, its potential in lexical suppletion, and the efforts made to enhance its status (1717: 273, 294–295).

The positioning of Gothic was crucial, even if at first only vaguely as a bridge between Old Testament patriarchs and Germanic pre-history (Brough 1985: 88–100, 133–140). Schottelius's knowledge of Gothic rested insecurely on Busbecq's 16th-century Crimean data (1663: 132 f.). Morhof (1682), with much more Gothic material available, venerated what he saw as the monosyllabism of its lexis, and identified it with the earliest stage of German. Understanding of affiliations slowly deepened and became more data-oriented, though political issues continued to colour debate. As open-minded a scholar as Morhof had difficulty in accepting the exclusive claims made for Swedish by Olof Rudbeck (*Atlantica*, 1679–1702). Leibniz saw the North Germanic antiquities rather as "belonging to us", and was particularly respectful of conservative Icelandic. Recognising the rift between Gothic and North Germanic, he inferred the existence of a proto-Germanic language, originating on the Baltic coast; from this had descended the "sisters" Gothic, Frankish and Saxon. Given the great antiquity of Germanic, he voiced the pressing need for an etymological dictionary (1717: 280–282), for which he was himself collecting (Schulenburg 1973: 108 ff., 225 ff.). More detailed again was Wachter's attempt to trace reflexes of Tacitus's tribal groups: "ab Ingevonibus habemus Linguam *Anglo-Saxonicam*, ab Istævonibus *Gothicam*, ab Herminvonibus *Francicam* & *Alamannicam*." Wachter saw Alemannic and Frankish as the "newest" dialects, with modern German their "verissima Filia", and Anglo-Saxon the fecund mother of English, Dutch, Norwegian, Icelandic, Danish and Swedish (1727: c4r ff., d6r).

6. The periodisation of German language history

Using Biblical and other data, Johannes Clajus set the antiquity of German at 3,784 years (1578: 2v ff.), an assumption which was to dominate language chronology for most of our period. As landmarks, scholars cited Tacitus's *Germania*, Charlemagne's German grammar, the legal use of German under Rudolf I (1218–1291), the patronage of Maximilian I (1459–1519), the development of printing, and the role attributed to Luther as linguistic reformer and purifier. Schottelius characterised five epochs or "Denkzeiten" (Rössing-Hager 1985: 1588 f.): (I) from origins to 800 AD; (II) 800–1250; (III) 1250–1500; (IV) 1500 to the present. A fifth and last "Denkzeit" lay for him in the future, when corrupting foreign influences would be removed and German restored to pristine purity and order (1663: 48 f.). Most of this periodisation reappeared, for example in Reimmann (1709: 10), who demarcated only four ages, the last running from 1500 to the present. Egenolff (1735/20 II: 149) assumed major linguistic changes every 300–400 years, though he made no use of linguistically defining features.

For Schottelius, German language history remained open-ended. Johann Christoph Gottsched took an opposing view (1762: 14–19), feeling that German of his day had attained a plateau of perfection which should be held indefinitely, arresting the diachronic process. Such classicising hopes did not survive the iconoclasm of Johann Gottfried Herder and the "Sturm und Drang". Herder's concept of language history with its three phases (poetic, prosaic, philosophical) operated historically to a depth well beyond Scriptural limits, and rejected the language of the Enlightenment in favour of older sources of vitality, including dialect and medieval literature: "the irruption of historicity into linguistic thought on the eve of the Revolution" (von Polenz 1994: 330–331).

7. Towards a understanding of German dialects

Impressionistic observation of dialect differences is found in German from medieval times. Among Humanist scholars, Beatus Rhenanus (1531) felt that High German dialects were 'rougher' than Low German, whilst Gesner (1555) was sensitive to Swiss-Swabian contrasts (Rössing-Hager 1985: 1575, 1581). Megiser's catalogue (1603) included specific references to the dialect enclave of Gottschee (Kočevje), also to a "common German", distinct from Upper German, East Frankish and Silesian, and widely current in Speyer, Augsburg, Strasbourg, Frankfurt and Cologne. Schottelius (1663: 152, 157) identified High German consonantism as the product of secondary development:

"wie dieselbe [...] sich des zz / tz / ß / an stat des t / oder d / [...] haben angefangen sich zubedienen / [...] da hergegen die alten Sachsen jhre alte rechte Ausrede / Ausspruch und Andeutung der Wörter behalten."

Himself a native speaker of Low German, Schottelius was caught between admiration for a consonantally conservative and etymologically valuable dialect, and an awareness that prestige and currency precluded any choice but High German: "unser männliches atticissirendes Tau muß allenthalben der sigmatisirenden Sprache weichen". Far from being fostered, dialect was subordinated in Schottelius's programme to the judgement of the learned: in ancient Greece, as Gesner had written (1555: 466), "illa communis putabatur, quam viri sapientes usurpabant"; and true German in its "Grundrichtigkeit" did not equal any existing variety in Schottelius's view, but was there to be sought as a supraregional, panchronic abstraction. The main linguistic thrust of the period was towards the establishment of a German standard, with dialectism culturally and sociolinguistically stigmatised. Yet a growing respect for dialects can also be traced. Schottelius's dictionary itself contained over 250 specifically Low German roots (more than 5 % of the total). Johannes Clauberg observed (1663, repr. Eckhart 1711) that dialects and antiquities could yield much of relevance to the origins of German. Distinctive again, underpinning his pioneering collection of Bavarian dialecticisms, was the view of Prasch (1686, 1689): words of Latin appearance, if current among rustics, are Germanic; and there are many such survivals in humble and remote places, where ancient Germania lies hidden like a residue of primeval gold. Working for the improvement of German, Leibniz likewise urged contemporaries to seek words, not only in High German, "sondern auch auff Plat-Teutsch, Märckisch, Ober-Sächsisch, Fränkisch, Bäyrisch, Oesterreichisch, Schwäbisch" and elsewhere (1717: 273). Dialects could always command respect: from Classical and Renaissance precedent (Attic Greek, Dante's Tuscan) and from recent example (Dutch), they were seen as potential bases for the establishment of languages (Zesen 1651b: 204); a case for Swiss German is explored by Bodmer & Breitinger (1746 II, 626–627). Even for Johann Christoph Adelung, belatedly standardising German on a high social variant, dialects could fill gaps in his semantic "ladders" (Reichmann 1993: 305).

8. Etymological speculation

Schottelius inherited a concept of *etymologia* as that part of grammar dealing with "the origins, nature, inflections, derivations and compounds" of words (1663: 181) (on the tradition, see Koerner 1995: 33). Our period already saw a strengthening of the diachronic component. Speculation was driven by historical enquiry and a search for underlying unity, but sometimes also by a desire to show that the German word was historically prior, or that its form might be perfected by understanding its genesis. Primarily at stake was the recognition of borrowing between *known* languages. Generalised etymological procedures were rarely made explicit. In the tradition of Quintilian, linguists from Bibliander (1548) to Gottsched (1762) used *additio, detractio, transpositio, permutatio* (occasionally with refinements) to cover phonological change, but essential instruments and controls (lexicographical coverage, genetic frameworks, models of linguistic change) were weak and uncertain. For a deeper understanding, we should do more than simply measure what retrospectively appears as the etymological success rate; but it is sometimes hard not to be judgmental, in what have been called the "dark ages of etymology" (Papp 1985).

Speculation was rife with key Germanic appellatives. According to the Revolutionary (ca. 1500) "hessen wier Tuschen in ollen sprochen Almans, wan for der zerstorung was Tusch alman sproch" (33b). *Alemanni* and *Germani* were taken as implying manly virtues: "Almanni [...] all mann / vnnd Germani [...] gar mann" (Franck 1539: 304 v). By association with *Heer-mann*, "Germani verò appellantur à fortitudine bellica, prima litera commutata" (Clajus 1578:)(3r). Other historical characteristics emerged: *Gotanen* "gut Ahnen", *Celtae* "Gehelden" (Brough 1985: 46). Schottelius derived *Germanen* from Germano-Celtic *Wehr* (1663: 291–292), and no less tendentiously accepted Gesner's etymology of *Kiev* (*Kuöw* = *Kuh* + *Aue*) (1561) as demonstrating the former extent of German (1663: 132). Debate over the name *deutsch* was predictably active. It was readily associated with the Tacitean *Tuisto*; *Tuiscones* was interpreted as *die* [article] *Ascanes* (Melanchthon 1538 in Schardius 1673: I, 77), and *de Askenas* (Clajus 1578:)(2v ff.). Schottelius (1663: 35–36) identified *Teut* with an Egyptian god, whence also Greek *deus, zeus, theos*, Latin *deus*, and the base *Diet-* in Germanic names (Kästner 1991; Gardt 1994: 350–351; 361–364).

17th-century etymological practice can be further illustrated with reference to selected figures. Georg Cruciger's *Harmonia* (1616) is a typographically ingenious, extensive and detailed attempt to display the formal interrelationships of Hebrew, Greek, Latin and German lexis, though the imprecision of his method, and his relegation of German to secondary status, found no favour with Schottelius or Eckhart. Tracing affinities between German and Latin, Redinger assumed that letters had emerged from Babel as "pura, commutata, addita, detracta, transjecta" or "inversa", and that they formed related sets: *b-p-f-ph-w*; *h-j-g-k-q-x*; *d-t-s-st-sch-z*; *l-m-n-r* (1659: 13 f.). A case apart is Zesen (1651b: A6r, 91 ff., 145 ff.), for whom words were the motivated product of sound symbolism and onomatopoeic creation, originating with Adam under the guidance of Nature (a "semanticisation of the phoneme", Blume 1978). Describing *a, e, u, o* and *b, d, l, s* as the original vowels and consonants, Zesen correlated them with water, earth, air and fire respectively, citing *Erde*, *Luft* and the root *-aa-* in German hydronyms, but also *Apollo* (*Ab* + *bolle* "waterball") and other fantasies. The sound *i* was a later development, invented to distinguish meaning; juxtaposed, *a* and *o* conflicted violently like water and fire, whilst *e* and *u* assumed a mediating function. Zesen identified as "flowing consonants" *l* and its derivatives *m, n*, and *r*. He presented a scale of "hardness", from *b* (the softest sound) through *v, p, f*, to *p*, all of which are "related by blood" (112). Further examples of Zesen's etymology may be cited: the convincing set *Geld, Gold, entgelten, gültig*; but also *West < gewest* "been", and *Bal(l) > Welt* (25, 175, 185). Having encountered fierce opposition in advocating the replacement of *Fenster* as a borrowing from Latin, he opportunistically reversed his argument (1651a: 75), deriving *Fenster* from German *fein*, whence also, he states, Latin *fenestra*.

Seeking in general to determine the direction of transferences, Schottelius concluded (1663: 143) that words originate only where there is "true cause". Proceeding from the concept of the primitive root, he defined prescriptively for German a threefold principle of segmentation and synthesis: a well-formed word consisted of stem (or root), derivational ending, and inflectional ending; elements might also be combined in derivatives and compounds, a mechanism of infinite expressive power (1663: 1247). Within the same paradigm, a fascinating creative and analytical tool was Georg Philipp Harsdörffer's "Fünffacher Denckring", consisting of five concentric rings: (I) 49 prefixes, (II) 60 initial clusters, (III) 12 vowels, (IV) 120 final clusters, (V) 24 inflectional and derivational suffixes (Gardt 1994: 207—208). Allowing for null positions on rings I and V, the device offers 108,000,000 permutations: "die gantze Deutsche Sprache auf einem Blätlein".

The Cartesian philosopher Johannes Clauberg was to win Leibniz's (qualified) admiration for his attempt to rationalise etymological method. Though seeing German as a sister or grand-daughter of Latin, and by no means sure-footed in his own etymologies, Clauberg formulated 24 rules (1663, repr. Eckhart 1711), which combine phonological, phonotactic, morphological and semantic observation. Formal resemblances, Clauberg states, are corroborated by semantic fit, though synonyms will not always correspond accurately. Vowels are freely interchangeable, *e* being the commonest in Germanic; 'greater' vowels tend to become 'lesser' ones, but Germans often prefer diphthongs where Greek and Latin have simple vowels. Long vowels compensate for the gemination of consonants, and vice versa. Consonants cannot all be conjoined with equal ease; 'gentle' consonants tend to combine, similarly 'rough' consonants; and Germans incline to the 'stronger' rather than the 'softer' pronunciation.

Another attempt to inject rigour was that of Prasch (1686), with six criteria for recognition of Germanic lexis: words considered barbarous in Classical Rome; names of objects native to or originating with Germani or Celts; words with demonstrable Germanic base forms; words common to all or most Germanic peoples; words used in remote regions; and words of Latin appearance if current among countryfolk. Prasch noted German-Latin resemblances in terminations (*pater—Vater*), also in comparative and superlative formation, verb conjugation and syntax. On differences between Bavarian and other varieties, he observed that letters had to be added, removed, murmured, transferred, exchanged, softened or roughened (1689: 15).

Planning the German etymological dictionary proposed by Leibniz, Eckhart set much store by the principles of Clauberg and Prasch (1711: 323 ff.), whilst Leibniz himself offered a foretaste of such a work, commenting that there was "nothing random in the world except to us in our ignorance" (1717: 282 f.). Proceeding from German *Welt*, earlier *werelt*, Leibniz cites as formally and semantically related *wirren*, *werre*, English *wire* and Greek *gyrus*, with the gloss "was in die Runde herum sich ziehet". He again finds the root *w* (implying motion) in German *wehen*, *Wind*, *Waage*, *Wogen*, *Wellen*, *Wirbel*, *Gewerrel*, *Querl*, *bewegen*, *winden*, *wenden*, *Welle*, *Waltze*, *Wild*, *Wald*, English *wheel*, French *vis*, Latin *volvo*, *verto*, *vortex*, and the names *Walen* and *Wallonen*. Characteristically, however, he is not yet willing to exclude an alternative derivation of *Werelt* from *währen*. Leibniz argued that the roots of a language are inaccessible from that language alone. Realising that borrowing was endemic to all periods, he felt that Clauberg and Prasch had over-estimated the inherited element in Germanic lexis (Schulenburg 1973: 59 f., 227 ff.).

Further refinement of method is at least implicit in Egenolff's German language history: in identifying roots in cognate languages, words must be semantically related, attention given to sound correspondences and other formal changes, including derivation, and various operations followed (e. g. deletion of affixes, reversal of sound changes undergone during transfer). On this basis, he links, for example, *ut/aus*, *Hut*, *Haus*, *Haut* and *Hütte*; he also recognises the frequency of *t/s* and *u/au* alternations, but without presenting them as historical change (Rössing-Hager 1985: 1600).

Crudely quantifying etymological success rates, Schmidt (1927) ranked Stieler lower than Helvigius, Kramer, Wachter or Frisch. Admittedly, several of Stieler's derivations survive only as curiosities, e. g. *Ader* < *Ahader (where *Aha-* = "water"); *Natur* < *Naht Ur* or *Nah d'Ur*. Yet he also offered in his great dictionary of 1691 (as Sonderegger showed in his reprint) many convincing derivations, e. g. for *Gift*, *Gunst*, *Hefe*, *Heu*, *Kunst*, *Macht* and *Mensch*. The growing list of successful etymological insights could be extended into the 18th century with an examination of Wachter, Frisch, Fulda, Adelung and others. A rise in standards is also seen negatively, for example in the healthy critique of uncontrolled etymologising by Matthias Kramer (1700), who cites as absurdities *Mareschal* < *Mars* + *Schalck*, and *Neckar* < *nekrós* (Gardt 1994: 362).

9. Conclusion

Over a range of themes, our sources show much interaction between commentators and the development of a metalinguistic descriptive resource, in lexis, idiom and imagery. The years 1600–1700 emerge as more than simply a transition from Renaissance to Enlightenment: they exhibit distinctive initiatives, as well as participating in broader continuities. Religious constraints and methodological weaknesses were sometimes recognised and challenged, with strengthening of empirical approaches. The shaping of a national agenda conditioned thought, but the matrix embraced language, ethics and culture, as well as politics. Users of German discovered and profiled their language's origin and identity, enriching it by available means, embracing unity and diversity, demarcating it from contiguous languages, and crystallising perceptions of these with stereotypes, hierarchies and genetic constructs. Before 1600 and decreasingly beyond, most perceptions reflected and developed Classical and Renaissance traditions. With improving communications and immersion in revitalised foreign cultures and languages, the passage of new linguistic ideas was intensified. By the early 18th century, in a process spanning Northern and Central Europe, a distinctive and varied set of positions, old and new, was on offer, including some harbingers of comparativism. "Giebt also die Untersuchung der Teutschen Sprach nicht nur ein Licht vor uns, sondern auch vor gantz Europa", wrote Leibniz (1717: 279), in words destined to achieve their fullest import belatedly, during the 19th century and beyond.

10. Bibliography

10.1. Primary sources

Annius, Ioannes. 1512. *Antiquitatu[m] variaru[m] volumina. XVII.* Paris: Parvus & Badius.

Besold, Christopher. 1619. *De natura populorum, ejusque pro loci positu, temporisq[ue] decursu variatione: Ac insimul etiam, de linguarum ortu et immutatione philologicus discursus.* Tubingæ: Cellius.

Bibliander, Theodor. 1548. *De ratione communi omnium linguarum & literaru[m] commentarius.* Tiguri: Froschauer.

Bödiker, Johann. 1690. *Grund-Sätze Der Deutschen Sprachen im Reden und Schreiben.* Cölln an der Spree: Liebpert.

–. 1746. *Grundsäze Der Teutschen Sprache Mit Dessen eigenen und Johann Leonhard Frischens vollständigen Anmerkungen. Durch neue Zusäze vermehret von Johann Jacob Wippel.* Berlin: Nicolai.

Bodmer, Johann Jakob & Johann Jakob Breitinger. 1746. *Der Mahler der Sitten.* Zürich: Orell.

Cruciger, Georg. 1616. *Harmonia linguarum quatuor cardinalium; Hebraicæ Græcæ Latinæ & Germanicæ.* Francofurti: Bringer & Tampach.

Eckhart, Johann Georg. 1711. *Historia studii etymologici linguae Germanicae hactenus impensi; ubi scriptores plerique recensentur und diiudicantur, qui in origines et antiquitates linguæ Teutonicæ, Saxonicæ, Belgicæ, Danicæ, Suecicæ, Norwegicæ et Islandicæ, veteris item Gothicæ, Francicæ atque Anglo-Saxonicæ inquisiverunt.* Hanoveræ: Förster.

Egenolff, Johann Augustin. 1735/20. *Historie, der Teutschen Sprache.* Leipzig: Martin.

Franck, Sebastian. 1539. *Chronica des gantzen Teütschen lands.* Bern: Apiarius.

Gesner, Conrad. 1555. *Mithridates. De differentiis lingvarum tvm vetervm tum quæ hodie apud diuersas nationes in toto orbe terraru[m] in usu sunt, Conradi Gesneri Tigurini Obseruationes.* Tiguri: Froschauer.

Goropius (Becanus), Ioannes. 1580. *Opera.* Antwerpiae: Plantin.

Gottsched, Johann Christoph. 1762. *Ausgewählte Werke,* hrsg. von P. M. Mitchell. Vol. 8, Parts 1–3: *Deutsche Sprachkunst,* bearbeitet von Herbert Penzl. Berlin & New York: de Gruyter, 1978, 1980.

Harsdörffer, Georg Philipp. 1646. *Specimen philologiæ Germanicæ.* Norimbergæ: Endter.

Helvigius, Andreas. 1611. *Etymologiæ, Sive origines dictionum germanicarum, ex tribus illis nobilibus antiquitatis eruditæ Linguis, Latina, Graeca, Hebraea, derivatarum.* Francofurti: Wolff & Humm.

Heppius, Joannes Michael. 1697. *Parallelismus et convenientia XII linguarum ex matrice Scytho-Celtica.* Wittebergae.

Hunger, Wolfgang. 1586. *Linguae germanicae vindicatio contra exoticas quasdam, quae complurium vocum & dictionum, merè Germanicarum, etymologias, ex sua petere sunt conati.* Argentorati: Jobin.

Jäger, Andreas. 1686. *Diss. philolog. de lingua vetustissima vernacula Europae Scytho-Celtica et Gothica.* Wittenbergae 1686. *Germaniae Litteratae Opuscula* by Johann Oelrichs, 1772–74, vol. II, 1–64. Bremae: Cramer.

Lazius, Wolfgang. 1557. *De gentium aliquot migrationibus.* Basileæ: Oporinus.

Leibniz, Gottfried Wilhelm. 1717. *Illustris viri Godofr. Guilielmi Leibnitii Collectanea etymologica, ilustrationi linguarum, veteris celticæ, germanicæ, gallicæ, aliarumque inservientia. Cum præfatione Jo. Georgii Eccardi.* Hanoveræ: Förster.

Luther, Martin. *Werke. Kritische Gesamtausgabe (Weimarer Ausgabe).* Weimar: Hermann Böhlaus Nachfolger, 1883 ff.

Morhof, Daniel Georg. 1682. *Unterricht Von Der Teutschen Sprache und Poesie / deren Uhrsprung / Fortgang und Lehrsätzen.* Kiel: Reumann.

Ponat, Georg Leopold. 1713. *Anleitung zur Harmonie der Sprachen / in welcher gezeiget wird wie die*

Hebräische / Chaldäische / Syrische / Arabische / Aegyptische und Persische / wie auch die Lateinische / Italiänische / Frantzösische und Englische Sprache / wenn man sie mit der Teutschen / oder mit der Griechischen zusammen hält und vergleichet / in gar kurtzer Zeit / und ohne grosse Mühe / glücklich könne erlernet werden. Braunschweig: Fickel.

Prasch, Johann Ludwig. 1686. *Dissertatio, de origine Germanica Latinæ linguæ.* Ratisbonæ: Hoffmann & Emmerich.

—. 1689. *Dissertatio altera, de origine Germanica Latinæ linguæ.* Ratisbonæ: Hoffmann.

Redinger, Johann Jakob. 1656. *Latinisher Runs der Tütschen Sprachkwäl / Oder: Latinish Tütshes Wortbüchlin: In welchem durch ainen lichten griff / mit etlich hundert bispilen gewisen wird / wie die Latinishe Sprach us der Tütshen geflossen.* Schaffhusen: Suter.

—. 1659. *Verwandschaft Der Teutschen und Lateinischen Sprache.* Hanoviae: Lasché.

Reimmann, Jakob Friedrich. 1709. *Versuch einer Einleitung in die Historiam Literariam Antediluvianam.* Halle: Renger.

Rhenanus, Beatus. 1531. *Rerum germanicarum libri tres.* Basileae: Froben.

Scaliger, Joseph Justus. 1610. *Opuscula varia antehac non edita.* Parisiis: Drouart.

Schottelius, Justus Georg. 1640. *Lamentatio Germaniae exspirantis.* Braunschweig: Gruber.

—. 1641. *Teutsche Sprachkunst.* Braunschweig: Gruber.

—. 1663. *Ausführliche Arbeit von der Teutschen HaubtSprache.* Braunschweig: Zilliger.

Struve, Burckhard Gotthelf. 1716. *Syntagma historiæ Germanicæ a prima gentis origine ad annum usque MDCCXVI.* Ienæ: Bielcke.

Wachter, Johann Georg. 1727. *Glossarium Germanicum continens origines et antiquitates linguæ Germanicæ hodiernæ.* Lipsiæ: Schuster.

Wack, Johann Conrad. 1713. *Kurtze Anzeigung / wie nemlich die uralte Teutsche Sprache Meistentheils Ihren Ursprung aus dem Celtisch- oder Chaldæischen habe / und das Beyrische vom Syrischen herkomme.* Regenspurg: Hagen.

Zedler, Johann Heinrich (publisher). 1732–52. *Grosses vollständiges Universal-Lexicon.* Halle & Leipzig: Zedler.

Zesen, Philipp von. 1651a. *Dichterische Jugend-Flammen.* Hamburg: Naumann.

—. 1651b. *Rosen-mând: das ist in ein und dreissig gesprächen Eröfnete Wunderschacht zum unerschätzlichen Steine der Weisen.* Hamburg: Papen.

10.2. Secondary sources (selected)

Blume, Herbert. 1978. "Sprachtheorie und Sprachenlegitimation im 17. Jahrhundert in Schweden und in Kontinentaleuropa". *Arkiv för Nordisk Filologi* 93. 205–218.

Bonfante, Giuliano. 1953. "Ideas on the Kinship of the European Languages from 1200 to 1800". *Cahiers d'Histoire Mondiale* 1. 679–699.

Borst, Arno. 1957–63. *Der Turmbau von Babel. Geschichte der Meinungen über Ursprung und Vielfalt der Sprachen und Völker.* Stuttgart: Hiersemann.

Brough, Sonia. 1985. *The Goths and the Concept of Gothic in Germany from 1500 to 1750: Culture, language and architecture.* Frankfurt etc.: Lang.

De Mauro, Tullio & Lia Formigari, eds. 1990. *Leibniz, Humboldt, and the Origins of Comparativism.* Amsterdam & Philadelphia: Benjamins.

Diedrichs, Eva Pauline. 1983. *Johann Bödikers Grundsätze der deutschen Sprache. Mit den Bearbeitungen von Johann Leonhard Frisch und Johann Jakob Wippel.* Heidelberg: Winter.

Garber, Jörn. 1989. "Trojaner – Römer – Franken – Deutsche. 'Nationale' Ableitungstheorien im Vorfeld der Nationalstaatsbildung". *Nation und Literatur im Europa der Frühen Neuzeit. Akten des 1. Internationalen Osnabrücker Kongresses zur Kulturgeschichte der Frühen Neuzeit* ed. by Klaus Garber, 108–163. Tübingen: Niemeyer.

Gardt, Andreas. 1994. *Sprachreflexion in Barock und Frühaufklärung: Entwürfe von Böhme bis Leibniz.* Berlin & New York: de Gruyter.

—. 1999. *Geschichte der Sprachwissenschaft in Deutschland: Vom Mittelalter bis ins 20. Jahrhundert.* Berlin & New York: de Gruyter.

Hoenigswald, Henry M. 1990. "Descent, Perfection and the Comparative Method since Leibniz". De Mauro & Formigari 1990. 119–132.

Koerner, Konrad. 1995. *Professing Linguistic Historiography.* Amsterdam & Philadelphia: Benjamins.

Jones, William Jervis. 1993. "König Deutsch zu Abrahams Zeiten: Some perceptions of the place of German within the family of languages from Aventinus to Zedler". *'Das unsichtbare Band der Sprache.' Studies in German Language and Linguistic History in Memory of Leslie Seiffert* ed. by John L. Flood et al., 189–213. Stuttgart: Heinz.

—. 1999. *Images of Language: Six essays on German attitudes to European languages from 1500 to 1800.* Amsterdam & Philadelphia: Benjamins.

Metcalf, George J. 1953. "Schottel and Historical Linguistics". *Germanic Review* 28. 113–125.

—. 1974. "The Indo-European Hypothesis in the 16th and 17th Centuries". *Studies in the History of Linguistics. Traditions and Paradigms* ed. by Dell Hymes, 233–257. Bloomington: Indiana Univ. Press.

Papp, Edgar. 1985. "Grundlagen etymologischer Forschung im 17. und 18. Jahrhundert". Wilfried Kürschner und Rüdiger Vogt (editors), unter Mitwirkung von S. Siebert-Nemann, *Akten des 19. Linguistischen Kolloquiums. Vechta 1984.* Vol. I. 15–22. Tübingen: Niemeyer.

Polenz, Peter von. 1994. *Deutsche Sprachgeschichte vom Spätmittelalter bis zur Gegenwart*. Vol. 2: *17. und 18. Jahrhundert*. Berlin & New York: de Gruyter.

Reichmann, Oskar. 1993. "Dialektale Verschiedenheit: zu ihrer Auffassung und Bewertung im 17. und 18. Jahrhundert". *Vielfalt des Deutschen. Festschrift für Werner Besch* ed. by Klaus J. Mattheier et al., 289–314. Frankfurt/M. etc.: Lang.

Robins, Robert H. 1990. "Leibniz and Wilhelm von Humboldt and the History of Comparative Linguistics". de Mauro & Formigari 1990. 85–102.

Rössing-Hager, Monika. 1985. "Ansätze zu einer deutschen Sprachgeschichtsschreibung vom Humanismus bis ins 18. Jahrhundert". *Sprachgeschichte. Ein Handbuch zur Geschichte der deutschen Sprache und ihrer Erforschung* ed. by Werner Besch, Oskar Reichmann & Stefan Sonderegger, vol. II: 1564–1614. Berlin & New York: de Gruyter.

Schmidt, Arthur. 1927. *Zum Fortschritt der etymologischen Erkenntnis des Deutschen in Wörterbüchern des 17. und 18. Jahrhunderts*. Berlin: Ebering.

Schulenburg, Sigrid von der. 1973. *Leibniz als Sprachforscher*. Mit einem Vorwort hrsg. von Kurt Müller. Frankfurt/M.: Klostermann.

Waterman, John T. 1963. "The Languages of the World: A classification by G. W. Leibniz". *Studies in Germanic Languages and Literatures In Memory of Fred O. Nolte. A collection of essays written by his colleagues and his former students* ed. by Erich Hofacker & Lieselotte Dieckmann, 27–34. St Louis: Washington Univ. Press.

William J. Jones, London (Great Britain)

147. Historical linguistics in the Low Countries: Lambert ten Kate

1. Introduction
2. The life and times of Lambert ten Kate
3. Ten Kate's linguistic works
4. Some methodological aspects
5. Competition, recognition and reception
6. Final remarks
7. Bibliography

1. Introduction

Lambert ten Kate Hermansz (1674–1731) is regarded as one of the greatest and most distinguished Dutch linguists. His reputation as a versatile scholar in the field of comparative historical linguistics has stood the test of time and what is more, it can be demonstrated that at the close of the 20th century the longstanding admiration for his works, in particular his voluminous *Aenleiding tot de kennisse van het verhevene deel der Nederduitsche sprake* [Introduction to the exalted part of the Dutch language] of 1723, is still growing. Whereas ten Kate's achievements enjoyed wide recognition in his native country, in other countries appreciation came late to his linguistic works. They long remained generally unknown in the international literature because they were not written in Latin but in the vernacular, in Dutch, and had never been reprinted. Quite apart from ten Kate's outspoken '*zugt*', his penchant, for the mother tongue, the magnitude of the task of translating such an opus magnum as the *Aenleiding* must have daunted its author.

As a consequence, until recently ten Kate was rarely mentioned in general histories of linguistics unlike his compatriot, the notorious Joannes Goropius Becanus (1519–1573), who published in Latin. Whereas Law (1990: 817) regards ten Kate's "remarkable work on Dutch", the *Aenleiding*, as the "high point" of comparative historical language study in the 18th century, Robins's authoritative *Short History of Linguistics* (1967[1], 1990[3]), for instance, does not refer to ten Kate's insights. The extended 1969 edition of Arens's seminal *Sprachwissenschaft* (1955[1]) provides only a few brief excerpts from ten Kate's works. However, it is only fair to point out here that in ten Kate's home country his work was '*meer geprezen dan gelezen*', i.e. it received much praise, but was little read.

It should not surprise us, then, that a comprehensive study of ten Kate has yet to be published. However, quite a number of monographs and papers are available to the interested reader. Detailed biographical and bibliographical data are given in ten Cate (1987); a bibliography of ten Kate's manuscripts and printed works can be found in van der Hoeven (1896: 169–176) and in ten Cate (1987: 29–89). Raumer's (1870) account of ten Kate's accomplishments as a comparative historical linguist is still useful. Knol (1977) gives an elaborate overview of the study of Dutch in the 18th century, to which de Bonth & Noordegraaf (1996) can be added. Ten Kate's merits for Dutch proper were duly appreciated by de Vooys (1923). A selection of Dutch and English papers on various aspects of ten Kate's works is included in the reference section of this contribution.

2. The life and times of Lambert ten Kate

Lambert ten Kate was born in Amsterdam on 23 January 1674 of Mennonite parents. His father, Herman ten Kate (1644–1706), was a corn merchant. Although Lambert became one of his father's partners in 1696, it seems that he did not like the corn trade very much, and he resigned from business in 1706. Ten Kate nevertheless remained a well-to-do citizen; following his father's death he lived on the ample income provided by the legacies of his parents and stepmother. The widely held opinion that he gave private tuition "in den angesehensten Häusern im Schreiben, Rechnen, Buchhalten und besonders in Geometrie und Algebra" in order to secure "den nöthigen Lebensunterhalt" (Raumer 1870: 139) is probably mistaken (cf. ten Cate 1987: 21–24). Ten Kate remained a bachelor all his life; he died on 14 December 1731 at the age of 57 as a consequence of 'eene slepende ziekte', a lingering disease (ten Cate 1987: 9); six days later he was buried in the Noorderkerk in Amsterdam.

When the German jurist and book collector Zacharias Conrad von Uffenbach (1683–1734) visited Amsterdam early in 1711 he also saw ten Kate's extensive art collection. Ten Kate, he noted, "handelt zwar eigentlich mit Korn, ist aber ein sehr höflicher, curiöser und dabey gelehrter Mann". Ten Kate appears to have been a versatile mind, a self-educated 18th-century 'Privatgelehrter' who was seriously engaged in various fields of both arts and sciences. He wrote, for example, an essay entitled 'Experiment on the division of the colours', imitating an experiment by Newton, and translated theological treatises from the French and the English. Far from being a scholarly recluse he kept in close contact with painters, poets and professors.

One of his older friends was Adriaen Verwer (c. 1655–1717), an Amsterdam Mennonite merchant who had written a Latin-medium grammar of Dutch, *Linguae belgicae grammatica, poetica, rhetorica* (1707[1], 1783[2]), which appeared under the pseudonym Anonymus Batavus (cf. van Driel 1992, 1996 for an introduction to this grammar). It is believed (Jongeneelen 1992: 203; de Bonth & Dibbets 1995: 115) that ten Kate participated in an early 18th-century Amsterdam linguistic circle, whose members included Verwer, ten Kate, and probably also Tiberius Hemsterhuis (1685–1766), professor at the Amsterdam Athenaeum Illustre from 1704 until 1717, and to become not only "the greatest Greek scholar of his time" (Lord Monboddo), but also the founding father of the 'Schola Hemsterhusiana', a group of Dutch classical scholars, consisting of Hemsterhuis and some of his pupils who followed his approach in the study of Greek. In addition to their literary and interpretative work, Hemsterhuis and his students developed their own etymological method of investigating language based on principles of reconstruction (cf. Noordegraaf 1995). As it appears, Hemsterhuis was acquainted with the results of ten Kate's linguistic investigations.

At any rate, it was Adriaen Verwer who encouraged ten Kate to engage himself in the study of Gothic. In the *praefatio* to his grammar, Verwer emphasized that it was of great importance "linguam nostram *ex origine* nosse" (1783 [1707]: viii), to know our language from its origin, and that this had become possible thanks to Franciscus Junius (1589–1677) and his ground-breaking edition of the Gothic *Codex Argenteus* (1665, 1684[2]). Verwer was a proponent of the 'gothica-genetrix' theory according to which Gothic was considered to be the mother of all Germanic languages (cf. Vanderheyden 1957: 666–667). As to the historical study of language ten Kate's achievements have been of much more importance than Verwer's; however, for his linguistic ideas ten Kate owed a lot to his mentor (Knol 1977: 102–103).

Ten Kate, a pious Mennonite, was also a prolific writer on religious matters. In 1732, for instance, his *Leven van onzen Heiland Jezus Christus* [Life of our Lord Jesus Christ] appeared, a voluminous book of some 1000 pages, presenting a harmony of the four gospels. His ideas on esthetics (cf. Prinsen 1936) were received all over Europe as the "discours préliminaire sur le beau idéal des peintres, sculpteurs et poètes" in the third volume of Jonathan Richardson's (1665–1745) *Traité de la peinture* (1728), which had been translated from the English by A. Rutgers "avec l'assistence de Monsieur ten Kate". The "discours", a translation of a Dutch *Verhandeling* written by ten Kate as early as 1720 (cf. Thijm 1869), clearly shows the religious dimensions of ten Kate's esthetics (cf. van Veen 1995).

3. Ten Kate's linguistic works

The year 1699 saw the completion of ten Kate's *Verhandeling over de Klankkunde* [Treatise on phonetics], in which he displayed his knowledge and understanding of the physical factors involved in the production of sound. The text remained unpublished but was revised and incorporated into the two-volume *Aenleiding* (for an extensive discussion of the *Verhandeling* cf. van der Hoeven 1896: 56−168). It has been suggested that the linguistic work of one of his acquaintances, the Haarlem apothecary Jan Trioen (1657−1721), served as a source of inspiration for ten Kate's *Verhandeling* (cf. Jongeneelen 1994). It was in connection with his linguistic investigations that ten Kate paid attention to the study of sounds. He was always keenly aware of the fact that, first and foremost, 'language' meant 'spoken language' (Van de Velde 1966: 212−213).

Inspired by his friend Adriaen Verwer, ten Kate composed his *Gemeenschap tussen de Gottische spraeke en de Nederduytsche* [The Relationship between the Gothic and Dutch languages] (1710). The *Gemeenschap* is a relatively short work of 84 pages which appeared anonymously because the author was uncertain about its reception. In this study, the 'overeenkomst' (conformity) between the Gothic and Dutch languages is 'vertoont' (demonstrated) in a letter, in a list of words, and on the basis of examples of Gothic declensions and conjugations. A thorough analysis of this work is given by Van de Velde 1966: 219−274.

The first part of the booklet consists of a letter to A. V., i.e. Adriaen Verwer, including a postcript (3−20). The second presents an alphabetical list of homonymous words in Dutch and Gothic (20−49). In the third and most important part (50−84) it is shown that the conjugation of verbs in Dutch and Gothic follows the same pattern, an insight which prompted ten Kate to divide the Gothic verbs into six 'classes' (Van der Hoeven 1896: 15−56, Rompelman 1952: 8−15). It is, indeed, in the verbal conjugation system that ten Kate recognized the regularity of vowel alternation, which eventually led him to the discovery of the phenomenon of what Jacob Grimm would later call Ablaut (cf. Polomé 1983b: 169−170).

Ten Kate was "durchdrungen von der Wichtigkeit dieser Entdeckung" (Raumer 1870: 142). Having nearly finished the manuscript of his study on the basis of Junius's *Gothicum Glossarium* he came across George Hicke's (1642−17129 *Linguarum Veterum Septentrionalium Thesaurus* (1705). Ten Kate (1710: 12) immediately noticed that his own treatment of the verbs was far superior to that of his English colleague, in particular with regard to the "unevenly flowing verbs", the strong verbs. All in all, the *Gemeenschap* includes a concise grammar of Gothic, which, on account of its systematicity, improved on Hicke's Gothic grammar (Van de Velde 1966: 272−274). Moreover, ten Kate drew interesting conclusions concerning the relationship between Germanic and other European languages, especially that between Gothic and Dutch, elegantly rejecting, for instance, the gothica-genetrix theory. Another of his discoveries was the identification of root stress as a defining characteristic of all Germanic languages (1710: 14; cf. Jongeneelen 1992: 214, n. 9). In all respects ten Kate's *Gemeenschap* has proved to be more valuable and more fruitful than the work of his English predecessor, Hickes (Van de Velde 1996: 274).

The years 1710−1723 saw the full development of these and other observations into the main body of ten Kate's *Aenleiding tot de kennisse van het verhevene deel der Nederduitsche sprake* of 1723. Among other matters, the classification of the Gothic verbs as presented in 1710, as elaborated here and applied to all the Germanic languages he knew. The *Aenleiding* consists of two volumes, each of approximately 750 pages, presenting the first historical grammar of Dutch, the concepts 'historical', 'grammar', and 'Dutch' being understood in a very broad sense (Rompelman 1952: 15−16). Note that this work originated and grew in ten Kate's interleaved copy of he 1642 edition of an important Dutch dictionary, the *Kilianus Auctus sive Dictionarium Teutonico-Latino-Gallicum*, in which, from 1712 onwards, ten Kate wrote his extensive notes on conceptions of language and etymological explanations.

The first volume includes a highly informative preface (reprinted both in Meinsma 1981b and de Bonth & Dibbets 1995: 121−155), which outlines the book and gives its contents. The book is, for the greater part, written in the form of 14 dialogues between N. (Adriaen Verwer) and L. (Lambert ten Kate), in which they discuss, among many other things, the importance of linguistics, the dispersion of languages in Europe, speech sounds, and the declensions and conjugations of Dutch. Besides eight appendices covering rather varied material one finds a fundamental essay (542−696) presenting a full comparative description of the irregular verb systems of Dutch (cf. de Bonth 1996: 120−122), Gothic, Old High German, Anglo-Saxon, New High German, and Icelandic. Ten Kate presented irrefutable proof that these verbs, far from representing an erratic type of conjugation, were subject to rules that obtained not only in Gothic, but were valid for all branches of Germanic. "Die Durchführung dieser Entdeckung [sc. daß die starken Verba den identischen Grundbau aller germanischen Sprachen bilden], bildet den wichtigsten Theil seiner *Aenleiding*" (Raumer 1870: 142).

The second volume provides an etymological dictionary, set up on the basis of the material collected in the first volume and according to the principles applied therein. Two introductory essays providing a 100-page discussion of the fundamentals of scientific etymology are followed by two long alphabetically arranged listings of Germanic words derived from strong verb roots. This specimen of a *Lexicon Etymologicum* (1723, II: 17) contains some 20,000 Dutch words and some 20,000 words from other languages. A full list of the sources mentioned in the *Aenleiding* is given in ten Cate 1987: 187−192.

Ten Kate's major work has many facets, including literary history (cf. Terpstra 1960; Heinrichs 1978); it may serve as a *Fundgrube* for linguists with varying historiographical interests. For instance, the *Aenleiding* contains many astute sociolinguistic observations concerning the state of contemporary Dutch and its manifold dialectological variations. Keenly aware of the close links between language and society, ten Kate paid ample attention to the cultural and historical dimensions of language (cf. Peeters 1990a: passim; Daan 1992). His achievements in phonetics are discussed by Eijkman 1924 and Meinsma 1981a, whereas Brink 1987 argues that ten Kate's underlying principles should be compared to the 20th-century generative school of phonology, concluding that it is justified to characterize ten Kate "as a precursor of generative phonology" (Brink 1987: 47).

With regard to ten Kate's contributions to morphology, in particular his 'panchronic' approach to the Germanic verbal system, Schultink (1994) pointed out that ten Kate operates with simple and implicit conceptions of morphological networks.

The reason why ten Kate payed so much attention to verbs, and to strong verbs in particular, had to do with his views on the ranking of the parts of speech. In 18th- and 19th-century Europe the relation of the principal parts of speech, the verb and the noun, was explicitly formulated as a genetic, rather than a logical problem (Stankiewicz 1974: 157). In ten Kate's work, genetic priority was decided in favour of the verb. To his mind, verbs were much older than other parts of speech, including nouns; and among the verbs, the strong verbs constituted "the very pinnacle of etymology" (cf. 1723, II: 11−13; cf. de Bonth 1996: 121−122).

4. Some methodological aspects

Junius, Hickes, and ten Kate are rightly considered to be the founding fathers of Germanic linguistics. However, due to the sophistication and the methodological rigour which characterize ten Kate's work (cf. Van de Velde 1980) the latter is much closer to a 19th-century scholar such as Jacob Grimm than to his older contemporary, George Hickes, whose work must be seen as the closing of a period (Rompelman 1952: 7). Ten Kate's main point was to provide an introduction to "the exalted part of the Dutch language", i.e. its etymology. In order to provide a firm theoretical basis for his etymologizing he set out the principles which should in his view underlie the 'geregelde afleiding' ('derivation according to fundamental rules') which should alone be relied upon for correct etymologies of the Germanic languages, rather than the traditional addition, removal, transposition and mutation of letters. Consequently, he promised "not to alter, shift, eliminate or add a single letter except on the strength of a consistent rule" (1723, I: 175; cf. 1723, II: 6). Rejecting the prevailing misconceptions about the subject, ten Kate gave short shrift of many of his predecessors: the only way to obtain a sound etymology, he argued, was to forget *anything* that had previously been said in this field of linguistics.

Abandoning the techniques of ancient etymology, ten Kate described and justified his own research methods very carefully (cf. Polomé 1983a: 8−9; de Bonth 1996: 116−117). He put forward a rigorous scientific approach: the linguist should *find* regularities, not *invent* them. To quote just one example:

"I have also observed in your words, and I approve of this, that speech is to be considered as a foster child of reason; and a comparison of the *laws of state* and of *language* has shown me distinctly, that although the authority of reason has to be considered as their foundation, they have become a *common law* when the custom and estimable usage which constitute the law, have their roots in centuries past. From this it may be easily concluded that, when one is looking back at this moment, *the laws of language must be discovered and not be made*; thus, reason does not seem to have a legitimate claim to their authorship […]" (ten Kate 1723, I: 13).

The frontispiece of the *Aenleiding* gives a splendid illustration of ten Kate's principles. In the left corner one sees a piece of ribbon on which is written 'Qui quaerit invenit', he who seeks will find; and in the foreground a cherub is tearing down a banner which reads: 'there is no rule without exception'. It was not without great satisfaction that ten Kate (1723, I: x) concluded that following his investigations "the common statement 'there is no rule without exception' no longer holds in our language". Ten Kate sought to formulate various 'streekhoudende dialect-regels' (1723, I: 165), i.e. consistent sound laws. It is evident, then, that his main concern was to find regularity in language, something akin to 'Ausnahmslosigkeit' (Rompelman 1952: 26). For ten Kate, to whom "regularity" was "the crown of a language" (1723, I: 543), could not believe that the so-called unevenly flowing verbs were as irregular as his contemporaries considered them his to be. To him, language was a "divine gift" (1723, I: 6); "fostered by the Milk of Reason" its development and extension had been left to Man (1723, I: 9−10). As Reason had been the "foster mother" of language (1723, I: 14), language must also be characterized by regularity and show logical coherence. Consequently, with the help of the researcher's reason, consistent rules could be discovered. As a matter of fact, there certainly is a relationship with the concept of *analogia*, 'regularity', as it was developed by the Hemsterhusians (cf. Verburg 1952: 430; Gerretzen 1940: 114). But how was one to find this regularity in the mass of historical grammatical phenomena with which ten Kate was confronted?

Although he might be called a rationalist in this respect (cf. Booij 1974), it can seriously be doubted whether ten Kate would have agreed with the statement "[q]ue la connaissance de ce qui se passe dans notre esprit, est necessaire pour comprendre les fondemens de la Grammaire", which the *Grammaire générale et raisonnée* (1660) presented to its readers (cf. Polomé 1983b: 163). Ten Kate was an adherent of 18th-century inductive functional rationalism, according to which reason is used for discovering and explaining the laws of language (Peeters 1990b: 154−155). His approach must be characterized as inductive and empirical. As it appears, this is a reaction to Cartesianism, partly on religious grounds, as will become clear from the following.

The year 1716 saw the publication of ten Kate's Dutch adaptation of George Cheyne's *Philosophical Principles of Natural Religion* (London 1705, 2nd ed. 1715), entitled *De Schepper en Zyn Bestier te kennen in Zyne Schepselen; Volgens het Licht der Reden en Wiskonst. Tot Opbouw van Eerbiedigen Godsdienst en Vernietiging van alle Grondslag van Altheistery* [The Creator and His Government revealed in His Creatures; according to the light of reason and mathematics. On behalf of the constitution of respectful religion and the destruction of every basis of atheism]. Eulogizing in the preface both his compatriot Christiaan Huygens (1629−1695) and the Englishman Isaac Newton (1643−1727), ten Kate attacked the Cartesian 'mechanismus': one had indulged in a mixture of untested conjectures, "sitting in one's study and speculating", whereas nothing should be accepted but what was to be proved by clear tests and experiments". In his criticizing the "harmful mechanism", which he considered to be abhorrent and dangerous, in particular for younger people, ten Kate revealed himself the pious Mennonite he had always been.

The background to ten Kate's views is to be found in the Newtonian approach then reigning supreme in the Netherlands (cf. Peeters 1990b; Jongeneelen 1992: 210; Noordegraaf 1996a: 226−231). Ten Kate can therefore be considered as a typical exponent of 18th century Dutch mainstream Enlightenment, the essence of which was "the overthrow of Cartesian deductive science and its replacement with *philosophia experimentalis*, a mania for scientific classification which spilled over beyond the realm of the natural sciences" (Israel 1995: 1045). Ten Kate's standpoint was lavishly praised by 19th and 20th-century Dutch scholars because it meant a strict adherence to empirical principles in linguistics. Ten Kate's merits were extolled by an older generation of Dutch historiographers because of his adherence to strict empirical principles. He was therefore considered to be a pioneer of the inductive method and a worthy predecessor of the great Jacob Grimm.

5. Competition, recognition and reception

In the 1760s a number of Leiden students and professors were seeking to promote the study of the mother tongue. To this end, a periodical was founded, *Tael- en dicht-kundige bydragen* (1758−1762), the first periodical to be devoted entirely to the study of Dutch language and literature. It was within this framework that the Orientalist Jan Jacob Schultens (1716−1778), professor at Leiden and son of the renowned Orientalist Albert Schultens (1686−1750), discussed the methods of etymology.

The occasion was the following. In December 1761, Meinard Tydeman (1741−1825), a student at Utrecht, published an essay on some Dutch "root parts", *Mengelwaarnemingen over eenige Worteldeelen der Nederduitsche Tael*, in the *Bydragen*. His essay was followed by a supplement, *Bylage over bel, bal, bol en belgen*, written by a certain H. v. B. (Herman van Breda), i. e. the Leiden student Herman Tollius (1742−1822). To this supplement a postcript was added, written by J. J. Schultens, in which the Leiden professor emphasized that Lambert ten Kate had done excellent work in examining "the origin and progress of our language" and had provided a "precious store of established and certain etymologies" in the second volume of his grand *Aenleiding*. Nevertheless, he argued, it ought to be possible for linguistic science to go further, penetrating more deeply into the foundations of language. As Schultens saw it, this could best be done with the help of Tiberius Hemsterhuis's method as refined by the latter's successor, Lodewijk Caspar Valckenaer (1715−1785). He therefore challenged the Leiden students to investigate whether the hypothesis of "the great Hemsterhuis, that the mighty copiousness of the Greek language sprung from the minutest germs", could also be applied to Dutch. In other words, what Schultens was advising was the application to the Dutch language of a method which had been developed for the analysis of Greek (de Buck 1931: 36−37). In 1763, it was again the Hemsterhuisian Herman Tollius − later, among other achievements, to become professor of Greek at Harderwijk University − who followed Schulten's advice by publishing an '*Essay of a new way of derivation from the parts of the roots* ta'en, te'en, ti'en, to'en, tu'en'. The lawyer and historian Hendrik van Wijn (1740−1831), who was also to become one of Jacob Grimm's correspondents, immediately followed with a similar treatise.

It can safely be concluded this is a clear case of extrapolation of the Hemsterhusian method to the Dutch language in an attempt to surpass ten Kate's method. I should like to note that the Hemsterhusian style efforts directed towards the etymology of Dutch were limited to the papers just mentioned (Knol 1977: 109), although the relationship between Grecists and students of Dutch had by no means come to an end (cf. Noordegraaf 1996b). All in all, it is abundantly clear which method eventually 'won'. In his concise 1882 overview of the study of the national language in the Netherlands, Willem H. van Helten (1849−1917), professor of Dutch at Groningen and a linguist of a neogrammarian creed, showed himself to be an ardent admirer of Lambert ten Kate. It comes as no surprise, therefore, that he made fun of the Hemsterhusian articles just mentioned (cf. van Helten 1882: 27−28).

In the Netherlands ten Kate was seen as a linguistic hero. For example, Jan Beckering Vinckers (1821−1892), professor of English at the University of Groningen (1885−1892), in translating William Dwight Whitney's (1827−1894) *Language and the Study of Language* (1867) into Dutch, inserted several pages on his compatriot into the first volume. He was of the opinion that it was ten Kate, not Grimm, who had laid the very first foundations of the comparative grammar of Germanic languages: "I for one am fully convinced that Grimm learned great deal from his study of ten Kate's work. What Bacon has meant for scientific research in general, ten Kate has meant for scientific language study in general" (Beckering Vinckers 1877: 37).

According to Hermann Paul (1891: 35), it was "unter allen älteren Forschern" Lambert ten Kate who succeeded "dem Standpunkt J. Grimms [*re* Ablaut] am nächsten zu kommen". Did Grimm ever recognize ten Kate's achievements? As early as 1812 Jacob Grimm's attention had been drawn to ten Kate's works by Hendrik W. Tydeman (1778−1863), one of his Dutch correspondents. Ten Kate, Tydeman wrote to Grimm, was held "to have achieved the same results regarding Dutch as A[lbert] Schultens had achieved concerning the Oriental languages, and [Tiberius] Hemsterhuis with regard to Greek". As it turned out, however, it was August Wilhelm Schlegel's (1767−1845) stinging review of the first volume of Jacob and Wilhelm Grimm's *Altdeutsche Wälder* in the *Heidelberger Jahrbuch* (1815), that prompted Grimm to actually study ten Kate. "Für die Geschichte unserer Grammatik", Schlegel argued,

"ist bisher durch Ausländern mehr geleistet worden als durch deutsche Gelehrte. Wir nennen hier vorzüglich ausser Hickes und [Edward] Lye [1694−1767], eine holländische Schrift: *Gemeenschap tussen de Gottische Spraeke en de Nederduytsche* von Lambert ten Kate. Sie umfasst nicht die ganze gothische Grammatik, sondern bloss die Konjugation und Deklination, diese sind aber meisterlich behandelt."

"[…] Lambert ten Kate hat den Satz durchgeführt, die sämmtliche Zeitwörter des Ulfilas nach Klassen geordnet und ihre Analogie bis in die feinsten Verzweigungen nachgewiesen." (Schlegel 1847 [1815]: 405−407; cf. Jongeneelen 1992: 212).

To Grimm, Schlegel's critique, which is generally considered to have led to his "Wendung zu strenger Wissenschaftlichkeit" (Raumer 1870: 452; Koerner 1989: 306), must have meant an exhortation to follow ten Kate's model of methodological rigour in historical linguistics. At any rate, Grimm managed to buy a copy of the *Aenleiding*. As he wrote to one of his Dutch friends on 15 December 1818: "Mit dem Ankauf des ten Kate für 6 f. bin ich sehr zufrieden, zum Nachschlagen wird es mir immer nützlich seyn wiewohl ich seit dem halben Jahre, dass ich mir ihn von der Göttinger Bibl. kommen lassen, wenig daraus gelernt habe" (cf. Jongeneelen 1992: 210). Be this as it may, Grimm must have studied ten Kate's work with more care in later years, although the references are decidedly scarce. It has been argued that some of Kate's insights concerning the problem of gender were adopted by Grimm in his *Deutsche Grammatik* (Dibbets 1996: 74). Furthermore, in his *Grammatik* (II, 1822−1837: 67) Grimm clearly acknowledged: "Ten Kate hat die Ablaute zuerst in ihrer Wichtigkeit hervorgehoben, nur die vocalunterschiede nicht strenge genug, am wenigsten die der consonanten beobachtet". Although Raumer argued that ten Kate "auf Grimms grammatische Forderungen einen besonders tiefgreifenden Einfluss geübt (hat)", I feel that his claim needs further substantiation (cf. Rompelman 1952: 271).

It is true to say that in his home country the much admired Lambert ten Kate had a strong impact on various 18th- and 19th-century students of Dutch (de Bonth 1996: 129; Jongeneelen 1996). However, it was the German Jacob Grimm who in the first half of the 19th century was to give the decisive impetus to the historical study of language in the Low Countries.

6. Final Remarks

A trustworthy informant at the end of the 18th century, the classical scholar Everhardus Scheidius (1742−1794), declared: "veras etymologiae rationes, hoc ipso demum ineunte saeculo, in Graecis reperit T. Hemsterhusius, in Orientalibus A. Schultensius, in Batavis L. ten Kate" [The true systematic etymologies were only found at the beginning of this very century, for Greek by Tiberius Hemsterhuis, for the Oriental languages by Albert Schultens and for Dutch by Lambert ten Kate] (Gerretzen 1940: 112). This statement may demonstrate that the autodidact ten Kate was considered to rank with distinguished university professors such as Hemsterhuis and Schultens.

In spite of the shortcomings it definitely also has (Van de Velde 1966: 273), the work of ten Kate stands out in the 18th century "as a unique contribution" (Polomé 1983b: 165) to the study of comparative historical linguistics, both in terms of its contents and its methodology.

7. Bibliography

7.1. Primary sources

ten Kate, Lambert. 1710. *Gemeenschap tussen de Gottische spraeke en de Nederduytsche.* Amsterdam: Jan Rieuwertsz.

−. 1716. *Den schepper in Zyn bestier te kennen in Zyne schepselen; Volgens het Licht der Reden en Wiskonst.* Amsterdam: Pieter Visser.

−. 1723. *Aenleiding tot de kennisse van het verhevene deel der Nederduitsche sprake.* 2 vols. Amsterdam: Rudolph & Gerard Wetstein.

Uffenbach, Zacharias Conrad von. 1754. *Merkwürdige reisen durch Niedersachsen, Holland und Engelland.* Ulm: Gaumisch.

Verwer, Adriaen. 1783. *Schets van de Nederlandse taal. Grammatica, poëtica en retorica.* Naar de editie van E. van Driel vertaald door J. Knol. Met een fotomechanische herdruk van Anonymus Batavus'

Idea Linguae Belgicae grammatica, poetica et rhetorica bezorgd door Everhardus van Driel, Leiden 1783 (1st ed. 1707). Bezorgd door Th. A. J. M. Janssen & J. Noordegraaf. Met als bijlage een *Lijst van bronnen* samengesteld door Henk Duits & Rob de Graaf. Amsterdam: Stichting Neerlandistiek VU; Münster: Nodus Publikationen 1996.

7.2. Secondary sources

Barnouw, Adriaan J. 1943. "Philology". *The Contribution of Holland to the Sciences* ed. by A. J. Barnouw & B. Landheer, 43−60. New York: Querido.

Beckering Vinckers, Jan. 1877. *Taal en Taalstudie. Voorlezingen over de gronden der wetenschappelijke taalbeoefening*, door W. D. Whitney. Volgens de derde uitgave voor Nederlandsers bewerkt. Eerste serie. Haarlem: F. Bohn.

van den Berg, B. 1975. "Lambert ten Kate's 'Gemeenlandsche Dialect". *Spel van zinnen: album A. van Loey* ed. by R. Jansen-Sieben, S. de Vriendt & R. Willemyns, 299−304. Brussel: Éditions de l'Université de Bruxelles.

de Bonth, Roland. 1996. "A Black Sheep and a White Crow. Carolus Tuinman (1659−1728) and Lambert ten Kate (1674−1731) on Etymology". *History and Rationality. The Skövde Papers in the Historiography of Linguistics* ed. by Klaus D. Dutz & Kjell-Åke Forsgen, 107−132. (= *Acta Universitatis Skodvensis. Series Linguistica*, 1.) Münster: Nodus.

− & Geert R. W. Dibbets, eds. 1995. *Voor rede vatbaar. Tien voorredes uit het grammaticale werk van Van Hoogstraten, Nyloë, Moonen, Sewel, Ten Kate, Huydecoper (1700−1730)*. Amsterdam: Stichting Neerlandistiek VU; Münster: Nodus.

− & Jan Noordegraaf. 1996. "Towards a Historiography of 18th century Dutch Linguistics". De Bonth & Noordegraaf 1996. 5−18.

− & Jan Noordegraaf, eds. 1996. *Linguistics in the Low Countries: The 18th century*. Amsterdam: Stichting Neerlandistiek VU; Münster Nodus.

Booij, Geert E. 1971. "Lambert ten Kate als voorloper van de TG-grammatica". *Spektator* 1. 74−78.

Brink, Daniel. 1986. "Lambert ten Kate as Indoeuropeanist". *Dutch Linguistics at Berkeley: Papers presented at the Dutch Linguistics Colloquium held at the University of California, Berkeley on November 9th, 1985* ed. by Jeanne van Oosten & Johan P. Snapper, 125−135. Berkeley: The Dutch Studies Program, U. C.

−. 1987. "Lambert ten Kate: A precursor of generative phonology". *Papers from the Second Interdisciplinary Conference on Netherlandic Studies held at Georgetown University, 7−9 June 1984* ed. by William H. Fletcher, 37−49. Lanham, Md.: Univ. Press of America.

de Buck, H. 1931. *De studie van het Middelnederlandsch tot in het midden der negentiende eeuw.* Groningen & Den Haag: J. B. Wolters.

ten Cate, C. L. 1987. *Lambert ten Kate Hermansz (1674−1731). Taalgeleerde en konst-minnaar.* Utrecht: Stichting "Genealogie ten Cate / ten Kate". Uitgave nr. 5.

Daan, Jo. 1992. "Wat is een dialect?: de betekenisnuances van dit woord in Nederland, bij Lambert ten Kate en in latere eeuwen". *Taal & Tongval* 44. 156−187.

−. 1994. "Lambert ten Kate gevierd, bewonderd en vergeten". *'Wat oars as mei in echte taal'. Fryske Stúdzjes ta gelegenheid fan it ôfskie fan prof. dr. A. Feitsma as heechlearaar Fryske Taal en Letterkunde* under redaksje fan Ph. Breuker, H. D. Meijering & J. Noordegraaf, 54−61. Ljouwert: Fryske Akademy.

Dibbets, Geert R. W. 1996. "De strijd om het genus in de achttiende-eeuwse grammatica van het Nederlands". De Bonth & Noordegraaf 1996. 57−90.

van Driel, L[odewijk] F[rans]. 1992. "Eene geauctoriseerde tale. Adriaen Verwer, koopman, jurist en taalliefhebber". *Voortgang, jaarboek voor de Neerlandistiek* 13. 121−143.

−. 1996. "Adriaen Verwer, koopman, jurist en schrijver van de *Idea*." Verwer 1783. 7−21.

Droixhe, Daniel. 1978. *La linguistique et l'appel de l'histoire (1600−1800). Rationalisme et révolutions positivistes.* Genève: Droz.

Eijkman, L. P. H. 1924. "Geschiedkundig overzicht van de klankleer in Nederland". *De Nieuwe Taalgids* 18. 17−33.

Gerretzen, Jan Gerard. 1940. *Schola Hemsterhusiana. De herleving der Grieksche studiën aan de Nederlandsche universiteiten in de achttiende eeuw van Perizonius tot en met Valckenaer.* Nijmegen & Utrecht: Dekker & Van de Vegt.

Heinrichs, Anne. 1978. "Von Ole Worm zu Lambert ten Kate. Frühe Rezeption der 'Krákumál". *Sprache in Gegenwart und Geschichte. Festschrift für Heinrich Matthias Heinrichs zum 65. Geburtstag* hg. von Dietrich Hartmann, Hansjürgen Linke & Otto Ludwig, 294−306. Köln: Böhlau.

Helten, Willem H. van. 1882. *Bijdrage tot een pragmatische geschiedenis der vaderlandsche-taalstudie in Nederland.* Groningen: J. B. Wolters.

van der Hoeven, Adrianus. 1896. *Lambert ten Kate (De 'Gemeenschap tussen de Gottische Spraeke en de Nederduytsche' en zijne onuitgegeven geschriften over klankkunde en versbouw.).* 's-Gravenhage: Martinus Nijhoff (Doct. diss. Univ. of Utrecht).

Israel, Jonathan. 1995. *The Dutch Republic. Its rise, greatness, and fall 1477−1806.* Oxford: Clarendon Press.

Jongeneelen, Gerrit H. 1992. "Lambert ten Kate and the Origin of 19th-Century Historical Linguistics". *The History of Linguistics in the Low Countries* ed. by Jan Noordegraaf, Kees Versteegh & Konrad Koerner, 201−219. Amsterdam & Philadelphia: Benjamins.

—. 1994. *Fonetiek en Verlichting. De 'Redeneringh over de talen' van Jan Trioen (1692)* Amsterdam: Stichting Neerlandistiek VU; Münster: Nodus.

—. 1996. "Huydecoper's Reception of ten Kate's Linguistic Theory. A first exploration". De Bonth & Noordegraaf 1996. 121–132.

Koerner, E. F. Konrad. 1989. "Jacob Grimm's Place in the Foundation of Linguistics as a Science". *Practicing Linguistic Historiography. Selected Essays* by Konrad Koerner, 303–323. Amsterdam: Benjamins.

Knol, Jan. 1977. "De grammatica in de achttiende eeuw". *Geschiedenis van de Nederlandse taalkunde* ed. by Dirk M. Bakker & Geert R. W. Dibbets, 64–112. Den Bosch: Malmberg.

Law, Vivien. 1990. "Language and its Students: The history of linguistics". *An Encyclopedia of Language* ed. by N. E. Collinge, 784–842. London & New York: Routledge.

Meinsma, G. L. 1981a. *The Phonetics of Lambert ten Kate. A textedition in reprint wih an introduction.* Amsterdam: Institute of Phonetic Sciences of the University of Amsterdam. Publication no. 69.

—, ed. 1981b. *Als de haen over de heete kolen? Lambert ten Kate. Teksten* [reprints from ten Kate's phonetics in *Aenleiding*, vol. I]. Amsterdam: Institute of Phonetic Sciences of the University of Amsterdam.

—. 1982–83. "Lambert ten Kate, an early phonetician". *Proceedings from the Institute of Phonetic Sciences of the University of Amsterdam* 7. 83–118.

Noordegraaf, Jan. 1995. "The 'Schola Hemsterhusiana' Revisited". *History and Rationality. The Skövde papers in the historiography of linguistics* hg. von Klaus D. Dutz & Kjell-Åke Forsgren, 133–158. Münster: Nodus. (Enlarged version in *The Dutch Pendulum. Linguistics in the Netherlands 1740–1900* by J. Noordegraaf, 23–55. Münster: Nodus, 1996.)

—. 1996a. "Dutch Philologists and General Linguistic Theory. Anglo-Dutch relationships in the 18th century". *Linguists and Their Diversions. A Festschrift for R. H. Robins on his 75th birthday* ed. by Vivien A. Law & Werner Hüllen, 211–243. Münster: Nodus.

—. 1996b. "From Greek to Dutch. The Schola Hemsterhusiana and the study of the mother tongue. A few remarks". De Bonth & Jan Noordegraaf. 33–56.

Paul, Hermann. 1891. "Geschichte der germanischen Philologie". *Grundriss der germanischen Philologie* hg. v. H. Paul. Vol. I, 9–151. Straßburg: Trübner.

Peeters, L[eopold]. 1990a. *Taalopbouw als Renaissance-ideaal: studies over taalopvattingen en taalpraktijk in de zestiende en zeventiende eeuw.* Amsterdam: Buijten & Schipperheijn.

—. 1990b. "Lambert ten Kate (1674–1731) en de achttiende-eeuwse taalwetenschap". *Traditie en progressie: Handelingen van het 40ste Nederlands Filologencongres*, 151–160. 's-Gravenhage: SDU Uitgeverij.

Polomé, Edgar C. 1983a. "Lambert ten Kate's Significance for the History of the Dutch Language". *Tijdschrift voor Nederlands en Afrikaans* 1, 2–14.

—. 1983b. "Netherlandic Contributions to the Debate on Language Change: From Lambert ten Kate to Josef Vercoullie". *Language Change* ed. by Irmengard Rauch & Gerald F. Carr, 163–173. Bloomington: Indiana Univ. Press.

Prinsen, M. M. 1936. "Lambert ten Kate als kunstkenner en aestheticus". *De Nieuwe Taalgids* 30. 53–66.

von Raumer, Rudolf. 1870. *Geschichte der germanischen Philologie, vorzugsweise in Deutschland.* München: R. Oldenbourg. (Repr. New York: Kraus, 1965.)

Rompelman, T. A. 1952. *Lambert ten Kate als germanist.* Mededelingen der Koninklijke Nederlandse Akademie van wetenschappen, Afd. Letterkunde. Nieuwe reeks, deel 15. Amsterdam: Noord-Hollandsche Uitgevers Maatschappij.

von Schlegel, August Wilhelm. 1847. *Sämmtliche Werke.* Hg. von Eduard Böcking. XII: *Vermischte und kritische Schriften*, 406. Leipzig: Weidmann Repr. Olms, Hildesheim & New York, 1971).

Schultink, H. 1989. "Regelmaat in onregelmatigheid: Ten Kate, Van Haeringen en de ANS in historisch perspectief". *Palaeogermanica et onomastica: Festschrift für J. A. Huisman zum 70. Geburtstag* hg. von Arend Quak & Florus van der Rhee, 229–242. (Amsterdamer Beiträge zur älteren Germanistik, 29).

—. 1994. "Lambert ten Kate en hedendaagse, Nederlandse morfologie". *Tijdschrift voor Nederlandse Taal- en Letterkunde* 110. 257–274.

Stankiewicz, Edward. 1974. "The Dirtyramb to the Verb in the 18th and 19th Century Linguistics". *Studies in the History of Linguistics. Traditions and paradigms* ed. by Dell Hymes, 157–190. Bloomington & London: Indiana Univ. Press.

Terpstra, J. U. 1960. "Ten Kate's Übersetzung von Ragnar Lodbroks Sterbelied (*Krákumál*) und ihre literarhistorische Bedeutung". *Neophilologus* 44. 135–146.

Thijm, Jos[ephus] A[lbertus] Alberdingk. 1869. "Over de ideale schoonheid, door Lambert Hermansz. ten Kate". *De Dietsche Warande* 8. 115–141.

van Veen, Henk Th. 1995. "Devotie en esthetiek bij Lambert ten Kate". *Doopsgezinde Bijdragen.* Nieuwe reeks 21. 63–96.

Vanderheyden, Jan-F. 1957. "Adriaen Verwer in de geschiedschrijving en over de geschiedenis van het Nederlands. Verwer en Zuid-Nederland". *Verslagen en Mededelingen Koninklijke Vlaamse Academie voor Taal- en Letterkunde* 1957, 617–671.

Van de Velde, Roger G. 1966. *De studie van het Gotisch in de Nederlanden. Bijdrage tot een status* quaestionis over de studie van het Gotisch en het Krimgotisch. Gent: Koninklijke Vlaamse Academie voor Taal- en Letterkunde.

—. 1990. "The Concept of 'Scientific' in the Development of the Language Sciences". *Progress in Linguistic Historiography: Papers from the international conference on the history of the language sciences (Ottawa, 28−31 August 1978)* ed. by Konrad Koerner, 395−402. Amsterdam: Benjamins.

Verburg, Pieter Adrianus. 1952. *Taal en Functionaliteit. Een historisch-critische studie over de opvattingen aangaande de functies der taal van de praehumanistische philologie van Orleans tot de rationalistische linguïstiek van Bopp*. Wageningen: Veenman. (Doctoral dissertation Vrije Universiteit Amsterdam, 1951.)

de Vooys, Cornelis G. N. 1923. "De taalbeschouwing van Lambert ten Kate". *De Nieuwe Taalgids* 17. 65−81. (Repr. in *Verzamelde taalkundige opstellen* by C. G. N. de Vooys, vol. I, 371−391. Groningen: Wolters, 1924.)

—. 1970. *Geschiedenis van de Nederlandsche taal*. Groningen: Wolters-Noordhoff.

Wal, Marijke van der. 1992. *Geschiedenis van het Nederlands* (in samenwerking met Cor van Bree). Utrecht: Het Spectrum.

Jan Noordegraaf, Alphen aan den Rijn (The Netherlands)

148. The study of early Germanic languages in Scandinavia: Ihre, Stiernhielm

1. Introduction
2. Denmark
3. Sweden
4 Bibliography

1. Introduction

Both descriptive and historical linguistics followed the same pattern in Scandinavia as elsewhere in Western Europe in the post-Renaissance period. What was special for Scandinavia was the extensive preoccupation with Old Norse, Gothic and especially the Runic script. Both in Denmark and Sweden the Runic script was considered to be extremely old (sometimes older than the Greek or Latin alphabet) and something in which one took great national pride. Both historians and grammarians were engrossed with the origin and interpretation of the Runic script. It was also quite fashionable to write Old Norse words in the Runic script, and in the first Icelandic dictionary (Ólafsson 1650) each entry is given both in the Runic and Latin alphabets. There were also a few more scholarly studies (e. g. Verelius 1675) which laid the foundations of runology as a linguistic discipline of great importance in Scandinavia in the 19th and 20th centuries.

2. Denmark

The Danish-Norwegian contributions to the field of diachronic linguistics and the study of early Germanic languages are few and insignificant. The study of the origin and diversity of languages was a favourite topic of linguistic dissertations at the University of Copenhagen in the 17th and 18th centuries, but all these dissertations are superficial and lack any original character. The basic text and the starting point for most of these studies on the origin of language as well as their diversity was Plato's *Cratylos*, which was the most frequently consulted book on linguistic information in Denmark in the 17th and 18th centuries. Concerning the origin of language, the dominant theory in Denmark (as opposed to Sweden) was that Hebrew was the first language and the origin, or at least the main source, of all other languages.

There are few comparative studies from this period in Denmark. Brunchmann (1756) was partly a comparative-contrastive grammar of German, Danish, and Swedish and partly a comparative-etymological vocabulary. The words are mainly explained as having originated from Hebrew, but also in a few cases from Latin and Greek. In addition, the author argues that borrowing between languages is a major reason for similarities in the vocabulary.

3. Sweden

The Swedish studies in this field were quantitatively more significant than in any other

European country. In the history of historical-comparative linguistics in Europe before 1800, Sweden has an important place.

3.1. Stiernhielm

The poet and founder of Swedish literature Georg Stiernhielm (1598−1672) was also the founder of Swedish historical-comparative linguistics. His most important linguistic work is Stiernhielm (1671) which is a preface to the first modern edition of Wulfila's Gothic Bible. Both the Gothic Bible and Stiernhielm's preface concerning the origin of languages became very influential in linguistic research in Sweden in the years after their publication.

Stiernhielm proposed as his basic thesis that all languages existing in the old world came from one language and could be reduced to one language. These languages came from Adam and Noah and the diversification of languages, and his classification into language families began with the three sons of Noah. Sem was the father of the Semitic languages like Hebrew, Arabic, and Syrian while Cham was the father of Egyptian, Ethiopian, Phoenician, etc. Stiernhielm clearly saw the relationship between the two groups, however, and gave the good and substantially correct survey of this language family, stressing that Hebrew was not the original language, but just like Syrian, Arabic etc. developed from a dialect of the original common language.

The third son, Japhet, was the father of Latin (and the Romance languages), Greek, Persian, Germanic and Slavonic. This is the Indo-European family which Stiernhielm called Scythian. Also lesser known languages like Phrygian and Thracian were included in this family grouping. Stiernhielm stressed the internal relationship between the Romance languages which had developed from dialects of Latin (which again developed from a dialect of Scythian) and similarly the development of Germanic into the dialects which became the modern Germanic languages. Furthermore, he gave one of the first primitive tabular representations of the relationship between the Germanic languages.

Stiernhielm concluded his preface with the Lord's Prayer in Latin and in the various Romance languages as an illustration of how languages could develop from a common source.

Stiernhielm was still convinced of the importance of Hebrew, however, and in some of his other works (e. g. Stiernhielm 1643?) we find a list of etymologies where Hebrew words are compared with words having a similar meaning and a more or less phonological resemblance in a haphazard collection of languages (Semitic, Indo-European, Turk, Finno-Ugric, etc.).

Stiernhielm assumed that certain sounds or sound combinations had certain specific meanings just as Plato had done in *Cratylos*, where, for example, *r* is said to indicate movement, *l* lightness, etc. The search for the true meaning of sounds is paralleled with a search for the fundamental dimensions of the world. Stiernhielm accepts Plato's opinion that *l* denotes life and light and finds confirmation in the Swedish words *lätt*, "easy" *le* "smile" and *leka* "play".

A number of rather speculative studies trying to prove that Swedish was the oldest language on earth, the language of Eden or the language most closely related to Hebrew appeared in this period, cf. Agrell 1955 for a thorough survey. A much referred to, and probably completely misunderstood, Swedish work concerning the origin of language is Kempe 1688. This work argues in a very general way for Swedish being the language of Paradise. There are no really linguistic arguments, no historical speculations and only very few etymologies. It is clearly a satirical work, and a very good and amusing one, making fun of Swedish speculations about Swedish as the language of Paradise.

3.2. The Rudbecks

Olaus Rudbeck (1630−1702), a world-famous physician who contributed much to the development of medicine both in Sweden and abroad, was also an authority on linguistics. He was met with great respect in his lifetime, and his prestige together with the impressiveness of his work (and that of his son as well) made him an authority to whom everybody could refer, especially the less they knew about languages and linguistics.

Rudbeck tried to contribute towards raising the status of Sweden and the Swedish language through his famous 4-volume work *Atland or Manheim*, published in 1679−1702. The work was originally written in Swedish but later translated into Latin. It is mainly a world history, albeit of a very small world, from the early beginnings of mankind based on all available sources. Rudbeck's intention was to show that Plato's island Atlantis was in fact Sweden and that Swedish was the language of Paradise mentioned in the Bible. The four volumes consist of about 3000 pages, a collection of all kinds of myths, which were considered to be historical facts and thus an empirical basis for historical studies, where all possible kinds of connections are drawn, not the least regarding etymology. The readers should take a look at the complete titles of Rudbeck's works in the bibliography. They, more than anything else, illustrate his megalomania.

Rudbeck started out with a conclusion, and his entire work is a manipulation of the facts to support this conclusion. In volume 1 he introduces some systematic comparisons between languages (1679: 19) with a random list of correspondences like Swedish F = Latin P, K = Latin C and K = G, the last illustrated by both Swedish *åker* "field" = Latin *ager* as well as Swedish *leka* "to play" = Danish *lege*. The letters of the alphabet had also supposedly originated in the Nordic countries, according to Rudbeck. He also proposed that the original language of mankind was monosyllabic (Rudbeck 1679: 31) and considers then Swedish to be a good candidate since no other language has more monosyllabic words than Swedish. The letters of the alphabet should also have originated in the Nordic countries according to him.

In Rudbeck (1698: 719–729) a list of almost 200 etymologies is presented to show that the Phoenician language is related to Swedish and Scythian. The words are also compared to Hebrew (which is closely related to Phoenician), but Rudbeck merely states that the similarities between Hebrew and Phoenician are due to borrowing since these two peoples were neighbours.

Rudbecks son Olavus Rudbeck Jr. (1660–1740) followed in his father's footsteps, both as professor of medicine and in continuing efforts to promote his father's over-patriotic ideas.

Rudbeck Jr.'s contribution to linguistics is a mixture of everything. His work from 1717 contains extensive lists which try to prove connections between Saami and Hebrew, Gothic and Chinese and Finnish and Hungarian, interspersed with all kinds of etymologies of Hebrew words which are compared with other Semitic languages, Greek, Italian, Gothic, Annamese, Bantu languages, etc. At the end, it is totally unclear which languages are related to which. Saami is related to both Finnish and Hungarian as well as to Hebrew. Such a wealth of examples from so many languages in various alphabets must have dumbfounded readers into becoming more and more impressed the less they understood.

Here are some examples of his Chinese-Swedish etymologies (Rudbeck 1717: 64–67):

Chinese/ Annamite	Gothic	Latin
çan f. *San*	*San, sanod* Lap.	*Respondeo* "I answer"
Chen chu	*San gu*	*Verus Deus* "True God"
Cym	*Thim, tima*	*Tempus* "time"
Dau	*Dau, du, dug*	*Pluvia* "rain"
Deeo	*Dei, deig*	*Mollis* "soft"

As we see, Sámi is considered a Gothic language. Furthermore, the Swedish forms given are frequently colloquial or dialectal variants chosen because they were most suitable for the comparison to Chinese!

Rudbeck Jr. also published a number of other works, all of which are filled to the brim with word lists or etymologies into which all kinds of languages could be drawn as long as a sound or two were identical and the meaning not too different.

In spite of their popularity, there were a few scholars in Sweden and some from abroad (e. g. Leibnitz) who saw the methodological weaknesses of the etymological speculations of Stiernhielm and the Rudbecks. In the introduction to his Swedish dictionary (Spegel 1712), the archbishop, administrator and poet Haquin Spegel (1645–1714) was very critical towards the etymological speculations of his day. Attempts to link living languages like Swedish or Dutch to Hebrew, the garden of Eden or the sons of Noah were ideas which he found both arbitrary and heretic.

3.3. Johan Ihre

Johan Ihre (1707–80), who was one of the most important and influential historical-comparative linguists in Europe in his day, marks the return to more sober methods. Ihre studied in Jena, Utrecht and Leiden. His first works are not that impressive. Ihre (1742–43) is a series of disssertations presenting a short laudatory history of the Swedish language. He gives a good survey of the opinions of others, relying heavily on Stiernhielm, and treats different layers of loan-words (from Latin and German), all the while condemning the extensive modern use of loan-words; however, the work is not particularly original. Ihre (1751) is a short treatise on Swedish orthography advocating a mild approach to phonological spelling. Furthermore, Ihre published numerous elementary and mainly unoriginal studies of Gothic morphology and lexicography as well as of the Gothic alphabet (Ihre 1753, 1767–

69). These studies are mainly synchronic and his morphological studies of Gothic lack any references to related forms in other Germanic languages.

With the exception of Rudbeck (1679–1702), Ihre (1769) is the most extensive (1260 pp.) linguistic work published in Scandinavia in this period. And compared with Rudbeck, it is much more systematic and methodologically sound. It is the major contribution to Swedish etymological research in the 17th and 18th centuries and was not without influence on the development of historical-comparative linguistics in the early 19th century. In many respects it is an uneven and even contradictory work. In the extensive introduction (Ihre 1769: i–xlviii) Ihre first gives a survey of the different languages to which he refers. Their history and relationship were analyzed mainly on the basis of mythical sources ranging from the Bible to Snorri Sturlasson's *Ynglingasaga*. The most prominent position was accorded to Hebrew, and to Scythian while of the Scythian languages, Swedish was the oldest, purest and most important member. For each language, word lists comparing the language to Swedish were given, but Ihre also maintained that Finnish and Saami were related to each other and to Hungarian, and that they were Hun languages spoken in The Nordic countries before Odin arrived. The numerous resemblances of Finnish and Saami words to words in various Germanic languages were attributed to borrowing, although Ihre found it hard to state the direction in which the borrowing had taken place. The concept of borrowing was, however, a very vague one to Ihre and he usually failed to distinguish between loanwords and inherited words.

The second part of the introduction consists of systematic lists of sound changes and sound correspondences (*mutationes litterarum*). Initially, Ihre states that one of his main purposes is to describe these sound changes, and that no one should engage in etymological research without doing so (Ihre 1769: ii). He has 96 lists of sound correspondences (Ihre 1769: xli–xliii), ordered alphabetically. The examples for each change are presented with an uncritical taxonomy of data, unsystematic and without any internal classification, i.e. regular changes and sporadic changes, diachronic changes within one language and comparative correspondences between languages, as well as optional synchronic variants, were all mixed together. In numerous cases, words were compared that were not etymologically related at all.

Here are some examples:

(1) Internal Swedish variation together with a unique (no other example exists) comparative correspondence (Ihre 1769: xlvii):

    T pro F
Hustru, mater familias "wife"   *Husfru.*
Torg "market place"   [Lat.] forum

(2) A correct correspondence illustrated with Swedish-Latin/Greek correspondences is compared to a Swedish-German correspondence illustrating a quite different phenomenon (Ihre 1769: xlvii)

    T pro D
Äta "to eat"   Edere [Lat.]
Bedja "to pray"   Beten Germ. & sic in plurimis aliis hujus Linguæ.
Dona "to thunder"   Tonare [Lat.]
MåtT "manner"   Modus [Lat.]
Sitta "to sit"   Sedere [Lat.]

(3) Loan words and – mostly wrong – etymologies are mixed together (Ihre 1769: xlvii):

    S pro C
Hwass "sharp"   Acer [Lat.]
Lysa "to light"   Lucere [Lat.]
Pensel "brush"   Penicillus [Lat.]
Sinnober "cinnabar"   κιννάβαρι [Grec.]

In spite of, or perhaps precisely due to, his overwhelming collection of data, Ihre seems to have understood very little of the principles of language change, language relationship and genetic classification. He did not see which correspondences were interesting and which were not. On the other hand, Agrell (1955) is undoubtedly right when he stresses the importance and uniqueness of the Swedish interest in sound correspondences. They were preoccupied with a trial and error procedure which finally lead to the emergence of the comparative grammar of the 19th century, and in this respect the Swedish contribution was unique.

If we, however, turn to the rest of the book, the wild etymologies are not very disturbing. Actually they comprise but a small part of the entries. What we find is an excellent Swedish dictionary with ample and mainly correct etymological connections to other Germanic languages indicated. Occasionally, we find comparisons with Latin and Greek, as well as reasonable comparisons with Finnish. There are few, of course all plainly wrong, Hebrew etymologies. For anyone studying Germanic languages or wanting to have a good etymological basis for comparing them with other languages, this was an excellent and most useful tool and a fundament for future diachronic studies. Without the support of Ihre (1769), both Rask and Grimm would have had problems in achieving what they did.

At the end of the 18th century, the dissatisfaction with the methods of Ihre and his predecessors was apparent in Sweden. The relationship between Semitic and Indo-European languages was categorically rejected by Thorberg (1785). After eliminating loan words and onomatopoetic words he concludes:

"Furthermore, it will necessarily be so that if you have a large number of words collected from various languages, at least a few ones will have some apparent similarity although they by their nature cannot be connected or can be considered as parallel forms." (Thorberg 1785: 2)

4. Bibliography

Agrell, Jan. 1955. *Studier i den äldre språkjämförelsens allmänna och svenska historia fram till 1827.* Uppsala Universitets Årsskrift 1955: 13. Uppsala: A.-B. Lundequistska bokhandelen.

Brunchmann, Andreas. 1756. *Harmonia lingvarum Teutonicæ. Danicæ, Sveticæ. Das ist: Allgemeine Zusammenstimmung Worinn Die Grammaticalischen Vesten, Besten und ersten Gründe deren Hoch-Teutschen, Dänischen und Schwetischen Sprachen.* Copenhagen: Gedruckt bey C. G. Glasinga nachgelassenen Wittwe, durch Nicolaus Möller.

Ihre, Johannes. 1742−43. *Dissertatio Academica De Mutationes linguæ Sueo-Gothicæ. I−II.* Upsaliæ & Holmiæ: Typis Nyströmianis.

−. 1753. *Specimen glossarii Ulphilani.* I−III. Ulsaliæ: L. M. Höjer.

−. 1761. *Utkast till Föreläsningar öfwer Swenska språket. och thes närmare kännedom.* Stockholm Upsala: Uti Kiesewetters Boklåda.

−. 1767−69. *Analecta Ulphilana.* I−X. Upsaliae: Johan. Edman.

−. 1769. *Glossarium Suiogothicum in quo tam hodierno usu frequentata vocabula, quam in legum patriarum tabulis aliisque ævi medii scriptis obvia explicantur, et ex dialectis cognatis, Moesogothica, Anglo-saxonica, Alemannica, Islandica ceterisque Gothicæ et Celtæ originis illustratur. I−II.* Upsaliæ: Typis Edmannianis.

−. 1773. *Scripta versionem Ulphilanam et lingua moeso-gothicam illustrantia.* Edita ab Antonio Friderico Büsching, Berolini: Ex officina typographica Bossiana.

[Kempe, Andreas] Simon Simplex. 1688. *Die Sprachen des Paradises, das ist, Begebene Anleitung der Natur zuerkennen, was vor Sprachen im ersten Anfange der Welt, im Paradeis, absonderlich beyin Fall Adams und Eve scynd* [sic!] *geredet worden. In einer Rede, von etlichen Hochgelehrten Persohnen, in ein Convent vorgehabt, und mit ihrer sämtlichen Vergnügung ausgeführet. Aus dem Schwedischen im Teutschen übersetzt von Albrecht Kopman.* [No place. No publisher.]

[Ólafsson, Mágnus] Magnus Olavius. 1650. *Specimen Lexici Runici, obscuriorum quarundam vocum quæ in priscis occurunt Historiis & Poetis Danicis, enodationem exhibens.* Nunc in ordinem redactum Auctum & Locupletatum ab Olao Wormio. Hafniæ: Melchior Martzan.

Rudbeck, Olavus. 1679. *Atland Eller Manheim Dedan Japhets afkomme, de förnemste Keyserlige och Kunglige Slecter ut till hela werlden, henne att styra, utgågne äro, så och desse eftersökande Folck utogade, nembligen Skyttar, Borbarn, Asar, Jettar, Giotar, Phryger, Trojaner, Amaizor, Traser, Lyder, Maurer, Tussar, Kaller, Kiempar, Kimrar, Saxer, German, Swear, Longobarder, Wandaler, Herular, Gepar, Tydskar, Anglor, Paitar, Danar, Sidkampar, och flera de som i werket wisas skola. / Atlantica Sive Manheim Vera Japheti posterorum sedes ac patria, ex qua non tantum Monarchæ & Reges ad totum fere orbem reliquum regendum ac domandum, Stirpesque suas in eo condendas, sed etiam Scythæ, Barbari, Asæ, Gigantes, Gothi, Phryges, Trojani, Amazones, Thraces, Libyes, Mauri, Tusci, Galli, Cimbri, Cimmerii, Saxones, Germani, Svevi, Longobardi, Vandali, Heruli, Gepidæ, Teutones, Angli, Pictones, Dani, Sicambri, aliique virtute clari & celebres populi olim exierunt.* Upsalæ: Henricus Curio.

−. 1689. *Atlands Eller Manheims. Andra deel Uti hwilken innehålles Månans och Jordennes Dyrkan, Sampt huruledes den aldraförst är begynt längst uppe uthi Swerige hoos Kimmi-boerne, och sedan uthspridd worden til störste delen af heela Werlden; Hwilket alt så wäl at the Fremmandes, som Wåre egnes Historier, i synnerheet af de Gamble och Underliga Gåtor, de der här till dagz aldrig warit af någon rätt förklarade, bewissadt warder. Och dessutun att effter Solennes och Månans lopp, Åretz rättelse omgång här andraförst achtad och uthräknad är, tillijka med monge andre märkelige ting, som alt här till legat fördolde. / Atlanticæ Sive Manheimii Pars Secunda In quâ Solis, Lunæ, ac Terræ cultus describitur, omnisque adeo Superstitionis hujusce origo parti Sveoniæ Septentrionali, Terræ puta Cimmeriorum vindicatur, ex quâ deinceps in Orbem reliqvum divulgata est: Idque Scriptorum non tantum domesticorum, Sed etiam exernorum, màxime vero veterum atque doctissimarum fabularum fide, qnatum [sic] explicatio, genuina nusquam ante hanc nostram in lucem prodiit. Accedunt demonstrationes certissimæ, quæ Septentrionales nostros, in maxime geminum Solis ac Lunæ motum, indeque pedentem accuratissimum temporum rationem, multo & prius & felicius, quam gentem aliam ullam olim penetrasse, ac etiam alia multa ad hanc usque diem incognita declarant.* Upsalæ: Henricus Curio.

—. 1698. *Atlands Eller Manheims Triie Del, Uti hwilcken beskrifwes Wåra Fäders äldsta Skrifter på Stenar, Böök och Näfwer, och när de detta begynt att giöra. sedan Gyllende Talets bemärkelse för hwart åhr, wåra himmels teckns ursprung och betydning, och huru de äro komme till the Greker och latiner. De sex första Tider eller Åldrar efter Noe flod, och huru wåra Atlänningars första regements skapnad warit, hwad uttåg och krig äro skiedde under Satur eller Bore och under hans sons Jofurs eller Thors regemente, och om wåras Schyters, Phenicers och Hamaifors uttåg under dem till Indo Schytien och Phenicien, eller in i Canaansoch Juda land, Förutan många artiga Gåtor uttrydde som här tills fördölgde legat. Atlanticæ seu Manheimii Pars tertia In qua vetustissima majorum nostrorum Atlantidum lapidus, fago atque cortici Runas suas incidendi ratio, unà cum tempore, quo illa primum cæperit, exponitur. Deinde Aurei Numeri singulis annis tributi, & Signorum Coelestium, quæ hinc ad Græcos & Latinos sunt translata, vera origo ac significatio traditur. Tum sex illæ a diluvio Noachi proximæ ætates, atque in illis prima. Atlantidum nostrorum reipub. forma describitur: quæ migrationes & bella sub Boreo seu Saturno ejusque filio Thoro seu Jove gesta sunt, recensentur; & denique Scytharum, Phænicum & Amazonum his ducibus in Indo-Scythiam & Phæniciam seu Palæstinam e Sveonia sacræ expeditiones enarrantur. Quibus omnibus mythologiæ perplures, quarum sensus in hunc usque diem incognitus heic demum detectus prodit, jucundæ sanè & perquem utiles adjungtur.* Upsalæ: Typis et impensis Auctoris.

—. 1702. *Atlands Eller Manheims Fjerde Del, Uti hwilcken beskrifwes åtskiliga Hendelsers tilsammanstemning i den Hälga Skrift mot de Hedniskes skrifter. Sedan Hwad wid Noachs tijds och under hans Barn och Barnabarn hafwer skiett A. M. 1600. Hwad An. M. 1800 skiedt är. Om hwad under Nachors, Tarachs och Mannens tijd och nästfölliande A. M. 1900 Händt är. Atlanticæ seu Manheimii Pars Quarta In qua agitur de consensu Sacri Codicis et scriptorum profanorum in rebus ultimæ antiquitatis. Deinde De rebus sub Diluvio et tempore huic proximo gestis A. M. 1600. De rebus ad Annum Mundi 1800 pertinentibus. De iis, quæ Nachori, Tarochi atque Manni, et quæ proxime sequebatur, ætate ad An. M. 1900 illustriora habentur. Reliqua capita, igne vorace combusta, desiderantur.* Upsalæ: Typis et impensis Auctoris.

Rudbeck, Olavus jr. 1705. *Ichthylogiæ Biblicæ Pars Prima De Ave Selav. Cujus mentio fit Numer. XI: 31. In qua Contra Cl. Bochartum & Ludolfum, non avem aliquam plumatam, nec Locustam fuisse, sed potius quoddam piscis genus, manifestis, demonstratur argumentis. Additâ Brevi, Hebræam inter & antiquam Gothicam lingvam, analogiâ, ex occasione vocum Hebraicarum loc. cit. occurrentium.* Upsalis: Johan. Henr. Werner.

—. 1717. *Specimen usus linguæ. Gothicæ. in Eruendis atque illustrandis obscurissimis quibusvis Sacræ Scripturæ locis: addita analogia linguæ Gothicæ Cum Sinica. Nec non Finnonicæ Cum Ungarica.* Upsalis: Joh. Henr. Werner.

Stiernhielm, Georg. [1643?]. *Magog Aramæo-Gothicus.* Upsaliæ: Eschillus Matthiæ.

—. 1671. *De linguarum origine.* In *D. N. Jesu Christi SS. Evangelia Ab Ulfila Gothorum in Moesia Episcopo Circa Annum à Nato Christo CCCLX ex Græco Gothicè translata, nunc cum Parallelis Versionibus, Sveo-Gothicâ, Norrænâ, seu Islandicâ, & vulgatâ Latinâ edita.* Stockholmiæ: Nicolaus Wankif.

Thorberg, Abraham. 1785. *Utkast til en critisk historia om österländska språket.* Upsala: Johan Edman.

Verelius, Olaus. 1675. *Compendiosa ad Runographiam Scandicam antiqvam recte intelligendam. / En kort underwijsning Om Then Gambla Swea-Götha Runa-Ristning.* Upsalæ: Henricus Curio.

—. 1691. *Index Lingvæ Veteris Scytho- Scandiæ sive Gothicæ ex vetusti ævi monumentis; maximam partem manuscriptis, collectus atqve opera Olai Rudbecki editus.* Upsalæ. [No printer].

Even Hovdhaugen, Oslo (Norway)

149. Investigating Older Germanic languages in England

1. Initial interest
2. A search for origins
3. Toward a dictionary of Old English
4. Anglo-Saxon grammar
5. Other Germanic languages
6. Bibliography

1. Initial interest

In the wake of the dissolution of the monasteries (1536−39) and the dispersal of their libraries under Henry VIII, some concern for the loss of manuscripts was felt by individual antiquarians such as John Leland (d. 1552), who noted some Anglo-Saxon ones in his *Itinerary* (Smith 1906−10), and John Talbot (d. 1558), who, like many later antiquaries, and Laurence Nowell (1530−ca. 1570) in particular, must have acquired his knowledge of the language on the basis of those Latin texts King Alfred (849−899) had translated into English, with the help of the English *Grammar* and *Glossary* of Latin by abbot Ælfric (*fl.* 1006) plus the glossaries individual monasteries had made from the interlinear and marginal glosses of manuscripts in their possession (Hetherington 1980: 6−8). Nowell, probably a member of Elizabeth's first parliament and, by the 1560s, certainly in the employ of Elizabeth's secretary of state, William Cecil, seems to have come to his interest in Old English via his topographic and cartographic interests (Berkhout 1998: 7). Nowell annotated his copy of Leland (1543) with Old English place names, made numerous transcriptions of a wide range of Old English texts, translated Ohthere's voyage from the Old English *Orosius*, contributed to the *Archaionomia*, an edition of the Anglo-Saxon laws, published in 1568 by William Lambarde (1536−1601) and produced the first dictionary of Old English, which he gave to Lambarde to assist him in his endeavours.

The first stirrings of a more general English interest in the language of the Anglo-Saxons date from 1568 when the Privy Council promulgated a general letter (now in Corpus Christi College Cambridge MS 114) to the effect that Elizabeth I of England was interested in the content and preservation of "auncient recordes or monuments written" and instructing her Archbishop of Canterbury, Matthew Parker (1504−1575) to collect all such manuscripts, to have them copied and returned to those owners who wanted them back. Apparently (Page 1975: 6), some forty of these contained texts in Old English. The Church in Anglo-Saxon times was seen to pre-date the deterioration claimed by the Protestants and therefore to be exemplary for the Church of England. Parker, in particular, took the opportunity to draw attention to features where both the Anglo-Saxon and the Elizabethan Church of England differed from the medieval Catholic Church such as encouraging Bible translation into the vernacular and permitting married priests. Parker and his secretaries, notably his Latin secretary, John Joscelyn (1529−1603), made considerable annotations to various manuscripts and, in answer to Parker's call for a grammar and a dictionary, Joscelyn and Parker's son John (1548−1618) produced an Old English-Latin dictionary which was never published (British Library MSS. Cotton Titus A. XV and A. XVI). Matthew Parker's efforts to defend the English church plus the diligence and the scholarship of his circle led to the publication of two works: *A Testimonie of Antiquitie* (1566), which contains a number of editions of Anglo-Saxon, ecclesiastical texts such as Ælfric's *Easter Homily*, the *Lord's Prayer*, the *Creed* and the *Ten Commandments*, and *The Gospels of the fower Euangelistes* (1571) (Gneuss 1996: 41).

From the very beginning of English text translation, the absence of any kind of apparatus and, in particular, the lack of a grammar and a dictionary, was perceived to hamper early progress severely. This article will, therefore, be mainly concerned with on the early development of these.

2. A search for origins

Gneuss (1996: 40) advances the rediscovery and first English translation of Tacitus' *Germania* (1598) as one of the principal impulses towards English interest in things Germanic, especially in view of the 1605 publications by Camden (1531−1623) and Richard Verstegan (alias Richard Rowlands) (*fl.* 1565−1620). Both these men recognised the Germanic nature of Old English and demonstrate familiarity with the work of the Dutch scholar. J. J. Scaliger (1540−1609) in their concern to refute any claim that the origin of the Germanic languages lay in the Persian based vocabulary similarities Scaliger had noted (Camden 1605: 24; Verstegan 1605: 26−7). Camden (1605−34) adduced fanciful Greek origins for several English words, but also demonstrated the capacity of the Anglo-Saxons to express Latin concepts without borrowing. Verstegan (1605: 206−239) added a list of 600 Old English words explaining them "by their moderne ortography" or by the 'French woords wee haue taken in steed of them'. To these he added some Old English etymologies based on Lambarde (1567).

Aylett Sammes (1636?−1689?) includes an edition of the laws of Ine in Sammes (1676). He proposed a Phoenician origin for English and put forward Old Gothick (or Runick) as the alphabet originally used by the Anglo-Saxons, Swedes and Danes (Sammes 1676: 410). His description of Old English manuscript punctuation under the alphabet indicates a limited acquaintance with the originals and, indeed, he notes that the Runick alphabet cited by Camden had no interpretation annexed.

Notwithstanding, whatever the ultimate origin of Old English may have been seen to be, it is clear that, by the 17th century, English scholars were aware of the general Germanic nature of Old English, probably as a result of contacts with Continental scholars such as Francis Junius (1590−1677). Indeed it is thought that Junius initially learned Old English in order to gain a better understanding of the nature of his native Dutch (Van Romburgh 2001a, b; Thomson 2000: 59).

3. Toward a dictionary of Old English

The influence of Norman administrations which England endured from the 11th century on and the loss of English as the language of both the aristocracy and officialdom meant that, by the 16th century, Old English had become incomprehensible. For political, ecclesiastical or intellectual reasons, several antiquarians felt the need to know something of the content of their holdings and a number of glossaries were produced. In addition to his list of these, while searching for Nowell's sources, Buckalew (1982: 22−3) traces the increasing sophistication of Leland's and Talbot's use of Ælfric's *Grammar* and *Glossary* to Nowell's transcript (now, Westminster Abbey MS 30) which the latter gave to William Lambarde in 1565.

Basing himself on a wide variety of prose sources including Ælfric's *Grammar* and *Glossary* (Buckalew 1982: 35), Nowell wrote the first Old English dictionary in English, the *Vocabularium Saxonicum*, but this had to wait for the 20th century before it was published (Marckwardt 1952). It has all the errors of a pioneering work, but is more or less consistently alphabetically ordered for the first three letters, of the stem where a prefix is recognised, gives a number of cognates from other languages, and draws attention to a number of Lancashire and other dialect words when these are perceived to be closer to Old English than the gloss given (Hetherington 1980: 16−21). Nevertheless it is clear that it circulated freely among interested scholars of the time, enabled Lambarde to append his glossary to the *Achaionomia*, and probably formed a basis for John Joscelyn's *Dictionarium*, a much larger work based on many more manuscripts, unfinished and unpublished, but left, like other manuscripts in Joscelyn's possession to Robert Cotton (1571−1631). Cotton's library at Westminster, the remains of which include the backbone of the British Library's collection of Anglo-Saxon manuscripts, was to form the focal point for the Society of Antiquities (*ca.*

1586−1608). One influential member, Sir Henry Spelman (1564?−1641?), compiled a glossary of Latin and Old English law terms (Spelman 1626) of which he was only able to publish the first volume (A to L). The second volume was published together with a re-edited first volume by his protegé William Dugdale (1605−1686), who had the expense defrayed by subscription (Adams 1917: 49). The proportion of Old English words in Dugdale (1664) is comparatively small and some time later Dugdale prepared a *Dictionarium Saxonicum*, some 328 folios containing material from charters, wills, and property transactions but also some poetry. While recognising his errors, Hetherington (1982: 83) commends his care in transcribing and recording variant forms from different manuscripts.

A year after meeting Spelman in 1630, Sir Simon D'Ewes (1602−1650) began work on a Saxon dictionary and Hetherington (1982: 83) credits him with introducing modern methodology to Old English lexicography. D'Ewes' endeavour had competition from a dictionary being written by the Dutch scholar, Johannes de Laet (1582−1649), whose knowledge of theology and Old English had impressed both Henry Spelman (Hetherington (1980: 98) and the antiquarian, John Morris (?1590−1658), who praised him for giving not merely a verbal translation but a paraphrase of A−S words and drawing attention to difficulties with medical botanical and legal terminology and for collecting cognates from other, mainly Teutonic languages (Bekkers (1970: xviv). Neither dictionary was ever published and De Laet's unfinished manuscript has been lost to us, as indeed has a considerable part of the Cotton collection, as a result of fires in 1728 at Copenhagen and 1731 at Westminster respectively.

In response to a more intellectual interest in Old English, Henry Spelman set up the first Saxon lectureship at Cambridge for orientalist Abraham Whelock (1593−1653) in 1640. The absence of published reference material meant that it took Whelock himself seven years to learn Old English and on Whelock's death the Spelman family arranged transfer of the stipend to endow William Somner's research (Douglas 1951: 53).

Matthew Parker's plea for a dictionary (Greg 1935−36: 246) had to wait almost a century before Somner (1659) was published in Oxford. Hetherington (1982: 86) points out that Somner's method was eclectic in that it relied on the material that had gone before and points to his use of Junius' transcription of Ælfric's *Glossary*, "not a scholar's or a theorist's dictionary, but a practical student's dictionary".

Somner (1659) was to serve its purpose well and support the efforts of the group of Saxonists around George Hickes (1642–1715) in Oxford, although the scarcity of copies led Thwaites (d. 1711) to complain that only one copy was available for his 15 students. In 1699 Thwaites had engaged in setting up the first school of language and literature at Queen's College Oxford, even though the posts he held were Professor of Greek and Reader in Moral Philosophy. Somner (1659) is not a pocketbook dictionary and attempts were made to produce a concise and inexpensive version for students. In 1701, Thomas Benson's, *Vocabularium Anglo-Saxonicum* appeared, but Thomas Hearne attributes it chiefly to Thwaites and his students of whom Benson was one. Hearne further analyses it as "[...] a compendium of Mr Somner, the additions being taken from Mr Junius' papers in the Bodleian".

Interest in the Old English language, if not in its literature, waned in 18th century England and the next substantial dictionary to be published was Bosworth (1898), again an unfinished work, but supplemented by Toller. This dictionary was very much on the lines of the massive 19th century compilations of the Philological Society (founded 1842), giving, as it does, etymologies, citations and locations for every entry. And, indeed, despite its deficiencies under certain letters, it is still in use to-day. Frederick Furnivall (1825–1910), a member of the Philological Society, then flourishing as a result of interest in the new philology in Germany, set up the Early English Text Society in 1864. The purpose of the new Society was to make editions of Old and Middle English texts so that these could be cut up and used for accurate quotations and etymological comparisons for what is now called the *Oxford English Dictionary*. Begun in 1862, the first volume of the *OED* was published in 1886. The Early English Text Society still exists, and, these days is concerned with making accurate text editions with full critical apparatus.

Even the two handbook dictionaries still in use date from the 19th century, namely Sweet (1897) and Clark (1894), but on the whole, lexicographical endeavour has moved away from England to Germany, America and, especially to Canada where the *Microfiche Concordance to Old English* has appeared Venezky & di Paulo (1980) and fascicles of the groundbreaking *Dictionary of Old English*, which gives all known locations and variants, are appearing. An entirely new approach to Old English lexicography is to be found in Roberts & Kay (1995).

4. Anglo-Saxon grammar

The production of an Anglo-Saxon grammar was just as beset with difficulties as those for a dictionary; successive compilers had access to more and more manuscripts, but were not necessarily successful in establishing underlying patterns. Whelock, for instance, had access to legal and historical texts and published the first English editions of Bede's *Ecclesiastical History* and the *Anglo-Saxon Chronicle* in addition to one of the *Anglo-Saxon Laws* providing information rather than adequate critical editions. Whelock published rules for the grammar of Old English in his edition of Bede (Whelock 1643) and these were included in Somner (1659) (Douglas 1951: 62–63).

Taught by the Dutchman, Francis Junius, who discovered many Old English manuscripts in England, Thomas Marshall (1621–1685) has left us only manuscript notes for an Old English grammar. Progress in the production of a grammar came with George Hickes, Dean of Worcester who pursued much of his work on the earlier Germanic languages while a political and ideological exile. Hickes first compiled a grammar of Anglo-Saxon and Gothic (Hickes 1689) and later his monumental *Thesaurus* of the septentrional languages (Hickes 1703–05) which contained and extension of both the earlier grammars, a grammar of Franconian, an Icelandic grammar, by Runólfur Jónsson, a dissertation on the justification for and techniques of investigating the northern languages, a description of Anglo-Saxon and Danish coins by Andrew Fontaine and, last but by no means least, the Catalogue of Manuscripts in English libraries by Humfrey Wanley (1672–1726). This catalogue had to serve Anglo-Saxonists until well into the 20th century when Ker (1957) was produced.

Hickes (1703–05) was far too bulky for classroom use and, in 1711, Edward Thwaites brought out a Latin epitome of the Old English grammar. Elizabeth Elstob (1683–1756) largely translated Thwaites (1711) into English for the benefit of a lady pupil who could not be expected to understand Latin. A full evaluation of both Hickes' and Elstob's Old English grammars is to be found in Hughes (1982).

The next grammar of Old English to be found in England came in the 19th century exposure to the new philology in Germany and Denmark via Benjamin Thorpe (1782–1870) and John Kemble (1807–1857). Thorpe translated Rask's Anglo-Saxon Grammar into English (Thorpe 1830) and Kemble, through his friendship with Grimm and knowledge of Grimm's philological work, brought the new scientific techniques to bear in his papers on aspects of Old English grammar. Further, the glossaries they published with their editions, were used in the preparation of Bosworth (1898) (Aarsleff 1983: 206–207).

The new philology and recognition of language families meant that, in England, such emphasis as there was shifted away from morphology and syntax to phonetic reconstruction, etymology and dialect studies, witness the efforts of Henry Sweet (1845–1912) in phonetics and Joseph Wright (1855–1930) in dialectology. Both men received extensive training in Germany and both produced grammars of Old English bearing the marks of this training. It was Sweet who made Old English accessible to the majority of 20th century students through his basic grammar, dictionary and editions of normalised texts many of which are still in use to-day.

But mainstream English interest was slow to recognise developments in Germany and focussed on the production of historical and literary material. In 1831, the Society of Antiquaries passed a resolution "for the publication of Anglo-Saxon and early English writers" (Aarsleff 1983: 188) and the fruits of English research are to be seen in the many 19th-century editions by Kemble, Thorpe, Cockayne, Stubbs and others.

Given the dissemination of interest in the 20th century and the lack of critical assessment, it seemed invidious and unbalanced to single out particular grammars simply because they were produced in England. The history of 20th century Anglo-Saxon language studies remains to be written.

5. Other Germanic languages

Despite the interest and enthusiasm with which German, Dutch and Flemish scholars were pursuing linguistic aspects of the older Germanic languages and the interest the Danes and Norwegians evinced in Icelandic and Old Norse from the end of the 16th century on, the English tended to restrict their investigations to a resurrection of the Anglo-Saxon legal code and a defence of the English Church, against the Catholics at first, but also against the Puritans in the later 17th century. What little there is of interest in Germanic languages other than English depends on those few scholars who travelled and had contacts with their Continental contemporaries, such as Henry Spelman who, in his correspondence with the Danish antiquary Ole Worm, made inquiries about Old Norse for use in Spelman (1626).

Francis Junius' pupil Thomas Marshall, graduate of and later to become rector of Lincoln College Oxford probably gained his fellowship on the basis of Marshall (1665), which he presented to Archbishop Sancroft as a "Copie of two ancient translations of the four Evangelists now published in the city of Dordrecht. The one, being Anglo-saxonique, is a monument of our English nation" (Green 1979: 276–277). Presumably while he was chaplain to the Merchant Adventures in Rotterdam and Dort, between 1648 and 1669, he collected a number of manuscripts including 17 in Middle Dutch ranging from Jan van Ruysbroek's 'Expositie van den Tabernacule' to a 15th century romance of Sydrac and Boctus. Although his interests had more to do with Arabic, Hebrew and Coptic, his collection also includes a 12 leaf autograph manuscript (Bodleian MS Marshall 78) containing rough notes for a Gothic grammar and one for an Anglo-Saxon grammar. Bodleian MSS Marshall 61 and 62 contain Latin notes comenting on Gothic collations and Old English words while Bodleian MS Marshall 114 is a 17th century transcript of the Icelandic Edda of Snorri Sturluson. It is likely that his interest in the septentrional languages were stimulated and sustained by his friendship with Junius and his circle. Junius not only published "editions of Caedmon (1655), of the Codex Argenteus and of the Moeso-Gothic version of Ulfilas" but sent Marshall an Icelandic dictionary in 1669 "not doubting but you shall then trie what the meaning of the Runik inscriptions Mr. Dugdale and your other antiquaries in England desire to knowe the interpretation" (Green 1979: 276–277). Junius, who had brought his fount of runic type to England, presented it to Oxford University Press where it was used for printing Hickes (1689) and Hickes (1703–05). Hickes himself gives Old Norse parallels in his Anglo-Saxon grammar.

One Robert Sheringham (1602–1678) had brought back to Cambridge from exile in Holland "a lively interest in Teutonic mythology" and produced (1670) *De Anglorum Gentis Disceptatio* described by William Nicolson *English Historical Library* (1736) as containing "many curious antiquities searched for in the most antient Saxon German and Danish authors" (Douglas 1939 [1951]: 53). Nevertheless, philological interest in Gothic and Icelandic appears to bear fruit in an edition by Edward Lye (1694–1767) of Junius (1743). Nevertheless, Lye (1772) was only published posthumously and a century was to pass before the publication of Cleasby & Vigfússon (1874). Richard Cleasby (1797–1847) collected materials for an Icelandic dictionary, but completion was left to the Icelander Guðbrandur Vigfússon.

The new philology gave rise to a few grammatical publications in England, such as Braune (1883) and Clark (1862), but these were either directly translated from German editions (Braune) or based on German; Clark (1862) was based on Bopp's *Vergleichende Grammatik*.

6. Bibliography

Aarsleff, Hans. 1983 [1967] *The Study of Language in England 1780–1860*, Minneapolis: Univ. of Minnesota Press; London: The Athlone Press.

Adams, Eleanor N. 1917. *Old English Scholarship in England from 1566–1800, Yale Studies in English.* Vol. 55. Yale: Yale University. (Repr. London: Archon Books, 1970.)

Ackerman, Gretchen P. 1982. "J. M. Kemble and Sir Frederic Madden: 'Conceit and Too Much Germanism?'". Berkhout & Gatch 1982. 167–181.

Bekkers, Johannes Antonius Frederik. 1970. *Correspondence of John Morris with Johannes de Laet.* Nijmegen: Van Gorcum – Dr. H. J. Prakke & H. M. G. Prakke.

Benson, Thomas. 1701. *Vocabularium Anglo-Saxonicum, lexico Gul. Somneri magna parte auctius* [...]. Oxford: at the Sheldon Theatre.

Berkhout, Carl T. 1998. "Laurence Nowell (1530–ca. 1570)". Damico 1998. 3–17.

– & Milton McC[ormick] Gatch. 1982. *Anglo-Saxon Scholarship; the First Three Centuries.* Boston, MA: Hall.

Bosworth, Joseph. 1898. *An Anglo-Saxon Dictionary, based on the Manuscript Collections of the late Joseph Bosworth, D. D., F. R. S. Rawlinson Professor of Anglo-Saxon in the University of Oxford.* Ed. & enlarged by T. Northcote Toller. London: Oxford Univ. Press.

Braune, Wilhelm, 1883. *Gothic Grammar with Selections for Reading and a Glossary.* Translated from the second German edition by G. H. Balg. London.

Brewer, Charlotte. 1998. "Walter William Skeat (1835–1912)". Damico 1998. 139–149.

Buckalew, Ronald E. 1982. "Nowell, Lambarde, and Leland: The Significance of Laurence Nowell's Transcript of Ælfric's *Grammar and Glossary*". Berkhout & Gatch 1982. 19–50.

Camden, William. 1605. *Remaines of a Greater Worke Concerning Britaine, the Inhabitants there of, their Languages, Names, Surnames, Empresses, wise Speeches Poesies, and Epitaphs.* London [as in section reprinted in W. F. Bolton ed. 1966 *The English Language; Essays by English and American Men of Letters 1490–1839.* Cambridge: Cambridge Univ. Press, v. 22–36.]

Clark, Thomas. 1862. *The Student's Handbook of Comparative Grammar, applied to the Sanskrit, Zend, Greek, Latin, Gothic, Anglo-Saxon, and English Languages.* London.

Cleasby, Richard & Vigfússon Guðbrandur. 1874. *An Icelandic-English Dictionary.* Oxford: Clarendon.

Damico, Helen, ed. (with Donald Fennema and Karmen Lenz). 1998. *Medieval Scholarship; Biographical Studies in the Formation of a Discipline.* Vol. I: *Literature and Philology.* New York & London: Garland.

Dekker, Cornelis [= Kees]. 1997. *'The Light under the Bushel' Old Germanic Studies in Methods of Jan van Vliet (1662–1666).* Leiden: privately printed.

Dickins, Bruce. 1939. "John Mitchell Kemble and Old English Scholarship". *Proceedings of the British Academy* 25: 51–84.

Douglas, David C[harles]. 1951 [1939]. *English Scholars 1669–1730.* Leiden: Eyre & Spottiswode.

Elstob, Elizabeth. 1715. *The Rudiments of Grammar for the English-Saxon Tongue, First Given in English: With an Apology for the Study of Northern Antiquities, Being Very Useful Towards the Understanding Our Ancient English Poets, and Other Writers.* London: Bowyer.

Gatch, Milton Mc[Cormick]. 1998. "Humfrey Wanley (1672–1726)". Damico 1998. 45–57.

Gneuss, Helmut. 1996. *English Language Scholarship: A Survey and Bibliography from the Beginnings to the End of the 19th Century. Medieval & Renaissance Texts & Studies.* Vol. 125. Binghamton, NY: Center for Medieval and Early Renaissance Studies, State University of New York at Binghamton.

Graham, Timothy, ed. 2000. *The Recovery of Old English: Anglo-Saxon studies in the sixteenth and seventeenth centuries.* Kalamazoo, Mich.: Medieval

Institute Publications, Western Michigan University.

Green, Vivian. 1979. *The Commonwealth of Lincoln College*. London: Oxford Univ. Press.

Greg, W. W. 1935–36. "Books and Bookmen in the Correspondence of Archbishop Parker". *The Library*, 4th ser. 16: 243–279.

Hall, J[ohn] R[ichard] Clark. 1894 [1916, 1931] *A Concise Anglo-Saxon Dictionary*. Cambridge: Cambridge Univ. Press.

Harris, Richard L., ed. 1992. *A Chorus of Grammars; The Correspondence of George Hickes and his Collaborators on the* Thesaurus linguarum septentrionalium. Toronto, Ontario: Pontifical Institute of Mediaeval Studies.

–. 1998. "George Hickes (1642–1715)". Damico 1998. 19–32.

Hearne, Thomas. 1885–1921. *Remarks and Collections of Thomas Hearne*. Ed. by C. E. Doble, D. W. Rannie & H. E. Salter. 11 vols. Oxford: Clarendon.

Hetherington, M[ary] Sue. 1980. *The Beginnings of Old English Lexicography*. Spicewood, Tex.: privately printed.

–. 1982. "The Recovery of the Anglo-Saxon Lexicon". Berkhout & Gatch 1982: 79–89.

Hickes, George. 1689. *Institutiones Grammaticae Anglo-Saxonicae et Moeso-Gothicae*. Oxford: at the Sheldon Theatre.

–. 1703–05. *Linguarum Vett. Septentrionalium Thesaurus Grammatico-Criticus et Archeologicus*. Oxford: at the Sheldon Theatre.

Hughes, Shaun F. D. 1982. "The Anglo-Saxon Grammars of George Hickes and Elizabeth Elstob". Berkhout & Gatch 1982. 119–147.

Junius, F[ranciscus] F. 1655. *Caedmonis monachi paraphrasis poetica genesios ac praecipuarum sacrae paginae historiarum, abhinc annos MLXX* […]. Amsterdam: C. Cunrad [etc.]

–. 1665a. *Quatuor D[omini] N[ostri] Jesu Christi evangeliorum versiones perentiquae duae, Goth. scil. et Anglo-Saxonica: quarum illam ex celeberrimo Codice Argenteo nunc primum depromsit Franciscus (Du Jon) Junius, F. F. Hanc autem ex Codicibus MSS. collatis emendatius reduci curavit Thom Mareschallus, Anglus: cujus etiam observationes in utramque versionem subnectuntur* […]. Amsterdam.

–. 1665b. *Gothicum glossarium quo pleraque argentei Codicus vocabula explicantur, atque ex linguis cognatis illustrantur*, Dordrecht: Hen. & Joan. Essaei.

–. 1743. *Etymologium Anglicanum*. Ed. by Edward Lye. Oxford: at the Sheldon Theatre.

Kemble, John M. 1991 [1840]. *Anglo-Saxon Runes*. Ed. & trans. by Bill Griffiths. Pinner, Middelsex: Anglo-Saxon Books.

Ker, N[eil] R[ipley]. 1957. *Catalogue of Manuscripts containing Anglo-Saxon*. Oxford: Clarendon.

Kiernan, Kevin S. 1998. "N. R. Ker (1908–1982)". Damico 1998. 425–437.

Lambarde, William, ed. & trans. 1568 *Archaionomia, sive De priscis Anglorum legibus libri, sermone anglico, vetustate antiquissimo, aliquot abhinc seculis conscripti, atq: nunc demum, magno iurisperitorum, & anantium antiquitatis omnium commodo, è tenebris in lucem vocati*. London: John Day.

Leland, John, 1543. *Genethliacon Illustrissimi Eaduerdi Principis Cambriae*. London: R. Wolfe.

Lye, Edward. 1772. *Dictionarium Saxonico et Gothico-Latinum* […]. Ed. by Owen Manning. London: Edm. Allen.

Madan, F., H. H. E. Craster & N. Denholm-Young, eds. 1895–1953. *A Summary Catalogue of Western Manuscripts in the Bodleian Library at Oxford*. 7 vols. Oxford: Clarendon.

Marckwardt, Albert H., ed. 1952. *Laurence Nowell's "Vocabularium Saxonicum"*. Ann Arbor, Mich.: University of Michigan Press.

Marshall, Thomas. 1665. *Observationes in Evangeliorum Versiones perantiquas duas Gothicas scil. et Anglo-Saxonicas*. Dordrecht.

Murphy, Michael. 1982. "Antiquary to Academic: The Progress of Anglo-Saxon Scholarship". Berkhout & Gatch 1982. 1–17.

[Page, Raymond, Ian]. 1975. *Matthew Parker's Legacy*. Cambridge: Corpus Christi College Cambridge.

Pearshall, Derek. 1998. "Frederick James Furnivall (1825–1910)". Damico 1998. 125–138.

Pulsiano, Philipp. 1998. "Benjamin Thorpe (1782–1870)". Damico 1998. 75–92.

Roberts, Jane & Christian Kay, with Lynne Grundy. 1995. *A Thesaurus of Old English, in two volumes*. Volume I.: *Introduction and Thesaurus*. Volume II.: *Index*. London: King's College London, Centre for Late Antique and Medieval Studies. *King's College Lonson Medieval Studies XI*.

Romburgh, Sophie van. 2001a. *'For my worthy Friend Mr. Franciscus Junius'. An edition of the complete correspondence of Francis Junius F. F. (1591–1677)*. Ph. D. dissertation. Leiden: Leiden Universdity.

–. 2001b. "Why Francis Junius (1591–1677) became an Anglo-Saxonist, or, the Study of Old English for the Elevation of Dutch". *Studies in Medievalism* 11.

Rosier, James L. 1960. "The Sources of John Joscelyn's Old English-Latin Dictionary". *Anglia* 78: 28–39.

Sammes, Aylett. 1676. *Britannia Antiqua Illustrata, or the Antiquities of Ancient Britain derived from Phænicians*. Vol. I. London.

Smith, Lucy Toulmin, ed. 1906–10. *The Itinerary of John Leland*. 5 vols. London.

Somner, William. 1659. *Dictionarium Saxonico-Latino-Anglicum. Voces phrasesque praecipuas Anglo-Saxonicas e libris sive manuscriptis, sive typis excusis aliisque monumentis [...] collectas [...]*. Oxford: William Hall.

Spelman, Henry. 1926. *Archeologus in modum glossarii ad rem antiquam posteriorem, continens Latino barbara peregrinus obsoleta [...]*. London: John Beale.

–. 1664. *Concilia, decreta, leges, constitutiones, in re ecclesiarum orbis Britannici*. Vol. 2: *From the Norman Conquest to the reign of Henry VIII* ed. by William Dugdale, London.

Sutherland, Kathryn. 1998. "Elizabeth Elstob (1683–1756)". Damico 1998. 59–73.

Sweet, Henry. 1876. *An Anglo-Saxon Reader in Prose and Verse: With Grammatical Introduction, Notes, and Glossary*. Oxford: Clarendon.

–. 1882. *An Anglo-Saxon Primer: With Grammar, Notes and Glossary*. Oxford: Clarendon.

–. 1886. *An Icelandic Primer: With Grammar, Notes and Glossary*. Oxford: Clarendon.

–. 1888 [1874]. *A History of English Sounds from the Earliest Period: Including an Investigation of the General Laws of Sound Change, and Full Word Lists*. London: Trübner.

–. 1897. *The Student's Dictionary of Anglo-Saxon*. Oxford: Clarendon.

Thomson, Karen. 2000. *An Historical Sketch of the Progress and Present State of Anglo-Saxon Literature in England by John Petheram 1840*. Edinburgh: The Stag Press.

Thorpe, Benjamin, trans. 1830 [1865]. *A Grammar of the Anglo-Saxon Tongue, with a Praxis [...]; A New Edition Enlarged and Improved by the Author. By Erasmus Rask*. Copenhagen: Møller. (2nd rev. ed. 1865, London: Trübner.)

Thwaites, Edward, ed. 1711. *Grammatica Anglo-Saxonica ex Hickesiano linguarum septentrionalium Thesauro excerpta*. Oxford: at the Sheldon Theatre.

Verstegan, Richard. 1605. *Restitution of Decayed Intelligence*. Antwerp: Robert Bruney.

Venezky, Richard Lawrence & Antoinette di Paolo Healey. 1980. *A Microfiche Concordance to Old English* (= *Publications of the Dictionary of Old English*, 1.). Toronto: Centre for Medieval Studies, University of Toronto.

Wheloc, Abraham. 1643. *Historiae ecclesiasticae gentis Anglorum libri V. A venerabili Beda presbytero [...]*. Cambridge.

Wiley, Raymond A., ed. 1971. *John Mitchell Kemble and Jakob Grimm: A Correspondence, 1832–1852*. Leiden: Brill.

Wright, Joseph & Elizabeth Mary Wright. 1908. *Old English Grammar*. London: Oxford Univ. Press.

Robin D. Smith, Leiden
(The Netherlands)

150. L'étude des langues slaves en Russie: M. L. Lomonosov

1. Introduction
2. Le roman de formation d'un futur linguiste
3. La carrière académique à Saint-Pétersbourg et les défis linguistique de l'époque
4. Lomonosov comme linguiste de la diachronie
5. Lomonosov comme linguiste de la synchronie
6. Conclusion
7. Bibliographie

1. Introduction

A l'époque de Lomonosov (1711–1765), la parenté qui unit les langues slaves était communément admise en Russie depuis le Moyen âge et la *Chronique de Nestor* (chapitre III); cette parenté linguistique paraissait encore plus évidente pour les étrangers, elle fondait le concept ethnique général de 'Slaves' bien mieux que tout autre argument historique, culturel ou pseudo-racial. Mais il manquait encore à cette intuition d'être assise sur des arguments scientifiques.

C'est dans le même halo d'imprécision que baignait le concept de 'langue russe'; dans le domaine de la codification, de la grammatisation de la langue, le russe accusait en effet un net retard par rapport à d'autres langues slaves telles que le polonais, le tchèque, le slovène, le croate qui avaient bénéficié de la promotion des langues vernaculaires initiée en Europe par la Réforme. Au XVIIe siècle, le prêtre catholique croate Jurij Križanić se plaignait déjà dans son *Etat russe au milieu du XVIIe siècle* de l'absence en russe d' "une bonne grammaire et d'un bon dictionnaire". Et si une grammaire allemande et une grammaire française avaient été publiées à Saint-Pétersbourg vers 1730, il faudra attendre encore un quart de siècle avant que n'y paraisse la première grammaire russe rédigée en russe que nous devons à Lomonosov. Les seules grammaires russes sont jusque là l'œuvre d'étrangers comme Ludolf (Ludolf 1696) ou de Russes qui rédigent en allemand comme Adodurov (Adodurov 1731). Ce retard est généralement attribué au rôle particulièrement important joué par le vieux slave, langue sacrée créée par les missionnaires Cyrille et Méthode au Xe siècle afin de répondre à la demande du prince de Moravie Rostislav qui voulait que l'on évangélise ses sujets en slave. La base de cette sorte d'espéranto slave était cependant le dialecte macédonien pratiqué par les deux apôtres, c'est-à-dire une langue slave du groupe méridional. En Russie, cette langue légèrement adaptée en 'slavon russe' se trouva utilisée en distribution complémentaire avec le russe qui appartenait au groupe oriental des langues slaves. On connaît l'affirmation célèbre de Heinrich Ludolf dans sa grammaire russe publiée à Oxford en 1696: "loquendum est Russice & scribendum est Slavonice" (Unbegaun 1959: [x]). Le slavon était effectivement en Russie la langue noble, pieusement préservée de toute évolution, réservée à la liturgie et aux genres littéraires élevés; le russe, au contraire, était utilitaire, d'usage quotidien, et donc soumis à l'érosion et à l'évolution. L'iconoclaste Unbegaun a donc pu suggérer qu'il y avait là une véritable diglossie (v. Ungebaun 1965), mais cette diglossie était vécue par l'usager comme deux simples niveaux de langue différents entre lesquels il ne cessait de faire le va-et-vient, aidé par le fait que ce slavon etait bien plus proche du russe que ne l'était alors le latin d'église des autres langues romanes. Jusqu'à la fin du XVIIe siècle, les seules grammaires publiées en terre russe ne concernaient donc que le slavon (v. Smotrickij 1619). Le rôle joué par l'orthodoxie, fondement de l'idéologie de l'état moscovite, ne pouvait qu'accentuer le retard pris par la réflexion linguistique en terre russe car l'Eglise considérait avec suspicion les arts de la parole (v. Bocadorova 1993: 60).

Cet équilibre entre slavon et russe va se trouver compromis par l'entrée de la Russie dans la modernité au XVIIe siècle et ne fera ensuite que s'accélérer avec Pierre le Grand. Techniques, sciences, modes nouvelles affluent en Russie, créant de nouveaux besoins terminologique. Le slavon se révèle incapable de les satisfaire et l'économie du système langagier entre en crise. Les influences étrangères se donnent libre cours dans le lexique avec des emprunts massifs (v. Comtet 1995: 25−31), et même dans la syntaxe qui tend à s'aligner sur le modèle latino-allemand d'ordre des mots. L'anarchie lexicale se donne libre cours avec souvent deux termes pour désigner une même notion, un terme étranger et un terme autochtone, entre lesquels l'usager peine à choisir.

Un besoin urgent se faisait donc sentir de rétablir l'harmonie dans la langue en usage en Russie, de la codifier afin de créer un outil de communication moderne qui réponde aux aspirations nationales du pays incarnées par Pierre le Grand. Cette quête de spécificité linguistique nationale ne pouvait s'opérer que par opposition, comparaison et distinction vis-à-vis des autres langues: slavon, autres langues slaves et langues d'Europe occidentale. Dans ce processus complexe de positionnement visant à normer une nouvelle langue moderne, le rôle de Lomonosov, le premier à avoir écrit une grammaire du russe en langue russe, a été fondamental. On peut se demander ce qui le préparait à jouer ce rôle de codificateur de la langue russe; chez cet être d'exception aux talents multiples, quel fil invisible pouvait bien relier le physicien, le chimiste, l'ingénieur, le géologue, le géographe, l'historien, le traducteur, l'homme de lettres, le théoricien du vers et le grammairien?

2. Le roman de formation d'un futur linguiste

Les circonstances de sa vie ont fait que, très tôt, Lomonosov a été confronté au babélisme universel. Il passa les dix-neuf premières années de sa vie dans un village de pêcheurs du Nord de la Russie où il était en contact avec les parlers finno-ougriens, carélien et lapon, en usage chez les allogènes de la région, parlers qu'on le voit ensuite désigner par le terme générique de "langues tchoudes": "Les Lapons [...] constituent avec les Finnois un peuple unique, qui regroupe aussi les Caréliens et quantité de peuplades sibériennes. Leur langue a une origine unique [...]." (Lomonosov 1950−59: 6, 361). A la même époque, l'un des premiers livres qu'il a entre les mains est la *Grammaire slavonne* de Metelij Smotrickij évoquée plus haut. Ensuite Lomonosov devait se rendre à Moscou; il réussit à se faire admettre à l'Académie slavo-gréco-latine où les études duraient cinq ans. Il y apprit le slavon et le latin qui devait obligatoirement pouvoir être parlé couramment dès la troisième année et il s'initia au grec en autodidacte. Il dut aussi prendre conscience à cette époque de la variablité spatiale du russe: il parlait un dialecte du Nord qu'il put confronter au dialecte moscovite ainsi qu'aux parlers russes méridionaux et à l'ukrainien (qu'on ne considérait encore à l'époque que comme un dialecte russe appelé symptomatiquement 'petit russien'); beaucoup de professeurs et d'élèves de l'Académie venaient en effet d'Ukraine, foyer culturel slave dont les confréries orthodoxes s'opposaient activement à la politique culturelle entreprenante menée par les Jésuites à partir de la Pologne et de la Lituanie.

Vint ensuite le séjour en Allemagne qui se prolongea jusqu'en 1741, d'abord à l'université de Marburg, puis à Freiberg en Saxe. L'Académie des sciences avait choisi Lomonosov et d'autres de ses condisciples pour y acquérir une formation scientifique et technique, en particulier comme ingénieur des mines; il s'agissait alors pour la Russie de former ces 'spécialistes' dont elle manquait cruellement et qu'elle était contrainte de faire venir de l'étranger. Lomonosov réussit fort bien tout ce qu'on attendait de lui, en particulier "acquérir des connaissances en russe, allemand, latin et français suffisantes afin de pouvoir couramment écrire et parler en ces langues". Lomonosov eut vite assimilé l'allemand et trois années plus tard il traduisait sans difficulté des odes du français en russe. A Marburg, il se frotte au hongrois (Papp 1998), à Freiberg il se montre capable d'imiter à la perfection le parler saxon local.

Il est possible aussi qu'il ait été confronté au slave de Lusace, le 'sorabe' ou 'serbe de Lusace', puisque Freiberg n'était distante que d'une centaine de kilomètres de Bautzen, centre du haut-sorabe; en tout cas, Lomonosov n'oubliera pas dans ses futurs tableaux linguistiques de mentionner cette langue sous son nom d'alors de 'wende'. Tout prouve par ailleurs qu'il a étudié alors le polonais; a pu jouer ici le fait que Freiberg avait pour suzerain Auguste II, à la fois Electeur de Saxe et roi de Pologne (Lomonosov assista à sa réception triomphale par la ville le 10 août 1739). Mais il a été amené à s'intéresser au polonais surtout du fait de ses recherches sur la versification russe; depuis le XVIIe siècle celle-ci s'inspirait du système polonais syllabique transmis par le relais ukrainien et Lomonosov s'était familiarisé avec ces *virši* à l'Académie slavo-gréco-latine. Vasilij Trediakovskij avait déjà proposé un nouveau modèle syllabo-tonique en 1735 mais il recommandait l'usage du trochée aux dépens des pieds ïambiques, ce qui montrait l'emprise du modèle syllabique polonais. Tout à son admiration pour les poèmes du grand poète baroque maudit Johann Christian Günther, Lomonosov a alors l'idée d'adapter sans restrictions la versification syllabo-tonique allemande au vers russe afin de tirer le meilleur parti possible des ressources prosodiques naturelles de sa langue. Il écrit donc en 1739 son *Epître sur les règles de la versification russe* [Pis'mo o pravilax rossijskogo stixotvorstva] (Lomonosov 1950–59: 7, 18) qu'il fait parvenir à l'Académie des sciences de Saint-Pétersbourg avec, en guise d'illustration, l'*Ode sur la prise de Xotin* [Oda na vzjatie Xotina] écrite en vers ïambiques pour bien se démarquer de Trediakovskij. L'*Epître* révèle que Lomonosov a étudié attentivement la 'prosodie polonaise' car il y critique l'usage systématique en russe des rimes féminines calquées du polonais dont l'accent de mot fixe sur la pénultième impose ce type de rime. Lomonosov illustrera ensuite sa compétence en polonais dans d'autres domaines; lors de l'affaire Miller, dont il sera question plus loin, on lui demandera de traduire en russe un extrait de l'historien polonais Długosz invoqué par l'académicien allemand à l'appui de sa thèse 'normaniste'; on sait aussi que Lomonosov a utilisé et annoté d'autres historiens polonais qu'il lisait dans le texte pour ses recherches historiques (Bernštejn 1979: 224–226). Cette compétence en polonais lui permettra plus tard de souligner l'influence que celui-ci a exercée sur l'ukrainien (Lomonosov 1950–59: 7, 608).

L'*Epître* amorce cependant aussi toute une réflexion sur l'accent de mot russe, que Lomonosov associe à la longueur, remettant du coup en cause la distinction que Smotrickij avait cru bon de faire entre des voyelles longues et brèves indépendantes de l'accent en russe (Lomonosov. 1950–59: 7, 10–11); ainsi n'hésite-t-il pas déjà à critiquer la tradition, souhaitant en bon scientifique considérer la langue russe telle qu'elle est, comme un objet débarrassé de toute idée préconçue.

3. La carrière académique à Saint-Pétersbourg et les défis linguistiques de l'époque

Lorsque Lomonosov revient dans la capitale russe en 1741, c'est en qualité de scientifique, de chimiste qu'il va bientôt être nommé avec le grade d'*ad"junkt* auprès de l'Académie des sciences. Mais son esprit encyclopédique saura toujours mener plusieurs activités de front et il n'oubliera jamais ses préoccupations philologiques et littéraires.

La Russie d'alors n'échappe pas au grand remue-ménage intellectuel initié par l'humanisme de la Renaissance relayé par la Réforme. La science du langage demeure alors soumise le plus souvent à un double présupposé qui empêche toute approche historique et comparative; à la thèse théologique de la monogenèse du langage à partir de l'hébreu langue mère s'ajoute la tradition aristotélicienne revivifiée par la *Grammaire générale et raisonnée* de Port-Royal avec ses prétentions universalistes: toute langue ne ferait que traduire les lois universelles de la pensée selon les lois d'une grammaire universelle. Cependant, ces postulats se heurtaient de plus en plus à la diversité des langues mise en évidence par les collectes et les descriptions systématiques des diférents idiomes. Dès le XVIe siècle apparaissent des études qui, bien qu'embryonnaires, peuvent déjà être qualifiées de pré-comparatistes (on présente ainsi les langues romanes comme ayant divergé à partir du latin par évolution naturelle, et non sous l'effet d'une corruption exercée par les langues germaniques). Les travaux de ce genre vont se multiplier au XVIIIe siècle où "tout le monde écrit sur le langage" (Mounin 1967: 141), jusqu'au philosophe Christian Wolf, maître de Lomonosov à Marburg. Dans le domaine slave, les travaux du prêtre catholique croate Jurij Križanić (1617–1693) s'inscrivaient déjà dans une optique comparatiste; écrite en 1666 et publiée seulement en 1848–1859 (Bodjanskij 1859), sa *Grammaire* proposait en effet une sorte d'espéranto slave en prétendant reconstituer un slave commun primitif; même si le résultat n'était qu'un mélange bâtard de russe, slavon et croate, le postulat de départ était déjà bien celui de la parenté génétique des langues slaves.

A son retour en Russie, Lomonosov retrouve aussi un pays en train de construire son identité nationale en grande partie par réaction aux influences allemandes; ces influences étaient dues au fait que la Russie engagée par Pierre le Grand sur la voie de la modernité ne pouvait se passer des spécialistes et des modèles que les pays germaniques étaient alors les mieux à même de lui fournir. Après avoir perdu du terrain sous le règne d'Elisabeth, ces influences devaient culminer sous le règne de Pierre III qui ne rêvait que d'inféoder la Russie à la Prusse de Frédéric II, en ayant au préalable converti ses sujets au protestantisme. C'est seulement dans les dernières années de la vie de Lomonosov que Catherine II, bien que princesse allemande, devait rompre avec cette tradition pro-germanique en orientant la Russie vers la France qui symbolisait alors la civilisation européenne. Tout pétri de culture germanique, époux d'une Allemande luthérienne, Lomonosov n'en était pas moins patriote et il critiquait vivement les excès de la présence allemande en Russie; il en avait surtout après les académiciens allemands de Saint-Pétersbourg dont il jalousait les prérogatives, les accusant de ne pas tenir suffisamment compte des intérêts de la Russie. Il s'était même laissé aller à les agresser physiquement, ce qui lui valut plus de cinq mois de mise aux arrêts en 1744. L'imprudence de l'un d'eux lui permit cependant de prendre bientôt sa revanche.

Le casus belli fut constitué par le discours de la séance solennelle d'ouverture de l'Académie confié à Fedor Ivanovič Miller (*alias* Gerhardt Friedrich Müller); celui-ci développait dans son *De origine nominum russorum* la thèse avancée une dizaine d'années plus tôt par un autre académicien allemand, Gottlieb Bayer (Bayer 1741), sur les origines varègues (ou 'normandes') de l'Etat et de la culture russes. Il s'ensuivit une grande polémique initiée par le petit groupe des académiciens russes, Miller fut sanctionné cependant que Trediakovskij et Lomonosov défendaient la cause nationale des origines russes de leur pays. Soutenant avec intolérance ce point de vue bien russe qui dénie aux étrangers le droit de parler de la Russie, Lomonosov ne pouvait pas plus supporter que l'académicien allemand Schlözer se permette à la même époque de composer une grammaire russe ou d'écrire une histoire de Russie comme Voltaire. On peut donc se risquer à affirmer que c'est la revendication nationaliste dans la droite ligne de l'héritage de Pierre le Grand qui va pousser Lomonosov à se faire historien avec son *Histoire de la Russie depuis l'origine de la nation russe, jusqu'à la mort du Grand Duc Iaroslav Premier* (Lomonosov 1766, édition post mortem) et grammairien avec la *Grammaire russienne* rédigée en 1754–55 (Lomonosov 1757) et pour laquelle il commença à amasser des matériaux dès la fin des années 1740.

On vérifie effectivement que le philologue et l'historien ont des préoccupations communes; dans la tradition de l'époque, Lomonosov invoque des arguments philologiques pour démontrer que la Russie a un très ancien passé de civilisation; il interroge par exemple la toponymie pour mieux cerner l'extension maximale du peuplement slave en Europe dans le passé, sa répartition entre les différentes ethnies. Il va donc être amené à mettre en perspective ces langues slaves selon une approche diachronique. En même temps, la polémique contre Schlözer lui permet d'affirmer que les premiers monuments écrits de la Russie comme la *Russkaja pravda* l'étaient en vieux russe et non en slavon. Et sa *Grammaire* donne au russe ses quartiers de noblesse, le hausse au niveau des grandes langues de civilisation; il la fera d'ailleurs traduire en allemand, dernier défi de l'élève à ses maîtres (Lomonoßow 1764). En s'appuyant sur la compilation scrupuleuse et préalable d'exemples tirés de la langue contemporaine il établit les bases d'une étude synchronique du russe qui se trouve enfin dégagé de l'hypothèque slavonne qui pesait sur lui. On relèvera que ce n'est exceptionnellement, contrairement à Trediakovskij, qu'il participe dans le feu de la polémique à la pseudo-scientifique 'guerre étymologique'; ainsi renvoie-t-il à l'occasion à Schlözer, coupable de proposer des étymologies offensantes tendant à prouver que les Russes étaient jadis subordonnés aux Germains (*knjaz'* "le prince" dérivé de *Knecht* "le domestique" ...) la filiation (imaginaire) du nom de la Prusse: *Preußen < Porus' < po Rus'* "qui jouxte la Russie" ... (Lomonosov 1950−59: 9, 426−427). Ce qui nous intéresse, c'est bien plutôt le corps de la doctrine linguistique de Lomonosov tel qu'il l'a exprimé dans une série d'ouvrages et dans des brouillons et matériaux qui n'ont été publiés qu'à l'époque actuelle (Lomonosov 1950−59); ces ouvrages sont les suivants: la *Lettre sur les règles de la versification russe* écrite en 1739 et déjà citée: la *Rhétorique* [Kratkoe rukovodstvo k krasnoreč'ju] composée en 1748 (Lomonosov 1950−59: 7, 89−378); la *Grammaire russienne* [Rossijskaja grammatika], écrite en 1754−1755 (Lomonosov. 1950−59: 7, 389−578); l'*Avant-propos sur l'utilité des livres du rituel pour la langue russe* [Predislovie o pol'ze knig cerkovnyx v rossijskom jazyke] écrit en 1757 (Lomonosov. 1950−59: 7, 585−594). Tous ces écrits ont été rédigés de 1739 à 1757, soit au cours d'une courte période de 18 ans, ce qui nous autorise à les traiter comme un corpus unique où nous avons pu vérifier que la pensée linguistique de l'auteur s'est peu à peu construite en progressant dans une direction unique sans jamais se contredire. Nous allons tenter d'en exposer la substance en suivant les deux grands axes de la diachronie et de la synchronie.

4. Lomonosov comme linguiste de la diachronie

On a malheureusement perdu les deux textes de Lomonosov intitulés *A propos de la ressemblance et des changements dans les langues* [O sxodstve i peremenax jazykov] et *A propos des langues parentes du russe* [O srodnyx jazykax rossijskomu] (Lomonosov 1950−59: 7, 761, 944). Mais l'ensemble de son œuvre permet de restituer sa pensée comparatiste. La réflexion de Lomonosov sur les rapports entre les langues slaves s'inscrit en effet dans une vision d'ensemble où il distingue entre langues 'parentes' (*srodstvennye*) et 'non parentes' (*nesrodstvennye*): cette approche moderne s'inscrit donc en faux contre les vieilles spéculations théologiques sur l'origine unique des langues; il est vrai que la parenté du russe avec les autres langues d'Europe occidentale était dans l'air du temps, elle avait déjà été avancée par Schlözer et le Français de Patron Baudan dans ses manuscrits conservés à Saint-Pétersbourg (Martel 1933: 22). Trediakovskij et Sumarokov reprennent cette idée avec une visée polémique puisque le slavon serait l'ancêtre de toutes les langues teutoniques pour le premier, tandis que pour le second le "celto-russe" serait plus ancien que le latin et le germanique.

Lomonosov, lui, est plus sobre, se contentant de noter la parenté des langues slaves avec ces langues que nous appelons 'indo-européennes'; cela lui permet de distinguer quatre groupes: slave (russe), grec, latin, allemand; il utilise beaucoup les numéraux dans la comparaison, méthode d'enquête favorite des futurs comparatistes. Lomonosov nous donne aussi des contre-exemples de langues non apparentées: le finnois, le 'mexicain' (aztèque), le hottentot et le chinois, ce qui témoigne de l'étendue de son information linguistique. Il range les langues baltiques avec le slave, annonçant ainsi l'hypothèse toujours à l'ordre du jour d'un chaînon intermédiaire balto-slave dans la filiation qui mène de l'indo-européen au slave commun d'une part, aux langues baltiques d'autre part. La même approche comparativiste se retrouve quand il traite des langues slaves; il en distingue sept:

le russe, le polonais, le bulgare, le serbe, le tchèque, le slovaque et le wende (le sorabe, v. *supra*); on note l'absence du slovène, peu connu, et du macédonien, du biélorussien et de l'ukrainien qui ne furent reconnus comme langues à part entière que bien plus tard. Lomonosov divise ce groupe slave en deux sous-ensembles, l'un sud-oriental (russe, bulgare et serbe), l'autre nord-oriental (polonais et tchèque) car il remarque à juste titre que le russe est en rapport plus étroit avec les langues "transdanubiennes" (*zadunajskie*) qu'avec le polonais et le tchèque; la linguistique actuelle n'a-t-elle pas créé un groupe 'léchitique' pour ce dernier ensemble? Lomonosov relève enfin l'influence des langues 'tchoudes' (finno-ougriennes) sur le russe, annonçant ainsi le concept de 'substrat finno-ougrien' qui sera développé plus tard à propos du russe, avec toutes les polémiques que cela a engendré (Lomonosov 1950–59: 7,608).

Nulle part il ne fait mention du sanskrit, omission d'autant plus surprenante que l'académicien allemand Gottlieb (Theofil) Bayer en avait publié une description à Saint-Pétersbourg dès 1732–1735 (Bayer 1732; Bayer 1735). Lomonosov aurait-il été aveuglé par sa hargne contre les Allemands de l'Académie au point de boycotter leurs écrits? la question demeure posée ... En tout cas, en rangeant les langues slaves avec les langues européennes, il faisait figure de précurseur; en 1786 Jones laisse les langues slaves de côté lorsqu'il établit l'origine commune du sanskrit, du gaulois, du grec, de l'allemand et du vieux perse; et il faut attendre 1833 pour que Bopp les intègre à l'arbre indo-européen. On comprend mieux ainsi la gestation du mythe herdérien sur le caractère exceptionnel, à la fois antique et novateur, de ce slave mystérieux qu'on avait mis si longtemps à redécouvrir.

5. Lomonosov comme linguiste de la synchronie

Cette approche historique des langues slaves permet en fait à Lomonosov de parvenir à une description correcte du russe contemporain; il ne cesse en effet d'appeler le slavon "ancienne langue morave" [*drevnij moravskij jazyk*], allusion évidente à la mission de Cyrille et Méthode en Moravie; cette dénomination étrangère permet de mieux le distinguer du russe qui retrouve ainsi sa pleine autonomie. Jusqu'alors les Russes considéraient en effet que le slavon était à l'origine de leur langue et on trouve encore cette affirmation chez Trediakovskij alors que Lomonosov met les deux langues sur un plan d'égalité. La levée de l'hypothèque slavonne permet donc à Lomonosov d'élaborer sa *Grammaire*. La longue préface, dans le goût du temps, rappelle encore les principes de la grammaire générale assimilés en Allemagne auprès de Christian Wolf puisqu'il y est question de la "parole humaine en général" et de ses lois. Mais cette approche philosophique cède vite le pas dans le corps de l'ouvrage à une approche plus linguistique.

La tâche de Lomonosov était ici particulièrement ardue; il lui fallait en effet donner le reflet le plus exact de ce qui existait mais aussi opérer la synthèse d'éléments divers car cette première grammaire russe se devait de fonder une nouvelle norme de l'usage, presque une nouvelle langue mise au service d'une authentique culture russe: l'observateur devait être aussi créateur. Dans l'usage, il existait en effet un fossé énorme entre les différentes langues écrites (liturgique, administrative, littéraire etc.) et les langues parlées à la Cour, dans les salons, le peuple, les provinces. Dans la collecte des faits linguistiques dont témoignent les matériaux préparatoires de la *Grammaire*, Lomonosov applique la méthode des sciences de la nature qu'il pratiquait par ailleurs en physique ou en chimie: à partir des observations dégager une théorie et par la théorie corriger les observations. Il voudrait aussi se garder, malgré ses références à la grammaire générale, d'appliquer des modèles étrangers, le grec en particulier, à la description du russe: "Beaucoup commettent l'erreur, en composant des grammaires, de les ramener de force aux autres langues. Ainsi en est-il des grécisants." (Lomonosov 1950–59: 7, 691). En fait, il reprend la terminilogie grammaticale fixée par Smotrickij (cf. *supra*) qui s'inspirait de la grammaire grecque byzantine et de la grammaire latine de Donat traduite en slavon en Russie en 1522; il emprunte également à la grammaire d'Adodurov (Adodurov 1731). On le voit aussi calquer le système temporel de l'allemand ou du français en distinguant dix temps en russe. C'est que en tout Lomonosov a été l'homme du compromis, de la combinaison (il est aussi chimiste) et de la synthèse.

Il fallait ensuite que Lomonosov opère deux grandes synthèses: tout d'abord celle des trois grands dialectes russes, même s'il rappelle que leurs différences n'entravent pas l'intercompréhension à l'intérieur de l'espace russe, au contraire des dialectes germaniques (flèche tirée contre le rival allemand); Lomonosov y distingue le dialecte 'pomore' [*pomorskij*], qui correspond aux parlers du Nord, le dialecte 'moscovite' [*moskovskoj*] où il range tous les parlers à *akan'e* (les /o/ se réalisent comme /a/ hors de l'accent de mot), l'ukrainien enfin [*malorossijskoj*] qui correspond aux parlers méridionaux (Lomonosov 1950−59: 7, 609). On voit ici la synthèse s'opérer au niveau de l'orthographe; contrairement à Trediakovskij qui préconisait une orthographe phonétique, Lomonosov prescrit d'écrire de telle sorte "que ne soient pas entièrement masquées les traces de l'origine et de la composition des mots." (Lomonosov 1950−59: 7, 430) Cette solution morphologique permet un consensus entre les divers parlers; ainsi *o* va-t-il noter /o/ en position non accentuée: cela correspond à la réalisation comme [o] dans les parlers du Nord cependant que les autres locuteurs qui réalisent ici [a] le feront spontanément en reconnaissant des racines 'familières' dans les textes écrits. La solution est phonologique avant la lettre, elle préfigure l'orthographe actuelle du russe.

La deuxième grande synthèse à faire était celle du slavon et du russe, car il n'était pas question de renoncer à la source inestimable de richesses lexicales et stylistiques du fond slavon qui avait assuré la pérennité de la culture russe au cours de l'histoire. Il est donc tenu compte par exemple de variantes slavonnes comme la distinction des genres au nominatif pluriel de l'adjectif, distinction qui n'existait pourtant pas à l'oral (voir le masculin *istinnye* en regard du féminin-neutre *istinnyja* 'véritables').

Mais Lomonosov met en valeur systématiquement la spécificité du russe; dans la morphologie du nom, il note des formes typiquement russes comme pour les masculins de la seconde déclinaison le génitif ou locatif singulier en /u/, le nominatif pluriel en /a/; il admet encore, sous l'influence de la tradition, un cas vocatif mais en s'empressant de relever que ce cas peut très bien être suppléé par le nominatif; et il note que le duel est en complète déshérence dans le système du russe contemporain; les substantifs animés épicènes du type *plaksa* "le pleurnicheur / la pleurnicheuse" n'échappent pas plus à sa perspicacité. Dans le système de l'aspect, il demeure visiblement embarrassé par le modèle franco-allemand et dilue la notion d'aspect en dix temps, faisant des suffixes itératifs ou imperfectivants des désinences temporelles; même si on a pu considérer qu'il a été en ce domaine moins avancé que Smotrickij (Mazon 1913: 347−348), on le voit noter cependant que la répétition et plus encore la durée sont associées à l'imperfectif; et sur le plan morphologique, il met en valeur le rôle perfectivant du préverbe qui fait basculer le temps du côté de l'accompli.

La synthèse russo-slavonne va le mieux s'exprimer dans le système stylistique proposé par Lomonosov dans l'*Avant-propos sur l'utilité des livres du rituel pour la langue russe*; il y transpose la théorie latine des trois styles en caractérisant ceux-ci par la différence du dosage russo-slavon dans le lexique et la morphologie; le style sublime utilise le maximum d'éléments slavons, richesse commune aux anciens Slaves et aux Russes d'aujourd'hui; il sera réservé aux grands genres littéraires, odes, épopées, sermons, discours solennels etc. Le style tempéré caractérise les comédies de mœurs, les satires, les églogues, les épîtres etc. Il inclut quelques slavonismes ainsi que le lexique russe utilisé par les Russes cultivés dans la conversation. Quant au style bas destiné aux comédies, à la conversation familière, il ne présente que des mots russes absents des textes slavons, avec souvent une coloration orale, familière. Mais le résultat final de cette ingénierie linguistique demeure une synthèse qui préserve l'existence de toutes les couches de la langue russe. Les écrivains russes vont donc disposer là d'une référence sûre pour s'orienter dans la langue de l'époque, quitte pour eux à s'affranchir ensuite des préceptes lomonossoviens dans leur création.

6. Conclusion

Le rôle de Lomonosov dans l'étude des langues slaves en Russie et la fondation du russe contemporain a bien été celui d'un éveilleur, d'un initiateur qui a posé les interrogations fondamentales auxquelles devaient ensuite répondre les linguistes russes du siècle suivant. Il a eu sur bien des problèmes des intuitions qui devaient ensuite être corroborées par le comparatisme: parenté et taxinomie des langues slaves, rôle du 'substrat finno-ougrien', 'adstrat' polonais en ukrainien. Il a surtout doté la langue russe d'une première grammaire basée beaucoup plus sur l'observation des faits linguistiques que sur des a priori, une sorte d'état des lieux qui va servir de référence au moins jusqu'à la moitié du XIXe siècle et permettre ainsi à la linguistique russe de se construire et de progresser. En même temps, cependant, il se veut patriote, a conscience de défendre la dignité du russe comme langue nationale face aux idiomes étrangers; le fait qu'il traduise sa grammaire russe en allemand participe de ce nationalisme ombrageux qui veut que seuls les Russes soient compétents pour parler des choses russes. Sa démarche rejoint donc celle des autres nations slaves pour qui la renaissance nationale passera bientôt obligatoirement par celle de la langue. Le bilan de son action dans le domaine de l'étude des langues slaves en Russie est donc tout à fait contrasté: Lomonosov participe du Siècle des Lumières par son ouverture sur la diversité langagière du monde, par sa méthode scientifique basée sur l'observation des faits, par son goût des synthèses ambitieuses qui rappelle l'esprit des Encyclopédistes; mais en même temps il tempère cet universalisme par des traits spécifiquement russes: respect de la tradition, nationalisme linguistique, génie pratique du compromis. On peut bien dire par là que Lomonosov a été le premier slaviste typiquement russe.

7. Bibliographie

Adodurov, Vasilij. 1731. "Anfangs-Gründe der Rußischen Sprache." Weismann, Ehrenreich. *Teutsch-Lateinisch- und Russisches Lexicon, samt denen Anfangsgründen der Russischen Sprache. Zu allgemeinen Nutzen bey der Kayserl. Academie der Wissenschaften zum Druck befördert [...]*. [Repr. dans Tschizevskij, Dimitrij in Zusammenarbeit mit Dietrich Gerhard, Hg., *Slavische Propyläen Text in Neu- und Nachdrucken*. Bd. 55, 1969: *Drei russische Grammatiker des 18. Jahrhunderts*. Nachdruck der Ausgaben von 1706, 1731 und 1750, mit einer Einleitung von B. O. Unbegaun. München: Fink. (Reproductions des textes en fac-similé, sans pagination. Le texte d'Adodurov est le deuxième du recueil.)]

Bayer, Gottlieb. 1741. *Origines russicæ*. Sankt-Petersburg: Izdatel'stvo Akademii nauk.

Bayer, Teofil. 1732. "Elementa literaturæ brahmanicæ, tangutanæ, mungalicæ. Cum 10 tabulis aeri incisis". *Commentarii Academiae Imperialis Petropolitanae* 3. 389−422. Sankt-Petersburg.

−. 1735. "Elementa brahmanica, tangutana, mungalica". *Commentarii Academiæ Imperialis Petropolitanæ* 4. 289−301. Sankt-Petersburg.

Bernštejn, Samuil Borisovič, éd. 1979. *Slavjanovedenie v dorevoljucionnoj Rossii. Biobibliografičeskij slovar'* [La slavistique dans la Russie prérévolutionnaire. Dictionnaire bio-bibliographique.] Moskva: "Nauka".

Bocadorova, Natalia. 1993. "Comparaison de la tradition linguistique russe et de la tradition des sciences du langage en Occident: X−XVIIe siècles". *Bulletin de la SHEL* 31. 59−60. Paris.

Bodjanskij, Osip Maksimovič, éd. 1859. Križanić, Jurij. *Gramatično izkazanje ob ruskom jeziku* [Exposé grammatical de la langue russe.] Sankt-Petersburg.

Comtet, Roger. 1995. "La tradition russe des dictionnaires des mots étrangers". *Slavica occitania* 1. 25−47. Toulouse.

Lomonosov, Mixail Vasil'evič. 1757. *Rossijskaja grammatika* [Grammaire russienne.] Sankt-Petersburg: Izdatel'stvo Akademii nauk.

−. 1766. *Drevnjaja rossijskaja istorija* [Histoire de la Russie ancienne.] Sankt-Petersburg: Izdatel'stvo Akademii nauk.

−. 1950−59. *Polnoe sobranie sočinenij* [Œuvres complètes.] Moskva & Leningrad: Izdatel'stvo Akademii nauk SSSR.

Lomonoßow, Michael. 1764. *Rußische Grammatik*. St. Petersburg: Akademie der Wissenschaften. (Repr. 1980. München: Otto Sagner.)

Ludolf, Heinrich. 1696. *Henrici Wilhelmi Ludolfii grammatica Russica Oxonii A. D. MDCXCVI*. (Repr. dans Unbegaun, Boris 1959.)

Martel, Antoine. 1913. *Michel Lomonosov et la langue littéraire russe*. Paris: Librairie ancienne Honoré Champion.

Mazon, André. 1913. "La notion morphologique de l'aspect des verbes chez les grammairiens russes". *Mélanges offerts à Monsieur Emile Picot*. Paris: Librairie Damascène Morgand, 343−367.

Mounin, Georges. 1967. *Histoire de la linguistique des origines au XXe siècle*. Paris: PUF.

Papp, Ferenc. 1998. "Mixail Vasil'evič Lomonosov (1711−1765), la langue hongroise et les Hongrois". *Slavica occitania* 6. 271−281. Toulouse.

Smotrickij, Meletij Gerasimovič. 1619. *Grammatiki slavenskija pravilnoe sintagma [...]* [Syntaxe régulière de la grammaire slave.] Vil'no. (repr. dans Horbatsch, Olexa, éd. 1974. Frankfurt/M.: Kubon & Sagner.)

Unbegaun, Boris, éd. 1959. *Henrici Wilhelmi Ludolfi Grammatica Russica Oxonii A. D. MDCXCVI*. Oxford: Oxford Univ. Press.

−. 1965. "Le russe littéraire est-il d'origine russe?". *Revue des études slaves* XLIV. 19−28. Paris.

Roger Comtet, Toulouse (France)

151. Die Entdeckung der Verwandtschaft der finnougrischen Sprachen

1. Sporadische Berichte, frühe Vermutungen
2. Die Schaffung der Grundlagen eines Sprachvergleichs
3. Die ersten Vergleichsversuche innerhalb der Sprachfamilie
4. Die Entdeckung der breiteren sprachlichen Verwandtschaft
5. Martin Fogels Feststellungen
6. Das Zeitalter der Expeditionen
7. Der Durchbruch in der Methode und im Inhalt: Sajnovics und Gyarmathi
8. Bibliographie

1. Sporadische Berichte, frühe Vermutungen

Die finnougrischen Sprachen werden wohl schon seit Tausenden von Jahren auf dem geographischen Gebiet Europas gesprochen, aber sie sind sehr lange im europäischen Bewußtsein nicht präsent gewesen. Weil sie selbst bis in das späte Mittelalter nur vorübergehend und eingeschränkt über eigene 'wissenschaftliche' Institutionen verfügten, waren sie bis zum späten 18. Jh. vornehmlich Objekte der Forschung fremder Kulturen. Entsprechend vage und problematisch fallen die ersten Aussagen über diese Sprachen und Völker aus.

So kommt bei Priskos Rhetor um 460 in einem Bericht der Name 'Onoguri' in bezug auf die Ungarn vor. In der *Germania* des Tacitus wird bereits im Jahre 98 über das Volk der 'Fenni' berichtet. Diese Bezeichnung kommt auch in der Anleitung zur *Erdbeschreibung* des Ptolemaios aus dem 2. Jh. in der Form 'φίννοι' vor, aber die Bedeutung dieser Angaben ist auch heute noch umstritten. Collinder (1960: 12) meint, das Ethnonym weise auf das Volk der Lappen hin, neuere Forschungen, wie Grünthal (1997: 277) betonen, daß der Name vielmehr ethnische Gruppen mit einer sammelnd-jagenden Lebensform bezeichnet habe.

Sporadisch kann man später auch andere Aufzeichnungen und Anmerkungen finden, welche mit den finnisch-ugrischen Völkern in Verbindung gebracht werden. Sie sind zwar meistens ohne Anspruch auf Wissenschaftlichkeit geschrieben worden bzw. geben oft bloße Vermutungen oder Behauptungen anderer Reisender wieder, aber sie bringen die Existenz dieser Völker und Sprachen ins Bewußtsein der Zeitgenossen. Ottar von Haalogaland, der Vasall des englischen Königs Alfreds des Großen (r. 871–899), zum Beispiel, bereiste das Gebiet von der Kola-Halbinsel bis zum Dwina-Fluß, wobei er auf das Volk der 'Bjarmos' traf. Dieser Begegnung verdanken wir die erste Aufzeichnung, welche zwei finnisch-ugrischen Sprachen (möglicherweise eine der permischen Sprachen und das Lappische) miteinander vergleicht: "Quod ad linguam attineret, eandem prope Bjarmorum ac Finnorum fuisse sibi visam" (zitiert nach Zsirai 1937: 475).

Ähnliche Kommentare haben wir den – vom ungarischen König Béla IV. (r. 1235–1270) mit Missionierungsaufgaben unter der Leitung von Julianus nach Rußland geschickten – Dominikanermönchen zu verdanken; in einem Brief des Fraters Riccardus an die päpstliche Kurie vom Frühjahr 1237 heißt es beispielsweise, Julianus habe auf seiner Reise ein Volk getroffen, dessen Sprache den Ungarn verständlich sei:

"Er fand sie nämlich am großen Strom Ethyl. Als sie ihn gesehen und erkannt hatten, daß er ein christlicher Ungar sei, freuten sie sich nicht wenig über seine Ankunft, führten ihn durch die Häuser und Dörfer und fragten ihn voll Vertrauen aus über den König und das Königreich der christlichen Ungarn, ihrer Brüder. Was er ihnen auch über Glauben und über andere Angelegenheiten vortrug, das hörten sie beflissen, da sie ja die ungarische Sprache benutzten; und sie verstanden ihn und er sie." (Göckenjan-Sweeney 1985: 79)

Über die weiter östlich lebenden Verwandten der Ungarn, die Wogulen und Ostjaken, bemerkt Wickman, daß sie:

"[...] were known among the Russians under the name of *Ugra* or *Jugra* since old times, and the Ugra people is mentioned already in the Nestor chronicle from the 11th century as living in the north-east." (Wickman 1988: 792–793)

Mehr Aufmerksamkeit für die finnougrischen Sprachen und erste Vergleichsversuche aufgrund genauerer Kenntnisse können wir erst seit der Renaissance vorzeigen. Die Informationen kommen aus Italien, wo ein Interesse an der Vielfalt der Sprachen zwar entstanden ist, aber Methoden zu ihrer Untersuchung zunächst noch fehlen. Die Verbindung zwischen den Bewohnern Ugriens und Ungarns stellt zum ersten Mal Aeneas Sylvius Piccolomini (1405–1464), der spätere Papst Pius II., her. In seiner 1458 geschriebenen und 1509 gedruckten *Cosmographia* konstatiert er:

Noster veronensis quem supra diximus ad ortum Thanais pervenisse, retulit populos in Asiatica scythia non longe a Thanai sedes habere, rudes homines et idolorum cultores; quorum eadem lingua sit cum hungaris pannoniam incolentibus." (zitiert nach Zsirai 1937: 477)

Diese Entdeckung hält er für so bedeutend, daß er sie an einer weiteren Stelle, in seinen autobiographischen *Commentarii* (erschienen Frankfurt, 1614), wiederholt und ergänzt: „Sie werden Ungarn genannt. Ihre Rede unterscheidet sich gar nicht von der, welche die jenseits der Ister [der Donau] Wohnenden gebrauchen. Sie nennen sich Verwandte [...]" (zitiert nach Stipa 1990: 29). Piccolominis Behauptungen werden in den folgenden Jahrzehnten von zahlreichen Autoren, besonders von ungarischen Geschichtsschreibern übernommen, ja, sie verkommt geradezu zu einem Gemeinplatz, weil sie sich dazu eignete, die 'ruhmreiche Vergangenheit der Ungarn', ihre skythische Abstammung zu belegen.

Noch einen Schritt weiter als Piccolomini geht in seinen Folgerungen der Gründer der ersten Akademie der Humanisten in Rom, Julius Pomponius Laetus (1425−1498), der 1479−1480 selbst 'nach Skythien' reiste. Seine Reiseerfahrungen sind in seinen Kommentaren zu Vergils Werken in drei Bänden 1487 erschienen. Hier weist Laetus eindeutig auf die Verwandtschaft der Völker hin:

"Der Hister wird Danubios genannt, nachdem er Ugria [d. h. Ungarn] erreicht hat. Sie [die Ungarn] haben ihren Ursprung von den Ugriern, die am Eismeer wohnen. Jetzt sind die Ugrier [die Ungarn] sehr mächtig." (Zitiert nach Stipa 1990: 31)

Bereits im 15. Jh. werden die Ideen des italienischen Humanismus von den kulturellen Zentren Mitteleuropas übernommen. In Prag, Krakau oder Wien ging dies mit einer Veränderung des 'Forschungsgegenstandes' einher: die Sprachen der Völker dieser Region finden zunehmend Berücksichtigung in den Werken der Gelehrten. Die oft erwähnten Beziehungen zwischen den Ungarn und den Ugriern werden zum Beispiel von dem Krakauer Professor Matthias de Miechow (1456−1523) in seinem 1517 erschienenen *Tractatus de duabus Sarmatiis, Asiana et Europiana et de contentis in eis* untersucht. Auffallend sind seine Hinweise auf die Herkunft der Ungarn, sowie seine Begründung für die slavischen Lehnwörter im Ungarischen:

[...] suntque eiusdem sermonis et loquele precise, nisi quod addiderunt nostri hungari aliqua vocabula ex Sclauonico idiomate, earum rerum quae in Scithia et Juhra non reperiuntur. (Zitiert nach Zsirai 1937: 479)

Auf den Spuren und unter dem Einfluß des Tractatus Miechows versucht der zweimalige kaiserliche Gesandte in Moskau, Siegmund Freiherr von Herberstein (1486−1556), in seinen 1549 gedruckten *Rerum Moscoviticarum Commentarii*, die ungarisch-ugrische Sprachverwandtschaft zu prüfen. Während sein Werk für lange Zeit als wichtigste Informationsquelle über Rußland und die dortigen Verhältnisse galt, mußte er seinen Plan, sprachliche Beweise für die Verwandtschaft zu sammeln, mangels geeigneter Gewährspersonen aufgeben:

"Aiunt Juharos in hunc diem eodem cum Hungaris idiomateuti, quod an verum sit, nescio. Nam etsi diligenter inquisierim, neminem tamen eius regionis hominem habere potui, quo cum famulus meus linguae Hungaricae peritus colloqui potuisset." (Zitiert nach Zsirai 1937: 477).

Trotzdem zögert von Herberstein nicht, in die der Ausgabe Venedig 1550 seiner *Rerum Moscoviticarum* [...] beigefügte Karte unter IYHRA (Jugra) einzutragen: "Horigine de Vngari(s)" (zitiert nach Stipa 1990: Abbildung 8).

Die im Norden Europas lebenden finnougrischen Völker und Sprachen werden im Laufe des 16. Jhs. zunehmend Objekte der Forschung. Sebastian Münster (1489−1552) veröffentlicht 1544 in Basel seine *Cosmographia universalis*, deren 4. Buch sich ausführlich mit den skandinavischen Ländern beschäftigt. Über das Finnische bemerkt er: "der innere[n] Finlender sprach ist gantz vnd gar vo[n] der Schwedier sprach gescheide[n] / hat auch kein gemeinschafft mit der Moscowyter sprache" (zitiert nach Stipa 1990: 78). In seinem Eifer, alles landeskundlich Bekannte in das Werk aufzunehmen, ebnet Münster den Weg späterer sprachwissenschaftlichen Forschungen, indem er den Text vom "Vatter vnser in Finlendischer vnd Pilappener sprach / deren sich etlich Lyflender gebrauchen" (zitiert nach Stipa 1990: 38) abdruckt. Dies sind die ersten bedeutenden Sprachproben ostseefinnischer Sprachen, welche durch die große Popularität von Münsters Werk für die Gelehrten Europas bis in die Zeit von Gottfried Wilhelm Leibniz (1646−1716) als Quelle dienen.

In dieselbe Richtung verweist das 1555 in Rom erschienene Buch *Historia de gentibus septentrionalibus* von Olaus Magnus (1490−1557). Er ist bemüht, ein richtiges Bild des Nordens anstelle der konfusen Darstellungen zu schaffen und weist bei der Schilderung der

Sprachen auf die vom Schwedischen abweichende Natur des Lappischen und Finnischen hin. Diese Unterschiede werden dann im *Orbis acrtoi nova et accurata delineatio* (Stockholm, 1626) grammatisch etwas detaillierter ausgeführt von Andreas Bureus (1571–1646). Er hebt für das Finnische das fehlende Genus, die Tendenz zur Vermeidung der Konsonantenhäufungen im Anlaut sowie die Postpositionen, die anstelle von Präpositionen gebraucht werden, hervor.

Um diese Zeit treten auch die anderen finnougrischen Völker und Sprachen zunehmend in wissenschaftlichen Schriften auf. So kommen z. B. in dem etwa 1618 erstellten handschriftlichen *Russian Vocabulary* von Richard James (1592–1638) "Unter den aufgezeichneten hauptsächlich russischen, aber auch einigen lappischen, syrjänischen und samojedischen Wörtern […] eine ganze Reihe ostseefinnischer Lehnwörter" (Stipa 1990: 50) vor. Einen noch deutlicheren Sprung hat das Lappische durch die 1648 erfolgte Veröffentlichung eines, von dem Pfarrer der Gemeinde Tornio, Johannes Torneaus (?–1681), zusammengestellten *Manuale Lapponicum* erfahren. Die Vorreiterrolle Schwedens in dieser Zeit erweist sich auch bei der Publikation der ersten größeren Monographie über die Lappen. Der aus Straßburg nach Uppsala berufene Autor Johannes Scheffer (1621–1679) faßt in seiner 1673 in Frankfurt erschienen *Lapponia* das Quellenmaterial der Lappmarktberichte zusammen, die von mit den Verhältnissen gut vertrauten Personen im Auftrag der schwedischen Regierung gesammelt worden waren, und schafft so das beste Kompendium seiner Epoche.

Die ersten vereinzelten Berichte über die übrigen kleineren finnougrischen Völker stammen aus sehr unterschiedlichen Zeiten. Der Hl. Stefan von Perm (1340–1396) hat z. B. 1372 versucht, eine eigene, von der kyrillischen abweichende Schrift für das Syrjänische zu schaffen. Diese Schriftlichkeit ist der Grund für die überraschende Tatsache, daß altsyrjänische Textaufzeichnungen (Ikonenaufschriften, Glossen) aus der Zeit des 15.–17. Jhs. neben dem Ungarischen die älteste Schicht finnougrischer Sprachdenkmäler darstellen. Die Tscheremissen und die Mordwinen treten auch in den bereits erwähnten Werken von Herbersteins auf, die Wogulen und die Ostjaken werden 1666 von Jurij Križanić in seiner *Historia de Sibiria sive Notitia Regnis Sibiriae et Litteris Oceani Clacialis et Orientalis* detaillierter geschildert (dieses Werk wurde erst 1890 in Moskau veröffentlicht). Auch die entferntesten Mitglieder der Sprachfamilie, die samojedischen Völker, werden gegen Ende des 16. Jhs. in Reiseberichten vorgestellt. Da diese Völker zu dieser Zeit bereits allesamt in Rußland oder in seinem unmittelbaren Machtbereich gelebt haben, kommen z. B. die Lappen, die Permier, die Wogulen und die Ostjaken auch gemeinsam in der Literatur vor, wie z. B. 1525 in der Beschreibung *Novocomensis libellus de legatione Basilii magni principis Moschouiae, ad Clementem VII pont. max.* […] von Paulus Jovius (1484–1552). Einen Vergleich ihrer Sprache finden wir aber in diesen Werken verständlicherweise nicht.

2. Die Schaffung der Grundlagen eines Sprachvergleichs

Um überhaupt zutreffende Aussagen über die Verwandtschaft der finnisch-ugrischen Sprachen machen zu können, war es unumgänglich, die einzelnen Sprachen systematisch zu erfassen. Die Ausarbeitung dieser wichtigen Voraussetzungen zum Sprachvergleich ist bei den einzelnen Völkern zu sehr unterschiedlichen Zeiten, hauptsächlich im 16.–19. Jh., erfolgt. An der chronologischen Spitze dieses Prozesses finden wir die Ungarn (→ Art. 137), gefolgt von den Finnen und den Esten, deren Entwicklung hier etwas eingehender geschildert werden soll.

In Finnland beginnt die Erarbeitung der Literatursprache mit der Tätigkeit des in Wittenberg ausgebildeten und in Turku sich für die Reformation einsetzenden Bischofs Michael Agricola (ca. 1510–1557), mit seinem 1543 veröffentlichten *ABC-kiria* ("ABC-Buch"). Agricolas rege Publikationstätigkeit (etwa 2.400 gedruckte Seiten) schafft die Grundlagen für die finnische Nationalsprache.

Die Initiative zur gedruckten Darstellung der Besonderheiten des Finnischen für die internationale Wissenschaft verdanken wir Erik Johann Schroderus (1608–1639), der im Jahre 1637 sein *Lexicon Latino-Scondicum* mit mehr als zweitausend finnischen Angaben in Stockholm veröffentlicht. Damit gelangt ein Teil des finnischen Wortschatzes in den Kreis der damals sehr populären lexikalischen Sammlungen. Dieser Umstand ist von großer Bedeutung, denn Mangels geeigneter Mittel und Methoden praktizierte man in dieser Zeit Sprachvergleiche in erster Linie aufgrund von Wortvergleichen (nach Pierre de la Ramée auch 'ramische' Methode genannt, vgl. Stipa 1990: 107). Zur Illustration der unabsehbaren Auswirkungen, die durch Zufall, durch Briefkontakte oder Bekanntschaften der Gelehrten und durch qualitative Unterschiede der Quellen (unter ihnen solide Arbeiten und höchst zweifelhafte Publikationen zugleich) in dieser kulturhistorisch so bedeutenden Epoche entstehen, seien hier zwei Beispiele erwähnt.

Die von Sebastian Münster in der *Cosmographia* 1544 zur Darstellung der Andersartigkeit des Finnischen abgedruckte finnische Liste von zwölf Wörtern wird, entsprechend der damaligen Praxis, 1603 von Hieronymus Megiser (1550−1616) in seinem *Thesaurus* nicht nur übernommen, sondern hinter den aus dem 1595 erschienenen *Dictionarium quinque nobilissimarum Europae linguarum* [...] von Faustus Verantius (1551−1617) sowie aus dem seit 1585 mit ungarischen Angaben ergänzten *Dictionarium* von Ambrosius Calepinus (1435−1511) abgeschriebenen ungarischen und lappischen Wörtern − möglicherweise ohne Absicht, aber trotzdem genetisch völlig korrekt − in der sechsten seiner zehn Tabellen unter den "Europäischen Sprachen" vorgestellt. Die Sprachproben sind bereits richtig 'plaziert', aber diese Tatsache führt zunächst zu keinen weitergehenden Feststellungen in bezug auf ihr genetisches Verhältnis.

Das andere Beispiel ist das 1664 in Stockholm anonym erschienene *Variarum rerum vocabula Latina, cum Svetica et Finnonica interpretatione*, von desesen 1668er Auflage mit einem Exemplar auf dem Schreibtisch von Martin Fogel (1634−1675) landet und bei der Entdeckung der sprachlichen Verwandtschaft der Ungarn und der Finnen ausschlaggebend wirkt.

Die Gründung der Universität Turku (1640) hat unmittelbare Auswirkungen auf die beginnende grammatische Aufarbeitung der finnischen Sprache. Für die 1649 in Turku erschienene *Linguae Finnicae brevis institutio* des Schweden Eskil Petraeus (1593−1657) hat die lateinische grammatische Tradition, aber wohl auch die bereits 1637 erschienene estnische Grammatik von Heinrich Stahl als Vorbild gedient. Auch wenn die für indogermanische Sprachen geeigneten Kategorien sich nur schwer auf finnougrische Sprachen anwenden lassen, war der Versuch von Petraeus von großer Bedeutung. Denn die erste wahrhaft finnische, von einem Muttersprachler geschriebene Grammatik wurde erst 1733 in Turku, zehn Jahre nach dem Tod ihres Verfassers Bartoldus Vhaël (1667−1723) veröffentlicht. Diese, auch in Turku erschienene, *Grammatica Fennica* berücksichtigt bereits in ihrer Struktur die Eigenarten des Finnischen.

"Das zeigt sich zum Teil in der Orthographie, aber mehr noch im Deklinationsparadigma − anstelle von 6 Kasus des Latein 14 finnische −, in der Behandlung der Personalendungen des Verbs und der Possessivsuffixe im Zusammenhang mit den Pronomina und überhaupt in dem Ziel, die eigenen Gesetze des Finnischen darzustellen." (Stipa 1990: 122)

Auch in Estland stellt die allererste Stufe der finnougrischen Sprachforschung die Entdeckung der eigenen Volkssprache dar. Hier, genauso wie in Finnland, übernehmen diese Aufgabe zunächst Fremde. Im Zuge der Reformation entsteht sogar die erste estnische Grammatik ein Jahrzehnt früher als die finnische, aber ihre Qualität zeigt die gravierenden Probleme eines solchen Unternehmens beinahe beispielhaft auf. Der Pastor Heinrich Stahl (ca. 1600−1657) hat seine zweisprachige Grammatik *Anführung zu der Esthnischen Sprach* (Revall [heute: Tallinn]: Verlag des Autors, 1637) zum Erlernen des Estnischen konzipiert. Zur Beschreibung des Estnischen hat Stahl nicht, wie damals üblich, das Lateinische, sondern die Grammatik einer Nationalsprache, nämlich des Deutschen, als Grundlage genommen und somit einen willkürlichen, jedoch nicht einmaligen Weg zur Beschreibung einer Sprache gewählt. Diese methodologische Vorentscheidung vermochte ein anderer Pastor, Johann Gutslaff (gest. 1657) in seinen *Observationes grammaticæ circa linguam esthonicam* (Dorpat [heute: Tartu]: Johannes Vogel, 1648) nur zum Teil zu revidieren.

"Die Sprache, die Stahl und Gutslaff schrieben, war eigentlich ein Estnisch nach deutschem Muster, vor allem mit deutsch geprägter Syntax, Phraseologie und einem mit deutschen Lehnwörtern und Lehnbildungen durchsetzten Lexikon [...]" (Haarmann 1976: 28−29).

Heinrich Gösekens (1612−1681) *Manuductio ad linguam Oesthonicam* (Reval [heute: Tallinn]: 1660) und Johann Hornungs (1660−1715) *Grammatica Esthonica* (Riga: Wilck, 1693) haben maßgeblich die Herausbildung der estnischen Schriftsprache mit der Übernahme vieler Elemente aus den verschiedenen estnischen Dialekten geprägt.

3. Die ersten Vergleichsversuche innerhalb der Sprachfamilie

Aufgrund ihrer geographischen Nähe und einer, die Verwandtschaft im Bewußtsein erhaltenden Tradition, wurden die Sprachen der ostseefinnischen Gruppe innerhalb der finnougrischen Sprachfamilie eher und mit mehr Erfolg miteinander in Verbindung gebracht als die entfernteren Vertreter der Sprachfamilie. Etwa hundert Jahre nach dem bereits erwähnten Hinweis auf die Zusammengehörigkeit des Finnischen und Estnischen bei Sebastian Münster erweiterte Michael Wexionius von Gyldenstolpe (1609–1670) den Umkreis der Forschungen. In dem 1650 in Turku veröffentlichten *Epistome descriptionis Sueciae, Gothiae, Fenningiae et subiectarum provinciarum* gelang es ihm "in a creditable, and surprisingly modern fashion, the relationship between Finnish, Estonian, Livonian and Lappish" (Korhonen 1986: 28) nachzuweisen. Seine Vorgehensweise bei der Beschreibung der behandelten Sprachen ist wirklich seiner Zeit weit voraus. Er geht über die gewöhnlichen Wortvergleiche hinaus und konzentriert sich auf die grammatischen Strukturen der Sprachen in einem beachtlich selbständigen System, welche von denen, die seine Quellen (hauptsächlich Petraeus, Stahl und Torneaus) nach lateinischem Muster aufgestellt haben, stark abweichen. Dank seiner enzyklopädischen Einstellung hat er eine systematische Darstellung der Grammatik dreier Sprachen geschaffen, deren Verwandtschaft sich „nicht bloß in Flexionsparadigmen (Nomen, Verb und Pronomen), sondern auch in Komparation, Konstruktion des Passivs und der Modi sowie anderer grammatischer Formen und Mittel" (Stipa 1990: 146) zeigt. Auch wenn das Werk von Wexionius sich nur mit dem als ostseefinnisch bezeichneten Zweig der Sprachfamilie befaßt, ist sein Werk der erste uns bekannte Schritt zur Anwendung vergleichender und auch die Struktur der Sprachen berücksichtigender Methoden in der finnougrischen Sprachforschung.

Die immer häufiger veröffentlichten Berichte über diese Sprachen rücken sie zunehmend ins Blickfeld einer bereits existierenden internationalen wissenschaftlichen Öffentlichkeit. Ohne klare linguistische Beweise werden von unterschiedlichen Autoren verschiedentlich Vermutungen bezüglich ihre Herkunft und Verwandtschaft geäußert. Gelehrte mit finnougrischen Muttersprachen sind jedoch zu dieser Zeit an diesem Prozeß noch nicht beteiligt.

Da geeignete vergleichende Methoden noch fehlen, führen die Darstellungen oft in die falsche Richtung bzw. zu falschen Ergebnissen. Ein Beispiel dafür stellt die 1666 in Nürnberg erschienene *Das alt und neue teutsche Dacia* von Johannes Tröster (?–?) dar. Der Autor hat sein Buch mit der Idee verfaßt, in Siebenbürgen habe es eine Art 'germanische Kontinuität' seit den Zeiten Attilas gegeben. Dementsprechend interpretiert er die Sprache der dort lebenden Ungarn auch als Mischsprache: „Die Ungariſche heutige Sprach / kan wol das halbe Theil / aus der Teutſchen erœrtert werden. Und ſolte einer die Mueh auf ſich nehmen / wuerde ſie gar Teutſch ſeyn" (Tröster 1666: 96–97). Diese Stellungnahme ist ganz klar und bewußt gegen die Einstellung ungarischer Gelehrter gerichtet, die zu dieser Zeit noch von der skythischen Herkunft der Ungarn und "daß ihre Sprach mit keiner Europaeiſchen etwas Gemeinſchafft habe / ſondern von denen allen weit entfrembdet ſeye" (Tröster 1666: 95) überzeugt gewesen waren. Um zu zeigen, wie sehr durchmischt der Wortschatz des Ungarischen ist, führt Tröster Beispiele auf, in denen er unter anderem auch finnische Wörter mit ungarischen vergleicht. Aus dem 1637 erschienenen *Lexicon Latino-Scondicum* von Schroderus zitiert er finnische Wörter, wie *VVaski, Terafs, Hærad, Mezæ* oder *Sopor*, damit allen klar werde, von wie weither das Ungarische Wörter habe holen müssen. Sehr wichtig ist festzustellen, daß Tröster hier nicht von der Verwandtschaft des Ungarischen mit dem Finnischen redet, wie es viele frühere Forscher (Setälä 1891: 31; Zsirai 1952: 11) getan haben:

"Da mœgen ſich nun die Ungariſchen Scribenten / als in einem Spiegel beſehen / wie falſch ſie ruehmen; die Ungariſche Sprach habe gar mit keiner Gemeinſchaft / ſondern ſey allein fuer ſich / eine Alt-Scythiſche Sprach; da doch vielleicht keine in Europa iſt / die nicht etwas bey der Ungariſchen abzuſondern hat." (Tröster 1666: 103)

4. Die Entdeckung der breiteren sprachlichen Verwandtschaft

Wer die sprachliche Verwandtschaft zwischen Finnisch und Ungarisch zu allererst festgestellt hat, ist umstritten. Es ist nicht leicht, hier eine 'Reihenfolge' aufzustellen, da im Laufe eines langen Prozesses unterschiedliche

Personen zu unterschiedlichen Zeiten unterschiedlich aussagekräftige Behauptungen gemacht haben und die Forschung diesbezüglich noch viel einschlägiges Archiv- und sonstiges Material untersuchen und erschließen muß. Außerdem handelt es sich hier nicht um einen zielgerichteten Prozeß, in dem eindeutig Positionen, Leistungen und Personen eingeordnet werden können. Die Entdeckung der Verwandtschaft unter den finnougrischen Sprachen im 17.–19. Jh. bietet ein deutliches Beispiel für die Zusammenarbeit der Forscher. Die Einzelnen haben natürlich Leistungen hervorgebracht, aber der Faden der individuellen Forschung wurde immer wieder von der Gemeinschaft der Gelehrten aufgenommen und weitergeführt. Lebhafte Korrespondenz (wie Fogel, Skytte, Stiernhielm oder Leibniz), Interesse an der Arbeit des Anderen und immer wieder die Fortsetzung der in Nachlässen zurückgebliebenen, nicht abgeschlossenen Materialien kennzeichnen diese Epoche. Dadurch werden Fehler korrigiert, falsche Einschätzungen revidiert, Forschungsmethoden fortentwickelt, und so wird eine der aufregendsten linguistischen Fragen der Zeit, das genetische Verhältnis und die sprachlich-geographische Ausbreitung der finnougrischen Sprachen, schrittweise geklärt.

In diesem Gesamtbild wird seit längerem und unter Hinweis auf Leibniz, der in mehrfacher Hinsicht eine entscheidende Rolle im Prozeß der Klärung der Verhätnisse zwischen den finnougrischen Sprachen gespielt hat, die Entdeckung der Verwandtschaft zweier finnougrischer Sprachen mit dem Namen Jan Amos Comenius (1592–1670) verbunden. In den 1768 in Genf erschienenen *Opera omnia* [...] von Leibniz stehen sogar zwei Hinweise auf Comenius: "Porrò nullam linguarum Europæarum Hungariæ æquè ac Finnica accedit, quod Comenius, quantum ſciam, primus notavit" (Bd. 2, 192). Einige Seiten später, in einer anderen Abhandlung, erweitert Leibniz den Kreis der Entdecker noch:

Hungaricum autem linguam in multis Fennonicæ conſentire jam Comenius in Didacticis & Sternielmius in argentei Codicis præfatione notarunt. (S. 204)

Diese von Leibniz zitierte Stelle wurde erst 1952 von András O. Vértes in den 1657 veröffentlichten *Opera didactica omnia* von Comenius gefunden, im Text der *Grammatica latino-vernacula*:

"Sunt ſanè Lingvæ, qvæ voculas ejuſmodi non præponunt, ſed poſtponunt; ut Hungarica & Finnica, ex Europæis: denominatio tamen fit à majori [...]" (S. 313, zitiert von Vértes O. 1952: 291).

Diese Bemerkung steht in jenen Aufzeichnungen des Comenius, die vor der Zeit seines Aufenthaltes in Ungarn, also von vor 1650 stammen. Diese Aufmerksamkeit den finnischen Postpositionen gegenüber kann weniger auf unmittelbare Erfahrungen während des Schweden-Aufenthaltes von Comenius zurückgeführt werden, als vielmehr auf Andreas Bureus, der in dem 1631 unter dem Namen Henricus Scoterus erschienenen Sammelwerk, *Suecia, ſiue de Suecorum Regis Dominiis et opibus* schreibt:

"Tertia ejus proprietas eſt, quod voculæ quæ in aliis linguis à præponendo præpoſitiones vocantur, in Finnonica lingua ſemper poſtponuntur" (zitiert nach Vértes O. 1952: 291).

Diese Besonderheit des Finnischen scheint für die Sprachforscher der Zeit am auffälligsten, und dank der Popularität des Werks von Bureus, auch am bekanntesten gewesen zu sein. Es muß jedoch unterstrichen werden, daß die oben zitierten Wörter von Comenius sich lediglich auf die Feststellung eines gemeinsamen Zuges der beiden Sprachen beschränken; von einer Verwandtschaft spricht er nicht.

Das obige Zitat von Leibniz erhält auch einen weiteren Hinweis auf die Arbeit von Georg Stiernhielm (1598–1672). In seinem Vorwort "Über den Ursprung der Sprachen", wo er die 'skytischen Primär- und Kardinalsprachen' in dem 1670 in Stockholm erschienenen *Glossarium Ulphila-Gothicum* schildert, stellt er folgendes fest:

"Von den bekannten nenne ich wenigstens zwei, Ungarisch und Finnisch, deren Ursprung bisher niemand aufhellen konnte. Weder auf das Slawische noch eine andere uns bekannte Sprache können sie zurückgeführt werden. Worüber ich mich am meisten wundere ist, daß im Wörterbuch Molnars [Molnár Szenczi, Albert: *Dictionarium Latino-hungaricum & Dictionarium Ungarolatinum*. Nürnberg 1604, sowie spätere, erweiterte Ausgaben – T. F.] recht viele ungarische Wörter gefunden habe, die auch den Finnen gemeinsam sind während doch die Völker himmelweit von einander entfernt sind." (Zitiert nach Stipa 1990: 144)

Stiernhielm erweitert also den Kreis der Ähnlichkeiten mit einem Hinweis auf den Wortschatz. Stipa (1990: 145) meint, daß er diese Erkenntnisse bereits seit 1652 systematisch verfolgt habe, aber seine Beobachtungen seien unveröffentlicht in seinem Nachlaß geblieben. Zwei Zettel wurden in der Sammlung *Miscellanea etymologica* gefunden, wobei der zweite den Titel "Ungarica convenientia cum Finnonica et Suethica" trägt. Wieweit diese Sammlung als Beweis für die Entdeckung der Sprachverwandtschaft dienen kann, ist fraglich, denn Stiernhielm hat auch das nichtverwandte Schwedische in seine Untersuchungen einbezogen. Auch estnische, lappische und andere Wörter stehen in dieser Liste, und wie Setälä (1892: 45−46) zeigt, haben sich viele von den aufgezeichneten lexikalischen Übereinstimmungen später bei der Entdeckung der Verwandtschaft tatsächlich als Beweismaterial erwiesen. So kommen u. a. ungarisch *eggy*, finnisch *ygs*, *yx* (eins); ungarisch *hal*, estnisch *kala* (Fisch); ungarisch *vay*, finnisch *woita* (Butter); ungarisch *fö*, estnisch *pä* (Kopf); ungarisch *kéz*, lappisch *ket*, *kiet* (Hand); ungarisch *tél*, estnisch *talwe* (Winter) in der Wortliste von Stiernhielm vor.

Der dritte Forscher, der ebenfalls von manchen Quellen zu den 'Entdeckern' der finnougrischen Sprachverwandtschaft gerechnet wird, ist der Schüler von Stiernhielm und Bekannte von Comenius, Bengt Skytte (1614−1683). Nach einer Begegnung mit ihm, im Jahre 1667, schreibt Leibniz, daß er "Non ignorabat consensum Finnonicæ et Hungaricæ" (Setälä 1891: 62). In Skyttes (unvollendetem und auch nicht veröffentlichtem) Lebenswerk, *Sol praecipiarum linguarum subsolarium*, spielen Wortvergleiche die zentrale Rolle, unter denen sich auch finnische, estnische und ungarische Belege befinden. Der Umfang dieses Manuskripts wurde erst 1921 bekannt, als in schwedischen Archiven insgesamt etwa 650 Seiten Material entdeckt wurden (siehe Grape 1921). Durch seine Lebensgeschichte gehört Skytte zu jener kleinen Gruppe von Gelehrten in der frühen Erforschung des Finnischen und des Ungarischen, welche nicht nur geschriebene Quellen benutzt hat, sondern "die Zusammengehörigkeit dieser beiden Sprachen bei der Materialbehandlung selbst beobachtet hatte" (Hormia 1965: 5). Gegen Ende seines Lebens plante Skytte noch eine Arbeit "Über Etymologie und Harmonie der Sprachen" zu verfassen, wo auch ungarische, finnische und lappische Wörter berücksichtigt werden sollten.

Skyttes Material haben nach seinem Tod und nach der Verteilung seines Nachlasses offensichtlich auch andere Forscher benutzen können. Sowohl Olaus Rudbeck der Ältere (1630−1702) als auch sein Sohn, Olaus Rudbeck der Jüngere (1660−1740), haben seine ungarischen Wortlisten in ihren Arbeiten benutzt. Von dem älteren Rudbeck ist erst im Jahre 1965 bekannt geworden, daß er gegen Ende seines Lebens ein umfangreiches finnisch-ungarisch-lappisches Wortmaterial mit offensichtlichem Vergleichszweck zusammengestellt hat. Aufgrund dieser Wortsammlung ist er auf einen Schlag "unter den Wissenschaftlern im Schweden des 17. Jhs. derjenige, von dem sich das meiste Material, gesammelt zur Klärung der Beziehungen zwischen Finnisch und Ungarisch, erhalten hat" geworden (Hormia 1965: 7).

Rudbeck d. J. hat die von Skytte und von seinem Vater gesammelten Wörter in seinem 1717 in Uppsala erschienenen *Specimen Usus linguae Gothicae* in einem hundert finnisch-ungarische Wortvergleiche umfassenden Anhang unter dem Titel "Analogia linguae Finnonicae cum Ungarica" veröffentlicht. Aufgrund dieser Publikation galt für lange Zeiten Rudbeck d. J. als Entdecker der finnisch-ungarischen Sprachverwandtschaft.

5. Martin Fogels Feststellungen

Wenn nicht nur der Zeitpunkt, sondern auch die Methode des Sprachvergleichs berücksichtigt wird, dann gilt zweifelsohne der Hamburger Arzt und Polyhistor Martin Fogel (1634−1675) als tatsächlicher Entdecker der finnisch-ungarischen Sprachverwandtschaft. Als besonders vielseitiger und begabter Gelehrter, der sich mit verschiedenen Fragen der Linguistik (Phonetik, Orthographie, Syntax, Etymologie) beschäftigt hat, kommt er in seinen Arbeiten ganz in die Nähe einer modernen sprachvergleichenden Methode. Er meinte, daß die 'Harmonie der Sprachen', die Erforschung der Universalien, sich nicht mehr auf bloße und sehr anfällige (meist auf schriftliche Überlieferungen gestützte) Wortvergleiche verlassen kann. Nach dem Vergleich unterschiedlicher Bestandteile von mehr als zwei Dutzend Sprachen kommt Fogel zur Ausarbeitung der Methode der 'Etymoscopia'. Dabei verfolgt er die Überzeugung, "ein Lexikon der Wörter genügt nicht, es muss ein Lexikon der besonderen Phrasen einer bestimmten Sprache zur Hilfe sein" (Kangro 1969: 30).

Diese neue Einstellung hängt sicherlich mit der Person Fogels stark zusammen, denn er hat die Sprachstudien nur als Teil seiner philosophisch-logischen Überlegungen betrachtet.

Fogel hat seine Überzeugung von der Notwendigkeit der "comparatio vocabulorum, phrasium et syntaxeos" (Kangro 1969: 30) 1669 konkret in dem Vorwort *De Finnicae Linguae indole observationes* zu seinem *Nomenclator Latino Finnicus* angewandt. In diesem Text ist zu lesen, "er habe die Verwandtschaft zwischen Finnisch und Ungarisch selbständig entdeckt, früher (im Anfang d. J. 1669) datiert als jeder andere Text, worin auf diese Verwandtschaft hingewiesen wird" (Hormia 1965: 1).

Diese Arbeit von Fogel wurde auf Bitte des Großherzogs der Toskana, Cosimo III., erstellt, der um ein finnisches Wörterbuch und eine Grammatik bat. Fogel besaß zwar ein 1668 gedrucktes Exemplar der zuerst 1644 anonym in Stockholm erschienenen *Vocabula Latina cum interpret. Suetica & Finnonica* (siehe den Auktionskatalog seiner Bibliothek in Veenker 1986: 58), hielt es aber für angemessener, den lateinisch-finnischen Teil dieses Werkes kalligraphisch abgeschrieben und mit einem eigens zusammengestellten grammatischen Überblick als Geschenk dem Herzog zukommen zu lassen. In dem so entstandenen *Nomenclator Latino Finnicus* sind seine bereits erwähnten "Observationes [...]" enthalten. Das nach Florenz geschickte Originalexemplar seines Werkes wurde erst 1893 veröffentlicht. In diesem stellte er vergleichende Wortlisten u. a. mit finnischen, ungarischen und auch lappischen Angaben zusammen. Insgesamt führt er 35 selbständige Wortstämme zur Illustration der Verwandtschaft auf. Da er sich bemüht, dabei die älteste Schicht des Wortschatzes zu berücksichtigen, kommen in seiner Liste 23 Wortidentifizierungen vor, die auch heute als richtig angesehen werden.

Angesichts der spärlichen gedruckten Quellen, die Fogel bei dieser Arbeit zur Verfügung standen (zur Erschließung ungarischen Materials bediente er sich u. a. des *Dictionarium* von Szenczi Molnár in einer Ausgabe von 1645, welche auch Stiernhielm benutzt hatte), ist es verständlich, daß ein Logiker, wie er es war, versuchte, sich durch strukturiertes Denken zu behelfen. Im Sinne des 'etymoscopischen Modells' richtet er seine Aufmerksamkeit − entgegen der allgemeinen Praxis seiner Zeit − auf grammatisch-strukturelle Komponenten in beiden Sprachen. Unter anderem stellt er fest, daß (1) beide Sprachen Postpositionen anstelle der Präpositionen verwenden, daß (2) das Possessivverhältnis in beiden Sprachen statt entsprechenden Pronomina mit Personalendungen ausgedrückt wird, daß (3) infolgedessen keine von ihnen ein Verb in der Bedeutung 'haben' besitzt, sondern das Besitzen mit Hilfe des Verbs *sein* ausdrückt, daß (4) sie kein grammatisches Geschlecht kennen, daß (5) ihre Wortstruktur ähnlich sei, und daß (6) "der 'Genius' der Sprachen im Suffixsystem und Flexion" (Stipa 1990: 143) ähnlich sei.

"Die strukturellen Übereinstimmungen der uralischen und der altaischen Sprachen wurden im Jahre 1838 von Ferdinand Johann Wiedemann in seinem Werke *Über die früheren Sitze der Tschudischen Völker und ihre Sprachverwandtschaft mit den Völkern Mittelhochasiens* in 14 Punkten zusammengefasst. Von den strukturellen Übereinstimmungen dieser Art, die zwischen der ungarischen und der finnischen Sprache festzustellen sind, bemerkte Fogelius bereits 170 Jahre früher nicht weniger als sieben, und dieser Umstand weist − besonders, wenn man berücksichtigt, dass Fogelius die finnisch-ugrischen Sprachen, die sozusagen zwischen dem Ungarischen und dem Finnischen stehen, nicht kannte − auf eine anerkennenswerte Beobachtungsfähigkeit hin." (Lakó 1969: 7−8)

Obwohl Fogel mit der Fertigstellung des *Nomenclators* seine Aufgabe erfüllt hatte, beschäftigte er sich weiter mit seinen eigenen Entdeckungen.

Fogel erweitert seinen Blick und ist bemüht, mehr vom Lappischen zu erfahren (Wis-Murena 1989), bezieht auch das Türkische in Zusammenhang mit dem Ungarischen in seine Untersuchungen hinein, aber sein früher Tod verhindert die Vollendung seiner Ideen. Seine Bibliothek samt Manuskripten wurde von Leibniz aufgekauft und wird bis heute in den Beständen des Nachlasses von Leibniz aufbewahrt. Für die Fortentwicklung der Finnougristik hat Fogel keine unmittelbare Wirkung haben können, da seine Manuskripte erst 1891 durch eingehende Forschungen von Emil Nestor Setälä (1864−1935) entdeckt wurden (Setälä 1891). Diese Feststellung bedarf allerdings weiterer Untersuchungen, denn Paul Hunfalvy (1810−1891) hat in einem früheren Artikel über ihn berichtet: "Dadurch [durch Comenius' Feststellung über die Verwandtschaft der Finnen mit den Ungarn aus dem Jahre 1657] aufmerksam gemacht, hätte ein Hamburger Arzt, Martinus Fogelius, das Finnische mit dem Ungarischen in Verbindung gebracht und sein Manuskript befände sich in der königlichen Bibliothek zu Hannover" (Hunfalvy 1877: 87). Fogels Arbeit hat also doch irgendwie das wissenschaftliche Denken seiner Nachfolger (aus Hunfalvys Formulierung "hätte" bzw. "befände sich" ist sichtbar, daß er nichts Konkreteres wußte) beeinflußt, nur diese Wege sind bis heute noch nicht ganz klar erschlossen.

Die wissenschaftliche Leistung Fogels wird noch deutlicher, wenn wir berücksichtigen, daß er "die Verwandtschaft dieser Sprachen erkannte, obwohl sie zu Fogelius' Zeit noch nicht beweisbar war." (Lakó 1969: 8)

6. Das Zeitalter der Expeditionen

Die Hinweise von Comenius, Stiernhielm, die Bemühungen Fogels, Skyttes, die Publikationen von Wexionius und Rudbeck d. J. haben zunächst nur wenig Einfluß auf die aktuelle Entwicklung des Sprachvergleichs ausüben können. In Ungarn "from the second part of the 17th century, Hungarian was grouped with the 'oriental' languages" (Szathmári 1972: 351). Auch in Finnland gab es ähnliche Versuche, die fast zur Mode gewordenen Vergleiche, bezüglich der 'convenientia' unterschiedlicher Sprachen, versperrten den Blick. Enevald Svenonius (1617−1688) stellt in seinem 1662 in Turku erschienenen *Gymnasium capiendae rationis humanae* Verbindungen zwischen dem Finnischen, dem Griechischen und dem Hebräischen her. Eric Cajanus (1675−1737) geht noch weiter, denn er "listed a number of grammatical features, after the Finnish-Hebrew etymologies, which he considered common to both languages" (Korhonen 1986: 26).

Die Polarisierung der Meinungen hat aber auch zur Entwicklung beigetragen; sie hat u. a. gezeigt, daß zu den richtigen Erkenntnissen mehr empirisches Material und neue Forschungsmethoden nötig sind. Auf den Spuren von Wexionius hatte bereits Scheffer 1673 versucht "Wortbildung- und -beugung, Vielfalt der Verbalflexion in den Tempora und Modi" (Stipa 1990: 147), zwischen Finnisch und Lappisch zu vergleichen und er fand dabei gerade den bei den übrigen Forschern der Zeit so beliebten Wortschatzvergleich hinderlich und widersprüchlich.

Inzwischen hatten Reisende das Spektrum der zu untersuchenden Sprachen bedeutend erweitert. Den wichtigsten Beitrag dazu leistete Nicolaes Witsen (1641−1717) mit seinem 1692 in Amsterdam erschienenen *Noord en Oost Tartarye*. Eine Leistung dieses Werkes besteht in der Überlieferung von Sprachmaterial, meistens verschiedener Vaterunser-Texte (z. B. auf Tscheremissisch, Sölkupisch, Wogulisch und Permisch), sowie Wörterverzeichnisse (Mordwinisch, Sölkupisch und Samojedisch). Die andere ist dadurch entstanden, daß von diesen Texten Witsen drei samojedische, den wogulischen und den syrjänischen an Leibniz geschickt hatte, der angesichts dieses Materials die Notwendigkeit des Sammelns in Rußland erkannte. Die dritte Leistung seiner ethnographisch-linguistischen Sammlung besteht in den von ihm angedeuteten Umrissen eines Gesamtbildes der finnougrischen Sprachen und Völker.

Zu Beginn des 18. Jhs. hat wieder einmal Leibniz der finnougrischen Forschung wegweisende Aufgaben gestellt. Seiner persönlichen Überzeugung "nihil maiorem ad antiquas populorum origines indagandas lucem praebeat, quam collatio linguarum" (Leibniz 1768, 6.2: 228) entsprechend hat er energisch zum Sammeln linguistischen Materials aufgefordert. Er hatte erkannt, daß es über die traditionellen europäischen Rahmen der sprachwissenschaftlichen Fragestellungen und Probleme hinaus weitere, bisher unberücksichtigte Phänomene gab. Um diese zu erschließen, versuchte er, die statisch-hierarchischen Vorstellungen über die Sprachen und ihre Verwandtschaft, die Völkergenealogien, durch eine dynamisch-empirische Auffassung zu ersetzen. Mit diesem Impuls hilft er, die materiellen Grundlagen der vergleichenden und historischen Sprachwissenschaft zu erstellen. Die finnougrischen Sprachen spielten in der Anwendung der neuen Methoden bei Leibniz eine zentrale Rolle. Die Verwandtschaftstheorie nach Leibniz wird von seinem Sekretär, Johann Georg von Eckart (1674−1730) in dem 1707 in Helmstedt herausgegebenen *De usu et praestantia Studii Etymologici in Historia* ganz nach den Vorstellungen von Leibniz dargestellt.

Diese Ansichten haben eine heute schwer vorstellbare, befreiende Wirkung auf die Forschung gehabt. Leibniz' Hinwendung zu den natürlichen Sprachen und seine Freundschaft mit dem Zaren Peter I. von Rußland haben die Erforschung der 'kleineren' finnougrischen Sprachen erheblich beschleunigt und dadurch zur Erkenntnis der Zusammenhänge innerhalb der Sprachfamilie beigetragen. Auch wenn die Berichte mancher Reisender, wie das *Memorabilia Russico-Asiatica* über die Mordwinen und Tscheremissen von I. D. Gottlob Schober (1670−1739) zum Teil verlorengegangen sind, kann der erhaltengebliebene Rest noch immer wichtige Informationen vermitteln (Müller 1732−64). Die Reisen zu den sibirischen Völkern erweitern das untersuchte Spektrum der Sprachen und helfen somit einerseits die Lücken der Sprachvergleiche zu füllen, andererseits tragen sie zur Herausbildung der modernen historischen Sprachwissenschaft bei.

Leibniz versuchte, die Sammeltätigkeit gleichzeitig durch seine gezielten inhaltlichen Empfehlungen für die Forscher etwas zu vereinheitlichen, damit Vergleiche wirklich möglich werden. Die Gründung der Akademie in St. Petersburg (1725), die regen Kontakte zu ihr und die persönliche Beteiligung vieler deutscher Gelehrter an ihrer Arbeit, sowie die Gründung der Universität in Göttingen (1737) unterstützten die bis dahin eher zufälligen wissenschaftlichen Kontakte institutionell.

Die erste große Expedition 1720–1727 zur Erschließung des russischen Nordens bringt für die finnougrische Forschung 1730 einen Wendepunkt, als Philipp Johann von Strahlenberg (1676–1747) in Stockholm und Leipzig sein *Das Nord- und Ostliche Theil von Europa und Asia* veröffentlicht. Dieser Reisebericht hat als Anhang ein erstes 'vergleichendes Wörterbuch', eine 'Tabula polyglotta', wo Strahlenberg, die Ideen seines Expeditionsleiters Daniel Gottlieb Messerschmidt (1685–1716) befolgend, einen Überblick über die Sprachen der Region präsentiert. Die Überschrift 'Harmonia Linguarum' erinnert an die frühere Tradition des Sprachvergleichs, aber im Inhalt spiegeln sich die leibniz'schen Ideen wieder. In der ersten von sechs Klassen werden Ungarisch (Székler), Finnisch, Wogulisch, Mordwinisch, Tscheremissisch, Permjakisch, Wotjakisch und Ostjakisch aufgeführt, da der Überschrift nach: "dieſe Völcker gehören alle ſämtlich in der Ober-Ungariſch- und Finniſchen Nation, welche mit einander einerley Dialect haben", neben ihnen, in der dritten Klasse, sind die entsprechenden Wörter aus fünf samojedischen Dialekten abgedruckt. Untereinander finden wir die folgenden Eintragungen: ung. *szem*; fi. *silmæ*; mord. *silma*; perm. *schin*; votj. *schi*; Ob-ostj. *say*; Czulim-ostj. *sfeul*; tawgi-sam. *seirne*; Jenisei-sam. *sea*. "He says quite explicitly that the Samoyeds must have had a common origin with the Hunnic" (i.e. Finno-Ugric) peoples (Wickman 1988: 797).

Diese bahnbrechenden Feststellungen werden im Laufe der folgenden Jahrzehnte durch großangelegte Wörtersammlungen zusätzlich untermauert. Die bedeutendste von ihnen ist das vollständig erst 1995 in Göttingen veröffentlichte, von Johann Eberhard Fischer (1697–1771) zusammengestellte *Vocabulorium Sibiricum*. Mit Hilfe der Materialien der 2. Kamtschatka-Expedition (1733–1743) ist es Fischer gelungen, die Idee von Leibniz über Sprachvergleichung zu verwirklichen, denn insgesamt 55 Sprachen werden bei der Erstellung von mehr als siebenhundert etymologischen Vergleichen berücksichtigt. Dieses Werk wird mengenmäßig nur von dem berühmten, 1787–1789 in St. Petersburg erschienenen zweibändigen *Linguarum totius orbis vocabularia comparativa* von Peter Simon Pallas übertroffen (in der vollständigen, vierbändigen Fassung sind 272 Sprachen mit jeweils 285 abgefragten Wörtern vertreten). Aber diese 'Vocabularia Comparativa'

"produced [...] by the dilettantism of a monarch [Zarin Katharina II.] not only gives a wrong picture of the relationship between the individual Finno-Ugrian languages, but also affords numerous regrettable examples of linguistic incompetence." (Gulya 1965: 167–168)

Zum Glück landete 1767 die erste Fassung von Fischers umfangreichem Material in Göttingen im "Institut der Historischen Wissenschaften" von J. C. Gatterer (1727–1799). Er schrieb 1770, wieder einmal im Sinne Leibniz':

"Während die Büchersprache in Form und Materie fast ebenso veränderlich ist wie die Kleidermode, so erhält sich oft Jahrtausende lang Form und Materie in dem Munde des gemeinen Mannes. Diese Sprachlehrer soll man aufmerksam hören. Ihre Sprache führt uns in die Jh. zurück, aus denen uns zu wenig geschriebene Denkmäler übrig sind." (Zitiert nach Stipa 1990: 196)

Diese Überzeugung im Einklang mit der klassifizierenden Tätigkeit von August Ludwig Schlözer (1735–1809) gab am Ende des Jhs. der finnougrischen Forschung jenen Ruck, wodurch sie in einer neuen Epoche anlangt.

7. Der Durchbruch in der Methode und im Inhalt: Sajnovics und Gyarmathi

Angeregt durch die Behauptungen über die lappisch-finnisch-ungarische Sprachverwandtschaft in Scheffers *Lapponia* und in Rudbeck d. Jn. *Specimen*, beschließt der Wiener kaiserliche Sternwart, Maximilian Hell (1720–1792) bei seiner Expedition 1769 auf die Insel Vardø zur Beobachtung einer besonderen Sonne-Venus Konstellation jemanden mitzunehmen, der in der Lage war, diese Annahmen glaubwürdig zu überprüfen. Aufgrund früherer Bekanntschaft wählt er seinen Kollegen János Sajnovics (1735–1785) dazu aus. Unterwegs versucht Sajnovics, sich auf die Aufgabe einzustellen, da er keine linguistische Fachausbildung hatte. Die Enttäuschung war dementsprechend groß, als sich beim ersten Treffen mit Lappen herausstellte, daß sie einander nicht verstanden.

Beim Anhören des Vaterunsers hatten sie zumindest den Eindruck, manche Wörter bzw. der Tonfall und Rhythmus habe Ähnlichkeiten aufzuweisen. Jetzt war der gelernte Mathematiker Sajnovics gefordert und innerhalb kürzester Zeit erarbeitet er ein Schema des Sprachvergleichs. Er zeichnete den nach dem Gehör selbst gesammelten Grundwortschatz von Gebirgslappen und Seelappen auf. Das so gewonnene Material bereitete er dann in einem halben Jahr auf, wobei er für die zukünftigen Forschungsmethoden mindestens zwei entscheidende Schritte wagt. Erstens zeigt seine Abstraktion, daß die konkreten Sprachen und Dialekte zwar unterschiedlich und deshalb für die einzelnen unverständlich sein können, sie aber trotzdem die gleiche Sprache sind. Zweitens baut er sein durch Sprachproben geprüftes Material direkt in seine Argumentation ein, ein damals ungewöhnlich stark sich auf die sprachliche Wirklichkeit stützendes Vorgehen.

Nach diesen methodologischen Überlegungen steht die sprachlich nach mathematischen Sprachgebrauch formulierte Schlußfolgerung klar vor ihm: *Demonstratio. Idioma Ungarorum et Lapponum idem esse.* Dieses 1770 in Kopenhagen und auch in Tyrnau (Nagyszombat, heute Trnava in der Slowakei) erschienene Werk bringt eindeutige Beweise für die lange vermutete sprachliche Verwandtschaft. Gerade dadurch, daß er die übliche Praxis des Sprachvergleichs nicht kennt, kann er neue Wege beschreiten. Er benutzt bei seiner Beweisführung weniger die Wörter und konzentriert sich statt dessen mehr auf morphologische Übereinstimmungen und geht in der Argumentation analytisch und abstrahierend vor. So stellt er fest, daß das Pluralzeichen -*k*, das Zeichen des Komparativs -*b*, die Personalendung des Sg. 1. -*m*, in beiden Sprachen identisch sind, daß die Aktionsarten des Verbs, seine Tempuszeichen, die Pronomina und Pronominalsuffixe, also die Kernelemente einer Sprache einander sehr nahestehen. Damit stuft er die beiden Sprachen aufgrund einer sprachlichen Analyse als etymologisch gleich ein. Dies stellt einen beispiellosen Vorgang dar, denn vergleichbare Leistungen in Bezug auf die indogermanischen Sprachen (Rasmus Rask) und die Methode des historischen Vergleichs (Franz Bopp) wird erst Jahrzehnte später ausgearbeitet und angewandt.

Es ist wichtig festzustellen, daß Sajnovics sich mit einer viel schwereren Aufgabe zurechtfinden mußte, da die finnougrischen Sprachen (mit Ausnahme des ostseefinnischen Zweigs) weiter auseinanderentwickelt sind, als die germanischen oder romanischen Sprachen. Zu einer Zeit ohne etablierte Forschungsmethode diese Ergebnisse zu präsentieren, ist "eine bahnbrechende Arbeit für die gesamte moderne vergleichende Sprachwissenschaft" (Pražák 1967: 72). Die Erkenntnisse von Sajnovics standen in so krassem Widerspruch zu den Überlegungen seiner ungarischen Zeitgenossen, daß diese hervorragende Arbeit und ihr Autor Gegenstand des Spottes und Zielscheibe des nationalen Aufbegehrens wurden.

Die Entdeckung der politischen Bedeutung einer Nationalsprache nach der Französischen Revolution und die daraus resultierende Bewegung, die ungarische Spracherneuerung nach 1772, führt auch zu einem Interesse an der Klärung der eigenen sprachlichen Vergangenheit. Angeregt von Josef Dobrovský (1753–1829) suchte Sámuel Gyarmathi (1751–1830) die Möglichkeit, die von Sajnovics eingeleiteten sprachvergleichenden Forschungen fortzusetzen. Es war ihm klar, daß dazu die Universität Göttingen und der dort dozierende von Schlözer, der mit dem in Uppsala tätigen Johannes Ihre (1707–1780) und durch ihn mit der St. Petersburger Akademie in Verbindung stand, die geeignetste Bildung geben konnte. So geht er 1796 nach Göttingen, wo er 1799 seine Dissertation *Affinitas lingvae hvngaricae cvm lingvis fennicae originis grammatice demonstrata* von Schlözer vorlegt. Diese aus drei Kapiteln und drei Appendices bestehende Arbeit folgt noch dem von Sajnovics aufgestellten Muster, hebt aber in ihrem Titel die Wichtigkeit der grammatischen Beweise hervor. Später und auf Schlözers Rat zieht er weitere finnougrische Sprachen, u. a. das Estnische, Ostjakische und auch das Samojedische, in seine Untersuchung ein.

"Sieben Punkte enthalten grammatische Vergleiche: Wortbildungsendungen, Deklination und Komparation, Bedeutung und Bildung der Pronomina, gesondert die Possessivsuffixe, allgemein Suffixe,

Konjugation, Adverbien wie auch Postpositionen, Syntax." (Stipa 1990: 215)

Daraus entsteht der erste, mit Hilfe des grammatischen Vergleichs untermauerte Versuch der Darstellung der gesamten Sprachfamilie; die Wortvergleiche im 'ramischen' Sinne spielten darin nur eine untergeordnete Rolle. Weil die *Affinitas* im Zentrum der damaligen sprachwissenschaftlichen Forschung, in Göttingen, erscheint, beschleunigt sie international die Anerkennung der Finnougristik als selbständige Disziplin. Diese Anerkennung trägt dazu bei, daß in den folgenden Jahrzehnten die nationalen Philologien in den finnougrischen Ländern sich herausbilden und die Finnougristik eine institutionalisierte Existenzgrundlage erhält.

8. Bibliographie

Collinder, Björn. 1962. *Comparative Grammar of the Uralic Languages.* Stockholm: Almquist & Wiksell.

Göckenjan, Hansgeorg & James R. Sweeney. 1985. *Der Mongolensturm: Berichte von Augenzeugen und Zeitgenossen 1235−1250.* Graz, Wien, Köln: Styria.

Grape, Andreas. 1921. "Riksråd − språkforskare [Reichsrat − Sprachforscher]". *Uppsala universitets-bibliotheks minnesskrift 1621−1921*, 329−372. Uppsala.

Grünthal, Riho. 1997. *Livvistä liiviin. Itämerensuomalaiset etnonyymit* [Vom Liwi zum Livi. Ostseefinnische Ethnonyme.] Helsinki: Suomalais-Ugrilainen Seura.

Gulya, János. 1965. "Some 18th Century Antecedents of the 19th Century Linguistics." *Acta Linguistica Hungarica* 15. 163−170. Budapest: Akadémiai Kiadó.

Haarmann, Harald. 1976. *Die estnischen Grammatiken des 17. Jahrhunderts.* Bd. 1−3. Hamburg: Buske.

Hegedűs, József. 1966. *A magyar nyelv összehasonlításának kezdetei az egykorú európai nyelvtudomány tükrében* [Die Anfänge des ungarischen Sprachvergleichs im Spiegel der zeitgenössischen europäischen Linguistik.] Budapest: Akadémiai.

Hormia, Osmo. 1965. "Über die fennougrischen Interessen von Olaus Rudbeck d. Ä." *Finnisch-Ugrische Forschungen* 35. 1−43. Helsinki.

Hunfalvy, Paul. 1877. "Die ungarische Sprachwissenschaft." *Literarische Berichte aus Ungarn*, hg. von Paul Hunfalvy, 75−106. Budapest: Franklin-Verein.

Kangro, Hans. 1969. "Martin Fogel aus Hamburg als Gelehrter des 17. Jahrhunderts". *Ural-Altaische Jahrbücher* 41. 1432. Wiesbaden: Harrasowitz.

Korhonen, Mikko. 1986. *Finno-ugrian Language Studies in Finnland 1828−1918.* Helsinki: Societas Scientiarum Fennica.

Lakó, György. 1969. "Martinus Fogelius' Verdienste bei der Entdeckung der finnougrischen Sprachverwandtschaft". *Ural-Altaische Jahrbücher* 41. 3−13. Wiesbaden: Harrasowitz.

Leibniz, Gottfried Wilhelm. 1768. *Leibnitii opera omnia 1−6*, hg. von L. Dutens. Genève: Tournes.

Müller, G. F. 1732−64. *Sammlung Russischer Gedichte* 1−9. St. Petersburg: Kaiserliche Akademie der Wissenschaften.

Pražák, Richard. 1967. *Josef Dobrovský als Hungarist und Finno-Ugrist.* Brno: Universita J. E. Purkyné.

Setälä, Emil Nestor. 1891. *Lisiä suomalais-ugrilaisen kielentutkimuksen historiaan* [Ergänzungen zur finnisch-ugrischen Sprachforschung.] Helsinki: Suomalaisen Kirjallisuuden Seura.

Stipa, Günter Johannes. 1990. *Finno-ugrische Sprachforschung von der Renaissance bis zum Positivismus.* Helsinki: Suomalais-Ugrilainen Seura.

Szathmári, István. 1972. "An Outline of the History of Hungarian Linguistics." *The Hungarian Language* hg. von Benkő, Loránd-Imre, Samu, 349−377. The Hague & Paris: Mouton.

Veenker, Wolfgang, Hg. 1986. *Memoriae Martini Fogelii Hamburgensis (1634−1675).* (= *Mitteilungen der Societas Uralo-Altaica*, 7). Hamburg: Als Ms. vervielfältigt.

Vértes O., András. 1952. "Comenius a magyar és a finn nyelv egy közös sajátságáról [Comenius über eine gemeinsame Besonderheit des Ungarischen und des Finnischen]". *Nyelvtudományi Közlemények* LIII. 290−291. Budapest.

Wickman, Bo. 1988. "The History of Uralic Linguistics". *The Uralic Languages: Description, history and foreign influences* hg. von Denis Sinor, 792−818. Leiden: Brill.

Wis-Murena, Cristina. 1989. "Martin Fogel Johannes Sajnovicsin edeltäjänä" [Martin Fogel als Vorläufer des Johannes Sajnovics.] *Virittäjä* 93. 1−10. Helsinki: Kotikielen Seura.

Zsirai, Miklós. 1937. *Finnugor rokonságunk* [Unsere finnougrische Verwandtschaft.] Budapest: Magyar Tudományos Akadémia.

−. 1952. *A modern nyelvtudomány magyar úttörői* [Die ungarischen Pioniere der modernen Sprachwissenschaft.] Budapest: Akadémiai Kiadó.

Tiborc Fazekas, Hamburg (Deutschland)

152. The knowledge of Sanskrit in Europe until 1800

1. The past up to 1583
2. Missionaries and merchants, 1583—1768
3. British colonials, 1768—1794
4. Stocktaking, 1790—1807
5. Bibliography

1. The past up to 1583

Ancient Greeks, notably Megasthenes, an ambassador at the court of Candragupta Maurya in 302—291 BCE, and his contemporary, the admiral Nearchos, wrote accounts of their travels to India which are preserved in the works of Arrian, Strabo, and Pliny. For all their highly positive reports on India's culture and polity and on the wisdom of its gymnosophists ("naked philosophers"), in keeping with the general lack of interest that Greeks showed for foreign, 'barbarian' tongues, they only noted that India features many different languages. Mercantile contacts between India and Rome, attested to by the discovery of Roman coins on the Indian coast and of Indian artifacts in Pompei, also failed to prompt observations of a linguistic nature. The account that the Venetian merchant Marco Polo gave of his travel in India in the late 13th century likewise failed to include remarks of linguistic import.

2. Missionaries and merchants, 1583—1768

Observations on India's languages, Sanskrit in particular, and on their apparent kinship with European languages began with missionary activities in the late 16th century. Yet this breaking information failed immediately to reach a wide audience. In 1583 the Jesuit missionary Thomas Stephens (Stevens), a scholar of Konkani — and the first Englishman known to have reached India via the Cape of Good Hope —, commented in a letter written from Goa to his brother in Paris on the structural similarity between Indian languages and Greek and Latin. This letter, which made no reference to Sanskrit, remained unpublished until 1957.

First to mention Sanskrit, as far as preserved documents allow us to ascertain, was the Florentine merchant and litterateur Filippo Sassetti. In a long report on Indian culture addressed from Cochin in 1585 to fellow Florentine Pier Vettori, Sassetti mentioned that all of India's sciences were written in a language so different from the vernacular that learning it required six years of study in an instructional mode that emphasized grammar. He characterized the language as "pleasant and euphonious" (*dilettevole e di bel suono*) and described it as based on 53 basic sounds which were difficult for Europeans to pronounce (1970: 420—421). In a fragment of a letter to Bernardo Davanzati apparently sent from Cochin in 1586, he referred to Sanskrit by name ("Sanscruta") and noted again its status as India's learned language. He observed that Indians learned it much as Europeans did Latin and Greek, but that they devoted much more time — six or seven years — to its study. He added that contemporary Indians could not say when Sanskrit was a spoken language, even though their recollection of past times stretched way back. He explained the meaning of the word Sanscruta (literally "perfected") as "well structured" (*bene articulata*) and pointed to lexical similarities with Italian, which persisted in the modern vernacular, notably in numerals 6, 7, 8, and 9, and in words for "god" and "snake" (1970: 501—502). A first edition of his letters appeared only in 1855.

The occasion for Sassetti's comments on Sanskrit in his letter to Davanzati was his description of a tree and of a medicine extracted from it, based on a Sanskrit *nighaṇṭu* (glossary). A similar interest in medicinal lore led to the composition in Cochin in 1673—1675 and the publication in Amsterdam in 1766—1771 of Henricus Van Rheede tot Draakenstein's monumental *Hortus Malabaricus*, an illustrated *materia medica* of South India. Prefixed to that work was a statement in Sanskrit in a script akin to Devanāgarī, with Latin translation via Malayalam and Portuguese, by the three pandits who provided the material. This statement and the names of plants in transliterated Sanskrit and Malayalam given throughout the work might have provided a first crude way to access Sanskrit in Europe. They did not. Contemporary European interest in India was not linguistic, but focused on matters of culture, society, and natural resources.

Sustained evangelical efforts, by Jesuits in particular, required a knowledge not only of Indian vernaculars, but also of the language of the high brahmanical tradition. Yet linguistic data were not transmitted immediately. Although the works of Roberto (de)

Nobili (1577–1656) bear clear evidence that he knew Sanskrit, they contain no linguistic observations. The first known author of a European grammar of Sanskrit was the German Jesuit Heinrich Roth. Contrary to most missionaries in Mughal North India, Roth noted that the majority of the people were not Muslim, but Hindu, and he set about learning their sacred language to further his proselytizing goals. The *Grammatica linguae Sanscretanae Bramanum Indiae orientalis* which he wrote in Agra between 1660 and 1662, in Latin with Sanskrit words in Devanāgarī script, follows traditional Indian terminology and analysis imparted by a pandit. It is nevertheless arranged in Western style in five chapters devoted to

(1) phonemics and morphophonemics,
(2) nominal and pronominal declensions,
(3) conjugations,
(4) participles and other nominal forms derived from verbs, and
(5) syntax, nominal composition, and indeclinables.

An appendix on metrics is based on the *Śrutabodha* traditionally attributed to Kālidāsa – misspelled and misunderstood as Kāladāsa. Roth's sophisticated grammar was brought to Rome with a companion manuscript which contains the texts of Veṇīdatta's *Pañcatattvaprakāśa*, a dictionary of Sanskrit synonyms, with Latin annotations by Roth, and of Sadānanda's philosophical treatise, the *Vedāntasāra*, with a marginal Latin translation by Roth. While in Rome, Roth contributed tables of Devanāgarī script and transliterations into Devanāgarī script of the Latin texts of the Lord's Prayer and of the Hail Mary to the *China Illustrata* of fellow Jesuit and polymath Athanasius Kircher (1667). The transliteration of the Lord's Prayer entered polyglot compilations from that by Andreas Müller (1680) to that of John Chamberlayne (1715). Unfortunately, Roth's grammar, which Kircher sought in vain to have published, disappeared in the early 1800s to be rediscovered only in 1967 by Arnulf Camps. The grammar and companion texts have since been published in a facsimile edition (Camps & Muller 1988). A copy of a grammar written in Kerala in the first third of the 18th century by another Jesuit, Johann Ernst Hanxleden, was brought to Rome together with a grammar of Malayalam and a Malayalam-Sanskrit-Portuguese dictionary by the same author, by Paulinus a Sancto Bartholomaeo and served as a basis for Paulinus's grammar before disappearing. It seems to have been rediscovered by Jean-Claude Muller (1985: 131–134) in the Italian National Library.

Protestant missionaries in Danish Tranquebar on the Coromandel coast also contributed information on Sanskrit, which appeared in a series of reports published in Halle, Germany, beginning in 1718. Most interesting was a letter of 1725 from Benjamin Schul(t)ze who stated that, when beginning to learn Sanskrit, he had been struck to find that Sanskrit numerals were "almost exclusively pure Latin words" (*fast lauter pure lateinische Wörter*) and he listed the Sanskrit numerals 1 to 20, 30, and 40, with equivalents in Latin for all, and in other European languages for some (1729: 708–710). In doing so, he claimed to do nothing more than follow up on a suggestion by an unnamed friend in Hamburg who had, as early as in 1714, intimated that many words in the Malabar calendar were pure Latin words. He thought of similarities in terms of borrowing, either from early contacts with Romans or more recently with Portuguese, yet he dismissed the latter possibility on the grounds that Sanskrit was unlikely to be only two centuries old or to have borrowed its numerical system this recently. He further provided for the *Orientalisch- und Occidentalischer Sprachmeister* (1748) translations of the Lord's Prayer in Sanskrit and other Indian languages, which were incorporated in Johann Christoph Adelung's *Mithridates* (1: 1806).

Of yet greater import was the publication of the *Lettres édifiantes et curieuses* of French Jesuit missionaries in Asia, which began in 1707 and knew multiple editions and translations. Foremost among these was a remarkably well-informed survey of Sanskrit literature sent by Jean-François Pons in 1740 and first published in 1743. Following Indian tradition, which makes of linguistics both the foundational and preeminent science, Pons gave pride of place to grammar in a description the importance of which warrants a modern translation:

"The grammar of the Brahmans can be ranked among the most brilliant sciences. Never has analysis and synthesis been better applied than in their grammatical treatises on the Samskret or Samskroutam language. I am inclined to believe that this language, which is remarkable for its harmony, copiousness, and power, used to be the living language in the countries in which the original Brahmans resided [...] [Pons, then in Karikal, on the Coromandel coast, accepts a North Indian, Gangetic origin for the Brahmans].

It is astounding that the human mind could have attained to the artistic perfection that bursts forth in these grammars. Their authors have analytically reduced the richest language in the world to a small number of primitive elements that may be taken as the *caput mortuum* of the language. These elements are not used by themselves, they have no actual meaning, they only relate to a notion, for example *kru* to the notion of action. The secondary elements that bear upon the primitive are the endings which make it a noun or verb; those which determine if it is to be declined or conjugated, a number of syllables that are to be inserted between the primitive element and the endings; a few prefixes; etc. When coming in contact with the secondary elements, the primitive element often changes its form [...] depending on what is added to it. The synthesis joins and combines all these elements in an infinite variety of terms of actual use. It is the rules of thus joining and combining these elements that grammar teaches, so that a mere schoolboy who might only know grammar can, by applying the rules to a root or primitive element, derive from it several thousand correct Samskret words. It is this art that has given its name to the language; indeed *samskret* means synthetic or composed." (1803 [1740]: 642–643).

For all its pre-linguistic terminology, Pons's account thus clearly established the close connection between the Sanskrit language and Indian linguistic analysis which was to fascinate and occasionally mislead contemporaries, and eventually shape Indo-European morphology. The works of Charles de Brosses, Alexander Dow, Jean-Rodolphe Sinner, Voltaire, Lord Monboddo, Nathaniel Brassey Halhed, Nicolas Beauzée, and Lorenzo Hervás y Panduro attest to its impact. As demonstrated by Hughes (1967), it was also plagiarized by John Cleland.

The French Royal Library was first to take advantage of missionary efforts to build Sanskrit collections. In 1718, its director, the Abbé Bignon, asked French missionaries in Asia to forward oriental manuscripts. In response, Pons sent from Bengal in 1732–1733 168 Sanskrit manuscripts which were promptly, though without special expertise, catalogued by Sinologist Etienne Fourmont (1739). Along with Indian manuscripts, Pons sent a grammar of Sanskrit he had composed in Latin, with Sanskrit words in Begali script. He was to write an additional chapter on syntax in his subsequent location in South India. This addition, in French with Sanskrit words partly in Telegu, partly in Roman script, was forwarded in 1772 by fellow Jesuit Gaston-Laurent Cœurdoux. Pons's grammar remained in manuscript form in the French Royal Library. By 1804, when Anquetil-Duperron sought to have it published, Paulinus a Sancto Bartholomaeo's first grammar had come out. Pons's grammar (described in Filliozat 1937; Muller 1985: 134–139) was nonetheless influential in that, in addition to being the source of the table of Bengali script in the *Encyclopédie*, it served as a primer for the first students of Sanskrit in Paris. Yet the Abbé Barthélemy of the Académie des Inscriptions and Belles Lettres seemed to be unaware of, or to dismiss, Pons's grammar when he requested Cœurdoux to send a grammar and dictionary of Sanskrit, without which, he said, no use could be made of the Sanskrit manuscripts in the Royal Library. Cœurdoux's response made tantalizing references to studies by himself and fellow Jesuits including Antoine Mosac, in Chandernagor, who learned Sanskrit at the famed panditic establishment of Nadiya in Bengal and has been credited by some with the authorship of the fake *Ezourvedam* that enthused Voltaire (cf. L. Rocher 1984: 45–47). Cœurdoux pleaded that missionaries had neither time to copy these studies nor money to have them copied for transmission to Europe. He nevertheless provided three lists of Sanskrit words with equivalent: (1a) words "closely resembling or identical" (*fort ressemblans ou les mêmes*) with Latin and Greek, (1b) "common" (*communs*) with Greek only, (2a) common with Latin (which included forms of the verb *as-* "to be" and pronouns), (2b) common with other languages, (2c) numerals in Sanskrit, Latin, and Greek, and (3) a basic French-Sanskrit lexicon. To these he appended astute notes which included a recognition of palatalization features: Sanskrit *ca* and *catur* (written *tcha* and *tchatour*) vs. Latin *que* and *quatuor*. After reviewing theories that might account for the large number of words common to Sanskrit with Latin and Greek, he concluded to a common origin in the biblical mode of post-Babel dispersion. Unfortunately, this memoir, handed over to Anquetil-Duperron in 1768, was read before the Académie only in 1786 and published only in 1808, as an appendix to a communication, and with footnotes, by Anquetil-Duperron (facsimile repr. appended to Mayrhofer 1983). The forty-year delay between receipt and publication of this account – a publication that coincided with that of Schlegel's *Ueber die Sprache und Weisheit der Indier*, which rendered it obsolete – denied this document the attention and influence it deserved. An account of Anquetil's early encounters with Sanskrit, including his collecting a few manuscripts and his abandoning a plan to study Sanskrit in favor of Avestan, is found in the narrative of his travels in India prefixed to his edition of the Zend-Avesta (1771).

Meanwhile, in Rome, the Sacred Congregation for the Propagation of the Faith was publishing descriptions of scripts collected by missionaries in different parts of the world. Besides scripts from Tibet and Burma, this collection included editions by Giovanni Cristoforo Amaduzzi of Cassiano Beligatti da Macerata's *Alphabetum brammhanicum seu Indostanum universitatis Kasi* (1771) and of Clemens a Iesu's *Alphabetum Grandonico-Malabaricum* (1772). An anonymous *Alphabetum Talenganicum* and an *Alphabetum Samscrdamicum litteris Granthamicis cum Latina pronuntiatione earum* by Ildephonsus a Praesentatione remained, however, in manuscript.

The first recorded observation of similarities between Sanskrit and Persian was not made in India but in Europe, by Maturin Veyssière de La Croze (1724), who noted among common traits between Indians and ancient Iranians a large number of similar words, but did not speculate on the cause of these similarities. Gottlieb Siegfried Bayer (1738) attributed commonalities between Greek, Persian, and Sanskrit numerals to borrowing from Greek in the Greek Bactrian kingdoms. Yet he acknowledged that the Tranquebar missionary Christoph Theodor Walther, whose memoir on the Indian computation of time (1733) he appended, indicated in his correspondence with him that he attributed such similarities to the common 'Scythian' origin propounded by Boxhorn, Saumaise, Jäger, Leibniz, and others. The French navy officer and traveler La Flotte (1769) similarly adopted a North Asian origin for the Brahmans, but the Berne librarian Jean-Rodolphe Sinner (1771) questioned La Flotte's claim that Sanskrit abounded in Greek expressions and rejected the Abbé Mignot's derivation of Sanskrit *devatā* from Latin *deus, deitas* on the grounds that neither Greek nor Latin could have been known in India. Even when similarities were accepted, and accepted for numerals and other basic vocabulary, i.e., vocabulary unlikely to have been borrowed according to the theories which de Laet, Grotius, Leibniz, and others had pioneered, scholars did not necessarily conclude to a common origin. When they did, it was sometimes made to fit in pet theories such as Jacques Le Brigant's (1787) promotion of Celtic. Other scholars such as the Président de Brosses (1765), bent on theoretical rather than comparative concerns, found Pons's report of Sanskrit's derivation from a handful of primitive elements of import for his language mechanics. Until the last third of the 18th century, not only were reports from India episodic and spotty, and their reception in Europe unevenly distributed through the scholarly world, but theories that accounted for, or utilized, its reported features were inconsistent.

3. British colonials, 1768−1794

In 1765, when the English East India Company obtained the administrative rights to Bengal, Bihar, and Orissa, a knowledge of India's culture became a colonial imperative. Among the first to seek panditic instruction in Sanskrit was Alexander Dow, who promptly concluded that he did not have enough years in India successfully to devote to its study and that he ought to devote his time primarily to Persian. In a "dissertation concerning the customs, manners, language, religion and philosophy of the Hindoos" prefixed to his translation of a Persian historical account, he hazarded remarks in which Sanskrit's perfection was viewed as possible evidence of artificiality:

"Whether the Shanscrita was, in any period of antiquity, the vulgar language of Hindostan, or was invented by the Brahmins to be a mysterious repository for their religion and philosophy, is difficult to determine. All other languages, it is true, were casually invented by mankind to express their ideas and wants; but the astonishing formation of the Shanscrita seems to be beyond the power of chance. In regularity of etymology and grammatical order, it far exceeds the Arabic. It in short bears evident marks, that it has been fixed upon rational principles, by a body of learned men, who studied regularity, harmony, and a wonderful simplicity and energy of expression." (Dow 1803 [1768], vol. I: xxvii)

This suggestion led Christoph Meiners (1780) to explain similarities with Greek as due to the Brahmans' deliberate patterning of Sanskrit after Greek.

Governor Warren Hastings's orientalist policies fostered a breakthrough. For the duration of his tenure, 1772 to 1785, and beyond, the cultivation of Sanskrit learning by servants of the East India Company was officially recognized as valuable and ways were found to publish the results of their studies. First and foremost among Hastings's projects was his commissioning the redaction of a code of Hindu laws by a group of pandits, and his ordering an English translation through the usual — and, in this case, particularly unsatisfactory — medium of a Persian rendering. This translation, which Hastings had the East India Company publish in London (1776), elicited considerable interest and underwent several editions, and translations into French and German (both 1778). In a long introduction, in which claims to Indian culture's "unfathomable" antiquity caused much controversy, the English translator Nathaniel Brassey Halhed gave information on Sanskrit which excited the interest of European scholars, Beauzée and Monboddo in particular. Halhed pursued his investigations on Sanskrit in a grammar of Bengali published in Bengal in 1778. Notwithstanding what might look like an inclusion of Arabic among Sanskrit's cognate languages — canceled by a further statement denying that Persian and Arabic "bear an original relation and consanguineity to each other" (p. xx) —, its preface spelled out the probative value of common basic vocabulary to establish common origin:

"I have been astonished to find the similitude of Shanscrit words with those of Persian and Arabic, and even of Latin and Greek: and those not in technical and metaphorical terms, which the mutuation of refined arts and improved manners might have occasionally introduced; but in the main groundwork of language, in monosyllables, in the names of numbers, and the appellation of such things as would be first discriminated on the immediate dawn of civilization." (vi–vii)

Less prominently displayed, but of greater value yet, were remarks in the body of the grammar which pointed to similarities in morphology, such as the conjugation in -*mi* in Sanskrit and Greek (p. 126), a remark which had particular resonance with Monboddo (cf. R. Rocher 1980a).

In a letter of 1779 (pr. R. Rocher 1983: 293–309), Halhed carried further an emphasis on morphology, noting commonalities between Sanskrit and Latin and Greek "in all the models of declination and inflexion of its words, in the use of genders, in the degrees of comparison, and every other part of grammatical analogy" (p. 309). Taking off from Monboddo's theory that Latin was more ancient than Greek, he developed an argument that gave precedence to morphological over lexical considerations:

"[I]f it could be clearly proved to the satisfaction of the learned, that there be any one language whatever, which having a certain degree of resemblance both to Greek and Latin, rather inclineth to the *latter* in those particulars wherein *that* appears to deviate from Greek [...], would there not be room for a conjecture that this third language had either been communicated to or borrowed from the other two, previous to the separation. I have often thought I could discover a resemblance of this kind in the Shanskrit; but have as often been puzzled to account for the existence of the dual number and the middle voice in this tongue and the Greek, which are totally absent from the Latin.

It must however be remembered, in favor of the pretensions to priority of original in the Shanscrit language, that it contains every part of speech, and every distinction which is to be found in Greek or in Latin, and that in some particulars it is more copious than either. For instance, a Shanscrit noun has 7 cases, without the vocative; had it borrowed this part of the system from Latin, it would have had but 5; if from Greek, but 4." (308–309)

Since, following on Monboddo, he was persuaded that "it is one of the last gradations of art to simplify a complex machine" (p. 295), he viewed Sanskrit's greater complexity as a sign of higher antiquity, and even as a basis for a "claim to the honour of a parent" (p. 309). Although these thoughts remained unpublished in his lifetime, Halhed must have shared them with his friend William Jones in the years that separated his return from, and Jones's departure for, India (cf. R. Rocher 1980b). In addition to references to Sanskrit's 'copiousness', already noted by Pons and Dow, and to its being particularly "refined" (Halhed 1776: 46), Halhed's new emphasis on morphology had a clear echo in the famous statement Jones made in 1786:

"The Sanskrit language, whatever be its antiquity, is of a wonderful structure; more perfect than the Greek, more copious than the Latin, and more exquisitely refined than either, yet bearing to both of them a stronger affinity, both in the roots of verbs and in the forms of grammar, than could possibly have been produced by accident; so strong indeed, that no philologer could examine them all three, without believing them to have sprung from some common source, which, perhaps, no longer exists." (Jones 1788: 422)

As Hoenigswald (1963: 3) has shown, Jones was of the opinion that Sanskrit's very perfection, which was owed to art and improvement, militated against its being the ancestor language, which had perforce to be primitive. The importance of Jones's statement, of which later generations were to make the founding document of comparative linguistics, lay in its impact more than its method. It affirmed, although it did not take pains to demonstrate, that Sanskrit and what were to be called the Indo-European languages were derived from a common source, and thereby put Sanskrit at the forefront of European interest. The author of this statement was not an obscure missionary, traveler, or East India company servant, but a scholar who had achieved eminence in Europe prior to assuming a seat on the bench of the Bengal Supreme Court; it could not be dismissed as the dream of an untutored enthusiast. It furthermore came enshrined as a presidential address in the proceedings of the Asiatic Society Jones had founded in Calcutta in 1784 and which provided a forum and encouragement for further enquiries by fellow Britishers in India and their Indian informants. The *Asiatick Researches*, which Jones edited until his death, were steadily to dispense to Europe, in reprints and in translations in French and German, the latest information on India from literature to botany and from history to climatic conditions. They included, among further contributions by Jones, a "Dissertation on the Orthography of Asiatick Words in Roman Letters" (1786), informed by the Indian tradition of phonetics, which set a standard for the transliteration of Sanskrit in Roman script, moving away from prior erratic renderings.

The encouragement of the Governor first, and of the Asiatic Society later, fostered in the 1780s and 1790s the revealing of Sanskrit literary treasures in translation no longer made from Persian intermediaries, but for the first time directly from Sanskrit. First among them was Charles Wilkins's pioneering translation (1785), under Governor Hastings's patronage, of the religio-philosophical poem *Bhagavadgītā* (from the epic *Mahābhārata*), a text the message of which had particular resonance in the climate of the Enlightenment. Wilkins continued, after his return to England, with a translation of the moral fables *Hitopadeśa* (1787). Jones, a gifted translator, followed suit with translations of Kālidāsa's play *Abhijñānaśāuntala* ("*Sacontala*", 1789), the erotic-mystical songs *Gītagovinda* of Jayadeva (1792), and the *Mānavadharmaśāstra* ("The Laws of Manu", 1794). These translations, which underwent multiple editions and translations into other European languages, elicited enthusiasm from the likes of Schopenhauer, Herder, Goethe, Schiller, Chateaubriand, and Lamartine, prompting what has been called the Oriental Renaissance (Schwab 1950: 64–71). Jones was also first to publish a Sanskrit text, the *Ṛtusaṃhāra*, a poetic description of the seasons attributed to Kālidāsa, in Devanāgarī script (1792). The first European edition of a Sanskrit text was not to appear before 1810, with Alexander Hamilton's edition of the *Hitopadeśa*, like Wilkins's *Grammar of the Sanskrita Language* (1808) intended as a textbook for students at the College founded by the English East India Company in 1806, where Hamilton was first to teach Sanskrit in Europe. Until Friedrich Schlegel's *Ueber die Sprache und Weisheit der Indier* (1808), information on Sanskrit originated exclusively from India or from scholars recently returned, Wilkins and Hamilton in Britain, and Paulinus a Sancto Bartholomaeo in Rome. Jones's untimely death in India in 1794 deprived Europe of the return of the most celebrated of all.

4. Stocktaking, 1790–1807

While discoveries were proceeding apace in India, Europe lagged significantly behind. Reflecting on the evidence provided by Pons, Dow, and Halhed, Michael Hissmann (1780) remained hostage to outdated assumptions that borrowing accounted for similarities with Western languages in Sanskrit. Nicolas Beauzée used the same corpus to update Diderot's paragraph about Sanskrit in the *Encyclopédie* (1765) into a five-page article in the *Encyclopédie méthodique* (1786), yet his primary concern was less Sanskrit proper or its kinship with European languages than using Sanskrit as a model in the development of an international scholarly language. The absurd suggestion that Sanskrit was a language made up by Brahmans on the model of Greek lingered on well into the 19th century with Dugald Stewart and Charles William Wall (1840). Yet, as the editor of his *Collected Works* noted, Stewart's manuscript conjectures on this subject were by then "so adverse to the harmonious opinion now entertained by those best qualified to judge" that he did not see the point of printing them (Stewart 1854–60, 4: 115).

It took a missionary returned from India knowledgeably to take stock of the state of Sanskrit and Indological scholarship at the end of the 18th century. Discalced Carmelite Paulinus a Sancto Bartholomaeo (born Philip(p) Wessdin (Vesdin) in Austria), who returned from Malabar in 1789, was extraordinarily well-read, although afflicted with an acerbic tongue. He devoted his retirement in Rome to publishing works in Latin on Indian scripts, languages, religion, and culture, primarily for the use of missionaries. First among these was a grammar, *Sidharubam seu grammatica Samscrdamica* (1790), the first grammar of Sanskrit ever printed. Based on a manuscript *Sidharubam* by Hanxleden, this grammar uses Western terminology and introduces Sanskrit words in Grantha script. It is organized, in Western manner, in four chapters on (1) declensions, (2) genders, adverbs, and conjunctions, (3) conjugations, and (4) syntax, between a syllabary and the prosodics of the śloka. It gives in an appendix the text of 14 stanzas from the *Bhāgavatapurāṇa*. In a prefatory "Dissertatio historico-critica in linguam samscrdamicam" which surveyed and critiqued current knowledge and opinion, Paulinus commented on the "elegance and majesty" of Sanskrit which "have been hampered by the almost unlimited difficulties of the idiom", likening them to "roses that are protected by large thorns" (L. Rocher 1977: 101). In spite of his knowledge of Dravidian languages, continued emphasis on lexical evidence led him to claim that Sanskrit was the parent of modern Indian languages that included Tamil and Malayalam ("Malabaric"). Issues of common religio-cultural origin were addressed in his *Systema Brahmanicum* (1791), based on documents in the Borgia Museum. He followed with *Alphabeta Indica* (1791) drawn from descriptions of Indian scripts in the library of the Sacred Congregation for the Propagation of the Faith, and followed with catalogues of Indic collections in the Congregation's library (1792) and in the Borgia Museum (1793). Collating three manuscripts allowed him to publish an edition of the first section of Amarasiṃha's dictionary (1798). He then turned to comparative philology with *De antiquitate et affinitate linguae Zendicae, Samscrdamicae, et Germanicae dissertatio* (1798), and *De Latini sermonis origine et cum orientalibus linguis connexione dissertatio* (1802), in which he rejected explanations of similarities by contact and borrowing or colonization, or by a northern 'Scythian' origin, and affirmed common oriental origin, albeit connected with the biblical dispersion myth. Although his evidence was primarily lexical, he also remarked on morphological features (cf. L. Rocher 1961: 349). Paulinus returned to grammar with a greatly expanded *Vyàcarana seu locupletissima Samscrdamicae linguae institutio* (1804) in seven chapters, which settled for the most part for Roman transliterations of Sanskrit words, but with sections in Grantha and occasional insertions of Devanāgarī. Dispensing with a lengthy introduction, this grammar offered two glossaries: Latin to Sanskrit by topics, and Sanskrit to Latin in slightly modified Roman alphabetical order. It also gave a list of verbs in Grantha script, Roman transliteration, and Latin translation, and a translation of the Lord's Prayer into Sanskrit. Paulinus's two grammars, and Pons's manuscript grammar in Paris, were the first means by which Sanskrit could be learned in Europe. Paulinus's other works also filled an important need and were much read and used, in particular by Hervás (1801) and Adelung (1, 1806). He further corrected Sanskrit words in the St. Petersburg vocabularies for Franz Carl Alter (1799), who published them along with his own corrections and their combined comparisons with other oriental languages.

International conditions in Europe unfortunately slowed scholarly advances. The richest collection of Sanskrit manuscripts was in Paris. Among them rested Pons's manuscript grammar of Sanskrit, which Antoine-Léonard de Chézy, destined to become in 1814 the first incumbent of a chair of Sanskrit on the continent, at the Collège de France, diligently studied. But learning a complex language on one's own, without the benefit of a tutor, was a struggle. Successfully learning Sanskrit still depended on the instruction of pandits, directly in India or mediately from Sanskrit scholars returned from India. The most profound Sanskrit scholars yet returned, Wilkins and Hamilton, were in England where Indophobia was rising. War conditions precluded travel between England and the continent, France in particular. Hamilton had to wait for the Peace of Amiens to be signed in 1802 to visit the Paris collections. The fact that the peace was promptly broken and Hamilton's ensuing detention in Paris created for the first time conditions that allowed avid scholars on the European continent to receive instruction from a member of Jones's Asiatic Society who had learned Sanskrit from pandits in India. Among these scholars (listed in R. Rocher 1968: 34−63) was Friedrich Schlegel, whose *Ueber die Sprache und Weisheit der Indier* (1808), based on Hamilton's instruction, was to open a new era in the history of the European knowledge of Sanskrit and comparative Indo-European linguistics. Hamilton's first informed catalogue of the Sanskrit manuscripts in the French Imperial Library, published jointly with their keeper, Louis-Matthieu Langlès (1807), gave scholars an added incentive to visit what was to remain a while longer the best collection in Europe. August Wilhelm Schlegel, destined to become the first holder of a chair of Sanskrit in Germany, in Bonn, was to make the Paris pilgrimage in the second decade of the 19th century. So did Franz Bopp, who went on to use the rapidly growing collections of the East India Company Library, the creation of which Wilkins brought about in 1800 and which he directed. From then on, European scholars became increasingly confident that a knowledge of Sanskrit could be acquired in Europe and that linguistic research and literary studies made in Europe were of a higher caliber than those conducted in India under the tutelage of pandits. The antagonism between British colonial scholars in India and antiquarian scholars in Europe, particularly in Germany, was to flare up on the occasion of the founding of the first chair of Sanskrit at a British university, the Boden chair at Oxford, in 1832, when its first incumbent, Horace Hayman Wilson, and August Wilhelm Schlegel locked in an acrimonious debate. Whatever the merits of that particular quarrel, the 19th century was essentially to reverse the pattern of scholarship prevalent in the 18th in that paradigmatic shifts in Sanskrit scholarship no longer emanated from India, but from the continent of Europe.

5. Bibliography

Camps, Arnulf & Jean-Claude Muller. 1988. *The Sanskrit Grammar and Manuscripts of Father Heinrich Roth S. J. (1620–68.)* Leiden: Brill.

Dow, Alexander. 1768. *History of Hindostan.* (new ed., 3 vol., 1803. London: Vernor & Hood.)

Filliozat, Jean. 1937. "Une grammaire sanscrite du XVIIIe siècle et les débuts de l'Indianisme en France". *Journal Asiatique* 229.275–284.

Halhed, Nathaniel Brassey. 1778. *A Grammar of the Bengal Language.* Hoogly in Bengal [: East India Company Press.]

Hoenigswald, Henry M. 1963. "On the History of the Comparative Method". *Anthropological Linguistics* 5: 1.1–10.

Hughes, S[haun] F. D. 1976. "John Cleland's Role in the History of Sanskrit Studies in Europe". *Archivum Linguisticum* 7.3–12.

Jones, Sir William. 1788. "The Third Anniversary Discourse: On the Hindus". *Asiatick Researches* 1.415–431.

Mayrhofer, Manfred. 1983. "Sanskrit und die Sprachen Alteuropas: Zwei Jahrhunderte von Entdeckungen und Irrtümern". *Nachrichten von der Akademie der Wissenschaften in Göttingen. Philologisch-historische Klasse* 5.123–153.

Muller, Jean-Claude. 1985. "Recherches sur les premières grammaires manuscrites du sanskrit". *Bulletin d'études indiennes* 3.125–144.

Pons, Jean-François. 1743. "Lettre au P. du Halde". *Lettres édifiantes et curieuses* (new ed., 1803, ed. L. Aimé-Martin, Paris: Desrez, 2.642–648.)

Rocher, Ludo. 1961. "Paulinus a Sancto Bartholomaeo on the Kinship of the Languages of India and Europe". *Brahmavidyā* 25.321–352.

—. 1977. *Paulinus a S. Bartholomaeo: Dissertation on the Sanskrit Language.* (= *Studies in the History of Linguistics*, 12.) Amsterdam: Benjamins.

—. 1984. *Ezourvedam: A French Veda of the Eighteenth Century.* (= *University of Pennsylvania Studies on South Asia*, 1.) Amsterdam & Philadelphia: Benjamins.

Rocher, Rosane. 1968. *Alexander Hamilton (1762–1824): A chapter in the early history of Sanskrit philology.* (= *American Oriental Series*, 51). New Haven, Ct.: American Oriental Society.

—. 1980a. "Lord Monboddo, Sanskrit, and Comparative Linguistics". *Journal of the American Oriental Society* 100.12–17.

—. 1980b. "Nathaniel Brassey Halhed, Sir William Jones, and Comparative Indo-European Linguistics". *Recherches de linguistique: Hommages à Maurice Leroy* ed. by Jean Bingen et al. 173–180. Brussels: Editions de l'Université de Bruxelles.

—. 1983. *Orientalism, Poetry, and the Millennium: The checkered life of Nathaniel Brassey Halhed 1751–1830.* Delhi: Motital Banarsidass.

Sassetti, Filippo. 1970. *Lettere da vari paesi 1570–1588* ed. by Vanni Bramanti. Milan: Longanesi.

Schulze, Benjamin. 1729. "Schreiben an Herrn Professor Francken". *Der Königlich Dänischen Missionarien aus Ost-Indien eingesandte ausführliche Berichte* 2: 21.708–10.

Schwab, Raymond. 1950. *La Renaissance orientale.* Paris: Payot.

Stewart, Dugald. 1854–60. *Collected Works.* Ed. by Sir William Hamilton, 4 vols. Edinburgh: Constable.

Rosane Rocher,
Philadelphia (U.S.A.)

XXIV. Historical and Comparative Linguistics of the Early 19th Century
Die historische und vergleichende Sprachwissenschaft zu Beginn des 19. Jahrhunderts
La linguistique historique et comparative au début du XIXe siècle

153. The renewal of the study of the classical languages within the university system, notably in Germany

1. Introduction
2. The classical languages in Europe in the Early Middle Ages
3. Classical languages and Humanism
4. Towards the establishment of classical scholarship as an independent science
5. 'The Age of Winckelmann': Development of classical studies during the eighteenth century
6. The attainment of ambitious goals: Classical studies in the nineteenth century and its impact on society in general
7. Conclusion
8. Bibliography

1. Introduction

The classical languages, Latin and Greek, used to be learned in high school and were extensively studied at the university. This is an accurate description of the conditions especially in Germany until at least the beginning of the 20th century. The university could concentrate on enlarging and refining the knowledge which the incoming students had acquired as pupils. Before they graduated with a Dr. phil. degree, they were capable of writing their 'Inaugural Dissertation' in Latin, in a manner 'not only grammatically correct, but also stylistically proficient and elegant' (Schonack 1914: 80−81), and most of them actually did. As a matter of fact, doctoral theses at least in the field of classical philology had to be written in Latin, with few well-founded exceptions. During the first hundred years of its existence from 1810 to 1910 the University of Berlin granted 641 doctoral diplomas in classical philology, and only 23 (about 3,6%) were written in German (Schonack, p. 82).

2. The classical languages in Europe in the Early Middle Ages

The study of languages in an academic setting from its very beginning was tied to the objectives of the Christian missionary work. In whatever country Christianity was introduced, the teaching and learning of Latin and Greek, and to a lesser extent also of Hebrew, from the early Middle Ages to the beginning of the 20th century played a vital role in the work of the Church. For Latin to become the language of the Church, extraordinary, elaborate, and world-wide procedures had to be put into place, had to be consistently upheld and developed with an exceptional endeavor and dedication over a long period of time to safeguard the eventual unprecedented success. Latin, Greek, and Hebrew were the vehicles that carried the Holy Scripture, and on the basis of this fact they were assigned a status of prominence which effectively eclipsed the significance of any other − so-called vernacular − languages.

Equally strong as the religious aspect was the general cultural dimension which the classical languages helped to create and vigorously expand within the framework of the carefully organized activities of the Christian Church. Christian culture comprised a multitude of values which depended upon the classical languages in order to be perceived and made explicit, to be propagated and to be preserved. Philosophy – throughout the Middle Ages and also in most of the centuries that followed – thrived by its relationship with the classical languages. They served, on the one hand, as the highly suitable tool which, by its association with the biblical scriptures, had been declared to be the most perfect tool for the expression and transmission of human thought, and they provided, on the other hand, an almost inexhaustible treasure of ancient writings which, after thorough probing and somewhat extensive adaptation, became for the greater part important ingredients of the Christian culture.

In the area of law the classical influence proved equally far-reaching. As is more obvious in this field, political and national considerations – besides religious and church-related issues – played a key role in exploring the riches of the classical languages and the substantive message which they carried. The reception of the Roman Law in its twofold shape – *Corpus iuris civilis* and *Corpus iuris canonici* – in the middle of the 15th century, after a lengthy process of scrutinizing, experimenting, adjusting, and also of discarding or marginalizing large portions of the Germanic law, is partially due to the widespread belief that the *Holy Roman Empire of the German Nation* as the successor state of the Roman Empire was destined to retain some of its most monumental features to which the structure of the Roman Law undoubtedly belonged. Even after the Roman Law was replaced in Germany by the *Bürgerliches Gesetzbuch* ('Civil Code') during the era of Bismarck and in Austria by the *Allgemeines Bürgerliches Gesetzbuch* ('General Civil Code') on January 1, 1900, the function of the Roman Law was diminished, but by no means eliminated, since both codes – the Austrian even more than the German – continued to rely heavily on the Roman Law.

Vital precondition for the spiritual might of the Church to unfold to unprecedented proportions was the presence of instruments that were both global in their applicability and universally effective and appealing by their unparalleled richness in content. Prior to the 19th century, the regional languages of Europe in general, and the languages of Germany in particular, were at no time a viable rival for the pervading force of the Latin language, and the fragmented German law, adapted from various Germanic sources, could not hold its own against the highly sophisticated codices of the Roman Law which had grown to a level of high perfection in conjunction with the development of a grandiose civilization. Much of the political systems of ancient Greece and Rome lived on in every single state of Europe, partially because it had become an integral part of the Christian culture, but partially also because it was vastly superior to equivalent indigenous institutions. And again it becomes apparent that the classical languages of necessity were considered indispensable for the attainment of the objectives of the Christian Church as well as those of other political and cultural institutions.

The gradually diminishing influence of the Church at the close of the Middle Ages and the beginning of modern times did not inflict any substantial damage to the status of the classical languages. Latin and Greek differed significantly in their status and importance for the modern world, but both continued to be safely established in various layers of modern society. The Christian Church and the classical languages, initially dependent upon each other a great deal for their rise to global prominence, could now develop with unremitting strength, but with only a minimal amount of mutual dependency.

Latin and Greek continued to constitute superior values for academic studies – and as a metalanguage for science – because of their formal structure and the content features to which they provide access. Whereas in previous times the significance of these content features was measured almost exclusively by religious criteria, they were now being examined more frequently in their own terms. Religious aspects remain important, but they share center stage with a growing number of other factors of equal or of even greater importance.

3. Classical languages and Humanism

Powerful movements and trends like the humanism of the 15th to the 16th century furthered the notion that any kind of advanced intellectual training presupposed extensive exposure to the classical languages and through them to classical literature and culture. Humanism as a movement started from ca. 1450 in Italy and spread from there to other European countries, notably to France and Germany. Church leaders in many countries were actively involved, yet not as originators and prime movers, but as ordinary participants, among many others.

The intended enrichment of intellectual and cultural life on a large scale was achieved best in Italy, and in Germany probably less than in any other country, as extended controversies among various theological and philosophical factions in Germany during the Reformation often resulted in personal feuds — to the disadvantage of the great and worthwhile issues that needed to be identified and solved.

The undisputed leaders of German humanism, Johannes Reuchlin (1455—1522) and Philipp Melanchthon (1497—1560), although both by no means uninvolved in stringent controversies, excelled as classical scholars and university teachers of classical languages, and both were prolific writers. Both scholars participated actively in the Reformation initiated by Luther: Melanchthon as a close ally of Luther, Reuchlin taking a firm stand in the opposite camp. Melanchthon, when appointed in 1518 as professor of Greek at the University of Wittenberg, demanded in his inaugural lecture *De corrigendis adolescentiae studiis* ('On what needs to be changed in university studies') that the study of classical languages should become the foundation of all other sciences, even of theology. With this demand, which he often reiterated and expanded by various specific activities, he greatly aided the process of establishing Greek as a regular university subject. As the *Praeceptor Germaniae* Melanchthon had earned the reputation of an outstanding teacher, perhaps "also to have been responsible for a certain classroom atmosphere which became characteristic of the later German humanism in contrast to that of France and England" (Pfeiffer 1976: 94).

Reuchlin taught briefly Greek and Hebrew at Ingolstadt after completing his university studies, being the first scholar to teach those languages in Germany (cf. Jahn 1868: 19). Thereafter he started to work as a lawyer for several decades. Shortly before his death he resumed teaching Greek and Hebrew at the University of Ingolstadt, which was founded in 1472 by Ludwig IX, Duke of Bavaria-Landshut (1417—1479), and changed location by moving to Landshut in 1802. It was in Ingolstadt that Humanism got its first foothold in Germany under Conrad Celtis (1459—1508). Like Melanchthon, Reuchlin furthered the study of classical languages by stressing their importance for general education. Apart from writing ground-breaking scholarly books especially on Hebrew, he also deserves praise for publishing Greek editions and translating Greek writers into Latin.

A contemporary of Reuchlin and Melanchthon, Desiderius Erasmus of Rotterdam (1467—1536), a Dutchman by birth, but a citizen of many European countries: France, Belgium, England, Germany, Italy, and Switzerland — and a citizen of the world by his own definition ("Ego mundi civis esse cupio" ['I desire to be a citizen of the world']) — had gained among his contemporaries the reputation of being the most eminent Humanist scholar of his time. His fame was already securely established when he published in 1516 the first printed edition of the New Testament in Greek (*Novum Testamentum omne*) in Basel. The motivation for his commitment to the classical languages was on the one hand clearly religious, but on the other also philosophical, in that he firmly believed in the teaching of Socrates that evil in man is driven out only by knowledge, that ignorance prevents or deteriorates spiritual life and that moral decline manifests itself in the decay of languages. Hence any strategy to increase the study of ancient languages is part if the service rendered to the implementation of the *Philosophia Christi*, which entails that classical, non-Christian *humanitas* and Medieval, Christian *pietas* must be combined to their mutual advantage.

Erasmus did not invent the notion of *Philosophia Christi*, but he held on to it tenaciously, advocated it strongly and fought for it all through his life. Christians, he was convinced, were charged with the obligation to "recognize, comprehend, and to know" (cognoscere, intellegere, scire). With this he laid the foundation for an approach to classical studies which was on an almost equal footing — and shared a number of objectives — with that of Christian religious and theological strategists. Erasmus, an annointed priest himself, did not view this slowly emerging 'branching off' into two autonomous domains where so far only one had existed with a single overriding objective, as a deviation from his Christian mission, even though he was frequently attacked by the Church for his emphasis on the need of Christians to expand their knowledge so as to be able, in his opinion, to be of greater service to God and to the Church. That the road from partial autonomy to total autonomy of classical studies proved to be a cumbersome and lengthy journey is largely due to the failure of Church authorities to realize that furthering a more intensive and more independent study of classical antiquity would hold great promise for achieving swiftly universal spiritual leadership in addition to religious dominance.

4. Towards the establishment of classical scholarship as an independent science

After Reuchlin, Melanchthon, and Erasmus the number of scholars in Germany who published on Greek and Roman writers and edited their works grew considerably. What was sorely lacking, however, were solid principles and directives how the works of the classical writers were to be approached and what methods were to be employed in bringing about editions that would do justice to the status of the works involved. A mere accumulation of works published with no discernible uniform criteria, although it seemed to be the order of the day, was far from being adequate. Nor was another aberration compatible with a worthwhile scientific methodology, the mere accumulation of knowledge on the classical world, without differentiating between what was important and what was not. Caspar von Barth's (1587–1667) escapades in this regard are referred to by Otto Jahn (1813–1869) as 'the most deterrent example' ("das abschreckendste Beispiel" [Jahn 1868: 22]), and Ulrich von Wilamowitz-Moellendorff (1848–1931) alludes to the dangers faced by those – at von Barth's time and now – who expose themselves to this kind of 'research': "One cannot read him without catching he infection of his muddled thinking and his muddled writing" (Wilamowitz 1982 [1921]: 67).

Martin Luther's Reformation and its aftermath had positive as well as negative consequences for classical language studies. On the one hand, both hostile camps, Protestants and Catholics, saw in classical studies an indispensable education tool which they were determined to put to maximum use. On the other hand, however, this use more often than not resulted in issues of classical scholarship being employed inappropriately in the ongoing public controversies and altercations between the two factions, and not even the best minds could refrain from participating or at least getting indirectly involved.

The devastating effects of the Thirty-Year War (1618–1648) interfered severely with the scholarly pursuits in every European country, but Germany seems to have been hit the hardest. The ravages of war and disease destroyed the lives of approximately 40% of the German population of 25 millions (cf. Freud 1985: 343), and those who were left had to fight for their survival with few material means and hardly any intellectual incentives at their disposal. Teaching and research in classical languages slowly regained a modicum of standards, but direction, objectives, and methodologies were largely chosen at random.

The desperately needed guidelines were finally provided by the English scholar Richard Bentley (1662–1742). His *Epistola ad Joannum Millium* ('Letter to John Mill' [1645–1707]; Principal of St. Edmund Hall, Oxford, prestigious editor of the New Testament, a close friend of Bentley) of 1691 contained observations which formed the basis for a critical scientific approach to the edition of classical texts. Bentley provided further substantial elaboration in the amended edition of his *Dissertation upon the Epistles of Phalaris* of 1699, "the first important work of classical scholarship written in a modern language" (cf. *Encyclopædia Britannica* 1993 xxvii: 27). While even the first edition of 98 pages exemplified what Bentley called an extensive procedure for dealing appropriately with ancient texts, the enlarged version of approximately 600 pages, written within a span of two years, focused comprehensively on a much larger number of issues and does it in a polemical fashion. In this regard Wilamowitz suggests that "the best way a German can characterize the *Dissertation* is by putting it on a level with the polemical writings of Lessing" (Wilamowitz 1982 [1921]: 8). The sum total of the issues Bentley raised amounts to the demand that in order to do full justice to the written piece of art by an ancient scholar or poet, the modern scholar has to make an all-out effort to establish and reconstruct the entire context for the work in question. This would involve not only an exquisite amount of knowledge of all aspects of grammar and style, of metrical phenomena and their relationship to grammatical features, and of historical facts and factors pertaining to the time period investigated, but would also require the ability and the courage to emend and reconstruct by reasoned conjectural work where the text material is suspected to be faulty or in need of supplementation. This list is by no means complete, but it may suffice to give an impression of the challenges which Bentley's demands had placed before the profession. The standard of classical scholarship was raised to a level which heretofore had never existed. Haphazard probing, mostly in accordance with individual predilection rather than the strict requirements of the text, were now replaced by the critical attitude of a sophisticated observer who determined his task on the basis of the nature of his object of inquiry and who employed objective criteria to derive rules from what he had observed and applied them to equivalent phenomena.

It is interesting to note that what Bentley put forward as a program for classical scholarship and illustrated in his two above-mentioned treatises as well as in others is by no means — on a purely theoretical level — different from, nor is it specific for, his particular field. His criteria are those that apply also to the scientific approach employed in any other field. But there is one important conclusion to be drawn from this. Bentley's venture for the first time established classical scholarship as an independent science, as a discipline that is no longer ancillary to other fields like theology or philosophy. Since Bentley's demands still had to be adopted and implemented by his fellow-researchers in England and in other countries throughout Europe, his envisioned mission was far from being completed. But the fact remains that the first step — and a very decisive step at that — had now been taken.

Even in England the recognition of the importance of Bentley's trend-setting procedure was slow to gain momentum, and much more so in Germany. Friedrich August Wolf (1759—1824), credited with having introduced into the debate the term *Alterthums-Wissenschaft* ('Science of the classics'), was the first in Germany to recognize and acknowledge the importance of Bentley's discovery (cf. Wilamowitz-Moellendorff 1982 [1921]: 81), and he saw to it that German classical scholars availed themselves of the fruits of Bentley's labors. Gottfried Hermann (1772—1848) and Karl Lachmann (1793—1851) were among the most prominent researchers to apply Bentley's methods to their own work. Wolf himself did little of that in his own editions, but exerted a profound influence on how classical scholarship should be conducted by both his highly effective teaching at the newly founded University of Berlin and by his methodological writings.

Bentley had his own predecessors, even in England. But there is a distinction to be made between what scholars do at a particular time and what effect they produce on their contemporary fellow-researchers and on those of a later time. While, for instance, Joseph Justus Scaliger (1540—1609) — in the opinion of many of the greatest philologist of the 16th century, who first served as professor of philosophy in Genf (1572—1574), then spent almost 20 years in France devoting his time to private studies and finally moved to Leiden in 1593 to occupy the chair in classical philosophy — can rightly be called to have been the first to approach classical antiquity from a holistic viewpoint and is credited with being the founder of scientific chronology (cf. his treatise *De emendatione temporum* ['On the Improvement of the Times'], 1583), he is but a link — though an important one — and a stepping stone in a continuous line of development. His efforts eventually led to a scholar like Bentley whose genius for combining intricate details with the ability to build the overall framework to which those details belong, propelled scientific standards to a much more advanced stage than could have been attained before. Subsequent endeavors by other scholars, especially in England and in Germany, would strive to consolidate the gains and search for ways to bring about further advances.

Bentley, appointed director of Trinity College in Cambridge in 1700 and elected Regius Professor of Divinity in 1717, did not produce any school of followers. Perhaps the main reason was his preoccupation with administrative matters and his eagerness to further his own numerous publishing plans. To what extent his religious duties interfered with his pursuit of classical studies — at least with regard to identifying and training a group of specially gifted students to become university teachers and potential implementers of his own innovative ideas — is hard to say. But outside the framework of a formal school Bentley's work over time gained widespread recognition in England, in spite of numerous polemical fights in which he was involved and which he conducted not only with intense energy and exhibiting a grandiose style, but also with a good amount of openly displayed delight. In Cambridge, more than in any other British university city, his work was continued by younger scholars, notably by Richard Porson (1759—1808). Bentley also reaped great praise, posthumously, from

Edward Gibbon (1737–1794), author of the six-volume *History of the Decline and Fall of the Roman Empire* (1774–88), who referred to Bentley as being "tremendous" (Pfeiffer 1976: 162).

Holland's reception of Bentley's ideas was almost immediate, although not all of the many outstanding Dutch classical scholars were willing to depart from the research procedures they had worked out on their own. Tiberius Hemsterhuis (1685–1766) had corresponded with Bentley. He and his most famous pupil, German-born David Ruhnken (1723–1798) [originally Ruhneken, latinized Ruhnkenius], as well as Lodewijk Kaspar Valckenaer (1715–1785), all of them teaching at the University of Leiden, endorsed Bentley's practices, and their work, in the opinion of Pfeiffer (1976: 163), "clearly shows how the study of the Greek lexicographers initiated by Bentley enabled his successors to produce better editions of the ancient Greek lexica and to recognize the idiomatic peculiarities of Greek, especially Attic, poets and writers". What has to be kept in mind, however, is that neither in England nor in Holland, and initially also not in Germany, were Bentley's initiatives taken up in all its aspects and ramifications and implemented to the fullest extent possible.

Even though war-torn 17th century Germany was slow in recovering from the huge, mostly man-made catastrophes, the rebuilding and strengthening of classical scholarship profited greatly from the fact that Greek and Latin language instruction had by and large been firmly entrenched in the German school system and had not been relegated to a purely academic pursuit at the university level. It also proved helpful that numerous school teachers of Latin and Greek simultaneously served as university instructors, and vice versa. While such an arrangement was largely dictated by economic considerations and brought with it serious drawbacks, it also had a favorable influence on the further development of classical studies in the country, and this for a variety of good reasons. One of the most important reasons was that the initial encounter with classical languages and literature, mediated by some of the most capable representatives of the teaching profession, left the minds of a considerable number of very young boys — during their most impressionable years of early adolescence — very favorably inclined towards classical studies. During their university years their level of interest could be raised, and very often was, to such an extent that many of them enthusiastically resolved to devote their entire lives to the learning and teaching of Greek and Latin. The ongoing trend towards the enlargement of the clientele being inspired to explore the 'new' old world of classical antiquity also involved a steadily increasing portion of the general public. This is due to the increased activity of a large number of intellectuals, and especially of writers and poets, who spoke out publicly in favor of, or wrote extensively on, the rewards to be reaped from acquiring a measure of familiarity with the ancient Romans and Greeks.

5. 'The Age of Winckelmann': Development of classical studies during the eighteenth century

Such a general endeavor did not and could not pursue academic objectives in itself, but it most certainly contributed significantly to the eventual success of the struggle of classical studies for wider recognition and greater influence in academia. Joseph Justus Scaliger's contention towards the end of the 16th century that — in the words of Rudolf Pfeiffer (1976: 118) — "the history of the ancient world had to be known as a whole, if at all" was his personal agendum which he set out to fulfill, but which needed more than a century to become accepted and acted upon by the majority of academic institutions where classical studies already were or were about to become part of their study program. Throughout this developmental process, non-academic considerations such as, for instance, the attitude of the general educated public, played a decisive role. The life and work of Johann Joachim Winckelmann (1717–1768) should serve as a convincing illustration. He learned Latin long before he began his university studies in 1738, first in Halle, then in Jena. Acquiring a first-rate command of classical languages for him was not an end in itself, but the indispensable means of gaining access to the world of art, especially that of ancient Greece. He entered professional life with teaching at a *Gymnasium* in 1743, and after a few years served for six years as a staff member in a private library near Dresden. His ardent desire to see the places rich in ancient, classical art was finally fulfilled when, in 1755, he was awarded a royal stipend that enabled him to travel to Rome. As he had converted to Catholicism the year before, he found easy access to employment opportunities in Church institutions, like the Vatican Library as *praefecto antiquitatum* − Superintendent of Antiquities −, which placed him in the unique position that he could fully realize his ultimate professional aim: to devote his life to the study and propagation of ancient art.

His extraordinary detailed knowledge of ancient art and its history, acquired over the years by avaricious reading habits and seeking out art treasures in Rome, Florence, Naples, Paestum, Herculaneum, and a number of other places, enabled him to develop useful guidelines for the approach to, and the evaluation of, Greek and Roman art. By his expertise he was in the position of not only determining criteria for the understanding and appreciation of an individual piece of art, but also placing it into its proper historical context. In addition, he could translate his seemingly limitless enthusiasm for the ancient art into written presentations which were appealing and even outright inspiring for large segments of the general public. Johann Wolfgang von Goethe (1749−1832) felt inclined − and with good reason − to call the 18th century 'the century of Winckelmann' (cf. "Skizzen zu einer Schilderung Winckelmanns" Goethe 1969 [1805]: 208−231).

Winckelmann's first and perhaps most important and certainly most influential publication appeared in 1755, the year of his first visit to Rome: This booklet of barely 40 pages on *Gedanken über die Nachahmung der griechischen Werke in der Malerei und Bildhauerkunst* ('Reflections on the Imitation of Greek Works in Painting and Sculpture') had a pervading influence inside and outside academia. It explained to those who could not possibly have developed on their own a motivation to explore the world of ancient art, why such an exploration would mean an enrichment of their personal lives beyond their wildest expectations: 'The only way for us to become great, or if this be possible, inimitable, is to imitate the ancients' ("Der einzige Weg für uns, gross, ja, wenn es möglich ist, unnachahmlich zu werden, ist die Nachahmung der Alten" [Winckelmann 1755: 4−5]).

With remarks like these a campaign was inaugurated which captivated the attention of the reading public. The ordinary citizens with a minimum of intellectual and artistic interests and inclination were touched as well as those who as writers and intellectuals had a stake in becoming aware of important new trends, examine them and then either endorse or reject them. Prominent representatives of the latter group were Gotthold Ephraim Lessing (1729−1781), Johann Gottfried Herder (1744−1803), and Friedrich von Schlegel (1772−1829), among many others. Those individuals in their turn spread the enthusiasm that Winckelmann had transmitted to them to their own clientele, thus adding on to the rising tide of public support for classical studies.

Winckelmann started out with developing a keen interest in the art of Greece. While this interest did never decrease, he vastly expanded its scope by also focusing on other important ancient cultures. His *History of Ancient Art*, which first appeared in 1764, included detailed discussions of Phoenician, Persian, and Egyptian art, in addition to Roman and Greek. The book, his *magnum opus*, 'is intended to show the origin, progress, change, and downfall of art, together with different styles of nations, periods, and artists, and to prove the whole, as far as it is possible, from the ancient monuments now in existence' (Winckelmann 1872, I: 149−150). It was enthusiastically received all over Europe and consolidated his fame as the founder of modern archeology and art history. Classical studies almost immediately felt the strong impact of his activities, most importantly by his impressive appeal to the general public − leading to a better understanding of and greater support for classical studies − and by making art and art history an integral part of any scientific approach to the ancient world. The latter part is aptly recognized by Goethe's remark that "seit Winckelmanns und seiner Nachfolger Bemühen ist Philologie ohne Kunstbegriff nur einäugig" ('since the endeavors of Winckelmann and his successors philology without the concept of art is only one-eyed' [quoted in Dobel 1991: 707]). Philology at that time was synonymous with classical philology.

Universities in Germany were by no means ready to lend all-out support to the establishment of chairs in Latin and Greek. But the tendency was there, and it grew steadily. It also helped that on numerous occasions researchers in classical studies emerged who produced superb editions of classical texts and wrote inspiring methodological treatises without being provided the appropriate employment at the university level.

One such researcher was Johann Jakob Reiske (1716–1774). His devotion to classical scholarship is unique in also this respect that, in addition to being appropriately called 'one of the first, if not the first, Greek scholar of the 18th century' (Foerster 1889b: 131), he is, furthermore, credited with being 'truly the founder of Arabic philology' (ibid.). With the unconditional support of his wife Ernestine Christine (1735–1798) whom he married in 1864, but hardly any other help from the outside world, he accomplished to produce an amazing amount of publications of extraordinary merit in the field of classical scholarship. He was greatest in preparing vastly improved editions of classical Greek writers — for instance, *Constantini Porfyrogeneti Libri duo de ceremoniis aulae Byzantinae* (2 vols., 1751–54) — and in writing commentaries on the texts themselves and the procedures he employed, either published as part of the editions or separately as *animadversiones*. The latter include *Animadversiones ad Sophoclem* (Leipzig, 1753) and the 8 volumes of *Animadversionum ad Graecos Auctores Volumen I* (Leipzig, 1759–66). Reiske confesses in his autobiography (cf. Foerster 1889b: 134) that 'most of my lifetime I have spent reading Greek authors'. With his elaborate textual criticism he surpassed the standards of his predessors and his contemporaries alike and served for several generations as a model. Last but not least, he also translated classical texts into German, for instance, the *Reden des Thukydides* (Leipzig, 1761) and in five volumes the speeches of Demosthenes and Aeschines (Lemgo, 1764–69).

It is also important to keep in mind that Reiske's outstanding credentials as Germany's first Arabic scholar and the expertise which he developed in that field was greatly beneficial for his later, almost exclusive preoccupation with research in classical languages. He had sharpened his understanding of the historical framework within which literary works have to be interpreted and saw the need to include in any interpretative approach facts and factors of as many other disciplines as were in his reach. We here see similarities to the concept of philology as they were envisioned by Richard Bentley and later on more elaborately presented by Friedrich August Wolf: that language phenomena and facts and factors of literature have to be viewed in the larger context of other cultural factors and must then be interpreted as integral parts of a structural whole.

It does not speak well of the state of classical studies in Germany at the time of Reiske that a scholar of his talents and accomplishments had to struggle through a mountain of adversities in order to reach and maintain the bare minimum of a living standard. Even if in view of his somewhat abrasive personality allowances have to be made concerning the difficulties created for him on purpose by some and not removed by others who could have easily interfered, the fact remains that even those who had highest praise for him — as, for instance, Gotthold Ephraim Lessing and even the Prussian King Frederick the Great (1712–1786) — were big in words, but small in supportive action.

The achievements and the sacrifices of scholars like Reiske were, however, in the long run not in vain. Lessing's great promise to Reiske's wife Christine (cf. her letter to Johann Gottlob Schneider (1750–1822), 5 March 1777: 'Certainly so far the life of no other scholar has been described more complete, better, and more beautiful than this one will be' [Foerster 1897: 897]) to detail the extraordinary accomplishments of Reiske in a 3-volume treatise on his life and work was for some unknown reason not even seriously begun, but word spread around. Recognition of the value of the scholarly discoveries in the ancient world was extended not only by colleagues working in the same field or in adjacent disciplines but also, and more significantly, by some of the greatest German *Denker und Dichter*. Johann Gottfried Herder had expressed his great admiration for Reiske (cf. Foerster 1889b: 131), and so has, among others, Theodor Mommsen (1817–1903), for whom Reiske was 'the incomparable one' ("der unvergleichliche") among 'the most insightful [classical] scholars' ("[unter den] einsichtigsten Forschern": cf. Mommsen, *Hermes* 6: 381 [1871]). Words of those intellectual giants carried weight with their peers as well as with the general public. Moreover, just as Lessing dealt extensively, especially in his theoretical writings for instance, in *Laokoon* [1766] and *Wie die Alten den Tod gebildet* [1769]) with the classical world, so did Friedrich Gottlieb Klopstock (1724–1803), the 'most German' among the poets of the classical period, who tried to find a common denominator for the classical and the German spirituality; Friedrich Hölderlin (1770–1843), who had high hopes that he could witness and actively participate in the revival of classical life and thought. His many contributions were in lyrical poetry (e. g., "Hyperions Schicksalslied"), in dramatic art (*Empedokles*), in translations from the Greek (*Ödipus* and *Antigone* by Sophocles) and a novel dealing with *Hyperion oder der Eremit in Griechenland* (2 vols., 1797–99). The greatest and longest-lasting impact came from Friedrich Schiller (1759–1805) and Goethe. Their poetry as well as their dramatic art is unthinkable without their exposure to the intellectual and artistic models they found in the classical world of Greek and Rome. But it is equally unthinkable that the revival of classical studies could have proceeded at the speed and intensity as it did without the 'popularizing' effect of Goethe and Schiller's poetry on the majority of their readers in Germany and beyond. Anselm Feuerbach's (1798–1851) well-known painting of the young Goethe looking at a distant 'classical' landscape, his state of mind being epitomised as "das Land der Griechen mit der Seele suchend" ('seeking out the land of the Greeks with his soul'), stands for numerous similar expressions of the widespread feelings of the Germans at the time that a great part of their heritage is tied to ancient Rome and Greece.

6. The attainment of ambitious goals: Classical studies in the nineteenth century and its impact on society in general

Towards the end of the 18th and the beginning of the 19th century the give-and-take between disciplines inside and outside academia in matters of formal and substantive aspects of classical antiquity kept growing by leaps and bounds. No field remained unaffected, and new special fields of interest and of academic studies emerged in response to the widening of scope. The Schlegel brothers August Wilhelm (1767–1845) and Friedrich (cf. Wilamowitz 1982: 107) were intellectual forces of global reach, especially by their work on classical esthetics, although mentioning just one area of their influence does by no means full justice to them. The older brother August Wilhelm's outstanding *Vorlesungen über dramatische Kunst und Literatur* ('Lectures on Dramatic Art and Literature', 2 parts, 1809–1811) and his *Theorie und Geschichte der bildenden Künste* ('Theory and History of the Visual Arts', 1827) were accepted as guidelines in many European countries, as they exemplified and made explicit how the values of classical art could be meaningfully employed to supplement and expand the esthetic notions prevailing at that time. Reading Schiller's essay "Über naive und sentimentalische Dichtung" ('On Naïve and Sentimental Poetry', 1795/96), which discusses and evaluates the esthetic principles of some of the ancient poets, was one decisive factor that inspired Schlegel to embark on his work in esthetics. Friedrich, the younger of the Schlegel brothers, was no less interested in classical Greek and Latin as he was in ancient Persia and India, as several publications of far-reaching influence do show, e. g., *Von den Schulen der griechischen Poesie* ('On the Schools of Greek Poetry', 1794) and *Geschichte der Poesie der Griechen und Römer* ('History of Greek and Roman Poetry', 1798). With Friedrich Schleiermacher's (1768–1834) annotated translation of the works of Plato, published from 1804 to 1828, "the earliest successful attempt to render a great writer of Greek prose in German of an artistic and literary type" (Sandys 1967 [1903–1908] III: 83), Greek philosophy gained ground in Germany and continued to prepare a larger group of the non-specialists for serious considerations of philosophical questions related to the ancient past and think about the relevance of those questions for the present time. Friedrich Schlegel played a role in enticing Schleiermacher to undertake the Plato translation.

What the Schlegel brothers by their joint effort together with Ludwig Tieck (1773–1853) have achieved with their brilliant translation of Shakepeare's works, Johann Heinrich Voss (1751–1826) brought about singlehandedly by his masterly and vastly influential translations of Homer's *Odyssee* (1781) and *Iliad* (1793) as well as a host of prestigious Latin writers, such as Ovid's *Metamorphoses* (2 vols., 1789), Vergil's *Georgica* (1789), *Hesiod und Orpheus* (1806), *Horaz* (2 vols., 1806), and *Tibull und Lygdamus* (1816).

The availability of knowledge of the classical Greek and Roman languages in modern Europe inevitably led to an encounter first with only selected segments of the classical culture, then with all aspects of it that came in sight. When the intensity of classical studies kept growing, the field of enquiry grew likewise, and so did the number of special subdisciplines devoted to the exploration of whatever characterized, in the opinion of the individual researchers, the life and work in the cradle of Western civilization. Visualizing life in Rome and Athens required enlightened reconstruction of reality on the basis of written accounts of a great variety and also of different value. Poetry alone could hardly be considered the exclusive guiding light on the lengthy expedition to recreate the reality of the ancient world in all its reachable spheres. The written word of necessity was supplemented by any kind of available artifacts, most importantly by archeology. Archeology, originally a part of the science of history, until the middle of the 18th century used to treat those conditions in the lives of peoples and nations that were not covered by 'history proper', i.e., political history, and was concerned primarily with the customs, laws, and myths of the people. After that, the term was used, for the first time by Johann August Ernesti (1707–1781) in 1768, in a more restricted way, referring to the 'knowledge of the monuments of art of classical antiquity'. Classical archeology, as we have stated before, has its founder and most significant proponent in Winckelmann. Important follow-up work was supplied by Karl Otfried Müller (1797–1840) who, as classical scholar and pupil of August Boeckh (1777–1855), published two highly significant books which provided convincing evidence for art history to be of necessity an integral part of classical studies. In 1830 *Archäologie der Kunst* ('Archeology of Art') and four years later *Denkmäler der alten Kunst* ('Monuments of the Ancient Art').

Boeckh drew the almost obvious conclusions from the theoretical and practical work of others, both contemporaries and predecessors. He had studied in Berlin under the classical scholar Friedrich August Wolf and attended lectures in philosophy by Schleiermacher. Both of these teachers left their deep impression on him. Equally strong was the influence he derived from the careful study of Winckelmann's writings. While considering the multifarious approaches of researchers from different fields and also weighing the findings from research work of his own, for instance, on the *Staatshaushalt der Athener* ('Public Economy of the Athenians', 2 vols., 1817) and on *Urkunden über das Seewesen des attischen Staates* ('Documents of the Navy of the Attic State', 1840) — both works devoted to the exploration of daily-life pursuits in ancient Greece — Boeckh felt the need to come up with a precise framework for all those endeavors that aimed, after all, at serving one and the same overriding purpose. This framework was the term "Philologie", massively enlarged by its definition as 'Wissenschaft von der gesamten antiken Kultur' ('science of the entire ancient culture'). 'Philologie', certainly filled with a meaning different from that of the English term 'philology', thus became identical with the term 'klassische Philologie' which had formerly been used.

Boeckh himself has not published about his concept of philology. One of the pupils, the philosopher Ernst Bratuschek (1837–1883), took it upon himself to transform the voluminous lecture notes of his teacher into a publishable treatise. It appeared in 1877 as *Enzyklopädie und Methodenlehre der philologischen Wissenschaften* ('Encyclopedia and Methodology of the Philological Sciences'). In the preface Bratuschek relates that from 1809 to 1865 Boeckh gave lectures in 26 semesters on the encyclopedia of philology, for which a total of 1696 students had registered (Boeckh 1877: iii). Between 1862 and 1866 he had himself attended those lectures as well as all other courses taught by Boeckh (ibid., iv).

Boeckh's definition of the concept of philology as "die Erkenntnis des Erkannten, also eine Wiedererkenntnis eines gegebenen Erkennens" ('recognition of what has been recognized, that is, acquiring again what is a given recognition' [1877: 53]) is the point of departure for a very elaborate enunciation of a system which in his opinion does full justice to the special status of the numerous branches of scientific inquieries into the world of antiquity, because their individual position within the overall structure as well as their relationship to each other had been carefully examined. He vigorously attacked Friedrich August Wolf's classification which comprises 24 main sections claiming: 'Both the individual disciplines that were set up and the overall structure which they are supposed to form lack, however, the scientific interrelationship' ("Es fehlt aber sowohl den einzelnen aufgestellten Disziplinen als auch dem Ganzen, das sie bilden sollen, der wissenschaftliche Zusammenhang" [Boeckh 1877: 40]). He does not find fault with his teacher's definition of philology as 'the embodiment of the knowledge and information that acquaint us with the actions and destinies, with the political, learned and domestic conditions of the Greeks and Romans, with their culture, their languages, arts, and sciences, customs, religions, national characters and modes of thinking' ("Inbegriff der Kenntnisse und Nachrichten, die uns mit den

Handlungen und Schicksalen, mit dem politischen, gelehrten und häuslichen Zustande der Griechen und Römer, mit ihrer Kultur, ihren Sprachen, Künsten und Wissenschaften, Sitten, Religionen, National-Charakteren und Denkarten bekannt machen" [Wolf 1807, I: 30]). But Wolf, although he was a great name at his time and his voice was heard and heeded by a large number of admirers inside and outside academia, did not provide much more than the term *Alterthumswissenschaft* and a general definition of it, whereas Boeckh embarked on an ambitious — and largely successful — expedition to present the newly established composite field in all its ramifications within the context of a workable program. The judgment of Ulrich von Wilamowitz-Moellendorff is harsh, but to the point when he evaluates Wolf's share in building a reputation for the University of Berlin, to which he transferred from Heidelberg one year after its foundation in 1810: "F. A. Wolf contributed the lustre of his name, but no more" (Wilamowitz 1982: 115). Of Boeckh's work, on the other hand, he speaks appreciatively in terms of 'Herkulean labours' (p. 129).

Alterthumswissenschaft as defined by either of the two main proponents was a field much larger than any other existing disciplines. Its challenge to the professional philologist was, not astonishingly, unprecedented. For Gottfried Hermann the proposed enlargement constituted a violation of the classicist's right and obligation to restrict himself to the more immediate tasks of dealing with classical language and literature (cf. Pfeiffer 1976: 181; Sandys 1967 [1903—1908] iii: 95). Other subject matter areas, he asserts, might have to be approached for consultation, but only occasionally, when a particular need arises, and by no means as part of a general procedure. Boeckh and his successors stated and publicly defended their position in favor of philology in its most comprehensive sense. Hermann and his followers did likewise, advocating, however, confinement of the classical scholar to strictly grammatical and text-critical studies.

The ensuing feud, mostly characterized by the clash of personalities, was hardly productive for either side, let alone for classical scholarship as a whole. If one looks, however, on the individual achievements of the participating key contenders, the verdict of Willamowitz captures with precision the most essential feature: "The importance of this battle of the schools is that it marked the close of an incomparably fruitful epoch" (Wilamowitz 1982: 129). The reference is to both the richness and the high quality of the chief representatives of both sides. I shall illustrate this by briefly discussing some essential works of Wolf and Müller on the one hand and Hermann and his star pupil Christian August Lobeck (1781—1860) on the other.

Wolf, entering Göttingen University in 1777 as the first student of philology at that institution (cf. Sandys 1967 [1903—08] iii: 52) laid the foundation for his 'big name' by his *Prolegomena ad Homerum* of 1765 which stimulated a lively discussion among classicists from many European countries, but also arose the interest of German poets like Schiller and Goethe as well as Klopstock and Wieland. Wilhelm von Humboldt and the Schlegel brothers and also Herder participated actively likewise in an extensive exchange of ideas on that subject, mostly in support of Wolf's views (cf. Sandys 1967 [1903—1908] iii: 57). In re-opening the 'Homeric question' Wolf contended that the Greek tradition on Homer was quite unreliable and that the origin of Homer's *Ilias* must be examined in the context of an existing oral tradition upon which Homer had relied. The work has won the distinction of being called "the first methodical and firmly based attempt at a history of an ancient text" (Pfeiffer 1976: 174) with a profound impact on all subsequent discussions of this topic.

Karl Otfried Müller, apart from the two books on art history mentioned above, proved his dedication to a wider concept of philology through earlier publications, among them a history of the Greek states, *Aegineticorum liber* (1817), *Geschichte der hellenischen Stämme und Städte* ('History of the Greek Tribes and *Cities*' [1820—24]), and *Prolegomena zu einer wissenschaftlichen Mythologie* ('Introduction to a Scientific Mythology' [1825]). He motivated the wideness of his range of inquiry by pointing out "that another race of men had already arisen, men who where asking the old world deeper questions than could be answered by any mere *Notengelehrsamkeit*" (Sandys 1967 [1903—1908] iii: 214). On the other side of the spectrum, Gottfried Hermann is almost dogmatic about defining his scientific field as narrowly as possible to safeguard that what for him are the essential components can be dealt with in the most meticulous manner, most significant among them metrical and grammatical studies, with works like *De metris poetarum* ('On the Metrics of the Poets' [1796]) and *De emendanda ratione grammaticae graecae* ('On How to Improve the Logical Approach to Greek Grammar' [1801]), and numerous editions, most importantly of *Orphica* ('*Orphic Hymns*' [1805]), where he unfolded the historical development of the text and its style from the oldest reachable time, including the area of Homer, and of which a contemporary critic "remarked that nothing had appeared in modern times more worthy of the genius of Bentley" (Sandys 1967 [1903–08] iii: 93). Lobeck tried to live up to the great expectations of his academic teacher Hermann, and he fully did. But this also implied that he tried to stay within the parameters set for the field by his master and seek scholarly excellence only there. Lobeck's editions of *Sophoclis Ajax* (1809) is the first in a long line of works every one of which showed him in full command of detailed knowledge of Greek language and literature as well as of a comprehensive methodology for his research procedure. He produced lengthy treatises on various grammatical aspects, such as *Paralipomena Grammaticae Graecae* (1837). Another brilliant piece of research was his two-volume work *Aglaophamus sive de theologiae mysticae Graecorum causis* (1829) which presents and interprets all available facts of the Greek mysteries.

In reviewing the theoretical positions and the practical achievements of these two groups of scholars, two significant questions emerge. Wolf and his group opted for the greatest possible extension of their field. Did they not, in view of the steadily increasing amount of knowledge to be mastered, by their very approach invite what they expressly had attempted to avoid: the splitting up of their field into many areas of specialization? And conversely, did Hermann and his group, in view of the steadily increasing need for supplementation of one field of knowledge by an adjacent field of knowledge, by their very approach not actually invite what they had expressly attempted to avoid: the growing together of neighboring fields into one area where supplementation of knowledge acquired in numerous fields is the pre-condition for the advancement of scholarship? The answer to both questions was at that time certainly not as apparent as it would be today. On the one hand, specialization, division of labor, was in the long run the unavoidable, most logical course of action. On the other hand, interdisciplinary studies, then largely a phenomenon of the future, would develop into a device and procedure which removes from the necessary specialization the imminent danger of isolation.

The major challenges and temptations to which classical philology was exposed to a steadily increasing degree during the first half of the 19th century were not not so much division of labor on the one hand, and interdisciplinary studies, on the other. They were essentially of a different kind. With the appearance of the works of Franz Bopp (1791–1867), Rasmus Rask (1787–1832), and Jacob Grimm (1785–1863) — just to name the major representatives of the emerging new disciplines of historical and comparative linguistics — the traditional study of classical languages lost its formerly held unchallenged position of the only possible study of languages that was worthwhile. The rise of comparative linguistics even brought with it the threat of marginalizing classical studies. Such a trend was by no means tied to the nature of the new approach. It was due almost exclusively to the unwillingness of many classicists to be open-minded and examine carefully how their own field could benefit from the new development. Gottfried Hermann and Christian August Lobeck are prime candidates for the dubious distinction of warding off any thought of accommodating comparative linguistics. This touched off another fruitless controversy among scholars who ought to have seen from early on that they are natural allies whenever potentially fruitful approaches to the study of languages are involved — no matter how different those approaches may appear.

The number of classical scholars who recognized the advantage of combining the merits of traditional philology within the innovations of comparative linguistics was initially rather small, but not for very long. Resistance was in evidence on both sides: Those who stood in the tradition of a well-established, time-honored scientific discipline — classical scholarship — could not easily bring themselves to share the widely-held belief that the newest had to be the best. Georg Curtius (1820–1885) grappled with this problem as late as the second half of the 19th century: 'No serious man of science is likely to give in to the illusion that the newest is always also the best, the most probable, even the absolute truth. The main question is where the truth lies.' ("Dem Wahne, dass das neueste auch immer das beste, wahrscheinlichste, ja das absolut wahre sei, wird sich ein ernster Mann der Wissenschaft doch nicht hingeben wollen. Die Hauptfrage ist die, wo die Wahrheit liegt." [Curtius 1885: 2]). Curtius was the most active and probably also the most prominent in a growing number of classical scholars who remained convinced that classical philology as the oldest and most developed of language science would and should retain its 'preferential position' (Curtius 1886, I: 127) if, and only if, it fully utilized its emerging supplementary relationship with historical and comparative linguistics. He regarded as the 'scholarly task of [his] life' to support 'the lively interplay' between the two branches of language studies (p. 149).

While praising Wolf as the originator of a classical philology which incorporates all aspects of scholarly investigations that could be expected to contribute to the overall objective, Curtius was also distinctly aware of the direction into which the development was headed: 'There is no single scholar any more who would be in the position to span all of these fields even in an approximate fashion. [...] A division of the indeterminable material has become unavoidable.' ("Es gibt keinen einzigen Gelehrten mehr, der alle diese Gebiete des Wissens auch nur einigermassen zu umspannen vermöchte. [...] Eine Theilung des unübersehlichen Stoffes ist unabweislich geworden" [p. 127]).

Hence, the greatness of the success of classical studies must not be looked for only in how those studies in the narrowest sense have produced remarkable results. Part of the success, maybe even its largest portions, would have to be identified in all those branches of science which where either created or intensely affected by the study of ancient Greece and Rome. Essential elements of classical studies found their way into all major branches of the learned world. In history, for instance, Barthold Georg Niebuhr (1776—1831), with his monumental three-volume work on *Römische Geschichte* (2nd edition, 1827—32) the founder of the critical-historical method, became an important trend setter in that he, contrary to previous methods, did not take for granted the facts as reported in the source material, but strove to get to objective facts by analyzing comparatively as many sources as were available. He combined, in successive stages, the life of a financial officer in various organizations with that of a university teacher and researcher first at the University of Berlin, which made him its first doctor shortly after its foundation in 1810, and then at the University of Bonn where he lectured, as he had in Berlin, on ancient history. He had a great successor in Theodor Mommsen who, after a three-year travel period in Italy and France and teaching positions in Leipzig, Zürich, and Breslau, settled for good in Berlin in 1858 as professor of Ancient History. Mommsen's major focus was the political system of Rome in which he amply published, beginning in 1843 with *De collegiis et sodaliciis Romanorum* ('On Communities and Sodalities of the Romans'). But his greatest achievement appeared to have been that he produced inspiring research work in a number of new branches of classical studies, e. g., in chronological research with *Römische Chronologie bis auf Cäsar* ('Roman Chronology to the Time of Cesar', 1858), and in numismatics with the *Geschichte des römischen Münzwesens* ('History of the Roman Monetary System', 1860). With his *Römisches Staatsrecht* ('Roman Public Law', 1893) he initiated an entirely new branch of science. The closeness of his major field with classical philology and their continued interdependence becomes apparent from Mommsen's large quantity of text editions of Latin writers from a great variety of fields, such as *Fragmenta juris antejustianium quae dicuntur Vaticana* ('Vatican Law Fragments Called anti-Justinian' [1861]), three books of Livius (1868), and the writings of Jordanes, *De origine actibusque Getarum* ('On the Origin and Activities of the Gothic People' [1862]).

As Mommsen illustrated by his research the interdependency of historical science and classical studies, so did Karl Lachmann with regard to his research work in Latin and in Germanistics. As a student he was exposed in Leipzig to the strong influence of Gottfried Hermann, but soon developed his own identity with almost exclusive concentration on Latin at the expense of Greek and a strong emphasis on rigorous textual criticism aiming at the reconstruction of authentic texts from the most reliable source material. After teaching at the University of Königsberg for seven years Lachmann came to Berlin in 1825 and two years later was appointed full professor of German and Classical Philology. The long list of critical Latin text editions began in 1816 with *Propertius*. One year before he died he published an edition of *Lucretius* (1850). Together with Jacob Grimm he founded Old German Philology. His many Middle High German text editions showed the same precision in applying text-critical criteria as were characteristic for his Latin editions. Inspired by Wolf's work on Homer, Lachmann tried to expand Wolf's findings and also to apply them to the German *Nibelungenlied*, which resulted in his *Betrachtungen über Homers Ilias* ('Thoughts on Homer's Ilias' [1847]) and several publications on the *Nibelungenlied*, including a text-critical edition of the Middle High German manuscript (1826). He even ventured into the field of modern literature with a critical edition of Lessing's works (1836–40).

It is strange, but not unusual, that classical scholarship like numerous other academic disciplines received unprecedented advancement by someone with much greater enthusiasm than formal academic training. Wilhelm von Humboldt (1767–1835), after a fleeting visit of one semester to the provincial University of Frankfurt/Oder, spent three semesters at the much larger and more sophisticated University of Göttingen, where he was supposed to devote his time to the study of law and economics. Instead, most of his endeavors were directed towards the study of classical philology and of philosophy. He was well prepared in Latin, as he had received extensive instruction by private tutors at his home, and during his brief stay in Frankfurt he was able to continue to expand significantly his knowledge of Greek with the help of a family friend, Prof. J. F. C. Löffler. Christian Gottlob Heyne (1729–1812), one of the most influential classical scholars of his time, became the greatest attraction for Humboldt during his stay in Göttingen. Later on Humboldt established close relationships with both Friedrich August Wolf and Gottfried Hermann. They and other influential classical scholars did not create, but solidly reinforced his belief that only through the thorough study of classical antiquity "could his inner objective of attaining perfect human intellectual refinement be obtained with such great immediacy" ('[sein Glaube ...] auf keinem anderen Wege so unmittelbar sein inneres Ziel vollendeter menschlicher Bildung erreichen zu können', Dove 1881: 79). Humboldt as a statesman, diplomat, and as a private citizen, being in touch with many of the most prominent intellectuals of his time, used his personal influence to propagate the study of classical antiquity. During his brief tenure as Prussian Minister of Education he exerted a profound influence on the shaping of secondary and university education, making sure that the study of Latin and Greek would become the center piece of a particular branch of high school, called *Humanistisches Gymnasium*. While he rated language instruction as highly essential, he insisted that particular emphasis be placed on cultural content rather than on grammatical knowledge as an end in itself. He also was most instrumental in establishing the University of Berlin in 1810 which became a model for all of Germany and was hailed as a great achievement by university authorities in numerous other European countries. It was due to Humboldt's personal initiative that many outstanding scholars were invited to join the faculty. The majority of them were either directly or indirectly involved in classical studies.

Humboldt's example shows to what extent the life of an intellectual who is not a professional classical scholar could be determined by extensive exposure to classical studies early in life, even prior to the beginning of university studies.

7. Conclusion

Classical Philology during the second half and particularly at the end of the 19th century is in a healthy state. There is no university in Germany without a vigorous program in classical studies, thanks to the excellent record of research work done by the *Altphilologen*, i. e., the scholars of Greek and Latin, as well as by researchers in the related fields, such as history, archeology, philosophy, esthetics, and many others. But classical studies are flourishing also because wide sections of the general public – as a result of a planned information campaign as well as the spontaneous emergence of trends favoring interest in the ancient world – are now sold to the idea that classical antiquity and its many values are ancestral to the modern Western world, and they matter as much to the individual life as the oldest ancestors matter in the life of a family.

One might, in conclusion, add another thought. In Europe outside Greece and Rome an abundance of artifacts has been unearthed that show us our past history in most magnificent terms. But no matter how far we may be able to reach back in time, our indigenous civilization is young, and most of its greatness has grown on seeds laid in Greek and Roman antiquity. When Heinrich Schliemann (1822−1890) in the 1870s and 1880s discovered the treasures of Troy and of other locations of ancient Greece, this extraordinary feat together with similar discoveries had an almost electrifying effect on both the scientific community and the public at large. What so far had been relegated to a realm of phantasy, of myth and fairy tales, was all of a sudden transformed into a world of concrete reality: Troy did exist after all! This revelation left the citizens of those days, most of them at least, with a desire to claim their share in these remarkable events, because they felt that this, too, was part of their ancestral heritage. Classical studies at that moment in time seemed to have stumbled upon the fountain of eternal youth.

8. Bibliography

Angermann, Constantin. 1886. "Georg Curtius". *Beiträge zur Kunde der indogermanischen Sprachen* 10.325−340.

Becker, Carl Heinrich. 1925. *Vom Wesen der deutschen Universität.* Leipzig: Quelle & Meyer.

−. 1931. *Das Erbe der Antike im Orient und Okzident.* Leipzig: Quelle & Meyer.

Benfey, Theodor. 1869. *Geschichte der Sprachwissenschaft und orientalischen Philologie in Deutschland seit dem Anfange des 19. Jahrhunderts mit einem Rückblick auf die früheren Zeiten.* München: Cotta.

Bentley, Richard. 1962 [1691]. *Epistola ad Joannem Millium.* (Repr. from the edition of Alexander Dyce, together with an introduction by George P. Goold.) Toronto: Univ. of Toronto Press.

−. 1699 [1697]. *A Dissertation upon the Epistles of Phalaris.* London: Hartley.

Bernays, Jacob. 1855. *Joseph Justus Scaliger.* Berlin: Hertz. (Repr., Osnabrück: Zeller, 1965.)

Bernhardy, Gottfried. 1832. *Grundlinien zur Encyklopädie der Philologie.* Halle: Anton.

Boeckh, August. ²1886 [1877]. *Enzyklopädie und Methodenlehre der philologischen Wissenschaften.* Ed. by Ernst Bratuschek. Leipzig: Teubner. (Repr., Stuttgart: Teubner, 1966.)

−. 1883. *Briefwechsel zwischen August Boeckh und Karl Otfried Müller.* Leipzig: Teubner.

Briggs, Ward W. & William Musgrave Calder III, eds. 1990. *Classical Scholarship: A biographical encyclopedia.* New York & London: Garland.

Brod, Max. 1965. *Johannes Reuchlin und sein Kampf: Eine historische Monographie.* Stuttgart: Kohlhammer.

Brugmann, Karl. 1885. *Zum heutigen Stand der Sprachwissenschaft.* Strassburg: Trübner. (See notably "Sprachwissenschaft und Philologie", 1−41.)

−. 1910. *Der Gymnasialunterricht in den beiden klassischen Sprachen und die Sprachwissenschaft.* Strassburg: Trübner.

− et. al. 1885. *Griechische und lateinische Sprachwissenschaft.* (Handbuch der klassischen Altertumswissenschaft, vol. II.) Nördlingen: Beck.

Bursian, Konrad. 1880a. "Johann Gottfried Hermann". *Allgemeine Deutsche Biographie* XII. 174−180. Berlin: Duncker & Humblot.

−. 1880b. "Christian Gottlob Heyne". *Ibid.*, 375−378.

−. 1883. *Geschichte der classischen Philologie in Deutschland von den Anfängen bis zur Gegenwart.* 2 vols. Leipzig & München: Oldenbourg.

Calder, William Musgrave III & Daniel J. Kramer. 1992 [1984]. *An Introductory Bibliography to the History of Classical Scholarship Chiefly in the XIXth and XXth Centuries.* [Napoli: Jovene Editore, 1984.] Hildesheim: Olms.

Clarke, Martin Lowther. 1959. *Classical Education in Britain, 1500−1900.* Cambridge: Cambridge Univ. Press.

−. 1986. *Greek Studies in England 1700−1830.* Amsterdam: Hakkert.

Clemm, Wilhelm. 1872. *Ueber Aufgabe und Stellung der classischen Philologie insbesondere ihr Verhältnis zur vergleichenden Sprachwissenschaft.* Giessen: Ricker.

Conrad, Johannes. 1884. *Das Universitätsstudium in Deutschland während der letzten 50 Jahre: Statistische Untersuchungen unter besonderer Berücksichtigung Preussens.* Jena: Fischer. (Transl. by John Hutchinson as *The German Universities for the Last Fifty Years*, Glasgow: Bryce & Son, 1885.)

Creuzer, Friedrich. 1854. *Zur Geschichte der classischen Philologie seit Wiederherstellung der Literatur, in biographischen Skizzen ihrer älteren Häupter und einer literarischen Übersicht ihrer neueren.* Frankfurt/M.: Baer.

Curtius, Georg. 1858−62. *Grundzüge der griechischen Etymologie.* 2 vols. Leipzig: Teubner. (5th ed., 1879.)

−. 1862. *Philologie und Sprachwissenschaft.* Leipzig: Teubner.

−. 1885. *Zur Kritik der neuesten Sprachforschung.* Leipzig: Hirzel.

−. 1886. *Kleine Schriften.* Ed. Ernst Windisch. Vol. I. *Ausgewählte Reden und Vorträge.* Vol. II: *Ausgewählte Abhandlungen wissenschaftlichen Inhalts.* Leipzig: Hirzel. (Repr., Hildesheim: Gerstenberg, 1972.)

Delbrück, Berthold. 1875. *Das Sprachstudium auf den deutschen Universitäten: Praktische Ratschläge für Studierende der Philologie.* Jena: Dufft.

Dobel, Richard, ed. 1991. *Lexikon der Goethe Zitate*. Augsburg: Weltbild Verlag.

Dove, Alfred. 1881. "Wilhelm von Humboldt". *Allgemeine Deutsche Biographie* XIII. 338–358. Berlin: Duncker & Humblot. (Repr. in *Portraits of Linguists*, ed. by Thomas A. Sebeok Vol. I, 71–101. Bloomington & London: Indiana Univ. Press.)

Eckstein, Friedrich August. 1871. *Nomenclator Philologorum*. Leipzig: Teubner. (Repr., Hildesheim: Olms, 1966.)

Flashar, Hellmut et al., eds. 1979. *Philologie und Hermeneutik im 19. Jahrhundert: Zur Geschichte und Methodologie der Geisteswissenschaften*. Göttingen: Vandenhoeck & Ruprecht.

Foerster, Richard. 1889a. *Die klassische Philologie der Gegenwart: Rede zum Antritt des Rektorates der Königlichen Christian-Albrecht-Universität zu Kiel am 5. März 1886 gehalten*. Kiel: Toeche.

–. 1889b. "Johann Jacob Reiske". *Allgemeine Deutsche Biographie* XXVIII. 129–140. Leipzig: Duncker & Humblot.

–, ed. 1897. *Johann Jacob Reiske's Briefe*. Leipzig: Hirzel.

–. 1911. *Das Erbe der Antike*. Breslau: Koebner.

Fraenkel, Eduard. 1926. *Die Stelle des Römertums in der humanistischen Bildung*. Leipzig: Quelle & Meyer.

–. 1964a. "Ulrich von Wilamowitz-Moellendorff". *Kleine Beiträge zur klassischen Philologie*. Vol. II, 555–562. Roma: Edizioni di storia e letteratura.

–. 1964b. "The Latin Studies of Hermann and Wilamowitz-Moellendorff". *Ibid.*, 563–576.

Freund, Michael. 1985. *Deutsche Geschichte: Von den Anfängen bis zur Gegenwart*. Bielefeld: Bertelsmann.

Fuhrmann, Manfred. 1982. *Brechungen: Wirkungsgeschichtliche Studien zur antik-europäischen Bildungstradition*. Stuttgart: Klett-Cotta.

Gaiser, Konrad. 1970. *Das Altertum und jedes neue Gute: Für Wolfgang Schadewaldt zum 15. März 1970*. Stuttgart: Kohlhammer.

Gercke, Alfred et al., eds. 1910. *Einleitung in die Altertumswissenschaft*. Vol. I: *Methodik – Sprache – Metrik – Griechische und römische Literatur*. Leipzig: Teubner.

Goethe, Johann Wolfgang von. 1969 [1805]. *Winckelmann und sein Jahrhundert in Briefen und Aufsätzen*. Leipzig: Seemann.

Grafton, Anthony. 1983. "Polyhistor into *Philolog*: Notes on the Transformation of German Classical Scholarship 1780–1850". *History of Universities* III. 159–192. Avebury, England: Avebury.

Gudeman, Alfred. [3]1897. *Outlines of the History of Classical Philology*. Boston: Ginn & Co. (First published in 1892 under the title *Syllabus on the History of Classical Philology.*)

–. [2]1909 [1907]. *Grundriss der Geschichte der klassischen Philologie*. Stuttgart: Teubner.

Haym, Rudolf. 1856. *Wilhelm von Humboldt: Lebensbild und Charakteristik*. Berlin: Gaertner. (Repr., Osnabrück: Zeller, 1965.)

Hentschke, Ada B. & Ulrich Muhlack. 1972. *Einführung in die Geschichte der klassischen Philologie*. Darmstadt: Wissenschaftliche Buchgemeinschaft.

Herbst, Wilhelm. 1872–76. *Johann Heinrich Voss*. 2 vols. Leipzig: Teubner. (Repr., Bern: Lang, 1970.)

Herder, Johann Gottfried. 1784–87. *Ideen zur Philosophie der Geschichte der Menschheit*: Berlin: Deutsche Bibliothek.

Hertz, Martin Julius. 1878. Review of Boeckh (1877). *Jenaer Literaturzeitung* 22. 334–337.

Hölscher, Uvo. 1965. *Die Chance des Unbehagens: Drei Essais zur Situation der klassischen Studien*. Göttingen: Vandenhoeck & Ruprecht.

Howald, Ernst. 1920. *Friedrich Nietzsche und die klassische Philologie*. Gotha: Perthes.

Hübner, Emil. 1876. *Grundriss zu Vorlesungen über die Geschichte und Encyklopädie der classischen Philologie*. Berlin: Weidmann.

–. [2]1889 [1876]. *Bibliographie der klassischen Alterthumswissenschaft: Grundriss zu Vorlesungen über die Geschichte und Encyklopädie der klassischen Philologie*. Berlin: Hertz.

Humboldt, Wilhelm von. 1961 [1793]. "Über das Studium des Alterthums und des griechischen insbesondere". *Werke* ed. by Andreas Flitner & Klaus Giel, vol. II. Darmstadt: Cotta, 1–24.

–. [1805] 1961. "Latium und Hellas oder Betrachtungen über das classische Alterthum". *Werke* ed. by Andreas Flitner & Klaus Giel, vol. II. Darmstadt: Cotta, 25–64.

–. 1836. *Über die Verschiedenheit des menschlichen Sprachbaus und ihren Einfluss auf die geistige Entwicklung des Menschengeschlechts*. *Werke* ed. by Andreas Flitner & Klaus Giel, vol. III, 368–756. Darmstadt: Cotta.

–. 1990. *Briefe an Friedrich August Wolf*. Ed. by Philip Mattson. Berlin & New York: De Gruyter.

Immisch, Otto. 1919. *Das Nachleben der Antike*. Leipzig: Dieterich.

Jäger, Gerhard. 1975. *Einführung in die Klassische Philologie*. München: Beck.

Jäger, Werner. 1960 [1914]. "Philologie und Historie". *Humanistische Reden und Vorträge*, 1–16. Berlin: de Gruyter.

–, ed. 1931. *Das Problem des Klassischen und die Antike: Acht Vorträge gehalten auf der Fachtagung der klassischen Altertumswissenschaft zu Naumburg 1930*. Leipzig: Teubner. (Repr., Darmstadt: Wissenschaftliche Buchgesellschaft, 1961.)

Jahn, Otto. 1868. "Bedeutung und Stellung der Alterthumsstudien in Deutschland". *Aus der Alterthumswissenschaft: Populäre Aufsätze*, 3–50. Bonn: Marcus.

Jankowsky, Kurt R. 1986. "Classical Philology, Comparative Studies, and the Emergence of Linguistic Science: The Case of Georg Curtius (1820–1885)". *The Twelfh LACUS Forum 1985* ed. by Mary C. Marino & Luis A. Pérez, 158–169. Lake Bluff, Ill.: LACUS.

Jens, Walter. 1973. "The Classical Tradition in Germany – Grandeur and Decay". *Upheaval and Continuity: A century of German history* ed. by E. J. Feuchtwanger, 67–82. London: Wolff.

Kaufmann, Georg. 1888, 1896. *Die Geschichte der deutschen Universitäten.* 2 vols. Stuttgart: Cotta.

Kent, Roland G. 1935. "Linguistic Science and the Orientalist". *Journal of the American Oriental Society* 55. 115–137.

Koechly, Hermann. 1874. *Gottfried Hermann: Zu seinem hunderjährigen Geburtstage.* Heidelberg: Winter.

Köpke, Ernst Rudolf. 1860. *Die Gründung der Königlichen Friedrich-Wilhelms-Universität zu Berlin.* Berlin: Schade.

Körner, Josef, ed. 1928. "Friedrich Schlegels 'Philosophie der Philologie' mit einer Einleitung herausgegeben". *Logos* 17. 1–72.

Kroll, Wilhelm. 1908. *Geschichte der klassischen Philologie.* Leipzig: Göschen. (2nd ed., Berlin: de Gruyter, 1919.)

Kusch, Horst, ed. 1953. *Festschrift Franz Dornseiff zum 65. Geburtstag.* Leipzig: VEB Bibliographisches Institut.

Lachmann, Karl. 1876. *Kleinere Schriften.* Vol. I: *Kleinere Schriften zur deutschen Philologie.* Ed. by Karl Müllenhoff. Vol. II: *Kleinere Schriften zur classischen Philologie.* Ed. by Johannes Vahlen. Berlin: Reimer. (Repr., Berlin: de Gruyter, 1974.)

Lange, Ludwig. 1855. *Die klassische Philologie in ihrer Stellung zum Gesamtgebiete der Wissenschaften und in ihrer innern Gliederung.* Prag: Tempsky.

Leitzmann, Albert, ed. 1929. *Wilhelm von Humboldts Briefe an Gottfried Hermann.* Weimar: Böhlau.

Lepsius, Richard. 1836. *Zwei sprachvergleichende Abhandlungen.* Berlin: Dümmler.

Lessing, Gotthold Ephraim. 1766. *Laokoon oder über die Grenzen der Malerei und Poesie.* Berlin: Voss.

Lexis, Wilhelm, ed. 1893. *Die deutschen Universitäten: Für die Universitätsausstellung in Chicago 1893.* 2 vols. Berlin: Asher & Co.

Linwood, William. 1845. *Remarks on the Present State of Classical Scholarship and Distinctions in the University of Oxford.* Oxford: Parker.

Lloyd-Jones, Hugh. 1982. *Blood for the Ghosts: Classical influences in the 19th and 20th centuries.* London: Duckworth.

–. 1982. *Classical Survivals: The classics in the modern world.* London: Duckworth.

Malden, Henry, 1831. *On the Study of the Greek and Latin Languages: An introductory lecture, delivered in the University of London, November 1, 1831.* London: Taylor.

Meister, Richard. 1947. *Geschichte der Akademie der Wissenschaften in Wien 1847–1947.* Wien: Holzhausen.

Mette, Benedikt. 1873. *Die vergleichende Sprachforschung in ihrer Bedeutung für die klassische Philologie.* Brilon: Friedländer.

Mommsen, Theodor. 1854–56. *Römische Geschichte.* 3 vols. Berlin: Weidmann. (Vol. V, 1885.)

–. 1871. "Bruchstücke des Johannes von Antiochia und des Johannes Malalas". *Hermes* 6. 323–383.

Müller, Iwan von et al., eds. 1886–1920. *Handbuch der klassischen Altertums-Wissenschaft in systematischer Darstellung, mit besonderer Rücksicht auf Geschichte und Methodik der einzelnen Disziplinen.* 9 vols. München: Beck.

Neckel, Gustav. 1925. "Germanische und klassische Philologie". *Neue Jahrbücher für Wissenschaft und Jugendbildung* 1: 46–53.

Nietzsche, Friedrich Wilhelm. 1909 [1872]. "Über die Zukunft unserer Bildungsanstalten". *Nietzsches Werke in zwei Bänden* ed. by Gerhard Stenzel, vol. II, 1047–1074. Salzburg: Das Bergland-Buch.

Oechsli, Wilhelm. 1915. *Briefwechsel Johann Kaspar Bluntschlis mit Savigny, Niebuhr, Leopold Ranke, Jakob Grimm und Ferdinand Meyer.* Frauenfeld: Huber & Co.

Oppert, Gustav. 1879. *On the Classification of Languages: A contribution to comparative philology.* Madras: Higginbotham & Co.; London: Trübner & Co.

Patzer, Harald. 1953. "Wilamowitz und die klassische Philologie". Kusch 1953. 244–257.

Paulsen, Friedrich. ³1919–21 [1896–97]. *Geschichte des gelehrten Unterrichts auf den deutschen Schulen und Universitäten vom Ausgang des Mittelalters bis zur Gegenwart. Mit besonderer Rücksicht auf den klassischen Unterricht.* 2 vols. Berlin & Leipzig: de Gruyter.

–. 1906. *The German Universities and University Studies.* Transl. by Frank Thilly & William W. Elwang New York: Charles Scribner's Sons.

Pauly, August Friedrich von (1796–1845). 1837–. *Paulys Realencyklopädie der classischen Altertumswissenschaft.* Ed. by Georg Wissowa (1859–1931) et al. [1893–1909.] 9 vols. München: Druckenmüller.

Pfeiffer, Rudolf. 1960. *Ausgewählte Schriften: Aufsätze und Vorträge zur griechischen Dichtung und zum Humanismus.* Ed. by Winfried Bühler. München: Beck.

–. 1976. *History of Classical Scholarship from 1300 to 1850.* Oxford: Clarendon.

Ranke, Friedrich. 1971. *Kleinere Schriften.* Ed. by Heinz Rupp & Eduard Studer. Bern & München: Francke.

Ranke, Karl Ferdinand. 1870. *Karl Otfried Müller: Ein Lebensbild.* Berlin: Hayns's Erben.

Ranke, Leopold, ed. 1832–36. *Historisch-politische Zeitschrift.* Hamburg: Friedrich Perthes; Berlin: Duncker & Humblot.

Robinson, George W. 1927. *Autobiography of Joseph Scaliger.* Cambridge, Mass.: Harvard Univ. Press.

Sandys, Sir John Edwin. 1967 [1903–08]. *A History of Classical Scholarship.* Vol. II: *From the Revival of Learning to the End of the 18th Century (in Italy, France, England, and the Netherlands).* Vol. III: *The 18th Century in Germany, and the 19th Century in Europe and the United States of America.* New York & London: Hafner.

Schliemann, Heinrich. 1875. *Troy and its Remains: A narrative of researches and discoveries made on the site of Ilium, and in the Trojan plain.* Ed. by Philip Smith. London: Murray. (Repr., New York: Arno Press, 1976.)

–. 1936 [1892]. *Selbstbiographie bis zu seinem Tode vervollständigt.* Ed. by Sophie Schliemann. Leipzig: Brockhaus.

Schonack, Wilhelm. 1914. *Ein Jahrhundert Berliner philologischer Dissertationen (1810–1910).* Hildesheim: Gerstenberg.

Schröder, Johann Friedrich. 1864. *Das Wiederaufblühen der klassischen Studien in Deutschland im 15. und zu Anfang des 16. Jahrhunderts und welche Männer es befördert haben.* Halle: Schwetschke.

Sellheim, Rudolf, ed. 1956. *Friedrich August Wolf: Ein Leben in Briefen.* Halle/S.: Niemeyer.

Steinmetz, Max, ed. 1965. *Bedeutende Gelehrte in Leipzig.* Leipzig: Karl-Marx-Universität.

Steinthal, Heymann. [4]1888 [1851]. "Wilhelm von Humboldt". *Ursprung der Sprache im Zusammenhang mit den letzten Fragen alles Wissens*, 58–81. Berlin: Dümmler. (Repr. in *Portraits of Linguists*, vol. I, 102–120, ed. by Thomas A. Sebeok. Bloomington & London: Indiana Univ. Press.)

Sweet, Paul R. 1978–80. *Wilhelm von Humboldt: A biography.* Vol. I: *1767–1808.* Volume II: *1808–1835.* Columbus: Ohio State Univ. Press.

Urlichs, Carl Ludwig von. 1892 [1886]. "Grundlegung und Geschichte der klassischen Altertumswissenschaft". Müller 1886–1920. Vol. I: 1–145.

Usener, Hermann. 1882. *Philologie und Geschichtswissenschaft.* Bonn: Cohen.

–, ed. 1885. *Gesammelte Abhandlungen von Jacob Bernays.* Berlin: Hertz.

Vahlen, Johannes, ed. 1892. *Karl Lachmanns Briefe an Moriz Haupt.* Berlin: Reimer.

Voigt, Georg. [3]1893 [1859]. *Die Wiederbelebung des classischen Altertums oder das erste Jahrhundert des Humanismus.* 2 vols. Berlin: Reimer. (4th ed., 1960.)

Wegner, Max. 1951. *Altertumskunde.* Freiburg & München: Alber.

Wilamowitz-Moellendorff, Ulrich von. 1893. "Klassische Philologie". *Die Deutschen Universitäten: Für die Universitätsausstellung in Chicago 1893* ed. by Wilhelm Lexis, vol. I, 457–475. Berlin: Asher & Co.

–. 1921. *Geschichte der Philologie.* Leipzig: Teubner.

–. 1967. *Reden und Vorträge.* Vol. I. Dublin & Zürich: Weidmann.

–. 1982 [1921]. *History of Classical Scholarship.* Transl. from the German by Alan Harris. Ed. by Hugh Lloyd-Jones. Baltimore, Md.: Johns Hopkins Univ. Press.

Winckelmann, Johann Joachim. 1764–67. *Geschichte der Kunst des Altertums.* Dresden: Walther. (Transl. by G. Henry Lodge as *The History of Ancient Art*, 4 vols., Boston: Osgood, 1872–73.)

–. 1987 [1755]. *Reflections on the Imitation of Greek Works in Painting and Sculpture.* La Salle, Ill.: Open Court. [Translation of *Gedanken über die Nachahmung der griechischen Werke in der Malerei und Bildhauerkunst.*]

Windisch, Ernst. 1886. "Georg Curtius". *Biographisches Jahrbuch für Altertumskunde* 9. 75–128. (Repr. in *Portraits of Linguists* ed. by Thomas A. Sebeok, vol. I, 311–373. Bloomington & London: Indiana Univ. Press, 1966.)

Wolf, Friedrich August. 1784. *Prolegomena ad Homerum, sive, De operum Homericorum prisca et genuina forma variisque mutationibus et probabili ratione emendandi.* Halle: Orphanotrophei. [Transl. as *Prolegomena to Homer* by Anthony Grafton et al. Princeton: Princeton Univ. Press, 1985.]

–. 1831–35. *Vorlesungen über die Alterthumswissenschaft.* 6 vols. Ed. by J. D. Gürtler & S. F. W. Hoffmann. Leipzig: Lehnhold.

– & Philipp Buttmann, eds. 1807–10. *Museum der Alterthums-Wissenschaft.* Vol. I: *Darstellung der Alterthums-Wissenschaft nach Begriff, Umfang, Zweck und Wert.* Berlin: Realschulbuchhandlung.

Wolff, Christian. 1860. *Briefe von Christian Wolff aus den Jahren 1719–1753. Ein Beitrag zur Geschichte der Kaiserlichen Academie der Wissenschaften zu St. Petersburg.* St. Petersburg: Kaiserliche Academie der Wissenschaften.

Kurt R. Jankowsky, Washington, D.C.
(U.S.A.)

154. The establishment of Oriental language studies in France, Britain, and Germany

1. Introduction
2. The beginning of the study of Oriental languages
3. Towards Oriental language studies as an independent academic discipline
4. Conclusion
5. Bibliography

1. Introduction

Oriental languages were sporadically studied as early as in the 12th century when the increased contacts between the Christian world and the Islamic-Arabic Orient created the necessity for an intensified preoccupation with those 'exotic' languages spoken there. The crusades, in spite of the extended hostile encounter between Oriental and Occidental cultures, also laid the foundation for widespread cultural exchanges and opened up avenues for lively commercial relations. One of the consequences in the subsequent time was the emergence of a large number of translations, both from Oriental languages and into Oriental languages. Initially, the motivation for this growing interest was the desire to fulfill the requirements which arose from an expansion and enhancement of the Christian missionary work. Looking upon Oriental languages as valuable objects of study in themselves took several more centuries to be brought about. Humanistic studies in the 16th century provided a substantial impetus towards that aim. Help also came from the steadily increasing commercial activities between the countries of the Western world and Oriental countries. Gradually study centers for learning Oriental languages and the training of teachers were instituted in various parts of Europe.

The study of language in ancient Greek and Rome has been in many respects a model for linguistic investigations during most of the centuries following the decline and eventual eclipse of the Roman Empire towards the middle of the first millennium. A. D. While there was much to be learned, and to be preserved, from the implementation of this model, as illustrated both by the ancient masters themselves and by their successors during the immediately following centuries, the model also endowed its implementers with what was initially embraced as a feature of excellence, but later on turned out to be a serious impediment. The Greeks focused on the study of their mother tongue, leaving hardly any room for interest in languages other than their own, which anyhow would have been mostly 'barbaric' languages, i. e., languages of people in conquered territories or in regions about which no reliable information was readily available. But the same attitude of utter disinterest in a foreign language was also applied by the Greeks towards the Latin language, and conversely by the Romans towards the Greek language. The Romans as well as the Greeks were bent on seeing their mother tongue unconditionally accepted by the subjugated people whose languages 'succumbed to the dominance of the Roman and Greek cultures and in some cases vanished entirely, in other cases came close to vanishing' (Benfey 1869: 171. — Translations from the German here and elsewhere are mine: KRJ).

The advancement of Christianity brought about substantial attitudinal changes, even though the status of these two classical languages as unrivaled in terms of excellence in form and substance was not only retained, but even significantly magnified. Hebrew joined the other two to form that long-lasting and all-powerful triad of the 'three holy languages' which did not let any other language grow to attain an even remotely comparable rank, since those three languages alone were deemed worthy to be carriers of the original Christian Scriptures.

But the Christian missionaries had to develop before long a much greater and more genuine interest in vernacular languages; the gospel, after all, was meant to reach all speakers of every language, regardless of their place in life and their station in society. Translations into vernacular languages and, later on, the composition of poetry and prose writings in vernacular languages, became an indispensable part of the missionaries' work. Wulfila's Gothic Bible in the 4th century A. D. and the Old Saxon epic poem Heliand of the 9th century are two prominent and very telling examples. The interest in the languages themselves at the initial stage was negligible, if it existed at all. Transmitting the message came first and last. But over time, inevitably the notion gained ground that the message was transmitted best if the language to be used was thoroughly understood and, therefore, could most effectively be employed. This lesson was learned and acted upon long before Martin Luther, but Luther's Bible translation is still one of the most impressive illustrations for the need of the Christian missionary to place the greatest possible emphasis on the cultivation of the vernacular language.

2. The beginning of the study of Oriental languages

While the study of classical languages all through the Middle Ages continued to emphasize, in spite of significant new initiatives, the investigation of the two languages in the tradition of classical antiquity, language study took on another dimension where predominantly missionary objectives were involved. The supreme interest in Hebrew as the language of the oldest Scriptures of Christianity necessitated paying nearly equal attention to other languages that assumedly played as important a role in the history of the Christian Church such as, e. g., Aramaic, a language vastly differnt from any familiar tongue spoken in Europe. Because of being closely affiliated with Christianity, such languages could by no means be perceived as 'barbaric', as they would have from a non-Christian Greek or Roman point of view. Although formal studies, i. e., research especially in grammar and lexicography, did not begin before the 10th century even in the case of Hebrew, the continued preoccupation with a number of biblical languages for many centuries laid the solid foundation for the eventual evolvement of scientific Oriental studies as they emerged towards the end of the 18th and the beginning of the 19th century. The numerous impediments to this development — which decreased over the centuries but never cased to exist — have to be viewed in the context of the beliefs and objectives which governed the work of the Christian missionaries. The most prominent of those beliefs was the notion that all languages had their origin in Hebrew. The first source for this belief is a pronouncement by the early Church theologian Origen (= Origenes Adamantios, c. 185–c. 253 A. D.), repeated by Hieronymus (Sophronius Eusebius, 331/340–420 A. D.) in a letter to Pope Damasus (cf. Benfey 1869: 179). Only Leibniz in the early 18th century took a firm stand against that dogmatic teaching, thus removing a major obstacle for conducting unrestricted research into the history and origin of languages.

The term 'Oriental Language Studies' means different things at different times, but even as early as 1874 it includes a large number of languages and concerns itself with matters other than languages as objects of study. In describing some aspects of the *Second International Congress of Orientalists*, held in London from 14th to 20th September, 1874, Robert Needham Cust (1821–1909) states that "from the domain of an Oriental Congress Europe and America are excluded, and the whole of Asia and North Africa as far as the Pillars of Hercules, are included. But it will be hard to exclude the Eastern, Southern, and Western shores of Africa from future Congresses" (Cust 1880: 413). From the sections he lists (ibid.) — 1) Arian; 2) Semitic; 3) Non-Arian; 4) Hamitic; 5) Archæological, and 6) Ethnological — it also becomes apparent that the Orientalists assembled in 1874 dealt with other disciplines as well, although these were obviously language-related. Oriental studies from the very start tended to be interdisciplinary. A comparison with Friedrich August Wolf's (1759–1824) re-definition of Classical philology as "the science of the entire intellectual life of the ancient cultured nations" (condensed from Wolf 1807: 30) comes to mind. The term 'Oriental philology' is in use since the beginning of the 19th century (cf. Boeckh 1886: 6), undoubtedly parallel to the range of meaning applied to 'Classical philology'.

The statutes of the *Royal Asiatic Society of Great Britain and Ireland*, founded in 1823, include the pronouncement, in the words of one of its founders, Horace Hayman Wilson (1786–1860), that "Our Society should concentrate information of whatever is produced, or illustrated, in respect of Asia, by the learning and industry of our countrymen, or residents in a foreign land" (Cust 1901: 3).

The German Orientalists had their first national meeting in October 1844 in Dresden, with the purpose of establishing a society, named *Deutsche Gesellschaft für die Kunde des Morgenlandes* or,

'somewhat shorter and handier' (*Jahresbericht 1846*: 131): 'Morgenländische Gesellschaft für Deutschland. [...] The general purpose of this society is: to further in all respects the knowledge of Asia and the countries that are closely related with it and to it and spread the interest in it to wider circles. Accordingly, the society will not only concern itself with the early Oriental history, but also with its modern history and with the current state of those countries.'

Two years later the *Zeitschrift der Deutschen Morgenländischen Gesellschaft* was founded and started publishing out of Leipzig. (It still exists today.)

France was by no means a latecomer in these endeavors. The *Société Asiatique* was established in Paris in 1821, and its first president for several years was Antoine Isaac Silvestre de Sacy (1758—1838), a scholar who has greatly influenced the course of Oriental studies in many countries, especially in France and Germany, by his pioneering work in Arabic studies.

The *OED* lists the term *Orientalist* in the sense of "one versed in Oriental languages and literature" as occurring first in 1779 and *Orientalism* as "Oriental scholarship; knowledge of Eastern languages" making its first appearance in writing in 1811. Oriental studies comprise a great deal of languages, and while the majority of the appropriate terms seem to have emerged only during the 19th century, the activity which they refer to are most likely to have been practiced at least several decades before. Again, according to the *OED*, the earliest English reference to an Oriental language is to *Sanskrit* as "the ancient and sacred language of India" in 1617, followed in 1634 by *Persia*, "the native land of the Persians". In general, the term referring to the practitioner seems more frequent and in some cases older than the term referring to what he practices; for instance, *Hebraist* (1755), *Arabist* (1847), *Sanskritist* (1864), *Semitist* (1885), *Indologian* (1897), *Turcolist* versus *Assyriology* (1828), *Egyptology* (1828), *Japanology* (1881), *Sinology* (1882) *Indology* (1888). For a large number of disciplines which would most certainly have to be included in *Oriental studies*, the *OED* does not cite one-word terms nor have such terms been formed in more recent times. Instead, compound forms with *studies* – and also *philology*, especially before the beginning of the 20th century – as the second component are used. This applies, e. g., to Abyssinian (= Ethiopic, Ethiopian), African, Altaic, Babylonian, Hittite, Iranian (Iranic), Mongolian, Tibetan, Turkic, Ural-Altaic *Studies* or *Philology*. The list is not complete. The French are equally reluctant to form one-word terms, whereas in German terms like *Afrikanistik, Altorientalistik, Arabistik, Hethitologie, Iranistik, Osmanistik, Tibetanistik, Turkologie* have been frequently used.

The general tendency towards specialization among academic subjects has also had its effect on all branches of Oriental studies, but much less so than on subjects with a substantially larger number of individual representatives. According to an Encyclopedia article of 1971 on *Orientalistik* (*Brockhaus Enzyklopädie* XIII, p. 806), the 'Orientalist' even in our time encompasses in teaching and research an area of knowledge 'comprising, sometimes over a period of several millennia, the problems of linguistics, [...] literature, history, geography, ethnography, religion, philosophy, jurisprudence, archaeology, art, etc., as well as to an increasing degree the problems of sociology and politology'.

The origin and development of Oriental studies is certainly tied to many more European countries than to those three which are dealt with here. National groups of Orientalists, as a rule, did not keep apart but cooperated actively with each other, and not only on the occasion of international congresses. Concerning the following survey of the prestages of the later, more systematized and institutionalized procedures in studying Oriental languages and cultures, it must be kept in mind that the impact and long-lasting effect of actions and decisions undertaken by single individuals was by no means restricted to the regional or national domain of the originator.

In 1143 Petrus (Mauritius) Venerabilis (c. 1092—1156), 9th Abbot of Cluny/France, arranged for the first translation of the Koran into Latin (cf. Glei 1985). Not much later a first Latin-Arabic glossary was compiled. Both works originated in Spain. The encounter of the Christian-Latin Occident with the Islamic-Arabic Orient during the Crusades produced inevitably an interest in, and most probably also a crucial need for, an extensive exchange of translations of written works between the opposing cultures. Numerous reports from the time provide ample documentation for the comprehensiveness and consistency of the effort to facilitate the preparation of such translations. Among the considerable number of scholars who worked incessantly for the implementation of these objectives, Raimundus Lullus (c. 1235—1315) deserves to be accorded a special place of prominence. Born in Palma/Mallorca, he taught philosophy and 'exact science' in

Paris, Montpellier, and Genoa. The greater part of his life, however, he spent attempting to convert Mohammedans to Christianity, with the Arabic language being his most important tool. He had learned Arabic himself and tried to engage the help of bishops and princes to arrange for Arabic lectureship so that translators could be trained. In traveling to Africa and to Asian countries in order to preach the gospel, he illustrated by his own example how compelling it was for the success of the missionary work to possess an adequate knowledge of the people's language.

For entirely different reasons Roger Bacon (c. 1214−c. 1292) had stressed the need to engage in serious studies of the Arabic language. He was one of the first to implement a strict separation of theology from philology and was convinced that Arabic philosophy and science would prove their worth if they were made available through adequate knowledge of the Arabic language. The *OED* lists under *Arabist* a quotation from 1753 stating that "Severinus gives all the surgeons in the 13th century the title Arabists".

A purely scholarly motivation such as that of Roger Bacon was rare, but the interest of the Church in furthering the study of languages based on a distinctly perceived usefulness for its missionary objectives continued to rise almost dramatically. At the 15th General Church Council, held from 1311 to 1312 in Vienne in the Départment Isère, Pope Clement V issued a decree that the Universities of Rome, Paris, Bologna, Oxford, and Salamanca establish Chairs for the teaching of Hebrew, Chaldee, and Arabic "in order to promote the study of the Oriental languages, and so to facilitate the conversion of the heathen" (Landon 1909: 271). Although this pronouncement remained largely ineffective until 1530, it is important to realize that as early as the beginning of the 14th century the highest authority of the Church had made unambiguously known its supportive attitude concerning this vital issue. One may also assume that the Pope's pronouncement contributed significantly to the improvement of the general conditions for the long-range development.

The 16th century brought numerous changes favorable to the development of the interest in studying Biblical, that is, Oriental languages. There were scholarly as well as commercial reasons involved, in addition to the purely religious motivation. The broadening of humanistic studies included a strong element for endorsing language studies in general, which undoubtedly strengthened the resolve to pursue Oriental language studies more vigorously than before. The opening of trade routes to various Oriental countries brought home from another point of view the advantage of, and the necessity for, enlarging the pool of knowledge about the distant countries and especially the usefulness of getting to know the languages involved. And last but not least, the Reformation, particularly the enormous success of the Luther Bible, demonstrated irrefutably how effective an excellent vernacular translation of the Scriptures could be. All of the approximately one hundred Bible translations in Germany before Luther were only partial translations. But more important than this is the fact that hardly any translation before Luther was even remotely comparable in quality to the Luther Bible. There was a crucial lesson to be learned, and it did not go unheeded.

In accordance with the decree of the Church Council of Vienne, the foundation of the *Collège de France* that took place in Paris in 1530 also saw the establishment of a Chair in Hebrew. A Chair in Arabic followed in 1587, one for Syriac in 1692, and those for Turkish and Persian in 1768. Chairs in Chinese and Sanskrit were added in 1814. In Rome two important institutions of international influence were established, the *Collegium Maronitarum* in 1584, and the *Collegium de Propaganda Fide* in 1627. Both foundations implied heavy reliance on the knowledge of Oriental languages in the pursuit of missionary work, in the first case in relation to the Maronites in Libanon, in the second case for missionary work in Oriental countries in general.

Meanwhile linguistic endeavors continued in other quarters. While the interest in Church matters remained the overriding motivation and concern, a trend began to emerge whose initiators also seriously considered Oriental language study as an objective in itself. The first French Arabist by several accounts (cf. Dugat 1868−1870, vol. I, p. xvii; Browne 1953, vol. I, 40−41) was Guillaume Postel (1510−1581) with his *Grammatica Arabica* of 1538. He is also credited with having been the first to provide Arabic types. His knowledge of several Semitic languages is extraordinary for his time and so is his attempt to compare those languages among themselves and with Hebrew. He also involved Latin and Greek in his research, dealing with altogether twelve languages.

Another early French Orientalist of remarkable accomplishments is Antoine Galland (1646–1715). From 1670 to 1675 he resided in Constantinople as an assistant to the French ambassador, utilizing his time to learn Arabic, Persian, and Turkish as well as writing a journal of his travels. He returned to the Orient in 1676 and 1679, when Louis XIV made him his *antiquaire*, specializing in the collection of coins and manuscripts. Galland became a member of the *Académie Royale des Inscriptions et Médaillles* in 1701, the year of its foundation, and started teaching Arabic at the *Collège Royale de France* in 1709. His numerous publications are both scholarly and popular, ranging from dictionary work, the translation of the Koran and academic papers, on the one hand, to collections of Oriental sayings and fables, on the other. He gained lasting fame and recognition by his *Arabian Nights*, a collection of over 300 Arabian tales with a long oral tradition, incorporating much older elements from a variety of Oriental countries other than Arabia, such as Persia, India, Iraq, and even Turkey and Egypt. Galland's source for his 12-volume translation, published in 1703–1717 as *Les mille & une nuits: Contes arabes traduit en Français*, was a 4-volume Arabic manuscript, first published in Calcutta in 1839–1842, supplemented among others by tales of a Syrian storyteller. Galland's *Arabian Nights* were an immediate success not only with the academic community, but also with the greater public both in France and abroad. It swiftly opened the door to the understanding of a distant world which so far had been an enigmatic entity at best. While some of the stories had been known in Italy since 1400, their impact outside Italy had remained negligible. Galland's collection, on the other hand, was immediately translated into German (Leipzig, 1719–1737), English (London, 13th ed., 1772), and several other languages. It continued to be the model for later editions until well into the 20th century. The wide-spread public appeal of the greater part of his work contributed significantly to the speed with which the development of Oriental studies in Europe proceeded. Its academic importance is underlined by the new edition which Silvestre de Sacy undertook, "Revus et corrigés sur l'édition princeps de 1704, augmentés d'une dissertation sur les Mille et une nuits", published in Paris in 1839–1840.

In Great Britain two noteworthy events added momentum to the development of Oriental studies there and also had repercussions far beyond the British Islands. One was the establishment of the *East India Trading Company* in 1600, the other was the funding of an Arabic Chair in both Cambridge in 1632 by Sir Thomas Adams (1586–1668) and in Oxford in 1636 by Archbishop William Laud (1573–1645), with Abraham Wheelocke (1593–1653) and Edward Pococke (1604–1691) as the first respective occupants. The motivation for the commercial initiative undertaken by British merchants, mostly from London, aimed at maximizing trade relations especially with the Indies. On Dec. 31, 1600 Queen Elizabeth I (1533–1603) by Royal Charter granted trade monopoly for the seaway to India to the group of London merchants who had formed a union in the year before. The Company had a checkered history, due partly to growing international competition, partly to internal opposition in political as well as in commercial matters, until it faded away in 1873. But the fact remains that the East India Company had sponsored and vigorously supported a considerable number of activities in the field of Oriental studies. For example, Max Müller's (1823–1900) printing of the highly influential 8-volume Rig-Veda edition could not have been achieved without the financial commitment on the part of the East India Company. The support amounted to £ 200 per year starting in 1847. Likewise, the Company helped Sir William Jones (1746–1794) in many ways, both before and during his 10-year stay as Chief Justice of the British Crown in Calcutta, especially by providing financial support for his translation of Mānava-Dharmaśāstra.

Political and trade relations with India and other Oriental countries soon gave rise to organizations and institutions whose initiators and administrators undoubtedly benefited from those affiliations, but developed and enthusiastically pursued cultural and scholarly objectives in which they were largely independent from any governmental or otherwise interfering authority. A case in point is the fruitful operation of the *Asiatick Society of Calcutta*, which Jones had founded in 1784 and of which he served as first president until his death in 1794. According to Garland Cannon, this society "rightly received the credit for inspiring the Oriental societies that followed, such as the Asiatic Society of Bombay (1804), Société Asiatique (1822), Royal Asiatic Society of Great Britain and Ireland (1823), and the American Oriental Society (1842)" (Cannon 1990: 204).

In most instances such societies did not only provide the opportunity to meet for formal and informal discussions and for the dissemination of scholarly papers, but often were also focal points for the collection of scientific materials and objects of art, which in some cases is already evident from the chosen name. In Jakarta, the *Batavia Society of Arts and Sciences*, founded in 1778, while owing — like many other societies of its kind — its existence to European colonial influence, fulfilled important cultural, scientific, and scholarly functions. Smaller societies were strengthened further by affiliating with larger societies. Thus, the *Literary Society of Bombay*, founded by Sir James Mackintosh (1765–1832), became in 1838 the *Bombay Branch of the Royal Asiatic Society* in London. The *Ceylon Society* joined in 1845 as another branch, and so did later on a similar society in Madras, founded by Sir Thomas John Newbolt (1807–1850) and Mr. Benjamin Guy Babington (1794–1866).

Commercial interests sometimes mingled effectively with scholarly asperations. Sir Charles Wilkins (1749/50–1836), for instance, came to India as "a senior merchant in the East India Company who had started studying Sanskrit in 1778" (Cannon 1990: 202–203). He served as secretary of the Company in Bengal from 1770 to 1786 and also as its librarian, beginning in 1800. Apart from being a most reliable attendee at the meetings of the Asiatick Society, listening, lecturing, and also publishing, he had earned the reputation of being one of the founders of Indian philology. His publications include *A Grammar of the Sanskrita Language* (1808) and *A Vocabulary, Persian, Arabic, and English* (1810). In Malda/Bengal he established in 1778 the first printing facility for Oriental languages, and his *Bhagvat-Gita or Dialogues of Krishna and Arjun* of 1785 constitutes the first Sanskrit translation printed in Europe.

France likewise tried its hand in establishing trade companies to boost its commercial relations with Oriental countries. Nominally, the first attempt was made by Cardinal Richelieu (1585–1642) in 1642, but only Jean-Baptiste Colbert (1619–1704), finance minister under Louis XIV (1638–1715), succeeded in establishing the *Companie Française des Indes Orientales* in 1664. In spite of prolonged personal commitment on the part of the King and Colbert's efforts to get the *Académie Française* actively involved, the net result was hardly more than a five-year span of satisfactory proceeds (1670–1675), largely due to the disinterest of the French merchants and the strong competition of the Dutch and the English trading companies. Under these circumstances no substantial gains for the cultural and scholarly sector could have been expected.

Germany's and Austria's endeavors to gain a foothold in the struggle for trade advantages with the Oriental world had much less tangible results than for the French, probably not only because of the two countries' lack of status as colonial powers. In spite of this apparent disadvantage, German-speaking scholars participated in the full range of explorations of the Oriental languages from the earliest days, when almost exclusively Biblical questions were investigated, to the 18th and 19th century, when progressively the interest had shifted more and more to linguistically-oriented objectives.

Johannes Reuchlin (1455–1522) laid the foundation for the scientific study of Hebrew by producing the first grammar, *De rudimentis Hebraicis* (1506) and the first lexicon of the Hebrew language, *De accentibus, et orthographia, linguae Hebraicae* (1518), materials which finally made it possible for scholars to fulfill the demands that Pope Clemens V had pronounced at the Council of Vienne in 1311/12. Johann Buxtorf's (1564–1629) edition of the *Biblia Sacra Hebraica* (1618–1619) as well as his *Lexicon Hebraicum et Chaldaicum* (1615) have had a profound influence on Biblical study for the next two hundred years, while the Jesuit Athanasius Kircher (1602–1680) decisively advanced the study of the Coptic grammar with two ground-breaking investigations which proved highly influential for all of Europe: *Prodromus Coptus sive Aegyptiacus* (Rome 1636), and *Lingua Aegyptiaca restituta* (Rome 1643). The French Egyptologist Jean-François Champollion (1790–1832), since 1832 holder of the first Chair in Egyptology at the *Collège de France*, benefited greatly from Kircher's work, when he succeeded in 1822 in deciphering in Egyptian hieroglyphs. Hiob Ludolf (1624–1704) is credited with being the originator of Ethiopian studies in Europe with his numerous treatises, including *Hi-*

storia Aethiopica (1681), *Lexicon Amharico-Latinum* (1698), and *Grammatica Aethiopica* (1661). He is also well known for his influence on Gottfried Wilhelm Leibniz (1646–1716) in matters of linguistic details. Leibniz, on the other hand, excelled by his ability, hardly surpassed by anyone at his time, to create comprehensive conceptual designs as is evidenced, e. g., in his "Brevis designatio meditationum de originibus gentium, ductis potissimum ex indicio linguarum" (1710), in which he surveyed most of the known languages of Europe and Asia as well as of Africa and also discussed briefly how they might be related. He came close to positing a common language of origin, but strenuously avoided naming Hebrew or any other known language as a possible 'proto-language'. In their development through time, Leibniz argued, languages were exposed to changes so drastic that in many instances original relationships might not be recognizable any longer.

With the support of Queen Sophie Charlotte of Prussia (1668–1705), Leibniz was able to establish in 1700 the 'Sozietät der Wissenschaften' in Berlin, which later on, through the initiative of King Frederick the Great (1712–1786), was to become the 'Akademie der Wissenschaften' in 1744. Leibniz' *Brevis designatio* was the first in a long series of treatises dealing with languages that were published by the Academy, of which he, incidently, was also the first President.

A scholar of extraordinary precision and sophistication, both as an Orientalist and as a Classical researcher, was Johann Jacob Reiske (1716–1774), since 1748 professor of Arabic at the University of Leipzig and principal of the Nicolai high school since 1758. Specially note-worthy among his works is his 5-volume edition of Abu'l-Feda's (1273–1331) *Annales muslemici arabice et latine* (1789–94), the work of a Kurdish aristocrat born in Damascus, who combined the profession of a soldier and with that of a scholar.

3. Towards Oriental language studies as an Independent academic discipline

By the middle of the 18th century the stage in Europe was set for an approach to the study of Oriental languages that viewed its object — at least for the larger part — as an entity worth being studied in its own right. The objectives of the Church were not discarded, and needed not be discarded, but they were thoroughly modified and adapted in accordance with the growing recognition that a comprehensive study of any language for its own sake was not necessarily detrimental to the overall aims and endeavors of the Church and was, moreover, extremely advantageous in many respects. This is not to say, however, that the numerous difficulties and obstacles that continued to exist — for instance, in matters of placing Oriental languages and the three 'holy' languages, Latin, Greek, and Hebrew, on the same level of importance — should be overlooked or even be entirely disregarded. But the certainty is there — and is also widely perceived — that an irreversible trend has been put into motion which eventually would lead to a fully developed scientific study of the Oriental world. The serious problems that still remained were of a different kind. By now oriental language studies had gained a firm foothold at many first-rate European universities, especially in England, France, and Germany. As attempts on behalf of other university subjects were made to expand their sphere of influence, the proponents of Oriental studies had now to see to it that the relevance of these studies was forcefully explained not only to colleagues of other disciplines, to university and governmental officials, but also to a wider general public. The publication of Antoine Galland's *Arabian Nights* in 1703–1717 as a translation which contained highly appealing cultural information from various Oriental languages, first in French, then in German and English as well as also in many other languages, was one event that had an enormously far-reaching effect. Arabists such as Silvestre de Sacy had made full use of it for the development of their field of study.

A similar event occurred in Germany about a century later, when Johann Wolfgang von Goethe in 1813 came across a complete edition of the Oriental works translated by Joseph Freiherr von Hammer-Purgstall (1774–1856). Greatly inspired by what he had read, Goethe engaged in serious Oriental studies of his own for several years, determined to incorporate the Oriental world into his own poetry much more copiously than he had done before. The result was the *West-östliche Divan*, Goethe's 125-page anthology of poems (cf. Richter 1898), accompanied by 121 pages of "Noten und Abhandlungen zu besserem Verständnis des West-östlichen Divans" ['notes and essays for better understanding of the *West-östliche Divan*']. The first poems were written in 1814, the first complete edition of the *Divan* appeared in 1820. The last page carries a four-liner in which Goethe dedicates the book to "Silvestre de Sacy, unserem Meister".

Goethe's enthusiasm for the Orient was not due to a sudden emotional eruption. It had built up slowly, but consistently over many years. Between 1762 and 1765, as a teenager, he studied Hebrew with a high school principal in Frankfurt, read part of Koran translations in 1771 and 1772 and was guided by Johann Gottfried Herder (1744–1803) to a full appreciation of Hebrew as well as Indian and Persian poetry. He also had followed closely the development in Calcutta, heaping praise on the work of Sir William Jones, but at the same time demanding that poetry must be evaluated in its own terms, not by comparing it to great poetry of other countries. According to Goethe, Jones

'knew, appreciated, loved his Orient and wanted to introduce its productions to old England [...] which could not be achieved in any way other than under the stamp of classical antiquity. All this is at present quite unnecessary, even harmful. We know how to appreciate the type of poetry of the Orientals, we grant them first-rate quality, but they should be compared to themselves, they should be honored in their own circle.' (Quoted in Richter 1898: 203)

Comparable to Goethe as well as Hammer-Purgstall and interacting with both of them was Friedrich Rückert (1788–1866). For some time he was professor of Oriental languages, first in Erlangen (1826), then in Berlin (1841–48). He combined teaching and research with creative writing and working on translations, all directed to his primary field of interest, the enigmatic world of the Orient. All three were creative writers, and all three contributed their share to the advancement of Oriental studies by interpreting a foreign world to their readers, thereby considerably increasing the involvement of the general educated public.

Higher education itself continued to expand, on the one hand, by enlarging existent institutions and adding on new ones, on the other, by intensified research leading to truly remarkable results. Paris saw the inauguration of the *École des Jeunes de Langue* for interpreters by Louis XIV in 1700 and of the *École nationale des langues orientales vivantes* in 1795. The need for the foundation of the second institution had been eloquently advocated by Louis Mathieu Langlès (1763–1824), since 1792 curator at the manuscript division of the National Library, in a petition entitled "De l'importance des langues orientales pour l'extension du commerce et le progrès des lettres et des sciences", in which he recommended the establishment of three chairs each in Paris and Marseille for Arabic, Persian, and Turkish. He was not the first and not the only one who emphasized the value of the practical aspects of academic appointments, but he probably went about it more vigorously and more persistently than many others before him, keeping up his efforts until he met with the desired success. The second time around the National Assembly granted his request, and Chairs were funded for Literary and Common Arabic, for Turkish and Crimean-Tartaric, and for Persian and Malayan. Silvestre de Sacy was appointed to the Arabic Chair, Langlès to the Chair for Persian and Malayan. They both began teaching their courses on 22 June 1796 (cf. Derenbourg 1887: vi). Part of the stipulations for conducting the affairs of the School was the obligation to include instruction on the political and economical situation of the Oriental countries involved.

Before long the 'National School of Living Oriental Languages' had acquired a solid international reputation. Students from many other European countries enrolled, especially from Germany, who were frequently sent to Paris by their government on a stipend. The long list of famous German linguists who have studied at the *École nationale* includes the following names: Franz Bopp (1791–1867); Othmar Frank (1770–1840); Julius von Mohl (1800–1876) who remained in France, became a citizen, and was appointed professor of Persian at the *Collège de France* in 1847. Other scholars on the list are Georg Wilhelm Friedrich Freytag (1788–1861); Johann Gottfried Ludwig Kosegarten (1792–1860); Heinrich Leberecht Fleischer (1801–1888); Gustav Flügel (1802–1870); and Maximilian Habicht (1775–1839).

The *Orientalische Akademie* (*Akademie für morgenländische Sprachen*, today *Hammer-Purgstall Gesellschaft*), founded in Vienna in 1754, developed into an excellent institution that admirably fulfilled the mainly academic objectives under which it had been established. A Chair for Oriental languages had already been in existence at the University of Vienna since 1674, but this enlargement of the facilities in the Austrian capital for the study of the Orient was certainly in keeping with the growing demand.

England's magnificent contribution of the century consisted in the 'discovery' by Sir William Jones in 1786 that some important languages of the Orient share common features with most of the European languages. Oriental studies thus became inextricably intertwined with the study of languages in general.

One of the members of Jones 'Asiatick Society in Calcutta was Alexander Hamilton (1762–1824), who was much more inclined to learn Sanskrit than to pursue his duties as a British soldier. It was Friedrich von Schlegel (1772–1829) who profited from Hamilton's knowledge of Sanskrit during a full year of instruction in Paris from 1803 to 1804. Schlegel acknowledges his indebtedness to Hamilton in the introduction to his book *Über die Sprache und Weisheit der Indier* (1808), in which he outlines for the first time ever the program of comparative grammar.

Two additional discoveries opened up entirely new avenues to the understanding of the World of the East. The first one is he deciphering of the cuneiform, the oldest type of writing in the Near East, by Georg Friedrich Grotefend (1775–1853), which he accomplished in 1802. He presented his findings to the *Göttinger Gesellschaft der Wissenschaften* in the same year, but a published account of what it entailed appeared only in 1824 (cf. Grotefend 1824–26). The second one is the decoding of the Egyptian hieroglyphs in 1822 by Champollion. In both cases the final result was possible only by a large-scale cooperative effort among numerous researchers from various countries. Of the many participants with significant contributions, those who deserve special acknowledgment are Christian Lassen (1800–1876), Sir Henry Creswicke Rawlinson (1810–1895), and Edward Hincks (1792–1866), in the case of cuneiform decipherment, and Thomas Young (1773–1829), Ippolito Rosellini (1800–1866), and Richard Lepsius (1810–1884), in the case of the solving of the hieroglyphic puzzle.

With the help of the cuneiform script access was gained to the Akkadian language, an East Semitic language mainly spoken in Babylonia and Assyria between 2500 to 1000 B. C., then being progressively replaced as colloquial language by Aramaic (cf. Soden 1952). The accessibility of Akkadian turned out to be extremely important as it cast new light on the Hebrew language 'which so far had been approachable only via Aramaic and Arabic', according to Carl Brockelmann (1868–1956) as cited in Hartmann & Scheel (1944: 3).

Another great discovery was due to the zeal and enthusiasm of Abraham Hyacinthe Anquetil-Duperron (1731–1805). Anquetil, who spent six years in India (1755–1761) studying and translating some 200 holy texts of the Iranian Parsees, became the founder of Iranian studies in Europe by his discovery of the Avesta, a collection of the laws and the teachings of the Old Zoroastrian religion. The collection, which originally comprised 21 books with a total of 815 chapters supposedly written in the 6th or 5th century B. C., had already been reduced through loss to 348 chapters by the 4th century A. D., and of these now only one fourth have survived. Anquetil's edition of 1769–1771, *Zend-Avesta, ouvrage de Zoroastre*, was immediately translated into German and proved to be of great influence on the emerging science of comparative religion. Anquetil had arrived in India well equipped with knowledge of Oriental languages. Apart from Hebrew he had mastered Arabic and Persian and had also acquired some familiarity with Avestan when he stumbled upon several manuscripts in that language at the Royal Library in Paris.

Sir William Jones, although well versed in classical Greek and Latin and having mastered a number of other European languages spoken at his time, had only one language priority during his 10-year stay in India: Sanskrit. He had written *A Grammar of the Persian Language* in 1771 which was hailed as a great achievement. Cannon speaks of him as the "Persian Jones" and makes it clear that Jones "deserved his name" (1990: 40). But although Jones continued to entertain a keen interest in Persia and the Persian language, his primary focus during the years from 1785 to 1794 was on India and on the "systematic study of Sanskrit, Jones's 'best' language" (Cannon 1990: xix). His definition of the genealogical relationship of languages as formulated in 1786, "the first known printed statement of the fundamental postulate of Indo-European comparative grammar, more than that, of comparative linguistics as a whole" (Edgerton 1946: 232), while providing a unique service to the European scholarly community, was for Jones himself first and foremost an achiement focussing on the productivity of Oriental studies. But even those pioneering European linguists who dwelt on Jones' hypothesis and expanded it to an all-encompassing theory of unprecedented proportion had to be at least part-time Orientalists as well in order to attain their scholarly objectives. The emergence of Indo-European linguistics cannot be dissociated from the existence of Oriental language studies.

From the work of Orientalists in general, and of Jones in particular, another important aspect arises. Even though Oriental studies succeeded in producing crucially important linguistic data, the cultural and intellectual information which was discovered and made available to the Western World, both to the academic specialists and to a much wider general public, was at least equal, if not of much greater significance. Its truly novel and unique nature left its mark on not only all European colonial countries, but also on a large number of organizations and institutions in any country of the Western world.

A striking example for the time before Jones is the above-mentioned Johann Jacob Reiske, who for some German linguists is 'the actual founder of Arabic philology' (Foerster 1889: 131). His motivation for embarking on Arab studies was from the very beginning not fueled by linguistic or theological criteria, but by the desire 'to explain and enrich [... with philological means] the history, geography, mathematics, physics, and medicine' as found in Arabic literature (ibid.). He posed the question as to 'how one could and should lend help to the Arabic literature' and provided the answer, which is as much promise and commitment as it is proven implementation, that his aim for delving into the Arabic language was 'to present the works of its literature in critical texts, to explain and evaluate them and to utilize them for history' (p. 132), i. e., placing them into a historical perspective, thereby securing their continued maximal effect.

Reiske's intentions were not a rarity, although the pursuit of theological and purely linguistic purposes were undoubtedly more frequent. A prominent example for endeavors along the lines of Reiske, only on a much larger scale and with incomparably greater repercussions, is the life and work of Friedrich Max Müller. Born and academically trained in Germany, he spent some time in France where Eugène Burnouf (1801–1852) decisively shaped his determination to devote his professional career to the study of Oriental languages and literatures. In 1846 he moved temporarily to London, and soon thereafter he settled for good in Oxford. No linguist of his time was awarded greater honors by a larger variety of sources from more parts of the world. Of his hundreds of small and large writings which touch upon our topic, only one, perhaps the most significant, should be mentioned here. In 1875 Müller began to devise a plan of bringing together a large number of outstanding scholars who specialized in the field of Oriental studies for the purpose of translating into English and editing, under the title of *The Sacred Books of the East*, "all the most important works of the seven non-Christian religions that have exercised a profound influence on the civilization of the continent of Asia" (Arthur Anthony MacDonnell [1854–1930] in the preface to vol. 50, p. vii). The ambitious project comprising a total of 50 volumes contained the sacred writings of: 1) Vedic-Brāhmanic Religion (21 vols.); 2) Buddhism (10 vols.); 3) Gaina Religion (2 vols.); 4) Confucianism (4 vols.); 5) Tāoism (2 vols.); 6) Parsi Religion (8 vols.); and 7) Islām (2 vols.). A total of 20 translators of various nationalities went to work. The editor himself translated all of four and part of two volumes, with a total of well over 2000 pages, thus being one of the four translators who carried the heaviest load of the project. The first volume appeared in 1879, the last in 1894. Vol. 50, *A General Index to the Names and Subject-Matter of the Sacred Books of the Eeast*, compiled and edited by Moriz Winternitz (1863–1937) in 1910, 10 years after Müller's death, is much more than a mere listing of names and titles. Instead, according to the general editor and the compilor, it was intended to be a "Manual of the History of Eastern Religions" (p. xii), and MacDonnell claims in his preface that he has "no hesitation in stating that it is the most comprehensive work of the kind that has yet been published. For it is not merely a complete index [...]. It also furnishes, in articles of any length, a scientific classification of the subject under various heads" (p. ix). A. A. MacDonnell, incidentally, was "Boden Professor of Sanskrit in the University of Oxford", a prestigious position which F. M. Müller had hoped to secure for himself in 1860, when the previous chair holder Horace Hayman Wilson (1786–1860) had died after a tenure of 28 years, but never received.

Müller achieved an enormous success in popularizing linguistic studies in general and Oriental studies in particular. The *Sacred Books* were only one instrument in this lifelong endeavor of global proportions, though a very important one. A conclusive indication of how great the influence of this publication has been, and still is today, is the fact that the work continues to be reprinted, e. g., in India under the sponsorship of UNESCO and the government of India (cf. Müller 1962—1973). The Indian edition carries in each volume the following dedication — dated 10 June 1962 — by Sarvepalli Radhakrishnan (1888—1975), at that time the President of India: "I am very glad to know that the Sacred Books of the East [...] which have been out-of-print for a number of years, will now be available to all students of religion and philosophy".

4. Conclusion

Oriental studies started out as academic endeavors ancillary to theological research. It took several centuries for those endeavors to avance through various stages to a point where Oriental languages were learned for their own sake and Oriental cultures were studied because of their own intrinsic value. In England, France, and Germany the development proceeded basically along similar lines, characterized by an interplay among several dynamic forces. Academic institutions were established because of a perceived public need. Those institutions produced results, often in accordance with expectations, sometimes transcending even the most optimistic anticipations. The favorable repercussions from quarters outside academia created the basis for obtaining the crucial authorization to expand research facilities, which inevitably led to more academic achievements and resulted in a greater amount of recognition by the general public.

During the 19th century every German university was eventually endowed with a chair in Oriental languages and literatures. The general trend in England and France was not altogether different. But whereas there the forces behind an academic expansion of this kind were likely to have been fueled for the greater part by political and commercial objectives and necessities, the enlargement of Oriental studies in Germany had much more to do with the emergence of particular philosophical and intellectual trends. Philosophers like Leibniz, Immanuel Kant (1724—1804), Friedrich Hegel (1770—1831), Friedrich Wilhelm Schelling (1775—1854), Arthur Schopenhauer (1788—1860), and Friedrich Nietzsche (1844—1900) played an influential role, as they all were extensively informed about various aspects of Asian philosophy and incorporated Oriental thought into their theorizing. Scholars and writers like Gotthold Ephraim Lessing (1729—1781), Johann Gottfried Herder, Goethe, Wilhelm von Humboldt (1767—1835), and Friedrich Rückert did their part in disseminating through their writings their profound enthusiasm for the Oriental world. What they offered to their public was appealing and convincing and had undoubtedly a lasting effect on how Oriental studies were valued and to what extent their continued growth was to be supported.

Oriental scholars have had regular meetings on a national level from the beginning of the 19th century onwards. The international cooperation flourished even before that time and continued to grow in the 1900s. The First International Congress of Orientalists (Congrès International des Orientalistes) was held in Paris in 1873, a full 55 years before the First International Congress of Linguists convened in The Hague in 1928. One may rightfully draw the conclusion that for the greater part of the 19th century general linguistics was second to Oriental linguistics, at least under a global perspective.

Oriental studies have as their center the study of Oriental languages. As we have emphasized, however, adjacent disciplines were always unavoidably near at hand and had to be at least marginally included into the research effort, not only for the sake of the neighboring disciplines, but also for the benefit of language study itself. Archaeological finds, for example, cast important light on language facts not obtainable through any other means. It is, therefore, not surprising that the *Deutsche Orient-Gesellschaft*, founded in January 1898 in Berlin and since 1901 under the protectorate of Emperor Wilhelm II, listed in its statutes (appended as a leaflet to Delitzsch 1898) as the first of its three objectives 'to further the study of Oriental antiquity in general, the exploration of the old cultural sites in Assyria, Babylonia, Mesopotamia and other West Asian countries as well as Egypt in particular'. That is to say, that conducting excavations had been accorded first priority. The Society revealed as its second objective 'to support the endeavors of the Royal Museum of Berlin — as well as, if need be, of other public collections in the German Empire — to acquire Oriental artifacts, monuments of art and of general culture'. As the third objective the wish was expressed 'to propagate in an appropriate manner the knowledge of the results of the research on Oriental antiquity and to enliven the interest in this part of the oldest culture of mankind'. The Society immediately got strong support from politicians and government officials as well as from high-level representatives of both the Catholic and Protestant Churches, and also from various branches of industry. University professors in general and Orientalists in particular were a minority among the large number of supporters. It seems that the all-out effort to disseminate information about the world of the Orient had at long last been extremely successful.

Britain and France had expanded their Oriental studies into a branch emphasizing archeology and excavations at a much earlier time. Political aims and scientific objectives in the three countries did not always coincide. But since excellent knowledge of the language and literature of all Oriental countries had been recognized by every authority which was involved as indispensable precondition for a broad-based Oriental Studies program, governmental participation in the enterprise proved more beneficial than harmful.

At the beginning of the 20th century Oriental studies in all three countries were well established and had achieved a status of excellence as academic programs, with numerous fully developed branches, by contributing greatly to our understanding of the Oriental World and proving that this knowledge constitutes a most welcome enrichment of our Occidental culture.

In 1828, five years after the Royal Asiatic Society was founded, it authorized the formation of an Oriental Translation Fund with the express purpose of providing "for the translation and publication of such works on Eastern history, science, and belles lettres as are inaccessible to the European public in M. S. form and indigenous language". *Ex oriente lux*, the motto adopted by this "London Translation Society" (cf. Schele de Vere 1853: 93), points fittingly to why ultimately Oriental studies were highly rewarding: There was new light to be seen and new insight to be gained from the exploration of the East.

5. Bibliography

Anquetil-Duperron, Abraham Hyacinthe. 1769—71. *Zend-Avesta, ouvrage de Zoroastre*. 3 vols. Paris: N. M. Tilliard.

Arberry, Arthur John. 1942. *British Contributions to Persian Studies*. London: Longmans, Green & Co.

—. 1943. *British Orientalists*. London: Collins.

—. 1946. *Asiatic Jones: The life and influence of Sir William Jones (1746—1794), pioneer of Indian studies*. London: Longmans, Green & Co.

—. 1960. *Oriental Essays: Portraits of seven scholars*. New York: Macmillan.

Babinger, Franz. 1957. "Ein Jahrhundert morgenländischer Studien an der Münchener Universität". *Zeitschrift der Deutschen Morgenländischen Gesellschaft* 107: 2. 241—269.

Bendall, Cecil B. 1900. "Wilkins, Sir Charles". *Dictionary of National Biography* 61. 259—260. London: Smith, Elder & Co.

Benfey, Theodor. 1869. *Geschichte der Sprachwissenschaft und orientalischen Philologie in Deutschland seit dem Anfange des 19. Jahrhunderts mit einem Rückblick auf die früheren Zeiten*. München: Cotta'sche Buchhandlung.

Boeckh, August. ^{2}1886 [1877]. *Enzyklopädie und Methodenlehre der philologischen Wissenschaften*. Ed. by Ernst Bratuschek. Leipzig: Teubner.

Böttger, Walter. 1964. "Gabelentz, Hans Georg Conon". *Neue Deutsche Biographie* VI.3. Berlin: Duncker & Humblot.

Brockelmann, Carl. 1944. "Stand und Aufgaben der Semitistik". Hartmann & Scheel 1944. 3—41.

Brockhaus Enzyklopädie in zwanzig Bänden. 1966—76. Wiesbaden: Brockhaus.

Browne, Edward Granville. 1953. *A Literary History of Persia*. 4 vols. London & Cambridge: Cambridge Univ. Press. (First published 1924.)

Buxtorf, Johann. 1609a. *Thesaurus grammaticus linguae sanctae Hebraeae*. 2 vols. Basileae: Impensis Ludovici Regis.

—. 1609b. *Lexicon Hebraicum et Chaldaicum*. 2 vols. Basileae: Typis Ludovici Regis.

—. 1615. *Grammaticae Chaldaicae et Syriacae*. 3 vols. Basileae: Typis Conradi Waldkirchi.

—. 1618—19. *Biblia Sacra Hebraica & Chaldaica*. 4 vols. Basileae: Sumptibus & typis Ludovici Regis.

Cannon, Garland. 1990. *The Life and Mind of Oriental Jones: Sir William Jones, the father of modern linguistics*. Cambridge: Cambridge Univ. Press.

— & Kevin R. Brine, eds. 1995. *Objects of Enquiry: The life, contributions, and influences of Sir William Jones, 1746—1794*. New York: New York Univ. Press.

Champollion, Jean-François. 1824. *Précis du système hiéroglyphique des anciens Egyptiens*. 2 vols. Paris: Treuttel et Wurtz.

Chatterjee, Sir Atul Chandra & Sir Richard Burn. 1943. *British Contribution to Indian Studies.* London: Longmans, Green & Co.

Conrad, Johannes. 1884. *Das Universitätsstudium in Deutschland während der letzten 50 Jahre: Statistische Untersuchungen unter besonderer Berücksichtigung Preussens.* Jena: G. Fischer. (Transl. by John Hutchinson as *The German Universities for the Last Fifty Years*, Glasgow: David Bryce & Son, 1885.)

Cust, Robert Needham. 1880–1904. *Linguistic and Oriental Essays: Written from the year 1840 to 1903.* 7 vols. in 8. London: Trübner & Co.; Luzac & Co.

—. 1880. *Linguistic and Oriental Essays: Written from the year 1846 to 1878.* First Series. London: K. Paul, Trench & Trübner. (Repr., New Delhi: Daya, 1985.)

—. 1891. *Linguistic and Oriental Essays: Written from the year 1847 to 1890.* Third Series. London: K. Paul, Trench & Trübner. (Repr., New Delhi: Daya, 1985.)

—. 1901. *Some Remarks on the Royal Asiatic Society of Great Britain and Ireland.* Hertford: Printed by Stephen Austin.

—. 1926. *List of Members of the Royal Asiatic Society of Great Britain and Ireland, Founded March, 1823.* London: Royal Asiatic Society of Great Britain and Ireland.

Delitzsch, Friedrich. 1898. *Ex Oriente lux: Ein Wort zur Förderung der Deutschen Orient-Gesellschaft.* Leipzig: J. C. Hinrichs'sche Buchhandlung.

Derenbourg, Hartwig. 1887. "Silvestre de Sacy: Une esquisse biographique". *Internationale Zeitschrift für allgemeine Sprachwissenschaft* 3. i–xxviii.

Dugat, Gustave. 1868–1870. *Histoire des orientalistes de l'Europe de XIIième au XIXième siècle, précédée d'une esquisse historique des études orientales: Série du XIXième siècle.* 2 vols. Paris: Maisonneuve.

École des langues orientales vivantes. 1883. *Notice historique sur l'École speciale des langues orientales vivantes.* Paris: E. Leroux.

École des langues orientales vivantes. 1885. *Centenaire de l'École des langues orientales vivantes 1795–1895.* Paris: Imprimerie nationale.

Edgerton, Franklin. 1946. "Sir William Jones: 1746–1794". *Journal of the American Oriental Society* 66. 230–239.

Falkenstein, Adam. 1960. *Denkschrift zur Lage der Orientalistik.* Wiesbaden: Franz Steiner.

Favre, Edouard. 1894. *Les études orientales à la Société d'histoire et d'archéologie de Genève 1838–1894.* Genève: Imprimé pour la Société d'histoire et d'archéologie.

Fleischer, Heinrich Leberecht. 1968 [1885–1888]. "Zu Rückerts Grammatik, Poetik und Rhetorik der Perser". *Kleinere Schriften*, gesammelt, durchgesehen und vermehrt. Vol. III. 531–605. Osnabrück: Biblio Verlag.

Foerster, Richard. 1889. "Johann Jacob Reiske". *Allgemeine Deutsche Biographie* 28. 129–140. Leipzig: Duncker & Humblot.

Friederici, Karl. 1877–1883. *Bibliotheca Orientalis or a Complete List of Books, Papers, Serials and Essays published in 1876 (to 1883) in England and the Colonies, Germany and France on the History, Languages, Religions, Antiquities, Literature and Geography of the East.* Leipzig: Otto Schulze; London: Trübner & Co.; Paris: E. Leroux; New York: Westermann & Co. (Continued by "Dr. Klatt [...] in Prof. *Kuhn's Literatur-Blatt für orientalische Philologie*". Cf. Friederici 1883, p. iii.)

Fück, Johann. 1953. "Geschichte der semitischen Sprachwissenschaft". *Handbuch der Orientalistik* ed. by Bertold Spuler, vol. III: *Semitistik*, 31–39. Leiden: Brill.

—. 1955. *Die arabischen Studien in Europa bis in den Anfang des 20. Jahrhunderts.* Leipzig: Harrassowitz.

Gabelentz, (Hans) Georg (Conon) von der. 1882. *Beiträge zur Kenntnis der melanesischen, mikronesischen und papuanischen Sprachen. Ein erster Beitrag zur Hans Conons von der Gabelentz Werke Die melanesischen Sprachen.* Leipzig: Hirzel.

—. 1891. *Die Sprachwissenschaft: Ihre Aufgaben, Methoden und bisherigen Ergebnisse.* Leipzig: T. O. Weigel. (2nd ed., prepared by Albrecht Graf von der Schulenburg, Leipzig: Tauchnitz, 1901.)

Galland, Antoine. 1694. *Les Paroles remarquables, les bons mots, et les maximes des Orientaux: Traduction de leurs ouvrages en arabe, en persan, & en turc. Avec des remarques.* Paris: S. Bernard.

—. 1703–17. *Les mille & une nuits: Contes arabes traduit en Français.* 12 vols. Paris: Chez la veuve de Claude Barbin. (Transl. into German as *Die Tausend und eine Nacht* [...] Leipzig: Moritz G. Weidmann, 1719–1937. Transl. into English as *Arabian Nights Entertainments: Consisting of one thousand and one stories told by the Sultaness of the Indies* [...] 13th ed. London: Longman [...], 1772.)

Glei, Reinhold. 1985. *Schriften zum Islam / Petrus Venerabilis.* Ediert, ins Deutsche übersetzt und kommentiert. Altenberge: CIS-Verlag.

Grotefend, Georg Friedrich. 1824–1826. ["Entzifferung der assyrischen Keilschrift"]. *Ideen über die Politik, den Verkehr und den Handel der vornehmsten Völker der alten Welt* ed. by Arnold Hermann Ludwig Heeren, Vol. I: 2. 345 ff. 4th ed., Göttingen: Vandenhoeck & Ruprecht.

—. 1835–39. *Rudimenta linguae Umbricae: ex inscriptionibus antiquis enodata.* Hannover: Hahn.

—. 1837. *Neue Beiträge zur Erläuterung der persepolitanischen Keilschrift.* Hannover: Hahn.

Grotefend, Hermann. 1879. "Grotefend, Georg Friedrich". *Allgemeine Deutsche Biographie* 9. 763–765. Leipzig: Duncker & Humblot.

Grube, Wilhelm. 1905. "Gabelentz: Hans Georg Conon von der". *Allgemeine Deutsche Biographie* 50. 548–555. Leipzig: Duncker & Humblot.

Hammerich, Louis Leonor. 1970. "Einige Jahrhunderte europäischen Kulturerbes". *Studies in General and Oriental Linguistics, Presented to Shirô Hattori on the occasion of his sixtieth birthday* ed. by Roman Jakobson & Shigeo Kawamoto,. 180–187. Tokyo: TEC Co.

Hammer-Purgstall, Joseph Freiherr von. 1804. *Encyklopädische Übersicht der Wissenschaften des Orients, aus sieben arabischen, persischen und türkischen Werken übersetzt.* Leipzig: Breitkopf & Härtel.

—. 1813. *Rosenol; oder, Sagen und Kunden des Morgenlandes aus arabischen, persischen und türkischen Quellen gesammelt.* Stuttgart: J. G. Cotta.

—. 1850–1856. *Literaturgeschichte der Araber.* 7 vols. Wien: Kaiserl.-Königl. Hof- und Staatsdruckerei.

Hartmann, Richard & Helmuth Scheel, eds. 1944. *Beiträge zur Arabistik, Semitistik und Islamwissenschaft.* Leipzig: Harrassowitz.

Hincks, Edward. 1863. *On the Polyphony of the Assyrio-Babylonian Cuneiform Writing: A letter to Professor Renouf.* Dublin: John F. Fowler.

Hsia, Adrian, ed. 1985. *Deutsche Denker über China.* Frankfurt/M.: Insel.

International Congress of Orientalists. 1876. *Transactions of the Second Session of the International Congress of Orientalists, Held in London in September, 1874* ed. by Robert K. Douglas. London: Trübner & Co.

Itkonen, Esa. 1991. *Universal History of Linguistics: India, China, Arabia, Europe.* Amsterdam & Philadelphia: Benjamins.

Jahresbericht der Deutschen Morgenländischen Gesellschaft für das Jahr 1845. Leipzig: Brockhaus & Avenarius, 1846.

Jahresbericht der Deutschen Morgenländischen Gesellschaft für das Jahr 1846. Leipzig: Brockhaus & Avenarius, 1847.

Jankowsky, Kurt R. 1979. "Max Mueller and the Development of Linguistic Science". *Historiographia Linguistica* 6. 339–359.

Jones, Sir William. 1792 [1788]. "Dissertation III on the Hindu's, Being the Third Anniversary Discourse Delivered to the Society Feb. 2, 1786". *Asiatick Researches or, Transactions of the Society Instituted in Bengal for Inquiring into the History and Antiquities, the Arts, Sciences, and Literatures, of Asia* 1. 95–117. London: G. Nicol.

Kircher, Athanasius, S. J. 1636. *Prodromus Coptus sive Aegyptiacus.* Romae: Typis S. Cong. de propaganda Fide.

—. 1643. *Lingua Aegyptiaca restituta.* Roma: Sumptibus Hermanni Scheus.

Kleuker, Johann Friedrich. 1776–77. *Zend-Avesta, Zoroasters lebendiges Wort.* 3 vols. Riga: J. F. Hartknoch.

Köpke, Ernst Rudolf Anastasius. 1860. *Die Gründung der Königlichen Friedrich-Wilhelms-Universität zu Berlin.* Berlin: Gustav Schade.

Landon, Edward H. 1909. *A Manual of Councils of the Holy Catholic Church.* Vol. II. Edinburgh: John Grant.

Langlès, Louis Mathieu. 1790. *Fables et contes indiens.* Nouvellement traduits, avec un discours préliminaire des notes sur la religion, la littérature, les mœurs, & c. des Hindoux. Paris: Royes.

—. 1817. *Monuments anciens et modernes de l'Hindoustan.* Paris: A. Boudeville.

Lassen, Christian. 1836. *Die altpersischen Keil-Inschriften von Persepolis: Entzifferung des Alphabets und Erklärung des Inhalts.* Bonn: Eduard Weber.

—. 1845. *Über die Kleininschriften der ersten und zweiten Gattung.* Bonn: H. B. König.

Leibniz, Gottfried Wilhelm. 1710. "Brevis designatio meditationum de originibus gentium, ductis potissimum ex indicio linguarum". *Miscellanea Berolinensia*, 1–16. Berolini: Sumptibus Johan. Christ. Papenii.

Lewis, Bernard. 1941. *British Contributions to Arabic Studies.* London: Longmans, Green & Co.

Lexis, Wilhelm. 1893. *Die deutschen Universitäten: Für die Universitätsausstellung in Chicago 1893.* 2 vols. Berlin: A. Asher & Co.

Littmann, Enno. 1942. *Der deutsche Beitrag zur Wissenschaft vom vorderen Orient.* Stuttgart: Kohlhammer.

—. 1955. *Ein Jahrhundert Orientalistik: Lebensbilder aus der Feder von Enno Littmann und Verzeichnis seiner Schriften. Zum achtzigsten Geburtstage am 16. September 1955.* Ed. by Rudi Paret & Anton Schall. Wiesbaden: Harrassowitz.

Ludolf, Hiob. 1661. *Grammatica Aethiopica.* Londini: Apud Thomam Roycroft. (Another ed., Frankfurt: J. D. Zunner, 1702.)

—. 1681. *Historia Aethiopica.* Frankfurt: J. D. Zunner.

—. 1698. *Lexicon Amharico-Latinum.* Frankfurt: J. D. Zunner.

M'Douall, Charles. 1849. *A Discourse on the Study of Oriental Languages and Literature.* Edinburgh: T. & T. Clark.

Mohl, Julius von. 1879–80. *Vingt-sept ans d'histoire des études orientales: Rapport faits à la Société asiatique de Paris de 1840 à 1867, par Jules Mohl. Ouvrage publié par sa veuve.* 2 vols. Paris: Reinwald.

Mommsen, Katharina. 1964. *Goethe und der Islam.* Stuttgart: Klett.

—. 1967. "Goethes Bild vom Orient". *Der Orient in der Forschung. Festschrift für Otto Spies zum*

5. April 1966 ed. by Wilhelm Hoenerbach, 453–470. Wiesbaden: Harrassowitz.

—. 1988. *Goethe und die arabische Welt.* Frankfurt/M.: Insel.

Morgenländische Forschungen: Festschrift Herrn Professor Dr. H. L. Fleischer zu seinem fünfzigjährigen Doctorjubiläum am 4. März 1874 gewidmet von seinen Schülern Hartwig Derenbourg, Hermann Ethe, Otto Loth, August Müller, Friedrich Wilhelm Martin Philippi, Bernhard Stade, Heinrich Thorbecke. Leipzig: F. A. Brockhaus, 1875.

Müller, Friedrich Max. 1876. "Address before the Aryan Section of the International Congress of Orientalists, held in London in September, 1874". *Transactions of the Second Session of the International Congress of Orientalists* ed. by Robert K. Douglas, 177–204. London: Trübner & Co.

—. 1893. "Inaugural Address". *Transactions of the Ninth International Congress of Orientalists (held in London, 5th to 12th September 1892)* ed. by E. Delmar Morgan, 1–44. Oxford: Oxford Univ. Press.

—, ed. 1900. *The Sacred Books of the East: Including selections from the Vedic Hymns, Zend-Avesta, Dhammapada, Upanishads, the Koran, and the Life of Buddha.* With critical and biographical sketches by Epiphanius Wilson. Rev. ed. New York: Colonial Press.

—, ed. 1962–73 [1879–1883]. *The Sacred Books of the East. Transl. by various Oriental scholars and edited by Friedrich Max Müller.* 50 vols. New ed. New Delhi: Motilal Banarsidass.

Paret, Rudi. 1966. *Arabistik und Islamkunde an deutschen Universitäten: Deutsche Orientalisten seit Theodor Nöldecke.* Wiesbaden: Steiner.

Pargiter, Frederick Eden. 1923. *Centenary Volume of the Royal Asiatic Society of Great Britain and Ireland, 1823–1923.* London: The Society.

Paulsen, Friedrich. 1906. *The German Universities and University Study.* Transl. by Frank Thilly & William W. Elwang. New York: Charles Scribner's Sons.

Pearson, James Douglas. 1966. *Oriental and Asian Bibliography: An introduction with some reference to Africa.* London: Lockwood; Hamden, Conn.: Archon Books.

Peers, E. Allison. 1929. *Ramon Lull: A biography.* London: Society for Promoting Christian Knowledge.

Postel, Guillaume. 1538. *Grammatica Arabica.* Parisiis: Apud P. Gromorsum.

Raumer, Rudolf von. 1864. *Herr Professor Schleicher in Jena und die Urverwandtschaft der semitischen und indoeuropäischen Sprachen: Ein kritisches Bedenken.* Frankfurt/M.: Heyder & Zimmer.

Rawlinson, Sir Henry Creswicke. 1850. *Commentary on the Cuneiform Inscriptions of Babylonia and Assyria: Including readings of the inscription on the Nimrud obelisk, and a brief notice on the ancient kings of Nineveh & Babylon.* London: J. W. Parker.

Reiske, Johann Jacob. 1789–94. *Abul-Fedae Annales muslemici arabice et latine.* 5 vols. Copenhague: F. W. Thiele.

Renan, Ernest. 1858. *Histoire générale et système comparé des langues sémitiques.* Paris: Imprimerie Impériale.

Reuchlin, Johannes. 1506. *De rudimentis Hebraicis.* Pforzheim: Thomae Anshelmi.

—. 1518. *De accentibus, et orthographia, linguae Hebraicae [...] libri tres.* Hagenau: in aedibus Thomae Anshelmi Badensis.

Richter, Eberhardt & Manfred Reichardt, eds. 1979. *Hans Georg Conon von der Gabelentz: Erbe und Verpflichtung.* Berlin: Akademie der Wissenschaften.

Richter, Rudolf, ed. 1898 [1820]. *Goethe, West-östlicher Divan nebst den Noten und Abhandlungen.* Leipzig: Bibliographisches Institut.

Royal Asiatic Society of Great Britain and Ireland, London. 1893. *Catalogue of the Library of the Royal Asiatic Society of Great Britain and Ireland.* London: The Society.

—. 1926. *List of Members of the Royal Asiatic Society of Great Britain and Ireland, Founded in 1823.* London: Royal Asiatic Society of Great Britain and Ireland.

Rückert, Friedrich. 1896. *Werke in sechs Bänden.* Ed. by Conrad Beyer. Leipzig: Max Hesse.

Sachau, Eduard. 1893. "Orientalische Philologie". *Lexis* 1893: 507–528.

Schele de Vere, Maximilian. 1853. *Outlines of Comparative Philology.* New York: G. P. Putnam.

Schimmel, Annemarie et al. 1985. *Rückert zu Ehren: Zwischen Orient und Okzident.* Schweinfurt: Rückert-Gesellschaft.

Schlegel, Friedrich von. 1808. *Über die Sprache und Weisheit der Indier: Ein Beitrag zur Begründung der Alterthumskunde.* Heidelberg: Mohr & Zimmer. (Repr., with an introd. by Sebastiano Timpanaro, Amsterdam: Benjamus, 1977.)

Silvestre de Sacy, Antoine Isaac. 1799. *Principes de grammaire générale, mis à la portée des enfans, et propres à servir d'introduction à l'étude de toutes les langues.* Paris: A. A. Lottin. (6th ed., Paris: Bélin, 1832. Repr., Stuttgart-Bad Cannstadt: Frommann–Holzboog, 1975.)

—. 1839–40. *Les mille & une nuits: Contes arabes traduit en Français par Antoine Galland.* [...] Revus et corrigés sur l'édition princeps de 1704, augmentés d'une dissertation sur les Mille et une nuits. Paris: Ernest Bourdin.

Singh, Janardan Prasad. 1982. *Sir William Jones: His mind and art.* New Delhi: Chand & Co.

Smith, Lucy Margaret. 1930. *Cluny in the 11th and 12th Centuries.* London: Allan & Co.

Société asiatique. 1922. *Le livre du centenaire (1822–1922)*. Paris: Geuthner.

Soden, Wolfram von. 1952. *Grundriss der akkadischen Grammatik*. Rome: Pontificium Institutum Biblicum.

Sternemann, Reinhard. 1984. *Franz Bopp und die vergleichende indoeuropäische Sprachwissenschaft*. Innsbruck: Institut der Sprachwissenschaft der Universität.

Young, Thomas. 1823. *An Account of Some Recent Discoveries in Hierogryphical Literature and Egyptian Antiquities: Including the author's original alphabet, as extended by Mr. Champollion*. London: J. Murray.

Wach, Joachim. 1951. *Types of Religious Experience Christian and Non-Christian*. Chicago: Univ. of Chicago Press.

–. 1958. *The Comparative Study of Religions*. Ed. with an introduction by Joseph M. Kitagawa. New York & London: Columbia Univ. Press.

–. 1988. *Essays in the History of Religions*. Ed. by Joseph M. Kitagawa & Gregory D. Alles. New York: Macmillan.

Wahl, Samuel Friedrich Gunther. 1784. *Allgemeine Geschichte der morgenländischen Sprachen und Litteraturen [...]. Nebst einem Anhang zur morgenländischen Schriftgeschichte, mit elf Tafeln in Kupfer gestochner Alphabete*. Leipzig: J. G. I. Breitkopf.

Wilkins, Sir Charles. 1785. *Bhagvat-Gita or Dialogues of Krishna and Arjun*. London: C. Nourse.

–. 1808. *A Grammar of the Sanskrita Language*. London: W. Bulmer & Co.

–, ed. 1810. *A Vocabulary, Persian, Arabic, and English: Abridged from the quarto edition of John Richardson's dictionary*. London: F. & C. Rivington.

Windisch, Ernst. 1917–1920. *Geschichte der Sanskrit-Philologie und indischen Altertumskunde*. 2 vols. Strassburg: K. J. Trübner.

–. 1921. *Philologie und Altertumskunde in Indien: Drei nachgelassene Kapitel des III. Teils der Geschichte der Sanskrit-Philologie und indischen Altertumskunde*. (= *Abhandlungen für die Kunde des Morgenlandes* 15: 3.) Leipzig: Brockhaus. (Repr., Nendeln: Kraus, 1966.)

Winternitz, Moriz. 1910. *A General Index to the Names and Subject-Matter of the Sacred Books of the East*. Oxford: Clarendon Press. (= Vol. 50 of Müller 1962–1973 [1879–1883].)

Wolf, Friedrich August & Philipp Buttmann, eds. 1807. *Museum der Alterthums-Wissenschaft*. Vol. I: Friedrich August Wolf, *Darstellung der Alterthums-Wissenschaft nach Begriff, Umfang, Zweck und Wert*. Berlin: Realschulbuchhandlung.

Kurt R. Jankowsky, Washington, D.C. (U.S.A.)

155. La genèse de la grammaire comparée

1. Un tournant théorique
2. Le témoignage de Humboldt
3. Des idées nouvelles
4. Les principes de Bopp
5. La perspective de l'histoire
6. La comparaison des langues
7. L'accueil des contemporains
8. Les raisons du succès
9. Le 'décollage' de la grammaire comparée
10. Bibliographie

1. Un tournant théorique

Si l'on admet que la grammaire comparée est une discipline s'employant à grouper des langues supposées partager une histoire commune d'après des concordances grammaticales impliquant une analyse des morphèmes, il est clair que les multiples entreprises comparatives menées jusque dans les dernières du XVIIIe siècle, et souvent retracées (Koerner 1975, Droixhe 1978, Collinge 1995), n'offrent que des exemples de regroupements fondés sur les analogies lexicales. Le privilège d'avoir assis la démonstration de la parenté des langues indo-européennes sur des preuves tirées de leur fonctionnement grammatical doit revenir sans conteste à Franz Bopp (Gipper & Schmitter 1975, Morpurgo-Davies 1975). La révolution théorique qu'il a, ce faisant, suscitée était en tout cas une évidence pour ses contemporains.

2. Le témoignage de Humboldt

Pour mesurer l'évolution rapide connue par la linguistique de Friedrich Schlegel (1772–1829) en 1808 à Jacob Grimm (1785–1863) en 1822, suivons un observateur attentif, Wilhelm von Humboldt (1767–1835), très exigeant quant à ses méthodes et ses résultats. En 1812, il évoque la comparaison génétique des langues – l'un de ses domaines de recherche – en un constat désabusé:

"Es fehlt noch an festen Grundsätzen, die Verwandtschaftsgrade der Sprachen zu bestimmen; man ist noch zu wenig einig über die Zeichen, welche die Abstammung verschiedener Völker von einander beurkunden; man begnügt sich noch viel zu häufig mit der fragmentarischen Vergleichung einzelner Sitten, und ein paar Dutzend auf gut Glück aus einer Sprache herausgerissener Wörter." (Humboldt 1903–36 *GS* III, p. 290 [1812b])

Pour lui, la question, "inwieweit die Verwandtschaft unter den Sprachen mit einiger Gewissheit bestimmt, und an welchen Kennzeichen dieselbe erkannt werden kann?" n'a pas encore de réponse (*GS* VII/2 630–631 [1812–1814]). Or, sur ces mêmes techniques, dix ans plus tard, son jugement a changé, ainsi qu'en témoigne sa lettre à August Wilhelm Schlegel (1767–1845) du 19 mai 1822: il y souligne "die Wichtigkeit des grammatischen Baues bei Beurtheilung der Sprachabstammung", et fait de la grammaire "das sichere Fundament" pour y parvenir. Il distingue trois composants "aus welchem der grammatische Bau besteht": 1) ce qui tient aux idées grammaticales et qu'on peut décrire sans citer un seul son de la langue (existence d'un verbe substantif, d'un passif, d'un impersonnel); 2) les moyens techniques désignant ces idées grammaticales (affixes, inflexion interne, redoublement); 3) "die wirklichen Laute, die grammatische Bildungssilben" (*a*-privatif, désinences). Un accord sur ces trois points ne laisse aucun doute sur une parenté, mais, dans le cas contraire, le troisième critère est seul décisif:

"Dieser Theil der Grammatik scheint mir am meisten für die Verwandtschaft, oder dagegen zu beweisen, weil er der speciellste ist, und die Aehnlichkeit, oder Verschiedenheit daher am wenigsten allgemeine Gründe haben kann, sondern auf zufälligeren historischen beruhen muss." (Leitzmann 1908: 50–52)

On tient là une des certitudes les plus indéfectibles de Humboldt, dès lors constamment réaffirmée (*GS* VI/1 21 [1827]; 43 [1828a]; 80 [1828b]; 252 [1827–1829]).

Certes, pour lui, la diversité des langues exige une approche plus complexe, mais son propre 'Sprachstudium' suppose malgré tout la résolution préalable des questions de genèse. Si donc une innovation s'est produite dans cette période, qui a fait changer d'avis Humboldt, on doit aussi lui faire crédit quant au responsable de ce progrès. Or, chaque fois qu'il se félicite de cette promotion des formes grammaticales concrètes pour juger des parentés linguistiques, il renvoie à Bopp (1791–1867), avec les mêmes éloges appuyés (*GS* VI/1 43 [1828a]; 81 [1828b]; 252 [1827–1829]). C'est donc vers ce dernier qu'on se tournera pour éclairer l'apparition d'une technique comparative à visée historique opérée à l'aide des éléments de formation grammaticaux.

Plus tard, le programme de travail de la grammaire comparée consistera à (1) confronter les morphèmes lexicaux et grammaticaux de deux ou plusieurs langues, et, en cas d'analogies récurrentes pour la forme et le sens, (2) ramenées à des séries de correspondances régulières, à expliquer les écarts constatables par (3) une évolution phonétique différenciée mais systématique éprouvée par un (4) original commun disparu qu'on (5) reconstruit. Mais si toutes ces composantes, aujourd'hui encore indispensables, n'étaient évidemment pas déjà présentes ensemble quand s'esquisse le projet comparatif dont Humboldt salue l'émergence chez Bopp, l'une au moins, la première citée, l'était, dont la dynamique fut assez puissante pour déclencher un processus cumulatif permettant à la stratégie de comparaison grammaticale de s'imposer aux yeux des contemporains comme une démarche rigoureuse, à la fois inédite et probante.

3. Des idées nouvelles

Au moment où Bopp commence à étudier le sanscrit, en 1812, des innovations sont déjà constatables sous trois points de vue différents qui vont venir converger dans son travail.

3.1. D'abord pour l'analyse de la morphologie des langues. Après une longue stagnation, des auteurs aux motivations et aux présupposés théoriques très divers, usent, sur plusieurs langues, d'une nouvelle technique: une forme verbale est décomposée en éléments constituants minimums, chacun porteur d'un sens dont la totalisation détermine la signification globale de la forme ainsi découpée; en outre, en s'unissant avec le même sens à d'autres éléments, chaque constituant se retrouve dans d'autres formes. Une langue apparaît donc comme une combinatoire d'éléments premiers cachés derrière des formes, insécables en apparence, mais susceptibles en fait d'être segmentées en unités isolables et recomposables à l'infini. Un tel découpage s'applique à des langues à la riche morphologie: grec, français, arabe et hébreu, ou basque.

L'analyse est radicalement neuve — avant Friedrich Wilhelm von Thiersch (1784—1860) en 1808, aucune grammaire grecque ne présentait les paradigmes avec des tirets séparant les morphèmes — et elle apparaît aussitôt aux observateurs comme supérieure aux pratiques antérieures. Pourtant, à la seule exception des langues sémitiques, bien connues de Bopp, ce type d'analyse des morphèmes grammaticaux, quel que soit son enracinement théorique, reste rigoureusement synchronique.

3.2. Deuxième innovation récente, celle qui concerne les preuves de la parenté historique par la comparaison. Au XVIIIe siècle d'incontestables réussites avaient été obtenues par la seule confrontation du lexique. Qu'il s'agisse des langues sibériennes, du domaine finno-ougrien, ou des langues néo-indiennes, rapprochées du tsigane, la comparaison s'effectuait par liste de mots et l'intervention de certaines données morphologiques (marques de flexions) était secondaire pour établir une preuve déjà fournie par le lexique, la stratégie comparative ne partant pas d'un découpage des éléments de formation qui mènerait à leur confrontation. Or, depuis peu, se multiplient les appels à l'utilisation de la grammaire. Par ses prises de position théoriques, Christian Jacob Kraus (1753—1807) en 1787 en est un bon témoin, mais dans sa propre pratique, sur le tsigane, on le voit se contenter de rapprocher l'existence de catégories (Biester 1793). F. Schlegel, à cet égard, n'innove pas. Sa comparaison est encore toute lexicale, malgré ses appels à recourir à l'"innerste Structur und Grammatik" (Schlegel 1808: 3; v. également pp. 4, 9), et, quand il en évoque les 'Grundbestandtheile', il désigne par là des particules (9—11). Reste que l'insatisfaction à l'égard du lexique a grandi et que se manifeste la volonté d'asseoir aussi la comparaison sur les faits de grammaire.

3.3. Dernier point, la reconnaissance de l'ancienneté d'une langue qui autorise des rapprochements sur un vaste domaine linguistique. La parenté du sanscrit avec grec, latin, germanique, persan, et sans doute d'autres encore, est passée à cette date en évidence, grâce à William Jones (1746—1794), puis F. Schlegel, même si la question de l'origine reste en suspens: un ancêtre commun disparu pour le premier, ou le sanscrit comme langue mère de toutes les autres pour le second.

4. Les principes de Bopp

Au départ de l'entreprise de Bopp il y a une connaissance du sanscrit bien supérieure à celle de F. Schlegel. Là où celui-ci n'avait qu'une définition de la racine à géométrie variable très imprécise — considérant les désinences comme internes à la Racine ou intégrant sous cette étiquette (Wurzel) toute la famille des mots reconnus comme analogues dans les langues parentes — Bopp suit les grammairiens indiens et ne pose que des racines orthodoxes (*shru-*, *tap-*, *ad-*, *rudh-*, *bhû-*, *stu-*, *dru-*, *tud-*, etc.).

4.1. Du même coup sa définition de l'inflexion se clarifie. Certes, la racine subit des transformations internes, mais en très petit nombre: "the only real inflections which I consider possible in a language whose elements are monosyllables, are the change of their vowels and the repetition of their radical consonants, otherwise called reduplication" (Bopp 1820: 12). Pour le reste, la complexité des formes verbales par rapport à la simplicité de la racine qui y est incluse s'explique par des additions (1816: 13), insertions (p. 14) pré- ou postpositions. Allant du plus simple au plus complexe, Bopp constate ainsi que le présent sanscrit est formé d'une racine verbale, "durch blosse Anhängung der Personskennzeichen" (p. 13), puis il décrit les autres temps et modes selon un accroissement successif de ces deux unités (racine + marque de personne) constituant la forme verbale minimum, chacune d'elles étant, soit transformée (changement vocalique), soit enrichie d'éléments adjoints.

Pour présenter rationnellement toutes ces formes, Bopp introduit aussi un puissant principe d'organisation. La simplicité de la construction du présent le conduit à interpréter le sens global de ce temps comme une proposition logique: les deux unités équivalant à Prédicat et Sujet, le verbe est une proposition en miniature. *Ad-ti* équivaut à "mange-il": "In dem tempus praesens wird die Bedeutung der Wurzel durch keine Nebenbestimmung beschränkt; das Subjekt ist im wirklichen Genusse des durch die Wurzel bezeichneten Prädikats" (p. 13), et peu après, plus nettement encore: "The Latin verb *dat* expresses the proposition he gives or he is giving, the letter *t*, indicating the third person, is the subject, *da* expresses the attribute of giving" (1820: 14).

Ce cadre logique qui fournit la contrepartie sémantique de la mécanique des formations verbales par additions au schéma élémentaire unifie leur description. Tout nouveau trait de signification exprimé s'incarne, selon sa nature, en une marque formelle rattachée, soit à la racine, pour les rapports de temps, soit à la personne, pour le nombre (1816: 26). Et, en corrélat, toute forme conjuguée s'analyse comme une somme de tels traits, conférant à chaque temps ou mode une valeur originale définie par une formule individualisée.

4.2. La cerner suppose qu'on ait préalablement décomposé les formes en une suite d'unités minimums caractérisées par une forme et un sens. L'exposé de Bopp montre sur ce point la force de ses convictions rationalistes. La langue étudiée est une mécanique gouvernée par des lois, et forme un système. Dans la régularité et la cohérence dont le sanscrit témoigne pour agencer et combiner les éléments premiers dont sont bâties les formes verbales, rien ou presque n'est fortuit ou arbitraire. Dans cette langue à l'ancienneté exceptionnelle, si proche d'une origine conçue comme une perfection, tout obéit encore à une motivation première préservée. Un principe de correspondance bi-univoque entre son et sens est ainsi posé qui guide l'investigation. Chaque unité minimum associe forme et valeur sémantique avec constance et Bopp se propose de donner "den Grund jeder Formänderung" (p. 12). Il part d'une certitude: tout changement de sens implique une modification de forme (p. 37), et inversement (p. 12); par exemple, "nie kann im Sanskrit der Vokal eines Wortes geändert werden, ohne dass dadurch die Bedeutung desselben eine Modifikation erleide" (p. 22). De plus — idéalement tout au moins, car la langue se dérobe parfois — un même trait de signification aura toujours la même traduction formelle (30 – 31):

"Gleiche Bedingungen und Verhältnisse können und sollen in der Sprache durch gleiche Formen ausgedrückt werden, und wir dürfen dieses hier vorzüglich von der indischen Sprache erwarten, weil sie in gar vielen Fallen ähnliche Modifikationen der Bedeutung durch ähnliche Formveränderungen andeutet".

La langue se ramène ainsi à un stock d'unités combinables selon des lois à retrouver.

4.3. Le repérage des éléments et celui de la structuration sémantique justifiant leur co-présence sont alors indissociables, opèrent en interaction par validation mutuelle des résultats. A partir du schéma 'Prédicat + Sujet', qu'incarnent 'Racine + Désinence personnelle', et en identifiant, par comparaison interne, recoupements et permutations, de nouveaux éléments minimums récurrents dans la conjugaison sanscrite, Bopp grossit progressivement la somme de formes et significations dont chaque temps ou mode se compose.

Pourquoi, par exemple dans le potentiel actif *adjât* de la racine *ad-*, "manger", analyser ce *-jâ-* comme résultant de *-î + â-*? La comparaison avec le moyen *adîta*, où le *â* qui précédait à l'actif la marque de personne *-t* a disparu, prouve que la caractéristique générale du potentiel est un *î*; on posera donc *î > j* par euphonie devant *â*; ce que confirme le rapprochement avec la conjugaison thématique qui joint toujours une voyelle *-a-* à la racine: *patsh-* donne, à l'actif, *patshaet*, derrière lequel par application d'une autre règle d'euphonie (*aî > ae*) on restitue *patshaît*. Bopp procède toujours en se donnant deux marges de manœuvre. Pour les sons, des identités avérées en matière de signification feront tolérer une variation dans les formes et derrière les altérations phonétiques éventuelles, laisseront dégager l'invariant, la marque formelle unique diversement modifiée selon son entourage. Pour l'interprétation sémantique, d'evidentes analogies dans des formes de sens différent obligeront à retrouver, au prix d'une réinterprétation du patron sémantique qui les soustend, et par delà les divergences, un trait de signification commun. Si, par comparaison des formes actives et moyennes, il identifie derrière le *-jâ-* du Potentiel un *-î-*, dont l'insertion est la caractéristique formelle de ce mode en ce qu'il marque que le lien entre Sujet et Prédicat n'est pas réel, "sondern bloss in dem Geiste des Redenden bestehe, welcher sie entweder möglich achtet, oder wünscht, oder als nothwendige Bedingung voraussetzt u. s. w." (1816: 14), et qu'il retrouve au Futur la présence d'un *-i-*, il l'explique alors par une "Sinnverwandtschaft" (p. 31) et reconstruit le Futur comme un Potentiel avec des terminaisons de Présent, tandis que le Potentiel, "der Form wie der Bedeutung nach" (p. 33) unit les caractéristiques de base du Futur à celles de Prétérit (l'augment). Guidé par cette exigence et progressant ainsi de proximités formelles en reconstruction d'un sens commun ou de parentés de sens en variantes phonétiques, Bopp fait de la morphologie verbale un réseau d'éléments constitutifs — les unités figurant dans diverses configurations sémantiques ou environnements phonétiques – pourvus d'une forme et d'un sens stable. Ce premier type d'analyse, issue d'un croisement entre les nécessités dictées par une racine aux limites fermes et son identification à un Prédicat, relié à un Sujet (Personskennzeichen), est déjà porteur d'une logique propre de reconnaissance et de reconstruction des éléments de formation présents dans les paradigmes du verbe sanscrit.

4.4. Mais, plus décisif, il s'y joint une autre conviction qui constitue la trouvaille fondamentale de Bopp en 1815 (Lefmann 1895, *Anhang* 18*–21*). Les finales de certains temps sanscrits présentent une identité avec les formes du verbe être, ainsi, pour le 2º Prét. avec celles, au même temps, mais débarrassées de l'augment, d'*asti* (ibid. p. 18*–19*). Autre composition mentionnée dans l'appendice, in extremis: "Es scheint mir keinem Zweifel mehr unterworfen zu seyn, dass die Buchstaben, die ich in diesem Versuche Kennzeichen der Personen zu nennen pflegte, wirkliche Pronomina seyen" (1816: 147). Du coup, certaines formes verbales s'analysent comme composées à partir d'unités existant par ailleurs dans la langue à l'état isolé et dans une autre fonction. A la différence des unités découpées de manière structurale qui n'avaient d'existence que théorique, dès qu'on peut reconnaître dans certains éléments de véritables mots, alors, en puissance, tout élément isolé par décomposition peut avoir aussi été un mot. Les formes mêmes où on identifie ce phénomène changent de nature et de statut, car le mécanisme de type logique valable pour exposer le cadre sémantique de la conjugaison, mais non, jusqu'ici, pour expliquer la constitution des formes, est lui aussi à repenser. Ce sera fait en 1820, quand le cadre Prédicat-Sujet recoupera l'union Racine-verbe substantif, ce dernier se voyant décomposé quant à sa marque de personne: *potest* devient alors *pot-es-t* = Prédicat + verbe abstrait + sujet. Mais d'ores et déjà (1816: 20, 18; cf. p. 34), une forme verbale unissant une racine (*Stammsylbe*) à un verbe auxiliaire s'explique par une composition effectuée à échelle historique, et observable dans la langue même. En plusieurs formes verbales, le procès de constitution de la langue devient lisible, sa structure fournit des informations sur son passé. Aussitôt le système d'explication de Schlegel est ruiné. Certes, Bopp continue, après lui, à déclarer que le sanscrit exprime ses rapports grammaticaux "auf wahrhaft organische Weise durch innere Umbiegung und Gestaltung der Stammsilbe" (p. 7), et à proclamer l'existence de Flexions organiques (p. 37), mais leur champ d'application en est très limité. Un autre principe de formation est promu, la Composition, que précisément F. Schlegel récusait pour le sanscrit et qu'il pensait caractéristique de langues appartenant à d'autres souches déclarées inférieures.

5. La perspective de l'histoire

L'important est que cette trouvaille et la conviction qu'elle induit ouvrent une nouvelle voie à la recherche. Le découpage interne qui, en synchronie et aidé de la logique, identifiait des éléments par permutations et substitutions, devient un simple préalable. Si certains des éléments reconnus sont en réalité des unités existant aussi à l'état autonome (pronom ou verbe être), tout élément signifiant découpé dans les verbes peut désormais être confronté avec un mot plein qui fournira sa vraie valeur, eu égard à son origine. Reconnaître comme actif dans la langue un principe de composition concurrent à celui de l'inflexion primitive impose un doute systématique quant à la nature propre de toute unité isolée. De toute part, la langue invite aux rapprochements: toute variation devient suspecte, tout écart est à réduire par une construction le justifiant.

Si, en faisant l'objet d'une composition, des mots pleins ont perdu leurs caractéristiques d'origine pour devenir des unités liées, l'analyse structurale et synchronique change de nature, car les produits du découpage sémantico-formel deviennent susceptibles d'une explication historique. Dans la perspective schlégélienne l'inflexion restait inexplicable, sinon comme surgissement miraculeux. Fruit d'une origine préservée, elle obligeait à faire l'éloge du primitif. Le découpage sémantique ajouté par Bopp laissait peu de place à la variation issue d'une évolution, les unités identifiées étant par essence stables. La composition, elle, trahit l'évolution subie par la langue qui, dans la profondeur de son passé, a effectué des opérations sur ses propres matériaux. Rapprocher des morphèmes liés avec des unités autonomes requiert, en cas de différence entre les formes, une justification en termes de conservation d'un côté, d'altération de l'autre, c'est-à-dire une perspective proprement évolutive expliquant la genèse des formes par des dérives, des altérations connues sous l'action du temps. Le principe de composition posé par Bopp pour le sanscrit suppose l'existence d'un état antérieur où la composition ne s'était pas encore produite, où les éléments à composer avaient encore telle ou telle forme, tel ou tel mode d'existence comme mots autonomes, avant d'aboutir à la situation actuelle livrée par l'état de langue observé. L'espace de l'investigation subit donc une transformation radicale. Son axe s'est déplacé d'une comparaison latérale des formes, interne à la langue et qui identifie des éléments identiques, à une autre confrontation, latérale elle aussi dans son principe, mais qui exige une explication des écarts éventuels dans une perspective verticale d'évolution historique. Toute l'analyse fondée sur la composition doit intégrer la composante d'une transformation inhérente aux langues désormais vues en mouvement.

5.1. L'articulation du découpage structural avec l'hypothèse compositionnelle a pour effet majeur de démultiplier les trouvailles sorties de chacune des analyses. Si, selon la première, les variations constatées se réglaient par des ajustements invoquant l'euphonie et le flou inhérent à la signification, sans perspective historique, le rapprochement d'éléments minimums avec des mots multiplie les disparités que seule une profondeur temporelle justifie avec son oubli des origines et l'effacement des opérations effectuées dans la langue. L'évolution subie se donne aussitôt comme un parcours à retracer.

Certes l'analyse morphématique permettait déjà de remonter dans le passé immédiat. Si, aux trois nombres, la marque de troisième personne est *T* (Bopp 1816: 13), et que l'on constate, pour le premier prétérit de la racine *ad*, "manger", une 3. sg. *âdat* (< *a* + *ad* + *at*), en face de 3. pl. *âdan*; alors, en les rapprochant des mêmes personnes du présent, 3. sg. *atti* (< (*)*ad-ti*) et 3. pl. *ad-anti*, la relation des deux personnes, commune à chaque temps (*âd-an* doit s'opposer à *âd-at* comme *ad-anti* à *ad-ti*), jointe au parallélisme des temps, impose que la finale de *âdan* (prét.) soit à *adanti* (présent) ce qu'au singulier *âd-at* est à (*)*ad-ti*, avec comme conclusion "dass das Kennzeichen *T* verloren gegangen; *an* drückt blos die Vielheit aus, und [...] dass ursprünglich *âdant* gestanden habe" (p. 17). La forme (*)*adant* est donc une reconstitution menée d'après le principe de la quatrième proportionnelle, une forme hypothétique à poser de par la seule force interne de la logique inhérente à un système morphologique postulé régulier. La rationalité supposée à la langue conduit à juger l'organisation des formes "gemäss der Sprachanalogie, die wir mit strenger Gesetzmässigkeit befolgt finden" (p. 128).

5.2. Mais quand l'analyse interne et la composition potentialisent leurs effets respectifs, on entre dans une dynamique cumulative et la recréation du passé se traduit par des reconstitutions en cascade où le sémantisme et l'hypothèse de formation par composition se prêtent mutuellement appui. Bopp, après avoir découvert dans les terminaisons du deuxième prétérit le prétérit d'*asti*, s'enhardit à retrouver ailleurs le verbe être incorporé. Ainsi au deuxième futur, construit "durch Anhängung der Sylbe *sjâ*", on a, pour la racine *sthâ-*: *sthâ-sjati, -sjâsi, -sjâti*. Bopp y reconnaît, non pas une forme analogue du verbe être, mais une forme postulée avoir existé et qu'il restitue, "*sjâti* halte ich für das Futurum der Wurzel *as*, welches isolirt nicht mehr vorkommt" (p. 30). Elle est reconstituée sur la base de l'analyse sémantique du potentiel, plus haut évoquée. On posera qu'au futur aussi "die Handlung nicht wirklich verrichtet ist, das Subjekt nicht in wirklicher Beziehung mit der ausgedrückten Eigenschaft ist", et que "die Verbindung zwischen Subject und Prädikat bloss im Geiste des Redenden gedacht wird" (ibid.). Or, si le potentiel d'*asti* est bien *sjât, sjâh, sjâm*, etc., alors, en vertu de la combinatoire sémantico-formelle, les finales *-sjâti, -sjâsi, sjâmi* doivent être "das Futur. des verb. abstract. seyn, das in Gemässheit der Sinnverwandtschaft auch in der Form mit dem Potential im Wesentlichen übereinstimmte" (p. 31). Cette première reconstruction en autorise une seconde, pour le conditionnel, où *asthâsjat* s'analyse comme un futur qui aurait aussi un augment et une désinence de premier prétérit. Non seulement Bopp y voit un composé dont il engendre la forme en reconstruisant son sémantisme – "dieser modus vereinigt, der Form wie der Bedeutung nach, den Charakter des Futurum mit dem Präteritum" (p. 33) – mais il invoque pour cela une forme du verbe être qu'il recrée en la dérivant d'une autre déjà postulée: dans le conditionnel *asthâsjat*, "*asjat* muss der modus condit. des verb. *Asti* gewesen seyn, der nicht mehr einzeln vorkommt" (ibid.). La reconstitution est de second degré, s'effectue à partir d'une forme de futur déjà restituée.

Plusieurs facteurs sont en convergence: la composition fournit un horizon d'attente et suggère une hypothèse pour interpréter une désinence; la proportion constante de la forme et du sens dans un cadre sémantique modulable permet de réinterpréter des catégories pour intégrer des différences apparentes (le -*i*- peut marquer potentiel et futur); l'analyse morphologique par substitutions et permutations fournit des matériaux (les marques de personnes repérables à d'autres temps ou modes) qui sont combinables dans une forme inédite légitimée par l'existence générale du principe de composition, et adossée à la comparaison interne. A quoi s'ajoute la caution extérieure du grec et du gotique. La reconstruction d'un état antérieur suivi d'une disparition de la forme du verbe être à l'état isolé constitue une hypothèse sur l'histoire de la langue et Bopp est conscient d'avoir cherché à établir une preuve "theoretisch" (p. 32).

6. La comparaison des langues

Jusque là, il faut le souligner, la méthode de Bopp et ses acquis ne doivent rien à la comparaison des langues. Sa trouvaille essentielle ne sort nullement d'une visée comparative et sa découverte du verbe substantif dissimulé dans les formes verbales sanscrites, couplée à une démarche rationaliste d'inspiration, a suffi à déclencher un mouvement d'investigation généralisée qui, d'abord appliquée au sanscrit, s'est ensuite portée sur des langues qui offraient a priori avec celui-ci assez d'analogies pour justifier le transfert d'une méthode déjà productive de résultats tangibles. L'essentiel des découvertes de Bopp s'est donc opéré par examen rigoureusement interne au sanscrit: repérer des éléments par décomposition et reconnaître dans les flexions des unités autonomes par ailleurs, dégager les identités dissimulées derrière des variations, proposer des découpages, isoler des morphèmes grammaticaux, tenter des restitutions, aucun de tous ces succès ne mobilise, dans le premier chapitre, une autre langue. La comparaison est seconde dans l'exposé comme elle l'a été dans l'ordre de la découverte.

Pourtant, fort de certitudes acquises en sanscrit, Bopp passe en revue les autres langues pour y reconnaître des faits similaires. Conformément à sa première démonstration et selon les mêmes méthodes, il suit deux pistes: l'existence d'un double système d'expression des formes grammaticales (l'un organique, l'autre par composition), et le découpage en unités significatives coordonnées par un patron logique. Mais comme le chemin a été frayé avec succès, l'investigation n'est plus que de reconnaissance. Rééditer l'analyse sur le grec, le latin ou le germanique ou projeter simplement des conclusions sanscrites en matière d'unités et de mécanismes, c'est tout un. En chaque langue examinée, Bopp retrouve le reflet d'éléments déjà isolés en sanscrit avec une fonction significative bien cernée, ainsi que l'omniprésence de la composition d'éléments jadis autonomes. Ces repérages valent aussi confirmation, car ils valident les analyses produites sur le sanscrit.

La comparaison transversale, de langue à langue, loin d'être un projet spécifique de Bopp est donc bien plutôt une conséquence fortuite de découvertes en sanscrit qui ne lui doivent rien, elle découle simplement de l'approche structurale déjà devenue historique du fait de la composition, dès qu'on l'applique à des langues reconnues depuis longtemps comme similaires. L'examen successif des autres langues est moins une comparaison par rapport au sanscrit qu'une comparution devant le système d'explication qu'il y a cerné. De ce point de vue l'innovation d'*Analytical Comparison* sera significative, car Bopp y bouleversera le plan du *Conjugationssystem*, les langues n'étant plus examinées séparément, mais traitées toutes ensemble pour chaque formation verbale. Ce qui constitue l'acte de naissance de la comparaison.

6.1. Partout où cela est possible, dès 1816, Bopp retrouve, en grec, latin, germanique ou persan, un correspondant à ce qu'il a constaté en sanscrit: racines ou éléments de formation. Les résultats du point de vue de la comparaison sont variables. Il peut s'agir de la reconnaissance d'une identité entre sanscrit et grec: *tan*/*tan*, *tup*/*tup* (Bopp 1816: 62), ou d'une projection à partir du sanscrit posant comme 'racine' en grec une forme (*da*-) que *didômi* n'impose pas et qui n'émane que du sanscrit, *dâ*- dans *dadâti* (ibid.), racine qui vaut comme reconstruction. Ou encore d'une équivalence entre forme grecque et sanscrite, intégrant une différence, selon une correspondance, c'est le cas des marques de participe: -*tar* (en sanscrit) / -*tor* (en latin) (p. 27). L'innovation est déjà perceptible quand le sanscrit propose dans un mécanisme de formation une proportionnalité attestée pour d'autres racines verbales. Quand Bopp reconstruit alors en grec une racine *phan-*, à partir de l'aoriste *ephêna*, il le fait sur la base de l'alternance constatée au prétérit 2 sanscrit: *shru-* / *ashrâvit* (p. 65) et il projette seulement sur le grec une *Bildungsweise* (par renforcement de la voyelle radicale) du sanscrit.

Mais surtout des formes sanscrites attestées ou restituées aimantent les analyses, dictant ce qu'il faut attendre, non par décalque dans des unités bien visibles, mais par restitution derrière celles qu'on constate. Deux perspectives de recherche sont alors en jeu, et en conjonction: l'analyse interne du grec ou du latin d'une part, selon la méthode qui, en sanscrit, repérait et rétablissait des formes au nom d'une cohérence interne; de l'autre, le modèle sanscrit qui, en tant qu'état à rejoindre, fournit, pour déchiffrer les formes disponibles dans les langues censées le refléter, un cadre à remplir. Quand une forme sanscrite existante conduit à poser, pour la forme grecque déclarée analogue, une forme antérieure – *edidôn* en face de l'indien *adadâm* exige un ancien (*)*edidôm* (p. 63) – la reconstitution interne est appelée par le sanscrit. mais le double gage de la logique interne et du modèle sanscrit vaut encore si ce dernier est le produit d'une reconstitution.

6.2. Lorsque Bopp cherche à prouver le transfert du principe de composition, son analyse s'autonomise, car les formes grecques ou latines n'ont pas de correspondant direct en sanscrit. Le latin *essem* est ainsi déclaré issu d'un hypothétique *esem* (à partir de *esam* ou *eram*), "durch Einfügung des den Conjunktiv bildenden *I*" (p. 92) et la forme *esa-i-m* est reconstruite sur la triple base d'un même principe actif dans les deux langues, de la parenté des sens en jeu dans les formes verbales des deux langues, et d'un élément *-I-* si bien attesté en sanscrit qu'on est fondé à le chercher partout où sa signification peut être impliquée dans la formation.

De même, dans l'aoriste grec *etup-sa, -sas, -se*, Bopp cherche d'abord un fait de composition: le *-s-* doit être, comme en sanscrit, le radical du verbe abstrait. Ensuite, aussi bien à l'aide du sanscrit *ataup-sam, -sah, -sat* que des terminaisons grecques de moyen *-sam-ên, -sas-o, -sat-o*, il retrouve derrière *-sa*, un ancien *-sam* et derrière *-se, -sat*. Se rencontrent ici la pression extérieure des formes sanscrites et l'application aux données du grec du principe de cohérence. Chez Bopp la reconstitution interne est souvent inséparable de la projection des données sanscrites. Ses reconstructions ne sortent donc pas d'un examen comparatif mené de forme à forme entre deux langues, elles s'appuient d'abord sur l'assise théorique élaborée pour le sanscrit. Bopp cherche en d'autres langues ce que le sanscrit a si bien illustré.

6.3. L'important est qu'il découvre parfois des données absentes en sanscrit. La logique des reconstructions une fois lancée, une véritable parité de statut entre les unités reconnues ou reconstituées en grec, latin, germanique ou en sanscrit tend à s'établir: en toute langue se retrouvent les échos d'un passé inégalement ou diversement conservé. Dès qu'on reconstruit des formes reflétant un même principe d'engendrement, la notion d'un passé commun à toutes les langues s'impose, car la suspicion devient forte qu'outre les exportations à partir du sanscrit et la généralisation du principe, on a également affaire à des différences produites dans un espace historique commun aux langues confrontées.

En 1816, Bopp ne parle du sanscrit qu'en terme d'*Ursprache* (p. 96), et les autres langues, "die mit dem Sanskrit in engster Verwandtschaft stehen" (p. 9), langues "mit dem Sanskrit verwandten" (p. 32), sont données comme "mit der altindischen gemeinschaftlichen Ursprunges" (p. 7). S'il entend montrer que "an allen Sprachen, die von dem Sanskrit, oder mit ihm von einer gemeinschaftlichen Mutter abstammen, keine Verhältnissbestimmung durch eine Flexion ausgedrückt werde, die ihnen nicht mit jener Ursprache gemein sey" (p. 9), le second terme de l'alternative reste théorique. Dans *Analytical Comparison*, quatre ans après, il rectifie sa position (Bopp 1820: 15):

"I do not believe that the Greek, Latin, and other European languages are to be considered as derived from the Sanskrit in the state in which we find it in Indian books; I feel rather inclined to consider them altogether as subsequent variations of one original tongue, which however, the Sanskrit has preserved more perfect than in its kindred dialects. [avec cette conséquence que] "whilst the Sanskrit has preserved many grammatical forms, which can be supposed to have formerly existed in Greek, Latin, Gothic & c. there are instances where the reverse is the case, where the grammatical forms, lost in the Sanskrit, have been preserved in Greek or Latin."

En pareil cas, si le grec conserve ce que le sanscrit a perdu, comme la désinence de moyen *-mai* qui oblige à reconstruire *b'avamê* derrière le *b'avê* sanscrit (p. 16), le sanscrit n'est plus qu'un témoin privilégié par son ancienneté. Il glisse de sa position initiale d'ancêtre du grec vers une autre, où il se tient à ses côtés, même si c'est en retrait chronologique. S'ouvre alors un nouvel espace de recherche pour toutes ces langues, comme auparavant il s'en était ouvert un pour le passé des formes sanscrites après l'analyse interne qui révélait le changement de statut d'unités passées de l'autonomie à la composition.

Le mérite essentiel de Bopp est d'avoir articulé la perspective évolutive et historique prise sur une langue donnée à l'aide des découpages structuraux avec l'approche comparative de langue à langue. A nouveau, les deux modes d'investigation s'épaulent mutuellement. Chaque langue apparentée est certes pourvue d'une histoire propre, d'une évolution particulière à retracer, mais toutes ensemble constituent des témoignages différents et d'intérêt analogue sur une histoire commune qu'elles contribuent à retracer. Elles révèlent un espace commun de variation parallèle et différenciée à partir d'une origine commune à reconstruire. On est loin de la vision linéaire d'une filiation verticale entre les données du sanscrit et celles des autres langues, qui allait de pair avec un fixisme projetant l'état d'une langue préservée sur l'écran de l'origine. Par rapport à F. Schlegel, l'ouverture de la perspective est donc double: une langue est prise dans deux axes, l'un historique et individuel, l'autre transversal, de similitude avec des langues congénères, et ces deux dimensions définissent un espace historique global, un lieu de convergence commune vers l'origine partagée et aussi, à partir de celle-ci, de divergence, à rendre cohérente en fonction de la solidarité des langues.

6.4. Pour l'heure, en 1816, aucune forme archétypale n'est encore issue directement d'une comparaison de langue à langue, du fait de la prééminence du sanscrit et de sa proximité par rapport à l'origine. A l'occasion, quand Bopp repère une identité, il la pose sous une forme synthétique: l'aoriste passif grec est dérivé d'un participe de sens passif "welches der indischen und allen ihr verwandten Sprachen gemeinschaftlich ist, und das aus der Wurzel durch Anhängung des Consonanten *T* ou *D* gebildet wird" (Bopp 1816: 68−69), celui qu'attestent les diverses langues, *Datah, dotheis, datus, dadêh*. L'identité première n'est pas retrouvée derrière une diversité qui serait vue comme caractérisée par une correspondance selon un écart constant.

Pourtant une confrontation générale des langues conduisant à une conclusion inédite pour chacune est déjà inscrite dans la pratique de Bopp, et dès que le sanscrit perd son privilège, glisse au statut de langue sœur aînée, l'émergence de formes primitives déterminées par les données de plusieurs langues devient possible. Le prétérit 2 sanscrit, *tutôpa* (1 et 3 sg.) *tutupa* (2 pl.), croisé avec le parfait grec dont le moyen conserve les "characteristics *m* and *t*, which are followed by the termination *ai*: *lelumai, lelegtai, lelutai, lelegtai*", conduit ainsi Bopp en 1820 à poser ceci (p. 35):

"[...] I consider that the omission of the pronominal signs in three different persons, in Sanskrit, was not a defect of the language in the primitive state, whilst Greek, Latin, Teutonic, Sanskrit, & c. still continued one and the same speech. In that remote age *tutôpa*м, *tutôpa*т, *tutupa*та, or *tutupi*та, or something similar, may perhaps have occupied the place of those mutilated forms we have mentioned. At least the Greek can boast of having preserved in the second person plural its usual τε; τετύπατε is therefore certainly older, and more in conformity with the constant analogy of the Greek and Sanskrit languages, than the Indian tutupa."

De même, Bopp touche à l'histoire des langues en général quand il constate "die allmählige und stufenweise Zerstörung des einfachen Sprachorganismus" (1816: 11) et l'inéluctable substitution à la Flexion du principe agglutinatif et des unions mécaniques. Il entrevoit alors une vision évolutionniste des types (pp. 95−96, 101, 104): une langue se définit non seulement par sa nature propre, mais encore par son degré d'avancement le long d'un parcours obligé.

Bopp s'est ainsi trouvé par hasard à la croisée de perspectives qui lui ouvraient, avec la voie de l'origine des flexions, également celle d'une comparaison réelle de langue à langue des structures grammaticales, appuyée qu'elle était sur un découpage en morphèmes. Mais en dernière instance c'est bien son analyse morphologique qui a été décisive pour le décollage de la linguistique comparative.

De ce point de vue ni les correspondances phonétiques incontestablement posées par Rasmus Rask (1787−1832) avant lui, ni l'écrasante supériorité des matériaux rassemblés par Grimm et les lois phonétiques qui en découlent dans la seconde édition du premier volume de sa *Deutsche Grammatik* en 1822, n'étaient, pour amorcer la réalisation du programme comparatif, porteurs de la même dynamique que l'analyse morphématique réalisée sur le sanscrit puis sur les langues apparentées.

7. L'accueil des contemporains

Les acquis de Bopp − ses décompositions − et leur cortège de révélations sur l'histoire des formes grammaticales étaient, dans leur principe heuristique, d'inspiration foncièrement rationaliste, sinon mécaniste. Or, ils seront reconnus comme valides par d'autres linguistes, dont les présupposés 'romantiques' sur le fonctionnement et la genèse du langage étaient, du moins en apparence, à l'opposé de la pratique positiviste de Bopp.

7.1. Il faut mentionner que Bopp, même sans jamais se référer à lui nommément, partage et évoque comme des évidences les conceptions de F. Schlegel sur le caractère, non seulement primitif, mais originellement motivé de la langue sanscrite. S'il ne pose pas un lien nécessaire entre la forme et le sens des racines, il souligne néanmoins le pouvoir signifiant autonome des syllabes de Flexion, "der lebendige Sinn und die wahre Bedeutsamkeit der grammatischen Formen" (Bopp 1816: 37), qu'elles tirent d'une motivation première (p. 95):

"Der Ursprung organischer Flexionen [...] muss so wie die Entstehung der bedeutenden Stammsylben bey dem frühesten Ursprung der Sprache gesucht werden, wenn man nicht annehmen will, dass man einer willkührlichen und zufälligen Zusammenstellung von Buchstaben diese oder jene Bedeutung gegeben habe, und dass die grammatischen Formen das Resultat einer getroffenen Uebereinkunft seyen."

Et, "wenn der Genius der Sprache mit bedachtsamer Vorsicht die einfachen Begriffe der Personen mit einfachen Zeichen dargestellt hat [...] so erhellet daraus, dass der Buchstabe ursprünglich Bedeutung hatte, und dass er seiner Urbedeutung getreu blieb" (p. 147), on s'explique aussi que, pour exprimer le concept de personne dans le verbe, ait été choisie la lettre "die, welche seit dem Ursprung der Sprache die ihm auszudrückenden Begriffe mit vollständiger Klarheit darstellten." (p. 148). Pour les unités composées, la motivation est même double: à une fondation première du sens de chacune s'ajoutent les raisons qui président à leur composition. D'où le soupçon qu'elle existait "schon in dem Fundamente der Sprache" (Lefmann 1895, *Anhang*, p. 32*), hypothèse qu'appuie le fait que l'esprit actuel de la langue sanscrite l'interdit (Bopp 1816: 30).

Bopp choisit donc de placer les Flexions dans la même couche chronologique de constitution de la langue que les Racines, contrairement à une longue tradition qui les déclarait postérieures. Tout élément repéré ou reconstruit est aussitôt porté au compte de l'origine. Un renversement fondamental s'opère alors. Au lieu d'une reconstruction *a priori* qui redescendait de l'origine postulée vers les formes disponibles, mais restait toujours impuissante à s'y incarner − approche favorite du XVIIIe siècle, mais encore saisissable chez Johann Christoph Adelung (1732−1806), A. I. Silvestre de Sacy (1758−1838) ou J.-P. Abel-Rémusat (1788−1832) − Bopp illustre la possibilité d'identifier toute unité découpée par analyse interne comme une parcelle de la langue originelle parvenue jusqu'à nous, plus ou moins altérée. En donnant à ses découpages rationnels incontestables comme une onction d'*Ursprache*, celle-ci paraissant valider ceux-là, Bopp les rendait acceptables aux lecteurs les plus épris de mystique primitive. Dans la mesure où les fragments reconnus par lui porteurs de signification leur apparaissaient aussi comme des éléments premiers pourvus de tous les traits d'une mythologie de l'origine, ceux de ses contemporains qui se revendiquaient de cette dernière ont pu, au prix d'une ambiguïté non clarifiée, approuver sans trouble une théorie dont les références avouées se rattachaient à des thèses familières et dont les conclusions se prêtaient aisément à une interprétation plus conforme à leurs désirs. Par là, Bopp a assuré à ses thèses une audience inattendue, et a permis que se rejoignent deux enracinements théoriques pourtant antagonistes − rencontre féconde qui a été l'une des conditions d'un essor rapide de la discipline. Par une équivoque fortuite, s'est donc trouvé dégagée une perspective pour la recherche morphologique dans un cadre mental qui, jusqu'alors, l'excluait.

7.2. Très peu d'années ont suffi pour que la technique d'analyse des formes en éléments constitutifs devienne d'évidence. Les auteurs qui, à des titres divers, détenaient une autorité à parler des questions de langues, W. v. Humboldt, August Wilhelm Schlegel et J. Grimm, entérinent, même sans en accepter tous les détails ni toutes les conséquences, la pratique de Bopp — souvent d'ailleurs en la mettant au compte des seuls grammairiens indiens, ce qui les dispense d'une allégeance trop directe — et surtout la considèrent comme indispensable à cette connaissance de la structure interne des langues qui est devenue leur premier souci.

Chacun de ces auteurs fait subir, à partir de 1816, à sa propre théorie des transformations souvent considérables et, par de nombreux remaniements, un corps de doctrine commun relativement homogène se cristallise rapidement. Humboldt abandonne l'hypothèse évolutionniste d'une filiation linéaire des langues par dépassement successif de différents stades de perfection; Grimm passe d'étymologies 'à la [Johann Arnold] Kanne [(1773−1834)], justement dénoncées par A. W. Schlegel en 1815, à une rigueur méthodologique faite d'exhaustivité dans la collecte de matériaux historiques; A. W. Schlegel, enfin, délaisse la référence à l'*Ursprache*, naguère encore omniprésente, pour la philologie indienne.

Tous, au-delà de réticences à l'encontre de Bopp qui tiennent à des motifs personnels, comme dans le cas de Schlegel, lui décernent un brevet de 'scientificité' qu'ils dénient à leurs prédécesseurs, et — point plus décisif encore — se le décernent mutuellement. Entre 1820 et 1826, soit de l'*Analytical Comparison* au tome II de la *Deutsche Grammatik*, avec les premiers morceaux de la *Vergleichende Zergliederung* de Bopp, les mémoires de Humboldt à l'Académie de Berlin, ainsi que les écrits de Schlegel recueillis dans son *Indische Bibliothek* (1820−1830) on pourrait mesurer, par de multiples éloges et citations réciproques, à quel point s'établit entre eux un véritable réseau de références croisées qui traduit une indéniable connivence théorique. Convaincus que ce qui les sépare en bloc de nombre de leurs contemporains, Johann Severin Vater (1772−1826) ou Julius Klaproth (1783−1835), est plus essentiel que ce qui peut les opposer sur des points de détails, et détenteurs d'une légitimité neuve, tous affirment qu'une étape vient d'être franchie, délimitant un avant et un après dans la recherche qui les occupe. A tous, qu'il s'agisse de Humboldt dans une importante lettre à A. W. Schlegel du 23 juillet 1821 (Leitzmann 1908: 15), d'A. W. Schlegel lui-même (1846−1847 XII 434 [1815]; 1913: 31−32 [1818−1819]), ou de Grimm (1822: 19), deux traits apparaissent comme essentiels: la connaissance de la structure du sanscrit a été déterminante dans les progrès décisifs récemment effectués; la dissection des formes et l'identification des unités minimales de signification les composant est le préalable de l'étude grammaticale.

7.3. Pour expliquer une reconnaissance aussi rapide, on peut certes invoquer l'évidence du vrai. Ce que repère Bopp en sanscrit, grec, latin ou gotique, avait le plus souvent, hormis des rapprochements aventureux, un fondement objectif dans la morphologie de ces langues. Mais l'adhésion d'une poignée de contemporains à une approche atomiste qui aurait dû heurter leurs convictions dépend surtout du fait qu'ils retrouvaient chez Bopp des présupposés identiques aux leurs et que ses 'mécanismes' grammaticaux semblaient s'en déduire, voire même venir les confirmer.

La figure de l'origine a en effet connu dans la seconde moitié du XVIIIe siècle une inversion majeure, puisqu'à l'image rationaliste de la table rase s'est substituée celle d'un surabondance première qui a plaqué sur les langues un modèle centré sur la profusion et la fécondité. Ces images, qui réhabilitaient la dignité du primitif, ont servi, au-delà, pour promouvoir les langues sur lesquelles était projetée cette priorité chronologique. Mieux encore, cette origine est parfois à portée de l'observation, exceptionnellement préservée. Chez Humboldt (*GS* III 323 [1812a]), August Wilhelm Schlegel (1913: 29−30 [1818−1819]) et Grimm (1822: 781) est clairement lisible la conviction que dans les langues éminemment anciennes, sanscrit, langues classiques ou gotique, certains éléments — lettres ou syllabes — ont une origine qui remonte à un enracinement primitif de la signification dans un lien naturel.

En outre, leur fondation première confère à ces fragments d'origine une valeur éminente qui leur assure une perpétuation surprenante à travers les âges et qui en fait de précieux témoignages d'une antériorité absolue (Humboldt *GS* IV 143 [1820−1821]; V 287 [1826]; A. W. Schlegel 1913: 25, 29−30 [1818−1819]).

Par rapport à cette adhésion commune, l'opposition, souvent soulignée, d'A. W. Schlegel à la thèse boppienne de la composition doit d'ailleurs être considérablement nuancée. Les syllabes flexionnelles ont bien, pour Schlegel, un sens propre, et, il n'y voit plus, comme son frère Friedrich, des modifications 'internes' de la racine, mais bien des éléments accolés à celle-ci (Leitzmann 1908: 63−74 [1822]). Simplement, il refuse de les expliquer comme provenant de mots auparavant employés isolément, considérant, là où de tels rapprochements sont possibles, que c'est au contraire par détachement que l'autonomisation s'est produite (p. 64).

Sur cette question de l'origine et sur sa présence tangible en certaines langues postulées primitives, les auteurs se retrouvent, par delà leurs préoccupations divergentes: Humboldt désireux de fonder en raison un discours sur les différences essentielles des langues, Schlegel d'asseoir sur les grammairiens indiens la philologie sanscrite, Grimm de retracer le développement des dialectes germaniques et de la langue allemande à patir du gotique. Or, dans les écrits de Bopp, le seul comparatiste pur, mais tout aussi imbu d'une mythologie de l'origine, ils identifiaient ces thèses devenues banales, et trouvaient en outre des unités de sens que lui-même rapportait à un fondement antérieur à toute expérience. Il n'est donc pas surprenant que, pour ses lecteurs, ces découpages, déjà validés par d'incontestables acquis, aient paru découler de leurs propres présupposés, alors qu'ils venaient d'un tout autre horizon conceptuel. L'illusion d'optique ainsi créée, qui rendait l'analyse morphologique indissociable d'un éloge de l'organisme primitif, dont elle constituait même la plus éclatante illustration, a servi à ménager une fusion sans heurts entre une approche d'esprit mécaniste, strictement rationaliste, et l'idéologie romantique. Grâce à ce malentendu infiniment fécond la technique de base de l'étude des structures grammaticales et, avec elle, la condition d'un exercice efficace de la comparaison, se sont donc diffusées quasi subrepticement, dans le sillage de ce qui pouvait passer pour une nouvelle conquête de la mystique de l'origine.

8. Les raisons du succès

Si l'on peut, avec quelque vraisemblance, attribuer à cette méprise la réception rapide de Bopp et l'accueil que lui réservèrent ceux qui avaient alors, plus que lui, autorité pour parler du langage — audience dont témoignent sa nomination à l'Université de Berlin, puis son élection à l'Académie, à l'initiative de Humboldt — il n'en est pas moins nécessaire d'évoquer les raisons d'ensemble qui ont pu muer des questions de langage, à la limite aussi infimes, en cette puissante discipline de l'institution universitaire allemande que fut tout au long du XIXe siècle la grammaire comparée des langues indo-germaniques.

Plusieurs facteurs d'ordre institutionnels et idéologiques paraissent pertinents pour cette explication. En premier lieu le vivier professoral de l'université allemande, suffisamment riche pour qu'y apparaissent des individus porteurs de mutations théoriques et que s'y diffusent des innovations. Deux domaines s'y prêtaient. Celui des 'langues orientales' d'abord, qui formaient un champ de recherche très productif: entre arabe, chaldéen, syriaque et hébreu s'effectuait un travail de comparaison grammaticale qui, initialement destiné à éclairer l'exégèse biblique, avait acquis son autonomie et possédait une tradition et des techniques propres, qu'attestent au XVIIIe siècle des dizaines de grammaires de ces langues récemment ramenées par August Ludwig von Schlözer (1735−1809) à l'unité 'sémitique'. Ensuite, l'essor d'une nouvelle discipline, l'histoire universelle, autour de l'école de Göttingen, qui fait de l'étude des langues une science auxiliaire de l'histoire en s'efforçant d'introduire dans leur utilisation la même rigueur à l'œuvre pour les autres documents, afin d'éclairer par elles l'origine des peuples, leurs mélanges et migrations.

De plus, en pays germanique, les nouvelles données linguistiques étaient placées dans un horizon valorisant systématiquement tout ce qui venait nourrir une vision du primitif assumant une fonction idéologique essentielle. Dans cette Allemagne des princes, morcelée à l'infini, s'était imposé, auprès des intellectuels, un besoin de compenser l'absence de perspective d'unification et l'impuissance de l'action politique. Il avait trouvé son exutoire et son refuge dans la constitution d'une figure idéale qui, reversée dans le passé, reprenait les traits de l'unité inatteignable ardemment désirée. Quelque part, à l'origine, dans une antériorité radicale, inaccessible à l'observation, était pourtant fondée la possibilité d'une Allemagne future et imaginaire, enfin réconciliée. Ce mythe d'origine extrêmement puissant cherchait à s'attirer tous les matériaux disponibles. C'est l'Inde qui, au premier chef, a bénéficié de ce mouvement d'assimilation hégémonique. D'abord par les secrets enfouis qu'elle pouvait révéler en matière de vérités philosophiques et religieuses d'ordre supérieur, puis par sa langue où se lit encore la révélation. Une identification naturelle de l'Allemagne à l'Inde (A. W. Schlegel 1884: 80 [1802−1803]) en résulta. Or, quant à la langue, les efforts entrepris pour constituer l'allemand en langue de culture à part entière, ainsi que pour en restituer le passé, efforts propres à tout mouvement de nationalisme linguistique, trouvèrent dans la langue indienne un moyen de liquider une oppression rendue encore plus insupportable depuis l'invation napoléonienne. La possibilité de poser une équation entre gotique et sanscrit offrit une occasion inespérée pour trancher le lien de subordination de l'allemand au français, et même au latin. La langue nationale se retrouva à parité d'ancienneté, de donc de perfection, avec grec ou sanscrit, grâce à toutes les vertus de l'origine dont elle pouvait, au même titre qu'elles, se parer. Les thèses sur la langue qui fleurissent alors dans les leçons berlinoises d'A. W. Schlegel, puis les adresses enflammées de Johann Gottlieb Fichte (1762−1814), ne sont rien d'autre qu'une continuation du mouvement d'émancipation de la Réforme par d'autres moyens. Aucun autre peuple ne puisait, à la même époque, dans l'étude d'une langue ancienne autant de satisfaction pour le besoin impérieux d'asseoir un discours valorisant sur sa propre langue.

9. Le 'décollage' de la grammaire comparée

C'est cette idéologie en effervescence qui explique finalement l'émergence rapide de la linguistique comparative et historique comme discipline reconnue et pratiquée par un nombre grandissant de professionnels. L'analyse morphologique de Bopp qui est à son principe s'est donc située dans une conjoncture spécifique qui a précisément fait défaut à des prédécesseurs comme Thiersch, insoucieux d'origine. Reliée qu'elle était à trois ensembles thématiques d'extension théorique croissante, l'approche de Bopp s'est assurée une assise de plus en plus large et une audience accrue. Ainsi, sa thèse de la Composition qui avait fait ses preuves sur les langues sémitiques eut d'abord pour lui le mérite de cautionner ses premiers découpages sanscrits. Ensuite, la conviction d'une origine privilégiée et organique des langues étudiées a relayé pour des interlocuteurs prestigieux ces premiers acquis, en autorisant une assimilation à leur propre démarche. Enfin, le désir exacerbé chez toute une génération de trouver dans la langue les voies d'un salut intellectuel les a poussés à saisir avidement ces résultats comme autant de confirmations de leurs vœux. Il est permis d'attribuer à ce processus d'articulation successive sur des vecteurs de puissance progressivement supérieure le 'décollage' de la grammaire comparée.

10. Bibliographie

Biester, Johann Erich. 1793. "I. Ueber die Zigeuner, besonders im Königreich Preussen; II. Von ihrer Sprache". *Berlinische Monatsschrift* 21.108−166, 360−393. [L'auteur en est C. J. Kraus.]

Bopp, Franz. 1816. *Ueber das Conjugationssystem der Sanskritsprache in Vergleichung mit jenem der griechischen, lateinischen, persischen und germanischen Sprache. Nebst Episoden des Ramajan und Mahabharat in genauen metrischen Uebersetzungen aus dem Originaltexte und einigen Abschnitten aus den Veda's.* Herausgegeben und mit Vorerinnerungen begleitet von K. J. Windischmann. Frankfurt am Main: Andreäische Buchhandlung. (Repr., Hildesheim: Georg Olms, 1975.)

−. 1820. "Analytical Comparison of the Sanskrit, Greek, Latin, and Teutonic Languages; shewing the original identity of their original structure". *Annals of Oriental Literature* 1.1−65. (Repr., avec une préface de E. F. K. Koerner, Amsterdam: John Benjamins, 1974: 2ᵉ éd., 1988.)

Collinge, N. E. 1995. "History of Comparative Linguisics"; "History of Historical Linguistics". *Concise History of the Language Sciences: From the Sumerians to the Cognitivists* éd. par E. F. K. Koerner & R. E. Asher, 195−202, 203−212.

Droixhe, Daniel. 1978. *La linguistique et l'appel de l'histoire (1600−1800): Rationalisme et révolutions positivistes.* Genève: Droz.

Gipper, Helmut & Schmitter, Peter. 1975. *Sprachwissenschaft und Sprachphilosophie im Zeitalter der Romantik: Ein Beitrag zur Historiographie der Linguistik.* 2. Aufl. Tübingen: Narr.

Grimm, Jacob. 1822. *Deutsche Grammatik.* Erster Theil. 2. Auflage Göttingen: Dieterich.

Humboldt, Wilhelm von. 1903−1936. *Gesammelte Schriften.* Hrsg. von der Königlich-Preussischen Akademie der Wissenschaften. Berlin: B. Behr's Verlag. 17 vols. I. Abt., Bd. 1−9, 13; *Werke*, hg. von Albert Leitzmann. Berlin: Behr. (Repr., Berlin: Walter de Gruyter, 1967−1968.) [= *GS.*]

−. [1812a]. Essai sur les langues du nouveau Continent. *GS* III 300−342.

−. [1812b]. Ankündigung einer Schrift über die vaskische Sprache und Nation, nebst Angabe des Gesichtspunctes und Inhalts derselben. *GS* III 288−300.

−. [1812−1814]. Ueber Sprachverwandtschaft. *GS* VII/2 629−636.

−. [1820−1821]. Prüfung der Untersuchungen über die Urbewohner Hispaniens vermittelst der vaskischen Sprache. *GS* IV 57−233.

−. [1826]. Lettre à Monsieur Abel-Rémusat, sur la nature des formes grammaticales en général, et sur le génie de la langue Chinoise en particulier. *GS* V 254–308.

—. [1827]. Ueber den Dualis. *GS* VI/1 4–30.

—. [1827–1829]. Ueber die Verschiedenheiten des menschlichen Sprachbaues. *GS* VI/1 111–303.

—. [1828a]. Ueber die Sprachen der Südseeinseln. *GS* VI/1 37–51.

—. [1828b]. An Essay on the best Means of ascertaining the Affinities of Oriental languages. *GS* VI/1 76–84.

Koerner, E. F. Konrad. 1975. "European Structuralism: Early Beginnings". *Current Trends in Linguistics* éd. par Thomas A. Sebeok, vol. XIII: *Historiography of Linguistics*, 717–727. The Hague: Mouton.

Kraus, Christian Jacob. 1787. Recension de "Peter Simon Pallas *Linguarum totius orbis Vocabularia comparativa I*". *Allgemeine Literatur Zeitung* N° 235: col. 1–8, 236: col. 9–16, 237: col. 17–24, 25–29 [Traduction partielle, introduction et notes, de Barbara Kaltz, 1985. "Christian Jacob Kraus' Review of *Linguarum totius orbis vocabularia comparativa*, ed. by Peter Simon Pallas (St. Petersburg, 1787)". *Historiographia Linguistica* 12. 299–260.

Lefmann, Salomon. 1891–1895. *Franz Bopp, sein Leben und seine Wissenschaft, mit [...] einem Anhang: Aus Briefen und anderen Schriften.* 2 vols. Berlin: Reimer.

Leitzmann, Albert, éd. 1908. *Briefwechsel zwischen Wilhelm von Humboldt und August Wilhelm Schlegel.* Halle: Niemeyer.

Morpurgo-Davies, Anna, 1975. "Language Classification in the Nineteenth Century". *Current Trends in Linguistics* ed. by Thomas A. Sebeok, vol. XIII: *Historiography of Linguistics*, 607–716. The Hague: Mouton.

Schlegel, August Wilhelm von. 1820–1830. *Indische Bibliothek.* 3 vols. Bonn: E. Weber.

—. 1846–1847. *Sämmtliche Werke.* Hg. von Eduard Böcking. 12 vols. Leipzig: Weidmann.

—. 1847 [1815]. Recension de "A. L. Chézy 1) Yadjnadatta-Badha. Paris 1814. 2) Discours prononcé au Collège Royal de France. Paris 1815". *SW* XII 427–437.

—. 1884. *Vorlesungen über schöne Litteratur und Kunst. Zweiter Teil (1802–1803): Geschichte der klassischen Litteratur.* Heilbronn: Henninger.

—. 1913. *Geschichte der Deutschen Sprache und Poesie.* Vorlesungen, gehalten an der Universität Bonn seit dem Wintersemester 1818/19. Hg. von Josef Körner. Berlin: Behr. (Repr., Nendeln/Liechtenstein: Kraus, 1968.)

Schlegel, Friedrich. 1808. *Ueber die Sprache und Weisheit der Indier. Ein Beitrag zur Begründung der Alterthumskund. Nebst metrischen Uebersetzungen indischer Gedichte.* Heidelberg: Mohr & Zimmer. (Repr., avec une introduction de Sebastiano Timpanaro, Amsterdam: John Benjamins, 1977.)

Thiersch, Friedrich. 1808. *Tabellen enthaltend eine Methode das Griechische Paradigma einfacher und gründlich zu lehren.* Göttingen: Dieterich.

Jean Rousseau, Paris (France)

156. The introduction of the historical principle into the study of languages: Grimm

1. Historical linguistics before Grimm
2. Jacob Grimm: Biography and background
3. Grimm's methodological contributions
4. Grimm's specific results
5. Grimm's stance on basic issues
6. Summary: Grimm's achievement
7. Bibliography

1. Historical linguistics before Grimm

1.1. It has been observed that each language must be (a) in some respects like *no* other language — hence its identity; (b) in some respects like *all* languages — hence our recognition of linguistic universals; and (c) in some respects like *some* other language(s). From likeness of type (c) comes the revelation that languages agree not only over individual features but in practise over blocks of them, so that they can be classified into relatively few typological sets. But this sort of likeness also spurs the natural human interest in discovering family connections; genealogy has its fascination. And because genealogy entails history (though the converse does not hold), there inevitably ensues a drive to present in historical fashion the data derived from crosslinguistic comparison. What had been achieved in the way of comparison by about 1810 fueled this interest. But enthusiasm derived from other sources (see below, 1.3.) really brought it to the point when it swept Jacob Grimm along on his career and dominated linguists' thinking for a century and a half.

1.2. Accessibility of comparanda began, for European scholars, when Conrad Gesner (1516−1565) inaugurated in 1555 that multilingual presentation of the Christian 'Lord's Prayer' which Leibniz later hailed (in a letter of 17 April 1692 to Ludolf) as most revealing in the comparing and contrasting of human speech, and which J. C. Adelung built up so richly in his *Mithridates* of 1806−1817 (J. S. Vater being his continuator). More and more copious collections of words and phrases compared across the languages of the known world followed, from Duret (1613), Pallas (1789), and Hervás y Panduro (1805). Cognate groupings naturally came into people's minds. As early as 1588 Filippo Sassetti linked Italian with Sanskrit, primarily via the names of numbers; and, after van Gorp's suggestion of 1569, the appellation 'Scythian' was given to the relevant language grouping, the nature of which busied people like Claude Saumaise (1643), Georg Stiernhielm (1671), and Andreas Jäger (1686 − he also applied the terminology of zoogenetic relations to linguistic cognateness). (On all these scholars, their names, dates and works, see Collinge 1995b: 196, 202; Jankowsky 1995.) These were at least attempts at real history. They were distinct from such ideological or religious exploitations of type (b) likeness (above) as the pious Judeo-Christian notion that Hebrew must be the mother of all tongues (an idea which, despite the hostility of Leibniz and J. J. Scaliger, persisted as late as Comenius (J. A. Komenský's *Janua Linguarum* of 1657). Such familial relations were built up from known or contemporary evidence; and the Germanic languages became especially an object of study after 1665 when Franciscus Junius (1589−1672) placed Gothic (previously tied to Celtic, as by Justus Schottelius only two years before) firmly within the Germanic group.

Linkage within the group was strengthened first by Lambert ten Kate (1674−1731) who did much to bridge the gap between Gothic and Dutch, then by Johan Ihre (1707−1780) who placed (Moeso-)Gothic on an early node in the tree whose later branches included Swedish and its closer cognates. But it was the work of Rasmus Rask (1787−1832), based mostly on sound correspondences across the Nordic languages, which laid the firm genealogical base not only for North Germanic but also, by ready extension, for the entire group. Research had led up to, and was poised to profit from, the famous 1786 declaration by William Jones (1746−1794) that a large-scale, multi-group family could perhaps be constructed out of the Indian, Hellenic, Italic, 'Gothic', and Celtic testimonia − a family which, after Thomas Young's use of the term in 1813, was known as 'Indo-European'. By 1733 progress had been made on the relevant Slavic group (by Vasilij Nikitič Tatiščev, 1686−1750); and a paradigm structure of cognateness was already elaborated by workers on the Finno-Ugric family (Martin Fogel, Johann Eberhard Fischer, János Sajnovics, and − with grammatical corroboration − Sámuel Gyarmathi) by the close of the 18th century. (On all this achievement consult → Art. 151; also Collinge 1995b: 196−197; Jankowsky 1995; and for input by British scholars like George Hickes (1705) and Edward Lhuyd (1707), see MacMahon 1995).

1.3. Even so, what actually happened between roughly 1820 and 1860 was curious. This was so in four ways. One cannot of course complain, given the coverage up to that point, that attention had not yet focussed on how a single language at a single time really functions, manipulating its sentence patterns and responding to its speakers' internal competence. True, a past *état de langue* (especially a closed data-set offered by a defunct language) seems an obvious field in which to test implications of operational theory or look for the essential presence of proposed universals; but much of the 20th century had to pass before thought came so far. It is stranger that philosophical approaches faded after the time of Leibniz and Locke (except for occasional figures like K. F. Becker in the mid-19th century). But these things *are* noteworthy: (1) the role of speech in social interaction did not gain the limelight until W. D. Whitney (1827−1894; → Art. 209) moved in that direction from the late 1860s (cf. G. de Tarde 1890), despite the suggested connection with language change; (2) language typology (see above) was a concern of Wilhelm von Humboldt (1767−1835) and the Schlegel brothers, August Wilhelm (1767−1845) and Friedrich (1772−1829), their aim being to relate the categories within sentences to the formal elements attached to or ordering words, and to suggest that the different strategies for doing so were subject to a trend towards improved efficiency − but then the topic lay dormant until revivified (and titled) by Georg von der Gabelentz (1840−1893) at the end of the 19th century; (3) the clear inference that a language family must descend from some 'mother' (described cautiously by William Jones in 1786 as 'some common source, which perhaps no longer exists') − was not picked up, and speculation on such an *Ursprache* ceased to engage scholars until August Schleicher (1821−1868) showed the way, from 1852 onwards, to reconstruct the prehistoric forms which may be justifiably argued as its necessary content (and which thereafter were set up, not altogether satisfactorily, by Brugmann and his coadjutors from 1886). Earlier 19th-century work was content to start with documented data, certainly from an increasingly rich base (after the contributions of F. Schlegel and Franz Bopp), but within the bounds of the known. Finally, (4) as from the time of Aristotle a major industry had been the listing and sorting of at least the formal elements of languages, (and 'parts of speech' and their affixal shapings), so this purely analytical 'stripping of parts' − a term familiar to those who practise gunnery, and the basic sense of the Sanskrit term vyākāraṇam, "grammar" − continued for some time in the form of a demonstration of the traceable evolution of those parts and shapes.

1.4. In these several negative ways linguists were constrained. Unexpected limits were imposed on theorizing about language, in all sectors for some fifty years and in others for over a hundred. Clearly, powerful causes must be sought for this conservative stance, a positive rationale rather than mere unconcern and timidity. In fact, two adequate causes were in the right place at the right time. There were (a) a favorable general climate of thought, and (b) an influential and charismatic advocate; more precisely, (a) the attitude of western Europe, especially Germany, and (b) Jacob Grimm (1785−1863). In Europe the immediately post-Napoleonic era was imbued with ideas and desires both released by, and reacting against, that emperor's achievements. Outside the reinforced autocracies (the Austrian and Russian empires), there was an upsurge of national awareness and mental confidence. In fashion were an antipathy to imposed ways of behaving and a suspicion of imposed ways of thinking. The previous century's 'Age of Enlightenment' and its controlled rationality were overtaken by a free-thinking enthusiasm. Wilhelm Scherer (1841−1886) enumerated in 1874 (pp. 340−341) thirteen contrasts between the earlier and the later mentalities, across what has been called a 'yawning gulf' (Morpurgo Davies 1975: 611). These may be summarized thus: active discovery of the demonstrable became prized over passive acceptance of the ideational; and that which seemed natural (and national) ousted the theoretical (and universal). People and peoples were anxious to assert their own identity in their own terms. They now saw contemporary usages and institutions as enshrining the national character and history of their users, and each as explaining the other. The past therefore loomed large. J. G. Herder (1744−1803) had already said (*Sämtliche Werke* VIII, 198; cf. Jendreieck 1975: 26) "was ich bin, bin ich geworden". In Germany more than elsewhere there developed an ethnic, empirical, and non-aprioristic stance, even within disciplines which had seemed theory-driven. Of this whole movement a leading and persuasive pair were Savigny and Grimm.

2. Jacob Grimm: Biography and background

2.1. The lawyer and savant Friedrich Carl von Savigny (1779−1861) espoused in all his legal teaching, and notably in his 1814 volume *Vom Beruf unsrer Zeit für Gesetzgebung und Rechtswissenschaft* (Our age's vocation for legislation and the study of law), the interpreting of legal statute and juridical process as the social expression of a national character, itself formed over many years. Montesquieu and Condillac had already had this view; and in 1808 Georg Friedrich Creuzer (1771−1858) had declared 'der Geist jedes Volkes' to be similarly illustrated by its mythology. The Savignian creed was easily extended to language. That the search for earlier and joint stages of closely related languages can be linked to ethnic behaviour was shown in 1816 by François Raynouard (1761−1836) in his handling of troubadour compositions in what is effectively the first comparative description of Provençal-Occitan. As comparative-historical essays had been published on Slavic and on sectors of Germanic, it was inevitable that attention be soon drawn to a Savignian sort of linguistics in Germany itself. Here enters Grimm.

2.2. Jacob Ludwig Karl Grimm lived from 4 January 1785 to 20 September 1863. As the son of a jurist he understandably trained as a lawyer, under the slightly senior Savigny; and in 1828 he produced his own history of German law (revised 1854). The training conspired with the times to whet his enthusiasm for nationalism and politics. He was successively secretary to Savigny in Paris and to the local defense department in Kassel, librarian and councillor there under Jerome Bonaparte, and thereafter an attender of the Congress of Vienna in 1814−1815. Typically, he was later (1837) one of the professorial 'Göttingen Seven' who were dismissed from that university, and some (including him) exiled, for opposing the untimely renewal of autocracy and breaking of constitutional promises by the king of Hanover. (For the details of his life, see the entry in *Neue Deutsche Biographie, sub nomine*; Jendreieck 1975: 50−65, 344−350.) The new creed, that only from knowledge of a people's evolution and character comes understanding of its institutions (or science or literature or language), and vice versa, propelled him into two fresh areas of research and publication. From 1812 to 1822, with his brother Wilhelm (1786−1859), he pressed on with the famous collection of *Kinder- und Hausmärchen* ('Grimms' Fairy Tales' in the English naming), followed in 1835 by Jacob's own *Deutsche Mythologie* (new edition 1844). But the inescapable relevance of language struck him early. Its study became the main preoccupation of his life. Etymology − the most undeniably historical of linguistic sectors − interested both brothers (who did not always see eye to eye). The fruits of their collaboration were the first three volumes (1854−1864) of the *Deutsches Wörterbuch*, to which their contribution was ended by Jacob's death, after treatment of the words up to *frucht* in the alphabet. This enterprise continued in the hands of others, the 16th and final volume appearing in 1961. But the zeal for describing a whole language as an evolutionary product made possible Jacob's own four detailed volumes of the *Deutsche Grammatik*, appearing between 1819 and 1837 (see the bibliographical list below for the sequence). Therein the facts of the German language, in its varied forms and with its cousins, over some fifteen stages, were minutely organized and technically labeled. It was from this historical opus, which as early as 1820 J. S. Vater (1772−1826) hailed as 'ein gewaltiges Werk' on the mere evidence of its first unrevised part, that Grimm's fame and influence really derived. (Hereafter these major publications will be denoted by the abbreviations *DW* and *DG*, respectively.)

3. Grimm's methodological contributions

3.1. It has become customary to divide Grimm's linguistic career into three epochs, although scholars disagree as to the precise date when one epoch ended and another began. Frankly, 'Grimm 3' does not significantly differ (if placed, as usual, after 1840) from what went just before. By then the great Germanic grammar had placed him at the head of the practical linguists of Europe, a position confirmed when in 1840 he and Wilhelm became professors in Berlin, both University and Academy. (For his further activities and honors, see the reference above, 2.2.) His early convictions − that language is among human and national achievements and that natural 'organic' cycles of growth and decay are irrelevant to it − remained his unaltering faith. His 1851 Academy address on language origins (glottogony), *Über den Ursprung der Sprache*, containing Herder-like notions of speech conditioned directly by man's needs, local in time and space, echoes this belief. His aim was always perceptive observation ('Beobachtung und Wahrnehmung'), despite the errors he might and did make. To anything which seemed to impede this empirical policy he was hostile. Yet, although it is fair to quote his defensive remark of 1822: "allgemeinen logischen Begriffen bin ich in der Grammatik feind" (*DG* ²I: vi), an apparent avoidance of theory does his practise less than justice. At its best his procedure avoided that divorce of analysis from actuality which J. R. Firth used to denounce, appealing plaintively for "a renewal of contact with the data". At its worst it could descend to concern for the insignificant ('Andacht zum Unbedeutenden' [Sulpitz Boisserée]) or even reverence for junk ('Ehrfurcht vor dem Trödel' [A. W. Schlegel]). In etymology, always an entrapping affair for the over-enthusiastic, Grimm's early "vague and wooly notions" and adhocery (to quote Ginschel 1967: 338−339) and the wildness which led A. W. Schlegel to judge him (in 1815) a stranger to his subject, these were not cleansed from his later *DW* articles (see Wyss 1979). So it is overdelicate to distinguish in him an *Aufbau* and an *Ausbau* period; all his working life after around 1816 (see below), his creed and his practise stayed essentially unchanged — and disparate. Hence 'Grimm 2' and 'Grimm 3' rather fuse.

3.2. On the other hand, one can see a distinct change in his analytical method in the years preceding the appearance of DG^1I, a setting on one side of his wordbased speculations. Rather than date the end of 'Grimm 1' so precisely as 19 November 1816 (as Ginschel does [1967: 361–363]), it makes sense to regard him in his early thirties as taking on board Indo-European genetics from Bopp (1816) as well as Indian evidence from Schlegel (1808) and Nordic data from Rask (1811–). From this brew he distilled four principles which controlled his later researches (although he never formulated them): (i) that linguistic evidence must be as full as possible, even if recourse is had to indirect sources of information; (ii) that evolutionary statements are weak if they ignore causation (an insight perhaps derived from Bredsdorff 1821); (iii) that compared items must show regularity in their mutual differences if deductions are to be valid; (iv) that one requires at least tacit acceptance of cognate languages in order to give a full account of 'descent' (for which term see Hoenigswald 1990: 122) for the tongue under examination. For all Grimm's Germanism, empiricism, and failure to codify his procedures, these tenets effectively provided his methodological underpinning.

As to (i), much information on early Germanic phonology, including that of Gothic, was gleaned from Grimm's survey of the rhyme practises of Middle High German poets (though rhyme evidence is often misleading). The weakness in (ii) was remedied by *inter alia* his belated recognition (which *was* in November 1816) of umlaut as part of German history and as infusing sense into many apparent sound shifts (see below, 4.2.1., 4.2.4.). Under (iii) credibility was given to comparatively based conclusions on changes by demonstrating regularity, a paradigm case being the set of equal movements linking common Germanic plosive consonants to their counterpart incidences in the same place in the same words in other Indo-European languages. This set forms the provisions of 'Grimm's Law' (on which see further below, 4.2.2.), a pronouncement which implies tenet (iv) and enforces the recognition of linguistic cognateness. As Grimm was in practise a unilingual explicator for the most part, his position on 'pure' versus genetic history needs to be clarified.

3.2.1. History's aspects include the intellectual, the utilitarian, and the sociological. The first is satisfied by the detecting of how things came to be as they are. But then it is also satisfying to find out how they work now, how they compete with rivals now, how they are subtly changing now. Few scientists are content with past states added to present phenomena. Even Savigny knew that (see Ginschel 1967: 15 n. 5); but Grimm's eyes were on yesterday always. Nor was he utilitarian, making clear to people of one age the successes and failures, paragons and monstrosities, shining paths and dead ends of their predecessors. He was neither creative nor normative, uninterested in language engineering or idiom cleansing. His was the sociological approach, and in an explanatory mode. His success in providing national evolutionary linguistics encouraged his followers to dominate the field for so long in Europe and North America. (See Pankow 1985 for the spin-off even in 19th century Russia.) Some mavericks wrote on subjects like 'the logic of grammar' (one thinks of K. F. Becker, J. N. Madvig, or H. Steinthal), but were denied the limelight. The 20th century has at last restored a balance between the study of the mechanics of language and that of its history, letting each fructify the other. The path to reconciliation has been tortuous and mutual understanding brittle. Yet that Holger Pedersen's 1924 (and third) rapportage on the Berlin–Göttingen–Leipzig historical heritage could be marketed under the English title *The Discovery of Language* as late as 1962 — that was strange then and is inconceivable nowadays. The spell of Grimm (and Bopp) has faded.

Furthermore, the notion that history controls shape may be applied easily enough to a people's politics or law or art or even humor; to interpret their langue so is harder. It may seem silly to label a speech group 'article conscious' or 'subjunctive prone'; still, blindness to the sequence of time characterizes Hopi, social distaste for using person markers to distance speaker from hearer is seen in some Australian languages, Sanskrit loves the passive, and so on. Whorfianism in its strongest form posits the converse: that speech forms constrain mental attitudes. It is then awkward that languages provably undergo fundamental changes, even in grammar. Where there is a documentary gap, from what traits does a diachronist decide whether, for instance, the three tense system under study is an elaboration of a previous two tense, or the dwindling of a five tense, operation? Given a clear line of descent, one may cogently describe the evolution; without it one must speculate. Grimm's vision did not cross gaps. When he went beyond Germanic into other and earlier languages he was in uncharted territory without light or sense of adventure. Even when in 1848 he accepted relationships based on categories such as numerals, kinship terms, and personal pronouns he set up no genealogical nodings from them (see Lötzsch 1985: 706−711).

3.2.2. The conclusion is that Grimm, although in general genealogical as to language, was not in a real sense genetic. As it is commonly claimed that he *was* genetic (as by Ginschel 1967: 362), a fine distinction must be drawn. Before his time linguistic genealogy had made considerable but erratic progress. There was at least no doubt that German (and not, for example, Finnish) is in the Indo-European family; and to have ignored the reflexes in Greek or Latin would have been perverse. The Indian evidence, hailed by Grimm as crucial, was in fact overtrusted. Yet this data had to be just that, given and agreed (as also for Savigny; cf. Ginschel 1967: 12). Grimm, like Bopp, worked chronologically downwards: from earlier forms he charted the descent to their later counterparts. Neither he nor his continuators were upwards men. Genetic linguistics, on the other hand, rests on a delicate interplay. The supposedly comparable data are justified as such by their sharing a no longer existent source; at the same time the prehistoric existence of that source itself (and its precise forms and their likely downward paths) must be deduced from a summarizing of the comparisons made. In language one does not thus arrive at genes, except metaphorically, and the analogy is only partial. But, as in comparative anatomy, there is a recognition of vanished but procreating entities. Within this model, however, Grimm did not grasp the retrodictive aspects or the speculative policy (nor did anyone until August Schleicher [1852: iv−v] pointed the way to reconstruction of prehistoric, 'starred', forms; → Art. 157). Reconstruction establishes *Urformen* which are really no more palpable than Platonic ideas; it is a probabilistic and suppositional exercise not too far removed from weather forecasting or higher finance. But Grimm's starting points had to be known and firm. His pre-Germanic array of obstruents (now debated) was taken on trust, essentially from Sanskrit, and his triad of inherited cardinal vowels a/i/u (falsified thereafter) derived from Gothic surface evidence (see Benware 1974), without due scepticism. He was an acceptor, not a reconstructer. This was not entirely because of lack of insight (in any case the methodology was not formulated until the 1950s by Hoenigswald), nor through timidity. If one seeks to provide explanation from the past for later *états de langue*, one's data must be given and secure, not proposed and merely probable. One cannot explain *ignotum per ignotius*.

4. Grimm's specific results

4.1. The details of his influential publications appear below (Bibliography, section A). As well as *DG* (1819−1837), the history of the German language (hereafter *GDS*; it came out in 1848, an appropriate year for a politically conscious work) and the etymological lexicon (*DW*, 1854−) all won much admiration in their own age. Revision, reprinting, and fresh reproduction have always come. Zeal was thus engendered for the diachronic study of German above all, its literature included. This, Grimm's chief legacy, found expression in descriptions of various stages of that language's history; for example, by August Schleicher (1860), Wilhelm Scherer (1868), Eduard Sievers (1874), Wilhelm Braune (1886), Adolf Noreen (1894), Friedrich Kluge (1920) − to cite a mere selection from a prolific and continuing tradition. Grimm's preoccupation was also echoed in Rudolf von Raumer's (1815−1876) *Vom deutschen Geist* (1848). Direct factual reliance on Grimm naturally weakened (the pedagogic influence of Friedrich Zarncke [1825−1891] becomes increasingly clear). But Grimm was the fount; and a warm mention of him is to be found as late as Kluge (1920: 339).

4.2. As noted above (3.2.), Grimm came to certain conclusions about diachronic study: that it must be adequately data-based, causative, and rely on regularity of correspondence. These led him to some findings which have remained famous even after being challenged, corrected or superseded. In the pursuit of full and reliable data he mostly avoided the etymological extravagances which always infected *DW*. Regularity of reflex equations, and local causes of notable disagreements, both found abiding expression in two pronouncements which became inextricably linked with his name, rather than that of the *primus inventor*. These were: the Germanic treatment of root vocalism (4.2.1.), and the phonetic features of some consonants in Germanic as compared with those in cognate forms elsewhere in Indo-European (4.2.2.). He also enriched the vocabulary of the trade with technical terms, of varying degrees of appropriateness (4.2.4.).

4.2.1. For vowel change in roots the abiding term was *Umlaut* (on its emergence see 4.2.4.). In previous use (e. g., by Lessing in 1779) it had covered any sound shift in a word's interior; and it was so employed by Grimm in 1812. But in 1816 he narrowed its sense, to signify the modifying of an inherited vowel or diphthong by the assimilating force of a vowel in a succeeding syllable, usually a grammatical marker. He had by then become convinced that solutions offered by others were correct and important. In 1811 Rasmus Rask had diagnosed in Nordic tongues (especially Icelandic) a backing and rounding effect triggered by the high and back nature of the next vowel to the right ('*u*-umlaut') — an idea derided by Grimm in 1812 as 'more clever than correct'. Then Georg Friedrich Benecke (1762 – 1844) convinced him of a like event in Middle High German with a high front trigger. The result is hailed by Ginschel, (1967: 361 – 362, 375 – 382) using Raumer's term 'Wendung', as a revolutionary switch. This '*i*-umlaut', actually noted in Nordic by Rask in 1814, was a characteristic of North and West Germanic and best shown by Old Saxon. A raised and fronted value was carried leftwards across an intervening consonant, but was blocked (according to dialect) by certain clusters. The effect is phonetically reasonable, Irish and Russian having like events; many languages show some form of intersyllabic harmony. Its recognition in Germanic demystified the evolution of many declensional and derivational relations: early *dat* versus *dati* underlies modern *Tat* versus *Täter*, *tätig*, *tätlich*. As late as the twelfth century the shift is shown in writing only in the case of $a > e$ (OHG singular *gast*, plural *gesti*); elsewhere graphic notation comes later if at all (so MHG has *briute* against OHG *brūti*). The affecting vowel is often lost (as in OHG *framadi* > MHG (*frem(e)de* > NHG *fremd*); the plural suffix has gone already in OE *fēt*, *gēs* (plurals of *fōt*, *gōs*, ModE *feet*, *geese*). If it had vanished in OHG too early to cause assimilation, MHG might extend the effect by analogy. For most of this complicated picture, plus the new transparency in grammatical history, Grimm deserves the credit, however late his conversion.

4.2.2. As to consonants, consistency in the formal differences within the 'same' words as between the Germanic and the other Indo-European languages must rest on a reconciliating statement. Rask had already presented in 1818 (p. 188) a set of phonetically ordered pairings, mostly between Icelandic and Greek and Latin. Except where Greek initial /h/ answers to /s/ elsewhere, the relevant consonants outside Germanic are all basically stops; they may have aspirated versions but they are not continuant or strident. The non-Germanic languages have an earlier *floruit*. On the basis of these facts, Grimm in 1822 (*DG* ²I) replaced Rask's correspondences with a more elaborate display of historical stages. He dropped the /s-/ case, a purely Greek phenomenon. Otherwise, his novelties were: (i) to relate the shifts to common Germanic; (ii) to adduce word-medial examples (Rask's Nordic testimonia had been almost entirely word-initial); (iii) to complete the symmetry by including etyma where apparently non-Germanic /b/ reflected as Germanic /p/ (usually so, as seen by Bredsdorff [1821: 21 – 22]; see below, 4.2.3.); (iv) to build in a further stage to account for the subsequent reshaping in canonic High German. He formulated two shifts (1822: 584 – 592) — or, more properly, one twofold shift, wherein OHG was seen as lowered by one level ('eine Stufe abwärts gesunken') from 'Gothic', here meaning Saxon, Frisian and North Germanic, just as was that level from Greek, Latin, and Sanskrit. The two stages needed nine rules to handle the series (labial, dental, velar) in the orders (voiceless, voiced, aspirated). The double shift was displayed thus (p. 584):

Gk	P.	B.	F.	T.	D.	TH.	K.	G.	CH.
Goth.	F.	P.	B.	TH.	T.	D.	—	K.	G.
OHG	B.(V)	F.	P.	D.	Z.	T.	G.	CH.	K.

The first movement, from Indo-European to Germanic, caters for points (i) to (iii) above. It has been called 'Grimm's Law', outside Germany, since at least 1838 (see Koerner 1989: 309 n. 3). Both Rask's and Grimm's handling of the matter are conveniently to be found (in English) in Lehmann (1967: 34, 52–60); for partial precursors see Morpurgo Davies (1975: 629). The scope, and the neatness, of Grimm's presentation may be exemplified within the dental series:

IE *dh-*; *-dh-*   : Gk. *thugátēr*; *méthu*
> Gmc. *d-*; *-d-*: Got. *daúhtar*; OE *mëdo*
IE *d-*; *-d-*   : Lat. *dent-*; *sed-*
> Gmc. *t-*; *-t-*: Got. *tunþus*; *sitan*
IE *t-*; *-t-*   : Gk. *taûros*; Lat. *frater*
> Gmc þ-; -þđ-: ON *þiór*; Got. *brōþar*/ON *broðer*

Respectively in the orders (allowing for Greek aspirate devoicing) Germanic seems to have lost inherited aspiration, voice, quick release. Many complications are hidden: relative chronology of the shifts, innovation versus conservation, secondary changes (as in Greek). But Grimm's package had appeal. This was true despite his confounding different phonation features (as aspiration with friction) and accepting as original the postclassical pronunciation of Greek *phi*; because of all this, the event was even seen as circular ('Kreislauf'); some have so justified it in this century (as Prokosch 1939: 49–52). Infelicitously, Grimm connects Latin *dies* with Germanic *dags*, and *iterum* with *widar* (*DG*²I, 586; 590). He also fails to state the environmental constraints on his shifts, such as preceding /s/, or second position in a cluster for /t/. Nor does he recognize a chronological order among the shifts. (See also Fourquet 1948.)

Yet it is no disgrace at that early stage to have not yet recognized the labialized velars of PIE, or the voicing variation in Germanic fricatives caused by the position of inherited but lost accent. The corrections by others over the next half-century (especially by Verner) are only fine tunings of an operable machine (see Morpurgo Davies 1994: 153 and n. 153). Grimm also knew when to have honest doubts: whether Latin *turba* should be linked with Gothic *paúrp* — the */b/ problem; or when to disqualify false evidence such as misleading loanwords (he warned '*scrīban* is *scribere* itself' (p. 588), and elsewhere noted loans between Celtic and Germanic). His often quoted readiness to allow that the plotted changes occurred only in the majority (p. 590) is not a sign of defeatism in face of the awkward. The Neogrammarians' later insistence on strict sound laws (with specific conditions to weed out the merely apparent exceptions) is perhaps responsible for unfairness to Grimm. Actually, he himself suggested three scenarios wherein sound shifts will either not occur or go awry: (a) where obstruent series vary by dialect, as 'five' in Ancient Greek is *pénte* in Ionic but *pémpe* in Aeolic (variant reflexes of a labiovelar, in fact); (b) where languages arbitrarily fluctuate in applying aspiration (as they notoriously do, although again Grimm offers fricative examples); and, most interestingly, (c) where individual words seem to have let the stream of innovation pass them by ("der Strom der Neuerung ist an ihnen vorbeigeflossen" [p. 590]). This last nonconformity, where a shift's progress across the vocabulary is impeded by extremes of a word's frequency or exigencies of its function or class membership, or just by analogy, was picked up by W. D. Whitney and has been a recent topic of research under the title 'lexical diffusion' (see Collinge 1995b: 208). Grimm's instances were inappropriate but his revelation defensible.

4.2.3. Grimm's third novelty was to include an inherited /b/ among the shifting consonants. He locates no confident examples, and Rask's asymmetric doubt seems simply to have offended his sense of pattern. It has been felt recently that although /b/ is rare in Proto-Indo-European, it should fit in, even if its phonetic awkwardness has to be established by new views on its phonation. A whole set of 'glottalic ejective' sounds has been proposed to replace the traditional legacy of plain voiced stops; here enters a possibly difficult */p'/. (It was the exceptional nature of the PIE system previously assumed that prompted this revising of when aspiration occurs and how breath source varies [on which see Vennemann 1989: 107–115; Salmons 1993 *passim*; but esp. 19–53, for the details]). Even those who are sceptical — for a summary, see Baldi (1999: 52–58) — tend to regard */b/ as a very late and sporadic IE arrival (so Matasović 1994). But whatever the phonetic nature of the segment, and in whichever direction the shift moves (for the new view allows Germanic mostly to reflect the earlier, rather than the shifted, forms), the correspondences are there; and that they point to historical events remains Grimm's valid discovery.

In passing, it is noteworthy that Rask and Grimm reviewed each other's work and exchanged letters (between 1811 and 1813, and again between 1823 and 1826 — i.e., when Rask was not in, or on his way to or from, India). Grimm made amends for his cool reception of Rask's 1811 opus both by his phonological expansion of *DG* I as a result of Rask 1818 and by his earlier acknowledgement (*DG* ¹I: xviii—xvix) of the Dane's achievement. Still, the sound shifts as historical testimony were for Grimm his own contribution; he made that clear to Rask in a letter in 1824, and Rask made no counter-claim nor used them as (in Grimm's phrase) a stiffener for etymology. But the correspondence remained distant; and Rask's view of *DG* I and II in 1830 was hardly kind. (On all this, see Baudusch 1985.)

Attempts were made (by Pedersen in 1916 and Jespersen in 1922) to re-name the first Germanic sound shift 'Rask's Law'. This may seem a "rather tiresome question" (Morpurgo Davies 1975: 629). The same has been suggested for umlaut in its more precise sense (by Antonsen 1962, 1987). But partial anticipation is a common occurrence (see Agrell 1955 on precursors to Grimm's Law; also Collinge 1995a: 28, 39—40).

4.2.4. Grimm's technical terms, in comparative-historical linguistics and in grammatical description, have had mixed success. Outside German, his phonological trio *Anlaut*, *Inlaut* and *Auslaut* (1822), for sounds found in initial, medial and final position respectively, has been sparingly adopted. They may mask crucial factors: whether the reference is to a syllabic onset or peak or coda as opposed to a separate segment standing on this or that side of others, or whether the placing is within a lexeme or a root or a stem or a compound. The terms *Umlaut* and *Ablaut* have fared better. The former seems to have been used first by the poet and amateur-linguist Friedrich Gottlieb Klopstock (1724—1803) in his *Gelehrten Republik* (1774: 229); on this work, which counselled trust in usage rather than normative description, see Jellinek (1913 I: 272—273 and n. 3). It was Grimm's illuminating demonstration of the assimilating process in Germanic (4.2.1.) that ensured its continued use, being kept in mind by the associated graphic device of superimposing a double-dot (or double-stroke) deictic on the unshifted vowel, abiding in German and borrowed elsewhere (as in Turkish *büyük*, *kötü*, etc.). The misleading compound *Rückumlaut* is rightly forgotten. It denoted a mythical 're-versal' of the process supposed to occur in some OHG and MHG verb preterites which really never underwent it at all (and occasionally survive in their original form unchanged even by analogy, as *kannte* from *kennen*).

Ablaut has had a professional life for a century and a half. It means the systematic variation, in roots and suffixes (both inflectional and derivational), of a basic IE front vowel which is taken as the datum. This variation may be of degree (absent/present/reinforced) or of articulatory place (front/back — though Grimm's deference to Sanskrit precluded recognition of the *e*/*o* alternation, there lost). Exemplary are the *-g(e/o)n-*values in Ancient Greek *gén-os*, *gí-gn-omai*, *gón-os* (from the root 'to engender'). The term 'vowel gradation' has, however, found much favor; and the two aspects are more conveniently distinguished as 'apophony' (of degree) and 'metaphony' (of place) — nor are they now seen, as Grimm supposed, as direct semantic markers. Yet 'ablaut' is still a concise morphophonological label. With another sort of local alternation Grimm was less adroit: the relation of *gibt* to *geben* he named 'breaking' ('Brechung'), which has not lasted as an appellation.

Grimm's most pervasive terms have been the pair 'strong' versus 'weak', as applied to rival formations realizing grammatical categories. These sometimes co-exist, syntax or style conditioning the choice; elsewhere they are mutually preclusive. Adjectival declension in German and Russian shows the former relation, verbal tense the latter (entire verb paradigms being so classified). The terms spread: in Ancient Greek, verbs usually possess either a 'strong' (thematic) or a 'weak' (athematic) aorist tense/aspect form. In Germanic, Grimm applied the strong rating to older and inherited types, the weak being the innovated. Certainly, the weak are more predictable as to shape; and while the strong verbs originally boasted seven subclasses the weak had only three in OHG and only one in MHG. Yet the weak type is by far the more productive: new, or borrowed, lexemes regularly follow weak formation, and old strong verbs may switch their allegiance, the reverse move being rarer. Hence a more neutral terminology would have been preferable.

5. Grimm's stance on basic issues

Fundamental questions for diachronists of the early 19th century were (i) where can one find within languages the richest and safest sets of comparanda? (ii) what is the relevance of scientific models? (iii) what is it that controls evolution in the forms and functions of speech?

5.1. A major body of opinion holds that a language's identity, and its most conservative behaviour, is to be found in its grammar and especially its morphology. Not all agree: there have always been those who believe that sharper historical and genealogical findings come from lexical comparison. But since the beginning of the 18th century a conviction had been growing that for diachronists grammar mattered most. Comparison of words is vitiated by the almost infinite range of semantic values and shades possible in any language, and by speakers' readiness freely to enrich their vocabulary with foreign borrowings. Grammar seemed more trustworthy. The credit for turning historians' attention that way is customarily given to the Ethiopianist Hiob Ludolf (1624–1704); so by Benfey (1869: 236 and n. 6; cf. Gray 1939: 432–433). It is sometimes pointed out that Wilhelm von Humboldt (in a letter to A. W. Schlegel dated 19 May 1822) distinguished three sorts of grammatical element (cf. Morpurgo Davies 1975: 611–612; Hoenigswald 1990: 127). These were: (a) categories, (b) mechanisms, (c) morphs — to use later terminology. The first two are, respectively, things like whether a language has verbs (and, if so, whether they have a passive voice), and the use of affixes, or umlaut, or reduplication as markers. These things place a language typologically. The third sort is that of the precise shape of a marker; it is likeness therein that most securely links the history of the tongues which share it. Ludolf's plea was on behalf of 'grammaticae ratio'. Some think that by that phrase he meant the structure of grammar (only (a) and (b) above); Arens' slanted translation "der grammatische Bau" (1969: 105–106) may have caused this; Benfey had used 'Gestaltung'. But Ludolf was writing over a century before Humboldt and was not making those subdivisions. He was rejecting blinkered reliance on random items of the lexicon, and commending attention to the functional organization of forms-plus-sounds — the combination of phonology and morphology (excluding syntax and lexis) which even quite recently has been called 'comparative grammar'; thus his prefatory 'dissertatio' in his 1702 grammar quotes "eadem coniugandi ratio" and "idem [...] declinandi modus" as the proofs of kinship of languages. (It is important also to dismiss the counterclaim on behalf of Johannes de Laet [1582–1649]. He did not anticipate 'Ludolf's Law' [Collinge 1995a: 30]. In order to contravert Hugo Grotius' ludicrous idea that native Amerindian languages are of Norse origin, de Laet did deplore uncontrolled recourse to sporadic lexical items — together with ad hoc 'letter changing', transposing of syllables, and so on — and did say that the 'genius' of a language lies in its pronunciation and syntax. But he still placed the greatest stress on items of vocabulary, provided that those chosen were near to the language's heart; he was the first to recommend numerals, kinship terms, and the names of body parts — exactly the major content of the lists of recent 'lexicostatistic' enthusiasts. It was on these, and not grammar, that he himself then relied to show how defeatingly wide a gap remained between, say, Algonquian and Norwegian [see Metcalf 1974: 246–248]. The new reliance on morphophonology came after him.)

Following the Ludolfian recommendation of grammar (but, *pace* Gray 1939: 432, not purely of morphology) a tussle ensued among historians of language. Some held that, as sounds are easily enumerable, describable, and relatable, genealogies should be based on them. For others it was more important to establish the sameness of mechanisms and markers, and/or the relevance of phonological comparanda, by congruent morphological environment. Rask was of the first group, Bopp of the second; Grimm wavered. His early leaning was to phonology (cf. Ginschel 1967: 367); but in 1819, no doubt under Bopp's spell, he offered a form based account of Germanic history. Then, counterpersuaded by Rask 1818 (note the time lag), he saw again the practicality of using sounds, and he recast *DG* I so that its 1822 version contained (in addition to the evidence from morphology) a new 596-page section on movement of sounds. The Raskian view continued to prevail. Schleicher was of that persuasion; and its practitioners became so complacent as to prompt the Neogrammarians' grim demand for exceptionless rigor. The old lexicalism, however, was demoted; Gyarmathi's titular "affinitas [...] grammatice demonstrata" (1799) became the keynote of Grimm's era, and etymology was now a separate enterprise.

5.2. The maxims of scientists fascinated 19th century linguists (see Morpurgo Davies

1994: 99–106); their response was often inconsistent. Friedrich Schlegel (1808: 28) led the way by identifying comparative anatomy as the discipline to copy: as the comparing of physical specimens leads to natural history, so linguistic comparison — especially, in his view, of morphologies — reveals the 'Naturgeschichte' of speech. Benecke reinforced the analogy in his review of *DG* ²I in 1822; but already in 1819 Grimm himself had gone so far as to claim, conversely, that among the sciences comparative anatomy alone rivals historical linguistics in arriving at conclusions which have safety, novelty, and even charm ("Reiz" [1819: xii]). Yet his attitudes were confused. It was a common opinion of the mid-to-late 19th century that language is a natural organism, with genera and species, a birth and a life marked by accelerating decay, and a possibly Darwinian progress. Schlegel and Schleicher both spoke of 'organisch'. Now Grimm already in his 1819 *Vorrede* listed seven major truths gleaned from his own previous research. Of these, the first, third and seventh respectively state that through time a language passes from being more pure to being less so, from formal richness to spareness, from greater to reduced variety. And yet he avoids terming this degeneracy; his attitude is therefore usually divorced from that which accepts *Verfall* (cf. Fowkes 1964: 59; Gessinger 1985: 654). Clearly it is hard to draw lines here. Grimm also noted how word meanings move from the transparent to the opaque, so that not only sclerosis but also inefficiency develops; and his second truth speaks of the loss of 'innocence' (Unschuld), his sixth of lost 'liveliness' (lebendige Form). Even so, he held to his creed that language changes in response to its users' evolution and that therefore scientific analyses are of little avail in charting its progress. His 1819 phrase "ein unvermerktes, unbewusstes Geheimnis" ("an unchronicled, subconscious mystery", *DG* ¹I: ix–x) really still applies to his view of human speech in his 1851 Academy address, wherein abstractness and non-stop change characterize its latest stages.

5.2.1. Another puzzle obtrudes itself. An evolutionary doctrine now called 'uniformitarianism' was first promulgated in 1785 by the geologist James Hutton (1726–1797), echoed by John Playfair (1748–1819), and given wider publicity by Charles Lyell (1797–1875) in his *Principles of Geology* of 1830–1833 (see Christy 1983). It has been termed "the major conceptual revolution in science between Newton and Einstein" (Lass in 1984, reviewing Christy). Positively, it provides that a process of the present day or the demonstrable past may be presumed in prehistory. Negatively, it precludes the diagnosis in prehistory of any development *not* documented in the subsequent evolution of the subject under study. William Whewell (1794–1866) recognized this as a salutary constraint on geological theory. He related it to language study too (1837: 516; 1840: 677–679), despite his general antipathy and his uncertainty of its application outside geology. Yet it was slow to commend itself to linguistic historians, for all Steinthal's stance, before its promotion by Whitney (1867) and Scherer (1868). The silence of earlier scholars, and especially of Grimm, is curious.

It has been noted (by Christy 1983: 95–96) that Brugmann differed from Grimm on the emergence of grammatical gender: Brugmann thought it a prime of grammar, Grimm believed it to be a late formalization of human sex-awareness. Now this typical Grimmian attitude was not 'non-uniformitarian' (*pace* Christy, p. 101); his process can be paralleled in several aspects of human mental development. Besides, Grimm's notion that only the past explains the usages of the present is simply the obverse of the Hutton-Lyell view that only the present justifies the processes attributed to the past. Again, the constraint does allow catastrophic change, but only if a similar event can be shown to happen in a body's later history (hence it cannot be assumed arbitrarily, as Whewell [1837: 513] pointed out). It rules out any theory of coming into being where that prime event is not matched afterwards (at least by death); if applied to cosmogony, it makes difficulties for any 'Big Bang' theory. But none of this can have bothered Grimm. He was not a reconstructionist, he did not pursue an *Ursprache*, he did not really speculate on the *birth* of language. As for the converse Hutton-Lyell implication, that a known event may be expected to recur, that is well exemplified by Grimm's own first and second *Lautverschiebungen*. Considering his applauding Schlegel's enthusiasm for science (cf. Gessinger 1985: 669), the fact that Grimm did not embrace (or even mention) uniformitarianism is at best a culpable oversight.

6. Summary: Grimm's achievement

Grimm gave linguists confidence in comparative study and devotion to a historical view.

He accepted that language change is unstoppable ('unaufhaltbar') and that it guarantees a tongue's individuality — these are the fourth and fifth of his 'Hauptsätze' of 1819 (p. xxvi). He also saw such change as a limiting and hardening process. On the other hand, he rejected the equation of language with a decaying natural organism possessed of a life cycle. He prized empirical methods, explanation through history, detailed linguistic description and labeling, and the need to excuse the irregular and exceptional. He was not a reconstructionist or a true geneticist, nor were his continuators; and he was only superficially guided by contemporary science.

Yet many of the criticisms leveled against him were unfair (A. W. Schlegel's in 1815 being the most vitriolic). Admittedly, he wrote of 'Buchstaben' ('letters') instead of 'Laute' ('sounds') when phonic values were under debate; but he declared this to be a mere convenience (see *DG* ²I: 3 and *GDS* I: 251). His errors can be counterbalanced by those of others (notably of Bopp); and to regard all that he contributed as simultaneously "large additions to positive science" and "the result of chance" (as did Ker 1915: 12) is merely bizarre. But, for all his 'monologic nature' (as Scherer called it), he could be clearly inconsistent even when he had not consciously changed his mind. His expressed attitude was often at variance with his actual achievement, notably in theory. In this, he was of his age: it has been well noted that "what characterizes [...] the nineteenth century are its immense achievements and its schizoid ways: what was done was one thing, what was said about what was done was another" (Hoenigswald 1990: 126).

Grimm owed much to others, not only to Rask and Bredsdorff in his age group but also to acknowledged precursors (for the details see Murpurgo Davies 1975: 618 n. 26; Koerner 1989: 306). Still, the construction of that powerful historical machine which for so long enslaved most scholarly endeavor and deflected inquiry from how language actually works — that was his own triumph and is his epitaph.

7. Bibliography

[Note: The *Zeitschrift für Phonetik, Sprachwissenschaft und Kommunikationsforschung* (= *ZSPK*) devoted parts of its vol. 38 (1985) to Jacob Grimm and Wilhelm von Humboldt; see fasc. 2: 112–120; fasc. 5: 462–610; fasc. 6: 654–721.]

7.1. Primary Sources

Benfey, Theodor. 1869. *Geschichte der Sprachwissenschaft und orientalischen Philologie in Deutschland seit dem Anfang des 19. Jahrhunderts mit einem Rückblick auf die früheren Zeiten.* Munich: J. G. Cotta.

Bopp, Franz. 1816. *Über das Conjugationssystem der Sanskritsprache in Vergleichung mit jenem der griechischen, lateinischen, persischen und germanischen Sprache.* Frankfurt/M.: Andreäische Buchhandlung. (Repr. Hildesheim: Olms, 1975. English version of linguistic portion [1820] repr. Amsterdam: Benjamins, 1974.)

Braune, Wilhelm. 1886. *Althochdeutsche Grammatik.* Halle: Max Niemeyer. (13th. ed., 1975.)

Bredsdorff, Jakob H. 1886 [1821]. *Om Aarsagerne til Sprogenes Forandringer* [On the causes of linguistic changes]. Republ. with introd. by Vilhelm Thomsen. Copenhagen: Gyldendal. (English transl. with an introduction by Henning Andersen in *Historiographia Linguistica* 9: 1, 2. 1–42 [1982].)

Grimm, Jacob. 1813–16. *Altdeutsche Wälder* (with Wilhelm Grimm). 3 vols. Vol. 1 Kassel: Thurneissen; vols. 2–3 Frankfurt/M.: Körner. (Repr. Darmstadt: Wissenschaftliche Buchgesellschaft, 1966.)

–. 1819. *Deutsche Grammatik.* I. Göttingen: Dieterich'sche Buchhandlung. (Repr., Hildesheim: Olms, 1995.)

–. 1822. Revised version of above. Ibid.

–. 1826, 1831, 1837. *Deutsche Grammatik.* Vols. II–IV. Ibid. (Revised ed. of all *DG* by Wilhelm Scherer, Gustav Roethe & Edward Schröder. Berlin & Gütersloh: C. Bertelsmann, 1870–1898; repr., Hildesheim: Olms, 1967 and again 1989–93.)

–. 1848. *Geschichte der deutschen Sprache.* 2 vols. Leipzig: Weidmann. (2nd rev. ed. Leipzig: S. Hirzel, 1853; 3rd ed., 1868; 4th ed., 1880; revised ed. by Elisabeth Feldbusch and Rosemarie Müller, Hildesheim: Olms, 1999.)

–. 1851. "Über den Ursprung der Sprache". Address to Berlin Academy, 9 January 1851. *Abhandlungen der Königlichen Akademie der Wissenschaften*, Philol.-Hist. Kl. 32; 2, Berlin: F. Dümmler. (5th ed., 1862; repr. as 1864 (below), I: 255–298. See also collected Academy addresses, Berlin: Akadem. Verlag, 1984; translated into English by Robert A. Wiley as *On the Origin of Language.* Leiden: Brill, 1984, 27 pp.)

–. 1854–. *Deutsches Wörterbuch* (with Wilhelm Grimm). Leipzig: S. Hirzel. (Vols. I–III reprinted by Olms, Hildesheim, 1999; Vols. IV–XVI by continuators, XVI appearing 1961.)

–. 1864–90. *Kleinere Schriften.* Vols. I–V ed. by Karl Müllenhoff. Berlin: F. Dümmler, 1864–71; vols. VI–VII ed. by Eduard Ippel, 1882–84; vol. VIII ed. by E. Ippel. Berlin & Gütersloh: C. Bertelsmann, 1890; repr. Hildesheim: Olms, 1991–1992.) [Vol. V (1871), 482–502, gives full list of Grimm's works.]

–. 1961. *Vorreden* [to GWB I & II (1854, 1860)]. Separate publ., with a foreword by Wilhelm Schoof. Darmstadt: Wissenschaftliche Buchgesellschaft.

—. 1968. *Vorreden* [to Grimm 1819 and 1822]. Separate publ., with a foreword by Hugo Steger. Darmstadt: Wissenschaftliche Buchgesellschaft.

Ihre, Johan. 1769. *Glossarium Suiogothicum*. Uppsala: Edmann.

Kate, Lambert ten. 1710. *Gemeenschap tussen de gottische spraeke en de neder duytsche vertoont*. Amsterdam: Jan Rieuwertz.

—. 1723. *Aenleiding tot de kennisse van het verherene deel der nederduitsche spraeke*. Amsterdam: R. & G. Wetstein.

Kluge, Friedrich. 1920. *Deutsche Sprachgeschichte; Werden und Wachstum unserer Muttersprache von ihren Anfängen bis zur Gegenwart*. Leipzig: Quelle & Meyer.

Ludolf, Hiob. 1702. *Grammatica Aethiopica*. Frankfurt/M.: Martin Jaquet.

Noreen, Adolf. 1894. *Abriss der urgermanischen Lautlehre*. Strasburg: Karl J. Trübner.

Rask, Rasmus K. 1811. *Vejledning til det Islandske eller gamle Nordiske sprog*. Copenhagen: Schubote.

—. 1818 [1814]. *Undersögelse om det gamle Nordiske eller Islandske sprogs oprindelse*. Copenhagen: Gyldendal.

Raumer, Rudolf von. 1848. *Vom deutschen Geiste*. Erlangen: Carl Heyder.

—. 1870. *Geschichte der germanischen Philologie*. Munich: J. G. Cotta.

Raynouard, François J. M. 1816. *Recherches sur l'origine et la formation de la langue romane*. Paris: Didot.

Scherer, Wilhelm. 1865. *Jacob Grimm*. Berlin: Reimer. (2nd ed., Berlin: Weidmann, 1885.)

—. 1868. *Zur Geschichte der deutschen Sprache*. Berlin: Duncker. (2nd ed. Berlin: Weidmann, 1878; new ed. of 1868 text, with an introd. by Kurt R. Jankowsky, Amsterdam & Philadelphia: Benjamins, 1995.)

—. 1874. *Vorträge und Aufsätze*. Berlin: Weidmann.

Schlegel, Friedrich. 1808. *Über die Sprache und Weisheit der Indier*. Heidelberg: Mohr & Zimmer. (New ed. by E. F. K. Koerner, with an introd. by Sebastiano Timpanaro, Amsterdam: Benjamins, 1977.)

Schleicher, August. 1852. *Die Formenlehre der kirchenslawischen Sprache*. Bonn: H. B. König.

—. 1860. *Die deutsche Sprache*. Stuttgart: J. G. Cotta. (5th ed., 1888.)

Sievers, Eduard. 1874. *Paradigmen zur deutschen Grammatik*. Halle: Max Niemeyer.

Whewell, William. 1837. *History of the Inductive Sciences*. 3 vols. London: Parker. (Esp. pp. 508–518.)

—. 1840. *The Philosophy of the Inductive Sciences, founded upon their history*. 2 vols. Cambridge: Deighton. (Esp. pp. 667–677. Both Whewell 1837 & 1840 had 2nd ed. in 1847.)

Whitney, William D. 1867. *Language and the Study of Language*. New York: Scribner; London: Trübner. (6th ed. 1896; repr., New York: AMS Press, 1971; Hildesheim: Olms, 1973.)

7.2. Secondary Sources

Agrell, Jan. 1955. *Studier i den äldre sprakjämforelsens Allmanna och Svenska historia fram til 1827*. Uppsala: Lundequist.

Antonsen, Elmer H. 1962. "Rasmus Rask and Jacob Grimm: Their relationship in the investigation of Germanic vocalism". *Scandinavian Studies* 34. 183–194.

—. 1987. Review of Collinge (1985). *Journal of English and Germanic Philology* 86. 590–592.

Arens, Hans. 1969. *Sprachwissenschaft*. 2nd enlarged ed. Freiburg & Munich: Alber.

Bahner, Werner. 1985. "Jacob Grimm im wissenschaftlichen und internationalen Kontext der deutschen Sprachwissenschaft in der ersten Hälfte des 19. Jahrhunderts". *ZPSK* 38. 462–480.

— & Werner Neumann, eds. 1985. *Sprachwissenschaftliche Germanistik*. Berlin: Akademie-Verlag. (On Grimm, pp. 125–150.)

Baldi, Philip. 1999. *The Foundations of Latin*. Berlin & New York: Mouton de Gruyter.

Baudusch, Renate. 1985. "Rasmus Rask und Jacob Grimm". *ZPSK* 38. 686–692.

Benware, Wilbur A. 1974. "Jacob Grimm's Vowel Triad: A brake on 19th century Indo-European research". *General Linguistics* 14. 71–85.

Cherubim, Dieter. 1985. "Hat Jacob Grimm die historische Sprachwissenschaft begründet?" *ZPSK* 38. 672–685.

Christy, T. Craig. 1983. *Uniformitarianism in Linguistics*. Amsterdam & Philadelphia: Benjamins.

Collinge, N. E. 1985. *The Laws of Indo-European*. Amsterdam & Philadelphia: Benjamins.

—. 1995a. "Further Laws of Indo-European". *On Languages and Language* ed. by Werner Winter, 27–52. Berlin: Mouton de Gruyter.

—. 1995b. "History of Comparative Linguistics" and "History of Historical Linguistics". Koerner & Asher 1995.195–212.

Fourquet, Jean. 1948. *Les mutations consonantiques du germanique: Essai de position des problèmes*. Paris: Les Belles Lettres.

Fowkes, Robert A. 1964. "The Linguistic Modernity of Jakob Grimm". *Linguistics* 8. 56–61.

Gessinger, Joachim. 1985. "Sprachursprung und Sprachverfall bei Jacob Grimm". *ZPSK* 38. 654–671.

Ginschel, Gunhild. 1967. *Der junge Jacob Grimm 1805–1819*. Berlin: Akademie-Verlag.

Gray, Louis H. 1939. *Foundations of Language*. New York: Macmillan.

Hoenigswald, Henry M. 1990. "Descent, Perfection, and the Comparative Method since Leibniz". *Leibniz, Humboldt, and the Origins of Comparativism* ed. by Tullio De Mauro & Lia Formigari, 119–131. Amsterdam & Philadelphia: Benjamins.

Jankowsky, Kurt R. 1995. "Early Historical and Comparative Studies in Scandinavia, the Low Countries, and German-speaking Lands". Koerner & Asher 1995. 179–182.

Jellinek, Max H. 1913–14. *Geschichte der neuhochdeutschen Grammatik.* 2 vols. Heidelberg: Carl Winter.

Jendreieck, Helmut. 1975. *Hegel und Jacob Grimm.* Berlin: Schmidt. (Esp. pp. 48–114, 254–283.)

Ker, William P. 1915. *Jacob Grimm.* (= Publications of the Philological Society, 7.) London.

Koerner, E. F. Konrad. 1989. *Practicing Linguistic Historiography.* Amsterdam & Philadelphia: Benjamins.

– & R. E. Asher, eds. 1995. *Concise History of the Language Sciences.* Oxford, New York & Tokyo: Pergamon, Elsevier Science.

Lehmann, Winfred P. 1967. *A Reader in Nineteenth Century Historical Indo-European Linguistics.* Bloomington & London: Indiana Univ. Press.

Lötzsch, Ronald. 1985. "Jacob Grimm über die Verwandtschaftnisse der indoeuropäischen, finnougrischen, baltischen und germanischen Sprachen und Dialekte". *ZPSK* 38. 704–711.

MacMahon, Michael K. C. 1995. "Beginnings of Comparative and Historical Studies in Britain". Koerner & Asher 1995. 183–184.

Matasović, Ranko. 1994. "Proto-Indo-European *b and the Glottalic Theory". *Journal of Indo-European Studies* 22. 133–149.

Metcalf, George J. 1974. "The Indo-European hypothesis in the sixteenth and seventeenth centuries". *Studies in the History of Linguistics* ed. by Dell Hymes, 233–257. Bloomington: Indiana Univ. Press.

Morpurgo Davies, A. 1975. "Language Classification in the Nineteenth Century". *Current Trends in Linguistics* ed. by Thomas A. Sebeok, vol. XIII: *Historiography of Linguistics,* 607–716. The Hague: Mouton.

–. 1994. "La linguistica dell'Ottocento". *Storia della linguistica* ed. by Giulio C. Lepschy, vol. III: 11–399. Bologna: Il Mulino. (English version, London: Longman, 1998.)

Neumann, Werner. 1985. "Zum Sprachbegriff Jacob Grimms". *ZPSK* 38. 500–518.

Pankow, Christiane. 1985. *Die Wirkung der Deutschen Grammatik von Jacob Grimm auf die grammatischen Ansichten russischer Sprachforscher im 19. Jahrhundert.* Tampere: Tampere Univ.

Pedersen, Holger. 1962 [1924]. *The Discovery of Language.* Transl. from the Danish by John W. Spargo. Bloomington: Indiana Univ. Press. (Orig. publ. as *Linguistic Science in the Nineteenth Century: Methods and results,* Cambridge, Mass.: Harvard Univ. Press, 1931.)

Prokosch, Eduard. 1939. *A Comparative Germanic Grammar.* Baltimore: Linguistic Society of America (for Yale Univ.)

Salmons, Joseph C. 1993. *The Glottalic Theory: Survey and Synthesis.* McLean, Va.: Institute for the Study of Man.

Vennemann, Theo, ed. 1989. *The New Sound of Indo-European.* Berlin: Mouton de Gruyter.

Wyss, Ulrich. 1979. *Die wilde Philologie: Jacob Grimm und der Historismus.* Munich: Beck.

N. E. Collinge, Cambridge (Great Britain)

157. The synthesis of comparative and historical Indo-European studies: August Schleicher

1. Schleicher's place in the history of liinguistics
2. Theory and method: The comparative method
3. Substantive issues: The 'new look' comparative Indo-European grammar
4. Bibliography

1. Schleicher's place in the history of linguistics

The 19th century produced three major syntheses of Indo-European comparative grammar: Franz Bopp's *Vergleichende Grammatik* of 1833–49, August Schleicher's *Compendium* of 1861–62, and the *Grundriss* by Karl Brugmann and Berthold Delbrück of 1892–1900. Bopp's synthesis continues to be revered as the first systematic exposition of the inherited grammatical forms in the major 'Indo-European' languages together with etymological explanations of their structure, and that of Brugmann is still used by practicing Indo-Europeanists today as a reliable handbook and the most comprehensive collection of comparable material. Schleicher's

Compendium, on the other hand, is now completely forgotten. Why? In the foreword to both the *Grundriss* (1886 [1897: v]) and the *Kurze Vergleichende Grammatik* (1933 [1904: iv]) Brugmann makes it clear that his own work was conceived as a replacement for Schleicher's 'excellent *Compendium*', which had by then become dated. Initial negotiations with the publishers had envisaged a one-volume work, like the *Compendium*, but the large amount of recent research to be assessed and integrated had made this impossible and the *Grundriss* grew to over four times the intended size. It was for this reason that, after its completion, Brugmann wrote the *Kurze Vergleichende Grammatik* (Brugmann 1933 [1904]) explicitly as a textbook to replace Schleicher's work. Note, however, that the *Compendium* had, in its time, served as the basic textbook for that very generation which included the Neogrammarians, who are credited with putting the comparative and historical grammar of the Indo-European languages on a truly scientific footing.

The immediate reason for the obsolescence of the *Compendium* must be sought in a series of substantive advances which had rapidly followed one another in the 1860s and 1870s and which, taken together, had had the effect of radically changing the 'look' of the parent language and, as a result, the nature of the changes assumed to have taken place in the individual daughter languages (a further reason will be discussed in section 3 below). By the late 1870s so much rewriting would have been necessary to update the work that its editors, August Leskien (1840–1916) and Johannes Schmidt (1843–1901), felt it was more than doubtful whether the result would have represented the intentions of their late teacher (Schleicher had died in 1868, at the age of 47).

August Schleicher, born on 19 February 1821 in Meiningen, read divinity and Oriental languages first at the University of Leipzig and then at Tübingen. Here he came under the influence of Hegel. From Tübingen he moved to Bonn, studying classics with Ritschl (1806–1876), from whom he learned strict method. He completed his doctorate there in 1846 and, in the same year, obtained the *venia legendi* in Indian language and literature and in comparative grammar. In 1850 he was appointed to his first academic post, which was converted in 1853 to a chair, at the University of Prague, where he became the colleague of Georg Curtius (1820–1885), who held the classics chair. In Prague Schleicher worked intensively on the synchronic and historical grammar of the Slavonic languages and on Lithuanian. From 1855 to his premature death in 1868, he was also, especially in matters Slavonic, a regular contributor to, and co-editor of, Adalbert Kuhn's *Beiträge zur vergleichenden Sprachforschung auf dem Gebiete der arischen, celtischen und slavischen Sprachen* (after 1876 merged with *Kuhn's Zeitschrift*, for which he also wrote prolifically). In 1857, for political reasons, he was obliged to leave Prague and accepted a hastily created and poorly paid post (*Honorarprofessur* in comparative linguistics and German philology) at the University of Jena. Although his poor salary obliged him to publish in order to live ("es ist zu hart, jährlich mindestens 400 Taler erschreiben zu müssen", Schmidt 1890: 410) he declined offers from St. Petersburg, Warsaw and Dorpat. It is ironic that, while he was recognized abroad as the top linguist in the field of Slavonic linguistics, in his own country he was not offered a chair. He died of pneumonia on 6 December 1868, before reaching his 48th birthday. His contributions to journals are too numerous to list here. The first volume of the *Beiträge* alone contains some twenty. His book-size publications comprise a cross-linguistic study of palatalization, a typological survey of the European languages, a history of the German language, grammars of Lithuanian, Old Church Slavonic and Polabian and, of course, the *Compendium* (see the References and Koerner 1989: 230–231, for details).

Historiographers of linguistics have not reached uniformity in their assessment of Schleicher's place in the history of the subject. There was hesitation last century and there is still disagreement today as to whether he should be ranked along with Bopp and Jacob Grimm among the founders of Indo-European comparative-historical grammar or whether he should rather be seen as the first of the Neogrammarians. Having sifted through all the relevant historiographic literature, Koerner (1981a, 1981b, 1983, 1987 = 1989: 86–92, 185–89, 211–231, 325–376) came down in favour of the latter position, crediting Schleicher with establishing "the 'disciplinary matrix' for subsequent generations of comparative-historical linguists" (Koerner 1989: 333). In his view it is Schleicher who represents the crucial turning point which brought about the Neogrammarian paradigm. Anna Morpurgo Davies (1998: 166–74) sees Schleicher's Indo-European work more closely integrated with that of his predecessors and colleagues, especially Bopp, Pott and Curtius, despite the fact that Schleicher took the 'organism metaphor' much more literally than they did. She sees the late 1850s as the gradual implementation of an existing paradigm (p. 167). As both Koerner and Morpurgo Davies have studied Schleicher from a wider perspective and within the context of his time, the present discussion will be more closely focused on the *Compendium* as a handbook of the comparative and historical grammar of the Indo-European languages.

The methodological framework Schleicher developed for comparative-historical linguistics has become standard in the subject and we have largely forgotten where it came from. But certain other aspects of his overall theory of language evolution definitely have not stood the test of time and were in fact even in his own day considered rather too extreme. For Schleicher had argued that structural innovation in language, such as the formation of new morphological forms, was confined to a prehistoric period of language youth in which agglutinating, and subsequently flectional, structure was capable of being formed out of isolating structure — that is to say, he saw the Humboldtian language types as successive stages in a *systema linguae* formed on the analogy of the *systema naturae* of the natural science of his time (see 2 below and Bynon 1986, for details and references). Thus, once a language had reached the highest, namely the flectional, stage it could from then on only decay. A new isolating stage following the break-down of flectional structure was not thinkable because even the most 'decayed' Indo-European language still held vestiges of true flection, where grammatical meaning is signalled by the internal modification of the root itself (as in *sang* and *song* alongside *sing*).

There can be little doubt that it was Schleicher who, without being directly named, was the chief target of criticism in the so-called 'Neogrammarian Manifesto' (Osthoff & Brugmann 1878, English translation in Lehmann 1967: 198–209). At least this is what his former pupil and loyal friend Johannes Schmidt (1842–1901) claimed, in print, and he was not contradicted (Schmidt 1886). One criticism implied there was Schleicher's pre-occupation with inferred proto-forms of the *Ursprache*. The 'Manifesto' argued that the principles governing the way languages 'live and change' should be based on the observation of living dialects and on recent well documented language history and not on inferred prehistoric change as Schleicher appeared to have done.

'Only that comparative linguist who for once emerges from the hypothesis-beclouded atmosphere of the workshop in which the original Indo-European forms are forged, and steps into the clear air of tangible reality and of the present in order to get information about those things which grey theory can never reveal to him, and only he who renounces forever that formerly widespread but still used method of investigation according to which people observe language only on paper and resolve everything into terminology, systems of rules, and grammatical formalism and believe they have then fathomed the essence of the phenomena when they have devised a name for the thing — only he can arrive at a correct idea of the way in which linguistic forms live and change, and only he can acquire those methodological principles without which no credible results can be obtained at all in investigations in historical linguistics and without which any penetration into the periods of the past which lie behind the historical tradition of a language is like a sea voyage without a compass.' (Osthoff & Brugmann 1878; English version from Lehmann 1967: 202)

Schmidt (1887: 304) notes the irony of this statement in view of the fact that Schleicher was a fluent speaker of several Slavonic languages and of Lithuanian, of which he had written a descriptive grammar based on his own field work. Schleicher's alleged non-adherence to the uniformitarian principle in fact goes only as far as the distinction between growth and decay; there is no trace of it *within* the 'decay' phase, as is shown by the following remark in relation to the Slavonic languages:

'We know in what direction the sounds of our languages change. This historical development of the sounds must be followed into prehistory on the basis of the same laws according to which we see them change in historical times, and in this way we will arrive at the sound system to which the sounds of all the Indo-European languages point as their common source.' (Schleicher 1858a: 4; my transl.: TB).

The reason why Schleicher's preoccupation was with corresponding forms from the *ear-*

liest stages of the individual Indo-European languages was simply that the so-called 'discovery' of Sanskrit by European scholars had, at a stroke, revealed the true relationship of Sanskrit to the European languages and of these to each other. A scholar educated in Greek and Latin and confronted with Sanskrit simply could not fail to see the fundamental identity of their grammatical forms and of a large number of their lexical roots. It was Sir William Jones (1746–1794) who, having studied Sanskrit texts with Indian scholars in India, drew on this experience when formulating, in 1786, the famous hypothesis:

"The Sanskrit language, whatever its antiquity, is of a wonderful structure; more perfect than the Greek, more copious than the Latin, and more exquisitely refined than either, yet bearing to both of them a stronger affinity, both in the roots of verbs and in the forms of grammar, than could possibly have been produced by accident; so strong indeed, that no philologer could examine them all three, without believing them to have sprung from some common source, which, perhaps, no longer exists: there is a similar reason, though not quite so forcible, for supposing that both the Gothic and the Celtic, though blended with a very different idiom, had the same origin with the Sanskrit; and the old Persian might be added to the same family […]" (Lehmann 1967: 13).

(We are concerned here only with the hypothesis of common origin and not with the concept of language perfection, which at the time was taken to have been achieved in the flectional language type in which lexical and grammatical meaning were considered to be fully integrated with each other in the structure of the word.)

It was in this context of geographically and linguistically separated, though historically related, languages that the phonological and morphological correspondences became apparent and that hypotheses could be formulated regarding the periods of separate development intervening between the postulated parent and each of the attested daughter languages. Bopp had identified the major morphological correspondences and referred to general laws (principles of morphological composition and 'sound laws') that would have caused them, but it was Schleicher who produced detailed internally consistent analyses by setting up the rules governing the sound changes specific to each of the languages compared. The result was the first historical phonology of the Indo-European languages and, together with it, the first systematic application of what has come to be known as 'the comparative method (of phonological reconstruction)' (Hoenigswald 1950; Koerner 1989: 360 ff.). The technique itself and the methodological framework within which it operates will be dealt with in the following section.

2. Theory and method: The 'comparative method'

2.1. Put in the form of a discovery procedure, the comparative method consists in assembling sets of postulated cognates, working out the rules that account for the differences in their phonological form, and in constructing for each such set a protoform, or base form, from which the respective forms in the individual languages can be derived by the application of the rules of sound change formulated for each respective language (see Fig. 157.1). The assumption underlying the

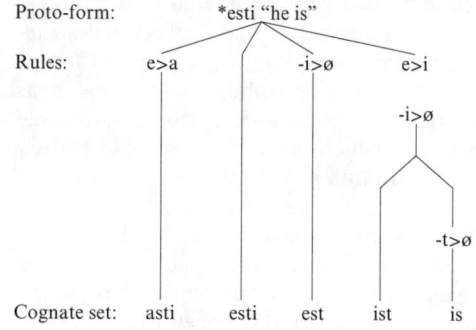

Fig. 157.1: Reflexes of PIE *esti.

comparative method is that inherited forms undergo rulegoverned phonological change so that, by working backwards through the changes that have occurred in the individual languages of the family, it is possible to infer (or 'reconstruct') the proto-form. The economy of the resulting analysis and the automatic nature of the rules involved can then be taken as proof of relatedness (cognation). There are, accordingly, three major components to the comparative method: protoforms, sound laws, and the family tree model (which specifies the lines of descent and hence the degrees of relatedness of the languages within the family).

2.2. The setting up of proto-forms or base forms is likely to be familar to the present-day student from Hockett's 'item and process' approach to synchronic morphological analysis and from the earlier versions of generative phonology. In these the linguist constructs an underlying representation or base form in such a way that all its variants can be derived from it by a maximally economical set of rules. Koerner (1989: 127) has produced evidence to suggest that Chomsky borrowed this method from his father's work on the historical grammar of Semitic. One major requirement of this procedure has come to be known as 'full accountability' (Hockett 1965), that is total coverage of the data by means of the most economical set of rules. It was this same principle which, in the form of the regularity postulate, underlay the diachronic analyses of the 19th century.

Schleicher interpreted the reconstructed proto-language as an integral part of the historical phonology of every Indo-European language, and the *Compendium* contains explicit reconstructions of *all* the forms which can be attributed to the parent language (Morpurgo Davies 1998: 168). Neither the aim of the method nor the premisses underlying reconstruction were, however, made explicit so that, when critics ridiculed Schleicher for attempting to reconstruct a lost language they entirely missed the methodological significance of reconstruction (i) as a means of extending the history of the individual languages into prehistory and (ii) as a test of cognation. For, if each set of putative cognates can be reduced to a single proto-form in accordance with language-specific sound laws, this form is the source and the compared forms are by definition cognates (unless there are good reasons otherwise, i. e. evidence which suggests that both are independent analogical innovations). Schleicher illustrated the procedure by tracing back Latin *generis* (gen. sg. of *genus* "family") and Greek *génous* (gen. sg. of *génos* "family"), each separately, to a proto-form *ganasas* (1876: 8, note). This form results from working back through the sound changes affecting Proto-Indo-European intervocalic -*s*-, which became -*r*- in Latin and was lost in Greek, but which is preserved in Sanskrit. The Sanskrit cognate *jánasas* also explains the reconstruction of two *a* vowels, in keeping with the state of the subject at the time.

'The disadvantage that in individual cases the forms of the proto-language which we have inferred are more or less doubtful could not possibly outweigh the advantages which flow from this presentation of the material.' (1876: 8, note; English version from Lehmann 1967: 94)

For, by operating with base forms from which the attested language forms are derivable by discrete sets of rules for each branch and individual language, Schleicher was able to set up testable hypotheses, thereby turning the comparative method into a diagnostic tool and comparative-historical grammar into a scientific enterprise.

2.3. The comparative method crucially depends on the regularity, or 'exceptionlessness' (Ausnahmslosigkeit) of the rules of sound change, or 'sound laws' (Lautgesetze). How Schleicher stood with regard to this regularity principle has been disputed despite the fact that his former pupil and loyal friend, Johannes Schmidt, stated with total clarity that

'Schleicher was the first to teach that all the modifications affecting Proto-Indo-European words, from the earliest times [Urzeit] to the present, are the result of two factors, sound laws operating without exception and, cutting across these, false analogies; these latter, too, were manifest already in the earliest phases of the development of these languages' (Schmidt 1886: 305; translation mine: TB).

But the Neogrammarian Manifesto gave the credit for first formulating the principle to August Leskien (another former student of Schleicher's) who, in the methodological introduction to his historical analysis of the nominal declension in Balto-Slavonic, made the point that allowing gratuitous deviations from a rule is inadmissable and that any such 'exception' will need accounting for, either in terms of some principle other than sound change (in practice, analogy) or in terms of a stricter, more sensitive formulation of the sound law itself (Leskien 1876: xxviii). This statement is not, however, made in the way one would proclaim some new principle; it merely spells out what the author took to be good method. The question of sound laws and 'exceptions' was widely discussed at the time. The authors of the 'Manifesto' chose Leskien's formulation from among many comparable ones quite as good as his (Hockett 1965). The 'Manifesto' formulates the regularity principle as follows:

'Every sound change, inasmuch as it occurs mechanically, takes place according to laws that admit no exception. That is, the direction of the sound shift is always the same for all the members of a linguistic community except where a split into dialects occurs: and all words in which the sound subjected to the change appears in the same relationship [i. e. context, position, TB] are affected by the change without exception.' (Osthoff & Brugmann 1978; English version from Lehmann 1967: 204)

A rule of sound change, in other words, is a language-specific input-output rule the scope of which is determined by the phonetic environment, e. g., PIE -s- > Greek zero and Latin -r-, PIE -m > Greek -n ('in Greek PIE intervocalic s is lost and in Latin it becomes r; in Greek word-final m becomes n').

Schleicher's awareness of, and adherence to, the regularity principle was first queried by Brugmann (1885, Anhang) on the grounds that he had never expressed it in print and that his practice did not point to uncompromising adherence to it either. Despite the vigorous defence on the part of Schmidt, Delbrück too was ambivalent on the matter, changing his mind between different editions of his *Einleitung*, published in six editions between 1880 and 1919. On the one hand, he says that Schleicher had generally been held to be its originator ("Man hat gemeint, Schleicher sei der Urheber") and that this would indeed seem to be in accordance with Schleicher's theoretical position, for 'he who considers language a natural object will presumably ascribe regularity to its changes' (Delbrück 1919: 174). (We shall turn to this natural science perspective under (3) below.) But on the other hand Delbrück wonders whether the fact that Schleicher had postulated 'exceptionless' sound changes safely excludes the possibility that he had also, as Bopp had done, accepted alongside these the possibility of there being irregular or sporadic sound changes (Delbrück 1919: 102). Careful reading of the *Compendium*, and the quotations assembled by Koerner (1989: 357—358) do not in fact leave any doubt regarding Schleicher's theoretical position. The following comment for instance relates to the exceptional occurrence of a labial for the expected velar (see below, section 3). Schleicher says that this change 'is not therefore conditioned by a generally valid sound law, for it occurs only exceptionally and independently of the neighbouring sounds' (1863a: 283). Brugmann would probably have expected him to add that there is an unresolved problem here. A bibliographical footnote in the introduction to the *Compendium* adds the following:

'At present two schools of thought oppose each other in Indo-European linguistics. The adherents of one have made strict adherence to the sound laws their basic principle (G. Curtius at Leipzig, Corssen in Berlin, the author of the present *Compendium*, and others); the other school of thought (Benfey at Göttingen, Leo Meyer at Dorpat, and others) do not feel the need to let their explanations of word forms be hindered by the sound laws hitherto discovered. This enables the adherents of this school to explain what to the others appears dark. [...] The future development of our discipline will show on which side the safe and truly scientific basis for the future thriving of linguistics is to be found.' (1876 [²1866]: 15—16; English version from Lehmann 1967: 87—88)

Brugmann (1885: 130—131) assembled a number of 'inconsistencies' in Schleicher's analyses, for instance his postulate on the one hand of a change of Greek *pheronts to phero:n and on the other of an exactly parallel *didonts to didoús. 'Nowhere does he ask what might have been the cause of the irregularity, nor does he note such cases as constituting problems yet to be solved.' In subsequent years the argument turned on Johannes Schmidt himself, and Brugmann (1885: 132) challenged some of his analyses too, whereupon Schmidt, in reply, attacked some of Brugmann's. The substance of their exchange centred on blaming each other for analyses which fell short of the strict regularity requirement, or which invoked analogy without giving proper arguments. Schmidt fully accepted the regularity principle but, to the challenge to come out clearly and say whether he was 'one of us', continued to refuse to join 'the party' (Schmidt 1887: 311, with further references). As regards Schleicher himself, Delbrück probably came closer to the true position when he identified as the main problem the state of the subject at the time. Many substantive issues had simply not yet been resolved and Schleicher was fighting hard to order and systematize what was known. It needs to be remembered that the substantive advances of the mid-1870s which revolutionized the 'look' of the proto-language and the shape of the sound changes operating in the branches of the family were still to come. When Schleicher wrote the *Compendium* neither the law of the palatals and with it the antiquity of the 'European' 5-vowel systems, nor the syllabic nasals and liquids had been discovered yet. In fact he could not possibly have given watertight conditions for the generally assumed split of PIE *a* into *e* and *o* in Greek and Latin if, as we now know, the change was in fact the other way round and Sanskrit had undergone an unconditioned merger! With hindsight it is thus easy to see that many of the sound changes and reconstructions postulated by Schleicher were not optimal, but not for lack of methodological rigour.

2.4. The degree of relatedness of the Indo-European languages Schleicher represented in the form of a family tree diagram (see Koerner [1989: 356 ff.] for a number of actual diagrams and for a history of the tree concept). This shows a threefold division of the parent language into an Asiatic, a south-western, and a north European branch, the Asiatic branch comprising Indo-Iranian, the south-western branch Greek (perhaps with Albanian), Italic and Celtic, and the northern European branch Balto-Slavonic and Germanic. The Indo-Iranian languages represented for him the most conservative group and the north European ones the least conservative one; on this basis he assumed that these latter would have left the common fold first while the other groups would have had less extensive periods of separate development. The family tree given in the *Compendium* is reproduced as Fig. 157.2. Note Schleicher's own interpretation: 'the length of the lines indicates time, the distance between the lines degree of relatedness' (Schleicher 1861: 7, 1876: 9; quotation from Lehmann 1967: 95).

The progressive differentiation which was to lead to the individual Slavonic languages ['dialects'] is divided into five chronological stages (Schleicher 1858 b):

(i) Slavonic as the Indo-European proto-language;
(ii) Slavonic as Balto-Slavonic-Germanic ('Slawodeutsch');
(iii) Slavonic as Balto-Slavonic ('Lettoslawisch');
(iv) Slavonic as a separate (intermediate) proto-language;
(v) Slavonic in the form of its individual dialects.

At stage one Slavonic had no separate existence, not even as a dialect, within Proto-Indo-European. What was to become Slavonic had the same inherent potential for change as all the other intermediate parent languages, that is to say, the conditions for its later emergence as a separate entity were no different from those for its sister languages: Proto-Indo-European was just as much Slavonic as it was Greek or Indo-Iranian. The split leading to the Balto-Slavonic-Germanic stage, and all subsequent splits, are based on progressive differentiation in the form of losses [sic!] and innovations.

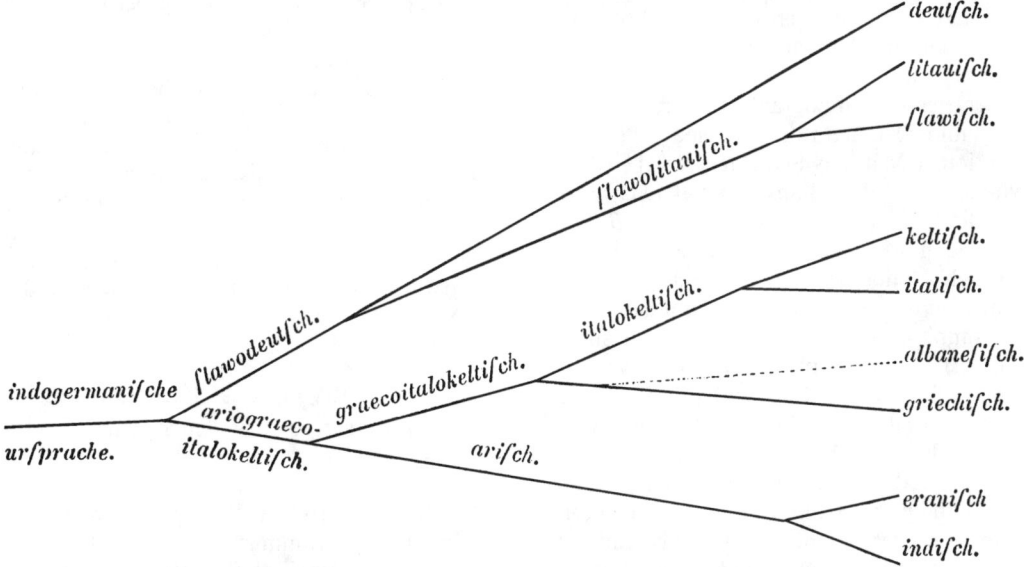

Fig. 157.2: One of Schleicher's genealogical trees (from 1876 [1861]: 9).

If Schleicher's work is seen in the context of the biological literature of his day, it is clear that he introduced the family tree model into historical-comparative linguistics for the same reason that biologists had done in their field, and that he was fully aware of the parallelism. Linguistics was for him part of the natural science of man, hence his deliberate use of such terms as 'organism', 'life', 'growth', 'decay', 'morphology', etc. Morpurgo Davies (1987) shows that these terms were current, at least as metaphors, in the linguistic literature of the time, and that the notion 'organism' in particular, inherently implied change. For Schleicher these notions were far from being mere metaphors. An optimal taxonomic classification was based on evolution, and 'the venerable old Lamarck' already had proclaimed that the natural order of the animals is the order in which they were formed (Lang 1904: 38). Schleicher's oft cited statement (e. g., Robins 1990 [1967]: 216, n. 75; Bynon 1986: 133) that adjacency in the system correlates with sequence in time makes the same point. Therefore, although it is true that trees had been used in linguistics before (Morpurgo Davies 1998: 185–86), for instance to display the 'affinities' among the languages of the world (Hoenigswald 1987, Auroux 1990), even the relationship of the Slavonic languages, and the manuscript history of a text (Koerner 1989: 356, n. 53), it is relatively unimportant whether or not Schleicher was aware of such earlier attempts. His trees have the quite specific purpose of mapping paths of evolutionary descent, as did those of both pre-Darwinian and Darwinian evolutionary biology.

Schleicher's bibliographical references to the biological literature are sparce but he mentioned Matthias Schleiden (1804–1881), who still held the botany chair at Jena in his day, and whose *Outline of Scientific Botany* (Schleiden 1842) was considered a breakthrough. Miocroscopic research had led Schleiden to make three important claims: (i) the simplest plant consists of only a single cell; (ii) the other plants are entirely composed of individual cells; (iii) the life of the plant as a whole is implicit in the individual cell (Schleiden 1842: 108). The cell itself was thus claimed to be a living organism, and the life of the entire plant was seen as no more than a 'higher potency' of it. This finds an immediate echo in Schleicher's view that the Indo-European Ursprache embodied the Indo-European languages not *für sich* but *an sich*, i. e., he contrasted in Hegelian terms the potential with the actual. For Schleicher the tree diagram of the Indo-European languages therefore implied that the proto-language was continued in every one of the descendant languages, whose future development was thus in some sense determined and constrained by their historical origin. Schleiden had sought to develop a scientific morphology based on the principle of evolution. Ernst Haeckel (1834–1919) was later to publish a *General Morphology of Organisms*, in which he developed the consequences of Darwin's theory of descent through natural selection (Lang 1904). Schleicher, who probably was the first to employ the term 'morphology' in linguistics had set himself comparable aims.

Haeckel had joined Jena University in 1861 and was, in later years, to become highly influential as 'the German Darwin'. His reading of Darwin's work had, at a stroke, 'removed the scales from his eyes' and he was to become an arduous defender and populariser of Darwin's ideas in Germany. It was he who had pressed Schleicher to read Darwin's *Origin of Species* when this had become accessible in German translation. He was in due course sent a copy of Schleicher's response fresh off the press, together with an invitation to tea (Koerner 1989: 210). It is well known that Schleicher was not unduly impressed by what he had read in Darwin because, in his view, evolutionary thinking was at least as advanced in linguistics as it was in biology (Schleicher 1863; Koerner 1989: 211 ff.). Although he credited Darwin with having identified natural selection as the mechanism which governed the evolutionary process in biology, sound laws and analogy had been identified as the corresponding mechanisms in linguistics. Koerner showed that Schleicher had published two family tree drawings as early as 1853, and six more in 1860, i. e., well before he had come across Darwin's work in 1863 (Koerner 1987, 1989: 37, 185–187).

3. Substantive issues: The 'new look' comparative Indo-European grammar

3.1. By comparison with Bopp's, Schleicher's comparative grammar is comparative *and historical*, so much so that Brugmann (1886, Preface) saw it as a series of individual historical grammars strung together. But it is at the same time an *Indo-European* grammar, in the sense of a grammar of the Indo-European parent language as the first stage of the historical grammar of each daughter language. Whereas Bopp took as his point of departure the situation in Sanskrit and then went on to show that the related languages too all reflected the single grammatical structure underlying them all, Schleicher took as his point of departure the inferred proto-language and derived the forms of the individual languages from it by language-specific sets of rules. His presentation was thus deductive, systematic and explicit, for which he offered pedagogic rather than theoretical reasons: presenting the reconstructed ('erschlossene') parent language alongside its oldest attested daughter languages will present the beginner with the current state of research in a concrete way and will make it easier for him to grasp the peculiarity of each individual language. The chosen method will also serve to refute the view still held by some that Sanskrit itself represented the ancestor of the Indo-European languages. The disadvantage that some reconstructed forms would be more doubtful than others would on balance be outweighed by the advantages (1876: 8, note). He might have added that, pedagogical considerations apart, this deductive approach was properly scientific because, by setting at the head of every set of cognate forms a base form ("eine auf die Lautstufe der idg. Ursprache zurückgeführte Form", 1876: 8, note) and by postulating a set of sound laws for each language, he had constructed explicit hypotheses capable of being tested against *all* the relevant material and thus to achieve 'full accountability'. Equally significantly in view of what has often been said, Schleicher made no claims regarding the historical reality of these postulated forms (1876: 8, note). The interest of comparative-historical grammar had never been merely antiquarian. Ever since Bopp it was considered an *explanatory* discipline because, in the individual languages, sound changes had over time obscured much of a once transparent morphological structure. Going back to the forms of the parent language would thus reveal the underlying grammar which, unlike the grammars of the daughter languages, would give direct access to the functions of the individual elements of the word. (This issue will be taken up below, 3.3.)

Schleicher's sources are discussed in a historiographically interesting note (1861: 12–13; 1876: 14–15. The list includes Bopp's *Comparative Grammar*, by then in its third edition (1868 ff.) but still lacking a historical phonology: phonology had become part of comparative grammar only with the entirely recast edition of volume I of Jacob Grimm's *Deutsche Grammatik* of 1822 and had been extended to the entire Indo-European domain by August Friedrich Pott in his *Etymologische Untersuchungen* (first edition 1833–36, second enlarged edition in six volumes, 1859–73). The detailed discovery of individual sound laws could be seen in the successive volumes of the *Zeitschrift für Vergleichende Sprachforschung* (since 1988 *Zeitschrift für Historische Sprachforschung*). Schleicher was a regular and most active contributor of essays and reviews to it and to the *Beiträge*, and these short publications sometimes give better insight into his thinking than the *Compendium*, which was conceived as a record of current knowledge. Other publications listed include, in the fourth edition, also Johannes Schmidt's own *History of IE vocalism* (Weimar 1871–75), which argues for the historical priority of the five-vowel systems of Greek and Latin over the three-vowel system of Sanskrit, a fact which had been discovered independently by several scholars more or less simultaneously (Collinge 1987).

The *Compendium* has two main sections, entitled respectively *Phonologie* and *Morphologie*, terms which became widely used in linguistics only much later. The other two parts which a grammar is expected to contain, *Funktionslehre* and *Syntax*, Schleicher considered not yet sufficiently well developed to be treated in a handbook of comparative grammar. The extreme conciseness of Schleicher's text is plain to see. It contains what he used to write on the board, dictate in class, or otherwise considered absolutely necessary for independent study. Discussion of controversial issues and personal opinion was deliberately excluded.

3.2. In Part I, Phonology, the phonological inventory of the protolanguage, in the form of a table arranged by place and manner of articulation (see Fig. 157.3), is followed, in nearly the familiar order, by the phonological inventories of the earliest attested *Einzelsprachen*. The sounds of the proto-language are defined as those sounds from which the

Übersicht der laute der indogermanischen ursprache,

	Consonanten				Vocale
	momentane laute		dauerlaute		
	nicht aspirierte stumm tön.	aspiratae tönend.	spiranten stumm tönend.	nasale tön.	r-laute tön.	
gutt.	k g	gh				a ⎫ aa āa
pal.			j			i ⎬ ai āi
lingu.					r	⎬ au āu
dent.	t d	dh	s	n		
lab.	p b	bh	v	m		u ⎭

Fig. 157.3: The consonants of PIE (according to Schleicher 1876 [1861]: 10).

sounds of the various Indo-European languages have arisen through the rules ('laws') of sound change which occur in the life of languages and to which they therefore point as their common source (1861: 8; 1876: 10). The sound laws are restricted to the domain of the word and are mainly rules of assimilation, elision, and rules affecting sounds in word-final position. Rules governing inter-word sandhi are excluded as belonging to the grammar of the individual language. What the modern reader will miss in many instances is a precise formulation of the phonetic conditions under which a particular rule applies. In some such cases Schleicher comments that we do not yet know the relevant sound law, but he does not always do so.

Vowels and consonants are treated separately. The vowels of the proto-language are still the basic three of Sanskrit. This poses no problems in identifying cognates but it does cause problems in specifying the conditions under which specific sound correspondences will apply. This is particularly so in the case of Greek and Italic, where the chief 'deviation' was considered to lie in the 'colouring' of *a* to *e* and *o*. Making reference to Curtius's study 'On the split of the a-sound in Greek and Latin' (Curtius 1864), Schleicher (1876: 55, note) puts forward a few rules of thumb, such that PIE *a* is represented by *e* mostly in roots and by *o* mostly in stem forming suffixes; and that Greek *o* is a reflex not only of PIE *a* but also of *a:* (compare Greek *phéretai* with Sanskrit and PIE *bhara-ti* "he carries", and Greek *phéromai* with Sanskrit and PIE *bhara:-mi* "I carry").

The system of vowel gradation (Steigerung) (see Fig. 157.4) of the proto-language reflects that of the Indian grammarians, i.e., three gradation series are postulated based respectively on the vowels *a*, *i*, and *u*. That *i* and *u*, unlike *a*, alternate with the corresponding 'sibilants' *y* and *v*, is well perceived. Vowel gradation is said to be employed to express grammatical meaning within the root itself, as behoves a flectional language. (Suffixes of course also express grammatical meaning; see 3.3.). The Germanic verb is singled out as having preserved the gradation system well as a means of expressing grammatical meaning.

The consonant system postulated for the proto-language is much simpler than that of Brugmann, lacking in particular the break-

Vocale der indogermanischen ursprache.

	grundvocal	erste steigerung	zweite steigerung.
1.	a-reihe *a*	a + a = aa	a + aa = āa
2.	i-reihe *i*	a + i = ai	a + ai = āi
3.	u-reihe *u*	a + u = au	a + au = āu

Fig. 157.4: The vowels of PIE (according to Schleicher 1876 [1861]: 11).

down of the 'gutturals' into palatals, velars and labiovelars. Again, this causes no problem for correctly identifying cognates but, significantly, Schleicher made no attempt at specifying the conditions governing the individual sound correspondences linking the proto-language and any one descendent. With hindsight we see that he was unable to do this because the phonological inventory he had postulated for the proto-language was underspecified, in keeping with the state of knowledge of his time. By way of an example we present Schleicher's list of PIE forms containing his undifferentiated unaspirated voiceless 'guttural' *k* (1861: 137; 1876: 159); we then break this list down into two separate sets, the first having a labiovelar and the second a palatal (the more marginal plain velar is ignored). With hindsight it is clear that there was no split at all for, already by the time of Brugmann's *Grundriss* it had become clear that Schleicher's undifferentiated 'guttural' was masking a contrast of two, or perhaps even three distinct sounds: palatal, labiovelar, and plain velar. Schleicher was in fact tantalizingly close to making this very discovery, when he envisaged an *an sich* division of the *k* containing roots in the proto-language into two sets depending on the nature of their reflex of *k* later on (Schleicher 1863a). (In the following data Schleicher's *j* for the palatal semivowel has been replaced by *y*, and Sanskrit forms are spelt in the familiar way; Schleicher does not place a hyphen after a root.)

PIE k: ka-s "who", ka "and" (Latin *-que*), katva:r-as "four", kankan "five", kard "heart", kak "cook", ki "lie", kru "hear", kruta-s "heard", vak "speak", dik "show", ruk "shine", dakan "ten", varka-s "wolf", etc.

Schleicher	Post-Schleicher
ka-s "who"	*qwo-s
-ka (Latin -que) "and"	*qwe
katva:r-as "four"	*qwetwor-es
kankan "five"	*penqwe
kak "cook"	*peqw-
varka-s "wolf"	*wḷqwo-s
vak "speak", va:k-s "speech"	*weqw-, wo:qw-s
kard "heart"	*k'erd-
dakan "ten"	*dek'm
kantam "hundred"	*k'mtom
ki "lie"	*k'ei-
kru "hear", kru-ta-s "heard"	*k'leu-, k'luto-s
dik "show"	*deik'-
ruk "shine"	*leuk'-

Schleicher's reconstructions reflecting PIE *k* and their post-Schleicherian counterparts:

Sanskrit: PIE k = Skr k, c, s, p (1861: 142–144; 1876: 164–166):

k = k: ká-s "who", kar "make", vŕka-s "wolf";
k = c: ca-ká:r-a "feci", ca "and", catvá:r-as "four", ruc "shine", vac "speak", vác-mi "I speak", but vákṣi, vák-ti, vá:c-am "vocem";
k = š: śi "lie", 3 sg śé:te: = Greek kéitai, śru "hear", diś "show", dašan- "ten" …; "s is favoured in particular before liquid consonants and v; ..k remains before s (with s to ṣ): á-dikṣat = Greek é-deik-se; dik-ṣu LocPl of diś- (NomSg dík for *dik-s, Gen diśás "sky region", DatPl dig-bhyás), …".
k = p: only sporadically. 'The change of original *k* into *p* is found in all the IE languages with the exception of Latin and Old Irish.' Ex.: pac "cook" for original kak, presumably with reduplication, preserved in Latin coc whereas Greek has two labials, pep; Skr pac and Slav. pek have changed the onset only while Lith kep has changed the coda only …; Skr páncan- "five" for PIE kankan; Skr sap appears to be a variant of sac (sequi).

Greek: PIE k = Gr k, p, t (ky = ss) (1861: 173–4, 1876: 202–203):

k = k: kard-ía "heart"; keĩ-mai "I lie", koíte: "bed", root ki, Skr śi; klu-tós "renowned", root klu "hear"; deík-numi "I show"; déka "ten", leuk-ós 'white', root luk, Skr ruc "shine";
k = p: pep "cook", in pé-pep-tai, pép-so: alongside pek in pésso: "I cook" = *pekyo:, originally kak; pénte/pémpe "five", poũ "where", põ:s "how", hep, hép-omai "follow"; Fep, Fépos "word", eĩpon "I said" = *FeFepon, Fóp-s = vo:c-s, but óssa "voice" = *Fokya with *k* retained (see the sound laws). 'According to Curtius, PIE *k* becomes Greek *p* in 17 cases whereas in 104 cases it has remained.'

k = t is mainly found in pronominal and numeral stems: tí-s "who", te "and", pénte "five", téssares "four".

Latin: Pie *k* remains unchanged (1861: 194–5, 1876: 232–4). It does not become *p* or *t* as in the other IE languages … Frequently, however, by a sound law not yet determined, the *k* generates a following *v* (see also Gothic): coctus / coquo "cook", quinque "five", quatuor "four", cord- "heart", quis "who", quid "what", deico "I show", decem "ten", etc.

Gothic: the PIE tenues become voiceless aspirates, the voiced aspirates voiced non-aspirates, and the voiced non-aspirates voiceless non-aspirates (consonant shift) (1861: 268–270; 1876: 314). Schleicher states that instead of the voiceless aspirate we sometimes find the voiced non-aspirate (i. e., PIE *k, p, t* to *g, d, b*) and that, as in Latin, there is the possibility of a *v* developing after the reflex of *k*.

All these examples show clearly that, with minor exceptions, Schleicher's pairings of proto-form and reflex are valid today but that he was not able to specifiy under which conditions his single PIE k becomes *c* or *š* or *k* in Sanskrit, or *p* or *t* or *k* in Greek. He had problems with two items in particular, the root for "cook", his proto-form *kak*, and the numeral "five", his proto-form *kankan,* items with a consonant constellation involving, in Brugmannian terms, a labial followed by a labiovelar. We now reconstruct **peqw-* "cook" and **penqwe* "five" plus different assimilations in the different languages. Schleicher's proto-forms *ka-k and *kan-kan may have been inspired by the Greek, Baltic and Slavonic forms. With regard to the velar and palatal plosive reflexes of PIE *k* in Sanskrit, Schleicher says that 'the law by which the gutturals become palatals is not yet worked out in detail; the fact that gutturals have palatal reduplications points to their late development' (1861: 141; 1876: 162–163). In pointing to the alternation of palatal and velar in *yu-yó:j-a* "iunxi" vs. *yó:g-a-s* "iunctio", he surmises that the physiologically determined alternation of guttural and palatal was later used to express a grammatical difference.

Leaving aside the gutturals, Schleicher's treatment of the sound laws responsible for the rich consonant inventory of Sanskrit is somewhat sketchy though in principle entirely modern: in addition to the 15 inherited consonants Sanskrit has 19 new ones, which are by origin variants of the original 15 and have come about, in the majority of cases, by recognizable sound laws operating in inherited words. (In principle these historical developments are reflected in synchronic morphological alternations well recognized in traditional Sanskrit grammar.) He postulates in addition influence from neighbouring Dravidian (1861: 141; 1876: 162–163).

The major sound changes of Greek Schleicher ascribed to the effect of the loss of the 'sibilants' *y, v* and *s* (treated as a class), which leads to a pile-up of vowels and subsequent contractions. An extensive footnote (1876: 56) analyses the 'multiple ambiguity' of the Greek vowels and diphthongs; for instance, the *ei* in *eimi* "I go" is identified as the result of gradation (root *i* "to go") whereas that in *eimí* "I am", "from *esmi, base from *as-mi* " [sic, Schleicher's asterisks] results from contraction following loss of *s*; *eĩpon* "I said" is from *eepon, *FeFepon, root *Fep, eĩe:n* 'I would be', opt. pres., from *esye:n, base form *as-ya:-m*; and *kteíno*: "I kill" from *ktenyo:. A similar exercise is undertaken for *ou*. This passage clearly illustrates Schleicher's use of the asterisk, which is placed relative to a specific sound law and systematically omitted in the case of PIE forms. – In the case of Germanic, the (first) consonant shift is presented in the form of the major sound correspondences followed by the remark that 'occasional malfunctionings of the consonant shift law are sometimes found without there being a visible cause' (1861: 268; 1876: 314), as when (Gothic) *b, d, g* (rather than the expected *f, th, h*) are found for PIE *p, t, k*.

This presentation of developments in the individual languages in the form of brief historical phonologies is followed by comprehensive tables summing up the major vowel and consonant correspondences, including those of the vowel gradation systems, across the languages discussed.

3.3. The second half of the *Compendium* is devoted to morphology. Here the difference to Bopp is more a matter of presentation than of substance. For Bopp had already sorted out innovations from retentions and had proposed morphological analyses of the inherited nominal and verbal forms. At first sight perhaps rather surprisingly, Schleicher also shares Bopp's aim of *explaining* these morphological forms by making reference to two levels of reconstruction: (i) base forms arrived at by phonological reconstruction alone, (ii) chronologically earlier base forms arrived at through morphological segmentation of those of (i) together with etymologies ('glottogonic' attributions) of the morphological segments thus isolated. Surprisingly, these two sets of reconstructed forms were placed side by side without being linked by any kind of rule. Sound laws were claimed not yet to exist in the parent language (1861: 11, 137; 1876: 13, 159). Their domain is the 'decay' phase of language evolution.

157. The synthesis of comparative and historical Indo-European studies: August Schleicher

The following analysed word forms of the proto-language illustrate the two layers of reconstruction (1862: 285 ff. passim, 1876: 495 ff. passim) the phonologically reconstructed form is given first (in italics):

va:k-s NomSg "vox", from *vak* "speak" + vowel gradation + demonstrative *sa* (weakened to *-s*);

as-mi 1sgPres "I am", from *as* "be" + *ma* "I, man, measure, think" (weakened to *mi*);

as-ti 3sgPres "he is", from *as* "be" + *ta* "he, that" (weakened to *ti*);

bhar-a-ti 3sgPres "he carries", from *bhar* "carry" + demonstrative *a* + *ta*;

bhar-a:-mi 1sgPres "I carry", from "carry" + strong grade of demonstrative *a* + *ma*.

These glottogonic analyses of the phonologically reconstructed forms are based on the theory of the prehistoric progression of language types. The root, as the bearer of the lexical meaning of the word, is taken to form the *oldest* component of the PIE word and to have itself previously been an independent word. The suffixes attached to the root are historically derived from roots which had become fused with the lexical root. They had lost their own lexical meanings when they had become downgraded to mark grammatical functions. Evidence for their former root status lies in the fact that they show vowel gradation. Every PIE word has thus developed from at least two roots; the first is the lexical root and the second tends to be a demonstrative pronoun in the case of nouns and a personal pronoun or auxiliary verb, in particular the verb 'to be', in the case of verbs. In essence this is Bopp's agglutination theory but with a fundamental difference in the interpretation of vowel gradation. While Bopp had, at least in his later work, come to the conclusion that internal flection/vowel gradation is the result of readjustments of syllable weights after grammatical elements had become fused into a single word (Morpurgo Davies 1998: 144, 176), Schleicher retained the older view expressed by Friedrich Schlegel that internal flection sprouts from the root as a means of 'organically' representing grammatical meaning − organically, because lexical and grammatical meaning are here fully integrated unlike in the case of affixation, which is merely mechanical, so that the affixes still show traces of their lexical origin. For Schleicher as for the Indian grammarians, the base form has the weakest vowel and the higher grades are formed from it by adding *a* (see Fig. 157.4).

'Word formation' deals with inflection and conjugation, i.e., the forms of nouns (including demonstrative and personal pronouns) and verbs as constituent parts of the sentence. Adverbs, prepositions, and conjunctions are outside the morphology although, etymologically, they may be case forms of nouns or verb forms. The (inflected) noun is formed from a stem which is itself neither nominal nor verbal by the addition of a case suffix, and the verb by the addition of a personal suffix to a tense or modal stem. The case suffixes are etymologically demonstratives (in the case of nominative and accusative) or postpositions (in the case of the local cases). The case forms of the plural contain the plural marker *-s(a)* added to the singular. The etymological derivation of the inflectional endings from independent words implies that all noun stems originally have a single set of case markers and all tenses and moods a single set of person and number markers. PIE *va:k-as* "voces" for instance is from *va:k-s-as*. Given that there is originally only a single base form to each case, all instrumental plural forms for instance are assumed to have ended in *-bhi-s*, from which are derived both Sanskrit *-bhis* and *-ais* together with their cognates in other languages as well as Balto-Slavonic and Germanic *-mis* (1862: 473 ff.; 1876: 565 ff.). All three sets of variants, namely,

(i) *-bhis* (in Sanskrit áśve:bhis, na:ubhís, Greek naũphi(n)),
(ii) *-ais* (in Skr áśva:is, Lith. vilkaís)
(iii) *-mis* (in Lith naktimìs, OBulg synŭmĭ, Go wulfam, gastim),

are thus all reduced to *-bhi-s* (instrumental + plural), despite the fact that phonologically neither the loss of *-bh-*, nor the change *-bh-* to *-m-* is in accordance with any known sound law.

In the case of the verb it is the person-number marker which turns the verb stem into a syntactic constituent. The person markers are the roots of the personal pronouns agglutinated to the verb stem (1862: 504 ff.; 1876: 644 ff.). A single first person singular suffix *-mi*, from *ma* "I", is postulated for both the athematic and thematic present (*asmi* "I am" and *bhara:mi* "I carry" respectively), i.e., the generalization of *-mi* found in the Sanskrit present tense is taken as the inherited pattern; in Greek and many other languages the -*mi* is assumed to have fallen after *a:*, that is to say, in the thematic verbs. The same -*ma* ending is attributed also to the perfect, with subsequent loss of -*m*-. The "secondary" variant of the suffix, -*m*, is found for instance in the first person singular optative, PIE *asya:-m* = Greek *eie:n* = Latin *sie:m*, and in the imperfect PIE *abharam* = Greek *épheron*. The first person plural ending -*masi* is analysed as -*ma-si* "I" [and] "thou", a so-called inclusive form (1862: 510−511; 1876: 647 ff.). Thus, for the "primary" variants:

PIE Active 1−3sg

Present		Perfect	Suffix
as-mi	bhara:-mi	vivaida	ma
as-si	bhara-si	vivaid-ta	tva/si
as-ti	bhara-ti	vivaida	ta

PIE Middle 1−3sg

| bhara-mai = bhara-ma-mi |
| bhara-sai = bhara-sa-si |
| bhara-tai = bhara-ta-ti |

In the second person, the discrepancy between the pronoun *tva* and the ending -*si* was not unproblematic. Brugmann was later (1885: 119) to reject his former teacher Georg Curtius' (1820−1885) derivation of -*si* from *t(v)a, dismissing his argument that

'the fact that we cannot verify a specific sound change for a historically attested period of the language does not in any way preclude the possibility that such a change might have occurred in an earlier period. Lacking knowledge of sound laws pertaining to the parent language makes this entire domain of investigation a much more slippery one than that of the later linguistic periods. In order to penetrate to the probable other analytic tools must be invoked in these circumstances. If the postulated sound changes in these instances involve such small and slight modifications as the assibilation of *t* before *v*, or a weakening of *a* to *i*, one cannot begrudge this as being especially daring.' (Curtius in 1876, cited from Brugmann 1885: 120; transl. mine: TB)

Brugmann argued that any proposed etymology will need to be supported by analogous instances and that all personal endings need not be old pronouns. A glottogonic analysis, in other words, needs to be justified.

The middle endings Schleicher derives, following Kuhn, from a sequence of two coreferential personal pronouns, namely, the object pronoun followed by the subject pronoun; thus, to Active *vagha-ti* "vehit" corresponds Mediopassive *vagha-ta-ti* "vehitur", later *vaghatai*. Similarly, Greek *phéromai* comes from *phero-ma-(m)i* "I carry (for) myself", etc. Forms such as *vagha-ma-ti* on the other hand are ruled out because they violate the coreferentiality constraint.

The tense and mood markers immediately follow the root. The possible morphological marking devices for tense and mood are, like in other categories, vowel grade, reduplication, and affixation, either singly or in combination. Other verbal affixes such as the causative/durative -*ya*-, and the past participle affix -*ta* are derived from pronominal roots. Schleicher's interpretation of the tense and mood system is as follows:

'When the Indo-European language was still in the earliest phase of formal structure, the root stood for what was later to be the entire word. At this early stage the only means of expressing grammatical meaning was repetition, in the first instance reduplication of the entire root. Thus, alongside *vid*, there would have existed *vid vid*. The function of reduplication is in general the same as that of gradation, its grammatical functions to be differentiated only later on, as for instance into intensive and iterative, as is still visible in the reduplicated aorist. Durative meaning finds expression in the reduplicated root of the reduplicated present stem; completive meaning in the perfect. We therefore assume, on the basis of the actually existing forms of the IE perfect, of the laws governing the life of language in general, and by way of analogy with the languages which have remained at older stages of language formation, that the oldest form of the stem of the perfect consisted in the reduplicated root, e. g., *vid vid* and, with encoding of the subject, e. g., 1sgPerf *vid vid ma*, 3sg *vid vid ta*. At the later agglutinating stage of the life of the parent language, these two roots would become attached to each other and to the personal pronoun, turning the latter into an affix; thus 1sg *vidvidma*, 3sg *vidvidta*. When the language had risen to the third stage, i. e., flection, gradation was added to the second occurrence of the root, and the entire complex was fused into a tighter unit through loss of the final consonant of the first occurrence of the root, whence *vivaidma*; the final form, following the loss of the initial consonant of the agglutinated pronoun, was *vivaida*' (1876 [1866]: 716; my transl.: TB).

It will be recalled that Schleicher had postulated a two-stage model of language evolution: a period of language growth in prehistory followed by a period of decay when the language enters history. Seen from this perspective, the Indo-European parent language is not an absolute beginning. Like any other flectional language it is supposed to have, in the growth phase, gone through an earlier agglutinating phase, and the agglutinating phase would in turn have followed an isolating phase. The Humboldtian language types, in other words, were seen as forming an evolutionary progression culminating in the perfect integration of lexical and grammatical meaning achieved in flection proper, i. e., the internal modification of the root realized in vowel gradation as a means of expressing grammatical meaning. These glottogonic analyses are thus justified by reference to the progression of language types. 'The earlier stages which we must presuppose for Proto-Indo-European can still be directly observed today in morphologically simpler languages' (1876: 331).

In the following illustration Schleicher traces both the structure and the substance of a Lithuanian sentence back through its prehistory, from the PIE flectional stage via the agglutinating stage right back to the isolating stage, as follows (1858: 8):

Lith vìlkas eíti ['wolf' Nom.sg. + 3sgPres of 'go'] (cf. Greek lúkos eîsi, Skr vŕka(s) e:ti)

PIE (flectional)	varkas aiti
PrePIE (agglutinating)	varkasa iti (ita)
PrePrePIE (isolating)	vark i / vark a i ta

We have already seen that *varkas* is formed from the root *vark* + stem formans/demonstrative *a* + NomSg/demonstrative *sa* (weakened to *s*). The verb form consists of the root *i* "go", with the first level of gradation to mark present tense, followed by the loosely attached third person singular/demonstrative pronoun *ta*, weakened to *ti*. Recall that Schleicher held to the Romantic view of gradation sprouting organically from the lexical root as a means of conveying relational meaning. The agglutinating predecessor of the above sentence would thus have been something like *varkasa iti* (or *ita*). At the preceding isolating stage grammatical meaning would either not be overtly expressed at all, or be expressed in the same manner as lexical meaning, namely by the juxtaposition of independent roots. The above sentence would at this stage have been simply *vark i* (or, more explicitly) *vark a i ta*.

Therefore, not only the higher types of language *structure* but the linguistic *substance* too which makes up the flectional Indo-European parent language would, in prehistoric times, have gone through these successive stages (1858a: 5).

It is on the face of it surprising that Schleicher made no attempt at relating by means of phonological rules the two layers of reconstruction. But sound laws were assumed to have not yet existed in the proto-language (1861: 11, 137; 1876: 13, 159). That is to say, forms such as *vaghatati* and *vaghatai, va:ksas* and *va:kas*, belong to the growth and decay phases, respectively, of the life of language. The parent language did not even have assimilation rules, so that the past participle of the root *yug-* "bind", Sanskrit *yukta*, Latin *junctus* (with the *-n-* marking present tense carried over) was assumed to have been still *yugta-* and not yet *yukta-* as in the daughter languages, and the instrumental plural of PIE *va:k-s* "speech", was still *va:k-bhis* and not yet *va:gbhis* as in Sanskrit. This would have been so because the parts of the word were not yet as tightly fused as later on. Schleicher's sound laws in other words are confined to the decay phase of language evolution, which is preceded by a kind of no man's land where "growth" and "decay" meet. Johannes Schmidt was later to argue that it was a natural step for the generation of scholars following Schleicher simply to discard the glottogonic reconstructions. He went even so far as to surmise that Schleicher himself, had he lived, would have come to the same conclusion (Schmidt 1890). Perhaps. The following generation were to practice strict adherence to the methodological principles of sound law and analogy, but from Schleicher's perspective such tightening of the procedure without the concomitant enquiry into sources of new morphology would probably have represented an unacceptable retrenchment. For it had the inevitable effect of reducing the explanatory power of the proto-language.

4. Bibliography

Auroux, Sylvain. 1990. "Representation and the Place of Linguistic Change before Comparative Grammar". *Leibniz, Humboldt and the Origins of Comparativism* ed. by Tullio De Mauro & Lia Formigari, 213–238. Amsterdam & Philadelphia: Benjamins.

Bopp, Franz. 1833–52. *Vergleichende Grammatik des Sanskrit, Zend, Griechischen, Lateinischen, Litauischen, Altslavischen, Gothischen und Deutschen.*

Berlin: Dümmler (2nd ed., 1857–61; 3rd ed. 1868 ff.)

Brugmann, Karl. 1933 [1904]. *Kurze Vergleichende Grammatik der indogermanischen Sprachen.* 3rd ed. Berlin & Leipzig: de Gruyter.

—. 1885. *Zum heutigen Stand der Sprachwissenschaft.* Straßburg: Trübner.

Brugmann, Karl & Berthold Delbrück. 1886–92. *Grundriss der vergleichenden Grammatik der indogermanischen Sprachen.* 5 vols. Straßburg: Trübner.

Bynon, Theodora. 1986. "August Schleicher". *Studies in the History of Western Linguistcs* ed. by Theodora Bynon & F. R. Palmer, 129–149. Cambridge: Cambridge Univ. Press.

Cardona, George & Norman H. Zide, eds. *Festschrift for Henry Hoenigswald.* Tübingen: Narr.

Collinge, Neville E. 1987. "Who Did Discover the Law of the Palatals?". Cardona & Zide 1987.73–80.

Christmann, Hans Helmut. 1977. *Sprachwissenschaft des 19. Jahrhunderts.* Darmstadt: Wissenschaftliche Buchgesellschaft.

Delbrück, Berthold. 1919 [1880]. *Einleitung in das Studium der indogermanischen Sprachen: Ein Beitrag zur Geschichte und Methodik der vergleichenden Sprachforschung.* 6th ed. Leipzig: Breitkopf & Härtel.

—. 1974 [1882]. *Introduction to the Study of Language.* Ed. by Konrad Koerner. Amsterdam: Benjamins.

Dyen, Isidore. 1987. "Genetic Classification in Linguistics and Biology". Cardona & Zide 1987. 257–267.

Hockett, Charles F. 1965. "Sound Change". *Language* 41.185–204.

Hoenigswald, Henry. 1950. "The Principal Step in Comparative Grammar". *Language* 26.357–364.

—. 1978. "The Annus Mirabilis 1876". *Transactions of the Philological Society* 1978.17–35.

—. 1987. "Language Family Trees, Topological and Metrical". Hoenigswald & Wiener 1987.257–267.

Hoenigswald, Henry M. & Linda Wiener, eds. 1987. *Biological Metaphor and Cladistic Classification: An interdisciplinary perspective.* London: Pinter.

Jones, Sir William. 1967 [1786]. "The Third Anniversary Discourse, on the Hindus". Lehmann 1967.10–20.

Koerner, Konrad. 1981a. "The Neogrammarian Doctrine: Breakthrough or extension of the Schleicherian paradigm". *Folia Linguistica Historica* 2.157–178.

—. 1981b. "Schleichers Einfluß auf Haeckel: Schlaglichter auf die wechselseitige Abhängigkeit zwischen linguistischen und biologischen Theorien im 19. Jahrhundert". *(Kuhns) Zeitschrift für Vergleichende Sprachforschung* 95.1–21.

—, ed. 1983a. *Linguistics and Evolutionary Theory: Three essays by August Schleicher, Ernst Haeckel and Wilhelm Bleek.* Amsterdam & Philadelphia: Benjamins.

—. 1983b. "August Schleicher and Linguistic Science in the Second Half of the 19th century". Introduction to Schleicher 1983 [1850]: xxii–lxxi.

—. 1987. "August Schleicher and Trees". Hoenigswald & Wiener 1987.109–113.

—. 1989. *Practicing Linguistic Historiography: Selected essays.* Amsterdam & Philadelphia: Benjamins.

Krahe, Hans. 1958/59. *Indogermanische Sprachwissenschaft.* Berlin: de Gruyter.

Lang, Arnold. 1904. *Ernst Haeckel als Forscher und Mensch.* (Reden gehalten bei der Feier des 70. Geburtstages Ernst Haeckels am 16. Februar 1904 in Zürich). Zürich: Albert Müller.

Lehmann, Winfred P., ed. & transl. 1967. *A Reader in Nineteenth-Century Historical Indo-European Linguistics.* Bloomington & London: Indiana Univ. Press.

Leskien, August. 1876. *Die Declination im Slavisch-Litauischen und Germanischen.* Leipzig: Hirzel.

Morpurgo Davies, Anna. 1987. "'Organic' and 'Organism' in Franz Bopp". Hoenigswald & Wiener 1987.81–107.

—. 1998. *Nineteenth-Century Linguistics.* (= *A History of Linguistics* ed. by Giulio Lepschy, vol. 4.) London: Longmans.

Robins, R. H. 1990. *A Short History of Linguistics.* 3rd ed. London: Longmans.

Schleicher, August. 1983 [1848]. *Sprachvergleichende Untersuchungen.* 2 vols. Reprint. Frankfurt/ M.: Minerva.

—. 1983 [1850]. *Die Sprachen Europas in systematischer Übersicht.* Ed. by Konrad Koerner. Amsterdam & Philadelphia: Benjamins.

—. 1852. *Die Formenlehre der altkirchenslavischen Sprache erklärend dargestellt.* Bonn: König.

—. 1856/57. *Handbuch der litauischen Sprache.* Prague: Calve.

—. 1858a. "Kurzer Abriss der Geschichte der slawischen Sprache". *Kuhn & Schleichers Beiträge* 1.1–26.

—. 1858b. "Das Auslautsgesetz des Altkirchenslawischen". *Kuhn & Schleichers Beiträge* 1.401–425.

—. 1861. "Sprachwissenschaft, Glottik". *Kuhn & Schleichers Beiträge* 2.127–128.

—. 1863a. "Das Ansichsein in der Sprache". *Kuhn & Schleichers Beiträge* 3.282–288.

—. 1977 [1863b]. "Die Darwinsche Theorie und die Sprachwissenschaft". Christmann 1977.85–105.

—. 1876 [1861–62]. *Compendium der vergleichenden Grammatik der indogermanischen Sprachen: Kurzer Abriss einer Laut- und Formenlehre der indogermanischen Ursprache, des Altindischen, Alteranischen,*

Altgriechischen, Altitalischen, Altkeltischen, Altslawischen, Litauischen und Altdeutschen. 4th ed. Weimar: Hermann Böhlau; 1876. (English translation from the third German edition by Herbert Bendall, London: Trübner, 1877.)

—. 1871. *Laut- und Formenlehre der polabischen Sprache.* Ed. by August Leskien. St. Petersburg: Eggers; Leipzig: Voss.

Schleiden, Matthias. 1842. *Grundzüge der wissenschaftlichen Botanik.* Leipzig: Wilhelm Engelmann.

Schmidt, Johannes. 1869—70. "Nachruf auf August Schleicher". *Kuhns Zeitschrift* 18.315—320 = *Kuhn & Schleicher's Beiträge* 6.251—256.

Schmidt, Johannes. 1887. "Schleichers Auffassung der Lautgesetze". *Kuhns Zeitschrift* 28.303—312.

Schmidt, Johannes. 1890. "August Schleicher". *Allgemeine Deutsche Biographie*, vol. XXXI, 402—415. (Reprinted in *Portraits of Linguists* ed. by Thomas Sebeok, vol. I, 374—395. Bloomington & London: Indiana Univ. Press, 1966.)

Theodora Bynon, London (Great Britain)

XXV. The Establishment of New Philologies in the 19th Century
Die Herausbildung neuer Philologien im 19. Jahrhundert
Le développement des nouvelley philologies au XIXe siècle

158. Die 'neuen Philologien', ihre Institutionen und Periodica: Eine Übersicht

1. Prämissen und Initiativen
2. Der Verein deutscher Philologen und Schulmänner
3. Die Universitäten: Professuren und Seminare
4. Fachzeitschriften
5. Bibliographie

1. Prämissen und Initiativen

Die Klassische Philologie hatte nach jahrhundertelangem Vorlauf in der ersten Hälfte des 19. Jhs. ihr Apogäum erreicht; das gilt in gleichem Maße für die hohe forscherische Leistung wie für den methodologischen Formenkreis Herrmannscher Ausrichtung mit der grammatischen Zentriertheit bzw. der Wolf-Böckhschen Observanz mit Grammatik, Textkritik und Hermeneutik als Triade umfassender Betrachtung der Antike. Die als gültig anerkannte Methodologie nahm den Charakter einer theoretischen Propädeutik für die sich in diesem Jh. herausbildenden Neuphilologien, also Germanistik, Romanistik, Anglistik und Slawistik, an. Allerdings stellten diese Neuphilologien im Unterschied zur Klassischen Philologie keine uneingeschränkt einheitliche Wissenschaften dar; ihre Gegenstandsbereiche gebieten später die Trennung in Sprach- und Literaturwissenschaft, die sich aber ohne jeden Zweifel gegenseitig bedingten, durchdrangen, stützten und im universitären Betrieb sich sogar in Personalunion überlagerten. Andererseits wiesen die grundlegenden Probleme der sprachwissenschaftlichen Neuphilologien einen weitgehend analogen Charakter auf, differenziert höchstens durch einzelsprachliche Spezifik und deren historische Bedingtheit.

Für den Neuansatz der Sprachwissenschaft des 19. Jhs. müssen weitere Faktoren in Rechnung gestellt werden:

(1) Die Wiederentdeckung des Sanskrit und die darauf aufbauenden orientalistischen Studien, die sich zunächst vor allem in Paris konzentrierten, führten zur umfassenden Begründung der genetischen oder historischen Sprachwissenschaft unter anderem durch Franz Bopp, der einen frühen geschichtlichen Punkt einer Sprachengruppe aneinanderstellte und damit die indoeuropäische Sprachverwandtschaft feststellte.

(2) Die Ausweitung des Boppschen Ansatzes durch Jacob Grimm auf die germanischen Sprachen mit der Besonderheit des diachronischen Vergleichs bestimmter paralleler Zustände dieser Sprachen, also in ihrer historischen Entwicklung. Diese genealogische oder historisch-vergleichende Sprachwissenschaft brachte die Entdeckung lautgeschichtlicher Gegebenheiten mit sich. Die theoretisch-methodologische Schlüssigkeit dieses germanistischen Ansatzes wirkte wiederum propädeutisch für andere Neuphilologien.

(3) Auf die romanische Philologie wandte Friedrich Diez (1794–1876) die historisch-vergleichende Methode an, wodurch er nach Vorarbeiten durch François Raynouard (1761–1836) und Lorenz Diefenbach (1806–1883) zum eigentlichen Begründer der Romanistik wurde.

Die Keltologie verdankt Kaspar Zeuss (1806–1856) mit dieser Methode ihre Begründung. Grundlegende Arbeiten zur Anglistik ergaben sich im Rahmen und aus der Weiterführung der Germanistik. Und die Slawistik konnte auf bedeutende Forschungen von Franz Miklosich (1813–1891), der die Grimmsche Methode anwandte, aufbauen.

(4) Impulse für die institutionelle Verankerung der neueren Sprachen in einem von den alten Sprachen geprägten Umfeld resultierten aus der Entwicklung eines gesteigerten bürgerlichen Selbstbewußtseins und der entsprechenden bildungspolitischen Erwartungen, auch im Hinblick auf kommerzielle und industrielle Belange. So nahm sich beispielsweise das Dessauer Philanthropinum Basedows im letzten Viertel des 18. Jhs. neuerer Sprachen an. Diese Dessauer Tradition wirkte noch nach, als in den vierziger Jahren des 19. Jhs. bestimmte Kreise der Schullehrerschaft eine Verstärkung des neusprachlichen Unterrichts auf Kosten des klassisch philologischen forderten. Symptomatisch hierfür waren die Engagements z. B. von Carl Mager (1810–1858) und August Fuchs (1818–1847), die im Angesicht des für geisteswissenschaftliche Lehrer obligatorischen Studiums der klassischen Philologie und/oder Theologie eine universitäre Ausbildung neuphilologischer Lehrer einklagten. Wegweisend und wissenschaftshistorisch bedeutsam war Magers Abhandlung *Die moderne Philologie und die deutschen Schulen* aus dem Jahre 1840 (in: *Pädagogische Revue*, Band 1, Seiten 1–80), in der aus der Sicht der Schule neben der klassischen und der orientalischen Philologie eine *moderne* Philologie, eine germanische und romanische, auch mit Blick auf die Lehrerbildung, an den Universitäten gefordert wird: die Neusprachenlehrer sollten die gleiche wissenschaftliche Ausbildung wie die Altsprachler erlangen. Wenige Jahre später veröffentlichte Mager dazu eine zweite programmatische Abhandlung *Über Wesen, Einrichtung und pädagogische Bedeutung des schulmäßigen Studiums der neuern Sprachen und Litteraturen und die Mittel ihm aufzuhelfen* (Zürich 1843). Darin liest man wiederum die Forderung nach der *modernen* Philologie, nämlich die germanische, romanische und slawische; und es werden entsprechende Professuren an den Universitäten eingefordert, auch eine Professur für englische Philologie. Diese Professorate würden sich um den wissenschaftlichen Nachwuchs, die Lehrerausbildung und der literarisch-sprachlichen Fortbildung der Studenten aller Fakultäten zu sorgen haben. Mager sieht sogar die Schaffung eines Seminars für moderne Philologie vor, wie sie ansatzweise schon 1839 in Rostock erfolgt war.

(5) Bezeichnend für das Bedürfnis der bereits etablierten Lehrerschaft nach neuphilologischer Aus- oder Weiterbildung war die Bildung von Lehrervereinen in vielen deutschen Ländern. So gründete sich 1815 in Berlin, wo gerade die jüngste deutsche Universität entstanden war, die Berlinische Gesellschaft für deutsche Sprache (vgl. H. Schmidt 1983) als Bindeglied zwischen Schule und Universität und als Ausdruck gewachsenen bürgerlichen Nationalbewußtseins, nicht zuletzt im Gefolge der Befreiungskriege. Entscheidende Impulse für ein neues Bildungskonzept, auch in Beziehung auf eine engere Bezogenheit von Schule und Universität, gingen auf die Bestrebungen Wilhelm von Humboldts zurück, als dieser 1809/10 als Leiter der geistlichen und Unterrichtsangelegenheiten solche Reformen, auch unter dem Einfluß Pestalozzis, anstieß und auf die Berlinische Gesellschaft einwirkte. Aufgabe der Gesellschaft, deren Mitgliedschaft sich im wesentlichen aus Berliner Schullehrern und -direktoren rekrutierte, waren eine kritische Bestandsaufnahme und Fortbildung der deutschen Sprache. Ein "Jahrbuch" erschien 1820 und enthielt eine eingehende Rezension von Jacob Grimms Grammatik durch August Zeune (1778–1853), der nach 1811, als von der Hagen nach Breslau ging, an der Universität die Germanistik bis 1824 vertrat; die Auseinandersetzung mit Grimm zeugt von der Rezeption der neuen sprachwissenschaftlichen Ideen der Germanistik.

2. Der Verein deutscher Philologen und Schulmänner

Er wurde im Jahre 1837 gegründet, vereinte die Schul- und Universitätslehrerschaft aller deutschsprachigen Länder, auch Österreichs und der Schweiz, und trug den Charakter einer Wandergesellschaft, die jedes Jahr in einer anderen Stadt tagte. Ursprüngliches Ziel war die Förderung klassisch-philologischer Studien und des gelehrten Schulunterrichts, organisiert in Form von Vorträgen, die protokollarisch jährlich in 'Verhandlungen' veröffentlicht wurden. Die quantitative Ausweitung der Versammlungen führte im Jahre 1844 zur Gründung einer orientalischen Sektion, 1845 einer pädagogischen Sektion, 1855 der archäologischen Sektion, 1862 der germanistischen Sektion, 1863 der germanistisch-romanistischen Sektion und der mathematisch-pädagogischen Sektion, 1865 der kritisch-exegetischen Sektion, 1877 als Sektion für klassische Philologie weitergeführt; und 1872 (ab 1880 regelmäßige Tagungen) Gründung der neusprachlichen Sektion (für Französisch und Englisch).

Ende der dreißiger Jahre war die klassische Philologie im Schulwesen die führende Disziplin. Das Französische oder Englische wurde von klassischen Philologen eher "nebenbei" übernommen und fand in Ermangelung einer universitären Ausbildung in der Regel auf niedrigem Niveau statt. Der aus Dessau gebürtige, Weseler Gymnasialdirektor [1823−1849] Ludwig Friedrich Christian Bischoff (1794−1867) führt in der Programmabhandlung des Weseler Gymnasiums 1838 lebhafte Klage:

"Wenn man von irgend einem Lehrgegenstande, welcher in den Kreis unserer Gymnasialstudien aufgenommen ist, sagen kann, er werde stiefmütterlich behandelt, so ist es der Unterricht in der *Französischen* Sprache."

Der Dessauer Schulmann, Alt- und Neuphilologe August Fuchs (1818−1847; vgl. Storost 1984), Teilnehmer an der Dresdner Philologenversammlung von 1844, gab in den *Blätter*[n] *für literarische Unterhaltung* (Leipzig 1844: 1245−1251) einen Bericht über diese Versammlung und forderte die Überwindung der Kluft zwischen Alt- und Neuphilologie, zwischen 'Philologen' und 'Linguisten':

"Das Vorurtheil, daß die Sprachforscher in Philologen, d. i. Forscher in griechischer und lateinischer Sprache, und Linguisten, d. i. Forscher in anderen Sprachen, zerfallen, muß niedergerissen werden [...], die 'Linguisten' haben in wenigen Jahren mehr für die allgemeine Sprachkunde, für das Sanskrit, für die germanischen und romanischen Sprachen u. s. w. gewonnen, als die 'Philologen' in einigen Jahrhunderten für die gründliche Erforschung der griechischen und lateinischen Sprache, die erst durch die neuere Sprachwissenschaft mittelbar und unmittelbar bedeutend weiter gefördert worden ist. Also weg mit dieser gehässigen und unwahren Scheidung zwischen Philologie und Linguistik, zwischen Philologen und Linguisten!" (Fuchs 1844: 1247)

Zur Stützung dieser Forderung hielt Fuchs auf der Hauptversammlung einen Vortrag "Über das Verhältniß der romanischen Sprachen zum Lateinischen" sowie in der Orientalistenversammlung einen Vortrag "Über den Einfluß des Arabischen auf die romanischen Sprachen", um bei beiden Fachgruppen Verständnis für die Neuphilologie zu wecken. Es war ein Anliegen von Fuchs, einem Vertreter der Evolutionstheorie bei der Herausbildung der romanischen Sprachen aus dem Lateinischen, den klassischen Philologen zu erklären, daß die romanischen Sprachen die 'erwachsene' lateinische Sprache seien und daß die 'Philologen' sie in ihre Studien einbeziehen müßten. Neueren Forschungen zufolge (Storost 1997) hat Fuchs sein Hauptwerk *Die romanischen Sprachen in ihrem Verhältnisse zum Lateinischen* (Halle 1949) als Einführung zur Diezschen Grammatik gedacht und dies auch dem Bonner Gelehrten so mitgeteilt.

Im Jahre 1861 stieß der Germanist Rudolf von Raumer (1815−1876) auf der 20. Philologenversammlung in Frankfurt/Main "in das gleiche Horn" wie Fuchs; er legte zwölf "Thesen über die Behandlung des Altdeutschen auf Gymnasien und über die Heranbildung der dazu nöthigen Lehrkräfte" (Raumer 1861) vor; von den klassischen Philologen wird verlangt, daß sie auch wissenschaftlich fundierten Unterricht im Alt- und Neuhochdeutschen erteilen können und die historische deutsche Grammatik und ältere deutsche Literatur kennen müssen. Die Diskussion dieser Thesen zeugt, auch behördlicherseits, von breiter Zustimmung. Es gingen wichtige hochschulpolitische Anstöße für die Germanistik davon aus. Seit 1866 gab es in den preußischen Prüfungskommissionen für Lehramtsanwärter einen Universitätsgermanisten, in Berlin war es Müllenhoff, in Halle Zacher, in Breslau Rückert, in Greifswald Hoefer, in Bonn Simrock, in Königsberg Schade, in Münster Storck.

Bei der ein neues Selbstbewußtsein der Neuphilologen bekundenden, aber auch deren Anerkennung verheißenden Gründung der germanistisch-romanistischen Sektion 1863 hielt der Berliner Lehrer und Gelehrte, Etymologe und Troubadour-Herausgeber Carl August Friedrich Mahn (1802−1887) den grundlegenden Vortrag "Über die Entstehung, Bedeutung, Zwecke und Ziele der romanischen Philologie" (vgl. Christmann 1986). Die zweite Auflage der 'Magna Charta der romanischen Sprachwissenschaft' (Trabant 1994) war schon erschienen ebenso wie das Diezsche *Etymologische Wörterbuch der romanischen Sprachen* (1853). Mahn nahm die Begründung der romanischen Philologie durch Diez als gegeben an und versuchte nun vor den versammelten Schulmännern, den Weg für die Anwendung, in der schulischen Praxis, der Vermittlung der romanischen Sprachen und des Englischen auf der Grundlage der historisch-vergleichenden Grammatik aufzuzeigen. Der Schüler könne die zu lernende Sprache besser behalten, wenn er die Wörter mit den nächsten verwandten Sprachen vergleicht. Mahn fordert eine Verstärkung von universitärer Forschung und Lehre im Hinblick auf die romanischen Sprachen und das Englische unter Berücksichtigung der neuen Methodologie. Seien erst einmal habilitierte Dozenten vorhanden, würden die Lehrstühle nicht auf sich warten lassen. Der Realist Mahn denkt zunächst an Doppelprofessuren für Englisch und Französisch, möglicherweise auch in Kombination mit Germanistik; am Ende müßten aber gesonderte Ordinariate für die einzelnen Fachrichtungen stehen. Die Forschungs- und Lehrinhalte müßten neben den literarhistorischen Untersuchungen mit Erklärung der Schriftsteller unter kritischen, sprachlichen und etymologischen Gesichtspunkten die historisch-vergleichende Grammatik der romanischen Sprachen und des Englischen auf der einen Seite und die wissenschaftliche Behandlung der einzelsprachlichen Grammatik sein. Die Programmatik ist vor dem Hintergrund der seit einigen Jahrzehnten bestehenden, bei den Kultusministerien unterstützten Forderung nach wissenschaftlicher Ausbildung der Lehrer für Neuphilologie auf der einen Seite und einer mehr auf wissenschaftliche Forschung ausgerichteten Universitätsprofessorenschaft auf der anderen Seite zu sehen. Auf dieses Verhältnis von Universität, Lehrerausbildung und gymnasialem Deutschunterricht hatte Adelbert von Keller schon 1842 in der programmatischen Tübinger Antrittsrede hingewiesen (*Inauguralrede über die Aufgabe der modernen Philologie*, Stuttgart 1842).

Eine besondere Vorliebe hatte Mahn für das Altprovenzalische (er war der Lehrer von Karl Bartsch), das als Verbindungsstück zwischen dem Lateinischen und den romanischen Sprachen anzusehen sei. Mahns Gedanken gipfeln in der Forderung nach Einrichtung philologischer Seminare für die Neuphilologie an den Universitäten, wie sie für die klassische Philologie seit langem gang und gäbe waren. Mahns Gedanken wurden unmittelbar von Gaston Paris (1839–1903) nach Frankreich getragen, der sie unter der Überschrift "La Philologie romane en Allemagne" in der Bibliothèque de l'École des Chartes, Jahrgang 25, Band 5. 433–445 (1864) veröffentlichte und klagte, daß Frankreich in der Akzeptanz einer romanischen Philologie noch weit hinter Deutschland zurückstehe; Paris hatte gerade mit der Übersetzung der Diezschen Grammatik begonnen und damit die Grundlagen der romanischen Philologie in Frankreich bekannt gemacht.

3. Die Universitäten: Lehrstühle, Professuren und Seminare

Bereits die Schaffung von Lehrstühlen für eine Disziplin bedeutete die Anerkennung als Lehrfach, mithin bereits eine gewisse Institutionalisierung; tatsächlich wurde aber ein Fach im Selbstverständnis der Universitäten erst mit der Einrichtung eines Ordinariats institutionalisiert. In der Institutionalisierungsphase der Neuphilologien bestand gemäß dem klassischen Philologiebegriff eine Einheit zwischen Literatur- und Sprachwissenschaft. Und in der Anfangsphase (wir verwenden diesen Begriff tatsächlich so unpräzise, weil die Vorgänge an den einzelnen Universitäten zeitlich höchst unterschiedlich verliefen) wurden die Lehrstühle, gerade in Beziehung auf die Deutsche Philologie, in der Regel von klassischen Philologen im Sinne einer Doppelprofessur mitvertreten. Aber auch bei den anderen Neuphilologien wird es zunächst zur Ausbildung von Doppelprofessuren in unterschiedlicher Kombination kommen: Germanistik-Anglistik, Germanistik-Romanistik, Romanistik-Anglistik.

3.1. Germanistik

Literaturgeschichtliche Vorlesungen und Übungen zum deutschen Stil im Sinn z. B. einer Hilfslehre für Juristen und Theologen finden sich realisiert oder angekündigt bereits im ausgehenden 18. Jh. an deutschsprachigen Universitäten, wobei die Beschäftigung mit dem Deutschen in der Regel nur einen Ausschnitt des Gesamtlehrprogramms polyhistorisch orientierter Professoren bildete. Zur eigenständigen Professionalisierung des Faches kam es an den verschiedenen Universitäten in der Zeit von 1810 bis 1850. Symptomatisch sind die Vorstellungen des preußischen Kultusministeriums von 1820 über die unbesetzte Professur der deutschen Sprache und Literatur an der Berliner Universität, in denen die historische und philosophische Behandlung der deutschen Sprache vom Mittelalter bis zur Gegenwart gefordert werden:

"Was der hiesigen Universität noch mangelt, ist ein Lehrer, welcher die deutsche Sprache und deren Literatur nebst den verwandten Mundarten mit eben so tiefer und umfassender historischer Kenntniß als philosophischer Kritik, und nicht bloß in Beziehung auf das Mittelalter und dessen Poesie, sondern in ihrem ganzen Umfange zu behandeln im Stande wäre [...]." (Zit. nach Meves 1994: 131).

In den dreißiger Jahren und danach massierten sich die Habilitationen, und die Privatdozenten drängten an die Universitäten, bereit, auf dem Gebiet ihrer Habilitationsspezialisierung (in Richtung der von Lachmann und Grimm vertretenen Disziplin) zu lehren. Die Bedeutung und Anerkennung der Germanistik wuchs am Ende der vierziger Jahre, was durch eine wachsende Zahl außerordentlicher Professuren evident wird, wiewohl sich die Entwicklung an den einzelnen Universitäten unaufhaltsam mit unterschiedlicher Förderung oder Intensität bis zu seinem vorläufigen Abschluß 1870, noch vor der Reichsgründung, vollzog. An den Universitäten ergab sich folgendes Bild:

Greifswald: 1785–1810 Jacob Wallenius (1761–1819), Orientalist, klassische Philologie, deutscher Stil; 1840 Albert Hoefer (1812–1883, 1838 Habilitation in Berlin: Sanskrit, Sprachvergleichung, altdeutsche Philologie): außerordentlicher (ao.) (1847 ordentlicher (o.) Prof. für Orientalistik mit altdeutscher Philologie als Teilaspekt;

Kiel: Seit 1789 Johann Adolph Nasser (1753–1828), Archäologie, römische und deutsche Literatur; 1841 PD Karl Müllenhoff (1818–1884), 1845 ao. (1854 o.) Professor der deutschen Sprachkunde, Altertumswissenschaft und Literatur; 1861 kam Karl Weinhold (1823–1901) aus Graz als Ordinarius für deutsche Sprache, Literatur und Altertümer; ihm folgte 1876 aus Breslau Friedrich Wilhelm Pfeiffer (1827–1893) als Ordinarius der deutschen Sprache und Literatur nach; infolge der besonderen Beziehungen Schleswig-Holsteins zu Dänemark war es natürlich, daß man sich an der Universität auch mit dem Dänischen beschäftigte. 1810 wurde im Zusammenhang mit der Dänisierung Holsteins ein Extraordinariat für dänische Sprache und Literatur geschaffen, das 1811 der dänische Dichter Jens Baggesen (1764–1826) erhielt, der jedoch infolge seiner Reisens und des Dichtens kaum Lehrveranstaltungen hielt, 1814 wurde er pensioniert; Nachfolger 1814 der Däne Henning Christopher Götzsche als Lektor, der bis 1822 blieb; sein Nachfolger von 1822 bis 1826 wurde Johann Ludwig Heiberg (1791–1860), dem von 1826 bis 1845 der Lektor der dänischen Sprache und Literatur Christian Flor (1792–1875) nachfolgte (1841 Professor), er las über Isländisch, Altnordisch und altnordische Mythologie; 1845 Einrichtung einer Professur für Nordisch, besetzt 1846–1848 mit dem Zoologen, Lyriker und Schriftsteller Johann Carsten Hauch (1790–1872); Nachfolger 1850–1852 Rochus von Liliencron (1820–1912) als Extraordinarius der nordischen Literatur und Sprache; Nachfolger 1853–1864 der dänische Dichter Christian Knut Frederik Molbech (1783–1857) als Extraordinarius (1857 Ordinarius) der dänischen und nordischen Literatur; Nachfolger 1865 Theodor Möbius (1821–1889) aus Leipzig als Ordinarius der nordischen Sprachen und Literatur, auch als Lektor für Dänisch; er las auch altenglische Grammatik und Literatur sowie Gotisch; Nachfolger 1889 der Hallenser Extraordinarius Hugo Gering (1847–1925) als Ordinarius der nordischen Philologie, er las über altnordische Grammatik und Literaturgeschichte, historische Grammatik des Dänischen und führte in die *Edda* ein.

Bern: 1805–1854 Carl Christian Jahn (1777–1854), er las auch über französische, italienische, spanische und englische Literatur.

Münster: Seit 1801 Johann Christoph Schlüter (1767–1841), deutscher Stil, deutsche Literatur; 1858 PD Wilhelm Storck (1829–1905), 1859 ao. (1868 o.) Prof. für deutsche Sprache und Literatur, bis 1892; Nachfolger Franz Jostes (1858–1925).

Göttingen: Seit 1805 George Friedrich Benecke (1762–1844), deutsche und englische Literatur und Sprache, nach klassisch philologischer Manier; 1829 Jacob Grimm wurde Ordentlicher Professor (er las nach klassisch philologischem Muster über deutsche Literaturgeschichte mit Sprachgeschichte und Altertumswissenschaft; 1831 Wilhelm Grimm wurde ao. Prof.; die Brüder mußten 1837 Göttingen verlassen; 1841 PD Wilhelm Müller (1812–1890), 1845 ao. (1856 o.) Professor.

Heidelberg: 1806–1811 Alois Wilhelm Schreiber 1763–1841), Professor der Ästhetik, las über deutschen Stil/Geschäftsstil; 1840 PD Karl August Hahn (1807−1857), 1847 Extraordinarius, ging 1849 nach Prag; 1852−1870 Adolf Holtzmann (1810−1870, Sanskritforscher, Sprachvergleicher, Theologe), Ordinarius für deutsche Sprache und Literatur.

Königsberg: Seit 1809 Johann Friedrich Ferdinand Delbrück (1772−1848), deutsche Literaturgeschichte und Mythologie, Rhetorik; 1816 Lachmann als ao. Professor für klassische und altdeutsche Philologie; 1824 Eberhard Gottlieb Graff (1780−1841, Autor des althochdeutschen Wörterbuchs) ao. (1827 o.) Prof. für deutsche Sprache und Literatur bis 1832; 1859 Julius Zacher (1816−1887), Ordinarius der deutschen Philologie bis 1863 (Halle); Nachfolger wurde 1863 Oskar Schade (1826−1906) (1860 PD in Halle).

Tübingen: 1811−1817 Salomon Michaelis (1769−1844), Lehrstuhlinhaber für deutsche Sprache und Literatur, zugleich seit 1810 Professor der französischen Sprache und Literatur; Vakanz bis 1829; 1829 wurde der Jurist Ludwig Uhland (1787−1862) ao. Prof. für deutsche Sprache und Literatur, er lehrte bis 1833; 1844 wurde Adelbert von Keller (1812−1883) Ordinarius für germanische Sprachen und Literatur.

Landshut (ab 1826 **München**): Seit 1804 Georg Aloys Dietl (1752−1809) Professor der Ästhetik, deutsche Klassiker und Stilübungen, Vorlesungen über Ossian und Shakespeare; ab 1809 Professor der Literaturgeschichte Johann Christian Siebenkees (1753−1851, seit 1776 Jurist und Historiker in Altdorf), deutsche Sprachlehre und Stilübungen; 1827 Johann Andreas Schmeller (1785−1829; 1828 ao. Prof. der altdeutschen Literatur und Sprache, im gleichen Jahr Versetzung an die Staatsbibliothek) und Hans Ferdinand Maßmann (1797−1874; 1828 Privatdozent für altdeutsche Sprache und Literatur), 1829 Nachfolger Schmellers, 1829 ao. (1835 o.) Prof. für ältere deutsche Sprache und Literatur [1. Ord. Professur in Bayern]) bis 1842, dann Berlin; 1853 Konrad Hofmann (1819−1890, Germanist und Romanist) Extraord. für indogermanische Sprachen und Literatur, 1856 Ordinarius für altdeutsche Sprache und Literatur.

Berlin: Nach dem kurzen, um wissenschaftlich philologische Durchdringung bemühten Wirken des Juristen und seit 1810 außerordentlichen Professors der deutschen Sprache Friedrich Heinrich von der Hagens (1780−1856) bis 1811 (deutsches Altertum) lag die deutsche Philologie (Geschichte der deutschen Sprache und Literatur, Nibelungenlied) von 1812 bis 1822 kontinuierlich in den Händen August Zeunes (1778−1853), eines Geographen, der in einer Zeit des aufbrechenden deutschen Patriotismus äußerst erfolgreich über das Nibelungenlied las und auch die gotische Bibelübersetzung besprach. 1824 kehrte von der Hagen aus Breslau als Ordentlicher Professor für deutsche Sprache und Literatur zurück, und Karl Lachmann kam 1825 als ao. Professor aus Königsberg; letzterer wurde 1827 Ordentlicher Professor der deutschen *und* klassischen Philologie. Während von der Hagen historisch-vergleichende deutsche Grammatik las und in das Mittelhochdeutsche einführte, lehrte Lachmann deutsche Grammatik und besprach das Nibelungenlied sowie altdeutsche Dichtung. Seit 1835 las Franz Bopp (1791−1867) über gotische und deutsche Grammatik sowie über deutsche Grammatik im Vergleich mit verwandten Sprachen. Das Eintreffen Jacob Grimms 1841 festigte die Position der sprachwissenschaftlichen Germanistik weiter, was durch die Nachfolger Lachmanns und von der Hagens, die klassischen Philologen und Germanisten Moriz Haupt bzw. Karl Müllenhoff noch unterstrichen wird. Berlin nahm gegenüber anderen deutschen Universitäten eine gewisse Vorreiterrolle ein, umso erstaunlicher ist es, daß erst 1887 unter Erich Schmidt (1853−1913) das Germanistische Seminar gegründet wurde.

Breslau: Seit 1811 von der Hagen, 1817 Ordentlicher Professor (erste wirkliche germanistische Professur in Preußen); 1835 Heinrich Hoffmann von Fallersleben (1798−1874), 1830 ao. (1835 o.) Prof.; 1836 Privatdozent Karl August Timotheus Kahlert (1807−1864), 1840 Extraordinarius, er las bis 1859 über Goethe, Schiller, Lessing; 1842 PD Gottschalk Eduard Guhrauer (1809−1854), 1843 Extraordinarius für Literaturgeschichte und Philosophie; 1848 der Berliner PD Theodor Mundt (1808−1861) wurde ao. Prof. für neuere Literatur und Literaturgeschichte (er ging 1850 wieder nach Berlin); 1852 Heinrich Rückert (1823−1875) Extraord. der deutschen Philologie.

Bonn: Seit 1818 Ferdinand Delbrück (1772−1848, Philosoph), o. Prof. für deutsche Literatur; 1818 Johann Gottlieb Radloff (1775−1846) Extraordinarius für allgemeine und deutsche Sprachkunde; 1823 Friedrich Diez (1794−1876), Extraordinarius (1830 Ordinarius) für mittlere und neuere Literaturen, er las auch über deutsche Literaturgeschichte bis zum 16. Jh., Nibelungenlied, Gotisch, Alt- und Mittelhochdeutsch und Angelsächsisch; 1837 PD Gottfried Kinkel (1815–1882), 1846 Extraordinarius für neuere Kunst-, Literatur- und Kulturgeschichte (bis 1849); 1850 Karl Simrock (1802–1876) ao. Prof. für die Geschichte der deutschen Literatur, 1852 Ordinarius für deutsche Sprache und Literatur (1. Bonner Professur dieser Art).

Rostock: 1837 Christian Wilbrandt (1810–1867), o. Prof. für Ästhetik und neuere Literatur, er vertrat europäische Literaturgeschichte: griechische, englische, deutsche (alt- und mittelhochdeutsche) Literatur, dazu Philosophiegeschichte, Kunstphilosophie, Ästhetik, 1852 entlassen; erst 1857 wurde die Germanistik mit Karl Bartsch (1832–1888) wieder aufgenommen.

Würzburg: 1840 Friedrich Anton Leopold Reuss (1810–1868, Mediziner) ao. Professor für Deutsche Philologie (Geschichte der deutschen Literatur, deutsche Altertumskunde, Diplomatik, Heraldik) bis 1855; 1856 Hermann Müller (1803–1876, Jurist), Ordinarius der deutschen Philologie bis 1868; 1868 Matthias Lexer (1830–1892) o. Prof. für deutsche Sprache und Literatur.

Leipzig: 1843 Moriz Haupt (1808–1874), o. Prof. der deutschen Sprache und Literatur (1837 Privatdozent für Klassische Philologie, 1838 ao. Prof. für Philosophie), 1851 entlassen; Friedrich Zarncke (1825–1891) wurde 1854 ao. (1858 o.) Professor für deutsche Sprache und Literatur.

Erlangen: Rudolf von Raumer (1815–1876), 1840 Habilitation, las über germanische Sprachen, allgemeine und deutsche Geschichte, 1846 ao. (1852 o.) Prof. (ohne Fachangabe);

Jena: 1845 Heinrich Rückert (1823–1875) Privatdozent (Geschichte des Mittelalters), 1848 ao. Prof.: Mythologie der Germanen, Deutsche Grammatik, Nibelungenlied bis 1852 (dann Breslau); 1852 Rochus von Liliencron (1820–1912, Extraord. f. nordische Sprache und Lit. in Kiel), Extraordinarius für deutsche Sprache und Literatur bis 1855; 1856 August Schleicher (1821–1868) Ordentlicher Honorarprofessor für deutsche Philologie und vergleichende Sprachkunde.

Marburg: 1838–1859 Privatdozent Franz Dietrich (1810–1883) für germanische und semitische Sprachen; 1844 ao. Prof für orientalische und germanische Sprachen, 1848 o. Prof. f. orientalische und altdeutsche Literatur; 1861 PD Ferdinand Justi (1837–1907) lehrte Germanistik, vergleichende Sprachwissenschaft und Orientalistik, 1865 ao. Professor der vergleichenden Grammatik und germanischen Philologie; 1868 Karl Lucae (1833–1888) Ordinarius für deutsche Sprache und Literatur.

Halle-Wittenberg: Der Vater der Halleschen Germanistik war der Extraordinarius (1830 Ordinarius) für Geschichte Heinrich Leo (1799–1878), er las 40 Jahre lang bis 1863 über mittelhochdeutsche Grammatik, das Nibelungenlied, althochdeutsche und angelsächsische Sprache, ab 1848 auch über das Keltische und die ältere irische Sprache, 1862 Grammatik des Kymrischen und Altnordischen; 1847 (bis 1857) PD Robert Prutz (1816–1872), 1849 Extraordinarius für Literaturgeschichte; ihm folgte 1860 als ao. (1868 o.) Prof. für Geschichte der deutschen Literatur Rudolf Haym (1821–1901) nach; schließlich kam 1863 der Ordinarius Julius Zacher (1816–1887) aus Königsberg nach Halle.

Münster (1786 als Universität gegründet, von 1818–1902 als Akademie fortgeführt, dann wieder Universität): 1858 PD Wilhelm Storck (1829–1905), 1859 (1868 Ordinarius) Extraord. für deutsche Sprache und Literatur.

Gießen: 1849 PD Karl Weigand (1804–1878), 1851 ao. (1867 o.) Professor des Deutschen.

Freiburg im Breisgau: Vor 1865 gab es keinen hauptamtlichen Vertreter des Fachs; einige Historiker griffen in die deutsche Philologie ein. 1865–1868 Matthias Lexer (1830–1892), 1868 ao. (1869 o.) Prof.; 1868–1874 PD (1866–1868 Heidelberg) Ernst Martin (1841–1910), 1868 Extraordinarius; 1874–1892 Hermann Paul (1846–1921), 1874 ao. (1877 o.) Prof.

Straßburg: Von 1872 bis 1877 vertrat der aus Wien gekommene Wilhelm Scherer (1841–1886) die Germanistik; ab 1877 Erich Schmidt (1853–1913) als Extraordinarius.

Graz: Der Lehrstuhl für deutsche Sprache wurde 1850 eingerichtet und mit Karl Weinhold (1823–1901) als Ordinarius der deutschen Sprache und Literatur bis 1861 besetzt; Nachfolger wurde Karl Tomaschek (1828–1878) als Ordinarius. Ihm folgte 1868 Richard Heinzel (1838–1905) bis 1873. Der Wiener PD Anton Emanuel Schönbach (1848–1911) wurde 1872/73 gerufen, 1873 zum Extraordinarius der deutschen Sprache und Literatur ernannt. Neben Schönbach lehrte Richard Maria Werner (1854–1913) als PD die deutsche Philologie. Weitere Lehrer waren: 1883–1886 der Extraordinarius

August Sauer (1855–1926), 1886–1924 Bernhard Seuffert (1853–1938; 1892 Ordinarius).

Prag: Deutsche Karl-Ferdinands-Universität: 1849 war eine Lehrkanzel für deutsche Sprache und Literatur mit Karl August Hahn (1807–1857) als Ordinarius eingerichtet worden; 1851 übernahm August Schleicher (1821–1868) die Lehrkanzel als Ordinarius der deutschen Sprache, der vergleichenden Sprachwissenschaft und des Sanskrits; Amtsnachfolger Schleichers wurde 1857–1899 Johann Kelle (1829–1909), der Ordinarius der deutschen Sprache und Literatur.

Innsbruck: 1858 Einrichtung einer Lehrkanzel für deutsche Philologie mit Ignaz Vinzenz Zingerle (1825–1892) als Professor der deutschen Sprache und Literatur. Bis 1890 las er über gotische Grammatik, Walter von der Vogelweide, Hermann von Aue und Schiller. 1887 wurde Josef Eduard Wackernell (1850–1920) als Extraordinarius berufen; er las über Geschichte der neueren Literatur.

Wien: 1859 Einrichtung einer Lehrkanzel für deutsche Sprache und Literatur mit Georg von Karajan (1810–1873); Nachfolger 1851 Oskar von Redwitz (1823–1891); Nachfolger 1853 Karl August Hahn, er lehrte ältere deutsche Philologie, während der 1855 habilitierte Karl Tomaschek (1828–1878) neuere deutsche Philologie und neuere Literaturgeschichte las. Nachfolger Hahns wurde von 1857–1868 Friedrich Pfeiffer (1815–1868), dem 1868 Wilhelm Scherer (1841–1886) als Ordinarius bis 1872 nachfolgte. Scherers Nachfolger wurde Richard Heinzel (1838–1905), der deutsche Grammatik, Altertumskunde, ältere deutsche Literaturgeschichte, Kritik, Metrik, Altnordisch und Angelsächsisch las, während Tomaschek das Gebiet der neueren Literatur, Kritik und Metrik lehrte.

Czernowitz: Von 1875 bis 1892 lehrte der Altgermanist Joseph Strobl (1843–1931) als ao. Professor (1880 Ordinarius); ihm folgte Oswald Zingerle von Summersberg (1855–1927) als Extraordinarius, 1894 Ordinarius der deutschen Sprache und Literatur bis 1918 nach.

Lemberg, Polnische Universität: Von 1851 bis 1871 las Johann Nepomuk Hloch über deutsche Mythologie, Mittelhochdeutsch und neuere deutsche Literaturgeschichte. Nachfolger in den siebziger Jahren wurde der polnische Schriftsteller Eugeniusz Arnold Janota (1823–1878). Von 1879 bis 1883 übernahm der Scherer-Schüler August Sauer (1855–1926) die wissenschaftliche Vertretung der deutschen Philologie; Nachfolger wurde 1883 der Extraordinarius Richard Maria Werner (1854–1913).

Krakau: 1850 Einrichtung einer ordentlichen Lehrkanzel für deutsche Philologie mit Karl Weinhold (1823–1901) als Ordinarius; Nachfolger wurde 1851 Frantiszek Tomasz Bratranek (1815–1884). Von 1883 bis 1913 Lehrte in Krakau der Zarncke-Schüler Wilhelm Creizenach (1851–1919).

Pest: 1850 Einrichtung einer ordentlichen Lehrkanzel für deutsche Philologie, die von 1852 bis 1860 mit Wilhelm Gärtner (1811–1875) besetzt war.

Bern: 1834 Karl Christian Jahn (1777–1854) als ao. Professor der schönen Literatur und der deutschen Sprache. 1853 Gymnasiallehrer Karl Pabst (1810–1873), 1856 Extraordinarius (1877 Ordinarius) für deutsche Sprache und Literatur. 1862 PD (1866 Extraordinarius) Ludwig Tobler (1827–1895), er lehrte allgemeine Sprachwissenschaft und germanische Philologie, altdeutsche und englische Sprache. 1874 kam als Nachfolger von Pabst der Züricher Germanist Ludwig Hirzel (1838–1897) als Ordinarius für deutsche Sprache und Literatur.

Basel: 1833 Wilhelm Wackernagel (1806–1868), Ordinarius der deutschen Sprache und Literatur, er las über die gesamte deutsche Philologie, incl. Altertumskunde, und über vergleichende Grammatik des Deutschen, Griechischen und Lateinischen. Nachfolger 1870 Moriz Heyne (1837–1906) bis 1883; ihm folgte Otto Behaghel (1854–1936) als Ordinarius der deutschen Sprache und Literatur bis 1888 nach.

Zürich: 1836–1842 und ab 1856 als Extraordinarius für altdeutsche Sprache und Literartur las Ludwig Ettmüller (1802–1877) über deutsche Literaturgeschichte, Altdeutsch, Altnordisch und Angelsächsisch. Nachfolger 1873 Ludwig Tobler, der 1878 Extraordinarius für altgermanische Sprache und Literatur wurde.

3.2. Romanistik und Anglistik

Vom Ende des 16. Jhs. (Guillaume Rabot seit 1571 in Wittenberg) bis zum Beginn des 19. Jhs. lag die neusprachliche studentische Ausbildung in der Regel in den Händen von 'Sprachmeistern', zumeist Muttersprachler, oft pädagogisch ungeschulte und unbegabte – wenn man von rühmlichen Ausnahmen wie François Roux († 1750) oder Matthias Kramer (ca. 1640–ca. 1729) absieht –, die in der sozialen Achtung neben die Reit-, Tanz- und Fechtlehrer der Universitäten gestellt waren. Daß hier die Abstellung von Mißständen und ein Umdenken notwendig war erkannte der preußische Kultusminister Altenstein 1819 in einem Schreiben an den Staatsminister Hardenberg (Zit. Risop 1910: 33):

"Es ist ein wesentlicher Mangel des grössten Teils der Universitäten, dass der Unterricht in den lebenden Sprachen auf solchen, nicht auf eine der Wissenschaft würdige Art erteilt und durch solchen nur die gewöhnlichste Sprachkenntnis bewirkt wird. Ein solcher Mangel ist für das gesamte Sprachstudium nachteilig. Ich habe mich bemüht, die Stellen für neuere Sprachen überall, soviel wie möglich, mit Männern von gründlicher wissenschaftlicher Bildung zu besetzen, um dadurch die Erlernung neuer Sprachen auch für das Studium der ganzen Literatur fruchtbarer zu machen und vorzüglich denen, welche sich zu Lehrern bilden wollen, gründlichere Kenntnisse zu verschaffen."

Dieser Prozeß bestimmte im wesentlichen die erste Hälfte des 19. Jhs.; oft traktierten Professoren anderer Disziplinen bestimmte Themen, zumeist literarische, der Neuphilologien. Das wurde bei der Behandlung der Germanistik deutlich, ist nicht minder bei den anderen Neuphilologien relevant. Das Englische, die angelsächsische Literatur (und ihre textkritische Edition) wurden zunächst als Teil der Germanistik begriffen. Der Göttinger germanistische Professor Benecke griff schon seit 1805 auf das Englische über, ohne daß es schon zu einer eigenständigen Wissenschaft wurde. Andere Germanisten, denken wir an Friedrich Diez (seit 1823 in Bonn), Adelbert von Keller (seit 1841 in Tübingen), Konrad Hofmann (seit 1853 in München), bezogen in ihre Forschung und Lehre die romanische Philologie mit ein. Kellers programmatische *Inauguralrede über die Aufgabe der modernen Philologie* von 1841 stellt an den Anfang der modernen Philologie, d. i. Neuphilologie, Jakob Grimms *Deutsche Grammatik* von 1819, François Raynouards *Grammaire comparée des langues de l'Europe latine* von 1821 und Friedrich Diez' *Grammatik der romanischen Sprachen* von 1836 ff. und postuliert über das reine Erlernen einer Fremdsprache hinaus die Einbeziehung ihres Werdens und die Feststellung ihrer Regelhaftigkeit — Gesichtspunkte, die in den zeitgenössischen Lehrbüchern vermißt werden — sowie die Herstellung wissenschaftlicher Wörterbücher, die der historischen Entwicklung der Sprache, der Etymologie nachgehen; über die historische Komponente nach Grimmschem und Diezschem Muster hinaus erwartet Keller auch die Betrachtung der gesprochenen Sprache, insbesondere der Mundarten, die manche älteren Sprachzustände bewahrt hätten. Auf dem Gebiet der Literatur dürften im Gegensatz zum Forschungsumfang der klasssischen Philologie nur die Werke der Belletristik und deren Geschichte, Kritik und Interpretation zum Auffinden des Volksgeistes Berücksichtigung finden. Keller (1842: 16) sieht und begründet das besonders enge Verhältnis zwischen germanischer und romanischer Philologie, wie es von ihm praktiziert wird:

"Die romanischen Völker sind durch Ursprung und Sitte, Religion und Wissenschaft nahe mit uns verwandt und wir haben an ihrer Bildung Theil, wie sie an der unsrigen. Ein durchdringendes Verständniß der romanischen Litteratur ohne die germanische und umgekehrt ist daher völlig unmöglich [...]."

Das Kellersche Dokument steht am Anfang eines schnellen Aufschwungs der romanischen und englischen (im Schoß der germanischen) Philologie, wie er durch sich häufende Habilitationen seitdem deutlich wird; Christmann (1985: 22) nennt: Berlin 1842: Nicolaus Delius; Göttingen 1845: Theodor Müller, Adolf Ebert; Tübingen 1847: Wilhelm Ludwig Holland; Bonn 1866: Bernhard ten Brink. Die Privatdozenten drängten auf Professorenstellen, die nach 1860 in der Regel als Doppelprofessuren für französische und englische Philologie eingerichtet wurden. Ein Widerspruch zwischen dem Anspruch dieser Professoren nach wissenschaftlicher Arbeit im Sinn der historischen Sprachbetrachtung und Textkritik auf der einen Seite und dem Anspruch der Ministerien und Schulen nach wissenschaftlicher Lehrerausbildung auf der anderen tat sich auf und wurde z. B. in den Philologenversammlungen diskutiert. Eine Trennung der Doppelprofessuren in eigenständige romanistische und anglistische Professuren wurde in dem Maße dringlich und gefordert, wie der Forschungs- und Wissensumfang größer wurde. Dieser Prozeß kennzeichnet die Zeit von 1870 bis zum Jahrhundertende.

Rostock: 1858 Karl Bartsch (1832—1888), Ordinarius für deutsche und neuere Literatur: er vertrat Germanistik *und* Romanistik; sein Nachfolger 1871 Reinhold Bechstein (1833—1894) war Ordinarius für Romanistik und Anglistik. 1891 Trennung der Doppelprofessur: Extraordinariat für Anglistik mit Felix Lindner (1849—1917), ao. Prof. für neuere Sprachen, 1899 ao. Prof. für englische

Philologie; 1897 Rudolf Zenker (1862–1941) Extraordinarius (1905 Ordinarius) für Romanistik (bis 1941).

Tübingen: 1844–1883 lehrte Adelbert von Keller (1841 Extraordinarius) germanische und romanische Philologie, er behandelte auch das Altenglische und Shakespeare; seit 1835 lehrte der PD (Privatdozent) Moriz Rapp (1803–1883, ab 1852 Extraordinarius für allgemeine Sprachwissenschaft und moderne ausländische Philologie, 1880 Emeritierung) Grammatik und Literaturgeschichte aller germanischen und romanischen Sprachen; der Extraordinarius Adolphe Peschier (1805–1878), 1844 Ordinarius für französische und englische Sprache und Literatur, lehrte seit 1837; ab 1847 lehrte der PD Wilhelm Ludwig Holland (1822–1891, 1853 Extraordinarius) deutsche und romanische Philologie; 1892 wurde Carl Voretzsch (1867–1947) als Professor der romanischen Philologie berufen. Die Anglistik wurde ab 1897 von dem Extraordinarius Wilhelm Franz (1859–1943, 1906 Ordinarius) vertreten.

Straßburg: 1872 Romanistik: Eduard Boehmer (1827–1906; 1879 em.); Anglistik: Bernhard ten Brink (1841–1892); ab 1895: Josef Schick (1859–1944).

Leipzig: 1862 Adolf Ebert (1820–1890), Ordinarius für Französisch und Englisch aus Marburg, 1873 wurde er Professor der romanischen Philologie; 1875 Richard Wülcker (1845–1918, ab 1884: Wülker), Extraordinarius (1880 Ordinarius) für englische Philologie.

Heidelberg: 1871 Karl Bartsch, Professor der germanischen und altromanischen Sprachen, insbesondere altfranzösischen Sprache und Literatur; 1869–1885 lehrte der Romanist Eugen Laur (*1825); 1885–1887 der Anglist Ferdinand Holthausen (1860–1956). Mit Anglistik befaßten sich: 1873–1901 der klassische Philologe Wilhelm Ihne (1821–1902), Extraordinarius der englischen Philologie, 1883 Honorarprofessor; 1878 liest Bartsch englische Sprachgeschichte, ebenso Otto Behaghel und der romanistische PD Fritz Neumann (1854–1934; 1881 Extraordinarius, ab 1882 Freiburg). 1894 Josef Schick (1859–1944) Extraordinarius für Anglistik, 1896 Nachfolger Johannes Hoops (1865–1949) als erster Ordinarius für englische Philologie bis 1949.

Freiburg im Breisgau: 1882 Fritz Neumann (1854–1934), Professor der romanischen Philologie; Arnold Schröer (1857–1935), 1900 Ordinarius der englischen Philologie.

Halle-Wittenberg: 1875 Hugo Schuchardt (1842–1927) Professor der romanischen Philologie; 1875 Carl Elze (1821–1889), ao. (1876 o.) Professor der englischen Philologie; Nachfolger Albrecht Wagner (1850–1909), 1887 ao. (1893 o.) Prof. für englische Philologie. Vorläufer der Romanistik waren: Ernst Wilhelm Gottlieb Wachsmuth (1784–1866), 1815 Lektor der italienischen Sprache, 1816 Extraordinarius bis 1920; 1822 Ludwig Gottfried Blanc (1781–1866), Dantephilologe, Extraordinarius der südeuropäischen Sprachen und Literaturen, 1833 Ordinarius der romanischen Sprachen und Literaturen; Nachfolger: PD der Theologie Eduard Boehmer (1827–1906), der seit 1865 romanistische Vorlesungen hielt, 1866 Extraordinarius, 1868 Ordinarius (1872 ging er nach Straßburg). Vor Elze wurde die Anglistik durch den Lektor Georg Hollmann († 1873) von 1834–1873 vertreten (er lehrte neben Englisch auch Französisch, Italienisch, Spanisch, Portugiesisch und Flämisch).

Kiel: 1872 Einrichtung eines Lehrstuhls für neuere, insbesondere romanische Sprachen, 1876 Albert Stimming (1846–1922), ao. (1879 o.) Professor (Doppelprofessur für Romanistik und Anglistik); 1884–1900 PD Gregor Sarrazin (1857–1915), 1889 Extraordinarius für Anglistik; Nachfolger Sarrazins wurde der Göteborger Ordinarius für englische Philologie Ferdinand Holthausen (1860–1956); Nachfolger Stimmings 1892 Gustav Körting (1845–1913) als Ordinarius für romanische Philologie.

Marburg: 1810 Friedrich Theodor Kühne (1758–1834) Professor der englischen und italienischen Sprache, er las über die "Theorie der französischen, italienischen, englischen und auf Verlangen spanischen Sprache" sowie über philosophische und allgemeine Grammatik, Interpretation englischer Literatur, und er hielt Übungen über englischen Stil; 1801–1813 las der Ordinarius Johann Friedrich Wachler (1767–1838) Literaturgeschichte der Italiener, Spanier, Portugiesen, Franzosen, Briten und Deutschen; 1810–1833 behandelte der Ordinarius der griechischen und römischen Literatur Karl Franz Christian Wagner (1760–1847) die Anfangsgründe der englischen Sprache sowie die Regeln der allgemeinen oder philosophischen Grammatik. Im Jahre 1836 kam aus Rostock der Ordinarius für neuere Literatur und Geschichte Victor Aimé Huber (1800–1869) als "ordentlicher Professor der abendländischen Literatur mit Ermächtigung zu

Vorlesungen über neuere Geschichte" und las Englisch, Französisch, Spanisch, Portugiesisch, Italienisch, englische Literaturgeschichte, Shakespeare, Dante (1843 ging er nach Berlin als Ordinarius der neueren Philologie); Nachfolger Hubers wurde Johann Carl Hinkel (1817–1894) von 1845–1854 als Extraordinarius der abendländischen Sprachen, er las französische Grammatik und Literatur, englische Anfangsgründe und Literatur sowie deutsche Literatur; dazu lehrte 1843–1853 der PD der klassischen Philologie Joseph Meier Hoffa (1805–1853) neuere Sprachen, englische Sprache und Literatur. 1849 kam als nostrifizierter (umhabilitierter) PD Adolf Ebert (1820–1890), 1856 Extraordinarius für neuere Sprachen, er las über englische, französische, italienische, spanische Sprache und Literatur; Nachfolger 1863 Ludwig Lemcke (1816–1884) als Extraordinarius (1865 Ordinarius) für neuere Sprachen und abendländische Literatur; 1867 Nachfolger PD Wilhelm Treitz (1838–1869) als Extraordinarius der abendländischen Sprachen. 1870 Bernhard ten Brink (1841–1892), Ordinarius der neueren Sprachen und abendländischen Literatur, er las englische Literaturgeschichte und gab eine Einführung in das Studium der englischen Sprache; Nachfolger 1873 Edmund Stengel (1845–1935) als Ordinarius der abendländischen Sprachen und Literaturen, als Doppelprofessor las er romanistische und anglistische Themen. 1880 wurde Stengel Professor der romanischen Philologie; 1884 kam Wilhelm Viëtor (1850–1918) als Extraordinarius (1894 Ordinarius) für englische Philologie. Nachfolger Stengels 1896 Eduard Koschwitz (1851–1904), dem wiederum 1901 der Königsberger Ordinarius für neuere Sprachen Alfons Kissner (1844–1928) als Ordinarius für romanische Philologie nachfolgte.

München: 1853 Konrad Hofmann (1819–1890), ao. Prof. für indogermanische Sprachen und Literatur, 1856 o. Prof. für altdeutsche Spache und Literatur, 1869 Prof. für altromanische Sprachen und Literatur, 1876 Doppelprofessur für Englisch und Französisch, im Seminar leitet er das Studium der mittelalterlichen französischen und englischen Sprache und Literatur, während Hermann Breymann (1843–1910) als Doppelprofessor für Englisch und Französisch das Neuenglische und Neufranzösische übernimmt; mit Trennung der beiden Lehrstühle des Seminars behielt 1896 Breymann die Romanistik, und der Heidelberger Extraordinarius für englische Philologie Josef Schick (1859–1944) erhielt 1896–1911 die Münchner Professur für englische Philologie. Nachfolger Breymanns wurde 1911 Karl Voßler (1872–1949). Ferner lehrte von 1873–1890 der Leipziger PD Michael Bernays (1836–1897) als Extraordinarius (1874 Ordinarius) für neuere Sprachen und Literaturen, er war vor allem Anglist, aber auch Romanist; von 1896 bis 1901 war der Belgier Julius Pirson (1870–1959) Lektor und PD der romanischen Sprachen.

Breslau: 1873 Gustav Gröber (1844–1911), Doppelprofessur für Französisch und Englisch; 1880 Adolf Gaspary (1849–1892), ao. (1883 o.) Prof. für Romanistik. 1873 wurde der PD für germanische Sprachen und Literaturen, insbesondere Nordisch, Eugen Kölbing (1846–1899), gerufen, der schließlich wie Zupitza zur Anglistik überwechselte und 1880 Extraordinarius (1886 Ordinarius) der englischen Sprache und Literatur wurde.

Greifswald: 1821–1833 Friedrich Kanngießer (1774–1833), Ordinarius für Geschichte und Lektor für Englisch, erteilt Englisch- und Italienisch-Unterricht; 1840–1853 Albert Hoefer (1812–1883), ao. Prof. Orientalistik, Komparatistik, altdeutsche Philologie, erteilt englischen Sprachunterricht und interpretiert englische Literatur. 1852–1881 Bern(h)ard Schmitz jun. (1818–1881), provisorischer (1854 definitiver) Lektor der neueren Sprachen: Englisch, Französisch; 1866 Extraordinarius für die neueren Sprachen: Französisch, Englisch, Italienisch, Spanisch, Holländisch, Dänisch, Schwedisch. 1787 Hermann Varnhagen (1850–1923), PD für romanische und englische Philologie, 1881 Extraordinarius (im gleichen Jahr ging er als Ordinarius nach Erlangen); Nachfolger 1882 Matthias Konrath (1843–1925) als Extraordinarius für englische Philologie, 1903 persönlicher Ordinarius, 1908 etatsmäßiger Ordinarius. 1881–1901 Heinrich Zimmer (1851–1910), Extraordinarius (1882 Ordinarius) für Keltologie und Anglistik, er las zu keltischer Thematik, über Altirisch, Irisch und Kymrisch, dazu auch Literaturgeschichte. 1881 wurde das Ordinariat für neuere Sprachen eingerichtet und mit Eduard Koschwitz (1851–1904) besetzt, der sich auf romanische Philologie beschränkte. 1881–1890 Dietrich Behrens (1859–1929), PD der romanischen Philologie (er ging 1890 als Extraordinarius nach Jena). 1896 kam es zu einem Romanistenaustausch mit der Marburger Universität: Koschwitz ging nach Marburg, und von dort kam Edmund Stengel (1845–1935), der 1913 emeritiert wurde.

158. Die 'neuen Philologien', ihre Institutionen und Periodica: Eine Übersicht

Bonn: 1822 kam der Indologe August Wilhelm Schlegel (1767–1845) nach Bonn und behandelte als *professor litterarum elegantiarum* die Literaturgeschichte Italiens, Spaniens, Frankreichs und Englands. 1821 Friedrich Diez (1794–1876), Lektor (für Italienisch, Spanisch, Portugiesisch), 1823 Extraordinarius für mittlere und neuere Literatur, 1830 Ordinarius für Geschichte der neueren Literatur; 1846–1865 Charles Monnard (1790–1865), Ordinarius für romanische Sprachen und Literaturen; 1846–1872 Nikolaus Delius (1813–1888) PD (1852 Lektor, 1855 Extraordinarius, 1866 Ordinarius, 1879 em.) für indische, englische und romanische Philologie. 1872–1888 Wilhelm Bischoff (1822–1888), Extraordinarius für französische und englische Sprache, zuständig für sprachpraktische Ausbildung. Nachfolger von Friedrich Diez wurde der Ordinarius Wendelin Foerster (1844–1915, 1908 em.). Das Altfranzösische und Rätische wurde 1882–1885 durch den PD Jakob Stürzinger (1855–1903) gelehrt. Die Anglistik wurde 1880 mit dem aus Leipzig gerufenen Professor der englischen Philologie Moritz Trautmann (1842–1920; 1912 em.) selbständig.

Gießen: 1823 Johann Valentin Adrian (1793–1864), Extraordinarius (1824 Ordinarius) der neueren Sprachen und Literatur; Nachfolger 1867–1884 Ludwig Lemcke (1816–1884) als Ordinarius der neueren Sprachen; ihm folgte 1884–1890 Adolf Birch-Hirschfeld (1849–1917) nach. 1888 Otto Behaghel (1854–1936), Ordinarius für germanische und romanische Philologie; 1891 Dietrich Behrens (1859–1929), Ordinarius der neueren Sprachen, und Ferdinand Holthausen (1860–1956), Extraordinarius der englischen Philologie.

Jena: 1826 Oscar Ludwig Bernhard Wolff (1799–1851), Extraordinarius für die Literatur der lebenden Sprachen, er unterrichtete Englisch, Französisch, Italienisch, Spanisch, Portugiesisch und las u. a. französische und englische Grammatik, Literaturgeschichte (europäische, deutsche, italienische Literatur: Dante, englische Literatur: Shakespeare); 1871–1883 Eduard Sievers (1850–1932), ao. Professor für deutsche Philologie mit Lehrauftrag für Romanistik, ab 1874 auch anglistische Lehrveranstaltungen, 1876 o. Prof. für deutsche Philologie; Nachfolger: 1883–1893 Friedrich Kluge (1856–1925), Extraord. (1885 Ord.) für deutsche und englische Philologie; und 1883–1886 PD Rudolf Thurneysen (1857–1940), 1884 Extraordinarius für romanische Philologie; Thurneysens Nachfolger wurden: 1886–1890 Wilhelm Meyer-Lübke (1861–1936), 1890–1891 Dietrich Behrens (1859–1929), 1891–1893 Eduard Schwan (1858–1893), 1893–1909 Wilhelm Cloëtta (1857–1911). Anglistischer Nachfolger Kluges wurde 1893–1897 Wilhelm Franz (1859–1944) als Extraordinarius der englischen Philologie.

Erlangen: 1827 wurde das englische Lektorat in Union mit einem spanischen gegründet, 1838 erfolgte die Vereinigung des englisch-spanischen Lektorats mit dem französischen. Das Lektorat endete 1884 mit dem Tod von Christian Martin Winterling (1800–1884; 1823 PD, 1834 ao. Prof. der neueren Sprachen), der von 1823 bis 1884 lehrte. 1874–1877 Alfons Kissner (1844–1928), Ordinarius für neuere Sprachen (Doppelprofessur für Französisch und Englisch; Nachfolger 1877–1881 Karl Vollmoeller (1848–1922), Extraord. für neuere Sprachen (ebenfalls Doppelprofessur); Nachfolger 1881 Hermann Varnhagen (1850–1923) als Ordinarius für neuere Sprachen. 1898 Trennung der Doppelprofessur: Varnhagen wurde Ordinarius für englische Philologie, während im gleichen Jahr Heinrich Schneegans (1863–1914) zum Ordinarius für romanische Philologie berufen wurde; dazu 1901 Julius Pirson (1870–1959) aus Belgien als Extraordinarius für Romanistik.

Königsberg: 1839–1869 Lektor Herbst, seit 1841 PD, für Französisch, Englisch, Italienisch, Spanisch. 1871–1876 Jakob Schipper (1842–1915) Extraordinarius (1872 Ordinarius) für neuere Sprachen (französisch-englische Doppelprofessur), 1877–1901 Alfons Kissner (1844–1928), Ordinarius für neuere Sprachen. Trennung der Doppelprofessur 1894: Max Kaluza (1856–1921), Extraordinarius (1902 Ordinarius) für englische Sprache und Literatur.

Berlin: 1820 Karl Friedrich Franceson (1782–1859), Lektor für Französisch, Italienisch und Spanisch, neben Sprachkursen hielt er literaturgeschichtliche Vorlesungen. Der wissenschaftlich-philologische Betrieb begann 1822 mit der Berufung des Extraordinarius Friedrich Wilhelm Valentin Schmidt (1787–1831), der über den Ursprung der romanischen Sprachen ebenso wie über französische, italienische und spanische Literaturgeschichte las. 1843–1851 Victor Aimé Huber (1800–1869), Ordinarius für neuere Philologie; er las englische, italienische und spanische Literaturgeschichte. Ab 1850 lehrte Hajim Steinthal (1823–1899) (1863 Extraordinarius für allgemeine Sprachwissenschaft) provenzalische Sprache und Literatur ebenso wie die historisch-psychologische Betrachtung der romanischen Sprachen im Anschluß an die Herbartsche Philosophie. – Das Englische war seit der Universitätsgründung kontinuierlich vertreten: 1812–1842 von D. [C.?] von Seymour († 1842), Lehrer (ab 1819 Lektor) des Englischen; 1843–1875 Thomas Solly (1816–1875), Lektor, 1860 Professor; wissenschaftliche Anglistik trieb ab 1842–1846 der PD Nicolaus Delius (1813–1888), der ein Lehramt für englische und französische Literatur innehatte; er las auch über vergleichende Grammatik der romanischen Sprachen; mit dem Weggang von Huber (1851) und Delius (1846) war die romanische und englische Philologie verwaist. Erst 1867 rief die Berliner Universität Adolf Tobler (1835–1910) als Ordinarius der romanischen Sprachen und Literatur. Und sogar erst 1876 wurde Julius Zupitza (1844–1895) als Ordinarius für englische Sprache und Literatur gewonnen.

Göttingen: 1845 habilitierte sich Theodor Müller (1816–1881) zum Privatdozenten für das Fach der neueren Sprachen und Literatur; er lehrte als PD Französisch, Englisch, Spanisch, Italienisch, Flämisch; 1852 Extraordinarius (1867 Ordinarius) für neuere Sprachen und Literatur (Doppelprofessur für Anglistik und Romanistik). 1881 wurde das Ordinariat getrennt: 1881–1891 Karl Vollmoeller (1848–1922), Ordinarius der romanischen Philologie, der aber auch anglistische Lehrverpflichtungen zu übernehmen hatte. 1881–1885 Arthur Napier (1853–1916), Extraordinarius für englische Philologie; 1885–1887 Albrecht Wagner (1850–1909), Extraordinarius für englische Philologie; 1887–1892 Alois Brandl (1855–1940), Ordinarius für englische Philologie.

Münster: 1865–1866 Wilhelm Treitz (1838–1869), Dozent für neuere Sprachen (Romanistik und Anglistik); 1866–1870 lehrte Bernhard ten Brink (1841–1892) als PD englische und französische Philologie; 1872–1873 der Philologe PD Carl Horstmann (*1847); 1873–1874 Eduard Mall (1843–1892), Extraordinarius für neuere Sprachen; 1875–1876 Hermann Suchier (1848–1914), Extraordinarius; 1877–1892 Gustav Körting (1845–1913), Ordinarius für die neueren Sprachen: er las Alt- und Mittelenglisch, Altfranzösisch, französische und englische Literaturgeschichte, trieb grammatische und sprachpraktische Übungen. Zu seiner Entlastung richtete er 1879 ein Lektorat für Englisch und Französisch ein, das mit dem Lektor Carl Deiters (1839–1904) besetzt wurde. Auch auf englisch-philologischem Gebiet entlastete sich Körting durch eine vollanglistische Dozentur, für die sich der Anglist Eugen Einenkel (1853–1930) 1883 habilitiert hatte. Körting las jedoch weiter zu anglistischer Thematik. 1892 wurde Einenkel Ordinarius der Anglistik, sein Nachfolger war 1900 der Breslauer Anglist Otto Jiriczek (1867–1941). Körtings Nachfolger wurde 1892 Hugo Andresen (1844–1918).

Würzburg: 1874–1890 Eduard Mall (1843–1892), Extraordinarius der Romanistik und Anglistik, er lehrte Provenzalisch, auch französische und spanische Literaturgeschichte und historische Grammatik des Französischen; 1890–1897 lehrte der PD Rudolf Zenker (1862–1941) neuere französische Literaturgeschichte. Nachfolger Malls 1893 Jacob Stürzinger (1853–1902), Professor für romanische und englische Philologie. 1898 Einrichtung eines anglistischen Extraordinariats, besetzt mit Max Förster (1869–1954), 1902 Ordinarius, 1909 ging er nach Halle. 1900 wurde Heinrich Schneegans (1863–1914) romanistischer Ordinarius.

Graz: 1876 Hugo Schuchardt (1842–1927), Ordinarius für Romanistik. 1891–1908 PD Karl Luick (1865–1935), 1893 Extraordinarius, 1898 Ordinarius für Anglistik.

Prag: Deutsche Karl-Ferdinands-Universität: 1842–1867 unterrichtete Felix Francesconi Italienisch und las über italienische und französische Literatur. 1858–1889 Anselm Ricard, Lektor der französischen Sprache und Literatur, er leitete 1871–1877 das Lektorat, das als *Séminaire pour la langue et la littérature françaises* bezeichnet wird. 1875–1876 Wendelin Foerster (1844–1915), Extraordinarius der romanischen Philologie; Nachfolger Jules Cornu (1849–1919), Ordinarius der romanischen Philologie. Die Anglistik wurde von den Germanisten Kelle und Martin mitverwaltet. Der erste Lehrstuhlinhaber wurde 1884–1888 Alois Brandl (1855–1940) als Extraordinarius der englischen Philologie; Nachfolger 1889–1908 Alois Pogatscher (1852–1935), Extraordinarius (1896 Ordinarius) für englische Sprache und Literatur.

Innsbruck: 1898 Theodor Gartner (1843–1925) Professor der romanischen Philologie. Vor ihm hatte sich schon Onorato Occioni (*30.3.1829 in Venedig, † 29.12.1925 in Padua) als Inhaber der Lehrkanzel für italienische Sprache und Literatur der romanischen

Philologie bis 1863 angenommen. Im Jahre 1893 habilitierte sich der Straßburger Privatdozent Rudolf Fischer (1860−1923) nach Innsbruck um, 1896 Extraordinarius (1902 persönlicher Ordinarius) für englische Philologie.

Wien: 1855 Adolfo Mussafia (1834−1905) Lehrer des Italienischen, 1860 Extraordinarius, 1867 Ordinarius. 1871 PD Ferdinand Lotheissen (1833−1887) für neuere französische Literatur, 1881−1887 Extraordinarius; Nachfolger 1890 Wilhelm Meyer-Lübke (1861−1936), Extraordinarius (1892 Ordinarius) für romanische Philologie. 1872−1876 Julius Zupitza (1844−1895), Extraordinarius der nordgermanischen Sprachen, er beschäftigte sich aber tatsächlich mit englischer Sprache, 1875 Ordinarius. 1876 Jakob Schipper (1842−1915), Ordinarius der englischen Philologie.

Czernowitz: Seit Gründung der Universität (1875) existierten zwei romanistische Ordinariate: eines für romanische Philologie und eines für rumänische Sprache und Literatur. Der erste Romanist war der Wiener Alexander Budinski (1844−1900) als ao. Professor, später Ordinarius, er blieb bis 1885. 1885 wurde der Romanist Theodor Gartner (1843−1925) als Professor der romanischen Philologie berufen (1899 ging er nach Innsbruck). Ihm folgte 1900 Mathias Friedwagner (1861−1940). Gartner und Friedwagner befaßten sich auch besonders mit dem Rumänischen. Der rumänische Lehrstuhl wurde 1875 mit Ion G. Sbiera (1836−1916) besetzt, 1881 Ordinarius; ihm folgte 1907 Sextil Puşcariu (1877−1948) nach. Als erster Extraordinarius für englische Philologie wurde 1904 (1909 Ordinarius) der Wiener PD Leon Kellner (1859−1928) berufen.

Bern: 1862 Einrichtung eines Lehrstuhls für französische Sprache und Literatur, 1863−1875 mit dem Extraordinarius (1873 Ordinarius) für französische Literatur und Sprache und für praktische Theologie, Albert Schaffter (1823−1897), besetzt; 1865 verzichtet er auf die theologische Professur und liest nur noch über französische Sprache und Literatur ebenso wie über englische und italienische Literatur. 1879 Heinrich Morf (1854−1921), Extraordinarius (1881 Ordinarius) für französische Sprache und Literatur. Ab 1881 las der Ordinarius für Dogmatik und Kirchengeschichte, Abbé Eugène Michaud (1839−1917; 1885 Ordinarius für neuere französische Literatur) besonders über französische Literaturgeschichte; wegen Kompetenzüberschneidungen mit Morf verließ dieser 1889 Bern, und Michaud wurde als Ordinarius für französische Sprache und Literatur Morfs Nachfolger. Seit 1881 lehrte der PD Eduard Müller (1853−1923), 1888 als Extraordinarius für Sanskrit, vergleichende Sprachlehre und englische Philologie, 1897 Ordinarius für orientalische Sprachen und englische Philologie.

Basel: Die Romanistik wurde zu Beginn des Jhs. von Alexandre Vinet (1797−1847) vertreten, der ab 1819 eine ao. (1835 o.) Professur für französische Sprache und Literatur innehatte. Das Italienische wurde ab 1825 von dem PD für Italienisch (1836 Professor) Luigi Picchioni-Troxler (1784−1869) gelehrt, der Sprachunterricht erteilte und Literaturvorlesungen hielt. Nachfolger Vinets wurde 1839 der Extraordinarius Charles François Girard (1811−1875), 1841−1875 Ordinarius für französische Sprache und Literatur. 1870−1871 PD Edmund Stengel (1845−1935), er las Geschichte der romanischen Sprachen, historische Grammatik des Französischen und Altprovenzalischen. 1877 wurde der Lektor der romanischen Sprachen, Jules Cornu (1849−1919), Extraordinarius, bis 1879; Nachfolger von Cornu wurde der Professor für romanische Philologie mit Lehrauftrag für Englisch, Gustave Soldan (1848−1902), er lehrte historische Grammatik und französische Literaturgeschichte, interpretierte altfranzösische und moderne Texte, las Englisch, Italienisch, Rätisch, Spanisch. Ab 1895 gehörte es zum Pflichtpensum der Professoren für romanische Philologie, nebenbei englische Sprache und Literatur zu lehren. So las auch der Germanist Gustav Binz (1865−1951) als PD ab 1895 (1900 Extraordinarius) altenglische Sprache und Literatur. Binz war der erste Vertreter der Anglistik bis 1908 in Basel.

Zürich: In der ersten Hälfte des 19. Jhds. war der Hauptträger der Romanistik der Ordinarius der klassischen Philologie Johann Kaspar von Orelli (1787−1849), der auch römische Literatur bis Petrarca las ebenso wie über Ariost und die Italiener der Renaissance. 1857−1872 lehrte der PD der romanischen Philologie Alfred Rochat (1833−1910) provenzalische Grammatik und französische Literaturgeschichte. 1869 las der klassische Philologe Eduard Wölfflin (1831−1908) über das Verhältnis von Volkslatein zu den romanischen Sprachen. Im Jahre 1870 wurde eine Professur für französische Sprache und Literatur eingerichtet und mit dem PD Gustav Gröber (1844−1911) besetzt, 1872 Extraordinarius. 1873 Ludwig Tobler (1827–1895), Extraordinarius für allgemeine Sprachwissenschaft und germanische Philologie, er füllte die Professur für romanische Philologie mit aus, ab 1878 las er auch Alt- und Mittelenglisch. Nachfolger Gröbers wurde 1874 PD Hermann Suchier (1848–1914); Nachfolger 1875 Heinrich Breitinger (1832–1889) als Ordinarius für romanische Philologie; 1878–1883 Gustav Settegast (1852–1932), Extraordinarius für romanische Philologie (ältere Periode); Nachfolger 1884–1887 PD Wilhelm Meyer-Lübke (1861–1936). 1889–1901 Heinrich Morf (1854–1921). Im Jahre 1889 erhielt der PD Theodor Vetter (1853–1922) einen Lehrauftrag für englische Sprache und Literatur, 1891 Extraordinarius der englischen Philologie.

3.3. Slawistik

Das Slawische als Teil der modernen Philologie wird von Mager (1843: 19) explizit genannt. Im *Jahrbuch der deutschen Universitäten* (Sommerhalbjahr 1842) wird unter dem Titel "Ueber die Nothwendigkeit auf den Universitäten Professuren der neueren Sprachen zu begründen" (S. 339–349) von Julius Heintze mit wissenschaftlichen Prämissen neben Professuren für den 'germanischen Sprachstamm' und den romanischen ausdrücklich eine solche für den 'slawischen Sprachstamm' (S. 348) postuliert. Gegenüber Germanistik, Romanistik und Anglistik entwickelte sich die Slawistik eher zögerlich. Das Deutsche Reich war durch eine ausgeprägte chauvinistische Überheblichkeit gegenüber den slawischen Völkern gekennzeichnet, was zu einer weitgehenden Vernachlässigung der Beschäftigung mit den slawischen Sprachen und Literaturen an den deutschen Universitäten führte. Die Beschäftigung mit den slawischen Sprachen fand lediglich eingebettet in die vergleichende Sprachwissenschaft im Rahmen der Indoeuropäistik statt. Noch am 11. Februar 1912 konnte sich der Leipziger Slawist August Leskien (1840–1916) bei dem Grazer Romanisten Hugo Schuchardt darüber beschweren, daß die Romanistik etwas in der Welt bedeute,

"die Slawistik, in Westeuropa wenigstens, fast nichts, in Deutschland überhaupt nichts. Ich habe seit Jahren fast keine deutschen Zuhörer mehr. [...] Außerdem stehe ich ganz allein." (Zit. Zeil 1988: 34)

Rostock: Im Rahmen des 1902 gegründeten Ordinariats für vergleichende und indogermanische Sprachwissenschaft: Gustav Herbig (1865–1925), 1913 Ordinarius für vergleichende Sprachwissenschaft, er lehrte von 1903–1921.

Leipzig: 1843 Schaffung eines Lektorats für slawische Sprachen und Literaturen, besetzt mit dem sorbischen Lektor Jan Petr Jordan (1818–1891); 1870 Einrichtung eines Lehrstuhls für slawische Sprachen und Literaturen, der 1871 mit dem Extraordinarius August Leskien besetzt wurde; im zur Seite standen der Lektor für Altbulgarisch Robert Scholvin (1850–1929), der Lektor für Literaturgeschichte Wilhelm Wollner (1851–1902), der Lektor Asmus Soerensen (1854–1912) für polnische und serbokroatische Literatur und Geschichte der Slawen, sowie Gustav Weigand (1860–1930), Lektor für Neubulgarisch; 1905 gründete Weigand das Institut für bulgarische Sprache in Verbindung mit dem 1893 von ihm geschaffenen Institut für rumänische Sprache.

Kiel: 1880/81 las der dänische Anglist Hermann Möller (1850–1923) über slawische Grammatik.

München: 1854–1867 Friedrich Bodenstedt (1819–1892) Honorarprofessor für slawische Sprache und Literatur, er las aber hauptsächlich über englische Literatur. Ein Lehrstuhl für slawische Philologie wurde erst 1911 eingerichtet: Erich Bernecker (1874–1937), er las über slawische und baltische Philologie. 1901–1914 las der Byzantinist Karl Krumbacher (1854–1909) über russische Sprache und Literatur (1892 Extraordinarius, 1897 Ordinarius).

Breslau: 1841 PD Wojciech Cybulski (1808–1867), polnischer Literarhistoriker, Lehrstuhl für Slawistik, 1860 Ordinarius. Nachfolger wurde 1868 der Posener polnische Gymnasiallehrer Władysław Nehring (1830–1909) als Ordinarius; ihm folgte 1807 der Ordinarius Erich Berneker (1874–1937) nach, der 1911 nach München ging; dessen Nachfolger wurde von 1911–1945 Paul Diels (1882–1963). Außerdem lehrte der Tscheche František Ladislav Čelakovský (1799–1852), seit 1842 Professor der slawischen Sprachen (1849 ging er nach Prag).

Greifswald: 1801/02 las der Petersburger Andreas Johannes Winter (1779–1805) über russische Sprache und Literatur, er war 1800 als Lektor für Schwedisch und Russisch gekommen. 1815 befaßte sich der Theologie-Professor Johann Gottfried Ludwig Kosegarten (1758–1818), der 1815 als Adjunkt für orientalische Sprachen und für Geschichte berufen worden war (1817 ging er als Prof. der orientalischen Sprachen nach Jena), mit der Erforschung der slawischen Personen- und Ortsnamen in Pommern, mit Kaschubistik sowie mit der Sprache der Sorben und Wenden. Ab 1894 lehrte der PD für Assyrisch und Äthiopisch Paul Rost (*1869) als Lektor der russischen Sprache in Anfänger- und Fortgeschrittenenkursen, er las über Altrussisch sowie russische Literaturgeschichte (1896 ging er als Lektor des Russischen nach Königsberg). 1902/03 beschäftigte sich Ernst Zupitza (1875–1917; 1900 PD für vergleichende Sprachwissenschaft, 1901 Extraordinarius) mit Altslawisch, Altbulgarisch und Litauisch.

Königsberg: Der Baltist Adalbert Bezzenberger (1851–1922) hatte schon in den 80er Jahren des 19. Jh. die Einrichtung eines slawistischen Lehrstuhls in K. gefordert. Doch erst 1914 wurde ein Extraordinariat für slawische Philologie geschaffen, das mit Paul Rost (*1869) besetzt wurde, der ab 1896 als Russisch-Lektor und Privatdozent für Assyriologie und slawische Philologie berufen wurde.

Berlin: 1841 Einrichtung eines slawistischen Lehrstuhls, der mit dem polnischen PD Wojciech Cybulski (1808–1867) besetzt wurde. Im 19. Jhd. war die Slawistik in der vergleichenden Sprachwissenschaft und Indoeuropäistik (Bopp) integriert. Ein eigenständiger slawistischer Lehrstuhl wurde 1873/74 gegründet und mit Vratoslav Jagić (1838–1923) besetzt; Nachfolger 1881 Alexander Brückner (1834–1896).

Münster: Seit 1876 las Gustav Körting (1845–1913), der Münsteraner Ordinarius der romanischen und englischen Philologie auch über russische Sprache und Literatur.

Graz: 1875 wurde ein Lehrstuhl für Slawistik geschaffen, der mit Gregor Krek (1840–1905) als Ordinarius besetzt wurde.

Wien: In den 40er bis 60er Jahren des 19. Jhds. lag auch hier die Slawistik in den Händen der Indoeuropäistik und der vergleichenden Sprachwissenschaft. 1849 wurden zwei Extraordinariate eingerichtet: eines für slawische Archäologie (Inhaber 1849: Johann Kollár (1793–1852)), ein anderes für slawische Philologie und Literatur, Inhaber 1849–1885 Franz Miklosich (1813–1891), der mit seiner vergleichender Grammatik der slawischen Sprachen die wissenschaftliche Slawistik begründete; Nachfolger: Vratoslav Jagić (1838–1923).

Bern: 1890 Friedrich Haag (1846–1914), der sich 1878 in Zürich für Slawistik und Sanskrit habilitiert hatte, Lehrauftrag für slawische Philologie, 1891 Ordinarius für klassische Philologie, allgemeine Pädagogik und Gymnasialpädagogik.

Basel: Ein Lektorat für slawische Sprache wurde erst 1923 eingerichtet; erste Lektorin war Elsa-Eugenie Mahler (* 28.12.1881 Moskau, † 30.6.1970 Basel), die sich 1928 zur Privatdozentin habilitierte, 1936 einen Lehrauftrag für russische Sprache und Literatur erhielt und 1938 Extraordinaria wurde.

Zürich: Der Privatdozent Friedrich Haag (1846–1914) las neben Sanskrit und Gotisch in den Jahren 1873, 1878–1883 auch slawische Sprachen: Russisch, Altbulgarisch, sowie Litauisch.

3.4. Seminargründungen

Die Idee von der Gründung neuphilologischer Seminare im Sinn von Institutsvorläufern basierte zum einen auf dem klassisch-philologischen und theologischen Vorbild – es sei an das berühmte Heyne-Seminar in Göttingen erinnert –, zum anderen auf der Institutionsvoraussetzung für die wissenschaftliche Lehrerbildung an der Universität. Zweck waren auf der einen Seite die Forschung, auf der anderen die aktive Einbeziehung und Beteiligung der Studenten am Ausbildungsprozeß, ihre Erziehung zur Selbständigkeit. Das war eine konsequente Fortsetzung früherer Bemühungen von Professorenvorlesungen mit anschließendem Übungsseminar. Lachmann las beispielsweise 1823 in Königsberg über die Anfangsgründe der älteren deutschen Sprache und schloß daran praktische Übungen an. Solche Übungen konnten unterschiedliche Formen annehmen, vom Kränzchen bis zur Gesellschaft, wie von Prutz in Halle in Form einer 'Deutschen Gesellschaft' versucht. Ziel der Seminare sollte in der Regel die Lehrerbildung sein, weswegen sie von den Kultusministerien Unterstützung und Förderung erfuhren. Sie wurden bis zum Ende des 19. Jhs. an allen deutschsprachigen Universitäten gegründet und durften

"unter institutionsgeschichtlichem Aspekt als Indikator der endgültigen Integration des Faches Deutsche Philologie in den Universitätsbetrieb [...] oder doch zumindest als vorläufiger Abschluß des Institutionalisierungsprozesses" (Meves 1994: 196)

gelten, was auch auf die neusprachlichen Seminare zu beziehen sein dürfte. Zugleich stellte die Gründungsphase, vor allem seit der

Reichseinigung, einen Indikator für die Arbeitsteilung in der neuphilologischen Landschaft dar.

Die erste neuphilologische Seminargründung fand im Jahre 1839 in **Rostock** als *philosophisch-ästhetisches Seminar* statt; der Initiator war Christian Wilbrandt (1801–1867), der Professor der Ästhetik und neueren Literatur; dieses Seminar, an dem vor allem Theologen und Juristen teilnahmen, arbeitete bis 1852. Behandelt wurden Themen der neueren deutschen Literatur, aber auch der altdeutschen und der französischen Literatur. Ein Student war der spätere Leipziger germanistische Ordinarius Friedrich Zarncke. Im Jahre 1858 kam es in Rostock zur Gründung eines *deutsch-philologischen Seminars* durch Karl Bartsch (1832–1888), den Ordinarius für deutsche und neuere Literatur, der die Germanistik und die Romanistik vertrat. Im Seminar wurden die ältere und neuere deutsche Literatur, deutsche Altertümer und Mythologie behandelt. Bartsch las auch über Provenzalisch und Altfranzösisch. Als Bartsch 1871 nach Heidelberg ging, wurde sein Nachfolger Reinhold Bechstein (1833–1894), der Ordinarius für Anglistik und Romanistik. Ein germanistischer Fachvertreter wurde erst wieder mit Wolfgang Golter (1863–1945) im Jahre 1895 gewonnen, der bis 1934 in Rostock lehrte. Die fachliche Differenzierung erfolgte ab 1891: der PD Felix Lindner (1849–1917) erhielt ein Extraordinariat (für neuere Sprachen), 1899 für englische Philologie; 1897 Rudolf Zenker (1862–1941) Extraordinarius für Romanistik (1905 Ordinarius), er lehrte bis 1941. Im Jahre 1905 wurde das *Romanisch-englische Seminar* unter der Leitung von Zenker gegründet.

Tübingen: 1867 *Seminar für neuere Sprachen*, mit germanistischer, romanistischer und anglistischer Orientierung, eingerichtet nach dem Rostocker Muster und geleitet (bis 1883) von Adelbert von Keller (1812–1883), nachgefolgt von Hermann von Fischer; Keller vertrat die Germanistik, während das Englische und Französische von Lektoren übernommen wurde. Umbenennung des Seminars 1901 in *Seminar für neuere Philologie* mit drei Abteilungen: eine deutsche, eine englische und eine romanische Abteilung, die 1906 als Seminare selbständig wurden.

Straßburg: 1872 *Seminar für deutsche Philologie* mit Wilhelm Scherer als Leiter; 1872 *Seminar für neuere Sprachen* unter Leitung von Eduard Boehmer (1827–1906; 1879 em.). 1873/74 Aufteilung in zwei Institute: das *romanische Seminar* mit Boehmer als Leiter und das *englische Seminar* mit ten Brink als Leiter.

Leipzig: 1873 *Deutsches Seminar*, Leiter Friedrich Zarncke, gefolgt 1892 von Eduard Sievers. 1891 gründete Richard Wülker (1845–1918) das *englische* und *romanische Seminar*; 1893 Gründung des *Instituts für rumänische Sprache* durch Gustav Weigand (1860–1930).

Heidelberg: 1873 *Seminar für neuere Sprachen* unter Karl Bartsch mit Behandlung des Deutschen, Französischen und Englischen, 1877 Umbenennung in *germanisch-romanisches Seminar*, 1923 Abtrennung des *Deutschen Seminars*, 1926 Auftrennung in ein *Englisches* und ein *Romanisches Seminar*.

Würzburg: 1873 *Seminar für deutsche Philologie* durch Matthias Lexer; 1893 wurde ein *romanisch-englisches Seminar* eingerichtet, 1902 wurden beide Teilbereiche selbständig.

Freiburg im Breisgau: 1874 *Seminar für neuere Sprachen*, Leiter Ernst Martin (1841–1910); 1874–1892 Leiter Extraordinarius (1877 Ordinarius) Hermann Paul, 1893–1919 Friedrich Kluge. 1883 trennte sich vom Seminar für neuere Sprachen ein *Romanisches Seminar* ab, das mit dem Heidelberger Romanisten Fritz Neumann (1854–1934) besetzt wurde. 1894 trennte sich vom germanistischen Seminar das *Englische Seminar*, Leiter: Honorarprofessor (1900 Ordinarius der englischen Philologie) Arnold Schröer (1857–1935).

Halle-Wittenberg: 1875 Gründung dreier Seminare: *Seminar für deutsche Philologie* mit Julius Zacher als Direktor, Nachfolger Eduard Sievers, 1887–1902 Konrad Burdach (1859–1936); *Seminar für romanische Philologie* mit Hugo Schuchardt, Nachfolger 1876 Hermann Suchier, ab 1914 Carl Voretzsch; *Seminar für englische Philologie* mit Carl Elze, Nachfolger 1887 Albrecht Wagner.

Kiel: 1875 *Seminar für germanistische Philologie* mit Karl Weinhold, Nachfolger 1876 Wilhelm Pfeiffer (1827–1893). 1885 Gründung eines *Romanisch-Englischen Seminars* durch Albert Stimming mit drei Abteilungen, der Romanischen unter Stimming, der Neufranzösischen unter einem Lektor und der Englischen unter Gregor Sarrazin; Nachfolger Stimmings wurde 1892 Gustav Körting; Teilung des Seminars 1911 in ein *Romanisches Seminar* mit Carl Voretzsch und ein *Englisches Seminar* mit Holthausen.

Marburg: Aus einer 1851 geschaffenen 'literatur-geschichtlichen Societät' und der 1852 daraus geformten 'deutschen Gesellschaft' entstand 1876 das *Seminar für deutsche Philologie* mit Karl Lucae als Gründer und Leiter, Nachfolger 1888 Edward Schröder. 1876 Gründung eines romanisch-englischen Doppelseminars unter Edmund Stengel, Nachfolger 1896 Eduard Koschwitz.

München: 1876 *Seminar für neuere Sprachen und Literaturen* mit zwei Abteilungen: die erste Abteilung befaßte sich mit dem Studium der älteren, anfangs der mittelalterlichen französischen und englischen Sprache und Literatur, 'Vorstand' der Abteilung wurde Konrad Hofmann; die zweite Abteilung für neuere französische und englische Literatur, Interpretation und Literaturgeschichte, mündliche und schriftliche Sprachübungen, 'Vorstand' wurde Hermann Breymann. Im Seminar gründete Oskar Brenner eine germanistische Bibliothek, aus der der Grundstock für das 1892 gegründete *Seminar für deutsche Philologie* hervorging, 'Vorstand' dieses Seminars wurde Matthias von Lexer, dessen Nachfolger 1893 Hermann Paul, der das Seminar bis 1916 leitete. Die beiden Lehrstühle des Seminars für neuere Sprachen wurden 1896 getrennt: Breymann behielt den romanistischen Lehrstuhl, 1911 Nachfolger Karl Voßler; Josef Schick erhielt 1896 die Professur der englischen Philologie. 1912 wurde ein *Seminar für slawische Philologie* mit Erich Bernecker als Leiter eingerichtet.

Breslau: 1876 wurde ein *germanistisches* und ein *romanisch-englisches Seminar* gegründet. Das germanistische leitete Karl Weinhold, und Eugen Kölbing war Leiter der englischen Abteilung des Seminars; Gustav Gröber leitete die romanische Abteilung..

Greifswald: 1876 gründete Wilhelm Wilmanns (1842–1911) das *deutsch-philologische Seminar* nach dem Muster des Hallenser und Kieler germanistischen Seminars; Nachfolger als Leiter wurde 1877 Alexander Reifferscheid (1847–1909). 1881/82 richtete Hermann Varnhagen ein provisorisches Seminar für neuere Sprachen (*romanisch-englische Societät*) ein, das als *Romanisch-Englisches Seminar* 1886 amtlich wurde. Nachfolger Varnhagens wurde 1882 Matthias Konrath. 1911 wurde das Seminar getrennt: es entstanden das *Romanische Seminar* und das *Englische Seminar*.

Bonn: 1878 richtete Wilhelm Wilmanns provisorisch ein *germanistisches Seminar* ein, das aber erst 1888 amtlich wurde. Mitdirektoren waren Johann Franck (27.4.1854–23.1.1914), der Niederländisch und Niederdeutsch lehrte, und Berthold Litzmann (1857–1926), der die deutsche Literatur vertrat. 1917 wurde eine niederländisch-niederdeutsche Abteilung des germanistischen Seminars eingerichtet, dessen Leiter Theodor Frings (1886–1968) wurde. 1878 wurde ein provisorisches *Seminar für romanische Sprachen* von Wendelin Foerster eingerichtet. Die Anglistik schuf sich 1881 eine *Englische Gesellschaft*, in der der Anglist Moritz Trautmann seminargleich arbeitete. Beide neusprachlichen Seminare wurden 1887 zu einem *Romanisch-Englischen Seminar* mit romanischer und englischer Abteilung vereinigt. Trautmann leitete die englische, Foerster die romanische Abteilung.

Jena: 1876 Gründung eines provisorischen germanistischen (deutsch-philologischen) Seminars durch Eduard Sievers, das 1879 halboffiziell wurde, d. h. von der Regierung finanziell unterstützt wurde; 1881 wurde das *Deutsche Seminar* offiziell. 1885 erfolgte die Gründung eines neusprachlichen Seminars (für Romanistik und Anglistik) durch Friedrich Kluge (anglistischer Leiter) und Rudolf Thurneysen (romanistischer Leiter).

Gießen: 1879 *Seminar für neuere Sprachen*, geleitet von Ludwig Pichler (1830–1911); 1886 *Deutsches Seminar* mit Wilhelm Braune (1850–1926). 1889 gründeten Adolf Birch-Hirschfeld und Otto Behaghel das *Romanisch-Englische Seminar*. 1908 wurde ein eigenständiges *englisches Seminar* eingerichtet.

Erlangen: 1883 *Deutsches Seminar* durch Elias von Steinmeyer, während das *Seminar für Romanische und Englische Philologie* erst 1890 (über die von Hermann Varnhagen 1885 eingerichtete *Romanisch-Englische Societät*) mit Varnhagen als Direktor installiert wurde. 1901 wurde ein unabhängiges *anglistisches Seminar* eingerichtet.

Königsberg: 1878 Alfons Kissner gründete das *Romanisch-Englische Seminar*. 1894 wurde die Einrichtung eines eigenständigen Lehrstuhls für englische Philogie durchgesetzt, mit Max Kaluza ab 1905 als Direktor. 1886 gründete Oskar Schade das *Deutsche Seminar*.

Berlin: 1887 wurde das *Germanistische Seminar* durch Erich Schmidt (Direktor) eröffnet; Schmidt leitete auch die neuere Abteilung, während ab 1889 Karl Weinhold mit der Leitung der älteren Abteilung betraut war, dessen Nachfolger 1902 Gustav Roethe (1859–1926) wurde. Aus einer von Adolf Tobler seit 1868 gepflegten romanischen Gesellschaft ging 1877 das *Romanisch-englische Seminar* hervor. Zur Aufgabe dieses Seminars heißt es in den Statuten von 1877 exemplarisch (zitiert nach Haenicke 1979: 245):

"den Studirenden Anleitung zum selbständigen wissenschaftlichen Studium der romanischen Sprachen (vorzugsweise des Französischen) und des Englischen, sowie der romanischen (namentlich der französischen) und der englischen Litteratur zu geben, Gelegenheit zur Uebung im mündlichen und schriftlichen Gebrauch der bezeichneten Sprachen zu gewähren und Anweisung zu derjenigen Behandlung der Grammatik des Französischen und des Englischen, sowie englischen und französischen Lesestoffes zu ertheilen, welche den Bedürfnissen der Gymnasien und Realschulen entspricht [...]."

Göttingen: 1889 gründete Gustav Roethe das *Germanistische Seminar*; 1889 wurde Moriz Heyne Direktor des *Seminars für deutsche Philologie*. 1882 gründete und leitete Theodor Müller das *Romanisch-Englische Seminar*.

Münster: 1894 gründeten Franz Jostes und Wilhelm Storck das *germanistische Seminar*. Seit 1902 leitete Julius Schwering (1863–1941) das Seminar. Romanistik und Anglistik fanden in Münster ihre seminaristische Institutionalisierung im Jahre 1886 durch die Gründung des *Romanisch-Englischen Seminars* mit einer romanistischen Anteilung unter Gustav Körting und einer anglistischen unter Eugen Einenkel. 1905 erfolgte die Trennung des Seminars in ein eigenständiges *Romanisches* und ein *Englisches Seminar*.

Graz: 1873 Einrichtung des *Seminars für deutsche Philologie* durch Anton Emanuel Schönbach; Mitvorstand war PD Richard Maria Werner. Ein *romanistisches Seminar* wurde erst 1901 eingerichtet, während das *englische Seminar* schon 1893 mit Karl Luick als Leiter gegründet worden war.

Prag: Deutsche Karl-Ferdinands-Universität: 1874 Gründung eines *Seminars für deutsche Sprache und Literatur* durch Johann Kelle. Die Prager Neuphilologie fand ihre Institutionalisierung 1875 mit der Schaffung eines *französisch-englischen Seminars*, das aus einer wissenschaftlichen und einer sprachpraktischen Abteilung bestand. Die wissenschaftliche Abteilung wurde in der Gründungsphase von Wendelin Foerster geleitet, der 1876 als Nachfolger von Diez nach Bonn ging; für ihn kam der Baseler Romanist Jules Cornu. Die Anglistik wurde im Rahmen des Seminars von den Germanisten Kelle und Martin mitverwaltet. Erster Extraordinarius wurde 1884 Alois Brandl, gefolgt 1889 von Alois Pogatscher. (Die tschechische Universität hatte sich 1887 ein germanistisches Seminar eingerichtet.)

Innsbruck: 1875 *Germanistisches Seminar*, Leiter: Ignaz Vinzenz Zingerle (er verwaltete die 'Lehrkanzel' für ältere deutsche Philologie und Literaturgeschichte, während die 'Lehrkanzel' für neuere deutsche Philologie und Literaturgeschichte 1887 von Josef Eduard Wackernell übernommen wurde). 1897 Gründung des *Englischen Seminars* (Leiter Rudolf Fischer) und 1904 des *Romanischen Seminars* (Leiter Theodor Gartner).

Wien: Um 1875 *Seminar für deutsche Philologie* unter Heinzel/Tomaschek. 1872 erfolgte schon die Einrichtung eines *Seminars für französische und englische Sprache* unter Adolfo Mussafia. Im Jahre 1894 wurde das französische Seminar, das 1890 aus der Trennung des Doppelseminars hervorgegangen war, als *Seminar für romanische Philologie* bezeichnet und von Mussafia und Meyer-Lübke geleitet. Die Anglistik vertrat Julius Zupitza bis 1876, er behandelte englische Literatur und Sprachgeschichte und sorgte sich um sprachpraktische Ausbildung; sein Nachfolger wurde Jakob Schipper. 1887 wurde das *Seminar für slawische Philologie* durch Vratoslav Jagiæ eingerichtet.

Czernowitz, gegründet 1875: 1876 wurde das *germanistische Seminar* von Joseph Strobl installiert; Nachfolger 1892 Oswald Zingerle. Die Romanistik, Rumänistik und Slawistik waren von der Gründung an durch Lehrkanzeln vertreten.

Lemberg, polnische Universität: 1873 *Deutsches Seminar* mit Eugen Janota (1823–1878) als Leiter.

Bern: 1859 Gründung eines *philologisch-pädagogischen Seminars* durch den klassischen Philologen Otto Ribbeck (1827–1898), in dem neben der Pädagogik die alte und neue Philologie, auch die Germanistik, in einer Institution zusammengefaßt wurden. 1885 kam es zur Gründung des *deutschen Seminars* durch Ludwig Hirzel (1838–1897) und Ferdinand Vetter (1847–1924). Im Jahre 1881 wurde durch den Romanisten Heinrich Morf (1854–1921) das *romanische Seminar* mit einer Sektion für ältere Sprachen und einer Sektion für neuere Sprachen gegründet. 1898 erfolgte die Gründung des *Englischen Seminars* durch den Sanskritisten, Komparatisten und Anglisten Eduard Müller-Hess (1853–1923).

Krakau: 1885 *Germanistisches Seminar* durch Wilhelm Creizenach.

Basel: 1885 wurde durch den Germanisten Otto Behaghel und den Romanisten Gustave Soldan ein *Germanisch-Romanisches Seminar* gegründet, das sich 1912 in eine sprachgeschichtliche und eine literargeschichtliche Abteilung schied. 1913 löste sich das *Deutsche Seminar* als selbständige Einheit mit einer Abteilung für deutsche Sprache und eine für deutsche Literatur heraus. Das *Slawische Seminar*, eine Unterabteilung des Seminars für indogermanische Sprachwissenschaft, wurde 1950 selbständig.

Zürich, gegründet 1833: 1887 Schaffung eines *Romanistisch-Anglistischen Seminars* durch Heinrich Breitinger; sein Nachfolger wurde 1889 Heinrich Morf, der 1894 das *romanische* und *englische Seminar* trennte. Ein *Deutsches Seminar* war von Ludwig Tobler 1886 gegründet worden.

4. Fachzeitschriften

Die relative Schnelligkeit, mit der sich in nur wenigen Jahrzehnten das besprochene Forschungsgebiet methodologisch und institutionell etablierte, war im Hinblick auf die sich mehrenden Erkenntnisse und Ergebnisse mit der Schaffung von Spezialzeitschriften vergesellschaftet (vgl. auch Storost 1990b). Im Rahmen der fachwissenschaftlichen Institutionalisierung sei auf drei Hauptgruppen von Periodika aufmerksam gemacht: die Schulzeitschriften, die germanistischen Fachblätter und die romanistischen/anglistischen/slawistischen Publikationsorgane, wobei wir hier auf die nicht unergiebigen Literaturzeitungen mit ihren Rezensionen und die neuphilologischen Reihen verzichten.

4.1. Schulzeitschriften

Sie machen das Ringen um die Gleichberechtigung von klassischer und Neuphilologie deutlich; es wird der konstruktive Beitrag versucht, der Neuphilologie einen Lehrinhalt und eine Methode zu schaffen, die historisch-vergleichende Sprachbetrachtung bis hin zur Nutzbarmachung von Physiologie und Psychologie in der Sprachforschung für die Schule zu erschließen, wobei man insbesondere die modernen Sprachen wie Französisch und Englisch sowie das Deutsche mit seinen phonetischen Problemen ins Auge faßte.

Archiv für das Studium der neueren Sprachen und Literaturen. 1846 von Ludwig Herrig (1816−1889) gegründet und gemeinhin als *Herrigs Archiv* bezeichnet: die älteste, heute noch existierende neuphilologische Zeitschrift. Diese Zeitschrift stand zunächst ganz im Dienst der Lehreraus- und weiterbildung, einer Idee, der sich Herrig in Berlin schon mit einem außeruniversitären Seminar für Lehrer der neueren Sprachen genähert hatte. Ganz im Sinne Carl Magers fühlte sich Herrig der Begründung der Neuphilologie verpflichtet; im Zentrum der Zeitschrift standen das Deutsche, das Französische und das Englische im Spannungsfeld zwischen Schule und Wissenschaft.

Zeitschrift für das Gymnasialwesen. Diese Berliner Zeitschriftengründung existierte von 1847 bis 1912 und fühlte sich der Öffnung des traditionellen Gymnasiums als einer reinen Gelehrtenschule in Richtung auf eine dem bürgerlichen Pragmatismus dienende Lehranstalt verpflichtet. Es wird allgemein der gymnasiale Schulsektor diskutiert; eine der Hauptstützen bleibt die klassische Philologie; gleichrangig werden aber die deutsche und französische Sprache und anderes aus dem Fächerkanon der Gymnasien besprochen. Da der Staat die Verantwortung für das Schulwesen trug, wurde von den Gründern, den Gymnasialprofessoren Wilhelm Julius Mützell (1807−1862) und Albert Gustav Heydemann (1808−1877), vorgesehen, die Seiten der Zeitschrift behördlichen Mitteilungen und deren Diskussion zu öffnen. − In Österreich wurde 1850 ein analoges Periodikum, die *Zeitschrift für österreichische Gymnasien* gegründet, die sich in den Dienst der österreichischen Gymnasialreform stellte und bis 1920 existierte. In ihr wurden unter anderem die neuesten philologischen Trends angesprochen, so die Diskussion um die Berechtigung der junggrammatischen Ansprüche.

Zeitschrift für den deutschen Unterricht. Die Germanisten Otto Lyon (1853−1912) und Rudolf Hildebrand (1824−1894) gründeten 1887 in Leipzig dieses Organ, das sich in konzentrierte Form dem Thema Schule und Germanistik zuwandte, das bislang in anderen Zeitschriften verstreut diskutiert wurde. Die Zeitschrift existierte bis 1943. Nationalistische Züge sind unverkennbar: das Deutsche als "Hauptmittel zur Förderung des Deutschtums überhaupt"; der Deutschunterricht dient der "Erziehung zu einer nationalen Bildung und Gesinnung" (so in Hildebrands *Einführung*). Die Zeitschrift strebt an, die wissenschaftlich fundierten Grundsätze der Germanistik mit der schulischen Praxis zu verknüpfen; die Theorien müßten die praktische Probe aushalten.

4.2. Germanistische Zeitschriften

Zeitschrift für deutsches Altertum. Diese heute noch existierende Zeitschrift wurde 1841 von Moriz Haupt (1808–1874) gegründet. In ihr erreichte die Beschäftigung mit dem deutschen Altertum einen ersten Höhepunkt. Mit Haupt war die Gewähr dafür gegeben, daß die klassisch-philologischen Bahnen, wie sie Gottfried Hermann (1772–1848) in der Ausrichtung auf die Betonung des Grammatischen und von Karl Lachmann (1893–1851) im Hinblick auf das Textkritische und Editorische praktiziert wurden, das methodologische Muster auch für die deutsche, gemeint ist die altdeutsche, Philologie abgaben. Die stürmischen Fortschritte in Beziehung auf neues altdeutsches Material, nach Lachmanns Methode konjekturiert, verlangten nach Öffentlichkeit; daher waren von Anfang an Texteditionen das Hauptanliegen von Haupts Zeitschrift, auch mit dem Motiv der Zuarbeit für die Sprachforschung. Die Zeitschrift wandte sich an den Kreis von Fachleuten, daher verzichtete sie weitgehend auf Erklärungshilfen und Kommentierungen im Sinn des Hermeneutischen.

Germania. Die wissenschaftliche Strenge und relative Enge des Lachmann/Hauptschen Editionsprogramms der *Zeitschrift für deutsches Altertum* führen zu einer Reaktionsbewegung, die 1856 in die Gründung der Zeitschrift *Germania. Vierteljahrsschrift für deutsche Alterthumskunde* durch Franz Pfeiffer (1815–1868) einmündete, die bis 1892 existierte und in der Anfangsphase vor dem Hintergrund der konträren Diskussion um die Nibelungenfrage zu verstehen ist. Die Zeitschrift orientierte sich an der Forschungsbreite der klassischen Philogie, wie sie von August Böckh (1785–1867) methodologisch repräsentiert wurde. Das bedeutete weniger Abdruck von Quellenschriften, dafür mehr Originalabhandlungen. Ziel ist (*Prospekt* der Zs.):

"Die deutsche Sprache in dem ganzen Umfang, in welchem sie in der deutschen Grammatik von Jacob Grimm behandelt ist. Dieses unsterbliche Werk ist die Grundlage geworden, auf welcher die ganze germanische Alterthumskunde ruht. Auch unsere Zeitschrift soll auf der Grundlage der Sprachforschung erbaut werden. Unsere Sprache in allen ihren Entwicklungen und Beziehungen soll Gegenstand unserer Studien sein, und alle den Sachen zugewandten Forschungen sollen mit der Sprachforschung Hand in Hand gehen."

Zeitschrift für deutsche Philologie. Gedacht als Ergänzung der *Zeitschrift für deutsches Altertum* gründeten Ernst Hoepfner (1836–1915) und Julius Zacher (1816–1887) wohl in Konkurrenz zur *Germania* 1868 diese heute noch existierende Zeitschrift, die vor allem Originalabhandlungen über sprachwissenschaftliche Themen (Sprachgeschichte, Lautgeschichte, Etymologie, Grammatik, Mundarten), der neueren Literatur (Textkritik, Textexegese) und der vergleichenden Mythologie sowie Rezensionen und Literaturübersichten drucken und sich dabei aus den Kontroversen, wie sie sich zwischen Haupts und Pfeiffers Zeitschrift rankten, heraushalten wollte. Mit dem Begriff 'deutsche Philologie' im Titel der Zeitschrift ist ein weiterer Fixpunkt auf dem Weg der Institutionalisierung der Germanistik markiert, der deutlich über das Konzept einer deutschen Altertumswissenschaft hinausweist. Als Rudolf von Raumer 1860 einen Artikel "Über den Begriff der deutschen Philologie" schrieb (Raumer 1860), versuchte er eine Einordnung der deutschen Philologie in die Reihe der anderen Philologien und eine Abgrenzung ihres Aufgabenbereichs. Während die Philologenversammlung mit ihrer Gründung einer germanistischen Sektion im Jahre 1862 und der germanistisch-romanistischen Sektion im Jahre 1864 eine neuphilologische Entwicklung nachvollzog und sanktionierte, schrieb Raumer schon 1860 von dem engen Verhältnis von germanischer und romanischer Philologie, die der klassischen Philologie gleichrangig und ebenbürtig geworden sei.

Beiträge zur Geschichte der deutschen Sprache und Literatur. Diese Zeitschriftengründung durch Hermann Paul und Wilhelm Braune im Jahre 1874, die noch heute existiert, wollte zunächst größere Abhandlungen wie Inauguraldissertationen abdrucken und sich dabei allen germanischen Sprachen öffnen. Ursprüngliche Absicht Pauls war es aber, seine eigenen Arbeiten möglichst schnell veröffentlichen zu können. Die *PBB* waren voll und ganz der junggrammatischen Forschungsmethode verpfichtet und in dieser Hinsicht sogar ein Kampfblatt.

4.3. Romanistische, anglistische und slawistische Zeitschriften

Jahrbuch für romanische und englische Literatur. Als Doppelzeitschrift für Anglistik und Romanistik und als wichtiger Schritt der Emanzipation dieser Wissenschaften 1859 von dem 'Doppelprofessor' Adolf Ebert (1820–1890) unter Mitwirkung des Iberoromanisten Ferdinand Wolf (1796–1866) gegründet, stand sie ab 1865 unter der Federführung von Ludwig Lemcke (1816–1884); bis 1871 erschienen 12 Bände. Lemcke setzte die Zeitschrift 1874–1876 als 'Neue Folge', jedoch mit dem erweiterten Titel *Jahrbuch für romanische und englische Sprache und Literatur* fort. Die Titelerweiterung entsprach Lemckes schon im Vorwort zu Band 6 vorgetragenem Anliegen, die Zeitschrift zur philologischen Seite hin auszuweiten, denn in den ersten Bänden beschränkte man sich "nur" auf Literatur, so daß im ersten Band die von Delius verfaßte Rezension der zweiten Auflage der Diezschen Grammatik fast wie ein Fremdkörper erscheint. Beiträger waren Diez, Wolf, Delius, Bartsch, Boehmer, ten Brink, Gröber, Mussafia, Adolf Tobler, Paris, Paul Meyer (1840–1917) und der spanische Romanist Manuel Milá y Fontanals (1818–1884). Neben der Behandlung altfranzösischer und altenglischer Fragen bringt die Zeitschrift Rezensionen sowie Übersichten über die neuere romanistische und anglistische Literatur von 1859–1874.

Jahrbuch der deutschen Dante-Gesellschaft. Die Dante-Gesellschaft war 1865 von dem Hallenser Danteforscher und -übersetzer Karl Witte (1800–1883), dem Hallenser Dante-Philologen Ludwig Gottfried Blanc (1781–1866) und Eduard Boehmer (1827–1906) unter dem Protektorat des Dante-Übersetzers, des Königs Johann von Sachsen (Philalethes, 1801–1873; Amtszeit 1854–1873) gegründet worden; ihr *Jahrbuch* erschien 1867–1877 in Leipzig in vier Bänden; Herausgeber waren Witte, Boehmer und der Schweizer Dante-Forscher Giovanni Andrea Scartazzini (1837–1901). 1920 wurde das *Jahrbuch* von dem Komponisten, Schriftsteller und Arzt Hugo Daffner (1882–1941) als *Deutsches Dante-Jahrbuch* mit Band 5 wieder aufgenommen; so existiert es heute noch. Daffner war Präsident der 1914 gegründeten Neuen Deutschen Dante-Gesellschaft und Herausgeber des *Jahrbuchs* bis 1927.

Romanische Studien. Eduard Boehmer edierte diese Zeitschrift von 1871–1895 in sechs Bänden (mit insgesamt 22 Heften) in Straßburg (ab Bd. 4 in Bonn). Sie bringt Editionen romanischer Texte sowie Abhandlungen zur Literatur, Grammatik und Etymologie. Die ersten neun Hefte (bis 1877) waren thematisch geordnet: 1. zu italienischen Dialekten; 2. Quæstiones grammaticæ et etymologicæ; 3. romanische Texte: engadinisch, greierzisch, altfranzösisch; 4. altfranzösischer Text, italienische Volkslieder; 6. altfranzösischer Text; 7. *Vosgien*, Rätoromanisch; 8. historische Grammatik; 9. Troubadourlyrik. Die nachfolgenden Hefte enthalten diverse romanistische Themen. Beiträger waren u. a. Witte, Boehmer, Cornu, Suchier, Stengel, Ernst Martin, Koschwitz, Foerster, Gröber, Morf, Vollmoeller, Eduard Schwan, Varnhagen.

Zeitschrift für romanische Philologie. Gustav Gröber (1844–1911) gründete diese heute älteste rein romanistische Zeitschrift der Welt 1877 im Anschluß an das Verschwinden von Lemckes Jahrbuch. Gröber war sich bewußt, daß das Erbe des gerade (1876) verstorbenen 'Meisters' Diez nicht geschmälert werden durfte und daß die von ihm begründete romanische Philologie in ihrer sich ständig ausweitenden Breite einen neuen Konzentrationspunkt nötig hatte. Im Prospekt (Band 1) spricht Gröber vom Abtragen einer Dankesschuld und einer Verpflichtung gegenüber dem Diezschen Werk sowie von einem notwendigen Mittel zur Förderung der jungen romanischen Philologie. Von Anfang an legte Gröber die Zeitschrift sehr breit an; es kam darauf an, 'durch Einzelforschungen die Einsicht in die Entwicklungsgeschichte der romanischen Sprachen und Literaturen' zu fördern und immer auf der Höhe der wissenschaftlichen Forschungen zu stehen. Im einzelnen führt Gröber im Prospekt zu den Aufgaben der Zeitschrift aus:

"Bei der beträchtlichen Ausdehnung des zu durchforschenden Gebietes, der grossen Zahl von Sprachen und Sprachnüancen und deren denkmalreichen Litteraturen kann die Aufgabe keine leichte erscheinen, und ausschliessen kann das neue Organ nur das Wenige, was in anderen eine speciellere Pflege erfährt. Es muss daher durch methodisch ausgeführte philologische, linguistische, litteraturhistorische Abhandlungen, durch Mittheilungen aus Handschriften, aus dem Sagen- und Sprachschatz der romanischen Völker, durch kleinere Beiträge zur Grammatik, Etymologie, Dialectologie, Textkritik, Exegese, Sprach- und Litteraturgeschichte etc. in einer der Wichtigkeit der verschiedenen romanischen Sprachen und ihrer Epochen entsprechenden Weise die Kenntniss von denselben und von ihren Litteraturen zu erweitern und durch eingehende Besprechungen aller wichtigen Arbeiten auf dem Gebiet der romanischen Philologie ein Bild von dem Fortschritt der Forschung Anderer zu geben suchen."

Von der ersten Nummer an schwört Gröber die Zeitschrift auf die sich herausbildende junggrammatische Methode ein: es geht um die Feststellung der 'Succession' der Lautgesetze, also die 'Chronologie der Entwicklung der romanischen Laute', insbesondere in der vorliterarischen Zeit, es geht um 'die lautphysiologische Erklärung für Vocal- und Consonantenwechsel'; schließlich geht es um die Beseitigung von Zweifeln 'an der ausnahmslosen Geltung der Lautgesetze' mit strenger linguistischer Argumentation. Auf dem Gebiet der Dialektologie stehen die Ausgrenzung der Dialekte in Vergangenheit und Gegenwart im Vordergrund sowie deren gegenseitige Beeinflussung, deren Alter und die Ursachen ihres Entstehens, die Frage nach Mischdialekten mit unterschiedlicher Lautbehandlung bei gleichen Bedingungen. Ferner macht Gröber auf das in der Grammatik oft vernachlässigte Gebiet der historischen Syntax und auf die mit methodischer Exegese begründete historische Lexikographie aufmerksam. Überdies geht es um den historischen Wortschatz der romanischen Völker, dessen begriffliche Ordnung und dessen Nutzung für die Kulturgeschichte der Völker sowie die Herausbildung der Semantik ('Onomatologie'). Gröber stellt darüber hinaus die Beschäftigung mit mittelalterlicher Lyrik heraus, insbesondere mit der Troubadourlyrik; er fragt nach dem Einfluß der provenzalischen Minnedichtung auf das lyrische Empfinden anderer romanischer und der germanischen Nationen und weist darauf hin, daß auch die Melodien dieses Gesangs nicht vernachlässigt werden dürfen. Nach klassisch-philologischem Muster insistiert Gröber auf kultur- und kunstgeschichtlichen Details in den literarischen Werken, nach Sitten, Gebräuchen, Anschauungen, Handwerk und Gewerbe in mittelalterlichen Dichtungen, alles Gesichtspunkte, die erkannt und beachtet werden müssen. Romanische Sprachstudien stehen für Gröber in enger Beziehung zu lateinischen Sprachstudien; beide können sich gegenseitig ergänzen. Der wechselseitige Einfluß der romanischen und germanischen Sprachen und Literaturen ist ebenfalls bekannt. Also werden Probleme, die Romanisten, Germanisten und klassische Philologen beschäftigen, in der Zeitschrift berücksichtigt werden. Eine Aufgabe der Zeitschrift sieht Gröber auch darin, die romanische Sprachen lehrende Schullehrerschaft mit der Fachwissenschaft vertraut zu machen. Der Service der Zeitschrift erstreckt sich hin bis auf eine umfassende romanistische Bibliographie, die von Anfang an in Supplementheften erschien. Außerdem wurden Beihefte mit Sondertiteln herausgegeben.

Englische Studien. Gröbers Breslauer germanistischer, romanistischer und anglistischer Kollege Eugen Kölbing (1846–1899) stieß nach dem Aufhören von Lemckes Jahrbuch in die damit entstandene anglistische Lücke und gründete 1877 die Zeitschrift *Englische Studien*, die 1944 mit Band 76 eingestellt wurde. Der Inhalt der Zeitschrift ist vorwiegend literaturgeschichtlich und textkritisch orientiert und bietet auch Rezensionen einen Platz.

Anglia. Der Leipziger Anglist Richard Paul Wülcker (1845–1910) und der nachmalige Bonner Anglist Moritz Trautmann (1842–1920) gründeten 1878 die *Anglia: Zeitschrift für englische Philologie enthaltend Beiträge zur Geschichte der englischen Sprache und Literatur,* die 1966 eingestellt wurde. Zur *Anglia* gab es ab 1890 eine Beilage unter dem Titel *Mitteilungen aus dem gesamten Gebiete der englischen Sprache und Literatrur: Monatsschrift für den englischen Unterricht*; die Beilage erschien mit später modifiziertem Titel bis 1944; sie sollte den Kern der Zeitschrift entlasten, der sich auf Originalbeiträge beschränken würde. Die *Mitteilungen* sollten die Rezensionen übernehmen und alle wichtigeren Erscheinungen und Strömungen der englischen und amerikanischen Literatur widerspiegeln sowie Fragen des englischen Unterrichts, z. B. auch Programme und Dissertationen, berücksichtigen. In der Anfangsphase brachte die *Anglia* Beiträge zur englischen Sprache und Literatur, Texte, Handschriften, Kollationen, Rezensionen und Anzeigen. Zu den ersten Beiträgern gehörten der Romanist Gottfried Baist (1853–1920), ten Brink, Delius, Elze, Sievers, Trautmann, Wülcker und Zupitza.

Zeitschrift für neufranzösische Sprache und Literatur. Gegründet 1879 durch Gustav Körting (1845–1913) und Eduard Koschwitz (1851–1904), berücksichtigte die Zeitschrift besonders den Französisch-Unterricht an den Schulen; sie erschien bis 1966 in 76 Bänden; von 1879 bis 1937 erschienen außerdem 15 Supplementhefte. Daß nun im Titel einer Zeitschrift 1879 zum ersten Mal das Neufranzösische erscheint, bedeutete, daß man sich über den Historismus in der Sprachwissenschaft hinausbegab und die nachmittelalterlichen Sprachen und Literaturen in die Forschung einbezog. Im *Prospekt* (1: ii, 1879) heißt es:

"Vielseitig und wesentlich ist die Ergänzung und Erweiterung, welche das Studium des Neufranzösischen der altfranzösischen Philologie zu verleihen mag, und erst aus dem Bündniss der beiden einander gleichberechtigten Schwestern, der alt- und neufranzösischen Philologie, wird als die höhere Einheit beider die (gesammt-) französische Philologie im vollsten und wahrsten Sinne gewonnen."

Über diesen gesamtphilologischen Aspekt hinaus gibt der Prospekt zu bedenken, daß auch die neufranzösische Sprache und Literatur um ihrer selbst willen und als kulturelle Weltphänomene zu betreiben sind. Gerade die neufranzösische Sprache sei im Gegensatz zu ihrer Literatur noch recht unzureichend erforscht.

"Noch sind die physiologischen und psychologischen Bedingungen der lautlichen Veränderungen in der neueren und neuesten französischen Sprache zu untersuchen [...]" (v).

Mit dieser junggrammatischen Prämisse betritt der Prospekt das Feld der neufranzösischen Grammatik, in der der Wandel grammatischer Formen, das Aufkommen neuer Wortbildungsmöglichkeiten und Redewendungen, auch in historischer Sicht, mit Kausalitätserklärungen zu berücksichtigen sind. Ein wichtiges Thema, das bislang weitgehend vernachlässigt wurde, bildet die Syntax des Neufranzösischen im Verein mit der Aufarbeitung der historischen Syntax. Und überdies

"fehlt es selbst noch an einer den Anforderungen des augenblicklichen Standes der Sprachwissenschaft entsprechenden Darstellung der gegenwärtigen hochfranzösischen Lautverhältnisse, der jetzt gültigen grammatischen und syntaktischen Normen" (vi).

Dazu nennt der Prospekt die Erforschung der neufranzösischen Mundarten, auch im Hinblick auf die Beschreibung der historischen Grammatik der französischen Sprache, sowie die historisch-genetische Lexikographie, Etymologie und Synonymik. Zum anderen weist das Neufranzösische im Titel der Zeitschrift auf pädagogische Zusammenhänge, einerseits mit Blick auf die Universitätsphilologie, andererseits bezüglich der Schule. Es geht um die Diskussion des Inhalts der Hochschulforschung, um die Frage, ob dort im wesentlichen die altfranzösischen Perioden oder auch die neufranzösischen Epochen eingezogen werden sollen. Nationalistisches Gedankengut fließt in den Prospekt ein, wenn gesagt wird, die neufranzösische Literatur 'nationalfranzösischen Lectoren' zu überlassen, 'deren Standpunkt natürlich den deutschen Studirenden nicht befriedigen kann und darf' (vi-vii). Ferner regt der Prospekt die Frage nach der Verwertung der Ergebnisse der französischen Philologie in Gymnasien und Realschulen an. Dem Nachwehen des klassisch philologischen Bildungsanspruchs wird der Anspruch entgegengestellt, daß der französische Unterricht ein Bildungsmittel sei, das über das Erlernen des Gebrauchs einer Fremdsprache weit hinausgeht.

Romanische Forschungen. Diese Zeitschrift wurde von Karl Vollmoeller (1848–1922) gegründet und erschien von 1883 bis 1950 in 62 Bänden. Eine Vorbemerkung zum ersten Heft charakterisiert sie so:

Die *Romanischen Forschungen* werden Untersuchungen aus dem Gesammtgebiet der romanischen Philologie einschliesslich des Mittellateins, Mitteilungen aus Handschriften, Nachkollationen und wichtige altromanische und mittellateinische Texte zur Veröffentlichung bringen. So dürfte das neue Organ als Repertorium für Mittellatein und für romanische Sprach- und Literaturgeschichte von dauerndem Wert sein.

Zu den Autoren der Anfangsphase dieses mediävistisch orientierten Blattes gehören u. a. Gottfried Baist, Vollmoeller, Foerster, Hugo Andresen und Konrad Hofmann.

Kritischer Jahresbericht über die Fortschritte der romanischen Philologie. Es ist schwierig, diese Zeitschrift in ein Schema einzuordnen, da sie in ihrer Art ein Novum darstellt: sie ist keine neuphilologische Zeitschrift im üblichen Sinn; sie ist auch keine Literaturzeitschrift im Sinne eines Rezensionsorgans. Ihr Anliegen war vielmehr die chronologische und ideengeschichtliche Aufarbeitung der aktuellen Romanistik als Wissenschaft und als Institution ebenso wie die kritische Beurteilung der zeitgenössischen romanistischen Fachliteratur. Vollmoeller (Einbandtext 1912) schreibt:

"Der romanische Jahresbericht ist die einzige romanistische Zeitschrift, welche alles, was erscheint, sicher bespricht, soweit es überhaupt zur Kenntnis der gelehrten Welt kommt."

Der *Jahresbericht* wurde 1892 gegründet (der erste Band enthält den Jahresbericht von 1890) und erschien bis 1915. Er war eng mit dem Namen seines Gründers, des Göttinger Romanisten Karl Vollmoeller (1848–1922), verbunden. An der Redaktion nahmen zahlreiche namhafte Fachwissenschaftler des In- und Auslandes teil, die über die Entwicklung ihrer speziellen Forschungsgebiete schrieben. Dem Philologiebegriff des 19. Jhs. entsprechend, ging die Einteilung der Zeitschrift von den Teilen *Sprachwissenschaft* und *Literaturwissenschaft* aus, zu denen sich der Teil *Grenz-*

wissenschaften gesellte, in dem randständige Gebiete wie Volkskunde, historische Geographie und Ethnographie, Kulturgeschichte, Kunstgeschichte, Rechts- und Philosophiegeschichte, Bibliothekswissenschaft, Paläographie und Handschriftenwesen abgehandelt wurden. In einem vierten Teil behandelte der *Jahresbericht* schließlich den 'Unterricht in den Romanischen Sprachen' mit den Bereichen: Universitäten, technische Hochschulen, höhere Lehranstalten, wobei die Universitätsberichte nach den deutschen Ländern geordnet wurden. Vor den einzelnen Teilen des *Jahresberichts* stand nach klassisch philologischem Muster zweckmäßigerweise ein einleitendes Kapitel über Enzyklopädie, Methodologie und Geschichte der Romanischen Philologie. Der Aufbau des sich anschließenden sprachwissenschaftlichen Teils ging von allgemeiner Sprachwissenschaft aus, enthielt also Sprachphilosophie, allgemeine und indoeuropäische Sprachwissenschaft und allgemeine Phonetik. Das nächste Kapitel war den Substraten und Superstraten des Romanischen gewidmet. Das Latein und den altitalischen Sprachen wurde ein eigenes Kapitel zugeordnet, in dem man über allgemeine lateinische Grammatik und Metrik, die Entwicklungsstufen des Lateinischen und über das Volkslatein handelte. In dem Kapitel über die speziellen romanischen Sprachen wurde alles das subsumiert, was den Forschungskanon ausmachte: Sprache, Dialekte, Textausgaben, Grammatik, Lexikographie, Phonetik, Alt- und Neusprachliches; aber auch die Kreolensprachen sowie Einwirkungen fremder Sprachen auf das Romanische und Auswirkungen romanischer Sprachen auf andere fanden ihren Platz. Diese Zeitschrift muß als Standardwerk für die Wissenschaftsgeschichte des von ihr berücksichtigten Zeitraums gewertet werden.

Archiv für slavische Philologie. Ein Ausdruck für den Aufschwung der Slawistik in der zweiten Hälfte des 19. Jhds. ist die Gründung dieser Fachzeitschrift in Berlin im Jahre 1876, die bis zum 42. Band im Jahre 1928 erschien. Die ersten 38 Bände wurden von dem serbokroatischen Slawisten Vratoslav Jagić (1838–1923) herausgegeben, ab Bd. 39 (1925) von dem Slawisten Erich Berneker (1874–1937). In der Anfangsphase der Zs. wurde Jagić von August Leskien und dem Slawisten Walter Nehring (1830–1909), ab Bd. 6 von dem in Berlin lehrenden polnischen Slawisten Aleksander Brückner (1856–1939) unterstützt. Von 1911 bis 1913 arbeiteten auch der Breslauer Slawist Paul Diels (1882–1963), der russische Sprachwissenschaftler Filipp Fortunatov (1848–1914) und der Wiener Slawist Constantin Jiraček (1854–1918) mit. In der Zeitschrift wurden von Anfang an Artikel zu literarischen Themen, zur Mythologie, zur Wissenschaftsgeschichte, zum Lautwandel (wobei die Brücke zu den Juggrammatikern von August Leskien geschlagen wurde) publiziert; ferner veröffentlichte das *Archiv* Rezensionen und eine aktuelle Bibliographie.

4.4. Schlußbemerkung

Die bei einem Handbuchartikel gebotene Kürze oder Beschränkung verbietet es, auf die einzelnen Zeitschriften genauer einzugehen; sie gebietet es sogar, auf bestimmte Aspekte völlig zu verzichten: genannt seien z. B. die Dialektzeitschriften wie die *Alemannia*, das *Jahrbuch des Vereins für niederdeutsche Sprachforschung*; *Bayerns Mundarten*; oder die *Zeitschrift für hochdeutsche Mundarten*. Ebenso verzichten wir auf die sprachpflegerischen Zeitschriften wie *Deutscher Sprachwart*; die *Zeitschrift des Allgemeinen Deutschen Sprachvereins*; oder die *Zeitschrift für deutsche Sprache*; germanistische Reihen wie die *Quellen und Forschungen zur Sprach- und Culturgeschichte der germanischen Völker*; die *Germanistischen Abhandlungen*; oder die *Göttinger Beiträge zur deutschen Philologie*. Gleichermaßen entgehen uns neuphilologische Reihen wie die *Altfranzösische Bibliothek*, die *Bibliotheca Normanncia*, die *Sammlung französischer Nachdrucke*, *Neuphilologische Studien*, die *Wiener Beiträge zur deutschen und englischen Philologie*, die *Romanische Bibliothek*, die *Münchner Beiträge zur romanischen und englischen Philologie*; die *Berliner Beiträge zur germanischen und romanischen Philologie*; oder die *Wiener Beiträge zur englischen Philologie*. Sie alle zeugen von dem außergewöhnlichen Aufschwung der Neuphilologien und ihrer Institutionalisierung in der zweiten Hälfte des 19. Jhs.

5. Bibliographie

Anrich, Ernst. 1891. "Geschichte der deutschen Universität Straßburg". *Zur Geschichte der deutschen Universität Straßburg*, 1–148. Straßburg.

Appel, Carl. 1909 [1905]. "Unterricht in den romanischen Sprachen und Literaturen an der Universität Breslau. Bis 1908". *Kritischer Jahresbericht über die Fortschritte der Romanischen Philologie* 9: 4. 23–26.

Arnold, Roland. 1967. "Aus der Geschichte der Greifswalder Anglistik: Matthias Konrath, der erste Direktor des englischen Seminars". *Wissenschaftliche Zeitschrift der Ernst-Moritz-Arndt-Universität Greifswald* 16. 183–188.

"Aus der Geschichte der Universität Heidelberg und ihrer Fakultäten 1386–1961". *Ruperto-Carola*, Sonderband 1961.

Bahner, Werner (in Zusammenarbeit mit Rudolf Fischer). 1959. "Die sprach- und literaturwissenschaftlichen Institute". *Festschrift zur 550-Jahr-Feier der Karl-Marx-Universität*, 81–86. Leipzig: Verlag Enzyklopädie.

Bahner, Werner et al., Hg. 1985. *Sprachwissenschaftliche Germanistik: Ihre Herausbildung und Begründung*. Berlin: Akademie-Verlag.

Bartsch, Karl. 1883 [1882]. "Über die Gründung germanischer und romanischer Seminare und die Methode kritischer Übungen". *Verhandlungen der 36. Versammlung deutscher Philologen und Schulmänner in Karlsruhe vom 27.–30. September 1882*, 237–245. Leipzig.

Baumgart, Peter, Hg. 1982. *400 Jahre Universität Würzburg. Eine Festschrift*. Neustadt/Aisch: Degener.

–. & Peter A. Süß Hg. 1995. *Lebensbilder bedeutender Würzburger Professoren*. (= *Quellen und Beiträge zur Geschichte der Universität Würzburg*, 8) Neustadt/Aisch: Degener.

Baur, Gerhard W. 1978. "Aus der Frühzeit der 'Beiträge'. Briefe der Herausgeber 1870–1885". *Beiträge zur Geschichte der deutschen Sprache und Literatur* 100. 337–368.

Bechstein, Reinhold. 1883. *Denkschrift zur Feier des fünfundzwanzigjährigen Bestehens des deutschphilologischen Seminars auf der Universität zu Rostock am 11. Juni 1883*. Rostock: Adler.

Behrens, Dietrich. 1907. "Zur Geschichte des neusprachlichen Unterrichts an der Universität Gießen". *Die Universität Gießen von 1607–1907. Beiträge zu ihrer Geschichte*. Festschrift zur dritten Jahrhundertfeier hg. von der Universität Gießen. Bd. II, 329–356. Gießen: A. Töpelmann.

Benfey, Theodor. 1869. *Geschichte der Sprachwissenschaft und orientalischen Philologie in Deutschland seit dem Anfang des 19. Jahrhunderts mit einem Rückblick auf die früheren Zeiten*. München: Oldenburg.

Bergeler, Alfred et al. 1937. *Das Germanische Seminar der Universität Berlin: Festschrift zu seinem 50jährigen Bestehen*. Berlin: de Gruyter.

Berndt, Rolf. 1970. "Das Institut für Anglistik an der Philosophischen Fakultät der Universität". *Wissenschaftliche Zeitschrift der Universität Rostock*, Gesellschafts- und Sprachwissenschaftliche Reihe 19: 5. 393–413.

Bezold, Friedrich von. 1933. *Geschichte der Rheinischen Friedrich-Wilhelms-Universität zu Bonn. Bd. II: Institute und Seminare 1818–1933*, Bonn: A. Marcus & E. Weber.

Bielfeld, Hans Holm. 1959–60. "Die Geschichte des Slawischen Instituts der Humboldt-Universität". *Wissenschaftliche Zeitschrift der Humboldt-Universität zu Berlin*. Beiheft zum Jubiläumsjahrgang 9. 35–43.

Bonjour, Edgar. 1960. *Die Universität Basel von den Anfängen bis zur Gegenwart 1460–1960*. Basel & Stuttgart: Helbing & Lichtenhahn.

Bonner Gelehrte: Beiträge zur Geschichte der Wissenschaften in Bonn. Band Sprachwissenschaften. Bonn: Bouvier; Röhrscheid, 1970.

Boucherie, Anatole. 1878. "L'enseignement de la philologie romane en France". *Revue des langues romanes* 14. 213–238.

Brüning, Eberhard. 1976. "Zur Geschichte des Lehrstuhls für englische Sprache und Literatur an der Karl-Marx-Universität Leipzig". *Aspekte der anglistischen Forschung in der DDR: Martin Lehnert zum 65. Geburtstag*. (Sitzungsberichte der Akademie der Wissenschaften der DDR. Ges.), 40–60. Berlin: Akademie-Verlag.

–. 1977. "Humanistische Tradition und progressives Erbe der Leipziger Anglistik/Amerikanistik: 100 Jahre Lehrstuhl für englische Sprache und Literatur an der Karl-Marx-Universität". *Abhandlungen der Sächsischen Akademie der Wissenschaften zu Leipzig*, Philologisch-historische Klasse 67: 1.

Bülck, Rudolf. 1951. "Karl Müllenhoff und die Anfänge des germanistischen Studiums an der Kieler Universität". *Zeitschrift der Gesellschaft für schleswig-holsteinische Geschichte* 74/75. 363–407.

Burkhardt, Ursula. 1976. *Germanistik in Südwestdeutschland: Die Geschichte einer Wissenschaft des 19. Jahrhunderts an den Universitäten Tübingen, Heidelberg und Freiburg*. Tübingen: Mohr.

Christmann, Hans Helmut, Hg. 1977. *Sprachwissenschaft des 19. Jahrhunderts*. Darmstadt: Wissenschaftliche Buchgesellschaft.

–. 1985. *Romanistik und Anglistik an der deutschen Universität im 19. Jahrhundert: Ihre Herausbildung als Fächer und ihr Verhältnis zu Germanistik und klassischer Philologie*. Stuttgart & Wiesbaden: Steiner.

–. 1986. "Programmatische Texte der Neuphilologie in der zweiten Hälfte des 19. Jahrhunderts: Mahn (1863), Breymann (1876)". *Zeitschrift für Phonetik, Sprachwissenschaft und Kommunikationsforschung* 39: 6. 656–668.

–. 1991. "Romanische Philologie an den Akademien der Wissenschaften des deutschen Sprachgebietes im 19. Jahrhundert". *Zeitschrift für Phonetik, Sprachwissenschaft und Kommunikationsforschung* 44: 1. 4–16.

–. 1994. "Linguistics and Modern Philology in Germany 1800–1840 as 'Scientific' Subjects and as University Disciplines". *Romanticisme in Science* hg. von Stefano Poggi & Maurizio Bossi, 203–214. Dordrecht: Kluwer.

Chronik des königlich deutschen Seminars an der Universität Leipzig 1873–1898. Festschrift zur

Feier seines fünfundzwanzigjährigen Bestehens. Leipzig: Vollrath, 1898.

Conrad, Ernst. 1960. *Die Lehrstühle der Universität Tübingen und ihre Inhaber 1477−1927*. (Zulassungsarbeit zur wissenschaftlichen Prüfung für das Lehramt an Gymnasien). Univ. Tübingen [masch.].

Conrad, Johannes. 1884. *Das Universitätsstudium in Deutschland während der letzten 50 Jahre*. Jena: G. Fischer.

Curtius, Georg. 1845. *Die Sprachvergleichung in ihrem Verhältniss zur classischen Philologie*. Programm, Vitzthumsches Gymnasium, Dresden.

Debus, Friedhelm. 1976. "Zur Entstehung und Geschichte des Germanistischen Seminars an der Christian-Albrechts-Universität Kiel". *Christiana Albertina*. Forschungsbericht und Halbjahresschrift der Universität Kiel, N. F. 4. 5−27.

Deuerlein, Ernst. 1927. *Geschichte der Universität Erlangen in zeitlicher Übersicht*, Erlangen: Palm & Enke.

Die deutsche Karl-Ferdinand-Universität zu Prag unter der Regierung seiner Majestät des Kaisers Franz Josef I. Prag: J. G. Calve, 1899.

Die Universität Gießen von 1607−1907. Festschrift zur dritten Jahrhundertfeier, 2 Bde. Gießen: A. Töpelmann, 1907.

Diesch, Karl. 1927. *Bibliographie der germanistischen Zeitschriften*. Leipzig: Hiersemann.

Dietrich, Gerhard. 1956. "Zur Geschichte der englischen Philologie an der Martin-Luther-Universität Halle-Wittenberg". *Wissenschaftliche Zeitschrift der Universität, Halle*. Gesellschafts- und Sprachwissenschaftliche Reihe 5.1041−1056.

Dietze, Joachim. 1966. *August Schleicher als Slawist: Sein Leben und sein Werk in der Sicht der Indogermanistik*. Berlin: Akademie-Verlag.

Dittschlag, Petra. 1984. "Die Gründung und Entwicklung sprachwissenschaftlicher Institute an der Universität Leipzig". *Linguistische Arbeitsberichte*. 42.

Eckardt, Eduard. 1925. "Die englische Philologie an der Universität Freiburg". *Aus der Werkstatt: Den Deutschen Bibliothekaren zu ihrer Tagung in Freiburg Pfingsten 1925 dargebracht von der Universitätsbibliothek*, 139−146. Freiburg i.Br.: Fr. Wagnersche Universitätsbuchhandlung.

Eichhorn, Eugen Klaus. 1957. *Geschichte des englischen Sprachunterrichts (Sprachmeister seit 1700) und der englischen Philologie an der Universität Jena bis zur Gründung des Extraordinariats für deutsche und englische Philologie (1884). Nebst einer Übersicht der Vertreter der englischen Philologie an der Universität Jena von 1884−1957*, Dissertation (masch.), Univ. Jena.

Erben, Wilhelm. 1913. "Die Entstehung der Universitätsseminare". *Internationale Monatsschrift für Wissenschaft, Kunst und Technik,* coll. 1247−1264, 1336−1348.

Feller, Richard. 1935. *Die Universität Bern 1834−1934*. Bern & Leipzig: Haupt.

Festschrift zur 500-Jahrfeier der Universität Greifswald 17.10.1956. Bd. II. Greifswald: Ernst-Moritz-Arndt-Universität, 1956.

Feyl, Othmar. 1980. *Die Universität Frankfurt (Oder) in der Bildungsgeschichte des östlichen Europa*. Frankfurt/Oder: Druck 'Neuer Tag'.

Fleischer, Wolfgang. 1984. "Zur Geschichte der germanistischen Sprachwissenschaft in Leipzig". *Deutsch als Fremdsprache* 21: 5. 257−264.

Fohrmann, Jürgen & Wilhelm Voßkamp, Hg. 1994. *Wissenschaftsgeschichte der Germanistik im 19. Jahrhundert*. Stuttgart & Weimar: Metzler.

Fuchs, August. 1844. "Die Versammlung deutscher Philologen und Schulmänner in Dresden am 1.−4. Oct. 1844". *Blätter für literarische Unterhaltung*, 1245−1247, 1249−1251.

Fuchs, Max & Max Born. 1932−33. "Zum 75jährigen Jubiläum der Berliner Gesellschaft für das Studium der neuern Sprachen". *Herrigs Archiv* 162. 1−12.

Gabka, Kurt et al. 1986. "Zur Geschichte der slawistischen Lehre und Forschung an der Universität Greifswald". *Wissenschaftliche Zeitschrift der Ernst-Moritz-Arndt-Universität* 35: 1/2. 15−19.

Gagliardi, Ernst (Bearbeiter). 1938. *Die Universität Zürich 1833−1933 und ihre Vorläufer: Festschrift zur Jahrhundertfeier*. Zürich: ohne Verlag, hg. vom Erziehungsrate des Kantons Zürich.

Germann, Dietrich. 1954. *Geschichte der Germanistik an der Friedrich-Schiller-Universität Jena auf archivalischer Grundlage dargestellt*, Dissertation (masch.), Univ. Jena.

−. 1957. "Eduard Sievers und die Gründung des Ordinariats für deutsche Philologie an der Universität Jena 1876". *Wissenschaftliche Annalen* 6. 485−491.

−. 1959. "Die Anfänge der deutschen Anglistik und die Entwicklung des Faches an der Universität Jena". *Archiv für Kulturgeschichte* 41. 183−200, 342−375.

Geschichte der Universität Rostock 1419−1969. Festschrift zur Fünfhundertfünfzig-Jahr-Feier der Universität. Bd. I: *Die Universität von 1419−1945*, Berlin: Deutscher Verlag der Wissenschaften, 1969; Bd. II: *Die Universität von 1945−1969*. Berlin: Deutscher Verlag der Wissenschaften, 1969.

Geschichte der Wiener Universität von 1848−1898, Wien: A. Hölder, 1898.

Goldmann, Karlheinz. 1967. *Verzeichnis der Hochschulen und hochschulartigen Gebilde sowie ihrer Vorläufer in deutsch- und gemischtsprachigen Gebieten unter besonderer Berücksichtigung ihrer (Haupt-) Matrikel*. Neustadt/Aisch: Degener.

Grabant, Gerhard. 1962. "Die Geschichte der Anglistik an der Friedrich-Wilhelms-Universität zu Berlin". *Deutsche Universitätszeitung* 12. 16−24.

Grau, Conrad. 1968. "Vratoslav Jagić und Reinhold Köhler: Zur Frühgeschichte des 'Archivs für slavische Philologie'". *Wissenschaftliche Zeitschrift der Humboldt-Universität zu Berlin.* Gesellschafts- und sprachwissenschaftliche Reihe 17. 229–233.

Gröber, Gustav. 1904. "Geschichte der romanischen Philologie". *Grundriß der romanischen Philologie,* 2. Auflage, Band 1, 1–185, hg. von Gustav Gröber. Straßburg: Karl J. Trübner.

Haenicke, Gunta. 1976. "Chronik des Englischen Seminars der Westfälischen Wilhelms-Universität von den Anfängen bis zur Übernahme des Lehrstuhls durch Edgar Mertner". *Edgar Mertner: Eine akademische Chronik,* Münster, 21–59. Als Manuskript gedruckt, Darmstadt: fotokop wilhelm weihert KG.

–. 1979. *Zur Geschichte der Anglistik an deutschsprachigen Universitäten 1850–1925.* Augsburg: Universität Augsburg.

–. 1981. *Biographisches und bibliographisches Lexikon zur Geschichte der Anglistik 1850–1925 (mit einem Anhang bis 1945).* Augsburg: Universität Augsburg.

–. Thomas Finkenstaedt. 1992. *Anglistenlexikon 1825–1990: Biographische und bibliographische Angaben zu 318 Anglisten.* Augsburg: Universität.

Hagen, Friedrich Heinrich von der. 1843. *Die Deutsche Sprache in der Königlichen Akademie der Wissenschaften zu Berlin.* Akademische Antrittsrede gehalten am Leibnitz-Tage, 8ten Juli 1841, Berlin.

Hämel, Adalbert. 1932. "Die romanische Philologie in Würzburg". *Aus der Vergangenheit der Universität Würzburg: Festschrift zum 350jährigen Bestehen der Universität* hg. von Max Buchner. 255–267. Würzburg: J. Springer.

Hartl, Eduard. 1926. "Das Seminar für deutsche Philologie". *Die wissenschaftlichen Anstalten der Ludwig-Maximilians-Universität zu München* hg. von Karl Alexander von Müller, 186–189. München: R. Oldenburg und Dr. C. Wolf & Sohn.

Häusler, Frank. 1986. "Vom Slawischen Seminar der Martin-Luther-Universität Halle-Wittenberg zur Sektion Germanistik/Slawistik der Pädagogischen Hochschule 'Erich Weinert' Magdeburg: Impulse und Ergebnisse". *40 Jahre Lehrstuhl für Slawische Philologie an der Martin-Luther-Universität Halle-Wittenberg (1945–1985),* Halle 63–67.

Heinsius, Theodor. 1848. *Die Germanologie auf deutschen Lehrstühlen: Deutschlands Unterrichtsbehörden zur geneigten Beachtung empfohlen.* Berlin: Mylinssche Verlagshandlung.

Heintze, Julius. 1942. "Ueber die Nothwendigkeit auf den Universitäten Professuren der neuern Sprachen zu begründen". *Jahrbuch der deutschen Universitäten,* Sommerhalbjahr 1842, 339–349.

Hermelink, Heinrich & Siegfried A. Kaehler. 1927. *Die Philipps-Universität zu Marburg 1527–1927.* Marburg: Elwert.

Hermes, Hans-Joachim. 1977. "Aus der Geschichte der Anglistik in Münster: Von den Anfängen bis zum 'Romanischen und englischen Seminar'". *Bibliotheksnachrichten* hg. von der Universitätsbibliothek Münster, Heft 197, 3–9.

–. 1980. "Die Anglistik an der Universität Münster: Von den Anfängen bis 1950". *Die Universität Münster 1780–1980* hg. von Heinz Dollinger. 383–395. Münster: Aschendorf.

Héron, Alexandre. 1884. "Du développement des études romanes en France". Discours de réception. *Précis analytique des travaux de l'Académie des sciences, belles-lettres et arts de Rouen pendant l'année 1882–1883,* 211–243. Rouen: E. Cagniard.

Herrig, Ludwig & Heinrich Viehoff.1848. "Wünsche für das Studium der neuren Sprachen". *Archiv für das Studium der neueren Sprachen und Literaturen (Herrigs Archiv)* 4. 225–234.

Hillebrand, Karl. 1865. "De la philologie en Allemagne dans la première moitié du siècle: L'école historique". *Revue moderne* 33. 239–268.

Hofmann, Erich. 1969. "Neuere fremde Sprachen". *Geschichte der Christian-Albrechts-Universität Kiel 1665–1965.* Bd. 5, Teil 1.2: *Geschichte der Philosophischen Fakultät.* Bearbeitet von Peter Rohs, Neumünster: Wachholtz.

–. 1969. "Philologien. IV. Germanistik". *Geschichte der Christian-Albrechts-Universität Kiel 1665–1965.* Bd. 5, Teil 2: *Geschichte der Philosophischen Fakultät,* 183–235. Neumünster: Wachholtz.

Hölbing, Franz. 1970. *300 Jahre Universitas Oenipotan: Die Leopold-Franzens-Universität zu Innsbruck und ihre Studenten.* Zur 300-Jahr-Feier hg. von der Österreichischen Hochschülerschaft an der Universität Innsbruck. Innsbruck: Verlag der 'Tiroler Nachrichten'.

Höppner, Wolfgang. 1987. "Germanistik als Universitätswissenschaft und staatstragende Institution in Preußen: Zur Vorgeschichte und Gründung des Germanischen Seminars in Berlin". *Wissenschaftliche Zeitschrift der Humboldt-Universität zu Berlin.* Gesellschaftswissenschaftliche Reihe 36: 9. 771–777.

Horn, Wilhelm, Gerhard Rohlfs & Georg Westermann Verlag. 1948. "Dem 100. Jahrgang (1945–1947) des 'Archiv' zum Geleit". *Archiv für das Studium der neueren Sprachen,* 100. Jahrgang, 185. 1–2.

Hübener, Gustav. 1933. "Das Englische Seminar". *Geschichte der Rheinischen Friedrich-Wilhelms-Universität zu Bonn,* Bd. II: *Institute und Seminare. 1818–1933.* 239–243. Bonn: Cohen.

Hübner, Walter. 1959. "Aus der Geschichte der 'Berliner Gesellschaft für das Studium der neueren Sprachen'". *Archiv für das Studium der neueren Sprachen mit Literaturblatt und Bibliographie,* 110. Jahrgang, 195. 27–31.

Jagoditsch, Rudolf. 1950. "Die Lehrkanzel für slavische Philologie an der Universität Wien 1849–1949". *Wiener Slavistisches Jahrbuch.* Bd. I: *Festschrift zur Hundertjahrfeier der Lehrkanzel für slavi-*

sche Philologie an der Universität Wien 1849–1949 hg. von R. Jagoditsch, 1–60. Wien: Sexl.

Janota, Johannes. 1980. *Eine Wissenschaft etabliert sich. 1810–1870*. Mit einer Einführung und hg. von Johannes Janota. Tübingen: Niemeyer.

Janßen, Matthias. 1995. "Oskar Schade (1826–1906)". *Die Albertus-Universität zu Königsberg und ihre Professoren: Aus Anlaß der Gründung der Albertus-Universität vor 450 Jahren* hg. von Dietrich Rauschning & Donata von Nerée. Berlin: Dunkker & Humblot.

Karg-Gasterstädt, Elisabeth. 1958/59. "Das alte Germanistische Institut". *Wissenschaftliche Zeitschrift der Universität Leipzig. Gesellschafts- und sprachwissenschaftliche Reihe* 8. 631–638.

Karl-Marx-Universität Leipzig. 1409–1959: Beiträge zur Universitätsgeschichte. 2 Bde., Leipzig: Verlag Enzyklopädie, 1959.

Kaufmann, Georg, Hg. 1911. *Festschrift zur Feier des hundertjährigen Bestehens der Universität Breslau*, Bd. II. Breslau: Hirt.

–. 1958. *Geschichte der deutschen Universitäten*, 2 Bde., Stuttgart: Cotta'sche Buchhandlung Nachfolger, 1888–96. (Neudruck 1958.)

Keller, Adelbert von. 1842. *Inauguralrede über die Aufgabe der modernen Philologie*. Stuttgart: Metzler.

Kirchner, Joachim, Hg. 1969–1977. *Bibliographie der Zeitschriften des deutschen Sprachgebiets bis 1900*. 3 Bde. Stuttgart: Hiersemann.

Klemperer, Victor. 1952. "Das romanische Katheder und Seminar". *450 Jahre Martin-Luther-Universität Halle-Wittenberg*, Bd. II, 315–320. Halle: Martin-Luther-Universität Halle-Wittenberg.

Knobloch, Johann. 1956. "Die Geschichte der sprachwissenschaftlichen Lehre und Forschung an der Ernst-Moritz-Arndt-Universität zu Greifswald". *Festschrift zur 500-Jahrfeier der Universität Greifswald, 17.10.1956*, Bd. II, 234–238. Greifswald: Ernst-Moritz-Arndt-Universität.

Koch, Herbert. 1950. *Geschichte der Romanistik an der Universität Jena*, Dissertation (Masch.), Universität Jena.

Kolde, Theodor. 1910. *Die Universität Erlangen unter dem Hause Wittelsbach 1810–1910: Festschrift zur Jahrhundertfeier der Verbindung mit der Krone Bayerns*. Leipzig: A. Deichert Nachfolger.

Kolk, Rainer. 1994. "Liebhaber, Gelehrte, Experten". *Wissenschaftsgeschichte der Germanistik im 19. Jahrhundert* hg. von Jürgen Fohrmann & Wilhelm Voßkamp, 48–114. Stuttgart & Weimar: Metzler.

Körner, Josef. 1935. "Deutsche Philologie". *Deutsch-Österreichische Literaturgeschichte* hg. von Eduard Castle, Bd. III. 48–89. Wien: Fromme.

Krause, Friedhilde. 1978. "Vratoslav Jagić und Richard Lepsius". *Zeitschrift für Slawistik* 23. 205–213.

–. 1987. "Vratoslav Jagić und Theodor Mommsen". *Zeitschrift für Slawistik* 32. 897–903.

Kurz, Josef. 1971. "Vratoslav Jagić in Berlin". *Zeitschrift für Slawistik* 16. 255–262.

Laubert, Karl. 1874. *Übersicht der Forschungen auf dem Gebiete der französischen Philologie*. Programm, Oberschule Frankfurt/Oder.

Lausberg, Heinrich. 1980. "Die Romanistik an der Universität Münster". *Die Universität Münster 1780–1980* hg. von Heinz Dollinger, 401–410. Münster: Aschendorf.

Lehmann, Jochen. 1967a. "Die germanischen Vorlesungen zwischen 1803 und 1900 an der Universität Heidelberg. Ein Beitrag zur Geschichte der Heidelberger Germanistik". *Ruperto Carola*, Jg. 21, 42 [recte 41]. 205–239.

–. 1967b. "Die germanistischen Vorlesungen zwischen 1803 und 1900 an der Universität Heidelberg". In: *Ruperto-Carola*, Jg. 19, 42. 205–239.

Leitner, Erich. 1973. *Die neuere deutsche Philologie an der Universität Graz 1851–1954: Ein Beitrag zur Geschichte der Germanistik in Österreich*. Graz: Akademische Druck- und Verlagsanstalt.

Lemmer, Manfred. 1955/56. "Julius Zacher und die Gründung des Seminars für deutsche Philologie an der Universität Halle". *Wissenschaftliche Zeitschrift der Martin-Luther-Universität Halle-Wittenberg. Gesellschafts- und sprachwissenschaftliche Reihe* 5: 4. 613–622.

–. 1958. "Vorläufer und Wegbereiter der hallischen Universitätsgermanistik". *Wissenschaftliche Zeitschrift der Martin-Luther-Universität Halle-Wittenberg. Gesellschafts- und sprachwissenschaftliche Reihe* 7: 6. 1111–1128.

–. 1959. "Die hallische Universitätsgermanistik". *Wissenschaftliche Zeitschrift der Martin-Luther-Universität Halle-Wittenberg. Gesellschafts- und sprachwissenschaftliche Reihe* 8: 3. 359–387.

Lenz, Max. 1910. *Geschichte der Königlichen Friedrich-Wilhelms-Universität zu Berlin*. Bd. III: *Wissenschaftliche Anstalten, Spruchkollegium, Statistik*, Halle/Saale: Buchhandlung des Waisenhauses.

–. 1914/15. "Die Anfänge der Germanistik an der Berliner Universität". *Das literarische Echo*, 17, Spalten 15–20.

Lepitre, Albert. 1891. "Les néo-grammairiens d'Allemagne". *Compte rendu du Congrès scientifique international des catholiques*, 5–23. Paris.

Mager, Carl. 1843. "Ueber Wesen, Einrichtung und pädagogische Bedeutung des schulmäßigen Studiums der neueren Sprachen und der Mittel, ihm aufzuhelfen". *Die modernen Humanitätsstudien*, Heft 2. Zürich: Meyer & Zeller.

–. 1848. "Wünsche für das Studium der neueren Sprachen". *Herrigs Archiv* 3. 225–234.

Mahn, Karl August Friedrich. 1863. *Über die Entstehung, Bedeutung, Zwecke und Ziele der romanischen Philologie. Ein Vortrag in der germanistisch-*

romanistischen Sektion der in Meiszen tagenden Versammlung deutscher Philologen und Schulmänner am 1. October 1863 gehalten, Berlin: Dümmler.

Mair, Walter N. 1982/83. "Die Romanische Philologie an der Universität Innsbruck bis 1918". *Tiroler Heimat*, Heft 46/47.

Martin, Ernst. 1872. *Das historische Studium der neueren Sprachen und seine Bedeutung für den Schulunterricht zunächst in Baden*. Freiburg: Wagner'sche Buchhandlung.

Meissner, Rudolf. 1933. "Das germanistische Seminar". Friedrich Bezold, *Geschichte der rheinischen Friedrich-Wilhelms-Universität zu Bonn. Bd. II: Institute und Seminare 1818–1933*. 214–238. Bonn.

Meves, Uwe. 1987. "Die Gründung germanistischer Seminare an den preußischen Universitäten (1875–1895)". *Deutsche Vierteljahrsschrift für Literaturwissenschaft und Geistesgeschichte*, 61. Jahrgang, Sonderheft, 69*–122*. Stuttgart: Metzler.

–. 1991. "Die Institutionalisierung der Germanistik als akademisches Fach an den Universitätsneugründungen in Preußen". *'Einsamkeit und Freiheit' neu besichtigt: Universitätsreformen und Disziplinenbildung in Preußen als Modell für Wissenschaftspolitik im Europa des 19. Jahrhunderts* hg. von Gert Schubring (= *Proceedings of the Symposium of the XVIIIth International Congress of History of Science at Hamburg–Munich, 1–9 August 1989*), 110–143. Stuttgart: Steiner.

–. 1993. "Emil Friedrich Julius Sommer (1819–1846), der erste 'zünftige' hallische Germanist: Dokumente aus seiner Privatdozentenzeit". *Von wyßheit würt der mensch geert… Festschrift für Manfred Lemmer* hg. von Ingrid Kühn & Gotthard Lerchner, 349–389. Frankfurt am Main: Lang.

–. 1994a. "Eberhard Gottlieb Graff (1780–1841)". *Jahrbuch der Albertus Universität zu Königsberg/Pr.* 29: 167–182.

–. 1994b. "Zur Namensgebung 'Germanist'". *Wissenschaftsgeschichte der Germanistik im 19. Jahrhundert* hg. von Jürgen Fohrmann & Wilhelm Voßkamp, 25–47. Stuttgart & Weimar: Metzler.

–. 1994c. "Zum Institutionalisierungsprozeß der Deutschen Philologie: Die Periode der Lehrstuhlerrichtung (von ca. 1810 bis zum Ende der 60er Jahre des 19. Jahrhunderts)". *Wissenschaftsgeschichte der Germanistik im 19. Jahrhundert* hg. von Jürgen Fohrmann & Wilhelm Voßkamp, 115–202. Stuttgart & Weimar: Metzler.

–. 1995a. Rez. von Joachim Burkhard Richter, *Hans Ferdinand Maßmann: Altdeutscher Patriotismus im 19. Jahrhundert*. (Berlin–New York: de Gruyter 1992). *Arbitrium: Zeitschrift für Rezensionen zur germanistischen Literaturwissenschaft* 1: 92–95.

–. 1995b. "Die Anfänge des Faches Deutsche Sprache und Literatur an der Universität Königsberg: Von Karl Lachmann bis zu Julius Zacher". *Zeitschrift für Deutsche Philologie* 114: 3, 376–393.

Meyer, Jürgen Bona. 1875. *Deutsche Universitätsentwicklungen. Vorzeit, Gegenwart und Zukunft*. Berlin: Habel.

Militz, Hans-Manfred. 1995. "Wegbereiter der Romanistik in Jena: Bernhard Wolff und Hermann Hettner". *Romanistik in Geschichte und Gegenwart* 1: 1. 33–42.

–. & Wolfgang Schweickard. 1995a. "Tradition und Perspektiven der Romanistik an der Friedrich-Schiller-Universität Jena". *Die Bedeutung der romanischen Sprachen im Europa der Zukunft: Romanistisches Kolloquium IX* hg. von W. Dahmen et al. 179–197. Tübingen: Gunter Narr.

Möller, Anneliese & Johann-Christoph Lohff. 1981. "Die Rostocker 'Zeitschrift für Orthographie' (1880–1885)". *Zeitschrift für Germanistik* 2. 411–422.

Morvay, Karin. 1975. "Die 'Zeitschrift für deutsches Altertum' unter ihren ersten Herausgebern Haupt, Müllenhoff, Steinmeyer und Scherer (1841–1890)". *Archiv für Geschichte des Buchwesens*. 15. Spalten 469–520.

Moser, Hugo. 1976. *Karl Simrock: Universitätslehrer und Poet, Germanist und Erneuerer von 'Volkspoesie' und Älterer 'Nationalliteratur'. Ein Stück Literatur-, Bildungs- und Wissenschaftsgeschichte des 19. Jahrhunderts*. Berlin: Schmidt.

Müller, Jörg Jochen. 1974. "Die ersten Germanistentage". *Germanistik und deutsche Nation 1806–1848: Zur Konstitution bürgerlichen Bewußtseins* hg. von Jörg Jochen Müller. 297–318. Stuttgart: Metzler; Stuttgart: Poeschel.

Müller, Karl Alexander von, Hg. 1926. *Die wissenschaftlichen Anstalten der Ludwig-Maximilians-Universität zu München: Chronik zur Jahrhundertfeier*. München: R. Oldenburg und Dr. C. Wolf & Sohn.

Müller, Oskar & Harald Raab. *Die Geschichte der slawistischen Studien und des Instituts für Slawistik an der Universität Rostock*. Universität Rostock (Manuskript, o. J.).

Müller, Rainer Albert. 1982. "Aspekte zur Geschichte der deutschen Philologie an der Universität Ingolstadt-Landshut-München (1799–1949)". *Die Ludwig-Maximilians-Universität in ihren Fakultäten* hg. von Laetitia Boehm & Johannes Spörl. Bd. II. 185–255. München: Duncker & Humblot.

Nauck, Ernst Theodor. 1956. *Die Privatdozenten der Universität Freiburg i. Br. 1818–1955*. Freiburg: Albert.

Obenaus, Sibylle. 1974. "Die deutschen allgemeinen kritischen Zeitschriften in der ersten Hälfte des 19. Jahrhunderts. Entwurf einer Gesamtdarstellung". *Archiv für Geschichte des Buchwesens* 14. 1–122. Frankfurt/M.

–. 1985. "Die Brüder Grimm als Rezensenten an allgemeinen kritischen Zeitschriften: Überlegungen zu Rezeptionsbedingungen von Literatur in den ersten Jahrzehnten des 19. Jahrhunderts". *Linguistische Studien* 130. 176–186.

Osthoff, Hermann. 1880. "Der grammatische Schulunterricht und die sprachwissenschaftliche Methode". *Zeitschrift für die österreichischen Gymnasien* 31. 55–72.

Paris, Gaston. 1864. "La philologie romane en Allemagne". *Bibliothèque de l'Ecole des Chartes* 25. 435–445.

Paul, Hermann. 1901. "Geschichte der Germanischen Philologie". *Grundriss der Germanischen Philologie*. Zweite, verbesserte und vermehrte Aufl., hg. von Hermann Paul, Bd. I, 9–158. Strassburg: Trübner.

Paulsen, Friedrich. 1897. *Geschichte des gelehrten Unterrichts auf den deutschen Schulen und Universitäten*, 2. Aufl., Bd. II. Leipzig: Veit.

Pischel, Joseph et al. Hg. 1983. *125 Jahre Germanistik an der Universität Rostock 1858–1983*. Rostock.

Pohrt, Heinz. 1968. "Die deutsche Slawistik im 19. Jahrhundert: Gedanken zu einer Darstellung ihrer Geschichte". *Wissenschaftliche Zeitschrift der Humboldt-Universität zu Berlin. Gesellschafts- und sprachwissenschaftliche Reihe* 17. 217–221.

–. 1976. "Vatroslav Jagić und die Slawistik in Berlin". *Zeitschrift für Slawistik* 21. 378–391.

–. 1977. "Die Anfänge der Polonistik an der Universität Berlin 1841 bis 1880". *Zeitschrift für Slawistik* 22. 219–226.

–. 1980. "Der Hochschullehrer der Berliner Universität [Aleksander Brückner]". *Zeitschrift für Slawistik* 25. 170–175.

–. 1982. "Zur Entwicklung der Slawistik und Baltistik in Deutschland gegen Ende des 19. Jahrhunderts". *Zeitschrift für Slawistik* 27. 700–709.

–. 1986. "Vasmer und die Anfänge des Slavischen Instituts an der Universität Berlin". *Zeitschrift für Slawistik* 31: 5. 654–662.

Prokopowitsch, Erich. 1955. *Gründung, Entwicklung und Ende der Franz-Josephs-Universität in Czernowitz (Bukowina-Buchenland)*. Clausthal-Zellerfeld: Pieper.

Prutz, Hans. 1894. *Die königliche Albertus-Universität zu Königsberg in Preußen im 19. Jahrhundert: Zur Feier ihres 350jährigen Bestehens*. Königsberg: Hartung.

Rahnenführer, Ilse. o.J. *Geschichte des Germanischen Instituts der Universität* Rostock, Germanistisches Institut der Universität Rostock (unveröffentlichtes Manuskript).

Raumer, Rudolf von. 1860. "Über den Begriff der deutschen Philologie". *Zeitschrift für die österreichischen Gymnasien* 11. 85–95.

–. 1863 [1861]. "Thesen über die Behandlung des Altdeutschen auf Gymnasien und über die Heranbildung der dazu nöthigen Lehrkräfte". *Verhandlungen der zwanzigsten Versammlung deutscher Philologen und Schulmänner in Frankfurt am Main vom 24. bis 27. September 1861*, 140–141. Leipzig. (Diskussionsbeiträge S. 141–174.)

–. 1870. *Geschichte der Germanischen Philologie vorzugsweise in Deutschland*. München: Oldenburg.

Rauschning, Dietrich & Donata von Nerée, Hgg. 1995. *Die Albertus-Universität zu Königsberg und ihre Professoren: Aus Anlaß der Gründung der Albertus-Universität vor 450 Jahren herausgegeben*. Berlin: Duncker & Humblot.

Richter, Joachim Burkhard. 1992. *Hans Ferdinand Maßmann: Altdeutscher Patriotismus im 19. Jahrhundert.* (= *Quellen und Forschungen zur Sprach- und Kulturgeschichte der germanischen Völker*, NF 100.) Berlin & New York: de Gruyter.

Richter, Werner. 1960. "Berliner Germanistik vor und nach dem hundertjährigen Jubiläum der Friedrich-Wilhelm-Universität". *Studium Berolinense: Aufsätze und Beiträge zu Problemen der Wissenschaft und zur Geschichte der Friedrich-Wilhelm-Universität zu Berlin* hg. von Hans Leussink et al., 490–506. Berlin: de Gruyter.

Risop, Alfred. 1910. *Die romanische Philologie an der Berliner Universität 1810–1910*. Erlangen: Fr. Junge.

Roethe, Gustav. 1910. "Das germanische Seminar". *Geschichte der Königlichen Friedrich-Wilhelms-Universität zu Berlin*, Bd. 3, 220–230, hg. von Max Lenz. Halle: Buchhandlung des Waisenhauses.

Rösel, Hubert. 1980. "Das Slavisch-Baltische Seminar der Westfälischen Wilhelms-Universität". *Die Universität Münster 1780–1980* hg. von Heinz Dollinger, 411–413. Münster: Aschendorf.

Röther, Klaus. 1980. *Die Germanistenverbände und ihre Tagungen: Ein Beitrag zur Germanistischen Organisations- und Wissenschaftsgeschichte*. Köln: Pahl-Rugenstein Verlag.

Schlawe, Fritz. 1959. "Die Berliner Jahrbücher für wissenschaftliche Kritik: Ein Beitrag zur Geschichte des Hegelianismus". *Zeitschrift für Religions- und Geistesgeschichte* 11. 240–258, 343–356.

Schmidt, Hartmut. 1983. "Die Berlinische Gesellschaft für deutsche Sprache an der Schwelle der germanistischen Sprachwissenschaft". *Zeitschrift für Germanistik* 4: 3. 278–289.

Schmidt, Immanuel. 1889. "Ludwig Herrig". *Herrigs Archiv* 82. i–xxiv.

Schneegans, Heinrich. 1911. "Unterricht in den romanischen Sprachen und Literaturen an der Universität Bonn 1818–1910/11". *Kritischer Jahresbericht über die Fortschritte der Romanischen Philologie* 11: 4. 1–45.

Schrey, Helmut. 1982. *Anglistisches Kaleidoskop: Zur Geschichte der Anglistik und des Englischunterrichts in Deutschland*. St. Augustin: Richarz.

Schubel, Friedrich. 1960. "Die neueren Sprachen". Ders. *Universität Greifswald*. Frankfurt/M.: Weidlich.

Seidel-Vollmann, Stefanie. 1977. *Die romanische Philologie an der Universität München 1826–1913*. Berlin: Duncker & Humblot.

Selle, Götz von. 1953. *Die Georg-August-Universität Göttingen: Wesen und Geschichte*. Göttingen: Musterschmidt.

–. 1956. *Geschichte der Albertus-Universität zu Königsberg in Preußen*. 2. durchgesehene u. verm. Auflage. Würzburg: Holzner.

Siebs, Theodor. 1911. "Deutsche Sprache und Literatur". *Festschrift zur Feier des 100jährigen Bestehens der Universität Breslau* hg. von Georg Kaufmann, Band II, 403–411. Breslau: Hirt.

–. 1911. "Zur Geschichte der germanistischen Studien in Breslau". *Zeitschrift für deutsche Philologie* 43. 202–234.

–. 1929. "Das Deutsche Institut der Breslauer Universität". *Schlesische Monatshefte*, 4. Juni 1929, 1–9.

Skarek, Willy. 1931. *Bestrebungen und Leistungen der österreichischen Frühgermanistik von Beginn des 19. Jahrhunderts bis zu dessen Mitte*. Dissertation (masch.), Universität Wien.

Staa, Meinhard von. 1930. "Aufbau und Bedeutung der deutschen Universitätsinstitute und -seminare". *Das akademische Deutschland* hg. von Michael Doeberl et al., Bd. III, 263–276. Berlin: Weller.

Stackmann, Karl. 1979. "Die Klassische Philologie und die Anfänge der Germanistik". *Philologie und Hermeneutik im 19. Jahrhundert: Zur Geschichte und Methodologie der Geisteswissenschaften* hg. von Hellmut Flashar et al., 240–259. Göttingen: Vandenhoeck & Ruprecht.

Steinmetz, Max (Hrsg.). 1958/62. *Geschichte der Universität Jena 1548/58–1958: Festgabe zum vierhundertjährigen Universitätsjubiläum*. Im Auftrag von Rektor und Senat verfaßt und hg. von einem Kollektiv des Historischen Instituts der Friedrich-Schiller-Universität Jena, 2 Bde. Jena: G. Fischer.

Stempel, Wolf-Dieter. 1964. "Zweihundert Bände 'Herrigs Archiv': Ein Rückblick". *Archiv für das Studium der neueren Sprachen und Literaturen* 115. Jahrgang, 200. 2–13.

Stimming, Albert. 1906. "Unterricht in den romanischen Sprachen und Literaturen an der Universität Göttingen". *Kritischer Jahresbericht über die Fortschritte der Romanischen Philologie* 10: 4. 116–141.

Stölzle, Remigius. 1914. "Seminarien der philosophischen Fakultät". *Würzburg hundert Jahre bayerisch: Ein Festbuch* hg. von der Stadt Würzburg. 225–230. Würzburg: Stürtz.

Storost, Jürgen. 1984. "'August Fuchs, Philolog': Ein Beitrag zur Auseinandersetzung zwischen Philologie und Linguistik in der ersten Hälfte des 19. Jahrhunderts". *Beiträge zur Romanischen Philologie* 23: 1. 95–108.

–. 1988. "Das sprachpflegerische Engagement von August Fuchs: Eine wissenschaftsgeschichtliche Studie zur Germanistik". *Beiträge zur Erforschung der deutschen Sprache* 8. 56–67.

–. 1989. "Die Diez-Stiftung. I: Zur Gründungsgeschichte". *Beiträge zur Romanischen Philologie* 23: 2. 301–316.

–. 1990a. "Die Diez-Stiftung. II: Zur Wirkungsgeschichte". *Beiträge zur Romanischen Philologie* 29: 1. 117–133.

–. 1990b. "Sechs maßgebende linguistische Fachzeitschriften in der zweiten Hälfte des 19. Jahrhunderts". *Zeitschrift für Germanistik* 11: 3. 257–384.

–. 1991a. "Zur germanistischen und junggrammatischen Position der Berliner und Münchner Akademie im 19. Jahrhundert". *Zeitschrift für Germanistik*, N. F., Heft 1. 82–98.

–. 1991b. "Zu germanistischen und junggrammatischen Positionen der wissenschaftlichen Akademien in Göttingen, Leipzig und Wien in der zweiten Hälfte des 19. Jahrhunderts". *Zeitschrift für Germanistik*. N. F., Heft 3. 555–567.

–. 1992. "Zu den Anfängen der Institutionalisierung von Germanistik und Neuphilologie (Romanistik) im Verein deutscher Philologen und Schulmänner". *Zeitschrift für Germanistik*. N. F., Heft 1. 75–89.

–. 1993. "Der Hispanist August Fuchs". Anhang: "August-Fuchs-Bibliographie". *Iberoromania*, 37. 116–137.

–. 1994a. "Der Allgemeine Deutsche Sprachverein". *Lingua et traditio: Geschichte der Sprachwissenschaft und der neueren Philologien: Festschrift für Hans Helmut Christmann zum 65. Geburtstag* hg. von Richard Baum et al. 827–843. Tübingen: Narr.

–. 1955 [1994b]. "Noch einmal: Zur Diez-Stiftung". *Romanistisches Jahrbuch* 45. 74–84.

–. 1997. "August Fuchs und Friedrich Diez: Zum 150. Todestag von August Fuchs am 8. Juni 1997". *Kontinuität und Innovation: Studien zur Geschichte der romanischen Sprachforschung vom 17. bis zum 19. Jahrhundert: Festschrift zum 70. Geburtstag von Werner Bahner* hg. von Gerda Haßler & Jürgen Storost, 259–274. Münster: Nodus.

Tobler, Adolf. 1899 [1890]. "Romanische Philologie an deutschen Universitäten" (Rektoratsrede Berlin 1890). Adolf Tobler, *Vermischte Beiträge zur französischen Grammatik*, 3. Reihe, 160–183. Leipzig: Hirzel.

Toma, Margit, o.J. *Das Romanische und das Lateinamerika-Institut der Universität Rostock*, Institut für Romanistik der Universität Rostock (Manuskript).

Trabant, Jürgen. 1994. "Magna Charta der romanischen Sprachwissenschaft: Zum 200. Geburtstag des Begründers der deutschen Romanistik, Friedrich Diez". *Der Tagesspiegel* (Berlin), 13. März.

Tschirch, Fritz. 1956. "Vor- und Frühgeschichte der Greifswalder Universitätsgermanistik". *Festschrift zur 500-Jahrfeier der Universität Greifswald 17.10.1956*, Bd. II, 136–199. Greifswald: Ernst-Moritz-Arndt-Universität.

Vogt, Walther Heinrich. 1940. "Die Gründung der Germanistik, der Deutschen und Nordischen Philologie an der Universität Kiel". *Festschrift zum 275jährigen Bestehen der Christian-Albrechts-Universität Kiel* hg. von Paul Ritterbusch, 295–308. Leipzig: S. Hirzel.

Voretzsch, Carl. 1904. *Die Anfänge der romanischen Philologie an den deutschen Universitäten und ihre Entwicklung an der Universität Tübingen*: Akademische Antrittsrede. Tübingen: Laupp.

–. 1905a. "Halle von den Anfängen bis 1905". *Kritischer Jahresbericht über die Fortschritte der Romanischen Philologie* 9: 4. 4–23.

–. 1905b. *Ernst W. G. Wachsmuth und Ludwig G. Blanc, die Begründer der romanistischen Professur an der Universität Halle*. Halle: Niemeyer.

–. 1912. "Unterricht in den romanischen Sprachen". *Kritischer Jahresbericht über die Fortschritte der Romanischen Philologie* 12: 4. 51–85.

–. 1926. *Das romanische Seminar der vereinigten Friedrichs-Universität Halle-Wittenberg im ersten Halbjahrhundert seines Bestehens*. Halle: Romanisches Seminar der Universität Halle.

Wagner, Rudolf, Hg. 1975. *Alma Mater Francisco Josephina: Die deutschsprachige Nationalitäten-Universität in Czernowitz*. Festschrift zum 100. Jahrestag ihrer Eröffnung 1875. München: Hans Meschendörfer.

Weyhe, Hans. 1944. "Aus hallischer Anglistik". *250 Jahre Universität Halle: Streifzüge durch ihre Geschichte in Forschung und Lehre*, 267–269. Halle/Saale: Niemeyer.

Weihs, Kurt. 1950. *Geschichte der Lehrkanzeln und des Seminars für romanische Philologie an der Universität Wien*. Dissertation (masch.), Universität Wien.

Weimar, Klaus. 1989. *Geschichte der deutschen Literaturwissenschaft bis zum Ende des 19. Jahrhunderts*. München: Fink.

Wenig, Otto, Hg. 1968. *Verzeichnis der Professoren und Dozenten der Rheinischen Friedrich-Wilhelms-Universität zu Bonn 1818–1968*. Bonn: Bouvier, Röhrscheid.

Weydt, Günther. 1980. "Die Germanistik an der Universität Münster". *Die Universität Münster 1780–1980* hg. von Heinz Dollinger, 375–382. Münster: Aschendorf.

Wiese, Leo. 1910. "Münster von den Anfängen bis 1908/09 [Geschichte der Romanistik]". *Kritischer Jahresbericht über die Fortschritte der Romanischen Philologie* 10: 4. 145–155.

Wilmotte, Maurice. 1886. *L'enseignement de la philologie romane à Paris et en Allemagne (1883–1885)*, 1–29. Bruxelles: Imprimerie de Polleunis, Ceuterick et Lefébure.

Zeil, Wilhelm. 1988. *Slawistik im deutschen Kaiserreich: Forschungen und Informationen über die Sprachen, Literaturen und Volkskulturen der slawischen Völker*, Habilitationsschrift, 3 Bde., Berlin: Humboldt-Universität, Gesellschaftswissenschaftliche Fakultät, Sektion Slawistik.

Ziemer, Hermann. 1881. "Die Stellungnahme des grammatischen Gymnasialunterrichts zur neueren sprachwissenschaftlichen Methode der sogenannten Junggrammatiker". *Zeitschrift für das Gymnasialwesen* 35.385–400.

Jürgen Storost, Berlin (Deutschland)

159. Les débuts et l'évolution de la philologie romane au XIXe siècle, surtout en Allemagne

1. Introduction
2. La naissance de la philologie romane
3. L'intégration de la philologie romane dans l'enseignement universitaire en Allemagne
4. Textes programmatiques de la 'nouvelle philologie'
5. Le transfert du modèle allemand
6. Bibliographie

1. Introduction

La philologie romane est une branche de la 'nouvelle philologie' (ou des 'nouvelles philologies' [*Neuphilologie(n)*], un ensemble disciplinaire (qui, progressivement, sera reconnu comme une matière 'académique', digne d'un enseignement universitaire) prenant naissance au XIXe siècle; cette nouvelle philologie se laisse principalement identifier par son opposition à la 'philologie classique'. La philologie romane, comme toutes les branches de la philologie 'moderne' (*moderne Philologie*; cf. Mager 1840), est d'abord – à l'instar de la philologie classique – une conjonction d'études littéraires (dont la part est prépondérante) et linguistiques (ou linguistico-grammaticales); ces études s'inscrivent dans un cadre de recherche historique (dont l'objet est le développement des cultures occidentales 'modernes', c'est-à-dire de celles qui font émergence au Moyen Âge) et plus globalement théorique (la philologie fait appel à des connaissances ethnologiques, culturelles, esthétiques et philosophiques). Science de textes − d'où aussi, chez certains auteurs, une conception restrictive de la philologie comme science de l'édition de textes (ou 'critique textuelle' ou encore 'ecdotique') − la philologie moderne mettra beaucoup de temps à se scinder en une branche littéraire et une branche linguistique; de plus, le dégagement de la philologie romane par rapport à la philologie germanique est un processus se déroulant sur plusieurs décennies (cf. ci-dessous § 3.).

L'objectif central de cet article est de retracer la naissance et l'évolution de la philologie romane en Allemagne, de définir le contenu scientifique qu'on a donné à cette 'nouvelle philologie' (cf. § 4.), et d'analyser comment le 'modèle allemand' a été transféré à d'autres pays, en prenant l'exemple de la France (§ 5.). Dans cet article, on s'intéressera surtout à la philologie romane dans son orientation linguistique, mais on signalera à quelques reprises son rattachement aux études littéraires.

Ce rattachement est inscrit dans l'histoire même du terme de 'philologie', qui avait évolué d'un sens général ("connaissance possédée par l'homme lettré") à un sens 'scientifique': l'étude systématique des langues et des littératures. C'est cette dernière signification, avec application au domaine roman, qu'on rencontre chez Fritz Neumann (1854−1934) en 1886 (*Die romanische Philologie: ein Grundriss*) et qui a été codifiée dans le *Grundriss* de Gustav Gröber (1844−1911; voir Gröber 1888: 140−154). Au XIXᵉ siècle, la philologie était profondément linguistique (comme le montre le sens du terme *philology* dans le monde anglo-saxon; cf. Bolling 1929; Malkiel 1960/61, 1966). Si elle débordait le cadre linguistique, c'était, d'une part, pour glisser vers une étude strictement littéraire (stylistique, étude des motifs ou des genres littéraires), mais, d'autre part, aussi pour s'ouvrir sur l'histoire des peuples et des cultures. Cette dernière perspective, tracée par Friedrich August Wolf (1759−1824) dans sa *Darstellung der Alterthumswissenschaft*, est celle qui est indiquée par Gröber; celui-ci, dans sa "Gliederung der romanischen Philologie", inclut l'ethnologie et l'histoire des peuples (1888: 152−153):

"Der Geschichtswissenschaftliche Teil, der die für die romanische Philologie wichtigsten Thatsachen der geschichtlichen Grenzwissenschaften zusammenfasst und die hauptsächlichsten Quellen und Hilfsmittel anführt, die für sie und zur Einführung in sie vorhanden sind, hebt naturgemäss an mit einem I. ETHNOLOGISCHEN Abschnitt, der von den Völkern, die romanische Länder bewohnten, nach ihrer physischen Seite und nach ihren geistigen Besonderheiten berichtet. Ein II. GESCHICHTLICHER Abschnitt gibt dagegen Kunde von den geistigen Äusserungen und Leistungen der Romanen ausser den sprachlichen und sprachkünstlerischen, also von A) der romanischen Staatengeschichte und den Schicksalen der romanischen Länder und Völker; B) von ihren Bildungszuständen, ihren Lebensformen, den bürgerlichen Einrichtungen, den Gewohnheiten, Sitten, Thätigkeiten, Unterhaltungen, wozu gehört, was die Volkskunde an Kenntniss über Glauben, Aberglauben, Gebräuche des Volkes u. s. w. ergibt (Culturgeschichte im engeren Sinne); C) von der kunstgeschichtlichen Thätigkeit der Romanen (Kunstgeschichte); D) der Wissenschaften (Geschichte der Wissenschaft)."

La philologie romane dans son orientation linguistique peut être définie comme l'étude synchronique, diachronique et comparative des structures des diverses langues romanes et comme l'étude des rapports entre ces structures linguistiques et l'histoire des peuples de la Romania; à un niveau 'réflexif', elle englobe l'histoire de ces études, sujet de description historiographique. [Sur le contenu du concept de 'philologie romane', voir Engels 1953; Tagliavini (1972: 1−2), Malkiel 1960/1961, Swiggers 1989); pour la scission entre la linguistique romane et les études littéraires romanes, voir Vidos 1956 et Gauger et al. (1981: 3); sur le rapport − souvent antagoniste − entre philologie et linguistique, voir Koerner 1982 et Swiggers 1998.]

2. La naissance de la philologie romane

2.1. Le contexte scientifique

Dans son contexte scientifique immédiat − celui de l'étude de langues et de leurs manifestations historiques −, la naissance de la philologie romane, comme discipline acquérant un certain prestige universitaire, ne peut être détachée de l'émergence de la grammaire comparée des langues indo-européennes. Celle-ci se définit progressivement par détachement de la comparaison typologique de langues; la grammaire comparée s'intéresse à l'étude de groupes génétiques de langues, dont le cours évolutif est articulé en termes de maintien et d'innovation de structures. (Sur les rapports entre grammaire comparée, typologie de langues et linguistique générale au début du XIXᵉ siècle, voir Swiggers 1996a, b; sur l'élaboration de la grammaire comparée, voir Morpurgo-Davies 1996, avec importante bibliographie, et Swiggers & Desmet 1996.)

Les bases théoriques de l'édifice de la grammaire comparée des langues indo-européennes sont posées par Franz Bopp (1791–1867) dans son *Über das Conjugationssystem der Sanskritsprache in Vergleichung mit jenem der griechischen, lateinischen, persischen und germanischen Sprache* (1816). L'objectif de ses recherches est le rapprochement des formes grammaticales des diverses langues indo-européennes en vue de remonter à un état primitif, dont le sanskrit se rapproche le plus par sa structure morphologique et qui permet d'expliquer les formes grammaticales rassemblées par le comparatiste. Devenu professeur à Berlin en 1821, Bopp poursuit ses recherches comparatistes, qu'il élargit aussitôt vers le domaine de la phonétique, ce qui lui permet d'entrevoir le mécanisme du changement phonétique régulier (en 1825 il utilisera pour la première fois le terme de *Lautgesetz*). Après de nombreuses études sur le sanskrit et sur des problèmes de grammaire comparée, Bopp publie le premier compendium de grammaire comparée des langues indo-européennes: *Vergleichende Grammatik des Sanskrit, Zend, Griechischen, Lateinischen, Lithauischen, Gothischen und Deutschen* (1833–1852), ouvrage de référence pour les premières générations de comparatistes.

Un autre pionnier de la grammaire comparée des langues indo-européennes fut le Danois Rasmus Rask (1787–1832). Dans ses *Undersøgelse om det gamle Nordiske eller Islandske Sprogs Oprindelse* (texte rédigé en 1814, mais publié seulement en 1818), Rask établit les rapports génétiques entre l'islandais, les langues scandinaves et germaniques, le latin et le grec, l'arménien, les langues baltiques et slaves. Dans son introduction, il donne une analyse de sa méthode; selon lui, la comparaison doit être fondée sur des critères morphologiques (le vocabulaire ne fournissant pas un appui fiable). L'originalité de Rask est qu'il introduit un second critère pour la détermination d'une relation génétique, à savoir les règles des changements de 'lettres'. Cette idée marquera le développement ultérieur de la grammaire historico-comparative, en montrant la nécessité d'établir des règles qui rendent compte de la transformation phon(ét)ique d'une langue en une autre. Dès 1814, Rask a entrevu le principe des lois phon(ét)iques, même s'il n'emploie pas ce terme (il se sert de la périphrase 'règles pour les transitions des lettres' [*Regler for Bogstavernes Overgange*]).

Chez Bopp et chez Rask la grammaire comparée reste avant tout un exercice de comparaison 'statique' ou 'achronique': l'intégration de l'histoire dans la grammaire comparée est due au travail qui sera investi dans l'étude de groupes linguistiques particuliers. L'apport décisif a été celui de Jacob Grimm (1785–1863), qui dans sa *Deutsche Grammatik* (1819–1847; premier volume 1819, avec une refonte importante en 1822, qui incorpore une phonétique détaillée pour laquelle l'auteur s'est inspiré des travaux de Rask) retrace l'évolution des langues germaniques à partir de l'indo-européen. La contribution fondamentale de Grimm est d'avoir souligné l'importance de la dimension historique en grammaire comparée (les correspondances sont interprétées en termes d'évolution) et d'avoir augmenté la précision des recherches comparatives, en les axant sur des groupes à l'intérieur de la famille indo-européenne, ce qui a permis de condenser l'espace chronologique de la différenciation et de travailler sur des rapports de parenté plus étroits.

C'est dans ce contexte intellectuel et scientifique que la linguistique comparée 'intra-indo-européenne' prend naissance et que la grammaire historico-comparative assume ses contours définitifs. Après l'œuvre fondatrice de Grimm pour les langues germaniques, Joseph Dobrovský (1753–1829) pose, en 1822, les bases de la grammaire comparée des langues slaves (*Institutiones linguae Slavicae*); en 1853, la *Grammatica celtica* de Johann Kaspar Zeuss (1806–1856) marque le début de la grammaire comparée des langues celtiques. Entre-temps, la linguistique romane avait pris naissance (cf. Swiggers 1997: 243–252).

2.2. Les figures fondatrices en Allemagne

Généralement, on fait commencer la linguistique romane avec la figure de Friedrich Diez (1794–1876). (Sur l'histoire et la 'préhistoire' de la philologie romane en Allemagne, voir Vàrvaro 1968, Niederehe & Schlieben-Lange 1987 et Bossong 1990.) En fait, l'origine de la linguistique romane constitue une problématique épineuse, à cause de plusieurs raisons:

(1) d'une part, un certain nombre de travaux du XVIIIᵉ siècle (comme par ex. ceux de Bonamy et de Turgot) préparent l'avènement de la 'philologie moderne' du XIXᵉ siècle, qui n'est donc pas le résultat d'une vraie rupture épistémologique (cf. Malkiel 1974; Swiggers 1997: 217−223);
(2) d'autre part, la philologie romane est à l'origine une discipline mixte, où l'histoire littéraire (et l'édition et le commentaire de textes) est côtoyée par l'histoire des langues romanes; d'ailleurs, le premier travail de grande envergure dans le domaine est l'œuvre d'un auteur qui est en premier lieu fasciné par la littérature (provençale), à savoir François-Juste-Marie Raynouard (1761−1836). Rappelons que sa *Grammaire de la langue romane ou langue des troubadours*, et sa *Grammaire comparée des langues de l'Europe latine, dans leurs rapports avec la langue des troubadours* sont insérées dans un ouvrage d'orientation littéraire, son *Choix des poésies originales des troubadours* (Paris, 1816−1821). (Sur l'œuvre et la personnalité de Raynouard, voir Körner 1913, Rettig 1976, Storost 1981 et Bossong 1990: 296−300).

Toutefois, en ce qui concerne l'émergence, en Allemagne, d'une pratique comparative appliquée aux langues romanes, l'œuvre et la personnalité de Friedrich Diez apparaissent comme fondatrices; ses travaux constituent la référence (marquée de 'scientificité') en linguistique romane pour ses contemporains et ses successeurs, en Allemagne et ailleurs. Diez doit son titre de fondateur de la linguistique romane en premier lieu à sa *Grammatik der romanischen Sprachen* (1836−1844), dans laquelle il compare six langues romanes (le roumain, l'italien, l'occitan, le français, l'espagnol et le portugais) et présente une analyse comparative des systèmes phonétique et morphologique des langues romanes. La perspective de Diez est une perspective proprement historico-comparative, alors que celle de François Raynouard respirait un comparatisme faussement historique et manquait d'une organisation grammaticale systématique.

Avant d'examiner l'apport fondamental de Diez, il importe toutefois de situer son œuvre par rapport au savoir acquis dans le domaine et surtout par rapport à ce qui avait été fait un peu avant lui en Allemagne. En effet, Diez a eu des précurseurs lointains (sur lesquels il s'est basé; cf. Malkiel 1974), comme Bernardo de Aldrete (1560−1641), Charles du Fresne Du Cange (1610−1688), Sebastián de Covarrubias (1539−1613) et Tomás Antonio Sánchez (1725−1802), et un précurseur immédiat dans la figure de Lorenz Diefenbach (1806−1883), qui en 1831 publie son ouvrage *Ueber die jetzigen romanischen Schriftsprachen, die spanische, portugiesische, rhätoromanische (in der Schweiz), französische, italiänische und dakoromanische (in mehren Ländern des östlichen Europa's) mit Vorbemerkungen über Entstehung, Verwandtschaft u. s. w. dieses Sprachstammes.* (Sur les conceptions linguistiques de Diefenbach, voir Swiggers 1995.) L'auteur y étudie les 'Schriftsprachen' − il s'agit des langues employées dans la littérature, dans l'administration, dans la religion, dans la correspondance savante − de la Romania, en les situant dans le contexte plus large des langues indo-européennes (cf. ci-dessus, 2.1.). Il réagit contre une philologie aride qui n'appréhende pas le langage comme phénomène humain, et il plaide pour un "rechtes, lebendiges Studium der Sprachen", qui intéresse à la fois le linguiste, le philosophe, le 'Geschichtsforscher' ("dem Geschichtsforscher zeigt es den Weg in unbekannten Räumen der Vergangenheit, besonders das vergleichende Sprachstudium" [1831: 1]), et tous ceux qui s'occupent de 'recherches empiriques'. Postulant une unité étroite entre grec et latin, Diefenbach accorde un grand poids à l'influence celtique sur le latin, mais la spécificité du latin est aussi expliquée par la continuation d'une variante dialectale dans la langue-ancêtre.

La portion centrale de l'ouvrage concerne le passage du latin aux langues romanes ("Die jetzigen romanischen Schriftsprachen im Allgemeinen" [1831: 21−35], et les caractéristiques des différentes *Schriftsprachen* romanes ("Die romanischen Schriftsprachen im Einzelnen" [1831: 36−51]). Les langues retenues sont l'espagnol, le portugais, le rhétoroman, le français, l'italien et le daco-roumain (valaque ou moldave, 'wlachisch oder moldauisch' [p. 21]). Diefenbach exclut de son examen l'occitan ('Provenzalsprache'; il y rattache, à côté du catalan, les patois francoprovençaux), le wallon, le catalan (rattaché du point de vue dialectal à l'occitan), le gallego (dialecte du portugais) et le génois.

Les langues romanes, issues du latin populaire qui s'est mêlé à d'autres langues, sont présentées, séparément, dans l'ordre suivant (1831: 36–51): espagnol (36–39), portugais (39–40), rhétoroman ('Churwalsch in Graubündten mit dem Ladin', 40–42), français (42–45), italien (46–49), daco-roumain (49–51). Le plan adopté est uniforme: Diefenbach considère d'abord le rapport particulier de la langue avec le latin, pour passer ensuite à son histoire externe (mélange avec tel substrat et tel superstrat), et il termine chaque fois par une brève 'Charakteristik' de la langue et quelques mots sur sa division dialectale. L'information n'est pas présentée sous une forme systématique, et Diefenbach n'approfondit guère les problèmes de substrat ou de superstrat. L'exposé sur les différentes langues romanes est suivi par des tableaux comparatifs, brièvement commentés, sur la prononciation des langues romanes (1831: 57–60, 65–71), sur certaines formes grammaticales, comme l'article (1831: 75–80) et les numéraux (1831: 83–86), sur le nom (1831: 89–94) et le verbe (1831: 105–118). Diefenbach combine un point de vue humboldtien — l'intérêt porté à la 'caractérisation' des langues — avec une démarche comparatiste (en synchronie), se concrétisant dans les tableaux où il juxtapose les formes des différentes *Schriftsprachen* de la Romania et dans son explication des formes du futur et du conditionnel dans les langues romanes (1831: 98–99). La liaison établie entre histoire de la langue et histoire des cultures fait que l'auteur est sensible aux phénomènes de mélange (*Mischung*) de langues, qu'il mentionne l'existence de créoles, et qu'il décèle les causes de l'évolution interne et externe d'une langue.

Si August-Wilhelm Schlegel (*Observations sur la langue et la littérature provençales*, 1818) — à l'échelle gallo-romane — et Diefenbach — ce dernier à l'échelle pan-romane — avaient ouvert des perspectives comparatistes (mais surtout typologiques, s'inscrivant dans le projet humboldtien de 'caractérologie' des langues), ce sera Friedrich Diez qui — profitant aussi des apports empiriques d'auteurs occitans (comme Raynouard, mais aussi Henri Pascal de Rochegude (1741–1834) [*Essai d'un glossaire occitanien*, 1819]) — établira la linguistique romane comme discipline scientifique (cf. Gauger et al. 1981: 14: "Der Begründer der romanischen Sprachwissenschaft — dies ist unbestritten — ist Friedrich Diez"). (Sur Diez, voir Curtius 1960 et surtout Baum 1993; sur l'importance de l'occitan pour les études comparatives et typologiques et sur la tradition 'occitanisante', voir Chambon & Swiggers 1994 et Baggioni & Martel 1997.)

Or, en quoi consiste l'apport de Diez? Il consiste dans l'application rigoureuse de la méthode comparative (de la grammaire comparée des langues indo-européennes) à des matériaux puisés dans l'ensemble des langues romanes, y compris les données dialectales. En effet, si Friedrich Diez — esprit imprégné du romantisme allemand, qui avait commencé par des études (de nature comparative) sur les littératures romanes médiévales — était un savant de cabinet, il se rendait bien compte de l'importance de l'étude des parlers vivants. Dans la préface de son *Etymologisches Wörterbuch der romanischen Sprachen*, on peut lire:

"Etwas habe ich durch vieljährige erfahrung auf diesem gebiete gelernt, was sich zwar von selbst versteht, aber nicht von allen verstanden sein will; daß zu wissenschaftlich sicherem urtheile sich nur *der* durcharbeitet, der den gesammten wortvorrath der sprache bis in ihre mundarten hinein zu bewältigen nicht ermüdet. Wer nicht so weit vorzudringen lust hat, der beklage sich nicht, wenn er jeden augenblick den boden verliert. Es ist kein wunder, wenn manche auf andern sprachgebieten ausgezeichnete forscher auf dem romanischen so oft fehlgreifen, da sie nur das einzelne in einer bestimmten gestalt auffassen, ohne seine geschichte und seine beziehungen nach allen seiten hin erkannt zu haben […]"
Die volksmundarten bieten der forschung ein unschätzbares nie zu erschöpfendes material, welches häufig über buchstabenverhältnisse und begriffsentwicklung überraschenden aufschluß gibt: ich habe sie daher überall zu rathe gezogen, so weit die mir gestatteten hülfsmittel ausreichten, ihnen auch zuweilen beispiels halber kleine artikel vergönnt." (Diez 1853: viii, xi)

La préface du dictionnaire étymologique de Diez comporte un autre passage très important pour notre propos: c'est celui, tout au début de la préface, où Diez oppose l'étymologie fantaisiste, non contrôlée, non critique, à l'étymologie critique:

"Die aufgabe der etymologie ist, ein gegebenes wort auf seinen ursprung zurückzuführen. Die zur lösung dieser aufgabe angewandte methode ist aber nicht überall dieselbe: leicht lässt sich eine kritische und eine unkritische wahrnehmen. Die unkritische nimmt ihre deutungen auf gut glück aus einer äusserlichen ähnlichkeit der form, oder erzwingt sie bei geringerer ähnlichkeit, ja selbst bei gänzlicher verschiedenheit derselben, durch eine reihe willkürlich geschaffener mittelglieder. Ein in seinem grundsatze so fehlerhaftes verfahren, dessen ungeachtet doch da, wo witz und divinationsgabe nicht fehlten, mancher treffliche wurf gelang, hat bei vielen die ganze etymologische kunst in miscredit gebracht, während sie sich andern durch die leichtigkeit ihrer ausübung, wozu sich jeder ohne beruf und vorbereitung aufgelegt fühlte, empfahl. Jene irren in ihrer abneigung, diese in ihrer zuneigung. Im gegensatze zur unkritischen methode unterwirft sich die kritische schlechthin den von der lautlehre aufgefundenen principien und regeln, ohne einen fußbreit davon abzugehen, sofern nicht klare thatsächliche ausnahmen dazu nöthigen; sie bestrebt sich dem genius der sprache auf der spur zu folgen, ihm seine geheimnisse abzugewinnen; sie wägt jeden buchstaben und sucht den ihm in jeder stellung zukommenden werth zu ermitteln. Und doch, wie wenig vermag sie oft, wie zweifelhaft sind ihre erfolge! Das höchste, was der etymologe erreicht, ist das bewußtsein wissenschaftlich gehandelt zu haben; für absolute gewißheit hat er keine gewähr, eine unbedeutende notiz kann ihm das mühsam erworbene zu seiner beschämung unversehens unter den füßen wegziehen. Dergleichen wird bei jeder forschung vorkommen, bei der etymologischen gehört es zu den täglichen erfahrungen, die auch dem scharfsinnigsten nicht erlassen werden. Darum bescheidenheit, selbst wo alles unsre deutungen zu unterstützen scheint!" (Diez 1853: vii−viii)

La 'méthode critique' dont parle Diez est celle de la grammaire historico-comparative, qui dans le cas de sa discipline, trouve un champ d'application gratifiant. L'avantage particulier que présente la romanistique par rapport à la grammaire comparée indo-européenne, à savoir l'accès plus direct *au terminus a quo* et la disponibilité d'une documentation plus étoffée dans le temps et dans l'espace, a eu pour résultat que la linguistique romane s'est développée comme une branche diachronique à valeur méthodologique exemplaire: l'abondance des données sur le latin et sur l'histoire ancienne des langues ainsi que sur les variétés dialectales romanes permet: de retracer les innovations et les maintiens entre le stade ancestral et les étapes ultérieures, de définir les critères de distinction entre la couche populaire et la couche savante dans le lexique, et de déterminer les rapports plus ou moins étroits de parenté. Le mérite de Diez, qui s'est inspiré de l'exemple de Jacob Grimm, est d'avoir compris les capacités de recréation et de restructuration d'un état de langue variable, d'avoir maîtrisé l'histoire complexe de langues constituant un ensemble plus ou moins unifié, défini par sa constitution historique, et d'avoir distingué entre phénomènes pan-romans et innovations 'plus locales'. Dans sa grammaire et dans son dictionnaire étymologique Diez a posé les bases de la linguistique romane comparée: il y identifie correctement la place des langues romanes à l'égard du latin (vulgaire), applique avec un vrai sens de méthode les lois phonétiques de la grammaire historique, reconnaît le mécanisme de l'analogie (dans la morphologie verbale) et distingue entre les mots hérités (*Naturproducte*) et les mots savants (*Kunstproducte*) − distinction qui sera ultérieurement précisée par Auguste Brachet dans sa *Grammaire historique de la langue française* (1867) et dans son *Dictionnaire des doublets ou doubles formes de la langue française* (1868).

Si Diez a codifié, pour son époque et pour les générations postérieures jusqu'à la fin du XIXe siècle, le savoir grammatical et lexical dans l'étude historico-comparative des langues romanes, il restait à montrer l'émergence et le développement continu des traits caractérisant les langues romanes, à partir de traces suivies dès les origines latines jusque dans les dialectes modernes. Ce sera l'œuvre d'une troisième figure importante dans l'histoire précoce de la linguistique romane en Allemagne. En 1849, August Fuchs (1818−1847), dans un ouvrage publié après sa mort prématurée, poursuit le but de montrer que l'évolution des langues romanes n'est pas l'effet de hasards externes, mais qu'elle répond à un processus de longue durée, qui caractérise le développement 'naturel' à partir d'un noyau commun. L'auteur place d'emblée sa recherche dans une perspective (humboldtienne) de linguistique générale.

"Unsere Aufgabe in diesem Bande ist es nun [...] nachzuweisen, wie das, worin die Romanischen Sprachen vom Lateinischen sich wesentlich zu unterscheiden scheinen, nur unentwikkelt und noch im Keime, schon im Lateinischen sich findet, und ob sich in diesen Erscheinungen der Romanischen Sprachen im Vergleiche zum Lateinischen wirklich ein Fortschritt zeigt. Eine derartige Untersuchung scheint mir aber nicht bloß für die Romanischen Sprachen wichtig, sondern für die Sprachkunde im Allgemeinen lehrreich zu sein, denn ganz derselbe Geist, welcher die Romanischen Sprachen aus den Römischen Volksmundarten hat hervorgehen lassen, scheint mir überhaupt bei der Entstehung aller sogenannten Tochtersprachen zu walten. Und dieser Geist, dieses Streben nach immer größerer Einfachheit, Klarheit und Verständlichkeit der Form und nach immer vollkommener Anpassung derselben an den sich fort und fort entwickelnden Gedanken, wirkt so gewaltig, daß keine äußern Verhältnisse ihn im Ganzen und Großen zu stören vermögen, und daß sich überall im Wesentlichen dieselben Erscheinungen finden. Was also hier vom Verhältnisse der Romanischen Sprachen zum Lateinischen gesagt ist, gilt in den Grundzügen auch von dem Verhältnisse der Prakritsprachen zum Sanskrit, des Neugriechischen zum Altgriechischen, des Neuhochdeutschen zum Althochdeutschen, des Englischen zum Angelsächsischen u. s. w. Darauf kommt es natürlich nicht an, daß die eine Sprache zur Bildung der Zukunft das Zeitwort *gehen*, die andere *wollen*, die dritte *werden*, die vierte *sollen*, die fünfte *haben* zu Hülfe nimmt, sondern die Hauptsache ist, daß allen diesen Ausdrukksweisen ein und derselbe Gedanke zum Grunde liegt: die ursprünglich aus Zusammensetzung entstandene, dem Streben nach Deutlichkeit nicht mehr genügende Zeitendung auf eine sinnlichere und verständlichere Weise auszudrükken. Auch die Erscheinung wiederholt sich in den Sprachen, daß oft sehr alte Formen, nachdem sie eine Zeitlang wie verschwunden gewesen sind, mit einem Male wieder auftauchen. In der That sind aber diese immer nur aus der Schriftsprache verschwunden, haben sich aber im Volksmunde fortwährend erhalten. Daher darf es uns nicht überraschen, wenn wir in den Romanischen Sprachen Wörter und Formen finden, die wir außerdem nur aus dem frühesten Lateinischen kennen; vielmehr bestätigen diese gerade erst recht den innigen Zusammenhang der Romanischen Sprachen mit der ältesten Lateinischen Volkssprache." (Fuchs 1849: 54–55)

L'apport de Fuchs – qui dédie son ouvrage au 'theurer Meister' Friedrich Diez – réside non seulement dans le vaste panorama qu'il dresse des langues et parlers de la Romania et dans l'examen synthétique et rigoureux de faits phonétiques, prosodiques, morphologiques (et indirectement syntaxiques) reliant le latin et les langues romanes, mais surtout dans la formulation du problème: celui de la détection de la 'romanité' des langues romanes dans l'histoire même de la langue latine, et cela dès les origines. En d'autres termes, c'est le schéma de 'reproduction familiale' qui est mis en question ici. Pour Fuchs, il n'y a pas, d'un côté, une langue-mère latine et, de l'autre, des langues-filles romanes: les langues romanes sont caractérisées comme la continuation naturelle de la langue vulgaire romaine. De plus, Fuchs montre que cette évolution n'est pas un processus de décadence, mais une marche vers une plus grande clarté et expressivité. Il est donc essentiel pour Fuchs que le latiniste et le romaniste partagent une partie de leurs connaissances et qu'entre la philologie et la linguistique il ne règne pas un esprit d'antagonisme, mais une volonté de collaboration (cf. aussi Fuchs 1844, analysé dans Swiggers 1989). En même temps, Fuchs met en relief la 'dignité scientifique' de la philologie moderne: les langues romanes modernes sont – du point de vue 'spirituel' – supérieures au latin. 'Wir sehen aber auch, daß die Romanischen Sprachen der geistigen Höhe ihrer Ausbildung nach der Lateinischen Sprache keineswegs weichen, sondern daß sie im Ganzen und Großen eben so hoch über derselben stehen, wie die geistige Ausbildung der jetzigen Romanischen Völker über der der alten Römer, denn – Geist und Sprache ist eins" (1849: 369). (Sur Fuchs, voir Malkiel 1967/68 et Storost 1984.)

3. L'intégration de la philologie romane dans l'enseignement universitaire en Allemagne

Après la description du 'savoir' qui constitue le noyau de la composante linguistique de la philologie romane, il faut examiner l'institutionnalisation, au sein des universités, de la discipline.

La philologie romane s'est établie comme matière académique et comme discipline institutionnalisée au cours du XIXe siècle. L'intégration au programme universitaire de l'enseignement des langues et des littératures romanes peut être décrite, à partir de l'époque de la Renaissance jusqu'à la fin du XIXe siècle, comme un processus comportant six étapes.

La première est celle qui englobe la période jusqu'à 1800 environ: elle se caractérise par un enseignement linguistique (et littéraire) à orientation pratique, qui prend pour objet les langues modernes (français, anglais, italien, espagnol), sans que celles-ci fassent l'objet d'une véritable reconnaissance académique (les cours de langues modernes sont fixés à des heures qui n'interfèrent pas avec les cours universitaires: *horis alias non legibilibus*).

La seconde phase, de 1790 à 1830 environ, a vu l'émergence d'un enseignement à propos des langues et cultures modernes, sous forme de conférences faites par des historiens et des philosophes, comme par exemple (dans le domaine des études romanes) les cours de August-Wilhelm Schlegel (1767–1845) à Bonn (1818–1845), de Valentin Schmidt (17??–1831) à Berlin (1819–1831), d'Ernst Wilhelm Gottlieb Wachsmuth (1784–1866) à Halle (1816–1820) et à Kiel (1820–1825) et, avant eux, de Johann Georg Jacobi (1740–1814) à Freiburg im Breisgau (1784–1814).

Ce n'est qu'à partir de la troisième phase, qu'on peut situer entre 1825 et 1850, que la philologie 'moderne' (les syntagmes *moderne*

Philologie et *romanische Philologie* sont attestés pour la première fois dans Mager 1840) s'intègre dans le programme universitaire, malgré les réticences des autorités académiques, comme en témoigne la déclaration officielle (en 1819) de la faculté de philosophie de l'Université de Berlin:

"Die philosophische Fakultät ist der festen Überzeugung, dass die neueren Sprachen und Literatur in den wissenschaftlichen Lehrplan nur dann aufzunehmen wären, wenn sich ein Lehrer derselben fände, der sie in einem grösseren Umfange und Zusammenhange von einem wissenschaftlichen historisch-philologischen oder ästhetisch-literarischen Standpunkte aus bearbeitete. Das Studium derselben, insofern es zu einem wahrhaft wissenschaftlichen Behufe getrieben wird – und nur in diesem Sinne kann es einer eigenen Professur bedürfen – würde nur durch einen solchen Mann wirklich gefördert werden; dagegen die Kenntnis einer einzelnen dieser Sprachen und ihrer Literatur, wäre sie auch mehr als gewöhnlich begründet und ausgeführt und von einem Sinn für die Schönheit beider begleitet, und ein dadurch bedingter Unterricht unseres Erachtens immer zu einseitig sein und vielleicht eine gar zu beschränkte spielende Beschäftigung mit diesen Gegenständen veranlassen würde, welche für den wesentlichen Zweck der Universitätsstudien eher störend als günstig ausfallen möchte." (Texte cité d'après Risop 1910: 62)

Cette philologie moderne englobe trois composantes: la comparaison (des langues et des littératures); l'histoire des langues et des littératures; la critique textuelle (= la philologie au sens restreint). Le haut prestige de la philologie classique explique qu'au départ la philologie moderne est confiée aux soins de grands philologues classiques comme Georg Friedrich Benecke (1762–1844) à Göttingen, Karl Lachmann (1793–1851) à Berlin et Moritz Haupt (1808–1874), successeur de Lachmann. C'est pendant cette période que les travaux fondateurs de Friedrich Diez (cf. ci-dessus 2.2.) voient le jour et que le champ de la philologie romane se construit. Les premières chaires de philologie moderne combinent les études germaniques et romanes: c'est le cas des professorats de Diez (à Bonn, 1823), d'Adelbert von Keller (1812–1883) à Tübingen en 1841 (cf. son texte programmatique de 1842), de Konrad Hofmann (1819–1890) à München en 1853 et de Karl Bartsch (1832–1888) à Rostock en 1858. Une exception notable est la création d'une chaire de langues et de littératures romanes à Halle en 1822 pour Ludwig Gottfried Blanc (1781–1866).

La quatrième phase, dont le début coïncide avec la dernière décennie de la troisième et qu'on peut situer entre 1840 et 1860, se caractérise par l'impact de l'école sur l'évolution de la philologie moderne. En effet, dans son texte de 1840, Carl Wilhelm Eduard Mager (1810–1858) avait exigé une formation scientifique pour les philogues modernes, futurs professeurs de lycée. C'est dans ce contexte qu'il faut voir la création, en 1846, de l'*Archiv für das Studium der neueren Sprachen* de Ludwig Herrig (1816–1889) et Heinrich Viehoff (1804–1886); leur revue réclame une formation historico-comparative et plaide pour une autonomisation de la philologie romane, de la philologie germanique et de la philologie slave. Il n'en reste pas moins que la plupart des chaires de philologie romane sont des chaires combinant études romanes et études anglaises: c'est le cas à Göttingen avec Theodor Müller (1816–1881), à Marburg avec Adolf Ebert (1820–1890), à Bonn avec Nicolaus Delius (1813–1888) et, à Münster et Strasbourg, avec Bernhard ten Brink (1841–1892).

Cette situation se prolonge dans la cinquième phase (1860–1875), qui voit se maintenir les professorats combinant la romanistique et les études anglaises, en dépit de protestations de la part des lycées. Les professorats nouvellement créés sont des *Doppelprofessuren* de romanistique et d'anglistique: Edmund Stengel (1845–1935) à Marburg en 1873, Eduard Mall (1843–1892) à Münster en 1873 et Würzburg en 1874, Gustav Gröber (Breslau 1874), Hermann Suchier (1848–1914) à Münster en 1875, Alfons Kissner (1844–1928) à Erlangen en 1875, Gustav Körting (1845–1913) à Münster en 1876, Karl Vollmöller (1848–1922) à Erlangen en 1877, Albert Stimming (1846–1922) à Kiel en 1876, Hermann Breymann (1843–1910) à Munich en 1881. L'approche historico-philologique domine toujours, ce qui explique le poids prépondérant de l'étude de textes médiévaux. À la fin des années 1860, on relève les premières traces de la séparation de la romanistique des études anglaises (et américaines).

La première chaire de philologie romane *sensu stricto* est celle créée à Berlin en 1867 pour Adolf Tobler (1835–1910). À partir de cette date, les universités allemandes instaurent des chaires de philologie romane qui ne comportent plus l'enseignement de la langue et de littérature anglaises. La liste des chaires créées entre 1867 et 1900 contient les noms de grands romanistes allemands de la seconde moitié du XIXe siècle: A. Tobler (Berlin, 1867), Eduard Boehmer (1927–1906) à Strasbourg,

(1872), A. Ebert (Leipzig, 1873), Wendelin Foerster (1844–1915) à Bonn en 1876, E. Stengel (Marburg, 1880), Eduard Koschwitz (1851–1904) à Greifswald en 1881 (en 1901 Koschwitz acceptera une chaire à Königsberg), Fritz Neumann (Freiburg im Breisgau, 1882), Rudolf Thurneysen (1857–1940) à Jéna en 1884, A. Stimming (Kiel, 1890), Carl Voretzsch (1867–1947) à Tubingue en 1892, Dietrich Behrens (1859–1929) à Giessen en 1896, Heinrich Schneegans (1863–1914) à Erlangen en 1898. Après une lente naissance dans la première moitié du XIXe siècle, la philologie romane est donc, enfin, reconnue comme discipline universitaire en Allemagne. (Sur l'histoire de la philologie/linguistique romane comme discipline universitaire en Allemagne et sur ses rapports avec d'autres philologies (modernes et classique), voir Stengel 1886, Voretzsch 1904, Schneegans 1912, Richert 1914 et Christmann 1985a, b; sur l'histoire des chaires de philologie romane dans des universités allemandes particulières, voir Risop 1910 et Seidel-Vollmann 1977; sur le contexte général de l'enseignement universitaire en Allemagne, voir Conrad 1884 et von Ferber 1956; pour le contenu des cours en philologie romane à l'Université de Bonn, voir Jaster 1993.)

4. Textes programmatiques de la 'nouvelle philologie'

Comme on l'a déjà vu, le XIXe siècle a vu se produire l'émergence de la philologie moderne et, plus tard – vers le milieu du siècle –, l'opposition entre philologie et linguistique (cf. Koerner 1982, Swiggers 1989). Tout au long du XIXe siècle, la philologie moderne s'est efforcée de définir son statut; la revendication de ses droits s'est faite dans une série de textes programmatiques, qu'il convient d'examiner brièvement (cf. Christmann 1986, 1987).

Pour la première moitié du siècle, trois textes sont à signaler.

(1) Karl W. E. Mager, *Die moderne Philologie und die deutsche Schulen* (1840): dans ce texte, Mager – ancien disciple de Raynouard (cf. Langbein 1858 pour une étude biographique) – propose une délimitation de la philologie par rapport à la linguistique et à l'histoire. La philologie est caractérisée par trois types d'activités: 'Kritik', 'Exegese' et 'Theorie der Dichtkunst und Beredsamkeit'.

(2) Adelbert (von) Keller, *Inauguralrede über die Aufgaben der modernen Philologie* (1842): ce texte lance un appel pour l'étude des dialectes (1842: 9), mais l'auteur se cantonne dans une définition traditionnelle de la philologie comme l'étude de langues et de littératures.

(3) Karl Elze (1821–1889), *Über Philologie als System* (1845): dans la lignée d'August Boeckh, Elze définit la philologie comme une science historique, qui a pour objet les manifestations de l'esprit humain.

Pour la période 1860–1880, époque à laquelle des chaires de philologie moderne à orientation didactique sont créées (cf. § 3.), il faut signaler deux textes:

(4) Carl August Friedrich Mahn (1802–1887), *Über die Entstehung, Bedeutung, Zwecke und Ziele der romanischen Philologie* (1863). L'auteur – romaniste et angliste, un des fondateurs du *Berliner Gesellschaft für das Studium der neueren Sprachen* et maître de Karl Bartsch – y plaide pour un soubassement scientifique (c'est-à-dire historico-comparatif) de la philologie moderne, dont le domaine englobe l'histoire littéraire, la grammaire historico-comparative et la grammaire 'scientifique' [au plan synchronique], et l'explication d'auteurs. Cette conception scientifique est recommandée non seulement pour les programmes universitaires, mais aussi pour les lycées et les gymnases. Le texte de Mahn devint très tôt une référence classique, grâce à l'exploitation qu'en a faite Gaston Paris (1864), qui dans son rapport sur la philologie romane en Allemagne incitait les Français à suivre l'exemple allemand: "En mettant sous les yeux des lecteurs français ce discours d'un Allemand à des Allemands, nous n'avons eu d'autre but que d'exciter en eux l'émulation, et de leur montrer ce qu'on fait ailleurs pour des études qu'ils devraient presque se réserver exclusivement" (Paris 1864: 444).

(5) Hermann Breymann, *Sprachwissenschaft und neuere Sprachen* (1876). Ce texte, qui commence par un éloge de la linguistique historico-comparative, définit la philologie comme l'étude de la vie culturelle de peuples dans l'histoire mondiale, rejoignant ainsi les conceptions de Boeckh et d'Elze. Breymann – grand philologue, mais également enseignant de français et

d'anglais — plaide pour l'intégration de la grammaire historico-comparative dans l'enseignement de langues, mais aussi pour un enseignement approfondi de langues vivantes. Dans cette optique, il préconise la séparation de la philologie romane, la philologie allemande ('germanique') et la philologie anglaise (cf. § 3.).

5. Le transfert du modèle allemand

La philologie romane, telle qu'elle avait pris forme en Allemagne et telle qu'elle avait été codifiée dans l'œuvre linguistique de Diez, a servi de modèle à l'élaboration d'une romanistique dans d'autres pays européens. On peut parler ici d'un 'transfert du modèle allemand', vu que dans ce pays (la Suisse et l'Italie, les pays scandinaves, la France, la Belgique et les Pays-Bas) on imite le système d'enseignement universitaire allemand et on propage le savoir et les méthodes des romanistes allemands. Ce transfert a entraîné des conflits entre les esprits convertis à la science allemande et les 'tradionalistes'; il est marqué par une politique de propagande scientifique et par la dénonciation de pratiques 'non scientifiques'; le cas de la France est instructif à cet égard. (Sur le contexte institutionnel français, voir Bergounioux 1984, 1994; Weisz 1983; pour un examen des attitudes de philologues et linguistes français, voir Swiggers 1991, 1993.)

La figure-clef dans le transfert du savoir philologique allemand à la science française fut Gaston Paris (1839–1903), le 'père des romanistes français'. À la fin des années 1850, le jeune Gaston Paris est envoyé en Allemagne par son père Paulin Paris. À Bonn, il fait la connaissance de Friedrich Diez, qu'il ne cessera de vénérer comme son maître. En 1857, G. Paris s'inscrit à l'Université de Goettingue. De retour à Paris, en 1858, il devient élève à l'École des Chartes. Muni d'une excellente formation, G. Paris n'hésite pas à critiquer le piètre état des études philologiques en France et à stigmatiser le retard scientifique et institutionnel de la France par rapport au système allemand. En 1864, Paris publie un article d'aperçu sur 'la philologie romane en Allemagne', où il retrace l'émergence de la philologie romane à l'intérieur de l'ensemble de la philologie moderne. En jouant habilement sur le sentiment national et anti-allemand des Français, il essaie de secouer les Français. Par son enseignement à l'École Pratique des Hautes Études (à partir de 1868) et au Collège de France (en 1866–67 et de 1869 à 1872 comme remplaçant, et à partir de 1872 comme titulaire), il diffuse la science allemande en France. Dans la *Revue critique d'histoire et de littérature* (1866–1935) et dans la *Romania* (1872–), deux revues qu'il a créées, G. Paris publie de nombreux comptes rendus philologiques et linguistiques qui répandent les exigences de la linguistique historico-comparative. En matière de philologie provençale, il aura son allié dans la personne de Paul Meyer (1840–1917), autre promoteur de la science allemande. Ces deux philologues adopteront d'ailleurs une position très ferme dans le débat autour de l'existence des dialectes. Paris et Meyer ont préféré conclure à l'impossibilité de tracer des frontières dialectales précises et nier même l'existence de dialectes plutôt que de remettre en question l'existence de lois phoniques infaillibles.

Autour d'eux, Gaston Paris et Paul Meyer ont constitué un groupe de romanistes qui modèlent la philologie romane sur un concept scientifique mettant à l'avant-plan deux critères: (1) le maniement d'un corpus de documentation aussi complet et aussi fiable que possible; (2) l'emploi d'une méthode historico-comparative qui respecte la régularité du développement des langues. C'est ce style de recherche scientifique qui est inculqué aux élèves qui fréquentent les cours de l'École Pratique des Hautes Études et de l'École des Chartes, et qui le dimanche matin se rendent chez Gaston Paris pour participer à son séminaire. Du coup, une nouvelle mentalité de recherche s'installe en philologie, et Gaston Paris, en harmonie avec son collègue classiciste et indo-européaniste Michel Bréal (1832–1915), s'en fait le porte-parole. Le glas a sonné pour la philologie à base impressionniste. En 1884, Gaston Paris éreinte dans un compte rendu très sec l'ouvrage d'Henri (Léonard) Bordier (1817–1888) sur *Philippe de Remi, sire de Beaumanoir, jurisconsulte et poète national de Beauvaisis*, en faisant observer que l'ouvrage ne répondait pas aux exigences de l'école philologique allemande, principes que Gaston Paris avait faits les siens. Et en réponse à des lettres de Bordier, Gaston Paris rétorqua qu'il n'acceptait aucune des étymologies de l'auteur:

"Quant aux étymologies de ce glossaire, outre qu'elles reposent le plus souvent sur une traduction erronée, elle dépassent en fantaisies déréglées tout ce qu'on avait jamais lu. Je regarde le point de vue où vous êtes comme aujourd'hui tout à fait dépassé (pardon du pédantisme que je suis obligé d'étaler, mais je ne sais pas parler autrement que sérieusement et sincèrement), et il me paraît inutile de le combattre. Nous formons des élèves qui sauront la phonétique et, pour ceux-là, les étymologies hasardées seront condamnées d'avance. Voilà pourquoi, tout en me croyant obligé de signaler les erreurs philologiques d'un historien éminent, je ne crois pas utile de les réfuter publiquement." (Cité d'après Swiggers 1990: 36)

Dans son approche linguistique, Gaston Paris se montra fidèle aux principes de l'école allemande (cf. Desmet & Swiggers 1996). Il acceptait la primauté de la grammaire historique (au détriment de l'orientation synchronique) et adhérait aux principes des lois phonétiques et de l'analogie. Dans son cours de 'Grammaire historique de la langue française', professé en 1868 à la Sorbonne, Gaston Paris affirme "que le développement du langage est *dirigé* par des lois qui lui sont propres, mais rigoureusement *déterminé* par des conditions historiques"; il répétera ce point de vue (Paris 1888, 1900):

"[Selon M. Eduard Wechssler (1869–1949)] il y a des lois phonétiques, et ces lois, comme telles, ne souffrent pas d'exception. Je n'ai pas besoin de dire, quant à moi, que j'adhère à cette solution; je la regarde même comme tellement évidente qu'il suffit de l'énoncer pour qu'elle s'impose. Tout ce qu'on lui a objecté repose sur un malentendu: les dérogations que l'on constate dans toute langue aux lois qui régissent, à un moment et dans un lieu donnés, les mutations phonétiques – car il ne s'agit que de cela –, sont innombrables; mais *elles n'ont jamais un caractère phonétique*; elles sont des perturbations apportées par des circonstances extrêmement diverses au jeu régulier des lois phonétiques. J'hésiterais davantage à assimiler les lois de mutation phonétique aux lois naturelles: celles-ci agissent toujours de même dans les mêmes conditions; celles-là ne peuvent subir cette épreuve, les conditions où elles agissent n'étant jamais deux fois les mêmes: elles ne sont que le résultat de constatations faites dans le passé; elles ne peuvent être appliquées à l'avenir. Il faut donc prendre ici le mot de *lois* dans un sens particulier et restreint (on trouverait des faits analogues dans la géologie par exemple); mais nier qu'il en existe ce serait admettre dans une évolution naturelle des faits fortuits, c'est-à-dire des effets sans cause, ce qui est absurde." (Paris 1900: 583–584)

Mais Gaston Paris demeura avant tout un philologue travaillant sur des textes et cela explique sa position théoriquement faible devant des problèmes théoriques, comme celui, mentionné ci-dessus, de l'existence de frontières dialectales (cf. Desmet & Swiggers 1996, pour une analyse de certaines contradictions). Heureusement, Gaston Paris était bien conscient de ses limites en tant que théoricien; il encouragera d'ailleurs les travaux dialectologiques de Jules Gilliéron (1854–1926), Jean-Pierre Rousselot (1846–1924), Jules Cornu (1849–1919), en suscitant aussi la collaboration d'amateurs, ceux-ci se confinant à un relevé de faits au plan synchronique (Paris 1888).

L'importance stratégique de Gaston Paris dans le transfert du modèle allemand ne se limita pas au contexte français: il fut aussi le maître de plusieurs élèves étrangers qui allaient devenir les premiers titulaires de chaires de philologie romane dans leur pays. (Sur les rapports de G. Paris et de P. Meyer avec la première génération de romanistes belges, voir Desmet & Swiggers 1990.)

À ce propos, il faut signaler un document 'sociohistoriographique' particulièrement intéressant, à savoir celui que Maurice Wilmotte (1861–1942) publia en 1886, comme rapport de mission sur un séjour d'étude en France (1883–1884, à Paris) et en Allemagne (1884–1885; semestre d'hiver à Halle; semestre d'été à Berlin; le mois d'août 1885 ayant été passé par Wilmotte à Bonn), auprès des 'maîtres' de la philologie romane (en l'occurrence: Gaston Paris, Paul Meyer et Arsène Darmesteter; Hermann Suchier, Adolf Tobler et Wendelin Foerster). (Sur l'enseignement de la philologie romane à Berlin et à Bonn, voir Risop 1910; Hirdt 1993, où on trouve des études sur l'œuvre et l'enseignement de F. Diez, de W. Foerster et de H. Schneegans; et Jaster 1993.) Wilmotte commence par rappeler qu'en France, le "véritable foyer scientifique", c'est Paris, alors qu'en Allemagne l'étude de la philologie romane est répartie sur toute la surface du territoire, quoique le progrès des études romanes soit le plus visible dans le nord du pays: "La Prusse compte aujourd'hui parmi les professeurs de ses Universités les trois représentants les plus remarquables de cette science: M. Tobler à Berlin, M. Foerster à Bonn et M. Suchier à Halle" (Wilmotte 1886: 5).

La description de l'enseignement de la philologie romane à Paris, à l'École Pratique des Hautes Études et au Collège de France, met à l'avant-plan l'activité de Gaston Paris, alors au sommet de sa carrière. Wilmotte (1886: 8) observe que les leçons de Gaston Paris "sont rédigées avec la précision et la conscience des meilleurs *Collegien* allemands. La bibliographie est nourrie; tout ce qui a été écrit sur la question traitée est énuméré, analysé et apprécié sommairement". Dans la description des cours, Wilmotte relève les noms de deux savants allemands auxquels G. Paris renvoie régulièrement: F. Diez et A. Tobler. L'enseignement de Paul Meyer est loué pour sa clarté et pour l'érudition qui y est étalée. Wilmotte fait remarquer que les cours à l'École des Chartes attirent aussi de jeunes étudiants allemands. Chez Arsène Darmesteter (1846–1888), Wilmotte apprécie la méthode sûre, basée sur la philologie allemande.

À propos de l'enseignement qu'il a pu observer en Allemagne, Wilmotte fait remarquer qu'il s'étaye sur des structures institutionnelles hiérarchisées: les professeurs sont entourés de *Privatdozente*, d'assistants et de 'lecteurs'. À Halle, chez Hermann Suchier — grand éditeur de textes en ancien français et spécialiste des anciens dialectes d'oïl — Wilmotte a pu apprécier l'organisation systématique des cours et des séminaires:

"Dans son séminaire philologique, dont les étudiants ne sont admis à faire partie qu'après un stage préparatoire et un examen quelque peu sommaire, M. Suchier occupait l'intervalle des *Vortraege* en dirigeant l'explication des poésies du troubadour *Zorzi* (Ed. Levy, Halle 1883.) Quant aux *Vortraege*, ils consistent généralement dans la lecture [...] d'un travail rédigé à domicile sur une question du domaine de la philologie romane. L'élève monte en chaire, et le professeur, qui a pris place sur l'un des bancs, se réserve le droit de critiquer, soit pendant la lecture, soit après qu'elle est achevée, la façon dont le sujet choisi a été traité. Ces *Vortraege* sont souvent la première rédaction d'une étude, qui, développée ensuite et remaniée soigneusement, constituera un sujet de thèse convenable." (Wilmotte 1886: 21)

L'enseignement de la philologie romane à Berlin a comme trait distinctif la grande variété des matières proposées aux étudiants, et enseignées avec "une conscience et une méthode impeccables" dans le cas d'Adolf Tobler. À la fin de son rapport, Wilmotte lance un appel au Ministre belge de l'Intérieur et de l'Instruction publique pour que la Belgique ne reste pas en retard sur les autres pays européens:

"Il [= notre pays, la Belgique] est le seul aujourd'hui qui n'ait pas de chaire officielle de philologie romane dans ses Universités; cependant, cette branche de science possède outre-Rhin autant de représentants que l'on compte d'Universités, et je néglige les *docenten* et les lecteurs très nombreux, qui constituent, en quelque sorte, l'état-major du professeur attitré. La France a suivi cet exemple en multipliant les chaires, non seulement à Paris, où nous trouvons MM. G. Paris, P. Meyer, A. Darmesteter, Gilliéron et Morel-Fatio, mais encore dans les facultés de province, où plusieurs maîtres, MM. Chabaneau, Joret, Thomas, Clédat, Constans, etc., sont en train de propager le goût sérieux d'études jadis dédaignées. La Suisse compte plusieurs professeurs de philologie romane: M. Morf à Berne, M. Ritter à Genève et M. J. Ulrich et W. Meyer à Zurich. L'Italie s'est associée à ce mouvement: il suffit de nommer Ascoli, qui a révolutionné les études de phonétique en publiant ses admirables *Saggi Ladini* et qui professe à l'Académie de Milan, MM. Rajna et Bartoli à l'Institut des Hautes-Études à Florence, M. d'Ancona à Pise, M. Monaci à Rome, M. d'Ovidio à Naples, etc. L'Espagne et le Portugal ont leur part dans ces efforts, ainsi que la Roumanie. Je nommerai MM. Braga, Coelho, Gaster. La Suède compte des romanistes comme MM. Lidforss, Wulf[f] et Vising à Lund, Geijer et Wahlund à Upsal, où M. de Feilitzen s'est également habilité en 1883; M. Storm enseigne cette science à Christiania et M. Wesselofsky à St-Pétersbourg. L'auteur du meilleur manuel de l'histoire de l'épopée française au moyen âge, M. K. Nyrop, est Danois. Enfin, notre sœur germanique, la Hollande, vient d'inaugurer un enseignement de ce genre à l'Université de Groningue, où le gouvernement a nommé M. Van Hamel, ancien élève de l'École des Hautes-Études à Paris." (Wilmotte 1886: 27–28)

Non seulement ce texte brosse un utile panorama du rayonnement de la conception et de la pratique 'allemandes' des études romanes à travers l'Europe, il est aussi un modèle pour la façon dont il faut approcher les instances officielles: en 1890 est créée la première chaire universitaire de philologie romane en Belgique, à Liège, dont le titulaire n'est personne d'autre que Maurice Wilmotte.

6. Bibliographie

Baggioni, Daniel & Philippe Martel, éds. 1997. *De François Raynouard à Auguste Brun: La contribution des Méridionaux aux premières études de linguistique romane* (= Lengas n° 42). Montpellier: Université Paul-Valéry Montpellier III.

Baum, Richard. 1993. "Friedrich Diez". Hirdt 1993 I, 45–140.

Bergounioux, Gabriel. 1984. "La science du langage en France de 1870 à 1885: Du marché civil au marché étatique". *Langue française* 63.7–41.

—. 1994. *Aux origines de la linguistique française.* Paris: Pocket.

Bolling, George M. 1929. "Linguistics and Philology". *Language* 5.27–32.

Bossong, Georg. 1990. *Sprachwissenschaft und Sprachphilosophie in der Romania. Von den Anfängen bis August Wilhelm Schlegel.* Tübingen: Narr.

Breymann, Hermann. 1876. *Sprachwissenschaft und neuere Sprachen.* München: Ackermann.

Chambon, Jean-Pierre & Pierre Swiggers. 1994. "Wilhelm von Humboldt et le provençal: avec l'édition d'une lettre à Jules Antoine Alexandre Fauris de Saint-Vincent". *Revue de Linguistique romane* 58.39–46.

Christmann, Hans Helmut. 1985a. *Romanistik und Anglistik an der deutschen Universität im 19. Jahrhundert. Ihre Herausbildung als Fächer und ihr Verhältnis zu Germanistik und klassischer Philologie.* (= Akademie der Wissenschaften und der Literatur, Abhandlungen der Geistes- und sozialwissenschaftlichen Klasse, Jg. 1985, Nr. 1.) Stuttgart: Steiner.

–. 1985b. "Klassische, germanische, englische und romanische Philologie der ersten Hälfte des 19. Jahrhunderts im Spannungsfeld von Universität, Schule und Ministerium". *Zeitschrift für Phonetik, Sprachwissenschaft und Kommunikationsforschung* 38.551–558.

–. 1986. "Programmatische Texte der Neuphilologie in der zweiten Hälfte des 19. Jahrhunderts: Mahn (1863), Breymann (1876)". *Zeitschrift für Phonetik, Sprachwissenschaft und Kommunikationsforschung* 39.656–668.

–. 1987. "Programmatische Texte der frühen Neuphilologie: Mager (1840), Keller (1842), Elze (1845)". Dans: *Bedeutungen und Ideen in Sprachen und Texten*, 51–65. Berlin: Akademie-Verlag.

Conrad, J. 1884. *Das Universitätsstudium in Deutschland während der letzten 50 Jahre. Statistische Untersuchungen unter besonderer Berücksichtigung Preussens.* Jena: Fischer.

Curtius, Ernst Robert. 1960. "Bonner Gedenkworte auf Friedrich Diez zum 15. März 1944". Dans: E. R. Curtius, *Gesammelte Aufsätze zur Romanischen Philologie*, 412–427. Bern & München: Francke.

Desmet, Piet & Pierre Swiggers. 1990. "Gaston Paris en zijn contacten met Belgische filologen". *De Brabantse folklore en geschiedenis* 265.64–71.

– & –. 1996. "Gaston Paris: aspects linguistiques d'une œuvre philologique". *Actas do XIX Congreso Internacional de Lingüística e Filoloxía Románicas, Universidade de Santiago de Compostela, 1989*, ed. por Ramón Lorenzo, vol. VIII, 207–232. La Coruña: Fundación "Pedro Barrié de la Maza, Conde de Fenosa".

Elze, Carl F. 1845. *Über Philologie als System: Ein andeutender Versuch.* Dessau: Aue.

Engels, Jozef. 1953. "Philologie romane – Linguistique – Études littéraires". *Neophilologus* 37.14–24.

Ferber, C. von. 1956. *Die Entwicklung des Lehrkörpers der deutschen Universitäten und Hochschulen 1864–1914.* Göttingen: Vandenhoeck & Ruprecht.

Fuchs, August. 1844. "Die Versammlung deutscher Sprachforscher und Schulmänner in Dresden am 1.–4. Oct. 1844". *Blätter für literarische Unterhaltung* 312.1245–1247; 313.1249–1251.

–. 1849. *Die romanischen Sprachen in ihrem Verhältnisse zum Lateinischen.* Halle: Schmidt.

Gauger, Hans-Martin, Wulf Oesterreicher & Rudolf Windisch. 1981. *Einführung in die romanische Sprachwissenschaft.* Darmstadt: Wissenschaftliche Buchgesellschaft.

Gröber, Gustav. 1888. *Grundriss der romanischen Philologie. I. Band: Geschichte und Aufgabe der romanischen Philologie – Quellen der romanischen Philologie und deren Behandlung – Romanische Sprachwissenschaft.* Strassburg: Trübner.

Hirdt, Willi, Hrsg., in Zusammenarbeit mit Richard Baum und Birgit Tappert. 1993. *Romanistik. Eine Bonner Erfindung.* 2 vols. Bonn: Bouvier.

Jaster, Barbara. 1993. "Bonner romanistische Lehrveranstaltungen und Doktorarbeiten (1818–1916)". Hirdt 1993 I, 321–456.

Keller, Heinrich Adelbert (von). 1842. *Inauguralrede über die Aufgabe der modernen Philologie.* Stuttgart: Cotta.

Koerner, Ernst Frideryk Konrad. 1982. "On the Historical Roots of the Philology/Linguistics Controversy". *Papers from the 5th International Conference on Historical Linguistics* éd. par Anders Ahlqvist, 404–413. Amsterdam & Philadelphia: Benjamins.

Körner, Josef. 1913. "François-Juste-Marie-Raynouard". *Germanisch-Romanische Monatsschrift* 5. 456–488.

Langbein, Wilhelm. 1858. "Dr. Carl Mager's Leben". *Pädagogische Revue* 49.309–388.

Mager, Carl W. E. 1840. "Die moderne Philologie und die deutschen Schulen". *Pädagogische Revue* 1.1–80.

Mahn, Carl August Friedrich. 1863. *Über die Entstehung, Bedeutung, Zwecke und Ziele der romanischen Philologie.* Berlin: Dümmler.

Malkiel, Yakov. 1960/61. "Three Definitions of Romance Linguistics". *Romance Philology* 15.1–7.

–. 1966. "Is there Room for 'General Philology'?". *Pacific Coast Philology* 1.3–11.

–. 1967/68. "Editorial Comment: August Fuchs (1818–1847), the Founder of Comparative Romance Dialectology". *Romance Philology* 21.285.

–. 1974. "Friedrich Diez's Debt to pre-1800 Linguistics". *Studies in the History of Linguistics. Traditions and Paradigms* éd. par Dell Hymes, 315–330. Bloomington & London: Indiana University Press.

Morpurgo-Davies, Anna. 1996. *La linguistica dell'Ottocento.* Bologna: Il Mulino.

Niederehe, Hans-Josef & Harald Haarmann, Hrsg. 1976. *In Memoriam Friedrich Diez. Akten des Kolloquiums zur Wissenschaftsgeschichte der Romanistik, Trier 2.–4. Okt. 1975.* Amsterdam: Benjamins.

— & Brigitte Schlieben-Lange, Hrsg. 1987. *Die Frühgeschichte der romanischen Philologie: von Dante bis Diez.* Tübingen: Narr.

Paris, Gaston. 1862. *Étude sur le rôle de l'accent latin dans la langue française.* Paris: Franck.

—. 1864. "La philologie romane en Allemagne". *Bibliothèque de l'École des Chartes* année 25: 5. 433–445.

—. 1868. Compte rendu d'Auguste Brachet, *Grammaire historique de la langue française* (Paris, 1867). *Revue critique* 3.23–31.

—. 1888. "Les parlers de France". *Revue des patois gallo-romans* 2.161–175.

—. 1990. Compte rendu de *Forschungen zur romanischen Philologie. Festgabe für Hermann Suchier.* Romania 29.579–585.

Rettig, Wolfgang. 1976. "Raynouard, Diez und die romanische Ursprache". Niederehe & Haarmann 1976.247–273.

Richert, Gertrud. 1914. *Die Anfänge der romanischen Philologie und die deutsche Romantik.* Halle a. S.: Niemeyer.

Risop, Alfred. 1910. *Die romanische Philologie an der Berliner Universität 1810–1910.* Erlangen (= *Kritischer Jahresbericht über die Fortschritte der romanischen Philologie* 10.1–116). (Réimpression dans: Dieter Heckelmann & Otto Büsch, Hrsg., *Wissenschaft und Stadt. Publikationen der Freien Universität aus Anlaß der 750-Jahr-Feier Berlins,* Bd. 6. Berlin: Colloquium Verlag, 1988).

Schneegans, Heinrich. 1912. *Studium und Unterricht der romanischen Philologie.* Heidelberg: Winter.

Seidel-Vollmann, S. S. 1977. *Die romanische Philologie an der Universität München (1826–1913): zur Geschichte einer Disziplin in ihrer Aufbauzeit.* Berlin: Duncker & Humblot.

Stengel, Edmund. 1886. *Beiträge zur Geschichte der romanischen Philologie in Deutschland.* Marburg: Elwert.

Storost, Jürgen. 1981. "Zur Stellung Raynouards in der Geschichte der romanischen Philologie". *Beiträge zur Romanischen Philologie* 20.195–212.

—. 1984. "August Fuchs, Philolog: Ein Beitrag zur Auseinandersetzung zwischen Philologie und Linguistik in der ersten Hälfte des 19. Jahrhunderts". *Beiträge zur Romanischen Philologie* 23.95–108.

Swiggers, Pierre. 1989. "Philologie (romane) et linguistique". *Actes du XVIIIe Congrès International de Linguistique et de Philologie Romanes (Trier 1986)* éd. par Dieter Kremer, vol. VII, 231–242. Tübingen: Niemeyer.

—. 1991. "Le travail étymologique: typologie historique et analytique, perspectives, effets". *Discours étymologiques. Actes du Colloque international organisé à l'occasion du centenaire de la naissance de Walther von Wartburg (Bâle, Freiburg i. Br., Mulhouse, 16–18 mai 1988)* éd. par Jean-Pierre Chambon & Georges Lüdi, 29–45. Tübingen: Niemeyer.

—. 1993. " 'Personne plus que moi ne reconnaît les droits de la discussion scientifique': À propos d'une lettre d'Émile Littré à Hugo Schuchardt". *Orbis* 36. 256–265.

—. 1995. "Une approche anthropologico-linguistique des langues romanes: *Ueber die jetzigen romanischen Schriftsprachen* (1831) de Lorenz Diefenbach". *Studi rumeni e romanzi: Omaggio a Florica Dimitrescu e Alexandru Niculescu* éd. par Coman Lupu & Lorenzo Renzi, vol. II, 662–674. Padova: UNIPRESS.

—. 1996a. "Les débuts de la 'philologie comparée' et la fin de la grammaire générale: Humboldt entre l'Europe et le Nouveau Monde". *Incontri Linguistici* 18.39–60.

—. 1996b. "L'éviction de la grammaire générale par la philologie comparée: relations intercontinentales, sédimentations mouvantes et rôle du français et des Français". *Travaux de linguistique. Revue internationale de linguistique française* 33.69–90.

—. 1997. *Histoire de la pensée linguistique. Analyse du langage et réflexion linguistique dans la culture occidentale, de l'Antiquité au XIXe siècle.* Paris: P. U. F.

—. 1998. "Filologia e Lingüística: Enlace, divórcio, reconciliação". *Filologia e Lingüística Portuguesa* 2.5–18.

Swiggers, Pierre & Piet Desmet. 1996. "L'élaboration de la linguistique comparative: Comparaison et typologie des langues jusqu'au début du XIXe siècle". *Sprachtheorien der Neuzeit* II: *Von der Grammaire de Port-Royal (1660) zur Konstitution moderner linguistischer Disziplinen* éd. par Peter Schmitter (= *Geschichte der Sprachtheorie,* 5), 122–177. Tübingen: Narr.

Tagliavini, Carlo. [6]1972. *Le origini delle lingue neolatine: Introduzione alla filologia romanza.* Bologna: Pàtron.

Vàrvaro, Alberto. [2]1980. *Storia, problemi e metodi della linguistica romanza.* Napoli: Liguori.

Vidos, Benedek E. 1956. *Handboek tot de Romaanse taalkunde.* 's-Hertogenbosch: Malmberg.

Voretzsch, Carl. 1904. *Die Anfänge der romanischen Philologie an den deutschen Universitäten und ihre Entwicklung an der Universität Tübingen.* Tübingen: Laupp.

Weisz, George. 1983. *The Emergence of Modern Universities in France, 1863–1914.* Princeton: Princeton University Press.

Wilmotte, Maurice. 1886. *L'enseignement de la philologie romane à Paris et en Allemagne (1883–1885). Rapport à M. le Ministre de l'Intérieur et de l'Instruction publique.* Bruxelles: Polleunis, Ceuterick & Lefébure.

Pierre Swiggers, Leuven & Liège (Belgique)

160. Die Entstehung und frühe Entwicklung der Germanischen Philologie

1. Zur Einführung
2. Der Institutionialisierungsprozeß an den Universitäten
3. Zur Binnendifferenzierung des Fachs
4. Bibliographie

1. Zur Einführung

Die Entstehung der Germanischen Philologie (im folgenden: Germ. Ph.) als wissenschaftliche und akademische Disziplin setzt zu Beginn des 19. Jhs. ein. Die zuvor entstandenen beachtlichen wissenschaftlichen Leistungen gingen von individuellen und punktuellen Bemühungen einzelner Gelehrter aus, entsprangen noch nicht der kontinuierlichen Bearbeitung abgrenzbarer Problemstellungen. Die Herausbildung der Germ. Ph. ist dabei eingebunden in übergreifende epochale Veränderungen im gesellschaftlichen, politischen und Wissenschaftssystem (Übergang von der gelehrten zur disziplinären Gemeinschaft, Auflösung der Hierarchie der Fakultäten, Reform der Universität mit ihrer Einheit von Forschung und Lehre, Durchsetzung des Forschungsimperativs, Autonomisierung der Fächer). Weder kann ihre Entstehung auf einen punktuellen Gründungsakt zurückgeführt werden noch verläuft ihre Entwicklung in einem einheitlichen und kontinuierlichen Prozeß. Für den Bereich der wissenschaftlichen Beschäftigung mit deutscher Sprache unterscheidet Schmidt (1985: 159 ff.) in der Initialphase drei konkurrierende Richtungen: die traditionelle Grammatik (Schulgrammatik), die nationale (deutsche) Philologie und die allgemeine (philosophische) Grammatik. Hunger (1987: 42 ff.) grenzt für den Bereich der altdeutschen Studien vier bzw. fünf unterschiedliche Forschungsrichtungen und methodische Ansätze idealtypisch voneinander ab: die Fortsetzung der Sammeltätigkeit, das literarisch-romantische Konzept mit einem literarästhetischen Ansatz (Ludwig Tieck, Joseph Görres, Ludwig Uhland), die nationalpolitisch-publikumsorientierte (durch die Napoleonische Herrschaft und die Befreiungskriege zusätzlich motivierte) Sichtweise (Friedrich Heinrich von der Hagen), die umfassende kulturhistorische Programmatik der germanischen Altertumskunde (Jacob Grimm) und das philologisch-textkritische Konzept (Georg Friedrich Benecke, Karl Lachmann). Daß es sich bei dieser Differenzierung lediglich um "abstrakte Positionen" (Hunger 1987: 43) handelt, die von den den Wissenschaftsprozeß tragenden Forschern in ihren Arbeiten unterschiedlich akzentuiert und miteinander verbunden werden können, veranschaulicht eindrucksvoll Jacob Grimms Werk (siehe Bluhm 1997: 45 ff., 129 ff.).

Einen zentralen Kristallisationspunkt für die Herausbildung der Disziplin bildete die Edition altdeutscher Texte, bei der altertumskundliche, sprachliche und literarische Interessen eng miteinander verbunden waren (vgl. Wyss 1988: 15). Das Beherrschen des von der Klassischen Philologie (im folgenden: Klass. Ph.) übernommenen philologischen Instrumentariums (Benecke, Lachmann) der (zu einer frühen institutionellen Verselbständigung führenden) historisch-vergleichenden Methode (Franz Bopp) und der Erkenntnisse der historischen Grammatik (J. Grimm 1819 ff.) sonderte dann seit den 20er Jahren zunehmend die Fachleute/Wissenschaftler von den Liebhabern/Dilettanten.

"Ungeachtet ihrer hervorragenden grammatischen Anfänge konstituiert sich die Deutsche Philologie als Einheit von Sprach- und Literaturwissenschaft, die sich vorzüglich in der Edition von Texten manifestiert, welche sowohl als Sprachdenkmäler wie als Kunstwerke fungieren können." (Dainat 1987: 306)

Philologisierung, Wissenschaftlichkeitsanspruch, Professionalisierung und Spezialisierung bilden die Schlüsselworte für die Anerkennung der Deutschen Philologie (im folgenden: Dt. Ph.) als wissenschaftliche Disziplin, die die (historische) Sprachwissenschaft als Teilbereich einbegreift, die Felder der Textinterpretation und der (neueren) Literaturgeschichte jedoch weitgehend unbestellt läßt. Die Klass. Ph. fungierte dabei als Leitdisziplin im methodisch-philologischen wie im personalen Bereich, in der Auseinandersetzung von Wort- und Sachphilologie, in der kontroversen Diskussion über die Bestimmung des Gegenstandsbereichs wie in der Zielsetzung der Disziplin. Sie bildete für die Dt. Ph. allerdings nicht nur "ihre ältere Schwester und Lehrerin", sondern auch eine (über-)mächtige Konkurrentin (Zarncke 1864: 63). Diese Konkurrenz spielte dann insbesondere eine Rolle im Hinblick auf ihren Stellenwert im Schul- und Beschäftigungssystem (siehe Kopp 1994: 695 ff.).

Wenn auch der Gegenstandsbereich der Dt. Ph. unterschiedlich weit gefaßt und in verschiedener Weise mit anderen Fächern verbunden werden konnte, so bildete doch die (alt-)deutsche Sprache und Literatur den Kernbereich der Disziplin. Als Disziplinbezeichnung dominierte in dieser Zeit der schon im 18. Jh. gebräuchliche Begriff 'Deutsche Philologie'; daneben finden sich z. B. 'Germanische Philologie', 'altdeutsche Philologie', 'deutsche Altertumswissenschaft', 'deutsche Literaturgeschichte' oder auch 'germanistische Philologie'. Die Fachvertreter wurden vereinzelt bereits gegen Ende der 30er Jahre als "Germanisten" bezeichnet, während die Fachbezeichnung 'Germanistik' erst in den 60er Jahren des 19. Jhs. aufkam. Auf der ersten Germanistenversammlung in Frankfurt am Main 1846 trat ihr Präsident Jacob Grimm dafür ein, den Namen 'Germanist' als übergreifende Bezeichnung für die Vertreter der "drei fächer" der "deutsche[n] philologie [...] des deutschen rechts und der deutschen geschichte" einzuführen. Als 'Germanist' zu gelten habe derjenige, "der das deutsche element in einem einzelnen theil oder seinem ganzen umfang sich erkoren habe" (1846: 573, 578). In dieser auch von dem Juristen Ludwig Reyscher (1802−1880), dem eigentlichen Initiator der Versammlung, propagierten Bedeutung bürgerte sich der Name "Germanist" nicht ein, doch blieb für das Selbstverständnis der Vertreter der Dt. Ph. der Bezug auf das "Deutsche" von zentraler Bedeutung (vgl. Meves 1994a: 25 ff.).

Als gegen Ende des 19. Jhs. Hermann Paul den *Grundriß der germanischen Philologie* (Bd. I, 1891) herausgab, hatte bereits eine neue Phase der Fachentwicklung begonnen. Er anerkannte darin in seiner Darstellung der "Geschichte der germanischen Philologie" die inzwischen durch "die wachsende Ausdehnung der Wissenschaft" notwendig gewordene Arbeitsteilung. Gerade deswegen warnte er aber zugleich − aus wissenschaftsimmanenten Gründen wie im Hinblick auf die Aufgabe der Deutschlehrerausbildung − vor einer "vollständigen Spaltung" des Faches infolge der immer mehr zunehmenden "einseitige[n] Beschränkung auf Sprachwissenschaft oder auf Literaturgeschichte" (Paul 1891: 151).

2. Der Institutionalisierungsprozeß an den Universitäten

2.1. Die Einrichtung von Fachprofessuren

Für die Institutionalisierung einer Disziplin an der Universität war die Einrichtung einer ordentlichen Professur von besonderer Bedeutung. Dieser Vorgang erstreckte sich für die Dt. Ph. über mehrere Jahrzehnte (und damit auch über verschiedene Phasen der nationalstaatlichen Entwicklung), verlief in den einzelnen Ländern und sogar von Universität zu Universität unterschiedlich, wobei die jeweiligen personalen, korporativen oder ökonomischen Faktoren einen wichtigen Einfluß ausüben konnten (siehe Meves 1994b: 115 ff.).

2.1.1. Die Konstituiuerungsphase

Um 1810 dominierten an den Universitäten noch die Generalistenprofessoren (Weimar 1989: 210 ff.), deren Lehrprogramm Rhetorik und Theorie des Stils mit praktischen Übungen ('akademischer Deutschunterricht'), Ästhetik und Poetik, 'Litterrär'- und Literaturgeschichte sowie vereinzelt Übungen in der Auslegung deutscher Dichtungen umfaßte (siehe z. B. Johann Christoph Schlüter, 1801−1841 Professor an der Akademie Münster). Einen Einschnitt markierte hier Beneckes (1805 ao., 1813 o. Professor an der Universität Göttingen) seit 1806 regelmäßig angebotene "Anleitung zur Kenntniß, zum sichern Verstehen und zur richtigen Beurtheilung der altdeutschen Dichter aus dem Schwäbischen Zeitalter". Das Schlüsselwort 'philologisch' kennzeichnet sein wissenschaftliches Programm; es besagt, daß die deutsche Literatur des Mittelalters "seit dem Auftreten Beneckes nicht anders behandelt werden soll als diejenige der klassischen Antike" (Stackmann 1991: 18 f.). Das von von der Hagen (1810 ao. Professor an der Universität Berlin, ab 1811 in Breslau) für den Inhaber der Professur der deutschen Sprache entworfene Vorlesungsprogramm signalisierte den Einfluß von Friedrich August Wolfs Konzeption der Altertumswissenschaft. Von der Hagens Themenkatalog konzentrierte sich auf die vaterländische Altertumskunde, womit zugleich eine inhaltliche Einschränkung des Gesamtbereichs der bisher an der Universität behandelten Gegenstände verbunden war, insofern die Sprachpflege (und damit die Standardsprache) und die Erklärung der neueren deutschen Literatur, aber auch Rhetorik, Poetik und Ästhetik sowie der akademische Deutschunterricht ausgespart blieben. Benecke und von der Hagen repräsentieren zwei unterschiedliche, für die Konzeption der Dt. Ph. in der Folgezeit wichtige Positionen, die auf den weiteren Rahmen der in der Klassischen Ph. von den Hauptkontrahenten Gottfried Hermann und August Friedrich Boeckh bestimmten 'Philologie'-Diskussion verweisen.

Während Hermann die Aufgabe des Philologen auf die kritische Wiederherstellung und Interpretation von antiken Texten beschränkt sehen wollte, hatte nach Boeckh die Philologie "bei jedem Volke seine gesammte geistige Entwickelung, die Geschichte seiner Cultur nach all ihren Richtungen darzustellen" (1877: 56). Beide Richtungen der jungen Disziplin waren an der Universität Berlin vertreten, an der von der Hagen das Ordinariat für deutsche Sprache und Literatur und Lachmann seit 1827 eine ordentliche Professur für Dt. und Klass. Ph. innehatten. Da ein philologisch gesicherter Text für Lachmann eine unverzichtbare Voraussetzung für die wissenschaftliche Beschäftigung mit der altdeutschen Dichtung bildete, konzentrierte er sich auf Editionen mhd. Dichtungen, für die er seine, an antiken Texten und am Neuen Testament gewonnenen, editorischen Erfahrungen sowie ein an der klassischen Textkritik geschultes methodisches Instrumentarium fruchtbar machte. Lachmanns für die Folgezeit maßgeblichen mhd. Editionen (u. a. *Iwein* [zusammen mit Benecke], 1827; *Die Gedichte Walthers von der Vogelweide*, 1827; *Wolfram von Eschenbach*, 1833) ging ein intensives Studium der Sprache der Dichtung voraus, das wiederum auf den von J. Grimm vorangetriebenen Erkenntnissen der historischen Grammatik und der historischen Lexikographie (Benecke) aufbauen konnte. Mit der Berufung J. Grimms zum Bibliothekar und ordentlichen Professor im Jahr 1829 und der Mitberufung seines Bruders Wilhelm an die Universität Göttingen übernahm diese die führende Stellung in der Disziplinentwicklung. Die neue Disziplin gewann an den Universitäten nur langsam an Bedeutung. 1829 gab es an den 20 (auf dem Territorium des späteren Dt. Reichs befindlichen) Universitäten mit den beiden Generalisten Schlüter in Münster und Johann Friedrich Ferdinand Delbrück (1772–1848) in Bonn sowie mit Benecke in Göttingen und von der Hagen in Breslau vier ordentliche Professuren. Zehn Jahre später waren die Ordinariate von Lachmann in Berlin und J. Grimm in Göttingen hinzugekommen. Dank beider Unterstützung erhielt Lachmanns Berliner Schüler Wilhelm Wackernagel (1806–1868) einen Ruf nach Basel, wo er 1835 zum ersten Ordinarius für deutsche Sprache und Literatur aufstieg (aber auch weiterhin Deutschunterricht am Pädagogium erteilte). Zusammen mit dem ebenfalls als Gymnasial- und als Universitätslehrer in Zürich wirkenden Ludwig Ettmüller (1833–1877), der sich insbesondere auch mit dem Altnordischen und Altenglischen befaßte, steht er am "Anfang einer schweizerischen Germanistik" (Wehrli 1993: 410).

Seit der Mitte der 30er Jahre wurden für die sich bildende Wissenschaft 'Deutsche Literaturgeschichte' zudem einige Professuren eingerichtet (Weimar 1989: 319 ff.), deren Inhaber zumeist ästhetisch-philosophisch oder historisch ausgerichtet waren (siehe z. B. Friedrich Theodor Vischer in Tübingen [1837] und Robert Prutz in Halle [1849]). Herausragende Werke auf diesem Gebiet schufen der Philosoph Karl Rosenkranz (*Geschichte der Deutschen Poesie im Mittelalter*, 1830) und insbesondere der Historiker Georg Gottfried Gervinus (1805–1871) mit seiner epochalen *Geschichte der poetischen National-Literatur der Deutschen* (5 Bde., 1835–1842). Bedeutsam für den universitären Etablierungsprozeß war das in den 30er Jahren einsetzende rapide Anwachsen der Habilitationen und die mit der Aufnahme der Privatdozententätigkeit verbundene Erwartung einer akademischen Karriere. Im folgenden Jahrzehnt nahm die Zahl der Habilitationen noch weiter zu, wobei jetzt die Mehrzahl der neuen Privatdozenten im wesentlichen den durch Lachmann und J. Grimm repräsentierten Richtungen zuzurechnen ist (Meves 1994b: 139 ff.). Die wachsende und sich festigende Bedeutung der Dt. Ph. zeigte sich auch in der Zunahme der Professuren. 1848/49 bestanden an knapp der Hälfte der deutschen Universitäten Ordinariate für das neue Fach, von denen ihm allerdings nur vier nominell gewidmet waren, während es in den anderen Fällen lediglich eines von zwei oder mehreren Fächern (Klass. Ph., Neuere Literatur, Orientalische Sprachen/Literatur, Vergleichende Sprachwissenschaft, Ästhetik) bildete. Der Begriff Germ. Ph. wurde zwar verschiedentlich in zeitgenössischen Abhandlungen, bei Lehrstuhldenominationen jedoch erst vereinzelt in der zweiten Hälfte des 19. Jhs. verwendet. Anfangs der 40er Jahre unterteilte z. B. der Pädagoge Karl Mager (1810–1858) die moderne Philologie in die (die deutsche und englische umfassende) germanische Philologie, in die romanische und slavische Philologie und forderte im Hinblick auf die gymnasiale Lehrerausbildung die Errichtung von drei Professuren für moderne Philologie an jeder Universität: "zwei ordentliche für einen Germanisten und einen Romanisten, und eine außerordentliche, bei deren Besetzung man vorzugsweise auf englische Philologie sehen könnte" (Mager 1843: 110). Über den Aufgabenbereich dieser modernen Philologie be-

160. Die Entstehung und frühe Entwicklung der Germanischen Philologie

standen schon zu Beginn der 40er Jahre verschiedene Auffassungen. Während Mager der Philologie die allseitige Erforschung der Existenz eines Volkes zuwies, wollte Adalbert von Keller (1812−1883) in seiner anläßlich der Ernennung zum außerordentlichen Professor der neueren Sprachen und Literatur in Tübingen gehaltenen programmatischen "Inauguralrede über die Aufgabe der modernen Philologie" diese auf die Erforschung der Sprache, ihrer historischen und physiologischen Seite sowie der lebenden Volksdialekte, und der schönen Literatur beschränken (Keller 1842: 9−10, 10−11). 1848/49 war das neue Fach an nunmehr 17 von 20 Universitäten mit Professuren vertreten, überwiegend jedoch erst im Status von Extraordinariaten. Sieht man einmal von den Generalisten, Literaturhistorikern und Ästhetikern ab, so sind selbst die Vertreter der Dt. Ph. extensional nicht ausschließlich auf 'Altdeutsches' (siehe z. B. Lachmanns Lessing-Ausgabe, 1838− 1840) und intensional nicht nur auf eine enge Verbindung von Grammatik, Metrik und Edition fixiert. J. Grimms *Deutsche Grammatik* (1819−1837) setzte neue sprachwissenschaftliche Standards und legte den Grund für die Konzentration auf die germanische und ältere deutsche Sprachgeschichte bei den universitären Fachvertretern. Unter diesen finden sich jedoch auch Forscher, die älteren Ansätzen gegenüber offen blieben, in methodisch unterschiedlicher Weise altertumswissenschaftlich ausgerichtet waren oder auch philosophische und dialektologische Ansätze verfolgten (siehe z. B. Johann Andreas Schmellers *Bayerische Grammatik* [1821] und sein *Bayerisches Wörterbuch* [1827−1837]).

2.1.2. Die Konsolidierungsphase

In Österreich setzte die Institutionalisierung der Dt. Ph. erst nach 1848 ein und stand in Verbindung mit der durchgreifenden Reform des höheren Bildungswesens (Egglmaier 1994: 204 ff.). Das in Deutschland entstandene Fächersystem und die in den einzelnen Fächern entwickelten wissenschaftskonstitutiven Standards dienten dabei den österreichischen Universitäten zur Orientierung (siehe Egglmaier 1994: 206):

"Zufolge des deutschen Vorbilds lag der Schwerpunkt des Fachs 'deutsche Sprache und Literatur' auf dessen älteren Partien. Als Germanisten bzw. Philologen galten nur jene, die sich mit der Bearbeitung und Edition alt- und mittelhochdeutscher Sprach- und Literaturdenkmäler beschäftigt hatten und beschäftigten. Nur sie wurden als Mitglieder der scientific community angesehen und verfügten als solche über die nötige Reputation, um während der ersten Phase der Reformbemühungen als Fachvertreter der deutschen Philologie für geeignet erachtet zu werden."

Von Anfang an erfolgten an den habsburgischen Universitäten die Ernennungen für das Fach deutsche Sprache und Literatur (1849 Prag: Karl August Hahn; 1850 Wien: Theodor von Karajan; 1850 Krakau: Karl Weinhold; 1851 Graz: Karl Weinhold), wobei die neuere deutsche Literatur mit in das Lehrangebot einbezogen wurde, bevor das neue Fach an allen Universitäten vertreten war.

In Deutschland führten die 1848er Ereignisse vereinzelt zum universitären Aufstieg (Prutz in Halle), in der Folge dann jedoch mehrfach zur politisch bedingten Amtsenthebung und/oder Stellenverlust (siehe z. B. Gottfried Kinkel [1815−1882] in Bonn, Moriz Haupt [1805−1879] in Leipzig, Julius Rupp [1809−1884] in Königsberg, Christian Willbrandt [1810−1867] in Rostock). Nach diesen Rückschlägen beschleunigte sich jedoch der Institutionalisierungsprozeß in den 50er Jahren merklich. Bestanden 1850 an acht Universitäten (des späteren Dt. Reiches) Ordinariate für das Fach, so war es 1860 bereits an dreizehn Universitäten mit ordentlichen Professuren vertreten. In der Diskussion um die (Wieder-)Einrichtung eines Ordinariats wurde jetzt verschiedentlich die Bedeutung der Dt. Ph. für die Lehrerausbildung bzw. die Bedeutung des gymnasialen Deutschunterrichts als Argument angeführt. 1859 motivierte die Königsberger Philosophische Fakultät ihr Votum für die Errichtung eines Lehrstuhls für deutsche Sprache und Literatur zunächst mit den gängigen Argumenten, dem Vorhandensein einer derartigen Professur "fast auf allen deutschen Universitäten", dem längst erreichten "Range einer selbstständigen Wissenschaft" (Meves 1994b: 169) und der innerwissenschaftlichen Bedeutung für die übrigen Sprach- und Geschichtswissenschaften, fügte dann aber einen für die Bestimmung des Gegenstandsbereichs des Faches bemerkenswerten Wunsch hinzu:

"[sie] würde es jedoch gern sehen, wenn der Vertreter dieses Fachs sich nicht zu exklusiv nur auf die aeltere Zeit beschränkte, sondern auch die Zeit seit der Reformation zum Gegenstand seiner Darstellung zu machen vermöchte, um auch solchen Studierenden, die sich nicht speciell der Philologie, sondern dem Schulfach oder dem Geschichtsstudium überhaupt widmen, oder auch, ohne Rücksicht auf ein spezielles Fach, ihre allgemeine Bildung gründlicher betreiben wollen, einen Anhalt zu gewähren." (Zit. nach Meves 1994b: 169)

Der Erlanger Germanist Rudolf von Raumer (1815–1876), Verfasser der ersten großen *Geschichte der Germanischen Philologie vorzugsweise in Deutschland* (1870), legte auf der 20. Versammlung deutscher Schulmänner und Philologen 1861 nicht nur zwölf intensiv diskutierte "Thesen über die Behandlung des Altdeutschen auf Gymnasien und über die Heranbildung der dazu nöthigen Lehrkräfte" (1863) vor, sondern initiierte zusammen mit seinen Rostocker und Baseler Kollegen Karl Bartsch und Wilhelm Wackernagel die Einrichtung einer germanistischen Sektion (1862) innerhalb des Philologenvereins. Nach dem zeitgenössischen Urteil Bechsteins hatte mit der Gründung dieser Sektion die "im engeren Sinne deutsche Philologie [...] also das mühsam erkämpfte Ziel erreicht, sie ist als streng wissenschaftliche Disziplin anerkannt und es ist ihr der pädagogische Einfluß zugestanden" (1865: 332).

Das Selbstbewußtsein (und die Anzahl) der Germanisten war aber noch nicht so groß, so daß auch die Vertreter der Romanischen und der Osteuropäischen Philologie in die der germanistische Sektion aufgenommen wurden. Diese formierte sich also eigentlich als eine Sektion für moderne Philologie, in Absetzung und Konkurrenz zur Klass. Ph. Im gleichen Jahr unterstützte das preußische Kultusministerium gegenüber dem Finanzministerium den Antrag der Universität Halle auf Errichtung einer ordentlichen Professur für deutsche Sprachkunde und Literatur:

"Dieselbe muß als wohl begründet anerkannt werden, indem es seit Erweckung der deutschen Sprachwissenschaft durch die Gebrüder *Grimm* und deren Ausbau durch eine Reihe der ausgezeichnetsten Philologen als eine Ehrensache anzusehen ist, daß den Studierenden auf deutschen Universitäten die Gelegenheit geboten werde, eine gründliche historische Kenntnis der Muttersprache zu erwerben, und eine solche namentlich den künftigen Gymnasial- und Realschullehrern nach dem jetzigen Stande der Wissenschaft durchaus unentbehrlich ist. *Halle* aber ist eine der wichtigsten Pflanzschulen für den Lehrerstand; es studieren dort etwa 100 junge Philologen." (Zit. nach Meves 1994b: 179)

Die hier zum Ausdruck kommende funktionale Verbindung zwischen dem Universitätsfach und der Deutschlehrerausbildung gewann in Preußen in den 60er Jahren zunehmend an Kontur. 1863 beantragte der Kultusminister die Erweiterung der Wissenschaftlichen Prüfungskommissionen um einen Prüfer für das Fach der deutschen Sprache und Literatur, das

"bisher immer mit dem Fach der Philosophie und Pädagogik verbunden gewesen [war], wobei, da das betreffende Kommissionsmitglied in der Regel ein Professor der Philosophie und kein Sprachgelehrter ist, die Geschichte der Entwicklung der deutschen Sprache und ihrer Gesetze unberücksichtigt zu bleiben pflegt. Es bedarf keiner weiteren Ausführung, daß dies ein wesentlicher Mangel ist, auf dessen Beseitigung auch im vaterländischen Interesse Bedacht zu nehmen ist. Die Lehrer des Deutschen in den obersten Classen der höheren Schulen müssen mit der alten Literatur unsers Volks und mit der Geschichte unserer Sprache bekannt sein, und Gelegenheit haben, sich bei der Prüfung für das Lehramt vor einem competenten Beurteiler darüber auszuweisen." (Zit. nach Meves: 1994b: 180)

Da das 'Altdeutsche' das entscheidende Kriterium für die Notwendigkeit universitärer Fachstudien künftiger Deutschlehrer an höheren Schulen bildete, mußten auch die Prüfungskommissionen personell entsprechend ausgestattet werden. 1866 waren zum ersten Mal alle Prüfungskommissionen in Preußen mit einem Hochschulgermanisten besetzt. Daß es sich hierbei um einen Aufstieg der Germanisten handelte, erwies sich nicht zuletzt an der Reaktion der Vertreter der das 'philologische Fach' noch immer dominierenden Disziplin Klass. Ph.

Das Ende 1866 erlassene neue *Reglement für die Prüfungen der Candidaten des höheren Schulamts* (1867) räumte bei der Zuerkennung der Lehrbefähigung für die oberen Klassen alternativ zu den altdeutschen Sprachkenntnissen den Nachweis von Philosophie-Kenntnissen ein, die zum Unterricht in der philosophischen Propädeutik befähigten. Auch nach Erlaß dieser Prüfungsordnung war ein germanistisches Fachstudium für den künftigen Deutschlehrer also noch nicht unumgänglich. Die in Bayern 1873 erlassene neue Prüfungsordnung erhöhte zwar zumindest theoretisch die Prüfungsanforderungen im Deutschen, änderte jedoch letztlich nichts an der den Deutschunterricht an den Gymnasien dominierenden Stellung der Altphilologen. So beklagte z. B. der Würzburger Professor Matthias Lexer, daß die Dt. Ph. "in Bezug auf ihre praktische Geltung als Berufswissenschaft" an den bayerischen Universitäten ganz hintanstehe (1877: 17).

In den 60er Jahren erhöhte sich die Anzahl der ordentlichen Professuren für das Fach der deutschen Sprache und Literatur wie noch in keinem Jahrzehnt zuvor. Bereits vor Gründung des Dt. Reiches 1870/71 war das Fach an 19 Universitäten mit Ordinariaten vertreten, so daß der Institutionalisierungsprozeß auf dieser Ebene als abgeschlossen gelten darf. Nur die Universität Jena hinkte dieser Entwicklung um einige Jahre hinterher. Der Antrag ihrer Philosophischen Fakultät aus dem Jahr 1876 auf Gründung einer ordentlichen Professur für das Lehrfach der Dt. Ph. bestätigte zugleich die Anerkennung dieses Fachs als Universitätsdisziplin und seine Einbindung in die Lehrerausbildung:

"In Erwägung, daß das Lehrfach der deutschen Philologie in der neueren Zeit eine früher nicht bekannte Ausbreitung und Bedeutung gewonnen hat, daß an allen deutschen Universitäten mit Einschluß Österreichs und der Schweiz ordentliche Professuren für deutsche Philologie bestehen, daß in den Prüfungskommissionen für das Oberlehrerexamen der Vertreter der deutschen Philologie überall einen Platz hat [...]" (Zit. nach Meves 1994b: 190−191)

2.2. Die Gründung von Seminaren

Zarncke hatte 1863 auf der 22. Philologen-Versammlung neben der Errichtung "einer ordentlichen Professur für germanische Philologie auch eine solche für die romanischen Sprachen" gefordert, sah aber erst dann "für unsere Wissenschaft eine feste Grundlage" erreicht, "wenn diesen beiden zur Seite ein wohlausgestattetes *Seminar* für das Studium der neueren Sprachen und Litteraturen stehen wird" (1863: 65). Schon lange vor der Gründung germanistischer Seminare zogen vereinzelt Fachvertreter ihre Studenten zur aktiven Mitarbeit in den Vorlesungen heran. Seit den 40er Jahren finden sich häufiger Ankündigungen von Übungen, oft in der Form von losen Kränzchen, Vereinigungen oder (Deutschen) Gesellschaften. Das erste deutsch-philologische Seminar in Rostock (1858) stand zwar wie sein Vorgänger den Studierenden aller Fakultäten offen, doch wurden insbesondere die Lehramtskandidaten zum Eintritt aufgefordert. Durch die Seminare sollten das Fachstudium intensiviert, die Studenten zum eigenständigen wissenschaftlichen Arbeiten angeleitet und zur Forschung hingeführt werden, womit verschiedentlich eine Förderung der deutsch-philologischen Ausbildung der künftigen Lehrer verbunden wurde. Insofern die Aufnahme in das Seminar in der Regel erst nach einer bestimmten Semesterzahl möglich war, oft eine Aufnahmeprüfung voraussetzte und eine Unterscheidung der Mitglieder in außerordentliche und ordentliche erfolgte, bewirkte die neue Institution eine Gliederung des Fachstudiums, die durch die Einführung eigener Proseminarveranstaltungen noch verstärkt wurde. Wollte der Student Mitglied des Seminars bleiben, mußte er zumeist jedes Semester eine schriftliche Arbeit anfertigen. Seit den 80er Jahren erhielten die germanistischen Seminare zunehmend auch eigene Räumlichkeiten. Gegen Ende des Jahrhunderts schlug sich die Verselbständigung des Gegenstandsbereichs neuere deutsche Literatur in der, an der Universität Straßburg bereits bei der Gründung des Seminars (1872/73) vorgenommenen, Aufteilung in eine ältere und neuere Abteilung nieder. Unter institutionsgeschichtlichem Aspekt bedeutete diese sich über die gesamte zweite Hälfte des 19. Jhs. erstreckende Gründungsphase (Rostock 1858, Münster 1895; siehe die Tabelle bei Meves 1987: 72*−73*.) die endgültige Integration des Fachs in den Universitätsbetrieb und den institutionellen Angleichungsprozeß an die Klass. Ph. In den 90er Jahren des 19. Jhs., in denen die letzten germanistischen Seminare gegründet wurden, erfolgte auch die entscheidende Aufwertung des Deutschunterrichts im gymnasialen Fächerkanon. Das Fach Dt. Ph. avancierte endgültig zu einer Berufswissenschaft für den künftigen Deutschlehrer an höheren Schulen.

3. Zur Binnendifferenzierung des Fachs

Für die Binnendifferenzierung des Fachs in verschiedene Gruppierungen spielte der wenige Jahre nach Lachmanns Tod (1851) einsetzende, erbittert geführte 'Nibelungenstreit', in dem nicht allein einzelne Forschungspositionen zum Nibelungenlied und der Textkritik, sondern das philologische Ethos Lachmanns selbst zur Diskussion standen (siehe Kolk 1990: 8 ff.), eine wichtige Rolle. Mit Haupts "Zeitschrift für deutsches Altertum" verfügten die 'Berliner' über ein Publikationsforum, dessen Gründung eine nachhaltige Aufwertung des Wissenschaftlichkeitsanspruchs und einen "Hinweis auf die Eigenständigkeit" des Forschungsbereichs der Dt. Ph. dokumentierte (Kolk 1994: 80). In Opposition zur Berliner Schule (Lachmann, Haupt, Müllenhoff) war der Wiener Ordinarius Franz Pfeiffer (ab 1857) bestrebt, deren philologische Verengung zu überwinden und mit dem von ihm initiierten Fachorgan "Germania: Vierteljahrsschrift für deutsche Altertumskunde" (1856–1892) einen weiteren Adressatenkreis zu erreichen. Mit der Gründung der "Zeitschrift für deutsche Philologie" (1869 ff.) wollte der Hallenser Ordinarius Julius Zacher (1816–1887), obgleich überzeugter Lachmannianer, sich von dem 'Partheitreiben' distanzieren und ein Publikationsorgan, das auch den Interessen der Deutschlehrer entgegenkommen sollte, für alle Gebiete der Dt. Ph. einschließlich der neueren deutschen Literatur bereitstellen. In entschiedener Abkehr von seinem Lehrer Haupt öffnete sich der Leipziger Ordinarius Friedrich Zarncke (1858 ff.) neuen wissenschaftlichen Richtungen. Aus seinem Schülerkreis gingen die Junggrammatiker Hermann Paul, Wilhelm Braune und Eduard Sievers hervor. Von der vergleichenden indogermanischen Sprachwissenschaft August Leskiens herkommend, stellten sie unter dem Einfluß der lautphysiologischen und psychologischen Sprachbetrachtung insbesondere den Lautwert der Schriftzeichen, die Lautgesetze und die Rolle der Analogie in den Mittelpunkt ihrer Untersuchungen. Mit ihren 1873 gegründeten Fachorgan "Beiträge zur Geschichte der deutschen Sprache und Literatur" schufen sie sich ein Forum für ihre 'junggrammatische Richtung', über die sie jedoch hinauswuchsen. Beispielhaft dafür steht Pauls Werk *Principien der Sprachgeschichte* (1880; ^{5}1920), das "theoretische Grundlagenwerk des Faches" (Henne 1995: 21).

Während Paul und Braune sich anfangs der 70er Jahre habilitierten, erhielt der 21jährige Sievers bereits kurz nach seiner Promotion eine außerordentliche Professur für Dt. Ph. in Jena (1871), zugleich mit einem Lehrauftrag für Romanische Philologie. Aus freien Stücken übernahm er zudem noch die Vertretung der Anglistik. Den Junggrammatikern gelang es jedoch nicht, ihre Richtung institutionell zu expandieren (Einhauser 1989: 258). Im Vergleich zu den vorangegangenen Jahrzehnten nahm die Zahl der Privatdozenten in Dt. Ph. in dem Jahrzehnt von 1870 bis 1880 außerordentlich stark zu (fast 30 Habilitationen). In diesem Anstieg kommen sowohl die Verfestigung der inneruniversitären Laufbahn – 1860 war die Hälfte der ordentlichen Professoren nicht habilitiert, 1870 gut ein Drittel – als auch die durch die zunehmende Binnendifferenzierung des Fachs steigenden Erwartungen des akademischen Nachwuchses auf eine Universitätskarriere zum Ausdruck. Zudem eröffnete die Habilitation auch die Möglichkeit, in dem sich zusehends verselbständigenden Fach Anglistik Fuß zu fassen. Julius Zupitza etwa habilitierte sich 1869 für Germ. Ph. in Breslau, erhielt 1872 eine außerordentliche Professur für nordgermanische Sprachen in Wien und stieg 1876 zum Ordinarius für englische Sprache und Literatur an der Universität Berlin auf.

Die Entstehung und allmähliche Etablierung der Neugermanistik bildete die wichtigste Folge der Binnendifferenzierung des Fachs im letzten Drittel des 19. Jhs. (siehe Weimar 1989: 429 ff.). Die Ansätze zu selbständigen Literaturgeschichts-Professuren (siehe 2.2.1.) fanden in den 50er Jahren, abgesehen von lokalen und personalen Sonderfällen, zunächst keine Fortsetzung. Der wohl von Hermann Hettner verfaßte Zeitungsartikel "Die deutschen Universitäten und die deutsche Litteratur" charakterisierte die 1857 bestehende Situation:

"die neuere deutsche Litteraturgeschichte ist ein Pariakind, von der Aristokratie der zunftmäßigen Facultätsstudien ausgestoßen. Keine einzige philosophische Facultät [...] hat eine statutenmäßige ordentliche Professur für deutsche Litteraturgeschichte."

Nach der Einrichtung vereinzelter Extraordinariate (Gießen 1863, Bern 1866) kam der Gründung eines zweiten Ordinariats für deutsche Sprache und Literatur an der Universität Wien (Karl Tomaschek) im Jahr 1868 eine richtungsweisende Bedeutung zu (Egglmair 1994: 216):

"Entscheidend dafür war, daß man sich ministeriellerseits der Argumentation [Franz Pfeiffers und Johannes Vahlens], daß 'das ausgebreitete Gebiet der modernen deutschen Literatur, das in Verbindung mit der modernen Culturentwicklung überhaupt sowie den Disciplinen der Poetik und Ästhetik behandelt, eine eigene Lehrkraft erfordert', nicht nur nicht entziehen konnte, sondern dies auch gar nicht wollte."

Die Einrichtung weiterer Ordinariate in Leipzig (1874), München (1874) und Berlin (1877) intensivierte die Anerkennung der neueren deutschen Literatur als eigenständigen wissenschaftlichen Gegenstandsbereich, die auch in der Gründung spezifischer Fachzeitschriften (ab 1870; seit 1894 erscheint der "Euphorion") zum Tragen kam.

Um ihre akademische Anerkennung zu erlangen, hatten die Neugermanisten zunächst die philologische Behandlung ihres Gegenstandes übernommen. Textkritik und Edition, Kommentar, Bibliographie und Biographie standen im Mittelpunkt ihrer Arbeit, ihr

Hauptgebiet bildete die Goethe-Philologie ("Goethe-Jahrbuch" seit 1880). Eine Sonderstellung nahm Wilhelm Scherer (1841–1888) ein, nicht allein im Hinblick auf die Teilung des Fachs und als Wissenschaftsorganisator, sondern ebenso durch seine publizistische Wirksamkeit und sein wissenschaftliches Werk (*Zur Geschichte der deutschen Sprache*, 1868; *Geschichte der deutschen Literatur*, 1883; *Poetik*, 1888) wie durch sein methodisch bewegliches und innovatives Verfahren (von der historisch-philologischen zur historisch-psychologischen Rekonstruktion). Nach einigen neuen Extraordinariaten in den 80er Jahren wurde zunehmend seit den 90er Jahren ein zweites Ordinariat gegründet und mit einem Neugermanisten besetzt (siehe die Tabelle bei Weimar 1989: 436 ff.). Da es an den Universitäten jedoch im allgemeinen höchstens zwei Ordinariate für das Gesamtgebiet gab, konnte sich die Sprachwissenschaft innerhalb des Faches institutionell noch nicht ausdifferenzieren. Die Verselbständigung der neueren deutschen Literatur erfolgte zu Lasten der germanistischen Sprachwissenschaft: Zwar lautete die Lehrstuhldenomination in der Regel "neuere deutsche Literatur und Sprache", doch blieb der Bereich Sprache an den deutschen Universitäten gewöhnlich bis in die 60er Jahre des 20. Jhs. (nicht jedoch in der DDR) mit der älteren deutschen Philologie verbunden.

4. Bibliographie

(siehe dazu das ausführliche Literaturverzeichnis zu dem Artikel 178)

Bahner, Werner & Werner Neumann, Hg. 1985. *Sprachwissenschaftliche Germanistik: Ihre Herausbildung und Begründung*. Berlin: Akademie-Verlag.

Bechstein, Reinhold. 1864, 1865. "Die deutsche Philologie in Jacob Grimm's Todesjahr". *Jahrbücher für Politik und Literatur* 11. 90–113; 12. 317–332.

Bluhm, Lothar. 1997. *Die Brüder Grimm und der Beginn der Deutschen Philologie*. Hildesheim: Weidmann.

Boeckh, August. 1877. *Enzyklopädie und Methodologie der philologischen Wissenschaften*. Hg. von Ernst Bratuschek. Leipzig: B. G. Teubner.

Dainat, Holger. 1987. "Veränderungen im Wissen über Wissenschaft". *Internationales Archiv für Sozialgeschichte der deutschen Literatur* 12. 296–307.

Egglmaier, Herbert H. 1994. "Entwicklungslinien der neueren deutschen Literaturwissenschaft in Österreich in der zweiten Hälfte des 19. Jahrhunderts und zu Beginn des 20. Jahrhunderts". Fohrmann & Voßkamp 1994. 204–235.

Einhauser, Eveline. 1989. *Die Junggrammatiker*. Trier: Wissenschaftlicher Verlag.

Finkenstaedt, Thomas. 1983. *Kleine Geschichte der Anglistik in Deutschland*. Darmstadt: Wissenschaftliche Buchgesellschaft.

Fohrmann, Jürgen & Wilhelm Voßkamp, Hg. 1991. *Wissenschaft und Nation*. München: Fink.

–, –, Hg. 1994. *Wissenschaftsgeschichte der Germanistik im 19. Jahrhundert*. Stuttgart: Metzler.

Grimm, Jacob. 1846. "Bericht über die Zusammenkunft der Germanisten in Frankfurt am 24., 25. und 26. Sept. 1846". Beilage zur *Allgemeinen Zeitung*, 22. Oktober 1846, 2353–2355. (Zit. nach Grimm, *Kleinere Schriften*, Bd. 7, 573–581. Berlin: Dümmler, 1884.)

Henne, Helmut. 1995. "Germanische und deutsche Philologie im Zeichen der Junggrammatiker". *Beiträge zur Methodengeschichte der neueren Philologien* hg. von Robert Harsch-Niemeyer, 1–30. Tübingen: Niemeyer.

[Hettner, Hermann]. 1857. "Die deutschen Universitäten und die deutsche Litteratur". *Allgemeine Zeitung Augsburg*. Nr. 304 vom 31. 10. 1857.

Hunger, Ulrich. 1987. "Romantische Germanistik und Textphilologie: Konzepte zur Erforschung mittelalterlicher Literatur zu Beginn des 19. Jahrhunderts". *Dt. Vierteljahrsschrift für Literaturwissenschaft und Geistesgeschichte*, 61. Jg., Sonderheft, 42*–68*.

–. 1994. "Die altdeutsche Literatur und das Verlangen nach Wissenschaft: Schöpfungsakt und Fortschrittsglaube in der Frühgermanistik". Fohrmann & Voßkamp 1994. 236–263.

–. 1995. "Gründung oder Prozeß: Die Entwicklung der wissenschaftlichen Germanistik, ein Werk Jacob Grimms?" *Jahrbuch der Brüder Grimm-Gesellschaft* 5. 153–176.

Janota, Johannes. 1980. *Eine Wissenschaft etabliert sich, 1810–1870*. Mit einer Einführung hg. von J. Janota. Tübingen: Niemeyer.

Keller, Adalbert von. 1842. *Inauguralrede über die Aufgabe der modernen Philologie*. Stuttgart: Metzler.

König, Christoph u. a., Hg. 2000. *Wissenschaftsgeschichte der Germanistik in Porträts*. Berlin & New York: de Gruyter.

Kolk, Rainer. 1990. *Berlin oder Leipzig? Eine Studie zur sozialen Organisation der Germanistik im "Nibelungenstreit"*. Tübingen: Niemeyer.

–. 1994. "Liebhaber, Gelehrte, Experten". Fohrmann & Voßkamp 1994. 48–114.

Kopp, Detlef. 1994. "(Deutsche) Philologie und Erziehungssystem". Fohrmann & Voßkamp 1994. 669–741.

Lexer, Matthias. 1877. *Rede zur Feier des 295. Stiftungstages der Kgl. Julius-Maximilians-Universität in Würzburg gehalten am 2. Januar 1877*. Würzburg: Thein'sche Druckerei.

Mager, [Karl]. 1843. "Ueber Wesen, Einrichtung und pädagogische Bedeutung des schulmäßigen Studiums der neueren Sprachen und Literaturen und die Mittel ihm aufzuhelfen". *Die modernen Humanitätsstudien*, Heft 2. Zürich: Meyer & Zeller.

Meves, Uwe. 1985. "Zur Einrichtung der ersten Professur für deutsche Sprache an der Berliner Universität (1810)". *Zeitschrift für dt. Philologie* 104. 161–184.

–. 1985. "Barthold Georg Niebuhrs Vorschläge zur Begründung einer wissenschaftlichen Disziplin 'Deutsche Philologie' (1812–1816)". *Zeitschrift für dt. Philologie* 104. 321–356.

–. 1987. "Die Gründung germanistischer Seminare an den preußischen Universitäten (1875–1895)". *Dt. Vierteljahresschrift für Literaturwissenschaft und Geistesgeschichte*, 61. Jg., Sonderheft. 69*–122*.

–. 1994a. "Zur Namensgebung 'Germanist'". Fohrmann & Voßkamp 1994. 25–47.

–. 1994b. "Zum Institutionalisierungsprozeß der Deutschen Philologie: Die Periode der Lehrstuhlerrichtung". Fohrmann & Voßkamp 1994. 115–203.

–. 1998. "Das Fach deutsche Sprache und Literatur an den deutschen Universitäten im Jahr 1846". *1846–1996: 150 Jahre Erste Germanistenversammlung in Frankfurt am Main. Zur Geschichte und Problematik der Nationalphilologien in Europa* hg. von Frank Fürbeth u. a., 85–103. Tübingen: Niemeyer.

Müller, Jörg Jochen, Hg. 1974. *Germanistik und deutsche Nation, 1806–1848*. Stuttgart: Metzler.

Paul, Hermann, Hg. 1891. *Grundriß der germanischen Philologie*. Bd. I. Straßburg: Karl J. Trübner.

Raumer, Rudolf von. 1863 [1861]. "Thesen über die Behandlung des Altdeutschen auf Gymnasien und über die Heranbildung der dazu nöthigen Lehrkräfte". *Verhandlungen der zwanzigsten Versammlung deutscher Philologen und Schulmänner in Frankfurt am Main vom 24. bis 27. September 1861*, 140–141 (Diskussionsbeiträge S. 141–174.) Leipzig: B. G. Teubner.

–. 1870. *Geschichte der Germanischen Philologie vorzugsweise in Deutschland*. München: R. Oldenbourg.

Reglement für die Prüfungen der Candidaten des höheren Schulamts. Amtlich. 1867. Berlin: Wilhelm Hertz.

Rompeltien, Bärbel. 1994. *Germanistik als Wissenschaft*. Opladen: Westdeutscher Verlag.

Schmidt, Hartmut. 1985. "Aspekte der Institutionalisierung: Zur Durchsetzung der neuen Denkmuster". Bahner & Neumann 1985. 151–248.

Stackmann, Karl. 1991. "Die Anfänge der Germanistik in Göttingen". *Drei Kapitel aus der Geschichte der Göttinger Germanistik* hg. von Karl Stackmann et al., 9–45. Göttingen: Vandenhoeck & Ruprecht.

Wehrli, Max. 1993. "Germanistik in der Schweiz. 1933–1945". *Jahrbuch der dt. Schillergesellschaft* 37. 409–422.

Weigel, Harald. 1989. *'Nur was du nie gesehn wird ewig dauern'. Carl Lachmann und die Entstehung der wissenschaftlichen Edition*. Freiburg: Rombach.

Weimar, Klaus. 1989. *Geschichte der deutschen Literaturwissenschaft bis zum Ende des 19. Jahrhunderts*. München: Fink.

Wyss, Ulrich. 1979. *Die wilde Philologie: Jacob Grimm und der Historismus*. München: Beck.

–. 1989. "Johann Andreas Schmellers und Jacob Grimms Literaturauffassung". *Johann Andreas Schmeller und der Beginn der Germanistik* hg. von Ludwig Eichinger & Bernd Naumann, 11–33. München: Oldenbourg.

Zarncke, Friedrich. 1864. "Rede zum Gedächtnis von Jacob Grimm und zur Eröffnung der germanistischen Section". *Verhandlungen der zweiundzwanzigsten Versammlung deutscher Philologen und Schulmänner in Meißen vom 30. September bis 2. Oktober 1863*, 62–66. Leipzig: Teubner.

Uwe Meves, Oldenburg (Deutschland)

161. Die Entstehung und frühe Geschichte der Slavischen Philologie

1. Bestimmung des Begriffs und Periodisierung
2. Objektbereich und Gegenstände
3. Beschreibung der slavischen Einzelsprachen
4. Vergleichende slavische Sprachwissenschaft
5. Literatur (in Auswahl)

1. Bestimmung des Begriffs und Periodisierung

1.1. 1875 bestimmte der Kroate Vatroslav Jagić (1838–1923), der bedeutendste Slavist des letzten Viertels des 19. und der ersten zwei Jahrzehnte des 20. Jh., die Slavische Philologie als Wissenschaft von den slavischen Sprachen, den Sprach- und Literaturdenkmälern, den 'Produkten des Volksgeistes' und dem literarischen Altertum (Jagić 1930–1934 I: 282). Seine Definition resümierte die Herausbildung der Slavischen Philologie und die Abgrenzung ihres Objektbereichs, d. h. den Verzicht auf die Einbeziehung der Geschichtswissenschaft, in Analogie zu den an-

161. Die Entstehung und frühe Geschichte der Slavischen Philologie

deren europäischen Philologien. Jagić nannte 'mit vollem Recht' das Studium der Sprachen an erster Stelle. Diese Priorität wurde auch schon 1841 von dem Slowaken Pavol Jozef Šafárik (tschechisch: Pavel Josef Šafařík) (1795−1861) gesetzt. In seiner Denkschrift zu den Aufgaben der in Berlin und Breslau zu schaffenden Professuren für Slavische Philologie nannte er als erste die Unterrichtung der Grammatik der 'vorzüglichsten slawischen Mundarten', darauf folgte die Geschichte der slavischen Literatur und als "Alles Übrige und nur am Rande die slavische Altertumskunde, die Interpretation einzelner Sprach- und Geistesdenkmäler u. a." (Rösel 1957: 165). Die Bedeutung der sprachwissenschaftlichen Studien ergab sich aus der Tatsache, daß die Sprache das einzige unbestreitbare gemeinsame und auffälligstes Merkmal aller Slaven war. Die Sprachwissenschaft war deshalb von Anfang an die wichtigste Komponente der Slavischen Philologie. Der 'Patriarch der Slavischen Philologie', der Tscheche Josef Dobrovský (1753−1829), ist vor allem Linguist gewesen, ebenso wie sein jüngerer russischer Zeitgenosse Aleksandr Xristoforovič Vostokov (1782−1864).

1.2. Die Slavische Philologie entstand in einem komplizierten Bedingungsgefüge von wissenschaftsexternen und wissenschaftsinternen Faktoren. Zu den wissenschaftsexternen Faktoren gehörten die Modernisierungsprozesse in Europa und die damit verbundene allmähliche Entstehung eines nationalen Bewußtseins. Der Slowake Ján (tschechisch: Jan) Kollár (1793−1852), der in den 30er Jahren des 19. Jh. die Konzeption der slavischen literarischen Wechselseitigkeit entwickelte, forderte von den Gebildeten die Kenntnis wenigstens der lebenden Dialekte, in denen Bücher gedruckt werden, und die Erarbeitung von "vergleichenden Sprachlehren und Wörterbüchern aller Mundarten, die den formellen oder materiellen Unterschied der Mundarten darstellen und so das Erlernen derselben erleichtern würden" (Kollár 1837: 125). Um die Dignität der Muttersprache als Mittel der Kommunikation in allen Bereichen nachzuweisen, mußten die Sprachpatrioten das historische Alter der Schriftsprachen sichtbar machen, die zeitgenössische Schriftform bzw. ihre Varianten ausbauen und ihren nationalen Charakter durch Sprachreinigung profilieren. Zur Sprachverteidigung kam das Streben nach Erkenntnissen über die Sprache und ihr Wesen. Neben der Suche nach ihren universalen Eigenschaften geriet auch die Vielfalt der Einzelsprachen in das Blickfeld der Gelehrten. Durch das Aufspüren von bisher kaum beachteten Idiomen in Europa selbst wie des aber schon 1756 ausgestorbenen Dravänopolabischen im Lüneburger Wendland und das Kennenlernen vieler neuer Sprachen während der kolonialen Eroberungen hatte sich der Kreis der Sprachen stark erweitert. Von besonderer Bedeutung war die Bekanntschaft mit dem Sanskrit und die Entdeckung seiner Verwandtschaft mit den klassischen, den germanischen und den keltischen Sprachen. Damit stellte sich auch die Frage nach der sprachlichen Zugehörigkeit der Slaven. Spätestens um 1800 galt der indogermanische Charakter des Slavischen als ziemlich sicher. Die Impulse, die von der historisch-vergleichenden Sprachwissenschaft ausgingen, wurden aber erst seit den dreißiger Jahren kräftiger, als ihre Rezeption mittels der Arbeiten Franz Bopps, Jacob Grimms und August Friedrich Potts in Rußland, bei den Tschechen und den Südslaven produktiv wurde. Ein wichtiger wissenschaftsinterner Faktor waren die biblische Textkritik der Aufklärung in Deutschland, durch die z. B. Dobrovský, der als Hebraist und Orientalist begonnen hatte, zur Beschäftigung mit den slavischen Bibelübersetzungen geführt wurde, und die historische Quellenkritik.

1.2. Die Periode der Entstehung und frühen Entwicklung der Slavischen Philologie gliedert sich in zwei Etappen, der die sog. Vorgeschichte vorangeht. Diese umfaßt etwa den Zeitraum vom Ende des 17. Jh. bis zum letzten Viertel des 18. Jh. und ist durch das Entstehen des wissenschaftlichen Interesses im Zeitalter der Aufklärung an den Slaven, wie es beispielhaft bei Gottfried Wilhelm Leibniz zu belegen ist, die ersten Versuche einer Gesamtdarstellung der slavischen Sprachen (Johann Leonhard Frisch) und ihrer historischen Schicksale (Karl Gottlob v. Anton), eifriges Sammeln von lexikalischem Material und Sprachproben (Johann Severin Vater) sowie die allmähliche Lösung der Grammatikschreibung von den Mustern für die klassischen Sprachen gekennzeichnet. (Zu den Genannten vgl. Eichler et al. 1993 sowie Zeil 1994.)

1.2.1. Die eigentliche Geschichte der Slavischen Philologie als kontinuierlich betriebener Forschung begann im letzten Viertel des 18. Jh. mit der Hinwendung Dobrovskýs zu slavistischen Gegenständen über die Bohemistik hinaus (vgl. vor allem Večerka 1995). Er veröffentlichte im Jahre 1791 die erste Fassung seiner *Geschichte der böhmischen Sprache (und Literatur)* und unternahm 1792/93 eine Reise nach Schweden und Rußland, um die dortigen slavischen Handschriften und frühen Drucke zu studieren. Die erste Etappe der Herausbildung der Slavischen Philologie endete ungefähr mit den 30er Jahren des 19. Jh. Sie wurde ideengeschichtlich zuerst von der Aufklärung, dann von der Romantik geprägt und weist einige charakteristische Merkmale auf, die sie sowohl von der Vorgeschichte als auch von der folgenden Etappe unterscheiden. Als erstes ist zu nennen die Herausbildung eines synkretistischen Paradigmas, d. h. von Leistungen und Zielsetzungen, die der Verbindung von philologischen, linguistischen, ethnographisch-folkloristischen und historischen Forschungen entsprangen. Typische Beispiele sind die Werke Šafáriks *Geschichte der slavischen Sprache und Literatur nach allen Mundarten* (1826), die *Slovanské starožitnosti* (1837; deutsch *Slawische Altertümer* 1843/44) und *Slovanský národopis* (1842) "Slawische Ethnographie". Zentrale Bedeutung hatten die Sammlung und Beschreibung von Sprach- und Literaturdenkmälern und historischen Quellen in handschriftlicher und gedruckter Form und ihre Interpretation. In der Sprachwissenschaft waren wichtige Gegenstände die Ermittlung der slavischen Einzelsprachen und ihre Ordnung, die grammatische Beschreibung der slavischen Sprachen und die vergleichende Darstellung ihres Wortschatzes. Der indogermanistische Bezug spielte vorerst nur eine geringe Rolle. Am Ende dieser Etappe wurde mit der Errichtung der ersten slavistischen Lehrstühle eine wichtige Stufe der Institutionalisierung erreicht.

1.2.2. In der zweiten Etappe, die etwa bis zu den 70er Jahren des 19. Jh. reichte, löste sich das synkretistische Paradigma der Slavischen Philologie allmählich auf. Sie wandelte sich von einer komplexen Wissenschaft zu einem Wissenschaftsverbund dieser Disziplinen mit jeweils spezifischen Theorien, Methoden, Aufgaben und Zielen. Seit den 40er Jahren zeichnete sich ein Paradigmenwechsel ab: das synkretistische Paradigma wurde durch einzelwissenschaftliche Paradigmen abgelöst. In der Sprachwissenschaft war dies das historisch-vergleichende Paradigma. In seiner frühen Phase bestand es aus Leistungen, die sich an den methodischen Prinzipien Bopps und Potts sowie J. Grimms und des Romanisten Friedrich Diez orientierten. Die von Bopp eingeleitete Einbeziehung des Slavischen in die Indogermanistik (in der zweiten Auflage seiner *Vergleichenden Grammatik*, 1835) drängte auf eine Hinwendung zur systematischen komparativistischen Betrachtung sowohl der slavischen Einzelsprachen als auch des Slavischen insgesamt und der anderen indogermanischen Sprachen. Sie wurde im Werk von Franz Miklosich insbesondere in *seiner Vergleichenden Grammatik der slavischen Sprachen* (seit 1852) und von August Schleicher in der *Formenlehre der kirchenslawischen Sprache* (1852) vollzogen und hob die Slavische Philologie auf einen vergleichbaren Forschungsstand mit der Germanistik und Romanistik. Besondere Aufmerksamkeit fanden nun auch die auffälligen Übereinstimmungen des Slavischen und des Baltischen. In diesen Rahmen gehört auch Aleksandr Afanas'evič Potebnja (1835–1891), der mit seiner Schrift über 'Denken und Sprache' (1862) den ersten bedeutenden originellen Beitrag zur allgemeinen Sprachwissenschaft in Rußland leistete. Die Aufnahme des Gedankenguts Humboldts und Steinthals führte ihn zur Einbeziehung des typologischen Kriteriums in die historische Syntaxforschung und zu Bemühungen um eine theoretisch fundierte Berücksichtigung der semantischen Komponente in der Etymologie; doch übernahm er auch methodische Grundsätze wie die Anerkennung von Lautgesetzen. Sein Hauptwerk mit dem bescheidenen Titel 'Aufzeichnungen zur russischen Grammatik' (1874–1899) dokumentiert seine Bemühungen um eine allgemeinlinguistische Deutung des Sprachwandels und die Resultate exakter Untersuchungen der slavischen Sprachen im indogermanischen Kontext.

1.3. Eine neue Periode der Geschichte der Slavischen Philologie begann mit dem letzten Drittel des 19. Jh.s, in dem sich die junggrammatische, positivistisch geprägte Modifikation der historisch-vergleichenden Sprachwissenschaft durchsetzte. Daran waren Slavisten wesentlich beteiligt. Zu nennen sind vor allem Jan Baudouin de Courtenay (1845–1929), der als erster das Prinzip der Analogie in einer konkreten Untersuchung beschrieb (1868), insgesamt aber eine weitgehend selbständige Forschungslinie außerhalb der junggrammatischen Richtung verfolgte, August Leskien (1840–1916), der das Zusammenwirken von Lautgesetzen und Analogie in der slavischen, baltischen und germanischen Deklination (1876) zeigte, und Filipp Fedorovič Fortunatov (1848–1914), der in seinen Vorlesungen seit etwa 1880 (veröffentlicht erst 1919) die Phonetik des Altkirchenslavischen unter Anwendung der neuen Kriterien konsequent unter Bezug auf die indogermanischen Verhältnisse beschrieb.

1.4. Neben der Eingrenzung des Objektbereichs, der Bestimmung von Forschungsgegenständen sowie der Übernahme bzw. Erarbeitung von theoretischen Positionen und Forschungsmethoden ist die Formierung eines Wissenschaftszweiges mit seiner Institutionalisierung verknüpft. In der ersten Etappe entwickelte sich die Slavische Philologie außerhalb der Universitäten. In ihren Zentren Prag, Wien, St. Petersburg und Moskau waren die institutionelle Basis Bibliotheken, Museen, wissenschaftliche Gesellschaften und von Mäzenaten geförderte Zirkel. Die slavischen Philologen waren Privatgelehrte wie Dobrovský oder Bibliothekare wie Vostokov (später Mitarbeiter der Russischen Akademie), Šafárik, der Slowene Bartholomäus [Jernej] Kopitar (1782–1844) sowie die Polen Jerzy Samuel Bandtkie (1768–1835) und Samuel Bogumił Linde (1771–1847). Zwischen ihnen bildete sich eine stabile wissenschaftliche Kommunikation heraus, die auch nichtslavische Gelehrte wie J. Grimm einbezog. Sie verlief zum einen über persönliche Begegnungen und einen Briefwechsel mit hohem wissenschaftlichen Wert, zum anderen über erste Versuche von Periodika, die entweder den Charakter von Almanachen hatten, z. B. Dobrovskýs *Slawin* (1806) und *Slovanka* (1814/1815), oder von Informations- und Rezensionsblättern, z. B. die von Kopitar in Wien redigierten *Jahrbücher der Literatur* und die *Bibliografičeskie listy*, die Petr Ivanovič Köppen [Keppen] 1825–1826 in St. Petersburg herausgab. Diese spiegelten wie der *Časopis českého museum* (erscheint seit 1823 bis heute mit wechselnden Titeln in Prag) den synkretischen Charakter der Slavischen Philologie wider.

Die zweite Etappe begann mit der Gründung von slavistischen Lehrstühlen. In Rußland wurden 1835 'Katheder für Geschichte und Literatur der slavischen Mundarten' in St. Petersburg, Moskau, Kazan' und Char'kov eingerichtet, die aber mit einer Ausnahme (Moskau) wegen des Fehlens ausgebildeter Slavisten zuerst nicht besetzt wurden. Deshalb schickte man Anwärter auf die Professuren, darunter Izmail Ivanovič Sreznevskij (1812–1880) und Viktor Ivanovič Grigorovič (1815–1876), auf längere Bildungsreisen, auf denen sie Sprachen, Dialekte und volkstümliche Lebensweise der Slaven kennenlernten, die Handschriftensammlungen studierten, Handschriften erwarben und Kontakt zu berühmten Slavisten und Sprachwissenschaftlern aufnahmen. Bereits 1841 erließ der preußische König Friedrich Wilhelm IV. eine Kabinettsorder, die die Errichtung von Lehrstühlen in Berlin und Breslau vorsah, doch konnte zunächst nur in Breslau eine Besetzung mit František Ladislav Čelakovský (1799–1852) erfolgen. In Österreich kam es 1849 zur Gründung von Lehrkanzeln in Wien, wohin Franz Miklosich berufen wurde, und Prag, wohin Čelakovský wechselte.

2. Objektbereich und Gegenstände

2.1. Besonders in der ersten Etappe der Geschichte der Slavischen Philologie wurde immer wieder die Frage erörtert, wieviel slavische Sprachen es überhaupt gebe, wie ihr gegenseitiges Verhältnis sei und ob es sich nicht vielleicht um eine slavische Sprache mit mehreren Dialekten handele. Die letztere Annahme reflektieren u. a. Titel wie Šafáriks *Geschichte der slawischen Sprache und Literatur*; auch Dobrovský sprach meist von der slavischen Sprache und ihren Mundarten usw. Neben der politischen Absicht, mit diesem Sprachgebrauch die Einheit der 'slavischen Stämme' bzw. der 'slavischen Nation' hervorzuheben, gab dazu auch die große materielle und strukturelle Nähe der Slavinen Veranlassung. Noch am Anfang des 19. Jh. waren zudem nicht einmal alle slavischen Idiome bekannt. Das Beispiel des Bulgarischen zeigt, daß die Wissensdefizite z. T. erst nach Jahrzehnten überwunden wurden. So reihte zwar August Ludwig von Schlözer (1735–1809) das Bulgarische schon 1771 in die slavischen 'Dialekte' ein, doch noch Dobrovský wußte wegen des Fehlens von Sprachdaten wenig mit ihm anzufangen. Erste Specimina eines Dialekts (von Razlog in Südwestbulgarien), die die Eigenständigkeit des Bulgarischen gegenüber dem Serbischen bezeugten, lieferte Vuk Karadžić (1787–1861) in einem *Nachtrag zu den St.-Petersburger vergleichenden Wörterbüchern* (1822). Die Kenntnis dieser Sprache nahm seit den 30er Jahren zu, aber erst 1852 erschien mit der *Grammatik der bulgarischen Sprache* der Brüder Anton (ca.

1823 – ca. 1866) und Dragan (1828 – 1911) Kiriak Cankof eine verläßliche Beschreibung. Wenn es im Falle des Bulgarischen darum ging, elementare Daten zu erhalten, so war ein anderes Problem wegen der ungeklärten strukturellen und funktionalen Kriterien kaum lösbar: das des Grades der Individualität und Selbständigkeit mehr oder minder gut bekannter Idiome, wie des Sorbischen, für das Kollár noch 1836/37 eine Überdachung durch die polnische oder tschechische Schriftsprache für empfehlenswert hielt, oder des Slowakischen, auf dessen spezifische Unterschiede zum Tschechischen die gebürtigen Slowaken Šafárik und Kollár in ihren Arbeiten zwar hingewiesen hatten, sich aber dennoch gegen den Ausbau einer selbständigen slowakischen Schriftsprache wandten, den Ĺudovit Štúr (1815 – 1856) 1846 nach dem gescheiterten Versuch von Anton Bernolák (1762 – 1813) am Ende des 18. Jh.s unternahm. Am Ende der ersten Etappe lag das Inventar der slavischen Einzelsprachen, denen allerdings ein verschiedener Status zuerkannt wurde, in Šafáriks 'Slavischer Ethnographie' (1842), die aber vor allem linguistische Themen behandelt, vollständig vor.

Eine erste Klassifikation der slavischen Sprachen in zwei 'Ordnungen' hatte Dobrovský bereits 1791 vorgenommen. Der Ordnung A teilte er die ost- und südslavischen Sprachen, der Ordnung B die westslavischen Sprachen zu. Bemerkenswert ist die ständige Vervollkommnung seiner Argumentation: während er sich bei der ersten Vorstellung der Klassifikation (1791 und 1792) mit einer bloßen Nennung der Sprachen begnügte, führte er später phonetische, morphologische und auch lexikalische Merkmale ein, die von fünf (1818, in der letzten Fassung der *Geschichte der böhmischen Sprache und älteren Literatur*) auf neun (1819, in der 2. Auflage des *Ausführlichen Lehrgebäudes*) und schließlich auf zehn (1822 in den *Institutiones*) vermehrt wurden. An der Zweiteilung der Slavia hielten Šafárik und auch Schleicher fest, der die Beziehungen in Form eines Stammbaums darstellte, doch schon 1820 machte Vostokov in seiner 'Abhandlung über die (altkirchen)slavische Sprache' darauf aufmerksam, daß im Russischen auch drei der von Dobrovský als nur westslavisch angesehenen Merkmale auftreten. Er wies dem Russischen eine Zwischenstellung zwischen Süd- und Westslavisch zu, wandte sich aber nicht grundsätzlich gegen die Dichotomie. Entschiedener für eine Dreiteilung der Slavia sprach sich J. Grimm 1823 in seiner Rezension zu Dobrovskýs *Institutiones* aus (Lötzsch 1984). Seit den 30er Jahren des 19. Jh.s wurde diese Klassifikation allmählich zur gängigen Lehrmeinung, wird aber bis in die Gegenwart immer wieder in Frage gestellt.

2.2. Im engen Zusammenhang mit den unter 2.1. erörterten Problemen stand die Diskussion um die Einordnung des Altkirchenslavischen, das in der ersten Etappe entsprechend dem Sprachnamen in den Quellen – slověnsk – meist einfach als Slavonische Mundart (Schlözer), slavonische Kirchensprache, lingua slavica dialecti veteris (Dobrovský) und ähnlich bezeichnet wurde. Schlözer gab offen zu: "Ich weis auch nicht, ob sich dieselbe zu den noch lebenden Dialekten verhalte wie eine alte Sprache zur neuen, wie Otfrid zu Luthern; oder ob sie ein ganz eigener Dialekt sei; Ist sie die Sprache, in der Cyrillus predigte und übersetzte, so muß man sie in der Bulgarey suchen". Dobrovský, der diese Stelle zitiert, bemerkte dazu: "Die slawonische Kirchensprache ist kein eigner, sondern der altservische Dialekt" (*Slovanka* 1814: 168). Damit wandte er sich auch gegen die Auffassung, daß das Altkirchenslavische als slavische 'Ursprache' anzusehen sei. 1817 schloß sich in Rußland Mixail Trofimovič Kačenovskij (1775 – 1842) dieser Meinung an; bekräftigt wurde sie von Vostokov (1820 in der 'Abhandlung'), der nachwies, daß auch Altkirchenslavisch und Russisch einander zwar sehr nahestehende, aber von Anfang verschiedene Sprachen sind. In seiner quellenkritischen Untersuchung zu Leben und Werk der Slavenlehrer Kyrill und Method kam Dobrovský (1823: 133) zu dem Schluß, daß die Sprache Kyrills der "alte, noch unvermischte serbisch-bulgarisch-macedonische Dialekt" gewesen sei. Vostokov brachte jedoch schon 1820 sprachliche Argumente für die bulgarische Grundlage der ältesten slavischen Schriftsprache vor (s. Keipert 1996). In der deutschen Slavistik bezeichnete sie Schleicher als Altbulgarisch, ihm folgte darin sein Schüler Leskien, doch konnte erst Jagić, gestützt auf die Resultate von Vatroslav Oblaks (1864 – 1896) Studien der slavischen Dialekte in der Nähe von Thessaloniki und auf seine eigene profunde Kenntnis des Altkirchenslavischen endgültig beweisen, daß die Sprache Kyrills und Methods eine bulgarisch-makedonische Grundlage hat (*Entstehungsgeschichte der kirchenslavischen Sprache* 1900; 2. Aufl. 1913). Unter den verschiedenen anderen Hypothesen über die sprachliche Zugehörigkeit des Altkirchenslavischen fand die 'pannonische Theorie' Kopitars die meisten Anhänger. Ihr Kern besteht in der Annahme, daß das Altkirchenslavische die älteste Sprachform des Slowenischen ist. Entsprechend wurde es auch Altslowenisch genannt. In Kopitars Beweisführung spielten insbesondere christliche Termini westlicher Herkunft, die auch im Slowenischen vorhanden sind, eine wichtige Rolle. Kopitars Hypothese übernahm sein Schüler Miklosich, der sie dahin gehend modifizierte, daß er auch das Bulgarische zur Tochtersprache des 'Altslowenischen' erklärte.

Im gesamten hier betrachteten Zeitraum waren das Werk der Slavenlehrer Kyrill und Method sowie die beiden alten slavischen Schriften — die kyrillische und die glagolitische —, die kirchenslavischen Sprach- und Literaturdenkmäler, ihre Sammlung, Beschreibung, Untersuchung und Interpretation Schlüsselgegenstände der Slavistik, und sie blieben auch danach wichtig, denn die meisten ältesten Sprachdenkmäler des Altkirchenslavischen wurden erst in der zweiten Hälfte des 19. und am Anfang des 20. Jh.s bekannt und in auch den Anforderungen der Linguistik genügenden Editionen allgemein zugänglich. Das Fundament der wissenschaftlichen Paläoslavistik hatten aber schon Dobrovský, Kopitar, Vostokov und Šafárik gelegt. Dobrovský verfaßte auf der Grundlage der ihm zugänglichen Quellen die erste wissenschaftliche Grammatik des Altkirchenslavischen, die *Institutiones* (1822, zu ihrer wissenschaftlichen Bedeutung vgl. Večerka 1995: 257). Vostokovs altkirchenslavische Grammatik erschien 1863 und wurde wegen ihrer rein deskriptiven, nichtkomparativistischen Zielsetzung von vielen schon als überholt betrachtet. Hohe wissenschaftliche Maßstäbe setzte seine Edition des Ostromir-Evangeliums, des ältesten in Rußland geschriebenen kirchenslavischen Denkmals (1056/57). Er begründete damit eine Tradition, die von Sreznevskij, Fedor Ivanovič Buslaev (1818–1897) u. a. fortgeführt wurde.

Im Gegensatz zu Dobrovský hielten Kopitar — er edierte 1836 den Glagolita Clozianus — und J. Grimm die Glagolica für mindestens ebenso alt wie die Kyrillica. Ihre Priorität wurde dann von Šafárik (1858) bewiesen (ausführlich dazu Jagić 1913: 182–205). Die Klärung des Alters der beiden Schriften zugunsten der Glagolica, deren Herkunft allerdings bis heute dunkel bleibt, hatte große linguistische Relevanz, erlaubte sie doch die Eingrenzung der Quellen, die den ältesten Zustand des Kirchenslavischen repräsentierten. Die kritisch-philologische Beschreibung dieses Zustandes war eine der wichtigsten Voraussetzungen für die Rekonstruktion des Urslavischen und damit für die Einbeziehung des slavischen Sprachmaterials in die vergleichende Untersuchung der indogermanischen Sprachen.

3. Beschreibung der slavischen Einzelsprachen

3.1. Seit Mitte des 18. Jh. nahmen Grammatikschreibung und Lexikographie einen sichtbaren Aufschwung. Das entsprach praktischen Bedürfnissen und hatte auch symbolischen Wert, denn das Vorhandensein von Grammatik und Wörterbuch wies eine Sprache als literarisches Idiom aus. Ein wichtiges Anliegen war die Kodifikation der Schriftsprache, die je nach dem Stand der Herauskristallisierung der Normen stärker präskriptiven oder stärker deskriptiven Charakter hatte. Viele Grammatiken sollten dabei als praktische Hilfsmittel einerseits die bessere Beherrschung der Muttersprache fördern, andererseits Sprechern anderer Sprachen das Erlernen der slavischen Sprache erleichtern. Theoretische Basis und Gegenstände der Grammatikschreibung lassen mehrere Traditionslinien erkennen. In Rußland hatte Mixail Vasil'evič Lomonosovs (1711–1765) *Rossijskaja grammatika* (1755/57; in deutscher Übersetzung von J. L. Stavenhagen als *Russische Grammatik* 1764) eine eigene Tradition begründet, die über Anton Alekseevič Barsov (1730–1791) zu Vostokovs Grammatiken (1831) führte. Im Habsburgerreich spielten deutsche Schulgrammatiken eine wichtige Vorbildrolle (Keipert 1991). Große Wirkung ging von Johann Christoph Adelungs *Umständlichem Lehrgebäude der Deutschen Sprache zur Erläuterung der deutschen Sprachlehre für Schulen* (1782) aus. Ihre Rezeption ist in Kopitars slowenischer Grammatik (1808) und auch in Vuk Karadžićs Grammatik des Serbischen (1814, erweiterte Fassung 1818; deutsche Übersetzung von J. Grimm 1824) offensichtlich. Dobrovskýs *Ausführliches Lehrgebäude der böhmischen Sprache* (1809; überarbeitete Fassung 1819) weist schon im Titel auf Adelung hin, dem Dobrovský in mancher Beziehung folgte. Es war die erste umfassende Deskription des

Baus des modernen Tschechischen. Dobrovský behandelte systematisch Phonetik, Wortbildung (in einer für eine slavische Sprache bislang nicht erreichten Vollständigkeit), Morphologie (mit einer neuen Ordnung der Deklinationstypen und Konjugationsklassen) und Syntax. Seine Grammatik wurde zum Vorbild für Grammatiken, z. B. des Slowenischen, Polnischen und des Russischen. Sie waren eine gute Grundlage für die vergleichende Untersuchung der slavischen Sprachen, denn sie boten trotz mancher präskriptiver Regeln eine adäquate Darstellung des Sprachsystems. Außerhalb des Paradigmas der Slavischen Philologie, aber mit großem Einfluß auf den Unterricht in den Schulen und z. T. auch rezipiert in der oben skizzierten Grammatikschreibung, lieferte etwa zwischen 1770 und 1830 die Universalgrammatik insbesondere in Polen (Urbańczyk 1993) sowie in Rußland (Biedermann & Freidhof 1988) die theoretische Basis zahlreicher Grammatiken.

Mit der allmählichen Durchsetzung des linguistischen historisch-vergleichenden Paradigmas wurde die Beschreibung der Gegenwartssprache mit sprachgeschichtlichen Erklärungen und inner- und außerslavischen Vergleichen verknüpft. Eine der frühesten und wichtigsten Grammatiken dieser Art ist der 'Versuch einer historischen Grammatik des Russischen' (1859) von Buslaev, die zwar viele neue Angaben über die Veränderungen der Laute und Formen des Russischen enthielt, tatsächlich aber eine Grammatik des modernen Russisch vor historisch-vergleichendem Hintergrund war. Die Muttersprache wurde im Unterschied zu den klassischen und den modernen Fremdsprachen nicht mehr als Mittel zum Textverständnis unterrichtet, sondern als wissenschaftlicher Gegenstand betrachtet, dessen Verständnis ohne Berücksichtigung seiner Geschichte unmöglich sei, wie Jagić in seiner kroatischen Schulgrammatik (1864) deklarierte.

3.2. Die lexikographische Erfassung des Wortschatzes der slavischen Sprachen von den Anfängen bis zur Gegenwart wird im Band *Wörterbücher* des HSK (Hausmann & al. 1990) ausführlich beschrieben. An dieser Stelle sollen einige Wörterbücher vorgestellt werden, die im Zusammenhang mit der Entstehung und frühen Entwicklung der Slavischen Philologie stehen, sich an ihren damaligen Fragestellungen und Aufgaben orientieren und heute noch wichtige Hilfsmittel sind.

Diese Wörterbücher unterscheiden sich entsprechend dem Stand der Slavistik und der sprachlichen Situation in den einzelnen slavischen Sprachräumen in Hinblick auf Merkmale wie präskriptiv/deskriptiv, schriftsprachlich/volkssprachlich ausgerichtet, die historische und vergleichende Dimension berücksichtigend/synchron-einzelsprachlich angelegt und im Aufbau der Wortartikel, insbesondere der Bedeutungsangaben. Ihnen allen ist gemeinsam, daß sie anders als die Lexika der vorangehenden Jahrhunderte nicht vorwiegend praktischen Bedürfnissen dienen sollten, sondern als philologisch-linguistische Nachschlagewerke konzipiert wurden.

Als erstes großes lexikographisches Werk, das der Periode der Herausbildung der Slavischen Philologie zuzurechnen ist, erschien 1807—1815 das 'Wörterbuch der polnischen Sprache' von Samuel Bogumił Linde mit ca. 60 000 Wörtern. Es hat deskriptiven Charakter, berücksichtigt vorzugsweise den Wortschatz des geschriebenen Polnisch zwischen 1550 und 1800 mit vielen Belegen und führt Parallelen aus anderen slavischen Sprachen an (Linde arbeitete später auch an einem vergleichenden slavischen Wörterbuch, von dem aber 1845 nur ein Probeheft erschien). Die Bedeutungserklärungen sind polnisch, oft werden auch deutsche Äquivalente genannt. Lindes Wörterbuch diente Josef Jungmann (1773—1847) als Vorbild für dessen 'Tschechisch-Deutsches Wörterbuch' (1835—1839). Auch hier wird älteres Wortgut, wenn auch in geringerem Maße als bei Linde, verzeichnet. Wesentlich stärker ist der präskriptive Aspekt ausgeprägt. Jungmann verfolgte mit seinem Wörterbuch vornehmlich das Ziel, zum Ausbau der Wortschatzes der tschechischen Standardsprache beizutragen. Es enthält deswegen auch zahlreiche Neologismen. Die Anführung deutscher Äquivalente sollte nicht nur die Bestimmung der Bedeutung erleichtern, sondern auch ihre Ersetzung durch das tschechische Stichwort fördern. Im Zusammenhang mit der von ihm eingeleiteten Reform der serbischen Schriftsprache entstand das 'Serbisch-Deutsch-Lateinische Wörterbuch' von Vuk Karadžić (1818; die erste Fassung enthielt über 26 000, die zweite von 1852 über 42 000 Wörter). Vuk, der die Schriftsprache auf eine volkssprachliche Basis stellte, verzichtete bis auf wenige Ausnahmen auf die damals im serbischen Schrifttum sehr verbreiteten kirchenslavischen bzw. russischen Lehnwörter und gab statt dessen der volkssprachlichen Lexik und dem Wortschatz der Folklore breiten Raum. Ganz auf die Standardsprache, insbesondere auf ihre buchsprachliche Schicht, orientierte dagegen das große Wörterbuch der kirchenslavischen und russischen Sprache der Russischen Akademie (*Slovar' cerkovno-slavjanskogo i russkogo jazyka*, 1847), das vor allem wegen der sorgfältigen Ausarbeitung der Wortartikel, insbesondere der grammatischen Angaben und der präzisen Bedeutungsangaben, als für seine Zeit bestes Wörterbuch bewertet wird. Kritisiert wurde allerdings die Aufnahme obsoleten kirchenslavischen Wortgutes und die spärliche Berücksichtigung der Lexik und des Wortgebrauchs der bedeutendsten zeitgenössischen Autoren (Rozanova 1998). Als Gegenstück zum präskriptiven Akademie-Wörterbuch legte Vladimir Ivanovič Dal' (1801–1872) sein 'Wörterbuch der lebenden großrussischen Sprache' (1863–1866) an, in dem er den Reichtum der russischen Volkssprache, d. h. der Dialekte, bei Berücksichtigung der volkstümlichen Fachausdrücke, zeigen wollte. Das Wörterbuch enthielt in seiner ersten Fassung etwa 200 000 Lexeme (in den späteren Auflagen etwa 220 000) und war für lange Zeit das größte Lexikon einer slavischen Sprache. Das Prinzip der Versammlung stammverwandter Wörter in einem Wortartikel ("Nestverfahren") hatte zum Ziel, die starke Entfaltung der Derivation im Russischen zu belegen, erschwerte aber die Benutzung des Wörterbuchs, so daß J. Baudouin de Courtenay in der 3. Auflage zusätzlich die alphabetische Anordnung der Wörter mit Verweisen auf das Wortnest einführte. Zu den lexikographischen Arbeiten der Russischen Akademie gehörten auch zwei Wörterbücher der (groß)russischen mundartlichen Lexik, bescheiden als 'Versuch ...' und 'Ergänzung zum Versuch ...' betitelt (1852 und 1858, zusammen etwa 40 000 Wörter), in denen die Verbreitung der Wörter angegeben wird. An den Dialektwörterbüchern war auch Vostokov, der spiritus rector des Akademie-Wörterbuches von 1847, beteiligt, ihre Konzeption war jedoch das Werk von Sreznevskij. Als russisches Dialektwörterbuch wurde auch das 'Wörterbuch der weißrussischen Mundart' (30 000 Wörter) betrachtet, das das Ergebnis jahrzehntelanger Sammelarbeit von Ivan Nosovič (1788–1877) war. Insgesamt befand sich die slavische Mundartlexikographie noch in den Anfängen. Volkstümliches Wortgut wurde zwar in einigen der beschriebenen Wörterbücher, z. T. vorrangig, gesammelt, aber in der Regel nicht mit dem Ziel, die räumliche Gliederung des Wortschatzes der jeweiligen Sprache darzustellen, sondern um Grundlagen für den Aufbau und die Bereicherung der standardsprachlichen Lexik zu schaffen. Das gilt auch für das deskriptive Wörterbuch der bulgarischen Volkssprache mit über 70 000 Wörtern von Najden Gerov (1823–1900). Er begann die Arbeit an dem Wörterbuch in den 50er Jahren, doch konnte es erst am Ende des 19. Jh.s erscheinen. Wie Vuks Wörterbuch ist es frei von puristischen Tendenzen – es werden z. B. zahlreiche türkische Entlehnungen dokumentiert (und ebenfalls besonders markiert) –, es belegt den Folklorewortschatz mit zahlreichen Zitaten, doch wird die Verbreitung der eigentlichen Dialektwörter nicht vermerkt. Eine Besonderheit des Lexikons ist die eigenwillige, etymologische Rechtschreibung.

Auf die Wörterbücher älterer Sprachzustände wird im folgenden Abschnitt eingegangen.

3.3. Im dem hier betrachteten Zeitraum zwischen 1780 und 1860 wurden sprachgeschichtliche Forschungen im engen Zusammenhang mit der Untersuchung der Sprachdenkmäler betrieben; denn schon bald wurde erkannt, daß die systematische Darstellung älterer Sprachzustände, die Nachzeichnung von Veränderungen im Sprachbau und im Wortschatz und die Sprachvergleichung unter Heranziehung der ältesten Belege nur nach gründlicher Kenntnis vieler Denkmäler und ihrer sprachlichen Eigenheiten möglich waren. Kennzeichnend dafür war der wissenschaftliche Weg Vostokovs, der in seinen frühen Jahren an einem etymologischen Wörterbuch des Russischen bzw. Slavischen arbeitete, dieses Vorhaben aber zugunsten der Beschäftigung mit den Sprachdenkmälern aufgab. Vostokov begründete in Rußland mit einer Grammatik und einem Wortindex zur Edition des Ostromir-Evangeliums (1843) das Genre der umfassenden sprachlichen Charakteristik von Texten. In der gleichen Forschungsrichtung standen Šafáriks *Serbische Lesekörner* (1833; er wies hier nach, daß das Altserbische und das Altkirchenslavische verschiedene Sprachen waren) und die *Počátkové staročeské mluvnice* (1845; deutsch 1847: *Elemente der altböhmischen Grammatik*), mit der Besonderheit, daß sie auf mehreren Texten beruhten, von denen sich einige später als patriotische Fälschungen herausstellten.

Die Aufgaben einer zu schaffenden Geschichte des Russischen wurden explizit von

Sreznevskij in seinen 'Gedanken zur Geschichte der russischen Sprache' (1849) formuliert. Es waren: eine vollständige komplexe Analyse jedes Sprachdenkmals; allseitige Beschreibung der Dialekte; grammatische, lexikalische und stilistische Beschreibung der modernen Sprachen; Vergleich der slavischen Sprachen mit den indogermanischen Sprachen. Die systematische Abarbeitung dieses Programms blieb der junggrammatischen Periode vorbehalten. Sreznevskij selbst leistete einen bedeutenden Beitrag mit zahlreichen Editionen und Untersuchungen von Handschriften, ganz besonders aber mit seinem bis heute nicht vollständig ersetzten Wörterbuch des Altrussischen, an dem er seit den 60er Jahren arbeitete; es erschien nach seinem Tode von 1893 bis 1912. Umfangreiche Wörterbücher des Altkirchenslavischen und späterer Redaktionen schufen Miklosich (1850; 1863) und Vostokov (1858–1863).

4. Vergleichende slavische Sprachwissenschaft

Elemente des Sprachvergleichs waren schon in der Versuchen einer Gruppierung der Einzelsprachen enthalten. 1820 entdeckte Vostokov in seiner Abhandlung über das (Altkirchen)slavische durch dessen Vergleich mit dem Polnischen und Polabischen, daß die altkirchenslavischen sog. Jus-Buchstaben Nasalvokale bezeichneten und wies nach, daß die sog. Jer-Buchstaben keineswegs nur graphische Zeichen wie im Russischen waren, sondern Lautwert besaßen. Für eine systematische vergleichende Darstellung der Grammatik mußte die empirische Forschung aber mehr Daten liefern (vgl. Abschnitt 3 und 4). In der ersten Etappe der Slavischen Philologie galt als vordringliche Aufgabe aber nicht eine vergleichende Grammatik, sondern ein allgemeines slavisches Etymologikon, ein Verzeichnis der Wurzelwörter und Stammsilben. Die Idee zu einem solchen Werk stammte noch aus der Zeit, als man Sprachverwandtschaft vor allem durch Wortgleichungen erweisen wollte. Diesem Anliegen widmete Dobrovský viel Zeit und Kraft, ohne das Werk vollenden zu können. Eine Fortsetzung versuchten Čelakovský und Šafárik. Vermutlich gab Šafárik, der in den 40er Jahren mehrere längere Aufsätze zur slavischen Phonetik und Struktur der Wurzeln veröffentlicht hatte, sein Vorhaben auf, als Miklosich mit seinen sprachvergleichenden Arbeiten, den *Radices linguae slovenicae veteris dialecti* (1845), in denen er die slavischen Wurzeln besonders mit ihren Entsprechungen im Sanskrit verglich, und vor allem mit der Vergleichenden Grammatik auf den Plan trat. Dieses umfangreiche, ungemein materialreiche Werk, in dem die Phonetik, Stammbildungs- und Formenlehre sowie die Syntax (im wesentlichen die Kasussyntax) der slavischen Sprachen unter Bezug auf die indogermanischen Gegebenheiten dargestellt wurden, markierte den Übergang zu einem autonomen linguistischen Paradigma. Das zweite programmatische Werk war die kirchenslavische Grammatik Schleichers. Lautlehre, Stammbildung und Formenlehre wurden hier zum ersten Mal an Hand des Materials von Miklosich (in den *Radices*, in der ersten Fassung seines kirchenslavischen Wörterbuchs (1850) und in der im gleichen Jahr erschienenen kirchenslavischen Laut- und Formenlehren) aus der Sicht des Indogermanistik interpretiert (Dietze 1966). Schleicher plante eine vergleichende Grammatik der slavischen Sprachen, "in welcher auch die reconstruction der slawischen grundsprache versucht werden soll" (Vorrede zur *Laut- und Formenlehre der polabischen Sprache* 1871: V), die er wegen seines frühen Todes jedoch nicht vollenden konnte.

5. Literatur (in Auswahl)

A. Primärliteratur

Baudouin de Courtenay, Jan. 1868. "Einige Fälle der Wirkung der Analogie in der polnischen Declination". *Beiträge zur Vergleichenden Sprachforschung* 6.19–88.

Buslaev, Fedor Ivanovič. 1859. *Opytističeskoj grammatiki ruskogo jazyka. Č. I. Ėtimologija. Č. II. Sintaksis.* Moskau: Universitetskaja tipografija (Nachdruck der 5. Aufl. 1881 mit dem Titel *Istoričeskaja grammatika russkogo jazyka* Moskau: Gosudarstvennoe izdatél'stvo učebno-pedagogičeskoj literatury Ministerstva prosveščenija RSFSR, 1959.)

Dal', Vladimir Ivanovič. 1863–1866. *Tolkovyj slovar' živogo velikorusskogo jazyka.* 4 Bde. Moskau. Bd. 1: Tipografija Semena; Bde. 2 & 3: Tipografija Lazarevskogo instituta vostočnych jazykov; Bd. 4: Tipografija Risa. (2. Aufl. St.-Petersburg & Moskau: Vol'f, 1880–1882; von dieser Ausgabe seit 1955 mehrere Nachdrucke; 3. Aufl. hrg. von J. Baudouin de Courtenay. St.-Petersburg & Moskau: Vol'f, 1903–1909, davon Nachdrucke in Rußland seit 1994.)

Dobrovský, Josef. 1791. "Geschichte der böhmischen Sprache". Prag: *Neuere Abhandlungen der k.*

böhmischen Gesellschaft der Wissenschaften: Abt. Zur Diplomatik. Altertumskunde und Geschichte, T. II. 311−364; 1792. *Geschichte der Böhmischen Sprache und Litteratur.* Prag: Johann Gottfried Calve; 1818. *Geschichte der Böhmischen Sprache und ältern Literatur.* Prag: Gottlieb Haase. (Edition als *Dějiny české řeči a literatury v redakcích z roku 1791, 1792 a 1818*, hrg. von Benjamin Jedlička. Prag: Nákladem komise pro vydávání spisů Josefa Dobrovského při Královské české společnosti nauk. V generální komisi nakladatelství Melantrich, 1936.)

−. 1809. *Ausführliches Lehrgebäude der Böhmischen Sprache, zur gründlichen Erlernung derselben für Deutsche, zur vollkommenern Kenntniß für Böhmen.* Prag: Johann Herrl; 1819. *Lehrgebäude der Böhmischen Sprache. Zum Teile verkürzt, zum Teile umgearbeitet und vermehrt.* Prag: Gottlieb Haase. (Edition als *Podrobná mluvnice jazyka českého v redakcích z roků 1809, 1819.* Prag. Nákladem Komise pro vydávání spisů Josefa Dobrovského při Královské české společnosti nauk. V generální komisi nakladatelství Melantrich, 1940.)

−. 1822. *Institutiones linguae slavicae dialecti veteris.* Wien: Antonius Schmid (Edition von Miloš Weingart, *Dobrovského "Institutiones".* 3 Bde. Bratislava: Universita Komenského, 1923−1925.)

−. 1823. *Cyrill und Method der Slawen Apostel. Ein historisch-kritischer Versuch.* Prag: Gottlieb Haase (Edition als *Cyril a Metod apoštolové slovanští.* Poznámkami opatřil Josef Vajs. Prag: Nákladem Komise pro vydávání spisů Josefa Dobrovského při Královské české společnosti nauk. V generální komisi nakladatelství Melantrich, 1948.)

Dopolnenie k Opytu oblastnogo velikorusskogo jazyka. St.-Petersburg: Tipografija Imperatorskoj akademii nauk, 1858. (Nachdruck, Leipzig: Zentralantiquariat der Deutschen Demokratischen Republik, 1970.)

Fortunatov, Filipp Fedorovič. 1919. *Lekcii po fonetike staroslavjanskogo (cerkovnoslavjanskogo) jazyka.* St.-Petersburg: Otdelenie russkogo jazyka i slovesnosti. Rossijskaja akademija nauk. (Nachdruck in: Fortunatov, F. F. *Izbrannye trudy*, T. 2:3−256. Moskau: Gosudarstvennoe izdatel'stvo učebno-pedagogičeskoj literatury Ministerstva prosveščenija RSFSR, 1957.)

Gerov, Najden. 1895−1908. *Rečnik na bălgarskij ezik s tălkuvanie rečite na bălgarski i na ruski.* 5 Bde. & Supplement. Plovdiv: Bde. 1−5: Pečatnica Săglasie; Supplement: Pečatnica Trud na Petko Beloveždov. (Nachdruck, Sofia: Bălgarski pisatel, 1975−1978.)

Jagić, Vatroslav. 1864. *Gramatika jezika hèrvatskoga, osnovana na starobugarskoj sloveňstini.* Dio pèrvi: *Glasovi.* Zagreb: A. Jakić.

Jungmann, Josef. 1835−1839. *Slovník česko-německý.* 5 Bde. Prag: V knížecí arcibiskupské knihtiskárně, u Josefy vdovy Fettlerlové, řízením Václava Špinky. (Nachdruck, hrg. von Jan Petr, Prag: Academia, 1989−1990.)

Karadžić, Vuk Stefanović. 1818. *Srpski rječnik istolkovan njemačkim i latinskim riječma.* Wien: bei den P. P. Armeniern, 1818. (2., wesentlich erweiterte Auflage Wien: Typis Congregationis mechitaristicae, 1852; 3. wiederum erweiterte, sog. Staatsausgabe, Belgrad: U Štamparije Kraljevine Srbije, 1898.)

[Karadžić, Vuk]. 1822. Stevanović, Vuk. *Dodatak k Sanktpeterburgskim Sravniteljnim rječnicima s osobitim ogledima bugarskog jezika.* Wien: o. V. (Nachdruck in *Sabrana dela Vuka Karadžića. Knj. 13. O jeziku i književnosti II*: 113−178, 540−545. Beograd: Prosveta, 1986.)

−. 1824. *Wuk's Stephanowitsch kleine Serbische Grammatik verdeutscht und mit einer Vorrede von Jacob Grimm.* Leipzig & Berlin: G. Reimer. (Nachdruck als Karadžić, Vuk Stefanović. *Kleine Serbische Grammatik übersetzt und mit einer Vorrede von Jacob Grimm [1824].* Neu hrsg. u. eingeleitet von Miljan Mojašević u. Peter Rehder. München: Sagner & Beograd: Prosveta, 1974.)

Kollár, Jan. 1837. *Über die literarische Wechselseitigkeit zwischen den verschiedenen Stämmen und Mundarten der slawischen Nation* (Aus dem Slawischen, in der Zeitschrift Hronka gedruckten [1836] und ins Deutsche übertragen und vermehrt vom Verfasser). Budapest: gedruckt mit von Trattner-Károlyischen Schriften. (Edition als Kollár, Jan. *Rozpravy o slovanské vzájemnosti. Souborné vydání* uspořádal Miloš Weingart. Prag: Slovanský ústav, 1929.)

Kopitar, Bartholomäus [Jernej]. 1808. *Grammatik der Slavischen Sprache in Krain, Kärnten und Steyermark.* Laibach [Ljubljana]: Heinrich Wilhelm Korn. (Nachdruck, München: Trofenik, 1970.)

Leskien, August. 1876. *Die Declination im Slavisch-Litauischen und Germanischen.* Leipzig. Hirzel. (Nachdruck, Leipzig. Zentralantiquariat der Deutschen Demokratischen Republik, 1963.)

Linde, Samuel Bogumił. 1807−1815. *Słownik języka polskiego.* 6 Bde. Warschau: 1807−1815. (2. erweiterte Aufl. Lemberg [Lwów]: W drukarni Zakładu Ossolińskich, 1854−1860; davon Nachdruck Warschau: Państwowy Instytut Wydawniczy, 1951.)

Miklosich, Franz. 1845. *Radices linguae slovenicae veteris dialecti.* Leipzig. (Nachdruck, Den Haag: Vaduz 1970.)

−. 1850. *Lautlehre der altslovenischen Sprache.* Wien: Braumüller. (2. Auflage 1852.)

Miklosich, Franz. 1850a. *Formenlehre der altslovenischen Sprache.* Wien: Braumüller. (2. Aufl. 1854.)

−. 1850b. *Lexicon linguae slovenicae veteris dialecti.* Wien: Braumüller. (Nachdruck, München 1970.)

−. *Vergleichende Grammatik der slavischen Sprachen.* Wien: Braumüller. 1852. I: *Vergleichende Lautlehre der slavischen Sprachen.* (2. Aufl. 1879); 1875. II: *Vergleichende Stammbildungslehre der sla-*

vischen Sprachen. (Nachdruck, Heidelberg: Carl Winters Universitätsbuchhandlung, 1926); 1856. III: *Vergleichende Formenlehre der slavischen Sprachen.* (2. Aufl. 1876); 1868. IV: *Vergleichende Syntax der slavischen Sprachen.* (2. Abdruck 1883; Nachdruck, Heidelberg: Winter, 1926.)

—. 1862/1865. *Lexicon palaeoslovenico-graeco-latinum.* Wien: Braumüller. (Nachdruck, Aalen: Biblio, 1963.)

Nosovič, Ivan Ivanovič. 1870. *Slovar' belorusskogo narečija.* St.-Petersburg: Tipografija Imperatorskoj akademii nauk. (Nachdrucke, Minsk: 'Belaruskaja Saveckaja ėncyklapedija', 1983; München: Sagner, 1984—1986.)

Opyt oblastnogo velikorusskogo slovarja. St.-Petersburg: Tipografija Imperatorskoj akademii nauk, 1852. (Nachdruck, Leipzig: Zentralantiquariat der Deutschen Demokratischen Republik, 1970.)

Potebnja, Aleksandr Afanas'evič. 1862. *Mysl' i jazyk.* St.-Petersburg: Tipografija Ogrizko (Nachdruck der 3. Auflage Char'kov: Tipografija Mirnyj trud, 1913, Kiev: SINTO, 1993.)

—. *Iz zapisok po russkoj grammatike.* 1874. I: *Vvedenie.* Voronež: Tipografija Goldštejna. 1874a. II: *Sostavnye členy predloženija i ich zameny v russkom jazyke.* Char'kov: Tipografija universiteta. 1899. III: *Ob izmenii značenija i zamenach suščestvitel'nogo.* Char'kov: Tipografija universiteta. 1941. IV: *Glagol. Mestoimenie. Čislitel'noe. Predlog.* Moskau: Izdatel'stvo Akademii nauk SSSR. (Nachdruck und Edition weiterer Texte: I.—II. der 2. Auflage 1888 — Moskau: Gosudarstvennoe izdatel'stvo učebno-pedagogičeskoj literatury Ministerstva prosveščenija RSFSR, 1958; III. Moskau: Prosveščenie, 1968; IV,1 Moskau: Prosveščenie, 1985; IV,2 Moskau: Prosveščenie, 1977.)

Šafárik, Pavol Jozef. 1826. *Geschichte der slawischen Sprache und Literatur nach allen Mundarten.* Ofen [Budapest]: Mit kön. ungar. Universitätsschriften. (Nachdruck, Bautzen: VEB Domowina-Verlag, 1983.)

—. 1833. *Serbische Lesekörner oder historisch-kritische Beleuchtung der serbischen Mundart. Ein Beitrag zur slawischen Sprachkunde.* Pesth [Budapest]: C. A. Hartleben. (Nachdruck, Novi Sad: Matica Srpska, 1957.)

—. 1836—1837. *Slovanské starožitnosti.* 2 Bde. Prag: Spurný. (2. Aufl., Prag: Tempský, 1862—1863.)

—. 1842. *Slovanský národopis.* Prag: Selbstverlag. (4. Aufl., erw. Edition Prag: Nakladatelství Československé akademie věd, 1955.)

—. 1845. *Počátkové staročeské mluvnice.* Prag: Matica česká, 1847. (2. Aufl., Prag: Tempský, 1867; deutsch Leipzig: Verlag der slavischen Buchhandlung, 1847.)

—. 1858. *Über den Ursprung und die Heimat des Glagolitismus.* Prag: o. V.

Schleicher, August. 1852. *Die Formenlehre der kirchenslavischen Sprache, erklärend und vergleichend dargestellt.* Bonn: König.

—. 1871. *Laut- und Formenlehre der polabischen Sprache.* St.-Petersburg: Druckerei der Kaiserlichen Akademie der Wissenschaften. (Nachdruck, Wiesbaden: Sändig, 1967.)

Slovar' cerkovno-slavjanskogo i russkogo jazyka. 4 Bde. St.-Petersburg: Tipografija Imperatorskoj akademii nauk, 1847. (2. Aufl. 1867; Nachdruck, Leipzig: Zentralantiquariat der Deutschen Demokratischen Republik, 1972.)

Sreznevskij, Izmail Ivanovič. 1849. *Mysli ob istorii russkogo jazyka. Biblioteka dlja čtenija,* T. 98, č. 1, otd. III:1—54; č. 2:117—198. (Petersburg: Tipografija voenno-učebnyx zavedenij, 1850, Nachdruck, Moskau: Gosudarstvennoe izdatel'stvo učebno-pedagogičeskoj literatury Ministerstva prosveščenija RSFSR, 1959.)

Vostokov, Aleksandr Xristoforovič. 1820. "Rassuždenie o Slavjanskom jazyke, služaščee vvedeniem k Grammatike sego jazyka sostavljaemoj po drevnejšim onogo pis'mennym pamjatnikam". *Trudy Obščestva ljubitelej rossijskoj slovesnosti,* 17:5—61 (wieder abgedruckt in: *Filologičeskie nabljudenija A. X. Vostokova,* hrg. von I. I. Sreznevskij: 1—27. St.-Petersburg: Tipografija Imperatorskij akademii nauk, 1865.)

—. 1831. *Russkja grammatika ... po načertaniju ego Sokraščennoj grammatiki polnee izložennaja.* St.-Petersburg: Tipografija Glazunova. (12. verb. Auflage 1874.)

—. 1843. *Ostromirovo evangelie 1056—1057 goda. S priloženiem grečeskogo teksta evangelij i s grammatičeskimi ob-jasneniejami.* St.-Petersburg: Tipografija Imperatorskoj akademii nauk. (Nachdruck, Wiesbaden: Harrassowitz, 1964.)

—. 1858—1861. *Slovar' cerkovnoslavjanskogo jazyka.* 2 Bde. St.-Petersburg: Tipografija Imperatorskoj akademii nauk.

—. 1863. *Grammatika cerkovno-slovenskogo jazyka izložennaja po drevnejšim onogo pis'mennym pamjatnikam.* St.-Petersburg: Tipografija Imperatorskoj akademii nauk. (Nachdruck, Leipzig: Zentralantiquariat der Deutschen Demokratischen Republik & Köln—Wien: Böhlau, 1980.)

B. Sekundärliteratur

Biedermann, Johann & Gerd Freidhof, eds. 1988. *Texts and Studies on Russian Universal Grammar 1806—1812.* Vol III: *Linguistische, philosophische und wissenschaftsgeschichtliche Grundlagen.* München: Sagner.

Bulaxov, M. G. 1976—1978. *Vostočnoslavjanskie jazykovedy. Biobliografičeskij slovar'.* 3 Bde. Minsk: Izdatel'stvo BGU im. I. V. Lenina

Bulič, S. K. 1904. *Očerk istorii jazykoznanija v Rossii.* T. I: XVIIIv. — 1825 g. St.-Petersburg: Tipografija M. Merkuševa. (Nachdruck, München: Sagner, 1989.)

Dietze, Joachim. 1966. *August Schleicher als Slawist. Sein Leben und sein Werk in der Sicht der Indogermanistik*. Berlin: Akademie-Verlag.

D'jakov, V. A., ed. 1979. *Slavjanovedenie v dorevoljucionnoj Rossii. Biobliografičeskij slovar'*. Moskva: Nauka.

Eichler, Ernst et al., eds. 1993. *Slawistik in Deutschland von den Anfängen bis 1945. Ein biographisches Lexikon*. Bautzen: Domowina-Verlag.

Gutschmidt, Karl. 1999. "Forscherpersönlichkeiten in der sprachwissenschaftlichen Russistik". *Handbuch der sprachwissenschaftlichen Russistik und ihrer Grenzdisziplinen* hg. von Helmut Jachnow, 1106–1137. Wiesbaden: Harrassowitz.

Hausmann, Franz Josef et al. 1990. *Wörterbücher. Ein internationales Handbuch zur Lexikographie*. Berlin–New York: de Gruyter.

Jachnow, Helmut. 1999. "Zur Geschichte der Sprachwissenschaft in Rußland, der UdSSR und den slavischen GUS-Staaten". *Handbuch der sprachwissenschaftlichen Russistik und ihrer Grenzdisziplinen* hg. von Helmut Jachnow, 1024–1049. Wiesbaden: Harrassowitz.

Jagić, Vatroslav. 1900. *Zur Entstehungsgeschichte der kirchenslavischen Sprache*. Wien.

Jagić, Ignatij Vikent'evič [Vatroslav]. 1910. *Istorija slavjanskoj filologii*. St.-Petersburg: Tipografija Imperatorskoj akademii nauk.

Jagić, Vatroslav. 1913. *Entstehungsgeschichte der kirchenslavischen Sprache*. Neue berichtigte und erweiterte Auflage. Berlin: Weidemannsche Buchhandlung.

–. 1930–1934. *Spomeni mojega života*. 2 Bde. Belgrad: Štamparija 'Sveti Sava'.

Keipert, Helmut. 1991. "Die 'Wiener Anleitung' in der slavischen Grammatikographie des ausgehenden 18. Jahrhunderts". *Zeitschrift für slavische Philologie* 51,23–59.

–. 1996. "A. Ch. Vostokov, die deutsche Slavenkunde und das Altbulgarische". *Palaeobulgarica* 20,1:99–114. Sofia.

Kudělka, Milan, Zdeněk Šimeček & kolektiv. 1972. *Československé práce o jazyce, dějinách a kultuře slovanských národů od r. 1760. Biograficko-bibliografický slovník*. Prag: Státní pedagogické nakladatelství.

Lötzsch, Ronald. 1984. "Jacob Grimm und die Klassifizierung der slawischen Sprachen". *Zeitschrift für Phonetik, Sprachwissenschaft und Kommunikationsforschung* 37.283–294.

Markov, D. F. & V. A. D'jakov (Hrg.) 1988. *Slavjanovedenie v dorevoljucionnoj Rossii. Izučenie južnyx i zapadnyx slavjan*. Moskva: Nauka.

Rösel, Hubert. 1957. *Dokumente zur Geschichte der Slawistik in Deutschland*. Teil I: *Die Universitäten Berlin und Breslau im 19. Jahrhundert*. Berlin. Akademie-Verlag.

Rozanova, V. V. 1998. "Slovar' cerkovnoslavjanskogo i russkogo jazyka". *Istorija russkoj leksikografii* hg. von F. B. Sorokoletov, 163–189. St.-Petersburg: Nauka.

Večerka, Radoslav. 1995. "Slovanská jazykověda". 230–295. Kudělka, Milan, Zdeněk Šimeček & Radoslav Večerka. *Česká slavistika v prvním období svého vývoje do počátku 60. let 19. století*. Prag: o. V. [Historický ústav].

–. 1996. *Die Anfänge der slavischen Sprachwissenschaft in den böhmischen Ländern*. Regensburg: Roderer.

Urbańczyk, Stanisław. *Dwieście lat polskiego językoznawstwa (1751–1950)*. Krakau: 'Secesja'.

Zeil, Wilhelm. 1994. *Slawistik in Deutschland: Forschungen und Informationen über die Sprachen, Literaturen und Volkskulturen slawischer Völker bis 1945*. Köln–Weimar–Wien: Böhlau.

Karl Gutschmidt, Dresden (Deutschland)

162. Finno-ugrische Philologie und vergleichende Grammatik

1. Kulturhistorische Zusammenhänge
2. Finno-ugrische Forschung in Ungarn
3. Finno-ugrische Forschung in Finnland
4. Finno-ugrische Forschung in Estland
5. Bibliographie

1. Kulturhistorische Zusammenhänge

Obwohl die Ansätze einer sprachvergleichenden Forschung bereits am Ende des 18. Jhs. wegweisende und richtige Kenntnisse über die Verwandtschaft der finnisch-ugrischen Sprachen geliefert haben, herrschten am Anfang des 19. Jhs. in den nationalen Philologien der finnisch-ugrischen Völker noch sehr unterschiedliche und recht verwirrte Verhältnisse. Auch die größten Vertreter der Sprachfamilie (Ungarn, Finnen, Esten) lebten in politischer Unfreiheit, als Teile von fremden Imperien war ihre kulturelle und wissenschaftliche Entwicklung stark eingeschränkt. Diese Situation hat die Rolle der Sprache innerhalb der Gesellschaft ganz anders definiert als das in den entwickelteren Gebieten Europas zu dieser Zeit bereits der Fall war: die Sprache ist politisches Programm, Träger der nationalen Identität, ja ein Revier der Freiheit und der Größe geworden, welches für sämtliche Erniedrigungen und Leiden die menschlichen Gemeinschaften entschädigen, trösten, belohnen sollte. Unter solchen Umständen war die Entwicklung einer objektiven, wissenschaftlichen Sprachbetrachtung außerordentlich schwierig und problematisch geworden. Um das zu verändern, hatte man nicht nur einzelne Forscher, sondern Forschungs- und Bildungsstätten, fachliche Publikationsfora und fruchtbare internationale Zusammenarbeit dringend nötig. Nicht in all diesen Bereichen und nicht in allen Ländern haben sich diese Vorbedingungen zur gleichen Zeit erfüllen können. Diese Lage wurde zusätzlich erschwert dadurch, daß die Aufgabe der wissenschaftlichen Erfassung, der grammatischen Beschreibung der eigenen Muttersprache mit der Forderung nach Entdeckung der genetischen und historischen Zusammenhänge einherging. Dieser Umstand stellte seine Aufgabe in zunächst drei Bereichen dar:

(1) wissenschaftliche/grammatische Erfassung der einzelnen finnisch-ugrischen Sprachen, Sammlung des dazu geeigneten Sprachmaterials über simple Wortangaben und Vergleiche hinaus;
(2) Erstellung einer eigenen Terminologie, eigener Kriterien und Methoden auch im historischen Bereich der Morphologie, um diese Sprachen mit anderen bekannten Sprachen vergleichen zu können;
(3) Anwendung dieser Methoden im historisch-vergleichenden Sinne, Schaffung einer finnisch-ugrischen Philologie als Disziplin.

Auch bei den entwickelteren Völkern der Sprachfamilie benötigte dieser Prozeß mehr als ein Jahrhundert, um sich vollständig auszubilden, bei den kleineren Sprachen ist die Entstehung der nationalen Philologien bis heute noch nicht abgeschlossen.

2. Finno-ugrische Forschung in Ungarn

Am deutlichsten können die Widersprüche dieser Entwicklung am Beispiel Ungarns und der ungarischen Sprache gezeigt werden. Bereits Ende des 18. Jhs. haben zwei grundlegende Werke die in Spuren schon vorhandene wissenschaftliche Öffentlichkeit im Lande über die wahre Verwandtschaft des Ungarischen informiert und zugleich erschüttert. Bis dahin herrschte nämlich die Ansicht, daß das unmittelbar mit keiner anderen Sprache vergleichbare Ungarisch eine orientalische Sprache, ein Abkömmling von berühmten Kulturen des Altertums (Skythen, Hebräer, u. a. m.) sei, wie es auch György Kalmár (1726−1781) in seinem, die orientalische Verwandtschaftshypothese vertretenden Werk, *Prodromus idiomatis Scythico-Mogorico-Chvno [sev Hvvno]-Avarici sive Adparatus criticus ad linguam Hungaricam* (Posonium [heutiger Name: Bratislava]: Lederer, 1770) schilderte.

Diese stolze Vorstellung wurde jedoch gründlich erschüttert, als János Sajnovics (1733−1785) in seiner *Demonstratio: Idioma Ungarorum et Lapponum idem esse* (Kopenhagen und auch Turnau [heutiger Name: Trnava], verlegt von der Akademie der Societas Jesu, 1770) handfeste Beweise beibrachte, welche die armen Nomaden, die Lappen, als sprachlich nächste Verwandte der Ungarn vorstellte. Durch diese Verbindung entstand unter den Gelehrten eine Spaltung, deren Spuren bezüglich der Herkunft des Ungarischen unter Ungarn mit unterschiedlichen Akzenten bis in unsere Tage hinein bestehen. Zunächst haben die Vertreter der orientalischen Orientierung ihre Argumente nochmals vorgebracht, die hauptsächlich in mehreren Schriften von Pál Beregszászi Nagy (ca. 1750−1828) ausgeführt, am deutlichsten in seinem Buch *Über die Ähnlichkeit der hungarischen Sprache mit den morgenländischen* (Leipzig, 1796) zusammengefaßt wurden. Mit wenig faktischem Erfolg, denn:

"These attempts at establishing correlations, like the contemporary Western experiments, failed to meet the requirements of science in a modern sense of the word, still they had the merit of raising the question and preparing for the next period by disseminating interest in matters of language." (Szathmári 1972: 351)

Die Herausbildung geeigneter wissenschaftlicher Methoden zum Sprachvergleich hat die Bedeutung der Grammatik gegenüber dem Wortschatz in der Argumentation gestärkt. Knapp drei Jahrzehnte nach Sajnovics brachte Sámuel Gyarmathi (1751−1830) in seinem *Affinitas lingvae hvngaricae cvm lingvis fennicae originis grammatice demonstrata* (Göttingen: Dieterich, 1799) weitere grammatische Beweise, die die Suche nach Verwandten in Richtung Norden richteten: "Außer dem Lappischen bezog er sämtliche finnougrische, ja, sogar die samojedischen Sprachen in seine vergleichenden Untersuchungen ein" (Hajdú & Domokos 1987: 411). Die Methoden des Sprachvergleichs, insbesondere für die nicht-indogermanischen Sprachen, waren zu dieser Zeit noch nicht etabliert, aber Gyarmathi, der 1795/96 in Göttingen, bei August Ludwig von Schlözer (1735—1809) studiert hatte, konnte jene Elemente der Forschungsarbeit kennenlernen und in seiner Tätigkeit auch erfolgreich verwenden, die später zur Herausbildung dieser Disziplin geführt haben:

"Sie zeigte sich in der Gliederung (1799: xii). Sieben Punkte enthalten grammatische Vergleiche: Wortbildungsendungen, Deklination und Komparation, Bedeutung und Bildung der Pronomina, gesondert die Possessivsuffixe, allgemein Suffixe, Konjugation, Adverbien wie auch Postpositionen, Syntax." (Stipa 1990: 215)

Fast zeitgleich mit der geschilderten Entwicklung in der internationalen Wissenschaft, waren starke emanzipatorische Bestrebungen auch in Ungarn in Gang gesetzt worden: die Phase der 'Spracherneuerung' nach 1772 führte zu Modernisierung und Vereinheitlichung des Ungarischen, bei Entdeckung ihrer Vergangenheit sowie gewisser Gesetzmäßigkeiten ihrer Entwicklung. Dieser Prozeß fand statt unter der Leitung von Schriftstellern und Gelehrten, wie Ferenc Kazinczy (1759—1831) und Ferenc Verseghy (1757—1822), die sich als Jakobiner für die Ideen der Französischen Revolution engagierten und dafür hohe Strafen erleiden mußten. Ihre philologische, sprachwissenschaftliche Tätigkeit hat vor allem neue Wörter ins Leben gerufen, welche jedoch den gerade entdeckten Gesetzmäßigkeiten des Ungarischen entsprechen mußten. Dieses wachsende Sprachbewußtsein und die allgemeinen gesellschaftlichen Bedingungen erforderten, daß die Nationalsprache endlich auf höchster Stufe unterrichtet wurde.

Die ungarische Sprache als Fach war an der Universität von Buda/Pest seit 1791 vertreten. Die Tätigkeit dieses Lehrstuhls wurde von seinem ersten Inhaber, Miklós Révai (1750—1807) maßgeblich geprägt, der in seiner dreibändigen *Elaboratior grammatica Hungarica* (Pest: Trattner, 1803, 1805, 1908), ein Jahrzehnt vor Bopp, eine historisch-vergleichende Methode auf das Ungarische angewendet hat. Révai hat auch das seit 1770 publizierte, bis heute als ältestes Sprachdenkmal der finnisch-ugrischen Sprachfamilie geltende, am Anfang des 13. Jhs. verfaßte *Halotti Beszéd* [Leichenrede], in seine Betrachtungen einbezogen. Mit diesem Vorgehen ist Révai methodologisch Jacob Grimm (1785—1863) um 15 Jahre vorausgegangen. Geradezu revolutionär ist seine Feststellung, daß der wahre Charakter des Ungarischen und seiner bereits bekannten Verwandten mit der klassischen Terminologie des Lateins nicht beschrieben werden könne; dazu sei die Fortentwicklung der wissenschaftlichen Apparatur und Betrachtung nötig.

Die bahnbrechenden Leistungen von Révai wurden nach seinem Tod nicht fortgesetzt. Sein Nachfolger, István Horvát (1784—1846), vertrat eine romantische, jeglicher philologischen Grundlagen entbehrende Schule der nationalen Geschichtsschreibung und erschwerte somit die Adoption der international bekannten Forschungsmethoden zunächst. Herausragende Talente, wie Sándor Kőrösi Csoma (1784—1842), der die Vorfahren der Ungarn im Rahmen einer Forschungsreise durch Indien und Tibet auf der Nordseite des Himalaja zu finden hoffte, konnten ihre wissenschaftliche Ausbildung nur im Ausland vollenden. Der andere große Sammler authentischen Sprachmaterials, Antal Reguly (1819—1858), mußte sein Wissen auch erst im Ausland ergänzen, ehe er sein umfangreiches Sprachmaterial von mehreren finnisch-ugrischen Sprachen aufzeichnen konnte.

Erst mit Paul Hunfalvy (1810—1891) tritt jene Persönlichkeit in Erscheinung, die sich auch für die Wissenschaftsorganisation zielbewußt eingesetzt hat. 1840 fing er an, sich mit Fragen der Sprachwissenschaft zu beschäftigen und stellte recht schnell fest, wie groß die Kluft zwischen dem Niveau des Auslands und der Kollegen in Ungarn war. Die Revolution und der Freiheitskampf von 1848/49 sowie die darauffolgende Vergeltung verursachten eine schmerzliche Unterbrechung dieser Entwicklung. Nach 1851 wird Hunfalvy leitender Bibliothekar der 1825 gegründeten Ungarischen Akademie der Wissenschaften. Er entfaltet eine weitgefächerte Aktivität, um die Grundlagen einer vergleichenden Sprachforschung zu schaffen. Einerseits versuchte er, die ungarische Sprachwissenschaft in die internationalen Forschungsaktivitäten zu integrieren, vor allem an die deutschen historischen (J. Grimm) und vergleichenden Schulen (W. Schott) anzuknüpfen. Andererseits war er stets bemüht, endlich die Feldforschung zu fördern. Aufgrund seiner eigenen Erfahrungen bei den ostseefinnischen Völkern im Jahre 1869 hat er die Notwendigkeit der Materialsammlung erkannt.

Eine ganze Generation von jüngeren ungarischen Forschern bekam durch sein Engagement gegen Ende des Jahrhunderts die Möglichkeit, bei den verwandten Völkern zu forschen. Diese Arbeit hat schließlich jene sprachwissenschaftliche Materialmenge entstehen lassen, wodurch eine ernste und verläßliche Untersuchung der Verwandtschaft dieser Sprachen begonnen werden konnte.

Eine zentrale Rolle spielten bei Hunfalvy die von ihm initiierten und zum Teil von ihm selbst redigierten Fachzeitschriften, wie *Magyar Nyelvtudomány* [Ungarische Sprachwissenschaft] (1856—1862) und *Nyelvtudományi Közlemények* [Sprachwissenschaftliche Mitteilungen], welche 1862 die vorige ablöst und die älteste, ununterbrochen erscheinende Fachzeitschrift der Finnougristik darstellt. Diese Fora ermöglichten endlich, daß kleinere Themen eingehend, unter Berücksichtigung der internationalen Quellen und vor den Augen einer wachsenden nationalen und internationalen Fachöffentlichkeit behandelt wurden. Diese vielseitigen und intensiven Aktivitäten führten 1872 zur Gründung des ersten Lehrstuhls für "vergleichende Altaische Sprachwissenschaft" (Finnougristik) der Welt an der Universität von Pest. Die Grundlagen einer nationalen Philologie wurden gelegt, denn, wie Hunfalvy formulierte (1877: 99): "Wir müssen zu der Ueberzeugung kommen, dass Niemand ungarischer Sprachgelehrter sein könne, der in den verwandten Sprachen nicht bewandert ist."

Der wohl wichtigste Beitrag Hunfalvys für die Entwicklung der Finnougristik in Ungarn war die direkte Anbindung an die Göttinger sprachwissenschaftliche Tradition durch die Einladung eines jungen deutschen Gelehrten, Joseph, später József, Budenz (1836—1892). Er absolvierte sein Studium der griechischlateinischen Philologie und der vergleichenden indogermanischen Sprachwissenschaft in Marburg und Göttingen. Von seinen Professoren wirkte auf ihn der Professor für Sanskrit und indogermanische vergleichende Sprachwissenschaft in Göttingen, Theodor Benfey (1809—1881), am stärksten:

"Seine Methode hatte aber Budenz nicht Benfey, sondern vielmehr dem Begründer der indoeuropäischen vergleichenden Sprachwissenschaft, Franz Bopp (1791—1867) zu verdanken." (Lakó 1974: 16)

Bopps Schriften zur Indogermanistik, insbesondere seine *Vergleichende Grammatik* (1833 ff.) eröffneten neue Perspektiven in der Methodik der Forschung. In Göttingen existierte bereits zur Studienzeit von Budenz auch eine Tradition des Interesses an nichtindogermanischen Sprachen. Die Werke Wilhelm Schotts (1807—1889) zu diesem Thema waren Budenz gut bekannt; seine Aufmerksamkeit wurde jedoch durch den ersten vergleichenden Sprachforscher der Universität Wien, Anton Boller (1811—1869), auf das Ungarische gelenkt.

Budenz traf 1858 auf Einladung Hunfalvys in Ungarn ein, um Ungarisch zu lernen. Nach 1860 lehrt er bereits in Pest, beschäftigt sich intensiv mit den türkischen und finnougrischen Sprachen, 1868 wird er Privatdozent der Universität Pest. Von 1872 an leitet er dort als ordentlicher Professor zwanzig Jahre lang den Lehrstuhl für 'Vergleichende Altaische Sprachwissenschaft' (Finnougristik). Seine Vorlesungen, Aufsätze und Bücher führen zur Herausbildung einer wissenschaftlichen Schule, die die Entstehung und Fortentwicklung der Finnougristik weltweit geprägt hat.

Neben zahlreichen kleineren Publikationen hat Budenz zwei wissenschaftliche Grundwerke geschaffen. Sein Hauptwerk, *Magyar-Ugor Összehasonlító Szótár* [Ungarisch-Ugrisches Vergleichendes Wörterbuch] ist zunächst in fünf Heften zwischen 1873—1881 erschienen. Diese Arbeit kann als großangelegter Beweis für die Anwendbarkeit der modernen philologischen Methoden, als die erste umfangreiche lexikalische Bearbeitung der finnougrischen Sprachfamilie angesehen werden. 996 Wortartikel beinhalten "auch die wichtigsten Tatsachen der finnisch-ugrischen vergleichenden Laut- und Formenlehre, wenngleich nicht systematisch geordnet, sondern sporadisch in den einzelnen Wortartikeln" (Lakó 1974: 21).

Die insgesamt sieben folgenden Ausgaben dieses Wörterbuchs zeigen seine enorme Bedeutung für die Entwicklung der finnischugrischen Philologie. Budenz selbst hat seine Ziele während dieser Arbeit höher gesetzt, die vielen morphologischen Angaben deuten darauf hin, daß er auf dem Wege zur Rekonstruktion der Grundsprache der Sprachfamilie die Bedeutung der Formlehre zunehmend erkannt hat.

Sein posthum vollendetes bahnbrechendes Werk, *Az ugor nyelvek összehasonlító alaktana* [Vergleichende Morphologie der ugrischen Sprachen] (1884—1894), zeigt eindeutig den Einfluß von August Schleicher (1821—1868). Damit hat er die Beweiskraft eines bis dahin in der Forschung im Vergleich zur

Lautlehre und Lexik weniger berücksichtigten Bereichs der sprachwissenschaftlichen Untersuchungen am Beispiel des ugrischen Zweiges der Sprachfamilie überzeugend demonstriert. Die morphologischen Beweise spielten während der 80er Jahre des 19. Jahrhunderts eine entscheidende Rolle in der wissenschaftlichen Diskussion von Budenz, in dem sogenannten 'Ugrisch-Türkischen Krieg', mit dem Turkologen, Ármin Vámbéry (1832−1913). Diese Auseinandersetzung hat unter anderem geklärt, daß sprachliche, kulturelle und anthropologische Merkmale eines Volkes bei der Suche nach Verwandtschaft durchaus in unterschiedliche Richtungen verweisen können, und daß die beiden Begriffe 'Sprache' und 'Volk', getrennt zu untersuchen seien. Auf jeden Fall ist es Budenz gelungen, der ungarischen Finnougristik nicht nur Leben einzuhauchen, sondern sie zugleich zum Mitglied eines regen und methodologisch fortschrittlichen internationalen wissenschaftlichen Lebens zu machen. Nach Budenz' Tod wurden seine grundlegenden Forschungen unter Anwendung seiner positivistischen Forschungsmethoden von seinen Schülern, József Szinnyei (1857−1943), Bernát Munkácsi (1860−1937), Ignác Halász (1855−1901), Béla Vikár (1859−1945), József Balassa (1864−1945) und anderen in den einzelnen Bereichen der finnougrischen Philologie fortgesetzt.

3. Finno-ugrische Forschung in Finnland

In Finnland hat dieselbe wissenschaftliche Entwicklung unter anderen gesellschaftlichen Bedingungen stattgefunden. Die Finnen, historisch und geographisch umgeben von mehr oder weniger verwandten Sprachen und Kulturen (Vepsen, Voten, Karelier, Esten, sogar Lappen), waren nicht so isoliert in bezug auf die Erforschung der Herkunft ihrer Sprache wie die Ungarn. Infolgedessen mußten sie auch keine weitführende, mythologisierende (und somit falsche) Forschung betreiben und konnten sich auf die tatsächlich vorhandenen Spuren sprachlicher Verwandtschaft konzentrieren. So entstand um ihre Sprache durch die Forschung ein immer breiter werdender Kreis des Wissens, welcher einerseits die Kenntnisse ständig erweiterte und bestätigte, andererseits fortwährend auch neue Aufgaben stellte. Im Gegensatz zu Ungarn, war dieser Prozeß durchgehend von der Empirie bestimmt worden. Emotionen spielten nur in wichtigen Phasen der finnischen Nationalgeschichte (wie zur Zeit der Reformation oder wie i. J. 1809, als Finnland von Schweden unabhängig wurde) eine zeitweilige Rolle.

Nach langem Kampf um die Anerkennung und Anwendung des Finnischen als Kultursprache, nimmt die finnisch-ugrische Philologie in Finnland erst mit der Tätigkeit des Historikers Henrik Gabriel Porthan (1739−1804) Konturen an. Als Ergebnis seiner eigenen Untersuchungen und der Feststellungen der *Demonstratio* von János Sajnovics faßt Porthan in dem *Prooemium* der Bischofschronik (1784−1800) auf zwei Tafeln den Grad der Verwandtschaft der finnisch-ugrischen Sprachen auf Grund ihrer gegenwärtigen geographischen Lage zusammen "der durch die Zusammengehörigkeit der an die Peripherie geratenen samojedischen Sprachen mit dem gleichsam den Gegenpol bildenden Ungarischen betont wird" (Stipa 1990: 227).

Die ersten Erkenntnisse der Sprachverwandtschaft haben auch in Finnland die Bedeutung der Feldforschung klar gezeigt. Einen epochalen Aufschwung erfährt sie durch die erste Publikation des finnischen Nationalepos, *Kalevala*, von Elias Lönnrot (1802−1884) im Jahre 1835. Begeistert von dem Erfolg des *Kalevala* und in Kenntnis der indogermanistischen Werke von Franz Bopp (1791−1867) und Rasmus Kristian Rask (1787−1832) beschließt Matthias Alexander Castrén (1813−1852), neue Materialien zu sammeln und bereist 1838 von Lappen bewohnten Gebiete, dann 1839 Karelien. Der Ertrag dieser Reisen macht den im Sinne des geisigen Erbes von Porthan tätigen Anders Johan Sjögren (1794−1855) auf Castrén aufmerksam. Sjögren ist nach 1848 Mitglied der Petersburger Akademie gewesen, und als solcher konnte er wichtige Forschungsreisen durchführen: 1824−26 zu den Ostseefinnen und Lappen; 1827−28 zu den Syrjänen und Tscheremissen sowie 1846 und 1852 zu den Liven. Seine Sprachbeschreibungen sind besonders wertvoll, weil Sjögren die Daten vor Ort gesammelt hatte.

In Kenntnis der Bedeutung der Feldforschung und der Größe der zu bewältigenden Aufgaben lädt Sjögren Castrén nach Rußland ein. In zwei Forschungsreisen gelang es Castrén trotz Krankheit, das umfangreichste Sprachmaterial der finnisch-ugrischen Völker, neben Regulys Sammlung, aufzuzeichnen: 1841−44 sammelte er unter Syrjänen und vornehmlich bei den samojedischen Völkern; 1845−49 sammelte er bei den Ostjaken und Samojeden und untersuchte türkisch-tatarische Sprachen. Als Anerkennung seiner Leistungen wird Castrén 1851 zum ersten Professor am Lehrstuhl für finnische Sprache und Literatur an der Universität Helsinki ernannt. Obwohl sein früher Tod die Aufarbeitung des Materials verhindert hat, sind die Schriften von Castrén bei der Erfassung der sprachverwandtschaftlichen Verhältnisse von grundlegender Bedeutung. Seine Doktorarbeit, *De nominum declinatione in lingua Syrjaena* (1844), seine beiden Grammatiken, *Elementa grammatices Syrjaenae* (Helsinki: Simelius, 1844) und *Elementa grammatices Tscheremissae* (Kuopio: Karsten, 1845), sind wichtige Beiträge zur Erweiterung des Wissens über die permischen und volgafinnischen Sprachen. Nach einer ostjakischen Sprachlehre wollte Castrén sein samojedisches Material bearbeiten; das mußte aber Franz Anton Schiefner (1817−1879) aus Castréns Nachlaß vollenden, mit der Herausgabe der *Grammatik der Samojedischen Sprachen* (St. Petersburg: Kaiserliche Akademie der Wissenschaften, 1854). Castréns Lebenswerk hatte schon in dieser unvollendeten Form einen enormen Anstoß für die finnische Sprachwissenschaft gegeben, aber seine samojedischen Studien haben auch dazu geführt, daß die samojedischen Sprachen auch als Verwandte der finnisch-ugrischen Sprachen anerkannt wurden.

Nach dem Tode Castréns leitete Lönnrot seinen Lehrstuhl in Helsinki weiter; ihm folgte 1863 August Ahlqvist (1826−1889) auf diesem Posten. Ahlqvist hatte bereits 1854 votische, estnische und vepsische Grammatiken verfaßt sowie 1856 Mokša-mordvinische Studien veröffentlicht. Als Autor einer systematischen finnischen Sprachbeschreibung, *Suomen kielen rakennus, vertaavia kieliopillisia tutkimuksia* [Die Struktur der finnischen Sprache, vergleichende grammatikalische Forschungen] i. J. 1877 und als Entdecker der kulturhistorischen Bedeutung der sogenannten 'Kulturwörter' in seinem erst 1871 vollständig herausgegebenem *De vestfinska språkens kulturord* (Helsinki: Suomalaisen Kirjallisuuden Seura [umgearb. deutsche Ausg.: *Die Kulturwörter der westfinnischen Sprachen*. Helsinki: Wasenius, 1875]) hat Ahlqvist in der Forschung wegweisend gewirkt, während er fast ein Vierteljahrhundert lang eine neue Generation von finnischen Linguisten ausbildete.

Ahlqvists pädagogisches Werk wurde von Arvid Genetz (1848−1915) fortgesetzt, der in der Sprachforschung vor allem durch komparatistische Arbeiten bekannt wurde. Seine Wirkung wurde durch die Tätigkeit von Otto Donner (1835−1909), dem Professor für Sanskrit und indogermanische Sprachwissenschaft an der Universität Helsinki, noch gestärkt. Donners dreibändiges *Vergleichendes Wörterbuch der Finnisch-Ugrischen Sprachen* (Helsinki: Finnische Literaturgesellschaft, 1874−1888) wurde auf Grund der 'Wurzel-Theorie' der Indogermanistik konzipiert und war somit für die finnisch-ugrische Sprachforschung weniger brauchbar als das entsprechende Wörterbuch von József Budenz. Aber seine große Synthese, *Die gegenseitige Verwandtschaft der finnisch-ugrischen Sprachen* (Helsinki: Acta Societatis Scientiarum Fennica, 1879), widerlegt die von Budenz erarbeitete Theorie über die Verzweigung der einzelnen Sprachen innerhalb der Sprachfamilie und stellt an ihrer Stelle das Stammbaum-Modell auf, das sich bis heute bewährt hat. Donner hat am 15. November 1883 die *Suomalais-ugrilainen Seura* (Finnisch-Ugrische Gesellschaft) ins Leben gerufen, um der Forschung weiteren Schwung zu verleihen. Mit seinen Vorgängern hat Donner in Finnland, ähnlich wie Budenz in Ungarn, für die Ausbildung einer neuen und sehr erfolgreichen Generation gesorgt, deren wichtigste Vertreter, wie Emil Nestor Setälä (1864−1935), Heikki Paasonen (1865−1919) oder Yrjö Wichmann (868−1932), die Finnougristik des 20. Jhs. maßgeblich geprägt haben.

4. Finno-ugrische Forschung in Estland

Anfang des 19. Jhs., fast zeitgleich zu Finnland, sind auch in Estland die ersten Anzeichen der Erforschung der Nationalsprache zu vermerken. Die Tatsache, daß zu dieser Zeit beide Völker Teile des Russischen Reiches waren und zum 'Wirkungskreis' der aufgeklärten Petersburger Akademie gehörten, hat sich genauso positiv auf diese Entwicklung ausgewirkt wie die traditionelle Bindung Estlands an Deutschland und die deutsche Wissenschaft.

Die 1838 erschienene vergleichende Untersuchung von Ferdinand Johann Wiedemann (1805−1887), *Über die früheren Sitze der tschudischen Völker und ihre Sprachverwandtschaft mit den Völkern Mittelhochasiens* (Reval [heute: Tallinn]), stellt den Anfang dieser Forschung dar. Die These, daß die Finnougrier (hier Tschuden) und die mandschumongol-tatarischen Völker und Sprachen verwandt sind, also daß eine ural-altaische Sprachverwandtschaft anzunehmen ist, gehört zu jenen Überlegungen, welche die Finnougristik seit ihrer Entstehung begleiten. Diesen vergleichenden Ansatz hat Wiedemann in seinen Grammatiken und Wörterbüchern (Syrjänisch, Tscheremissisch, Votjakisch und Erzä-Mordvinisch) befolgt; da er aber dabei nur fremde und nicht besonders gute Quellen aufgearbeitet hat, können diese Werke in ihrer Bedeutung mit seinem *Esthnisch-deutschen Wörterbuch* (St. Petersburg: Kaiserl. Akademie der Wissenschaften, 1869), das bis heute die umfangreichste Phraseologie- und Dialektwortsammlung darstellt, und vor allem mit der *Grammatik der ehstnischen Sprache* (St. Petersburg: Kaiserl. Akademie der Wissenschaften, 1875) nicht gleichgestellt werden. Wiedemann hat auch gestaltend in die Prozesse eingegriffen: die votische Literatursprache wurde unter seiner Mitwirkung erarbeitet.

Ähnlich wie Wiedemann hat sich auch Nikolaj Ivanovič Anderson (1845−1905) hauptsächlich mit vergleichender Forschung befaßt, in seinen 1879 publizierten *Studien zur Vergleichung der indogermanischen und finnisch-ugrischen Sprachen* (Dorpat [heute: Tartu]: Laakmann) hat er wichtige, jedoch oft umstrittene Feststellungen zu diesen historisch so prägenden Kontakten der finnisch-ugrischen Sprachen gemacht.

Diese vielversprechenden Anfänge haben aber noch die wissenschaftliche und bildungspolitische Hilfe Finnlands und auch Ungarns sowie die nationale Selbständigkeit des Landes benötigt, um im 20. Jh. eine ausgedehnte und intensive Entwicklung der estnischen sprachwissenschaftlichen Forschung und des Hochschulunterrichtes zu ermöglichen.

5. Bibliographie

Gyarmathi, Sámuel. 1968 [1799]. *Affinitas lingvae Hvngaricae cvm lingvis Fennicae originis grammatice demonstrata*. (= Indiana University Publications; Uralic and Altaic Series, 95.) Bloomington, Ind.; The Hague: Mouton.

Hajdú, Péter-Domokos, Péter. 1987. *Die uralischen Sprachen und Literaturen*. (= Bibliotheca Uralica, 8.) Hamburg: Buske; Budapest: Akadémiai Kiadó.

Hanzeli, Victor E., ed. & transl. 1983. *Sámuel Gyarmathi, Grammatical Proof of the Affinity of the Hungarian Language with Languages of Fennic Origin*. With an Introduction. Amsterdam & Philadelphia: Benjamins.

Hunfalvy, Paul. 1877. "Die ungarische Sprachwissenschaft". *Literarische Berichte aus Ungarn*, 75−106. Budapest: Druck des Franklin-Vereins.

Lakó, György. 1974. *József Budenz und die zeitgenössische vergleichende Sprachwissenschaft*. (= Annales Universitatis Scientiarum Budapestinensis de Rolando Eötvös nominatæ, 5.), 13−42. Budapest.

Stipa, Günter Johannes. 1990. *Finnisch-ugrische Sprachforschung*. (= Mémoires de la Société Finno-Ougrienne, 206.) Helsinki: Suomalais-Ugrilainen Seura.

Sajnovics, Joannis. 1968 [1770]. *Demonstratio idioma Ungarum et Lapporum idem esse*. (= Indiana University Publications; Uralic and Altaic Series, 91.) Bloomington, Ind.; The Hague: Mouton.

Szathmári, István. 1972. "An Outline of the History of Hungarian Linguistics". *The Hungarian Language* hg. von Loránd Benkő & Samu Imre, 349−377. The Hague: Mouton.

Tiborc Fazekas, Hamburg (Deutschland)

163. Semitische Philologie und vergleichende Grammatik: Geschichte der vergleichenden Semitistik

1. Einleitende Bemerkungen
2. Die mittelalterliche hebräische Sprachwissenschaft
3. Die frühneuzeitliche lateinischsprachige Sprachwissenschaft
4. Die vergleichende Sprachwissenschaft im 18. Jh.
5. Die vergleichende Sprachwissenschaft im 19. bis 20. Jh.
6. Literatur

1. Einleitende Bemerkungen

Die semitischen Sprachen werden im Vorderen Orient und Nordafrika gesprochen. Neben den erloschenen Sprachen und Schriftkulturen, die im wesentlichen erst durch Inschriftenfunde und Ausgrabungen seit dem 19. Jh. bekannt geworden sind, wie dem Akkadischen (Babylonisch-Assyrischen), dem Altsüdarabischen, dem Phönizischen und den Sprachen der aramäischen Inschriften, stehen die semitischen Sprachen und Schriftkulturen: das Hebräische, Jüdisch-Aramäische, Syrische, Arabische, Äthiopische, Mandäische u. a. Wegen des niemals abgebrochenen Kontaktes zwischen Orient und Okzident waren diese Sprachen fast immer in mehr oder weniger großem Umfang in Europa bekannt. Es waren vor allem die Juden, die zur Kenntnis des Hebräischen und Talmudischen in Europa beitrugen. Die angestrebte Bekehrung der orthodoxen Syrer und Äthiopier förderte die Kenntnis des klassischen Syrisch und des Äthiopischen. Durch die christliche Mission und das Interesse an der arabischen Wissenschaft wurde das Studium des Arabischen begünstigt.

2. Die mittelalterliche hebräische Sprachwissenschaft

Wenn man von einigen neueren Idiomen absieht, sind die semitischen Sprachen recht eng miteinander verwandt, so daß es keiner besonderen Methode bedarf, um deren engen Zusammenhang zu erkennen. So war es bereits Hieronymus (um 347–419/420) aufgefallen, daß das Aramäische ("chaldaico sermone") im Buch Daniel "cum arabica lingua habere plurimam societatem" (1981: 6).

Es waren später die in arabischen Ländern lebenden jüdischen Gelehrten, die, des Hebräischen und Jüdisch-Aramäischen mächtig, den etymologischen Zusammenhang dieser Sprachen mit dem Arabischen zuerst beschrieben. Jehûdâ Ibn-Quraiš (10. Jh.), ein nordafrikanischer Jude (aus Tahert), scheint der erste gewesen zu sein, der in seinen Schriften einen Vergleich des Hebräischen mit dem Arabischen anstellte und zur Erklärung schwerverständlicher biblischer Ausdrücke das Arabische heranzog. Sein Hauptwerk ist die jüdisch-arabische Schrift Risâlah (Wetzstein 1842, Bargès & Goldberg 1857, Becker 1984), das 'Sendschreiben an die Gemeinde der Juden in Fâs'. Darin begründet er die große Ähnlichkeit der drei Sprachen durch "die Nähe der Wohnsitze und der Stammverwandtschaft der Völker" (Bacher 1892: 142–143): *wa-s-sabab fî hāδâ l-imtizâǧ qurb al-muǧâu̯arah fî l-bilâd wa-l-muqârabah fî n-nasab.* Dabei habe die "Ähnlichkeit der Sprachen" "schon vor der Vermischung" bestanden: *fa-tašâbahat al-luγât min qabl al-mumâsaǧah* (Wetzstein 1842: 26–27). Selbst die Regelmäßigkeit der Lautentsprechungen war ihm schon aufgefallen; denn es bestehe "zwischen dem Hebräischen und Arabischen kein Unterschied außer dem, der durch die Verwendung des [hebr.] *ṣ* und [arab.] *ḍ* [mit einem markierten *ṣ* geschrieben], *g* und *ǧ*, *t* und *δ* [mit einem markierten *t* geschrieben], *ʕ* und *γ* [mit einem markierten *g* geschrieben], *ħ* und *h* [mit einem markierten *k* geschrieben], *z* und *δ* [mit einem markierten *d* geschrieben] erzeugt sei" (Wetzstein 1842: 25–26): *ħattâ lâ i̯akûn bai̯na l-ʕibrânī̯ī wa-l-ʕarabī̯ī fî δâlika min al-iħtilâf illâ mâ bai̯na btidâl aṣ-ṣâd wa-ḍ-ḍâd, wa-l-gîmel wa-l-ǧîm, wa-t̯-t̯êt wa-t̯-t̯â, wa-l-ʕai̯n wa-l-gai̯n, wa-l-ħê wa-l-ḳâ, wa-z-zâi̯ wa-δ-δâl* (Becker 1984: 117). Die Gültigkeit dieser Lautgesetze wird im lexikalischen Teil anhand von hunderten von Beispielen unter Beweis gestellt.

Für Dûnaš ben-Labrâṭ (aus Baghdad, lebte in Fâs und Cordoba, Mitte 10. Jh.) sind die beiden Sprachen Hebräisch und Arabisch *dômôt* "gleich". Man hat damals schon erkannt, daß alle Nomina und Verba von einer dreiradikaligen Wurzel gebildet und so strukturiert sind, daß bestimmten Schemata eine Bedeutung zukommt, die die der Wurzel modifiziert. Ein jüngerer Zeitgenosse von Ibn-Quraiš, Dûnaš Ibn-Tamîm (aus Qairawân, ca. 890–nach 955/956), versuchte in einem nicht erhaltenen jüdisch-arabischen Werk nachzuweisen, daß die hebräische Sprache eigentlich nur ein reineres Arabisch sei (s. del Valle 1981: 257–263). Dem Sprachvergleich ist auch das teilweise erhaltene jüdisch-arabische Werk *Kitâb al-muwâzanah baina l-luγah al-ʕibrânīi̯ah wa-l-ʕarabīi̯a* von Ibn-Barûn (um 1100) gewidmet (Bacher 1894, van Bekkum 1981).

Die jüdischen wie die christlichen Wissenschaftler hielten das Hebräische für die Sprache des Paradieses. Ein Argument dafür war die in Genesis 2, 23 berichtete Ableitung des Wortes für 'Frau' (*'iššâʰ*, im Lutherdeutsch "Männin") von dem für 'Mann' (*'îš*), welche nur für das Hebräische stimmt. Diese wohl älteste Volksetymologie wurde durch die moderne Sprachvergleichung nicht bestätigt; es liegen vielmehr die beiden nicht verwandten Wurzeln $*\sqrt{\mathcal{P}n\theta}$ "weiblich" bzw. $*\sqrt{\mathcal{P}i\mathfrak{s}_1}$ "Mann" vor.

3. Die frühneuzeitliche lateinischsprachige vergleichende Semitistik

Die europäischen Theologen haben über jüdische Wissenschaftler und christliche Orientalen Zugang zu den anderen semitischen Sprachen gefunden, diese in Grammatiken und Wörterbüchern beschrieben sowie grammatische und lexikalische Parallelen und Unterschiede zwischen ihnen behandelt. Eine kritische Würdigung dieser umfangreichen Literatur steht noch aus (s. jedoch Eichhorn 1807: 404−411).

Eine Zusammenfassung der Kenntnis der 'orientalischen Dialecte' bietet im 16. Jh. Pierre Victor Palme Cayet (1525−1610), d. i. Petrus Victorius Caietanus Palma: *Paradigmata de IV linguis orientalibus praecipuis, Arabica, Armenica, Syra, Aethiopica* (Paris: Prevosteau, 1596). Wichtig ist auch Angelus Caninius (1521−1557): (*Didûqâ d-liššān 'ărāmay*) *Institutiones linguæ Syriacæ, Assyriacæ atque Thalmudicæ, una cum Æthiopicæ, atque Arabicæ collatione* [...] (Paris: Stephan, 1554). In dieser aramäischen Grammatik wird das Aramäische mit dem Hebräischen, Arabischen und Äthiopischen verglichen. Zwischen Aram. und Hebr. stellt er eine "mutatio literarum" fest, z. B. "Mem in fine tantùm in Nun, (*ṭôbîm*) (*ṭābîn*)" (mit Hinweis auf den Lautwandel m > n vom Latein zum Französischen in *alumen, alun,* "Alaun"), "Sade in Aain, (*'ęręṣ*) (*'ăraʕ*)", "Sin in Thau raphatum, (*šāloš*) (*tlāt*), ἀγαθός, ἀγασός". Es werden einige Paradigmen des Arabischen und Äthiopischen in vokalisierter hebräischer Schrift geboten.

In dem hebräisch-lateinischen Wörterbuch von Johann Habermann, d. i. Johannes Avenarius (1520−1590): (*Sępęr haš-šårāšîm*) *Hoc est Liber radicum seu Lexicon ebraicum* (Wittenberg: Crato, 1568; ²1589), wird das Hebräische nicht mit anderen semitischen Sprachen, sondern mit dem Griechischen (sowie Latein. und Dt.) verglichen, z. B. hebr. "[*šāqap*] − σκοπέω, [*māsak*] − μίσγω, misceo, mischen; [*'ābîb*] − ἡβάω, ἡβάσκω, pubeo, Bub, Büble."

In den drei folgenden Wörterbüchern werden jeweils fünf bzw. sechs semitische Sprachen vergleichend angeführt: Valentin Schindler (gest. 1604): *Lexicon pentaglotton, Hebraicum, Chaldaicum, Syriacum, Talmudo-Rabbinicum & Arabicum* [...] (Hannover: Hennëus 1612), Johann Heinrich Hottinger (1620−1667): *Etymologicum Orientale sive Lexicon harmonicum EʹΠΤΑΓʹΛΩΤΤΟΝ* [...] (Frankfurt am Main: Ammonius & Serlinus, 1661) − es werden außer den Sprachen in Schindlers *Lexicon* auch das Samaritanische und Altäthiopische berücksichtigt, und − mit Persisch als siebter Sprache − Edmund Castell(us) (1606−1685): *Lexicon heptaglotton, Hebraicum, Chaldaicum, Syriacum, Samaritanum, Aethiopicum, Arabicum, conjunctim, et Persicum, separatim* [...]; *Cui accessit brevis & harmonica* [...] *grammaticæ, omnium præcedentium linguarum delineatio,* tomus I−II, London: Roycroft & Scott, (1669); ²1686. (Nachdr., Graz: Akademische Druck- und Verlagsanstalt, 1970.)

Bei diesen Werken sind folgende Besonderheiten hervorzuheben:

− Alle Bereiche der Grammatik (vom Lautlichen bis zum Semantischen) werden behandelt.
− Es wird jeweils viel Material angeführt. Es wird Vollständigkeit angestrebt.
− Die Vorgehensweise ist methodisch. Es werden die Verfahrensschritte benannt.
− Es werden − viel mehr, als heute üblich − die Sprachbeispiele in der jeweiligen Nationalschrift geboten (d. h. Hebr. und Jüdisch-Aramäisch in hebr., Syrisch in syr., Arabisch in arab., Samaritanisch in samar. und Altäthiopisch in äth. Schrift).
− Die Präsentation des Materials ist oftmals didaktisch. Beliebt sind Zusammenstellungen in Tabellenform.

Die Methodik betreffend läßt sich feststellen:

− Der Primat des Hebräischen ist unbestritten. Die anderen Sprachen sind jedoch in sprachvergleichender Hinsicht von gleichem Gewicht. Hottinger (1661, Vorwort) spricht davon, daß "inter dialectos ἰσοτιμία" herrsche, die Dialekte also gleiches Gewicht hätten.
− Es wird das Wurzelprinzip beachtet, d. h. alle Wörter der Sprache sind von einer meist dreiradikaligen Wurzel gebildet.
− Die Sprachvergleichung bemüht sich um die "harmonia matris Hebrææ cum filiabus Chald., Syra, Talmud-Rabb., Samarit., Arab., Aethiop." (Hottinger 1661, Einleitung), d. i. die Übereinstimmung der Ursprache mit den Tochtersprachen (nämlich den semitischen Sprachen außer dem Hebräischen).
− Es werden auch solche Wurzeln semitischer Sprachen, die nicht im Hebräischen bezeugt sind, auf das Hebräische bezogen. So wird regelmäßig eine "radix inusitata" angeführt, wenn sie "ex aliis linguis vicinis restituenda" sei (Hottinger 1661); damit ist allerdings die rekonstruierte zweiradikalige Urwurzel gemeint.
− In Hottinger (1661) werden alle dreiradikaligen Wurzeln des Hebräischen (und damit des Semitischen) auf eine zweiradikalige Form zurückgeführt (Prinzip des 'Biradikalismus'). Diese Art Wurzelbildung wird von ihm 'Rhizologia' genannt. So

wird die hebr. Wurzel √rgl, von der *rę́gęl* "Fuß" gebildet ist, von einer zweiradikaligen Urwurzel √rg abgeleitet, die folgende Wurzelerweiterungen an den Tag lege:

rg + ʾ (z. B. (d) arab. √rǵu̯, raǵā "hoffen"),
rg + b (z. B. (a) hebr. *rę́gęb* "Schollen", (c) äth. *rəgb* "Taube"),
rg + g (z. B. (d) arab. *raǵǵa* "erschüttern, rütteln", *raǵraǵa* "erzittern lassen"),
rg + z (z. B. (a) hebr. *rāgaz* "erbeben", (d) äth. *rägäzä* "durchbohren"),
rg + l ("Fuß"),
rg + m (z. B. (a) hebr. *rigmâ* "coetus", (c) äth. *rägämä* "fluchen"),
rg + n (z. B. (a) hebr. √rgn "murren"),
rg + ʕ (z. B. (a) hebr. √rgʕ, (d) arab. *raǵaʕa* "zurückkehren"),
rg + p (z. B. (c) arab. *raǵafa* "zittern"),
rg + š (z. B. √syr. *rgaš* "fühlen").

Für alle zehn Wurzelderivationen werden zahlreiche Belege angeführt, die in dem Wörterbuch fast zwei Seiten (S. 458—459) füllen. Bei allen angeführten dreiradikaligen Wurzeln wird jeweils unterschieden, ob diese (a) im Hebräischen bezeugt sind, (b) von der Bedeutung her eine Entsprechung im Hebräischen haben, (c) nur eine Verwandtschaft unter sich aufweisen, ohne daß das Hebräische beteiligt wäre ("Harmonia filiarum inter se, vel omnium, vel quarundam, exclusa Hebræa"), oder (d) jeweils einzelsprachlich ganz eigene Bedeutungen aufweisen.

Solche biradikalistischen Thesen werden auch heute wieder von einigen vertreten, auch wenn sie einer methodischen Kritik nicht standhalten (s. Voigt 1988).

4. Die vergleichende Sprachwissenschaft im 18. Jh.

Der Übergang zur — aus heutiger Sicht — 'modernen' vergleichenden Sprachwissenschaft wurde im 18. Jh. gelegt, als man sich von der Idee des Hebräischen als Ursprache des Menschengeschlechtes (also nicht nur des Semitischen) und der Vorstellung des göttlichen Ursprungs der Sprache (s. Herder 1772) zu lösen begann. Von der Konzeption her trat an die Stelle des Hebräischen mit seinen Tochtersprachen die semitische Sprachgruppe. In der aus der alttestamentlichen Völkertafel übernommenen Bezeichnung ist schon das genealogische (Stammbaum-)Prinzip zu erkennen; denn Sem (hebr. *Šēm*) ist neben Ham und Japhet einer der drei Ahnen der nachsindflutlichen Menschheit.

Von den 'Semi, Chamique' spricht Gottfried Wilhelm Leibniz (1646—1716) bei der Behandlung der damals bekannten Sprachzweige, wobei er das Hebräische nur noch als „dialectum quandam majoris linguae" (1710: 4) bezeichnet. A. W. Schlözer (1735—1809) redet von dem "Semitischen Sprach- und VölkerBezirke" (*sic*), in der "Eine Sprache" herrsche, "die ich das Semitische nenne" (1781: 161). Es folgt ein Hinweis auf das Jafetische (d. i. Indogermanische) als zweite große "HauptSprache" eines "HauptVolkes" "in ganz VorderAsien", die "vielleicht auch gar" die Sprache der "OstIndier" umfasse (ibid.). Dabei wird auf die bengalische Grammatik von N. B. Halhed (1778) verwiesen, in der — also vor William Jones 1786 — auf bemerkenswerte Ähnlichkeiten zwischen dem 'Shanscrit' und dem Lateinischen und Griechischen hingewiesen wird. Johann Gottfried Eichhorn (1752—1827) hält das Hebräische für einen "Dialect der weit ausgebreiteten Semitischen Sprache" (1790: 45). Die "Morgenländischen Sprachen" des semitischen "Sprachgebiets" solle man genauer "Sprachen der Semiten" nennen (Eichhorn 1807: 404—405).

5. Die vergleichende Sprachwissenschaft im 19. und 20. Jahrhundert

Mit der Entdeckung des Akkadischen und Altsüdarabischen im 19. Jh. und des Ugaritischen im 20. Jh. und mit der Einbeziehung der vorher kaum bekannten gesprochenen Sprachen (und Dialekte des Arabischen, Neuaramäischen, Neusüdarabischen und Äthiopischen) ist der Gegenstand der Semitistik in einem unvorhersehbaren Umfang angewachsen. Von daher ist es verständlich, daß die Beschreibung all dieser Sprachen und deren lexikographische Erfassung die Sprachvergleichung etwas in den Hintergrund gedrängt hat.

In der Semitistik hat sich die sprachvergleichende Methode am Anfang an der entwickelteren Indogermanistik orientiert. Den Höhepunkt markieren die sprachvergleichenden Arbeiten von Jacob Barth (1851—1914), Theodor Nöldeke (1836—1930) und Carl Brockelmann (1886—1956). Der zweibändige *Grundriß der vergleichenden Grammatik* von Brockelmann (1908—1913) ist bislang nicht durch eine neuere Darstellung ersetzt worden. Kürzere, aber gehaltvolle vergleichende Grammatiken liegen in Wright (1890), Lindberg (1897), Zimmern (1898), Gray (1934) und Bergsträßer (1928; engl. 1983) vor. Die vielbenutzte Darstellung von Moscati (1964) wurde wegen ihres Materialmangels und die von Lipinski (1997) wegen der fehlenden wissenschaftlichen Diskussion kritisiert.

Es gibt zahllose komparatistische Einzeldarstellungen. Es seien hier wenigstens die wichtigsten Namen mit jeweils einem Werk genannt: Hupfeld (1839), Ewald (1871), Philippi (1871), Hommel (1883, 1892), de Lagarde (1889−91), König (1901), Reckendorf (1909), Růžička (1909), Christian (1919−20), Nyberg (1920), M. Cohen (1924), Ungnad (1925), Sarauw (1939), Rössler (1950, engl. 1981), Rundgren (1955, 1959), Petráček (1960−64), Kuryłowicz (1962, 1973), Lekiašwili (1963), Polotsky (1964), Blau (1970, 1998), Corriente (1971), Hetzron (1972), Garbini (1972; ²1984), Bravmann (1977), Ullendorff (1977), Steiner (1977), Majzel' (1983), D. Cohen (1984), Voigt (1988) und Goldenberg (1998).

Zu den wichtigsten Themen der vergleichenden Semitistik gehört die Frage der internen Gliederung der Sprachgruppe, angefangen mit Heinrich Ewald (1871). Ein neuer Ansatz stellt die Gliederung des Semitischen von Robert Hetzron (1974) dar, der das Arabische vom Äthiopischen und Neusüdarabischen trennte und es zum sog. Zentralsemitischen schlug (vgl. Voigt 1987).

Die verbale Morphologie spielt bei allen Gliederungen die entscheidende Rolle. Hier gibt es eine lange Tradition, die dem Akkadischen, Äthiopischen und Neusüdarabischen gemeinsame Präsensform (im Grundstamm $iVparrVs$) dem Ursemitischen zuzuweisen (Rössler 1950, Greenberg 1952, Polotsky 1964). Ebenso stark wird dieser Zusammenhang bestritten (Rundgren 1959).

Das Verbum im Hebräischen wird in jeder Generation erneut von verschiedenen Gesichtspunkten aus dargestellt. Ein ganz neuer Ansatz geht auf Rössler (1977) zurück, der das ursemitische Präsens auch im Hebräischen nachweisen konnte. Der entscheidende Beweis, nämlich die unterschiedliche Funktion von $iṣr$ ($iiṣṣor$)- und $inṣr$ ($*iinaṣṣVr$)-Formen, ist bislang unbegreiflicherweise nicht akzeptiert worden. Die Diskussion scheint hier noch nicht abgeschlossen zu sein.

Die vergleichende Semitistik ist bis ins 20. Jh. namentlich von Hebraisten betrieben worden. Die hebräischen Grammatiken enthalten von daher oftmals einen mehr oder weniger umfangreichen semitistischen Teil, s. Gesenius (1813; ²⁸1909), Ewald (1838), König (1881−1897), Bergsträßer (1918−1929), Bauer & Leander (1922) und Meyer (1966−1972).

Ein der historisch-vergleichenden Sprachwissenschaft verpflichtetes vergleichendes Wörterbuch der semitischen Sprachen steht noch aus. Einen Ersatz bieten die Wörterbücher semitischer Einzelsprachen, die etymologische Hinweise enthalten, wie zum Syrischen Brockelmann (²1928), zum Mandäischen Drower & Macuch (1963), zum Hebräischen Gesenius (²1847; ¹⁷1915 u. ö.), Murtonen (1986−1990) und Koehler & Baumgartner (³1967−1996) und zum Altäthiopischen Leslau (1987), mit dem zur Zeit umfassendsten etymologischen Wörterbuch. Das *Dictionnaire des racines sémitiques* von D. Cohen u. a. (1970−) "n'est pas un dictionnaire étymologique" (1970: vii), sondern eine Kompilation aller in semitischen Sprachen bezeugten Wurzeln.

Allgemein läßt sich sagen, daß die Methodik der Sprachvergleichung seit Brockelmann der allgemeinen und indogermanischen Sprachwissenschaft hinterherhinkt.

6. Literatur (außer Werken des 16./17. Jahrhunderts, s. § 3.)

Bacher, Wilhelm. 1892. *Die hebräische Sprachwissenschaft (vom 10. bis zum 16. Jh.)*. Trier: Mayer. (Nachdr. m. a. Werken, Amsterdam: Benjamins, 1974.)

−. 1894. "Die hebräisch-arabische Sprachvergleichung des Abû Ibrahîm Ibn Barûn". *Zeitschrift für die Alttestamentliche Wissenschaft* 14.223−249.

−. 1907. "Aus einem alten Werke hebräisch-arabischer Sprachvergleichung". *Zeitschrift der Deutschen Morgenländischen Gesellschaft* 61.700−704.

Bargès, J. J. L. & D. B. Goldberg. 1857. R. Jehuda ben Koreisch [...] *Ad synagogam Judæorum civitatis Fez Epistola de studii Targum utilitate et de linguæ Chaldaicæ, Misnicæ, Talmudicæ [...] convenientia cum Hebræa*. Paris: Duprat & Maisonneuve.

Barth, Jacob. ²1894: *Die Nominalbildung in den semitischen Sprachen*. Leipzig: Hinrichs. (Nachdr., Hildesheim: Olms 1967.)

−. 1907−1911. *Sprachwissenschaftliche Untersuchungen zum Semitischen*. T. 1−2, Leipzig: Hinrichs.

−. 1913. *Die Pronominalbildung in den semitischen Sprachen*. Leipzig: Hinrichs. (Nachdr., Hildesheim: Olms, 1967.)

Bauer, Hans & Pontus Leander. 1922. *Historische Grammatik der hebräischen Sprache des Alten Testaments*. Halle/Saale: Niemeyer. (Nachdr., Hildesheim: Olms, 1965.)

van Bekkum, W. Jacques. 1981. "The 'Risala' of Yehuda ibn Quraysh and its Place in Hebrew Linguistics". *Historiographia Linguistica* 8.307−327.

Beqer [Becker], Dan. 1984. *Ha-'Risâlah' šel Jehûdah ben Quraiš: mahadûrah bîqqôrtît*. Tel Aviv: Universîtâ.

Bergsträßer, Gotthelf. 1928. *Einführung in die semitischen Sprachen*. München: Hueber. (Nachdr., Darmstadt: Wissenschaftliche Buchgesellschaft, 1963 u. ö.; *Introduction to the Semitic languages*, transl. with notes [...] by Peter T. Daniels. Winona Lake: Eisenbrauns, 1983.)

−. 1918−1929. *Hebräische Grammatik*. Teil I−II, Leipzig: Vogel. (Nachdr. mit Gesenius & Kautzsch [^{28}1909], Darmstadt: Wissenschaftliche Buchgesellschaft, 1985.)

Blau, Joshua. 1970. *On Pseudo-Corrections in Some Semitic Languages*. Jerusalem: The Israel Academy of Sciences and Humanities.

−. 1998. *Topics in Hebrew and Semitic Linguistics*. Jerusalem: Magnes.

Bravmann, Max M[eïr]. 1977. *Studies in Semitic Philology*. Leiden: Brill.

Brockelmann, Carl. 1908−1913. *Grundriß der vergleichenden Grammatik der semitischen Sprachen*; I: *Laut- und Formenlehre*, II: *Syntax*. Berlin: Reuther & Reichard. (Nachdr., Hildesheim: Olms, 1966.)

−. ^{2}1928. *Lexicon Syriacum*. Halle: Niemeyer. (Nachdr., Hildesheim: Olms, 1966.)

Christian, Viktor. 1919−20. "Akkader und Südaraber als ältere Semitenschichte [*sic*]". *Anthropos* 14−15.729−739.

Cohen, David. 1984. *La phrase nominale et l'évolution du système verbal sémitique*. Löwen & Paris: Peeters.

− & Fr. Bron & A. Lonnet. 1970−1999 [noch nicht abgeschl.]. *Dictionnaire des racines sémitiques ou attestées dans les langues sémitiques*. [I.], II. Paris − La Haye: Mouton, [später] Leuven: Peeters.

Cohen, Marcel. 1924. *Le système verbal sémitique et l'expression du temps*. Paris: Leroux.

Corriente, Federico. 1971. *Problematica de la pluralidad in semítico: El plural fracto*. Madrid: Consejo superior de investigaciones científicas.

Drower, E. S. & Rudolf Macuch. 1963. *A Mandaic Dictionary*. Oxford: Clarendon.

Eichhorn, Johann Gottfried. ^{2}1790. *Einleitung in das Alte Testament*. 1. Th. Reutlingen: Grözinger.

−. 1794. "Semitische Sprachen". *Eichhorn's Allgemeine Bibliothek der biblischen Litteratur* 6:1.772−776.

−. 1807. *Geschichte der Litteratur von ihrem Anfang bis auf die neuesten Zeiten*. 5. Bd., I. Abth. Göttingen: Vandenhoek & Ruprecht.

Ewald, Heinrich. ^{3}1838. *Grammatik der hebräischen Sprache des Alten Testaments*. Leipzig: Hahn.

−. 1870 [1871]. "(Sprachwissenschaftliche Abhandlung, 3:) Abhandlung über die geschichtliche Folge der semitischen Sprachen". *Abhandlungen der königlichen Gesellschaft der Wissenschaften zu Göttingen* 15.157−219.

Garbini, Giovanni. 1972. ^{2}1984. *Le lingue semitiche: Studi di storia linguistica*. Neapel: Istituto Orientale.

Gesenius. Wilhelm. 1813. *Hebräische Grammatik*. Halle: Renger. (Völlig umgearb. von Emil Kautzsch. Leipzig: Vogel, ^{26}1896, ^{28}1909; Nachdr. mit Bergsträßer [1918−1929], Darmstadt: Wissenschaftliche Buchgesellschaft, 1985.)

−. 1835−1853. *Thesaurus philologicus criticus lingvae hebraeae et chaldaeae Veteris Testamenti*. Bd. I−III, [IV]. Leipzig: Vogel.

−. ^{2}1847. *Lexicon manuale Hebraicum et Chaldaicum*. Leipzig.

−. ^{17}1915. *Hebräisches und aramäisches Handwörterbuch*. Leipzig: Vogel. (Nachdr., Berlin: Springer, 1962.)

Goldenberg, Gideon. 1998. *Studies in Semitic Linguistics: Selected writings*. Jerusalem: The Hebrew University.

Gray, Louis H. 1934. *Introduction to Semitic Comparative Linguistics*. New York: Columbia University Press. (Nachdr., Amsterdam: Philo, 1971.)

Greenberg, Joseph H. 1952. "The Afro-Asiatic (Hamito-Semitic) Present". *Journal of the American Oriental Society* 72.1−9

Herder, Johann Gottfried. 1772. ^{2}1789. *Abhandlung über den Ursprung der Sprache*. Berlin: Voß.

Hetzron, Robert. 1972. *Ethiopian Semitic: Studies in classification*. Manchester: University.

−. 1974. "La division des langues sémitiques". *Actes du premier congrès international de linguistique sémitique et chamito-sémitique (Paris 1969)*, 182−194. Den Haag: Mouton.

Hieronymus. 1981. *Liber Danihelis, ex interpretatione Sancti Hieronymi cum praefationibus [...]*. Rom: Typis Polyglottis Vaticanis.

Hommel, Fritz. 1883. *Die semitischen Völker und Sprachen*. Leipzig: Schulze.

−. 1892. *Aufsätze und Abhandlungen arabistisch-semitologischen Inhalts*. München: Franz.

Hupfeld, Hermann. 1839. "System der Semitischen Demonstrativbildung und der damit zusammenhängenden Pronominal- und Partikelnbildung". *Zeitschrift für die Kunde des Morgenlandes* 2.124−163, 427−482.

Jehuda ben Koreisch, R.: s. Wetzstein (1842), Bargès & Goldberg (1857) und Beqer [Becker] (1984).

Koehler, Ludwig & Walter Baumgartner. 1967−1996. *Hebräisches und aramäisches Lexikon zum Alten Testament*. 3. Aufl., Lfg. 1−5, [6.]. Leiden: Brill.

König, Friedrich Eduard. 1881−1897. *Historisch-kritisches Lehrgebäude der hebräischen Sprache*.

Bd. 1−3, Leipzig: Hinrichs. (Nachdr., Hildesheim: Olms, 1979.)

−. 1901. *Hebräisch und Semitisch: Prolegomena und Grundlinien einer Geschichte der semitischen Sprachen.* Berlin: Reuther & Reichard.

Kuryłowicz, Jerzy. 1962. *L'apophonie en sémitique.* Breslau [usw.]: Polsk. Akadem. Nauk; Den Haag: Mouton.

−. 1973. *Studies in Semitic Grammar and Metrics.* Breslau [usw.]: Polsk. Akadem. Nauk; London: Curzon.

de Lagarde, Paul. 1972 [1889−1891]. *Übersicht über die im Aramäischen, Arabischen und Hebräischen übliche Bildung der Nomina.* Nachdruck. Osnabrück: Zeller.

Leibniz, Gottfried Wilhelm. 1710. "Brevis designatio meditationum de Originibus Gentium, ductis potissimum ex indicio linguarum". *Miscellanea Berolinensia ad incrementum scientiarum* [...], [1.]. 1−16. Berlin.

Lekiašwili, Alekhsi. 1963. *Saḥeltha skhesisa da riçhwis çarmoeba semitur enebši / Obrazovanie form roda i čisla imen v semitskich jazykach / La formation du genre et du nombre des noms en sémitique.* Tiflis: Universit.

Leslau, Wolf. 1987. *Comparative Dictionary of Geᶜez (Classical Ethiopic)* [...]. Wiesbaden: Harrassowitz.

Lindberg, O. E. 1897. *Vergleichende Grammatik der semitischen Sprachen.* Göteborg: Wettergren & Kerber.

Lipiński, Edward. 1997. *Semitic Languages: Outline of a comparative grammar.* Löwen: Peeters.

Majzel', Solomon S. 1983. *Puty razvitija kornevogo fonda semitskich jazykov.* Moskau: Nauka.

Meyer, Rudolf. 1966−1972. *Hebräische Grammatik.* Bd. I−IV. Berlin: de Gruyter.

Moscati, Sabatino [ohne 'u. a.']. 1964. *An Introduction to the Comparative Grammar of the Semitic Languages.* Wiesbaden: Harrassowitz.

Murtonen, A. 1986−1990. *Hebrew in its West Semitic Setting: A comparative survey of non-Masoretic Hebrew dialects and traditions.* 4 Bde. Leiden: Brill.

Nöldeke, Theodor. 1904. *Beiträge zur semitischen Sprachwissenschaft.* Straßburg: Trübner.

−. 1910. *Neue Beiträge zur semitischen Sprachwissenschaft.* Straßburg: Trübner.

Nyberg, H. S. 1920. "Wortbildung mit Präfixen in den semitischen Sprachen". *Le Monde Oriental* 14.177−291.

Petráček, Karel. 1960−1964. "Die innere Flexion in den semitischen Sprachen". *Archív orientální* 28−32.

Philippi, Friedrich Wilh. M. 1871. *Wesen und Ursprung des status constructus im Hebräischen.* Weimar: Böhlau.

Polotsky, Hans J. 1964. "Semitics". *At the Dawn of Civilisations* [...], 99−111, 357−358. London: Allen.

Reckendorf, Hermann. 1909. *Über Paronomasie in den semitischen Sprachen.* Gießen: Töpelmann.

Rössler, Otto: s. u. → Art. 163a (1950)

−. 1977. "Zum althebräischen Tempussystem: Eine morpho-syntaktische Untersuchung". *Hebraica*, 33−57. Berlin: Reimer.

Rundgren, Frithiof. 1955. *Über Bildungen mit s/š- und n-t-Bildungen im Semitischen.* Uppsala: Almqvist & Wiksell.

−. 1959. *Intensiv und Aspektkorrelation: Studien zur äthiopischen und akkadischen Verbalstammbildung.* Uppsala: Lundequist; Wiesbaden: Harrassowitz.

Růžička, Rudolf. 1909. *Konsonantische Dissimilation in den semitischen Sprachen.* Leipzig: Hinrichs; Baltimore: Johns Hopkins Univ. Press.

Sarauw, Chr. 1939. *Über Akzent und Silbenbildung in den älteren semitischen Sprachen.* Kopenhagen: Munksgaard.

Schlözer, August Ludwig (von). 1781. "Von den Chaldäern". *Repertorium für Biblische und Morgenländische Litteratur* 8.113−176.

Steiner, Richard C. 1977. *The Case for Fricative Laterals in Proto-Semitic.* New Haven: American Oriental Society.

Ullendorff, Edward. 1977. *Is Biblical Hebrew a Language? Studies in Semitic languages and civilizations.* Wiesbaden: Harrassowitz.

Ungnad, Arthur. 1925. *Das Wesen des Ursemitischen.* Leipzig: Pfeiffer.

del Valle Rodriguez, C. 1981. *La escuela hebrea de Córdoba.* Madrid: Nacional.

Vater, Johann Severin. 1817. *Handbuch der Hebräischen, Syrischen, Chaldäischen und Arabischen Grammatik.* Leipzig: Vogel.

Voigt, Rainer. 1987. "The classification of Central Semitic". *Journal of Semitic Studies* 32.1−21.

−. 1988. *Die infirmen Verbaltypen des Arabischen und das Biradikalismus-Problem.* Stuttgart: Steiner.

Wetzstein, Joh. Gottfr. 1842. "Hebräische Lexikographie: Schreiben des Jehuda ben Qarisch [sic] an [...]". *Der Orient: Berichte, Studien und Kritiken* 3:2.17−30.

Wright, William. 1890. *Lectures on the Comparative Grammar of the Semitic Languages.* Cambridge: Cambridge University Press. (Nachdr., Amsterdam: Philo, 1966.)

Zimmern, Heinrich. 1898. *Vergleichende Grammatik der semitischen Sprachen.* Berlin: Reuther & Reichard.

Rainer Voigt, Berlin (Deutschland)

163a. Semitohamitische Philologie und vergleichende Grammatik: Geschichte der vergleichenden Semitohamitistik

1. Einleitende Bemerkungen
2. Erste sprachvergleichende Beobachtungen
3. Beginn der semitohamitischen Sprachwissenschaft
4. Die klassische Periode (Müller, Reinisch, Meinhof)
5. Die nachklassische Periode
6. Der Komparatismus Otto Rösslers
7. Der 'neue' Komparatismus
8. Literatur

1. Einleitende Bemerkungen

Nach der alttestamentlichen Völkertafel sind die Söhne Hams (*Ḥām*): *Kûš* "Kusch", *Miṣrajim* "Ägypten", *Pûṭ* "Libyen(?)" und *Kənaʕan* "Kanaʿan. Danach umfaßt, wenn man das nach heutiger Auffassung deplazierte Kanaʿan herausnimmt, die in der Folge so benannte 'hamitische' Sprachgruppe das Kuschitische, Ägyptische und Berberische. Diesen Sprachgruppen ist heute lediglich noch das Tschadische hinzuzufügen. Anstelle des alten Terminus 'semitohamitisch' (oder 'hamitosemitisch') wird, einer Mode folgend, gerne 'afroasiatisch', 'afrasisch' u. ä. verwendet. Unabhängig von der Bezeichnung, rechnet heute kaum jemand mit einer Zweiteilung der Großsprachgruppe. Gelegentlich wurde einfach 'semitisch' anstelle von 'semitohamitisch' verwendet, ohne daß dadurch die Besonderheiten des 'Hamitischen' in Abrede gestellt wurden.

Die Einbeziehung der afrikanischen Sprachgruppen ging von der Semitistik aus, die den anderen Disziplinen inbezug auf das methodische Rüstzeug und die Breite und Tiefe der bezeugten Sprachen voraus ist.

2. Erste vergleichende Beobachtungen

In der frühen Phase ging es nicht um die Einsicht in die semitohamitische (= sh.) Großsprachgruppe, sondern um die Beobachtung einzelner semitischer Züge in verwandten nicht-semitischen Sprachgruppen. Der nordafrikanische jüdische Gelehrte Jehûdâ Ibn-Quraiš (10. Jh.), der als Begründer der vergleichenden Semitistik gilt (→ Art. 163), bringt in seiner *Risâlah* auch gelegentlich Vergleiche mit dem Berberischen. So wird das hebräische Hapaxlegomenon *kåmûs* "aufbewahrt" mit der berberischen Form "*km(m?)ûs*" (d. i. *akəmmus*) "Ballen" (der berb. Wurzel $\sqrt{kms}$ "sammeln") verglichen und dadurch erklärt. Genauso findet die seltene hebr. Form *u̯ai-îp* "er wurde schön" ($\sqrt{ipi}$) in berb. *yif* "er ist besser" (Becker 1984: 356–357) eine – auch heute noch überzeugende – Parallele. Dabei muß Jehûdâ schon die Ähnlichkeit der Personalpräfixe *y-, t-, n-* in den Präfixkonjugationen aufgefallen sein. Es ist jedoch nicht bekannt, ob dies auch einen Niederschlag in seinen Schriften gefunden hat.

In dem Umfang, wie im 17. Jh. außereuropäische Sprachen bekannt wurden, hat man auch die Ähnlichkeit kuschitischer, berberischer und tschadischer Wörter mit dem Semitischen (d. i. insbesondere mit dem Hebräischen) festgestellt. Eine Zusammenfassung dieser Beobachtungen bringt der *Mithridates* von Johann Christoph Adelung (1732–1806) und dem Orientalisten Johann Severin Vater (1771–1826) (vgl. Vater 1817). Das Berberische zeigt danach "eine starke Verwandtschaft mit den semitischen Dialekten" (Adelung & Vater 1812 III: 1: 46), die sich u. a. in den identischen Personalpräfixen zeige.

3. Beginn der semitohamitischen Sprachwissenschaft

Das Werk von Adelung & Vater steht an der Grenze zu der Epoche, die durch die Entwicklung der indogermanischen, historisch-vergleichenden Sprachwissenschaft gekennzeichnet ist. Verglichen mit solchen Meisterwerken wie Franz Bopps *Conjugationssystem* (1816), nehmen sich die Anfänge der vergleichenden Semitohamitistik bescheiden aus. Diese neue Disziplin etabliert sich mit zwei Artikeln von Francis William Newman (1805–1897) d. J. 1845. In diesen kurzen Beiträgen werden u.a. folgende Bereiche der Grammatik behandelt (Voigt 1995):

(a) die Personalpronomina des Berberischen, Semitischen, Koptischen und Hausa (Tschadischen);
(b) die Demonstrativa des Berberischen, Semitischen und Hausa;
(c) die innere und äußere Pluralbildung des Sem. und Berb. (sem. *-ūna* = berb. *-ən*); es wird sogar die Identität der plurali-

schen Affixe am Nomen und am Verb festgestellt;

(d) die einfache Präfixkonjugation des Berb., Sem. und Hausa: das Afformativ der 1. sg. berb. *y* = altäth. *k* (d. i. -*ku*), hausa *yakira, takira* (d. i. *yaa kiraa, taa kiraa*) 'er rief, sie rief' = hebr. "*yaqra, taqra*" (d. i. *i̯iqrå', tiqrå'*) "er ruft, sie ruft" = berb. *yaqqar, θoqqar* (d. i. kabyl. *yəqqaṛ, ṯəqqaṛ*) "er sagt, sie sagt" — diese Gleichung wird von einigen wenigen Tschadisten mit Hinweis auf die angebliche Unmöglichkeit eines Vergleiches mit dem Semitischen abgelehnt.

(e) die Verbalstammableitungen des Berb. und Sem.: das 'causative Verbum' auf *s*, das "reciproke oder reflektive Verbum" auf *m*, das "Passivum" mit *t*;

(f) der Wortschatz aller Sprachgruppen (z. B. hausa *sha* (d. i. *shaa*) = berb. *aswa, iswa* (d. i. kabyl. *yəswa*) = kopt. *si* (d. i. *sō, se-*) "trinken"). Bemerkenswert ist die Gleichung berb. *illa* = amh. *ala* (d. i. *allä*) "er ist" — die identische Wurzel wird jedoch, wie wir heute wissen, unterschiedlich konjugiert, im Berb. präfigierend, im Amhar. suffigierend.

Schließlich wird darauf hingewiesen, daß im Berberischen und Semitischen die "allgemeinen Principien der Inflexion, der Euphonik und der Wurzelbuchstaben identisch" sind. Das Berberische bezeichnet Newman als "hebräo-afrikanische Sprache, wie das Ghyz und das Amharische". Die "Berbern" seien also "von alter Zeit her mit den Canaanitern und Aethiopiern blutsverwandt" (Newman 1845: 646). Wenn Newman von den Sprachen der 'hebräischen Familie' spricht, meint er das Semitische bzw. in Erweiterung derselben das Semitohamitische.

Die einzige semitohamitische Sprachgruppe, die bei Newman nur kurz erwähnt wird, ist das Kuschitische. Die ersten Nachrichten über diese umfangreiche Sprachgruppe stammen von Antoine d'Abbadie (1810–1897), der 1843 auch eine — wenig sinnvolle — Gliederung der Sprachen des Raumes unternimmt. Danach ist nur das 'gööz' (d. i. das Altäthiopische) echt semitisch, während 'tögr-yañ' (d. i. das Tigrinische) und 'tögrăy' (d. i. das Tigre) als "langues présumées sémitiques" und Amharisch, Gurage, Harari, Gafat, "l'ilmorma, langue parlée par les Gallas", "A'far", Saho und Somali als "langues sous-sémitiques" bezeichnet werden.

Die erste kuschitistische Arbeit stammt von Heinrich von Ewald (1803–1875), der — zu Recht — in den 'Fürwörtern' (d. s. Personalpronomina), in dem "semitischen Imperfectum" (*ane, tane, jane* "ich bin, du bist, er ist" bzw. *ekke, tekke, jekke* "ich war, du warst, er war" = arab. *(lam) i̯aku(n)*), in dem sibilantischen Kausativ und in der inneren Pluralbildung semitische Züge erkennt. Die spezifische kuschitische Konjugation (d. i. Verbalnomen + Hilfsverb in der Präfixkonjugation) ist ihm verborgen geblieben, obwohl er die Formen (*bete, bette, bete* [d. s. **beet-'ee, beet-tee, beet-yee*] "ich aß, du aßest, er aß") anführt und sich um eine Erklärung bemüht. Das Saho bezeichnet er als "wurzelhaft semitische Sprache"; "so lernen wir nun, dass es in Africa selbst höchst verschiedene Zweige des Semitischen gibt, welche sich schon in einer für uns bis jetzt unermesslichen Urzeit getrennt haben müssen" (Ewald 1844: 421).

In dem semitohamitistisch bedeutsamen Jahr 1844 erschien auch Theodor Benfeys (1809–1881) Arbeit über das Verhältnis des Ägyptischen zum Semitischen.

Der später so gängige Begriff 'hamitisch' taucht in der frühen Zeit noch nicht bzw. noch nicht in der späteren Bedeutung auf. A. d'Abbadie scheint diesen Terminus zum ersten Mal verwendet zu haben. Er nennt "the important family of Ethiopian languages" "Chamitic, either on account of the traditions which ascribe their origin to Cham, or because the first of its languages which I studied is Khamtigna (i. e. Kham's tongue)" (1845); diese Etymologie ist inzwischen überholt. Wenige Jahre später faßt er unter der "famille kamitique" neben den Agausprachen auch "Yamma, Pays des Janjaro", Gonga, Kafa und viele andere Sprachen zusammen, während er das Kambata, Galla, Saho, ᶜAfar, Somali, Hadiya u. a. einer 'famille sous-kamitique' zurechnet (1848: 373).

Bei Wilhelm Bleek (1827–1875) findet sich der Terminus "Semito-Afrikaner', der später durch 'Semito(-)hamiten' ersetzt wurde. Von ihm stammt eine der ersten Gliederungen afrikanischer Genussprachen. Die 'Semito-Africani' umfassen die Semiten, 'Gallaei' (d. s. Kuschiten) und die Berber. Die 'Copti' bilden mit den Indogermanen und den Semito-Africani die nördliche Genussprachfamilie (1851: 59):

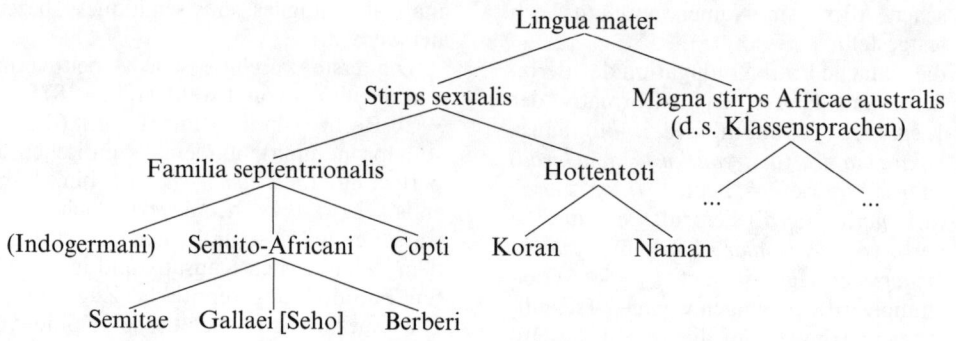

Ein etwas modifiziertes Bild gibt Bleek (1853: 39). Sein "Nördlicher Zweig" des "Sexuellen Sprachstammes", dem der "Großafricanische Sprachstamm" gegenübersteht, umfaßt jetzt folgende (fünf) Gruppen:

hair" sprächen für eine Zugehörigkeit zur kaukasischen Rasse. "So, beginning with the Shemite of full Caucasian type, the descending scale towards the Negro would be this: Shemite − Berber − Galla − Egyptian. It

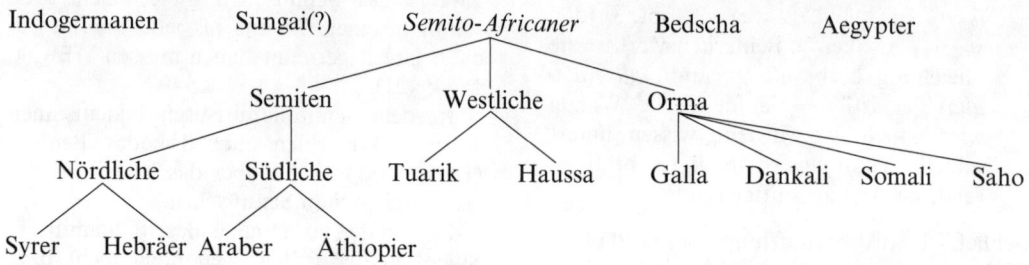

Der gut geeignete Terminus 'Semito-Afrikaner' hat sich wohl wegen seiner Verwechslungsmöglichkeit mit den Äthiopiern (= Äthiosemiten) nicht durchsetzen können.

Einen ganz ähnlichen Stammbaum entwirft Lottner (1860/61), der die mit dem Semitischen verwandten afrikanischen Sprach(grupp)en als „African sisterfamilies" des Semitischen bezeichnet hat. Der Terminus 'hamitisch', welcher immer noch auf einen Teil der äthiopischen Sprachen beschränkt ist, fehlt bei ihm nicht deshalb, weil er − wie man gemeint hat − rassistische Konnotationen vermeiden wollte. Carl Lottner (1843−1873) hat − wie andere auch − die beiden wissenschaftlichen Konzepte der Sprache und der Rasse miteinander verbinden wollen. Nach ihm unterscheiden sich die vier "sisterfamilies of language", die er in Afrika annimmt, in rassischer Hinsicht stark. "Nearest to the Shemite in the form of the skull and in colour, is the Berber; farther removed, the Egyptian. The Gallas are generally called negroes", aber "the form of the skull, the high, open forehead, the straight (not woolly)

is remarkable that the grammatical similarity with the Semitic decreases in the same ratio" (1860/1861: 123−124). Im Unterschied zu Lottner konnte Bleek der 'Race' nicht ein so großes Gewicht beimessen, da er meinte, daß die hottentotische Sprache, deren Sprecher "nach den meisten Autoritäten noch eine Stufe tiefer als Neger und Mongolen" stünden, doch wegen der "treuen Beibehaltung alterthümlicher Formen" "im ganzen Sexuellen Stamm ungefähr dieselbe Stelle" einnähme, "wie etwa das Sanskrit in der indogermanischen Sprachfamilie" (1852/1853: 33).

Aus der wachsenden Anzahl von neuentdeckten Sprachen in Afrika und dem gestiegenen Interesse an der Sprachgruppengliederung erwuchs die Notwendigkeit einer einheitlichen Benennung. Wenn man nicht von den 'afrikanischen Zweigen' des Semitischen reden wollte, bot sich die Bezeichnung 'hamitisch' (s. o.) an. Richard Lepsius (1810−1881) hat in der zweiten Auflage seines *Standard Alphabets* (²1863) als erster im linguistischen Sinne von hamitischen Sprachen geredet. Er hat sich dabei weder an A. d'Abbadie, der damit eine äthiopische Sprachgruppe meinte (s. o.), noch an Johann Ludwig Krapf (1810−1881) i. J. 1850, der damit auf die Bantusprachen abzielte, orientiert, sondern an der alttestamentlichen Völkertafel.

Das erste Kriterium bei der Gliederung der Sprachen der Welt war das Genus. Genussprachen sind die Sprachen der Söhne Noahs (d. s. nach Genesis 10: Sem, Ham und Japhet). Es ergibt sich bei Lepsius folgende Gliederung der Sprachen der Welt (^{2}1863: 301−308):

LITERARY LANGUAGES
  A. Gender languages
    I. Japhetic (Indogermanic) languages
    II. Semitic languages
    III. Hamitic languages
  B. No-gender languages
    I. Asiatic languages
      1. Tataric languages
      2. Monosyllabic languages
      3. Isolated languages
    II. Polynesian or Malayan (Oceanic) languages

ILLITERATE LANGUAGES
    III. Australian or Papuan languages
    IV. African languages
    V. American languages

Zu den 'hamitischen' Sprachen zählt Lepsius alle Sprachgruppen, die wir auch heute als − politisch korrekt ausgedrückt − nicht-semitische Vertreter der semitohamitischen (oder afroasiatischen) Großsprachgruppe ansehen, d. s. Ägyptisch(-Koptisch), 'Äthiopisch' (d. i. Kuschitisch), Libysch (Berberisch) und Hausa (von den anderen tschadischen Sprachen war damals wenig bekannt). Nur in einem Punkt kann man Lepsius heute nicht mehr folgen. Das Hottentottische und die Buschmansprachen (heute als Khoisansprachen bekannt) werden jetzt nicht mehr zum Semitohamitischen gerechnet.

Die Einteilung der Großsprachgruppe in einen semitischen und einen hamitischen Zweig wurde in der Folge von vielen übernommen, aber nur teilweise im Sinne einer strikten Dichotomie interpretiert. Denn es ist sehr schwierig, sprachliche Züge zu finden, die allen sh. Sprachen außer dem Semitischen zu eigen sind. Eine überzeugende interne Gliederung des Semitohamitischen wurde bislang nicht vorgelegt.

Von der Semitistik wurde diese Ausweitung der Sprachgruppe nach Afrika nur teilweise aufgegriffen. So wird in dem Werk über die Geschichte der semitischen Sprachen von Renan (1855, ^{3}1863) eher der Verwandtschaft des Semitischen mit dem Indogermanischen als mit dem SH. nachgegangen.

4. Die klassische Periode (Müller, Reinisch, Meinhof)

Den dritten Abschnitt möchte ich die klassische Periode nennen, weil in ihr die grundlegenden Werke geschaffen wurden, auf denen auch heute noch jede vergleichende semitohamitische Arbeit aufbaut.

Friedrich Müller (1834−1898) verdanken wir die erste vergleichende Grammatik der semitohamitischen Sprachen. Sie verbirgt sich in seinem monumentalen sechsbändigen *Grundriß der Sprachwissenschaft* (Wien 1876−1888). In der 2. Abt. (*Die Sprachen der mittelländischen Rasse*, 1887) des 3. Bandes (*Die Sprachen der lockenhaarigen Rassen*) werden auf 200 Seiten fast alle Gebiete der Grammatik miteinander verglichen (eine Kurzfassung liegt in Müller 1867 vor). Leider ist diese Darstellung wenig bekannt geworden. Es scheint, als hätten die dem späteren Verständnis widerstrebenden Titel der Einzelbände die verdiente Rezeption verhindert. Ein vergleichbares Werk ist erst 1965 mit Diakonoffs *Semito-Hamitic languages* erschienen.

Leo Reinisch (1832−1919), der Grammatiken und Wörterbücher von zehn kuschitischen Sprachen (Irob, Bilin, Chamir, Quara, Afar, Saho, Kafa, Beḍauye, Somali und Dschäbärti-Somali) vorgelegt hat, behandelt in seinem Werk über *Das persönliche Fürwort und die Verbalflexion in den chamito-semitischen Sprachen* (1909) vor allem den Bau des Verbums in allen fünf Zweigen mit einem Material- und Ideenreichtum, der in der Geschichte dieser Wissenschaft einmalig ist. Er legte auch die erste detaillierte etymologische Studie (über das *Zahlwort vier und neun*) vor (1890). Nicht alle seine Ideen (z. B. die Einbeziehung des Barea und Kunama und bestimmte omnikomparatistische Etymologien) wurden in der Folgezeit von anderen Forschern aufgegriffen. Reinischs Werke sind noch immer voll von Anregungen, die allerdings jeweils methodisch hinterfragt werden müssen (s. Reinisch 1987).

Den spezifischen Charakter der kuschitischen Suffixkonjugation (heute das Kriterium zur Ausgliederung des Kuschitischen) erkannte zuerst Praetorius (1894), indem er diese als zusammengesetzte Bildung aus Verbalnomen und präfigierend konjugiertem Hilfsverb betrachtete.

Schließlich ist Carl Meinhof (1857—1944) zu nennen, dessen Werk *Die Sprachen der Hamiten* (1912) in vielen Einzelpunkten über das seiner Vorgänger hinausgeht. In einem wesentlichen Punkt bleibt es aber hinter ihnen zurück. Das Konzept des Semitohamitischen wird durch die Einbeziehung des Ful, Masai und Nama verwischt. Andrerseits hat Meinhof stärker als andere das Semitohamitische in die afrikanische Sprachenwelt einbezogen. Diesem Konzept folgend könnte in Zukunft noch mit Revisionen des traditionellen Bildes zu rechnen sein. Wenn er das Nama als sh. Sprache bezeichnet, zeigt dies, daß bei ihm rassische Kriterien nicht die entscheidende Rolle spielen. Das Werk bildet den Höhepunkt der klassischen Periode der sh. Sprachvergleichung.

5. Die nachklassische Periode

Die Forschung nach Meinhof strebte nicht einen Ausbau seines Systems an, sondern stellte Einzelprobleme und -vergleiche in den Mittelpunkt. Dies fiel umso leichter, als Meinhof schon 1921/22 seine Hamitentheorie deutlich modifiziert hatte. "Hottentottensprachen", "nilotische Hamiten-Sprachen", das "proto-hamitische Ful" und das Hausa möchte er jetzt etwas "beiseite" stellen, da sie "den Semitensprachen bereits ferner" stünden (1921/22: 242). Das Modell, das er nun aufstellt, ist komplexer und methodisch klarer als das von 1912. Die aspektuelle Hauptopposition zwischen den Vokalen i und a, wie sie in der sekundären Konjugation des Kuschitischen auftritt, gilt danach auch in den Sprachen, die über Präfixkonjugationen verfügen. Man beachte: je eingehender die Untersuchungen werden, umso mehr tritt der 'hamitische' Gedanke zurück.

Die Epoche, die zwischen Meinhofs Hamitenbuch und Otto Rössler liegt, möchte ich mit Marcel Cohens (1884—1974) *Essai comparatif* (1947) abschließen lassen. Die Bedeutung dieses Werks liegt weniger in den vorgeführten Wortgleichungen als in seinem programmatischen Charakter. Eine vergleichende Betrachtung des sh. Sprachschatzes erscheint von nun an als lohnendes Ziel. Dabei hat Cohen die Aufgabe aber bei weitem unterschätzt, indem er nur verschiedene Gleichungen zusammenstellte, ohne die lautgesetzlichen Besonderheiten der Sprachgruppen zu beachten.

6. Der Komparatismus Otto Rösslers

Mit dem Werk Otto Rösslers (1907—1991) beginnt in zweierlei Hinsicht ein neuer Abschnitt der sh. Sprachvergleichung. Zum einen wurden von ihm (1971) zum ersten Mal die Lautentsprechungen zwischen Ägyptisch und Semitisch auf der Basis eines gemeinsamen Konsonantenblocks untersucht. Es werden die Lautgesetze nicht isoliert betrachtet; vielmehr werden die Phoneme der beiden Sprach(grupp)en auf ein ursprachliches Konsonantensystem bezogen. Auch aufgrund der Inkompatibilität von Lauten in einer ägyptischen Wurzel kommt Rössler zu der Schlußfolgerung, daß ᶜ (ᶜA(y)in) kein Laryngal sein kann, weil er — wie in ᶜḥᶜ "stehen" — in einer Wurzel neben einem echten Laryngal auftreten kann. Teilweise neue Gleichungen zwischen Ägyptisch und Semitisch führen Rössler zu der Einsicht, daß ᶜ nur ein Zerfallsprodukt von Dentalen und affrizierten Sibilanten (der rekonstruierten ägyptosemitischen Ursprache) sein kann. Erst später wird er im Äg. zu dem Laryngal, den wir aus dem Hebräischen und Arabischen kennen. Diese wichtige Einsicht (sowie der emphatische Charakter von äg. d /$ṭ$/ und d /$č̣$/) wird inzwischen von fast allen Ägyptologen (aber nicht von den 'neuen' Komparativisten, s. u.) anerkannt.

Eine neue Dimension hat die Semitohamitistik in einem programmatischen Artikel *Verbalbau und Verbalflexion* (Rössler 1950) gefunden, der das Verbum in den Mittelpunkt der sprachvergleichenden Bemühungen stellt. Dem Ansatz von Reinisch und Viktor Christian (1887—1963) folgend, werden zum ersten Mal die aspektuellen Bildungen der wichtigsten sh. Sprachen in ein historisches Modell gebracht. Kernpunkt ist die Anerkennung von zwei verschiedenen Präfixkonjugationen (z. B. im Grundstamm Durativ $iVkattVl$ und Narrativ $iVktVlu$ / Konsekutiv $iVktVl$) neben der Suffixkonjugation. Die Ausprägungen in den Einzelsprachen werden auch anhand der verschiedenen Verbalstammableitungen aufgezeigt. Gegen diesen Ansatz haben insbesondere diejenigen argumentiert, die für die — als primitiv konzipierte — Ursprache nur eine einzige Aspektform annehmen wollen, bzw. überhaupt einem Vergleich im sh. Rahmen skeptisch gegenüberstehen.

Der Rösslersche Ansatz wurde von Voigt weiter ausgebaut, der das ursprachliche Aspektsystem um eine weitere Kategorie erweitert hat. Neben dem Aorist (= Rösslers Narrativ/Konsekutiv) und dem Präsens (= Durativ) steht als dritte Präfixkonjugation das Perfekt (≠ ws. Perfekt), das sich im akkadischen Perfekt sowie im Berberischen und im Kuschitischen erhalten hat (Voigt 1990). Dem Beḍauye kommt dabei eine besondere Bedeutung zu (s. den geschichtlichen Abriß in Voigt 1988). In dieser Frage vertritt Zaborski (1975) ein anderes Konzept.

7. Der 'neue' Komparatismus

Die etymologische Arbeit am SH. wurde insbesondere von Werner Vycichl betrieben. Wichtig ist sein Beitrag "Hausa und Ägyptisch" (1934) sowie sein etymologisches Wörterbuch des Koptischen (1983).

Die etymologischen Studien haben in den 80er und 90er Jahren einen ungeheuren Aufschwung durch die teilweise nostratisch ausgerichteten Forscher aus Osteuropa und Amerika genommen. Russische Wissenschaftler (A. G. Belova, A. Ju. Militarëv, V. Ja. Porchomovskij, O. V. Stolbova) haben unter Leitung von Igor' M. D'jakonov (1915–1999) 1981–1986 ein – im Westen kaum bekanntes – vergleichendes Wörterbuch vorgelegt, das seit 1993 im *St. Petersburg Journal of African Studies* in einer erweiterten Fassung auf Englisch ("Historical Comparative Vocabulary of Afrasian") herauskommt. Im Jahre 1995 sind zwei Wörterbücher dieser Art erschienen, das *Hamito-Semitic Etymological Dictionary* von Orel & Stolbova und der Band *Reconstructing Proto-Afrosiatic* von Ehret. Das Wörterbuch von Takács (1999) geht vom Ägyptischen aus. Von diesen vier Werken sind drei biradikalistisch angelegt, insofern bei Ehret alle, bei D'jakonov u. a. fast alle dreiradikaligen Wurzeln auf eine zweiradikalige Basis zurückgeführt werden. Nur Orel & Stolbova und Takács anerkennen in großem Umfang dreiradikalige neben zweiradikaligen Wurzeln. Trotz vieler interessanter Etymologien besteht auch bei dieser Arbeit ein Haupteinwand darin, daß die Frage der Lautentsprechungen nicht hinreichend untersucht wird. Es bekennen sich zwar alle Autoren zur Notwendigkeit regelmäßiger Lautentsprechungen und glauben auch, dies zu beachten. Sieht man sich jedoch die Tabelle der Lautkorrespondenzen an, so entspricht z. B. ein ursprachliches *d einem d im Sem., Berb., Ägypt. (dies gegen Rössler), den verschiedenen Zweigen des Tschadischen usw. Das gleiche gilt für viele andere ursprachliche Laute. Nach allem, was wir aus den entwickelteren Disziplinen, wie der Indogermanistik, wissen, verändern sich die Laute im Laufe der Zeit z. T. beträchtlich. Angesichts der vielen Jahrtausende, die wir rekonstruierend bis zum ursemitohamitischen Knoten überbrücken, müssen stärkere Lautveränderungen stattgefunden haben, als die 'neuen' Komparatisten gewöhnlich annehmen.

Ein anderer Einwand betrifft die allgemein unterentwickelte Rekonstruktionsarbeit innerhalb der sh. Einzelzweige. Um die interne Rekonstruktion verdient gemacht haben sich Dolgopolskij (1973) für das Kuschitische, Sasse (1979) für das Ostkuschitische sowie Jungraithmayr & Shimizu (1981), Jungraithmayr & Ibriszimow (1994) und Stolbova (1996) für das Tschadische. Es müßte noch mehr in dieser Richtung gearbeitet werden, um eine größere Verläßlichkeit sh. Rekonstruktionsarbeit zu erreichen.

Das gestiegene Interesse an sh. Forschung belegen die sechs *Internationalen Hamitosemitistenkongresse*, die bisher abgehalten wurden: 1-A. Paris 1969 (Akten 1974), 1-B. (Akten 1975), 2. Florenz 1974 (Akten 1978), 3. London 1978 (Akten 1984), 4. Marburg/Lahn 1983 (Akten 1987), 5. Wien 1987 (Akten 1990), 6. Moskau 1994 (Akten nicht erschienen). Es gibt auch in Italien eine sh. Kongreßreihe, z. B. 7. Mailand 1993 (Akten 1994), 8. Neapel 1996 (Akten 1997), 9. Triest 1998 (Akten 1999).

Das beste Handbuch zur sh. Sprachwissenschaft ist das zweibändige Werk *Afrazijskie jazyki* (1991); demgegenüber ist der Band *Les langues chamito-sémitiques* (1988) kaum sprachhistorisch ausgerichtet und vernachlässigt – einer französischen Tradition folgend – vollständig das Tschadische.

Das SH. ist (als 'noachische Sprache') schon immer mit dem Indogermanischen (der Sprache Japhets) verglichen worden, wie in dem über 800 S. umfassenden *Hebräische[n] Wurzelwörterbuch* (1845) von Ernst Heinrich Meier (1813–1866). In jüngster Zeit wird – nach einer Zeit der Marginalisierung – das SH. wieder verstärkt auch im Rahmen des Nostratischen erfaßt und verglichen, s. z. B. Dolgopolskij (1998).

8. Literatur

d'Abbadie, Antoine. 1843. "Lettres [...] à M. Jules Mohl: I. Sur les langues éthiopiennes, II. Sur la langue saho". *Journal asiatique* 4. série, tome II (= 43). 102–118.

—. 1845. "Ethiopian Family of Languages". *The Athenaeum*, 18.359–360; *Journal of the Royal Asiatic Society of Bengal: Bombay branch* 2.219–223.

—. 1848. "Lettre [...] à M. Mohl". *Journal asiatique* 12.370–376.

Abel, Carl. 1886. *Einleitung in ein ägyptisch-semitisch-indogermanisches Wurzelwörterbuch.* Leipzig: Friedrich.

Adelung, Johann Christoph. 1812. *Mithridates oder allgemeine Sprachenkunde, mit dem Vater Unser als Sprachprobe in beynahe 5000 Sprachen und Mundarten.* Fortges. u. bearb. v. Johann Severin Vater. 3. Theil, 1. Abth., Berlin: Voss. (Nachdr., Hildesheim: Olms, 1970).

Afrazijskie jazyki. 1991. Kn. 1. *Semitskie jazyki*, kn. 2. *Kušitskie jazyki, livijsko-guančskie jazyki, egipetskij jazyk, čadskie jazyki.* (= *Jazyki Azii i Afriki*, 4, 1–2.) Moskau: Glavnaja redakcija vostočnaja literatura.

Benfey, Theodor. 1844. *Über das Verhältnis der ägyptischen Sprache zum semitischen Sprachstamm.* Leipzig: Brockhaus.

Bleek, Wilhelm. 1851. *De nominum generibus linguarum Africae australis, copticae, semiticarum aliorumque sexualium.* Bonn: Georg.

—. 1852/53. "Über africanische Sprachverwandtschaft". *Monatsberichte über die Verhandlungen der Gesellschaft für Erdkunde zu Berlin* 14.18–40.

Bopp, Franz. 1816. *Über das Conjugationssystem der Sanskritsprache in Vergleichung mit jenem der griechischen, lateinischen, persischen und germanischen Sprache.* Frankfurt am Main: Andreä.

Burrini, Gabriele. 1978–79. "Profilo storico degli studi sul camito-semitico". *Annali dell'Istituto Orientale di Napoli* 38.113–153; 39.351–384.

Cohen, Marcel. 1947. *Essai comparatif sur le vocabulaire et la phonétique du chamito-sémitique.* Paris: Champion.

Diakonoff, Igor. 1965. *Semito-Hamitic Languages.* Moskau: "Nauka".

—. 1988. *Afrasian Languages.* Moskau: "Nauka".

— (Hrsg.). 1993–1997. "Historical Comparative Vocabulary of Afrasian". *St. Petersburg Journal of African Studies*, vol. 2–6 [noch nicht abgeschlossen].

D'jakonov, Igor' M. (Hrsg.). 1981–1986. *Stravnitel'no-istoričeskij slovar' afrazijskich jazykov.* Moskau: "Nauka".

Dolgopolskij, A(ha)ron B. 1973. *Sravnitel'no-istoričeskaja fonetika kušitskich jazykov.* Moskau: Nauka.

—. 1998. *The Nostratic: Macrofamily and Linguistic Palaeontology.* Cambridge: The MacDonald Institute for Archaeological Research.

Ehret, Christopher. 1995. *Reconstructing Proto-Afroasiatic (Proto-Afrasian): Vowels, Tone, Consonants, and Vocabulary.* Berkeley: University of California Press.

Ewald, Heinrich von. 1844. "Über die Saho-Sprache in Äthiopien". *Zeitschrift für die Kunde des Morgenlandes* 5.410–424.

Jungraithmayr, Herrmann & Kiyoshi Shimizu. 1981. *Chadic Lexical Roots.* Vol. II. Berlin: Reimer.

Jungraithmayr, Herrmann & Dymitr Ibriszimow. 1994. *Chadic Lexical Roots.* 2 Bde. Berlin: Reimer.

Köhler, Oswin. 1975. "Geschichte und Probleme der Gliederung der Sprachen Afrikas". *Die Völker Afrikas und ihre traditionellen Kulturen.* Teil 1, 135–373. Wiesbaden: Steiner.

Les langues chamito-sémitiques. Textes réunis par David Cohen. Paris: Centre National de la Recherche Scientifique, 1988.

Lepsius, C. [Karl] R. ²1863. *Standard Alphabet for Reducing Unwritten Languages and Foreign Graphic Systems.* London: Williams & Norgate; Berlin: Hertz. (Nachdr., Amsterdam: Benjamins, 1981.)

Lottner, C. 1860/1861. "On Sisterfamilies of Languages, Especially those Connected with the Semitic Family". *Transactions of the Philological Society* 20–27, 112–132.

Meier, Ernst. 1845. *Hebräisches Wurzelwörterbuch – nebst drei Anhängen [...] und über das Verhältnis des ägyptischen Sprachstammes zum Semitischen.* Mannheim: Bassermann.

Meinhof, Carl. 1912. *Die Sprachen der Hamiten.* Hamburg: Friedrichsen.

—. 1921/1922. "Was können uns die Hamitensprachen für den Bau des semitischen Verbum lehren?" *Zeitschrift für Eingeborenensprachen* 12.241–275.

Müller, Friedrich. 1867. "Hamitische Sprachen". *Reise der österreichischen Fregatte Novara um die Erde in den Jahren 1857 [...]. Linguistischer Theil* von Fr. Müller, 51–70. Wien: Gerold's Sohn in Comm.

—. 1887. "Der hamito-semitische Sprachstamm". *Die Sprachen der lockenhaarigen Rassen*, 2. Abt. *Die Sprachen der mittelländischen Rasse*, 224–419. Wien: Hölder.

Newman, Francis William. 1845. "Über die Struktur der Berbernsprache [sic]". *Naturgeschichte des Menschengeschlechts*, von J. C. Prichard, nach der 3. Aufl. des engl. Originals [von 1844] mit Anm. u. Zusätzen hrsg. v. R. Wagner und F. Will, Bd. 3: 2, 636–646. Leipzig: Voss.

—. 1845. "Bemerkungen über die Haussa-Sprache mit Zugrundelegung des Vocabularium derselben mit grammatischen Elementen von J. J. Schön, 1843". Ibid., 647–652.

Praetorius, Franz. 1894. "Über die hamitischen Sprachen Ostafrika's". *Beiträge zur Assyriologie und vergleichenden Sprachwissenschaft* 2.312–341.

Reinisch, Leo. 1890. *Das Zalwort [sic] vier und neun in den chamitisch-semitischen Sprachen.* (= *Sitzungsberichte der phil.-hist. Cl. der kaiserlichen Akademie der Wissenschaften* 121, XII.). Wien: Temsky in Comm.

—. 1909. *Das persönliche Fürwort und die Verbalflexion in den chamito-semitischen Sprachen.* Wien: Hölder in Komm.

—. 1987. *Leo Reinisch: Werk und Erbe.* Hrsg. v. Hans G. Mukarovsky. Wien: Österreichische Akademie der Wissenschaften.

Renan, Ernest. 1855, ³1863. *Histoire générale et système comparé des langues sémitiques*, Teil I: *Histoire générale des langues sémitiques.* Paris: L'Imprimerie Impériale.

Rössler, Otto. 1950. "Verbalbau und Verbalflexion in den semitohamitischen Sprachen: Vorstudien zu einer vergleichenden semitohamitischen Grammatik". *Zeitschrift der Deutschen Morgenländischen Gesellschaft* 100.461–514.

—. 1971. "Das Ägyptische als semitische Sprache". *Christentum am Roten Meer* Bd. 1, hrsg. v. Fr. Altheim & R. Stiehl, 263–326. Berlin: de Gruyter.

Sasse, Hans-Jürgen. 1979. *The Consonant Phonemes of Proto-East-Cushitic.* (= *Afroasiatic Linguistics*, 7: 1). Malibu, Cal.: Undena.

Stolbova, Olga. 1996. *Studies in Chadic Comparative Phonology.* Moskau: Diaphragma.

— & Vladimir Orel. 1995. *Hamito-Semitic Etymological Dictionary.* Leiden–New York–Köln: Brill.

Takács, Gábor. 1999. *Etymological Dictionary of Egyptian.* Vol. I. Leiden: Brill.

Vater, Johann Severin: s. Adelung (1812).

—. 1817. *Handbuch der Hebräischen, Syrischen, Chaldäischen und Arabischen Grammatik.* 2. Ausg. Leipzig: Vogel.

Voigt, Rainer. 1988. "Zur Bildung des Präsens im Beḍauye". *Cushitic–Omotic*, 379–407. Hamburg: Buske.

—. 1990. "Die drei Aspekte des Semitohamitischen und des Indogermanischen". *Proceedings of the 5th International Hamito-Semitic Congress*, Bd. 1. 87–102. Wien: Institute für Afrikanistik und Ägyptologie.

—. 1995. "Zur Geschichte und den Grundlagen der vergleichenden Semitohamitistik". *Studia Chadica et Hamitosemitica: Akten des intern. Symposiums zur Tschadsprachenforschung*, 1–9. Köln: Köppe.

Vycichl, Werner. 1934. "Hausa und Ägyptisch". *Mitteilungen des Seminars für Orientalische Sprachen [...] zu Berlin*, 3. Abt., 36.36–116.

—. 1983. *Dictionnaire étymologique de la langue copte.* Löwen: Peeters.

Zaborski, Andrzej. 1975. *The Verb in Cushitic.* Krakau: Uniwersytet Jagielloński.

Rainer Voigt, Berlin (Deutschland)

XXVI. Indo-European Philology and Historical Linguistics and their Legacy
Indo-europäische Philologie, Historische Sprachwissenschaft und ihr Erbe
La philologie indo-européenne et la linguistique historique et leurs legs

164. The crisis of historical-comparative linguistics in the 1860s

1. Introduction
2. Schleicher's heritage
3. The emerging problems
4. Need for rebuilding Indo-European phonology
5. Successful crisis management
6. Conclusion
7. Bibliography

1. Introduction

By the middle of the 19th century, linguists from many, mostly European countries had good reason to rejoice, when surveying the achievements in the field of Indo-European language studies which had been attained during the first half of the century. Ambitious projects had yielded results that surpassed in many instances even the most optimistic expectations. The majority of those who pursued the study of language − trying to compete with the successful procedures of the natural sciences − grew confident that this competition would eventually reach a stage where optimal results could become the general rule rather than merely be the singular exception. Nothing less than the attainment of such a goal was expected of 'their science', historical-comparative linguistics, which was described by one of its practitioners, Hermann B. Rumpelt (1821−1881), − and in similar terms by numerous others − as 'one of the greatest scientific accomplishments of our century' ("eine der grössten wissenschaftlichen Errungenschaften unseres Jahrhunderts" [Rumpelt 1869: 3]). Franz Bopp (1791−1867), the acknowledged founding father of Indo-European linguistics, in the words of one of his most devoted followers, Johannes Schmidt (1843−1901), 'has left [us] a science whose foundations were safely established by him for all time' ("hat eine Wissenschaft hinterlassen, deren Grundlagen durch ihn für alle Zeiten sicher gestellt sind" [Schmidt 1870: 251]). Theodor Benfey (1809−1881), in particular, praised Bopp's *Vergleichende Grammatik* (1833−1852) because of its "Fülle des Stoffes und der genialen Behandlung [....], welche dieses Werk, trotz aller seiner Mängel, zu dem grossartigsten aller auf dem Gebiete der Sprachforschung jemals erschienenen stempelt" ('wealth of material and brilliant treatment [...], which make this work, in spite of all of its shortcomings, the most magnificent of all that have ever appeared in the field of linguistic research' [1869: 506]). The extraordinary results of Bopp's investigations in his *Vergleichende Grammatik* as well as those of other researchers of his time "verdankte man wesentlich der geschichtlichen und vergleichenden Durchforschung der indogermanischen Sprachen" ('was essentially due to the historical and comparative exploration of the Indo-European languages' [Benfey, p. 554]).

Whereas the satisfaction with both what had been achieved and what was envisioned as immediate objectives was entirely legitimate, it was just a question of time until the workers in the field would realize that, with the rapid advancement and programmatic enlargement of the research agenda, a far-reaching reassessment of goals as well as of procedures would before long have to become an unavoidable necessity.

2. Schleicher's heritage

By the beginning of the 1860s an enormous amount of information on the study of Indo-European languages had been accumulated. August Schleicher (1821–1868) felt that time had come to provide what he thought was long overdue and badly needed, namely to write a 'compendium of the comparative grammar of the Indo-European languages' (Schleicher 1861–1862 [⁴1876]: i). "Ich denke, wir brauchen ein solches Buch […] – es ist nöthig, dass wir einmal Bilanz machen und in systematisch kurzer Uebersicht mit zwingender Anschaulichkeit die Resultate und Ergebnisse reinlich darlegen" (Schleicher on 28 January 1860; quoted in Schmidt 1890: 411). He strove for completeness and clarity, paired with a strictly scientific attitude, and he is convinced that the emerging science has already produced an abundance of valuable research which would withstand the test of time. 'After leaving aside what is still doubtful, there remains a rich quantity of insights, comprising the various sides which language offers to scientific observation, insights which in our judgment will stand secured for all time' (Schleicher 1861–1862 [⁴1876]: i).

To be sure, Schleicher's work, much as he deserves credit for his painstaking and valuable stock-taking effort, goes far beyond the mere accumulation of data. In the words of Fritz Bechtel (1855–1924), writing twenty-four years after Schleicher's untimely death, his creativity is manifested above all in a methodological innovation

'in the attempt to pursue all phenomena of the most important historical languages to prehistorical time […]. By this type of language investigation Schleicher has become the founder of a method which is still characteristic for our procedure today. Each estimation of the gain achieved since his time has to be linked to Schleicher.' (Bechtel 1892: 1)

Only a few years after the appearance of its second edition (1866), Schleicher's *Compendium* was referred to as 'one of the most meritorious works in this field, by which the study of this branch of knowledge is extraordinarily facilitated and furthered' (Benfey 1869: 588). Statements like this one assured the book's long-lasting success. Henry Hoenigswald, writing one hundred years later, (1963: 5–6) measures the differences between Bopp's *Vergleichende Grammatik* (1833–1852) and Schleicher's *Compendium* and finds them "profound. In a sense they mark the step from 'comparative grammar' in the literal sense to the 'Comparative Method'."

Furthermore, Schleicher was the first to be seriously engaged in the reconstruction of the Indo-European proto-language, and "his authority in his day was paramount; there was no competing doctrine of reconstruction" (Lehmann & Zgusta 1979: 459). According to him, historical linguistic research was not possible without the reconstruction of non-attested language stages. Programmatic statements to this effect were made by him as early as 1848: 'A comparative grammar […] always presupposes a historical-linguistic act, by which the oldest forms of the linguistic stocks suitable for comparison have to be either identified or reconstructed. Systematic linguistic investigation begins its work only after these have been found' (1848: 27). And again in 1850: 'We must trace the entire way [of development] covered by a language until we view it in its oldest state, or if this is not possible for lack of linguistic documents […], that oldest state must be reconstructed in analogy to other languages as best as possible; only then can we successfully compare the language which we have selected as our starting point, with other languages' (1850: 22). As to the nature of the proto-language, he asserted that 'a comparison of the oldest forms, of the languages underlying the families, establishes proof of the common origin of all these languages from an Indo-European stem mother, whose essential features can only be reconstructed from all of these daughters' (1850: 124). Antoine Meillet (1866–1936), discussing the impact of the *Compendium*, which went through four editions in less than 15 years, points to Schleicher's advancement over Bopp and Pott in that "Schleicher a posé la langue commune, en a déterminé les traits essentiels et l'évolution; […] la méthode qu'il a instituée a été dès lors celle de tous les linguistes et a dominé le développement ultérieur de la science" (⁷1934 [1903]: 465). As Theodora Bynon (1986: 12) reminds us, Schleicher's *Compendium* "was in his day accepted as the unrivaled textbook on the subject". However, by 1882, Henry Sweet (1845–1912) proclaimed that "Schleicher's Compendium is now so utterly antiquated that no one thinks of using it except for the sake of its word-lists and inflection tables" (quoted after Morpurgo Davies 1986: 150).

Schleicher consolidated the large number of phonological and morphological descriptions of individual Indo-European languages into a unified system and designed 'the first comparative phonology of the Indo-European languages' (Schmidt 1890: 411). His historical reconstruction presupposed adherence to the belief in the regularity principle — that sound changes proceed with regularity — which he applied more rigorously and more consistently than any of his predecessors. He was also well on his way to fully comprehend the importance of analogy as a second significant factor to be reckoned with in determining the course of language development (cf., for instance, Schleicher 1860 [^{3}1874]: 60−61 and 65).

Bechtel (1892: 1) referred to Schleicher's *Compendium der vergleichenden Grammatik der indogermanischen Sprachen* as both the conclusion of an epoch in linguistic science and the beginning of a new one, and he provided several reasons for this evaluation. As to the second observation, we may direct the attention to an additional important factor mentioned by Schleicher himself. It illustrates his superb ability to proceed both innovatingly and with supreme caution:

'Wheras in former times the system was readied first and then an attempt was made to accommodate the object into the system, the procedure today is the opposite. Above all, great emphasis is placed on the most detailed investigation of the object without envisioning a systematic construction of the overall framework [...] based on the conviction that [...] the attempt to produce [a system] would have to be postponed until [...] a sufficient quantity of reliable observations [...] became available.' (Schleicher 1863 [^{2}1873]: 8−9)

["Während man einst zuerst das System fertig machte und dann das Objekt darauf hin bearbeitete es ins System zu bringen, verfährt man jetzt umgekehrt. Vor allem versenkt man sich in das genaueste Einzelstudium des Objektes, ohne an einen systematischen Aufbau des Ganzen zu denken [...] in der Überzeugung, dass [...] mit dem Versuch der Herstellung [eines Systems] gewartet werden müsse, bis [...] eine genügende Fülle zuverlässiger Beobachtungen [...] vorliegt."]

Schleicher's general interest in the natural sciences — manifested among other things in his preference for the inductive method — and his special interest in botany is sustained throughout his career. From early on he maintained that 'the method of linguistics [...] aligns itself essentially with the method of the other natural sciences" ("die Methode der Linguistik [...] schliesst sich wesentlich der Methode der übrigen Naturwissenschaften an" [1850: 2]).

He continued along similar lines in *Deutsche Sprache* (1860 [^{3}1874]: 37):

"[...] das Leben der Sprache [unterscheidet sich] durchaus nicht wesentlich von dem aller anderen lebenden Organismen, der Pflanzen und Tiere. Es hat wie diese eine Periode des Wachstums von den einfachsten Anfängen an zu den zusammengesetzteren Formen und eine Periode des Alterns, in welcher sich die Sprachen von der erreichten höchsten Stufe der Ausbildung allmählich mehr und mehr entfernen [...]. Die Naturforscher nennen dies die rückschreitende Metamorphose."

['[...] the life of language is by no means essentially different from that of all other living organisms, of plants and of animals. It has like those a period of growth from the simplest beginnings to the more composite forms and a period of aging, in which languages gradually remove themselves more and more from the highest attained stage of development [...]. Natural scientists call this retrogressive metamorphosis.']

Schleicher further elaborated on his attitude towards the natural sciences in his essay on *Die Darwinsche Theorie und die Sprachwissenschaft* (1863 [^{2}1873]: 7). Languages, as organisms of nature, 'without being definable by the will of man, rose and developed according to definite laws'. Linguistic investigators have to determine their research procedure in accordance with those facts. "Nur die genaue Beobachtung der Organismen und ihre Lebensgesetze [...] soll die Grundlage auch unserer Disziplin bilden" (ibid., p. 6). We encounter a similar passage in the introduction to Schleicher's *Compendium* (^{4}1876 [1861−1862: 1]) where he stated that the methodology of linguistics "ist im wesentlichen die der Naturwissenschaften überhaupt; sie besteht in genauer Beobachtung des Objektes und in Schlüssen, welche auf die Beobachtung gebaut sind". (Here and in other citations in German, from Schleicher and others, the spelling has been modified in order to agree with current usage: KRJ.) Considerations like those led Schleicher inevitably to a greater strictness in dealing with the laws of language in general, with sound laws in particular, than had been customary for his predecessors.

His bow toward Charles Darwin's (1809−1882) findings in passages like the following should not be surprising:

"Diejenigen Sachen, die wir, wenn wir uns der Ausdrucksweise der Botaniker und Zoologen bedienten, als Arten einer Gattung bezeichnen würden, gelten uns als Töchter einer gemeinsamen Grundsprache, aus welcher sie durch allmähliche Veränderungen hervorgingen. Von Sprachsippen, die uns genau bekannt sind, stellen wir ebenso Stammbäume auf, wie dies Darwin für die Arten von Pflanzen und Tieren versucht hat." (1863 [^{2}1873]: 15)

['Those languages which, if we use the terminology of botanists and zoologists, we would call species of a genus, are considered by us as daughters of a common proto-language from which they developed by gradual variation. Of the language groups with which we are very familiar we draw up family trees like those that Darwin has tried to set up for the species of plants and animals.']

Last but not least, when focussing on Schleicher we cannot fail to refer also to his family-tree concept, his 'Stammbaum-Theorie' (first published in Schleicher 1853; cf. Koerner in new ed. of Schleicher 1983 [1850]: xlviii*; Collinge 1995a: 198), the intellectual legacy by which he is known first and foremost in linguistic circles past and present (cf. Schleicher 1861−1862 [⁴1876]: 7). The concept summarized the endeavors of a long period of development in linguistic research. 'Schleicher was more a conclusion and a completion than a new beginning' (Arens ²1969 [1955]: 250), is one example of numerous similar assessments. Leonard Bloomfield (1887−1949) noted that "the earlier students of Indo-European did not realize that the family-tree diagram was merely a statement of their method; they accepted the uniform parent languages and their sudden and clearcut splitting, as historical realities" (1933: 311).

At the same time, the family tree also signaled, perhaps merely implicitly, a new beginning, even though Schleicher did not, or could not, spell out in any detail as to where this new beginning might lead. A new beginning, certainly different from what Schleicher had envisioned, was ushered in by Schleicher's star pupil Johannes Schmidt. He proposed to replace the idea of Schleicher's family tree by 'the image of the wave which expands in concentric circles that decrease in strength with increasing distance from the center' (Schmidt 1872: 27), thus inaugurating what came to be known as his 'wave theory' ("Wellen-Theorie"). The family-tree concept accurately depicts some crucial aspects in the development of Indo-European languages − for instance, the emergence of individual languages by younger languages separating from older languages − but leaves out other aspects that may be of equal importance − disregarding the possibilities for indvidual languages to influence each other after separation (cf. the modern terms of 'language contact' and 'Sprachbünde'). The same must be said for the concept that Schmidt had intended to be the all-comprehensive replacement of the *Stammbaum*. In reality, however, Schleicher's and Schmidt's models complement each other in various respects. In Schleicher's model, the emphasis lies on illustrating the retention and development of Proto-Indo-European features in the succession of the individual Indo-European languages, irrespective of the incorporation of features due to mutual influences of sister languages after they had separated. In Schmidt's model, the developmental aspect is, on the one hand, taken for granted as far as the language features of the ancestor language are concerned; on the other hand, that aspect is more realistically illustrated by the emphasis on how and to what extent languages after separation can influence each other when their speakers remain in contact. Thus in Schmidt's model, the focus is not on inherited language material but on later contact phenomena between individual branches. For the mutual influence in Schmidt's sense to occur, he presupposes, in addition to a mother-daughter relationship of languages, a relationship of 'languages in contact', i. e., interacting stages of sister languages (p. 19), with no differentiation being made between inherited and adopted language elements.

'We will have to acknowledge that the languages geographically closest to each other have more in common than those positioned at a greater distance, that therefore a continuous transfer leads from the Indian through the Iranian languages to Slavic and from there to the Lithuanian language, that Slavic contains more Aryan features than Lithuanian, Iranian more Slavic features than Sanskrit.' (Schmidt 1872: 15−16)

In an appendix Schmidt listed 498 word correspondences of adjacent languages for which in his opinion the conditions of continuous mutual influence applied (1872: 36−68).

August Leskien (1840−1916) rightly contended that the two theories supplement each other (1876: xxi). This view was endorsed by Brugmann (1884: 229−230) − who used the more descriptive terms 'Spaltungstheorie' and 'Übergangstheorie', respectively, for Schleicher's and Schmidt's concepts (ibid.), and later on by Bloomfield (1933: 318) who proclaimed that "today we view the wave process and the splitting process merely as two types − perhaps the principal types − of historical processes that lead to linguistic differentiation". (For more current views cf., e. g., Pulgram 1953, and also the discussion of Morpurgo Davies [1998: 286].) In contrast, Bechtel (1892: 6) makes the claim that with the discovery of the law of the palatals the family-tree concept loses its validity.

One might add, historiographically, that both concepts served extremely well within the time frame of their occurrence in that Schleicher's 'Spaltungstheorie' accurately depicts the focus of his own endeavor as well as that of his predecessors since Bopp, whereas Schmidt's 'Übergangstheorie' illustrates the transition to a distinctly different emphasis of investigation.

3. The emerging problems

During the last years of Schleicher's life and the first decade thereafter, his elaborate edifice did not crumble, but, apart from continued strong endorsements, it also encountered severe criticism, even outright rejection. Among his staunchest supporters were Johannes Schmidt and Hermann Collitz (1855–1935). They both were discerning enough to distance themselves from Schleicher's shortcomings; for instance, from his differentiation between the prehistorical period of development and the historical period of decay (cf. Schleicher 1861–1862 [^{4}1876]: 3). Collitz agreed with Schmidt that, on balance, Schleicher deserved their full support:

'I believe Schmidt was right when he occasionally stated in his lectures that Schleicher's methods contained in themselves the means for their correction. What in my opinion separates us from Schleicher is by far inferior to what unites us with him.' (Collitz 1886: 212)

("Ich glaube, Schmidt hatte recht, wenn er in seinen Vorlesungen gelegentlich sagte, Schleichers Methode trage die Mittel zu ihrer Korrektur in sich selber. Was uns von Schleicher trennt, steht nach meiner Überzeugung zurück hinter dem, was uns mit ihm vereint."]

By the 1870s, the number of Schleicher's opponents was greater than that of his supporters. A few years before and after Scleicher's death, important new discoveries had been made. The palatal law, first published in 1878 (see below), as well as the findings of Hermann Grassmann (1809–1877) in 1863 and of Karl Verner (1846–1896) in 1876, to name only the most influential achievements, presented substantial problems for some of Schleicher's data and procedures as codified in his *Compendium*. Valuable as this handbook continued to be 'by its excellent collection of examples, by the strictness of its methodology and the appropriateness of its arrangement' (durch die ausgezeichnete Beispielsammlung, durch Schärfe der Methode und zweckmäßige Einrichtung" [Leskien & Schmidt as co-editors of the posthumous 4th edition, 1874: ix]), it grew increasingly dated with every edition.

Only with the publication of Brugmann's *Grundriss*, beginning in 1886 with the first volume, did a more current and more comprehensive manual of Indo-European studies become available. Its second edition of 1897–1916 was still called in 1933 'the standard work of reference today' (Bloomfield 1933: 15). But in the meantime various attacks were launched against Schleicher, and they were also directed against several of Schleicher's basic tenets. Karl Brugmann (1849–1919) and Hermann Osthoff (1847–1909), Ferdinand de Saussure (1857–1913), Baudouin de Courtenay (1845–1929) were among his most outspoken critics (cf. also Koerner 1983: xii*–xiii* and Koerner 1989c: 328–329 for details of the attack on Schleicher). In the "Vorwort" to their *Morphologische Untersuchungen*, for instance, while Wilhelm Scherer and his book *Zur Geschichte der deutschen Sprache* (1868) is highly praised by Osthoff & Brugmann (1878: xi) as having had a substantial and lasting influence on "wie die sprachlichen Umgestaltungen und Neugestaltungen sich vollziehen" ('how the linguistic changes and innovations come about'), Schleicher, though only indirectly mentioned by reference to the 'ältere Sprachforschung', is frequently, and rather aggressively, taken to task (cf. Jankowsky [1972: 131–137]).

Schleicher's success in his pioneering attempt of reconstructing not only the Indo-European proto-language, but also as many non-attested linguistic forms of older language stages as was possible on the basis of extant texts, depended upon his strict adherence to regular sound-change laws. That this principle – which later on the Neogrammarians claimed to have been the first to endorse and which they have made the cornerstone of their research procedure (cf., e. g., Delbrück 1880 [^{6}1919: 101 ff.) – was fully embraced by Schleicher, is asserted by Schleicher himself (cf. Schleicher 1861–1862 [^{4}1876]: 13, note) and corroborated by Johannes Schmidt (1890: 411), who took great pains to point out that Schleicher had not only designed 'the first comparative phonology of the Indo-European languages', but also 'demanded exceptionless status for its rigorously determined laws. This demand had so far not been made before thus strictly and cogently by anyone.' Schmidt's formulation had been even more forceful in his obituary of Schleicher: 'He freely acknowledged that he was the slave of the sound laws which he observed to the very last detail, but he never lost sight of the overall framework' (Schmidt 1870: 253).

In weighing those two opposing viewpoints concerning Schleicher's position to the sound-law concept against each other, one has to take into account that the Neogrammarians greatly benefitted from Verner's removal of the last exception to Grimm's Law (cf. Verner 1876) in their assertion that 'sound laws suffer no exception', which placed them in a much better position than Schleicher had been. For Schleicher's system of Indo-European phonology, on the other hand, Verner's discovery, eight years after Schleicher's death, was one of several important events which necessitated changes of far-reaching consequences. The others included two revolutionary discoveries of Brugmann. The first of those involved the expansion of the Indo-European vowel system by positing the existence of two types of IE **a** (Brugmann's law; cf. Collinge 1985: 13−21 and Morpurgo Davies 1998: 242); the second brought to light syllabic nasals and liquids in the Proto-Indo-European language (cf. Bechtel 1892: 118, 125; Collinge 1995b: 205−206).

Osthoff & Brugmann (1878: xi) made it very clear that in their opinion an all-out revision was imperative: 'Before additional work is undertaken, the entire structure, as far as it has been completed so far, is in need of a thorough revision. Even the foundation walls contain numerous places that require repairs.' The needed repair work was not to be restricted to a few items only. Many of the aspects identified as causing severe problems were specifically referred to in the "Vorwort" to the *Morphologische Untersuchungen* (1878: iii−xx). Perhaps the most important one concerned the place of language development within the framework of cultural history. Schleicher's division of development into a prehistorical stage of language formation and a historical stage of language decay had prevailed for quite some time. Jacob Grimm (1785−1863) and many of his followers had entertained that same belief. Friedrich Max Müller (1823−1900), e. g., stated (1880 [1861−1864] I, p. 272): "On the whole, the history of all the Aryan languages is nothing but a gradual decay." For Schleicher (1850: 12) it became a cornerstone of his linguistic theory. 'History and language formation are activities of the human intellect that supercede each other.' This was often repeated by him, for instance, in his *Deutsche Sprache* (1860 [³1874]: 35) as well as in his *Compendium* (1861−1862 [⁴1876]: 3), where he subdivided the life of language in the two main stages: "1. Entwicklung der Sprache, vorhistorische Periode" and "2. Verfall der Sprache [...] historische Periode"; and lastly in his treatise *Über die Bedeutung der Sprache für die Naturgeschichte des Menschen* (1865: 27). Historical-comparative research reaches back to the earliest attestable forms and possibly beyond that through the method of reconstruction with the help of sound laws. Once the proto-language is reached, the most abstract stage of language, its highest point of development is attained, a stage not 'marred' by sound laws. Streitberg (1897: 371−372) draws the obvious conclusion from Schleicher's position:

'The Indo-European proto-language is, therefore, as Schleicher believes, necessarily a perfect ideal language, which does not know, cannot know anything of 'sound laws'. For at the very moment when the first sound law would begin to take effect or, to put it differently, when the first sign of decay would be perceivable, it would cease to be the "proto-language".'

It was Wilhelm Scherer (1841−1886) who successfully demolished the notion of pre-historical language development and historical language decay in his book *Zur Geschichte der deutschen Sprache* of 1868: 'I for my part have noticed only development, only history' (Scherer 1868: x).

4. Need for rebuilding Indo-European phonology

In general, Brugmann and Osthoff, as did other prominent members of the neogrammarian group (cf., e. g., Jankowsky 1972: 127 ff.), have certainly overstated their case. Yet they as well as most members of the group found ample reason for their highly critical attitude towards past practices as well as for their confidence with which they embarked upon their 'new approach'. How new it was, in their own estimation, is probably clarified best by quoting what Brugmann (1885: 125) had to say about this, nearly ten years after the Neogrammarians had formed their loosely-knit group: 'As far as I am concerned, I have always regarded the newer approaches as nothing else but the organic and consistent development of the older endeavors, and this view has grown stronger with me year after year.' Koerner (1989b: 96) lists several valid reasons for the continuity of the transition from the 'older approaches' to the practices of the Neogrammarians:

"[...] the *Junggrammatiker* [...] continued, by and large, to work within the framework established by Schleicher and others before 1879. In sum, while noting the cumulative progress and the refinement in methodology that began with the year 1876, I dare to assert that there was nothing like a revolution taking place in linguistics in the 1870s as is frequently claimed."

And it should also be stressed that with the numerous controversies which the Neogrammarians encountered, their actual positive research work fared much better than the theoretical pronouncements which they themselves had provided.

Brugmann's two articles of 1876, on "Nasalis sonans in der indogermanischen Grundsprache" and "Zur Geschichte der stammabstufenden Declination' (Brugmann 1876a, b), focus on crucial issues of the transition period from the time after Schleicher to the time when frustration and uncertainty gave way to the claim that a considerable amount of rebuilding and consolidation had been achieved. Brugmann certainly made use of Schleicher's technique, but he fully utilized the implications of Verner's discovery in that he showed the role of the accent in the determination of Indo-European vowels. Closely related to the two Brugmann articles is Osthoff's treatise "Zur Frage des Ursprungs der germanischen n-Declination", also published in 1876, in which Osthoff pursued a similar objective by attempting to prove that the differentiation between strong and weak declension is tied to the difference in accentuation. In an article published three years later, Brugmann (1879: 1–99) uses the first eight pages to provide a brief summary of what his two earlier articles, and implicitly also the 1876 article by Osthoff, are mainly concerned with and at what results they have arrived. By positing the existence of a Proto-Indo-European vowel **a** with three alternants **a$_1$, a$_2$, a$_3$** which would correspond in other Indo-European languages as **a, e, o**, Brugmann increased significantly the regularity of correspondences between the proto-language and the resultant daughter languages (cf. Collinge 1985: 13–21) and identified the Indo-European accentuation as the cause for the vowel alterations (Bechtel 1892: 43–44). He and Osthoff asserted for the proto-language the existence of nasals and liquids with syllabic function (cf. Bechtel 1892: 124–129), a discovery with far-reaching consequences for the understanding of the *ablaut* system. Winfred Lehmann (1967: 190), specifically referring to Brugmann's first article, comments that "it illustrates the growing control over articulatory phonetics; it reflects that the phonological and morphological levels are distinct, and that the one can be examined for insights into the other". In the opinion of Morpurgo Davis (1998: 242), the effect of both discoveries amounted to nothing less than that "at one blow a number of apparently arbitrary correspondences were removed while the origin of another set of morphophonemic alternations was explained".

Of the three linguistic components, phonology, morphology, and syntax, the first two were almost exhaustively treated in Schleicher's *Compendium*. Phonology was the more important of the two, since any significant progress in morphological research presupposed reliable phonological data.

For Schleicher, as the initiator of reconstruction, going from the oldest attestable language stage of as many Indo-European languages as possible to their non-attested, but scientifically reconstructed common ancestral stage was not so much a matter of choice as it was the fulfillment of a scientific ambition. In phonology his efforts centered around the establishment of a phonetic system of Indo-European. The work with consonants proved to be much less problematic than that with vowels. But even here to arrive at solid results required the full comprehension of both the ingredients and the implications of Grassmann's law, which was not available before 1863 and of which Schleicher did not seem to have fully recognized its importance. Only after the results of both Verner's law and of the law of the palatals were utilized in the mid-1870s, did a consonantal system evolve which has not substantially changed to this very day. "After some debatable points were cleared up in the sixties and seventies of the 19th century, the consonants were pretty well established as we today reconstruct them" (Lehmann 1955: 1).

The vowel system, on the other hand, posed a real problem, for Schleicher even more than for his predecessors, as he was bent on reconstructing the sound system of the parent language. Schleicher's vowel system of the Indo-European proto-language, which "developed over a period of several years" (Benware 1974: 75), took its lead from Jacob Grimm's assumption that the vowels of the triad **a i u** "were the basic vowels for Germanic at its earliest stage [...]. Although this statement applied to Germanic, it is clear that Grimm considered it valid for the history of all languages" (Benware 1974: 7).

This assumption goes together with the belief, which Schleicher shared, that in the evolution of languages the simplex comes before the complex. Hence he recognized — based on Sanskrit as presumably the oldest of the Indo-European languages — only three basic vowels: **a i u**, each endowed with two 'augmentations', which Schleicher called "erste Steigerung, zweite Steigerung" (Schleicher 1861–1862 [⁴1876]: 9):

Grund-vokal	erste Steigerung	zweite Steigerung
1. a-Reihe a	a + a = aa (â)	a + aa = âa (â)
2. i-Reihe i	a + i = ai	a + ai = âi
3. u-Reihe u	a + u = au	a + au = âu

Schleicher's comment on this arrangement (1860 [³1874]: 135): 'Extremely simple, but also extremely regular and strictly symmetrical' sounds fascinating, yet it also spelled trouble. The 'augmentations', meant to account for the vowel alternations of Grimm's ablaut (cf. Benware 1974: 76 ff.), did by no means fit all facts. Since Schleicher applied the same symmetry to the consonantal system, one might assume as, for instance, Pedersen (1931: 271) and Benware (1974: 77) do, that his overriding concern was "diese eigentümlichen Zahlenverhältnisse in der Anzahl der Laute" (1861–1862 [⁴1876] :9), in addition to his reluctance to compromise his idea of the Indo-European proto-language as being the perfect, ideal language. Hence, the starting point of any irregularity had to be assigned to the historical period, the period of continuous decay.

Schleicher's table of consonants as listed in the *Compendium* (⁴1876 [1861–1862]: 10) is as follows:

veränderungen [...] hervorgegangen sind, und auf welche sie demnach als auf ihre gemeinsame Quelle hinführen" ('from which the sounds of the various Indo-European languages have developed in accordance with the laws of sound changes and to which they therefore lead back as to their common source' [ibid.]). Most important is his explanation in a footnote (p. 11), which again establishes 'Symmetrie der Zahlenverhältnisse':

"Ursprünglich besass [...] das Indogermanische wahrscheinlich sechs momentane Laute, nämlich drei stumme und drei tönende; sechs konsonantische Dauerlaute, nämlich drei Spiranten und drei sogenannte Liquidae, d. h. die beiden Nasale n, m und r (l ist eine sekundäre Abart des r), und sechs Vokale. Im späteren Stande der Sprache, kurz vor der ersten Trennung, gab es neun momentane Laute und neun vokalische Laute."

['Most probably Indo-European [...] had six momentaneous sounds, i. e., three mute and three sonorous; six consonantal continuants, i. e., three spirants and three socalled liquids, that is the two nasals n, m and r (l is a secondary variant of r), and six vowels. At the later stage of the language, shortly before the first separation, there were nine momentaneous sounds and nine vocalic sounds'.]

For Schleicher this stage was apparently the end of the line. In spite of his assertion that 'the explanation of the facts of sound history can only be expected from the physiology of the speech organs' (1860 [³1874]: 50), he had reached an impasse, which he could not have overcome with the means at his disposal. Nor could have any individual linguist at his time, as Pedersen (1931: 271) with good reason asserts in connection with just one significant factor: "Schleicher's system may pass as an expression of the current opinion of his time. Not only for Schleicher, but for all his contempo-

	Momentane Laute			Dauerlaute			
	nicht aspirierte		Aspiratae	Spiranten		Nasale	r-Laute
	stumm	tönend	tönend	stumm	tönend	tönend	tönend
Gutt.	k	g	gh				
Pal.					j		
Lingu.							r
Dent.	t	d	dh	s		n	
Lab.	p	b	bh		v	m	

He identifies the sounds of the Indo-European proto-language as those sounds, "aus welchen die Laute der verschiedenen indogermanischen Sprachen nach den Gesetzen der Laut-

raries, Sanskrit was of sufficient importance to assure the acceptance of the triad a, i, u in spite of the protest of the languages of the European branches." The solution of the crisis was brought about by a group of linguistic scholars, some of them collaborating, most of them sharing the fruits of their labors, thus making the final result a truly cooperative undertaking.

5. Successful crisis management

In the continued search for more regularity, the irregularities identified in the oldest attestable forms of Indo-European languages had to be aligned with more realistically reconstructed forms in the proto-language than Schleicher had been able to produce. With more reliable data of individual languages becoming available and a constant refinement of the methods employed, Schleicher's successors were in a much better position to advance beyond the untenable position he had held, as they had gained, from good results, the insight, "dass es sich verlohne, die Vergleichung der idg. Sprachen bis in das feinste Detail zu treiben [...] mit besseren Hilfsmitteln und verschärfter Methode" ('that it yields good results to pursue the comparison of the Indo-European languages to the very minute detail [...] with better means and a more rigorous method' [Delbrück ^{6}1919 [1880]: 126]).

G. J. Ascoli (1829–1907) discovered in 1870 that, on the basis of comparing Sanskrit, Old Bactrian, and Aryan, the proto-language must have contained three k series instead of only one (Ascoli 1872: 49–79; cf. also Fick 1873: 3–34, Collitz 1879, and Schmidt 1881: 64 ff.). For Collinge (1985: 135) this amounts to Ascoli, besides Benfey and Arthur Amelung (1840–1874), having done 'spade work' on the way to the discovery of the law of the palatals which, according to Bechtel (1892: 62), entails:

"dass vor demjenigen arischen a, dem in Europa e gegenüberliegt, die Gutturale behandelt werden, wie vor i und y, d. h. Palatisierung erfahren; dass sie aber unverändert bleiben, wenn dem arischen a in Europa ein a oder o entspricht."

['that the gutturals occurring before that Aryan a, which corresponds in Europe with e, are treated as if occurring before i and y, that is, incur palatalization, but that they remain unchanged, if the Aryan a corresponds in Europe with a or o.']

This law is unique in that it has no single author. It became known between 1874 and 1878 and was first published by Hermann Collitz in 1878 (cf. Morpurgo Davies 1998: 243). Collinge (1985: 135–136) lists six candidates who might have had a share in its discovery and formulation, including Verner, Collitz, Saussure, and Schmidt. While Collinge elaborates (pp. 136–139) on their individual contributions, he refrains from determining a rank order: "The reader must judge personally" (p. 136).

Brugmann's two articles of 1876, mentioned above, together with Osthoff's study of the same year, broke new ground. It was now proposed that the proto-language must have contained liquids and nasals with syllabic function. Osthoff (1876) claimed the existence of sonant liquids l and r, Brugmann had asserted to have proven sonant nasals m n ŋ as part of the Indo-European inventory. Streitberg's (1919: 144) evaluation gives an impression of its immediate effect:

"Brugmann [...] löste durch diese Annahme mit einem Schlag eine ganze Reihe von Rätseln des idg. Vokalismus wie der idg. Stammbildung; Ordnung und Gesetz wurden sichtbar, wo eben noch Willkür und Verwirrung zu herrschen schien, und nach allen Seiten eröffneten sich der Forschung weite Ausblicke."

['Brugmann [...] by this assumption at one blow solved a whole series of puzzles of the IE vocalism as well as of the IE stem formation; order and law became visible where just a short while ago arbitrariness and confusion seemed to prevail, and wide prospects for research opened up in all directions.']

Brugmann's most significant discovery, however, is tied to his investigation of the Proto-Indo-European vowel system. A comparison of all Indo-European languages in a more detailed and more methodologically rigorous manner than Schleicher had done and without holding on to preconceived ideas as to the position of Sanskrit, led him to the belief that the vowel inventory of the proto-language also contained **e** and **o**, due to splitting of **a**. By replacing Schleicher's triad of 3 basic vowels with a 5-vowel theory, Brugmann had effectively broken the deadlock and shown the way leading out of the crisis. One additional and very important contribution surfaced in 1878 through the work of Ferdinand de Saussure, then 21, with his article on 'Les liquides et nasales consonantes' — chapter 1 of his *Mémoire sur le système primitif des voyelles dans les langues indo-européennes* — in which he elaborated on the findings of Brugmann and Osthoff (cf. Hübschmann 1885: 1–2). It must be mentioned in this connection that the splitting of **a** had been discovered, more or less intensely, for about two decades, yet the focus of those discussions was not the proto-language, but the individual daughter languages where the splitting was observed (cf. Delbrück ^{6}1919 [1880]: 127). Georg Curtius (1820–1885) had been the first to direct the attention to the possibility of a proto-language — the European proto-language — being involved (Curtius 1864). His findings, though constituting an important stepping stone, remained inconclusive.

The investigation of the individual sounds of a language began to pick up speed in the second half of the 19th century, intensified during the intervening decades until the mid-1870s, when it reached its undeniable peak in Eduard Sievers' *Grundzüge der Lautphysiologie zur Einführung in das Studium der Lautlehre der indogermanischen Sprachen* of 1876. This work, "by any standard an important event" (Hoenigswald 1978: 19), furnished comprehensive proof, what numerous other studies in the previous decades had sporadically, selectively, and also merely somewhat half-heartedly attempted to prove: that knowledge of all aspects of phonetics — articulatory, acoustic, auditory — can provide important, if not essential information for a thorough understanding of how sounds change and why. In addition to stressing the need to study living languages and dialects (Sievers 1876: 5), Sievers emphasizes the fact that 'in general it is not the single sound that incurs changes according to certain laws valid everywhere, but there is normally a corresponding development of corresponding sound series' (p. 4). Sievers also published a number of highly influential articles on the role of accent in the Germanic languages (Sievers 1877–1878). In Brugmann's and Osthoff's investigation into the vocalic function of nasals and liquids Siever's *Grundzüge* played a crucial role because it was he who "had established that nasals and liquids can have syllabic function" (Koerner 1976: 196). Brugmann also was aided by the research of Arthur Amelung (1871), who 'was the first [...] to plead for the assumption of several *a*-sounds in the [IE] proto-language" (Bechtel 1892: 24).

With the publication of the first volume of Brugmann's *Grundriss* in 1886, the revision of the entire sound system of the Indo-European proto-language began to take shape. The new system was to look dramatically different from what we find in Schleicher's *Compendium*. The following table, adapted from the second edition of the *Grundriss* where Brugmann presents the "Lautbestand der idg. Ursprache" (1897: 92), illustrates the 'new look' of PIE at the end of the 19th century:

Vokale, in sonantischer Funktion	i ī, u ū, e ē, o ō, å ǻ, a ā, ə
in konsonantischer Funktion	i̯, u̯
Diphthonge (Kurzdiphthonge)	ei oi åi ai əi, eu ou åu au əu
(Langdiphthonge)	ēi ōi ǻi āi ēu ōu ǻu āu
Nasale, in konsonantischer Funktion	m (labial), n (dental), ñ (palatal), ŋ (velar)
in sonantischer Funktion	m̥ m̥̄, n̥ n̥̄, ñ̥ ñ̥̄, ŋ̥ ŋ̥̄
Liquidae, in konsonantischer Funktion	r, l
in sonantischer Funktion	r̥ r̥̄, l̥ l̥̄
Verschlusslaute (Explosivae):	
p p^h b b^h	(labial, genauer bilabial),
t t^h d d^h	(dental, genauer vermutlich alveolar),
k̂ k̂^{h} ĝ ĝ^h	(palatal),
q q^h g g^h	(rein velar)
q^u q^{uh} g^u g^{uh}	(labiovelar)
Reibelaute (Spiranten)	s und š (stimmlos), z und ž (stimmhaft)
	þ und þ^h (stimmlos), ð und ð^h (stimmhaft); j.

6. Conclusion

The solution to the crisis of historical-comparative linguistics was brought about, as we have shown, by a thorough revision of the Proto-Indo-European sound system which necessitated far-reaching changes and adjustments in the grammatical analysis of all individual Indo-European languages. Just as Schleicher's *Compendium* superseded Bopp's *Vergleichende Grammatik*, so did Brugmann's *Grundriss* outdistance Schleicher's remarkable achievements.

Further advances of the linguistic profession — those that have already been made since the last edition of Brugmann's *Grundriss* and those that the future still holds in store — have all one simple, but essential feature in common: they will have to be built on the accomplishments of the past.

7. Bibliography

Amelung, Arthur. 1871. *Die Bildung der Tempusstämme durch Vocalsteigerung im Deutschen: Eine sprachgeschichtliche Untersuchung.* Berlin: Weidmann.

Arens, Hans. ²1969 [1955]. *Sprachwissenschaft: Der Gang ihrer Entwicklung von der Antike bis zur Gegenwart.* Freiburg: Alber.

Ascoli, Graziadio Isaia. 1872. *Vorlesungen über die vergleichende Lautlehre des Sanskrit, des Griechischen und des Lateinischen.* Transl. from the Italian by Johann Bazzigher & Heinrich Schweizer-Sidler. Halle: Buchhandlung des Waisenhauses.

Bechtel, Fritz. 1892. *Die Hauptprobleme der indogermanischen Lautlehre seit Schleicher.* Göttingen: Vandenhoeck & Ruprecht.

Benfey, Theodor. 1869. *Geschichte der Sprachwissenschaft und orientalischen Philologie in Deutschland seit dem Anfange des 19. Jahrhunderts mit einem Rückblick auf die früheren Zeiten.* München: Cotta'sche Buchhandlung.

Benware, Wilbur A. 1974. *The Study of Indo-European Vocalism in the 19th Century: From the beginnings to Whitney and Scherer.* Amsterdam: Benjamins.

Bloomfield, Leonard. 1933. *Language.* New York: Holt, Rinehart & Winston.

Bopp, Franz. 1816. *Ueber das Conjugationssystem der Sanskritsprache in Vergleichung mit jenem der griechischen, lateinischen, persischen und germanischen Sprachen; hrsg. und mit Vorerinnerungen begleitet von Karl Joseph Windischmann.* Frankfurt/Main: Andreä. (Repr., Hildesheim: Olms, 1975.)

–. 1883–1852. *Vergleichende Grammatik des Sanskrit, Send, Armenischen, Griechischen, Lateinischen, Litauischen, Altslavischen, Gothischen und Deutschen.* Berlin: Dümmler. (2nd ed., 1857–1861.)

Brugmann, Karl. 1876a. "Nasalis sonans in der indogermanischen Grundsprache". *Studien zur griechischen und lateinischen Grammatik* 9.285–338.

–. 1876b. "Zur Geschichte der stammabstufenden Declination". *Studien zur griechischen und lateinischen Grammatik* 9.363–406.

–. 1879. "Zur Geschichte der Nominalsuffixe **-as-**, **-jas-** und **-vas-**". *Zeitschrift für vergleichende Sprachforschung* 24.1–99.

–. 1884. "Zur Frage nach den Verwandtschaftsverhältnissen der indogermanischen Sprachen". *Internationale Zeitschrift für Allgemeine Sprachwissenschaft* 1.226–256.

–. 1885. *Zum heutigen Stand der Sprachwissenschaft.* Strassburg: Trübner. (Repr. in Wilbur 1977.)

–. 1886 [²1897]. *Vergleichende Laut-, Stammbildungs- und Flexionslehre der indogermanischen Sprachen.* Vol. I of Karl Brugmann & Berthold Delbrück, *Grundriss der vergleichenden Grammatik der indogermanischen Sprachen.* Strassburg: Trübner. (5 vols., 1886–1895 [²1897–1916].)

Bynon, Theodora. 1986. "August Schleicher: Indo-Europeanist and general linguist". Bynon & Palmer 1986.29–149.

– & Frank R. Palmer, eds. 1986. *Studies in the History of Western Linguistics: In honour of R. H. Robins.* Cambridge: Cambridge University Press.

Collinge, Neville E. 1985. *The Laws of Indo-European.* Amsterdam & Philadelphia: Benjamins.

–. 1995a. "History of Comparative Linguistics". Koerner & Asher 1995.195–202.

–. 1995b. "History of Historical Linguistics". Koerner & Asher 1995.203–212.

Collitz, Hermann. 1878. "Über die Annahme mehrerer grundsprachlicher *a*-Laute". *Beiträge zur Kunde der indogermanischen Sprachen* 2.291–305.

–. 1879. "Die Entstehung der indo-iranischen Palatalreihe". *Beiträge zur Kunde der indogermanischen Sprachen* 3.177–234.

–. 1886. "Die neueste Sprachforschung und die Erklärung des indogermanischen Ablautes". *Beiträge zur Kunde der indogermanischen Sprachen* 11. 203–242. (Repr. in Wilbur 1977.)

Curtius, Georg. 1864. "Ueber die Spaltung des a-Lautes im Griechischen und Lateinischen mit Vergleichung der übrigen europäischen Glieder des indogermanischen Sprachstammes". *Berichte der Königl. Sächs. Gesellschaft der Wissenschaften, Philolog.-Histor. Classe*, 9–42. Leipzig: Teubner. (Repr. in Georg Curtius, *Kleine Schriften* ed. by Ernst Windisch. Vol. 2: *Ausgewählte Abhandlungen wissenschaftlichen Inhalts*, 13–49. Leipzig: Hirzel, 1866.)

Delbrück, Berthold. 1880 [⁶1919]. *Einleitung in das Sprachstudium: Ein Beitrag zur Geschichte und Methodik der vergleichenden Sprachforschung.* Leipzig: Breitkopf & Härtel. (6th ed.: *Einleitung in das Studium der indogermanischen Sprachen.* Repr., Hildesheim: Olms, 1976.)

Fick, August. 1873. *Die ehemalige Spracheinheit der Indogermanen Europas.* Göttingen: Vandenhoeck & Ruprecht.

Grassmann, Hermann. 1863. "Über die Aspiraten und ihr gleichzeitiges Vorhandensein im An- und Auslaute der Wurzeln". *Zeitschrift für vergleichende Sprachforschung* 12.81–138.

Hoenigswald, Henry. 1963. "On the History of the Comparative Method". *Anthropological Linguistics* 5.1–11.

–. 1978. "The *annus mirabilis* and Posterity". *Transactions of the Philological Society 1978. Commemorative Volume: The Neogrammarians*, 17–35. Oxford: Blackwell.

Hübschmann, Heinrich. 1885. *Das indogermanische Vocalsystem.* Strassburg: Trübner. (Repr., Amsterdam: Oriental Press, 1975.)

Jankowsky, Kurt R. 1972. *The Neogrammarians: A re-evaluation of their place in the development of linguistic science.* The Hague: Mouton. (Repr., Berlin: Mouton de Gruyter, 1992.)

—. 1990. "The Neogrammarian Hypothesis". *Research Guide on Language Change* ed. by Edgar C. Polomé, 223–239. Berlin: Mouton de Gruyter.

Koerner, E. F. K. 1976. "1876 as a Turning Point in the History of Linguistics". *Journal of Indo-European Studies* 4:4.333–353. (Repr. in Koerner 1978.189–209.)

—. 1978. *Toward a Historiography of Linguistics: Selected essays.* Amsterdam: Benjamins.

—. 1983. *August Schleicher: Die Sprachen Europas in systematischer Übersicht.* Cf. Schleicher 1850.

—. 1989a. *Practicing Linguistic Historiography: Selected essays.* Amsterdam & Philadelphia: Benjamins.

—. 1989b. "The Neogrammarian Doctrine: Breakthrough or extension of the Schleicherian paradigm: A problem in linguistic historiography". Koerner 1989a.79–100.

—. 1989c. "August Schleicher and Linguistic Science in the Second Half of the 19th Century". Koerner 1989a.325–375.

— & R. E. Asher, eds. 1995. *Concise History of the Language Sciences: From the Sumerians to the Cognitivists.* Oxford & New York: Pergamon.

Lehmann, Winfred P. 1955. *Proto-Indo-European Phonology.* Austin: University of Texas Press.

—, ed. 1967. *A Reader in 19th-Century Historical Indo-European Linguistics.* Bloomingston: Indiana University Press.

— & Ladislav Zgusta. 1979. "Schleicher's Tale after a Century". *Studies in Diachronic, Synchronic, and Typological Linguistics: Festschrift für Oswald Szemerényi on the occasion of his 65th birthday* ed. by Bela Brogyanyi, 445–466. Amsterdam: Benjamins.

Leskien, August. 1876. *Die Declination im Slavisch-Litauischen und Germanischen.* Leipzig: Hirzel. (Repr., Leipzig: Zentralantiquariat der DDR, 1963.)

Meillet, Antoine. ^{7}1934 [1903]. *Introduction à l'étude comparative des langues indo-européennes.* Paris: Hachette.

Morpurgo Davies, Anna. 1986. "Karl Brugmann and Late Nineteenth-Century Linguistics". Bynon & Palmer 1986.150–171.

—. 1998. *Nineteenth-Century Linguistics.* (= *History of Linguistics*, 4.) London & New York: Longman.

Müller, Friedrich Max. 1880 [1861–1864]. *Lectures on the Science of Language.* 2 vols. London: Longmans, Green.

Osthoff, Hermann. 1876. "Zur Frage des Ursprungs der germanischen n-Declination. (Nebst einer Theorie über die ursprüngliche Unterscheidung starker und schwacher casus im Indogermanischen". *Beiträge zur Geschichte der deutschen Sprache und Literatur* 3.1–89.

— & Karl Brugmann. 1878. "Vorwort". *Morphologische Untersuchungen auf dem Gebiete der indogermanischen Sprachen* 1.iii–xx. Leipzig: Hirzel.

Pedersen, Holger. 1931. *Linguistic Science in the 19th Century.* Transl. by John Webster Spargo. Cambridge, Mass.: Harvard University Press.

Pulgram, Ernst. 1953. "Family Tree, Wave Theory, and Dialectology". *Orbis* 2:1.67–72.

Rumpelt, Hermann B. 1869. *Das natürliche System der Sprachlaute und sein Verhältnis zu den wichtigsten Cultursprachen mit besonderer Rücksicht auf deutsche Grammatik und Orthographie.* Halle: Buchhandlung des Waisenhauses.

Saussure, Ferdinand de. 1879 [1878]. *Mémoire sur le système primitif des voyelles dans les langues indo-européennes.* Leipzig: Teubner (Repr., Hildesheim: Olms, 1968.)

Scherer, Wilhelm. 1868. *Zur Geschichte der deutschen Sprache.* Berlin: Duncker. (New ed., with an introductory article by Kurt R. Jankowsky. Amsterdam & Philadelphia: Benjamins, 1995.)

Schleicher, August. 1848, 1850. *Sprachvergleichende* [Vol. II: *Linguistische*] *Untersuchungen.* Vol. I: *Zur vergleichenden Sprachengeschichte.* Vol. II: *Die Sprachen Europas in systematischer Uebersicht.* Bonn: König.

—. 1850. *Die Sprachen Europas in systematischer Übersicht.* Bonn: König. (New ed. with an introductory article by Konrad Koerner, Amsterdam & Philadelphia: Benjamins, 1983.)

—. 1853. "Die ersten Spaltungen des indogermanischen Urvolkes". *Allgemeine Monatsschrift für Wissenschaft und Literatur* 3.786–787.

—. 1860 [^{3}1874]. *Die Deutsche Sprache.* Stuttgart: Cotta'sche Buchhandlung. (Repr., Wiesbaden: Sändig, 1973.)

—. 1861–1862 [^{4}1876]. *Compendium der vergleichenden Grammatik der indogermanischen Sprachen.* 4th ed. prepared by Johannes Schmidt & August Leskien, 1876. Weimar: Böhlau.

—. 1863 [^{2}1873]. *Die Darwinsche Theorie und die Sprachwissenschaft: Offnes Sendschreiben an Herrn Dr. Ernst Häckel.* Weimar: Böhlau.

—. 1865. *Über die Bedeutung der Sprache für die Naturgeschichte des Menschen.* Weimar: Böhlau.

Schmidt, Johannes. 1870. "Nachruf: August Schleicher". *Beiträge zur vergleichenden Sprachforschung* 6.251–256.

—. 1872. *Die Verwantschaftsverhältnisse [sic] der indogermanischen Sprachen.* Weimar: Böhlau.

—. 1881. "Zwei arische **a**-Laute und die Palatalen". *Zeitschrift für vergleichende Sprachforschung* 25.1–179.

—. 1887. "Schleichers Auffassung der Lautgesetze". *Zeitschrift für vergleichende Sprachforschung* 28.303—312.

—. 1890. "Schleicher". *Allgemeine Deutsche Biographie* 31.402—416. Berlin: Duncker & Humblot. (Repr. in Sebeok 1966.374—395.)

Sebeok, Thomas A., ed. 1966. *Portrait of Linguistics: A biographical source book for the history of Western linguistics, 1746—1963.* Vol. I: *From Sir William Jones to Karl Brugmann.* Bloomington: Indiana University Press.

Sievers, Eduard. 1876 [²1881]. *Grundzüge der Lautphysiologie zur Einführung in das Studium der Lautlehre der indogermanischen Sprachen.* Leipzig: Breitkopf & Härtel. (2nd ed.: *Grundzüge der Phonetik.*)

—. 1877—1878. "Zur Akzent- und Lautlehre der germanischen Sprachen i—iii". *Beiträge zur Geschichte der deutschen Sprache und Literatur* 4.522—539; 5.63—163.

Streitberg, Wilhelm. 1897. "Schleichers Auffassung von der Stellung der Sprachwissenschaft". *Indogermanische Forschungen* 7.360—372.

—. 1919. "Karl Brugmann". *Indogermanisches Jahrbuch* 7.143—148. (Repr. in Sebeok 1966.575—580.)

Verner, Karl. 1876. "Eine Ausnahme der ersten Lautverschiebung". *Zeitschrift für vergleichende Sprachforschung* 23.97—130.

Wilbur, Terence H., ed. 1977. *The Lautgesetz-Controversy: A documentation (1885—86).* Amsterdam: Benjamins.

Kurt R. Jankowsky, Washington, D.C. (U.S.A.)

165. Die Entstehung und frühe Entwicklung des junggrammatischen Forschungsprogramms

1. Einleitung
2. Die Vertreter des junggrammatischen Forschungsprogramms
3. Die Benennung einer Forschungsrichtung
4. Entstehung und Inhalt des Forschungsprogramms
5. Resümee
6. Bibliographie

1. Einleitung

Die Junggrammatiker: Selten hat es in der Geschichte der Sprachwissenschaft eine Gruppe von Forschern gegeben, die mit einem so griffigen Namen bedacht wurde, und selten ist eine Gruppe von Anfang an so umstritten gewesen wie diese. Noch heute — 120 Jahre nach der Herausbildung des junggrammatischen Forschungsprogramms — schwanken die Urteile zwischen begeisterter Anerkennung einerseits und einem Infragestellen ihrer Leistungen andererseits. Einige sehen in den Junggrammatikern die Wegbereiter für die moderne, postsaussureanische Linguistik, andere sind der Überzeugung, daß ihr Forschungsprogramm sich kaum von dem ihrer Vorgänger unterscheidet. Im folgenden wird der Frage nachzugehen sein, wie sich diese kontroverse Beurteilung erklärt. Zuvor soll jedoch auf die in diesem Zusammenhang nicht unwichtige Namensgebung sowie auf die Konstellation der Gruppe eingegangen werden.

2. Die Vertreter des junggrammatischen Forschungsprogramms

Man muß unterscheiden zwischen Junggrammatikern im engeren Sinne, die intensiv an der Herausbildung des neuen Ansatzes beteiligt waren, und Vertretern der 'junggrammatischen Richtung', die sich als Kollegen oder als Schüler dem Forschungsprogramm der Kerngruppe angeschlossen haben.

Zur zentralen Gruppe gehören die Indogermanisten Karl Brugmann (1849—1919), Hermann Osthoff (1847—1909) und Berthold Delbrück (1842—1922) sowie die Germanisten Wilhelm Braune (1850—1926), Hermann Paul (1845—1921) und Eduard Sievers (1850—1936). Mit Ausnahme von Delbrück gehören sie alle einer Altersstufe an und haben einen engen Bezug zur Universität Leipzig, da sie dort Ende der 60er/Anfang der 70er Jahre des 19. Jhs. studiert und/oder ihre universitäre Laufbahn fortgesetzt und dabei den persönlichen Einfluß von August Leskien (1840—1916) erfahren haben. Dieser war maßgeblich an der Herausbildung der 'junggrammatischen Richtung' beteiligt und darf als der eigentliche Lehrer der Junggrammatiker gelten.

Delbrück nimmt insofern eher eine Randstellung ein, als er als etwas älterer der Generation Leskiens angehört. Außerdem hat er nicht in Leipzig, sondern in Halle (sowie ein Jahr in Berlin) studiert und sich später dort auch habilitiert. Von 1870 an wurde Jena zu seiner Wirkungsstätte, von wo aus er sich um einen regen Austausch mit seinen Leipziger Kollegen bemühte. Darüber hinaus erhält der gerade 20 Jahre alte Sievers 1871 einen Ruf nach Jena, so daß ein direkter Kontakt gegeben ist. Wie kein anderer seiner Generation hat Delbrück die Grundsätze des junggrammatischen Ansatzes vertreten und auch gegenüber Kritikern verteidigt (s. dazu seine *Einleitung in das Sprachstudium* (1880) sowie die Replik auf Curtius' *Kritik der neuesten Sprachforschung* (1885)): Ihn zum engsten Kreis hinzuzuzählen erscheint insofern berechtigt.

Nicht selten werden neben den bereits Genannten auch Otto Behaghel (1859—1936), Friedrich Kluge (1856—1926), Wilhelm Streitberg (1865—1925) u. a. als Junggrammatiker bezeichnet. Dies erweist sich jedoch als problematisch, da sie alle der Schülergeneration angehören. Sie waren also an der Entstehung des junggrammatischen Forschungsprogramms nicht direkt beteiligt und sollten deshalb lediglich als Vertreter der sich bereits konsolidierenden junggrammatischen Richtung angesehen werden. Daß sie sich sehr verdient gemacht haben um den neuen Ansatz, wird damit keinesfalls bestritten.

Überdies wird die Bezeichnung Junggrammatiker gelegentlich auf Wilhelm Scherer (1841—1886) und sogar auf Ferdinand de Saussure (1857—1913) ausgeweitet. Doch wenngleich Scherer mit der ersten Auflage seines Werkes *Zur Geschichte der deutschen Sprache* (1868) einen Impuls für einen methodischen Richtungswechsel gegeben haben mag, ist er als einer der zentralen Widersacher der Junggrammatiker sicher nicht zu dieser Gruppe zu zählen. Saussure dagegen kann lediglich als Vertreter der junggrammatischen Richtung angesehen werden — wie Behaghel, Kluge und Streitberg gehörte auch er der Schülergeneration an —, und das auch nur in seinen Anfängen.

Zur inneren Struktur der Kerngruppe ist zu sagen, daß die Indogermanisten einerseits und die Germanisten andererseits, die sich damals durchaus noch als Philologen im umfassenden Sinne verstanden, zunächst unabhängig voneinander einen neuen Weg in der Erforschung älterer Sprachstufen einschlugen (s. 4.; eine leicht abweichende Sicht findet sich bei Jankowsky (1972), der die Indogermanisten als die ursprüngliche Gruppe ansieht, der sich die Germanisten später anschlossen; selbst bei Collinge (1994: 1561) werden die Germanisten — einschließlich Paul — noch zu "close adherents" gegenüber den indogermanistischen "major voices" degradiert). Die Germanisten konnten dabei neben Leskien Friedrich Zarncke (1825—1891) zu ihren Lehrern zählen, auf den höchstwahrscheinlich auch die Prägung des Namens Junggrammatiker zurückzuführen ist (s. 3.). Das eigentliche Bindeglied zwischen den Germanisten und den Indogermanisten bildete Hermann Paul, den man aus heutiger Sicht als den zentralen Kopf der Junggrammatiker bezeichnen muß. Da er sich nicht auf germanistische Fragestellungen beschränkte, sondern sich grundsätzlich mit den *Principien der Sprachgeschichte* auseinandersetzte (1. Aufl. 1880; die letzte von Paul redigierte 5. Aufl. datiert von 1920), stand er den von vornherein sprachwissenschaftlich orientierten Indogermanisten fachlich näher als Braune und Sievers. Dies gilt vor allem für die Anfangszeit, in der Brugmann und Osthoff mit ihren *Morphologischen Untersuchungen* und Paul mit seinen *Principien* der in der Entwicklung begriffenen neuen Richtung erst einmal eine theoretische Basis liefern. (Zu den persönlichen Beziehungen zwischen den Jungrammatikern s. Einhauser 1989, Kap. 1; speziell zu Osthoff und Brugmann dies. 1992).

3. Die Benennung einer Forschungsrichtung

Wem die Idee zuzuschreiben ist, eine Reihe von jungen Sprachwissenschaftlern, die in den 70er Jahren des 19. Jhs. in Leipzig studierten und freundschaftlich miteinander verbunden waren, als Junggrammatiker beziehungsweise ihren Ansatz als junggrammatisch zu bezeichnen, wird sich nicht mehr mit endgültiger Sicherheit klären lassen. Belegt ist, daß Friedrich Zarncke 1878 in einem Dissertationsgutachten den Begriff 'junggrammatische Schule' verwendet hat; ob dagegen die Behauptung ebenfalls zutrifft, er habe den Namen mündlich auch bereits vorher in seinen Vorlesungen benutzt, läßt sich nicht mehr nachweisen (Zarncke selbst bezweifelte dies). Auf jeden Fall ist davon auszugehen, daß der Begriff in Anlehnung an eine in den 30er Jahren des vorigen Jahrhunderts aufgekommene Oppositionsbewegung gebildet wurde, die als Junges Deutschland bezeichnet wurde: So wie die Mitglieder dieser Bewegung gegen die politisch-gesellschaftlichen Verhältnisse ihrer Zeit aufbegehrten, suchten die Junggrammatiker die zu ihrer Zeit üblichen philologischen Forschungsmethoden zu optimieren und vor allem die Sprachwissenschaft in neue Bahnen zu lenken (s. 4.).

Da die Junggrammatiker selbst hinsichtlich der Benennung ihrer Gruppe keine einheitliche Linie vertraten, konnte bei Außenstehenden leicht der Eindruck entstehen, sie würden die Verwendung des Begriffs junggrammatisch beziehungsweise Junggrammatiker befürworten, ihn gleichsam als werbewirksames Schlagwort für ihren Ansatz benutzen, um so zugleich ihr Zusammengehörigkeitsgefühl zum Ausdruck bringen zu können. Insbesondere der Ton des von Brugmann verfaßten Vorworts zum ersten Band der gemeinsam mit Osthoff herausgegebenen "Morphologischen Untersuchungen auf dem Gebiete der indogermanischen Sprachen" (1878) und die darin mehrfach enthaltene Formulierung 'junggrammatische Richtung' vermittelt diesen Eindruck. Brugmann bereute zwar seine Vorgehensweise später und vermied den weiteren Gebrauch der Bezeichnung, doch der einmal ins Rollen gebrachte Stein ließ sich nicht mehr bremsen. Viele derjenigen, die nicht diesem leicht elitär erscheinenden Kreis angehörten, fühlten sich durch den zweifellos etwas überheblichen Ton brüskiert. Das galt sowohl für einige Vertreter der Lehrergeneration, hier vor allem Georg Curtius (1820–1885) und Johannes Schmidt (1843–1901), als auch für etliche, die, wie die Junggrammatiker selbst, noch dem wissenschaftlichen Nachwuchs zuzurechnen waren und – frisch promoviert oder bereits habilitiert – am Beginn ihrer Universitätskarriere und von daher per se in einem Konkurrenzverhältnis zu den Junggrammatikern standen. Das trifft insbesondere auf die Indogermanisten Adalbert Bezzenberger (1851–1922), Hermann Collitz (1855–1935) sowie Friedrich Bechtel (1855–1924) und mit Einschränkung auf den Germanisten Wilhelm Scherer zu sowie dessen Schüler Konrad Burdach, Gustav Roethe, Erich Schmidt und Edward Schröder. Scherer hatte zwar bereits seit 1868 einen Lehrstuhl inne (ab 1877 in Berlin), doch durch eine anhaltende Auseinandersetzung zwischen seinem Lehrer Karl Müllenhoff (1818–1884) und Friedrich Zarncke (sog. Nibelungenstreit) war er mit in den Konflikt hineingeraten. Sachliche wie persönliche Aspekte trugen dazu bei, daß er (und mit ihm seine Schüler) sogar zu einem der vehementesten Gegner der Junggrammatiker wurde.

Diese Gegner nun versuchten, das Schlagwort junggrammatisch neu zu besetzen, indem sie es in neue Kontexte stellten. Nicht mehr von der junggrammatischen Richtung war jetzt die Rede, sondern von der junggrammatischen Partei. Unterstützt wird dieses Bild durch entsprechende Komposita wie "Parteinahme", "Parteitreiben" und "Parteigenossen" (s. z. B. Bezzenberger 1879). Von der 'Junggrammatik' wird in dieser Zeit noch nicht gesprochen, sieht man einmal von einer entsprechenden brieflichen Äußerung von Osthoff (Osthoff an Brugmann, ohne Datum, ca. Febr. 1879) ab. Dies ist eine Formulierung, die man erst in der späteren Geschichtsschreibung häufiger findet, die jedoch, wie Henne (1995: 29–30) zu Recht betont, aufgrund der Polysemie des Begriffs abzulehnen ist. Das gleiche gilt im übrigen für die in wissenschaftsgeschichtlichen Darstellungen vereinzelt immer wieder einmal begegnenden Substantivierungen 'Junggrammatikertum' und 'Junggrammatismus' sowie die erst jüngst wieder von Bartschat (1996) verwendete Formulierung 'junggrammatische Schule', die von den Junggrammatikern selbst ausdrücklich zurückgewiesen wurde (s. etwa Paul 1886).

Die Unzufriedenheit mit dem "dummen Cliquennamen" ("hermed nok om dette dumme klikenavn", Holger Pedersen (1867–1951) 1916 zit. nach Schuchardt 1976 [1928]: 452) hielt noch lange an, nicht nur bei einigen der Junggrammatiker selbst, sondern auch bei späteren Geschichtsschreibern. So schlägt Pedersen vor, junggrammatisch durch 'jungleipzigisch' ("ung-leipzgsk") oder 'jungcurtiusisch' ("ung-curtius'sk") zu ersetzen, um damit zum Ausdruck zu bringen, daß die Junggrammatiker weit weniger innovativ waren, als durch den Namen suggeriert wird. Für ihn konnte junggrammatisch nicht als "die Bezeichnung einer bestimmten Richtung, sondern nur eines bestimmten Kreises von Sprachforschern" gelten (Pedersen auf einer Postkarte an Hugo Schuchardt (1842–1927) vom 16. 11. 1922, zit. nach Swiggers 1992: 160), und das sollte mit einer Bezeichnung wie jungleipzigisch zum Ausdruck kommen. Weiter fährt er fort (ebd.):

"Die Bezeichnung "ung-curtius'sk" ist allerdings etwas boshaft; wenn man aber ableugnet, dass die Junggrammatiker eine besondere Richtung darstellten und sie einfach als einen bestimmten Kreis von Personen bestimmt, warum sollte man sie dann nicht nach ihrem Lehrer benennen können?"

Ganz im Gegensatz dazu regt Hermann Ziemer (1845–1910), der als ein Anhänger der junggrammatischen Richtung gelten kann, bereits 1882 die Verwendung der Bezeichnung Neugrammatiker als die in seinen Augen bessere Alternative an (Ziemer 1883 [1882]). Die mit Junggrammatiker verbundenen Konnotationen einer "aufrührerischen Oppositionspartei" kommen hier nicht zum Tragen, die von Pedersen und anderen in Abrede gestellte Neuheit des Ansatzes wird hingegen um so stärker akzentuiert. Doch schon Anfang der 80er Jahre scheint sich der Name Junggrammatiker so weit durchgesetzt zu haben, daß Ziemers Vorschlag im deutschsprachigen Raum keine Chance auf Realisierung mehr hat. In anderen Sprachen hat man *jung* dagegen mit dem ebenfalls unbelasteteren *neo* übersetzt (engl. *Neogrammarians*, franz. *néogrammairiens*, ital. *neogrammatici* usw.). Dies führt hin zu der Frage, wie neu die Erkenntnisse der Junggrammatiker, wie innovativ die Änderungen der bis dahin üblichen Forschungspraxis denn eigentlich waren.

4. Entstehung und Inhalt des junggrammatischen Forschungsprogramms

Den stärksten Anstoß zur Herausbildung ihrer Richtung haben die Junggrammatiker von August Leskien erfahren, der weniger durch seine Schriften als vielmehr durch seine akademische Lehre wirksam wurde. Als Schüler von August Schleicher (1821–1868) ging er über diesen insofern hinaus, als er die Ansicht vertrat, lautliche Veränderungen würden sich in der geschichtlichen Entwicklung einer Sprache so vollziehen, daß es keine Abweichungen gibt. Vereinfacht ausgedrückt: Wenn aus dem Laut x in einem Wort y auf dem Weg von Stufe a zu Stufe b einer Sprache der Laut z wird, dann ist davon auszugehen, daß dieser Laut in allen anderen Wörtern, in denen er erscheint, genau die gleiche Veränderung erfährt. Sollte dies in Einzelfällen nicht zutreffen, so läßt sich dies entweder durch abweichende lautliche Bedingungen (andere Betonung, anderer Kontext etc.) erklären, die dazu führen, daß ein anderes Lautgesetz zum Tragen kommt, oder aber durch psychisch bedingte Analogiebildungen zu anderen Formen, die die erwartbare Entwicklung stören: die These von der Ausnahmslosigkeit der Lautgesetze war geboren.

Neu an dieser These war nicht die Vorstellung, daß sich in der sprachlichen Entwicklung gesetzmäßige Veränderungen vollziehen – spätestens seit Jacob Grimm gehörte diese Annahme zum Allgemeingut sprachwissenschaftlicher Forschung –, sondern die Behauptung, daß diese 'Gesetze' ausnahmslos wirkten, da es für jede scheinbare Ausnahme eine Erklärung gebe. Möglicherweise wäre die These nie in dieser Schärfe formuliert und von den Schülern Leskiens in geradezu absolutistischer Weise vertreten worden, wenn nicht gerade Mitte der 70er Jahre des vergangenen Jahrhunderts überraschende Erklärungen für einige bis dahin ungeklärt gebliebene Ausnahmen gefunden worden wären. Von besonderer Überzeugungskraft war in diesem Zusammenhang das sogenannte Vernersche Gesetz. Neben einigen anderen, die unabhängig von ihm die gleiche Entdeckung machten, vermochte der Däne Karl Verner (1846–1896) in seinem 1876 erschienenen Aufsatz "Eine Ausnahme der ersten Lautverschiebung" nachzuweisen, daß die bis dahin als willkürlich angesehenen Ausnahmen der von Grimm entdeckten Ersten Lautverschiebung einer gesetzmäßigen Entwicklung unterliegen. Im Laufe des Jahres 1876 erschienen zahlreiche weitere Publikationen (u. a. von Leskien, Brugmann, Osthoff, Sievers und Winteler; s. Literaturverzeichnis), die Aufschluß über bis dahin ungeklärte Lautentwicklungen gaben beziehungsweise grundsätzlich zum Ausbau der theoretischen Grundlagen im Bereich der Phonetik beitrugen, so daß das Jahr 1876 in der Regel als das Jahr angesehen wird, in dem der Siegeszug des junggrammatischen Ansatzes seinen Anfang nahm (s. dazu ausführlicher Koerner 1976; Hoenigswald 1978).

4.1. Das junggrammatische "glaubensbekenntnis"

1878 gaben Osthoff und Brugmann den ersten Band der *Morphologischen Untersuchungen* heraus, begleitet von einem Vorwort, in dem sie die Ziele und Methoden der neuen Richtung in Abgrenzung von der bis dahin üblichen Forschungspraxis darlegten:

(1) Vornehmstes Ziel der vergleichenden Sprachwissenschaft müsse die Erforschung des "menschlichen sprechmechanismus" sein, wobei man sich nicht nur auf physiologische Aspekte beschränken dürfe (insofern erscheint der Mechanismus-Begriff etwas unglücklich gewählt), sondern auch die psychische Komponente berücksichtigen müsse. Die ältere Sprachforschung habe "zwar eifrigst die

sprachen, aber viel zu wenig den sprechenden menschen" erforscht (Osthoff & Brugmann 1878: iii). Außerdem habe sie nur die schriftlich fixierte Sprache im Blick gehabt und konnte insofern gar nicht erkennen, "was sprachlich überhaupt möglich ist" (ebd.), sie konnte nicht erklären, wie sprachliche Veränderungen zustande kommen, sie konnte keine dem Objekt angemessene Untersuchungsmethode entwickeln (vgl. ebd.: iii−iv).

(2) Die vergleichende Sprachwissenschaft dürfe ihr Hauptaugenmerk nicht auf die Rekonstruktion der indogermanischen Grundsprache richten und dementsprechend vornehmlich den Vergleich der ältesten, der Grundsprache besonders nahestehenden Sprachen bzw. Sprachstufen (Altindisch, Altiranisch, Altgriechisch etc.) in den Mittelpunkt ihrer Untersuchungen stellen. Vielmehr gelte:

"[...] von der ursprache ab und der gegenwart zuwenden muss der vergleichende sprachforscher den blick, wenn er zu einer richtigen vorstellung von der art der fortentwicklung der sprache gelangen will [...]" (Osthoff & Brugmann 1878: vii)

Das heißt zugleich: nicht Literatursprache, sondern "das echte, naturwüchsige, reflexionslose alltagssprechen" (ebd.: vii−viii) gilt es zu untersuchen. Die Notwendigkeit eines solchen methodischen Richtungswechsels ergibt sich Brugmann zufolge zum einen aus der Tatsache, daß die Buchstaben nur sehr bedingt Rückschlüsse auf die Qualität der Laute zulassen, die sie repräsentieren. Zum anderen führt er als Beleg für seine Hypothese die Beobachtung an, daß lautliche Veränderungen in den Mundarten viel konsequenter durchgeführt werden, als man es aufgrund der Untersuchungen nur in schriftlicher Form erhaltener Sprachen hätte erwarten dürfen (vgl. ebd.: viii−ix).

(3) Sprachforscher müßten sich bewußt machen, daß sie, wenn sie von der "sprache" sprechen, eigentlich "die sprechenden menschen" meinen (ebd.: vii, Anm. 1). Der Begriff 'Sprache' verleite dazu, dieselbe als etwas unabhängig von den Menschen Existierendes zu betrachten und dabei zu vergessen, daß sie "nur im individuum ihre wahre existenz hat, und dass somit alle veränderungen im sprachleben nur von den sprechenden individuen ausgehen können" (ebd.: xii).

(4) Da man annehmen müsse, daß die psychischen und physischen Prozesse, die bei der Aneignung, der Reproduktion und der Neugestaltung einer Sprache durch die sprechenden Menschen beobachtbar sind, früher dieselben waren wie heute, sei die Annahme älterer Sprachforscher zurückzuweisen, für ältere Sprachstufen seien weniger Analogiebildungen anzusetzen als für jüngere, weil die Sprecher in älteren Sprachperioden noch ein besseres Sprachgefühl oder Sprachbewußtsein gehabt hätten (vgl. ebd.: xi−xii, xv).

Daraus ergeben sich die beiden zentralen methodischen Grundsätze der junggrammatischen Richtung:

"Erstens. Aller lautwandel, so weit er mechanisch vor sich geht, vollzieht sich nach ausnahmslosen gesetzen, [...]
Zweitens. Da sich klar herausstellt, dass die formassociation, d. h. die Neubildung von sprachformen auf dem wege der analogie, im leben der neueren sprachen eine sehr bedeutende rolle spielt, so ist diese art von sprachneuerung unbedenklich auch für die älteren und ältesten perioden anzuerkennen [...]" (Osthoff & Brugmann 1878: xiii)

Bereits 1874, also vier Jahre vor dem Erscheinen der *Morphologischen Untersuchungen*, hatten auch die Germanisten ein Organ für ihre Forschungsergebnisse gegründet, die heute noch erscheinenden "Beiträge zur Geschichte der deutschen Sprache und Literatur" mit einer wechselnden, zum Teil gemeinsamen Herausgeberschaft von Paul, Braune und Sievers (s. hierzu ausführlich Henne 1995: 1−10). Zur theoretischen Fundierung des Ansatzes haben jedoch vor allem Pauls 1880 veröffentlichte *Principien der sprachgeschichte* beigetragen, die bei den germanistischen wie bei den indogermanistischen Freunden gleichermaßen auf großen Respekt stießen. Mit Blick auf die Diskussion und die Aufbruchstimmung der 70er Jahre wird mit diesem Werk gewissermaßen ein Schlußpunkt gesetzt und die Phase der Konsolidierung des junggrammatischen Ansatzes eingeleitet.

Im folgenden soll ein kurzer Vergleich der ersten Auflage der *Principien* mit der vorjunggrammatischen Sprachwissenschaft, wie sie vor allem durch August Schleicher repräsentiert wurde, den sprachtheoretischen und methodischen Fortschritt der Junggrammatiker gegenüber ihren Vorgängern deutlich machen. Dabei werden auch die Anregungen berücksichtigt, die von Wilhelm Scherer ausgegangen sind.

4.2. August Schleicher und Hermann Paul im Vergleich

August Schleicher darf als zentraler Repräsentant jener Sprachwissenschaftlergeneration angesehen werden, von der sich die Junggrammatiker abzugrenzen suchten. Wenngleich nicht namentlich erwähnt, sind einige der von Brugmann in der Einleitung zum ersten Band der *Morphologischen Untersuchungen* angeführten Kritikpunkte offensichtlich direkt gegen seinen Ansatz gerichtet, so z. B. wenn die Verwendung der "so gemeinschädlichen ausdrücke 'jugendalter' und 'greisenalter der sprachen'" angeprangert wird (Osthoff & Brugmann 1878: xv). Die folgende Gegenüberstellung von Schleichers 1860 erschienenem Werk *Die Deutsche Sprache* (im folgenden wird aus der nur leicht abweichenden 5. Auflage von 1888 zitiert), in dem er sich im Vergleich zu seinen anderen Arbeiten am ausführlichsten mit theoretischen Fragestellungen auseinandersetzt, sowie einigen weiteren Veröffentlichungen Schleichers mit Pauls *Principien* konzentriert sich auf vier zentrale Aspekte: (1) das den Theorien jeweils zugrundeliegende Sprachkonzept, (2) die Auffassungen zum Phänomen des Sprachwandels, (3) die Ansichten über die Aufgaben und Methoden der Sprachwissenschaft sowie (4) die Einordnung der Sprachwissenschaft in das Gesamtspektrum der Wissenschaften.

(1) Das jeweilige Sprachkonzept

Mit Schleicher erlebt die durchaus nicht neue Organismus-Metapher ihren Höhepunkt. Er definiert Sprachen als

"[...] Naturorganismen, die, ohne vom Willen des Menschen bestimmbar zu sein, entstunden, nach bestimmten Gesetzen wuchsen und sich entwickelten und wiederum altern und absterben; auch ihnen ist jene Reihe von Erscheinungen eigen, die man unter dem Namen 'Leben' zu verstehen pflegt." (Schleicher 1863: 6−7; zur jüngsten Renaissance des Organismusbegriffs vgl. Schmitter 1992)

Wenngleich es Paul nicht immer gelingt, sich der Metapher vom 'Leben der Sprache' zu enthalten, distanziert er sich doch deutlich von der Organismus-Vorstellung, indem er − wie zuvor Brugmann − den Blick auf die Benutzer der Sprache lenkt. Aufgrund dieser neuen, auf dem individualpsychologischen Ansatz Johann Friedrich Herbarts (1776−1841) beruhenden Sichtweise gelingt ihm denn auch später die Differenzierung zwischen dem "Sprachusus" einerseits und der "individuellen Sprechtätigkeit" (Paul 1920 [1880]: 30) andererseits, womit er der Unterscheidung de Saussures zwischen *Langue* und *Parole* immerhin nahekommt (s. hierzu ausführlicher Meriggi 1966: 1; Koerner 1972, 1973 u. 1975 sowie Scheerer 1980: 143−144). Dabei ist ihm durchaus bewußt, daß der Usus nichts real Existierendes, sondern vielmehr eine Abstraktion ist (vgl. Paul 1920 [1880], Kap. II, ansatzweise auch schon in der 1. Aufl. sowie in den Erläuterungen zur Künstlichkeit der auf dem Usus beruhenden Gemeinsprache in Kap. XIV). Zwar taucht auch bei Paul der Begriff des "Sprachorganismus" auf, jedoch wird damit anders als bei Schleicher ein "psychischer organismus" (Paul 1880: 33) bezeichnet, ein individueller, weitgehend im Unterbewußtsein anzusiedelnder "organismus von vorstellungsgruppen" (Paul 1880: 29, 31), der sich bei jedem Mitglied einer Sprachgemeinschaft über den Kontakt zu anderen sprechenden Individuen herausbildet, sich ständig verändert (in der Kindheit stärker als im Alter) und damit eine zentrale Rolle für den Sprachwandel spielt (vgl. ebda. 31 ff.).

(2) Das Phänomen des Sprachwandels

Gemäß seiner Vorstellung von Sprachen als 'natürlichen', Pflanzen und Tieren vergleichbaren Organismen liegt die Veränderung von Sprache Schleicher zufolge gewissermaßen in der Natur der Sache; und wie die Pflanzen und Tiere durchlaufen die Sprachen seiner Ansicht nach auch eine Phase der Entwicklung und eine des Verfalls. In beiden Phasen kommen neben regelmäßigen Veränderungen, wie sie in jedem geschichtlichen Prozeß zu beobachten sind, v. a. auch Lautgesetze zum Tragen. Diese sind für ihn "physische Gesetze" (Schleicher 1983 [1850]: 15; s. a. Schleicher 1888: 50 ff.) insofern, als sie ihren "Grund in der Natur der menschlichen Sprachorgane" haben (Schleicher 1848: 120). Die Lautgesetze sind also Naturgesetze, die von außen, über die Sprachorgane auf die Sprache Einfluß nehmen. Da aber Naturgesetze regelmäßig sind, müssen auch Lautgesetze "von allgemeiner Geltung" sein (ebd.). Daneben nimmt Schleicher jedoch auch nicht-gesetzmäßige Lautveränderungen an, die im Naturorganismus Sprache von vornherein angelegt sind, vergleichbar mit dem genetischen Programm anderer Lebewesen. Johannes Schmidts (1887, 1893) Behauptung, daß schon Schleicher von der Ausnahmslosigkeit der Lautgesetze ausging, findet in seinen Schriften demnach keine Bestätigung (s. dazu ausführlicher Einhauser 1989: 200 ff.).

Mit Scherer als Zwischenstufe, der die Lautgesetze als historische Gesetze interpretierte und eine strengere Handhabung derselben forderte, sind es eben doch erst die Junggrammatiker, die die These von der Ausnahmslosigkeit der Lautgesetze aufstellen, wobei es sich, das muß immer wieder betont werden — in erster Linie um ein methodisches Postulat handelt, das als solches bis heute anerkannt wird. Bezüglich des Lautgesetz-Begriffs selbst war man sich auch unter den Junggrammatikern keineswegs einig (vgl. Schneider 1973: 19—53 sowie Einhauser 1989: 219—226). So war zunächst nicht nur bei Osthoff & Brugmann (1878) sondern auch bei Paul (1877) eine relativ große Nähe zu Schleichers Auffassung vom Lautgesetz als Naturgesetz erkennbar. Doch schon in der ersten Auflage seiner *Principien* wird das Lautgesetz von Paul "als beschreibende Formel für geschichtliche Tatsachen" definiert, wie Schneider (1973: 46) es formuliert:

"Das lautgesetz sagt nicht aus, was unter gewissen allgemeinen bedingungen immer wieder eintreten muss, sondern es constatiert nur die gleichmässigkeit innerhalb einer gruppe bestimmter historischer erscheinungen." (Paul 1880: 55; im Orig. gesperrt)

Wie erwähnt, bildet die Annahme, daß neben den Lautgesetzen Analogiebildungen starken Einfluß auf die Entwicklung einer Sprache nehmen, sozusagen das zweite Standbein der junggrammatischen Methode. Während Schleicher eher beiläufig auf diesen Faktor eingeht und zudem davon ausgeht, daß Analogiebildungen — wie die Lautgesetze — den Verfall einer Sprache bewirken, weil mit zunehmender Entfernung von den ursprünglichen Formen das Gefühl für ihre Bedeutung verloren gehe (vgl. Schleicher 1888 [1860]: 64—65), wird diese Position bereits von Scherer abgelehnt. Wie der von ihm geschätzte amerikanische Sprachwissenschaftler William Dwight Whitney (1827—1894) geht auch Scherer davon aus, daß man bei der Beschreibung sprachlicher Veränderungen nicht zwischen Entwicklungs- und Verfallsperioden differenzieren dürfe, daß die psychologischen und physiologischen Grundlagen sprachlicher Veränderungen vielmehr von jeher dieselben sind. Von Paul nun wird die Analogiebildung sogar als notwendige 'Gegenspielerin' zu den Lautgesetzen angesehen, ohne die eine Sprache aufgrund der lautlichen Veränderungen nach und nach an Zusammenhang verlieren und schließlich ihre Verständlichkeit einbüßen würde (vgl. Paul 1880: 100). Er geht sogar so weit zu behaupten, daß jeder auf einem Lautgesetz beruhende Lautwandel Analogiebildungen nach sich ziehe, um das Gleichgewicht wieder herzustellen, ohne daß diese jedoch mit der gleichen Regelmäßigkeit durchgeführt würden wie die Lautgesetze (vgl. Paul 1880: 104—105). Vor allem das Gedächtnis — das Ins-Bewußtsein-Treten einer traditionellen Form — trägt nach Ansicht Pauls dazu bei, daß die schöpferische Kraft, die in einer Neubildung enthalten ist, sich möglicherweise nicht durchsetzen kann (vgl. Paul 1880: 106 ff.). In der Erklärung dieses Phänomens zeigt sich, daß der Zugang zur Sprache zwanzig Jahre nach Schleicher nicht mehr unter dem Einfluß der Naturwissenschaften steht, sondern unter dem der sich als wissenschaftliche Disziplin gerade etablierenden Psychologie. Die Analogie wird bei den Junggrammatikern also zum psychologischen Pendant zu den rein physiologisch bedingten Lautgesetzen (zum Analogie-Konzept der Junggrammatiker s. auch Amsterdamska [1987: 106—109] sowie den "Ahnen"-Überblick bei Jankowsky 1990: 228—232).

Der Einfluß der Psychologie zeigt sich gleichermaßen in den grundsätzlichen Erörterungen zum Thema Sprachwandel. In diesem Punkt geht Paul weit über Schleicher hinaus, dessen Überlegungen zum Sprachwandelprozeß naturgemäß von seiner Organismusvorstellung geprägt waren: Sprache verändert sich, weil sie ein Naturorganismus ist; der individuelle Sprecher hat keinen Einfluß auf die Veränderungsprozesse.

Paul hingegen sieht den Auslöser für Veränderungen in dem Spannungsverhältnis, in dem der Sprachusus und die individuelle Sprechtätigkeit auf der Grundlage der individuellen psychischen Organismen zueinander stehen. Ansatzweise ist diese Überzeugung bereits in der ersten Auflage erkennbar (s. Paul 1880: 34), eine detailliertere Darstellung findet sich jedoch erst in den späteren Auflagen (1886, 1898 u. ö.). Demnach ergibt sich der Sprachusus einerseits aus den physischen Produkten der einzelnen Organismen der Sprecher einer Sprachgemeinschaft, andererseits ist er ausschlaggebend für die Grundkonstellation der jeweiligen psychischen Organismen. Dabei bleibt jedoch immer ein nicht unbeträchtliches Maß an individueller Freiheit erhalten, die es ermöglicht, Veränderungen des Usus herbeizuführen, der seinerseits wiederum auf die einzelnen Organismen einwirkt (vgl. Paul ^{5}1920: 29 ff.). Kurz: es ist die "gewöhnliche Sprechtätigkeit", durch die

Veränderungen des Usus verursacht werden, ohne daß dabei eine willentliche oder auch nur bewußte Einflußnahme vorläge. Ausschlaggebend ist vielmehr die Zweckmäßigkeit des neuen Sprachgebildes, das allein aus dem Bedürfnis heraus entstanden ist, sich verständlich zu machen. Paul schließt zwar bewußt vorgenommene Eingriffe nicht vollkommen aus, mißt ihnen jedoch eine höchst geringe Bedeutung bei (Paul ⁵1920: 32). Besonderes Gewicht kommt nach Ansicht Pauls der Phase des Spracherwerbs zu, denn in dieser Zeit ist das Individuum dem Einfluß der es umgebenden Sprecher am stärksten ausgesetzt, verhält sich jedoch noch schwankend hinsichtlich der Nachahmung und Anwendung der durch die ältere Generation gemachten Vorgaben, so daß Abweichungen beziehungsweise Neuerungen entstehen, die sowohl auf den Vorstellungsorganismus des Sprechers als auch auf den des Hörers wirken.

Das für Schleicher so zentrale Thema der Sprachspaltung mag hier ausgespart bleiben, da Paul sich ihm erst in späteren Auflagen zuwendet.

(3) Die Aufgaben und Methoden der Sprachwissenschaft

Für Schleicher umfaßt die Sprachwissenschaft zwei Bereiche, die "Grammatik" und die "Glottik". Zwar ist Schleicher bewußt, daß man eine Sprache auch "abgesehen von den Veränderungen", also synchronisch betrachten kann, doch ist diese Blickrichtung für ihn nur von Interesse, wenn es um die Beschreibung einer Sprache in der Phase ihrer "höchsten Entfaltung" (Schleicher 1888 [1860]: 124) geht, eine Voraussetzung, wie sie etwa im Fall der indogermanischen Ursprache gegeben wäre. Wichtiger erscheint ihm ohne Zweifel die Untersuchung der historischen Entwicklung einer Sprache, die "geschichtliche Grammatik oder Sprachengeschichte (Geschichte der Laute, der Form, der Function, des Satzbaues)" (ebd.). Der Glottik kommt die Aufgabe zu, die Verwandtschaftsverhältnisse zwischen den Sprachen aufzudecken, wobei sie sich auf die Ergebnisse der "geschichtlichen Grammatik" stützen kann. Vor allem diese vergleichende Sprachbetrachtung, wie sie üblicherweise genannt wird, nimmt in Schleichers Werk eine zentrale Rolle ein. Man kann sagen: Sprachwissenschaft ist für ihn Vergleichende Sprachengeschichte (wie auch eines seiner Werke betitelt ist) mit dem Ziel, ausgehend von der indoeuropäischen Ursprache einen 'genealogischen Stammbaum' zu erstellen, aus dem ersichtlich wird, wie und wann es von den Anfängen bis heute zu Sprachspaltungen gekommen ist, welchem Sprachtyp die einzelnen Sprachen angehören und in welchem Verhältnis sie zueinander stehen, d. h., welchen Zweigen sie innerhalb der "Gesamtfamilie" zuzuordnen sind. Die Ergebnisse seiner Forschungen münden schließlich in dem 1861−62 erschienenen *Compendium der vergleichenden Grammatik der indogermanischen Sprachen: Kurzer Abriss einer Laut- und Formenlehre der indogermanischen Ursprache, des Altindischen, Alteranischen, Altgriechischen, Altitalienischen, Altkeltischen, Altslawischen, Litauischen und Altdeutschen* (2 Bde., Weimar: Böhlau; 4. Aufl., 1876). Theoretische Grundlage ist die von ihm entwickelte Stammbaumtheorie, der Paul ebenso wenig zustimmte wie der Auffassung, man müsse bei der − lediglich rekonstruierten hypothetischen − Ursprache mit dem Vergleich beginnen. Ganz im Gegenteil: die Gegenwartssprache müsse der Ausgangspunkt sein, die Stufe in der Entwicklung einer Sprache also, die direkt − und das heißt auch: in ihrer mündlichen Existenzform − beobachtbar ist.

Doch darüber hinaus hat sich der Blickwinkel bei den Junggrammatikern auch grundsätzlich verändert. Neben das Was tritt verstärkt die Frage nach dem Wie und dem Warum. Mit dem bloßen 'Sammeln von Lautgesetzen', dem Anhäufen immer weiterer historischer Fakten allein mag man sich nicht mehr zufrieden geben. Daneben kommt zunehmend das Bedürfnis auf, differenziertere Erklärungen für die zu beobachtenden Fakten zu finden und letztlich das Phänomen Sprache in seiner Gesamtheit besser zu begreifen, letzteres allerdings nicht mit Hilfe einer eingeschränkten, rein synchronischen Sichtweise, sondern indem diese als integraler Bestandteil der nach wie vor grundsätzlich historisch orientierten Blickrichtung verstanden wird. So stellt Paul in einer seiner meistzitierten Äußerungen fest:

"Ich habe noch kurz zu rechtfertigen, dass ich den Titel Prinzipien der Sprachgeschichte gewählt habe. Es ist eingewendet, dass es noch eine andere wissenschaftliche Betrachtung der Sprache gäbe, als die geschichtliche. Ich muss das in Abrede stellen. Was man für eine nichtgeschichtliche und doch wissenschaftliche Betrachtung der Sprache erklärt, ist im Grunde nichts als eine unvollkommen geschichtliche, unvollkommen teils durch Schuld des Betrachters, teils durch Schuld des Beobachtungsmaterials. Sobald man über das bloße Konstatieren von Einzelheiten hinausgeht, sobald man versucht den Zusammenhang zu erfassen, die Erscheinungen zu begreifen, so betritt man auch den geschichtlichen Boden, wenn auch vielleicht ohne sich klar darüber zu sein." (Paul 1920 [²1886]: 20)

Dieser Passus ist zwar in der ersten Auflage noch nicht enthalten, sondern erst als Reaktion auf entsprechende Kritik formuliert worden, aber die hier so vehement verteidigte Sichtweise lag den *Principien* von Anfang an zugrunde.

Bedauerlicherweise ist Pauls Ansatz in der Sprachwissenschaftsgeschichtsschreibung häufig auf dieses Zitat reduziert worden, die deutliche Entwicklung, die in den *Principien* gegenüber Schleicher erkennbar ist (und auch gegenüber Scherer, der ja nur punktuelle Anstöße gab, ohne diese durch ein theoretisches Fundament abgesichert zu haben), wurden vielfach übersehen. Bereits in der ersten Auflage begründet Paul die Notwendigkeit, die Gegenwartssprache zum Ausgangspunkt sprachwissenschaftlicher Untersuchungen zu machen:

"Ohne sorgfältige achtsamkeit auf unsere eigene sprechtätigkeit und die unserer verkehrsgenossen ist gar keine anschauung von der entwicklungsweise der sprache zu gewinnen." (Paul 1880: 24; im Orig. gesperrt)

Zugleich erkennt er die Grenzen einer im strengen Sinne wissenschaftlichen Analyse, denn die ideale Grundlage wird dem Sprachforscher nie zur Verfügung stehen:

"Das wahre object für den sprachforscher sind […] sämmtliche äusserungen der sprachtätigkeit an sämmtlichen individuen in ihrer wechselwirkung auf einander." (Paul 1880: 28; im Orig. gesperrt)

Er betont wiederholt die Bedeutung der Psychologie für die Sprachwissenschaft, denn Veränderungen finden im Kopf statt, im Bereich des Unbewußten: "Das wirklich gesprochene hat gar keine entwickelung" (Paul 1880: 32; im Orig. gesperrt). Der physischen Seite des Sprechens wird also eine deutlich nachgeordnete Rolle zugewiesen, sie dient lediglich der Vermittlung zwischen den "psychischen organismen" (vgl. Paul 1880: 33). Und gerade diese neue 'psychologische' Sichtweise scheint es auch zu sein, die bei Paul zu einer differenzierteren Sichtweise der Sprache führt. Die Unterscheidung zwischen Sprachusus und individueller Sprechtätigkeit wird in der ersten Auflage zwar noch nicht explizit getroffen, aber immerhin wird hier bereits an der "bloss deskriptiven grammatik" kritisiert, daß sie immer nur "die *abstraction des der zeit üblichen* im auge" habe, wenn sie von Veränderungen der Sprache spricht (Paul 1880: 34; Hervorhebung von mir, E. E.) und daß das, "was die deskriptive grammatik eine sprache nennt", nicht mehr als eine "zusammenfassung des usuellen" sei und somit überhaupt keine reale Existenz habe (Paul 1880: 266). Dagegen setzt Paul immer wieder die Bedeutung der Sprach- bzw. Sprechtätigkeit (s. z. B. Paul 1880: 30 u. 34). Die Begriffe werden hier offensichtlich synonym verwendet, was — wie der noch fehlende Begriff des Sprachusus — deutlich macht, wie allmählich sich die später explizite begriffliche Differenzierung bei Paul entwickelt.

(4) Die Einordnung der Sprachwissenschaft
Nach anfänglichen Unsicherheiten — in der *Vergleichenden Sprachengeschichte* von 1848 hatte er die Sprachwissenschaft noch als eine Geschichtswissenschaft angesehen (zu den Gründen s. u. a. Streitberg 1899) — steht für Schleicher bereits zwei Jahre später fest, daß die Sprachwissenschaft gemäß seiner Annahme, die Sprache sei ein Naturorganismus, den Naturwissenschaften zuzuordnen ist (s. Schleicher 1983 [1850]: 1 ff., 10—11, Anm.), und diese Auffassung behält er dann auch in späteren Werken konsequent bei (s. 1888 [1860]: 120; 1863: 5 ff.). Damit einher geht eine strikte Abgrenzung von der Sprachphilosophie einerseits, die sich als nicht-empirische Wissenschaft zur Sprachwissenschaft verhalte wie die Naturphilosophie zu den Naturwissenschaften, und von der Philologie andererseits, die er, wie ursprünglich auch die Sprachwissenschaft selbst, den historischen Wissenschaften zuordnet (vgl. Schleicher 1888 [1860]: 119 ff.).

Schleichers Auffassung wird bereits von Scherer zurückgewiesen, begründet wird die daraus resultierende Zuordnung der Sprachwissenschaft zu den Geisteswissenschaften allerdings erst bei Paul. Paul spricht in diesem Zusammenhang jedoch nicht von Geistes-, sondern von Kulturwissenschaften. Ihm mißfällt die mit der Gegenüberstellung von Natur- und Geisteswissenschaften verbundene Vorstellung (wie sie sich z. B. bei Dilthey findet), bei den Naturwissenschaften handele es sich um erklärende Gesetzeswissenschaften, während die Geisteswissenschaften stets historisch ausgerichtete hermeneutische Gesellschaftswissenschaften seien. Das würde bedeuten, daß gesetzmäßige Prozesse einzig und allein Gegenstand der Naturwissenschaften sind, während sich die Geisteswissenschaften auf die Beobachtung geschichtlicher Entwicklungen beschränken. Da geschichtliche Entwicklungen jedoch nie allein auf psychischen, sondern immer auch auf physischen Faktoren beruhen, bevorzugt Paul den Begriff der Kulturwissenschaft. Die Sprachwissenschaft nun, die wie jede andere Kulturwissenschaft neben der allgemeinen Geschichtsforschung, deren Aufgabe es ist, historische Fakten zu sammeln, eine Prinzipienwissenschaft umfaßt, die die allgemeinen Bedingungen der sprachgeschichtlichen Entwicklung erforscht (s. Abb. 165.1), also gewissermaßen das theoretische Fundament für die Geschichtsforschung liefert, sei die unter den Geschichtswissenschaften methodisch am weitesten fortgeschrittene, woraus sich die im Vergleich mit den übrigen Geschichtswissenschaften größte Nähe zu den Naturwissenschaften ergebe. Das dürfe jedoch nicht dazu führen, sie mit diesen gleichzusetzen (1920: 5−6; zu diesem Thema insgesamt s. ebd., Einleitung). In diesem Zusammenhang weist Paul ausdrücklich auf die Leistungen der Junggrammatiker hin, wenn er betont, daß trotz der Sonderstellung, die der Sprachwissenschaft unter den Kulturwissenschaften von jeher aufgrund der vergleichsweise guten Beobachtbarkeit ihres Forschungsgegenstandes zukommt, noch viel daran zu fehlen scheine,

[...] dass ihre methode schon bis zu demjenigen grade der vollkommenheit ausgebildet wäre, dessen sie fähig ist. Eben jetzt sucht sich eine richtung bahn zu brechen, die auf eine tiefgreifende umgestaltung der methode hindrängt. Bei dem streite, der sich darüber entsponnen hat, ist deutlich zu tage getreten, wie gross noch bei vielen sprachforschern die unklarheit über die elemente ihrer wissenschaft ist. (Paul 1880: 7; Hervorhebung im Orig.)

In der fünften Auflage erscheint diese Passage so umformuliert, daß das Ziel der Vervollkommnung der Methode − dank der Junggrammatiker − offensichtlich als erreicht angesehen wird (s. Paul 1920: 5−6).

5. Resümee

Die historische sprachwissenschaftliche Forschung des 19. Jhs. findet ihren Höhepunkt

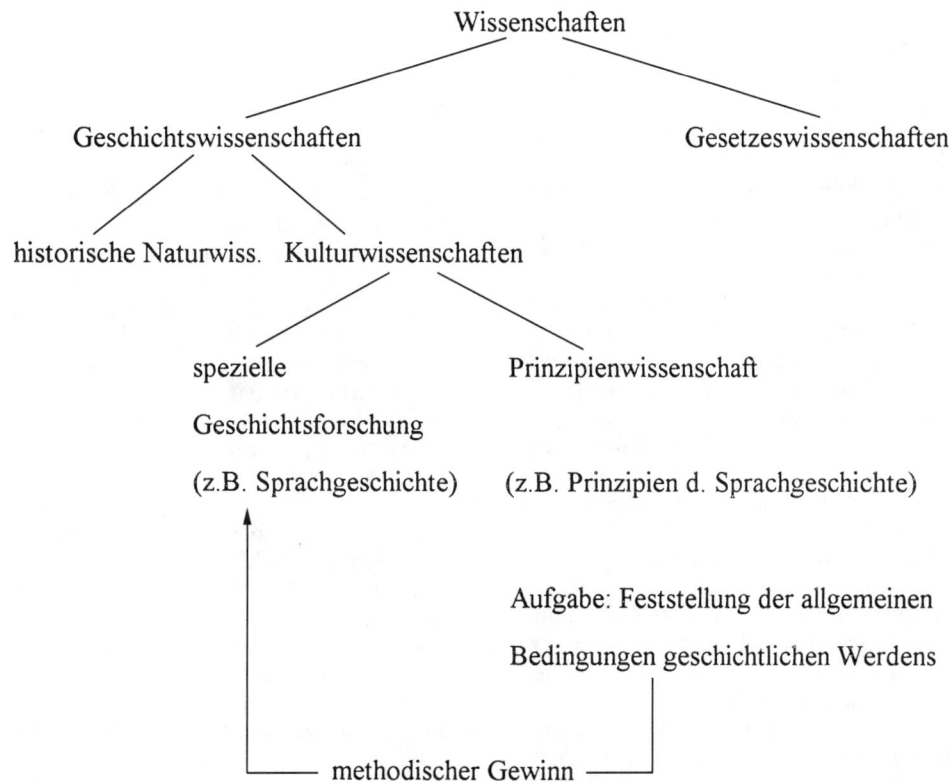

Abb. 165.1: Einordnung der Sprachwissenschaft nach Hermann Paul (1880: 7 ff.).

mit der Herausbildung der junggrammatischen Richtung. Nicht zuletzt aufgrund der Impulse, die in der zweiten Hälfte des 19. Jhs. von der Phonetik einerseits und der Psychologie andererseits ausgingen, ist bei den Junggrammatikern ein deutlicher Fortschritt gegenüber ihren Vorgängern zu verzeichnen, wobei vor allem folgende Punkte ins Gewicht fallen:

– eine bis dahin nicht dagewesene Rigorosität in der Handhabung der Lautgesetzfrage;
– eine größere Gewichtung psychologischer Faktoren sowie eine damit einhergehende verstärkte Anwendung des Prinzips der Analogie;
– die Aufwertung der Gegenwartssprache als einzige der direkten Beobachtung zugängliche Sprachstufe, die als Korrektiv bei der Untersuchung nur schriftlich überlieferter Sprachstufen dient, und
– ein im Ansatz erkennbares Bewußtsein von der Systemhaftigkeit der Sprache sowie ein verändertes Forschungsziel, das weniger auf die Beschreibung als auf die Erklärung sprachlichen Wandels ausgerichtet ist.

Was bleibt, ist die grundsätzlich historische Ausrichtung des Ansatzes, denn die 'Fähigkeit' zum Wandel wird als eine elementare Eigenschaft der Sprache angesehen. Eine Sprachbetrachtung, die diesen zentralen Aspekt unberücksichtigt läßt, die sich also auf die Beschreibung von Sprachzuständen beschränkt, ohne den historischen Kontext zu berücksichtigen, ist in den Augen der Junggrammatiker unwissenschaftlich. Allerdings stehen sich synchronische und diachronische Sprachbetrachtung nicht als unvereinbare Gegensätze gegenüber, wie dies aufgrund der Gleichsetzung der Begriffe 'diachronisch' und 'historisch' oft behauptet wird, vielmehr werden beide im Rahmen des Geschichtsbegriffs, wie er von Paul verstanden wird, vereint (s. hierzu Reis 1978: 183 sowie Albrecht 1988: 140). Trotzdem läßt sich nicht leugnen, daß die synchronische Sprachforschung nur als notwendige Vorstufe zur diachronischen Analyse verstanden wird, und in dieser Auffassung liegt denn auch der zentrale Unterschied zur strukturalistischen Sprachwissenschaft des 20. Jhs. begründet.

Sie bot selbst Wissenschaftlern, die den Junggrammatikern zunächst nahestanden (etwa Saussure oder Baudouin de Courtenay), wiederholt Anlaß zur Kritik. Das gleiche gilt für die trotz gegenteiliger Zielsetzungen doch vergleichsweise starke Konzentration auf die Laut- und Formenlehre sowie die einseitige Orientierung an der Individualpsychologie und die entsprechende Mißachtung der Völkerpsychologie, wie sie von Lazarus und Steinthal sowie später von Wundt vertreten wurde (s. dazu auch Bartschat 1996: 24–30). Darüber hinaus begegnet – bei den zeitgenössischen Kritikern ebenso wie in einer Vielzahl wissenschaftsgeschichtlicher Abhandlungen – unter dem Stichwort 'Positivismus' immer wieder das Pauschalurteil, mit dem die gesamte Sprachwissenschaft des 19. Jhs. bedacht wurde. Wie ungerechtfertigt diese Einschätzung in bezug auf die Junggrammatiker ist, wird in überzeugender Weise von Albrecht (1994) nachgewiesen. Eines darf allerdings bei der Bewertung der junggrammatischen Leistungen nicht außer acht gelassen werden: die praktische Umsetzung der eigenen theoretischen Sichtweise und der daraus resultierenden methodischen Forderungen kam etwas zu kurz. Trotzdem ist der folgenden Feststellung Amsterdamskas (1987: 101) zuzustimmen:

"If the Neogrammarians' proclamation of methodological innovations were more rhetorical than descriptive of their actual practice, nevertheless their understanding of the nature of language and of its history, their conception of linguistics as a science, and their justifications of the adopted research practice were new."

Im übrigen sind auch die Erfolge auf der Anwendungsebene beachtlich. Sie schlagen sich nicht nur in den zahlreichen Einzeluntersuchungen nieder, die unter dem Einfluß des junggrammatischen Ansatzes im letzten Drittel des 19. Jhs. und darüber hinaus durchgeführt wurden, sondern ebenso in der Vielzahl der Grammatiken, die die 'junggrammatische Handschrift' trugen beziehungsweise zum Teil bis heute tragen – und dies nicht nur im deutschsprachigen Raum (s. dazu Henne 1995: 11–21; Einhauser 1996).

Eine kritische Sichtung der zahlreichen Abhandlungen über die Junggrammatiker findet sich bei Einhauser (1989, Kap. 3). Daß sich diese Gruppe nach wie vor des Interesses der Wissenschaftsgeschichtsschreiber erfreut, läßt sich an den entsprechenden Veröffentlichungen der letzten Jahre erkennen. Neben den bereits erwähnten von Jankowsky (1990), Swiggers (1992), Albrecht (1994) und Henne (1995) sei außerdem auf den 1988 erschienenen Aufsatz "Luoghi comuni su Hermann Paul (e la scuola neogrammatica)" von Graffi hingewiesen sowie auf den von Jankowsky veröffentlichten Artikel über "Development of Historical Linguistics from Rask and Grimm to the Neogrammarians" (1996), der sich als ergänzende Lektüre zu diesem Beitrag empfiehlt.

6. Bibliographie

Ahlquist, Anders, Hg. 1992. *Diversions of Galway: Papers on the History of Linguistics from ICHoLS V, Galway, Ireland, 1–6 Septembre 1990*. Amsterdam & Philadelphia: Benjamins.

Albrecht, Jörn. 1988. *Europäischer Strukturalismus: Ein forschungsgeschichtlicher Überblick*. Darmstadt: Wissenschaftliche Buchgesellschaft.

–. 1994. "Hermann Paul, ein Strukturalist ante litteram?". Baum et al. 1994.393–408.

Amsterdamska, Olga. 1987. *Schools of Thought: The development of linguistics from Bopp to Saussure*. Dordrecht: Reidel.

Asher, R. E. & J. M. Y. Simpson, Hgg. 1994. *The Encyclopaedia of Language and Linguistics*. Vol. III. Oxford: Pergamon Press.

Bartschat, Brigitte. 1996. *Methoden der Sprachwissenschaft: Von Hermann Paul bis Noam Chomsky*. Berlin: Schmidt.

Baum, Richard, Klaus Böckle, Franz Josef Hausmann & Franz Lebsaft, Hgg. 1994. *Lingua et Traditio: Geschichte der Sprachwissenschaft und der neueren Philologien: Festschrift für Hans Helmut Christmann zum 65. Geburtstag*. Tübingen: Narr.

Bezzenberger, Adalbert. 1879. Rezension von Osthoff & Brugmann (1878). *Göttingische gelehrte Anzeigen* 2.641–681.

Brugmann, Karl. 1876. "Nasalis sonans in der indogermanischen Grundsprache". *Studien zur griechischen und lateinischen Grammatik* 9.285–338.

Christmann, Hans Helmut. 1977. *Sprachwissenschaft im 19. Jahrhundert*. Darmstadt: Wissenschaftliche Buchgesellschaft.

Collinge, N. E. 1994. "Historical Linguistics: History". Asher & Simpson 1994 III, 1559–1567.

Delbrück, Hermann. 1880. *Einleitung in das Sprachstudium: Ein Beitrag zur Geschichte und Methodik der vergleichenden Sprachforschung*. Leipzig: Breitkopf & Härtel.

–. 1885. *Die neueste Sprachforschung: Betrachtungen über Georg Curtius Schrift 'Zur Kritik der neuesten Sprachforschung'*. Leipzig: Breitkopf & Härtel. (Wiederabdruck in Wilbur 1977.)

Einhauser, Eveline. 1989. *Die Junggrammatiker: Ein Problem für die Sprachwissenschaftsgeschichtsschreibung*. Trier: Wissenschaftlicher Verlag Trier.

–, Hg. 1992. *Lieber freund ... Die Briefe Hermann Osthoffs an Karl Brugman, 1875–1904*. Trier: Wissenschaftlicher Verlag Trier.

–. 1996. "Grammatikschreibung in der Tradition der Historischen Grammatik: Ein Ausblick auf das 20. Jahrhundert". Schmitter 1996.216–243.

Graffi, Giorgio. 1988. "Luoghi comuni su Hermann Paul (e la scuola neogrammatica)". *Lingua e Stile* 23: 2.211–234.

Harsch-Niemeyer, Robert, Hg. 1995. *Beiträge zur Methodengeschichte der neueren Philologien: Zum 125jährigen Bestehen des Max Niemeyer Verlages*. Tübingen: Niemeyer.

Henne, Helmut. 1995. "Germanische und deutsche Philologie im Zeichen der Junggrammatiker". Harsch-Niemeyer 1995.1–30.

Hoenigswald, Henry M. 1978. "The Annus Mirabilis 1876 and Prosterity". *Transactions of the Philological Society. Commemorative Volume: The Neogrammarians*, 17–35. London.

Jankowsky, Kurt R. 1972. *The Neogrammarians: A re-evaluation of their place in the development of linguistic science*. The Hague: Mouton.

–. 1990. "Theoretical Models of Change: The Neogrammarian Hypothesis". Polomé 1990.223–239.

–. 1996. "Development of Historical Linguistics from Rask and Grimm to the Neogrammarians". Schmitter 1996.193–208.

Koerner, E. F. Konrad. 1972. "Hermann Paul and Synchronic Linguistics". *Lingua* 29.274–307. (Wiederabdruck in Koerner 1978.73–106.)

–. 1973. *Ferdinand de Saussure: Origin and Development of His Linguistic Thought in Western Studies of Language*. Braunschweig: Vieweg.

–. 1975. "European Structuralism: Early beginnings". Sebeok 1975.717–827.

–. 1976. "1876 as a Turning Point in the History of Linguistics". *Journal of Indo-European Studies* 4.333–353. (Wiederabdruck in Koerner 1978.189–209.)

–. 1978. *Toward a Historiography of Linguistics: Selected essays*. Amsterdam: Benjamins.

Leskien, August. 1876. *Die Declination im Slavisch-Litauischen und Germanischen*. Leipzig: Hirzel.

Meriggi, Piero. 1966. "Die Junggrammatiker und die heutige Sprachwissenschaft". *Sprache* 12.1–15.

Osthoff, Hermann. 1876. "Zur frage des ursprungs der germanischen N-declination (Nebst einer theorie über die ursprüngliche unterscheidung starker und schwacher casus im indogermanischen.)". *Beiträge zur Geschichte der deutschen Sprache und Literatur* 3.1–89.

Osthoff, Hermann & Karl Brugmann. 1878. *Morphologische Untersuchungen auf dem Gebiete der indogermanischen Sprachen* Bd. I. Leipzig: Hirzel. (Nachdruck, Hildesheim: Olms, 1974. Vorwort zu Band I auch wieder in Christmann 1977.190–206.

Paul, Hermann. 1880. *Principien der Sprachgeschichte*. Halle: Niemeyer.

—. 1920. *Prinzipien der Sprachgeschichte.* 5. Aufl. Halle/S.: Niemeyer. (Wiederabdruck, Tübingen: Niemeyer, 1975.)

Polomé, Edgar C., Hg. 1990. *Research Guide on Language Change.* Berlin & New York: Mouton de Gruyter.

Reis, Marga. 1978. "Hermann Paul". *Beiträge zur Geschichte der deutschen Sprache und Literatur* 100: 2.159–204.

Scheerer, Thomas M. 1980. *Ferdinand de Saussure: Rezeption und Kritik.* Darmstadt: Wissenschaftliche Buchgesellschaft.

Scherer, Wilhelm. 1868. *Zur Geschichte der deutschen Sprache.* Berlin: Duncker. (New ed., with an Introd. by Kurt R. Jankowsky, Amsterdam & Philadelphia: Benjamins, 1995.)

Schleicher, August. 1848. *Zur vergleichenden Sprachengeschichte.* Bonn: König.

—. 1983 [1850]. *Die Sprachen Europas in systematischer Übersicht: Linguistische Untersuchungen.* New edition with an introductory article by Konrad Koerner. Amsterdam & Philadelphia: John Benjamins.

—. 1863. *Die Darwinsche Theorie und die Sprachwissenschaft: Offenes Sendschreiben an Herrn Dr. Ernst Häckel* [...] Weimar: Böhlau. (Wiederabdruck in Christmann 1977.85–105.)

—. 1888 [1860]. *Die deutsche Sprache.* 4. Aufl. Stuttgart: Cotta.

Schmidt, Johannes. 1887, 1893. "Schleichers Auffassung der Lautgesetze". *Zeitschrift für vergleichende Sprachforschung* 28.303–312, 32.419–420.

Schmitter, Peter. 1992. "'Maschine' vs. 'Organismus': Einige Überlegungen zur Geistes- und Sprachwissenschaftsgeschichte im 18. und 19. Jahrhundert". Ahlquist 1992.291–307.

—. Hg. 1996. *Sprachtheorien der Neuzeit II: Von der Grammaire de Port-Royal (1660) zur Konstitution moderner linguistischer Disziplinen.* (= Geschichte der Sprachtheorie, 5.) Tübingen: Narr.

Schneider, Gisela. 1973. *Zum Begriff des Lautgesetzes in der Sprachwissenschaft seit den Junggrammatikern.* Tübingen: Narr.

Schuchardt, Hugo. 1928 [1922]. *Hugo Schuchardt-Brevier: Ein Vademecum der allgemeinen Sprachwissenschaft.* Zusammengestellt und eingeleitet von Leo Spitzer. 2. erw. Aufl. (Wiederabdruck, Darmstadt: Wissenschaftliche Buchgesellschaft, 1976.)

Sebeok, Thomas A., Hg. 1975. *Current Trends in Linguistics.* Bd. 13: *Historiography of Linguistics.* The Hague: Mouton.

Sievers, Eduard. 1876. *Grundzüge der Lautphysiologie zur Einiführung in das Studium der Lautlehre der indogermanischen Sprachen.* Leipzig: Breitkopf & Härtel.

—. 1877. "Zur accent- und lautlehre der germanischen sprachen". *Beiträge zur Geschichte der deutschen Sprache und Literatur* 4.522–539.

Streitberg, Wilhelm. 1899. "Schleichers Auffassung von der Stellung der Sprachwissenschaft". *Indogermanische Forschungen* 7.360–372.

Swiggers, Pierre. 1992. "A propos du terme 'junggrammatisch': Une lettre de Holger Pedersen à Hugo Schuchardt". *Historische Sprachforschung* 105.155–160.

Verner, Karl. 1876. "Eine Ausnahme der ersten Lautverschiebung". *Zeitschrift für vergleichende Sprachforschung auf dem Gebiete der indogermanischen Sprachen* 23.97–130.

Wilbur, Terence H., Hg. 1977. *The Lautgesetz-Controversy: A documentation (1885–1886).* Amsterdam: Benjamins.

Winteler, Jost. 1876. *Die Kerenzer Mundart des Kantons Glarus in ihren Grundzügen dargestellt.* Leipzig & Heidelberg: Winter.

Ziemer, Hermann. 1883. *Junggrammatische Streifzüge im Gebiete der Syntax.* Colberg: Post'sche Buchhandlung. (1. Aufl., 1882.)

Eveline Einhauser, Köln (Deutschland)

166. The consolidation of the neogrammarian framework

1. Introduction
2. Initial pronouncements of neogrammarian objectives
3. Converting programmatic statements into exemplary publications
4. Neogrammarian accomplishments gaining ground
5. Sound laws, analogy and beyond
6. Consolidating the neogrammarian 'paradigm'
7. Conclusion
8. Bibliography

1. Introduction

The Neogrammarians – or 'Young Grammarians' in a more appropriate translation of the original term *Junggrammatiker* – were a fairly loosely-knit group of linguists who, during the last quarter of the 19th century, had acquired, mostly through the excellence of their individual work, a reputation which no other group of linguistic scholars had been able to achieve in Germany at that time, probably at any time. 'The Neogrammarians stand out in their time in the linguistic world' (Růžička 1977: 5). In all likelihood the group members had exchanged ideas about what was to be publicly announced (cf. Norman 1972: 84), and they certainly stayed in touch with one another for most of their lives, even though it is doubtful that they at any time considered any special arrangement to become much more than an informal group of friends and colleagues who shared professional objectives important to them (cf. Brugmann 1900: 131–132). The original group is mostly defined (cf. Jankowsky 1972: 127–128) as consisting of the Indo-Europeanists Karl Brugmann (1849–1919), August Leskien (1840–1916), Hermann Osthoff (1847–1909), Berthold Delbrück (1842–1922) and the Germanists Hermann Paul (1846–1921), Eduard Sievers (1850–1932), Wilhelm Braune (1850–1926), and Friedrich Kluge (1856–1926). In 1876, the year referred to by Henry Hoenigswald (1978) as *annus mirabilis*, they started to proclaim an ambitious program which amounted to no less than the demand for a radical change of previous practices. They were very young indeed. At the beginning of their campaign, only Leskien was older than 30, and Kluge, with 20 years of age, was the youngest, still a graduate student by our terms today. On account of his young age in 1876 he might have to be called a latecomer to the group, but he certainly showed great familiarity with neogrammarian thought already in the first major work, his doctoral dissertation of 1879, which won special praise from Hermann Osthoff even one year before it was published (cf. Einhauser 1992: 79). Apart from their unbounded enthusiasm and great academic promise, they had luck on their side. The large number of their predecessors had readied the stage for them to act boldly and, as they thought, for fairly good reasons. Ever since the beginning of Indo-European studies in the first quarter of the 19th century, linguists had yearned to achieve results – as well as prestige – comparable to those obtained in the natural sciences. While such achievements had largely remained wishful thinking, notable advances were made on several fronts. Most significant among them was the discovery of Karl Verner (1846–1896) in 1875, published in April 1876. What he had found, in the words of W. P. Lehmann (1967: 132), "may be the single most influential publication in linguistics" in that it "solved the most troublesome contemporary problem – 'the last set of exceptions to Grimm's law'."

From 1876 onwards, spurred by Verner's discovery, The Neogrammarians, notably Brugmann and Osthoff, became extremely active in producing statements regarding their objectives as well as an abundance of scholarly work by which they sought to implement assiduously their various programmatic announcements. The immediate outbreak of controversy between the older, more conservative generation of linguists – represented notably by Georg Curtius (1820–1885), but also Johannes Schmidt (1843–1901) as well as others – and the somewhat radical 'Young Turks' (Hockett 1965: 186–187) was as least as much a clash of personalities as it was a dispute over accomplished research. Although somewhat pointedly phrased, one might agree with Labov's endorsement of Hoenigswald's view that "the time and ink devoted [by commentators too numerous to mention] to the Lautgesetzfrage has been spilt on a misunderstanding" (Labov 1981: 272). At least their earlier statements were somewhat vague, almost casual, sometimes outright abrasive, showing little or no regard at all for the accomplishments of some of their predecessors, and above all lacking effective coordination.

Hardly any of these problems have affected adversely the nature of their publications, however. Graziadio Isaia Ascoli (1829–1907), basically well disposed towards the Neogrammmarians, but on occasions also one of their harshest critics (cf. Ascoli 1886), later provided a sober-minded evaluation at the time when the storm had reached its peak: 'When checking into the entire controversy thoroughly and comprehensively without bias, it seems indeed almost impossible that it could ever have existed' ("In der Tat erscheint es bei einer unbefangenen umfassenden und eingehenden Prüfung der gesamten Kontroverse fast unmöglich, dass sie jemals existieren konnte" [Ascoli 1887: 171]).

2. Initial pronouncements of neogrammarian objectives

The introduction to Leskien's *Declination im Slavisch-Litauischen und Germanischen*, published in 1876, contains the following passage (p. xxxiv):

'In this investigation I have taken my lead [...] from the principle that the form of a casus as it has come down to us is never based on an exception to otherwise observed sound laws. [...]: if one understands exceptions as such cases where the expected sound change has not occurred because of certain recognizable circumstances, then there can of course no objections be raised against the statement that the sound laws are not without exceptions.'

["Bei der Untersuchung bin ich [...] von dem Grundsatz ausgegangen, dass die uns überlieferte Gestalt eines Casus niemals auf einer Ausnahme von den sonst befolgten Lautgesetzen beruhe. [...]: versteht man unter Ausnahmen solche Fälle, in denen der zu erwartende Lautwandel aus bestimmten erkennbaren Umständen nicht eingetreten ist [...], so ist gegen den Satz, die Lautgesetze seien nicht ausnahmslos, natürlich nichts einzuwenden." — Translation from the German, here and elsewhere, are mine: KRJ. Where necessary and feasible, the spelling has been adjusted in accordance to current practices.]

Needless to say, this statement, tucked away in a lengthy discussion of what Leskien intended to present in the main part of his treatise and specifically dealing with Johannes Schmidt's 'Wave Theory' ("Wellentheorie"; cf. Schmidt 1872: 27 ff.) in comparison with Schleicher's (1821–1868) 'Family-Tree Theory' ("Stammbaumtheorie"; cf. Schleicher ^{3}1874 [1860]: 72 ff.; 1861–1862 [^{4}1876]: 6–7; ^{2}1873 [1863]: 18 ff., 34–35), was far from being elaborate and had to give rise almost automatically to serious objections by linguists who so far had worked under somewhat different premises, mainly due to the fact that they followed the time-honored tradition of classical language studies. Georg Curtius, for instance, the teacher of most of the *Junggrammatiker*, had always maintained 'that the future of both sciences [classical philology and comparative-historical linguistics] rests on their adequate and vigorous interrelation' (Curtius ^{2}1848 [1845]: 26). But even if Leskien's wording, "that curiously undigested lump of wisdom" (Hoenigswald 1878: 24), did indeed "cause intellectual discomfort" (ibid.), one has also to acknowledge the assertion of Eduard Hermann (1869–1950) 'that Leskien's statement of the exceptionless operation of the sound laws has had an extraordinarily healthy effect in linguistic science. It has sharpened the eyes of the linguists in an unprecedented way' (1931: 5). And Hermann, a student of Delbrück, was by no means favorably inclined towards the Neogrammarians. He not only questioned Paul's treatment of analogy, but also remarked that in the course of time his 'doubts as to the exceptionless operation of the sound laws too had become stronger and stronger' (Hermann 1931: iii).

The second important pronouncement of the principles that should guide the historical linguist, the 18-page "Vorwort" to vol. I of *Morphologische Untersuchungen* by Osthoff and Brugmann, left hardly anything to be desired as far as clarity and comprehensiveness of the neogrammarian objectives are concerned. But it also contained a number of assertions that were openly aggressive and were bound to raise vociferous objections from a number of linguists who, with a more factual and less emotionally charged approach, could have easily been won over to their position. (This *Manifesto*, although signed by Osthoff and Brugmann, was in effect written by Brugmann; about two decades later Brugmann [1900: 131] revealed that Osthoff's role consisted in no more than dissecting 'one or two of my sentences which had turned out to be too long' ["eine oder zwei meiner Perioden, die zu lang ausgefallen waren"].) More importantly, while the contents of the "Vorwort" had certainly been discussed among the group participants, there is no evidence that the other group members contributed any substantial portion of it. They could hardly have been unaware of any of the major factual components, however, though it is safe to assume that none of them, with the exception of Osthoff, would have made use of the same aggressive tone that Brugmann had employed. It should also be mentioned at this point that Brugmann and his academic teacher and mentor Georg Curtius had broken off relations over a dispute concerning the publication of two papers of Brugmann's in Curtius' *Studien zur griechischen und lateinischen Grammatik*, of which Curtius had made his star pupil the co-editor for the last two volumes. In a brief "Nachwort" to *Studien* 9 (1876) Curtius let it be known that he had entertained considerable doubts as to the 'direction and method of investigation' as manifested in the contributions of his co-editor to the current issue, but could not take action in time 'due to an extended absence from Leipzig' (Curtius 1876: 468). As an immediate reaction, Curtius informed Brugmann in a personal letter that his co-editorship of the *Studien* would be terminated (Streitberg 1921: 29), and the journal was discontinued in the following year. In response, Brugmann together with Osthoff founded *Morphologische Untersuchungen* in 1878. (The first five volumes appeared between 1878 and 1890, a sixth and last volume was published only in 1910.) The two co-founders were the sole contributors. The following passage in a letter from Osthoff to Brugmann, dated 2 April, 1877, shows the intensity and bitterness of the dispute (as well as Osthoff's sense that history was being made):

'If I were you I would [...] carefully preserve the correspondence with C[urtius]: it may very well serve for posterity, when we have been in our graves for a long time, as a valuable document in the history of linguistics, insofar as it illustrates not only a personal conflict, but more importantly the fight of a ground-breaking new trend with one that is old and rotten.' (Einhauser 1992: 31)

["Die Korrespondenz mit C[urtius] würde ich [...] an Deiner Stelle sorgfältig aufbewahren: sie kann vielleicht der Nachwelt, wenn wir längst im Grabe liegen, als wertvolles Dokument in der Geschichte der Sprachwissenschaft dienen, insofern als sie nicht nur einen persönlichen Konflikt, vielmehr den Kampf einer sich Bahn brechenden neuen Richtung mit einer alten verrotteten illustriert."]

In a later section I will deal with the large number of programmatic statements made in this 'Neogrammarian *Credo*'. Here I will briefly examine how the Neogrammarians looked upon the achievements of the past. They certainly acknowledged previous accomplishments, but their verdict, especially with regard to contemporary linguists, was probably overstated. The availability of new insights into historical processes, for instance Wilhelm Scherer's (1841–1886) equation of conditions that prevailed in prehistorical and in historical times (cf. Scherer 1868 [^{2}1878]: x), required a thorough reassessment of current procedures, and even if the necessary reorientation was somewhat slow in gaining ground, there was no need to embark on a crusade-like campaign against all those who had achieved a great deal in the past and were now somewhat hesitant to change course without being sufficiently convinced of its necessity. (Indeed, a similar atmosphere and open warfare between the older generation and the younger linguists reigned during the 1960s when Chomsky and his followers and associates did battle with the 'structuralists'.) Curtius, for one, when he elaborated his position concerning the four major items of disagreement with his younger colleagues — (1) Sound Laws, (2) analogy, (3) the origin of the Indo-European vocalism, and (4) the emergence of the Indo-European linguistic forms — had stated unequivocally in his 161-page treatise that 'nobody will expect that these deliberations will result in a retraction of the views which I had formed in younger years in connection with the founders of our science [i. e., Bopp and his generation]' (Curtius 1885: 5). No doubt, he wanted his position to be heard and maintained and his work acknowledged. It may be argued that, had the Neogrammarians strictly stated facts and refrained from taking recourse to repeated invectives, their pronouncements would have generated far more desirable results — at least in relation to their teachers. One example of the aggressive language used in the *Manifesto* may suffice:

'Only that comparative linguist who for once emerges from the hypotheses-beclouded atmosphere of the workshop, in which the original Indo-European forms are forced, and steps into the clear air of tangible reality and of the present in order to get information about those things which gray theory can never reveal to him, and only he who renounces forever that formerly widespread but still used method of investigation according to which people observe language only on paper and resolve everything into terminology, systems of rules, and grammatical formalism and believe they have then fathomed the essence of the phenomena when they have devised a name for the thing — only he can arrive at a correct idea of the way in which linguistic forms live and change, and only he can acquire those methodological principles without which no credible results can be obtained at all in investigations in historical linguistics and without which any penetration into the periods of the past which lie behind the historical tradition of a language is like a sea voyage without a compass.' (Osthoff & Brugmann 1878: ix–x; quoted after Lehmann 1967: 202)

["Nur derjenige vergleichende Sprachforscher, welcher aus dem hypothesentrüben Dunstkreis der Werkstätte, in der man die indogermanischen Grundformen schmiedet, einmal heraustritt in die klare Luft der greifbaren Wirklichkeit und Gegenwart, um sich hier Belehrung zu holen über das, was ihm die graue Theorie nimmer erkennen lässt, und nur derjenige, welcher sich für immer lossagt von jener früherhin weit verbreiteten, aber auch jetzt noch anzutreffenden Forschungsweise, nach der man die Sprache nur auf dem Papier betrachtet, alles in Terminologie, Formelwesen und grammatischen Schematismus aufgehen lässt und das Wesen der Erscheinungsform immer schon dann ergründet zu haben glaubt, wenn man einen Namen für die Sache ausfindig gemacht hat: — nur der kann zu einer richtigen Vorstellung von der Lebens- und Umbildungsweise der sprachlichen Formen gelangen und diejenigen methodischen Prinzipien gewinnen, ohne welche man überhaupt bei sprachgeschichtlichen Forschungen keine glaubwürdigen Resultate erlangen kann und ohne welche im besonderen ein Vordringen in die hinter der Sprachüberlieferung zurückliegenden Zeiträume einer Meerfahrt ohne Kompass gleicht."]

If the aggressive tone is disregarded and the focus is placed on the general argument in favor of a new methodology, the passage contains mostly legitimate proposals. But the text as a whole had to come across to the majority of fellow linguists not associated with the group as extremely provocative, especially since the tone used in that passage is just one example of their obviously arrogant behavior. This was bound to upset especially the senior members of the profession.

3. Converting programmatic statements into exemplary publications

Of several other pronouncements made between 1876 and 1878, those of Brugmann (1876a: 317 ff.), Paul (1877: 321 ff.), and Osthoff (1878: vii–viii) are the most noteworthy, although especially those by Brugmann and by Osthoff show an aggressive flavor similar to that of the *Manifesto*. In the subsequent years, however, the formulations became much more factual and much less emotion-laden. The provocative tone was replaced by a tendency to explain and convince their skeptics. To defuse criticism, an attempt was made to characterize the encountered opposition as due to a lack of understanding of the neogrammarian position. Hermann Paul, for instance, had no difficulty finding the appropriate words:

'The idea of sound-law is not to be understood in the sense in which we speak of 'laws' in Physics or Chemistry [...]. Sound-law does not pretend to state what must always under certain general conditions regularly recur, but merely expresses the reign of uniformity within a group of definite historical phenomena.' (Paul ⁵1920 [1880]: 68; English translation quoted after Strong 1890: 57)

["In dem Sinne, wie wir in der Physik oder Chemie von Gesetzen reden [...], ist der Begriff 'Lautgesetz' nicht zu verstehen. Das Lautgesetz sagt nicht aus, was unter gewissen allgemeinen Bedingungen immer wieder eintreten muss, sondern es konstatiert nur die Gleichmässigkeit innerhalb einer Gruppe bestimmter historischer Erscheinungen."]

This wording is a clarifying formulation, which ought to have been suitable to pour oil on the troubled waters. Statements like these have been forthcoming regularly also from other Neogrammarians from 1880 onwards. They caught the attention of some, but were disregarded by many others who continued to consider the formulations in the "Vorwort" of 1878 as the 'official' neogrammarian *Credo*, since that statement was never expressly withdrawn. How formulations changed over the years is illustrated best by a quotation from Paul (1879a: 166), where he maintained the Brugmann-Osthoff line 'that each sound law functions with absolute necessity, that it permits an exception no less than a chemical or physical law' ("dass jedes Lautgesetz mit absoluter Notwendigkeit wirkt, dass es ebenso wenig eine Ausnahme gestattet, wie ein chemisches oder physikalisches Gesetz"). Delbrück, the self-appointed historian of the Neogrammarians – specializing in morphology and syntax rather than in phonology – was, according to the stated objective of his *Einleitung in das Sprachstudium*, interested 'to facilitate [...] the comprehension of comparative philology in its newest shape' ("das Verständnis der vergleichenden Sprachforschung in ihrer neuesten Gestalt zu erleichtern" [Delbrück 1880: v]; English translation quoted after Delbrück 1882: v). The author proved to be quite capable of handling even the most delicate subjects – such as the notion of sound law – with insightful caution and without any concessions to clarity: 'The phontic laws [...] are [...] nothing but uniformities which appear in a certain language and period, for which alone they are valid' ("Die Lautgesetze [...] sind [...] nichts anderes als Gleichmässigkeiten, welche in einer gewissen Sprache und Zeit auftreten, und nur für diese Zeit Gültigkeit haben" [Delbrück 1880: 128] and Delbrück 1882: 130). In his rejoinder to Georg Curtius' *Zur Kritik der neuesten Sprachforschung*, Delbrück goes even one step further: 'It has been [...] repeatedly stressed that it would be preferable not to speak of laws, but instead, more modestly, of historical regularities' ("Es ist [...] wiederholt hervorgehoben worden, dass man besser thäte, nicht von Gesetzen, sondern bescheidener von geschichtlichen Gleichmässigkeiten zu reden" [Delbrück 1885: 17]).

The 1880 quotation is from a lengthy chapter on "Die Lautgesetze" ('Phonetic Laws') which deals extensively with numerous aspects that are important not only for the neogrammarian position, but also for removing objections raised by their critics and potential opponents, including notably the group of linguists around August Fick (1833–1916) in Göttingen, for instance, Hermann Collitz (1855–1935). Delbrück took care to acknowledge the achievements of various predecessors, including Schleicher and Curtius (cf. Delbrück 1880: 101–128). Still much later, in 1902, he did additional noteworthy public-relation work with a 31-page article on "Das Wesen der Lautgesetze" ('The Nature of the Sound Laws'). That, however, happened at a time when the neogrammarian framework was already well established. Here his theoretical presentation is backed up with ample data from actual research. He also refers the reader to Eduard Wechssler's treatise on *Gibt es Lautgesetze?* (1900) which discusses the considerable amount of literature that had appeared until 1900, and does it, according to Konrad Burdach (1934: 108), both objectively and comprehensively: 'The factual core of the oftentimes heated debates has been described most impartially and most distinctly by the Romanist Eduard Wechssler.'

Not all linguists outside the close circle of friends found fault with the abrasive flavor of the "Vorwort". I would like to mention Franz Misteli (1841–1903) as one scholar who was capable of looking beyond the annoying language of the *Credo* and write a very constructive review of the "Vorwort" and other recent writings by members of the Leipzig circle in a 137-page paper published in 1879 and 1880. Starting with an evaluation of the *Credo*, Misteli expands his review article to include not only the 290 pages of research papers in the first volume of *Morphologische Untersuchungen* (3 by Brugmann, 2 by Osthoff), but he also refers to other works by the same authors as well as other Neogrammarians, thus presenting a comprehensive picture of what the 'new movement' aimed at and had achieved so far.

Misteli does not hold back criticism, but he approaches his task in every instance constructively, arriving in the end at a rather positive evaluation of what the Neogrammarians had proposed and what they actually had attained to date:

'The purpose of the article is to have voiced and as I believe also proved that the main propositions of the Neogrammarians can claim full recognition, even if they do not constitute a revolution, but a development of linguistic science.' (Misteli 1879–1880: 25)

["Der Zweck der Abhandlung ist, die Ueberzeugung ausgesprochen und ich, ich glaube, auch begründet zu haben, dass die Hauptsätze der junggrammatischen Schule volle Anerkennung verlangen dürfen, wenn sie gleich keinen Umschwung, sondern eine Entwicklung der Sprachwissenschaft darstellen."]

Statements like these definitely helped spread a better understanding of what the Neogrammarians were trying to do much more effectively than the Neogrammarians themselves have initially been able to.

The *Manifesto* of 1878 undoubtedly conveyed the impression that its writers thought of their movement as a major breakthrough, as a discontinuity with earlier methods that had outlasted their usefulness. Only two years later, Delbrück (1880: 55; English version 1882: 56) could correctly assert that 'a new tendency began to gain ground, which was partly a continuation of the previous endeavors, partly an attempt to oppose, ameliorate and expand them'.

Statements like the following by Hermann Collitz reflect the angry reaction by many contemporary linguists – even among some of the younger generation:

'It seems to me an injustice and an unparalleled arrogance that Brugmann attempts to withhold credit for having founded once for all the method of historical linguistics from those men [Bopp, Grimm, W. von Humboldt, Pott, Benfey, Schleicher and others], in order to assign this credit to the neogrammarian school' (Collitz 1886: 219).

In the wake of Verner's (1876) discovery, the extraordinary enthusiasm it created, and the mixture of justified and perhaps unrealistic hopes it brought to the fore, the overstatement on the part of Brugmann and others was an almost natural expression. Yet by the time his *Grammar of Greek* (1885b) was to appear, Brugmann wrote in a clearly conciliatory tone: 'I for my part have always taken the newer viewpoints as only the organic and consistent development of the older endeavors, and this attitude has become stronger in me from year to year.' ("Ich für meine Person habe die neueren Anschauungen immer nur für die organische und folgerechte Fortentwicklung der älteren Bestrebungen gehalten, und diese Ansicht hat sich mir von Jahr zu Jahr mehr befestigt" (Brugmann 1885a: 125].)

Koerner, evaluating the accomplishments of the Neogrammarians, devotes an article to the question as to whether "The Neogrammarian Doctrine [is a] Breakthrough or Extension of the Schleicherian Paradigm" and arrives at the conclusiuon that the Neogrammarians "continued, by and large, to work within the framework established by Schleicher and others before 1870. [...] while noting the cumulative progress and the refinement in methodology that began with the year 1876, I dare to assert that there was nothing like a revolution taking place in linguistics in the 1870s as is frequently claimed" (Koerner 1989 [1982]: 96).

Hugo Schuchardt (1842–1927), the distinguished Romance scholar and one of the most outspoken critics of the Neogrammarians, is a good example for the type of general criticism leveled against them. Again the opposition is directed much more against the formulation of the theory than against its practical implementations. In Schuchardt's scholarly work the sound law principle is made use of practically as often and in much the same way as by the Neogrammarians themselves: 'But in other respects [leaving out the theoretical formulations] I am not aware of any basic difference with the Neogrammarians: if we talk about a new movement, which, however, can not be dated as beginning with the 1878 program, we others deserve to be called men of the new movement with the same right as the Neogrammarians' (Schuchardt 1886: 1558, quoted after Wheeler 1887: 42). However, Schuchardt's refusal to bury the hatchet goes far beyond the sound law controversy. For one, he strongly objects to the assumed neogrammarian claim that they have invented a whole set of new principles: 'The only sentence that the so-called neogrammarian school can claim as its exclusive property is that of the exceptionless effect of the sound laws' ("Der einzige Satz, den die sog. junggrammatische Schule als ihr ausschliessliches Eigentum betrachten darf, ist der von der ausnahmslosen Wirkung der Lautgesetze" [Schuchardt 1885: 1]), he asserts. But even this verdict does not apply any more after Brugmann's clarification of the same year. Yet Schuchardt's complaints reach deeper; they are concerned 'with the position of linguistics within the framework of the sciences [...], and I do not believe that the reconciliation desired by him [= Brugmann] will be possible before we have discarded the name of philology' ("mit der [...] Stellung der Sprachwissenschaft im Kreise der Wissenschaften [...], und ich glaube nicht, dass die von ihn [= Brugmann] ersehnte Verständigung möglich sein wird, ehe wir uns nicht des Namens 'Philologie' entäussert haben" [Schuchardt 1885: 37]). Schuchardt does not feel comfortable with the alignment of linguistics with traditional philology as practiced by the Classicists. From a methodological point of view it would make much more sense to him if a particular science would deal with the linguistic (sprachwissenschaftlich) aspect of language and its development 'never mind how distant from each other they may be' ("mögen sie auch noch so weit auseinander liegen" [Schuchardt 1885: 37]).

And conversely, another science would deal exclusively with the philological aspects of different languages. 'The identity of the research procedure carries a greater weight than the coherence of heterogeneous objects of investigation' ("Die Identität der Forschungsmethode fällt schwerer ins Gewicht als der Zusammenhang heterogener Untersuchungsobjekte" [ibid.]). Thus defined, a newly established linguistic science would make traditional 'Philologie' disposable. Schuchardt draws – like his teacher Schleicher – on the practices of natural scientists for his visionary demands: '[...] linguists should, following the example of the natural scientists, more often, take a walk around the world for the sake of a particular phenomenon or group of phenomena' ("[...] die Linguisten sollten, dem Beispiele der Naturforscher folgend, häufiger, irgend einer Erscheinung oder Erscheinungsgruppe zu lieb Spaziergänge um die Welt machen" [Schuchardt 1885: 38]). Schleicher (1860 [³1874]: 119) had already stressed that the linguist 'needs to have knowledge of all languages or at least of the main structures, the characteristic elements of the classes of linguistic organisms'.

The precise delineation of the terms *Philologie* and *Linguistik/Sprachwissenschaft* presented a problem not only for Schuchardt, but for many of his contemporaries as well. This problem was greatly compounded by the existence of similar terms in French (*philologie-linguistique*) and English (*philology-linguistics*) with differences that did not coincide necessarily with those of the corresponding German terms. An extensive investigation of the history of these two competing terms has been provided by Koerner (1997: 167–175).

Schuchardt thus widens the scope of the discussion considerably. He broaches numerous subjects other than sound law and analogy, raising some very pertinent questions, which go far beyond the main topic. This monograph *Über die Lautgesetze* with its subtitle: "Gegen die Junggrammatiker" not only responded to what he regards as the Neogrammarians' inadequate or even overstated formulation of their objectives, but also dealt with much more substantive matters of the discipline as a whole.

For example, Schuchardt takes Brugmann and his fellow linguists to task for limiting language comparison to genealogically related languages: 'Brugmann, and most [of his colleagues] with him, do not think much of comparing unrelated languages' ("Brugmann, und die meisten mit ihm, geben nicht viel auf Vergleichungen zwischen unverwandten Sprachen" [Schuchardt 1885: 38]). The Neogrammarians could of course have truthfully responded that for now they were fully occupied with doing an adequate job analyzing the genealogically related languages within the Indo-European language family.

4. Neogrammarian accomplishments gaining ground

Examining the various early statements as to how the Neogrammarians viewed the achievements of the past and how they related those to what they themselves intended to do should have shown that the greater part of their messages were in need of further elaboration. They certainly intended to get through with their message, but mostly they did not, at least not initially, because of the tone in which it had been cast. While it may have slowed down the spreading of the substantive part of their message, it did hardly interfere with their positive work.

As far as the publication of their research is concerned, the Neogrammarians avoided the mistakes that were made concerning the propagation of their objectives. They created — apart from the *Morphologische Untersuchungen* in 1878 — two powerful instruments for the spreading of their research; first, in 1874, by launching the *Beiträge zur Geschichte der deutschen Sprache und Literatur*, founded and co-edited by Braune, Paul, and Sievers. Later, in 1891, they started another periodical, *Indogermanische Forschungen*, edited by Brugmann and his student Wilhelm Streitberg (1864—1925). During the first 10 years in the life of the *Beiträge*, the Neogrammarians Osthoff, Braune, Kluge, Paul, and Sievers contributed a total of 90 papers of about 2½ thousand printed pages (cf. Jankowsky 1983: 241). They also published articles in a large number of other periodicals, in addition to a great quantity of books, most of which had a determining influence on the course of Germanic and Indo-European studies, in Germany as well as in many other countries, since German was then as much the language of scholarly expression as English is today. Brugmann from the very beginning emerged as the principal 'spokesperson' of the group. His publications number approximately 400 (cf. Streitberg 1909, 1919b). His 5-volume *Grundriss der vergleichenden Grammatik der indogermanischen Sprachen*, co-authored by Delbrück, started to appear in 1886 and did retain its predominant position well into the middle of the 20th century. Within Germanic philology, the voluminous *Grundriss der germanischen Philologie*, edited by Hermann Paul, which appeared a few years later, in 1891, had a comparable success (2nd ed., 1900—1909). Other books on various Germanic and Indo-European languages followed in quick succession, and within a relatively short time no room was left for any doubt that the Neogrammarians were setting the tone, not so much by programmatic writings but by continuously producing serious research.

Since the evolving crisis in historical and Indo-European linguistics during the 1860s had created an especially urgent need for new guidance in the fields of phonetics and general methodology (→ 163), two monographs, Eduard Sievers' *Grundzüge der Lautphysiologie* (since 1881: *Phonetik*) of 1876, which had its 5th ed. in 1901, and Hermann Paul's *Prinzipien der Sprachgeschichte* of 1880, which had its 4th ed. in 1909, proved to be most powerful and influential guidelines for the reorientation of linguistic research in that both monographs offered an abundance of detailed methodological reflection unavailable through any other existing publication. The primary beneficiaries were not only fellow Neogrammarians, but also new converts as well as a sizeable number of erstwhile critics who came to recognize the value of the materials for their own research, even if they continued to have reservations with certain formulations of the neogrammarian *Credo*. Hugo Schuchardt's cautious acknowledgment of 'the value of the accomplishments achieved by the individual [Neogrammarians]' (Schuchardt 1885: 35) is not a rare occurrence. Between 1880 and 1890, the Neogrammarians had become the unchallenged leaders in their fields, and students from other parts of Germany, from Europe and beyond flocked to their lectures, whether at the foremost center of neogrammarian thought, the University of Leipzig, or at other distinguished universities like Jena, Freiburg, Halle, Munich or Heidelberg. Four of the original Neogrammarians taught at Leipzig: Braune only for three years (1877—1880), Leskien for his entire professional life (following his appointment in 1870), Sievers for 31 years (1892—1923), Brugmann for 39 years (1877—1884 and 1887—1919). The neighboring University of Jena ranked second in importance. Delbrück taught there —

after a three-year stint in Halle — from 1870 to 1913. Sievers started his teaching career in Jena (1871–1883), then moved to Tübingen for four years and subsequently to Halle (1887–1892), until he finally settled for good in Leipzig. In 1893, when Kluge arrived at Freiburg as his final place of work, his two neogrammarian colleagues had already left: Paul, who had started teaching there in 1874, had moved to Munich (1893–1916), and Brugmann had returned to Leipzig in 1887. Heidelberg was the one and only place for Osthoff's teaching career which comprised the 30 years from 1877 to 1907. Heidelberg is also the university where Braune, coming in from Giessen (1880–1888), taught for many years (1888–1919). The following table provides a synoptical view of where and when the original eight Neogrammarians have taught.

Tab. 116.1

	Leipzig	Halle	Jena	Tübingen	Freiburg	München	Gießen	Straßburg	Heidelberg
Braune	1877–80						1880–88		1888–1919
Brugmann	1877–84 1887–1919				1884–87				
Delbrück		1867–70	1870–1913						
Kluge			1884–93		1893–1916			1880–84	
Leskien	1870–1913								
Osthoff				1869–70					1877–1907
Paul					1874–93	1893–1916			
Sievers	1892–1923	1887–92	1871–83	1883–87					

The enormous scholarly output, which is characteristic of all of the Neogrammarians, did not prevent them from devoting a great deal of their time and energy to their teaching duties and their guidance of students. Friedrich Kluge's list of publications — to take the example of a very early associate — starting in 1879 with *Beiträge zur Geschichte der germanischen Conjugation*, his doctoral dissertation, shows (mostly multiple) entries every single year between 1879 and 1926 (cf. Dammann 1926: 5–20). Franz Specht (1888–1949) gave credit to Kluge, next to Sievers, Paul and Braune, for the "gewaltigen Aufschwung" ('huge upswing') of Germanic studies (Specht 1948: 246), mentioning specifically Kluge's *Urgermanisch* and his *Nominale Stammbildungslehre der altgermanischen Dialekte* as having been 'extremely valuable for the Germanist and general linguist' (ibid.). Collinge (1995: 204) also stresses the Kluge's productivity, placing him likewise side by side with Sievers, Paul and Braune as having "helped to produce from 1891 [publication date of the first volume of Paul's *Grundriss*] a comprehensive survey of the linguistic history of that [neogrammarian] group". But Kluge also served, as Basler (1927: 281) relates, as supervisor for over 100 doctoral dissertations. Heavy involvement in working with students, besides continuous scholarly output, was of course not only characteristic of Kluge, but was equally true for most of the Neogrammarians as well as for many other distinguished contemporary linguists, since they all subscribed to the same scholarly ethos.

5. Sound laws, analogy and beyond

In the "Vorwort" to *Morphologische Untersuchungen*, the authors had pointed to '[t]he two most important principles of the *neogrammarian movement*' (Osthoff & Brugmann 1878: xiii), namely, that sound laws suffer no exception and that any change which cannot be explained by the effect of sound laws must be due to processes of analogical formation. For the Neogrammarians these are valid statements, but by prominently listing those two features, essential as they are, without showing explicitly how they fit into their overall theory of language change and without acknowledging the respective contributions of their predecessors and other contemporaries, the Neogrammarians had opened the door for justified criticism. Their teacher Curtius had stated as early as 1870 that 'there are two [...] basic concepts of greatest importance for language investigation, that of analogy and that of the sound law' (1886 [1870]: 52), which suggests that Brugmann's and Osthoff's ideas were not all that original. Delbrück (1880: 38–39 and 101–105), shows much greater readiness than Osthoff and Brugmann to give due credit to Curtius' achievements, criticizing him only moderately for his reluctance to be as rigorous as the Neogrammarians in matters of the twin principles of sound laws and analogy. Hermann Paul, in his *Prinzipien der Sprachgeschichte* of 1880, "elaborates the neogrammarian linguistic theory as a whole within which each particular neogrammarian doctrine finds its proper place" (Norman 1972: 116), thus providing — better and more convincingly than any other neogrammarian — an essential instrument to convince critics and skeptics alike that the 'sound law and analogy' principles of the neogrammarian *Credo* were an integral part of their comprehensive methodological framework. Paul's methodology, in spite of some initial harsh criticism by, e. g., Schuchardt (1885: 24, 34), Misteli (1882), Bezzenberger (1881: 845–846), and others, gained wide acceptance almost immediately and retained its strong influence, even outside Indo-European linguistics, well into the 20th century. Otto Jespersen's (1860–1943) comments may serve as an illustration of the positive evaluations of Paul's *Prinzipien* by contemporary linguists which by far outnumber the critical voices: 'I feel obliged [...] to express my reverence for the leaders [of the Neogrammarians] and especially emphasize with admiration how much I owe to Paul's *Prinzipien der Sprachgeschichte*: This book stimulated me first to seriously think about the multifarious phenomena of the life of language and it has been of greatest significance for the direction of my studies' (Jespersen 1886: 160). Even a much more recent evaluation, that of the American Indo-Europeanist George S. Lane (1902–1981), amounts to a strong endorsement: "Hermann Paul's *Prinzipien der Sprachgeschichte* from the time of its publication in 1880 remained the codification of linguistic doctrine for half a century" (Lane 1945: 465).

That Osthoff and Brugmann, in youthful arrogance, had identified, for at least the greater part, 'the older [representatives of] linguistic science' (1878: v) for their negligence or indifference or outright incompetence, was not exactly helpful to the Neogrammarians' cause. No names were mentioned. "Die ältere Sprachforschung", sometimes termed even broader as "die vergleichende Sprachwissenschaft", served as a general stand-in for a research methodology that was in need of substantial revision, to be brought about by 'especially younger researchers' (xii), unmistakably identified as members of the *junggrammatische Richtung*.

Polemics aside, the *Credo* also acknowledged important contributions by some predecessors and contemporaries. Wilhelm Scherer leads the list, since 'with the appearance of Scherer's book "Zur Geschichte der deutschen Sprache" [...] and essentially by the impulses emanating from this book, the physiognomy of comparative linguistics has changed not insignificantly' (iii). Scherer is credited with having pointed researchers in the right direction when he suggested that elements other than purely physical matters are involved in sound change (p. xi), thus stressing the importance of psychological considerations for language change. Wheeler's (1887: 47) assessment of how Scherer dealt with the concept of analogy — which accounts for psychologically conditioned changes, changes other than those due to the 'mechanical' operation of the sound laws — illustrates the stage of the general discussion at Scherer's time, that is, before the Neogrammarians took the lead: "[Scherer] made frequent, though sometimes erroneous, always instructive use of the explanation of analogy, without reaching any general statement concerning the nature and limitations of the principle."

However, when Scherer published a second edition of *Geschichte der deutschen Sprache* (^{2}1878), Osthoff wrote a devastating review. Expecting great things of this second edition, Osthoff experienced, instead, '[...] a strange disappointment! It became apparent that Scherer was, so to say, actually personally innocent of all the new and the very best that he has achieved in linguistic science' (1880: 109). He missed in him 'serious headwork, steadfast pursuance of what is found to its utmost consequences' (ibid.). Since 'there is in Scherer not the slightest trace of all this', he cannot be accorded lasting recognition for 'what his ingenious instinct lets him find in a lucky moment' (ibid.). Paul (1879b: 307–308) arrived at a similar verdict, although he was much more factual and, in spite of all his harsh criticism, also provided a long list of praising comments on what Scherer had achieved with his first edition in 1868 (ibid.).

Next to Scherer, Heymann Steinthal (1823–1899) received recognition as an important representative of 'a science whose first basic outlines were drawn up by Steinthal in the article "Assimilation and Attraktion, psychologisch beleuchtet" which so far has met with little attention on the part of linguistic science and sound physiology' (Osthoff & Brugmann 1878: iv). This praise is almost verbatim repeated by an early convert,

Hermann Ziemer (1882 [²1883]: 4−5), a high school teacher hundreds of miles away from Leipzig, who deserves some credit for spreading the neogrammarian teachings especially among his colleagues, a role acknowledged by Brugmann in his review of Ziemer's *Junggrammatische Streifzüge* (1882: 401−402).

Osthoff and Brugmann (1878: iv) stress that the results of sound physiology or phonetics 'have been made use of even by the older linguistic science, since about the 1850s'. (Eduard Sievers is not mentioned by name, but his *Grundzüge der Lautphysiologie* of 1876 have undoubtedly provided background information for that passage, and probably many others, in the *Manifesto*.) Only if, in addition to considering 'the purely physical aspect of speech mechanism' (ibid.), the psychological factor is brought to bear, can '[e]ven the most common sound changes, like, for instance, the transition of *nb* to *mb*, of *bn* to *mm*' (ibid.) be sufficiently explained. Acknowledging, however, the relevance of these factors is tied to the discovery of the individual speaker as the originator of changes in speech — even though these individually initiated changes still have to be endorsed by the speech community — and hence the only one who directly affects language change.

One of the major consequences of identifying the individual speaker as the initiator of language change was that the Neogrammarians held out the study of actual speech as indispensable, since it provides the most accurate model for the comprehension of major aspects of language change and the reconstruction of older forms:

'In all living popular speech varieties the sound shapes peculiar to the dialect appear throughout the entire vocabulary by far more consistently implemented and upheld in their speech by the members of the speech community than what one should expect from the study of languages which are accessible merely through the written medium.' (p. ix)

["In allen lebenden Volksmundarten erscheinen die dem Dialekt eigenen Lautgestaltungen bei weitem konsequenter durch den ganzen Sprachstoff durchgeführt und von den Angehörigen der Sprachgemeinschaft bei ihrem Sprechen inne gehalten als man es vom Studium der älteren bloss durch das Medium der Schrift zugänglichen Sprachen her erwarten sollte."]

Brugmann and Osthoff refer to Jost Winteler's (1846−1929) work on *Die Kerenzer Mundart des Kantons Glarus* (1876) as a compelling example of what the minute study of contemporary speech can teach the historical linguist so that s/he is much better prepared than ever before to explain changes in earlier language stages. The study of the actual speech sound has to gain priority over the study of the written letter: 'The letters are, after all, always only rough and clumsy and very often even misleading reflections of the audible sound; to obtain a precise idea of the process involved in a sound transition in, for instance, an ancient Greek or Latin dialect is outright impossible' (viii). One year after the publication of the *Manifesto*, Osthoff elaborated in a 48-page popularizing essay on *The Physiological and Psychological Moment in the Formation of Linguistic Forms* (1879), pursuing the objective 'to create general interest in the two methodological principles of modern linguistic science [...] as the highest and most important guiding norms of research' (p. 3), namely, the exceptionless functioning of the sound laws and the changes brought about by the effect of analogy.

The second part of this quotation throws light on why the Neogrammarians believe that, in view of the necessity to concentrate on the physiological as well as psychological evidence which only current languages can provide, '[l]anguage areas such as Germanic, Romance, Slavic are without any doubt those, where comparative linguistics can develop in the best possible way its methodological principles' (p. vii). Those language groups qualify for two reasons. First, there is enough language material available, covering language stages from the most ancient to the most modern times, to trace developments almost uninterruptedly. Second, in the written documents of Indo-European languages like Sanskrit, Greek, and Latin the researcher is confronted with a kind of 'speech influenced in such a way and to such an extent by literature [...] that we hardly have a chance to come to know the natural, spontaneous, everyday-speech of the Old Indians, the Greeks, and the Romans' (Osthoff & Brugmann 1878: vii−viii), whereas in the three named language groups 'we deal, to a much higher degree [...], with the genuine language of the common people, with the speech in normal communication and everyday situations' (p. vii). Researchers who continue to start their investigation with the oldest attestable language form without having previously studied the life of the living popular languages with their rich dialectal variations cannot, in the opinion of the Neogrammarians, gain adequate insight into how languages change. Already in the "Vorwort" the belief is expressed 'that the psychic and physical activity of people in acquiring the language inherited from their ancestors and in reproducing and reshaping the sound images received into their consciousness must have been essentially the same at all times (Osthoff & Brugmann 1878: xiii). The underlying principle of uniformitarianism (cf. Morpurgo Davies 1998: 190−192, 231−233) is implicitly present in Scherer (1868: x) [and specifically discussed much later in Scherer (^{2}1878: 16)]. The Neogrammarians followed the example of Scherer and more particularly of William D. Whitney (1827−1894) "who made uniformitarianism the guiding principle of his book *Language and the Study of Language* (1867)" (Christy 1983: x), when they came to realize the value of the principle for historical linguistics.

As we have seen, the authors of the *Credo*, while they are not hesitant to severely criticize current practitioners of comparative linguistics, are also keen on spelling out a program that reaches far beyond the parameters of the sound law and analogy principles. Whether they focus on the speaking individual vs. the written language or on the observation of living dialects vs. the 'reconstruction of the Indo-European proto-language [...] as the main objective and center of the entire comparative linguistic research' (p. v), they invariably aim at pointing to a larger framework, such as, for instance, the development of a comprehensive research methodology based on a more realistic picture of the life of language. Some of the future tasks for the profession were addressed in the *Credo*, for instance, the need for further elaboration and consolidation of the work on sound physiology which was recognized in its full potential after the publication of Sievers' *Lautphysiologie* (1876) and was assumed to grow rapidly and substantially in the near future. Eventually, its combination with the psychological aspects of language production and language change was expected to yield worth-while results. Hermann Paul (^{5}1920 [1880]: 7), in the opening section of his *Prinzipien der Sprachgeschichte*, defined as one of the main tasks for the "Prinzipienlehre der Kulturwissenschaft" 'to present the general conditions under which the psychological and physical factors, following their individual rules, come to work together for a common purpose'.

6. Consolidating the neogrammarian 'paradigm'

What can be defined as neogrammarian achievements independent of what was discussed in connection with the *Credo*?

The first item to be listed, it seems to me, is one that cannot be repeated often enough. The intended or unintended effect of the *Credo* and the many other public discussions of the neogrammarian principles between 1876 and 1878, from brief casual mentioning to more elaborate presentations − all listed in a footnote on page xiii of *Morphologische Untersuchungen* − was that the neogrammarian view of the state of linguistic science had become an issue of great importance for the members of the profession as well as for many scholars of neighboring disciplines. "[...] few historical linguists or general linguists have escaped neogrammarian influence" (Robins 1978: 10). And the influence kept growing and expanding: "Bloomfield, Brugmann's and Leskien's pupil in the years 1913−14, applied with striking success neogrammarian principles to a family of languages about as far removed in cultural milieu as possible from the Indo-European of the founding fathers" (Robins 1978: 10−11).

In 1876, "the year in which everything seemed to happen at once" (Hoenigswald 1978: 17; cf. Koerner 1976, for a documentation), seemingly miraculous things had occurred indeed: Karl Verner's article on the effect of Proto-Indo-European accentuation on the expected sound changes according to Grimm's Law; Eduard Sievers' *Grundzüge*, systematically presenting a comprehensive picture of sound physiology and its application to historical linguistics and how this newly expanded field can be used to explain the transition of sounds; Jost Winteler's careful analysis of a German dialect; August Leskien's brief discussion of the sound law principle in his *Declination im Slavisch-Litauischen*; Brugmann's treatises on "Nasalis sonans" and on "Geschichte der stammabstufenden Declination"; and Osthoff's paper "Zur Frage des Ursprungs der germanischen n-Declination": they all appeared in 1876. And their appearance certainly did not go unnoticed, the less so as there were several stages in the development of the doctrines involved: Leskien had regularly explained his version of the sound law principle in his lectures; Verner's discovery was being hotly discussed with some of his German colleagues at least since early 1876 (cf. Brugmann 1897: 269; Schröder 1910: 328); Brugmann and Osthoff used to exchange ideas about their research between themselves and with others (cf. Einhauser 1992). Furthermore, whenever opportunities for explaining their views in public lectures presented themselves, many Neogrammarians made good use of them. Thus Osthoff's treatise on *Das physiologische und psychologische Moment in der sprachlichen Formenbildung* (1879) started out as a lecture at the 1878 meeting of philologists in Gera. 'The hope to increase in this way the benevolent attachment in wider circles of the educated for the linguistic science and linguistic methods seems to come true' (Ziemer 1882 [²1883]: 11).

This situation had changed fundamentally and dramatically during the next 10 to 15 years. For one, the publications mentioned and the large number which were continuously produced by neogrammarian authors now afforded ample opportunities for the profession to throughly evaluate the research results of the 'movement'. Secondly, we have to take note of the fact that no other group of linguists existed that came even remotely close to the visibility and the productivity of the Neogrammarians, quantitatively as well as qualitatively. Thirdly, in the 1880s and the beginning 1890s, after many years of consistent planning and painstaking labor, a series of seminal works appeared which established beyond any doubt that the neogrammarian accomplishments had progressed from mere promise to certain fulfillment. The number of handbooks and grammars (e. g., Brugmann's grammar on Greek, Leskien's grammar on Old Church Slavic), some of them widely used to this very day, which have earned their place of distinction in linguistic science, is far too large to be enumerated here, let alone be even cursorily discussed. We will mention, instead, only two of them, Brugmann & Delbrück's *Grundriss der vergleichenden Grammatik der indogermanischen Sprachen* (1886–1895), and Hermann Paul's *Grundriss der germanischen Philologie* (1891–1893), both summarizing the then current state of neogrammarian research.

Brugmann is the author of the first two volumes of the *Grundriss*, dealing with phonology in volume I and with morphology in volume II. Delbrück's responsibility lay with comparative syntax, *Vergleichende Syntax der indogermanischen Sprachen*, the next three volumes.

In the introduction to vol. I of the first edition (1886), Brugmann takes great care to establish a link to 'the excellent Compendium of Schleicher' (Brugmann & Delbrück ²1897–1910 [1886–1895] I. v). But since later editions, the fourth and last appearing in 1876, after Schleicher's death, had only been minimally revised, and since even the two new editors of the work, Leskien and Schmidt, had expressed the opinion that a complete revision of the *Compendium* was required, Brugmann stated that, in view of the vast progress of Indo-European studies during the last ten years, no expert would have any doubts 'that the entire multi-sectioned and widely-ramified scientific discipline has again to be summarized, even if only in its major characteristics, and to be readied for a uniform overall presentation' (Preface, p. v). The progress involved the availability of a much larger amount of data, which at that time required a profound revision in the fields of phonology and morphology based on the need for a 'more thorough reflection on the actual factors and the general conditions of language development' (Brugmann 1885a: 31). One of the most important of these factors was the utilization of the insight that 'language does not exist except in the individual where it lives as an organism of associations ("Vorstellungsgruppen") and [that] only in the psychic organization of man lie the foundations of its historical development' (Brugmann 1885a: 22).

In the original planning session with the publisher in 1880, Brugmann had anticipated that his *Grundriss* would be of a size comparable to that of Schleicher's *Compendium* and that the work would be concluded in about three years. As it turned out, readying just the first volume for publication required double as much time as had been originally estimated, and the final 5-volume *opus* was about 4½ times the size of Schleicher's work.

The *Grundriss* is a thoroughly neogrammarian publication, yet in Brugmann's understanding this does not mean that he restricts himself to presenting only the neogrammarian viewpoint. In the preface to the first edition he stated:

'I took what is good wherever I was convinced that I would find it; all trends of Indo-European research get a hearing at various places. Thus I hope, even if I might have overlooked a number of valuable building blocks, that I have come, nevertheless, close to the objective that I have set myself: presenting the current state of our knowledge in broad outlines and highlighting all that is of greater importance.' (Brugmann & Delbrück ²1897–1910 [1886–1895]: vi)

He was also keen on providing an agenda for the future, hoping that 'by pointing to what had not yet developed beyond the stage of a task and an hypothesis, I would be able to encourage the readers to embark on research of their own' (p. vii).

Only a few years later, a second edition was prepared. Brugmann related: '[...] the considerable enlargement and more thorough treatment that our knowledge of sound changes has experienced since 1886 in nearly all sections of the Indo-European field, necessitated the inclusion of a large number of new accomplishments' (Preface to the 2nd ed. [1897: ix−x]).

He greatly expanded the section "Zum kombinatorischen Lautwandel", perhaps in responce to strong criticism by Hugo Schuchardt in his treatise *Über die Lautgesetze* (1885: 36), where Schuchardt had complained: 'What sense do all those thousands of sound laws make as long as they remain isolated, as long as they do not become part of a higher order?' Brugmann (1897: xi) took this criticism graciously, noting that those 'excellent words of Schuchardt' ought to have been placed as the motto before that chapter, newly revised according to Schuchardt's critical remarks. He also commented quite objectively on Schuchardt's verdict in *Über die Lautgesetze* against the 'axiom of the general validity of the sound laws': 'The objection raised has been reduced by Wundt to its proper proportion' (Brugmann ^{2}1897: 72), subsequently quoting from the Leipzig psychologist Wilhelm Wundt (1832−1920):

'The essential and at the same time undeniably significant feature of the views which have gained effect in the newer linguistic science is based on the fact that the exception is not admitted as an obvious occurrence and as one that does not need any further explorations, but that, instead, the stipulation is made to search for the intervening causes which explain the exception' (Wundt 1886: 212).

The *Grundriss* was frequently reprinted and swiftly translated into French and English. The English translation of the 2nd edition was reprinted as recently as 1972 in Varanasi/India as vol. 84 of the *Chowkhamba Sanskrit Studies Series*.

In 1904 Brugmann published a one-volume *Kurze vergleichende Grammatik der indogermanischen Sprachen*, condensed from the 5-volume edition and likewise dealing with all three grammatical components, phonology, morphology, and syntax. Brugmann argued that such a brief presentation, while impossible 15 years ago, would now be fully appropriate since a much greater amount of troublesome linguistic phenomena have been treated adequately, '[...] so that in regard to them we may confidently speak of a *communis opinio*' (Brugmann 1904: iv).

Hermann Paul's *Grundriss der germanischen Philologie* started as a 2-volume edition (1891−1893) and was enlarged in the 2nd version (1900−1909) to 3 volumes with many subsections. True to the 'philology' part in its title, the range of subjects treated goes far beyond the actual linguistic domain. Fields selected include, apart from the individual Germanic languages, e. g., Germanic civilization, law, music, mythology, medieval military history and art, epic poetry, folklore, chivalry, social life, and customs. Accordingly, the number of scholars participating in the ambitious project amounted to almost three dozens − 35 to be exact.

Paul's *Grundriss* with its large number of contributing scholars is the best illustration of the most important feature in the development of linguistic science during the last decades of the 19th century. For all practical purposes, there is no dividing line any more between the neogrammarian approach and that of the rest of the linguistic profession. What counts is the expertise of the individual scholar, and those perhaps eight original Neogrammarians have done their lion's share in the consolidation of the neogrammarian framework and, with it, in advancing the cause of linguistic science in general. Their position had become 'mainstream' by the end of the 19th century.

The 'Neogrammarian School' which formally never existed, had faded away, or, in the words of Brugmann (1900: 132), 'has today become, thank heavens, only part of history'. Paul, himself studiously avoiding the term 'Junggrammatiker', somewhat angrily proclaimed in his review of Schuchardt (1885) that 'a neogrammarian *school* does not exist. One may talk of a neogrammarian *direction* ("junggrammatische *Richtung*") though, if by all means one has to have such a troublesome name' (Paul 1886: 3). More or less intensive personal relationships continued among most of them until their death, but they were not conspicuous by any particular professional link that had bound them together from the mid-1870s to the mid-1890s. Much more characteristic for all of them is the fact that they remained extremely productive scholars to the very end of their lives, excelling through scholarly works which have made a lasting impact on our general procedures in conducting historical linguistic research. Even in the field of syntax they produced works that became models for fellow linguists not only of their home country. Delbrück's 5 volumes of *Syntaktische Forschungen* (1871–1888) and his *Germanische Syntax* (1910–1918), Brugmann's *Griechische Grammatik* (1885b) and his posthumous *Syntax des einfachen Satzes* (1925) are cases in point. Whitney's (1892) enthusiastic review of *Altindische Syntax* (vol. 5 of Delbrück's *Syntaktische Forschungen*) may serve as an example of how well those works were received.

Eduard Hermann, a student of Delbrück's, could safely state in 1931: 'Gradually, not only many a Romanist converted to the sound law principle, but practically all theoretical opponents have professed to be followers of Leskien's principle in the actual conduct of their phonological research. [...] Opponents of the Neogrammarians in theory and practice are rarely found today' (Hermann 1931: 6).

Concerning Hermann Paul and his importance for general linguistics, it is interesting to note that — in spite of his claim that no scientific investigation of language was possible other than via an historical approach (Paul ^{5}1920 [^{2}1886]: 20) — there are elements in his theory which had an impact on the formation of structural ideas at the turn of the 20th century. Koerner's findings in this regard are much more than casual assumptions:

"We [...] think it to be appropriate to consider Paul as one source, albeit an important one, of Saussure's linguistic inspiration, his *Prinzipien* reflecting in a number of respects the ideas current in the last decades of the 19th century when Saussure's theory began to take its shape. In setting up a list of terminological and conceptual parallels between Paul's ideas and Saussure's notions we intend [...] to support our claim that Paul's *Prinzipien* had in fact a profound influence on the development of Saussure's linguistic thought." (Koerner 1972: 301)

7. Conclusion

In 1932, Leonard Bloomfield who, as was mentioned above, had successfully applied the sound law principle to non-Indo-European languages, proposed a reformulation of the sound law hypothesis which ought to be generally acceptable even today: "[W]e realize that a linguistic change is not a 'law', but a historical event, and that the term 'exception', accordingly, is irrelevant. We formulate this type of change, rather, by saying that *phonemes change*. This is an assumption" (1932: 227; emphasis is in the original).

While reviewing the results of recent research in historical linguistics, William Labov arrived at an interesting conclusion. For him, the 'Neogrammarian controversy' lingers on, but he is convinced that the value of the underlying assumptions and practical applications cannot be questioned:

"My resolution of the Neogrammarian controversy is a proposal for a shift of research strategies. I would strike from our agenda the questions, 'Does every word have its own history?', 'Is it phonemes that change?', 'Are the Neogrammarians right or wrong?' and start a research program of a different sort. We begin with respect for the achievements of our predecessors; but that does not mean that we rest content with the data they have gathered. An appreciation of their work is shown, not by the re-manipulation of the original observations, but by adding a wider and deeper set of inquiries that will display the value and the limitations of these initial results." (Labov 1981: 304)

This constructive recommendation may not be the last word to be heard about the Neogrammarians and the assessment of their work, but it is good enough to prove that the neogrammarian framework, consolidated in the 1880s, is still taken seriously and considered useful and important one hundred years later.

8. Bibliography

Ascoli, Graziadio Isaia. 1886. "Dei Neogrammatici. − Lettera al prof. Pietro Merlo". *Archivio Glottologico Italiano* 10.18−73.

−. 1887. *Sprachwissenschaftliche Briefe.* Transl. by Bruno Güterbeck. Leipzig: Hirzel.

Basler, Otto. 1927. "Friedrich Kluge". *Journal of English and Germanic Philology* 26.281−283.

Bezzenberger, Adalbert. 1881. Review of Paul (1880). *Deutsche Litteraturzeitung* 21.845−846.

Bloomfield, Leonard. 1932. Review of Hermann (1931). *Language* 8.220−233.

Brugmann, Karl. 1876a. "Nasalis sonans in der indogermanischen Grundsprache". *Studien zur griechischen und lateinischen Grammatik* 9.285−338.

−. 1876b. "Zur Geschichte der stammabstufenden Declination". *Studien zur griechischen und lateinischen Grammatik* 9.363−406.

−. 1882. Review of Ziemer (1882). *Literarisches Centralblatt für Deutschland* 1882.401−402.

—. 1885a. *Zum heutigen Stand der Sprachwissenschaft.* Strassburg: Trübner. (Repr. in Wilbur 1977.)

—. 1885b. *Griechische Grammatik (Lautlehre, Stammbildungs- und Flexionslehre und Syntax).* München: Beck.

—. 1897. "Karl Verner†". *Indogermanische Forschungen (Anzeiger)* 7.269–270.

—. 1900. "Zu dem 'Vorwort' zu Band 1 der *Morphologischen Untersuchungen* von Osthoff und Brugmann". *Indogermanische Forschungen (Anzeiger)* 11.131–132.

—. 1904. *Kurze vergleichende Grammatik der indogermanischen Sprachen.* Strassburg: Trübner.

—. 1925. *Die Syntax des einfachen Satzes im Indogermanischen.* Berlin: de Gruyter.

— & Berthold Delbrück. ²1897–1910 [1886–1895]. *Grundriss der vergleichenden Grammatik der indogermanischen Sprachen.* 5 vols. Strassburg: Trübner. (2nd ed. by Brugmann alone.) [Vol. I: *Vergleichende Laut-, Stammbildungs- und Flexionslehre.* – Note that Delbrück did not contribute to the second edition.]

Burdach, Konrad. 1934. *Die Wissenschaft von deutscher Sprache.* Berlin: de Gruyter.

Christy, T. Craig. 1983. *Uniformitarianism in Linguistics.* Amsterdam & Philadelphia: Benjamins.

Collinge, Neville E. 1985. *The Laws of Indo-European.* Amsterdam & Philadelphia: Benjamins.

—. 1995. "History of Historical Linguistics". Koerner & Asher 1995.203–212.

Collitz, Hermann. 1886. "Die neueste Sprachforschung und die Erklärung des indogermanischen Ablautes". *Beiträge zur Kunde der indogermanischen Sprachen* 11.203–242. (Repr. in Wilbur 1977.)

Curtius, Georg. ²1848 [1845]. *Die Sprachvergleichung in ihrem Verhältnis zur klassischen Philologie.* Berlin: Besser.

—, ed. 1868–1877. *Studien zur griechischen und lateinischen Grammatik.* 10 vols. Leipzig: Hirzel. (Repr., Hildesheim: Olms, 1972.) [Vols. 9 & 10 co-edited with Karl Brugmann.]

—. 1886 [1870]. "Bemerkungen über die Tragweite der Lautgesetze, insbesondere im Griechischen und Lateinischen". *Kleine Schriften* ed. by Ernst Windisch, 50–94. Leipzig: Hirzel.

—. 1876. "Nachwort". *Studien zur griechischen und lateinischen Grammatik* 9.468.

—. 1885. *Zur Kritik der neuesten Sprachforschung.* Leipzig: Hirzel. (Repr. in Wilbur 1977.)

Dammann, Oswald. 1926. "Verzeichnis der Schriften Friedrich Kluges 1879–1926". *Festschrift Friedrich Kluge zum 70. Geburtstage am 21. Juni 1926* ed. by Wilhelm Franz, 5–20. Tübingen: Englisches Seminar.

Delbrück, Berthold. 1871–1888. *Syntaktische Forschungen.* 5 vols. Halle: Buchhandlung des Waisenhauses.

—. 1880 [⁶1919]. *Einleitung in das Sprachstudium: Ein Beitrag zur Geschichte und Methodik der vergleichenden Sprachforschung.* Leipzig: Breitkopf & Härtel.

—. 1882. *Introduction to the Study of Language: A critical survey of the history and methods of comparative philology of Indo-European languages.* New ed., with an introductory article by E. F. K. Koerner. Amsterdam: Benjamins, 1974.

—. 1885. *Die neueste Sprachforschung: Betrachtungen über Georg Curtius' Schrift "Zur Kritik der neuesten Sprachforschung".* Leipzig: Breitkopf & Härtel. (Repr. in Wilbur 1977.)

—. 1902. "Das Wesen der Lautgesetze". *Annalen der Naturphilosophie* 1.277–308.

—. 1910–1918. *Germanische Syntax.* 4 vols. Leipzig: Teubner.

Einhauser, Eveline. 1989. *Die Junggrammatiker: Ein Problem für die Sprachwissenschaftsgeschichtsschreibung.* Trier: Wissenschaftlicher Verlag Trier.

—, ed. 1992. *Lieber Freund …: Die Briefe Hermann Osthoffs an Karl Brugmann, 1875–1904.* Trier: Wissenschaftlicher Verlag Trier.

Hermann, Eduard. 1931. *Lautgesetz und Analogie.* Berlin: Weidmann.

Hockett, Charles F. 1965. "Sound Change". *Language* 41.185–204.

Hoenigswald, Henry. 1978. "The *annus mirabilis* and Posterity". *Transactions of the Philological Society 1978. Commemorative Volume: The Neogrammarians*, 17–35. Oxford: Blackwell.

Jankowsky, Kurt R. 1972. *The Neogrammarians: A re-evaluation of their place in the development of linguistic science.* The Hague: Mouton. (Repr., Berlin: Mouton de Gruyter, 1992.)

—. 1983. Review of *Beiträge zur Geschichte der deutschen Sprache und Literatur* volume 100 (Tübingen: Niemeyer, 1978). *Forum Linguisticum* 7: 3.239–259.

—. 1990. "The Neogrammarian Hypothesis". *Research Guide on Language Change* ed. by Edgar C. Polomé, 223–239. Berlin: Mouton de Gruyter.

Jespersen, Otto. 1933 [1886]. "Zur Lautgesetzfrage". *Linguistica: Selected papers*, 160–228. Copenhagen: Levin & Munksgaard. (Repr. in Wilbur 1977.)

Kluge, Friedrich, 1879. *Beiträge zur Geschichte der germanischen Conjugation.* Strassburg: Trübner.

—. 1886. *Nominale Stammbildungslehre der altgermanischen Dialekte.* Halle: Niemeyer.

—. ³1913 [1889]. *Urgermanisch: Vorgeschichte der altgermanischen Dialekte.* Strassburg: Trübner. (2nd ed. 1897.)

Koerner, E. F. K. 1972. "Hermann Paul and Synchronic Linguistics". *Lingua* 29.274–307. (Repr. in Koerner 1978.73–106.)

—. 1976. "1876 as a Turning Point in the History of Linguistics". *Journal of Indo-European Studies* 4: 4.333–353. (Repr. in Koerner 1978.189–209.)

—. 1978. *Toward a Historiography of Linguistics: Selected essays.* Amsterdam: Benjamins.

—. 1982. "The Neogrammarian Doctrine: Breakthrough or extension of the Schleicherian paradigm: A problem in linguistic historiography". *Papers from the Third Internationial Conference on Historical Linguistics* ed. by J. Peter Maher, Allan R. Bomhard & E. F. K. Koerner, 129–152. (Repr. in Koerner 1989.79–100.)

—. 1989. *Practicing Linguistic Historiography: Selected essays.* Amsterdam & Philadelphia: Benjamins.

—. 1997. "Linguistics vs Philology: Self-definition of a field or rhetorical stance?". *Language Sciences* 19: 2.167–175.

— & R. E. Asher, eds. 1995. *Concise History of the Language Sciences: From the Sumerians to the cognitivists.* Oxford & New York: Pergamon.

Labov, William. 1981. "Resolving the Neogrammarian Controversy". *Language* 57: 2.267–308.

Lane, George S. 1945. "Changes of Emphasis in Linguistics with Particular Reference to Paul and Bloomfield". *Studies in Philology* 42.465–483.

Lehmann, Winfred P. 1967. *A Reader in Nineteenth-Century Historical Indo-European Linguistics.* Bloomington & London: Indiana University Press.

Leskien, August. 1876. *Die Declination im Slavisch-Litauischen und Germanischen.* Leipzig: Hirzel. (Repr., Leipzig: Zentral-Antiquariat der DDR, 1963.)

Misteli, Franz. 1879–80. "Lautgesetz und Analogie: Methodologisch-psychologische Abhandlung". *Zeitschrift für Völkerpsychologie* 11.365–475 and 12.1–27. [On the occasion of Osthoff & Brugmann (1878).]

—. 1882. Review of Paul (1880). *Zeitschrift für Völkerpsychologie* 13.376–409. ([Partially] repr. in Hans Helmut Christmann, *Sprachwissenschaft des 19. Jahrhunderts,* 226–245. Darmstadt: Wissenschaftliche Buchgesellschaft, 1977.)

Morpurgo Davies, Anna. 1998. *Nineteenth-Century Linguistics.* (= *History of Linguistics*, 4.) London & New York: Longman.

Norman, William M. 1972. *The Neogrammarians and Comparative Linguistics.* Ann Arbor, Mich.: University Microfilms. (Doctoral dissertation, Princeton University.)

Osthoff, Hermann. 1876. "Zur Frage des Ursprungs der germanischen n-Declination. (Nebst einer Theorie über die ursprüngliche Unterscheidung starker und schwacher casus im Indogermanischen)". *Beiträge zur Geschichte der deutschen Sprache und Literatur* 3.1–89.

—. 1878. *Das Verbum in der Nominalcomposition im Deutschen, Griechischen, Slavischen und Romanischen.* Jena: Costenoble.

—. 1879. *Das physiologische und psychologische Moment in der sprachlichen Formenbildung.* Berlin: Habel.

—. 1880. Review of Scherer (^{2}1878). *Germania (Vierteljahrsschrift)* 25.109–113.

—. 1886. *Die neueste Sprachforschung und die Erklärung des indogermanischen Ablautes: Antwort auf die gleichnamige Schrift von Dr. Hermann Collitz.* Heidelberg: Petters. (Repr. in Wilbur 1977.)

— & Karl Brugmann. 1878. "Vorwort". *Morphologische Untersuchungen auf dem Gebiete der indogermanischen Sprachen* I.iii–xx. Leipzig: Hirzel. (Transl. in Lehmann 1967.197–209.)

— & Karl Brugmann. 1878–1910. *Morphologische Untersuchungen auf dem Gebiete der indogermanischen Sprachen.* 6 vols. Leipzig: Hirzel. (Repr., Hildesheim: Olms, 1974.)

Paul, Hermann. 1877. "Die Vokale der Flexions- und Ableitungssilben in den ältesten germanischen Dialekten". *Beiträge zur Geschichte der deutschen Sprache und Literatur* 4.315–475.

—. 1879a. *Untersuchungen über den germanischen Vokalismus.* Halle: Niemeyer.

—. 1879b. Review of Scherer (^{2}1878). *Jenaer Literaturzeitung* (NF) 12: 22.307–311.

—. 1880. *Prinzipien der Sprachgeschichte.* Tübingen: Niemeyer. (2nd ed. 1886, transl. as *Principles of the History of Language* by Herbert A. Strong. New and rev. ed. London: Sonnenschein, 1890. – 5th ed., 1920.)

—. 1886. Review of Schuchardt (1885). *Literaturblatt für germanische und romanische Philologie* 7.1–6.

—, ed. 1891–1893. *Grundriss der germanischen Philologie.* 2 vols. in 3. Strassburg: Trübner. (2nd rev. and enlarged ed., 3 vols. in 4, 1900–1909.)

Robins, Robert H. 1978. "The Neogrammarians and Their Nineteenth-Century Predecessors". *Transactions of the Philological Society 1978. Commemorative Volume: The Neogrammarians,* 1–16. Oxford: Blackwell.

Růžička, Rudolf. 1977. *Historie und Historizität der Junggrammatiker.* Berlin: Akademie-Verlag.

Scherer, Wilhelm. 1868 [^{2}1878]. *Zur Geschichte der deutschen Sprache.* Berlin: Duncker. (New ed., with an introductory article by Kurt R. Jankowsky, Amsterdam & Philadelphia: Benjamins, 1995.)

Schleicher, August. 1860 [^{3}1874]. *Die Deutsche Sprache.* Stuttgart: Cotta'sche Buchhandlung. (3rd ed. repr., Wiesbaden: Sändig, 1973.)

—. 1861–1862 [^{4}1876]. *Compendium der vergleichenden Grammatik der indogermanischen Sprachen.* 2

vols. 4th ed. prepared by Johannes Schmidt & August Leskien. Weimar: Böhlau.

—. ²1873 [1863]. *Die Darwinsche Theorie und die Sprachwissenschaft: Offenes Sendschreiben an Herrn Dr. Ernst Häckel.* Weimar: Böhlau.

Schmidt, Johannes. 1872. *Die Verwantschaftsverhältnisse der indogermanischen Sprachen.* Weimar: Böhlau.

Schröder, Eduard. 1910. "Karl Verner". *Allgemeine Deutsche Biographie* 55 (Nachträge bis 1899: *Wandersleb–Zwirner*), 326–330. Berlin: Duncker & Humblot.

Schuchardt, Hugo. 1885. *Über die Lautgesetze. Gegen die Junggrammatiker.* Berlin: Oppenheim. (Repr. in Wilbur 1977.)

—. 1886. Review of Otto Jespersen (1886) [*Til Sprögsmålet om Lydlove*] and Jacob Hornemann Bredsdorff, *Om Aarsagerne til Sprogenes Forandringer* (Copenhagen: Gyldendal, 1886). *Deutsche Literaturzeitung* 7.1556–1559.

Sievers, Eduard. 1876 [²1881]. *Grundzüge der Lautphysiologie: Zur Einführung in das Studium der indogermanischen Sprachen.* Leipzig: Breitkopf & Härtel. (2nd ed.: *Grundzüge der Phonetik*; 5th ed., 1901.)

Specht, Franz. 1948. "Die 'indogermanische' Sprachwissenschaft von den Junggrammatikern bis zum 1. Weltkrieg". *Lexis* 1.229–263.

Steinthal, Heymann. 1860. "Assimilation und Attraktion, psychologisch beleuchtet". *Zeitschrift für Völkerpsychologie* 1.93–179.

Streitberg, Wilhelm. 1909. "Karl Brugmanns Schriften, 1871–1909". *Indogermanische Forschungen* 26.425–440.

—. 1919a. "Karl Brugmann". *Indogermanisches Jahrbuch* 7.143–148. (Repr. in *Portraits of Linguistics: A biographical source book for the history of Western linguistics, 1746–1963* ed. by Thomas A. Sebeok. Vol. I: *From Sir William Jones to Karl Brugmann*, 575–580. Bloomington & London: Indiana University Press, 1966.)

—. 1919b. "Karl Brugmanns Schriften, 1909–1919". *Indogermanisches Jahrbuch* 7.148–152.

—. 1921. "Worte zum Gedächtnis an Karl Brugmann". *Berichte der sächsischen Akademie der Wissenschaften. Philologisch-historische Klasse* 73.29.

Strong, Herbert A. 1890. See Paul, 1880.

Verner, Karl. 1876. "Eine ausnahme der ersten lautverschiebung". *Zeitschrift für vergleichende Sprachforschung* 23: 2.97–130.

Wechssler, Eduard. 1900. "Gibt es Lautgesetze?". *Festgabe für Hermann Suchier*, 349–538. Halle: Niemeyer. [Published also as a monograph, Halle a. S.: Niemeyer, 1900.]

Wheeler, Benjamin Ide. 1887. *Analogy and the Scope of Its Application in Language.* Cambridge, Mass.: Wilson & Son. (Repr., New York: Johnson, 1965.)

Whitney, William D. 1867. *Language and the Study of Language.* New York: Scribner.

—. 1892. "On Delbrück's Vedic Syntax". (Review of Delbrück, *Altindische Syntax* [= vol. 5 of *Syntaktische Forschungen*]. Halle: Buchhandlung des Waisenhauses, 1888). *American Journal of Philology* 13.217–306.

Wilbur, Terence H., ed. 1977. *The Lautgesetz-Controversy: A documentation (1885–86).* Amsterdam: Benjamins.

Winteler, Jost. 1876. *Die Kerenzer Mundart des Kantons Glarus in ihren Grundzügen dargestellt.* Leipzig & Heidelberg: Winter.

Wundt, Wilhelm. 1886. "Über den Begriff des Gesetzes, mit Rücksicht auf die Frage der Ausnahmslosigkeit der Lautgesetze". *Philosophische Studien* 3.195–215.

Ziemer, Hermann. 1882 [²1883]. *Junggrammatische Streifzüge im Gebiete der Syntax.* Colberg: Post.

Kurt R. Jankowsky Washington, D. C.
(U.S.A.)

167. Die Anwendung der vergleichenden Methode auf afrikanische Sprachen

1. Wissenschaftsgeschichtlicher Überblick
2. Induktive Methode nach Meinhof
3. Zweistufen-Methode nach Guthrie
4. Massenvergleich nach Greenberg
5. Lexikostatistik
6. Rezeption moderner strukturalistischer Methoden
7. Sprachgeographischer und dialektologischer Sprachvergleich
8. Schlußbemerkung
9. Bibliographie

1. Wissenschaftsgeschichtlicher Überblick

Bereits in der ersten Hälfte des 19. Jhs. wurde von europäischen Reisenden und Gelehrten erkannt, daß die Mehrheit der Sprachen Schwarzafrikas untereinander in Lexikon und Grammatik große Übereinstimmungen aufweisen. Man interpretierte dies allgemein als ein Indiz für enge sprachverwandtschaftliche Beziehungen. Besonders auffällig erwiesen sich in dieser Hinsicht die Sprachen des südlichen Subkontinents. Wilhelm Heinrich Immanuel Bleek (1827−1875), einer der Begründer der Afrikanistik, bezeichnete sie nach einem weitverbreiteten Wortstamm mit der Bedeutung "Menschen" als 'Bantu'-Sprachen und widmete ihnen eine erste, wenn auch unvollständig gebliebene, vergleichende Grammatik (Bleek 1862−69). Die seither als Bantuistik bekannte Teildisziplin übernahm hinsichtlich Anpassung und Entwicklung vergleichender Methoden bis in die jüngste Vergangenheit hinein in der Afrikanistik eine Vorreiterstellung. Vermittelt durch Carl Meinhof (1857−1944), der an den Universitäten von Halle, Erlangen und Greifswald neben Theologie und Hebräisch auch Germanistik studiert hatte, fand eine erste Rezeption junggrammatischer Methoden statt. Meinhof adaptierte sie an die besonderen Verhältnisse der Sprachen Afrikas. Im Vergleich zu den indogermanischen Sprachen sind die afrikanischen Sprachen vor allem dadurch gekennzeichnet, daß sie, von wenigen Ausnahmen abgesehen, bis zum Beginn der Kolonialzeit schriftlos waren und folglich auch so gut wie keine Sprachdenkmäler besitzen. Meinhof rekonstruierte dennoch (^{2}1910; ^{2}1948) das Inventar der hypothetischen Protosprache aller rezenten Bantusprachen, die er 'Urbantu' nannte. Mit seiner Methode (s. 2.) übte er viele Jahrzehnte lang einen beherrschenden Einfluß auf die gesamte Afrikanistik und darüber hinaus sogar auf die Austronesistik (Dempwolff 1934−38) aus.

Die Ära Meinhofs ging erst zu Ende, als in den sechziger Jahren der Brite Malcolm Guthrie (1903−1972) mit seiner sogenannten 'Zweistufen-Methode' hervortrat. Sie stellte im Vergleich zu Meinhofs Methoden einen erheblichen Fortschritt dar (s. 3.). Die Publikation des vierbändigen Hauptwerks (Guthrie 1967−71) fiel allerdings in eine Phase, als sich die Afrikanistik erstmals einer breiten Rezeption strukturalistischer Methoden einschließlich der Methode der internen Rekonstruktion (vgl. 6.) öffnete. Das führte dazu, daß Guthries Methode vor diesem neuen Hintergrund alsbald heftiger Kritik ausgesetzt war und selbst in der Bantuistik niemals eine uneingeschränkte Akzeptanz erfuhr.

Mit dem Ziel einer genealogischen Sprachgliederung entwickelte der Amerikaner Joseph H. Greenberg (geb. 1915) in den fünfziger Jahren die Methode des sogenannten sprachlichen Massenvergleichs (s. 4.). Mit ihrer Hilfe gelang es ihm, alle afrikanischen Sprachen zu nur vier Sprachfamilien zusammenzufassen. Sein Werk (Greenberg 1963) gilt heute noch als wichtiges Referenzwerk, insbesondere außerhalb der sprachlichen Afrikaforschung, auch wenn die historischen Implikationen inzwischen weitgehend überholt sind.

Ähnlich verhält es sich mit genetischen Sprachgliederungen auf lexikostatistischer Grundlage (s. 5.), die von einigen Afrikanisten hauptsächlich während der siebziger und achtziger Jahre erstellt wurden (Coupez et al. 1975; Ehret 1971; Heine 1972−73; Nurse 1979). Manche benutzten diese Methode auch nur als eine Art diagnostisches Vorverfahren, um Sprachverwandtschaft überhaupt festzustellen. Im weiteren Verlauf ihrer Studien wandten sie dann auf die lexikostatistisch definierten 'Sprachfamilien' vergleichende Methoden an (Rottland 1982, Vossen 1982).

Die gegenwärtige Entwicklung ist durch zwei Hauptströmungen gekennzeichnet. Zum einen versucht man, durch Verbreiterung und Verfeinerung der empirischen Datengrundlage die Voraussetzungen für die Anwendung moderner komparatistischer Methoden zu verbessern (s. 6.). Zum anderen ist man bestrebt, durch Kombination dieser Methoden mit dialektologischen Methoden neben den Divergenzerscheinungen auch die Konvergenz- und Überschichtungsprozesse in der Geschichte der afrikanischen Sprachen zu entschlüsseln (s. 7.).

Im übrigen diente die Anwendung historisch-vergleichender Methoden zu allen Epochen der afrikanistischen Wissenschaftsgeschichte nicht nur der Rekonstruktion früherer Sprachzustände, sondern stets auch der Sprachgliederung. Nicht selten wurden sprachhistorische Rekonstruktionen als Quellen für kulturhistorische Prozesse verwendet (Ehret 1967; 1968; 1971) oder sogar von benachbarten Disziplinen zur Grundlage eigener historischer Schlüsse gemacht (Phillipson 1977). Vor allem aber versuchte man, die verwirrende Fülle von über 1.600 Einzelsprachen mit unzähligen Dialektvarianten auf möglichst einfache Weise zu ordnen und damit überschaubar zu machen. Wenn die herrschende Meinung der auf Afrika spezialisierten Prähistoriker zutrifft, daß die gesamte Menschheit vor etwa 150.000 Jahren in der afrikanischen Savanne ihren Ursprung nahm

(Leakey & Lewin 1992: 203 ff.) und menschliche Sprache seit etwa 100.000 Jahren besteht (s. 274), dann ist Afrika der Kontinent mit der längsten Sprachgeschichte. Sie umfaßt nach den prähistorischen Zahlenvorgaben 4.000 bis 6.000 Generationen in ununterbrochener genetischer Folge. Es ist schlichtweg absurd sich vorzustellen, daß diese lange Kulturgeschichte jemals auf letzte Ursprachen zurückgeführt werden kann. Komplizierte und komplexe Verhältnisse erfordern ebensolche Entwicklungsmodelle. Das sollte die Perspektive der zukünftigen Entwicklung in der Afrikanistik auf sprachhistorischem Gebiet sein.

2. Induktive Methode nach Meinhof

Meinhof vertrat die Auffassung, daß die Bantusprachen aus einer Vermischung hauptsächlich von nigritischen, klassenlosen Tonsprachen und hamitischen druckakzentuierenden Klassensprachen entstanden seien (1910: 18). In welcher Weise diese Vermischung im einzelnen geschah, war ihm zwar nicht klar, er hielt es dennoch für möglich, Urformen einer hypothetischen Ursprache zu rekonstruieren in der Erwartung, die darin enthaltenen Mischungsverhältnisse später aufhellen zu können. Er erachtete ein solches Vorgehen trotz des spekulativen Charakters für nützlich, weil die rekonstruierten Urformen im Hinblick auf die Strukturbeschreibung einzelner Bantusprachen seiner Meinung nach einen hohen Erklärungswert hatten (Meinhof 1910: 20). Kernstück seiner Methode war eine möglichst genaue Feststellung der Lautverschiebungsgesetze. Da Meinhof seine Methode nur in einem heute schwer zugänglichen und daher weithin unbekannten Aufsatz darlegte (Meinhof 1895), wird von seinen Kritikern häufig übersehen, daß seine Vorgehensweise nicht auf Intuition oder gar Spekulation beruhte, sondern nach Art eines Versuchs- und Irrtumsverfahrens angelegt war. Der von ihm selbst in Publikationen weithin bekanntgemachten Deduktionsstufe ging eine induktive Stufe voraus. Zunächst zog er nur drei besonders gut beschriebene Bantusprachen für einen historischen Vergleich heran: Herero, Zulu und Swahili. Aus diesen Sprachen stellte er ihm identisch scheinende Verbalstämme zusammen, wobei er sich vom Gleichklang und der Bedeutungsgleichheit leiten ließ. Auf diese Weise erhielt er bereits eine ganze Reihe von regelmäßig wiederkehrenden Lautensprechungen. Danach untersuchte er auch andere Wortstämme und erschloß sich allmählich auch solche Lautensprechungen, die nicht an der phonetischen Oberfläche liegen. Allgemeine Erfahrungswerte aus der Indogermanistik dienten ihm als Richtschnur, die regelmäßigen Lautensprechungen auf ihre wahrscheinlichen Urlaute zurückzuführen. Das so gefundene Lautsystem wurde in einer zweiten, deduktiven Phase als historisches Bezugssystem verwendet, um die Lautsysteme anderer Bantusprachen regelhaft daraus abzuleiten. Nach dieser Methode rekonstruierte Meinhof für das Urbantu 7 Vokale, 2 Halbvokale, 9 Konsonanten und 10 sogenannte Nasalverbindungen, dazu fast 600 Proto-Lexeme und eine Fülle von Morphemen vor allem aus dem Nominal- und Pronominalbereich. Die beiden Werke, in denen er seine Ergebnisse veröffentlichte (Meinhof ²1910; ²1948), waren nach Art eines systematischen Lehrbuchs zur Darstellung bisher noch nicht erfaßter Sprachen aufgebaut. Über 50 Jahre dienten sie nachfolgenden Afrikanisten als Modell zur monographischen Beschreibung rezenter Bantusprachen (als spätes Beispiel vgl. Dammann 1957).

Angeregt durch Meinhof, versuchte der Berliner Afrikanist Diedrich Westermann (1875−1956) mittels der induktiven Methode die sprachhistorischen Zusammenhänge innerhalb der westlichen Sudansprachen sowie zwischen diesen und dem Urbantu herauszuarbeiten (Westermann 1911; 1927). Er rekonstruierte ein sogenanntes Ur-Sudan, bestehend aus 380 lexikalischen Wurzeln sowie bestimmten strukturellen und phonologischen Merkmalen. Im Vergleich zu den Bantusprachen mußte er sich allerdings mit sehr viel divergenteren Sprachen befassen. Dies führte ihn dazu, konsequenter als Meinhof von einem Vermischungs- und Substrat-Modell (1927: 5) auszugehen. Noch in seinen letzten wissenschaftlichen Äußerungen zu dieser Frage (1949: 16) sprach er nur von einer "Urverwandtschaft zwischen westlichen Sudan- und Bantusprachen, die durch Überlagerungen und andere Vorgänge überdeckt und dadurch weniger deutlich geworden ist". Sein Schüler Oswin Köhler (1911−1996) folgte ihm in dieser Sichtweise und zog es daher vor, statt von 'Sprachfamilien' im genetischen Sinne, von 'Sprachbereichen' (Köhler 1975: 184) zu sprechen.

3. Zweistufen-Methode nach Guthrie

In den vierziger und fünfziger Jahren hatte sich die Kenntnis der Bantusprachen wesentlich erweitert. Aus allen Teilen des weiten Verbreitungsgebiets lagen nun detaillierte Sprachbeschreibungen und Wörterbücher vor. Außerdem setzten sich unter dem Einfluß der britischen Schule strukturalistische Prinzipien in der Afrkanistik durch und damit auch der Grundsatz Saussures, in der Sprachbeschreibung die rezente von der historischen Perspektive zu trennen. Wie schon Meinhof, so war auch Guthrie mit dem Problem fehlender Sprachdenkmäler aus früheren Phasen der Bantu-Sprachgeschichte konfrontiert. Anders als Meinhof, der aus dem Vergleich der rezenten Einzelsprachen unter Einsatz des gesunden Menschenverstandes und allgemeiner sprachhistorischer Erfahrungen unmittelbar Inventar und Struktur der hypothetischen Ursprache abgeleitet hatte, wählte Guthrie ein zweistufiges Verfahren, das die empirisch nachprüfbaren Ergebnisse des Sprachvergleichs (Stufe I) von den letztlich spekulativen Rekonstruktionen in der historischen Dimension (Stufe II) strikt trennte. In der ersten Stufe wurden die Sprachdaten nach dem Prinzip der regelmäßigen Formentsprechungen zusammengestellt und sprachgeographisch sowie statistisch aufbereitet. Das Ergebnis war ein Korpus von über 2.000 Konstrukten, das Guthrie als 'Common Bantu' (Gemein-Bantu) bezeichnete. Es faßte formelhaft die Sprachelemente mit allgemeiner oder regional begrenzter Verbreitung unter den Bantusprachen auf einer diasprachlichen Ebene zusammen. Lange Zeit war Guthrie überhaupt abgeneigt, seine vergleichenden Forschungen in einer historischen Perspektive zu sehen. Erst Mitte der fünfziger Jahre trat allmählich ein Sinneswandel bei ihm ein (Flight 1980: 87). Unter der Prämisse, daß das Gemein-Bantu ein Ergebnis vieler paralleler Divergenzprozesse nach dem Stammbaumprinzip sei, ergänzte Guthrie seine bis dahin rigoros empirisch ausgerichtete Methode um eine historische Deduktionsstufe. Auf der Grundlage einer gemischten, aber transparent gemachten Argumentation interpretierte er sein Gemein-Bantu im Sinne einer Abfolge verschiedener Protosprachen, deren älteste Stufe er als 'Proto-Bantu X' bezeichnete. Seine sprachhistorischen Hypothesen wurden mit ganz unterschiedlichen Argumenten schon bald nach ihrer Veröffentlichung widerlegt (Möhlig 1976, 1979; Flight 1980). Das Korpus seiner Konstrukte zum Gemein-Bantu überdauerte jedoch und wird noch heute als allgemeines Referenzsystem benutzt.

4. Massenvergleich nach Greenberg

Unabhängig von den methodologischen Problemen, mit denen die empirisch in Afrika arbeitenden Linguisten befaßt waren, führte Joseph H. Greenberg in den fünfziger Jahren eine kombinierte Methode, beruhend auf dem Massenvergleich (mass comparison) und dem Prinzip der formalen Ähnlichkeit sozusagen von außen in die Afrikanistik ein. Nach Greenbergs eigenen Ausführungen (1963: 1) basiert seine Methode insbesondere auf folgenden drei Prinzipien: (1) Die verglichenen Formen müssen sowohl in Form als auch Bedeutung ähnlich sein. (2) Zur Vermeidung von Übereinstimmungen, die auf Zufall oder Entlehnung beruhen, wird statt des üblichen Paarvergleichs eine Vielzahl von Sprachen gleichzeitig miteinander verglichen. (3) Es werden nur linguistische Fakten in Betracht gezogen.

Das nur auf der Grundlage detaillierter phonologischer Studien zu verwirklichende Prinzip der regelmäßigen Lautentsprechung wird in Greenbergs Ansatz durch das laienhafte Ähnlichkeitsprinzip ersetzt. Angesichts der vielen einsilbigen Vergleichsformen und der komplizierten morphophonologischen Veränderungen im morphologischen und lexikalischen Inventar der afrikanischen Sprachen kann der Verzicht des von Meinhof und Guthrie befolgten Grundsatzes der regelmäßigen Lautentsprechung nur als ein methodologischer Rückschritt gewertet werden, der auch durch das neue Prinzip des Massenvergleichs anstelle des Paarvergleichs nicht wettgemacht wird. Im übrigen ist auch bei oberflächlicher Lektüre der methodologischen Ausführungen Greenbergs leicht festzustellen, daß weder die Dreizahl seiner Prinzipien, noch das Prinzip der ausschließlichen Relevanz linguistischer Kriterien zutreffen. Bei der Erläuterung des Massenvergleichs (Greenberg 1963: 2) schiebt er nämlich implizit ein viertes sprachgeographisches Prinzip nach, indem er fordert, daß sich die Vielheit der Vergleichssprachen über weite und voneinander getrennte Verbreitungsgebiete erstrecken müsse. Ohne selbst Feldforschungen in Afrika durchzuführen, ging Greenberg von dem Sprachmaterial aus, das andere bis in die fünfziger Jahren hinein publiziert hatten. Auf dieser qualitativ uneinheitlichen Datengrundlge rekonstruierte er eine 'vollständige genetische Gliederung der Sprachen Afrikas' (Greenberg 1963: 3). Seine Methoden wurden alsbald heftig angegriffen (Fodor 1966, 1982). Trotzdem wird seine Gliederung heute allenthalben − vor allem von benachbarten Disziplinen − als Referenzsystem verwendet. Selbst die von ihm definierten Unterfamilien sind noch aktueller Gegenstand wissenschaftlicher Diskussion (vgl. z. B. Bender 1996). Die Beliebtheit seiner Gliederung läßt sich nur so erklären, daß sie trotz aller methodologischer Schwächen doch größere sprachhistorische, nicht unbedingt auch sprachgenetische Zusammenhänge sichtbar macht, was bei einem rein geographischen oder alphabetischen Referenzsystem nicht der Fall wäre.

5. Lexikostatistik

Die auf den Amerikaner Morris Swadesh (1909−1967) zurückgehende Methode der Lexikostatistik wurde seit den siebziger Jahren in der Afrikanistik ebenfalls angewendet (s. o.). Diese Methode beruht auf der Annahme, daß Sprachen umso enger genetisch verwandt sind, je höher ihr gemeinsamer Anteil am Grundwortschatz ist. Die mit unterschiedlichen statistischen Verfahren berechneten Prozentsätze werden in unilineare, genealogische Stammbäume umgesetzt. Die mit dieser "schnellen" Methode erzielten Ergebnisse ließen sich allerdings im nachhinein mit den zeit- und materialaufwendigen vergleichenden Methoden zumeist nicht bestätigen.

6. Rezeption moderner strukturalistischer Methoden

Im Zuge der allgemeinen Öffnung der Afrikanistik gegenüber den modernen linguistischen Methoden, die in den sechziger Jahren einsetzte, wurden auch die neueren historisch-vergleichenden Methoden einschließlich der Methode der internen Rekonstruktion rezipiert. Eine Richtung versuchte seither, diese Methoden an die sprachhistorische Tradition der Afrikanistik anzubinden (Gerhardt 1968−69; Kastenholz 1996; Miehe 1991; Rottland 1982; Voßen 1982, 1997). Im Bereich der Tschadischen Sprachen konnte vor kurzem auf dieser Grundlage ein Kompendium von etwa 170 lexikalischen Wurzelmorphemen des Grund- und Kulturwortschatzes erarbeitet werden (Jungraithmayr & Ibriszimow 1994). Aufbauend auf den Vorarbeiten von Dimmendaal (1988), Reh (1985, 1996), Rottland (1982) und Voßen (1982) wurde von Hall & Hall (1996) unlängst der Versuch unternommen, das Laut- und Forminventar der Protosprache der nilotischen Unterfamilie zu rekonstruieren.

Trotz methodologischer Stringenz und der Verwendung linguistischen Grundmaterials, das allen modernen Ansprüchen gerecht wird, gehen die meisten dieser Studien immer noch von der Prämisse einer unilinear-genetischen Entwicklung aus. Die damit einhergehende Vernachlässigung konvergenter sprachhistorischer Prozesse ist vermutlich eine späte Folge der Sprachgliederung Greenbergs. Das gedankliche Erbe der älteren Afrikanistiktradition Meinhofs und Westermanns wurde darüber stillschweigend, d. h. ohne jemals mit wissenschaftlichen Gründen widerlegt worden zu sein, beiseite gelegt.

7. Sprachgeographischer und dialektologischer Sprachvergleich

Was schon Westermann (1927: 5) hinsichtlich der Sudansprachen Westafrikas feststellte, hat sich inzwischen auch für die als eng verwandt angesehenen Bantusprachen erwiesen: Die Konvergenzfaktoren in der Sprachgeschichte Afrikas sind bei weitem wirksamer als die der Divergenz. Entlehnungs-, Verschmelzungs- und Überschichtungsprozesse, vor allem zwischen bereits affinen Sprachen und Dialekten, treten deutlich zutage, wenn man die komparativen Methoden in zusammenhängenden Spracharealen, also mit dialektologischen Methoden kombiniert (Möhlig 1978). Ausgehend von dem Prinzip, daß die Uhren des Sprachwandels in benachbarten Dialekten verschieden schnell gehen, lassen sich nicht nur Lautentsprechungen mit Blick auf ein hypothetisches Protosystem, sondern darüber hinaus Lautverschiebungen als Prozesse mit verschiedenen Zwischenstadien rekonstruieren (Möhlig 1980: 38 ff.). Führt man schrittweise die verglichenen Lautsysteme insgesamt auf immer fernere Protostufen zurück, gelangt man im Ergebnis selbst bei eng verwandten Sprachen nicht zu einer gemeinsamen Ursprache, sondern zu einer Vielheit von Ursprachen, die sich mit der vergleichenden Methode trotz aller typologischer Ähnlichkeiten nicht weiter im Sinne des Stammbaum-Modells voneinander ableiten oder miteinander verbinden lassen. Für die Bantusprachen kann dies nur bedeuten, daß sie insgesamt nicht nach dem Divergenzprinzip aus einem einzigen Urbantu oder einer Hierarchie von Proto-Bantu-Stufen hervorgegangen sind, sondern aus vielen Protosprachen, die parallel oder auf untrerschiedlichen Zeithorizonten existiert haben. Mit historisch ausgerichteten dialektologischen Methoden lassen sich viele der sprachhistorischen Prozesse sowohl hinsichtlich ihrer auslösenden Faktoren, als auch ihres Verlaufs im einzelnen plausibel rekonstruieren (Möhlig 1992: 157), wobei diese Prozesse infolge ihrer geringen Zeitentiefe häufig durch außerlinguistische Quellen verifiziert werden können. Zur Darstellung der komplexen sprachhistorischen Vorgänge dienen Fließdiagramme und Kartogramme (Möhlig 1984/85, Voßen 1988).

8. Schlußbemerkung

Die derzeitige Lage in der historisch orientierten Afrikanistik ist durch Spezialisierung auf Teilbereiche gekennzeichnet. Den Bantuisten, die fast ein Jahrhundert lang die sprachhistorische Forschung in der Afrikanistik bestimmten, sind inzwischen die Tschadisten, Kuschitisten, Mandeisten, Nilotisten usw. an die Seite getreten. Jede dieser afrikanistischen Teildisziplinen hat ihre eigene Wissenschaftstradition mit spezifischen Fragestellungen entwickelt. Die derzeitigen Studien zeigen mehrheitlich, daß selbst in vergleichsweise homogenen Unterfamilien Afrikas das genealogische Interpretationsmodell nicht zur Bildung eindeutiger Theorien der Sprachgeschichte führt. Ein weiterer methodologischer Mangel, der erst in jüngster Zeit sichtbar wird, besteht darin, daß man bisher beim lexikalischen oder grammatischen Vergleich von einzelnen Lexemen oder Grammemen anstatt von Paradigmen oder semantisch-konzeptual defnierten Feldern ausgegangen ist. Die Wichtigkeit des System- und Sinnzusammenhangs einzelner Sprachelemente als methodologische Komponente des Sprachvergleichs hat sich in Studien, die sich auf den Vergleich von Lautsystemen oder grammatischen Paradigmen beschränkten (Möhlig 1982; Weier 1985; 1986) deutlich herausgestellt. Auf dieser Grundlage ließen sich in der Tat erstmals stratifikatorische protosprachliche Zustände rekonstruieren. Analoge Ergebnisse konnten indessen auf lexikalischer Grundlage bisher nicht erzielt werden.

Die Wissenschaftsgeschichte der Afrikanistik hat gezeigt, daß es auf eine einfache Rezeption der historisch-vergleichenden Methoden, wie sie etwa an romanischen oder germanischen Sprachen entwickelt wurden, allein nicht ankommt. Auch die im Vergleich zu den Zeiten Meinhofs und Westermanns erheblich verbesserte Datengrundlage vermag die zur Zeit unbefriedigende Situation der sprachgeschichtlichen Forschung in Afrika nicht zu überwinden. Es kommt zusätzlich auf die Entwicklung neuer Methoden an, die in der Lage sind, neben den divergenten auch die konvergenten Prozesse der Sprachgeschichte zu erfassen. Darüber hinaus bedarf es plausibler theoretischer Entwicklungsmodelle, die die empirisch faßbaren synchronen Faktoren des Sprachwandels in Afrika mit einbeziehen. Der tragende Grundsatz jeder historischen Extrapolation, die mangels Sprachzeugnisse aus früheren Epochen von der gegenwärtigen Sprachsituation ausgehen muß, kann nur wie folgt lauten: Es darf vorausgesetzt werden, daß die in der Gegenwart beobachtbaren Verhältnisse, Bedingungen, Kräfte und Bewegungsabläufe des Sprachwandels auch in der Vergangenheit in ihrer rezenten Ausgestaltung schon existierten und wirksam waren, es sei denn, konkrete Beweise legen einen anderen Schluß nahe (Möhlig 1978: 148). Diejenigen, die ihre sprachhistorischen Extrapolationen nach dem Stammbaum-Modell vornehmen, verkehren diese von der Empirie vorgegebene Beweislastregel, ohne einen wissenschaftlichen Grund dafür anzugeben.

9. Bibliographie

Bender, M. Lionel. 1996. "Nilo-Saharan 1995". *Proceedings of the Sixth International Nilo-Saharan Linguistics Conference Santa Monica 1995, March 27−29* hg. von M. Lionel Bender & Thomas J. Hinnebusch, 1−25. Köln: Institut für Afrikanistik, Univ. zu Köln.

Bleek, Wilhelm Heinrich Immanuel. 1862−1869. *A Comparative Grammar of South African Languages*. Part I: *Phonology* (1862); Part II: *The Concord*, Sect. 1: *The Noun* (1869). London: Trübner.

Coupez, André, É. Evrard & Jan Vansina. 1975. "Classification d'un échantillon de langues bantoues d'après la lexicostatistique". *Africana Linguistica* 6.131–158.

Dammann, Ernst. 1957. *Studien zum Kwangali: Grammatik, Texte, Glossar.* Hamburg: Cram, de Gruyter.

Dimmendaal, Gerrit Jan. 1988. "The Lexical Reconstruction of Proto-Nilotic: A first reconnaissance". *Afrikanistische Arbeitspapiere* 16.5–67. Köln.

Dempwolff, Otto. 1934–38. *Vergleichende Lautlehre des Austronesischen Wortschatzes.* 3 Bde. Berlin: Reimer.

Ehret, Christopher. 1967. "Cattle Keeping and Milking in Eastern and Southern Africa". *Journal of African History* 8.1–17.

–. 1971a. "Sheep and Central Sudanic Peoples in Southern Africa". *Journal of African History* 9.213–221.

–. 1971b. *Southern Nilotic History: Linguistic approaches to the study of the past.* Evanston: Northwestern Univ. Press.

Flight, Collin. 1980. "Malcolm Guthrie and the Reconstruction of Bantu Prehistory". *History in Africa* 7.81–118.

Fodor, István. 1966. *The Problems in the Classification of the African Languages.* Budapest: Center for Afro-Asian Research of the Hungarian Academy of Sciences.

–. 1982. *A Fallacy of Contemporary Linguistics: J. H. Greenberg's classification of the African languages and his "Comparative Method".* Hamburg: Buske.

Gerhardt, Ludwig. 1968–69. "Analytische und vergleichende Untersuchungen zu einigen zentralnigerianischen Klassensprachen". *Afrika und Übersee* 51.161–198; 52.23–57, 125–143, 207–242; 53.44–65.

Greenberg, Joseph H. 1963. *The Languages of Africa.* Den Haag & Bloomington: Mouton. (3. Aufl., 1971.)

Guthrie, Malcolm. 1967–71. *Comparative Bantu: An introduction to the comparative linguistics and prehistory of the Bantu languages.* 4 Bde. Farnborough: Gregg Press.

Hall, Beatrice & R. M. R. Hall. 1996. "From Cognate Set to Etymology in the Reconstruction of Proto-Nilotic". *Proceedings of the Sixth International Nilo-Saharan Linguistics Conference Santa Monica 1995, March 27–29,* hg. von M. Lionel Bender & Thomas J. Hinnebusch, 151–175. Köln: Institut für Afrikamistik, Univ. zu Köln.

Heine, Bernd. 1972/73. "Zur genetischen Gliederung der Bantu-Sprachen". *Afrika und Übersee* 56.164–185.

Jungraithmayr, Herrmann & Dymitr Ibriszimow. 1994. *Chadic Lexical Roots.* Berlin: Reimer.

Kastenholz, Raimund. 1996. *Sprachgeschichte im West-Mande: Methoden und Rekonstruktionen.* Köln: Köppe.

Köhler, Oswin. 1975. "Geschichte und Probleme der Gliederung der Sprachen Afrikas: Von den Anfängen bis zur Gegenwart". *Die Völker Afrikas und ihre traditionellen Kulturen.* Teil I: *Allgemeiner Teil und südliches Afrika* hg. von Hermann Baumann, 135–373. Wiesbaden: Steiner.

Leakey, Richard & Roger Lewin. 1992. *Origins Reconsidered: In search of what makes us human.* Hew York & London: Doubleday.

Meinhof, Carl. 1895. "Vorbemerkungen zu einem vergleichenden Wörterbuch der Bantusprachen". *Zeitschrift für afrikanische und oceanische Sprachen* 1.268–281.

–. ^{2}1910 [1899]. *Grundriß einer Lautlehre der Bantusprachen.* Berlin: Reimer.

–. ^{2}1948 [1906]. *Grundzüge einer vergleichenden Grammatik der Bantusprachen.* Hamburg: Eckardt & Messtorff.

Miehe, Gudrun. 1991. *Die Präfixnasale im Benue-Congo und im Kwa: Versuch einer Widerlegung der Hypothese von der Nasalinnovation des Bantu.* Berlin: Reimer.

Möhlig, Wilhelm J. G. 1976. "Guthries Beitrag zur Bantuistik aus heutiger Sicht. *Anthropos* 71.673–715.

–. 1978. "Synchrone Faktoren des Sprachwandels im Savannen-Bantu". *Struktur und Wandel afrikanischer Sprachen* hg. von Herrmann Jungraithmayr, 132–150. Berlin: Reimer.

–. 1979. "The Bantu Nucleus: Its conditional nature and its prehistorical significance". *Sprache und Geschichte in Afrika SUGIA* 1.109–141.

–. 1980. "Bantu languages". *Language and Dialect Atlas of Kenya.* Bd. I: *Geographical and Historical Introduction. Language and society. Selected bibliography* hg. von Bernd Heine & Wilhelm J. G. Möhlig, 11–53. Berlin: Reimer.

–. 1984/85. "The Swahili Dialects of Kenya in Relation to Mijikenda and to the Bantu idioms of the Tana Valley". *Sprache und Geschichte in Afrika SUGIA* 6.253–308.

–. 1992. "Language Death and the Origin of Strata: Two case studies of Swahili dialects". *Language Death: Factual and theoretical explorations with special reference to East Africa* hg. von Matthias Brenzinger, 157–179. Berlin & New York: Mouton de Gruyter.

Nurse, Derek. 1979. *Classification of the Chaga Dialects: Language and history on Kilimanjaro, the Taita Hills, and the Pare Mountains.* Hamburg: Buske.

Phillipspon, David W. 1977. *The Later Prehistory of Eastern and Southern Africa.* London: Heinemann.

Reh, Mechthild. 1985. *Reconstructing Proto-Western Nilotic and Proto-Nilotic Lexicon.* MS. Cologne: Institute of Africanistics.

—. 1996. *Anywa Language: Analysis and internal reconstructions.* Köln: Köppe.

Rottland, Franz. 1982. *Die Südnilotischen Sprachen: Beschreibung, Vergleichung und Rekonstruktion.* Berlin: Reimer.

Voßen, Rainer. 1982. *The Eastern Nilotes: Linguistic and historical reconstructions.* Berlin: Reimer.

—. 1988. *Towards a Comparative Study of the Maa Dialects of Kenya and Tanzania.* Hamburg: Buske.

—. 1997. *Die Khoe-Sprachen: Ein Beitrag zur Erforschung der Sprachgeschichte Afrikas.* Köln: Köppe.

Weier, Hans-Ingolf. 1985. *Basisdemonstrativa im Bantu.* Hamburg: Buske.

—. 1986. *Substitutiv und Possessiv im Bantu.* Berlin: Reimer.

Westermann, Diedrich. 1911. *Die Sudansprachen: Eine sprachvergleichende Studie.* Hamburg: Friederichsen.

—. 1927. *Die westlichen Sudansprachen und ihre Beziehungen zum Bantu.* Berlin: de Gruyter.

—. 1949. *Sprachbeziehungen und Sprachverwandtschaft in Afrika.* (= Sitzungsbericht der Deutschen Akademie der Wissenschaften zu Berlin; Phil.-hist. Klasse, Jahrgang 1948, Nr. 1.) Berlin.

Wilhelm J. G. Möhlig, Köln (Deutschland)

168. The comparative method applied to Austronesian languages

1. The Comparative Method
2. The Austronesian language family
3. Soubgrouping
4. Phonology
5. Morphology and syntax
6. Lexicon
7. Summary
8. Bibliography

1. The Comparative Method

The Comparative Method (CM) has occupied a central position in linguistic methodology for over a century and a half. However, because it was a by-product of the establishment of the Indo-European language family, its universality has been questioned. Bloomfield (1925, 1928) provided an early test of the universality of the CM. More recently this issue was addressed at the Workshop on Linguistic Change and Reconstruction Methodology held at Stanford University, 1987 (Baldi 1991).

Broadly speaking, the CM is concerned with three methodologically distinguishable aspects of linguistic history: (1) the establishment of genetic relationship, (2) the reconstruction of proto-languages, and (3) the subgrouping of related languages. This brief presentation will be concerned only with the latter two aspects. The discussion of linguistic reconstruction will be divided into three subfields: phonology, morphology and syntax, and lexicon.

2. The Austronesian language family

The Austronesian (AN) language family may be the world's largest in number of languages, and evidently was the first geographically extensive language family for which a common origin was recognized. Ruhlen (1987) lists 959 AN languages, and Grimes et al. (1995) give 1,202. Prior to the European colonial expansions of the past four centuries AN languages had the greatest territorial range of any language family on earth, extending some 206 degrees of longitude from Madagascar to Easter Island, and over 70 degrees of latitude from northern Taiwan to the South Island of New Zealand. These facts of numbers and geography have had two significant consequences for the comparative study of AN languages. First, many languages remain poorly described or not described at all. Second, the descriptive literature on these languages presents problems of access because of the variety of languages in which it is written.

The relationship of Malagasy to Malay and other languages of island Southeast Asia was recognized in print less than a decade after the first Dutch expedition to the East Indies departed via the Cape route in 1595 (Houtman 1603). A century later Adrian Reland (1676–1708) was able to demonstrate a historical connection between Malay and various Pacific languages even though only the sketchiest descriptive materials were then available for the latter (Reland 1706–1708).

European knowledge of the Austronesian languages of the Pacific increased significantly during the second voyage of James Cook (1772–1775), when vocabularies were collected from various parts of Melanesia and Polynesia (Förster 1778). As a result of the fuller information provided by Cook's voyages it was shown convincingly that this still unnamed language family extends from the western edge of the Indian Ocean (Madagascar) to the last inhabitable landfall west of South America (Easter Island). Some six decades later Wilhelm von Humboldt (1767–1835) combined Malay, the name of the best-known Austronesian language of island Southeast Asia, with that of the best-known group of languages in the Pacific (at that time considered to be a single language) to create a new language-family name: 'Malayo-Polynesian' (Humboldt 1836–1839).

During the second half of the 19th century several Dutch scholars initiated the first tentative comparative work on the Austronesian languages of island Southeast Asia. The most important of these were: (1) Hermann Neubronner van der Tuuk (1824–1894), (2) Jan Lourens Andries Brandes (1857–1905), and (3) Hendrik Kern (1833–1917). Van der Tuuk (1865, 1872) pointed out three phonetically variable sound correspondences holding between some of the better-known languages of western Indonesia and the Philippines. He did not attempt reconstruction, and he confounded two correspondences which later scholarship has proved to be distinct, but his work stands nonetheless as a brilliant pioneering effort in a previously undeveloped field. Brandes (1884) separated the languages of Indonesia into western and eastern divisions on the basis of shared typological traits, a division that has not subsequently proved to correlate with the evidence of exclusively shared innovations. Kern (1886, 1889) was the first scholar (and still one of the few) to include the entire sweep of Austronesian under his scholarly purview. He made important contributions to establishing the Austronesian affinity of some of the languages of Melanesia, and to addressing the question of the Austronesian homeland. With regard to reconstruction, however, he lacked a sense of method, often resorting to Old Javanese forms of a millennium ago as representative of Proto-Austronesian, a language which must have been spoken some five millennia earlier.

Shortly after the beginning of the 20th century the Austrian linguist and ethnologist Wilhelm Schmidt (1845–1921) presented evidence that the Munda languages of eastern India and the Mon-Khmer languages of mainland Southeast Asia, despite great typological divergence, form a single family which he named 'Austroasiatic' (Schmidt 1906). At the same time he suggested that the Austroasiatic and Malayo-Polynesian languages form a larger genetic unit which he called 'Austric'. Both in the interest of terminological uniformity, and because the name 'Malayo-Polynesian' had implied a bridge from Southeast Asia to Polynesia which bypasses Melanesia, Schmidt suggested that the name 'Malayo-Polynesian' be replaced with 'Austronesian'. At least since the work of Dempwolff in the mid 1930s 'Austronesian' has come to be the generally accepted designation for this family of languages.

Despite the significant descriptive lacunae that remain to be filled there are adequate, and in some cases excellent grammars and dictionaries for perhaps 100 AN languages, as well as shorter descriptions for a number of others. Much of the literature on the aboriginal languages of Taiwan is in Japanese or Chinese, although the more significant publications during the second half of the 20th century have been in English. The earliest descriptions of Philippine languages were in Spanish, but the great bulk of publications since about 1900 have been in English, with some in Tagalog or other Philippine languages. Publications on Malagasy, the AN languages of Vietnam and Kampuchea and various French possessions in the Pacific (French Polynesia, New Caledonia and the Loyalty Islands) have been predominantly in French, with a smaller number in English. Much of the work on the languages of Indonesia until the middle of this century was published in Dutch, with a smaller output in German. In more recent decades the National Language Centers in Indonesia and Malaysia have issued a number of linguistic descriptions in Malay (Bahasa Indonesia and Bahasa Malaysia).

3. Subgrouping

As recently as the late 1930s it was common to speak of Indonesian, Melanesian, Micronesian and Polynesian branches of the AN language family. Dempwolff (1934–38) showed that all of the AN languages of the latter three areas apart from Palauan and Chamorro in Micronesia belong to a single enormous subgroup which contains well over 400 languages. This group, now commonly known as 'Oceanic' (OC) has been so well-established by subsequent research that it can no longer be considered controversial.

However, the position of Oceanic within Austronesian resisted analysis considerably longer. The following subgrouping of AN is now widely accepted: (1) AN divides into several primary branches in Taiwan and a Malayo-Polynesian (MP) branch which includes all other languages; (2) MP divides into Western (WMP) and Central-Eastern (CEMP) branches, the former represented in the Philippines, western Indonesia, mainland Southeast Asia, Madagascar and western Micronesia (Palauan and Chamorro); (3) CEMP divides into Central and Eastern branches, the former represented in the Lesser Sundas and the southern and Central Moluccas of eastern Indonesia; (4) EMP divides into South Halmahera-West New Guinea and Oceanic (OC), the former represented in the northern Moluccas and coastal portions of western New Guinea. Principal publications presenting evidence for this picture are Blust (1978, 1993, 1995, 1999).

Within Oceanic Grace (1955) recognized 19 primary branches, most of which are confined to western Melanesia. His group (4), which involved the immediate relationships of Polynesian, had the greatest internal structure. Specifically, he proposed a grouping of Rotuman, Fijian and Polynesian as one primary branch of a larger grouping which included many of the languages of central and northwestern Vanuatu (then called the 'New Hebrides'). This entire grouping in turn was one of four primary branches of a still larger grouping which included all other languages of Vanuatu, and possibly the Nuclear Micronesian languages.

Pawley (1972) argued for an 'Eastern Oceanic' grouping which included the languages of the Southeastern Solomons together with the membership of Grace's group (4) minus Southern Vanuatu and Nuclear Micronesian. Lynch and Tryon (1985) argued for an expanded 'Central-Eastern Oceanic' which includes southern Vanuatu and the AN languages of the Santa Cruz Islands.

Within Polynesia the classification of Pawley (1966, 1967) is widely accepted: (1) the first split separates Tongan and Niue ('Tongic') from the rest ('Nuclear Polynesian'); (2) the second split separates Samoan and the Polynesian Outlier languages of Micronesia and Melanesia ('Samoic-Outlier') from the rest ('Eastern Polynesian'); (3) the third split separates Eastern Polynesian into Easter Island and the rest; (4) the fourth split separates the rest into Tahitic and Marquesic branches (with Hawaiian in the latter). More recently Ross (1988) has proposed several large groupings in western Melanesia, bringing some measure of order into what had earlier appeared to be an almost intractable problem.

The implications of these subgrouping proposals for primary centers of dispersal and prehistoric migration routes have not been lost on archaeologists: the AN migrations must have begun from Taiwan or the adjacent coast of southern China about 4,000 BC, from there moving southward into the Philippines and Indonesia. In Indonesia there was a split into a western stream ancestral to WMP, and an eastern stream ancestral to the rest. CEMP in turn split somewhere in northeastern Indonesia, one branch (CMP) moving south and west through the Lesser Sundas, the other settling the northern Moluccas before in turn splitting into a relatively sedentary South Halmahera-West Guinea group and a more mobile group which moved around the north coast of New Guinea to give rise to the proto-Oceanic speech community and the Lapita archaeological culture (Pawley & Green 1985, Bellwood 1991). Proto-Oceanic speakers then split up and fanned out rapidly, settling all of Melanesia, western Polynesia (Samoa-Tonga) and probably parts of Micronesia within three or four centuries of the earliest settlements in the Bismarck Archipelago around 1600 BC.

4. Phonology

As already noted in passing, important early work on phonological correspondences between various languages of Indonesia and the Philippnes was carried out by the Dutch linguist H. N. van der Tuuk (1824–1894) prior to the time of the Neogrammarian revolution in Indo-European studies (1865, 1872). By the early part of this century the Swiss linguist Renward Brandstetter (1860–1942) had reconstructed much of the sound system and a preliminary vocabulary of what he called 'Original Indonesia' (Brandstetter 1906, 1916), and by the 1930s the German medical doctor and linguist Otto Dempwolff (1871–1938) had reconstructed a complete sound system and a lexicon of over 2,200 base forms for what he called 'Original Austronesian'. Dempwolff's reconstruction was particularly noteworthy for its attention to methodology, and was praised by such notable scholars as Leonard Bloomfield (1936).

Dempwolff's reconstruction of the PAN sound system was in turn improved by the American linguist Isidore Dyen (1953, 1965). Since the mid 1960s the major issues in phonological reconstruction have been settled to the satisfaction of most scholars. In a number of publications Isidore Dyen has proposed additional consonants by splittling earlier single phonemes into numerous phonetically vacuous varieties (*R$_1$ through *R$_4$, *S$_1$ through *S$_6$, *x$_1$ through *x$_3$, etc, but it is generally agreed that these distinctions have little relationship to PAN, or to general scientific requirements of independent evidentiary support. At least partly in reaction to Dyen's abandonment of realism in reconstruction, Wolff (1988) has moved to the opposite extreme, proposing that a number of plausible consonant distinctions proposed by Dempwolff be abandoned.

4.1. Consonants

PAN had labials *p, *b, *m, and *w (labiovelar), dentals *t, *d, *n, *S, *l *r, *C and *N, palatals *c, *z, *ñ, *s, and *y, velars *k, *g, *j and *ŋ, a uvular *R, a pharyngeal *q and glottals *ʔ and *h. The labials had their expected phonetic values. Among the dentals the following phonetic values are probable, but by no means universally accepted: *t (postdental), *d and *n (alveolar), *S (postdental or alveolar), *l (alveolar) *r (alveolar flap), *C (alveolar affricate), *N (voiceless alveolar lateral). For the palatal series *c and *z probably were palatal affricates, and *s a palatal fricative. The velars had their expected phonetic values except that *j probably was a palatalized velar [g^y], and formed an island in the phonological system. Ross (1992) provides a closely argued interpretation of the phonetics of the PAN phoneme system which differs in some details from that given here. The most controversial consonants are *r, *c, *g and *ʔ. Wolff (1988) has questioned each of the first three, but there is unimpeachable evidence for *g, and good circumstantial evidence for *r and *c. PAN *ʔ has been proposed by Zorc (1982), who offers interesting arguments and supporting evidence, but who cannot account for numerous irregularities in the correspondences.

Space does not permit a full review of the reconstruction of lower-order AN protolanguages. Some of the more notable examples, however, include Proto-Tsouic, the reconstructed ancestor of a small group of languages in central Taiwan (Tsuchida 1976), Proto-Minahasan and Proto-Sangiric, ancestral to modern languages in northern Sulawesi (Sneddon 1978, 1984), Proto-Malayo-Javanic, a putative ancestor of Malay, Javanese, Sundanese and Madurese which has occasioned considerable debate (Nothofer 1975; Blust 1981), Proto-Central Pacific (Geraghty 1983), and Proto-Polynesian (Walsh & Biggs 1966).

Consonant change in the AN languages is quite varied, but many changes follow the familiar 'erosion sequences' *p > /f/ > /h/ > zero, and *k > /h/ > zero (for examples cf. Blust 1991a, b). Another common consonant change is the loss of contrast in final position through a series of steps including 1) devoicing, 2) merger of all stops as glottal stop and all nasals as the velar nasal, and 3) loss of all final consonants. The latter change is unknown in Taiwan or the Philippines, and occurs in only a few languages of Indonesia, but is very common in Oceanic languages, which often favor an open-syllable typology either through loss of the final consonant or through the addition of a final echo vowel. A recurrent conditioned change is *t > /s/ before *i, which is found scattered through many languages from the northern Philippines to western Polynesia.

Typologically unusual, or phonetically opaque consonant changes include the recurrent change *t > /k/ independently in three Polynesian languages (Hawaiian, Samoan, Luangiua), in New Caledonia, in several languages of the Admiralty Islands of northwest Melanesia, in Kisar of eastern Indonesia, and in Enggano of western Indonesia, the change *l > /ŋg/ in the Polynesian Outlier language of Rennell Island in the central Solomons, the change of intervocalic *b to /k/ in some of the Berawan dialects of northern Sarawak, and the change of *w to /c/-, -/nc/- in Sundanese and some Sumatran dialects of Malay. To these we might add changes which resulted in typologically unusual outcomes, as with the recurrent development of preploded final nasals in various languages of Borneo, Sumatra, and mainland Southeast Asia (e. g., *malem̩ /malapm/, *bulan > /buretn/ in Mentu Land Dayak of Sarawak). A striking example of such a change is the development of an apico-labial series with stops, fricatives and nasals in some of the languages of Vanuatu, an articulation type which appears to be unique among the world's languages (Tryon 1976; Maddieson 1987).

The change of *t to /k/ in AN languages is perhaps the single most widespread change which has puzzled theoreticians. In Hawaiian it is the end point of a drag chain which began with the loss of Proto-Polynesian PPN *? and the subsequent change *k > /?/: PPN *?atu > Hwn /aku/ "bonito, tuna", *ta?ane > /kāne/ "man, male", *kata > /?aka/ "to laugh". One dialect of Hawaiian (Ni'ihau) has not undergone the change. Much the same set of preconditions exists in Samoan, but here the change is in progress and forms part of a set of stylistic shifts which distinguish speech registers (/t/ and /n/ of formal register corresponding to /k/ and /ŋ/ of casual register). In other languages the change is conditioned, as in several languages of the Admiralty Islands, where *t which came to be final as the result of loss of a final vowel shifted to /k/, but a non-final *t did not: POC *kutu > /kuk/ "louse", *mʷata > /mʷak/ "snake", but *tama > /tama-/ "father", *pitaquR > /putow/ "a tree: Callophyllum inophyllum". In no case is there any indication that *t was anything other than a voiceless unaspirated postdental or alveolar stop immediately prior to its change to a velar.

4.2. Vowels and diphthongs

Proto-Austronesian had four vowels: *a, *i, *u and *e (schwa), and four diphthongs: *-ay, *-aw, *-uy and *-iw. In general AN vowels are far more stable than the vowels of Indo-European languages. Diachronically the most variable vowel is *e, which has merged with each of the other vowels either conditionally or unconditionally in various languages, and has become /e/ (mid-front) or /o/ in other languages (e.g., PAN *enem > Paiwan /enem/, Isneg /annám/, Tagalog /ánim/, Cebuano Bisayan /unúm/, Malagasy /enina/, Toba Batak /onom/, Fijian /ono/ "six"). The vowel next most likely to change is *a, which is rounded or centralized in final position in a number of the languages of island Southeast Asia, and which assimilates to neighboring high vowels many languages throughout the family. In some languages *u has been fronted in particular environments, but apart from some lowering in narrowly defined environments *i rarely changes. There have been few controversies concerning the reconstruction of the vowels.

The most common change to the diphthongs is monophthongization, sometimes singly, as where Malay merged *-uy and *-iw with *-i but left *-ay and *-aw intact, or as a group, as where Proto-Oceanic merged *-uy and *-iw with *-i, and then created two new vowels through monophthongization of *-ay (> *e) and *-aw (> *o). In two widely separated areas diphthongs have been truncated by loss of the glide: (1) Taokas, Favorlang-Babuza, Hoanya and Papora have truncated final *y (the same change appears to be in progress in Thao); (2) many of the languages of the central and southern Moluccas and the Lesser Sunda islands of eastern Indonesia have truncated both final *y and *w in diphthongs (e.g., PMP *matay > Ngadha /mata/ "die, dead", *lakaw > /la?a/ "walk, go").

4.3. The Regularity Hypothesis

Sound change in AN languages in overwhelmingly regular, and reaffirms the universal validity of the CM. However, there are areas of irregularity which continue to resist adequate explanation. These areas include sporadic fronting of *u in a number of Oceanic languages and a few WMP languages (Blust 1970a), sporadic prenasalization or denasalization in many languages of western Indonesia, the Philippines, and the Pacific, sporadic voicing interchange in the velar stops (Blust 1996), multiple apparently unconditioned reflexes of *R in many widely scattered languages and a pervasive unconditioned split into 'fortis' and 'lenis' reflexes of non-prenasalized prevocalic stops in many OC languages (Ross 1988).

Because it is perhaps the single most pervasive type of extra-paradigmatic phonological change in AN languages sporadic prenasalization will be illustrated with a few examples. Many of the languages of the Philippines and Indonesia reflect *pusej "navel", but Balinese has /puŋsed/. Since many of the languages which have a cognate form allow medial prenasalization in many other words it must be assumed that Balinese has sporadically added a preconsonantal nasal in this form. Similarly, many AN languages reflect *qudaŋ "shrimp, lobster", but Iban has /undaŋ/. Since Balinese has /udaŋ/ "shrimp, lobster" and Iban has /pusat/ "navel", and since such cases can be miltiplied hundreds of times over it is clear that sporadic prenasalization is a type of *pandemic* irregularity — a species of change which is not rule-governed (at least in any sense that is currently understood), and which moreover is shared by an entire population of related languages. To date all attempts to explain medial prenasalization as a product of fossilized morphology or conditioned phonological change have failed (Blust 1996).

4.4. Drift

The concept of 'drift', or parallel development motivated by the independent operation of inherited structural pressures, was first clearly elucidated by Edward Sapir (1921) on the basis of examples from the Germanic languages. Austronesian languages provide many more examples of surprising changes which have occurred independently, sometimes in languages within the same geographical region, and some in widely separated languages (Blust 1977, 1990, 1994; Rehg 1991; Sneddon 1993). Some of these recurrent changes affect only the phonology (e.g., *t > /k/ in at least seven independent cases), while others involve the interaction of phonological and syntactic change, as where haplology took place in the suffixed reflexes of earlier reduplicated monosyllables (e.g., *tutuk-i > /tuki/), but not in their non-suffixed forms (e.g., *tutuk > /tutu/), thereby giving rise to a correlation between reduplication and transitivity independently in many OC languages (Blust 1977).

4.5. Areal phenomena

The subject of areal phenomena in AN languages can only be touched on here. It is normally the case that areal traits are clearest when the languages which share them do not share a demonstrable genetic relationship; this does not mean, however, that languages which share a common ancestor do not also share many similarities as a result of contact and borrowing.

Two geographical areas provide particularly clear indications of areal phenomena in AN languages. The first of these is the Chamic group of AN languages, found in Vietnam, Kampuchea and on Hainan island in southern China. These languages have acquired many typological traits typical of neighboring Mon-Khmer languages, or in the case of Tsat, spoken on Hainan, of neighboring Tai-Kadai languages and Chinese. Such traits include a tendency to monosyllabic or 'sesquisyllabic' canonical form, contrastively aspirated and preglottalized stops, word-initial consonant clusters of stops or nasals plus liquids, register (Western Cham) or tone (Eastern Cham and Tsat), and an increased number of diphthongs (Maddieson & Pang 1993; Thurgood 1993, 1999).

Many of the AN languages of coastal New Guinea have acquired SOV word order as a result of intensive contact with neighboring Papuan languages, and some have acquired other, perhaps more surprising features. Gapapaiwa, spoken in southeastern New Guinea, for example, has replaced the PAN (and POC) decimal system of counting with a far more cumbersome system 1, 2, 2 + 1, 2 + 2, 2 + 2 + 1 under influence from Papuan languages which have similar systems.

5. Morphology and syntax

Superficially AN languages exhibit a wide range of syntactic types. Dempwolff (1934: 13) went so far as to say that, by contrast with such languages groups as Semitic or Bantu, AN languages have no 'common grammar', and that grammatical comparison would therefore prove fruitless. Subsequent researchers have come to regard Dempwolff's position on this matter as overly pessimistic.

Many of the AN languages of Taiwan and the Philippines, and others scattered over a wide area either possess or show evidence of having once possessed a morphological system of voice-marking in the verb which afforded three possibilities of focusing sentence constituents other than the actor. Wolff (1973) reconstructed the essential morphological elements of this system, although Starosta, Pawley & Reid (1982) offer an alternative syntactic interpretatioin. The following Tagalog examples illustrate how a focus system works (where AF = Actor Focus, PF = Patient Focus, LF = Locative Focus, BF = Benefactive Focus, and IF = Instrumental Focus):

(1) AF: b-um-ilí nang kotse ang lalake 'the man bought a/the car'
(2) PF: b-in-ilí nang lalake ang kotse 'a/the man bought the car'
(3) LF: b-in-ilh-án nang lalake nang isdá^{ʔ} ang báta^{ʔ} 'a/the man bought some fish from the child'
(4) BF: i-b-in-ilí nang lalake nang isdá^{ʔ} ang báta^{ʔ} 'a/the man bought some fish for the child'
(5) IF: i-b-in-ilí nang lalake nang isdá^{ʔ} ang pera 'a/the man bought some fish with the money'

In Tagalog the particle /ang/ marks an NP as having a 'focused' case relation to the verb. The nature of that relationship is specified by the focus affix on the verb (AF: -um-, PF: -in in non-perfective constructions, zero in perfective constructions marked by the infix -in-, LF: -an, BF and IF: i-). The *choice* of focus in a given sentence is determined by the thread of discourse: /ang/ phrases are definite, implying that they are old information. Hence the focus-marking apparatus provides a morphological means of tracking reference. But the complexities of the system are by no means exhausted through simple reference to the use of these affixes in verbal inflection, since the same affixes also serve as nominalizers, and here their role more closely resembles that of derivational affixes in languages such as English.

PAN appears to have had a focus system of the general 'Philippine' type. As a rule focus languages underwent the fewest syntactic changes in areas nearest the probable AN homeland in Taiwan. A notable exception is Malagasy, which left southeast Borneo between 1000 and 1500 years ago, at a time when the syntactic typology of languages in Borneo must have been much more Philippine-like than is the case today (Dahl 1951, 1991; Adelaar 1989).

Although much of the focus-marking apparatus of PAN was lost in POC, some features of the original grammatical system were retained and elaborated in new ways. Pawley (1973) provides an outline grammar of Proto-Oceanic, and many other details are filled in by Ross (1988).

Before leaving the subject of morphology one other topic should be briefly mentioned. Brandstetter (1916) drew attention to the occurrence of submorphemic meaning-bearing syllables in a number of the languages of island Southeast Asia, and this matter has been taken up in greater detail by Blust (1988), Nothofer (1990, 1991), Zorc (1990) and others. Blust (1988) presents 231 examples of sound-meaning associations which are defined by recurrent association (but not by paradigmatic contrast) and which are independently attested in at least four morphemes. Examples include -/pit/ "approximation of two surfaces" in such forms as Malay /(h)apit/ "pressure between two disconnected surfaces", /capit/ "pincers", /men-ce-pit/ "to nip", /dempit/ "pressed together", /(h)empit/ "pressure between two unconnected surfaces", /gapit/ "nipper, clamp", /(h)im-pit/ "squeezing pressure", and /jepit/ "to nip, catch between pincers". What is notable about such forms is that they exhibit a recurrent sound-meaning association much like the /gl/- in English *gleam, glitter, glow, glisten* and the like, but typically consist of an entire morpheme-final syllable. Moreover, unlike English or German phonesthemes these submorphemic elements are not restricted to a single language, but cognate roots are shared by literally hundreds of languages. In summary, roots constitute a unit of structure intermediate between the phoneme and the morpheme which is difficult to ignore in describing or comparing AN languages.

6. Lexicon

The reconstructed lexicon of early AN is probably as advanced as that of any other language family studied to date, a fact which remains almost completely unknown to most scholars in other fields. To make my point a few comparisons are perhaps in order. The standard Indo-European etymological dictionary of Pokorny (1959) consists of two volumes. The first of these contains 1183 pages of Indo-European etymologies together with reconstructed prototypes. The second contains 495 pages of cross-references which cite the material of the first volume language-by-language. All told there are approximately 3,150 etymologies proposed, some of which contain subparts based on differing vowel grades. There is no annotation apart from the most passing remarks. The rather differently organized dictionary of Buck (1949) contains about 1,100 sets of synonyms from the major Indo-European languages. The most important feature of this dictionary is its copious annotation, since it is in the notes that Buck distinguishes cognate from non-cognate forms, mentions PIE etyma, discusses semantic evolution, and the like.

The Dravidian etymological dictionary of Burrow & Emeneau (1984) contains some 5,557 proposed cognate sets. However, no reconstructed forms are proposed, and there is no annotation. A list of some 61 widely distributed Indo-Aryan loanwords in Dravidian languages in appended.

Published work on Austronesian includes the standard dictionary of Dempwolff (1938), which contains some 2,223 entries, and a series of publications by the writer of which the most important are Blust (1970b, 1980, 1983/84, 1986, 1989) which have added over 3,000 more items to Dempwolff's material. A new and far more comprehensive comparative dictionary of the Austronesian languages has been in preparation by the writer since

1990. Material has been drawn from over 150 languages, and to date somewhat more than 2,000 pages have been completed. The work done so far includes over 3,600 reconstructed base forms with supporting evidence (for some individual etymologies drawn from over 100 languages), and more than 7,500 total forms, since in addition to unaffixed base forms many affixed forms are also reconstructed. Reconstructions are distinguished by level of proto-language, close attention is paid to semantic inferences, and there is extensive annotation, amounting in some cases to several pages. There are several appendices, including one for widely distributed loanwords (over 300 identified so far), another for monosyllabic roots (submorphemes), and a third for 'noise' (convergent similarities).

It should be noted that the recently published *Comparative Austronesian Dictionary* (Tryon 1995) is a misnomer, as it is neither comparative nor a dictionary in the usual sense of either word, but rather is a set of raw materials for comparison.

7. Summary

The Austronesian languages have played a key part in the development of a general Comparative Method for historical linguistics. Their interrelationships were recognized earlier than those of the Indo-European languages, and with the work of the Dutch scholar H. N. van der Tuuk in the 1860s and 1870s they were among the first languages for which systematic sound correspondences were established. Today lexical reconstruction in AN probably is unparalleled in the field of historical linguistics. Surprisingly, some Indo-Europeanists remain remarkably ignorant of these developments. Lehmann (1992: 88) for example, asserts that AN is a subbranch of an 'Austric' family (roughly equivalent to claiming that Indo-European is a subbranch of a 'Nostratic' family), and maintains with respect to 'Austric' that "the evidence for reconstructing even the proto-languages of its assumed subgroups is small". Such a statement was untrue even in the first decade of this century, and was explicitly repudiated by Leonard Bloomfield (1936) in his defense of Dempwolff against a now long forgotten critic. For it to be made in the 1990s, when the reconstructed lexicon of the earlier stages of Austronesian rivals or surpasses that of Indo-European both in quantity and in precision is simply absurd.

8. Bibliography

Adelaar, K. Alexander. 1989. "Malay Influence on Malagasy: Linguistic and culture-historical implications". *Oceanic Linguistics* 28.1−46.

Baldi, Philip, ed. 1991. *Patterns of Change, Change of Patterns: Linguistic change and reconstruction methodology.* Berlin: Mouton de Gruyter.

Bellwood, Peter. 1991. "The Austronesian Dispersal and the Origin of Languages". *Scientific American* 255: 1.88−93.

Bloomfield, Leonard. 1925. "On the Sound System of Central Algonquian". *Language* 1.130−156.

−. 1928. "A Note on Sound Change". *Language* 5.99−100.

−. 1936. "On Laves' Review of Dempwolff". *Language* 12.52−53.

Blust, Robert. 1970a. "i and u in the Austronesian Languages". *Working Papers in Linguistics* 2: 6. 113−145. Honolulu: Department of Linguistics, Univ. of Hawaii.

−. 1970b. "Proto-Austronesian Addenda". *Oceanic Linguistics* 9.104−162.

−. 1977. "A Rediscovered Austronesian Comparative Paradigm". *Oceanic Linguistics* 16.1−51.

−. 1978. "Eastern Malayo-Polynesian: A subgrouping argument". *Second International Conference on Austronesian Linguistics* ed. by Stephen A. Wurm & Lois Carrington, Fascicle 1, 181−234. Canberra: Department of Linguistics, Research School of Pacific Studies, Australian National Univ.

−. 1980. "Austronesian Etymologies". *Oceanic Linguistics* 19.1−181.

−. 1981. "The Reconstruction of Proto-Malayo-Javanic: An appreciation". *Bijdragen tot de Taal-, Land- en Volkenkunde* 137: 4.456−469.

−. 1983/84. "Austronesian Etymologies − II". *Oceanic Linguistics* 22/23.29−149.

−. 1986. "Austronesian Etymologies − III". *Oceanic Linguistics* 25.1−123.

−. 1988. *Austronesian Root Theory: An essay on the limits of morphology.* Amsterdam & Philadelphia: Benjamins.

−. 1989. "Austronesian Etymologies − IV". *Oceanic Linguistics* 28.111−180.

−. 1990. "Three Recurrent Changes in Oceanic Languages". *Pacific Island Languages: Essays in honour of G. B. Milner* ed. by J. H. C. S. Davidson, 7−28. London: School of Oriental and African Studies, Univ. of London.

−. 1991a. "Patterns of Sound Change in the Austronesian Languages". Baldi 1991.129−165.

−. 1991b. "Sound Change and Migration Distance". *Currents in Pacific Linguistics: Papers on Austronesian languages and ethnolinguistics in honour of George W. Grace* ed. by Robert Blust,

27–42. Canberra: Department of Linguistics, Research School of Pacific Studies, Australian National Univ.

—. 1993. "Central and Central-Eastern Malayo-Polynesian". *Oceanic Linguistics* 32.241–293.

—. 1994. "Austronesian Sibling Terms and Culture History". *Austronesian Terminologies: Continuity and change* ed. by Andrew K. Pawley & M. D. Ross, 31–72. Canberra: Department of Linguistics, Research School of Pacific Studies, Australian National Univ.

—. 1995. "The Position of the Formosan Aboriginal Languages: Method and theory in Austronesian comparative linguistics". *Proceedings of the International Symposium on Austronesian Studies Relating to Taiwan* ed. by Paul J-K Li et al., 585–650. Taipei: Institute of History and Philology, Academia Sinica.

—. 1996. "The Neogrammarian Hypothesis and Pandemic Irregularity." *The Comparative Method Reviewed* ed. by Mark Durie & M. D. Ross, 135–156. Oxford: Oxford Univ. Press.

—. 1999. "Subgrouping, Circularity and Extinction: Some issues in Austronesian comparative linguistics". *Selected Papers from the Eighth International Conference on Austronesian Linguistics* ed. by Elizabeth Zeitoun & Paul Jen-Kuei Li, 31–94. Taipei: Institute of Linguistics, Academia Sinica.

Brandes, Jan Lourens Andries. 1884. *Bijdrage tot de vergelijkende klankleer der Westersche afdeeling van de Maleisch-Polynesische taalfamilie*. Utrecht: P. W. van de Weijer.

Brandstetter, Renward. 1906. *Ein Prodromus zu einem vergleichenden Wörterbuch der malaio-polynesischen Sprachen für Sprachforscher und Ethnographen*. Luzern: anthor.

—. 1916. *An Introduction to Indonesian Linguistics*. Transl. by C. O. Blagden. London: The Royal Asiatic Society.

Buck, Carl Darling. 1949. *A Dictionary of Selected Synonyms in the Principal Indo-European Languages: A contribution to the history of ideas*. Chicago: Univ. of Chicago Press.

Burrow, Thomas & Murray B. Emeneau. 1984. *A Dravidian Etymological Dictionary*. 2nd ed. Oxford: Clarendon Press.

Dahl, Otto Chr. 1951. *Malgache et Maanjan: Une comparaison linguistique*. Oslo: Egede Instituttet.

—. 1991. *Migration from Kalimantan to Madagascar*. Oslo: The Institute for Comparative Research in Human Culture.

Dempwolff, Otto. 1934–38. *Vergleichende Lautlehre des austronesischen Wortschatzes*. 3 vols. (= *Zeitschrift für Eingeborenen-Sprachen*; Supplements 15, 17, 19.) I: *Induktiver Aufbau einer indonesischen Ursprache* (1934); II: *Deduktive Anwendung des Urindonesischen auf austronesische Einzelsprachen* (1937); III: *Austronesisches Wörterverzeichnis* (1938). Berlin: Reimer.

Dyen, Isidore. 1953. *The Proto-Malayo-Polynesian Laryngeals*. Baltimore: Linguistic Society of America.

—. 1965. "Formosan Evidence for Some New Proto-Austronesian Phonemes". *Lingua* 14.285–305.

Förster, John Reinhold. 1778. *Observations Made during a Voyage round the World*. London.

Geraghty, Paul A. 1983. *The History of the Fijian Languages*. Honolulu: Univ. of Hawaii Press.

Grace, George W. 1955. "Subgrouping of Malayo-Polynesian: A report of tentative findings". *American Anthropologist* 57.337–339.

Grimes, Barbara F. et al. 1995. "Listing of Austronesian Languages". *Comparative Austronesian Dictionary: An introduction to Austronesian studies* ed. by Darrell T. Tryon, Part 1, Fascicle 1.121–279. Berlin: Mouton de Gruyter.

Houtman, Frederick de. 1603. *Spraeck ende woordboeck: Inde Maleysche ende Madagaskarsche Talen met vele Arabische ende Turcsche woorden*. Amsterdam: Cloppenburch.

Humboldt, Wilhelm von. 1836–1839. *Über die Kawi-Sprache auf der Insel Java*. Ed. by Joh. Carl Eduard Buschmann. 3 vols. Berlin: Druckerei der Königlichen Akademie.

Kern, Hendrik. 1886. "De Fidji-taal vergeleken met hare verwanten in Indonesië en Polynesië". *Verhandelingen van de Koninklijke Nederlandsche Akademie van Wetenschappen; Afdeeling Letterkunde*, Nieuwe reeks, 16.1–242.

—. 1889. "Taalkundige gegevens ter bepaling van het stamland der Maleisch-Polynesische volken". *Verslagen en Mededeelingen der Koninklijke Akademie van Wetenschappen; Afdeeling Letterkunde*, 3de reeks, 6.270–287.

Lehmann, Winfred P. 1992. *Historical Linguistics: An introduction*. 3rd ed. London: Routledge.

Lynch, John & D. T. Tryon. 1985. "Central-Eastern Oceanic: A subgrouping hypothesis". *Austronesian Linguistics at the 15th Pacific Science Congress* ed. by Andrew Pawley & Lois Carrington, 31–52. Canberra: Department of Linguistics, Research School of Pacific Studies, Australian National Univ.

Maddieson, Ian. 1987. *Patterns of Sounds*. Cambridge: Cambridge Univ. Press.

— & Keng-fong Pang. 1993. "Tone in Utsat". *Tonality in Austronesian Languages* ed. by Jerold A. Edmondson & Kenneth J. Gregerson, 75–89. Honolulu: Univ. of Hawaii Press.

Nothofer, Bernd. 1975. *The Reconstruction of Proto-Malayo-Javanic*. The Hague: Nijhoff.

—. 1990. Review of Blust (1988). *Oceanic Linguistics* 29.132–152.

—. 1991. "More on Austronesian Radicals (or Roots)". *Oceanic Linguistics* 30.223–258.

Pawley, Andrew K. 1966. "Polynesian Languages: A subgrouping based on shared innovations in morphology". *Journal of the Polynesian Society* 75.37–62.

–. 1967. The Relationships of Polynesian Outlier Languages". *Journal of the Polynesian Society* 76.259–296.

–. 1972. "On the Internal Relationships of Eastern Oceanic Languages". *Studies in Oceanic Culture History* ed. by R. C. Green & M. Kelly, vol. III, 1–142. Honolulu: Bernice P. Bishop Museum.

–. 1973. "Some Problems in Proto-Oceanic Grammar". *Oceanic Linguistics* 12.103–188.

– & Roger C. Green. 1985. "The Proto-Oceanic Language Community". *Out of Asia: Peopling the Americas and the Pacific* ed. by Robert Kirk & Emöke Szathmary, 123–146. Canberra: The Journal of Pacific History.

Pokorny, Julius. 1959. *Indogermanisches etymologisches Wörterbuch*. 2 vols. Bern: Franke.

Rehg, Kenneth L. 1991. "Final Vowel Lenition in Micronesian Languages: An exploration of the dynamics of drift". *Currents in Pacific Linguistics: Papers on Austronesian languages and ethnolinguistics in honour of George W. Grace* ed. by Robert Blust, 383–401. Canberra: Department of Linguistics, Research School of Pacific Studies, Australian National Univ.

Reland, Adrianus. 1706–1708. *Dissertationum miscellanearum*. 3 vols. Trajecti ad Rhenum (= Utrecht]: G. Broedelet.

Ross, Malcolm D. 1988. *Proto Oceanic and the Austronesian Languages of Western Melanesia*. Canberra: Department of Linguistics, Research School of Pacific Studies, Australian National Univ.

–. 1992. "The Sound of Proto-Austronesian: An outsider's view of the Formosan evidence". *Oceanic Linguistics* 31.23–64.

Ruhlen, Merritt. 1987. *A Guide to the World's Languages*. Vol. I: *Classification*. Stanford, Calif.: Stanford Univ. Press.

Sapir, Edward. 1921. *Language: An introduction to the study of speech*. New York: Harcourt, Brace & Co.

Schmidt, Wilhelm. 1906. *Die Mon-Khmer Völker: Ein Bindeglied zwischen Völkern Zentralasiens und Austronesiens*. Braunschweig: Friedrich Vieweg & Sohn.

Sneddon, J. N. 1978. *Proto-Minahasan: Phonology, morphology and wordlist*. Canberra: Department of Linguistics, Research School of Pacific Studies, Australian National Univ.

–. 1984. *Proto-Sangiric and the Sangiric Languages*. Canberra: Department of Linguistics, Research School of Pacific Studies, Australian National Univ.

–. 1993. "The Drift towards Open Final Syllables in Sulawesi Languages". *Oceanic Linguistics* 32.1–44.

Starosta, Stanley, Andrew K. Pawley & Lawrence A. Reid. 1982. "The Evolution of Focus in Austronesian". *Papers from the Third International Conference on Austronesian Linguistics* ed. by Stephen A. Wurm & Lois Carrington, vol. II, 145–170. Canberra: Department of Linguistics, Research School of Pacific Studies, Australian National Univ.

Thurgood, Graham. 1993. "Phan Rang Cham and Utsat: Tonogenetic themes and variants". *Tonality in Austronesian Languages* ed. by Jerold A. Edmondson & Kenneth J. Gregerson, 91–106. Honolulu: Univ. of Hawaii Press.

–. 1999. *From Ancient Cham to Modern Dialects: Two thousand years of language contact and change*. (= *Oceanic Linguistics*, Special Publication, 28.) Honolulu: Univ. of Hawaii Press.

Tryon, Darrell T. 1976. *New Hebrides Languages: An internal classification*. Canberra: Department of Linguistics, Research School of Pacific Studies, Australian National Univ.

–, ed. 1995. *Comparative Austronesian Dictionary: An introduction to Austronesian studies*. 4 parts. Berlin: Mouton de Gruyter.

Tsuchida, Shigeru. 1976. *Reconstruction of Proto-Tsouic Phonology*. Tokyo: Institute for the Study of Languages and Dultures of Asia and Africa.

Tuuk, Herman N. van der. 1865. "Note on the Relation of the Kawi to the Javanese". *Journal of the Royal Asiatic Society* 1.442–446.

–. 1872. "'t Lampongsch en zijne tongvallen". *Tijdschrift voor Indische Taal-, Land-, en Volkenkunde* 18.118–156.

Walsh, D. S. & Bruce Biggs. 1966. *Proto-Polynesian Word List I*. Auckland: Linguistic Society of New Zealand.

Wolff, John U. 1973. "Verbal Inflection in Proto-Austronesian". *Parangal Kay Cecilio Lopez* ed. by Andrew B. Gonzalez, 71–91. Quezon City: Linguistic Society of the Philippines.

–. 1988. "The PAN Consonant System". *Studies in Austronesian Linguistics* ed. by Richard McGinn, 125–147. Athens, Ohio.

Zorc, R. David. 1982. "Where, o Where, Have the Laryngeals Gone? Austronesian laryngeals re-examined". *Papers from the Third International Conference on Austronesian Linguistics* ed. by Amran Halim, Lois Carrington & Stephen A. Wurm, vol. II, 111–144. Canberra: Department of Linguistics, Research School of Pacific Studies, Australian National Univ.

–. 1990. "The Austronesian Monosyllabic Root, Radical or Phonestheme". *Linguistic Change and Reconstruction Methodology* ed. by Philip Baldi, 175–194. Berlin: Mouton de Gruyter.

Robert A. Blust, Honolulu (U.S.A.)

169. The comparative method applied to Amerindian: The reconstruction of Proto-Algonkian

1. Introduction
2. Regularity of sound change
3. Sapir and Michelson
4. Bloomfield's 1925 reconstruction
5. Bloomfield's 'Sketch' of 1946
6. PA studies after Bloomfield
7. Comparative reconstruction by computer
8. Completing the picture
9. Bibliography

1. Introduction

This chapter will concentrate on the sequence of events that led to the application of the comparative method to the Algonkian family of languages, and to the various stages of the reconstruction of Proto-Algonkian. The Algonkian family, languages of which are found from the Atlantic to the Rockies, and from the Arctic to the Southern United States, was the most widespread and diverse of the four linguistic groupings (Inuktitut, Algonkian, Iroquois, and the Muskogean languages of the southern U. S.) encountered by the Europeans at the time of the earliest contacts in North America; it has some of the oldest documentation and some of the earliest comparative studies. The 400-year history of Algonkian studies is consequently the most complete model for the kind of work that has been done or is being done or can be done with other Amerindian groupings, from all parts of the American continent.

2. Regularity of sound change

Comparative reconstruction, as a scientific procedure, is necessarily based on the regularity of sound change: reconstructions are only acceptable if they are coherently based on documented sound changes, which give coherent correspondences in cognate words from different languages. Since the languages of the Algonkian and Iroquoian families were those of the Eastern seaboard, the Great Lakes, and the St. Lawrence River system, these were the first language families to be encountered by the Europeans from early contact onwards. Inuktitut, encountered on the most northerly coast of the Eastern seaboard, had but recently spread across the Arctic from the West, and had consequently but little dialectal variation.

The earliest explorers and missionaries recognized that Algonkian languages were related, even if no longer mutually comprehensible, and that the Iroquoian languages were similarly members of a closely related family. Roger Williams (1603–1683), in his description of the Algonkian language that he had learned in New England (1643) mentions, in fact, a regular sound shift: that the word for 'dog' was pronounced regionally in four different ways: anùm, ayím, arùm, alùm. As Mary Haas comments (1967: 817): "Eliot (1666) makes a similar observation, except for *y*, when he states: 'We *Massachusetts* pronounce the *n*. The *Nipmuck* Indians pronounce *l*. And the *Northern* Indians pronounce R'".

The American scholar John Pickering (1777–1846) in his notes to Sébastian Rasles' (1657–1724) *Dictionary to the Abenaki Language* (1833, ms. from 1690s) quotes the above information from both Williams and John Eliot (1604–1690), but does not understand the nature of these correspondences, since this is too soon after the publication of Jacob Grimm's *Deutsche Grammatik*, the 1822 edition of Volume I of which gave "an exact statement of how the sounds of the various dialects corresponded to one another" (Pedersen 1962: 38), and provided a first introduction to the technology of comparative linguistics.

Peter Stephen Duponceau's (1760–1844) *Mémoire sur le système grammatical des langues de quelques nations indiennes de l'Amérique du Nord* (1838) although it contained an appendix of the comparative vocabulary of Algonkian and Iroquoian languages to show that the two families were completely unrelated, and another comprising a comparative survey of the vocabulary of 30 Algonkian languages, had likewise no insight into the nature of the sound correspondences.

With the push of new immigrants westward in the late 19th century, more and more languages and language families were encountered and documented, so that by the end of the century an important first attempt at classification of North American Indian languages had been made by John Wesley Powell (1834–1902) for the newly founded Bureau of American Ethnology in Washington, D. C., Powell (1891) recognized 58 distinct families, which were later reduced to 55, and eventually reduced to six major stocks in a bold and sweeping classification prepared for the *Encyclopedia Britannica* in 1929 by Edward Sapir.

3. Sapir and Michelson

Sapir (1884–1939) had already created a stir in 1913 by suggesting that Wiyot and Yurok (known collectively as Ritwan), two languages of California, geographically distant from the normal Algonkian domain of prairies and East, were related to the Algonkian family. This was roundly rejected by Truman Michelson (1879–1938) who, a year earlier, had himself made a classification of Algonkian languages, based on considerable personal field work (1912). Michelson had noted the sound shift mentioned by Williams and Eliot (without reference to them), but although he had done his apprenticeship in comparative linguistics in Germany, he made no more sense of the data than did Duponceau or Pickering. Sapir in his 1913 article was the first to perceive the nature of this sound shift, which was relevant to his demonstration of the relatedness of Wiyot and Yurok to Algonkian. He noted Michelson's failure to see the systemic regularities in the data (1913: 640–641):

"Michelson seems to assume that Algonki[a]n originally possessed only *n*, and that, under undefined circumstances, it developed into *l* in several dialects. Inasmuch as *l* occurs in all positions [...] as distinct from *n*; and as Cheyenne seems to have *t* or its palatalized reflex *ts*, not *n*, where Eastern dialects have *l*, [...]. I prefer to believe that original Algonki[a]n had both *l* and *n* and that these sounds were leveled to *n* in several Central dialects".

Here we have the first proper understanding of the comparative method and its application to the data of the Algonkian family. Michelson, a proud and prickly individual (see, for example his 1923 "Rejoinder" to Bloomfield's 1922 review of his *The Owl Sacred Pack of the Fox Indians* (1921), and his disparaging condemnation of Speck's phonetic transcription of Montagnais (1937), fault-finding that he later was forced to retract (1938) on the evidence of his own field work – but without apologizing), obviously took umbrage, and poured scorn on Sapir's proposal, claiming that it was based on no more than chance resemblances (Michelson 1914).

Although some scholars went on record in support of Sapir's proposal (Dixon & Kroeber 1919; Radin 1919), the result of Michelson's intervention was that for 50 years the phylum relationship (as it turns out to be) between Algonkian, on the one hand, and Ritwan (the supposed family of which the only known exponents are Wiyot and Yurok) on the other, was considered controversial, with scholars unwilling to make a categorical judgment for or against the proposal.

It was left to Mary Haas (1910–1996), who had been one of Sapir's own doctoral students, to demonstrate the validity of Sapir's proposal. She used the trail-blazing comparative work of Bloomfield (1925, 1946), and the field work of Robins (1958) and Teeter (1964), to show (Haas 1960, 1966) that Sapir had been right in his proposal that Wiyot and Yurok are related to Algonkian, but that it is a phylum, not a family relationship. Haas's amalgam of the work of Sapir and Bloomfield, the two great names in American linguistics in the early part of this century, underlines the fact that these two very different individuals, the mentalist and generalist Sapir, and the anti-mentalist and particularist Bloomfield, were both deeply involved in Algonkian studies. Sapir surveyed an enormous range of North American languages, and made his own brilliant synthesis of their relationships; Bloomfield was wont to comment that the most one could do in a lifetime was a competent description of two or three languages. They even differed in their spellings: Sapir used the modified spelling *Algonkian*, given that the older form *Algonquian* was from a French spelling, that the traditional pronunciation had always been *-kian*, and that *Esquimau* had already been standardized to *Eskimo*. Bloomfield, however, maintained the traditional spellings *Algonquin* (a dialect of Ojibway), *Algonquian* (the whole family).

4. Bloomfield's 1925 reconstruction

In the very first edition of *Language* (1925), the journal of the newly founded Linguistic Society of America, Bloomfield made a major breakthrough in Amerindian linguistics by applying the comparative method in detail to the study of Algonkian languages, showing the correspondences of four central groups of languages, which he hoped would be "a basis for further discussion" (1925: 130). He added, in a solitary but now famous footnote on the same page:

"I hope, also to help dispose of the notion that the usual processes of linguistic change are suspended on the American continent (Meillet and Cohen, *Les langues du monde*, Paris 1924, p. 9). If there exists anywhere a language in which these processes do not occur (sound-change independent of meaning, analogic change, etc.), then they will not explain the history of Indo-European or of any other language. A principle such as the regularity of phonetic change is not a part of the specific tradition handed on to each new speaker of a given language, but is either a universal trait of human speech or nothing at all, an error."

This is clearly a manifesto, and it was supported by Bloomfield's devastatingly punctilious demonstration of the regularity of sound change in Algonkian languages: in the polysyllabic words of his examples every single segmental phoneme was a regular correspondence to the phonemes in the cognate words, and a regular reflex of the phonemes in the reconstructions. It was a resounding answer to Meillet's comment (Meillet & Cohen 1924: 9):

"[...] one may well ask whether the languages of America (which are for the most part poorly known and insufficiently studied from a comparative point of view) will ever lend themselves to exact, exhausting comparative treatment; the samples offered so far hold scant promise [...]" (My transl.: JH)

The most interesting feature of the P(roto)-A(lgonkian) sound system is the variety of consonant clusters. There are three main sets: pre-aspirated, pre-glottalized, and pre-nasalized, and clusters of other minor groupings.

The following sets of correspondences show the reflexes for pre-glottalized and pre-aspirated */θ/ and */t/.

PA	Cree	Fox	Menomini	Ojibway
*ʔθ	st	s	ʔn	ss
*ʔt	st	ht	ʔt	tt
*hθ	ht	s	hn	ss
*ht	ht	ht	ht	tt

The coherence of these sets are illustrated by the following.

(1)   *pema:ʔθenwi   *neʔθwi
              it is blown   three
    C   pima:stan   nisto
    F   pema:senwi   neswi
    M   pemɛ:ʔnen   nɛʔniw
    O   pima:ssin   nisswi

Other regular changes in (1): C and O merge */e/ and */i/; C and M lose the final vowel; O also loses the preceding /w/, as do C and M after consonants (see (2)). The /-an/ of C is a morphological variant. M has varieties of tamber and length that require special explanation (see below).

(2)   *a:ʔtawe:wa   *meʔtekwi   *api:ʔtamwa
        extinguished   stick   sit near
   C   a:stawi:w   mistik   api:stam
   F   mehtekwi   api:htamwa
   M   a:ʔtawɛw   mɛʔtek   api:ʔtam
   O   a:ttawe: mittik   otapi:tta:n

*a:ʔtawe:wa is an intransitive verb; *api:ʔtamwa is transitive, O using a different conjugation.

(3)   *pemohθe:wa   *tahθwi   *ešihθenwi
        he walks   so many   it lies so
   C   pimohte:w   tahto   isihtin
   F   pemose:wa   taswi   išisenwi
   M   pemo:hnɛw   tahni:-   ese:hnen
   O   pimosse: tasso   išissin

*/wi/ is allophonically reduced to /o/ in C and O. In C and M *š and *s merged.

(4)   *a:pehtawi   *ki:šihta:wa   *te:pehtawe:wa
        half   he completes it   he hears him
   C   a:pihtaw   ki:sihta:w   te:pihtawe:w
   F   a:pehtawi   ki:šihto:wa   te:pehtawe:wa
   M   a:pɛhtaw   ke:sehtaw   tɛ:pɛhtawɛ:w
   O   a:pitta   oki:šitto:n   ote:pittawa:n

Bloomfield describes *ki:šihta:wa as a pseudo-transitive verb (anti-passive), with morphological variants *hto:/hta: in its conjugation, an alternation which the languages levelled differently.

The greatest challenge to Bloomfield's reconstruction of the PA sound system was the variation of length and timbre in Menomini, which proved to be somewhat of a Gordian knot to unravel. At first Bloomfield (1925: 131) reconstructed five PA timbres long and short, because of Menomini, whereas the other languages show a maximum of four. He also comments on the "complex but regular alternation of long and short vowels" in M. Later, in a volume dedicated to the memory of Trubetzkoy (1939), he gives a morphophonemic description of M vowel length in a set of statements that, although purely descriptive, nevertheless "approximate the historical development from Proto-Algonquian to present day Menomini" (1939: 105). In 1946 (see next section) he reduces the PA vowel timbres to four, short and long, from which six M timbres are derived. The final details of the phonological history of M are ultimately clarified by Hockett (1981).

5. Bloomfield's 'Sketch' of 1946

During the next twenty years Bloomfield's 1925 sketch of the sound system of PA was fleshed out by the work of other scholars (e. g., Michelson 1935, 1939; Siebert 1941), so that when he came to make a fuller statement on PA phonology and morphology he was able to comment (Bloomfield 1946: 85):

"Our reconstructions are based, to begin with, on the four best-known languages: Fox, Cree, Menomini, and Ojibwa. Michelson's brilliant [1935] study of the divergent western languages (Blackfoot, Cheyenne, and the Arapaho group) showed that these reconstructions will, in the main, fit all the languages and can accordingly be viewed as Proto-Algonquian".

This 1946 work known to Algonkianists as 'Bloomfield's Sketch', is a remarkable document, full of detailed information, and a typical example of the compressed style of Bloomfield's late descriptive work, as in his posthumous *The Menomini Language* (1962). It is a chapter of only 45 pages. It contains 404 numbered reconstructions, and further economy is achieved by cross reference to these numbers instead of repeatedly adding examples.

There are some two dozen Algonkian languages, yet Bloomfield was able to do successful reconstructions with only four. The reason for this is that the four central languages that he chose (on three of which he did field work, Fox being the exception) were all conservative, and consequently retained distinctive elements from the protolanguage. Fox, for example, retained final vowels, and reflexes of all four short vowels. Cree was essential for determining *θ and *l, both levelled to /n/ in the other three languages, and also had /sk/ as a reflex for determining *θk and *xk clusters — which, as Siebert (1941) had shown, then required evidence from Eastern Algonkian to distinguish *θk from *xk. Menomini retained the pre-glottalized clusters, and Ojibway the pre-nasalized clusters. This facility for reconstructing from selected conservative languages was later exploited by Hewson (1993) to carry out computerized reconstruction (see Section 7 below).

6. PA studies after Bloomfield

Much of Bloomfield's Algonkian work was left unpublished, in manuscript form, on his early death in 1949; these manuscripts were inherited by Charles Hockett, to whom we owe the publication of the Menomini grammar (1962) and dictionary (1975), and the monograph on Eastern Ojibway (1958). On the basis of Bloomfield's unpublished lexicons of Fox (drawn from the published reports of William Jones (1874–1909) and Michelson and eventually published (1994) in a critical edition by Goddard), Cree, Menomini, and Ojibway, Hockett began the most important task left undone by Bloomfield: the creation of a Proto-Algonkian dictionary.

In 1957 Hockett published 404 reconstructed items in /k-/, which, he indicated, might "be regarded as the first instalment of a Central Algonquian comparative dictionary". Hockett reverts to Bloomfield's 1925 term 'Proto-Central-Algonquian' because he did not use the evidence of an Eastern language to resolve the handful *θk/*xk clusters in the data; this could have been done, since there are several missionary dictionaries dating back to Rasles (1833) which would have provided the necessary data.

In the 1950s Haas was active in probing the relationship of the Algonkian family to other to other Amerindian groupings. Having finally put an end to the controversy over the relationship to Ritwan (see Section 3 above), she proceeded to supply some comparative evidence of a relationship to the Gulf languages (1958) and to Tonkawa (1959), and a resume (1960) in which she states a fourfold purpose:

"(1) to validate the Algonkian-Ritwan connection, (2) to show that the possibility of an Algonkian-Mosan affiliation merits further investigation, (3) to show that the Gulf languages and Tonkawa are also related to Algonkian, and (4) to suggest that all these languages are probably related to one another." (Haas 1960: 989)

In 1964 an important meeting was held at the National Museum of Canada in Ottawa to bring together scholars working on Algonkian languages. Among the published proceedings (1967) were two significant comparativist papers. Frank T. Siebert (1912–1998) presented reconstructions of the names of flora and fauna and demonstrated their geographical range in North America, and concluded that the Proto-Algonkian homeland was in the region of the Great Lakes (1967: 13–47). Goddard presented a reconstruction of the categories of the PA verb, based on evidence from all the major Algonkian languages (using missionary grammars when no other evidence was available). He showed for the first time that Bloomfield's reconstruction of the transitive verb morphology was based on Fox, Cree, and Menomini, whereas Ojibway (where the morphological differences had been treated by Bloomfield [1946: 98—99] as a reshaping) and other languages showed clearly that F, C, and M had merged two earlier paradigms (1967: 66—106).

From that meeting came a plan to hold an annual Algonkian conference, the first of which was in 1968 at Wakefield, in the Laurentians to the north of Ottawa. These have been held annually since, with publication of the *Papers* from the mid-1970s onwards. It was at this time that I was having difficulty investigating the possible relationship of Beothuk (language of the extinct Indians of Newfoundland) to Algonkian because what few PA reconstructions existed were scattered throughout the literature. It was also at this time that George Aubin and Hong Bae Lee collected these scattered items and produced (Brown University mimeo, 1968) *An Etymological Word-list of Reconstructed Proto-Algonquian*, which Aubin later expanded, completely revised, and published (1975), providing an essential reference work for comparative Algonkian studies.

7. Comparative reconstruction by computer

Given that a protolanguage dictionary, done by traditional methods of reconstruction, can take the whole lifetime of a scholar to prepare, and given the extraordinary regularity of sound correspondences in Bloomfield's four central languages, I began to envision the possibility, in the early 1970s, of streamlining the process by doing comparative reconstruction on the computer. Through the generosity of Charles Hockett, I was able to procure copies of Bloomfield's manuscript lexicons of Cree, Fox, and Menomini (all still unpublished at that point) to add to the word list in his *Eastern Ojibwa* (1958), which was then supplemented by the Ojibway word list of Piggott & Kaye (1973). Altogether some 30,000 lexical items from these four languages were put into machine readable form. With the aid of a Canada Council Research Grant we were successful in setting up a computer system to carry out comparative reconstruction. The description of how this is achieved, and the operation of the various programmes in the system has been reported on in a variety of articles (Hewson 1974, 1977, 1989).

The computer strategy that was developed in this work is, in fact, so simple, that it can be stated in a simple sentence (Hewson 1993: iv): "From the data of the daughter languages generate all possible protoforms, then sort alphabetically, and examine all sets of identical protoforms collocated by the sort." Each line of the sort begins with the potential protoform generated automatically from the known reflexes, followed by the native word identified by language. Where words from different languages produce identical protoforms, these items are thrown together by the sort, a step which eliminates the time-consuming and sometimes frustrating dictionary search for cognates. By this technique enormous amounts of low level reconstruction can be done.

This new dictionary (Hewson 1993) also incorporated cross references to the numbered glosses in Aubin's (1975) PA dictionary (see 6. above) and to the numbered glosses in Siebert (1975), 263 significant reconstructions which appeared too late to be included in Aubin's work. In this way the computerized reconstructions are correlated with all previous known reconstructions.

The end product is a protolanguage dictionary that is very different from the typical dictionaries produced in the past, which would normally be processed section by section, and produced in fascicles, with vast amounts of particular and atomistic detail. The computer generated dictionary produces only the low level reconstruction of what is perfectly regular; the detailed research on particular items must be added later. But it has the enormous advantage of producing several thousand words which are immediately available for comparative work inside and outside the language family, materials that would not be otherwise available.

This early work was done on a mainframe, when only an ASCII alphabet in capital letters was available. Since then the technology has been improved enormously, to the point where Martine Mazaudon and John Lowe (1991) have now developed a Reconstruction Engine sophisticated enough to be adapted to the reconstruction of any language family: dealing with a family of tone languages, for example, they devised a means to represent tone, and the reflexes of the tones.

8. Completing the picture

The last fifty years has seen the creation of modern dictionaries and grammars and other materials of almost all the extant Algonkian languages. This has been accompanied by a great deal of comparative and historical work on individual languages. There are now published or unpublished statements on the phonological reflexes of all the extant languages. There are also sketches of the historical phonology of the most deviant languages, notably Goddard's work on Arapaho (1974), and Proulx's work on Blackfoot (1989). Proulx has also pursued the comparative reconstruction to the phylum level, proposing proto-forms for Proto-Algic (1984, 1985), which covers both the Algonkian and Ritwan families. Interesting contributions to the reconstruction of Proto-Algic have also been made by Berman, who shows, for example, that much that was puzzling can be explained by the proposal that ablaut was "a productive process" in Proto-Algic (1984: 341).

The computer work has continued with research on the word formatives, covered briefly by Bloomfield in the *Sketch* (1946: 103 ff.). From the residue of some 20,000 words of the original data, some 6,000 items were given etymologies on the basis of their transparent word formatives, with hyphens placed between the formatives in the reconstructed forms. The result will be a dictionary of reconstructed 'singletons', where each formative has many cognates elsewhere (an unusual form of internal reconstruction). A further volume will be a concordance made on all items between hyphens, a process which will display the collocations and the range of usage of each word formative, by collating the words in which each formative element is found.

A further computer project, undertaken for an M. A. thesis by Towhid bin Muzzafar (1997), entails adding the data of further languages to the computerized protolanguage dictionary. The language chosen was Shawnee, whose phonological history is slightly complex, but without extensive sound change, and the experiment was carried out with a segment of the published Shawnee vocabulary. Using phono software devised originally by Steven Lee Hartman to derive Spanish forms from Latin, and adapted with Hartman's collaboration, potential Shawnee forms were derived from the protolanguage dictionary and the dictionary of 'singletons', and compared by computer sort with the extant Shawnee data. As well as providing new materials for the protolanguage dictionary (where the sets matched), this procedure also showed where there are problems with the reconstructions, and irregularities in the phonological history.

Meanwhile David Pentland has been working for many years at the preparation of a PA dictionary that will include not only the early reconstructions recorded by Aubin, the results of the computerized reconstructions, and the data of other Algonkian languages, but also a philological commentary on the aberrations and variations in the data. Begun on a mainframe computer in the early 1980s, it will represent the culmination of almost a century of intense work by many individuals.

9. Bibliography

Aubin, George F. 1975. *A Proto-Alonquian Dictionary.* (= *Canadian Ethnology Service Paper*, 29.) Ottawa: National Museums of Canada.

Berman, Howard. 1984. "Proto-Algonquian-Ritwan Verbal Roots". *International Journal of American Linguistics* 50.335–42.

Bloomfield, Leonard. 1922. Review of Michelson (1921). *American Journal of Philology* 43.276–281.

—. 1925. "On the Sound System of Central Algonquian". *Language* 1.130–156.

—. 1939. "Memomini Morphophonemics". *Études phonologiques dédiées à la mémoire de N. S. Trubetzkoy* (= *Travaux du Cercle Linguistique de Prague*, 8), 105–115. (Repr. in Bloomfield 1970.351–362.)

—. 1946. "Algonquian". *Linguistic Structures of Native America* ed. by Harry Hoijer et al., 85–129. New York: Viking Fund Publications in Anthropology 6.

—. 1958. *Eastern Ojibwa: Grammatical sketch, texts, and word list.* Ed. by C. F. Hockett. Ann Arbor: Univ. of Michigan Press.

—. 1962. *The Menomini Language.* New Haven: Yale Univ. Press.

—. 1970. *A Leonard Bloomfield Anthology.* Ed. by C. F. Hockett. Bloomington: Indiana Univ. Press.

—. 1975. *Menomini Dictionary.* Milwaukee: Public Museum Press.

Dixon, Roland Burrage & Alfred Louis Kroeber. 1919. "Linguistic families of California". *University of California Publications in American Archaeology and Ethnology* 16.47–118. [On Ritwan, 112–113.]

Duponceau, Pierre-Étienne. 1838. *Mémoire sur le système grammatical des langues de quelques nations indiennes de l'Amérique du Nord.* Paris: Pihan de la Forest.

Eliot, John. 1666. *The Indian Grammar Begun.* Cambridge, Mass.: Marmaduke Johnson. (Repr., Boston: Massachusetts Historical Society, 1822.)

Goddard, Ives. 1967. "The Algonquian Independent Indicative". *National Museum of Canada Bulletin* 214.66–106.

—. 1974. "An Outline of the Historical Phonology of Arapaho and Atsina". *International Journal of American Linguistics* 40.102–116.

—. 1994. *Leonard Bloomfield's Fox Lexicon.* Critical Edition. (= *Algonquian and Iroquoian Linguistics Memoir*, 12.) Winnipeg: Univ. of Manitoba.

Grimm, Jacob. 1967 [1822]. *Deutsche Grammatik.* Vol. I., 2nd ed. Hildesheim: Olms.

Haas, Mary R. 1958. "A New Linguistic Relationship in North America: Algonkian and the Gulf languages". *Southwest Journal of Anthropology* 14.231–246.

—. 1959. "Tonkawa and Algonkian". *Anthropological Linguistics* 1: 1.1–6.

—. 1960. "Some Genetic Affiliations of Algonkian". *Culture in History: Essays in honor of Paul Radin* ed. by Stanley Diamond, 977–992. New York: Columbia Univ. Press.

—. 1966. "Wiyot-Yurok-Algonkian and Problems of Comparative Algonkian". *International Journal of American Linguistics* 32.101–107.

—. 1967. "Roger Williams's Sound Shift: A study in Algonkian". *To Honor Roman Jakobson*, vol. I, 816–832. The Hague: Mouton.

Hewson, John. 1974. "Comparative Reconstruction on the Computer". *Historical Linguistics: Proceedings of the first international congress on historical linguistics* ed. by John M. Anderson & Charles Jones, 191–197. Amsterdam: North-Holland.

—. 1977. "Reconstructing Prehistoric Languages on the Computer: The triumph of the electronic neogrammarian". *Proceedings of the 4th International Conference on Computational Linguistics* ed. by Antonio Zampolli, 263–273. Firenze: Olschki.

—. 1989. "Computer-Aided Research in Comparative and Historical Linguistics". *Computational Linguistics/Computerlinguiustik* ed. by Istvan S. Bátori, Winfried Lenders & Wolfgang Putschke, 576–580. Berlin & New York: de Gruyter.

—. 1993. *A Computer-Generated Dictionary of Proto-Algonquian.* (= *Canadian Ethnology Service; Mercury Series Paper*, 125.) Ottawa: Canadian Museum of Civilization.

Hockett, Charles F. 1957. "Central Algonquian Vocabulary: Stems in /k-/". *International Journal of American Linguistics* 23.247–268.

—. 1981. "The Phonological History of Memonini". *Anthropological Linguistics* 23.51–87.

Mazaudon, Martine & John B. Lowe. 1991. "Du bon usage de l'informatique en linguistique historique". *Bulletin de la Société Linguistique de Paris* 86.49–87.

Meillet, Antoine & Marcel Cohen. 1924. *Les langues du monde.* Paris: Champion. (2nd ed., 1952).

Michelson, Truman. 1912. "Preliminary Report on the Linguistic Classification of Algonquian Tribes". *BAE Annual Report* 28: 221–280. Washington, D. C.

—. 1914. "Two Alleged Algonquian Languages of California". *American Anthropologist* 16.361–367.

—. 1921. *The Owl Sacred Pack of the Fox Indians.* (= *Bureau of American Ethnology Bulletin*, 72.) Washington, D. C.

—. 1923. "Rejoinder [to Bloomfield 1922]". *American Journal of Philology* 44.285–286. (Repr. in Bloomfield 1970.101.)

—. 1935. "Phonetic Shifts in Algonquian Languages". *International Journal of American Linguistics* 8.131–171.

—. 1937. "Some Linguistic Features of Speck's Naskapi". *American Anthropologist* 39.370–372.

—. 1938. "Studies among the Montagnais-Naskapi Indians of the Northern Shore of the St. Lawrence River". *Explorations and Fieldwork of the Smithsonian Institution in 1937*, 119–122. Washington, D. C.

—. 1939. "Contributions to Algonquian Linguistics". *International Journal of American Linguistics* 10.75–85.

Muzzafar, Towhid bin. 1997. "Computer Simulation of Shawnee Historical Phonology". Unpublished M. A. thesis, Memorial University of Newfoundland.

Pedersen, Holger. 1962 [1931]. *The Discovery of Language: Linguistic science in the nineteenth century.* Transl. by John Webster Spargo. Bloomington: Indiana Univ. Press.

Pickering, John. 1833. "Introductory Memoir". *A Dictionary of the Abenaki Language* by Sebastian Rasles. Cambridge, Mass.: Harvard Univ. Printer.

Piggott, Glyne & Jonathan Kaye. 1973. *Odawa Language Project, Second Report.* Mimeo, Univ. of Toronto.

Powell, John Wesley. 1891. "Indian Linguistic Families North of Mexico". *BAE Annual Report* 7.1–142. Washington, D. C.

Proulx, Paul. 1989. "A Sketch of Blackfoot Historical Phonology". *International Journal of American Linguistics* 55.43–82.

—. 1984. "Proto-Algic I: Phonological sketch". *International Journal of American Linguistics* 50.165–207.

—. 1985. "Proto-Algic II: Verbs". *International Journal of American Linguistics* 51.59–93.

Radin, Paul. 1919. "The Genetic Relationship of the North American Languages". *University of California Publications in Archaeology and Ethnology* 14.489–502.

Rasles, Sébastien, s.j. 1833 [ms. in French from 1691 onwards]. *A Dictionary of the Abenaki Language.* Cambridge, Mass.: Harvard Univ. Printer.

Robins, Robert H. 1958. *The Yurok Language.* Berkeley: Univ. of California Press.

Sapir, Edward. 1913. "Wiyot and Yurok, Algonkin Languages of California". *American Anthropologist* 15.617–646.

—. 1929. "Central and North American Languages". *Encyclopedia Britannica*, 14th ed., Vol. 5.138–141. (Repr. in Sapir 1949: 169–178.)

—. 1949. *Selected Writings of Edward Sapir.* Ed. by David G. Mandelbaum. Berkeley: Univ. of California Press.

Siebert, Frank T. 1941. "Certain Proto-Algonquian Consonant Clusters". *Language* 17.298–303.

—. 1967. "The Original Home of the Proto-Algonquian People". *National Museum of Canada Bulletin* 214.13–47.

—. 1975. "Resurrecting Virginia Algonquian from the Dead". *Studies in Southeastern Languages* ed. by James M. Crawford, 285–453. Athens: Univ. of Georgia Press.

Speck, Frank Gouldsmith. 1935. *Naskapi: Savage hunters of the Labrador peninsula.* Norman: Univ. of Oklahoma Press.

Teeter, Karl V. 1964. *The Wiyot Language.* Berkeley: Univ. of California Press.

Williams, Roger. 1643. *A Key into the Language of America.* London: Gregory Dexter. (Repr. Menston, Yorks.: Scolar Press, 1971.)

John Hewson, St. John's (Canada)

170. The comparative method as applied to other Non-Indo-European language families

1. Introduction
2. Finno-Ugric
3. Algonquian
4. Uto-Aztecan
5. Dravidian
6. Mayan
7. The applicability of the CM to so-called 'exotic' languages
8. Bibliography

1. Introduction

While the comparative method (henceforth: CM) was developed in work on the Finno-Ugric (FU) and Indo-European (IE) families, it has been applied to many other language families with success, and some of these, in turn, have contributed to further understanding of comparative linguistics and historical linguistic change in general. Here we survey briefly the history of the application of the CM to a few of these families where the work of comparative reconstruction has been particularly successful and in some cases has contributed to the history of linguistics: Finno-Ugric, Algonquian, Uto-Aztecan, Dravidian, and Mayan. (For others, → Art. 167–169.)

There are literally hundreds of language families in the world, though historical linguistic research is advanced in only a few (see table 170.1). For example, Sino-Tibetan (ca. 300 languages) is an extremely important family, with the largest number of speakers, but comparative research in it is in a relatively undeveloped state: "It is sobering to realize that Sino-Tibetan linguistics is only about 50 years old, and has been a flourishing field of inquiry for only the past 25 years" (Matisoff 1991: 469). The classification has been and continues to be a controversial, with many Chinese scholars including in the family also Hmong-Mien (Miao-Yao) and Tai-Kadai, where most Western scholars limit the family to the two branches of Chinese and Tibeto-Burman. (For a thorough review of the field and its current standing, see Matisoff 1991.)

Table 170.1: Distribution of language families in the world

Americas:	150+ language families, 2,000+ languages
New Guinea (Papuan):	60+ language families, 750–800 languages
Australia:	26 language families, ca. 250 languages
Africa:	20+ families, 2500+ languages
Europe + Asia:	37 families (18 = isolates)
Europe:	3 surviving families (IE, Uralic, Basque; formerly Etruscan)

A few of the better-known of these families, with an indication of the state of comparative linguistic research in them, are: Austronesian (ca. 800 languages, relatively advanced), Bantu (ca. 400 languages, moderate), Chadic (ca. 140 languages, work needed), Otomanguean (ca. 40 languages, good), North Caucasian (30–35 languages, research needed), Turkic (25–35 languages, moderate), Athabaskan (ca. 30 languages, relatively good), Munda (ca. 25 languages, much needed), Semitic (20–25 languages, moderately good), Salishan (23 languages, good), Siouan (ca. 20 languages, good); Chibchan (ca. 20 languages, moderately good), Hmong-Mien (Miao-Yao; ca. 15 languages, much needed), and Kartvelian (South Caucasian, 4 languages, quite good).

The CM's earliest history is open to interpretation; this explains why the following at one time or another have all been considered 'fathers' – or at least precursors – of comparative linguistics: Giraldus Cambrensis 1194, Dante 1305, Gelenius 1537, Ges[s]ner 1555, Sassetti 1585, J. J. Scaliger 1610 [1599], Boxhorn ca. 1648, Comenius 1657, Stiernhielm 1671, Jäger 1686, Leibniz 1697, 1710, 1710; Ludolf 1702, Relander [Relandus] 1706, Lluyd 1707, Ten Kate 1723, von Strahlenberg 1730, Turgot 1753, Ihre 1769, Sajnovics 1770, Jones 1786, Kraus 1787, Gyarmathi 1799, Bopp 1816, 1833; Rask 1818, Grimm 1819, 1822, among others. Many see Bopp's comparative grammar as the earliest truly comparative work, and yet, on the one hand, Bopp himself acknowledge his predecessors, in particular Gyarmathi and members of the Dutch etymological school, and, on the other, relied little on the regular sound correspondences so characteristic of current understanding of the CM. All this raises the question of when the history of the CM in various families begins. We will rely on Hoenigswald's (1990: 119–120) summary (an interpretation perhaps not shared by all scholars of linguistic historiography) of the points upon which 17th- and 18th-century scholars agreed in lieu of a definitive answer to that question:

"First, [...] there was 'the concept of a no longer spoken parent language which in turn produced the major linguistic groups of Asia and Europe'. Then there was [...] 'a concept of the development of languages into dialects and of dialects into new independent languages'. Third came 'certain minimum standards for determining what words are borrowed and what words are ancestral in a language', and, fourth, 'an insistence that not a few random items, but a large number of words from the basic vocabulary should form the basis of comparison' [...] fifth, the doctrine that 'grammar' is even more important than words; sixth, the idea that for an etymology to be valid the differences in sound – or in 'letters' – must recur, under a principle sometimes referred to as 'analogia'."

2. Finno-Ugric

While the CM is often closely associated with IE, the Finno-Ugric (FU) language family was established before IE and the CM developed here inspired later work in IE. For example, Rask asserted the success of his IE comparisons on the basis of their favorable comparison with Sajnovics' FU standard. We mention only highlights of the history of FU here (see Stipa 1990, for details).

Johann Eberhard Fischer's (1697–1771) *Vocabularium Sibiricum* (ca. 1756 [published in Schlözer 1768, 1802]) is often called the oldest FU etymological dictionary. Fischer, a professional philologist, was interested in sound correspondences (and not just the similarity among letters which sometimes impressed lay persons). The Hungarian Jesuit mathematician Johannis [János] Sajnovics (1735–1780) demonstrated in 1770 the relationship between Lapp, Finnish, and Hungarian. In his method grammatical comparison was given a central role, and morphosyntactic correspondences were considered essential for proving relationship among languages, though sound correspondences also played a role in Sajnovics' work. Sajnovics' work was so well-known and influential that Rask (1993 [1818]: 283) argued that his own evidence of Germanic kinship with Greek and Latin should be considered compelling because it compared favorably with Sajnovics' "proof that the Hungarian and Lappish languages are the same [which] no one has denied since his day."

Sámuel Gyarmathi's (1757–1830) very influential *Affinitas linguae Hungaricae cum linguis Fennicae originis grammatice demonstrata* (1799) both reflected and led the intellectual concerns of the day. While others had advocated and used grammatical comparisons, Gyarmathi's procedures were the most thorough and consistent to that date. Significantly, he warned against arguing for a genetic relationship based on shared syntactic similarities which are actually aspects of universal grammar and, as such, cannot be used to establish a genetic relationship (Gyarmathi 1983 [1799]: 33.) Gyarmathi's work was cited as a model by comparativists for decades afterwards.

In short, the Uralic family (FU plus Samoyed, some 25 languages) was thoroughly established and comparative linguistic methods reasonably refined before the well-known early IE comparative research of Schlegel, Rask, Grimm, and Bopp.

Rather intense FU (and broader: Uralic) historical linguistic research has continued up to the present and the field is remarkably advanced, with excellent reconstructions of the phonology (Sammallahti 1988), morphosyntax (Janhunen 1982), etymological dictionaries (Sammallahti 1988, Rédei 1986–1988, with remarkable breadth and depth in the historical study of many of the individual languages and linguistic prehistory of the family — one of the crowning success stories for the CM.

3. Algonquian

Algonquian (a family of about 30 languages) has a long record of comparative work, which has contributed to historical linguistics. Algonquian historical linguistics is advanced. Before Sir William Jones' famous third discourse was published (delivered 1786, published 1788), Jonathan Edwards, Jr. (1745–1801) reported the family relationship among the Algonquian languages. Edwards (1788 [1787]) presented vocabulary lists and grammatical features in support — Jones presented no actual linguistic evidence for his thesis. Leonard Bloomfield's (1887–1949) famous Algonquian proof of 1925 demonstrated the applicability of the CM to and the regularity of sound change in so-called exotic languages once and for all. It was based on phonological correspondence sets and reconstructions for Proto-Central Algonquian (PCA). He reconstructed *çk for one particular set distinct from the others based on scant evidence but relying on the assumption that sound change is regular. He concluded the difference in this correspondence set (though only sounds already found in the other correspondence sets were involved, though in different combinations) could be explained only as the reflex of a PCA sound different from those reflected by the other correspondence sets. This decision was confirmed when Swampy Cree was discovered to contain the correspondence *htk* for the *çk set, distinct in Swampy Cree from the reflexes of the other reconstructed sounds. Based on this Bloomfield (1928: 100) concluded:

"As an assumption, however, the postulate of sound-change without exception yields, as a matter of mere routine, predictions which otherwise would be impossible. In other words, the statement that phonemes change (sound-changes have no exceptions) is a tested hypothesis: in so far as one may speak of such a thing, it is a proved truth."

Bloomfield's reconstructed sketch of Central Algonquian (1946) is still considered a model of excellence in historical linguistic research; "it has formed a reliable basis for work in the field of Algonquian historical lilnguistics and will continue to do so" (Goddard 1987: 206). His demonstration that sound change is regular also in unwritten and so-called exotic languages (Bloomfield 1925, 1928), and that hence the comparative method is fully applicable to such languages, is generally conceded to be a major contribution. Algonquian's pedigree is as respectable as IE, and comparative work in the family remained up to date with the latest developments in IE and contributed to the history of comparative linguistics in general. It is one of the better known language families in the world; for details and current status, see Goddard (1979, 1987, 1990, 1994).

4. Uto-Aztecan

According to Lamb (1964: 109), "there are only a few linguistic groups in North America that have been favored enough by the attentions of scholars during the last century and a half to require a historical survey. Uto-Aztecan is one of them." There are ca. 35 Uto-Aztecan (UA) languages. In the early part of the 18th century, various scholars contributed to the postulation of the Shoshonean subgroup of UA: Albert Gallatin (1761–1849) in 1848; Horatio Hale (1817–1896), who collected a good deal of data on the languages of western North America in the years 1838–1842; Henry Rowe Schoolcraft (1793–1864) and, Robert Gordon Latham (1812–1888), each in 1853, and William Wadden Turner (1810–1859) in the same year (see also Turner 1856). Eduard Buschmann's (1805–1880) works on UA (see Buschmann 1857, 1859) were a major contribution. Through comparison of lexicon and morphology, Buschmann related the Sonoran languages to each other and to Pima and

Shoshonean. He also presented lexical and morphological similarities between Aztec and Sonoran, but equivocated on whether they were genetically related, favoring borrowing as the account of the resemblances. Francisco Pimentel (1823–1893) presented in 1874 the first "scientic classification of Mexican Indian languages based on comparative philology" (vol. I, p. xi), in which he recognized UA, which he called 'Mexicano-Ópata'. His methods were those standard in European linguistic studies; he especially emphasized grammatical evidence, but also utilized basic vocabulary. Daniel Garrison Brinton (1837–1899) united the known UA languages and coined the name 'Uto-Aztecan' (1891), though John Wesley Powell's (1832–1902) famous classification of North American Indian languages rejected UA (1891), generally accepted by others at the time, based on his belief that grammar was the result merely of the stage of social evolution attained by speakers of languages and that genetic relationships should rely only on lexical evidence – Brinton had favored grammatical evidence. Alfred L. Kroeber's (1876–1960) 1907 classification of the northern UA languages also gave evidence for the validity of the family, but it was Edward Sapir (1884–1939) who, during 1913–1919, conclusively established UA. In this early extensive application of the CM to a group of Native American languages, Sapir worked out the sound correspondences and reconstructed the sound system, and this work remains the foundation for all subsequent historical work in UA. Ultimately it was his rigorous application of the CM which proved Powell wrong and successfully demonstrated the relationship among the UA languages. Sapir's UA work, coupled with Bloomfield's in Algonquian, confirmed that the CM method is fully applicable to so-called 'exotic' languages, that the question of written versus unwritten language is irrelevant for the CM, and that sound change is regular also in unwritten or so-called 'primitive' languages. (See Campbell 1997, for details.)

5. Dravidian

Francis Whyte Ellis (ca. 1778–1819), British civil servant, is credited for recognizing the Dravidian language family (ca. 25 languages). Based mostly on lexical and grammatical evidence, Ellis (1816) argued that Tamil, Telugu, and Kannada "form a distinct family of languages". He tried to show that, in spite of a common belief that all the languages of Indian descended from Sanskrit, "the Sanscrit has, in later times, especially intermixed, but with which it [his Southern India, i.e., Dravidian, family] has no radical [genetic] connexion" (Krishnamurti 1969: 312). Others also made preliminary comparisons among these languages (e.g., Lassen 1844; Elliot 1847). However, Robert Caldwell (1814–1891) is seen as the definitive founder of comparative Dravidian (see Caldwell 1856). The demonstration of Dravidian genetic relationship, as in the case of other language families, was not a one-time discovery of a kinship; rather, new Dravidian languages continued to be discovered (several came to light during the 1960s and 1970s from more remote jungle and mountainous areas). With limited sources, Caldwell proved the family relationship, relying on phonological and morphological evidence, as well as disproved the common assumption of a Sanskrit origin for Dravidian (cf. Krishnamurti 1969, 1994; Zvelebil 1990).

Caldwell's (1913 [1856]: 1) method relied on comparing "grammatical principles and forms", and he held the Dravidian languages to be related "because of the essential and distinctive grammatical characteristics which they all possess in common, and in virtue of which, joined to the possession in common of a large number of roots of primary importance, they justly claim to be considered as springing from a common origin, and as forming a distinct family of tongues." (Caldwell 1913 [1856]: 3) While sound correspondences were not given any particular emphasis in Caldwell's study, he does occasionally cite sound correspondences among the evidence for particular language relationship. Though much remains to be done within Dravidian, the historical phonology and much of the grammar of Proto-Dravidian has been worked out, and there is an etymological dictionary (Burrow & Emeneau 1984), though it lacks lexical reconstructions. Lexical borrowing and areal linguistic diffusion are prominent topics in Dravidian linguistics, and much attention is devoted to the postulated Dravidian connection with Harappan civilization and to a variety of proposed but as yet not fully accepted hypotheses of more remote linguistic kinship with Dravidian languages. (For recent overviews of Dravidian comparative linguistics, see Krishnamurti 1994 and Zvelebil 1990.)

6. Mayan

There are 31 Mayan languages. Mayan historical linguistics (with a time depth of about 4,000 years), has a long and successful history and seems always to have been up to date with general thinking. Historical linguistic findings began almost immediately with first Spanish contact. For example, by 1700 Francisco Ximénez (1667–1730), a Dominican missionary, had a clear understanding of the relationship among languages of the Mayan family:

'All the languages of this Kingdom of Guatemala [ten are named, others alluded to] ... which are spoken in diverse places, were all a single one, and in different provinces and towns they corrupted them in different ways; but the roots of the verbs and nouns, for the most part, are still the same; and it is no miracle, since we see it in our own Castilian language – the languages of Europe being daughters of Latin, which the Italians have corrupted in one way, the French in another, and the Spanish in another.' (Ximénez ca. 1702: 1)

Lorenzo Hervás y Panduro (1735–1809) in his famous catalogue of languages compared words and 'not a little of their grammatical structure' among a number of the Mayan languages and determined that they were related to one another (1800: 304), and Adelung & Vater (1806–1817) recognized the genetic relationship, including Huastec for the first time. Hyacinthe, Comte de Charencey (1832–1916) used sound correspondences to classify and subgroup the Mayan languages (1870); his 1872 and 1883 papers include several accurate Mayan correspondences sets and sound changes. Otto Stoll (1849–1922), too, presented a number of sound correspondences and associated sound changes among Mayan languages in neogrammarian style: "These changes follow regular phonetic laws and bear a strong affinity to the principle of 'Lautverschiebung' (Grimm's law), long ago known as an agent of most extensive application in the morphology of the Indo-Germanic languages" (1885: 257).

Not only was the role of sound change well-known and utilized early in comparative Mayan work, the study of Mayan historical syntax was contemporary with that of IE. Eduard Seler (1849–1922), the renowned authority on Mesoamerican antiquities, was trained in comparative linguistics and his dissertation (Seler 1887) was on comparative Mayan grammar. This study of the historical morphology and syntax of Mayan languages was squarely within the IE tradition, but in fact appeared even before Delbrück's celebrated works (1888, 1893) which are the foundation of neogrammarian historical syntax.

Reconstruction of Proto-Mayan (PM) is very advanced, one of the most successful of any of the world's language families. There is general consensus concerning the historical phonology; many aspects of PM syntax have been reconstructed; Mayan subgrouping is well understood, with few remaining disagreements; and the diversification of the family and its homeland and prehistory have largely been worked out. There is a rich written documentation in many of these languages beginning with early European contact, extending over 450 years in some cases, and its philological study is contributing to documenting changes in the languages. Mayan hieroglyphic writing, the decipherment of which is now very advanced, is yielding rich philological and historical linguistic information (see Campbell & Kaufman 1985).

7. The applicability of the CM to so-called 'exotic' languages

There is no longer any doubt about the applicability of the CM to 'exotic' languages, though this was questioned based on misconceptions concerning so-called 'primitive' languages. Meillet & Cohen (1924: 9) expressed misgivings in their famous *Les Langues du Monde*, and Rivet (1925: 26) considered it possible that such languages might not conform to 'rules as strict as those found in the Indo-European language.' That is, the regularity of sound change was questioned and, since this is a cornerstone of the CM, the applicability of the CM to exotic languages was sometimes doubted as well. Bloomfield directed his famous article against these sentiments (1925: 130):

"I hope, also, to help dispose of the notion that the usual processes of linguistic change are suspended on the American continent. (Meillet and Cohen, [...] p. 9). If there exists anywhere a language in which these processes do not occur (sound-change independent of meaning, analogic change, etc.), then they will not explain the history of Indo-European or any other language. A principle such as the regularity of phonetic change is not part of the specific tradition handed on to each new speaker of a given language, but is either a universal trait of human speech or nothing at all, an error."

Sapir summarized the now almost universal attitude (1949 [1931]: 74):

"Is there any reason to believe that the process of regular phonetic change is any less applicable to the languages of primitive peoples than to the languages of the more civilized nations? This question must be answered in the negative [...]. If these laws are more difficult to discover in primitive languages, this is not due to any special characteristic which these languages possess but merely to the inadequate technique of some who have tried to study them."

"The methods developed by the Indo-Europeanists have been applied with marked success to other groups of languages. It is abundantly clear that they apply just as rigorously to the unwritten primitive languages of Africa and America as to the better known forms of speech of the more sophisticated peoples [...]. The more we devote ourselves to the comparative study of the languages of a primitive linguistic stock, the more clearly we realize that phonetic law and analogical leveling are the only satisfactory key to the unraveling of the development of dialects and languages from a common base [...]. There can be no doubt that the methods first developed in the field of Indo-European linguistics are destined to play a consistently important role in the study of all other groups of languages." (Sapir 1949 [1929]: 160–161.)

Some doubts about the applicability of the CM to exotic languages seem to rely on a belief that change in exotic languages may somehow be fundamentally different from that recognized in IE. For example, Boretzky (1984) contrasts Aranta (Australia) and Kâte (New Guinea) with Slavic and Romance and claims that in exotic languages semantic slots are likely to be filled either by morphs which are difficult to relate or that the phonological differences are so small (in Arandic) that reconstruction by the CM is impossible; he asserts that change in the Arandic languages proceeds more by abrupt lexical replacement through borrowing than by gradual phonological change. Even if true, however, this would in no way invalidate the CM for these languages. Rather, "it is quite clear that Australian languages change in a regular fashion, in the same way as Indo-European and other families" (Dixon 1990: 398) and it was through discovery of regular sound changes that Hale (1964, 1976) was able to show that the languages of northeastern Queensland with many monosyllabic words, formerly thought to be quite aberrant, developed regularly and belong together with the Pama-Nyungan languages. Borrowing is a fact of linguistic life that the CM has to contend with everywhere, not just in Australia or New Guinea. Comparative work in a number of families (some surveyed here), not just IE, has contributed to the development of the CM and to greater understanding of linguistic change in general.

8. Bibliography

Adelung, Johann Christoph [& Johann Severin Vater]. 1806–17. *Mithridates, oder allgemeine Sprachenkunde mit dem Vater Unser als Sprachprobe in bey nahe fünfhundert Sprachen und Mundarten.* Berlin: Voss. [4 vols., 1 completed in Adelung's life; the remaining 3 were completed by Johann Severin Vater.]

Baldi, Philip, ed. 1990. *Linguistic Change and Reconstruction Methodology.* Berlin: Mouton de Gruyter.

Bloomfield, Leonard. 1925. "On the Sound System of Central Algonquian". *Language* 1.130–56.

–. 1928. "A Note on Sound-Change". *Language* 4.99–100.

–. 1946. "Algonquian". *Linguistic Structures of Native America* ed. by Harry Hoijer, 85–129. New York: The Viking Fund.

Boretzky, Norbert. 1984. "The Indo-European Model of Sound Change and Genetic Affinity and Change in Exotic Languages". *Diachronica* 1.1–51.

Brinton, Daniel G. 1891. *The American Race.* New York: Hodges.

Burrow, Thomas & Murray Emeneau. 1984. *A Dravidian Etymological Dictionary.* 2nd ed. Oxford: Clarendon Press.

Buschmann, Johann Carl Eduard. 1857. "Die Pima-Sprache und die Sprache der Koloschen". *Abhandlungen der Königlichen Akademie der Wissenschaften zu Berlin* 1856.321–432.

–. 1859. *Die Spuren der aztekischen Sprache im nördlichen Mexico und höheren amerikanischen Norden.* (*Abhandlungen aus dem Jahre 1854 der Königlichen Akademie der Wissenschaften zu Berlin*, Supplement-Band 2.) Berlin.

Caldwell, Robert. 1856. *A Comparative Grammar of the Dravidian or South-Indian Family of Languages.* London: Harrison. (3rd ed., London: Routledge & Kegan Paul, 1913.)

Campbell, Lyle. 1997. *American Indian Languages: The historical linguistics of Native America.* New York & Oxford: Oxford Univ. Press.

– & Terrence Kaufman. 1985. "Mayan Linguistics: Where are we now?" *Annual Review of Anthropology* 14.187–198.

Charencey, Hyacinthe de. 1870. *Notice sur quelques familles de langues du Méxique.* Havre: Imprimerie Lepellatier.

–. 1872. *Recherches sur les lois phonétiques dans les idiomes de la famille mame-huastèque.* Paris: Maisonneuve.

—. 1883. *Mélanges de philologie et de paléographie américaines.* Paris: Ernest.

Dixon, Robert M. W. 1980. *The Languages of Australia.* Cambridge: Cambridge Univ. Press.

—. 1990. "Summary Report: Linguistic change and reconstruction in the Australian language family". Baldi 1990.393–401.

Delbrück, Berthold. 1888. *Altindische Syntax.* Halle/S.: Niemeyer.

—. 1893–1900. *Vergleichende Syntax der indogermanischen Sprachen.* (Teil 3 of Karl Brugmann & Berthold Delbrück, *Grundriss der vergleichenden Grammatik der indogermanischen Sprachen.*) Straßburg: Trübner.

Edwards, Jonathan, Jr. 1788 [1787]. *Observations on the Language of the Muhhekaneew Indians; In which the extent of that language in North America is shewn; its genius is grammatically traced; some of its peculiarities, and some instances of analogy between that and the Hebrew are pointed out.* (Communicated to the Connecticut Society of Arts and Sciences, and published at the request of the Society.) New Haven: Josiah Meigs. (Repr., London: W. Justins, Shoemaker-Row, Blackfriars; 1788, also repr. with notes by John Pickering, in the Massachusetts Historical Society Collection, second series, 10.81–160, and Boston: Phelps and Farnham, 1823.)

Elliot, Walter. 1847. "Observations on the Language of the Gonds and the Identity of Many of Its Terms with Telugu, Tamil and Canarese". *Journal of the Asiatic Society of Bengal* 16, part 2.

Ellis, Francis Whyte. 1816. Note to the Introduction of *A Grammar of the Teloogoo Language* by Alexander Duncan Campbell, 1–32. Madras.

Goddard, Ives. 1979a. "Comparative Algonquian". *The Languages of Native America: An historical and comparative assessment* ed. by Lyle Campbell & Marianne Mithun, 70–132. Austin: Univ. of Texas Press.

—. 1987. "Leonard Bloomfield's Descriptive and Comparative Studies of Algonquian". *Historiographia Linguistica* 14.179–217.

—. 1990. "Algonquian Linguistic Change and Reconstruction". Baldi 1990.99–114.

—. 1994. "The West-to East Cline in Algonquian Dialectology". *Actes du vingt-cinquième Congrès des algonquinistes* ed. by William Cowan, 187–211. Ottawa: Carleton Univ.

Gyarmathi, Sámuel. 1799. *Affinitas linguae Hungaricae cum linguis Fennicae originis grammatice demonstrata.* Göttingen: Johann Christian Dieterich. (English translation, *Grammatical Proof of the Affinity of the Hungarian Language with Languages of Fennic Origin*, translated, annotated, and introduced by Victor E. Hanzeli, Amsterdam & Philadelphia: Benjamins, 1983.)

Hale, Kenneth. 1964. "Classification of the Northern Paman Languages, Cape York Peninsula, Australia: A research report". *Oceanic Linguistics* 3.248–265.

—. 1976. "Phonological Developments in Particular Northern Paman Languages, and, Phonological Developments in a Northern Paman Language: Uradhi". *Languages of Cape York* ed. by Peter Sutton, 7–49. Canberra: Australian Institute of Aboriginal Studies.

Hervás y Panduro, Lorenzo. 1800. *Catálogo de las lenguas de las naciones conocidas y numeracion, division, y clases de estas segun la diversidad de sus idiomas y dialectos.* Vol. I. Madrid: Administracion del Real Arbitrio de Beneficiencia.

Hoenigswald, Henry M. 1990. "Is the 'Comparative' Method General or Family Specific?". Baldi 1990.375–383.

Jones, Sir William. 1788 [1786]. "Third Anniversary Discourse: On the Hindus". *Asiatick Researches* 1.415–431.

Janhunen, Juha. 1982. "On the Structure of Proto-Uralic". *Finno-Ugrische Forschungen* 44.23–42.

Krishnamurti, Bh. 1969. "Comparative Dravidian Studies". *Current Trends in Linguistics* ed. by Thomas A. Sebeok, vol. V: *Linguistics in South Asia*, 309–333. The Hague: Mouton.

—. 1994. "Dravidian Languages". *International Encyclopedia of Linguistics* ed. by William Bright, vol. I, 337–338. Oxford: Oxford Univ. Press.

Kroeber, Alfred L. 1907. "Shoshonean Dialects of California". *University of California Publications in American Archaeology and Ethnology* 4.65–165.

Lamb, Sydney M. 1964 "The Classification of the Uto-Aztecan Languages: A historical survey". *Studies in California Linguistics* ed. by William Bright, 106–125. Berkeley & Los Angeles: Univ. California Press.

Lassen, Christian. 1844. "Die Brahui und ihre Sprache". *Zeitschrift für die Kunde des Morgenlandes* 5.337–409.

Matisoff, James A. 1991. "Sino-Tibetan Linguistics: Present state and future prospects". *Annual Review of Anthropology* 20.469–504.

Meillet, Antoine & Marcel Cohen. 1924. *Les langues du monde.* Paris: Champion. (2nd ed., 1950.)

Miller, Wick R. 1986. "Numic Languages". *Handbook of North American Indians.* Vol. XI: *Great Basin* ed. by Warren L. D'Azevedo, 98–106. Washington, D. C.: Smithsonian Institution.

Pimentel, Francisco. 1862, 1865. *Cuadro descriptivo y comparativo de las lenguas de México.* Mexico: Andrade y Escalante. (2nd ed., 1874.)

Powell, John Wesley. 1891. "Indian Linguistic Families of America North of Mexico". *Seventh Annual Report, Bureau of American Ethnology*, 1–142. Washington, D. C.: Government Printing Office.

Rask, Rasmus Kristian. 1818 [1814]. *Undersögelse om det Gamle Nordiske eller Islandiske Sprogs*

Oprindelse. Copenhagen: Gyldendal. (English translation by Niels Ege, *Inivestigations of the Origin of the Old Norse or Icelandic language.* Copenhagen: The Linguistic Circle of Copenhagen, 1993.)

Rédei, Károly. 1986—88. *Uralisches etymologisches Wörterbuch.* 7 fascicles. Budapest: Akadémiai Kiadó.

Rivet, Paul. 1925. "Les Australiens en Amérique". *Journal de la Société Linguistique de Paris* 26.23—63.

Sajnovics, Jo[h]annis [János]. 1770. *Demonstratio idioma Ungarorum et Lapponum idem esse.* Copenhagen: Typis Collegi Societatis Iesu. (2nd ed., Trnava [Tyrnau], Hungary, 1770; photolithic repro. Bloomington: Indiana Univ.; The Hague: Mouton, 1968; German translation by M. Ehlers, Wiesbaden: Harrassowitz, 1972.)

Sammallahti, Pekka. 1988. "Historical Phonology of the Uralic Languages". *The Uralic Languages: Description, history, and foreign influences* ed. by Denis Sinor, 478—554. Leiden: Brill.

Sapir, Edward. 1913—19. "Southern Paiute and Nahuatl: A study in Uto-Aztecan". *Journal de la Société des Américanists de Paris*, Part 1, 10.379—425, Part 2, 11.433—438. (Part 2 also printed in *American Anthropologist* 17.98—120, 1915.)

—. 1929. "The Status of Linguistics as a Science". *Language* 5.207—214. (Repr. in *Selected Writings of Edward Sapir in Language, Culture, and Personality* ed. by David G. Mandelbaum, 160—166. Berkeley: Univ. of California Press, 1949.)

—. 1931. "The Concept of Phonetic Law as Tested in Primitive Languages by Leonard Bloomfield". *Methods in Social Science: A case book* ed. by Stuart A. Rice, 297—306. Chicago: Univ. of Chicago Press. (Repr. in *Selected Writings of Edward Sapir* ... [etc.], 73—82.)

Schlözer, August Ludwig von. 1768. *Probe russischer Annalen.* Bremen & Göttingen.

—. 1802—1809. *Nestor: Russische Annalen in ihrer slavonischen Grundsprache verglichen und erklärt.* 5 vols. Göttingen.

Seler, Eduard. 1887. *Das Konjugationssystem der Mayasprachen.* Berlin: Unger. (Repr. in Eduard Seler, *Gesammelte Abhandlungen zur Amerikanischen Sprach- und Altertumskunde* 1.65—126. Berlin: Ascher; 1902; reissued, Graz: Akademische Druck- und Verlagsanstalt, 1960.)

Stipa, Günter Johannes. 1990. *Finnisch-ugrische Sprachforschung.* Helsinki: Suomalais-Ugrilainen Seura.

Stoll, Otto. 1885. "Supplementary Remarks to the Grammar of the Cakchiquel Language. Ed. by Daniel G. Brinton". *Proceedings of the American Philosophical Society* 22.255—268.

Turner, William Wadden. 1853. "The Aborigines of New Mexico and the Surrounding Regions". *Transactions of the American Ethnological Society* 3.159—166.

—. 1856. "The Apaches: A paper read before the American Ethnological Society". *Literary World* (17 April 1856), 281—282.

Ximénez, Francisco. ca. 1702. *Arte de las tres lenguas cakchiquel, quiche y tzutuhil.* Guatemala.

Zvelebil, Kamil V. 1990. *Dravidian Linguistics: An introduction.* Pondicherry: Pondicherry Institute of Linguistics and Culture.

Cathy Bereznak, Baton Rouge (U.S.A.)/
Lyle Campbell, Christchurch (New Zealand)

XXVII. Language Typology, Language Classification, and the Search for Universals
Sprachtypologie, die Klassifizierung der Sprachen und die Suche nach sprachlichen Universalien
La typologie linguistique, la classification des langues et la recherche des universaux

171. Typology by the end of the 18th century

1. The programme
2. Two themes for variation: The 17th century
3. Variations on a few themes: The 18th century
4. Eclipse of the Enlightenment
5. Bibliography

1. The programme

Typology is a research programme aimed at mapping cross-linguistic diversity and distinguishing what is systematic about it from what is random. Typological research commences by identifying differences among languages, as opposed to traits shared universally. Typology's remit then is to determine whether these individual differences are interrelated or independent of each other, steering clear of such interrelationships as are due to logical necessity, historical contingency (common heritage or joint borrowing), or chance.

Typology, thus, is not so much about the classification of languages as about the distributions of individual traits — units, categories, constructions, rules of all kinds — across the linguistic universe; these distributions, not languages as such, are the primary objects of comparison. (This has been insufficiently appreciated by historians of linguistics, including Robins (1973), Monreal-Wickert (1977), Droixhe (1978), and Qasim (1985), whose otherwise valuable surveys of early comparative efforts thus tend to pass over the very sort of detail that typology thrives on.) Given two logically independent traits, p and q, it is possible for languages to have both (p & q), to have neither ($-p$ & $-q$), or to have only one (p & $-q$, $-p$ & q); if one of the last two combinations is unattested or comparatively infrequent, this points to a relationship between the two traits in the form of an implication (*if p then q*, or *if q then p*, categorically or with more than chance frequency). Implications are the laws which typology is out to discover.

Although inevitably theory-driven (as well as theory-driving), typology is an empirical, inductive enterprise, methodically checking possibilities against reality. Unlike curio-collecting, it requires a vision of system. Therefore it was only able to get seriously going as the theorizing about what is universal and particular was beginning to be informed by detailed factual knowledge (or sometimes factually inspired conjectures) about how languages differed, and as some such individual differences were beginning to be perceived as being implicationally related. It was only in the 17th century, as the diversity of languages was turning from a subject of belief into one of inquiry and after much collecting, inventorying, and classifying of specimens, that a tradition of research was gropingly and haltingly inaugurated in Europe whose focus was on the systematic nature of cross-linguistic grammatical variation. Firmly established by the end of the 18th century, though professionally long marginalized by comparative endeavours of far narrower scope, centred upon single families such as Germanic or Indo-European, it has continued unbroken until today.

2. Two themes for variation: The 17th century

A considerable amount of information on the languages of the Old World and the less familiar idioms of distant civilizations and wildernesses was accumulating during the 16th and 17th centuries. Grammars were published, albeit usually in small editions, on many languages which had hitherto been undescribed or descriptions of which had only been circulated privately (e. g., among missionaries). Good indicators of the extent and depth of knowledge about languages which was becoming generally available were the language thesauri or *trésors* and the encyclopedias which began to proliferate a little later. However, among those who, for one reason or another, compared languages, few would take notice and revise standard preconceptions about their diversity and unity accordingly.

2.1. To inflect or not to inflect

Possessing some knowledge of major ancient and modern literary languages of Europe and perhaps the Near East, and given to generalizing, it is not unreasonable to conclude that, in essence if not in every detail, grammars are variations on no more than two themes. In order to relate words to each other and to anchor utterances in the speech-act (which are the tasks of grammar), either these words themselves will be inflected, obviating the need to press their mere arrangement into grammatical service, or there will be special grammatical words (such as adpositions, auxiliaries, and pronouns) assisting in the combination of lexical words when their rigid linear ordering alone affords insufficient distinctive power. Indeed, in the 17th century, once grammars began to be compared rather than only sounds (or letters) and words, it quickly became a popular conclusion, promulgated in such influential general works as Francis Bacon's *De dignitate et augmentis scientiarum* (1623) or John Locke's *Some Thoughts Concerning Education* (1693), that languages will either be inflecting and free to invert words or non-inflecting and non-inverting, in ancient and modern style respectively.

First impressions proved long-lasting, although they were evidently rather too sweeping. A closer look at just about any ancient or modern language nearby would have taught moderation to those maintaining the generalization that the business of grammar IN ITS ENTIRETY will be entrusted either to inflectional morphology or jointly to function words and word order, and will never be divided between morphology and syntax.

2.2. Which kinds of words to inflect, and for what

Sometimes the received wisdom was indeed found wanting and perfectible, especially when newly acquired knowledge was brought to bear on it. While his fellow philosophical grammarians were continuing the habit of lifting supposedly general categories, especially those of the parts of speech and their inflections, from the grammars of particular languages, viz. the classical ones, Tommaso Campanella (1568—1629), the author of *La città del sole* who devoted the first part of his *Philosophia rationalis* (1638) to grammar, would only accept as truly general what was compatible with all languages — and his linguistic universe included Hebrew, Chaldean, Arabic, Turkish, Ancient Greek, Latin, the contemporary Romance vernaculars (Italian, French, Spanish), as well as Chinese and Vietnamese.

In this factual light it was wrong to define a noun as that part of speech which inflected for case, for there were languages (the Romance vernaculars, Hebrew, and, erroneously, Arabic were mentioned by Campanella) where nouns, instead of showing morphological case variations, were accompanied by special function words (i. e., were *articulabilis* or *particulabilis*). And, less crucially, there were also languages such as Ancient Greek where nouns were both inflected for case and accompanied by the definite article. Similarly, although verbs frequently were those parts of speech which inflected for tense, person-number, and possibly further categories, this was too specific as a general definition since there were languages such as Chinese and Vietnamese whose verbs were invariable and whose categories of accidence were expressed by separate words, viz. adverbial *notulae* and personal pronouns. Nominal inflection could not be defined as necessarily comprising both case and number, for there were languages such as the Romance vernaculars and Hebrew where nouns inflected only for number.

Campanella's empirically inspired corrections of such traditional views of parts of speech and inflectional systems amounted to a rejection of the idea that languages *in toto* can only be *declinabilis* (inflecting) or *(p)articulabilis* (non-inflecting). He saw that nominal and verbal grammar need not be cast in entirely the same mould: in Romance verbs inflected rather profusely as compared to nouns, which at most inflected for number (but not for case). Thus, not only were nominal and verbal inflection variables rather than universals, they were also interrelated. As Campanella was unaware of languages with case-inflecting nouns but entirely uninflected verbs, while the three other combinations of case and verbal inflection and non-inflection were attested in languages he was aware of, the pattern he had found, summarized in Table 171.1, consisted in the inflection of verbs (for any category) being implied by the inflection of nouns for case. Likewise, since nouns were observed either to inflect for both case and number, to inflect only for number, or not to inflect at all, but not to inflect only for case, as summarized in Table 171.2, these two nominal inflectional categories were also interrelated, with case being implied by number.

Table 171.1: Domains of inflection, according to Campanella (1638)

NOMINAL CASE INFLECTION	VERBAL INFLECTION	combination attested in
+	+	Latin, Greek, Turkish
+	−	
−	+	Italien, French, Spanish, Hebrew
−	−	Chinese, Vietnamese

Table 171.2: Categories of inflection, according to Campanella (1638)

CASE INFLECTION	NUMBER INFLECTION	combination attested in
+	+	Latin, Greek, Turkish
+	−	
−	+	Italien, French, Spanish, Hebrew
−	−	Chinese, Vietnamese

No offence was caused by these grammatical heresies of Fra Tommaso, however.

2.3. How to order words of various kinds

More explicit in the actual statement of implications than Campanella was François (de) Mesgnien (or, in Polish, Meninski; c. 1623−1698), author of what Campanella would have called *grammaticae civiles* of French, Italian, and Polish, but expert above all on the Orient. After many years in Polish and Austrian diplomatic service at the Ottoman court at Constantinople, Mesgnien published, at his own oriental press at the court of Vienna, his *magnum opus*, the *Thesaurus linguarum orientalium*, which was accompanied by a contrastive grammar, *Linguarum orientalium turcicæ, arabicæ, persicæ institutiones seu Grammatica turcica* (1680, re-edited in 1756). The focus of this grammar indeed was on Turkish, Arabic, and Persian, but further languages, including Greek, Latin, French, Italian, German, Polish, and Hungarian, were also drawn into the comparison.

What emerged from Mesgnien's comparative survey of inflectional morphology (*etymologia*, Parts 2−5) was that languages were much more variable on this count than it had seemed to many a general philosophical grammarian. Among the parts of speech and inflectional categories which were highlighted as not being universal were definite articles, prepositions, personal and possessive pronouns, and genders, most cases, and adjective agreement.

But it was only in Part 6, *De syntaxi*, Section 2, *De ordine constructionis* (1680: 146−148), that Mesgnien actually emphasized interrelations between variables. Here he examined the linear order of constituents in a number of constructions: (i) subject, object, and verb, (ii) nominal attribute and head noun, (iii) adjectival attribute and head noun, (iv) adposition and noun phrase, (v) particle (especially conjunctions and interrogative words) and clause, (vi) subject and verb in interrogative clauses, (vii) indirect object, direct object, and subject, (viii) core and circumstantial actants. As Mesgnien observed, with particular reference to Turkish, Hungarian, and German, on the one hand, and Arabic, on the other, the normal orders did not vary randomly from one construction to another. At least for those constructions involving a constituent governing another, the ordering tended to be harmonious: governors uniformly either followed or preceded their governees in all relevant constructions. Mesgnien in fact gave two general ordering rules, but it is plain that they have a common denominator in the relationship of government.

1. Regens debet semper postponi suo recto, seu casui quem regit, ideoque Verbum, quòd omnia regere videatur, ultimum orationis locum obtinet.

2. Substantivum Adjectivo suo postponitur, ut & alteri Substantivo quod regit in genitivo [...]. Sed horum ferè omnium contrarium evenit in lingua Arabica [...]. (1680: 147)

Admittedly, the mutual implications between linear orders across construction types would not quite hold without all reservations. Thus, Persian seemed to Mesgnien to be less rigid in its arrangements, but the preference still was for governors to precede governees, as in Arabic. Arabic, moreover, admitted subject-verb-object as an alternative to verb-subject-object, and the former was the first choice in Persian as well.

3. Variations on a few themes: The 18th century

The second half of the 18th century saw the typological programme gaining momentum. This was in the wake of a new wave of European expansion, but the exploration of more and more languages of those parts of the globe recently appropriated by the secular and ecclesiastical powers of Europe was an almost negligible factor, at least initially. When comparatists did venture further afield in search of system, they were prone to lose their bearings and to find systems which were only imagination. In fact, most of the less fantastic typological themes had already been introduced earlier; they were now varied and expanded on – or also forgotten and independently rediscovered. Above all, typology was coming to be recognised as a research programme in its own right, typically tied up, though, with the kindred subject of the evolution of language(s).

3.1. Inflection or order

The choices languages had in expressing overtly how the words being combined were to be related to each other – rigid linear order, special grammatical words, inflections – continued to be regarded as interpedendent, often in global schemes less subtle than that of Campanella. The explanatory reasoning was that, lest there be unnecessary confusion in communication, it was advisable to use some kind of overt grammatical marking, but to use several kinds in concert would be unnecessarily uneconomical; it tended to find empirical confirmation, depending on what languages one was looking at and how closely.

The Abbé Gabriel Girard's (c. 1677–1748) practical intention in his *Les vrais principes de la langue françoise: ou La parole réduite en méthode, conformément aux loix de l'usage* (1747) was to provide a genuine grammar of French, contrasting it to Latin in order to emphasize how different the two languages are. It was only *en passant* that mention was also made of Italian, Spanish, (Muscovite) Russian, Polish, Church Slavonic, Croat, Ancient Greek, "Teutonic" (presumably comprising German and its relatives and predecessors), and Hebrew – none very exotic even by contemporary standards, but that sufficed to add a typological dimension to a contrastive pedagogical grammar.

Concerning the expression of grammatical relations expecially of nominals by rigid order, case inflection, and prepositions, Girard found only two of eight possible combinations attested, as shown in Table 171.3. This pointed to these mutual implications: if constituent order is rigid, then cases are absent, and vice versa; if cases are absent, then the use of prepositions, especially for nominals in circumstantial relations, is extensive, and vice versa; if order is rigid, then the use of prepositions is extensive, and vice versa; if, on the other hand, constituent order is flexible, then cases are present, and vice versa; if cases are present, then the use of prepositions is sparse, and vice versa; if order is flexible, then the use of prepositions is sparse, and vice versa.

Table 171.3: Means of expressing grammatical relations, according to Girard (1747)

ORDER	CASES	PREPO-SITIONS	combination attested in
rigid	absent	extensive	French, Italian, Spanish
rigid	absent	sparse	———
rigid	present	extensive	———
rigid	present	sparse	———
flexible	absent	extensive	———
flexible	absent	sparse	———
flexible	present	extensive	———
flexible	present	sparse	Latin, Russian, Church Slavonic, Ancient Greek, Germanic

The presence or absence of agreement between nouns and adjectives, especially in case, was assumed to be a trait correlating with the use or non-use of inflection on nouns. So was the mode of adjective comparison, by inflections or grammatical words, although this trait seemed less conspicuous to Girard, whose emphasis was on the marking of grammatical relations.

Although Girard's scheme can be seen as but continuing the old motif of the global two-way contrast between languages favouring and disfavouring inflections, his names for his types (or *génies*) were inspired by the two corresponding modes of ordering. For him, languages such as French, Italian, and Spanish, lacking nominal case marking, represented the *génie analogue*, with the linear order of major clause constituents mirroring the 'natural' progression of ideas expressed in the clause, with the agent (subject) coming first, followed by the action (verb), followed in turn by whatever is acted on or aimed at or otherwise involved in the action (objects, adverbial phrases). Latin, Russian, and Church Slavonic, all inflecting for case, were Girard's type specimens of the *génie transpositif*, where constituent order is arbitrary and flexible, unrestrained by the natural order of ideas and instead following the speaker's momentary imagination.

It was arguably Girard's familiarity with Slavonic which suggested to him the potential significance of the definite article. There was none in any of his transpositive languages, while all his analogous languages had one. But he also knew that Ancient Greek and Germanic had a definite article too, sharing this separate part of speech with the analogous languages, while with regard to inflections and givenness to word-order inversions they were of a more transpositive bent. These, then, were representatives of a *génie mixte* or *amphilogique*. Theoretically there was yet another possibility of such a mixture: no definite article and rigidly natural order plus lack of (case) inflection; but there was no such language known to Girard. Translating Table 171.4 into an implication, what Girard had induced was that if languages had rigid order and no cases, they also had a definite article, both not vice versa. Incidentally, Campanella, in whose scheme articles had also played a role, owing to their involvement in relational marking and their occasional fusion with prepositions, had known two relevant languages whose word order was rigid and which lacked cases: Vietnamese and Chinese; it might have disappointed Girard that both also lacked a definite article, thus filling the empty line in Table 171.4 and disproving his categorical implication.

Table 171.4: Expression of relations and of definiteness, according to Girard (1747)

CASES & FREE ORDER	DEFINITE ARTICLE	combination attested in
+	+	Ancient Greek, Germanic
+	−	Latin, Russian, Church Slavonic
−	+	French, Italian, Spanish
−	−	

3.2. Word orders in harmony

The notions of an *ordo artificialis* and an *ordo naturalis* are of Scholastic provenience, and it was in a Scholastic spirit, rather than in that of Mesgnien (who was only remembered by William Jones and a few fellow orientalists, and not for his typological merits), that Girard and those adopting his distinction between transpositive and analogous languages continued to determine what was natural/analogous when word order was rigid rather than artificial/inverted. One of Mesgnien's lessons had not been learnt when Girard and others, relying on cognitive speculation rather than the cross-linguistic evidence by then available, took for granted that subject-verb-object, as in French, was the only natural order of these constituents.

However, Mesgnien's other lesson, that orders in different kinds of constructions are not independent, though lost on Girard himself, was relearnt by his most effective propagator, Nicolas Beauzée (1717–1789), the chief linguistic contributor to what has rightly been called the central document of the Enlightenment, Diderot and d'Alembert's *Encyclopédie, ou Dictionnaire raisonné des sciences, des arts et des métiers*. The expression of grammatical relations by word order, as opposed to inflections, was a leading topic in several of Beauzée's articles in the *Encyclopédie* (especially that on *Langue*), re-appearing much revised and expanded in the three grammatical and literary volumes of the *Encyclopédie méthodique* (1782–1786) which Beauzée co-edited, as well as in his textbook (for unlike the typologizing philosophers, diplomats, abbés, and judges, he actually taught this subject at the new École Royale Militaire at Paris), *Grammaire générale, ou Exposition raisonnée des éléments nécessaires du langage* (1767).

While Girard had only been concerned with the clause-level ordering of subject, verb, and object or other verbal complements, Beauzée looked at a wider range of constructions at clause- and phrase-level, namely all those involving the relationship of *détermination*. These were at least six:

DETERMINED	DETERMINING
subject	predicate
verb	complement (objects, prepositional phrases)
preposition	complement (noun phrase)
head noun	attributive adjective
head noun	relative clause
head noun	complement (prepositional phrase)

In transpositive languages all potentially declinable kinds of nominal words of determining constituents – nouns, pronouns, adjectives (including articles) – had to be declined at least for case, the cardinal relational category; and since there were inflections guaranteeing clarity, order everywhere admitted of inversions. In analogous languages, on the other hand, linear order in all these constructions was (relatively) rigid, and the determined constituents uniformly preceded the determining ones in all of them. Thus, for Beauzée, there were mutual implications between verb-object and preposition-NP, noun-adjective, etc. Had he been more open-minded about how the succession of ideas is expressed by none-too-inverted constituent order in analogous languages other than French, he might have re-discovered that determined constituents (Mesgnien's governors) could in equally uniform manner follow determining ones (governees) instead.

But then, this was not really what would have been suggested to Beauzée, as unmistakably as it had been to Mesgnien, by the languages he was comparing – staple fare such as French, Italian, Spanish, English, German, Latin, Ancient Greek, and Hebrew, blended with extras such as Portugese, Swedish, Breton, Irish, Polish, Basque, Lapp, Arabic, Aramaic, Chinese, and (Peruvian) Quechua. Also, Beauzée's second- or third-hand knowledge especially about these latter, less commonly compared languages was slight. Among the many things he seems to have been unaware of in such languages were basic word orders other than subject-verb-object. Often he would only ascertain from published grammars whether one or the other morphological category (such as the dual or cases) was present or lacking. And he was not very systematic either in extracting cross-linguistic generalizations, despite his programmatic conviction that even the differences among languages, far from being random anomalies, are "limitées, fondées en raison, réductibles à des points fixes" (1767: I, xvii). Defective though his sources often were, they could have been exploited more fully in Beauzée's quest for *points fixes* to which all variety could be reduced.

What indeed was suggested to Beauzée by his evidence was that the distinction between the analogous and transpositive modes of ordering was only gradual. Among analogous languages some appeared to him to be more liberal than others in admitting deviations from the rigid natural order (the notorious 'inversions'), and these he distinguished as *libre* and *uniforme*. Likewise, among transpositive languages some appeared to him to be more prone than others to adopt, in certain constructions, the rigid linear order mirroring the order of ideas, hence could also be distinguished as 'uniform' and 'free'. Thus, as shown in Table 171.5, while the uniform analogous class and the free transpositive one remained diametrically opposed to one another, differing on all relevant counts, the free analogous class and the uniform transpositive one were primarily distinguishable only on the criterion of nominal inflection.

Table 171.5: Rapprochement of types owing to the rigid-to-free order continuum, according to Beauzée (1765, 1767)

	ANALOGOUS		TRANSPOSITIVE	
	UNIFORM	FREE	UNIFORM	FREE
ORDER DECLENSION	rigid absent	rigid, but inversions absent	free within limits present	free present

As a result of these subclassifications Girard's correlations between rigid/flexible order and the absence/presence of inflectional morphology were effectively replaced by these one-way implications: if constituent order is free without limits, then nominal words will be inflected, but not vice versa (because of the uniform transpositive type); if constituent order is rigid without inversions, then there will be no nominal inflection, but again not vice versa (because of the free analogous type). The remaining ordering possibility (or possibilities) — neither entirely rigid or entirely free — was found both in the absence and the presence of nominal inflection, hence could not be implicationally related to either. In this sense the regulation of constituent order, in all relevant constructions alike, was more fundamental than the presence or absence of nominal inflection in Beauzée's scheme, for it had implications and was not merely an *implicatum*.

Girard's *génie mixte* was tacitly abandoned. When Beauzée disregarded the use or non-use of a definite article as a trait potentially interrelated with others, it does not, however, seem to have been on the evidence of one of his languages, Chinese — which was impeccably analogous, except that it was lacking a definite article, an obligatory equipment of this type according to Girard.

3.3. The division of expressive labour between lexicon, parts of speech, and inflections

Although there had always been differences of opinion about which parts of speech there were and how best to define them, even for vernaculars not diverging too widely from the classical mould, there was initially no question that all languages had essentially the same. Even the more recent view of universal grammar as a fund from which particular grammars make their choices (rather than as the largest common denominator of all particular grammars) did not perforce entail the idea that adopting or spurning some part of speech might be contingent on, or be of any consequence for, anything else.

The recognition that variability here might not be an independent variable began with minor parts of speech. Special grammatical words such as adpositions, auxiliaries, personal and also possessive pronouns, and certain adverbs were seen as functional analogues of inflections for categories such as case, tense, mood, voice, person and number, and comparative and superlative. For reasons of economy they would therefore be dispensable to the extent that a language had inflections for essentially the same categories of accidence at its disposal (and rich inflection would in turn give word order free rein), and vice versa. By the time of Girard and Beauzée it was beyond question that inflections and the corresponding kinds of grammatical words were essentially in complementary distribution across languages.

When Girard highlighted the definite article as another part of speech that could be missing, the novelty was that it was not an inflection specifically for definiteness but word order and inflection as such, especially for marking grammatical relations of noun phrases, that the article's obligatoriness or optionality (in the analogous and transpositive types, respectively) was claimed to depend on.

Eventually doubts arose whether even the major lexical parts of speech of noun, verb, and adjective were compulsory. But no matter how radical the permissible differences among languages as to their parts of speech, they were assumed to be regular rather than random, following from the division of expressive labour not only between inflection and syntax but also, and more fundamentally, between grammar and lexicon.

The most influential typological scheme along such lines was that of Adam Smith (1723–1790). In a short essay on the most popular of contemporary topics, *Considerations concerning the first formation of languages, and the different genius of original and compounded languages* (first published in 1761, but frequently reprinted and translated), the moral philosopher and economic theorist sketched a scenario for the origin and progress of language where parts of speech and the form of inflections played key roles in characterizing developmental stages (cf. Plank 1992).

Although the genre of the *Considerations* was that of 'conjectural history', Smith's aim as an actual historian was to confirm the ancient ancestry of modern languages. This might seem a self-evident supposition, but it had been questioned, notably by Girard's insistence on the immutability of types (precluding analogous French from having developed from transpositive Latin, for example), and also by all those who took the dearth or even absence of inflections (as in Chinese) for conclusive proof of the originality of such a language. Still, in his demonstration that the structural mechanisms of the ancient languages could be traced further back in time than those of modern languages, and that there were plausible ways and means how ancient structures could have been transformed into modern ones, especially into those of 'compounded' (i. e., mixed) languages, no great effort was made by Smith to compare in any detail the few languages mentioned in passing and often rather vaguely — Ancient and Modern Greek, Etruscan, Latin, Gothic, the older Germanic tongues of the Lombards, Franks, and Saxons, French, Italian, (Old) Armenian, Hebrew, the languages of some savage nations Smith had read of, and above all English. It was through stringent deduction from assumptions about cognitive capacities and limitations that Smith was lead to postulate, not only elements of a diachronic theory, but also richer and subtler systemic interrelations than could be found in his sources (including Girard's *Vrais principes*).

The primordial mode of denotation in Smith's conjectural history was holistic: originally, complete events were denoted by atomic expressions without any internal grammatical structure. Although such event denotations were reminiscent of impersonal verbs such as *pluit* "it rains" or *turbatur* "there is a confusion" in Latin, there was no unit of a 'sentence' as separate from that of a 'word' at this early stage of language formation. And with a language only consisting of a (growing) lexicon of event denotations and of no grammar, there could be no differentiation of parts of speech either.

It was the mental operation of abstraction that was credited with adding a grammar to the lexicon. With the power of abstraction improving, events would be analysed into their elements, viz. substances and attributes, and these would be denoted by nouns substantive and personal verbs respectively. Subjects would only be the first substances to be divided from attributes, with objects coming next, yielding doubly unsaturated, or bivalent or transitive, personal verbs. The two new parts of speech, each in its own way semantically less comprehensive than the original event denotations, could be freely combined with each other, whereas the earlier, purely lexical mode of denotation had been so uneconomical as to call for separate expressions regardless of whether events were wholly distinct or shared the substances or attributes with one another.

Subsequently, upon the transformation, by the mental operations of comparison and generalization, of the original proper names of particular substances into common nouns substantive denoting multitudes of substances of the same kind (as in *another Thames* or *a Newton*, with former proper names now applying to any big river or any philosopher), there would be the necessity to distinguish substances from others of the same kind, now sharing the same general denotation; this would be accomplished by the recognition of qualities peculiar to them. Once events had been analysed into their constituent parts, substances would also be distinguished as to their syntagmatic relations to attributes or other substances (such as agent, patient, recipient, instrument, or subject, object, adverbial). A third sort of difference, suggested by comparison and discrimination, would consist in the quantities in which substances occur. Reflecting gradations in cognitive complexity, quality distinctions would be attained before relational ones, which in turn would precede quantity distinctions. Likewise, distinctions such as those of animacy, sex, size, or colour would be attained before other quality distinctions; distinctions such as local ones would appear before other relational distinctions; and distinctions such as those between individuals, pairs, and larger groups would be the first quantity distinctions.

In order to be able to express all such cognitive distinctions, a multitude of distinct expressions of the class of nouns substantive could be coined, each holistically denoting a particular substance or kind of substance together with the respective quality, relation, and quantity. This, however, would soon overburden the speakers' memory, and would also run counter their "love of analogy" (§§ 16, 25), aiming at relationships between *denotata* to be diagrammatically mirrored in the form of their denotations. On both grounds a grammatical, combinatory solution would again be preferable to a lexical one. By means of distributing the expressive labour between basic lexical units and grammatical elements with a distinguishing functional, novel composite expressions could be produced for the different qualities, relations, and quantities of one and the same substance as well as for the same qualities, relations, and quantities of different substances, which would partially resemble one another in form corresponding to the partial identities between their *denotata*.

Smith now envisaged two variants of the grammatical solution. One consisted in the innovation of new classes of basic expressions for the newly distinguished classes of denotata, viz. of nouns adjective for qualities, prepositions for relations, and quantifiers (including numerals) for quantities, syntactically recombinable to yield complex substance expressions. The other was to create morphological complexity, consisting in the formal variation of the inherited nouns substantive themselves. It was the morphological variant which seemed to him more congenial to language formers not yet at the height of their comparing and especially abstracting powers.

Smith's contention that it required less comparative and abstractive effort to express categories of accidence by formal variations of nouns substantive than by separate words predisposed him to ascribe peculiar formal properties to inflections; these will be the subject of the next section. At any rate, with abstraction and comparison maturing even further, and with syntax being found more economical than even regularized inflection especially by adult learners in the ubiquitous circumstances of languages in contact, language reformers would eventually switch from the morphological to the syntactic mode of composite denotation: they would abandon (i.e., give up learning) inflections and instead employ special parts of speech.

Considering that sex and animacy are only two of a huge number of qualities potentially qualifying kinds of substances, the creation of a special word class, noun adjective, would virtually be inevitable for economical reasons alone. Certain kinds of qualities, in particular sex or animacy, representing the "most extensive species of qualifications" (§ 8), might nevertheless continue to be distinguished inflectionally. When nouns adjective then accompany nouns substantive in syntactic construction, speakers, out of "love of similarity of sound" and "delight in the returns of the same syllables" (§ 10), would make them agree in the inflectional variations exhibited by the substance denotations; owing to such overt indication of their connectedness, substantives and adjectives would not need to be placed next to each other. Among relations it would be the least abstract and general ones, especially those to do with spatial qualifications, which would first find expression in a word class of their own, viz. as prepositions; the more abstract and general ones (such as those denoted by *to*, *from*, *by*, *for*, *with*, and especially *of* in English) would continue longer to be expressed by case inflections or also by rigid constituent order. Quantity, the most abstract and general category of all, would continue longest in the inflectional mode, minimally in the form of a two-way opposition between singular and plural, notwithstanding the availability of separate quantity words in a class of their own.

The elaboration of attributes would proceed along the same lines. In particular, like nouns substantive, personal verbs would need to be further diversified, owing to the multiplication of their *denotata* by comparison and abstraction. Abstract though the idea of three speech-act roles is, it would sooner or later be grasped that attributes can hold of the speaker, the addressee, or a nonparticipant in the speech act, or of any combinations of these. It would likewise be recognized that attributes may be ascribed to substances involved in the event in different capacities such as agent or patient; that events may be localized in time as anterior, simultaneous, or posterior to the speech act; and that attributions may be affirmed or denied or put forward as a request, wish, or mere possibility. At first separate personal verbs would be coined, and individually memorized, to express all such distinctions (such as those between "the lion comes", "the bear comes", "the wolf comes", "I came", "you came", "he came", "it came", "we came", "ye came", "I should have come", etc.). But eventually the lexical mode of denotation would be superseded by the inflectional one, where, more economically as well as diagramatically, the terminations of personal verbs would be varied to express distinctions of speech-act roles and of number of the substance and of voice, tense, and mood of the attribution. Verbal inflections could be expected to have the same formal properties as their nominal counterparts, and to be to some extent regulated by successive generations of improvers. Eventually, although probably later than in the nominal domain, they would seize on the syntactic mode of combination, giving up on verbal inflections especially when having to learn a new language and instead availing themselves of entirely new classes of words specifically to denote person and number (personal pronouns) and voice, tense, and mood (auxiliaries).

In Smith's scheme implications between structural traits, rather than constraining change, fell out from assumptions about gradual developments, as determined by gradations of cognitive complexity. Also, his developmental perspective was conducive to seeing continua rather than stark across-the-board contrasts.

In line with the traditional position that languages were either inflecting or uninflecting — effectively claiming that either all or none of the WORDS of a class of words potentially susceptible to inflection (i.e., nouns, adjectives, verbs) had to be inflected, and that either all or none of the CLASSES of potentially inflectable words had to be inflected — nominal and verbal inflection was to be expected to flourish or to wilt in unison on Smith's principles. (That this was in fact not what they always did, with verbal inflections often being richer and more robust than nominal ones, had been an insight of Campanella's, by now forgotten.)

Where Smith instead saw gradual differences between older and younger original (i.e., non-compounded) languages and also between original and even multiply mixed languages, was in their more plentiful or more meagre supply of inflectional categories and categorial differentiations. Since, in accordance with their increasing abstractness and generality, quality inflections (gender) would appear first, followed by relational inflections (case), followed in turn by quantity inflections (number), there should be original languages with the category combinations shown in Table 171.6 — interpreted implicationally: number implies case, which in turn implies gender. However, this would only hold for phases of inflectional expansion; during the gradual take-over of function words, gender would be destined to go first, followed by case, with number as the longest-lasting inflectional survivor. The permissible and impermissible combinations in phases of inflectional reduction are set out in Table 171.7, reversing the expansional implications: gender implies case, which in turn implies number. And for this phase of inflectional reduction and concomitant expansion of the fund of function words, there would be a corresponding chain of implications between different classes of such innovated words: numerals/quantifiers imply prepositions, which in turn imply adjectives — which in turn imply the presence of nouns substantive, and these only exist by virtue of being in contrast to the other class of principal words, (personal) verbs.

Table 171.6: Combinations of categories during inflectional expansion, according to Smith (1761)

GENDER	CASE	NUMBER	combination assumed to be
−	−	−	possible
+	−	−	possible
+	+	−	possible
+	+	+	possible
−	+	+	impossible
−	−	+	impossible
−	+	−	impossible
+	−	+	impossible

Table 171.7: Combinations of categories during inflectional reduction, according to Smith (1761)

GENDER	CASE	NUMBER	combination assumed to be
+	+	+	possible
−	+	+	possible
−	−	+	possible
−	−	−	possible
+	−	+	impossible
+	+	−	impossible
−	+	−	impossible
+	−	−	impossible

Implications between the terms realizing individual inflectional categories would be equally phase-specific. For instance, during inflectional expansion subject, object, and attributive cases would imply local and other adverbial cases, being more abstract, hence later, than these; while during inflectional reduction this implication would again be reversed, with the more abstract relations retaining inflectional marking longest. By the same logic, the dual inflection would appear, and then disappear again, before the plural inflection, the dual being the less general of these two numbers; thus, plural implies dual during expansion, while dual implies plural during reduction.

Further interrelations between the inflections of different parts of speech follow from Smith's explanation of the analogical creation of agreement through rhyme. Thus, there would be no dual number with personal verbs unless there was also one with nouns substantive, the only source from which the respective inflections could originate. And there would be no inflections of nouns adjective which were not also found on nouns substantive, the only source from which they could be copied.

As the threshold was crossed from a pure lexicon-language to a grammar-language, the differentiation of attribute and substance denotations (or verbs and nouns) as the first parts of speech had been due to holistic event denotations being analysed into a subject part and a rest; only subsequently would the rest in turn be divided up into an object part and a rest. Thus, bivalent (or transitive) verbs, this ultimate rest, imply monovalent (or intransitive) verbs. When it was recognized a little later, by Peter Stephen Duponceau (1766–1844) and other Americanists, that event denotations in languages with sentence-words were not really atomic but had internal structure, if perhaps of a morphological rather than syntactic kind, this analytic asymmetry was seen to correspond to a synthetic one: the incorporation of subjects implies that of objects. In acknowledgment of Adam Smith's conjectural inspiration, though strongly disapproving of the cognitive-linguistic history he had conjectured, such languages going to extremes in practising the opposite of analysis were named 'polysynthetic'.

3.4. Four allied properties of inflections

In grammars of languages such as Turkish (including the comparative one of Mesgnien) it had long been noted that inflections were not always exactly like those of Latin or Greek, insofar as categories were kept apart whose exponents could not be separated in endings in the classical languages, such as number and case of nouns. Occasionally, especially with languages like Turkish serving as a foil, the classical inflectional languages had further been found deficient insofar as meanings were not always related to forms in inflections in an orderly one-to-one-fashion: one form could express more than one meaning, resulting in inflectional homonymy (or syncretism), and one meaning could be expressed by more than one form, with such synonymy giving rise to inflection classes.

But it was only Adam Smith who, through conjecture rather than induction, envisaged such perfections or imperfections of inflectional systems as being interrelated. The origin and progress of inflectional variations accounted for what exactly was meant when Smith characterized them, seemingly impressionistically, as "thoroughly mixed and blended" (§ 14) with the words they were varying.

Smith's contention was that inflections involved less metaphysical analysis and correspondingly less formal separation than function words, hence would come first in language formation. By way of what was later dubbed 'excrescence' in contradistinction to 'coalescence', inflectional variations would actually grow out of invariable words. Varying parts of the original words, especially their terminations, in themselves meaningless, language formers would thereby create paradigmatic contrasts and imbue the variable parts with meaning. For example (using Latin forms in lieu of the irrecoverably lost ones from linguistic prehistory), by altering the two final sounds of an originally invariable, basic noun substantive such as *lupus* "wolf" a pair of words could be produced, *lupus* and, say, *lupa*, containing an invariable core, *lup-*, and variable terminations, *-us* and *-a*; and this paradigmatic contrast could be used to express distinctions such as the qualitative one between wolves of male and female sex. Originating in this manner, the cohesion between inflections and invariable word-parts would naturally be tight.

Given a stock of basic words differing randomly in their shape, formal variations thus semanticized would differ a great deal from one word to the other, at least initially, prior to the attainment of general notions and corresponding formal generalizations. For example, given two nouns substantive such as *lupus* "he-wolf" and *arbor* "tree", when their terminations were varied to express relational contrasts, the sets of their inflections would naturally be different, consisting, say, of *-us/-i/-o/-um/-o/-e* with *lup-* and of *-Ø/-is/-i/-em/-e/-Ø* with *arbor-*.

When basic words needed to be simultaneously varied for more than one category, the necessary changes could be made in different places. Smith tacitly assumed, however, that all distinctions would be expressed cumulatively in the termination. For example, in association with *lup-* "wolf" a single final sound *-o*, contrasting with *-ae*, on the one hand, with *-us/-i/-um/-e*, on the other, and finally with *-is*, could thus be made to differentiate gender (masculine, with *-ae* expressing the corresponding feminine), case (dative, with *-us/-i/-um/-e* expressing the corresponding nominative/genitive/accusative/vocative), and number (singular, with *-is* expressing the corresponding plural). Consequently, with the qualities, relations, and quantities proliferating, the variations of the terminations of nouns substantive needed to express them would multiply; and mutatis mutandis for verbs and nouns adjective. If there were as few as three genders (which was the maximum Smith had encountered), ten cases (as supposedly in Old Armenian), and three numbers (as in Greek, Gothic, and Hebrew, possessing a dual in addition to singular and plural), a word would need as many as ninety variants to distinguish them all cumulatively by contrasts in its termination. And the non-uniformity of these terminal inflections across different words further increased the formal variations that needed to be memorized at this stage of linguistic evolution.

Owing to the haphazard manner of their creation, such inflectional systems would be liable to grow unwieldy, unless regularized. From love of analogy, the near-random variety of the set of inflections associated with words of the same class would be made more uniform, presumably by the transference of one inflectional set to words which had previously been inflected differently or not been inflected at all. Cumulatively expressed inflectional categories would eventually be divided up between separate variable parts of words, with one portion of the termination of nouns substantive, for example, denoting number and another denoting case. If there were two numbers and six cases, eight forms would then suffice to make all distinctions (since the singular suffix could now be combined with the nominative, accusative, genitive, and other case suffixes, and likewise the plural suffix), as opposed to the twelve forms needed as long as number expression was not disentangled from case expression. This transition from chaos to order and from profusion to economy would be effectuated "insensibly, and by slow degrees" (§ 33) and "without any intention or foresight in those who first set the example, and who never meant to establish any generale rule" (§ 16) — as if led by an invisible hand.

One might have expected the invisible hand also to lead to the tight links between the invariable part of words and their inflections being loosened and eventually severed in the wake of improving abstraction. Thus, morphological constituents of words, i. e., inflections, would ultimately be transformed into syntactic constituents of nominal and verbal phrases, i. e., into words of their own: quality words (adjectives), relation words (prepositions) quantity words (quantifiers, numerals), person-number words (personal pronouns) and voice, tense, and mood words (auxiliaries, perhaps adverbs). However, in the absence of any evidence for such an origin of function words from inflections, Smith invoked language mixture to account for the major discontinuity in his story: at the hands of adult learners of languages in contact, inflections would not be further regularized but simply be abandoned. The function words replacing them, in concert with rigid order (in itself not a prominent parameter in Smith's scheme), would be less tightly bound and, like improved inflections, uniform and non-cumulative.

Blending Smith's scheme with Beauzée's, though with the evaluation of ancient and modern European languages rather than their evolution as his main concern, the anonymous author of the article *Language* in the first edition of the *Encyclopædia Britannica* (1771) — presumably the editor himself, William Smellie (1740–1795) — derived a further systemic correlate from a supposedly inbuilt deficiency of inflectional systems.

On the criteria of variety of expression and accuracy in the distinction of meanings the transpositive type was deemed inferior to the analogous one, like on that of simplicity. Equipped with not too many personal pronouns, auxiliaries, and prepositions, analogous languages should have no difficulty varying their expressions to distinguish all kinds of even subtle nuances of meaning. Their function words were separately stressable and could in principle be inverted, if only in violation of the rules of natural order. Thus, the permutations and stress variations of as few as three words — *I*, *do*, and *write* — enabled analogous English to distinguish as many as fifteen semantic nuances (evidently Anonymous was not troubled by petty normative regulations): *I write, I do write, Write I do, Write do I*, and with contrastive stress, *Í write, I wríte, Í do write, I dó write, I do wríte, Write I do, Write Í do, Write I dó, Write do I, Write dó I, Write do Í*. In transpositive languages inflectional endings were bound to their stems, hence were not invertable and hardly individually stressable at will. Thus, the Latin translation of *I (do) write, scribo*, though less prolix, was also much more limited in its expressive potential, even if an independent pronoun was added for emphasis. A multitude of distinct forms would have been needed to express all corresponding nuances inflectionally. And there already was a profusion of forms taxing the speakers' memories, owing to inflections cumulating categories and coming in several declensions and conjugations (as had been observed by Smith).

Ensnared in this dilemma, transpositive languages would typically sacrifice accuracy in the distinction of meanings. They would cut down on the number of inflections by making "the same word serve a double, treble, or even quadruple office" (1771: 867) — i.e., by neutralizing or syncretizing distinctions in inflectional paradigms. For example, in the cumulative inflection for case and number, virtually all declensions of Latin nouns and adjectives were seen to economize by neutralizing one or the other paradigmatic distinction. Thus, the single word form *domini* took the office of genitive singular, nominative and vocative plural, and *puellae* even of genitive, dative, and ablative singular and nominative and vocative plural.

Thanks to Adam Smith and Anonymous of the *Encyclopædia* (most likely William Smellie), there were now four parameters on record along which the expressions of categories of accidence could vary: the cohesion of primary word and accidence expression could be tight (morphological) or loose (syntactic); the expression of different categories could be cumulative or separate; one category (or category bundle) could be expressed by alternative, synonymous exponents with different primary words or by only a single uniform exponent; and the exponents of different categories (or category bundles) could be homonymous or distinct. Although the logically possible combinations of values for these parameters were numerous (to be precise, sixteen, as seen in Table 171.8), only two were considered real, following from general explanatory principles of evolution or evaluation.

Table 171.8: Parameters of accidence, according to Smith (1761) and Anonymous (1771)

COHESION	CUMULATION	SYNONYMY	HOMONYMY	assumed to be real
+	+	+	+	yes
+	+	+	−	no
+	+	−	−	no
+	−	−	−	no
−	−	−	+	no
−	−	+	+	no
−	+	+	+	no
+	+	−	+	no
+	−	+	+	no
+	−	−	+	no
+	−	+	−	no
−	+	−	+	no
−	+	+	−	no
−	+	−	−	no
−	−	+	−	no
−	−	−	−	yes

Thus, four traits of systems of accidence expression were assumed mutually to imply one another, by "moral" rather than "physical necessity" (as Anonymous emphasized). Smith's and Anonymous's perception of these traits was certainly inspired by the classical languages, and on the strength of their principles they took their interrelatedness for granted. If their acquaintance with Turkish, one of the languages that at least Smith mentioned in passing, had been closer, they would have noticed that the declensions and conjugations there were more or less uniform, that there was very little homonymy among its inflections, that there was virtually no inflectional cumulation, and that its inflections were far less thoroughly mixed and blended with stems. On these parameters the inflections of languages such as Turkish, thus, resembled function words — except that they were still part of morphological rather than syntactic constructions, if less close-knit ones. This type of morphology *alla turca* later came to be known as agglutinative. Unlike fourteen other moral possibilities it would have had a natural place in the scheme of Smith and Anonymous, requiring only the recognition of the parameter of cohesion as admitting of gradual variation within the domain of morphology itself.

3.5. *Tout se tient*, owing to parallel articulation

The late 18th and early 19th century witnessed a new wave of world-wide language compiling, alongside ever more systematic genetic and areal comparisons. Often, what out-of-the-way languages were like could still only be gleaned from short haphazard wordlists and perhaps translations of the Lord's Prayer; therefore, some large-scale collaborative collecting was now undertaken to give comparisons a more solid footing. The items collected en masse used to be words (as in the project initiated by Catherine the Great), but some were equally curious about grammars, notably Hartwich Ludwig Christian Bacmeister (1730−1806, also of St. Petersburg), whose multilingual, Russian-French-Latin-German questionnaire − requesting a translation of 23 everyday sentences, properly glossed, phonologically described, and grammatically annotated − was filled in by his obliging correspondents for no less than about a hundred languages.

Prone to merely reiterate the classifications of old or to rest content with such gross master distinctions as that between monosyllabic and polysyllabic languages, the collectors themselves − including Lorenzo Hervás (1735−1809), Peter Simon Pallas (1741−1811), Johann Christoph Adelung (1732−1806) and Johann Severin Vater (1772−1826), and Adriano Balbi (1781−1841) (Bacmeister wearied of his questionnaires and shelved them forever [Adelung 1815: 23−32]) − were rarely able to exploit their riches to good typological advantage. Still, this was a climate where observation increasingly superseded conjecture in comparative grammar, with the realm of the variable expanding at the expense of what used to be taken for granted as universally invariant. As if not to be overwhelmed by diversity, the faith deepened that ALL variation had system.

The apogee of 18th-century system-seeking were arguably the six volumes each of *Of the Origin and Progress of Language* (1773−92) and *Antient Metaphysics* (1779−99), published anonymously by a judge at the High Court of Scotland, James Burnett, better known as Lord Monboddo (1714−1799). Burnett's ambition was comprehensiveness. Confident that some familiarity with all ancient and modern languages presently known was not beyond his grasp, he managed to make reference to some fifty and to deal in some detail with Greenlandic Eskimo, Huron, Albinaqu(o)is, Galibi, Island Carib (of the Arawakan family, unrelated to Carib), Guaraní, Tahitian, Chinese, Sanskrit, Ancient Greek, Latin, Italian, French, Gothic, Icelandic, and English.

Burnett's preoccupation was with origins, progress, and decay, not only of languages, and he sought to reduce the infinite variety which existed, or was reliably reported to have existed, to order from an evolutionary perspective. As in the scheme of his Edinburgh contemporary, Adam Smith, typological co-variation of structural traits was the result of their co-evolution. In Burnett's scenario of the evolution of languages, mainly elaborated in the first two volumes of the *Origin and Progress* series (1773/74) and in the fourth volume of *Antient Metaphysics* (1795), and in many respects reminiscent of Smith's, five major stages are discernible: (i) natural communication, (ii) more or less barbarous languages, (iii) mixed barbarous-artificial languages, (iv) overartificial languages, and (v) languages of less or more art. The criteria defining these stages, ultimately only partitions of a developmental and diffusional continuum, were to do with both 'matter' (i.e., sound structure) and 'form' ('sounds considered as significant'): linguistic evolution consisted essentially in the 'articulation' of matter and form, in the imposing of structure upon the unstructured, in the analysis of wholes into recombinable parts.

Crucially, as befitted true systems, material and formal articulation were assumed to proceed in tandem. And there were few structural traits which Burnett did not see implicated in articulation. To name only his major clusters of parameters, material articulation consisted in (i) the elaboration of sound inventories, (ii) the complexity of syllable structures, (iii) word length, and (iv) accentual differentiation (as opposed to not-so-articulated tonal modulation), and formal articulation in (i) the differentiation of parts of speech, (ii) the elaboration of inflectional and derivational morphology, and (iii) analytic syntax (as opposed to synthesis and even more so to polysynthesis). Burnett would feel reassured in his vision of parallel double articulation when encountering languages (such as Huron, of Outer Iroquoian affiliation) which were so defective on the formal side as not to articulate their sentences into words (which meant they practised incorporation), while at the same time they were so lacking in material articulation as not to have labial consonants. (For Burnett, labial consonants implied velar and guttural ones, rather than the other way round, as later phonological typologists would have it.)

Inevitably, the indefatigable Burnett found the sort of languages that his theory predisposed him to look for — and indeed a few rather less expected ones, causing honest confusion. Patching up the theory in light of such contrary evidence, material and formal articulation as such were not observed by Burnett ever to be so wildly out of step as to question whether matter and form really were to be expected to be articulated in parallel to begin with. But then the web of structural interdepencies woven by double articulation was so intricate that flaws in the weaving could easily remain undetected.

4. Eclipse of the Enlightenment

By the end of the 18th century there were landmarks and leading lights in the search for system in the realm of language which were hard not to notice in the intellectual landscape of enlightened Europe. As the Enlightenment was shading off into Romanticism, the typological programme was paramount among the unfinished business guaranteeing continuity. The search for a hopefully limited number of groundplans upon which languages can be constructed was indeed being continued with essentially the same leitmotifs and in exactly the same somewhat free style. It was only that the new protagonists, chief among them Friedrich and August Wilhelm Schlegel, were ideological antagonists of the *literati* and *lumières* who had gathered around the great encyclopedias, where linguistic typology had found its most prominent platform. They were understandably reluctant to present themselves as their heirs and debtors, or indeed reincarnations.

5. Bibliography

Adelung, Friedrich. 1815. *Catherinens der Grossen Verdienste um die vergleichende Sprachenkunde.* St. Petersburg: F. Drechsler. (Repr., with an introduction by Harald Haarmann, Hamburg: Buske, 1976.)

[Anonymous.] 1771. "Language". *Encyclopædia Britannica; or, a Dictionary of Arts and Sciences, Compiled upon a New Plan [...], by a Society of Gentlemen in Scotland,* vol. II, 863–880. Edinburgh: A. Bell & C. Macfarquhar.

Bacmeister, Hartwich Ludwig Christian. 1773. *Nachricht und Bitte wegen einer Sammlung von Sprachproben [...].* St. Petersburg: Akademie der Wissenschaften.

Bacon, Francis. 1623. *Opera Francisci Baronis de Verulamio, vice-comitis Sancti Albani, tomus primus. Qui continet de augmentis scientiarum Libros IX.* London: Haviland.

Beauzée, Nicolas. 1765. "Langue". *Encyclopédie, ou Dictionnaire raisonné des sciences, des arts et des métiers,* ed. by Denis Diderot & Jean le Rond d'Alembert, vol. IX, 249–266. Paris: Briasson. (Repr. in *Encyclopédie méthodique ou par ordre de matières,* par une Société de Gens de Lettres, de Savants, et d'Artistes, *Grammaire et littérature,* vol. II, 400–444. Paris: Panckoucke; Liège: Plomteux, 1784.)

—. 1767. *Grammaire générale, ou Exposition raisonnée des éléments nécessaires du langage, pour servir de fondement à l'étude de toutes les langues.* 2 vols. Paris: J. Barbou. (New, revised edition, Paris: Delalain, 1819. Reprint of 1767 edition, Stuttgart: Frommann, 1974.)

[Burnett, James.] 1773/74. *Of the Origin and Progress of Language,* vols. I/II. Edinburgh: A. Kincaid & W. Creech/J. Balfour; London: T. Cadell. (Repr., second editions of vol. I [1774] and II [1809], with a new preface by Regna Darnell, New York: AMS Press, 1973.)

—. 1795. *Antient Metaphysics. Volume Fourth. Containing the History of Man [...].* Edinburgh: Bell & Bradfute; London: T. Cadell. (Repr., New York: Garland, 1977.)

Campanella, Tommaso. 1638. *Philosophiæ rationalis partes quinque. Videlicet: Grammatica, dialectica, rhetorica, poetica, historiographia, iuxta propria principia. Suorum operum tomus I.* Paris: Ioannes du Bray.

Droixhe, Daniel. 1978. *La linguistique et l'appel de l'histoire (1600–1800).* Genève: Droz.

Girard, Gabriel. 1747. *Les vrais principes de la langue françoise: ou La parole réduite en méthode, conformément aux loix de l'usage.* 2 vols. Paris: Le Breton; 1 vol. Amsterdam: J. Wetstein. (Repr., with an introduction by Pierre Swiggers, Genève: Slatkine, 1982.)

Locke, John. 1693. *Some Thoughts Concerning Education.* London: A. & J. Churchill. (Repr. in *The Educational Writings of John Locke,* ed. by J. L. Axtell, 111–138. Cambridge: Cambridge University Press, 1968.)

Mesgnien Meninski, Franciscus à. 1680. *Linguarum orientalium turcicæ, arabicæ, persicæ institutiones seu Grammatica turcica ...* Windobonæ: Operâ, typis, & sumptibus Francisci à Mesgnien Meninski. (Re-edited as *Institutiones linguae Turciae.* Windobonae: Kollar, 1756.)

Monreal-Wickert, Irene. 1977. *Die Sprachforschung der Aufklärung im Spiegel der großen französischen Enzyklopädie.* Tübingen: Narr.

Plank, Frans. 1992. "Adam Smith: Grammatical economist". *Adam Smith Reviewed,* ed. by Peter Jones & Andrew S. Skinner, 21–55. Edinburgh: Edinburgh University Press.

Qasim, Erika. 1985. *Vorgeschichte und frühe Geschichte der Sprachtypologie 1500–1835*. Doctoral dissertation, Universität München.

Robins, R. H. 1973. "The History of Language Classification". *Current Trends in Linguistics*, ed. by Thomas A. Sebeok, vol. XI: *Diachronic, Areal, and Typological Linguistics*, 3–41. The Hague: Mouton.

Smith, Adam. 1761. "Considerations concerning the first formation of languages, and the different genius of original and compounded languages". *The Philological Miscellany [...]*, vol. I, 440–479. (Repr. in the 3rd and subsequent editions of *The Theory of Moral Sentiments*, London and Edinburgh: T. Cadell, 1767 ff.; paragraph references to the *Glasgow Edition of the Works and Correspondence of Adam Smith*, vol. IV: *Lectures on Rhetoric and Belles Lettres*, ed. by J. C. Bryce, 201–226. Oxford: Clarendon Press, 1983.)

Frans Plank, Konstanz (Germany)

172. La classification des langues au début du XIXe siècle

1. Typologie et grammaire comparée
2. Les frères Schlegel
3. Wilhelm von Humboldt
4. Conclusion
5. Bibliographie

1. Typologie et grammaire comparée

Depuis le début du XIXe siècle se pratique un mode de classification des langues d'après les seuls traits de structure grammaticale (Koerner 1995a, Robins 1973). Cette approche, baptisée 'typologie', a deux caractéristiques essentielles: elle se propose d'entrer dans l'analyse interne des langues pour traiter de leur fonctionnement morpologique; elle refuse de prendre en compte l'éventuelle parenté historique des langues ainsi comparées. Aussi fallait-il que la grammaire comparée soit déjà constituée pour qu'une classification des langues par types grammaticaux devienne possible. Sans un mode d'analyse des langues inconnu jusque là – celui que pratiquent communément Franz Bopp (1791–1867) et Wilhelm von Humboldt (1767–1835) et qui manipule les morphèmes des langues étudiées – et sans l'ouverture temporelle sur le passé de celles-ci qui rend souvent difficile pour un groupe de langues d'articuler un héritage commun ou une évolution continue avec l'existence – ou l'absence – de similitudes structurelles, une perspective strictement typologique, c'est-à-dire affranchie de toute référence historique, n'aurait pu émerger et s'autonomiser.

Pour les mêmes raisons, les ébauches de répartition du XVIIIe siècle, celle de l'abbé Gabriel Girard (1677–1748) de 1747, fondée sur la morphologie et l'ordre de mots, entre langues analogues, transpositives et amphilogiques, ou celle plus historique proposée par Adam Smith (1723–1790) en 1761 entre langues simples et composées – ou langues mélangées – parce qu'elles ne dissocient nullement les approches historique et typologique, ne relèvent pas à proprement parler de cette dernière. L'histoire des tentatives de classification et leurs composantes idéologiques a été souvent retracée (Koerner 1995b). Mais comme c'est l'essor de la comparaison génétique menée sur des bases morphologiques qui a vu naître la dimension typologique proprement dite, ce sont les premiers acteurs de la grammaire comparée qui seront ici privilégiés: les frères Schlegel et surtout Humboldt.

Ce dernier affectionnait deux métaphores pour évoquer la difficulté à entrer dans l'individualité d'une langue – indéniable de loin, mais inassignable de plus près à des détails précis – celle du nuage (Humboldt 1903–1936 *GS* III 167 [1806]; III 318, 330 [1812a]; IV 36 [1821c]; VII/2 623 [1810–1811]; VII/2 634 [1812–1814]; VIII 129 [1816]), puis du visage (VI/1 246 [1827–1829a]; VII/2 388 [1827–1829b]; VII/1 48 [1830–1835]). Mais justement, la génération qui avait déjà classé les nuages en 1803 avec Luke Howard (1772–1864) et célébrait la physiognomonie de Johann Caspar Lavater (1741–1801) ne pouvait manquer de classer aussi les langues. Humboldt s'y est employé, après Friedrich et August Wilhelm von Schlegel, et souvent contre eux. Car il émet cette réserve, paradoxale, mais fondamentale: selon lui, plus on analyse une langue en détail et plus on perd l'impression d'ensemble de son caractère (V 372 [1824–1826]), plus s'éloignent son individualité (V 472 [1824–1826]; VII/1 278 [1830–1835]), son principe vital (VI/2 388, 394, 397 [1827–1829b]), bref, ce qui seul importe et doit fonder la classification. Après les esquisses des frères Schlegel, on retracera donc le projet humboldtien de classement des langues dans son développement, mais aussi d'après l'aporie qu'illustre le retour de ses deux métaphores.

2. Les frères Schlegel

2.1. Friedrich Schlegel (1772–1829)

En 1808, avec son *Ueber die Sprache und Weisheit der Indier*, F. Schlegel entend d'abord démontrer la parenté historique des langues germaniques, du latin, grec, et persan avec le sanscrit. Des racines analogues (Schlegel 1808: 6–26) désignent déjà le sanscrit comme étant l'*Ursprache* (p. 66), l'origine commune (p. 27) de ces langues. Mais pour Schlegel la perfection (p. 42) du sanscrit trahit aussi une origine non naturelle (p. 60–69), suppose une révélation (105–106). L'étude de la structure interne, ou grammaire comparative (p. 28), a ainsi deux objectifs: trouver dans la morphologie du sanscrit un fonctionnement spécifique, absent des autres langues, qui en fasse une langue à part, mais aussi prouver que les langues parentes du sanscrit en partagent la perfection. Parmi les faits morphologiques dignes d'éloge, Schlegel doit donc accueillir ceux du sanscrit et des langues filles, tout en excluant les modes d'expression de toutes les autres langues. Schlegel, en plaçant la flexion au centre d'une démonstration de la supériorité du sanscrit, pour en tirer un classement des langues, impose à ce procédé grammatical de rendre compatibles faits de structure et données génétiques. La flexion, définie comme modification interne de la racine (pp. 35, 45, 50) est propriété exclusive du sanscrit et des langues parentes. Or, sous sa plume, la racine désigne parfois un mot entier, qui, s'il est modifié par une désinence ou un suffixe, constitue toujours une altération interne de la racine (p. 33). Grâce à cette définition élastique de la racine, la flexion – apophonie vraie (*Ablaut*), ou inflexions – couvre des marques de différente nature, avec comme seule restriction qu'elles n'aient pas de signification propre à l'état isolé (p. 45). Le critère permet de regrouper les langues unies au sanscrit par une parenté génétique, et elles seules. Ce classement de toutes les langues en deux groupes principaux (pp. 45, 54), effectué au nom de la flexion, achève donc de démontrer l'origine commune d'un groupe de langues (51–52). En face, les langues, très variées (p. 52, 54), ne sont unies que par une double absence: du principe flexionnel et de parenté, mais Schlegel les caractérise comme ayant une grammaire par adjonction (p. 48) d'affixes (pp. 54, 56), éléments porteurs de relations grammaticales et pourvus d'un sens avant leur emploi grammatical.

La description de chacun des deux groupes est pourtant plus nuancée. Celui qui est privé de flexion connaît une marche progressive (pp. 49, 56), depuis le chinois ou le malais, avec leurs mots pleins indépendants et juxtaposés (pp. 45, 49), jusqu'aux langues américaines et au basque, avec mots et particules ajoutés (46–47), puis à l'arabe enfin, où la fusion confine à la flexion (48–49). Les langues progressent par paliers (p. 49) vers un idéal de coalescence (p. 56) incarné par les langues à flexion. Pour celles-ci, une évolution inverse est postulée, selon un fatalisme historique. La perfection première tend, comme par entropie, à perdre sa vigueur native et à se simplifier, à mesure que s'éloigne l'origine (p. 56). L'allemand excepté (p. 32), les langues issues des langues anciennes à flexion (anglais, langues scandinaves, romanes et néo-indiennes) prennent un caractère moderne, conjuguent par verbes auxiliaires, déclinent par prépositions (p. 34–35). Or, en tant qu'il découle d'une loi générale, ce caractère dépasse l'opposition entre les langues à flexion et les autres, puisque le celtique en offre les traits (p. 50) sans venir du sanscrit. De même, l'opposition entre procédé organique et additions mécaniques (p. 51), qui distingue langues à flexion et langues à affixes, passe aussi à l'intérieur même des langues issues du sanscrit. Parmi elles, des langues modernes, identifiables par là (p. 39), usent de particules ajoutées, ce qui est une formation mécanique (p. 41). Elles ont beau venir de langues à flexion, elles n'en ont plus toutes les caractéristiques, et ne sont plus assimilables aux langues anciennes qui, comme sanscrit, grec ou latin, sont à flexions organiques pures. Au sein de la descendance du sanscrit, des langues dont le principe est celui de la nouvelle grammaire (p. 34) s'opposent donc à celles dont la grammaire ancienne a pour principe d'exclure de l'expression grammaticale tout mot ou particule (p. 35). Ces divers clivages traversent la distinction fondamentale des deux groupes de langues et ne manquent pas de travailler la théorie. A la fin de son livre, plus rarement lue, Schlegel évoque les effets qu'ont, pour le style, la structure des langues et les "Grundverschiedenheiten der Grammatik" (p. 215). Il énumère bien alors (p. 216) – le fait est passé inaperçu – *trois* types de langues: 1) celles qui forment leur grammaire "durch Suffixa und

Präfixa", à savoir les plus exemplaires des langues à affixes (langues américaines et basque), souvent étiquetées de même (pp. 47, 49); 2) les langues à verbe auxiliaire et prépositions: les langues modernes sorties des langues à flexion (langues romanes, mais aussi celtiques dont l'origine est indécise); 3) les langues "durch innere Flexion der Wurzeln".

2.2. August Wilhelm von Schlegel (1767–1845)

Il n'est donc pas étonnant qu'A. W. Schlegel dans ses *Observations sur la langue et la littérature provençales* (1818) donne sa propre "classification fondamentale" des langues comme déjà "développée" par son frère (Schlegel 1846 II 213 [1818]; cf. p. 128 [1816]; 1913: 25 [1818/1819]). Il pose en effet "trois classes" (Schlegel 1846 II 158 [1818]) avec quelques innovations. S'il conserve la classe des langues "qui emploient des affixes", il range dans une classe à part entière, les langues "sans aucune structure grammaticale", comme le chinois (p. 159). Surtout, il subdivise "en deux genres" la classe des "langues à inflexions": en langues synthétiques et analytiques (p. 160) – distinction faite depuis peu (Schlegel 1846–1847 XII 407 [1815]). Mais seules les synthétiques sont de vraies langues à inflexions, qui marquent la liaison des idées par des syllabes qui "considérées séparément n'ont point de signification": déclinaison et conjugaison permettent "d'énoncer en un seul mot l'idée principale […] avec tout son cortège d'idées accessoires et de relations variables" (Schlegel 1846 II 160 [1818]; cf. p. 131–133 [1816]). Les langues analytiques, en recourant aux articles, pronoms personnels, prépositions, adverbes, etc. (p. 160 [1818]) n'entrent plus sous sa définition des langues à inflexions, tandis que des langues synthétiques il suffit de dire qu'elles "se passent de tous ces moyens de circonlocution" (ibid.). Cette distinction secondaire reste de pure forme, puisque la dissymétrie du traitement ne lève pas la difficulté rencontrée par son frère. Les langues analytiques ne doivent qu'à leur genèse d'être rangées sous les langues à inflexions dont elles sont issues, mais dont elles n'illustrent plus la définition, puisque seules les synthétiques épousent parfaitement le caractère flexionnel. Les langues analytiques sont produites par "décomposition" des langues synthétiques (p. 161).

Pour la classe des langues à inflexions, faits de structure et considérations génétiques sont donc indissociables. Les deux perspectives se mêlent et les classes de Schlegel coiffent les données historiques qui, placées sous elles, ne peuvent les intersecter. Classes de langues, familles, langues principales et dialectes sont rangés par subordination décroissante (Schlegel 1913: 25 [1818/1819]). Et s'il souligne que des langues de même classe – construites d'après le même système grammatical – n'ont pas toujours l'affinité de famille qui exige des analogies plus étroites (Schlegel 1820–1830 II 198 [1827]), il n'envisage pas que cette affinité puisse coexister avec une différence de classe.

Quant à savoir "si les langues peuvent ou non graduellement changer de nature et passer de la première classe à la seconde et de la seconde à la troisième" (Schlegel 1846 II 214 [1818]), rien ne l'atteste (Schlegel 1846 II 133 [1816]; 1913: 25 [1818/1819];) et il préfère poser une barrière infranchissable. Tout passage de l'une à l'autre est impossible (Schlegel 1820–1830 II 196 [1827]), les langues des classes inférieures restant toujours dans leur sphère (Schlegel 1846 II 130 [1816]). Cette séparation se fonde sur la conviction que la formation des langues parfaites dépend d'une autre phase de l'esprit humain, suppose un instinct admirable (Schlegel 1820–1830 II 196, 206 [1827]). Et la différence de dignité implique celle de l'origine (Schlegel 1913: 30 [1818/1819]), qui est, en certains cas, extraordinaire et privilégiée (Schlegel 1846 I 307 [1805]; II 128 [1816]). Avec cette vision inégalitaire est posé en principe que les langues, loin de se former par le cours du temps, se déforment (Schlegel 1846 II 130 [1816]; 1913: 66 [1818/1819]): une langue originairement de la troisième classe n'élèvera plus sa grammaire "à un autre système" (Schlegel 1846 II 136 [1816]), mais devra essayer de compenser les pertes subies.

Chez les deux frères Schlegel la classification reste donc très liée à la découverte de la parenté du sanscrit avec les langues classiques. La perfection morphologique et l'origine mythique qui lui est prêtée impliquent une théorie du classement des langues qui se contente de prolonger les données génétiques sans les contredire. C'est à Humboldt qu'il reviendra de faire une part plus grande à l'histoire et aux langues méconnues, sans préjudice d'exigences théoriques infiniment plus complexes.

3. Wilhelm von Humboldt (1767–1835)

La question de la classification des langues n'est pas, chez Humboldt, centrale, elle reste à la marge d'exposés dont le propos, plus vaste, a varié en quarante ans d'études. Chacune des synthèses théoriques qu'il a successivement tentées sort ainsi de l'examen attentif d'une langue précise. Le fonctionnement général du langage s'y dévoile et impose un traitement de la diversité linguistique privilégiant la perspective dont cette langue vient de révéler l'importance. Humboldt échafaude alors une stratégie globale de comparaison qui suggère un mode de classement. Familier de nombreuses langues, dont il tenait certaines pour exemplaires, il est ainsi passé par plusieurs moments théoriques à l'égard de la classification linguistique. Mais, malgré des oscillations, ses conclusions s'articulent toujours à quelques convictions immuables.

3.1. Basque, encyclopédie, classes de langues

Humboldt est entré en linguistique en 1799 avec le basque. Désireux d'en faire ressortir toute l'originalité, il voulu en présenter la morphologie (erratique au regard du grec ou du latin) en liaison avec les autres langues. Son rationalisme universaliste lui suggérait un plan unitaire pour déployer cet éventail de la diversité des formes. Et la Grammaire générale, avec ses catégories tirées de la logique, lui parut dès 1801 fournir le cadre propre à traiter la variété sans masquer les écarts ni non plus les grossir. Son projet d'encyclopédie systématique des langues (VII/2 598 [1801–1802]; III 295 [1812b]) consiste à juxtaposer les analyses des langues particulières — amérindiennes après 1804 — pour pratiquer sur elles une comparaison générale et raisonnée menant à une classification des langues (III 298 [1812b]). En passant en revue les problèmes que toute langue doit résoudre (VII/2 601 [1801–1802]; III 312 [1812a]), Humboldt se propose donc de ranger les solutions apportées par chacune, en les ordonnant des plus communément adoptées aux plus singulières (III 326 [1812a]). Chaque caractéristique d'une langue apparaîtra alors à côté de celles des autres langues, et de manière différentielle, révélant le degré exact de proximité ou d'éloignement que toutes manifestent entre elles (VII/2 601 [1801–1802]). Mais, comme c'est à partir des grandes fonctions dictées par l'esprit humain que tous les traits d'une langue seront ainsi distribués, celle-ci n'est saisie comme système complet que dispersée sous les divers têtes de chapitre de la Grammaire générale. Vu le nombre des entrées, les points de ressemblance repérables, qui amèneraient à grouper les langues d'après des traits partagés, seront multipliés pour chaque langue. On découvrira donc des classes naturelles de langues, indépendantes des affinités historiques (III 326 [1812a]), et ces classes, établies sous différents points de vue, seront si variées qu'une langue pourra parfaitement appartenir à plusieurs à la fois (III 312 [1812a]; IV 246 [1821b]).

Certes, cet exposé objectif des ressemblances doit faciliter la comparaison historique, mais Humboldt souligne surtout les limites de l'encyclopédie qu'il projette. Son vrai but, plus ambitieux, est de cerner le caractère individuel de chaque langue. Or, non seulement il ne se déduit pas des qualités particulières d'une langue et de leur réunion, mais s'en tenir à des traits distinctifs qui ne touchent pas à l'essentiel ferait perdre de vue le principe vital qui anime toute langue (III 330 [1812a]). En effet, le caractère à définir échappe, par essence, au raisonnement (III 338 [1812a]): les différentes qualités d'une langue forment un ensemble tel qu'on ne s'aperçoit pas même de l'absence de celles qui lui manquent (III 340 [1812a]), la variété de caractères offerte par les langues ne connaît pas l'imperfection et les nuances perceptibles entre ces caractères éludent toute description objective. Dès qu'il touche aux caractères, le projet d'établir des classes pour les y ranger systématiquement (III 337 [1812a]) est donc vide de sens, ou gros d'erreurs.

3.2. L'hypothèse de l'évolution

L'étude du sanscrit, après 1819, déplace le centre de gravité de l'enquête vers la définition des formes grammaticales authentiques en condamnant le projet d'encyclopédie. A partir du fait central que révèle la grammaire sanscrite, la flexion, Humboldt pose et résout deux questions. Tant dans ses lettres à A. W. Schlegel ou à F. Bopp que dans un mémoire daté de 1821 (IV 285–313 [1821a]), il soutient qu'il est inutile de supposer à la flexion une origine quasi miraculeuse, car elle s'est, pour l'essentiel, formée à partir d'une agglutination préalable. En quoi toutes les langues se ressemblent, car l'adjonction (*Anfügung*) de syllabes signifiantes constitue toujours le principal moyen de bâtir des formes grammaticales (IV 299 [1821a]). Du coup, un classement des langues en deux groupes, ou genres, d'après un procédé, qui, adjonction ou flexion, serait, dès leur origine, exclusif, devient intenable, et la dichotomie des Schlegel, simpliste et aveugle aux développements historiques encore observables, est fermement et définitivement condamnée (IV 298 [1821a];

VI/1 260, 275 [1827−1829a]); VI/2 418 [1827−1829b]; VII/1 131 note [1830−1835]).

Pour autant, le passage, indéniable, de l'agglutination à la flexion ne cautionne pas une sorte de transformisme. Car il n'est ni systématique (si les langues à flexion l'ont éprouvé c'est parce qu'elles avaient aussi des flexions primitives), ni généralisable. Humboldt refuse de poser une évolution globale du langage humain dont on restituerait le parcours à l'aide de langues représentatives d'états d'avancement successif le long d'une voie unique de progrès. Sa mise au point a d'autant plus d'importance que la perfection flexionnelle du sanscrit, comparée aux langues américaines, inférieures, paraissait favoriser cette hypothèse. Par une sorte de récapitulation − l'ontogenèse reproduisant la phylogenèse − les langues achevées seraient passées par différents stades illustrés par d'autres langues qui, elles, auraient stagné à un degré moindre de développement. Il avait de fait, un temps (IV 17−18 [1820]), cru à une répartition linéaire des formes grammaticales lisible comme un schéma d'évolution à voie unique du langage, et avait relié la chronologie propre à chaque langue à des stades de formation de la grammaire valables pour toutes les histoires particulières (III 265 [1811]; 303, 306 [1812a]; IV 207 [1820−1821]). Avec des rythmes différents d'évolution et des progressions inégales, mais selon un ordre identique, il n'y aurait eu alors, en superposant les développements individuels, qu'un seul procès constitutif du langage, dont le passé de certaines langues résumerait tous les moments, d'autres ayant cessé plus tôt de progresser.

En 1821 cependant Humboldt récuse nettement ce schéma unique de formation des langues et affirme l'indépendance des parcours individuels: les souches primitives de la Grèce ou de l'Inde n'ont pas nécessairement commencé par l'état présent des langues d'Amérique (IV 286 [1821]). Les langues ne passent pas d'un stade à un autre supposé plus avancé; le chinois ne pourrait se mettre à ressembler au tahitien, celui-ci au copte, lequel deviendrait du sémitique et ce dernier du sanscrit ou du grec (VI/1 275 [1827−1829a]). Désormais, la diversité des formes linguistiques présentée en succession ne vaudra pour lui ni comme suite chronologique (VI/2 387 [1827−1829b]) pour la formation du langage, ni comme engendrement effectif de chacune par la précédente (VI/1 275 [1827−1829a]; VII/1 274 [1830−1835]). Les concepts temporels, tranchera-t-il, ne s'appliquent pas au développement d'une langue (VII/1 149 [1830−1835]).

3.3. Flexion sanscrite et bipartition

A cette étape de sa réflexion, une conviction fonde la théorie de Humboldt: la flexion en grec ou sanscrit est unique, non par son origine, agglutinative, mais par son fonctionnement. Formulée dès 1821, la thèse s'affirme encore en 1826 (V 254−308 [1826a]) où Humboldt justifie la supériorité de ce mode d'expression des rapports grammaticaux sur trois points: la relation grammaticale n'y est pas implicite, ajoutée par la pensée, mais effectivement désignée par la langue; la forme de la pensée s'exprime par un signe non matériel, privé de tout contenu concret accessoire (IV 291−292, 299−300, 306, 309 [1821a]), puisque les inflexions des mots indiquent les formes grammaticales d'une manière directe (V 242 [1826b]); et surtout, le procédé flexionnel exprime lui aussi synthétiquement la synthèse du sujet et du prédicat − fonction propre du verbe − effectuée par l'opération d'imposition d'existence propre au sujet parlant (V 261 [1826a]; VII/2 648 [1827]).

Ce fonctionnement fait de la flexion un point d'accomplissement unique dans la réalisation de la faculté de langage, et Humboldt décrit en 1821 (IV 305−306 [1821a]) le déploiement de la formalité grammaticale comme autant de stades préalables à cet achèvement: 1) les objets sont simplement désignés, les rapports ajoutés par la pensée ou encore exprimés par la position ou des mots servant pour les objets et les choses: 2) la désignation grammaticale s'opère par des positions stables et les mots tendent à perdre leur désignation matérielle; 3) au stade des analogues de formes, les mots à signification formelle deviennent des affixes; 4) au plus haut degré, le mot n'est plus modifié que par un son de flexion, les mots désignant la forme sont de pures expressions de rapports. Plus tard (VI/1 140−141 [1827−1829a]), il donnera cette présentation qui prend la forme d'une genèse pour un simple moyen de représenter la diversité des configurations grammaticales et la relation unissant chacune au concept accompli de la forme grammaticale. En revanche, selon l'écart qui les sépare de la perfection, ces moyens d'expression grammaticale sont bien à lire comme les étapes d'un progrès (IV 285−286 [1821a]). Malgré tout, aucun de ces quatre modes d'expression des rapports grammaticaux n'est un simple équivalent d'une langue donnée. Aucune langue surtout n'incarne complètement le degré ultime d'achèvement (IV 310 [1821a]; VI/2 364, 388 [1827−1829b]).

Pourtant, la flexion offre une différence qualitative qui fournit un critère absolu de discrimination des langues pour apprécier, d'après leur fonctionnement, leur réussite dans la réalisation de l'idéal grammatical. L'écart entre la grammaire accomplie et les états qui la précèdent tient du gouffre (IV 294 [1821a]) et, quand le procédé flexionnel est bien implanté dans une langue, elle a un degré supérieur de formalité qui la distingue radicalement de celles qui n'y atteignent pas (IV 301 [1821a]). La distance est telle qu'elle amène à séparer les langues en deux classes: celles qui, grammaticalement formées, produisent un effet en retour de la langue sur l'esprit, suscitent l'éveil des locuteurs à la formalité et les mènent au progrès spirituel, et, d'un autre côté, toutes celles qui échouent à satisfaire pleinement les exigences de la pensée (IV 307−310 [1821a]). Cette coupure, désormais constamment réaffirmée par Humboldt, est en effet absolue (VI/2 355 [1827−1829b]) et, faute de s'y référer, tout jugement sur les langues se priverait du seul fondement certain dont on dispose pour mener l'étude historico-philosophique du langage et des langues (V 471 [1824−1826]).

3.4. Chinois et tripartition

L'arrivée du chinois dans le champ des études de Humboldt en 1823, à l'occasion d'un débat avec J.-P. Abel-Rémusat (1788−1832), a eu deux conséquences. D'abord sur l'interprétation des stades de développement grammatical en termes de progrès. Le chinois montre un refus délibéré de marquer la catégorie ou la valeur grammaticale des mots (V 281, 257 [1826a]). Ce choix, qui reflète une tendance à s'affranchir des vertus du langage (p. 291), poussé qu'il est à la limite, se renverse en positivité. Renonçant à un avantage commun à toutes les autres langues, le chinois en acquiert un autre, unique (p. 288). La langue chinoise diffère donc des langues imparfaites par la conséquence et la régularité de son système grammatical (p. 289), en acquérant sa propre perfection (p. 306, 288). L'ancien schéma d'un progrès linéaire de la grammaire n'est dès lors plus viable. L'isolement des mots et le recours à la position, censés, en 1821 encore, caractériser le degré inférieur des formes grammaticales, deviennent compatibles avec une perfection inédite. Désormais, la liste des divers mécanismes grammaticaux ne figurera plus un accomplissement de la structure grammaticale par paliers successifs, et cette répartition ordonnée ne décrira plus que le degré, en chaque langue, d'inscription de l'idée grammaticale dans la matière sensible de la parole (VI/2 387 [1827−1829b]). La notion de progrès cesse ainsi d'aimanter les efforts de Humboldt pour distinguer les formes grammaticales. Cependant, compte tenu des mérites indubitables de la flexion, l'ecart entre tout autre procédé et l'accomplissement flexionnel permet toujours de voir dans leurs degrés variés d'éloignement comme une marche progressive (VI/1 141 [1827−1829a]), mais affranchie, dorénavant, de tout jugement de valeur.

La perfection chinoise contraint également Humboldt à réaménager sa dichotomie. Puisque les mérites du chinois tiennent à un autre système que celui des langues classiques (V 282, 289 [1826a]), le champ linguistique ne s'organise plus exclusivement autour du critère des vraies formes grammaticales. Après l'intervention d'un autre principe possible, une structuration plus complexe se dessine. Chinois et sanscrit incarnent maintenant, chacun à un titre différent, deux termes indépassables du langage, définis, conjointement et positivement, par rapport à toute autre langue. Le chinois, par la netteté et la pureté avec lesquelles il applique son système grammatical (V 282, 289 [1826a]; V 321 [1826c]), rejoint les langues classiques (V 382, 461 [1824−1826]; V 300 [1826a]; V 321 [1826c]; VII/1 274 [1830−1835]). Mais comme l'explication de ce phénomène diffère dans les deux cas, tant le rapport de ces deux langues entre elles qui celui de chacune d'elle à toutes les autres est à aborder sous deux angles. Le chinois ayant un système opposé (V 289 [1826a]) aux langues classiques, si le critère est celui du degré d'élaboration de la grammaire explicite, alors le sanscrit demeure le seul pôle positif, et placées sur un seul axe, l'étagement des langues se fera dans sa direction, à partir d'une absence bien assumée, en chinois, puis en passant par les divers mécanismes morphologiques inaboutis des autres langues. De ce point de vue, le chinois reste, comme organe de la pensée (p. 292), inférieur aux langues à formes grammaticales accomplies (p. 294), et moins propre qu'elles au développement de l'esprit (VII/1 274 [1830−1835]). Si, en revanche, on privilégie le choix d'une tension exclusive vers la pensée pure, dépouillée des ressources du langage, alors la positivité est, cette fois sans gradation, du côté du seul chinois, dont l'avantage est étranger (V 292 [1826a]) à toute autre langue, sans exception. Nulle part ailleurs qu'en chinois les rapports logiques ne sont saisis de manière aussi pure et aussi nette (ibid.), ne produisent un plaisir si purement intellectuel (V 321 [1826c]). Sans varier quant à la prééminence du sanscrit, Humboldt a donc ajouté à sa première répartition – toujours valide et finalement seule déterminante – une autre, de nature différente, quoique d'une pertinence moindre.

Dédoublant les critères et les superposant, il en tire une nouvelle partition des langues en trois genres (V 282 [1826a]; 321 [1826c]). Fondé sur les deux langues les plus opposées qui soient (VII/1 271 [1830−1835]) et comme situées aux bornes du domaine des langues (VII/1 274, 344 [1830−1835]), ce partage inégal ne laisse entre les deux pôles nulle place pour un troisième terme qui serait de validité équivalente (VI/1 142 [1827−1829a]). La double polarité détermine trois classes. Dans l'une, la langue chinoise est seule; dans l'autre, figurent langues sanscritiques et classiques (V 282−283 note [1826a]), et plus tard sémitiques (VII/1 274 [1830−1835]). Et, par rapport à ces deux ensembles si bien identifiés par leur caractère exceptionnel, le reste des langues ne se définit que par la privation des deux traits positifs déjà reconnus: elles n'ont ni flexion ni refus de toute désignation grammaticale. Cette caractéristique commune, purement négative, leur vaut de se trouver toutes comprises entre ces deux limites. Très différentes entre elles, n'ayant rien en partage et n'étant réunies par aucun principe concurrent (VII/1 276 note [1830−1835]), elles sont versées en bloc dans une classe unique (VII/1 274 [1830−1835]). Le recoupement de deux dichotomies produit donc une typologie à trois entrées qui, jusqu'au bout (VII/1 344 [1830−1835]), lui paraîtra le cadre le plus adéquat pour maîtriser la diversité des langues, en dépit de la disproportion notable des ensembles ainsi composés: le seul chinois / une ou deux familles de langues / toutes les autres.

3.5. Deux logiques et deux objections

En 1826, avec son schéma des stades de développement de la grammaire et sa définition des langues à flexion comme modèle de perfection, Humboldt a approché de deux manières la classification des langues et a acquis des certitudes dont il ne s'écartera plus, mais qu'il composera diversement.

Selon une première logique, le classement des langues découle de l'étude détaillée de langues précises dont les caractéristiques illustrent des tendances propres à l'esprit humain incarné dans le langage. A l'état pur, au degré extrême, ces langues livrent des virtualités inscrites dans la faculté de langage et, à ce titre, communes aussi à toutes les autres langues, mais alors inégalement réparties. Le caractère asymptotique de langues exemplaires permet d'apprécier les autres en fonction de la distance qui les en sépare. Organiser l'ensemble des faits de langue autour de ces tendances implique que les langues réalisant ces principes idéaux soient promues, tandis que les autres, exclues d'un tel accomplissement, ne seront regroupées que pour leur échec et resteront à peu près indifférenciées. D'où des dichotomies d'extension inégale: à un pôle d'absolu s'oppose un ensemble hétéroclite uni par la seule absence d'un trait décisif. Dans cette perspective les langues doivent avant tout permettre de remonter á ce qui les fonde dans l'esprit humain et faire entrevoir les limites idéales de son fonctionnement, et, à cette fin, très peu d'entre elles suffisent.

Plus empirique, face à la diversité des faits de grammaire repérés dans de multiples langues, qu'il s'agit d'abord de décrire et d'identifier, l'autre logique consiste à restituer la variété des mécanismes grammaticaux en visant à l'exhaustivité. Tous ces traits de structure sont autant de moyens d'expression à la disposition de toute langue. Non hiérarchisés, ils sont dissociés des langues: aucun n'est hégémonique dans une langue donnée, et presque toujours la grammaire d'une langue en fait coexister plusieurs. Certaines langues pourtant, parce qu'un procédé y prédomine et s'illustre particulièrement, en tirent leur désignation et fournissent le type d'un procédé grammatical. C'est le cas du sanscrit comme langue flexionnelle. Mais la démarche inverse est illégitime. Car, quand bien même on aura relevé les diverses techniques en jeu dans une langue, elle ne sera pas décrite pour autant, puisque sa nature profonde ne se ramène pas à l'ensemble de ses caractéristiques. Seul l'usage qui est fait de ses divers procédés et leur combinaison sont déterminants en tant qu'ils se fondent sur un principe spirituel commandant l'organisation globale des formes grammaticales. Les langues offrent une forme d'individualité dont l'idiosyncrasie tient à l'essence idéale qui les anime et résiste à tout principe de classement. Ce caractère singulier forme la limite indépassable des analyses concrètes.

Contre tout essai de classification des langues, s'élèvent en effet deux objections de principe qui tiennent à la nature des classes comme à celle des objets à regrouper. Pour rassembler des langues en une classe, il faudrait qu'elles soient, par toutes leurs caractéristiques, analogues entre elles et différentes de toutes les autres (VI/1 150 [1827−1829a]). Or on trouve des flexions dans des langues américaines (IV 299 [1821a]) et des formes non flexionnelles en sanscrit (VI/2 388 [1827−1829b]). La diversité des langues livre ainsi un continuum de propriétés qui est de l'ordre du plus ou moins, et le vrai caractère de chaque langue consiste dans l'union de ces propriétés (VI/1 150 [1827−1829a]). Poser des classes pour y placer les langues, c'est aussi méconnaître l'individualité vivante de toute langue (V 472 [1824−1826]), contredire sa nature même (VI/1 150 [1827−1829a]). Car ces classes supposent un traitement analytique ou anatomique de la langue. Or celle-ci n'est pas un corps naturel, mais une fonction, un procès spirituel, avec une action vivante (VI/1 146 [1827−1829a]; V 369−370 [1824−1826]). L'individualité d'une langue n'est sentie qu'en acte et ne peut devenir objet de connaissance (V 371−372 [1824−1826]), son caractère ne se laissant pas saisir par des concepts (VI/1 150, 246 [1827−1829a]). Une classification d'après le vrai caractère grammatical de la langue est en contradiction avec l'essence de celle-ci qui, déterminée de toute part par un principe inhérent, n'est pas plus susceptible d'entrer dans des genres qu'un homme ou un visage humain (VI/2 388 [1827−1829b]; VI/1 246 (1827−1829a]). Finalement, classer les langues exigerait de les appréhender dans leur essence spirituelle, laquelle élude toute description: "Die einzelnen Sprachen sind nicht als Gattungen, sondern als Individuen verschieden, ihr Charakter ist kein Gattungscharakter, sondern ein individueller. Das Individuum, als solches genommen, füllt aber allemal eine Classe für sich" (VI/1 150 [1827−1829a]). C'est entre ces limites et dans ces deux directions fixées par une vision du langage et des langues comme des formes idéales, que Humboldt proposera encore, après 1826, quatre essais de classement.

3.6. Unité du mot: isolement, flexion, agglutination

Un concept dénoté par un mot entre dans des catégories plus générales de la pensée ou de la parole. Aux trois termes décrivant cette opération, isolement, agglutination et flexion (VII/1 109 [1830−1835]), Humboldt préfère ses propres catégories. Sauf quand les mots ne peuvent subir de transformation, une modification n'est possible que par changement interne ou par accroissement externe (p. 111). Dans ce dernier cas, une distinction s'impose encore entre simple composition (*Zusammensetzung, Anfügung*) et transformation par accrétion (*Anbildung*) (p. 112), qui obéit, elle, à un principe différent, de nature organique (p. 113) et tend à l'unité du mot. L'accrétion se sépare donc de la composition et rejoint l'altération interne (*Umänderung*) (p. 115), pour constituer avec elle la flexion. A l'opposition entre flexion interne et adjonction extérieure de F. Schlegel, Humboldt substitue donc une césure entre flexion organique (interne ou par accrétion), et addition mécanique (p. 117).

Dès lors, l'absence d'indication des catégories du mot (en chinois) et la flexion (en sanscrit), sont les deux seuls choix possibles, compatibles avec une pure organisation des langues, et la composition n'est qu'une flexion avortée, privée de la pureté de fonctionnement des deux autres: la composition ne renonce pas à la flexion, mais faute d'y parvenir, la trahit irrémédiablement. Cette troisième voie, qui n'en est une que par impuissance, est un hybride, depuis peu dénommé, précise Humboldt, 'agglutination' (ibid.). Certes, les langues qui, sans imiter le chinois, ont un sens flexionnel insuffisant, sont exclues de la perfection, mais avec deux correctifs importants. Ces langues visent toujours l'indication grammaticale, ont parfois des flexions internes, et les compositions ressemblent alors si bien aux flexions qu'il est souvent difficile de les en distinguer (117−118). Cette difficulté pratique sera levée par un examen global de leur structure (118−119) qui permet de trancher entre langues où domine la flexion et langues qui y prétendent en vain. Mais cette différence ne se mesurera plus alors qu'en terme d'éloignement relatif, car l'échec même des langues agglutinantes traduit de leur part une tension positive, d'intensité variable, vers l'idéal flexionnel. Finalement, entre elles et les langues à flexion, la différence, incontestable, n'est que de degré et ne suffit pas pour les constituer en deux genres distincts. Ce qui est le cas en revanche pour les langues flexionnelles face au chinois.

Coexistent donc, à propos de la formation du mot, deux approches pour répartir les langues. Soit privilégier deux pôles positifs, le chinois et la flexion, incarnant chacun un principe dans toute sa pureté et sa cohérence, et donc exclure les autres procédés privés de cette clarté de fonctionnement. Soit ne traiter les langues que du point de vue de l'idéal et considérer qu'à l'exception chinoise près, toutes sont attirées par lui, ont un sens de la flexion plus ou moins développé et réussissent plus ou moins à le rejoindre. Dans cette vision scalaire, la coupure demeure entre les langues purement formées et les autres, mais il est permis de saluer dans les langues agglutinantes l'idéal flexionnel inabouti qui les anime aussi (118−119). Ces langues, orientées vers un terme absolu qu'elles visent sans l'atteindre et dont elles partagent obscurément le principe sans parvenir à l'incarner, ne sont pas condamnées, comme chez les Schlegel. L'ensemble des langues (sauf une, le chinois) se trouve alors placé dans un espace unique, vectorisé par la flexion en tant qu'unique pôle positif, approché à des degrés divers.

3.7. Unité de la phrase: trois méthodes chinois, flexion, incorporation

Pour étudier comment le mot entre dans la phrase, des langues modèles sont à nouveau examinées. Que le sanscrit entrelace dans l'unité du mot ses liens à la phrase ou que le chinois laisse chaque mot intact (VII/1 143 [1830−1835]), l'unité de la phrase se construit toujours à partir des données fournies par les mots − explicitement en sanscrit, de manière non phonétique en chinois (p. 150). Les deux moyens n'en font qu'un, opposé à un troisième, qui consiste, en mexicain, à maintenir l'unité de la phrase pour l'entendement en la traitant, non comme un tout composé de mots, mais comme un mot unique (p. 143). Une première dichotomie sépare ainsi les langues qui vont du mot à la phrase de celles qui, tournées exclusivement vers la phrase, n'en défont pas l'unité. Le chinois, qui renonce à toute indication formelle, s'efface là derrière le sanscrit qui, plus exemplaire d'une centration sur le mot, s'oppose nettement à la méthode d'incorporation du mexicain (p. 158).

Un autre type de rapport unit aussi les trois langues en cause. Le mexicain reporte les limites de l'unité du mot au niveau de la phrase sans différencier ces deux plans; le chinois, fermé sur les mots, ne marque pas dans les mots leurs relations à la phrase et n'éveille pas le sentiment de son unité. En regard de cette double dissymétrie, les langues flexionnelles distinguent entre unité de la phrase et unité du mot. La flexion, qui maintient l'équilibre entre mot et phrase, est donc le pôle positif, flanqué de deux pôles négatifs, opposés par le fonctionnement, quand en chinois prédomine le mot, et en mexicain, la phrase. Les trois méthodes ne sont pas concurrentes, une seule, la flexion, est valide, qui, par sa légalité formelle, atteste le principe pur de construction grammaticale. Les deux autres sont des écarts, en deux directions, mais également condamnables (162−163). Une tripartition apparente revient donc toujours à privilégier un fonctionnement achevé qui renvoie les langues qui en sont exclues à leur infériorité. Pour trois langues sont ainsi isolées des options fondamentales: trois méthodes ou procédés (p. 144), qui sont l'incorporation (pp. 147−148, 150, 155, 163), le procédé sanscrit ou méthode de flexion (pp. 148, 163) et celui du chinois ou système d'absence d'indication (p. 148).

En présentant ces procédés dans des langues qui les exhibent à l'état le plus pur, Humboldt, plus qu'à classer les langues, vise à définir des limites de fonctionnement, à cerner les diverses solutions adoptées pour constituer la phrase en unité. Du champ des langues il propose une triangulation fondée, non sur ces sommets formés par trois langues précises, mais sur les méthodes abstraites qu'elles révèlent. Sanscrit et chinois n'encadrent plus à eux seuls l'amplitude du langage humain, car, dans l'entre-deux, le mexicain est aussi nettement caractérisé que les deux autres. C'est entre chacun des trois termes extrêmes que le gros des langues se situe et il reste à examiner pour chaque langue son rapport spécifique aux trois méthodes types.

Des trois langues est tiré le procédé que chacune préfère, mais la méthode reconnue n'est pas équivalente à la langue concrète qui l'exhibe. Les trois méthodes sont des limites idéales, des formes types (p. 254), jamais incarnées totalement dans une langue, surtout pour la flexion (162−163). En corollaire, on trouve en toute langue des traces plus ou moins nettes des trois méthodes (p. 144): il y a de l'incorporation en sémitique et même en sanscrit (p. 156), tout comme le mexicain tend à l'unité du mot (p. 150). Il est vrai qu'en sanscrit, chinois, ou mexicain une méthode donnée l'emporte et devient le centre de gravité de l'organisme en recomposant autour d'elle toute la structure (p. 144), mais pour toute autre langue, il faudra chercher quelle méthode est adoptée de préférence et apprécier sa distance à la langue type (p. 150), ou tenter de définir de quel mélange original des trois méthodes possibles chaque langue est la combinaison inédite.

3.8. Quadripartition: chinois, forme fléchissante, agglutinante, incorporante

Quand il résume ses acquis essentiels Humboldt énumère encore des méthodes (VII/1 160−164, 250−257 [1830−1835]). La flexion, seule forme en accord avec les fins du langage (p. 252), continue à être au centre du champ des langues, car sa méthode garde le pur principe de structure (p. 162). Et, même si la méthode flexionelle ne s'inscrit pas en totalité dans les langues sanscritiques, elles en restent la meilleure approximation (p. 253), fournissent un point de référence absolue. Les autres langues ont une forme déviante (162−163), qu'on apprécie par rapport à cette forme repère (p. 252). Trois sortes de défaillances sont possibles relativement à la flexion: l'absence de désignations de relations, la tendance à les ajouter et à les ériger en flexions, enfin l'expédient de traiter comme mot ce que la parole présenterait en une phrase (p. 163), autrement dit les stratégies du chinois, de l'agglutination et de l'incorporation. L'énumération rompt donc ici avec les deux classements proposés auparavant, d'abord pour le mot, puis pour la phrase. Plus loin encore, Humboldt superpose des distinctions qu'il établissait auparavant sur deux plans différents, quand il dira avoir posé − outre le chinois, qui se prive de toute forme grammaticale − trois formes possibles pour les langues, "die flectirende, agglutinirende und die einverleibende" (p. 254). Or sa liste, qu'il destine dans ce passage à traiter la construction de la phrase, ne devrait pas inclure la forme agglutinante, puisque, du point de vue de la constitution de la phrase en unité, il est indifférent qu'au niveau du mot il y ait flexion ou agglutination − distinction seulement pertinente pour assurer l'unité du mot. Tout en s'affichant comme orientée seulement sur la phrase, la distribution en quatre formes types écrase ainsi en un seul les deux classements auparavant établis sur deux plans distincts.

Ce télescopage, et la quadripartition qu'il implique, ont deux explications. Humboldt a conclu que le seul point de vue déterminant pour saisir la structure d'une langue est celui de la phrase, qui, plus puissant, commande en fait l'organisation des autres éléments placés sous lui (p. 257). En même temps, comme il s'emploie toujours à prouver la supériorité absolue de la flexion, il est poussé à décrire les formes grammaticales d'après cet idéal, donc à rassembler toutes celles qui s'en écartent et ont en commun de s'expliquer, soit comme refus, soit comme impuissance par rapport à la flexion. En conséquence, même si le critère affiché est d'ordre syntaxique, l'agglutination, sans y répondre, figure pourtant dans la liste, à titre de non-flexion, parce que la flexion sert de référence. Le spectre de la grammaire est alors à quatre foyers, dont trois sont des manières de faillir à celui qui incarne l'idéal. Mais, comme le chinois se singularise par sa dérobade, Humboldt n'évoque les diverses *Sprachmethoden* que comme trois types de procédés (p. 257), qui sont flexion, agglutination et incorporation. Tri- ou (avec le chinois) quadripartition qui restera longtemps canonique.

Dans sa description des langues par quelques formes types, Humboldt distingue les formes de langues abstraites possibles et les formes concrètes (p. 254). Parmi les premières, "die flectirende" est la seule légitime et fonde une opposition décisive entre langues à légalité pure et langues dont la forme s'en écarte (p. 256). Mais cela ne condamne pas les langues concrètes où une seule de ces formes ne règne jamais exclusivement et qui s'efforcent toujours de rejoindre la forme correcte (p. 254). Si toutes les langues portent en elles une ou plusieurs de ces formes abstraites (pp. 254, 144), il faut, pour peser les mérites d'une langue, se demander quel principe préside à leur assimilation ou mélange (p. 254), principe qui n'émerge qu'après avènement d'une individualité radicale. Les formes abstraites sont ainsi un moyen d'apprécier les langues, à la fois décisif, quand on y identifie la forme pure, et secondaire dans les autres cas, où il importe plutôt de découvrir dans les langues la forme originale qu'elles confèrent à l'esprit et selon laquelle elles se présentent à lui intérieurement (p. 257).

3.9. Six méthodes grammaticales

Vers 1827−1829, Humboldt avait aussi classé les méthodes grammaticales (VI/2 337−486 [1827−1829b]), en les présentant en succession sur une échelle, graduée d'après le degré croissant d'insertion dans la parole − donc d'expression matérielle dans les sons − du type grammatical. Si on l'examine quant à son exhaustivité et à sa formalité, cette pénétration de l'expression grammaticale dans le phonétisme offre une gradation, de l'avarice jusqu'à la plus grande richesse (386–387). L'idée grammaticale vient s'inscrire dans la langue de six façons, décrites (ibid.), puis nommées (p. 387–397): I, les rapports grammaticaux, non désignés, sont ajoutés par la pensée: méthode de la grammaire implicite; II, on les indique par la position: méthode de la grammaire non phonétique; III, on leur consacre des mots particuliers avec un sens propre qui restent isolés: méthode par désignation matérielle et séparée; IV, ces mots se lient aux radicaux en une unité phonétique et perdent leur désignation matérielle première: méthode d'adjonction (*anfügende*); V, la désignation matérielle cède devant la forme grammaticale authentique, mais celle-ci n'est visée que dans quelques mots servant de formes: méthode des mots auxiliaires; VI. enfin la forme est générale, les sons caractéristiques des rapports n'ont de signification que grammaticale, la richesse en formes phonétiques excède le besoin de désignation: méthode de formation authentique qui fournit à la réunion des pensées un vrai symbole dans l'unité phonétique, ou méthode de flexion.

Cette série de six méthodes combine donc les quatre stades décrits en 1821 et les divers classements du *Kawi-Werk*. Mais comme elle privilégie la progression de l'investissement phonétique des rapports grammaticaux, en marche vers une fusion et une prise de possession complète, tout se joue autour du mot et la liste n'inclut donc pas l'incorporation, puisque celle-ci est, à la limite, proche de la flexion (p. 398). Les méthodes sont en tout cas distinguées avec soin des langues qui, dans leur grammaire, utilisent normalement toutes ces méthodes à la fois, ou du moins les principales, même si, en adoptant plutôt une méthode donnée, quelques langues en portent alors le caractère. Apprécier comment une langue synthétise plusieurs méthodes est nécessaire pour comprendre le type d'action exercé par sa structure grammaticale et en expliquer la genèse (p. 388).

Sans viser une classification, Humboldt veut d'abord rapporter les langues particulières aux méthodes possibles de structure grammaticale puis, au-delà, au type idéal que l'une d'entre elles incarne et qui est la référence, l'étalon général auquel toutes les langues doivent être comparées (pp. 397, 391). L'analyse opérera en cercles concentriques: à partir de la méthode la plus achevée, puis, à défaut, de celle qui, inférieure, reste pourtant clairement définie, en mesurant dans les deux cas la distance par rapport à la réussite absolue. Pour les langues à peu près fidèles à la flexion, on cherchera les exceptions. Pour celles qui suivent une autre méthode, on pèsera ce qui les rapproche de la forme idéale. Mais si des langues, parce qu'elles ne suivent pas une seule méthode, s'éloignent doublement des modèles-types, on essaiera de déterminer la méthode principale (p. 397). Humboldt donne un exemple de langue pour chaque méthode qui, en y étant dominante, autorise l'identification: chinois (II), polynésien (III), delaware (IV), sanscrit (V) (ibid.). Au second degré, on trouve des langues qui, soit portent le même caractère, soit se situent entre l'une ou l'autre méthode (p. 398). Sa typologie empirique se fonde donc sur un petit nombre de formes grammaticales tirées de l'étude de langues précises qui, elles, ne se laissent ramener qu'exceptionnellement aux méthodes ainsi isolées. Les enjeux spirituels de l'enquête sur les méthodes grammaticales l'emportent sur tout effort de classification, théoriquement invalidée par ailleurs. Les certitudes acquises sur les principales méthodes adoptées par une structure grammaticale, fournissent à l'analyse des langues et à leur comparaison un point fixe précieux. Ces convictions ont aussi des effets sur les recherches d'ordre historique, avec des recoupements, mais aussi des interférences.

3.10. Classes de langues, typologie et genèse

Un autre écrit exactement contemporain (VI/1 111–303 [1827–1829a]) définit ainsi les classes de langues: sont de la même classe les langues qui n'ont en commun ni des désignations grammaticales ni des mots, mais seulement une identité ou une analogie de la vision grammaticale — c'est-à-dire la forme de la langue saisie en concept (p. 294). Si, pour être de même classe, deux langues doivent n'avoir aucune parenté historique tout en offrant une analogie générale du fonctionnement grammatical, la définition de Humboldt permet de rassembler légitimement les langues sanscritiques et sémitiques qui, sans partager de morphèmes grammaticaux, recourent à la flexion, mais elle devrait aussi interdire à des langues unies par une parenté génétique (prouvée par des désignations grammaticales concrètes analogues) d'appartenir à la même classe. Or les langues du domaine indo-européen illustrent parfaitement ce contre-exemple.

En fait, la thèse de Humboldt est ici que l'analogie de vision grammaticale, ou 'Sprachform' abstraite, est, *à elle seule*, la condition nécessaire et suffisante pour poser une classe de langues. Contrairement à ce que sa définition, trop rapide, donne à entendre, l'absence de marques grammaticales communes n'est nullement requise en sus. Il présente d'ailleurs comme un cas particulier le fait que des langues de même souche puissent appartenir à des classes différentes (p. 301), ce qui revient à poser, *a contrario*, que, d'ordinaire, il en va autrement, et de fait, il déclare explicitement que grec et sanscrit, unis par une étroite parenté historique, appartiennent à la même classe (p. 262). En revanche, grec ancien et grec moderne, ou latin et langues romanes, ayant des formes de langue très différentes, forment deux classes séparées (261–262). Appartenir à une même souche n'implique donc pas pour deux langues d'être de même classe; pas davantage il n'est requis, dans l'esprit de Humboldt, que seules des langues sans aucune parenté génétique puissent être de même classe. Sanscrit, grec et sémitique sont bien de même classe, mais les deux premiers sont aussi de même souche, alors que, du grec ancien, malgré la continuité, est issue, en grec moderne, une nouvelle forme (255–256), avec un changement de classe. En dépit donc d'une formulation malencontreuse, les deux critères, historique et typologique, sont parfaitement dissociés pour Humboldt, et il en use en pratique de manière indépendante. Son originalité est même d'avoir, le premier, distingué les faits prouvant la parenté génétique des traits permettant de décrire les structures grammaticales in abstracto. A la différence des Schlegel, des langues de même origine seront ou non de même classe, et, inversement, des langues de même classe seront, selon le cas, de même origine ou non.

Cette inadvertance passagère dans la définition des classes tient à leur présence parmi les autres degrés de parenté unissant des langues. En fait Humboldt cherche de quel type de groupement, du plus étroit au plus lâche, les langues sont susceptibles: une même souche ou famille, un même domaine (*Gebiet*), une même classe. A chaque fois, si le critère valable au niveau supérieur fait défaut, il en introduit un nouveau qui définit alors un mode de liaison moins puissant et plus large qu'aux stades précédents. Dans son développement, les classes forment le troisième recours possible: même des langues sans parenté historique (ni de même souche ni de même domaine) peuvent être néanmoins de structure grammaticale analogue. Sinon, en dernier ressort, elles ont encore en commun ce qui est propre à toute langue (p. 294), car, d'un certain point de vue, dans le genre humain il n'est qu'une seule langue (p. 301). Dans un exposé centré sur la parenté historique, la classe n'est ainsi qu'un critère par défaut, alors que, dans les constructions précédentes, la classe se fondait sur le seul critère d'une identité de *Sprachform*, qui, n'ayant pas à pallier une défaillance des preuves historiques, constituait d'emblée un trait positif pour organiser la diversité des formes.

4. Conclusion

Après la découverte par les frères Schlegel de l'exception du sanscrit et l'exploitation de sa morphologie à des fins de discrimination, Humboldt a donc continué à faire tourner la classification des langues autour de la flexion. Mais, en reportant la justification de sa perfection à un autre niveau d'explication qu'une origine fabuleuse, il a ouvert à la question des rapports du langage et de la pensée des voies qui restent encore aujourd'hui à frayer. Il a surtout séparé définitivement les deux ordres de la genèse historique et de la typologie. Par sa réévaluation du poids des évolutions et sa croyance en l'individualité spirituelle des langues il a ainsi libéré les langues du fixisme des espèces sans postuler un transformisme généralisé. En restituant la complexité des formes d'un grand nombre de langues il a aussi plaidé pour leur égale dignité, et son traitement de la diversité restera valide pendant plus d'un siècle, comme l'atteste la fortune des concepts qu'il a soit forgés (langues isolantes, à incorporation) soit définis avec une rigueur nouvelle (flexion et agglutination).

5. Bibliographie

Girard, Gabriel. 1747. *Les vrais principes de la langue francoise ou La parole réduite en méthode, conformément aux lois de l'usage, en seize discours*. 2 vols. Paris: Le Breton. (repr., avec introduction et bibliographie, par Pierre Swiggers, Genève: Droz, 1982.)

Howard, Luke. 1803. "On the Modification of Clouds", *Philosophical Magazine*. XVI. London. (Repr., *Neudrucke von Schriften und Karten über Meteorologie und Erdmagnetismus*, éd. par G. Hellmann, N° 3, Berlin, 1894. [Repr., Nendeln/Liechtenstein: Kraus, 1969].)

Humboldt, Wilhelm von. 1903–1936. *Gesammelte Schriften.* Hrsg. von der Königlich-Preussischen Akademie der Wissenschaften. Berlin: Behr (Repr., Berlin: De Gruyter, 1967–1968.) 17 vols. I. Abt., Bd. 1–9, 13; Werke, hg. von Albert Leitzmann. Berlin: B. Behr. [= *GS.*]

–. [1801–1802]. "Fragmente der Monographie über die Basken". *GS* VII/2 593–603.

–. [1806]. "Latium und Hellas oder Betrachtungen über das classische Alterthum". *GS* III 136–170.

–. [1810–1811]. "Einleitung in das gesammte Sprachstudium". *GS* VII/2 619–629.

–. [1811]. "Berichtigungen und Zusätze zum ersten Abschnitte des zweiten Bandes des Mithridates über die Cantabrische oder baskische Sprache". *GS* III 222–287.

–. [1812a]. "Essai sur les langues du nouveau Continent". *GS* III 300–342.

–. [1812b]. "Ankündigungen einer Schrift über die vaskische Sprache und Nation, nebst Angabe des Gesichtspunctes und Inhalts derselben". *GS* III 288–300.

–. [1812–1814]. "Ueber Sprachverwandtschaft". *GS* VII/2 629–636.

–. [1816]. "Aeschylos Agamemnon metrisch übersetzt". *GS* VIII 117–230.

–. [1820]. "Ueber das vergleichende Sprachstudium in Beziehung auf die verschiedenen Epochen der Sprachentwicklung". *GS* IV 1–35.

–. [1820–1821]. "Prüfung der Untersuchungen über die Urbewohner Hispaniens vermittelst der vaskischen Sprache". *GS* IV 57–233.

–. [1821a]. "Ueber das Entstehen der grammatischen Formen, und ihren Einfluss auf die Ideenentwicklung". *GS* IV 285–313.

–. [1821b]. "Versuch einer Analyse der mexicanischen Sprache". *GS* IV 233–284.

–. [1821c]. "Ueber die Aufgabe des Geschichtsschreibers". *GS* IV 35–56.

–. [1824–1826]. "Grundzüge des allgemeinen Sprachtypus". *GS* V 364–475.

–. [1826a]. *Lettre à Monsieur Abel-Rémusat, sur la nature des formes grammaticales en général, et sur le génie de la langue Chinoise en particulier. GS* V 254–308.

–. [1826b] "Notice d'une grammaire Japonoise imprimée à Mexico". *GS* V 237–247.

–. [1826c]. "Ueber den grammatischen Bau der chinesischen Sprache". *GS* V 309–324.

–. [1827]. "Erwiderung auf einen Aufsatz von Guido Görres". *GS* VII/2 645–652.

–. [1827–1829a]. "Ueber die Verschiedenheiten des menschlichen Sprachbaues". *GS* VI/1 111–303.

–. [1827–1829b]. "Von dem grammatischen Baue der Sprachen". *GS* VI/2 337–486.

–. [1830–1835]. *Ueber die Verschiedenheit des menschlichen Sprachbaues und ihren Einfluss auf die geistige Entwicklung des Menschengeschlechts. GS* VII/1–344.

Koerner, E. F. K[onrad]. 1995a. "History of Typology and Language Classification". *Concise History of the Language Sciences: From the Sumerians to the Cognitivists* ed. by E. F. K. Koerner & R. E. Asher, 212–217. Oxford & New York: Pergamon.

–. 1995b. "Toward a History of Linguistic Typology". *Professing Linguistic Historiography* par Koerner, 151–170. Amsterdam & Philadelphia: Benjamins.

Robins, Robert H. 1973. "The History of Language Classification". *Current Trends in Linguistics* ed. by Thomas A. Sebeok, vol. XI: *Diachronic, Areal and Typological Linguistics,* 3–41. The Hague: Mouton.

Schlegel, August Wilhelm von, Hg. 1820–1830. *Indische Bibliothek.* 3 vols. Bonn: Weber.

–. [1827]. "Antwort des Herausgebers." *Indische Bibliothek* 2.189–207.

–. 1846–1847. *Sämmtliche Werke* hg. von Eduard Böcking. 12 vols. Leipzig: Weidmann. (= *SW.*)

–. [1815]. Recension de 'Altdeutsche Wälder, hg. durch die Brüder Grimm'. *SW* XII 383–426.

–. 1846. *Œuvres écrites en francais* et publiées par Edouard Bocking. 3 vols. Leipzig: Weidmann. (= *OEF.*)

–. [1805]. Considérations sur la civilisation en général. *OEF* I.277–316.

–. [1816]. De l'étymologie en général. *OEF* II.103–141.

–. [1818]. Observations sur la langue et la littérature provençales. *OEF* II.149–250.

–. 1913. *Geschichte der Deutschen Sprache und Poesie.* Vorlesungen, gehalten an der Universität Bonn seit dem Wintersemester 1818/19 hg. von Josef Körner. Berlin: Behr. (Repr., Nendeln/Liechtenstein: Kraus, 1968.)

Schlegel, Friedrich von. 1808. *Ueber die Sprache und Weisheit der Indier. Ein Beitrag zur Begründung der Alterthumskund. Nebst metrischen Uebersetzungen indischer Gedichte.* Heidelberg: Mohr & Zimmer. (Repr., avec une introduction de Sebastiano Timpanaro, Amsterdam: Benjamins, 1977.)

Smith, Adam 1761. "Considerations concerning the First Formation of Languages, and the Different Genius of Original and Compounded Languages". *The Philological Miscellany* 1.440–479. London. (Repr. dans A. Smith, *The Theory of Moral Sentiments, To which is added A Dissertation on the Origin of Languages,* 3ᵉ éd. London: A. Millar; Edinburgh: A. Kincaid & A. Bell. 1767; repr., Gunter Narr ed., avec un article de Eugenio Coseriu, "Adam Smith und die Anfänge der Sprachtypologie", et un article de A. R. Serbati, "Kritik der glottogonischen Theorie Adam Smiths". Tübingen: TBL Verlag, 1970.)

Jean Rousseau, Paris (France)

173. Die Klassifizierung der Sprachen in der Mitte des neunzehnten Jahrhunderts

1. Einleitung
2. Morphologische Klassifikation
3. Die neuphilologische Nische
4. Ethnographische Impulse
5. Humboldtianische Klassifikation: Steinthal
6. Bibliographie

1. Einleitung

1.1. Anlehnung an Humboldt

Das Arbeitsgebiet der Sprachklassifikation fiel der Sprachforschung des 19. Jhs. in dem Bearbeitungsstand zu, den ihm Wilhelm von Humboldt gegeben hatte, den man mit Pott (1833: xxiii) "im Besitze der ausgebreitetsten, seltensten und zugleich von ächter Sprachphilosophie durchdrungenen Sprachkenntniß, wie kein Lebender" sah, was noch lange nach seinem Ableben zutraf: Der Kreis der für Humboldt (1836) verfügbaren Sprachen (vgl. das Sprachenregister in Mueller-Vollmer 1993: 454—460) wurde in der Forschung erst gegen Ende des 19. Jhs. wesentlich überschritten. Das Arbeitsfeld selbst wird in den Humboldt-Rezensionen von Pott (1837) und Bopp (1840) als bei Humboldt vorfindlich gesehen: "Abgesehen von historischer Verwandtschaft, lassen sich die Sprachen in drei Klassen eintheilen, je nachdem sie entweder der Isolirung, der Flexion oder Agglutination sich bedienen; dies sind, wie der Verf. bemerkt, die Angelpunkte, um welche sich die Vollkommenheit des Sprach-Organismus dreht", sagt Bopp (1840: 719), sich auf Humboldt (1836: 119) beziehend. Pott (1837: 492) sagt, daß Humboldt sich bei der "charakteristischen Unterscheidung der Hauptklassen von Sprachen" besonders auf den Satzbau gestützt habe; es geht um "vornehmlich vier Hauptunterschiede [...]: Isolirung oder das Auseinander im Monosyllabismus; Agglutination; Flexion; Einverleibung oder massenhafte Aufhäufung im Polysynthetismus, und diesen entsprechen, [...] wenigstens im Allgemeinen und nach der Hauptrichtung ebensoviele, dadurch abgesonderte Sprachklassen" (Pott 1837: 495). Für Pott stand dies als das auch von Humboldt Gemeinte fest. Schleicher (1858: 3—4, Anm.) hat Potts Überblicksdarstellung von 1848 gelesen und nach den geläufigen drei (statt Potts vier) Klassen korrigiert; seiner Meinung nach "gebührt die priorität in der aufstellung dieser drei classen mir", er habe sie "nach genauem studium des Humboldt'schen werkes (einleitung zur kawisprache) und nach mühsamer durchforschung aller mir zugänglichen grammatiken sehr vieler sprachen zuerst aufgestellt" (Schleicher 1858: 4, mit Bezug auf Schleicher 1848). Diesen Anspruch hat er erst, als er auf A. W. Schlegel (1818) hingewiesen worden war, zurückgenommen (Schleicher 1861: 258). Steinthal schließlich fand bei Humboldt (1836: 119—132) eine "Zweitheilung der Sprachen" (Steinthal 1852: 10), die er mit seinen eigenen klassifikatorischen Entwürfen nur verdeutlichen wollte. Er ging Humboldt gegenüber so weit, daß er schließlich in seiner Humboldt-Ausgabe (1884: 654, vgl. Humboldt 1836: 326) eine Überschrift "Classification der Sprachen" einführte, was aber nur zeigt, wie unsicher auch sein Anschluß an Humboldt in dieser Sache ist.

1.2. Arbeitsinteressen

Der seit Ende des 19. Jhs. hervorstechende Gegensatz zwischen genealogischer und negativ von daher bestimmter typologischer Klassifikation wurde in der nachhumboldtischen Sprachforschung durchaus gesehen, er spielte aber eine auffallend geringe Rolle. Man ging davon aus, daß der Herkunft nach verwandte Sprachen auch ihrem Bau nach ähnlich waren, und umgekehrt wich man der Kenntnisnahme der doch beträchtlichen Struktur-Unterschiede zwischen den alten und neuen europäischen Sprachen aus, weil sie ja gleichen Ursprungs waren. Der Umkehrschluß von der strukturellen Ähnlichkeit auf die Herkunftsgemeinschaft muß nahegelegen haben, und zumindest für das mittlere Drittel des 19. Jhs. fällt die Fülle von Arbeiten auf, die sich mit Großgruppen über das Indogermanische hinaus beschäftigen. Meist ging es um das Semitische (vgl. als Überblick Delitzsch 1873: 4—21), aber es gab auch prominente Beispiele in anderer Richtung, namentlich Bopps Versuche, das Malaiische und die südkaukasischen Sprachen als mit dem Indogermanischen verwandt zu erweisen. Es ist nun gewiß kein Zufall, daß diese Versuche in eine Zeit der letzten Nachblüte der sog. 'allgemeinen Grammatik', zumindest im Bereich der Schullehrbücher, fallen. Die Linguisten waren tatsächlich bis weit ins 19. Jh. hinein von dieser Tradition geprägt, die auch auf ihre Auffassung von der Sprachklassifikation Einfluß hatte: Von da her erklärt sich die Ausrichtung der aufgestellten Typenreihen auf einen Kulminationspunkt hin, in dem die klassischen Schulsprachen (Latein, Griechisch) einen Zustand vertreten, wo die von der 'allgemeinen Grammatik' betonten kognitiven Leistungen sprachlicher Strukturelemente optimal realisiert erscheinen. Auch Steinthal, der 1855 sich nicht gegen die allgemeine Grammatik überhaupt wandte, sondern gegen eine naiv naturalistische Spielart von ihr, verstand die Klassifikation der Sprachen ausdrücklich als "die wahre allgemeine Grammatik" (Steinthal 1855: 387); sein Klassifikationsentwurf von 1860 erweist sich als Rekonstruktion des allgemeingrammatischen Arbeitsprogramms, wo die Sprache selbst den logischen Maßstab hervorbringt, an dem der Kulminationspunkt der 'Sprachvollendung' abgelesen werden kann.

Im Gegensatz zu diesen einfachen Linearisierungen steht das Modell des sprachstrukturellen Kreis- oder Spirallaufs, wie Georg von der Gabelentz es vertreten hat (Gabelentz 1891: 250). Hier ist die Feststellung einer Strukturierungsform nicht mehr zugleich eine Einordnung in einen einmaligen Entwicklungsgang, denn die gleiche Strukturierung kann immer wieder erreicht werden. Eine solche Sichtweise ist schon bei Jacob Grimm angedeutet, wenn er die Entsprechungen im indogermanischen, germanischen und hochdeutschen Konsonantismus als 'Verschiebung' von Zuordnungen innerhalb eines begrenzten Inventars deutet und anmerkt: "Die begonnene bewegung hat nicht eingehalten, sondern ihren kreis erst in der hochdeutschen mundart erfüllt" (Grimm 1822: 8). Schleicher (1860: 70—71) jedoch hielt die Annahme, die Sprachentwicklung führe durch "große Kreisläufe von Isolirung zu Flexion, von Flexion zu Isolirung und so fort" zwar für "etwas bestechendes", dem aber die Erfahrung widerspreche. Mehr als dies ist es freilich die geschichtsphilosophisch begründete (vgl. Jaritz 1992) Annahme, daß "Sprachbildung und Geschichte [...] sich ablösende Thätigkeiten des Menschen" seien (Schleicher 1860: 35) und daß strukturelle Komplexität nur einmal, vorhistorisch, aufgebaut und dann nur noch abgebaut werde: Die Sprachgeschichte wird auch in struktureller Hinsicht unumkehrbar.

1.3. Periodisierung

Es lassen sich also drei Generationen (d. h. Altersgruppen von Linguisten) auseinanderhalten, in denen das Arbeitsthema der Sprachklassifikation von der einfachen Anlehnung an das bei Humboldt Abgelesene wegentwickelt wurde. In der ersten Generation kam Pott (1802—1887) zu einer ersten Formulierung des recht schlichten Inventars (vgl. Pott 1848: 186—187), während der mit Humboldt wenigstens in indologischen Dingen im Gedankenaustausch stehende Bopp (1791—1867) auf diesem Grundmodell stillschweigend aufbaute. Bereits Pott (1833: xxvi) sah, "daß der Classification ein doppelter Eintheilungsgrund untergelegt werden kann; — ich möchte sie den physiologischen und den genealogischen nennen"; aber in der Praxis war die 'physiologische' Klassifikation nur für den groben Rahmen gut, innerhalb dessen strukturell als einheitlich gesehene 'Sprachfamilien' genealogisch dargestellt wurden. Der zweiten Generation ging es stärker um Einpassung der gefundenen Typenfolge in einen (ideal-)historischen Ablauf, wobei Schleicher (1821—1868) beim Grundmodell ansetzte, während Steinthal (1823—1899) dem seine eigene, seiner Ansicht nach enger an Humboldt angelehnte Klassifikation entgegensetzte. Bei beiden ist die in den Sprachtypen durchlaufene Geschichte kurz und auf den Gipfelpunkt der klassischen indogermanischen Sprachen hinzielend, wie es den geschichtsphilosophischen Erwartungen ihrer Zeit entsprach. Die dritte Generation ließ die geschichtsphilosophischen Schematismen hinter sich, behielt aber die Konzeption der Typenreihe als nicht mehr einmalige, sondern zyklisch wiederholbare Abfolge bei. Gabelentz (1840—1893) hatte im "Spirallauf der Sprachgeschichte" (Gabelentz 1891: 250) die Eigenständigkeit der nun 'typologisch' genannten Sprachverschiedenheit gegenüber der nur voranschreitenden genealogischen Diversifizierung anschaulich gemacht. Delbrück (1901: 47) sagte: "Wie bekannt, hatten sich die Sprachforscher einmal dahin geeinigt, die Sprachen nach ihrem Bau in isolierende, einverleibende, agglutinierende und flektierende einzuteilen. Aber diese Klassifikation ist uns allmählich unter den Händen zerronnen", und er wußte, daß zwischen 'agglutinierenden' und 'flektierenden' Sprachen "ein grundsätzlicher Unterschied nicht besteht", daß Einverleibung auch außerhalb der dafür angeführten Beispielsprachen vorkommt "und (was vielleicht das Wichtigste ist) daß die isolierende chinesische Sprache einst eine flektierende war" (ebda.). Bezeichnend für diese ganze Generation ist, daß er "an der

Aufstellung einer alle Sprachen umfassenden Klassifikation verzweifelt" (Delbrück 1901: 48). Im folgenden ist zunächst nur von der ersten und zweiten Generation zu reden.

2. Morphologische Klassifikation

2.1. Pott

In seinem Referat von 1848 geht es Pott, zwischen einer "philosophischen Seite" der Sprachwissenschaft und einer "eigentlichen Philologie" der Sprachen mit einer Literatur (Pott 1848: 185, 188), um zwei Arten von "Eintheilung und Gruppirung der Sprachen des Erdbodens, ungefähr nach Weise der Naturkundigen" und "zu ermitteln durch die sprachvergleichende Methode" (S. 185), nämlich erstens "Nach physiologischen Unterschieden in dem Sprachbaue" (S. 186) und zweitens "Nach genealogischen Verwandtschaften oder Nichtverwandtheit", wobei erst dies "Eigentliche Linguistik als Gegenbild und Grundlage der Ethnographie" ist (S. 187). Für Humboldt (1836: 105) war die Sprache insofern ein "vollständig durchgeführter Organismus", als sich an ihr nicht nur in quasi anatomischer Operation Teile, "sondern auch Gesetze des Verfahrens, oder [...] vielmehr Richtungen und Bestrebungen desselben" feststellen ließen, die er im gleichen medizinischen Bild vom lebenden Körper "mit den physiologischen Gesetzen vergleichen" wollte. Nur steht bei Humboldt dieser Gedanke gerade im Gegensatz zu dem an eine Klassifikation (vgl. Borsche 1981: 216). Trotzdem ist die Einteilung in vier Arten von Sprachen ausdrücklich "Nach W. v. Humboldt" (Pott 1848: 186). Es sind dies

1) die isolierenden Sprachen, "in welchen noch Stoff (Wurzel: Hauptbegriff) und Form (Ableitungs- und Abbiegungsmomente: Nebenbegriffe, Bestimmung) in völliger Getrenntheit beharren";
2) die agglutinierenden Sprachen, "worin Stoff und Form fast nur äußerlich an einander kleben";
3) "Eigentlich Flexivische Sprachen, in denen innige Durchdringung von Stoff und Form stattfindet, so daß beide sich zur unauflöslichen Einheit verschmelzen" (S. 186);
4) "Einverleibende, durch Aggregation namentlich den Kern des Satzes, das Verbum, überlastende Sprachen" (S. 187), eine Klasse, als deren besonderes Merkmal noch "Polysynthese" angegeben wird.

Wenn "Nr. 3 die eigentliche Norm" ist, die in 1) und 2) unterschritten wird, kann Pott (S. 186) sich noch auf Humboldt berufen, daß aber 4) "transnormal" sein soll, leuchtete schon Zeitgenossen nicht ein. Schleicher (1848: 9–10, Anm.) hatte sicherlich recht, wenn er zwischen 2) und 4) keinen "wesentlichen Unterschied" sah: Was im Bau des einzelnen Wortes als Agglutination erscheint, ist im Satzbau als Einverleibung bestimmbar (vgl. Coseriu 1972: 130). Potts Beispiele für isolierende Sprachen sind Chinesisch und "die sog. Indochinesischen Idiome" (Pott 1848: 186), also von Humboldt behandelte Sprachen. Dagegen spielen seine Beispiele für agglutinierende Sprachen, "die sogenannten Tartarischen Sprachen", keine Rolle bei Humboldt, der sich an entlegenen Stellen auf die agglutinierenden Sprachen, "wie fast alle Amerikanischen sind" (Humboldt 1836–39 II, 283), bezog, also auf Potts einverleibende Beispielsprachen. Als die flexivischen Sprachen werden bei Humboldt und bei Pott die indogermanischen und die semitischen Sprachen behandelt. Was Pott als Einverleibung überhaupt den amerikanischen Sprachen zuschreibt, wurde bei Humboldt (1836: 169) nur am 'Mexikanischen' (Aztekischen) als "Mexicanische Einverleibungsmethode" abgelesen, war aber nicht als auf diese Sprache, auch nicht auf die amerikanischen Sprachen allein bezogen, sondern als strukturelle Möglichkeit grundsätzlich aller Sprachen zu verstehen (vgl. Coseriu 1972: 122–123). Pott ist offensichtlich im Unrecht, wenn er Humboldts 'physiologisches', auf ein Sprachganzes ausgehendes Interesse für die Sprachklassifikation reklamiert (vgl. Borsche 1981: 215–216) und mit den Überlegungen zu strukturellen 'Methoden' zusammenführt.

2.2. Bopp

Diese Ineinssetzung ist ihm nicht gedankenlos unterlaufen; vielmehr geht es um ein ganzes Arbeitsprogramm, wo es nicht auf partielle Beschreibung vieler verschiedener Sprachen ankam, sondern auf klare Verhältnisse in einigen wenigen Sprachen. Die Reihe von Sprachklassen konnte erstens als Folge von Schritten in einer strukturellen Entwicklung gelesen werden, und zweitens hatten in ihr die indogermanischen Sprachen einen wohldefinierten Platz. Bei Humboldt war es um Flexion als Wortformung und "Act des selbstthätigen Setzens durch Zusammenfassung" (Humboldt 1836: 250) und um "Auffindung des synthetischen Actes im Sprachbaue" in

Unterscheidung von der "Ersetzung durch unadäquate Analoga" von Formen (S. 251) gegangen. Nunmehr wurde die Verbindung der indogermanischen Flexion mit einem vorflexivischen Zustand interessant, weil sie die Grundlage dafür war, die von Friedrich Schlegel aufgebrachte Deutung der Flexion als 'innere Modifikation der Wurzel' (die "Schlegelsche Evolutionstheorie" [Delbrück 1919: 163]) zugunsten der als die "Boppsche Theorie" bekannten "Zusammensetzungs- oder Agglutinationstheorie" (Delbrück 1919: 70−71) zurückzuweisen.

Bopp selbst hat allerdings eine andere Klassifikation vorgeschlagen, die ohne Bemühung Humboldts allein aus dem Widerspruch gegen die Schlegelschen Klassifikationen entwickelt ist. Sie nimmt ausdrücklich drei Klassen an,

1) "Sprachen ohne eigentliche Wurzeln und ohne Fähigkeit zur Zusammensetzung und daher ohne Organismus, ohne Grammatik" (Bopp 1868−71 I, 204) mit der Beispielsprache Chinesisch;
2) "Sprachen mit einsylbigen Wurzeln, die der Zusammensetzung fähig sind, und fast einzig auf diesem Wege ihren Organismus, ihre Grammatik gewinnen" (S. 205−206). Hierunter fallen "die indo-europäische Sprachfamilie, und außerdem alle übrigen Sprachen, sofern sie nicht unter 1 oder 3 begriffen sind, und in einem Zustande sich erhalten haben, der eine Zurückführung der Wortformen auf ihre einfachsten Elemente möglich macht" (S. 206). Es ist also noch mit einer vierten Klasse zu rechnen, dem Rest von Sprachen, die nicht historisch-vergleichend behandelt und nicht klassifiziert werden können.
3) "Sprachen mit zweisylbigen Verbalwurzeln und drei nothwendigen Consonanten als einzigen Trägern der Grundbedeutung". Dies ist die Klasse und Familie der semitischen Sprachen; sie "erzeugt ihre grammatischen Formen nicht bloß durch Zusammensetzung, wie die zweite, sondern auch durch bloße innere Modification der Wurzeln" (ebda.).

Bopp wendet sich gegen den von Friedrich Schlegel im Blick auf das Indogermanische vorgetragenen Gedanken "von Flexionen als für sich bedeutungslosen Sylben" (ebda.), weil er darin den Versuch sieht, indogermanische und semitische Flexion gleich zu behandeln, aber eben damit verabschiedet er Humboldts Deutung der Flexion als wahrer Form, wo "gar nicht zwei Elemente, sondern nur Eines, in eine bestimmte Kategorie versetztes, das Doppelte ausmacht", das, "wenn man es auseinanderlegt, nicht gleicher, sondern verschiedener Natur ist, und verschiedenen Sphären angehört" (Humboldt 1836: 121). Bopp hat mit seinem eigenen Klassifikationsvorschlag keinen Anklang gefunden, aber man kann sicher sein, daß er, was die Gestalt der allgemein akzeptierten Klassifikation angeht, umso einflußreicher gewesen ist.

2.3. Schleicher

Der Orientalist (nicht nur Indologe) Böhtlingk, der es für nötig erachtete, seiner Beschreibung des Jakutischen ein paar Seiten über Sprachklassifikation vorauszuschicken, bezog sich noch allein auf Pott (1848) und das sich gegen Pott wendende Buch Steinthals von 1850 (Böhtlingk 1851: xxvii). Bald aber trat in Handbüchern und Einleitungen eine noch einfachere Klassifikation hervor, so bei Benloew (1858: 67) in

1) langues monosyllabiques;
2) langues agglutinantes ou agglutinatives ("qui combinent une série de mots primitifs, mais sans les fondre en un tout véritablement organique");
3) langues à flexion ("où la combinaison a amené cette fusion, et où la trace des éléments constitutifs du mot s'est effacée pour tout autre que pour un linguiste expérimenté" [S. 67−68]).

Benloew nennt keinen Namen, aber der Linguist, der diese Klassifikation vollends zum Gemeingut gemacht hat, war August Schleicher (vgl. Schleicher 1848: 6−12; 1850a: 7−10; 1860: 11−26). Er betrachtete als eine Hauptaufgabe der Sprachwissenschaft "die ermittelung und beschreibung der sprachlichen sippen oder sprachstämme, d. h. der von einer und der selben ursprache ab stammenden sprachen und die anordnung diser sippen nach einem natürlichen systeme" (Schleicher 1861−62, I: 1). Auch sein Gegner Steinthal redete einmal von einer Klassifikation der Sprachen "nach Art des Pflanzensystems von Jussieu" (Steinthal 1970 [1850b]: 134, Anm.): Die "Methode des Jussieu" (Jussieu 1844, IV/1: 38, gemeint ist Antoine Laurent de Jussieu) arbeitet mit dem Prinzip der "Unterordnung der Kennzeichen" (subordination des caractères), d. h., der Bündelung kopräsenter Merkmale, die jeweils so durch ein einziges Merkmal vertreten werden, "daß ein Theil der Organisation einer Pflanze im voraus durch einen einzigen

Punkt angezeigt ist" (S. 39); sie verspricht, das Geschäft des Zusammenordnens weit über die augenfälligen Ähnlichkeiten einzelner Arten zu größeren Einheiten hin voranzutreiben: "Die Kenntniß aller dieser constanten Verhältnisse zwischen den verschiedenen Theilen, welche es möglich machen, von dem Theile auf das Ganze, wie von dem Ganzen auf den Theil zu schließen, ist die Grundlage der natürlichen Methode, und wenn diese Kenntniß vollkommen wäre, so könnte man sagen, daß die Methode die Wissenschaft selbst sei" (S. 40). Auf sprachliche Verhältnisse übertragen deutet das Bild vom 'natürlichen System' also ein sehr anspruchsvolles Programm der zusammenhängenden Beschreibung an, und Schleicher sieht ein: er kann die Sprachen "vorläufig am leichtesten nach irer morphologischen beschaffenheit an ordnen" (Schleicher 1861–62, I: 3). Neben der Morphologie (als "lere von der äußeren lautlichen form der sprache") steht die "lere von der function der einzelnen teile des wortes und des wortes selbst", wo es besonders um den "gegensatz von nomen und verb" geht: "In den kreiß dieser ins innerste wesen der sprache vor dringenden forschung zu treten, wage ich zur zeit noch nicht, da es mir hier an leitenden grundanschauungen und an methode noch gebricht" (Schleicher 1859: 1). Später hat er es gewagt (Schleicher 1865), wobei das Vorbild Steinthals leitend geworden zu sein scheint (vgl. entsprechende Vorhaltungen, Steinthal 1865).

Schleichers Morphologie rechnet mit Wörtern und einer Teilung "in zwei elemente, in bedeutung und beziehung; beide kommen in der sprache nur vereint vor und bilden zusammen das wort" (Schleicher 1859: 2). Es besteht einerseits aus der Wurzel, die für Schleicher durchaus "den lautlichen außdruck der bedeutung" leistet (ebda.). Ist die 'Beziehung' ohne Lautform, nur als 'Funktion' nachgewiesen, "fält sie nicht ins gebiet der morphologie" (S. 3, Anm.). Schleichers Notation rechnet außer mit Wurzeln (einfache Majuskeln: A) mit Beziehungsausdruck durch "wurzeln (worte) algemeinerer bedeutung" (ebda.) ($\acute{A}$), unterschieden vom spezialisierten "beziehungslaut" (einfache Minuskeln: a). Dieser "kann in die wurzel hinein treten" (ebda.) ($\acute{A}$); anderseits kann sich die Wurzel "zum zwecke des beziehungsaußdruckes regelmäßig verändern, so daß also die beziehung nunmer symbolisch bezeichnet wird" (S. 3–4) (A^a). Den ersten Fall ($\acute{A}$) vertritt z. B. das Nasal-Infix des indogermanischen Verbs im Präsens (lat. *rump-it*, 'bricht', *rup-it*, 'brach'), wo der Lautbestand der Wurzel bleibt; im zweiten Fall (A^a) geht es um den Ablaut, wo ein veränderter Lautbestand der 'Wurzel' Wortinhalt und 'Beziehung' darstellt. Weiter ist an Veränderung des Lautbestands "nicht sowol zum zwecke des beziehungsaußdruckes, als vilmer um die bedeutung in gewisser weise zu ändern" (S. 7) ($\underline{A}$), etwa durch Negation. Schließlich ist beim Beziehungsausdruck bedacht, daß "die den wortstamm bildenden elemente" (als a usw.) unterschieden werden "von den casussuffixen, personalbezeichnungen des verbi und verwantem" (ebda.) (als α usw.): das ist, durch europäische Leser seit Friedrich Schlegel vermittelt, die *vibhakti* der Sanskritgrammatik (Pāṇini 1.4.104; Böthlingk [1887: 42] spricht von "Personal- und Casusendungen"), die Bestandteil einer Wortdefinition ist (Pāṇini 1.4.14).

Der ersten, isolierenden Klasse entsprechen die morphologischen Formeln A und $A + \acute{A}$ (sowie $\acute{A} + A$ und $A + A + \acute{B}$) mit Beispielen aus dem Chinesischen (das sich aber mit einigen Erscheinungen "nicht nur nach classe II. sondern auch nach classe III. neigt" [Schleicher 1859: 11]), dem Kassia (d. h. Khasi), Namaqua (d. h. Nama, Hottentottisch) und Birmanisch (nach Humboldt 1836: § 24).

Der zweiten, "zusammen fügenden" Klasse entspricht die Formel Aa und $Aa\alpha$, mit zahlreichen Beispielsprachen: Ungarisch, Türkisch, Jakutisch, Mandschu, Samojedisch. Die "südafrikanischen" Sprachen (d. h. Bantusprachen) stehen für Formeln wie $\acute{A} + Aa$ oder $Aa + Ab$, in denen die als pronominal gewerteten Präfixe des Verbs und Nomens erfaßt sind. Ähnlich ($aA + \acute{A}$ usw.) wird das Tibetische gedeutet. Schleicher (1859: 4) spricht hier von einer besonderen "combinierenden" Klasse, aber nur als "eine besondere Abart der zweiten, der anfügenden Classe" (Schleicher 1860: 15).

Die beiden Sprachgruppen der dritten, flektierenden Klasse, Semitisch und Indogermanisch, unterscheiden sich so in ihren Formeln, daß Semitisch mehrere Möglichkeiten (A^a, aA^a, aA^ab, A^aa, bA^a) realisiert, Indogermanisch dagegen fast nur die Formel A^aa.

Von dem "morphologischen systeme der sprachen" hält Schleicher (1859: 37) "die historische, die (wenn ich so sagen darf) leibliche verwantschaft der sprachen" getrennt: "Denkbarer weise können selbst verwante sprachen, sprachen, die von einer grundsprache ab stammen, verschidene morphologische form haben" (ebda.). Er meint dabei aber nichts Indogermanisches, sondern "den so genanten [sic] finnisch-tatarischen sprachstamm, dem man auch die drawidischen sprachen, das japanische und villeicht noch anderes bei geselt" (1859: 38, Anm.).

3. Die neuphilologische Nische

Die Indogermanistik vertraute auf die Transparenz möglichst früher Sprachzustände und war an der strukturellen Charakteristik späterer Zustände wenig interessiert. Schleicher verlegte die "Entwicklung der Sprache" mit vollständigem oder teilweisem Durchlaufen der drei Sprachklassen in die Vorgeschichte (Schleicher 1848: 21—22). Für die Verfallsgeschichte dagegen bietet sich "der allgemeine Gegensatz synthetischer und analytischer Sprachen, ferner speciell das Beispiel der romanischen Sprachen und des Prakrit, die sich aus Latein und Sanskrit auf eine überraschend ähnliche Weise entwickelt haben", was ihn vermuten läßt, daß "sämmtliche indogermanische Sprachen, ja Sprachen nicht indogermanischen Stammes einen im wesentlichen übereinstimmenden Verlauf [...] zeigen" (Schleicher 1848: 26). Eine solche Periodisierung setzt eine ziemlich kurze Verlaufszeit voraus. Jacob Grimm sah die ältesten Sprachdenkmäler "um viele jahrtausende", also keine Jahrzehntausende, "von dem wirklichen ursprung der sprache oder der schöpfung des menschengeschlechts auf erden" getrennt (Grimm 1864: 259); es bleibt Zeit nur für einmaligen Auf- und Abbau. So ist im Neuindischen, Neupersischen, Neugriechischen und Romanischen "die innere Kraft und Gelenkigkeit der Flexion meistens aufgegeben und gestört, zum Teil durch äußere Mittel und Behelfe wieder eingebracht" (S. 281). Besonders die romanischen Sprachen führen immer wieder auf die an romanischem Material entwickelte inner-indogermanische Klassifikation in synthetische und analytische Sprachen (A. W. Schlegel 1818: 16). Humboldt (1836: 284) kennt die "analytische Methode", und Diez (1836—44, III: vii) sieht "bereits gewisse analytische Erscheinungen im Latein" und nicht nur "die Grammatik synthetischer Sprachen" (Diez ²1856—60, II: 3). Daneben zeigt sich in Ansätzen eine konkurrierende Redeweise, die von der Charakterisierung dieser Sprachen als der "Lateinischen Töchtersprachen" durch Humboldt (1836: 286, 290, 294) ausgeht, der einmal das Latein als ihre "fremde Muttersprache" bezeichnet (S. 294). Wenn Bopp (1840: 698) behauptet, "daß der Malayisch-Polynesische Sprachzweig ein Abkömmling des Sanskrit-Stammes ist, daß er zu demselben in einem töchterlichen Verhältnisse steht, während die meisten Europäischen Sprachklassen dem Sanskrit schwesterlich die Hand reichen", meint Schwesternschaft strukturelle Ähnlichkeit und Tochterschaft das Gegenteil davon. Schleicher (1860: 28) ignoriert diese Implikation für die "Tochtersprachen" und "Enkelsprachen" des Sprachenstammbaums; Steinthal (1849: 368) dagegen definiert die Tochtersprache als "eine Sprache, welche von einem andern Volke, als dem sie ursprünglich angehört, oder auch von letzterm, aber mit fremden sehr einflussreichen Stämmen vermischte Volke, nach einem neuen Principe entwickelt, d. h. umgeformt worden ist", und er schlägt vor, "Töchtersprachen" wie die romanischen und "secundaire Sprachen" ohne Umformung wie das Deutsche als die analytischen Sprachen zusammenzufassen (ebda.). Aber keiner dieser Begriffe hat in der damaligen Fachdiskussion eine Rolle gespielt.

4. Ethnographische Impulse

Max Müller, ein literaturwissenschaftlich arbeitender Sanskritist und in der Sprachwissenschaft ein nach außen wirkungsvoller, von den Fachkollegen aber nicht besonders ernstgenommener Popularisierer (vgl. Delbrück 1919: 94), findet in der Geschichte der Naturwissenschaften, "in deren Reihe die Sprachwissenschaft jetzt zum ersten Mal eingefügt zu werden beansprucht" (M. Müller 1863—1866, I: 4), eine empirische, klassifizierende und theoretische Periode (ebda.): Es werden "Thatsachen gesammelt" und geordnet, und zuletzt "fragt [...] der Forscher, woher dies alles stamme und was es bedeute" (S. 16). Die Klassifikation steht im Schatten der Ursprungsthematik; unter Klassifikation ist einfach das Vergleichen zu verstehen, weshalb das Sanskrit einen "vollständigen Umschwung in dem classificatorischen Studium der Sprachen" herbeiführen konnte (S. 139). Genealogische Klassifikation sei nur in "absterbenden Sprachen" möglich, wo es nur um "das Fortschreiten der phonetischen Corruption" geht (S. 145), während alle Sprachen auf Wurzeln reduziert und in morphologische Klassen (radikal oder isolierend: mit unverbundenen Wurzeln, terminational oder agglutinativ: von zwei verbundenen Wurzeln wird eine unselbständig, inflektional: beide werden unselbständig) geteilt werden können. Die so festgestellten Einheiten, etwa die (agglutinierenden) turanischen Sprachen, sollen zugleich genealogisch zusammenhängen (S. 243—244). Dies ist aber nur eine Oberfläche, denn mit Berufung auf Humboldt, daß nämlich "language is the outward expression of what he calls the spirit or individuality of a nation" (M. Müller 1854: 22) werden die drei Klassen als "'Family', 'Nomad' and 'State' languages" interpretiert (ebda.). Eine Nomadensprache etwa ist agglutinierend, damit "sie vielen verständlich bleibe" (M. Müller 1863—66, I: 247), wo immer der Nomade hinkommt.

Bei Max Müller wird neben den Sprechergruppen die Sprachstruktur zur unselbständigen Variablen, und die drei Sprachklassen fügen sich dem auffallend gut. Das hat damit zu tun, daß sie nicht bloß Strukturen beschreiben, sondern sie auf das flektierte Wort 'unserer' klassischen Sprachen hin orientieren. Erst der Zustrom von Sprachmaterial aus Übersee veränderte die Verhältnisse so, daß ein Bearbeiter von solchem Material fragen konnte: "was ist unsere Sprachforschung oder Linguistik heut zu Tage mehr als eine einseitige Betrachtung der flectirenden Sprachen?" (F. Müller 1867: 5).

5. Humboldtianische Klassifikation: Steinthal

Die von Steinthal (1850a, 1852, 1860) vertretene Sprachklassifikation trifft sich mit der morphologischen Klassifikation in der Anlehnung an Humboldt, und sie ist besonders deutlich in der Fortsetzung allgemeingrammatischer Anliegen wie der Bewertung von Sprachen und der Erhebung der Flexion zum Kriterium dafür. Aber sie nimmt die modernen indogermanischen Sprachen zur Kenntnis. Und sie stellt sich entschieden gegen die morphologische Klassifikation und versucht stattdessen, geleitet von dem Konzept der 'inneren Sprachform', die Sprachen als ganze zu erfassen. Steinthal bestimmt die 'innere Sprachform' zwar, im Anschluß an Äußerungen Humboldts (1836: 103) bezüglich "der nothwendigen Synthesis der äußeren und inneren Sprachform", als Verbindung von Laut und Anschauung bzw. Vorstellung (Steinthal 1855: 204), aber er nimmt für sie ein dialektisches Fortschreiten vom fast bloßen Laut zur fast bloßen Vorstellung an (vgl. Ringmacher 1996: 106—110), das nach durchlaufenem Zyklus keinen anderen Zugang als die Introspektion offenläßt. Steinthal galt bei seinen Zeitgenossen als unverständlich, als "ein schwer verständlicher Philosoph" (Delbrück 1919: 111), und ein Gipfel der Unverständlichkeit ist sein Konzept der Formsprache, für ihn "der Kern der Classification der Sprachen" (Steinthal 1855: 363).

Er hat drei Anläufe zu einer Sprachklassifikation unternommen, von denen zwei (Steinthal 1850a, 1860) hier zu besprechen sind. Die erste Klassifikation, das "System der Sprachen als die Entwicklung der Sprachidee" (Steinthal 1850a: 82), stützt sich auf 13 Sprachgruppen: I. die hinterindischen Sprachen ("nebensetzend"), II. der malajo-polynesische Stamm ("Inhaltsbestimmungen durch Wortformung ausdrückend"), III. die Sprache der Kaffern- und Congo-Stämme [also Bantu] ("Beziehung der Wörter durch Präfixe ausdrückend"), IV. Mandschuisch, Mongolisch ("Formbestimmungen durch den Wurzeln angefügte Stoffwörter ausdrückend"), V. die türkischen Dialekte ("durch Zusammensetzung der Wurzel mit dem Verbum substantivum conjugirend"), VI. der uralische oder finnische Stamm ("den Wurzeln Endungen anbildend"), VII. das Chinesische ("nebensetzend"), VIII. das Mexikanische ("einverleibend"), IX. die nordamerikanischen Sprachen ("vielzusammensetzend"), X. das Vaskische ("vielanbildend"), XI. das Aegyptische ("anfügend"), XII. das Semitische ("beugend" und "innerlich symbolisch abwandelnd"), XIII. das Sanskritische [Indogermanische] ("beugend" und "anbildend"). I.—VI. sind "Stoff und Form vermischend", I.—IV. "ohne Kategorien", II.—IV. "abwandelnd", V.—VI. "die Kategorien des Seins und der Thätigkeit scheidend", VII.—XIII. "Stoff und Form scheidend", VII.—IX. "Nomen und Verbum nicht scheidend", X.—XIII. "Nomen und Verbum scheidend". Zugleich sind I.—IV. "Sprachen unvollkommener Form", V.—XIII. "Sprachen vollkommenerer Form", I.—IX. "Formlose Sprachen", X.—XIII. "Sprachen mit Formen" (ebda.). An diesem Schema ist vor allem bemerkenswert, daß Steinthal (1850a: 14) "alle vorgängigen Classificationen in der meinigen" repräsentiert sieht: VII.—XIII. erinnert ihn an A. W. Schlegel, das Verhältnis von Semitisch (XII) und Indogermanisch (XIII) an Bopp, alles übrige an Humboldt. Die Tafel von 1860 ist viel übersichtlicher, sie umfaßt nur noch acht Sprachgruppen: I. Die hinterindischen Sprachen, II: Die polynesischen, III. Die ural-altaischen, IV. Die amerikanischen, V. Das Chinesische, VI. Das Aegyptische, VII. Das Semitische, VIII. Das Sanskritische (Steinthal 1860: 327). I.–IV. sind "formlose Sprachen", V.–VIII. "Form-Sprachen", I. und V. "nebensetzend", II.–IV. und VI.–VIII. "abwandelnd". Natürlich ist damit nicht die Gesamtheit der Sprachen der Welt abgedeckt. Man wird es so zu verstehen haben, daß die vier Gruppen von Formsprachen den Kernbestand ausmachen und die vier genannten formlosen Gruppen nur die nächstliegenden Fälle von 'Scheinformen' sind. Dem Hinweis von 1850 folgend findet man in den Formsprachen das gängige Dreierschema wieder, mit einer (äußerlich) isolierenden (Chinesisch), einer (äußerlich) agglutinierenden (Ägyptisch) und zwei flektierenden Gruppen, und für die "formlosen" Sprachen hat Steinthal Humboldts Rede von "vollkommneren" und "unvollkommneren" Sprachen von ihrer Gradualität (vgl. Humboldt 1836: 301) befreit. Er läßt sich nicht beirren durch Hinweise auf chinesische "Unvollkommenheit der Sprachbildung" (S. 285) und die Unterscheidung "der von dem wahren Begriff der grammatischen Formen ausgehenden (flectirenden) und der unvollkommen zu ihnen hinstrebenden (agglutinirenden) Sprachen" (S. 255), denn er liest an den Flexionsformen etwas ab, das er auf die innere Geformtheit der Sprachen bezieht. Ihm geht es um kongruierende Formen wie den indogermanischen Nominativ (auf -s) und die Personen-Endungen des Verbs (vgl. Ringmacher 1996: 138, 141). Für die Formsprachlichkeit des Ägyptischen ist maßgeblich, daß es ein grammatisches Genus und eine auf Kongruenz aufbauende Satzsyntax hat (Ringmacher 1996: 174). Chinesisch als Formsprache ohne Formen erreicht einen geformten Satz ohne die Hilfe geformter Wörter (Steinthal 1860: 113), wobei die Stellung des direkten Objekts nach dem Prädikat, im Gegensatz zur Voranstellung von Attributen, wichtig wird (S. 115).

Steinthal lehnt einen allgemeinen (und allgemein bleibenden) Begriff von Sprache ab (denn er führt ihn dialektisch weiter in die Bestimmtheit als Einzelsprache, dann Rede) und setzt dagegen die "Sprachidee" (Steinthal 1850a: 58) als Gesamtheit der die gleichen Ausdrucksleistungen erfüllenden Sprachen, so daß "nach dem Verhältnisse der einzelnen Sprachen zu den allgemeinen Forderungen der Sprache überhaupt" (S. 24) zu fragen ist. Auf die Bewältigung der Forderungen hin betrachtet ist sie "Idee der Sprachvollendung", wobei die Vollendung darin liegen soll, daß die erfolgreichsten Sprachen, die indogermanischen (eigentlich das Griechische) das begriffliche Denken aus sich entlassen und damit den Maßstab für die Beurteilung aller Sprachen liefern (vgl. Ringmacher 1996: 176). Dieser schwierige Gedankengang zielt auf den Versuch, einen offensichtlich von der allgemeinen Grammatik herkommenden 'sprachkritischen' Impuls vor dem Vorwurf des Arbeitens mit unangemessenen Kriterien zu schützen. Da zur Zeit, als das vorgetragen wurde, die allgemeine Grammatik von der rein historischen Forschung aus dem Feld anerkannter linguistischer Arbeitsinteressen verdrängt wurde, kann man es so sehen, daß die Sprachklassifikation, in ihren beiden von Schleicher und Steinthal verantworteten Großformen, einen historischen Moment lang und gewissermaßen nebenher der alleinige Vertreter einer strukturell interessierten allgemeinen Linguistik und insoweit sicherlich zukunftweisend war.

6. Bibliographie

Benloew, Louis. 1858. *Aperçu général de la science comparative des langues pour servir d'introduction à un traité comparé des langues indo-européennes*. Paris: Durand.

Böhtlingk, Otto von. 1851. *Über die Sprache der Jakuten. 1, Einleitung. Jakutischer Text. Jakutische Grammatik*. St. Petersburg: Akademie der Wissenschaften.

—. 1887. *Pâṇini's Grammatik*. Leipzig: Haessel.

Bopp, Franz. 1840. [Rezension von Humboldt (1836–39)]. *Jahrbücher für wissenschaftliche Kritik*. Jahrgang 1840. 697–741.

—. 1868–71. *Vergleichende Grammatik des Sanskrit, Zend, Armenischen, Griechischen, Lateinischen, Litthauischen, Altslavischen, Gothischen und Deutschen*. 3. Auflage, 3 Bände. Berlin: Dümmler.

Borsche, Tilman. 1981. *Sprachansichten: Der Begriff der menschlichen Rede in der Sprachphilosophie Wilhelm von Humboldts*. Stuttgart: Klett-Cotta.

Coseriu, Eugenio. 1972. "Über die Sprachtypologie Wilhelm von Humboldts: Ein Beitrag zur Kritik der sprachwissenschaftlichen Überlieferung". *Beiträge zur vergleichenden Literaturgeschichte. Festschrift für Kurt Wais zum 65. Geburtstag* hg. von Johannes Hösle, 107–135. Tübingen: Niemeyer.

Delbrück, Berthold. 1880. *Einleitung in das Sprachstudium: Ein Beitrag zur Geschichte und Methodik der vergleichenden Sprachforschung*. Leipzig: Breitkopf & Härtel. (6. Auflage, Leipzig 1919.)

—. 1901. *Grundfragen der Sprachforschung mit Rücksicht auf W. Wundts Sprachpsychologie erörtert*. Straßburg: Trübner.

Delitzsch, Friedrich. 1873. *Studien über indogermanisch-semitische Wurzelverwandtschaft*. Leipzig: Hinrichs.

Diez, Friedrich. 1836—44. *Grammatik der romanischen Sprachen*. 3 Bände. Bonn: Weber. (2. Auflage. Bonn 1856—60.)

Fuchs, August. 1849. *Die romanischen Sprachen in ihrem Verhältnisse zum Lateinischen*. Halle: Schmidt.

Gabelentz, Georg von der. 1891. *Die Sprachwissenschaft, ihre Aufgaben, Methoden und bisherigen Ergebnisse*. Leipzig: Weigel.

Grimm, Jacob. 1822. *Deutsche Grammatik*. Erster Theil, zweite Ausgabe. Göttingen: Dieterich.

—. 1851. "Über den Ursprung der Sprache". *Abhandlungen der Königlichen Akademie der Wissenschaften zu Berlin*. 1851. (Zitiert nach *Kleinere Schriften* I, 255—298. Berlin: Dümmler, 1864.)

Humboldt, Wilhelm von. 1836. *Über die Verschiedenheit des menschlichen Sprachbaues und ihren Einfluß auf die geistige Entwickelung des Menschengeschlechts*. Hg. von Eduard Buschmann. Berlin: Dümmler.

—. 1836—39. *Über die Kawi-Sprache auf der Insel Java*. Hg. von Eduard Buschmann. 3 Bände. Berlin: Akademie der Wissenschaften.

—. 1884. *Die sprachphilosophischen Werke*. Hg. von H. Steinthal. Berlin: Dümmler.

Jaritz, Peter. 1992. "August Schleicher und Hegel, der viel geschmähte Meister". *Beiträge zur Geschichte der Sprachwissenschaft* 2. 57—76.

Jussieu, Adrian von [Adrien de]. 1844. *Die Botanik*. Übersetzt von G[eorg Matthias] Kißling. 4 Bände in 6 Teilen. Stuttgart: Scheible, Rieger und Sattler.

Lehmann, Winfred P. 1991. "Franz Bopp's Use of Typology". *Zeitschrift für Phonetik, Sprachwissenschaft und Kommunikationsforschung* 44. 275—284

Morpurgo Davies, Anna. 1998. *History of Linguistics*. Bd. IV: *Nineteenth-century Linguistics*. London: Longman.

Müller, Friedrich. 1867. *Reise der österreichischen Fregatte Novara um die Erde in den Jahren 1857, 1858, 1859, unter den Befehlen des Commodore B. von Wüllerstorf-Urbair, Linguistischer Theil*. Wien: Hof- und Staatsdruckerei.

Müller, Max. [1854]. *Letter to Chevalier Bunsen, on the Classification of the Turanian Languages*. London: Longman, Brown, Green & Longmans.

—. 1863—66. *Vorlesungen über die Wissenschaft der Sprache*, für das deutsche Publikum bearbeitet von Carl Böttger. 2 Bände. Leipzig: Mayer.

Mueller-Vollmer, Kurt. 1993. *Wilhelm von Humboldts Sprachwissenschaft. Ein kommentiertes Verzeichnis seines sprachwissenschaftlichen Nachlasses*. Paderborn: Schöningh.

Plank, Frans. 1991. "Hypology, Typology: The Gabelentz puzzle". *Folia linguistica* 25: 421—458.

Pott, August Friedrich. 1833. *Etymologische Forschungen auf dem Gebiete der Indo-Germanischen Sprachen, mit besonderem Bezug auf die Lautumwandlung im Sanskrit, Griechischen, Lateinischen, Littauischen und Gothischen*. Band 1. Lemgo: Meyer.

—. 1837. [Rezension von Humboldt (1836)]. *Allgemeine Literaturzeitung auf das Jahr 1837*, April, Nr. 60—65. 475—519.

—. 1848. "Die wissenschaftliche Gliederung der Sprachwissenschaft: Eine Skizze". *Jahrbuch der freien deutschen Akademie* 1. 185—190.

Ringmacher, Manfred. 1996. *Organismus der Sprachidee: H. Steinthals Weg von Humboldt zu Humboldt*. Paderborn: Schöningh.

Schlegel, August Wilhelm de. 1818. *Observations sur la langue et la littérature provençales*. Paris: Librairie grecque-latine-allemande.

Schleicher, August. 1848. *Sprachvergleichende Untersuchungen*, Bd. I: *Zur vergleichenden Sprachengeschichte*. Bonn: König.

—. 1850. *Linguistische Untersuchungen*, Bd. II: *Die Sprachen Europas in systematischer Übersicht*. Bonn: König. (Wiederabdruck, Amsterdam: Benjamins, 1983.)

—. 1858. "Kurzer abriß der geschichte der slawischen sprache". *Beiträge zur vergleichenden Sprachforschung auf dem Gebiete der arischen, celtischen und slawischen Sprachen* 1. 1—27.

—. 1859. *Zur Morphologie der Sprache*. St. Petersburg: Akademie der Wissenschaften. (*Mémoires de l'Académie impériale de St.-Pétersbourg*, 7. Reihe, Band I, Nr. 7.)

—. 1860. *Die deutsche Sprache*. Stuttgart: Cotta.

—. 1861. "Zur Morphologie der Sprachen". *Beiträge zur vergleichenden Sprachforschung auf dem Gebiete der arischen, celtischen und slawischen Sprachen* 2. 256—260, 460—463.

—. 1861—62. *Compendium der vergleichenden Grammatik der indogermanischen Sprachen*. Weimar: Böhlau.

—. 1865. "Die Unterscheidung von Nomen und Verbum in ihrer lautlichen Form". *Abhandlungen der Königlich sächsischen Gesellschaft der Wissenschaften*, Phil.-hist. Klasse 1865: 495—587.

Steinthal, H. 1849. [Rezension von Fuchs (1849)], *Allgemeine Literaturzeitung*, 1849, 189, col. 353—355, 190, col. 366—368.

—. 1850a. *Die Classification der Sprachen dargestellt als die Entwickelung der Sprachidee*. Berlin: Dümmler.

—. 1850b. "Der heutige Zustand der Sprachwissenschaft". *Allgemeine Monatsschrift für Literatur* 1, 1850: 208–217. (Zitiert nach *Kleine sprachtheoretische Schriften* hg. von Waltraud Bumann, 114–138. Hildesheim: Olms)

—. 1852. *Die Entwicklung der Schrift, nebst einem offenen Sendschreiben an Herrn Prof. Pott.* Berlin: Dümmler.

—. 1855. *Grammatik, Logik und Psychologie, ihre Prinzipien und ihr Verhältniß zueinander.* Berlin: Dümmler.

—. 1860. *Charakteristik der hauptsächlichsten Typen des Sprachbaues.* Berlin: Dümmler.

—. 1865. [Rezension von Schleicher (1865)]. *Zeitschrift für Völkerpsychologie und Sprachwissenschaft* 3. 497–506

Veldre, Georgia. 1992. "Zur Diskussion über den Begriff 'Tochtersprache' im 19. Jahrhundert". *Historiographia Linguistica* 19. 65–96.

Manfred Ringmacher, Berlin (Deutschland)

174. Sprachtypologie und Ethnologie in Europa am Ende des 19. Jahrhunderts

1. Einleitung
2. Im Umkreis der Völkerpsychologie
3. Zwischenbilanzen
4. Georg von der Gabelentz
5. Bibliographie

1. Einleitung

Das letzte Viertel des 19. Jhs. als die Zeit, in der die vergleichende Bearbeitung der indogermanischen Sprachen im Kanon des akademischen Unterrichts Fuß faßt, ist zugleich die Epoche, in der die Bemühungen, die auf einen Strukturvergleich von Sprachen ausgehen, aus der zerfallenden Einheit der vergleichenden Linguistik hinaus in die disziplinäre Selbständigkeit entlassen werden. Gabelentz hat dann vorgeschlagen, das neue Arbeitsgebiet "Typologie" zu nennen (Gabelentz 1894; vgl. Plank 1991). Unter den gegebenen Umständen war dies ein Weg in die Bedeutungslosigkeit: Zwischen lauter Einzelsprachen und genetisch verbundenen Sprachgruppen war eine allgemeine Linguistik leicht zu vergessen. Insbesondere aber war die Suche nach strukturellen Ähnlichkeiten zwischen Sprachen nur noch als Bestätigung genetischer Gruppierungen geduldet, und die allzu kühnen Vergleichungen begannen, gerade weil als Behauptungen weitgreifender genealogischer Zusammenhänge gemeint, peinlich zu werden und dem Spott der Fachwelt anheimzufallen; das hat etwa der Afrikanist Leo Reinisch (1832–1919) erfahren, als er die "Sprachen der alten Welt" miteinander in Verbindung brachte (Reinisch 1873). Grundsätzlich wurde das Thema der Strukturverschiedenheit der Sprachen an die Ränder des Gesamtfaches abgedrängt, insbesondere in die Beschreibung außereuropäischer Sprachen, die gerade in dieser Zeit des weltweiten wirtschaftlichen und administrativen Ausgreifens der europäischen Staaten in steigender Anzahl in Europa bekannt wurden, auch wenn weiterhin galt: "Sprachforscher von Fach kommen selten in die Lage, an Ort und Stelle Materialien sammeln zu können" (Gabelentz 1892: 1). Für das, was Ende des 19. Jhs. in dieser Hinsicht möglich geworden war, steht beispielhaft Friedrich Müller (1834–1898), Professor für vergleichende Sprachwissenschaft und Sanskrit in Wien, aber auch Bearbeiter des linguistischen und des ethnographischen Teils der "Reise der österreichischen Fregatte Novara um die Erde" (Müller 1867, 1868) und Autor eines *Grundrisses der Sprachwissenschaft* (Müller 1878–88), in dem er sich zwar über die bestehenden Sprachklassifikationen wohlinformiert zeigt, selbst aber im Gang der Darstellung ("aus dem einfachen Grunde, dass sowohl die morphologische als auch die psychologische Classification [der Sprachen] in letzter Instanz behufs der wissenschaftlichen Anordnung ihres Stoffes auf die genealogische Classification sich beziehen müssen" [Müller 1876: 82]) sich an der Einteilung der Sprecher in Rassen orientiert. Bemerkenswerterweise interessiert er sich auch für Humboldt "als einen Sprachforscher […], der, was Sorgfalt und Gründlichkeit der Forschung anlangt, von keinem erreicht, geschweige denn übertroffen wird" (Müller 1867: v). Er läßt sich Manuskripte Humboldts schicken, muß dann aber gestehen, dem Gelesenen habe er "leider nur Weniges entnehmen können, da die Notizen Humboldt's über mehrere südamerikanische Sprachen entweder auf gedruckte Quellen zurückgehen oder aus denselben Handschriften stammen, welche Vater seinerzeit für seinen Mithridates benutzt hatte" (Müller 1882: viii). Denn gerade eine ethnographisch interessierte Linguistik hat inzwischen hohe Ansprüche an die Verläßlichkeit von gesammelten Sprachzeugnissen, seitdem auch außereuropäische Feldforschung möglich geworden ist. Trotz alledem zieht er sich aber das scharfe Urteil Saussures zu, Leute wie er hätten die Linguistik kein Stück weitergebracht (Godel 1954: 66). Es ist Ende des 19. Jhs. noch weit bis zur Anerkennung ethnolinguistischer Forschung und auch bis zur Anerkennung der Sprachtypologie. Hugo Schuchardts 1892 vorgetragene Einschätzung, der "wirkliche, der innere Fortschritt der Sprachwissenschaft" scheine ihm "in d[...]er anthropologisch-ethnologischen Richtung zu liegen, nur in ihr" (Spitzer 1928: 104), steht im Widerspruch zur allgemeinen Überzeugung. Doch gerade unter den ungünstigen Bedingungen dieser Zeit gibt es unübersehbare Manifestationen eines sprachtypologischen Interesses, das nicht nur mit einem verspäteten Arbeitsanliegen hinter dem damaligen Desinteresse herhinkte, sondern dem kommenden Interessenumschwung vorausgeeilt ist.

2.1. Im Umkreis der Völkerpsychologie: Neubeginn bei Wundt

Die 'Völkerpsychologie' war sicherlich ein Arbeitsgebiet, von dem erwartet werden konnte, daß es inmitten der indogermanistischen Begeisterung nicht einfach untergehen würde. Sie hatte von ihrer anfänglichen Prägung durch Steinthal nicht nur die Absicht, über die Sprache hinaus die Gesamttätigkeit der Gemeinschaften von Sprechern zu würdigen, sondern auch ein ausgeprägtes klassifikatorisch-typologisches Interesse an den Sprachen mitbekommen. Allerdings war ihr Verhältnis zur Sprachwissenschaft immer ein gespanntes, und die von Steinthal erreichte Einheit wurde bald wieder in Frage gestellt. Psychologie und Linguistik gehen dabei ganz verschiedene Wege.

In der Psychologie ist das Weitere dadurch bestimmt, daß Wilhelm Wundt (1832—1920) die Beschränkung auf Individualpsychologie in einer "ergänzenden Untersuchung der an das Zusammenleben der Menschen gebundenen psychischen Vorgänge" überwinden will (Wundt 1900: 1: 1), die er "Völkerpsychologie" nennt, weil diese Bezeichnung "nun einmal eingeführt ist" (S. 3). Aus dem Gegenstandsbereich seiner Völkerpsychologie schließt er aber die vorgefundene "spezielle Völkerpsychologie", die "Analyse der geistigen Eigenthümlichkeiten der einzelnen Rassen und Völker" (ebda.), als psychische Ethnologie aus, ebenso "auch andere Gebiete menschlicher Geistesthätigkeit", insbesondere alle "Erscheinungen [...], die zwar das gesellschaftliche Dasein des Menschen zu ihrer Grundlage haben, selbst aber durch das persönliche Eingreifen Einzelner zu Stande kommen" (S. 4). Als Gegenstände bleiben die Sprache, der Mythos (und die "Anfänge der Religion"), die Sitte (und "die Ursprünge und allgemeinen Entwicklungsformen der Cultur"), als "Gebiete gemeinsamen Vorstellens, Fühlens und Wollens" betrachtet, ohne Rücksicht auf den "Einfluss hervorragender Individuen, welche die überlieferten Formen willkürlich gestalten" (S. 24—25). Wundt sagt über die Sprache grundsätzlich, was er als Nichtfachmann bei den Fachleuten vorfindet, weshalb ihm auch vorgehalten worden ist, daß er "sich in dem einen oder anderen Falle zu wenig mit der neueren Forschung in Fühlung gehalten hat" (Delbrück 1901: 175). Umso bezeichnender ist darum, wie beiläufig er im Kapitel über "Wortbildung" den "Sprachtypus" als "eine bestimmte Art der Verbindung und der Entwicklung der Sprachwurzeln" (Wundt 1900 I: 1, S. 549) und als eine überwundene Sache der Vergangenheit von sich weist. "Noch undurchführbarer" erscheint ihm aber, wenn die Art der Unterscheidung von Stoff- und Formelementen in einer Sprache zur Grundlage ihrer Bewertung gemacht wird (S. 551): Für Wundt sind die Klassifikationen von Schleicher wie von Steinthal (→ Art. 174) etwas Überwundenes.

2.2. Beschränkung auf Linguistik: Misteli, Winkler

Als der Basler Indogermanist Franz Misteli (1841—1903) Steinthals Buch über Sprachklassifikation (Steinthal 1860) neu bearbeitete, ging es ihm nur um allgemeine Sprachwissenschaft und darum, sich "auf das Wissbare und rein Sprachliche einzuschränken, wiewohl auch so noch die Völkerpsychologie nicht leer ausgeht und zweifelsohne manchem die eine oder andere Stelle mystisch genug klingen mag" (Misteli 1893: viii). In seiner Neubearbeitung war er bestrebt, sich in allen behandelten "Sprachstämmen eine selbständige Auffassung zu erwerben, nicht sowohl durch das Studium der Wörterbücher und Grammatiken, [...] als zumeist der Texte, deren Studium namentlich in Sprachen, die noch keine eindringende grammatische Behandlung erfahren, einzig richtige Wege weist" (ebda.). Er gesteht zu, "das von Steinthal gegebene Sprachmaterial habe hier Veränderung und Vermehrung erfahren, wenn auch der Geist der Bearbeitung derselbe geblieben" (S. ix), aber Treue in dieser Hinsicht kann er allenfalls für die einzelnen Sprachdarstellungen beanspruchen, während die von ihm hinzugefügte Einleitung das Ganze zu einem sehr selbständigen Werk macht. Hier unterscheidet er

1) die "flectirenden oder ächtwortigen" Sprachen (Semitisch und Indogermanisch), die ihm "wegen des richtigen Verhältnisses von Wort und Satz, insofern nämlich Subject und Prädicat, Prädicat und Object, Attribut und Regens gesondert auseinander treten, als Formsprachen" gelten (S. 99);
2) die "agglutinirenden oder scheinwortigen Sprachen" ("uralaltaische" und dravidische Sprachen), die "wegen des schwankenden Verhältnisses von Wort und Satz" formlose Sprachen seien (S. 100);
3) die "einverleibenden oder satzwortigen Sprachen" (Mexikanisch, Grönländisch), "ohne Frage" auch formlos (ebda.), und
4) einen "nichtwortigen" Rest in drei Gruppen: (a) die "Wurzel-isolirenden" (Chinesisch, Siamesisch [Thai], vielleicht "Barmanisch"); (b) die "Stammisolirenden" (Malaiisch und Dajak); (c) die "anreihenden" Sprachen (Ägyptisch und Bantusprachen) (ebda.).

Davon werden Chinesisch und Ägyptisch "wegen der befriedigenden Gestaltung des ganzen Satzes, obschon sie nicht ein wahres Verb besitzen" (S. 107) als Formsprachen anerkannt.

Das Endergebnis respektiert also zwar äußerlich Steinthals Klassifikation bis hin zu dessen vier Formsprachen, aber Misteli interessiert sich viel mehr für die sechs Strukturtypen, in denen er einen bei Steinthal neben der Bestimmung von Formsprachlichkeit herlaufenden Aspekt der Sprachtypen in den Vordergrund hebt. Als Finnougrist und Kenner des Ungarischen und Finnischen (vgl. Simonyi 1911) lehnt er Steinthals Schluß von der Formsprachlichkeit auf die Eignung als "Cultursprache" ab: "Dagegen auf psychische Typen weisen die verschiedenen Sprachstämme allerdings und damit auf die Pflege verschiedener Culturzweige, wenn sie überhaupt zu Cultursprachen sich ausbilden" (Misteli 1893: 109).

Im Gegensatz zu Mistelis Bedenken gegenüber dem Begriff der Formsprache baut Heinrich Winkler (1849−1930) seine Bemühung um die "fundamentalen Verschiedenheiten des indogermanischen und des uralaltaischen Sprachbaues" (Winkler 1888: 257) ganz von diesem Konzept her auf. Er betont, er habe sich in seiner Arbeit "wenig oder gar nicht an die Lehrbücher gehalten, sondern den umständlicheren Weg gewählt, mich durch das Studium der für die einzelnen Sprachen gesammelten Sprachproben in den Geist dieser Sprachen einzuleben", und dabei sei in ihm die "unerschütterliche Überzeugung" entstanden, daß das Finnische zu den altaischen Sprachen gehöre bzw. "dass es denselben Geist atmet" wie diese (Winkler 1909: iii). Und zwar findet er am altaischen Sprachbau eine "Richtung [...], die fast ohne alle die in unseren Sprachen des Westens üblichen flexivischen Mittel im wesentlichen dasselbe wie diese erreicht durch die Stellung der Satzteile und durch Antreten deutender Vollwörter an den näher zu bestimmenden Hauptausdruck" (S. 122). Die Betrachtung einzelner Sprachen dient nicht mehr dazu, bloß eine Klassifikation zu illustrieren, und Winkler findet zu der alten Aufgabe der Sprachcharakteristik zurück, die ihn unter den Bedingungen der großräumigen Erreichbarkeit von Sprachproben auf Ähnlichkeiten benachbarter Sprachen führt. Lewy (1961: 699) wollte Winkler zum "Begründer d[...]er linguistisch-geographischen Betrachtungsweise" erklären, was sicher übertrieben ist; aber zweifellos wurde in Winklers Generation den Forschern der areale Aspekt der Verschiedenheit im Sprachbau bewußt, zumal wenn sie sich, wie Winkler und nach ihm Finck (vgl. besonders Finck 1910), auf die Charakterisierung einzelner exotischer Sprachen einließen. Richard Lepsius (1810−1884) hielt seine Klassifikation der afrikanischen Sprachen in Bantu-Sprachen, hamitische Sprachen und Sprachen einer Übergangs- und strukturellen Mischungszone, zu der auch das von ihm beschriebene Nubisch gehörte, für eine „genealogische Gruppirung" (Lepsius 1880: xvi); er sah areale Zusammenhänge noch nicht als Problem.

2.3. Eine andere Psychologie: Byrne, Finck

In einem von der Entwicklung in der Völkerpsychologie ganz unabhängigen Entwurf betrachtet James Byrne (1820−1897) "the languages of mankind [...] with reference to the magnitude of the parts inito which they break up thought, that is, the extent of the thought or largeness of the view which is present at once to the mind of the speaker" (Byrne 1892 II, S. 276), und er findet als dem zugrundeliegend in "the mental character of the various races" einen Unterschied in der psychischen Reaktionsgeschwindigkeit, einerseits "quickness and mobility of thought", andererseits "slowness and persistence" (S. 277). Schnelle Erregbarkeit, die er in afrikanischen Völkern findet, "tends to cause language to be broken into small fragments which are thought lightly, and are ready to join as thought passes from one to another" (S. ix); die etwas verminderte Erregbarkeit, die zusammen mit "a concrete habit of thought" bei den ozeanischen und dravidischen Völkern auftritt, "tends to produce disyllabic roots" (S. x), und langsame Erregbarkeit wie in den amerikanischen Völkern "tends to form massive aggregates of elements in which the mind retains the first elements while it thinks the other" (ebda.). Nicht ganz so langsam reagieren die zentral- und nordasiatischen Völker, zwischen langsam und schnell liegen ostasiatische und "syro-arabische" Völker (ihr Reaktionsmuster "tends to divide language into single integers"), zwischen ihnen und dem ozeanischen und dravidischen Reaktionsmaß liegen die Indogermanen, von denen wiederum die Kelten am schnellsten seien. Der Parameter der Reaktionsschnelligkeit ist die Grundlage einer, Byrnes Einschätzung nach, 'natürlichen' Klassifikation, die große geographisch zusammenhängende Einheiten liefert; damit überkreuzt sich die Äußerung von "mental power"; sie "tends to unify combined elements, to give more subjectivity to the verb, and to note gender in the noun" (S. ix). Mit beiden Parametern kommt diese Klassifikation unübersehbar her von einem bis ins 19. Jhs. unangefochtenen Theoriefossil der Psychologie, der Lehre von den vier humoralen Temperamenten, die immer wieder zur Beschreibung individueller Charaktere herangezogen wurde und hier, nicht zum erstenmal, der Charakterisierung von Menschengruppen und ihren Sprachen dienstbar gemacht wird.

Misteli (1893: 109) kennt diese Psychologie; vor allem aber stützt sich auf sie Franz Nikolaus Finck (1867−1910), der ausdrücklich von vier Temperamenten spricht und sie nach 1. großer oder geringer Reizbarkeit, 2. Vorherrschen von [passiv registrierten] Empfindungen oder [aktiv zum Ausdruck drängenden] Gefühlen klassifiziert (Finck 1901: 10−11). Er nennt Byrnes Sprachen mit "quick excitability" (die afrikanischen) *anreihend*, die mit "less slow excitability" (die zentral- und nordasiatischen) *agglutinierend*, die mit "slow excitability" (die amerikanischen) *einverleibend*, bei denen mit "intermediate excitability" unterscheidet er die *wurzelisolierenden* (Chinesisch und 'Indochinesisch') und die semitischen Sprachen; nur bei der Gruppe mit "less quick excitability" (ozeanische und dravidische Sprachen) fällt Finck die Umrechnung auf Mistelis Terminologie schwerer: die ozeanischen Sprachen sind *stammisolierend* oder gehören zu den *anreihenden* Sprachen, die dravidischen Sprachen weist er den *agglutinierenden* Sprachen zu (S. 16−17). Das Merkmal, nach dem die semitischen und indogermanischen Sprachen bei Byrne als *flektierend* zusammengefaßt sind, sieht Finck (S. 19) als in Widerspruch zu den Merkmalen der übrigen Klassen stehend. Er antwortet mit dem "Vorschlag" (S. 25) einer zweidimensionalen Klassifikation (S. 27), mit

1) "Vorherrschen von Empfindungen" und "großer Reizbarkeit" (anreihende Sprachen, in Afrika);
2) "Vorherrschen von Empfindungen" und "mittlerer Reizbarkeit" (wurzelisolierende Sprachen, in Hinterindien und China);
3) "Vorherrschen von Empfindungen" und "geringer Reizbarkeit" (agglutinierende Sprachen, in Zentral- und Nordasien, Südindien);
4) "annähernd gleicher Stärke von Empfindungen und Gefühlen" und mittlerer bis großer Reizbarkeit (indogermanische Sprachen);
5) "annähernd gleicher Stärke von Empfindungen und Gefühlen" und mittlerer bis geringer Reizbarkeit (kaukasische Sprachen und Baskisch);
6) "Vorherrschen von Gefühlen" und großer Reizbarkeit (stammisolierende Sprachen in Ozeanien und Australien);
7) "Vorherrschen von Gefühlen" und mittlerer Reizbarkeit (vokalisierende Sprachen, die semitischen Sprachen);
8) "Vorherrschen von Gefühlen" und geringer Reizbarkeit (einverleibende Sprachen, die "Sprachen der amerikanischen Rasse" und Grönländisch).

Finck hat später nicht mehr ausdrücklich von den Sprechertemperamenten als Grundlage dieser Klassifikation gesprochen, ist aber bei eben diesen acht Bautypen geblieben. Winkler, der sich von der Psychologie der Temperamente immer ferngehalten hat, möchte denn auch "eine ungleich größere Menge von ähnlichen Haupttypen annehmen" (Winkler 1911: 60). Schuchardt (1902: 274) sieht seine Erwartung "dass geistige Eigenart ["das Temperament der Sprachträger"] und Weltanschauung ["innere Sprachform"] wirklich scharf auseinandergehalten und als mittelbare und unmittelbare Grundlage des Sprachbaus erörtert werden" von Fincks Entwurf nicht erfüllt. Tatsächlich ist nicht so sehr die zugrundegelegte Psychologie wie das schlichte aufzählbare Ganze der Finckschen Klassifikation und vor allem die exemplarische Charakterisierung einzelner Sprachen (Finck 1910) wirksam geblieben.

3. Zwischenbilanzen

In den zeitgenössischen Überblicksdarstellungen zur Klassifikation der Sprachen äußert sich ein Unbehagen gegenüber den verfügbaren Klassifikationen; fast immer wird Beschränkung auf die genealogische Klassifikation, wie von F. Müller vorgeführt, empfohlen. Zwar will Abel Hovelacque (1843–1898), den Adam (1881: 229) zu den Anhängern Schleichers zählt, allein die klassische morphologische Klassifikation gelten lassen (Hovelacque 1878: 54), aber wenn er sich gegen die genealogische Klassifikation wendet, meint er nur Friedrich Müller, dessen Gleichsetzung von Sprachklasse und Menschenrasse er für dem Fortschritt in der Anthropologie und der *ethnologie linguistique* schädlich hält (S. 55). Seine auf Schleicher (1859) aufbauende Typologie (Hovelacque [1883–1889]) findet allerdings bei den Anthropologen keinen Anklang. – Der Amerikanist Lucien Adam (1833–1918) geht ebenfalls von den selbstverständlich gewordenen drei morphologischen Typen (Adam 1881: 217) aus, referiert die Diskussionen um die Flexion, wo er vorschlägt, die Wortveränderungen in den semitischen Sprachen nicht 'Flexion', sondern 'Version' zu nennen, und entscheidet sich für eine korrigierte Liste (Adam 1881: 245):

1) Isolierende Sprachen (Chinesisch, Annamitisch [Vietnamesisch], Siamesisch [Thai], Birmanisch, Tibetisch);
2) Versionelle Sprachen (Semitisch);
3) Agglutinierende Sprachen (alle, die nicht unter 1. 2. 4. 5. fallen);
4) Harmonische Sprachen (Uralaltaisch [wegen der Vokalharmonie]);
5) Flexionssprachen (Indogermanisch).

In freier Anlehnung an Whitney (1875: 174), der andere Klassifikationen gar nicht erst erwägt, kommt er zu der Einschätzung, nur die genealogische Klassifikation sei auch eine natürliche Klassifikation, aber er folgert weiter, daß die morphologische Klassifikation an dieser Qualität teilhat, wenn ihre Klassen zugleich Stadien der Sprachentwicklung sind (Adam 1881: 246). Er verteidigt die genealogische Klassifikation gegen Max Müllers Zweifel an ihrer Möglichkeit außerhalb der indogermanischen und semitischen Sprachen (S. 262), und nimmt an, die Wissenschaft werde auch die widerspenstigsten Idiome noch meistern (S. 263).

Raoul de la Grasserie (1839–1914), ein anderer aufmerksamer Beobachter der laufenden Diskussionen mit einem Arbeitsschwerpunkt in nichteuropäischen Sprachen, kommt schließlich zu einer detaillierten Klassifikation der Sprachklassifikationen, wo die Hauptunterscheidung die zwischen der Klassifikation verwandter und nichtverwandter Sprachen ist (La Grasserie 1889–1890: 375). Grundsätzlich auf beiden Seiten ist die 'allein wahre, die genealogische' Klassifikation; die partiellen und subjektiven Klassifikationen werden nur vorläufig, in Ermangelung von Besserem, geduldet (ebda.). Bei den verwandten Sprachen ist das Ziel, die vollständige und objektive Klassifikation, erreicht oder in greifbare Nähe gerückt (S. 377). Aber auch auf der Seite der nichtverwandten Sprachen will sich La Grasserie nicht mit den vielen möglichen Teilklassifikationen begnügen. Er verweist auf 'das große Prinzip der *subordination des caractères*' in der Biologie (S. 297) und hält es auch in der Linguistik für anwendbar, derart, daß Sprachen, die in wesentlichen Dingen übereinstimmen, dies auch in anderer Hinsicht tun (S. 298): Die uralischen und die altaischen Sprachen stimmen in der Vokalharmonie überein, und zu dieser phonetischen Dominante kommen als untergeordnete Übereinstimmungen hinzu in morphologischer Hinsicht die Agglutination und in 'psychischer' Hinsicht das 'Umhüllen' (ebda., auf S. 303 ist die Rede von einem "ordre [...] enveloppant qui imite l'unité de racine"; gemeint sind suffixal abgeleitete, den Grundstamm 'umhüllende' Wortstämme), und auf dieser Grundlage läßt sich eine 'objektive' und doch nicht genealogische Familie der uralaltaischen Sprachen aufstellen. La Grasserie bleibt unschlüssig, ob der *air de famille*, die Familienähnlichkeit, nicht doch nur die letzte Spur einer sonst nicht mehr nachweisbaren alten Verwandtschaft ist, ein Spiel des Zufalls oder ein undeutliches Zeugnis gemeinsamer Herkunft (S. 338). Aber ihn trennt nur ein sehr kleiner Schritt von der Anerkennung des neuen Arbeitsfeldes, dem Gabelentz den Namen geben wird.

4. Georg von der Gabelentz

Die Erfahrung in der Sinologie (vgl. Gabelentz 1881) und der Bearbeitung zahlreicher weiterer nichtindogeranischer Sprachen hat sich bei Georg von der Gabelentz (1840–1893) in wichtigen Beiträgen zur allgemeinen Linguistik niedergeschlagen. Wenn er etwa mit den Begriffen des psychologischen Subjekts und Prädikats ("ich nenne das, woran, worüber ich den Angeredeten denken lassen will, das psychologische Subject, das, was er darüber denken soll, das psychologische Prädicat" [Gabelentz 1869: 378]) eine lebhafte Diskussion angestoßen hat, so ist er damit sicher nicht, wie angenommen worden ist (vgl. Knobloch 1988: 218, Anm. 19; S. 323), von Weil (1844) abhängig, der vielmehr im geäußerten Satz nur "eine *notion initiale*, qui est également présente et à celui qui parle et à celui qui écoute" und "une autre partie du discours, qui forme l'*énonciation* proprement dite" bzw. "le *but du discours*" (Weil 1879 [1844]: 20–21) unterschieden hatte. Er sagt, er sei von "Beobachtungen an Sprachen [...] wie die indochinesische[n], das Mandschu, das Japanische und die malaiischen und polynesischen" (Gabelentz 1875: 140–141) ausgegangen, während Weil es so sieht, daß Gabelentz im Grundsätzlichen "ne dit rien que je n'aie exposé vingt-cinq ans avant lui" (Weil 1879: viii). Gabelentz ist sicherlich auch als Vermittler älterer allgemein-linguistischer Konzepte von Bedeutung, aber das ist kein Grund, ihm die Fähigkeit zu einleuchtenden Neuansätzen abzusprechen. Was die Namengebung im Fall der Sprachtypologie angeht, ist seine Initiative (Gabelentz 1894) wegen eines Lese- und Druckfehlers (*Hypologie* statt *Typologie*) in dem postum veröffentlichten Text wirkungslos geblieben, und in dem Passus der zweiten Auflage von *Sprachwissenschaft*, wo von *Typologie* die Rede ist (Gabelentz 1901: 481), bleibt die Urheberschaft problematisch. Plank (1991: 424–428) wägt die Argumente für Gabelentz und den Herausgeber Schulenburg ab; Bartschat (1996: 91, Anm. 4) deutet an, daß ein Handexemplar eine Rolle gespielt haben kann. In Frage steht nur der Wortlaut, wo Eingriffe des Herausgebers wahrscheinlich sind, sondern noch mehr die Einordnung in den systematischen Zusammenhang des Lehrbuchs.

Es geht um die einzelne Sprache und um allgemeine Sprachwissenschaft, denn: "In der schildernden Darstellung werden die Einzelsprachen und Sprachfamilien unter den Gesichtspunkt der allgemeinen Sprachwissenschaft gerückt" (Gabelentz 1901: 479) – so beginnt das Kapitel "Die allgemeine Grammatik", in das der Absatz über Typologie eingeschoben ist. Zugleich wird die Sprachschilderung ganz auf die "Wechselbeziehungen zwischen Volksthum und Sprache" bzw. zwischen "der völker- und sprachenkundlichen [Seite]" (S. 476–477) bezogen verstanden, so daß alles Sammeln von Sprachmaterial eine "Induction" ist, die außerhalb der Sprache zu ihrem Ziel kommt. Doch in anderen Zusammenhängen kommt Gabelentz ohne solche Grenzüberschreitung aus:

"Lassen wir die historischen Sprachvergleicher noch eine geraume Weile weiterarbeiten und die anderen grossen Sprachfamilien ähnlich sorgfältig untersuchen, wie die unsere. Dann darf man hoffen, auf Grund eines reichen Inductionsmaterials Erfahrungssätze zu gewinnen, die besagen, dass im Leben der Sprachen die und die Tendenzen einander parallel gehen: 'je mehr so, desto mehr oder weniger so'" (S. 178).

Die Ausführungen von 1894 und 1901 zur Typologie korrigieren also offenbar eine Einseitigkeit der Darstellung, indem sie eine Sprachschilderung empfehlen, in der strukturelle Merkmale einer Sprache nicht mit Eigenheiten der Sprecher, sondern mit anderen strukturellen Merkmalen dieser Sprache korreliert werden. Die Sprachen, heißt es 1894, "sind freie organische Gebilde, und weil und insoweit sie dies sind, stehen alle ihre Teile zueinander in notwendigem Zusammenhange" (Gabelentz 1894: 4), doch wer diesem Zusammenhang nachgehen wollte, wäre wie die "Zigeunerin [...], die aus den Zügen der Handfläche den ganzen Menschen deutet" oder wie "Cuvier, dessen Geist aus dem einzelnen Knochen das ganze Tier aufbaute", erwiesenermaßen zum Scheitern verurteilt, denn Gabelentz kennt einen fehlgeschlagenen "ersten Versuch" (ebda.). Er meint sicher

Steinthals Vorstellung von der einen Form einer ganzen Sprache (zu Cuvier vgl. Plank 1991: 433−434). 1901 wird in dem Ansinnen, daß "wir, wie es kühne Botaniker wohl versucht haben, aus dem Lindenblatte den Lindenbaum construiren könnten", ohne Rückblicke auf frühere Versuche nur noch eine Aufgabe gesehen, der die allgemeine Sprachwissenschaft "mit ihren heutigen Mitteln" gewachsen sein müßte (Gabelentz 1901: 481). 1894 wird von "statistischer" Arbeitsform und von einer "Statistik der Konjunkturen" gesprochen (Gabelentz 1894: 4, 6), 1901 von "ziffermäßig bestimmten Formeln" (Gabelentz 1901: 481), und das Ergebnis wäre, daß "wir in untadelig exakter Weise zur Erkenntnis wahrhaft typisch entscheidender Züge gelangen" (Gabelentz 1894: 6). Die "Konjunkturen" struktureller Merkmale verweisen voraus auf die implikationelle Typologie des 20. Jhs., während auf der anderen Seite Cuviers Knochen und das Lindenblatt auch in der biologischen Einkleidung auf den Humboldtschen Gedanken vom Gesamteindruck einer Sprache zurückverweisen:

"Die charakteristische Form der Sprachen hängt an jedem einzelnen ihrer kleinsten Elemente; jedes wird durch sie, wie unerklärlich es im Einzelnen sei, auf irgend eine Weise bestimmt",

hatte Humboldt (1836: 43) gesagt. Sowohl der Gedanke einer Vernetzung der strukturellen Merkmale und der Gesichtspunkt der einzelnen Sprachen als auch der Verzicht auf den ethnologischen Seitenblick prägen das Erscheinungsbild der von Gabelentz vorgeschlagenen Sprachtypologie.

5. Bibliographie

Adam, Lucien. 1881. "Les classifications de la linguistique". *Revue de linguistique et de philologie comparée* 13.217−268.

−. 1882. *Les classifications, l'objet, la méthode, les conclusions de la linguistique.* Paris: Maisonneuve.

Bartschat, Brigitte. 1996. "Sprachwissenschaft und Sprachforschung bei Georg von der Gabelentz". *Sprachwissenschaftsgeschichte und Sprachforschung. Ost-West-Kolloquium Berlin 1995. Sprachform und Sprachformen: Humboldt, Gabelentz, Sekiguchi.* Hrsg. von Eugenio Coseriu, Kennosuke Ezawa & Wilfried Kürschner. 87−95. Tübingen: Niemeyer.

Byrne, James. 1885. *General Principles of the Structure of Language.* 2 Bände. London: Trübner. (2. Auflage, 1892.)

Delbrück, Berthold. 1901. *Grundfragen der Sprachforschung mit Rücksicht auf W. Wundts Sprachpsychologie erörtert.* Straßburg: Trübner.

Finck, Franz Nikolaus. 1899. *Der deutsche Sprachbau als Ausdruck deutscher Weltanschauung. Acht Vorträge.* Marburg: Elwert.

−. 1901. *Die Klassifikation der Sprachen.* Marburg: Elwert.

−. 1910. *Die Haupttypen des Sprachbaus.* Leipzig: Teubner. (3. unveränderte Auflage, 1936.)

Gabelentz, Georg von der. 1869. "Ideen zu einer vergleichenden Syntax: Wort- und Satzstellungen". *Zeitschrift für Völkerpsychologie und Sprachwissenschaft* 6.376−384.

−. 1875. "Weiteres zur vergleichenden Syntax: Wort- und Satzstellung". *Zeitschrift für Völkerpsychologie und Sprachwissenschaft* 8.129−165, 300−338.

−. 1881. *Chinesische Grammatik. Mit Ausschluß des niederen Stils und der heutigen Umgangssprache.* Leipzig: Weigel.

−. 1891. *Die Sprachwissenschaft. Ihre Aufgaben, Methoden und bisherigen Ergebnisse.* Leipzig: Weigel. (2. Auflage, herausgegeben von Albrecht Graf von der Schulenburg, Leipzig: Tauchnitz, 1901; Nachdruck der 2. Auflage, Tübingen: Narr, 1969, 3. Auflage des Nachdrucks, 1984.)

−. 1892. *Handbuch zur Aufnahme fremder Sprachen.* Im Auftrage der Kolonial-Abtheilung des Auswärtigen Amtes bearbeitet. Berlin: Mittler.

−. 1894. "Hypologie der Sprachen, eine neue Aufgabe der Linguistik". *Indogermanische Forschungen* 4.1−7.

Godel, Robert. Hrsg. 1954. "Notes inédites de F. de Saussure". *Cahiers Ferdinand de Saussure* 12.49−71.

Hovelacque, Abel. 1878. "La classification des langues en anthropologie". *Revue d'anthropologie* 7.47−55.

−. [1883−1889]. "Agglutination". "Flexion". *Dictionnaire des sciences anthropologiques. Anatomie, crâniologie, archéologique, préhistorique, ethnographie (mœurs, arts, industrie), démographie, langues, religions.* Herausgegeben von A. Bertillon u. a. 22−24, 493−494. Paris: Doin.

Humboldt, Wilhelm von. 1836. *Über die Verschiedenheit des menschlichen Sprachbaues und ihren Einfluß auf die geistige Entwickelung des Menschengeschlechts.* Herausgegeben von Eduard Buschmann. Berlin: Dümmler. (Nachdruck, herausgegeben von Donatella Di Cesare. Paderborn: UTB, 1998.)

Knobloch, Clemens. 1988. *Geschichte der psychologischen Sprachauffassung in Deutschland von 1850 bis 1920.* Tübingen: Niemeyer.

La Grasserie, Raoul de. 1889−1890. "De la classification des langues". *Internationale Zeitschrift für allgemeine Sprachwissenschaft* 4.374−387; 5.296−338.

Lepsius, Richard. 1880. *Nubische Grammatik. Mit einer Einleitung über die Völker und Sprachen Afrika's.* Berlin: Hertz.

Lewy, Ernst. 1961 [1952]. "Heinrich Winkler". *Kleine Schriften*, 697–700. Berlin: Akademie-Verlag.

Misteli, Franz. 1893. *Charakteristik der hauptsächlichsten Typen des Sprachbaues. Neubearbeitung des Werkes von Prof. H. Steinthal (1861)*. Berlin: Dümmler.

Müller, Friedrich. 1867. 1868. *Reise der österreichischen Fregatte Novara um die Erde in den Jahren 1857, 1858, 1859, unter den Befehlen des Commodore B. von Wüllerstorf-Urbair, Linguistischer Theil; Ethnographischer Theil*. Wien: Hof- und Staatsdruckerei.

–. 1876–88. *Grundriss der Sprachwissenschaft*. I. Band, I. Abtheilung, *Einleitung in die Sprachwissenschaft*. 1876. II. Band, *Die Sprachen der schlichthaarigen Rassen*, 1. Abtheilung, *Die Sprachen der australischen, der hyperboreischen und der amerikanischen Rasse*. 1882. Wien: Hölder.

Plank, Frans. 1991. "Hypology, Typology: The Gabelentz Puzzle". *Folia Linguistica* 25.421–458.

Reinisch, Leo. 1873. *Der einheitliche Ursprung der Sprachen der alten Welt nachgewiesen durch Vergleichung der Afrikanischen, Erythräischen und Indogermanischen Sprachen mit Zugrundelegung des Teda*. Wien: Gerold.

Schleicher, August. 1859. *Zur Morphologie der Sprache*. (= *Mémoires de l'Académie impériale de St.-Pétersbourg*, 7. Reihe, Band I, Nr. 7.) St. Petersburg: Akademie der Wissenschaften.

Schuchardt, Hugo. 1902. [Rezension von Finck 1899 und 1901.] *Literaturblatt für germanische und romanische Philologie* 23.273–279.

Simonyi, Siegmund [Zsigmond]. 1911. *Franz Misteli: Denkrede in der Gesamtsitzung der Ungarischen Akademie der Wissenschaften am 29. Mai 1911*. Leipzig: Harrassowitz.

Spitzer, Leo. Hrsg. 1928. *Hugo Schuchardt-Brevier: Ein Vademecum der allgemeinen Sprachwissenschaft*. 2. Auflage. Halle: Niemeyer.

Steinthal, H. 1860. *Charakteristik der hauptsächlichsten Typen des Sprachbaues*. Berlin: Dümmler.

Weil, Henri. 1844. *De l'ordre des mots dans les langues anciennes comparées aux langues modernes: Question de grammaire générale*. Paris: Joubert. (3. Auflage, Paris: Vieweg. 1879.)

Whitney, William Dwight. 1875. *The Life and Growth of Language*. London: Kegan Paul, Trench, Trübner & Co.

Winkler, Heinrich. 1888. "Sprachliche Formung und Formlosigkeit". *Philologische Abhandlungen, Martin Hertz zum siebzigsten Geburtstage von ehemaligen Schülern dargebracht*, 257–270. Berlin: Hertz.

–. 1909. *Der Uralaltaische Sprachstamm, das Finnische und das Japanische*. Berlin: Dümmler.

–. 1911. "Über die Haupttypen des Sprachbaues". *Memnon* 5.59–80.

Wundt, Wilhelm. 1900. *Völkerpsychologie: Eine Untersuchung der Entwicklungsgesetze von Sprache, Mythus und Sitte*. Erster Band: *Die Sprache*. 2 Teile. Leipzig: Engelmann.

Manfred Ringmacher, Berlin (Deutschland)

175. Language typology and ethnology in 19th-century North America: Gallatin, Brinton, Powell

1. Introduction: The study of the American Indian
2. Albert Gallatin
3. Daniel Garrison Brinton
4. John Wesley Powell
5. Conclusion
6. Bibliography

1. Introduction: The study of the American Indian

The question of language typology has been intertwined inextricably with emerging ethnological interpretation as well as descriptive data about the aborigines of North America. Anthropology and linguistics have developed in North America as mutual handmaidens resulting from their common subject matter in the study of the natural and social history of the New World. The characteristic four-subdiscipline approach of American anthropology — including physical anthropology, cultural anthropology or ethnology, linguistics and prehistoric archaeology — has usually been attributed to the unity and ubiquitous presence of the American Indian subject (e.g., Hallowell 1960).

Only in North America did anthropology emerge 'in the field' with the scholars and the subjects of their study sharing the same land and eventually independent nation-state. This meant that the Americans had urgent motives for studying the Indians among whom their own society emerged: pressures of land on the expanding frontier, ongoing hostilities between Indians and whites, persistent policies of assimilation and Christianization, and federal government responsibility for the welfare of the first peoples of the continent in a rapidly changing world. By the 18th century, the study of the American Indian was a major component of the scholarly effort emanating from Europe to describe and categorize all of the world's languages. American scholars were in correspondence with their counterparts in France, Germany, Russia and England. As indigenous scholars, they were the experts on the languages of the Indians (though this was hardly the way the Indians saw them). Early observers focused on the typological similarities of the American languages in contrast to more familiar grammatical categories of Indo-European languages. The inflectional or polysynthetic character of the American languages was taken as clear evidence that the Indians were fundamentally different from Europeans. This masked the considerable differences among the American Indian languages.

1.1. Professionalization of American anthropology

The relationship between language typology and language history in American anthropology and its linguistic sub-branch has been a dynamic one, closely tied to the emerging professionalization of the discipline from the mid-18th through the end of the 19th century. The three major figures in the study of language typology − Gallatin, Brinton and Powell − represent an increasingly professional attitude toward science and its institutionalization within American society.

Swiss-born Albert Gallatin (1761−1849) was the most distinguished among a generation of Americanist scholars building on the Enlightenment comparativist and progressivist tradition (Bieder 1986: 17; Wolfart 1967). He was a statesman whose scientific work was strictly amateur. His reference group was a scholarship of language typology based in Europe, although also pursued by a number of other distinguished American scholars. The American Philosophical Society founded by Benjamin Franklin (1706−1790) in 1769 was modelled directly on the Royal Society in London; Gallatin was elected in 1821, Brinton in 1869, and Powell in 1889 (Andresen 1990: 52−53). The Society included American Indian languages among the interests of its historical and literary committee by 1815, largely through the efforts of Stephen Peter Duponceau (1760−1844) and John Pickering (1777−1846).

Daniel Garrison Brinton (1837−1899) was also an amateur ethnologist and linguist, but he used his association with the American Philosophical Society as a way to pursue interests of publication and lecturing in both ethnology and linguistics that were not available to Gallatin a generation earlier. Brinton attempted to develop professional anthropology within museum and university contexts in Philadelphia and defined himself as an anthropologist for much of his career. Nonetheless, he never held a paying position as an anthropologist and was self-educated in his avocational field. Like Gallatin, he was deeply immersed in European scholarship, and served to introduce the work of Wilhelm von Humboldt to a North American audience (Brinton 1885).

John Wesley Powell (1843−1902), founder of the Bureau of American Ethnology in 1879, was the first person to organize a professional institution employing anthropologists. The Bureau depended on government funding and its mandate was constrained by practical uses of ethnological and linguistic information. Increasingly, during the late 19th and early 20th centuries, museums and universities developed professional anthropological research and publication programs as well als providing professional training on the German model of graduate education (Darnell 1998).

Institutions for dissemination of anthropological information were developing during the same period. Albert Gallatin was one of the key founders of the American Ethnological Society, located in New York City, in 1842 and served as its first president. The members shared a commitment to monogenesis and progress as explanations of cultural and linguistic diversity. Meetings were held at Gallatin's home in deference to his poor health and he subsidized the Society's first two publications (Gallatin 1845, 1848). This position gave Gallatin the status of America's foremost ethnologist (Bieder & Tax 1976). A generation later, Franz Boas was able to build a power base independent of Powell's Bureau of American Ethnology by revitalizing the long-dormant American Ethnological Society. The Society's base in New York was ideal for Boas after he moved to Columbia University in 1896. The Anthropological Society of Washington, associated with the Bureau of American Anthropology and other individuals and government organizations with ethnological interests, provided the base for a national journal, the new series of the *American Anthropologist* beginning in 1898. A national association, the American Anthropological Association, followed in 1903, a year after the death of Powell. Linguistics was much slower to develop disciplinary autonomy, with the Linguistic Society of America and its journal *Language* both beginning in 1925. During the crucial years of professionalization of science throughout North America, the mid to late 19th century, therefore, the language sciences were pursued through anthropology or in literature. The latter did not involve cross-cultural or ethnological interests and contributed little to the study of language typology.

1.2. Language typology and ethnology

Enlightenment views of language focused on documenting the diversity of human languages as evidence for a universal grammar which would represent the concepts at the basis of human rationality. So-called primitive languages, because they were believed to be simpler and older in form than those of civilized Europe, would lead scholars to the origins of language itself. In the Americas, absence of written records rendered the history of the Indians inaccessible to direct study. The problem of American Indian origins was crucial to the larger Enlightenment agenda of placing all peoples within a framework of universal reason. In this context, philology seemed to have an explanatory force that other sciences could not offer. This framing of the question, of course, was based on European scholarship and adapted to the North American environment.

There was considerable debate among Enlightenment scholars as to whether the actual Indians encountered during American geographical expansion were fully rational. Even within the thought of the same scholars, there was considerable ambivalence: on the one hand, the 'wonderful structures' of the American languages, and, on the other, the primitive nature of the Indian customs. Duponceau in 1819 coined the term 'polysynthetic' to refer to the property thought to be shared by all American Indian languages. He reconciled the absence of advanced civilization as a result of degeneration from a past that fit the sophistication of the polysynthetic languages (Bieder 1986: 28).

There were close connections between European and American scholarship. Alexander von Humboldt (1769–1859) met with Duponceau and Benjamin Smith Barton (1766–1813) in Philadelphia and with Gallatin, Thomas Jefferson (1743–1826), and James Madison (1751–1836) in 1804 (Andresen 1990: 24). This group of statesmen and avocational scholars formed the core of the early American language typology work. Wilhelm von Humboldt was interested in obtaining American data for the researches of Johann Christoph Adelung (1732–1806) and Johann Severin Vater (1772–1826) for their forthcoming overview of the world's languages; *Mithridates* appeared between 1806 and 1817, with Humboldt contributing to its last volume an analysis of Basque. The notion of a "global inventory" was not American (Andresen 1990: 25), though the American scholars willingly contributed data. American patriotism necessitated inclusion of New World data produced by home-grown scholars.

During the crucial years between 1770 and 1830, linguistics was emerging in Germany in both historical and comparative schools of thought; Sanskrit rather than American Indian languages were at the centre of the effort to inventory the world's languages (Andresen 1990: 44). Linguistic relativism vied with universalism based on rationalism. Ethnology came to be associated with the former and attracted the major attention of the American scholars in their efforts to keep up with and contribute to the new sciences in Europe.

2. Albert Gallatin

Albert Gallatin (1761–1849) was the most distinguished among the Enlightenment scholars, also including Benjamin Smith Barton, Peter Stephen Duponceau, John Pickering, Henry Rowe Schoolcraft (1793–1864), Lewis Cass (1782–1866) and Thomas Jefferson. They were statesmen and patriots as well as scholars, dedicating themselves to classifying and organizing systematic collections representing the new American environment and including its aboriginal peoples alongside its natural phenomena. Language was one of the ways of bringing order to this chaotic diversity.

The contributions of the loose group of American scholars were quite diverse. Duponceau (1760–1844) proposed a universal phonetic alphabet and postulated a single typological character for all of the Indian languages in 1819 (quoted in Andresen 1990: 101): "a wonderful organization which distinguishes the languages of the aborigines of this country from all other idioms of the known world". He believed that these forms were found everywhere from "Greenland to Cape Horn". Pickering (1777–1846) proposed a uniform orthography for the Indian languages of North America in 1820. Duponceau specialized in Algonquian languages, was based in Philadelphia and pursued French scholarly ties, whereas Pickering studied Cherokee, an Iroquoian language, was based in Boston and preferred German scholarship (Andresen 1990: 105). Both combined interests in language typology and language history. Gallatin's particular contribution was his effort to classify the languages of the American Indians. His effort in 1836 lasted until superseded by Powell in 1891.

Gallatin had left his native French-speaking Switzerland for America in 1780. After dabbling unsuccessfully in land ventures, he turned to a political career, serving for three terms in the legislature for western Pennsylvania, a brief term in the United States Senate, and six years in the House of Representatives, becoming secretary of the treasury under President Thomas Jefferson in 1801, a position he also held under Jefferson's successor, James Madison. Jefferson was wont to consult Gallatin on matters of geography, e. g., the Lewis and Clark Expedition and the acquisition of the Louisiana Territory, and on Indian affairs. Gallatin foresaw education producing full participation of Indians in the emerging American society. Land issues, in particular, depended on scientists producing accurate surveys; a stickler for detail, Gallatin carried out some of these surveys personally. He resigned as secretary of the treasury in 1813, in the midst of a war with Britain, to undertake a diplomatic mission to Russia. Gallatin remained in Europe as ambassador to France until 1823, feeling somewhat alienated from the American movement away from the agrarian liberalism which had motivated his own fiscal policies. He retired from his Pennsylvania farm to Baltimore, taking on a diplomatic mission to England in 1826. He returned to New York to devote himself to Science, particularly philology.

Methodology quickly became crucial to Gallatin's philology. He was usually forced to rely on unreliable data from untrained observers travelling among the Indians. Nonetheless, in 1823 he began working toward a classification of the Indian languages, persuading the Secretary of War to send a circular to Indian agents and missionaries enlisting their help. The government hoped for a return in terms of practical clarification of tribal units and geographical boundaries. Gallatin had more success, however, in eliciting data through the Bureau of Indian Affairs and Michigan governor Lewis Cass. *A Table of Indian Languages of the United States* (Gallatin 1826) provided the first classification based on philological principles and accompanied by a map of American tribes. Gallatin himself considered the work preliminary and in need of revision.

Synopsis of the Indian Tribes of North America (Gallatin 1836) was published by the American Antiquarian Society. This work moved fully from historical classification of languages into language typology. Gallatin took for granted the distribution throughout the American continents of what Duponceau had characterized as polysynthetic languages; all Indians would eventually progress from savagery to barbarism to civilization because of the unity of the whole human species. Gallatin elaborated on the methods and evidence implicit in his 1826 chart; he presented grammatical patterns, comparative vocabularies and sentence lists in appendices. Gallatin grouped 81 vocabularies into 28 linguistic families postulated to share a common origin. He declined to reduce them to a single origin, in Asia or elsewhere, and argued that his perspective was consistent both with Old World origins of the American Indians and with the Mosaic chronology. Gallatin opposed the increasingly popular argument that polysynthesis implied degeneration of the Indians, a conclusion further confirmed by evidence from mound builder archaeology. In contrast, Gallatin argued that the polysynthetic languages of the Indians were characteristic of a primitive level of civilization. Interestingly, he emphasized geography in his philological treatise, especially subsistence patterns in relation to degree of social progress. Agriculture was the key step toward civilization and individual Indians could adopt it as their life style.

During the 1840s, a scientific racism based on concepts of polygenesis and degeneration increasingly challenged Gallatin's Enlightenment views. *Notes on the Semi-Civilized Nations of Mexico, Yucatan and Central America* (Gallatin 1845) and his monograph-length "Introduction" to *Hale's Indians of North-west America* (Gallatin 1848) cited achievements of the American civilizations of Central and South America as evidence that further progress was possible. Asian migration could not be demonstrated directly by vocabularies, although the shared structures of all American languages and the monogenetic origin of the human species made it likely. American democracy, in his view, was to include the Indians. He spoke out against the racism which was increasingly evident in America.

3. Daniel Garrison Brinton

Daniel Garrison Brinton (1837–1899) was a prominent Philadelphia Quaker physician who turned to ethnology as an avocation. He received a B. A. from Yale University in 1858 and graduated from Jefferson Medical School in 1860. He served as a surgeon in the Union Army during the Civil War. In 1874, Brinton retired from active medical practice to edit the weekly *Medical and Surgical Reporter*, a periodical contributing to the professionalization of American medicine. In 1887, he retired from business to devote himself entirely to ethnology. Brinton carried over his scientific interests and training from medicine into ethnology.

Brinton also concerned himself with the professionalization of anthropology, attempting to establish it as a field of study at the University of Pennsylvania. Technically, Brinton held the first American professorship of anthropology, but he received no salary and had no students (Darnell 1988). The largest portion of Brinton's ethnological work was presented and published through the American Philosophical Society in Philadelphia. The members, in the tradition of Gallatin, Duponceau and Jefferson, were scholars whose interests ranged widely across the social and human sciences. Brinton, in spite of his failure ever to hold paid employment as an ethnologist, was one of only four 19th-century anthropologists to serve as president of the American Association for the Advancement of Science. He was also president of the International Congress of Anthropology in Chicago in 1893. His stature as the foremost (amateur) ethnologist and linguist of his generation, at the brink of professional anthropology, is without question – in spite of the movement toward new credentials and scholarly standards in the ensuing generation.

Brinton's ethnological and linguistic interests remained consistent over his long career. His basic ideas about the psychic unity of mankind are already present in *Myths of the New World* (Brinton 1868). His lectures to the Academy of Natural Sciences in Philadelphia were published as *Races and Peoples* (Brinton 1890b) and *The American Race* (Brinton 1891). These two works clarify Brinton's fundamental ambivalence about the role of the American Indian in human evolution (Darnell 1988). On the one hand, he placed the European and the Chinese ahead of the American Indian in progress, leaving the Negro race as the exemplar of savagery. On the other hand, within the American continent, including Middle and South America, Brinton praised the many progressive accomplishments of the Indians. His *Library of Aboriginal American Literature* produced eight volumes of texts, mostly his own work on Central American languages, set a new expectation for expressive richness in so-called primitive languages (Hallowell 1960: 43). Not surprisingly, given this approach, Brinton was most interested in the languages and cultures of the high cultures of the Americas. Here, written languages and literary traditions provided documents expressing the universal human spirit in ways that were intelligible to Euro-American observers. Brinton was a distinguished bibliophile, purchasing the complete libraries of several scholars, including Abbé Brasseur de Bourbourg, and Carl Hermann Berendt. His library remains a separate collection at the University of Pennsylvania Museum.

Brinton's reputation has been much eclipsed because of dramatic changes taking place in anthropology and other American sciences at the end of the 19th century. He was an amateur in an era of increasing professionalization. His evolutionary theory was being replaced rapidly by the historical particularism of Franz Boas and his academically trained students. Poor health prevented Brinton from considering fieldwork, in an era when first-hand research increasingly defined professional status within the discipline of anthropology.

Brinton assumed that the American Indians constituted a single entity, in racial, linguistic, historical and ethnic terms. He debunked the degenerationist notion that the Mound Builders were not the ancestors of the present Mississippi Valley Indians and defended a monogenetic origin for the Indians. He was a pioneer in arguing for a phonetic basis to the Mayan script.

In line with his views on the psychic unity of mankind, Brinton believed that the origin of language could never be fully reconstructed. All present languages possessed the characteristics of rational thought which were universal among human cultures. Religion, likewise, was universal on the basis of its psychological functioning; his position is consistent with his own Quaker beliefs which were open to the possibility of individual spiritual perception through dreams and visions. He was far less interested in dogmas which separated religions.

Language was a crucial tool for ethnology in Brinton's anthropology. *The American Race* (Brinton 1891) distinguished in its subtitle "ethnographic description" and "linguistic classification". That is, Brinton adopted the comparative method of Indo-European philology in order to interpret the descriptive data of ethnology; he reasoned that both were products of the human mind and therefore comparable (Darnell 1988: 81). Like Max Müller, Edward Tylor and the Grimm brothers, Brinton assumed that mythology and philology were, in similar ways, evidence of the thoughts of so-called primitive man. This perspective, of course, led Brinton away from historical interpretations of myth and toward a universalist or structural view (an intriguing precursor of the mythological studies of Claude Lévi-Strauss). The creative thought characterizing a group of people was to be found in language, both vocabulary and grammar being crucial to explicating culture-specific meanings. Brinton held much more stringent standards for diffusion or borrowing as an explanation of cultural similarity than for psychic unity. For example, he argued (Brinton 1868) that the similarities between Iroquoian and Algonquian myths arose independently in spite of the contiguous geography location of these traditional enemies who spoke different languages.

Relying on psychic unity, Brinton argued against universal laws of language growth. Each language embodied a particular worldview. Brinton found Wilhelm von Humboldt's concept of 'inner form' a congenial way to describe language as a universal symbolic resource. Accordingly, Brinton, like Gallatin, emphasized grammar more than vocabulary, in the European mode. Another advantage of the relative emphasis on grammar, for both Brinton and Humboldt, was in "differential intuitive awareness" held by speakers, who could "reflect on lexical meanings" but would not be able to distort embedded beliefs and ideologies in the grammar (Lucy 1992: 37−38); the relation between language, thought and reality, therefore, resided primarily in grammar.

Brinton attempted to make the work of Humboldt better known in America by translating his essay on the structure of the American verb in 1885. Brinton included this paper prominently in his selected essays (Brinton 1890a). Humboldt saw "each language as an organism", with its parts tied to "the intellectual and emotional development of the nationality speaking it" so that "the fundamental laws of articulate speech" produce a philosophy of language which in turn leads to a philosophy of history because these laws "are also the laws of human thought" (Brinton 1890a: 330−331). Brinton wanted to study logical relations as expressed in languages, particularly the polysynthetic ones. He criticized the reliance of John Wesley Powell on mechanical inspection of vocabulary for ignoring the 'structural plan' of the American languages (i.e., Duponceau's polysynthetic process): "This is indeed the play of 'Hamlet' with the part of Hamlet omitted" (Brinton 1890a: 358). The world's languages would fall into "a few great classes or groups" according to their processes of word formation (Brinton 1890b). Most American Indian languages were more incorporative than analytical. Thus, they inserted accessory words within the verb so that the sentence appeared to be a single word. In his later work, Brinton acknowledged that there were some at least partial exceptions: Otomi, Maya and Sahaptin had some analytical tendencies. He denied, however, that the geographic distribution of these exceptions could shed light on the history of particular languages within the polysynthetic type. Preferences for verbs, frequency of generic particles and development of pronouns were characteristic of the American languages (Brinton 1891: 55). He was critical of Max Müller as well as Powell for seeking genetic connections without foregrounding the typological idea of incorporation or polysynthesis.

In a process akin to that of biological evolution, the typological categories of language were assumed not to be fully discrete. Following Humboldt, Brinton saw progress, as in organic evolution, by what he characterized as 'imperceptible gradations'. The standard for evaluating the different forms was the morphological flexibility of the so-called 'inflectional' languages (i.e., the Indo-European). Again, there is an ambivalence between cultural relativism and evolutionary racism.

In line with Brinton's notions of progress, he believed that linguistic change could be beneficial, by challenging the individual ability to think which was potential in every human language. Dramatic culture change often meant that "the limitations of thought imposed by the genius of the language are violently broken down" so that "the mind is thus given wider play for its faculties" (Brinton 1890a: 323). This did not, however, imply a single evolutionary sequence. For example, the Aryan languages were superior for certain purposes. Brinton wanted an analytical and grammatically simple Aryan base for an international language, in line with the natural trend of human psychic development. He proposed mixing the features of the languages of the half dozen "most cultivated nations in the world", all Aryan (1890b: 34). It was reasonable and acceptable to Brinton that the number of languages spoken in the world was decreasing. The inflected Indo-European languages would provide a basis for the internationalism of the future. It was left to individual aboriginal people to profit from culture contact and participate in the new forms.

Brinton's typological work depended on a pre-evolutionary model of types which were part of the structure of the universal mind. All of this changed dramatically with the incorporation of Darwinian thought into the language sciences. Thereafter, only historical classifications were considered non-arbitrary (Greenberg 1957: 68). By the end of Brinton's lifetime, the centre of gravity in North American linguistics and ethnology had shifted away from language typology and toward genetic relationship and language as a tool to time perspective in cultures without writing (cf. Darnell [1990: 91–96] for the continuity of such concerns in the work of Edward Sapir and other Boasian anthropologists).

Brinton's most extensive foray into historical work was in *The American Race* (Brinton 1891), the first linguistic classification to include all of North and South America. Most of the linguistic material is contained in the Linguistic Appendix with its 120 vocabularies from Mexico, Central and South America. The index includes 1400 tribal names. Geographical locations are noted, though there is no systematic map. In practice, the classification is less detailed than Gallatin's for some North American tribes and mixes ethnological and linguistic criteria in some groupings. Brinton's most significant substantive proposal was the relationship of Ute and Shoshone to Nahuatl, based on his reading of the German sources; this connection was accepted slowly because of the apparent cultural gaps between these tribes. Crucially, however, Brinton's historical work remained framed within the typological model of the larger unity of all American Indian languages.

4. John Wesley Powell

The government anthropology of John Wesley Powell (1834–1902) was built explicitly on the legacy of Gallatin, Jefferson and Lewis Henry Morgan (1818–1881). Powell was a natural history teacher from Illinois who reached the rank of Major in the Union Army during the Civil War, losing an arm in the process. In 1869 he mounted an expedition to explore the Colorado River, resulting in his appointment seven years later to head the United States Geological and Geographical Survey of the Rocky Mountain Region. Powell quickly distinguished his Survey from three larger ones under federal government auspices by his emphasis on the aboriginal cultures of the desert Southwest, working first-hand with the Ute and Shoshone languages. His argument that environment can only be understood in interaction with culture and technology for its exploitation culminated in a report on the arid lands which opposed homesteading of standard-sized parcels regardless of attention to the avilability of water resources (Powell 1878). This political position earned Powell the enmity of Congress and of the powerful land speculators who often dominated Congressional debate. Powell decided upon a strategic retreat to the newly established Bureau of American Ethnology in 1879, protected from overt political interference by the umbrella of the Smithsonian Institution, founded as the scientific arm of the United States government in 1846. Powell was free to explore ethnological diversity brought to light in the course of his geological explorations and chose to do so in the first instance on the basis of language.

Powell was committed to the idea of social evolution, a model drawn more from Herbert Spencer (1820–1881) than from Charles Darwin (1809–1881). The ethnologist who mediated these ideas in their relation to the American Indian was Lewis Henry Morgan. Powell accepted Morgan's sequence of savagery, barbarism and civilization, adding a fourth stage, enlightenment, to distinguish European civilization from all other human developments. Within such a sequence, the American Indians were seen as having reached a slightly variable range of developmental stages near the border of savagery and barbarism in spite of the surface differences between the root-gathering savages of the southwestern desert and the so-called high civilizations of Mexico and Peru.

Powell read this evolutionary framework back onto issues of linguistic typology which had lacked such connotations in their original formulation by Wilhelm von Humboldt and others. All American Indians had the same polysynthetic or incorporative languages. Therefore, grammar was not an issue in the practical task of classifying cultural diversity. It was in the realm of vocabulary that distinctions could be made among American Indian tribes and linguistic families. Oddly enough, Powell believed that grammar could change more rapidly than vocabulary with progress as a result of European contact. In fact, he assumed that evolutionary progress was tending "toward unification and mutual intelligibility", a "linguistic integration" attained through history (Andresen 1990: 195).

Powell was a self-taught linguist. His staff at the Bureau of American Ethnology, with the exception of Swiss-born Albert Samuel Gatschet (1832–1907), also were not trained in Indo-European philology. The vocabulary inspection method of linguistic classification, therefore, had the additional advantage that an amateur linguist could identify cognates indicative of prior historical relationship of two contemporary languages. Although Haas (1969) assumes that the choice of grammatical or lexical emphasis in assigning linguistic relationship was made on theoretical grounds, it is clear that Powell and his staff were constrained by their lack of linguistic training as well as by theory. Moreover, the theory of most concern to them was not linguistic at all. Social evolutionism had origins independent of the European tradition of linguistic typology. The link between grammatical evidence for genetic relationship of languages and the language typology tradition was much clearer in the work of Gallatin and to some extent Brinton. Powell's chief assistant, self-trained ethnologist William J. McGee (in Goode 1897: 377–378), expressed the overlapping and only partially linguistic reasons for basing the emerging classification of the American Indians on language:

"[...] the linguistic characters have been found to be interrelated with other characters, including those expressed in arts, industries, institutions, and beliefs, and were used in the classification only because of the essentially collective or demotic features of the Indians, they were most easily ascertained [...] the several categories of characters represented by language have been found, through study of traditions and direct survivals, to express the actual phylogenetic development of the tribes and stocks. Accordingly, each linguistic character is treated not merely as an external adventive feature, but as a product of evolution, a record of the past, and a precursor of the future. The classification of American Indians devised and applied by the bureau is accordingly a condensed expression of the sum of present knowledge concerning the origin and development of the native American people."

The Bureau of American Ethnology operated under considerable financial constraint and its mandate was explicitly pragmatic. Congress funded the Bureau in hope of practical information about the distribution and relationship of the various tribes, e. g., to enable settling appropriate tribes together on reservations. Powell and his staff were expected to produce some order in the apparent diversity of languages. In 1879 there was no map of tribal locations and no agreement on which groups were referred to by which terms. Powell therefore embarked on a series of classificatory projects. Powell revised Gallatin's questionnaires in a further public call for comparative vocabulary lists (Powell 1877, 1880), using his position as Chief Ethnologist of the Bureau to solicit informal (and unpaid) collaboration.

The various classificatory projects envisioned by Powell depended on the resources of the Smithsonian Institution, the standard repository of government manuscripts and artifacts regarding the Indians. Powell inherited 670 linguistic manuscripts in 1877 as the Bureau was being established. This gave him a data base far superior to that of Gallatin when he did his classification a generation earlier. There was never any intention to publish the full collection, which was highly technical and restricted in use to the Bureau staff and their collaborators. Powell stated proudly (Powell 1897: lxxxii): "the manuscripts constantly accessible for purposes of study are abundant — richer, it is believed, than for any other body of linguistic records of a primitive people."

Powell put James Constantine Pilling to work on a series of bibliographies cataloguing what was known about the Indians of various parts of the United States, arranged according to culture areas and linguistic families (the limitation of the Bureau's mandate). These bibliographies were never published, being intended for internal use. The entire staff worked on the 'Synonymy', a project attempting to make order within the overlapping terminologies from consecutive visitors to Indian country over the period since contact; it included brief tribal sketches as well as geographic, tribal and linguistic terms. This part of the project produced the *Handbook of American Indians North of Mexico* ed. by Frederick Webb Hodge (1864–1956) in two parts (1906, 1910). The *pièce de résistance* of the classificatory enterprise demonstrating the practical uses of science to the democratic nation was to be the linguistic classification which finally appeared under Powell's name in 1891. (Additional syntheses were planned on mortuary customs, sign language, medical practices, tribal government and mythology. The theme was one of mapping the aboriginal peoples on the basis of all possible features.)

Powell and his unacknowledged colleagues proposed 55 independent linguistic stocks, later modified by the Bureau to 58. This classification supplemented gaps in Gallatin's earlier version with systematic fieldwork by various members of the Bureau staff. In his discussion, Powell presented no linguistic evidence, although he did mention proposed connections which he had decided were not sufficiently well proven to be included. Most prominent among these were consolidations proposed by the Bureau's occasional linguistic collaborator Franz Boas for the Northwest Coast and the connection proposed by Brinton between Ute and Shoshone with Nahuatl. Powell's rejection of the latter is particularly interesting since he had personal experience with Ute and Shoshone. His linguistic analyses remained at the superficial level, even when he was personally familiar with the material. The 1891 classification must be read, in retrospect, as something of a heuristic device. Powell was interested in useful classifications of closely related peoples, not in the reconstruction of long-range historical relationships. Relative time depth was not of much interest given the assumption of typological unity throughout the Americas.

5. Conclusion

Powell's attitude toward the importance of linguistic classification, whether typological or genetic, therefore, poses a sharp contrast to work which came both before and after. Gallatin looked to the typological pattern of all or almost all American Indian languages as part of his search for their shared worldview, taking a place among the other major races of humankind; he assumed such patterns to have considerable time depth and consistency over time. In the 20th century, Boas and his students, particularly Edward Sapir, would emphasize a smaller number of historically independent linguistic families which held the potential for understanding the culture histories of tribes without writing. Both typological and genetic methods were applied to these questions. The *Handbook of American Indian Languages* (Boas, ed. 1911, 1922) returned to typological concerns, although Boas preferred to call his classification 'psychological' (which he opposed to 'historical'). The grammatical sketches presented in the first two volumes of this *Handbook* attempted to show how grammatical categories encapsulated the patterns of thought of various North American tribes. Each language family was understood to have a distinctive psychological pattern. No attempt was made to generalize about all American Indian languages. Throughout his career, Boas preferred this movement between psychology or typology and history, which for him was based on the distribution of cultural traits within particular culture areas. He spoke out against the more dramatic historical connections of linguistic families of North America proposed by his former students in the early 20th century, particularly Sapir (Darnell 1990, 1998). Although much of this work was published under Bureau of American Ethnology auspices, Powell died before it became clear that his own focus on superficial genetic relationship was adequate only in the short term. What came to substitute for it returned in many ways to the earlier typological framework.

6. Bibliography

Adelung, Johann Christoph & Johann Severin Vater. 1806–1817. *Mithridates oder allgemeine Sprachenkunde.* 6 vols. Berlin: Voss.

Andresen, Julie Tetel. 1990. *Linguistics in America, 1769–1924.* New York: Routledge.

Bieder, Robert. 1986. *Science Encounters the Indian, 1820–1880: The early years of American ethnology.* Norman & London: Univ. of Oklahoma Press.

– & Thomas Tax. 1976. "From Ethnologists to Anthropologists: A brief history of the American Ethnological Society". *American Anthropology: The early years* ed. by John Murra, 11–21. New York: American Ethnological Society.

Boas, Franz. 1911. "Introduction". *Handbook of American Indian Languages.* Ed. by Franz Boas, vol. I (= *Bureau of American Ethnology Bulletin*, 40), 1–83. Washington, D. C.

–, ed. 1922. *Handbook [...].* Part 2.

Brinton, Daniel Garrison. 1868. *Myths of the New World.* New York: Leypoldt & Holt.

–. 1885. "The Philosophic Grammar of American Languages as set forth by Wilhelm von Humboldt, with a translation of an unpublished memoir by him on the American verb". (= *Proceedings of the American Philosophical Society*, 22), 306–354. Philadelphia.

–. 1890a. *Essays of an Americanist.* Philadelphia: Porter & Coates.

–. 1890b. *Races and Peoples: Lectures on the science of ethnography.* New York: N. D. C. Hodges.

–. 1891. *The American Race: A linguistic classification and ethnographic description of the native tribes of North America.* New York: N. D. C. Hodges.

Darnell, Regna. 1988. *Daniel Garrison Brinton: The 'Fearless Critic' of Philadelphia.* (= *University of Pennsylvania Department of Anthropology Monograph*, 3), 1–194. Philadelphia.

–. 1990. *Edward Sapir: Linguist, anthropologist, humanist.* Berkeley & Los Angeles: Univ. of California Press.

–. 1998. *And Along Came Boas: Continuity and revolution in Americanist anthropology.* Amsterdam & Philadelphia: Benjamins.

Gallatin, Albert. 1826. *A Table of the Indian Languages of the United States. East of the Stony Mountains, arranged according to languages and dialects.* Washington, D. C.

–. 1836. *A Synopsis of the Indian Tribes of North America.* (= *Transactions and Collections of the American Antiquarian Society*, 2), 1–422. Cambridge, Mass.

–. 1845. *Notes on the Semi-Civilized Nations of Mexico, Yucatan and Central America.* (= *Transactions of the American Ethnological Society*, 1), 1–352. New York.

–. 1848. "Introduction" to *Hale's Indians of Northwest America and Vocabularies of North America.* (= *Transactions of the American Ethnological Society*, 2), xxiii–clxxx, 1–130.

Greenberg, Joseph. 1957. "The Nature and Use of Linguistic Typologies". *IJAL* 23.68–70.

Haas, Mary. 1969. "Grammar or Lexicon? The American Indian Side of the Question from Duponceau to Powell". *IJAL* 35.239–255.

Hallowell, A. Irving. 1960. "The Beginnings of Anthropology in America". *Selected Papers from the American Anthropologist, 1888–1920* ed. by Frederica de Laguna, 1–90. Washington, D. C.: American Anthropological Association.

Hodge, Frederick Webb, ed. 1906, 1910. *Handbook of American Indians.* 2 parts. (= *Bureau of American Ethnology Bulletin*, 30). Washington, D. C.

Lucy, John. 1992. *Language Diversity and Thought: A reformulation of the linguistic relativity Hypothesis.* Cambridge: Cambridge Univ. Press.

McGee, W. J. 1897. "The Bureau of American Ethnology". *The Smithsonian Institution 1846–96: The History of its First Half Century* ed. by G. Brown Goode, 367–396. Washington, D. C.: Devine Press.

Murray, Stephen O. 1994. *Theory Groups and the Study of Language in North America: A social history.* Amsterdam & Philadelphia: Benjamins.

Powell, John Wesley. 1877. *Introduction to the Study of Indian Languages.* Washington, D. C.: Smithsonian Institution.

–. 1968 [1878]. *Report on the Arid Region of the United States.* New York: Belknap Press.

–. 1880. *Introduction to the Study of Indian Languages.* 2nd enl. ed. Washington, D. C.: Smithsonian Institution.

–. 1891. *Indian Linguistic Families of America North of Mexico.* (= *Bureau of American Ethnology Annual Report 7 for 1885–86)*, 7–139. Washington, D. C.

–. 1897. *15th Annual Report for 1893–94.* Washington, D. C.: Bureau of American Ethnology.

Wolfart, H. C. 1967. "Notes on the Early History of American Indian Linguistics". *Folia Linguistica* 1.153–171.

Regna Darnell, London, Ontario (Canada)

176. Language typology in the 20th century from Sapir to late 20th-century approaches

1. Introduction
2. Sapir's approach
3. Jakobson and the Prague School
4. Greenberg
5. Later work on word order typology
6. Head-marking and dependent-marking
7. Recent results
8. Functionalists versus generativists
9. Bibliography

1. Introduction

Typology, broadly speaking, is the classification of languages according to linguistic traits and the comparison or classification of linguistic patterns (structures) across languages. More specifically, typology is understood in different ways, among them, as the *classification* of structural types cross-linguistically, as investigation of cross-linguistic *generalizations* concerning patterns among linguistic traits, and as a general approach to linguistics which attempts to *explain* the patterns and classification through appeal to language function in cross-linguistic comparison — the relation between linguistic form and semantic/pragmatic function (see Comrie 1989 [1981]; Croft 1990; Givón 1984; 1990; Mallinson & Blake 1981). There are typological classifications involving phonological, morphological, syntactic, semantic, lexical, discourse, and even socio-cultural attributes of languages (e. g., typologies for multilingualism, endangered and dying languages, ethnography of communication traits, and so on). Languages can be typologized according to almost any linguistic trait, and indeed classifications based on widely varied attributes exist. For example, the Leipzig psychologist Wilhelm Wundt (1832–1920) dealt with twelve oppositions or types, including prefixing versus suffixing languages, free versus fixed word-order languages, and languages with more elaborated verbal versus more elaborate nominal forms (Wundt 100: 436). Important studies in phonological typology include Trubetzkoy (1929, 1931, 1939), Hockett (1955), and Maddieson (1984), among others; in semantics Ullmann (1953, 1963) and Berlin (1972). Nevertheless, the emphasis in typology has been on morphosyntax. Throughout the 19th century, typological studies were primarily morphological — the structure of the word alone (morphology) determined a language's whole character, its typological classification. Typology today is closely associated with the study of linguistic universals, which investigates common characteristics in the world's languages, usually with the goal of providing insight into the fundamental nature of human language.

2. Sapir's approach

Morphological typology in the 20th century has been dominated by Edward Sapir's (1884–1939) treatment, in Chapter 6 of his *Language* (1921), though Sapir's typology rests on a tradition extending from the 18th and 19th centuries represented by the Schlegel brothers, Adam Smith, Franz Bopp, Wilhelm von Humboldt, August Schleicher, Friedrich Müller, Heymann Steinthal, Franz Niklaus Finck, Wilhelm Wundt, and others (see Koerner 1994), and on into the 20th century by, for example, Nikolaj J. Marr (1865–1934), who dominated linguistics in the early Soviet Union. In particular, Sapir was influenced by Humboldt and Steinthal. For many in the Schlegel-Humboldtian tradition, the typological categories — isolating, agglutinative, flexional, and incorporating — were taken as reflecting the level of social evolution attained by the speakers of the language (a typical equation was isolating = savagery, agglutinative = barbarianism, inflectional = civilization). For Friedrich Müller (1834–1898), for example, social evolution, racial type, and language type were correlated, so that, for example, hair shape and linguistic morphology were correlated (Müller 1876–88). Sapir rejected the evolutionary prejudice that typified traditional typological studies: "all attempts to connect particular types of linguistic morphology with certain correlated stages of cultural development [...] are rubbish" (1921: 219). He did not accept the notion of significant racial differences in the "fundamental conformation of thought", that the variability of linguistic forms (the actual processes of thought) could be indexed to racial differences. However, Sapir did uphold the psychological orientation of the Humboldtian tradition, and his own approach maintained that there was an intimate connection between the content of language and culture/experience. A version of this notion was made popular by Sapir's student, Benjamin Lee Whorf (1897–1941), known variously as the (Sapir-)Whorf Hypothesis, Whorfianism, world view theory, cognitive orientation, and so on: a speaker's perception of the world is organized or constrained by the linguistic categories his or her language offers.

Sapir refined and redirected the typology of the Humboldt tradition, divorcing it of its historical and evolutionary associations. He incoporated Humboldt's four-part morphological typology in his own framework, which utilized the following four intersecting dimensions.

(1) *Pure Relational versus Mixed-relational languages.* Pure relational languages express syntactic relationships by means of the position of one element in relation to another; thus, the syntactic form of a sentence gives it its grammatical significance and relates the concrete elements to one another. In contrast, mixed-relational languages express some syntactic relationships by means of elements that have some concrete significance, such as objects, actions and qualities.

(2) *Simple versus Complex.* Simple languages do not modify the meanings or relationships of their radical concepts (i. e., nouns, verbs, etc.) by means of affixation or internal changes, but complex languages do.

(3) *Morphological Technique or Processes.* Sapir classified languages in four morphological types: (i) *Isolating* (analytic) — the words consist of a single morpheme; (ii) *Agglutinative* — words consist of a root and invariant affixes that are separable and encode a single grammatical concept; (iii) *Fusional* — this contrasts with the agglutinative type in that the affixes have variable forms and may encode several grammatical contrasts simultaneously; and (iv) *Symbolic* — which utilizes internal changes such as reduplication, vowel and consonant changes, and changes in stress and pitch as a means of marking grammatical contrasts.

(4) *Degree of Synthesis.* Three types of categories were involved: (i) *Analytic* languages have little or no tendency to combine more than one grammatical concept into single words or morphemes; (ii) *Syn-* *thetic* languages combine several grammatical concepts to form polymorphemic words; and (iii) *Polysynthetic* languages combine long strings of bound morphemes into a single word form that may be translated as whole clauses in English. Here, Sapir comes closest to the Humboldtian categories, though in Sapir's scheme there is no direct analogue of the 'inflecting' type of the traditional typologies.

Sapir's four categories, in addition to morphological, incorporate semantic and syntactic criteria, and thus they add a dimension of complexity to morphological typology that far outstripped that of his predecessors. In Sapir's approach, a language may exploit a variety of dimensions, rather than being classified, as in the Humboldtian tradition, as belonging uniquely to one particular type, and languages are arranged on a scale, for example, as more or less agglutinative rather than categorically either agglutinative or non-agglutinative (Carstairs-McCarthy 1994; Greenberg 1973: 153). Sapir is the foundation for 20th-century approaches to typology, though few pursued his ideas directly (though see Greenberg 1954, who suggested how the position of a language on each of Sapir's dimensions could be quantified).

3. Jakobson and the Prague School

Several concepts fundamental to modern approaches to typology come from the Prague School and especially from Roman Jakobson. For example, Nikolaj S. Trubetzkoy's (1890–1938) classification of vowel systems, consonants, and phonological types, with its emphasis on structural comparisons, oppositions and relations, and markedness (see Trubetzkoy 1929, 1931, 1939), was to become fundamental in modern typological and theoretical thinking. Implicational universals (if a language has a trait x, then it is expected also to have a trait y) in connection with language types were discussed already by Jakobson (1941: 59) and Skalička (1941: 4), and Jakobson's (1958) article brought implicational universals and their relation to language types to broader attention. In many ways, this article is the beginning of present-day typology and universals. The Prague School is also the inspiration for André Martinet's (1908–1999) influential work (see for example Martinet 1962). Markedness, developed by the Prague School linguists, plays a major role in both the generativist and typological approaches. The notions of *rheme* (topic) versus *theme* (comment) and 'new' versus 'old/given' information were also developed by the Prague School linguists, Vilém Mathesius (1929) in particular. These play an important role in Michael Halliday's 'Systemic Grammar' (see, for example, Halliday 1967), and they are basic ingredients of discourse analysis and typological thinking today (see Chafe 1976).

4. Greenberg

Joseph H. Greenberg (1915—2001) is generally considered the founder of modern typology. In his paper on morpheme and word order universals (Greenberg 1966 [1963]), he formulated 45 universals for the associations among a variety of syntactic, semantic, and morphological characteristics of languages which he observed in his sample of 30 languages. Most of these were in the form of implicational universals. Greenberg deals with relationships of *order* (e.g., Universal 2: In languages with prepositions, the genitive almost always follows the governing noun, while in languages with postpositions it almost always precedes) and *hierarchy* (e.g., Universal 34: no language has a trial number unless it has a dual; no language has a dual unless it has a plural); these relationships are not part of Sapir's typology (Carstairs-McCarthy 1994: 4819). Of the six logically possible orders of subject, object, and verb — SVO, SOV, VSO, VOS, OVS, OSV —, Greenberg (1966 [1963]: 76) found the first three were common cross-linguistically, but the last three "do not occur at all, or at least are excessively rare". His first universal reflects this observation: "Universal 1: In declarative sentences with nominal subject and object, the dominant order is almost always one in which the subject precedes the object" (p. 77). Soon, however, languages with VOS order and later with OSV and OVS order were pointed out, forcing this universal to be abandoned. The other orders of elements important in Greenberg's study are: prepositions as opposed to postpositions (Pr-N/N-Po), the position of qualifying adjectives in relation to nouns (AN/NA), and the position of the genitive in relation to the head noun (GN/NG). The possible combinations of these yield 24 logically possible word-order types, of which only 15 are attested in Greenberg's sample. Four were most frequent in the languages of his sample: (1) SVO / Prep / NG / NA, (2) SOV / Post / GN / AN, (3) SOV / Post / GN / NA, and (4) VSO / Prep / NG / NA. Subsequent research has revealed representatives of several of the 24 logically possible types which were not attested in Greenberg's sample (Hawkins 1983; Campbell et al. 1988; Dryer 1988, 1992). The existence of these languages requires several other of Greenberg's (and later of Hawkins') preposed universals to be abandoned or reformulated.

The Stanford Universal Universals Project applied Greenberg's approach to many other areas of grammar (see Greenberg et al. 1978).

One of the merits of Greenberg's work is that he did not pick any one typological parameter as deterministic; instead, he established (sometimes complex) correlations among the various parameters. For example, Universal 2 (cited above) does not mention S, V, or O at all, but rather treats a complex relationship involving preposition/postposition and NG/GN (Greenberg 1966: 76). A limitation of Greenberg's work is that few explanations are offered for the universals that are postulated. For example, this Universal 2, a valid observation of distributions, does not explain why the position of adpositions plays a role in determining the order of the genitive relative to the head noun. However, this sort of explanation was not a goal of Greenberg's research, though central to others.

5. Later work on word order typology

Theo Vennemann (1974a, b) and Winfred Lehmann (1973) did seek such explanations. Vennemann's Natural Serialization Principle held that a language tends to serialize (to order) all 'operator-operand' (modifier-modified, adjunct-head) pairs unidirectionally, with the order operator-operand or the order operand-operator throughout. He did not establish any new word-order correlations. The generalization is problematic in that it is itself in need of explanation and several of the languages in Greenberg's sample do not conform completely. Vennemann's hypothesis predicts that the tendency towards natural serialization will eventually result in changes in ordering which will make the exceptional languages fit expectations. Lehmann proposed a 'fundamental principle' governing word order patterns which reduces the six logically possible word order types to two — OV and VO — the position of the subject is not important from a typological standpoint. He argued that the verb and object are primary concomitants of one another and that modifiers are positioned on the opposite side of a constituent from its primary concomitant. Thus, in OV languages adjectives and other nominal modifiers occur to the left of the object and verbal modifiers are positioned to the right of the verb; in VO languages nominal modifiers are placed to the right of the object and the verbal modifiers are found to the left of the verb. Lehmann did attempt to draw additional correlations, between word order and other linguistic parameters, including phonological phenomena; however, these must be investigated in a wider range of languages. A problem with Lehmann's formulation, as with Vennemann's, is that the inconsistent languages fall outside the analysis; for instance, Mallinson & Blake (1981: 379) estimate that only about 40% of languages are consistent. In Lehmann's and Vennemann's treatments, the inconsistencies can be accounted for only as the result of assumed but often unattested diachronic changes which are presumed to confirm to the tendency for changes to be in the direction of greater consistency. The use of consistency for historical reconstruction has been much criticized (see Harris & Campbell 1995: 195–239, for details). In the Lehmann and Vennemann views, all universals become statistical (tendencies); none are absolute and therefore they fail to reflect that VSO languages are always prepositional.

John A. Hawkins (1983) attempted to reduce the exceptions in Greenberg's data, arguing against the statistical universals (that languages tend to display the property in question with much greater than chance frequency). This he did by formulating many of the word-order universals in terms of double conditions, as in Greenberg's Universal 5: If a language has dominant SOV order and the genitive follows the governing noun, then the adjective likewise follows the noun (in Hawkins' formulation: SOV ⊃ (AN ⊃ GN)). Hawkins' expanded sample included 336 languages; he corrected some misassignments of languages to Greenberg's 24 types, though later work again has corrected mistaken attributions of languages in Hawkins' sample. Hawkins proposed two principles to account for word order patterns which are frequent but not in conformity to expectations of harmony. The *Heaviness Serialization Principle* for instance recognizes that languages (especially prepositional ones) tend to place 'lighter' constituents (Dem, Num) to the left of Head, 'heavier' (relative clause, adjective phrases, etc.) to the right, where heaviness is defined in terms of, for example, length and number of morphemes, number of words, and syntactic branching, as illustrated in English by AN with simple ('lighter' adjectives ("the yellow book"), but NA with 'heavier' adjectives/adjective phrases ("the book yellow with age"). The *Mobility Principle* recognizes (especially in postpositional languages) that Adj, Dem, and Num are more mobile than Gen and Rel and can move around their heads more easily, producing unexpected serializations. Hawkins proposed functional explanations for these principles and for the word order universals in general. The earlier the head appears in NP, the easier for hearers to process the construction; so, heavier modifiers are placed after the head. For example, prenominal relative clauses delay recognition of the head, and so serialize readily to right, after the head noun. Hawkins (1990, 1995) has sought various functional and psychological explanations for his findings.

6. Head-marking and dependent-marking

A major contribution to typology which has not yet been integrated into the general functional-typological approach is Johanna Nichols' (1986, 1992) head-marking and dependent-marking, a taxonomy of morphosyntactic marking which relies on the notions of *head* (which determines the syntactic type of the entire constituent) and *dependent* (non-head members of the constituent). English *Jane's dog* is an instance of dependent marking, where the morphological indicator of possession (-'s here) is marked on the dependent constituent *Jane* (the possessor) and not on *dog* (the head); whereas in K'iche' *u-ts'iʔ ʃuan* "John's dog", literally "his-dog John", has the marker of possession *u-* is on the head constituent *ts'iʔ* "dog" (the possessed) and not on dependent *ʃuan*. The head-dependent distinction classifies the syntactic constituents of a language, and correlations among this trait across constructions typologizes languages cross-linguistically. Nichols goes further and attempts to correlate the geographical distribution of head-marking and dependent-marking languages with linguistic prehistory and ancient population movements — a more controversial aspect of her work.

7. Recent results

Some of the principal participants in the on-going typological research from about 1975 to the present are Barry Blake, Robert M. W. Dixon, Joan Bybee, Wallace Chafe, Bernard Comrie, William Croft, Scott DeLancey, John DuBois, Talmy Givón, Joseph Greenberg, John Haiman, Bernd Heine, Paul Hopper, Christian Lehmann, Charles Li, Marianne Mithun, Doris Payne, Frans Plank, Masayoshi Shibatani, and Elizabeth Closs Traugott. Their contributions on the whole involve the identification of a grammatical phenomenon based on semantic/pragmatic/functional grounds external to any given language and the comparison/classification of the structures found cross-linguistically to express/signal the various phenomena so defined. In this way, contributions have been made in the understanding of subject; transitivity; types of alignment — ergative-absolutive, nominative-accusative, active-stative; noun-incorporation; voice; lexical categories — noun, verb, adjective, etc.; case marking, grammatical agreement, pronominals; relative clause types; tense-aspect-modality; topicality and focus; new versus old/given information; foregrounding and backgrounding; argument chaining, clause chaining; information flow; switch-reference; markedness, iconicity, pragmatic motivations; the roles of grammatical hierarchies and prototypes, animacy, accessibility; and of course word order, to mention some of the main ones.

In this approach, languages are not generally classified as belonging uniquely to one type or another, but rather often utilize more than one structural type (often called a *strategy*) for a given construction, as is the case in English with both GN genitive order (e. g., "Betty's wish") and NG genitives (e. g., "the wish of the people"). Often it is possible to determine which strategy is *basic* (unmarked). However, for many typological relationships, the 'either-or' (binary) categorization of traditional markedness is not sufficient, and many are describe in terms of *hierarchies* and *prototypes*. Hierarchies (scales) involve grammatical categories which have more than two values (relative markedness) in a chain of intersecting implicational universals — a ranking of members of a grammatical category. For example, Greenberg's Universal 34 (no language has a trial number unless it has a dual; no language has a dual unless it has a plural) can be restated, adding later findings, as a hierarchy; Singular ⊂ Plural ⊂ Dual ⊂ Trial/Paucal, i. e., the presence of a category 'trial' in a language implies that the language will also have all the categories lower on the hierarchy as well ('dual', 'plural', 'singular'); the presence of a 'dual' implies 'plural' and 'singular' in the language, which may or may not have a 'trial'; and 'plural' implies 'singular', but 'singular' can exist with or without the presence of all the others. Some other grammatical hierarchies that have been proposes are: the Noun-Phrase accessibility hierarchy (subject ⊂ direct object ⊂ direct object ⊂ oblique), the animacy hierarchy (1st/2nd person pronoun ⊂ third person pronoun ⊂ human NP ⊂ animate NP ⊂ inanimate NP). Hierarchies have also been used to state other such implicational chains that hold among related grammatical categories, e. g., color universals, ethnobiological nomenclature, and sonority in phonology. The notion of *prototype* is used in typology to refer to categories which have a cluster of traits; members of the category which exhibit all of 'core' properties of the category are 'prototypical'; other members which have fewer of the defining properties are more peripheral (less prototypical) members of the category. For example, the more prototypical transitive clauses in Hopper & Thompson's (1980) formulation exhibit more of the following traits, less prototypical ones fewer: two or more participants, visible action, punctual, volitional, realis, highly agentive, totally affected object, etc. A clause with a verb like "kill" typically exhibits many of these cross-linguistically, while "smell" has fewer (no visible action, object is not perceptible affected, and so on) and consequently cross-linguistically "smell" is coded as a transitive verb less frequently than "kill" is (often verbs of perception are coded more intransitively, in constructions equivalent to, for example, "it smells to me" or "to me smells" for what English codes as transitive "I smell it"). The notion of prototype has been utilized in the definitions of 'noun', 'verb', 'transitivity', 'subject', 'object', 'agent', 'patient', 'ergativity', 'color categories', among others.

A concern in this typological research is the *sample* of languages upon which cross-linguistic generalizations are based. It should be sufficiently broad to represent the range of different means by which the phenomenon in question can be signalled, and it should avoid non-typological sources of cross-liniguistic similarity (such as a bias in the sample from too many languages which are genetically related to one another or from too many from the same linguistic area which may share structural traits due to diffusion and borrowing). For example, Bybee (and associates), Dryer, Hawkins, and Nichols, have constructed quite large representative samples, with roughly 200—350 languages each, upon which their work is based. However, William Croft (1990: 19—20) argues that a sample of from 40 to 100 languages is adequate for formulating hypotheses, which the linguistic community at large can then test against larger numbers. Results are also limited by the quality of data available for given languages, but this is improving constantly.

Linguists of this typological persuasion explain the structure of language on the basis of function; for them, function drives shape, that is, the way grammatical constructions are packaged reflects their function, their role in communication. The functional explanations offered often involve assumptions about perception and production, about what would facilitate the hearer's being able to process (parse) what he/she hears and about what would aid the speaker to produce (package) the intended message. Among types of functional explanations, currently much discussed are those involving *iconicity*. Iconicity has to do with claims that the structure of language somehow reflects the structure of the world (or the speaker's experience with or perception of the real world). For example, we say in English (and equivalently in almost all languages) "Ruth came in and she sat on the couch", where the order of the clauses reflects the temporal sequence in the real-world events, with Ruth first entering and then subsequently sitting — we cannot say "Ruth sat on the couch and she came in" for the entering-sitting sequence. The fact that the linguistic order reflects the order of events as they transpired in the world is said to be iconic. This has been called the 'linear order principle': The order of clauses in coherent discourse will tend to correspond to the temporal order of the occurrence of the depicted events (Givón 1990: 971). Iconic motivations have been proposed for many pieces of grammar and for correspondences among pieces of grammar (see Haiman 1985; Croft 1990; Givón 1990). Some 'quantity' (or 'economy') iconic principles are: (1) A larger chunk of information will be given a larger chunk of code; (2) Less predictable information will be given more coding material; and (3) More important information will be given more coding material. 'Proximity' iconic principles are: (4) Entities that are closer together functionally, conceptually, or cognitively will be placed closer together at the code level, i.e. temporally or spatially; and (5) Functional operators will be placed closest, temporally or spatially at the code level, to the conceptual unit to which they are most relevant (Givón 1990: 969—970). Many others have been proposed. One difficulty with proposed iconic explanations is that the structural categories of the world, or of how it is experienced, are not established in such a way to permit easy comparison between these and grammatical categories (Croft 1990: 171).

Typological research incorporates many diachronic assumptions about pathways of change and in turn typological insights have been valuable for understanding linguistic change and for constraining reconstructions. This work is too extensive and varied to be evaluated here in detail (see Comrie 1989: 201—226; Croft 1990: 203—259; Harris & Campbell 1995; Hawkins 1983). Suffice it to mention *grammaticalization*, the subject of extensive discussion. Meillet (1912) introduced the term 'grammaticalization', by which he meant changes in which an original independent word with independent meaning (*mot autonome*) develops into an 'auxiliary word' and ends up as a grammatical marker (*élément grammaticale*). Kuryłowicz's (1965: 52) definition was, "Grammaticalization consists in the increase of the range of a morpheme advancing from a lexical to a grammatical or from a less grammatical to a more grammatical status, e.g. from a derivative formant to an inflectional one". Grammaticalization in more recent literature deals with changes which are seen as the result of language fulfilling discourse and communicative functions involving two related processes: (1) lexical-to-grammatical-morpheme changes, which undergo change from independent word to clitic or affix; and (2) discourse-structure-to-morphosyntactic-marking changes, i. e., the fixing of discourse strategies in syntactic and morphological structure (Traugott & Heine 1991: 2). Both kinds of grammaticalization are typically associated with 'semantic bleaching' and 'phonological reduction'. That grammaticalization is often associated with 'semantic bleaching' is hardly remarkable, since the concept of the semantic bleaching, the shift from more lexical to more grammatical content, virtually follows from the definition of grammaticalization. In a much cited example, English *will* (originally "want") was grammaticalized as 'future' and semantically bleached of its lexical content "want". Many see grammaticalization as a form of reanalysis (Harris & Campbell 1995: 92; Hopper & Traugott 1993: 32), though there are reanalyses which are not grammaticalizations (reanalyses involving word-order changes, affixes becoming independent words, changes from one grammatical structure to another, and so on).

8. Functionalists versus generativists

It has become almost a convention in the literature to contrast the 'generativist' approach associated with Noam Chomsky and his followers with that of the 'typological' (sometimes called the functional-typological or 'Greenbergian') approach. The role of typology in generativist theories is not discussed here, though many parallels and points of contact are found in their view of universals and in the parameters which define permitted ranges of variation for certain grammatical phenomena. Fundamental points of difference between the two include the following. (1) Typologists rely on a wide range of languages for their generalizations; generativist research has relied on fewer languages but investigated in greater detail. (2) Typologists' generalizations are presented in mainly concrete terms involving 'surface-structure' sorts of things (although a degree of abstraction is involved in their definition of many of the concepts with which they deal, e. g., the notion of 'subject'); generativist universals typically involve much greater abstraction, constraining the relation between (abstract) universal grammar and constructions of individual grammars. (3) Typologists favor functionalist explanations, based on discourse, communicative needs, pragmatic factors, and iconicity. The shape of grammar is driven by the functions it fulfills. Generativist universals and parametric variation are explained by reference to human biology (cognition), as part of the genetic endowment. The shape of the grammar is determined by built-in innate properties of the mind which mediate language acquisition which determines what can and cannot show up in the structure of a given language.

9. Bibliography

Berlin, Brent. 1972. "Speculations on the Growth of Ethnobotanical Nomenclature". *Language in Society* 1.51–98.

Campbell, Lyle, Vit Bubenik & Leslie Saxon. 1988. "Word Order Universals: Refinements and clarifications". *Canadian Journal of Linguistics* 33. 209–230.

Carstairs-McCarthy, Andrew. 1994. "Typology, Morphological". *The Encyclopedia of Language and Linguistics* ed. by R. E. Asher & J. M. Y. Simpson, vol. IX, 4817–4820. Oxford & New York: Pergamon Press.

Chafe, Wallace. 1976. "Givenness, Contrastiveness, Definiteness, Subjects, Topics, and Point of View". *Subject and Topic* ed. by Charles N. Li, 25–55. New York: Academic Press.

Comrie, Bernard. 1989 [1981]. *Language Universals & Linguistic Typology: Syntax and morphology.* 2nd ed. Chicago: Univ. of Chicago Press.

Croft, William. 1990. *Typology and Universals.* Cambridge: Cambridge Univ. Press.

Dryer, Matthew S. 1988. "Object-Verb Order and Adjective-Noun Order: Dispelling a myth". *Lingua* 74.185–217.

–. 1992. "The Greenbergian Word Order Correlations". *Language* 63.815–855.

Givón, Talmy. 1984, 1990. *Syntax: A functional-typological introduction.* 2 vols. Amsterdam & Philadelphia: Benjamins.

Greenberg, Joseph H. 1954. "A Quantitative Approach to the Morphological Typology of Language". *Method and Perspective in Anthropology* ed. by Robert F. Spencer, 192–220. Minneapolis: Univ. of Minnesota Press. (Repr. in *IJAL* 23. 178–194 (1954).)

–. 1966 [1963]. "Some Universals of Grammar with Particular Reference to the Order of Meaningful Elements". *Universals of Language* ed. by Joseph H. Greenberg, 2nd ed., 73–113. Cambridge, Mass.: MIT Press.

–. 1973. "The Typological Method". *Current Trends in Linguistics* ed. by Thomas A. Sebeok, vol. 11: *Diachronic, Areal, and Typological Linguistics*, 149–193. The Hague: Mouton.

–. Charles A. Ferguson & Edith A. Moravcsik, eds. 1978. *Universals of Human Language.* 4 vols. Stanford, Calif.: Stanford Univ. Press.

Haiman, John, ed. 1985. *Iconicity in Syntax*. Amsterdam & Philadelphia: Benjamins.

Halliday, M. A. K. 1967. "Notes on Transitivity and Theme in English Part I, II.". *Journal of Linguistics* 3.37–81, 199–244.

Harris, Alice C. & Lyle Campbell. 1995. *Historical Syntax in Cross-Linguistic Perspective*. Cambridge: Cambridge Univ. Press.

Hawkins, John A. 1983. *Word Order Universals*. New York: Academic Press.

—. 1990. "A Parsing Theory of Word Order Universals". *Linguistic Inquiry* 21.223–261.

—. 1995. *A Performance Theory of Order and Constituency*. Cambridge: Cambridge Univ. Press.

Hockett, Charles F. 1955. *A Manual of Phonology*. Bloomington: Indiana Univ.

Hopper, Paul & Sandra Thompson. 1980. "Transitivity in Grammar and Discourse". *Language* 56.251–299.

Hopper, Paul & Elizabeth Closs Traugott. 1993. *Grammaticalization*. Cambridge: Cambridge Univ. Press.

Jakobson, Roman. 1941. *Kindersprache, Aphasie und allgemeine Lautgesetze*. Uppsala: Språkvetenskapliga Sällskapets i Uppsala Förhandlingar. (English transl. by Allan R. Keiler, *Child Language, Aphasia, and Phonological Universals*, The Hague: Mouton, 1968.)

—. 1958. "Typological Studies and Their Contribution to Historical Comparative Linguistics". *Proceedings of the Eighth International Congress of Linguists* ed. by Eva Sivertsen, Carl J. Borgstøm, Aarne Gallis & Alf Sommerfelt, 17–25. Oslo: Oslo Univ. Press.

Koerner, Konrad. 1994. "Typology and Language Classification: History". *The Encyclopedia of Language and Linguistics* ed. by R. E. Asher & J. M. Y. Simpson, vol. IX, 4813–4817. Oxford & New York: Pergamon Press.

Kuryłowicz, Jerzy. 1965. "The Evolution of Grammatical Categories". *Esquisses Linguistiques II* by J. Kuryłowicz, 38–54. Munich: Fink.

Lehmann, Winfred. 1973. "A Structural Principle of Language and Its Implications". *Language* 49.47–66.

Maddieson, Ian. 1984. *Patterns of Sounds*. Cambridge: Cambridge Univ. Press.

Mallison, Graham & Barry J. Blake. 1981. *Language Typology: Cross-linguistic studies in syntax*. Amsterdam: North-Holland.

Martinet, André. 1962. *A Functional View of Language*. Oxford: Oxford Univ. Press.

Mathesius, Vilém. 1929. "Zur Satzperspektive im modernen Englisch". *Archiv für das Studium der Neueren Sprachen und Literaturen* 155.202.210.

Meillet, Antoine. 1912. "L'évolution des formes grammaticales". *Scientia* 12, No. 26 (Milan). (Repr. in Meillet, *Linguistique historique et linguistique générale*, vol. I, 130–148. Paris: Klincksieck, 1951.

Müller, Friedrich. 1876–88. *Grundriss der Sprachwissenschaft*. 4 parts in 6 vols. Vienna: A. Hölder.

Nichols, Johanna. 1986. "Head-Marking and Dependent-Marking Grammar". *Language* 62.56–119.

—. 1992. *Linguistic Diversity in Time and Space*. Chicago: Univ. of Chicago Press.

Sapir, Edward. 1921. *Language: An introduction to the study of speech*. New York: Harcourt, Brace & Co.

Skalička, Vladimír. 1941. *Vývoj české deklinace: Studie typologická*. (*Studie Pražaského kroužku*, 4.) Prague: Jednota českých matemaatikú a lysiku.

Traugott, Elizabeth Closs & Bernd Heine. 1991. "Introduction". *Approaches to Grammaticalization* ed. by E. C. Traugott & B. Heine, 1–14. Amsterdam & Philadelphia: Benjamins.

Trubetzkoy, Nikolaj S. 1929. "Zur allgemeinen Theorie der phonologischen Vokalsysteme". *Travaux du Cercle Linguistique de Prague* 1.39–67.

—. 1931. "Die phonologischen Systeme". *Travaux du Cercle Linguistique de Prague* 4.96–116.

—. 1939. *Grundzüge der Phonologie*. (= *Travaux du Cercle Linguistique de Prague*, 7.) Prague.

Ullmann, Stephen. 1953. "Descriptive Semantics and Linguistic Typology". *Word* 9.225–240.

—. 1963. "Semantic Universals". *Universals of Language* ed. by Joseph Greenberg, 217–262. Cambridge, Mass: MIT Press.

Vennemann, Theo. 1974a. "Analogy in Generative Grammar: The origin of word order". *Proceedings of the Eleventh International Congress of Linguistics* ed. by Luigi Heilmann, vol. II, 79–83. Bologna: Il Mulino.

—. 1974b. "Topics, Subjects and Word Order: From SXV to SVX via TVX". *Proceedings of the First International Conference on Historical Linguistics* ed. by John M. Anderson & Charles Jones, vol. I: *Syntax, Morphology, Internal and Comparative Reconstruction*, 339–376. Amsterdam: North-Holland.

Wundt, Wilhelm. 1900. *Völkerpsychologie*. Tome II: *Die Sprache*. 2 vols. Leipzig: Engelmann.

George Yonek, Pittsburgh (U.S.A.)
Lyle Campbell, Christchurch (New Zealand)

177. Theories of universal grammar in the late 20th century

1. Introduction: Typological and generative approaches
2. The search for typological parameters
3. The search for an explanatory basis
4. Conclusion
5. Bibliography

1. Introduction: Typological and generative approaches

The late 20th century is unusual in having two at times radically different approaches to the investigation of language universals, which we may label the typological and the generative approaches. Our emphasis here will be on the typological approach, though there will also be reference to the generative approach, to draw out both similarities and differences. Both share the view that there are universal properties of human language, by which we mean properties that are necessarily characteristic of the human language potential (rather than, for instance, being the result of historical accident). Both are thus distinguished from the Boas tradition in earlier American linguistics, which claimed that languages can vary without limit from one another. But the two current approaches are also characterized by considerable differences.

Perhaps the best way of describing the consistent difference between them is that generative grammar is primarily theory-driven, while typology is primarily data-driven, though this should not be taken to mean that generative grammar ignores data or that typology is anti-theoretical. Generative grammar, especially in its mainstream manifestations, is concerned with investigating language to throw light on the structure of the human mind, and interest in data is subordinated to this goal. Typology is concerned more directly with trying to ascertain the extent and limitations of variation across languages by investigating cross-linguistic similarities and differences. (For general accounts of typology, see Comrie 1989 and Croft 1991. A summary of a number of important contemporary typological approaches is provided in Shibatani & Bynon 1995.)

Since around 1980, there has been a period when typological and generative approaches grew close to one another, followed by a more recent period in which they seem to be growing apart again. During the Principles and Parameters (or Government and Binding) period of generative grammar (e.g., Chomsky 1981), both approaches were driven by a shared vision of the importance of principled syntactic variation among languages, and this is reflected in the discussion of section 2. With the rise of Minimalism (e.g., Chomsky 1995), and especially of Antisymmetry (Kayne 1994) − with its view that all languages are underlyingly subject-verb-object − the interests of typology and generative grammar have diverged. Only the future will tell whether and, if so, how they will converge again.

2. The search for typological parameters

One of the main characteristics of language universals research, from both typological and generative (Principles and Parameters) approaches, during the late 20th century has been the search for typological parameters, in particular for typological parameters of wide-ranging effect. The extreme search of this kind would be for a single parameter in terms of which one could characterize the whole syntax of a language, a so-called holistic typology (cf. Comrie 1991). In the relevant period, claims about typological parameters have usually been more modest − the search for partial typologies − although at least within the Principles and Parameters approach the aim was to find a *small* number of parameters that would characterize cross-linguistic syntactic variation. In the sub-sections of this section, I will discuss briefly a number of parameters that were suggested, taking examples from both typological and generative work. The constraints of space unfortunately have meant the exclusion of many other interesting proposals, such as Hawkins's (1986) 'semantic typology', dealing with differences in the closeness of fit between semantic and surface syntactic representations. The lack of further discussion of the Pro-drop parameter, a major component of generative discussion in the 1980s, reflects two facts: The parameter was always greeted with some skepticism by typologists, and it seems now to have dropped out of mainstream generative discussion as well.

2.1. Word order

Word order, or more accurately constituent order, has played at least an important historical role in typological work in that it was essentially with constituent order that Greenberg (1966a) inaugurated the current mainstream interest in universals and typology. In keeping with the general aims of the conference that forms the basis of Greenberg (1966b), this work is concerned primarily with establishing quite specific universals, rather than with establishing overall parameters of great generality, but some generalizations emerge even by inspection from the data collections that form the appendix to Greenberg (1966a), for instance that verb-initial languages tend strongly to have prepositions and postnominal genitives, while verb-final languages tend strongly to have postpositions and prenominal genitives. These tendencies were then taken as the bases of more extensive constituent-order typologies, for instance in the work of Vennemann (1974), where these constituent-order differences are subsumed into two general types, head-initial (VSO, PrNP, NGen, etc.) versus head-final (SOV, NPPo, GenN, etc.) — to use the terms that became more widespread with the incorporation of these ideas into generative grammar, with head-initial and head-final being the two choices on a major parameter.

The extent to which constituent order is a significant determinant of other aspects of cross-linguistic typological variation remains a hotly debated issue. The empirical problems with such generalizations as the head-final versus head-initial parameter are considerable, and while attempts to establish other principles and parameters that interact with this parameter to give rise to the exceptions can to some extent 'save' the parameter, they equally do much to undermine its empirical testability. In generative grammar, for instance, a new parameter of direction of case assignment was introduced, so that Mandarin Chinese, for example, can remain head-final despite its VO word order, since case assignment is to the right, i.e. the object must stand to the right of its verb. In typology, an independent principle seems to be at work preferring that attributive adjectives follow their head noun (Dryer 1989), so that NAdj is preferred even in otherwise basically head-final languages. As we shall see in section 3.2., Hawkins (1995) suggests that the correlations observed between different instances of constituent order, such as between position of verb relative to the object and position of the adposition relative to its noun phrase, may be epiphenomenal, the accidental result of principles of a quite different kind.

But despite these reservations, there are still a number of logically independent factors that seem to correlate with constituent order. To mention just one example, drawn to my attention by Maria Polinsky, the phenomenon of light verbs seems to correlate particularly strongly with verb-final constituent order. In the light verb construction, the lexical meaning of the predicate is carried by an invariable verb form (often one borrowed from another language), while verb categories are marked on a semantically empty or almost empty auxiliary verb, the 'light verb', often 'do' or 'become'. This phenomenon is found in such areally diverse verb-final languages as Japanese, Hindi, Tsez (Daghestanian branch of Northeast Caucasian), and Haruai (a Papuan language). Constituent order is thus an area that promises to reveal further riches, even if we do not yet understand how to unify them into a single coherent whole.

2.2. Configurationality

Configurationality emerged in the early 1980s as one of the most exciting typological parameters proposed within generative grammar, perhaps somewhat ironically as a parameter that was taken up more readily, in the long run, by typologists than by generativists, whose interest in the parameter had waned by the second half of the decade. The parameter would divide languages into configurational and non-configurational languages. Configurational languages have a hierarchical phrase structure, as represented for instance in phrase markers, while non-configurational languages would, at least ideally, lack all such hierarchical structure. Since much of mainstream current formal syntactic theory depends crucially on syntactic configuration — for instance, the definition of key notions like c-command — the difference between configurational and non-configurational languages would be great indeed. The positing of non-configurationality arose from Hale's work on the Australian Aboriginal language Warlpiri (e.g., Hale 1982), which has the following distinctive characteristics: word order is syntactically completely free, in particular words that seem to belong together semantically can be separated from one another, their relationship to one another being shown by the rich case morphology (so that an ergative adjective must belong with an ergative noun); unstressed pronouns can be freely omitted, i.e., there is no requirement that syntactic arguments be expressed by means of a noun phrase. These and other features led Hale to posit that the phrase structure of a Warlpiri sentence is simply a string of words.

While later work has considerably restricted the set of distinctions between Warlpiri and canonical configurational languages like English, many typologists are still happy with configurationality as a parameter that describes the degree to which a language is characterized by hierarchical syntactic structure. In Warlpiri, it turns out that there is some hierarchical structure; for instance, multi-clause sentences clearly consist of a number of clauses, each dominated by the matrix sentence-node and itself dominating a number of words; second-position clitics suggest that certain clusters of words in clause-initial position do form a single phrase. Yet it is still true that many languages seem to provide no evidence of the kind that leads syntacticians investigating English to posit a VP node, i.e. a constituent that includes the verb and its objects but not its subject. This would point to a difference in degree of hierarchical organization in the structure of the clause depending on the presence versus absence of a VP node intervening between the sentence-node and the argument-nodes.

2.3. Head-marking versus dependent-marking

A question that arises perennially when two languages are found to differ in an apparently substantial way from one another is whether this difference should rather be viewed as superficial variations on a common theme. The distinction between head-marking and dependent-marking, developed most explicitly by Nichols (1986), is a good case in point.

It has been known for some time that some languages mark the relationship between constituents of a construction primarily by marking the head, while others do so primarily by marking the dependent. Japanese *hito ga kodomo o butta*, literally "man NOMINATIVE boy ACCUSATIVE hit", i.e. 'the man hit the child', indicates subject and object of the predicate by marking the dependent noun phrases with nominative *ga* and accusative *o*, respectively. Swahili *mtu a-li-wa-piga watoto*, literally "man he-PAST-them-hit children", i.e., "the man hit the children", marks subject and object by pronominal prefixes on the verb (the head); note that *a-li-wa-piga* is a complete well-formed Swahili sentence, meaning "he hit them". (In addition, there are mixed types. Thus English *he hits them* shows both case marking of the dependents and minimal marking of the person-number of the subject by the verb inflection. English *the man struck the children* shows neither case marking of the dependents nor head marking on the verb.)

In early work in generative grammar (and not only there), the dependent-marking variant was taken as underlying all languages, and the head-marking type was derived by first making the head agree with the relevant dependents, and then if necessary deleting the dependents, as for instance in the Swahili sentence *a-li-wa-piga*. Nichols (1986) argues that there is no a priori justification for this approach, which simply deems dependent marking — the usual option in the major European languages — to be the norm, head marking to be treated as a deviation therefrom. Indeed, since head-marking seems to be at least as frequent cross-linguistically as dependent-marking, it is at least as plausible that one should adopt the inverse derivation, or perhaps treat both as equal variants. (Some implications of this for argument structure are discussed in Comrie 1993.)

But Nichols goes beyond the mere establishment of the distinction between head-marking and dependent-marking types and discussion of the theoretical implications of this distinction, she also shows that there are correlations between the head-marking versus dependent-marking parameter and other parameters of cross-linguistic variation, and suggests explanations for some of these correlations, a point that looks ahead to section 3. For instance, Nichols notes that, in her data-base, there is a correlation between head-marking and verb-initial constituent order, and suggests that this may be a means of early signalling of the basic relations within the clause, something which in a verb-final language can done by means of the case marking on the dependents. (Even if a verb-initial language has case marking of noun phrases, one would have to wait until those noun phrases appear to work out the basic relations of major constituents within the clause.) It is interesting in this connection, and again looking forward to section 3., that Nichols does not suggest 'mystical' connections between the head-marking/dependent-marking and other parameters; rather the correlations follow naturally from the interaction of independent properties of the various constructions.

3. The search for an explanatory basis

In the work from the earlier part of our period from a typological viewpoint, there was in general little concern with explanation. Indeed, in Greenberg (1966b) some of the contributors noted explicitly that, in their view, the most urgent task for language universals research was the reliable documentation of as large a number of language universals as possible, with explanation for these universals being viewed very much as a secondary concern, for later research. By contrast, work from a generative viewpoint, given its concern with language universals as a window on the human mind, was very much interested in explanation, such explanation being sought, of course, in the structure of the human mind, and more specifically of the language faculty as a separate module or modules of the human mind. Indeed, part of the early skirmishing between typological and generative approaches centered on the latter's claim that the former was not explanatory. And it should be noted that some typological approaches still in general pay little attention to explanation, such as the Leningrad–St. Petersburg school; yet despite this, this school has made enormous contributions to our understanding of language universals, in part precisely through careful empirical documentation of universal patterns of cross-linguistic variation that have then provided input to more explanatorily oriented studies. (In addition to the overview of the Leningrad–St. Petersburg school contained in Shibatani & Bynon 1995, Nedjalkov 1988 can serve as an excellent illustration of the methodology, accessible to English-speaking readers.)

In more recent work on language universals from the typological viewpoint, however, the question of explanation has loomed large, and the main difference between generative and typological approaches lies not so much in whether explanation is considered important, but rather in what kinds of explanations are entertained, with typologists prepared to consider a wider range of explanations as significant factors constraining cross-linguistic variation. Section 3.1. below is concerned with the kind of explanation favored in generative grammar (and not a priori excluded by typologists), while sections 3.2. and 3.3. are concerned rather with the kinds of explanations that typologists have favored.

3.1. Formal generalizations and the structure of the mind

Given that generative grammar sees itself as seeking a window onto the nature of the human mind, it is inevitable that this approach to language universals has concentrated on universals that seem to point in this direction. And although typologists would in general deny that this is the only source of explanations for language universals – admitting some of the possibilities suggested in sections 3.2. and 3.3. – typologists would also not in general deny that at least some universals may simply reflect properties of the structure of the human mind.

Consider, for instance, the claim, first made explicit in generative grammar, that the syntactic processes in human languages are structure-dependent. To understand the distinction intended between structure-dependent and structure-independent, it will be useful to consider a handful of syntactic processes found in real and imaginary languages. In English, yes-no questions are formed by inverting the subject and the first auxiliary verb, as in the relation between the statement *the aging professor can still remember the students' names* and the question *can the aging professor still remember the students' names?* Crucially, this process – or, more neutrally, this systematic relation between related sentence-types – requires identification of pieces of syntactic structure, in this case of the subject of the sentence, which may range from a single word (as when *the aging professor* is replaced by *he*) or a long string (as when this noun phrase is replaced by *the professor who had recently celebrated his eightieth birthday*). The need to recognize bits of syntactic structure is what is meant by structure-dependent. In an imaginary language that formed yes-no questions without the constraint of structure-dependence, one possibility would be to form the question corresponding to a statement by simply inverting the order of words in the statement, to give for instance *names students' the remember still can professor aging the?* In the purely formal terms of automata theory, it is actually much simpler to create an automaton that will carry out this structure-independent transformation than to create one that will carry out the actual transformation that is found in the English examples, which requires parsing the sentence to identify its subject. Nonetheless, human language operates, at least overwhelmingly, in terms of structure-dependent rather than structure-independent processes (relations). This is therefore a significant fact about the structure of human language, one that does not have any obvious functional advantage, and one that is therefore likely simply to reflect an arbitrary, but nonetheless deep-seated, property of the human mind.

More strictly, one might say: a property of the human language faculty, and many working within the generative framework would emphasize this, given their view that the language faculty is a distinct module or set of modules within the human mind. At least with this particular example, however, it is not clear that there is a restriction to language, since greater ease in dealing in real time with structured strings than with unstructured strings seems to be a general property of human cognition. The precise delimination of those formal properties of language that are unique to language, versus being more general properties of cognition, thus emerges as an interesting question for future research.

3.2. Processing explanations

While the explanations discussed in section 3.1. are concerned with the structure of the human language faculty (and perhaps more generally of the human cognitive faculty), the discussion in this section concerns explanations that relate rather to the operation of that faculty. One of the interesting psycholinguistic results of early generative grammar was that reiteration of the process of embedding a dependent clause inside another dependent clause of the same type, though apparently violating no grammatical rule of the language, rapidly leads to loss of acceptability, as can be seen in the process of English relative clause formation that leads from *the man called the boy* to *the boy that the man called caught the dog* to *the dog that the boy that the man called caught escaped.* On at least one account, the grammar of English allows this last sentence, but processing constraints result in its being characterized as of low acceptability. Given this, one might expect that languages would devise means of avoiding such configurations, for instance by being constructed in ways that avoid dependent clauses embedded centrally inside (rather than at the left or right periphery) of the matrix clause, or by allowing such clauses to be moved to the left or right periphery, given that such peripherally located embedded clauses are known not to cause similar processing problems (as in *the rat that ate the malt that lay in the house that Jack built*). And indeed we find, for instance, that English allows relative clauses to be 'extraposed', i. e., to appear clause-finally rather than adjacent to a clause-medial head noun, as in *I met a student yesterday who wanted to talk about studying linguistics.*

An extensive development of ideas similar to these is presented in Hawkins (1995), which is concerned with a wide range of constituent order phenomena. Hawkins' basic claim is that preferences for particular orders of constituents, both among options available within a particular language and in the determination of language-particular required orders from among universally available options, is determined primarily by the need to identify syntactic constituents as soon as possible while the sentence is being presented linearly. In other words, the basic determinant of constituent order is the need for sentences to be readily parsable. And certainly a large number of constituent order phenomena fall under this generalization. Interestingly, if Hawkins is correct, then it is seen that the kinds of explanations suggested in earlier work for universals of constituent order by and large fall by the wayside, since they are at best accidental results of the operation of a single, more general principle – and, of course, the numerous exceptions to those earlier explanations are no longer problematic, to the extent that they fit in with Hawkins' generalization.

3.3. Functional explanations

In this section I will be concerned with explanations that relate directly to the function of language, as a means of communication. A number of current approaches to language, including in particular language universals, are explicitly functional in orientation, such as the model of Functional Grammar developed by the late Simon Dik, and the UNITYP approach to language universals developed by Hansjakob Seiler, the latter summarized in Seiler's contribution to Shibatani &

Bynon (1995). In this section, I want to take just one simple example of how a functional approach can contribute to our understanding of cross-linguistic variation.

This example concerns the phenomenon of reference-tracking, i.e., the various ways in which languages keep track of which participant is being referred to by various linguistic elements, such as pronouns, pronominal affixes on verbs, sometimes other features of verb morphology, etc. Many reference-tracking devices turn out to show, either within a particular language or cross-linguistically, sensitivity to grammatical person. In nearly all cases where such sensitivity to grammatical person is shown, the third person has the greatest range of distinctions. Where gender is used as a reference-tracking device, as with singular pronouns in English, the distinction is most likely to be found in the third person; indeed, in English it is only found here. Where distinct reflexive pronouns are found only in some grammatical persons, they are always found in the third person, and sometimes, as in French, only there. The phenomenon of obviation in Algonquian languages, which allows two participants in a discourse segment to be distinguished consistently as proximate versus obviative, operates only in the third person. A particular language may, of course, extend a particular distinction to non-third persons, as English extends the reflexive/non-reflexive distinction to all grammatical persons, but crucially we do not find languages that have, for instance, distinct reflexives only in the non-third person. From a formal viewpoint, there is no reason why we should find this pattern rather than its inverse. But once we ask about the function of reference-tracking devices, then an explanation for the observed distribution is obvious. First and second person pronominal devices refer to the speaker and the hearer respectively, and it is highly unusual for speaker or hearer to change in mid-sentence or mid-utterance, therefore there is no overwhelming need, from a reference-tracking viewpoint, for distinctions to be made within the first and second persons. By contrast, the third person covers all other potential referents in the universe of discourse, and grammatical distinctions relevant to reference-tracking are therefore particularly useful in the third person, precisely where they are found, empirically, to be richest.

For a more extensive discussion of ways in which language function can contribute explanatorily to language universals research, reference may be made to Givón (1984, 1991).

4. Conclusion

In this brief survey, it has been possible only to touch the surface of some of the issues arising in current approaches to language universals research, especially in such research from a typological viewpoint, and to draw, in part at random, on a few individual pieces of work as illustrations. This should, however, have given some idea of the exciting nature of current research in this area, which is both rich in its empirical bases and provocative in its search for explanation.

5. Bibliography

Chomsky, Noam. 1981. *Lectures on Government and Binding.* Dordrecht: Foris.

—. 1995. *The Minimalist Program.* Cambridge, Mass.: MIT Press.

Comrie, Bernard. 1989. *Language Universals and Linguistic Typology.* 2nd ed. Oxford; Blackwell; Chicago: Univ. of Chicago Press.

—. 1991. "Holistic versus Partial Typologies". *Proceedings of the Fourteenth International Congress of Linguists* ed. by Werner Bahner, Joachim Schildt & Dieter Viehweger, vol. I, 139–148. Berlin: Akademie-Verlag.

—. 1993. "Argument Structure". *Syntax: Ein internationales Handbuch zeitgenössischer Forschung/An International Handbook of Contemporary Research* ed. by Joachim Jacobs, Arnim von Stechow, Wolfgang Sternefeld & Theo Vennemann, Tome I, 905–914. Berlin & New York: de Gruyter.

Croft, William. 1991. *Typology and Universals.* Cambridge: Cambridge Univ. Press.

Dryer, Matthew S. 1989. "Large Linguistic Areas and Language Sampling". *Studies in Language* 13.257–292.

Givón, Talmy. 1984, 1991. *Syntax: A functional-typological introduction.* 2 vols. Amsterdam & Philadelphia: Benjamins.

Greenberg, Joseph H. 1966a. "Some Universals of Grammar with Particular Reference to the Order of Meaningful Constituents". Greenberg 1966b.73–113.

—, ed. 1966b. *Universals of Language.* 2nd ed. Cambridge, Mass: MIT Press.

Hale, Kenneth. 1982. "Preliminary Remarks on Configurationality". *Proceedings of the 12th Annual Meeting of the North Eastern Linguistic Society* ed. by James Pustejovsky & Peter Sells, 86–96.

Amherst, Mass.: Graduate Linguistics Association, Univ. of Massachusetts.

Hawkins, John A. 1986. *A Comparative Typology of English and German: Unifying the contrasts.* London: Croom Helm.

—. 1995. *A Performance Theory of Order and Constituency.* Cambridge: Cambridge Univ. Press.

Kayne, Richard S. 1994. *The Antisymmetry of Syntax.* Cambridge, Mass.: MIT Press.

Nedjalkov, Vladimir, ed. 1988. *Typology of Resultative Constructions.* Amsterdam & Philadelphia: Benjamins.

Nichols, Johanna. 1986. "Head-Marking and Dependent-Marking Grammar". *Language* 62.56–119.

Shibatani, Masayoshi & Theodora Bynon, eds. 1995. *Approaches to Language Typology.* Oxford: Clarendon Press.

Vennemann, Theo. 1974. "Analogy in Generative Grammar: The origin of word order". *Proceedings of the Eleventh International Congress of Linguists* ed. by Luigi Heilmann, vol. I, 339–376. Bologna: Il Mulino.

Bernard Comrie, Leipzig (Germany).

XXVIII. The Analysis of Speech and Unwritten Languages in the 19th Century and its Continuation in the 20th Century
Die Erforschung der lautlichen Äußerung und nicht verschrifteter Sprachen im 19. und ihre Fortsetzung im 20. Jahrhundert
L'étude de la parole et des langues non-écrites pendant le XIXe siècle et sa continuation au XXe siècle

178. The development of phonetics from the late 18th to the late 19th century

1. Introduction
2. Early treatments of non-segmental features
3. The vowel triangle
4. The beginnings of experimental phonetics
5. Developments in traditional approaches
6. Germany: communication theory and a new terminology
7. The International Phonetic Association and its founders
8. Conclusion
9. Bibliography

1. Introduction

The period dealt with by this section saw enormous strides forward in knowledge of the speech mechanism and ways of describing it and of recording speech sounds. Nevertheless, one must not forget the valuable work done in earlier centuries, notably in the 17th century, when scientific research flowered in many areas and saw the founding of academies and societies, such as the Royal Society in England, intended to further this research. Even before that there were perceptive accounts of the formation of speech, for instance by John Hart († 1574) in England, and by the Dane, Jacob Madsen (1538–1586). Petrus Montanus (1594/95–1638) in the Netherlands published his *De Spreeckonst* in 1635, though it remained little known until relatively recently (see Hulsker 1988). Foremost among English 17th-century writers on speech sounds were John Wallis (1616–1703) the famous mathematician and William Holder (1616–1698). At the end of the century the Swiss-born doctor, Conrad Amman (1669–1730) was working in the Netherlands and published works on speech. All of the last three mentioned were motivated in part by their work as teachers of the deaf. In the early 18th century Denys Dodart (1634–1707) and Antoine Ferrein (1693–1769) gave perceptive accounts of the mechanism of phonation, till then little understood.

(For further accounts of these early works see Kemp 1994: 3102 ff. and biographical articles in Asher 1994. A recent bibliography of works relating to the history of phonetics may be found in E. F. K. Koerner's introduction to the two works reproduced in Panconcelli-Calzia 1940. These works of Panconcelli-Calzia are particularly informative in tracing the development of early experimental phonetic techniques.)

2. Early treatments of non-segmental features

Thus by the late 18th century many of the elements of a proper science of phonetics were already present. However, one area which had hitherto only received rather summary treatment was the analysis of non-segmental features, such as rhythm and intonation.

2.1. At the age of 75 Joshua Steele (1700–1791) wrote a remarkable work on the non-segmental aspects of speech (Steele 1775). One of his chief contributions was to clarify and expand the use of certain terms: 'accent', 'quantity' 'pause', 'emphasis', also called 'poise' or 'cadence', and 'force'. Steele uses a musical notation to record many of these features. 'Quantity' (= duration) is shown by semiquavers, quavers, etc., and 'accent' (= pitch variation) by rising or falling oblique lines attached to the stems of these notes, corresponding to the 'slides' which the voice makes in speech. Steele suggested some of the functions of pitch patterns — a final fall for completion, and a rise for non-completion. An increase in the extent of a movement could indicate greater emotional involvement. 'Pause' is indicated by musical rests. 'Emphasis' is more complex. Speech, he says, is made up of 'cadences' or emphatical divisions, each cadence, like a musical bar, being marked by a pulsation or 'thesis' followed by an 'arsis' or remission. The pulsation may sometimes fall on a pause rather than a syllable, and be followed by one or more syllables in the remission. He marks the thesis with a small triangle and the unemphatic syllables with two or three dots. The speaker/hearer instinctively feels the pulsations, and the alternation of 'heavy' and 'light', or emphatic and non-emphatic. Emphasis is not the same as 'force' (= loudness) because it may fall on pause (i.e., silence) or on a whispered syllable. The following is one of his examples:

Oh,	|happiness|	our
|Δ	|Δ .. ∴ |	Δ ∴
|beings	|end and	|aim
|Δ ∴	|Δ ∴	|Δ

In the third cadence the thesis falls on a pause and the syllable *our* is in the arsis. In spite of the varying number of syllables each cadence has the same quantity. What Steele calls the 'measure' of speech or 'rhythmus' consists of the number of cadences in a line or sentence. Steele's attempt at analysis of non-segmental features is ahead of its time, and in spite of some inconsistencies it deserves to be accorded an important place in phonetic history, notably in its 'temporal' approach to rhythm, hotly disputed by some traditional prosodists.

2.2. Another stimulus to phonetics came from the elocutionists. Public speaking had deteriorated to a disastrous degree, and in addition, there was increasing pressure in Britain (notably in Scotland) for educated people to speak with an English accent, conforming to what was established as the prestigious accent of the time. The Irish actor Thomas Sheridan (1719–1788), father of the playwright Richard Brinsley Sheridan, and Walker (1732–1807), who also started his career as an actor, both taught elocution. Sheridan's contribution to phonetics lies partly in the description of speech contained in his very popular *Lectures on Elocution* (1762) and partly in his *General Dictionary of the English Language* (1780). Like Steele, he was concerned to emphasise the importance of the non-segmental features of speech, which he rightly believed were crucial to effective public speaking, and much of the *Lectures* is concerned with the proper use of intonation. The importance of the *Dictionary* for phonetics lies in his attempt to record pronunciations, with the idea of establishing a standard accent which would replace local varieties. This required him to develop a system of transcription, which consisted in a respelling of each word, using numeral diacritics to disambiguate confusable letters. Walker's *Elements of Elocution* (1781) adopts a much more formal approach than Sheridan in presenting rules for the use of intonation in English, relating it to pauses and to grammatical constructions. He was almost certainly influenced by knowledge of Steele's work. His *Critical Pronouncing Dictionary* (1791) had outstanding success, and provides invaluable evidence as to what Walker considered a 'proper' pronunciation at that time.

3. The vowel triangle

By the middle of the 19th century it had become fairly common to show the relationship of vowels to each other by using a diagram — most commonly in the form of a triangle. One of the earliest examples of this in print appeared in the *Dissertatio physiologico-medica de Formatione Loquelae* (1781) by Christoph Friedrich Hellwag (1754–1835) — (see Viëtor 1886). Hellwag took ⟨a⟩ to be the principal vowel. In 1780 he had presented the diagram with ⟨a⟩ to the left and a branching path extending to the right and ending in ⟨u⟩

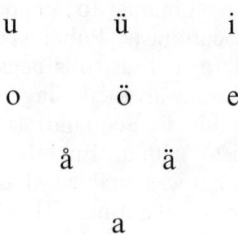

Fig. 178.1: Hellwag's vowel triangle of 1781.

and ⟨i⟩ (see Fig. 178.1). In between these three vowels are six others, said to be equally spaced from each other. In 1781 he turned the diagram to put ⟨a⟩ at the bottom. Hellwag claimed that his order and positioning of the vowels was not only auditory in its basis but also physiological, and gave short descriptions of the tongue and lip positions. The vowels ⟨ü⟩ and ⟨ö⟩ are placed centrally, sharing as they do with ⟨i⟩ and ⟨e⟩ respectively the same tongue position and with ⟨u⟩ and ⟨o⟩ the same lip position.

Hellwag allows that an infinite number of other vowels may be interpolated between those symbolised, and envisages the possibility of a mathematical model of all the vowels that the human vocal apparatus can produce. Interestingly, in describing ⟨u⟩ he noted that it can be produced without the normal close lip rounding if the root of the tongue is retracted to constrict the pharynx. He also observed that if the vowels are whispered one can detect a musical scale (corresponding to what are later called 'formants') extending from low to high in ⟨u, o, å, a, ä, e, i⟩, which is noticeably altered if the vowels are pronounced with the velum open. Many of the later vowel diagrams retain the triangular form with ⟨a⟩ at one angle and ⟨i⟩ and ⟨u⟩ at the others, but with different orientations, and they often appear to have become conventionalised, and to reflect simply an auditory impression rather than a physiological relationship. For a robust critique of these diagrams in the light of X-ray investigation see Russell (1928, Chap. 13), and for examples of analogies of vowel sounds with colours see Lepsius (1981 [1863], 51*−55*).

4. The beginnings of experimental phonetics

While simple experiments to investigate aspects of speech had been carried out earlier (e. g., by Dodart and Ferrein in the early 18th century, using excised larynxes) it was not till the end of that century that pioneering experiments were made in an attempt to produce speech sounds artificially. The apparatus devised by Christian Gottlieb Kratzenstein (1723−1795) and Wolfgang von Kempelen (1734−1804) is described elsewhere (→ Art. 180). By the early 19th century, with the advent of more sophisticated apparatus, it had become increasingly possible to analyse speech experimentally.

4.1. Investigations of the acoustics of speech sounds

Early descriptions of speech tend to identify different vowel sounds either by reference to the aperture of the lips or the internal cavity of the mouth, or to give them auditory labels such as 'thin', 'fat', 'clear', 'dark'. Hellwag had recognised that vowels have a characteristic musical 'pitch', as had others prior to the 19th century, but a theory to account for it was lacking. The German physicist Ernst Florens Friedrich Chladni (1756−1827) published his important *Die Akustik* in 1802. One should also note his *Über die Hervorbringung der menschlichen Sprache* (On the Production of Human Language) published in 1824, which is one of the earliest works to attempt to set out an articulatory theory of phonetics (MacMahon 1984).

After a general account of the numerical aspects of vibrations and an explanation of terms he goes on to describe the vibrations of resonating strings and air, and in due course to vowel sounds. His ten vowels are arranged in three series, the first involving a progressive narrowing of the lips, the second a progressive narrowing of the interior cavity of the mouth, and the third combining the characteristic of the other two. They are arranged digrammatically in a similar form to Hellwag's, but vertically reversed. Chladni discusses the vibrations of closed and open pipes and concludes that their shape is unimportant. He examines the vibrations of plates, and the nodal lines involved, and finally discusses the propagation of sounds and the sensation of sound.

Robert Willis (1800−1875) and Charles Wheatstone (1802−1875), both British physicists, pursued further investigations. Willis (1830) fitted a cylindrical tube with a reed, and by attaching further tubes to it was able to vary the total length. In this way he discovered that a simple increase in the length could produce the series of vowels ⟨i, e, a, o, u⟩, without any change in the diameter or shape of the tubes. Moreover, he observed that the quality of the vowel was independent of the note produced by the reed and concluded that it derived from damped vibrations resulting from the reflections of the original wave at the extremity of the tube. This theory came to be known as the 'inharmonic' or 'transient' theory. Wheatstone (1837–38), on repeating Willis's experiments, found that there was not only one resonance per vowel but several. The column of air in the tubes vibrated not only when it was capable of producing the same sound as the reed, but also when the number of vibrations it was capable of producing was any simple multiple of the vibration produced by the reed – i.e. when it corresponded to a harmonic of the original sound. The same was true of the cavity of the mouth acting as a resonator, responding to the vibrations of the vocal cords. Wheatstone's theory appears to be the origin of the 'harmonic cavity tone' theory, later developed by Helmholtz. Wheatstone also constructed a speaking machine on the basis of von Kempelen's description, with some modifications. His account of the vowels takes the "aw" vowel in *fall* as his starting point, and constructs three series, not far different from Chladni's. Hermann von Helmholtz (1821–1894) published his *Die Lehre von den Tonempfindungen* in 1863 (translated into English by A. J. Ellis – cf. 5.1.). He had previously experimented with cylindrical resonators, but later substituted spherical ones made of glass or of brass, with two openings, one with a neck which could be inserted into the ear (see Fig. 178.2). Using the resonators and tuning forks he analysed the components of the German vowels, separating them into two classes – ⟨u, o, a⟩ specified by one resonance, and ⟨ü, ö, ä, i, e⟩ specified by two resonances, one of which he attributed to the pharynx and the other to the mouth cavity. These correspond closely to modern definitions of the first two formants. Helmholtz then synthesised the vowels by combining the output of the appropriate tuning forks. This was the earliest effective speech synthesis using acoustic methods, and exercised a major influence on later acoustic research (Köster 1973: 159 ff.). A device called a 'phonautograph' was invented by Édouard Léon Scott in 1857 (see Fig. 178.3). This enabled the investigator to record graphically the frequency vibrations produced by tuning forks and by the vocal cords, for instance during the production of various vowel sounds. Another such device was the manometric flame developed by Rudolf Koenig from 1862 (Koenig 1872), which was connected to resonators and produced varying patterns on a mirror according to the resonances of the sounds detected see Fig. 178.4). In 1889 Ludimar Hermann (1838–1914) published *Phonophotographische Untersuchungen*, in which he analysed the wave forms of vowels, supporting the 'inharmonic' theory proposed by Willis as opposed to Helmholtz's 'harmonic' theory. He is credited with the invention of the term 'formant'. Work on consonants progressed more slowly, but during the 1870s the significance of the vowel like transition associated with consonants was realised, and Charles Rosapelly (ca. 1850–1913) coined the name 'vocaloid' for it. By the end of the century more sophisticated devices had been developed to give graphic representations of the acoustics of speech sounds (Marey 1878; Wendeler 1887; Pipping 1890). See further in Tillmann (1995: 414).

Fig. 178.2: A. Helmholtz resonator (from Rousselot 1897–1908: 162).

Fig. 178.3: Scott's phonautograph (from Rousselot 1897–1908: 110).

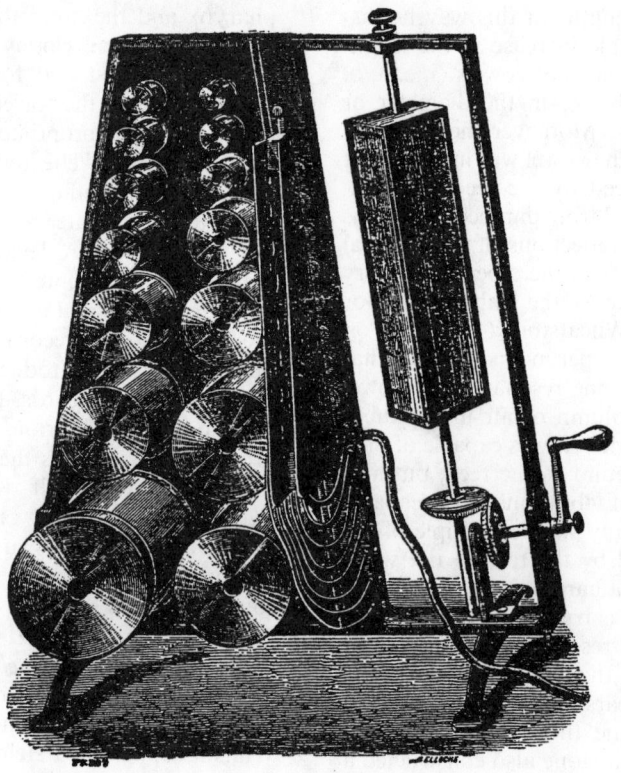

Fig. 178.4: Koenig's manometric flame apparatus (from Rousselot 1897–1908: 164).

4.2. Instrumental investigation of speech articulations

Erasmus Darwin, grandfather of Charles Darwin, in his book *Temple of Nature* (1803) described how he inserted cylinders made of tinfoil in the mouth, and deduced from the impressions made on them the part of the mouth involved in the formation of each vowel. This technique was an anticipation of the form of palatography first developed in 1879 by the New York dentist Norman William Kingsley (1829–1913), using an artificial palate. The palate was painted with a substance which was wiped off when the informant produced an utterance. The palate could then be removed and the wipe-off examined and related to the articulations. It required a careful selection of the utterance, and a fair degree of practice with the palate to allow a reasonably natural articulation. Some seven years earlier a London dentist, James Oakley Coles (1845–1906), had solved part of this problem by painting a mixture of gum and flour directly on the roof of his mouth. He then observed where the mixture had been wiped off after a particular sound had been produced, and transferred the pattern to a pre-prepared drawing of the palate and tongue (see Fig. 178.5). However his knowledge of phonetics was insufficient to allow him to obtain convincing results. Palatography became a popular technique in the latter part of the century, being used, among others, by Paul Grützner, Rudolf Lenz, Friedrich Techmer, and Abbé Rousselot, and has remained a useful method of investigation through the 20th century. It has been largely replaced in recent years by electropalatography, which also uses an artificial palate, but gives a much more detailed picture of speech, including the precise timing of articulations. (See further on these techniques Abercrombie 1957; Hardcastle et al. 1989.) Similar investigations were made of tongue contacts with the palate by painting the tongue itself to give linguograms (Grützner 1879). Palatography in its early stages was confined to the examination of carefully selected brief utterances. In order to be able to observe continuous speech, and to make

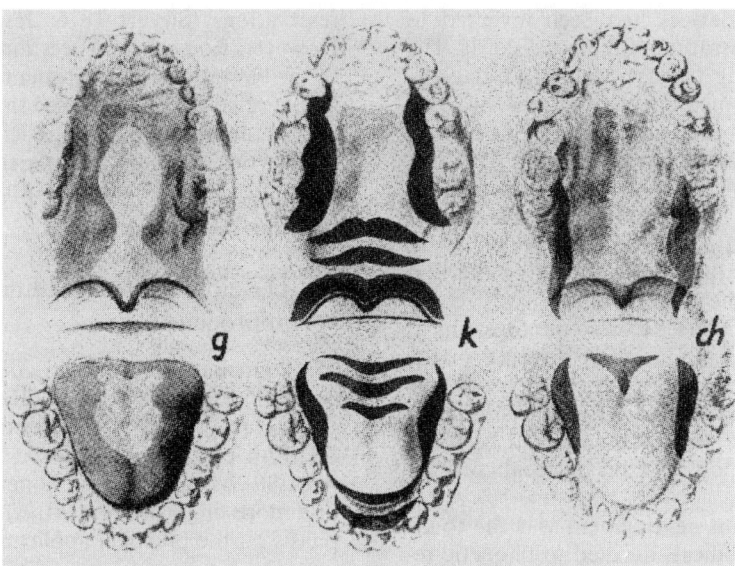

Fig. 178.5: Examples of Oakley Coles's palatograms (from Panconcelli-Calzia 1940: 55).

quantitative observations and measurements of it, a way of converting it into a continuous graphic form was needed. In 1734 a clockwork device had been invented to record wind speeds by means of a scriber resting on continuous sheets of paper on a revolving drum. Some hundred years later Karl Ludwig used a similar device to record the pattern of respiration, and the technique, known as kymography, provided a vital step forward in investigating various aspects of speech over time. The precise methodology varied, but in its developed form it consisted in obtaining an analogue on paper of the variations in air pressure during speech over time, conveyed to membranes via tubes from mouth and nose. Attached to the membranes were scribers which were moved by the air to give curves on a revolving drum covered in smoked paper (see Fig. 178.6). The technique was widely used by Pierre Jean Rousselot (1846–1924), both in his dissertation on the Gallo-Roman dialect, and in his *Principes de phonétique expérimentale* (1897–1908), but it had its limitations and these were carefully analysed by E. A. Meyer (1898). By the mid-

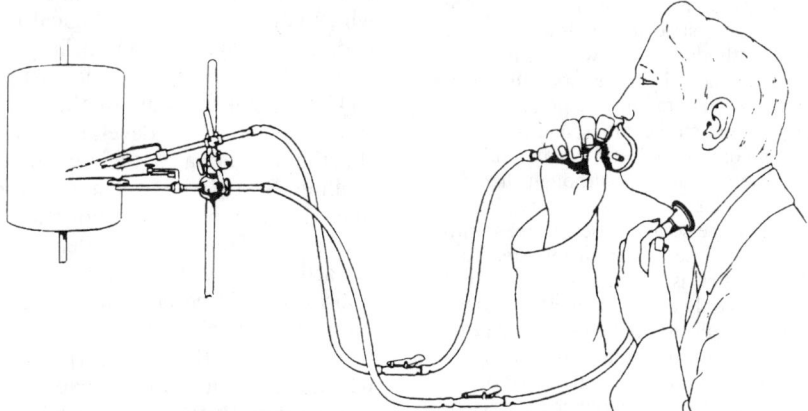

Fig. 178.6: Kymographic apparatus for recording mouth airstream and glottal vibration (from Panconcelli-Calzia. 1924. *Die experimentelle Phonetik in ihrer Anwendung auf die Sprachwissenschaft.* Berlin: de Gruyter).

19th century devices had been invented to observe the operation of the vocal cords. The Spanish singing teacher Manuel Garcia demonstrated a method of observing his own vocal cords in 1855, using a dentist's mirror. Within the next few years Johann Czermak (1828−1873) developed an apparatus enabling him to observe other people's vocal cords by the use of reflected artificial light, and published his results, including the first diagrams of the activity of the vocal cords in living informants, and also photographs of them. This marked a major advance in the understanding of the functioning of the mechanism of phonation. By the last quarter of the century the stroboscope had been enlisted to make observation of vocal cord activity easier.

An important development was the foundation of periodicals devoted to phonetic research. In the 1880s Wilhelm Viëtor (1850−1918) founded the *Zeitschrift für Orthographie* and *Phonetische Studien* (later entitled *Die neueren Sprachen*), and Friedrich Techmer (1843−1891) founded the *Internationale Zeitschrift für Allgemeine Sprachwissenschaft* (1884), which regrettably ceased publication on his death. The rapid development of the natural sciences in the 19th century with the consequent emphasis on experimentation gave a great impetus to those who believed that this was the way ahead for phonetic research. However, some had reservations. We find these expressed in the article for the 11th edition of *Encyclopædia Britannica* (1911) by Henry Sweet. Having mentioned such techniques as laryngoscopy and palatography he goes on:

"The methods hitherto considered are all comparatively simple. They require no special knowledge or training, and are accessible to all. But there are more elaborate methods − with which the name 'experimental phonetics' is more specially connected − giving special training in practical and theoretical physics and mathematics, and requiring the help of often complicated and costly, and not easily accessible apparatus [...]. Although their results are often of value, they must always be received with caution: the sources of error are so numerous [...]. It cannot be too often repeated that instrumental phonetics is, strictly speaking, not phonetics at all. It is only a help: it supplies materials which are useless till they have been tested and accepted from the linguistic phonetician's point of view. The final arbiter in all phonetic questions is the trained ear of a practical phonetician." (Henderson 1971: 37)

Eduard Sievers (1850−1932) and Otto Jespersen (1860−1943) had expressed similar reservations (Sievers 1876; Jespersen 1904). However, Rousselot was certainly well aware of the limitations of experimental techniques, and in retrospect one can see that the opposition of the traditional phoneticians may have unduly delayed the development of the new techniques and the funding of phonetic laboratories.

5. Developments in traditional approaches

The contribution of the physiologists in continental Europe, notably Rapp, Merkel, Brücke and Sievers, to phonetic research in the 19th century is discussed elsewhere (→ Art. 180). Within Britain phonetics developed in a more linguistic context, with strong emphasis on the practical applications.

5.1. Alexander John Ellis (1814−1890) came of a middle class family, and was fortunate enough to have an independent income as a result of a legacy, which allowed him to pursue his own research. He graduated with a first class degree in mathematics from Cambridge, but his many interests included music and phonetics. He grew up in a part of London where Cockney was heard every day, and his time at Shrewsbury School and at Cambridge exposed him to other more prestigious accents. It was a trip to Italy which made him conscious of the need for a system to record dialectal differences in a consistent way. He decided to study the available works on phonetics, and to extend his knowledge of languages. He was particularly influenced by Karl Moritz Rapp's (1803−1883) *Versuch einer Physiologie der Sprache* (1836−41), which combined a physiological basis with a wide knowledge of modern languages and a very keen ear for phonetic distinctions. In 1843 Ellis got to know of the work of Isaac Pitman directed at developing a system of shorthand, and also the reform of English spelling. By 1845 he was in a position to produce a major work on phonetics − *The Alphabet of Nature* − intended to contribute towards a more accurate analysis and symbolisation of speech. Three years later he published *The Essentials of Phonetics*, printed throughout in the Phonotypic transcription which Ellis and Pitman had devised. This also focuses chiefly on the problem of devising a universal alphabet. (Further details of his partnership with Pitman and his development of new systems of transcription are to be found in Art. 186.) Ellis defined phonetics as a branch of acoustics, and acknowledged a debt to von Kempelen, Willis and Wheatstone, and also to Robert Gordon Latham's (1812−1888) *Handbook of the English Language* (1st ed., 1841). Willis is quoted at length. In his description of speech sounds Ellis praises Rapp's account of the vowels, which displayed them in a triangular diagram of 11 vowels, with the open vowel ⟨a⟩ at the bottom, and three series radiating from it, similar to earlier diagrams (cf. 3.). However, his *Urvokal* ("basic vowel") ⟨ə⟩ is immediately above ⟨a⟩, in the centre of the diagram, representing "unentwickelte Indifferenz" (absence of differentiating form) − that is, a neutral (schwa-like) form as opposed to the distinct vowels which surrounded it. Ellis's diagram contains 17 vowels, and he places his 'original' vowel (symbolised ⟨ë⟩) at the base while retaining the three series radiating from it, which he relates to Willis's acoustic scale. The division of vowels into long, brief (short in an open syllable) or stopped (short in a closed syllable) is clearly English-based (see Kelly 1981: 254 ff.). Ellis's classification of consonants shows few advances on 17th-century systems such as that of Wallis (1653). The terms 'spoken' and 'whispered' are used to separate voiced and voiceless. There are some oddities, such as his description of ⟨l⟩ as having vibration of the sides of the tongue. Clucks (= clicks) are described as produced by "smacking the tongue". In 1849 Ellis became prostrated by overwork but he later produced further publications on transcription (→ Art. 186). However, the work which has brought him the most attention and recognition is the five-part *Early English Pronunciation* (1869−89). In his later years he had become deeply involved with the history of English pronunciation, and this work was an attempt to give an account of it from medieval times up to his own time. It contains a fascinating collection of data, much of it derived from a large army of informants in Britain and abroad, and goes well beyond anything attempted before in the field of English dialectology, though in many cases it is far from easy to interpret Ellis's transcriptions in his Palaeotype system (see Local 1983; Shorrocks 1991). Ellis's expertise in the area of acoustics and music is exemplified by his edition of Helmholtz's *Die Lehre von den Tonempfindungen*, under the title *On the Sensations of Tone* (2nd ed., 1885) which included much original work by Ellis. His contribution to the development of theoretical phonetics perhaps lies more in the stimulus he gave to later workers in the field than in his own ideas, but there is no questioning his broad scholarship and meticulous research.

5.2. The practical aspect of phonetics is nowhere more evident than in the life and work of Alexander Melville Bell (1819−1905). His contribution to the development of an iconic system of transcription is described elsewhere (→ Art. 207). Bell was a teacher of elocution, like his father before him − a Scot, who practised in Edinburgh and London between 1843 and 1870, and subsequently in the USA and Canada. His pupils included native English speakers and foreigners from various parts of the world, including some who suffered from speech defects. The fund of practical experience resulting from his acquaintance with such a wide range of speech sounds stimulated Bell to produce a new and improved method of describing and transcribing them. The scope of phonetics for him was not confined to the traditional vowels and consonants but included "all oral effects in speech and their graphic representation". His major contribution, apart from the new system of transcription, was in his description of vowels. In his early work he had followed in the tradition of previous descriptions, dividing his 22 vowels into three parallel groups of 7: 'labial', 'lingual' and 'labio-lingual', together with the vowel "ah". Bell was dissatisfied with this scheme, and in his major work *Visible Speech* (1867) he presented a revised analysis. His earlier description had recognised the part played in vowel formation by the height of the tongue and the shape of the oral aperture, but he now specifies the precise point at which the tongue is at its highest, emphasising the fact that the whole of the oral passage is involved in vowel production. Three horizontal positions are defined, labelled "front', 'back' and 'mixed' (midway between front and back), and three vertical grades of height: 'high', 'mid' and 'low'. This gave nine 'cardinal degrees', as he described them. All of these vowels, irrespective of their tongue position, were subject to "rounding", which involved a modification of the guttural passage and the buccal cavities as well as the lips. Bell also introduced a distinction labelled 'primary' and 'wide'. Primary vowels were nearest to consonants, involving a narrowing of the pharynx, whereas for the wide vowels the pharynx and guttural passage were fully expanded. This gave 36 vowels in all. He also ordered the vowels acoustically, according to their 'pitch', but it was his refining of the physiological basis which constituted a major contribution and influenced all subsequent descriptions. In the light of later experimental research the extent to which Bell's description tallies with the physiological facts has been called into question, but even accepting that his analysis had an auditory or proprioceptive basis, the framework he provided proved to be an effective practical tool. In 1880 Sweet commented:

"Bell's analysis of the vowels is so perfect that after ten years' incessant testing and application to a variety of languages, I see no reason for modifying its general framework." (Henderson 1971: 241).

Bell also revised his earlier consonant scheme, basing it on five places of articulation — throat (= glottal), back (= velar), front or top (= palatal), point (= dental/alveolar), lip (= labial). In terms of manner of articulation he divided into primary (= central oral), divided (= lateral oral), nasal, and shut (= stop). He wrongly classed [f, v, θ, ð] as 'divided' (i.e., lateral consonants). Sweet attributed this to "an attempt to uphold the symmetry of the system, even where its ground plan is defective", pointing out that if Bell had provided a sign for the teeth-position [θ] and [f] would fall into their natural places 'point-teeth' and 'lip-teeth' respectively. 'Mixed' consonants are those said to have a compression at two points. One example given is [s], described as 'front-mixed', because both the front and the point of the tongue are raised. Apart from 'breath' and 'voice', modifications at the larynx include aspiration, whisper, hoarseness, and the "catch" (= [ʔ]). Like Ellis, Bell introduces "glides" as a third category, intermediate to vowels and consonants, said to be formed

"when the configurative channel is so far expanded as to remove compression or buzzing from the voice [...] These elements are only *transitional* sounds. If they had a fixed configuration, they would be vowels, and would form syllables." (Henderson 1971: 265)

Having quoted this passage Sweet comments

"This view of 'glides' being intermediate to consonants and vowels is the result of confusion between the two distinct divisions of sounds, namely, that of syllabic and non-syllabic and that of consonant and vowel. The latter is entirely the result of the *position* of the organs, while the former is purely relative, dependent mainly on stress, secondarily on quantity. Any sound, whether consonant or vowel, may be either *syllabic*, that is, a syllable former, or the contrary." (Henderson 1971: 266)

Kenneth Pike (1943: 78) later introduced the terms 'vocoid' and 'contoid' precisely to solve this problem. Bell recognised that clicks involve suction, and identified four types. Modifiers are provided for nasalisation, trilling, protrusion, accent, hiatus etc., and also marks for five tonal variants. Ellis's approval of Bell's *Visible Speech* is quoted at length by Bell in his 1867 book. In 1880 Sweet gave a detailed account of it with critical comments before setting out his revised version of it — the Organic Alphabet (Henderson 1971: 256−270).

5.3. Apart from his fame as inventor of the telephone Alexander Graham Bell (1847−1922) deserves mention for his work in teaching the deaf using the *Visible Speech* method invented by his father. He was also inspired by seeing the operation of Wheatstone's reconstruction of the speaking machine invented by Wolfgang von Kempelen to construct a complex physiologically based automaton of his own, which could apparently produce vowels and nasals and a few simple utterances. In 1879 he published a paper entitled "Vowel Theories".

5.4. Henry Sweet (1845−1912) was in his early twenties when Bell's *Visible Speech* was published, and it stimulated what was already a strong interest in languages. He took lessons from Bell, and was well acquainted with the earlier tradition in phonetics. In 1877 he published his *Handbook of Phonetics*, which had a major impact on phonetics in Britain, and an even greater one on the continent of Europe. He placed phonetics firmly in the context of language study rather than adopting the physiological approach characterising many continental writers (→ Art. 180 and MacMahon 1991). In his view it was "the indispensable foundation of all study of language" (1877: v), and he himself acquired a wide knowledge of the phonetics of languages, particularly those of northern Europe. The system he put forward in the *Handbook* differed from Bell's in a number of ways. We saw that he corrected Bell's faulty analysis of [f, v, θ, ð], by adding the category "teeth". He also took issue with Bell's distinction of 'primary' and 'wide' vowels, attributed to a change in the shape of the pharynx. Sweet substituted the terms 'narrow' and 'wide', extending them to consonants, and relating the distinction to the shape of the tongue rather than the pharynx. For narrow sounds the tongue is said to be under tension, and relatively convex through being 'bunched up lengthwise', narrowing the oral passage, whereas for wide sounds it was relaxed and flattened. Sweet emphasised that this did not depend on tongue height. He contrasted the high-front-narrow vowel in French *si* with the high-front-wide vowel in English *bit*. However, one of his major innovations in the *Handbook* is the introduction of a broad division into analysis and synthesis. He writes:

"Analysis regards each sound as a fixed, stationary point, synthesis as a momentary point in a stream of incessant change. Synthesis looks mainly at the beginning and end of each sound, as the points where it is linked on to other sounds, while analysis concerns itself only with the middle of the fully developed sound." (Henderson 1971: 44)

And later:

"From a purely phonetic point of view words do not exist [...] We see, then, that there are two ways of dealing with languages: (1) the synthetic, which starts from the sentence; (2) the analytic, which starts from the word." (Henderson 1971: 43)

Glides are an essential aspect of synthesis. Sweet rejected Bell's classification of glides as a third category alongside vowels and consonants, and confined the term 'glide' to the vowels. Diphthongs are held to be a combination of glide vowel and full vowel, or possibly of two full vowels. Other aspects of synthesis are: force, which he later called stress, quantity or length, syllable division, and intonation. In the *Handbook* Sweet confesses to a lack of competence to deal with intonation (Henderson 1971: 175), but he does his best to grapple with it, and with stress and tone. Word-tone in languages such as Chinese is distinguished from the sentence-tone of English, and word-stress from sentence-stress (= tonic placement). In spite of the emphasis which Sweet gave to synthesis most of his successors tended to neglect it. Another of his innovative terms, "organic basis", is a particularly interesting phenomenon. To quote him:

"Every language has certain general tendencies which control its organic movements and positions, constituting its organic basis or basis of articulation. A knowledge of the organic basis is a great help in acquiring the pronunciation of a language." Henderson 1971: 184—185)

These tendencies were largely ignored prior to the appearance of Beatrice Honikman's article "Articulatory Settings" in 1964.

In 1890 Sweet published his *Primer of Phonetics*, clarifying and expanding the material in the *Handbook*. Instead of the Roman-based phonetic notation of the *Handbook* ('Romic'), he now uses his revised version of Bell's Visible Speech — the Organic Alphabet (→ Art. 186, for further descriptions of these notations). However, the most striking change came in the 1906 edition of the *Primer*. Sweet decided that the 36 vowel classification did not account satisfactorily for the way certain vowel sounds were produced. His earlier assumption had been that the back vowels had a backward slope of the tongue, and the front vowels a forward slope, while for the mixed vowels the tongue was flat. Now he became persuaded that for some vowels the tongue was 'shifted' forwards or backwards while retaining the slope. Thus, the mixed vowel could be shifted back while retaining its flatshape, the back vowel could be shifted forward while retaining its back slope, and the front vowel shifted back, retaining its front slope. This gave him a system of 72 vowels. Sweet's objective was to give precise instructions for producing the sounds concerned, though he may well have originally identified them by a combination of auditory, tactile and proprioceptive sensations. Later experimental investigations have shown that many of the articulatory descriptions found in Bell, Sweet and others do not tally with the picture as revealed by X-rays (e. g., Russell 1928; Wood 1982).

Sweet's cautionary remarks about the techniques of experimental phonetics have already been quoted (cf. 4.2.), and perhaps it is regrettable that he was not more receptive to them. However, now that the instrumental, and particularly the acoustic, aspects of phonetics have come almost to dominate the scene, it is salutary to remind ourselves of the insights that are to be found in the *Handbook* and the *Primer*. Sweet's achievements in advancing phonetic theory, in the study of the English language and in the practical teaching of languages were given more ready recognition during his lifetime outside Britain than within it, but there can be few who would now question his crucial influence in the development of the science of phonetics.

6. Germany: communication theory and a new terminology

6.1. Friedrich Techmer's (1843—1891) scientific background, together with his wide knowledge of languages, made him particularly suited to undertake the reconciliation of the different traditions in phonetics, classical and experimental. His foundation of the *Internationale Zeitschrift für allgemeine Sprachwissenschaft* was mentioned earlier. Volume 1 (pp. 69—192) contained a valuable survey of the various experimental techniques used to investigate speech, a set of German technical terms for phonetics, and also an attempt to formulate a scientific theory to deal with all phonetic speech communication, covering analysis and synthesis. He distinguished seven interrelated stages dealing with speech, proceeding first from outside to inside — a physical-acoustic analysis, then from inside to outside — an anatomical and a physiological-productive analysis. Physiologically sounds are divided into 'mouth-openers' (Mundöffner) and 'mouth-closers' (Mundschließer), physically they are either "noises" (Geräuschlaute) or 'tones' (Klanglaute), and perceptually they are either syllabic (Phon) or non-syllabic (Symphon). So, for instance, vowels are characterised as 'mouth-openers, tones and syllabic'. Techmer was highly critical of mistakes he claimed to have detected in Melville Bell's and Paul Passy's work, and in turn came under attack from Sweet and Storm, who asserted that he provided too little evidence for his theory from languages, and failed to explain the theory adequately.

6.2. Moritz Trautmann (1842—1920) published his book *Die Sprachlaute im Allgemeinen und die Laute des Englischen, Französischen und Deutschen im Besonderen* (The Sounds of Speech in general and in particular the sounds of English, French and German) about the same time as Techmer's theory of speech communication (1884—86). One of his objectives was to provide the basis for a German school of phonetics, introducing new terminology and putting the emphasis on an acoustic approach to vowel description rather than the articulatory one adopted by the British and Scandinavian phoneticians. Unfortunately his presentation is often obscure and lacking in the exemplification from languages which could have clarified it, especially considering that he intended it for use by language teachers.

7. The International Phonetic Association and its founders

It is well known that the International Phonetic Association (IPA) sprang out of an association concerned with the teaching of languages. Further details of its origin and growth can be found in MacMahon (1986). However, it may be appropriate to include here some brief remarks on the contributions to phonetic theory of several of those who were instrumental in the establishment of the IPA, namely Johan Storm, Otto Jespersen, Wilhelm Viëtor and Paul Passy. Their contributions to the application of phonetics to language teaching and their involvement in the IPA are dealt with in detail in art. 208. Henry Sweet's work is described in 5.4. above. Johan Storm (1836—1920) was a brilliant practical phonetician, who developed a new system for transcribing the dialects of his native country Norway, still in use today. He was a close friend of Henry Sweet, and encouraged him to produce a new work giving the main results of Bell's investigations with suitable additions and alterations. This resulted in Sweet's *Handbook* (cf. 5.4.). However, Storm lacked Sweet's ability to set out his investigations in a systematic way, and his wider reputation rests on his undoubtedly strong influence on contemporary phoneticians, notably Sweet and Eduard Sievers. The Danish scholar Otto Jespersen (1860—1943) made important contributions to many aspects of linguistics. Influenced by Sweet's *Handbook* and by his Norwegian friend Johan Storm he developed an early interest in phonetics. In 1889 he published his analphabetic system for phonetic transcription (→ Art. 186), involving a detailed analysis of the various sound types. His book *Fonetik* (1897—1898; republished in German as *Phonetische Grundfragen* and *Lehrbuch der Phonetik*, both 1904) gives a thorough account of descriptive phonetics, based on his own personal observations. The Danish edition provides a new set of phonetic terms for Danish. Like Sweet he was not an advocate of the new experimental methods in phonetics, being particularly critical of those who favoured an acoustic approach over the articulatory one. He made important contributions to the phonetics of Danish, including the invention of a dialect alphabet 'Dania', which is still in use in Denmark. A planned English edition of his textbook on general phonetics never reached fruition (Rischel 1989: 56). Wilhelm Viëtor (1850—1918) was a pioneer of reform in language teaching, and made an important contribution to the study of phonetics in Germany. He founded the periodical *Phonetische Studien*, later continued as *Die Neueren Sprachen*, published a textbook in phonetics containing a valuable summary of the work of his predecessors (Viëtor 1884), and was one of the founder members of the IPA. Paul Passy (1859–1940) like Viëtor was a founder member of the IPA – and also shared with him the determination to reform the teaching of languages and in particular their phonetic aspect. His doctoral thesis on historical phonetics won the Prix Volney (Passy 1890), and his brilliant teaching brought him a wide influence both within and outside France.

8. Conclusion

The 19th century, and particularly the second half, was an exciting and stimulating time for those working in the field of phonetics. It saw the establishment of the traditional side, with its auditory/articulatory theory, as a discipline, and the rapid development of the experimental approach, in spite of the scepticism of many phoneticians. Any attempt in a limited space to summarise these developments will inevitably leave gaps. The birth and growth of phonology is closely linked with the study of phonetics, but falls outside the scope of this article. The focus is concentrated, one hopes not unduly, on western Europe and the USA, as it was there that the major developments took place.

9. Bibliography

Abercrombie, David. 1957. "Direct Palatography". *Zeitschrift für Phonetik* 10.21–25. (Repr. in *Studies in Phonetics and Linguistics* by D. Abercrombie, 125–130. London: Oxford Univ. Press, 1965.)

Asher, Ronald E., ed. 1994. *The Encyclopedia of Language and Linguistics.* Oxford: Pergamon Press.

Austerlitz, Robert. 1975. "Historiography of Phonetics: A bibliography". *Current Trends in Linguistics* ed. by Thomas A. Sebeok, vol. XIII: *Historiography of Linguistics*, 1179–1209. The Hague: Mouton.

Bell, Alexander Melville. 1867. *Visible Speech: The Science of Universal Alphabetics.* London: Simpkin, Marshall & Co.

Breymann, Hermann. 1897. *Die phonetische Literatur von 1876–1895: Eine bibliographisch-kritische Übersicht.* Leipzig: A. Deichert.

Chladni, E. F. F. 1802. *Die Akustik.* Leipzig: Breitkopf & Härtel.

Danielsson, Bror, ed. 1955. *John Hart's Works.* Stockholm: Almqvist & Wiksell.

Darwin, Erasmus. 1803. *The Temple of Nature or the Origin of Society.* London: J. Johnson. (Facsimile repr., Menston: Scolar Press 1973).

Ellis, Alexander J. 1845. *The Alphabet of Nature.* Bath: I. Pitman.

–. 1848. *The Essentials of Phonetics.* London: F. Pitman.

Grützner, Paul. 1879–83. "Physiologie der Stimme und Sprache". *Hermanns Handbuch der Physiologie.* Band I. Teil II. Leipzig: Vogel.

Hardcastle, William et al. 1989. "New Developments in Electropalatography: A state-of-the-art report". *Clinical Linguistics and Phonetics* 3:1.1–38.

Hellwag, Christoph F. 1781. *Dissertatio physiologico-medica de Formatione Loquelae.* Tübingen.

Helmholtz, Hermann. 1863. *Die Lehre von den Tonempfindungen.* Braunschweig: Vieweg. (English transl., by A. J. Ellis *On the Sensations of Tone*, 2nd ed. London: Longmans Green 1885.)

Henderson, Eugénie J. A. 1971. *The Indispensable Foundation: A selection from the writings of Henry Sweet.* London: Oxford Univ. Press.

Honikman, Beatrice. 1964. "Articulatory Settings". *In Honour of Daniel Jones*, 73–84. London: Longmans.

Hulsker, J. L. M. 1988. "Petrus Montanus as a Phonetician and Theoretician". *Historiographia Linguistica* 15:1/2.85–108.

Jespersen, Otto. 1904. *Lehrbuch der Phonetik.* Leipzig & Berlin: Teubner.

Kemp, J. Alan. 1994. "Phonetics: Precursors of Modern Approaches". Koerner & Asher 1995. 371–388.

König, Rudolf. 1872. "Die manometrischen Flammen". *Annalen der Physik und Chemie* 146.161 ff.

Koerner, E. F. K. & R. E. Asher, eds. 1995. *Concise History of the Language Sciences.* Oxford & New York: Pergamon.

Köster, Jens-Peter. 1973. *Historische Entwicklung von Syntheseapparaten.* Hamburg: Buske.

Lepsius, Carl Richard. 1981 [1863]. *Standard Alphabet for Reducing Unwritten Languages and Foreign Graphic Systems to a Uniform Orthography in European Letters.* 2nd rev. ed. prepared by J. Alan Kemp. Amsterdam: Benjamins.

Local, John K. 1983. "Making a Transcription: The evolution of A. J. Ellis's Palaeotype". *Journal of the International Phonetic Association* 13:1.2–12.

MacMahon, Michael K. C. 1984. "Phonetics and Medicine in the Early 19th Century (Abstract)". *Henry Sweet Society Newsletter* No. 2, Nov. 1984, p. 16. Oxford.

–. 1986. "The International Phonetic Association: The first 100 years". *Journal of the International Phonetic Association* 16.30–38 (1987).

–. 1991. "Sweet, Europe and Phonetics". *Henry Sweet Society Newsletter* No. 17, Nov. 1991, 12–18.

Marey, Étienne Jules. 1878. *La méthode graphique dans les sciences expérimentales.* Paris: Masson.

Meyer, Ernst Alfred. 1898. "Die Silbe". *Die neueren Sprachen* 6.479–493.

Panconcelli-Calzia, Giulio. 1940. *Quellenatlas zur Geschichte der Phonetik.* Hamburg: Hansischer Gildenverlag. (Repr., together with Panconcelli-Calzia (1941), and an English introduction by Konrad Koerner, Amsterdam & Philadelphia: Benjamins, 1993.)

–. 1941. *Geschichtszahlen der Phonetik: 3000 Jahre Phonetik.* Hamburg: Hansischer Gildenverlag. (Reprinted in the 1993 ed. of Panconcelli-Calzia 1940.)

Passy, Paul. 1890. *Études sur les changements phonétiques.* Paris: Firmin-Didot.

Pipping, Hugo. 1890. *Om Klangfärgen hos sjungna vokaler.* Helsingfors: Frenkell & Son. (Transl. into German as "Zur Klangfarbe der gesungenen Vokale", *Zeitschrift für Biologie* 27, 1890, 77 ff.)

Rapp, Karl M. 1836–41. *Versuch einer Physiologie der Sprache.* 4 vols. Stuttgart & Tübingen: Cotta.

Rischel, Jørgen. 1989. "Otto Jespersen's Contribution to Danish and General Phonetics". *Otto Jespersen: Facets of his life and work* ed. by Arne Juul & Hans F. Nielsen, 43–60. Amsterdam & Philadelphia: Benjamins.

Rousselot, Pierre Jean. 1897–1908. *Principes de phonétique expérimentale.* 2 vols. Paris: Welter.

Sheridan, Thomas. 1780. *A General Dictionary of the English language.* London: Dodsley. (Facsimile ed. Menston: Scolar Press, 1967.)

Shorrocks, Graham. 1991. "A. J. Ellis as Dialectologist". *Historiographia Linguistica* 18:2/3.321–334.

Sievers, Eduard. 1876. *Grundzüge der Lautphysiologie.* Leipzig: Breitkopf & Härtel.

Steele, Joshua. 1775. *An Essay towards Establishing the Melody and Measure of Speech.* London: J. Almon. (2nd ed. *Prosodia Rationalis*, 1779; Facsimile ed., Menston: Scolar Press, 1969.)

Tillmann, Hans Günter. 1995. "Phonetics: Early modern, especially instrumental and experimental work". Koerner & Asher 1995.401–416.

Viëtor, Wilhelm. 1884. *Elemente der Phonetik des Deutschen, Englischen und Französischen.* Heilbronn: Gebr. Henninger. (4th ed., 1898.)

–, ed. 1886. *Christoph Friedrich Hellwag: Dissertatio inauguralis physiologico-medica de formatione loquelae.* New edition of 1781 Univ. of Tübingen thesis, with commentary. Heilbronn: Gebr. Henninger.

Walker, John. 1781. *Elements of Elocution.* 2 vols. London: Robinson. (Facsimile repr. Menston: Scolar Press, 1969.)

–. 1791. *A Critical Pronouncing Dictionary and Expositor of the English Language.* London: G. G. J. & J. Robinson. (Facsimile repr., Menston: Scolar Press, 1968.)

Wendeler, Paul. 1887. "Ein Versuch die Schallbewegung einiger Konsonanten und anderer Geräusche mit dem Hensen'schen Sprachzeichener graphisch darzustellen". *Zeitschrift für Biologie* 23.303–320.

Wheatstone, Charles. 1837–38. Review of Willis (1830), *Le mécanisme de la parole* by W. von Kempelen and *Tentamen coronatum de voce* by C. G. Kratzenstein. *London & Westminster Review* 28 (1837), 27–41, and 29 (1838), 27.

Willis, Robert. 1830. "On the Vowel Sounds, and on Reed Organ Pipes". *Transactions of the Cambridge Philosophical Society* 3.231–268.

Wood, Sidney. 1982. *X-Ray and Model Studies of Vowel Articulation.* Lund: Dept. of Linguistics, Univ. of Lund.

J. Alan Kemp, Edinburgh (Great Britain)

179. Field work and data-elicitation of unwritten languages for descriptive and comparative purposes: Strahlenberg, Sjögren, Castrén, Böhtlingk

1. Before 1800
2. The Finnish tradition
3. Otto Böhtlingk
4. Field work and comparative Indo-European linguistics
5. Bibliography

1. Before 1800

Field work and data elicitation from informants (cf. Samarin 1967) are probably as old as any human engagement in the study of language. However, it was largely an individual matter and not a part of the methodology of linguistics. This applies also to the intensive activity – largely by missionaries – after 1500 to learn and describe the numerous indigenous language of Africa, the Americas, Asia and later on Oceania (cf. Wonderly & Nida 1963; Hovdhaugen 1996). Many of these missionary linguistics were first class field linguists (and of course, many others failed on almost every paragraph in the non-existing handbook). Nonetheless, they did not consider this as a part of the explicit methodology of their linguistic research which consisted mainly of grammar and dictionary writing and translation (cf. also Hovdhaugen 1996).

Data collection for comparative purposes started with Conrad Gesner's (1516–1665) *Mithridates* (1555) and similar projects in the 16th century consisting mainly of more or less reliable translations of The Lord's Prayer as well as short word lists. In this case there was a kind of generally accepted methodology, but it was quite naïve and in many cases led to distorted data often being a direct word-for-word translation.

A work to profoundly influence the methodology and use of field work in comparative linguistics was Strahlenberg (1730). This work by the former Swedish officer and prisoner of war in Russia, Philipp Johann von Strahlenberg [Stralenberg, born Tabbert] (1676–1747) was translated into all the major European languages. Strahlenberg was one of the more than 20,000 Swedish soldiers and officers taken prisoner by the Russians after the defeat at Poltava in 1709. Strahlenberg returned to Sweden from his involuntary stay in Russia in 1723.

Most of Strahlenberg's success is undoubtedly due to his field work methods. He collected his material during his extensive travels in Russia, and where languages were concerned he chose the numerals from 1 to 10 as his basis. He rejected the practice of others, who collected words for abstract religious terms or translations of The Lord's Prayer as the basis for comparison, because such translations would be difficult to obtain and unnatural since abstract concepts might be lacking in the language. On the basis of his collection of numerals and a few other lexical items he arrived at a classification of 32 languages, among them 5 Caucasian languages with material he had from other sources. He classified the languages into groups or nations, and with the exception of the subclassification of Caucasian languages and the grouping together of the Tungusian and Paleo-Siberian languages, he arrived at a classification quite identical to the results of modern comparative research.

2. The Finnish traditioin

For centuries Russia had attracted the interest of scholars due to its great linguistic variaty, and in the 18th century numerous foreign travelers (Finnish, Dutch, German, and Swedish) collected shorter or longer word lists from some of these languages. There were also more systematic and organized collections of linguistic data like those organized by the philosopher Leibniz and especially those by Empress Catherina II (1729–1796), cf. Adelung (1815). The most impressive result of this organized vocabulary collection was Pallas (1787–89) edited by the German naturalist (!) Peter Simon Pallas (1741–1811).

All these linguistic studies were carried out in the spirit of the enlightenment, during which time words were collected just like plants on the basis of Linné's model. The words were classified from a comparative perspective, but without any interest for the grammar and the overall description of the languages studied, or rather collected.

The idea of sending expeditions into Russia to study the Finno-Ugric languages there in search of roots was first put forward by the influential Finnish polyhistorian Henrik Gabriel Porthan (1739–1804). Porthan launched the idea around 1780, specifically as a concern for determining the lexical resources of Finnish on the basis of comparison with related languages. Little was known about eastern Finno-Ugric languages when Porthan articulated his view. However, János Sajnovics (1735–1785) had already in his famous comparison of Saami and Hungarian from 1770 showed the importance of material gathered from native informants for comparative studies. In the 1820s the Russians, or more precisely the Academy in St. Petersburg, became interested in the idea and asked the Finnish scholar Sjögren to conduct these investigations.

Anders Johan Sjögren (1794–1855) was the first of the great Finno-Ugric field linguists, making his main expedition in 1824–1829 with the broad aim of collecting and investigating materials related to Finno-Ugric languages, history, archeology, geography, agriculture, etc. (cf. Branch 1973). This trip covered more than 20,000 km and brought him to areas where, among others, Carelian, Saami, Mari, Komi, and Udmurt were spoken. Most of his material remained unpublished, but his grammatical and comparative sketch of Komi (Sjögren 1832) became a model for similar studies.

Sjögren's methods in field work were many faceted. One important point distinguishing him from most of his predecessors was that he always tried to get an active command of the languages he studied. Furthermore, he based his descriptions of a language on information received from several informants preferably representing different dialects or at least locations.

Sjögren spent the years 1835–1838 in the Caucasus, curing his eye that had been badly injured. During his stay he studied Georgian, Persian, Turkish, Cabardian, and especially Ossetic. His Ossetic grammar and dictionary from 1844 based on his own field work rightly gained him international recognition. It is indeed a masterpiece and one of the great grammars of the time. The grammar contains a thorough phonological section with very accurate phonetic descriptions of the articulation of Ossetic sounds, based on a surprisingly good insight into articulatory phonetics. The phonology is followed by an orderly word and paradigm morphology and a good treatment of most aspects of the syntax. The whole grammar is based on the pattern of Latin grammar, but since Ossetic is an Indo-European language, this is not very problematic. Moreover, the author did not feel totally bound by the framework of Latin grammar and departed from it when the structure of Ossetic makes it necessary or advisable. With his Finnish background Sjögren was well-equipped to handle the rich, by Indo-European standards, set of local cases in Ossetic.

Sjögren was the (often underestimated) pioneer of empirical Finno-Ugric studies and the one who started to implement Porthan's vision. Part of this oversight is due to the fact that Sjögren spent his whole career in St. Petersburg and was, therefore, frequently treated with suspicion by scholars residing in Finland. In any case, long trips and extensive fieldwork became one of the dominant characteristics of Finno-Ugric studies for almost a century.

When the Imperial Academy of Sciences in St. Petersburg wanted to send new expeditions to carry on the successful linguistic field work initiated by Sjögren, Sjögren felt himself to be too old, and his choice fell on Matthias Alexander Castrén (1813–1852) who was appointed in 1844. Castrén had previously done field work in Lapland and Karelia 1838 and 1839 and had already started work in Russia in 1843 and also made a long field journey to Lapland and Western Siberia in 1841–1844. Even if he was experienced with travelling in the Far North, the conditions of this first long trip had been so tough that he was found to suffer from tuberculosis in 1844 forcing him to terminate his journey and return home.

By then Sjögren had managed to provide adequate financial support from the Imperial Academy for the decisive long journey. It was to last for about 5 years and to extend over Siberia beyond the Jenissei, from the coastal tundra of the Arctic Sea all the way to the Chinese border. What Castrén managed to accomplish during this trip is truly amazing. Besides extensive archaeological and ethnographic material, he collected material on all the Samoyed languages, material sufficient to write a thorough grammar for all of them (Castrén 1854, 1855, both published posthumously), on Khanty (Ostyak), on the totally isolated and extremely difficult Jenissei-Ostyak languages Ket and Kott, on two dialects of the Turkic language Khakas, on Buryat Mongolian and on Evenki (Tungusian). And all his work was carried out under tough climatic conditions with him being ill most of the time.

An idea of how his field work took place can be gained from his own description of how he wrote his grammar of Komi.

'In that town [Kolwa] I settled down for the rest of the summer and got as a place to stay one of the worst poky holes there where I was continuously pestered by heat and humidity, by mosquitos, vermin and a noisy crowd of children. Although I was accustomed to working under many different circumstances, I had great difficulties in keeping my thoughts together and had to take refuge in a cellar under the poky hole. In this subterranean living place I wrote my Komi grammar although I was even here disturbed both by rats and mice. The study of Samoyed which was the main purpose of my visit to Kolwa had to be done on the upper floor since my teachers were a bit nervous about the lower regions [of the place] and did not like to enter them. Beside this I strolled every day around in the woods and the fields, shot some ducks, collected cloudberreis and in a word tried to acquire some better food than what the Samoyeds used to serve me.' (Castrén 1852: 263–264; translated from the Swedish by E. H.)

Castrén managed to publish very few grammatical descriptions before his death. His grammar of Komi (Castrén 1844) is based on several months' field work. He is very critical towards older studies which were replete with errors, simplifications and gaps, and is very careful in explaining the languages' pronunciation, continuous making comparisons with Finnish. On his death bed Castrén managed to finish his grammar of Samoyed

(Castrén 1854), but the rest of his material consisting of grammars of Ket and Kott, Khakas, Buryat Mongolian and Evenki was edited and published by the famous orientalist Franz Anton von Schiefner (1817–1879) at the St. Petersburg Academy. Schiefner, who was a specialist of Tibetan, later rendered a similar service to linguistics by editing the material on the Caucasian languages collected by Peter Baron von Uslar [Petr Karlovič Uslar] (1816–1875) and many others.

It is not easy to evalute Castrén. His linguistic works are uneven. He was very interested in phonetics, but as he lacked a phonetic alphabet and an understanding of articulatory phonetics, his phonetic descriptions of the languages he investigated are mostly unclear and inaccurate. He was basically a comparativist, collected his language material and wrote his grammar as a basis for comparative studies. He was completely uninterested in syntax, and none of his grammars, not even this extensive grammar of Samoyed (Castrén 1854), contains any syntax.

Sjögren and Castrén started an Age of Explorers, a Finnish tradition of making long and cumbersome scientific journeys to the East, especially Siberia. An important methodological result of this approach was that Finnish linguists started to analyse genuine vernacular speech much earlier than linguists in most other countries.

The ultimate consolidation of field work efforts was performed by Otto Donner (1835–1909), an excellent organizer, on whose initiative the Finno-Ugric Society was founded in 1883. Donner outlined a systematic programme for the Society to promote Finno-Ugric research and field work, and he raised most of the money needed for implementing the long journeys and other plans. Starting in 1884, the Society sent numerous field workers and researchers all over the Uralic area (cf. Korhonen 1989: 247–248). Much work was also done on neighbouring non-Uralic languages.

This period of intensive field work lasted 30 years, from 1884 to 1914. No less than 41 scholars participated in the systematically organized journeys. The Russian revolution and Finland's independence in 1917 changed the situation, the borders were closed, and after the early 1920s no more explorers were let into the young Soviet Union.

3. Otto Böhtlingk

To some extent the Finnish contribution to field linguistics was more on the quantitative than on the qualitative level and the descriptive studies were, with the exception of Sjögren (1844), not on the level of the great descriptive grammars of the 19th century like Otto Böhtlingk's (1815–1904) grammar of Yakut of 1851 and Samuel Kleinschmidt's (1814–1886) grammar of Kalaallisut (Greenlandic) of 1851. Kleinschmidt had learned Kalaallisut as a child and wrote the grammar largely based on his own intuitions as the main source of data (cf. Nowak 1987, 1992). But Böhtlingk's Yakut grammar belongs to the milestones of descriptive linguistics and of field work methodology. Böhtlingk, who is mainly known for his work on Sanskrit grammar and lexicography, received in 1845 the linguistic material of Yakut gathered by the German explorer and naturalist Alexander Theodor von Middendorff (1815–1894). Shortly afterwards, Böhtlingh located a native speaker of Yakut in St. Petersburg, Uvarovskij, and with his help he collected text material for his grammar and checked all his Yakut material. Bloomfield (1933: 18–19) rightly regarded Böhtlingk's grammar as a forerunner of descriptive linguistics of the 20th century. A few quotes from the introduction illustrate well Böhtlingk's methodological consciousness and sophistication which was quite unique for his time:

"Dieses Wörterverzeichniss begann ich nun vor Allem mit Uwarowskij durchzugehen und zwar auf die Weise, dass ich ihm nicht das jakutische Wort zur Prüfung vorlegte, sondern das dem russischen Worte entsprechende jakutische ausfragte. Bei dieser Arbeit wurden alle offenbar falschen Wortformen ausgeschieden; [...]" (Böhtlingk 1851: xlix)

"Uwarowskij ist ein Mann von gesundem Verstande, aber ohne gelehrte Bildung: er spricht und schreibt das Jakutische eben so geläufig wie das Russische, kennt aber die Sprache natürlich nur *ex usu.* Jede Regel habe ich mir selbst abziehen müssen und vor dem Lehrer immer zu verbergen gesucht, damit er nicht befangen wurde und mir zu Gefallen der Theorie vor der Praxis den Vortritt gestattete. Nicht selten indessen errieth der begabte Lehrer, auch ohne alle Andeutung von Seiten des Schülers, diejenige Form, welche dieser nach der Analogie zu hören erwartete. Traf die Erwartung des Schülers in dergleichen Fällen zu, so durfte die auf solche Weise gewonnene Form erst dann als in der Wirklichkeit vorhanden betrachtet werden, wenn sie nach Verlauf von einiger Zeit vom Lehrer, der inzwischen seine frühere Unbefangenheit wiedererlegt hatte, bestätigt wurde." (Böhtlingk 1851: 1)

Böhtlingk was, however, very familiar with the works of Strahlenberg and Castrén, and Finnish linguistics in general. His sophisticated field work methodology built on a solid tradition.

4. Field work and comparative Indo-European linguistics

In the first decades of comparative Indo-European linguistics the focus was solely on written sources, mainly of dead languages. It was only in the second part of the the 19th century that Indo-Europeanists started to get interested in material from living, and partly undescribed, languages. The first living language to attract field workers was Lithuanian especially due to its archaic tonal system which was not reflected in the written language and older sources. August Schleicher (1821–1868), followed later by August Leskieni (1840–1916), started the study of Lithuanian dialects and prosody, a field that was later on cultivated by, e.g., Ferdinand de Saussure and Louis Hjelmslev. Celtic languages and Albanian were also included due to the scarcity of (old) texts and the importance of the modern languages or dialects for comparative studies. The Indo-Europeanists did not, however, develop any methods of field linguistics that went beyond the works of the Finnish linguists and Böhtlingk. Linguistic field work methodology in general, and its use in comparative linguistics in particular, is based on a continuous development from Strahlenberg via Sjögren and Castrén to its perfection by Böhtlingk.

5. Bibliography

Adelung, Friedrich. 1815. *Catherinens der Grossen Verdienste um die vergleichende Sprachenkunde.* St. Petersburg: Friedrich Drechsler. (Repr., Hamburg: Buske, 1976.)

Bloomfield, Leonard. 1933. *Language.* New York: Holt & Co.

Branch, Michael. 1973. *A. J. Sjögren, Studies of the North.* (= *Mémoires de la société finno-ougrienne,* 152.) Helsinki: Suomalais-ugrilainen seura.

Böhtlingk, Otto Nicolaus von. 1851. *Über die Sprache der Jakuten.* [= *Dr. A. Th. von Middendorffs Reise in den äussersten Norden und Osten Sibiriens.* Band III.] St. Petersburg: Gedruckt bei der kaiserlichen Akademie der Wissenschaften. (Repr. with a foreword by John R. Krüger, The Hague: Mouton, 1964.)

Castrén, Matthias Alexander. 1844. *Elementa Grammatices Syrjaenae.* Helsingforsiae: Ex officina typographica heredum Simelii.

—. 1852. *Nordiska resor och forskningar.* I. Helsingfors: Finska Litteratur-Sällskapets Tryckeri.

—. 1854. *Grammatik der samojedischen Sprachen.* Herausgegeben von Anton Schiefner. St. Petersburg: Eggers & Co.

—. 1855. *Wörterverzeichnisse aus den samojedischen Sprachen.* Bearbeitet von Anton Schiefner. St. Petersburg: Eggers & Co.

Ges(s)ner, Conrad. 1555. *Mithridates: De differentiis linguarum tum veterum tum quae hodie apud diversas nationes in toto orbe terrarum in usu sunt.* Zürich: Excudebat Froschoverus.

Hovdhaugen, Even. 1996. *... and the Word was God: Missionary linguistics and missionary grammar.* Münster: Nodus.

Kleinschmidt, Samuel. 1851. *Grammatik der grönländischen Sprache mit teilweisem Einschluss des Labradordialekts.* Berlin: Reimer. (Repr., Hildesheim: Olms, 1968.)

Korhonen, Mikko. 1986. *Finno-Ugrian Language Studies in Finland 1828–1918.* Helsinki: Societas Scientiarum Fennica.

Nowak, Elke. 1987. *Samuel Kleinschmidts 'Grammatik der Grönländischen Sprache'.* Hildesheim: Olms.

—. 1992. "How to 'Improve' a Language: The case of eighteenth-century descriptions of Greenlandic". *Diversions of Galway: Papers on the History of Linguistics from ICHoLS V, Galway, Ireland, 1–6 September 1990* ed. by Anders Ahlqvist, 759–771. Amsterdam: Benjamins.

Pallas, Peter Simon, Hg. 1787–89. *Linguarum totius orbis vocabularia comparativa.* 2 vols. St. Petersburg: Schnoor.

Sajnovics, Johannes. 1770. *Demonstratio: Idioma Ungarorum et Lapponum idem esse.* Regiæ scientiarum societati Danicæ prælecta. Hafniæ mense Januario. Hafniæ: Gerhard Giese Salicath. (Repr., Turnau 1771.)

Samarin, William J. 1967. *Field Linguistics: A guide to linguistic field work.* New York: Holt, Rinehart & Winston.

Sjögren, Andreas Johan. 1832. *Ueber den grammatischen Bau der syrjänischen Sprache mit Rücksicht auf die finnische.* (= *Mémoires de l'Académie de St. Petersburg,* sixième série. Tome I, 149–169.) St. Petersburg: Akademie der Wissenschaften zu St. Petersburg.

—. 1844. IRON ÆVZAGAXUR *das ist ossetische Sprachlehre nebst kurzen ossetisch-deutschen und deutsch-ossetischen Wörterbuche.* St. Petersburg: Gedruckt bei der kaiserlichen Akademie der Wissenschaften.

Strahlenberg, Philipp Johann von. 1730. *Das Nord- und Ostliche Theil von Europa und Asia. In so weit solches Das ganze Russische Reich mit Sibirien und das grossen Tatarey in sich begriffet, In einer Historisch-Geographischen Beschreibung der alten und neuern Zeiten, und vielen andern unbekannten Nachrichten vorgestellet, Nebst einer noch niemals ans Licht gegebenen Tabula Polyglotta von zwey und dreyssigerley Arten Tatarischer Völcker Sprachen und einem Kalmuckischen Vocabulario. Sonderlich aber Einer grossen richtigen Land-Charte von den benannten Ländern und von verschiedenen Kupfferstichen, so die Asiatische-Scythische Antiquität betreffen; Bey Gelegenheit der Schwedischen Kriegs-Gefangenschaft in Russland, aus eigener sorgfältigen Erkundigung, auf denen verstatteten weitten Reisen zusammen gebracht und ausgefertiget*. Stockholm: In Verlegung des Autoris.

Wonderly, William L. & Eugene A. Nida. 1963, "Linguistics and Christian Missions". *Anthropological Linguistics* 5:1.104–144.

Even Hovdhaugen, Oslo (Norway)

180. Physiologie de la parole et phonétique appliquée au XIXe et au début du XXe siècle

1. Initroduction
2. De la physiologie des sons à la phonétique
3. Le dernier quart du siècle
4. Des applications de la phonétique physiologique
5. Phonétique physiologique et phonologie
6. Bibliographie

1. Introduction

Il suffit de feuilleter *Geschichtszahlen der Phonetik: 3000 Jahre Phonetik*, le répertoire chronologique méticuleux établi par Giulio Panconcelli Calzia (1941) pour se rendre compte du long chemin parcouru depuis trois mille ans dans la voie de la connaissance des organes de la phonation et de leurs fonctions. Depuis les planches anatomiques (de Leonardo da Vinci [1452–1519] à Julio Casserio (c. 1552–1616] à Court de Gébelin [1725–1784]) jusqu'à la recherche du point d'articulation des voyelles (Erasmus Darwin 1803) sans oublier le prototype du triangle vocalique moderne (Christoph Hellwag 1781), les médecins, anatomistes, physiologistes, physiciens, travaillaient inconsciemment à la construction d'un savoir qui allait aboutir, d'autres circonstances favorables aidant, à la naissance d'une discipline linguistique autonome: la phonétique (Ohala 1991). En fait, c'est par extension que Panconcelli Calzia utilise le mot 'phonétique' avant la lettre, pour indiquer toutes les études qui on trait à la voix et à l'appareil phonatoire quelle que soit leur origine. Et lorsque dans son célèbre tableau statistique (1941: 81) il attribue à l'Allemagne 40% des contributions à la science phonétique du XIXe siècle (contre 30% à la France, 15% à l'Angleterre, 3,3% aux U.S.A. et à l'Autriche, 2,8% à la Hollande, 2% à la Suisse et au Danemark, 0,896% à l'Italie et à la Belgique), il inclut dans son calcul l'apport des physiologistes, des physiciens, des techniciens. Car les progrès de la phonétique, à ses débuts, sont dus aux médecins qui après maints tâtonnements sont parvenus à une représentation physiologique correcte des organes de la phonation suivie, plus tard, d'une interprétation fonctionnelle (Auroux 1992).

Hermann Breymann (1843–1910) recense pour la période 1876–1895, quelque 700 titres consacrés à la phonétique, toutes approches confondues: linguistiques, physiologiques, physiques … (1897). La physiologie des sons, discipline extralinguistique, remonte au moins au milieu du XIXe siècle. Mais le succès de la physiologie et de ses méthodes d'investigation se situe bien avant: le XIXe siècle est le théâtre du rapide développement de la technique d'analyse physiologique. Dans la première moitié du siècle la méthode expérimentale, souveraine dans les sciences physico-chimiques, avait rencontré des difficultés particulières à s'introduire dans les sciences biologiques. C'est Claude Bernard (1813–1878) qui posa les bases de la méthode expérimentale en physiologie, grâce à la renommée internationale de ses découvertes et de son enseignement oral et écrit. Dans la deuxième moitié du siècle, à Paris, un autre médecin, Etienne Jules Marey (1830–1904), se livra au perfectionnement de la méthode graphique inaugurée par les physiologistes allemands. La méthode expérimentale, appliquée dans les sciences exactes, en médecine, en physiologie et même en littérature (cf. les Physiologies, très en vogue au début du XIXe siècle), apparaissait comme le seul garant d'objectivité. Ainsi que Claude Bernard l'avait écrit "Dans l'investigation scientifique, les moindres procédés sont de la plus haute importance" (1865: 27).

Après le succès des travaux du naturaliste suédois Carl von Linné (1707−1778) et du zoologiste français Georges Cuvier (1769−1832), les sciences naturelles jouissaient d'un très grand prestige dont le développement de la phonétique n'est qu'une manifestation parmi d'autres. En utilisant en phonétique les méthodes de ces dernières, le courant expérimental de plus en plus actif vers la fin du siècle, croyait faire de la linguistique une science exacte, rigoureuse, du même type que les sciences naturelles (pour l'influence des sciences sur la linguistique du XIXe siècle, cf. Koerner 1989, chap. 12, 13 et 15; 1995, chap. 3). Les appareils des laboratoires de physiologie étaient destinés à meubler les premiers laboratoires de phonétique à la suite des expériences faites par le docteur Charles-Léopold Rosapelly (c. 1850−1913) dans le laboratoire de physiologie de Marey à Paris (1875), expériences reprises en 1885 par Rousselot (1846−1924) à la recherche d'un moyen d'expression exacte des sons lors de son projet de recherche diachronique sur le patois de Cellefrouin. En commentant les expériences faites en commun dans le Laboratoire de Marey par Rosapelly et Louis Havet (représentant de la commission nommée en 1874 par la Société de Linguistique de Paris) Rousselot écrivait (1897: 50): "Si les compétences propres à chacun des deux collaborateurs, celle du physiologiste et celle du linguiste, s'étaient trouvées réunies dans la même personne, la phonétique expérimentale était fondée."

1.1. Linguistique comparée et phonétique

La littérature phonétique antérieure à 1875, provenant des horizons les plus disparates, est riche mais souvent peu scientifique si l'on en croit le jugement sévère porté par Henry Sweet: "It becomes more indigestible every year" (Breymann 1897: 128). Il paraît curieux et intéressant à la fois, que pendant 50 ans la linguistique comparative ait pu travailler sur la parenté entre les langues et sur les lois de l'évolution sans bien connaître les sons, leurs mécanismes de production et de combinaison. La découverte du Sanskrit n'avait pas eu d'effets immédiats sur la réflexion phonétique européenne et cela en dépit des analyses articulatoires très fines faites par les grammairiens hindous. Par ailleurs, aucun élément n'avait été absorbé d'autres domaines où une réflexion avait eu lieu dans un but strictement pratique, à savoir la Réforme de l'orthographe et l'enseignement des langues aux sourds-muets.

Autour de 1850, une certaine phonétique fait son entrée dans la linguistique comparée qui, au départ, l'avait presque totalement ignorée. A partir de ce moment, la phonétique physiologique va se développer très rapidement. La découverte de la réalité physique qui se cachait derrière les lettres avait fait croire aux linguistes qu'en étudiant la substance sonore on expliquerait plus facilement l'évolution des sons et que l'on acquerrait ainsi une meilleure compréhension de l'histoire de la langue. Tout illusoire qu'il est, cet espoir est à l'origine du développement impétueux de la phonétique, une phonétique résolument articulatoire, en accord avec l'orientation génétique de la linguistique dominante (Jakobson 1976, Malmberg 1991). Les limites d'une approche purement organique des sons ne tardèrent pas à se révéler provoquant le franchissement d'une nouvelle étape dans la perspective d'une analyse linguistique objectivement mesurable. Néanmoins, répondant aux critiques avancées notamment par Hugo Pipping (1894), Rousselot insistait sur l'importance de l'analyse physiologique de la parole, le complément indispensable de l'analyse physique. Il avait d'ailleurs envisagé pour le nouvel enseignement inauguré en 1889 à l'Institut Catholique de Paris l'appellation "Phonétique physiologique" avant d'arrêter son choix sur "Phonétique expérimentale", cette dernière lui paraissant plus extensif (1911: 11).

2. De la physiologie des sons à la phonétique

L'étude des sons en tant que discipline scientifique prit naissance au début du XIXe siècle. Ses progrès furent extrêmement lents jusqu'au jour où des physiologistes et des physiciens appliquèrent leurs connaissances à l'étude des sons du langage. Elle fut, au départ, essentiellement physiologie du son − un chapitre de la physiologie générale − et tel fut son nom. Les expériences techniques de savants géniaux étaient les prémisses de son introduction dans les volumes de physiologie.

2.1. Les machines parlantes

Le mécanisme de la phonation, fascinant et longtemps résistant à l'analyse, fut exploré au

XVIIIe siècle à l'aide d'automates (les ancêtres des synthétiseurs modernes) construits à l'imitatioin de l'appareil phonatoire humain (Vaïsse 1878). Des sons synthétiques sont produits à l'aide de mécanismes simulant l'activité des organes de la parole, ce qui supposait une bonne analyse de la phonation. Christian Gottlieb Kratzenstein (1723−1795) professeur de physiologie à Copenhague, gagna le concours de l'Académie des Sciences de St.-Pétersbourg (1779) ayant pour objet les différences physiologiques des voyelles AEIOU et la fabrication d'un mécanisme capable de les produire. Il présenta cinq résonateurs reproduisant les dimensions et la forme de la cavité buccale lors de la production des cinq voyelles. La machine est décrite dans un essai de 1781 qui illustre les mécanismes de production de la voix et contient une description détaillée (chiffrée) de la position des organes dans la production des voyelles. En France, en 1783, l'Abbé Mical (1730−1789) présentait à l'Académie des Sciences deux têtes parlantes dont les diagrammes ne nous sont malheureusement pas parvenus.

Vers 1780, après deux décennies d'investigations physiologiques patientes, un noble hongrois, Wolfgang von Kempelen (1734−1804), inventeur talentueux, constructeur génial du célèbre joueur d'échec, présenta la machine parlante décrite dans un ouvrage de 1791 *Mechanismus der menschlichen Sprache*, où l'auteur traite d'abord de questions générales telles que l'origine du langage, des mécanismes de la phonation, des sons des principales langues européennes. Les sons vocaliques sont caractérisés par les ouvertures des lèvres et du canal de la langue, chacune ayant cinq degrés correspondant aux cinq voyelles. Le modèle anthropomorphe adopté (complètement libéré de l'apparence humanoïde) se compose d'un soufflet (courant d'air venant des poumons), d'une mince plaque d'ivoire recouverte de peau vibrant à différentes vitesses (cordes vocales), d'une cavité avec deux ouvertures variables (cavités buccale et canal de la langue). La machine est manœuvrée par les acrobaties manuelles d'un opérateur devant savoir se servir habilement de ses dix doigts (pour une description détaillée de la production des différents sons, cf. Dudley & Tarnoczy 1950). D'après l'inventeur, on pouvait apprendre à utiliser la machine en trois semaines si l'on s'en tenait au Latin, au Français et à l'Italien tandis que l'Allemand présentait plus de difficultés à cause du nombre élevé de consonnes (la machine pouvait en produire 19). Par la finesse des analyses et la variété des phénomènes sonores analysés (cris d'animaux, défauts de prononciation, sons et bruits humains non linguistiques tels que la toux, les ronflements, les reniflements, les nasillements, les baisers …), cet ouvrage est à considérer comme le meilleur jusqu'à son époque, et son auteur le véritable pionnier de la phonétique expérimentale.

Après Kempelen, Joseph Faber, professeur de mathématiques à Vienne, créa Euphonia (1835) machine pourvue de langue et de mâchoires en matériau flexible et de six diaphragmes modifiant pour chaque son la forme du canal buccal (Liénard 1991, Gessinger 1994).

L'intensification de ces tentatives dans le siècle des automates (cf. la série de chefs-d'œuvre automatiques de Vaucanson [1709−1782]) n'est pas le fait du hasard. Bien au contraire, l'on peut considérer que, par-delà la question des sourds-muets à laquelle von Kempelen n'était pas indifférent, elles sont l'aboutissement d'une curiosité scientifique croissante pour la compréhension et l'imitation des phénomènes naturels, doublée d'un goût pour l'expérimentation profondément ressenti à l'époque.

2.2. Les physiologistes

De leur côté, les physiologistes visaient la description et le rôle des organes intervenant dans la formation de la voix (en particulier le rôle de la glotte, cf. Dodart [1634−1707] *Sur les causes de la voix de l'homme, et de ses différens tons*, 1700 et surtout Ferrein [1693−1769] qui élabora le concept de 'cordes vocales' en 1741) ainsi que la définition et le classement des sons à partir de données purement articulatoires: lieux et modes d'articulation pour les consonnes; distance et position de la langue par rapport au palais, activité des lèvres, pour les voyelles (Panconcelli Calzia 1940 et 1941).

Les ouvrages qui ont établi les fondements scientifiques de la physiologie du son sont restés célèbres: Brücke, *Grundzüge der Physiologie und Systematik der Sprachlaute für Linguisten und Taubstummenlehrer* (1856); Merkel, *Anatomie und Physiologie des menschlichen Stimm- und Sprach-Organs (Anthropophonik)* (1857); Helmholtz, *Die Lehre von den Tonempfindungen als physiologische Grundlage für die Theorie der Musik* (1863). Ce dernier constitue la première étude acoustique scientifique des sons de la parole tandis que le physiologiste viennois Ernest Brücke (1819−

1892) pose les bases d'une description articulatoire rationnelle et devient le point de référence des philologues allemands. Un ouvrage antérieur en quatre volumes de Karl Rapp (1803–1883), *Versuch einer Physiologie der Sprache nebst historischer Entwickelung der abendländischen Idiome nach physiologischen Grundsätzen* (1836–41) n'avait pas été bien accueilli par la linguistique dominante plus portée à souligner ses défauts qu'à intégrer ses aspects novateurs. Philologue mais néanmoins polyglotte — ce qui était plutôt rare à l'époque — avec une sensibilité linguistique particulière cultivée depuis l'enfance, Rapp a le mérite d'avoir le premier mis la phonétique à la base de son vaste projet d'étude diachronique. De par sa conception de la phonétique, il entra nécessairement en collision avec ses contemporains et notamment avec la théorie des lettres de Grimm qu'il critiqua d'un ton "stürmisch und anmassend" (tempétueux et arrogant) ce qui explique sans doute que son œuvre soit tombée dans l'oubli (Jespersen 1933: 59).

L'ouvrage de Brücke, qui passe en revue les articulations des principales langues modernes et fait une analyse critique comparative des systèmes phonétiques élaborés par les Grecs, les Hindous, les Arabes, marque une étape fondamentale et est destiné à avoir un grand succès international. Son point de vue est strictement génétique et statique, les sons étant avant tout le produit de l'activité des organes phonateurs. Systématique et clair, réduisant les données anatomiques et acoustiques à l'essentiel, cet ouvrage est supérieur à celui de Merkel, professeur de médecine à Leipzig, qui noie l'identité des sons dans une masse énorme de détails empiriques (anatomiques, physiologiques, acoustiques). Le second, auquel allaient les préférences de Sievers et de Sweet (dans la version abrégée et corrigée de 1866), analyse pourtant avec finesse les phénomènes suprasegmentaux que le premier ne fait qu'effleurer. Les deux ne manquent pas d'interprétations erronées ni de déductions abusives dues au fait que tout n'était pas résolu en physiologie de la parole et que les langues modernes ne leur étaient pas familières (cf. Jespersen 1933; Kohler 1981; Kemp 1995).

Dans la perspective des sciences naturelles (anatomie, physiologie, physique), ces physiologistes s'intéressaient aux lois générales du langage, et donc de la phonation, tandis que les linguistes cherchaient à étudier ces lois telles qu'elles fonctionnent dans les différentes langues et dans les dialectes. Les premiers ne disposaient pas des données empiriques spécifiques indispensables aux seconds. Leur classification des sons à ambition universelle basée sur des déductions plus que sur l'observation et la connaissance réelle des langues est loin d'être parfaite. L'étude des sons resta longtemps un domaine de recherche spécialisé, les échanges entre les chercheurs étant rares et difficiles. En effet, d'après Sievers

"[...] linguistics had learned, or wanted to learn, too little from natural sciences, and vice versa, and where a mutual exchange of knowledge had taken place it was often accompanied by misunderstanding at the receiving end." (Kohler 1981: 162)

En 1880, G.-H. von Meyer (1815–1892), professeur d'anatomie à l'Université de Zurich, écrivait:

"L'étude de la structure et des dispositions des organes de la parole s'impose au philologue avec un caractère de nécessité qui devient de jour en jour plus marqué; chaque jour, en effet, on voit s'affermir cette conviction qu'une intelligence exacte des lois relatives à la modification des lois du langage dans la formation des dialectes et des langues dérivées, ne peut s'acquérir sans le secours des lois physiologiques de la production des sons. Les manuels ordinaires d'anatomie ne répondent pas entièrement aux besoins de cette étude [...]. De même aussi, dans les manuels de physiologie, on ne consacre à ce sujet qu'une place restreinte."
"Je me propose de donner dans le présent ouvrage une exposition d'ensemble portant sur la structure et sur les dispositions des organes de la parole et entreprise principalement en vue des recherches philologiques." (Cité d'après l'éd. française, 1885, p. xxiii)

Mais cette sorte de dépendance ne dura pas longtemps.

2.2.1. La transcription phonétique 'organique'. L'imitation des sons par la reproduction des caractéristiques physiologiques qui, tout au long des siècles, a tenté savants et philosophes, peut s'adresser à l'ouïe (2.2.) ou à la vue. L'idée que l'alphabet doit peindre les mouvements phonateurs — née au XVIIe siècle parallèlement à la quête d'un alphabet universel (Becher 1661, von Helmont 1667, Wilkins 1668) — fut prise en charge par le XVIIIe siècle (De Brosses 1765) et transmise en héritage au siècle suivant pendant lequel elle terminera sa trajectoire se révélant tout à la fois féconde et sans avenir (pour une analyse complète, → Art. 186).

La définition articulatoire des sons, très débattue parmi les physiologistes et les linguistes, est à la base d'un système de transcription génial mais apparemment peu fortuné — une version rajeunie de l'alphabet organique de De Brosses — élaboré par Brücke (1863), dont les symboles, de véritables consignes articulatoires, représentent les lieux et les modes d'articulation. La tentative de Brücke, accueillie avec enthousiasme parce qu'elle rompait avec la tradition de l'écriture alphabétique, était destinée à l'échec car elle était nécessairement le reflet des opinions de l'auteur en matière de physiologie des sons (cf. les issues divergentes de Merkel 1866; Rumpelt 1869) et, en tout cas, d'un état des connaissances transitoire, l'accord définitif entre les spécialistes étant loin d'être fait dans le domaine. L'idée de Brücke eut un meilleur accueil en Angleterre (Bell 1867; Sweet 1880−81). Alexander Melville Bell (1819−1905) n'était pas linguiste au sens propre du terme. Tout comme Alexander John Ellis (1814−1890), il fonda son classement des voyelles sur des bases strictement articulatoires et tenta de réaliser un alphabet phonétique à base physiologique. Dans la perspective d'enseignement qui l'intéressait, il poussa son intuition jusqu'à croire qu'une représentation graphique conçue comme une image fidèle de l'articulation pourrait remplacer la perception auditive. Contrairement à Moritz Taushing (1838−1884), qui exprima des réserves et proposa un système de notation musicale original, Sweet se montrait optimiste quant aux acquis physiologiques (surtout pour les consonnes) et donc favorable à une écriture organique. Il est à l'origine d'une vague d'intérêt pour le *Visible Speech* (1867) de Bell qui ne manqua pourtant pas d'adversaires. Parmi les plus réputés, Otto Jespersen (1860−1943) qui s'opposa nettement au système Bell−Sweet et refusa en bloc toutes les tentatives précédentes fondées sur l'emploi des lettres qui, d'après lui, en dépit de l'imagination graphique déployée dans leur modification, ne sauraient en aucun cas traduire la complexité de l'articulation. La transcription analphabétique imaginée par Jespersen (1889) ressemblant fort aux formules chimiques, est la résultante de deux options fondamentales: le choix d'un alphabet autre que celui de l'orthographe, la représentation minutieuse des gestes articulatoires qui composent chaque son à l'aide de lettres latines et grecques et de chiffres indiquant les lieux d'articulation, les articulateurs, l'action du larynx, le rapprochement des organes ... Elle présente des analogies avec la notation musicale des articulations proposée par Techmer (1880).

La conférence de Copenhague (1925), réunissant les savants les plus éminents dans tous les domaines de la recherche linguistique chargés de mettre de l'ordre dans le labyrinthe des notations, marquait la fin d'une époque révolue car elle décrétait l'abandon de la transcription organique tandis qu'avançait l'idée d'une transcription des phonèmes s'ouvrant aux nouvelles perspectives fonctionnelles (pour une discussion cf. Laziczius 1961: 16−37; Gessinger 1994).

3. Le dernier quart du siècle

S'il est convenu de dater l'entrée des linguistes dans la science des sons vingt ans après Brücke, il ne faut toutefois pas oublier les grands précurseurs anglais: A. J. Ellis et A. M. Bell (→ Art. 198). On doit aux disciples de Bell, James A. H. Murray (1837−1915) et surtout Henry Sweet (1845−1912), l'application de ses idées à la linguistique. Autour de ce dernier se groupa une véritable école qui comprenait les Scandinaves Johan Storm (1836−1920), Adolf Noreen (1854−1925), Johan August Lundell (1851−1940), August Western (1856−1940), très à l'avant-garde en la matière. Ils seront suivis par le danois Otto Jespersen (1860−1943) et, en France, par Paul Passy (1859−1940).

En Allemagne à côté de Sievers une nombreuse école héritière d'une forte traditon physiologique réunira Moritz Trautmann (1842−1920), Friedrich Techmer (1843−1891), Wilhelm Viëtor (1850−1918), Otto Bremer (1862−1936), que suivront beaucoup d'autres. Cette base physiologique approfondie était appréciée par Sweet qui considérait Sievers "by far the soundest of German phoneticians":

"The most important feature of German phonetics is that it is based on a sound and minute physiology of the vocal organs. The laryngoscopic study of the glottal sounds begun by Garcia, and carried out more fully by Czermak and Merkel, has yielded most valuable results." (*Academy*, 28th April 1877).

Le défaut de l'école allemande était, d'après lui, l'excès de théorie: "the defect of German phonetics is that it is hardly practical enough [...]" ("Seventh Adress to the Philological Society", 1878, cité d'après Wyld 1913: 106).

De son côté, Sievers appréciait à sa juste valeur l'école anglaise. Dès la deuxième édition de son ouvrage, il reconnaissait l'apport fondamental de Ellis, Bell, Sweet, Storm, qu'il ne connaissait pas lors de la première édition de 1876.

La collaboration réelle des linguistes ne commença donc qu'en 1876. A cette date, deux ouvrages écrits par deux amis, Jost Winteler (1846–1929), *Die Kerenzer Mundart des Cantons Glarus* et Eduard Sievers (1850–1932), *Grundzüge der Lautphysiologie*, marquent un tournant dans la méthode de recherche en linguistique par la prise en charge des données physiologiques et font de la phonétique une science linguistique indépendante. D'après Sievers, le mérite de Winteler avait été de montrer que, bien qu'il soit possible d'étudier des lois physiologiques générales du langage, le plus important pour le linguiste c'est d'étudier les sons à l'intérieur des différentes langues et dialectes. Moins connu, mais fondé sur des principes analogues, l'ouvrage de J. H. A. Murray *Dialect of the Southern Counties of Scotland* (1873) fait apparaître une convergence intéressante des deux côtés de la Manche (Sweet 1877, cité d'après Wyld 1913: 87).

L'une des raisons qui font de 1876 une année mémorable, c'est la publication de l'article de K. Brugmann sur le 'nasalis sonans'. Une autre raison tient à la publication de l'ouvrage de Sievers qui supplanta Brücke car, dans son article, Brugmann renvoie au volume de Sievers, ce dernier étant très proche du jeune cercle de Leipzig (cf. Pedersen 1931, cité dans Wells 1974: 444).

Par ailleurs, une vague de 'revendication phonétique' envahit l'Europe toute entière. En 1877, encouragé par le linguiste norvégien Johan Storm, Henry Sweet publie son *Handbook of Phonetics* où il indique clairement la phonétique comme le fondement indispensable de toute étude linguistique, théorique et pratique, en langue maternelle ou étrangère. Cet ouvrage fondamental "taught phonetics to Europe and made England the birthplace of the modern science" (Wrenn 1966 [1946]: 517). En 1879, dans *Englische Philologie,* Storm écrivait: "Die Phonetik oder Lautphysiologie, eine Wissenschaft, die noch zu wenig beachtet ist". En 1885 paraîtra *Elementarbuch des gesprochenen Englisch* de Sweet impatiemment attendu par tous les phonéticiens (Passy 1887: 10–11). Par son originalité, son indépendance scientifique, son ouverture, ce grand novateur anticipe des parcours de recherche qui stimulent encore le lecteur d'aujourd'hui: la définition des bases articulatoires de chaque langue qui renvoie aux modes phonatoires de Pierre Delattre (1953), l'idée d'écoute anticipatrice non sans liens avec l'approche paysagiste des langues (Lhote 1990), l'intérêt pour les langues parlées et l'attention pour les phénomènes prosodiques qui le déterminèrent à privilégier l'approche synthétique négligée par ses contemporains trop (é)pris par la description analytique des sons.

Sur le continent, le changement de titre de l'ouvrage de Sievers dès sa deuxième édition (*Grundzüge der Phonetik*, 1881) est révélateur d'une (r)évolution en cours. Le sous-titre (*Zur Einführung in das Studium der Lautlehre der indogermanischen Sprachen*) indique clairement ses liens avec la linguistique historique de l'époque (Kohler 1981). Ses *Grundzüge der Phonetik* eurent le mérite de donner une base physiologique exacte aux recherches de phonétique et ont servi de modèle aux manuels de phonétique postérieurs. Cet ouvrage a été pendant de longues années le manuel de phonétique de tous ceux qui faisaient de la grammaire comparée. Dans la deuxième partie de sa vie, Sievers montra un intérêt croissant pour les phénomènes prosodiques aboutissant à une contribution originale à la phonostylistique du texte (*Schallanalyse*, 1912). Kohler (1981) a reconstruit dans le détail le développement de la science des sons en Allemagne au XIXe siècle, en faisant ressortir les contributions majeures des médecins, des linguistes et des pédagogues et la bifurcation de Sievers par rapport à Brücke et Merkel qu'il connaissait à fond. Sievers figure parmi les chercheurs qui assurèrent la transition entre physiologie et linguistique. A l'opposé de la parabole, Jespersen représente le sommet et l'achèvement de la phonétique classique (Malmberg 1971). Dans les mains des linguistes, la physiologie du son s'était transformée en phonétique.

3.1. L'avènement de la phonétique expérimentale

Au tournant du siècle, une véritable révolution se produisit dans les méthodes de recherche en phonétique car l'approche subjective partielle, pratiquée notamment par les philologues, fut l'objet de critiques de plus en plus nombreuses. La nécessité d'un changement découlant de l'insuffisance de l'analyse organique subjective, intuitive et trop souvent approximative, était apparue clairement à des linguistes clairvoyants tels que Schuchardt, Sweet, Storm, Bréal, Paris. Pour que la phonétique progresse, pour qu'elle ne s'enlise pas dans un cumul stérile de détails encombrants, il fallait que le linguiste joigne ses efforts à ceux du physicien et du physiologiste. Rappelons à ce propos que Gaston Paris poussa le linguiste à pénétrer dans les laboratoires de physiologie: c'est grâce à lui que Rousselot découvrit en 1885 le laboratoire de Marey à Paris et qu'il renoua avec les expériences faites dix ans plus tôt par un médecin, le docteur Rosapelly. Dialectologue et linguiste doué d'un génie technologique toujours en éveil, Rousselot inaugurait ainsi la phonétique expérimentale dont il est considéré à juste titre comme le père fondateur. L'exploration des mécanismes de la phonation fut poursuivie de manière systématique à l'aide d'appareils de plus en plus perfectionnés. Dans les premières recherches sur la physiologie du son, un rôle important avait été joué par la méthode palatographique utilisée, entre autres, par Rudolf Lenz (1863−1935), Paul Grützner (1847−1919), Friedrich Techmer (1843−1891). En 1855 Manuel V. Garcia (1805−1906) inventa le laryngoscope. C'est à l'aide de cet appareil que le médecin tchèque Czermak étudia le fonctionnement des cordes vocales et du voile du palais (1860). Il est intéressant de rappeler également le kymographe inventé en 1847 par le physiologiste allemand Karl Ludwig (1815−1895) et utilisé par Brücke (→ Art. 178).

Dans la dernière décade du siècle, le débat autour de la légitimité de l'approche expérimentale battait son plein. Néophites enthousiastes, abstentionnistes, sceptiques ou franchement contraires, les phonéticiens n'étaient pas indifférents à la rumeur que les recherches de l'abbé Rousselot avaient suscitée dans le monde scientifique international. Parmi les phonéticiens classiques, tous polyglottes et doués d'une oreille extrêmement fine, certains ne s'écartèrent guère de l'approche génético-articulatoire traditionnelle, tandis que d'autres se laissèrent gagner aux nouvelles technologies. Parmi ces derniers, Viëtor dont le disciple Ernst Alfred Meyer (1873−1953) se rendit dès sa jeunesse en Suède et introduisit à l'Université d'Uppsala la méthode kymographique de son maître. Giulio Panconcelli Calzia (1878−1966), élève de Rousselot et, plus tard, directeur du laboratoire de phonétique de Hambourg, adopta résolument l'approche expérimentale, mais la phonétique resta toujours pour lui une partie de la physiologie, l'approche articulatoire restant dominante. Gabriel Bergounioux (1995) a bien visualisé la phonétique tripartite de la fin du siècle: universitaire, pédagogique, dialectologique, poursuivant des objectifs partiellement communs, cultivés parfois par le même savant comme dans le cas de Rousselot.

En soulignant l'importance de l'analyse scientifique approfondie des patois pour la grammaire historique et comparée, Eduard Koschwitz (1851−1904) observait que pour bien étudier les patois, il fallait être un véritable phonéticien, c'est-à-dire "un phonéticien naturaliste, physicien et physiologiste" (1892: 134). Etre phonéticien signifiait posséder des connaissances approfondies d'anatomie et de physiologie, maîtriser l'acoustique et la musique, posséder une oreille musicale, connaître la biologie et la psychologie, savoir manipuler les appareils. De plus, ce bagage de connaissances devait être complété par la connaissance pratique de plusieurs langues. Il s'agit de talents et de connaissances que l'on ne trouve qu'exceptionnellement réunis dans la même personne: Rousselot fut l'une de ces exceptions. Si pendant longtemps le dialogue entre linguistes et physiologues ne s'engagea pas, c'est bien parce que chacun d'eux ne possédait qu'une partie de cette étendue de compétences que toute étude phonétique complète requiert.

4. Des applications de la phonétique physiologique

Le grand essor que la physiologie de la parole a connu dans la deuxième moitié du XIXe siècle est prouvé par différents domaines d'application: elle montrait de nouveaux itinéraires à tous les professionnels de la voix, professeurs de chants et d'élocution, pour l'hygiène de la voix parlée et chantée, dans le traitement des pathologies. C'est l'origine d'un grand nombre de traités de diction, d'ouvrages sur l'art de réciter, de lire à haute voix, parmi lesquels *Pronunciation for singers* de A. J. Ellis (1877) et le très fortuné *L'art de la lecture* (1877) d'Ernest Legouvé (1807−1903), fondé sur le travail corporel (respiration, gestuelle, mimique etc.).

Mais l'enseignement des langues vivantes (maternelle et étrangères) en situation normale et pathologique est sans doute le domaine qui a davantage bénéficié des acquis de la jeune discipline à partir du moment où se réalisa cette révolution copernicienne qui consistait à affirmer la primauté de l'apprentissage oral sur l'écrit dominant depuis toujours (→ Art. 187). Avant la Réforme, déclenchée par le pamphlet de Wilhelm Viëtor

(1882), les compétences orales requises/apprises en langue étrangère n'allaient pas au-delà du 'reading knowledge', exercice où la prononciation n'était surtout pas une priorité: chacun prononçait à sa manière. Après 1886, l'"avalanche de la phonétique est en branle" (Passy 1887: 37).

Pour étrange que cela puisse paraître, le progrès social était le but ultime de l'action phonétique de Paul Passy, un 'socialiste chrétien' engagé qui consacra à ce projet pédagogique et humanitaire toutes ses énergies (Galazzi 1992). De même, au tournant du siècle, l'ambition de Rousselot consiste à mettre la phonétique au service du bien en s'attaquant à tous les défauts de prononciation généralement liés à des vices organiques qui nécessitent une rééducation spécifique (zézaiements, nasonnements ...). Les phénomèmes physiologiques fixés par les appareils sont le point de départ d'applications pédagogiques et thérapeutiques très célèbres (Passy 1903).

4.1. L'action des phonéticiens-pédagogues

L'approche organo-génétique qui marqua les débuts de la phonétique, trouva dans le domaine des langues vivantes son champ d'application le plus fécond grâce à l'action déterminée et passionnée des jeunes phonéticiens rassemblés à Stockholm en 1886 (Passy 1887) et bientôt réunis en un réseau international très actif, l'Association Phonétique Internationale (MacMahon 1986; Galazzi 1992). Les phonéticiens-pédagogues qui étaient à l'origine de ce vaste mouvement de réforme de l'enseignement (Viëtor, Jespersen, Passy) suivaient la tradition pratique venant d'Angleterre tout en restant très influencés par la littérature physiologique allemande (cf. Klinghardt 1885). Viëtor, nourri de la tradition allemande, adopta avec enthousiasme l'orientation pratique anglaise. A son tour, Sweet reconnaissait sa dette envers Storm tandis que Passy assimilait les traditions allemande et anglaise grâce à la lecture personnelle des 'aînés' (Sweet, Sievers, Storm, Lundell). Tout un savoir descriptif concernant les organes de la parole s'était accumulé et constituait un patrimoine destiné à passer dans les manuels. Le célèbre ouvrage de Viëtor *Elemente der Phonetik und Orthoepie des Deutschen, Englischen und Französischen* (1884), répondait aux besoins pratiques d'étudiants et d'enseignants aux prises avec les sons d'une langue étrangère. L'optique contrastive adoptée était destinée à rester dans les manuels successifs auxquels il servit de modèle.

Une importance non négligeable dans la diffusion des nouvelles idées, et notamment de la physiologie de l'appareil phonatoire, revient à de nombreuses revues trop souvent éphémères, liées aux noms célèbres de Viëtor, Passy, Rousselot: *Zeitschrift für Orthographie, Orthoepie und Sprachphysiologie* (1880−1885), *Phonetische Studien* (1887−1893), *Die Neueren Sprachen* (1893−1943), *La parole* (1899−1905), *Le Maître phonétique* (1886−1970), *La revue de phonétique* (1911−1929/30) et encore: *Verdandi* (1883−1927), *Internationale Zeitschrift für Allgemeine Sprachwissenschaft* (1884−1890), *Archives néerlandaises de physiologie de l'homme et des animaux* (1916−1927), *Bollettino di filologia moderna* (1894−1895; 1901−1909).

La contribution des cours d'été (Greifswald, Paris, Édimbourg, Genève, Grenoble ...), fut, elle aussi, fondamentale. Rappelons en particulier ceux de Marburg, la ville de Viëtor, où un public d'enseignants cosmopolite s'initiait aux applications pédagogiques de la phonétique physiologique sous la direction de conférenciers prestigieux (Galazzi 1996a). La phonétique jouant le même rôle que la connaissance de l'anatomie en gymnastique, l'accent était mis sur l'"organic training' qui amenait à la production correcte du son étranger. Mais la phonétique physiologique était un savoir pour le maître plus que pour l'apprenant. Ainsi Passy, qui faisait autorité en la matière, distinguait-il deux sortes de phonétique (1901b):

"Le professeur, lui, doit avoir une prononciation aussi parfaite que possible. Pour y arriver, il faut qu'il connaisse à fond et les sons de sa langue maternelle et ceux de la langue qu'il doit enseigner. Même un séjour très prolongé à l'étranger n'y suffit pas; on n'y arrive que par la phonétique. [...] Il faut étudier scientifiquement les sons, habituer son oreille à saisir les moindres nuances, exercer ses organes à reproduire tous les sons. Mais l'élève, bien entendu, n'a pas besoin de tout cet appareil scientifique, c'est l'art du professeur de lui faire savoir, sans trop de théorie, ce dont il a besoin pour se rendre compte de ses difficultés de prononciation et pour les corriger, chose indispensable pour povoir goûter plus tard la poésie et les œuvres littéraires aussi bien que pour converser avec les étrangers."

C'était un point de vue largement répandu parmi les phonéticiens-pédagogues (Klinghardt 1885). L'étude organique, susceptible d'être pratiquée de deux manières différentes, allait faire naître deux courants dont les partisans, d'accord sur les buts à atteindre, s'opposaient quant aux procédés d'investigation à employer. Les adaptes de la méthode directe (appelés parfois phonéticiens 'classiques') préconisaient l'observation immédiate par les sens; les tenants de la méthode expérimentale faisaient appel aux appareils aussi bien pour l'analyse de la parole que pour la mise en place des organes de l'apprenant.

4.2. La méthode physiologique pure

A la suite de Storm, Henry Sweet avait placé la phonétique au centre de l'apprentissage linguistique. Sa raison d'être était de servir de base pour l'étude du langage.

"[...] if our present wretched system of studying modern languages is ever to be reformed, it must be on the basis of a preliminary training in general phonetics, wich would at the same time lay the foundation for a thorough practical study of the pronuncation and elocution of our own language-subject which are totally ignored in our present scheme of education." (1877: v−vi)

Le crédo de l'époque − héritage de siècles entiers de recherches physiologiques − est bien exprimé par Schumann (1855−1927):

"Pour apprendre la prononciation correcte d'une langue étrangère trois conditions sont à remplir. En premier lieu il faut connaître les organes de la parole, leur fonctionnement et leur utilité; il faut savoir ensuite comment on emploie ces organes pour produire les sons de la langue maternelle et enfin quel usage il convient d'en faire pour prononcer la langue étrangère avec l'accent qui la caractérise." (Schumann 1896 [1884]: 3, cité d'après Zünd-Burguet 1902: 13)

Pour les tenants de la Réforme, la toute première leçon en langue étrangère était une initiation à l'univers des sons, élémentaire, concrète et épurée de tout jargon technique (Jespersen 1953 [1902]: 117−145). Une telle introduction était naturellement abrégée si elle avait déjà eu lieu en langue maternelle − comme cela était souhaitable et souhaité − ou en rapport avec une autre langue étrangère. Il s'agissait d'exercices phonétiques préliminaires d'exploration des organes et de prise de conscience des mécanismes à l'aide du toucher, de la vue et de l'ouïe alternant avec des vocalises individuels ou en chœur.

L'emploi d'images, de tableaux des sons, de dessins ou de schémas au tableau noir pour visualiser l'appareil phonatoire et ses différentes parties était assez courant depuis les *Lauttafeln* de Viëtor (1884 et 1892). Des planches anatomiques figuraient souvent dans les ouvrages théoriques (cf. Techmer 1885, Michaëlis & Passy 1897, etc.) et parfois dans les manuels scolaires.

La prise de contact par le toucher (à l'aide des doigts ou de la langue pour les parties internes) héritait de pratiques courantes dans la rééducation des sourds-muets (toucher les cordes vocales pour matérialiser la vibration; boucher les oreilles, les fosses nasales ...) Un petit miroir très efficace permettait d'accéder à certains aspects moins visibles à l'œil.

Trautmann prétendait faire passer les explications phonétiques essentielles en une heure ce qui paraissait utopique tout comme l'opinion d'autres phonéticiens qui voulaient apprendre dès la première leçon la position 'indifférente' de la langue et la 'base d'articulation' de la langue étrangère.

Au tournant du siècle, au moment où l'on voit se multiplier les publications sur l'apprentissage de la prononciation, le manuel de Kristoffer Nyrop (1858−1931) est un excellent représentant de la méthode physiologique tout court: réfléchie, systématique, comparative mais non instrumentale. Ce manuel, illustré des planches anatomiques habituelles, est centré sur la physiologie du phonème dont l'apprenant doit avoir une idée exacte. L'auteur conseille des exercices phonétiques méthodiques et surveillés qui mènent à la maîtrise des organes de la parole tout en développant 'la souplesse du gosier et la finesse de l'ouïe'. Ponctué de remarques savantes et agrémenté d'anecdotes, de quiproquos phonétiques et d'exemples d'exercices souvent drôles, ce manuel sait merveilleusement instruire en amusant. Ses références pour le français sont Passy, Legouvé, Dupont-Vernon (1844−1898), Koschwitz. La phonétique articulatoire lui inspire une confiance totale:

"[...] il n'y a pas de moyen plus rationnel, et en même temps plus simple et plus facile de faire apprendre à un étranger la prononciation d'un phonème inconnu que de lui donner des notions exactes sur le lieu et le mode d'articulation." (Nyrop 1902: vi)

4.3. La méthode phonotechnique

Les tracés graphiques enregistrant l'activité organique sont à la base de *l'enseignement par la vue* brillamment illustré par Rousselot dans une série d'articles publiés dans *La Parole* en 1901 et 1902 (Galazzi 1995). Dans le manuel écrit en collaboration avec son neveu Fauste Laclotte (1902), Rousselot déclare avoir voulu profiter de tous les moyens offerts par la science pour peindre aux yeux, faute de pouvoir parler à l'oreille, la prononciation du français. Le paragraphe III (*Parole − Organes de la parole − Moyen de les explo-*

rer et d'en montrer le fonctionnement), ne laisse aucun doute sur les choix opérés:

"L'analyse physique des vibrations de la voix est sans utilité pratique dans l'enseignement, sauf pour guider l'éducation d'une oreille insuffisante. Nous n'en dirons donc rien ici. Plus précieuses sont, pour le but que nous nous proposons, les données fournies par l'analyse physiologique des mouvements organiques." (1913 [1902]: 13)

Les pages suivantes indiquent les moyens d'investigation, des plus sophistiqués aux plus rudimentaires: le manomètre à eau que peuvent remplacer une allumette ou une bougie, placés à quelques centimètres de la bouche pour étudier le régime du souffle; l'explorateur du larynx, un bout de crayon appliqué sur le cartilage thyroïde ou simplement les doigts pour les vibrations des cordes vocales; une olive nasale ou le toucher (ailettes du nez) pour la nasalité; le palais artificiel, le tambour indicateur et les ampoules, ou encore simplement le petit doigt, pour l'exploration de la langue. Tout n'était pas neuf: la distribution de miroirs de poche et le 'test de l'allumette' étaient très en vogue; et l'emploi d'un appareil phonatoire en papier mâché était connu en Allemagne.

Si pour Rousselot les appareils avaient représenté surtout − et de son propre aveu − des moyens d'investigation, un de ses disciples, Adolphe Zünd-Burguet, voulut en faire des instrument spécifiques d'apprentissage dans la classe (Galazzi 1993). Parfaitement cohérent avec lui-même et avec les acquis de son temps, il publia tour à tour une *Méthode pratique, physiologique et comparée de prononciation française* (1902), des *Exercices pratiques et méthodiques de prononciation française* (1901) et un opuscule, *Les organes de la parole en trois langues* (anglais, français et allemand, 1905) qui accompagnait une Carte murale des organes de la parole en chromolithographie.

Les fondements de sa méthode qui se veut descriptive, comparative et raisonnée sont: la prise de conscience du fonctionnement de l'appareil phonatoire, la description des articulations sur la base des données fournies par l'analyse expérimentale, l'optique contrastive. Le livret de 1902, illustration complète de l'approche physiologique, est composé de deux parties: une description des sons divisés en 5 groupes d'après leur parenté organique avec des dessins des articulations et des empreintes au palais artificiel et une plaquette d'illustrations. Dans celle-ci, après quelques planches du larynx et de la bouche, les figures 10 à 44 représentent le visage d'une jeune parisienne de 14 ans dont la gestuelle phonatoire est prise comme 'modèle visuel' de prononciation. Zünd-Burguet appliqua ses talents multiples à tous les domaines s'intéressant à la voix humaine (parole, chant, pathologies). Preuve en est le *Gymnase de la voix: parole-chant-respiration* qu'il dirigea 48, rue de Rome à Paris, centre polyvalent qui ne manquait pas d'attraits:

"Guérison rapide et sûre de tous les défauts de Prononciation
Formation, Rectification et Développement de la voix pour le chant
Enseignement de la parole aux muets et sourds muets
Éducation linguistique des enfants arriérés."

Cohérent avec l'enseignement de son maître, il mit au point une méthode vociphonique pour la rééducation des mal entendants (1913, 1914) qui, par certains côtés, paraît anticiper le SUVAG Lingua de Peter Guberina (n. 1913). L'optimisme du fondateur du *Gymnase de la voix* était loin d'être universellement partagé; toutefois les avancées technologiques étaient indéniablement à même d'offrir des supports de plus en plus fiables dont l'enseignement allait tirer grand profit. Dès 1904, à Grenoble, Théodore Rosset (1877−19??) proposait un enseignement de la prononciation qui faisait en quelque sorte la synthèse des deux approches précédentes. Il comprenait un cours théorique de phonétique, un laboratoire de phonétique expérimentale, un enseignement pratique des articulations et de la diction (Galazzi 1996b).

4.4. L'oralisation des sourds-muets

Une longue tradition de description des sons des différentes langues existait dans le domaine de l'enseignement aux sourds-muets. Depuis le XVIe siècle, la littérature du genre avait produit essentiellement des dissertations sur les éléments de la parole et sur l'analyse phonétique des sons du langage, c'est-à-dire de l'alphabet physiologique. Parmi ces travaux pionniers visant à apprendre aux sourds-muets à parler et à comprendre en interprétant les mouvements articulatoires, rappelons ceux de J. P. Bonet pour le catalan (1620), J. Bulwer (1648), J. Wallis (1653) et J. Holder (1669) pour l'Anglais (cf. Wollock 1996), F. M. Van Helmont (1667) pour l'hébreu, J. C. Amman (1692−1700) pour l'allemand.

Les premières descriptions de physiologie des organes sensoriels nous viennent des amphithéâtres d'anatomie, notamment celui de Padoue. Les ouvrages de Hieronymus Fabricius ab Aquapendente (1600) et de Julio Casserio (1601) attirèrent l'attention des savants sur les pathologies des organes de la parole (Panconcelli-Calzia 1940, 1941). Pendant de longues années, on crut à la nécessité de l'apprentissage articulatoire par l'imitation des mouvements visibles et invisibles des organes de la parole. La connaissance de l'anatomie et de la physiologie de ces organes ainsi que celle des mécanismes de production des sons (points et modes d'articulation) était à la base d'un tel enseignement. Avec la diffusion de la méthode mimique et des alphabets manuels liée au succès de l'école française (abbé de l'Epée [1712–1789], abbé Sicard [1742–1822]), l'urgence des références phonétiques s'estompa et le soin des pathologies fut laissée aux médecins. Néanmoins, vers 1870 on décèle les indices d'une inversion de tendance. En 1872, Alexander Graham Bell mit au point un système d'enseignement fondé sur le 'Visible Speech' de son père: *Visible Speech as a Means of Communicating Articulation to Deaf Mutes*. Le retour à l'enseignement oral triompha au Congrès International de Milan (1880) où l'on imposa l'oralisation à l'exclusion de tout langage gestuel. L'ambition des tenants de la méthode orale était de faire en sorte que la langue parlée soit pour le sourd, comme pour tout autre locuteur, une activité organique. Tels étaient les espoirs que les avancées en physiologie avaient fait naître (O. Claveau, introduction à von Meyer 1885).

5. Phonétique physiologique et phonologie

Loin d'être décrits une fois pour toutes, les mouvements articulatoires n'ont cessé d'être explorés, interrogés, fixés par les chercheurs à l'aide de moyens technologiques de plus en plus sophistiqués donnant lieu aux applications les plus diverses (cf. Demeny 1891). Le développement spectaculaire de la branche 'organogénétique' selon l'appellation proposée dans le *Projet de terminologie phonologique standardisée* d'après Stumpf (*Travaux du Cercle Linguistique de Prague* 4: 310 [1931]), cachait les germes du changement qui allait inéluctablement se produire marquant le passage d'une linguistique de la production vers une linguistique de la compréhension/perception. Car le renouveau touchant les sciences du langage dans les années 1920 est paradoxalement lié à une sorte de malaise provoqué par le développement rapide et intense de la phonétique (Nerlich 1991). Cette nouvelle science physiologique et physique, déroutante par son cumul de détails de plus en plus impressionnant, élaborait une définition des sons d'une inextricable complexité mais négligeant l'essentiel, à savoir leur rôle fonctionnel communicatif. L'affinement des observations portant sur les caractéristiques matérielles des sons (physiologiques et physiques) fait surgir un besoin impérieux de hiérarchisation qui annonce la phonologie déjà pressentie par des phonéticiens tels que Sweet, Passy, Sievers. Après avoir quitté les lettres pour les sons, il s'agissait de lâcher le son concret, héritage de la 'Lautphysiologie', pour partir à la recherche d'un principe organisateur.

Après cinquante ans de recherches minutieuses en phonétique physiologique, il n'est pas étonnant qu'au premier Congrès des Linguistes à La Haye en 1928, Mathesius ait pu affirmer qu'une nouvelle école, la phonologie, était venue libérer la linguistique russe du poids de la physiologie du son (*Xenia Pragensia* 1929: 433, cité dans Dieth 1950: 16). Mais, ainsi que l'écrit Jespersen (1933 [1897]: 231) "Ohne Phonetik (Lautphysiologie) gibt es keine Phonologie".

6. Bibliographie

Abercrombie, David. 1965. *Studies in Phonetics and Linguistics.* London: Oxford Univ. Press.

Asher, Ronald E. & Eugénie J. A. Henderson, éds. 1981. *Towards a History of Phonetics.* Edinburgh: Edinburgh Univ. Press.

Auroux, Sylvain. 1992. "Note sur les progrès de la phonétique au XVIIIe siècle, Appendice 3" *Histoire des idées linguistiques*, vol. II, 598–606. Liège: Mardaga.

Bergounioux, Gabriel. 1996. "Phonétique et dialectologie au XIXe siècle". *L'analisi linguistica e letteraria,* anno IV, 1.27–46. Milano: Vita e Pensiero.

Bernard, Claude. 1865. *Introduction à l'étude de la médecine expérimentale.* Paris: J.-B. Ballière et fils.

Bouton, Charles P. 1984. *Discours physique du langage: Genèse et histoire de la neurolinguistique.* Paris: Klincksieck.

Breymann, Hermann. 1897. *Die Phonetische Literatur von 1876–1895.* Leipzig: Deichert.

Brücke, Ernst. 1856. *Grundzüge der Physiologie und Systematik der Sprachlaute für Linguisten und Taubstummenlehrer.* Wien: C. Gerold's Sohn (2e éd., revue, 1876.)

—. 1871. *Die physiologischen Grundlagen der neuhochdeutschen Verskunst.* Wien: C. Gerold.

Claveau, Octave. 1885. "L'enseignement de la parole aux sourds-muets". Préface à Meyer 1885: vii–xxiv.

Czermak, Johann Nepomuk. 1879. *Gesammelte Schriften.* Leipzig: Engelmann.

Demeny, Georges. 1891. "Analyse des mouvements de la parole par la chronophotographie". *Comptes-rendus de l'Académie des Sciences* 113.216–217.

Dieth, Eugen. 1950. *Vademekum der Phonetik.* Bern: Franke.

Dodart, Denis. 1700. "Sur les causes de la voix de l'homme, et de ses differens tons". *Mémoires de l'Académie Royale des Sciences* (Paris), 238–267.

Dudley, Homer & Tamás H. Tarnoczy. 1950. "The Speaking Machine of Wolfgang von Kempelen". *Journal of the Acoustical Society of America* 22: 2.151–166.

Ferrein, Antoine. 1741. "De la formation de la voix de l'homme". *Mémoires de l'Académie Royale des Sciences* (Paris), 409–432.

Galazzi, Enrica. 1992. "1880–1914. Le combat des jeunes phonéticiens: Paul Passy". *Cahiers Ferdinand de Saussure* 46.115–129.

–. 1993. "Machines qui apprennent à parler, machines qui parlent: Un rêve technologique d'autrefois". *Études de Linguistique Appliquée* 90.73–84.

–. 1995. "Phonétique/Université/Enseignement des langues à la fin du XIXe siècle". *Histoire Epistémologie Langage* 17:1.95–114.

–. 1996a. "Physiologie de la parole et enseignement de la prononciation fin XIXe/début XXe siècles". Relation présentée au Colloque Int. de la SIHFLES, *Phonétique et pratiques de prononciation*, Linköping, 22–25 mai 1996. (Publié dans *Documents* de la SIHFLES No. 19.166–183. Paris, 1997.)

–. 1996b. "Théodore Rosset: Une méthode originale pour l'enseignement de la prononciation française à l'Université de Grenoble dès 1904". Relation présentée au Colloque Int. CUEF-SIHFLES sur le thème *L'apport des centres de français langue étrangère à la didactique des langues*, Univ. Stendhal-Grenoble 3, 26–28 septembre 1996. (Publié dans *Documents* de la SIHFLES No. 20. 37–53. Paris, 1997.)

–. 1996c. "L'Aphabet Phonétique International à ses débuts; Transcription universelle et variations". *L'analisi linguistica e letteraria*, anno IV, 1.47–64.

–. 2000. "L'Association Phonétique Internationale". *Histoire des idées linguistiques* dirigée par Sylvain Auroux, vol. III, 499–516. Liège: Mardaga.

Gessinger, Joachim. 1994. *Auge & Ohr: Studien zur Erforschung der Sprache am Menschen, 1700–1850.* Berlin & New York: de Gruyter.

Jakobson, Roman. 1976. *Six leçons sur le son et le sens.* Paris: Éditions de Minuit.

Jespersen, Otto. 1889. *The Articulations of Speech Sounds Represented by Means of Analphabetic Symbols.* Marburg: Elwert.

–. 1933 [1897]. "Zur Geschichte der Älteren Phonetik". *Linguistica: Selected papers in English, French and German*, 40–80. Copenhagen: Levin & Munksgaard.

–. 1953 [1902]. *Come si insegna una lingua straniera.* Firenze: Sansoni.

Juul, Arne & Hans F. Nielsen, eds. 1989. *Otto Jespersen: Facets of his life and work.* Amsterdam & Philadelphia: Benjamins.

Kemp, J. Alan. 1995. "Phonetics: Precursors of modern approaches". *Concise History of the Language Sciences* éd. par E. F. K. Koerner & R. E. Asher, 371–388. Oxford & New York: Pergamon Press.

Klinghardt, Hermann. 1885. "Lautphysiologie in der Schule". *Englische Studien* 8.287–323.

Koerner, E. F. Konrad. 1973. *The Importance of F. Techmer's Internationale Zeitschrift für Allgemeine Sprachwissenschaft in the Development of General Linguistics.* Amsterdam: Benjamins.

–. 1989. *Practicing Linguistic Historiography.* Amsterdam & Philadelphia: Benjamins.

–. 1995. *Professing Linguistic Historiography.* Amsterdam & Philadelphia: Benjamins.

Kohler, Klaus. "Three Trends in Phonetics: The development of the discipline in Germany since the nineteenth century". Asher & Henderson 1981. 161–178.

Koschwitz, Eduard. 1888. *Neufranzösische Formenlehre nach ihrem Lautstande dargestellt.* Oppeln: Franck.

–. 1892. *Zur Aussprache des Französischen in Genf und Frankreich.* Berlin: Gronau.

Laziczius, Julius. 1961. *Lehrbuch der Phonetik.* Berlin: Akademie-Verlag.

Lenz, Rudolf. 1887. *Zur Physiologie und Geschichte der Palaten.* Diss. Bonn. (Gütersloh: Bertelsmann.)

Lhote, Elisabeth. 1991. *Le paysage sonore d'une langue, le français.* Hamburg: Buske.

Liénard, Jean-Sylvain. 1991. "From Speaking Machine to Speech Synthesis". *Actes du XIIème Congrès International des Sciences Phonétiques, Aix-en Provence, 19–24 Août 1991*, vol. I, 18–27. Aix-en-Provence: Université de Provence. Service des Publications.

MacMahon, Michael K. C. 1986. "The International Phonetic Asdociation: The first 100 years". *Journal of the International Phonetic Association* 16.30–38.

Malmberg, Bertil. 1991. "La phonétique dans la science du langage au 19ème et au 20ème siècles: une comparaison idéologique". Relation présentée au XIIe Congrès International des Sciences Phonétiques, Aix-en Provence, 19–24 août 1991.

Marey, Étienne Jules. 1878. *La méthode graphique dans les sciences expérimentales et particulièrement en physiologie et en médecine.* Paris: Masson.

Merkel, Carl Ludwig. 1857. *Anatomie und Physiologie des menschlichen Stimm- und Sprach-Organs (Anthropophonik): Nach eigenen Beobachtungen und Versuchen wissenschaftlich begründet und für Studierende und ausübende Ärzte, Physiologen, Akustiker, Sänger, Gesanglehrer, Tonsetzer, öffentliche Redner, Pädagogen und Sprachforscher dargestellt.* Leipzig: Abel.

Meyer, Georg Hermann von. 1880. *Unsere Sprachwerkzeuge und ihre Verwendung zur Bildung der Sprachlaute.* Leipzig: Brockhaus (Trad. française, *Les organes de la parole et leur emploi pour la formation des sons du langage.* Paris: Felix Alcan, 1885.)

Michaëlis, Hermann & Paul Passy. 1897. *Dictionnaire phonétique de la langue française.* Hannover & Berlin: Meyer.

Nerlich, Brigitte. 1991. "De la phonétique à la phonologie: Éléments pour une histoire de la 'Science des sons'". *La Licorne* 19.45–69.

Nyrop, Kristoffer. 1902 [1893]. *Manuel phonétique du français parlé.* 2e éd. traduite et remaniée par Emmanuel Philipot. Paris: Picard; Leipzig: Harrassowitz.

Ohala, John J. 1991. "The Integration of Phonetics and Phonology". *Proceedings of the XIIth Int. Congress of Phonetics Sciences, Aix-en-Provence, August 19–24, 1991*, vol. I, 2–16. Aix-en-Provence: Université de Provence, Service des Publications.

Panconcelli-Calzia, Giulio. 1993. *Geschichtszahlen der Phonetik* (1941), together with *Quellenatlas der Phonetik* (1940). New ed., with an introduction by Konrad Koerner. Amsterdam & Philadelphia: Benjamins.

Passy, Paul. 1887. *Les sons du français, leur formation, leur combinaison, leur représentation.* Paris: Firmin-Didot.

—. 1887. *Le phonétisme au Congrès philologique de Stockholm en 1886.* Rapport présenté au Ministère de l'Instruction Publique. Paris: Delagrave.

—. 1901a. *Petite phonétique comparée des principales langues européennes.* Leipzig & Berlin: Teubner.

—. 1901b. "Conférences de phonétique à Copenhague". *Le Maître Phonétique*, oct.–nov. 1901, 128–129.

—. 1929. *La phonétique et ses applicatioins.* Leipzig: Teubner.

Pedersen, Holger. 1931. *Linguistic Science in the Nineteenth Century.* Cambridge, Mass.: Harvard Univ. Press. (Repr. comme *The Discovery of Language*, Bloomington: Indiana Univ. Press, 1962.)

Pipping, Hugo. 1894. *Ueber die Theorie der Vocale.* Helsinki: Finnische Literaturgesellschaft.

Rapp, Karl Moritz. 1836–1841. *Versuch einer Physiologie der Sprache nebst historischer Entwicklung der abendländischen Idiome nach physiologischen Grundsätzen.* 4 vols. Stuttgart & Tübingen: Cotta.

Rosapelly, Charles Léopold. 1876. "Inscription des mouvements phonétiques". *Travaux du laboratoire de M. Etienne Jules Marey.* Paris: Masson.

Rosset, Théodore. 1905. *Exercices pratiques d'articulation et de diction composés pour l'enseignement de la langue française aux étrangers.* Grenoble: Gratier.

Rousselot, abbé Pierre Jean. 1892. *Les modifications phonétiques du langage, étudiées dans le patois d'une famille de Cellefrouin (Charente).* Paris: Welter.

—. 1897, 1908. *Principes de phonétique expérimentale.* 2 vols, Paris & Leipzig: Welter.

—. 1899. "Applications pratiques de la phonétique expérimentale". *Revue de l'Institut Catholique de Paris* No. 3.193–210.

—. 1903. *Education de l'oreille dans la surdité.* Clermont: Daix frères.

—. 1911. "Phonétique expérimentale et 'Instrumentalphonetik'". *Revue de Phonétique* 1.11–16.

— & Fauste Laclotte. 1902. *Précis de prononciation française.* Paris & Leipzig: Welter.

Schumann, Paul. 1884. *Französische Lautlehre für Mitteldeutsche, insbesondere für Sachsen.* Dresden.

Sievers, Eduard. 1881 [1876]. *Grundzüge der Phonetik zur Einführung in das Studium der Lautlehre der indogermanischen Sprachen.* 2e éd. Leipzig: Breitkopf & Haertel.

Storm, Johan. 1881 [1879]. *Englische Philologie.* Heilbronn: Henninger.

Sweet, Henry. 1877. *A Handbook of Phonetics, including a Popular Exposition of the Principles of Spelling Reform.* Oxford: Clarendon.

—. 1885. *Elementarbuch des gesprochenen Englisch.* Oxford: Clarendon; Leipzig: Weigel.

—. 1890. *A Primer of Phonetics.* Oxford: Clarendon.

—. 1899. *The Practical Study of Languages.* London: Clarendon; New York: Holt.

Techmer, Friedrich. 1880. *Phonetik: Zur vergleichenden Physiologie der Stimme und Sprache.* 2 vols. Leipzig: Engelmann.

—. 1885. *Zur Veranschaulichung der Lautbildung.* Leipzig: Barth.

Transkription und Translitteration, Phonetische. Nach den Verhandlungen der Kopenhagener Konferentz im April 1925. Oxford: Clarendon; Heidelberg: Winter, 1926.

Trautmann, Moritz. 1884–86. *Die Sprachlaute im Allgemeinen und die Laute des Englischen, Französischen und Deutschen im Besonderen.* 2 vols. Leipzig: Fock.

Vaïsse, Léon. 1878. "Notes pour servir à l'histoire des machines parlantes". *Mémoires de la Société de Linguistique de Paris* 3.257–268.

Viëtor, Wilhelm. 1882. *Der Sprachunterricht muss umkehren! Ein Beitrag zur Überbürdungsfrage.* Heilbronn: Henninger.

—. 1884. *Elemente der Phonetik und Orthoepie des Deutschen, Englischen und Französischen mit Rücksicht auf die Bedürfnisse der Lehrpraxis.* Mit 14 Figuren. Heilbronn: Henninger.

—. 1897. *Kleine Phonetik des Deutschen, Englischen und Französischen.* Leipzig: Reisland.

Wells, Rulon. 1974. "Phonemics in the Nineteenth Century, 1876—1900". *Studies in the History of Linguistics* éd. par Dell Hymes, 434—453. Bloomington & London: Indiana Univ. Press.

Wollock, Jeffrey. 1996. "John Bulwer's (1606—1656) Place in the History of the Deaf". *Historiographia Linguistica* 23:1/2.1—46.

Wrenn, Charles L. 1966 [1946]. "Henry Sweet". *Portraits of Linguists* éd. par Thomas A. Sebeok, vol. I, 512—532. Bloomington: Indiana Univ. Press.

Wyld, H. C. K., éd. 1913. *Collected Papers of Henry Sweet.* Oxford: Clarendon.

Zünd-Burguet, Adolphe. 1902. "L'enseignement de la prononciation d'après la méthode expérimentale I". *Die Neueren Sprachen* 10.1—14; Paris: Gymnase de la voix (extrait).

—. 1902. *Méthode pratique, physiologique et comparée de prononciation française.* (Accompagné d'un livret d'illustrations: 18 planches hors texte et 69 figures). Paris: Gymnase de la voix; Genève: Kündig; Marburg: Elwert.

—. 1906 [1901]. *Exercices pratiques et méthodiques de prononciation française spécialement arrangés pour les études pratiques aux universités et les cours de vacances.* Marburg: Elwert.

—. 1914. *Conduction sonore et audition: Étude historique, critique et expérimentale.* Paris: Maloine.

Enrica Galazzi, Milan (Italie)

181. Die Dialektologie, ihr Beitrag zur historischen Sprachwissenschaft im 19. Jahrhundert und ihre Kritik am junggrammatischen Programm

1. Vorbemerkung zu methodischen und terminologischen Schwierigkeiten
2. Disziplinäre Entwicklungslinien von historischer Sprachwissenschaft und Dialektologie
3. Dialektologie als Wegbereiterin für die theoretische Neuorientierung der historischen Sprachwissenschaft
4. Beiträge der Dialektologie zur historischen Sprachwissenschaft
5. Dialektologie als Kritikerin an dem junggrammatischen Programm der historischen Sprachwissenschaft
6. Bibliographie

1. Vorbemerkung zu methodischen und terminologischen Schwierigkeiten

Die methodischen Schwierigkeiten dieses Themas bestehen im wesentlichen darin, daß die Einwirkungen der Dialektologie auf die historische Sprachwissenschaft zumeist nicht direkt zu belegen sind, so daß prinzipiell nur mögliche Zusammenhänge leitender Ideen zu rekonstruieren sind; ihre kausale Verknüpfung kann lediglich postuliert bzw. plausibel gemacht werden (vgl. allgemein Brekle 1985: 1—33; Koerner 1978a und 1995a). Diese Problematik zeigt sich deutlich bei der Konstituierung der Phonetik: waren es die praktischen Bedürfnisse der genauen dialektologischen Notation Johann Andreas Schmellers (1821) oder die theoretischen Forderungen des junggrammatischen Programms von Hermann Osthoff und Karl Brugmann (1878) nach Einbeziehung der gesprochenen Sprache oder lediglich eine disziplininterne Weiterentwicklung der Ansätze Rudolf von Raumers (1837) und ihrer Fortsetzungen bei Ernst Brücke (1856), die Sievers (1850—1932) Lautphysiologie 1876 bedingten? In gleicher Weise ist die Frage, ob Georg Wenker (1852—1911) mit seinen dialektgeographischen Erhebungen die Ausnahmslosigkeit der Lautgesetze beweisen oder widerlegen wollte, zu einem nahezu klassischen Streitfall in der germanistischen Wissenschaftsgeschichte geworden.

Es muß zunächst offen bleiben, ob diese Sachlage dem gegenwärtigen Forschungsstand in der Geschichtsschreibung der Sprachwissenschaft geschuldet ist oder ob die Quellensituation tatsächlich so spärlich ist, daß nur in seltenen Fällen belegbare Zusammenhänge hergestellt werden können, wie dies beispielsweise bei August Schleicher (1821—1868) und Ernst Haeckel (1834—1919) der

Fall ist (vgl. Koerner 1981). Ein möglicher weiterführender Aufschluß ist vielleicht aus der Briefliteratur zu erwarten, die bisher aber offensichtlich recht wenig herangezogen wurde (vgl. als Ausnahme Einhauser 1989).

Zu diesen Schwierigkeiten sind gleichfalls terminologische Probleme zu stellen. Dies betrifft weniger den Begriff der historischen Sprachwissenschaft, obwohl auch in diesem Bereich das Verhältnis zu der vergleichenden Sprachwissenschaft näher zu bestimmen wäre, um gesicherte Klarheit über das gemeinte und in Bezug zu setzende Wissenschaftsgebiet zu erreichen. Wesentlich problematischer ist der Begriff der Dialektologie, wobei es nicht in erster Linie um eine Abgrenzung zur Mundart[en]forschung geht, die hier als synonyme Termini verstanden werden, sondern um die Frage, wann die dialektologischen Arbeiten eine so weitgehende Eigenständigkeit erlangt haben, um eine selbständige Disziplin unter diesen Namen ansetzen zu können, weil von der Beantwortung der Vergleichszeitraum abhängig ist. Der Artikel folgt hier der am häufigsten anzutreffenden Auffassung, die Johann Andreas Schmeller (1785–1852) als "Begründer der wissenschaftlichen Dialektforschung" ansieht (Streitberg & Michels 1927: 145; Bach 1950: 16; vgl. auch Schirmunski 1962: 59; Markey 1977: 4; Wagner 1988: 51–52); der Auffassung von Amirova et al. (1980: 417): "Den Junggrammatikern ist das Entstehen der Dialektologie zu verdanken und später auch der Sprachgeographie", kann hier auf Grund der angeführten Fakten nicht gefolgt werden, so daß mit dem Erscheinen seiner Arbeit über *Die Mundarten Bayerns* im Jahr 1821 die idealisierte Konstituierung der Dialektologie als wissenschaftliche Disziplin festzulegen ist. Diese retrospektive Sicht ist sicher berechtigt, dennoch setzt sich ein allgemeines Bewußtsein und eine dementsprechende Anerkennung für dieses neue und selbständige Teilgebiet nur sehr langsam durch, noch 1878 wird Jost Winteler als "lautphysiologe" von Hermann Osthoff (1847–1909) und Karl Brugmann (1849–1919) bezeichnet (vgl. Osthoff & Brugmann 1878: ix, Anm. 1). Die zeitgenössischen Darstellungen der Sprachwissenschaft erwähnen Johann Andreas Schmeller und die Dialektologie zumeist nicht (vgl. z. B. Delbrück 1880); eine Ausnahme macht Rudolf von Raumer (1815–1876), der die "Erforschung der deutschen Volksmundarten" (1870: 721) wenigstens in kleineren Abschnitten behandelt (1870: 242–247, 487–492 und 721–725) sowie Johann Andreas Schmeller unter die "Mitforscher der Brüder Grimm" stellt und seine Arbeiten ausführlich in einem eigenständigen Abschnitt darstellt und würdigt (1870: 555–566).

2. Disziplinäre Entwicklungslinien von historischer Sprachwissenschaft und Dialektologie

Die allmähliche Herausbildung der Sprachwissenschaft und der Dialektologie im 19. Jh. wirft jeweils Fragen nach dem Zeitraum ihrer Konstituierung, dem Grad ihrer Eigenständigkeit und ihrem Entwicklungsverlauf auf, deren Beantwortung wiederum konstitutiv für das Aufzeigen von Einwirkungen und Beeinflussungen ist. Der allgemeine Umriß hierfür wird in den einleitenden bzw. allgemeinen Teilen der → Artikel 182–185 gegeben; da jedoch die thematische Isolierung nur bedingt die Verflechtungen erkennen läßt, ist eine kurze Skizzierung der dialektologischen und sprachhistorischen Entwicklungslinien erforderlich.

Der anfängliche Verlauf beider Disziplinen geht weitgehend getrennt vonstatten: die frühen mundartlichen Wortschatzsammlungen des 18. Jhs. in Form der Idiotika und das von Johann Andreas Schmeller 1827 herausgegebene *Bayerische Wörterbuch* sowie die unmittelbaren Nachfolgeprojekte (Schmid 1844 [1831], Stürenburg 1857, Kehrein 1862, Lexer 1862 und Vilmar 1868; vgl. auch 4.2.1.) bilden die Grundlage für eine in der weiteren Entwicklung sich breit entfaltenden Dialektlexikographie, führen aber zu keiner nennenswerten Einflußnahme auf die frühe historische Sprachwissenschaft, die sich nur gelegentlich für Wörter interessiert, die nicht in den Hochsprachen und den historischen Quellen belegt sind. In ähnlicher Weise fanden auch die frühen grammatischen Dialektbeschreibungen, die von Johann Andreas Schmellers bahnbrechenden Werk *Die Mundarten Bayerns* (1821) ausgingen (vgl. 4.2.2.) und die eine grundlegende Basis der späteren Dialektologie darstellen, keine erwähnenswerte Beachtung in der frühen historischen Sprachwissenschaft und konnten dementsprechend auch keinen unmittelbaren Einfluß auf ihre Konzeptionierung ausüben, obwohl Johann Andreas Schmeller zum ersten Mal nachgewiesen hatte, daß die Mundarten eine gesetzmäßige sprachliche Entwicklung aufweisen und keine Entstellung der Hochsprache erkennen lassen (vgl. Jankowsky 1996: 201−202).

In der ersten Entwicklungsphase bis etwa zur Mitte des 19. Jhs. können die Forschungsarbeiten der Dialektologie offensichtlich keinen direkten Niederschlag in der historischen Sprachwissenschaft erzielen; die geschichtliche Betrachtung der Dialekte und die Dominanz der Lautlehre lassen das herrschende historische Paradigma dieser Forschungsepoche und damit eher eine Einflußnahme in umgekehrter Richtung erkennen. Die Dialektologie scheint aber dennoch indirekt gewirkt zu haben, denn wesentliche Aspekte in dem junggrammatischen "glaubensbekenntniss" (1878: xix), das eine graduelle bzw. partielle Neuorientierung der historischen Sprachwissenschaft formuliert, lassen sich unmittelbar auf den Gegenstandsbereich der Dialektologie und insbesondere ihre Methoden und Ergebnisse zurückführen.

Das neue junggrammatische Programm basierte im wesentlichen auf axiomatisch aufgestellten Positionen (→ Art. 165 und Putschke 1984, 1998; Einhauser 1989, 1996); neben der postulierten Ausnahmslosigkeit der Lautgesetze, die in der nachfolgenden vehementen Kontroverse zu dem hauptsächlichen Unterscheidungsmerkmal hochstilisiert wurde, stellt die Forderung nach dem Einbezug des sprechenden Menschen und seiner Gegenwartssprache eine wesentlich grundlegendere Veränderung in der theoretischen Ausrichtung der historischen Sprachwissenschaft dar; Wagner (1988: 47) sieht in diesem Aspekt eine wesentliche Grundlage für "den Übergang zum zweiten sprachwissenschaftlichen Paradigma des 19. Jahrhunderts".

In dieser partiellen Übereinstimmung des Objektbereiches kreuzen sich zum ersten Mal die Entwicklungslinien von Dialektologie und historischer Sprachwissenschaft in einem grundlegenden Bereich.

Von diesem Kreuzungspunkt an bleibt die Dialektologie eine weiterhin eigenständige aber durchaus komplementäre Disziplin zur historischen Sprachwissenschaft und erst von diesem Zeitpunkt an kann die Frage nach möglichen Beiträgen der Dialektologie gestellt werden. Neben ihrem ergänzenden Beitrag wird die Dialektologie aber im weiteren Forschungsverlauf auch zunehmend zu einer Kritikerin der junggrammatischen Ausrichtung.

3. Dialektologie als Wegbereiterin für die theoretische Neuorientierung der historischen Sprachwissenschaft

Am Anfang der wissenschaftlichen Dialektforschung steht eine grundsätzliche Abwendung von der Buchstabenorientierung der historischen Sprachwissenschaft: "Eine Sprache besteht aus Lauten und Lautverbindungen [...]" stellt Johann Andreas Schmeller (1929 [1821]: 1) gleich im ersten Satz seiner grammatischen Darstellung der Mundarten Bayerns fest. Schmellers Erhebung des dialektalen Materials durch direkte Befragung der Mundartsprecher und die damit verbundene fehlende Schriftlichkeit waren wohl der Anstoß zu dieser grundlegend neuen Ausrichtung. In konsequenter Fortführung dieses Ansatzes zeigte sich, daß die Alphabetschrift zur Fixierung der mundartlichen Äußerungen nicht differenzierend bzw. exakt genug war, so daß Schmeller eine besondere Transkription entwickeln mußte, die er als "etymologische" Schreibung (Schmeller 1929 [1821]: 11) bezeichnete; so konnte er beispielsweise durch spezielle Diakritika bereits unterschiedliche vokalische Öffnungsgrade, die Nasalität und den Reduktionsvokal ausdrücken. Der Einfluß Grimms war aber in diesem Zeitraum offensichtlich noch so beherrschend, daß diese grundlegende Veränderung zunächst nicht beachtet und schon gar nicht übernommen wurde, obwohl Jacob Grimm (1785−1863) in der Vorrede zu seiner Deutschen Grammatik 1822 die Arbeit von Schmeller "allen nachfolgern zum muster" empfiehlt und die "gelungene faßung des schwierigen ausdrucks" besonders hervorhebt (1967 [1822]: xi).

Aber auch von lautphysiologischer Seite aus konnte gegen die Vorherrschaft der Buchstabenbetrachtung kein entscheidender Durchbruch erreicht werden. Obwohl ausgearbeitete Konzeptionen vorlagen, war dennoch das historische Paradigma in diesem Bereich so dominant, daß auch Rudolf von Raumer "nicht die verdiente Beachtung gefunden" hat (Delbrück 1904: 103).

Eine erste Auswirkung dieser phonetischen Sichtweise auf die historische Sprachwissenschaft ist erst bei Wilhelm Scherer (1841−1886) *Zur Geschichte der deutschen Sprache* (1868) belegbar, der den "Physiologische[n] Grundlagen" einen eigenen Abschnitt widmet (1868: 33−62), in dem er die Ergebnisse von Ernst Brücke (1819−1892) und Rudolf von Raumer zusammenfaßt und gegen die Ansichten von Carl Ludwig Merkel (1866) verteidigt. Allerdings scheint er sich der eingeschränkten Verbreitung dieser Kenntnisse durchaus bewußt zu sein, wenn er in der Einleitung fragt: "Steht durchweg oder wenigstens in ihren hervorragendsten Vertretern die philologische und linguistische Behandlung der Lautlehre auf derjenigen Höhe, welche sie vermöge der Vermehrung unserer physiologischen Einsicht bereits erklommen haben könnte?" (1868: 4).

Es ist jedoch mit großer Wahrscheinlichkeit davon auszugehen, daß auch August Leskien (1840—1916) in seinen Vorlesungen diese Betonung des Sprechlautes vertreten hat; direkte Zeugnisse hierfür liegen aber offenbar nicht vor (vgl. Koerner 1978a: 193 und 197—198). Diese neue Auffassung scheint in direkter Linie aus der Dialektologie in das junggrammatische Programm Eingang gefunden zu haben — obwohl dieser Zusammenhang in der Sprachgeschichtsschreibung bisher wenig Beachtung gefunden hat (vgl. z. B. Bartschat 1996: 15—17, die aus der Dialektologie keine "unmittelbare[n] Denkanstöße für die Junggrammatiker" sieht, vgl. auch Bahner & Neumann [1985: 346—349], die die Dialektologie bei der "lautphysiologische[n] Fundierung" zwar nennen, aber ihren Anteil nicht genauer herausarbeiten; einige Formulierungen in diesem junggrammatischen Programm zeigen auffällige inhaltliche Übereinstimmungen mit Passagen bei Schmeller 1827: 8) — und entfaltet von hier seine Wirksamkeit, auch wenn diese zunächst eher eine theoretische Forderung darstellte, denn praktische Konsequenzen sind nicht unmittelbar zu erkennen:

"Die ältere sprachforschung trat, [...] an ihr untersuchungsobjekt, [...] heran, ohne sich zuvor eine klare vorstellung davon gemacht zu haben, wie überhaupt menschliche sprache lebt und sich weiterbildet, welche factoren beim sprechen thätig sind und wie diese factoren in gemeinsamer arbeit die fortbewegung und umbildung des sprachstoffes bewirken. Man erforschte zwar eifrigst die sprache, aber viel zu wenig den sprechenden menschen. Der menschliche sprechmechanismus hat eine doppelte seite, eine psychische und eine leibliche. Ueber die art seiner thätigkeit ins klare zu kommen muss ein hauptziel des vergleichenden sprachforschers sein. Denn nur auf grund einer genaueren kenntniss der einrichtung und der wirkungsweise dieses seelisch-leiblichen mechanismus kann er sich eine vorstellung davon machen, was sprachlich überhaupt möglich ist [...]" (Osthoff & Brugmann 1878: iii; zur Geschichtsschreibung der Phonetik vgl. Koerner 1995b: 171—202 mit einer ausführlichen Bibliographie).

Für die historische Sprachwissenschaft kündigt sich damit im theoretischen Bereich eine grundlegende Neuorientierung an, die in einem nicht unerheblichen Maße durch die Dialektologie vorbereitet und mit bewirkt wurde (vgl. z. B. Jankowsky 1996: 201—202) und die im wesentlichen darin bestand, "dass die Sprache nicht ein selbständiger Organismus ist, der wächst, verfällt und stirbt, sondern dass sie nur in und mit den Menschen lebt, die sie sprechen, und dass die Faktoren, die ihr Leben im ganzen, ihre Bildung, ihre Überlieferung und ihre Veränderungen bedingen, zu allen Zeiten dieselben gewesen sind" (Thomsen 1927: 83).

Damit war die bisher gültige Bewertung, die "die jüngeren sprachentwicklungen [...] mit einer gewissen geringschätzung, als verkommene, gesunkene, alternde phasen möglichst unberücksichtigt gelassen" hatte (Osthoff & Brugmann 1878: vi; vgl. auch Osthoff 1883: 15), nicht nur grundsätzlich in Frage gestellt, sondern in ihr Gegenteil gewendet worden: "Gerade die jüngsten phasen der neueren indogermanischen sprachen, die lebenden volksmundarten, sind [...] von hoher bedeutung für die methodologie der vergleichenden sprachwissenschaft." (Osthoff & Brugmann 1878: viii).

Diese zunächst formale Abwendung von der Organismusvorstellung: "Wenn es nur jemand fertig brächte, die so gemeinschädlichen ausdrücke 'jugendalter' und 'greisenalter der sprachen', an denen [...] bisher fast nur fluch und kaum ein segen gehaftet hat, für immer aus der welt zu schaffen!" (Osthoff & Brugmann 1878: xv), hatte weitreichende theoretische und praktische Folgen.

3.1. Der *Objektbereich* der historischen Sprachwissenschaft war nicht mehr in der vorherigen Ausschließlichkeit auf die Rekonstruktion der Ursprache gerichtet, sondern bezog die Gegenwartssprachen und vor allem die Dialekte mit ein: "Also von der ursprache ab und der gegenwart zuwenden muss der vergleichende sprachforscher den blick, wenn er zu einer richtigen vorstellung von der art der fortentwicklung der sprache gelangen will, [...]" (Osthoff & Brugmann 1878: vii). Die noch von Schleicher (1821—1868) vertretene Abwertung der neueren Sprachperioden als Verfallsprodukte (1861: 3—4) hatte mit der neuen Auffassung von Sprache als psychophysische Tätigkeit des Menschen ihre herrschende Gültigkeit verloren.

3.2. Der *Datenbereich* der historischen Sprachwissenschaft mußte entsprechend der Erweiterung des Untersuchungsgegenstandes ebenfalls ausgedehnt werden.

"In allen lebenden volksmundarten erscheinen die dem dialect eigenen lautgestaltungen jedesmal bei weitem consequenter durch den ganzen sprachstoff durchgeführt und von den angehörigen der sprachgenossenschaft bei ihrem sprechen inne gehalten als man es vom studium der älteren bloss durch das medium der schrift zugänglichen sprachen her erwarten sollte; diese consequenz erstreckt sich oft bis in die feinsten lautschattierungen hinein" (Osthoff & Brugmann 1878: ix).

Somit kam dem sprachlichen Material der Dialektologie, das sie in ihren Dialektgrammatiken und Dialektwörterbüchern — zunächst im Sinne ihrer eigenen wissenschaftlichen Zielvorstellung — gesammelt hatte, ein gänzlich neuer Stellenwert in der historischen Sprachwissenschaft zu. Die ausschließliche Berücksichtigung schriftlicher Quellen hatte damit ihre bis dahin herrschende Vorrangstellung eingebüßt.

3.3. Der *Methodenbereich* der historischen Sprachwissenschaft hatte sich durch diese Veränderung der Blickrichtung ebenfalls neu zu orientieren, denn die gegenwärtige Sprache bildet nunmehr den Ausgangspunkt für die Analyse "der im volksmund sich vollziehenden umgestaltung der sprache" (Osthoff & Brugmann 1878: viii); aber auch in Hinsicht auf eine angemessene Deutung ist diese neue Grundlage von Bedeutung, "weil uns die lebendigen laute der gegenwart die möglichkeit an die hand geben, die schriftzeichen, durch die der Deutsche in vergangenen jahrhunderten den laut zu fixieren suchte, richtig zu verstehen. Die buchstaben sind ja immer nur rohe und unbeholfene und sehr oft geradezu irre leitende abbilder des klingenden lautes" (Osthoff & Brugmann 1878: viii). Erst die so gewonnenen Erkenntnisse ermöglichen ein direktes Vordringen in ältere Sprachperioden und die Rekonstruktion protosprachlicher Laute und Formen.

So steht die Dialektologie in einer Linie, die sie zur Wegbereiterin für die theoretische Neuorientierung der historischen Sprachwissenschaft werden ließ. In gleicher Weise urteilt Wrede (1863–1934):

"wir wissen heute [1917 bzw. 1919], daß auch die Mundartenforschung in den verflossenen hundert Jahren der deutschen Philologie die Wege mit hat ebenen dürfen, ja daß darüber hinaus gerade sie der allgemeinen Sprachwissenschaft oft Richtung gegeben und mindestens prinzipielle Bausteine geliefert hat. [...] Kam Grimm vom deutschen Altertum her und suchte er die Sprache der alten Handschriften oder der gedruckten Bücher zu organisieren, so setzt Schmeller bei der gesprochenen und gehörten Sprache der Gegenwart ein; jeder von beiden erfaßt das Problem der heimatlichen Rede am andern Ende, und beide schaffen so zu gleichen Teilen den Unterbau für die kommende deutsche Sprachwissenschaft" (Wrede 1919: 3–4).

4. Beiträge der Dialektologie zur historischen Sprachwissenschaft

Die neuen Einsichten in das Wesen der Sprache und die damit verbundene Abkehr von der Organismusvorstellung gelangte zu einer neuen und positiven Bewertung der gegenwärtigen Sprachen und führte auch zu einer Anerkennung der Mundarten, so daß dadurch das Ansehen der Dialektologie als eine durchaus komplementäre Disziplin wuchs und ihr Einfluß auf die historische Sprachwissenschaft zunahm. Die dialektologischen Beiträge zur historischen Sprachwissenschaft sind in der Hauptsache in den oben genannten Bereichen (vgl. 3.1.–3.3.) zu suchen, die mit der Neuorientierung im junggrammatischen Programm in enger Verbindung stehen.

4.1. Dialektologie als Objekterweiterin

Diese positive Bewertung der Mundarten hatte zwangsläufig zur Folge, daß die Dialektologie einen neuen und zunehmend bedeutenderen Gegenstandsbereich für die historische Sprachwissenschaft darstellte, die "somit das wichtigste Objekt ihrer Forschung erkannte, — alles dieses hat dazu geführt, dass der Laut- und Flexionslehre der Dialekte grosser Eifer zugewandt wurde" (Siebs 1902: xxxii).

Der Beitrag der Dialektologie in diesem Bereich bestand im wesentlichen darin, einen überschaubaren Beobachtungsraum für die neuen sprachwissenschaftlichen Fragestellungen und Untersuchungen zur Verfügung zu stellen. Hier konnten einerseits die theoretischen Vorstellungen über sprachliche Veränderungsvorgänge und sprachhistorischen Entwicklungsprozesse überprüft werden; Osthoff (1883: 15) umreißt diese Erweiterung zusammenfassend:

"Wir wollen wissen, wie menschliche Sprache überhaupt sich entwickelt, welche Gesetze bei der Veränderung der Sprache zu walten pflegen und ihre Geschicke bestimmen; wir wünschen so den richtigen Begriff von dem allgemeinen Wesen der

Sprache zu gewinnen. [...] da ist es einzig und allein der Volksmund, dessen ungekünstelter und unverfälschter Rede wir aufmerksam [...] zu lauschen haben, um über das geheimnißvolle Walten und Weben des Sprachgeistes ungeahnte Wahrheit zu erkunden."

Andererseits ließen sich die Dialekte in ein historisches Kontinuum zu den älteren Sprachperioden stellen, wodurch eine nicht unerhebliche Komplettierung der Sprachgeschichte insgesamt erreicht wurde. "Die Volksmundarten verfolgen ihren Stammbaum in ununterbrochener Reihe bis auf die historischen Anfänge des germanischen Volksthums zurück; in den Adern der Volkssprache fließt reines, seit Jahrtausenden unvermischtes Blut" (Osthoff 1883: 15). Dieser Zusammenhang ließ sich in umgekehrter Richtung auch zur Heimatbestimmung alter Schriftdenkmäler nutzen, um auf diese Weise weitere einzelne Mosaiksteine zu einer Sprachgeschichte zusammenzutragen (vgl. z. B. Berthold 1927).

Dieser dialektologische Einfluß unterstützte allerdings die Verkürzung von Sprache auf den Laut- und Formenbereich, die bereits in der historischen Sprachwissenschaft als deutliche Tendenz vorhanden war; im Prinzip ist es erst die strukturalistische Ausrichtung des 20. Jhs., die diesen linguistischen Objektraum durch eine stärkere Einbeziehung von Syntax erweiterte. Bei einer solchen Beurteilung ist jedoch zu berücksichtigen, daß einerseits auch von einigen Junggrammatikern (vgl. vor allem Delbrück [1842−1922] und Brugmann) beachtliche syntaktische Arbeiten vorliegen, während andererseits die sogenannten Strukturalisten wegen der bei ihnen fehlenden Einbeziehung der Syntax kritisiert wurden (vgl. beispielsweise de Saussure). Unter Einbezug einzelner Arbeiten relativiert sich selbstverständlich diese allgemeine Beurteilung, dennoch ist eine durchgängige Schwerpunktsetzung in Hinsicht auf eine junggrammatische Laut- und Formenlehre und eine strukturalistische Syntax deutlich zu erkennen.

Durch diese Neubewertung "macht die Sprachwissenschaft vollen Ernst mit dem eindringlichen Studium der Dialekte" (Osthoff 1883: 32). Dieser Einbezug in die laufenden sprachhistorischen Forschungsarbeiten läßt sich an der praktischen Arbeit einer ganzen Reihe von Linguisten aufzeigen; Osthoff geht sogar so weit, seine "sprachvergleicherischen Neigungen" auf das "frühzeitig entgegentretende [...] Verhältniß volksmundartlichen Mutterlautes und in der Schule erlernter Schriftsprache" (1883: 33) zurückzuführen. Anschaulich läßt sich dieser Zusammenhang in einem besonders frühen Fall an dem Werk August Schleichers demonstrieren: vor seinem *Compendium* (1861) publizierte er eine Grammatik und ein Wörterbuch seiner Heimatstadt Sonneberg im Meininger Oberlande (1858). Noch ist das Hauptziel in einer bewahrenden Dokumentation zu sehen (1858: iii); eine Bewertung dieser Mundart als Verfallserscheinung − wie es seiner grundsätzlichen Organismusvorstellung entspräche − läßt sich hier nicht finden, sondern eher das Gegenteil, nämlich eine liebevolle Einschätzung in Erinnerung an seine Kindheit (Schleicher 1858: v). Darüber hinaus stellt er fest: "auch ist wol hier und da etwas zu wißenschaftlichen zwecken verwertbares in derselben enthalten" (Schleicher 1858: iii); von seiner Grammatik aber sagt er ausdrücklich, daß sie "mer für den sprachforscher bestimt" (Schleicher 1858: vi) ist.

Von Interesse ist hier die Verwendung einer phonetischen Schreibung "nach der außsprache" (Schleicher 1858: 1) und in der Lautlehre die praktische Ausarbeitung des sprachhistorischen Zusammenhangs von der indogermanischen Grundsprache bis zum Sonnebergischen (vgl. Schleicher 1858: 20−25 für den Vokalismus), die Kontrastierung zur Schriftsprache (vgl. Schleicher 1858: 25−27) und das Aufstellen von vokalischen und konsonantischen Lautgesetzen innerhalb der Mundart (vgl. Schleicher 1858: 27−33); für die Frage nach dem terminologischen Erstgebrauch von 'Lautgesetz' (vgl. Schleicher 1858: 25−33) und die Behauptung seiner Ausnahmslosigkeit sind vielleicht die folgenden Belege von Wichtigkeit: "das gesetz scheint früher außnamsloser gewesen zu sein" (Schleicher 1858: 29) und "Ein außnamsloses lautgesetz ist die verwandlung von s nach r in sch [...]" [Schleicher 1858: 30]).

4.2. Dialektologie als Datengeberin

Mit der grundlegenden Neubewertung der gegenwärtigen Sprachen und in deren Gefolge der Mundarten um die Mitte des 19. Jhs. erhielt einerseits das bisher gesammelte dialektologische Material einen neuen Stellenwert, indem es zu einer zunehmend wichtigeren Datenquelle für die historische Sprachwissenschaft wurde ("Die dialecte bieten der gesamten sprachforschung wichtiges material" [Wegener 1880: 452]) und andererseits führte die Zusammenarbeit zu einer Weiterentwicklung der Dialektologie selbst, wobei insbesondere die Fortschritte der Lautphysiologie daran einen maßgeblichen Anteil hatten (vgl. allgemein hierzu Lehmann 1969: 103−120).

Der Datenzuwachs bezog sich im wesentlichen auf zwei Gebiete (4.2.1−2).

4.2.1. Die *Mundartwörterbücher* stellten der historischen Sprachwissenschaft ein reichhaltiges lexikalisches Material zur Verfügung, wobei insbesondere die bevorzugte Auswahl von nichtstandardsprachlichen Wörtern ihren sprachhistorischen Interessen entgegenkam; auch das Bayerische Wörterbuch von Johann Andreas Schmeller (1827) als erste wissenschaftliche lexikographische Arbeit stand noch in der Tradition der Idiotika (vgl. z. B. Scholz 1933; Werlen 1996: 432−436), wenn im Untertitel formuliert wurde: "Sammlung von Wörtern [...] die in den lebenden Mundarten [...] vorkommen [...] und in der heutigen allgemein=deutschen Schriftsprache entweder gar nicht, oder nicht in denselben Bedeutungen üblich sind". Dadurch erschloß sich der Sprachwissenschaft ein großes zusätzliches Vergleichsmaterial für ihre sprachhistorischen Rekonstruktionen. In der Nachfolge von Johann Andreas Schmeller − jedoch mit der Tendenz nunmehr den gesamten lexikalischen Bestand einer Mundart zu dokumentieren − stehen die im 19. Jh. begonnenen und zum Teil auch abgeschlossenen Wörterbücher für das Thüringische von Ludwig Hertel (1895), für das Oberhessische von Wilhelm Crecelius (1897−1899), für das Elsaß von Ernst Martin (1841−1910) und Hans Lienhart (1899−1907), für das Pfälzische von Georg Autenrieth (1899), für das Schwäbische von Hermann Fischer (1901−1936) und für das Schleswig-Holsteinische von Otto Mensing (1927−1935) sowie das Schweizerische Idiotikon von Franz Joseph Stalder (1806−1812) sowie seit 1881. Diese Gruppe von Wörterbüchern wird durch kleine zumeist lokal ausgerichtete Wörterbücher (vgl. Schirmunski 1962: 99−102; Bach 1950: 50−51) bis hin zu großen landschaftlich orientierten Wörterbuchunternehmen (vgl. Niebaum 1979, Friebertshäuser 1983) im 20. Jh. fortgeführt. Ihr lexikalisches Material findet als sprachhistorische Belege Eingang in die linguistischen Untersuchungen und wird ebenso in die etymologischen Wörterbücher eingearbeitet; dies ist vor allem deutlich an den Quellenverzeichnissen abzulesen; in diesem Zusammenhang kann beispielsweise Oskar Schade (1872−82) angeführt werden, der in seinem Abkürzungsverzeichnis (lxiv−cxv) unter der benutzten Literatur eine Vielzahl dialektologischer Wörterbücher und Grammatiken nennt und in seinem Einleitungstext (v−lxiii) ausdrücklich auf die Einbeziehung des mundartlichen Materials hinweist: "Nun sind aber auch die lebendigen deutschen Mundarten viel reichlicher herbeigezogen worden, als dies in der 1. Auflage [1866] geschehen war; gehoben ist dieser Schatz noch lange nicht" (Schade 1872−1882: xxii) und "Welchen Wert Schmellers bairisches Wörterbuch nicht bloß für die neueren Mundarten in Baiern, auch fürs Mittel- und Althochdeutsche hat, [...] braucht hier nicht wieder gesagt zu werden" (Schade, S. xxi).

4.2.2. Die *Mundartgrammatiken* stehen im wesentlichen ebenfalls in der Nachfolge von Johann Andreas Schmeller und bieten der historisch-vergleichenden Sprachwissenschaft gleichfalls eine breite Materialbasis sowohl für ihre Rekonstruktionen des Laut- und Formenbestandes als auch für ihre Untersuchungen sprachlicher Veränderungsprozesse. In die Anfangsperiode gehören beispielsweise die folgenden Arbeiten: Müllenhoff (1854) über den dithmarscher und Weinhold (1853) über den schlesischen Dialekt, Regel (1868) über Ruhla, Schröer (1868) über die Gottschee, Nerger (1869) über die mecklenburgische, Heinzerling (1871) über die siegerländische Mundart und Jellinghaus (1877) über die Mundart von Ravensberg. Eine nicht unerhebliche Schwierigkeit dieser frühen dialektologischen Grammatiken stellt das Fehlen einer einheitlichen Lautschrift dar, so daß man gezwungen war, jeweils spezielle Zeicheninventare zu entwerfen; hier eröffneten die Fortschritte der Lautphysiologie (vgl. Sievers 1876) neue Beschreibungsmöglichkeiten und bereiten so auch den Weg zu einer vereinheitlichten Transkriptionsschrift.

Den Durchbruch von dialektologischer Seite aus erreichte Jost Winteler (1876, bereits 1875 erschienen) mit seiner bei Eduard Sievers angefertigten Dissertation über seinen Heimatort *Die Kerenzer Mundart des Kantons Glarus*, die bereits Hermann Osthoff und Karl Brugmann (1878: ix) in ihrem Vorwort lobend hervorhoben und als eine "vortreffliche schrift" sowie eine empfehlenswerte Informationsquelle bezeichneten. Die Einschränkung auf einen einzigen Ort (vgl. Winteler 1876: vii) entsprach durchaus den junggrammatischen Idealvorstellungen, nämlich "die Grenze für den Ausdruck Dialekt so eng als möglich, wo möglich nicht über eine

Stadt, ein einziges Dorf hinaus zu ziehen" (Osthoff 1883: 17) und darüber hinaus sollte es auch noch die "heimatliche [...] mundart" (Osthoff & Brugmann 1878: ix) sein; die dennoch bestehenden Schwierigkeiten einer genauen Exploration und Notation werden erkannt und ausführlich erörtert (Winteler 1876: 35−37). "Es ist Wintelers Buch [...], das die modernen Forderungen zum erstenmal und sofort in ausgezeichneter Weise erfüllt hat" (Wrede 1919: 7; vgl. Streitberg & Michels 1927: 149−151; Schirmunski 1962: 65−68; Koerner 1978a: 197).

Der Vorbildcharakter dieser Arbeit basiert:

(a) Auf einer strikten Einbeziehung der sich etablierenden *Lautphysiologie* in theoretischer wie auch praktischer Hinsicht bei der Beschreibung der einzelnen Laute und kommt dabei im Konsonantismus zu dem grundlegenden Ergebnis, daß "das noch keineswegs in allen Theilen gelöste Problem der Lautverschiebungen noch einmal gründlich und nach allen Seiten hin von dem neuen Boden aus durchzuarbeiten" ist, wobei hauptsächlich von "den gegebenen oder zu erschließenden Lautwerthen" auszugehen ist (Winteler 1876: 30); vor allem bei den Unterschieden zwischen Mediae und Tenues, Fortes und Lenes zeigten sich die weitreichenden Konsequenzen einer lautphysiologischen Beschreibung gegenüber der Buchstabenbetrachtung, die solche diffizilen Verschiedenheiten verdeckte. Im Vokalismus gelangte er zur Aufstellung eines Vokalschemas auf der Grundlage der Klangqualitäten (vgl. Winteler 1876: 105), das eine systematische Ordnung der Vokale erreicht, die sich durchaus mit einem phonetischen Vierecksystem vergleichen lassen kann; darüber hinaus basiert das Ermittlungsverfahren an entscheidenden Stellen auf dem Minimalpaarvergleich der späteren Phonologie (vgl. Winteler 1876: 103−105; Trubetzkoj 1962 [1939]: 7 "von den Zeitgenossen Wintelers [...] ist sein Gedanke von der Unterscheidung zweier Arten von Lautgegensätzen gar nicht beachtet, vielleicht sogar gar nicht bemerkt worden.").
(b) Auf einer *'etymologischen' Einordnung* des mundartlichen Lautbestandes, die auf der Basis eines umfangreichen Beleg- und Vergleichsmaterials eine überzeugende sprachhistorische Kontinuität des Dialektes aufzeigen kann.
(c) Auf der Herausarbeitung *lautgesetzlicher Zusammenhänge*, die in überzeugender Weise den Systemcharakter der Mundart beweisen und belegen damit die Auffassung der Junggrammatiker, daß "die dem Dialekt eigenen Lautgestaltungen [...] mit vollster Consequenz und Ausnahmslosigkeit durch den ganzen Sprachstoff durchgeführt erscheinen" (Osthoff 1883: 17).

Nach dem Beispiel von Jost Winteler entstanden zahlreiche Ortsgrammatiken, die zumeist nur den Lautstand und seine sprachhistorische Einordnung beschreiben: beispielsweise Ferdinand Holthausen (1886: Soest), Andreas Heusler (1888: Basel), Philipp Wagner (1889−1891: Reutlingen), Joseph Schatz (1897: Imst/Tirol), Victor Henry (1900: Kolmar) und Primus Lessiak (1903: Pernegg/Kärnten), die heute von den dialektologischen Handbüchern als die führenden Arbeiten dieser Periode angesehen werden. Darüber hinaus entstanden − zumeist als Dissertationen − eine Vielzahl weiterer Ortsuntersuchungen; größere Dialektgebiete werden nur bearbeitet von Friedrich Kauffmann (1890: schwäbisch), Joseph Schatz (1903: tirolisch), Ferdinand Münch (1904: ripuarisch-fränkisch) und Wolf von Unwerth (1908: schlesisch). Damit "hat die deutsche Mundartforschung seit der zweiten Hälfte des 19. Jhs. ein sehr umfangreiches Material deskriptiver Monographien fast aller Lokalmundarten der deutschen Sprache zusammengetragen" (Schirmunski 1962: 145).

Im gleichen Zeitraum, in dem die Arbeit von Jost Winteler erschien, publizierte auch Georg Wenker seine Dissertation *Über die Verschiebung des Stammsilben-Auslauts im Germanischen* (1876), in der er die vielleicht früheste Integration umfangreicher dialektaler Daten in die sprachhistorische Forschung vornahm. Die gesamte Untersuchung bezieht ständig dialektale Belege − überwiegend aus dem westdeutschen Raum − als Vergleichs- oder Bestätigungsmaterial in die Argumentation ein. Dies wird besonders bei der Erörterung des Verschiebungsvorgangs der ursprachlichen inlautenden Tenues deutlich, wenn "ein zweiter thatsächlicher Beweis für diese Möglichkeit aus dem phonetischen Stande der Consonantenaussprache in den heutigen Mundarten" (Wenker 1876: 126−127) herangezogen wird. Von besonderem Interesse für die Beurteilung dieser und der späteren Arbeiten Georg Wenkers ist der Hinweis auf "genaue [...] persönliche [...] Untersuchungen und Beobachtungen, die in einer Reihe von Städten Westdeutschlands (deren nördlichste Osnabrück und Minden, deren südlichste Basel und Zürich sind) angestellt wurden und die demnächst anderseitig verwendet werden sollen." Ursprünglich war eine vollständigere Aufnahme dieses Materials vorgesehen gewesen, "welche Absicht erst nachträglich in Rücksicht auf den Umfang des Ganzen aufgegeben wurde" (Wenker 1876: 126, Anm. 1). Über die Form einer solchen Einziehung finden sich keine Angaben, aber es wäre durchaus denkbar, die gesamte tabellarische Dokumentation des historischen

Sprachmaterials um eine Spalte mit den mundartlichen Belegen zu ergänzen; eine solche mögliche Anordnung der geographisch orientierten Erhebungsdaten zeigt bereits hier die Nähe zu einer kartographischen Darstellung.

Trotz dieses umfangreichen Datenzuwachses beurteilt Frings (1921: 9) die Einbeziehung dialektologischer Daten in die Grammatikschreibung insgesamt durchaus kritisch: "in Francks Grammatiken wagt sich die Mundart gelegentlich hervor; erst Behaghel hat der Verknüpfung von geschichtlicher Überlieferung und neuzeitlichem Bestand breiten Raum gegeben. Aber die Verknüpfung ist noch nicht enge, noch nicht organisch genug" (vgl. auch Einhauser 1996: 217).

4.3. Dialektologie als Methodenförderin

Die junggrammatische Verabsolutierung der Ausnahmslosigkeit der Lautgesetze und die strikte Einbeziehung der Analogie erforderten für ihre allgemeine Anerkennung eine überzeugende Beweisführung am konkreten Sprachmaterial (vgl. Amirova et al. 1980: 378). Hier bot die Dialektologie mit ihren mundartlichen Ortsuntersuchungen einen realen und überschaubaren Laborraum, der durchaus der Funktion des Korpus in der strukturellen Linguistik vergleichbar ist; damit unterstützte die Dialektologie die methodische Axiomatik der Junggrammatiker und trug in einem nicht unerheblichen Maße zu ihrer praktischen Durchsetzung und theoretischen Gültigkeit bei.

Dieses methodische Zusammengehen bewirkte einerseits eine prinzipielle Bestätigung der neuen Auffassungen über die Mundarten und andererseits eine Übertragung der hier gewonnenen neuen Ansichten auf die sprachhistorischen Perioden – dies betraf vor allem die Wirksamkeit der Analogie (vgl. z. B. Delbrück 1904: 161–171) und die Annahme unterschiedlicher Dialekte auf den historischen Sprachstufen (vgl. z. B. Lehmann 1969: 117–118).

Eine wesentliche Neuerung im methodischen Bereich entwickelte die Dialektologie mit ihrer sprachgeographischen Kartierung (vgl. Siebs 1902: xxxii; Werlen 1996: 436–446) und schuf damit eine grundsätzlich neue Perspektive: die bisher ausschließlich geltende historische Sichtweise ("Es ist eingewendet, dass es noch eine andere wissenschaftliche betrachtung der sprache gäbe, als die geschichtliche. Ich muss das in abrede stellen" [Paul 1886: 19]) wird nun mit einem räumlichen Gesichtspunkt konfrontiert. Damit wird die Methodik der Sprachveränderung um die Methodik der Sprachverbreitung erweitert (vgl. Berner 1948: 33–41). Dieser Gegensatz bestand jedoch nur in der Anfangsphase, denn das historische Paradigma war wohl noch immer so dominant, daß sich die Sprachgeographie schon sehr bald einer geschichtlichen Interpretation der synchronen Kartenbilder zuwandte, wobei sowohl die Verbreitungsformen als auch die Koinzidenz von Sprachgrenzen mit außersprachlichen Linienverläufen als wesentliche Datierungsverfahren benutzt wurden (vgl. Putschke 1974). Erst dadurch wurde die kartographische Methode zu einer weiterführenden Ergänzung der sprachhistorischen Methodik.

Ein Beispiel für das Zusammenwirken beider Methoden kann in Ferdinand Wredes Ingwäonentheorie gesehen werden, die eine grundlegend neue Auffassung über das Verhältnis der westgermanischen Sprachen vorschlägt und somit zu einer durchgreifenden – allerdings hypothetischen – Modifikation der deutschen Sprachgeschichte gelangt (vgl. hierzu Haindl 1950: 2–22).

Dieser Einbezug der sprachgeographischen Betrachtungsweise bewirkte auch eine Überprüfung der sogenannten Stammeshypothese. Die in der historischen Sprachwissenschaft vorherrschende Auffassung ging davon aus, daß die rezenten Dialektgrenzen im wesentlichen die Grenzen der frühzeitlichen deutschen Stammesgebiete wiedergaben (vgl. Bach 1950: 25–26, 64, 95–96; Schirmunski 1962: 69–70). Die sprachgeographischen Untersuchungen zeigten jedoch, daß die Dialektgrenzen allenfalls auf die Territorialgrenzen des späteren Mittelalters (Bach 1950: 124–126) zurückzuführen waren, so daß damit die Stammeshypothese endgültig aufgegeben werden mußte (vgl. Schirmunski 1962: 131–145).

Die Integration der sprachgeographischen Methode bedingte auch ein andersartiges Erklärungsverfahren für sprachliche Entwicklungsprozesse: die historische Sprachwissenschaft hatte die lautlichen Veränderungen im sprachgeschichtlichen Ablauf auf die Wirkung von Lautgesetzen und Analogien zurückgeführt und das Zustandekommen dieser inneren Gesetzlichkeiten auf sprachphysiologische und -psychologische Mechanismen zurückgeführt (Osthoff & Brugmann 1878: iii–v). Demgegenüber hatte die Sprachgeographie erkannt, daß die Ursache für räumliche Entwicklungen vor allem in außersprachlichen Faktoren wie Sprachmischung, Sprachausgleich und sprachlicher Verdrängung zu suchen seien und übertrug dieses Deutungsschema auch auf geschichtliche Veränderungsvorgänge. Damit erweiterte sich die individuallinguistische Erklärungsmethode um ein soziallinguistisches Begründungsverfahren; die unterschiedliche Explikation der nhd. Diphthongierung ist ein Beispiel für diese beiden Interpretationsmuster, die auch im weiteren Fortgang in keine übergeordnete Symbiose aufgelöst wurden, sondern sich eher konfrontativ gegenüberstanden. Denn "es [gab] keine Antwort auf die Frage, inwieweit außersprachliche und innersprachliche Bedingungen als Impuls für die Entstehung von Lautveränderungen wechselseitig zusammenwirken bzw. die Bedingungen herstellen, die für den Ablauf einer Lautveränderung erforderlich sind und sie schließlich auch beenden" (Amirova et al. 1980: 380).

5. Dialektologie als Kritikerin an dem junggrammatischen Programm der historischen Sprachwissenschaft

Mit dem Einbezug der sprachgeographischen Methode in die historische Sprachwissenschaft ist neben einer bedeutenden Ergänzung des Methodenarsenals auch gleichzeitig der Beginn einer konfrontativen Auseinandersetzung verbunden (vgl. z. B. Stroh 1952: 418–419; Ivić 1971: 54 und 70–73; Robins 1973: 50–52.

Die gängige Geschichtsschreibung stellt die Kritik der Dialektologie – im engeren Sinne der Sprachgeographie – an dem junggrammatischen Programm recht übereinstimmend und im Kern in folgender Weise dar: Georg Wenker wollte mit seinen sprachgeographischen Erhebungen die Ausnahmslosigkeit der Lautgesetze empirisch beweisen (Bach 1950: 40: "Was er [Wenker] wollte, war dies: das Axiom von der Ausnahmslosigkeit der Lautgesetze durch die lebenden Mdaa. [Mundarten] zu erweisen [...]"). Als aber bereits die ersten Sprachkarten divergierende Linienführungen für die mundartlichen Vertretungen der gesetzmäßigen Lautveränderungen zeigten, wurde diese Tatsache als Gegenbeweis für das junggrammatische Prinzip gewertet und damit diese methodische Grundannahme der historischen Sprachwissenschaft für widerlegt erachtet (vgl. beispielsweise Wrede 1908; Mitzka 1943: 8–9; Stroh 1952: 418; Schirmunski 1962: 84–85; 127–131; Arens 1969: 331; Agricola et al. 1969: 350; Helbig 1971: 27; Markey 1977: 5–6; eine differenzierte Ansicht vertritt Haag 1929; zu einer generellen Kritik an dem junggrammatischen Programm, vgl. Bartschat 1996: 29–30). Als ein Beispiel für diesen sprachgeographischen Befund wird häufig der sogenannte rheinische Fächer angeführt.

Ein Überprüfung dieser Kritikpunkte bezieht sich in der Hauptsache auf die folgenden Fragen: ob die Zielvorstellung Georg Wenkers überhaupt zutrifft, ob das junggrammatische Programm das Axiom der Ausnahmslosigkeit der Lautgesetze auch auf Dialekte bezogen hat und ob die empirischen Ergebnisse der Sprachgeographie überhaupt als Gegenbeweis gelten können.

5.1. Die geäußerte Auffassung über die sprachwissenschaftliche *Zielsetzung Georg Wenkers* wird offensichtlich den tatsächlichen Gegebenheiten nicht gerecht, worauf Werner H. Veith (1970: 393–399) als erster aufmerksam gemacht hat (vgl. auch die Ergänzungen bei Wiegand & Harras [1971: 11–13, besonders Anm. 23] und die Darlegung der weiteren Entwicklungsphasen [1971: 13–25]): es ist erwiesenermaßen keine Äußerung Georg Wenkers zu finden – weder in seinen Veröffentlichungen noch in den Archivmaterialien des Forschungsinstituts für deutsche Sprache (Marburg) – die diese Absicht bestätigt (vgl. Knoop et al. 1982: 51). Auch die Darstellung und Auswertung seiner ersten Enquete (Wenker 1877) und insbesondere seiner *Sprach-Karte der Rheinprovinz nördlich der Mosel* lassen eine solche Intention ebenfalls nicht erkennen; die kartographische Eintragung von 'Mischmundarten' und 'Uebergangs-Mundarten' spricht eher gegen den Versuch, das junggrammatische Axiom auf mundartlicher Ebene beweisen zu wollen, sondern ist weit mehr ein Beleg für seine wirkliche Zielvorstellung, die er ganz offensichtlich in einer sprachwissenschaftlich fundierten Herausarbeitung der dialektalen Gliederung der Rheinprovinz gesehen hat. Diese Sichtweise wird später (1885) durch Wenker selbst bestätigt: "Als ich [...] die Mundart meiner Heimatprovinz in Untersuchung zog, that ich es hauptsächlich, um eine Anzahl wichtiger und im allgemeinen Ansehen stehender Eigenthümlichkeiten der dortigen Dialekte schärfer als bisher abzugrenzen und festzustellen" (Wenker 1886: 89).

Der Initiator dieser irreführenden Behauptung ist mit hoher Wahrscheinlichkeit Ferdinand Wrede, wenn er 1903 diesen unterstellten Zusammenhang hier allerdings noch als Frage formuliert:

"1876 ist Leskiens *Deklination im Slavisch-Litauischen und im Germanischen* erschienen mit der unumwundenen Formulierung, daß die Wirkung der Lautgesetze ausnahmslos sei. [...] Im selben Jahre 1876 aber schickt Wenker seine ersten Fragebogen aus und bereitet so, gegenüber jenem Streit um Theorie und Prinzip, eine sachliche Anschauung des Tatbestandes, wenigstens auf deutschem Sprachgebiet, vor. Ist dieser Zusammenfall beider Daten lediglich Zufall gewesen?" (Wrede 1963 [1903]: 310)

Schon 1908 beantwortete er diese Frage in der Zueignung des ersten Bandes der Deutschen Dialektgeographie an Georg Wenker:

"Es war kein Zufall, dass grade im Jahre 1876, wo das lange vorbereitete und dann so folgenschwere Wort von der Ausnahmslosigkeit der Lautgesetze geprägt ward, Ihre [Wenkers] ersten dialektischen Fragebogen ausgesandt wurden: der Streit um das sprachwissenschaftliche Dogma hat Ihren Sprachatlas geboren" (Wrede 1908: vii).

Nach Wenkers Tod (1911) bestätigt er noch einmal seine Sichtweise, die ihm zunehmend zur Gewißheit wird:

"In dem Bestreben nun, diesem Axiom, für das eigentlich nur mit theoretischen Waffen gekämpft wurde und gekämpft werden konnte, auch von der praktischen Seite, d. h. induktiv, beizukommen, liegt der Anfang der modernen Dialektgeographie [...] Auf geographische Anschaulichkeit übertragen bedeutet diese Forderung, daß die Sprachgrenze, welche auf der Landkarte das Gebiet des dialektischen *haus* gegen das des dialektischen *hus* abtrennt, zugleich unverändert die Grenze sei zwischen *us* und *aus, lut* und *laut* usw. Den Beweis dafür wollte Wenker liefern" (Wrede 1919: 8–9).

Von nun an galt Ferdinand Wredes Behauptung als unverrückbare Lehrmeinung und wurde von vielen Darstellungen und Handbüchern zur Geschichte der Dialektologie und der Sprachwissenschaft ungeprüft übernommen (vgl. beispielsweise: Agricola et al. 1969: 349; Arens 1969: 331; Bretschneider 1934: 96; Helbig 1971: 20, 26−29; Henzen 1954: 159; Markey 1977: 5−6; Martin 1939: 83, 1959: 87; Mitzka 1943: 8−9; Schwarz 1950: 43−44; Stroh 1952: 418−419; zur grundsätzlichen Kritik an der Geschichtsschreibung der Linguistik vgl. Koerner 1981: 2−3); eine Ausnahme macht Schirmunski (1962: 70), der sich zu diesen Zusammenhängen direkt nicht äußert, sondern lediglich hervorhebt, daß Wenker "nicht mit den Junggrammatikern in Verbindung" stand.

5.2. Um die Berechtigung der kolportierten Kritik zu überprüfen, ist sicher auch der Frage nachzugehen, ob das junggrammatische Programm das *Axiom der Ausnahmslosigkeit der Lautgesetze* überhaupt auch *auf Dialekte bezogen* hat. Die Vorstellungen der Junggrammatiker gehen tendenziell schon in die Richtung, daß "in allen lebenden volksmundarten [...] die dem dialect eigenen lautgestaltungen jedesmal bei weitem consequenter durch den ganzen sprachstoff durchgeführt" wurden (Osthoff & Brugmann 1878: ix), so daß ihre Prinzipien auch für die Dialekte zu gelten haben (vgl. Paul 1886 [1880]: 64). Im junggrammatischen Programm werden aber keine Aussagen über das Zusammenspiel der Mundarten in der geographischen Dimension getroffen; lediglich in ihrem ersten methodischen Grundsatz wird die Ausnahmslosigkeit der lautgesetzlichen Entwicklungen für den Fall der Dialektspaltung ausdrücklich aufgehoben (vgl. Osthoff & Brugmann 1878: xiii). Demgegenüber äußert sich Hermann Paul (1846−1921) bereits 1880 mit einer verblüffenden Sachkenntnis über die geographische Verteilung: "Ziehen wir daher in einem zusammenhängenden sprachgebiete die grenzen für alle vorkommenden dialectischen eigentümlichkeiten, so erhalten wir ein sehr kompliziertes system mannigfach sich kreuzender linien" (Paul [1880: 238, zit. nach Schirmunski 1962: 65] 1886: 40). Damit verlagert sich die Problemstellung auf die Frage nach den Ursachen von Dialektgrenzen und hier erkennen Hermann Paul (1880) und Georg Wenker (1886) schon sehr früh, daß es vor allem Ausgleichsprozesse zwischen den Mundarten sind, die Abweichungen von der erwarteten einheitlichen Lautlinie bewirken; so kommt insbesondere Georg Wenker schon bei seiner ersten Kartierung 1877 zur Festlegung von Misch- und Übergangsdialekten (vgl. 5.1. und hierzu die ähnlichen Ergebnisse von Fischer 1895). Aus diesen Zusammenhängen ergibt sich der folgende Schluß: weil das junggrammatische Programm keine unmittelbaren Aussagen über dialektale Gliederungen trifft und die historische Sprachwissenschaft ebenfalls hierüber kaum direkte Vorstellungen vertreten hat, kann auch der erreichte sprachgeographische Befund nicht als Gegenargument oder Kritik vorgebracht werden.

5.3. Wenn das junggrammatische Programm keine Vorstellungen genauerer Art an die dialektale Raumgliederung formulierte und wenn Georg Wenkers Absicht nicht in dem Nachweis der Ausnahmslosigkeit dialektaler Lautentwicklungen bestand, dann stellt sich die Frage, ob die *empirischen Ergebnisse der Sprachgeographie* losgelöst von den zunächst angenommenen Umständen überhaupt *als Gegenbeweis* gelten können.

Eine Übertragung der junggrammatischen Forderung nach Ausnahmslosigkeit der Lautgesetze auf die sprachgeographische Kartierung könnte nur dann einheitliche Lautlinien fordern, wenn sich die Dialektgrenzen seit der Periode der betreffenden Lautentwicklungen nicht verändert hätten ("Die Lautgesetze wirken in der Endkonsequenz ausnahmslos in den Grenzen einer bestimmten Sprache oder einer Gruppe von Sprache innerhalb einer umschriebenen zeitlichen Periode" [Amirova et al. 1980: 380]). Dies würde beispielsweise im Falle der hochdeutschen Lautverschiebung eine im wesentlichen ununterbrochene Konstanz der Dialektgebiete seit dem 5.–7. Jh. n. Chr. voraussetzen. Eine solche Annahme aber wäre nur bei Befürwortung der sogenannten Stammeshypothese vorstellbar, deren Ablehnung sich allerdings erst in Folge der sprachgeographischen Erkenntnissen durchsetzte, so daß beispielsweise Bach (1950: 40) behaupten konnte, daß Georg Wenker noch mit seinen ersten Kartierungen neben der Ausnahmslosigkeit der Lautgesetze auch belegen wollte, "daß die Mda. [Mundart]-Grenzen in alter und neuer Zeit sich im wesentlichen als die gleichen darstellten". Die sprachgeographischen Untersuchungen haben aber schon sehr früh erkennen lassen, daß die rezenten Dialektgrenzen ihre Ursachen in den politischen Gliederungen des 14.–18. Jhs. haben (vgl. z. B. Haindl 1950: 77–93; Schirmunski 1962: 89). "Daraus ergibt sich aber die wichtige weitere Folgerung, daß die heutigen Sprachlinien wesentlich jünger sind als die den Lautwandel bedingenden Lautgesetze" (Wrede 1919: 10; vgl. auch Frings 1921: 5–9). Auf der Grundlage dieser sprachgeschichtlichen Vorstellungen waren auf den Sprachkarten ohnehin nur Linienbündel zu erwarten gewesen (zu deren Deutung als Durchbrechungen der konsequenten Lautgesetze vgl. Wenker 1895: 40–41) – die strikte Grenzlinie stellt unter diesen Bedingungen die Ausnahme dar und sie erfordert eigentlich eine zusätzliche Begründung (zur Raum-Zeitproblematik der Sprachkarte vgl. Putschke 1983).

Aus dieser gegenseitigen Abhängigkeit folgt, daß eine Beurteilung der sprachkartographischen Ergebnisse als Beweis oder Gegenbeweis an den jeweiligen Kenntnisstand – Ablehnung oder Anerkennung der Stammeshypothese – gebunden ist. Generell ergibt sich aber aus diesen Zusammenhängen die Schlußfolgerung, daß die sprachgeographischen Kartenbilder überhaupt nicht in Verbindung mit den junggrammatischen Prinzipien über die Ausnahmslosigkeit der Lautgesetze zu bringen sind und so weder einen Beweis noch einen Gegenbeweis liefern können.

Diese Irrelevanz der sprachgeographischen Ergebnisse für eine Kritik an der historischen Sprachwissenschaft und insbesondere an dem junggrammatischen Programm hat in der relativ breiten Diskussion um die Position Georg Wenkers und die entstehende Dialektgeographie fast keine Beachtung gefunden, lediglich Leo Jutz formuliert seine Bedenken gegen die damals in der Marburger Schule herrschende Meinung, wenn er die Linienbündel der Sprachkarten "als Grundlage für die Ablehnung der Ausnahmslosigkeit der Lautgesetze nicht als zureichend anerkennen" (Jutz 1932: 477) kann.

Diese herkömmliche Kritik erweist sich also bei einer genaueren Überprüfung als Scheinkritik und somit ist der Schluß zu ziehen, daß die Dialektologie – und auch die Sprachgeographie – an dem junggrammatischen Programm keine stichhaltige Kritik geltend machen konnten.

In letzter Konsequenz aber ist die Neuorientierung der Junggrammatiker selbst für das Ende der historischen Sprachwissenschaft verantwortlich: mit der Erweiterung ihres Objektbereiches in Richtung auf die gegenwärtigen Sprachen und Dialekte ließ sich die alte historische Sichtweise als die einzig mögliche nicht mehr aufrechterhalten und damit reichten auch dann die alten methodischen Instrumente zur Deskription und Explikation nicht mehr aus; hier war bereits der Keim für das Ende der historischen Sprachwissenschaft und der Beginn der strukturellen Sprachwissenschaft gelegt.

6. Bibliographie

Agricola, Erhard, et al. 1969. *Die deutsche Sprache. Kleine Enzyklopädie.* Bd. I. Leipzig: VEB Bibliographisches Institut.

Amirova, T. A., B. A. Ol'chovikov & Ju. V. Roždestvenskij. 1980. *Abriß der Geschichte der Linguistik.* Ins Deutsche übersetzt von Barbara Meier, hg. von Georg Friedrich Meier. Leipzig: Bibliographisches Institut.

Arens, Hans. 1974 [1969]. *Sprachwissenschaft. Der Gang ihrer Entwicklung von der Antike bis zur Gegenwart,* Bd. 1: *Von der Antike bis zum Ausgang des 19. Jahrhunderts,* Bd. 2: *Das 20. Jahrhundert.* Frankfurt/M.: Athenäum Fischer.

Autenrieth, Georg. o. J. [1899]. *Pfälzisches Idiotikon: Ein Versuch.* Kaiserslautern: Crusius.

Bach, Adolf. 1950 [1934]. *Deutsche Mundartforschung. Ihre Wege: Ergebnisse und Aufgaben.* Mit 58 Karten im Text. 2. Aufl. Heidelberg: Winter.

Bahner, Werner & Werner Neumann, Hg. 1985. *Sprachwissenschaftliche Germanistik: Ihre Herausbildung und Begründung.* Berlin: Akademie-Verlag.

Bartschat, Brigitte. 1996. *Methoden der Sprachwissenschaft von Hermann Paul bis Noam Chomsky.* Berlin: Schmidt.

Berner, Gertraud. 1948. *Die Entfaltung der dialektgeographischen Methoden von Wenker bis zur Gegenwart in der deutschen Forschung.* Hausarbeit für die Lehramtsprüfung, Univ. Innsbruck.

Berthold, Luise. 1927. *Alter Text und moderne Mundart.* (= Rheinische Beiträge und Hülfsbücher zur germanischen Philologie und Volkskunde, 13.) Bonn: Klopp.

– et al., Hg. 1934. *Von Wenker zu Wrede: Dem Herausgeber des "Deutschen Sprachatlas" Ferdinand Wrede zum siebzigsten Geburtstage von seinen Marburger Mitstreitern.* 2. Aufl. Marburg: Elwert.

Brekle, Herbert Ernst. 1985. *Einführung in die Geschichte der Sprachwissenschaft.* Darmstadt: Wissenschaftliche Buchgesellschaft.

Bretschneider, Anneliese. 1934. *Deutsche Mundartenkunde.* Marburg: Elwert.

Brugman[n], Karl & Hermann Osthoff. 1878. *Morphologische Untersuchungen auf dem Gebiete der indogermanischen Sprachen.* Bd. I. Leipzig: Hirzel.

Bursian, Conrad. 1883. *Geschichte der classischen Philologie in Deutschland von den Anfängen bis zur Gegenwart.* München & Leipzig: Oldenbourg.

Crecelius, Wilhelm. 1897–99. *Oberhessisches Wörterbuch.* Auf Grund von Vorarbeiten Weigands, Diefenbachs und Hainebachs sowie eigener Materialien. 2 Bde. Darmstadt: Historischer Verein für das Großherzogtum Hessen.

Delbrück, B[erthold]. 1904 [1880]. *Einleitung in das Studium der indogermanischen Sprachen: Ein Beitrag zur Geschichte und Methodik der vergleichenden Sprachforschung.* 4. völlig umgearbeitete Aufl. Leipzig: Breitkopf & Härtel.

Einhauser, Eveline. 1989. *Die Junggrammatiker: Ein Problem für die Sprachwissenschaftsgeschichtsschreibung.* Trier: Wissenschaftlicher Verlag.

–. 1996. "Grammatikschreibung in der Tradition der Historischen Grammatik: Ein Ausblick auf das 20. Jahrhundert". *Sprachtheorie der Neuzeit,* Bd. II: *Von der Grammaire de Port-Royal (1660) zur Konstitution moderner linguistischer Disziplinen* hg. von Peter Schmitter, 216–243. Tübingen: Narr.

Fischer, Hermann. 1895. *Geographie der schwäbischen Mundart. Mit einem Atlas von 28 Karten.* Tübingen: Laupp.

–. 1901–24, 1936. *Schwäbisches Wörterbuch.* Auf Grund der von Adelbert v. Keller begonnenen Sammlungen. 6 Bde. Bd. 6, 2: *Nachträge*, 1936. Tübingen: Laupp.

Friebertshäuser, Hans, Hg. 1976. *Dialektlexikographie: Berichte über Stand und Methoden deutscher Dialektwörterbücher. Festgabe für Luise Berthold zum 85. Geburtstag am 27. 1. 1976.* Wiesbaden: Steiner.

–. 1983. "Die großlandschaftlichen Wörterbücher der deutschen Dialekte: Areale und lexikalische Beschreibung". *Dialektologie: Ein Handbuch zur deutschen und allgemeinen Dialektforschung* hg. von Werner Besch, Ulrich Knoop, Wolfgang Putschke, Herbert Ernst Wiegand. Zweiter Halbbd., 1283–1295. Berlin & New York: de Gruyter.

Frings, Theodor. 1921. "Die deutsche Sprachwissenschaft und die deutsche Mundartenforschung: Ein Wort zum Geleit". *Zeitschrift für deutsche Mundarten* 1921.2–12.

Grimm, Jacob. 1967 [1819, 1822]. *Deutsche Grammatik.* Hg. von Wilhelm Scherer. Hildesheim: Olms.

Haag, Karl. 1929. "Sprachwandel im Lichte der Mundartgrenzen". *Teuthonista* 6.1–35.

Haindl, Angela. 1950. *Ergebnisse der dialektgeographischen Forschung für die deutsche Sprachgeschichte.* Hausarbeit für die Lehramtsprüfung, Univ. Innsbruck.

Heinzerling, Jak[ob]. 1871. *Ueber den Vocalismus und Consonantismus der Siegerländer Mundart: Eine sprachgeschichtliche Untersuchung.* Marburg: Pfeil.

Helbig, Gerhard. 1971. *Geschichte der neueren Sprachwissenschaft. Unter dem besonderen Aspekt der Grammatik-Theorie.* München: Hueber.

Henry, Victor. 1900. *Le dialecte alaman de Colmar (Haute-Alsace) en 1870. Grammaire et lexique* (= Bibiothèque de la faculté des lettres, 11.) Paris: Alcan.

Henzen, Walter. 1954. *Schriftsprache und Mundarten: Ein Überblick über ihr Verhältnis und ihre Zwischenstufen im Deutschen.* 2. neu bearbeitete Aufl. Bern: Francke.

Hertel, L[udwig]. 1895. *Thüringer Sprachschatz. Sammlung mundartlicher Ausdrücke aus Thüringen nebst Einleitung, Sprachkarte und Sprachproben.* Weimar: Böhlaus Nachfolger.

Heusler, Andreas. 1888. *Der alemanische Consonantismus in der Mundart von Baselstadt.* Strassburg: Trübner.

Holthausen, Ferdinand. 1886. *Die Soester Mundart: Laut- und Formenlehre nebst Texten.* Norden & Leipzig: Soltau.

Ivić, Milka. 1971. *Wege der Sprachwissenschaft.* Übersetzt von Matthias Rammelmeyer. München: Hueber.

Jankowsky, Kurt R. 1996. "Development of Historical Linguistics from Rask and Grimm to the Neogrammarians". *Sprachtheorien der Neuzeit.* Bd. II: *Von der Grammaire de Port-Royal (1660) zur Konstitution moderner linguistischer Disziplinen* hg. von Peter Schmitter, 193−215. Tübingen: Narr.

Jellinghaus, Hermann. 1877. *Westfälische Grammatik: Die Laute und Flexionen der Ravensbergischen Mundart mit einem Wörterbuche.* Bremen: Kühtmann.

Jutz, Leo. 1932. "Grundzüge der deutschen Mundartforschung". *Zeitschrift für Deutschkunde* 46. 465−488.

Kauffmann, Friedrich. 1890. *Geschichte der schwäbischen Mundart im Mittelalter und in der Neuzeit. Mit Textproben und einer Geschichte der Schriftsprache in Schwaben.* Strassburg: Trübner.

Kehrein, Joseph. 1872 [1860−62]. *Volkssprache und Volkssitte in Nassau [im Herzogthum Nassau]. Ein Beitrag zu deren Kenntniß.* Neue Ausgabe, Bd. I. Bonn: Habicht.

Knoop, Ulrich, Wolfgang Putschke & Herbert Ernst Wiegand. 1982. "Die Marburger Schule: Entstehung und frühe Entwicklung der Dialektgeographie". *Dialektologie: Ein Handbuch zur deutschen und allgemeinen Dialektforschung.* hg. von Werner Besch, Ulrich Knoop, Wolfgang Putschke & Herbert Ernst Wiegand. Erster Halbbd., 38−92. Berlin & New York: de Gruyter.

Koerner, E. F. K[onrad]. 1978a. *Toward a Historiography of Linguistics: Selected essays.* Amsterdam: Benjamins.

−. 1978b. *Western Histories of Linguistic Thought: An annoteted chronological bibliography. 1822−1976.* Amsterdam: Benjamins.

−. 1981. "Schleichers Einfluß auf Haeckel: Schlaglichter auf die wechselseitige Abhängigkeit zwischen linguistischen und biologischen Theorien im 19. Jahrhundert". *Zeitschrift für Vergleichende Sprachforschung* 95.1−21.

−. 1995a. "Historiography of Linguistics". *Concise History of the Language Science from the Sumerians to the Cognitivists* hg. von E. F. K. Koerner & R. E. Asher, 7−16 Oxford & New York: Pergamon.

−. 1995b. *Professing Linguistic Historiography.* Amsterdam & Philadelphia: Benjamins.

Lehmann, Winfred F. 1969. *Einführung in die historische Linguistik.* Autorisierte, vom Verfasser durchgesehene Übersetzung von Rudolf Freudenberg. Heidelberg: Winter.

Lessiak, Primus. 1963 [1903]. *Die Mundart von Pernegg in Kärnten.* Marburg: Elwert.

Lexer, Matthias. 1862. *Kärntisches Wörterbuch. Mit einem Anhange: Weihnacht-Spiele und Lieder aus Kärnten.* Leipzig: Hirzel.

Markey, Thomas L. 1977. *Prinzipien der Dialektologie: Einführung in die deutsche Dialektforschung. Mit einer ausführlichen Bibliographie.* (= Giessener Beiträge zur Sprachwissenschaft, 8.) Grossen-Linden: Hoffmann.

Martin, Bernhard. 1959 [1939]. *Die deutschen Mundarten mit 21 Karten im Text.* 2., neubearbeitete Aufl. Marburg: Elwert.

Martin, E[rnst] & H[ans] Lienhart. 1899−1907. *Wörterbuch der elsässischen Mundarten.* Bd. 1−2. Strassburg: Trübner.

Mensing, Otto. 1927−35. *Schleswig-Holsteinisches Wörterbuch.* (Volksausgabe) Bd. 1−5. Neumünster: Wachholtz.

Merkel, Carl Ludw[ig]. 1866. *Physiologie der menschlichen Sprache (physiologische Laletik.)* Leipzig: Wigand.

Mitzka, Walther. 1943. *Deutsche Mundarten. Mit 11 Karten.* (= Studienführer, Gruppe I: Kulturwissenschaft, 24.) Heidelberg: Winter.

−. 1952. *Handbuch zum Deutschen Sprachatlas.* Marburg: Elwert.

Müllenhoff, Karl. 1854. *Quickborn: Volksleben in plattdeutschen Gedichten ditmarscher Mundart von Klaus Groth.* Mit einem Glossar nebst Einleitung von Karl Müllenhoff. 6. sehr vermehrte und verbesserte Aufl., 259−277. Hamburg: Perthes=Besser & Mauke.

Münch, Ferdinand. 1904. *Grammatik der ripuarisch-fränkischen Mundart.* Bonn: Cohen.

Nerger, Karl. 1869. *Grammatik des meklenburgischen Dialektes älterer und neuerer Zeit: Laut- und Flexionslehre.* Leipzig: Brockhaus.

Niebaum, Hermann. 1979. "Deutsche Dialektwörterbücher". *Deutsche Sprache* 7.345−373.

Osthoff, Hermann. 1883. *Schriftsprache und Volksmundart.* Berlin: Habel.

− & Karl Brugman[n]. 1878. *Morphologische Untersuchungen auf dem Gebiete der indogermanischen Sprachen.* Erster Theil. Leipzig: Hirzel.

Paul, Hermann. 1886 [1880]. *Principien der Sprachgeschichte.* 2. erweiterte Aufl. Halle: Niemeyer.

Putschke, Wolfgang. 1974. "Dialektologie". *Grundzüge der Literatur- und Sprachwissenschaft,* Bd. 2: *Sprachwissenschaft* hg. von Heinz Ludwig Arnold & Volker Sinemus in Zusammenarbeit mit Rolf Dietrich & Siegfried Kanngießer, 328−369. München: dtv.

−. 1983. "Sprachgeographie: Irrtum oder Forschungsinstrument?". *Aspekte der Dialekttheorie* hg. von Klaus J. Mattheier, 83−102. Tübingen: Niemeyer.

−. 1998 [1984]. "Die Arbeiten der Junggrammatiker und ihr Beitrag zur Sprachgeschichtsforschung". *Sprachgeschichte: Ein Handbuch zur Ge-*

schichte der deutschen Sprache und ihrer Erforschung hg. von Werner Besch et al. 1.331–347. 2. Aufl. 1998, 474–494. Berlin & New York: de Gruyter.

Raumer, Rudolf von. 1870. *Geschichte der Germanischen Philologie vorzugsweise in Deutschland.* München: Oldenbourg.

Regel, Karl. 1868. *Die Ruhlaer Mundart.* Weimar: Boehlau.

Robins, R[obert] H[enry]. 1973. *Ideen- und Problemgeschichte der Sprachwissenschaft. Mit besonderer Berücksichtigung des 19. und 20. Jahrhunderts.* Autorisierte, mit einem Nachwort versehene Übersetzung aus dem Englischen von Christoph Gutknecht & Klaus-Uwe Panther. Frankfurt/M.: Athenäum.

Schade, Oskar. 1872–82 [1866]. *Altdeutsches Wörterbuch.* 2. umgearbeitete und vermehrte Aufl. Halle: Verlag der Buchhandlung des Waisenhauses. (Altdeutsches Lesebuch. Gothisch, altsächsisch, alt- und mittelhochdeutsch. Mit literarischen Nachweisen und einem Wörterbuch. 2. Theil: Altdeutsches Wörterbuch.)

Schatz, Joseph. 1897. *Mundart von Imst: Laut- und Flexionslehre.* Strassburg: Trübner.

–. 1903. *Die tirolische Mundart.* Innsbruck: Wagner.

Scherer, Wilhelm. 1868. *Zur Geschichte der deutschen Sprache.* Berlin: Duncker. (Neuausgabe, mit einer Einleitung von Kurt R. Jankowsky, Amsterdam & Philadelphia: Benjamins, 1995.)

Schirmunski, V[iktor] M. 1962. *Deutsche Mundartkunde: Vergleichende Laut- und Formenlehre der deutschen Mundarten.* Berlin: Akademie-Verlag.

Schleicher, August 1858. *Volkstümliches aus Sonneberg im Meininger Oberlande.* Weimar: Böhlau.

–. 1861–62. *Compendium der vergleichenden Grammatik der indogermanischen Sprachen,* Bd. I: *Kurzer Abriss einer Lautlehre [...],* Bd. II: *Kurzer Abriss einer Formenlehre [...]* Weimar: Böhlau.

Schmeller, J[ohann] Andreas. 1821. *Die Mundarten Bayerns grammatisch dargestellt.* München: Thienemann. (Neudruck, München: Hueber, 1929.)

–. 1827. *Ueber das Studium der altdeutschen Sprache und ihrer Denkmäler.* München: Leutner.

–. 1827–37. *Bayerisches Wörterbuch. Sammlung von Wörtern und Ausdrücken, die in den lebendigen Mundarten sowohl, als in der ältern und ältesten Provincial-Litteratur des Königreichs Bayern, besonders seiner ältern Lande, vorkommen, und in der heutigen allgemein-deutschen Schriftsprache entweder gar nicht, oder nicht in denselben Bedeutungen üblich sind, mit urkundlichen Belegen, nach Stammsylben etymologisch-alphabetisch geordnet.* Vier Theile. Stuttgart & Tübingen: Cotta.

Schmid, Johann Christoph von. 1844 [1831]. *Schwäbisches Wörterbuch mit etymologischen und historischen Anmerkungen.* 2. Ausg. Stuttgart: Schweizerbart.

Scholz, Adolf. 1933. *Deutsche Mundarten-Wörterbücher: Versuch einer Darstellung ihres systematisch-historischen Werdeganges von Anbeginn bis zum Ende des Achtzehnten Jahrhunderts.* Leipzig: Eichblatt.

Schröer, K[arl] J[ulius]. 1868. "Ein Ausflug nach Gottschee: Beitrag zur Erforschung der Gottscheewer Mundart". *Sitzungsberichte der Philosophisch-Historischen Classe der kaiserlichen Akademie der Wissenschaften,* Bd. 60.165–288. Wien, 1869.

–. 1870. "Weitere Mittheilungen über die Mundart von Gottschee". *Sitzungsberichte der Philosophisch-Historischen Classe der kaiserlichen Akademie der Wissenschaften,* Bd. 65.391–510. Wien.

Schwarz, Ernst. 1950. *Die deutschen Mundarten. Mit 20 Abbildungen und 2 Karten.* Göttingen: Vandenhoeck & Ruprecht.

Siebs, Theodor. 1902. *Die Entwicklung der germanistischen Wissenschaft im letzten Viertel des neunzehnten Jahrhunderts. Einleitung zur Festschrift der Gesellschaft für deutsche Philologie.* Leipzig: Reisland.

Sievers, Eduard. 1893 [1876]. *Grundzüge der Phonetik [Lautphysiologie] zur Einführung in das Studium der Lautlehre der indogermanischen Sprachen.* 4. verbesserte Aufl. Leipzig: Breitkopf & Härtel.

Stalder, Franz Joseph. 1806–12. *Versuch eines Schweizerischen Idiotikons mit etymologischen Bemerkungen untermischt. Samt einer Skizze einer Schweizerischen Dialektologie.* Aarau: Sauerländer.

–. 1819. *Die Landessprachen der Schweiz oder Schweizerische Dialektologie mit kritischen Sprachbemerkungen beleuchtet. Nebst der Gleichnißrede von dem verlorenen Sohne in allen Schweizermundarten.* Aarau: Sauerländer.

Streitberg, Wilhelm & Victor Michels. 1927. *Germanisch.* (= *Grundriß der indogermanischen Sprach- und Altertumskunde* hg. von Albert Debrunner & Ferdinand Sommer, Bd. 2.) Berlin & Leipzig: de Gruyter.

Stroh, Friedrich. 1952. *Handbuch der Germanischen Philologie.* Berlin: de Gruyter.

Stürenburg, Cirk Heinrich. 1862 [1857]. *Ostfriesisches Wörterbuch.* Aurich: Spielmeyer.

Thomsen, Vilhelm. 1927 [1902]. *Geschichte der Sprachwissenschaft bis zum Ausgang des 19. Jahrhunderts: Kurzgefasste Darstellung der Hauptpunkte.* Übersetzt von Hans Pollak. Halle: Niemeyer.

Trubetzkoj, N[ikolaj] S[ergeevič]. 1962 [1939]. *Grundzüge der Phonologie.* (= *Travaux du Cercle Linguistique de Prague,* 7.) 3., durchgesehene Aufl. Göttingen: Vandenhoeck & Ruprecht.

Unwerth, Wolf von. 1908. *Die Schlesische Mundart in ihren Lautverhältnissen grammatisch und geographisch dargestellt.* (= *Wort und Brauch. Volkskundliche Arbeiten,* 3). Breslau: Marcus.

Veith, Werner H. 1970. "[-explikative, +applikative, +komputative] Dialektkartographie. Ihre wissenschaftlichen Voraussetzungen und Möglichkeiten in der Phonologie auf der Grundlage der kontrastiv-transformationellen Methode und der automatischen Datenverarbeitung". *Germanistische Linguistik* 4.385–497.

Vilmar, A[ugust] F[riedrich] C[hristian]. 1868. *Idiotikon von Hessen.* Marburg & Leipzig: Elwert.

Wagner, Peter. 1988. *Untersuchungen zur Methodologie und Methodik der Dialektologie.* Marburg: Elwert.

Wagner, Philipp. 1889–91. *Der gegenwärtige Lautbestand des Schwäbischen in der Mundart von Reutlingen.* Fest-Schrift der K. Realanstalt zu Reutlingen zur Feier der 25jährigen Regierungszeit Sr. Majestät des Königs. Erste Hälfte 1889, Teil 2. Beilage zum Programm der Königlichen Real-Anstalt zu Reutlingen, 1891. Leipzig: Fock.

Wegener, Philipp. 1880. "Über deutsche Dialectforschung". *Zeitschrift für deutsche Philologie* 11.450–480.

Weinhold, Karl. 1853. *Ueber deutsche Dialectforschung: Die Laut- und Wortbildung und die Formen der schlesischen Mundart. Mit Rücksicht auf Verwantes in deutschen Dialecten. Ein Versuch.* Wien: Gerold & Sohn.

Wenker, Georg. 1876. *Über die Verschiebung des Stammsilben-Auslauts im Germanischen. Tabellen und Untersuchungen.* Bonn: Marcus.

–. 1877. *Das rheinische Platt: Den Lehrern des Rheinlandes gewidmet.* Düsseldorf: Selbstverlag.

–. 1886 [1885]. [Vortrag über das Sprachatlasunternehmen, mit Vorzeigung von Karten.] *Verhandlungen der 38. Versammlung deutscher Philologen und Schulmänner in Gießen vom 30. September bis 3. Oktober 1885*, 187–193. Leipzig.

–. 1895. "Über den Sprachatlas des Deutschen Reiches". *Verhandlungen der 43. Versammlung deutscher Philologen und Schulmänner in Köln [am 27. September] 1895*, 34–43. Leipzig.

Werlen, Iwar. 1996. "Dialektologie und Sprachgeographie vom 13. bis 20. Jahrhundert". *Sprachtheorien der Neuzeit*, Bd. II: *Von der Grammaire de Port-Royal (1660) zur Konstitution moderner linguistischer Disziplinen* hg. von Peter Schmitter, 427–458. Tübingen: Narr.

Wiegand, Herbert Ernst & Gisela Harras. 1971. "Zur wissenschaftshistorischen Einordnung und linguistischen Beurteilung des Deutschen Wortatlas". *Germanistische Linguistik* 1–2.

Winteler, Jost. 1876 [1875]. *Die Kerenzer Mundart des Kantons Glarus in ihren Grundzügen dargestellt.* Leipzig & Heidelberg: Winter.

Wrede, Ferd[inand]. 1908. "An Georg Wenker". *Deutsche Dialektgeographie: Berichte und Studien über G. Wenkers Sprachatlas des Deutschen Reichs* hg. von Ferdinand Wrede, vii–xiii. Marburg: Elwert.

–. 1919. "Zur Entwicklungsgeschichte der deutschen Mundartenforschung". *Zeitschrift für deutsche Mundarten* 1919.3–18.

–. 1963 [1903]. "Der Sprachatlas des Deutschen Reichs und die elsässische Dialektforschung". *Ferdinand Wrede. Kleine Schriften.* (= *Archiv für das Studium der neueren Sprachen und Literaturen* 111 [1903], 29–48), hg. von Luise Berthold, Bernhard Martin & Walther Mitzka, 309–324. Marburg: Elwert.

Wolfgang Putschke, Marburg (Deutschland)

182. Die Dialektologie des Deutschen

1. Einleitendes
2. Die Vorgeschichte der Dialektologie des Deutschen
3. Die Grundlegung der Dialektologie des Deutschen
4. Gegenstandskonstitution im neunzehnten Jahrhundert: Der pluridimensionale Dialekt
5. Die klassisch-monodimensionale Dialektologie
6. Ansätze zu einer pluridimensionalen Dialektologie im zwanzigsten Jahrhundert
7. Bibliographie

1. Einleitendes

Die notwendige historische Bedingung für die Herausbildung der Dialektologie als wissenschaftliche Disziplin war die Existenz eines Bewußtseins von der Heterogenität des Objektbereichs 'Sprache'. Die tatsächliche Grundlegung der Dialektologie bestand dann in der Fokussierung einer bestimmten, nämlich der arealen Variationsdimension als wissenschaftlicher Gegenstand. Diese Fokussierung der arealen Dimension des heterogenen Objektbereiches 'Sprache' hat sich von Anfang an als problematisch erwiesen: Erstens war es schon zu Beginn schwierig und konnte erst in einem langwierigen theoretischen Ausdifferenzierungsprozeß gelingen, bestimmte, als 'dialektal' anzusprechende sprachliche Varianten von anderen – etwa von soziolektalen oder situativen – abzuheben. In diesem Bemühen wurde in der Forschungsgeschichte der deutschen Dialektologie besonders des 19. Jhs. der

Dialektbegriff immer enger gefaßt, so daß zuletzt 'Dialekt' praktisch identifiziert wurde mit den areal differenten, jeweils homogen gedachten, von der ältesten Generation der Landbevölkerung gesprochenen Varietäten. Man darf in dieser immer rigideren Fokussierung eines immer schmaleren Sektors des Objektbereiches eine beachtliche, theoretisch motivierte Dynamik des wissenschaftlichen Gegenstandes 'Dialekt' sehen. Zweitens unterlag jedoch von Anfang an auch der Objektbereich der Dialektologie selbst einer beachtlichen Dynamik. Zunächst die industrielle Revolution und später die Etablierung der Massenmedien hatten im 19. und 20. Jh. für die arealen Varietäten funktionale und systemische Auswirkungen, die schon früh plakativ als 'Auflösung der Dialekte' bezeichnet worden sind.

Beide Aspekte, die Dynamik der Theoriebildung und die Dynamik des Objektbereiches, sind verantwortlich für eine gewisse Gegenstandsungewißheit, die von den Anfängen bis auf den heutigen Tag für die Dialektologie kennzeichnend ist und die einen Gutteil der Krise der Dialektologie ausmacht, von der gesprochen worden ist. Es ist vor diesem Hintergrund jedoch keineswegs angemessen, die Dialektologie allgemein als wissenschaftliche Disziplin mit einem sich verflüchtigenden Gegenstand zu sehen. Angemessener erscheint es, die Dialektologie als eine wissenschaftliche Disziplin zu betrachten, die theoriegeschichtlich durch den Versuch gekennzeichnet war, schrittweise einen immer schärfer abgegrenzten Sektor des heterogenen Objektbereiches 'Sprache' als ihren Gegenstand zu fokussieren, nämlich die als homogen gedachten Basisdialekte. Aufgrund dieser im Ergebnis verengten Konzeption des wissenschaftlichen Gegenstandes der Dialektologie und aufgrund der – in Gestalt eines System- und Funktionswandels der Basisdialekte – gleichzeitig zu konstatierenden hohen historischen Dynamik des Objektbereiches mußte der Eindruck entstehen, Objektbereich und Gegenstand der Disziplin verflüchtigten sich gleichermaßen. Rezente Entwicklungen der dialektologischen Theoriebildung versuchen hier Abhilfe zu schaffen: Indem der Gegenstand der Dialektologie wieder weiter gefaßt wird, wird Raum geschaffen für eine adäquate wissenschaftliche Beschreibung der arealen und anderer Variationsdimensionen des dynamisch sich verändernden Objektbereichs 'Sprache'.

Um die sehr unterschiedlichen Begriffsbildungen in den Blick nehmen zu können, die die Dialektologie im 19. und 20. Jh. kennzeichnen, ist es notwendig, im folgenden zunächst einen weiten Dialektbegriff zugrunde zu legen. Unter 'Dialekt' wird daher eine muttersprachlich erworbene Varietät eines Gesamtsprachsystems verstanden, die sich durch einen Teil ihrer sprachlichen Elemente einerseits horizontal abhebt von Nachbarvarietäten anderer arealer Erstreckung, die sich andererseits vertikal abhebt von überdachenden Varietäten des Gesamtsprachsystems, namentlich von der Standardsprache. Dialektologie ist dementsprechend diejenige sprachwissenschaftliche Teildisziplin, die die Struktur und Funktion der so verstandenen Dialekte zum Gegenstand hat.

Obwohl die Geschichte der Dialektologie des Deutschen nicht in allen Teilen als gut erforscht gelten darf, sind verschiedene Darstellungen erschienen, die einen zuverlässigen Überblick besonders über die klassische Dialektologie des Deutschen ermöglichen. Auf diese Darstellungen kann im folgenden verwiesen werden (vgl. z. B. Schirmunski 1962: 56−151; Goossens 1977: 109−143; Knoop 1982; Knoop et al. 1982; Niebaum & Macha 1999: 48−75).

2. Die Vorgeschichte der Dialektologie des Deutschen

Ein allgemeines Bewußtsein der arealen Differenziertheit der Sprache existiert − nicht nur für das Deutsche − von alters her, wie schon das alttestamentarische (Richter 12,6) Stigmawort *sibboleth* (für *schibboleth*) belegt. In der deutschen Literatur des Mittelalters finden sich zahlreiche Beispiele für ein Bewußtsein der arealen Differenziertheit der Sprache: "Swâbe ir wörter spaltent / Die Franken ein teil si valtent / [...]" (Hugo von Trimberg [c. 1230−1310], "Der Renner", 1290−1300). Mit diesem Bewußtsein arealer Differenziertheit scheint jedoch weder eine sprachliche noch eine soziale Bewertung verbunden gewesen zu sein. Eine Abwertung des Dialektalen fand nicht statt, im Gegenteil, literarische Belege lassen sich mitunter als Plädoyer für Dialektloyalität lesen: "Ich bin ein Durenc von art geborn. / Hêt ich die sprâche nû verkorn / und hête mîne zungen / an ander wort getwungen, / war zuo wêre mir daz guot? / Ich wêne, er effenlîche tuot, / der sich der sprâche zucket an, / der er nicht gefuogen kan" (Ebernand von Erfurt [Anfang 13. Jh.], "Heinrich und Kunigunde", v. 4467 ff.). Der Grund für diese Toleranz gegenüber sprachlicher Arealität ist in der Tatsache zu suchen, daß die mittelalterlichen Tendenzen zu überregionalem sprachlichem Ausgleich sich zunächst nur in der Literalität vollzogen. Die Oralisierung dieser überregionalen Ausgleichssprache erfolgte mittels der arealsprachlichen phonetisch-phonologischen Systeme, die insofern zur überregional-literalen Norm nicht in Konkurrenz traten.

Diese Situation änderte sich mit der beginnenden Neuzeit. Mit der schrittweisen Etablierung einer überregionalen Ausgleichsvarietät (neuhochdeutsche Standardsprache), besonders aber durch die Herausbildung einer eigenen Oralisierungsnorm dieser Varietät, erhielten die Dialekte erst den Gegenpol, der sie als systemisch different und areal begrenzt ins Bewußtsein treten ließ. "Von Volksmundarten kann nur da die Rede sein, wo eine Gemeinsprache sich gebildet hat" (Raumer 1870: 242; vgl. Knoop 1982: 5). Dem entspricht, daß einige der ersten Veröffentlichungen, die Dialekte in ihrer Arealität zum Gegenstand haben, im 18. Jh. im niederdeutschen Norden Deutschlands erschienen (vgl. Richey 1754, Dähnert 1781). Hier waren nicht nur die systemischen Differenzen zwischen − niederdeutschem − Dialekt und überregionaler − mitteldeutsch-oberdeutscher − Ausgleichsvarietät besonders augenfällig, sondern hier entwickelte sich auch zuerst eine Oralisierungskonvention für die auf literalem Wege übernommene, hochdeutsch fundierte überregionale Ausgleichsvarietät.

Parallel zu der Etablierung einer überregionalen Ausgleichsvarietät vollzog sich − nicht allein − im Deutschen eine Abwertung des Dialektalen. Der nun mögliche Vergleich der Dialekte mit der im Entstehen begriffenen neuhochdeutschen Standardsprache, gekennzeichnet durch überregionale Geltung, prestigebesetzte Verwendungsdomänen, sozial elitäre Trägerschicht und nun sowohl oraler als auch literaler Realisierung, ließ die Dialekte als sozial, areal und medial restringiert erscheinen (vgl. Alinei 1980). Aus der Identifikation von Dialektverwendung und Illiteralität, auch aus der sozialen Abwertung der Bauernschaft ergab sich ein erster Ansatzpunkt der negativen Bewertung der Dialekte. Ein zweiter Ansatzpunkt der Abwertung der Dialekte ist in Deutschland bis ins 18. Jh. hinein in dem Versuch zu sehen, die begonnene Standardisierung des Neuhochdeutschen zum Abschluß zu bringen, und zwar durch Eliminierung von − nicht nur, aber in erster Linie − arealsprachlichen Varianten. Standardisierung wurde nicht zuletzt als Ausmerzung des eng Regionalen begriffen (vgl. Henzen 1954; Knoop 1980−82). Die "Mundart" erschien nun als "die unedle, nachlässige und unbearbeitete Sprache des gemeinen Volkes" (ADB 1765; vgl. Knoop 1982: 4), die einer geradezu moralischen Abwertung unterlag und Gegenstand des Sprachspottes wurde. Nach Walter Henzen (1954: 124) ist spätestens mit diesen Abwertungstendenzen des Dialektgebrauchs der Prozeß der Etablierung der neuhochdeutschen Standardsprache irreversibel geworden und ein Prozeß des Dialektabbaus eingeleitet. Der Standardisierungsprozeß des Neuhochdeutschen war also nicht nur die historische Bedingung der Wahrnehmung des Dialektes als arealer Varietät des Deutschen, sondern er war zugleich Auslöser für die Verlagerung des Domänenspektrums des Dialektes. Die oben angesprochene Dynamik des Objektbereiches der Dialektologie war schon in dem Moment eingeleitet oder fortgeschritten, in dem dieser Objektbereich überhaupt als denkbarer wissenschaftlicher Gegenstand ins Bewußtsein trat.

3. Die Grundlegung der Dialektologie des Deutschen

Der im 18. Jh. als Folge der Bemühungen um Standardisierung des Neuhochdeutschen zu konstatierende Versuch der Ausmerzung des Dialektes war zugleich Ausgangspunkt für Gegenbewegungen, die für die spätere Dialektologie des Deutschen grundlegend werden sollten. Zum einen gaben eine Reihe von Autoren ihrer Befürchtung Ausdruck, die Bemühungen um Zurückdrängung der Dialekte könnten erfolgreich sein und damit die Dialekte gänzlich abgebaut werden. Zu dieser Vermutung gelangten Autoren nicht zuletzt durch von ihnen beobachtete Veränderungen der Varietätenpräferenz, die − oft voreilig − in die Zukunft extrapoliert wurden und als Indiz für Dialektabbau gewertet wurden. Der Hamburger Michael Richey (1678−1761) machte 1754 den Anfang, wenn er sein Hamburger Idiotikon im Vorwort (S. xliii−xliv) wie folgt legitimiert:

"Es dürfte überdem hohe Zeit seyn, dergleichen zu bewerckstelligen, wofern man noch der Nachwelt, von der jetztlebenden [...] Sprache einen Begriff zu machen gedencket. Unsere Mund-Art geräth ja von Tage zu Tage in Abnahme, indem das Hoch-Teutsche schon längst nicht allein in öffentlichen Handlungen und Schriften, sondern auch im gemeinen Umgange Besitz genommen, daß auch der Bauer selbst mit einem halb-Hoch-Teutschen Worte sich schon vornehmer düncket; folglich zu vermuthen ist, daß die wahre und eigentliche Landes-Sprache, in welcher niemand mehr öffentlich redet oder schreibet, mit der Zeit sich nicht allein vermischen und verstellen, sondern allmählig gar verlieren werde."

War hier bei Richey − wie bei zahlreichen seiner Nachfolger − offensichtlich ein 'antiquarisches' Interesse (vgl. Löffler 1980) motivierend, das wenigstens wissenschaftlich dokumentiert sehen wollte, was dem Untergang geweiht schien, so sind bei anderen Sammlern und Dokumentaren der dialektalen Lexik auch andere Motive auszumachen, beispielsweise das Bestreben, durch Nutzung der Dialektlexik die Lexik der Standardsprache um indigenes Lexemmaterial zu bereichern (vgl. Haas 1994b: 349−353). Es entstanden in der Nachfolge Richeys eine Fülle landschaftlicher Wortschatzsammlungen, so daß sich die erste Traditionslinie einer deutschen Dialektologie primär als Idiotikographie darstellt. Diese frühen Wortschatzsammlungen bieten hinsichtlich Umfang, arealer Erstreckung und methodologischer Reflexion ein sehr heterogenes Bild, das von vollständigen Wörterbüchern bis zu − mitunter unveröffentlichten − Idiomatismenlisten reicht (vgl. Haas 1994a, b).

Eine zweite, dann besonders theoriegeschichtlich bedeutende Traditionslinie der frühen Dialektologie geht auf die Sprachwissenschaft der Romantik zurück. Schon zuvor hatte Herder sich gegen die monistischen Tendenzen der normativen Sprachwissenschaft seiner Zeit gewendet und den Blick auf die Heterogenität der natürlichen Sprache gelenkt: "In einer natürlichen Sprache müssen uneigentliche Wörter, Synonymen, Inversionen, Idiotismen sein" (Herder 1965 [1772]: 34; vgl. Knoop 1982: 5). Diese Orientierung auf die Natürlichkeit der gesprochenen Sprache verband sich mit einem neuen historischen Interesse, wie es dann für die Sprachwissenschaft des 19. Jhs. grundlegend werden sollte. Die Dialekte erschienen als natürliche, historisch gewachsene Ausdrucksmittel, die besonders auch deshalb wissenschaftlich interessant erschienen, weil hier Bestände greifbar zu werden schienen, die in der Standardsprache verlorengegangen oder bewußt eliminiert worden waren. Entscheidend ist die Entstehung der Dialektologie als wissenschaftliche Disziplin dann aber von der Wende zur historischen Sprachwissenschaft geprägt, die von der Sprachwissenschaft der Romantik ausgeht. Bedeutend als Anreger dialektologischer Forschung ist hier besonders Jacob Grimm geworden. Obwohl Grimm selbst nicht als Dialektologe in Erscheinung getreten ist, förderte er die dialektologische Forschung zum einen persönlich und wurde zum anderen auf dem Wege der Rezeption seines sprach- und kulturhistorischen Werks maßstabsetzend für die Dialektologie. In historisch-vergleichender Intention richtete die Sprachwissenschaft der Romantik ihren Blick auf das Gesamtspektrum der empirisch erhebbaren Quellen. Die Lebendigkeit und Differenziertheit des 'Volksgeistes' in seiner Heterogenität wurde so zum Objekt der wissenschaftlichen Beschreibung:

"Für Jacob Grimm heißt das Gesetz des Lebens in der Sprache wie in der Natur unendliche Differenzierung, und die Differenziertheit der Sprache in die Vielzahl einzelner Mundarten galt ihm als Beweis für den Naturcharakter der Sprache; die 'Abweichungen und Unregelmäßigkeiten' sind Produkte des in der Sprache wirkenden 'Naturgesetzes' und Qualitäten der lebendigen Individualität der Sprache." (Jendreieck 1975: 262)

Mit einer historischen Sprachauffassung löste Grimm den zuvor so gesehenen Gegensatz zwischen den arealen Varietäten und der Standardvarietät "dahin auf, daß es nur *eine* Sprache gibt, die − vielfältig wie das Leben − nicht nach Regeln, sondern nach ihrem lebendigen Brauch beobachtet werden soll. Folgerichtig ist sein ganzer Sinn historisch, auf Erforschung des Gegebenen gerichtet" (Knoop 1982: 13). Die entstehende Dialektologie im 19. Jh. ist dieser zugleich empirisch und historisch orientierten Wissenschaftsauffassung zunächst vollständig verpflichtet. Die Dialektologie ist also am Anfang − und für beachtliche Zeit − in ihrer Methodologie Empirie und in ihrem Forschungsziel Sprachgeschichte. Jacob Grimm hebt in verschiedenen Äußerungen besonders die Forschungen zweier Dialektologen positiv hervor: Es handelt sich zum einen um den Schweizer Franz Josef Stalder (1768−1843; vgl. Stalder 1806, 1812), bei dem Ansätze vorliegen, die frühere bloße Idiotikographie zu einer vergleichenden Laut- und Formenlehre auszubauen. Der andere Dialektologe ist Johann Andreas Schmeller (1785–1852; vgl. Schmeller 1821, 1827–37), dessen Werk für die Dialektologie als Wissenschaft fundamentalen Charakter hat.

4. Gegenstandskonstitution im neunzehnten Jahrhundert: Der pluridimensionale Dialekt

Schmeller hatte die frühen dialektologischen Ansätze – insbesondere die Idiotikographie – zur Kenntnis genomnen, gelangte aber auf dieser Grundlage in mehrfacher Hinsicht zu grundlegenden Neuansätzen, die ihn auch aus heutiger Sicht in der Geschichte der Disziplin hervorheben. In Schmellers Werk finden sich die Hauptforschungsrichtungen der Dialektologie: Dialektgeographie, Dialektgrammatik und Dialektlexikographie, anhand des – noch unscharf abgegrenzten – Bairischen exemplarisch behandelt. Der Forschungstopos, Schmeller sei der Begründer der modernen Dialektologie, ist insofern durchaus berechtigt. Schmellers Ausnahmestellung dokumentiert sich zum einen in seinem 'Bayerischen Wörterbuch' (vgl. Schmeller 1827–37, 1872–77), das zwar anfangs, in der Planungsphase, noch in die idiotographische Tradition gestellt war (1816: "Gedanken über ein zu bearbeitendes bairisches Idiotikon"), das dann aber von Schmeller zurecht in 'Wörterbuch' umbenannt wird, da es die dialektale Lexik in neuer Systematik darstellt und sprachhistorisch einordnet. Schmellers Wörterbuch wurde somit zu einem Ausgangspunkt einer neuen, wissenschaftlichen Dialektlexikographie. Schon in der Planungsphase des Wörterbuches hatte Schmeller aber erkannt, daß eine Dialektlexikographie der Ergänzung durch eine Laut- und Formenlehre bedurfte. Die Ausweitung einer solchen Laut- und Formenlehre zu einer Dialektgrammatik war entscheidend durch Jacob Grimms *Deutsche Grammatik* beeinflußt, die Schmeller 1819 rezipierte: "Grimms historisch begründete Deutsche Grammatik, die manches meiner Hirngespinste auseinanderbläst – beschäftigt mich sehr" (Tagebuch vom 16. 7. 1819; vgl. Ruf 1954: 408). Auf der Grundlage der Beschäftigung mit Grimms vergleichender historischer Grammatik der germanischen Sprachen gelangte Schmeller zu einer zukunftsweisenden Neukonzeption der Dialektologie. Sein Werk "Die Mundarten Bayerns grammatisch dargestellt [...]" von 1821 begreift die Dialekte dann als eigenständige, anderen sprachlichen Ausprägungen prinzipiell gleichberechtigte Resultate sprachhistorischer Entwicklungen, die auch eigener wissenschaftlicher Beschreibung würdig sind. Diese Beschreibung ist bei Schmeller zugleich historisch, geographisch, grammatisch und in Ansätzen soziolinguistisch angelegt (vgl. Knoop 1982: 14–15): Erstens wird Dialekt als sprachhistorisches Phänomen begriffen und beschrieben. Zweitens wird Dialekt als areallinguistische Einheit gefaßt und beschrieben: Schmellers *'Mundarten Bayerns'* ist erstmals eine Sprachkarte beigegeben, so daß von hier auch die Sprachgeographie als dialektologische Methode ihren Ausgang nimmt. Drittens beschreibt Schmeller die Grammatik der bairischen Dialekte, wobei eine synchronisch-deskriptive Perspektive vorherrscht. Viertens gelangt Schmeller auch schon zu einer ansatzweise soziolinguistischen Charakterisierung dialektaler Sprechweisen, indem er sprachliche Varianten als charakteristisch für bestimmte soziale Kategorien markiert. Es wird unterschieden eine "gemeine ländliche Aussprache" von der Aussprache "der Bürgerclasse in (Märkten und) Städten" und der "Aussprache der Gebildetern" (Schmeller 1821: 21).

Mit dem Blick zugleich auf die Historizität, Arealität, Systematizität und soziale Differenziertheit des Dialektes gelangte Schmeller schon in der Phase der Fundierung der Dialektologie als wissenschaftliche Disziplin zu einem Begriff der Pluridimensionalität des Dialektes. Auf der Grundlage des in der Sprachwissenschaft der Romantik herausgearbeiteten Bewußtseins für die Vielgestaltigkeit, für die natürliche Heterogenität der Sprache konstituiert Schmeller den wissenschaftlichen Gegenstand Dialekt variationslinguistisch, das heißt mehrdimensional. Dies geschieht explizit im Hinblick auf die diatopische und die diastratische Variationsdimension. (Die diachronische Variationsdimension ist bei Schmeller aufgrund seiner sprachhistorischen Ausrichtung gleichermaßen präsent.) Günter Bellmann hat darauf hingewiesen, daß dieses bei Schmeller vorhandene Konzept des pluridimensionalen, zumindest zweidimensionalen Dialektes in der frühen deutschen Dialektologie (Karl Christian Ludwig Schmidt, Rudolf von Raumer, Philipp Wegener) als Gemeingut angesehen werden konnte und bis zu Johann Christoph Adelung (1732–1806) zurückverfolgt werden kann (vgl. Bellmann 1986: 5–25).

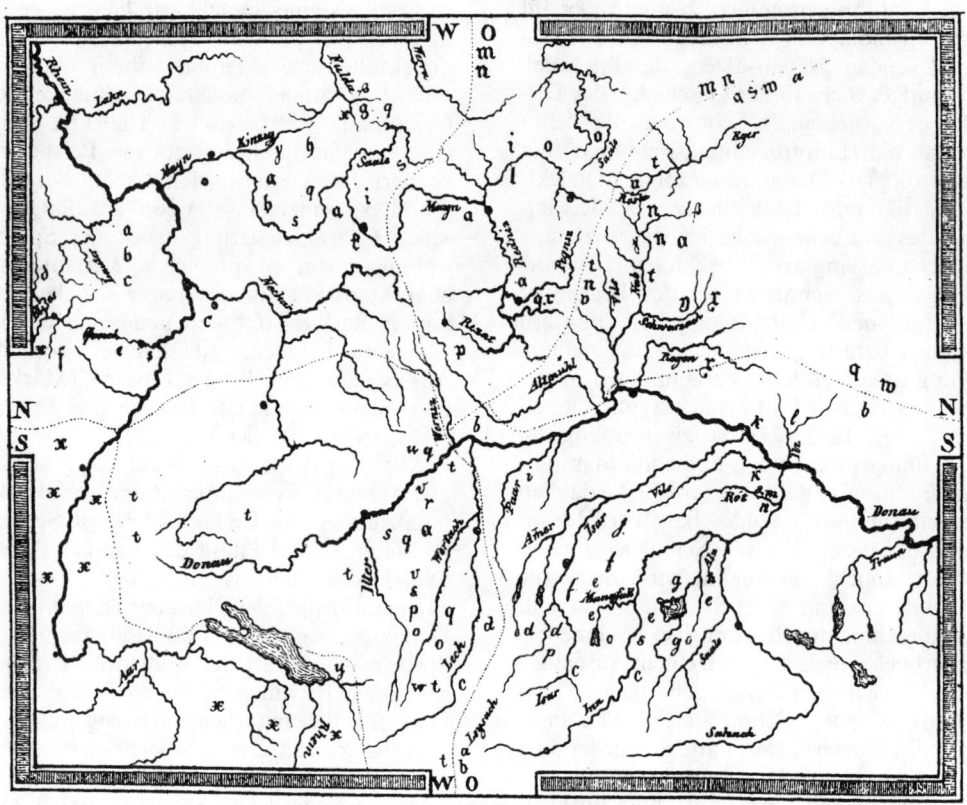

Abb. 182.1: Johann Andreas Schmellers Übersichtskarte zu den Mundarten Bayerns (Schmeller 1821: Faltkarte als Anhang).

5. Die klassisch-monodimensionale Dialektologie

5.1. Festigung der Dialektologie als Disziplin

Die weitere Entwicklung im 19. Jh. resultierte in der Stabilisierung der Dialektologie als sprachwissenschaftliche Disziplin, was zum einen an der Entwicklung eines methodologischen Kanons, zum anderen an der Erarbeitung von umfangreichem Faktenwissen über den Objektbereich und zum dritten an der ansatzweisen Ausarbeitung einer Dialekttheorie ablesbar war. Die Erkenntnisfortschritte der Dialektologie treten dabei im 19. Jh. keineswegs zufällig auf, sondern sie resultierten aus den sehr rasch sich vollziehenden Erkenntnisfortschritten der Sprachwissenschaft als ganzer. Besonders die Weiterentwicklung der zunächst in der Romantik fundierten historischen Sprachwissenschaft in die sprachtheoretisch und methodologisch avancierte junggrammatische Schule hat sich hier anregend ausgewirkt. Und im Kontext der junggrammatischen Sprachwissenschaft waren es ganz besonders die methodologische Hinwendung zur gesprochenen Sprache sowie die Ausarbeitung einer wissenschaftlichen Phonetik (vgl. Sievers 1876; Putschke 1984), die ihre Auswirkungen auf die Dialektologie nicht verfehlt haben. Der Entwicklungsschub, den die Dialektologie beginnend mit dem als 'Epochenjahr' bezeichneten Jahr 1876 verzeichnet, ist ohne diese theoretischen und methodologischen Anregungen im weiteren Kontext der junggrammatischen Schule nicht erklärbar.

Andererseits sahen sich die Dialektologen des 19. Jhs. Umstrukturierungen ihres Objektbereiches gegenüber, die es erschwerten, den wissenschaftlichen Gegenstand Dialekt zu fokussieren. Waren schon zu Beginn dialektologischen Interesses die arealen Varietäten als dynamisch sich verändernde ins Bewußtsein getreten, insbesondere im Hinblick auf die ihren Funktionsbereich ausweitende Standardsprache, so verstärkte sich diese Dynamik im 19. Jh. spürbar.

"Dieser Sprachwissenschaft wächst ein zunehmend problemgeladener Objektbereich entgegen: Von den Zeitgenossen wurde vor allem die Verbreitung der Schulbildung auch unter der Landbevölkerung registriert. Mehr noch haben Bauernbefreiung sowie Entstehung und Entwicklung der Industriegesellschaft tiefgreifende Veränderungen im Sozialleben, so u. a. erste Wellen der Mobilität und der Verstädterung zur Folge gehabt, die sich ihrerseits auf das Sprechverhalten immer größerer Bevölkerungsteile und auf die Sprache selbst auszuwirken beginnen. Die auf diese Weise ausgelösten Veränderungen, die zuvor eher punktuell, etwa in den Städten auftraten, äußern sich nunmehr flächenhaft." (Bellmann 1986: 23)

Diese sprachexternen Faktoren wirkten sich auf die Dynamik des Objektbereichs der Dialektologie aus durch einen hinsichtlich Spreceranzahl und Verwendungssituationen zunehmenden Standardsprachgebrauch, durch Verringerung des systemischen Abstands der arealen Varietäten von der Standardsprache (Dialektalität), durch sich anbahnende Tendenzen vom Lokal- zum Regionaldialekt und durch eine zunehmende diastratisch und diasituativ gesteuerte Variabilisierung der Dialektverwendung.

Diese Tatsache war den Dialektologen des ausgehenden 19. Jhs. sehr wohl bewußt. Georg Wenker beispielsweise war der Meinung, daß die "Mundarten durch Vermischung untereinander und mit dem Hochdeutschen mehr und mehr ihrer Reinheit und Ursprünglichkeit verlustig gehen [...]" (Wenker 1878, zit. nach Bellmann 1986: 27). Die Reaktion auf diese Wahrnehmung einer sich verstärkenden Variabilität war nun aber nicht mehr, wie noch zu Beginn des Jahrhunderts bei Schmeller und anderen, daß diese Variabilität zum Gegenstand gemacht worden und begrifflich gefaßt worden wäre. Im Gegenteil, Georg Wenker und andere Forscher seiner Zeit reagierten auf die als störend empfundene Pluridimensionalität der Sprachvariation mit einem heuristisch motivierten Akt der Komplexitätsreduktion, indem Dialekt nämlich bloß eindimensional, rein diatopisch variierend konzeptioniert und empirisch auch nur eindimensional erhoben wurde. In der — nach Schmellers vorzeitigem Entwurf — von Georg Wenker begründeten Sprachgeographie liegt die Eindimensionalität des Dialekts schon in der Erhebungsmethode begründet: Indem pro Belegortspunkt nur ein Fragebogen erhoben wurde und die Sozialdaten der Informanten nicht festgehalten wurden, war qua Erhebung der Dialekt als eindimensionaler, als nur diatopisch variierender konstituiert. Die methodische Vorgehensweise der weit überwiegenden Zahl der zu gleicher Zeit entstehenden lokalen Dialektgrammatiken war in gleicher Weise dazu angetan, Dialekt als eindimensional, nur diatopisch variierend zu erweisen: Oft wurden Grammatiken pro Ort aufgrund der Dialektkenntnis eines einzelnen Informanten, meist des Grammatikographen selbst, erstellt, so daß auch hier sozial oder situativ indizierte Variation methodisch ausgeblendet wurde.

Daß der wissenschaftliche Gegenstand 'Dialekt' sowohl in der Dialektgeographie als auch in der Dialektgrammatikographie als diastratisch und diasituativ homogen, nur allein diatopisch variierend, erscheinen konnte, war also zunächst heuristisch motiviert und methodologisch konstituiert, indem nämlich andere als die diatopische Variation nicht erhoben wurde. Es ist festzuhalten, daß die Dialektologie, die im letzten Viertel des 19. Jhs. einen glänzenden Aufschwung nahm und eine Fülle neuer Forschungsergebnisse erarbeitete, diesen Aufschwung durch eine in anderer Hinsicht mißliche Komplexitätsreduktion erkaufte, die im Vergleich zu der Dialektologie des Jahrhundertbeginns Dialekt nur noch als eindimensional-diatopisch variierend kannte. Da diese Homogenisierung des Objektbereiches schon durch die Erhebungsmethode bewirkt war, konnte sie auch durch spätere sprachexterne Interpretationstechniken nicht wettgemacht werden. Da diese Komplexitätsreduktion aber zugleich wissenschaftlich höchst ertragreich war — es wurde auf der Grundlage des eindimensionalen Dialektbegriffes ein Großteil der Forschungsergebnisse der deutschen Dialektologie erarbeitet — konnte sie über lange Zeit, bis weit ins 20. Jh. hinein, methodologisch bestimmend bleiben. Es kann deshalb von einer klassisch-monodimensionalen Dialektologie gesprochen werden.

5.2. Die Dialektgeographie

Nach der Vorläuferschaft Schmellers kam es erst ab 1876 zu einer systematisch betriebenen Dialektgeographie, und zwar ausgehend von dem Forschungsansatz des Marburger Bibliothekars Georg Wenker (1852—1911). Im Gegensatz zum früher verbreiteten Forschungstopos, Georg Wenker habe durch seine sprachgeographischen Unternehmen den junggrammatischen Satz von der Ausnahmslosigkeit der Lautgesetze beweisen wollen, ist inzwischen bekannt (vgl. Veith 1970: 393 ff.), daß Wenker nirgends behauptet oder den Schluß nahegelegt hat, er wolle die Ausnahmslosigkeit der Lautgesetze nachweisen. Wenkers Forschungsinteresse war anders gelagert und veränderte sich im Laufe der Arbeiten mehrfach. In einer ersten Forschungsphase ging es Wenker um das Auffinden als gegeben angenommener, klar in Erscheinung tretender Dialektgrenzen (vgl. zum folgenden Knoop et al. 1982: 46—68):

"Ich lebte noch in der schönen und beruhigenden Überzeugung, diese Charakteristika müssten ganz oder nahezu ganz einträchtiglich zusammengehn und so eine klare Dialektgrenze ergeben, der zufolge jeder Ort entweder dem einen oder dem anderen Dialektgebiete zugewiesen werden könnte." (Wenker 1886, zit. nach Wiegand & Harras 1971: 12)

Mit dem Fortgang der Arbeiten stellte sich Wenker die Situation bald wesentlich komplexer dar (ebda.).

"Und je weiter die Arbeit [...] vorrückte, um so bunter ward die Verwirrung, um so verwickelter zeigte sich der Lauf der Linien in ihrer Gesamtheit. [...] Da vollzog sich die erste durchgreifende Umwandlung der alten naiven Vorstellung von Dialektgrenzen. Diese mußte aufgegeben werden gegen eine neue, und diese mußte gesucht werden."

In einer zweiten Phase verlagerte sich das Forschungsziel also hin zu einer aufgrund der unübersichtlichen Datenlage als notwendig erachteten Dialektabgrenzung durch den Forscher. Zuletzt, in einer dritten Phase, wurde auch diese Zielbestimmung der Dialektabgrenzung als zu eng angesehen. Das Ziel dialektgeographischer Arbeit wurde schließlich in der Datendokumentation gesehen, so daß der Sprachatlas als Forschungsinstrument nun einer Vielzahl im einzelnen sehr unterschiedlich gelagerter Forschungsinteressen offenstünde.

Zunächst jedenfalls, in der Gründungsphase um 1876, dominierte Wenkers Interesse an der Auffindung der als gegeben vorausgesetzten Dialektgrenzen. Der empirische Ansatz, den Wenker zur Erreichung dieses Zieles entwickelte, sollte für die deutsche Dialektologie zentrale Bedeutung erlangen. Die auf Wenkers Ansatz zurückgehende "Marburger dialektologische Schule" erwies sich in Erhebungsmethode und Dateninterpretation als das bestimmende Forschungsparadigma der deutschen Dialektologie — bis weit in das 20. Jh. hinein.

Dies gilt zuallererst für das Sprachatlasunternehmen, das unter Wenkers Protagonistentum schrittweise — und gegen Widrigkeiten und Widerstände unterschiedlichster Art — sich herausbildete. 1876 arbeitete Wenker einen ersten Fragebogen aus, den er an die Lehrer der nördlichen Rheinprovinz verschickte. Der Fragebogen umfaßte 42 standardsprachlich abgefaßte Sätze, die mithilfe des gebräuchlichen Alphabets durch die Lehrer in den ortsüblichen Dialekt 'übersetzt' werden sollten. Wenkers Fragebogenaktion war erfolgreich, so daß er schon 1877 seine — den Informanten dedizierte — Schrift *Das rheinische Platt* (Wenker 1877) vorlegen konnte, die eine Einteilung der rheinischen Dialekte (nördlich der Mosel) enthält. In dieser Schrift darf nun die eigentliche Grundlage der Dialektologie als areallinguistische Disziplin gesehen werden. Wenker begann im gleichen Jahr, die areale Basis seiner Sprachdatenerhebung zu verbreitern, indem er noch 1877 eine zweite Fragebogenaktion startete. Inzwischen an der Universitätsbibliothek in Marburg in untergeordneter Position angestellt, versandte Wenker einen modifizierten Fragebogen — nun 38 Sätze — an die westfälischen Schulorte. Die 1876 erhobenen Daten wurden durch Wenker handschriftlich zu Sprachkarten umgezeichnet, die dann zu einem *Sprach-Atlas der Rheinprovinz nördlich der Mosel sowie des Kreises Siegen* zusammengestellt wurden, dem ersten deutschen Sprachatlas (1878). Hatte Wenker bis zu diesem Zeitpunkt die Sprachgeographie des Deutschen als Privatforschung betrieben, so erforderte die von ihm in der Folge intendierte Verbreiterung der arealen Basis des Unternehmens — ganz Preußen sollte sprachgeographisch erforscht werden — nun aber institutionelle Unterstützung. Diese suchte Wenker 1878 zu erreichen, gestützt auf ein Gutachten der Marburger Universität. Die staatliche Unterstützung wurde Wenker — in sehr bescheidenem Umfange — 1879 auch gewährt, so daß mit diesem Datum der Beginn des Sprachatlasunternehmens als staatlich geförderte Institution anzusetzen ist.

Die Berliner Akademie der Wissenschaften, die vom preußischen Kultusministerium als Gutachter herangezogen worden war, hatte jedoch die Begrenzung des Sprachatlasunternehmens nur auf Preußen kritisiert und eine Ausweitung verlangt. Wenker stimmte dem zu, so daß nun — mit erneut umgearbeitetem Fragebogen (40 Sätze) — ein Sprachatlas von Nord- und Mitteldeutschland ins Auge gefaßt werden konnte. Die ungeheuren

1. Im Winter fliegen die trocknen Blätter durch die Luft herum. — 2. Es hört gleich auf zu schneien, dann wird das Wetter wieder besser. — 3. Thu Kohlen in den Ofen, daß die Milch bald an zu kochen fängt. — 4. Der gute alte Mann ist mit dem Pferde durch's Eis gebrochen und in das kalte Wasser gefallen. — 5. Er ist vor vier oder sechs Wochen gestorben. — 6. Das Feuer war zu heiß, die Kuchen sind ja unten ganz schwarz gebrannt. — 7. Er ißt die Eier immer ohne Salz und Pfeffer. — 8. Die Füße thun mir sehr weh, ich glaube, ich habe sie durchgelaufen. — 9. Ich bin bei der Frau gewesen und habe es ihr gesagt, und sie sagte, sie wollte es auch ihrer Tochter sagen. — 10. Ich will es auch nicht mehr wieder thun. — 11. Ich schlage Dich gleich mit dem Kochlöffel um die Ohren, Du Affe! — 12. Wo gehst Du hin, sollen wir mit Dir gehn? — 13. Es sind schlechte Zeiten! — 14. Mein liebes Kind, bleib hier unten stehn, die bösen Gänse beißen Dich todt. — 15. Du hast heute am meisten gelernt und bist artig gewesen, Du darfst früher nach Hause gehn als die Andern. — 16. Du bist noch nicht groß genug, um eine Flasche Wein auszutrinken, Du mußt erst noch ein Ende wachsen und größer werden. — 17. Geh, sei so gut und sag Deiner Schwester, sie sollte die Kleider für eure Mutter fertig nähen und mit der Bürste rein machen. — 18. Hättest Du ihn gekannt! dann wäre es anders gekommen, und es thäte besser um ihn stehn. — 19. Wer hat mir meinen Korb mit Fleisch gestohlen? — 20. Er that so, als hätten sie ihn zum dreschen bestellt; sie haben es aber selbst gethan. — 21. Wem hat er die neue Geschichte erzählt. — 22. Man muß laut schreien, sonst versteht er uns nicht. — 23. Wir sind müde und haben Durst. — 24. Als wir gestern Abend zurück kamen, da lagen die Andern schon zu Bett und waren fest am schlafen. — 25. Der Schnee ist diese Nacht bei uns liegen geblieben, aber heute Morgen ist er geschmolzen. — 26. Hinter unserm Hause stehen drei schöne Apfelbäumchen mit rothen Aepfelchen. — 27. Könnt ihr nicht noch ein Augenblickchen auf uns warten, dann gehn wir mit euch. — 28. Ihr dürft nicht solche Kindereien treiben. — 29. Unsere Berge sind nicht sehr hoch, die euren sind viel höher. — 30. Wieviel Pfund Wurst und wieviel Brod wollt ihr haben? — 31. Ich verstehe euch nicht, ihr müßt ein bißchen lauter sprechen. — 32. Habt ihr kein Stückchen weiße Seife für mich auf meinem Tische gefunden? — 33. Sein Bruder will sich zwei schöne neue Häuser in eurem Garten bauen. — 34. Das Wort kam ihm vom Herzen! — 35. Das war recht von ihnen! — 36. Was sitzen da für Vögelchen oben auf dem Mäuerchen? — 37. Die Bauern hatten fünf Ochsen und neun Kühe und zwölf Schäfchen vor das Dorf gebracht, die wollten sie verkaufen. — 38. Die Leute sind heute alle draußen auf dem Felde und mähen. — 39. Geh nur, der braune Hund thut Dir nichts. — 40. Ich bin mit den Leuten da hinten über die Wiese ins Korn gefahren. —

Abb. 182.2: Die 40 Sätze Georg Wenkers (Walther Mitzka: Handbuch zum Deutschen Sprachatlas. Marburg: Elwert 1952: 13—14).

Materialmengen, die zu bearbeiten waren – es lag aus jedem Schulort ein Fragebogen vor –, stellten Wenker dann allerdings trotz der staatlichen Förderung vor kaum zu bewältigende Auswertungsprobleme, so daß von diesem *Sprachatlas von Nord- und Mitteldeutschland* nur eine einzige Lieferung erscheinen konnte. Daß es Wenker – wie zuvor – möglich sein sollte, praktisch als Einzelner die Materialien auszuwerten, war praktisch auszuschließen. In dieser Situation richtete die Philologenversammlung in Gießen 1885 den Antrag an das Reichkanzleramt, das Sprachatlasunternehmen, das dann allerdings erneut auszuweiten wäre zu einem "Sprachatlas des deutschen Reichs", finanziell zu unterstützen. Diese Unterstützung wurde zuletzt gewährt, jedoch verlor Wenker damit auch seine Urheberrechte an dem Projekt. Der Sprachatlas wurde nun – unter erneuter Ausdehnung auf Süddeutschland – als staatliches Projekt geführt und finanziert, die Materialien wurden zugleich Staatseigentum und Wenker wurde dazu verpflichtet, auf eigene Forschung zu verzichten und ausschließlich an der Kartenherstellung zu arbeiten. Auch eine Publikation der Sprachkarten sollte vorerst unterbleiben. In dieser Weise konnten nun die Arbeiten fortgeführt und unter Wenkers Nachfolger Ferdinand Wrede auch abgeschlossen werden.

Der so entstandene *Sprachatlas des Deutschen Reichs* liegt in zwei durchweg farbig gezeichneten Manuskript-Exemplaren vor. Das deutsche Sprachgebiet wird jeweils auf drei Einzelblättern im Maßstab 1 : 1.000.000 (Nordwest-, Nordost- und Südwestblatt) projiziert. Auf insgesamt 1646 Teilkarten sind 339 sprachliche Erscheinungen kartiert. Ein bis auf den heutigen Tag zu beklagendes Desiderat ist in der Tatsache zu sehen, daß diese umfassende, auch anschauliche Version des Sprachatlasses bislang nicht publiziert werden konnte, weil die aufwendige Farbreproduktion nicht realisierbar erschien. Ferdinand Wrede (1863–1934) konnte mit dem *Deutschen Sprachatlas* (DSA) lediglich eine Teilveröffentlichung (1927–56) erreichen, die jedoch, was das dargebotene Material angeht, stark reduziert war. Es handelt sich um letztlich nur 79 kartierte Erscheinungen, teilweise allerdings in mehreren Teilkarten dargeboten. Auch auf die Mehrfarbigkeit des Originals mußte verzichtet werden, was einen enormen Verlust an Anschaulichkeit zur Folge hatte. In jüngster Zeit ist dann eine umfangreichere Publikation gelungen, und zwar in Gestalt des *Kleinen Deutschen Sprachatlasses* (Veith & Putschke 1984 ff.). Hier werden die durch das Sprachatlasmaterial beschreibbaren linguistischen Phänomene in einiger Vollständigkeit analysiert und kartographiert – allerdings bei einer beträchtlichen Ausdünnung des sehr dichten Belegnetzes, das für Wenkers Erhebung kennzeichnend war. Gegenwart lassen es inzwischen zu, die aufwendig gezeichneten Farb-Originale des "Sprachatlasses des Deutschen Reichs" virtuell im Internet zu publizieren. Dies ist Gegenstand des Projektes "DiWA" ("Digitaler Wenker-Atlas"). Im Rahmen dieses Projektes werden nicht nur die Original-Farbkarten publiziert, sondern auch die Original-Fragebogen, verschiedene Tondokumente, eine interaktiv nutzbare dialektologische Bibliographie, Karten aktueller Regionalatlanten des Deutschen und anderes mehr. Im Entstehen ist somit hier ein interaktives dialektologisches Informationssystem (http://www.deutscher-sprachatlas.de).

Die Forschungsaktivitäten des "Forschungsinstitutes für Deutsche Sprache 'Deutscher Sprachatlas'" in Marburg, das aus Wenkers Ein-Mann-Projekt entstanden ist, erschöpften sich in der Zeit nach Wenker bei weitem nicht in der Auswertung und Teilpublikation der einmal erhobenen Daten.

Zum einen gelang es schrittweise, die deutschen Dialekte mittels der Marburger Erhebungsmethode in einer gewissen Vollständigkeit zu erfassen. Zunächst konnte das Sprachatlas-Material durch eine 1888 durchgeführte Befragung in Luxemburg ergänzt werden. Von 1926–1933 veranlaßte dann Wrede die Abfragung der Wenker-Sätze in der Schweiz, in Liechtenstein, in Österreich, im Burgenland und in der deutschsprachigen Tschechoslowakei. Zuletzt erreichte Wredes Nachfolger Walther Mitzka die Abfragung der Wenker-Sätze in deutschsprachigen Orten Polens und in Südtirol. Es resultierte aus diesen verschiedenen Fragebogenaussendungen im Ergebnis ein Material von 51.480 lokalen Antwortbögen, ein unschätzbarer Datenfundus, der aktuell – unter Jürgen Erich Schmidt als Sprachatlasdirektor – digitalisiert wird, so daß er im Rahmen des Projekts 'DiWa' (s. o.) der Öffentlichkeit per Internet zur Verfügung steht.

Zum zweiten darf man zumindest eine Ergänzung und Vervollständigung des Wenker'schen Laut- und Formenatlasses in Walther Mitzkas (1888–1976) *Deutschem Wortatlas*

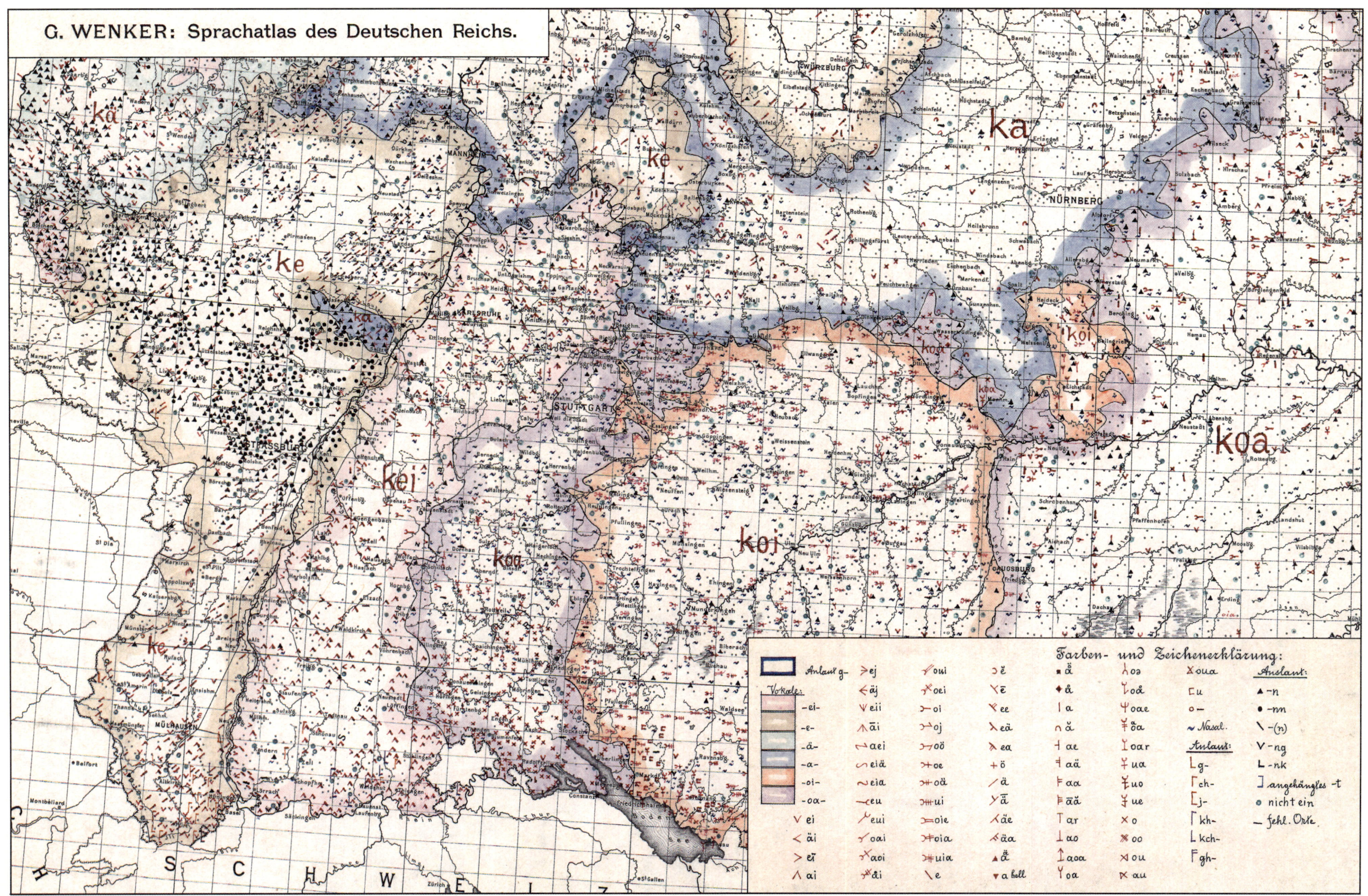

Abb. 182.3: Georg Wenker: Sprachatlas des Deutschen Reichs, Ausschnitt aus der Karte *kein* (Elektronische Publikation des Gesamtwerks im Rahmen von DiWA: http://www.deutscher-sprachatlas.de).

(DWA) sehen, der ab 1938 am Marburger Forschungsinstitut entstand. Mit gleicher Methode wie die Laut- und Formenlehre wurde nun hier bis 1942 der Wortschatz erhoben, und zwar gleichfalls mit den Lehrern als Laien-Exploratoren bzw. Informanten. Das Ortsnetz war auch hier extrem dicht (48.381 Orte), jedoch gelang nun, nachdem Erfahrungen der Vergangenheit bedacht werden konnten und das Institut personell ausgebaut worden war, eine Publikation innerhalb vergleichsweise kurzer Zeit (1951—73).

Drittens wurden die Arbeiten an den Sprachatlanten in Marburg flankiert durch eine Vielzahl von im Kontext des Sprachatlasses erarbeiteten Monographien, die die gesamtareal-diatopische Verfahrensweise der Großraumatlanten durch — syntopische — Ortsgrammatiken oder durch kleinraumdiatopische areale Analysen ergänzten. Es handelte sich hier um die noch durch F. Wrede gegründete Reihe "Deutsche Dialektgeographie" (DDG) (vgl. Wagener 1988) sowie um die Reihen "Deutsche Wortforschung in europäischen Bezügen" (DWEB) (1958—1972), "(Gießener) Beiträge zur deutschen Philologie" (BdPh) (seit 1922), und "Marburger Beiträge zur Germanistik" (seit 1962).

Die Marburger Unternehmen haben die deutsche Dialektologie nachhaltig bestimmt. Die Grundzüge der dialektalen Gliederung des deutschen Sprachraumes sowie wesentliche Ergebnisse der Laut- und Formengeschichte des Deutschen sind aufgrund der Sprachatlasmaterialen erarbeitet worden, so daß die Relevanz der Dialektologie, speziell des Marburger Forschungsinstituts, für die — speziell historische — Sprachwissenschaft des Deutschen als nicht zu gering veranschlagt werden darf.

Noch entscheidender als im Inhaltlichen dürfte der Einfluß der Marburger Dialektologie im Methodischen gewesen sein. Der spezifische methodische Zugang der zentralen Marburger Forschungsunternehmen hat — möglicherweise auch durch die frühe "Verstaatlichung" und institutionelle Expansion des Marburger Forschungsprojektes — für die Dialektologie des Deutschen eine bestimmende Rolle erlangt. Die methodologische Typik der Marburger Schule erweist sich erstens in der Datenerhebung, zweitens aber auch in der Datenauswertung und nicht zuletzt in der Dateninterpretation.

Die Erhebungsmethode der Marburger Schule folgt zunächst dem Prinzip der hohen Belegnetzdichte: Zumindest die Großraumatlanten Marburger Prägung haben angestrebt, möglichst jeden (Schul-)Ort des Erhebungsareals als Belegort zu führen, d. h. es wurde eine maximale Erhebungsortdichte zumindest angestrebt. Des weiteren ist die Marburger Erhebungsmethode durch indirekte Datenerhebung gekennzeichnet: Die Daten wurden mittels Fragebogenaussendungen erhoben, wobei die linguistischen Fragen in der Aufforderung bestanden, standardsprachliche Sätze in den Ortsdialekt zu 'übersetzen'. Ein weiteres Erhebungsprinzip bestand darin, pro Erhebungsort nur einen Fragebogen ausfüllen zu lassen, der dann für den Lokaldialekt als repräsentativ angesehen wurde. Die Exploratoren, die den Fragebogen erhielten, waren die (Volksschul-)Lehrer. Man muß also im Hinblick auf die komplexen Erfordernisse einer wissenschaftlichen Sprachdatenerhebung von dem Prinzip der Laien-Exploration sprechen. Eine Informantenverifikation fand nicht statt. Es blieb den Lehrern überlassen, ob sie — wenn sie beispielsweise selbst Sprecher des zu erhebenden Dialektes waren — selbst als Informanten dienen wollten oder ob sie sich — bei einem Bewußtsein dialektaler Unsicherheit — Schülern als — möglicherweise dialektsicherer — Informanten bedienen wollten. Die Sozialdaten dieser Informanten wurden nicht festgehalten, so daß eine nachträgliche Einschätzung der Informantenkompetenz kaum möglich war. Die Transkription erfolgte, wie bei dem Verfahren der indirekten Datenerhebung durch Laien nicht anders möglich, durch die den Lehrern geläufige Standardorthographie, mit der sie versuchten, die dialektalen Lautungen abzubilden.

Die Datenauswertung zielte in den Marburger Großprojekten auf die Kartierung der erhobenen Sprachbelege. Hierzu wurden zunächst die Fragebogen kontrolliert, dann die Transkripte segmentiert und zuletzt kartiert. Die Kartierung erfolgte in Flächendarstellung mit dem Leitformverfahren, was sich schon aufgrund der großen Belegnetzdichte anbot; eine Originalformkartierung wäre schon aus Platzgründen unmöglich gewesen.

Die Dateninterpretation zielte zunächst, wie ausgeführt, auf das Ziel der Dialekteinteilung ab, ein Ziel, das auch erreicht werden konnte. Auch wenn in neuerer Sicht die Dialekteinteilung nach den Sprachatlasdaten ergänzungs-, z. T. revisionsbedürftig erscheint (vgl. Wiesinger 1970, 1983a), ist die Grund-struktur der Einteilung der deutschen Dialekte doch ein Hauptertrag der Sprachatlasinterpretation. Des weiteren dienten die erstellten Sprachkarten dann der sprachhistorischen Interpretation, wobei die dargestellten Sprachdaten mit außersprachlichen Daten korreliert wurden (vgl. z. B. Frings 1956, 1957).

Die Methodik der Marburger Großraumatlanten war zu keinem Zeitpunkt unumstritten. So richtete sich die scharfe Polemik, mit der Otto Bremer (1862−1936), ein Schüler Eduard Sievers', 1895 Wenkers dialektgeographischen Ansatz überzog, gleich gegen mehrere der angeführten methodischen Festlegungen Wenkers (vgl. Bremer 1895; Schirmunski 1962: 78−84): Ein erster Haupteinwand monierte Wenkers zweifellos hochökonomisches Prinzip der Laien-Transkription, das aus junggrammatischer Perspektive, besonders aus der Perspektive der im Entstehen begriffenen wissenschaftlichen Phonetik, als völlig unangemessenes Erhebungsverfahren erscheinen mußte. Zum zweiten richtete sich schon Bremers Kritik gegen die homogenisierende Tendenz von Wenkers Erhebung, die einen Fragebogen pro Ort als repräsentativ ansetzte. Bremer bemängelte, daß hier existierende sprachliche Varianten unterdrückt wurden und, was möglicherweise noch schwerer wiegt, daß aufgrund der fehlenden Informantenkontrolle im Sprachatlas noch nicht einmal erkennbar ist, welcher sozialen Schicht erhobene Dialektvarianten jeweils zuzuordnen seien: Mäanderierende Linien auf den Sprachkarten, so Bremer, bildeten eher dialektale Variationszonen ab als − wie es den Anschein haben mußte − wirkliche Dialektgrenzen. Aus heutiger Sicht läßt sich sagen, daß Bremers Kritik in wesentlichen Punkten berechtigt ist. Zum einen sind die Laien-Schreibungen nur für einen Teil der zu untersuchenden lautlichen und flexivischen Phänomene aussagekräftig: Nicht wenige Dialekterscheinungen (z. B. Vokaldauer, Akzentuierung, Konsonantenschwächung) entziehen sich dem Zugriff des Sprachatlasses weitgehend. Zum anderen ist auch die Kritik an der zufallsgesteuerten Informantenauswahl und an der fehlenden Fixierung der Sozialdaten der Informanten berechtigt. Allerdings hat man auch darauf hingewiesen (vgl. Goossens 1977: 115), daß der Sprachatlas − zieht man die Spezifika seiner Erhebungsmethode bei einer sorgfältigen Dateninterpretation in Rechnung − durchaus zuverlässige Fakten liefert, wenn auch nur für einen begrenzten Teil der Phänomene, nämlich diejenigen, die durch Laien-Schreibungen erfaßt werden können.

Die Spezifika des Wenker'schen Sprachatlasprojekts treten nicht zuletzt im Vergleich zu dem nahezu synchron erhobenen *Atlas linguistique de la France* von Jules Gilliéron (1854−1926) hervor, der in mehrfacher Hinsicht eine methodologische Alternative darstellt. Gilliéron gab der direkten Datenerhebung durch nur einen Explorator den Vorzug. Nur eine Person, der ohrenphonetisch geschulte Explorator Edmond Edmont (1849−1926), führte von 1897 bis 1901 die gesamte Erhebung durch. Hierdurch konnte eine präzise phonetische Transkription erfolgen, allerdings − dies ist eine erhebungsökonomische Konsequenz aus der direkten Aufnahmemethode − es mußte das Ortsnetz sehr viel grobmaschiger ausfallen als bei Wenker (639 Orte statt 40.000). Ein Vorteil der so gewonnenen überschaubareren Datenmenge war dann wieder die Möglichkeit, die Auswertung ökonomischer durchzuführen: Gilliéron konnte den gesamten Atlas, der nicht nur die Lautlehre, sondern auch die Grammatik und den Wortschatz der französischen Dialekte zum Gegenstand hat, innerhalb von 12 Jahren nach dem Ende der Erhebung publizieren. Hierbei mag auch die leichter zu bewältigende Methode der Originalformkartierung hilfreich gewesen sein, die durch das großmaschige Ortsnetz möglich wurde, aber auch aus Gründen der möglichst neutralen Datenpräsentation erwünscht war.

Die weitere methodologische Entwicklung, nicht nur international, sondern auch in Deutschland, ist dem französischen Modell gefolgt. Wenkers Pionierleistung hat der deutschen Dialektologie zwar unschätzbare Informationen über die deutschen Dialekte eingebracht. Der methodische Ansatz Wenkers, der der Ökonomie und Vollständigkeit der Datenerfassung den Vorrang vor der Präzision der Datenerfassung und der Ökonomie der Datenauswertung eingeräumt hat, sollte sich aber nicht durchsetzen.

Schon die in Marburg in der von Ludwig Erich Schmitt (1908−1994) herausgegebenen Reihe "Deutscher Sprachatlas, Regionale Sprachatlanten" (RSA) erschienenen Regionalatlanten waren bestrebt, die Vorteile der französischen und der deutschen Methode miteinander zu verbinden. Meist in direkter Erhebung wurden und werden in diesen Regionalatlanten überschaubarere Areale untersucht, so daß wegen der geringeren Gebietsgröße trotz der direkten Erhebungstechnik vertretbare Ortsnetzdichten erreicht werden können. Man darf eine Konvergenzerscheinung der zeitweise unversöhnlichen romanistischen und germanistischen dialektologischen Forschungsansätze darin sehen, daß auch in der Romania in entsprechender Weise ein Netz von Regionalatlanten entstanden ist, die gleichfalls versuchen, die Vorteile der zunächst als alternativ angesehenen methodischen Ansätze zu verbinden. (Vgl. zu den abgeschlossenen und laufenden deutschen und internationalen Projekten die Übersicht bei Veith & Putschke 1989, bes. S. 416−434.)

5.3. Die Dialektgrammatikographie

In das Jahr 1876, in dem Wenker seine sprachgeographischen Arbeiten aufnahm, fällt auch die eigentliche Begründung einer zweiten methodologischen Traditionslinie der deutschen Dialektologie, die Forschungtradition der Dialektgrammatik. Auch was die Dialektgrammatik angeht, ist zwar das ältere Vorbild Schmellers ins Gedächtnis zu rufen, jedoch waren im letzten Viertel des 19. Jhs. durch die junggrammatische Sprachtheorie mit ihrer naturwissenschaftlichen Orientierung, ihrer Hinwendung zur empirischen Phonetik und ihrer − entgegen weitverbreiteten Ansichten − ansatzweise strukturbezogenen Orientierung verbesserte Voraussetzungen für die Dialektgrammatikographie gegeben. Höchste wissenschaftshistorische Relevanz kommt hier aufgrund ihres Modellcharakters Jost Wintelers (1846−1929) Grammatik *Die Kerenzer Mundart des Kantons Glarus* (1876) zu. Wintelers Grammatik entspricht im wesentlichen der junggrammatischen Methodologie, auch wenn sie in wesentlichen Zügen unabhängig erstellt worden war, bevor Winteler in Jena mit den Überlegungen besonders Sievers' konfrontiert wurde. Wintelers Ziel war die Beschreibung der Lautlehre und des Flexionssystems eines gesprochenen Ortsdialektes. Hierbei verweist Wintelers Grammatik weit ins 20. Jh., wenn er − leider in diesem Punkte zu wenig rezipiert − vom Primat der Synchronie ausgeht und bedeutende Elemente einer strukturalistischen Analyse vorwegnimmt. Andererseits verfährt auch Winteler, was seine Datengrundlage angeht, stark reduktionistisch, indem er die Kompetenz eines einzelnen Individuums, nämlich des Verfassers selbst, als repräsentativ für den zu untersuchenden Ortsdialekt ansetzt. Gerade diese reduktionistische, die reale Sprachvariation stark homogenisierende Verfahrensweise ist von nachfolgenden Dialektgrammatiken − in vielen Fällen Dissertationen, in denen der Verfasser seinen Heimatdialekt erforscht − übernommen worden, so daß die Tradition der Dialektgrammatik nicht anders als die der Dialektgeographie von einer stark homogenisierenden Tendenz geprägt erscheint.

Eine dialektgrammatographische Tradition ist im übrigen entstanden, obwohl das junggrammatisch orientierte grammatikographische Forschungsprogramm, das Philipp Wegener (1848−1916) 1879 vorlegte, nicht realisiert worden ist: Wegener regte an, das gesamte deutsche Sprachgebiet durch eine Kette ortsdialektal bzw. kleinregional orientierter Dialektgrammatiken systematisch zu erforschen. Diese sollten nach dem gleichen, der junggrammatischen Methodologie entlehnten Muster aufgebaut sein, d. h. zunächst eine empirisch gestützte phonetische Deskription der dialektalen Laute, sodann eine diachronisch orientierte Laut- und Flexionslehre enthalten. Obwohl zunächst zustimmend aufgenommen, ist dieses Programm nicht in den Rang eines nationalen Forschungsprojektes erhoben worden, das dem Sprachatlasprojekt vergleichbar gewesen wäre. Trotzdem entstanden in der Folge, auf Wintelers Modell aufbauend, eine Fülle von Ortsgrammatiken, später oft ausgedehnt zu kleinregionalen Gebietsmonographien. Zahlreiche dieser Arbeiten sind unter Wredes Herausgeberschaft in der Reihe "Deutsche Dialektgeographie" erschienen (vgl. Wagener 1988). Einige Dialektgrammatiken sind auch, angeregt durch den Sprachatlas-Kritiker O. Bremer, in der von ihm herausgegebenen Reihe "Sammlung kurzer Grammatiken deutscher Mundarten" erschienen. Insgesamt läßt sich feststellen, daß ein Großteil des deutschen Sprachraumes heute durch Dialektgrammatiken erschlossen ist (vgl. hierzu die Zusammenstellung, bes. die Übersichtskarten, bei Wiesinger & Raffin 1982). Wenn diese Grammatiken auch je syntopisch orientiert sind, so ermöglichen sie, wie Peter Wiesinger gezeigt hat, bei sorgsamer diatopisch-vergleichender Analyse doch eine Einschätzung der dialektalen Gliederung des Deutschen, die dem Ertrag des Sprachatlasses nicht nachsteht, ihm in mancher Hinsicht sogar überlegen ist (vgl. Wiesinger 1970, 1983a). Genau wie der Sprachatlas Wenkers monodimensional homogenisierend, ermöglichen die Dialektgrammatiken aufgrund der höheren deskriptiven Präzision des Explorators vor Ort in vielen Fällen ein präziseres Bild der dialektalen Verhältnisse, als der Sprachatlas es — bei größerer arealer Vollständigkeit freilich — bietet.

5.4. Die Dialektlexikographie

Wie oben angesprochen, weist die Dialektlexikographie innerhalb der deutschen Dialektologie die am weitesten zurückreichende Tradition auf: Die ersten dialektologischen Darstellungen, die für das Deutsche existieren, waren Wortschatzsammlungen, zunächst in der Form von Idiotika, also der Darstellung des von der Schrift- bzw. Standardsprache abweichenden dialektalen Sonderbestandes. Hier ist der Anfang durch Johann Ludwig Praschs (1637—1690) 1689 erschienenes *Glossarium Bavaricum* markiert und dann im 18. Jh. durch das o. a. *Idioticon Hamburgense* Michael Richeys. Die — im einzelnen sehr unterschiedlich motivierte — Tradition der Idiotismensammlung und -publikation hat über die Geschichte der Dialektologie des Deutschen Bestand, wobei die entstandenen Idiotika an Umfang und Qualität erheblich differieren und insoweit ein heterogenes Bild ergeben (vgl. Haas 1994a, b). Aufbauend auf den Idiotismensammlungen ist dann eine Tradition auszumachen, die zum wissenschaftlichen Dialektwörterbuch führt, also zur Erhebung und Darstellung des Dialektwortschatzes einschließlich derjenigen Elemente, die lexikalisch mit der Standardsprache übereinstimmen. Mit seinem *Bayerischen Wörterbuch* (1827—37, 1872—77) steht Johann Andreas Schmeller auch hier — weit vorzeitig — am Anfang der Tradition einer wissenschaftlichen Dialektlexikographie. Diese umfaßt dann besonders im 20. Jh. eine Fülle von Projekten zur Orts- und Regionallexikographie. Anders als bei der Sprachgeographie entstanden also hier, bei der Dialektlexikographie, zuerst die regionalen Untersuchungen, die aufgrund der — relativen — Begrenztheit der Untersuchungsareale eine intensivere Durchdringung des Materials anstreben konnten. Bei aller Vielgestaltigkeit der Methoden und Publikationsformen ermöglichen die erschienenen und im Erscheinen begriffenen Regionallexika inzwischen einen praktisch lückenlosen Überblick über die Lexik der deutschen Dialekte (vgl. Niebaum 1979, 1994; Friebertshäuser 1983). Die Entwicklung der Dialektlexikographie ist durch eine zunehmende Hinwendung zur nicht bloß lexikalischen, sondern gleichzeitig sprachgeographischen Darstellung der Dialektwortschätze gekennzeichnet, so daß zahlreiche Dialektwörterbücher auch Wortkarten enthalten. Mit dieser auch diatopischen Orientierung begibt sich die Dialektlexikographie in die Nähe zur lexikalischen Dialektgeographie des Deutschen (vgl. z. B. als Großraumprojekte den o. a. *Deutschen Wortatlas* oder den *Wortatlas der deutschen Umgangssprachen*; vgl. Eichhoff 1977—78; als Kleinraumprojekte die regionalen Wortatlanten des Deutschen; vgl. Veith & Putschke 1989).

5.5. Datenerhebung und Dateninterpretation: Ergebnisse der klassisch-monodimensionalen Dialektologie

Es ist bei dem hier zur Verfügung stehenden Raum ausgeschlossen, einen inhaltlichen Überblick über die reichen Ergebnisse der klassisch-monodimensionalen Dialektologie auch nur andeuten zu können. Es muß und kann zu diesem Zweck auf die vorliegenden Handbücher (vgl. Schirmunski 1962, Besch 1982, 1983) und Forschungsberichte (vgl. Mattheier & Wiesinger 1994) verwiesen werden. Tatsächlich liegen heute in Gestalt von großräumigen, regionalen und lokalen Untersuchungen eine Fülle von Arbeitsergebnissen vor, die eine Einschätzung der dialektalen Verhältnisse des Deutschen auf den verschiedenen Ebenen linguistischer Beschreibung — Phonetik, Phonologie, Morphologie, Syntax, Lexik, Semantik und Pragmalinguistik — ermöglichen. Da die Dialektologie historisch ihren Ausgangspunkt im Kontext der junggrammatischen Schule nahm, verwundert es nicht, daß besonders die phonetisch-phonologischen und morphologischen Beschreibungen besonders stark vertreten sind, gefolgt von den lexikalischen, während die Dialektsyntax und besonders die Dialektpragmatik nach wie vor wissenschaftliche Desiderate darstellen.

Die Eigenständigkeit der Dialektologie in der Untersuchung dieser verschiedenen linguistischen Teilsysteme lag zu allen Zeiten einmal in ihrem spezifischen Gegenstand begründet, der diatopischen Variation. Eigenständig ist die Dialektologie auch stets in ihrer Methodologie gewesen, besonders was die Erhebungsverfahren gesprochener Sprache angeht, die sie zuerst entwickelt und ständig verfeinert hat. Und eigenständig war die Dialektologie zweifellos auch in ihren sprachgeographischen Darstellungsverfahren, besonders der Sprachkarte, weshalb der dialektgeographische Ansatz hier auch ausführlicher als andere gewürdigt worden ist.

Die Geschichte der Forschungsfragen, die die Dialektologie des Deutschen behandelt hat, ist im übrigen − besonders was die sprachtheoretischen Zugänge zu den erhobenen Daten angeht − vor dem Hintergrund der Theorieentwicklung der Sprachwissenschaft insgesamt zu sehen. Die über lange Zeit monodimensional-diatopisch erhobenen dialektalen Daten sind in der Geschichte der Dialektologie jeweils entsprechend den aktuellen sprachwissenschaftlichen Konzepten befragt und interpretiert worden. In der Diskussion befindliche sprachwissenschaftliche Theorieansätze sind zu allen Zeiten − nicht zuletzt in akademischen Qualifikationsarbeiten − an dialektalem Datenmaterial erprobt worden, so daß die Dialektologie sich gleichzeitig als ein dynamisches sprachwissenschaftliches Laboratorium darstellt. Für alle Phasen der Dialektologiegeschichte kann man daher geradezu von einer Tradition sprachwissenschaftlicher Modernität sprechen.

Dies gilt schon für die Konstitutions- und Festigungsphase der Disziplin im 19. Jh., in der die Sprachgeschichte das umfassende sprachwissenschaftliche Paradigma darstellte. Die Sprachgeschichte war auch für die Dialektologie der Fluchtpunkt ihrer Dateninterpretation, so daß man die klassische Dialektologie auch als Teildisziplin der historischen Sprachwissenschaft bezeichnet hat (vgl. Putschke 1982). Die erhobenen dialektalen Varianten wurden in den Darstellungen in aller Regel zu den entsprechenden Formen des jeweiligen historischen Protosystems in Beziehung gesetzt. In der Aufdeckung dieser Beziehungen sah die Dialektologie über weite Zeitabschnitte ihren Gegenstand. Ihre Ergebnisse wurden insofern als Elemente einer empirisch gegründeten Geschichte der deutschen Sprache angesehen. Die Interpretation dialektaler Daten im Sinne eines sprachhistorischen Beschreibungsparadigmas ging dabei vielmals auch weit über die bloße sprachhistorische Klassifikation hinaus, wenn etwa die in Sprachkarten erkennbaren dialektalen Lagerungen als Ausdruck sprachhistorischer Dynamik interpretiert wurden. Im Verbund mit der Interpretation areal distribuierter außersprachlicher Faktoren konnten diese dialektalen Lagerungen dann auch bezüglich der Herausbildung der neuhochdeutschen Standardsprache interpretiert werden, indem durchgreifende historische Sprachveränderungsprozesse auf der Grundlage der aktuell erhobenen dialektalen Daten interpretiert wurden (vgl. z. B. Frings 1956, 1957). Erst später entstand, in Abkehr von dieser methodisch problematischen Rückprojektion rezenter Dialektstrukturen in die Geschichte, eine 'Historische Dialektologie', die unter Nutzung neu erschlossener literaler Quellentypen Informationen über die Dialektstrukturen zurückliegender Epochen erarbeitete (vgl. Schützeichel 1976, Kleiber 1994).

War die Dialektologie im 19. Jh. insofern modern, als sie ihre Fragestellungen in den Kontext des damals vorherrschenden sprachwissenschaftlichen Paradigmas stellte, so zeigte sich diese Orientierung auf die jeweils aktuellen sprachtheoretischen Konzepte auch in späteren Phasen der Wissenschaftsgeschichte. Beispielsweise fand der Strukturalismus, der sich ausgehend von der Saussure-Rezeption im beginnenden 20. Jh. vehement durchsetzte, sehr bald Eingang in die dialektologische Datenanalyse. Hierbei kann daran erinnert werden, daß mit Wintelers Ortsgrammatik schon zu einem sehr frühen Zeitpunkt strukturalistische Methoden in der Dialektbeschreibung zum Einsatz kamen. Im 20. Jh. wurden strukturalistische Verfahrensweisen nun auch erfolgreich eingesetzt, um intern-linguistische Erklärungen für einmal dialektale Raumstrukturen (vgl. Weinreich 1954, Moulton 1963, Goossens 1969, Jongen 1982) oder dialektale Veränderungsprozesse andeuten zu können. Der klassisch-monodimensionalen Dialektologie sind die strukturalistischen Ansätze trotzdem zuzuordnen, da sie zwar in systemischer Sicht eine Datenverknüpfung leisten, jedoch die Datengrundlage nach wie vor dieselbe ist, nämlich der monodimensional, allein diatopisch variierende Basisdialekt.

Eine spätere generative Dialektologie nutzte das Beschreibungsinventar der generativen Grammatik, um diatopisch kontrastierende dialektale Sprachsysteme mittels je unterschiedlicher Regelbestände oder Regelanwendungen auf bestimmte Bezugssysteme abbilden zu können. Dialektverschiedenheit konnte innerhalb einer so verfahrenden Dialektologie als Differenz von Ersetzungsregeln verstanden werden, Dialektkarten wurden zu Regelkarten (vgl. Veith 1972, 1982).

Ein 'Forschungsabschluß' der klassisch-monodimensionalen Dialektologie ist insofern trotz der hohen Dichte der erarbeiteten Ergebnisse nicht unbedingt zu erwarten, da auch in der Zukunft innovative sprachwissenschaftliche Beschreibungsansätze es notwendig machen werden, neue Fragen an monodimensional erhobene dialektale Daten zu stellen. Zum anderen existieren auch heute noch gewisse 'weiße Flecken' in der Kenntnis der alten Basisdialekte, die mit klassisch-monodimensionalen Methoden auszufüllen sind.

Andererseits zeigt es sich, daß eine Fülle aktueller Forschungsfragen im Rahmen der klassisch-monodimensionalen Dialektologie nicht mehr angegangen werden können, die bestimmt war durch das konstitutive Merkmal der monodimensional-arealen Datenerhebung, begleitet unter Umständen durch spätere korrelationistisch-mehrdimensionale Dateninterpretation. Diese traditionelle Verfahrensweise scheint in der Gegenwart nicht mehr hinzureichen, und zwar erstens aus Gründen der aktuellen Dynamik des Objektbereiches der Dialektologie, zweitens aus Gründen grundsätzlich veränderter wissenschaftlicher Fragestellungen, die neue Formen der Datengewinnung notwendig machen.

Der Objektbereich der Dialektologie war nie durch Konstanz oder Homogenität geprägt, sondern stets durch Dynamik und Heterogenität. Die methodologische Homogenisierung des Dialektes und seine Reduktion auf die Diatopik war stets eine möglicherweise heuristisch sinnvolle dialektologische Fiktion. Unter den Bedingungen der Gegenwart jedoch ist die Dynamik der Dialekte in einer Weise ausgeprägt, daß die vertraute Fiktion ihre heuristische Leistung eingebüßt hat: In Teilgebieten des Deutschen, besonders im Niederdeutschen, im Ruhrgebiet und in bestimmten Städten, beginnt der traditionelle Gegenstand der Dialektologie, d. h. der standardfernste Basisdialekt, sich aufzulösen oder er ist bereits aufgelöst. Er wird ersetzt durch ein situativ variierendes, durchaus auch areal differierendes Variationsspektrum, das angemessen durch den Begriff 'Substandard' angesprochen worden ist (vgl. Bellmann 1983; Holtus & Radtke 1986 ff.).

Zum zweiten sieht sich die Sprachwissenschaft der Gegenwart auch mit veränderten theoretischen Fragestellungen konfrontiert, die eine bloße Fortschreibung monodimensional-diatopischer Untersuchungsdesigns als unangemessen erscheinen lassen. Spätestens seit der sogenannten 'kommunikativ-pragmatischen Wende' in der Sprachwissenschaft der siebziger Jahre dieses Jahrhunderts erscheint es interessant und geboten, die Beschreibung nicht mehr auf methodologisch wohlabgegrenzte Sprachsysteme zu beschränken, sondern diejenigen Strukturen zu untersuchen, die den variativen Sprachgebrauch interagierender Menschen bestimmen. Was die Dialektologie angeht, so deutet sich als Konsequenz aus beiden Einflußfaktoren an, eine klassisch-monodimensionale Dialektologie abzulösen bzw. zu ergänzen durch eine pluridimensionale Dialektologie, die schon im Moment der Datenerhebung mehrdimensional vorgeht und sich insofern einen Weg zum variierenden Sprachgebrauch der Dialektsprecher und darüber hinaus auch zu den Veränderungstendenzen des Dialektes erschließt.

6. Ansätze zu einer pluridimensionalen Dialektologie im zwanzigsten Jahrhundert

Ansätze zu pluridimensionalen Verfahrensweisen in der Dialektologie gab es, wie zu Beginn gezeigt, schon früh; sie wurden dann aber durch eine sich durchsetzende Monodimensionalität verdrängt, die zum bestimmenden Forschungsparadigma wurde. Pluridimensionale Fragestellungen werden innerhalb dieses von der Marburger Methodologie bestimmten Paradigmas eher am Rande diskutiert (vgl. Kuhn 1934, von Polenz 1960, Hildebrandt 1968; vgl. hierzu Mattheier 1980; Bellmann 1986: 31–42). Auch von außerhalb, beispielsweise von Forschern der fortschrittlichen Wiener (vgl. Pfalz 1928; Wiesinger 1983) oder der Württembergischen (vgl. Ruoff 1982; Auer 1993: 13–18) dialektologischen Schule, werden früh pluridimensionale Ansätze verfolgt. Aber erst in jüngerer Zeit, beeinflußt durch kommunikativ-pragmatische Fragestellungen in der Sprachwissenschaft allgemein, begann die Dialektologie, die Dynamik ihres Gegenstandes auch methodologisch ernst zu nehmen und die Fixierung auf den jeweils tiefsten Dialekt zu überwinden. Der Dialektwandel und das gesamte Spektrum arealer Sprachvariation zwischen Standardsprache und tiefstem Dialekt wird so zum zentralen Forschungsgegenstand. Solche Ansätze belegen, daß es sich bei der Dialektologie keineswegs um eine wissenschaftsgeschichtlich überholte Disziplin handelt, sondern daß eine Dialektologie, die das gesamte Spektrum der Sprachvariation zwischen den Polen Basisdialekt und Standardsprache in den Blick nimmt und die Dynamik des Gegenstandes zur Forschungsaufgabe macht, eine Disziplin ist, die nicht nur einen sprecher- und hörerseitig höchst relevanten Sektor des Gegenwartsdeutschen behandelt, sondern die angesichts des gewaltigen Aufgabenfeldes erst am Anfang steht.

Das Hauptproblem einer pluridimensionalen Dialektologie stellt sich − wie schon für Wenker und Gilliéron im 19. Jh. − als methodologisches und forschungspraktisches dar: Das Gesamtspektrum der Dialekt/Standard-Variation, das die verschiedensten sozial definierten Sprechergruppen aus den verschiedensten Spracharealen in den unterschiedlichsten Sprechsituationen umfaßt, läßt sich für das gesamte deutsche Spracharal mit traditionellen dialektologischen Methoden der Sprachdatenerhebung nicht erfassen. Eine im Entstehen begriffene pluridimensionale Dialektologie ist deshalb darauf angewiesen, entweder nur Teilspektren der Dialekt/Standard-Variation exemplarisch zu beschreiben, oder aber das Gesamtspektrum mit neuen Methoden in den Blick zu nehmen.

Den zweiten Weg, das Gesamtspektrum mit neuen Methoden zu erforschen, gehen verschiedene Ansätze, die subjektive Daten erheben, also Einschätzungen der je eigenen Sprachverwendung durch die Informanten selbst. Besonders Arbeiten, die in Teilarealen oder auf das Gesamtareal bezogen zu einem deutschen Dialektzensus beitragen, sind hier anzuführen. Zwar müssen solche subjektiven Daten im Vergleich zur direkten Beobachtung des Sprachverhaltens durch den Forscher immer unter dem Vorbehalt gesehen werden, daß die subjektiven Einschätzungen das tatsächliche Sprachverhalten nicht unmittelbar widerspiegeln. Andererseits können − bei sorgsamer Interpretation − auf diese Weise Daten zum variativen Sprachverhalten gewonnen werden, die auf andere Weise nicht ermittelbar wären. Die vorliegenden Analysen subjektiver Daten haben jedenfalls zukunftsweisende Ergebnisse erbracht, so daß auch von den weiteren Bestrebungen um einen deutschen Dialektzensus aufschlußreiche Resultate zu erhoffen sind (vgl. Stellmacher 1987, 1995; Friebertshäuser & Dingeldein 1989, Dingeldein 1994, Mattheier 1994).

Die Erhebung objektiver Daten zum Variationsspektrum muß sich hingegen auf Teilaspekte beschränken. Als sehr ergiebig hat sich hier − in gewisser Anlehnung an die Tradition der Dialektgrammatik − der Verzicht auf die diatopische Variationsdimension erwiesen. Syntopisch angelegte Arbeiten, die ihren Blick auf lokale Variationsspektren richten, haben hier gezeigt, daß vertiefende Einblicke in die kommunikative Nutzung des Dialekt/Standard-Kontinuums durch die Sprecher möglich sind. Besonders die Forschungen zur Sprachvariation in ländlichen Gemeinden, aber auch die neuere Stadtsprachenforschung haben sich hier als ergiebig gezeigt (vgl. z. B. Besch 1981, 1983; Schlobinski 1987, Frank-Cyrus 1991, Macha 1991, Auburger 1993, Lausberg 1993, Kallmeyer 1994, Steiner 1994, Davies 1995; Keim 1995, Hofer 1997).

Soll hingegen bei pluridimensionalen Ansätzen die Diatopik berücksichtigt werden, so ist es unabdingbar, die areale Kontrastierung zu beschränken, indem nur Teilareale untersucht werden, nicht alle Teilgegenstände der Sprache in den Blick genommen werden oder die Untersuchung auf wenige variative Register beschränkt wird. Einige neuere Sprachatlasprojekte belegen hier, daß es durchaus mit Gewinn möglich ist, pluridimensional zu verfahren, d. h. gleichzeitig mit der diatopischen Dimension auch weitere, z. B. die soziale oder die situative Dimension, zu erfassen. Solche Versuche wurden und werden beispielsweise unternommen in Projekten wie dem Atlas zur Wortgeographie der städtischen Alltagssprache in Hessen (vgl. Friebertshäuser & Dingeldein 1988), dem Atlas zur regional gefärbten Standardsprache (vgl. König 1989), dem Sprachatlas von Oberösterreich (vgl. Scheuringer 1992), dem Mittelrheinischen Sprachatlas (vgl. Bellmann 1994; Bellmann et al. 1994 ff.) oder dem Sprachatlas vom Bayerisch Schwaben (vgl. König 1997). Es zeigt sich, daß sich mit der integrierten Untersuchung der diatopischen und weiterer Dimensionen der rezenten Sprachvariation auch die Wandlungstendenzen, denen die Dialekte der Gegenwart unterliegen, untersuchen lassen. Die Dialektologie hat sich also im ausgehenden 20. Jh. mit einer methodologischen Neuorientierung Zugänge zu einem Forschungsfeld erschlossen, dessen Dimensionen bis jetzt noch kaum abgesteckt sind. Die vorliegenden Ergebnisse ermutigen jedoch dazu, auf diesem Wege weiterzugehen.

(Mit Jürgen Erich Schmidt, Marburg, wurde der hier vertretene wissenschaftshistorische Ansatz intensiv diskutiert, wofür ich an dieser Stelle ausdrücklich danken möchte.)

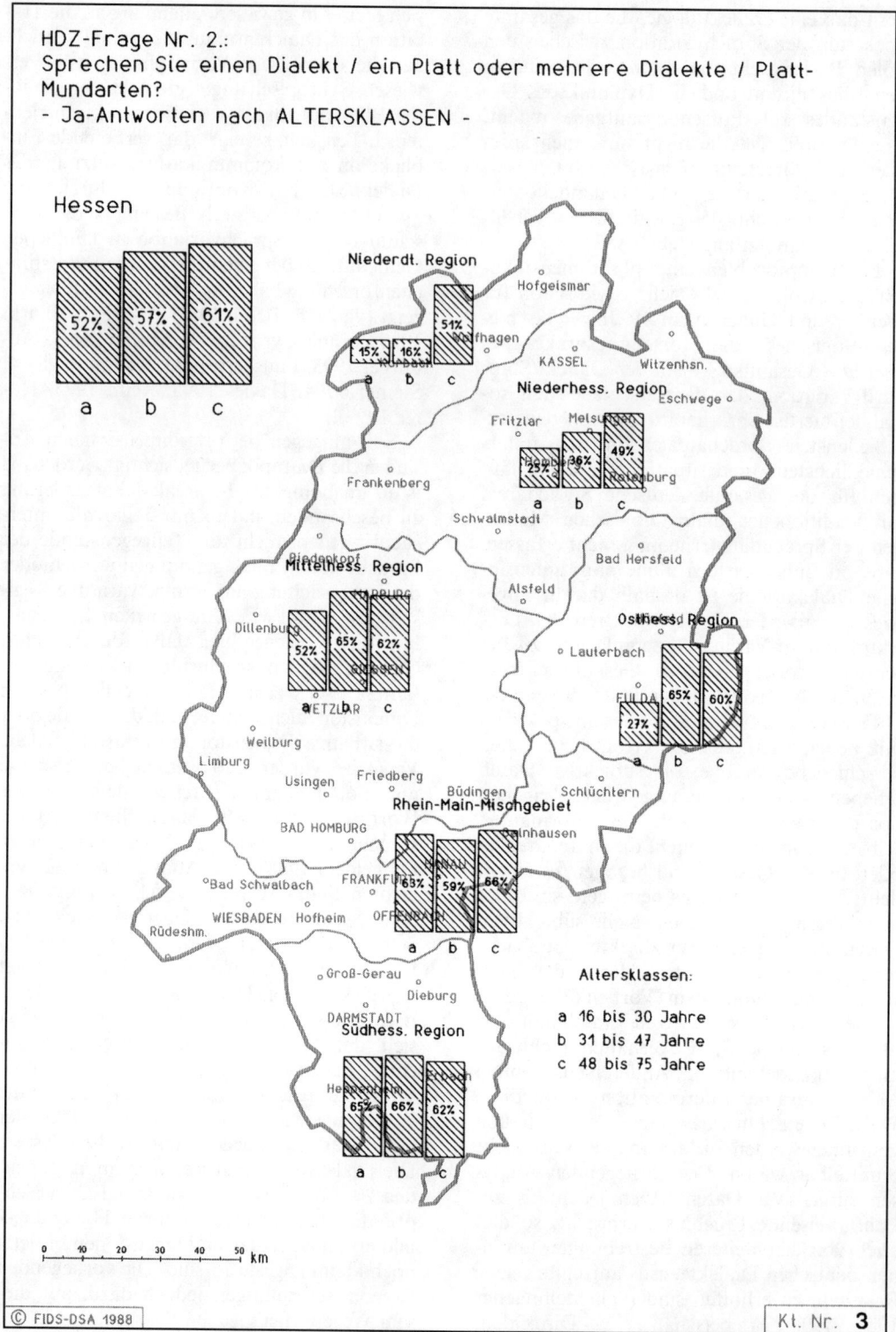

Abb. 182.4: Hessischer Dialektzensus, Karte 3 (Friebertshäuser & Dingeldein 1989).

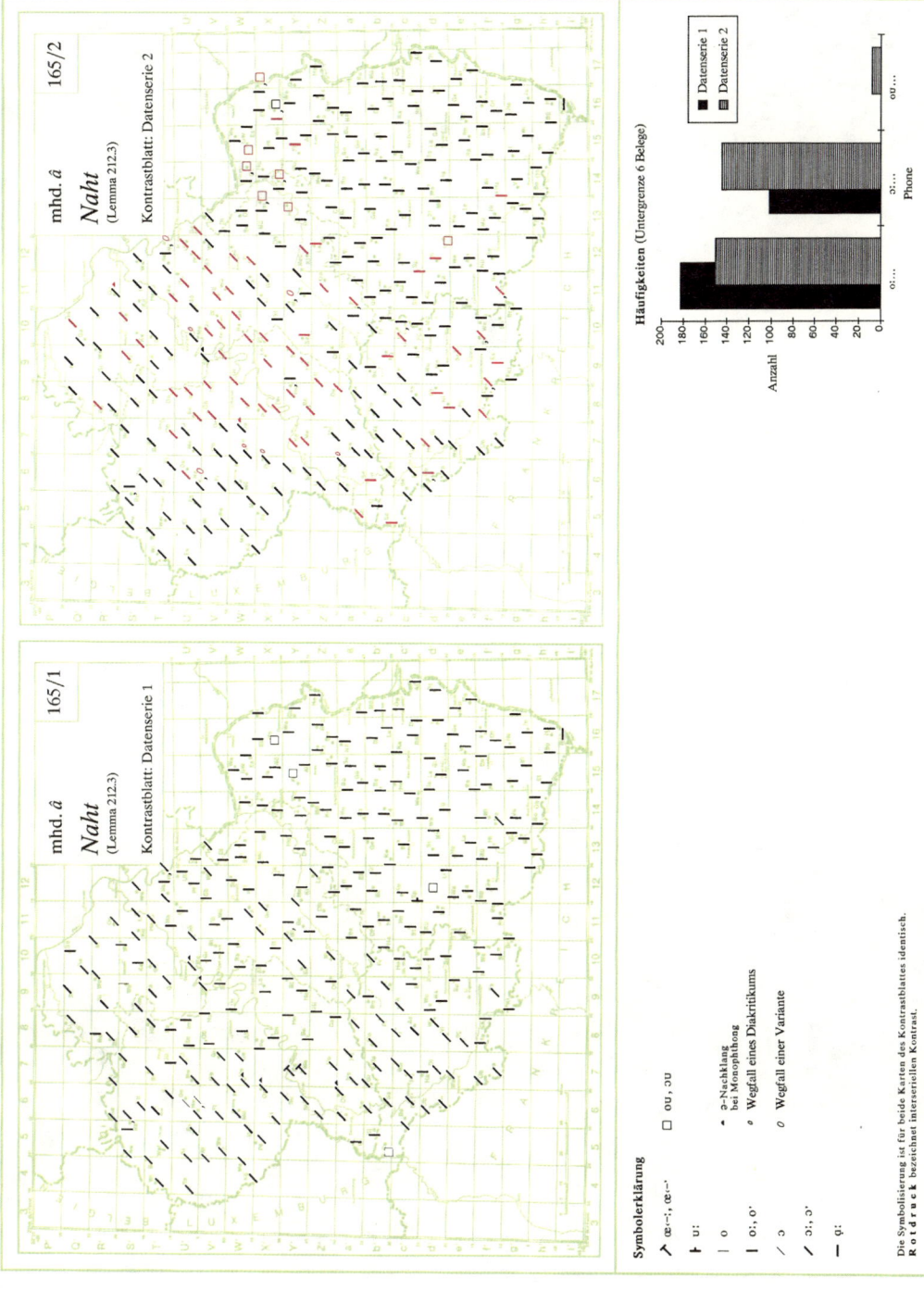

Abb. 182.5: Mittelrheinischer Sprachatlas, Karte 165/1–2 *Naht* (Bellmann et al. 1994–2000, Bd. 2).

7. Bibliographie

Alinei, Mario. 1980. "Dialect: A dialectical approach". *Dialekt und Dialektologie* hg. von Joachim Göschel et al., 11–42. Wiesbaden: Steiner.

Auer, Peter. 1993. "Zweidimensionale Modelle für die Analyse von Standard/Dialekt-Variation und ihre Vorläufer in der deutschen Dialektologie. Ein Beitrag zur historischen Kontinuität". *Verhandlungen des internationalen Dialektologenkongresses. Bamberg, 29. 7.–4. 8. 1990. Bd. II: Historische Dialektologie und Sprachwandel. Sprachatlanten und Wörterbücher* hg. von Wolfgang Viereck, 12–22. Stuttgart: Steiner.

Atlas linguistique de la France. Publié par Jules Gilliéron & Edmond Edmont. 10 Lieferungen. 1902–20. Paris: Champion. (ALF).

Aubin, Hermann et al. 1926. *Kulturströmungen und Kulturprovinzen in den Rheinlanden: Geschichte, Sprache, Volkskunde.* Bonn: Inst. für geschichtliche Landeskunde, Univ. Bonn.

Auburger, Leopold. 1993. *Sprachvarianten und ihr Status in den Sprachsystemen.* Hildesheim: Olms.

Bach, Adolf. 1969 [1950]. *Deutsche Mundartforschung. Ihre Wege, Ergebnisse und Aufgaben.* 3. Aufl. Heidelberg: Winter.

Bellmann, Günter. 1983. "Probleme des Substandards im Deutschen". *Aspekte der Dialekttheorie* hg. von Klaus J. Mattheier, 105–130. Tübingen: Niemeyer.

–. 1985. "Substandard als Regionalsprache". *Germanistik – Forschungsstand und Perspektiven: Vorträge des Deutschen Germanistentages 1984*, 1. Teil, hg. von Georg Stötzel, 211–218. Berlin & New York: de Gruyter.

–. 1986. "Zweidimensionale Dialektologie". *Beiträge zur Dialektologie am Mittelrhein* hg. von G. Bellmann, 1–55. Stuttgart: Steiner.

–. 1994. *Einführung in den Mittelrheinischen Sprachatlas.* Tübingen: Niemeyer.

–, Joachim Herrgen & Jürgen Erich Schmidt. 1994–99. *Mittelrheinischer Sprachatlas (MRhSA).* Bde. 1–4. Tübingen: Niemeyer.

Besch, Werner, Hg. 1981, 1983. *Sprachverhalten in ländlichen Gemeinden: Forschungsbericht Erp-Projekt. Bd. I: Ansätze zur Theorie und Methode. Bd. II: Dialekt und Standardsprache im Sprecherurteil.* Berlin: Schmidt.

–. 1983. "Dialekt, Schreibdialekt, Schriftsprache, Standardsprache. Exemplarische Skizze ihrer historischen Ausprägung im Deutschen". Besch et al. 1983.961–990.

–, Ulrich Knoop, Wolfgang Putschke & Herbert Ernst Wiegand, Hg. 1982, 1983. *Dialektologie: Ein Handbuch zur deutschen und allgemeinen Dialektforschung.* 2 Bde. Berlin & New York: de Gruyter.

Bremer, Otto. 1895. *Beiträge zur Geographie der deutschen Mundarten in Form einer Kritik von Wenkers Sprachatlas des deutschen Reichs.* Leipzig: Breitkopf & Härtel.

Brunner, Richard J. 1971. *Johann Andreas Schmeller. Sprachwissenschaftler und Philologe.* Innsbruck: Institut für Vergleichende Sprachwissenschaft der Universität Innsbruck.

Chambers, J. K. & Peter Trudgill. 1990 [1981]. *Dialectology.* 2. Aufl. Cambridge: Cambridge Univ. Press.

Christen, Helen. 1997. "Koiné-Tendenzen im Schweizerdeutschen?". *Varietäten des Deutschen: Regional- und Umgangssprachen* hg. von Gerhard Stickel, 346–363. Berlin & New York: de Gruyter.

Cornelissen, Georg. 1992. "Zur Erforschung des 'Sprachwandels im Dialekt von Krefeld'". *Rheinische Vierteljahrsblätter* 56.338–345.

Dähnert, Johann Carl. 1781. *Platt-Deutsches Wörter-Buch nach der alten und neuen Pommerschen und Rügischen Mundart.* Stralsund: Struck.

Davies, Winifred V. 1995. *Linguistic Variation and Language Attitudes in Mannheim-Neckarau.* Stuttgart: Steiner.

Debus, Friedhelm. 1983. "Deutsche Dialektgebiete in älterer Zeit: Probleme und Ergebnisse ihrer Rekonstruktion". Besch et al. 1983.930–960.

Deutscher Sprachatlas auf Grund des Sprachatlas des deutschen Reichs. 1927–56. Von Georg Wenker, begonnen v. Ferdinand Wrede, fortgesetzt v. Walther Mitzka u. Bernhard Martin. Marburg: Elwert. (DSA.)

Deutscher Wortatlas. 1951–80. Von Walther Mitzka. (Bd. 5ff. von Walther Mitzka und Ludwig Erich Schmitt, Bde. 21 u. 22 hg. v. Reiner Hildebrandt.) Gießen: Schmitz. (DWA.)

Dingeldein, Heinrich J. 1991. *Studien zur Wortgeographie der städtischen Alltagssprache in Hessen. Areale, stratische und diachron-kontrastive Analysen.* Tübingen: Francke.

–. 1994. "Befragungen zum Sprachgebrauch als Problem der Dialektologie". Mattheier & Wiesinger 1994.393–411.

Dünninger, Josef. 1954. "Johann Ludwig Prasch und sein *Glossarium Bavaricum* von 1689". *Bayerisches Jahrbuch für Volkskunde*, 185–190.

Eichhoff, Jürgen. 1977–78. *Wortatlas der deutschen Umgangssprachen.* 2 Bde. Bern & München: Francke.

Fischer, Hermann. 1895. *Geographie der schwäbischen Mundart.* Tübingen: Laupp.

Frank-Cyrus, Karin M. 1991. *Subjektive Varietätenwahl in pfälzischen Dorfgemeinschaften unter besonderer Berücksichtigung geschlechtsspezifischer Dialektverwendung.* Frankfurt/M.: Haag & Herchen.

Friebertshäuser, Hans. 1983. "Die großlandschaftlichen Wörterbücher der deutschen Dialekte. Areale und lexikologische Beschreibung". Besch et al. 1983.1283−1295.

− & Heinrich J. Dingeldein. 1988. *Wortgeographie der städtischen Alltagssprache in Hessen.* Graphisch-computative Bearbeitung: Harald Händler und Wolfgang Putschke. Tübingen: Francke.

−. 1989. *Hessischer Dialektzensus. Statistischer Atlas zum Sprachgebrauch.* Tübingen: Francke.

Frings, Theodor. 1956. *Sprache und Geschichte.* 3 Bde. Halle/Saale: Niemeyer.

−. 1957. *Grundlegung einer Geschichte der deutschen Sprache.* 3. Aufl. Halle/Saale: Niemeyer.

Gilliéron, Jules & Mario Roques. 1912. *Études de géographie linguistique.* Paris: Champion.

Goebl, Hans. 1994. "Dialektometrie und Dialektgeographie. Ergebnisse und Desiderate". Mattheier & Wiesinger 1994.171−191.

Goossens, Jan. 1969. *Strukturelle Sprachgeographie. Eine Einführung in Methodik und Ergebnisse.* Heidelberg: Winter.

−. 1977. *Deutsche Dialektologie.* Mit 13 Karten und 4 Abbildungen. Berlin & New York: de Gruyter.

Götz, Ursula. 1995. "Regionale grammatische Varianten des Standarddeutschen". *Sprachwissenschaft* 20.222−238.

Grimm, Jacob. 1819−37. *Deutsche Grammatik.* 4 Bde. Göttingen: Dieterich.

Grober-Glück, Gerda. 1982. "Die Leistungen der kulturmorphologischen Betrachtungsweise im Rahmen dialektgeographischer Interpretationsverfahren". Besch et al. 1982.92−113.

Grosse, Rudolf. 1993. "Beiträge der Dialektgeographie zur Sprachgeschichtsschreibung". *Verhandlungen des internationalen Dialektologenkongresses.* Bamberg, 29. 7.−4. 8. 1990 hg. von Wolfgang Viereck. Bd. II: *Historische Dialektologie und Sprachwandel. Sprachatlanten und Wörterbücher,* 98−107. Stuttgart: Steiner.

Haag, Karl. 1898. *Die Mundarten des oberen Nekkar- und Donaulandes. (Schwäbisch-alemannisches Grenzgebiet: Baarmundarten.)* Reutlingen: Hutzler.

Haas, Walter. 1981. *Das Wörterbuch der schweizerdeutschen Sprache. Versuch über eine nationale Institution.* Hg. von der Redaktion des Schweizerdeutschen Wörterbuchs. Frauenfeld: Huber.

−. 1992. "Mundart und Standardsprache in der deutschen Schweiz". *Dialect and Standard Language in the English, Dutch, German and Norwegian Language Areas* hg. von J. A. van Leuvensteijn & J. B. Berns, 312−336. Amsterdam: North-Holland.

−, Hg. 1994a. *Provinzialwörter. Deutsche Idiotismensammlungen des 18. Jahrhunderts.* Berlin & New York: de Gruyter.

−. 1994b. "'Die Jagd auf Provinzial-Wörter'. Die Anfänge der wissenschaftlichen Beschäftigung mit den deutschen Mundarten im 17. und 18. Jahrhundert". Mattheier & Wiesinger 1994.329−365.

Hagen, Anton M. & Tom Boves. 1994. "Soziophonetik und Dialektologie". Mattheier & Wiesinger 1994.443−455.

Henzen, Walter. 1954. *Schriftsprache und Mundarten. Ein Überblick über ihr Verhältnis und ihre Zwischenstufen im Deutschen.* 2. Aufl. Bern: Francke.

Herder, Johann Gottfried. 1965 [1772]. *Abhandlung über den Ursprung der Sprache.* Johann Gottfried Herder, Sprachphilosophische Schriften. Aus dem Gesamtwerk ausgewählt, mit einer Einleitung, Anmerkungen und Registern versehen von Erich Heintel. 2. Aufl., 3−87. Hamburg: Meiner.

Herrgen, Joachim. 1994. "Kontrastive Dialektkartographie". Mattheier & Wiesinger 1994.131−163.

− & Jürgen Erich Schmidt. 1985. "Systemkontrast und Hörerurteil. Zwei Dialektalitätsbegriffe und die ihnen entsprechenden Meßverfahren". *Zeitschrift für Dialektologie und Linguistik* 52.20−42.

Hildebrandt, Reiner. 1968. "Der Deutsche Wortatlas als Forschungsmittel der Sprachsoziologie". *Wortgeographie und Gesellschaft: Festgabe für Ludwig Erich Schmitt* hg. von Walther Mitzka, 149−169. Berlin: de Gruyter.

Hofer, Lorenz. 1997. *Sprachwandel im städtischen Dialektrepertoire: Eine variationslinguistische Untersuchung am Beispiel des Baseldeutschen.* Tübingen & Basel: Francke.

Holtus, Günter & Edgar Radtke, Hg. 1986. *Sprachlicher Substandard.* Tübingen: Niemeyer.

Hotzenköcherle, Rudolf. 1962. *Einführung in den Sprachatlas der deutschen Schweiz.* Bern: Francke.

Humboldt, Wilhelm von. 1836. *Über die Verschiedenheit des menschlichen Sprachbaues und ihren Einfluß auf die geistige Entwicklung des Menschengeschlechts.* Berlin: Akademie der Wissenschaften. (Nachdruck, Bonn: Dümmler, 1960.)

Jendreieck, Helmut. 1975. *Hegel und Jacob Grimm. Ein Beitrag zur Geschichte der Wissenschaftstheorie.* Berlin: Schmidt.

Jongen, René. 1982. "Theoriebildung der strukturellen Dialektologie". Besch et al. 1982.248−277.

Kallmeyer, Werner, Hg. 1994. *Kommunikation in der Stadt. Teil 1: Exemplarische Analysen des Sprachverhaltens in Mannheim.* Berlin & New York: de Gruyter.

Karch, Dieter. 1975. *Mannheim, Umgangssprache.* Tübingen: Niemeyer.

Keim, Inken. 1995. *Kommunikative Stilistik einer sozialen Welt "kleiner Leute" in der Mannheimer Innenstadt.* Mit zwei Beiträgen von Werner Kallmeyer. Berlin & New York: de Gruyter.

Kleiber, Wolfgang. 1994. "Historische Dialektologie unter besonderer Berücksichtigung der historischen Dialektkartographie". Mattheier & Wiesinger 1994.259–322.

Kleiner Deutscher Sprachatlas. 1984 ff. Im Auftrag des Forschungsinstituts für deutsche Sprache – Deutscher Sprachatlas – Marburg/Lahn. Dialektologisch bearb. von Werner H. Veith. Computativ bearb. von Wolfgang Putschke. Tübingen: Niemeyer.

Knoop, Ulrich. 1982. "Das Interesse an den Mundarten und die Grundlegung der Dialektologie". Besch et al. 1982.1–23.

– et al. 1982. "Die Marburger Schule: Entstehung und frühe Entwicklung der Dialektgeographie". Besch et al. 1982.38–92.

König, Werner. 1989. *Atlas zur Aussprache des Schriftdeutschen in der Bundesrepublik Deutschland.* 2 Bde. Ismaning: Hueber.

–. 1997. *Sprachatlas von Bayerisch-Schwaben.* Bd. I: *Einführung.* Kartographie: Sabine Ihle. Exploration: Edith Funk et al. Heidelberg: Winter.

Kuhn, Hans. 1934. "Spaltung und Ausgleich in der Entwicklung der deutschen Mundarten in den 6 ersten Lieferungen des Deutschen Sprachatlasses". *Von Wenker zu Wrede: Dem Herausgeber des "Deutschen Sprachatlas" Ferdinand Wrede zum 70. Geburtstag von seinen Marburger Mitarbeitern,* 38–54. Marburg: Elwert.

Kunze, Konrad. 1982. "Der 'Historische Südwestdeutsche Sprachatlas' als Muster historischer Dialektgeographie". Besch et al. 1982.169–177.

Lausberg, Helmut. 1993. *Situative und individuelle Sprachvariation im Rheinland. Variablenbezogene Untersuchung anhand von Tonbandaufnahmen aus Erftstadt-Erp.* Köln: Böhlau.

Lerchner, Gotthard et al. Hg. 1995. *Chronologische, areale und situative Varietäten des Deutschen in der Sprachhistoriographie.* Festschrift für Rudolf Große. Frankfurt/M.: Lang.

Löffler, Heinrich. 1990. *Probleme der Dialektologie. Eine Einführung.* 3. Aufl. Darmstadt: Wissenschaftliche Buchgesellschaft.

–. 1994. "Zukunftsperspektiven der historischen Sprachgeographie". Mattheier & Wiesinger 1994. 323–328.

Macha, Jürgen. 1991. *Der flexible Sprecher. Untersuchungen zu Sprache und Sprachbewußtsein rheinischer Handwerksmeister.* Köln: Böhlau.

–. 1992. "Dialekt und Standardsprache. Ausprägung und Gebrauch bei rheinisch-ripuarischen Sprechern". *Dialect and Standard Language in the English, Dutch, German and Norwegian Language Areas* hg. von J. A. van Leuvensteijn & J. B. Berns, 271–289. Amsterdam: North-Holland.

Martin, Bernhard. 1934. "Georg Wenkers Kampf um seinen Sprachatlas". *Von Wenker zu Wrede:* Dem Herausgeber des "Deutschen Sprachatlas" Ferdinand Wrede zum 70. Geburtstag von seinen Marburger Mitarbeitern, 1–37. Marburg: Elwert.

Mattheier, Klaus J. 1980. *Pragmatik und Soziologie der Dialekte. Einführung in die kommunikative Dialektologie des Deutschen.* Heidelberg: Quelle & Meyer.

–. 1994. "Varietätenzensus. Über die Möglichkeiten, die Verbreitung und Verwendung von Sprachvarietäten in Deutschland festzustellen". Mattheier & Wiesinger 1994.413–442.

–, Hg. 1983. *Aspekte der Dialekttheorie.* Tübingen: Niemeyer.

– & Peter Wiesinger, Hg. 1994. *Dialektologie des Deutschen. Forschungsstand und Entwicklungstendenzen.* Tübingen: Niemeyer.

Menge, Heinz H. 1997. "Noch einmal von vorn? Zur Systematisierung der sprachlichen Variation im Ruhrgebiet". *Sprache und Literatur an der Ruhr* hg. von Konrad Ehlich et al. Redaktion: Stephan Schlickau, 39–55. 2. Aufl. Essen: Klartext Verlag.

Mihm, Arend. 1997. "Die Realität des Ruhrdeutschen – soziale Funktion und sozialer Ort einer Gebietssprache." *Ebda.*, 19–38. 2. Aufl.

Moulton, William. 1963. "Phonologie und Dialekteinteilung". *Sprachleben der Schweiz: Sprachwissenschaft, Namenforschung, Volkskunde. Festschrift für Rudolf Hotzenköcherle* hg. von Paul Zinsli et al., 75–86. Bern: Francke.

Niebaum, Hermann. 1979. "Deutsche Dialektwörterbücher". *Die deutsche Sprache* 7.345–373.

–. 1994. "Lexikalische Dialektbeschreibung". Mattheier & Wiesinger 1994.77–91.

– Jürgen Macha. 1999. *Einführung in die Dialektologie des Deutschen.* Tübingen: Niemeyer.

Paul, Hermann. 1920 [1880]. *Prinzipien der Sprachgeschichte.* 5. Aufl. Halle/Saale: Niemeyer.

Pfalz, Anton. 1928. "Formenwucher". *Festschrift Max H. Jellinek zum 29. Mai 1928 dargebracht,* 97–104. Wien & Leipzig: Österreichischer Bundesverlag für Unterricht, Wissenschaft und Kunst. (Nachdruck in: *Die Wiener dialektologische Schule: Grundsätzliche Studien aus 70 Jahren Forschung* hg. von Peter Wiesinger, 209–216. Wien: Halosar, 1983.)

Polenz, Peter von. 1960. "Mundart, Umgangssprache und Hochsprache am Beispiel der mehrschichtigen Wortkarte 'voriges Jahr'". *Hessische Blätter für Volkskunde* 51/52.224–234.

Prasch, Johann Ludwig. 1689. *Dissertatio altera, de origine germanica latinae, una cum onomastico germanico-latino, aliquatenus suppletur & explicatur, adeoque via aperitur novo Etymologico. Accedit glossarium bavaricum.* Ratisbonae: Emmerich.

Protze, Helmut. 1969, 1970. "Die deutschen Mundarten". *Die deutsche Sprache.* 2 Bde. hg. von Erhard Agricola et al., 312–422. Leipzig: VEB Bibliographisches Institut.

Putschke, Wolfgang. 1982. "Theoriebildung der 'klassischen' Dialektologie". Besch et al. 1982. 232–247.

–. 1984. "Die Arbeiten der Junggrammatiker und ihr Beitrag zur Sprachgeschichtsforschung". *Sprachgeschichte: Ein Handbuch zur Geschichte der deutschen Sprache und ihrer Erforschung* hg. von Werner Besch et al. 1. Halbbd., 331–347. Berlin & New York: de Gruyter.

Raumer, Rudolf von. 1857. "Mundartliche Dichtungen und Sprachproben. Offener Brief an den Herausgeber der Zeitschrift für die deutschen Mundarten". *Die deutschen Mundarten* 4.390–394.

–. 1870. *Geschichte der Germanischen Philologie, vorzugsweise in Deutschland.* München: Oldenbourg.

Reiffenstein, Ingo. 1982. "Das phonetische Beschreibungsprinzip als Ergebnis junggrammatischer und dialektologischer Forschungsarbeiten". Besch et al. 1982.23–38.

Richey, Michael. 1754. *Idioticon Hamburgense oder Wörterbuch zur Erklärung der eigenen, in und um Hamburg gebräuchlichen, Nieder-Sächsischen Mund-Art. Jetzo vielfältig vermehret, und mit Anmerckungen und Zusätzen Zweener berühmten Männer, nebst einem Vierfachen Anhange, ausgefertiget.* Hamburg: Conrad König.

Ruf, Paul, Hg. 1954–57. *Johann Andreas Schmeller. Tagebücher 1801–1852.* 3 Bde. München: Beck.

Ruoff, Arno. 1982. "Die Forschungstätigkeit der Württembergischen Schule als Beispiel regionaler Dialektologie". Besch et al. 1982.127–144.

Scheuringer, Hermann. 1992. "Der Sprachatlas von Oberösterreich (SAO): Ein neuer Dialektatlas im Zentrum des bairischen Raumes". *Zeitschrift für Dialektologie und Linguistik* 59.257–274.

Scheutz, Hannes & Peter Haudum. 1982. "Theorieansätze einer kommunikativen Dialektologie". Besch et al. 1982.295–315.

Schirmunski, Viktor M. 1962. *Deutsche Mundartkunde: Vergleichende Laut- und Formenlehre der deutschen Mundarten.* Aus dem Russischen übersetzt und wissenschaftlich bearbeitet von Wolfgang Fleischer. Berlin: Akademie-Verlag.

Schlobinski, Peter. 1987. *Stadtsprache Berlin. Eine soziolinguistische Untersuchung.* Berlin & New York: de Gruyter.

Schmeller, Johann Andreas. 1886 [1816]. "Sprache der Baiern. Gedanken über ein zu bearbeitendes bairisches Idiotikon, oder Sammlung des Eigenthümlichen der baierischen Volkssprache". *An der Wiege der bayerischen Mundart-Grammatik und des bayerischen Wörterbuches* hg. von Ludwig Rockinger, 69–85. München: Wolf. (Neudruck, hg. von Robert Hinderling. Aalen: Scientia, 1985.)

–. 1821. *Die Mundarten Bayerns grammatisch dargestellt* von Joh. Andreas Schmeller. Beygegeben ist eine Sammlung von Mundart-Proben, d. i. kleinen Erzählungen, Gesprächen, Sing-Stücken, figürlichen Redensarten u. dergl. in den verschiedenen Dialekten des Königreichs, nebst einem Kärtchen zur geographischen Uebersicht dieser Dialekte. München: Thienemann; (Neudruck, Wiesbaden: Sändig, 1968.)

–. 1827–37. *Bayerisches Wörterbuch mit urkundlichen Belegen.* 4 Bde. Stuttgart & Tübingen: Cotta'sche Verlagsbuchhandlung. (2. Aufl., bearb. v. Georg Karl Frommann, München: Oldenbourg, 1872–77.)

Schmid, Johann Christoph. 1795. *Versuch eines schwäbischen Idiotikon, oder Sammlung der in verschiedenen schwäbischen Ländern und Städten gebräuchlichen Idiotismmen; mit etymologischen Anmerkungen.* Berlin & Stettin: Nicolai.

Scholten, Beate. 1988. *Standard und städtischer Substandard bei Heranwachsenden im Ruhrgebiet.* Tübingen: Niemeyer.

Schützeichel, Rudolf. 1976. *Die Grundlagen des westlichen Mitteldeutschen: Studien zur historischen Sprachgeographie.* 2. Aufl. Tübingen: Niemeyer.

Sievers, Eduard. 1876. *Grundzüge der Lautphysiologie. Zur Einführung in das Studium der indogermanischen Sprachen.* Leipzig: Breitkopf & Härtel. (ab 2. Aufl. 1881: *Grundzüge der Phonetik.*)

Socin, Adolf. 1888. *Schriftsprache und Dialekte im Deutschen nach Zeugnissen alter und neuer Zeit. Beiträge zur Geschichte der deutschen Sprache.* Heilbronn: Henninger. (Nachdruck, Hildesheim: Olms, 1970.)

Sprach-Atlas der Rheinprovinz nördlich der Mosel sowie des Kreises Siegen. 1878. Nach systematisch aus ca. 1500 Orten gesammelten Material zusammengestellt, entworfen und gezeichnet von Dr. Georg Wenker. Marburg.

Sprachatlas der deutschen Schweiz. 1962 ff. Begründet von Heinrich Baumgartner und Rudolf Hotzenköcherle hg. v. Rudolf Hotzenköcherle. Bern: Francke. (SDS.)

Sprach-Atlas von Nord- und Mitteldeutschland. 1881. Auf Grund von systematisch mit Hilfe der Volksschullehrer gesammeltem Material aus circa 30 000 Orten bearbeitet, entworfen und gezeichnet von Georg Wenker. Abth. I, Lief. 1. Straßburg & London: Trübner.

Stalder, Franz Josef. 1806, 1812. *Versuch eines Schweizerischen Idiotikon mit etymologischen Bemerkungen untermischt. Samt einer Skizze einer Schweizerischen Dialektologie.* 2 Bde. Aarau: Sauerländer.

Steiner, Christiane. 1994. *Sprachvariation in Mainz. Quantitative und qualitative Analysen.* Stuttgart: Steiner.

Stellmacher, Dieter. 1987. *Wer spricht Platt? Zur Lage des Niederdeutschen heute. Eine kurzgefaßte Bestandsaufnahme.* Leer: Schuster.

–. 1995. *Niedersächsischer Dialektzensus: Statistisches zum Sprachgebrauch im Bundesland Niedersachsen.* Stuttgart: Steiner.

—, Hg. 2000. *Dialektologie zwischen Tradition und Neuansätzen: Beiträge der Internationalen Dialektologentagung, 19.–21. Oktober 1998.* Stuttgart: Steiner.

Stickel, Gerhard, Hg. 1997. *Varietäten des Deutschen: Regional- und Umgangssprachen.* Berlin & New York: de Gruyter.

Trümpy, Hans. 1955. *Schweizerdeutsche Sprache und Literatur im 17. und 18. Jahrhundert (auf Grund der gedruckten Quellen).* Basel: Krebs.

Veith, Werner H. 1970. "-Explikative +applikative +komputative Dialektkartographie: Ihre wissenschaftlichen Voraussetzungen und Möglichkeiten in der Phonologie auf der Grundlage der kontrastiv-transformationellen Methode und der automatischen Datenverarbeitung". *Germanistische Linguistik* 4.387–497.

—. 1972. *Intersystemare Phonologie.* Berlin & New York: de Gruyter.

—. 1982. "Theorieansätze einer generativen Dialektologie". Besch et al. 1982.277–295.

—. 1994. "Quantitative Dialektologie. Computerkartographie". Mattheier & Wiesinger 1994.193–244.

—. & Wolfgang Putschke, Hg. 1989. *Sprachatlanten des Deutschen: Laufende Projekte.* Tübingen: Niemeyer.

Viereck, Wolfgang, Hg. 1993–95. *Verhandlungen des internationalen Dialektologenkongresses. Bamberg, 29.7.–4.8.1990.* Bd. II: *Historische Dialektologie und Sprachwandel. Sprachatlanten und Wörterbücher.* Bd. III: *Regionalsprachliche Variation, Umgangs- und Standardsprachen.* Bd. IV: *Soziolinguistische Variation, Bilingualismus, Multilingualismus, Sprachkontakt, Sprachvergleich, Dialektgebrauch und Einstellungen zu Sprechervarietäten.* Stuttgart: Steiner.

Wagener, Peter. 1988. *Untersuchungen zur Methodologie und Methodik der Dialektologie.* Marburg: Elwert.

Wagner, Kurt. 1927. *Deutsche Sprachlandschaften.* Marburg: Elwert.

Wegener, Philipp. 1880. "Über deutsche Dialectforschung". *Zeitschrift für deutsche Philologie* 11.450–480.

Weinreich, Uriel. 1954. "Is a Structural Dialectology Possible?". *Word* 10.388–400.

Wenker, Georg. 1876. *Über die Verschiebung des Stammsilben-Auslauts im Germanischen.* Bonn: Marcus.

—. 1877. *Das rheinische Platt. Den Lehrern des Rheinlandes gewidmet.* Düsseldorf: Selbstverlag.

Werlen, Iwar. 1994. "Neuere Fragestellungen in der Erforschung der Syntax deutscher Dialekte". Mattheier & Wiesinger 1994.49–75.

Wiegand, Herbert Ernst & Gisela Harras. 1971. "Zur wissenschaftshistorischen Einordnung und linguistischen Beurteilung des Deutschen Wortatlas". *Germanistische Linguistik* 1–2.

Wiesinger, Peter. 1970. *Phonetisch-phonologische Untersuchungen zur Vokalentwicklung in den deutschen Dialekten.* Bd. I: *Die Langvokale im Hochdeutschen.* Bd. II: *Die Diphthonge im Hochdeutschen.* Berlin: de Gruyter.

—. 1979. "Johann Andreas Schmeller als Sprachsoziologe". *Linguistic Method. Essays in Honor of Herbert Penzl* hg. von Irmengard Rauch & Gerald F. Carr, 585–599. The Hague: Mouton.

—. 1983a. "Die Einteilung der deutschen Dialekte". Besch et al. 1983.807–900.

—. 1983b. "Die Wiener dialektologische Schule in ihren grundsätzlichen Schriften". *Die Wiener dialektologische Schule: Grundsätzliche Studien aus 70 Jahren Forschung* hg. von Peter Wiesinger, 1–21. Wien: Halosar.

—. 1987. *Bibliographie zur Grammatik der deutschen Dialekte: Laut-, Formen-, Wortbildungs- und Satzlehre 1981 bis 1985 und Nachträge aus früheren Jahren.* Bern: Lang.

—. 1994. "Zum gegenwärtigen Stand der phonetisch-phonologischen Dialektbeschreibung". Mattheier & Wiesinger 1994.3–27.

—. 1997. "Sprachliche Varietäten – Gestern und Heute". *Varietäten des Deutschen. Regional- und Umgangssprachen* hg. von Gerhard Stickel, 9–45. Berlin & New York: de Gruyter.

— & Elisabeth Raffin. 1982. *Bibliographie zur Grammatik der deutschen Dialekte. Laut-, Formen-, Wortbildungs- und Satzlehre 1800 bis 1980.* Unter Mitarbeit von Gertraude Voigt. Bern & Frankfurt/M.: Lang.

Winteler, Jost. 1876. *Die Kerenzer Mundart des Kantons Glarus in ihren Grundzügen dargestellt.* Leipzig & Heidelberg: Winter.

Zender, Matthias. 1982. "Prinzipien und Praxis dialektaler Lexikographie am Beispiel des Rheinischen Wörterbuchs". Besch et al. 1982.113–126.

Zimmermann, Gerhard. 1992. "Das Sächsische: Sprachliche und außersprachliche Einschätzungen der sächsischen Umgangssprache". *Muttersprache* 102.97–113.

Joachim Herrgen, Mainz (Deutschland)

183. The dialectology of Dutch

1. Introduction
2. Forerunners of Dutch dialectology
3. The Romantic period (1830–1879)
4. Dialectgeography in the Aufbau phase (1879–1920)
5. Institutionalization and outstanding dialectologists (1920–1960)
6. Expansion and decline of dialectology (1960–present)
7. Bibliography

1. Introduction

Dutch dialectology can be defined as the research of the dialects that are spoken in the Dutch-speaking language area. This area covers the part of Belgium north of the French-Flemish language boundary and the Netherlands with the exception of Friesland, where Frisian is spoken. Frisian is considered a separate language since it has its own grammar and spelling system. The history of the status of Dutch in the Netherlands is quite different from the one in Belgium. In the Netherlands, Dutch has the official function of the standard language since human memory, whereas in Belgium it has a comparable status only from the very end of the 19th century. Before that time French was the official language. Since 1898 there are, at least on paper, two official languages in Belgium: Dutch and French. In real terms, however, French remained the language of the administration until 1932–1935. From then on it was possible to complete a Dutch education up to the university level.

It goes without saying that when dialects of the same language are spoken in different countries with a different linguistic past, the history of the dialectology in those countries also differs. Therefore, we will deal with the history of Dutch dialectology in the Netherlands and in Belgium separately. The history of dialectology of Dutch will be treated chronologically as much as possible. For each period, we will first deal with the dialectological history in the Netherlands and subsequently with the one in Belgium. We have chosen this order since the evolution of dialectology in the Netherlands proceeds — especially in the beginning — somewhat faster than in Belgium. Five periods in the evolution of Dutch dialectology are distinguished. In Section 2 we deal briefly with the predecessors of dialectological research. Section 3 treats dialectology during the romantic movement (1830–1879). Section 4 shows the beginning of the third period, marked by the first dialect questionnaire that was sent out in the Netherlands (1879), and ending after World War I (1920). Section 5 covers the period 1920–1960, a period in which dialectology becomes institutionalized in both countries and in which several important dialectologists played a leading role. The last section of this article is devoted to the period from 1960 to the present. Until the seventies there was considerable financial support contributing to the launching of many dialect projects. In the eighties funding has, however, become a scarce commodity. Nowadays there is hardly any money available left for dialectological research.

It is not possible to write a history of a scientific discipline without relying heavily on those who did so before. This survey is based largely on the histories of Dutch dialectology written by Van Ginneken (1943), Weijnen (1966: 1–18), Goossens (1977a: 106–160; 1977b), Noordegraaf (1979), Van der Horst (1979), Hagen (1992), and Foolen & Noordegraaf (1996).

2. Forerunners of Dutch dialectology

The interest in dialect phenomena did not appear out of the blue. Dialect variation in the Dutch-speaking language area did not escape notice of many Dutch linguists. We already find remarks on dialect variation in the first orthographies, dictionaries and grammars of Dutch (16th century). Dialect variants do not, however, play a major role in those publications. The authors mention them in relation to the standardization of Dutch. They explicitly point out that those dialect variants do not belong to the standard language (cf. Hagen 1992: 330–331). In the literary production of the 16th and the 17th-century dialect variation is dealt with correspondingly: it is used to characterize simple, funny, or mean persons. Just as elsewhere in Europe, the systematic study of dialects in the Dutch-speaking language area was inspired by Romanticism, a movement that can be seen as a reaction to the hard and fast rules of Classicism. During the Romantic period writers became interested in the unspoiled, the natural, even the miraculous, and dialects were one of the things that could be qualified as such. The first publications on Dutch dialects are, however, a direct outcome of the movement that preceded Romanticism: Classicism. The *Maatschapppij der Nederlandse Letterkunde* (Society of Netherlandic Literature), or the *Maatschappij* for short, was founded in Leiden (the Netherlands) in 1766. The society followed the example of the objectives of the Académie Française and other such academies in Europe. The eleven members were especially intruiged by the academies' contributions to the standardization of spoken languages. In 1773 the Society therefore decided to leave no stone unturned in order to compile a dictionary of the Dutch language. The design was prepared and the members of the Society were called upon to hand over their notes on the vocabulary of Dutch and to collect more words (Van Sterkenburg 1992: 11 – 12). Unfortunately, this undertaking was soon stranded. Only some word-lists were published, but no dictionary. These lists, however, mark the — humble — beginning of the systematic study of dialects in the Dutch-speaking language area, since they contain words of the dialect of Groningen (Halsema 1776; Van Bolhuis 1783).

3. The Romantic period (1830–1875)

3.1. Word-lists

It took more than another half a century before other dialectological studies appeared. At first the dialects were not studied by linguistically skilled persons, but by painstaking laymen, to put it in the words of Goossens (1977a: 106). They studied the linguistic level that seemed to express most clearly a national character and that seemed to them rather easy to describe: the lexicon. Dictionaries of dialects written by laymen began to appear from the end of the 1830s, especially in the Netherlands. Goossens (1977a: 107) gives a survey. The first periodical devoted to the study of dialects, *Taalkundig Magazijn* (1837–1842), appears in the same period. Initially, the purpose of the journal was to collect data for a dictionary of the Dutch language, but again only lists of dialect words were published.

The modest interest for dialects in the last quarter of the 18th century and in the first of the 19th was primarily a Dutch affair. In that period, Dutch-speaking Belgium was totally involved in the struggle against French domination. After the French revolution, French had gained a firm foothold in the Dutch-speaking part of Belgium. Reaction against this influence culminated in the *Vlaamse Beweging* (Flemish Movement). When Dutch became one of the two official languages of Belgium (1830), the *Vlaamse Beweging* tried to make the Belgian speakers of Dutch aware of the important contribution Belgium had made to Dutch language and literature. The founder of the *Vlaamse Beweging*, Jan Frans Willems (1793–1846), started his examples of Belgian Dutch dialects in the first volume of the journal *Belgisch Museum*, in 1837.

The quality of these early dialect word-lists was not very high neither in Belgium or in the Netherlands. In both countries the authors were inspired by romantic sentiments, much more than linguistic accuracy. As a consequence, the collections of dialect words were no more than an array of curiosities. They do not give much insight into the dialect, since the pronunciation was not indicated; forms were adapted to Standard Dutch and doubtful etymologies were given. For that matter, the Belgians were not only inspired by romanticism, but they also had the secret desire to have the Flemish words accepted in the national lexicon. When proposals were made in the Netherlands to produce a comprehensive general Dutch dictionary, the Belgians feared that the dictionary would turn out to be too 'Hollandic' and therefore started collecting their own regional words for a general Flemish dictionary. Their particularistic attitude ws strengthened by the foundation in 1870 of the *Zuidnederlandsche Maatschappij van Taalkunde* (South Netherlandic Society of Linguistics), which firmly fostered the compilation of regional Flemish dictionaries.

3.2. Dialect grammars

The first dialect grammars appear in the Netherlands in the second quarter of the 19th century. J. Sonius Swaagman (1827) writes an essay in Latin (!) about the dialect of Groningen. The study of Behrns (1840) about the dialect of Twente is of a higher scientific value. The author applies the methodology of comparative linguistics to the vowels of the dialect, and he joins in the work of important German Indo-Europeanists like Grimm and Bopp. However, the majority of the dialect grammars appears much later: from 1880 onwards. This is not surprising since writing a dialect grammar requires considerable linguistic training and experience. (In Section 4 we will come back to the production of dialect grammars.)

3.3. Dialect texts

The Romantic interest for dialects not only resulted in dictionaries and at least one dialect grammar, but also in the collection of texts written in dialect. We find such collections in the Netherlands from the 1830s. The impulses to collect those data came from Germany and France. In Germany, J. M. Firmenich (1808−1889) was looking for Dutch dialect texts for his collection *Germaniens Völkerstimmen* (1843−1867). In France Jacques Le Brigant (1720−1804) had already started in 1779 to collect translations of the Parable of the Prodigal Son in Celtic. The French scholar Charles-Etienne Coquebert de Montbret used the same text in 1807 for a dialect survey in the whole French Empire, to which the Netherlands belonged in 1810. Unfortunately, only the translation into Frisian has come down to us. The collecting of translations of the Parable of the Prodigal Son also appeared later on in countries outside the French empire: Germany (Radlof 1817), Switzerland (Stalder 1819; Schott 1840), Italy, Bulgaria, Transylvania (Biondelli 1853), and again in Belgium and the Netherlands: Jan Frans Willems published the Parable in 16 Northern and Southern Dutch dialects in the first four volumes of his *Belgisch Museum* (1837−1840). Johan Winkler (1840−1926) published a collection of translations of the Parable in 186 Northern and Southern Dutch dialects (1874). The latter publication is the most comprehensive in the Dutch-speaking language area and it is considered to be an important help in defining and characterizing Dutch dialects.

3.4. A linguistic map of the Netherlands

The translations of one and the same text into different dialects of a standard language are also an important means in dialect geographical research. A first attempt at a dialect geographical description of the Netherlands was made in the middle of the 19th century. The general assembly of the *Maatschappij der Nederlandse letterkunde* held a competition in 1852 for making the best linguistic map of the Netherlands indicating dialect boundaries. The competition was highly inspired by the publication of the second edition of Karl Bernhardi's (1803−1883) *Sprachkarte von Deutschland* (1849). Unfortunately, the Maatschappij had to record in 1857 that the competition had fallen through: not a single contribution was received by then. Thereupon the Maatschaapij decided to enclose in the minutes of their meeting a dialect questionnaire asking members to complete it. Again, the response was apathetic, as only a few forms were returned. Yet another attempt of making a dialect geographical description of the Netherlands proved unsuccessful. Serious dialect geographical research got off the ground in the Netherlands and in Belgium only in the last quarter of the 19th century, just as elsewhere in Europe.

4. Dialect geography in the Aufbau phase (1879−1920)

4.1. The birth of dialect geography

The first large-scale dialect survey in the Dutch-speaking language area was held in 1879 by the *Aardrijkskundig Genootschap* (Dutch Geographical Society). Johan Hendrik Kern (1833−1917), professor of Sanskrit in the University of Leiden, was the driving force behind this dialect survey. In 1866 he had become a member of the committee of the *Maatschappij der Nederlandse Letterkunde* that had held the unsuccessfull dialect competition (cf. 3.4.), and he revived the old dialect enterprise. Kern was a polyglot, an Indo-Europeanist who had also published articles about Dutch and Dutch dialects. At the 13th Nederlandsch Taal en Letterkundig Congres held in 1873, he made a plea for the compilation of word-lists and grammars of all Dutch, Franconian and Saxon dialects. He justified his proposal by saying that the study of the dialects of a language is of general importance for a country, especially for its folklore. He was convinced that tribe and dialect borders would coincide and he was eager to demonstrate this to be so. His last argument for conducting a large-scale dialect survey precisely in the 1870s is that typical dialect characteristics were disappearing due to the development of important new means of transport such as steamers, steam trams and trains, which led to increasing contacts with speakers of other dialects and speakers of Standard Dutch. During the meeting a committee was put together in order to start the project. The committee consisted of Belgian and Dutch members, and was to survey the dialects of the whole Dutch speaking language area.

At the meeting of the congress in 1875, Kern had to confess that the project had not made any progress. It is unclear what happened precisely, but it is noteworthy that when Kern requested the *Aardrijkskundig Genootschap* to participate in the dialect survey he only spoke about the Netherlands. In 1878 Kern adressed this Geographical Society and argued that dialect geography was a part of geographical science and that therefore geographers should play a role in mapping dialects in the Netherlands. The *Aardrijkskundig Genootschap* had been founded only in 1873, and the ideas about what did and did not belong to geography were not yet clearly defined: geography described the whole earth with everything in and on it. To geographers of that time it was no problem that they should accept the task of studying dialects. By contrast, later dialectologists had serious problems with the fact that the first large-scale dialect survey was performed by geographers and not by dialectologists. Kloeke (1926: 16) for example writes that this attitude is typical, but depressing and shameful (cf. 5.3.). In 1879 the Society distributed a dialect questionnaire among its members, all living in the Netherlands, and asked them to answer the questions in the dialect of their place of residence (Gerritsen 1979: 14–18).

Although this Dutch survey was held only three years after the first dialect survey ever, Georg Wenkers' (1852–1911) 1876 survey of dialects in the Rhineland, the driving force behind the Dutch survey was quite a different one. Wenkers' undertaking was highly inspired by the linguistic theory of his time. He wanted to prove the neogrammarian theory that sound change is exceptionless, the so-called *Ausnahmlosigkeit der Lautgesetze*. The Dutch survey, however, was hardly theoretically inspired. Kern was acquainted with the theory of the Neogrammarians, but according to Uhlenbeck (1918: 36), he regarded it as narrow-minded and soul-less. Due to his knowledge of many languages Kern realized that countless factors could affect language change and therefore he considered it vain to base a theory of sound change on one language family only and to capture the whole process of sound change on the basis of merely two mechanisms: sound laws and analogical leveling.

280 questionnaires of the 1879 survey were returned. The analysis of the data was, however, a long time coming. In 1892 Jan te Winkel (1847–1927) was appointed in the University of Amsterdam for Dutch philology, and the *Aardrijkskundig Genootschap* asked him to draw a linguistic map of the Netherlands on the basis of the answers to the 1879 questionnaires. Te Winkel accepted the invitation, but the enterprise failed for several reasons. The answers were not written down clearly, the completed lists had not been evenly distributed over the Netherlands, and Te Winkel believed that the wrong questions had been posed, at least for testing the theories of the Neogrammarians. Although that theory had been criticized vehemently in the last quarter of the 19th century, Te Winkel still was in favor of this theory and wanted to do his research within the framework of this theory. The *Aardrijkskundig Genootschap* allowed him to send out a new questionnaire in 1895. On the basis of the 209 returned lists, Te Winkel's *Noordnederlandse tongvallen* (1899–1901) was published. This book included two linguistic maps with commentary, one of the reflexes of the west-Germanic *âe*, the other of *î*. Inspired by his belief in sound laws, Te Winkel intended to publish a map with commentary for each west-Germanic vowel. Only two maps appared, however. Goossens (1977: 128) ascribes this failure to the fact that Te Winkel did not realize that he could only make a map of the reflexes of a west-Germanic vowel after having drawn maps for a number of single words with that vowel. According to Goossens this faulty approach to the data is the reason Te Winkels' undertaking was less fruitful than similar approaches in Germany (Wenker) and France (Gilliéron).

Te Winkel (1899–1901) had a definite neogrammarian slant, but nods in the direction of other theories were made too. For example, he indicated tribe borders on his maps. In his later work he seemed to be less faithful to the neogrammarian theory. In Te Winkel (1904), for example, he stressed the fact that language change needs a description that goes further than laws, that considers also such mechanisms as analogy, economy and aesthetics. There was certainly a discrepancy between Te Winkel's theoretical insights and the practice of his dialect research (Hagen 1992: 334).

Dialect geographical surveys were held somewhat later in Dutch-speaking Belgium. In 1886 Pieter Willems (1840–1898), professor of Latin Philology at Leuven University, organized a dialect survey in 337 localities in order to collect the data for his intended study of the phonetics and morphology of the 'Franconian'. His questionnaire contained more than 2000 items. Willems' study was not successful, but the data of his survey proved to be very useful for later research.

The surveys of the *Aardrijkskundig Genootschap* and of Willems marked the beginnings of the scientific dialect geographic study of Dutch dialects.

4.2. A favourable climate for the study of spoken language

The interest in dialects at the end of the 19th century was driven not only by romantic feelings and the testing of linguistic theories, but also a consequence of the increasing interest in the spoken language at the time. The spoken word did not only fascinate linguists; writers from the second half of the 19th century complained of the distortion of the written language and advocated the use of 'normal' language. Multatuli (pseudonym of Eduard Douwes Dekker [1820–1887], one of the most famous Dutch writers of the 19th century) wrote, for example, "I try to write living Dutch, but I went to school". The *Tachtigers*, Dutch writers who were active around 1880, strove to reflect the spoken language as much as possible in their writings. Albert Verweij's (1865–1937) highest ambition was, for example, "to write in such a way that my readers have the feeling that I am speaking".

The discussion about spelling reforms in the Netherlands, but also elsewhere in Europe, that took place in the same period cannot be seen apart from this literary interest in the spoken word. One aimed at reflecting the spoken language in the spelling. Those who taught English as a second language also aimed at reflecting spoken English exactly. As a result, The International Phonetic Association was founded in 1886. At Otto Jespersen's request, this association devised in 1889 a phonetic alphabet which should be applicable to all languages. The International Phonetic Alphabet (IPA), used world-wide today, resulted from this effort.

The interest in spoken languages arose during a period in which a number of technical innovations brought the spoken word into completely new roles in society. Alexander Graham Bell (1847–1922) invented the telephone in 1876. From then on it was – at least for some people – possible to communicate orally over long distances. Another innovation that offered a new way of recording the human voice, was the microphone. Emil Berliner (1851–1929) succeeded in 1877 and David Edward Hughes (1831–1900) in 1878, to amplify the human voice by means of a microphone. From then onwards it became easier to convey information with the human voice to mass audiences. At the same time, still other inventions made it possible to capture spoken language. In 1877 Thomas Edison (1847–1931) launched the phonograph, a machine which could record and then reproduce sound. These inventions made it possible to analyze spoken language in greater detail. In the Dutch-speaking language area, however, it was not until the 1950s that dialect studies used these new technologies on a large scale (cf. 5.5.). Although dialects were not studied with the help of all these technical innovations available, they were studied intensively as will be shown in the following sections.

4.3. Dictionaries

From 1875 onwards a number of dialect lexicons were published (cf. Goossens 1977: 113). In this period we also find the first specialist dialect dictionaries, dictionaries about the dialect used in a special trade, the dialect of the black smith, the carpenter, the bricklayer. These dictionaries were published especially in Dutch-speaking Belgium. The *Koninklijke Vlaamse Academie voor Taal- en Letterkunde* (Royal Flemish Academy for Language and Literature), called on its members in 1890 to submit word-lists of the various professions. The Academy feared that due to the fact that French was the language of education in Dutch-speaking Belgium, new professions would not acquire a Dutch terminology and traditional professions would lose their indigenous words. At first, it was not the purpose of the Vlaamse Academie to collect and publish lists with dialect words, but it happened to go in that direction, thanks to the growing recognition that it was not necessary to produce a Standard Dutch specialist terminology since the Netherlands did already have one.

Such specialist dictionaries appear in the Netherlands at the end of the 1950s. The regional dictionaries (cf. 6.1.) are to some extent also specialist dictionaries.

4.4. Dialect monographs

The stream of dialect monographs began to flow from about 1880 in both the Netherlands and Belgium. Goossens (1977: 117–

126) gives an extensive list. The majority of the monographs were writen under the auspices of two schools, the Amsterdam school of Jan te Winkel (see end of 4.1. above) and the Louvainian of Philemon Colinet (1833–1917). There are two important differences between the two. The Belgian Dutch grammars describe dialects of cities and towns, while the Netherlandic grammars describe village dialects. This difference is a result of the fact that dialects were spoken much less in the Netherlands than in Belgium. In Belgian cities dialects were still spoken, but not so in the Netherlands. This is due to the fact that a kind of Standard Dutch has always been the only official language in the Netherlands. In Dutch cities the members of the upper class who spoke Standard Dutch played an important role in the leveling out and even the disappearance of dialects. In Dutch-speaking Belgium there were, however, two official languages and the upper class spoke French. As a consequence, the dialects spoken by the lower classes, were not affected by Standard Dutch. A second difference between the Netherlandic and the Belgian monographs is that the former were designed in line with the German model, tracing the developments from early Western Germanic to modern dialect variants according to sound laws. The Belgian Dutch grammars are designed after the French model, directed first of all to precise synchronic descriptions. The dialect monographs of this period mainly deal with phonetics and phonology and very little with morphology and syntax.

4.5. Dialect texts

The most important collection of Dutch dialect texts of this period is the work by Johan A. and L. Leopold (1882), which also contains texts of the North-German and Frisian dialects. The most scientific publication of Dutch dialect texts of this period however, is Frings & Vandenheuvel (1921), in which we find among other things the 40 sentences that Wenker used for the first dialect survey in the world. They are translated and phonetically described in 56 southern Dutch dialects (cf. 5.4. below).

4.6. Classification maps

At the end of the 19th century dialectologists had acquired so much insight into the Dutch dialects that they dared to draw a map on which the dialects were delineated. The first was drawn by Hermann Jellinghaus (1892).

He discussed his classification and gave a short comparative phonological and phonetic description, mainly based on the dialect texts that were published until then.

Te Winkel (1898) published a second classification map in his contribution to the second enlarged edition of Hermann Paul's *Grundriss* (1896–1909). The maps were also published in later works of Te Winkel (1899–1901, 1904). Both te Winkel and Jellinghaus took the traditional standpoint that dialect borders reflect tribe borders (cf. 4.1.).

The innovations in classification of dialects that Wenker and, later, Wrede had introduced in Germany from the 1880s onwards were picked up by the Dutch Indo-Europeanist Jozef Schrijnen (1869–1938). He draws the course of Wenker's Bernrather line (the italicized phonemes in the following examples: ma*ch*en–ma*k*en, la*ss*en–la*t*en, scha*tz*–scha*t*, a*pf*el–a*pp*el, scha*f*–schaa*p*) and Ürdinger line (only the following two words: *ich*–*ik* and *auch*–*ook*) through the Netherlands and Belgium (Schrijnen 1902). Schrijnen was the first in the Netherlands who investigated the path of isoglosses.

The third important dialect classification map of the Netherlands appeared in 1913 in Jacques van Ginneken's (1877–1945) handbook of the Dutch language and its sociological structure (1913–1914). The work consists of two volumes of more than one thousand pages. For its time this *magnum opus* undoubtedly represented, also by international standards, a quite exceptional documentation of the regional and social variation in Dutch (Hagen 1992: 337). It contains a description of the varieties of Dutch along three 'language circles', i.e., 'local language circles' (differentiation in dialects), 'familial language circles' (differentiation according to family, sex and age), and 'social language circles' (differentiation in terms of social class, profession, political party, and religion) (cf. 5.1.). More than 200 pages are devoted to the dialects in the Netherlands and Belgium. Van Ginneken discusses these dialects with a dialect classification map as point of departure. His map is a compromise between the classification according to tribes, by Jellinghaus and Te Winkel, and the one according to isoglosses by Schrijnen. Goossens (1977: 131) states that Van Ginneken's map shows an enormous erudition, but that it also shows that he did not realize the importance of the developments in dialectology such as the theories about expansions (cf. 5.3.) that occurred in Germany and in the Netherlands precisely in the period in which he wrote his handbook. These new developments were still not even incorporated into the second edition of the handbook published in 1928.

5. Institutionalization and outstanding dialectologists (1920–1960)

We have seen in Section 4 that the dialectology of Dutch was flourishing at the end of the 19th century and at the beginning of the 20th. Dialectology was, however, not yet institutionalized. Those who contributed to Dutch dialectology were mostly more prominent in other disciplines. Philemon Colinet for example was an important phonetician and Jan te Winkel enjoyed great fame with the five volumes that he wrote about the development of Dutch literature (Te Winkel 1908–1919).

The institutionalization of dialectology came about in the Netherlands and Belgium after World War I. Four linguists play an important part in this: Van Ginneken and Kloeke in the Netherlands and Blancquaert and Grootaers in Belgium. These four scholars lived and worked at about the same time. Jacques van Ginneken and Edgar Blancquaert (1894–1964) pleaded for an approach to dialectology modelled after French dialectology, and Gesinus Kloeke (1887–1963) and Ludovic Grootaers (1885–1965) for one modelled in accord with German dialectology. In order to give some insight into the role that those linguists played in the development of Dutch dialectology, we will offer a sketch on their dialectological work. We will first deal with those who worked in the line of French dialectology, Van Ginneken (5.1.) and Blancquaert (5.2.), and subsequently with those who promoted the German approach: Kloeke (5.3.) and Grootaers (5.4.).

5.1. Jacques Van Ginneken

We have shown in 4.5. that a great part of Van Ginneken's main work (1913–1914) was devoted to dialects. But he represented himself as a dialectologist in other matters as well. He organized together with Schrijnen and J. J. Verbeeten a dialect survey in North-Brabant and Netherlandic-Limburg. On the basis of 170 returned questionnaires, Schrijnen wrote, among other things, his publication about the isoglosses of Ramisch (Schrijnen 1920) and, earlier Schrijnen (1917) in which he published the first lexical map in the Dutch-speaking language area: *vlinder* (butterfly). Theodor Frings (1886–1968) had used the data of this survey, together with data collected during World War I with the help of Flemish prisoners of war, in Frings & Van Ginneken (1919). Frings demonstrated in this article that the areal spread of a number of dialect phenomena in Belgium and the Netherlands can be explained by expansion from Cologne. This publication has had an important impact to the use of the concept of 'expansions' as an explanatory device for the spread of dialect phenomena (cf. 5.3.).

In 1918 Van Ginneken qualified for succeeding Jan te Winkel, who was 70 by then and had retired, as professor of Dutch philology in the University of Amsterdam. But van Ginneken did not get the chair for several reasons. An important political point was that he was blamed for antisemitism on the basis of the chapter devoted to the language of the Jews in his handbook (Van Ginneken 1913–1914). A second reason was that he was clearly opposed to the regularity principle held by Te Winkel and therefore would not have carried on in the dialectological tradition adhered to by Te Winkel. Van Ginneken was convinced that the fresh and new spirit in linguistics was blowing from France and not from Germany (Hagen 1992: 340). Just like the French-oriented linguists, he adhered to the Romanist Hugo Schuchardt's (1885) the criticism of the Neogrammarians. Van Ginneken was not only French-oriented in his attitude towards the Neogrammarians, but he had also great interest in the development of Romance linguistics, especially in the French sociological school of linguistics. His idea to write a handbook on the sociological structure of the Dutch language (Van Ginneken 1913–1914) was probably inspired by Antoine Meillet. Yet Van Ginneken did not entirely disapprove of the German approach, as appears from the fact that he published a study together with Frings (Frings & van Ginneken 1919). Van Ginneken, however, did receive a professorship in 1923. He was appointed to the chair in Dutch Philology, Indo-European and Sanskrit at the newly founded University of Nijmegen.

Van Ginneken took the view that language was a complex phenomenon which could only be understood through an interdisciplinary approach. He opted for a combination of social, psychological and biological methods.

We can find this opinion clearly in his dialectological work, especially in the investigations he did together with Louise Kaiser in and around the Zuiderzee, the area that was impoldered in the 1930s (cf. 5.5.). He held the view that the spread of linguistic phenomena could be explained by biological factors. He states for example in Van Ginneken (1943: 40—79) that phonetic differences between dialects are a results of differences in what he calls 'articulatiebasis' (articulatory setting), whether one speaks with an open or a closed mouth and whether one has full or thin lips. Such theories encountered much resistance among his colleagues since it tended toward racial typing of speakers.

Van Ginneken can be considered a linguistic jack-of-all-trades, with a creative, well-rounded approach. He studied far more aspects of linguistics than dialectology alone, including language psychology, child-language acquisition, and spelling. He also played an important role in the internationalization of linguistics in the Netherlands. Thus, he took part in the organization of the First International Conference of Linguists (The Hague, 1928) and the First International Phonetic Congress (Amsterdam, 1932). Thanks to him, Dutch linguists became acqainted with linguistic surveys elsewhere in the world, and the rest of the world had the opportunity to learn about Dutch linguistics. Where his merits for dialectology are concerned, the opinions diverge. According to almost everyone (Hagen 1992: 337) he is not always very accurate in his work. Nevertheless, Hagen (1992: 337—340) attributes to him almost as much importance as to Kloeke (cf. 5.3.). Goossens (1977: 133) appreciation is much less favourable. He states that Van Ginneken did not open new vistas for dialectology, but that by popularizing dialectological research he made it an attractive discipline for both philologists and lay persons. His great personality attracted doctoral students who wrote dissertations about dialect geographical phenomena. Through his work the University of Nijmegen became one of the most authoritative dialectological institutes in the Netherlands.

According to Jo Daan (1964), Van Ginneken claimed to be the leading man in Dutch dialectology. For that matter, Kloeke had the same opinion about his own position. There was always a certain tension between these two rivals. Some of the dissertations (e. g., Janssen 1941) written under the supervision of Van Ginneken were straight attacks on the theory that Kloeke (1927) advocated (cf. 5.3.).

5.2. Edgar Blancquaert

Edgar Blancquaert (1894—1964) studied in Gent, Brussels and Paris. At the latter he followed the courses of Jules Gilliéron (1854—1926) and Albert Dauzat (1877—1955). Those courses had an important influence on his dialectological work, which was clearly French-oriented. As grammar school teacher from 1922—1925 he made recordings for a regional dialect atlas, the *Dialectatlas of Klein-Brabant* (Blancquaert 1925). This atlas was highly inspired by Gilliéron's *Atlas linguistique de la France* with regard to both the presentation of the results and the method of the fieldwork. Blancquaert had collected his data by direct oral elicitation procedures and documented in narrow phonetic transcriptions. The atlas consists of a text with maps. For each place the text gives a translation of all the 141 sentences in a narrow phonetic transcription. The maps show the areal spread of a number of the items occurring in the questions. They are drawn in a way similar to the maps of the French atlas: next to each place a word or a phrase is written down phonetically, and dialect areas are not delimited by isoglosses.

Blancquaert became assistant professor in Gent in 1925, and full professor in 1930. At that moment he saw the opportunity to implement a plan that he had always dreamed of: to publish a series of areal atlases following the model of his *Dialectatlas of Klein-Brabant* which would cover the whole Dutch speaking language area (Blancquaert 1925). Although many linguists were rather sceptical about his enterprise, Blancquaert succeeded in inspiring enough colleagues to realize the whole ambitious project. His successor in Gent, Willem Pée (1903—1986), in particular made great afforts to complete the project. The atlas was published under the name of both Blancquaert and Pée. When Blancquaert died in 1964, 10 of the planned 16 volumes had been published and the data collection for the other 6 volumes was nearly finished. The project was completed in 1982 in the Series "Nederlandse Dialectatlassen" (1930—1982). The atlases contain a phonetic reflection of the transcription of 141 sentences in the dialect of more than 2500 places in the Netherlands and Belgium. They have proved to be a real treasure for phonetic, morphological, lexical, and syntactic studies.

5.3. Gesinus Gerardus Kloeke

Gesinus Kloeke (1881–1963) studied German philology. He received his doctoral degree from the University of Leipzig and his *habilitation* from the University of Hamburg. During his study in Germany he became acquainted with the methodology of the Marburgian school of Wenker and Wrede. In 1914, he returned to the Netherlands as a grammar school teacher. During school holidays he did dialectological fieldwork, publishing the results. In this period he met Grootaers (cf. 5.4.). Together they made a plea for a dialect atlas of the whole Dutch-speaking language area, following the model of Wenker's German atlas. They designed a basic map with indexes (Grootaers & Kloeke 1926). In 1934, Kloeke was appointed professor in Dutch Linguistics at the University of Leiden. Grootaers was appointed to the same position in Louvain in 1935. They continued their good teamwork and published a mainly lexical geographic Atlas of Northern and Southern Netherlands (Kloeke & Grootaers 1939–1972; cf. 5.5., 6.1.).

In addition to the basic map and the atlas, Kloeke's special contribution to dialectology was that of theoretical enrichment. In his research, he brings together several disciplines: dialect geography, sociolinguistics – *avant la lettre* – and theories on language change. We already find keen sociolinguistic analyses in his early publications, such as his studies on forms of address (Kloeke 1920) and of hypercorrections (Kloeke 1924). Since those publications were written in Dutch and never translated into another language, they had no influence upon linguistics elsewhere in the world. However, thanks to Bloomfield's (1935 [1933]: 328–331) discussion on Kloeke's (1927) master piece in Dutch dialectology, devoting an entire section in the former's *Language*, Kloeke did achieve an important influence on international dialectology. According to Bloomfield, Kloeke's book about the Hollandic expansion in the 16th and 17th century and its reflection in 20th-century Dutch dialects, *Expansie* for short, contains good examples of theory-building and hypothesis-testing in dialectology. Kloeke's study described the geographical distribution of the west-Germanic *û* in the words *huis* (house) and *muis* (mouse) in the Dutch-speaking language area. The study's emphasis was on the change from [u:] to [y:], showing that the change probably originated in Flanders and spread during the Middle Ages over a large part of the country, including the central district, which today pronounces a diphthong [oey]. He demonstrated that new variants 'jumped' from town to town before spreading out to the countryside. Since the geographical distribution of the change coincided with the boundaries of the Republic of the United Low Countries in 1589, Kloeke attributed the spread to influence from Holland, the most powerful province in the Republic. He showed that the change took place by a process of borrowing from the upper classes, and that therefore social prestige was the motivating factor in the diffusion. He makes this explanation more plausible by indicating that he could observe the same mechanism at work in the year 1920: people in the [u]-area used [y] in words like *huis* and *muis* in situations in which they tried to speak Standard Dutch. De facto Kloeke applied in this argument Labov's (1972: 274) Uniformitarian Principle, stating that language change in the past can be explained by language patterns in the present. By using social factors as a motivation for language change and by applying the uniformitarian principle in his explanations, he proves himself to be a true sociolinguist *avant la lettre* (cf. Hagen 1988: 273; Koerner 1995: 124).

Kloeke made a contribution to a theory of language change through his explanation of the fact that the change from [u] to [y] proceeds quicker in *huis* than in *muis*. According to him, this lexical diffusion is a result of a difference in frequency of occurrence between the words: it occurs faster in *huis*, a word that was frequently used in everyday communication with the people from Holland, the most powerful district of the republic, than in *muis*, a word that was seldom used. Kloeke demonstrated that sound change does not occur at the same time in all words. However, he was not adherent of Schuchardt's or other scholars' argument (first stated by Jacob Grimm in 1819) according to which each word has a history of its own, as Bloomfield (1933: 328) suggests. Kloeke took the view that the pressure of the sound laws plays the principal part in the diffusion of sound change (Kloeke 1921: 42), but that there are exceptions and restrictions too. Nevertheless, Kloeke did feel attracted to the idea of every word having its own history. This is evident from both the fact that the motto of the introduction to Kloeke (1927) originated from Schuchardt and that Schuchardt is described in the introduction as he "who more than anyone else influenced the ideas of younger linguists" (Kloeke 1927: 3).

We should point out here, however, that the idea of the spread of linguistic phenomena caused by expansion of a prestige form was not invented by Kloeke, but by his friend Theodor Frings (1886–1968) (see 5.1.). In the 1920s Frings worked at the University of Bonn. This job gave him plenty of time to do research but due to strong inflation not enough money to support his family. In the same period, Kloeke worked as teacher of German at the Leiden gymnasium, spending long hours, but making lots of money. Being a bachelor at that time Kloeke could afford to wish more time for research than money. In light of their respective circumstances, the two arranged to switch places during 1921–1922. In his new situation in Bonn period Kloeke became well acquainted with the concept of 'expansion' as an explanatory device (W. U. S. Kloeke, p. c.). The German masterpiece of this approach, Frings (1926) appeared one year before Kloeke's *Expansie*.

In Kloeke's second important publication, on the origin and evolution of *Afrikaans* (Kloeke 1950), we find sociolinguistic ideas similar to those as in his *Expansie*. He shows, on the basis of a detailed study of the dialects of Holland and Zeeland, that *Afrikaans* is based on *Zuidhollands*, the dialects spoken in the area south of Amsterdam and north of Rotterdam. Kloeke became interested in the origin of Afrikaans during a tour of South African universities at the end of the 1930s, but only during World War II did he get the opportunity to investigate this problem. Kloeke was one of the first professors at the University of Leiden to resign from his post when Jewish colleagues were dismissed. Since Kloeke had lived quite a long time in Germany and knew many Germanists, among others Jan van Dam, the head of the *Kulturkammer*, it was of great importance to him to demonstrate that he stood on the side of the Dutch and not with the Germans. Following his resignation Kloeke went underground for nine months, got arrested, was put first into prison, and then into a kind of concentration camp. Half-way during the war he was set free, but the occupying force prohibited him to enter the western part of the Netherlands. He stayed, therefore, until 1945 with a friend who had lived a long time in South-Africa and had a library with an extensive collection of publications on Afrikaans. There, in exile, he wrote his study on the origin and evolution of Afrikaans (W. U. S. Kloeke, p. c.).

Besides Kloeke's important theoretical contributions to Dutch dialectology, he also made a practical contribution. He wanted to found a dialect centre in the Netherlands similar to the *Zuidnederlandse dialectencentrale* (Southern Netherlandic Dialect Centre) founded by Grootaers in Belgium (see 5.4.). He managed to convince the literary section of the Koninklijke Nederlandse Akademie van Wetenschappen of the importance of financing the centralization of Netherlandic dialect activities, and thus the *Dialectenbureau* was founded in 1930. Kloeke intented to become the director of the *Dialectenbureau*. He could not accept the job, however, as the salary was too low for supporting a family. Rumour has it that Van Ginneken (cf. 5.1.), a member of the committee supervising the Dialectenbureau, had deliberately arranged to set the salary for the post lower than Kloeke could possibly accept, thus effectively depriving him of such an important position in the organization of Dutch dialectology (Jo Daan, p. c.). Instead, the Netherlands specialist, Pieter Jacobus Meertens (1899–1985), was appointed. As has been said, Kloeke was appointed somewhat later (1934) to a professorship of Dutch linguistics at Leiden University. He brought with him the *Taalatlas van Noord- en Zuidnederland* (Kloeke & Grootaers 1939–1972). The *Dialectenbureau* took charge of the atlas only after the sixth fascible had appeared in 1956 (cf. 5.5., 6.1.).

5.4. Ludovic Grootaers

Ludovic Grootaers (1885–1956) studied German philology in Louvain and received his doctorate in 1907 on account of a dissertation about the dialect of Tongeren (Belgium). From 1924 on he was assistant professor in Louvain. He became acquainted with experimental phonetics in the phonetic laboratory of his teacher Philemon Colinet and he applied those experimental phonetic methods to the analysis of dialects. Like Kloeke (cf. 5.3.), he was a proponent of the German approach to dialectology. He became interested in this approach since the innovative German dialect publications were largely devoted to the Lower Rhinish and Ripuarian dialects, and those dialects were related to the Limburgian dialects which he investigated (Tongeren, Hasselt). We have already mentioned in 5.3. that he made a plea for an atlas analoguous to the German one and that, together with Kloeke, he drew a basic map with indexes (Grootaers & Kloeke 1926) and published the word atlas of Northern and Southern Netherlands (Kloeke & Grootaers 1939–1972).

In 1935, Grootaers was appointed to a professorship at the University of Louvain. In addition to the Atlas, he gave other important stimulations to dialectology of Dutch. He had tried in 1920 to make an atlas on the basis of the Dutch dialect translations of the Wenker sentences (cf. 4.5.). The enterprise failed however. He decided thereupon to send out his own questionnaires and to found his own Flemish dialectological institute, de Zuidnederlandse Dialectencentrale. The centre distributed dialect questionnaires throughout the whole Dutch-speaking part of Belgium. Data from these questionnaires served as important material for Kloeke & Grootaers (1939–1972) and for a projected large-scale Flemish dialect dictionary; but it took until the 1960s for this type of lexicographic dialect project to materialize (cf. 6.1.).

Grootaers stimulated dialectology in still quite another way: under his supervision an enormous number of dissertations were written in which dialectological problems were approached in the framework of the Marburg school.

5.5. Other developments

In the 1930s the Dutch were reclaiming land from the sea called de Zuiderzee. Scholars from different disciplines, including linguists, realized that this was an unique laboratory-like situation for investigating processes of assimilation between the autochthonous population of the rather isolated islands and the new inhabitants of the newly reclaimed land (called *polder*), who were recruited from all over the Netherlands. The *Stichting voor het Bevolkingsonderzoek in de drooggelegde Zuiderzeepolders* (Society for Research into the Population of the reclaimed Zuiderzeepolders) was founded in order to investigate this assimilation process in a number of ways, including dialects. It is remarkable that all the dialect surveys performed within the scope of the land reclamation are innovative. Louise Kaiser (1891–1973) performed not only quantitative investigations into phonetic aspects of the dialects (1940–1949), but she also took into consideration biological aspects like stature, hair and eye colour (cf. 5.1.). Meertens & Kaiser (1942), Daan (1950) and Van Ginneken (1954) give a complete picture of the dialects, but they also describe every-day life on the islands on the basis of the dialect lexicon. As with the word-field theory of the German linguist Jost Trier (1894–1970), the lexicon is structured on the basis of semantic word fields, and the meaning of the words are organized according to the context in which they are introduced. Word concordances are added in order to make these systematic dialect dictionaries better accessible. Van de Ven (1969) is the first sociolinguistic study in the Netherlands in the narrower Labovian sense. Only this type of dialect study is continued later on in the Dutch-speaking language area.

Compared with the often vehement theoretically-oriented discussions between the proponents of the French and the German methods of dialect research, dialectology was on the theoretical sidelines around World War II. Theories were discussed, especially the expansion theory of Kloeke, violently attacked by Hellinga (1938), but more time was devoted to data collection, establishing journals, such as *Onze Taaltuin* (1932–1942), *Taal en Tongval* (1949–), *Driemaandelijkse bladen* (1949–) and preparing Atlases (cf. 5.2.) and the atlas of Kloeke and Grootaers (cf. 5.3. and 5.4.). During World War II two insightful dialectological handbooks were written: Weijnen (1941) and Van Ginneken (1943).

At the same time a number of young dialectologists, later appointed to important linguistic positions in the Netherlands and Belgium, published their dissertations. Pauwels (1933), Heeroma (1935), Pée (1936–1938), Weijnen (1937), Van den Berg (1938) and Hellinga (1938) wrote dialect geographical studies, while Overdiep (1940), Sassen (1953) and Vanacker (1948) wrote dialect monographs. The latter paid especially attention to syntax, a subject that was rather neglected until then. Around 1960 almost all university chairs in Dutch linguistics were held by professors with qualifications in dialectology.

The *Dialectenbureau* acquired more than one thousand respondents all over the Netherlands who filled in at least one questionnaire yearly. After Grootaers' death (1956) the *Dialectenbureau* also took care of the respondents of his centre (cf. 5.4.) and continued sending questionnares all over Dutch-speaking Belgium. Furthermore the *Dialectenbureau* started collecting tape recordings of dialects. As of 1996 they have recordings with transcriptions of more than 1000 local dialects.

Along with the official central dialect institutes in the Netherlands and Belgium, research centers for dialectology were also founded at the universities of Groningen, Nijmegen, Leuven, and Gent. That does not imply that dialect research has not been performed elsewhere. On the contrary, dialectology held a dominant position in Dutch linguistics during the period 1930–1960.

6. Expansion and decline of dialectology: 1960–present

This section traces developments in Dutch dialectology in the period from 1960 to the present. The first section (6.1.) deals with the large-scale projects that were set up or completed in this period. 6.2. discusses the relationship between linguistic theory and dialectology in this period, and the last section is devoted to speculations about the future of dialectology (6.3.)

6.1. Generous funding and large-scale projects

Dutch universities flourished in the 1960s. This was partly due to the great number of children born just after World War II, which necessitated an expansion of the post-secondary education system. These so-called baby-boomers entered into higher education in the sixties. The flourishing of the universities in the Netherlands was also a result of the discovery of enormous natural gas reserves in the country which appeared to sustain this system. Therefore there seemed to be oceans of money. The universities and the dialect centres appointed many dialectologists and large-scale projects were started or completed. And in the first place, the production of atlases.

The linguistic atlas of Northern and Southern Netherlands (Kloeke & Grootaers 1939–1972) (cf. 5.3., 5.4. and 5.5.) continued and was completed as was the series of Dutch dialectatlases ten years later (Blancquaert & Pée 1930–1982) (cf. 5.2.). A number of new atlases were started. Klaas Heeroma set up a linguistic atlas of the eastern part of the Netherlands, including the neighbouring areas (Heeroma 1963). The purpose of this atlas was to demonstrate the so-called 'Westphalian expansion', the spread of Westphalian words all over the northeastern part of the Netherlands. Daan & Francken (1972–1977) made an atlas of the evolution of sounds in the Dutch-speaking language area and Gerritsen (1991) about the spread of syntactic phenomena. Goossens (1981) published an atlas about lexical, morphological and phonological aspects of the northern Rhineland and the south-eastern part of the Netherlands. Atlases of Dutch dialects of the past were also published, such as Berteloot (1984), on phonetic and phonological aspects of 13th-century Dutch dialects, and Mooijaert (1992), on morphological and lexical aspects of those dialects. Ton Goeman, Johan Taeldeman, Piet van Reenen and Jan Goossens set up a project for collecting, transcribing and computerizing data for a large-scale morphological and phonological atlas.

Hagen (1992: 344) stated that by its position in the delta of Europe, the Netherlands, situated between the powerful languages and cultures of France, Germany and England, seemed predestined to play an important role in interlingual dialectology. Indeed we find already pleas for a European dialectology in Kloeke (1927), and later on Van Ginneken and Heeroma too point in this direction. It is therefore not surprising that the later *Atlas Linguarum Europae* was initiated in the Netherlands in the 1960s (Weijnen et al. 1975).

Other large-scale projects begun in this period were the areal dictionaries. We have seen in 5.4. that Grootaers had the intention of writing a dictionary of Flemish, but for want of help, he did not succeed. The data Grootaers collected however, are being published together with more recently collected data, in three areal dictionaries initiated and supervised in the Netherlands by Weijnen of Nijmegen University, and by Willem Pée, of the University of Gent and later on, by Valeer Frits Vanacker (b. 1921) of the same university: *Woordenboek van de Brabantse dialecten* (1967–), *Woordenboek van de Limburgse dialecten* (1983–), *Woordenboek van de Vlaamse dialecten* (1979–). The first two dictionaries cover an area in The Netherlands and in Belgium, the latter covers only Belgium. The three dictionaries are so-called systematic onomasiological dictionaries. They are set up according to the same principles and the same design. The first volume always deals with the agricultural lexicon, the second with non-agricultural specialist terminology, and the third with the general lexicon. The places where the dialect words are found are carefully documented. Each volume contains numerous lexical maps. These three dictionaries will be completed at the beginning of the next millenium. One dictionary already completed along these modern lines of dialect lexicography is the dictionary of the Zeeland dialects (Ghijsen 1959–1964).

In this period two important handbooks on dialectology were published. Weijnen (1966) is a comprehensive reference book. Goossens (1977a) is a convenient, clearly written book often used for courses in Dutch dialectology. Jo Daan draws an important new dialect classification map (Daan & Blok 1968) based not only on isoglosses but also on which dialects dialect speakers experience as similar to their own dialect and which as different. Today this map is considered the most insightful dialect classification map of the Dutch-speaking language area (cf. 3.4. and 4.6.).

6.2. Linguistic theory and dialectology

We have seen in 4.1. (above) that the regularist theory of the neogrammarians gave an important impulse to dialect geography. Theories were tested and refined on the basis of dialect data. The expansion theory was an important driving force of dialect research in the 1920s. The spread of linguistic phenomena was explained by means of external linguistic factors such as social, cultural and historical aspects (cf. 5.3., 6.1.). The connection with linguistic theories became, however, somewhat looser later on (cf. 5.5.). Dialectologists no longer used dialect data to test and refine linguistic theories, but they concentrated on collecting data: atlases, dictionaries and dialect centres distributing and evaluating dialect questionnaires. Many dialectologists got bogged down in gathering data. The collectors' mania was especially stimulated by the idea that dialects were dying out (Weijnen 1958) and that as much dialect data as possible had to be collected before dialects had been wiped out completely. Only some dialectologists tried to approach dialects from a theoretical point of view. It is remarkable that those theories were more linguistically than sociologically oriented in the 1960s Already Weijnen (1951), the most prominent dialectological successor of Van Ginneken in Nijmegen, for example, made a plea for the explanation of the spread of dialect phenomena using internal linguistic factors – similar to Gilliéron's *gallus-cattus* map. Jan Goossens (b. 1930), professor of Dutch philology in Louvain, and since 1969 in Münster, demonstrated that a similar structural approach to dialect phenomena could also be very fruitful in the Dutch-speaking language area. His dissertation (Goossens 1963) is an example of this program on the lexical level. Goossens (1969) shows the possibilities of applying structural theory to dialect geography, especially phonological data.

Generative linguistics has not strongly influenced Dutch dialectology. The generative mechanisms of description are used, but the theories are rarely tested. There are, however, some exceptions: Hoppenbrouwens (1982) and Taeldeman (1985). It is striking that the generative approach to Dutch dialects is seldom used in dialect syntax, but more often in phonology. Gerritsen (1991) tries to explain the spread of syntactic phenomena with the help of generative theories, but she did not succeed since the data she collected proved too complex. Only one or two generative linguists studied isolated dialect phenomena, but a systematic generative analysis of Dutch dialects has never been made. Nevertheless, generative linguistics has had some influence on Dutch dialectology. First, it stimulated research into dialect syntax. As a result, dialectologists became interested in syntactic characteristics of dialects. The investigations into the areal spread of syntactic phenomena by Cor van Bree (1981) of Leiden University, inspired by generative linguistics, has been an important impulse for dialect geographical surveys into syntax (Gerritsen 1991) and for the study of syntactic phenomena in a certain area (Cornips 1994; Voortman 1994). Generative linguistics also stimulated dialectology not only because it was very expansive, but also because, for many younger linguists, it was the only legitimate approach to linguistics. However, the increasing distance between real language use and the more and more abstract generative descriptions caused a reaction. The actual language use, in this case the dialects, was investigated in order to demonstrate that speech performance was not as heterogenous as the generativists suggested.

This reaction to abstract theorizing led to an intense growth of sociolinguistics. Van Ginneken (cf. 4.6. and 5.1.), and Kloeke (cf. 5.3.) had already emphasized the importance of the study of social aspects of language use. Jo Daan in Daan & Weijnen (1967) translated the Labovian approach for the Dutch-speaking language area. Weijnen, in the same publication (1967), offered a sociological analysis of dialect use in Limburg. Some years earlier Nuytens (1962) had made a big plash with his study of the bilinguals in Borne (a village in the north-east of the Netherlands).

Sociolinguistics attracted especially the younger generation of linguists in the 1970s and the 1980s. It seemed to come to a break between dialectologists and sociolinguists in the 1970s. Had there been sufficient financial means it would probably not have come that far, but there were financial problems. This was due, on the one hand, to the economic recession following the first world oil crisis in 1973 and, on the other, to the fact that universities had to economize as the number of students decreased due to the lower birth rate in the 1970s. The struggle for research funds led to a schism between dialectologists and sociolinguists, as the major part was employed for sociolinguistic projects. The sociolinguistic projects seemed to bear more relevance for society than the dialect projects. One of those important sociolinguistic projects was, for example, the so-called Kerkrade project (Kerkrade is a town near the German-Dutch border in the south of The Netherlands). This project investigated whether speaking a dialect has consequences for success in school. When it turned out that dialect speaking children were less successful than children speaking Standard Dutch, methods were developed to teach the standard language to dialect speakers (Hagen 1981). Dialectologists and sociolinguists were reconciled when the problems of dialect-speaking children were pushed aside by the still more serious problems of children from foreign workers in The Netherlands (Marrocans, Turks). A lot of the financial resources consequently went to projects in which the linguistic and communicative problems of foreign workers were analyzed.

Nowadays dialect geographers successfully apply sociolinguistic methods. Kruijsen (1995) used them in his study of the spread of French elements in the area just north of the French-Flemish border. Earlier, Gerritsen & Jansen (1982) used data collected with a sociolinguistic methodology and with a quantitative analysis for their investigation of the expansion of the Amsterdam dialect in the area around Amsterdam. The classic dialect monograph giving a qualitative description of nearly all dialect characteristics of a dialect is nowadays replaced by the thorough quantitative sociolinguistic study of a small number of dialect phenomena (Van Hout 1989, Brouwer 1989). Not only the dialect of the lower classes is investigated, but also the dialect of the élite. Voortman (1994), for example, gives a thorough description of the language of the upper class in a number of places in the Netherlands. The psycholinguistic approach to language variation that is frequently used in sociolinguistics, the study of language attitudes and the domains in which varieties are used, is also applied to Dutch dialects (van Hout & Knops 1988). Summarizing, we can say that sociolinguistics has contributed highly to methodological innovations in dialectology.

In addition to sociolinguistics, theories of language change, especially those developed in the paradigm of Weinreich, Labov & Herzog (1968), have contributed to dialectological research. Not only because the spread of a linguistic element tells us something about its history, but also because the dialects have been recorded carefully in the past. By doing this in the same way today, we can study dialect change in real time and thus put theories on language change to a test. There have been a number of such projects in the Dutch-speaking language area.

The first dialect survey ever held in the Netherlands (1879, cf. 4.1.) was repeated 100 year later in the same way (Gerritsen 1979). A number of dialectologists traced the changes in the answers to the questions between the 1879 survey and the 1979 survey on the lexical, phonological and morphological levels. Some adaptations to Standard Dutch were found, but the majority of the aspects that were investigated showed no change. The results of the survey indicated that the dialects are much more stable than had ever been imagined. In 1995 a similar project was carried out using the questionnaire of 1895 (cf. 4.1.); it yielded similar results. In 1995, the Dialectenbureau, since 1979 Department of dialectology of the P. J. Meertens-Institute in Amsterdam (P. J. Meertens was the first director of the Dialectenbureau, cf. 5.3.) began again collecting translations of the Parabel of the Prodigal Son in a number of dialects in the Dutch-speaking language area and in Germany in order to compare the results with those published by Winkler in 1874 (cf. 3.3.). A remarkably similar project is the survey that Harrie Scholtmeyer (1992) performed in the reclaimed Zuiderzeepolders (cf. 5.5.). Contrary to expectation, the population did not yet speak Standard Dutch by 1990, but it had adapted its language to the dialects spoken on the nearest mainland.

Theories of the linguistic and sociolinguistic mechanisms of language change have also been tested in Dutch dialects with the help of the apparent-time method. In this method one studies at a certain moment the speech of people of different ages and one interprets differences between the age groups as changes. Insightful studies included, for example, Van Bree (1985) on the adaptations to Standard Dutch in the dialect of Haaksbergen, Gerritsen (1999) on standardization in three similar dialects under influence of three different standard languages, and Vousten (1995) on the acquisition of the Venray dialect by adolescents who had acquired Standard Dutch as their first language.

6.3. The future of Dutch dialectology

We noted earlier in (5.5.) that during the 1960s almost all professors in linguistics had some association with dialectology. That almost a guaranteed that courses in dialectology would be given and that dialectological research would be promoted. There are nowadays still some professors in linguistics who work in dialectology, Cor van Bree in Leiden, Toon Hagen in Nijmegen, Johan Taeldeman in Gent, Georges de Schutter in Antwerpen, and Herman Niebaum in Groningen, but most of them are on the point of retiring. Due to the fact that universities have to economize, it is almost certain that they will not be succeeded by a dialectologist, provided that their post will be filled after their retirement at all. This means that the transfer of dialectological knowledge is not secure. All the more since the reorganization of higher education will decerease the number of disciplines. The large-scale atlas and dictionary projects will have to be completed before the 21th century, because future financial support is in doubt.

The unfavourable position for the future of dialectology can be seen in terms of the absence of chairs, general education and large-scale projects. The main hope may lie with the involvement of lay persons. Every self-respecting local historical circle has a dialect branch writing a traditional dialect monograph or a dictionary of the local dialect. There is a flourishing *Stichting Nederlandse Dialecten* (Dutch Dialects Foundation) that organizes every two years much frequented dialect days. Each province partly finances the dictionaries in their area. The interest in the dialect of a particular place or area can be seen also as a reaction to the over-all unity and linguistic stream-lining for which the European Community strives. People want to emphasize the characteristics and the uniqueness of their own area. This reaction has aroused interest in the regional culture, food, and also, language. Proposals for the development of spelling systems for the dialects and education in the dialect have to be considered from this point of view.

Weijnen (1975) said that a dialectologist at a Dutch university feels lonely. This is certainly very true today, but s/he can find solace in the vitality of dialect speakers themselves.

7. Bibliography

Behrns, Johannes Henricus. 1840. "Twentsche vocalen en klankwijzigingen". *Taalkundig Magazijn* 3.331–390.

Bernhardi, Karl Christian Sigismund. 1849. *Sprachkarte von Deutschland.* Kassel: Bohne.

Berteloot, Amand. 1984. *Bijdrage tot een klankatlas van het dertiende-eeuwse Middelnederlands.* 2 vols. [Vol. 1: texts; vol. 2: maps]. Gent: Koninklijke Nederlandse Academie voor Taal- en Letterkunde.

Biondelli, Bernardino. 1853. *Saggio sui dialetti gallo-italici.* Milano: Hoepli.

Blancquaert, Edgar. 1925. *Dialectatlas van Klein-Brabant.* Antwerpen: De Sikkel.

– & Willem Pée. 1930–1982. *Reeks Nederlandse Dialectatlassen.* 16 vols. Antwerpen: De Sikkel.

Bloomfield, Leonard. 1935 [1933]. *Language.* London: Allen & Unwin.

Brouwer, Dédé. 1989. *Gender Variation in Dutch.* Dordrecht: Foris.

Cornips, Leonie. 1994. *Syntactische variatie in het Algemeen Nederlands van Heerlen.* Dordrecht: ICG Printing.

Daan, Jo. 1950. *Wieringer land en leven in de taal.* Alphen aan den Rijn: Samsom. (2nd ed., Heerhugowaard: "Acca" Drukkerijen, 1981.)

–. 1964. "G. G. Kloeke 1877–1963". *Orbis* 13. 622–629.

– & Antonius A. Weijnen. 1967. *Taalsociologie.* Amsterdam: Noord-Hollandse Uitgeversmaatschappij.

– & D. P. Blok. 1968. *Van Randstad tot landrand: Toelichting bij de kaart: Dialecten en naamkunde.* Amsterdam: Noord-Hollandse Uitgeversmaatschappij.

– & M. J. Francken. 1972, 1974. *Atlas van de Nederlandse klankontwikkeling.* 2 vols. Amsterdam: Noord-Hollandse Uitgeversmaatschappij.

Firmenich, Johannes Mathias. 1843–1866. *Germaniens Völkerstimmen.* 4 vols. Berlin: Schmitt.

Foolen, Ad & Jan Noordegraaf, eds. 1996. *De taal is kennis van de ziel. Opstellen over Jac. van Ginneken (1877–1945)*. Münster: Nodus.

Frings, Theodor. 1926. "Sprache". *Kulturströmungen und Kulturprovinzen in den Rheinlanden* ed. by Hermann Aubin, Theodor Frings & Josef Müller, 90–185. Bonn: Verlag Ludwig Roehrscheid. (Repr. in Frings, *Sprache und Geschichte* vol. II.40–146. Halle/Saale: Niemeyer, 1956.)

– & J. Vandenheuvel. 1921. *Die südniederländischen Mundarten: Texte. Untersuchungen. Karten.* Teil I: *Texte*. Marburg: Elwert.

– & Jacques van Ginneken. 1919. "Zur Geschichte des Niederfränkischen in Limburg". *Zeitschrift für deutsche Mundarten* 3/4.97–208.

Gerritsen, Marinel, ed. 1979. *Taalverandering in Nederlandse dialekten*. Muiderberg: Coutinho.

–. 1991. *Atlas van de Nederlandse Dialectsyntaxis.* Amsterdam: P. J. Meertens-Instituut.

–. 1999. "Standardization in a Linguistic Laboratory around the Belgian-Dutch-German Border: Three similar dialects under influence of three different standard languages". *Language Variation and Change* 11.43–67.

– & Frank Janssen. 1982. "The Interplay between Diachronic Linguistics and Dialectology: Some refinements of Trudgill's formula". *Papers from the Third International Conference on Historical Linguistics* ed. by J. Peter Maher et al., 11–38. Amsterdam: Benjamins.

Ghijsen, Ha. C. M. 1959–1964. *Woordenboek der Zeeuwse dialecten*. 2 vols. The Hague: Van Goor.

Goossens, Jan. 1963. *Semantische vraagstukken uit de taal van het landbouwbedrijf in Belgisch-Limburg*. 2 vols. Antwerpen: De Nederlandsche boekhandel.

–. 1969. *Strukturelle Sprachgeographie*. Heidelberg: Winter.

–. 1977a. "Geschiedenis van de Nederlandse dialectstudie". *Geschiedenis van de Nederlandse taalkunde* ed. by D. M. Bakker & Geert R. W. Dibbets, 285–311. s'Hertogenbosch: Malmberg.

–. 1977b. *Inleiding tot de Nederlandse Dialectologie*. Groningen: Wolters-Noordhoff.

Grootaers, Ludovic & Gesinus G. Kloeke. 1926. *Handleiding bij het Noord- en Zuid-Nederlandsch dialectonderzoek*. The Hague: Nijhoff.

Hagen, Antonius Maria. 1981. *Standaardtaal en dialectsprekende kinderen*. Muiderberg: Coutinho.

–. 1988. "Sociolinguistic Aspects in Dialectology". *Sociolinguistics/Soziolinguistik: An International Handbook of the Science of Language and Society* ed. by Ulrich Ammon, Norbert Dittmar & Klaus J. Mattheier, Tome I, 402–413. Berlin & New York: de Gruyter.

–. 1992. "Dutch Dialectology: The national and the international perspective". *The History of Linguistics in the Low Countries* ed. by Jan Noordegraaf, Kees Versteegh & Konrad Koerner, 331–353. Amsterdam & Philadelphia: Benjamins.

Heeroma, Klaas. 1935. *Hollandse dialektstudies*. Groningen: Wolters.

–. 1963. *Taalatlas van Oost-Nederland en aangrenzende gebieden*. Assen: Van Gorcum.

Hellinga, W. Gs. 1938. *De opbouw van de algemeen beschaafde uitspraak van het Nederlands*. Amsterdam: Noord-Hollandse Uitgeversmaatschappij.

Hoppenbrouwers, Cor. 1982. *Language Change: A study of phonetic and analogical change with particular reference to S. E. Dutch dialects*. Meppel: Boom.

Janssen, W. A. F. 1941. *De verbreiding van de uu-uitspraak voor Westgermaanse û in zuidoost Nederland*. Maastricht: Ernest van Aelst.

Jellinghaus, Hermann. 1892. *Die niederländischen Volksmundarten nach den Aufzeichnungen der Niederländer*. Norden: Dietrich Soltau.

Kaiser, Louise. 1940–1949. *Phonotypologische beschrijving van de bevolking der Wieringermeer*. 2 vols. Alphen aan den Rijn: Samsom.

Kloeke, Gesinus Gerardus. 1920. "Dialectogeografische onderzoekingen I: De aanspreekvormen in de dialecten onzer Noordelijke provinciën [with two maps]". *Tijdschrift voor Nederlandse Taal- en Letterkunde* 39.238–266.

–. 1924. "Klankoverdrijving en goedbedoelde (hypercorrecte) taalvormen". *Tijdschrift voor Nederlandsche Taal en letterkunde* 43.161–188.

–. 1926. "Geschiedenis van het Noord-Nederlandsch dialectonderzoek". *Handleiding bij het Noord- en Zuidnederlandsch dialectonderzoek* ed. by L. Grootaers & G. G. Kloeke, 1–26. The Hague: Nijhoff.

–. 1927. *De Hollandsche expansie in de zestiende en zeventiende eeuw en haar weerspiegeling in de hedendaagsche Nederlandsche dialecten*. The Hague: Nijhoff.

–. 1950. *Herkomst en groei van het Afrikaans*. Amsterdam: Noord-Hollandse Uitgeversmaatschappij.

– & Ludovicus Grootaers. 1939–1972. *Taalatlas van Noord- en Zuid-Nederland*. 9 vols. Leiden: Brill.

Koerner, Konrad. 1995. *Professing Linguistic Historiography*. Amsterdam & Philadelphia: Benjamins.

Kruijsen, Joep. 1995. *Geografische patronen in taalcontact: Romaans leengoed in de Limburgse dialecten van Haspengouw*. Amsterdam: P. J. Meertens-Instituut.

Labov, William. 1972. *Sociolinguistic Patterns*. Philadelphia: Univ. of Pennsylvania Press.

Leopold, J. A. & L. Leopold. 1882. *Van de Schelde tot de Weichsel*. Groningen: Wolters.

Meertens, Pieter J. & Louise Kaiser. 1942. *Het eiland Urk*. Alphen aan de Rijn: Samsom.

Mooyaart, Marijke. 1992. *Atlas van Vroegmiddelnederlandse Taalvarianten.* Utrecht: LEd.

Noordegraaf, Jan. 1979. "Eene linguïstische kaart van Nederland: Rondom de dialectenquête van 1879". Gerritsen 1979.36–51.

Nuijtens, Emile Theophile Gerardus. 1962. *De tweetalige mens: Een taalsociologisch onderzoek naar het gebruik van dialect en cultuurtaal in Borne.* Assen: Van Gorcum.

Overdiep, Gerrit S. 1940. *De volkstaal van Katwijk aan Zee.* With the collaboration of C. Varkeviser. Antwerpen: Standaard boekhandel.

Paul, Hermann, ed. 1896–1909. *Grundriss der germanischen Philologie.* 2nd enlarged ed., 3 vols. Strassburg: Trübner.

Pauwels, J. L. 1933. *Enkele bloemnamen in de Zuidnederlandsche dialecten.* The Hague: Nijhoff.

Pée, Willem. 1936–1938. *Dialectgeographie der Nederlandsche diminutiva.* 2 vols. Tongeren: Michiels.

– et al. 1979. *Woordenboek van de Vlaamse dialecten.* Gent & Tongeren: Michiels.

Radlof, Johan Gottlieb. 1817. *Die Sprachen der Germanen in ihren sämmtlichen Mundarten dargestellt.* Frankfurt/M.

Sassen, Albert. 1953. *Het Drents van Ruinen.* Assen: Van Gorcum.

Scholtmeijer, Harrie. 1992. *Het Nederlands van de IJsselmeerpolders.* Kampen: Mondiss.

Schott, Albert. 1840. *Die Deutschen am Monte-Rosa.* Zürich.

Schrijnen, Jozef Karel Frans Hubert. 1920. *De isoglossen van Ramisch in Nederland.* Bussum: Brand.

–. 1902. "Benrather, Uerdinger en Panningerlinie". *Tijdschrift voor Nederlandse taal en Letterkunde* 21.249–252.

–. 1917. "Vlindernamen: Proeve van taalgeografie". *De Beiaard* 2.26–37.

Schuchardt, Hugo. 1885. *Über die Lautgesetze: Gegen die Junggrammatiker.* Berlin: Oppenheim.

Stadler, Franz Joseph. 1819. *Die Landessprachen der Schweiz.* Aarau.

Swaagman, J. Sonius. 1827. *Commentatio de dialecto Groningana.* Groningen: Oomkens.

Te Winkel, Jan. 1899–1901. *Noordnederlandse tongvallen. Atlas van taalkaarten met tekst.* 2 vols. Leiden: Brill.

–. 1904. *Inleiding tot de geschiedenis der Nederlandse taal.* Culemborg: Blom & Olivierse.

–. 1908–1919. *De ontwikkelingsgang der Nederlandsche Letterkunde.* 5 vols. Haarlem: De Erven F. Bohn.

Uhlenbeck, Christianus Cornelius. 1918. "Johan Hendrik Caspar Kern 6 april 1833–4 juli 1917". *Jaarboek Koninklijke Akademie van Wetenschappen* 1917.15–44. Amsterdam.

Vanacker, Valeer Frits. 1948. *Syntaxis van het Aalsters dialect.* Tongeren.

Van Bolhuis, Lambertus. 1783. *Groningerlandsche Woorden.* Groningen.

Van Bree, Cor. 1981. *Hebben-constructies en datiefconstructies binnen het Nederlandsche taalgebied: Een taalgeografisch onderzoek.* Hendrik Ido Ambacht: Intercontinental Graphics.

–. 1985. "Structuurverlies en structuurbehoud in het dialect van Haaksbergen en Enschede, een onderzoek naar verschillen in resistentie". *Leuvense Bijdragen* 74.1–35.

Van den Berg, Berend. 1938. *Oude tegenstellingen op Nederlands taalgebied.* Leiden: Dubbeldeman.

Van der Horst, Joop. 1979. "Van organisme naar mechanisme". Gerritsen 1979.21–34.

Van de Ven, M. Ch. H. J. 1969. *Taal in Noordoostpolder: Een sociolinguïstisch onderzoek.* Amsterdam: Publicaties van de Stichting voor het bevolkingsonderzoek in de drooggelegde zuiderzeepolders.

Van Ginneken, Jacques. 1913–1914. *Handboek der Nederlandse Taal: De sociologische structuur der Nederlandse taal.* 2 vols. 's Hertogenbosch: Malmberg.

–. 1943. *De studie der Nederlandse streektalen.* Amsterdam: Elsevier.

–. 1954. *Drie Waterlandse dialecten.* Vol. I: *Grammatica, phonologie, klankleer,* bezorgd door Antonius A. Weijnen. Vol. II: *De structuur van de woordenschat,* bezorgd door Maria van den Hombergh-Bot. Alphen aan den Rijn: Samsom.

Van Halsema, Diderik Frederik Johan. 1776. *Groninger woordenlijst.* Unpub. ms. Leiden Univ. Library.

Van Hout, Roeland. 1989. *De structuur van taalvariatie. Een sociolinguïstisch onderzoek naar het stadsialect van Nijmegen.* Dordrecht: Foris.

– & Uus Knops, eds. 1988. *Language Attitudes in the Dutch Language Area.* Dordrecht & Providence, R. I.: Foris.

Van Sterkenburg, Petrus G. J. 1992. *Het Woordenboek der Nederlandsche Taal: Portret van een Taalmonument.* The Hague: SDU.

Voortman, Berber. 1994. *Regionale variatie in het taalgebruik van notabelen: Een sociolinguïstisch onderzoek in Middelburg, Roermond en Zutphen.* Amsterdam: IFOTT.

Vousten, Rob. 1995. *Dialect als tweede taal: Linguïstische en extralinguïstische aspecten van de verwerving van een Noordlimburgs dialect door standaardtalige jongeren.* Amsterdam: Thesis Publishers.

Weinreich, Uriel, William Labov & Marvin I. Herzog. 1968. "Empirical Foundations for a Theory of Language Change". *Directions for Historical Linguistics* ed. by Winfred P. Lehmann & Yakov Malkiel, 95–189. Austin & London: Univ. of Texas Press.

Weijnen, Antonius A. 1937. *Onderzoek naar de dialectgrenzen in Noord-Brabant in aansluiting aan geografie, geschiedenis en volksleven.* Bergen op Zoom: Gebroeders Juten.

–. 1941. *De Nederlandse dialecten.* Groningen: Noordhoff.

–. 1951. *Taalgeografie en interne taalkunde.* (= Bijdragen en Mededelingen van de Dialectencommissie, 12.) Amsterdam: Noord-Hollandsche Uitgeversmij.

–. 1966. *Nederlandse dialectkunde.* Assen: Van Gorcum.

– et al. 1967–. *Woordenboek van de Brabantse dialecten.* Assen: Van Gorcum.

–. 1975. *Atlas Linguarum Europae: Introduction.* Assen: Van Gorcum.

– et al. 1983–. *Woordenboek van de Limburgse dialecten.* Assen: Van Gorcum.

Winkler, Johan. 1874. *Algemeen Nederduitsch en Friesch Dialecticon.* 2 vols. The Hague: Nijhoff.

Marinel Gerritsen, Nijmegen
(The Netherlands)

184. The dialectology of English in the British Isles

1. Standard versus nonstandard
2. The 17th century
3. The 18th century as a prelude to the 19th
4. The 19th century
5. Into the 20th century
6. Bibliography

1. Standard versus nonstandard

A standard variety of written English may be dated from the 15th century with the rise of the dialect of London, which had gained enormous prestige. Görlach (1995a: 192) observes:

"The early spread of the written standard brought with it a stigmatization of regional dialects, which became restricted to literary niches as in pastoral poetry, satire and substandard stage diction (in stereotypical form) before their scope was widened again in 18th-century Scotland and 19th-century England [i. e., through new forms of writing in Scots and English dialects]".

Early attitudes to dialects are revealed in Puttenham (1589, cited after Wakelin 1977: 27), who advised people to adopt as a standard "the vsuall speach of the Court, and that of London and the shires lying about London within lx. myles, and not much aboue". There were some in any shire who spoke in the approved manner, "but not the common people of euery shire, to whom the gentlemen, and also their learned clarkes do for the most part condescend". We may note here Puttenham's awareness of social variation and attitudes to dialects as well as regional variation. Words such as 'barbarous' and 'vulgar' become common from the 16th century on as epithets describing nonstandard speech. However, Renaissance nationalism fostered historical interest in the English language, and that interest included local speech. It was a part of the wider fascination with antiquities, the Society of Antiquaries being founded in 1572. Thus Dean Laurence Nowell's (c. 1514–1576) *Vocabularium Saxonicum* (c. 1565) cited nonstandard words to help illuminate Old English texts (see Marckwardt 1952).

2. The 17th century

The study of regional dialects in England began during the 17th century. Although the 19th century is our focus here, we cannot simply begin in the year 1800, for 19th-century dialectologists were working in part within a long-established tradition. Alexander Gill (1565–1635) attempted the first, admittedly very broad, classification of the Modern English dialects: "There are six major dialects: the general, the Northern, the Southern, the Eastern, the Western, and the Poetic" (1619 II, 102). He outlined the main characteristics of each. As Ihalainen (1994: 199) comments, Gill, a schoolmaster, was probably motivated chiefly by a "desire to eradicate provincialisms from the language of his young scholars" rather than by any profound interest in Dialectology.

Some dictionaries of the English language included 'hard' words whose distributions were regionally restricted, but more importantly for dialect lexicology, John Ray (1627–1705) compiled *A Collection of English Words Not Generally Used* (1674), which was the first general English dialect dictionary. Words are defined, and sometimes their area of provenance is indicated by county, town, or wider area. The book is divided into "North-Country" and "South & East-Country". According to his prefatory remarks, Ray compiled his glossary for three reasons: (1) because nobody had done anything like it before; (2) to assist those travelling in the Northern counties; and (3) to afford diversion to the curious. Görlach (1995b: 83) observes that Ray "showed an almost modern descriptive interest in local dialects", while Ihalainen (1994: 200) suggests that Ray "became interested in dialects partly because of the regional variation in names of plants he was studying".

The 17th century also saw the compilation of several specialized (occupational) and regional vocabularies. For instance in 1677 Bishop William Nicolson (1655–1727) compiled his "Glossarium Brigantinum", a collection of 327 Cumberland dialect words. George Meriton's (1634–1711) *A Yorkshire Dialogue* of 1683, written wholly in a Yorkshire dialect, was the first in the dialect dialogue genre that would subsequently prove so popular. The second and third editions have a glossary appended. On the one hand, the work fits into a European literary genre of writings about trickery and roguery. On the other, it reflects renewed interest in antiquities and the English language after the founding of the Royal Society in 1645.

3. The 18th century as a prelude to the 19th

In the 18th century we see a development of several earlier trends. There was interest in dialect words in some general English dictionaries, especially Nathan(iel) Bailey's (d. 1742) *An Universal Etymological English Dictionary* (1721); manuscript glossaries were compiled for a number of dialects (see Wakelin 1977: 43); and Francis Grose (1731–1791) compiled *A Provincial Glossary* (1787), the second general English dialect dictionary. Grose offers definitions, occasionally quotes earlier forms and gives a general idea of the provenance of a term: North, South, West, Common, or sometimes the county. He has no words that are distinctively East. He refers to the usefulness of such a provincial dictionary in helping to gloss older authors. The late 18th century saw a number of printed local dialect glossaries too. Particularly noteworthy is that appended to the Rev. John Hutton's *A Tour to the Caves* (1780). His prefatory remarks explain the uses of such a glossary: in the interpretation of older texts; as an aid to business transactions and travel in the North, and to the understanding of court evidence there; in etymology; for amusement or diversion; and to help the reader avoid provincial words and pronunciations in polite society.

18th-century dialect literature ranged from the Rev. Josiah Relph's (1712–1743) pastorals in the Cumberland dialect, published posthumously in his *Poems* (1747), to several dialogues that were essentially specimens illustrative of local dialects: e. g., *"An Exmoor Scolding"* of 1727, which was reprinted in the *Gentleman's Magazine* of 1746 along with the "Exmoor Courtship" and John Collier's (1706–1786) *A View of the Lancashire Dialect*. This last piece proved so popular that it eventually ran to over 100 editions. On the one hand, it is a specimen of a local dialect, as its title and the appended glossary suggest, and of local manners and customs; on the other it is, like its Yorkshire predecessor (cf. 2.), a literary piece within the genre of writings about trickery and roguery. Many 19th-century compositions would reflect this same mix of humorous entertainment and antiquarian specimen.

A further motivation for dialect study in the 18th and 19th centuries was a religious one. Whitehall (1933: 261–262) drew attention to the role played by the clergy from 1700 onwards. In an effort to understand their parishioners better, clergymen began to learn local dialects; such knowledge helped them perform their educational and pastoral duties more effectively. Whitehall (1933: 262) comments: "From this point it was an easy step to scholarly interest in dialectology and the sponsoring of dialect publications. Under clerical support dialect study and dialect literature flourished until the economic upheavals of the Industrial Revolution brought about the influx of a strong current toward secularization." A didactic element is unmistakeable in the Rev. William Hutton's (1762–1811) *A Bran New Wark* of 1785, a curious piece written in a mixture of literary English and Westmorland dialect. Hutton explained in his introductory remarks that his parishioners were more likely to heed his homilies if these were written in the local dialect.

4. The 19th century

4.1. General

There is in the 19th century on the one hand a clear continuation of earlier antiquarian trends, with increased production of dialect glossaries, specimens of local manners and customs (including speech), curiosities or literary diversions, and pieces highlighting provincialisms, whether for purposes of travel or so that provincials would know what to avoid in high society. Some authors of dialect specimens, it is true, took a positive view of dialect, but for the greater part dialect was viewed as a curiosity, and the clergymen and other antiquarians who compiled local glossaries were convinced of the superiority of the classical languages; as Levitt (1989: 9) writes: "They would not themselves wittingly speak in anything but the accents of what they considered the best society. Amateurs in both senses of the word, one can detect in the very titles of many of their collections a sentimental, kindly but essentially patronising spirit." However, despite frequently negative social attitudes to nonstandard speech, there was no clear programme to eradicate the provincial dialects until after the Education Act of 1870, and the effects of that were neither so far-reaching nor so rapid as scholars have typically assumed. Most of the population continued to speak a regional dialect throughout the century, and indeed one major shift *vis-à-vis* the 18th century lies in the evolution of dialect literatures to meet the needs of the new urban populations brought about by the industrialization of the North of England (cf. 4.5.). We also witness a development of the 18th-century sense of provincial consciousness into a much stronger local patriotism, and an increased concern with local antiquities. These interests were furthered by the founding of local learned societies, a number of which promoted dialect study and writing. Examples include the Manchester Literary Club, the Cumberland & Westmorland Antiquarian & Archaeological Society, and the Rochdale Literary & Scientific Society.

On the other hand, the 19th century is of course notable for a revolutionary development in scientific modes of thinking in most fields of inquiry. The application to language study of methods from the physical sciences led to a concern with the comparison and classification of languages, and with the history of languages and the mechanisms of linguistic change. Philologists also became concerned about the quality of their data. A scientific Dialectology arose as part of this more general development. There were obvious influences from Romanticism, which led to a positive reassessment of dialect-speakers and dialect speech as well as fostering linguistic nationalism and directing attention to modern languages and dialects (Robert Burns' 18th-century Scots vernacular poems were very influential in 19th-century England); from Comparative Philology, which saw dialects as being linguistically important and worthy of study; from the Neogrammarians, whose work provided one impetus for linguistic geography and inspired a more scientific historically-based dialect monograph; from Positivism; and from developments in phonetics. Similarly out of the former ragbag of manners and customs more definite conceptions of Folklore and Folk Life began to arise in the 19th century. While the scientific advances in 19th-century Philology and Dialectology are reflected in ample measure in the works of such English dialect scholars as Alexander John Ellis (1814–1890) and Joseph Wright (1855–1930), that fact is not to deny that attitudes towards nonstandard dialects were often negative in the British Isles, nor that much work on English dialects remained altogether amateurish.

4.2. Early lexicology

The close link that antiquarians felt existed between the ancient and the dialectal is made explicit in the titles of two mid-19th-century dictionaries: James Orchard Halliwell's (1820–1889) *Dictionary of Archaic & Provincial Words* (1st ed., 1847) and Thomas Wright's (1810–1887) *Dictionary of Obsolete & Provincial English* (1857). Halliwell (1847: vii) had no doubts about his own motivations: "So many archaisms are undoubtedly still preserved by our rural population, that it was thought the incorporation of a glossary of provincialisms would render the work a more useful guide than one restricted to known archaisms." He wrote that "the only sufficient reason for preserving" provincial words was "the important assistance they continually afford in glossing the works of our early writers". His dictionary contains over 51,000 headwords prefaced by an essay on the English dialects, arranged on a county basis. A remarkably large number of printed glossaries covering more restricted areas appeared during the 19th century. Garnett (1836) reviewed some early dialect glossaries and dictionaries, while J. Wright covered most of the glossaries to 1889 in an important state-of-the-art report, "Englische Mundarten" ["English Dialects"] (1891, transl. in Shorrocks 1988), written at a critical time just before his own works were to change the face of English Dialectology. We are warned that, although the dictionaries of Halliwell (1847) and T. Wright (1857) are valuable, they fail to distinguish living terms from obsolete (1891: 976), and that many of the local glossaries are unscientific. Wright goes on to list what he takes to be the most useful and reliable dictionaries and glossaries. Scots, Hiberno-English and Welsh English are included. Glossaries are also listed in the Bibliography in vol. VI of Wright (1898–1905).

4.3. The English Dialect Society: Wright's Dictionary and Grammar

In 1870 William Aldis Wright (1836–1914) made a plea for the formation of a dialect society and the collection of the 'provincial', i. e., regional lexicon on a national scale: "It has long been my conviction that some systematic effort ought to be made for the collection and preservation of our provincial words. In a few years it will be too late. Railroads and certified teachers are doing their work" (Wright 1870: 271). The idea that "in a few years it will be too late" is one that we find repeated by J. Wright, Ellis (who called for the founding of an English Dialect Society in Part III of *On Early English Pronunciation*, p. xii), the Rev. William Walter Skeat (1835–1912), and others. The changes brought about by urbanization and industrialization, cheap printing and advances in transportation and education appeared at the time to be levelling the regional dialects very rapidly (though the rate of levelling has generally been overestimated somewhat by scholars). Inspired by the urgent need to collect the regional lexicon and by a desire to help Ellis with Part IV of *On Early English Pronunciation* (which was at first to have contained the account of English dialects before the true size of the project became apparent), Skeat, Professor of Anglo-Saxon at Cambridge, founded the English Dialect Society (EDS) in 1873. (Cf. the founding of the Folklore Society in 1878 and the Folk-Song Society in 1898 – also to collect and preserve what would otherwise be lost.) Further impetus was no doubt provided by the Philological Society's (founded 1842) earlier instigation of the *New English Dictionary* (now *Oxford English Dictionary*) in 1857–1858.

The EDS was an initiative of enormous proportions. It collected nonstandard words, phrases, and expressions (including proverbs and technical terms) from all over the British Isles, and published 80 volumes in four series from 1873–1896: (1) Bibliographies; (2) Reprints of Existing Glossaries; (3) New Glossaries; (4) Miscellanies. The Society's Bibliography (Skeat & Nodal 1873–1877) was an important work that incorporated and superseded existing county bibliographies and the earlier general bibliography of English dialects put out by the publisher John Russell Smith (1839). Most of the rest of the Society's volumes are glossaries, reflecting its primary interest in lexis (though the series New Glossaries did include Wright's (1892) pioneering Windhill grammar). G. L. Brook (1910–1987) remarked with justification that "the material is too often arranged by counties. It is only rarely that county boundaries coincide with dialect boundaries" (1978: 155). Arguably the best of its glossaries is Nodal & Milner (1875–1882), still the standard Lancashire glossary. Etymologies, with which Skeat assisted, were only included in this glossary where the editors felt on reasonably safe ground. Around 1879 the Society began to think of its collecting and publishing activities as constituting preparation for what would rapidly become its ultimate goal: the compilation of an *English Dialect Dictionary*. Accordingly it assembled a huge library of over 800 linguistic and dialectal books and pamphlets that were excerpted for the Dictionary. The English Dialect Library is still intact, and held in the Central Free Library, Manchester.

It took Skeat a long time to find a suitable Editor for the Dictionary. Eventually Joseph Wright was found, a man who was by then a brilliant philologist but who had been unable to read until well into his teens, so that he had learned a Yorkshire dialect thoroughly before he ever encountered Standard English. He became Secretary of the Society and Editor of the *English Dialect Dictionary* in 1895, whereupon the Society disbanded the next year, feeling that, as work was now underway on the Dictionary, its task was complete. The Dictionary was promptly published in six large volumes (1898–1905), consisting of

c. 5,000 pages, 100,000 headwords and 500,000 quotations and references to published sources (to project from figures available for vol. I). The aim of the Dictionary was to record all the dialect words then in use in the British Isles, or known to have been in use within the previous 200 years. It attests eloquently to the great advances that had been made in British lexicography during the second half of the 19th century, evincing a remarkable improvement in systematicity, thoroughness and historical scholarship. Each entry contains some or all of the following in the order given here: (1) headword; (2) part of speech; (3) usage note (e. g., *obsolete*); (4) geographical distribution; (5) alternative spellings; (6) pronunciation in broad phonetic script; (7) definition(s), with sources and distribution; (8) supporting quotations from oral and published sources, with sources and distribution; (9) cross-references; (10) derived forms, compounds, idioms, proverbs, etc.; (11) etymology, broken down into (i) quotations from early English literature; (ii) cognate forms and/or comparisons from other European languages and dialects; (iii) word formation. Superscript numbers attached to county abbreviations refer the reader to specific sources listed in the Bibliography. The Dictionary has been criticized on a number of counts: the wide time span of its coverage; vague localization and uneven geographical coverage; the unreliability of dialect literature as linguistic evidence; debatable etymologies; the requirement of written authority for the entries; inexpert correspondents and intermediaries; lack of information about individual informants; and the fact that the commonness or rarity of entries is not usually given. These are fair points, as long as they are tempered by knowledge of the circumstances under which Wright worked and the resources available to him. Generally the Dictionary has been very well received and acknowledged to be an indispensable reference work of enviable magnitude and craftsmanship.

By way of summation and complement Wright added, at Skeat's instigation, the *English Dialect Grammar*, which was published as a part of vol. VI, and separately (1905). It is devoted chiefly to historical phonology (with an extensive lexical index); the *grammar*, in the narrower sense of the word, is mainly inflectional morphology, with little on other aspects of syntax, though that is unsurprising given the date of the work. Like the Dictionary, it covered the dialects of all parts of the British Isles where English was habitually spoken at the time. Wright himself thought it philologically more significant than the Dictionary, and some later scholars have echoed that view. Certainly, it is a remarkable synthesis, and has been generally well received. It is of course not without its faults and criticisms similar to those made of the Dictionary have inevitably been directed at the Grammar too, for — notwithstanding extra work undertaken for the latter — they share both corpus and methodology. Particular concern has been expressed about the use of intermediaries, many correspondents' inability to cope with the phonetic alphabet, and unevenness of coverage. Some have also claimed that it bore the hallmarks of a rushed job. Brook, who admired Wright's achievement, observed in a more temperate fashion that the Grammar was a "less satisfactory" work than the Dictionary, and that "it could with advantage be replaced by an entirely new work, making use of the material recorded in the Survey of English Dialects" (1969: 18). While there is something to that, it must be countered that the Questionnaire of the Survey of English Dialects was less than ideal for purposes of eliciting grammar (the recently-published *Survey of English Dialects: The dictionary & grammar* (Upton et al. 1994) is not what Brook had in mind, since the grammatical component is an index rather than a synthesis), and that the time difference between the two surveys is of such an order that Wright's Grammar would still remain valuable for its coverage of an earlier period.

Most scholars have found the decision to disband the EDS in 1896 unfortunate, incomprehensible or even naive and complacent (Petyt 1980: 78 ff.). Granted there was still much to be done, but it must be appreciated that the members of the Society were not full-time dialectologists; and that a dialect society with an expensive subscription (half a guinea per annum for the years 1873–1876, and one guinea per annum for the years 1877–1896) could not go on indefinitely. Rather, to facilitate the completion of their huge undertaking, the members were asked by Skeat to transfer their subscriptions to the Dictionary (see Skeat 1896: 1). Further, Wright himself had weighty duties as Professor of Comparative Philology at Oxford (he succeeded Max

Müller to the Chair in 1901), and heavy research commitments in other areas, notably a series of historical and comparative teaching grammars. To blame Wright personally for the winding-up of the EDS, and to charge him with having abandoned Dialectology after the Dictionary and Grammar because he thought there was nothing more to be done, i.e., in effect to have done less for English Dialectology, than he might have done — a line taken by a number of scholars, some of them quite obviously following Dieth (1947) — is both unappreciative and historiographically unreasonable. Wright had published an important but overlooked survey article on English dialects (1891), a pioneering monograph on the Windhill dialect (1892), and then brought out the enormous *English Dialect Dictionary* between 1898 and 1905, having assumed the Editorship as late as 1895. This was a truly gargantuan task, whatever the help from his wife, for Wright assumed huge secretarial and financial burdens in connection with the Dictionary (see E. M. Wright 1932 for a detailed account of the work on the Dictionary). It is even more remarkable that he could be persuaded to add the *English Dialect Grammar*. Neither of these works — whatever their shortcomings — has been superseded yet. In addition, Wright saw to it that the EDS's enthusiastic Yorkshire Committee of Workers went on with its work by founding the Yorkshire Dialect Society in 1897. Dieth's complaints about the deficiencies of Wright's contribution to the discipline twice drew a deserved rebuke from Brook (1981: 5—6; 1969: 22), who justly estimated that Wright's work in English Dialectology was "four or five times as great in quantity and importance as a reasonably productive scholar might expect to accomplish in the course of a life-time" (1981: 6).

In discussing Wright's supposed abandonment of Dialectology, scholars seem repeatedly to attribute to him a certain self-satisfaction with what he had already done, and/or a conviction of doubtful merit that 'pure' dialect was in its death throes by 1905. But too much, it seems to the present writer, is being made here of prefatory remarks in the Dictionary (1898 I: v) and Grammar (1905: vii) about the rate of change in the traditional vernaculars, and how it would soon be too late to address certain questions about the state of the regional dialects in the late 19th century. No doubt Wright did, like many another, overestimate the rate of levelling of the regional dialects. But it does *not* follow from these remarks that Wright therefore thought there was nothing more to be done. In a letter of 21 Nov. 1924 to his longtime friend, Ferdinand Holthausen, Wright wrote: "There is an enormous amount still to be done in dialectology in most Germanic countries, and if I were a younger man — with plenty of leisure — I should devote all my spare time and energies to English dialects" (E. M. Wright 1932 II, 481). This is unequivocal, and establishes beyond a doubt that the man who had already carried out so very much work on English dialects knew full well how much remained to be done; it also points up the relevant practical considerations. Similarly Wright was quite convinced of the need for a more modern (i.e., post-Ellis 1889) geographical survey of English dialects. Wright & Wright (1923: 2—3) commented that we would never establish Middle English dialect boundaries properly until we had a good atlas of the present-day dialects.

4.4. Linguistic geography

Though Gill (cf. 2.) had produced a broad classification of the English dialects, linguistic or dialect geography is very much a 19th-century phenomenon. Garnett (1836) and Guest (1838) commented briefly on the division of the dialects in the Middle and Old English periods. But the first attempt at a somewhat more detailed classification of the Modern English dialects was made by Prince Louis-Lucien Bonaparte (1813—1891), nephew of Napoleon I and an independent linguistic scholar who resided in London, in 1877. He had commissioned numerous translations of the *Song of Solomon* into regional English dialects by way of linguistic specimens. Bonaparte made his findings available to Ellis, a gentleman-scholar of private means, whose work completely superseded his own. Ellis, who had been involved with the Early English Text Society (EETS), was working on a definitive history of the English language, *On Early English Pronunciation* (1869—1889), when he realized that much of historical interest was preserved in the regional vernaculars rather than in writing or educated speech. He therefore undertook a survey of regional English, published in the main as Part V of his *magnum opus*, and subtitled "The Existing Phonology of English Dialects Compared with That of West Saxon

Speech" (1889). (Note that, although dialectologists typically cite only Part V of *On Early English Pronunciation*, discussion of dialects actually begins in Part IV (1875), which includes the English spoken in America and Ireland.) The Philological Society, the Chaucer Society and the EETS all lent support. It is the first detailed, reasonably systematic, wide-ranging, geographical survey of English dialects, including varieties spoken in England, Scotland, Wales, and part of Ireland, as well as some observatons on certain overseas varieties; and it is based upon spoken materials, collected using both the direct and indirect methods. Ellis was well ahead of his time in using the former. From a remarkable wealth of data (there are 835 closely-printed pages in Part V alone), a classification of the English dialects — never since superseded — is distilled, and summarized in cartographic form. Ellis divides the dialects of England and Lowland Scotland into six *Divisions*, subdivided into forty-two *Districts*. Within each District, the dialect is further subdivided into a number of Varieties (and even Sub-varieties). Interestingly (and correctly), his 'transverse lines' or isoglosses in the extreme North of England do not coincide exactly with the political border between England and Scotland. The work is also characterized by a pioneering use of highly-detailed phonetic transcription. As no system of phonetic notation adequate to Ellis' needs was available at the time, he invented his own, the *palaeotype*. As one familiar with printing, and as one who had published extensively on spelling, phonetics, music, and physics, he was singularly well-qualified to undertake such a task.

Ellis's work has often been criticized, e.g., by Dieth (1947: 76, 85), for such things as inaccuracies, the use of the indirect method (though he used the direct method too), failure to present his findings in cartographic form (despite the two summary maps), and for the difficult palaeotype. The present writer has suggested elsewhere (Shorrocks 1991: 324 ff.) that Ellis's work is currently undervalued and that modern research often confirms Ellis's findings. The materials and analyses for the Northwest of England are generally very good, with Thomas Hallam (1819–1895) having done much fieldwork of value on the North Midland dialects and John George Goodchild (1844–1906) on the West Northern. Both had an excellent command of the palaeotype. Ellis's work was pioneering in both dialect geography and phonetics. Unfortunately, in a sense, his phonetic notation was overtaken almost as soon as *The Existing Phonology of English Dialects* appeared in 1889 because of the publication of the International Phonetic Association's more accessible alphabet in August 1888.

4.5. Dialect literature

In the late 18th and early 19th centuries dialect literatures developed chiefly in the industrialized North of England to meet the needs of the new urban populations created by the Industrial Revolution. Lancashire and Yorkshire have the strongest traditions of such writing, which grew out of earlier oral traditions via street literature. Dialect poetry, plays and prose were written in large quantities from around the middle of the 19th century, as well as journals, newspapers and almanacs. Although John Collier (cf. 3.) is looked upon as the founder of Lancashire dialect writing, he is actually quite different from the 19th-century dialect authors, despite the fact that they admired and emulated him, taking over many of his orthographical conventions in the process. Collier had essentially written an antiquarian specimen with his *A View of the Lancashire Dialect* (1746). The new literature was different in that it grew in part out of working-class (to use a somewhat anachronistic term) culture and was directed at a dialect-speaking readership or audience. Indeed much of this early dialect literature was performed in schools, at penny readings or union meetings, in churches and at other social gatherings, or read out aloud by whoever *could* read in pubs and homes. Certainly a 'higher' dialect literature continued too in the form of specimens of interest to antiquarians and philologists; but what is really new about 19th-century dialect literature is the evolution of a substantial literature written specifically for dialect speakers. (On the nature of this new dialect literature see further Shorrocks 1996, 1999.)

The study of dialect literature began in the 19th century, with bibliographies, annotated anthologies, discussions of the suitability of dialect as a literary medium, essays devoted to particular writers, etc. Literary dialect (in works otherwise written in standard English) found new outlets during the 19th century in the novels of Brontë, Gaskell, Eliot, Hardy and others. We witness a new concern for the social, economic and moral conditions of the working class in writers such as Elizabeth

Gaskell. Dialect literature and literary dialect became important to dialectologists as corpora of linguistic evidence, and study of them began in the 19th century. Nicolai (1876) is an interesting early essay in which a brief grammatical and phonological sketch is attempted for each of four main dialects. He includes a few remarks on lexis and there are comments too on phonetic processes such as assimilation and metathesis. The author consciously restricts himself to those dialects that have a literature: (1) Lancashire; (2) Somerset; (3) Yorkshire; (4) Scottish, noting that, whereas poetry is only an occasional phenomenon in the English dialects, "der schottische Dialekt" has a more substantial literary tradition, having been more like a separate language than a dialect for a long time. There is however a quite startling omission from Nicolai's survey, viz. the Cumberland and Westmorland dialects, which had a very rich published literature by as early as 1839.

4.6. Miscellaneous

The last three decades of the 19th century are noteworthy for the compilation of general county bibliographies and specialized dialect bibliographies arranged by county or author, in addition to the EDS's Bibliography (cf. 4.3.). Endeavours of interest in the neighbouring field of Folklore (not always distinguishable as a discipline at the time) include antiquarian collections of folk-songs and ballads, folklore and folk-tales, superstitions, customs, proverbs and sayings, as well as more specific items such as a dictionary of folk-names of birds. Occupational dialects were studied in small measure, e. g., the special sheepscoring numerals used by shepherds. Scientific writings on regional botany, fauna, etc. often contained local names. The transactions of local learned societies are important here, as also in the case of other onomastic studies of local personal and place-names, though their roles in furthering dialectology remain relatively unexplored. Particularly thorough and scientific is Goodchild's "Traditional Names of Places in Edenside" (1883), based on nearly 14 years' work with the Government Geological Survey of Cumberland and Westmorland north of the Lake District Watershed. Goodchild, who did excellent fieldwork for Ellis (1889), employed the palaeotype to record the local pronunciation of Edenside names precisely. (Dialect was also used in ephemeral advertising materials and in the related field of political election campaigning in the 19th and early 20th centuries, but dialectologists have yet to study such sources.)

5. Into the 20th century

Towards the end of the 19th century, sounder etymological studies began to appear, with some emphasis on the Scandinavian element in English dialects; though this impulse carried over into 20th-century English Dialectology, work on the lexicon was in total less marked than before. Antiquarianism remained a significant driving force for some time to come; bibliographical endeavours continued briefly; and a little more attention was devoted to occupational dialects, some of it in connection with studies in Folk Life. There was an increased amount of work devoted to dialect literature and literary dialect, especially in the early 20th century; and a decided increase in onomastic studies, especially with the work of the English Place Name Society.

As we have seen, Ellis (1889) had begun a descriptive phonetic survey of the English dialects for historical purposes, and similar sentiments would inspire the 20th-century Survey of English Dialects, which was historical and phonetic in orientation, as were many of the monographs associated with it. Concern with sound change and its regularity inspired not only the development of linguistic geography, but also J. Wright's monograph on the dialect of Windhill (1892), the first truly scientific monograph on an English dialect. Earlier monographs had been relatively unsystematic, with only Murray's (1873) study of the dialects of the Southern counties of Scotland being historical; and the phonological and grammatical components of most glossaries had been largely unsatisfactory, as detailed in Wright (1891: 975), not least because their authors lacked phonetic training. Now in 1892 Wright, who had studied under the Neogrammarians in Germany, produced an exemplary monograph on the Windhill dialect, notable for its emphasis on diachronic phonology and inflectional morphology. A vigorous local monograph tradition grew up patterned after it, except that Middle rather than Old English was later used as the basis for the historical description. In addition Luick (1896) provided a stimulus for a small amount of comparative historical work on the Modern dialects and work in Old and Middle English dialectology in the 20th century.

Reflecting on the state of English Dialectology at the beginning of the 20th century, Wyld (1904) distinguished an early, pre-scientific, antiquarian-sentimental phase in dialect study from a more systematic, scientific, modern phase associated with the development of Comparative Philology. In the latter, the value of dialect study for philological purposes is recognized: general principles of linguistic change can be better deduced from living dialects — a point that recent work in sociolinguistics shows signs of returning to. He is disturbed by the thin numbers of native scholars in the more rigorous kind of study, and criticizes the disbanding of the EDS. Skeat (1911: 105) by contrast wrote in his *English Dialects* (the first book devoted exclusively to a survey of the English dialects and English Dialectology): "The fulness of the vocabulary in the Dictionary [Wright 1898–1905], and the minuteness of the account of the phonology and accidence in the Grammar [Wright 1905], leave nothing to desire. Certainly no other country can give so good an account of its dialects." It is perhaps this statement more than any other that has caused some commentators to accuse English Dialectologists of naivety and complacency: Petyt refers to "this complacent attitude" on the part of the EDS members, and blames them squarely for Britain's late start on more modern dialect atlases (1980: 78–79, 81). The truth lies somewhere in between, for Skeat is being uncritical, Wyld selective, and Petyt is arguing purely from a modern perspective. British Dialectologists were unlikely to begin a new survey in the early 20th century, when the work of Ellis and Wright was still reasonably fresh. It must also be emphasized that results of surveys carried out in other countries were not instantly available in published form, so that some of the inadequacies of 19th-century British work only became apparent later.

6. Bibliography

Bailey, N[athaniel]. 1721. *An Universal Etymological English Dictionary.* — See William E[dward] A[rmytage] Axon, ed. *English Dialect Words of the Eighteenth Century as Shown in the Universal Etymological Dictionary of Nathaniel Bailey.* (= EDS, 41.) London: Trübner & Co. for EDS, 1883.

Bonaparte, Prince Louis-Lucien. 1877. "On the Dialects of Monmouthshire [...] with a New Classification of the English Dialects". *Transactions of the Philological Society* 1875–1876.570–581.

Brook, G[eorge] L[eslie]. 1969. "The Future of English Dialect Studies". *Studies in Honour of Harold Orton on the Occasion of his Seventieth Birthday* ed. by Stanley Ellis, 15–22. [Leeds:] School of English, Univ. of Leeds.

—. 1978. *English Dialects.* 3rd ed. London: André Deutsch.

—. 1981. "Dialect Societies in England". *Journal of the Lancashire Dialect Society* 30.3–11.

[Collier, John. 1746.] *A View of the Lancashire Dialect.* Manchester: booksellers.

Dieth, Eugen. 1947 [1946]. "A New Survey of English Dialects". *Essays & Studies* 32.74–104.

Ellis, Alexander J[ohn]. 1869–89. *On Early English Pronunciation.* 5 vols. (= *Publications of the Chaucer Soc.*, EETS, and Phil. Soc.) London. Part III, 1871. Part IV, 1875. Part V, *The Existing Phonology of English Dialects Compared with That of West Saxon Speech,* 1889.

"Exmoor Courtship" and "An Exmoor Scolding". 1746. *Gentleman's Magazine* 16.297–300, 352–355.

[Garnett, Rev. Richard]. 1836. "Art[icle] III". *Quarterly Review.* 55: 110 (Feb.).354–387.

Gill, Alexander. 1619. — See Bror Danielsson & Arvid Gabrielson. *Alexander Gill's Logonomia Anglica (1619).* 2 vols. (= *Acta Universitatis Stockholmiensis*; Stockholm Studies in English, 26–27.) Stockholm: Almqvist & Wiksell, 1972.

Goodchild, J[ohn] G. 1883 [1881–82]. "Traditional Names of Places in Edenside". *Transactions of the Cumberland & Westmorland Antiquarian & Archaeological Society* o. s. 6.50–76.

Görlach, Manfred. 1995a. "English in Nineteenth-Century England". *New Studies in the History of English* by M. Görlach, 190–234. Heidelberg: Winter.

—. 1995b. "Dialect Lexis in Early Modern English Dictionaries". *New Studies in the History of English* by M. Görlach, 82–127. Heidelberg: Winter.

Grose, Francis. 1787. *A Provincial Glossary; with a collection of local proverbs, & popular superstitions.* London: S. Hooper.

Guest, Edwin. 1838. *A History of English Rhythms.* — See *A New Edition* ed. by the Rev. Walter W. Skeat, 1882. (Repr., New York: Haskell House, 1968.)

Halliwell, James Orchard. 1847. *Dictionary of Archaic & Provincial Words.* London: Russell Smith.

H[utton], [Rev.] J[ohn]. 1780. *A Tour to the Caves, in the Environs of Ingleborough & Settle, in the West Riding of Yorkshire.* London: booksellers.

[Hutton, Rev. William]. 1785. *A Bran New Wark, by William de Worfat.* Kendal: W. Pennington.

Ihalainen, Ossi. 1994. "The Dialects of England since 1776". *The Cambridge History of the English Language,* vol. V: *English in Britain & Overseas* ed. by Robert Burchfield, 197–274. Cambridge: Cambridge Univ. Press.

Levitt, John. 1989. "Dialect Study Then and Now". *Journal of the Lancashire Dialect Society* 38.7–16.

Luick, Karl. 1896. *Untersuchungen zur englischen Lautgeschichte.* Straßburg: Trübner.

Marckwardt, Albert H. 1952. *Laurence Nowell's Vocabularium Saxonicum.* Ann Arbor: Univ. of Michigan Press; London: Geoffrey Cumberlege for Oxford Univ. Press.

M[eriton], G[eorge]. 1683. – See A. C. Cawley, ed., *George Meriton's "A Yorkshire Dialogue" (1683).* (= *Yorkshire Dialect Soc. Reprint*, 2.) Kendal: Titus Wilson for YDS, 1959.

Murray, James A. H. 1873. *The Dialect of the Southern Counties of Scotland.* Berlin & London: Asher & Co. for Philological Society.

Nicolai, A. F. 1876. "Über die Dialekte der englischen Sprache". *Archiv für das Studium der neueren Sprachen und Literaturen* 55.383–406.

Nicolson, Bishop William. 1677. "Glossarium Brigantinum". – See Rev. Mackenzie E[dward] C[harles] Walcott, *Glossary of Words in the Cumbrian Dialect* [London: 1869?].

Nodal, John H[oward] & George Milner. 1875–82. *A Glossary of the Lancashire Dialect.* 2 Parts. (= *Publications of the Manchester Literary Club;* EDS 10, 35.) Manchester & London.

Petyt, K[eith] M[alcolm]. 1980. *The Study of Dialect: An introduction to Dialectology.* London: André Deutsch.

Ray, John. 1691 [1674]. *A Collection of English Words Not Generally Used.* 2nd augmented ed. London: Christopher Wilkinson.

Relph, Rev. Josiah. 1747. *A Miscellany of Poems.* Glasgow: Robert Foulis for Mr. Thomlinson in Wigton.

Shorrocks, Graham. 1988. "English Dialects: A Translation of Joseph Wright's "Englische Mundarten". *JEL* 21: 2.127–136.

–. 1991. "A. J. Ellis as Dialectologist: A reassessment". *HL* 18/2–3.321–334.

–. 1996. "Non-Standard Dialect Literature and Popular Culture". *Speech Past & Present: Studies in English dialectology in memory of Ossi Ihalainen* ed. by Juhani Klemola, Merja Kytö & Matti Rissanen, 385–411. Frankfurt/M.: Lang.

–. 1999. "Working-class Literature in Working-class Language: The North of England". *English Literature and the Other Languages* ed. by Ton [= A. J.] Hoenselaars & Marius Buning. With an Afterword by N. F. Blake, 87–96. (= *DQR [Dutch Quarterly Review] Studies in Literature*, 24.) Amsterdam & Atlanta: Rodopi.

Skeat, Rev. Walter W[illiam]. 1896. "The English Dialect Society's Last Notice". 31 Dec. 1896. [Seemingly issued as a single folded leaf of 3 pp.]

–. 1911. *English Dialects from the Eighth Century to the Present Day.* (= *Cambridge Manuals of Science & Literature.*) Cambridge: Cambridge Univ. Press.

– & J[ohn] H[oward] Nodal, eds. 1873–1877. *A Bibliographical List of the Works that have been Published, or are Known to Exist in MS, Illustrative of the Various Dialects of English.* (= EDS 2; 8; 18. Series A. Bibliographical, 1.) London: Trübner & Co. for EDS.

Smith, John Russell, comp. 1839. *A Bibliographical List of the Works that have been Published, towards Illustrating the Provincial Dialects of England.* London: Russell Smith.

Upton, Clive, David Parry & J[ohn] D. A. Widdowson. 1994. *Survey of English Dialects: The dictionary & grammar.* London & New York: Routledge.

Wakelin, Martyn F. 1977. *English Dialects: An introduction.* Rev. ed. London: Athlone Press.

Whitehall, Harold. 1933. "Thomas Shadwell and the Lancashire Dialect". *Michigan University Publications, Language & Literature, Studies in English & Comparative Literature* 10.261–278.

Wright, Elizabeth Mary. 1932. *The Life of Joseph Wright.* 2 vols. London: Oxford Univ. Press.

Wright, Joseph. 1891. "Englische Mundarten". *Grundriß der germanischen Philologie* ed. by Hermann Paul, vol. I, 975–981. Straßburg: Trübner.

–. 1892. *A Grammar of the Dialect of Windhill, in the West Riding of Yorkshire.* (= EDS, 67.) London: Kegan, Paul, Trench, Trübner & Co. for EDS.

–, ed. 1898–1905. *The English Dialect Dictionary.* 6 vols. London & Oxford: Henry Frowde for EDS; New York: G. P. Putnam's Sons.

–. 1905. *The English Dialect Grammar.* Oxford: Henry Frowde.

– & Elizabeth Mary Wright. 1923. *An Elementary Middle English Grammar.* London: Humphrey Milford for Oxford Univ. Press.

Wright, Thomas, comp. 1857. *Dictionary of Obsolete & Provincial English.* London: Henry G. Bohn.

Wright, William Aldis. 1870. "Provincial Glossary". *Notes & Queries* 4th ser. 5, 12 March, 271.

[Wyld, Henry Cecil]. 1904. "The Study of Living Popular Dialects and Its Place in the Modern Science of Language". *Transactions of the Yorkshire Dialect Society* part 6, vol. I.5–31.

Graham Shorrocks, St. John's (Canada)

185. Dialectology in the Slavic countries: An overview from its beginnings to the early twentieth century

1. Introduction
2. General developments
3. Individual Slavic lands
4. Summary
5. Bibliography

1. Introduction

1.1. Historical limits

The historical limits for this survey are defined as follows. The point of departure is 'fuzzy': dialectology in the Slavic lands did not begin at a certain date, but developed slowly from other undertakings; since one major initial impetus was in ethnography, we begin with the influential folktext collections of the period 1810–1830; comments on dialects had been made from time to time by writers before this, but only in the 19th century did they begin to have a proper linguistic foundation. The finishing point is arbitrarily set at 1914: World War One was a turningpoint in the cultural history of many Slavic countries. Political developments during this period should be kept in mind: in particular, the relative stability and ease of travel in the Austrian and Russian Empires, and the enormous instability in the Balkan countries, where the gradual Turkish withdrawal and its aftermath focussed both political and cultural attention on Serbia, Macedonia and Bulgaria, which became gradually more accessible.

1.2. Geographical scope and terms

The 'Slavic countries' are defined as those European lands where Slavic languages are now spoken; this includes minority Slavic idioms in non-Slavic jurisdictions, e. g., Sorbian in Germany. The definition of 'dialect' is more challenging, for most of the contemporary National Standard Slavic languages were generally considered 'dialects' in the mid-19th century. Many Ukrainians, for example, will disagree with having the language of the classics of their literature called a 'dialect'; but many descriptions of the time referred to it as a 'Little [or, South] Russian dialect'. An arbitrary definitioni is therefore essential. We consider the object of description a 'dialect' if that idiom was not (yet) standardized in the sense used by Stewart (1968). The dialects are identified, as far as possible, according to their current geographic affiliation to a standard Slavic language, as listed in Comrie & Corbett (1993): thus the dialect of Prilep in Macedonia is here called a 'Macedonian dialect' even though Stoilov (1893–1894) referred to it as 'Bulgarian'. Given the uncertainty of some borders and of some contemporary developments toward standardizartion, all dialects spoken before 1914 in what later became the Serbo-Croatian-speaking republics of the now former Yugoslavia are here termed 'Serbo-Croatian' (in quotation marks). In Section 3, the various Slavic lands are labelled according to language headings as defined and following the nomenclature in Comrie & Corbett (1993); Polabian is not considered at all, having died out in the 18th century.

2. General developments

2.1. Introduction

In this section we treat developments and their causes, which were common to more than one Slavic land. Some, like the ethnographic impetus (2.2.) and the links to diachronic linguistics (2.3.), were more general; others, such as the needs of those concerned with language standardization (2.4.), were more localized. In some countries only one impetus was important; in others we have to consider a plurality. We also mention the intrusion of politics into dialectology (2.5.) and other general considerations (2.6.).

2.2. Ethnography and Romanticism

The interest in folk poetry which had developed in the 18th century grew enormously in the 19th, and resulted in an enterprise with a characteristic impact on the development of Slavic dialectology: the well-documented collaboration between Goethe, Jacob Grimm, Talvj [pseud. for *Teresa A. L. von Jakob* (1797–1870)], Jernej Kopitar (1780–1844), and Vuk Karadžić (1773–1864) in the years 1813–1826, which resulted in the publication of Karadžić's first Serbian folksong collectons (1814/15) and their translations into German and later English and French (on Kopitar's pivotal role, see Butler 1982; on

Karadžić, see 3.3.). Similar, but less well-known folk-text collections were published in the Russian Empire, Poland, and in the Czech and Slovene lands in the 1820s and 1830s (and elsewhere in following decades) by persons interested in folk culture and its potential contributions to literature, many of them dilettantes but some with academic credentials. They led in turn, sooner or later, to a scholarly interest in the language in which the folksongs were written, since the authenticity of orally-transmitted literature was considered so important. Much of the early interest in Slavic dialects was thus an indirect by-product of the work of poets and translators. As interest in the 'folk' became more and more scholarly, dialect descriptions began to be seen as integral to general ethnographic field reports.

2.3. Requirements for historical linguistics

We assume that the general 19th-century emphasis on diachrony was not originally inimical to dialectology, indeed that there was no incompatibility prior to the 1870s clash between the assumed outcome of 'sound laws' (i.e., geographically-exceptionless reflexes) and what was in fact observed in the field. Through the 1860s and later, four diachronic considerations encouraged dialect investigations. First, any 'scientific' approach required the use of actually-observed data, and the opacity of orthographies (especially, of Russian) prompted recourse to spoken materials. Second, it became clear that the process of standardizing 'literary' languages had obscured the traces of natural development, which could only be observed by looking at dialects. Third, analyses of older texts were demanded which were written in localized variants. And fourth (and this became increasingly more vital) historical reconstruction was often made simpler, and sometimes even was made feasible, by recourse to dialect data. Towards the end of the century, when the above-mentioned incompatibility became more and more apparent, those who reacted to the so-called 'exceptionlessness of sound laws' had an even more pressing need for dialect data (Wolf 1975: 1–33; Petyt 1980: 37–43).

2.4. Practical needs for language standardization

The concerns of many language planners in Slavic lands without standardized 'literary' languages — of which at the beginning of the 19th century there were in effect but two: Russian and Polish — required dialect descriptions. In several countries one of the fundamental decisions about the new literary language was the choice of its territorial basis; to engage in any discussion of the competing claims of already-existing literary forms, a knowledge of their dialect bases was essential.

2.5. Political considerations

In a few instances, politics intruded into linguistics: the political status of a particular territory or region was considered dependent on the dialects spoken by its inhabitants and the relationships of these dialects to 'languages' in neighbouring regions; descriptions were therefore essential.

2.6. Other general considerations

The role of a number of academic establishments as centres of Slavic dialectology should not go unremarked. Some universities, e.g., Prague, that were famous in this period for other work in Slavic linguistics happen to have made little or no contribution to dialectology. Others became important with the appointment of a specific linguist, e.g., Lucjan Malinowski (1839–1898) in Kraków, 1877 (see 3.8.); so also St. Petersburg in 1868–1870, when Baudouin de Courtenay worked there with I. I. Sreznevskij (1812–1880), had a long-lasting influence (see 3.4.). Vienna was especially important, first as the place where Karadžić and Kopitar collaborated in the 1830s, and then again after the establishment of the Slavic department by Franz Miklosich (1813–1891) in 1849; here several dialectologists were trained, many expeditions for fieldwork were funded, and a great deal was published, e.g., in the series *Schriften der Balkankommission: Linguistische Abteilung, I: Südslavische Dialektstudien* from 1900.

Contributions to local dialectology by non-native dialectologists represent another major consideration; so, for example, Baudouin de Courtenay, Vasilij Bogorodickij (1857–1939), and L. V. Ščerba (1880–1944) received commissions from authorities in Russia to describe Slovene and Sorbian dialects; and without the work of the German Hermann Hirt (1865–1936) and the Norwegian Olaf Broch (1867–1961) the dialectology of several Slavic languages would have been much poorer. Two of these deserve special mention: Baudouin de Courtenay (see 3.4., 3.8., 3.9.), and Broch. The latter was trained in Leipzig (August Leskien) and Vienna (Jagić); his phonetic accuracy was legendary ("Jamais jusqu'alors l'étude des parlers, dans le domaine slave, n'avait bénéficié d'une finesse et d'une sûreté comparables à celles de ce disciple de Sweet et de Sievers" [Mazon 1962: 374]); he conducted fieldwork on Slovak/Ukrainian transitional dialects (2 books), on Serbian/Bulgarian transitional dialects (1 book) and in both North and South Russia (2 books – see Gallis & Egeberg 1961).

3. Individual Slavic lands

We now treat the Slavic lands in turn. Note that citations of dialectological works are selections only: e.g., we cite two works by Nitsch from this linguist's 10 dialectological books and articles published between 1905 and 1914. It is assumed that the earliest dialect descriptions in each Slavic land tended to be impressionistic, and that since detailed descriptions of individual dialects are required before successful analysis, the first attempts at generalization and analysis likewise tended to be naturally more imperfect than those that came later. With a very few exceptions, we do not try to characterize the quality of dialectological works. The major source for all these sections is Jagić (1910).

3.1. Bulgarian

None other than Karadžić is credited with the publication of the first Bulgarian folksongs (1822); although until the late 1870s Turkish rule was not conducive for linguistic fieldwork (Miklosich 1856 being a description of a Bulgarian émigré community), many collections of folk materials were published, mostly by visiting scholars, but few pretended to linguistic accuracy before the 1880s. From 1890, and especially after 1900, Bulgarian linguists made up for lost ground with a spate of descriptions; one impetus came from work on the codification of the standard language, which required consideration of data from competing (eastern versus western) dialect bases; also, there were problems in the delimitation of Bulgarian vs. Serbian dialects (see Mladenov 1901). Noteworthy landmarks were the works of Conev (1890–1891), who was very much concerned with diachrony; Miletič (1903); Mladenov (1911). *Sources:* Gerčev (1911), Stojkov (1962).

3.2. Macedonian

As in the Bulgarian lands, linguistic fieldwork in Macedonia was difficult before the late 1870s; there were some folksong collections and occasional dialect notes in journals during the 1860s but the first descriptions date from the next decade. With the withdrawal of the Turks competing claims to Macedonian territory were made by her neighbours; the claims of the Serbs and of the Bulgarians were in large part linguistic, i.e., that the Macedonian dialects were closer to Serbian or to Bulgarian respectively; hence, dialectology became suddenly very important, and many studies (of both a descriptive and, to demonstrate such similarities, an historical nature) were published between 1885 and 1914, some by Serbs (e.g., Novaković 1890–1892), the overwhelming majority by Bulgarians (e.g., Georgiev 1904; Grigorov 1907), and a few by other Slavists (e.g., Oblak 1896). *Source:* Gerčev (1911).

3.3. 'Serbo-Croatian'

The "außerordentlich talentierte" (Ivić 1958: 15) Karadžić was not only a collector of folktexts (cf. 2.2.); he *inter alia* wrote the first grammar of Serbian and almost single-handedly reformed the literary language and orthography. Already his *Srpski Rječnik [Serbian Dictionary]* of 1818 contained a preface entitled "O srpskom književnom jeziku i pravopisu i o srpskim dialektima [On the Serbian literary language and orthography and on Serbian dialects]": there were several already-existing literary forms based on different dialects, and reference to the latter was essential. Karadžić's dialect materials were fragmentary and never the prime object of his research, but in publications for over 40 years he kept adducing new, personally-observed data, and in effect produced his own classification of these dialects.

A period of virtually total stagnation in dialectology followed; competent linguists were more concerned with textological studies and/or with problems of standardization. In particular, there were protracted disputes among supporters and opponents of the 'Illyrian Movement' about various 'literary dialects' of Croatian: e.g., one factor was the prestige of 16th- and 17th-century literature written in the dialect of Dubrovnik. Hence, the titles of, e.g., Babukić (1836) and Daničić (1857) mention the word 'dialect', but are concerned with the establishment of Croatian and/or Serbian literary norms. Descriptions of dialects were made, but these were generally inferior. By 1900, however, the picture had changed: with contributions from Sla-

vists based, mostly, in Vienna (Valjavec 1885, Oblak 1894, Broch 1903, Hirt 1903) local dialectology was reinvigorated and Rešetar (1900, 1907), Belić (1905a, 1908) and Ivšić (1914) brought dialect descriptions up to the level achieved elsewhere in the Slavic world.
Source: Ivić (1958).

3.4. Slovene

The Slovene dialects are known to show more variation than those of any other Slavic language. 19th-century Slovene dialectology, which was extraordinarily fruitful, developed not from other interests (although it was sometimes linked to ethnography, e. g., by Matija Valjavec in the 1850s) but directly through the personal involvement of linguists. It boasted the earliest competent Slavic dialectological study, Sreznevskij (1841); indeed, it was the individuality of the Slovene dialects that encouraged this scholar in his work; and he not only made copious notes, but produced a classification of the Slovene dialects. At the same time, Urban Jarnik (1842) published the first ever description of a single Slavic dialect. Sreznevskij directly influenced Baudouin de Courtenay's choice of Slovenia for dialectological field-work, which provided data for the latter's views on the 'sound-law vs. variability' controversy (Stankiewicz 1976: 21−22); it is also noteworthy that much of the data for Schuchardt's major (and only much later appreciated) work of 1884 derived from his observation of Slovene (and Czech) dialects. Of Baudouin de Courtenay's 40-odd publications on Slovene, at least 25 are on dialects; we mention here just two (1875, 1904); his 'Turanian theory' aside, he raised Slovene and Slavic dialectology to a high level, and in Slovenia developed the methodology which he taught his students (Tolstoj 1960). His contemporaries, Janez Scheinigg (1881−1882) and Karl Štrekelj (1886), produced descriptions of equal quality; and the tradition was continued by Oblak (1890−1895) and then Ramovš (1914).
Source: Toporišič (1962).

3.5. Slovak

Most of the Slovak lands were under Hungarian jurisdiction during the period in question, and the use of Slovak was discouraged; nevertheless, the language was being codified by mid-century, and the discussions about the base of the standard (central vs. western dialects) required dialectological work. Jan Kollár's (1793−1852) and Ľudovit Štur's (1815− 1856) collections of folksongs in the 1830s and 1840s did not (as elsewhere) lead directly to dialectology in the Slovak lands; the first descriptions of the Slovak dialects came from Prague (Šafárik and Šembera, cf. 3.6.). The rest of the period until 1914 saw much energy devoted to folklore collection but very little to dialectology: apart from contributions from the Czech František Pastrnek (1853−1940) and the Norwegian Broch only one name stands out, that of Samo Czambel (1906).
Sources: Kondrašov (1951); Kudělka & Šimeček (1972).

3.6. Czech

The Czech lands were in the first half of the 19th century a centre not only for diachronic Slavic linguistics (for which they are best known), but also for ethnography: for Pavel Šafárik (1795−1861), František Čelakovský (1799−1852), and others the history of the Slavic languages and of the people who spoke them and their culture were all interconnected; thus Šafárik (1826) includes a classification of the Czech and Slovak dialects. The first Czech dialectologist of note, Šembera, was also an historian of culture and literature; his first articles appeared in the 1830s, and his exhaustive (if necessary superficial) survey of all the dialects of Czech and Slovak in 1864. The 1860s also saw useful publications by Josef Jireček (1825−1888) and Josef Kouble (1855−1921); diachronic considerations were important. After a lean period in the 1880s efforts were renewed: important names were Josef Neoral (1852− 19??), Josef Bartocha (1859−1927), and, with descriptions of a very high quality, Bartoš (1886/95, 1906). A very large number of publications appeared right up to World War One. *Sources:* Bělič (1972); Kudělka & Šimeček (1972).

3.7. Sorbian, Upper and Lower

Whereas Upper Sorbian was more or less fully standardized during the 19th century, Lower Sorbian has had a permanently precarious existence as a standard language. Most early-19th-century descriptions of any varieties of the former, and virtually all descriptions before 1914 of any of the latter, referred to them as 'dialects'. Prominent figures involved in mid-century descriptions, and in analyses of dialect differences among the Sorbs, were the language activist Jan Smoler (1841 − note: his dialect data were published in a folksong collection), Michał Hórnik

(1869), Josef Wjelan (1869). The culmination of all this work is seen in the monumental Muka (1891) and an influential monograph by the Russian Ščerba (1915). *Source:* Jenč (1977).

3.8. Polish

Dialectology in Poland was slow in developing, compared to the early date of the first dialect descriptions in neighbouring Slavic lands and Germany. Here as much as elsewhere the incentive came from collectors of folktexts: inspired by Karadžić, Polish scholars – e.g., Kazimierz Wójcicki (1830s) and especially Oskar Kolberg (1850s–1890s) – produced monumental collections. Jan Karłowicz (1836–1903), another folktext collector, became in 1887 the editor of the ethnographic journal *Wisła*, in which large numbers of texts appeared; from these, Karłowicz collated dialect lexica and published them in six volumes (1900–1911). Meanwhile, Malinowski, a student of Schleicher's, was appointed in 1877 to the Chair of Slavic Dialects in Kraków University and set about ably filling the gap in this area of scholarship; his 1873 book was the first good linguistic dialect description in Poland, and his students produced several valuable descriptions and diachronic analyses. Among these students, late in Malinowski's career, was Kazimierz Nitsch, who also attended lectures by Baudouin de Courtenay in Kraków following the latter's fieldwork in Slovenia (cf. 3.4.). Kazimierz Nitsch (1874–1958) became the preeminent Polish dialectologist: starting with localised fieldwork and descriptions of small dialect areas, he expanded into synthetic analyses. His writings, which were prolific, are still mostly valid, e.g., Nitsch (1907, 1911). *Sources:* Handke & Rzetelska-Feleszko (1977), Gruszecka-Nitschowa (1977); Urbańczyk (1993).

3.9. Cassubian

In the 19th century (as today) the status of Cassubian was uncertain; most but not all linguists considered it a dialect of Polish. Many dialectologists, including Baudouin de Courtenay and Nitsch (see 3.8.), entered into this debate, which had political overtones: a criterion for the separation of the Cassubian lands from, or their union with, Poland was linguistic (dis)similarity; hence the fact that the dialects in this small territory attracted a great deal of attention, compared to the ('other') dialects of Polish. Strictly linguistic descriptions of these dialects date from Alexander Hilferding (1861), and included major works by Franz Tetzner (1863–1919) and Stefan Ramułt (1859–1913), and especially Nitsch's first major publication of 1905. *Sources:* as for 3.8.

3.10. Belorussian

As the Belorussian lands were part of the Russian Empire, their dialects were generally considered 'Russian' during this period. Among the folklorists of the Russian Empire (see 3.11.) with major collections of Belorussian folksongs were I. I. Nosovič (1874) and P. V. Šejn (1887–1892), the latter with linguistic data included. As with Russian and Ukrainian dialects, diachronic considerations became a guiding force in the latter part of the century, but the leading exponent for Belorussian, E. F. Karskij (1860–1931), was equally involved in systematic synchronic description. His numerous publications include strictly linguistic books (Karskij 1897–1910) and a three-volume ethnographic encyclopedia which had great reliance on dialect data (1903–1922), including maps. Karskij may be said to have virtually single-handedly brought Belorussian dialectology to the level of work produced on Polish and on Russian dialects. *Source:* Blinava & Mjacel'skaja (1980).

3.11. Russian

Nowhere in the Slavic lands in the 19th century were folk-texts collected with more zeal than in the Russian Empire. This tradition, which had been founded in the 18th century, had numerous representatives with links to literary figures; especially prolific were Nikolaj Nadeždin (1830s), Petr Kireevskij (1860s–1870s) and V. I. Dal' (1801–1872). The latter's dictionary included an long introductory chapter (1880: xlix–xciii) on Russian dialects, classified according to phonological and lexical features; this was a painstaking continuation of classificatory attempts that had been started 100 years earlier. Ethnography in general was well-funded and under royal patronage from 1855. Most of the thrust in 'philology' at Russian universities in the 1870s and 1880s was directed to ethnographic and cultural history; individual scholars however used their fieldwork commissions for more descriptive purposes; thus, with close attention to phonetic accuracy, Kolosov (1877). Gradually, dialects came to be considered also a prime source for data for historical analyses; thus A. I. Sobolevskij (1897) noted dialect data with both folkloristic and diachronic aims. Two outstanding linguists were active in diachronic dialectology before the end of the century: A. A. Potebnja (1865) — see 3.12. — and A. A. Šaxmatov (1899), who initiated a project for the systematic description of the dialects of Russian, and was the main organizer of the Moscow Dialectological Committee of the Academy of Sciences (1904—) and also of sets of instructions for fieldworkers and of postal questionnaires. The Committee's first great achievement was the first dialect map of Russian (Durnovo, Sokolov & Ušakov 1915). Mention should also be made of the successful work of linguists, such as Broch (1907), who treated dialects solely as objects of synchronic analysis. *Source:* Kuznecov (1973).

3.12. Ukrainian

Prominent among the folklorists mentioned in 3.11. was Myxajlo Maksymovyč (1804—1873), rector of Kiev University, who published collections of Ukrainian folksongs in the 1820s and 1830s. It should be recalled that the Ukrainian lands were politically divided, their language not officially standardized, and their dialects therefore considered either 'Polish' or 'Russian'. In (Austro-Hungarian) Western Ukraine, Jakov Holovac'kyj (1849) published the first survey and classification of Ukrainian dialects; another active figure was I. H. Verxrac'kyj (1892/94), and several of the scholars who were active in Polish ethnography and dialectology, especially Kolberg (see 3.8.), also worked on Ukrainian. In Eastern Ukraine, much of the work was in part political, with the aim of demonstrating that the Ukrainian dialects were not 'Little [or Southern] Russian dialects of Russian', especially given the official ban on the term 'Ukrainian'. Thus even Potebnja's dialectological writings (e. g., 1871), which were linked to his diachronic reconstructions of Ukrainian phonology, were considered in some quarters as 'separatist'. Ethnographic work continued with its centre in Kiev and several serial publications; strictly linguistic work, like that on Russian dialects, had mostly diachronic aims, thus Žytec'kyj (1876) and Myxal'čuk (1872). Works of a more strictly synchronic nature appeared in the 1900s, e. g., Jarošenko (1909).
Source: Żylko (1955).

4. Summary

4.1. General trends

It is clear that the impetus on dialectology from ethnography was very important for all the Slavic languages except Slovene, which was selected for its intrinsic linguistic interest by Sreznevskij and Baudouin de Courtenay; that the link to diachronic studies was particularly important in Russian, Polish, Czech and 'Serbo-Croatian' dialectology; that language standardization had an important impact on descriptions of Bulgarian, Slovak and especially 'Serbo-Croatian' dialects; and that political considerations had an impact on the development of the dialectology of Macedonian, of Ukrainian, of Cassubian, and to a lesser extent that of Bulgarian.

4.2. Methodology and cartography

Little has been written about the development of methodology; we know that Baudouin de Courtenay was very much concerned with instructing his students in correct fieldwork methods (see Lencek 1992: 351—352) and that Šaxmatov (3.11.) and Malinowski (3.8.) were also much involved, but no doubt this held true for others. As for linguistic cartography, we speculate that Myxal'čuk (1872) may be the first publication to include a map showing the geographical extent of any Slavic dialects (see Korolevyč 1966); by the turn of the century, such maps were much more common (see Miletič 1903; Broch 1903). As for the earliest attempts to show isoglosses, Belić (1905b) is a map whereon the major dialect boundaries coincide by default with isoglosses (since the traditional 'Serbo-Croatian' divisions were according to one set of lexical and one set of phonological reflexes); Frinta (1916), who attempted to map the consonant /v/ for the whole Slavic-speaking territory, may be the earliest attempt at isogloss cartography without reference to dialect areas.

5. Bibliography

Babukić, Věkoslav. 1836. *Osnova slovnice slavjanske narěčja ilirskoga* [Fundamentals of the Slavic grammar of the Illyrian dialect]. Zagreb: Hirschfeld.

Bartoš, František. 1886—1895. *Dialektologie moravské.* 1: *Nářečí slovenské, dolské, valašské a lašské;* 2: *Nářečí hanacké a české.* [Moravian dialectology. 1: The Slovak, Dol, Valach and Lach Dialects; 2: The Hanak and Bohemian dialects]. Brno: Matica moravská.

—. 1906. *Dialektický slovník moravský* [Moravian dialect dictionary]. (= *Archiv pro lexikologii a dialektologii* 6, 8.] Prague: Nákl. české akademie Císaře Františka Josefa pro vědy, slovesnost a úmění.

Baudouin de Courtenay, Jan Ignacy Niecisław. 1875. *Opyt fonetiki rez'janskix govorov* [Sketch of the phonetics of the Resia sub-dialects]. Warsaw & St. Petersburg: Kožančikov.

—. 1904. *Materialien zur südslavischen Dialektologie und Ethnographie. II: Sprachproben in den Mundarten der Slaven von Torre im Nordöstlichen Italien* (= *Sbornik Otdelenija russkogo jazyka i slovesnosti Akademii nauk*, 78: 2). St. Petersburg: Akademie der Wissenschaften.

Belić, Aleksandar. 1905a. *Dijalekti istočne i južne Srbije* [The dialects of East and South Serbia]. Belgrade: Srpska akademia.

—. 1905b. "Dialektologičeskaja karta serbskogo jazyka [Dialectological map of the Serbian language]." *Stat'i po slavjanovedeniju* (St. Petersburg), 1–59.

—. 1908. "O srpskim ili hrvatskim dijalektima [On Serbian or Croatian dialects]". *Glas* 78.660–664.

Bělič, Jaromír. 1972. *Nástin české dialektologie* [Outline of Czech dialectology]. Prague: Státní Pedagogické Nakladatelství.

Blinava, Èvelina Danilawna & Ewdakija Scjapanawna Mjacel'skaja. 1980. *Belaruskaja Dyjalektolohija* [Belorussian dialectology]. 2nd ed. Minsk: Vyšèjšaja Škola.

Broch, Olaf. 1903. *Die Dialekte des südlichsten Serbiens. Mit einer Dialektkarte.* (= *Schriften der Balkankommission; Linguistische Abteilung, I: Südslavische Dialektstudien,* 3.) Vienna: A. Hölder.

— [Brok, O.]. 1907. *Opisanie odnogo govora iz jugozapadnoj časti Totemskogo uezda* [Description of one Sub-dialect from the Southwestern Part of the Tot'ma Ujezd]. St. Petersburg: Akademija Nauk.

Butler, Thomas. 1982. "Jernej Kopitar and South Slavic Folklore". *To Honor Jernej Kopitar 1780–1980* ed. by Rado L. Lencek & Henry R. Cooper, Jr. (= *Papers in Slavic Philology*, 2), 109–121. Ann Arbor, Mich.: Univ. of Michigan.

Comrie, Bernard & Greville G. Corbett. 1993. *The Slavonic Languages.* London: Routledge.

Conev, Ben'o. 1890–91. "Za istočnobălgarskija vokalizăm [On East Bulgarian vocalism]". *Sbornik na narodni umotvorenija, nauka i knižnina* 3.283–323, 4.484–528.

Czambel, Samo. 1906. *Slovenská a jej miesto v rodine slovanských jazykov. I: Východno-slovenské nárečie* [The Slovak Language and its Place in the Family of Slavic Languages. I: The Eastern Slovak Dialect]. Turčiansky Sv. Martín: Nákl. vlastné.

Dal', Vladimir Ivanovič. 1880. *Tolkovyj slovar' živogo velikorusskogo jazyka* [Explanatory dictionary of the living Great Russian language). Vol. I: *A–Z.* 2nd rev ed. St. Petersburg: Vol'f.

Daničić, Djuro. 1857. "Razlike izmedju srpskoga jezika (štokavskog dijalekta) i hrvatskoga (čakavskog dijalekta) [The differences between the Serbian language (Štokavian dialect) and the Croatian language (Čakavian dialect)]". *Glasnik Društva srpske slovesnosti* 9.1–57.

Durnovo, Nikolaj Nikolaevič, Nikolaj Nikolaevič Sokolov & Dmitrij Nikolaevič Ušakov. 1915. *Opyt dialektologičeskoj karty russkogo jazyka v Evrope s priloženiem očerka russkoj dialektologii* [Attempt of a dialectological map of the Russian language in Europe with an attached sketch of Russian dialectology]. Moscow: Akademija Nauk.

Frinta, Antonín. 1916. *Fonetická povaha a historický vývoj souhlásky 'v' ve slovanštině* [The phonetic nature and historical development of the consonant 'v' in Slavic]. Prague: Česká akademie věd a úmění.

Gallis, Arne & Erik Egeberg. 1985. "Die Slawistik in Norwegen". *Beiträge zur Geschichte der Slawistik in nichtslawischen Ländern* ed. by Josef Hamm & Günther Wytrzens, 417–438. Vienna: Verlag der österreichischen Akademie der Wissenschaften.

Georgiev, Jordan A. 1904. "Materiali za rečnika po veleškija govor [Materials for a vocabulary of the Veles dialect]". *Sbornik na narodni umotvorenija, nauka i knižnina* 20.1–85.

Gerčev, Xristo. 1911. "Pogled vărxu razvoja na bălgarskata dijalektologija: Istorikobibliografičen pregled [A glance at the development of Bulgarian dialectology: An historical-bibliographic survey]". *Izvestija na Seminara po slavjanskata filologija pri Univerziteta v Sofia* 3.607–674.

Grigorov, Milko. 1907. "Govorăt na malorekancite (mijacite) v Debărsko [The dialect of the Malorekanci (Mijaci) in Debar]". *Izvestija na Seminara po slavjanskata filologija pri Univerziteta v Sofia* 2.201–304.

Gruszecka-Nitschowa, Aniela. 1977. *Całe życie nad przyrodą mowy polskiej: Kazimierz Nitsch i jego prace* [A whole life on the nature of Polish speech: Kazimierz Nitsch and his work]. Kraków: Wydawnictwo Literackie.

Handke, Kwiryna & Ewa Rzetelska-Feleszko. 1977. *Przewodnik o językoznawstwie polskim* [Guide to Polilsh linguistics]. Wrocław: Ossolineum.

Hilferding, Alexander. 1861. *Ostatki Slavjan na južnom beregu Bal'tijskogo morja* [Remnants of the Slavs on the South coast of the Baltic Sea]. St. Petersburg.

Hirt, Hermann. 1903. *Der ikavische Dialekt im Königreich Serbiens.* Vienna: C. Gerald's Sohn.

Holovac'kyj, Jakov. 1849. "Rozprava o jazyci južnorusskom i eho naričijax [A treatment of the South Russian language and its dialects]". *Istoryčeskyj očerk osnovanija halicko-russkoj matici [Historical sketch of the foundation of the Galician-Rus' Matica].* L'viv: Halicko-russka matica.

Hórnik, Michał. 1869. "Přikład Mužakowskeje podryče [An example of the Mužakow sub-dialect]". *Časopis Maćicy Serbskeje* 22:2.119–121.

Ivić, Pavle. 1958. *Die Serbokroatischen Dialekte: Ihre Struktur und Entwicklung. I: Allgemeines und die štokavische Dialektgruppe*. The Hague: Mouton.

Ivšić, Stjepan. 1914. *Nacrt za istraživanje hrvatskih i srpskih narječja* [A plan for the investigation of the Croatian and Serbian dialects]. Zagreb: no publisher.

Jagić, Ignatij Vikent'evič. 1910. *Istorija slavjanskoj filologii* [History of Slavic philology]. St. Petersburg: Akademija Nauk.

Jarnik, Urban. 1842. "Obraz slovenskoga narečja u Koruškoj [The form of the Slovene dialect in Carinthia]". *Kolo* 1.41–57.

Jarošenko, Volodymyr. 1909. "Ukrainskaja skazka v fonetičeskoj transkripcii [A Ukrainian folktale in phonetic transcription]". *Izvestija Otdelenija russkogo jazyka i slovesnosti Akademii Nauk* 14:1. 237–240.

Jenč, Helmut. 1977. "Wuwiće a problematika sorabistiskeje dialektologije [The development and problematics of Sorbian dialectology]". *Sorabistiske přednoški 1977 [Sorbian Papers 1977]*, 54–62. Bautzen: Ludowe nakładnistwo Domowina Budyšin.

Karadžić, Vuk Stefanović. 1814. *Mala prostonarodna Slaveno-Serbska Pesnarica* [Small Slaveno-Serbian songbook of the common people]. Vienna: Johann Schnierer.

–. 1815. *Narodna Srbska Pesnarica. Čast vtora*. [Serbian songbook of the people. Part Two]. Vienna: Johann Schnierer.

–. 1818. *Srpski Rječnik, istolkovan njemačkim i latinskim riječma* [Serbian dictionary, translated into German and Latin words]. Vienna: bei den P. P. Armeniern.

–. 1822. *Dodatak k Sanktpeterburgskim sravniteljnim rječnicima sviju jezika i narječja, s osobitim ogledima bugarskog jezika* [Addendum to the St. Petersburg comparative dictionaries of all the languages and dialects, with special attention to the Bulgarian language]. Vienna: no publisher.

Karłowicz, Jan A. 1900–1911. *Słownik gwar polskich, I–VI* [Dictionary of the Polish dialects, I–VI]. Kraków: Akademia Umiejętności.

Karskij, Evfimij Fedorovič. 1897–1910. *Materialy dlja izučenija belorusskix govorov* [Materials for the study of the Belorussian Dialects]. Vols. I–VI. 1897, 1898, 1900, 1903, 1908, 1910. St. Petersburg: Akademija Nauk.

–. 1903–22. *Belorusy* [The Belorussians]. I, Warsaw, 1903; II.1, Warsaw, 1908; II.2, Warsaw, 1911; II.3., Warsaw, 1912; III.1., Moscow 1916; III.2., Prague 1921; III.3., Prague 1922.

Kolosov, Mitrofan Alekseevič. 1877. *Zametki o jazyke i narodnoj poèzii v oblasti severnorusskogo narečija* [Notes on the language and folk poetry in the area of the North Russian dialect]. St. Petersburg: Akademija Nauk.

Korolevič, N. F. 1966. "Rozvytok ukrajins'koji linhvistyčnojni heohrafiji [The development of Ukrainian linguistic geography]". *Ukrajins'ka linhvistyčna heohrafija [Ukrainian Linguistic Geography]* ed. by I. O. Varčenko et al., 143–151. Kiev: Naukova dumka.

Kondrašov, N. A. 1951. "Očerk po istorii slovackoj dialektologii [Sketch of the history of Slovak dialectology]". *Slavjanskaja filologija 1951*, 98–107. Moscow: Moskovskij gosudarstvennyj universitet.

Kudělka, Milan & Zdeněk Šimeček. 1972. *Československé práce o jazyce, dějinách a kultuře slovanských národů od r. 1760* [Czechoslovak works on the language, history and culture of the Slavic peoples from 1760]. Prague: Státní Pedagogické Nakladatelství.

Kuznecov, Petr Savvič, ed. 1973. *Russkaja dialektologija* [Russian dialectology]. Moscow: Prosveščenie.

Lencek, Rado L. 1992. *The Beginnings of the Scientific Study of Minor Slavic Languages: The correspondence between Jan Baudouin de Courtenay (1845–1929) and Vatroslav Oblak (1864–1896)*. Munich: Slavica.

Malinowski, Lucjan. 1873. *Beiträge zur slavischen Dialektologie. Vol. I: Über die Oppelnsche Mundart in Oberschlesien*. Leipzig: Bar & Hermann.

Mazon, André. 1962. "Nécrologie: Olaf Broch (1867–1961)". *Revue des études slaves* 41.374–375.

Miklosich, Franz. 1856. "Die Sprache der Bulgaren in Siebenbürgen". *Denkschriften der Kaiserlichen Akademie der Wissenschaften; Philosophisch-Historische Classe* 7.105–146. Vienna.

Miletič, Ljubomir. 1903. *Das Ostbulgarische. Mit einer Karte*. (= *Schriften der Balkankommission; Linguistische Abteilung, I: Südslavische Dialektstudien*, 2) Vienna: A. Hölder.

Mladenov, Stefan. 1901. "Kăm voprosa za ezika i nacionalnata prinadležnost na Novo Selo (Vidinsko) [On the question of the language and national affiliation of Novo Selo (Vidin region)]". *Sbornik na narodni umotvorenija, nauka i knižnina* 18. 471–507.

–. 1911. "Zur bulgarischen Dialektologie. 1: Aus den Forschungen auf dem Gebiet des Ostbulgarischen". *Rocznik sławistyczny* 4.97–121.

Muka, Arnošt. 1891. *Historische und vergleichende Laut- und Formenlehre der niedersorbischen (niederlausitzisch-wendischen) Sprache. Mit besonderer Berücksichtigung der Grenzdialekte und des Obersorbischen*. Leipzig: Hirzel.

Myxal'čuk, Konstantyn Petrovyč. 1872. "Narečija, podnarečija i govory Južnoj Rossii v svjazi s narečijami Galičiny [Dialects, sub-dialects and local idioms of Southern Russia in connection with the dialects of Galicia]". *Trudy ètnografičesko-statisti-*

českoj èkspedicii v Zapadno-russkij kraj: Materialy i issledovanija 7.453–512. St. Petersburg: Imperatorskoe russkoe geografičeskoe obščestvo.

Nitsch, Kazimierz. 1905. "Dialekty polskie Prus Zachodnich. Cz I: Dialekty po lewej stronie Wisły [The Polish dialects in West Prussia. Pt. I: The dialects on the left bank of the Vistula]". *Materiali i prace Komisji Językowej Akademii Umiejętności w Krakowie* 1905: 1/2.101–284.

—. 1907. "Dialekty polskie Prus Zachodnich. Cz. II: Dialekty po prawej stronie Wisły [... Pt. II: The dialects on the right bank of the Vistula]". *Materiali i prace Komisji Językowej Akademii Umiejętności w Krakowie* 1907:3.305–395.

—. 1911. *Mowa ludu polskiego [The speech of the Polish people]*. Kraków: L. Frommer.

Nosovič, Ivan Ivanovič. 1874. *Belorusskie pesni* [Belorussian songs]. (= *Gosudarstvennoe russkoe geografičeskoe občestvo; Otdelenie ètnografii, Zapiski*, 5.) St. Petersburg: no publisher.

Novaković, Stojan. 1890–1892. "Ein Beitrag zur Kunde der macedonischen Dialecte: Der Dialect von Veles-Prilep". *Archiv für slavische Philologie* 12.78–94, 13.543–557, 14.360–373.

Oblak, Vatroslav. 1890–95. "Doneski k historični slovenski dialektologiji [Contributions to historical Slovene dialectology]". *Letopis Matice Slovenske* 1890.180–236, 1891.66–153, 1892.222–223, 1894.203–219, 1895.234–246.

—. 1894. "Der Dialekt von Lastovo". *Archiv für slavische Philologie* 16.426–450.

—. 1896. *Macedonische Studien. Die slavischen Dialekte des südlichen und nordwestlichen Macedoniens*. Vienna: C. Gerold's Sohn.

Petyt, K. M. 1980. *The Study of Dialect: An introduction to dialectology*. London: Deutsch.

Potebnja, Aleksandr Afanas'evič. 1865. "O zvukovyx osobennostjax russkix narečij [On phonetic peculiarities of Russian dialects]". *Filologičeskie zapiski* (Voronež) 1865:1.49–94, 1865:2–3.95–158.

—. 1871. "Zametki o malorusskom narečii [Notes on the Little-Russian dialect]". *Filologičeskie zapiski* (Voronež) 1870:1.1–136.

Ramovš, Fran. 1914. "Zur slovenischen Dialektforschung". *Archiv für slavische Philologie* 35.329–337.

Rešetar, Milan. 1900. *Die serbokroatische Betonung südwestlicher Mundarten*. (= *Schriften der Balkankommission; Linguistische Abteilung, I: Südslavische Dialektstudien*, 1.) Vienna: A. Holder.

—. 1907. *Der štokavische Dialekt*. (= *Schriften der Balkankommission;* [...], 8.) Vienna: A. Holder.

Scheinigg, Janez. 1881–82. "Obraz rožanskega narečja na Koroškem [The form of the Rož dialect in Carinthia]". *Kres* 1.412–415, 459–465, 525–527, 561–563, 617–621, 663–667; 2.427–431, 475–479, 529–532, 582–585, 628–630.

Schuchardt, Hugo. 1884. *Slawo-deutsches und slawo-italienisches*. Graz: Leuschner & Lubensky.

Smoler, Jan Arnošt. 1841. "Dyalektyske Wšelakosćje Serbskeje Rečje. Die dialektischen Unterschiede in der Wendischen Sprache". *Volkslieder der Wenden in der Ober- und Niederlausitz: Aus Volksmunde aufgezeichnet* ed. by J. E. Schmaler & Joachim Leopold Haupt, 277–282. Grimma: Gebhardt.

Sobolevskij, Aleksej Ivanovič. 1897. *Opyt russkoj dialektologii* [Sketch of a Russian dialectology]. St. Petersburg: Merkušev.

Sreznevskij, Izmail Ivanovič. 1841. "O slavjanskix narečijax [On Slavic dialects]". *Žurnal Minsterstva narodnogo prosveščenija* 1841:9.133–164.

Stankiewicz, Edward. 1976. *Baudouin de Courtenay and the Foundations of Structural Linguistics*. Lisse/Holland: Peter de Ridder.

Stewart, William A. 1968. "Sociolinguistic Typology of Multilingualism". *Readings in the Sociology of Language* ed. by Joshua A. Fishman, 530–545. The Hague: Mouton.

Stoilov, Anton P. 1893–94. "Material za bălgarski rečnik ot grad Prilep [Material for a Bulgarian dictionary of the town of Prilep]." *Periodičesko spisanie na Bălgarskoto kniževn o društestvo v Sofia* 43.149–152, 47.817–820.

Stojkov, Stojko. 1962. *Bălgarska dialektologija* [Bulgarian dialectology.] Sofia: Nauka i izkustvo.

Šafárik [Šafařík], Pavel. 1826. *Geschichte der slavischen Sprachen und Literatur nach allen Mundarten*. Ofen: Königl. ungarische Universitäts-Schriften.

Šaxmatov, Aleksej Aleksandrovič. 1899. "K voprosu ob obrazovanii russkix narečij i russkix narodnostej [On the question of the formation of the Russian dialects and the Russian nationalities]". *Žurnal Minísterstva narodnogo prosveščenija* 1899:4. 324–384.

Šejn, Pavel Vasil'evič. 1887–92. *Materialy dlja izučenija byta i jazyka russkogo naselenija Severno-Zapadnogo kraja* [Materials for the study of the way of Life and the Language of the Russian Population of the North-Western Region]. I.1 (1887), I.2 (1890), II (1893), III (1894). St. Petersburg: Akademija nauk.

Šembera, Alois Vojtěch. 1864. *Základové dialektologie československé* [Fundamental Czechoslovak dialectology.] Vienna: no publisher.

Ščerba, Lev Vladimirovič. 1915. *Vostočnolužickoe narečie* [The East Lusatian dialect]. Petrograd: Kollins.

Štrekelj, Karel. 1886. "Morphologie des Görzer Mittelkarstdialectes mit besonderer Berücksichtigung der Betonungsverhältnisse". *Sitzungsberichte der Kaiserlichen Akademie der Wissenschaften, Philosophisch-Historische Classe* 113.374–496. Vienna: C. Gerold's Sohn.

Tolstoj, Nikita Ill'ič. 1960. "O rabotax I. A. Boduèna de Kurtenè po slovenskomu jazyku [On I. A. Baudouin de Courtenay's works on the Slovene language]". *I. A. Boduèn de Kurtenè (k 30-letiju so* dnja smerti) [I. A. Baudouin de Courtenay (On the 30th Anniversary of his Death)] ed. by S. B. Bernštejn, 67−81. Moscow: Akademija Nauk SSR.

Toporišič, Jože. 1962. "Die slowenische Dialektforschung". *ZSlPh* 30.383−416.

Urbańczyk, Stanisław. 1993. *Sto lat polskiego językoznawstwa* [One hundred years of Polish linguistics]. Kraków: Akademia Umiejętności.

Valjavec, Matija. 1885. "Mitteilungen aus dem kroatischen kaj-Dialecte". *Archiv für slavische Philologie* 8.399−409.

Verxrac'kyj, Ivan Hryhor'evyč. 1892−94. "Über die Mundart der galizischen Lemken: Ein Beitrag zur slavischen Dialektologie". *Archiv für slavische Philologie* 14.587−612; 15.46−73; 16.1−41.

Wjelan, Josef E. 1869. "Namjezno-Mužakowska wotnožka serbšćin [The Namjezno-Mužakow portion of the Sorbian language]". *Časopis Maćicy Serbskeje* 22:2.57−93.

Wolf, Lothar. 1975. *Aspekte der Dialektologie: Eine Darstellung von Methoden auf französischer Grundlage*. Tübingen: Niemeyer.

Žylko, Fedot Trofymovyč. 1955. *Narysy z dialektolohiji ukrajins'koji movy* [Sketches from the dialectology of the Ukrainian language]. Kiev: Radjans'ka Škola.

Žytec'kyj, Pavel Ignat'evič. 1876. *Očerk zvukovoj istorii malorusskogo narečija* [Sketch of the phonetic history of the Little-Russian dialect]. Kiev: Universitetskaja tipografija.

Tom Priestly, Edmonton (Canada)

186. The history and development of a universal phonetic alphabet in the 19th century: from the beginnings to the establishment of the IPA

1. Introduction
2. Approaches to transcription
3. Universal Alphabetic schemes
4. Analphabetic notations
5. Dialect alphabets
6. Conclusion
7. Bibliography

(Note: Where it is necessary to refer to specific sounds the alphabet of the International Phonetic Association (IPA) will be used, enclosed in square brackets.)

1. Introduction

The idea of a universal alphabet has been around for many centuries. Among those interested in it one finds spelling reformers, map-makers, traders, language learners and teachers, all with reasons for wanting a method of writing foreign languages which can be widely understood and interpreted. 18th-century social reformers such as Thomas Sheridan (1719−1788), and William Thornton (1759−1828) in the United States, saw that their cause would be helped if they could make it easier for people to 'improve' their way of speaking, and so tried to devise new methods of indicating pronunciatioin. However, the search for a universal alphabet is fraught with difficulties (see Rousseau 1985).

2. Approaches to transcription

In the following sections the term 'notation' will be used when referring to ways of noting down individual sounds, reserving 'transcription' for pieces of connected speech. Two broad types of transcription can be distinguished − "impressionistic" and "systematic" (Abercrombie 1967: 127−128). In an impressionistic transcription the transcriber attempts to note down all the nuances of sounds that can be detected, for instance in recording the sounds of a language previously uninvestigated. It requires a large number of symbols, and is almost certain to differ to some extent for each transcriber. However, when the investigator is familiar with the language it should be possible to identify those features which are crucial in conveying its meaning, and to establish a limited set of symbols − a 'systematic' transcription. Many of the early inventors of phonetic alphabets aimed to provide symbols for all the sounds that could be heard in any language. However, in applying them to specific languages they were often guided by an intuitive awareness of the linguistic system, so that they arrived at what was in effect a systematic transcription. In their notation, however, they often adopted conventions based on their own language's orthography, with the result that one finds very different versions of one and the same name, for example on maps.

2.1. One of the major difficulties facing devisers of a new phonetic system of notation is of finding sufficient different symbols to convey all the necessary sounds unambiguously, since no existing alphabet on its own can do this. Certain basic principles need to be observed in deciding on solutions to this: (a) The symbols chosen should each be capable of representing one sound unambiguously, and no more than one sound (or in some cases a larger unit such as one syllable). The symbol ⟨c⟩ as used in English does not conform to this. It represents either [s], as in ⟨city⟩ or [k] as in ⟨cat⟩. Conversely, a particular sound should always be represented by one, and no more than one, particular symbol. Once again English orthography fails this test − the sound [s] may be represented by either ⟨s⟩, as in ⟨sit⟩ or ⟨c⟩ as in ⟨city⟩. (b) To facilitate reading, the symbols should be clearly differentiated, but should harmonise with each other. For example, mixing roman type with black letter or even italic will detract from legibility. Ideally the symbols should be familiar ones. (c) The symbol system should be capable of expansion to allow for the incorporation of sounds newly detected.

2.2. The commonest type of notation is based on the *alphabetic* principle, each successive sound segment being represented by one symbol. The roman alphabet is an obvious example. Some phonetic alphabets contain symbols which are devised so as to suggest by their shape the nature of the sound and its relation to similar sounds. These are known as *iconic* symbols (for examples see 3.1., 3.9.). Where they are based on articulations they may be called *organic* (see 3.10.). A more unusual type of notation is called *analphabetic* (i.e. non-alphabetic). Sounds are represented by a group of symbols, each one relating to one element of the sound concerned. Chemical formulae are symbols of this kind (cf. 4.)

2.3. If the roman alphabet is to be used for a phonetic notation it needs to be augmented. Various possibilities exist: (a) Use of some of its symbols with a new phonetic value. For instance, the symbol ⟨x⟩ in English represents the two sounds [ks], so it is redundant and may be used, as in the IPA alphabet, to represent a voiceless velar fricative (e.g., the final sound of Scottish *loch*). (b) Inverting or reversing existing symbols, e.g. using [ɔ] for a back vowel, or [ɹ] for a certain type of r-sound. (c) Adding diacritical marks to existing symbols. They may be joined to the original, as in [ç], or separate, as in [ñ]. However, if used widely they may interfere with legibility, and prior to the advent of computer technology were expensive to produce if not readily available to printers. (d) Borrowing letters from other alphabets, for example Greek, or Old English, either with their original sound value or giving them a new value. Other symbols that may be borrowed include @, !, &, %, and numerals. (e) Using digraphs, as English uses ⟨sh⟩ to represent the first consonant in ⟨she⟩. (f) Using upper case letters (where they are clearly different in shape from the lower case) with a new value, e.g., IPA [ɴ] for a voiced uvular nasal. (g) Inventing new symbols. The obvious disadvantage of this is their unfamiliarity. Examples include John Hart's ð = IPA [θ]) and ǥ (= IPA [tʃ]) (Hart 1569).

2.4. To make an alphabet widely usable its symbols need to be clearly linked to the sounds referred to. Sometimes early phonetic alphabets supplied examples from languages to illustrate the sounds, but this still left areas of doubt, because of dialectal and other variations. Many used auditory labels, such as 'thin', 'fat', 'liquid' − difficult to interpret unless one actually hears the sounds. The alternative was articulatory labels, based on the way it was believed the sounds were formed.

2.5. To make it clear that symbols in a text are part of a phonetic transcription the IPA convention encloses them in square brackets or in slashes, but underlining, italics, and curved brackets have also been used. Normally spaces at word boundaries are retained, even though no phonetic feature may be signalled by them.

2.6. Early descriptions and transcriptions of speech tend to neglect features associated with longer stretches of speech, such as pitch variation and stress, and duration in vowels and consonants, though they are often crucial for understanding. Where they are noticed these features are usually indicated by diacritical marks or by punctuation marks assigned to stretches such as syllable, word, clause etc. Sometimes a musical notation is used to show pitch change and duration. An early examples of this can be found in Steele 1775 (for further details → Art. 178, 2.1.). An acute accent on the vowel is often used to indicate stress, and diacritics written to the right of the vowel for tones. Sometimes numbers have been used to indicate specific tones.

3. Universal Alphabetic schemes

Prior to the 19th century the most notable attempts at a universal alphabet were those of John Wilkins (1614–1672) in 1668, Francis Lodwick (1619–1694) in 1686, Charles de Brosses (1709–1777) in 1765, Sir William Jones (1746–1794) in 1788, and William Thornton (1759–1828) in 1793. Accounts of these and other early systems may be found in Kemp (1995). Various things combined in the early 19th century to give additional impetus to the search for a universal way of transcribing the languages of the world. Colonial empires expanded and administrators had to find ways of writing the names of the peoples and places that came under their jurisdiction. Christian missionaries needed a consistent method for writing the Bible down in the various languages they encountered. Those wishing to learn languages with non-roman scripts, or with no written form, looked for a satisfactory romanised transcription of them.

3.1. John Pickering (1777–1846), a lawyer by training, and first President of the American Oriental Society, acquired a working knowledge of all the principal European and Semitic languages and of Chinese. Strictly, like Sir William Jones, he falls outside our remit, since he did not intend his alphabet for universal use. However, in writing his essay "On the Adoption of a Uniform Orthography for the Indian Languages of North America" (1818), he was following suggestions made as to a possible universal alphabet by the famous American linguist Peter Du Ponceau in an article which he published in 1817 entitled "English Phonology". Pickering, in words reminiscent of the later phoneme theory, says he aimed to record the "fundamental sounds of the principal Indian languages", not "the delicate modifications of speech which the nicest ear shall be able to discover in the different dialects". Du Ponceau had recommended using the Greek alphabet, but Pickering chose the roman, employing a number of digraphs, like Jones. He is unusual in employing subscript numerals as diacritics rather than dots, lines, etc.

3.2. It was probably during his visit to America (1795–1798) that the French statesman, oriental scholar and reformer Constantin François Chassebœuf, Comte de Volney (1757–1820), conceived the idea of a writing system that could be universally applied. Volney's interest in this sprang from his conviction of the need to improve the methods employed for teaching and learning oriental languages. A vital tool, in his view, was a system for converting oriental orthographies into roman script. In America he made the acquaintance of William Thornton and also became familiar with the transcription system of Sir William Jones (Jones 1788). In *Simplification des langues orientales* (1795) he attempted to tackle the problem, limiting himself to a few oriental languages. He assumed that a firm basis for the transcription would require a knowledge of the anatomy of the vocal organs, but in fact he includes little information of this kind. He limits the sounds to be described to those which could make a difference of meaning — a foretaste of the phonemic criterion to be formulated later in the century. The roman alphabet is supplemented by Greek letters and by some completely new symbols for the representation of the Arabic emphatic consonants. Digraphs are avoided, in accordance with the 'one sound/one symbol' principle (cf. 2.1.). In *L'alphabet européen appliqué aux langues asiatiques* (1819), Volney added further oriental languages. The notation has been simplified, and now excludes Greek symbols, but allows some diacritics. Volney made no use of digraphs or turned letters.

3.3. Aware of the deficiencies in his own attempts Volney left a sum of 24,000 francs in his will to the French Academies to establish a Prize "de provoquer et encourager tout travail tendant à donner suite et exécution à ma méthode de transcrire les langues asiatiques en langues européennes regulièrement organisées". In the "programme" of the first competition (1821) the Commission appointed by the Academies to organise it rejected the idea of including universal schemes. They justified this on the grounds that to allow such a wide scope would delay the much-needed solution. Several of the contenders for the prize, such as one whom we know only as de Brière (1832?), and even members of the Commission itself, such as Destutt de Tracy, were bitterly critical, seeing this as a betrayal of Volney's true intentions. In the end Destutt resigned from the Commission in protest. However, for the 1827 competition the Commission actually invited participants to put forward a universal scheme, but then awarded the prize to Andreas Schleiermacher whose alphabet was intended for the transliteration of some 32 languages, not for a system of transcription, much less a universal one. Although universal alphabets were put forward for the Prize over the next 20 years (for example by de Brière in 1831) none was successful. For further details and a reproduction of some of the prize-winning submissions see Kemp 1996 (?).

3.4. In Britain an unusual but highly fruitful partnership between Isaac Pitman (1813–1897) and Alexander John Ellis (1814–1890) led to important advances in the devising of phonetic alphabets, some of which were later incorporated in the alphabet of the IPA. Pitman's early experiences as a schoolmaster of relatively humble origins led him to commit himself to social reform. He became convinced that the cause of wider education could only be given greater impetus by making it easier to read English. This meant reform of English spelling. Prior to his work on this he had developed a system of shorthand, based not on written symbols but on the sounds of the language (Pitman 1837), acknowledging a debt both to John Walker's analysis of the sound system of English in his *Critical Pronouncing Dictionary* (1791) and to the characters used in Samuel Taylor's "Stenography" (1786). He later called it "Phonography". Between 1840 and 1847 seven new editions of Pitman's system appeared with modifications. By 1842 he had produced experimental alphabets which he called 'phonotypic', intended for universal use in transcribing languages, and in 1843 he decided that the symbols should be roman in basis. This is the point at which Pitman's contact with Ellis started. Ellis came from a very different background. He was educated at a public school and was a Cambridge graduate in mathematics. A legacy enabled him to spend his time in research (→ Art. 178, 4.1.). Following a visit to Italy he became interested in devising a precise method for recording the sounds of Italian dialects, and hearing of Pitman's efforts at publicising spelling reform (another of his interests) he wrote to him, and sent him several alphabets to comment on. They agreed to use the roman alphabet as a basis, and while Pitman pursued the more practical aspects of publicising their enterprise Ellis had time to read widely on phonetic topics, including the work of German writers such as Karl Mori(t)z Rapp (1803–1883), who influenced him greatly (cf. 3.7.1.). He acquired a knowledge of French, German and Italian and took lessons in at least nine other languages, including Arabic and Russian. The "1847 Alphabet" was the final result of his collaboration with Pitman (see further in Kelly 1981). It was not a universal alphabet, but it laid the foundations for Ellis's more ambitious schemes.

3.5. Ellis's research led him to publish *The Alphabet of Nature* (1845) and *The Essentials of Phonetics, containing the theory of a universal alphabet* (1848). The latter was entirely printed in the Pitman-Ellis Phonotypic alphabet and contained his 'ethnical' alphabet. Ellis describes the alphabet of nature as

"a series of symbols representing certain mechanical conditions requisite for the production of the sensations termed spoken sounds, allowing someone else to reproduce these sensations."

He thought it impossible at that time to do more than produce an approximation to this. The 'ethnical alphabet' contained 17 basic vowels, 9 'breathings', and 37 basic consonants, but through various supplements Ellis provided for 313 elements. The notation was roman but with various modifications – turned letters, digraphs, trigraphs, and a few diacritics. Among the symbols derived from the Phonotypic alphabet were the vowels ⟨ɛ, ɯ, ɵ, ω⟩ (= IPA [i, u, ɔ, o]), and the consonants ⟨ʃ, ʒ, ŋ⟩ (in their IPA values). In 1853 Ellis published a pamphlet entitled *English Phonetics* which contained his "New Universal Latinic Alphabet". This alphabet is later included in his *Universal Writing and Printing with Ordinary Letters* (1856) together with the 'Digraphic' alphabet. He called them "temporary scientific instruments", entirely composed of roman letters, and not to be used to replace existing orthographies. As the names suggest, the Digraphic alphabet makes frequent use of two-letter combinations to represent single sounds, whereas the Latinic alphabet employs, where possible, symbols of the Latin alphabet in their original values or analogous ones, supplementing them by using small capitals as well as lower case, and turned letters. Ellis also allowed for the Digraphic to use turned letters and diacritics. In the same publication he proposed an entirely new series of letters to supplement the roman alphabet, — a 'Panethnic' alphabet, though he recognised that it might require half a century to a century before a standard alphabet became practicable, "for it must grow from popular feeling and use" (1856: 15). He is highly critical of Lepsius's system both for perceived inaccuracies and for its excessive use of diacritics (cf. 3.8.). Ellis favoured the use of "diacritic letters", not attached to the symbol being modified but simply adjacent to it. His examples include ⟨c⟩ = more guttural or cerebral (= retroflex), ⟨j⟩ = more palatal, ⟨n⟩ = nasalised. Thus ⟨kc⟩ = IPA [q], ⟨tc⟩ = IPA [ṭ]. Ellis also provided a "practical approximative alphabet" — a simplified form of the Digraphic for the use of travellers and others. His best known system of notation is 'Palaeotype', so named because its principle was to use the "old Latin alphabet", excluding diacritical marks and typefaces other than roman or Italic (see Ellis 1867; Local 1983). By this time Alexander Melville Bell had put forward his iconic system cf. 3.9.), but Ellis, while considering such a system to be "indispensable for a complete solution of the problem" (1867: 3) believed that for philological purposes his own 'makeshift' system was to be preferred, both because not enough was yet known about the formation of sounds, and also because philologists were often "ill-qualified, withhout special training, to use a very refined instrument". However, as Local points out (1983: 5 ff.) the alphabet is a mixture. The attempt at completeness of coverage suggests that it is providing for an impressionistic transcription (cf. 2.), but some symbols appear to be based on a prior systematic analysis of a language. 20 letters are retained in their Latin use and 3 in their English values — ⟨v, w, z⟩. The symbols ⟨c, q, x⟩ are given new values = IPA [θ, ŋ, x], and ⟨h, j⟩ are used as diacritic letters, as in ⟨dh⟩ (= IPA [ð] and ⟨nj⟩ (= IPA [ɲ]. A few turned letters are used — ⟨ɔ, ə, ɹ⟩, and "occasionally" some groups of letters, such as ⟨krh⟩, which he identifies as "Swiss *ch*". In addition Ellis uses many small capitals, as he had earlier in Latinic, but often with different values. Thus ⟨ĸ⟩ in Latinic = IPA [x], in Palaeotype = IPA [q]. Altogether, including a number of "non-literal" symbols, such as turned numerals (used for clicks) there are about 250 separate symbols. Length is shown by duplication, and accent and tones are shown by dots in various combinations. Palaeotype was chosen by Ellis for use in recording dialects in his monumental *On Early English Pronunciation* (EEP) (1869—89), with some addition and modification of the symbols, notably in Part 5, where he is concerned with English dialects (for an appraisal of this see Shorrocks 1991 and Local 1983). He also provided an 'approximative' form of it, confined to about 46 symbols, each letter being used

"for two or three nearly related sounds, indifferently, either because the distinction is unimportant for the discussion in hand, or is unknown." (Ellis 1867: 8)

(cf. Henry Sweet's "broad" transcription, 3.10.). Although some of Ellis's symbols are to be found in the IPA alphabet with the same values, none of his alphabets was adopted widely, but his guiding principles had a lasting effect on phonetics in Britain. For some examples of his alphabets, see Table 186.1.

Table 186.1: Comparative table of some symbols from A. J. Ellis's alphabets

Digraphic	Latinic	Panethnic	Palaeotype	IPA
ng	N	ŋ	q	ŋ
kh	ĸ	x	kh	x
zh	Ɉ	Ɉ	zh	ʒ
wh	ɯ	ɯ̂	wh	ʍ
oe	ə	ɵ	œ	ø

3.6. Across the Atlantic once again, Samuel Haldeman (1812—1880), Professor of Zoology and Natural History and later Professor of Comparative Philology at the University of Pennsylvania, wrote an essay entitled *Analytic Othography* (1858: separately published 1860). It won the prize instituted by the President of the Phonetic Society of Great Britain, Sir Walter Trevelyan, to bring about "a reform in the spelling of the English language". Haldeman was an excellent observer, with a thorough knowledge of native American languages, and brought his scientific background to bear on the problem. Moreover he was fully familiar with the work done in this area by Pitman, Ellis, Sir William Jones, Lepsius and Melville Bell, and subsequently worked closely with Ellis and Bell. One of the conditions of the Prize was that the essay should use as few as possible new types. Haldeman therefore used the roman alphabet as the basis, and rigidly confined the symbols to their original Latin values. So ⟨v⟩ has the value of IPA [w] and ⟨z⟩ is rejected. He supplements the alphabet with some new or modified characters, diacritics and turned letters, including small capitals. One unsatisfactory device is his use of 'broken' letters (e. g., ⟨u⟩ with part of the second vertical missing). Ellis also disliked his use of varying widths of characters to show different durations. His phonetic classification is sound and includes a good description of clicks, though in general he does not describe the physiological formation of the sounds.

3.7. In continental Europe a number of scholars brought their physiological training to bear on phonetic description and notation. To the extent that it was backed by a knowledge of languages, and an awareness of linguistic relationships between sounds, this was beneficial to the development of phonetics as a discipline. However, this was not always the case. Most of them attempted to provide a basis for transcribing any sound of human speech, but often their lack of familiarity with sounds in actual languages led to errors, and the attempt to make the notation iconic gave it undue rigidity and made it less legible. (For more detail of the background → Art. 180.)

3.7.1. We have noted that Karl Moritz Rapp influenced Ellis (cf. 3.4.). His *Versuch einer Physiologie der Sprache* (1836—41) contains accounts of about a dozen languages. Rapp believed that the analysis of speech and language should be the responsibility of the natural scientist, but he had a keen ear for sounds and a first hand knowledge of many of the languages which he includes. His emphasis on spoken sounds rather than written letters was a reaction against the *Buchstabenlehre* ("letter-based doctrine") of Jacob Grimm. It led him to develop a system of phonetic notation using the roman alphabet, with half a dozen Greek symbols and a few diacritics.

3.7.2. Ernst Brücke (1819—1892) was a distinguished Viennese physiologist and doctor. In *Grundzüge der Physiologie* (1856) he sets out clearly and succinctly his analysis of speech sounds and the mechanism of speech production, with diagrams of the vocal tract. Some errors of description result from his comparative lack of knowledge of languages, and although in theory his system takes in all human speech sounds he admits it cannot cope with clicks, which were known to him only through travellers' tales. He put forward a new roman-based notation and developed an iconic system in a subsequent publication (Brücke 1863). The roman system is supplemented by a few Greek letters and by the use of raised numerals as diacritics. Thus the IPA series [t, ṭ, tʲ, t̞] would be symbolised as ⟨t¹, t², t³, t⁴⟩. The iconic system is based on articulations in the consonant symbols and acoustic resonances in the vowel symbols. Each symbol is built up from separate components, representing factors in the sound's production. Brücke believed this would aid learning and also help to illustrate the process of sound change. The components of the consonant symbols represent place, manner and larynx activity, in a specific combination based on 3 vertical areas. Thus the raised hook ⟨'⟩ = labial, and raised ⟨'⟩ = labio-dental, while lowered ⟨(⟩ = closed glottis, and ⟨)⟩ = creak. Voiced sounds are unmarked, so that IPA [b] would be represneted by the raised labial hook with an attached medial hook representing 'stop', i. e. ⟨'(⟩. IPA [p] would have an additional stroke to show wide open glottis (Brücke allows for 9 states of the glottis). The 14 vowel symbols are designed to occupy the middle area only, so as to be distinct from the consonants (see Fig. 186.1). Like other iconic systems it has

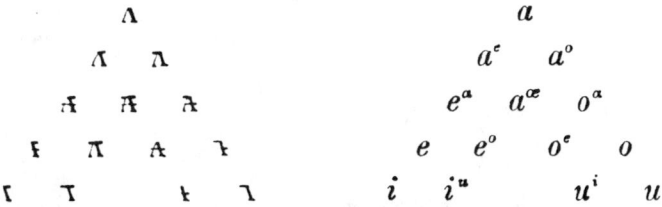

Fig. 186.1: Brücke's iconic vowel symbols.

the disadvantage of being difficult to expand and only applicable to sounds whose articulatory formation is understood. Moreover, its symbols are easily confusable — more so than those of Bell (cf. 3.9.).

3.7.3. Carl Merkel (1812–1876), Professor of Medicine in Leipzig, and Brücke exchanged criticisms of each other's systems over several years. Merkel's first major work (Merkel 1857), was intended for a wide variety of readers, including doctors, singers, teachers and linguists. Like Brücke he had a limited acquaintance with languages, but unlike him Merkel submerges the reader in a mass of anatomical and physiological detail. His phonetic classification is flawed in a number of ways, notably in his failure to understand the mechanism of voicing, but it improves on Brücke's in attempting to deal with characteristics of sounds in longer units — syllables, words, sentences. He devised a notation intended to encompass all the sounds possible to the human vocal apparatus. In his later work — *Physiologie der menschlichen Sprache (physiologische Laletik)* 1866 — he details a number of omissions in Brücke and corrects some of his own earlier mistakes. His iconic script is no more legible than Brücke's, though perhaps easier to write (see Fig. 186.2).

3.7.4. Moritz Thausing's (1838–1884) *Das natürliche Lautsystem der menschlichen Sprache* (1863) is confessedly based on Brücke. It describes speech sounds in terms of their departure in degree of stricture from the 'Naturlaut', ⟨a⟩, defined as the earliest and easiest sound for humans to produce, since it involves the least 'damping' (*Verdumpfung*) in its passage through the vocal tract. Other sounds diverge from it in three directions, each path having 7 'grades'. He uses the pyramid as a model, with ⟨a⟩ at the summit. His system of notation is a novel one, based on a musical notation within a staff of four lines and three spaces, corresponding to the 7 grades, each set having a characteristic shape for its notes. The fact that the symbols are not iconic is seen by Thausing as a virtue, since there is no necessity for him to identify the articulatory formation.

3.7.5. After a life-time of interest in languages, Félix du Bois-Reymond (1782–1865), a clockmaker by trade, finally published his book *Kadmus* in 1862 when he was 80, stimulated by the works of Lepsius (cf. 3.8.) and Brücke. It includes a useful summary of earlier systems, and gives a reasonably accurate account of speech sounds in acoustic and articulatory terms. His notation

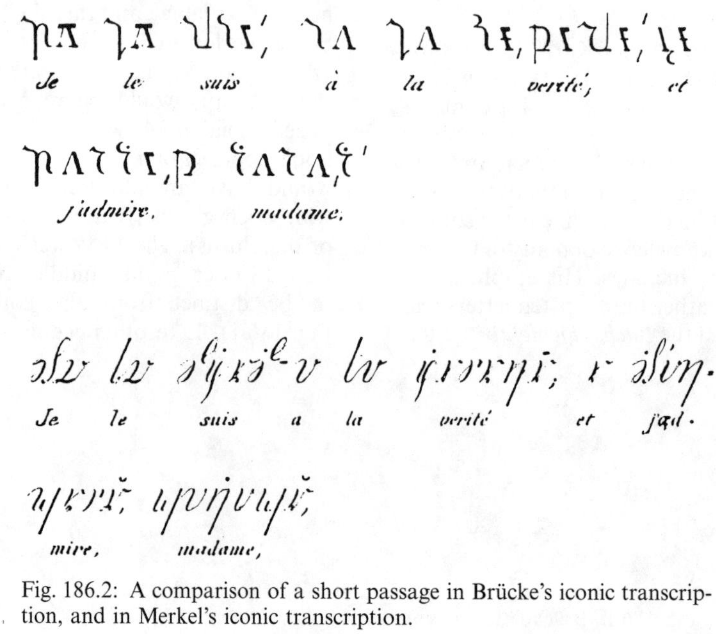

Fig. 186.2: A comparison of a short passage in Brücke's iconic transcription, and in Merkel's iconic transcription.

uses some roman symbols. Like Brücke he makes use of three vertical areas. The symbols for voiceless consonants extend below the middle area, and those for voiced ones above it. Vowels are confined to the middle area, as with Brücke. He attempts to give letters an iconic value, so, for example, to preserve the sameness of place of articulation and difference in voicing which he sees symbolised in the letters ⟨p⟩ and its inversion ⟨b⟩, he proposes to replace the symbol ⟨t⟩ with ⟨q⟩, to pair with its inversion ⟨d⟩.

3.8. In 1848 the Church Missionary Society (CMS) produced a pamphlet to assist their missionaries when faced with languages lacking writing systems, but it was only a stopgap, and in 1852 they asked Carl Richard Lepsius (1810–1884) to produce a new system of transcription. Lepsius was a philologist and Egyptologist by training, and had for some time had a strong interest in writing systems. By 1853 he had persuaded a committee of the Royal Academy of Berlin to have a new alphabet cut and cast. In the following year an Alphabetical Conference was held in London, largely inspired by the Prussian ambassador, Carl Bunsen, with the purpose of reaching agreement on a new system for representing all languages in writing (see Lepsius 1981 [1863]: 28*–32*). It was attended by representatives of missionary societies, learned societies and distinguished linguistic scholars. Foremost among these were Lepsius and Friedrich Max Müller (1823–1900). In spite of his pioneering work in this area A. J. Ellis was not invited. The Conference adopted resolutions to the effect that the basis for any alphabet must be physiological; it must be limited to the 'typical' sounds of human speech; the notation must be rational, consistent, suited to writing and printing, and roman-based, with necessary supplements; and it must form a standard in relation to which other alphabets might be assessed. Lepsius's new alphabet and Max Müller's *Missionary Alphabet* (published in 1854), which relied heavily on the mixing of italic script with roman, were both considered, but no decision was reached. Shortly afterwards the CMS committed itself to Lepsius's alphabet, and the first edition of it was published in both German (1854) and English (1855); see Lepsius 1981 [1863]: 32*–34*. Lepsius considered that "a comprehensive exposition of the physiological basis would be out of place" (ibid. 46), though he was fully acquainted with such a basis from Brücke and others. He believed that the intended users were non-specialists, who would not be helped by technical details, but would benefit more from having available a large collection of alphabets of different languages expressed in his own Standard Alphabet. With this in mind the collection of 54 languages in the first edition (19 pages) is expanded to cover 117 languages (222 pages) in the second edition of 1863. Lepsius uses four symbols from the Greek alphabet – ⟨χ, θ, γ, δ⟩ (= IPA [x, θ, γ, ð], but the chief characteristic of the notation, and one that has been widely criticised, is its heavy reliance on diacritical marks (31 in all). The advantage of these is chiefly the possibility of characterising whole groups of related sounds by marking them with the same diacritic. For instance nasal vowels are marked with ⟨˜⟩, palatals with ⟨´⟩, retroflexes with ⟨.⟩, and so on. The disadvantages are the ease with which small marks of this kind can be omitted or displaced, the cost of cutting special types, and the interference with legibility. Ellis (1867: 6) noted that 17 diacritics were used above and 14 below the body of the letters, and calculated that some 200 out of a total of 286 characters would have to be specially cut. He also pointed out that Lepsius sometimes provides several symbols for one sound, for etymological or other reasons. Sweet later echoed some of his criticisms. Brücke called Lepsius's system a symbol conversion rather than a transcription, and in America Haldeman, perhaps somewhat harshly, described it as "unphilosophic, inconsistent, vacillating and superficial". On the grounds of 'practical utility' Lepsius followed the order of the roman alphabet in the presentation of his symbols, rather than grouping them according to their articulation (see Fig. 186.3). Like Ellis, he envisaged situations in which the full alphabet would not be necessary, and others where extra diacritical marks could be added "if further essential differences should be shown". Although the Standard Alphabet never attained universal acceptance, it had some success, at least in Africa, and was used by Carl Meinhof (1857–1944), the distinguished Africanist, and the missionary Karl Endemann (1836–1919) with some modifications. The "Anthropos Alphabet" (1907) devised by the missionary Wilhelm Schmidt (1845–1921) was also based on Lepsius's symbols.

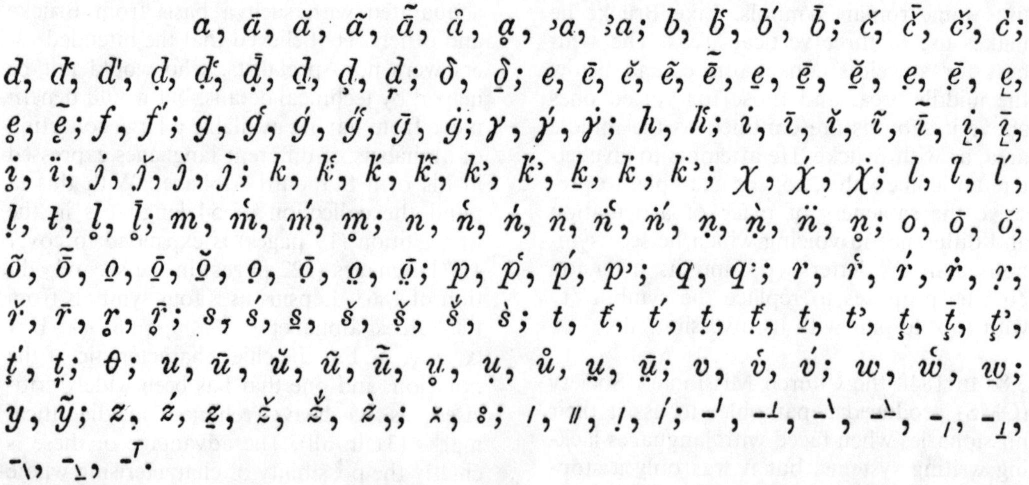

$a, \bar{a}, \breve{a}, \tilde{a}, \utilde{a}, \mathring{a}, a̧, \text{'}a, \text{'}a; b, ƀ, b', \bar{b}; č, ć, č̓, ċ;$
$d, đ, d', ḍ, ḍ̇, ḓ, \underline{d}, d̦, ḓ; ð, ð̣; e, ē, ĕ, ẽ, \utilde{e}, ẹ, ẹ̄, ẹ̆, ę̣, ē̦, e̦,$
$e̱, \bar{e̱}; f, f'; g, ǵ, ġ, ǧ, ḡ, ġ; γ, γ́, γ̇; h, ħ; i, ī, ĭ, ĩ, \utilde{i}, i̧, ī̧,$
$i̱, ï; j, ǰ, j̦, j̄; k, k̄, ḱ, k̂, k̓, k̓̄, \underline{k}, ķ, k̓̔; χ, χ́, χ̇; l, ḷ, l',$
$l̦, ł, ḻ, l̤; m, ṁ, ḿ, m̦; n, ṅ, ń, ṇ, n̂, ń̇, ṋ, ǹ, n̈, n̦; o, ō, ŏ,$
$õ, \utilde{o}, ǫ, ǭ, ǫ̆, o̦, ō̦, o̱, ō̱; p, ṕ, p̓, p'; q, q'; r, ŕ, ŕ, ṙ, ṛ,$
$ř, r̄, r̦, r̦̄; s, ś, ṣ, š, ṣ̌, ṧ, ṡ; t, ṭ, t', ţ, ṱ, \underline{t}, t', ṭ̦, ț̄, t̓̄,$
$t̓, ț; θ; u, ū, ŭ, ũ, \utilde{u}, u̧, u̯, ů, u̦, ū̦; v, v̇, v́; w, ŵ, \underline{w};$
$y, ỹ; z, ź, ẓ, ž, ẓ̌, ż,,; x, ʒ; /, //, !, /; -́, -̱́, -̀, -̱̀, -̦̂, -̱̂,$
$-̦̀, -̱̀, -̦̄^T.$

Fig. 186.3: The symbols of Lepsius's Standard Alphabet.

3.9. Alexander Melville Bell's (1819—1905) contribution to phonetics sprang from his work as a teacher of elocution, which he had begun as an assistant to his father. Bell was a highly gifted observer of speech, and had great success with his pupils. His system was ostensibly 'physiological' — based on articulations, and the treatment of the vowels as well as consonants in these terms was largely a new one. (For further details → Art. 198.) Courses were provided for language learners and for those with speech problems, and Bell became convinced that his work would greatly benefit from a precise 'scientific' system for writing down all sounds that the human vocal apparatus was capable of producing, including inarticulate sounds such as sneezing and yawning. The symbols used were to convey by their shape the way in which the sounds were formed and so be 'self-interpreting' (i. e., give instructions to do something). He saw this alphabet among other things as a tool for the foreign language teacher and for children learning their own language, for teaching the deaf to speak and the blind to read, for correcting speech defects, and ultimately to help in establishing a universal language. It was first advertised in 1864, but Bell's efforts to interest the British Government in it failed. In 1867 he published the system under the title *Visible Speech, the Science of Universal Alphabetics*. It is based on a sagittal diagram of the head and vocal organs facing right, unlike the typical diagram now used which faces left. Bell proposed 28 'radical symbols', which could be combined to symbolise any sound. Ten of these are for the consonants and vowels, and are reversible "to show kindred sounds of different organic formation". Thus the radical consonant symbol C represents "part of the mouth contracted". The same symbol is given a specific value of "back", representing IPA [x], while the front labial continuant [ɸ] is symbolised by the same symbol reversed — Ɔ. The intermediate dental articulation (IPA [θ]) has the same symbol with the open segment facing upwards — ∪, and the palatal [ç] has it facing downwards — ∩. All these are voiceless; the corresponding voiced sounds have a voice bar, so Ꞓ (from the radical C) represents [ɣ], Ə represents [β], and so on. The corresponding stop consonants have the 'shut' symbol, so [k] is represented by Ɑ, [g] by Ꞝ and [p] by Ɒ. The radical symbol Ɛ represents "part of the mouth divided" (i. e., a lateral), which in different orientations can represent labial, palatal, alveolar and velar places of articulation. Further diacritics include indications of double and secondary articulations, trilling, nasalisation, accent, and airstream direction. Detailed notations are provided for a wide range of non-speech sounds, such as hiccough, various kinds of cough, moan, gasp, clearing the throat. The vowels are based on the vertical voice bar — I. This is modified by diacritics to give a total of 36 vowels (see Fig. 186.4), with 3 horizontal tongue positions, 3 vertical apertures,

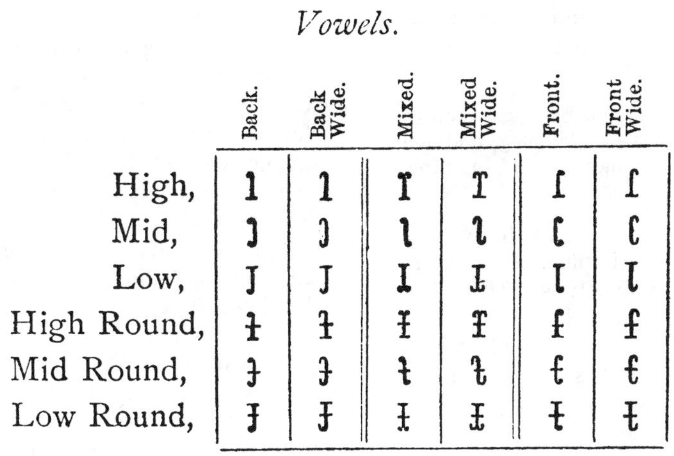

Vowels.

	Back.	Back Wide.	Mixed.	Mixed Wide.	Front.	Front Wide.
High,	1	1	ɪ	ɪ	ɪ	ɪ
Mid,	]	]	ι	ι	ϲ	ϲ
Low,	J	J	ɪ	ɪ	ɩ	ɩ
High Round,	ł	ł	ɨ	ɨ	ɟ	ɟ
Mid Round,	ʒ	ʒ	ι	ι	ɛ	ɛ
Low Round,	ɟ	ɟ	ɨ	ɨ	ŧ	ŧ

Fig. 186.4: The table of vowels in Melville Bell's *Visible Speech*.

lip rounding/unrounding, and primary/wide (based on supposed differences in the pharyngal configuration). The notation is presented with a square type body, giving the appearance of capitals (for an example, see Fig. 186.5), but in some publications Bell used a lower-case style with an oblong body, so that the vowels project above and below the consonants, thus indicating the syllables. Ellis gave his qualified approval to the scheme, in spite of the inconvenience involved in any system requiring new types. As we shall see, Henry Sweet used Bell's scheme as a basis for his own Organic Alphabet, but neither Bell's nor Sweet's version of the alphabet gained acceptance outside a small circle. In 1869 Bell published a transcription system called 'line-writing', which in its initial form is very similar to his shorthand system (steno-phonography). The symbols are sometimes reminiscent of one of the transcription systems devised by John Wilkins whose work Bell may well have known (cf. 3.1.). Like Visible Speech it is iconic and is based on the same phonetic analysis. In 1888 he published a new simplified system entitled "World-English", intended primarily as an aid in the teaching of reading, and based on the assumption that English being so widespread would form the most suitable basis.

3.10. To quote Henderson (1971: ix), Henry Sweet (1845–1912), "as an 'all-round' linguist, [...] has seldom been equalled and never surpassed". His first major work on phonetics was his *Handbook of Phonetics* (1877). He was a pupil of Melville Bell and the book is intended largely as an exposition of Bell's phonetic framework. However, Sweet used a roman-based notation, instead of Bell's iconic one, because he believed that new discoveries in phonetics were certain to be made, and these would require revisions to Bell's iconic scheme, whereas they could be accommodated by the roman alphabet, because of the arbitrary nature of relations between its symbols and the sounds they represent. Sweet took Ellis's Palaeotype as his model, but modified the vowel symbols to make them less arbitrary, rejecting Ellis's idea of trying to provide for all possible sounds. He believed that having chosen to use the roman alphabet, as a temporary measure,

"all that is necessary is to find signs for the fundamental distinctions, and the minuter or exceptional ones can easily be supplied by simple description." (Henderson 1971: 230)

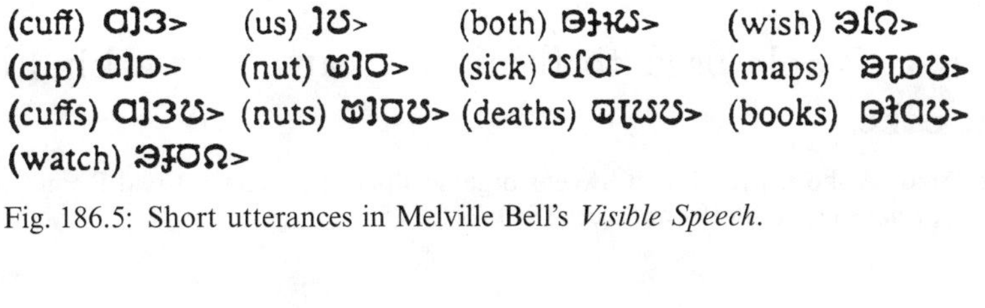

(cuff) ɑ]ɜ>   (us)]ʊ>   (both) ɘɟɪʊ>   (wish) ɘſΩ>
(cup) ɑ]ɒ>   (nut) ʊ]ʊ>   (sick) ʊſɑ>   (maps) ɘ]ɒʊ>
(cuffs) ɑ]ɜʊ>   (nuts) ʊ]ɒʊ>   (deaths) ʊ[ɪʊ>   (books) ɘɟɑʊ>
(watch) ɘɟɒΩ>

Fig. 186.5: Short utterances in Melville Bell's *Visible Speech*.

He calls the alphabet 'Romic' and distinguishes two varieties. The first, 'Broad Romic' (see Fig. 186.6)

"is one which makes only the practically necessary distinctions of sound in each language and makes them in the simplest manner possible, omitting all that is superfluous." (Henderson 1971: 242)

This corresponds very closely to what has later been called a "simple phonemic transcription" (Abercrombie 1964: 17 ff.). Where minuter detail is required the second variety, "Narrow Romic", is to be used (see Fig. 186.6). Sweet particularly stresses the need to retain the general associations of letters and the international character of the systems. Non-segmentals are catered for, but he is against the retention of spaces between words. In a later article written in 1878 (Henderson 1971: 235) he emphasises the need for "elasticity", to avoid having to cast new types "for every insignificant shade of sound". Where diacritics are used they should be cut on separate types, to avoid the cutting of a number of subordinate types for every new letter (he may well have Lepsius's notation in mind). However, in his article "Sound Notation" (1880) summing up the problems involved in devising a 'general alphabet', Sweet outlines the deficiencies of the roman alphabet in comparison with Bell's Visible Speech (Henderson 1971: 231—241). He now puts forward his own modified version of Bell's system which he calls an "Organic Alphabet", developed with the help and advice of H. Nicol, A. J. Ellis and J. A. H. Murray, and subsequently used in his *Primer of Phonetics* (1890) and other works. He counters his own earlier objections to this system by claiming that "the great majority of the [phonetic] facts are really as firmly established as anything can well be" (Henderson 1971: 241). After setting out Bell's system with general criticisms Sweet goes on to specify changes made in his Organic Alphabet. These fall into two types: (a) those dealing with the shapes of letters, and (b) those resulting from a difference of analysis. Under the former heading he adopts Bell's alternative of an aoblong body for the types rather than a square one. The symbols for the nasal consonants are simplified to make them more different from the corresponding stops. Under the latter heading, Sweet introduces a special symbol for the 'teeth' position, ∪, and for 'blade', S, neither of which Bell had provided. He also makes a number of changes to modifying symbols. However, the system is basically still that of Visible Speech in terms of its intention and its notation (see Fig. 186.6). In his article of 1880 Sweet also introduced some changes to his Romic notation of 1877. Capitals are eliminated, various letters from non-roman alphabets and Pitman's Phonotypy are introduced to replace digraphs, e. g., ⟨β, ç, ð, ɸ, ȝ⟩, and italics are restricted mostly to functioning as modifiers. Sweet's Romic transcription was one of the bases for the Alphabet of the IPA, the first version of which appeared in 1888 (cf. 6. below).

4. Analphabetic notations

Sweet sums up the 'analphabetic' type of notation as follows:

"a group of symbols resembling a chemical formula, each symbol representing not a sound, but an element of a sound: the part of the palate, tongue, etc., where the sound is formed, the degree of separation (openness) of the organs of speech, and so on. The two great advantages of such a system are that it allows perfect freedom in selecting and combining the elements and that it can be built up on the foundation of a small number of generally accessible signs." (Henderson 1971: 255)

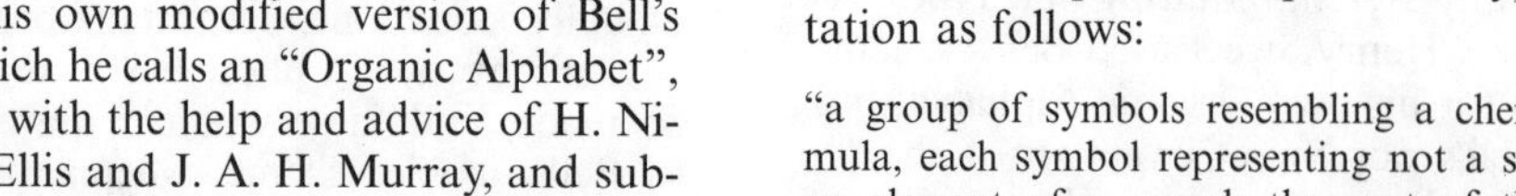

224. ːɒɟɷɒɷ ·ɷɬɔs -ɔʇ ·ʋɟɑ -ʍɟ- ·ɪʋ -ɘʇs -ʇ ːɑ}₊ɾɷ -ʇɘ ·ϡɷɟɔ ·ɑʄɾɑˋ-

225. ːpijpl ·juws -tə ·þiŋk -ði ·əəþ -wəz -ə ːkaind -əv ·flæt ·keikˋ

226. People used to think the earth was a kind of flat cake.

Fig. 186.6: A short utterance in Sweet's organic alphabet, Sweet's Broad Romic, and normal English spelling (from Sweet 1880: 244, 225, 266).

Erasmus Darwin, grand father of Charles, had proposed such a system in 1803, and Thomas Wright Hill (1763–1851) a Birmingham schoolmaster with little or no phonetic training, devised a scheme (only published in 1860 after his death) using numerals to express the places of articulation. The numerator represented the passive articulator and the denominator the active: 1 = lips, so $\frac{1}{1}$ = bilabial, 2 = teeth, so $\frac{2}{1}$ = labio-dental, 3 = tongue tip, so $\frac{2}{3}$ = dental, and so on. Degree of stricture and state of the glottis were shown by the shape of the line between the figures, and vowels were distinguished by having a double line instead of a single one. However, the best known and most elaborated 19th-century example is Otto Jespersen's (1860–1943) analphabetic notation (he later renamed it "antalphabetic"), contained in Jespersen 1889. Greek letters are used to represent the active articulators and roman letters the passive. Numerals show the relative stricture of the articulators. He also uses heavy type, and subscript and superscript letters. Thus $\beta 1^{fe}\delta 0\epsilon 3$ represents a single segment — one kind of [s], where β = tongue tip, 1 = close stricture, ^{fe} = in the area of the alveolar ridge/hard palate, $\delta 0$ = velic closure, and $\epsilon 3$ = open vocal cords. Jespersen illustrates its use for transcribing continuous text in a matrix form, but clearly its application is limited to minute phonetic analysis. Friedrich Techmer (1843–1891) put forward an analphabetic notation of a different type (Techmer 1880). It resembles a musical score, with five horizontal lines, which, together with the spaces between them, indicate the main places of articulation. The manners of articulation are shown by musical-type notes (cf. Thausing, 3.7.4.). However, Techmer never envisaged its widespread use. In contrast, his roman-based system (in Techmer 1884) was considered by the distinguished Norwegian phonetician Johan Storm (1836–1920) to be the best of the German systems of notation, and was used as a basis for Emil Nestor Setälä's (1864–1935) 1901 transcription of Finno-Ugric languages. It is a complex scheme, taking italic script for its basic notation, and utilising upper and lower case, with diacritics underneath or to the right of the main symbols.

5. Dialect alphabets

These are usually designed for specific languages and do not claim to be universal, but some of them have had a wider use. The Swedish Dialect Alphabet (*landsmålsalfabetet*) devised by Johan August Lundell (1851–1940) was published in 1879, with the intention of bringing some order into the comparative chaos of competing systems at that time in Sweden. Lundell had a scientific training, and had subsequently studied phonetics and various proposals for a universal alphabet, as well as being acquainted with a number of languages "outside the ordinary curriculum of academic studies" (Lundell 1928: 2). Like Techmer he uses italic for the basic script, on the grounds that it suits cursive writing as well as printing. Lundell disliked unattached diacritics, except to represent non-segmentals, preferring newly created symbols, mostly involving the addition of loops or hooks to his basic symbols. Sweet criticised the fact that for Swedish alone it uses as many as 88 basic letters and a large number of diacritics, which could lead to a total of some thousands of types if its use were extended to all languages (Henderson 1971: 238). In correspondence with Johan Storm he encouraged him not to follow Lundell's example in devising a Norwegian dialect alphabet. Storm, however, was enthusiastic about Lundell's alphabet, much to Sweet's disgust!

6. Conclusion

The culmination of 19th-century transcription systems is reached in 1888 with the alphabet of the IPA, based on a modified form of the Pitman-Ellis alphabet of 1847 (cf. 3.4., and for the foundation of the International Phonetic Association (→ Art. 198, 7.). The intention behind it from the start was to be a practical tool for language teaching, so its symbols were chosen with a view to clarity, familiarity and economy. There was to be a separate sign for each distinctive sound (i. e., for each phoneme) and in supplementing the roman alphabet the use of diacritics was discouraged. An iconic principle can also be seen in the stipulation that new symbols "should be suggestive of the sound they represent, by their resemblance to the old ones". So, for example, additional symbols for nasal consonants have retained the basic ⟨n⟩ shape. The Alphabet has been revised a number of times, most recently following the Kiel Convention of 1989 (see further in Mac-Mahon 1990).

7. Bibliography

Abercrombie, David. 1964. *English Phonetic Texts*. London: Faber & Faber.

—. 1967. *Elements of General Phonetics*. Edinburgh: Edinburgh Univ. Press.

Bell, Alexander Melville. 1867. *Visible Speech: The science of universal alphabetics*. London: Simpkin, Marshall & Co.

Brière, de. 1832 (?). *Histoire du prix fondé par le Comte de Volney*. Paris: Dondey-Dupré.

Brücke, Ernst Wilhelm. 1856. *Grundzüge der Physiologie und Systematik der Sprachlaute*. Vienna: C. Gerold's Sohn. (2nd enlarged ed., 1876.)

—. 1863. "Über eine neue Methode der phonetischen Transcription". *Sitzungsberichte der Wiener Akademie der Wissenschaften; Phil.-hist. Classe* 41:2. 222–85.

De Brosses, Charles. 1765. *Traité de la formation mécanique des langues*. Paris: Saillant.

Du Bois-Reymond, Félix Henri. 1862. *Kadmus oder Allgemeine Alphabetik*. Berlin: F. Dümmler.

Ellis, Alexander J. 1853. *English Phonetics*. London: F. Pitman.

—. 1856. *Universal Writing and Printing with Ordinary Letters*. Edinburgh: R. Seton.

—. 1867. "On Palaeotype". *Transactions of the Philological Society*, Supplement II, 1–52.

—. 1869–89. *On Early English Pronunciation*. London: Asher & Co.

Haldeman, Samuel S. 1860. *Analytic Orthography*. Philadelphia: J. B. Lippincott & Co.

Hart, John. 1569. *An Orthographie*. London: William Seres.

Henderson, Eugénie J. A., ed. 1971. *The Indispensable Foundation: A selection of the writings of Henry Sweet*, London: Oxford Univ. Press.

Jespersen, Otto. 1889. *The Articulations of Speech Sounds*. Marburg: Elwert.

Jones, Sir William. 1788. "Dissertation on the Orthography of Asiatick Words in Roman Letters". *Asiatic Researches* 1.1–56.

Kelly, John. 1981. "The 1847 Alphabet: An episode of phonotypy". *Towards a History of Phonetics* ed. by R. E. Asher & E. J. A. Henderson, 248–264. Edinburgh: Edinburgh Univ. Press.

Kemp, J. Alan. 1995. "History of Phonetic Transcription". *Concise History of the Language Sciences* ed. by E. F. K. Koerner & R. E. Asher, 388–401.

—. 1999. "Transcription, Transliteration, and the Idea of a Universal Alphabet". *Prix Volney Essay Series* ed. by Joan Leopold, vol. I:2, 476–571. Dordrecht: Kluwer.

Lepsius, Carl Richard. 1981 [1863]. *Standard Alphabet for Reducing Unwritten Languages and Foreign Graphic Systems to a Uniform Orthography in European Letters*. 2nd rev. ed. Repr., with an introduction by J. A. Kemp. Amsterdam: Benjamins.

Local, John K. 1983. "Making a Transcription: The evolution of A. J. Ellis's Palaeotype". *Journal of the International Phonetic Association* 13:1.2–12.

Lundell, Johan A. 1879. "Det svenska landsmålsalphabetet". *Nyare Bidrag till kännedom om de Svenska landsmål* 1.13–158.

—. 1928. "The Swedish Dialect Alphabet". *Studia Neophilologica* 1.1–17.

MacMahon, M. K. C. 1990. "Rewriting the Alphabet: The IPA and the last 100 years". *Henry Sweet Society Newsletter* No. 14, May/June 1990, 11–14. Oxford.

Merkel, Carl Ludwig. 1857. *Anatomie und Physiologie des menschlichen Stimm- und Sprach-Organs (Anthropophonik)*. Leipzig: Abel.

Pickering, John. 1818. "On the Adoption of a Uniform Orthography for the Indian Languages of North America". *Memoirs of the American Academy of Arts and Sciences* 4:2.319–360. (Repr., Cambridge Mass., 1820.)

Pike, Kenneth. 1943. *Phonetics*. Ann Arbor: Univ. of Michigan Press.

Pitman, Isaac. 1837. *Stenographic Sound-hand*. London: Samuel Bagster.

Rapp, Karl M. 1836–41. *Versuch einer Physiologie der Sprache*. 4 vols. Stuttgart & Tübingen: J. G. Cotta.

Rousseau, Jean. 1985. "On a Universal Alphabet – A Letter of W. von Humboldt to G. Bancroft (Sept. 17, 1821). *Topoi* 4.171–180.

Shorrocks, Graham. 1991. "A. J. Ellis as Dialectologist". *Historiographia Linguistica* 18:2/3.321–334.

Sweet, Henry. 1880. "Sound Notation". *Transaction of the Philological Society* 1880. 177–235.

—. 1890. *A Primer of Phonetics*. Oxford: Clarendon Press.

Techmer, Friedrich. 1880. *Zur vergleichenden Physiologie der Stimme und Sprache: Phonetik*. Leipzig: Engelmann.

—. 1884. "Transskription mittels der lateinischen Kursivschrift". *Internationale Zeitschrift für Allgemeine Sprachwissenschaft* 1.171–185.

Thausing, Moritz. 1863. *Das natürliche Lautsystem der menschlichen Sprache*. Leipzig: W. Engelmann.

Thornton, William. 1793. "Cadmus, or a Treatise on the Elements of written Language". *Transactions of the American Philosophical Society* 3, 262–319.

Volney, C. F. F. 1795. *Simplification des langues orientales*. Paris: Imprimerie de la République.

—. 1819. *L'alfabet européen appliqué aux langues asiatiques*. Paris: Didot.

Walker, John. 1791. *A Critical Pronouncing Dictionary*. London: G. G. J. & J. Robinson. (Facs. repr., Menston: Scolar Press, 1968.)

J. Alan Kemp, Edinburgh (Great Britain)

187. Modern Language Instruction and Phonetics in the Later 19th Century

1. Laying the foundations: the 1870s and early 1880s
2. The establishment of the IPA and the consequences
3. 'Quousque Tandem': Person, pamphlet, pressure-group and periodical
4. Felix Franke
5. The Phonetic Method of Language Teaching and Henry Sweet's 'Elementarbuch'
6. After the 'Elementarbuch'
7. Texts for students
8. Phonetics on vacation
9. Paul Passy and French by the Phonetic Method
10. Sweet's 'The Practical Study of Languages'
11. Conclusions
12. Bibliography

1. Laying the foundations: the 1870s and early 1880s

Great strides were made in Europe during the 1870s in the study of language and languages, most notably by the Neogrammarians in their hypothesis concerning the regularity of sound-change. There were, however, other developments afoot, some of which would not come to fruition until the 1880s. In 1876, the German phonetician Eduard Sievers (1850–1932) published his *Grundzüge der Lautphysiologie* (later to be re-titled *Grundzüge der Phonetik* in the 1881 and subsequent editions; → Art. 198). The following year, in Britain, Henry Sweet (1845–1912) published his *Handbook of Phonetics* (1877). Both he and Sievers tackled questions of general phonetics, of phonetic analysis and categorisation, of phonetic notation, and of the place of phonetics within science and the humanities. Both works were aimed at diverse readerships.

In Sweet's *Handbook*, there are strong hints of another topic, which he does not deal with explicitly in the work. They anticipate what was shortly to be a relatively new development in applying a knowledge of phonetics. In the Preface, he writes that no-one should "delude himself with the idea that he has already acquired French pronunciation at school or elsewhere: in nine cases out of ten a little methodical study of sounds will convince him that he does not pronounce a single French sound correctly" (Sweet 1877: xiii). He also notes that if the spelling of English were to be reformed, then school-inspectors would in future be "examin[ing] not in spelling but in pronunciation, elocution, and intelligent reading". These, he adds, are "subjects which are now absolutely ignored as branches of general education" (p. 196).

Another major contribution to general phonetics was Friedrich Techmer's (1843–1891) 2-volume *Phonetik*, published in 1880. Although not dealing specifically with phonetics in relation to language teaching and learning, the work was, like Sievers's and Sweet's, important for helping to provide the intellectual foundations on which the study of the application of phonetics in modern language teaching contexts could be built. Within a short time, Sievers, Sweet, and Techmer were being quoted as the authorities on phonetics to whom the classroom-teacher could turn for necessary information on the pronunciation of various languages.

1884 saw the publication of two other works, adding to the growing literature on phonetics: the first part of Moritz Trautmann's (1842–1920) *Die Sprachlaute im Allgemeinen,* and Wilhelm Viëtor's (1850–1918) *Elemente der Phonetik und Orthoepie des Deutschen, Englischen und Französischen.* Both books were quickly recognised, alongside those of Sievers, Sweet and Techmer, as intelligible and accessible accounts of phonetic theory — although each had an identifiable drawback: the absence of any agreement on the type of phonetic notation that should be used by phoneticians and language-teachers (cf. Breymann 1897: 27–29).

In retrospect, one sees, from the mid-1870s onwards, publications on phonetic topics in five different, but sometimes overlapping, areas. Firstly, 'general phonetics' — though the term was understood in a wider sense than it is today, to take account also of clinical and pathological phonetic phenomena. Secondly, descriptions for the general public of the phonetics of individual languages; the main languages were English, French, and German. Thirdly, descriptions of the pronunciation of a particular language for the express use of schoolchildren. Fourthly, equivalent descriptions for their teachers. And lastly, phonetics for those wishing to teach themselves the pronunciation of a language. By far the largest number of publications were in 'general phonetics' (as defined above), followed by descriptions of French, German and English. Less frequent were publications on the phonetics of other languages, such as Dutch, Danish, Norwegian, Swedish, Spanish, Portuguese and Hungarian. (See the entries in Breymann 1897 and MacMahon [forthcoming].)

The problem of phonetic notation, which until the mid-1880s was a matter of personal preference, had still not been resolved. Writers could choose from a variety of systems of British, European and American origins, including Sweet's 'Romic' systems, the 'Visible Speech' system of Alexander Melville Bell (1819—1905), the various 'Glossic' systems of Alexander Ellis (1814—1890), the 'Standard Alphabet' of Richard Lepsius (1810—1884), and the 'Analytic Orthography' of Samuel Haldeman (1812—1880). Luckily, the emergence and relatively rapid development of what is now the International Phonetic Association, together with its associated Alphabet, narrowed the choice of notational systems and provided a rallying-point for the growing number of language-teachers who professed varying degrees of interest in phonetics.

2. The establishment of the IPA and the consequences

The Association was founded in Paris in 1886 and was initially called *Dhi Fonètik Tîtcerz' Asóciécon* (i. e., the Fonetic Teachers' Association — FTA). In 1889, it became *L'Association Phonétique des Professeurs de Langues Vivantes* (AP), and, in 1897, *L'Association Phonétique Internationale* (API) — in English, the *International Phonetic Association* (IPA). There were two aims: firstly, to encourage teachers to use phonetic notation as a way of helping young children to read. Secondly, to press for phonetic notation to be used in schools to help children acquire realistic pronunciations of foreign languages. On the history of the IPA generally, see Albright (1958) and MacMahon (1986). The founder and dominant personality in the Association for many years was Paul Passy (1859—1940), a language-teacher and phonetician in Paris (see, further, Section 9. below).

In its first month of its existence, the Association had only eleven members, most of them in France. Word soon spread, however, across Europe and beyond about the Association's activities, and the membership figures quickly rose. By 1914, the high point of the Association's existence in terms of membership and influence in educational circles, there were more than 1750 members in 40 countries. The majority of them were language-teachers in schools. (For the changing patterns of membership between 1886 and 1906, see the tabular summary in *Le Maître Phonétique* 1906: 58.)

The Association's first journal was *Dhi Fonètik Tîtcer* (FT), the mainstay of the Association's activities from May 1886 onwards. So much material was being offered for publication that for many years the journal appeared monthly. In January 1889, its name was changed to *Le Maître Phonétique*, at the same time as French became the Association's official language. In 1971 the title was changed again, to the *Journal of the International Phonetic Association*.

From 1886 until 1970, almost all of the journal was printed in various types of phonetic notation, since this was regarded as both the key to a conscious appreciation of what normal adult pronunciation sounded like and the means by which learners could improve their own pronunciation. The proviso 'various types of phonetic notation' is important. Phonetic notation was seen as a flexible tool; at least in the early days of the Association, teachers experimented with a large variety of phonetic notations — depending on the language being taught, the level of the child or adult learners, and their linguistic, particularly orthographic, backgrounds.

Parallel to the application of phonetic principles in the classroom was a second concern for the Association, namely the establishment of an agreed set of phonetic symbols to be used as an international standard for the notation of speech, of whatever language, dialect or accent. Eventually, this factor, the development of the International Phonetic Alphabet (IPA), was to overshadow the original motivations for the Association. Academic phonetics, with its interests in describing languages and developing a theory of general phonetics, became gradually more central to the Association's activities than the language-teaching concerns which had given rise to the Association in the first place.

3. 'Quousque Tandem': Person, pamphlet, pressure-group and periodical

Wilhelm Viëtor (1850−1918), a German phonetician and later to be professor of English at the University of Marburg, had seen, and heard, for himself the limitations of contemporary language-teaching theories and methods, both as a learner and as a teacher. He decided to take a stand in favour of radical change. In 1882 he published pseudonymously a pamphlet *Der Sprachunterricht muß umkehren!* ('Language teaching must start afresh!'), in which he argued passionately for the teaching of modern languages in German schools to be fundamentally restructured. Phonetics should play a major rôle in directing attention away from the written, especially literary, language and onto the contemporary spoken language. By 'spoken language', he meant not the translation of isolated words or short sentences, but genuine communication between speakers. (For an English version of the pamphlet, see Howatt 1984: 340−363.)

Viëtor's pseudonym was 'Quousque Tandem' (i.e., 'How much longer'), a phrase from one of Cicero's speeches. In the summer of 1886, just two months after the founding of the FTA, a group of Scandinavian teachers and phonetician-linguists established a society, also called Quousque Tandem, whose aims were very similar to Viëtor's. In 1888, their society's periodical, *Quousque Tandem Revy*, began publication.

In his pamphlet, Viëtor castigated the errors of his contemporaries in the language-teaching world in terms which left little to the imagination: "appalling confusion [...] nonsense [...] rubbish [...] wrongheadedness [...] dreadful methods [...] gruesome [...] fraudulent [...] stupidity [...] rubble of the past" (Howatt 1984: 345 et passim). Howatt's summary of contemporary language-teaching books (at least in England) expresses the nub of the problem thus: there was "a jungle of obscure rules, endless lists of gender classes and gender-class exceptions, self-conscious 'literary' archaisms, snippets of philology, and a total loss of genuine feeling for living language" (Howatt, p. 136). Viëtor, despite his accurate diagnosis of the state of language-teaching, did not provide any detailed model syllabi for a truly 'reformed' language-learning class. These were to follow in his later publications and in those of his fellow-reformers. For the wider historical background to the changes he and his colleagues had been advocating, including antecedents in earlier centuries, see Viëtor (1902), Widgery (1888).

An example of a somewhat unsuccessful attempt to apply phonetics was August Western's (1856−1940) textbook on English pronunciation. The first edition appeared in 1882, in Norwegian, and was sub-titled 'for skoler' (i.e., for schools); the second appeared in 1885, in German, and was 'for students and teachers'. (Some copies of the Norwegian edition of 1882 have 'for Studerende og Lærere', i.e., for students and teachers, as the sub-title.) Although phonetic notation is used, language is regarded mainly as lists of words; their pronunciation is explained at some length but is categorised according to the orthography. In the 1882 edition, there are no texts in a phonetic notation − but there are two pages of personal and geographical names. The 1885 edition is marginally better: over five pages of names and two-and-a-half pages of texts!

Arnold Schröer's (1857−1935) publication, *Einleitung und Paradigmen zur Lehre von der Aussprache und Wortbildung* (1885), based on his own experiences of teaching in both class-rooms and lecture-rooms, reflects Viëtor's thinking more fully. It begins with a description of the organs of speech, followed by sections on vowels, consonants, and grammar (especially morphology). There are lists of words in a phonetic notation. But a mixture of roman and italic fonts are used for the symbols; some have diacritics positioned above and below them. The result is visually complex and, to the unskilled reader, potentially confusing.

4. Felix Franke

1884 saw the publication of the short but significant work *Die praktische Spracherlernung auf Grund der Psychologie und der Physiologie der Sprache dargestellt* by a young German language-teacher from Sorau in Silesia (now Zary in western Poland), Felix Franke (1860−1886). An indication of both its popularity and the importance of its content is that it passed through several editions (including a Danish translation by Otto Jespersen); the last was in 1927. Franke, like Viëtor, argued for a major revision of the methodology of foreign-language teaching. There should be only a minimal amount of grammar, he said, and in any case it should be relevant to the learner's needs; translation work was acceptable, but it should be kept to a minimum. Phonetic terminology and phonetic notation, on the other hand, should be consciously used in the class-room. An illustration of his theory was his *Phrases de tous les jours* (1886), which was quickly adopted as a standard item for teaching French in the class-room. The work passed through 12 editions between 1886 and 1928. On Franke's contributions to language teaching, see Jespersen (1995 [1938]: 47−52).

5. The Phonetic Method of Language Teaching and Henry Sweet's 'Elementarbuch'

Viëtor's 'Quousque Tandem' pamphlet and Franke's *Die praktische Spracherlernung* have always been regarded as the starting-points for the so-called 'Phonetic Method' (or 'Reform Method') of modern-language teaching in the late 19th century; a more extensive formulation of the background to the method can be found in the historical review of language-teaching methodologies (1888) by William Widgery (1856−1891), a language-teacher and philologist in London, who was highly active on behalf of the Phonetic Method. (See also Breymann 1895; Howatt 1984: 336−337.)

It was Henry Sweet who was to publish the most influential textbook of the reformers, the *Elementarbuch des gesprochenen Englisch* of 1885. The work provides a practical exemplification of the theory − although much of the thinking is attributable to Sweet alone and antedates the 1880s, having its origins in his own experiences of language-learning and language-teaching. Ironically, the experience of teaching English to non-native speakers was limited to adult (or near-adult) learners, mostly university students from outside Britain who took private lessons with him.

Even though the Clarendon Press in Oxford, arguably the world's most distinguished publishing-house at that time, were the publishers, the work rejects the traditional and hallowed methods of teaching languages. It is truly radical: it turns the learning of English on its head. Students do no translation work; nor are there any grammar exercises. There is not even one word in traditional English orthography. Instead, all English words are in a phonemic transcription − even those in the *Glossary*. (The German equivalents of the English words are, however, given in orthographic German.) Sweet says that his aim is "das rein practische studium des gesprochenen Englisch", i. e., a thoroughly practical study of spoken English (1885: iii). He deliberately avoids anything that is linguistically idiosyncratic or unusual, and he aims to introduce the learner to the commonest idiomatic expressions, all logically organised.

The introductory phonetics section in Sweet's book covers the essential points about the speech organs, quantity, stress, pitch, articulatory basis, vowels, consonants, liaison, strong and weak forms, and intonation. His phonemic transcription, although at times somewhat out-of-line with what one would expect to see nowadays, involves the use of only seven non-roman symbols. It is much easier on the eye than the one Schröer had used in his *Einleitung*. (See the reproductions of two pages from the book in Atherton 1996: 4−5.)

Sweet placed great stress on the series of texts in the book, 40 pages in all, which are transcribed phonemically, with stress and various intonation features also being added. Traditional word-division is illusory: a white space before a 'word' normally means that the following string of phonemic units is stressed. Thus confronted with the following sentence in a (modernised) phonemic transcription, /ʃiː siːmztə sɪŋk mɔːrən mɔːrɪntəðə wɔːtə, tɪlət laːstwiːkənsiː nʌθɪŋbətðə tɒpsə(v)ðə maːsts/ in traditional orthography, "she seems to sink more and more into the water, till at last we can see nothing but the tops of the masts" (Sweet 1885: 1), a child would know (a) which syllables to stress, (b) which sounds to make, and (c) which words require a weak, not a strong, form (i. e., 'to', 'the', 'at', 'can', 'but', 'of'). Since the essential features of the intonation pattern are also included as diacritics within the transcription − they are not marked here − a learner could be expected to achieve even greater realism in his or her pronunciation of English. Throughout, the emphasis is on getting the learner to communicate in sentences (or even larger units), using the real-world pronunciations of middle-class Londoners. The contrast could not be starker between this and the older method, with its emphasis on grammar and translation, which meant that most children would have got as far as reproducing — usually badly — lists of isolated words or short syntactic strings.

Reaction to Sweet's book was mixed. There were those — not all of them pedants or prescriptivists — who condemned the style of pronunciation that Sweet had used. It was 'slovenly'; "no teacher should use [it] as a model"; it was "a blow aimed at correctness of speech" (see Breymann 1897: 107—108). Others enthusiastically embraced both the theoretical orientation and the contents of the work. Epithets such as 'trail-blazing' and 'epoch-making' were used (see Breymann, ibid.). In Passy's opinion, the book summed up the views of allegedly many practising teachers:

> I would say [...] that whoever has gone through the 40 pages of texts once or twice has done more, by this practical work, to perfect his pronunciation, especially as regards tone and stress, than he could have done with the best theoretical books, and learned more than the best native English teacher could have taught him. (Passy 1886: [4])

Many years later, in 1938, Jespersen went so far as to say that the *Elementarbuch* had "not [been] surpassed by any book on any major language" (Jespersen 1995 [1938]: 50). An English translation of much of the substance of the *Elementarbuch* can be found in Sweet's *Primer of Spoken English* (1890).

6. After the 'Elementarbuch'

The Phonetic Method was practised by only a minority of teachers; educational politics, rather than ignorance of the theory, may have prevented some of the others from using it. Otto Jespersen (1860—1943), writing in 1889, some 4 years after the publication of the *Elementarbuch*, pointed out that he appeared to be the only teacher using it in Denmark: he had five pupils studying English (Jespersen 1889: 18). In France, on the other hand, 165 pupils were using it — although in only three schools (Passy 1889: 94—95). Regardless of numbers, the enthusiasm of the language-teachers and phoneticians remained high. The methodology was discussed, modified, and incorporated into school textbooks — the term 'Reformlesebuch', for example, became popular in Germany. In the pages of *The Phonetic Teacher* and *Le Maître Phonétique*, colleagues reported successes from various countries, mostly in Western Europe: from Britain, France, Belgium, Germany, Austria-Hungary, Switzerland, Spain, Denmark and Finland; and further afield, from Madagascar, Japan, the United States of America, Brazil and Chile. However, the system was used for teaching only three languages: English, French and German.

One of the class-room teachers who did most to espouse the Phonetic Method and to publicise its clear advantages over more traditional techniques, especially the Grammar-Translation method, was Hermann Klinghardt (1847—1926), a teacher in Reichenbach, south of Leipzig. In a series of publications (e. g., Klinghardt 1888, 1892), he described the success of his language-teaching methods, which were based mainly on Sweet's methodology. He had been given the opportunity, in an enlightened educational setting, to use Sweet's *Elementarbuch*. His superiors backed him, especially when they saw — and heard — for themselves the speed and fluency in English achieved by 16 year-old schoolchildren (cf. Klinghardt 1891: 12; Howatt 1984: 173—175; Kohler 1981: 170—174).

Max Walter (1857—c. 1935), a teacher in Kassel and Frankfurt, was also an enthusiastic supporter of the Phonetic Method. Like several of his contemporaries, he published a textbook on teaching English by the method (Walter 1899). His colleague, Karl Quiehl (1857—post 1912) was the author of a very popular course on French (for German students) based on practical experience of using the Phonetic Method in the classroom (Quiehl 1889).

Otto Jespersen was a committed supporter of Sweet's ideas (cf., e. g., Jespersen 1886), maintaining that a thorough training in sounds, backed up by a simple, systematic transcription, was the essential first step in teaching a foreign language. In his view, phonemic transcription should continue to be used for at least a year before traditional orthography was introduced to school-children. Like Sweet, he argued for natural sentences to be included within inherently interesting connected texts. Grammar, he said, should not be taught formally, but left to the deductive powers of the learners to establish for themselves.

Inspired by the example of Sweet, the Austrian language-teacher Wilhelm Swoboda (fl. 1888—1899) produced in 1889 his *Englische Leselehre nach neuer Methode*, which was closely modelled on the *Elementarbuch*. Approximately half of it is devoted to texts in phonemic transcription, the remainder to phonetic theory (consonants, vowels, stress, intonation). Words are assigned to stress-groups (as in Sweet 1885), but, within these, the orthographic units are also shown. The glossary, too, makes a concession to orthography, listing the phonemic form, then the orthographic, then the German translation of each word. Swoboda's aim was, simply, to make phonetics more accessible to the schoolchild (and teacher!) than Sweet's *Elementarbuch* had done, for in his opinion: "Die Phonetik wird zur Zeit noch als ein Gespenst gefürchtet" (Swoboda 1889: iv).

The Australian-born phonetician and language-teacher William Tilly (earlier: Tilley, 1860–1935) established his 'Institut Tilly' in Germany, first in Marburg, then in Berlin and other cities. It taught foreign languages (mainly to native English speakers) by the Phonetic Method (cf. Jones 1935, Glass 1977). The British phonetician Daniel Jones was first taught phonetics by Tilly. In 1918, Tilly was appointed professor of phonetics at Columbia University, New York City.

Inevitably, not all language-teachers who sympathised with the concept of a phonetically-inspired course were in agreement with the views of writers such as Sweet, Jespersen and Klinghardt. For example, Charles Colbeck (1847–1903), a teacher at Harrow School in England, was in favour of reading being taught before children attempted pronunciation (Colbeck 1887). Johan Storm (1836–1920), professor of English in Oslo, although a committed phonetician, favoured an intermediate position between the old school of grammar-translation and the Phonetic Method (Storm 1887). François Guex (b. 1861) reported on his idiosyncratic use of the Phonetic Method (1890) − modified so that it contained *no* phonemically-transcribed texts. He had decided to avoid them for fear of his learners confusing orthography and phonetic symbols. Johann Zimmermann (1819–post 1889) rejected phonetic notation on the grounds that the results in the classroom did not justify the time and effort that went into learning it (Zimmermann 1889: v). Many years later, the British phonetician Elizabeth Robson (fl. 1903–1939) was to make the shrewd remark that a principal fault to be avoided by the teacher using phonetics was "to put some funny little squiggle on the B[lack] B[oard] and imagine that you have thereby corrected a sound" (Robson 1929: 70). Similarly: "never teach a phonetic script as a new and queer spelling; I have caught students at that game" (p. 73). The English primary school-teacher, Laura Soames (1840–1895), a late convert to phonetics, found phonetic notation to be of greatest use in the teaching of reading to young children (cf. MacMahon 1994).

7. Texts for students

The relative absence of texts in phonemic notation in many of the publications was quickly remedied by the format of *The Phonetic Teacher* and its successor *Le Maître Phonétique*. In practically every issue, from 1886 to as late as 1966, transcriptions were published of texts specially selected as being appropriate for language-teaching in schools and, later, universities; they were known simply as 'spécimens'. Passy set aside space for them in what he called the "Learners' Corner" (subsequently re-named "Partie des élèves") of the journal. In the first year (May 1886 to April 1887), only texts in English were published; from May 1887 onwards, texts in French and German were added. These three languages were to provide the bulk of the transcriptions for 80 years, up until 1966 when the "Partie des élèves" ceased to be included in the journal. The content varied from nursery rhymes and songs to extracts from books on history and geography; some passages were simply re-prints from textbooks written by phonetician/language-teachers. A mark of the importance attached to phonemic texts for language-learners, at least 70 and more years ago, was the series of *Textes pour nos élèves* which the IPA published in pamphlet form between 1921 and 1925.

Between 1886 and 1896, many more languages than English, French and German appeared in the "Learners' Corner". The list includes Moroccan Arabic, Armenian, Mandarin Chinese, Danish, Dutch, Finnish, Hungarian, Italian, Norwegian, Portuguese, Spanish and Swedish. Altogether, between 1886 and 1966, over a thousand such 'spécimens' for language-learners were published.

8. Phonetics on vacation

Phonetics was part of the curriculum for modern-language teachers in training, at least in certain countries (cf., e.g., Althaus 1911 for details of the curricula in England). Vacation courses provided a further opportunity for practising teachers to acquaint themselves with the new methodology, or to undertake refresher courses in it. Numerous such vacation courses were held, particularly in the 1890s and 1900s, in Britain, France, Germany and Switzerland. The programme for the one held at Amherst College in Massachusetts, U.S.A., in 1888, noted that

> the time is coming when a knowledge of the manner in which sounds are produced will be required of every teacher of modern languages. Not only must the ear be trained to distinguish between correct and incorrect sounds, but the teacher must be able to describe to the learner the position that the organs of speech must take in order to pronounce correctly. (Spanhoofd 1888: 315)

In the summer of 1913, no less than 16 such courses were held at which phonetics in relation to language-teaching was discussed and demonstrated: in London, Ramsgate, St Malo, St Servan, Caen, Honfleur, Le Havre, Boulogne-sur-Mer, Lisieux, Paris, Versailles, Rouen, Marburg, Jena, Neuchâtel, and Geneva (*Le Maître Phonétique* 1913: 77).

9. Paul Passy and French by the Phonetic Method

It is impossible to overestimate the contribution that Paul Passy made, both to the development of phonetics in the later 19th century and to the methodology of language teaching (cf. Gimson 1977; Galazzi 1992, 1995). His prodigious physical and mental energies were devoted to many issues — not all of them linguistic. He was involved from the very start in the International Phonetic Association, and for many years was the editor of its journal. He published extensively within the wider field of linguistics, his work covering a wide range of topics such as historical sound-change, the comparative phonetics of the major European languages, spelling reform, French dialects, Old Norse, and the teaching of reading to young children. The driving-force in his life was, ironically, not phonetics or linguistics, but Christianity.

Passy's major description of French pronunciation was *Les sons du français* (1887), which had been preceded in 1885 by a selection of extracts, clearly drawing on the pattern of the Phonetic Method, *Le Français parlé, morceaux choisis à l'usage des étrangers avec la prononciation figurée*. The clearest example of his work in the tradition of the Phonetic Method, however, was his *Elementarbuch des gesprochenen Französisch* (1893), so obviously modelled, both in title and content, on Sweet's *Elementarbuch* of 1885. It was co-authored with Franz Beyer (1849–1927), a language-teacher (latterly 'königlicher Professor') in Munich. Beyer had himself published a work on French phonetics in 1887, *Das Lautsystem des Neufranzösischen*, which Passy regarded as the first systematic description of French pronunciation that had yet appeared. Its sub-title ("Kapitel über Aussprachereform und Bemerkungen für die Unterrichtspraxis") indicates its relevance to the teacher and learner of French from a German perspective (cf. also Beyer 1888).

Another collaborator with Passy was the Oslo school-teacher Thalla Tostrup (fl. 1894–post 1901). Together they produced numerous French 'spécimens' in phonemic transcription for the benefit of Norwegian schoolgirls learning French. These were serialised in *Le Maître Phonétique*, and later published separately as Passy & Tostrup (1895).

Like many of the other University academics who involved themselves in the Phonetic Method, Krystoffer Nyrop (1858–1931), professor of Romance languages at Copenhagen, was first and foremost an historical linguist. His *Kortfattet Fransk Lydlære* (1893), written for Danish teachers and learners of French, followed what was by now a familiar Sweetian pattern: introductory materials on the speech organs, consonants, vowels, suprasegmentals and assimilation and liaison, followed by texts in a phonemic notation marked with an appropriate intonation pattern.

10. Sweet's 'The Practical Study of Languages'

The *Practical Study of Languages* (1899) is the distillation of Sweet's thinking over more than twenty years about "the whole field of the practical study of languages" (Sweet 1899: v). During the late 1870s, he had reached certain conclusions on how languages should be studied — and, in particular, taught. In his Presidential address to the Philological Society in 1877, for example, he had highlighted some of the deficiencies in language-teaching, and had argued that improvements would only come about by making the central concept of language-teaching the "natural sentence, which will [...] be presented in a purely phonetic form" (Sweet 1877–79: 15). The antithesis of the natural sentence was the "arithmetical sentence" in which words were simply added to one another to form such curiosities as "The philosopher pulled the lower jaw of the hen" (an example from Sweet's schooldays studying Greek). Various papers on 'the practical study of languages' followed over the next 18 years, but it was not until 1899 that he set out his ideas in their fullest form.

Sweet takes the subject in a wide sense, to include not only the teaching of West-European languages in schools and universities, but also Oriental languages and dead languages, as well as the analysis of hitherto unwritten languages – the sort of tasks that missionaries were confronted with. His central dictum is that the study of any language has to be based on phonetics, in the sense that, since other elements of language-structure make direct reference to sound-structure, phonetics has to take precedence over them (cf. Sweet 1899, Chaps. 2–7, passim).

In the context of language-teaching, this means that a learner has to be provided with an appropriate phonetic transcription so that s/he will appreciate the "significant sound-distinctions" as Sweet calls them (i.e., the phonemic contrasts). The learner should not be expected to try to imitate the pronunciation (even of a native speaker) on the off-chance that s/he will somehow achieve an acceptable pronunciation. Instead, the phonemic transcription will give specific guidance on those features to pay particular attention to. Predictably, Sweet argues strongly for the spoken language to be taught before the written. Furthermore, he draws attention to the need to clarify what style or styles of the spoken language are to be acquired by the learner. On the question of audio-visual aids in the class-room, he is fairly circumspect – in part because of the quality of the apparatus then available. Phonetic dictation in the foreign language is, he believes, an admirable way of training the learner's ear and should be regarded as an integral part of the teaching and learning process.

On certain matters, he adopts a middle-of-the-road view ("a mean between unyielding conservatism on the one hand and reckless radicalism on the other" [Sweet 1899: vii]), preferring, contrary to some of his younger colleagues, to include both translation work and the formal exposition of grammatical structures in the learning process (cf. Véronique 1992: 177–182). His ideas in the fifteen years since the *Elementarbuch* had clearly undergone some revision.

11. Conclusions

Jespersen writes of a "campaign waged over several years" to change the methodology of modern-language teaching (Jespersen 1995 [1938]: 47). Facing the reformers were the twin forces of pedagogical tradition and questions of school management. Many schoolteachers held firmly to the view that since English, German, French, etc. were languages with similarities to Latin and Greek, they should be taught in similar ways to Latin and Greek. The Grammar-Translation method seemed to work successfully for Latin and Greek: *ergo*, it would work for English and the other languages too. What is more, any intended upheaval in modern-language teaching methods in schools would bring logistical problems in its wake: the training of the teachers, the assessment of the subject-matter, the provision of appropriate materials, etc.

Ranged against the conservatives were the reformers. For them, the essential features of the Phonetic Method which made it superior to traditional styles of teaching were: a deliberately heavy emphasis on the conversational registers of spoken language, often to the exclusion – at least in the early stages of learning – of the written language; the employment in the classroom of certain aspects of articulatory phonetic theory; the use of a phonetic notation which pointed up the phonemic contrasts of the language; a minimal amount of overt grammatical instruction; and relatively little translation work.

The problem remained, however, of how to persuade sceptical teachers that a conscious knowledge, on the part of themselves and their pupils alike, of such things as the action of the soft palate, fricatives, plosives, back vowels and rising intonation patterns could – and would – lead to a significant improvement in the foreign-language skills of the learners. With hindsight, the reformers never appeared to have answered this criticism in such a way that it ceased to become an obstacle to change. On the other hand, the relatively rapid agreement that emerged on the format of the International Phonetic Alphabet in the late 1880s meant that one of the objections to the Phonetic Method, namely its reliance on many apparently self-contradictory and arcane notational systems, quickly disappeared. Furthermore, since the Phonetic Method was used almost exclusively with only three languages, English, French and German, there was the potential for almost all schoolchildren or students studying a foreign language, at least in Western Europe, to benefit from its practices.

Despite opposition, the proponents of the Phonetic Method did achieve a considerable amount. In this, they were helped by the unswerving commitment to their cause of able and strong-willed individuals: academics such as Sweet, Passy, and Viëtor, and teachers holding senior positions in schools or educational organisations such as Klinghardt, Walter, and Widgery. Inevitably, local disagreements arose as to how precisely the Method was to be realised in practical schoolroom situations, but the fundamental loyalty to the 'cause' remained unchanged. Few teachers, it seems, recanted and rejoined the conservative side.

Of critical importance in promulgating the thesis of the Phonetic Method, as well as in maintaining its momentum, was the founding and development of the International Phonetic Association and, especially, its journal. An extensive network existed of like-minded colleagues in schools and universities. Passy regularly published lists of members, thus providing information about who in the next town, city or even country might be consulted for advice and support. The monthly issues of *The Phonetic Teacher* and *Le Maître Phonétique* ensured that teachers across many countries in Europe and beyond were kept up-to-date with details of experiments in the use of the Phonetic Method, and with the latest publications aimed at the schoolroom.

World War I and its aftermath wreaked havoc with the Association and its work. The membership figures declined rapidly; many of the leading lights from the 1880s had either died or had retired from active teaching by the time the journal was re-started in 1923. The need for the Phonetic Method to pioneer change in the methodology of modern-language teaching was no longer as urgent as it had once been. The 'campaign' had indeed been won − at least on some fronts. Its legacy today is the acceptance of the priority of spoken over written language in classroom methodologies, and of the requirement for a high level of proficiency in pronunciation − although, of course, this is now usually achievable by dint of audio-visual technologies rather than by the conscious deployment of phonetic terminology and notation.

12. Bibliography

Albright, Robert W. 1958. *The International Phonetic Alphabet: Its backgrounds and development.* (= *Publication of the Indiana University Research Center in Anthropology, Folklore, and Linguistics,* 7); also Part III of *International Journal of American Linguistics,* Vol. 24, No. 1. B.

Althaus, L. H. 1911. "The Means of Training in Phonetics Available for Modern Language Teachers". *Modern Language Teaching* 7.39−58. (Repr. in *Le Maître Phonétique*, Supplement to juillet-août 1911.1−28.)

Atherton, Mark. 1996. "Being Scientific and Relevant in the Language Textbook: Henry Sweet's primers for learning colloquial English". *Paradigm* 20.1−20.

Beyer, Franz. 1887. *Das Lautsystem des Neufranzösischen. Mit einem Kapitel über Aussprachereform und Bemerkungen für die Unterrichtspraxis.* Cöthen: Otto Schulze.

−. 1888. *Französische Phonetik für Lehrer und Studierende.* Cöthen: Otto Schulze.

− & Paul Passy. 1893. *Elementarbuch des gesprochenen Französisch.* Cöthen: Otto Schulze.

Breymann, Hermann. 1895. *Die Neusprachliche Reformliteratur von 1876−1895: Eine bibliographisch-kritische Übersicht.* Leipzig: A. Deichert.

−. 1897. *Die Phonetische Literatur von 1876−1895: Eine bibliographisch-kritische Übersicht.* Leipzig: A. Deichert (Georg Böhme).

Colbeck, Charles. 1887. *On the Teaching of Modern Languages in Theory and Practice.* Cambridge: Cambridge Univ. Press.

Franke, Felix. 1884. *Die praktische Spracherlernung auf Grund der Psychologie und der Physiologie der Sprache dargestellt.* Leipzig: Reisland.

−. 1886. *Phrases de tous les jours: Dialogues journaliers avec transcription phonétique.* Heilbronn: Henniger frères.

Galazzi, Enrica. 1992. "1880−1914: Le combat des jeunes phonéticiens: Paul Passy". *Cahiers Ferdinand de Saussure* 46.115−129.

−. 1995. "Phonétique/université/enseignement des langues à la fin du XIXe siècle". *Histoire Epistémologie Langage* 17:1.95−114.

Gimson, Alfred C. 1977. "Passy, Paul". *A Biographical Dictionary of the Phonetic Sciences* ed. by Arthur J. Bronstein et al., 160−161. New York: The Press of Lehman College.

Glass, Johanna B. 1977. "Tilly, William". *A Biographical Dictionary of the Phonetic Sciences* ed. by Arthur J. Bronstein et al., 211. New York: The Press of Lehman College.

Guex, François. 1890. *Des recherches phonétiques et de leurs applications à l'enseignement des langues vivantes. Wissenschaftliche Beilage zum Programm der Kantonschule in Zürich.* Zürich: Zürcher & Furrer.

Howatt, Anthony P. R. 1984. *A History of English Language Teaching.* Oxford: Oxford Univ. Press.

Jespersen, Otto. 1886. "Den nye sprogundervisnings program". *Vor Ungdom*, 356–381.

—. 1889. [Letter to the Editor]. *Le Maître Phonétique*, février 1889.18.

—. 1995 [1938]. *A Linguist's Life.* An English translation of Otto Jespersen's Autobiography with notes, photos and a bibliography ed. by Arne Juul, Hans F. Nielsen & Jørgen Erik Nielsen. Odense: Odense Univ. Press.

Jones, Daniel. 1935. "William Tilly †". *Le Maître Phonétique* octobre–décembre 1935.61–63.

Klinghardt, Hermann. 1888. *Ein Jahr Erfahrungen mit der neuen Methode: Bericht über den englischen Unterricht mit einer englischen Anfängerklasse im Schuljahre 1887–88. Zugleich eine Anleitung für jüngere Fachgenoßen.* Marburg: N. G. Elwert.

—. 1891. [Letter to the Editor]. *Le Maître Phonétique*, 1891.11–13.

—. 1892. *Drei weitere Jahre Erfahrungen mit der imitativen Methode. Obertertia bis Obersecunda; ein Bericht aus der Praxis des neusprachlichen Unterrichts.* Marburg: N. G. Elwert.

Kohler, Klaus. 1981. "Three Trends in Phonetics: The development of phonetics as a discipline in Germany since the nineteenth century". *Towards a History of Phonetics* ed. by Ronald E. Asher & Eugénie J. A. Henderson, 161–178. Edinburgh: Edinburgh Univ. Press.

MacMahon, Michael K. C. 1986. "The International Phonetic Association: The first 100 years". *Journal of the International Phonetic Association* 16.30–38.

—. 1994. "Laura Soames' Contribution to Phonetics". *Historiographia Linguistica* 21.103–121.

—. (forthcoming). *Analytical Index to the Publications of the International Phonetic Association 1886–2000.*

Nyrop, Kristoffer. 1893. *Kortfattet Fransk Lydlære, til Brug for Lærere og Studerende.* København: P. G. Philipsen.

Passy, Paul. 1885. *Le Français parlé, morceaux choisis à l'usage des étrangers avec la prononciation figurée.* Heilbronn: Henninger.

—. 1886. Review of Henry Sweet, *Elementarbuch des gesprochenen Englisch (Grammatik, Texte und Glossar).* 2nd ed. (1886) *Dhi Fonètik Tîtcer* April 1886. 24.

—. 1887. *Les sons du français, leur formation, leur combinaison, leur representation.* Paris: Firmin-Didot.

—. 1889. "Note". *Le Maître Phonétique*, novembre 1889.94–95.

Passy, Paul & Thalla Tostrup. 1895. *Leçons de choses en transcription phonétique pour servir au premier enseignement du français.* Paris: Firmin-Didot.

Quiehl, Karl. 1889. *Die Einführung in die französische Aussprache: Lautliche Schulung, Lautschrift und Sprechübungen im Klassenunterricht. Auf Grund von Unterrichtsversuchen.* Marburg: N. C. Elwert.

Robson, Elizabeth H. A. 1929. *How Shall We Train the Teacher of Modern Languages? A textbook on modern language method for use in training colleges, and for all interested in the study and teaching of modern languages.* Cambridge: W. Heffer & Sons.

Schröer, Arnold. 1885. *Einleitung und Paradigmen zur Lehre von der Aussprache und Wortbildung (Supplement zur Englischen Schulgrammatik).* Wien: Alfred Hölder.

Sievers, Eduard. 1876. *Grundzüge der Lautphysiologie.* Leipzig: Breitkopf & Härtel. (2nd ed., 1881; 5th ed., 1901.)

Spanhoofd, [E.] 1888. [Letter to the Editor]. *The Phonetic Teacher*, July 1888.315.

Storm, Johan. 1887. "Om en forbedret undervisning i levende Sprog". *Universitets-og skole-annaler*, 11–13.

Sweet, Henry. 1877. *A Handbook of Phonetics: Including a popular exposition of the principles of spelling reform.* Oxford: Clarendon Press.

—. 1877–79. "Sixth Annual Address of the President to the Philological Society, delivered at the Anniversary meeting, Friday, the 18th of May, 1877". *Transactions of the Philological Society*, 1–122.

—. 1885. *Elementarbuch des gesprochenen Englisch (Grammatik, Texte und Glossar).* Oxford: Clarendon Press. (2nd ed., 1886; 3rd ed., 1891.)

—. 1890. *A Primer of Spoken English.* Oxford: Clarendon Press.

—. 1899. *The Practical Study of Languages: A guide for teachers and learners.* London: J. M. Dent & Co. (Repr., with preface by Ronald Mackin, Oxford: Oxford Univ. Press, 1964.)

Swoboda, Wilhelm. 1889. *Englische Leselehre nach neuer Methode.* Wien: Alfred Hölder.

Techmer, Friedrich. 1880. *Phonetik: Zur vergleichenden Physiologie der Stimme und Sprache.* 2 vols. Leipzig: W. Engelmann.

Trautmann, Moritz. 1884.–86. *Die Sprachlaute im Allgemeinen und die Laute des Englischen, Französischen und Deutschen im Besonderen.* 2 parts. Leipzig: G. Fock.

Véronique, Daniel. 1992. "Sweet et Palmer: Des précurseurs de la linguistique appliquée à la didactique des langues?". *Cahiers Ferdinand de Saussure* 46.173–190.

[Viëtor, Wilhelm.] 1882. *Der Sprachunterricht muß umkehren! Ein Beitrag zur Überbürdungsfrage von Quousque Tandem.* Heilbronn: Gebr. Henninger.

Viëtor, Wilhelm. 1884. *Elemente der Phonetik und Orthoepie des Deutschen, Englischen und Französischen, mit Rücksicht auf die Bedürfnisse der Lehrpraxis.* Heilbronn: Gebr. Henninger.

—. 1902. *Die Methodik des neusprachlichen Unterrichts: Ein geschichtlicher Überblick in vier Vorträgen.* Leipzig & New York: Teubner, Lemcke & Buechner.

Walter, Max. 1899. *Englisch nach dem Frankfurter Reformplan. Lehrgang während der ersten 2 Unterrichtsjahre.* Marburg: N. G. Elwert.

Western, August. 1882. *Engelsk Lydlære for Skoler.* Kristiania: P. T. Mallings.

—. 1885. *Englische Lautlehre für Studierende und Lehrer.* Heilbronn: Gebr. Henninger.

Widgery, William H. 1888. *The Teaching of Languages in Schools.* London: D. Nutt.

[Zimmermann, Johann Wilhelm.] 1889. *Die englische Aussprache auf phonetischer Grundlage methodisch bearbeitet für den Schul- und Selbstunterricht. Von einem Schulmanne.* Braunschweig: Oskar Löbbecke.

*Michael K. C. MacMahon, Glasgow
(Great Britain)*

XXIX. Approaches to Semantics in the 19th and the First Third of the 20th Century
Ansätze zur Semantik im 19. und im ersten Drittel des 20. Jahrhunderts
Les approches à la sémantique au XIXe et au premier tiers du XXe siècle

188. The renewal of semantic questions in the 19th century: The work of Karl Christian Reisig and his successors

1. Introduction
2. The beginnings of semasiology
3. The transformation of Reisig's semasiology
4. Bibliography

1. Introduction

Until the beginning of the 19th century semantic questions had predominantly been treated by philosophers, rhetoricians, etymologists, and lexicographers. From the 17th century onwards one can notice a gradual sharpening of semantic and semiotic awareness amongst philosophers and scholars studying the fields of literature and language. John Locke's (1632–1704) semiotic revolution and his remarks on the metaphorical origin of abstract and mentalistic concepts filtered through to poetics and rhetoric in England, where one can observe a shift from representational semantics to a semantics of usage and habit (Formigari 1993). In France this Lockian revolution led to the foundation for a new logic of ideas (Auroux 1993) and a semiotically based experimental metaphysics in which the relation between the sign and the idea was of paramount importance (Auroux 1995). Semiotics also spilled over to Germany where it culminated in the (1764) work of Johann Heinrich Lambert (1728–1777) and inspired many minor treatises on language, the psychology of language, and anthropology (Formigari 1994). The reflection on synonyms, advanced by Abbé Gabriel Girard's (1677–1748) insight that two words in a given language can never have exactly the same meaning or value, became a thriving field in French linguistics, growing up in parallel with new insights into tropes initiated by the work of César Chesneau Du Marsais (1676–1756) (Haßler 1991) and ending in Ferdinand de Saussure's (1857–1913) linguistics, where a language is a sign system based on oppositions and differences. Both fields also raised the awareness of a difference between the value or meaning of a sign *in abstracto*, that is in the language system, and *in concreto*, that is in language use, leading up to a semantics of use and context (Nerlich 1992).

In Germany, insights into the synonymic structure of the lexicon were deepened in the work of Johann August Eberhardt (1739–1809) which again fostered semantic insights. But most importantly, Immanuel Kant's (1724–1804) seemingly a-linguistic philosophy stimulated linguistic and especially semantic research on two sides. There were those who tried to apply to linguistic topics Kant's insights into the spontaneity of the subject and into mental categories (for example August Ferdinand Bernhardi [1769–1820] and Christian Karl Reisig [see further below]), and there were those who opposed Kant's exclusion of language from philosophy and demanded a new philosophy based on a 'critique of language' (for example Johann Georg Hamann [1730–1788] and Johann Gottfried Herder [1744–1803]; Cloeren 1988, Coffa 1991; Formigari 1994). Preceding Kant, one also has to take into consideration the work of Gottfried Wilhelm von Leibniz (1646–1716) which stimulated not only research into symbolic cognition, but also more empirical research into etymology and semantics and the role of the figures of speech in semantic change.

Finally, there were several other impulses that made it possible to establish semantics as a linguistic discipline in Germany. They came from Friedrich August Wolf's (1759—1824) new foundations of classical philology, from reflections on the limits and prospects of Latin lexicography, and, most importantly, from the establishment of a new type of hermeneutics which started with Johann August Ernesti (1707—1781) and culminated in Friedrich Daniel Ernst Schleiermacher's work (1768—1834). (On the development of semantics as a discipline, consult Gordon 1982; Nerlich 1992; Morpurgo Davies 1994; Schmitter 1987, 1995.)

2. The beginnings of semasiology

The new semiotic awareness inspired by Locke, the new rhetoric and synonymics imported from France, the new lexicography, the new hermeneutics, and the new classical philology rooted in a German tradition of thought, inspired a host of treatises on lexical and philological semantics. We shall only look at three of them which seem to have led up to the 'critical mass' when philosophical and philological speculation turned into a new linguistic discipline: *semasiology*. In 1817 the Biblical scholar Ernst August Philipp Mahn (1787—1854) wrote in his hermeneutically inspired *Darstellung der Lexicographie*:

"Der genaue Sprachforscher hat — um die Nüancen der Synonyme zu bemerken, die Kraft jedes Wortes zu fühlen, die Bedeutung desselben in jeder Stylart, in jedem Gebrauche, und jedem Zeitalter genau zu fassen — das ganze Leben der Nation *historisch-critisch* zu ergründen." (Mahn 1817: 48; italics mine: BN)

"Das Lexicon [...] erhält den Namen *Sprachdeutungsbuch*. [...] Er [the lexicographer, BN] muss nämlich erstlich die Bedeutungen der Worte *historisch-logisch* auffassen, d. h. die Urbedeutung vermittelst der Etymologie [...] ergründen, und wo dies ihn verlässt, dem Genius der Sprache, wie darinn die Bedeutungen der Wörter analogisch auseinander hergeleitet werden, gemäss, die nächste Bedeutung aufnehmen." (Mahn, p. 82; italics mine: BN)

A few years later Georg David Koeler (1758—1818) wrote in his little treatise on a thesaurus of the Latin language which has recently been rediscovered by Schmitter (1995):

"So wäre denn alles Wesentlich aufgezählt, was erforderlich ist, einen Thesaurus seiner würdig zu behandeln, und wir werden nun zu summiren im Stande sein. Jeder Artikel wird, mit Ausnahme nur weniger, in *drei Haupttheile* zerfallen, von denen der erste die *Formenlehre*, der andere die *Bedeutungslehre oder Hermeneutik*, der dritte die *Verbindungslehre oder Syntaxis* betrifft." (Koeler 1820: 359; quoted in Schmitter 1995: 597; italics in the original)

Some years later still, Reisig (1792—1829) translated *Bedeutungslehre* by *Semasiologie*. In doing so, Reisig established a new *linguistic* discipline. This he did in his lectures on Latin Grammar (held in 1822) and later on Latin *linguistics* (delivered in 1824), which were devoted to etymology or *Formenlehre*, semasiology or *Bedeutungslehre*, and syntax. Like Koeler and Mahn, Reisig too was dissatisfied with the existing Latin dictionaries and complained that they were rather deficient and did not provide any systematic derivation of meanings one from the other (Reisig 1890: 2). Again in concordance with Koeler and Mahn, who had advocated a logico-historical derivation of meanings, Reisig wished to base this systematic derivation of meanings on the "Entwicklungsgang[.] des menschlichen Geistes" (Koeler 1820: 361), on logical principles inherent in human thought. Unlike Mahn and Koeler, however, Reisig makes explicit reference to Kant who, according to him, had discovered the laws of human thought. Reisig claims that the evolution of a particular language is determined by free language use within the limits set by the general laws of language, and these general laws are Kant's laws of pure intuition (space and time), and his categories. Reisig also took over from Kant the representational view of meaning according to which words stand for ideas or presentations and the ideas are the meanings of the words. This representational semasiology indeed held sway in Germany until well into the 20th century, when it was finally replaced by a relational or structural type of semantics. For Reisig the three basic mechanisms of association between ideas or meanings, already identified in rhetoric, are synecdoche, metonymy and metaphor. He claims, here following in the footsteps of Du Marsais as well as Bernhardi, that these figures of speech are not only used for purely aesthetic aims but pervade the normal use of speech and underlie the gradual changes in meaning that can be observed and recorded in a dictionary. They are the *logico-rhetorical* laws of semantic change. However, Reisig's semasiology cannot be reduced to a theory of semantic change alone. Like Mahn and Koeler, Reisig is interested in synonyms, and gives the study of synonyms a new disciplinary title: *synonymology*. Reisig points out that the meaning of a word is not only constituted by its function of representing an idea, but that it is also determined by the state of the language in general and by the use of the word in a certain style or register. In dealing with the stylistic problem of choosing the right word from a range of words with the 'same' meaning, Reisig reshapes the unidimensional definition of the word as signifying one concept and opens up a synchronic approach to semasiology alongside the diachronic one. Finally, like Koeler before him and Michel Bréal (1832–1915) after him, Reisig, the semasiologist, is also interested in syntax, that is the syntagmatic relations into which a word can enter and which might change its value. In creating semasiology as part of (Latin) grammar or linguistics, Reisig brought to a synthesis the rhetorical tradition and the hermeneutical tradition and gave them a historical and philosophical foundation inside classical philology.

3. The transformation of Reisig's semasiology

The semasiology which Reisig had postulated as part and parcel of Latin linguistics, was transformed and to some extent deformed in the work that he inspired in his successors: Albert Agathon Benary (1807–1861) (Benary 1834), a former student of Reisig, Friedrich Haase (1808–1867) (Haase 1874–1880), also a former student of Reisig and the first editor of his work (see Reisig 1839), and Ferdinand Heerdegen (1845–1930) (Heerdegen 1875; 1878; 1881) who reedited the semasiological part of Reisig's work in 1890. All three: Benary, Haase, and Heerdegen give Reisig the merit of having put semasiology on the linguistic map, but also criticise him in various ways. Haase criticises Reisig in three ways. He replaces Reisig's conception of grammar, which was quite philosophical and stood in the tradition of the 18th century, by the new 19th-century historical model. Second, he replaces Reisig's representational model of the sign, where the sign signifies an idea, by a bilateral model of the sign, where the meaning is an integral part of the sign (cf. Schmitter 1987: 155 ff.). And finally, he replaces the inner logical principles guiding the transitions between meanings and semantic change by historical ones. Like Reisig he still looked at the stylistic variation of meaning brought about by contextual factors, something that Heerdegen was to reject.

Heerdegen too redefined grammar, but in a more systematic way then Haase. Using the form/function distinction, introduced by Bréal in 1866, he establishes the following hierarchy of grammatical theories. Grammar is split between the theory of the word and the theory of the sentence. The theory of the word is subdivided into etymology (form) and semasiology (function); the theory of the sentence into the theory of inflection (form) and syntax (function). He thereby gave semasiology an official place inside grammar. Like his predecessors Heerdegen also studied semantic change. Trying to emulate the achievements in phonetics or the study of sound laws, he distinguished between unconditoned semantic change and conditioned semantic change. On the level of unconditioned semantic change he distinguished between restriction or specialisation of meaning and semantic transfer; on the level of conditioned semantic change he studied substitution (caused for example by synonyms). Like the representatives of the new generation of linguists, these classical philologists tried to reshape semasiology so that it would fit into the new historical comparative mould, cutting off the by then 'ideologically unsound' philosophical trimmings and the stylistic (that is, the more co-textual and synchronic) parts of Reisig's semasiology.

Two other followers, Oskar Hey (1866–1911) in 1894 and Max Hecht (1857–19??) in 1888 moved semasiology towards a more modern, psychological, approach to meanings. Haase, Heerdegen, Hey and to a lesser degree Hecht formed the backbone of what came to be known as the 'classical' logico-rhetorical tradition of German semasiology, concentrating on establishing typologies of semantic change rather than looking for the causes of semantic change (cf. Gordon 1982, chap. 1; Schmitter 1987: 154 ff.; 1988; Nerlich 1992: 43–52). If we follow the chronology, there is a gap in publications on semasiological problems between 1839 and 1874, the (again posthumous) publication of Haase's semasiological work. The gap is filled by what one could call the 'etymological interlude', represented by the works of Jacob Grimm (1785–1863) (Grimm 1854), August

Friedrich Pott (1802−1887) (Pott 1836; cf. Bologna 1995a, b) and Georg Curtius (1820−1885) (Curtius 1858), who all tried to integrate, albeit critically, the new semasiological ideas into their conceptions of etymology, that is, to take into account the 'letter' and the 'spirit', the form and the (multiple) meaning(s) of words.

By the end of the 19th century the Reisig-Heerdegen type of semasiology had become outdated and was gradually replaced by more psychological approaches, such as advocated for example by Karl Otto Erdmann (1858−1931) in 1910 and Hans Sperber (1885−1960) in 1923 (→ Art. 189). The semantic study of the classical languages Latin and Greek was extended to the semantic study of modern, living languages. The death knell for German semasiology of the classical or logico-rhetorical and typological type was sounded by Leo Weisgerber (1899−1984) in 1927. Influenced by Saussure, he proclaimed that the purely lexicographical study of the meaning of words and their changes is a dead end and must be replaced by more psychological and structural approaches to meaning. This heralded a new era in German semantics, namely, the study of semantic fields (→ Art. 193).

4. Bibliography

Auroux, Sylvain. 1993. *La logique des idées.* Paris: Vrin.

−. 1995. "The Semiological Sources of Semantics". *Historical Roots of Linguistic Theories* ed. by Lia Formigari & Daniele Gambarara, 221−231. Amsterdam & Philadelphia: Benjamins.

Benary, Agathon. 1934. [Review of] "Wissenschaft der Grammatik: Ein Handbuch zu academischen Vorlesungen, sowie zum Unterricht in den höheren Klassen der Gymnasien von J. C. Staedler. Berlin 1833. Verlag von Bechtold und Harje". *Jahrbücher für wissenschaftliche Kritik* 9. Juli. 65−69; 10. Juli. 73−75.

Bréal, Michel. 1866. "De la forme et de la fonction des mots". *Revue des cours littéraires de la France et de l'étranger*, 4ᵉ année (1866−1867), 65−71.

Bologna, Maria Patrizia. 1995a. "Langage et expressivité chez August Friedrich Pott". *Historiographia Linguistica* 22:1/2.75−90.

−. 1995b. "Riflessioni sul rapporto fra ricerca etimologica e teoria semantica nella linguistica tedesca dell'Ottocento". *Scritti Linguistici e Filologici in Onore di Tristano Bolelli*, 121−137. Pacini Editore.

Cloeren, Hermann J. 1988. *Language and Thought: German approaches to analytical philosophy in the 18th and 19th centuries.* Berlin & New York: de Gruyter.

Coffa, J. Alberto. 1991. *The Semantic Tradition from Kant to Carnap. To the Vienna Station.* Ed. by Linda Wessels. Cambridge: Cambridge Univ. Press.

Curtius, Georg. 1858. *Grundzüge der griechischen Etymologie.* Erster Theil. Leipzig: Teubner.

Du Marsais, César Chesneau de. 1757 [1730]. *Des tropes ou des différens sens dans lesquels on peut prendre un même mot dans une même langue.* Paris: chez David. (1st ed., Paris: Brocas, 1730; 5th rev. ed. and augmented by M. l'Abbé Sicard, Paris: Laurens, an XI [1803].)

Eberhardt, Johann August. 1795. *Versuch einer allgemeinen deutschen Synonymik in einem kritisch-philosophischen Wörterbuche der sinnverwandten Wörter der hochdeutschen Mundart.* Erster Theil: A−C. Nebst einem Versuche einer Theorie der Synonymik. Halle & Leipzig: Ruff.

Erdmann, Karl Otto. 1910 [1900]. *Die Bedeutung des Wortes: Aufsätze aus dem Grenzgebiet der Sprachpsychologie und Logik.* 2nd ed. Leipzig: Avenarius. (4th ed., 1925.)

Formigari, Lia. 1993. *Signs, Science and Politics: Philosophies of language in Europe 1700−1830.* Amsterdam & Philadelphia: Benjamins.

−. 1994. *La sémiotique empiriste face au kantisme.* Traduit par Mathilde Anquetil. Liège: Mardaga.

Girard, Abbé Gabriel. 1718. *La justesse de la langue françoise, ou les Différentes significations des mots qui passent pour synonymes.* Paris: d'Houry. (Reedited, extended, etc. by Fabre d'Olivet, Beauzée etc. until 1855; adaptation to the English language, 1776.)

Gordon, W. Terrence. 1982. *A History of Semantics.* Amsterdam & Philadelpia: Benjamins.

Grimm, Jacob. 1854. [Preface]. *Deutsches Wörterbuch*, ii−lxvii. Vol. I: *A-Biermolke.* Leipzig: Hirzel.

Haase, (Heinrich Gottlob) Friedrich (Christian). 1874−1880. *Vorlesungen über lateinische Sprachwissenschaft, gehalten ab 1840.* Vol. I: *Einleitung und Bedeutungslehre 1. Teil* ed. by Friedr[ich] Aug[ust] Eckstein; Vol. II: *Bedeutungslehre 2. Teil* ed. by Hermann Peter. Leipzig: Simmel.

Haßler, Gerda. 1991. *Der semantische Wertbegriff in Sprachtheorien vom 18. zum 20. Jahrhundert.* Berlin: Akademie-Verlag.

Hecht, Max. 1888. *Die griechische Bedeutungslehre: Eine Aufgabe der klassischen Philologie.* Leipzig: Teubner.

Heerdegen, Ferdinand. 1875−1881. *Ueber Umfang und Gliederung der Sprachwissenschaft im Allgemeinen und der lateinischen Grammatik insbesondere. Versuch einer systematischen Einleitung zur lateinischen Semasiologie.* Erlangen: Deichert. [Drei Hefte.]

Hey, Oskar. 1894—1896. "Die Semasiologie: Rückblick und Ausblick". *Archiv für Lateinische Lexicographie und Grammatik* 9.193—230.

K[oeler], G[eorg] D[avid]. "Über die Einrichtung eines Thesaurus der Lateinischen Sprache". *Litterarische Analekten* 4.307—369.

Lambert, Johann Heinrich. 1764. *Neues Organon, oder Gedanken über die Erforschung und Bezeichnung des Wahren und dessen Unterscheidung vom Irrthum und Schein.* 2 vols. Leipzig: Wendler. (Repr., Hildesheim: Olms, 1965—69.)

Mahn, Ernst August Philipp. 1817. *Darstellung der Lexicographie nach allen ihren Seiten.* Rudolstadt: Froebel.

Morpurgo Davies, Anna. 1994. "La linguistica dell'Ottocento". *Storia della linguistica* ed. by Guilio. C. Lepschy, vol. III, 11—399. Bologna: Il Mulino.

Nerlich, Brigitte. 1992. *Semantic Theories in Europe 1830—1930: From etymology to contextuality.* Amsterdam & Philadelphia: Benjamins.

Pott, Aug[ust] Friedr[ich]. 1833—36. *Etymologische Forschungen auf dem Gebiete der Indo-Germanischen Sprachen, mit besonderem Bezug auf die Lautumwandlung im Sanskrit, Griechischen, Lateinischen, Littauischen und Gothischen.* 2 vols. Lemgo: Meyer.

Reisig, Christian Karl. 1839. *Vorlesungen über lateinische Sprachwissenschaft.* Herausgegeben mit Anmerkungen von Dr. Friedrich Haase. Leipzig: Lehnhold.

—. 1890. *Vorlesungen über lateinische Sprachwissenschaft.* Vol. II: *Semasiologie oder Bedeutungslehre.* Mit den Anmerkungen von Ferdinand Heerdegen. Berlin: Calvary.

Schmitter, Peter. 1987. *Das sprachliche Zeichen: Studien zur Zeichen- und Bedeutungstheorie in der griechischen Antike sowie im 19. und 20. Jahrhundert.* Münster: Institut für Allgemeine Sprachwissenschaft der Westfälischen Wilhelms-Universität.

—. 1995. "Von der Hermeneutik zur Semasiologie: Aspekte der Entwicklung von semantischen Forschungsprogrammen in der Zeit um 1800". *Panorama der Lexikalischen Semantik. Thematische Festschrift aus Anlaß des 60. Geburtstags von Horst Geckeler* ed. by Ulrich Hoinkes, 589—603. Tübingen: Narr.

Sperber, Hans. 1923. *Einführung in die Bedeutungslehre.* Leipzig: K. Schroeder.

Weisgerber, Leo. 1927. "Die Bedeutungslehre: Ein Irrweg der Sprachwissenschaft?" *Germanisch-Romanische Monatschrift* 15.161—183.

Brigitte Nerlich, Nottingham (Great Britain)

189. The development of semasiology in Europe: A survey from the second half of the 19th to the first third of the 20th century

1. Introduction
2. General overview
3. The philosophical roots of the semasiological traditions in Europe
4. Semasiological achievements in Europe
5. Bibliography

1. Introduction

The development of semasiology in Europe (cf. Jaberg 1901; Quadri 1950; Kronasser 1952; Baldinger 1957; Kretzmann 1967; Land 1974; Gordon 1982; Schmitter 1991; Haßler 1991; Nerlich 1992a, 1996a; Warren 1992) will be surveyed in three telescopic steps: first a general overview of the situation of semantics in Europe from the second half of the 19th to the first third of the 20th century will be provided. This will be followed by a closer look at the philosophical roots of the three main traditions, the German, French and English one. Finally, the particular achievements of German, French and English speaking semanticists will be analysed.

2. General overview

In article → 188 the birth and development of semasiology in Germany have been charted and with it the development of the semantic tradition known as the *logico-classificatory or logico-rhetorical* one. In Germany, this tradition was gradually superseded by the *psychologico-explanatory* approach, a tradition which itself was woven from various psychological strands of thought from the social-psychological (völkerpsychologisch) to the Jungian ones. In France too the logico-classificatory tradition had still prevailed in the 1853—57 work of Auguste de Chevallet (1812—1858) for example (Nerlich 1996b) and to some extent in that of Arsène Darmesteter (1846—1888). The psychological approach to semantic change was fostered by Michel Bréal (1832—1915). In France one can also observe a *naturalistic* or biological tradition in semantics which competed with the more psychological approaches (cf. Desmet

1994). After 1900, however, the semantic scene in Germany and France changed quite dramatically under the influence of Ferdinand de Saussure's (1857–1913) sign theory, his emphasis on the systematicity of language and the distinctions between *langue* and *parole, synchrony* and *diachrony.* The Bréalian tradition of semantics underwent a Bergsonian transformation in the stylistics advocated by Charles Bally (1865–1947), and a Durkheimiain transformation in the sociological school of semantics inaugurated by Antoine Meillet (1866–1936). But despite introducing sociological ideas into semantic research, Meillet still worked in the older paradigm of historical-comparative linguistics which Saussure had tried to supplement by a synchronic theory of signs and language as a system of signs, and which Bréal had tried to supplement with a both descriptive and historical theory of signs and meanings in use. In Britain the middle of the 19th century saw the emergence of *sign-theoretical* approaches proposed by Benjamin Humphrey Smart (1786–1872), on the one hand, and of a new type of *historical lexicography* in the form of the Oxford English Dictionary project, on the other. Both, Smart's semiotic theory of signs and knowledge and the lexicographical semantics advocated by James Murray (1837–1915) were initially called *sematology.* Lexical semantic questions were part and parcel of historical lexicography and would remain so well into the 20th century. However, in the first two decades of the 20th century questions concerning the status of the linguistic sign and the 'meaning of meaning' resurfaced in philosophical and psychologically inspired circles under the influence of new developments in logic and mathematics. These new philosophies of 'meaning' later split into those treating semantic questions from a formal and truth-conditional point of view and those treating semantic questions from the point of view of ordinary language.

Linguistic semantics came under the influence of German linguistics and anthropology and a functional and contextual approach to semantics emerged. The terms *sematology* and *semasiology*, which was used alongside sematology in the English speaking world to refer to the science of meaning and of the changes of meaning, were gradually replaced by the term *semantics*, as proposed in the most central work of that period: Bréal's *Essai de sémantique*, published in French in 1897, and translated into English in 1900.

The purely sign-theoretical reflections were now carried out under the banners of *semiotics* in America or *significs* in England (cf. Read 1948). The reflection on 'meaning' in general and the 'meaning of meaning' became central to a new philosophy of language. All over Europe 19th-century semantics was heavily influenced by philosophical, logical or psychological conceptions of the mind, or as it was more often called the 'soul', a term inherited from the early phase of German Semasiology. The soul was regarded as a container of either ideas, concepts (*Begriffe*) or presentations (*Vorstellungen*) which were equated with the meanings attached to sounds, words or sound-presentations (*Lautvorstellungen*). The meaning of words was sought in mental representations. Adopting this conception unquestioned as the basis for historical semantics, most of the semanticists of that time forgot to question the real nature of *linguistic* meaning. Typologies of semantic change replaced, or better, stood for theories. Linguists also failed to think through the difference between *Bedeutung* (or 'conventional meaning') and *Bezeichnung* (or the *use* of a word with a conventional meaning to mean something in particular in a given situation). Only by the end of the 19th century was this semantics of representation slowly overcome and replaced by a semantics of communication, where meaning is seen as constructed through linguistic interaction, and is not just given as a mental representation waiting to be labelled. Here the work of Hermann Paul (1846–1921) can be regarded as a watershed (→ Art. 191). The unquestioned correlation between word and idea was further problematised under the influence of Saussure's new sign-theory and his distinction between *signifié* and *signifiant*. From at least 1927 onwards, when Leo Weisgerber (1899–1984) gave a summary and critique of the old *psychological* and *diachronic* type of semasiology, a new, more *synchronic* and *structural* type of semantics was developed by those studying semantic fields. One of the first to propose such a type of study was Richard Moritz Meyer (1860–1914) in 1910. The most famous work in this tradition was produced by Jost Trier (1894–1970) in 1931. However, the new synchronic semantics developed after Saussure had its hidden roots in linguistic works carried out before Saussure. In France Raoul de la Grasserie (1839–1914) advocated for example a non-historical semantics which was however still based on the old model of an association between word and idea. In Germany the turn of the 19th to the 20th century saw a wave of synchronic and/or psychological studies of meaning by Franz Brentano's (1838–1917) act-psychology and Edmund Husserl's (1859–1938) phenomenology, culminating in Anton Marty's (1847–1914) functional and descriptive semasiology (Marty 1908). In his review article of 1906, the Wundtian psychologist of language Ottmar Dittrich (1865–1952) quotes approvingly from the philosophical work of Eduard Martinak (1859–1943):

"Auch die ausdrücklich starke Betonung der Tatsache, daß die sprachlichen Bedeutungsphänomene mit dem Bedeutungswandel nicht erschöpft sind, sondern daß 'die Abgrenzung des Begriffes Bedeutungslehre insofern erweitert werden muß, als sie nicht ausschließlich auf das historische Werden und sich Verändern der Bedeutungen Rücksicht zu nehmen, sondern die psychischen Vorgänge und Gesetzmäßigkeiten in der gegenwärtigen, tatsächlichen Handhabung der Sprache, wie wir sie tagtäglich vollziehen, ebensogut, ja in erster Linie, ihrer Betrachtung zu unterwerfen habe." (Martinak 1901: 79, quoted in Dittrich 1906: 3).

3. The philosophical roots of the semasiological traditions in Europe

After this more general overview, it is important to point out in how far the different European strands of semasiology were influenced by different philosophical traditions on the one hand, by different sciences on the other.

In the case of German semasiology, German hermeneutics and idealism, as well the Romantic movement influenced early German semasiology (→ Art. 188). Semasiology after Christian Karl Reisig (1792–1829) was very much attached to the predominant paradigm in linguistic science, that is to historical-comparative philology. This might be the reason why the term *semasiology*, as designating one branch of a prospering and internationally respected discipline, was at first so successful. Things were different in France, where Bréal, from 1866 onwards, used semantic research as a way to *challenge* the German supremacy in linguistics (cf. the collection of Bréal's texts on semantic by Desmet & Swiggers 1995). It is therefore not astonishing to find that German semasiologists and French semanticists did not see eye to eye. Oskar Hey (1866–1911) dismissed Bréal's *sémantique* to some extent as practical school-semasiology, part of practical stylistics (Hey 1898: 89–90, note 2), whereas the Egyptologist and friend of Bréal Gaston Maspero (1846–1916) emphasised that Bréal, unlike his German colleagues, not only studied word forms but also their meanings and the evolution of meaning, "ce que les Allemands affublaient du nom de *sémasiologie*" (Maspero 1916: 269). However, German *Semasiologie*, just like the French tradition of *la sémantique*, came under the influence of philosophies and psychologies which made these two traditions move closer together. French semantics, especially the Bréalian version, was influenced by the German philosophy of language promoted by Wilhelm von Humboldt (1767–1835) and the psychology of language rooted in the work of Johann Friedrich Herbart (1776–1841) and Heymann Steinthal (1823–1899). Its specifically French basis had its roots in the work of Etienne Bonnot de Condillac (1714–1780) and his followers, the *Idéologues* who studied words as signs (Auroux & Delesalle 1990), as well as the French research into synonyms and tropes (Auroux 1995).

Despite some of his reservations against the formal and phonetic bias in German historical comparative philology, Bréal was also an avid follower of Franz Bopp (1791–1867) and promoted his methodology in France. Bréal, Gaston Paris (1839–1903), and Victor Henry (1850–1907) first expressed their conviction that semantics should be a psychological and historical science in their reviews of the seminal book, *La Vie des mots*, written in 1887 by Darmesteter. Darmesteter had derived his theory of semantic change from biological models, such as Charles Darwin's (1809–1882) theory of evolution and August Schleicher's (1821–1868) model of language as an evolving organism and of languages as organised into family trees, changing independently from the speakers of the language. Darmesteter applied this conception to words and the semantic changes they undergo. It is therefore not surprising to find that Darmesteter's work contains a host of biological metaphors about the birth, life and death of words, their struggle for survival, etc. This metaphorical basis of Darmesteter's theory was noted with scepticism by his colleagues and friends. But they all agreed that his book was the first really sound attempt at analysing how and why words change their meanings. To integrate Darmesteter's insights into his own theoretical framework, Bréal had only to replace the picture of the autonomous changes of meaning affecting by words, by the axiom that words change their meaning because the speakers and hearers use them in different ways, in different situations, according to their experiences and feelings (cf. Delesalle 1987; Nerlich 1990). For Bréal words are not organisms that live and die but *signs*, as the *Idéologues* had pointed out at the end of the 18th century, used to convey meaning. However, the French movement of 'Ideology' inspired not only Bréal, but also a rival movement in French linguistics. The Belgian linguist Honorée Chavée (1815–1877), and the French linguists Abel Hovelacque (1843–1896) and Julien Vinson (1843–1926) were in competition with Bréal's approach. In a more radical way than Darmesteter, they were influenced by Schleicher's naturalism and combined this naturalism with the philosophy of the *Idéologues* who had studied the evolution of ideas as expressed in language. According to this mixture of influences, they called their semantic enterprise *idéologie* (cf. Chavée 1867, 1878) and opposed it, just like Bréal did with his *sémantique*, to phonetics (cf. already Ackermann 1840).

The English tradition of semantics emerged from philosophical and semiotic discussions about *words* in the 17th and 18th century (John Locke, 1632–1704), and a kind of practical etymology as developed by John Horne Tooke (1736–1812) who sought to find truth and the foundation for moral actions in the original meaning of words. Semantics in its broadest sense was also used at first to underpin religious arguments about the divine origin of language. The most famous figure in what one might call religious semantics, was Richard Chenevix Trench (1807–1886), an Anglican ecclesiast, who wrote numerous books on the history of the English language and lexicography. His new ideas about dictionaries provoked the Philological Society in London to the create the *New English Dictionary*, later called the *Oxford English Dictionary*, which is nowadays the richest sourcebook for those who want to study semantic change in the English language. At the turn of the 19th to the 20th century one can observe in England a rapid increase in books on *words* and their meanings, the trivial literature of semantics so to speak (cf. Nerlich 1992b). But there was also the beginning of a more thoroughly philosophical reflection on meaning in the wake of Charles Kay Ogden (1889–1952) & Ivor Armstrong Richards' (1893–1979) book *The Meaning of Meaning* (1923), as well as the start of a new tradition of contextualism in the work of (Sir) Alan Henderson Gardiner (1879–1963) and John Rupert Firth (1890–1960), mainly influenced by the works of the German linguist Philipp Wegener (1848–1916) and the Polish-born anthropologist Bronislaw Malinowski (1884–1942).

4. Semasiological achievements in Europe

We shall now take a closer look at the advancements in semasiology made in German, French and English speaking countries in Europe. As pointed out above, a new impetus to the study of meaning came from the rise of psychological thought in Germany, especially under the influence of Herbart, Steinthal, Moritz Lazarus (1824–1903), and Wilhelm Wundt (1832–1920), the latter three fostering a return to Humboldt's philosophy of language. As early as 1855 Steinthal had written a book in which he tried to refute the belief held by some of his fellow linguists that language is based on logical principles and that grammar must therefore be based on logic. According to Steinthal language resides on psychological principles, and these principles are largely of a semantic nature. Criticising the view inherited from Reisig that grammar has three parts (etymology, semasiology, and syntax), he claims that there is meaning in etymology as well as syntax. Semasiology should therefore be part of etymology and syntax, not be separated from them (1855: xxi–xxii). Steinthal thereby gave us a truer reading of Reisig's intentions than Reisig's most immediate followers. Using the Humboldtian dichotomy of inner and outer form, Steinthal wanted to study grammar (etymology and syntax) from two points of view: semasiology and phonetics. This approach to semantics is very similar to that advocated by Bréal from 1866 onwards. Steinthal and later Lazarus also turned the linguists' attention to the *hermeneutic* problem of understanding. Just as Reisig had been influenced by the classical philologist Friedrich August Wolf (1759–1824), so Steinthal and Lazarus were influenced by Philipp August Boeckh (1785–1867). For Steinthal (1871) the origins of language and of consciousness lie in fact in *understanding*. This principle would be very important to Wegener (1885) who fostered a new approach to semantics, no longer a mere word semantics, but a semantics of communication and understanding (Nerlich 1990). A further step toward such a semantics was taken by Hermann Paul. Paul is often regarded as one of the leading figures in the neogrammarian movement, and his book, the *Prinzipien der Sprachgeschichte*, first published in 1880, is regarded by some as the bible of the Neogrammarians. It is true that Paul intended his book at first to be just that. But from the second edition onwards (1886), having read Wegener amongst many others, Paul elaborated his at first rather patchy thoughts on semantic topics. Bréal — normally rather critical of neogrammarian thought, especially their phonetic bias — could therefore say in his review of the second edition (Bréal 1887: 307; integrated into the *Essai*) that Paul's book constituted a major contribution to semantics. All three, Bréal, Wegener and Paul, insisted on the fact that the emergence of meaning and the change of meaning are based on the interaction between speaker and hearer; here again their indeptedness to Steinthal is clear, as clear as their opposition to another very influential psychologist of language, namely, Wundt, who, despite his socio-psychological ideology, reduced language to the unidimensional phenomenon of individual expression (cf. Vonk 1995). Paul's immediate intention was to get rid of abstractions such as the 'soul of a people' or '*the* language', ghosts that Wundt, and even Steinthal, still tried to catch in their 'folk' psychologies. These entities, if indeed they are entities, escape the grasp of any science that wants to be empirical. What can be observed, from a psychological and genetic perspective, are only the psychological activities of individuals, but individuals that interact with others. This interaction is mediated by physiological factors: the production and reception of sounds, and by psychological factors: the association of ideas. Historical linguistics (and all linguistics should be 'historical' in Paul's eyes) as a science based on principles is therefore closely related to two other disciplines: physiology and the psychology of the individual. From this perspective, language use (*Sprachusus*) does not change autonomously as it had been believed by a previous generation of linguists, but it can neither be changed by an individual act of will. It evolves through the cumulative changes which happen in the speech activity (*Sprechtätigkeit*) of individuals interacting with other individuals. This speech activity normally proceeds unconsciously — we are only conscious of what we want to say, not of how we say it or how we change what we use in our speech activity: the sounds and the meanings. Accordingly, Paul devotes one chapter to sound change, one to semantic change, and one to analogy (concerned with the changes in word forms). The most important dichotomy that Paul introduced into the study of semantics was that of usual and occasional meaning (*usuelle und okkasionelle Bedeutung*). The usual meaning is the accumulated sedimentation of occasional meanings, the occasional meaning, based on the usual meaning, is imbued with the intention of the speaker and reshaped by being embedded in the context of discourse. Contextual clues facilitate the understanding of words which might be ambiguous or polysemous in their usual signification (but Paul does not use term *polysemy*, which had been introduced by Bréal in 1887). Like so many linguists of the 19th century, Paul also tried to state the main types of changes of meaning. However, this classification is a rather patchy one which stays within the limits of the logico-classificatory framework, as inaugurated by Reisig (→ Art. 188). The elaboration and development of Paul's theory of semantic change is be charted in article 191. In the following I shall only indicate very briefly the major lines of development that semantic theory in general took in Germany after Paul.

Many classical philologists as well as schoolteachers continued the tradition started by Reisig. However, by the end of the century the influence of psychology on semantics increased strongly, as can be seen in the works of Karl Otto Erdmann (1858–1931) of 1900 and Hans Sperber (1885–1960) of 1923 who deal with emotional or affective meaning on a diachronic as well as synchronic level. Erdmann tried to answer the question as to what language can achieve as a means of communication; Sperber tried to discover from where a certain meaning receives the psychological impulse to supplant another. But then as now psychology was not a unified doctrine. Apart from Herbarts's psychology of mechanical association, which had a certain influence on Steinthal and hence Wegener and Paul, and apart from some more incidental influences from Sigmund Freud

(1856–1939) and Carl Gustav Jung (1875–1961) on Sperber for example, the most important development in the field of psychology was Wundt's *Völkerpsychologie*. Two volumes of his monumental work on the psychology of such collective phenomena as language, myth and custom were devoted to language (Wundt 1900), and of these a considerable part was concerned with semantic change (on the psychology of language in Germany, cf. Knobloch 1988; on Wundt, cf. Knobloch 1992; Nerlich & Clarke 1998). Wundt distinguished between regular semantic change based on social processes or, as he said, the psyche of the people, and singular semantic change, based on the psyche of the individual. He divided the first class into 'assimilative' change and 'complicative' change, the second into name-making according to individual (or singular) associations, individual (or singular) transfer of names, and metaphorically used words. In short, the different types of semantic change were mainly based on different types of association processes. But even before 1900 Wundt had attracted students and followers who worked on semantic change, such as Alfred Rosenstein (1857–19??) who wrote a thesis in 1884 with the title *Die psychologischen Bedingungen des Bedeutungswandels der Wörter*, based on Wundt's work on logic.

However, Wundt's reputation and fame went far beyond his laboratory at Leipzig. Hanns Oertel (1886–1952) in the United States was strongly influenced by Wundt, so were Gustaf Stern (1882–1948) in Denmark (1931) and Cornelius Gerritt Nicolaas de Vooys (1873–1955) in Holland (Vooys 1907). Yet, Wundt's doctrine was by no means left unchallenged. Paul and Wegener argued against his psychology on the basis of Steinthal's psychology, Léonce Roudet (1861–post-1928) in France (1923) criticised Wundt, and Erik Wellander (1884–1977) in Sweden used Adolf Noreen's (1858–1925) insights into semantics to refute Wundt in 1917. Wundt's staunchest enemy was Marty, who developed his descriptive semasiology in opposition to Wundt's historical and Steinthal's 'innatist' approach. But the final blow to Wundt's psychology of linguistic expression came from the Würzburg school of psychology and then most decisively from Karl Bühler (1879–1963) (Bühler 1934). By then historical semantics had given way to a more structural-oriented study of semantic fields in the works of Weisgerber (1927), Walter Porzig (1895–1961) in 1923, and Trier (1931); cf. Nerlich & Clarke (2000). Gradually semantics detached itself from its historical and psychological roots and became 'autonomous'. It was only in the 1980s that the historical and psychological roots of meaning were rediscovered by cognitive linguists in particular (see Nerlich & Clarke, in prep.).

After this sketch of the evolution of semasiology in German speaking countries, we now come to French speaking countries, where a rather different doctrine was being developed by Bréal, the most famous of French semanticists. But Bréal was by no means the only one interested in semantic questions. Lexicographers and etymologists, such as Emile Littré (1801–1881) and later Darmesteter and Adolphe Hatzfeld (1824–1900), as well as Léon Clédat (1851–1930) and August Brachet (1844–1898), contributed to the discussion of semantic questions. Littré was one of the first to advocate uniformitarian principles in linguistics (1863 [1855]: 27), which became so important to Darmesteter and Bréal. According to the uniformitarian view the laws of language change now in operation, which can be observed in living languages, are the same that produced language change in the past. Hence, one can explain past changes by laws now in operation. Darmesteter was the first to put forward a programme for semantics which resembles in its broad scope that of Reisig before him and Bréal after him, and, in his emphasis on history, that of Paul. He wanted to find the causes and the laws of semantic change, and regarded figures of speech as providing the pointers towards such laws, stressing however, that these figures not only underlie changes in word meaning but also the grammatical forms and syntactic construction found in human languages. But as early as 1840, even before Littré and Darmesteter, the immediate predecessors of Bréal, another group of linguists had started to approach semantic problems under the heading of *idéologie* (cf. above), or as one of its members later called it *fonctologie*, a term influenced by Schleicher's distinction between form, function and relation (Schleicher 1860). French semantics of this type focused, like the later German semasiology, on the isolated word and the idea or meaning it incarnates, and excluded from its investigation the sentential or other contexts. Later on, in 1899 and 1908, de la Grasserie proposed an *integral semantics* based on this framework.

He was (with Marty) the first to point out the difference between synchronic and diachronic semantics, or as he called it 'la sémantique statique' and 'la sémantique dynamique'. However, the real winner in this 'struggle for survival' between opposing approaches to semantics, the 'naturalists' and the 'humanists' as one might call them, was the school surrounding Bréal. Language was no longer regarded as an organism, nor did words 'live and die'. The focus was now on the language users, their psychological make-up and the process of mutual understanding. It was in this process that 'words changed their meanings'. Hence the laws of semantic change were no longer regarded as 'natural' or 'logical' laws, but as 'intellectual' laws (cf. Bréal 1883), or what one would nowadays call cognitive principles. This new psychological approach to semantic problems, most forcefully developed in Bréal's *Essai de sémantique* (1897), resembles that advocated in Germany by Steinthal, Paul and Wegener. Paul, Wegener, Darmesteter, and Bréal all stressed that the meaning of a word is not determined by its etymological ancestry, but by the value it has in current usage, a point of view that moved 19th-century semantics slowly from a largely 'diachronic' to a more 'synchronic' and functional perspective (cf. also Madvig 1875). Bréal also stressed that semantic change is a phenomenon not only of the word or idea, but must be observed at the morphological and syntactical level, too. The evolution of grammar or syntax is thus an integral part of semantics. But Bréal's semantics did not remain unchallenged. It was criticised not only by the naturalists, but also by some of Bréal's associates. In an 1897 review of Victor Henry's (1850–1907) book on linguistic antinomies (1896) and in an article entitled "Comment les mots changent de sens" (Meillet 1897, 1905), Meillet stressed the role of *collective* forces, such as social groups, over and above the individual will of the speaker, an idea which was important for the development of a new trend in 20th-century French semantics: *sociosemantics*. Henry himself was critical of Bréal's insistence on consciousness, or at least certain degrees of consciousness, as factors in language change. Instead, he held the view that all changes in language are the result of unconsciously applied procedures, a view he defended in his 1896 booklet on linguistic antinomies, and in his 1901 study of a case of glossolalia (Chiss & Puech 1987). At the end of the century one can observe, just as in Germany, an increase in psychological approaches, the psychology of the unconscious included. There was also, just as in Germany, a trend to study emotional meaning, a trend particularly well illustrated by the work of the Swiss linguist Bally, a linguistic enterprise which he called *stylistics*, but which constitutes in fact the systematic exploration of the instruments of expression used in *parole* (Bally 1909, 1932; cf. Chiss & Puech 1987). This period of expansion was followed by a period of syntheses, of which the work of the Belgian writer Albert Joseph Carnoy (1878–1961) is the best example (Carnoy 1927; cf. Geeraerts 1997). After the 1930s the influence of Saussure made itself felt and diachronic word semantics was gradually replaced by a synchronic semantics, as advocated for example by the follower of Meillet, Joseph Vendryes (1875–1960), in his article on 'static etymology'. As Vendryes said. "L'histoire est rigoureusement exclue de l'étymologie statique, dont la tâche est de fixer la valeur sémantique des mots à l'intérieur d'une langue et à un moment donné strictement limité" (Vendryes 1953: 7; quoted in Bologna 1995b: 121, n. 3). Influenced amongst others by British contextualism, a contextual and communicational approach to semantics was exemplified in the work of Emile Benveniste (1902–1976). A semiotic approach culminated in the work of Algirdas Julien Greimas (1917–1992). And finally, modern structural semantics, a semantics of relations instead of a semantics of ideas, was advocated in 1964 by Bernard Pottier (b. 1924).

In English-speaking countries the study of semasiology was linked for a long time to a kind of etymology that sought to discover the true origins of words not only for their own sake but for the sake of epistemology, religion and ethics. Genuinely philological and lexicographical considerations only came to dominate the scene by the middle of the 19th century with the creation of the Philological Society of London in 1842, and its proposal to create a *New English Dictionary*. The influence of Locke's *Essay Concerning Human Understanding* (1690) and especially of the chapter "On Words", on English thinking had been immense, strengthened by John Horne Tooke's widely read *Diversions of Purley* (cf. Tooke 1786–1805). Tooke's theory of meaning can be summarised in the slogan "one word – one meaning". Etymology has to find this true and primitive meaning. Measured against this yardstick any use deviating from it was then regarded as 'wrong', linguistically and morally. Up to the 1830s Tooke was much in vogue. His doctrine was however challenged by two philosophers: Dugald Stewart (1753–1828) and, following him to some extent, by the rhetorician Smart. In his 1810 essay *On the Tendency of Some Late Philological Speculations*, "Stewart attacked", as Aarsleff points out, "what might be called the atomistic theory of meaning, the notion that each single word has a precise idea affixed to it and that the total meaning of a sentence is, so to speak, the sum of these meanings." He "went to the heart of the matter, asserting that words gain meaning only in context, that many have none apart from it" (Aarsleff 1967: 103). This contextual view of meaning was endorsed by Smart in his anonymously published *An Outline of Sematology or an Essay towards establishing a new theory of grammar, logic and rhetoric* (1831, cf. Eschbach 1978). According to Smart, words do not derive their meanings from ideas arbitrarily associated with them, but from the use made of them in con-text. Language is no longer seen as transferring notions from the head of the speaker to the head of the hearer. Instead we use words in such a way that we adapt them to what the hearer already knows. It is therefore not astonishing to find a praise of tropes and figures of speech in the third chapter of the *Outline*, devoted to rhetoric. Smart claims that tropes are not only nice, but necessary. Tropes and figures of speech "are the original texture of language" (1831: 214). This is a view similar to that expressed by Gustav Gerber (1820–1901) in his doctrine of language as art (Gerber 1871–74). Smart's conception of the construction of meaning seems to have had little influence on English linguistic thought in the 19th century. He left however an impression on philosophers and psychologists of language, such as Victoria Lady Welby (1837–1912) and George Frederick Stout (1860–1944) who developed not so much a theory of semantic change but a theory of meaning as part of a theory of signs, as part of semiotics, or as Lady Welby called it in 1911: *significs*.

What Murray later called *sematology*, that is the use of semantics in lexicography, received its impulses from the progress in philology and dictionary writing in Germany and from the dissatisfaction with English dictionary writing. This dissatisfaction was first expressed by Richard Garnett (1789–1850) in 1835. He attacked English lexicographers for relying much too heavily on Horne Tooke and for overlooking the achievements made in historical-comparative philology. The next to point out certain deficiencies in dictionaries was the man who became a popular arbiter on semantic matters: Bishop Richard Chenevix Trench (1807–1886). His most popular book was *On the Study of Words* (1851). Trench is central to the English semantic tradition which has its roots in Locke's reflections 'on words'. However, as Aarsleff (1967: 238) has pointed out, although

"he shared with the Lockeian school, Tooke and the Utilitarians, the belief that words contained information about thought, feeling, and experience [...] he did not use this information to seek knowledge of the original, philosophical constitution of the mind, but only as evidence of what had been present to the conscious awareness of the users of words within recent centuries; this interest was not in etymological metaphysics, not in conjectural history; not in material philosophy, but in the spiritual and moral life of the speakers of English."

His presentation of semantic changes was intended to be at the same time a historical record and a lesson in changing morals and history. Set aside the religious lessons which one would nowadays overlook, but which were so important for Trench, one is surprised to find here some important insights into the nature of semantic change which would later on be treated more fully by Darmesteter and Bréal. It also surprises us to find that language is for Trench "a collection of faded metaphors" (1890 [1851]: 48), that words are for him fossilised poetry (for very similar views, cf. Greenough & Kittredge 1902). One might here detect the influence of post-Lockian literary theory and rhetoric (cf. Nerlich & Clarke, in press). Trench also writes about what we would nowadays call the amelioration or pejorisation of word-meaning, about the changes in meaning due to social factors such as politics, commerce, the influence of the church, on the rise of new words according to the needs and thoughts of the speakers, and finally we find a chapter "On the Distinction of Words", which deals with the differentiation of synonyms. Trench's books, which became highly popular, must have sharpened every educated Englishman's and Englishwoman's awareness for all kinds and sorts of semantic changes. On a more scientific level Trench's influence was even more important.

As Murray writes in the *Preface* to the first volume of the *New English Dictionary* (1884), the "scheme originated in a resolution of the Philological Society, passed in 1857, at the suggestion of the late Archbishop Trench, then Dean of Westminster" (p. iv). In this dictionary the new historical method in philology was for the first time applied to the "life and use of words" (p. v). English semantics joined forces with German historical comparative philology and lexicography and endeavoured "to treat the etymology of each word strictly on the basis of historical fact, and in accordance with the methods and results of modern philological science" (p. vi). Etymology was no longer seen as an instrument to get insights into the workings of the human mind, as philosophers in France and England had believed at the end of the 18th century, or to discover the truly original meaning of a word. Following in the footsteps of August Friedrich Pott (1802–1887) and Jacob Grimm (1785–1863), etymology was put on a purely scientific, i. e., historical, footing. Just as the new comparative philology studied language in itself and for itself, so the new etymology studied semantic changes in themselves and for themselves. The program laid down for the *New English Dictionary* is in fact a good summary of semasiological trends in Germany and England up to the end of the 19th century. But, as we have seen, by then a new approach to semantics, fostered by Steinthal and Bréal under the influence of psychological thought, brought back considerations of the human mind, of the speaker, and of communication, opening up semantics from the study of the history of words in and for themselves to the study of semantic change in the context of psychology and sociology. Influenced by Wegener and Malinowski, Gardiner and then Firth tried to develop a new contextualist *technique of semantics* (cf. Gardiner 1932; Firth 1935). However, by the 1960s England, like the rest of Europe, began to feel the influence of structuralism. Stephan Ullmann (1914–1976) tried to bridge the gap between the old (French and German) type of historical-psychological and the new type of structural semantics in his most influential books on semantics written in 1951 and 1962. Although brought up in the tradition of Gardiner and Firth, John Lyons (b. 1932) finally swept away the old type of semantics and advocated the new 'structural semantics' in 1963.

5. Bibliography

Aarsleff, Hans. 1983 [1967]. *The Study of Language in England 1780–1860.* London: Athlone.

Ackermann, Paul. 1840. "Examen de quelques faits relatifs à la formation et à la culture de la langue française". *Journal de la langue française et des langues en général*, 3 série, 3.105–130.

Auroux, Sylvain. 1995. "The Semiological Sources of Semantics". *Historical Roots of Linguistic Theories* ed. by Lia Formigari & Daniele Gambarara, 221–231. Amsterdam & Philadelphia: Benjamins.

–. & Simone Delesalle. 1990. "French Semantics of the Late Nineteenth Century and Lady Welby's Significs". *Essays on Significs: Papers presented on the occasion of the 150th anniversary of the birth of Victoria Lady Welby (1837–1912)* ed. by H. Walter Schmitz, 105–131. Amsterdam & Philadelphia: Benjamins.

Baldinger, Kurt. 1957. *Die Semasiologie: Versuch eines Überblicks.* Berlin: Akademie-Verlag.

Bally, Charles. 1951 [1909]. *Traité de stylistique française.* 3e éd. Nouveau tirage. 2 vols. Genève: George; Paris: Klincksieck. (1st ed., Heidelberg: Winter; Paris: Klincksieck, 1909.)

–. 1965 [1932]. *Linguistique générale et linguistique française.* 4e éd. revue et corrigée. Berne: Francke.

Bologna, Maria Patrizia. 1995a. "Langage et Expressivité chez August Friedrich Pott". *Historiographia Linguistica* 22.75–90.

Bréal, Michel. 1883. "Les lois intellectuelles du langage: Fragment de sémantique". *Annuaire de l'Association pour l'encouragement des études grecques en France* 17.132–142.

–. 1887. "L'histoire des mots". *Revue des deux mondes* (1 juillet 1887) 82.187–212.

–. 1897. *Essai de sémantique (Science des significations).* Paris: Hachette.

–. 1924 [1897]. *Essai de sémantique (Science des significations).* Paris: Gérard Monfort. [Reprint of the 4th ed. of 1908.]

–. 1964 [1900]. *Semantics: Studies in the science of meaning.* Transl. by Mrs. Henry [i. e., Nina] Cust. With a new Introduction by Joshua Whatmough. New York: Dover Publications.

Carnoy, Albert J[oseph]. 1927. *La science du mot: Traité de sémantique.* Louvain: Eds. "Universitas".

Chavée, Honoré. 1867. "Les familles naturelles des idées verbales". *Revue de linguistique et de philologie comparée* 1.32–45.

–. 1878. *Idéologie lexicologique des langues indo-européennes.* Œuvre posthume publiée par les soins de sa veuve, Mme Harriett Harrisson. Paris: Maisonneuve.

Chevallet, A[lbin d'Abel] de. 1853–1857. *Origine et formation de la langue française.* 2 parties en 3 vols. Paris: Dumoulin.

Chiss, Jean-Louis & Christian Puech. 1987. *Fondations de la linguistique: Etudes d'histoire et d'épistémologie*. Bruxelles: Boeck-Wesmael.

Clédat, Léon. 1895. "Les lois de la dérivation des sens appliquées au français". *Revue de Philologie* 9.49–55.

Darmesteter, Arsène. 1887. *La vie des mots étudiée dans leurs significations.* Paris: Delagrave.

Delesalle, Simone. 1987. "Vie des mots et science des significations: Arsène Darmesteter et Michel Bréal". *DRLAV: Revue de linguistique* 36–37. 265–314.

Desmet, Piet. 1990. "The Role of Semantics in the Development of Historical Linguistics in France". *Belgian Journal of Linguistics* 5.133–158.

–. 1994. "La *Revue de linguistique et de philologie comparée* (1867–1916) – organe de la linguistique naturaliste en France". *Beiträge zur Geschichte der Sprachwissenschaft* 4:1.49–80.

– & Pierre Swiggers, eds. 1995. *De la grammaire comparée à la sémantique: Textes de Michel Bréal publiés entre 1864 et 1898.* Introduction, commentaires et bibliographie. Leuven & Paris: Peeters.

Dittrich, Ottmar. 1906. Review of Martinak (1901) [as well as works by Erdmann, Waag, Rittershaus, Rozwadowski, Freudenberger and Mauthner]. *Indogermanische Forschungen: Anzeiger für Indogermanische Sprach- und Altertumskunde* 19.1–15.

Du Marsais, César Chesneau de. 1757 [1730]. *Des tropes ou des différens sens dans lesquels on peut prendre un même mot dans une même langue.* Paris: chez David. (1st ed., Paris: Brocas 1730; 5th rev. ed. and augmented by M. l'Abbé Sicard, Paris: Laurens, an XI [1803].)

Erdmann, Karl Otto. 1910 [1900]. *Die Bedeutung des Wortes: Aufsätze aus dem Grenzgebiet der Sprachpsychologie und Logik.* 2nd ed. Leipzig: Avenarius. (4th ed., 1925.)

Eschbach, Achim. 1978. *Benjamin Humphrey Smart Grundlagen der Zeichentheorie: Grammatik, Logik, Rhetorik.* Aus dem Englischen und mit einer Einleitung hrsg. von Achim Eschbach. Frankfurt/M.: Syndikat.

Firth, John Rupert. 1957 [1935]. "The Technique of Semantics". *Papers in Linguistics 1934–1951*, 7–33. London: Oxford Univ. Press.

Gardiner, (Sir) Alan Henderson. 1951 [1932]. *The Theory of Speech and Language.* Oxford: Clarendon Press. (2nd ed., with additions [pp. 328–344], 1951; repr., 1963.)

Garnett, Richard. 1835. "English Lexicography". *Quarterly Review* 54.294–330.

Geeraerts, Dirk. 1997. "Albert Carnoy's *La Science du mot*". *L'Histoire de la sémantique préstructurale: Quatre études* ed. by Piet Desmet et al., 45–57. Leuven. Katholieke Univ. Leuven.

Gerber, Gustav. 1871–74. *Die Sprache als Kunst.* 2 Bde. (Bd. 2 in zwei Teilen). Bromberg: Heyfleder.

(2nd ed. [2 vols. in one], 1885; repr. Hildesheim: Olms, 1961.)

Girard, Abbé Gabriel. 1718. *La justesse de la langue françoise, ou les Différentes significations des mots qui passent pour synonymes.* Paris: d'Houry. (Reedited, extended, etc. by abbé Fabre d'Olivet, Beauzée etc. until 1855; adaptation to the English language 1776.)

Gordon, W. Terrence. 1982. *A History of Semantics.* Amsterdam & Philadelphhia: Benjamins.

Grasserie, Raoul de la. 1899. "Des mouvements alternants des idées révélés par les mots". *Revue Philosophique* 48.391–416, 495–504.

–. *Essai d'une sémantique intégrale.* Paris: Leroux.

Greenough, James & George Kittredge. 1902. *Words and Their Ways in English Speech.* London: Macmillan.

Haßler, Gerda. 1991. *Der semantische Wertbegriff in Sprachtheorien vom 18. zum 20. Jahrhundert.* Berlin: Akademie-Verlag.

Henry, Victor. 1896. *Antinomies linguistiques.* Paris: Alcan.

–. 1901. *Le langage Martien.* Paris: Maisonneuve. (Repr., with *Antinomies.* Preface by Jean-Louis Chiss & Christian Puech. Paris: Didier Erudition, 1987.)

Hey, Oskar. 1898. Review of Bréal (1897). *Archiv für Lateinische Lexicographie und Grammatik* 10.551–555.

Jaberg, Karl. 1901. "Pejorative Bedeutungsentwicklung im Französischen. Mit Berücksichtigung allgemeiner Fragen der Semasiologie. Erster Teil. Einleitung". *Zeitschrift für Romanische Philologie* 25.561–601.

Knobloch, Clemens. 1988. *Geschichte der psychologischen Sprachauffassung in Deutschland von 1850 bis 1920.* Tübingen: Niemeyer.

–. 1992. "Wilhelm Wundt (1832–1920)". *Sprachphilosophie. Philosophy of Language. La philosophie du langage: Ein internationales Handbuch zeitgenössischer Forschung* ed. by Dietfried Gerhardus, Kuno Lorenz & Georg Meggle, vol. I, part 1, 412–431. Berlin & New York: de Gruyter.

Kretzmann, Normann. 1967. "Semantics, History of". *The Encyclopedia of Philosophy* ed. by Paul Edwards, vol. VII, 358–406. New York & London: Macmillan.

Kronasser, Heinz. 1952. *Handbuch der Semasiologie: Kurze Einführung in die Geschichte, Problematik und Terminologie der Bedeutungslehre.* Heidelberg: Winter. (2nd ed., 1968.)

Land, Stephen K. 1974. *From Signs to Propositions: The concept of form in eighteenth-century semantic theory.* London: Longman.

Littré, Emile. 1880. "Pathologie verbale ou lésion de certains mots dans le cours de l'usage". *Études et glanures pour faire suite à l'Histoire de la Langue Française*, 1–68. Paris: Didier.

Locke, John. 1975 [1690]. *Essay on Human Understanding.* Ed. by P. H. Nidditch. Oxford: Oxford Univ. Press.

Lyons, John. 1963. *Structural Semantics.* Oxford: Blackwell.

Madvig, Johann Nikolai. 1875. *Kleine philologische Schriften.* Leipzig: Teubner. (Repr. Hildesheim: Olms, 1966.)

Martinak, Eduard. 1901. *Psychologische Untersuchungen zur Bedeutungslehre.* Leipzig: Barth.

Marty, Anton. 1908. *Untersuchungen zur Grundlegung der allgemeinen Grammatik und Sprachphilosophie,* vol. I. Halle/S.: Niemeyer.

Maspero, Gaston. 1917. "L'œuvre scientifique de Michel Bréal". *Revue internationale de l'enseignement* 71.181–192, 268–273.

Meillet, Antoine. 1897. Review of Henry (1896). *Revue critique* 14.261–263 (5 avril 1897).

–. 1905. "Comment les mots changent de sens". *Année sociologique* 9.230–271. (Repr. in Meillet, *Linguistique historique et linguistique générale* I, 230–271. Paris: Champion.)

Meyer, Richard Moritz. 1910. "Bedeutungssysteme". *Zeitschrift für vergleichende Sprachforschung* 43.352–368.

Murray, (Sir) James A[ugustus] H[enry], ed. 1884. *A New English Dictionary: On historical principles; founded mainly on the materials collected by The Philological Society.* Vol. I. Oxford: Clarendon Press. [Read notably the Preface.]

Nerlich, Brigitte. 1990. *Change in Language: Whitney, Bréal and Wegener.* London: Routledge.

–. 1992a. *Semantic Theories in Europe 1830–1930: From etymology to contextuality.* Amsterdam & Philadelphia: Benjamins.

–. 1992b. "La sémantique: 'Éducation et Récréation'". *Cahiers Ferdinand de Saussure* 46.159–171.

–. 1996a. "Semantics in the XIXth Century". *Geschichte der Sprachtheorie* ed. by Peter Schmitter, vol. V: *Sprachtheorien der Neuzeit II: Von der 'Grammaire de Port-Royal' (1660) zur Konstitution moderner linguistischer Disziplinen,* 395–426. Tübingen: Narr.

–, 1966b. "Un chaînon manquant entre la rhétorique et la sémantique: L'œuvre d'Auguste de Chevallet". *Travaux de Linguistique* 33.115–131.

– & David D. Clarke. 1998. "The Linguistic Repudiation of Wundt". *History of Psychology* 1:3. 179–204.

– & –. 2000. "Semantic Fields and Frames: Historical explorations of the interface between language, action and cognition." *Journal of Pragmatics* 32:2.125–150.

– & –, in press. "Mind, Meaning, and Metaphor: The philosophy and psychology of metaphor in nineteenth-century Germany". *History of the Human Sciences.*

– & –, in prep. "Cognitive Linguistics and the History of Linguistics: Forerunners and influences". *Handbook of Cognitive Linguistics* ed. by Dirk Geeraerts and Hubert Cuyckens. Oxford: Oxford Univ. Press.

Ogden, C[harles] K[ay] & I[vor] A[rmstrong] Richards. 1923. *The Meaning of Meaning: A study of the influence of language upon thought and of the science of symbolilsm.* With supplementary essays by B. Malinowski & F. G. Crookshank. London: Kegan Paul, Trench, Trübner & Co. (8th ed., 1948); repr., New York: Harcourt Brace Jovanovich, 1989.) [For details, see Gordon (1982: 270).]

Oertel, Hanns. 1902. *Lectures on the Study of Language.* New York: Charles Scribner's Sons; London: Arnold.

Paul, Hermann. 1880. *Principien der Sprachgeschichte.* Halle/S.: Niemeyer. (2nd rev. ed., 1886; 3rd rev. ed., 1898; 4th rev. ed., 1909; 5th ed., 1920.)

Porzig, Walter. 1934. "Wesenhafte Bedeutungsbeziehungen". *Beiträge zur Geschichte der Deutschen Sprache und Literatur* 58.70–97.

Pottier, Bernard. 1964. "Vers une sémantique moderne". *Travaux de Linguistique et de Littérature* 2.107–137.

Quadri, Bruno. 1952. *Aufgaben und Methoden der onomasiologischen Forschung: Eine entwicklungsgeschichtliche Darstellung.* Bern: Francke.

Read, Allen Walker. 1948. "An Account of the Word 'Semantics'". *Word* 4:2.78–97.

Reisig, Christian Karl. 1839. *Vorlesungen über lateinische Sprachwissenschaft.* Ed. with notes by Friedrich Haase. Leipzig: Lehnhold.

Rosenstein, Alfred. 1884. *Die psychologischen Bedingungen des Bedeutungswechsels der Wörter.* Danzig: Kafemann.

Roudet, Léonce. 1921. "Sur la classification psychologique des changements sémantiques". *Journal de psychologie normale et pathologique* 18.676–692.

Schleicher, August. 1860. *Die Deutsche Sprache.* Stuttgart: Cotta.

Schmitter, Peter, ed. 1990. *Essays towards a History of Semantics.* Münster: Nodus.

Smart, Benjamin H[umphrey]. 1831. *An Outline of Sematology: Or an essay towards establishing a new theory of grammar, logic, and rhetoric.* London: Richardson.

Steinthal, Heymann. 1855. *Grammatik, Logik und Psychologie: Ihre Prinzipien und ihr Verhältnis zueinander.* Berlin: Dümmler. (Repr., Hildesheim: Olms, 1968.)

–. 1871. *Abriss der Sprachwissenschaft.* Erster Teil: *Die Sprache im allgemeinen: Einleitung in die Psychologie und Sprachwissenschaft.* Berlin: Dümmler.

Stern, Gustaf. 1931. *Meaning and Change of Meaning. With special reference to the English language.* Göteborg: Elander. (Repr., Bloomington: Indiana Univ. Press, 1968.)

Stewart, Dugald. 1810. *Philosophical Essays.* Edinburgh: Creech.

Tooke, John Horne. 1798−1805. *Epea ptepoenta; or, the Diversions of Purley.* 2nd ed. 2 vols. London: printed for the author.

Trench, Richard Chenevix. 1890 [1851]. *On the Study of Words.* 21st ed. revised by The Rev. A. L. Mayhew. London: Kegan Paul, Trench, Trübner & Co.

Trier, Jost. 1931. *Der deutsche Wortschatz im Sinnbezirk des Verstandes: Die Geschichte eines sprachlichen Feldes.* Heidelberg: Winter.

Ullmann, Stephan. 1951. *The Principles of Semantics: A linguistic approach to meaning.* Glasgow: Jackson. (2nd enlarged ed. Glasgow: Jackson; Oxford: Blackwell, 1957.)

−. 1962. *Semantics.* Oxford: Blackwell.

Vendryes, Joseph. 1953. "Pour une étymologie statique". *Bulletin de la Société de Linguistique de Paris* 49: 1.1−19.

Vonk, Frank. 1995. "The 'Vocal Gesture' from Wundt to Mead: A chapter in the historiography of the psychology and sociology of language". *History of Linguistics 1993* ed. by Kurt R. Jankowsky, 235−244. Amsterdam & Philadelphia: Benjamins.

Vooys, C[ornelius] G[errit] N[icolaas] de 1907. "De psychologiese beschouwing van de betekenisverandering". *De Nieuwe Taalgids* 1.20−31.

Warren, Beatrice. 1992. *Sense Developments: A contrastive study of the development of slang senses and novel standard senses in English.* Stockholm: Almqvist & Wiksell.

Wegener, Philipp. 1991 [1885]. *Untersuchungen über die Grundfragen des Sprachlebens.* Halle/S.: Niemeyer. (New ed. by E. F. Konrad Koerner with an introduction by Clemens Knobloch, Amsterdam & Philadelphia: Benjamins, 1991.)

Weisgerber, Leo. 1927. "Die Bedeutungslehre: Ein Irrweg der Sprachwissenschaft?". *Germanisch-Romanische Monatschrift* 15.161−183.

Welby, Victoria Lady. 1911. *Signifcs and Language: The articulate form of our expressive and interpretative resources.* London: Macmillan (Repr., with an introd. by H. Walter Schmitz, Amsterdam & Philadelphia: Benjamins, 1985.)

Wellander, Erik. 1917. *Studien zum Bedeutungswandel im Deutschen.* Uppsala: Uppsala Universitets Arsskrift.

Wundt, Wilhelm. 1900. *Völkerpsychologie.* Vol. I: *Die Sprache.* Leipzig: Engelmann.

Brigitte Nerlich, Nottingham (Great Britain)

190. Die frühe Entwicklung des onomasiologischen Ansatzes in der Sprachwissenschaft und Lexikographie des 19. Jahrhunderts

1. Definition
2. Vorgeschichte
3. Theoretische Überlegungen zur Onomasiologie im 19. Jahrhundert
4. Arbeiten onomasiologischen Charakters im 19. Jahrhundert
5. Auf dem Wege zur onomasiologischen Methode
6. Bibliographie

1. Definition

Thema der Onomasiologie ist die Erfassung der Sachen durch die Wörter: Ausgangspunkt sind Gegebenheiten der außersprachlichen Wirklichkeit, und gefragt wird, mit welchen sprachlichen Zeichen sie benannt werden. Den Ausdruck 'Onomasiologie' hat in diesem Sinne Adolf Zauner (1870−1943) geprägt (1903: 340), wobei das griechische ὀνομαστικόν als Terminus technicus für eine nach Gegenstandsbereichen geordnete Wortliste (belegt seit Pollux im 2. Jh. n. Chr.) den Anknüpfungspunkt darstellt.

2. Vorgeschichte

Nach Sachgruppen geordnete kleinere oder größere Wortlisten gibt es, seit Menschen Wörter verschiedener Art zusammenstellen. So gibt es chinesische, indische und babylonische Synomyma-Listen (Dornseiff 1970: 29−30).

Ob im Griechischen schon der Vorsokratiker Heraklit von Ephesos (c. 540−475 v. Chr.) eine Ordnung des Wortschatzes nach sachlichen Kriterien versucht hat, ist angesichts der schlechten Überlieferungslage nicht endgültig zu entscheiden, aber jedenfalls sammelte Prodikos von Keos (c. 460−390 v. Chr.) Synonyme und Quasi-Synonyme. Die alexandrinischen Philologen schufen dann mit ihren Glossensammlungen Zusammenstellungen verschiedener Bezeichnungen für Körperteile, Lebensalter, Verwandtschaftsgrade usw. Als es im Zuge des Attizismus wichtig wurde, für alles mögliche gut attische Ausdrücke zur Verfügung zu haben, stellte

Iulius Pollux (2. Jh. n. Chr.) aus Naukratis in Ägypten sein ganz nach Sachgebieten (Götter; Menschen; Lebensbereiche der Menschen) geordnetes ὀνομαστικόν zusammen, das erhalten ist. Auch die dem Schulinteresse verpflichteten Glossare, beispielsweise die zweisprachigen *Hermeneumata*, bieten den Wortschatz nach Sachgruppen, um den Lernenden das Vokabular für einen Lebensbereich nach dem anderen zur Verfügung zu stellen (Kramer 1996: 35−36). Auch Isidor von Sevilla (560−636 n. Chr.) folgt in Teilen seiner *Origines* der Ordnung nach Sachen (Codoñer 1996: 57−58).

Für das Mittelalter wurden auf der höheren Ebene vor allem Isidors Werk (Codoñer 1996: 75), in der Schul- und Gebrauchssphäre die *Hermeneumata* traditionsstiftend (Nebbiai-dalla Guarda 1996: 149). Das erfolgreichste onomasiologischen Gesichtspunkten verpflichtete Werk der frühen Neuzeit war zweifellos das erste Buch des − oft aufgelegten − Traktats *De duplici copia verborum et rerum et verborum* von Erasmus von Rotterdam (1469−1536) von 1512 (in: *Opera omnia* I, Leiden: van der Aa, 1703: 3−74).

Die von Comenius (Jan Amos Komenský, 1592−1670) im Jahre 1631 als *Janua linguarum reserata* und 1633 auf tschechisch als *Dvéře jazyků odevřené* sachlich geordnete Einführung in den lateinischen Wortschatz (kritisch-synoptische Ausgabe: Comenius 1959), die ihrerseits von der thematisch geordneten lateinisch-spanischen (1611) und lateinisch-englischen (1615) *Janua linguarum* des irischen Jesuiten William Bathe (1564−1614) abhängt (McArthur 1986: 163), ist in gewisser Weise eine modernisierte Ausführung der *hermeneumata*.

3. Theoretische Überlegungen zur Onomasiologie im 19. Jahrhundert

Das erste größere Werk, das nach unseren Begriffen onomasiologisch vorgeht, ist das erste umfangreiche Synonymenwörterbuch des Deutschen, das an der Wende vom 18. zum 19. Jh. von Johann August Eberhard (1739−1809) vorgelegt wurde (1795−1802; Kurzfassung 1802, bis 1910 siebzehn Auflagen). Die Wörter, die Dinge bezeichnen, die in der Realität gemeinsam auftreten, weisen nach Eberhard auch in der Sprache semantische Gemeinsamkeiten auf, wobei einzelne unterscheidende Züge die semantische Feingliederung ermöglichen; Aufgabe der Synonymik sei es, die Spezifika dieser onomasiologisch begründeten Wortschatzstruktur festzulegen.

Karl Friedrich Becker (1775−1849) sah die Sprache als Organismus, in dem auch die Wortbildung organisch geschieht. "Das Wort ist der in Lauten leiblich gewordene Begriff. [...] Indem der Mensch die reale Welt außer ihm in eine geistige Welt von Gedanken und Begriffen in ihm verwandelt, werden Gedanken und Begriffe sogleich wieder leiblich in der Sprache" (Becker 1841: 62). Ursprünglich sei "das Sein unter einer Thätigkeit begriffen" worden, weswegen "die ganze Entwickelung der Begriffe von den Thätigkeitsbegriffen als den Wurzelbegriffen" ausgehe und daher "in allen Sprachen die Wurzelwörter Verben und die Substantiven von Verben abgeleitet seien" (S. 70). Alle Begriffe und also auch der sie ausdrückende Wortschatz könne kein "Aggregat von Einzeldingen" sein, sondern es sei anzunehmen, "das allgemeine Arten von Begriffen sich durch eine fortschreitende Individualisierung in besondere Arten, und diese in ihre Unterarten scheiden, und daß die ganze Geamtheit der Begriffe sich durch eine fortschreitende Individualisierung in besondere Arten, und diese in ihre Unterarten scheiden, und daß die ganze Gesammtheit der Begriffe sich auf diese Weise in einem organischen System von Begriffen entwickelt" (S. 71). Für Becker war die Bewegung der Urbegriff, der schon "uranfänglich schon in mannigfaltigen Wörtern hervortritt, in denen mannigfaltige konkrete Besonderheiten der Bewegung geschieden sind" (S. 72). Bei der Ausbildung der Verben und dann Nomina, Präpositionen, Kasus usw. spielt jeweils die Systematik der "besondern Gegensätze der objektiven Beziehungen" (S. 76) die entscheidende Rolle. Becker hat die Hierarchie seines binären Begriffssystems nicht konkret ausgeführt; es bleibt aber festzuhalten, daß seiner Meinung nach die Systemhaftigkeit der Realität in der Wortschatzgliederung wiederzufinden sei.

Den wohl wichtigsten Beitrag zur Theorie der Onomasiologie lieferte der Londoner Arzt Peter Mark Roget (1779−1869), in dessen 1852 zum ersten Male erschienenen und immer wieder neu aufgelegten *Thesaurus of English Words and Phrases* eine Begriffstafel von 1000 Nummern, verteilt auf 6 Gruppen, vorkommt. Abgesehen davon, daß die Termini noch nicht vorkommen, liefert P. M. Roget am Anfang seiner "Introduction" eine tadellose Definition des Unterschiedes zwischen dem "semasiologischen" und dem 'onomasiologischen' Ansatz (Roget 1962 [= 1852], xxiii):

"The purpose of an ordinary dictionary is simply to explain the meaning of the words; and the problem of which it professes to furnish the solution may be stated thus: – The word being given, to find its signification, or the idea it is intended to convey. The object aimed at in the present undertaking is exactly the converse of this: namely, – The idea being given, to find the word, or words, by which that idea may be most fitly and aptly expressed".

Rogets "six primary Classes of Categories" umfassen: 1. "Abstract Relations among things, such as Existence, Resemblance, Quantity, Order, Number, Time, Power"; 2. "Space and its various relations, including Motion, or changing of place"; 3. "Material World"; 4. "Intellect and its operations"; 5. "ideas derived from the exercise of volition"; 6. "ideas derived from the operation of our Sentient and Moral Powers" (S. xxvi). Innerhalb der einzelnen Gruppen werden Gegensatzpaare einander – sozusagen nach einem Plus-Minus-System – gegenübergestellt (z. B. *order – disorder* oder *form – amorphism*), und "in many cases, two ideas which are completely opposed to each other, admit of an intermediate or neutral idea, equidistant from both: [...] *identity – difference – contrariety*; *beginning – middle – end*; *past – present – future*" (S. xxviii).

Dem Ordnungsprinzip von Peter Mark Roget war ein großer Erfolg beschieden: Anton Schlessing (1828–1910) wandte es 1881 auf das Deutsche an, und das 1872 in Hamburg erschienene *Wörterbuch deutscher Synonyme* von Daniel Sanders (1819–1897) ist ebenfalls davon abhängig.

Für den Bereich der Romanistik hat der Begründer des Faches, Friedrich Diez (1794–1876), das onomasiologische Ordnungsprinzip herangezogen, um die Grundtendenzen der Wortschatzentwicklung vom Lateinischen zu den romanischen Einzelsprachen zu beleuchten: Seine als Anhang zur *Grammatik der romanischen Sprachen* konzipierte Schrift über die romanische Wortschöpfung (Diez 1875) umreißt den Plan einer vergleichenden Gesamtdarstellung der Geschichte des romanischen Wortschatzes, wobei er die Grundfrage stellt: "Wie hat der Sprachgenius mit dem römischen Erbtheil geschaltet?" (S. vi). Zur Beantwortung teilt er den Wortschatz "nach dem allgemeinen Ordnungssinne" in 27 Begriffsklassen ein: "I. Gott-Herr; II. Weltgebäude, Jahreszeiten, Tageszeiten, Naturereignisse; III. Oberfläche der Erde; IV. Mensch; V. Körper des Menschen; VI. Seele des Menschen; VII. Altersstufen; VIII. Verwandtschaft; IX. Tierwelt; X. Pflanzenreich; XI. Mineralreich; XII. Gartengewächse; XIII. Ackerbau; XIV. Schiffahrt; XV. Krieg, Kampf; XVI. Heer, Krieger; XVII. Des Kriegers Ausrüstung; XVIII. Pferderüstung; XIX. Bürgerliches Gewerbe; XX. Kunst und Wissenschaft; XXI. Stadt; XXII. Kirche; XXIII. Haus; XXIV. Im Hause, Mobiliar; XXV. Kleidung; XXVI. Speise und Trank; XXVIII. Tischgeräte". Bei jedem dieser Begriffsklassen steht zunächst der lateinische Ausdruck, dann folgen die Bezeichnungen der romanischen Sprachen; es ergeben sich neben den nicht wenigen Beispielen ungebrochener Kontinuität andere Fälle, in denen das lateinische Wort durch romanische Neuschöpfungen oder durch Entlehnungen ersetzt wurde. Bruno Quadri (*1917) hebt die Verschiedenheit der Wortschatzzusammensetzung der einzelnen romanischen Sprachen hervor (1952: 45):

"So zeigt es sich, daß von allen romanischen Sprachen das Italienische die lateinische Tradition am treuesten fortsetzt, während das Französische durch zahlreiche Neubildungen gekennzeichnet ist. Das Iberoromanische und erst recht die von Rom frühzeitig isolierte Sprache Rumäniens ging immer wieder ihre eigenen Wege".

In seinen Bemühungen, die lateinischen Bestandteile des rumänischen Wortschatzes gegenüber den fremden Elementen herauszustreichen, hat auch Ion Heliade-Rădulescu (1802–1872) onomasiologische Ansätze herangezogen. Bei seinem Vergleich von über 1300 rumänischen Wörtern mit ihren italienischen Entsprechungen unterteilt er den Wortschatz in zwei Hauptgruppen, 'physische' und 'moralische' Wörter ("vorbe ... fizice ... și morale" [1973 [1840]: 218]), d. h. Bezeichnungen für Konkreta und Abstrakta, die ihrerseits wieder in 'geläufige oder häufiger verwendete' und 'technische' ("vorbe ... uzuale sau mai des întrebuințate și tehnice" [ibid.]) zu unterteilen sind. Die erstgenannte Gruppe ist besonders stabil und zeigt normalerweise aus dem Lateinischen ererbte Wörter; Änderungen treten nur auf, wenn die Realität sich ändert. In diesem Zusammenhang "plädiert Heliade dafür, die Benennungen derselben Dinge in den diversen rumänischen Regionen zu vergleichen, eine Forderung, die erst viel später nach Entstehen der Sprachatlanten in Europa erfüllt werden konnte" (Frisch 1983: 94).

Daß der onomasiologische Ansatz eine notwendige Ergänzung jeder semasiologischen Arbeit bilden müsse, hob besonders Gaston Paris (1839–1903) hervor, der dafür plädierte, daß man untersuchen müsse, "comment les idées nouvelles s'arrangent pour trouver leur expression dans les mots. Cette étude qu'on a guère abordée encore, serait d'un sérieux intérêt: elle nous ferait connaître quelles sont les conditions internes favorables à l'admission de sens nouveaux dans la langue" (1887: 72–73 = 1909: 289).

Ernst Tappolet (1870–1939) hat mit seiner Abhandlung über die romanischen Verwandtschaftsnamen nicht nur die erste größere romanistische Arbeit geschrieben, die der Untersuchung eines Wortfeldes gewidmet ist, sondern er hat darin auch theoretische Überlegungen angestellt. Er stellt sich in Gegensatz zu den bis dahin herrschenden Ansätzen, die von einer Gegebenheit des Lateinischen ausgehen und deren Weg ins Romanische verfolgen; das Forschungsobjekt seiner neuen Disziplin, die er "Vergleichende Lexikologie" nennt (Tappolet 1895: 3), soll vielmehr das "Begriffliche" sein, also "das, was der Sprache zu Grunde liegt, zu dessen Ausdruck sie nur Mittel ist" (S. 2); "im Vordergrund steht [...] die Grundfrage: Wie drückt die Sprache einer bestimmten Zeit, eines bestimmten Ortes den gegebenen Begriff aus? d. h. hat sie den von einer früheren Periode übernommenen Ausdruck beibehalten oder hat sie ihn durch eine Neuschöpfung ersetzt?" Tappolets Ansatz ist also innerhalb des onomasiologischen Rahmens diachron und diatopisch, und sein Erkenntnisziel ist sprachbiologisch geprägt: Wie Friedrich Diez unterscheidet er zwischen 'lateinischer Tradition' und 'romanischer Wortschöpfung', wobei bei letzterer nach Bildungsart und Ursache dafür gliedert. Er suchte Auskünfte "über die Lebenskräftigkeit, über die zeitliche und örtliche Gültigkeitssphäre" (S. 4) der Wörter, und vermutete: "Je bestimmter und allgemeiner ein Begriff, desto länger wird die einmal geschaffene Bezeichnung sich erhalten, desto größerem Gebiet wird er sich mitteilen; und andererseits: Je unbestimmter oder je spezieller er ist, desto mehr wird die Bezeichnung nach Zeit und Ort variieren" (S. 5).

Hugo Schuchardt (1842–1927), der bekanntlich immer quer zu den herrschenden Strömungen stand, hat in seiner etymologischen Arbeit zu *trouver* Ansätze zu einer onomasiologische Studie zu "finden" geliefert (Schuchardt 1899: 68–75), freilich nicht als Selbstzweck, sondern als Bestandteil einer eigentlich semasiologisch orientierten Arbeit. Für die spätere Entwicklung wichtig sind aber seine Ausführungen, in denen er darlegt, daß ohne gründliche Kenntnis der Wortbedeutung, die auch Sachverstand impliziert, keine zuverlässige Etymologie erstellt werden kann.

4. Arbeiten onomasiologischen Charakters im 19. Jahrhundert

Zahlreicher als die theoretischen Überlegungen zu dem, was man später Onomasiologie nennen würde, waren die im 19. Jh. entstandenen Arbeiten, die in irgendeiner Weise mit diesem Konzept zu verbinden sind: die praktischen Aktivitäten richteten sich entweder auf nach Sachgebieten geordnete Gesamtwörterbücher oder auf einzelne Begriffsfelder.

4.1. Onomasiologische Wörterbücher

Zunächst einmal sind die Wörterbücher zu nennen, die darauf abzielten, den Gesamtwortschatz einer Sprache nach Sachgebieten geordnet darzubieten.

Das Deutsche ist vertreten durch die Veröffentlichungen von Johann August Eberhard (1739–1809) der Jahre 1796–1802, Friedrich Ludwig Karl Weigand (1804–1878) von 1837 und 1844 besonders von Daniel Sanders (1819–1897) der Jahre 1872 u. 1875.

Im Englischen beherrscht der erfolgreiche *Thesaurus* von Peter Mark Roget von 1852 so vollkommen die Szene, daß daneben kein Raum mehr für andere Werke blieb.

Für das Französische versuchte Gustave de Ponton d'Amécourt (1825–1888) 1853 eine Klassifizierung nach 'familles intéllectuelles', aber sein kompliziertes Werk fand kaum Beachtung, weil wenig später (1859) Théodore Robertson (1803–1871) eine Adaptation von Rogets *Thesaurus* lieferte.

4.2. Onomasiologische Einzelstudien

Die ersten Einzelstudien, die wir der Onomasiologie zurechnen würden, stammen aus dem Bereich der Germanistik und sind mit dem Namen Jacob Grimm (1785–1863) verbunden. Für ihn haben die um die Jahrhundertmitte abgefaßten Studien zu den Wörtern des Besitzes (1864: 113–144), zu den Namen des Donners (1865: 402–438) oder zu den Bezeichnungen für die fünf Sinne (1884: 193–207) allerdings nicht das Ziel, den Wortschatz der entsprechenden Bereiche synchron zu erfassen und zu strukturieren, sondern die Ausrichtung ist etymologisch-altertumskundlich: "Das Sprachliche wird nicht um seiner selbst willen untersucht, sondern es dient als Kriterium zur Aufdeckung eines alten Kulturzustandes" (Quadri 1952: 39).

Eine ähnliche Zielsetzung haben − notwendigerweise − Arbeiten, die in der frühen Indogermanistik entstehen: Es geht stets um eine Rekonstruktion der Verhältnisse zur Zeit indogermanischen Urgemeinschaft und der unmittelbar darauf folgenden Periode der ältesten Wanderungen. Die Bezeichnungen für Tiere und Pflanzen (Löwe: Pauli 1873; Birke und Buche: Krause 1892), der sprachliche Ausdruck von Verwandtschaftsbeziehungen (Delbrück 1889), die Benennung der Körperteile (Pauli 1867) oder auch die Verben des Befehlens (Hintner 1893) finden stets nur als "Beitrag zur vergleichenden Altertumskunde" (Delbrück 1889: 392) Aufmerksamkeit. Letztlich gilt diese Zielsetzung auch für die frühen Arbeiten von Rudolf Meringer (1859−1931), in denen bemerkenswerte Sachkenntnis über urtümliche Hausformen eingesetzt wird, um ein wortgeschichtliches Problem, die nach Meinung des Autors in gotisch *wandus* "Rute" zu fassende Grundbedeutung von deutsch *Wand*, zu lösen (1891−1895; 1898).

In der deutschen Mundartforschung finden sich seit der Mitte des 19. Jh. erste onomasiologische Arbeiten; sie sind Tiernamen (Kater: Höfer 1857; Storch: Stegmann 1868; Murmeltier: Meyer 1874−75; Eule: Branky 1893; Hahn: Menges 1894; Kröte, Frosch, Regenwurm: Schwartz 1895), Pflanzennamen (Ulme: Krause 1887−88) und Krankheitsbezeichnungen (Rochholz 1871) gewidmet und behandeln, meist in knappem Rahmen, die Beziehungen zwischen sachlichen Gegebenheiten und sprachlichen Benennungen, normalerweise mit dem Akzent auf reichhaltiger Sammlung lexikalischen Materials, wobei theoretischen Überlegungen kein Raum gewährt wird. Diese Arbeiten bilden wichtige Meilensteine für die Entwicklung der Arbeitsweise der Dialektologie (besonders in Punkto Enquête-Technik), aber neue methodische Anstöße für die Onomasiologie ergeben sich kaum.

In der Romanistik beginnt die große Zeit der onomasiologischen Einzelstudien, die ja ein beliebtes Thema für Dissertationen waren, erst zu Beginn des 20. Jh. Dennoch sind einige frühere Arbeiten zu nennen. In den meisten Fällen handelt es sich, dem Zeitgeist entsprechend, um dialektologische Arbeiten junggrammatischer Ausrichtung, bei denen das jeweils im Titel genannte Wortfeld lediglich den Begrenzungsrahmen für die zu behandelnden Wörter abgibt. Eine gewisser Beliebtheit erfreuten sich Pflanzennamen (Wacholder, Artischocke: Bonaparte 1882−84; Pappel: Puitspelu 1888), Tierbezeichnungen (Reptilien: Bonaparte 1882−84; Maikäfer: Puitspelu 1889; Wiesel: Flechia 1876; Eidechse: Flechia 1878; Leuchtwürmchen: Salvioni 1892; Fledermaus: Forsyth Major 1893) und Tagesnamen (v. Reinsberg-Düringsfeld 1864; Babad 1893), während Speisen und Getränke (Wein: Bonaparte 1882−84) oder landwirtschaftliche Geräte (Pflug: Thomas 1894) noch unterrepräsentiert sind.

5. Auf dem Wege zur onomasiologischen Methode

Zusammenfassend läßt sich sagen, daß die Sprachwissenschaft im 19. Jh. bis an die Türe der onomasiologischen Methode kommt, diese aber noch nicht aufzuschließen weiß. Im Bereich der Einzelstudien bilden die Sachgruppen noch primär ein bequemes Abgrenzungskriterium, um die Stoffmenge in den Griff zu bekommen, und bei den Versuchen, den gesamten Wortschatz onomasiologisch zu gliedern, stehen trotz teilweise beachtlicher Schärfe der Reflexion (wie etwa bei Peter Mark Roget) eindeutig praktisch-didaktische Absichten im Vordergrund. Angesichts der Tatsache, daß historische Fragestellungen tonangebend sind, ist es nicht verwunderlich, daß auch onomasiologische Ansätze mit der vorherrschenden etymologischen Wortforschung kombiniert und so in den Dienst der Erforschung der Vergangenheit gestellt werden, beispielsweise um zur Lösung der Frage nach der Urheimat der Indogermanen durch Abgrenzung des grundsprachlichen Pflanzen- und Tiernamenrepertoires beizutragen oder um zu zeigen, daß bei den romanischen Sprachen der Anteil der ererbten lateinischen Elemente in den Bedeutungsbereichen am höchsten ist, die für das Alltagsleben am wichtigsten sind. Eine wirkliche methodische Selbständigkeit und eine Herauslösung aus der noch alles überschattenden etymologischen Blickrichtung erfolgt erst in den ersten Jahren des 20. Jh.: "Wörter und Sachen" von Rudolf Meringer (1904), "Sachen und Wörter" von Hugo Schuchardt (1905) und 'géographie linguistique' im Sinne von Jules Gilliéron (1902) sind hier die Schlagwörter, die die neuen Horizonte andeuten.

Die Geschichte der Onomasiologie ist erfreulich gut aufgearbeitet: Für die Zeit bis zum Anfang der fünfziger Jahre liegt mit Quadri (1952) einer hervorragend informierte und umsichtige Bestandsaufnahme vor für die folgende zwei Jahrzehnte gibt es mit De Gorog (1973) zumindest eine Ergänzung für das Französische.

6. Bibliographie

Babad, Jonas. 1893. "Französische Etymologien: *Samedi*". *Zeitschrift für romanische Philologie* 17. 563–566.

Bathe, William. 1611. *Ianua linguarum, seu modus maxime accommodatus, quo patefit aditus ad omnes linguas intelligendas*. Salamanca: Franciscus de Cea Tesa.

Becker, Karl Ferdinand. 1841. *Organism der Sprache*. Frankfurt: G. F. Kettembeil.

Bonaparte, Luis Lucien. 1882/1884a. "Words Connected with the Vine in Latin and the Neo-Latin Dialects". *Transactions of the Philological Society* 1884.251–311.

–. 1882/1884b. "Names of European Reptiles in the Living Neo-Latin Languages". *Ibid.*, 312–354.

Branky, Franz. 1983. "Vulgärnamen der Eule". *Zeitschrift für deutsche Philologie* 26.540–547.

Codoñer, Carmen. 1996. "Isidore de Séville: différences et vocabulaires". Hamesse 1996.57–77.

Comenius, Iohannes Amos. 1959 [1631]. *Janua linguarum reserata*. Editio synoptica et critica quinque authenticos textus Latinos necnon Janualem Comenii textum Bohemicum continens, curavit Jaromír Červenka. Praha: Státní pedagogické naklada-telství.

De Gorog, Ralph. 1973. "Bibliographie des études de l'onomasiologie dans le domaine du français". *Revue de linguistique romane* 37.419–446.

Delbrück, Berthold. 1889. *Die indogermanischen Verwandtschaftsnamen: Ein Beitrag zur vergleichenden Alterthumskunde*. Leipzig: Hirzel.

Diez, Friedrich. 1875. *Romanische Wortschöpfung*. Bonn: Marcus.

Dornseiff, Franz. [7]1970 [[1]1934]. *Der deutsche Wortschatz nach Sachgruppen*. Berlin: de Gruyter.

Eberhard, Johann August. 1795–1802. *Versuch einer allgemeinen deutschen Synonymik in einem kritisch-philosophischen Wörterbuche der sinnverwandten Wörter der hochdeutschen Mundart*. 6 Bde. Halle: Buff.

–. [17]1910 [[1]1802]. *Synonymisches Handwörterbuch*. Halle: Buff.

Flechia, Giovanni. 1876. "Postille etimologiche II". *Archivio glottologico italiano* 2.49–52.

–. 1878. "Postille etimologiche III". *Archivio glottologico italiano* 3.159–163.

Forsyth Major, C. J. 1893. "Italienische Vulgärnamen der Fledermaus". *Zeitschrift für romanische Philologie* 17.148–160.

Frisch, Helmuth. 1983. *Beiträge zu den Beziehungen zwischen der europäischen und der rumänischen Linguistik*. Bochum: Brockmeyer; Bukarest: Meridiane.

Hamesse, Jacqueline, Hg. 1996. *Les manuscrits des lexiques et glossaires de l'Antiquité tardive à la fin du Moyen Âge*. Louvain-la-Neuve: Fédération Internationale des Instituts d'Études Médiévales.

Heliade-Rădulescu, Ion. 1973 [1840]. "Paralelism între limba rumână și italiană". *Scrieri lingvistice* hg. von Ion Popescu-Sireteanu, 181–250. București: Editura științifică.

Hintner, Victor. 1893. "Die Verba des Befehlens in den indogermanischen Sprachen". *Xenia Austriaca: Festschrift der österreichischen Mittelschulen zur 42. Versammlung deutscher Philologen und Schulmänner in Wien*, Bd. I, 167–190. Wien.

Höfer, Albert. 1857. "Deutsche Namen des Katers". *Germania* 2.168–171.

Kramer, Johannes. 1996. "I glossari tardo-antichi di tradizione papiracea". Hamesse 1996.23–55.

Krause, Ernst Hans Ludwig. 1887–88. "Die niederdeutschen Namen der Ulme". *Niederdeutsches Korrespondenzblatt* 12.67–69; 13.59–60.

–. 1892. "Die indogermanischen Namen der Birke und Buche in ihrer Beziehung zur Urgeschichte". *Globus* 62.153–157; 161–168.

McArthur, Tom. 1986. "Thematic Lexicography". *The History of Lexicography* ed. by R. R. K. Hartmann, 157–166. Amsterdam & Philadelphia: Benjamins.

Menges, Heinrich. 1894. "Der Name des Haushahns in der Schriftsprache und im Elsässischen". *Zeitschrift für den deutschen Unterricht* 8.578–584.

Meringer, Rudolf. 1891–95. "Studien zur germanischen Volkskunde: Das Bauernhaus und dessen Einrichtung". *Mitteilungen der Anthropologischen Gesellschaft Wien*. Jg. XXI–XXV.

–. 1898. "Etymologien zum geflochtenen Haus". *Festgabe für Richard Heinzel*, 173–188. Halle: Niemeyer.

–. 1904. "Wörter und Sachen". *Indogermanische Forschungen* 16.101–196.

Meyer, Karl. 1874/1875. "Die deutschen Benennungen des Murmeltiers". *Jahrbuch des Schweizer Alpenclub* 10.589–594.

Nebbiai-dalla Guarda, Donatella. 1996. "Les glossaires et dictionnaires dans les bibliothèques médiévales". Hamesse 1996.145–204.

Paris, Gaston. 1887. "La vie des mots". *Journal des Savants* 1887.65–77; 149–156; 241–249.

–. 1909. *Mélanges linguistiques*. Éd. par Mario Roques. Paris: Protat.

Pauli, Carl. 1867. *Über die Benennung der Körpertheile bei den Indogermanen*. Berlin: Dümmler.

—. 1873. *Die Benennung des Löwen bei den Indogermanen: Ein Beitrag zur Lösung der Streitfrage über die Heimat des indogermanischen Urvolks.* Münden: Augustin.

Ponton d'Amécourt, Gustave de. 1853. *Le panorama des mots: Nouveau dictionnaire de synonymes.* Paris: Lecoffre.

Puitspelu, Nizier du. 1888. "Le peuplier dans les langues romanes". *Revue des langues romanes* 32.289–292.

—. 1889. "Le hanneton dans les dialectes modernes". *Revue des langues romanes* 33.288–291.

Quadri, Bruno. 1952. *Aufgaben und Methoden der onomasiologischen Forschung.* Bern: Francke.

Reinsberg-Düringsfeld, Otto von. 1864. "Volkstümliche Benennungen von Monaten und Tagen bei den Romanen". *Jahrbuch für romanische und englische Literatur* 5.361–392.

Robertson, Théodore. 1859. *Dictionnaire idéologique: Recueil des mots, des phrases, des idiotismes et des proverbes de la langue française classés selon l'ordre des idées.* Paris: Derache.

Rochholz, Ernst Ludwig. 1871. "Mundartliche Namen des Cretinismus". *Zeitschrift für deutsche Philologie* 3.331–342.

Roget, Peter Mark. 1962 [1852]. *Thesaurus of English Words and Phrases.* Ed. by Robert A. Dutch. London: Longman.

Salvioni, Carlo. 1892. *Lampyris italica: Saggio intorno ai nomi della lucciola in Italia.* Bellinzona: Privatdruck.

Sanders, Daniel. 1871 [²1882]. *Wörterbuch deutscher Synonymen.* Hamburg: Hoffmann & Campe.

—. 1875. *Deutscher Sprachschatz geordnet nach Begriffen.* 2 Bde. Hamburg: Hoffmann & Campe.

Schlessing, Anton. 1881. *Deutscher Wortschatz, oder: Der passende Ausdruck.* Stuttgart: Neff.

Schuchardt, Hugo. 1899. "Franz. *trouver*, prov. *trobar*, ital. *trovare* 'finden', graub.-lad. *truvar* 'richten' < lat. *turbare*". *Sitzungsberichte der Kaiserlichen Akademie der Wissenschaften zu Wien* 141:3.54–187.

—. 1905. "Sachen und Wörter". *Zeitschrift für romanische Philologie* 29.620–622.

Schwartz, Wilhelm. 1895. "Die volkstümlichen Namen für Kröte, Frosch und Regenwurm in Nord-Deutschland nach ihren landschaftlichen Gruppierungen (mit den einzelnen Ortsangaben)". *Zeitschrift des Vereins für Volkskunde* 5.246–264.

Stegmann, H. 1868. "Über deutsche Storchnamen". *Deutscher Sprachwart* 3.116–118.

Thomas, Antoine. 1894. "Sur les noms de la charrue". *Bulletin de la Société des parlers de France* 1.105–108.

Weigand, Friedrich Ludwig Karl. 1837. *Versuch einer Unterscheidung sinnverwandter Wörter der deutschen Sprache nach dem gängigen Stande der deutschen Sprachforschung.* Gießen: Ricker.

—. 1844. *Wörterbuch der deutschen Synonyme.* 3 Bde. Mainz: Kupferberg.

Zauner, Adolf. 1903. "Die romanischen Bezeichnungen der Körperteile". *Romanische Forschungen* 14.339–530.

Johannes Kramer, Trier (Deutschland)

191. The study of meaning change from Reisig to Bréal

1. Introduction
2. Typologies of semantic change (Germany)
3. Lexicographical and semiotic reflections on meaning (England)
4. Theories of semantic change
5. Bibliography

1. Introduction

In this article we shall follow the development of semantics from the 1830s to the 1890s as it progressed from a historicistic subdiscipline of grammar and aid to etymology and lexicography to an independent study of meaning at all levels of language. We shall first look at semasiology in Germany, where typologies of semantic change were produced in great numbers, first classifying types of semantic change according to logico-rhetorical and later to psychologico-causal criteria. In a next section we shall look at England where the links between semantics, semiotics and lexicography were strongest, and in the last section we shall see how a 'theory' of semantic change was developed in France, again in several phases, a rhetorical, lexicographical, biological and psycho-sociological one (cf. Nerlich 1992a; 1996a).

2. Typologies of semantic change (Germany)

Since Leo Weisgerber's (1899–1984) paper on the errors of semasiology (1927; cf. also Baldinger 1957), it has become customary to distinguish between two great trends in the history of 19th-century German semantics:

(1) a logico-classificatory one and
(2) a psychologico-explanatory or teleological one.

Those who followed the first trend wanted to find a neat classification of general types or 'laws' of semantic changes at the level of the word, taking 'sound laws' as a model, without wishing to know what actually brought about individual changes as such. Those who preferred the second approach aimed not only at finding a classification of types of semantic change, but at providing a list of causes of semantic change, causes that were presumed to be historical, psychological or cultural in nature. Only this second approach was regarded as being able to *explain* particular semantic changes that had actually taken place and could be verified in the given texts. This new approach to semantic change also led to an increased examination of co-textual and contextual factors that might contribute to changes in word-meaning.

The first type of approach received its epithet 'logical' from the fact that it generally used the figures of speech (for example metaphor, metonymy, and synecdoche) as well as two general semantic 'movements' (restriction and generalisation of meaning), as tools to classify types of semantic change. In the case of the restriction of meaning (provoked perhaps by synecdoche), the extension of a term shrinks whereas the intension increases; in the case of the generalisation of meaning (provoked perhaps by metaphor or metonymy), the extension increases and the intension shrinks. To describe semantic change in these or similar terms is to subordinate it to logic.

The work of Christian Karl Reisig's (1792–1829) and his immediate followers has been briefly summarised in article 211. I shall therefore only refer to some points not mentioned in this overview regarding what one can call the four H's: Haase, Heerdegen, Hey, and Hecht, all four classical philologists. Friedrich Haase (1808–1867) and Ferdinand Heerdegen (1845–1930) both reedited Reisig's work and produced original texts in the field of semasiology, replacing however Reisig's philosophical emphasis by a historical-comparative one. Their work came to constitute the backbone of the logico-rhetorical tradition of German semasiology. Max Hecht (1857–19??) and Oskar Hey (1866–1911) later contributed to the psychologico-explanatory strand.

Contrary to Reisig and all the other 19th-century semanticists, Haase's model of the linguistic sign, developed in his lectures on Latin linguistics, is bilateral; the meaning is an integral part of the word (cf. Schmitter 1987: 155f.), not a mental appendix to it. This is why Haase was excluded from the general criticism that Weisgerber (1927) was to level against 19th-century German semasiology, a semantics that Knobloch (1988) calls 'Vorstellungsemantik', or semantics of representations. Like Reisig, Haase wants to discover the laws or principles that govern the transitions between meaning$_1$ and meaning$_n$ of a word, but unlike Reisig these different principles or types of transitions are not deduced from general 'logical' laws of the human mind, but are induced from historical records. Haase therefore speaks only of the natural or historical, not the inner or logical order. Haase agrees however with Reisig in his semasiological usage of the terms provided by rhetoric to classify tropes. But he wants to transform the figures of speech to meaningful laws that have a true life in a language (cf. Haase 1874: 128, 172). Like Arsène Darmesteter (1846–1888) one year after him (1890 [1875]), he regards these laws or regularities as productive procedures in the 'life of a language', and this life is seen as progress, in accordance here with Georg Wilhelm Friedrich Hegel's (1770–1831) philosophy of history, and again in line with the later work of Darmesteter and Michel Bréal (1832–1915). This progressive view of the history of language was not shared by other German and French scholars, in particular those following August Schleicher (1821–1868), who regarded the history of language, especially sound change, as a process of decay.

Unlike Reisig and Haase, Heerdegen's (1875) conception of grammar is four-fold, and he subsumes both phonetics and morphology under etymology (*Laut- und Formenlehre*). Grammar has two parts: *Satzlehre* and *Wortlehre*, which again split into two branches each. *Satzlehre* subsumes *Etymologie* (formal group) and *Semasiologie* (functional group). Semasiology is thereby given an official place inside classical philology based on historical principles. Heerdegen's form/function distinction was influenced by Schleicher (1861) who distinguished between *Formenlehre* or morphology (a term he introduced to linguistics) and *Funktionslehre* or the study of meaning. But Heerdegen also refers to both of Bréal's seminal lectures on the form and function of words (1866) and on latent ideas (1868) (cf. Heerdegen 1878: 16 note). However, whereas semasiology in Heerdegen's sense deals only with part of the 'mental' or functional group of phenomena, Bréal's *sémantique* strives to cover the whole of the mental group and part of the formal one as well. Heerdegen's classification of *types* of semantic change can be found in the second part of his work on Latin grammar (Heerdegen 1878), a classification which he reformulates and reshapes in 1890 (cf. Kronasser 1968 [1952]: 33). In 1890 Heerdegen postulates the following basic principles of all semantic development. He distinguishes between unconditioned semantic change and conditioned semantic change. On the level of unconditioned semantic change he distinguished between restriction or specialisation of meaning and semantic transfer; on the level of conditioned semantic change he studied substitution (caused for example by synonyms) (cf. Heerdegen 1890: 65 ff.). Like Wilhelm Wundt (1832–1920) in 1900, Heerdegen apparently wished to emulate very closely the achievements of phonetics, where one normally distinguished between two forms of change: isolated and combinatorial sound change. Again, Bréal attempted to avoid casting the intellectual or psychological laws of semantic change in the mould of the (physiological) laws of sound change, in this comparable to the next two scholars: Hecht and Hey.

Haase and Heerdegen had both been strongly influenced by historical comparative linguistics. Hecht und Hey's work, by contrast, shows a steady psychologisation of semantics, which had begun in the 1860s under the influence of Heymann Steinthal's (1823–1899) psychology of language. We shall therefore first look at the forgotten classification of types of semantic changes proposed by one of Steinthal's followers, Ludwig Tobler (1827–1895). Tobler was also influenced by Wilhelm von Humboldt (1767–1835), Georg Curtius (1820–1885), and others. He does not refer to Reisig, and does not use the term 'Semasiologie', but speaks instead of a 'system of etymology'. His goal was to provide systematic principles (*Grundsätze*) for the transitions between concepts (*Begriffsübergänge*), so as to establish a 'science' of etymology (Tobler 1860: 354). Like Reisig, Steinthal and many others he confused thoughts, concepts, ideas or representations (*Vorstellungen*) with the meanings of words, a confusion only lifted by Ferdinand de Saussure (1857–1913), and then still not completely (he still employed the term 'concept' to refer to the conceptual part of his bilateral sign). Tobler believed that he could base a science of etymology on a systematisation of the possible transitions between concepts. He also thought (with Humboldt) that the vocabulary of a nation represents its framework of thought, and (with Curtius) that the original meanings of the original stock of roots form the 'inner form' of a language. Like Steinthal, Tobler believed semasiology to be an instrument for revealing the inner form or conceptual framework of a language and the mind of a nation, its constitution as well as its evolution. His classification of types of semantic change is logical, based on a priori dichotomies. It has in fact no proven psychological validity, nor can it claim to represent any real principles for meaning-transitions, a fact pointed out by Steinthal (1977 [1860]: 61) and by Hecht (1888: 6–7). Hecht would in fact fulfil a wish Steinthal had expressed in his review of Curtius's *Grundzüge der griechischen Etymologie* (1858) that, taking this excellent work as a basis, somebody should outline a Greek etymology from a psychological perspective (cf. Steinthal 1977 [1860]: 50–51). Tobler distinguished between two broad types of semantic change: immanent psychological semantic change, and accidental historical change. Immanent semantic change can proceed in (gradual) steps or in jumps. When it is gradual, it can be real or conjectural (*scheinbar*). And finally, real gradual psychological semantic change can be subdivided into two large groups: material semantic change, where one can observe the transfer of meaning to another conceptual sphere, and formal semantic change where one can observe restriction or extension inside the same conceptual sphere. So we have here in embryo the classical distinction between semantic change based on metaphor and metonymy, on the one hand, and restriction and extension, on the other, a classification that can still be found in Hermann Paul's (1846–1921) work. Although Tobler belonged to those linguists that were influenced by Steinthal's psychology of language, he did not produce a causal or psychological classification of semantic changes. This challenge was taken up by Hecht and Hey in a thoroughly psychological semasiology.

As an example of the way the relation between semantics, lexicography, etymology, and psychology was seen from Hecht and Hey up to about 1920, I provide an extract from Max Hecht's *Greek Semasiology* of 1888:

"Insofern sie [die Semantik] zugunsten der Lexikographie die Bedeutungen in zeitlicher Folge ordnet und im Interesse der Etymologie die Gesetze der Bedeutungsänderung aufstellt, hat sie sprachwissenschaftlichen Wert. Soweit sie aber diese Gesetze aus der Natur des Geistes herleitet und eine Geschichte der Vorstellungen gibt — *Bedeutungen sind Vorstellungen* —, fällt sie auf das Gebiet der empirischen Psychologie." (Hecht 1888: 5; italics mine: BN)

This approach was endorsed by Hey in the introduction to his semantic studies (Hey 1892), which provide at one and the same time a history of German semasiology and a critique of Haase and Heerdegen. Hey fully approved of Hecht's distinction between three basic perspectives that one can apply to the study of semantic change, two of which were very similar to Darmesteter's (1887). The three types of semantic change are: (1) objective semantic change, caused by changes external to the individual soul, as Hey puts it, historical or cultural changes; (2) subjective semantic change, caused by acts of the soul itself; and (3) a mixture of both (cf. Hey 1892: 101—102). Just as Hey had asked Heerdegen whether there can be any unconditioned semantic change at all (cf. pp. 92—93), one has to ask Hecht and Hey whether there can be a semantic change initiated by an independent act of the soul, or whether this act is not itself to some extent determined by historical or cultural circumstances. But on the positive side, one has to concede that in following Hecht, Hey definitely broke the logico-classificatory spell in German semasiology and introduced psychological as well as more global cultural considerations into the study of historical semantics (cf. Kronasser 1986 [1952]: 34). This provoked a boom in new causal and psychological typologies of semantic change, produced not only by academics but also by school teachers. The best examples here are the typologies of semantic change established by a certain Robert Thomas and Karl Schmidt (1859—19??), both in 1894 (cf. Nerlich 1992a: 68—72, for details).

3. Lexicographical and semiotic reflections on meaning (England)

English semantics in the 19th century was not a theoretically well established field, like German semasiology or French semantics. It consisted of two disjointed and never really amalgamated strands of thought: sematology and semasiology. The first type of semantics was a predominantly philosophical one, which emerged from a line of thinkers such as John Locke (1632—1704), John Horne Tooke (1736—1812), Dugald Stewart (1753—1828) and culminated in the work of Benjamin Humphrey Smart (1786—1872) of 1831. The second was a predominantly practical one which sprang from a long line of lexicographers and etymologists, such as Samuel Johnson (1709—1784), Noah Webster (1758—1843), Charles Richardson (1775—1865), Richard Garnett (1789—1850), and culminated in the works of Richard Chenevix Trench (1807—1886) and the first editor of the *Oxford English Dictionary* James H. A. Murray (1837—1915). One of the rare contributions to the question of semantic change, so hotly debated in Germany and France, came from the general linguist Archibald Henry Sayce (1845—1933) — and he only repeated an early classification by August Friedrich Pott (1802—1887). It is significant that he used the terms sematology and semasiology interchangeably. Later writers such as James Bradstreet Greenough (1833—1901) and George Lyman Kittredge (1860—1944), Ernest Weekley (18—19), and Eric Partridge (1894—1982) did not do much to advance the theory of semantics, but took pleasure in supplying more and more examples for German or French classifications of semantic changes. To find more significant contributions to the study of semantic change, one has to look across the ocean and read William Dwight Whitney (1827—1894) and Hanns Oertel (1868—1952), for example. By the end of the century, Lady Victoria Welby (1837—1912) rekindled the philosophical interest in semantic questions which had been sparked off by Locke's semiotic philosophy of language and fostered an entirely new approach to the problem of meaning. This approach also constituted a return to Smart's sematology, which included a contextual theory of meaning and reflections on semiotic matters, and it linked up with 'semiotics' as a general sign theory developed under this title on the other side of the Atlantic by

Charles Sanders Peirce (1839–1914). What Lady Welby called 'significs' lifted American semiotics and European sematology, semasiology, and 'la sémantique' onto a higher psychological, moral and ethical plane (cf. Welby 1985 [1911]). This way of thinking was continued in the 20th century by Charles Kay Ogden (1889–1957) and Ivor Armstrong Richards' (1893–1979) thoughts on the meaning of meaning (Ogden & Richards 1923), and by the Dutch signific movement.

4. Theories of semantic change

In Germany semasiology had emerged from a theoretical synthesis based on insights from rhetoric, hermeneutics, Kantian philosophy and classical philology. In France semantics was also rooted in rhetoric, but rhetorical ideas were merged with insights into the history of the French language, a living language, to provoke first systematic thoughts on semantic change in the work of Joseph-Balthasar-Auguste-Albin d'Abel baron de Chevallet (1812–1858). Emile Littré (1801–1881) later looked at semantic change from the point of view of the lexicographer and collector of semantically interesting titbits. Darmesteter came under the spell of Schleicher, his organicism and biological metaphors of the life and death of words, but he produced the first full treatise of semantic change and made a first step in emancipating semantics from rhetoric, but attached it instead to psychology. Bréal, by contrast, developed a fully independent semantics as a type of cognitive linguistics from 1866 onwards, an effort that culminated in his 1897 *Essai de sémantique*, which can be regarded as the declaration of independence for the discipline of semantics, independent from rhetoric, etymology, lexicography, phonetics, and historical comparative linguistics.

I shall focus here on the line of development that leads from rhetoric to semantics in France, leaving aside the type of semantics developed by the French 'naturalists', whose work has been well studied by Piet Desmet (cf. Desmet 1994, 1997). Desmet summarises the work of the leader of this school, Honorée Chavée (1815–1877), in the following way:

"[...] ce linguiste belge d'origine namuroise a été l'un des premiers à plaider pour l'étude simultanée de l'évolution phonétique et (idéo)logique du langage. Dès sa première publication, Chavée (1843) combine l'étude des "variations des sons dans les mots" avec celle des "variations du sens dans les mots", disciplines qu'il appelle respectivement la *phonologie lexiologique* et l'*idéologie lexiologique*. Le but de cette idéologie lexiologique est d'étudier les lois qui président aux variations (idéo)logiques que les mots des différentes langues sœurs ont connues pour reconstituer le sémantisme des mots primitifs de la langue mère." (Desmet 1997: 17)

This type of reconstructive semantics was influenced by the positivism of Auguste Comte (1798–1857) as well was the naturalism of Schleicher. Semantics was therefore regarded as a positive or natural science, a view that Bréal later rejected in favour of a more descriptive and 'humanistic' semantics. Chavée himself stated his research programme in the following way:

"Pour la science lexiologique, l'étude comparative et approfondie des vocabulaires n'est qu'un moyen d'arriver par l'analyse à la connaissance et à la classification des vocables simples ou primitifs dans chaque système de langues. Ces mots élémentaires une fois trouvés, elle les compare entre eux, sous le double rapport du sens et du son, pour découvrir leurs analogies et les grouper en familles naturelles, etc." (Chavée 1849: x)

A very different approach to semantic change, and a much more familiar one, was proposed by Chevallet (cf. Nerlich 1996b) in his *De l'Origine et la Formation de la langue française* (1853). This work stands in the tradition of Anne Robert Jacques Turgot's (1727–1781) cognitive etymology and above all César Chesneau Dumarsais's (1676–1756) rhetoric of ordinary language. Taking four classical tropes as a starting point, Chevallet distinguished between four parameters of semantic change: (1) the *general causes* of semantic change which are either cognitive or social ones; (2) the *procedures* of innovation and semantic change: metaphor (semantic transfer based on comparison), metonymy (cause for effect, etc.), synecdoche (genus for species, etc.), metalepsis (antecedent for consequent); (3) the eventual *results* of the use of tropes, such as the restriction and extension of meaning and the deterioration of meaning (Chevallet does not mention amelioration); (4) the *psychological conditions* of semantic change, that is the individual reasons for using a procedure of semantic innovation which can eventually lead to semantic change: they are our vivid imagination, the need for precision and the necessity to fill semantic gaps. Chevallet stresses that the use of a figure of speech is not a 'semantic change' in itself. One can only speak of semantic change when the original meaning has been forgotten (1853: 199), an insight also found later in the works of Darmesteter and Bréal. Chevallet also pointed out that semantic change is normally some kind of 'chain reaction' (p. 200).

"Mais un mot qui a déjà passé à une acception dérivée, en vertu d'un trope, passe quelquefois de cette seconde acception à une troisième, puis à une quatrième, et, de la sorte, à plusieurs autres successivement, sans qu'on puisse déterminer le point où devront s'arrêter des évolutions indéfinies."

And a final point; he exemplifies all these processes by examples taken from the living French language. Although not mentioned by either Darmesteter or Bréal, Chevallet's work must be regarded as a step towards a semantics that was rhetorically inspired but was in fact an independent linguistic discipline, a development that Darmesteter himself summarised as follows:

"Depuis longtemps, les diverses transformations du sens dans les mots ont été étudiées par les auteurs de rhétorique, qui leur donnent le nom grec de tropes. Les grammariens français depuis le XVIIIe siècle en ont fait une analyse détaillée, en particulier Du Marsais, dans un ouvrage resté célèbre. Mais ils se placent au point de vue de l'art d'écrire, non au point de vue linguistique. Or c'est cette dernière considération qui seule importe." (Darmesteter 1887: 45)

At the same time as Chavée was speculating about semantics from an naturalistic point of view and when Chevallet contributed to semantics from a rhetoric point of view, Littré began to think about semantic change from the point of view of a lexicographer. Littré, medical doctor, politician, journalist, lexicographer and positivistic thinker, began to speculate about what Darmesteter and Bréal later on called the evolution and transformation of language. In an article on etymology, first published in the *Journal des Savants* in 1855 and reprinted in his *Histoire de la langue française* (1863), Littré tried to apply to etymology notions borrowed from natural history (cf. Littré 1863: 28). For him, the main feature of a language is that it is never and can never be fixed (cf. p. 25), that it evolves all the time to make sure that progressively new thoughts can be expressed. A language, like any other institution, is in a state of constant evolution. One can see that Littré's naturalism was not as naïve as those of his 'ideological' colleagues. In using the term 'institution', not 'organism' to refer to language, he was much more in line with the ideas later expressed by Whitney than with his French colleagues. Like Whitney, he adhered to the doctrine of (geological) uniformitarianism fostered by Sir Charles Lyell (1797–1875), and he therefore claimed that 'the faculty that transforms is of the same nature as the faculty that creates' (cf. Littré 1863: 27). Littré's remarks on the evolution and transformation of language must have left a profound impression on the thoughts of Darmesteter and Bréal. It is therefore regrettable that the famous article on 'verbal pathology' written by Littré for his *Études et Glanures* in 1880, and reprinted separately in 1888 with a preface by Bréal and a new title "Comment les mots changent de sens", is nothing more than an enumeration of linguistic curiosities and abnormalities. Words that change their meaning are regarded as aberrations or illnesses of the language, rather than as results of the normal 'transformation' of language in every-day use. In his review of Littré's booklet, Gaston Paris (1839–1903) approved (with some reservations) of Bréal's decision to abandon the title "Pathologie verbale", but he argued that the new title was not ideal either, as it suggests a theory of semantic change, which the booklet does not provide (cf. Paris 1888). The first sketch of a theory of semantic change can, however, be found in a book by Darmesteter, published one year earlier, under an equally unfortunate title: *La vie des mots*, and which Paris mentioned approvingly in his review of Littré. In spite of its shortcomings, the title of Littré's work, *Comment les mots changent de sens*, was used by other linguists for different purposes, as for example in Meillet's sociological account of semantic change (→ art. 254). The view that change is illness, but that language heals itself by its own therapeutic means, too, was not forgotten. It was continued by Jules Gilliéron (1854–1926) in his work on dialects and linguistic atlases, the change of meanings and the spread of words in social and geographical space.

Around the same time that Chevallet, Littré and others speculated on semantic change, Bréal began his crusade to free semantics from logico-rhetorical, lexicographical, etymological and historical-comparative shackles, and we shall come to his research programme soon. Before this, we shall look at Darmesteter's seminal work of 1887, in which semantics was first put on the linguistic map. There is, however, one difference between Bréal and Darmesteter, which I would like to stress from the outset: Darmesteter seems to use 'semantics' to study the history of the human mind, what he calls a 'historical psychology' (Darmesteter 1877: 7), whereas Bréal used psychology to establish (historical) semantics. Darmesteter's famous book was published first in English under the title *The Life of Words as Symbols of Ideas* (1886), as a result of lectures that Darmesteter had delivered in London (cf. Bergougnioux 1987; Delesalle 1987). The most striking fact about the book is the constant use of metaphors, such as the life and death of words, the struggle for survival, etc., which demonstrates the influence of Darwin, Schleicher, and possibly Chavée. Darmesteter wrote in the English edition that "the absolute truth of the Darwinian theory as applied to [...] language evolution by natural selection is a fact" (Darmesteter 1886: 19). Darmesteter mentioned as his linguistic sources of inspiration the work of Littré and Bréal in France, of Whitney in the United States, but also a minor work by a German semasiologist, Heimbert Lehmann (1860–19??), on semantic change in the French language, published in 1884, and based mainly on Paul's work (cf. Nerlich 1996b: 127). For Darmesteter languages and words themselves are organisms, the life of which is however purely intellectual. This life consists in an ongoing evolution. But this evolution does not lead to inevitable chaos. A certain equilibrium is maintained by the interaction of two forces: a conservative force and a revolutionary force (cf. Darmesteter 1886: 6). Language itself has two main features, it is physical and intellectual, or, physiological and psychological in character. From the first trait stem phonetic alterations, from the second alterations in grammar (analogical change) and lexicon (neologisms). The following passage expresses Darmesteter's linguistics credo:

"Language is a resonant matter that human thought transforms insensibly and aimlessly, under the unconscious action of the struggle for survival and natural selection." (Darmesteter 1886: 27)

Darmesteter wanted to study thought through the traces it leaves in language, especially through the use of metaphor, metonymy, synecdoche, catachresis and their results: the multiplication of meanings, what Bréal called a year later 'polysemy'.

Darmesteter's book is divided into three parts: one examines how words are born, another how they live together, and the third how they die. Words are born in two ways: by the creation of new words (neologism 'of words') or by the creation of new meanings, neologism 'of meaning' (Darmesteter 1886: 23). They change their meaning under the pressure of what Darmesteter calls *logical conditions, psychological actions*, and *philological* or linguistic *conditions*. Again the figures of speech, such as metaphor and metonymy, are the most important procedures of (logical) semantic change. They bring about the 'birth' of new word meanings. But Darmesteter went further than some of his German colleagues, who also used these figures for a 'logical' account of semantic change, when he wrote that the condition for these figures to work efficiently is the forgetting of the etymological meaning.

"[...] the *process* of metaphor comprises two stages: one, where the metaphor is still visible, and the name, in designating the second object, still evokes the image of the first; another when, through the forgetting of the first image, the name designates the second object alone and becomes adequate to it." (Darmesteter 1886: 63)

Darmesteter also distinguished between two longterm semantic processes which are the result of this forgetting: *concatenation* and *radiation* (cf. p. 76). In the case of radiation a word accumulates meanings around a core, that is, becomes polysemous; in the case of concatenation a word develops a polysemous chain of meanings, where the first links in the chain might be lost or forgotten. As an example of 'radiation' one can analyse what would be called nowadays the radial set of meanings surrounding the word *head* for example. In the case of French *tête* (head) one can extract the following essential features or properties from the prototype: 'upper part of the human body', 'round form', and 'the part of your body which contains the brain'. Each of these properties lends itself to metaphorical or metonymical extensions. Based on the first property we get *tête de ligne, tête de pont*, etc.; based on the second we get *tête d'un arbre, tête d'un clou*, etc. (all based on metaphor); based on the third we get: *tête de folle, tête dure* (metonymy), *payer tant par tête* (synecdoche), etc.

An example of metonymy-based 'concatenation' is the word *bureau*, where the meaning travels from a type of cloth covering a table, to the table, the room and the people habitually populating the room. Both radiation and concatenation are the result of the use of certain figures of speech. Having thus described some *types* of semantic change (the figures of speech), which are basically synchronic phenomena, and the effect they have when reiterated, thus producing diachronic changes (concatenation and radiation), Darmesteter asked what were the *causes* of semantic change. The causes are described under the heading of 'actions psychologiques'. He does not deny that the emergence of neologisms has, just like any other fact of language, its cause in individual actions (p. 89). But as these arbitrary and voluntary phenomena escape the grasp of science, he only wanted to study the other facet of these facts: their ratification by the masses, that is, their collective side. Darmesteter distinguishes between two causes of semantic change: objective (external) causes, which depend on the history of the speakers and on the history of ideas, and subjective (internal) causes, which depend on what he calls "popular psychology" (p. 90). This distinction had a decisive influence on German semasiology, after having been adopted by Hecht (1888), Hey (1892), and Schmidt (1894). It was criticised by Paris and Bréal in their respective reviews of Darmesteter's work (cf. Bréal 1887; Paris 1888), but most decisively by Carl Svedelius (1861–1951) in 1891. In the second part of his book, on the 'linguistic' life and 'interaction' between words, Darmesteter speaks of mutual semantic 'contamination', of semantic reactions and the struggle of survival between (synonymous) words, all topics later taken up in other terms by Bréal. Finally, in the third part, on the death of words, Darmesteter gives an account of the result of the stuggle for survival, causing the drop-out of some, the survival of other words. The most common causes of the death of words are the disappearance of referents or the replacement of one word by another better or fitter one.

Unlike many of his colleagues in Germany and France, Bréal abhorred the biological metaphors that still floated around; he also rejected any modelling of semantic laws on the laws of sound change. Bréal was perhaps the first who regarded semantics as an out and out psychological and to some extent sociological enterprise, which he opposed to the physiological enterprise of phonetics. Semantics therefore deals not only with word meanings and their changes over time, but also with aspects of morphology and syntax, even with aspects of pragmatics (speech acts, modality) and with aspects of discourse analysis, cognitive semantics and language acquisition. That is to say, his semantics, developed between 1866 and 1897, was a psychological study of synchronic and diachronic aspects of language change, language use and language evolution.

At the time when Littré published the first volume of his famous dictionary of the French language in 1863 (cf. Littré 1873), the young Bréal, just freshly arrived from Germany, published his first major work, a long essay on comparative mythology, *Hercule et Cacus* (Bréal 1877 [1863]). His goal was to analyse the origin and history of the fable or myth of Hercules and Cacus and more generally to find out the laws underlying the development or transformation of the fable. To achieve this goal mere interpretation — Bréal (1877 [1863]: 6) speaks of 'hermeneutics' — is not enough; one has to find the reason why every sign was attributed the value it has (p. 3). To find out the meaning of fables it is not enough to sepculate, one has to look carefully at the words used and the names given to gods and goddesses, and ask why they meant what they meant, why they were created and used. Like language itself, these names were a 'popular' creation (p. 5), not the inspired product of poetic minds. At the beginning they were quite transparent with no hidden meaning, but slowly this original meaning was forgotten and with the forgetting of etymology, the gates were opened to change. What had once designated a force of nature, like the sun, became the name for a god. And as there were many synonymous names for the sun, the forgetting of the original use of these names led again to change. They were ordered into families of gods and goddesses (p. 13) — a myth was created. Errors in understanding brought about ever new variations of these myths. And finally when the origin of a name became totally obscured, the people tried to reinterpret it and in doing so it created a new myth: it gave the name a history, made up a story to explain it.

In this early work Bréal expressed not only novel ideas about the origin and evolution of myths (a topic also explored by Max Müller of Oxford, a friend and colleague of Bréal's), but prepared the ground for his new view of semantic change. Bréal claimed that language is created and changed by the people in ways which the philologist has only to describe. There is nothing mysterious about it. The precondition of semantic change (and the precondition of the study of semantic change) is (the acknowledgement of) one important fact: the forgetting of the etymological meaning. The rest is reinterpretation by folk etymology, accumulation of synonyms, and the distribution of synonyms, all processes of semantic change which Bréal explored in more detail in the *Essai*. These processes were what interested Bréal, not 'la recherche d'un sens original perdu'! At the beginning stands improvisation, followed by progress towards more complexity. After this youthful outpouring of his semantic convictions came a time of consolidation for Bréal.

In 1866 Bréal started to translate the second edition of Franz Bopp's (1791–1867) Comparative Grammar, a project he finished by 1874 (cf. Bopp 1866–74). But at the time when Bréal was importing German comparative philology to France, he also wrote two revolutionary 'declarations for the right of meaning', that is for a semantics based on historical and psychological principles. They were his lectures on *La forme et la fonction des mots* (1866) and on *Les idées latentes du langage* (1868), and here German philologists, even Bopp, were sharply criticised for their narrow focus on linguistic form and their neglect of the function of words in discourse. Bréal still speaks, like Littré, of the transformation and evolution of language, in this respect faithful to a certain Lamarckism fashionable in the France of that time, but he underlined strongly the relationship between language and the human mind. In these two lectures the first cornerstones for Bréal's future semantics were laid. He did not want to study language in itself and for itself, like Schleicher and the French 'naturalists', but he wanted to study the place and influence of the human being (*l'homme*) in language, in his psychological make-up, in his social relations with other human beings, and all this in a proper historical setting. For Bréal, it is the human being who is the real force behind all language change, and not language itself as a quasi-human organism. In 1883 Bréal gave this new enterprise a new name: 'sémantique' (cf. Bréal 1883: 133). A further milestone in Bréal's elaboration of a new semantics was his joint review of Darmesteter's 1887 book and the second edition of Paul's *Prinzipien der Sprachgeschichte* of 1886 (cf. Bréal 1887a), which he later integrated into the *Essai*. In the same year, 1887, Bréal also published an article on how languages repair weak points in their grammar (in this case the genitive plural in Latin), and he pointed out:

"Si la linguistique s'est appliquée à observer les modifications subies par le mécanisme grammatical, elle n'a pas cherché avec le même soin les causes intellectuelles pour lesquelles ce mécanisme se modifie et se renouvelle. [...] Cependant, en renonçant à une telle recherche notre science serait incomplète. Les langues seraient, en quelque sorte privée de leur premier moteur." (Bréal 1887b: 233)

What drives language change and produces language structure is human *need*. Linguistic forms do not change autonomously or organically, they change because they are used for ever different purposes, because they are adapted to different functions.

The relation between form and function had been the topic of his 1866 and 1868 lectures. In 1866 he had pointed out that the meaning or function of words could survive the alteration of form. In the 1868 lecture he wanted to show that form and meaning do not have to correspond exactly, that there can be gaps in the form which do no harm to the understanding of the meaning. The force that 'repairs' the alterations and that fills the gaps (ellipsis) is human intelligence, the human mind. In the 1866 lecture Bréal had stressed that the history of a language was not just an internal history, but it was intimately linked to political, intellectual and social history, where creation and change are at any moment our own work.

Under Bréal, French semantics was slowly moving away from the study of isolated words towards a semantics of communication and understanding. All these new insights were integrated in his famous *Essai* of 1897. But the *Essai* also contains a more traditional approach to semantic change. Whereas Bréal studies morpho-semantic aspects of semantic change in the first part of the *Essai* and syntactico-pragmatic ones in the third part, the second part of the *Essai* explores the usual types of semantic change, such as the extension and restriction of meaning, metaphor, and metonymy (which he calls the 'thickening of meaning'), and 'tendencies' of words, that is the amelioration or pejorisation of meaning. But as always Bréal goes beyond these narrow typologies, especially when he analyses a novel semantic phenomen, namely 'polysemy', the multiplicity of meaning (cf. Nerlich & Clarke 1997). Bréal had invented this term in 1887 in his review of Darmesteter's book and he made it famous in his *Essai* published 10 years later. Bréal did not only analyse polysemy as lexicographers did when trying to cope with the multiplicity of meaning in entries for their dictionaries, but focused instead on the emergence of polysemy, on the understanding of polysemous words in discourse and also on the cognitive and structural aspects of multiple meanings. He thereby stepped outside diachronic word semantics and into synchronic cognitive semantics.

Bréal no longer explores how one meaning replaces another in the semantic development of word but how meanings are structured around a core and how they can be accessed by speakers and hearers. The thread that runs through Bréal's semantic work is the following insight: To understand the evolution and the structure of languages we should not focus so much on the forms and sounds but on the functions and meanings of words and constructions, used and built up by human beings under the influence of their will and intelligence, on the one hand, and the influence of the society they live and talk in, on the other. Unlike some of his contemporaries, Bréal therefore looked at how ideas, how our knowledge of a language and our knowledge of the world, shape the words we use. However, he was also acutely aware of the fact that this semantic and cognitive side of language studies was not yet on a par with the advances made in the study of phonetics, of the more physiological side of language. In his 1884 article "Comment les mots sont classés dans notre esprit", Bréal therefore appeals to the future to supply us with insights into the cognitive aspects of human language and writes:

"When we compare intelligence to a file cabinet in which ideas are arranged in order, or to a photographic plate on which images are deposited, or to an instrument whose various strings vibrate in turn, it is clear that these are merely analogies. In fact, the true nature of intellectual phenomena is unknown to us. We perceive the effects, but the cause remains hidden. We are obliged to transpose facts of a higher order into the language of the five senses. To be precise, we should speak neither of ideas nor of words, for there are no such things: there are only states, the habits of our brain and the movements of our vocal apparatus. But if we spoke in this way no one would understand us. Thus it is better to speak in an approximate way, while waiting for the establishment of the science of human intelligence which one of our former colleagues, one of the great figures of the Institute, Claude Bernard [(1813–1878)], liked to call the science of the twentieth century." (Bréal 1991 [1884]: 151)

With Bréal semantics as a linguistic discipline made a first step into this future, a future in which we are still participating and to which we are still contributing at the beginning of the 21st century.

5. Bibliography

Baldinger, Kurt. 1957. *Die Semasiologie: Versuch eines Überblicks.* Berlin: Akademie-Verlag.

Bergounioux, Gabriel. 1987. "Comment la sémantique se fit un nom, à propos de *la Vie des mots* d'Arsène Darmesteter". *Ornicar?: Revue du champ freudien* 42.12–44.

Bopp, Franz. 1866–1874. *Grammaire comparée des langues indo-européennes.* Transl. by Michel Bréal. 5 vols. Paris: Imprimerie Impériale/Nationale.

Bréal, Michel. 1866. "De la forme et de la fonction des mots. (Leçon faite au Collège de France pour la réouverture du cours de grammaire comparée)". *Revue des cours littéraires de la France et de l'étranger*, 4ème année, No. 5 (29 déc. 1866), 65–71. (Repr. in Bréal 1995: 89–96.)

–. 1868. *Les idées latentes du langage.* Leçon faite au Collège de France pour la réouverture du cours de grammaire comparée, le 7 déc. 1868. Paris: Hachette. (Repr. in Bréal 1995: 184–213.)

–. 1883. "Les lois intellectuelles du langage: Fragment de sémantique". *Annuaire de l'Association pour l'avancement des études grecques en France* 17.132–142. (Repr. in Bréal 1995: 271–282.)

–. 1887a. "L'histoire des mots" [Review of Darmesteter (1887) and Paul (1886)]. *Revue des Deux Mondes* 82:4.187–212.

–. 1887b. "Comment les langues réparent les points faibles de leur grammaire". *Mélanges Renier (= Bibliothèque de l'École des Hautes Etudes. Sciences philologiques et historiques*, fasc. 73), 233–239. Paris: F. Vieweg.

–. 1924 [1897]. *Essai de sémantique (Science des significations).* Reprint of the 4th ed. of 1908. Paris: Gérard Monfort.

–. 1991. *The Beginnings of Semantics: Essays, lectures and reviews*, ed. and transl. by George Wolf. London: Duckworth.

–. 1995. *De la grammaire comparée à la sémantique.* Textes de Michel Bréal publiés entre 1864 et 1898. Introduction, commentaires et bibliographie par Piet Desmet et Pierre Swiggers. Leuven & Paris: Peeters.

Chavée, Honoré. 1849. *Lexiologie indoeuropéenne.* Paris: A. Franck.

Christmann, Hans Helmut, ed. 1977. *Sprachwissenschaft im 19. Jahrhundert.* Darmstadt: Wissenschaftliche Buchgesellschaft.

Curtius, Georg. 1858. *Grundzüge der griechischen Etymologie.* Erster Theil. Leipzig: Teubner.

Darmesteter, Arsène. 1877. *De la création actuelle de mots nouveaux dans la langue française et les lois qui la régissent.* Paris: F. Vieweg. (Repr., Geneva: Slatkine, 1972.)

—. 1886. *The Life of Words as Symbols of Ideas.* London: Kegan Paul, Trench & Co.

—. 1887. *La vie des mots étudiée dans leurs significations.* Paris: Delagrave.

—. 1890 [1875]. Review of A. Chaignet, *La philosophie de la science du langage étudiée dans la formation des mots* (Paris, 1875). *Reliques scientifiques: Recueillies par son frère,* vol. II, 77–87. Paris: Librairie Léopold Cerf. [First published in the *Revue critique* 52, 1875.]

Delesalle, Simone. 1987. "Vie des mots et science des significations: Arsène Darmesteter et Michel Bréal". *DRLAV: Revue de linguistique* 36–37. 265–314.

Desmet, Piet. 1994. "La *Revue de linguistique et de philologie comparée* (1867–1916) – organe de la linguistique naturaliste en France". *Beiträge zur Geschichte der Sprachwissenschaft* 4:1.49–80.

—. 1997. "L'*idéologie lexioloque* d'Honoré Chavée ou l'étude des lois qui président aux variations logiques des mots". *L'Histoire de la Sémantique préstructurale: Quatre études* ed. by Piet Desmet, Dirk Geeraerts & Pierre Swiggers, 17–44. Leuven: Katholieke Universiteit Leuven.

Haase, Friedrich. 1874–1880. *Vorlesungen über lateinische Sprachwissenschaft, gehalten ab 1840.* Bd. I: *Einleitung und Bedeutungslehre* 1. Teil, ed. by Friedrich August Eckstein. Leipzig: Simmel; Bd. II: *Bedeutungslehre* 2. Teil, ed. by Hermann Peter. Leipzig: Simmel.

Hecht, Max. 1888. *Die griechische Bedeutungslehre: Eine Aufgabe der klassischen Philologie.* Leipzig: Teubner.

Heerdegen, Ferdinand. 1875–1881. *Ueber Umfang und Gliederung der Sprachwissenschaft im Allgemeinen und der lateinischen Grammatik insbesondere. Versuch einer systematischen Einleitung zur lateinischen Semasiologie.* Drei Hefte. Erlangen: Deichert.

—. 1890. "Grundzüge der lateinischen Bedeutungslehre". Reisig 1881–1890 III, 39–154.

Hey, Oskar. 1892. "Semasiologische Studien". *Jahrbücher für Classische Philologie,* Suppl. 18.83–212.

—. 1894/1896. "Die Semasiologie: Rückblick und Ausblick". *Archiv für Lateinische Lexikographie und Grammatik* 9.193–230.

Knobloch, Clemens. 1988. *Geschichte der psychologischen Sprachauffassung in Deutschland von 1850 bis 1920.* Tübingen: Niemeyer.

Kronasser, Heinz. 1952. *Handbuch der Semasiologie: Kurze Einführung in die Geschichte, Problematik und Terminologie der Bedeutungslehre.* Heidelberg: Winter. (2nd ed., 1968.)

Littré, Emile. 1863. *Histoire de la langue française: Études sur les origines, l'étymologie, la grammaire, les dialectes, la versification et les lettres au moyen âge.* Paris: Didier & Cie.

—. 1873. *Dictionnaire de la langue française contenant [...], la nomenclature, la grammaire, la signification des mots [...].* 4 vols. Paris: Hachette. [First ed., 30 parts, 1863–72.]

—. 1880. "Pathologie verbale ou lésion de certains mots dans le cours de l'usage". *Études et glanures pour faire suite à l'Histoire de la Langue Française,* 1–68. Paris: Didier.

—. 1888. *Comment les mots changent de sens.* Avec un avant-propos et des notes par Michel Bréal. Paris: Delagrave.

Nerlich, Brigitte. 1992a. *Semantic Theories in Europe 1830–1930: From etymology to contextuality.* Amsterdam & Philadelphia: Benjamins.

—. 1992b. "La sémantique: 'Éducation et récréation'". *Cahiers Ferdinand de Saussure* 46.159–171.

—. 1996a. "Semantics in the XIXth Century". *Geschichte der Sprachtheorie* ed. by Peter Schmitter, Bd. v: *Sprachtheorien der Neuzeit II: Von der 'Grammaire de Port-Royal' (1660) zur Konstitution moderner linguistischer Disziplinen,* 395–426. Tübingen: Narr.

—. 1996b. "Un chaînon manquant entre rhétorique et sémantique: L'œuvre d'Auguste de Chevallet". *Travaux de Linguistique* 33 ("Langue et linguistique: mouvements croisés et alternés [1790–1860]"), 115–131.

— & David D. Clarke. 1997. "Polysemy: Patterns in meaning and patterns in history". *Historiographia Linguistica* 24:3.359–385.

Oertel, Hanns. 1902. *Lectures on the Study of Language.* New York: Charles Scribner's Sons; London: Arnold.

Ogden, C[harles] K[ay] & I[vor] A[rmstrong] Richards. 1985 [1923]. *The Meaning of Meaning: A study of the influence of language upon thought and of the science of symbolism.* Repr., without the supplements. London, Boston & Henley: ARK Paperbacks. (With supplementary essays by Bronislaw Malinowski & Frederick G. Crookshank, London: Routledge & Kegan Paul, 1923 (10th ed. = second impression, 1953; repr., New York: Harcourt, Brace, Jovanovich, 1989.)

Paris, Gaston. 1888. Review of Littré (1888). *Revue Critique* N. S. 26.411–413.

Paul, Hermann. 1880. *Principien der Sprachgeschichte.* Halle/S.: Niemeyer. (2nd rev. ed., 1886; 3rd rev. ed., 1898; 4th rev. ed., 1909; 5th ed., 1920.)

Reisig, Christian Karl. 1839. *Vorlesungen über lateinische Sprachwissenschaft.* Herausgegeben mit Anmerkungen von Dr. Friedrich Haase. Leipzig: Lehnhold.

—. 1881–1890. *Vorlesungen über lateinische Sprachwissenschaft.* Herausgegeben mit Anmerkungen von Ferdinand Heerdegen, 3 vols. Berlin: Calvary.

Schleicher, August. 1861. *Compendium der vergleichenden Grammatik der indogermanischen Sprachen.* Vol. I. Weimar: Böhlau.

Schmidt, Karl. 1894. *Die Gründe des Bedeutungswandels: Ein semasiologischer Versuch.* Berlin: Hayn's Erben.

Schmitter, Peter. 1987. *Das sprachliche Zeichen: Studien zur Zeichen- und Bedeutungstheorie in der griechischen Antike sowie im 19. und 20. Jahrhundert.* Münster: Institut für Allgemeine Sprachwissenschaft der Westfälischen Wilhelms-Universität.

Smart, Benjamin H[umphrey]. 1831. *An Outline of Sematology: Or an essay towards establishing a new theory of grammar, logic, and rhetoric.* London: Richardson. [Published anonymously.]

Steinthal, Heymann. 1860. "Ueber den Wandel der Laute und Begriffe". *Zeitschrift für Völkerpsychologie und Sprachwissenschaft* 1.416–432. (Repr. in Christmann 1977.50–64.)

Svedelius, Carl. 1891. *Étude sur la sémantique.* Upsala: Josephsons Antikvariat.

Thomas, Robert. 1894, 1896. "Ueber die Möglichkeiten des Bedeutungswandels I". *Bayrische Blätter für das Gymnasialwesen* 30.705–732; 32.1–27.

Weisgerber, Leo. 1927. "Die Bedeutungslehre: Ein Irrweg der Sprachwissenschaft?". *Germanisch-Romanische Monatschrift* 15.161–183.

Welby, Victoria Lady. 1911. *Significs and Language: The articulate form of our expressive and interpretative resources.* London: Macmillan & Co. (Repr., with an introd. by H. Walter Schmitz, Amsterdam & Philadelphia: Benjamins, 1985.)

Brigitte Nerlich, Nottingham (Great Britain)

192. Die Forschungsrichtung "Wörter und Sachen"

1. Die Forschungsrichtung
2. Entstehung eines Konzepts
3. Die Zeitschrift "Wörter und Sachen"
4. Die Methode "Wörter und Sachen"
5. Umsetzung des Konzepts
6. Zentren und Schulen der Sachwortforschung
7. Ausblick
8. Bibliographie

1. Die Forschungsrichtung

Die überwiegend im deutschsprachigen Raum betriebene Forschungsrichtung "Wörter und Sachen" (im Folgenden: W & S) wird in der Literatur als "Richtung" (Vidos 1968: 80), "Methode" (Iordan 1962: 84) oder "Schule" (Amirova et al. 1980: 430 ff.) bezeichnet. Sie praktizierte eine empirische Sprachwissenschaft mit stark volks- und sachkundlichem Bezug.

Ihr Name ist mit der 1909 von Rudolf Meringer begründeten gleichnamigen Zeitschrift (im folgenden: *WuS*) verbunden, die bis 1944 in 23 Bänden erschien. Diese "Kulturhistorische Zeitschrift für Sprach- und Sachforschung" — so ihr ursprünglicher Untertitel — war das Organ einer Sprachforschung, die im Gegensatz zum dominanten Lautbezug der Junggrammatiker die Rolle inhalts- und refernzsemantischer Aspekte von Sprache sowie außersprachlicher Faktoren untersuchte. Sie folgte damit vor allem der von Hugo Schuchardt 1885 in dem Beitrag *Über die Lautgesetze: Gegen die Junggrammatiker* vorgetragenen Kritik (Schneider 1973; Wilbur 1977). In Meringers Slogan "Bedeutungswandel ist Sachwandel [...] und Sachwandel ist Kulturwandel" (Meringer 1912: 26) kam das nicht völlig neue Konzept (2.1.) einer Zeitschrift (3.) mit neuen Methoden (4.) und Gegenständen zum Ausdruck. Innovativ war ihre stark visuelle Prägung (4.4.), die sich vom ersten Heft an in dem Einbezug von Abbildungen (Photographien, Zeichnungen, Schaubilder) niederschlug. Die Beiträge aus verschiedenen Fächern (5.) von Autoren mit z. T. unterschiedlichen Konzeptionen (3.1.) stießen neben Kritik auch auf breite positive Resonanz, vor allem in der Volkskunde (6.1.) und in der Romanistik, wo eigene Schulen und Projekte entstanden (6.2.; 6.3.). Als sich nach 1933 in der Zeitschrift einige Vertreter der Forschungsrichtung dezidiert in den Dienst der nationalsozialistischen Wissenschaft stellten, orientierten die neuen Herausgeber (3.2.) die Zeitschrift 1938 um. Wie in der Volkskunde fanden hier die ideologischen Implikationen einer dominant an der Sach- und Volkskultur orientierten Forschung ihren negativen Ausdruck. Das Kriegsende führte zur Einstellung der Zeitschrift. Während die Forschungsrichtung danach weniger Beachtung fand, wurde mit Leo Weisgerber einer der Herausgeber zu einer zentralen Gestalt in der deutschen Sprachwissenschaft nach 1945. In den späten sechziger Jahren wurde mit der Schaffung zahlreicher Professuren die Linguistik verstärkt als Hochschuldisziplin etabliert. Die meisten neuen Vertreter lehnten die als traditionell verstandene Sprachwissenschaft zumeist aus inhaltlichen und teils aus politischen Gründen ab. In Reaktion auf einen Beitrag von Weisgerber (1970) setzten sich Baumann (1970) und Wienold (1970) programmatisch von dessen Vorstellungen und damit auch von W & S ab. Es kam dabei zu ersten kritischen fachgeschichtlichen Auseinandersetzungen mit den nationalsozialistischen Verflechtungen von Sprachwissenschaftlern; so in dem Kommentar von Römer (1971) zu Weisgerber (1971).

Erst in neuerer Zeit fand W & S vor allem wegen einiger ethnographischer Daten wieder Beachtung. Angesichts der semantischen Diskussion der fünfziger und sechziger Jahre (7.1.) sowie neuerer Bestrebungen innerhalb kognitiv orientierter Semantiken (7.2.) könnte sich das systematische und fachgeschichtliche Interesse an den Konzepten dieser Forschungsrichtung verstärken. Die Auseinandersetzung mit ihr weist darauf hin, daß Körperlichkeit, Technik und Medialität als wesentliche Faktoren der Bildung sprachwissenschaftlicher Theorien, Methoden und Gegenstände bei der fachgeschichtlichen Rekonstruktion berücksichtigt werden müssen.

2. Entstehung eines Konzepts

Im dritten Heft von *WuS* nahm Rudolf Meringer (1859−1931) zu Kritiken an den ersten beiden Bänden Stellung und legte das Konzept von Zeitschrift und Forschungsrichtung ausführlich dar. In Teilen griff er dabei auf Argumente zurück, welche bei den Junggrammatikern das Fehlen semantischer und psychologischer Aspekte kritisierten. Hugo Schuchardt (1842−1927) hatte schon 1885 einige für W & S zentrale Kritikpunkte konzeptionell und in fachgeschichtlicher Perspektive formuliert. Für ihn bedeutete "die Aufstellung des junggrammatischen Prinzips [...] keinen Umschwung in der Geschichte der Sprachwissenschaft, mit dem sie sicherer und rascher fortzuschreiten begonnen hätte" (Schuchardt 1976 [1912]: 81−82).

Vielmehr sieht er in der "Geschichte dieses blendenden Sophismus" die Fortsetzung

"der früheren Ansicht, welche die Sprache vom Menschen loslöste, ihr ein selbständiges Leben lieh und welche zuerst in romantisch-mystischer, dann in streng naturwissenschaftlicher Färbung auftrat." (Schuchardt 1976 [1912]: 82)

In der für die damalige Zeit aktuellen Opposition stellt er der von ihm favorisierten geisteswissenschaftlichen die veraltete naturwissenschaftliche Orientierung der Sprachwissenschaft entgegen.

"Diese ragt wie eine Antiquität aus jener Epoche in die heutige hinein, welche der Sprachwissenschaft den Charakter einer Geisteswissenschaft zuerkennt, welche in der Sprache keinen natürlichen Organismus, sondern ein soziales Produkt erblickt." (Ebda.)

Mit der Betonung des sozialen und kulturellen Charakters von Sprache befand sich W & S in einer geistes- und kulturwissenschaftlichen Strömung der Sprachwissenschaft, die um die Jahrhundertwende ihren Aufschwung genommen hatte. Zu ihr zählt auch Vosslers neoidealistischer Ansatz. Diesen neuen Strömungen bot Carl Winter in Heidelberg (Carl Winter, Universitätsverlag 1954) mit seinen philologischen Reihen und Publikationen eine Plattform. Er startete 1909 neben *WuS* die "Germanisch-Romanische Monatsschrift" mit Wilhelm Meyer-Lübke als Mitherausgeber, brachte zahlreiche volkskundlich orientierte Arbeiten heraus und hatte schon 1904 die programmatische Schrift *Positivismus und Idealismus in der Sprachwissenschaft* Vosslers und danach weitere seiner Arbeiten veröffentlicht. Der Winter-Verlag zählte damit eine ganze Reihe jüngerer Sprachwissenschaftler mit neuen und modernen Ansätzen zu seinen Autoren. Hier erschienen zugleich die Romanischen Elementar- und Handbücher von W. Meyer-Lübke, und mit Murko und Mikkola publizierten zwei weitere Herausgeber von *WuS* einige Arbeiten. Dem Verlag, der auch Bally und Meillet zu seinen Autoren zählte, kam so eine wichtige markt- und produktstrategische Funktion bei der Entwicklung der Sprachwissenschaft zu Beginn des 20. Jhs. zu.

Meringer selbst hatte seit den neunziger Jahren des 19. Jhs. eine Reihe sach- und volkskundlicher Hausstudien und 1904 einen umfangreichen Beitrag mit dem Titel *Wörter und Sachen* sowie einige Folgebeiträge (Lochner von Hüttenbach 1976: 33) publiziert. Dem Verständnis ihrer Hauptvertreter nach hatte die neue Richtung verschiedene Vorläufer, deren Nennung dazu geeignet war, den neuen Ansatz in der fachlichen Auseinandersetzung mit Junggrammatikern zu profilieren und zu legitimieren. So sieht Meringer in Grimm und Hermann Usener Vorläufer, während Schuchardt auf "stofflich geordnete Glossare" (Schuchardt 1976: 122) und den *Orbis sensualium pictus* (1658) des Comenius verweist, der "das Bild systematisch dem sprachlichen Zweck dienstbar gemacht" (S. 123) hat. Er zieht ferner eine Verbindungslinie zu enzyklopädischen Wörterbüchern — bis hin zum *Nouveau Larousse* —, in denen Bilder die „Sachen zur Anschauung" bringen. Dabei schwebt ihm ein holistischer, onomasiologischer Ansatz für eine

"ethnographisch orientierte Sprachforschung vor, welche die Wörter, ihren Gebrauch, ihre Bedeutung und ihren Wandel in Verbindung zu den Sachen bringt, die sie bezeichnen." (Settekorn 1993: 197)

Besser noch als in einem Bilderatlas könnten ganzheitliche Szenen in einem ethnographischen Museum dargestellt werden. Dieser Ansatz war gegen "den Atomismus der junggrammatischen Richtung mit ihrem naiven, letztlich biologistischen Sprachverständnis" gerichtet und sollte "die kulturell artikulierte Sprachpraxis gemeinsam mit Nachbardisziplinen [...] erforschen" (Maas 1988: 261).

2.1. Fachgeschichtliche Stellung von W & S

Mit theoretischen Überlegungen und praktischen Arbeiten haben Meringer und Schuchardt ihre Ansichten zu Status, Grundlagen und Methoden der Sprachwissenschaft vorgestellt und als Wortführer intensiv die Konzeption der Richtung W & S beeinflußt. Beide folgten verstärkt geistes- und kulturgeschichtlichen Ausrichtungen, die sich dezidiert von einer naturwissenschaftlich orientierten Sprachwissenschaft absetzten, für die vor allem Schleicher und dann die junggrammatische Schule mit dem zentralen Konzept der Lautgesetze standen. Der Einführung von W & S kamen zudem Bemühungen um eine Intensivierung und Differenzierung kultur- und sozialwissenschaftlicher empirischer Arbeit entgegen, die sich im Verlauf des 19. Jhs. verstärkt hatten. Schon zu dessen Beginn zeitigte die fortschreitende Industrialisierung erhebliche gesellschaftliche Umbrüche und führte zu einer wachsenden Auseinandersetzung mit den eigenen Volksgruppen, mit der gerade in Deutschland die Suche nach den Grundlagen einer nationalen deutschen Identität einherging. Auf dem Weg zur nationalen Einheit gab es seit den Brüdern Grimm immer wieder Bemühungen um eine Erfassung und Erforschung der kulturellen Grundlagen des deutschen Volkes. Nach der Jahrhundertmitte spielte dabei Wilhelm Riehl (1823—1897) eine wichtige Rolle, der nach eigenem Bekunden durch die Revolution von 1848 zum bewußten Konservativen geworden war. Ihm gelang es, unter dem Namen 'Volkskunde' eine eigene empirische Wissenschaft vom deutschen Volk als akademische Disziplin zu etablieren. Im letzten Viertel des 19. Jhs. wurden Ansätze volkskundlicher Beschreibung auch auf die Sprachen und Kulturen anderer Völker übertragen und in den Rahmen der internationalen Folkloreforschung gestellt. Parallel zu diesen nationalen und internationalen Bemühungen um binnenethnographische Forschung verlief der vor allem von den Kolonialmächten betriebene Auf- und Ausbau der Ethnologie und anderer einschlägiger Disziplinen zur Erforschung der Kolonien.

Vor diesem Hintergrund war um die Jahrhundertwende die Forderung nach einer ethnographisch und kulturwissenschaftlich fundierten Sprachwissenschaft doppelt aktuell: innerdisziplinär war es der Versuch, durch einen inhaltlich fundierten Angriff auf eine als bekannt und anerkannt vorausgesetzte Schule die konkurrierende Richtung mit eigenem Gegenstandsverständnis zu etablieren und dies unter Bezug auf inhaltlich wie methodisch ähnliche oder gleichlaufende Ansätze aus anderen Disziplinen zu tun. Zugleich bot die neue Richtung die Chance, sich nach außen im größeren ethnographischen und ethnologischen sowie allgemeinen kulturwissenschaftlichen Rahmen zu bewegen, der Anknüpfungspunkte und Kooperationsmöglichkeiten versprach. So verweist Meringer in seiner programmatischen Auseinandersetzung "Zur Aufgabe und zum Namen unserer Zeitschrift" (Meringer 1911) ausdrücklich auf inhaltliche Bezüge zur Psychologie, die sich in der noch heute beachteten Arbeit *Versprechen und Verlesen* (Meringer & Meyer 1895 [1978]) niedergeschlagen hatten.

Bei Versuchen der Etablierung und wissenschaftlichen Situierung einer Richtung oder Disziplin markiert die Gründung einer eigenen Zeitschrift (Weingart 1976) eine wichtige wissenschaftshistorische Etappe. Dies gilt in besonderem Maß, wenn deren Name — wie bei *WuS* — für das Programm der neuen Richtung steht und die Herausgeber als deren erste und wichtigste Vertreter gelten. Im Fall von *WuS* hatten Meringer und Schuchardt mit ihren Arbeiten das Terrain für die neue Richtung vorbereitet, und Meringer war nach eigenem Bekunden (1912: 36) von der Streitschrift *Über die Lautgesetze* (1885) seines Grazer Amtskollegen beeindruckt. Dennoch kam es zwischen den beiden Wegbereitern von *WuS* zu einer heftigen Auseinanderzung (4.1.). Sie hatte sich u. a. am Namen und am Konzept der neuen Zeitschrift entzündet, in der Schuchardt nie veröffentlichte.

Die fachhistorische Einschätzung dieser beiden wichtigen Vertreter von W & S ist unterschiedlich. Konnte Meringer als Hauptherausgeber von *WuS* bis zu seinem Lebensende den Gang der Richtung an maßgeblicher Position beeinflussen (Lochner von Hüttenbach 1992), wurde Schuchardt 1922 anläßlich seines achtzigsten Geburtstages von Spitzer mit der Herausgabe des *Schuchardt-Brevier* geehrt, das wichtige seiner über viele Zeitschriften zerstreuten Beiträge einem breiteren Publikum einfacher zugänglich gemacht hat. Amirova et al. (1980) konzentrieren die Darstellung von *WuS* weitgehend auf seine Arbeiten und verbinden diese Richtung hauptsächlich mit Schuchardt.

Während Schuchardt in den 70er und 80er Jahren des 20. Jhs. nicht zuletzt wegen seiner Kreolstudien Aktualität erhielt, gerieten die Arbeiten von Meringer wie *WuS* in Deutschland weitgehend in Vergessenheit. Zweifellos haben dazu neben der inhaltlichen Kritik an einer zu starken Sachorientierung auch die politischen Implikationen der Zeitschrift und mancher ihrer Autoren beigetragen (3.2.; 6.3.). Anders verlief die in der Schweiz von Jaberg und Jud gestiftete Traditionslinie (6.2.).

3. Die Zeitschrift "Wörter und Sachen"

Von der Jahreszeitschrift *Wörter und Sachen: Kulturhistorische Zeitschrift für Sprach- und Sachforschung* erschienen von 1909 bis 1937 insgesamt nur 18 Bände, mit einer kriegsbedingten fünfjährigen Pause zwischen den Bänden 6 (1914/15) und 7 (1921). Ab 1938 erschien eine Neue Folge mit geändertem Untertitel: *Zeitschrift für indogermanische Sprachwissenschaft, Volksforschung und Kulturgeschichte*. Sie brachte die Bände 19 bis 23 (1943/44) hervor, die zugleich als Neue Folge I bis V gezählt wurden. Zwischen 1913 und 1933 erschienen sechs, 1942 und 1943 zwei weitere Beihefte. Neben dem Indogermanisten R. Meringer (Graz) gehörten der Romanist W. Meyer-Lübke (Wien, später Bonn), der Germanist R. Much (Wien) und die Slavisten J. J. Mikkola (Helsinki) und M. Murko (Graz) zu den ursprünglichen Herausgebern der Zeitschrift. Die erhaltenen, unveröffentlichten 'Copierbücher' der Verlagskorrespondenz zeigen, daß der Verleger Otto Winter die Neugründung in enger Abstimmung mit Meringer parallel zu jener der *Germanisch Romanischen Monatsschrift* betrieb, in der auch einige Beiträge zu *WuS* erschienen (z. B. Wagner 1920). Mit weiteren Publikationsreihen waren beide Zeitschriften neue Produkte eines Wissenschaftsverlags, der in den beiden ersten Jahrzehnten des 20. Jhs. im sprachwissenschaftlichen Sektor expandierte und internationales Ansehen erwerben konnte.

Mitte 1908 standen Format und Umfang der Zeitschrift sowie die vorläufige Verpflichtung des Verlags zur Publikation von drei Jahresbänden zu einem Subscriptionspreis von "20 Mark" pro Band fest. Die Honorare beliefen sich für die ersten 400 Subscribenten auf 50 Mark pro Bogen, davon 32 Mark,

"also 4 Mark pro Seite für den Verfasser und 10 Mark für den Herausgeber sowie den Mitherausgebern jeweils für die von ihnen herausgegebenen Bogen 8 Mark" (Winter an Meringer 12. 06. 1908)

und sollten bei höheren Zahlen steigen. Geregelt war auch die Verwendung von Abbildungen. Diese "sollen in Zinkographie oder Autotypie im Text beigegeben werden. Die Vorlagen dazu sind dem Verlag von den Verfassern in reproduktionsfähigem Zustand zu liefern." (Ebda.)

"Dass der Raum für die Abbildungen honoriert wird ist selbstverständlich" (Winter an Meringer 1. 7. 1908). Winter weist ausdrücklich darauf hin, daß "reicher Abbildungsschmuck" förderlich sein wird und gerade der erste Band "Beiträge von Bedeutung wie Meyer-Lübke" (Winter an Meringer 9. 10. 1908) enthalten solle, weigert sich aber, Beiträge von Friedrich Kluge zu drucken, der "sich gegen meinen Verlag jederzeit [...] feindlich" (Winter an Meringer 10. 11. 1908) benommen hat. Die Reaktionen und Rezensionen fielen insgesamt positiver aus (Lochner von Hüttenbach 1976: 33; 1992: 73 f.) als es Meringers Reaktion auf kritische Einwände vermuten läßt.

3.1. Auseinandersetzungen und Strategien

Daß die Reaktion Meringers teilweise heftig ausfiel, mag an den Auseinandersetzungen gelegen haben, welche die Gründung der Zeitschrift begleiteten; in den unveröffentlichten Briefen des Verlegers an Meringer werden sie offen angesprochen. Dabei tritt neben inhaltlichen und formalen Aspekten ganz deutlich die geschäftliche Seite eines

Unternehmens zutage, das seinem Verleger einiges Geschick bei der Finanzierung abverlangte. Der Fall von *WuS* zeigt die ökonomischen Implikationen wissenschaftlicher Auseinandersetzung. Wissenschaftlicher Streit kann die Aufmerksamkeit der Fachgemeinschaft auf die Kontrahenten ziehen und das Geschäft beleben. Er gibt zugleich Gelegenheit zur Klärung der Positionen und verschafft die Möglichkeit, sie inhaltlich zu untermauern und sie fachhistorisch durch Verweis auf einschlägige Vorgänger historisch zu situieren und zu legitimieren. Bei der Einführung von *WuS* kommt zu den verlegerischen Strategien die unverkennbare Streitbarkeit Meringers hinzu, der sich immer wieder und in *WuS* gleich vom ersten Heft an mit Kritikern seiner Untersuchungen und deren Ansatz auseinandergesetzt hat. So mit C. C. Uhlenbeck, dem er vorhält, er solle "nicht Klage über meine Heftigkeit" führen, sondern sich vergegenwärtigen, "in welcher er mich angegriffen hat", nicht ohne von sich zu behaupten, "daß persönliche Gehässigkeit mir fremd ist und daß ich gern von ihm lerne" (1990a: 206, 207—208). Meringers nach außen gerichtete Auseinandersetzungen dienten der Festigung des neuen Ansatzes, während es bei dem sehr polemisch geführten Disput mit Schuchardt um die Behauptung und den Ausbau der Führungsposition innerhalb der neuen Richtung ging.

Winter nimmt gegenüber Meringer mit Bedauern zur Kenntnis, daß "Herr Hofrat Schuchardt nicht mittun will", und schlägt vor: "Keine Notiz davon nehmen und sich nach wie vor freundschaftlich zeigen in den Beiträgen ist die beste Antwort darauf" (Winter an Meringer, 11. 1. 1909). Gegen Ende des gleichen Monats schreibt Winter über die inzwischen eskalierte Auseinandersetzung an Meringer:

"Ich höre dass Herr Schuchardt wegen der W & S. ein Rundschreiben erlassen und dass Sie geantwortet haben. Es tut mir herzlich leid, dass das Unternehmen mit solchen Geburtswehen geplagt ist. Geschäftlich macht es garnichts aber ich hoffe dass Sie nicht zu viel Aerger erleben. Falls sie ein Exemplar der Schriftstücke übrig haben so wird mich der Inhalt natürlich sehr interessieren." (Winter an Meringer, 23. 1. 1909)

Sogleich bestätigt Winter den Eingang der erbetenen Exemplare und stellt fest:

"[…] auch ein Mann wie Sch. darf sich nicht über das was man gute Sitte nennt hinwegsetzen […]. Er [muss] sie aber stark verletzt haben denn sie sprachen mir noch im Frühjahr in Graz von Sch. mit größter Verehrung wie ich mich erinnere." (Winter an Meringer 28. 1. 1909)

Am 27. 02. übersendet Winter Meringer die ersten drei fertigen Exemplare mit der Bitte, "eines Herrn Prof. Murko zu übergeben", und teilt ihm die Namen der Zeitschriften mit, die ein Rezensionsexemplar des ersten Bandes erhalten sollen; er schlägt vor, daß die Verfasser der Artikel aus ihren 20 Separata Exemplare den "interessierten Spezialzeitschriften (den romanischen, slawischen etc.)" zukommen lassen. Der Verlag sorgt für die Werbung und Prospekte und erwartet Erfolg:

"[…] wenn die Beiträge stets auf der Höhe des ersten Bandes bleiben. Lieber etwas zurücksenden als nicht erstklassiches [sic!] abdrucken. Besonders Aufsätze mit Abbildungen, wie z. B. der Ihrige werden ziehen und sollen ja die Eigenart des Unternehmens äusserlich kennzeichnen." (Winter an Meringer 27. 2. 1909)

Positive Besprechungen gehen zahlreicher ein als Bestellungen. Den Gedanken an Beihefte stellt der Verleger zunächst zurück; das "Verkaufen von solchen monographischen Arbeiten ist ein[e] schwierige Aufgabe", denn "alles was monographischer streng wissenschaftlicher Natur ist, hat Blei an den Verkaufsfüssen und kann den Weg vom Lager des Verlegers weg garnicht finden." (Winter an Meringer 13. 3. 1909). Als Schuchardt gar den Preis der Zeitschrift kritisiert, reagiert Winter:

"Wenn Herr Schuchardt sich berechnet was die Herstellung der W. & S. kosten muss so wird er uns den Vorwurf zu teuer zu sein nicht weiter machen. Für etwas Gutes darf man aber auch überall einen entsprechenden Preis fordern." (Winter an Meringer 29. 3. 1909)

Im September 1909 wird die neue Zeitschrift auf dem Philologentag vorgestellt, und nachdem erste positive Besprechungen eingetroffen sind, macht das Unternehmen zaghafte Fortschritte, wie Winter am 3. 1. 1910 in seinem Neujahrsgruß an Meringer feststellt; zu Beginn dieses Jahres hat die Zeitschrift 193 Abonnenten, was "noch ein Stück Weg bis zur geschäftlichen Balance" bedeutet. Meringers Streit mit Schuchardt begleitet den weiteren Start der Zeitschrift. So bemerkt Winter:

"Dass Herr Schuchardt vielleicht contre cœur uns hilft ist ja sehr schön. Aber ist es wirklich nötig, dass Sie ihm antworten? Schweigen wäre vielleicht die beste Antwort, wenn er dann noch einmal anfängt, können Sie dann mit Begründung ganz fest zufassen. Aber einstweilen würde ich schweigen, wobei ich sehr gut verstehe, dass es Ihnen nicht leicht wird, aber in Anbetracht des Alters Ihres Gegners kann einem ei[n] Schweigen niemand falsch auslegen." (Winter an Meringer 30. 3. 1909)

Wie stark der Streit zwischen Meringer und Schuchardt letztlich zum Erfolg der Zeitschrift beigetragen hat, läßt sich nicht empirisch belegen, doch hat er ihr beim interessierten Fachpublikum zusätzliche Publizität verschafft.

Für die insgesamt positive Einschätzung des neuen Organs spricht auch das breite Spektrum der Beiträger. Neben rein volkskundlich und ethnographisch orientierten Autoren finden sich Sprachwissenschaftler aus unterschiedlichen Disziplinen: aus der allgemeinen Sprachwissenschaft und Indogermanistik, aus Germanistik, Romanistik und Slavistik. Allerdings ist nicht zu verkennen, daß die volks- und sachkundlich orientierten Beiträge anfänglich deutlich dominierten. Unter Meringers Leitung und mit der Gründergeneration der Herausgeber praktizierte die Zeitschrift ein vorwiegend materielles Sachkonzept. Dies entsprach einem in den zwanziger Jahren des 20. Jhs. zusehends durch Projekte zu Sprach- und Sachatlanten geprägten sprachwissenschaftlichen Kontext. Es entstand in diesem Bereich ein breiter Markt, auf dem sich neue sprachwissenschaftliche Zeitschriften mit entsprechender Ausrichtung, wie das am Romanischen Seminar der Universität Hamburg herausgegebene *Volkstum und Kultur der Romanen*, etablieren konnte (6.3.).

3.2. Die Zeitschrift im Nationalsozialismus

Der Weg vieler Vertreter der volkskundlichen und kulturmorphologischen Sprachwissenschaft führte zu völkischen und rassistischbiologischen Vorstellungen (Maas 1988; Simon 1985a). Wo sie nicht aus den Universitäten verdrängt wurden (Beckmann 1994; Christmann/Hausmann 1989; Hausmann 1991; 1993; Maas 1992), schlossen sich nach 1933 die meisten Sprachwissenschaftler dem nationalsozialistischen System an oder stellten sich — wie zahlreiche Vertreter von W & S und Autoren der Zeitschrift — explizit in dessen Dienst.

Um die Zeit des staatlich-politischen Umsturzes in Deutschland gab es bei den Herausgebern von *WuS* entscheidende Änderungen: ab Bd. 9 (1926) waren Güntert und nach Meringers Tod 1931 ab Bd. 15 (1933) Weisgerber Mitherausgeber geworden. Als 1936 mit Meyer-Lübke und Much weitere Mitglieder der Gründergeneration starben, kam es 1938 zu einer Neuorientierung der Zeitschrift. In diesem und im nächsten Jahr war Güntert Hauptherausgeber, von 1940–1943/44 hatte der Indologe Walter Wüst diese Funktion inne. R. von Kienle, H. Kuen, K. Stegmann v. Pritzwald, W. Porzig und L. Weisgerber waren Mitherausgeber der Neuen Folge (= NF) von *WuS*. In deren erstem Band (NF I), der zugleich als Band 19 firmiert, wies Güntert der Zeitschrift und der Richtung in seinem programmatischen Vorwort *Neue Zeit, neues Ziel* den Weg in den Nationalsozialismus, indem er die Orientierung auf die "geistigen Kräfte", die Abwendung von einer auf die materiellen Gegenstände konzentrierten Forschung, die Konzentration auf die völkische Sprachgemeinschaft fordert. Die Sprachwissenschaft solle "grundlegende Beiträge zur Erkenntnis unseres völkischen Wesens und unserer völkischen Eigenart" liefern und die einzelnen Beiträge "sich zusammenschließen im Sinn der großen nationalpolitischen Aufgaben der Gegenwart unter dem gemeinsamen Leitspruch: Dienst an unserem Volk" (Güntert 1938: 11).

Man mag in diesen Ausführungen einen geradezu exemplarischen Beitrag zu einer völkischen und rassistischen Sprachwissenschaft (Römer 1985) oder zugleich einen Versuch sehen, Konzept und Zeitschrift mit dem neuen Regime kompatibel zu halten (Maas 1988). Wie in anderen Zeitschriften auch wurden zum einen jüdische und politisch unliebsame Autoren ausgeschlossen, zum anderen geriet *WuS* mit Walter Wüst als Hauptherausgeber vollends ins Fahrwasser des neuen Regimes und der SS (Kater 1974). Die damals übliche Anpassung einer wissenschaftlichen Zeitschrift an die Gegebenheiten des Marktes war im Fall von *WuS* eindeutig politisch bestimmt. Wüsts Position als nationalsozialistischer Funktionsträger beeinträchtigte zwar seine Herausgebertätigkeit, sicherte aber trotz des seit 1941 chronischen Papiermangels das Erscheinen von *WuS*, das erst 1944 angesichts der "totalen Kriegsmaßnahmen" (Brief Anders an Winter 26. 10. 1944) auf Erlaß der Reichsschrifttumkammer eingestellt wurde. Einem Antrag auf Wiederaufnahme von *WuS* war nach Kriegsende kein Erfolg beschert. Als schließlich 1950 der Verlag ein Ersuchen Weisgerbers auf Neugründung bzw. Wiederaufnahme ablehnte (Müller 1991), war das endgültige Aus der Zeitschrift besiegelt.

4. Die Methode "Wörter und Sachen"

Der Titel der Zeitschrift bringt ein eigenes Konzept von Gegenstand und Methoden sprachwissenschaftlicher Arbeiten (4.1.) zum Ausdruck. Mit dezidiert kulturhistorischem Einschlag (4.2.) setzten die an W & S orientierten Arbeiten ein eigenes Emperieverständnis (4.3.) um. Bei der oft multimedialen (4.4.) Erfassung und Präsentation von Sach- und Sprachdaten in Wort und Bild folgten sie einer spezifischen Methodologie (4.5.). Die Kritik an einem vereinfachten unilateralen Zeichenmodell und einer vorwiegend auf die materiellen Sachen gerichteten Forschungspraxis führte zur Forderung nach einer methodischen Umorientierung (4.6.).

4.1. Sachen und Wörter, Wörter und Sachen

Der Name von Forschungsrichtung und Zeitschrift war für Rudolf Meringer (Biographisches bei Lochner von Hüttenbach (1976: 25−45) Slogan, 'Losungswort' und Programm: nicht allein Wörter und Wortformen, sondern auch deren Referenzobjekte sollten Gegenstand sprachwissenschaftlicher Arbeit sein, Sprachwandel sei nicht nur als Laut-, sondern auch als Bedeutungswandel zu untersuchen. Er vertrat die Auffassung, daß die "Sprachwissenschaft nur Teil der Kulturwissenschaft ist, daß die Sprachgeschichte zur Wortgeschichte der Sachgeschichte bedarf" (Meringer 1909a: 1). So einfach und eingängig der Slogan auch war, die Termini 'Wort' und 'Sache' sowie ihr durch 'und' bezeichnetes Verhältnis bedurften einer Klärung.

Im Vorwort zum ersten Band von *WuS* geht Meringer auf die beiden zentralen Begriffe des gewählten Namens ein. Er versteht hier unter "Sachen" konkrete, materielle Dinge wie solche des geistigen und sozialen Lebens, und das heißt für ihn "nicht nur die räumlichen Gegenstände, sondern ebensowohl Gedanken, Vorstellungen und Institutionen, die in irgendeinem Worte ihren sprachlichen Ausdruck finden." (Meringer 1912: 50) Dabei sollen, wie er später präzisiert (ebda.) "die dem Sprecher zugrunde liegenden psychischen Phänomene [...] ebenso als 'Sachen' gelten, wie die Gegenstände des Raumes, von denen wir auch nur die psychischen Bilder in unserer Seele kennen."

Zunächst befaßten sich die Beiträge in *WuS* jedoch vor allem mit dem materiellen, greifbaren Referenten und suchten aus onomasiologischer Sicht Bezeichnungen für die vorgegebenen Sachen, die in Wort und oft auch im Bild präsentiert wurden. Dies kommt in den Titeln exemplarischer Beiträge zum Ausdruck wie: *"Die Werkzeuge der pinsere-Reihe und ihre Namen (Keule, Stampfe, Hammer, Anke) mit 35 Abbildungen und Sprachlich-sachliche Probleme. Mit 40 Abbildungen* von R. Meringer, *"Das Bauernhaus der Gegend von Köflach in der Steiermark. Mit 47 Textabbildungen"* von J. R. Bünker, *"Zur Geschichte der Dreschgeräte. Mit 40 Abbildungen und Karte"* von W. Meyer-Lübke − alle in Band 1 −, sowie in Band 6 *"Die Terminologie der Marmorindustrie in Carrara"* von G. Bottiglioni (1914/15) mit 19 Photos und 90 Zeichnungen. Da schon die Titelblätter von *WuS* die Zahl der Abbildungen des jeweiligen Bandes ankündigten, sind dies typische Beispiele. Mit dieser für philologische und sprachwissenschaftliche Zeitschriften innovativen sowie aufwendigen und kostspieligen Bildorientierung wurden Sach- und Kulturbezug der neuen Forschungsrichtung augenfällig. Dem Einsatz von Bildern galten eigene methodologische Überlegungen (4.5.), denn die Bilder sollten mit der Einsicht in die Sachen und ihre Kontexte einen unmittelbaren, authentischen Zugang ermöglichen. Da auch die Sprachatlanten mit ihren synoptischen Karten über die rein geschriebene oder gedruckte Repräsentation von Schrifttexten mit einem eigenen Modus visueller Darstellung hinausgingen, wurde um die Jahrhundertwende − der *Atlas linguistique de la France* von J. Gilliéron und E. Edmont erschien zwischen 1902 und 1910 − das Auge neben dem Ohr auf neue Art zentrales Organ sprachwissenschaftlicher Wahrnehmung, Darstellung und Erkenntnis. Die Erarbeitung kombinierter Sprach- und Sachatlanten wie die des AIS (6.2.) war ein weiterer konsequenter Schritt in diese Richtung. W & S zog dabei *ein einfaches Zeichenmodell* heran, "in dem Wort und Sache ohne eine Zwischengröße in einer direkten Verbindung miteinander stehen" (Schmidt-Wiegand 1992: 26). Mit dieser einfachen referenzsemantischen Auffassung wurden der bildlichen Repräsentation der Referenten die entsprechenden Wortformen zugeordnet.

Für den sachbezogenen Ansatz von W & S gab es sprachgeschichtliche und etymologische Argumente: so war etwa eine Reihe romanischer Bezeichnungen für "Leber" (u. a. ital. *fegato*; frz. *foie*; span. *hígado*) lautgeschichtlich nicht aus dem grch.-lat. Stamm *hepar*, sondern nur aus dem lat. *ficatum* abzuleiten; den Weg zu diesem Etymon ebnete erst die Sachkenntnis jener Tierzuchtpraxis, die durch Verfütterung von Feigen besonders großen Lebern erzielte. Solche und zahlreiche eigene Befunde ließen Meringer feststellen: "Bedeutungswandel ist Sachwandel [...] und Sachwandel ist Kulturwandel" (1912: 26). Wie Schuchardt tat er dies in Opposition zur junggrammatischen Auffassung, daß Sprachwandel sich als Lautwandel auf der Grundlage von Lautgesetzen vollziehe, doch gaben beide unterschiedliche Antworten auf die Frage nach dem Verhältnis von Wort und Sache.

Die Titelblätter von *WuS* zierte bis 1938 ein Jacob Grimm entnommenes Motto:

"Sprachforschung, der ich anhänge und von der ich ausgehe, hat mich doch nie in der Weise befriedigen können, daß ich nicht immer gern von den Wörtern zu den Sachen gelangt wäre."

Dieses Motto hatte eine Legitimationsfunktion: es verweist auf die Autorität eines bekannten sowie anerkannten Sprachwissenschaftlers und übernimmt dessen Reihenfolge der Kernbegriffe, die eine Dominanzrelation nahelegt. Zusammen mit der Frage, wer zuerst den Einbezug von Bildern in die Sprachwissenschaft gefordert habe, stand diese Beziehung im Mittelpunkt des Prioritätsstreites zwischen dem Indogermanisten Meringer und dem Romanisten Schuchardt. Beide lehrten an der Universität Graz, Schuchardt seit 1876 und Meringer seit 1899. Dieser hatte indogermanische Sprachstudien betrieben und sich "der methodischen Sachforschung und der Volkskunde zugewendet" (Lochner von Hüttenbach 1980: 30), mehrere Reisen auf den Balkan mit volkskundlichen Studien unternommen und 1904 einen ersten programmatischen Aufsatz mit dem Titel *Wörter und Sachen* publiziert.

Der unveröffentlichte Briefwechsel des Herausgebers Meringer mit seinem Verleger zeigt, daß der von Lochner von Hüttenbach (1976; 1980; 1992) im Detail dokumentierte und von Zeitgenossen als "peinlich" (Spitzer 1929: 370) empfundene Prioritätenstreit sich längerfristig angebahnt und bei der Gründung von *WuS* verschärft hatte. Bei der Auseinandersetzung spielten mehrere Ebenen eine Rolle, die allgemeinere Strukturen fachgeschichtlicher Auseinandersetzungen erkennen lassen.

Inhaltlich ging es zum einen um den Zeichenbegriff. Wie Weisgerber (1974) rückblickend unterstreicht, verband Schuchardt in der Tat mit der Formulierung "Sachen und Wörter" eine andere Konzeption als Meringer, denn er forderte, daß "die Vorstellungen bei dem Verhältnis von Sachen und Wörtern nicht bloß eine gelegentliche, sondern eine regelmäßige und notwendige Rolle" spielen (Schuchardt 1976 [1912]: 126).

Meringer dagegen zog die Begriffs- oder Konzeptebene, ohne sie auszuschließen, eher beiläufig in Betracht. Beide waren sich über den *Einbezug von Bildern* und im *onomasiologischen Ansatz* einig. So hatte Schuchardt 1904 von einem Bilderatlas und einem ethnographischen romanischen Museum gesprochen, in dem

"Szenen aus dem alltäglichen wie dem festlichen Leben des Volkes in Rundbildern dargestellt und dadurch uns viele sachliche Beziehungen erst klar gemacht [werden] und mit ihnen wiederum sprachliche Beziehungen." (Schuchardt, S. 119)

Bei der Frage, wer zuerst derlei Forderungen erhoben und Bilder in sprachwissenschaftlichen Arbeiten benutzt habe, treten zu den inhaltlichen auch *persönliche* und *soziologische* Aspekte. Dies gilt nicht zuletzt, wenn Meringer eine Art Urheberschutz für das 'Markenzeichen' W & S reklamiert. Daß beide Forscher unterschiedliche Charaktere hatten, stand lange einer eher freundschaftlich-wissenschaftlichen Beziehung nicht entgegen, in welcher der Jüngere dem Älteren Respekt bekundete, doch dürfte die räumlich-institutionelle wie persönliche Nähe den Konflikt der beiden vertieft haben, der bei der Gründung der Zeitschrift eskalierte.

Soziologisch gesehen ist die Auseinandersetzung der beiden Sprachwissenschaftler einer jener Kämpfe um die öffentlich anerkannte Spitzenstellung (Bourdieu 1979: 543 ff.), welche häufig die Einführung neuer wissenschaftlicher Richtungen oder Paradigmen begleiten. Durch die neue Zeitschrift mit programmatischem Titel institutionalisierte sich die neue Richtung (Weingart 1976) auf dem sprach- und geisteswissenschaftlichen Markt; die Namengebung war dazu geeignet, dem Ansatz und seinem Gegenstand volle soziale Anerkennung zu verschaffen, dabei zugleich den Herausgeber zu legitimieren, seinen Bekanntheitsgrad und sein Ansehen zu erweitern. Die Herausgeberschaft manifestierte zusätzlich die Anerkennung durch die Vertreter einer neuen Richtung, die mit ihrer Offenheit für andere Disziplinen eine wachsende und breite Anhängerschaft erwarten ließ.

4.2. Kulturhistorische Ausrichtung und ethnologischer Kontext

Das Vorwort zum ersten Band von *WuS* vermerkt, daß "Sprachwissenschaft nur ein Teil der Kulturwissenschaft" sei und "in der Vereinigung von Sprachwissenschaft und Sachwissenschaft die Zukunft der Kulturwissenschaft liegt". Diese Position wurde später in *WuS* mehrmals bekräftigt (Meringer 1912, Sperber 1929), aber auch gezielt umgedeutet (Güntert 1938).

Die Einführung der sprachwissenschaftlichen Methode "Wörter und Sachen" fand dem Sachverständnis ihrer Protagonisten nach in einem umfassenderen gleichlaufenden ethnographisch-volkskundlichen Kontext statt. Die kulturgeschichtliche Ausrichtung — Meringer konzipierte unter Anlehnung an die Wellentheorie des Sprachwandels seines Lehrers Johannes Schmidt (vgl. Lochner von Hüttenbach 1976) — setzte die Änderung und Ausbreitung von Sprache mit der im Bereich der Ideen und der Sachen parallel:

"Neben den Sprachwellen sind die Sachwellen zu konstatieren. Beide zusammen kann man Kulturwellen nennen, denn jegliche Neuerung, jeglicher Fortschritt vollzieht sich im Sinn der Wellentheorie." (Meringer 1904: 191)

Entsprechend sollte W & S "Material zu einer umfassenden Kulturgeschichte der indogermanischen Völker herbeischaffen" (ebda.). Zugleich war W & S an der Volkskunde (Emmerich 1971; Brückner & Beitl 1983; Brednich 1988; Roth 1992) orientiert, die Wilhelm Heinrich Riehl (1823–1897) maßgeblich als spezifisch deutsche und deutschsprachige Variante der Binnenethnographie herausgebildet und institutionalisiert hatte. Riehl hatte seine *Naturgeschichte des deutschen Volkes als Grundlage einer deutschen Sozialpolitik* konzipiert. Beobachtungen "historisch entstandener Lebensgewohnheiten" (Steinbach 1976: 6), die er vor Ort auf Wanderungen gesammelt hatte und denen er einen ähnlichen Status wie Schriftzeugnissen zubilligte, waren die wesentliche Quelle seiner konservativen Gesellschaftskonzeption (Emmerich 1971: 56 ff.), die Familie und Bauerntum eine tragende gesellschaftliche Rolle zuordnete. Viele Volkskundler, für die Riehl Gründervater ihrer Disziplin war, griffen sie auf und führten sie fort. Im Nationalsozialismus galt Riehl als ein Vorläufer der Blut-und-Boden-Ideologie.

Wie die Volkskunde verfolgte W & S grundlegend konservativ-konservatorische Zielsetzungen. Diese galten vor allem den durch technischen Fortschritt und Industrialisierung im Umbruch befindlichen bäuerlichen Kulturen, deren geographisch und klimatisch bedingten Lebensweisen, den Wohn- und Produktionsverhältnissen, den Geräten, Arbeitsprozessen und Gebräuchen sowie ihren regional unterschiedlichen sprachlichen Bezeichnungen.

Zielsetzungen, Überzeugungen, Methoden und Praktiken der Volkskunde ähnelten denen der Ethnologie, die mit der zunehmenden Ausbreitung der Kolonialmächte seit dem letzten Viertel des 19. Jhs. an Bedeutung und Umfang gewonnen und zu umfangreichen ethnologischen Beschreibungen angesetzt hatte (Theye 1984; 1989). Meringer weist auf diesen Zusammenhang hin:

"Folklore und Volkskunde sind in letzter Linie das wissenschaftliche Ergebnis des britischen Weltreichs, der Herrschaft Britanniens über seine Kolonien." (1909b: 209)

Im Bemühen um optimale Nutzung der überseeischen Ressourcen hatte die Geographie der Kolonien und die Beschreibung ihrer Völker einen raschen Aufschwung erfahren. Es kam zu zahlreichen völkerkundlichen Expeditionen, bei denen die modernsten Verfahren der Datenerhebung, darunter Photoapparat und Phonograph, Verwendung fanden (Fischer 1981). Einschlägige Forschungseinrichtungen wurden gegründet, so das Hamburger Kolonialinstitut, aber auch Museen (Theye 1989: 19), welche die Ergebnisse ethnologischer Arbeit anschaulich zur Darstellung brachten.

Wie all diese Unterfangen hatte auch W & S *ein spezifisches Gegenstandsverständnis*: mit einer dominant raum-zeitlichen Orientierung, ging man von der kulturellen Gleichzeitigkeit des Ungleichzeitigen sowie davon aus, daß in der Gegenwart der Sachen die Kulturgeschichte präsent sei. Die vor Ort erhobenen Daten galten als Zeugnisse traditioneller Kultur- und Sprachpraktiken, die in Wort und Bild einzeln, in Reihen oder in ihrer geographischen Verbreitung auf Karten eingestellt wurden. Für die entsprechende Kulturraumforschung und Kulturmorphologie war die "Anwendung des Prinzips 'Wörter und Sachen'" (Schmidt-Wiegand 1992: 41) wertvolle Ergänzung, wo nicht Voraussetzung. Zugleich strebte diese ethnographische Forschung ganzheitliche Präsentationsformen an, und Schuchardts Traum von einem romanischen Museum erfüllte sich zumindest ansatzweise in dem *Musée Arlatan* von Arles, für dessen Errichtung Frédéric Mistral

(1830—1914) Mittel aus dem ihm 1904 verliehenen Literaturnobelpreis bereitgestellt hatte. Einige Vitrinen veranschaulichen dort in Lebensgröße und mit allem Zubehör ganzheitliche Szenen aus dem provenzalischen Alltagsleben (Krüger 1927b). In der gleichen Zeit fanden in Nordeuropa vermehrt Gründungen von Freilichtmuseen (Zippelius 1974) statt, in denen vergangene oder vergehende bäuerliche Kultur auch unter Vorführung ausgewählter Arbeits- und Produktionstechniken präsentiert wurde. Da diese Gründungen in vielen Fällen als Beitrag zur Herausbildung eines regionalen oder nationalen Bewußtseins gedacht waren, verwundert es nicht, daß in Deutschland gleichlaufende Bemühungen in den Dienst nationalkonservativer und nationalsozialistischer Kulturpolitik gerieten.

4.3. Empirieverständnis

Wie für Ethnologen und Volkskundler galten auch für die Vertreter von W & S das Reisen und Studieren vor Ort zumal dann als unabdingbar, wenn es sich um fremde Sprachen und Kulturen handelte. So spielen Reisen — und bei den Fremdsprachenphilologen besonders die Auslandsaufenthalte — in den wissenschaftlichen Biographien vieler kultur- und sachkundlicher Sprachwissenschaftler eine zentrale Rolle. Auf Reisen wird das geeignete und karriereträchtige Material gesucht und zumeist auch gefunden, es werden mit Terrains symbolisch auch Grenzen für Spezial- und Forschungsgebiete abgesteckt und Verbindungen geknüpft. Weil Reisen insgesamt bei der Blick- und Gegenstandskonstitution eine zentrale Rolle spielen, sind Hinweise auf Forschungsreisen und Auslandsaufenthalte bei Bewerbungen, Laudationes und Nachrufen wichtiger Bestandteil der wissenschaftlichen Biographien. So auch Elise Richter in einem langen Nachruf auf Schuchardt. Sie liefert hier ein prägnantes Beispiel für den engen Zusammenhang zwischen Reisen, Volks-, Sprach- und Sachstudien:

"Er setzte sich zu den Kutschern in ihre Kneipen, nahm an allen Volksbelustigungen teil, ging täglich in die Predigt oder ins Theater, besuchte bürgerliche und aristokratische Salons und war bemüht, sich der Art der Leute anzupassen, unter denen er lebte [...]. Der Zweck der Reise sind nicht die 'Baedekersehenswürdigkeiten', Bilder und Bibliotheken. Ein großer Genießer und guter Beurteiler von Gemälden [...] hält er es doch nicht aus, mehr als ein Dutzend auf einmal zu sehen. Hingegen wird er nicht müde, Bilder des Strassenlebens, der Volkssitte aufzunehmen." (Richter 1928: 239)

Diese Darstellung bekundet zugleich jenes Empirieverständnis, dem Wilhelm Riehl (1869) in seinem Wanderbuch Ausdruck verliehen hatte. Dort empfiehlt er systematisch beobachtendes Wandern als empirische Methode der Volkskunde. Er fordert dazu auf, Bibliotheken und Archive, Pergamente und Bücher zu verlassen und sich ins richtige Leben zu begeben, um so Auskunft über die wahren Zustände zu erhalten. Entsprechende Forderungen brachte Meringer für *WuS* polemisch auf den Punkt:

"Ich füge hinzu, daß für mich der Stubenhocker oft ebensowenig ein Forscher ist, als der Tintenkleckser, der die Sau mit dem Löschpapier fängt, ein Jäger ist. Weg mit der Überschätzung der Bücherwelt: Was uns das Leben lehren kann, soll man nicht aus Büchern zusammensuchen." (Meringer 1912: 30)

Wenn er allerdings "die Sachstudien [...], aber nicht nur die Studien bei gedruckten Quellen, sondern vornehmlich die Sachstudien im Volke" (1909a: 1) fördern wollte, dann galt dies nicht der breiteren Volksbildung, sondern der volkskundlichen Forschung vor Ort. Die Rede vom 'Hinausgehen ins Land, ins Feld, ins reale Leben, zum Volk', gründet auf einem soziologisch geprägten Gegenstands- und Empirieverständnis, das mit der Konstruktion eines vorgeblich neutralen, objektivierenden Standpunktes (Bourdieu 1980) den — in der Regel akademischen — Ausgangspunkt der Forscher außer- oder oberhalb des geographischen und sozialen Raumes der Betrachtungsgegenstände ansiedelt und von dort ein als objektiv ausgegebenes Bild der Situation gewinnt und liefert. In aller Regel wird dabei der eigene Standpunkt ebenso wenig bedacht wie die Bedingungen für die Erarbeitung des entsprechenden wissenschaftlichen Wissen (Settekorn 1993).

Was bei W & S unter polemischer Absetzung von den 'Junggrammatikern' und 'Positivisten' als Volksnähe formuliert wurde, ließ sich zugleich auch mit jenen natur- und volksbezogenen Auffassungen verbinden, die wissenschaftlich in der Volkskunde (Brückner 1983; Emmerich 1971; Roth 1992) und gesellschaftlich in der Jugendbewegung ihren breiten Ausdruck fanden, bevor sie von der NS-Ideologie vereinnahmt wurden. Ihr Empirie- und Gegenstandsverständnis machte es vielen Anhängern von W & S leicht, sich mit dem national-sozialistischen System zu arrangieren oder aktiv in ihm mitzuarbeiten.

4.4. Multimedialität

Das Programm von W & S implizierte neue Bereiche der Perzeption und Repräsentation. Neben dem Ohr wurde das auf die 'Sachen' gerichtete Auge zu einem zentralen Organ der kulturwissenschaftlich ausgerichteten Sprachwissenschaft. Abbildungen der behandelten Sachen waren für den onomasiologisch-ganzheitlichen Ansatz W & S von zentralem Interesse. Als augenfälliges Merkmal dienten sie der Distinktion nach außen gegenüber wort- und buchorientierten Ansätzen; nach innen hatten sie durch die Übernahme einer gemeinsamen Form sprachwissenschaftlicher Praxis eine Integrationsfunktion. Der Streit zwischen Schuchardt und Meringer zeigt deutlich, daß die Verwendung von Abbildungen als Markenzeichen der Richtung und der Zeitschrift galt, die neben den schon in der Sprachgeographie üblichen Karten, neben Zeichnungen und schematischen Darstellungen (Aufrisse, Ausschnitte, Skizzen) gerade auch Photographien brachte. Daß dies in einer sprachwissenschaftlichen Zeitschrift erst gut 65 Jahre nach Erfindung der Photographie geschah, lag an der Entwicklung der Phototechnik. Da sie die praktische Umsetzung des Konzepts von W & S ermöglichte, trug sie wesentlich zu dessen Herausbildung bei. Die Nutzung von Photographien zu sprach- und wissenschaftlichen Zwecken war technisch möglich geworden, nachdem sich in den achtziger Jahren mit der Erfindung von Trockenplattenverfahren und Rollfilm Größe und Gewicht der photographischen Ausrüstung soweit verringert hatten, daß Transport und Bedienung von Kameras auch für Laiennutzer bei der sprach- und sachwissenschaftlichen Feldarbeit weitgehend unproblematisch geworden waren (Lederbogen 1989; Settekorn 1993). Denn die Bezahlung geeigneter Berufsphotographen für die Datenerhebung hätte größere Forschungsbudgets der interessierten Sprachwissenschaftler erfordert. Wissenschaftspolitisch hatte die Nutzung von Photos einen doppelt symbolischen Wert: neben dem hohen Maß an Authentizität des Darstellungsverfahrens wiesen sie auf die Aktualität der Arbeiten und Modernität ihrer Verfasser hin. So kann der multimediale Zugriff von W & S für die Zeitverhältnisse als in hohem Maß technisch fortschrittlich gelten.

4.5. Methoden der Sachforschung

Der Einsatz neuer Techniken der Erhebung, Verarbeitung und Präsentation sprach- und sachkundlicher Daten erforderte eine eigene methodische Reflexion darüber, welche Mittel unter welchen Bedingungen wie einzusetzen seien. In Teilen übernahmen die Vertreter von W & S Vorgehensweisen der Sprachgeographie, wenn auch über die jeweilige Form von Fragebüchern und die Auswahl von Meßpunkten in jedem Fall einzeln zu entscheiden war (Scheuermeier 1926). Dagegen mußte auf die Frage nach dem Einsatz von Photoapparat und Zeichnung sowie für die Kombination von Bild- und Sprachdaten eine eigene Antwort gefunden werden. In seinem Beitrag *Methoden der Sachforschung* spricht Scheuermeier (1936) die Möglichkeiten und Methoden einer multimedial konzipierten Sachforschung bei der Erörterung einer am Prinzip W & S orientierten Feldforschung geradezu mustergültig an. Daß es sich dabei um einen Vortrag vor den Mitarbeitern des *Atlas der deutschen Volkskunde* handelt, weist auf das Interesse deutscher Volkskundler an den Vorgehensweisen ihrer schweizerischen wort- und sachkundlichen Kollegen und auf grenzüberschreitende gemeinsame Fragestellungen hin. Scheuermeier hatte als Explorator im Dienste des AIS einschlägige Erfahrungen gesammelt. In der programmatischen Schrift *Der Sprachatlas als Forschungsinstrument* hatten Jaberg & Jud (1928) "die wissenschaftliche Einstellung, die unserer Arbeit zugrunde liegt" (Scheuermeier 1936: 334) dargestellt (vgl. Iordan 1962: 252 ff., 289 ff.; Goebl 1992: 260 ff.). Mit der Dominanz des Wortschatzes vor der Phonetik, dem gezielten Einbezug von Photographien und Zeichnungen sowie mit der onomasiologischen Strukturierung von Fragebüchern und Karten kam der kulturwissenschaftlich geprägte Ansatz dieses Atlasses zum Ausdruck, der mit seiner Konzeption spezifische Anforderungen an die sach- und sprachgeographische Datenerhebung stellte. Diese Tätigkeit erforderte "die nötige physische Widerstandskraft" (Iordan 1962: 290) der Exploratoren sowie deren Fähigkeit, sich bei der Befragung sympathetisch auf die ländliche Bevölkerung einzustellen. Nicht selten wurde dies mit der ländlichen Herkunft von Exploratoren begründet. Zur möglichst repräsentativen Datenerhebung (Scheuermeier 1926) mußte eine hinreichend dichte Zahl von Meßpunkten abgearbeitet werden. Besonders bei weit auseinander liegenden und abgelegenen Orten in schwer zugänglichen Regionen brachte dies beschwerliche Wege mit sich. Scheuermeiers Bedauern darüber, daß er bei seiner sachkundlichen Feldarbeit kein Automobil zur Verfügung hatte und auf die Benutzung öffentlicher Verkehrsmittel angewiesen war, verweist auf die ökonomischen und materiellen Grenzen des groß angelegten Unternehmens. Die von ihm und den beiden anderen Exploratoren — G. Rohlfs in Süditalien und M. L. Wagner auf Sardinien (Wagner 1921) — praktizierte Feldforschung war in großen Teilen auch körperliche Aneignung des Gegenstandes, die mit dem gezielten Einsatz der auch im Wortsinn gewichtigen methodischen und technischen Instrumente einherging. Die Rede von den 'Wanderromanisten' gibt damit ein gutes Stück Forschungsrealität wieder.

Die einheitlich onomasiologisch aufgebauten Fragebücher sicherten die einheitliche Befragung nach den Bereichen des materiellen und geistigen Lebens der Befragten. Die Photographien sollten sowohl ganzheitliche Szenen als auch Details und Zusammenstellung ausgewählter Geräte und Gegenstände und Arbeitsvorgänge veranschaulichen, während die Zeichnungen die Darstellung von Perspektiven, Schnitten und solche Einblicke erlaubten, die sich der photographischen Erfassung verwehrten. Die Sprachaufnahmen sollten möglichst naturgetreu in phonetischer Umschrift wiedergegeben werden, um Aussprachevarianten mit höchster Genauigkeit zu erfassen. Den Bildern wurde eine Legende mit den am jeweiligen Ort üblichen Benennungen der dargestellten Gegenstände beigegeben. Die Auswahl und Verarbeitung der vor Ort von den Exploratoren gesammelten Daten zu den Karten des Atlas erfolgten an zentralem Ort in der Schweiz, wobei die Trennung zwischen der Feldarbeit und der Auswertung, wie schon im Fall von Edmont und Gilliéron bei der Erarbeitung des ALF, weitgehend der von Hand- und Kopfarbeit mit den entsprechenden Bewertungen entsprach. Diese Sicht klingt bei Iordan dort an, wo er es für Scheuermeier — bezeichnenderweise in einer Anmerkung — angebracht hält,

"einige Arbeiten dieses Forschers zu erwähnen, der, indem er sich die Konzeption der Initiatoren des AIS aneignete, die Wörter mit den Sachen studiert oder, anders gesagt, zugleich Sprachgeschichte und Geschichte der materiellen Kultur betreibt." (Iordan 1962: 291)

Der umfassenden, methodisch differenzierten und wohlbedachten wort- und sachkundlichen Datenerhebung wurde der Status einer unabdingbaren Vorarbeit zugesprochen. Nicht weniger, aber auch nicht mehr. Angesichts der allein in diesem Bereich zu bewältigenden Probleme mag es verständlich erscheinen, daß man der Sachforschung ein um so größeres Gewicht beilegte, als die zunehmende Industrialisierung das schnelle Verschwinden althergebrachter Gegenstände und sozialer Praktiken und der entsprechenden Terminologie nach sich zog. In der Schweiz wurde diese Arbeit mit dem AIS und den beiden großen Publikationen von Scheuermeier zielstrebig zu einem gut dokumentierten einheitlichen Ergebnis geführt. Doch war es auch bei der von Scheuermeier präsentierten methodischen Ausdifferenzierung gerade die Konzentration auf die materiellen, in Wort und Bild erfaßbaren Sachen, die innerhalb von W & S zu einer methodischen Neuorientierung und zu einem gewandelten Gegenstandsverständnis führte.

4.6. Methodische Umorientierungen

In der zweiten Hälfte der zwanziger Jahre verstärkten sich Ansätze zu konzeptionellen Umorientierungen, die schließlich mit der Einrichtung der Neuen Folge von *WuS* auch in der formalen wie inhaltlichen Umgestaltung der Zeitschrift ihren Ausdruck fanden. Dieser Wandel ging mit Veränderungen in der Herausgeberschaft einher. Er setzte ein, als 1926 Hermann Güntert (1886—1948) Mitherausgeber wurde, und er verstärkte sich nach dem Tod der beiden einflußreichen Herausgeber. Meringer († 1931) und Meyer-Lübke († 1936). Die Einbeziehung Günterts sollte die Verbindung zwischen "sprachlicher und allgemeiner kultureller Entwicklung" (*WuS* 9: iii) stärken, denn die anfänglich dominierende Orientierung auf materielle Sachen stieß bei der Untersuchung solcher Erscheinungen des geistigen und gesellschaftlichen Lebens (Brauchtum, Recht, Sitte etc.) auf Schwierigkeiten, die weder konkret faßbar noch direkt abbildbar waren. Anders als Meringer vertrat Güntert einen auf die "Sachen des Geistigen" (Weisgerber 1974: 354), auf Vorstellungen und Ideen gerichteten Sachbegriff.

Mit Leo Weisgerber (1899—1984) wurde 1933 ein Vertreter der jüngeren Generation allgemeiner Sprachwissenschaftler Mitherausgeber, der in mehreren Beiträgen (Weisgerber 1929; 1932; 1933; 1934; 1974; Nerlich 1992: 116 ff.) für einen weitreichenden inhaltlichen und konzeptionellen Wandel von *WuS* plädierte. Schon 1929 und 1932 hatte er in *WuS* mit dem Hinweis, daß der vereinfachte unilaterale Zeichenbegriff aufzugeben und die Begriffsebene in die Sprachbetrachtung einzubeziehen sei, eine grundlegende Kritik am onomasiologischen Ansatz formuliert. Er vertiefte sie an gleicher Stelle mit dem in zwei Teilen 1933 und 1934 erschienenen langen Beitrag *Die Stellung der Sprache im Aufbau der Gesamtkultur*. Weisgerber orientierte sich an W. v. Humboldt, für den das Wort "nicht Abdruck des Gegenstandes an sich, sondern des von diesem in der Seele erzeugten Bildes" (Humboldt 1883/84: 287) war, und er plädierte für eine Begriffslehre, um Probleme und Schwierigkeiten des semasiologischen (Bedeutungslehre) und des onomasiologischen (Bezeichnungslehre) Zugriffs zu überwinden. Da Weisgerber auch sprachpsychologische Aspekte einbezog, setzte er jene von Meringer schon in den Arbeiten zur Sprachproduktion hergestellten Kontakte zwischen Sprachwissenschaft und Psychologie (Maas 1988) fort, weshalb er auch ausdrücklich als geeigneter Mitherausgeber begrüßt wurde. Weisgerber betonte rückblickend, daß W & S die Konzept- und Begriffsebene ausgeblendet habe. Deren Hervorhebung führte zu einem sozial und kulturell geprägten Sprachbegriff, der einen engen Bezug zwischen Sprache und Weltsicht herstellte. Weisgerber ging unter Anschluß an das, "was sich seit 1916 weltweit als Vermächtnis von F. de Saussure Beachtung verschaffte", um

"das Hinzugewinnen der geistigen Sprachseite für die übermäßig lautbezogene Forschung, mit dem notwendig verbunden war die Aufwertung der allzusehr von der geschichtlichen Methode überdeckten beschreibenden Sprachbetrachtung." (Weisgerber 1974: 354)

Neben Weisgerber wandten sich Jost Trier und Walter Porzig der Sprachinhaltsforschung zu.

5. Umsetzung des Konzepts

Die Gründung der Zeitschrift war für die Entwicklung der Richtung von entscheidender Bedeutung, da sie Vertretern unterschiedlicher Disziplinen eine Publikationsmöglichkeit bot (Lochner von Hüttenbach 1992). Die Auswahl der Beiträge läßt deutlich die Handschrift Meringers als Hauptherausgeber und die des angesehenen Romanisten Meyer-Lübke erkennen. Gleich im ersten Heft haben beide mit exemplarischen Aufsätzen der Zeitschrift ihre spezifische Richtung gewiesen und sie in späteren Beiträgen bekräftigt. Dies gilt vor allem für Meringer, der neben seinem programmatischen Aufsatz "Zur Aufgabe und zum Namen unserer Zeitschrift" (*WuS* 3: 22—56) 14 größere und 12 kleinere Beiträge lieferte, während Meyer-Lübke mit 4 größeren und 10 kleineren Beiträgen vertreten war. Die anderen Herausgeber publizierten weitaus weniger in *WuS*: Mikkola war mit 3 kleineren, Much mit einem größeren und zwei kleineren, Murko mit 3 größeren Beiträgen vertreten. Dieses Verhältnis spiegelt ungefähr die Gewichtung der Wahl von Verfassern und Themen in der alten Folge wider. So standen in den ersten 18 Bänden der Zeitschrift neben zahlreichen volkskundlichen Arbeiten im sprachwissenschaftlichen Bereich vor allem indogermanistische, allgemein sprachwissenschaftliche und romanistische Beiträge im Vordergrund; slavistische und germanistische Arbeiten traten dagegen deutlich zurück (Lochner von Hüttenbach 1992; Moser 1992; Schmidt-Wiegand 1981). Einen Schwerpunkt bildeten auf Gegenstände der Sach- und Volkskultur bezogene diachrone wie diatopische Arbeiten mit mehr oder weniger reicher Illustration; so die des Meringer-Schülers von Geramb (Lochner von Hüttenbach 1976: 41) zu den *Feuerstätten des volkstümlichen Hauses in Österreich-Ungarn* (1912) oder zur *Kulturgeschichte der Rauchstuben* (1926). Andere Arbeiten, wie die von Bottiglioni (1914/15) versuchten, spezifische Arbeitsbereiche ganzheitlich in Wort und Bild in Entsprechung zu den Abläufen der untersuchten Tätigkeiten oder für einzelne Regionen zu dokumentieren. So Giese (1932) für Korsika (Ravis-Giordani 1992), Krüger (1927a) für *Die nordwestiberische Volkskultur* oder Wagner (1921) für Sardinien. Die Briefe des Verlegers an Meringer und Meyer-Lübke zeigen, welche Sorgfalt man nicht nur auf die Wahl der Autoren, sondern vor allem auch auf die Auswahl der Illustrationen richtete. Daneben wurden zahlreiche etymologische und sprachhistorische Einzelstudien publiziert. Nicht zuletzt finden sich immer wieder allgemeine und grundsätzliche Arbeiten zu unterschiedlichen theoretischen und methodischen Fragen der Volkskunde (Pessler 1912, 1933) oder der Sprachwissenschaft. Hierzu zählen Güntert *Zum heutigen Stand der Sprachforschung* (1929), Sperber *Sprachwissenschaft und Geistesgeschichte* (1929) sowie die Arbeiten von Weisgerber (1929; 1932; 1933; 1934); in der Neuen Folge zielten die Grundsatzbeiträge von Güntert (1938), Stegmann von Pritzwald (1938) oder Gläser (1939) auf eine in Theorie und Praxis dem

Nationalsozialismus angepaßte Sprachwissenschaft (Maas 1988; Simon 1985a, b). Insgesamt lassen besonders die Beiträge der ersten 18 Bände erkennen, daß die Herausgeber sich um ein relativ weites Spektrum nationaler und internationaler Mitarbeiter bemühten und dabei zugleich Beziehungen zu den zentralen Orten der an W & S orientierten Forschung pflegten.

6. Zentren und Schulen der Sachwortforschung

Die Zentren der überwiegend deutschsprachigen Sachwortforschung lagen in Österreich an der Universität Graz (Moser 1992), wo Schuchardt als Romanist und Meringer als Indogermanist arbeiteten. Meringer betrieb mit seiner Lehr- und Publikationstätigkeit sowie mit seinen Außenkontakten die Durchsetzung und Verbreitung der Methode W & S; unter seiner Federführung wurde die Zeitschrift zu einem europäischen Sammelbecken der Sachwortforschung (Lochner von Hüttenbach 1976; 1992). Des weiteren hat der seinerzeit einflußreiche Romanist Meyer-Lübke als Mitherausgeber der Zeitschrift zahlreiche romanistische Beiträge aufgenommen und damit der sachwortbezogenen Forschung zu romanischen Sprachen und Kulturen einen Weg geebnet. So hat Leo Spitzer dort zwischen 1912 und 1926 sieben kleinere, einen größeren (Spitzer 1912) sowie einen Gemeinschaftsbeitrag mit J. Jud (Jud & Spitzer 1914/15) veröffentlicht. Neben Jaberg (1926) und Jaberg & Jud (1926) waren die Mitarbeiter am schweizerischen Projekt durch M. L. Wagner (1910; 1914/15) vertreten, der 1921 in einem Beiheft von *WuS Das ländliche Leben Sardiniens im Spiegel der Sprache* und damit jenen Bereich behandelte, den er für den AIS explorierte. Mit Krüger (1927a) und Giese (1928; 1932 (— dazu: Ravis-Giordani 1992; Giese 1934) kamen Vertreter der Hamburger Schule zu Wort. Gleiches gilt für E. Richter (1929) sowie für Griera (1925) vor seiner Kritik an Meyer-Lübkes Buch zum Katalanischen (1925; vgl. Iordan 1962: 272—273). Schon diese Namen weisen auf einen ursprünglich breiteren romanistischen Bezug von *WuS* und auf Querverbindungen zu exponierten Vertretern der romanistischen Sachwortforschung hin (vgl. Quadri 1952; Georg 1973; Goebl 1992). Nach dem Tod von Meyer-Lübke und in der Neuen Folge schwächte sich diese Tendenz zusammen mit der inhaltlichen und politischen Neuorientierung deutlich ab.

Es kam hinzu, daß sich in der Schweiz an den Romanischen Seminaren der Universitäten Bern (Jaberg) und Zürich (Jud) und in Deutschland am Romanischen Seminar der Universität Hamburg (Giese, Krüger) unabhängige Zentren einer stark volks- und sachkundlich orientierten Forschung mit eigenen Projekten und Publikationsmöglichkeiten herausgebildet hatten. In Deutschland sind die rheinische kulturmorphologische Schule und die Arbeiten am *Atlas der deutschen Volkskunde* (Cox 1992; Schmidt-Wiegand 1992) allenfalls bedingt der Richtung von W & S zuzurechnen.

6.1. Sprachwissenschaft und Volkskunde in Graz

Angesichts der Auseinandersetzung zwischen Meringer und Schuchardt kann aus sprachwissenschaftlicher Sicht von einer einheitlichen Grazer Schule (Lochner von Hüttenbach 1992) nur dann die Rede sein, wenn man die örtliche und institutionelle Nähe der beiden Sprachwissenschaftler sowie die methodischen Übereinstimmungen und ihre gemeinsame Absetzung von den Junggrammatikern bedenkt. So dürften es auch Zeitgenossen wie Spitzer gesehen haben, denn für ihn ist in beider Sprachauffassung die "'Wörter und Sachen'-Forschung so fest verankert, daß der eine wie der andere Gelehrte der Richtung Gevatter stehen können" (Spitzer 1929: 370). Die konzeptionellen Unterschiede (4.1.) führten zwar zu methodischen Umorientierungen und zu einer starken Hinwendung zu der von Schuchardt betonten kognitiven Sprachdimension, doch vollzog sie sich im Innern und unter dem Namen der Richtung W & S. Unverkennbar ist auch, daß von den beiden Grazer Hauptfiguren viele unterschiedliche Anregungen ausgingen. Jedoch fehlte ein einheitliches, für Graz spezifisches Publikationsorgan. Denn zum einen publizierte Schuchardt gerade nicht in *WuS* und zum anderen war diese Zeitschrift mit ihrer Offenheit das wichtigste übergreifende Organ der ganzen Richtung mit ihren vielfältigen Überschneidungen von Volkskunde und Sprachwissenschaft. Aus volkskundlicher Sicht ist allerdings die Rede von einer Grazer Schule der Volkskunde angebracht, zu deren zentralen Personen der durch Meringer geförderte Gründer des *Steirischen Volkskundemuseums* von Geramb gehörte (Moser 1992).

Die beiden weiteren Zentren der Sachwortforschung waren dagegen personell und institutionell an romanische Universitätsseminare gebunden und hatten ein weitaus homogeneres Gegenstands- und Praxiskonzept. Durch Zahl und Gewicht ihrer Arbeiten stellen sie bei der Umsetzung der auf die Sachkultur konzentrierten Richtung von W & S zwei wichtige Stränge dar.

6.2. Das Schweizer Projekt des "Sprach- und Sachatlas Italiens und der Südschweiz" (AIS)

Der AIS ist ein eigenes schweizerisches Projekt. Seine Betreiber waren Karl Jaberg (1877–1958) und Jakob Jud (1882–1952). Sie haben nach eigenem Bekunden (Jaberg & Jud 1928: 4–5) schon in ihrer Studentenzeit an einen Atlas für Italien und die italienische Schweiz gedacht. Beide waren in ihrem sprachgeographischen Denken und Forschen stark von J. Gilliéron beeinflußt, den sie bei ihren Studienaufenthalten in Paris kennengelernt hatten. Aus dieser Zeit stammte auch die Freundschaft zu Max Leopold Wagner (1880–1962), dem späteren Explorator für den AIS. Wie er und die beiden anderen Exploratoren, Gerhard Rohlfs (1892–1986) und Paul Scheuermeier (1888–1973), hatten auch Jaberg und Jud auf Studien- und Forschungsreisen Einblick in die sprachliche und dialektale Situation unterschiedlicher Länder der Romania gewonnen.

Die Entstehungsgeschichte des AIS hat Karin Rautmann (1993) unter Einbezug der umfangreichen, unveröffentlichten Korrespondenz in einer Magisterarbeit detailliert nachgezeichnet. Dabei wird ersichtlich, daß das Projekt mit der sprachgeographischen Erfassung des italophonen Bereichs die räumliche Lücke schließen sollte zwischen den 1902–1910 publizierten neun Bänden des *Atlas linguistique de la France* (ALF) von Edmont und Gilliéron und dem von Griera konzipierten katalanischen Sprachatlas. Die Subskriptionseinladung zum AIS bekundet weiterreichende Ziele des neuen Atlasses, die eine starke konzeptionelle Nähe zur Methode W & S (vgl. 4.1.–4.5.) erkennen lassen:

"Dem Fortschritt der letzten Jahre folgend, will er nicht nur der Sprachwissenschaft, sondern in weitgehendem Masse auch der Sachgeschichte dienen. Geographen, Ethnographen, Folkloristen, Historikern, Prähistorikern und Archäologen will er in Wort und Bild Material liefern, die, heute noch als Relikte längst vergangener Kulturepochen erhalten, mit der gerade in Italien immer rascher fortschreitende Modernisierung des Lebens in kurzer Zeit verschwinden werden. Die noch lebenden sachlichen und sprachlichen Zeugen der Vergangenheit aufzurufen, bevor sie ganz verstummen, ist in dem Lande eine besonders dringende Aufgabe, das seine Sprache und seine Kultur einem grossen Teil des Abendlandes mitgeteilt hat." (Jaberg & Jud 1927)

Die Wahl des italienischen Bezugsbereichs (zunächst Gesamtitalien, dann nur Oberitalien, schließlich doch ganz Italien) hing ebenso wie die Frage, ob überhaupt und wenn ja, wieviele Exploratoren einsetzbar waren, von der Entwicklung der Finanzierungsquellen ab. Daß schließlich mit Rohlfs, Scheuermeier und Wagner drei ausgewiesene Sprachwissenschaftler die Sprach- und Sachaufnahmen durchführten, unterscheidet den AIS von seinem französischen Vorbild. Das zentrale sprachgeographische Arbeitsinstrument, das Fragebuch, erarbeiteten Jaberg und Jud mit viel Sorgfalt. Da der AIS als Teil eines umfassenden romanischen Sprachatlasses konzipiert war, wurde zur Vergleichbarkeit der einzelnen Sprachbereiche das Gilliéronsche Fragebuch partiell übernommen und den spezifischen Verhältnissen der Untersuchungsgebiete angepaßt. Bei Fragen nach Elementen der bäuerlichen Kultur griff man auf einschlägige Literatur wie Gilliéron & Mongin (1907) Meyer-Lübke (1909) und Schuchardt (1910) oder auf eigene Erfahrung vor Ort zurück. Dies brachte eine ganzheitliche Konzeption mit sich:

"Dann lag mir aber vor allem daran, sachlich mich recht einzuleben; mit dem Bauern, welcher ein einfacher, aber mit gutem natürlichen Verstande begabter Mann ist, kletterte ich im ganzen Haus herum, um alle Teile kennen zu lernen; er demonstrierte mir den ganzen Vorgang des Spinnens und Webens, er erklärte mir einlässlich die ganze Alpenwirtschaft, so dass ich nach 'Meringer' nun auch allmählich sachlich mit bilde." (Jud an Jaberg am 1. 7. 1907)

Auf diese Art wird die subjektive vorwissenschaftliche Erfahrung objektiviert und zur Grundlage wissenschaftlicher Arbeit; zugleich sollte die Beibehaltung der Probandenperspektive die Fragepraxis erleichtern. Die Dichte der Meßpunkte war in Norditalien höher als in Mittel-, Süditalien und Sizilien; dies lag nicht zuletzt daran, daß zwischenzeitlich die Einbeziehung des Südens in Frage gestellt wurde und Rohlfs als Explorator begrenzt zur Verfügung stand. Die Korrespondenz zum Projekt zeigt, daß die Aufnahmen auf Sardinien durch andere äußere Formen

(Witterung, Gesundheit des Explorators, Schwierigkeiten mit der Fremdenpolizei, politische Situation) erschwert wurden. Man bevorzugte Orte, deren Sprecher möglichst wenig von der Regional- oder Schriftsprache beeinflußt waren, aber "auch stark modernisierte Mundarten" (Jaberg & Jud 1928: 186) fanden Berücksichtigung, sofern sie für eine Region typisch waren. Die definitive Wahl trafen die Exploratoren an Ort und Stelle. Da pro Ort nur eine Gewährsperson befragt werden sollte, galt deren Auswahl eine um so größere Sorgfalt, als für die Sprach- und Sachaufnahmen jeweils drei Tage zu veranschlagen waren. Daß die Exploratoren des AIS nach Gehör transkribierten, obwohl zur Erhebungszeit bei Dialektarbeiten Tonaufnahmegeräte bekannt waren (Veken 1984), lag neben deren oft eingeschränkter Aufnahmequalität vor allem auch an ihrem Gewicht: denn Fragebuch, Photoausrüstung und persönliches Gepäck brachten den ohne Auto reisenden Dialektologen schon genügend Transportprobleme. Nach einer Reihe von Schwierigkeiten bei der Datenerhebung, der Finanzierung und der Suche nach einem geeigneten Verlag erschien 1928 der erste und 1940 der abschließende achte Band des AIS. Im Erscheinungsjahr des ersten Bandes gaben Jaberg und Jud mit *Der Sprachatlas als Forschungsinstrument. Kritische Grundlegung und Einführung in den Sprach- und Sachatlas Italiens und der Südschweiz* eine quasi offizielle Auskunft über Genese und Aufbau ihres gemeinsamen Hauptwerks. Im Gesamtaufbau und in der Anlage der einzelnen Karten folgt der AIS dem Prinzip von W & S. Seine 1705 Karten sind onomasiologisch nach den Begriffs- bzw. Sachgruppen der benutzten Fragebücher geordnet, damit "sich beim Durchblättern eines Bandes sofort ein Gesamtüberblick" (Jaberg & Jud 1928: 15) ergibt. Die einzelnen Atlasblätter enthalten das jeweilige Stichwort in italienischer, deutscher und französischer Sprache. Kernstück der Blätter sind die Karten mit den Angaben zur phonetischen Realisierung der an den 990 Meßpunkten üblichen Bezeichnungen für die jeweilige Sache, bzw. den jeweiligen Begriff. Bei Bedarf sind, teilweise auf eigenen Blättern, Zeichnungen der Gegenstände beigegeben. Am linken Blattrand finden sich ggf. Verweise auf verwandte Publikationen zum Stichwort sowie eine Legende mit Hinweisen auf Besonderheiten der Aufnahmesituation. Erst 1960, und damit nach dem Tod von Jaberg und Jud, findet deren Lebenswerk mit dem Erscheinen eines Index zum schnellen Finden eines gesuchten Wortes seinen endgültigen Abschluß. Eine vor allem sachkundliche Ergänzung liefert Scheuermeiers Arbeit *Bauernwerk in Italien* (1943; 1956), dessen Bände reich mit Photographien sowie mit Holzschnitten des eigens für diese Arbeit gewonnenen Malers Paul Boesch illustriert sind. Noch heute findet diese Arbeit Beachtung in der Volkskunde.

6.3. Die Hamburger Schule

Schon vor der Gründung der Universität Hamburg (1919) gab es seit 1911 am Hamburger Kolonialinstitut ein Romanisches Seminar mit Bernhard Schädel (1878−1926) als erstem Leiter. Er war mit seinen Arbeiten zum Katalanischen (1904; 1905; 1908; 1909) ein Gründervater der deutschen Katalanistik. Er hatte 1908 die *Société de Dialectologie Romane* und die *Revue de Dialectologie Romane* mit ihren Beiheften *Bulletin de Dialectologie Romane* ins Leben gerufen, von denen zwischen 1909 und 1914 je sechs Bände erschienen. Er praktizierte eine kultur- und landeskundlich orientierte Romanistik mit einer für die reichsdeutsche Romanistik außergewöhnlichen iberischen und ibero-amerikanischen Schwerpunktsetzung und pflegte enge Kontakte zu Vertretern von Wirtschaft, Handel und Politik. Während des Ersten Weltkriegs konnten Seminarmitglieder ihre landeskundlichen Fähigkeiten nachrichtendienstlich für das Außenministerium bei der Informationsauswertung über lateinamerikanische Staaten einsetzen (Settekorn 1990). So auch Fritz Krüger (1889−1974), der nach 1928 nach Schädels Tod als dessen Nachfolger zum Ordinarius ernannt worden war. Bis zur Amtsenthebung Walther Küchlers (1877−1953) zum Ende des Jahres 1933 teilte er sich die Leitung des Seminars (Settekorn 1991; 1992a) mit ihm. Er hatte sie danach bis zu seiner Entnazifizierung 1945 allein inne. Am Romanischen Seminar gab Fritz Krüger von 1928 bis 1944 die 16 Jahrgänge der Zeitschrift *Volkstum und Kultur der Romanen* (= *VKR*) heraus, bis 1934 mit Küchler als Mitherausgeber. *VKR* hatte die Zusatzreihe *Hamburger Studien zu Volkstum und Kultur der Romanen* mit 37 Bänden zwischen 1929 und 1945. Beide Titel benennen schlagwortartig das für die Hamburger Schule prägende kultur- und volkskundliche Programm. Es lieferte für zahlreiche unter Krügers Leitung angefertigte Dissertationen zu unterschiedlichen Regionen der Gallo- und Iberoromania eine ebenso einheitliche wie verläßliche Produktionslogik der ethnographischen und sachwortbezogenen Erfassung vorwiegend bäuerlicher Kulturen. Viele dieser Arbeiten wurden in den *Hamburger Studien* publiziert. Das sachlich Greifbare, bildhaft Erfaßbare (Deutschmann 1992b) stand dabei im Mittelpunkt der empirisch-ethnographischen Arbeit vor Ort. Krüger benennt sie 1914 im Titel seiner Arbeit *Studien zur Lautgeschichte westspanischer Mundarten auf Grund von Untersuchungen an Ort und Stelle*. Reisen, Wandern, die direkte Anschauung und das durch ein einheitliches Fragebuch geleitete Erfassen sprachlicher und sachlicher Daten vor Ort waren auch hier Methode des empirischen Arbeitens, dessen Ergebnisse man in Wort und Bild präsentierte: dazu gab es am Seminar einen eigenen Zeichner. Nach Fritz Krüger, der unter zahlreichen Arbeiten von 1935 bis 1939 die sechsbändige, vorwiegend volkskundliche Studie *Die Hochpyrenäen* und 1950 seine *Géographie des Traditions Populaires en France* publiziert hatte (vgl. *Homenaje a Fritz Krüger*; Moldenhauer 1959), war Wilhelm Giese (1895–1990) ein weiterer prominenter Vertreter der Hamburger Schule; von ihm stammen neben der Habilitationsschrift *Volkskundliches aus den Hochalpen des Dauphiné* (1932) zahlreiche Arbeiten zu Sprach- und Sachkultur – nicht nur – der Romania (vgl. Haarmann & Studemund 1971: 547–590). Giese, der im Zuge seiner zahlreichen wissenschaftlichen Reisen und Wanderungen eine große Sammlung eigener geo- und ethnographischer Photographien angefertigt hatte, sah sich, wie die meisten anderen Mitglieder der Hamburger Schule, dem Prinzip von W & S verpflichtet: neben den Wörtern sollten deren Referenzobjekten in ihrer Situierung und ihren Zusammenhängen durch Bilder anschaulich gemacht und auf diese Art vor ihrem Verschwinden dokumentiert werden.

Während sich die Forschungsarbeit auf das methodische orientierte, theoretisch aber wenig reflektierte Sammeln, Zusammenstellen und Aufbereiten von Sprach- und Sachdaten zu romanischen Volkskulturen konzentrierte und die Publikationen – anders als in *WuS* – keine massiven politischen Einschläge erkennen lassen, war die allgemeine politische wie die hochschulpolitische Praxis der Hauptvertreter der Hamburger Schule rechtskonservativ (Deutschmann 1992a; b) bis nationalsozialistisch; die Verbindungen des Hamburger Seminars zu den Diktaturen der iberischen Halbinsel funktionierten bestens (Settekorn 1991). Nach 1945 kam es im Zuge der Entnazifizierung zu Amtsenthebungen. Krüger bekam durch Vermittlung seines ehemaligen Schülers Dornheim ein Ordinariat an der Universität Mendoza (Argentinien), sein langjähriger Assistent Giese wurde nicht mehr am Romanischen Seminar angestellt, unterrichtete jedoch bald wieder im Bereich der Allgemeinen Sprachwissenschaft. Zwar setzten beide nach 1945 ihre Publikations- und Lehrtätigkeit fort, doch bedeuteten die Einstellung von *VKR* durch die britische Militärverwaltung und die Emigration Krügers de facto das Ende der Hamburger Schule.

Deren frankreichbezogene Arbeiten stießen Ende der achtziger Jahre deshalb auf das Interesse französischer Ethnographen, weil sie in der Tat Dokumente der französischen Volkskultur enthalten, über die die französische Ethnographie selbst nicht verfügt (Bromberger 1991). Die posthume Veröffentlichung der französischen Übersetzung (1991) von Gieses Habilitationsschrift (Giese 1932) weist darauf hin, daß einige der nach der Methode von W & S erstellten Arbeiten ihr selbstgesetztes ethnographisch-konservatorisches Ziel in der Tat erreichten. Gerade deshalb sind die fachgeschichtliche Rekonstruktion, Würdigung und Kritik sprachwissenschaftlicher Praktiken unter Einbezug ihrer politischen und ideologischen Implikationen erforderlich. Dabei sind auch interessante und faszinierende Neuentdeckungen zu machen, wie der in Vergessenheit geratene Aufsatz "Die katalanische Terminologie der Korkstopfenerzeugung" in der *Revue de Dialectologie Romane*, mit dem R. Marx (1915) das methodische Prinzip W & S geradezu vorbildlich umgesetzt hat. Seine umfassende sachliche, historische, sprachgeschichtliche und lexikologische Auseinandersetzung mit einem spezifischen, nach wie vor aktuellen Bereich landwirtschaftlicher Produktion erfüllt in seiner Anlage viele Bedingungen eines Expertensystems.

7. Ausblick

Neben der rein fachgeschichtlichen Rekonstruktion bietet die Auseinandersetzung mit W & S Anlaß zur Reflexion über zwei allgemeinere Bereiche: über die vernachlässigten und in ihrer grundlegenden Bedeutung meist verkannten körperlichen, materiellen, technischen und medialen Faktoren der Sprachwissenschaftsgeschichte (7.1.) sowie über Verbindungslinien zu aktuellen Positionen ganzheitlicher Semantiken (7.2.).

7.1. Körperlichkeit, Materialität und Medialität in der Geschichte der Sprachwissenschaft

Die Konzeption von Gegenstand, Methode und Praxis der Forschung war bei dem onomasiologischen, sachwortbezogenen Ansatz von W & S sehr stark an die Formen des empirischen Arbeitens und an deren technisch-mediale Mittel gebunden. Mit der für W & S spezifischen Form der Inkorporation des sachwortlichen Wissens entwickelte sich ein sprachwissenschaftlicher Habitus (Bourdieu 1970; 1980; 1984: 134−135), den man in der Auseinandersetzung mit konkurrierenden Schulen als authentisch, lebensnah und praxisbezogen verstanden wissen wollte. Der mit Fragebuch, Kamera und Zeichenstift ausgerüstete Sprachwissenschaftler wollte sich dezidiert vom Schreibtisch- und Bibliotheksgelehrten unterscheiden. Der rege, nur in Teilen veröffentlichte Briefwechsel, der die Erarbeitung des AIS begleitete (Rautmann 1993), zeigt deutlich, welch große Rolle die Körperlichkeit der Exploratoren und die materiellen, technischen wie medialen Bedingungen für sich und in Verbindung miteinander bei der empirischen Arbeit spielten. Zwar treten diese Aspekte bei W & S besonders deutlich zutage, doch ist zu vermuten, daß ihnen nicht nur in der Geschichte der Sprachwissenschaft (Gessinger 1994; Schlieben-Lange 1993; Settekorn 1993), sondern allgemein in der Wissenschaftsgeschichte eine bislang unterschätzte Rolle zukommt (Kauß 1990; Knorr-Cetina 1984; Kutschmann 1986; Shilling 1993). Es sind Faktoren, die wesentlich zur Konstitution des 'point de vue' und damit des sprachwissenschaftlichen Gegenstandes beitragen.

7.2. Vom Begriffssystem zu holistischen Semantiken

Bei Kriegsende mußten mit *WuS* und *VKR* zwei zentrale Publikationsorgane ihr Erscheinen einstellen und einige Sachwortforscher aus politischen Gründen ihre Universitätsstellen räumen. Gleichwohl gibt es neben der über das Kriegsende hin fortgesetzten, politisch nicht belasteten Arbeit der Schweizer am AIS die onomasiologisch orientierte Traditionslinie. Dabei handelt es sich zum einen um die Feldtheorie von J. Trier und die von Weisgerber und Porzig seit den vierziger Jahren entwickelten Ansätze zur Sprachinhalts- und Wortfeldforschung, die gut zwanzig Jahre später von Coseriu aufgegriffen wurden (vgl. Geckeler 1971: 131 ff.). Zum anderen lösten Hallig und v. Wartburg mit ihrem Vorschlag zu einem *Begriffssystem als Grundlage der Lexikographie* (1952) vor allem in der Romanistik eine rege Diskussion (vgl. Iordan 1962: 479 f.) um zeichentheoretische und semantische Grundbegriffe aus. Vor allem Baldinger (1960; 1964; 1966) und Heger (1964; 1966; 1968; 1971) trugen ihre eigenen theoretischen wie methodischen Überlegungen vor. Bei dieser Diskussion spielte es keine Rolle, daß das Begriffssystem von Hallig und Wartburg auf dem für die empirische Arbeit vorgesehenen Fragebuch des Romanischen Seminars der Universität Leipzig aufbaute. Somit geriet die fachgeschichtliche Einbettung dieses Vorschlags nicht in den Blick. Die ihm zugrunde liegende onomasiologische Orientierung tauchte jedoch im Verlauf der Diskussion in gewandelter Form wieder auf. So entwickelte Heger in mehreren Etappen schrittweise einen Ansatz, der bei allen Unterschieden konzeptionelle Ähnlichkeiten zu den kasustheoretischen Ansätzen (vgl. Dirven & Radden 1987) hatte, die Fillmore (1987) selbst in den holistischen Ansatz der Rahmentheorie (vgl. Müller 1984) überführte. Diese Entwicklung vollzog sich im Kontext einer semantischen Diskussion, die zusehends an der maschinellen Erfassung und Bearbeitung von strukturierten Wissensmengen (Settekorn 1971; Wettler 1980; Morik 1982) sowie an Fragen der Konzeptualisierung interessiert (vgl. Aitchison 1987) war. Für die in den achtziger Jahren hervortretende kognitive Wende war nach Gardner neben der Annahme mentaler Repräsentationen die Überzeugung konstitutiv, "daß der Elektronenrechner für unser Verständnis des menschlichen Denkens von zentraler Bedeutung ist" (Gardner 1989: 18). Auch hier zeigt sich, daß und auf welche Weise Orientierung an neuen technologischen Entwicklungen in die sprachwissenschaftliche Gegenstandsbildung eingeht. Bei dieser Entwicklung traten, wenn auch unter fortgeschrittenen theoretischen, methodischen und technologischen Voraussetzungen, Fragen nach der auf Erfahrung basierten Strukturierung und dem Inhalt der konzeptuellen Einheiten (Frame, Scene, Schema, Scenario) wieder auf. Im Titel des grundlegenden Artikels fragte Tannen (1979) *What's in a frame?*. Allerdings wurden die vorgeschlagenen Strukturierungen nun nicht wie bei Hallig und v. Wartburg auf ihre lexikologische Anwendbarkeit, sondern auf ihre Möglichkeit zur Modellierung von Verstehensprozessen oder ihre maschinelle Implementierung hin befragt.

Daß Kognition, sprachliche Konzeptualisierung und Wissen in hohem Maße kulturell (Lakoff 1987; Lakoff & Johnson 1980) beeinflußt sind und auf primär körperlicher Erfahrung basieren, kommt als Grundannahme der Schule von Berkeley im Titel des Buches von Johnson (1987) *The Body in the Mind: The bodily basis of meaning, imagination and reason* zum Ausdruck. Die Befassung mit W & S zeigt, daß dies auch für den fachgeschichtlichen Blick auf die Konzeption von Gegenstand, Theorie und Methoden der Sprachwissenschaft zutrifft und dabei zugleich die medialen und technischen Möglichkeiten sprachwissenschaftlichen Arbeitens eine zentrale Rolle spielen.

8. Bibliographie

Aitchison, Jean. 1987. *Words in the Mind: An introduction to the mental lexicon.* London: Blackwell.

Amirova, T[amara] A[leksandrovna] & B[oris] A[dreevič] Ol'xovikov & Ju[rij] V[ladimirovič] Roždestvenskij. 1980 [1975]. *Abriß der Geschichte der Linguistik.* Ins Deutsche übersetzt von Barbara Meier, hg. von Georg Friedrich Meier. Leipzig: VEB Bibliographisches Institut.

Baldinger, Kurt. 1960. "Alphabetisch oder begrifflich gegliedertes Wörterbuch?" *ZRPh* 76.521–536.

—. 1964. "Sémasiologie et onomasiologie". *Revue de linguistique romane* 28.249–272.

—. 1966. "Sémantique et structure conceptuelle (Le concept de 'se souvenir')". *Cahiers de Lexicologie* 8.1–46.

Baumann, Hans-Heinrich. 1970. "Sprachwissenschaft oder Sprachwesenschaft?". *Linguistische Berichte* 10.84–87.

Beckmann, Friedhelm. 1994. 'Von Opfern und Wendehälsen, Mitläufern und Widerständlern: Nochmals zur Romanistik der Jahre 1930 bis 1950". *Romanistische Zeitschrift für Literaturgeschichte* 18.219–239.

Beitl, Klaus. 1992. "Das Wort, die Sache, der Vergleich: Österreichische Beiträge zur Volkskunde von Frankreich". Beitl & Chiva 1992, 105–122.

— & Isac Chiva, Hg. 1992. *Wörter und Sachen: Österreichische und deutsche Beiträge zur Ethnographie und Dialektologie Frankreichs. Ein französisch-österreichisches Projekt.* Wien: Verlag d. österr. Akademie d. Wiss.

Bottiglioni, Gino. 1914/15. "Die Terminologie der Marmorindustrie in Carrara". *WuS* 6.89–115.

Bourdieu, Pierre. 1979. *La distinction: Critique sociale du jugement.* Paris: Les Éditions de Minuit.

—. 1980. *Le sens pratique.* Paris: Les Editions de Minuit.

—. 1984. *Questions de sociologie.* Paris: Les Editions de Minuit.

Brednich, Rolf W., Hg. 1988. *Grundriß der Volkskunde: Eine Einführung in die Forschungsrichtung der Europäischen Ethnologie.* Berlin: Reimer.

Bromberger, Christian. 1991. "Un demi-siècle après ... . Redécouvrir les travaux de l'école romaniste de Hambourg". Giese 1991.9–20.

Brückner, Wolfgang & Klaus Beitl, Hg. 1983. *Volkskunde als akademische Disziplin: Studien zur Institutionsbildung.* Wien: Verlag d. österr. Akademie d. Wiss.

Bünker, J. R. 1909. "Das Bauernhaus der Gegend von Köflach in Steiermark. Mit 47 Textabbildungen". *WuS* 1.121–162.

Carl Winter Universitätsverlag. 1954. *Verlagskatalog, 1822–1954.* Heidelberg: Winter.

Christmann, Hans Helmut & Frank-Rutger Hausmann, Hg. 1989. *Deutsche und österreichische Romanisten als Verfolgte des Nationalsozialismus.* Tübingen: Staufenberg.

Cox, Heinrich Leonard. 1992. "Möglichkeiten und Grenzen einer Wort- und Sachforschung auf Grund der Sammlungen des Atlas der deutschen Volkskunde". Beitl & Chiva 1992.227–248.

Deutschmann, Olaf. 1992a. "Fritz Krüger 1931–1945: Ein Aide-mémoire". Beitl & Chiva 1992. 167–172.

—. 1992b. "Bericht über die Hamburger Schule". Beitl & Chiva 1992.173–180.

Dirven, René & Günter Radden, Hg. 1987. *Concepts of Case.* Tübingen: Narr.

Emmerich, Wolfgang. 1971. *Zur Kritik der Volkstumsideologie.* Frankfurt/M.: Suhrkamp.

Fillmore, Charles J. 1987. "A Private History of the Concept 'Frame'". Dirven & Radden 1987. 28–36.

Fischer, Hans. 1981. *Die Hamburger Südsee-Expedition: Über Ethnographie und Kolonialismus.* Frankfurt/M.: Syndikat.

Gardner, Howard. 1989 [1985]. *Dem Denken auf der Spur: Der Weg der Kognitionswissenschaft.* Aus dem Amerikanischen von Ebba D. Drolshagen. Stuttgart: Klett-Cotta.

Geckeler, Horst. 1971. *Zur Wortfelddiskussion: Untersuchungen zur Gliederung des Wortfeldes 'alt–jung–neu' im heutigen Französisch.* München: Fink.

Geramb, Viktor R. von. 1912. "Die Feuerstätten des volkstümlichen Hauses in Österreich-Ungarn". *WuS* 3.1–22.

—. 1926. "Die Kulturgeschichte der Rauchstuben: Ein Beitrag zur Hausforschung". *WuS* 9.1–67.

Gessinger, Joachim. 1994. *Auge & Ohr: Studien zur Erforschung der Sprache am Menschen.* Berlin & New York: de Gruyter.

Giese, Wilhelm. 1928. "Über portugiesische Brunnen". *WuS* 11.109–145.

—. 1932. "Die volkstümliche Kultur des Niolo (Korsika)". *WuS* 14.65–73.

—. 1934. "Apulische Brunnenschöpfräder". *WuS* 14.90–92.

—. 1991 [1932]. *Mots et choses en haut-Dauphiné dans les années 30.* Traduit de l'allemand par Paul Aimès et Jean Courtois. Avec une présentation de Christian Bromberger. (= *Le monde alpin et rhodanien*, 3–4.) Grenoble: Centre alpin et rhodanien d'ethnologie.

Gilliéron, Jules & J. Mongin. 1907. *Étude de géographie linguistique: "Scier" dans la Gaule romane du sud et de l'est.* Paris: Champion.

Glässer, Edgar. 1939. "Sprachräume, Völkertümer und Nationalitätenpolitik: Ein grundsätzlicher Beitrag zur sprachwissenschaftlichen Volksforschung". *WuS* 20 (= N.F. 2).158–182.

Goebl, Hans. 1992. "Die Sprachatlanten der europäischen Romania". Beitl & Chiva 1992. 249–287.

Gorog, Ralph de. 1973. "Bibliographie des études de l'onomasiologie dans le domaine du français". *Revue de linguistique romane* 37.419–444.

Griera, Antoni. 1925. "Castellà-Català-Provençal: Observacions sobre el libre de W. Meyer-Lübke *Das Katalanische*". *ZRPh* 45.198–254.

Güntert, Hermann. 1929. "Zum heutigen Stand der Sprachwissenschaft". *WuS* 11.386–397.

—. 1938. "Neue Zeit – neues Ziel". *WuS* N.F. 19.1–11.

Haarmann, Harald & Michael Studemund, Hg. 1971. *Beiträge zur Romanistik und Allgemeinen Sprachwissenschaft: Festschrift Wilhelm Giese.* Hamburg: Buske.

Hahn, Edmund. 1911. "Wörter und Sachen". *Zeitschrift für Ethnologie*, Jg. 1911, Heft 1, 177–178; Heft 2, 376–379.

Hallig, Rudolf & Walther von Wartburg. 1952. *Begriffsystem als Grundlage für die Lexikographie. Versuch eines Ordnungsschemas.* Berlin: Akademie-Verlag.

—. 1954. "Zum Aufbau eines Ordnungsschemas für Wortschatzdarstellungen". *ZRPh* 80.249–256.

Hausmann, Frank-Rutger. 1991. "Vertriebene und Gebliebene: Ein Forschungsbericht der deutschsprachigen Romanistik von 1933–1945". *Romanistische Zeitschrift für Literaturgeschichte* 15.164–180.

—. 1993. *"Aus dem Reich der seelischen Hungersnot". Briefe und Dokumente zur Fachgeschichte der Romanistik im Dritten Reich.* Würzburg: Königshausen & Neumann.

Heger, Klaus. 1964. "Die methodologischen Voraussetzungen von Onomasiologie und begrifflicher Gliederung". *ZRPh* 80.486–516.

—. 1966. "Valenz, Diathese und Kasus". *ZRPh* 83. 138–170.

—. 1968. "Structures immanentes et structures conceptuelles". *Probleme der Semantik* hg. von W. Theodor Elwert, 17–24. Wiesbaden: Steiner.

—. 1971. *Monem, Wort und Satz.* Tübingen: Niemeyer.

Homenaje a Fritz Krüger. 2 Bde. Mendoza, Argentinien: Faculdad de Filosofia y Letras, Univ. Nacional de Cuyo, 1951, 1954.

Humboldt, Wilhelm von. 1883/84. *Die sprachphilosophischen Werke Wilhelm's von Humboldt.* Hg. von Heymann Steinthal. Berlin: Dümmler.

Hüpper-Dröge, Dagmar. 1983. *Schild und Speer: Waffen und ihre Bezeichnung im frühen Mittelalter.* Frankfurt/M., Bern & New York: Lang.

Iordan, Iorgu. 1962 [1932]. *Einführung in die Geschichte und Methoden der romanischen Sprachwissenschaft.* Ins Deutsche übertragen, ergänzt und teilweise neubearbeitet von Werner Bahner. Berlin: Akademie-Verlag.

Jaberg, Karl. 1926. "Zur Sach- und Bezeichnungsgeschichte der Beinbekleidung in der Zentralromania". *WuS* 9.137–172.

— & Jakob Jud. 1926. "Ein Sprach- und Sachatlas Italiens und der Südschweiz". *WuS* 9.126–129.

—. 1927. *Subskriptionseinladung: Sprach- und Sachatlas Italiens und der Südschweiz von K. Jaberg und J. Jud.* Die Mundartaufnahmen wurden durchgeführt von P. Scheuermeier, G. Rohlfs und M. L. Wagner. 8 Bände. Gedruckt mit Unterstützung der Gesellschaft für wissenschaftliche Forschung an der Universität Zürich und privater Freunde des Werkes von der Verlagsanstalt Ringier & Cie in Zofingen (Schweiz). Zofingen.

—. 1928. *Der Sprachatlas als Forschungsinstrument. Kritische Grundlegung und Einführung in den Sprach- und Sachatlas Italiens und der Südschweiz.* Halle/S.: Niemeyer. (Ital. Übersetzung, *L'atlante linguistico come strumento di ricerca: Fondamenti critici e introduzione*, Mailand, 1987.)

—. 1928–1940. *Sprach- und Sachatlas Italiens und der Südschweiz.* 8 Bde. Zofingen: Verlagsanstalt Ringier.

Januschek, Franz, Hg. 1985. *Politische Sprachwissenschaft: Zur Analyse von Sprache und Kultur als kultureller Praxis.* Opladen: Westdeutscher Verlag.

Johnson, Mark. 1987. *The Body in the Mind: The bodily basis of meaning, imagination, and reason.* Chicago & London: Univ. of Chicago Press.

Jud, Jakob. 1908. "Poutre: eine sprachgeographische Untersuchung". *Archiv für das Studium der neueren Sprachen* 120.72–95.

— & Spitzer, Leo. 1914/15. "Zur Lokalisierung des sogenannten Capitulare de villis". *WuS* 6.116–140.

Kater, Michael. 1974. *Das "Ahnenerbe" der SS 1935–1945: Ein Beitrag zur Kulturpolitik des Dritten Reichs.* Stuttgart: Deutsche Verlagsanstalt.

Klauß, Henning. 1990. *Zur Konstitution der Sinnlichkeit in der Wissenschaft. Eine soziologische Analyse der Wandlungen des Subjekt-Objekt-Verhältnisses.* Rheda-Wiedenbrück: Daedalus.

Knorr-Cetina, Karin. 1984. *Die Fabrikation der Erkenntnis: Zur Anthropologie der Naturwissenschaft.* Frankfurt/M.: Suhrkamp.

Krause, Eckart & Ludwig Huber & Holger Fischer, Hg. 1991. *Hochschulalltag im "Dritten Reich": Die Hamburger Universität 1933–1945.* 3 Bde. Berlin & Hamburg: Reimer.

Krüger, Fritz. 1927a. "Die nordwestiberische Volkskultur". *WuS* 10.45–137.

—. 1927b. "Volkskundliches aus der Provence: Das Museum Frederi Mistrals". *Philologische Studien: Karl Voretzsch zum 60. Geburtstag und zum Gedenken an seine erste akademische Berufung vor 35 Jahren* hg. von Bernhard Schädel & Werner Mulertt, 285–349. Halle: Niemeyer.

Kutschmann, Werner. 1986. *Der Naturwissenschaftler und sein Körper: Die Rolle der inneren Natur in der experimentellen Naturwissenschaft der frühen Neuzeit.* Frankfurt/M.: Suhrkamp.

Lakoff, George. 1987. *Women, Fire, and Dangerous Things: What categories reveal about the mind.* Chicago & London: Univ. of Chicago Press.

— & Mark Johnson. 1980. *Metaphors We Live By.* Chicago & London: Univ. of Chicago Press.

Lederbogen, Jan. 1989. "Technikgeschichte der Fotografie. Fotoausrüstungen und Fotografieranleitungen für Forschungsreisende". Theye 1989. 490–505.

Lochner von Hüttenbach, Fritz. 1976. *Das Fach vergleichende Sprachwissenschaft an der Universität Graz.* Graz: Universitätsverlag.

—. 1980. "Sachen und Wörter – Wörter und Sachen". *Hugo von Schuchardt (Gotha 1842 – Graz 1927): Schuchardt-Symposium 1977 in Graz. Vorträge und Aufsätze* hg. von Klaus Lichem & Hans-Joachim Simon, 159–169. Wien: Verlag d. österr. Akademie d. Wiss.

—. 1992. "Die Grazer Schule – Meringer und Schuchardt". Beitl & Chiva 1992.61–84.

Maas, Utz. 1988. "Die Entwicklung der deutschsprachigen Sprachwissenschaft von 1900 bis 1950 zwischen Professionalisierung und Politisierung". *Zeitschrift für Germanistische Linguistik* 16.253–290.

—. 1992. "Die vom Faschismus verdrängten Sprachwissenschaftler: Repräsentanten einer anderen Sprachwissenschaft?". *Die Künste und die Wissenschaften im Exil 1933–1945* hg. von Edith Böhme & Wolfgang Motzkau-Valeton, 551–621.

Marx, Rainer. 1915. "Die katalanische Terminologie der Korkstopfenerzeugung". *Revue de Dialectologie Romane* 6.1–80.

Meringer, Rudolf. 1904a. "Wörter und Sachen". *Indogermanische Forschungen* 16.101–196.

—. 1904b. Wörter und Sachen I. *Ibid.*, p. 191. [Zitat bei Iordan 1962: 87; cf. Schriftenverz. Meringers in *WuS* 14 (1932).

—. 1909a. "Die Werkzeuge der *pinsere*-Reihe und ihr Namen (Keule, Stampfe, Hammer, Anke) mit 35 Abbildungen". *WuS* 1.3–28.

—. 1909b. "Sprachlich-sachliche Probleme. Mit 40 Abbildungen". *WuS* 1.121–210.

—. 1911. "Zur Aufgabe und zum Namen unserer Zeitschrift". *WuS* 3.22–56.

—. 1921. "Die innere Sprache in der Erregung". *WuS* 7.50–80.

— & Karl Mayer. 1978 [1895]. *Versprechen und Verlesen: Eine psychologisch-linguistische Studie.* With a new introduction by Anne Cutler & David Fay. Amsterdam: Benjamins.

Meyer-Lübke, Wilhelm. 1909. "Zur Geschichte der Dreschgeräte. Mit 40 Abbildungen und einer Karte". *WuS* 1.211–244.

Moldenhauer, Gerardo. 1959. *Notice bibliographique et biographique.* (= *Biographies et Conférences*, 17.) Louvain: Centre International de Dialectologie près de l'Université Catholique de Louvain.

Morik, Katharina. 1982. *Überzeugungssysteme der künstlichen Intelligenz: Validierung vor dem Hintergrund linguistischer Theorien über implizite Annahmen.* Tübingen: Niemeyer.

Moser, Hans. 1992. "'Wörter und Sachen'. Die Geschichte der Sachen und die Grazer volkskundliche Schule". Beitl & Chiva 1992.85–104.

Müller, Claudia. 1991. *"Wörter und Sachen", eine sprachwissenschaftliche Methode und ihre Zeitschrift. Fachgeschichtliche Untersuchungen.* Wissenschaftliche Hausarbeit. Univ. Hamburg (unveröff.).

Müller, Klaus. 1984. *Rahmenanalyse des Dialogs. Aspekte des Sprachverstehens in Alltagssituationen.* Tübingen: Narr.

Nerlich, Brigitte. 1992. *Semantic Theories in Europe 1830–1930: From etymology to contextuality.* Amsterdam & Philadelphia: Benjamins.

Pessler, Wilhelm. 1912. "Ziele und Wege einer umfassenden deutschen Ethnographie". *WuS* 3.56–65.

—. 1933. "Deutsche Wortgeographie: Wesen und Werden, Wollen und Weg". *WuS* 15.1–80.

Quadri, Bruno. 1952. *Aufgaben und Methoden der onomasiologischen Forschung: Eine entwicklungsgeschichtliche Darstellung.* Bern: Francke.

Rautmann, Karin. 1993. *Die Entstehung des 'Sprach- und Sachatlas Italiens und der Südschweiz' (AIS): Ein Einblick in einen Forschungsprozeß.* Magisterarbeit, Univ. Hamburg (unveröff.).

Richter, Elise. 1928. "Hugo Schuchardt. 1842–1927". *Archiv für das Studium der Neueren Sprachen und Literaturen.* 83. Jg. 154.224–258.

Riehl, Wilhelm Heinrich. 1869. *Wanderbuch als zweiter Theil zu "Land und Leute".* (= *Naturgeschichte des Volkes als Grundlage einer deutschen Social-Politik,* 4.) Stuttgart: Cotta.

—. 1976. *Die bürgerliche Gesellschaft.* Herausgegeben und eingeleitet von Peter Steinbach. Frankfurt/M., Berlin & Wien: Ullstein.

Römer, Ruth. 1971. "Mit Mutter Sprache gegen die Nazis?". *Linguistische Berichte* 14.68–69.

—. 1985. *Sprachwissenschaft und Rassenideologie in Deutschland.* München: Fink.

Roth, Martin. 1992. "Volkskunde der 1920er und 1930er Jahre: Ideologiegeschichtliche Implikationen". Beitl & Chiva 1992.45–57.

Schädel, Bernhard. 1904. *Untersuchungen zur katalanischen Lautentwicklung.* Halle/S.: Erhard Karras.

—. 1905. *Mundartliches aus Mallorca.* Halle/S.: Rudolf Haupt.

—. 1908a. *Manual de fonètica catalana.* Cöthen: Otto Schulze.

—. 1908b. "La frontière entre le gascon et le catalan". *Romania* 37.140–156.

—. 1909. *Die katalanischen Pyrenäendialekte.* Cöthen: Otto Schulze.

Scheuermeier, Paul. 1926. "Im Dienste des Sprach- und Sachatlasses Italiens und der Südschweiz". *Festschrift Louis Gauchat,* 317–321. Aarau: Sauerländer.

—. 1936. "Methoden der Sachforschung: Zur sachlichen Materialsammlung für den Sprach- und Sachatlas Italiens und der Südschweiz". *Vox Romanica* 1.334–369.

—. 1943. *Bauernwerk in Italien, der italienischen und rätoromanischen Schweiz.* Vol. I: *Eine sprach- und sachkundliche Darstellung landwirtschaftlicher Arbeiten und Geräte.* Erlenbach & Zürich: Rentsch.

—. 1956. *Bauernwerk in Italien, der italienischen und rätoromanischen Schweiz.* Vol. II: *Eine sprach- und sachkundliche Darstellung häuslichen Lebens und ländlicher Geräte.* Bern: Stämpli.

Schlieben-Lange, Brigitte, Hg. 1993. *Materiale Bedingungen der Sprachwissenschaft.* Stuttgart: Klett.

Schmidt-Wiegand, Ruth. 1981. *Wörter und Sachen. Zur Bedeutung für die Frühmittelalterforschung.* Berlin & New York: de Gruyter.

—. 1992. "'Wörter und Sachen'. Forschungsrichtung – Forschungsinteresse – Forschungsaufgabe". Beitl & Civa 1992.21–44.

Schneider, Gisela. 1973. *Zum Begriff des Lautgesetzes in der Sprachwissenschaft seit den Junggrammatikern.* Tübingen: Narr.

Schuchardt, Hugo. 1905. "Zur Methodik der Wortgeschichte". *ZRPh* 38.316–325.

—. 1910. "Sachwortgeschichtliches über den Dreschflegel". *ZRPh* 34.257–294.

—. 1976 [1922]. *Hugo-Schuchardt-Brevier. Ein Vademecum der allgemeinen Sprachwissenschaft.* Zusammengestellt und eingeleitet von Leo Spitzer. Unveränderter reprografischer Nachdruck der 2., erweiterten Auflage, Halle 1928. Darmstadt: Wissenschaftliche Buchgesellschaft.

Settekorn, Wolfgang. 1971. "Akzeptabilität, Kontext und Konsituation". *Muttersprache* 81.209–223.

—. 1990. "Die frühe Hamburger Iberoromanistik und der Krieg". *Iberoamericana* 39.32–94.

—. 1991. "Romanistik an der Hamburger Universität: Untersuchungen zu ihrer Geschichte von 1933 bis 1945". Krause et al. Bd. II, 757–774.

—. 1992a. "Die Hamburger Schule: Wissenschaftliche und ideologische Implikationen: Beitl & Chiva 1992.139–166.

—. 1992b. "Theorie – Geschichte – Praxis: Skizze eines Resümees". Beitl & Chiva 1992.327–338.

—. 1993. "Das Auge und der Körper des Linguisten: Argumente für eine Medien-, Technik- und Sozialgeschichte (nicht nur) der Sprachwissenschaft". *Zeitschrift für Literaturwissenschaft und Linguistik* 90/91.195–234.

Shilling, Chris. 1993. *The Body and Social Theory.* London & New Delhi: Sage.

Simon, Gerd. 1979. *Sprachwissenschaft und politisches Engagement: Zur Problem- und Sozialgeschichte einiger sprachtheoretischer, sprachdidaktischer und sprachpflegerischer Ansätze in der Germanistik des 19. und 20. Jahrhunderts.* Weinheim & Basel: Belz.

—. 1982. "Zündschnur zum Sprengstoff: Leo Weisgerbers keltologische Forschungen und seine Tätigkeit als Zensuroffizier in Rennens während des 2. Weltkrieges". *Linguistische Berichte* 79.30–52.

—. 1985a. "Sprachwissenschaft im Dritten Reich: Ein erster Überblick". *Politische Sprachwissenschaft* hg. von Franz Januschek, 97–141. Opladen: Westdeutscher Verlag.

—. 1985b. "Die sprachsoziologische Abteilung der SS". *Sprachtheorie, Pragmatik, Interdisziplinäres. Akten des 19. Linguistischen Kolloquiums Vechta 1984* hg. von Wilfried Kürschner, Rüdiger Vogt & Sabine Siebert-Nemann, Bd. II, 375–396. Tübingen: Niemeyer.

Sperber, Hans. 1912. "Sprachwissenschaft und Geistesgeschichte". *WuS* 3.173–186.

Spitzer, Leo. 1912. "Die Namengebung bei neuen Kulturpflanzen im Französischen". *WuS* 6.122–165.

—, Hg. 1929. *Meisterwerke der romanischen Sprachwissenschaft.* Bd. I. München: Hueber.

Stegmann von Pritzwald, Kurt. 1938. "Sprachwissenschaftliche Minderheitenforschung: Ein Arbeitsplan und eine Statistik". *WuS* 19.52–71.

Steinbach, Peter. 1976. "Einleitung". Riehl 1976. 7–53.

Tannen, Deborah. 1979. "What's in a Frame? Surface evidence for underlying expectations". *New Directions in Discourse Processing* hg. von Roy O. Freedle, 137–182. Norwood, N. J.: Ablex.

Theye, Thomas. 1984. *Optische Trophäen: Vom Holzschnitt zum Foto-Album: Eine Bildgeschichte der Wilden. Einblicke in eine kannibalische Beziehung.* Reinbek: Rowohlt.

–, Hg. 1989. *Der geraubte Schatten: Die Photographie als ethnographisches Dokument. Eine Ausstellung des Münchener Stadtmuseums in Zusammenarbeit mit dem Haus der Kulturen der Welt.* München & Luzern: Bucher.

Veken, Cyril. 1984. "Le phonographe en terrain: La mission Brunot-Bruneau dans les Ardennes en 1912". *Recherches sur les français parlé* 6.45–71.

Vidos, Benedik Elemér. 1968. *Handbuch der romanischen Sprachwissenschaft.* München: Hueber.

Vossler, Karl. 1904. *Positivismus und Idealismus in der Sprachwissenschaft.* Heidelberg: Winter.

Wagner, Max Leopold. 1910. "Sardische Etymologien". *WuS* 2.241–244.

–. 1914/15. "Neusardisch *pinzus*". *WuS* 6.199–201.

–. 1920. "Die Beziehung zwischen Wort- und Sachforschung". *Germanisch-Romanische Monatsschrift* 8.45–58.

–. 1921. *Das ländliche Leben Sardiniens im Spiegel der Sprache.* (= *WuS*, Beiheft 4.) Heidelberg: Winter.

Weingart, Peter. 1976. *Wissensproduktion und soziale Struktur.* Frankfurt/M.: Suhrkamp.

Weisgerber, Leo. 1929. "Adjektivische und verbale Auffassungen der Gesichtsempfindungen". *WuS* 12.197–226.

–. 1932. "Weiteres über das Zusammenarbeiten von Sprachwissenschaft: Psychologie, Physiologie und Chemie an den Problemen der Sinnesempfindungen". *WuS* 14.99–106.

–. 1933. "Die Stellung der Sprache im Aufbau der Gesamtkultur". *WuS* 15.134–224.

–. 1934. "Die Stellung der Sprache im Aufbau der Gesamtkultur. Zweiter Teil". *WuS* 16.97–236.

–. 1970. "Muß die Linguistik die Sprachwissenschaft bekämpfen?". *Linguistische Berichte* 9.58–63.

–. 1971. "Von der Untheorisierbarkeit und der sprachlichen Kreativität des Menschen". *Muttersprache* 81.98–102.

–. 1974. "Treffpunkt Wort-Sachforschung". *Antiquitates Indogermanica: Gedenkschrift für Hermann Güntert* hg. von Manfred Mayrhofer, Wolfgang Meid, Bernfried Schlerath & Rüdiger Schmidt, 353–359. Innsbruck: Inst. für Sprachwissenschaft, Univ. Innsbruck.

Wettler, Manfred. 1980. *Sprache, Gedächtnis, Verstehen.* Berlin & New York: de Gruyter.

Wienold, Götz. 1970. "Weisgerber-Linguistik und Hochschulreform". *Linguistische Berichte* 10.81–83.

Wilbur, Terence H., Hg. 1977. *The Lautgesetz Controversy: A documentation.* Mit einer Einleitung des Hg. Amsterdam: Benjamins.

Zippelius, Adelhart. 1974. *Handbuch der europäischen Freilichtmuseen.* Köln: Rheinland-Verlag.

Wolfgang Settekorn, Hamburg (Deutschland)

193. The origin and development of the theory of the semantic field

1. Forerunners and founders
2. Jost Trier's concept of the semantic field
3. Alternatives to Trier's field theory
4. Georges Matoré (1908–197?)
5. Morpho-semantic field theory
6. Conclusion
7. Bibliography

1. Forerunners and founders

1.1. From Plato to Kant

The long and rich history of the principle of organic unity can be traced back at least to Plato and Aristotle, where the concept of organism was transferred from living beings and applied to various branches of aesthetics – primarily literary criticism and principles of literary composition (Orsini 1972). Aristotle's usage differs from modern usage in two respects. Firstly, 'organic unity' and 'mechanical unity' define each other as opposites and denote, respectively, elements of a whole which are intrinsically and extrinsically joined: "Organic as distinct from mechanical unity: not the homogeneous sameness of the sandheap, but unity combined with variety" (Butcher 1904: 192). Secondly, the root word of 'organic' being *órganon*, meaning "instrument", the derivative retains for Aristotle the primary meaning of "instrumental". It applied more frequently, therefore, to the parts of a body than to the whole, insofar as the parts were viewed as instruments or tools of the whole. While this usage was retained through the Middle Ages, the 18th century saw the emergence of the concept of organism which is still familiar today. This was the addition of the property of life, which has dominated the concept of organic unity ever since. The primary influence for this change can be ascribed to Kant and his classic definition of the teleology of the living organism as "one in which every part is reciprocally means and end" (Eucken 1913: 165–166).

1.2. Karl Christian Reisig (1792–1829)

It may be argued that the history of linguistic semantics in the 19th century begins with Reisig, whose posthumously published *Vorlesungen über lateinische Sprachwissenschaft* (1839) added to the two traditional divisions of philology (etymology and syntax) a third, which Reisig called 'Semasiologie' (*"semasiology"*) or 'Bedeutungslehre' (*"the doctrine of meaning"*). While there is no hint of theories of the semantic field as such in the *Vorlesungen*, the Semasiologie section of the work is the only one characterized by abstract and generalized observations on language, of the type that led to 20th-century linguistic semantics. Reisig was aware of the essential dynamism of language, the very quality, he argued, that necessitated the addition of Semasiologie as a distinct branch of philology. In this respect, the new direction in Reisig's approach to philology represents the impulses that would lead to the development of semantic field theory.

1.3. Friedrich Haase (1808–1867)

As the editor responsible for the posthumous publications of Reisig's *Vorlesungen*, Haase recognized both strengths and weaknesses in his teacher's work. While the innovativeness of Reisig's 'Semasiologie' was beyond question for Haase, he criticizes Reisig and many other scholars in whose work he perceives two dominant features. Each of these brings us back to the question of organicism and its development from antiquity to Hegel. In the first place, Haase notes, organic growth as a metaphor for the evolution of language pervades the work for the comparative grammarians. As Haase uses the metaphor himself from the early pages of his own *Vorlesungen* (the continuation of Reisig's work), it is not surprising that he minimizes his criticisms of the tradition to which it belongs. But for the second trend which he identifies, that of historical research 'contaminated' by philosophical speculation, Haase has harsh words. He charges, in essence, that the historical investigation of language declined as a result of a misguided application of Hegelian philosophy. Haase finds the influence of Kant equally insidious and pervasive in a series of philological works that include Reisig's *Vorlesungen*. In this respect, Haase views Reisig not as the beginning but as the end of a tradition. Discussing Gottfried Hermann's (1772–1848) *Abhandlung über Pleonasmus und Ellipsis*, Haase makes clear that his opposition to Hermann's Kantian position is in respect to its treatment of idioms and figures of speech as receiving their meaning in a negative way, that is, in 'opposition to law-governed usage' (Gesetzwidrigkeit). Kant is thus made the scapegoat (albeit indirectly) for Hermann's work insofar as it embodies the antithesis of 19th-century historical linguistics – but this does not imply any opposition to Kantian teleology (see 1.1.) – and there is, thus, no contradiction in assigning to both Kant and Haase a place in the history of the idea examined here.

1.4. Ferdinand Heerdegen (1845–1930)

Like Haase, Heerdegen was critical of Reisig's *Vorlesungen*, charging that it confuses meaning and stylistics (in spite of Reisig's preliminary remarks on semasiology that attempt to forestall such criticism), that it confuses meaning and syntax (in spite of Heerdegen's own excursions into the interpenetration of these two domains), and that it reveals nothing about the historical development of Latin. In respect to the latter, Heerdegen's criticism of Reisig, like those of Haase, is based in the perception that Reisig is not upholding the tradition of 19th-century historical linguistics. This is also the basis of Heerdegen's critical remarks regarding Reisig's 'synonymology', which focuses on complete word groups rather than on individual Latin words. Yet the paradox already noted above – Heerdegen proceeding to investigate the connection of semantics to syntax after having criticized Reisig for the same initiative – arises again, and in more pronounced fashion, in the matter of adhering to historical perspective. For although Heerdegen repeatedly emphasizes the distinction between change of meaning (Bedeutungswechsel), a historical process, and complex meaning at any stage in the development of a language (Bedeutungsumfang), he fails to establish any criteria for maintaining such a distinction.

Moreover, if, as Heerdegen implies, only change of meaning is a valid study, this view is at odds with the substantial speculation of a synchronic nature to be found in his own work. What came to be designated much later as the 'atomistic' view of word-meaning in 19th-century linguistics, while it is highly characteristic of Heerdegen's writings, is tempered by a perspective which foreshadows the 'field' view of meaning. In his conclusion, Heerdegen declares that Reising was not the founder of semantics but a precursor. In this respect, Heerdegen's judgement is at odds with that of Haase, who considered Reisig's work as the end of a tradition of philological exegesis, rather than as the beginning of a new tradition of linguistic theory. Overriding this contrast in the views of Haase and Heerdegen is the preoccupation of both scholars with the conventions of 19th-century historical linguistics. Their primary concern was to see the groundwork of semasiology laid by Reisig developed in a fashion which would be compatible with those conventions. Michel Bréal rose to this challenge.

1.5. Bréal (1832−1915) and Darmesteter (1846−1888)

When Bréal was at the height of his scholarly productivity, it was the *Junggrammatiker* and their discussion of phonetic laws which dominated linguistics, even to the extent of influencing developments in the emerging field of semantics. Yet it is Arsène Darmesteter, fourteen years Bréal's junior, whose work reflects the excesses of this influence in his indiscriminate adoption of neogrammarian and pre-neogrammarian assumptions. Darmesteter's work is laden with analogies, particularly to the natural sciences, and his dominant metaphor, evident in the title of his influential book (Darmesteter 1886; 1910), is the metaphor which Saussure would later criticize − that of the organism. Koerner (1975: 733) has suggested that whereas mechanistic models were used in 19th-century linguistics to classify data, the organic model served to explain data. This coincides with the view of Phillips (1970), who attributes the rise of the organic model to the explanatory inadequacy of mechanistic models. In fact, this notion of a mechanistic-classificational/organicist-explanatory dichotomy is, in some measure, substantiated from Darmesteter himself (1886: vii−viii). Darmesteter's analogies and metaphors lead him into error in the many instances where there is simply no basis for them. There is no valid sense, for example, in which the original meaning of a word can be compared to the origin of a species, nor an earlier meaning compared to parents. Yet Darmesteter does not use such metaphors without reflection. On the contrary, he speculates that the metaphor of organism for linguistic change dates from the time of the discovery of Sanskrit and the resulting shift away from the study of classical languages to that of modern languages. Darmesteter goes so far as to concede the ultimate banality of the organic metaphor, but he maintains that it is nonetheless accurate (1886: 3). The use of the organicist model in linguistics was not limited to the life and growth of languages but applied also to their decline and death. This is already evident in Haase (1874: 4) as well as in the organisation of Darmesteter's book, where the closing chapters deal with the 'death' of word-meaning. Far from abandoning organicism, Darmesteter extends it in his concluding chapter, thus depriving it of its descriptive force and debasing its explanatory value.

Reaction against such a state of affairs was inevitable and soon found its expression in Bréal's writings. The disjunction between Darmesteter and Bréal does not mark the end of organicism in linguistics but rather a turning point in the life of the idea. The well-known passage from Saussure's *Cours de linguistique générale*, outlining the distinction between *signification* and *valeur* with the example of *redouter, craindre, avoir peur*, and concluding "si *redouter* n'existait pas, tout son contenu irait à ses concurrents" (p. 160), is not so far removed from Darmesteter's 'cell' absorbing a neighboring one. But in Saussure, as in Bréal before him and in Trier and others after him, the expression of the principle of part-whole relations is no longer slavishly tied to the metaphor of organism. Bréal speaks of the emptiness of this metaphor, of how it has distracted linguists from seeking primary causes for language change. At the same time, it is Bréal who offers a succinct explanation of organicism as a reaction to the word-as-spirit view, which dominated an earlier generation of linguists (particularly in Germany), and which was in turn a reaction against the excesses of 17th-century rationalism (Bréal 1924 [1897]: 310−313). Bréal's opposition to organicism is less important in itself, less important even in demonstrating the contrast between his work and Darmesteter's, than in revealing its decisive role in ensuring the historical basis of his own method of semantic investigation (Bréal 1924 [1897]: 256). Bréal's two overriding objectives in elaborating his semantics, detectable already in his programmatic article of 1883, were to complete or complement the existing framework of philosophical investigation and to determine the laws governing change of meaning. In articulating these objectives, Bréal commits himself to a 'field' view of language — a statement of the part-whole relationship of linguistic elements free of underlying organicist implication. A synchronic and paradigmatic view are also already evident in his formulations:

"On considère trop les mots isolément: il est si aisé de prendre un mot à part et d'en retracer l'histoire, comme s'il n'avait pas été comprimé, mis en relief, légèrement nuancé ou tout à fait transformé par les autres mots du vocabulaire, au milieu desquels il se trouve placé et dont il ressent l'influence voisine ou lointaine." (Bréal 1883: 133)

1.6. Ferdinand de Saussure (1857−1913)

Stephen Ullmann's *Semantics* (1962: 238) identifies Saussure's treatment of associative relations in the lexicon (1972 [1916]: 170 ff.) with the first of three possible approaches to structural semantics: through individual words, semantic fields, and the lexicon as a whole. In fact, the three approaches are neither necessarily distinct from each other nor mutually incompatible, as Ullmann's presentation might lead a reader to believe. Thus, for example, the second of the four types of lexical relations outlined by Saussure, based solely on meaning that words share ("la seule analogie des signifiés"), is fundamentally akin to a semantic field. And Saussure's third series, where words are linked to each other by both meaning and form, anticipates, in rudimentary form, the concept of the morphosemantic field, to be discussed below. Notwithstanding these similarities, it is pertinent to recall that Saussure did not intend his remarks on associative relations as a contribution to semantics. The relevance of the *Cours* to semantic theory, the influence it exerted on scholars after Saussure, such as Jost Trier, is to be found principally in the elaboration of the duality *signification/valeur*. The *Cours* evokes the notion of value in defining the systematic nature of language: "La langue est un système dont tous les termes sont solidaires et où la valeur de l'un ne résulte que de la présence simultanée des autres" (1972 [1916]: 159). In the same section of the work, Saussure calls attention to the complementarity of *valeur* and *signification*, noting that it would be misleading to characterize a word as nothing more than sound linked to a concept:

"Le définir ainsi, ce serait l'isoler du système dont il fait partie; ce serait croire qu'on peut commencer par les termes et construire le système en en faisant la somme alors qu'au contraire c'est du tout solidaire qu'il faut partir pour obtenir par analyse les éléments qu'il renferme." (Saussure 1972 [1916]: 157)

Here is a passage which will find strong echoes in semantic field theory, particularly as developed by Jost Trier.

2. Jost Trier's concept of the semantic field

2.1. Background

During the 1930s, Jost Trier (1894−1970) developed his theory about conceptually related areas of the vocabulary. Though the impetus toward this type of study grew steadily among the scholars whose work we have already examined in these pages, it remains most commonly associated with Trier's name, and most frequently designated as 'semantic field theory'. However, as we shall see shortly, this designation fails to reflect the terminological distinction between lexical and conceptual fields which is fundamental in the work of Trier himself. In fact, the term 'field theory' migrated from physics to Gestalt psychology under the influence of Wolfgang Köhler, a physicist turned psychologist (Sturrock 1986: 38), and was probably first used in linguistics by Esais Tegnér (1843−1928) − cf. Öhman (1951: 73). Trier's scholarship has been subjected to much scrutiny and has gained both advocates and adversaries. Following World War II, his thought continued to exert a major influence on European linguists. Trier follows Gunther Ipsen in beginning with the basic premise that the words in a language's lexicon fall into meaning-groups which are totally independent of etymology. In what may be an oblique reference to Saussure (Trier 1932b: 418−419), he also emphasizes that the word groups which are the subject of his study are not 'chains of association'. Such chains, after all, form open-ended series (Saussure indicated this feature by an 'etc.' attached to each of them), whereas Trier will claim for the word groups of his study an internal structure analogous to a mosaic, with its component pieces interlocking perfectly (Trier 1932b: 419). Trier's writings on semantic fields spanned nearly four decades, from the publication of his first book (1931) to his final article on the theoretical aspects of semantics, just two years before his death (Trier 1968). Trier acknowledges his debt to Saussure for the notion of language as elements in opposition and to Wilhelm von Humboldt for the notion of language as a dynamic system (1931: 11 ff.). Humboldt presents the latter concept by way of the contrast between *ergon* (product) and *ernergeia* (active force). Language is comparable to *energeia*, in Humboldt's view, which Trier followed. As for Saussure, he provides Trier with two notions which are ultimately more important than the one Trier acknowledged, for they characterize the very essence of theory and method, as developed by Trier. This common ground between Saussure and Trier becomes clear from a comparison of the key passage from the *Cours* exemplifying the concept of *valeur* (1972 [1916]: 157, quoted in 1.6 above) and such key passages as Trier (1932a: 625). Clearly central for both Saussure and Trier are the two fundamental notions of commutual delimitation of content and analysis beginning with the whole and working toward its constituent parts. Together, these two notions provide the framework for Trier's comparative and contrastive studies of structures in the German lexicon at different periods. As noted previously, the field view of meaning was implicit or latent in the work of scholars as early as Haase and Heerdegen, but still largely undeveloped by the time of Bréal. While there is no mention or indication in Trier's published work that he detected the germ of the field theory in Haase or Heerdegen, it is nevertheless worthy of note that the latter discussed the semantic development of *Kunst* and conceptually related terms (Heerdegen 1890: 103) — precisely the semantic domain which Trier would study in his best-known work. Likewise, Bréal discussed *Kunst, List* (1924: 101) and *Witz, wizzen* (p. 114).

2.2. Theory and practice

The field theory developed by Trier recognizes what is often referred to in linguistics as the Sapir-Whorf Hypothesis — the principle that every language imposes its own arbitrary divisions on the continua of the physical world (1934a: 185). The semantic dimension of language is thus a structure of representative elements of reality which are necessary and sufficient to provide speakers with a coherent and comprehensive means of referring to that reality (Trier 1934b: 429). Despite the fact that such representation is selective with respect to what it designates ("dem Sein gegenüber ein Auswahlsystem" [ibid.]), and in this sense *discontinuous*, Trier stresses that the representational system of language as a whole is a *continuum*: "Es enthält keine Lücken und blinden Flecke" (ibid.). A second key feature of Trier's field theory is the distinction between conceptual and lexical fields. A lexical field comprises a given word and all its conceptually related terms. In conformity with his first principle of the continuity of language as a representational system, Trier asserts that a lexical field articulates the entire conceptual field, or area of thought. The dominant feature of a field is that its constituent words form an interdependent whole. As a dynamic system, the field is functional in the production of speech, and it can only function as a whole. This proves to be the case, according to Trier, even in the transitional states he examines, where certain usages are clearly in a state of flux (1934a: 183). Such are the most basic features of Trier's conception of linguistic fields; more specific details will be noted in 2.3. (infra). In Trier's view, semantic field theory offers the only useful and productive context for the study of word-content (1934b: 430). It provides an insight not afforded by other methods such as traditional etymology. Trier applies his method to the intellectual vocabulary of medieval German. Taking as his corpus the courtly poetry written around 1200 A. D., he compares its terms for the concept of 'knowing' with those for the same concept, a century later, in the work of the famous mystic and scholastic, Meister (Johannes) Eckhart (c. 1260–1327). This study reveals two distinct structures, organized along fundamentally different lines. In 1200 the key words of the semantic field are *kunst, list, wisheit*. A semantic opposition underpins the pair *kunst/list*, where *kunst* designates all courtly skills and attainments, and *list* refers to activities outside the courtly realm. The use of either word automatically entails social and ethical judgement. At the same time, *wisheit* is a hypernym, covering the meanings of both *kunst* and *list* and admissible as an alternative term for one or the other. But by 1300, the semantic field of 'knowing' had been restructured around the three key terms *kunst*, *wizzen*, and *wisheit*. As for *list*, the sense of "non-courtly skills" had been replaced by that of "trick" or "cunning" with negative connotations. With *list* displaced as a key term, the opposition between *kunst* and *list* inevitably disappeared as well. As for *wisheit*, it lost the status of hypernym it had held in 1200, remaining in use only in reference to religious and mystical experiences.

2.3. Critical reception of Trier's field theory

Harsh criticism of Trier has come from many quarters. Apresjan (1966: 46) denied any innovativeness in Trier's work, charging that the methods by which Trier sought to verify his field hypothesis were outdated, that Trier's method is completely intuitive, non-structural, speculative, and devoid of formal criteria. Similarly, Miller (1968) concludes that Trier's methodology rests on nothing more than intuition, and that the semantic fields identified by Trier are established on a logical basis, rather than on any inherent features of the linguistic data. Miller adds that Trier depends on the techniques of philology, introspection, and *Sprachgefühl*. These are the outdated methods allued to by Apresjan. The criticisms of both Apresjan and Miller hinge on the absence in Trier's work of the formal linguistic procedures which characterize methodologies developed in linguistics after the period to which Trier's earliest writing belong – most notably in componential analysis. Among other critics, Hans Schwarz (1959) charges that Trier's study is completely devoid of method. Behind such adverse criticism there is at least one common error, illustrated by Spence (1961: 92), who reads Trier as contending that "the single word gets its meaning only in distinguishing itself from its field neighbours". Many critics have interpreted Trier in the same way and then proceeded to dispute the point (*inter alia* Oksaar 1958: 14). But, in fact, Trier does not maintain that the meaning of a term is established exclusively by commutual delimination, for he is as mindful as Saussure of the *signification/valeur* duality. The semantic field determines the exact extension of a word relative to other words (*valeur*), but the word can be used meaningfully without a knowledge of all its conceptual cogantes (Trier 1932a: 625). It is reasonable to assume that in some cases, perhaps most, a speaker will know only partial fields. This notion is not incompatible with Trier's view as stated elsewhere (1932b: 417).

2.4. The connection with componential analysis

Goodenough (1956) was the first publication to formalize a method of semantic investigation under the same of 'componential analysis', but well-known works of earlier date anticipate such procedures. These include Jakobson (1936), Harris (1948), and Lotz (1949). Bendix (1966: 15) traces the thread from Saussure through the work of the field theorists to Goodenough. Weinreich (1963: 152–153) views the development from Wilhelm von Humboldt to Goodenough as continuous. The objective in componential analysis is to describe the relations among the lexical items taken as data. Moreover, statements about related lexical items, in terms of their inclusion or exclusion with respect to a set of analytical semantic features, are considered preferable to an item-by-item characterization of meaning. Lehrer (1974: 46) notes that componential analysis *presupposes* aspects of semantic field theory but also emphasizes (66 ff.) fundamental differences between the two methods. In the first place, componential analysis subdivides word meanings in order to discover relations among words, whereas in the case of Trier's semantic fields, subdivisions are not part of the analysis but assumed to be inherent in the language. The results of the discovery procedure of componential analysis are sometimes said to fill 'semantic space', a metaphor implying a three-dimensional reality. By contrast, Trier's mosaic metaphor conceives of semantic space as two-dimensional. Such statements do not describe the results of the study, as in componential analysis, but rather a preliminary supposition about the nature of the semantic field. Moreover, complete delimination within a field and distinct limits for a field are assumptions on Trier's part; in componential analysis the indeterminacy of a field's limits are recognized. The componential analyst opts between adding dimensions to the analytic framework, in order to expand the semantic field under study, and eliminating dimensions, in order to discriminate the maximum number of terms by a minimum number of components of meaning. As a result of this choice, the semantic space under study may have open areas in its semantic representation, comparable to the gaps in the distinctive feature matrix of a phonological system. In phonology, this is the case because no language utilizes all the combinations made possible by the matrix; in semantic analysis, depending on the lexical domain under analysis, every possible combination in the feature matrix may also be logically possible. If so, there will be no gaps in the semantic space. One such example occurs in McKaughan's (1959) analysis of the Maranao pronoun system. In other instances, such as Bendix's (1966) analysis of a set of English verbs, some features are irrelevant to some lexemes of the data, with the result that there are empty areas in the semantic space. Though both componential analysis and Trier's approach to semantic fields work from the field as a whole to its parts, it is only the former which incorporates a procedure for verifying the validity of its results.

In componential analysis, the whole of a field is initially tentative, as is the selection of the individual lexical items comprising it. A set of shared component features of meaning then determines whether or not all and only those items which properly belong together have been selected. Conversely, the coherence of the data provides a measure of the suitability of the features of meaning used for the analysis. By contrast, in Trier's work, the methodology includes no self-checking mechanism, in spite of Trier's apparent claim to the contrary: "Das Feld ist uns immer etwas, was über sich hinausweist" (1934b: 449). Trier's semantic fields are arbitrarily established but presented as though they represent fixed groupings determined by the language itself. Trier's field method does not discover anything, it merely arranges data. In the absence of components of meaning below the level of the word, it is impossible to make any discoveries. Data and analytic features provide mutually functioning checks in componential analysis, but the arbitrary whole and arbitrary parts of Trier's field method cannot.

3. Alternatives to Trier's field theory

The theoretical and methodological aspects of Trier's approach to semantic fields is distinct from those of his contemporaries. He was aware of this and called attention to it in his writings, which frequently offer critical commentary on the work of other scholars such as Ipsen, Porzig, von Wartburg, and Weisgerber.

3.1. Gunther Ipsen (1899–1984)

Despite some similarity between Ipsen's (1932) conception of linguistic fields and Trier's view, Trier does not consider himself a disciple of Ipsen, for the latter never articulated the claim, so important to Trier, that lexical fields delimit the entire vocabulary: "In den Feldern ergliedern sich die Worte, aber die Felder selbst ergliedern sich – nach Ipsen –nicht mehr aus übergeordneten Grössen, sondern liegen frei, nicht lückenlos aneinandergrenzend, an bevorzugten Stellen des Wortganzen" (Trier 1934a: 443). Furthermore, Ipsen's view evolved over the years, and he ultimately adopted a position which Trier found unacceptable. Ipsen's later theory based semantic fields on formal features as well as conceptual relation. For example, in Indo-European the names for the metals were acquired by borrowing; since the oldest of these was neuter, all subsequent borrowing within this semantic field were made neuter. They arranged themselves as attributes around a nucleus word until finally they were regarded as colour adjectives and accordingly became altered as to sound (Öhman 1953: 125). Trier thought that this type of field concept would be of use only in studying remote periods of Indo-European. Moreover, as Ipsen's methodological innovation can only be applied to words exhibiting both formal and semantic similarity, Trier considered it doubtful that much suitable material would ever be found for such a study. Trier's method, imposing fewer restrictions on its subject matter, is applicable to any period or culture from which written texts are available.

3.2. Walter Porzig (1895–1961)

In reviewing Porzig's work, Trier concedes that words which can occur in a given context may legitimately be designated and treated as areas of the lexicon, even when, unlike the terms *kunst*, *list*, *wisheit*, etc. of his own study, they are not unified by a single, inherent element of meaning. But he objects to Porzig calling such word groups 'semantic fields'. The notion of total delimitation of the lexicon, i.e., that of the entire lexicon subdividing into fields, a fundamental component of Trier's field theory, is missing from Porzig's semantic analysis, as it was also from Ipsen's. Trier condemned the work of both scholars as a failure, because they imply discontinuity of the linguistic universe (Trier 1934a: 198). Trier's criticism appears not to have influenced Porzig, for even twenty years later his goals and procedures remain substantially the same.

3.3. Walther von Wartburg (1888–1971)

Trier attempts to demonstrate the relevance of field structure for von Wartburg's work. His point of departure is the example, first introduced by Gilliéron, of the development of Classical Latin *gallus* ("rooster") and Vulgar Latin *cattus* ("cat"). (As Latin crystallized into Romance, phonetic development of final *-ll* to *-t* in the speech of the Gascony region of France caused the two forms to become identical. *Gat* survived as the term for "cat", and to avoid confusion, the rooster was redesignated by the terms *faisan* or *vicaire*, and the latter ultimately developed into *bigey*.) Trier observes (1934a: 178) that von Wartburg failed to take account of any changes which may have occurred in the conceptual structure to which the two terms belong. Trier's own objective of providing a comprehensive account of language-content leads him to view von Wartburg's method as inadequate. He concludes that it is not possible to discuss the case without reference to the conceptual field in question. While it is true that the causes of change were both phonetic and semantic, the semantic factor was incidental rather than concomitant. Trier seems to admit this in spite of himself when he uses phrases such as "rein lautlichen Vorgang" and "äusserliche lautliche Zufälligkeiten". Had it not been for the phonetic convergence of the two forms, the matter of semantic differentiation would never have arisen. Trier's error is in thinking of *gat* and *bigey* as a pair of words in the same way that *kunst* and *list* formed a pair in his own study. It is evident that such an analogy exists for him, when he speaks of "Das Stück Weltbild das im Sprachzustand A mit *cattus* und *gallus* erschlossen war." But *cattus* and *gallus* and their subsequent equivalents are not mutually delimiting terms, as *kunst* und *list* were in their domain. Rather, they are remotely connected terms within the conceptual domain of animals, whereas *kunst* and *list* were two key terms in 12th-century feudal society. Von Wartburg is not explicit about the semantic relationship of *gat* and *bigey*, nor does Trier show us precisely the nature of that relationship to the over-all structure of the 'animal' field. But we do not need to know anything about that relationship to demonstrate that semantic structures are irrelevant in this case. It is sufficient to observe that at the intermediate stage, where homonyms coexist, what has changed is not the relationship of signified to signified (Saussure's *valeur* and Trier's commutual delimination) but the signifier-signified relation, in that it has become ambiguous for the form *gat*. The fact that the Gascony dialect imported *bigey* suggests that it sought to maintain the original condition where two distinct concepts were represented by two distinct signifiers. The type of analysis upon which Trier insists is superfluous for von Wartburg's example. It could be applied in the rare instances where homonymy is reinterpreted as polysemy, but this is an entirely different matter.

3.4. Leo Weisgerber (1899–1984)

Weisgerber, whose work is admirably reviewed by Bynon (1966), concedes the possibility of semantic field studies, but he is keenly aware of the shortcomings in Trier's work. He pays greater attention than Trier to theoretical questions and recognizes the need for adjustment in Trier's theory (Weisgerber 1962: 271). Weisgerber proposes a three-way classification of semantic fields into *Feld*, *Teilfeld*, *Grossfeld*, demonstrating that this is the necessary consequence of Trier's proposition concerning the structure of semantic fields. Another problem which Weisgerber discerns in Trier's approach is the inter-play of linguistic and extra-linguistic factors: "Die Frage wie bei dieser Gestaltung die sprachlichen und die aussersprachlichen Bedingungen sich zueinander verhalten, ist bei Trier nicht ausdrücklich aufgenommen" (1962: 275). This refers to the fact that linguistic fields (Sprachfelder) and conceptual domains (Sinnbezirke) are not rigidly differentiated by Trier. Indeed, he seems to suggest that the terms are interchangeable. One of the most positive aspects of Weisgerber's work is the thorough fashion in which he deals with preliminaries to his analysis, thus reducing the possibility of ambiguity at a later stage. For example, Weisgerber differentiates linguistic and logical concepts, a distinction to which few of his predecessors had paid attention.

Weisgerber deals more positively with certain aspects of semantics than did Trier. For example, homonymy, so problematic for the field theory, is dismissed by Trier (1934a: 180) as a curiosity and an impediment, but Weisgerber (1962: 203) offers a method for handling it.

4. Georges Matoré (1908–*post* 1972)

Despite the fact that Matoré disavowed any connection with earlier studies in elaborating his *La Méthode en lexicologie* (1953), a study of the French lexicon as an explanation of social facts, the work shows some similarities in theory and method to that of Trier. According to Sumpf (1968: 6) this affinity is to be explained by an intellectual current common to England and France: "En gros, on peut dire que le problème des relations entre la sociologie et la linguistique, se situe en France, comme en Allemagne d'ailleurs, dans le cadre de l'identification au XIXe siècle entre histoire-langue-culture-nation." The general orientation of method and the recurrence of terms such as 'explication totale', 'ensembles', and 'organismes' in Matoré are reminiscent of Trier and his predecessors. It is not surprising, therefore, that Matoré makes direct reference to Trier's work calling it a "contribution très précieuse" (Matoré 1953: 15). But Matoré has criticism as well as praise for Trier. Indeed, he views all semantic fields theories as failures in one respect, namely, in not limiting themselves to precisely established periods of time. As a result, he says, those studies provide only partial explanations – and questionable ones at that.

The notions of dividing history into periods and establishing key dates as parameters for the study of the lexicon are fundamental to Matoré's method and distinguish it from Trier's. His approach is also distinct from Trier's in that he restricts his study to the modern language. By and large, however, similarities seem to outweigh differences between the two scholars, for these are similarities of approach and basic conceptions. Thus, for example, the notion of an inter-related lexical structure which varies at different periods but always remains an inter-related whole is common to Matoré and Trier. More important still is Matoré's idea of the *mot-témoin*, a coordinating term which allows a hierarchy to form in the lexicon. While Trier did not propose a corresponding term, he did use the notion of a coordinating concept or set of such concepts. This was the function of *kunst*, *list*, and *wisheit* in the intellectual vocabulary at the first stage of medieval German in Trier's (1931) study. Both Trier and Matoré develop an analysis working from whole to part. Trier repeatedly insisted that analysis must proceed in this fashion and that a study which begins with constituent parts will fail to reveal the structure to which they belong. Similarly, Matoré established a hierarchy of progressively subordinate units – the lexicon as a whole, conceptual fields, *mot-clé* (a lexical unit expressive of a given period or segment of society) *mot-témoin*, and individual words.

5. Morpho-semantic field theory

5.1. Pierre Guiraud (1912–1983)

In an apparently radical departure from semantic field theories in the tradition of Trier and his contemporaries, Pierre Guiraud began to develop his concept of the *champ morpho-sémantique* during the 1950s. Guiraud cited a host of influences in the development of this idea, beginning with Saussure, and including scholars as diverse in their orientations as Louis Hjelmslev (1899–1965) and Gustave Guillaume (1883–1960). Guiraud gradually came to recognize that the dualities used by Saussure as the framework for the *Cours* could be applied specifically as a means of providing a fuller and more accurate description of the lexicon. In explaining the reference to external and internal criteria for etymology in the title of his first publication on the subject of morpho-semantic fields (Guiraud 1956), he makes the case for supplementing the exclusively diachronic approach of traditional etymology by a synchronic description of the creative forces of language, such as paranoymic attraction, derivation, reduplication, substitution, etc. This is the most fundamental feature of Guiraud's method, which culminated in the publication of his *Dictionnaire des étymologies obscures* in 1982. Though Guiraud developed morpho-semantic analysis as an etymological tool, its usefulness in synchronic analysis is evident, for it reveals the highest degree of systematicity in the lexicon by examining the correlation of recurring overt formal features and semantic features. Guiraud (1967: 33) indicates that the entire objective of his approach is to describe the structural interaction of formal features of the lexicon: "Il s'agit finalement d'établir la convergence entre la forme des catégories signifiantes et celle des catégories signifiées."

Morpho-semantic fields, as defined by Guiraud, are, therefore, those areas of the lexicon where specific sub-morphemic features and specific semantic features coalesce, forming a type of paradigm. The effect of this grouping is to attract and integrate other words (the metathesis in the development of Old English *thirl* to *thrill* may be viewed as an example of the attraction of the morpho-semantic field of *drill*, *shrill*, *grill*, etc.). The morphological features which the constituents of a morpho-semantic field share give the field its unity; the semantic features which those constituents share make the field distinct from other fields. But morpho-semantic fields are also connected to each other, according to Guiraud. This is particularly true of the morpho-semantic fields based on root-forming expressive phoneme patterns, such as the field of *tiquer*, *toquer*, *taquer*, etc., where /t-k/ conveys the idea of movement and the vowel specifies the particular type of movement. Here an entire network develops among the forms /kl-k/, /kl-p/, /kr-k/, /š-k/, /s-p/, /p-k/, which all prove to be morpho-semantically related, but the strongest correlation is between /kr-k/ and /š-k/ (*croquer*, *chiquer*, etc.). Guiraud does not ascribe expressive values directly to the root forms of morpho-semantic fields but directly to the phonological system of the language: "Les valeurs phono-expressives sont des faits de structure qui procèdent beaucoup plus du système de la langue que de la figure phonique de l'étymon" (1960: 153). A root, therefore, is at an intermediate level between potentially onomatopoeic elements and the forms in which they are actualized. The immediate connection in expressive words is between the images which they convey, whether they be acoustic or kinetic, and the distinctive features of the constituent phonemes, *not* the phonemes themselves. This accounts for the notion of a network of expressive roots. Since expressive properties reside within distinctive features, the roots with phonemes which share those features will have a common expressive property.

The expressive aspect of the terms in Guiraud's morpho-semantic fields is evident from any sample of sense characterizations taken from his studies. For example (Guiraud 1962: 115): *tic* – mouvement convulsif; *tac* – fièvre accompagnée d'une toux fatigante; *taquer* – train ou véhicule bruyants et cahotants. It is possible, therefore, to contrast morpho-semantic fields of onomatopoeic roots with semantic fields, such as those described by Trier, and to characterize that contrast in terms of the marked/unmarked dichotomy. Thus, within the semantic field of 'movement', forms with expressive roots such as those with /t-k/, /š-k/, cited above, constitute the marked members and all others constitute the unmarked members. In the context of the only three possible types of general systems (diacritic, taxonomic, and lexical), morpho-semantic fields are represented by the zones of intersection in the lexical type. Such intersection must occur by virtue of the system type and validates Guiraud's claim that expressive roots from a network among themselves.

5.2. The contributions of other scholars

Before Guiraud's studies of the morpho-semantic field, Leonard Bloomfield (1933: 145–146) dealt marginally with the same phenomenon under the name of *root-forming morphemes*. A more extensive treatment occurs in the work of J. R. Firth (1935) under the heading of *phonesthemes*. Bolinger also discusses the phenomenon in two essays which predate Guiraud's publications (Bolinger 1949, 1950). More recently, numerous studies converging in subject matter with those of Guiraud (but designated by widely diverging terminologies – Gordon 1980: 120–127; 1987: 111–113; 1992: 185–187) have appeared. Inevitably, these studies also diverge widely as to purpose, though their common ground with Guiraud's orientation remains apparent. Thus Jones (1978: 278):

"Given a lexicon where the items are expressed as phonological features and feature products, it is possible to show that the underlying variables of such a phonological matrix correlate with the semantic categories of the lexicon."

Jones's conclusions are radical: "There will be no lexicon in the traditional sense, but a word will be coined afresh from its semantic specifications whenever it is used" (Jones 1978: 278). They are also reminiscent of Guiraud's preoccupations:

"The strength of this explanation is that it draws together coherently a number of otherwise unexplained facts about languages: the frequencies of phonemes and their combinations, the fact that homonyms are common and synonyms unusual, and the fact that words that are semantically alike may be very different in their phonological features." (Jones 1978: 278)

In Robert Lord (1970a, b; Lord & Chang 1987, 1992; Lord 1996) the work of Guiraud,

Bolinger and others is synthesized and developed further. Lord also offers illuminating lessons on the connections between morpho-semantic theory and the Chinese philological tradition (dating from the second century A. D.) of *sheng-xun*, or explanation for the original sense of words by the study of semantically cognate homophones, as well as the 11th century right-radical theory, deriving word meaning from the phonetic radical attached to the right side of the written character representing it. Lord's insight was that Chinese provides an ideal test case for morpho-semantic theory, because it is virtually free of affixes and inflectional morphology, thus eliminating the possibility of relations between bound morphemes and quasi-morphemes, which troubles morpho-semantic investigation of English, for example. The one-to-one correspondence between characters and syllables in Chinese also facilitates the study, and the dominant CVC syllable type allows the study to extend to overlapping initial and final segments as morpho-semantic units. Lord calls the covert lexical feature isolated by his study *morpho-semantic concurrence* (hence-forth: MSC), defining it as "a set of lexical items which are closely similar (synonymic) or opposite (antonymic) in *meaning* and which share an *initial* or *final* lexical segment (or both, resulting in homonyms)" (Lord & Chang 1992: 353). In extending the MSC to include relations of antonymy, Lord goes well beyond Guiraud, but in other respects his orientation conforms closely to Guiraud's. Thus:

"The MSC is maintained in provisional equilibium and held together by paronymic atraction. But it is impermanent, to the extent that (a) the set of lexical items it subtends, (b) its common (initial or final) morphological segment, and (c) its semantic value are all subject to change; *not* arbitrarily, but in accordance with the internal dynamics of the lexicon." (Lord & Chang 1992: 353)

Among the interesting results of Lord's studies are that (1) homonymic counterparts of MSCs occur in other semantic categories, and therefore the polysemy of a particular item becomes distributed through as many different semantic categories as there are polysemantic variants of the item; (2) in Cantonese a single MSC for a final segment usually serves to interconnect two or more MSC initial segments within the same category; (3) nesting within semantic categories tends to find a parallel in the phonology of MSCs; (4) patterns of semantically superordinate MSCs emerge.

6. Conclusion

It is impossible within the limited space available here to survey the range of rich developments relating to semantic field theory over the past thirty years. Readers are invited to consult Gordon (1980, 1987, 1992).

7. Bibliography

Apresjan, Jurij D. 1966. "Analyses distributionnelles des significations". *Langages* 1.44–74.

Bendix, Herman. 1966. *Componential Analysis of General Vocabulary.* Bloomington: Indiana University Research Center in Anthropology, Folklore and Linguistics.

Bloomfield, Leonard. 1933. *Language.* New York: Holt & Co.

Bolinger, Dwight. 1949. "The Sign is not Arbitrary". *Boletin del Instituto Caro y Cuervo* 5.52–62.

–. 1950. "Rime, Assonance, and Morpheme Analysis". *Word* 6.117–136.

Bréal, Michel. 1883. "Les lois intellectuelles du langage: Fragment de sémantique". *Annuaire de l'Association pour l'encouragement des études grecques en France* 17.132–142.

–. 1924 [1897]. *Essai de sémantique: Science des significations.* Paris: Hachette.

Butcher, Samuel Henry. 1904. *Harvard Lectures on Greek Subjects.* London: Macmillan.

Bynon, Theodora. 1966. "Leo Weisgerber's Four Stages in Linguistic Analysis". *Man* 1966/1.468–483.

Darmesteter, Arsène. 1883. "Cours de littérature française du moyen âge et d'histoire de la langue française". *Revue internationale de l'enseignement* (Paris, 15 Dec.), 111–114.

–. 1886. *La Vie des mots étudiés dans leurs significations.* Paris: Delagrave.

Eucken, Rudolf. 1913. *Main Currents of Modern Thought.* London: Unwin.

Firth, John Rupert. 1935. "The Use and Distribution of Certain English Sounds". *English Studies* 17: 1.2–12.

Goodenough, Ward H. 1956. "Componential Analysis and the Study of Meaning". *Language* 32. 195–216.

Gordon, William Terrence. 1980. *Semantics: A Bibliography 1965–1978.* Metuchen: N. J.: Scarecrow.

–. 1987. *Semantics: A bibliography 1979–1985.* Metuchen, N. J.: Scarecrow.

–. 1992. *Semantics: A bibliography 1986–1991.* Metuchen, N. J.: Scarecrow.

Guiraud, Pierre. 1956. "Les champs morphosémantiques". *Bulletin de la Société de Linguistique de Paris* 52. 265–288.

—. 1960. "Le champ morpho-sémantique du verbe chiquer". *Bulletin de la Société de Linguistique de Paris* 55.134—154.

—. 1962. "Le champ morpho-sémantique de la racine T. K.". *Bulletin de la Société de Linguistique de Paris* 57.103—125.

—. 1967. *Structure étymologique du lexique français.* Paris: Larousse.

—. 1982. *Dictionnaire des étymologies obscures.* Paris: Payot.

Haase, Friedrich. 1874, 1880. *Vorlesungen über lateinische Sprachwissenschaft, gehalten ab 1840.* Ed. by Friedrich August Eckstein and Hermann Peter, respectively. 2 vols. Leipzig: Simmel.

Harris, Zellig S. 1948. "Componential Analysis of a Hebrew Paradigm". *Language* 24.87—91.

Heerdegen, Ferdinand. 1890. *Vorlesungen über lateinische Sprachwissenschaft von Karl Christian Reisig.* Vol. II: *Lateinische Semasiologie oder Bedeutungslehre.* Berlin: S. Calvary.

Ipsen, Gunther. 1932. "Der neue Sprachbegriff". *Zeitschrift für Deutschkunde* 46.1—18. (Repr. in Schmidt 1973.55—77.)

Jakobson, Roman. 1936. "Beitrag zur allgemeinen Kasuslehre". *Travaux du Cercle Linguistique de Prague* 6.240—288.

Jones, Alex I. 1978. "Form and Meaning in an Australian Language". *Language and Speech* 21. 264—278.

Koerner, E. F. Konrad. 1975. "European Structuralism: Early beginnings". *Current Trends in Linguistics* ed. by Thomas A. Sebeok, vol. XIII: *Historiography of Linguistics*, 717—827. The Hague: Mouton.

Lehrer, Adrienne. 1974. *Semantic Fields and Lexical Structures.* Amsterdam: North-Holland.

Lord, Robert. 1970a. "Lexico-Semantic Categories". *Studia Linguistica* 24.17—42.

—. 1970b. "A New Concept in Structural Semantics: The homoneme". *Actes du Xe Congrès International des Linguistes* ed. by Alexandru Graur, vol. II, 433—442. Bucharest: Éditions de l'Académie de la République Socialiste de Roumanie.

—. 1996. *Words: A hermeneutical approach to the study of language.* Lanham, Md.: Univ. Press of America.

— & T. Z. Chang. 1987. "Morphosemantic Categories in Chinese: An interim report". *Journal of the Atlantic Provinces Linguistic Association* 9. 123—157.

— & —. 1992. "How Does the Lexicon Work?". *Word* 43: 3.349—373.

Lotz, John. 1949. "The Semantic Analysis of the Nominal Bases in Hungarian". *Travaux du Cercle Linguistique de Copenhague* 5.187—197.

Lounsbury, Floyd G. 1956. "A Semantic Analysis of the Pawnee Kinship Usage". *Language* 32. 158—194.

Lyons, John. 1963. *Structural Semantics: An analysis of part of the vocabulary of Plato.* Oxford: Blackwell.

Matoré, Georges. 1953. *La Méthode en lexicologie.* Paris: Didier.

McKaughan, Howard. 1959. "Semantic Components of Pronoun Systems". *Word* 15.101—102.

Miller, Robert Lee. 1968. *The Linguistic Relativity Principle and Humboldtian Ethnolinguistics.* The Hague: Mouton.

Öhman, Suzanne. 1951. *Wortinhalt und Weltbild: Vergleichende und methodologische Studien zur Bedeutungslehre und Wortfeldtheorie.* Stockholm: Norstedt.

—. 1953. "Theories of the Linguistic Field". *Word* 9.123—134. (German transl. by author in Schmidt 1973.288—317.)

Oksaar, Els. 1958. *Semantische Studien im Sinnbereich der Schnelligkeit.* Stockholm: Almqvist & Wiksell.

Orsini, G. N. 1972. "The Ancient Roots of a Modern Idea". *Organic Form: The life of an idea* ed. by G. S. Rousseau, 8—23. London: Routledge & Kegan Paul.

Phillips, D. C. 1970. "Organicism in the Late Nineteenth and Early Twentieth Centuries". *Journal of the History of Ideas* 31.413—432.

Porzig, Walter. 1957. *Das Wunder der Sprache.* Berne: Francke.

Reisig, Karl Christian. 1839. *Vorlesungen über lateinische Sprachwissenschaft.* Ed. posthumously by Friedrich Haase. Leipzig: Lehnhold.

Saussure, Ferdinand de. 1972 [1916]. *Cours de linguistique générale.* Paris: Payot.

Schmidt, Lothar, ed. 1973. *Wortfeldforschung: Zur Geschichte und Theorie des sprachlichen Feldes.* Darmstadt: Wissenschaftliche Buchgesellschaft. [Rich bib. (465—483).]

Schwarz, Hans. 1959. *Sprache — Schlüssel zur Welt.* Düsseldorf: Schwann.

Spence, N. C. W. 1961. "Linguistic Fields, Conceptual Systems, and the *Weltbild*". *Transactions of the Philological Society* 1961.87—106.

Sturrock, John. 1986. *Structuralism.* London: Collins.

Sumpf, Josef. 1968. "Linguistique et sociologie". *Langages* No. 11.3—35.

Trier, Jost. 1931. *Der deutsche Wortschatz im Sinnbezirk des Verstandes.* Heidelberg: Winter.

—. 1932a. "Die Idee der Klugheit in ihrer sprachlichen Entfaltung". *Zeitschrift für Deutschkunde* 46.625—635. (Repr. in Schmidt 1973.41—54.)

—. 1932b. "Sprachliche Felder". *Zeitschrift für deutsche Bildung* 8.417—427.

—. 1934a. "Deutsche Bedeutungsforschung". *Germanische Philologie I: Ergebnisse und Aufgaben. Festschrift für Otto Behaghel* ed. by Alfred Goetze et al., 173–200. Heidelberg: Winter. (Repr. in Schmidt 1973.116–128.)

–. 1934b. "Das sprachliche Feld: Eine Auseinandersetzung". *Neue Jahrbücher für Wissenschaft und Jugendbildung* 10.428–449. (Repr. in Schmidt 1973. 129–161.)

–. 1968. *Altes und neues vom sprachlichen Feld.* Mannheim & Zürich: Bibliographisches Inst.

Ullmann, Stephen. 1964. *Semantics: An introduction to the science of meaning.* Oxford: Blackwell.

Weinreich, Uriel. 1963. "On the Semantic Structure of Language". *Universals of Language* ed. by Joseph H. Greenberg, 114–171. Cambridge, Mass.: MIT Press.

Weisgerber, Leo. 1927. "Die Bedeutungslehre – Ein Irrweg der Sprachwissenschaft". *Germanisch-Romanische Monatsschrift* 9.161–183.

–. 1962. *Sprachliche Gestaltung der Welt.* Düsseldorf: Schwann.

W. Terrence Gordon, Halifax (Canada)

XXX. Psychology and Physiology in 19th-Century Linguistics
Psychologische und physiologische Ansätze in der Sprachwissenschaft des 19. Jahrhunderts
La psychologie et la physiologie dans la linguistique du XIXe siècle

194. Die Beziehungen zwischen Sprache und Denken: Die Ideen Wilhelm von Humboldts und die Anfänge der sprachpsychologischen Forschung

1. Vorbemerkungen
2. Literaturbericht und Forschungsstand
3. Die Anfänge der psychologischen Richtung: Grammatik, Logik und Psychologie
4. Theoriearchitektonische Probleme: die Vorzüge der Psychologie
5. Die Hauptprobleme der frühen Sprachpsychologie: ein Aufriß
6. Apperzeption und psychologische Semantik: eine Fallstudie
7. Schlußbemerkung
8. Bibliographie

1. Vorbemerkungen

Daß Werk und Wirkung weit auseinanderfallen, ist bei den Gründerfiguren sprachwissenschaftlicher Epochen die Regel. Offenbar besteht deren Funktion weit eher darin, daß sie beschworen als daß sie gelesen und ihre Ratschläge in praxi beherzigt werden. Sie wirken wie mythische Stifter, nicht wie gemeine Wissenschaftler. So kann man die Wirkungsgeschichte Wilhelm von Humboldts im 19. Jh. schreiben, ohne ihn zu lesen, weil sie nicht auf seinem Werk beruht, sondern auf seinem Ansehen, und die unglaublich breite philologische Rekonstruktion der 'eigentlichen' Gedanken Humboldts muß durchaus gegen den tatsächlich rezipierten Autor gleichen Namens erfolgen, sie gewissermaßen als ein großes Mißverständnis ansehen. Daß die eigentlich sprachwissenschaftlichen Hauptwerke Humboldts bis heute nicht vollständig ediert sind, paßt da nur zu gut. Spott ist jedoch nicht am Platze, zumal das 20. Jh. auch einen solchen Humboldt hat, der Ferdinand de Saussure heißt und mit seinem großen Vor- gänger gemeinsam hat, daß auch er die vielseitigen Widersprüche des Gegenstands 'Sprache' nach allen Seiten ausgemessen — und sie dann stehengelassen hat. Demzufolge verblassen die fachlich-intellektuellen Wirkungen solcher Gründerfiguren um so mehr, je genauer man ihnen nachspürt, und es ist Berthold Delbrück (1842—1922) hoch anzurechnen, daß er diesen Umstand offen ausspricht:

"Überhaupt ist nichts schwieriger, als mit deutlichen Worten anzugeben, worin die Einwirkung besteht, welche Humboldt gerade auf die indogermanische Sprachforschung ausgeübt hat." (Delbrück 1893: 27)

Selbst wenn man die historisch-vergleichende Sprachwissenschaft des 19. Jhs. als 'Vereinseitigung' Humboldtscher Interessen ansehen wollte, wäre das nicht mehr als eine *façon de parler*, welche den Unterschied zwischen der robusten, erfolgreichen und institutionell eigenständigen Praxis dieser Richtung und dem esoterisch-umstrittenen Werk ihres 'Gründers' verwischt. Auch die Sprachpsychologie des 19. Jhs. ist bestenfalls eine solche 'Vereinseitigung', wiewohl institutioneller Erfolg und dauerhafte Organisationsformen ihr nicht beschieden waren. Sie ist allein eine geistesgeschichtliche, keine institutionelle Realität. Ihre Träger waren Philosophen/Psychologen wie Moritz Lazarus (1824—1903), Sprachforscher wie Heymann Steinthal (1823—1899), Gymnasiallehrer wie Ludwig Noiré (1829—1889) und Philipp Wegener (1848—1916). Den intellektuellen Einfluß Humboldts hat sie bestenfalls über Steinthal aufgenommen, aber gerade da, wo dessen Sprachlehre psychologisch wird, entfernt sie sich vielleicht am weitesten von Humboldt (zum tatsächlichen Einfluß Humboldts auf die historisch-vergleichende Sprachforschung vgl. auch Trabant 1986: 160 ff.). Indessen gehört der Streit um Humboldts Präsenz in der Sprachforschung der Jahrhundertmitte zu den Gründungsdokumenten der Sprachpsychologie: Steinthal streitet ab, daß es eine wirkliche Auseinandersetzung mit Humboldt gebe oder gegeben habe (darauf antwortet Pott 1880) und reklamiert damit das eigene Werk, das sich von Anfang an kritisch-bewundernd an Humboldt mißt, als exklusiv (vgl. auch Di Cesare 1996).

Wirklich involviert in die sprachpsychologische Diskussion hat dagegen die (vornehmlich junggrammatischen) Indogermanisten erst das Werk von Wilhelm Wundt (1832–1920), nachdem zuvor schon Hermann Paul (1846–1921) in seinen Prinzipien der Sprachgeschichte auf die Psychologie zurückgegriffen hatte. Von den drei großen Richtungen des 19. Jhs. ist die Sprachpsychologie die kleinste, die am wenigsten institutionell verankerte, am wenigsten wirkungsmächtige. Die historisch-vergleichende Richtung gilt noch heute als eigentlich repräsentativ für das Jh.; die schulgrammatische, abgestützt durch die gesellschaftliche Wirkungsmacht namentlich der Gymnasien, ist weniger bekannt und gilt vielen als unergiebig, wiewohl nur sie das kategoriale Instrumentarium der Grammatik auf die Höhe gebracht hat, an welcher der synchronische Strukturalismus des 20. Jhs. anknüpfen konnte (vgl. Forsgren 1985, Erlinger, Knobloch & Meyer 1989). Diesen beiden Strömungen gegenüber bleibt die Einheit der 'Sprachpsychologie' diffus und problematisch.

2. Literaturbericht und Forschungsstand

Im Literaturbericht bleiben konsequent die Arbeiten ausgespart, die sich allein oder primär auf das Werk Humboldts beziehen. Es wäre dies ein anderes Thema, das nicht auf die Anfänge der Sprachpsychologie hin zu ordnen (oder gar zu beschränken) ist. Speziell die Anfänge der völkerpsychologischen Sprachauffassung thematisieren Waltraud Bumann (1965) in ihrer Monographie über Steinthal und Ingrid Belke (1971 ff.) in ihrer reich kommentierten Ausgabe des Briefwechsels von Lazarus und Steinthal. Eine sehr brauchbare Einordnung der frühen Völkerpsychologie in die allgemein- und wissenschaftspolitische Situation der Jahrhundertmitte gibt Schmidt (1987). Arens (1969: 277 ff.) ordnet die frühe Sprachpsychologie (zusammen mit den physiologischen Ansätzen) einer theoretischen "Neubegründung im Zeichen der Naturwissenschaft" ein und hat damit, wie zu zeigen sein wird, durchaus Recht. Eine problemgeschichtlich geordnete Gesamtdarstellung der (deutschen) Sprachpsychologie bis 1920 versucht Knobloch (1988). Jaritz (1990) thematisiert (neben Bopp und Schleicher) auch Steinthal und die Junggrammatiker im Zusammenhang mit den wechselnden theoretischen Hintergründen und Bezugssystemen für die Praxis der historisch-vergleichenden Sprachforschung. Damit sind zugleich zwei Betrachtungsweisen der Sprachpsychologie im 19. Jh. angedeutet: einmal als Lieferant für Begründungszusammenhänge der herrschenden historisch-vergleichenden Praxis (vgl. 3. und 4.) und einmal als eigenständiger Problemraum (vgl. 5. und 6.).

Für eine erste Orientierung im Bereich der psychologischen Semantik mag Kronasser (1952) genügen, aber den großen geschichtlichen Zusammenhang auch für die psychologisch-semantischen Strömungen gibt Nerlich (1992), deren Buch auch die bei weitem umfangreichste und vollständigste Bibliographie für die Semantik des 19. Jhs. enthält.

Nicht uninteressant als Quellen für die Erforschung der frühen Sprachpsychologie sind auch die Selbstthematisierungen der Zeit, so z. B. Benfey (1869), der Steinthal zwar voller Achtung, aber im Appendix zur Allgemeinen Sprachwissenschaft eher unter den curiosa abhandelt, Paul (1920 [1880]), der (zweifellos nach dem Vorbild von Steinthal 1864) den Dienst zu bestimmen versucht, welchen die Psychologie der historischen Sprachforschung leisten kann, Delbrück (1893), der u. a. Steinthals Einfluß zu rekonstruieren sucht. Ein vortreffliches Korrektiv für die durchweg interessierten Selbstbilder der Epoche bietet die sperrige und sprunghafte, jedoch immer treffende Abhandlung von August Friedrich Pott (1880). Man darf nicht vergessen, daß wir es mit einer geschichtsphilosophisch geschulten Generation von Forschern zu tun haben, die immer auch darauf bedacht war, schon zu Lebzeiten den eigenen Platz in der Fachgeschichte auf Dauer einzurichten.

Zu den besten einschlägigen Vorarbeiten gehört das sprachtheoretische Werk Karl Bühlers (1879–1963), der im 20. Jh. kritisch anknüpft an das Werk der sprachpsychologischen Pioniere, das er in diesem Zusammenhang mit viel Sinn für wissenschaftsgeschichtliche Logiken aspektiv nachzeichnet (u. a. in Bühler 1927, 1933, 1934). Ebenfalls systematisch verarbeitet wird die Sprachpsychologie des 19. Jhs. bei Cassirer (1923), Funke (1927), Dempe (1930), Ammann (1925–1928), kurz: bei den sprachtheoretischen Autoren, welche die Traditionen der frühen Sprachpsychologie mit den Mitteln des frühen 20. Jhs. kontinuieren wollen.

Darüber hinaus sind etliche Sprachpsychologen des Untersuchungszeitraums monographisch bearbeitet worden. Darunter sind folgende wichtig: Wilhelm Wundt von Ungeheuer (1984) und Knobloch (1992), K. W. L. Heyse von Petzet & Herbig (1913), Ludwig Noire (1829–1889), von Berg (1918), Gustav Gerber (1820–1901) von Simonis (1959) und Anton Marty (1847–1914) von Raynaud (1982). Über Philipp Wegener ist die "Introduction" zur Neuausgabe von Wegener (1990 [1885]) zu vergleichen. Eine umfangreiche Bibliographie der frühen Sprachpsychologie und Hinweise zur Biographie ihrer Hauptakteure enthält Knobloch (1988).

3. Die Anfänge der psychologischen Richtung: Grammatik, Logik und Psychologie

Psychologiehistorisch fallen die Anfänge der Sprachpsychologie in "jene durchaus nüchterne, erfahrungsnahe, naturwissenschaftliche Phase" (Bühler 1927: 1), die auf den Zerfal des Hegelschen Systems folgt. Zur gleichen Zeit befindet sich die akademische Sprachwissenschaft, die einige Jahrzehnte "romantische Geisteswissenschaft" gewesen ist (Arens 1969: 170 ff.), im Zeichen einer naturwissenschaftlichen Neufundierung, welche das Selbstverständnis der historisch-vergleichenden Forscher stärker erfaßt als ihre tatsächliche Praxis.

Mit Recht gilt Steinthals (1855) vehemente Kritik an Karl Ferdinand Becker (1775–1849) als die Geburtsurkunde der psychologischen Richtung. Mit Becker, dessen Ansehen in der gebildeten Öffentlichkeit dem der beiden Grimms nicht um viel nachstand, sollte aber die ganze Allgemeingrammatische Richtung, von Steinthal auch als 'logisch' apostrophiert, getroffen werden. Die hatte sich nämlich neben der sich universitär etablierenden historisch-vergleichenden Sprachforschung als durchaus lebenskräftig und erneuerungsfähig erwiesen. Aus der apriorischen Richtung des (von Humboldt hoch geschätzten) August Ferdinand Bernhardi (1768–1820; vgl. Bernhardi 1801–1803, 1805) und der eher empirisch-vergleichenden Allgemeinen Grammatik von Johann Severin Vater (1771–1826) waren im Werk von Bekker, Simon Heinrich Adolf Herling (1780–1849) oder Karl Wilhelm Ludwig Heyse (1797–1855) neue Allgemeingrammatische Synthesen entstanden, die, wenigstens dem Anspruch nach, auch den rasch wachsenden Stoff der historisch-vergleichenden Sprachforschung einzubeziehen und theoretisch zu synthetisieren versprachen. Just diesen Anspruch einer neuen theoretischen Synthese, welche auch die geschichtliche Sprachforschung umfaßt, erhebt aber auch Steinthal selbst für die Sprachpsychologie. Das Etikett für seine Gegner liefert die 'Logik', welche in den grammatischen Kategorien den notwendigen Ausdruck ewiger und allen Menschen gemeinsamer Denkgesetze sieht. Ein unvoreingenommener Blick auf die Allgemeingrammatische Tradition von Bernhardi bis Becker hätte diese polemische Ansicht jedenfalls relativiert (vgl. Forsgren 1985). Im Rückblick kann man Beckers aktualgenetische Interpretation des Satzes als Denkprodukt durchaus auch psychologisch deuten, nicht logisch (vgl. Haselbach 1966: 57 ff.). Daß sie bei Wundt im psychologischen Gewande, aber substantiell unverändert, wieder auftaucht, ist da gewiß kein Zufall (vgl. Knobloch 1988: 434 ff.).

Steinthals Bemühen geht jedoch dahin nachzuweisen, daß näherhin die Sprache überhaupt ein aktiv formender und bedingender Faktor allen höheren Seelenlebens ist und fernerhin auch der völkerpsychologisch ausgeprägte Sprachtypus und Entwicklungsstand der Sprache (im Blick auf die logische Entfaltung der "Sprachidee" in der Geschichte) die Richtung der höheren seelischen Prozesse bestimmt. Dieses Unternehmen prägt Steinthals Verhältnis zur Psychologie, die keineswegs bloß als Hilfswissenschaft oder gar als Rückversicherung für die historisch-vergleichende Praxis (wie später bei den Junggrammatikern; vgl. Jaritz 1990: 94) ins Spiel kommt. Vielmehr ist der Titel von Steinthals theoretischer Hauptschrift Einleitung in die Psychologie und Sprachwissenschaft durchaus wörtlich und programmatisch zu nehmen (Steinthal 1881 [1871]). Die Sprachforschung erhebt darin den Anspruch, ihren eigenen Gegenstand als auch konstitutiv für die Psychologie der höheren Seelentätigkeit nachzuweisen. Steinthal ist also durchaus nicht herbartianisch in dem Sinne, in dem es die herbartianische Pädagogik und Psychologie der Jahrhundertmitte war. Seine Sprachauffassung ist der Johann Friedrich Herbarts (1776–1841) entgegengesetzt (vgl. Misteli 1880), und wo die Psychologiegeschichte Herbart als den nüchternen Empiriker und Realisten versteht, der die Statik und Mechanik der Vorstellungen erstmals als autonomes Forschungsgebiet statuiert und mathematisch beschrieben hat, da geht Steinthals Bemühen eigentlich darauf, diese Autonomie als sprachlich gestiftet nachzuweisen. Soweit das Programm völkerpsychologisch ausgerichtet ist, enthält es auch den Anspruch, der unreflektierten nationalphilologischen Praxis der ersten Jahrhunderthälfte ein modernes psychologisches Fundament zu geben.

Den Anspruch, Sprache sei der repräsentative Gegenstand und eigentliche Prüfstein der höheren Psychologie, kann man bis in die Magazine des späten 18. Jhs. zurückverfolgen. Karl Philipp Moritz erhebt ihn ebenso wie verschiedene seiner Zeitgenossen. Bei Wundt ist er gegen Ende des 19. Jhs. mit Händen zu greifen: Die Sprache bildet den ersten Band der Völkerpsychologie, und schon in seinem ersten Leipziger Semester liest der bis dato fast nur als Physiologe hervorgetretene Wundt über Sprache − in der Hauptstadt der Junggrammatiker (vgl. Ungeheuer 1984). Es ist dieser Anspruch, der die Gereiztheiten und Koalitionen stiftet, die nach 1900 die Debatte um Wundts *Sprache* begleiten (Delbrück 1901, Wundt 1901, Sütterlin 1902, Wegener 1902). Der launige Streit darum, wer der Gebende und wer der Nehmende sei zwischen Psychologie und Sprachwissenschaft, bezeugt, daß beide Seiten einander hier gar nicht verstanden haben. Für Wundt sind die Sprachen geformt vorliegender, objektivierter, Ausdruck seelischen Geschehens, weshalb er von der Sprachforschung zu nehmen glaubt. Für Delbrück (1901) hingegen, der mit Herbarts und mit Wundts Psychologie leben kann, ist Seelenlehre nur interessant als Hypothese über die Verbindung historisch disparater Sprachformen. Der Wundtsche Anspruch klingt nach selbst im Werk Karl Bühlers, das wohl niemand ernsthaft auf die Alternative 'Psychologie oder Sprachtheorie' festlegen mag. Auch für ihn ist die Sprache der Prüfstein der psychologischen Theoriebildung.

Steinthals Kampfschrift gegen Becker versucht erstlich den Boden zu räumen, auf dem dann das Gebäude der Sprachpsychologie errichtet werden soll. Ein Jahr später, 1856, ediert Steinthal Heyses *System der Sprachwissenschaft* nach dessen Tode. Mit Heyse war Steinthal freundschaftlich verbunden, und während er Beckers sprachtheoretische Ansichten vehement ablehnt, versucht er seine Psychologie an den Systemgedanken Heyses, diesen echt hegelianisch 'aufhebend', anzuschließen. Heyses Standpunkt ist insgesamt der, welcher von Steinthal auch Humboldt unterstellt wird: auch die historische Sprachforschung kommt zu einer allgemeinen Grammatik, welche aber die Gestalt einer vergleichenden Sprachenkunde hat. Die philosophisch allgemeine Grammatik liefert die essentiellen, notwendigen und wesentlichen Eigenschaften der 'Sprachidee'. Indem beide Seiten gewissermaßen abgeglichen werden, bestimmt die Klassifikation der Sprachen ihr jeweiliges Verhältnis zur Sprachidee. Die (relative) Berechtigung der alten, allgemein-philosophischen Grammatik bleibt dabei erhalten. Steinthal will aber die Psychologie an ihre Stelle setzen (vgl. auch Pott 1880: 174 ff. über die Ursprünge dieses Konzeptes).

Die Völkerpsychologie ist dagegen schon in Steinthal (1855) das, was sie im Ganzen auch bleiben wird: ein programmatischer Appendix von wenigen Seiten (1855: 387−392), eingeführt da, wo die Psychologie der Sprache überhaupt (und mit ihr die 'Sprachidee') in Vereinzelung und Besonderung übertritt, als Korrelat für die Klassifikation der Sprachen.

Von Anfang an ist es das Verhältnis der Sprache zum 'geistigen Leben', das auf dem Spiel steht in der Schlacht gegen Becker. Der Hauptfehler der bisherigen Sprachphilosophie (und namentlich der Allgemeinen Grammatik) besteht aus Steinthals Sicht darin, dieses geistige Leben so invariant zu setzen, daß seine eigenen Gesetzmäßigkeiten im Bau der Sprachen lediglich zum Ausdruck kommen und die Verschiedenheit der Sprachen dabei ebenso zu einer bloß äußerlichen Angelegenheit herabgesetzt wird wie die aktive Mitwirkung der Sprache an diesem. Steinthals Formel lautet: die Sprachen sind nicht invarianter Ausdruck des (gar noch: logischen) Denkens, sondern je autonome Darstellungen des

Gedachten und in dieses nicht aufzulösen. Auch entwirft Steinthal (1881 [1871]: 51) eine in sich differenziertere Theorie von der Sprachabhängigkeit des Denkens: dieses sei nämlich in seiner elementaren, anschaulichbildlichen Stufe zunächst sprachunabhängig, dann sprachgebunden und sprachgeformt in seiner gewöhnlich-alltäglichen Stufe, schließlich in seiner höchsten, wissenschaftlichen Form suche es sich wieder von den Präformationen der Sprache zu lösen.

Gesucht wird der Punkt in der psychischen Entwicklungslogik, an welchem das 'Seelenleben vor der Sprache' notwendig umschlägt und Sprache für sich erzeugt, so daß sie auf allen höheren Stufen der seelischen Tätigkeit als formans nicht mehr wegzudenken ist. Das ist die neue Klammer, mit der Steinthal die Probleme des Sprachursprungs, des kindlichen Spracherwerbs und des jedesmaligen Sprechens zu verbinden sucht. Denn da die Sprache nichts fertig in uns Liegendes ist, sondern beständig neu erzeugt werden muß, gibt es eigentlich kein vom jedesmaligen Sprechen verschiedenes Ursprungsproblem.

4. Theoriearchitektonische Probleme: die Vorzüge der Psychologie

Was waren nun die Vorzüge, welche die Psychologie um die Jahrhundertmitte für Sprachtheoretiker plötzlich interessant erscheinen ließen? Ich beschränke mich zunächst auf die Fundierungs- und Begründungsprobleme, die beständig neben der historisch-vergleichenden Praxis herliefen. Steinthal wird nicht müde zu betonen, daß das, was ihn und seine Zeitgenossen über Humboldt und dessen Erkenntnismöglichkeiten hinaushebt, die Verfügung über eine wissenschaftliche Psychologie sei (z. B. Steinthal 1881 [1871]: 78; vgl. die ironische Diskussion in Pott 1880: 37 ff). Mit Hilfe dieser Psychologie vor allem glaubt Steinthal aus den Widersprüchen herauszufinden, in denen Humboldt seiner Ansicht nach steckengeblieben ist.

Zuerst einmal gilt, daß die Psychologie als einzige philosophienahe Disziplin den Verschleiß der idealistischen Systeme einigermaßen schadlos überstanden hat (und ergo als zeitgemäße wissenschaftliche Alternative zur diskreditierten Philosophie passieren kann). Weiterhin hat sie eine Reihe von Vermittlungen anzubieten, deren die historisch-vergleichende Sprachforschung dringend bedarf.

Die steht einmal vor dem Problem, daß für ihre Praxis nur der schriftlich überlieferte, gleichsam philologische, Materialfundus zur Verfügung steht, während der Erklärungsanspruch weit über das Material hinausreicht. Keine Theorie des 19. Jhs. kann an diesem Problem achtlos vorübergehen; da alle Sprachen gewissermaßen 'fertig' in die geschichtliche Überlieferung eintreten, kann man einen strikten Gegensatz zwischen naturgeschichtlicher Gewordenheit und historischer Entwicklung aufmachen, man kann aber auch die geschichtliche Überlieferung naturalisieren oder die Natur- und Vorgeschichte historisieren oder beides. August Schleichers kurzer Weg von Hegel zu Haeckel durchläuft (und mischt) alle diese Möglichkeiten, und auch die psychologischen Theorieprogramme sind auf dieses theoriearchitektonische Problem der Epoche ausgerichtet (und folglich mit dem Ende dieser Konstellation verschwunden). Die Psychologie verspricht ein naturwissenschaftliches Fundament für die vorgeschichtliche Zeit und eine zeitlose Methodologie für die geschichtliche. Darin liegt die relative Äquivalenz evolutionistischer und psychologischer Begründungen für die historische Sprachforschung (und ihr gemeinsamer Gegensatz etwa gegen die Boppsche 'Zergliederungsmethode', die trotz organisch-naturwissenschaftlicher Metaphorik dem philosophischen Programm der Allgemeinen Grammatik verbunden bleibt; vgl. Jaritz 1990). Am Ende besteht ja die junggrammatische Pointe auch nur darin, die naturgeschichtliche Zwangsläufigkeit der 'Lautgesetze' methodisch auch für die geschichtlichen Zeiten zu veranschlagen und damit die Methodologie für Gegenwart, belegte Vergangenheit und Vorgeschichte einheitlich zu naturalisieren. Deswegen hat man Wilhelm Scherer als Vorläufer für sie in Anspruch genommen, der solche Ansprüche rhetorisch brilliant eingesetzt hat (Scherer 1875), oder auch August Schleicher, der die geschichtsphilosophische Einheit seiner Konstruktion am Ende ebenfalls gern in evolutionistische Naturmetaphern kleidete. Und was die allgemeine Reputation (vermeintlich) präziser naturwissenschaftlicher Methoden betrifft, so ist es im Rückblick schwer, einen klaren Trennungsstrich zwischen methodischen Idealen und Hypostatisierungen über den Gegenstand zu ziehen. Offenbar bestand die Fortschrittserwartung der Sprachforschung weithin darin, daß immer größere Teile des Materials quasi-naturwissenschaftlichen Verfahren unterworfen werden könnten.

Für Steinthal kommt die Psychologie zweimal in Betracht. Einmal behandelt die "psychologische Ethnologie" (ein Zweig der Völkerpsychologie; vgl. Steinthal 1881: 41) die Sprachen der vorgeschichtlichen Naturvölker, sie springt da ein und vertritt die Philologie, wo es sie mangels überlieferten Stoffes nicht geben kann. Die Sprachwissenschaft, so Steinthal (1881: 39) greift als vergleichende Grammatik weit über die geschichtliche Zeit (und damit über die Philologie) hinaus. Dann kommt die Psychologie aber auch noch in Betracht als prinzipienwissenschaftliches Fundament für die Philologie selbst (unverkennbar folgt Steinthal hier modernisierend der hermeneutischen Tradition von Schleiermacher und Boeckh). Man geht gewiß nicht fehl darin, daß es gerade diese janusköpfige Anlage der Psychologie gewesen ist, die sie für die Sprachforschung interessant gemacht hat, ihr Anspruch, Natur- und Geistesgeschichte zu verschränken. Und wer im Rückblick die Entwürfe studiert, die aus Steinthals umfassendem Programm hervorgegangen sind: von der kruden junggrammatischen Komplementarität zwischen physiologisch-naturgesetzlichen und analogisch-psychologischen Faktoren im Sprachwandel bis hin zu Wundts subtiler Verklammerung von natürlich-physiologischer und historisch objektivierter Ausdrucksevolution in der Sprache (Wundt 1921−1933 [1900]), der wird wenigstens finden müssen, daß alles sich auf diesem Terrain bewegt, was auf Resonanz in der historisch-vergleichenden Hauptströmung angelegt war. Es mußte ja durchaus so scheinen, als ob die Psychologie als 'Naturwissenschaft des Geistigen' die leidige Alternative zwischen Philologie und organischem Naturgesetz synthetisch überbrücken könnte.

Was schließlich die psychologischen Schulen selbst betrifft, deren Dienste die Sprachforschung in Anspruch nehmen konnte, so war die Herbartsche Lehre eine Sache der Praktiker, der Pädagogen und Schulmänner, die Fechner-Wundtsche psychophysische Tradition dagegen genoß mehr Reputation in der akademischen Welt der Mandarine. Sie war die modernere und anspruchsvollere Theorie.

Und noch ein weiteres Vermittlungsangebot bringt die Psychologie in ihre Verbindung zur Sprachforschung ein: Nachdem die Semiotik des 18. Jhs. jeglichen Kredit verloren hatte, war sie die einzige Disziplin, die den seelisch-körperlichen Doppelcharakter der Sprache wissenschaftlich zu fassen versprach. Mit Recht nennen die Historiographen sie in einem Atemzug mit der Physiologie, die ebenfalls metaphorisch bemüht wurde in der Sprachforschung und in der psycho-physischen Richtung von Weber, Fechner und Wundt mit ihr auf eine Weise zusammengebunden wurde, die auch über die Verbindung von geistig-seelischem Gehalt und körperlicher Artikulation in der Sprache Aufschluß versprach. Bei Steinthal gibt es einen klaren Primat der seelischen Seite in der Sprache: "Das Erste, das wahrhaft Thätige und Regierende, bleibt natürlich die Seele, und so beginnen wir hier mit ihrer Entwickelung", schreibt er (1855: 235) in der ersten Skizze seines psychologischen Programms. Herbart, der sich selbst als empirischen Realisten sah (vgl. Hehlmann 1967: 134), ist für diesen Idealismus der schöpferischen Seele ein nicht weniger problematischer Gewährsmann als Steinthal selbst, der nun die proklamierte Autonomie der Vorstellungen an den Sprachlaut zurückbinden möchte. Steinthal glaubt damit unanfechtbar wissenschaftlich zu fundieren, was er bei Humboldt bloß als apercu über die intime Verwobenheit der Sprache mit dem Vorstellungleben der Völker gefunden hat (und was ihn in scharfen Widerspruch zu Humboldts Neigung stellt, an einer allgemein-philosophischen Grammatik und an einer empirisch-vergleichenden Durchführung der historischen Grammatik als Gegenstück zu Individualität und Verschiedenheit der Sprachen festzuhalten).

5. Die Hauptprobleme der frühen Sprachpsychologie: ein Aufriß

Es ist üblich, die frühe Sprachpsychologie im Bezugssystem der historisch-vergleichenden Sprachforschung und ihrer Fundierungsprobleme zu situieren und darzustellen (vgl. Arens 1969: 277 ff., Jaritz 1990). Das ist durchaus begründet, zumal die Hauptakteure von Steinthal bis Paul und Wundt dieses Verhältnis durchaus im Blick hatten. Darüber hinaus ist aber auch anzuerkennen, daß die psychologische Richtung mehr zu bieten hatte als ideologische Hilfsdienste für die übermächtig erfolgreiche Indogermanistik. Karl Bühler, der die psychologische Sprachauffassung im 20. Jh. erneuert, bescheinigt zwar den Protagonisten des 19. Jhs. (Steinthal, Lazarus, Paul, Wundt), daß in ihren Werken „noch alles offen und so gut wie nichts erledigt" und "die Bewegung auf der ganzen Linie im Nebensächlichen" stecken geblieben sei (Bühler 1927: 30). Das ist jedoch der Hochmut desjenigen, der sich selbst weiter weiß, weil er die Beschränkungen der bewußtseins- und erlebnispsychologischen Axiomatik in der Psychologie überwunden und den Übergang der Sprachwissenschaft von Stoff- zum Form-, Funktions- und Systemdenken aktiv miterlebt hat.

Unter den Problemen, an denen die frühe Sprachpsychologie sich abgearbeitet hat, ist der Sprachursprung naturgemäß am unergiebigsten, was positive und dauerhafte Ergebnisse betrifft. Weil aber nirgends die Axiome und Prämissen einer Theorie ungestörter sich entfalten als da, wo ihr störende Tatsachen durchaus nicht in die Quere kommen können, ist der Sprachursprung für die Theoriegeschichte vielleicht das einträglichste Problem (vgl. Knobloch 1988: 93−181). Für die Epoche sind Ursprungsfragen Wesensfragen (und vice versa), der Sprachursprung bildet also kein reizvolles Seitenthema, er ist das Thema schlechthin. Das stoffliche Interesse der Indogermanistik an 'Ursprachen' ist sein praktisches Korrelat, und einige Sprachpsychologen sind verwegen genug, auf der stofflichen Seite nach Anschluß zu suchen (Lazarus Geiger, Ludwig Noire und vor allem Max Müller; vgl. Knobloch 1988: 126−138). Steinthal hat sein Buch über den Sprachursprung von 1851 bis 1888 beständig erweitert, ergänzt und ausgebaut (Steinthal 1888), was bezeugt, wie wichtig ihm die Sache war. Es dokumentiert die Lehrmeinungen von Herder an aus der Sicht desjenigen, der glaubt, mit seinem Modell des 'Sprachreflexes' das Problem ein für alle Male gelöst zu haben. Dieses Modell bündelt eine Reihe von höchst widersprüchlichen Denktraditionen zu einer Synthese, die erkennen läßt, was dem Zeitgeist plausibel und teuer war. Es enthält eine hegelianische Entwicklungslogik der menschlichen Seele, die an einer bestimmten Stelle Sprache hervorbringen muß, es enthält die Annahme eines natürlichen, den starken Eindruck pathognomisch nachbildenden Sprachreflexes, der romantische und naturwissenschaftlich-nüchterne Motive bis in die Wortwahl hinein reizvoll verbindet, und es enthält schließlich den Humboldtschen Gedanken der (selbst sich entwickelnden) inneren Form als der jeweiligen Verbindungslogik von Ausdrückendem und Ausgedrücktem (vgl. 6.). Schließlich ist Steinthals Theorie, ganz im Einklang mit den dominierenden antipraktischen Motiven der Zeit, auf die Leistung der Sprache für das (Selbst-)Bewußtsein des Sprechenden abgestellt, nicht auf Kommunikation und Sozialität, wie man von einem 'Völkerpsychologen' vielleicht erwarten könnte.

Unmittelbar auf Humboldt zurück führt gleich mehrfach das Geflecht von Problemen, das unter dem Stichwort der 'Völkerpsychologie' abgehandelt wird (meist in ausdrücklichem Gegensatz zur 'Individualpsychologie', die nach Meinung der Opponenten die einzig wirkliche ist). Es betrifft einmal die Zurechnungsinstanz für sprachliche Erscheinungen: Gehört eine Sprache ausschließlich dem sprechenden Individuum (mit der junggrammatischen Konsequenz, daß 'die Sprache' zu einer Abstraktion wird und lediglich 'Individualsprachen' Realität haben) oder gehört sie der Gesellschaft, für deren Mitglieder sie verbindlich normiert ist? Trotz großer Differenzen im Detail gilt für die Völkerpsychologen von Steinthal bis Wundt, daß sie das Sprechen als individuelle Leistung an die gesellschaftlich vorliegende eigengesetzliche Objektivation binden. Dann gehört in diesen Problemkreis auch die Streitfrage: Spiegeln die Sprachen in ihren Struktur- und Gebildeordnungen allgemeine und notwendige Eigenschaften der geistigen und/oder kommunikativen Tätigkeit oder prägen sie diese je nach ihrer eigentümlichen Bildung? Hierin steckt freilich eine stillschweigende Gleichsetzung verschiedener Bedeutungen von 'Sprache': des Sprechens als einer individuellen Aktivität mit der Sprache als einer verbindlichen Ordnung von Darstellungstechniken, wie aus Lazarus' popolärer Formulierung deutlich wird:

"Wie die Sprache des Individuums Ausdruck und Maßstab seines individuellen Geistes ist, so ist die Sprache des Volkes, als gemeinsames Eigenthum Aller, Ausdruck und Maßstab des Volksgeistes." (Lazarus 1884: 400)

Indirekt hängt am Völkerpsychologieproblem noch die axiomatisch höchst wichtige Frage nach dem Ursprung und Quellpunkt der sprachlichen Semantik (vgl. die Diskussion bei Bühler 1927; Freyer 1923). Wenn nämlich die Zurechnung auf das Individuum mit seinen 'Vorstellungen' das letzte Wort sein soll, dann wird die Ableitung gemeinsam geteilter Bedeutungen unmöglich. Gemeinsame Bedeutungen muß man dann entweder anderswo verankern (in der Gleichartigkeit der psychischen Prozesse überhaupt etc.)

oder als bloße Illusion geißeln. Prägt dagegen die gesellschaftlich verbindlich vorgegebene Sprache das Vorstellungsleben des Individuums, dann sind geteilte Bedeutungen von vornherein selbstverständlich gegeben. In beiden Sichtweisen wird die sprachliche Kommunikation problematisch. Für radikale Skeptiker und Individualisten wird sie unmöglich (vgl. z. B. Mauthner 1923 [1900–1902]), für radikale Kollektivisten wird sie unnötig. Aus diesem Kreis treten nur diejenigen Sprachforscher heraus, die ihr Bezugssystem von vornherein zwischen den Extremen 'Individuum' und 'Volk' wählen: in der Kommunikation selbst (z. B. Wegener 1885; Madvig 1875).

Die Praxis zur völkerpsychologischen Theorie ist, wenn es überhaupt eine gibt, die Klassifikation der Sprachen. In deren Neigung, die klassifizierten Sprachen auch zu bewerten, lebt ein Bündel vorwissenschaftlicher Motive fort: Sprachnationalismus, Griechenbegeisterung, romantischer Organizismus etc. Soweit ich sehe, hat kein ausdrücklicher Gegner der Völkerpsychologie typologische Klassifikation der Sprachen betrieben (Pott wieder einmal ausgenommen), obwohl man das völkerpsychologische Fundament der Typologie ohne Substanzverlust abstreichen kann. Die Absätze, in denen etwa Misteli (1893) über die vergleichende Beschreibung von Lautlehre und Morphosyntax hinausgeht, tragen zur Sache eigentlich kaum etwas bei: "Unter den Völkern, welche die indogermanischen Sprachen reden, befinden sich unläugbar die begabtesten Völker der Erde" (Misteli 1893: 487) etc. Aber selbst ein so nüchterner und vielseitiger Sprachkenner wie Georg von der Gabelentz (1840–1893) bleibt in diesen Dingen widersprüchlich. Im ganzen hält er an der Korrelation von Sprachbau und Kulturwert der Völker fest, obwohl er die Einzelheiten, auf denen diese Deutung ruht, in höchst ironischen Passagen verwirft (vgl. Gabelentz 1891: 371 ff.), um dann aber, ganz gegen seine eigene Beweisführung, zu schließen:

"Und doch bleibt es dabei: soweit die Gesittung oder Rohheit der Völker von ihrer geistigen Beanlagung abhängig ist, muss jenen der Werth der Sprachen entsprechen." (Gabelentz 1891: 376)

Die Psychologie erbt (von Logik und Philosophie) die Zuständigkeit für die innere Seite der Sprache(n). Im stofforientierten 19. Jh. war das kein sonderlich reizvolles Erbe. Akademische Reputation war weithin an die Bedingung geknüpft, neue stoffliche Zusammenhänge zu entdecken oder bekannte und bestehende anders zu erklären. Die Semantik bleibt ein Mauerblümchen im 19. Jh., wiewohl man ohne semantische Theorie keine Etymologie betreiben kann, die doch eifrig betrieben wurde, u. a. von Leuten wie Pott! Faßliche Gestalt gewinnt die Semantik denn auch zuerst als Lehre vom Bedeutungswandel (vgl. Nerlich 1988, 1990, 1992). Den verspäteten Abschluß dieser Tradition bildet, wie Nerlich (1992: 118) herausstellt, Stern (1931). Ein Außenseiter wie Madvig, der schon 1871 darauf hinweist, daß auch die konstruierten Verwandtschaften der Form auf weitreichenden, aber nie thematisierten Annahmen über 'gleiche' oder 'veränderte' Bedeutung beruhen, wird nicht gehört. So ist es eine undankbare Aufgabe, die rezipierte psychologische Semantik systematisch und im Detail zu rekonstruieren. Ihr Kern war der (polemisch gegen die 'Logik' gewendete und nur in dieser Wendung sinnvolle) Satz, die Bedeutung eines Ausdrucks, das seien die mit ihm verbundenen Vorstellungen, wobei beinahe jeder unter 'Vorstellung' etwas anderes verstand, kaum einer jedoch zwischen dem Wort des Lexikons und dem Wort der Rede unterschied. Eine Reihe von indirekten Gründen rechtfertigt es jedoch, gleichwohl einen genaueren Blick auf die Seitenstränge der psychologischen Semantik zu werfen. Da ist einmal, wie Nerlich (1992: 8) betont, der Umstand, daß aus den konzeptionslosen und ärmlichen Versuchen, den Bedeutungswandel zu systematisieren, im Laufe der Zeit recht differenzierte Theorien über die verschiedenen Aspekte von Sinn, Bedeutung und Referenz herausgewachsen sind. Da ist zum anderen aber auch die Tatsache, daß es an der Peripherie der Debatte eine Reihe von interessanten Autoren gab, die damals wie späterhin ohne angemessene Resonanz geblieben sind, deren Wiederentdeckung sich aber durchaus lohnt (vgl. 6.).

Bedeutendes geleistet hat die frühe Sprachpsychologie auch auf dem Gebiet der Grammatik, wenn auch ihre Produktivität und Innovationskraft weit hinter der Schulgrammatik zurückbleibt, von der sie jedoch (ganz im Gegensatz zur historisch-vergleichenden Sprachforschung) auch Anregungen aufnimmt. In Betracht kommen hier vor allem Überlegungen über das Wechselverhältnis zwischen grammatisch-festen und psychologisch-dynamischen Kategorien des Sprechens. Den Motiven der fortschreitenden Psychologisierung grammatischer Kategorien geht Elffers-van Ketel (1991) nach. Verbunden haben sich diese Lehren mit einer viel älteren Tradition der Psychologisierung der Wortfolge (als Spiegel des Vorstellungsverlaufs). Die stammen vor allem aus der Grammatik der französischen Aufklärung, von wo sie zu den deutschen Schulgrammatikern der ersten Jahrhunderthälfte gelangten (Becker und Herling). Von denen wiederum hat Weil (1844) Anregungen bezogen. Gabelentz (1869—1875), dem gewöhnlich der Gedanke des psychologischen Subjektes und Prädikates zugeschrieben wird, hat dem bloß eine etwas andere (und keineswegs glückliche) Richtung gegeben (vgl. Knobloch 1988: 336—340).

Weil (1844) löst die Einheit der grammatischen Kategorien auf in zwei nicht notwendig synchrone Reihen von Bewegungen im Satz:

"There are in the proposition two different movements: an objective movement, which is expressed by syntactical relations; and a subjective movement, which is expressed by the order of words."
(Weil 1978 [1844]: 30)

Im Prinzip kann jedes grammatische Satzglied die Funktion des 'subjektiven' Ausgangspunktes, des Themas, übernehmen, es gibt allerdings teils allgemeine, teils einzelsprachliche, mit der syntaktischen Ausnutzung der Konstituentenfolge zusammenhängende limitierende Faktoren. Die Thema-Rhema-Forschung nimmt hier ihren Anfang. Bei Wegener (1885) tauchen ähnliche Überlegungen auf, jedoch nicht mehr mit Bezug auf Serialisierung und Strukturbildung allein, sondern vor dem Hintergrund einer funktionalen Zweigliederung der Äußerung in einen expositorischen, das Verständnis vorbereitenden, einbettenden und absichernden und einen für die Mitteilung zentralen Teil (das "logische Prädikat", wie es bei Wegener [1885: 29—34] unglücklich heißt). Diese dynamische Funktionsverschiedenheit dient Wegener als historisches Motiv für bestimmte Typen der grammatischen Strukturbildung:

"alle Formen des pronominalen Nebensatzes sind aus der nachträglichen Correctur einer Mitteilung ohne genügende Exposition hervorgegangen."
(Wegener 1885: 40)

Der Sprecher realisiert, daß bestimmte Ausdrücke für den Hörer nicht ohne weiteres verständlich sind, und aus der allmählichen Grammatikalisierung 'nachträglicher Correkturen' werden Muster der Subordination. So beginnt in der psychologischen Grammatik des 19. Jhs. das Nachdenken über Dinge, die man heute der funktionalen Motivierung grammatischer Strukturbildung zurechnen würde. Während Weil (1844) an der Wort- und Konstituentenfolge typologische Syntax betreibt, sucht Wegener allenthalben die funktional-kommunikativen Fundamente grammatischer Strukturbildung und deren Einsatz beim Sprechen, das von entgegengesetzten Motiven beherrscht ist: einmal hat der Sprecher die Tendenz rasch und ohne Umschweife auf den (rhematischen) Kern der Mitteilung zu kommen, dann hat er aber auch den (zivilisierten) Wunsch, die Verständlichkeit und Beziehbarkeit dieses rhematischen Kerns durch vorausgehende Exposition abzusichern. Strukturen und Reihenfolgebeziehungen müssen flexibel genug sein, um diese beiden Motive in allen Lebenslagen ausgleichen zu können.

Sachdienliches trägt zu dieser Diskussion auch Marty (1897) bei, der die grammatische Funktion des Subjekts doppelt verankern möchte: einmal im naturgemäßen Fortgang des Denkens vom Bekannten zum Unbekannten und dann auch im Dynamismus der Mitteilung, welcher festlegt, worauf der Hörende zuerst seine Aufmerksamkeit richten soll. Daß beide Reihen nicht notwendig parallel sind, korrigiert die monologische Perspektive Hermann Pauls (1920 [1880]: 127) in dieser Angelegenheit (vgl. auch Sandmann 1979: 7—45, 77—126; Elffers-van Ketel 1991, Knobloch 1988: 332 ff.).

Was schließlich das Verhältnis von Denken und Sprechen betrifft, so ist schon angeklungen, daß die mächtige Opposition Steinthals gegen Becker und seine Schule auch auf gemeinsamen Anliegen und Prämissen beruht. Coseriu (1975) notiert, daß sich die Denkfehler der 'Logizisten' und der 'Antilogizisten' in der Grammatik bisweilen gleichen, bisweilen aber auch ergänzen. Zwar trennt Steinthal einigermaßen konsequent die sprachliche Form (der Vorstellung oder Darstellung) von den Inhalten des Denkens und vom sprachlich Dargestellten, doch bleibt auch ihm am Ende nur der (völkerpsychologische) Schluß von der ausdrucksseitigen Organisation auf den ausgedrückten Inhalt. Ein praktisches Korrelat der Auseinandersetzung zwischen Steinthal und Becker ist (wie immer, wenn Logizisten und Antilogizisten zusammenstoßen) das Problem der Universalität der Kategorien: Becker fordert sie für den Satz auf der Grundlage seiner 'tiefen' Satzglieduniversalien, und Steinthal leugnet sie auf der Grundlage der morphosyntaktischen Verschiedenheit der Sprachen (die er in Formsprachen und formlose Sprachen einteilt). Zunächst scheint der Differenzierungsgewinn ganz auf Steinthals Seite zu sein: er kann die Logik (als 'Ethik des Denkens') ganz von der Sprachform ablösen. Aber auch Becker hat einen Vorteil von seiner Konstruktion: die Anatomie der Satzgliedverhältnisse ist ganz unabhängig von den Details ihrer morphosyntaktischen Realisierung, die er somit in verschiedenen Sprachen vergleichen kann. Steinthal steht hingegen streng genommen für den Sprachvergleich, die vornehmste Aufgabe der Disziplin, völlig mittellos da, weil er die Universalität der Kategorien nicht anerkennt (es ist leicht zu zeigen, daß er sie in praxi anerkennen muß: er beschreibt die Mande-Negersprachen (ausgerechnet) mit der Beckerschen Satzgliedlehre). Pott (1863: 214) notiert spöttisch, Steinthal selbst habe eine Monographie über den Infinitiv in möglichst vielen Sprachen versprochen.

Das Problem Sprache und Denken hat indessen noch eine Vielzahl anderer Facetten. Es tangiert die psychologische Semantik als Frage nach dem Verhältnis zwischen den begriffsähnlichen Sprachbedeutungen und den Erkenntnisbegriffen (vgl. 6.). Von der jeweiligen Fassung, die dieser Problemlösung gegeben wird, hängt wiederum die Selbstbeschreibung ab, die Etymologen von ihrem Geschäft geben. Setzt man Wortbedeutung und Erkenntnisbegriff gleich (wie Müller 1888, Noiré und Geiger folgend), dann wird die Sprachgeschichte zur Vernunft- und Erkenntnisgeschichte geadelt.

Die 'Psychologisierung der Logik' steht ebenfalls im Zusammenhang mit veränderten Vorstellungen über das Verhältnis von Sprache und Denken. In der 2. Hälfte des 19. Jhs. verwandelt sich die Logik von einer Normwissenschaft für richtiges Schließen und Urteilen (dem Anspruch nach) zu einer empirischen Wissenschaft von den Denk- und Urteilsprozessen und der Begriffsbildung, zu einer vorempirischen Denkpsychologie gewissermaßen. Wer die Logiken von Lotze, Wundt oder Sigwart aufschlägt, der wird feststellen, daß diese Lehren wiederum die Vorstellung verändert haben, die sich Psychologen von der Satzbildung gemacht haben (vgl. Knobloch 1988: 441−453). Eine sowohl sprach- als auch logikunabhängige (introspektive) Denkpsychologie entwickelt sich erst aus der Külpe-Schule und aus der Opposition gegen Wundt und die psychologistische Logik um 1900. Ihre sprachpsychologische Ausfolgerung beginnt erst mit Bühler und Otto Selz (1881−1943).

Der wirkliche Umschwung in der Frühphase der Sprachpsychologie betrifft jedoch auch ihre Gegner. Verändert hat sich die Herangehensweise dergestalt, daß die geordneten Produkte und Techniken des Sprechens als Indikatoren für die Genese und Aktualgenese der in ihnen verlaufenden Denkprozesse genommen werden. Das ist gegenüber der alten Allgemeinen Grammatik ein Zugewinn an empirischer Gesinnung. Man nimmt die Sprachtatsachen als gegeben und fragt sich, "wie die Denkvorgänge beschaffen sein müßten, wenn jene [die Sprachtatsachen: C. K.] aus ihnen verständlich werden sollten", und, so fährt Bühler fort:

"logisch wäre gegen dieses Verfahren nun gar nichts einzuwenden, wenn nur jene engen Beziehungen zwischen Denken und Sprechen, die es voraussetzt, tatsächlich bestünden." (Bühler 1907−1908 I: 298)

Daran zweifelt der Külpe-Schüler natürlich sehr, und er vergißt auch nicht darauf hinzuweisen, daß diese zweifelhafte Axiomatik nicht nur bei Steinthal und Lazarus, sondern auch bei Wundt vorherrscht.

6. Apperzeption und psychologische Semantik: eine Fallstudie

Wer sich der frühen Sprachpsychologie begriffsgeschichtlich nähern wollte, der käme am Begriff der "Apperzeption" nicht vorbei. Niemand glaubte, ohne diesen Begriff auskommen zu können, jeder hat ihn für sich eigens neu bestimmt und definiert. Kurz: es handelt sich um einen rechten Grundbegriff, evaluativ eindeutig und kognitiv unklar. Die Verzweigungen und Verästelungen der Begriffsgeschichte müssen wir auf sich beruhen lassen (vgl. für Einzelheiten Staude 1882 und Janke 1971). Es gibt jedoch von Leibniz bis Wundt auch ein Stück gemeinsamen Boden, auf welchem sich die Debatte um den Begriff bewegt hat. Der Hauptdisput (zwischen Wundt und den Herbartianern) dreht sich um die Frage, ob Apperzeption als epistemisch-kognitiver Akt verstanden werden soll (wie in der Tradition Leibniz−Herbart) oder eher als ein voluntaristisches 'nehmen − für' (wie es Wundt vorschwebte). Es ist aus heutiger Sicht leicht, das als Scheinalternative abzutun. Damit würde man jedoch dem polemischen Charakter derartiger Grundbegriffe in der Geistesgeschichte nicht gerecht. Wir beschränken uns auf den sprachpsychologischen Ausgangspunkt des Begriffs, auf Steinthals Version der 'Apperzeption' und ihre Auswirkungen auf einige Vertreter psychologisch-semantischer Positionen.

Hier, bei Steinthal, organisiert der Begriff zuerst die Disjunktion zwischen der Sprache als einer Technik der Auffassung und Darstellung auf der einen, den solchermaßen aufgefaßten Begriffen oder Sachen auf der anderen Seite. Was der Sprachlaut (nebst der 'inneren Form') in diesen Vorgang einbringt, das ist die aktive apperzipierende Masse, die selbst nicht wieder apperzipiert wird. Nach der Herbartschen Tradition (und hier ist Steinthal Herbartianer) schafft die Apperzeption einen Zuwachs neuer Vorstellungen durch die Auffassung, Einordnung und Bewußtmachung aktueller Perzeptionen im Lichte der organisierten vergangenen. Die Eindrücke, welche die Bühne des Bewußtseins bevölkern, können nur dann bewußt werden, wenn sie von einer anderen Vorstellung apperzipiert werden (vgl. Janke 1971: 454). Als diese 'andere' Vorstellungsreihe präsentiert Steinthal den Sprachlaut, der also eigentlich als Mittel und Werkzeug des bewußten Seelenlebens in diesen Zusammenhang eintritt. Die Sprache ist, so könnte man mit der Marxschen Formel sagen, das praktische Bewußtsein der Menschen, weil nur vermittels der sprachlichen Apperzeption wirklich und willkürlich dem Bewußtsein verfügbar wird, was es an Eindrücken aufnimmt und an Konzepten bildet.

Steinthals auf den ersten Blick höchst seltsame, beinahe groteske Bedeutungstheorie wird nur vor diesem Hintergrund verständlich. Zur 'Bedeutung' und somit zur Sprache rechnet er nur das Apperzipierende und durchaus nicht, was im Einklang mit dem sprachlichen common sense wäre, auch das Apperzipierte. Bedeutung ist für ihn 'innere Form', und das Aufgefaßte wird selbst nur in dem Maße Teil der Sprache als es dazu dient, seinerseits wiederum anderes aufzufassen. Das Bedeutete rechnet ansonsten nur zum sprachlichen Prozeß, als es durch diesen aufgefaßt ist (das unterscheidet Steinthal etwa von Martys entgegengesetzter Terminologie, wonach Bedeutung das nichtsprachliche, sprachlich nur dargestellte Seelenleben ist, innere Form nur die Technik seiner Darstellung).

Steinthal muß nach seiner Position folgerichtig behaupten, daß es eigentlich weder Polysemie noch Homonymie noch autochthonen Bedeutungswandel gibt (vgl. Steinthal 1860). Das Apperzipierende ist und bleibt das Etymon, und lediglich das Apperzipierte unterliegt dem ständigen Wechsel. Diese Lage wird jedoch insofern beständig kompliziert, als etablierte und eingelebte Apperzeptionen das Apperzipierte nach und nach dem Apperzipierenden einverleiben. Das gewohnheitsmäßig Aufgenommene wechselt gleichsam die Seiten und wird seinerseits zum Aufnehmenden.

Daß diese Lehre der historischen Sprachforschung mehr als nur entgegenkam, daß sie ihr gleichsam auf den Leib geschnitten war, liegt auf der Hand. Sie adelt das Etymon eines historisch belegten Wortes als dessen eigentliche, durch mannigfachen Gebrauch bloß korrumpierte Bedeutung. Sie erlaubt es, dieses Etymon festzuschreiben und als sprachspezifische Auffassungsweise für Sachen und Begriffe völkerpsychologisch zu deuten. Abbilden läßt sie sich auch auf den historischen Prozeß des Vergessens und Verblassens etymologischer Bedeutungen. Das Etymon muß rekonstruiert werden. Denn

"Da der Repräsentant nicht durch sich und nicht als er selbst, sondern durch und für andres gilt, so tritt auch das Apperzeptionsmittel wenig ins Bewußtsein [...] und kann endlich vergessen werden." (Steinthal 1860, zitiert nach Christmann 1977: 61)

Die Semantik ist prozessualisiert, da jedes Erzeugnis eines Apperzeptionsprozesses selbst wieder zum Werkzeug neuer Apperzeptionen werden kann, und sie hat ein Endziel im Etymon (wie die Formengeschichte ein Endziel in der 'Ursprache' hat). Gleichzeitig liefern die Kategorien und Weisen der Apperzeption, wie Herbart sie gibt, einen Schlüssel und eine Systematik für die Beschreibung des Bedeutungswandels (vgl. Nerlich 1992: 56 ff.), einen Schlüssel freilich, mit dem auch die Nachfolger Steinthals auf diesem Gebiet nur mit mäßigem Erfolg hantiert haben.

Die Paradoxie, welche in der Suche nach einem Etymon für alle Bezeichnungen liegt, hat selbst ein mißtrauischer Mann wie Pott nicht ganz entschlüsselt. Der schreibt vielmehr (1880 II: 433) in seinen Anmerkungen zu Humboldts Kawi-Einleitung, alle Benennungen seien synekdochisch und wählten nur ein einziges Merkmal für die Bezeichnung, alle anderen Merkmale des Bezeichneten Gegenstandes blieben unbezeichnet, würden jedoch mitverstanden. Diese (auf Gerber zurückgehende; s. u.) Ansicht geht stillschweigend davon aus, daß alle Benennungen einer Sprache letztlich auf Prädikate derselben Sprache zurückgeführt werden können und insofern 'deskriptive Benennungen' (Seiler

1975) sind. So verfährt Pott selbst, wenn er die 43 Bezeichnungen des Sanskrit für 'Erde' auf solche Prädikate zurückführt. Das geht an für Sprachen, welche die Gewohnheit haben, ihre Bezeichnungen aus Prädikaten zu bilden, enthält aber auch die starke Hypothese, daß es letztlich immer so sein müsse.

Dennoch markiert der Steinthalsche Apperzeptionsbegriff in der frühen Sprachpsychologie bei weitem die differenzierteste und komplexeste semantische Position. Zum einen sind Bezeichnendes und Bezeichnetes von Anfang an so polarisiert, daß das Bezeichnende nicht allein Laut ist und auch kein fertiger Begriff, sondern ein vom Bezeichneten genommenes Merkmal, das auf das Bezeichnende übergeht. Zum anderen ist die Bedeutungsrelation gleich dynamisch angelegt. Ein Aspekt des Bezeichneten geht auf das Bezeichnende über und kann dann selbst wieder charakterisierend in andere Bezeichnungsverhältnisse eintreten (die "charakterisierende innere Sprachform"; Steinthal 1881: 425–428). Aufgrund dieser dynamischen Eigenschaften ist Steinthals Modell der Bedeutungsrelation eine Quelle für spätere Neuerungen geworden. Unter diesen seien Gerber (1871–1874) und Wegener (1885) noch kurz erwähnt, weil beide ganz unterschiedliche Potentiale der Umdeutung offenbaren, die in diesem Modell stecken.

Während sich die Grenze zwischen Apperzepierendem und Apperzipiertem bei Steinthal ständig verschiebt, ist doch klar, daß nur das Apperzipierende eigentlich zur Sprache gehört. Die Grenze zwischen Darstellung und Dargestelltem wird daher nicht allein von unkundigen Linguisten, sondern von der Sprachentwicklung selbst beständig verschoben und verwischt. Das scheint mir ein realistischer Zug seiner Semantik zu sein.

Ein Aspekt dieser beständigen Grenzverschiebung zwischen apperzipierender und apperzipierter Vorstellung ist aber auch, daß sich das Bewußtsein der speziellen Auffassungsweise mechanisiert und schließlich verliert, wenn die Verwendung eines Ausdrucks einigermaßen regelmäßig und geordnet ist (was zu Steinthals dritter Stufe der inneren Sprachform, dem mechanisierten "Sprachgebrauch" führt; vgl. Steinthal 1881 [1871]: 428 ff.) Die eigentlich sprachliche Vermittlung verschwindet für das Bewußtsein des Sprechenden, und das Band zwischen Laut und Bezeichnetem scheint so direkt und umweglos wie ein bloßes Zeichen. Das ist darum wichtig, weil spätere funktions- und kommunikationsorientierte Semantiker wie Wegener, Bréal und Whitney dieses Vergessen des Etymon, das 'Kongruentwerden' der Namen, als Errungenschaft schätzen (vgl. Nerlich 1992: 226 ff.). Der Gedanke ist bei Steinthal vorhanden, gehört da aber in die Geschichte von Verfall und Niedergang der historischen Sprachen.

Für die jeweilige Kommunikation kommen aber Apperzipierendes und Apperzipiertes nur als Einheit in Betracht, dieses wird nur im Lichte von jenem bewußt. Das ist der Einsatzpunkt für Gerbers (1871–74) 'ästhetische' Semantiktheorie, die außer Pott (1880: 34, 211) und Nietzsche (vgl. Ungeheuer 1983) von den Zeitgenossen niemand recht zu schätzen wußte (Pott notiert auch als einzigen kongenialen Anreger für Gerber August Ferdiand Bernhardi). Sie beruht auf der streng durchgeführten Ansicht, daß alle sprachlichen Bedeutungseinheiten nach ihrer Redebedeutung Tropen seien. Die Tropisierung ist der eigentliche Funktionsmechanismus des (wasbestimmten) Wortes in der Kommunikation. Das Wort zeigt immer 'etwas' als 'etwas anderes' oder 'im Lichte von' etwas anderem. Darüber hinaus ist das Wort nach seiner lautlichen Seite phonetisch-grammatische Figur, nach seinen syntagmatischen Beziehungen syntaktisch-grammatische Figur (Gerber 1871 I: 332 ff.). Figurativ oder bildlich sind alle Aspekte des Wortes in Funktion. Zwischen dem, was ein Wort an sich selbst ist, und seiner fallweisen Verwendung weiß Gerber sehr wohl zu unterscheiden (1871 I: 336). Die relative Bestimmtheit eines Wortes in seinen Verwendungen kann sich als 'usus' (der Ausdruck wird ganz so gebraucht wie später von Hermann Paul) oder habituelle Bezeichnung festsetzen, aber nicht so fest, daß die Möglichkeit ganz entfiele, Ähnliches, Verwandtes, Analoges fallweise auch mit dem solchermaßen usuell fixierten Ausdruck zu bezeichnen. Steinthals Abfolge der inneren Form wird gewissermaßen entzeitlicht, in die Synchronie der Funktionsmechanismen projiziert, und da zeigt sich, daß die 'charakterisierende' Stufe niemals wirklich untergehen kann. Auch wenn die Worte uns wie bloße Bezeichnungen der Dinge vorkommen, sind es doch untergründig immer unsere Beziehungen zu den Dingen, die in Worte gefaßt werden (wenn einer wirklich Humboldt fortgesetzt hat in diesen Dingen, dann war es Gerber!).

Die dominierende Rolle, welche das Bild, der Tropus, in Gerbers Lehre spielt, führt dazu, daß man eine andere, bedeutende Leistung leicht übersieht: Gerber entthront nämlich die Vorstellungssemantik in dem Punkt, wo sie auf der sensualistischen Prämisse der Verarbeitung von Perzeptionen, Wahrnehmungen, Sinneseindrücken beruht. Er sagt ausdrücklich, "daß die Bedeutungen der isolierten Wörter so vorgestellt werden müssen, wie ihnen in der Wahrnehmung nichts entspricht" (Gerber 1884: 103) und daß auch die Übertragung keineswegs von anschaulichen Ähnlichkeiten der bezeichneten Dinge getragen sein muß. Regulativ und begrenzend ist allein die aspektive Verbindbarkeit des Gemeinten mit der eigenen Bildsphäre des Ausdrucks, und deren Grenzen weiten sich umso mehr, wenn ein Ausdruck von Identifikationsaufgaben entlastet ist. Sprachverständnis und Gegenstandserkenntnis hängen nun notwendig an solchen selbsterzeugten Formen und Figuren. Das ist eine Position, die leicht zu sprachkritischen und erkenntnisskeptischen Weiterungen führt, weshalb Gerber auch in der Geschichte der sprachkritischen Philosophie kein Unbekannter ist (vgl. Schmidt 1968, 1971; Cloeren 1988). Beim Sprechen kann der Redende das Einzelne und Individuelle meinen, "nie aber kann er es sagen" (Gerber 1871 I: 249), individuelle Bezüge muß der Hörer aus dem Kontext, aus den Redeumständen, aus seinem Wissen ergänzen, sie lassen sich nicht eigentlich sprachlich darstellen.

Aus dem Dynamismus der Apperzeption ist so eine höchst originelle semantische Theorie erwachsen, deren Reflexionsniveau so schnell nicht wieder erreicht wurde. Steinthals apodiktisches und mißverständliches Axiom, ein Wort habe immer nur eine Bedeutung, hat sich zu dem Satz gewandelt:

"Die Wörter haben nicht eine Bedeutung, sondern sie vertreten Bedeutungsgebiete, deren Umkreis beständig gezogen wird, niemals aber gezogen ist, so lange die Sprache des Wortes lebt." (Gerber 1884: 161)

Die Fiktion einer 'eigentlichen' Grundbedeutung, die es lediglich aufzusuchen gelte, kann Gerber nicht aufrechterhalten (darauf verweist schon Ludwig Tobler (1827–1895) 1871–1875, sicherlich der kundigste Rezensent der *Sprache als Kunst*). Auch die naive Gleichsetzung des Tropus mit dem Erkenntnisbegriff und mit dem Denken überhaupt (wie sie in der Traditionslinie von Geiger, Noiré und Müller zu finden ist) steht Gerber nicht zu Gebote, weil das 'Wort in Funktion' im Aufgefaßten immer einen (und sei es fiktiven, weil sprachlich nicht darstellbaren) Gegenhalt hat (vgl. Knobloch 1988: 259–268, 423–430). Auch für den Eindruck des Festen und Beständigen, den die Wörter den Sprechenden vermitteln, gibt Gerber eine Erklärung. Er macht dafür das proportionale Gefüge von syntaktischer Beziehung und Bezeichnung verantwortlich, das ein Wort so zu halten scheint, daß jede neue Bedeutung einleuchtet, als wäre sie nur eine Spielart der alten (vgl. Gerber 1871: 355 et pass.).

Nach einer anderen Seite wird der Dynamismus der Apperzeption fruchtbar gemacht in Wegeners Situationstheorie des Sprechens und der Sprache. Im Gegensatz zum wortsemantischen Gerber verfügt Wegener über eine dynamische Theorie des Satzes (d. i. bei ihm: der kommunikativen Äußerung), die auch für ausdrucksseitig einfache Gebilde eine funktionale Zweiteilung unterstellt. Die Exposition (s. o. 5.) ist gewissermaßen eine Konzession des Sprechers an den Hörer (Nerlich 1992: 84), die dieser aber nur machen muß, wenn die Beziehbarkeiten des 'logischen Prädikates' sich nicht aus der Situation von selbst verstehen. Was bei Steinthal eine (in der Diachronie) bewegliche Konstellation von Apperzipierendem und Apperzipiertem war, das wird bei Wegener (1885) eine bewegliche kommunikative Matrix, bei der das gesprochene Wort zunächst an die Situation(en) seiner bisherigen Verwendung erinnert. Nach und nach kommandiert und differenziert aber das Wort selbst die Bezüge, zu deren Verständnis ursprünglich die Verwendungssituation unentbehrlich war, so daß die Last des Redeverstehens immer mehr bei den Worten und Sätzen selbst zu liegen scheint. Gleichzeitig differenzieren sich im Satz zwei entgegengesetzte Weisen der Apperzeption: eine expositorische, welche die Anknüpfungspunkte für das 'logische Prädikat' identifiziert und gewissermaßen das Erbe der situativen Beziehbarkeiten sprachlich verwaltet und ordnet, und eine prädizierende, welche solche Beziehbarkeiten einfach voraussetzt.

Von der Anlage ist Wegeners Semantik um das Problem der Hörerinstruktion herum gebaut. Sprachzeichen sind im Kern fragmentarische Anweisungen für den Hörer. Mit ihrer Hilfe, aber niemals aus ihnen allein, kann er gemeinten Sinn und Bezüge rekonstruieren. Aber nur die aktuelle Verflechtung der Zeichen mit verschiedenen Quellen des geteilten Wissens (von der gemeinsamen Anschauung und Praxis bis hin zum allgemeinen und kulturellen Hintergrund) führt zur hinreichenden Aggregation von Sinn in der sprachlichen Kommunikation. Aus der dynamischen Apperzeptionslehre ist hier (wie schon ansatzweise bei Lazarus 1884) eine Sprecher-Hörer-Dynamik geworden, weshalb Nerlich (1992: 87) den pragmatischen Charakter von Wegeners Semantik betont.

Am Ende dieses Abschnitts muß man herausstellen, daß hier durchaus nicht die Geschichte der psychologischen Semantik in systematischer Form reproduziert wurde, eher im Gegenteil. Wir haben nur einige Theoreme ausgeführt, die von den Zeitgenossen weitgehend ignoriert wurden und ohne die Aktivität der Historiographen wahrscheinlich völlig vergessen wären. In der Praxis der Etymologie dominierte eine andere, dürr taxonomische Tradition (vgl. Nerlich 1992: 73 ff. et pass.). Es handelt sich hier um die Abart der Wissenschaftsgeschichte, die man passend als 'Wiedergutmachung' bezeichnen könnte.

7. Schluß

Ohne Zweifel ist der frühen Sprachpsychologie die zeitliche und ideologische Nähe der historisch-vergleichenden Sprachforschung nicht gut bekommen. Sie ist mit dieser verschwunden, und auch historiographisch fällt auf sie nur das indirekte Licht, das von der allseits ausgeleuchteten Indogermanistik reflektiert wird. Die Mandarine der Sprachforschung haben das Werk der Psychologen darauf geprüft, ob es als Metatheorie und Rechtfertigung für ihre eigene Praxis taugt. Und nur wer selbst ein Mandarin war, wie Wundt, konnte seinerseits den Stoff der Sprachforschung einfach als Material für eine Psychologie der höheren Ausdrucksprozesse reklamieren. Man kann das im Nachhinein psychologisch als mangelndes Selbstbewußtsein der Psychologen deuten oder soziologisch als mangelhafte (oder gescheiterte) Ausdifferenzierung der Sprachpsychologie aus dem Feld einer institutionell mächtigen Praxis. Ganz gleich, welche Erklärung man für das Schicksal der frühen Sprachpsychologie vorzieht, entstanden ist sie aus dem Versuch, die ehemals philosophische Zuständigkeit für das 'Innen' der Sprachen zeitgemäß naturwissenschaftlich zu modernisieren. Den Mangel der Allgemeinen und Philosophischen Grammatik mußten alle spüren, die von Humboldt das Interesse an den inneren Folgen der Sprachverschiedenheit geerbt hatten. Für die historisch-vergleichende Indogermanistik war dies kein vordringliches Problem. Sie ist ja ohne weiteres mit den tradierten Kategorien der lateinischen Grammatik ausgekommen. Ihr Interesse konzentrierte sich auf den historischen Stoff. Das psychische 'Innen' wurde erst dann interessant, als Hermann Paul und die Junggrammatiker realisierten, daß die einzige Verbindung zweier historisch belegter Sprachformen über die Psyche der Sprecher führte. Damit beginnt die Vereinnahmung der (bis dahin weitgehend ignorierten) Psychologie als "Rückversicherung" (Jaritz 1990: 94). Diese Psychologie durfte dann aber keinesfalls historisch relativ und selbst das Produkt des (veränderlichen) Sprachbaues sein! Als Fundament der historisch-vergleichenden Praxis taugte sie nur, insofern sie selbst zeitlos, unhistorisch, unwandelbar und vor allem: von der Sprache unabhängig war, weshalb auch kein Junggrammatiker von Steinthals Völkerpsychologie etwas wissen wollte. Von dieser Sekundärverwertung der Herbartschen Psychologie fällt ein bezeichnendes Licht auf einen Sachverhalt, den schon Wundt (1888) scharfsinnig notiert: Steinthals völkerpsychologische Weiterungen sind mit dem zeitlosen Gerüst der Herbartschen Seelenmechanik völlig unvereinbar.

Alle genuin sprachpsychologischen Probleme und Lösungen waren dagegen in der akademischen Hauptströmung der Linguistik kaum resonanzfähig. Ausnahmen gibt es natürlich auch hier: Hermann Paul hat Wegener, August Friedrich Pott hat Gerber rezipiert und Friedrich Max Müller hat die Hauptgedanken zu seiner *Science of Thought* von Geiger und Noiré. Dennoch kann von eigentlich sprachpsychologischer Forschung im Untersuchungszeitraum nicht die Rede sein, sondern nur von sprachpsychologischer Theoriebildung. Zwar wird die Psychophysik mit den Schwellenmessungen um die Jahrhundertmitte so etwas wie eine experimentell forschende Naturwissenschaft, aber noch Wundt bietet seine ganze Reputation auf für die Argumentation, daß sprachliche Prozesse nicht solchermaßen experimentell untersucht werden können, sondern in ihrer Logik den (völkerpsychologischen) Vergegenständlichungen abgelesen werden müssen.

8. Bibliographie

Ammann, Hermann. 1925—28. *Die menschliche Rede: Sprachphilosophische Untersuchungen.* Lahr im Schwarzwald: Moritz Schauenburg. (Nachdruck Darmstadt: Wissenschaftliche Buchgesellschaft 1974.)

Arens, Hans. 1969. *Sprachwissenschaft: Der Gang ihrer Entwicklung von der Antike bis zur Gegenwart.* 2. Aufl. Freiburg: Alber.

Becker, Karl Ferdinand. 1827. *Organism der Sprache als Einleitung zur deutschen Grammatik.* Frankfurt/M.: Ludwig Reinherz. (2. überarbeitete Aufl. Frankfurt/M. 1841.)

Belke, Ingrid. 1971–1986. *Moritz Lazarus und Heymann Steinthal: Die Begründer der Völkerpsychologie in ihren Briefen.* 3 Bde. Tübingen: Mohr.

Benfey, Theodor. 1869. *Geschichte der Sprachwissenschaft und orientalischen Philologie in Deutschland seit dem Anfange des 19. Jahrhunderts, mit einem Rückblick auf die früheren Zeiten.* München: Cotta'sche Buchhandlung.

Berg, Anton. 1918. *Die Anschauungen L. Noirés Über Ursprung und Wesen von Sprache und Vernunft.* Diss. Gießen & Darmstadt: Bender.

Bernhardi, August Ferdinand. 1801–1803. *Sprachlehre.* 2 Bde. Berlin: Frölich. (Nachdruck, Hildesheim: Olms, 1973.)

—. 1805. *Anfangsgründe der Sprachwissenschaft.* Berlin: Frölich.

Bühler, Karl. 1907–1908. "Tatsachen und Probleme zu einer Psychologie der Denkvorgänge". *Archiv für die gesamte Psychologie* 9.1907.297–365; 12. 1908. 1–92.

—. 1927. *Die Krise der Psychologie.* Jena: Fischer.

—. 1933. *Ausdruckstheorie: Das System an der Geschichte aufgezeigt.* Jena: Fischer.

—. 1934. *Sprachtheorie. Die Darstellungsfunktion der Sprache.* Jena. Fischer.

Bumann, Waltraud. 1965. *Die Sprachtheorie Heymann Steinthals.* Meisenheim a. Gl.: Hain.

Cassirer, Ernst. 1923. *Philosophie der symbolischen Formen*, Teil 1: Die Sprache. Berlin: B. Cassirer. (2. Aufl. Darmstadt: Wiss. Buchgesellschaft, 1953.)

Christmann, Hans Helmut, Hg. 1977. *Sprachwissenschaft des 19. Jahrhunderts.* Darmstadt: Wissenschaftliche Buchgesellschaft.

Cloeren, Hermann J. 1988. *Language and Thought: German approaches to analytic philosophy in the 18th and 19th centuries.* Berlin: de Gruyter.

Coseriu, Eugenio. 1975 [1957]. "Logizismus und Antilogizismus in der Grammatik". Ders.: *Sprachtheorie und allgemeine Sprachwissenschaft*, 210–233. München: Fink.

Delbrück, Berthold. 1893. *Einleitung in das Sprachstudium: Ein Beitrag zur Geschichte und Methodik der vergleichenden Sprachforschung.* 3. erw. Aufl. Leipzig: Breitkopf & Härtel.

—. 1901. *Grundfragen der Sprachforschung, mit Rücksicht auf W. Wundts Sprachpsychologie erörtert.* Strassburg: Trübner.

—. 1919. *Einleitung in das Studium der indogermanischen Sprachen.* 6. Aufl. Leipzig: Breitkopf & Härtel. [Stark überarbeitete Fassung von Delbrück 1893.]

Dempe, Helmuth. 1930. *Was ist Sprache? Eine sprachphilosophische Untersuchung im Anschluß an die Sprachtheorie Karl Bühlers.* Weimar: Böhlaus Nachfolger.

Di Cesare, Donatella. 1996. "'Innere Sprachform': Humboldts Grenzbegriff, Steinthals Begriffsgrenze". *Historiographia Linguistica* 23: 3.321–346.

Elffers-van Ketel, Els. 1991. *The Historiography of Grammatical Concepts. 19th and 20th-century changes in the subject-predicate conception and the problem of their historical reconstruction.* Amsterdam & Atlanta: Rodopi.

Erlinger, Hans Dieter, Clemens Knobloch & Hartmut Meyer. 1989. *Satzlehre – Denkschulung – Nationalsprache: Deutsche Schulgrammatik zwischen 1800 und 1850.* Münster: Nodus.

Forsgren, Kjell-Ake. 1985. *Die deutsche Satzgliedlehre 1780 bis 1830.* Göteborg: Acta Universitatis Gothoburgensis.

Freyer, Hans. 1923. *Theorie des objektiven Geistes. Eine Einleitung in die Kulturphilosophie.* Leipzig & Berlin: Teubner. (3. Aufl. Leipzig, Berlin: Teubner, 1934.)

Funk, Otto. 1927. *Studien zur Geschichte der Sprachphilosophie.* Bern: Francke.

Gabelentz, Georg von der. 1869–75. "Ideen zu einer vergleichenden Syntax. Wort- und Satzstellung". *Zeitschrift für Völkerpsychologie und Sprachwissenschaft* 6.376–384; 8.129–165 und 300–338. (Teil II und III unter dem Titel: "Weiteres zur vergleichenden Syntax".)

—. 1891. *Die Sprachwissenschaft, ihre Aufgaben, Methoden und bisherigen Ergebnisse.* Leipzig: T. O. Weigel Nachfolger.

Geiger, Lazarus. 1868–74. *Ursprung und Entwicklung der menschlichen Sprache und Vernunft.* 2 Bde. Stuttgart: Cotta'sche Buchhandlung.

Gerber, Gustav. 1871–74. *Die Sprache als Kunst.* 2 Bde. (2. Bd. in zwei Teilen.) Bromberg: Mittler'sche Buchhandlung (2. Aufl. Berlin, 1885.)

—. 1884. *Die Sprache und das Erkennen.* Berlin: Gaertner.

Haselbach, Gerhard. 1966. *Grammatik und Sprachstruktur: Karl Ferdinand Beckers Beitrag zur allgemeinen Sprachwissenschaft in historischer und systematischer Hinsicht.* Berlin: de Gruyter.

Hehlmann, Wilhelm. 1967. *Geschichte der Psychologie.* Stuttgart: Kröner.

Heyse, Carl Wilhelm Ludwig. 1856. *System der Sprachwissenschaft*, hg. von Heymann Steinthal. Berlin: Dümmler.

Janke, W. 1971. Artikel "Apperzeption". *Historisches Wörterbuch der Philosophie* hg. von Joachim Ritter & Karlfried Gründer, Bd. 1, 448–455. Darmstadt: Wissenschaftliche Buchgesellschaft.

Jaritz, Peter. 1990. *Sprachwissenschaft und Psychologie.* (= Beiheft 10 der *Osnabrücker Beiträge zur Sprachtheorie.*) Osnabrück: Univ. Osnabrück.

Knobloch, Clemens. 1988. *Geschichte der psychologischen Sprachauffassung in Deutschland von 1850 bis 1920.* Tübingen: Niemeyer.

—. 1992. "Wilhelm Wundt". Sprachphilosophie: Ein internationales Handbuch hg. von Marcelo Oascal, Gottfried Gerhardus, Kuno Lorenz & Georg Meggle, 1. Halbband, 412−431. Berlin & New York: de Gruyter.

Kronasser, Heinz. 1952. *Handbuch der Semasiologie: Kurze Einführung in die Geschichte, Problematik und Terminologie der Bedeutungslehre.* Heidelberg: Winter.

Lazarus, Moritz. 1884. *Geist und Sprache.* 3. Aufl. Berlin: Dümmler (1. Aufl., 1856.)

Madvig, Johann Nicolai. 1871. "Einige der Voraussetzungen der Etymologie und ihre Aufgabe". Madvig 1975.319−355.

—. 1875. *Kleine philologische Schriften.* Leipzig: B. G. Teubner. (Nachdruck Hildesheim: Olms, 1966.)

Marty, Anton. 1897. "Über die Scheidung von grammatischem, logischem und psychologischem Subjekt resp. Prädikat". *Archiv für systematische Philosophie* 3.294−333.

Mauthner, Fritz. 1923 [1901−1902]. *Beiträge zu einer Kritik der Sprache.* 3 Bde. Nachdruck der 2. Aufl. Berlin & Wien: Ullstein.

Misteli, Franz. 1880. "Herbarts Sprachauffassung im Zusammenhang seines Systems". *Zeitschrift für Völkerpsychologie und Sprachwissenschaft* 12. 407−451.

—. 1893. *Charakteristik der hauptsächlichsten Typen des Sprachbaues.* Berlin: Ferdinand Dümmler. [= Neubearbeitung von Steinthals gleichnamigem Werk von 1861.]

Müller, Friedrich Max. 1888. *Das Denken im Lichte der Sprache.* Leipzig: Wilhelm Engelmann.

Nerlich, Brigitte. 1988. "Théories du changement sémantique en Allemagne au XIXe siècle: Stöckmann, Sperber et Leumann". *Histoire Epistémologie Langage* 10: 1.101−112.

—. 1990. *Change in Language: Whitney, Bréal and Wegener.* London: Routledge.

—. 1992. *Semantic Theories in Europe 1830−1930.* Amsterdam & Philadelphia: Benjamins.

Noiré, Ludwig. 1877. *Der Ursprung der Sprache.* Mainz: Victor v. Zabern.

—. 1885. *Logos. Ursprung und Wesen der Begriffe.* Leipzig: Wilhelm Engelmann.

Paul, Hermann. 1920 [1880]. *Prinzipien der Sprachgeschichte.* 5. Aufl. Halle a. S.: Niemeyer.

Petzet, E. & G. Herbig. 1913. "C. W. L. Heyse und sein System der Sprachwissenschaft". *Sitzungsberichte der Königlich-Bayerischen Akademie der Wissenschaften, philosophisch-philologische und historische Klasse,* 7. Abhandlung. München.

Pott, August Friedrich. 1863. "Zur Geschichte und Kritik der sog. Allgemeinen Grammatik". *Zeitschrift für Philosophie und philosophische Kritik,* N. F. 43.102−141, 185−245.

—. 1880. I−II. *Wilhelm von Humboldt und die Sprachwissenschaft.* (Nachdruck Hildesheim: Olms, 1974.) 2. Aufl. Berlin: S. Calvary. (I = Einleitung und erster Band zu W. V. Humboldt: Über die Verschiedenheit des menschlichen Sprachbaues und ihren Einfluss auf die geistige Entwicklung des Menschengeschlechtes; II = Humboldt-Text mit Anmerkungen.)

Raynaud, Savina. 1982. *Anton Marty, filosofo del linguaggio: Uno strutturalismo presaussureano.* Rom: La Goliardica editrice.

Sandmann, Manfred. 1979 [1954]. *Subject and Predicate: A contribution to the theory of syntax.* 2. Aufl. Heidelberg: Winter.

Scherer, Willhelm. 1875. "Rezension von W. D. Whitney: *Die Sprachwissenschaft*" (München: W. Ackermann 1874). *Preußische Jahrbücher* 35.106−111. (Wiederabgedruckt in Christmann 1977: 181−188.)

Schmidt, Gunther. 1987. "Steinthal und Lazarus − Berliner 'Talente dritten Ranges'? Die wissenschaftshistorische Einordnung der Sprach- und Völkerpsychologie in ihrer Anfangsphase". *Linguistische Studien Reihe A*: Arbeitsberichte Nr. 162, 109−147. Berlin: Akademie-Verlag.

Schmidt, Siegfried J. 1968. *Sprache und Denken als sprachphilosophisches Problem von Locke bis Wittgenstein.* Den Haag. Mouton.

—, Hg. 1971. *Philosophie als Sprachkritik im 19. Jahrhundert.* Textauswahl II. Stuttgart: Frommann-Holzboog.

Seiler, Hansjakob. 1975. "Die Prinzipien der deskriptiven und der etikettierenden Benennung". *Linguistic Workshop II: Arbeiten des Kölner Universalienprojekts* hg. von H. Seiler, 2−57. München: Fink.

Simonis, Hans. 1959. *Die Sprachphilosophie O. F. Gruppes und G. Gerbers nach ihrer Bedeutung für die Erkenntnistheorie.* Diss., Univ. Bonn.

Staude, Otto. "Der Begriff der Apperzeption in der neueren Psychologie". *Philosophische Studien* 1: 2.149−212.

Steinthal, Heymann. 1855. *Grammatik, Logik und Psychologie, ihre Prinzipien und ihr Verhältnis zueinander.* Berlin: Dümmler (Nachdruck: Hildesheim: Olms, 1968.)

—. 1860. "Über den Wandel der Laute und des Begriffs". *Zeitschrift für Völkerpsychologie und Sprachwissenschaft* 1.416−432. (Wiederabgedruckt in Christmann 1977: 5−65.)

—. 1970 [1864]. "Philologie, Geschichte und Psychologie in ihren gegenseitigen Beziehungen". *Kleine sprachtheoretische Schriften.* Neu zusammengestellt und mit einer Einleitung versehen von Waltraud Bumann, 436−511. Hildesheim: Olms.

−. 1881 [1871]. *Einleitung in die Psychologie und Sprachwissenschaft*. 2. Aufl. Berlin: Dümmler.

−. 1888. *Der Ursprung der Sprache, im Zusammenhang mit den letzten Fragen alles Wissens*. 4. Aufl. Berlin: F. Dümmler. (3. Aufl. 1877; 2. Aufl. 1858, 1. Aufl., 1851.)

Stern, Gustaf. 1931. *Meaning and Change of Meaning. With special reference to the English language*. Göteborg. (Nachdruck Bloomington & London: Indiana Univ. Press, 1968.)

Sütterlin, Ludwig. 1902. *Das Wesen der sprachlichen Gebilde*. Heidelberg: Winter.

Tobler, Ludwig. 1871−75. Besprechung von Gerber (1871−74). *Zeitschrift für Völkerpsychologie und Sprachwissenschaft* 7.418−447 und 8.372−377.

Trabant, Jürgen. 1986. *Apeliotes oder der Sinn der Sprache. Wilhelm von Humboldts Sprach-Bild*. München: Fink.

Ungeheuer, Gerold. 1983. "Nietzsche über Sprache und Sprechen, über Wahrheit und Traum". *Internationales Jahrbuch für die Nietzsche-Forschung* 12, 134−213. Berlin: de Gruyter.

−. 1984. "Bühler und Wundt". *Bühler-Studien* hg. von Achim Eschbach, Bd. II, 9−67. Frankfurt/ M.: Suhrkamp.

Wegener, Philipp. 1885. *Untersuchungen über die Grundfragen des Sprachlebens*. Halle a. S.: Niemeyer. (Nachdruck mit einer Einleitung von Clemens Knobloch, hg. von Konrad Koerner, Amsterdam & Philadelphia: Benjamins, 1991.)

−. 1902. Anzeige von Delbrück (1901). *Literarisches Centralblatt* vom 22. 3. 1902.401−410.

Weil, Henri. 1844. *De l'ordre des mots dans les langues anciennes comparées aux langues modernes*. Paris: Joubert. (Nachdruck der engl. Übersetzung: *The Order of Words in the Ancient Languages Compared with that of the Modern Languages*, mit einer Einleitung von Aldo Scaglione, Amsterdam: Benjamins, 1978.)

Wundt, Wilhelm. 1888. "Über Ziele und Wege der Völkerpsychologie". *Philosophische Studien* 4. 1−27.

−. 1901. *Sprachgeschichte und Sprachpsychologie, mit Rücksicht auf B. Delbrücks 'Grundfragen der Sprachforschung'*. Leipzig: Engelmann.

−. 1921−22 [1900]: *Völkerpsychologie Band 1: Die Sprache*, erster und zweiter Halbband. 4. Aufl. Stuttgart: Kröner.

Clemens Knobloch, Siegen (Deutschland)

195. Language and psychology: 19th-century developments outside the Germany: A survey

1. Introduction
2. 19th-century studies outside Germany of developmental psycholinguistics
3. 19th-century views outside Germany on the relationship between language and thought
4. Biological and social aspects of psycholinguistics: 19th-century research outside Germany
5. Conclusion
6. Bibliography

1. Introduction

In the opening lecture of a series devoted to the 'science of language' delivered in English at the Royal Institute of Great Britain in April, May and June 1861, the German-born Oxford professor F. Max Müller (1866: 3−4) said,

"the science of language is a science of very modern date. […] We hear it spoken of as Comparative Philology, Scientific Etymology, Phonology, and Glossology. In France it has received the convenient, but somewhat barbarous, name of *Linguistique*."

He would probably have considered the term 'psycholinguistics' even more barbarous; its first appearance in the title of an article was provided by Nicholas Henry Pronko (b. 1908) in 1946 and in a book-title by Osgood & Sebeok (1954). However, Pronko (letter to author, 1 Aug. 1996) states that the word was in regular use in a research community at Indiana University led by Jacob Robert Kantor (1888−1984) and Hilgard (1987: 251) noted that Kantor used the word as early as 1936 in his book *An Objektive Psychology of Grammar*.

Since the publication of Osgood's and Sebeok's text, there have been many others of which we may consider that of Kess (1992) as one of the most scholarly and comprehensive. Yet in his historical account of modern psycholinguistics Kess covers only the period 1951 to 1990 (Kess 1992: 16−28). If we turn to another text at the start of this period, we find that Carroll (1953) did not even attempt to cover the history of what he called 'linguistic psychology'. But he referred the reader to four extremely useful reviews of the literature that all appeared in the *Psychological Bulletin* in the first half of the 20th century. These included, in backward chronological order, the article by Pronko (1946); a paper by McGranahan (1936), whose references to work from the previous century are restricted to the names of Max Müller (1823–1900), Ludwig Noiré (1829–1889), Hermann Paul (1846–1921), and George J. Romanes (1848–1894); a paper by Adams & Powers (1929) who nowhere refer to 19th-century ideas about language; and a summary by Mead (1904) of the work of Wilhelm Wundt (1832–1920) on language with casual mention of the other German writers of the late 19th century. However, the history of psycholinguistics in Germany in the 19th century has recently been described in great detail by Knobloch (1988), of which an English summary was provided by Murray (1990).

My premonition of the unexpected difficulty of writing this article was confirmed by two searches carried out in the Stauffer Library of Queen's University at Kingston. Between 1965 and 1994 the *Journal of the History of the Behavioral Sciences* contained one article only on late 19th-century language science, an article on Max Müller by Knoll (1986), while a search through some six shelves' worth of books on language in the *Psychology* section of the library yielded no systematic history of 19th-century *psycholinguistics*. It seems, therefore, that the present article has to be seen as an original research contribution, and, therefore, of limited value at this stage of our historical knowledge.

This being the case, we have to define the subject matter with which we shall be concerned. A particularly useful modern text is that of Deese (1970) who begins by making the point that the word 'psycholinguistics' clearly applies both to *parole* as defined by F. de Saussure (1857–1913) and to 'performance' as defined by N. Chomsky. Deese (1970: 4) discusses de Saussure's famous distinction by defining *langue* as "the system – both grammatic and semantic – that makes speech possible" and *parole* as the "actual vocal output of a speaker". And his definition (Deese 1970: 6) of Chomsky's 'competence' is: "each of our heads evidently contains a device that can both generate and interpret sentences according to rules"; while his definition of Chomsky's 'performance' is: "an account of what we actually do. Our speech is determined by habit and a host of other things unrelated to linguistic competence." Deese then goes on to discuss the latter distinction in his second chapter, while his remaining three chapters are devoted to linguistic development, the role of language in thinking, and the biological/social context of language. These last three issues also constitute the main topics to which 19th-century writers on psycholinguistics contributed. The issues of *la langue* and linguistic competence will therefore be addressed minimally in the following survey, which is ordered under the same headings as those used by Deese in his final three chapters.

2. 19th-century studies outside Germany of developmental psycholinguistics

The first studies of how children acquire linguistic skills were based on the diary method, that is, an observer would keep a written record of the behaviour of a growing child from birth onwards for perhaps two or three years. Usually the observer was a parent; in the late 18th century, following the observations reported by Dietrich Tiedemann (1748–1803) in 1787, a number of German scientists wrote short reports on the development of psychical and mental capacities in the child and later in the 1830s some mothers in the United States and in England reported similar observations with a view to improving child care. None of these focussed particularly on language development and are reviewed in more detail by Wallace, Franklin & Keegan (1994: 10).

The first diary to be devoted exclusively to language development appears to be that concerning a little girl by the famous French psychologist Hippolyte Taine (1828–1893). His account (Taine 1877), was followed by the publication in 1877 of a sketch of a diary concerning his own son by Charles Darwin (1809–1882); the diary itself actually dated back from thirty-seven years earlier and devotes only a paragraph' to 'communication' in the infant. Then F. Pollock (1878) wrote another account of language development in an infant that was at least as detailed as that of Taine, while minor contributions along these lines were added by James Sully (1880) and Champneys (1881). An outstanding summary incorporating data from these various diaries, as well as from later 19th-century records kept by a number of American or Canadian academics, was produced as a Ph. D. thesis by Frederick Tracy (1893); the thesis topic was suggested by James Mark Baldwin (1861–1934) and Stanley Hall (1844–1924) at Clark University. It represents one of the first major American contributions to the academic discipline of child psychology. Tracy's review also included the well-known observations of Wilhelm Preyer (1841–1899) in 1882 in Germany.

Few of the diarists concerned with speech development said much about the first few months of life. Taine (1877: 252), following a line of argument familiarized in 1855 by the evolutionist Herbert Spencer (1820–1903), suggested that the outset of his article that something like natural selection determines the course of language learning:

"It is out of the enormous number of movements, constantly essayed, that there will be evolved by gradual selection the intentional movements having an object and attaining it [...]. There is the same spontaneous apprenticeship for cries as for movements. The progress of the vocal organ goes on just like that of the limbs; the child learn to omit such or such a sound as it learns to turn its head or its eyes, that is to say by grouping and constant attempts."

Taine noted that in the first 6 months vowels first emerge, while by 12 months the child is making a large number of spontaneous sounds which Tracy (1893: 112) called "babble", a word which has since become standard, while the translator of Taine called it "twittering". By this time consonants are also included; both Taine and Pollock found that *mm* was among the first consonants, and Darwin's baby seemed unusually precocious in using the syllabel *mum* to mean "give me food". When the child utters such a sound, the child also expresses emotion in the intonation of the sound, a fact which particularly interested Darwin. In his *Expression of the Emotions in Animals and Man* (Darwin 1872) had argued that human ways of expressing emotion through crying, gesture, and facial expression had their roots in an evolutionary process extending back to animals.

Taine's infant at 14 months also asked for food using her own word (*ham*) but only after several other words had been learned; and Taine (1877: 257) suggested that the actual sounds in the word may have been selected because of their relationship to the process of eating; the sound "begins with a guttural aspirate like a bark, and ends with a closing of the lips as if food were seized and swallowed". Champneys (1881: 106) added that the use of *m* in the word 'mama' to mean 'mother' also indicates the naturalness with which the infant produces this sound. Sully (1880) found that his infant subject was producing not only *m* but also *b* and *n* as early as 7 months; while Pollock (1878: 393) noted that his baby also used *mm* to mean 'want' but that this expression had disappeared by 15 months then reappeared at 18 months in two forms, *ma* [*a* as in 'fAll'] and *mama* [*a* as in bAnk], with his subject's first sentence being formed from these two words to mean "more food, mother". Incidentally, Sully's infant could pronounce *r* at 7 months, whereas Pollock's infant was having difficulty in pronouncing *r* as late as 20 months.

Clearly we cannot go on at this level of detail to summarize the events reported in the diaries but several generalizations can be derived from their contents, as follows.

(a) The first compound sounds, usually produced around the end of the first year of life, consist of consonants followed by vowels; the addition to the vocabulary of words possessing final consonants may not occur until a child is about 18 months old. This finding was supported with additional evidence by Tracy (1893), and Clark & Clark (1977: 388) have a table summarizing 20th-century evidence on the subject.

(b) Whenever a new compound sound is produced, its meaning at first extends to a variety of objects and desires and only gradually does the sound come to mean particular objects or desires. I emphasize the difference between 'objects' and 'desires' because it is central in the theory of language development put forward by Burrhus Frederic Skinner (1957); and Karl Bühler (1930: 54–59) argued that language is *first* used to express desires and only later to indicate or refer to objects. We have observed how Taine's and Darwin's infants used *mm* to mean "want food".

Concerning objects, for example, Pollock showed how the sound *baba*, which may have emerged from babbling, initially represented any living things in the baby's household including the cat. A month later, at 13 months, the sound seemed to differentiate into *wah wah* ("dog" or "cat"), *náná* ("nurse"), and *dádá* ("father"). However by 15 months *wah wah* had come to mean "dog" only, the "cat" now being called *miau*. And at about the same time the new sound *bébi*, which was imitated from adults with their encouragement, came to mean "baby" and a month later the subject herself. The first 'real' word taught to the child, according to Pollock (1878: 394) was *ni* meaning "knee".

However, the child's initial usage of *ni* was actually to express a desire, namely, "take me on your knee and show me pictures". Another example where words representing objects are uttered with the intention of expressing a desire occurs much later in Pollock's narrative. By 20 months the child had acquired words containing a wide variety of consonants (and occasionally disyllables, including her own name, *A—si*, standing for 'Alice'). Among the first word combinations she used were *zat sig* meaning "that thing"; but it was uttered as an expression of desire, namely "tell me the name of that thing".

The gradual narrowing down in meaning or referent of uttered words as language learning progressed received a great deal of support from other scholars, and Murray (1990: 377) gave a long quotation from V. M. Bexterev's (1857—1927) 1918 study (Bexterev 1932) showing that this French, British and North American evidence on how the meaning of words becomes focussed over time was known in Russia at the time that conditioned reflexes were first being investigated experimentally.

(c) Taine, in particular, stressed that children's linguistic utterances appear to consistent with an anthropomorphic view of the external world. For example, when his subject, at about the age of 17 months, asked where the moon had gone, she was told that it had set. In French this is rendered as "est allée se coucher" which also means in French "to go to bed". So the child asked where the moon's maid was. On another occasion, when her toy carriage would not move, she accused it of being naughty. At the same time, Pollock (1878: 399) noted that his subject, when she talked to a doll, apparently seemed to know that the doll was indeed a toy and not a real baby.

(d) None of the diaries took the period of study beyond about 23 months, and, of course, the observations reported were very selective. It is therefore only at the end of the various diaries that we get references to the acquisition of grammar. Taine says hardly anything on the topic. Pollock (1878: 399) says that his subject's first verbal inflexion occurred at 22 months when she used "*klaid*" and "*comed*" for "came". This last is an interesting example of the use of analogical reasoning in ontogenetic development. Thumb & Marbe (1901) argued that the laws of language-change within the evolution of any single language were also the consequence of analogical and other kinds of associative reasoning on the part of the language's users. However, Bernhard Perez (1878) wrote a book on the first *three* years of child development and Tracy (1893) analysed the grammatical content of children's first words, noting that the majority were nouns, hardly any of which were abstract. Nonetheless, there was a shortage of evidence from the 19th century concerning the acquisition of grammatical rules by children.

It may be noted that the first observations of how children learn to write were reported by Baldwin (1895: 59—103) in the course of his formulation of a theoretical approach to child development. This approach in part foreshadowed that of Jean Piaget (1896—1980), as has been shown by Broughton (1981), although Woodward (1979) indicates how Piaget's psychology also had its sources in the writing of the generation of French psychologists immediately preceding his.

3. 19th-century views outside Germany on the relationship between language and thought

Consider the following lengthy paragraph from Bloom (1981: 1):

"Does the fact that the Chinese lexicon carves up the English word "reason" into a highly differentiated set of lexical concepts imply that the Chinese reason about reason and reasons in a more differentiated fashion than English speakers do? Does the fact that the Chinese lexicon includes words roughly equivalent to the English terms "suggestion", "mental perspective", and "meaning" but has no term directly equivalent to the English word "idea" imply that English speakers have an idea that Chinese speakers do not share? Does the fact that the Chinese language, unlike English, commonly uses distinct terms to distinguish "if–then" relationships from "if-and-only-if-then" relationships imply that Chinese students are, on that score at least, better fitted for first-year logic than their American counterparts? Does the fact that the English language, unlike Chinese, provides a distinct means for shifting from the talk of people or acts being "sincere", to the talk of "sincerity" as an abstracted property imply that English speakers are inclined to think about being sincere in a more detached way?"

This quotation illustrates extremely well the first great problem concerning the relationship of language to thought that has obsessed psycholinguists. Let us call it the question of 'language and clear thinking'.

Now consider the fact that Weiskrantz (1988) has recently edited a book entitled *Thought without Language*. It includes essays on the extraordinary abilities of non-speaking animals at remembering places where food has been previously found, where another member of the species has been seen, landmarks on migration routes, etc. It includes an account by a professor of electrical engineering who does all his calculation concerning electric circuits in terms of visual images of the circuitry, he himself is dyslexic and cannot 'think' very well in terms of words; and it contains other articles concerning case histories where people with brain damage of the type known as 'aphasia' who can, nevertheless, carry out many everyday tasks involving motor skills, visual imagery, and other kinds of memory. A particularly well-known case of this last kind was reported by Lecours and Joanette (1980). Weiskrantz's book in an attempted answer to what we may call the question: "Is *all* thought dependent on language?" We now discuss these two questions in order.

3.1. Language and clear thinking

Although histories of linguistics such as that of Robins (1990) generally start with ancient writings, there is some consensus that the discussion of the relationship of thought to clear thinking has its modern origins in Locke's *Essay Concerning Human Understanding* (1690). The work is in four parts, devoted to innate notions, ideas, words, and knowledge, respectively. In the section on words, Locke has a discussion of 'abuses' of words; among these are words used vaguely or inconsistently, employed without clear definition, applied inappropriately, and ambiguous in referent (e. g., does an embryo have 'life'?). Another abuse of words concerns the tendency to think that, because we can make a word whose referent is an abstract concept, then the referent has reality in the way that real objects in the external world do. We now call this the error of 'reification' and Locke made a major contribution to psychology as a science when he argued that the abstract nouns 'the will' and 'the self' do not have this kind of reality.

Not only did Locke thereby start a movement within philosophy to show how philosophical errors can result from the uncritical use of everyday language, a movement that has culminated in 20th-century linguistic analysis, but he also foreshadowed a movement in linguistics whose concern was to show that linguistic relativity and language change were also an outcome of such erroneous thinking. Condillac (1971 [1746]: 78–91) reiterated Locke's views and Smith (1976) has described how, in 1760, the German scholar Johann David Michaelis (1717–1791) wrote a dissertation on the subject; and at the beginning of the 19th century, the English-born Alexander Bryan Johnson (1786–1867), who emigrated to Utica in New York State when he was fifteen, wrote a strikingly original *A Treatise on Language* (1947 [1836]). Johnson argued as forcefully as he could that the typical thinking we associate with Western philosophy has been seriously misguided by the way we use language to refer to nature. All we know about nature, he argued, is through our senses; language is thus a distorting mirror held up to nature.

For the rest of the 19th century, this question was written about by almost all linguists. Nerlich (1991: 335) noted that "in 19th-century England the study of the semantic side of language was either part of philosophy [...] or part of etymology and lexicography". We have only space to pick out one example of a well-known psychologist deeply concerned with the role of language in clear thinking, George Frederick Stout (1860–1944). According to Nerlich (1991: 337),

"Stout argues that although we can think without language, it is only through language that our intentions can be turned into concepts and thus become the object of attention and of what Stout call 'apperception'. This term is borrowed from the German tradition of psychology, namely, that of

Johann Friedrich Herbart (1776–1841) and Heymann Steinthal (1823–1899), who in turn had inherited it from Gottfried Wilhelm Leibniz and Immanuel Kant. *Apperception* is a concept that dominated European psychology until it was eventually superceded by more fashionable terms such as *Gestalt*."

One consequence of the fact that language allows us to represent in memory the outcomes of acts of selective attention will necessarily be a lack of consistency in the exact 'meaning' of individual words and, hence, that the 'meaning' of a word, to quote Nerlich (1991: 344) again, is "nothing fixed once and for all, but rather a fuzzy territory delimited vaguely by the usual meaning". Stout's views were expressed particularly in an article published in 1891 in the British journal *Mind*, founded in 1876 by the Scottish psychologist Alexander Bain (1818–1903).

3.2. Is *all* thought dependent on language?

This section will be devoted especially to the writings of two academic scholars who worked outside Germany, namely, F. Max Müller and Ivan Mixajlovič Sexenov (1829–1905). Though German-born, Müller became professor of comparative philosophy at Oxford and, because of his fascinatingly good ability to write readable English, had an enormous impact on academic studies of the language sciences in Britain and North America. Sexenov studied physiology in Germany with Hermann von Helmholtz (1821–1894) and others before returning to Russia where he continued his physiological research on the nervous system.

Max Müller assured his fame with his *Lectures on the Science of Language* (1866) referred to at the start of this article; their chief burden was to prove that the Indo-European languages, as well as other languages groups, derived from a common ancestor some 10,000 years ago of which Sanskrit was an early exponent; Müller's reputation was as an expert not only on philosophy but also on near-Eastern religions. But the gem of the book is his demonstration that when we totally alter the meaning of a sentence by adding one letter (e. g. by changing 'I love' to 'I loved'), the letter to be added, in his case *d*, had its roots in words describing real *things* in the ancient source language. Müller went on to argue that language and thought are inextricable in the sense that the actual words we use have word-ancestors which denoted events in the external world, and, therefore, reflecting the 'thinking' of our human ancestors. In particular, he claimed all written languages are based on ancient word-elements called 'roots', not with nouns or verbs from more recent languages (e. g., Latin in the case of most European languages). By 'roots' he meants, "the last residuum of grammatical analysis" and in his *Science of Thought* (1887), he listed 121 Sanskrit roots, referring mainly to actions rather than things, that formed the basis from which thousands of words in the Indo-European and other languages evolved. However, Rieber & Vetter (1980: 16) claimed that Michel Bréal (1832–1915) showed that many of these verb-like roots actually originated as nouns denoting things. Müller (1887: 543) concluded that, "No one, I believe, will be able in future to dispute the fact that thought without language is impossible". But, again this argument had been earlier contested by William Dwight Whitney (1827–1894) who, in his *Language and the Study of Language* (1867), argued that no advance can be made on this topic without a close analysis of the word 'thought'. Müller and Whitney continued their debate for over 20 years, and Valone (1996) has described how de Saussure came to prefer Whitney's views to those of Müller, a fact which may explain in part why Müller's work has tended to be neglected in the 20th century.

However, research in this century has clearly shown that humans are indeed helped enormously to think about things and events that are not actually physically present by making use of language. With respect to recalling material that has just been presented, there is ample evidence that preventing speech reduces immediate recall. For example, Murray (1967) showed that if a person says something else aloud while trying to retain visually presented sequences of eight letters, there is a fourfold reduction in the immediate recall of the letters as compared with the recall resulting from reading the sequence silently; similar experiments had first been reported in the 19th century by Münsterberg (1890), Smith (1896) and Cohn (1897).

The idea that 'thought' was coterminous with 'language' was raised quite independently by I. M. Sexenov, whose early research had included the discovery that if, in frogs, the brain was sectioned at the level of the optic thalami, then stimulating the sectioned areas could *inhibit* certain reflexes such as the scratch reflex. He was led from this to publish his extraordinary *Reflexes of the Brain* (1965 [1863]) in which he argued that 'thought' was basically speaking with the final explosion of air through the vocal cords and vocal cavity *inhibited* to such an extent that the speech was for practical purposes 'silent'. In the following passage, Sexenov (1965 [1863]: 86) forcefully expressed his opinion:

Thus man not only learns to group his movements reflexes, he, at the same time, acquires (also by means of reflexes) capacity to inhibit them ... I shall now show the reader the first and most important result of man's capacity to inhibit the last member of a reflex. This can be summarized as the ability to think, meditate, and reason [...] a thought is the first two-thirds of a psychical reflex."

Two comments are necessary. First, Sexenov used the word 'reflex' to refer to any kind of action sequence that takes place semi-automatically with little conscious effort involved. Thus, with this definition, sneezing or laughing are unlearned vocal reflexes; the automatic utterance of a swear word in a frustrating situation is a learned reflex. Sexenov, therefore, is arguing not only that language utterances consist to some extent of learned reflexes but also that silent thought consists of learned reflexes that include the learned inhibition of overt enunciation. Second, Sexenov's views exerted a strong influence on the opinions of Ivan Petrovič Pavlov (1849–1936), who came to conceive of language as a second type of representation of the external world additional to the representation via immediate perception of that world.

One of Pavlov's most important successors was Aleksander N. Sokolov whose book entitled *Inner Speech and Thought* (1972 [1968]) started with a general review of the topic of thought and language that included only a mildly critical account of Max Müller's beliefs, and a statement that, although 'wordless' thought (e. g., visual imagery) might exist, he is sceptical of the value of introspective evidence for visual imagery even when such evidence was reported by scientists of the calibre of Albert Einstein. Sokolov preferred to focus on establishing as much as possible experimentally about the role of inner speech in thinking and produced a valuable review of evidence that, when child and adult subjects were thinking, involuntary movements of the muscles of the tongue, lips and larynx could be demonstrated, imperceptible to the subjects themselves. Sokolov himself carried out a number of experiments using articulatory or motor interference to study their deleterious effect on various intellectual tasks. One of the final conclusions expressed by Sokolov (1972 [1968]: 263) was strikingly consistent with the claim that had been made over 100 years earlier by Sexenov:

"As learning takes root and mental operations become increasingly automatized, however, the need for external verbalization (enunciation aloud) arises no longer, and it is replaced by reduced, abbreviated verbalization — inner speech which underlies the so-called internalization of mental actions, or their implementation on an internal (mental) plane, the motor speech reactions being maximally reduced but not totally eliminated."

In the 1860s, therefore, Müller in England and Sexenov in Russia represented the 'no thought without language' school. However, Whitney (1872) had argued that this claim cannot be made without a closer analysis of the meaning of the word 'thought' and the same argument was updated, making use of 20th-century evidence on imagery and on movement learning, by Murray (1990).

4. Biological and social aspects of psycholinguists: 19th-century research outside Germany

We shall restrict our discussion to biological and social origins of language, questions concerning the way language is processed in the brain are discussed in the following chapter. However, it may be noted that, at the end of the 19th century, there was considerable discussion of the thought-processes of people with serious sensory deficits such as blindness or deafness. A useful review of the history of speech therapy as applied to the deaf has been provided by Rieber and Vetter (1980: 24–40). According to these authors, both Sir Francis Galton (1822–1911) and Darwin's disciple George J. Romanes attacked Max Müller's view that there was 'no thought without language' on the grounds that deaf people were clearly capable of sophisticated problem solving and other kinds of intellectual functioning.

Speculation as to how language originated goes back to ancient times and includes the so-called 'Adamist' view, expressed in the Book of Genesis, according to which the first man, Adam, invented language. This early history is reviewed in Robins (1990: 21–23) and in Marx (1967: 443−453); from our point of view, the single most important figure in generating the 19th-century theories of the origin of language was the Abbé Etienne Bonnot de Condillac (1715−1780). A follower of Locke, Condillac, in the second part of his *Essai sur l'origine des connaissances humaines* (1746), suggested that language arose when natural tones and vocal sounds, e. g., grunts of pain, were combined with natural gestures to communicate emotions between individuals. These sounds and gestures were initially instinctive but Condillac (1971 [1746]: 173) claimed that

"insensibly [individuals] learned to do by reflection what they had hitherto done merely by instinct [...]. For example, he who saw a place in which he had been frightened mimicked those cries and movements which were the signs of fear in order to warn the other not to expose himself to the same danger."

Condillac tried to bolster his argument by reference to Greek and Latin and foreshadowed Wundt (and Chomsky) by stressing how the rules of word order were flexible enough so that the same proposition could be expressed in different ways. His ideas were propagated to Germany partly because Wilhelm von Humboldt (1767−1835) learned of his theories during an extended stay in Paris (Aarsleff 1982: 335−355) and partly because similar ideas were expressed in a famous 1770 essay by Herder (Robins 1990: 164−168; Marx 1967: 453−459; Aarsleff 1982: 146−209).

But in the 19th century outside Germany the question of the origins of language were discussed by many biologists as well as by philosophers. The views of Herbert Spencer have been well summarized by Tulviste (1991: 11−16); he believed that humans were capable of more 'abstract' thought than were animals. Max Müller believed that language started when certain key ideas (which themselves would nowadays be expressed as sentences) took shape in the form of single-word 'roots'. In so doing, he dismissed the theories that language evolved from onomatopaeic and interjectional sources, to which might be added the theory suggested by Karl W. L. Heyse (1797−1855) in 1856 and propagated by Ludwig Noiré (1829−1889) in 1877 according to which articulate sounds also originated in the noises, songs, etc. uttered when humans were engaged in physical labour or marching.

Quite the opposite conclusion to Müller's was arrived at by Charles Darwin himself. Howard Gruber (1981: 178−242) has shown how Darwin's views on the evolution of humans gradually took shape over the 20 years or so between the end of the voyage of the *Beagle* and the publication of the *Origin of Species* (1859). But in that book there is little reference to language. For that we must turn to *The Descent of Man* (1871), a book considerably added to in the second edition used here (Darwin 1899). Arguing that higher animals shared so many features with humans that it will be reasonable to suppose humans to have evolved from more primitive forms of mammals, Darwin stressed that human language as such must necessarily have evolved in a species intellectually more sophisticated than any other species because several species *can* communicate by articulate sounds, and many species *can* recognize the meaning of particular sounds, but they still do not possess what we would call language. Darwin (1899 [1871]: 855−856) wrote,

"that which distinguishes man from the lower animals is not the understanding of articulate sounds, for, as everyone knows, dogs understand many words and sentences. In this respect they are at the same stage of development as infants, between the ages of ten and twelve months, who understand many words and short sentences, but cannot yet utter a single word. It is not the mere articulation which is our distinguishing character, for parrots and other birds possess this power. Nor is it the mere capacity of connecting definite sounds with definite ideas, for it is certain that some parrots, which have been taught to speak, connect unerringly words with things, and persons with events. The lower animals differ from man solely in his almost infinitely larger power of associating together the most diversified sounds and ideas; and this obviously depends on the high development of his mental powers."

Darwin disagreed with Müller that an impossible barrier exists between animals and humans because the former do not have the power of forming general concepts. Darwin (1899: 89) thought that animals did possess such a power:

"... at least in a rude and incipient degree. As far as concerns infants of from ten to eleven months, old, and deaf-mutes, it seems to me incredible that they should be able to connect certain sounds with certain general ideas as quickly as they do, unless such ideas were already formed in their minds."

This sentence indicates that Darwin probably thought that an understanding of the origins of language was as likely to be attained from a study of how a baby attains speech as from a study of comparative philology. It was the task of his close friend Romanes, born in Kingston, Canada, but resident in England from infancy, to amplify Darwin's hypothesis and attempt to demonstrate that it was scientifically confirmable.

This amplification consisted of the remarkable book *Mental Evolution in Man* (1889). To arrive at this point, Romanes first had to demonstrate that humans represented a level of development of intellect that exceeded those of all other species. In his two books, *Animal Intelligence* (1882) and *Mental Evolution in Animals* (1884), Romanes collected observations on behaviour in species ranging from protozoa to invertebrates to birds and mammals, and argued that the increasing ability to solve problems and to express a wide variety of emotions was reflected not only in a 'branching tree' representing the branches of emotion, will and intellect evolving from a common trunk of 'neurility' subserving simple unlearned reflexes, but also in the parallel development of the human infant over the first few years of life. His diagram showing both of these has been reproduced by Murray (1988: 266–267) and by Boakes (1984: 29). For example, Romanes claimed that memory, as well as simple sensations of pain and pleasure, first appear in animals at the level of echinoderms (e. g., starfish and sea anemones) with the human baby being of roughly the same level of development at the time of birth; recognition of offspring and of conspecific animals, as well as association by similarity and contiguity, present their appearance in fish, reptiles and cephalopods (e. g., octopus, squid); a human baby aged about 4 months corresponds to this level. Recognition of pictures, responses to the sounds of words, tool use, and emotions we normally connect with reward and punishment, are present in the apes and the domestic dog; a human baby of 15 months is at about the same intellectual level but is on the fringe of acquiring a grasp of language that will enable it to outdo all other species in the ability to think abstractly. When the baby does begin to communicate in speech beyond this level, he has crossed the barrier between animals and humans, a barrier that Max Müller (1866: 392) defined as: "Man speaks, and no brute has ever uttered a word. Language is our Rubicon, and no brute will dare to cross it."

The detailed working out of Romanes' argument took place in the *Mental Evolution of Man*, which argued that Darwin's theory of the origin of language was plausible given that parallels to the evolution of language across species could be found (a) in acquisition by human infants of language, and (b) in a 'new look' at the evidence from philology. However, in order to express the argument clearly, Romanes was forced to invent a new word, which has not been given currency since his time presumably because his book has been so little read.

The word Romanes had to invent was 'receptual', from which the abstract noun 'recept' can be derived. It is easier, however, to compare the meaning of 'receptual' and 'conceptual' than is the case for 'recept' and 'concept'. Romanes invented the word 'receptual' to refer to a process (involving memory) that can occur when one of the 'higher' animals or a human child (and, of course, a human adult) is confronted with a sensory situation which it recognizes to be familiar; coordinated with this sense of familiarity (which is a feeling), there may also be the elicitation of an appropriate response based on the 'meaning' or significance of the sensory situation, a meaning that had been determined on the previous occasions in which it had been encountered. Thus, a dog might be taken down a particular street for the *second* time in its life, and not only have a sense of familiarity but 'remember' that it had seen another dog on the street on the first visit to that street. Of course, it was this kind of 'recognition' that Darwin had in mind when he talked about parrots that could not only 'recognize' ('know') a visitor but also 'know' what sound to articulate in order to be fed; it may be noted parenthetically that the relationship between different kinds of 'knowing' processes has recently been made a focus of extensive research in the literature on human recognition (Tulving 1985). The point Romanes wished to make was that receptual experiences (i. e., 'recepts') are, so to speak, stepping-stones on the way to conceptual experiences (i. e., 'concept' formation), and that language can only be learned if the mind has evolved to such an extent that 'receptual' memory has been complemented by 'conceptual' memory, so that propositions can be mentally formed that can be expressed by combinations of words into sentences.

To be more precise, Romanes distinguished five stages in the use of sounds for the purpose of communication, with only the higher stages being worthy of being called 'language' as opposed to 'communication'. These stages are as follows:

(1) *The indicative stage*: gestures, tones or word expressive of emotional states and simple desires.
(2) *The denotative stage*: the enunciation of a sound so that it "affixes a vocal mark to a particular object quality or action" (Romanes 1889: 159).
(3) *The connotative stage*: the same as using a denotative name but now adding some quality that describes the thing being named; to do this clearly requires the ability to compare that thing with others that the animal or child has experienced, i.e., it requires 'receptual processing'.
(4) *The denominative stage*: an extension of a denotative name to cover a class of objects.
(5) *The predicative stage*: where there is a putting together of two denominative terms to express what we normally call a 'proposition'.

Romanes chose to illustrate these five stages by referring to the way in which a child requires language, and he made good use of the diaries of language growth provided by Taine, Darwin, Preyer and others (but not, alas, Pollock) as well as of his own children. The five stages can be represented respectively by (1) a child's first use of a hand-wave to say goodbye or the utterance *mm* to express a desire for food; (2) the first use of a sound such as *baba* to name the household cat; (3) the extension of the use of a sound like *baba* not only to denote the household cat but also to describe one or more of its attributes; (4) the use of words like *star* to develop a general concept of 'starness' which itself can be an object of thought; and (5) the use of a word like "star" along with another word in a sentence such as "the star is bright".

To this classification, Romanes applied his new word 'receptual' and basically said that the first four stages involved receptual activity but only the final stage, the predicative, involved the conceptual. He then went on, having provided another tree diagram, classifying 'signs' as having various branches growing from a trunk with the last four of the above stages being twigs on an 'intellectual' branch, to assert that Müller's Rubicon was crossed when we moved from the third to the fourth stage and, furthermore, that Müller may have been right in a somewhat unexpected way, namely, that when he had stressed the importance of 'roots' in his theory of the origin of language, he had also stated those roots originally expressed *predicates*. Only species capable of using predicative signs, according to Romanes, could develop a language.

Having thus analysed exactly what made human language different from animal communication, Romanes went on to explain how, once the child had achieved a predicative use of language, a by-product of this new level of sophistication in the way the world was *represented* in the child's mind was the development of a mental representation of the child himself or herself in addition to the representation of other concepts. Romanes (1889: 175) argued that the human can "set one state of mind before another state", and contemplate the relation between them; ideas are enabled "to exist *beside* the judgment, not *in* it". Ideas themselves, therefore, become objects of thought and the power to 'think' is "the power which is given by introspective reflection in the light of self-consciousness". As an example of the difference between receptual thinking and thinking in terms of concepts which have themselves become objects of knowledge (even though those concepts originally derived from recepts), Romanes (1889: 176) went on to write:

"The diving bird, which avoids a rock and fearlessly plunges into the sea, unquestionably displays a receptual knowledge of certain 'things', 'relations', and 'truths'; but it does not know any of them *as such*: although it knows them, it does not *know that it knows them*: however well it knows them it does not think them or regard the things, the relations, or regard the things, the relations and the truths which it perceives as *themselves the objects of perception*."

Romanes (1889: 218−220) described how his own daughter moved through the various stages of linguistic performance corresponding to the shift from the receptual to the conceptual and surmised that the origin of the child's idea of having a self might occur in a sudden leap of progress; he noted that Wundt believed that a definite memory of such a moment might be laid down as one's 'first memory'. Whether or not this is true, modern research does tend to support the analyses by Romanes of the link between language performance and the formation of a self-concept (Howe & Courage 1993).

Romanes then turned to the study of philology, classifying various languages into six types and noting that spoken language goes so far back in time that the 121 'roots' of Müller are rather late developments in language history. He speculated, cautiously, that in certain warm climates (particularly California and Brazil) any children accidentally separated from their parents might form small groups who could develop their own language much as individual children nowadays can develop a self-invented language. It was this, he believed, that explains the multiplicity of complicated languages on the American continent in particular; he also argued that 'isolating' languages in which a single word can stand for a noun, verb or other part of speech are not necessarily to be judged as somehow 'primitive'; Chinese is such a language and the reader will recall the passage at the start of section 3 on the sophistication of Chinese.

Romanes, therefore, was compelled to agree with Darwin when he concluded that onomatopoeia, interjection, and work-related articulations were indeed the original basis of human language, and in so doing, he also agreed with Condillac.

At the very end of the book, Romanes dared to differ from Darwin insofar as Darwin had suggested that modern humans had evolved without an intermediary species (extinct) between the higher apes and humans. Romanes (1889: 376) on the other hand believed that a third species which he called *homo alalus* formed a 'connecting link' between the apes and humans. (Perhaps this is where the popular expression 'the missing link' originated.) This creature would have been more human than 'ape-like' and would have communicated to other members of his tribe or society "the logic of his recepts by means of gesture-signs, facial expressions and vocal tones". Romanes (1889: 439) concluded that, by studying both the psychogenesis of a child and the history of languages, we could bridge "the psychological distance which separates the gorilla from the gentleman".

Throughout the book Romanes referred both to the literature (mainly in English) on animal behaviour and also to the literature (mainly in German) on linguistics and philology. However, any reader who wishes to evaluate how far Romanes was ahead of his time must also peruse the late 20th-century literature not only on animal behaviour or linguistics, but also on the experimental and physiological study of memory. Good starting points include the article by Howe & Courage (1993) mentioned above, and a book by Searleman & Herrmann (1994). Explanations for the neglect, by 20th-century memory scientists, of the psychological ideas of Romanes have been offered by Murray, Kilgour & Wasylkiw (2000) and by Thomas (2000).

5. Conclusion

It is impossible to state that the 19th-century literature on psycholinguistics emanating from non-German sources has the unity and continuity of the equivalent German literature so well summarized by Knobloch (1988). Nevertheless, a unity was given to the former in the writings of Romanes, whose place in the history of comparative psychology (but not in the history of psycholinguistics) has been evaluated by Boakes (1984: 23−32) and by Richards (1987: 331−408). By tying together the observations of 19th-century scientists on children's language development, communication in animals, and languages from all over the globe (Condillac had been restricted to Greek and Latin), and also by a clever analysis of the role played by recognition in the growth of the child's mind (as demonstrated by his invention of the term 'receptual'). Romanes provided a unity to psycholinguistics that has unjustifiably been forgotten. He himself had hoped to add more information on language use in what he called 'savage' societies, but that book was never written; and in his final years he had the misfortune to see his works neglected because they displayed some adherence to Lamarckianism. On the other hand, if we turn to a late 20th-century theory of how the evolution of the human *brain* ran parallel to the evolution of language, that of Donald (1991), we find that Donald, like Romanes, also claimed that a theory of memory was indispensable to a theory of language development. Donald also had to invent a new word; here, he wished to express his conviction that, between apes and humans, there was an intermediate species possessing in particular a highly developed memory for gestures and movements; his new word for this kind of memory was 'mimetic memory'. The 19th-century psycholinguists influenced by Darwin would have appreciated this.

6. Bibliography

Aarsleff, Hans. 1982. *From Locke to Saussure: Essays on the study of language and intellectual history.* Minneapolis: Univ. of Minnesota Press.

Adams, Sidney & Francis F. Powers. 1929. "The Psychology of Language". *Psychological Bulletin* 25.241–260.

Baldwin, James Mark. 1895. *Mental Development in the Child and the Race.* New York & Macmillan & Co.

Bexterev, Vladimir Mixajlovič. 1918. *Obščee osnovi refleksologii čeloveka.* St. Petersburg. (English transl. of 4th ed. by Emma & William Murphy, *General Principles of Human Reflexology*, New York: International Publishers, 1933.)

Boakes, Robert. 1984. *From Darwin to Behaviourism: Psychology and the minds of animals.* Cambridge: Cambridge Univ. Press.

Bloom, Alfred H. 1981. *The Linguistic Shaping of Thought: A Study in the impact of language on thinking in China and the West.* Hillsdale, N. J.: Lawrence Erlbaum.

Broughton, John M. 1981. "The Genetic Psychology of James Mark Baldwin". *American Psychologist* 36.396–407.

Bühler, Karl. 1930. *The Mental Development of the Child.* Transl. by Oscar Oersep. London: Kegan Paul, Trench, Trübner & Co.; New York: Harcourt, Brace & Co.

Carroll, John B. 1953. *The Study of Language.* Cambridge, Mass.: Harvard Univ. Press.

Champneys, F. G. 1881. "Notes on an Infant". *Mind* 6.104–107.

Clark, Herbert H. & Eve V. Clark. 1977. *Psychology and Language.* New York: Harcourt Brace Jovanovich.

Cohn, Jonas. 1897. "Experimentelle Untersuchungen über das Zusammenwirken des akustisch-motorischen und des visuellen Gedächtnisses". *Zeitschrift für Psychologie* 15.161–184.

Condillac, *Abbé* Etienne Bonnot de. 1746. *Essai sur l'origine des connaissances humaines: Ouvrage où l'on réduit à un seul principe tout ce qui concerne l'entendement humain.* Amsterdam: Pierre Mortier. (Facs. ed. of the English translation by Thomas Nugent, 1756, with an introd. by Robert G. Weyant, *An Essay on the Origin of Human Knowledge.* Gainesville, Fla.: Scholars' Facsimiles & Reprints, 1971.)

Darwin, Charles. 1859. *Origin of Species by Means of Natural Selection or the Preservation of Favored Races in the Struggle for Life.* London: John Murray.

—. 1871. *The Descent of Man and Selection in Relation to Sex.* London: John Murray. (2nd ed., revised and augmented, 1874; repr., London: John Murray, 1899.)

—. 1872. *The Expression of Emotions in Man and Animals.* London: John Murray.

Deese, James. 1970. *Psycholinguistics.* Boston: Allyn & Bacon.

Donald, Merlin. 1991. *Origins of the Modern Mind.* Cambridge, Mass. & London: Harvard Univ. Press.

Gruber, Howard E. 1981. *Darwin on Man: A psychological study of scientific creativity.* 2nd ed. Chicago: Univ. of Chicago Press.

Herder, Johannes G. 1772. *Abhandlung über den Ursprung der Sprache, welche den von der Königl. Academie der Wissenschaften für das Jahr 1770 gesetzten Preis erhalten hat.* Berlin: C. F. Voss.

Heyse, Karl Wilhelm Ludwig. 1856. *System der Sprachwissenschaft.* Ed. by H. Steinthal. Berlin: F. Dümmler.

Hilgard, Ernest R. 1987. *Psychology in America. A historical survey.* New York: Harcourt Brace Jovanovich.

Howe, Michael L. & Mary L. Courage. 1993. "On Resolving the Enigma of Infantile Amnesia". *Psychological Bulletin* 113.305–326.

Johnson, Alexander Bryan. 1836. *A Treatise on Language.* New York: Harper & Bros. (Newly edited, with a critical essay on his philosophy of language, by David Rynin, Berkeley & Los Angeles: Univ. of California Press, 1947.)

Kantor, Jacob Robert. 1936. *An Objective Psychology of Grammar.* Bloomington, Indiana: The Principia Press. (Reissued, 1952.)

Kess, Joseph F. 1992. *Psycholinguistics: Psychology, linguistics and the study of natural language.* Amsterdam & Philadelphia: Benjamins.

Knobloch, Clemens. 1988. *Geschichte der psychologischen Sprachauffassung in Deutschland von 1850 bis 1920.* Tübingen: Niemeyer.

Knoll, Elizabeth. 1986. "The Science of Language and the Evolution of Mind: Max Müller's quarrel with Darwinism". *Journal of the History of the Behavioral Sciences* 22.3–22.

Lecours, André Roch & Yves Joanette. 1980. "Linguistic and Other Psychological Aspects of Paroxysmal Aphasia". *Brain and Language* 10.1–23.

Locke, John. 1700 [1690]. *An Essay Concerning Human Understanding.* 4th ed. London: Printed for Awnsham John Churchil [et al.]. (Repr. and abridged as *An Essay Concerning Human Understanding*, London: Dent (Everyman Edition), 1961.)

Marx, Otto. 1967. "The History of the Biological Basis of Language". *Biological Foundations of Language* by Eric H. Lenneberg, 443–469. New York: Wiley & Sons.

Mead, George H. 1904. "The Relations of Psychology and Philology". *Psychological Bulletin* 1.375–391.

McGranahan, Donald V. 1936. "The Psychology of Language". *Psychological Bulletin* 33.178–216.

Müller, F. Max. 1866. *Lectures on the Science of Language.* London: Longmans, Green & Co.

—. 1887. *The Science of Thought.* 2 vols. New York: Charles Scribner's Sons.

Münsterberg, Hugo. 1890. "Die Association successiver Vorstellungen". *Zeitschrift für Psychologie* 1.99–107.

Murray, David J. 1967. "The Role of Speech Responses in Short-Term Memory". *Canadian Journal of Psychology* 21.263–276.

—. 1988. *A History of Western Psychology.* 2nd ed. Englewood Cliff, N. J.: Prentice-Hall.

—. 1990. "On the Early History of Psycholinguistics". *Historiographia Linguistica* 17.369–381.

—, Andrea R. Kilgour & Louise Wasylkiw. 2000. "Conflicts and Missed Signals in Psychoanalysis, Behaviorism and Gestalt Psychology". *American Psychologist* 55.422–426.

Nerlich, Brigitte. 1991. "The Place of G. F. Stout's "Thought and Language" (1891) in the History of English Semantics". *Historiographia Linguistica* 18. 335–347.

Noiré, Ludwig. 1877. *Der Ursprung der Sprache.* Mainz: Franz von Zabern.

Osgood, Charles E. & Thomas A. Sebeok, eds. 1954. *Psycholinguistics: A survey of theory and research problems.* (= Indiana University Publications in Anthropology and Linguistics; Memoir, 10.) Bloomington, Ind.

Perez, Bernard. 1878. *Les trois premières aneès de l'enfant.* Paris: Baillière & Co. (Published in English transl. by A. M. Cristie as *The First Three Years of Childhood.* New York: Kellogg, 1888. Repr., New York: Arno Press, 1975.)

Pollock, F. 1878. "An Infant's Progress in Language". *Mind* 3:392–401.

Preyer, Wilhelm. 1882. *Die Seele des Kindes.* Leipzig: Grieben. Published in English trans. by H. W. Brown as *The Mind of the Child*, Parts 1 and 2, New York: Appleton, 1888–89. Repr., New York: Arno Press, 1973.)

Pronko, Nicholas Henry. 1946. "Language and Psycholinguistics: A review". *Psychological Bulletin* 43.189–239.

Richards, Robert J. 1987. *Darwin and the Emergence of Evolutionary Theories of Mind and Behavior.* Chicago: Univ. of Chicago Press.

Rieber, Robert W. & Harold Vetter. 1980. "Theoretical and Historical Roots of Psycholinguistics Research". *Psychology of Language and Thought* ed. by R. W. Rieber, 3–49. New York: Plenum Press.

Robins, Robert Henry. 1990. *A Short History of Linguistics.* 3rd ed. London & New York: Longman.

Romanes, George John. 1882. *Animal Intelligence.* London: Kegan Paul, Trench & Co.

—. 1884. *Mental Evolution in Animals.* New York: D. Appleton & Co.

—. 1889. *Mental Evolution in Man.* New York: D. Appleton & Co.

Searleman, Alan & Douglas Herrmann. 1991. *Memory from a Broader Perspective.* New York: McGraw-Hill.

Sexenov, Ivan Mixajlovič. 1866 [1863]. *Refleksy solovnogo mozga.* Published separately from "Medicinskij Vestnik". St. Petersburg. (2nd ed., 1871, English transl. by S. Belsky, *Reflexes of the Brain*, Cambridge, Mass.: MIT Press, 1965.)

Skinner, Burrhus Frederick. 1957. *Verbal Behavior.* Englewood Cliffs, N. J.: Prentice-Hall.

Smith, Raoul N. 1976. "The Sociology of Language in Johann David Michaelis's Dissertation of 1760". *The Journal of the History of the Behavioral Sciences* 12.338–346.

Smith, W. G. 1895. "The Relation of Attention to Memory". *Mind* 4.47–73.

Sokolov, Aleksandr N. 1968. *Vnutrennjaja reč' i myšlenie.* Moscow: Izd. Prosvescenie. (English transl. by George T. Onischenko, ed. by Donald B. Lindsley, *Inner Speech and Thought*, New York & London: Plenum Press, 1972.)

Spencer, Herbert. 1890 [1855]. *Principles of Psychology.* 3rd ed. London: Williams & Norgate.

Stout, George Frederick. 1891. "Thought and Language". *Mind* 16.181–197.

Sully, James. 1880. "Mental Development in Children". *Mind* 5. 385–386.

Taine, Hippolyte. 1877. "M. Taine on the Acquisition of Language by Children". *Mind* 2.252–259. (Originally published in French in *Revue Philosophique*, Jan. 1876, 1.3–23.)

Thomas, Roger K. 2000. "Romanes, George John". *Encyclopedia of Psychology* ed. by Alan E. Kazdin, vol. VII, 113–115. Washington, D. C.: American Psychological Association; New York: Oxford Univ. Press.

Thumb, Albert & Karl Marbe. 1901. *Experimentelle Untersuchungen über die psychologischen Grundlagen der sprachlichen Analogiebildung.* Leipzig: W. Engelmann. (Repr., with an introduction by David J. Murray, Amsterdam: Benjamins, 1978.)

Tiedemann, Dietrich. 1787. "Beobachtungen über die Entwicklung der Seelenfähigkeiten bei Kindern". *Hessische Beiträge zur Gelehrsamkeit und Kunst* 2.313–315; 3.486–488.

Tracy, Frederick. 1893. "The Language of Childhood". *American Journal of Psychology* 6.107–138. (Repr. in F. Tracy, *The Psychology of Childhood*, 115–160. Boston: D. C. Heath, 1907.)

Tulving, Endel. 1985. "Memory and Consciousness". *Canadian Journal of Psychology* 26.1–12.

Tulviste, Peeter. 1991. *The Cultural-Historical Development of Verbal Thinking*. Transl. by Marie Jaroszewska Hall. Commack, N. Y.: Nova Science Publishers.

Valone, David A. 1996. "Language, Race, and History: The origin of the Whitney-Müller debate and the transformation of the human sciences". *Journal of the History of the Behavioral Sciences* 32:2.119–134.

Wallace, Doris B., Margery B. Franklin & Robert T. Kegan. 1994. "The Observing Eye: A century of baby diaries". *Human Development* 37.1–29.

Weiskrantz, Lawrence. 1988. *Thought without Language*. Oxford: Clarendon Press, New York: Oxford Univ. Press.

Whitney, William Dwight 1872 [1867]. *Language and the Study of Language: Twelve Lectures on the Principles of Linguistic Science*. 5th ed. New York: Scribner & Co.

Woodward, William R. 1979. "Young Piaget Revisited: From the grasp of consciousness to décalage". *Genetic Psychology Monographs* 99.131–161.

David J. Murray, Kingston (Canada)

196. Le langage et le cerveau: La localisation de la faculté du langage et l'étude des aphasies

1. Introduction
2. Les origines: Gall et sa postérité
3. Les commencements: de Broca (1861) à Wernicke (1874)
4. Progrès de la neurologie
5. L'école allemande (1876–1886)
6. L'école française (1876–1900)
7. L'école anglaise: Jackson (1864–1893)
8. La critique de l'école française: P. Marie et Ch. Foix (1906–1916)
9. Le renouveau de l'école allemande: Pick et von Monakow (1913–1914)
10. L'école anglaise: Henry Head (1926)
11. Le courant phénoménologique
12. Du structuralisme à la neurolinguistique
13. Bibliographie

1. Introduction

La localisation cérébrale concerne l'ensemble des fonctions, des dispositions et des capacités contrôlées par l'encéphale. Le rôle des systèmes d'expression symbolique (notamment de la parole) y figurerait comme un élément parmi d'autres si ce n'était en déterminant une localisation pour la faculté du langage que l'investigation clinique, à partir de Broca (1861), n'avait commencé à dresser le relevé scientifique des aires corticales. L'inscription du linguistique dans le cerveau bénéficie de ce fait d'une forme de priorité chronologique dans l'histoire de la neurologie.

Depuis la plus haute Antiquité, une série de témoignages et d'observations avait permis d'entrevoir qu'une relation particulière existait entre le langage et le cerveau. Cependant, l'ignorance de la topologie corticale (dont la description, entreprise à la Renaissance, restait encore très sommaire au milieu du XIXe siècle) d'une part et le développement séparé des connaissances sur la nature du langage d'autre part empêchaient que se dessine l'hypothèse 'parallèliste' dont le programme se résumerait à ce que telle zone du cerveau déterminerait le contrôle de telle faculté. Pour qu'une corrélation systématique soit établie entre un point du cortex et une affection du langage, il fallait préalablement que la médecine distingue entre deux plans: la forme du trouble et sa cause organique, autrement dit le 'séméiologique' (l'expression des symptômes) et l'''étiologie' (source de la lésion). Il fallait ensuite qu'à une conception holistique du cerveau qui avait été de règle à travers tout le XVIIIe siècle succède une différenciation des territoires corticaux dont Gall (1809) proposa la première classification. Il fallait surtout que les affections du langage — les aphasies–, longtemps tenues pour des formes de démence ou d'idiotie, soient caractérisées comme des pathologies préservant, pour l'essentiel, l'intelligence, voire la parole intérieure.

Du début du XIXe siecle à la fin des années 1930, les découvertes concernant l'aphasie semblent relever de champs scientifiquement et géographiquement disjoints:

(1) Géographiquement, malgré l'internationalisation des échanges, la dominance médicale de la problématique dans tous les pays et l'unification progressive de la recherche en Europe, le type d'approche de l'aphasie (et les conditions matérielles

du débat) reflètent des traditions nationales; en schématisant, le principe explicatif est plus volontiers attendu de la philosophie en Angleterre, de la clinique en France et de l'expérimentation en Allemagne.

(2) Scientifiquement, les disciplines impliquées dans la définition du syndrome aphasique appartiennent à des domaines séparés: les sciences de la vie (anatomie, histologie), la médecine hospitalière (clinique, chirurgie) et les sciences de l'homme, encore balbutiantes (anthropologie, psychologie). Dans ce partage, une discipline fait continûment défaut, et non la moindre: la linguistique. Pourquoi? On peut penser qu'attachés à la définition des familles de langues et à la reconstruction, les linguistes du XIXe — qui sont presque tous de formation littéraire classique — privilégient une approche comparatiste et qu'à ce titre ils se situent du côté des langues et de leur diversité plutôt qu'ils ne s'interrogent sur la faculté universelle du langage. S'ils cherchent l'empreinte des mots, c'est dans les textes, les mythes voire les formations sociales et non dans les replis du cerveau. Ils se consacrent au temps, au changement, à l'histoire et non au corps, à l'espèce humaine ou aux facultés. Aussi l'aphasie n'implique pas, dans ses commencements, la science du langage.

2. Les origines: Gall et sa postérité

2.1. Gall (1809)

Franz Joseph Gall (1758—1828), dans une série d'études publiées au début du XIXe siècle, notamment avec Gaspard Spurzheim (1776—1832), exploita son travail de recherche anatomique et neurologique pour fonder une discipline nouvelle: la 'phrénologie'. Il identifia dans le cortex (qu'il disséquait en suivant son expansion à partir du bulbe — et non plus, comme on l'avait fait avant lui, par coupes) la partie essentielle du cerveau. Elargissant à la conformation osseuse les leçons de la physiognomonie, il établit, à partir de la morphologie du crâne, un relevé des saillies du cerveau, assignant chacune des vingt-sept facultés innées qu'il avait distinguées dans l'esprit à un domaine particulier reconnaissable par les reliefs de la boîte crânienne.

Les vingt-sept facultés étaient déterminées a priori, sans esprit de système, et si les huit dernières étaient spécifiquement dévolues à l'espèce humaine, la 'mémoire verbale' (faculté n° XIV) et le 'sens du langage et de la parole' (faculté n° XV) appartenaient à une série commune à l'ensemble des vertébrés supérieurs, y compris l'homme. Il était moins question de situer une faculté de langage intrinsèque qu'une capacité à communiquer un message ou à conserver l'interprétation d'un signal, ce dont sont capables les animaux. Les capacités associées au langage se situaient, selon Gall, vers les lobes antérieurs, ce qu'il justifiait par l'anatomie comparée, la configuration crânienne de certains modèles biographiques censés avoir eu au plus haut point l'aptitude en question et surtout la cranioscopie. Gall refusait l'introspection, prétendant n'accéder à la connaissance des capacités qu'à l'aide de mesures physiques externes, objectives.

2.2. Critiques philosophiques et critiques médicales

Si caduques qu'elles soient aujourd'hui, ces thèses rencontrèrent en leur temps un profond mouvement d'intérêt dont témoignèrent les discussions auxquelles elles donnèrent lieu de la part de philosophes tels Maine de Biran (*Observations sur les divisions organiques du cerveau*), Hegel (*Phénoménologie de l'Esprit*) et Auguste Comte (*Cours de philosophie positive*). L'enjeu était crucial qui déterminait l'articulation d'une capacité mentale et d'un organe physique, un nouveau dialogue de l'âme et du corps dont, paradoxalement, la langue et la parole étaient pratiquement exclues.

Dans une perspective médicale, le projet analytique de Gall fut attaqué par Pierre Flourens (1794—1867) qui récusait l'idée d'une division physiologique du cortex et admettait seulement des spécialisations fonctionnelles dont l'inscription n'était pas déterminée a priori. Une polémique sévère opposa les partisans de Flourens — les 'unitaires' —, dominants dans l'Université, et les élèves de Gall — les 'localisateurs'. Les uns et les autres cherchèrent à étayer leur argumentation par des preuves tirées d'une meilleure connaissance du cerveau. Alors que Magendie s'attachait à démontrer l'indistinction du cortex, d'autres anatomistes (Burdach, Rolando, Leuret et al.) proposèrent un système de description par lobes et par plis dont Gratiolet, un élève de Leuret, systématisa les subdivisions en recourant à l'anatomie comparée. Il existait désormais des repères, une topographie dans la plicature apparente du cortex: la discussion, vive quant aux facultés sensori-motrices, s'accordait sur des principes anatomiques descriptifs.

Parallèlement, une description histologique était faite, à la suite des travaux de Félix Vicq d'Azyr (1748−1794), par Baillarger en 1840 (sur la structure feuilletée du cortex), Remak en 1844 (interpénétration de la substance blanche et de la substance grise et, plus tard, description de l'axone) et Kölliker en 1852 (étude des cellules nerveuses et des ganglions), complétée par une recherche anatomo-clinique dominée par Bouillaud.

2.3. Bouillaud (1825)

Le chef de file de ceux qui, de 1825 à 1865, soutinrent le théma de la localisation en justifiant leur démonstration par l'exemple de la faculté de langage située, selon eux, vers l'avant du cerveau, fut Jean-Baptiste Bouillaud (1796−1881). Renonçant aux facultés trop restrictives de Gall, il fondait sa conviction sur le fait que l'homme, qui parle, est aussi le seul chez qui le déverrouillage frontal ait provoqué, à la différence des primates, un fort développement des lobes antérieurs. Bouillard opérait une distinction entre la conservation de la motilité des organes concourant à la voix et leur dysfonctionnement au service de la parole; à la perte de la parole comme profération, il opposait la perte du langage comme 'mémoire des mots'.

3. Les commencements: De Broca (1861) à Wernicke (1874)

3.1. École française: Broca (1861−1865)

Dans le dernier tiers du XIXe siècle, les progrès de la description ont fixé à quatre lobes (frontal, temporal, pariétal, occipital), cinq si l'on y rattache l'insula, et à une série de circonvolutions − quatre pour le lobe frontal par exemple − la division du cerveau (cf. fig. 196.1 et 196.2). Les discussions scientifiques se sont accordées sur une analyse, pressentie par Jacques Lordat (1773−1870), qui distinguait deux processus dans le langage: "l'idéation' et la réalisation articulatoire.

Dans ce contexte, la communication de Paul Broca (1824−1880) devant la Société d'Anthropologie de Paris (avril 1861) présentant le résultat de l'observation et de l'autopsie d'un de ses patients, Leborgne − surnommé 'Tan' − atteint d''aphémie' consti-

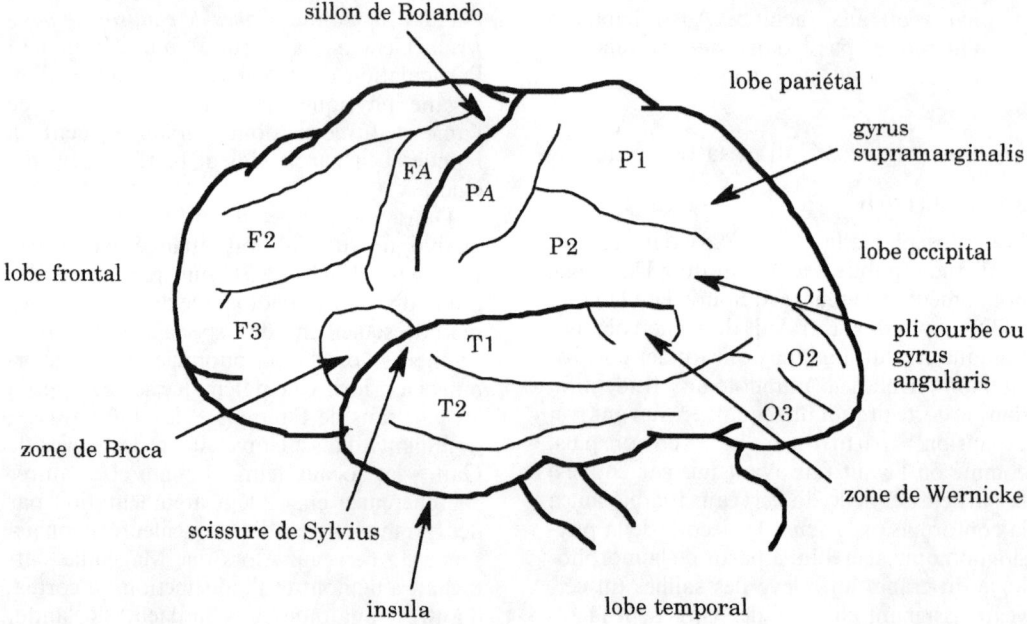

F: circonvolutions frontales (FA: frontale ascendante)
P: circonvolutions pariétales (PA: pariétale ascendante)
T: circonvolutions temporales
O: circonvolutions occipitales

Fig. 196.1: Topographie corticale

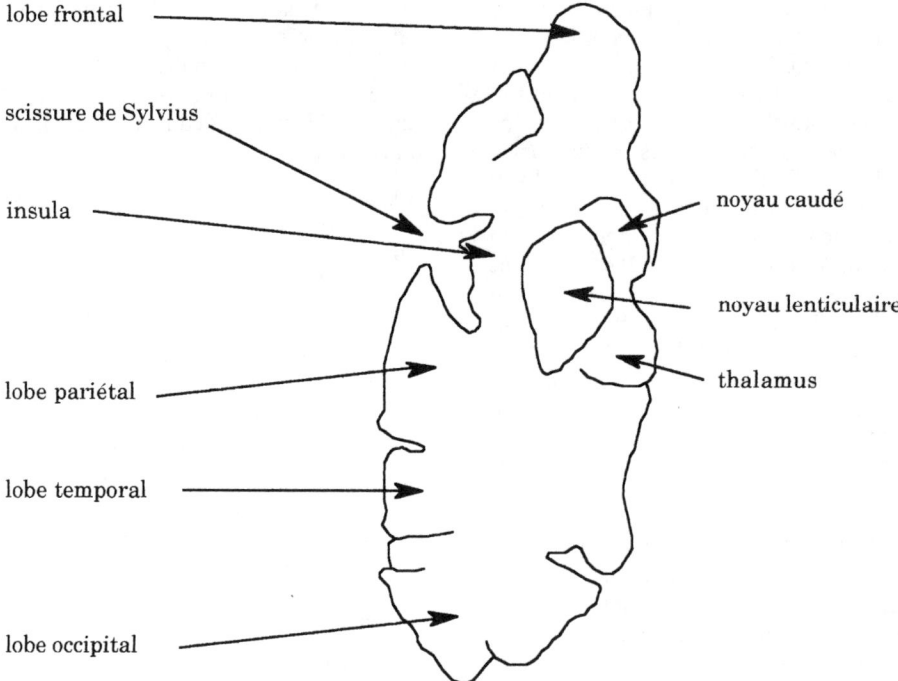

Fig. 196.2: Coupe du cerveau

tuait l'aboutissement d'une recherche orientée vers l'aphasie comme corrélation d'une lésion corticale et d'un dysfonctionnement grave des organes phonateurs. Les débats qui s'ensuivirent opposèrent unitaristes et localisationnistes, chacun argumentant par la présentation de nouveaux cas, souvent contradictoires, jusqu'à un premier bilan, en 1865, au terme duquel Broca développait les trois thèses qui signèrent une définition clinique de la première forme d'aphasie recensée:

(1) une assignation précise de la zone du langage au pied de la troisième circonvolution frontale (F3, aire de Broca);
(2) la priorité donnée à une localisation fondée sur les circonvolutions;
(3) l'affirmation du principe de la dominance hémisphérique: la faculté de langage est située à gauche.

Broca est resté comme le fondateur d'une nouvelle analyse des relations entre lésion et symptôme. Pourtant, il revint à l'un de ses adversaires, Trousseau, de baptiser *aphasie* l'affection décrite. En même temps, celui-ci rappelait d'autres aspects de la pathologie, notamment son caractère amnésique. Des critiques furent aussi formulées par Falret (1864), Fleury (1966), Gairdner (1866), Ogle (1867) et d'autres.

Bien que ses deux premières hypthèses aient été depuis nuancées. Broca demeure le premier à avoir affirmé publiquement — même si, en 1836, Marc Dax l'avait précédé dans une communication demeurée inédite — la dissymétrie hémisphérique du contrôle cortical du langage. La fondation d'une anthropologie qui accapara Broca et sa mort prématurée interrompirent son apport à l'aphasiologie. L'échec d'une école linguistique inspirée de son œuvre, menée par Abel Hovelacque (1843–1896) autour de la *Revue de Linguistique et de Philologie comparée* (1869–1916), ne permit pas non plus qu'un lien durable s'établît entre neurologues et linguistes.

3.2. École anglaise: Bastian (1869) et Broadbent (1872)

En Angleterre, où la découverte de Broca connut un retentissement immédiat, Henry Charles Bastian (1837–1915) suggéra d'étendre à l'ensemble des usages langagiers une répartition en centres dont Broca aurait désigné seulement le premier élément: il proposa, dès 1869, à partir d'un modèle associationniste purement théorique, de distinguer un centre visuel verbal, un centre auditif verbal, un centre d'écriture (centre 'chéiro-kinesthésique') et un centre moteur de la parole ('glosso-kinesthésique'). Figurés dans un schéma qui dessinait un demi-cercle autour du sillon de Rolando, les deux premiers centres constituaient des sous-ensembles finalisés d'un centre visuel (occipital) et d'un centre auditif (temporal), cependant que l'aire de Broca commandait les organes phonateurs.

En 1872, William Henry Broadbent (1835−1907) reprit ces distinctions en conjecturant l'existence d'un centre intellectuel qui subsumerait les quatre autres. Partant d'une dizaine d'observations cliniques, il proposait de simplifier le tableau des aphasies en les corrélant à une lésion soit des centres perceptifs, soit du centre intellectuel, soit de leur liaison. Le centre intellectuel lui-même était par la suite décomposé en un centre de dénomination (naming centre) et un centre de phraséologie (propositioning centre).

3.3. École allemande: Wernicke (1874)

En 1870, Karl Maria Finkelnburg (1832−1896) avait proposé de restituer à l'aphasie sa dimension signifiante en réunissant dans un seul ensemble nosographique les troubles du langage et la perte des fonctions symboliques sous le nom d'"asymbolie". Tout en restreignant à l'atteinte langagière le déficit, Carl Wernicke (1848−1905) reprit cette idée lorsqu'il publia, en 1874, *Der aphasische Symptomencomplex* dans lequel il séparait ce qui relève du langage (des mots) et de la pensée. Il projetait sur une représentation du cortex un quadrilatère a, a1, b, b1 défini par les terminaisons nerveuses (cf. fig. 196.3). Le point *a* marque l'entrée dans le bulbe de la terminaison du nerf auditif et *a1* la terminaison corticale des voies acoustiques, *b* le centre des images motrices verbales et *b1* la sortie bulbaire des voies motrices centrifuges. De ce schéma, Wernicke déduisit différentes sortes d'aphasie:

(a) si la liaison $a-a1$ est interrompue, il y a surdité;
(b) si *a1* (situé dans la portion antérieure du lobe temporal gauche) est touché, la représentation acoustique des mots devient impossible (aphasie de réception);
(c) si $a1-b1$ est lésé (insula), la compréhension de la parole et l'articulation sont intactes mais le patient est dans l'incapacité de coordonner son expression;
(d) si *b*, le centre moteur situé dans le lobe frontal est atteint, c'est une aphasie de Broca;
(e) et de même pour $b-b1$ (atteinte des commandes de motricité, aphasie de production).

Parallèlement à la zone émettrice du langage (aphasie motrice de Broca), une zone réceptrice située au voisinage de l'aire de projection des afférences auditives décidait le principe d'une nouvelle forme d'aphasie, dénommée ultérieurement 'aphasie de Wernicke', cependant qu'un troisième type semblait prédictible en cas de rupture entre les zones dites de Broca et de Wernicke, autour de la scissure de Sylvius.

Wernicke eut le souci d'étayer ses hypothèses par une démonstration clinique avant de

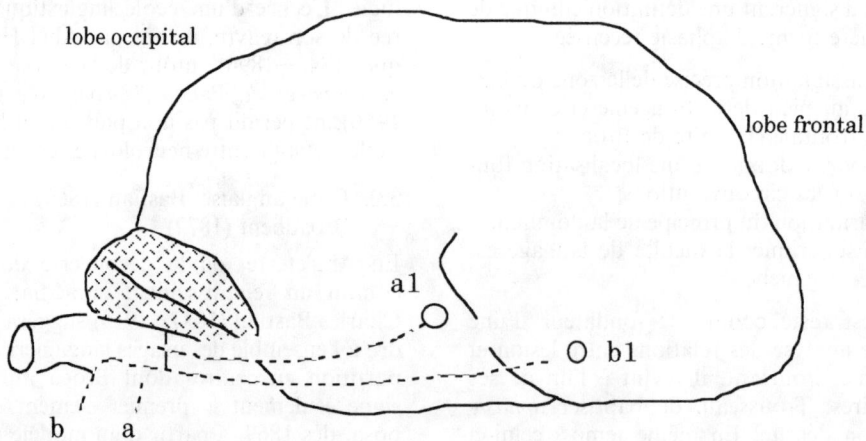

a: pénétration de la voie acoustique dans le bulbe
a1: terminaison centrale de la voie acoustique
b: voie motrice centrifuge
b1: centre frontal de représentation des mouvements de la parole

Fig. 196.3: Représentation du Wernicke (1874)

développer une théorie qui privilégiait les liaisons entre les différentes zones du langage, distinguant une aphasie motrice dans le lobe frontal, une aphasie sensorielle dans le lobe temporal et une aphasie de conduction dans l'insula. L'agraphie, qui ne constituait pas un symptôme autonome, demeurait selon lui une conséquence de l'aphasie.

4. Progrès de la neurologie

4.1. Les aires: Meynert (1867)

Dès lors que la théorie localisationniste morcelait les facultés en plusieurs compétences afférant à des centres individualisés, l'affinement nosographique dépendait aussi de la recherche neurologique: le langage était concerné pour autant que son fonctionnement était lié aux capacités sensorielles (délimitation de l'aire de l'audition) et motrices (commandes corticales des organes phonateurs). Après Rudolf Berlin (1858), Theodor Meynert (1833–1892), à partir de 1867, après avoir distingué cinq couches (substances blanche et grise) constitutives dans le cortex, imposa la distinction entre les aires de projection et les aires d'association en fonction de leur structure interne. Il aboutit à une représentation du cortex comme 'le champ sur lequel le corps de l'animal est projeté par les nerfs', avec des liaisons entre toutes les parties, figurant un corps anamorphosé à la surface du cerveau.

Traitant plus particulièrement du langage, Meynert en assigna l'aire à la scissure de Sylvius et à l'insula à partir d'une description exhaustive des couches corticales et des fibres d'association de cette zone, insistant sur la corrélation de l'aphasie avec la perturbation de l'audition. Flechsig poursuivit cette investigation en s'intéressant à la progressivité de la myélinisation; il définit par ailleurs trois centres d'association: l'atteinte du centre postérieur (temporo-pariéto-occipital) et du centre moyen (insula), si elle est située à gauche, devait aboutir à une perturbation du langage.

4.2. Les centres: Fritsch & Hitzig (1870)

Les expériences de Fritsch et Hitzig, en 1870, démontrèrent, par application d'un courant électrique, qu'il existe réellement une localisation corticale. L'application d'électrodes en un point donné du cortex d'un chien déclenchait une réaction musculaire précise vérifiée en laboratoire: la corrélation entre tel segment du cortex et une partie du corps permettait de désigner des 'centres'. L'excitabilité semblait limitée à la partie antérieure du cerveau, liée à la motricité, alors qu'une électrode posée dans la partie postérieure ne provoquait aucune réaction. Ces observations furent confirmées par les carences motrices résultant d'ablations infimes du lobe opérées par vivisection. Le théma localisationniste était devenu irréfutable.

4.3. Localisations: Ferrier (1873) et Munk (1878)

David Ferrier (1843–1928), qui fut l'élève de Bain et un disciple de Spencer, situa en 1873 le centre auditif proposé par Bastian dans la première circonvolution temporale et, en 1878, il établit une cartographie des centres corticaux de la motilité chez le singe en utilisant les méthodes de Hitzig. Il soutint l'hypothèse que le substrat sensoriel des lobes antérieurs aurait conditionné le développement des fonctions intellectuelles et il opéra des différenciations dans le cerveau entre zones d'afférences et zones d'efférences – dans le corps strié et le thalamus, limitant au cortex la partie consciente de l'activité sensitive, idéative et émotive. Dans son analyse, il réservait à la psychologie l'interprétation des données biologiques.

H. Munk s'opposa à Ferrier dans une œuvre qui, dès 1878, soutint que le cortex contrôlait une motricité sous-corticale mais qu'il était seulement sensoriel. En 1880, il apportait d'autres preuves concernant la zone de l'audition, étendant ensuite sa démonstration à la 'cécité psychique' en 1890 (un chien ayant subi l'ablation d'une zone déterminée du cerveau peut éviter des obstacles – ce qui prouve la conservation de sa vision – sans pouvoir reconnaître son maître). Il refusait d'assigner une localisation particulière pour l'intelligence qu'il estimait présente dans l'ensemble du cortex.

Em 1879, Tamburini et Luciani insistèrent sur le caractère sensori-moteur du cortex et contribuèrent à la détermination de la zone de l'audition. V. Horsley (1875), A. S. F. Grünbaum et Charles S. Sherrington (1902), par des expérimentations sur le chimpanzé, parvinrent à dresser la carte détaillée des zones motrices le long du sillon de Rolando. Ces recherches furent confirmées par les premières tentatives neurochirurgicales.

4.4. Histologie: Ramon y Cajal (1900)

En histologie, les découvertes essentielles furent celles de Golgi (1886) qui distingua les 'cylindraxes' (ou axones) en fonction de leur taille et de leur ramifications, en deux groupes, identifiant l'un à l'ensemble des cellules à fonction motrice, l'autre aux cellules à fonction sensorielle. Santiago Ramón y Cajal (1900) établit définitivement l'organisation cytoarchitechtonique du cortex en découvrant le neurone. K. Brodmann (1909) dessina, à partir de la différenciation histologique, une nouvelle représentation corticale qui sert de base à la cartographie actuelle.

5. L'école allemande (1876–1886)

5.1. Kussmaul (1876) et Exner (1881)

Trouvant dans les travaux allemands une confirmation de ses hypothèses, Broadbent avait conforté sa conviction qu'un centre intellectuel (qu'il situait dans la sous-jacence de la zone du langage dessinée par le quadrilatère de Wernicke) avait sa place dans le graphe de l'encéphale. Cette conception fut illustrée en 1876 par Adolf Kussmaul (1822–1902) qui entendait restituer aux troubles du langage leur dimension symbolique (c'est-à-dire intellectuelle) en leur assignant un 'centre de conception' ou 'idéogène'; il distingua six types d'aphasie:

(1) aphasie ataxique ou anarthrie verbale dans la troisième frontale et l'insula;
(2) aphasie amnésique (ou aphasie proprement dite, incapacité à se rappeler les mots) dans le gyrus angulaire;
(3) surdité verbale (incapacité à comprendre le langage sans qu'il y ait surdité);
(4) cécité verbale (incapacité à lire l'écriture);
(5) paraphasie (incapacité à faire correspondre les idées aux mots);
(6) agrammatisme (incapacité à organiser syntaxiquement le discours).

Kussmaul restait très circonspect quant aux localisations, insistant sur le caractère pédagogique de ces subdivisions. En revanche, il proposait d'opérer une distinction, dans l'observation des symptômes, entre le traitement des substantifs et celui des autres mots, introduisant une dimension grammaticale dans sa description.

Une autre approche fut tentée par Sigmund Exner (1846–1926) qui, en 1881, proposa de localiser un centre graphique au pied de la deuxième circonvolution frontale. Il en avait conjecturé l'existence en procédant à un maillage de l'écorce cérébrale comprenant trois cent soixante-sept cases délimitées par le tracé des lobes et des sillons; faisant la recension de toutes les autopsies d'aphasiques, il quantifiait la relation de chaque symptôme à l'une ou plusieurs de ces cases pour aboutir à une prédiction de localisation qu'invalidaient par avance l'insuffisance des sources et une topographie trop sommaire.

5.2. Lichtheim (1884)

Ludwig Lichtheim (1845–1928) publia en 1884 une synthèse qui établissait une corrélation entre apprentissage de la langue et aphasie. Il déduisait de la progression de l'écholalie enfantine au langage volontaire l'existence de trois centres distincts (auditif, moteur, intellectuel) figurés sur un diagramme.

Il dessinait un patron adopté ensuite par nombre d'aphasiologues qui y ajouteront des éléments ou en varieront les composantes mais qui en conserveront le principe. À des lésions affectant les centres (ou 'aphasies nucléaires'), Lichtheim opposait des 'aphasies de conduction'. Il déterminait, à partir du

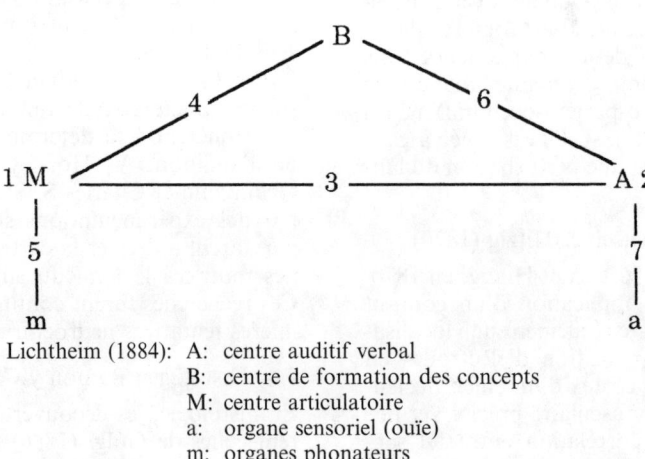

Lichtheim (1884): A: centre auditif verbal
B: centre de formation des concepts
M: centre articulatoire
a: organe sensoriel (ouïe)
m: organes phonateurs

Fig. 196.4: Lésions et localisations selon Lichtheim (1884)

point de lésion, sept formes d'aphasie (fig. 196.4):

(1) centre articulatoire: aphasie motrice corticale (aphasie de Broca);
(2) centre auditif verbal: aphasie sensorielle (aphasie de Wernicke);
(3) liaison des centres articulatoire et auditif: aphasie de conduction de Wernicke;
(4) liaison des centres articulatoire et intellectuel: aphasie motrice transcorticale;
(5) liaison du centre articulatoire aux organes: aphasie motrice sous-corticale;
(6) liaison des centres auditif et intellectuel: aphasie sensorielle transcorticale;
(7) liaison de l'ouïe au centre auditif verbal: surdité verbale (décrite par Kussmaul).

Dans un second schéma, Lichtheim introduisit un centre de l'écriture dominé par les centres du langage et reliant le centre des représentations visuelles au centre de commande des organes moteurs.

5.4. Grashey (1885)

Partant de la monographie d'un de ses patients qui lui avait révélé l'importance de la durée et de la mémoire dans les processus langagiers, Grashey proposa une alternative à une étiologie aphasique par lésion de centres ou de voies de conduction. Il postula l'existence d'une perturbation du langage due au dysfonctionnement de la mémoire courte. Selon sa théorie, l'émission de "lettres" (sons) serait tellement ralentie qu'une rupture de la chaîne sonore se produirait. Il opposait, à l'intérieur des processus d'intégration temporelle des sensations, la perception visuelle – qui est instantanée pour des formes ou des objets caractérisés – et la perception auditive qui est progressive. Ce serait dans la désynchronisation des opérations que s'originerait la perturbation aphasique plus que dans la rupture de coordination des centres visuel et auditif. La détermination de localisations n'avait plus qu'une importance secondaire.

5.5. Wernicke (1885)

En 1885–1886, Wernicke, devenu le fondateur de l'école de Breslau, dans une recension de la littérature médicale concernant l'aphasiologie, rendit un hommage appuyé à Grashey mais il élaborait un schéma plus complexe, réintégrant l'ensemble de l'imagerie mentale dans un graphe à deux étages comprenant une strate idéative où se sommerait l'ensemble des opérations intellectuelles et une strate linguistique où, en reprenant pour l'essentiel la nomenclature de Lichtheim, il imposait les dénominations d'"aphasie sensorielle corticale', 'sous-corticale' et 'transcorticale', d'"aphasie motrice corticale', 'sous-corticale', et 'transcorticale' et d'"aphasie de conduction'. Le lien à l'anatomie, circonscrit en 1874 dans l'équivalence avec la projection des aires, s'étendait désormais à la stratification du cortex comme l'indiquait la tripartition des aphasies motrices et sensorielles.

6. L'école française (1876–1900)

6.1. Charcot (1876)

Jean-Martin Charcot (1825–1893), qui s'est revendiqué bruyamment de la méthode anatomo-clinique, notamment dans le travail entrepris avec Pitres sur les localisations cérébrales (1876–1880), procéda à une reconstruction de l'aphasie par déduction d'un schéma dont il eut quelque difficulté à trouver, au chevet du malade, l'illustration. Le principe en était emprunté, avec une discrétion exagérée, à l'école allemande.

Charcot commença par limiter la faculté de langage à une collection de vocables stockés dans l'encéphale; sa conception du mot se bornait à la catégorie des noms d'objet concret (son exemple favori est le mot *cloche*), suivant une tradition réductrice commune en psychologie du langage dont Saussure stigmatisera la méthode, dans ses notes, en la qualifiant d'*onymique*. Pour Charcot, le mot était un 'complexus', la somme de quatre images distribuées chacune dans un centre (centre auditif des mots, centre visuel des mots, centre du langage articulé, centre du langage écrit) et toutes rassemblées par un centre d'idéation qui les subsumait.

De cette organisation procédaient quatre types d'aphasie:

(1) surdité verbale (aphasie de Wernicke);
(2) cécité verbale;
(3) aphasie motrice (aphasie de Broca);
(4) agraphie.

Chaque aphasie recevait une localisation hypothétique, plus souvent empruntée à la littérature médicale qu'à une autopsie de première main, bien que les présentations faites à la Salpêtrière aient été censées justifier les leçons cliniques. De l'importance relative de chacun des centres, Charcot concluait qu'il devait exister trois grands types de caractères – les moteurs, les visuels et les auditifs –, proposant d'édifier les principes d'une psychologie des aptitudes sur l'organisation corticale. Ses élèves, notamment Ballet, Bernard, Grasset et Ferrand, reprirent et complexifièrent ce schéma.

6.2. Déjerine (1900)

Jules Déjerine (1849−1917), dans les premières années du XXe siècle − ses conclusions sont reprises dans son traité paru en 1914 −, proposa de remanier les taxinomies en distinguant trois niveaux de perturbation du langage selon qu'étaient lésés les fonctions intellectuelles, le langage proprement dit ou sa réception et sa profération. L'aphasie ne concernerait que le second domaine et se subdiviserait en deux groupes:

(1) les aphasies pures qui n'impliqueraient que des lésions périphériques;
(2) les aphasies vraies (la lésion de la zone du langage entraîne une perturbation de la parole intérieure) qui se décomposeraient en 'aphasies d'expression' (les aphasies motrices) et en 'aphasies de compréhension' (les aphasies sensorielles), leur combinaison aboutissant à l'"aphasie totale'.

Déjerine résumait les acquis de la clinique dans sa définition d'une 'zone du langage' qu'il représentait comme un dépôt des images du langage situé au pied de la troisième frontale, dans le gyrus et la partie postérieure de la première circonvolution temporale. L'ensemble recouvrait toute les parties corticales attenantes à la scissure de Sylvius, dans les lobes frontal, temporal et pariétal, constituant un ensemble interdépendant à l'intérieur duquel l'atteinte d'une partie entraînerait des répercussions sur toutes les autres.

Déjerine confirmait l'idée que les centres verbaux seraient apparus par spécialisation des zones générales de la motricité et de la sensorialité. Il récusait l'idée d'un centre graphique. La rectification qu'il entreprit avec ses élèves tint avant tout à l'exigence d'observations anatomiques précises qui ratifiaient la distinction opérée entre les zones corticale et sous-corticale.

Au début du XXe siècle, et au travers de la discussion poursuivie entre la France et l'Allemagne, une certaine doxa s'était établie. Les cliniciens s'accordaient sur l'existence de quatre à six types d'aphasie, avec des symptômes bien différenciés, correspondant à autant de localisations particulières. Soulevée par la psychologie, la question du centre organisateur, c'est-à-dire de l'intelligence, apparaissait comme la dernière difficulté d'une pensée localisationniste que tout semblait devoir conforter; les relevés topographiques du cortex, l'histologie, l'expérimentation animale et la chirurgie recoupaient les divisions fonctionnelles assignées à des circonvolutions subdivisées en aires ou en centres. Cette assurance allait être minée par les critiques jacksonienne et, à un moindre degré, freudienne.

7. L'école anglaise: Jackson (1864−1893)

Présenté, conformément à la psychologie de l'époque, tantôt sous forme d'une collection de mots enregistrés dans le cerveau (les images verbales), tantôt comme un schème complexe, sensori-moteur, intégré au dispositif cortical (théorie des constructeurs de diagrammes), le modèle mental de la langue pâtissait d'une approche réductrice contredite en 1891 par l'analyse originale de Sigmund Freud (1856−1939) et bien avant par Jackson.

Les propositions de John Hughlings Jackson (1834−1911) en Angleterre ne rencontrèrent pas un succès comparable à celles de Broca, de Wernicke, de Lichtheim ou de Charcot. Parue entre 1864 et 1893, sa contribution connut une notoriété grandissante seulement après sa mort. La personnalité de leur auteur, la publication de ses travaux dans des revues dispersées occultèrent la nouveauté d'une pensée qui demeura en dehors des idées communes développées sur le continent. Privilégiant les atteintes à l'usage du langage plus que l'étude des lésions, Jackson se situait à l'opposé de la définition d'une faculté conçue comme centre moteur ou centre d'analyse sensoriel et servant le plus souvent à ratifier des théories localisationnistes.

Jackson reprenait la distinction faite en 1865 par Jules Baillarger (1806−1891) entre la conservation des usages automatiques (réflexes et actes automatiques) et la perte des usages volontaires d'une fonction dont il enrichissait la définition par l'apport de Spencer. Selon Jackson, l'atteinte d'une fonction (car le langage doit être pensé plutôt comme une fonction que comme une faculté) est un phénomène régressif, une dissolution qui suit un processus inverse de celui de l'apprentissage, du plus organisé (inférieur, inné) au moins organisé (supérieur, acquis), du plus simple au plus complexe et du plus automatique au plus volontaire. Le déficit apparu avec la maladie entraînerait une compensation, notamment par la levée des inhibitions qui s'exerçaient sur les fonctions inférieures et qui vont supplanter, dans l'expression, les émissions volontaires.

Jackson refusa d'opérer une distinction tranchée entre les localisations et d'opposer les zones en sensorielles et motrices, nuançant néanmoins sa position après avoir pris connaissance des résultats de Fritsch et Hitzig (1870). Il s'intéressa à la parole intérieure comme activité dissociée: réalisée mentalement, elle ne différerait que par le degré de mobilisation des centres inférieurs impliqués dans l'action, ce qui exclut toute opposition ou distinction avec la parole proférée.

Pour Jackson, la classification des aphasies dépendrait de trois paramètres:

(1) du degré d'atteinte des fonctions volontaires du langage,
(2) du caractère local ou général de l'affection,
(3) de la classification des symptômes selon qu'ils manifestent une destruction (déficit) ou une décharge (compensation).

Il simplifia la typologie des aphasies de la façon suivante:

(a) Dégradation de la phraséologie (*propositioning*) par répercussion d'une atteinte corticale compromettant la compréhension et la réalisation motrice, les symptômes s'échelonnant de la stéréotypie (plus motrice) à la jargonophasie (plus sensorielle);
(b) altération des capacités représentationnelles par disjonction des termes et de leur référent;
(c) conjonction des deux formes d'aphasie.

Tout en reconnaissant la prééminence de la partie postérieure de la troisième circonvolution frontale gauche, Jackson se refusait à circonscrire dans un domaine aussi restreint les compétences mobilisées par la langue, résumant en une formule son jugement: "Localiser la lésion qui détruit le langage et localiser le langage sont deux choses différentes". La fonction du langage ne se réduisait pas au stockage de mots puisqu'il y avait, au centre du dispositif, la proposition comme processus phraséologique (*propositioning*) et qu'il fallait opposer au langage supérieur (volontaire) des formes de langage inférieures tels le discours archaïque et le discours de confection (notamment les 'stéréotypes', fixés quelquefois au moment de l'ictus) ou la parole émotionnelle.

Jackson distingua en outre le comportement verbal issu de l'hémisphère droit (automatique) de celui produit volontairement par les zones déjà identifiées dans l'hémisphère gauche, s'autorisant de cette opposition pour refuser la séparation de l'activité linguistique et de l'activité intellectuelle. En effet, la compensation et l'inhibition des fonctions inférieures par les fonctions supérieures déterminaient le développement du discours de façon plus fondamentale qu'un mécanisme de perception, de conceptualisation ou de réalisation.

8. La critique de l'école française: P. Marie et Ch. Foix (1906–1928)

Une tradition anti-localisationniste s'était conservée en médecine, représentée en France par Vulpian et Brown-Sequard et en Allemagne par Goltz, mais les recoupements de l'anatomie, de l'histologie et de l'expérimentation interdisaient une remise en cause décisive. Peut-être la contradiction eût été malaisée si une révision philosophique n'avait amoindri la position sous-jacente des 'matérialistes', de ceux qui n'accordaient à la pensée (et au langage) d'autre existence que celle d'une production corticale. Contre la philosophie positiviste universitaire, Henri Bergson (1859–1940), accusant les conclusions de sa thèse sur *Les Données immédiates de la conscience* (1889) s'opposa, dans *Matière et mémoire* (1896), à la double réduction du langage aux mots et des mots à des images d'objet. Il affirmait la primauté d'une pensée intuitive et continuiste, d'une pensée 'mouvante' qui échapperait, dans son fonctionnement comme dans son origine, à la localisation.

8.1. P. Marie (1906)

Dans le champ médical, Pierre Marie (1853–1940) imposa une révision du même ordre dans la conception 'classique' de l'aphasie. Il résuma, en trois articles violemment polémiques parus en 1906, ses critiques contre le schématisme et le localisationnisme. Il distinguait préalablement l'anarthrie' (perte de la coordination des mouvements d'articulation) de l''aphasie', faisant de celle-ci un trouble intellectuel marqué par une diminution globale des capacités mentales, manifeste dans la difficulté de compréhension du langage parlé. L'aphasique n'est pas pour autant un dément car l'intelligence est diverse et ne se réduit pas au langage.

Dès lors, selon Marie, l'aphasie est une et une sa localisation assignée à l'aire de Wernicke (dans le pli courbe et au pied des deux premières temporales). Quant à l'anarthrie, elle est due, selon Marie, à une lésion de la zone lenticulaire gauche. L'aphasie de Broca devenait, dans cette conception, un mixte d'aphasie et d'anarthrie, ce qui autorisait à titrer le premier des quatre articles: "La troisième circonvolution frontale ne joue aucun rôle spécial dans la fonction du langage'. Le débat avec Déjerine fut passionné qui se conclut à l'avantage de Marie.

8.2. Foix (1916)

Charles Foix, dans une série de publications échelonnées de 1916 à 1928, reprit à nouveaux frais cette théorie en distinguant trois paramètres dans l'aphasie: un élément amnésique, un élément agnosique et un élément dysphasique. Sa contribution déterminante fut de rapporter les effets de la lésion aux territoires artériels concernés par l'hémorragie ou, plus fréquemment, par le ramollissement. Il profita d'une abondance de cas, liés aux traumatismes de la Première Guerre Mondiale, pour dessiner une nouvelle topologie: l'aphasie de Wernicke est assignée au territoire postérieur de la sylvienne, dans le lobe temporal gauche. Si la scissure de Sylvius et la zone rolandique sont atteintes, l'anarthrie domine.

9. Le renouveau de l'école allemande: Pick et von Monakow (1913–1914)

9.1. Influence de l'école de Wurzbourg

Alors que les meilleurs spécialistes de l'anatomie du cerveau étaient de langue allemande, ce fut néanmoins le développement des recherches psychologiques, notamment celles de l'École de Wurzbourg (Marbe, Ach, K. Bühler), qui autorisèrent une approche nouvelle de l'aphasie en Allemagne. L'expérimentation sur la compétence langagière, initiée par Wundt et son école de psychologie du langage, démontrait la complexité des constructions préludant à la mise en œuvre de processus d'analyse et de production linguistique. Selon l'hypothèse de Stern, le rôle des 'attitudes de conscience' (*Bewussteinslagen*) dans la communication mais aussi – notamment dans les cas de persévération – sur la prégnance des images visuelles et des formules verbales était crucial. Les recherches de Bühler sur la compréhension des phrases complexes mettaient en évidence que l'analyse des énoncés ne procédait pas par un mot à mot associationniste mais supposait une construction interprétative de type métalinguistique.

9.2. Pick (1913)

En 1913, Arnold Pick (1851–1924) publiait un ouvrage programmatique, inspiré de Jackson, dont la partie d'application n'a jamais paru. Exploitant le parallèle du langage enfantin et de la parole aphasique, Pick dressait le registre des moyens d'expression affectés par 'l'agrammatisme', en distinguant un niveau 'musical' (rythme et intonation) et un niveau 'verbal', celui-ci se subdivisant à son tour selon que le trouble porterait sur les mots-outils ou sur les mots 'pleins'. L'importance différentielle de ces critères conduisait Pick à proposer une aphasie 'vernaculaire', dont les contours épouseraient les moyens d'expression de chaque langue.

Pick distinguait un temps intellectuel en deçà du temps linguistique, ce dernier comprenant un temps de structuration de l'énoncé et un temps de remplissage par les unités lexicales. Un dysfonctionnement du moment intellectuel s'apparenterait à l'aphasie transcorticale cependant que les symptômes du moment linguistique seraient tantôt une jargonophasie, tantôt le style télégraphique. Pick restait réservé quant aux localisations, affirmant qu"il n'est pas nécessaire que la lésion et la fonction coïncident; il maintenait la distinction entre le caractère expressif d'une aphasie correspondant à une lésion située dans le lobe frontal et son caractère réceptif dans le cas d'une lésion dans le lobe temporal, celle-ci aboutissant à une jargonophasie.

La disjonction du temps intellectuel et du temps linguistique, médiés par une maîtrise de schèmes spatio-temporels, sera reprise par Van Woerkom en 1921, la problématique de l'agrammatisme (style télégraphique et jargonophasie) par Isserlin en 1922.

9.3. Von Monakow (1914)

A partir de 1914, Constantin von Monakow (1853–1930) proposa une autre explication fondée sur le concept de *diaschise*: l'affection suivrait l'organisation synaptique et retentirait dans le cortex selon les montages d'intégration et de concaténation requis par l'organisation dynamique (temporelle) de la parole organiseée en 'mélodies cinétiques'. Le discours de l'aphasique résulterait de perturbations liées à l'élévation des seuils d'excitabilité ou à la persévération. Analyser l'aphasie supposerait de récapituler l'enchaînement chronologique des actes de langage pour déterminer à quelle étape du processus serait intervenue la perturbation: phase intellectuelle (rapport à l'allocutaire et au contexte), phase préverbale (sélection lexicale et mélodique), phase 'ecphorique' (de la constitution des phrases à leur articulation). En élevant les seuils de réception et de commande, la lésion entraînant l'aphasie déclencherait des réactions d'évitement et une recherche de l'économie. La théorie d'un effacement des images verbales par l'aphasie était remplacée par celle d'une rétention d''engrammes' (schémas) sensori-moteurs disposés chronologiquement dont l'ecphorie serait empêchée.

10. L'école anglaise: Henry Head (1926)

Henry Head (1861–1940) a joué un rôle polémique important dans son attaque contre ses prédécesseurs qu'il traita de 'faiseurs de diagrammes'. Il est l'éditeur des articles dispersés de Jackson dont il fit son guide dans l'analyse de l'aphasie. Il remplaça en 1926, dans *Aphasia and Kindred Disorders of Speech*, la notion de 'centres' par celle de 'foyers', pour insister sur le caractère approximatif des localisations. Il démontra, par des séries de tests effectués auprès de ses patients, que la nosographie élaborée était, dans ses principes mêmes, inopérante, qu'il s'agisse de l'opposition aphasie de Broca / aphasie de Wernicke ou des distinctions aphasies corticales / transcorticales / sous-corticales.

Pour Head, l'aphasie mettait en cause le fonctionnemenet symbolique tout entier, ce qui préludait à une analyse globale du fonctionnement mental. Pour classer les aphasies, il proposait de partir non plus de la clinique ou de l'anatomie mais des niveaux de l'analyse linguistique, opposant:

(1) l'*aphasie verbale* liée à la phonétique (aphasie motrice),
(2) l'*aphasie syntaxique* (agrammatisme),
(3) l'*aphasie nominale* (incapacité à nommer les objets) et
(4) l'*aphasie sémantique* (incapacité à comprendre les mots hors contexte).

Il précisait cependant qu'il récusait toute correspondance terme à terme entre les processus neurologiques et les unités constituant l'acte de parole.

En résumé, les localisations proposées par Head étaient:

(a) pour l'aphasie verbale, la partie inférieure des circonvolutions pré et post-centrales;
(b) pour l'aphasie syntaxique, les circonvolutions du lobe temporal;
(c) pour l'aphasie nominale, le pli courbe;
(d) pour l'aphasie sémantique, le gyrus angulaire.

Ces localisations reprenaient en fait des recherches antérieures que Head avait si justement critiquées, révélant une certaine ambivalence de sa démarche. Etait sous-jacente à cette classification la distinction opérée selon que le trouble porte sur l'utilisation (aphasies verbale et syntaxique) ou sur la signification (aphasies nominale et sémantique), avec une interdépendance de ces deux fonctions, la nomenclature reflétant les tests qui étaient au principe de la partition.

11. Le courant phénoménologique

La phénoménologie a marqué de son empreinte le travail de Kurt Goldstein (1878–1965) et Adhemar Gelb (1887–1936). Goldstein partait de l'hypothèse que l'organisme réagit comme un tout et que, face à la diminution de ses facultés, il se contraint dans un fonctionnement économique de la relation linguistique ('réaction de catastrophe'). Dans la distinction de la forme et du fond qui est au principe de l'existence de la langue et de sa Gestalt, l'aphasie estomperait le contraste et tendrait vers une confusion généralisée, variable selon les usages répertoriés du langage (représentatif, émotionnel, usuel ou savoir verbal) et particulièrement sensible dans une parole intérieure dominée par la paraphasie.

Goldstein, par des tests, a mis en évidence comment le déficit verbal se révélait à travers une certaine incapacité à exprimer des conceptions mentales, notamment dans l'aphasie amnésique. Il y a, dans le discours du patient, une perte générique de l'attitude catégorielle, celle qui permet dans des conditions ordinaires d'opérer par le langage un classement des qualités et des substances. Il ne demeure plus que des définitions concrètes ou des références prises dans l'environnement immédiat ou familier. Ce point de vue noétique sera confirmé par plusieurs travaux de Lotmar.

12. Du structuralisme à la neurolinguistique

Un dernier renouvellement de l'aphasiologie s'articule, dans les premières années du XXe siècle, à la linguistique psychologique (théorie de l'apprentissage et pathologie) et à la linguistique structurale qui a inspiré les protocoles de recherche d'Andreï Luria (1902–1982). Formé à l'école d'Ivan Pavlov, proche d'Alexis Leontiev (1903–1979), Luria a confronté ses hypothèses à celles de Roman Jakobson (1896–1982), de la même façon que Théophile Alajouanine et André Ombredane (1950), faisaient appel à la phonéticienne Marguerite Durand pour établir le 'syndrome de désintégration' dans l'aphasie. Dans un ordre d'idées voisin, on peut mentionner l'œuvre de MacDonald Critchley (1970).

Depuis ses débuts, la relation que la clinique cherche à établir entre le langage et la topographie corticale est déterminée par la double souffrance – mentale et physique – de l'aphasique. Les témoignages de médecins affectés par une perte provisoire de leurs capacités linguistiques (Lordat 1843; Saloz 1918; Forel 1927) en témoignent: le malade, retranché de ses semblables, est victime d'une lésion corporelle, située dans l'encéphale, dont l'effet est psychique bien que les capacités cognitives ne semblent pas, a priori, trop diminuées. L'aphasiologie est à mi-chemin des deux ordres de la réalité cartésienne, de la *res extensa* et de la *res cogitans*, impliquée dans la connaissance neurologique et les découvertes cliniques d'une part mais associée au développement de la psychologie et à l'expérimentation par tests d'autre part.

L'aphasiologie a représenté, au cours du XIXᵉ siècle, en regard d'une linguistique vouée au comparatisme et à l'étude des langues, la constance d'une sollicitude pour une capacité universelle de langage en quoi l'humanité manifestait sa spécificité anthropologique. Par là, elle établissait un rapport conflictuel mais heuristique entre les sciences de l'homme et la médecine. Aujourd'hui, alors que des progrès réels ont été faits dans la description des symptômes et l'identification de foyers de lésion, la nosographie demeure hésitante et la thérapeutique accompagne le malade dans son entreprise de recouvrement de la parole plus qu'elle ne le soigne. Si l'investigation de l'encéphale est restée une affaire de médecins, l'aphasiologie a semblé condamnée à échouer dans une problématique localisationniste, jusqu'à ce que la linguistique ou la psychologie en aient renouvelé l'approche par une analyse en terme de 'fonction' (Jackson), par une taxinomie décalquant les niveaux de langue (Head), par une synthèse établissant le parallèle avec l'acquisition (Jakobson) ou par une réflexion générale sur la forme (Goldstein).

13. Bibliographie

Baillarger, Jules. 1865. *De l'Aphasie au point de vue psychologique.* Paris: Masson.

Bastian, Henry Charlton. 1869. "On the Various Forms of Loss of Speech in Cerebral Disease". *British and Foreign Medical and Chirurgical Review* 43.209–236, 470–492.

–. 1898. *A Treatise on Aphasia and Other Speech Defects.* Londres: H. K. Lewis.

Bouillaud, Jean-Baptiste. 1825. "Recherches cliniques propres à démontrer que la perte de la parole correspond à la lésion des lobules antérieurs du cerveau". *Archives générales de Médecine* 8.25–45.

Bouton, Charles. 1984. *Discours physique du langage.* Paris: Klincksieck.

Broadbent, William Henry. 1872. "On the Cerebral Mechanism of Speech and Thought". *Medical and Chirurgical Transaction* 55.145–194.

Broca, Paul. 1961a. "Remarques sur le siège de la faculté du langage articulé, suivies d'une observation d'aphémie (perte de la parole)". *Bulletin de la Société Anatomique* 6.398–407.

–. 1861b. "Perte de la parole: Ramollissement chronique et destruction partielle du lobe antérieur gauche du cerveau". *Bulletin de la Societé d'Anthropologie* 2.235–238.

–. 1865. "Sur le siège de la faculté du langage articulé". *Bulletin de la Société d'Anthropologie* 6. 377–393.

Charcot, Jean-Martin. 1876. *Leçons sur les localisations dans les maladies du cerveau.* Paris: Progrès Médical.

–. 1884. *Differenti forme d'afasia.* Milan: Francesco Vallardi.

–. 1885. *Malattie del sistema nervoso.* Milan: Francesco Vallardi.

Critchley, MacDonald. 1970. *Aphasiology and other Aspects of Language.* London: Edward Arnold.

Déjerine, Jules 1906. "L'aphasie sensorielle; sa localisation et sa physiologie pathologique". *Progrès Médical* 14.437–439, 453–457.

–. 1914. *Sémiologie des affections du système nerveux.* Paris: Masson & Cie.

Dubois, Jean & Henri Hécaen. 1969. *La naissance de la neuropsychologie du langage.* Paris: Flammarion.

Eling, Paul, ed. 1994. *Reader in the History of Aphasia.* (= *Classics in Psycholinguistics,* 4.) Amsterdam & Philadelphia: Benjamins.

Ferrier, David. 1886. *The Functions of the Brain.* London: Smith, Elder & Co.

Foix, Charles. 1928. "Aphasies". *Nouveau Traité de Médecine* éd. par G. Roger, F. Widal & P. J. Teissier, XVIII.135–213. Paris: Masson & Cie.

Freud, Sigmund. 1891. *Zur Auffassung der Aphasien.* Wien: Deuticke.

Gall, Franz Joseph. 1808. *Discours d'ouverture lu par Monsieur le Dr Gall à la première séance de son cours public sur la physiologie du cerveau.* Paris: F. Didot, Lefort et F. Schœll.

—. 1825. *Sur les fonctions du cerveau et sur celles de chacune de ses parties.* Paris: J. B. Baillière.

Geschwind, Norman. 1974. *Selected Papers on Language and the Brain.* Dordrecht: Reidel.

Goldstein, Kurt. 1906. "Ein Beitrag zur Lehre von der Aphasie". *Journal für Psychologie und Neurologie* 7.172–188.

—. 1910. "Über Aphasie". *Beihefte zur medizinischen Klinik* 6.1–32.

—. 1934. *Der Aufbau des Organismus: Einführung in die Biologie unter besonderer Berücksichtigung der Erfahrungen am kranken Menschen.* La Haye: Martinus Nijhoff.

Head, Henry. 1926. *Aphasia and Kindred Disorders of Speech.* Cambridge: Cambridge Univ. Press.

Hécaen, Henri & Georges Lantéri-Laura. 1977. *Evolution des connaissances et des doctrines sur les localisations cérébrales.* Paris: Desclée de Brouwer.

Jackson, John Hughlings. 1931. *Selected Writings.* Vol. II: *Speech.* Éd. par James Taylor. Londres: Hodder & Soughton.

Kussmaul, Adolf. 1876. *Die Störungen der Sprache.* Leipzig: Vogel.

Lichtheim, Ludwig. 1885. "Ueber Aphasie". *Deutsches Archiv für Klinische Medizin* 36.204–268.

Marie, Pierre. 1906a. "Révision de la question de l'aphasie: La troisième circonvolution frontale ne joue aucun rôle spécial dans la fonction du langage". *La Semaine Médicale* 26.241–247.

—. 1906b. "Que faut-il penser des aphasies sous-corticales (aphasies pures)?" *La Semaine Médicale* 26.493–500.

—. 1906c. "L'aphasie de 1861 à 1866. Essai de critique historique sur la genèse de la doctrine de Broca". *La Semaine Médicale* 26.565–571.

— & Charles Foix. 1917. "Les aphasies de guerre". *Revue Neurologique* 25.53–87.

Monakow, Constantin von. 1914. *Die Lokalisation im Grosshirn.* Wiesbaden: Bergmann.

Ombredane, André. 1950. *L'aphasie et l'élaboration de la pensée explicite.* Paris: PUF.

Osgood, Charles E. & Murray S. Miron, eds. 1963. *Approaches to the Study of Aphasia.* Urbana & Chicago: Univ. of Illinois Press.

Pick, Arnold. 1913. *Die agrammatischen Sprachstörungen.* Berlin: Springer.

Schiller, Francis. 1979. *Paul Broca, Founder of French Anthropology, Explorer of the Brain.* Berkeley & Los Angeles: Univ. of California Press.

Wernicke, Carl. 1874. *Der aphasische Symptomencomplex: Eine psychologische Studie auf anatomischer Basis.* Breslau: Cohn & Weigert.

—. 1885–1886. "Einige neuere Arbeiten über Aphasie". *Fortschritte der Medizin* 3.824–830; 4.371–377, 463–469.

Gabriel Bergounioux, Orléans (France)

197. Psychologische Ansätze bei der Erforschung des frühkindlichen Spracherwerbs

1. Forschungsstand, Literaturbericht, Periodisierung
2. Unsystematische Beobachtung: von 1850–1880
3. 'Intellektualismus' vs. 'Voluntarismus': Die erste Blüte der Kindersprachforschung (1880–1907)
4. Bedeutungsentwicklung: Eine Fallstudie
5. Schlußbemerkung
6. Bibliographie

1. Forschungsstand, Literaturbericht, Periodisierung

Eine zusammenhängende Geschichte der Spracherwerbsforschung gibt es nicht. Einige ihrer frühen Protagonisten haben die Bemühungen ihrer Vorläufer summarisch kolportiert und ohne historiographischen Anspruch gewürdigt (Ament 1899, 1902; Stern & Stern 1928 [1907]). Eine zweite Quelle bilden diejenigen Autoren, die in der ersten Hälfte des 20. Jhs. die Erforschung der Kindersprache gefördert und dabei auch ihre Anfänge kritisch gesichtet haben (Bühler 1918, 1922; Piaget 1923; Wygotski 1934; Leopold 1948). Schließlich sind noch neuere Lehr- und Handbücher der Spracherwerbsforschung zu nennen, die gleichfalls auf die Geschichte der Zunft eingehen (z. B. Kegel 1984; Oksaar 1977). Diese letzteren fußen, wie alle neueren Bearbeitungen des Themas, auf dem Reader von Bar-Adon & Leopold (1971), der wichtige Quellentexte auszugsweise nachdruckt und kommentiert. Ebenso wie Leopold (1948a) beruht auch der Reader weitgehend auf den Vorarbeiten von Richter (1927). Dieses Werk kann als eigentliche Quelle für das herrschende Verständnis der frühen Kindersprachforschung gelten. Ich habe in der neueren Literatur kaum eine Aussage gefunden, die nicht auch schon bei Richter (1927) stünde. Richter sympathisiert mit der Position von Wundt und Meumann (s. u.), aber seine sorgfältige Studie ist auch heute keineswegs überholt. Von den zahlreichen Bibliographien zur Spracherwerbsforschung enthält lediglich Leopold (1952) auch die wichtigsten Arbeiten des 19. Jhs.; sie finden sich aber beinahe alle bereits in der Bibliographie von Richter (1927). Die einzige zusammenhängende Darstellung der Annahmen über Bedeutungs- und Begriffsentwicklung in der Kindersprache gibt Köhler (1929). Eine brauchbare und umfangreiche Zusammenstellung der frühen wortschatzstatistischen Untersuchungen in den U.S.A. (75 Titel) liefert das Literaturverzeichnis von Smith (1926).

Bei der Periodisierung des Untersuchungszeitraumes empfiehlt sich folgendes Vorgehen: Den Auftakt bilden einige wenige Arbeiten des ausgehenden 18. Jhs. Sie stammen aus dem Umkreis der Philantropisten und der psychognostischen Magazine, deren bedeutendes das 1783 von Karl Philipp Moritz (1756−1793) gegründete *Magazin zur Erfahrungsseelenkunde* ist. Nicht untypisch für diesen Kontext ist der Beitrag von Carl Friedrich Pockels (1757−1814), 1784−85, dessen erster Teil ausschließlich phylogenetische Spekulationen enthält, während der zweite aus bemerkenswerten Beobachtungen über Verständnis, Nachahmung und Ideenentwicklung in der frühen Kindersprache besteht. Den wirkungsgeschichtlich herausragenden Beitrag aus dieser Zeit bilden Dietrich Tiedemanns (1748−1803) *Beobachtungen über die Entwicklung der Seelenfähigkeit bei Kindern* von 1787. Wiederaufgenommen wird das Thema Kindersprache dann erst in der Mitte des 19. Jhs. Die Protagonisten sind zunächst: Mediziner, Physiologen, Pädagogen auf der einen, Völkerpsychologen auf der anderen Seite. Die Einflüsse stammen zunächst von Herbart, dann, im Zuge der Darwinrezeption, aus dem Evolutionsparadigma. Charakteristisch für diese zweite "Phase der unsystematischen Beobachtungen" ist, daß die Kindersprache nicht um ihrer selbst willen beobachtet wird, sondern vor dem Hintergrund einer Variante von Haeckels 'biogenetischem Grundgesetz': man erwartete Aufschluß über Sprachursprung und Menschwerdung:

"Die Erforschung des Kindes, d. h. die Aufstellung ontogenetischer Datenfolgen, sollte Lücken in der phylogenetischen Reihe schließen helfen, die Lücke zum primitiven menschlichen Vorfahren ebenso wie zum Anthropoiden." (Kegel 1974: 20)

Ab etwa 1880 bemächtigen sich die Psychologen des Themas. Es erscheinen die ersten systematischen Längsschnittuntersuchungen, sorgfältige Aufzeichnungen über die ersten drei Lebensjahre des Kindes (Perez 1878; Egger 1878; Preyer 1882; Compayré 1897). Es beginnt eine stürmische Entwicklung der Kindersprachforschung mit lebhaften Diskussionen und rasch akkumulierten Tatsachen. In diesen Jahren wird auch Tiedemann als Vorläufer entdeckt, übersetzt und neu herausgegeben. Summa und Abschluß dieser Sturm- und Drangperiode bildet das Werk von Stern & Stern (1907). Auch in dieser Phase erwarten viele Autoren (namentlich Linguisten) von der Spracherwerbsforschung noch Aufschluß über ganz andere Dinge: über die Gesetze des Sprachwandels oder über die Funktionsweise 'primitiver' Sprachen.

Erst in dieser Zeit werden methodische Standards für die Kinderbeobachtung etabliert: biographische Langzeittagebücher, regelmäßige Beobachtung mit unmittelbarer Aufzeichnung, natürliche Sprechsituationen, zurückhaltende Beobachtung, statistische Vergleiche und vorsichtiges Experimentieren. Kinderpsychologische Institute und Zeitschriften schießen wie Pilze aus dem Boden. Zwischen 1891 und 1914 werden 21 einschlägige Zeitschriften und mehr als 25 Institute gegründet, hauptsächlich im englisch-, französisch- und deutschsprachigen Gebiet (Bühler & Hetzer 1929: 219−220).

Die akademische Institutionalisierung der Psychologie und ihre beinahe gleichzeitige 'krisenhafte' Ausdifferenzierung in Schulen und Lehrmeinungen bilden den Hintergrund für die erste Blüte der Spracherwerbsforschung zwischen 1880 und dem Ersten Weltkrieg. Ausgetragen überwiegend in der klassischen, immer wieder neu aufgelegten Kontroverse zwischen Empirismus und Nativismus (vgl. Abschnitt 3), nachahmendem Lernen oder organischer Entfaltung einer natürlichen Anlage, sind die Hauptprobleme des Zeitraums: das Verhältnis von Sprechen und Denken, die lautliche Entwicklung, Wortformen und Wortbildung, Wortbedeutung und Sprachverstehen. Syntax und Grammatik spielen zunächst keine große Rolle. Umfassende Studien zum Erwerb von Syntax und grammatischen Formen findet man nicht vor Ivan Gheorgov (1862−1936) d. J. 1908 und Stern & Stern (1907).

Spracherwerbsforschung ist in erster Linie ein Beobachtungsproblem. Im historiographischen Rückblick wird einerseits deutlich, wie sehr es von theoretischen Konzeptionen und praktischen Vor-Urteilen über Sprache abhängt, was als was beobachtet werden kann, andererseits erscheint im Rückblick interessant, wer die naiven und theoretischen Prägungen der Beobachtung als solche reflektiert.

2. Unsystematische Beobachtung: von 1850 bis 1880

Zwischen der empirischen Psychologie des späten 18. Jhs. (Tiedemann 1787; Pockels 1784−1785) und den ersten systematischen Längsschnitt-Studien aus den Jahren um 1880 (Perez 1878; Preyer 1882) liegt etwa ein halbes Jahrhundert, aus dem nichts Nennenswertes zu berichten ist (wenige Ausnahmen nennt Richter 1927: 8 ff.), und ein Zeitraum von 30 Jahren, der eine ganze Reihe von meist unsystematischen Theorien und Materialsammlungen zum kindlichen Spracherwerb hervorgebracht hat. Anregungen gehen zunächst ebenso von Herbarts Psychologie wie vom allgemeinen Prestige der Sprachforschung aus, dann aber, mit der breiten Darwinrezeption, übernimmt der Entwicklungsgedanke die Führung.

Wir beginnen mit den Völkerpsychologen Moritz Lazarus (1824−1903) und Heymann Steinthal (1823−1899) (vgl. auch → Art. 194). Bei diesen findet man eine ganz eigentümliche Variante des biogenetischen Grundgesetzes. Man könnte ihr den Namen 'Aktualismus' beilegen. Ihre gültige Formulierung steht bei Steinthal (1881: 82 ff.). Sie besteht in der (mit den Autoritäten Wilhelm von Humboldt und Herbart unterfütterten) Ansicht, daß es zwischen der ursprünglichen Sprachschöpfung, dem kindlichen Spracherwerb und sogar dem jedesmaligen Sprechakt keinen fundamentalen Unterschied gebe. Die Neu- und Nacherzeugung einer Sprachform für den auszudrückenden Gedanken ist im Kern ein und derselbe Akt, da die Sprache niemals ein Ergon, etwas fertig im Sprecher Liegendes, ist. Im Spracherwerb trifft zwar die angeborene Bereitschaft zur Spracherzeugung auf die gesellschaftlich vorgebahnten Formen der Sprache, sie muß sich aber in ihnen aus eigener Kraft bewegen. Die Völkerpsychologen erwarten aus der Beobachtung des kindlichen Spracherwerbs also Aufschluß über die allgemeine Evolution der Sprache, über das allmähliche Werden der 'Sprachidee'.

"Kinder sind starke Analogisten", notiert Lazarus (1884 [1857]: 174). Die kindliche Formenbildung gegen die Norm, aber mit analogem Vorbild, belegt für ihn die quasi-instinktive Eigentätigkeit des sprechenden Kindes. Für Steinthal (1881 [1871]) ist die Lauterzeugung ursprünglich reflexhaft und spontan, sie kann nicht gelehrt werden. Die Sprache entspringt im Kind wie ein Naturprozeß. Wir lehren das Kind bestenfalls *unsere* Sprache, nicht aber *die* Sprache (Lazarus 1884 [1857]: 168). Die Fähigkeit, Sprache zu erzeugen, muß es selbst mitbringen und selbst üben. Das spärliche Beobachtungsmaterial, das Steinthal präsentiert, soll in erster Linie spontane, vorbildlose Laut- und Wortschöpfungen des Kindes exemplifizieren. Steinthal wünscht, seine ersten Stufen der Sprachbildung in den spontanen Produktionen des Kindes wiederzufinden: den pathognomischen Reflexlaut, die gestische Schallnachahmung (vgl. Steinthal 1881 [1871]: 382−383) und die charakterisierende Stufe der Bezeichnung nach einem Merkmal und dessen spontane Übertragung (vgl. Steinthal 1881 [1871]: 403−404, 366−432).

Klar und bedeutsam (besonders in der populären Version von Lazarus 1884) sind die Differenzierungen der Völkerpsychologen, wo es um Wort, Vorstellung, Bedeutung und Begriff in der Kindersprache geht. Der Gegensatz zur späteren Begriffsverwirrung (vgl. 4.) ist schlagend. Lazarus (1884: 181 ff.) versteht die vom Kind aufgenommenen Worte als *Veranlassung*, Vorstellungen zu bilden, nicht als deren Ursache. Erst ganz allmählich wird die Vorstellung vom Wort ablösbar und damit definierbar, Bedeutung. "Das Wort selbst leistet gleichsam Hebammendienste bei der Geburt des Gedankens" (1884: 189). Während die Wörter nach ihrer lautlichen Seite und nach ihrer allgemeinen Beziehung auf die Sache nach einiger Zeit recht stabil werden, durchlaufen sie mit Bezug auf den (heute würde man sagen): kognitiven Inhalt, auf die Bedeutungsorganisation, in die sie eintreten, die gesamte Entwicklung eines Menschen (1884: 365). In der praktischen Verständigung deutet das Wort auf einen variablen Gedankeninhalt, auf der Seite des Denkens hingegen gibt es immer den Überschuß des Gedanklichen über die bloße Lautform. Niemals stehen Lautformen exklusiv für nur einen Gedanken (1884: 375) Begriffe hingegen gehen über das Wort immer hinaus, sie bestehen in geordneten (prädikativen) Explikationen, und das Wort kann im günstigsten Falle für sie als Kürzel dienen. Das empirische Material besteht jedoch auch bei Lazarus nur aus einzelnen Beobachtungen, die in den theoretischen Gedankengang eingeflochten sind.

Herbartianer findet man nicht nur unter den Völkerpsychologen, sondern auch in der anderen Fraktion der 'unsystematischen Beobachtung'. Die Mediziner Berthold Sigismund (1819—1864) und J. E. Löbisch (1795—1853), der Pädagoge Ludwig Strümpell (Lebensdaten nicht ermittelt), sie alle veröffentlichen ihre Beobachtungen über den Spracherwerb in den Jahren nach 1850. Sie sind geprägt durch den quasi-naturwissenschaftlichen Duktus der physiologischen Psychologie und interessiert vor allem an allgemeinen Gesetzlichkeiten und Erklärungen der lautlich-physiologischen Seite des Sprechens. Originell ist Sigismund (1856), dessen nüchterne und klare Beobachtungen von den Nachfolgern gelobt werden. Überhaupt sind in dieser Gruppe die Beobachtungen reicher und geordneter, die theoretischen Erklärungen aber sehr viel anspruchsloser als bei den Völkerpsychologen.

Zu erwähnen sind noch die (spärlichen) Beiträge von Sprachwissenschaftlern (August Schleicher 1861 und Baudouin de Courtenay 1869). Schleicher beobachtet die Lautartikulation seiner Kinder und notiert ihre Analogiebildungen. Baudouin berichtet von (eigenen und fremden) Beobachtungen an polnischen Kindern, geordnet nach den Abteilungen: Lautliches, Stammbildung, Wortbildung, Syntaktisches, Lexikalisches. Bei beiden handelt es sich um präzise Expertenbeobachtungen, angestellt jedoch vor dem Hintergrund des laut- und sprachgeschichtlichen Interesses. Baudouin notiert nicht einmal das Alter der Kinder, hat aber einen sehr sicheren Blick für die Eigenheiten der kindlichen Artikulation und Formenbildung. Wofür er sich jedoch eigentlich interessiert, erhellt aus der folgenden Beobachtung:

"Ein russisches mädchen, wenn man es lateinisches *ecclesia* auszusprechen aufforderte, konnte es auf keine weise aussprechen, sondern sprach immer dafür *kjeza*, ganz genau wie italienisches *chiesa*." (Baudouin 1869: 218)

3. Nativismus vs. Empirismus: die erste Blüte der Kindersprachforschung

Die Anfänge der systematischen Spracherwerbsforschung fallen zusammen mit den Anfängen der Entwicklungspsychologie überhaupt. William Thierry Preyer (1841—1897) d. J. 1882 und seine Zeitgenossen beobachten und protokollieren die kindliche Gesamtentwicklung von der Geburt an und benötigen ergo, um Sprachanfänge beobachten zu können, Hypothesen über den Zusammenhang des Sprechens mit dieser Gesamtentwicklung. Alle nennenswerten Streitfragen der Epoche betreffen diesen Zusammenhang, während die 'nackten' Tatsachen rasch akkumuliert werden und relativ unstrittig bleiben. William Thierry Preyer, von Hause aus Physiologe, etabliert nüchterne Maximen für die Beobachtung kleiner Kinder: dreimal täglich möge man dasselbe Kind beobachten, Abrichtung und künstliche Beeinflussung möge man vermeiden, das Kind möglichst nicht unterbrechen, Beobachtungen sofort notieren etc. (Preyer 1882: 309 ff.). Das Fundament seiner Beobachtungen bilden Hypothesen über Aufbau und Funktionsweise des Gehirns und über die Dominanz der Verstandesentwicklung im Spracherwerb (vgl. die gründliche Darstellung in Kegel 1974: 17—23). Was ihm den Vorwurf des 'Intellektualismus' einträgt, ist seine Gleichsetzung jeder praktischen Generalisierung mit 'Begriffsbildung'. Solche Generalisierung hält er für elementar und vorsprachlich. Das Wort spielt bei ihrer Bildung keine aktive Rolle: "das gesprochene [...] Wort ist nur ein Zeichen, welches die Mitteilung des Begriffs ermöglicht" (Preyer 1882: 348). Dabei macht er es seinen Gegnern leicht, wenn er den "Begriff" der Nahrung umstandslos durch das "Hungergefühl" entstehen läßt (S. 255) oder die in einer passenden Situation nachgeplapperte Warnung 'Heiß!" emphatisch als das "erste gesprochene Urteil" feiert (S. 291). Weitgehend akzeptiert bleiben dagegen, was Preyer über die Dialektik von Sprechen und Verstehen mitteilt: In den Frühphasen des Spracherwerbs wiederholen Kinder bereitwillig Ausdrücke, die sie durchaus nicht verstehen können, und sie "verstehen" (auf welchem Niveau auch immer) sichtlich Ausdrücke, die zu wiederholen sie keinerlei Anstalten machen. Noch Wilhelm Wundt (1832—1920) (1921 [1900] I: 298) wird die allmähliche Verbindung dieser beiden Fähigkeiten für den Hauptmotor der kindlichen Sprachentwicklung erklären. In der (nativismusrelevanten) Streitfrage, ob das Kind aus eigenem Antrieb Wörter präge oder erfinde, die kein Vorbild in der Erwachsenensprache haben, ist Preyer (1882: 295) nüchtern: Er hat solche Bildungen nicht finden können und führt die äußeren Formen des Sprechens, Analogiebildungen eingeschlossen, auf den Verkehr des Kindes mit seiner sprechenden Umgebung zurück. Auch in diesem Punkt knüpft der (psychologisch viel subtilere) Wundt, der ja gleichfalls von der physiologischen Psychologie her kommt, an ihn an. Wundt radikalisiert noch den Empirismus Preyers, indem er die vermeintlich genuin kindlichen Eigenbildungen der Ammen- und Kindersprache (Reduplikationen, Onomatopoetika, einfache Silben) auf Motive der erwachsenen Sprecher zurückführt. Die haben nämlich, so Wundt (1900 I: 311), allen Grund, kindgemäße Ausdrücke eigens für den Verkehr mit den Kleinen zu erzeugen und zu tradieren, erstens um die eigene Sprache dem Laut- und Silbenvorrat der Kinder anzugleichen, zweitens um Ausdrücke möglichst so zu bilden, daß sie von selbst verständlich sind.

Was dann noch übrigbleibt an nicht erklärbaren (und einigermaßen konsistent gebrauchten) Eigenbildungen, das führen Wundt und Preyer als "bis zur Unkenntlichkeit verzerrte Nachahmungen" (Richter 1927: 63), während die nativistische Fraktion (die ansonsten so unterschiedliche Forscher wie Darwin, Steinthal, Taine, Ament und Strümpell umfaßt) diese Bildungen als Beleg für die autonome sprachschöpferische Kraft des Kindes nimmt. Prominent werden in dieser Debatte die Beobachtungen, die Carl Stumpf (1901) über die eigenartige Privatsprache seines Sohnes zwischen 1;11 und 3;3 veröffentlicht. Der nämlich verwendet in dieser Zeit fast ausschließlich Wörter und Kombinationen, zu denen sich Vorbilder in der sprechenden Umgebung nur schwer finden lassen. Stumpf selbst, Schüler Franz Brentanos und einer der interessantesten Psychologen der Zeit, lehnt die nativistische Erfindungstheorie jedoch ab, weil 'Erfindung' für ihn ein Ziel, einen Willen und klare Mittel-Zweck-Beziehungen involviert. Stattdessen konstatiert er eine Mischung aus mißlungenen Nachahmungen, Onomatopoetika, spielerischen Umformungen des Lautmaterials und eigensinnigen Kombinationsvorlieben; deren Ansatz und Material jedoch stammen durchaus von der sprechenden Umgebung, der sein Sohn schon 18 Monate ausgesetzt war, als er seinen Sonderweg zu beschreiten begann.

Aber gerade diese Züge spontan-willkürlicher Kreativität im Umgang mit dem Material, das die sprechende Umgebung darbietet, sind für Wilhelm Ament (1899, 1902) ein Zeichen angeborener sprachschöpferischer Fähigkeit. Der Ausdruck 'Erfindung' ist semantisch so versatil, daß man auf der einen Seite jede vorbildlose Anwendung einer nachgeahmten Form dem spontanen Sprachtrieb (und damit der 'Erfindung') zurechnen kann, auf der anderen Seite kann man aber auch jede Äußerung, der Beziehbarkeiten auf gehörte Vorbilder anhaften, kraft dieser Tatsache zur 'Nachahmung' rechnen, und sei ihr Gebrauch noch so eigenwillig. Stumpf (1901) hat hier zweifellos die Fronten etwas geklärt, wie kurz nach ihm Ament (1902). In den Jahren um 1900 folgen die Abhandlungen zur Kindersprache einander in immer kürzeren Abständen, das Prestige des Themas ist groß, ebenso das öffentliche Interesse, wie die mitlaufende Menge populärer Darstellungen (z. B. Schädel 1905) belegt. Ament (1902) nun systematisiert, im Anschluß an Compayré, die verschiedenen Lesarten schöpferischer Eigentätigkeit des Kindes. Den ersten Präzedenzfall bildet die spontane, umfassende und vorbildlose Lautproduktion der Kinder in der Lallphase, die freilich sowohl präsemiotisch als auch vor-willkürlich ist, den letzten die Tatsache, daß alle Kinder am Ende weitgehend so sprechen wie ihre Umgebung. Zwischen diesen beiden Polen gibt es folgende Möglichkeiten der nativistischen 'Erfindung':

"1. Das Kind liefert von selbst den Laut oder das Wort, aber die Eltern geben den ohne besondere Absicht artikulierten Silben einen Sinn. 2. Das Kind erfindet das Wort und fixiert zugleich dessen Bedeutung. Dies ist der merkwürdigste, seltenste und zugleich am meisten umstrittene Fall. 3. In andern, sehr häufigen Fällen liefern die Eltern die Wörter; aber das Kind, das sie wiederholt, deutet sie in seiner Weise und benutzt sie in anderem Sinne." (Ament 1902: 209)

Aments Aufstellung bezieht sich auf die semantische Seite der Kindersprache, alte Streitfälle, wie etwa die analogen Formenbildungen nach starken Mustern ("gehte, gegeht, bringte, gebringt") und die Eigenheiten der kindlichen Syntax, bleiben unerledigt. In der Regel warten die Nativisten mit Beispielen auf, die sie für genuine Worterfindungen im Sinne von (2) halten: Steinthal, Taine, Darwin, Ament. Empiristen hingegen (wie Geiger, Preyer, Lindner, Wundt, Paul oder

Meumann) können solche Worterfindungen nicht feststellen. Sie beobachten lediglich Nachahmungen, die für die Erwachsenen nicht ohne weiteres wiederzuerkennen sind, und/oder Semantisierung spielerischer Lautproduktionen durch die Erwachsenen.

Noch ein Stück tiefer als Stumpf und Ament dringt Ernst Meumann (1862–1915) in das Dickicht ein, das Nachahmung und spontane Eigentätigkeit im kindlichen Sprechen bilden (Meumann 1903). Der nämlich konstatiert (in seiner Zurückweisung von Fritz Schultzes (1846–1908) Gesetz d. J. 1880 des geringsten Kraftaufwandes in der Lautproduktion), daß die Nachahmung fremder Laute zunächst für das Kind komplexer ist als die spontane Artikulation, daß Kinder eine Zeitlang Laute und Lautfolgen nicht nachahmen können, die sie spontan scheinbar mühelos erzeugen (Meumann 1903: 22). Ganz offenbar ist es eine beträchtliche Errungenschaft, wenn Kinder anfangen, ihre Lautproduktion unter die systematische Kontrolle äußerer Vorbilder zu stellen. Ganz analoge Verhältnisse postuliert Meumann (S. 29) auch für die innere Seite des kindlichen Sprechens: Was bei unzureichender Beobachtung für Worterfindung gelten könne, das müsse als spontane Kombinations- und Assoziationstätigkeit der Kinder aufgefaßt werden, bevor es allmählich und schrittweise unter die Kontrolle der sprechenden Umgebung gerät.

Es versteht sich von selbst, daß gerade aus diesen Befunden auch eine nativistische Gegenposition Honig saugen kann. Wenn nämlich die geordnete Nachahmung 'schwerer', voraussetzungsreicher ist als die spontane Erzeugung entsprechender Lautfolgen, dann liegt es nahe, die Eigenheiten der 'Ammensprache' den Kindern zurechnen und den Erwachsenen lediglich deren Nachahmung und Tradierung. So hat es Ament (1899, 1902) denn auch verstanden wissen wollen. Im Streit um die Ammensprache stehen sich Nativisten und Empiristen unversöhnlich gegenüber. Auffallend ist, daß unter den professionellen Linguisten keiner die schöpferische Autonomie der Kinder gelten läßt. Dem nüchtern-positivistischen Geist der Junggrammatiker und ihrer Zeitgenossen kommt der Nativismus vor wie ein Relikt romantischer Ursprungserklärung, wie eine enthusiastisch-blinde Überhöhung des schöpferischen Kindes. "Das Jahrhundert des Kindes ist auch das Jahrhundert der kindischen Erwachsenen", schreibt Rudolf Meringer (1859–1931) gegen Ament (Meringer 1908: 107).

Und Wundt, Paul und Delbrück, die sich sonst kaum in einem Detail einig sind, kommen mühelos darin überein, die Kindersprache mit all ihren Eigenheiten den Ammen und Müttern zuzurechnen. Wer − wen? heißt hier die entscheidende Frage. Nativist ist, wer die *ham-*, *heia-* und *teiti-*Sprache von den Kindern erzeugen und von den Erwachsenen nachahmen und tradieren läßt; Empirist ist, wer umgekehrt in diesen Ausdrücken Anpassungen der Erwachsenen an das Artikulations- und Fassungsvermögen der Kinder sieht. Die Übereinstimmung der Linguisten (Steinthal ist die einzige Ausnahme, gehört aber zur älteren Generation) ist auch insofern überraschend, als ansonsten die Parteiungen im Kindersprachstreit vertrauten und anderweitig etablierten Mustern folgen: Ament ist Schüler Oswald Külpes und kämpft, wie alle Külpe-Schüler, in der Hauptsache gegen den alles beherrschenden Wundt. Der wieder hat in Ernst Meumann und Heinrich Anton Idelberger (1873–19??) treue Schüler, die trotz ihrer vorzüglichen Beobachtungen doch immer bemüht sind, die Dinge in gutem Einklang mit der Wundtschen Systemarchitektonik zu halten: sie betonen den anfänglich vorherrschenden Gefühlsausdruck und die allmähliche Trennung von Laut- und Gebärdensprache, welche anfangs nur zusammen auftreten etc.

Im allgemeinen wird die Monographie von Stern & Stern (1907) als Schlichtungsspruch im Nativismusstreit akzeptiert. Sie ist in allen Aspekten der frühen Kindersprachforschung die sorgfältigste und durchdachteste Studie, und den Autoren wächst die Meinungsführerschaft auf diesem Gebiete beinahe von selbst zu. Gegenüber Preyer sind die Beobachtungsmethoden wesentlich verfeinert (vgl. Kegel 1974: 29 ff.). Die Tagebuch-Methode ist zu hoher Vollkommenheit entwickelt (vgl. Behrens & Deutsch 1991, Deutsch 1994a, b). Die Monographie ist dreigeteilt und beginnt mit den detaillierten Biographien der Stern-Kinder, bevor dann die Psychologie der Kindersprache und die Linguistik der Kindersprache getrennt entfaltet werden. In einer gründlichen Diskussion der in der Literatur erwähnten kindlichen 'Urschöpfungen' kommen sie zu dem Ergebnis:

"Die wahre Spontaneität der kindlichen Wortbildung äußert sich nicht im Schaffen aus dem Nichts, sondern im freien Schalten und Walten mit dem gegebenen Material." (Stern & Stern 1928 [1907]: 385)

Die starre Disjunktion von Schöpfung oder Nachahmung ist aufgelöst zugunsten einer minutiösen Erhebung dessen, was das Kind an Expressivität, Sozialität und Intentionalität mitbringt und was es zur spontan-aktiven Auseinandersetzung mit der Sprache seiner Umgebung befähigt (Stern & Stern 1928 [1907]: 124 ff). Die Kindersprache ist Produkt der 'Konvergenz' dieser beiden Reihen, und diese 'Konvergenzformel' der Sterns ist angebahnt und vorbereitet durch Ament, der zuvor definiert hatte:

"Unter Kindersprache verstehe ich demnach die Gesamtheit der aus dem Konflikt zwischen dem spontanen Sprachtrieb des Kindes und den zeitlich fest bestimmten Formen der Muttersprache resultierenden Erscheinungen." (Ament 1902: 229)

Es ist schwierig, den Nativismuskonflikt in der frühen Kindersprachforschung abschließend zu beurteilen. Auch wenn es sich zu nicht geringen Teilen um einen Wortstreit handelt, induziert von der variablen Semantik und den paradoxen Konsequenzen, die das Wort 'Erfindung' entfaltet, wenn man es auf die Gegebenheiten des Sprechens anwendet (im Humboldt-Steinthalschen Sinne ist jeder *Sprechakt* eine 'Erfindung', aber da man nur zur *Sprache* rechnen kann, was soziale Geltung hat, kann es individuelle 'Erfindungen' in einer Sprache gar nicht geben!), bleibt doch ein durchaus interessanter Rest, zumal die heutige Spracherwerbsforschung noch immer in ähnlichen Denkmustern befangen ist. Nimmt man den Spracherwerb als einen speziellen kommunikativen Zusammenhang, der aufgebaut wird, wenn Kinder sich in die vorgeordnete Sphäre des Sprechens einschalten, dann kann ein wissenschaftlicher Beobachter die Eigenheiten dieses Kommunikationssystems prima facie nur eben diesem System zurechnen. Theoretische Zwänge der psychologischen Modellbildung und tiefsitzende praktische Gewohnheiten verleiten aber offenbar (bis heute) dazu, vermeintlich differenzierter zuzurechnen. Man legt es darauf an, die Anteile des Kindes und die der sprechenden Umgebung an diesen Prozessen in der Zurechnung säuberlich zu entmischen. Dieses Verfahren entspringt der praktischen Gewohnheit, Sinneffekte in den gemeinten Sinn des Sprechers und den verstandenen Sinn des Hörers zu zerlegen, es löst praktische Probleme der Kommunikation, u. a. das Problem des Anschlußhandelns und der Intention, aber im Kontext der wissenschaftlichen, der theoretischen Beobachtung des Spracherwerbs bringt es die emergenten Eigenschaften dieser Kommunikationsprozesse zum Verschwinden. Und gerade in deren Aneignung besteht eine Pointe des Primärspracherwerbs. Auch hier kommt allein bei den Sterns zum Ausdruck, daß der Streit um die differenzierte Zurechnung eigentlich müßig ist. Über die Ausdrücke der Ammensprache schreiben sie:

"Entweder greift er [der Erwachsene: C. K.] die vom Kinde tatsächlich erzeugten Äußerungsformen auf und gibt sie ihm als Sprachgut zurück (Beispiel *mama*); oder er schafft selbst Ausdrücke, die, wenn auch im Einzelfalle vom Kinde noch nicht spontan erzeugt, dennoch "kindgemäß" sind, d. h. der kindlichen Tendenz zur natürlichen Symbolik entsprechen (Beispiel *wauwau*)." (Stern & Stern 1928 [1907]: 131)

Die Beherrschung der grammatischen Formen, der Wortarten und der syntaktischen Fügung ist beinahe ebenso schwierig zu beobachten wie die semantische Entwicklung. Obwohl schon Dewey (1894) den Sinn der allgemein geübten Praxis bezweifelt, Statistiken über die Wortartenzugehörigkeit der Kinderausdrücke in der Grammatik der Erwachsenensprache zu führen, obwohl Gale & Gale (1900) und Ament (1899) zusätzlich detaillierte *Gebrauchsstatistiken* über die frühen Kinderwörter anlegen, bleibt doch die Praxis vorherrschend, von der Erwachsenengrammatik auszugehen und das Auftreten von deren Einheiten in der Kindersprache einfach zu konstatieren (vgl. die Diskussion in Meumann 1903: 67–76). Noch Gheorgov (1908), sicher die umfassendste Studie zum Erwerb der grammatischen Formen (zweier bulgarisch sprechender Kinder), bleibt in den Grenzen dieses Verfahrens. Sein Buch ist aufgebaut wie eine junggrammatische Grammatik: Unter jeder grammatischen Kategorie sind die Belege aufgeführt, datiert und kommentiert. Auch die allgemein-kognitive Periodisierung von Stern & Stern (1928 [1907]): Substanzstadium – Aktionsstadium – Relations- und Merkmalsstadium trägt überdeutlich die Spuren der je involvierten Wortarten: Substantiv – Verb – Präposition, Konjunktion und Adjektiv. Eine solche strikt grammatische Beobachtungspraxis führt zu einer Überschätzung der einzelnen grammatischen Form, welche umstandslos mit der Bedeutung oder Funktion gleichgesetzt wird, die ihr doch, wenn überhaupt, erst im Ensemble aller grammatischen Optionen der Erwachsenensprache zukommt. Wirklich umgewälzt wird diese Sichtweise erst von Bühler (1922).

4. Bedeutungsentwicklung: eine Fallstudie

In allen Phasen der Kindersprachforschung spielen Hypothesen über den Zusammenhang von Sprache und Denken eine wichtige Rolle. Spätestens bei der Frage nach den Bedeutungen indiziert das Sprechen nicht mehr nur sich selbst, sondern einen (an sich nicht beobachtbaren) Denkakt. Ganz überwiegend orientiert sich die Beobachtung der semantischen Entwicklung am (unterstellten) *Gegenstandsbezug* der Wörter. Aus dessen Invarianzmuster wird auf einen Modus der kindlichen 'Begriffsbildung' geschlossen, wobei die Verwendung des Ausdrucks 'Begriff' höchst strittig und uneinheitlich bleibt. Sie schwankt zwischen einer maximalen, logisch-epistemischen Lesart und einer minimalen, die jede generalisierte Reaktion einschließt. Zwischen 'Vorstellung', 'Bedeutung' und 'Begriff' gibt es alle Varianten der Gleichsetzung und der Opposition, weshalb Leopold (1948b) den Disput um die Begriffsbildung im Kern für einen Wortstreit hält. 'Intellektualistisch' heißt in der deutschsprachigen Diskussion diejenige Fraktion (Preyer, Lindner, Ament), welche im kindlichen Wort allein die verstandesmäßige Generalisierung sehen möchte.

Für Preyer (1882) ist die Begriffsbildung selbst ganz unabhängig vom sprachlichen Ausdruck. Das Sprachzeichen macht den vorsprachlich gebildeten Begriff lediglich kommunikabel, mitteilbar. Schon Löbisch (1851) hatte dagegen vermutet, daß der Name anfänglich so sehr zur Sache gehört, daß diese ohne ihn gar nicht völlig scharf aufgefaßt werden kann (und schon Sigismund [1856: 95—96] notiert, der 'voluntaristischen' Gegenposition vorgreifend, die Ursprache sei "nichts als ein vernehmlich gemachter Wille".) Ob das Sprachzeichen nur Ausdruck oder auch Mittel der begrifflichen Generalisierung sei, war höchst strittig. Von Max Müller z. B. übernimmt Taine (1876) die (radikal erst in Müller 1888 publizierte) Ansicht, daß es ohne Sprache gar keine begriffliche Generalisierung geben könne. Das begriffliche Denken gilt ihm als insgesamt sprachlich erzeugt. Zwischen diesen beiden Polen gibt es auch mittlere und mäßige Ansichten, die z. B. auf das Mißverhältnis zwischen dem bescheidenen kindlichen Wortvorrat und den gewaltigen Nennbedürfnissen der Kommunikation verweisen, welche die Kinder dazu zwingen, auf eigene Faust Generalisierungen zu entwerfen und kommunikativ zu erproben (z. B. Perez 1878). Auch Sully (1896) beobachtet vorsichtiger und will die aktiv verwendeten nachgeahmten Wörter zunächst als bloße Zeichen des Wiedererkennens verstanden wissen (vgl. Köhler 1929).

Wirklich in Bewegung kommt die Bedeutungsdiskussion aber erst um die Jahrhundertwende. Die Protagonisten sind, wie schon oben, Ament, Wundt und Meumann. Letzterer, in der Theorie abhängig von Wundt als dessen Schüler, in der kritischen Systematisierung des Bedeutungsproblems aber durchaus unabhängig von ihm, lehnt seine Vorläufer mehrheitlich als 'intellektualistisch' ab, Ament eingeschlossen (s. u.). Es gebe durchaus keinen Grund, die frühen Wörter der Kinder als Namen von großer Allgemeinheit, als epistemologisch unzulängliche Verallgemeinerungen, aufzufassen. Stattdessen handele es sich um affektiv-volitive Äußerungen des Begehrens, deren innerer Zusammenhang keiner der involvierten Sachen, sondern vielmehr einer der involvierten Strebungen und Affekte sei. Wie Wundt (1921 [1900] I: 299) führt er die vermeintliche Begrifflichkeit der kindlichen Bildungen auf reflexionspsychologische Fehlschlüsse zurück: der Erwachsene vergleicht die verschiedenen Verwendungen des Wortes untereinander und mit der Erwachsenensprache, konstatiert "Verengungen", "Erweiterungen" etc., die er dann in den Kopf des Kindes verlegt (vgl. Meumann 1903: 56).

Erst viel später erfolge die schrittweise Intellektualisierung der Affektwörter. 'Begrifflich' indessen seien auch die deutlich gegenstandsbezogenen und nennenden Wörter des Kindes noch lange nicht, da man ihre Anatomie wesentlich einfacher durch assoziative Reproduktion auf der Basis vager Ähnlichkeiten erklären könne. Was dem Beobachter als konsistente Leistung in der Ebene der symbolischen Darstellung erscheint, das ist psychologisch sehr viel einfacher und bleibt im Kern noch lange synkretisch. Angelegt sind Meumanns (1902, 1903) Beobachtungen auf die Übereinstimmung mit Wundts ausdruckspsychologischem System (vgl. Knobloch 1992). Auch die Sensibilität für 'reflexionspsychologische' Entgleisungen teilt Meumann mit seinem äußerst methodenbewußten Lehrer. Seine Prinzipien lauten: möglichst einfache Erklärungen, wenn möglich im Hinblick auf spätere Entwicklungsstufen, nie etwas unterstellen, was auch später noch sichtlich fehlt oder unsicher ist (Meumann 1902: 156). Er ist es auch, der den Weg freimacht für eine realistische Verwendung der

Ausdrücke 'Wort' und 'Satz' in der Kindersprachforschung: Alle Wörter des Kindes sind ursprünglich 'Satzwörter', und die eigentlichen Wortfunktionen, die Nennfunktion eingeschlossen, differenzieren sich grammatisch und semantisch erst dann aus, wenn das Kind Mehrwortäußerungen verwendet. Psychologisch ist das Wort ein Produkt des Satzes und der Satz (als Äußerungs-, nicht als Gebildeeinheit) eine ursprüngliche Funktion des Wortes (Meumann 1903: 67). Meumann postuliert, "daß *alle* ersten Wörter des Kindes Satzwörter sein *müssen* und erst durch eine Einschränkung dieser ursprünglichen Funktion und durch eine Intellektualisierung [...] die eigentliche Wortfunktion" entsteht (ebda.). Mit der Entdeckung des Satzcharakters der kindlichen Äußerung kreditiert er Romanes (1893). Für die sich bildende Tradition der Spracherwerbsforschung mag dieser Hinweis berechtigt sein. Außerhalb derselben findet man eine präzise Systematisierung derjenigen Beziehbarkeiten, die das kindliche Wort zum Satz machen, z. B. bei Wegener (1885: 11–19), der gleichfalls die affektiven und 'imperativischen' Kontexte des frühen Sprechens herausstellt. Erst durch die allmähliche Abblassung und Neutralisierung werden die Affektwörter zu neutralen Bezeichnungen. Was Wegener dem Wundt-Schüler Meumann voraus hat, das ist der versierte Sinn für die treibende Dynamik der Kommunikation: An den differenzierenden Verstehensreaktionen der Erwachsenen differenziert sich auch erst die Grammatikalisierung des Meinens (Wegener 1885: 15). Auch wenn Wegener das Stoffkorpus der Spracherwerbsforschung nicht durch eigene systematische Beobachtungen bereichert hat, darf er in keiner Geschichte der Zunft fehlen.

Indirekt gefördert wurde die Untersuchung der Bedeutungsentwicklung auch durch die besonders in den USA zahlreichen wortstatistischen Untersuchungen (Tracy 1893; Dewey 1894; Gale & Gale 1900, 1902). Einen besonderen Fortschritt markieren die Arbeiten der Gales, die neben der kategorialen Einordnung der Wörter in die konventionellen grammatischen Klassen auch genaue Gebrauchsprotokolle führten und statistisch auszuwerten versuchten (vgl. Meumann 1903: 69–70). Dabei konnte man nicht übersehen, was Dewey (1894) notiert: daß es anfänglich gar keine Berechtigung dafür gibt, die Wörter der Kinder nach den Wortarten der Erwachsenengrammatik zu klassifizieren, weil auch bei den (vermeintlichen) Nenn- und Eigenschaftswörtern noch lange Zeit der Aktionssinn, der pragmatische Bezug auf einen laufenden oder zu initiierenden sozialen Handlungskomplex überwiegt. Grammatische Gebrauchseigenschaften der Wörter können sich ohnehin erst in der syntagmatischen Verkettung und der damit einhergehenden Funktionsdifferenzierung der Satzteile entwickeln. Im Deutschen stammen die ersten präzisen und konsequenten Gebrauchsprotokolle von Ament (1899). Ich komme darauf zurück.

Daß Meumann die Bedeutungsdiskussion bis zur Jahrhundertwende nicht nur kritisch resümiert, sondern auch ein gutes Stück weitergebracht hat, darüber sind sich die Autoren einig (vgl. Richter 1927: 70–73; Köhler 1929: 187 ff.). Zu Meumanns Erkenntnissen gehört auch, was in der späteren Egozentrismusdebatte (ausgelöst durch Piaget 1923) nicht hinreichend bedacht, wohl aber implizit anerkannt wurde: daß die rein sprachliche 'Mitteilung' ein anspruchsvolles und bereits 'intellektuelles' Motiv des kindlichen Sprechens ist, das aus der praktischen, affektiv und assoziativ gesteuerten Teilhabe an den Aktionskontexten der Kommunikation erst allmählich herauswächst.

Fast alle einfachen Verstehensleistungen des Kindes interpretiert Meumann (1902: 173 ff.) als 'Wiedererkennen'. Als weitere wichtige Verstehensquelle nennt er die kleinen Dressuren und Routinen, in die Kinder von den Erwachsenen verwickelt werden und die ihren Äußerungen und Aktionen einen schematischen Kontext bieten (1902: 177–178). Bruner (1987) hat diese 'Interaktionsformate' in jüngster Zeit wieder in die Diskussion gebracht. Das Gebärdenverstehen hält mit dem Sprachverstehen Schritt oder eilt ihm voran (hier hält es Meumann mit Wundt, seinem Lehrer). Mit dem bloßen Wortverstehen verbinden sich alsbald die aktiven 'Wunschwörter', die jeweils auf eine konkrete Konstellation zielen. Der Schein von Verallgemeinerung entsteht nur für den Erwachsenen, der die Verwendungen auf seine Weise vergleicht. Meumann entzaubert die ratiomorphe Oberfläche der Kindersprache. Dafür schätzen ihn alle 'Anti-Intellektualisten' bis hin zu Wygotski (1956 [1934]). Ohne das spontane Sprechen gibt es, so vermutet Meumann (1902: 167), keine willkürliche Reproduktion von Vorstellungen. Zu den Motiven, die das Kind über die ersten Stufen der Wortbedeutung hinaustreiben, rechnet er (1902: 209): die Norm der Erwachsenensprache, den Zwang zur Differenzierung der Verständigung, die genauere Wahrnehmung und schließlich die zunehmende Organisation der Assoziationen beim Kinde.

Eine Sonderstellung in der Bedeutungsdiskussion hat weiterhin Ament (1899). Meumann (1902) rechnet ihn umstandslos zu den 'Intellektualisten', mit denen er abrechnet, und dieses Etikett ist, nicht ganz zu Recht, an ihm haftengeblieben. Ament, der eine eigenständige 'Kindersprachwissenschaft' begründen und als erklärende Wissenschaft von bloßer Beschreibung und (pädagogischer) Nutzanwendung abtrennen möchte (Ament 1899: 26), ist, da er seinen Krieg in der Hauptsache gegen die Wundt-Schule führt, Parteigänger der Nativisten und dürfte deren Position nach Steinthal und Lazarus am beredtesten vertreten haben. Sehr mißverständlich und etwas schillernd sind seine Ausführungen über das 'Begriffliche' in der Kindersprache. Was er als kindliche 'Urbegriffe' bezeichnet, die Schritt für Schritt differenziert und gelernt werden müssen, das ist die "Bedeutung eines Wortes, welches mit einer undifferenzierten Vorstellung verknüpft ist" (Ament 1899: 150), also durchaus kein 'Begriff' im Sinne der Intellektualisten. Auch deren Neigung, jede Verallgemeinerung für einen Begriff zu erklären, teilt er nicht. Vielmehr besteht seine durchaus eigenständige Pointe gerade darin, daß er den genuin begrifflichen Charakter nicht nur bei der Kindersprache, sondern auch in den gängigen Verallgemeinerungen und Übertragungen der Erwachsenensprache bezweifelt (Ament 1902: 273). In diesem Punkt war Ament bahnbrechend für das Studium der semantischen Entwicklung im Kindesalter: Die Sprachbedeutungen sind bei Kindern so wenig 'Begriffe' wie bei Erwachsenen, sie haben aber die Eigenschaft, über ihre eigene vage und ungeordnete (kommunikative) Invarianzbildung zum *Instrument* der Begriffsbildung werden zu können. "Das Kind erwirbt sich die Begriffe des täglichen Lebens, indem es die Begriffswörter der Umgangssprache richtig verstehen und anwenden lernt", schreibt Bühler (1918: 361), und die Rolle des Wortes als eines Mittels zur Bildung und Fixierung von Invarianzen bis hin zum eigentlichen 'Begriff' findet man später gewürdigt bei Ach (1921) und Wygotski (1956 [1934]).

In diesem Zusammenhang sind Aments (1899: 76 ff.) feine Verwendungsprotokolle für die ersten 200 Wörter eines Kindes zu erwähnen. Aus ihnen geht die seltsam-pauschale und assoziative Invarianzextraktion der situativen Einwortäußerungen deutlich hervor. Die Konstellationen der Wortverwendung sind genau nachgezeichnet, ohne daß Ament, wie die Mehrzahl seiner Zeitgenossen, den Kindern ganz selbstverständlich nominative Motive unterstellt. Noch Bühler (1918: 402) würdigt den Wert dieser Protokolle, aber Ament bringt sich selbst durch "vorschnelle Theoretisierung" (Köhler 1929: 185) und mißverständliche Verallgemeinerung um die Ernte seiner Beobachtungen. Der Weg von den 'Urbegriffen' über 'Einzelbegriffe' (eine an sich schon monströse Wortbildung!) zu 'Allgemeinbegriffen" ist schon terminologisch so präjudizierend, daß der Reflexionspsychologie-Vorwurf der Wundt-Schule nicht lange auf sich warten läßt.

Im Jahre 1909 veröffentlicht Ament noch ein Postskript zur Debatte um Intellektualismus und Voluntarismus, das aber weitgehend wirkungslos bleibt, nicht zuletzt, weil die vermittelnde, auf 'Konvergenz' eingestellte Position von Stern & Stern (1907) den Disput im Bewußtsein der Zeitgenossen erledigt hat. Erwähnenswert ist noch, daß Ament den schematischen Charakter der Kinderzeichnungen für die Anatomie der frühkindlichen Begriffsbildung heranzieht (vgl. Köhler 1929: 185).

Auch Lindners (1905) Postskript zur Intellektualismus-Debatte ist kaum zur Kenntnis genommen worden, wiewohl es Bedenkenswertes enthält und in jeder Hinsicht gewichtiger ist als Ament (1909). Der Autor, ein Gefolgsmann Preyers und mit diesem immer den 'Intellektualisten' zugerechnet, stellt sich ebenfalls auf den Standpunkt, Begriffe im emphatischen Sinne der Logik (als epistemisch geordnete Zusammenfassung wesentlicher Gegenstandsmerkmale) seien auch in der Sprache des Erwachsenen durchaus nicht anzutreffen. Weder er noch Preyer habe jemals derartige Ansichten vertreten, vielmehr stünde 'Begriff' nur für intellektuelle Verallgemeinerungen überhaupt, für Denkinhalte (Lindner 1905: 342). Vom 'Voluntarismus' zeigt er sich durchaus unbeeindruckt. Daß Trieb und Affekt das Verhalten des Kindes beherrschen, hält er zwar für selbstverständlich (S. 347), keineswegs aber, daß auch die ersten Worte im Dienst von Trieb und Affekt stehen. Jedes Wort enthält für ihn notwendig einen Akt der Verallgemeinerung. Seine Kritik an Ament und Meumann ist scharf — und meistens sehr treffend, wenn auch nicht immer fair. Viel Aufhebens macht er von Aments jugendlichem Alter (der war erst 22 Jahre, als seine Abhandlung gedruckt wurde, und es ist nicht ganz klar, wer die Beobachtungen angestellt hat, auf denen seine Arbeit fußt) sowie von Idelbergers (in der Tat etwas lächerlichen) Experimenten (Idelberger 1904), die nur ersonnen sind, um Meumann zu bestätigen. Der Text Lindners gibt Einblick in die kleinliche Hinterbühne des Streits um den kindlichen Spracherwerb.

Woran Lindner (1905) jedoch (m. E. mit einem gewissen Recht) festhält, ist: daß die Generalisierungen und Umfangserweiterungen, denen wir im frühen kindlichen Sprechen begegnen, von der gleichen Art sind wie die in der Norm der Erwachsenensprache unauffälligen und dort als 'Polysemie' kodifizierten. Es ist allein die Abweichung von der Norm der Erwachsenensprache, welche uns diese Bildungen so auffällig macht wie die (falschen) Analogien der kindlichen Formenbildung.

Weniger epistemologisch aufgeladen ist die Bedeutungsdiskussion in Frankreich (vgl. Köhler 1929: 177 ff.), wenngleich sich die Positionen und Probleme ähneln. Taine (1876) haben wir oben bereits erwähnt. Deville (1890−91) gibt eine klare und präzise Beschreibung des Sprechens in den ersten beiden Lebensjahren eines Kindes. Jedes Kapitel enthält eine Übersicht über die bis dahin sinnvoll gebrauchten Wörter, einschließlich der Umstände ihrer Verwendung. Erfrischend gegenüber der Begriffshuberei ist auch Compayré (1893), der unkonventionelle Generalisierungen und improvisierte Wortverwendungen auf den kargen Symbolvorrat des Kindes zurückführt, auf die momentane Ausdrucksnot, der aber die sichere Unterscheidung der gleich benannten Gegenstände korrespondiert (vgl. zur englischen und französischen Diskussion Richter 1927: 78−93 und Köhler 1929). Claparède (1905) sei nur erwähnt, da die Wirkungsgeschichte dieses Autors ganz ins 20. Jh. gehört.

Stark beeinflußt hat die Bedeutungsdiskussion der in Kanada geborene britische Evolutionist Romanes (1889), der eine regelrechte Stufenfolge von der tierischen zur menschlichen Symbol- und Objektivitätsfähigkeit aufstellt. Sie wird in den U.S.A. von James Mark Baldwin übernommen und kehrt partiell in der Konzeption Piagets wieder. In frühen Stadien der Wortverallgemeinerung stehen die besonderen und einzelnen Erfahrungen, in denen das Wort erworben wird, für alles Ähnliche, woran sich der Organismus durch das Wort akkommodiert, und sie liefern die Vorlage, an welche ähnliche Erfahrungen wenn möglich assimiliert werden (Köhler 1929: 182). Für Romanes beginnt das sprachliche Signalement mit indikativer Gestik zur Vermittlung von Wünschen und Bedürfnissen (indikative Stufe). Denotativ nennt er die einfach-mechanischen Wortdressuren, zu denen auch Papageien in der Lage sind. Konnotativ heißt schließlich die Stufe der spontanen Verallgemeinerung solcher Zeichen. Mit der Zeit gelangt die Entwicklung auf die Stufe der Denomination, dann nämlich, wenn das Zeichen beginnt, die für Vergleich und Generalisierung relevanten Merkmale des Zeichens zu bedeuten (Stufe der Vorbegriffe). Um zu den Stufenfolgen der Bedeutungs- und Begriffsentwicklung zu gelangen, wie man sie später bei Wygotski (1956 [1934]) findet, muß man eigentlich nur die unterstellte Parallele zur Phylogenese abstreichen, die aber für den Evolutionisten natürlich essentiell ist.

In der deutschsprachigen Diskussion war die Wirkung von Romanes zunächst gering. Daß die innere Logik der kindlichen Wortbedeutung selbst in den wenigen Jahren der frühen Kindheit Umbrüche erfährt und raschen Wandel des Organisationsniveaus, das erkennt zwar die voluntaristische Fraktion an, wenn sie von einer stufenweisen Intellektualisierung der Wortbedeutungen ausgeht (z. B. Meumann 1902, 1903), aber eine frühe und differenzierte Fassung dieses Gedankens findet man lediglich bei dem auch ansonsten originellen und eigensinnigen Carl Franke (1854−1925). Dessen Arbeit, ebenfalls interessiert am Haeckelschen Parallelismus, unterscheidet folgende Niveaus, sichtlich an Romanes angelehnt:

(1) Stufe der Satzwörter: Imperative, Vokative nach ihrer Funktion; dazu gehören auch vermeintliche 'Urteile' wie "Heiß!";
(2) denotative Stufe; Beziehung des Wiedererkennens von Kontexten, Handlungen, Gegenständen, Eigenschaften im Wort;
(3) konnotative oder verallgemeinernde Stufe; Namen;
(4) prädikative Stufe; Satzbildung (Franke 1908 [1899]: 759−760)

Dieses Instrumentarium führt jedenfalls über den 'Intellektualismus' weit hinaus. Namentlich das konstellative Wiedererkennen ist von der Namensbildung deutlich abgesetzt, und anerkannt ist auch, daß die (eigentliche) Satzbildung mit ihrer Disjunktion von nominativer und prädikativer Teilhandlung die semantische Logik auf eine völlig neue Grundlage stellt. Aber Franke (1908 [1899]) ist kaum rezipiert worden, möglicherweise auch seines pädagogischen Publikationskontextes wegen, der nicht in die Zeit der institutionellen Fächerdifferenzierung paßt. Dabei muten auch seine eigenwilligen Ansichten zur lautlichen Entwicklung, zu den 'Kernkonsonanten' und 'Kernvokalen', die von Kindern zuerst erworben werden und in keiner Sprache fehlen, an wie merkwürdige Vorboten von Jakobson (1941), der in seiner Bibliographie auf Franke verweist. Bar-Adon & Leopold (1971: 40−42) publizieren eine Reaktion Frankes auf die lautlichen Beobachtungen von Stern & Stern (1907).

5. Schlußbemerkung

Wiewohl auch Stern & Stern (1907) noch ein ausführliches Kapitel auf das verwenden, was der kindliche Spracherwerb (vermeintlich) über Sprachursprung, Sprachwandel und Tiersprache lehrt, kann die Spracherwerbsforschung um diese Zeit als 'autonom' gelten. Eine Reihe einflußreicher Autoren, unter ihnen Wundt, bezweifelt die Tragweite Haeckelscher Erwartungen, wiewohl auch Wundt noch allenthalben, wenn auch vorsichtiger, Parallelen zwischen der Kindersprache und der 'Sprache der Primitiven' zieht. Den Einfluß des kindlichen Spracherwerbs auf die Sprachentwicklung bezweifeln die Linguisten mehrheitlich (vgl. Meringer 1908; Jespersen 1925). Die großen Konfliktlinien der Jahrhundertwende (Nativismus vs. Empirismus, Intellektualismus vs. Voluntarismus) sind zwar so wenig bereinigt wie solche Dispute je wirklich geklärt werden: sie sind abgearbeitet, erschöpft, es gibt keine neuen Argumente. Aber allgemein gelten die ausgleichenden Formulierungen von Stern & Stern (1907) als Grundlage der weiteren Arbeit. Wenn man deren 1. Auflage von 1907 mit der letzten (heute noch gedruckten) von 1928 vergleicht − die 2. und 3. sind textgleich mit der 1. und lediglich um kurze Anhänge zur neueren Literatur erweitert − dann ist zu erkennen, wie schon die neuen Konfliktlinien der folgenden Jahrzehnte sich abzuzeichnen beginnen. Sie betreffen (immer wieder) das Verhältnis des kindlichen Sprechens zum Denken, zur Begriffsbildung, zur kognitiven Entwicklung, dann aber auch, eng damit verbunden, das Verhältnis zwischen äußerer Sprachfertigkeit (Beherrschung von Formensystem, Syntax, Konjunktionen, Pronomina etc.) und innerer semantischer Entwicklung. Auch für diese findet man bei den Sterns weitsichtige Formeln, wie die von der 'Ausgliederung', der schrittweisen 'Abhebung' und Differenzierung einmal des Sprechens vom Gesamtverhalten, dann aber auch der Einheiten, aus denen es selbst sich aufbaut (Stern & Stern 1928: 123−124, 179−180). Auch die Formel von der "allmähliche[n] Vereindeutigung des ursprünglich Vagen und Vieldeutigen" (S. 123) läßt zumindest Platz für ein bewegliches Zusammenspiel von kommunikativ-sprachlicher und allgemein-kognitiver Entwicklung, für die Erkenntnis, daß die Kopplung beider Seiten weder eindeutig noch statisch ist. Man kann also weder, wie es die 'Intellektualisten' getan haben, vom Wort oder der Konstruktion her auf die Beherrschung 'entsprechender' kognitiver Domänen schließen noch umgekehrt die völlige Unabhängigkeit beider Seiten behaupten. Wie sich das Sprechen selbst nur allmählich automatisiert, so setzen sich auch die kognitiven Operationen nur schrittweise von der sprachlichen Form ab, die sie zu organisieren und für den Sprecher bewußt zu machen helfen. Aber auch die alten Feindetiketten bleiben in Gebrauch. Wer etwa Wygotskis (1956 [1934]: 65−74) Kritik an den Sterns aufschlägt, der findet, daß auch sie im Vorwurf des 'Intellektualismus' gipfelt, den schon Meumann mit nicht mehr Recht gegen Ament geschleudert hatte. Der Vorwurf bezieht sich auf das, was die Sterns etwas unglücklich als die 'Entdeckung' der Symbolfunktion durch das Kind im ersten Fragealter bezeichnen (und was ohne Zweifel besser als Nenn- und Namensfunktion bezeichnet wäre, weil die Konnotationen von 'Symbol' zu den Verwechslungen einladen, in denen Wygotski schwelgt). Wer jedoch genauer liest, der entdeckt die seltsamsten Züge in Wygotskis Text. Man hat als Leser den Eindruck, daß der große Psychologe auf der Vorderbühne lauthals und pflichtgemäß gegen Idealismus, Intellektualismus und Personalismus wettert, um in den Sachfragen stillschweigend da weiterzumachen, wo die Sterns aufhören. Anders lassen sich die Widersprüche kaum erklären, will man nicht von Übersetzungsfehlern ausgehen. So macht Wygotski (1956 [1934]: 72) gegen Stern geltend, was dieser ausdrücklich fordert: man müsse die Einwortäußerungen im Kontext von Gebärde und Handlung interpretieren:

"Ursprünglich kommt die Art, wie ein Mensch sich in irgend einer Situation gibt, in einer Gesamtaktion des Organismus zum Ausdruck, in welcher Gebärdung, Mimik und Handlung mit den begleitenden Lauten eine untrennbare Ganzheit bildet. Man macht es sich meist viel zu wenig klar, daß die aus dieser organischen Einbettung herausgelöste bloße "Lautsprache" [...] erst eine sehr späte Etappe, ja eigentlich überhaupt nur eine künstliche Abstraktion bildet." (Stern & Stern 1928: 123)

Die Konvergenzannahme, über die Wygotski (1956 [1934]: 72) spottet, wird schon im 'nächsten' Kapitel (Die Abfolge der Kapitel von *Denken und Sprechen* stammt nicht von Wygotski selbst) ein Eckstein der kulturhistorischen Auffassung — und so geht es weiter.

6. Bibliographie

Ament, Wilhelm. 1899. *Die Entwicklung von Denken und Sprechen beim Kinde.* Leipzig: Wunderlich.

—. 1902. *Begriff und Begriffe der Kindersprache.* (= Sammlungen von Abhandlungen aus dem Gebiete der pädagogischen Psychologie und Physiologie, V: 4.) Berlin: Reuther & Richard.

—. 1909. *Zur Geschichte der Deutung der ersten Kinderworte.* Bamberg: Buchner.

Baldwin, James Mark. 1895. *Mental development in the child and the race: Methods and processes.* New York: Macmillan.

Bar-Adon, Aaron & Werner F. Leopold, eds. 1971. *Child language: A book of readings.* Englewood Cliffs, N. J.: Prentice-Hall.

Baudouin de Courtenay, Jan. 1869. "Einige beobachtungen an kindern". *Beiträge zur vergleichenden Sprachforschung* 6.215—220.

Behrens, H. & W. Deutsch. 1991. "Die Tagebücher von Clara und William Stern". *Theorien und Methoden psychologiegeschichtlicher Forschung* hg. von H. E. Lück & R. Miller, 66—76. Göttingen: Hogrefe.

Bühler, Karl. 1918. *Die geistige Entwicklung des Kindes.* Jena: Fischer. (2. Aufl., 1921.)

—. 1922. "Vom Wesen der Syntax". *Idealistische Neuphilologie: Festschrift für Karl Vossler,* 54—84. Heidelberg: Winter.

Bühler, Charlotte & Hildegard Hetzer. 1929. "Zur Geschichte der Kinderpsychologie". *Beiträge zur Problemgeschichte der Psychologie: Festschrift zu Karl Bühlers 50. Geburtstag,* 204—224. Jena: Fischer.

Claparède, Edouard. 1905. *Psychologie de l'enfant et pédagogie experimentale.* Genève: Kündig.

Compayré, Gabriel. 1893. *L'évolution intellectuelle et morale de l'enfant.* Paris: Hachette.

Deutsch, Werner. 1994a. "The Observing Eye: A century of baby diaries. Commentary". *Human Development* 37.30—35.

—. 1994b. "Nicht nur Frau und Mutter — Clara Sterns Platz in der Geschichte der Psychologie". *Psychologie und Geschichte* 5:3/4.171—182.

Deville, Gabriel. 1890—1891. "Notes sur le développement du langage". *Revue de Linguistique et de philologie comparée* 23.330—343; und 24.10—42, 128—143, 242—257, 300—320.

Dewey, John. 1894. "The Psychology of Infant Language". *The Psychological Review* 1.63 ff.

Egger, Emile. 1879. *Observations et réflexions sur le développement de l'intelligence et du langage chez les enfants.* Paris: Picard.

Franke, Carl. 1908. "Sprachentwicklung der Kinder und der Menschheit". *Encyklopädisches Handbuch der Pädagogik* hg. von W. Rein, Band 8, 2. Aufl., 742—780. Langensalza. Beyer & Mann. (Auch als Separatum, 1899.)

Gheorgov, Ivan A. 1908. *Ein Beitrag zur grammatischen Entwicklung der Kindersprache.* Leipzig: Engelmann. (Auch in *Archiv für die gesamte Psychologie* 2:3.205—395 [1908].)

Idelberger, Heinrich Anton. 1904. *Hauptprobleme der kindlichen Sprachentwicklung nach eigener Beobachtung behandelt.* Diss. Berlin: Walter.

Jespersen, Otto. 1925 [1922]. *Die Sprache, ihre Natur, Entwicklung und Entstehung.* Heidelberg: Winter.

Kegel, Gerd. 1974. *Sprache und Sprechen des Kindes.* Reinbek: Rowohlt.

Knobloch, Clemens. 1988. *Geschichte der psychologischen Sprachauffassung in Deutschland von 1850—1920.* Tübingen: Niemeyer.

—. 1992. "Wilhelm Wundt". *Sprachphilosophie: Ein internationales Handbuch* hg. von Marcelo Dascal, Gottfried Gerhardus, Kuno Lorenz & Georg Meggle, 1. Halbband, 412—431. Berlin & New York: de Gruyter.

Köhler, Elsa. 1929. "Kindersprache und Begriffsbildung: Ein Beitrag zur Problemgeschichte". *Beiträge zur Problemgeschichte der Psychologie: Festschrift zu Karl Bühlers 50. Geburtstag,* 173—203. Jena: Fischer.

Leopold, Werner F. 1948a. "The Study of Child Language and Infant Bilingualism". *Word* 4.1—17. (Wiederabgedruckt in Bar-Aron & Leopold 1971:1—13.)

—. 1948b. "Semantic Learning in Infant Language". *Word* 4.173—180. (Wiederabgedruckt in Bar-Adon & Leopold 1971: 96—102.)

Lindner, Gustav. 1898. *Aus dem Naturgarten der Kindersprache.* Leipzig: Grieben.

—. 1905. "Neuere Forschungen und Anschauungen über die Sprache des Kindes". *Zeitschrift für pädagogische Psychologie, Pathologie und Hygiene* 7:5/6.337—392.

Meringer, Rudolf. 1908. *Aus dem Leben der Sprache: Versprechen, Kindersprache, Nachahmungstrieb.* Berlin: Behr.

Meumann, Ernst. 1902. "Die Entstehung der ersten Wortbedeutungen beim Kinde". *Philosophische Studien* 20.152−214.

−. 1903. *Die Sprache des Kindes.* Zürich: Zürcher & Furrer.

Oksaar, Els. 1977. *Spracherwerb im Vorschulalter: Einführung in die Pädolinguistik.* Stuttgart: Kohlhammer.

Perez, Bernard. 1878. *La psychologie de l'enfant: Les trois premières années de l'enfant.* Paris: Picard.

Piaget, Jean. 1923. *Le langage et la pensée chez l'enfant.* Neuchâtel: Delachaux & Niestlé.

Pockels, Carl F. 1784−1785. "Über den Anfang der Wortsprache in psychologischer Rücksicht". *Magazin zur Erfahrungsseelenkunde,* II. Band, 3. Stück, 267−275; III. Band 1. Stück, 60−69.

Preyer, Wilhelm. 1882. *Die Seele des Kindes.* Leipzig: Grieben. (9. Aufl., 1923.)

Richter, Friedrich. 1927. *Die Entwicklung der psychologischen Kindersprachforschung bis zum Beginn des 20. Jahrhunderts: Ein Beitrag zur Geschichte der Kinderseelenkunde.* Münster: Münsterverlag.

Romanes, G. John. 1889. *Mental Evolution in Man: Origin of human faculty.* London: Kegan, Paul, Trench.

Schädel, E. 1905. *Das Sprechenlernen unserer Kinder.* Leipzig: Brandstetter.

Schleicher, August. 1861. "Einige Beobachtungen an Kindern". *Beiträge zur vergleichenden Sprachforschung* 2.497−498 (Engl. Übersetzung in Bar-Adon & Leopold 1971:19−20.)

Schultze, Fritz. 1880. *Die Sprache des Kindes: Eine Anregung zur Erforschung des Gegenstandes.* Leipzig: Günther.

Smith, Madorah Elizabeth. 1926. "An Investigation of the Development of the Sentence and the Extent of Vocabulary of Young Children". (= *University of Iowa Studies* (Studies in Child Welfare), V: 5.) Ames, Iowa.

Stern, Clara & Stern, William. 1907. *Die Kindersprache: Eine psychologische und sprachtheoretische Untersuchung.* Leipzig: Barth (4. Aufl., 1928; Nachdruck der 4. Aufl., Darmstadt: Wissenschaftliche Buchgesellschaft 1975.)

Steinthal, Heyman. 1881 [1871]. *Einleitung in die Psychologie und Sprachwissenschaft.* 2. Aufl. Berlin: Dümmler.

Stumpf, Carl. 1901. "Eigenartige sprachliche Entwicklung eines Kindes". *Zeitschrift für pädagogische Psychologie und Pathologie* 3:6.419−447.

Tiedemann, Dietrich. 1787. "Beobachtungen über die Entwicklung der Seelenfähigkeiten bei Kindern". *Hessische Beiträge zur Gelehrsamkeit und Kunst,* Bd. II, 313 ff.; Bd. III, 486 ff. (Neu hg. von Chr. Ufer, Altenburg: Oskar Bonde, 1897.)

Wegener, Philipp. 1885. *Untersuchungen über die Grundfragen des Sprachlebens.* Halle a. S.: Niemeyer. (Neudruck, mit einer Einleitung von Clemens Knobloch, Amsterdam & Philadelphia: Benjamins, 1991.)

Wundt, Wilhelm. 1900. *Die Sprache,* erster Halbband. Stuttgart: Kröner. (4. Aufl., 1921.)

Wygotski, Lew Semonowitsch. 1956 [1934]. *Denken und Sprechen.* Berlin: Akademie-Verlag.

Clemens Knobloch, Siegen (Deutschland)

XXXI. Structural Linguistics in the 20th Century
Der europäische Strukturalismus im 20. Jahrhundert
Le structuralisme européen au XXe siècle

198. Die Wurzeln des Strukturalismus in der Sprachwissenschaft des 19. Jahrhunderts

1. 'Strukturalismus', 'Struktur', 'System', 'Organismus'
2. Sprachtheoretische Organismuskonzeptionen
3. Systemhaftigkeit im lautsprachlichen Zusammenhang
4. Die Rekonstruktion der indogermanischen Ursprache
5. 'Junggrammatischer Atomismus' vs. 'strukturale Methode'
6. Bibliographie

1. 'Strukturalismus', 'Struktur', 'System', 'Organismus'

Angesichts der heutzutage herrschenden Überzeugung, daß eine jede Sprache unweigerlich 'strukturell organisiert' sei und daß die Linguistik somit notgedrungen eben diese 'Struktur(en)' der Sprache(n) widerspiegeln müsse, besteht die Gefahr nivellierender historiographischer Einschätzungen, gemäß derer eine strukturbezogene linguistische Sichtweise über die Zeiten hinweg unausweichlich und letztlich überall vorhanden gewesen sei (vgl. z. B. Lehmann 1994). Eine besondere Verwurzelung des linguistischen Strukturalismus des 20. Jhs. in der Sprachwissenschaft des 19. Jhs. ließe sich demzufolge gar nicht feststellen, sondern sie ergäbe sich einfach aus der Natur des Gegenstands 'Sprache' selbst. Um solche fragwürdigen Generalisierungen von vornherein auszuschließen, tut man gut daran, sich zunächst jener Art von linguistischem 'Strukturalismus' des 20. Jhs., um dessen 'Wurzeln' im vorigen Jh. es geht, genauer zu vergewissern.

Schwierig ist ein solches Unternehmen insbes. deshalb, weil das 20. Jh. überaus viele unterschiedliche Formen und Spielarten *von* Strukturalismus mit mehr oder minder stark ausgeprägten Familienähnlichkeiten kennt (und das Netz der Beziehungen reicht dabei selbst noch weit in den sog. 'Poststrukturalismus' hinein). Eine bündige und zugleich allgemein anerkannte Definition *des* 'Strukturalismus' hingegen existiert u. W. nicht → Art. 207. Was im folgenden genannt werden kann, ist demzufolge nur eine Sammlung von relevanten Punkten, deren — vollständige oder auch bloß überwiegende — Vereinigung und Zusammenschau im 20. Jh. (und insbes. in dessen zweitem Drittel) dazu geführt haben, daß man den jeweiligen linguistischen Arbeiten eine gewisse 'strukturalistische' Ausrichtung attestiert hat.

Als wesentlich sehen wir dabei vor allem Folgendes an: (a) Eine jegliche 'Struktur' ist eine nach außen abgeschlossene, als selbständig identifizierbare Ganzheit, (b) die besagte 'Ganzheit' ist zudem zerleg- und somit analysierbar, wobei (c) gemäß einer althergebrachten Formulierung 'das Ganze mehr ist als die Summe seiner Teile' (so daß, gleichsam in technischer Übersetzung, nicht nur die einzelnen Elemente, sondern zugleich und gerade auch die Relationen zwischen den Einheiten der betr. Ganzheit wesentlich sind). Weiterhin gilt, daß (d) eine solche 'Struktur' der Sprache selbst immanent ist oder zumindest qua Zuschreibung immanent sein soll und daß (e) weder die sprachlichen Einheiten selbst noch die zwischen ihnen bestehenden Beziehungen empirisch direkt zugänglich sind, sondern sich nur im Rekurs auf konkrete sprachliche Äußerungen 'aufdecken' lassen; zudem ist festzuhalten, daß (f) eine besondere Art der materiellen Vergegenständlichung der betr. sprachlichen Elemente gerade *nicht* von Bedeutung ist. Vor allem aber sind (g) diese 'Strukturen' wesentlich einzelsprachlich gebunden (auch wenn sie bisweilen als Instantiierungen einer übergreifenden, universellen 'Sprachstruktur insgesamt' begriffen werden mögen), und zwar (h) insbes. an den Zustand der betr. Einzelsprache zu einer bestimmten Zeit.

Die meisten dieser Punkte bedürfen eigentlich umfänglicher Erläuterungen, wie sie hier nur kurz angedeutet werden können. Hinsichtlich des Punkts (c) ist etwa zu vermerken, daß bloße Berufungen auf einen Satz wie 'das Ganze ist mehr als die Summe seiner Teile' (vgl. z. B. Jakobson 1931: 247), die oftmals als Ausweis eines besonderen strukturalistischen Denkens gewertet werden, letztlich nur plakativ sind und einer genaueren Bestimmung bedürfen (vgl. schon Schlick 1935); bzgl. des Punkts (f) ist z. B. darauf hinzuweisen, daß das Problem des Postulats einer einzigen Struktur einer Einzelsprache angesichts zweier unterschiedlicher Existenzweisen ein und derselben Sprache zu gewissen Zeiten, nämlich sowohl in lautlicher als auch in schriftlicher Form, auch heutzutage immer noch besteht (s. Kohrt 1985: 356 ff.), und ob nun gemäß Punkt (d) die besagte 'Struktur' in der Sprache selbst angelegt ist oder ob sie nur als postuliert zu gelten hat, war auch unter den Strukturalisten im 20. Jh. notorisch strittig. All dies und anderes sei hier wissentlich vernachlässigt – angenommen sei nur, daß diejenigen, die sämtlichen o. g. Punkten (a)–(h) anhingen oder anhängen, als 'Strukturalisten' *katexochen* zu gelten haben. An dem solchermaßen gesetzten Prototyp wollen wir uns im folgenden orientieren und anhand der genannten Punkte herauszuarbeiten suchen, inwiefern Verbindungen zu sprachwissenschaftlichen Anschauungen des 19. Jhs. bestehen.

In den letzten Jahrzehnten ist nicht selten grundsätzlich bestritten worden, daß es solche Verbindungen zwischen der Linguistik des 19. und des 20. Jhs. überhaupt oder in nennenswertem Umfang gebe und daß sie sich allenfalls über einzelne 'Vorläufer' herstellen ließen. Im Anschluß an plakative propagandistische Versuche früher Strukturalisten, sich mit Schlagworten wie dem von einer "junggrammatischen atomistisch-isolierenden Methode" (so etwa Jakobson 1931: 247) prononciert von der vorherigen Geschichte der Sprachwissenschaft abzusetzen, hat man insbes. den Junggrammatikern, tendenziell aber auch ihren Vorgängern im 19. Jh. unterstellt, daß sie schon die o. g. Punkte (a)–(d) bei der linguistischen Analyse grundsätzlich ignoriert hätten, so daß demgemäß "die Sprache in eine Fülle von formalen und lautlichen Einzelheiten [zerfallen]" sei (so z. B. Helbig 1971: 17). Mit vollem Recht ist gegen solch überzogene Sichtweisen geltend gemacht worden, daß der grundsätzliche Zusammenhang zwischen den einzelnen sprachlichen Einheiten überhaupt nicht 'übersehen' werden könne (vgl. z. B. Koerner 1975: 724, 805; Lehmann 1994), und er wurde im 19. Jh. faktisch auch durchaus anerkannt: Es handelte sich dabei um eine ebenso einfache wie elementare Grundüberzeugung, die gerade wegen ihrer Selbstverständlichkeit im fachwissenschaftlichen Diskurs normalerweise nicht jeweils noch einmal eigens thematisiert werden mußte, sondern allenfalls dort, wo man es mit Fachfremden und/oder Fachfremdem zu tun hatte. Es ist somit durchaus nicht zufällig, daß eine Formulierung wie "Jede Sprache ist [...] ein bewundernswürdiges Gewebe, in dem alle Fäden unter einander zusammenhängen, [...], durch tausend Fäden mit andern Sprachen verknüpft" (Curtius 1886: 172) gerade in einem populären Vortrag (von 1868) erscheint, und es ist ebensowenig zufällig, daß z. B. Sievers (1876: 1) in expliziter Abgrenzung zu den naturwissenschaftlichen Disziplinen der Physik und der Physiologie hervorhebt, daß für den Sprachwissenschaftler "nicht der einzelne Laut einen Werth [habe], sondern die Lautsysteme der einzelnen Spracheinheiten". Als ein Konglomerat isolierter Einzelphänomene ist die Sprache keinem einzigen Linguisten des 19. Jhs. erschienen, sondern sie galt jeweils von vornherein als ein zusammenhängendes Ganzes. Die Feststellung einer generellen Gültigkeit der Punkte (a)–(d) für jene Zeit ist allerdings letztlich trivial und unspektakulär; es handelt sich nur um eine grundsätzliche Basis, von der aus den Verbindungen zu späteren strukturalistischen Anschauungen des 20. Jhs. überhaupt erst genauer nachgegangen werden kann.

Zwar ist die Behauptung von Benveniste (1962: 32), daß Ferdinand de Saussure (1916) im *Cours de linguistique générale* das Wort *structure* niemals gebraucht hätte, faktisch nicht zu halten, und es ist auch fraglich, ob Saussure dessen Verwendung dort bewußt 'vermieden' hat (so Koerner 1987: xxx) – richtig aber ist auf alle Fälle, daß ein fachsprachlicher Gebrauch von Begriffen wie 'Struktur', 'strukturell/struktural' usw. im Sinne einer Vereinigung der o. g. Punkte (a)–(h) erst seit Ende der 20er Jahre des 20. Jhs. zu konstatieren ist (vgl. z. B. Thèses 1929: 10–11, Jakobson & Slotty 1930: 386–387) und daß er sich dann seit den 30er und 40er

Jahren in Europa und den USA weiter ausbreitete. Im Kontext des 19. Jhs. hingegen stellte der Strukturbegriff im wesentlichen "a general morphological term" (Koerner 1975: 723) dar, dessen Anwendung nicht zuletzt sprachtypologisch ausgebeutet wurde (vgl. schon Friedrich Schlegels [1808: 28] Verweis auf eine "innre Structur der Sprachen"). Zur Kennzeichnung jener Zusammenhänge, die wir heute als 'strukturell' zu bezeichnen gewohnt sind, wurde hingegen sowohl von Saussure (1916) als auch von den frühen Strukturalisten um 1930 vor allem der Begriff des 'Systems' verwendet, der bereits in der Linguistik des 19. Jhs. durchaus gebräuchlich war. Mit dem Systembegriff eng verbunden muß der damals ebenfalls stark verbreitete Begriff des 'Organismus' gesehen werden (vgl. z. B. Steinthal 1855: 84–85, 379–380); noch bei Saussure und in seiner direkten Nachfolge wird z. T. von *organisme* im Sinne von *système* gesprochen (vgl. z. B. Saussure 1922 [1916]: 40; Bally 1952 [1913]: 155).

'Organismus' und 'System', nicht aber 'Struktur' sind also wesentliche allgemeine Schlüsselbegriffe für eine Nachzeichnung der Vorgeschichte des Strukturalismus im 19. Jh. Allerdings muß man dabei grundsätzlich in Rechnung stellen, daß gerade im 19. Jh. ein durchaus anderes Verhältnis von Theorie und Praxis herrschte, als wir es heutzutage gewohnt sind. Es ist oft genug bemerkt worden, daß die damalige sprachwissenschaftliche Forschung primär 'datenorientiert', wenn nicht gar 'datenverliebt' war und daß theoretischen und/oder methodologischen Überlegungen normalerweise ein deutlich geringerer Stellenwert zukam. Generelle theoretisch-methodologische Sätze finden sich z. T. in recht allgemein gehaltenen Entwürfen (insbes. in Vorworten zu Monographien), und ihre globalen Vorgaben haben dann für die faktische(n) Analyse(n) nicht selten genug bloß begrenzte Auswirkung; z. T. sind sie auch an eher versteckter Stelle, in Randbemerkungen oder in Fußnoten, zu finden, wo ein einzelnes praktisches Problem ad hoc nach grundsätzlicherer Reflexion und Selbstvergewisserung verlangte — aber gerade auch dann mochten solche allgemeineren Überlegungen womöglich schon beim übernächsten Analysefall einfach ignoriert werden, bis hin zum Extrem einer expliziten provokatorischen Behauptung wie "Jeder Einzelfall hat seine eigene Methodik" (J. Schmidt 1885: 342).

Bei Versuchen einer Rekonstruktion der Vorgeschichte des Strukturalismus im 19. Jh. darf man sein Augenmerk also nicht einseitig nur auf explizite theoretische und methodologische Aussagen der damaligen Zeit richten; insbes. für dieses Jahrhundert gilt, daß gerade und vor allem "die Praxis Bewertungsmaßstäbe liefert" (Reis 1978: 179), und zwar in Verbindung mit — und evtl. gar jenseits von — zeitgenössischen Äußerungen genereller Art. Hinsichtlich der letzteren darf zudem nicht vergessen werden, daß eine auch nur einigermaßen festgefügte sprachwissenschaftliche Terminologie damals allenfalls in Ansätzen bestand und daß gerade die Verwendungen globaler Termini wie 'Sprache', 'System', 'Organismus' usw. jeweils einer möglichst sensiblen Ausdeutung bedürfen. Die folgende Darstellung beruht auf dem Bemühen, diesen Faktoren Rechnung zu tragen, auch wenn in dem hier vorgegebenen engen Rahmen die Explizierungen und Nachweise notwendigerweise skizzenhaft bleiben müssen.

2. Sprachtheoretische Organismuskonzeptionen

Sowohl die sprachwissenschaftlichen als auch die sprachphilosophischen Arbeiten des ausgehenden 18. und eines großen Teils des 19. Jhs. weisen einen überaus frequenten Gebrauch der Organismusmetaphorik auf. Die Gebrauchshäufigkeit der zur Illustration von Sprachverwandtschaften und zur Darstellung sprachlicher Entwicklungen verwendeten Ausdrücke *Organismus, organisch, lebendig* etc. ging jedoch zeitgleich mit der Etablierung der Junggrammatiker stark zurück, deren Verdienst es u. a. war, "[qu'] on ne vit plus dans la langue un organisme qui se développe par lui-même" (Saussure 1922 [1916]: 19). Der — bei aller Distanzierung — jedoch auch noch nach 1870 anzutreffende Gebrauch der 'beliebten aber vieldeutigen' Metaphorik (vgl. schon Osthoff 1875: 17) zeigt, daß die Ausdrücke *organisch, Organismus, lebendig* etc. verschiedenen Ansprüchen an eine sprachwissenschaftliche Terminologie genügten. Die ausgesprochen unbestimmte Metapher des Organischen nämlich, die nur vordergründig Einheitlichkeit beschwor, erschien durch ihre Vagheit gerade dazu prädestiniert, gänzlich unterschiedliche Sprachkonzeptionen zu illustrieren. Zum einen weckte der Gebrauch des Ausdrucks *Organ* erwünschte artikulatorisch- und auditiv-phonetische Konnotationen etwa bzgl. des *Sprachorgans* (vgl.

Kohrt 1990: 597) und einer damit verbundenen physiologischen Ursprünglichkeit, die schon früh in Herders berühmter "Abhandlung über den Ursprung der Sprache" (1891 [1772]), einer primär lautphysiologischen Sprachursprungstheorie, zum Tragen kam und die später in den physiologischen Arbeiten von Rapp (1836−41) eine zentrale Rolle spielte.

Zum anderen ist für den Gebrauch der Metaphorik der den Ausdrücken *organisch*, *Organismus* etc. inhärente und (hier) über das Konzept der 'Lebendigkeit' transportierte Ganzheitsgedanke (vgl. (a), (b) und (c) in Abschnitt 1) wesentlich. Dieser Grundsatz, der seit Aristoteles bis hin zum 21. Jh. als 'abendländische Gemeinphilosophie' angesehen werden muß, wurde und wird − bewußt oder unbewußt − durch die jeweilige Verwendung der Organismusmetaphorik aufgerufen. Gleichzeitig werden dabei Vorstellungen von einer prozeßartigen 'dynamischen' Entwicklung des zu betrachtenden Gegenstandes (hier: der Sprache) aktiviert, die zudem den 'energeia-Gedanken' sowie eine teleologische Orientierung dieses Prozesses implizieren. Ein entscheidender Grund dafür, neu erforschte Sprachphänomene oder -entwicklungen mit dem Attribut *organisch* zu charakterisieren, bestand insofern gerade in dem Vertrauen darauf, durch den Rekurs auf ein allgemein be- und anerkanntes Konzept Neues verständlicher erscheinen zu lassen. So konnten etwa Friedrich Schlegel (1808: 51), der den morphologischen Bau flektierender Sprachen bekanntlich als "organisches Gewebe" bezeichnete, Jacob Grimm (1822: 591), der die ahd. Lautverschiebung "als etwas *unorganisches*" auffaßte oder Karl Ferdinand Becker (1827) mit seiner berühmten Arbeit *Organism der Sprache* relativ unbesorgt davon ausgehen, daß ihre jeweiligen Aussagen zumindest *cum grano salis* verstanden wurden. In diesem Sinne konnte − trotz aller Kritik − auch noch Saussure (vgl. etwa 1922 [1916]: 41−42) die verbreitete und allgemeinverständliche Metaphorik gebrauchen, indem er gleichzeitig als *organisme* nur das verstand, was kompatibel war mit seinen eigenen Vorstellungen eines (Sprach-)Systems.

Die Kehrseite der Medaille, nämlich die in Kauf genommene Vagheit der Metaphorik, die sich bereits in der Gegenüberstellung der o. a. Zitate von Fr. Schlegel und J. Grimm abzeichnet, ist jedoch nicht gleichzusetzen mit einer Beliebigkeit der Verwendung. Weder wurde die Organismusmetaphorik im 19. Jh. wahllos eingesetzt noch war ihr Gebrauch wesentlich an ein einziges sprachwissenschaftliches resp. sprachphilosophisches Konzept des 19. Jhs. gebunden − wie fälschlich immer wieder kolportiert wird. Tatsächlich ist zu konstatieren, daß die Metaphorik gerade auf Grund der oben dargelegten Beliebtheit im Rahmen unterschiedlicher Sprachkonzeptionen unterschiedliche Zwecke erfüllte und sich − bei ausdrucksseitiger Homogenität − auf inhaltsseitig gänzlich unterschiedliche Konzeptionen bezog (vgl. Kucharczik 1998).

Im folgenden werden drei distinkte sprachtheoretische Organismuskonzeptionen des 19. Jhs. vorgestellt; dabei wird nicht auf die − im 18. und 19. Jh. ungemein verbreiteten − allgemeinen naturmetaphorischen Sprachkonzeptionen eingegangen, sondern wesentlich auf die zentralen und expliziten sprachtheoretischen Organismuskonzeptionen des 19. Jhs. (vgl. zur Unterscheidung Kucharczik 1995: 79 ff.). Von eher marginalem Wert sind dabei allzu generelle Einschätzungen wie etwa diejenigen von Wilhelm von Humboldt (1962 [1795]: 150) in einem Brief an Friedrich Schiller, "daß die Sprache selbst ein organisches Ganzes [sei]"; diese frühen Belege (vgl. auch die Briefe resp. Arbeiten von Fr. Schlegel 1987 [1795]: 264−265; A. W. Schlegel 1846 [1798]: 266; 1846 [1808]:157) verweisen lediglich auf den hohen Gebrauchswert der − hier noch recht unspezifisch gebrauchten − Metaphorik vor ihrer Etablierung als Quasi-Terminologie. Zentral dagegen sind (mindestens) die drei folgenden Konzepte: der Gebrauch der Organismusmetaphorik zum einen in sprachtypologisch-morphologischem Kontext, zum anderen zur Illustration einer diachronen Relation und zum dritten die (vermeintlich) wörtlich genommene Metapher. Diese drei Konzeptionen werden im folgenden kurz vorgestellt.

Prädestiniert schien der Gebrauch des Attributs *organisch* zunächst für den Bereich der Morphologie und der Typologie zu sein; Fr. Schlegel (1808: 51) etwa nutzte die Metaphorik zur morphologisch-typologischen Unterscheidung von einerseits flektierenden Sprachen, die "organisch entstanden s[ind] und ein organisches Gewebe bilden", sowie andererseits affigierenden Sprachen, deren "Zusammenhang eigentlich kein andrer [sei], als ein bloß mechanischer durch äussere Anfügung". Neu an dieser Typologie war insbesondere, daß die von Schlegel vorgenommene Sprachvergleichung nicht (mehr) auf lexikologischer, sondern auf morphologischer Ähnlichkeit der miteinander verglichenen Sprachen basierte; ein *organisches* 'Gewebe' war demnach das Ergebnis eines morphologischen Prozesses (hier: allein der Flexionssprachen). Der "Begriff des Organischen [war] nicht mehr in allgemeiner Weise auf den Charakter der Sprache und jeder Sprache bezogen" (H. Schmidt 1986: 69), sondern diente nunmehr wesentlich der Charakterisierung der "innre[n] Structur" (Schlegel 1808: 28) flektierender Sprachen, also ihres grammatischen (resp. hier: morphologischen) Aufbaus. Kennzeichnend für diese typologische Terminologie war zudem die mit der Verwendung der Ausdrücke *organisch* und *mechanisch* einhergehende Wertung der einzelnen Sprachen und Sprachtypen: Schlegel (1808: 51) würdigte zum einen den "Reichthum", die "Bestandheit und Dauerhaftigkeit" der flektierenden Sprachen, während er zum anderen den affigierenden Sprachen vorwarf, daß ihre Wurzeln "nur wie ein Haufen Atome" seien, und diese Sprachen charakterisierte als "immer schwer, leicht verworren und oft noch besonders ausgezeichnet durch einen eigensinnig willkührlichen, subjektiv sonderbaren und mangelhaften Charakter" (S. 52).

Die von August Wilhelm Schlegel (1818: 14) zehn Jahre später vorgenommene Erweiterung der Sprachtypologie in die drei Klassen: "les langues sans aucune structure grammaticale, les langues qui empoient des affixes, et les langues a [*sic!*] inflexions" sowie die Übernahme dieser Dreiteilung durch W. v. Humboldt (vgl. etwa 1979 [1822]: 46) hatte zunächst keine deutliche Veränderung im Gebrauch der Organismusmetaphorik zur Folge; auch Humboldt (vgl. 1836: 148, 171) charakterisierte im wesentlichen die flektierenden Einzelsprachen als 'organisch' und würdigte die "Flexionsmethode" als "ein geniales, aus der wahren Intution der Sprache hervorgehendes Princip" (S. 204). Die bei Fr. Schlegel noch offen zutage tretende Wertung stand für Humboldt allerdings nicht mehr derartig im Vordergrund; dennoch charakterisierte auch er Flexionssprachen als "Sprachen [...] glücklichen Baues" (S. 261) sowie einer "vollendeten Sprachbildung" (S. 197). Allerdings gebrauchte Humboldt die Metapher unter anderen Vorzeichen als Fr. Schlegel, indem er sich nämlich auf die Erkenntnisse von Bopp (1816) stützen konnte, der Schlegels Auffassung von Flexion als Spiegel organischer Einheit dahingehend korrigierte, daß Flexion nichts anderes sei als das Resultat zugrundeliegender Zusammensetzung (letztlich also eines mechanischen Prozesses im Schlegelschen Sinne). Humboldt (1979 [1822]: 47—48) adaptierte diese Agglutinationstheorie und inkorpierte sie in seine eigene Anschauung von einer — historischen — Entstehung 'grammatischer Formen': eine historisch ausgerichtete Typologie, die "die Verschiedenheit der Sprachen", ausgehend von den isolierenden Sprachtypen über die affigierenden Sprachtypen bis hin zu den Flexionssprachen "als Stufen in ihrem Fortschreiten" (Humboldt 1979 [1822]: 31) auffaßte. Diese 'diachrone Typologie' unterschied sich insofern in einem wesentlichen Punkt von Fr. Schlegels typologischer Klassifikation; dennoch gebrauchte auch Humboldt die Organismusmetapher weiterhin in bezug auf die Flexionssprachen, und zwar nicht nur das Adjektiv *organisch*, sondern auch das Substantiv, indem er etwa der "Sanskrit Sprache" eine "Vollständigkeit des Organismus" bescheinigte (Humboldt 1979 [1822]: 63).

Die Verwendung der Lebendigkeitsmetaphorik zur Charakterisierung eines Sprachtyps, der letztlich auf Zusammensetzung beruht, mußte jedoch kontraintuitiv erscheinen, weil die Metaphorik dadurch ad absurdum geführt wurde; insofern war es sicherlich kein Zufall, daß die Organismusmetaphorik nicht mehr zur typologischen Klassifikation eingesetzt wurde, sondern wieder frei war, um (z. T. zeitgleich, z. T. chronologisch später) gänzlich andersartige Sprachphänomene zu illustrieren. So diente die Organismusmetaphorik J. Grimm primär zur Kennzeichnung regelhafter historischer Prozesse im Rahmen seiner Systematisierung des germanischen Laut- und Formeninventars. Löther (1984: 13) hat bereits darauf hingewiesen, daß Grimm die Organismusmetaphorik gerade nicht pauschal auf die Sprache an sich bezog (wie fälschlich auch in neueren Arbeiten immer wieder angenommen wird), sondern daß *organisch* bei Grimm synonym stand für 'regelhaft' und 'gesetzmäßig'.

Die angenommenen Regeln, Gesetze resp. "internal laws" (Morpurgo Davies 1998: 87), die die Entwicklung eines lebendigen Organismus (und damit im Sinne der Sprachauffassung des 19. Jhs. auch eines sprachlichen Organismus) determinierten, waren jedoch nicht allein ausschlaggebend dafür, daß sprachliche Phänomene als 'organisch' bezeichnet wurden. Grimm, der die Organismusmetapher seit 1812 regelmäßig und ausgesprochen häufig gebrauchte (vgl. Kucharczik 1998: 92 ff.), faßte bei weitem nicht alle regelhaften sprachlichen Erscheinungen und

Entwicklungen als 'organisch' auf und bezeichnete weder das Althochdeutsche noch gar das Mittelhochdeutsche oder sogar Neuhochdeutsche als sprachlichen 'Organismus'. Sieht man sich etwa einmal seine Einschätzung der Lautverschiebungsregeln der germanischen Sprachen an (und niemand wird bezweifeln können, daß es sich bei den verschiedenen Regeln um — *cum grano salis* — regelhafte Entwicklungen handelt!), dann wird ganz offensichtlich, daß Grimm (1831: 322) einerseits zwar die germanische Lautverschiebungsregel als "organische lautverschiebung" bezeichnete, andererseits die "alth[ochdeutsche] lautverschiebung als etwas *unorganisches*" ansah (Grimm 1822: 591). Zu verstehen ist diese merkwürdig erscheinende Auffassung, die u. a. dazu führte, daß bestimmte sprachliche Phänomene als 'organischer' eingeschätzt wurden als andere, nur dadurch, daß Grimm unter 'organisch' zwar 'regelmäßig' verstand, aber daß er zudem eine klare zeitliche Grenze setzte, vor der Lautentwicklungen — und vermittelt damit auch morphologische Entwicklungen — noch als organisch anzusehen waren. Diese Grenze lag für ihn *vor* der althochdeutschen Lautverschiebung, und zudem galt, daß alle Sprachorganismen, die vor dieser "althochd[eutschen] augenscheinlichen verwirrung" (Grimm 1927 [1821]: 293) bereits bestanden hatten, als vollständiger, vollkommener und 'organischer' galten, je älter sie waren. Insofern galt Grimm (ebda.) das Gotische zwar als 'organische' Sprachstufe; in — diachroner — Relation zum Altgriechischen und Lateinischen jedoch müsse man, so Grimm (1822: 591), "das gothische für ebenso unorganisch halten". Diese Dichotomie 'organisch' vs. 'unorganisch' ist in keiner Weise mit der Schlegelschen Dichotomie 'organisch' vs. 'mechanisch' in Beziehung zu setzen und zeigt deutlich die unterschiedlichen Anwendungsbereiche der Organismusmetaphorik.

Nachdem hier zwei distinkte sprachtheoretische Organismuskonzeptionen vorgestellt wurden, die sich zum einen primär auf die morphologische Struktur der Flexionssprachen, zum anderen auf Lautgesetzmäßigkeiten vor der althochdeutschen Lautverschiebung bezogen haben, soll abschließend kurz auf eine dritte und gleichzeitig völlig andere Organismuskonzeption des 19. Jhs. verwiesen werden, die wesentlich mit dem Indogermanisten Schleicher in Zusammenhang stand. Schleichers (1865: 3) Auffassung von Sprachen als "materielle[n] Existenzen, als reale[n] Naturwesen" sowie seine schon seit 1850 vielfach erhobene Forderung, Sprachwissenschaft sei als eine Naturwissenschaft aufzufassen und zu betreiben (vgl. Schleicher 1863: 88), hatte einen — aus heutiger Sicht — fast kurios anmutenden Gebrauch der Organismusmetaphorik zur Folge, indem Sprache nämlich — völlig theoriekonsistent — als realer, natürlicher Organismus aufgefaßt wurde (vgl. auch Morpurgo Davies 1998: 196). Schleicher nahm insofern die Organismusmetapher wörtlich, als er propagierte, daß Sprachen nicht nur mit Entstehung, Entwicklung und Verfall der Naturorganismen zu vergleichen seien, sondern daß sie wie die "anderen Naturorganismen" auch (Schleicher 1860: 4) reale Organismen darstellten, daß sie in Arten und Gattungen zu unterteilen seien, einer Sprachsippe angehörten, daß ihr Wachstum gesetzmäßig verlaufe und sie einem natürlichen Verfall unterlägen. Die dieser Annahme zugrundeliegende — und durchaus berechtigte — Auffassung, daß das Untersuchungsobjekt einer naturwissenschaftlichen Disziplin (hier der Sprachwissenschaft resp. 'Glottik') auch ein reales, natürliches sein sollte, stieß jedoch bereits in Schleichers eigenen Arbeiten an Grenzen; so verfällt Schleicher (1860: 17) in sprachtypologische Wertungen Schlegelscher Prägung, wenn er den morphologischen Aufbau von Wörtern affigierender Sprachen als "Anhäufung von einzelnen Elementen", nämlich "Stücken eines Conglomerates", charakterisiert und diesen Sprachen gleichzeitig abspricht, einen "organisch gegliederte[n] Organismus" auszubilden. Einem (vermeintlich) realen Organismus seine Organizität völlig abzusprechen, stellt allerdings eine "extreme form" einer Theorie des organischen Lebens der Sprache mit "extreme consequences" dar (Whitney 1871: 37). Whitneys Auffassung, Sprachen seien "far from being natural organisms, [but] the gradually elaborated products of the application by human beings" (S. 50), setzte sich in den Folgejahren durch und führte auch dazu, daß die Organismusmetaphorik zur Beschreibung von Sprachphänomenen und sprachlichen Entwicklungen durch andere Terminologien verdrängt wurde.

3. Systemhaftigkeit im lautsprachlichen Zusammenhang

Die Nachzeichnung der Verwendungen des Organismusbegriffs in der Sprachwissenschaft des 19. Jhs. hat gezeigt, daß man sich in dieser Zeit über das Bestehen sprachlicher Beziehungen systematischer Art zwar durchaus im klaren war — daß aber der Verweis darauf oft genug eher bloß global geschah und daß dabei dann nicht selten ganz unterschiedliche Aspekte fraglos ineinandergeblendet wurden. In dieser Allgemeinheit finden wir entsprechende Äußerungen bis zum Ende des 19. Jhs. und auch darüber hinaus, indem etwa im Einklang mit der oben in Abschnitt 1 bereits zitierten Äußerung von Curtius (1886 [1868]: 172) erklärt wird, daß in der Sprache "die verschiedenartigsten Faktoren in gegenseitiger Abhängigkeit zusammenwirken, bei [ihr] im Grunde alles durch alles bedingt ist" (Brugmann 1904: viii), oder daß man, "[s]obald man über das blosse constatieren von einzelheiten hinausgeht [und] den zusammenhang zu erfassen [versucht]", notwendigerweise zugleich "auch den geschichtlichen boden [betritt]" (Paul 1886: 19−20). Bei einer derart globalen Anerkennung jedweder systematischer Zusammenhänge, die vermeintlich zwischen allem und jedem bestehen, droht dann allerdings letztlich gar die Geltung des eingangs genannten elementaren Punkts (a) fragwürdig zu werden, nämlich die Geschlossenheit des Systems, die im Endeffekt nur noch in einer Abgrenzung des 'Sprachlichen insgesamt' vom Bereich des Nicht-Sprachlichen gegeben wäre. Um die wirklichen Wurzeln des Strukturalismus in der Sprachwissenschaft des 19. Jhs. freizulegen, wird man sich demzufolge nicht wesentlich auf solch allgemeine Überzeugungen der damaligen Zeit beziehen können, sondern man wird vielmehr auf deren begrenztere und konkrete Umsetzung in einzelnen sprachwissenschaftlichen Bereichen achten müssen.

Ihre größten Erfolge hat die historisch-vergleichende Sprachwissenschaft im 19. Jh. bekanntlich auf dem Gebiet der sog. 'Lautlehre' erzielt; diese rückte sehr schnell in jene Position einer zentralen Teildisziplin, die anfangs (bei Fr. Schlegel, F. Bopp u. a. m.) noch die 'Formenlehre', also die Morphologie, eingenommen hatte. Zugleich darf nicht vergessen werden, daß seit dem Ende der 20er Jahre des 20. Jhs. insbes. die neu entwickelte 'Phonologie' geradezu als 'Paradedisziplin' für die Demonstration der Sinnhaftigkeit strukturalistischer Ansätze galt. Es gibt also überaus gute Gründe, zunächst gerade in diesem Bereich nach wesentlichen Verbindungen zwischen der Linguistik des 19. und der des 20. Jhs. Ausschau zu halten.

Das spezifische Interesse der Sprachwissenschaftler des 19. Jhs. galt bekanntlich zentral dem diachronen Phänomen des lautlichen Wandels, und bei seiner Erforschung ist im Laufe des Jhs. sowohl eine kontinuierliche Verbesserung des Analyseinstrumentariums als auch eine fortschreitende Verschärfung der Methode zu beobachten (von bloßen Konstatierungen regelmäßiger 'Buchstabenübergänge' bis hin zum Postulat einer Ausnahmslosigkeit von Lautgesetzen). Beide Entwicklungsaspekte sind im gegenwärtigen Zusammenhang gleichermaßen von Bedeutung: der erste deshalb, weil erst durch die Einbeziehung lautphysiologischer Erkenntnisse ein Bewußtsein für die Existenz einzelsprachlicher (synchroner) Lautsysteme geschaffen und dann weiter geschärft werden konnte, und der zweite deshalb, weil erst die Herausarbeitung einer möglichst durchgängigen Regelhaftigkeit der lautlichen Wandelprozesse überhaupt die Einsicht dafür eröffnen konnte, daß man es nicht mit isolierten, wahllosen und sporadischen Veränderungen einzelner Ausdrucksgestalten, sondern mit Umgestaltungen von in sich ebenfalls regelhaften sprachlichen Systemen zu tun hatte.

Wenn Sprachwissenschaftler wie Bopp, Grimm, Pott oder Rask im ersten Drittel des 19. Jhs. in bezug auf den Wandel von Ausdrucksformen den Begriff des 'Buchstabens' verwandten, so waren dennoch im wesentlichen 'Laute' gemeint (s. dazu genauer Kohrt 1985: 4 ff.). Die lautphysiologischen Kenntnisse der einzelnen Linguisten blieben zunächst allerdings sehr beschränkt und begannen sich erst im zweiten Drittel des 19. Jhs. wesentlich und dann immer weiter fortschreitend zu verbessern. Anfänglich wurden einfach nur regelmäßige lautliche Entsprechungen zwischen den Elementen von historisch miteinander vermittelten Ausdrucksgestalten verschiedener Sprachen vergleichend registriert, ohne besonders nach dem Wie oder Warum des Wandels zu fragen, und es wurde zunächst ebenso frag- und klaglos hingenommen, daß die betr. 'Lautgesetze' − "sowie jede Regel" (von Raumer 1837: 13) − Ausnahmen haben (vgl. schon Grimm [1822: 590]: "die lautverschiebung erfolgt in der masse, thut sich aber im einzelnen niemahls rein ab"). Eine offenkundig rigidere Position entwickelte sich erst seit der Mitte des 19. Jhs.: Ohne es theoretisch öffentlich zu verkünden, ging wohl schon Schleicher bei der praktischen Analyse grundsätzlich davon aus, daß Lautgesetze ausnahmslos gelten (s.

J. Schmidt 1887), und bereits Curtius (1858: 68) meinte explizit, im lautlichen Bereich "feste Gesetze erkennen [zu können], die sich mit der Consequenz von Naturkräften geltend machen". Im Einklang mit Bopps (1833: 1, 274) früherer Scheidung von "zwei Arten von euphonischen Veränderungen in allen Sprachen" erkannte Curtius (1858: 701) neben einem solchen 'wesentlichen', 'durchgreifenden' Lautwandel allerdings ausdrücklich auch noch 'unwesentliche', bloß 'sporadische' lautliche Veränderungen an und setzte diese Trennung explizit mit der "Unterscheidung der Regel von der Ausnahme" in Beziehung (so daß den Ausnahmen damit quasi ein eigenständiger theoretischer Status zugebilligt wurde).

Nicht zuletzt an eben dieser bloßen 'Papierkorbkategorie' eines sog. 'sporadischen' Lautwandels entzündete sich die Kritik jener Curtius-Schüler, die später als 'Junggrammatiker' bekannt werden sollten, und die betr. 'Aufräumaktion' bestand im wesentlichen darin, daß der Inhalt dieses 'Papierkorbs' möglichst vollständig entweder in die bereits existierende Schublade des 'durchgreifenden' Lautwandels oder in die nun nicht neu, aber anders eingerichtete Schublade der Analogie eingeordnet werden sollte (vgl. Leskien 1876: 2; Osthoff 1879: 8 ff.; differenzierter später Brugmann 1885: 53 ff.). Der legendäre Streit zwischen den Junggrammatikern und ihren Gegnern um die Ausnahmslosigkeit der Lautgesetze mit all seinen Nebenkriegsschauplätzen und Scheingefechten (vgl. dazu Schneider 1973, Wilbur 1977) braucht hier nicht eigens nochmals aufgerollt zu werden; im gegenwärtigen Zusammenhang ist allein relevant, daß durch das theoretisch-methodologische Bemühen, eine Ausnahme denkbarer isolierter Veränderungen von Ausdrucksformen konsequent zugunsten des Postulats jeweils regulärer, systematischer Wandelprozesse (per Lautgesetz oder Analogie) auszuschließen, zugleich implizit auch eine interne Regularität der jeweiligen lautlichen Ausgangs- und Endverhältnisse unterstellt werden mußte.

Ende der 30er Jahre des 19. Jhs. wurde von Benfey (1837: 910) die grundsätzliche "Wichtigkeit einer in das Wesen und die Funktionen der Laute selbst eindringenden Untersuchung" hervorgehoben, und im selben Jahre forderte unabhängig davon von Raumer (1837: 2), daß "mit aller klaren Etymologie phonetische Untersuchungen Hand in Hand gehen [müssen]", "da die Umwandlung der Wörter nicht auf den geschriebenen Zeichen beruht und auf den Aehnlichkeiten derselben, sondern auf den gesprochenen Lauten". Für eine stärkere Einbeziehung der Lautphysiologie in die historische Sprachwissenschaft gab es gleich zwei wesentliche Motivationshintergründe. Zum einen ging es darum, durch den Rekurs auf phonetische Faktoren die jeweiligen Prozesse des lautlichen Wandels überhaupt plausibel zu machen; eine "plötzlich eingedrungene Vertauschung [zweier] Laute" sei letztlich undenkbar, und nur durch differenzierte lautphysiologische Beschreibungen ließe sich das "Allmälige der Lautverwandlungen" begreifen (von Raumer 1837: 5). Zum anderen und im Verbund damit war es darum zu tun, jene "wilde etymologie [zu] bändigen" (Grimm 1853: 293), die letztlich dazu tendiert, "aus allem alles zu machen" (so Benfey [1837: 910] in seiner Kritik an Pott 1833−1836). Etabliert werden sollte also ein strenges Korrektiv, das eine "unerbittliche Kritik" an den "kühnsten Constructionen über den Ursprung der Formen" ermöglichte: "zahllose Etymologien [fragwürdiger Art] zerschellen an den scharfen Ecken der Lautgesetze und methodischen Formenzerlegung" (Curtius 1862: 10).

Die grundsätzliche Feststellung, daß die lautlichen Erscheinungen letztlich unendlich vielfältig seien und daß bei der phonetischen Deskription jeweils nur gewisse 'Grenzpunkte' oder 'Grundlaute' ausgemacht werden könnten, durchzieht geradezu als Topos (vgl. Mugdan 1996: 263) die gesamte sprachwissenschaftliche Literatur des 19. Jhs., von Benfey (1837: 911) und von Raumer (1837: 3−4) über Schleicher (1848: 30 ff.) bis zu Paul (1880a: 43) und darüber hinaus. Ebenso topisch ist in der Historiographie des 20. Jhs. die Behauptung, daß die Analyse und Verzeichnung von Mengen solcher 'Grundlaute' in der Linguistik des 19. Jhs. generell nur zu einer bloßen "Klassifikation" (Reis 1974: 41) bei der Aufstellung von einfachen "Lautinventaren" (Mugdan 1996: 261) geführt habe. Ein oberflächlicher Rekurs auf damalige Redeweisen wie die von einem "spoken alphabet" bei Whitney (1867: 91) mag dies auf den ersten Blick plausibel erscheinen lassen, aber zugleich wird dort ausdrücklich von einem "orderly system of articulations, with ties of relationship running through it in every direction" gesprochen, und alles andere als zufällig ist "spoken alphabet" dann von Leskien auch mit "Lautsystem" ins Deutsche übersetzt worden (s. Whitney 1876: 142; zum Hintergrund vgl. Kohrt 1989). Und Sievers' (1876: 1) Betonung der linguistischen Relevanz von "Lautsystemen" war – entgegen Scheerer (1980: 145) – damals weder neu noch besonders bemerkenswert, denn der explizite Rekurs auf ein "System der Sprachlaute mit Bezugnahme auf die Sprachorgane" (so Schleicher 1848: 120) war schon in den sprachwissenschaftlichen Schriften des zweiten Drittels des 19. Jhs. völlig kommun (vgl. Kohrt 1990: 592 ff.).

Es gibt keinen triftigen Grund, solchen erklärten 'Lautsystemen' im Nachhinein ihre Systemhaftigkeit einfach abzusprechen, denn sie genügten jeweils ohne weiteres den in Abschn. 1 genannten Kriterien (a)–(d) und darüber hinaus gar noch dem Punkt (g), sofern sie für eine gewisse Einzelsprache aufgestellt wurden. Allerdings wurden sie dann (im Einklang mit der frühen allgemeinen Phonetik vor 1800) nur sehr bedingt als idiosynkratisch aufgefaßt, indem sie nämlich im wesentlichen als bloße Adaptionen eines 'universalen', dem Anspruch nach 'natürlichen' lautlichen Systems angesehen wurden; eine "allgemeine Lautlehre" bildete also die Basis für die verschiedenen "speciellen Lautlehren" (Schleicher 1860: 125) und sicherte dabei die durchgängige Vergleichbarkeit der Einzelsysteme bei der historischen Analyse (s. z. B. Schleicher 1861–62: 8). Zugleich gab es – entgegen Punkt (h) – keinerlei spezifischen Rekurs auf einzelsprachliche Zustände zu einer gewissen Zeit, und auch die Punkte (e) und (f) spielten bei dieser Betrachtungsweise keine besondere Rolle: Der lautliche Bereich galt grundsätzlich als empirisch direkt zugänglich (z. B. durch Selbstbeobachtung wie bei Schleicher 1848: 121–122), und es war erklärtermaßen gerade um die jeweils besondere materielle Erscheinungsweise der lautlichen Einheiten zu tun, die es wissenschaftlich möglichst differenziert zu erfassen galt. Auf einem ganz anderen Blatt hingegen stand die während des gesamten 19. Jhs. immer wieder reflektierte Tatsache, daß das nur in geschriebener Form historisch Bezeugte nur in begrenztem Maße Rückschlüsse auf die lautliche Entwicklung zuließ; diese unvermeidliche Beschränkung gab allerdings normalerweise nur zur Vorsicht bei der Interpretation Anlaß und stellte selbst bei Rekonstruktionen den grundsätzlichen Ansatz vermeintlich nicht in Frage (vgl. jedoch die Differenzierungen in Abschn. 4).

Im letzten Viertel des 19. Jhs. wurden dann allerdings einzelne Ansätze entwickelt, bei deren Konzipierung lautlicher Systeme auch schon die o. g. Punkte (e) und (f) relevant wurden; die betr. Überlegungen gehörten jeweils erkennbar nicht einfach dem 'main stream' der damaligen linguistischen Forschung an. Zwei miteinander verbundene, dennoch aber unterschiedliche Aspekte sind in diesem Zusammenhang von Bedeutung: zum einen eine psychologisierende Sichtweise, bei der zwischen der materiellen Erscheinung der Laute einerseits und ihrer mentalen Existenz andererseits unterschieden wurde (wie man es bis Anfang der 30er Jahre des 20. Jhs. auch in der frühen Prager Phonologie noch tat, vgl. Kohrt 1985: 263 ff.), und zum zweiten das aus dem Bemühen um eine praktisch verwendbare phonetische Transkription heraus entwickelte Konzept der 'Distinktivität' (das man in der Rückschau später nicht selten als "das den Strukturalismus beherrschende [...] Prinzip" angesehen hat, s. Reis 1978: 178).

Unter Berufung auf Steinthal (1860) hatten Osthoff & Brugmann (1878: iv) grundsätzlich die Einbeziehung "psychische[r] factoren" in die sprachwissenschaftliche Analyse gefordert, und Paul (1880a: 40 ff.) setzte dies konsequent auch im Bereich des Lautlichen um, wobei jedoch, wie auch bei Osthoff (1879: 13–14), davon ausgegangen wurde, daß das Bewußtsein in diesem Bereich keine wesentliche Rolle spiele. Wenige Jahre zuvor hatte hingegen schon Winteler (1876: 22) in einer 'mentalistischen' Absetzung von der vorherigen Lautphysiologie dafür plädiert, unterschiedliche Lautsysteme im jeweiligen "Bewußtsein des Sprechers" bzw. in dessen "Sprachgefühl" anzunehmen, so daß ein und dasselbe, lautphysiologisch eindeutig zu charakterisierende Element dort auf Grund seiner spezifischen Einbettung in einen psychischen Gesamtzusammenhang jeweils einen anderen Stellenwert erhalten könne (vgl. Kohrt 1984: 28 ff.). Ein solcher Rekurs auf das 'Sprachgefühl', durch das die Laute anders wahrgenommen werden, als es ihrer lautphysiologischen Charakterisierung entspricht, findet sich seit den 70er Jahren des 19. Jhs. auch bei Baudouin de Courtenay (s. Mugdan 1996: 294–295) und wird dann schließlich mit dessen grundsätzlicher Trennung des 'Lauts' als faktischem Schallereignis von dem 'Phonem' als einem "psychische[n] Aequivalent des Sprachlautes" (Baudouin de Courtenay 1895: 9) auch terminologisch festgeschrieben (zu unterschiedlichen Einschätzungen der Hintergründe vgl. Kohrt 1985:

119 ff. und Mugdan 1984: 61 ff.; 1996: 266 ff., 293 ff.).

In der historiographischen Literatur der letzten Jahrzehnte hat man sowohl Winteler als auch Baudouin de Courtenay nur allzu oft unterstellt, daß sie bereits systematisch Gebrauch vom Distinktivitätsprinzip gemacht hätten — was nachweislich nicht den Tatsachen entspricht (vgl. Kohrt 1984: 22 ff., 1985: 221 ff.; Mugdan 1996: 271 ff.). Inzwischen ist allgemein bekannt, daß dieses Kriterium der 'Bedeutungsunterscheidung' von Sweet (1877) entwickelt worden ist; seiner Meinung nach war im Zusammenhang einer Transkription von Lauten einer Einzelsprache jeweils zu unterscheiden "between those differences which are *distinctive*, that is, to which differences of meaning correspond, and those which are not" (S. 182). Der Entstehungskontext dieser Konzeption war dabei eindeutig der einer praktischen, angewandten Phonetik, nicht der einer für wissenschaftliche Zwecke bestimmten Lautphysiologie, und nur im erstgenannten Zusammenhang, nicht aber in der Sprachwissenschaft selbst wurde der Distinktivitätsgedanke in der Folgezeit zunächst aufgenommen und verbreitet (s. Kohrt 1985: 244 ff.; Mugdan 1996: 278 ff.). Es ist demzufolge auch geradezu symptomatisch, daß der Aspekt der Bedeutungsunterscheidung z. B. von Paul (1880b: 9) ausgerechnet in einer kleinen populären Schrift "Zur orthographischen Frage" aufgegriffen wurde — wie er zuvor schon bei Sweet (1877) wesentlich in den Kontext einer 'spelling reform' eingebettet gewesen war.

4. Die Rekonstruktion der indogermanischen Ursprache

Die obige Diskussion hat gezeigt, daß es in der historisch-vergleichenden Sprachwissenschaft des 19. Jhs. auf Grund einer fortschreitenden Einbeziehung lautphysiologischer Faktoren durchaus Ansätze gab, von denen her man zur Ausbildung strukturalistischer Theorien und Methoden gemäß den oben in Abschnitt 1 aufgeführten Punkten (a)–(h) hätte gelangen können. Zugleich aber ist auch deutlich geworden, daß eben dieser Weg in mehrfacher Hinsicht verstellt war — indem man sich nämlich weiterhin primär auf die vergleichende Analyse einzelner historisch überlieferter Daten und Datengruppen konzentrierte und 'systematische' Aspekte im wesentlichen nur sekundär und sprachübergreifend in Anschlag brachte, um die betr. Analysen methodologisch besser zu unterfüttern. Allerdings mußte diese Haltung — zumindest partiell — notgedrungen dort aufgegeben werden, wo keinerlei direkte historische Daten mehr zur Verfügung standen, nämlich bei dem Versuch der Rekonstruktion der indogermanischen Ursprache. In diesem Bereich liegen u. E. die entscheidenden Wurzeln des Strukturalismus in der Sprachwissenschaft des 19. Jhs., und besonders wesentlich ist dabei der oben in Abschnitt 1 angeführte Punkt (d), nämlich das Problem einer 'realistischen' vs. einer 'formalistischen', 'konstruktivistischen' Konzeption sprachlicher Systeme/ Strukturen.

Daß für sprachvergleichende Zwecke eine Rekonstruktion der indogermanischen Ursprache sinnvoll und gar notwendig sei, war bereits im ersten Drittel des 19. Jhs. deutlich geworden (vgl. Morpurgo Davies 1998: 167 ff.). Erst Schleicher (1861–62) aber lieferte eine umfassende Darstellung des idg. Lautsystems und begründete sie wenig später in zweifacher Hinsicht: Eine solche Rekonstruktion sei zum einen didaktisch sinnvoll, weil von ihr aus eine systematisch geordnete Darstellung der weiteren Ausdifferenzierung der idg. Sprachen möglich werde, und sie schalte zum anderen von vornherein die irrige Vorstellung aus, daß das Sanskrit als Protosprache anzusehen sei (s. Schleicher 1866: 8–9). Obwohl Schleicher ausdrücklich einräumte, "daß in einzelnen fällen die von uns erschloßenen formen der indogermanischen ursprache mehr oder minder zweifelhaft sind" (ebd.), nahm er dennoch grundsätzlich einen 'realistischen' Standpunkt ein, indem er seine Übersicht der idg. Laute in systematischer Form, nämlich "lautphysiologisch an geordnet" präsentierte, "mit den etwa nötigen bemerkungen über außsprache und dergl." (Schleicher 1861–62: 8, 1866: 10). Wenig später jedoch, kurz vor seinem Tode, modifizierte er seine Einstellung, indem er als Nachtrag zur 2. Aufl. des *Compendiums* notierte: "Daß dise [rekonstruierten idg.] grundformen wirklich einmal vorhanden gewesen sind, wird durch die aufstellung der selben nicht behauptet" (Schleicher 1869: 342). Es ist durchaus denkbar, wenn nicht gar wahrscheinlich, daß Schleichers Schüler (Leskien und) J. Schmidt an diesem Sinneswandel nicht ganz unbeteiligt war(en), denn der letztere erklärte kurz danach ganz prononciert, daß die rekonstruierte idg. Ursprache nicht mehr als "eine wissenschaftliche fiction" darstelle, die die "forschung [...] allerdings wesentlich erleichter[e]" (J. Schmidt 1872: 17).

Eine derartige strikt 'formalistische' Position wurde im weiteren auch von anderen Linguisten vertreten; so war etwa für Delbrück (1880: 53) "die Ursprache nichts [...] als eine Formel", die nur die "wechselnden Ansichten der Gelehrten" widerspiegle und deren Repräsentationen nur "dazu [dienten], das Erkannte zu veranschaulichen". Zugleich aber war jene 'realistische' Position, derzufolge die rekonstruierte idg. Ursprache ein "wirkliches Gebilde" darstelle (so noch Hirt 1939: 112), von vornherein bereits in zweifacher Hinsicht gebrochen: Zum einen mußte unzweifelhaft sein, daß die rekonstruierten idg. Formen jeweils nur hypothetisch gesetzt sein konnten und daß somit nur ein behaupteter Realitätsanspruch bestand (vgl. Bezzenberger 1879: 666), und zum anderen war gleichermaßen klar, daß sich eine solche unterstellte 'Wirklichkeit' phonetisch bestenfalls in Ansätzen konkretisieren ließ. Wenn es schon bei nur schriftlich bezeugten "todten Sprachen [...] oft unmöglich [ist], den Lautwert eines Zeichens genau zu bestimmen" (so Brugmann 1886: 24), dann muß dies natürlich erst recht für bloß rekonstruierte Formen gelten (vgl. dazu schon die überaus vorsichtigen Bemerkungen bei Benfey 1837: 910–911). Und wer es gar wie Paul (1880a: 6) schon für eine bloße "selbsttäuschung" hielt, "wenn man meint[,] das einfachste historische factum ohne eine zutat von speculation constatieren zu können", der mußte sich erst recht darüber im klaren sein, daß dann das Maß an Spekulation bei Rekonstrukten als notwendigerweise ahistorischen, nicht raumzeitlich gebundenen Entitäten (s. Pulgram 1959) ganz besonders hoch anzusetzen war und daß sich spezifische lautphysiologische Konkretisierungen dort nur sehr schwer begründen ließen.

An dieser Stelle ist es sinnvoll, sich kurz die generellen Implikationen eines derartigen rekonstruktiven Vorgehens zu vergegenwärtigen. Daß das betr. Rekonstrukt grundsätzlich den im Abschnitt 1 genannten Punkten (a)–(d) genügen muß, bedarf keiner Frage, denn nur dann können die rekonstruierten Elemente überhaupt der postulierten Ursprache angehören. (Daß die einzelnen Rekonstruktionsteile jeweils nur mehr oder minder gut begründet und mit gewissen Zweifeln behaftet sein mögen – vgl. Hermann 1907 –, steht auf einem anderen Blatt.) Die Ursprache selbst ist, im Einklang mit Punkt (e), nicht direkt empirisch zugänglich, sondern sie muß notwendigerweise erst erschlossen werden; über eine besondere Art ihrer materiellen Vergegenständlichung läßt sich – vgl. Punkt (f) – von einer 'formalistischen' Warte aus gesehen nichts wirklich Gültiges, aus einer 'realistischen' Position heraus allenfalls wenig Konkretes sagen. Es handelt sich bei einem derartigen Konstrukt gemäß Punkt (g) notwendigerweise zudem um eine (hier: hypothetische) Einzelsprache, die als grundsätzlich homogen und uniform angenommen werden muß. Zwar ist die in Frage stehende Ursprache raumzeitlich nicht konkret situierbar, aber dennoch muß zumindest die Möglichkeit einer Fixierung bzgl. Zeit und Raum bei der Rekonstruktion grundsätzlich mitgedacht bleiben; in zeitlicher Hinsicht spiegelt das Rekonstrukt demnach letzlich – im Einklang mit Punkt (h) – den Zustand einer (postulierten) Einzelsprache zu einer gewissen, hier allerdings nicht genau spezifizierbaren Zeit wider (vgl. Hjelmslev 1968: 148). Kurzum: Die Idee einer Rekonstruktion der idg. Ursprache implizierte in wesentlichen Teilen bereits eine 'strukturalistische' Betrachtungsweise, die es nur konsequent umzusetzen galt.

Im gegenwärtigen Zusammenhang ist dabei vor allem die schon durch Schleicher eingeleitete Abkehr von einer 'realistischen' Interpretation sprachlicher Rekonstrukte in Richtung auf 'formalistische', 'konstruktivistische' Auffassungen wesentlich, die sich in der damaligen Analysepraxis in dem Moment ganz deutlich zeigte, wo Mitte der 70er Jahre des 19. Jhs. Schleichers vorheriges Rekonstrukt der idg. Ursprache grundsätzlich in Zweifel gezogen wurde. Relevant ist dabei zunächst ein scheinbar bloß oberflächliches Phänomen, nämlich die Verwendung einer 'algebraischen' Notation (neuer Art) bei der Transkription elementarer Ausdruckseinheiten der idg. Ursprache. Generell gesehen waren die dabei verwandten Repräsentationsweisen nichts Neues in der Sprachwissenschaft: Konkretisierend hatte zuvor z. B. schon Brücke (1856: 34ff.) in seinen Transkripten einzelnen Buchstaben Ziffern als Superskripte hinzugesetzt, um gewisse lautphysiologische Binnenklassifizierungen zu verdeutlichen (was Scherer 1868: 42ff. u. a. m. dann adaptierten), und Schleicher (1861–62: 3) hatte bereits abstrahierend Schreibweisen wie "W^x (W^1, W^2, W^3 u. s. f.)" im morphologischen Zusammenhang zur Darstellung einer "regelmäßig veränderliche[n] Wurzel" verwandt. Der im gegenwärtigen Zusammenhang wesentliche Schritt aber bestand darin, daß dann Brugmann (1876: 367−368) Subskriptnotationen wie ⟨a₁⟩, ⟨a₂⟩ usw. zur Bezeichnung rekonstruierter Ausdruckselemente der idg. Ursprache verwandte, "deren genauere [lautphysiologische] Qualität und Quantität [...] unberücksichtigt" bleiben sollte. Es handelte sich also um elementare Einheiten, deren eigenständige Existenz im Ausdruckssystem der idg. Ursprache postuliert wurde, ohne daß sie phonetisch eindeutig zu spezifizieren waren. Dies hinderte Brugmann (1876: 380−381) allerdings nicht daran, zumindest gewisse Spekulationen über eine genauere phonetische Charakterisierung dieser Elemente anzustellen, und er zog sich wenig später, trotz anfänglicher Bedenken und wohl nicht zuletzt auch auf Grund des Drängens von Osthoff (s. Einhäuser 1992: 96), auf jene 'realistische' Position zurück, derzufolge a_1 mit e und a_2 mit o zu identifizieren seien (s. Brugmann 1879).

Die in Ansätzen abstrahierende, 'formalistische' Sichtweise, die Brugmann zuvor nur zögerlich und eher notgedrungen eingenommen und schon kurze Zeit darauf bereits wieder aufgegeben hatte, wurde direkt im Anschluß daran von Saussure (1879 [1878]) in seinem *Mémoire sur le système primitif des voyelles dans les langues indo-européennes* aufgenommen, und aus ihr wurden nun strikte Konsequenzen gezogen. Die verwickelte Rezeptionsgeschichte dieses komplexen und nur schwer zugänglichen Buchs im Rahmen der Indogermanistik ist erst in jüngster Zeit systematisch aufgearbeitet worden (vgl. Gmür 1986; Mayrhofer 1981, 1988), und mittlerweile hat man auch seine Relevanz für die Vorgeschichte des Strukturalismus erkannt (auf die zuvor bereits Hjelmslev [1968: 149 ff.] hingewiesen hatte). In dieser Arbeit entwickelt Saussure, ausgehend von Brugmanns vorheriger Trennung von a_1 und a_2, ein ausgebautes algebraisches Notationssystem für die Bezeichnung rekonstruierter Einheiten, die als Bestandteile des Ausdruckssystems der idg. Ursprache anzusehen waren, ohne daß hinsichtlich ihrer phonetischen Konkretisierung irgendetwas präjudiziert werden sollte. Damit ging eine terminologische Präzisierung einher, die in Saussures Arbeit zwar konsequent durchgeführt, aber theoretisch nicht eigens expliziert wurde: Es wurde nämlich systematisch zwischen *son* als einem konkreten, lautphysiologisch klar zu bestimmenden Element und *phonème* als einem abstrakten Element eines (einzel)sprachlichen Ausdruckssystems unterschieden, das allein auf Grund vergleichender Analyse zu etablieren war (vgl. Kohrt 1985: 84 ff.). Für die besagten 'Phoneme' war allein wesentlich, daß sie sich als "*distincts l'un de l'autre et distincts de tous autres phonèmes*" des betr. Ausdruckssystems nachweisen ließen (Saussure 1879: 121), und als solche 'Phoneme' kamen sowohl einfache als auch segmental komplexe Einheiten in Betracht (vgl. z. B. Saussure 1879: 19).

Die Relevanz von Saussures *Mémoire* innerhalb der Vorgeschichte des Strukturalismus darf man keinesfalls unterschätzen. Formulierungen aus dem *Cours* wie "*dans la langue il n'y a que des différences*" (Saussure 1922 [1916]: 166), sie sei "*une forme et non une substance*" (S. 169) sind im 20. Jh. immer wieder als zentrale strukturalistische Einsichten angesehen worden. Faktisch stammen die betreffenden Passagen, wie wir inzwischen wissen, erst aus Saussures dritter Vorlesung zur allgemeinen Sprachwissenschaft von 1910/11 (vgl. Saussure 1968: 270; 276), während der Grundgedanke jedoch bereits in der ersten Vorlesung von 1907, und zwar in direktem Zusammenhang mit der Rekonstruktionsproblematik, entwickelt worden war (s. Godel 1957: 65, De Mauro 1972: 475); die Reorganisation der Grundlagentexte, die die Herausgeber des *Cours* vorgenommen haben und durch die der Abschnitt zur Rekonstruktion an das Ende des Buchs geriet, hatte diese direkte Verbindung zunächst unkenntlich gemacht. Zudem war die Tatsache, daß bei Saussure (1879) auch segmental komplexe Ausdruckseinheiten als 'Phoneme' gewertet wurden, im Rahmen der komplexen Geschichte des Phonembegriffs, die bis zur strukturellen Phonologie Prager Prägung führt, alles andere als unwesentlich (s. dazu detailliert Kohrt 1985: 119 ff. sowie Mugdan 1996: 286 ff.). Auf der anderen Seite aber muß man notwendigerweise den besonderen Kontext im Auge behalten, in dem das *Mémoire* entstanden ist. Das Vorgehen von Saussure (1879) spiegelt weder ein "grundsätzliches Desinteresse für die tatsächliche Beschaffenheit einer prähistorischen indoeuropäischen Grundsprache" wider (so Scheerer 1980: 20) noch war "Saussure's notion of a linguistic system [...] drastically different from that of his predecessors" (so Amsterdamska 1987: 230) und er selbst gar "the first abstract phonologist in that he was operating with hypothetical construct and indirect (distributional) evidence" (so Koerner 1987:

207). Was Saussure von seinen Zeitgenossen unterschied, war zunächst nur die strikte Konsequenz, Subtilität und Vorsicht zugleich, mit der er bei der Rekonstruktion der idg. Ursprache zu Werke ging, und später dann die Tatsache, daß er die dabei gewonnenen Erfahrungen und Einsichten auch für die Analyse von Einzelsprachen nutzbar zu machen suchte, die nicht mehr rekonstruiert werden mußten, sondern direkt empirisch gegeben waren.

5. 'Junggrammatischer Atomismus' vs. 'strukturale Methode'

Ende der 20er Jahre des 20. Jhs. entstand das positive, von Neuaufbruch kündende Wort von einer 'strukturalen Methode', die im Gegensatz zu Früherem auf Zusammenhänge bedacht sei (s. Jakobson & Slotty 1930: 386−387); antithetisch wurde der vorherigen Sprachwissenschaft zugleich eine bloß 'atomistische', nur auf isolierte Einzelheiten fixierte Vorgehensweise unterstellt, die bereits damals als spezifisch 'junggrammatisch' apostrophiert wurde (s. z. B. Jakobson 1931: 247). Eben diese Redeweise von einem 'junggrammatischen Atomismus', der von einem strukturalistischen Vorgehen grundverschieden sei, ist mittlerweile in der Historiographie der Linguistik geradezu topisch geworden. Dabei blieb unberücksichtigt, daß kein Sprachwissenschaftler des 19. Jhs. jemals theoretisch die Position vertreten hat, daß es einzig und allein auf isolierte Einzelheiten ankäme; sie waren sich vielmehr allesamt bewußt, daß die untersuchten sprachlichen Einzelphänomene jeweils Teile eines übergreifenden Ganzen waren. Nicht um theoretische Ansichten, sondern allenfalls um die faktische Analysepraxis kann es also zu tun sein, wenn man einen Gegensatz zwischen 'isolierender' und 'systematisierender' Betrachtungsweise postulieren will. In dieser Hinsicht wirkt die spezielle Verbindung von 'atomistisch' und 'junggrammatisch' jedoch eher befremdlich − denn die Junggrammatiker waren bekanntlich nicht mehr und nicht weniger datenorientiert als ihre damaligen Gegner (s. Morpurgo Davies 1986: 157), und ein auch nur kurzer Blick in die Arbeiten von Sprachwissenschaftlern aus der ersten Hälfte des 19. Jhs. wie Bopp, Grimm, Pott u. a. zeigt zur Genüge, daß der besagte 'Atomismus'-Vorwurf gegen sie mühelos ebenfalls erhoben werden könnte.

Eine sehr viel generellere, nicht eigens auf die Junggrammatiker beschränkte Einschätzung, daß es sich nämlich bei der gesamten Sprachwissenschaft des 19. Jhs. im wesentlichen um "a field of mere data gathering and ordering, a barren positivistic enterprise" gehandelt habe (so Koerner 1987: 213), scheint durchaus berechtigt − wenngleich es, wie man oben gesehen hat, auch verschiedene Ansätze gab, die schon damals den Systemaspekt stärker in den Vordergrund stellten. Eben diese Ansätze aber gerieten Ende des 19. Jhs. vor allem durch den dominanten Einfluß der Junggrammatiker weitestgehend aus dem Blickfeld, und zwar sowohl in theoretischer Hinsicht als auch unter praktischen Gesichtspunkten. In dem einflußreichsten theoretischen Buch der damaligen Zeit, H. Pauls *Prinzipien der Sprachgeschichte*, wurde bekanntlich ein rein individualisierender Ansatz propagiert, bei dem schon der Sprachusus nur noch als eine "Durchschnittsbildung über ihrerseits punktuellen individuellen Realitäten" (Reis 1978: 189) in den Blick kam; das "wahre object für den sprachforscher" sollten letztendlich *sämmtliche äusserungen der sprachtätigkeit an sämmtlichen individuen in ihrer wechselwirkung auf einander* sein, und ausdrücklich kritisiert wurde ein vorheriges Vorgehen der historischen Linguistik, bei dem "nur eine reihe von descriptiven grammatiken parallel an einander gefügt" worden seien (Paul 1880a: 27−28). Was damit abgelehnt wurde, war die von Schleicher (1861−62) gewählte Darstellungsart, bei der − beginnend mit der rekonstruierten idg. Ursprache − nacheinander die Ausdruckssysteme der einzelnen Sprachen (resp. Sprachstufen) präsentiert wurden. Brugmann (1886) löste im ersten Band seines *Grundrisses*, dem in der Folgezeit übermächtig wirksamen Handbuch, diesen systematischen Zusammenhalt dann grundsätzlich auf, indem er die Entwicklung der (rekonstruierten) idg. Laute jeweils einzeln nacheinander durch die verschiedenen Sprach(grupp)en hindurchverfolgte − in dem erklärten Bemühen, die vermeintlichen "Vorzüge" der Darstellungsweisen von Bopp und von Schleicher "zu vereinigen" (s. Brugmann 1886: vi-vii).

Angesichts dieser Umstände ist das spätere geflügelte Wort vom 'junggrammatischen Atomismus' ohne weiteres zu verstehen − aber im 19. Jh. insgesamt gab es keineswegs nur eine Betrachtung isolierter sprachlicher Erscheinungen, sondern daneben auch, wenngleich weniger evident und zunächst weniger verbreitet und einflußreich, stärker systemorientierte Ansätze, die dann allerdings erst im linguistischen Strukturalismus des 20. Jhs. wirklich entfaltet wurden. Aber schon für das 19. Jh. gilt, wenngleich weniger ausgeprägt, die Einsicht, "daß in der historischen Sprachwissenschaft die Antinomie zwischen Systematikern und Historikern einprogrammiert ist" (Untermann, zitiert nach Mayrhofer 1986: 88), und beides findet man, wenngleich in jeweils anderer Ausprägung und unterschiedlichen Schwerpunkten der Verteilung, sowohl im 19. als auch im 20. Jahrhundert.

6. Bibliographie

Amsterdamska, Olga. 1987. *Schools of Thought. The development of linguistics from Bopp to Saussure.* Dordrecht & Boston: Reidel.

Bally, Charles. 1952 [1913]. "Ferdinand de Saussure et l'état actuel des études linguistiques". *Le langage et la vie*, von Charles Bally, 3. Aufl. 147–160. Genève: Droz; Lille: Giard.

Baudouin de Courtenay, Jan. 1895. *Versuch einer Theorie phonetischer Alternationen: Ein Capitel aus der Psychophonetik.* Straßburg: Trübner.

Becker, Karl Ferdinand. 1827. *Organism der Sprache, als Einleitung zur deutschen Grammatik.* Frankfurt/M.: Hermann'sche Buchhandlung (Kettembeil.)

Benfey, Theodor. 1837. Rezension von August Friedrich Pott. *Etymologische Forschungen auf dem Gebiete der Indo=Germanischen Sprachen.* 2 Bde. (Lemgo: Meyer, 1833–36). *Ergänzungsblätter zur Allgemeinen Literatur-Zeitung* 1837.905–933.

Benveniste, Émile. 1962. " 'Structure' en linguistique". *Sens et usages du terme structure dans les sciences humaines et sociales* hg. von Roger Bastide, 31–39. The Hague: Mouton.

Bezzenberger, Adalbert. 1879. Rezension von Hermann Osthoff & Karl Brugmann, *Morphologische Untersuchungen auf dem Gebiet der indogermanischen Sprachen.* Erster Theil. (Leipzig: Hirzel, 1878). *Göttingische Gelehrte Anzeigen* 2.641–681.

Bopp, Franz. 1816. *Über das Conjugationssystem der Sanskritsprache in Vergleichung mit jenem der griechischen, lateinischen, persischen und germanischen Sprache.* Hg. und mit Vorerinnerungen begleitet von Karl Josef Windischmann. Frankfurt/M.: Andreä.

–. 1833. *Vergleichende Grammatik des Sanskrit, Zend, Griechischen, Lateinischen, Litthauischen, Gothischen und Deutschen.* [Erste Abtheilung.] Berlin: Dümmler.

Brücke, Ernst. 1856. "Physiologie und Systematik der Sprachlaute". *Zeitschrift für die österreichischen Gymnasien* 7.505–545, 589–632, 686–700.

Brugmann, Karl. 1876. "Zur Geschichte der stammabstufenden Declinationen. Erste Abhandlung: Die Nomina auf -*ar*- und -*tar*-". *Studien zur griechischen und lateinischen Grammatik* 9.361–406.

–. 1879. "Vorwort". *Morphologische Untersuchungen auf dem Gebiete der indogermanischen Sprachen*, von Hermann Osthoff & Karl Brugmann. Zweiter Theil, v–vi. Leipzig: Hirzel.

–. 1880. "Zur beurtheilung der europäischen vocale *a, e, o*". *Morphologische Untersuchungen auf dem Gebiete der indogermanischen Sprachen*, von Hermann Osthoff & Karl Brugmann. Dritter Theil, 91–130. Leipzig: Hirzel.

–. 1885. *Zum heutigen Stand der Sprachwissenschaft.* Straßburg: Trübner. (Wieder abgedruckt in Wilbur 1977.)

–. 1886. *Grundriß der vergleichenden Grammatik der indogermanischen Sprachen.* 1. Bd.: *Einleitung und Lautlehre.* Straßburg: Trübner.

–. 1904. *Kurze vergleichende Grammatik der indogermanischen Sprachen.* Straßburg: Trübner.

Collitz, Hermann. 1878. "Ueber die annahme mehrerer grundsprachlicher a-laute". *Beiträge zur Kunde der indogermanischen Sprachen* 2.291–305.

Curtius, Georg. 1858. *Grundzüge der griechischen Etymologie.* Leipzig: Teubner.

–. 1862. *Philologie und Sprachwissenschaft.* Leipzig: Teubner.

–. 1886. *Ausgewählte Reden und Vorträge.* Leipzig: Hirzel.

Delbrück, Berthold. 1880. *Einleitung in das Sprachstudium.* Leipzig: Breitkopf & Härtel.

De Mauro, Tullio. 1972. "Notes". *Cours de linguistique générale* de Ferdinand de Saussure, édition critique préparée par Tullio de Mauro, 405–477. Paris: Payot.

Einhauser, Eveline. 1989. *Die Junggrammatiker: Ein Problem für die Sprachwissenschaftsgeschichtsschreibung.* Trier: Wissenschaftlicher Verlag.

–, Hg. 1992. *Lieber Freund ... Die Briefe Hermann Osthoffs an Karl Brugmann, 1875–1904.* Trier: Wissenschaftlicher Verlag.

Gmür, Remo. 1986. *Das Schicksal von F. de Saussures "Mémoire": Eine Rezeptionsgeschichte.* Bern: Institut für Sprachwissenschaft der Universität Bern.

Godel, Robert. 1957. *Les sources manuscrites du Cours de linguistique générale de F. de Saussure.* Genève: Droz.

Grimm, Jacob. 1927 [1821]. "Brief an Karl Lachmann vom 1. 4. 1821". *Briefwechsel der Brüder Jacob und Wilhelm Grimm mit Karl Lachmann* hg. von Albert Leitzmann, Bd. I, 292–294. Jena: Frommann.

–. 1822. *Deutsche Grammatik.* Erster Theil. Zweite Ausgabe. Göttingen: Dieterich.

—. 1831. *Deutsche Grammatik.* Dritter Theil. Göttingen: Dieterich.

—. 1853 [1848]. *Geschichte der deutschen Sprache.* 2. Auflage. Leipzig: Hirzel.

Helbig, Gerhard. 1971. *Geschichte der neueren Sprachwissenschaft unter dem besonderen Aspekt der Grammatiktheorie.* München: Hueber.

Herder, Johann Gottfried. 1891 [1772]. "Abhandlung über den Ursprung der Sprache". *Herders Sämmtliche Werke* hg. von Bernhard Suphan, Bd. V, 1–154. Berlin: Weidmann.

Hermann, Eduard. 1907. "Über das Rekonstruieren". *Zeitschrift für vergleichende Sprachforschung* 41.1–64.

Hirt, Herman. 1939. *Die Hauptprobleme der indogermanischen Sprachwissenschaft.* Halle: Niemeyer.

Hjelmslev, Louis. 1968 [1963]. *Sprache: Eine Einführung.* Übers. von Otmar Werner. Darmstadt: Wissenschaftliche Buchgesellschaft.

Humboldt, Wilhelm von. 1962 [1795]. "Brief an Friedrich Schiller vom 14. 9. 1795". *Der Briefwechsel zwischen Friedrich Schiller und Wilhelm von Humboldt* hg. von Siegfried Seidel, Bd. I, 147–151. Berlin: Aufbau-Verlag.

—. 1979 [1822]. "Ueber das Entstehen der grammatischen Formen und ihren Einfluss auf die Ideenentwicklung". *Wilhelm von Humboldt. Werke in fünf Bänden* hg. von Andreas Flitner & Klaus Giel, Bd. III, 31–63. Stuttgart: Cotta.

—. 1836. *Über die Verschiedenheit des menschlichen Sprachbaues und ihren Einfluß auf die geistige Entwickelung des Menschengeschlechts.* Berlin: Dümmler. (Faks.-Nachdrucke: Berlin: Schneider 1935; Bonn: Dümmler, 1960.)

Jakobson, Roman. 1931. "Prinzipien der historischen Phonologie". *Travaux du Cercle linguistique de Prague* 4.247–267.

— & Friedrich Slotty. 1930. "Die Sprachwissenschaft auf dem 1. Slavistenkongreß in Prag vom 6. bis 13. Oktober 1929". *Indogermanisches Jahrbuch* 14.384–391.

Koerner, E. F. Konrad. 1975. "European Structuralism: Early Beginnings". *Current Trends in Linguistics* hg. von Thomas A. Sebeok, Vol. XIII: *Historiography of Linguistics*, 717–827. The Hague: Mouton.

—. 1987. "Mikołaj Kruszewski's Contribution to General Linguistics". *Mikołaj Kruszewski, Writings in General Linguistics*, vi–xxxiv. Amsterdam & Philadelphia: Benjamins.

Kohrt, Manfred. 1984. *Phonetik, Phonologie und die "Relativität der Verhältnisse": Zur Stellung Jost Winterers in der Geschichte der Wissenschaft.* Stuttgart: Steiner.

—. 1985. *Problemgeschichte des Graphembegriffs und des frühen Phonembegriffs.* Tübingen: Niemeyer.

—. 1989. "William Dwight Whitney und die Vorgeschichte der strukturellen Phonologie". *Varia linguistica* hg. von Manfred Kohrt & Klaus Robering, 17–58. Berlin: Institut für Linguistik der TU Berlin.

—. 1990. "'Sound Inventory' and 'Sound System' in 19th Century Linguistics". *History and Historiography of Linguistics: Papers from the Fourth International Conference on the History of the Language Sciences (ICHoLS IV), Trier, 24–28 August 1987* hg. von Konrad Koerner & Hans-Josef Niederehe, 589–603. Amsterdam: Benjamins.

Kucharczik, Kerstin. 1995. *Der Organismusbegriff in der Sprachwissenschaft des 19. Jahrhunderts.* Diss. phil., Technische Universität Berlin.

—. 1998. "*Organisch* – 'um den beliebten aber vieldeutigen ausdruck zu gebrauchen'. Zur Organismusmetaphorik in der Sprachwissenschaft des 19. Jahrhunderts". *Sprachwissenschaft* 23.85–111.

Lehmann, Winfred P. 1994. "The Continuity of Theory in Linguistics". *Miscellanea di studi linguistici in onore di Walter Bellardi* hg. von Palmira Cipriano et al. Bd. II, 985–1011. Rom: Il Calamo.

Leskien, August. 1876. *Die Declination im Slavisch-Litauischen und im Germanischen.* Leipzig: Hirzel.

Löther, Burkhard. 1984. "Zum Organismus-Begriff bei Jacob Grimm". *Zeitschrift für Phonetik, Sprachwissenschaft und Kommunikationsforschung* 37. 11–18.

Mayrhofer, Manfred. 1981. *Nach hundert Jahren: Ferdinand de Saussures Frühwerk und seine Rezeption durch die heutige Indogermanistik.* Heidelberg: Winter.

—. 1988. "Zum Weiterwirken von Saussures 'Mémoire'". *Kratylos* 33.1–15.

—, Hg. 1986. *Indogermanische Grammatik.* Bd. I. Heidelberg: Winter.

Morpurgo Davies, Anna. 1986. "Karl Brugmann and Late Nineteenth-century Linguistics". *Studies in the History of Western Linguistics: In honour of R. H. Robins* hg. von Theodora Bynon & F. R. Palmer, 150–171. Cambridge: Cambridge Univ. Press.

—. 1998. *Nineteenth-century Linguistics.* London & New York: Longman.

Mugdan, Joachim. 1984. *Jan Baudouin de Courtenay (1845–1929): Leben und Werk.* München: Fink.

—. 1996. "Die Anfänge der Phonologie". *Sprachtheorien der Neuzeit II* hg. von Peter Schmitter, 247–318. Tübingen: Narr.

Nüsse, Heinrich. 1962. *Die Sprachtheorie Friedrich Schlegels.* Heidelberg: Winter.

Osthoff, Hermann. 1875. *Zur geschichte des schwachen deutschen adjectivums.* Habilitationsschrift. Leipzig: Universität Leipzig [Teildruck].

—. 1879. *Das physiologische und psychologische Moment in der sprachlichen Formenbildung.* Berlin: Habel.

— & Karl Brugmann. 1878. "Vorwort". *Morphologische Untersuchungen auf dem Gebiete der indoger-*

manischen Sprachen von Hermann Osthoff & Karl Brugmann. Erster Theil, iii–xx. Leipzig: Hirzel.

Paul, Hermann. 1880a. *Principien der Sprachgeschichte*. Halle: Niemeyer.

—. 1880b. *Zur orthographischen Frage.* (= *Deutsche Zeit- und Streit-Fragen*, 143.) Berlin: Habel.

—. 1886. *Principien der Sprachgeschichte.* 2. Aufl. Halle: Niemeyer.

Pedersen, Holger. 1962 [1931]. *The Discovery of Language. Linguistic science in the nineteenth century.* Bloomington & London: Indiana Univ. Press.

Pott, August Friedrich. 1833–36. *Etymologische Forschungen auf dem Gebiete der Indo-Germanischen Sprachen.* 2 Bde. Lemgo: Meyer.

Pulgram, Ernst. 1959. "Proto-Indo-European Reality and Reconstruction". *Language* 35.421–426.

Rapp, Karl Moritz. 1836–41. *Versuch einer Physiologie der Sprache nebst historischer Entwicklung der abendländischen Idiome nach physiologischen Grundsätzen.* 4 Bde. Stuttgart & Tübingen: Cotta.

Raumer, Rudolf von. 1837. *Die Aspiration und die Lautverschiebung.* Leipzig: Brockhaus.

Reis, Marga. 1974. *Lauttheorie und Lautgeschichte: Untersuchungen am Beispiel der Dehnungs- und Kürzungsvorgänge im Deutschen.* München: Fink.

—. 1978. "Hermann Paul". *Beiträge zur Geschichte der deutschen Sprache* 100.159–204.

Saussure, Ferdinand de. 1879. *Mémoire sur le système primitif des voyelles dans les langues indo-européennes.* Leipzig: Teubner.

—. 1922 [1916]. *Cours de linguistique générale.* 2. Aufl. Paris [& Lausanne]: Payot.

—. 1968. *Cours de linguistique générale.* Édition critique par Rudolf Engler. Bd. I. Wiesbaden: Harrassowitz.

Scheerer, Thomas. 1980. *Ferdinand de Saussure: Rezeption und Kritik.* Darmstadt: Wissenschaftliche Buchgesellschaft.

Scherer, Wilhelm. 1868. *Zur Geschichte der deutschen Sprache.* Berlin: Weidmann. (Neudruck, mit einer Einleitung von Kurt R. Jankowsky, Amsterdam & Philadelphia: Benjamins, 1995.)

Schlegel, August Wilhelm. 1846 [1798]. "Der Wettstreit der Sprachen: Ein Gespräch über Klopstocks grammatische Gespräche". *August Wilhelm von Schlegel's Sämmtliche Werke* hg. von Eduard Böcking, Bd. VII, 197–268. Leipzig: Weidmann.

—. 1846 [1809]. "Vorlesungen über dramatische Kunst und Literatur". *August Wilhelm von Schlegel's Sämmtliche Werke* hg. von Eduard Böcking, Bd. V u. VI. Leipzig: Weidmann.

—. 1818. *Observations sur la langue et la littérature provençales.* Paris: Librairie Grecque – Latine – Allemande.

Schlegel, Friedrich. 1987 [1795]. "Brief an A. W. Schlegel vom 23. 12. 1795". *Kritische Friedrich-Schlegel-Ausgabe* hg. von Ernst Behler, Bd. XXIII, 263–267. Paderborn, München & Wien: Schöningh; Zürich: Thomas.

—. 1808. *Über die Sprache und Weisheit der Indier: Ein Beitrag zur Begründung der Alterthumskunde.* Heidelberg: Mohr & Zimmer. (Repr., mit einer Einleitung von Sebastiano Timpanaro, Amsterdam: Benjamins, 1977.)

Schleicher, August. 1848. *Zur vergleichenden Sprachgeschichte.* Bonn: König.

—. 1860. *Die Deutsche Sprache.* Stuttgart: Cotta.

—. 1861–62. *Compendium der vergleichenden Grammatik der indogermanischen Sprachen.* 2 Bde. Weimar: Böhlau.

—. 1863. *Die Darwinsche Theorie und die Sprachwissenschaft. Offenes Sendschreiben an Herrn Dr. Ernst Häckel.* Weimar: Böhlau.

—. 1865. *Über die Bedeutung der Sprache für die Naturgeschichte des Menschen.* Weimar: Böhlau.

—. 1866. *Compendium der vergleichenden Grammatik der indogermanischen Sprachen.* 2. Aufl. Weimar: Böhlau.

—. 1869. *Indogermanische Chrestomathie.* Weimar: Böhlau.

Schlick, Moritz. 1935. "Über den Begriff der Ganzheit". *Erkenntnis* 5.52–55.

Schmidt, Hartmut. 1986. *Die lebendige Sprache: Zur Entstehung des Organismuskonzepts.* (= *Linguistische Studien*; Reihe A: Arbeitsberichte, 151.) Berlin: Akademie der Wissenschaften der DDR, Zentralinstitut für Sprachwissenschaft.

Schmidt, Johannes. 1872. *Die Verwantschaftsverhältnisse* [sic] *der indogermanischen Sprachen.* Weimar: Böhlau.

—. 1885. Rezension von Georg Curtius, *Zur Kritik der neuesten Sprachforschung* (Leipzig: Hirzel, 1885.) *Deutsche Literaturzeitung* 1885.339–344.

—. 1887. "Schleichers Auffassung der Lautgesetze". *Zeitschrift für vergleichende Sprachforschung* 28.303–312.

Schneider, Gisela. 1973. *Zum Begriff des Lautgesetzes in der Sprachwissenschaft seit den Junggrammatikern.* Tübingen: Narr.

Sievers, Eduard. 1876. *Grundzüge der Lautphysiologie zur Einführung in das Studium der Lautlehre der indogermanischen Sprachen.* Leipzig: Breitkopf & Härtel.

Steinthal, Heymann. 1855. *Grammatik, Logik und Psychologie: Ihre Principien und ihr Verhältniss zu einander.* Berlin: Dümmler.

—. Assimilation und Attraction psychologisch beleuchtet. *Zeitschrift für Völkerpsychologie und Sprachwissenschaft* 1.93–179.

Sweet, Henry. 1877. *A Handbook of Phonetics, Including a Popular Exposition of the Principles of Spelling Reform.* Oxford: Clarendon.

Thèses. 1929. "Thèses présentées au premier congrès des philologues slaves". *Travaux du Cercle Linguistique de Prague* 1.7–29.

Watkins, Calvert. 1978. "Remarques sur la méthode de Ferdinand de Saussure comparatiste". *Cahiers Ferdinand de Saussure* 32.59–69.

Whitney, William Dwight. 1867. *Language and the Study of Language*. London: Trübner.

—. 1871. "Strictures on the Views of August Schleicher Respecting the Nature of Language and Kindred Subjects". *Transactions of the American Philological Association* 2.35–64.

—. 1875. *The Life and Growth of Language*. London: King; New York: Appleton.

—. 1876. *Leben und Wachsthum der Sprache*. Übers. von August Leskien. Leipzig: Brockhaus.

Wilbur, Terence H., Hg. 1977. *The Lautgesetz-Controversy: A documentation*. Amsterdam: Benjamins.

Winteler, Jost. 1876. *Die Kerenzer Mundart des Kantons Glarus in ihren Grundzügen dargestellt*. Leipzig & Heidelberg: Winter.

Manfred Kohrt, Bonn
Kerstin Kucharczik, Bochum
(Deutschland)

199. La dimension synchronique dans la théorie linguistique de Saussure

"Il existe une distinction sans laquelle les faits ne seront compris à aucun degré, si ce n'est par illusion, sans laquelle ils ne peuvent même pas être fixés, saisis, sans laquelle il n'y a aucune clarté possible. Telle est en linguistique la distinction de l'état et de l'événement." (Saussure, N. 12; *CLG/E* II 29a)

1. Définition et délimitation
2. La dimension synchronique dans la pratique comparatiste de Saussure
3. La dimension synchronique dans les réflexions méthodologiques de Saussure
4. L'émergence de la priorité logique et sémiologique de la dimension synchronique
5. Le rôle de la dimension synchronique dans la théorie linguistique de Saussure
6. Conclusion
7. Bibliographie

1. Définition et délimitation

1.1. Selon le *Dictionnaire de la langue française* d'Émile Littré (1801–1881), l'adjectif *synchronique* "se dit des phénomènes qui s'accomplissent en même temps", et il est relatif au *synchronisme*, c'est-à-dire au "rapport d'événements arrivés dans le même temps", ou à la "simultanéité de deux phénomènes" (^{2}1877 IV, p. 2115a).

Saussure connaissait évidemment ces définitions quand il a, d'une part, retenu l'adjectif *synchronique* et, d'autre part, forgé le substantif abstrait *synchronie* pour caractériser "ce qui appartient à un instant déterminé de la langue" (*CLG/E* 201, n° 1508be), c'est-à-dire l'ensemble des "termes coexistants" (*CLG/E* 181, n° 1346bd), par opposition aux "faits se passant à travers le temps (ibid., n° 1346e), c'est-à-dire l'ensemble des "faits évolutifs" (*CLG/E* 179, n° 1335bde), pour quoi il a créé symétriquement *diachronique* et *diachronie*. Pour lui, synchronie et diachronie désignent un couple de concepts mutuellement déterminés, dont il serait illégitime, dans un exposé théorique, de considérer les membres séparément; mais dans un exposé historique et descriptif, l'étude de la seule dimension synchronique envisagée pour elle-même ne devrait pas être trop dommageable, moyennant quelques précautions et quelques empiètements sur des articles différents.

1.2. Un bilan des travaux consacrés au couple synchronie ~ diachronie aurait en principe sa place dans un pareil exposé, mais le modèle en ce genre, le rapport critique que Rudolf Engler (1962) a consacré à l'arbitraire du signe, montre que l'étude serait beaucoup trop longue, si même, dans l'état actuel des choses, elle dût être possible; on y a donc nécessairement renoncé. En revanche, on ne saurait examiner la dimension synchronique dans la seule théorie linguistique de Saussure. Au moins deux motifs imposent l'élargissement du champ étudié: (a) les conditions particulières dans lesquelles les conceptions saussuriennes nous sont connues, qui font que l'exposé systématique de sa théorie linguistique suppose une large part de reconstruction, soumise aux risques de subjectivité inhérents à une telle entreprise (Bally et Sechehaye, qui ont rédigé le *CLG* en retenant, de la documentation manuscrite qui leur était accessible, ce qui, entre 1913 et 1915 et vu l'état de la linguistique du temps, leur paraissait essentiel, étaient bien conscients de ces risques, et ne méritent certainement pas les reproches que parfois on leur adresse *a posteriori*: sans leur travail, on ne connaîtrait rien de Saussure théoricien du langage, et sans leurs interprétations, nous n'aurions pas les moyens de tenter les nôtres); (b) la nécessité, qui résulte du point précédent, de suivre pas à pas, chez Saussure lui-même, l'émergence, dans sa pratique de comparatiste, d'un point de vue méthodologique qui ne sera exposé publiquement comme tel que dans ses trois cours de linguistique générale de 1907, 1908−1909 et 1910−1911.

Le plan du présent article et la démarche qu'on y a suivie résultent des remarques précédentes; bien loin de prétendre tenir compte de l'immense littérature secondaire consacrée au sujet, on y citera essentiellement les textes originaux, en abordant successivement: 1) La dimension synchronique dans la pratique comparatiste de Saussure; 2) la dimension synchronique dans ses réflexions méthodologiques; 3) l'émergence de la priorité logique et sémiologique de la dimension synchronique; 4) le rôle de la dimension synchronique dans la théorie linguistique. On verra, chemin faisant, la focalisation épistémologique se déplacer de l'objet d'abord supposé donné à l'objet construit par le linguiste, puis de l'objet construit par le linguiste à l'objet produit et utilisé par le sujet parlant; on verra du même coup le rapport entre synchronie et diachronie passer de la simple distinction mutuelle à un emboîtement paradoxal, et de l'emboîtement paradoxal à la subordination définitive de la diachronie relativement à la synchronie.

2. La dimension synchronique dans la pratique comparatiste de Saussure

Une digression s'avère d'emblée nécessaire. Sous le titre de grammaire comparée, on range des études disparates qui s'appliquent tantôt à une seule langue attestée dont on suit l'histoire, tantôt à un groupe de langues parentes dont la source attestée est relativement bien connue (telles les langues romanes, issues du latin vulgaire), tantôt enfin à un groupe de langues attestées présumées parentes dont la source, non attestée, est hypothétique (telles les langues indo-européennes, re-lativement à l'indo-européen reconstitué). En outre, selon les cas, le linguiste s'intéresse à des données parallèles, c'est-à-dire comparables entre elles, indice d'un lien de parenté (p. ex. sanscrit *pitā́* = grec *patèr* = latin *pater* "père"); soit il s'attache aux changements qui ont affecté une unité entre deux de ses attestations (p. ex. latin *patrem* > espagnol *padre*); soit encore il se sert des parallèles présumés pour en induire hypothétiquement le lien de parenté dont il suppose qu'ils sont l'indice, et tente par là de ramener à une unité, non attestée mais reconstruite, la diversité des données comparées.

Enfin, pour ce qui est des unités considérées, la grammaire comparée s'est attachée d'abord aux mots entiers, puis aux sous-unités constitutives des mots (racines et morphèmes d'une part, phonèmes d'autre part), enfin à la structure même des mots. Or si le statut méthodologique des unités et des sous-unités est ambigu (en ce qu'on les extrait d'un état de langue pour en étudier l'histoire, souvent même en sortant de cette langue), en revanche le statut méthodologique de la structure du mot, qui se définit entre des éléments constitutifs coprésents, est clair: la structure est par définition synchronique (l'intérêt pour les structures morphologiques prend d'ailleurs une importance considérable à partir du milieu des années 1870, comme en témoignent à partir de 1878 la série des *Morphologische Untersuchungen* de Karl Brugmann et Hermann Osthoff).

À cet égard − et paradoxalement − la grammaire comparée se sert donc inévitablement de la synchronie pour réaliser son programme diachronique. Selon Hermann Paul (1846−1921), théoricien de la linguistique historique, cette nécessité est tout au plus un pis-aller pratique, "das praktische Bedürfnis, welches für systematische Darstellung ein solches Verfahren gefordert hat" (^{8}1968 [^{2}1886]: 23); en particullier, cette démarche ne permet pas d'avoir une juste vue de l'évolution de la langue, parce que, si à chaque étape la "deskriptive Grammatik" révèle même "eine gewisse Regelmässigkeit in dem gegenseitigen Verhältnis" des faits de langue, la succession des états décrits n'explique pas l'évolution; car l'évolution relève pour lui de la causalité matérielle, alors que la description synchronique n'est qu'une "Abstraktion aus den beobachteten Tatsachen"; or "zwischen Abstraktionen gibt es überhaupt keinen Kausalnexus" (Paul ^{8}1968 [^{2}1886]: 24; cf. Koerner 1988 [1972]: 26−27).

Quand Saussure s'initie à la grammaire comparée, ses premières recherches étymologiques portent sur des mots entiers (Saussure 1988 [1876–77]; mais les considérations morphologiques retiennent aussi très tôt son attention. Dès son premier article publié (Saussure 1877a, lu le 27 mai 1876 à la Société de Linguistique de Paris, quand l'auteur n'avait pas 19 ans), il distingue ce qu'il appelle les "deux modes d'emploi" du suffixe -t- (il entend par là les deux manières dont le suffixe se joint à la racine dans le mots considérés) et la "fonction [...] active ou passive" dudit suffixe (R 339); foncièrement, il opère avec une structure grammaticale définie par une propriété formelle et une fonction sémantique: plusieurs des ingrédients qui seront propres à la dimension synchronique des faits de langue se trouvent ici en germe, peut-être à l'insu de l'auteur.

Un an plus tard, la conscience méthodologique de Saussure se manifeste en revanche avec netteté, quoique fort brièvement et sans motivation apparente (Saussure 1877b). Voici, en effet, comment il conclut une petite recherche qui s'est révélée peu fructueuse: "Ni grammaticalement, par conséquent, ni étymologiquement nous ne pouvons rattacher l'une à l'autre la formation latine en -*eo* et celle du passif en skr." (R 364), remarque qu'il explique ainsi en note (au moyen d'exemples erronés qu'il vaut mieux ne pas citer): "Ramener" tel mot latin et tel mot sanscrit non analysés "à une forme indoeurop[éenne]" également inanalysée "est une identification que nous appellerons *étymologique*; dire simplement qu'ils s'équivalent comme formés tous deux" des éléments $a + b$ "sera une identification *grammaticale*" (R 364–365). Si l'identification étymologique est foncièrement diachronique, l'identification grammaticale, qui repose sur l'analyse structurale (en $a + b$) des mots de deux langues attestées, est tout aussi clairement non diachronique en son principe.

Puis vient le célèbre *Mémoire* (Saussure 1878), qu'il serait trop long d'analyser ici. On relèvera simplement que, sous le couvert d'un problème de phonétique historique, Saussure se fonde sur l'étude éminemment structurale de divers phénomènes morphophonémiques des langues attestées (sanscrit et grec surtout) pour supposer l'existence, en indo-européen, de deux "coefficients sonantiques" inconnus jusque là (qu'il note A et Q, deux des futures laryngales de la grammaire comparée moderne). Ces "phonèmes" – distincts entre eux indépendamment du "son" – qu'ils "devaient avoir" (p. 122) – ne se manifestent que par "leur rôle dans l'organisme grammatical" (p. 123; au 'rôle grammatical' est réservé tout le chapitre V du *Mémoire*, qui constitue à lui seul plus de quarante pour cent du livre). Autrement dit, l'analyse synchronique a une valeur heuristique relativement à A et à Q, et ces phonèmes ont une valeur explicative quand il s'agit de reconstruire les fonctions morphologiques, c'est-à-dire synchroniques, des diverses "formes que peut prendre la racine" en indo-européen (p. 135).

Moins de trois ans après le *Mémoire*, Saussure publie sa thèse de doctorat (Saussure 1881). Comme il s'agissait d'étudier une construction grammaticale (le génitif absolu du sanscrit) envisagée dans son emploi textuel, la perspective synchronique s'imposait, du moins en ce qui concerne la description du tour syntaxique en question (Saussure ne consacre qu'une page et demie à l'"extension du génitif absolu" dans les genres littéraires et au cours du temps). Ce qui frappe, ce n'est pas seulement que Saussure s'attache à un fait de syntaxe, mais qu'il le définit en retenant ses "particularités caractéristiques" (R 275), qui contrastent avec celles de son concurrent, le locatif absolu (cf. De Mauro 1972 [1967]: 330–331). En cela, il détermine ce qui fait négativement l'unité du tour, à la fois syntaxiquement et surtout sémantiquement: "Sur chacun de ces différents points [syntaxiques] nous l'avons trouvé assujetti à certaines limites étroites, où l'usage n'a jamais enfermé le locatif absolu"; "en ce qui concerne le *rapport logique* avec l'action principale, [...] le locatif offre plus de latitude que le génitif absolu" (R 277).

La thèse de 1881 contient l'unique description synchronique, appliquée à une langue attestée, que Saussure ait publiée. Sa manière d'aborder les faits, qui annonce déjà les enseignements de la maturité, tranche nettement, sur le fond, avec la technique descriptive que les grammairiens des langues anciennes pratiquaient alors – voir p. ex. les grammaires du grec et du latin de Raphael Kühner (1802–1878) qui, dans leurs versions révisées au début du siècle respectivement par Friedrich Bernhard Gerth (1844–1911) et par Carl Friedrich Ludwig Anton Stegmann (1852–1929), sont d'ailleurs aujourd'hui encore précieuses au philologue. Néanmoins, sa présentation des exemples suit le modèle ordinaire, non par conviction, mais par commodité: "Si nous faisons une classification, c'est uniquement pour introduire un ordre dans nos exemples. Ce qui précède montre en effet qu'il n'y a pas différentes valeurs propres du génitif absolu. Nous ne pouvons qu'inscrire des catégories logiques, en mettant en regard de chacune d'elles des exemples qui en dépendent" (*R* 280); les "catégories logiques" se superposent donc à l'unicité linguistique de la valeur du tour (le rapport qu'il y a entre logique et langue chez Saussure mériterait d'être étudié spécialement).

De 1881 à 1891, avec une interruption d'un an, Saussure enseigne à l'École Pratique des Hautes Études de Paris; de ces années date certainement un approfondissement de ses réflexions méthodologiques, encore que les publications de cette époque en montrent rarement la trace; on mentionnera l'importance du rythme quantitatif (Saussure 1884) ou de la syllabation (Saussure 1887a), problème qui l'a par la suite beaucoup préoccupé (cf. les notes N 14a−c, dans *CLG/E* II 30a−35a, probablement de 1897) et l'identification d'un "système" particulier ou 'groupe morphologique' ancien dans le "germanique antédialectal" (Saussure 1887b). À cet égard, le témoignage d'Antoine Meillet, quoique rendu quelque vingt-cinq ans plus tard, est formel: "Les doctrines qu'il a enseignées dans ces cours de linguistique générale sont celles dont s'inspirait déjà l'enseignement de grammaire comparée qu'il a donné [...] à l'École des Hautes Études [...]. Je les retrouve telles qu'il était souvent possible de les deviner" (Meillet 1916: 33, cité par De Mauro 1972 [1967]: 338).

La distinction entre synchronie et diachronie était sûrement l'une de ces 'doctrines'. Dans le rapport sur son cours de 1882−1883, Saussure précisait que "le commençant doit composer lui-même sa grammaire d'après un texte déterminé, dont il se fera une loi de ne pas sortir" (Fleury 1965: 57, cité par De Mauro 1972 [1967]: 337). La même idée revient, différemment exprimée, une dizaine d'années plus tard: "La valeur d'une forme est tout entière dans le texte où on la puise" (Saussure 1894: 514, cité par De Mauro, p. 342).

3. La dimension synchronique dans les réflexions méthodologiques de Saussure

Chez Saussure comparatiste, la dimension synchronique est donc indéniablement présente, et prégnante. La vraie manière de poser la question n'est pourtant pas de constater simplement que l'état et l'évolution de la langue sont distincts en fait (Hermann Paul faisait la même constatation, mais dans une tout autre perspective, comme on l'a vu), elle est de déterminer comment synchronie et diachronie s'articulent entre elles méthodologiquement et théoriquement. Saussure commence par hésiter, accordant la primauté méthodologique tantôt à l'une, tantôt à l'autre.

Les premières réflexions à nous accessibles que Saussure ait consacrées à cette question remontent à ses leçons inaugurales genevoises de 1891 (N 1.1−3). Elles mettent au premier rang des principes linguistiques le "facteur *Temps*" (*CLG/E* II 10b): "L'ensemble des considérations de ce genre se résumait pour nous dans le principe universel de l'*absolue continuité* de la langue dans le temps. Avec ce premier principe venait se combiner le second, de la *continuelle transformation* de la langue dans le temps" (ibid. 12a; le troisième principe est celui de la "différenciation dans l'espace", aussi important pour Saussure que la "différenciation dans le temps" [12a−13a]). C'est dans cette perspective radicalement diachronique qu'apparaît la notion d'état, nettement subordonnée à celle de transition: "Il n'y a jamais de caractères permanents, mais seulement transitoires et de plus délimités dans le temps; il n'y a que des états de langue qui sont perpétuellement la transition entre l'état de la veille et celui du lendemain" (ibid. 11b).

Auparavant, Saussure a opposé les "deux espèces distinctes" de phénomènes diachroniques, "d'une part le changement *phonétique* et d'autre part le changement [...] *analogique*" (ibid. 9a), dont "on peut dire que l'un attaque la forme par le côté du son et que l'autre l'attaque par le côté de l'idée" (ibid. 9a−b). Le changement analogique (qu'il soit sanctionné par l'usage, comme *je trouve* qui a remplacé *je treuve*, ou non, comme *je venirai* chez un petit enfant) est en un sens une "transformation", encore que "tous les éléments de *venirai* [soient] contenus et donnés dans des formes existantes fournies par la mémoire: *punirai, punir*, ou bien si l'on veut le suffixe *-ir*, le suffixe *-irai*, et leur rapport de signification" (ibid. 9b).

La perspective est donc ici différente; s'agissant de l'analogie, Saussure subordonne nettement l'innovation diachronique à l'état synchronique: "Il n'y aura donc jamais de création *ex nihilo*, mais chaque innovation ne sera qu'une application nouvelle d'éléments fournis par l'état antérieur du langage" (ibid.). En même temps, la mention de la mémoire suppose évidemment le cerveau et la psychologie d'un sujet parlant, dont on a ici l'une des toutes premières apparitions explicites chez Saussure.

Si donc le "facteur *Temps*", c'est-à-dire l'évolution diachronique, est en principe premier, le changement analogique est en revanche second relativement à l'état synchronique. Incohérence ou paradoxe? On est loin en tout cas des positions d'Hermann Paul, qui, au nom de l'explication causale de l'histoire de la langue, ravalait l'état grammatical au rang de pis-aller abstrait.

En 1891, Saussure n'a peut-être pas encore pris la pleine mesure du paradoxe – ou de l'incohérence? – des positions qu'illustrent ses leçons d'ouverture du cours d'histoire et comparaison des langues indo-européennes. En tout cas, dans une publication rarement citée (Saussure 1897), il répète fortement la thèse selon laquelle le synchronique est subordonné au diachronique, tout en insistant sur la différence des deux dimensions:

"Quand on fera pour la première fois une théorie vraie de la langue, un des tout premiers principes qu'on y inscrira est que jamais, en aucun cas, une règle qui a pour caractère de se mouvoir dans un *état de langue* (= entre 2 termes contemporains), et non dans un *événement phonétique* (= 2 termes successifs) ne peut avoir plus qu'une validié de hasard. [...] Et dans tous les cas, pour poser la règle sous son vrai sens, il faudra reprendre le terme antérieur au lieu du terme contemporain." (*R* 540)

Cette "constatation" méthodologique de Saussure est-elle "diamétralement opposée à ses réflexions personnelles pendant les années 1890", comme le veut Koerner (1988 [1980]: 94)? Il se peut qu'elle montre plutôt que Saussure n'avait pas encore réglé théoriquement la question des rapports paradoxaux entre les deux dimensions. En tout cas l'exemple d''événement phonétique' qu'il donne 'comme indication du procédé' suppose non pas un changement phonétique au sens courant du terme, mais ce qu'il appelle 'expulsion' d'un *e* (due vraisemblablement au déplacement du ton) dans certaines formes de la déclinaison, c'est-à-dire un fait foncièrement grammatical, et par là même synchronique; l'explication du paradoxe ne tient donc pas, ici du moins, au caractère spécifique des changement phonétiques.

Il faut peut-être malgré tout chercher la raison de cette fluctuation dans la différence entre le changement phonétique, qui est diachroniquement premier et aveugle, d'une part, et la transformation analogique, dont le mécanisme est synchroniquement premier et psychologique, d'autre part, selon un double emboîtement hiérarchique paradoxal.

Ce n'est pourtant pas la voie que Saussure a d'abord suivie. Souvent, en effet, il se contente de distinguer les deux perspectives, sans se déterminer sur leurs rapports mutuels. C'est ce qu'il fait notamment, peu après 1894 (cf. Godel 1957: 37) dans la note N 11, sur l'état et le mouvement de la langue (*status* et *motus*, *CLG*/*E* II 26a–b), dans un passage où il insiste sur la symétrie de ces deux aspects: "Tous les phénomènes particuliers ou généraux dont la langue peut être le théâtre, ou bien font partie d'un *état* qu'ils caractérisent chacun dans leur moment ou bien se présentent à nos yeux sous la forme d'un *événement*. [...] Pourquoi, parmi les cent et un principes de distinction possibles en linguistique, accorder une importance particulière à celui qui sépare l'état de l'événement, l'événement de l'état?" (ibid. 26b). La réponse à cette question tient probablement au fait que cette distinction est, pour Saussure, la seule fondée en réalité, puisque les idiomes varient effectivement dans le temps tout en restant effectivement les mêmes pour les sujets parlants.

La symétrie du *status* et du *motus*, qui suffit à "nous faire voir dans la langue deux objets entièrement différents, nécessitant deux sciences" (ibid. 29a) – les futures linguistiques synchronique et diachronique –, résulte donc d'une constatation de nature positiviste, censée porter sur l'objet complexe qu'est la langue. Telle qu'elle est ici présentée par Saussure, l'attitude du linguiste qui prétend à l'objectivité autorise en soi le passage au premier plan soit de la synchronie (quand il s'agit de grammaire ou d'analogie) soit de la diachronie (quand il s'agit d'expliquer causalement un fait de langue): "L'événement est la cause de l'état et ce qui l'explique (dans un certain sens)" (ibid.), tandis que, dans un autre sens, la transformation analogique a son principe "dans des formes existantes fournies par la mémoire", dont la coexistence est alors la cause de l'événement et ce qui l'explique.

4. L'émergence de la priorité logique et sémiologique de la dimension synchronique

Pour le théoricien, l'indétermination du rapport entre le *status* et le *motus*, ou, pis encore, le caractère paradoxal de leur relation, est pourtant intenable: suivant "une pente qu'il faut croire naturelle de notre esprit", écrit-il peu après 1894 (cf. Godel 1957: 37), "[...] l'attention va [d'elle]-même aux événements et tend à se désintéresser des états. Soit que ce trait aille jusqu'à une abolition complète [...] du sens de ce que peut être un état, soit qu'on se borne à ne pas attribuer aux états de rôle particulier à côté des événements dont ils sont issus" (N 12, *CLG/E* II 26b); il y a là une "disproportion de l'esprit" qui "met le trouble dans la linguistique" (ibid. 26b–27a).

En vue de définir logiquement le rapport entre synchronie et diachronie, Saussure – dans ses méditations du milieu des années 90 – tente deux approches distinctes. D'une part, grâce au "théorème épistémologique des points de vue" (selon le mot d'Engler 1995: 2), il théorise l'équivalence entre la considération du *status* et celle du *motus*, pour justifier en droit la symétrie observée en fait; ce faisant, il doit abandonner la position positiviste – chimérique lorsqu'il s'agit d'une langue – selon laquelle la linguistique aurait affaire à un objet déterminé indépendamment de l'observateur linguiste. D'autre part, il identifie des évidences immanentes qui lui permettent de fonder la prééminence hiérachique de la synchronie sur la diachronie; pour ce faire, il finit par substituer, au point de vue du linguiste, le point de vue des sujets parlants.

4.1. Le théorème des points de vue

La position méthodologique d'abord adoptée par Saussure est donc tacitement celle de l'observateur qui considère la langue comme objet d'étude extérieur dont il constate qu'elle est le lieu de phénomènes qui apparaissent comme hétérogènes. Cherchant à déterminer ce qui est affecté par lesdits phénomènes, Saussure (vers 1894) se persuade toutefois que la langue n'est pas constituée d'objets donnés d'avance – ni mot (tel que le latin *eqvos*, N 9.2, *CLG/E* 26e, n° 131) ni même "figure vocale" (telle que *nü* ou *kan-ta-re*, N 9.1, *CLG/E* 25f et 26c, n° 129), tant il est vrai que "absolument rien ne saurait déterminer où est l'objet immédiat offert à la connaissance dans la langue (ce qui est la fatalité de cette science [la linguistique])" (N 12, *CLG/E* II 27b). En linguistique, il n'y a pas de "premier objet tangible [...] antérieur à l'analyse" (ibid.); autrement dit, le positivisme linguistique est ici radicalement battu en brèche.

De manière concomitante, et toujours à la même époque de ses réflexions, la position de Saussure, de méthodologique, se fait épistémologique. Le terme-clé est ici 'point de vue': "Il n'y a rien, c'est-à-dire non seulement rien qui soit déterminé d'avance hors d'un point de vue, mais pas même un point de vue qui soit plus indiqué que les autres. Il n'y a d'abord que la critique comparative des points de vue" (N 9.1, *CLG/E* 26c, n° 129).

Cette conception foncièrement et radicalement relativiste se traduit dans la formule fameuse du *Cours*: "Bien loin que l'objet précède le point de vue, on dirait que c'est le point de vue qui crée l'objet" (*CLG* 23), laquelle pourtant édulcore sensiblement l'expression que Saussure lui a donnée dans la source de ce passage, à savoir l'ébauche du livre auquel il travaillait vers 1895 (cf. Godel 1957: 36–37): "Il nous est interdit en linguistique, quoique nous ne cessions de le faire, de parler '*d'une chose*' à différents points de vue, ou d'une chose en général, parce que c'est le point de vue qui FAIT la chose" (N 9.2, *CLG/E* 26e, n° 131).

Précisément, le point de vue choisi permet au linguiste de déterminer, en fixant les rapports qui s'établissent entre elles, les unités avec lesquelles il opérera: "À mesure qu'on approfondit la matière proposée à l'étude linguistique, on se convainc davantage de cette vérité qui donne, il serait inutile de le dissimuler, singulièrement à réfléchir: que le lien qu'on établit entre les choses préexiste, dans ce domaine, *aux choses elles-mêmes*, et sert à les déterminer" (N 9.2, *CLG/E* 26d, n° 130).

Le premier 'lien', le rapport à chaque fois fondateur de l'unité, c'est la "relation d'identité": "Il y a différents genres d'identité. C'est ce qui crée différents ordres de faits linguistiques. Hors d'une relation quelconque d'identité, un fait linguistique n'existe pas. Mais la relation d'identité dépend d'un point de vue variable, qu'on décide d'adopter; il n'y a aucun rudiment de fait linguistique hors du point de vue défini qui préside aux distinctions" (N 9.1, *CLG/E* 26c, n° 129). Mais y a-t-il un point de vue privilégié, qui permettrait de restreindre l'absolu relativisme qu'on a signalé ci-dessus? Saussure semble bien en retenir deux comme théoriquement fondamentaux, ou peut-être seulement comme descriptivement principaux.

Pour revenir à l'argument de cet article, c'est en ce sens, en effet, que la synchronie et la diachronie sont définies, en 1897 ou peu après (cf. Godel 1957: 37), comme des points de vue: "Partout l'état historique et l'état conscient sont deux états qui s'opposent. Ce sont les deux voies du signe. D'où la difficulté, mais la nécessité, de ne les mélanger nulle part en rien. Ils s'opposent comme les deux états possibles d'un mot, et avant le choix desquels le mot n'*est rien*. Chaque mot est à l'intersection du point de vue diachronique et synchronique" (N 15.17, *CLG/E* II

40b). On retiendra l'allusion, encore fugitive, au signe, dans des réflexions qui se font implicitement sémiologiques.

La question du rapport théorique entre les deux axes, ainsi réinterprétée en des termes épistémologiques qui supposent l'intervention essentielle (par le choix du point de vue) de l'observateur sur l'objet à observer, trouvera sa réponse définitive quand Saussure aura reconnu que l'identité foncière garante d'une entité observable est son identité avec elle-même, et qu'il aura développé les principaux corollaires sémiologiques de cette thèse (à cet égard, on sera attentif, dans la citation qui va suivre, à la longue incise ici détachée du reste par des tirets).

Les diverses sortes d'identité – fussent-elles restreintes aux "deux états possibles" des mots – ne sont pas équipollentes:

"Considérons par exemple la suite de sons vocaux *alka*, qui après un certain temps, en passant de bouche en bouche, est devenue *ôk* – et remarquons que, pour simplifier, nous nous abstenons absolument de faire intervenir la valeur significative de *alka* ou *ôk*, quoique sans elle il n'y ait pas même le commencement d'un fait de langage proprement dit –. Donc *alka*, moyennant le facteur TEMPS se trouve être *ôk*. Au fond, où est le LIEN entre *alka* et *ôk*? Si nous entrons dans cette voie, *et il est inflexiblement nécessaire d'y entrer*, nous verrons bientôt qu'il faudra se demander où est le LIEN entre *alka* et *alka* lui-même". (N 9.2, *CLG/E* 26d, n° 131)

Ainsi, vers 1895, Saussure met en évidence le fait que, pour établir le lien qui met en relation d'identité une entité avec elle-même, on doit faire intervenir la 'valeur significative' de l'entité en question. Or tenir compte de la valeur suppose qu'on envisage l'entité en sa qualité de signe, c'est-à-dire d'unité bifaciale. C'est donc, peut-on conclure, le point de vue sémiologique qui va permettre à Saussure d'établir finalement la prééminence logique de la synchronie.

4.2. Les évidences immanentes

Quant aux évidences que Saussure retient en vue d'établir l'éventuel rapport de dépendance entre synchronie et diachronie, il y en a deux. La première peut être qualifiée d'historique ou de causale: "Comment n'est il pas évident que tout ce qui est dans l'état est contenu d'avance dans l'événement: que si l'on a quelque part *gero* : *gestus* (état), c'est parce que l'événement avait fait de *geso gero?" (N 11, *CLG/E* II 26b; exemple latin sur un verbe significant "porter" [*je porte* : *porté*], dans lequel *s* est devenu *r* par rhotacisme entre voyelles, mais s'est conservé devant consonne).

L'évidence de la causalité historique accorde ainsi au *motus*, à la diachronique, une priorité qui semble trancher la question: "C'est à ce point qu'en est la linguistique" (ibid.). Mais elle le fait en sacrifiant l'"indépendante valeur" du *status*, pour laquelle Saussure dégage une seconde évidence, d'ordre sémiologique, qui se révèlera déterminante (le terme de sémiologie intervient explicitement plus bas dans la même note, ibid. 27b, dans le cadre des réflexions sur l'objet de la linguistique). Elle accorde au *status* le "rôle particulier qui le distingue comme état" (ibid., 27a), et que Saussure semble bien se considérer ici comme seul à identifier dans toute son importance: "Il se trouve que dans la langue, c'est aux états, et à ceux-ci seuls, qu'appartient le pouvoir de signifier" (ibid., cité par Godel 1957: 138); en d'autres termes: "Tout fait statique est par opposition aux faits diachroniques accompagné de signification (et par là d'un autre caractère fondamental' (ibid., 28b).

A posteriori, souligner l'évidence sémantique de la langue comme un 'caractère fondamental' paraît éminemment trivial, et pourtant c'est à cette banalité que tient le renversement du rapport hiérachique entre synchronie et diachronie. En effet, "la langue hors de ce pouvoir ⟨de⟩ signifier cesserait d'être quoi que ce soit" (ibid.). Or il faut bien entendu que la langue soit quelque chose pour que les événements qui l'affectent soient simplement concevables; récipoquement, l'absence de signification fait des changements diachroniques, hors de l'état qu'ils affectent, un non-être linguistique, de sorte que, l'évidence historique n'étant possible que dans le cadre défini par l'évidence sémiologique, la priorité logique revient nécessairement à l'état, c'est-à-dire à la synchronie. Il y a donc bien un point de vue privilégié: c'est celui du signe et de son 'pouvoir de signifier', autrement dit le point de vue de la communication, qui est en fin de compte celui des sujets parlants; le relativisme absolu, qui résultait de la focalisation épistémologique sur l'observateur linguiste, fait place à une hiérarchie focalisée sur l'usager même de la langue.

Cette façon de voir intéresse au premier chef la nature des analyses morphologiques auxquelles se livre le linguiste: soit, par un "procédé détestable" (N 7 [probablement de 1894–1895], *CLG/E* II 18a), il "ne voit que l'état le plus primitif et applique imperturbablement l'analyse du premier jour aux périodes subséquentes" (ibid., p. 18b), divisant par exemple *gantier* en *gant + ier*, soit au contraire, sachant bien "que l'analyse de la langue peut reposer sur un rapport apparent des formes [...] qui n'est pas justifié par l'étymologie" (ibid., p. 18a), il divise le même mot en *gan + tier* (ce que prouve *clou-tier*), "car c'est là l'analyse de la langue [c'est-à-dire des sujets parlants], et cette analyse est son seul guide" (ibid., exemple changé). Dans le premier cas, l'analyse est, comme le dit le *CLG* (p. 251), "objective", réservée au grammairien et sans valeur pour les sujets parlants; dans le deuxième cas, elle est "subjective" et synchronique: "La morphologie ne peut jamais combiner et mêler plusieurs époques différentes; [...] elle doit exercer son activité au sein de chaque époque" (*CLG/E* II 18a).

Si donc l'observateur prétend décrire la langue, il doit adopter le point de vue privilégié du sujet parlant, puisque "tout ce qui est dans le sentiment des sujets parlants est phénomène réel" (ibid.). C'est ce que Saussure dira on ne peut plus clairement dans le deuxième cours, en décembre 1908: "Dans l'ordre synchronique, il n'y a qu'une [...] méthode possible. Cette perspective du grammairien, du linguiste a pour étalon, pour prototype, la perspective des sujets parlants" (*CLG/E* 200, n° 1503b); "pour savoir dans quelle mesure une chose *est*, il faudra se demander quelle signification elle a. Donc une seule méthode: savoir ce qui est ressenti par les sujets parlants" (ibid., n° 1504d; cf. *CLG* 128). Enfin, en juin 1911, l'identification du linguiste au sujet parlant, dans la perspective synchronique, est affirmée comme telle: "Il est important de remarquer que la perspective statique concerne à la fois les sujets parlants et le linguiste, soit la masse parlante soit les grammairiens" (*CLG/E* 198, n° 1496 bde combinés).

La priorité logique ainsi acquise, théoriquement justifiée par l'évidence sémiologique, a donné aux études synchroniques une dignité renouvelée (la grammaire descriptive, qu'elle ait été utilitaire ou logicisante, était certes déjà foncièrement synchronique, mais, ignorant les conditions d'existence du signe — en particulier celles de sa transmission — ne pouvait pas, aux yeux de Saussure, rendre un compte satisfaisant de la langue dans sa totalité (cf. N 8 [non datée, vraisemblablement toujours du milieu des années 90], *CLG/E* II 21a]). Dans la formulation qu'en a donnée le *CLG*, la prééminence ainsi reconnue à la synchronie a ouvert la voie à toute la linguistique structurale du XXe siècle: "Le rôle caractéristique de la langue vis-à-vis de la pensée n'est pas de créer un moyen phonique matériel pour l'expression des idées, mais de servir d'intermédiaire entre la pensée et le son, dans des conditions telles que leur union aboutit nécessairement à des délimitations réciproques d'unités" (*CLG* 156), les "délimitations réciproques" étant par définition synchroniques.

Mais, à considérer ce qu'est devenue la linguistique structurale, on peut douter que Saussure s'y fût reconnu, car pour lui la priorité logique de la synchronie n'en comportait assurément pas la considération exclusive. Au contraire, la position de certains structuralistes dogmatiques (ceux pour qui le système est une totalité dont on ne sort pas) lui aurait sans doute paru, par son caractère unilatéral, refléter une 'disproportion de l'esprit' symétrique à celle des historiens du XIXe siècle, allant "jusqu'à une abolition complète du sens de ce que peut être" le *motus* de la langue.

En effet, la prééminence logique du synchronique ne signifie aucunement que le diachronique doive s'effacer comme accessoire ou non pertinent. Saussure, dès le milieu des années 90, est formel: "Ce qu'il y a de particulier dans le signe *conventionnel*, c'est que les disciplines qui pourraient avoir à s'en occuper [la philosophie et la psychologie] ne se sont pas doutées que ce signe était (2°) *transmissible*, et par là doté d'une seconde vie" (N 12, *CLG/E* II 28b); cf. encore, dans un contexte analogue et probablement contemporain: "Le système sémiologique 'langue' est le seul [...] qui ait eu à affronter cette épreuve de se trouver en présence du *Temps*, qui ne soit pas simplement fondé de voisin à voisin par mutuel consentement, mais aussi de père en fils par impérative tradition et *au hasard de ce qui arriverait en cette tradition* (N 24a, *CLG/E* II 47a; le consentement est bien entendu la convention du texte précédent, le futur arbitraire du *CLG*).

'La transmission et la tradition' du signe — et plus généralement de la langue comme 'système sémiologique' — sont "dominées [...] par les forces mécaniques" (N 12, *CLG/E* II 28b), tandis que "là où le conventionnel se retrouve, c'est quand on voit que tout signe repose purement sur un co-status négatif" (ibid.), c'est-à-dire sur la délimitation réciproque et arbitraire des valeurs dans le système synchronique.

5. Le rôle de la dimension synchronique dans la théorie linguistique de Saussure

Ainsi, après bien des hésitations, Saussure en arrive, une dizaine d'années avant ses cours de linguistique générale, à une conception sémiologique de la synchronie, dont le caractère essentiel est évidemment de concerner des signes et donc de reposer en fin de compte sur la signification: "Tout ce qui concourt à la signification d'une manière quelconque est statique" (N 12, *CLG/E* II 28b). À cet égard, il faut le répéter, la synchronie est focalisée sur le sujet parlant: "La synchronie ne connaît qu'une perspective, celle des sujets parlants, et toute sa méthode consiste à recueillir leur témoignage" (*CLG* 128). Selon le théorème des points de vue, c'est la perspective des sujets parlants — qui est celui de la communication intersubjective — qui crée l'objet 'langue', d'après la dialectique du code (= la langue) et des messages (= la parole), incarnée dans le "circuit de la parole" (*CLG* 27−28) qu'il vaudrait d'ailleurs mieux appeler 'circuit de la communication'. Dans la postérité saussurienne, c'est principalement Luis Jorge Prieto (1926−1996) qui a étudié les implications de cette dialectique (cf. p. ex. Prieto 1960, 1968).

À son tour, la distinction de la langue et de la parole suppose la question des identités (cf. ci-dessus), essentielle à la détermination de ce qui est significatif, c'est-à-dire pertinent, dans chaque état de langue; ainsi, le genre grammatical ou le sexe du possesseur à la troisième personne du singulier n'est pas pertinent en français, qui n'a que *son*, tandis qu'il l'est en anglais, qui distingue *his* et *her*, de même, le français régional distingue les voyelles nasales de *brun* et *brin*, tandis que le français parisien les confond.

Cette question des identités, quoique foncièrement synchronique, n'en est pas moins un préalable, une sorte d'évidence de départ à partir de laquelle se construit la thérie, elle "a dû représenter pour Saussure l'aspect philosophique du problème du langage: c'est de la réflexion sur les 'différents genres d'identités' que procèdent les 'distinctions premières', la détermination des points de vue justes, créateurs d'ordres de faits qui correspondent à des réalités" (Godel 1957: 136−137).

On comprend donc que, dans la théorie linguistique de Saussure, la dimension synchronique occupe une place assez difficile à situer exactement. D'une part, en effet, le point de vue des sujets parlants, qui sert à définir la synchronie sémiologique, est l'unique garant de la langue, de sorte que cette dimension non seulement est première de fait relativement à la diachronie, mais encore devrait être première en principe dans la construction théorique du linguiste. Mais, d'autre part, dans le plan idéal de la théorie tel que Godel (1957: 135) l'a esquissé en se fondant sur les indications données dans le troisième cours, la synchronie linguistique, qui se définit dans un idiome donné (et que Saussure a parfois appelée *idiosynchronie*), se situe nettement en seconde position, après la distinction langue ~ parole.

Il s'agit peut-être là d'un problème particulier d'organisation de la théorie linguistique: "Ce qui fait la difficulté du sujet, c'est qu'on peut le prendre, comme certains théorèmes de géométrie, de plusieurs côtés: tout est corollaire l'un de l'autre en linguistique statique" (entretien avec Albert Riedlinger, de janvier 1909, dans Godel 1957: 29). Mais il est possible aussi que cette divergence s'explique par la différence implicite des niveaux théoriques auxquels se place Saussure quand il parle, notamment, de synchronie, niveaux qu'on a désignés dans l'alinéa précédent par les qualificatifs de sémiologique et de linguistique, le linguistique proprement dit étant emboîté dans le sémiologique (sur cette différence, cf. Godel 1967; Amacker 1975: 129−130). Ainsi, pour ne donner qu'un premier exemple, la linéarité est une propriété nécessaire des expressions linguistiques, alors que d'autres systèmes sémiologiques, tels que la signalisation routière, ne la connaissent pas.

La distinction de ces deux niveaux, que Saussure n'a pas toujours faite explicitement, est nécessaire à l'interprétation de ce qu'il a dit de spécifique, à la fin du troisième cours (en juin 1911), concernant la 'linguistique statique', c'est-à-dire la synchronie proprement linguistique. C'est ainsi seulement, en particulier, que s'explique un changement terminologique autrement peu justifié relatif à l'arbitraire, d'une part, et une contradiction dangereuse, portant sur la parole, d'autre part.

5.1. Arbitraire sémiologique et immotivé linguistique

Dans la perspective sémiologique, Saussure a distingué l'arbitraire 'onymique' (ou nomenclaturiste) de l'arbitraire radical. Le premier concerne le caractère conventionnel des seules désignations, considérées comme les étiquettes, variables *ad libitum*, de choses naturellement données; pour la conception nomenclaturiste, c'est un même objet qui s'appelle par exemple *gant* en français, *glove* en anglais ou *Handschuh* (c'est-à-dire littéralement chaussure [*Schuh*] de la main [*Hand*]) en allemand. Pour Saussure, cette sorte d'arbitraire, qu'on illustre en citant "toujours des exemples de mot [*sic*] comme *arbre, pierre, vache*" est "ce qu'il y a de plus grossier dans la sémiologie: le cas où elle est (par le hasard des objets qu'on choisit pour être désignés), une simple onymique, c'est-à-dire, car là est la particularité de l'onymique dans l'ensemble de la sémiologie, le cas où il y a [outre le *mot* et son *sens*] un *troisième* élément incontestable dans l'association psychologique du sème, la conscience qu'il s'applique à un être extérieur assez défini en lui-même pour *échapper* à la loi générale du signe" (N 15.7.1 [datant de 1897 ou après], *CLG/E* II 36b–37a).

La 'loi générale du signe', en revanche, veut que soient conventionnels non seulement les désignants, mais aussi les désignés, en vertu de la définition réciproque des unités: "Tout signe repose purement sur un co-status négatif" (N 12, *CLG/E* II 28b); comme l'interprète le *CLG* (p. 166): "Ce qu'il y a d'idée ou de matière phonique dans un signe importe moins que ce qu'il y a autour de lui dans les autres signes."

Tel que Saussure le conçoit en juin 1911, l'arbitraire radical n'est rien d'autre que l'expression de ce 'co-status négatif' reconnu aux deux faces du signe, et notamment au signifié: "La valeur d'un mot ne sera jamais déterminée que par le concours des termes coexistants qui le limitent" (*CLG/E* 260, n° 1874bce), thèse qu'il illustrait en novembre 1908, entre autres, par l'exemple des synonymes, tels *craindre* et *redouter*, qui "n'existent que l'un à côté de l'autre; *craindre* s'enrichira de tout le contenu de *redouter* tant que *redouter* n'existera pas" (*CLG/E* 261, n° 1881b; cf. *CLG* 160).

Dans cette discussion, les mots (pris isolément) sont considérés comme des exemples de signes; et d'ailleurs il s'agit justement de définir quelles sont leurs propriétés sémiologiques, dont l'arbitraire radical. Mais "s'il ne s'agit plus de mots isolés" (*CLG/E* 39, n° 212bd [avril 1911]), c'est-à-dire, vraisemblablement, dès qu'on les envisage comme des entités proprement linguistiques, la perspective change, et Saussure modifie expressément sa terminologie en conséquence: "Au lieu d'arbitraire nous pouvons dire *immotivé*" (*CLG/E* 297, n° 209le [mai 1911]). Et dans la mesure même où les mots et expressions linguistiques sont complexes et donc en principe analysables, ils cessent d'être totalement immotivés pour devenir relativement motivés (*CLG* 180–181), tout en restant par définition, en ce qui concerne leur nature de signes, (sémiologiquement) arbitraires. L'analysabilité, c'est-à-dire la motivation relative, dépend du "mécanisme de la langue" (*CLG* 176–184), qui implique le jeu des rapports associatifs – dits aussi parfois, moins heureusement, paradigmatiques – et des rapports syntagmatiques; mais on sort décidément ici des confins d'un article sur la synchronie.

5.2. La parole dans les perspectives sémiologique et linguistique

Pour la sémiologie, la parole est la réalisation concrète du signe, dans une circonstance donnée, par un sujet parlant déterminé (c'est d'ailleurs justement dans la parole ainsi conçue que se pose pour le récepteur le problème des identités, au niveau des sons réalisant le signifiant comme au niveau des sens réalisant le signifié). En revanche, dans la perspective proprement linguistique, l'expression est en principe complexe et analysable; le signe n'est plus une monade. Ici aussi le passage d'un niveau à l'autre semble apparemment conscient chez Saussure (en avril 1911): "Si nous prenons les mots, les formes grammaticales [comme signes], tout cela est bien fixé dans un état, donné dans la langue. Mais il y a toujours cet élément individuel qu'est la combinaison laissée au choix de chacun pour exprimer sa pensée dans une phrase" (*CLG/E* 285–586, n° 2022e), c'est-à-dire dans une unité complexe servant à la communication.

Ici, abusé peut-être par le fait que dans les deux cas c'est l'individu qui intervient, Saussure commet une confusion regrettable entre l'exécution concrète du signe et la formation d'une entité linguistique complexe; quoique cette dernière soit potentielle comme tout signe, et aussi indépendante de sa réalisation concrète que l'est par exemple une symphonie (selon une comparaison d'avril 1911 [*CLG/E* 53, n° 330be, *CLG* 36]), Saussure dit pourtant: "Cette combinaison appartient à la parole, car c'est une exécution" (*CLG/E* 285, n° 2022e suite), c'est "l'usage individuel du code de langue" (ibid., n° 2022d). Or cette confusion, qui repose sur l'identification erronée et abusive de la réalisation du signe (au niveau sémiologique) et de la combinaison de la phrase (au niveau proprement linguistique), se traduit immédiatement par ce que Saussure appelle pudiquement un 'flottement', flottement qui non seulement contredit, mais encore ébranle dans ses fondements mêmes la distinction pourtant cruciale entre langue et parole, et qui plus est à propos d'un phénomène linguistique aussi essentiel que la syntaxe: "Cette partie-là (2° *usage individuel du code de langue*) soulève une question: ce n'est que dans la syntaxe en somme que se présentera un certain flottement ici entre ce qui est donné dans la langue et ce qui est laissé à l'initiative individuelle. La délimitation est difficile à faire" (*CLG/E* 286, n° 2022e, suite).

S'il est vrai que, au niveau linguistique, les sujets parlants forment leurs phrases avec plus ou moins d'originalité, en recourant aussi plus ou moins à des combinaisons toutes faites, il n'en est pas moins vrai que, au niveau sémiologique, toutes les phrases possibles, toutes les unités complexes produites par le 'mécanisme de la langue' sont des signes que réalisera concrètement l'acte de parole où ils seront utilisés dans le circuit de la communication. C'est pourquoi, avec Éric Buyssens (cf., p. ex., 1943), on se servira avantageusement, pour désigner le lieu métaphorique des phrases, d'un terme comme discours: les unités complexes et les phrases, en tant qu'unités de discours, sont certes le produit de l'activité individuelle, mais restent virtuelles tant qu'elles ne sont pas actualisées dans la parole, bref! quoique articulés, ce sont des signes.

6. Conclusion

Saussure n'a étudié pour elle-même la dimension synchronique de sa théorie que brièvement et selon deux perspectives distinctes: selon la perspective sémiologique dans l'introduction du deuxième cours (cf. Saussure 1957), et selon la perspective proprement linguistique à la fin du troisième cours.

Comme par ailleurs il n'a pas donné de forme définitive à ses idées, c'est à la postérité que revient le soin de les interpréter au mieux et d'en saisir si possible le caractère systématique. Le cas de l'arbitraire et celui de la parole sont deux exemples qui montrent, positivement pour le premier et négativement pour le second, qu'il nous faut introduire, dans nos reconstructions, la distinction des deux perspectives examinées au point 4, dont l'étude de la dimension synchronique a permis d'établir le rôle d'abord heuristique puis théorique chez Saussure.

7. Bibliographie

a) Abréviations:

CFS = *Cahiers Ferdinand de Saussure*. Genève: Droz, 1941–.

CLG = [Ferdinand de Saussure], *Cours de linguistique générale*. Publié par Charles Bally et Albert Sechehaye avec la collaboration d'Albert Riedlinger. Paris: Payot, ^{3}1931 (^{1}1916).

CLG/D = [Ferdinand de Saussure], *Cours de linguistique générale*. Édition critique [*en fait*: commentée] préparée par Tullio De Mauro. Paris: Payot, 1972. [Traduction française (p. I à XVIII et 319 à 495) par L.-J. Calvet de l'"Introduzione" et du "Commento" de T. De Mauro dans Ferdinand de Saussure, *Corso di linguistica generale* (Bari: Laterza ^{1}1967), p. v à XXIII et 283–482.]

CLG/E = [Ferdinand de Saussure], *Cours de linguistique générale*. Édition critique par Rudolf Engler. Wiesbaden: O. Harrassowitz, 1968 (tome I) et 1974 (tome II, fasc. 4 = *CLG/E* II).

MSL = *Mémoires de la Société de Linguistique de Paris*. Paris: A. Franck [*puis* Champion], 1868–1935.

R = *Recueil des publications scientifiques de Ferdinand de Saussure*. Publié par Charles Bally et Léopold Gautier. Genève: Éditions Sonor, 1922.

b) Ouvrages et articles:

Amacker, René. 1975. *Linguistique saussurienne*. Genève: Droz.

Buyssens, Éric. 1943. *Les langages et le discours*. Bruxelles: Office de la Publicité.

De Mauro, Tullio. 1972. "Introduction" et "Notes biographiques et critiques sur F. de Saussure". *CLG/D*. I–XVIII et 319–404.

Engler, Rudolf. 1962. "Théorie et critique d'un principe saussurien: L'arbitraire du signe". *CFS* 19.5–66.

–. 1995. "La forme idéale de la linguistique saussurienne". *Saussure and Linguistics Today* ed. by Tullio De Mauro & Shigeaki Sugeta, 17–40. Tokyo: Waseda Univ.; Rome: Bulzoni.

Fleury, Michel. 1965. "Notes et documents sur Ferdinand de Saussure (1880–1891)". *École Pratique des Hautes Études, IVe Section. Annuaire 1964–1965*, 35–67. Paris: École Pratique des Hautes Études.

Godel, Robert. 1957. *Les sources manuscrites du Cours de linguistique générale de F. de Saussure*. Genève: Droz.

–. 1967. "De la théorie du signe aux termes du système". *CFS* 22.53–68.

Koerner, E. F. K[onrad]. 1972. "Hermann Paul and Synchronic Linguistics". *Lingua* 29. 274–307. (= Koerner 1988.17–50.)

—. 1980. "Sur l'origine du concept et du terme de 'synchronique' en linguistique". *Recherches de linguistique / Hommages à Maurice Leroy* éd. par Francine Mawet et al., 100–109. Bruxelles: Éditions de l'Université de Bruxelles. (= Koerner 1988. 89–98.)

—. 1988. *Saussurean Studies / Études saussuriennes.* Genève: Slatkine.

Littré, Émile. ²1877. *Dictionnaire de la langue française.* 4 tomes. Paris: Hachette.

Meillet, Antoine. 1916. Compte rendu du *CLG. Bulletin de la Société de Linguistique de Paris* 20 (fasc. 64), 32–36.

Paul, Hermann. ⁸1968 [¹1880; ²1886]. *Prinzipien der Sprachgeschichte.* Tübingen: Niemeyer.

Prieto, Luis J[orge]. 1968. "La sémiologie". *Le langage*, sous la direction d'André Martinet, 93–144. Paris: Gallimard.

— 1960. "À propos de la commutation". *CFS* 17. 55–63.

Saussure, Ferdinand de. 1877a. "Le suffixe -*t*-". *MSL* 3.197–209. (= *R* 339–352.)

—. 1877b. "Sur une classe de verbes latins en -*eo*". *MSL* 3.279–293. (= *R* 353–369.)

—. 1878. *Mémoire sur le système primitif des voyelles dans les langues indo-européennes.* Leipsick [sic]: B. G. Teubner [antidaté 1879] (= *R* 1–268.)

—. 1881. *De l'emploi du génitif absolu en sanscrit.* Genève: Fick. (= *R* 269–338.)

—. 1884. "Une loi rythmique de la langue grecque". *Mélanges Graux: Recueil de travaux d'érudition classique dédié à la mémoire de Charles Graux* publiés par Gaston Boissier, Alfred Croiset, Louis Havet, Ernest Lavisse, Henri Weil, 737–748. Paris. Ernest Thorin. (= *R* 464–476.)

—. 1887a. "Sur un point de la phonétique des consonnes en indo-européen". *MSL* 6, 1889.246–257. (= *R* 420–432.)

—. 1887b. "Comparatifs et superlatifs germaniques de la forme *inferus, infimus*". *Mélanges Renier: Recueil de travaux publiés* [sic] *par l'École Pratique des Hautes Études (Section des sciences historiques et philologiques) en mémoire de son président Léon Renier* publié par Ernest Desjardins et al., 385–393. Paris: École Pratique des Hautes Études. (= *R* 481–491.)

—. 1894. "Sur le nominatif pluriel et le génitif singulier de la déclinaison consonantique en lituanien". *Indogermanische Forschungen* 4.456–470. (= *R* 513–525.)

—. 1897. Compte rendu de Johannes Schmidt, *Kritik der Sonantentheorie: Eine sprachwissenschaftliche Untersuchung* (Weimar: H. Böhlau, 1895). *Indogermanische Forschungen, Anzeiger* 7.216–218. (= *R* 539–541.)

—. 1957. "Cours de linguistique générale (1908–1909. Introduction (d'après des notes d'étudiants)". Publié par Robert Godel. *CFS* 15.6–103. [Présentation, pp. 3–5.]

—. 1988 [1876–77]. "Dix-huit notes étymologiques". Éd. par René Amacker et Simon Bouquet. *CFS* 42.227–237. [Introd. (215–226); commentaire (237–244).]

René Amacker, Genève (Suisse)

200. Le développement des idées saussuriennes par l'École de Genève

"Le *Cours de Linguistique* n'est pas une œuvre achevée; c'est un commencement." (Sechehaye 1927: 224)

1. L'École genevoise de linguistique générale
2. Le *Cours de linguistique générale*
3. Charles Bally (1865–1947)
4. Charles-Albert Sechehaye (1870–1946)
5. Conclusion
6. Bibliographie

1. L'École genevoise de linguistique générale

C'est Michel Bréal (1832–1915) qui a utilisé pour la première fois la formule d'"École genevoise de linguistique", à l'occasion du dixième Congrès international des orientalistes organisé par Saussure à Genève en septembre 1894. La formule revient le 14 juillet 1908, dans le discours que Charles Bally (1865–1947) prononce en remettant à Saussure le volume de *Mélanges* publié en son honneur; le texte de ce discours paraît le 18 juillet dans le *Journal de Genève*, sous le titre de "Maître et disciples". L'expression 'École de Genève' concerne non seulement Saussure (en tant que professeur d'histoire et de comparaison des langues indo-européennes et de sanscrit), mais aussi en particulier ses deux collègues privat-docents à l'Université, Charles Bally et Albert Sechehaye (1870–1946), qui ont tous les deux un livre de linguistique et quelques autres publications à leur actif.

Après la mort de Saussure, la formule est en quelque sorte consacrée par Sechehaye (1927: 217), mais c'est en décembre 1940 seulement que l'École genevoise accède à un statut institutionnel (sous la forme d'une Société genevoise de linguistique, dissoute en décembre 1956) et prend une importance décisive dans la vie académique par la création d'une revue de linguistique générale, les *Cahiers Ferdinand de Saussure*, dont le premier numéro paraît en 1941 et qui existe toujours. Quoique l'on mentionne volontiers trois générations de linguistes plus ou moins étroitement rattachés à l'École genevoise, seule la première, qui ne compte que Bally et Sechehaye, mérite véritablement ce nom, la seconde génération — celle de Serge Karcevski (1884–1955), d'Henri Frei (1899–1980) et de Robert Godel (1902–1984) — ayant déjà commencé le retour critique et interprétatif sur les sources du *Cours de linguistique générale* (ci-après *CLG*), notamment avec la publication de l'ouvrage de Godel (1957).

Il ne saurait être question, dans le cadre d'un article d'encyclopédie, d'étudier l'ensemble de la production scientifique de Bally et de Sechehaye. L'examen se bornera aux contributions théoriques essentielles, en tant qu'elles constituent potentiellement ou véritablement un développement des idées saussuriennes, et notamment des points suivants: la distinction langage ~ langue ~ parole, l'opposition entre synchronie et diachronie, la langue comme système de valeurs, les rapports associatifs et syntagmatiques. Les applications, notamment didactiques, ne seront mentionnées qu'à l'occasion et très brièvement. Le présent article est du reste la version abrégée d'une étude publiée séparément (Amacker 2000).

Bally et Sechehaye, en désignant Saussure dès la "Préface" du *CLG* comme leur "maître" (p. 9), sont à l'origine d'un malentendu sans cesse entretenu depuis 1916, et qu'une foule de mises au point n'a jamais réussi à dissiper: non! ils n'ont pas été auditeurs des cours de linguistique générale (cf. *CLG*, p. 8; Godel 1957: 95). Cet hommage à un collègue d'une dizaine d'année leur aîné est rendu à Saussure professeur de grammaire comparée et de sanscrit. C'est surtout le considérable "travail d'assimilation et de reconstitution" exigé par la mise au point du *CLG* qui a donné aux deux linguistes l'occasion de "pénétr[er] jusqu'au fond de chaque pensée particulière", en s'efforçant, "à la lumière du système tout entier, [...] de la voir sous sa forme définitive" (p. 9).

Certes, à plusieurs reprises Bally fait état des entretiens qu'il avait eus avec Saussure et qu'il "regretter[a] toujours de n'avoir pas notés" (1913b: 17), tout comme Sechehaye de son côté déclare que c'est de Saussure qu'il tient l'intérêt qu'il porte "aux problèmes généraux de la linguistique" et qu'il a reçu "plusieurs des principes qui ont éclairé [sa] route dans ces recherches" (1908: [v]); mais cette influence privée des idées saussuriennes sur leurs premiers travaux reste discrète et partiale; d'ailleurs, tout bien pesé, même le *CLG* n'a pas laissé, dans leurs œuvres, la trace qu'on attendrait.

2. Le *Cours de linguistique générale*

Le travail d'assimilation et de reconstitution de l'enseignement donné par Saussure en 1907, en 1908–1909 et en 1910–1911 constitue à la fois la première — et indispensable — interprétation des aperçus théoriques de Saussure et le premier témoignage du développement de ses idées dans l'École genevoise. On a déjà souvent signalé certaines des difficultés que le plan choisi a comportées (ainsi Godel 1957: 98–102, 135–136), voire certains des gauchissements de fond qui résultent d'une décision peu heureuse de la part de Bally et de Sechehaye (ainsi De Mauro 1972: 464, note 228, montre que les éditeurs ont renversé l'ordre théorique réciproque de l'arbitraire et de la relativité des valeurs). On se bornera ici à un seul exemple, pour illustrer l'influence négative qu'exerçait sur les rédacteurs du *CLG* leur formation traditionnelle.

Présentant le sujet difficile des "entités abstraites en grammaire", et notamment au point de vue associatif, les éditeurs introduisent correctement l'exemple des diverses désinences du génitif en latin, mutuellement "rattachées par le sentiment d'une valeur commune qui dicte un emploi identique" (*CLG*, p. 190), mais en tirent une conclusion peut-être imprudente: "C'est ainsi que la notion de génitif en soi prend place dans la langue"; de fait, ce qui n'est encore ici que le soupçon d'une intrusion de grammaire générale devient une certitude quelques lignes plus loin, où Bally et Sechehaye généralisent indûment la formule de Saussure, selon laquelle "on peut même avoir association avec tous les substantifs" (*CLG/E* unité n° 2181), en ajoutant de leur cru que "des associations du même genre [...] fixent la notion des parties du discours" (*CLG*, p. 190). Or les vieilles parties du discours appartiennent indubitablement à ces "cadres usuels de la linguistique synchronique" que les rapports associatifs et syntagmatiques devaient remplacer une fois adoptées les "divisions rationnelles" de la grammaire (*CLG*, pp. 188, 187). En mettant au nom de Saussure, trois pages après l'exposé des principes qui devaient à ses yeux renouveler l'étude de la grammaire, une doctrine qui ignore − voire contredit − ces principes, les éditeurs montrent qu'ils n'ont apparemment pas été en mesure d'apprécier en tout point l'originalité des thèses de leur collègue.

3. Charles Bally (1865–1947)

L'influence exercée par Saussure − et que j'ai dite privée − sur Bally avant 1913 est difficile à apprécier. Quand Bally publie le *Précis de stylistique*, il a quarante ans et une longue expérience de l'enseignement; en outre, il a beaucoup lu, notamment les psychologues autrichiens, au premier rang desquels Alexius Meinong (1853–1920), qui soutient l'idée (que Bally fait sienne dès le *Précis*) que le jugement s'accompagne toujours d'une 'signification impressive caractéristique' (*charakteristische Gefühlsbedeutung* [Meinong 1894: 32]). Comme introduction à Bally, on consultera Durrer (1998).

3.1. Le *Précis de stylistique* (1905)

Il m'est toutefois difficile d'identifier les sources éventuelles de Bally et, par conséquente, de dire à quel point il est original, quand, présentant le *Précis* comme "l'esquisse d'une méthode" (selon le sous-titre, formule reprise p. 3), il souligne que "les observations qu'on va lire ne constituent pas un système fermé" et décrit son ambition en des termes qui semblent annoncer la fameuse phrase conclusive du *CLG*: "Mon but est [...] d'amener à une conception rationnelle d'une langue vivante, quelle qu'elle soit, prise en elle-même et étudiée pour elle-même" (ibid.); mais je me plais à penser que Saussure n'est peut-être pas totalement étranger à ces formules, qui se laissent somme toute assez mal encadrer par ailleurs dans le psychologisme de l'auteur. Sa méthode, consistant à étudier "la manière dont nos pensées arrivent à leur expression", de même que sa définition de la langue comme "un ensemble d'opérations *psychologiques* qu'il faut étudier autant par le sens de la vie que par les lois et les méthodes scientifiques", sont, je crois, bien peu saussuriennes (p. 2; je reproduis les mises en relief voulues par les auteurs dans tous les textes que je cite).

On trouve aussi, dans l'ouvrage de 1905, une conception systémique de la langue, mais si particulière qu'il me semble impossible de la déclarer saussurienne, malgré certaines apparences. Ainsi, Bally admet, il est vrai, que "le sens d'un mot est [...] toujours, quoique de façon imperceptible dans une foule de cas, solidaire" de son entourage, par quoi il entend les "éléments pensés ou exprimés en même temps que lui" (p. 9). Faut-il voir ici une application de ce que seront dans le *CLG* les rapports associatifs et syntagmatiques? Il est difficile de répondre, car l'auteur semble bien plutôt songer à une théorie de l'ellipse dans le discours; en effet, il "part du principe que *notre pensée ne se formule jamais par des mots isolés, mais par des groupes de mots;* les éléments de ces groupes sont, les uns parlés, d'autres simplement pensés, ce qui donne souvent l'illusion de phrases n'ayant qu'un mot, comme: *oui! non! venez! debout!* etc ...". Autrement dit, pour Bally, les phrases réelles, non illusoires, ne sont pas celles que l'on observe: on ne peut pas être plus anti-saussurien!

Même l'insistance sur l'aspect synchronique de la stylistique ne répond pas parfaitement à la rigueur de la position exposée dans le *CLG*. Bally est certes péremptoire: "On ne peut assez insister sur le caractère non-historique de notre science" (p. 10); mais il dit aussi: "Que cette remarque ne donne pas l'idée que nous voudrions exclure la méthode historique de l'étude des langues modernes; elle apparaît plus nécessaire que jamais, et l'on n'a pas une connaissance solide d'un idiome sans avoir étudié son passé" (ibid.).

Enfin, la nature même de la stylistique mérite un commentaire dans la perspective de cet article, étant donné qu'il y a lieu de la considérer comme une discipline s'occupant essentiellement du discours, c.à.d. de la parole comme libre combinaison des unités de langue, et non pas comme réalisation concrète (sur ces deux acceptions, cf. *CLG*, p. 31): "La stylistique étudie les *moyens d'expression* dont dispose une langue, les procédés généraux employés par elle pour rendre par la parole les phénomènes du monde extérieur aussi bien que les idées, les sentiments et en général tous les mouvements de notre vie intérieure" (p. 7). Néanmoins, il définit aussi son travail par l'opposition entre l'individuel et le collectif: "La tâche de la stylistique est d'extraire ce qu'il y a de *général* dans les caprices de l'expression personnelle et d'en dégager les tendances communes" (p. 12).

Par là, Bally semble anticiper l'"usage individuel du code de langue selon la pensée individuelle", qui définit un des aspects de la parole dans la leçon de Saussure du 25 avril 1911 (*CLG/E*, unité n° 247); en même temps, il affirme que les moyens d'expression forment un système: "Le système expressif d'un idiome est parfaitement reconnaissable à travers les styles individuels" (Bally 1905: 12).

L'ambition future de la stylistique de Bally, qui se lit seulement en filigrane dans le *Précis de stylistique*, a un aspect humboldtien qui, à ma connaissance, est tout à fait étranger à Saussure; il s'agirait, en effet, de déterminer le 'caractère' d'une langue, tâche qui est encore, en 1905, hors de portée: "Non seulement aucune des langues modernes n'a encore été caractérisée par les procédés scientifiques, mais la méthode d'investigation n'est pas fixée dans ses traits essentiels" (p. 13).

3.2. Le *Traité de stylistique française* (1909)

Le *Traité* se trouve, à l'égard des idées de Saussure, dans le même rapport ambigu que l'était le *Précis*, dont il "marque la continuation" (p. vii). Et de fait, l'ambition typologique reste la même, et tout aussi chimérique encore: "Il y a une chose que ce livre ne peut donner: c'est une caractéristique du français d'aujourd'hui" (ibid.). Au point de vue du présent article, l'examen du *Traité* n'apporte donc guère d'éléments nouveaux. La perspective synchronique y est néanmoins bien plus fermement affirmée: "Le sujet qui parle spontanément sa langue maternelle a tout le temps conscience d'un *état*, nullement d'une *évolution* ni d'une perspective dans le temps. [...] Ainsi la stylistique, ne pouvant adopter aucune méthode contraire aux opérations naturelles du langage, ne saurait être historique" (p. 21).

En indiquant un parallélisme entre la méthode et l'objet de la stylistique, Bally se trouve épistémologiquement saussurien, si je puis dire. En effet, comme je le montre dans l'article consacré à la dimension synchronique chez Saussure, il est possible de reconstruire chez lui une évolution théorique qui fait de la langue d'abord un objet donné (extérieur à l'observateur), puis un objet problématique (dépendant du point de vue arbitrairement choisi pour l'étudier), enfin un objet qui relève de la connaissance du sujet parlant (l'observateur devant s'identifier au locuteur). Quand Bally prétend que sa discipline doit adopter une méthode conforme "aux opérations naturelles du langage", il veut évidemment dire conforme à ce qui "donne la conscience et fait la réalité d'un état de langue chez les sujets parlants" (p. 21), selon la troisième des positions épistémologiques successives de Saussure que je viens de rappeler. Mais faut-il voir dans ce rapprochement, tout indubitable qu'il est, le produit d'une influence, fût-elle secrète? Ce qu'il y a de sûr, c'est que Bally proclame son originalité: "Mes idées sur le sujet se sont développées par l'expérience [de l'enseignement] et l'observation personnelles, en dehors de toute influence étrangère" (1909 I: x), de sorte que l'on ne peut rien tirer à cet égard de la dédicace de l'ouvrage ("A mon maître Ferdinand de Saussure, hommage respectueux"), qui n'est peut-être qu'une manière de revendiquer ostensiblement son rattachement à l'École genevoise.

Bally présente dans le *Traité* une conception de la bifacialité des phénomènes linguistiques qui doit apparemment plus à la tradition stoïcienne qu'à l'enseignement de Saussure: "Le langage est pour nous un ensemble de moyens d'expression *simultanés* aux faits de pensée, dont ils ne sont qu'une autre face, la face tournée vers le dehors" (p. 12); d'ailleurs, pour distinguer la stylistique de la linguistique, il introduit une seconde dualité, encore moins saussurienne que la première: "Le langage réel présente [...], dans toutes ses manifestations, un côté intellectuel et un côté affectif, ces faces de l'expression surgissant avec une intensité très variable selon la disposition du sujet parlant, la situation et le milieu" (*ibid.*).

L'équivalent approximatif de la distinction entre le langage, la langue et la parole s'exprime dans l'opposition entre "les trois stylistiques": "Devons-nous entendre par moyens d'expression les tendances universelles de l'esprit humain, telles qu'elles se reflètent dans la parole articulée, ou bien nous attacherons-nous à caractériser celles d'un idiome particulier, ou encore chercherons-nous le reflet d'une personnalité dans le parler d'un individu quelconque?" (Bally 1909: 17). Si la première éventualité est exclue, Bally soutient que "la recherche doit se porter de préférence sur un idiome particulier", notamment la langue maternelle, car "c'est là que la correspondance entre la parole et la pensée se manifeste de la façon la plus claire et la plus aisée" (p. 20).

Quelques remarques concernant le rôle de l'individu dans l'évolution linguistique anticipent Saussure (cf. *CLG/E*, unité n° 350). Bally est précis: "Chaque individu a sa manière propre d'employer son idiome maternel; il lui fait subir, dans certaines circonstances ou habituellement, des déviations portant sur la grammaire, la construction des phrases, le système expressif [...]. Ces particularités sont en général peu apparentes, mais elles ne sont pas entièrement négligeables [...] parce que ces déviations du parler individuel peuvent amener à la longue des changements dans la langue du groupe, si des circonstances favorables font adopter par la collectivité les innovations individuelles" (1909: 18).

L'aspect résolument synchronique de la stylistique tient au fait que "le fondement de son étude est dans les relations constantes entre le langage et la pensée". C'est là, pour Bally, l'occasion d'insister sur le caractère systémique de son objet: "Ce qui fait la réalité d'un état de langage chez les sujets parlants, c'est l'action réciproque des faits de langage, leur solidarité les uns vis-à-vis des autres. [...] Les moyens d'expression sont entre eux dans un état de relativité; ils ne forment pas un *ensemble* par leur nombre, mais un *système* par leur groupement et leur pénétration réciproque" (1909: 21–22).

Sur ce point, on croirait lire la définition relative des valeurs telle qu'elle s'exprime dans le *CLG*, à savoir: "Son contenu [celui du mot] n'est vraiment déterminé que par le concours de ce qui existe en dehors de lui. Faisant partie d'un système, il est revêtu, non seulement d'une signification, mais aussi et surtout d'une valeur" (*CLG* 159). Comme le dit Bally, "les symboles linguistiques n'ont de *signification* et ne comportent d'*effet* qu'en vertu d'une réaction générale et simultanée des faits de langage, qui se limitent et se définissent les uns par les autres; les mots ne sont *compris* et *sentis* que par une *comparaison* incessante et inconsciente qui se fait entre eux dans notre cerveau" (1909: 22).

Et encore: "L'important est que chez le même sujet, le mot soit relié par association à d'autres mots, plus précis ou plus généraux, plus abstraits ou plus concrets, plus ou moins propres à exciter la sensibilité, ou à évoquer un milieu social plutôt qu'un autre" (p. 22).

Une influence saussurienne secrète s'est probablement exercée ici sur Bally; c'est du moins l'hypothèse que la comparaison qui suit, avec son vocabulaire typique de Saussure, me suggère: "Sans la vue très nette de cette *relativité synchronique* des moyens d'expression, il n'y a pas de stylistique possible, pas plus qu'il ne peut exister de système grammatical" (*ibid.*).

Il est vrai que Bally, afin d'assurer à la stylistique la place qu'il revendique pour elle, modifie la conception qu'il hérite vraisemblablement de Saussure en la complétant: il ajoute à la valeur sémantique des mots leurs effets stylistiques, comme il précise que le mécanisme selon lequel ils sont compris – la "*comparaison* incessante et inconsciente qui se fait entre eux dans notre cerveau" – est également celui en vertu duquel ils sont 'sentis', notamment comme "plus ou moins propres à exciter la sensibilité, ou à évoquer un milieu social plutôt qu'un autre".

Cet ajustement de la conception apparemment saussurienne du système linguistique s'accompagne d'un prolongement qui la dénature assez sérieusement. Dans l'"Introduction", il ne s'agit que d'une phrase: "Ce qui maintient la cohésion de ce système, c'est que les 'compartiments' dont il se compose correspondent aux catégories habituelles de notre pensée" (1909: 22); dans le corps de l'ouvrage, en revanche, les 'compartiments' en question sont définis par les principes de classement du dictionnaire idéologique auquel Bally a travaillé toute sa vie (cf. le "Tableau synoptique des termes d'identification et de leurs principaux synonymes" [1909 II, p. 223–264]). Or ces principes reposent sur l'analyse logique des notions, et non pas sur les rapports linguistiques des mots: "Il est bien clair [...] que les termes fondamentaux qui formeront les têtes de rubriques et marqueront le plan général de l'ouvrage ne doivent pas être cherchés dans un drame de Victor Hugo [...]; il faudra commencer par dépouiller de bons traités de logique, de psychologie, de sciences naturelles, de classification des sciences, etc." (p. 132); on ne saurait mieux souligner le caractère cette fois-ci non immanent du système descriptif auquel songe Bally: bien loin d'adopter la langue comme norme d'elle-même, il arrête son choix sur des disciplines non linguistiques.

Pourtant, comme Saussure l'aurait fait, Bally insiste ici encore sur l'identité de principe qui doit régner entre le savoir du sujet et la description qu'en fait le linguiste: "Les faits d'expression reposent dans notre esprit par groupes et se présentent de la même façon à notre conscience quand nous parlons. C'est là le germe de tout le travail d'identification [...]; l'identification est [...] l'utilisation systématique et le traitement méthodique d'un processus naturel. Nous suivrons la même marche que le sujet parlant dans l'usage spontané de la langue" (1909: 98–99).

Bally fait un usage assez fréquent de la notion de système. Mais ses rares indications précises — au delà des proclamations de principe — vont toutes dans le même sens, à savoir une conception non immanente du système, qu'il soit lexical comme dans les textes cités ci-dessus ou 'expressif', comme dans l'unique détermination que j'en aie trouvée; à propos du renforcement expressif des termes de négation (*pas un chat, pas l'ombre d'un doute,* etc.), Bally écrit (1909: 297): "Ce sont ces petits faits-là qui montrent le mieux ce qu'est au fond un système expressif, c. à. d. un système de catégories affectives qui cherchent leur expression dans le langage".

3.3. Les textes de 1913

Le même mixte d'inspiration et de terminologie saussuriennes d'une part et de psychologie du langage originale d'autre part se retrouve encore chez Bally après la mort de Saussure. Je n'en retiendrai que deux exemples: son opuscule *Le langage et la vie*, du printemps 1913 (Bally 1913a), et sa leçon inaugurale du 27 octobre 1913 (Bally 1913b).

Le premier texte, qui atteste une connaissance élémentaire des notes des étudiants de Saussure, expose pour l'essentiel les vues de Bally concernant les présupposés de sa stylistique: "Je pense que le langage naturel et spontané, instrument d'expression et d'action dans la vie réelle, mérite d'être étudié dans ce qui fait son essence, c'est-à-dire son contenu subjectif et affectif" (1913a: 47). Pourtant, sous le titre de "Fonctionnement du langage", l'auteur consacre quelques lignes au "système d'une langue", qu'il définit d'une manière très saussurienne comme l'ensemble "des associations et des oppositions synchroniques qui unissent ses divers éléments dans la conscience des sujets parlants" (p. 41) et qui se présente tout autrement que chez les grammairiens, qui "tous prétendent nous donner un tableau de la structure de l'idiome étudié" (ibid.), alors qu'il s'agit en fait d'"un tableau [...] où l'on a peint séparément des détails impossibles à raccorder dans une vue d'ensemble" (41–42).

Dans le même chapitre de son opuscule, Bally fait allusion à la théorie de la valeur, qui exclut l'histoire, puisque les "systèmes linguistiques [...] reposent tout entiers sur l'opposition simultanée, synchronique, de symboles linguistiques, qui, à chaque moment, reçoivent de cette opposition seule, et de nulle autre source, leur signification et leurs valeurs diverses" (1913a: 42). Encore une fois, Bally expose ici un principe saussurien, tout en se servant d'une terminologie en partie non saussurienne (on aura remarqué *symboles* pour *signes*, et *valeurs* au pluriel au lieu du singulier, témoignant de l'usage non technique de ce mot).

Enfin, Bally semble admettre, toujours dans le même chapitre, une certaine distinction entre le programme de la stylistique, à savoir "l'étude expérimentale du fonctionnement du langage" (1913a: 41), et l'étude du système linguistique pur et simple, qui supposerait que le linguiste "ne saurait ni lire ni écrire la langue qu'il étudierait" (p. 42) et qu'il renoncerait "à la rattacher à la civilisation et à l'organisation sociale qu'elle représente, afin que son attention se portât tout entière sur l'action réciproque des symboles. Alors il aurait quelque chance de saisir le système dans sa réalité" (42–43), résultat que Bally, peut-être instruit par sa propre expérience, semble ici exclure définitivement.

Passons au deuxième texte, plus souvent cité, où Bally présente différemment ce qui est au fond la même opposition. Quoique plongé dans les notes des étudiants de Saussure, il n'abandonne aucunement la part d'originalité qu'il s'est réservée depuis 1905. Il choisit même sa leçon inaugurale pour marquer ce qui distingue sa position de celle de son prédécesseur. Il commence par affirmer que "Ferdinand de Saussure était un intellectualiste convaincu [...]. Pour lui la langue est l'œuvre de l'intelligence collective, c'est un organisme intellectuel" (1913b: 23. 24), puis il décrit sa propre démarche: "Quant à moi, les circonstances ont voulu que je rencontre sa pensée [celle de Saussure] en partant de l'extrémité opposée du champ d'observation. Dans mes leçons [...] je fus amené à étudier les valeurs expressives du langage spontané, naturel, dépouillé de tout vêtement littéraire, de la langue parlée dans la vie réelle. C'est à propos de cette face de la langue, et en pensant à la distinction saussurienne entre la parole et la langue, qu'un doute m'est venu" (p. 24).

Ce doute peut se résumer comme il suit: si la langue parlée courante est "profondément affective et subjective dans ses moyens d'expression et d'action" (1913b: 24), elle devrait être décidément du côté de l'individu, c'est-à-dire de la parole (comme réalisation de la langue); mais "ce serait supposer que l'homme qui se sert de la langue parlée dans la vie journalière est un perpétuel improvisateur, qu'il crée à mesure ce que la langue normale ne lui offre pas pour l'expression de ses sentiments, de ses désirs, de ses volontés" (p. 24). Or Bally constate que "celui qui parle pour exprimer une émotion, pour prier, pour ordonner, n'a presque jamais besoin d'inventer pour être expressif: il trouve des moyens d'expression tout prêts dans la langue parlée, ce sont même les premiers qui lui viennent à l'esprit" (p. 26); donc "c'est bien de la langue et non de la parole" (ibid.).

Sa solution du problème passe par une sorte de compromis: "En somme, je reste fidèle à la distinction saussurienne entre la langue et la parole, mais j'annexe au domaine de la langue une province qu'on a beaucoup de peine à lui attribuer: la langue parlée envisagée dans son contenu affectif et subjectif" (1913b: 26).

Utilisant une autre image, Bally semble considérer la 'langue affective' comme une zone de transition entre langue et parole, puisqu'elle lui "apparaît [...], dans le globe de la langue tout entière, comme une zone périphérique qui enveloppe la langue normale; elle participe de son caractère social, puisque tous les individus s'accordent sur les valeurs qu'elle contient", mais elle a avec la parole "une affinité indéniable" (ibid.). C'est ce caractère 'périphérique', joint à l'aspect psychologique de l'affectivité et de la subjectivité qui font que la langue parlée "réclame une étude spéciale: [...] la stylistique", qui "s'emboîte dans la linguistique générale" (ibid.).

Ce compromis résulte à mon avis du désir académique éprouvé par Bally de réserver une place à sa stylistique dans la chaire de linguistique générale qu'il inaugure, tout en se distinguant de son prédécesseur, plutôt que de l'intention théorique d'élaborer pour son compte la distinction langue-parole.

3.4. Après le *CLG*

Des textes que Bally a publiés après la publication du *CLG*, je dirai peu de choses. Dans son article de 1921 sur "Langage naturel et langage artificiel", Bally souligne d'emblée qu'il va distinguer entre "la langue en tant que système, et la parole ou langue en action [... et] entre les faits propres à l'assimilation de la langue par les sujets et ceux qui concernent le fonctionnement habituel et normal" (1926 [1921]: 186). Incidemment, peut-être suivant Sechehaye (cf. plus bas, § 4.7), il relève que "les sujets parlants et les sujets entendants n'ont pas la même attitude dans l'exercice de la parole" (ibid.).

Enfin, quoique l'ouvrage essentiel de la période considérée, *Linguistique générale et linguistique française*, soit mieux connu, il faut en dire quelques mots. D'emblée, l'auteur y annonce que "le point d'aboutissement" de son étude est "la caractéristique du français d'aujourd'hui" (1965 [1932]: 8); par là, il réalise enfin le projet qu'il caressait depuis plus d'un quart de siècle, d'abord comme idéal (1905: 13), puis comme but, mais encore hors de sa portée (1909: vii). Quant aux "théories de linguistique générale", elles s'y présentent explicitement comme un ensemble de "principes de base" et de "questions de méthode" (1965 [1932]: 8), abordés à l'occasion de "deux sujets fondamentaux": "la théorie de l'énonciation [cf. Ducrot 1986], et la technique des signes matériels (ou *signifiants*) dans leurs rapports avec les valeurs (ou *signifiés*)" (ibid.).

Bally rattache à sa théorie de l'énonciation un chapitre alors très nouveau sur le rôle de l'intonation en syntaxe (1965 [1932]: 56−75), les courbes mélodiques et la pause éventuelle distinguant la phrase coordonnée (type *il a échoué*; *à son examen*) de la phrase segmentée (type: *il a échoué, à son examen*, avec pause et intonation basse du second élément) et de la phrase liée (type: *il a échoué à son examen*, sans pause, et avec un contour intonationnel unique). La théorie de la phrase segmentée, qui comporte un 'thème' antéposé ou postposé, caractérisé chacun par une intonation caractéristique, et un 'propos' qui a le contour intonationnel d'une phrase liée normale, doit être considérée comme l'ancêtre de tous les développements postérieurs concernant la thématisation et le dynamisme rhématique de la phrase. La notion de phrase segmentée figurait d'ailleurs déjà dans le *Traité*, sous la désignation de "dislocation des membres de phrase" (1909: 311−316); Bally, qui avait signalé le rôle syntaxique de l'intonation dès ce même ouvrage (1909: 93−95, 267−270), y reviendra dans un article de 1941.

Quant au deuxième point, il donne à Bally l'occasion de présenter à sa manière "la théorie de l'arbitraire et de la motivation, telle qu'elle est formulée par Saussure" (1965 [1932]: 128). La question est difficile, car le texte semble bien résulter de la systématisation en partie artificielle de doctrines présaussuriennes et d'interprétations personnelles des thèses du *CLG*. Avant tout, il faut préciser que, Saussure se bornant à définir les grandes lignes d'une épistémologie de la linguistique, il est indispensable à qui souhaite décrire une langue ou un fragment de langue de se créer une méthode; or dès avant la mise au point du *CLG* Bally disposait de sa méthode propre, illustrée en particulier dans le *Traité* (il mentionne lui-même le lien entre les deux ouvrages [1965 (1932): 188–189]). Si un partisan d'un saussurisme idéal peut regretter que cette méthode doive peu aux thèses les plus novatrices du *CLG*, un juge objectif doit en revanche saluer la tentative de Bally et reconnaître tout le prix des observations qu'il systématise dans son ouvrage.

Les deux piliers sur lesquels s'appuie l'édifice théorique sont, d'une part, la "non-linéarité ou dystaxie" (1965 [1932]: 146–171) et, d'autre part, la "polysémie" (p. 171–185). Au titre de la dystaxie, Bally compte non seulement les signes fractionnés, par exemple des locutions comme *tout à coup* (p. 164), ou la disjonction (p. 169–170), mais aussi un grand nombre de phénomènes fondés sur le caractère implicite d'éléments jugés nécessaires à l'interprétation; ainsi "*capitale* pour *ville capitale*, *tailleur*, pour *tailleur d'habits*" résulteraient de "l'agglutination de syntagmes implicites renfermant originairement l'ellipse d'un des termes" (p. 147).

Au nombre de ces phénomènes, on rencontre le cumul des signifiés (149–153), que l'auteur illustre par *jument* (femelle du cheval), *pire* (plus mauvais), *du* (de le), *moi* (la personne qui parle), *la* (article, féminin, singulier), *donc* (en conséquence de cela), etc. On trouve en outre surtout la sous-entente, phénomène de langue (p. 159), l'ellipse, phénomène de parole (ibid.), le signe zéro (160–164), illustré par *marche-0* (à côté des noms d'action dérivés par suffixation explicite, type *form-ation*, *lav-age*, *règle-ment*, etc.) et l'hypostase (165–168), définie comme "la combinaison d'un signe explicite complet et autonome avec un autre qui, sans être exprimé, est nécessaire au sens. L'hypostase est – répétons-le – un syntagme dont la partie explicite est le déterminant, l'idée catégorielle le déterminé" (p. 165, exemple *le beau*, c'est-à-dire 'la notion de beau').

Sans revenir sur tous les problèmes que posent ces idées, je discuterai seulement le recours à l'implicite, réservant au cumul une observation conclusive. Parler, comme fait Bally, de 'syntagme implicite', unissant un mot et, par exemple, une idée catégorielle, contredit absolument la définition saussurienne: "Le syntagme se compose […] toujours de deux ou plusieurs unités consécutives" (*CLG*, p. 170), nécessairement 'concrètes' et coprésentes dans le dicours. Quant aux diverses manifestations de la sous-entente (au sens large), Saussure au fond les récusait toutes: "Le seul mot d'*ellipse* a un sens qui devrait faire réfléchir. Un tel terme paraît supposer que nous savons initialement de combien de termes *devrait* se composer la phrase, et que nous y comparons les termes dont, en fait, elle se compose, pour constater les déficits […]. L'ellipse n'est autre chose que le surplus de valeur" (note *Item* N 15.3 = *CLG/E* II, p. 35b, n° 3308).

La notion de 'cumul des signifiés' (1965 [1932]: 149–153) est de celles dont l'interprétation est embarrassante. A côté d'exemples indubitables (*la* article actualisateur féminin singulier [p. 149]), on en trouve qui laissent perplexe (*donc* = "en conséquence de cela" [p. 150]), voire qui paraissent tirés par les cheveux ("dans *faire une chose par amitié*, *par* cumule l'idée de rapport rectionnel pur et simple avec celle de motif" [ibid.]). Visiblement, Bally n'a pas su faire rigoureusement la différence entre les valeurs lexicales, issues du découpage arbitraire, selon les rapports associatifs, de la "matière à signifier" (note *Item* N 15.9.3 = *CLG/E* II, p. 37a, n° 3314.3) et les valeurs grammaticales qui s'y superposent nécessairement dès que les signes ont des catégorisations variables; quant à ces dernières, elles sont corrélatives aux restrictions de coprésence des termes dans la chaîne du discours en vertu de la linéarité (selon les rapports syntagmatiques). De toute manière, ce que Bally prend pour un cumul de signifiés ne peut être qu'un cumul de valeurs; et à mon avis, les valeurs lexicales ne se cumulent pas.

Concluons. Les nombreux éléments nettement non saussuriens que l'on peut sans peine relever chez Bally, notamment après 1913, tiennent au fait qu'il a développé sa propre linguistique générale sans trop se préoccuper de savoir si elle correspondait ou non à la doctrine exposée dans le *CLG*. Il a souvent revêtu de la terminologie saussurienne des idées qu'il avait développées pour l'essentiel avant 1912, dans le cadre de la stylistique; tout compte fait, l'écho saussurien le plus intéressant chez lui reste donc celui qui provient de l'influence privée que Saussure a pu exercer sur lui avant sa mort.

4. Charles-Albert Sechehaye (1870–1946)

Il en va assez différemment de Sechehaye, dont les productions scientifiques sont plus faciles à analyser que celles de Bally, en particulier à cause du fait que ses idées s'y expriment avec une netteté en général remarquable. En outre, comme il se prononce bien plus souvent que Bally sur les questions théoriques, il n'est presque pas de texte de lui que l'on puisse laisser hors de considération. Il existe une monographie consacrée à Sechehaye, notamment à l'*Essai* de 1926 (Fryba-Reber 1994).

4.1. La systématisation des sciences du langage

Se décrivant lui-même comme partageant avec Saussure "le goût [...] des grandes abstractions et de ces vues de l'esprit qui dépassent et dominent les faits", il définit sa propre particularité en affirmant qu'à cela lui-même "ajoute une préoccupation d'organisation et de système" (1927: 18). Cette préoccupation se manifeste notamment dans le souci qu'il a toujours manifesté, dès *Programme et méthodes de la linguistique théorique* (1908), de construire un ensemble logiquement cohérent des sciences du langage, en les emboîtant (le terme est de lui), d'une part, les unes dans les autres et, d'autre part, toutes ensemble, dans la psychologie (1908: 55–65). Au niveau linguistique, la science du "langage grammatical" ou "organisé" s'emboîte dans la science du "langage prégrammatical" ou "affectif" (cf. 1908: 67–83); les "disciplines évolutives", à savoir "morphologie évolutive" et "phonétique", s'emboîtent dans les "disciplines statiques", à savoir "morphologie statique" et "phonologie" (122–130); enfin, on a "emboîtement de la phonologie dans la morphologie statique" (131–134) et "emboîtement de la phonétique dans la morphologie évolutive" (titre du grand chapitre XIII, p. 161–214]).

Revenant, près de vingt ans plus tard et dix ans après la publication du *CLG*, sur son premier livre, il ne trouve qu'une critique à faire à cet égard: "Ce qui a manqué à la classification que nous avons proposée, c'est la conception claire de la science de la parole comme lien nécessaire entre la connaissance des états de langue et celle des évolutions. Or c'est par là justement que le système des disciplines linguistiques trouve son entière perfection et s'adapte complètement et définitivement à son objet. Cette vue peut se ramener au schéma:

Prégrammatical
        > Parole organisée > Évolution,
Grammatical

qui constitue le corps même de toute classification des disciplines linguistiques" (1926a: 221–222). Ainsi complétée, la doctrine de 1908 représente, pour son auteur lui-même, "un système complet" (1908b: 172), "un système bien agencé impliquant des rapports logiques qui constituent la structure interne de toute pensée linguistique rigoureusement méthodique" (1927: 19).

Dans son analyse du *CLG*, dix ans plus tôt, Sechehaye a enchaîné, aussi logiquement que possible, les thèses principales de Saussure. Un simple montage du libellé de ces thèses montre les rapports qu'il a tenus pour pertinents: "Dans l'ensemble mal déterminé des phénomènes que l'on désigne sous le nom de langage, il faut distinguer deux choses: la langue et la parole" (1917: 11); "la langue n'est qu'un cas particulier [...] d'un cas général, et les problèmes qui la concernent doivent être considérés avant tout comme des problèmes de sémiologie" (12–13); "toute sémiologie est essentiellement une science des valeurs" (p. 13); "la quatrième thèse [...] affirme le caractère solidaire, c'est-à-dire strictement *différentiel*, des valeurs linguistiques" (p. 16); "la langue [...] est dans sa nature la plus essentielle une combinaison arbitraire de sens et de sons [...]. Par ce qu'elle contient d'arbitraire, la langue échappe aux prises de l'esprit; ce n'est pas une organisation qu'il puisse modifier [...]. Par contre, et pour la même raison, les éléments qui entrent dans la constitution de la langue sont très susceptibles d'être affectés par des agents quelconques, étrangers au mécanisme de la langue" (p. 22); "il y a deux problèmes linguistiques: le problème synchronique, qui concerne les états de la langue [...] et le problème diachronique, qui concerne les transformations dont toutes les parties de la langue sont le théâtre. Le savant ne confondra jamais ces deux ordres de questions, qui sont par nature étrangères et irréductibles les unes aux autres" (p. 23); "la langue est à chaque moment un état fortuit de cette combinaison arbitraire des sons et des idées qui la constitue" (p. 25).

Plus tard, Sechehaye insiste pourtant sur la différence qu'il y a entre son point de vue systématique et celui de Saussure: "Le *Cours de Linguistique générale* ne tire de ses distinctions aucun principe de classement rigoureux et met plutôt en évidence les relations de réciprocité qui s'établissent entre les divers aspects du fait linguistique. Ainsi pour Ferdinand de Saussure la langue existe pour la parole, mais elle naît aussi de la parole [...], et rien ne nous force à mettre l'une devant l'autre ou au-dessus de l'autre. C'est un complexe que seule l'abstraction analyse. Pour nous, au contraire, dans cette abstraction même nous apercevons un principe de subordination et de classement et nous mettons la parole, sous sa forme prégrammaticale, avant la langue. Il en est ainsi sur tous les points, et nous croyons toujours qu'il doit en être ainsi" (Sechehaye 1926a: 219).

4.2. Langage, langue et parole

Qu'est-ce que Sechehaye entend en 1926 par 'parole'? D'une part, il s'agit encore, comme en 1908, de toute manifestation expressive, quelle qu'elle soit, servant à la communication. Sous son aspect prégrammatical, cela se définit comme "un langage sans règle", par exemple lorsque "l'homme improvise la mimique, le geste ou les sons qui lui semblent les plus propres à faire entendre par intuition ce qu'il veut dire" (1908a: 69), en recourant au "moyen naturel d'expression" (p. 70); c'est la "parole sous sa forme prégrammaticale" de 1926. D'autre part, il s'agit de l'activité langagière ordinaire, organisée par la grammaire, "le *langage organisé*, c'est-à-dire celui où l'élément grammatical entre pour quelque chose" (1908: 70), la "parole organisée" de 1926 (p. 220).

Une comparaison chère à l'auteur montre comment il conçoit la différence entre les deux aspects de la parole: "*Prégrammatical* et *extragrammatical* ne diffèrent que par l'absence ou la présence d'une relation avec la grammaire, c'est comme la chimie prise en dehors de la vie organique ou observée chez elle. La vie en se manifestant au sein de la matière, ne change rien aux affinités ou aux propriétés physiques de celle-ci; elle les fait seulement servir à ses propres fins. De même, l'être psychologique qui se crée ou qui acquiert une grammaire, ne subit aucune modification essentielle dans sa nature. Toutes les lois qui pouvaient présider à son langage spontané subsistent; elles se réalisent seulement dans des conditions qui ont été modifiées par un agent nouveau, dont le principe est en dehors d'elles" (p. 70−71). Cette même comparaison revient dans la contribution de Sechehaye aux *Mélanges Saussure* (1908b: 173) − dans cet article bien surprenant, qui consiste en une analyse de la stylistique de Bally et de la linguistique théorique de l'auteur et constitue un véritable manifeste publicitaire *pro domo* (j'ai signalé naguère [Amacker 1992: 68−69] que Sechehaye s'y montrait assez condescendant à l'égard de Bally; aux textes que je citais, on ajoutera par exemple celui auquel je renvoie ici même).

En 1926, Sechehaye complète donc le dispositif théorique de *Programme et méthodes* par la 'science de la parole'. Mais le fait qu'il reconnaît ne pas avoir eu une "conception claire" de cette science "comme lien nécessaire entre la connaissance des états de langue et celle des évolutions" (1926a: 220) n'implique pas qu'il ait ignoré 'parole' en 1908; il pourrait y avoir du reste là une manifestation de l'influence privée de Saussure (qui pourtant n'a présenté l'"opposition de langue et de parole" que dans une leçon du printemps 1907 [Godel 1957: 57, 145]). En effet, on trouve en 1908 plusieurs passages qui semblent correspondre plus ou moins à la teneur des cours de linguistique générale sur cette matière.

Dans le premier passage, 'grammaire' est un avatar de 'langue': "La grammaire existe dans notre vie psychique et physique au même titre que tous les autres facteurs qui concourent à la production de la parole, et c'est pur arbitraire que d'en vouloir faire abstraction" (Sechehaye 1908a: 25). La 'production de la parole', quant à elle, est un acte individuel concret, rapporté au 'système abstrait du langage' (c.à.d. de la langue); à propos de l'injonction non propositionnelle *ici!* (que le locuteur ne distingue pas par une "analyse plus complète de sa pensée" de l'injonction propositionelle *viens!*), Sechehaye précise que, en revanche, "la grammaire fait cette analyse": "C'est dans le système abstrait du langage, et non pas nécessairement dans un acte psychologique isolé de quelque sujet, que se trouvent le principe et la consécration de cette différence" (40−41). Le rapport entre la langue (comme organisme grammatical) et la parole qui la réalise suppose un plein engagement du locuteur: "Le plus parfait organisme grammatical ne saurait à lui seul constituer un langage. Il est seulement à la disposition du sujet parlant, qui en use par un acte de volonté et sous le contrôle de son intelligence. Toute parole suppose donc à côté de la disposition à laquelle elle doit sa forme, l'intervention libre du sujet, sa volonté et son attention, qui seules la réalisent" (p. 52). Bref! les "signes reçus ou symboles", comme Sechehaye les appelle, "existant en idée [c. à. d. abstraitement] en dehors des réalisations concrètes qui se produisent dans la parole, [...] ont une forme stéréotypée moyenne, normale, dont les mots de la langue ne sont que des reproductions plus ou moins parfaites. Etant fixes, ils sont nécessairement dans une certaine mesure conventionnels" (p. 82). En termes psychologisants, on a là l'essentiel de la thèse saussurienne exposée dans sa première leçon du deuxième cours (début novembre 1908, après la publication de *Programme et méthodes*): "Donc *la langue* est un ensemble de conventions nécessaires adoptées par le corps social pour permettre l'usage de la faculté du langage chez les individus. [...] Par la *parole* on désigne l'acte de l'individu réalisant sa faculté au moyen de la convention sociale qu'est la langue" (*CLG/E* unité n° 160; cf. *CLG*, p. 25).

Dans l'article des *Mélanges Saussure*, l'emploi 'saussurien' de parole disparaît en revanche comme terme technique; là où on l'attendrait, Sechehaye emploie maintenant *langage*, *parole* étant le nom générique réservé à l'expression sémiologique au moyen d'un idiome, tandis que *langue* fait son apparition dans une acception déjà quasiment saussurienne: "Il ne faut pas confondre la langue, ensemble de dispositions acquises par un individu, avec le langage, qui est la langue mise en œuvre dans la parole par celui qui possède ces dispositions" (1908b: 183, imprimé en italiques), "principe de distinction" qui permet d'esquisser le "fonctionnement" du langage (ibid.).

Plus précisément encore: "Chaque personne a sa langue, son état grammatical. Une langue, dans le sens ordinaire, est un état moyen [...]. Le *langage*, c'est la langue mise en œuvre; son siège c'est l'individu devenu volontairement actif [...]. Le langage est à chaque moment une création originale, l'application de procédés abstraits et généraux à une fin spéciale [...]" (1908b: 184); ici encore, la rencontre avec Saussure — mais le Saussure du troisième cours — est remarquable: "L'acte social ne peut résider que chez les individus additionnés les uns aux autres, mais comme pour tout fait social, il ne peut être considéré hors de l'individu. Le fait social, ce sera une certaine moyenne qui s'établira, qui ne sera sans doute complète chez aucun individu" (*CLG/E*, unité n° 218–219, du 25 avril 1911; cf. *CLG*, p. 29).

Enfin, dans un article pourtant écrit pendant l'établissement du *CLG* (et qui a bénéficié de la connaissance des notes des étudiants au moins pour la distinction entre langue et parole (cf. Sechehaye 1914: 292, n. 2), Sechehaye recourt à un autre substitut de cette distinction. Il s'agit de 'la grammaire proprement dite', d'une part, et de 'la vie et les individus', d'autre part, dans la remarque suivante, relative aux limites "que la syntaxe descriptive ne doit pas chercher à franchir" et aux "conflits de règles": "Contentons-nous [...] d'énoncer les principes [c. à. d. les règles] évidents, en nous remettant à la vie et aux individus pour tout ce qui échappe à la grammaire proprement dite" (1914: 347). En 1926, la même équivalence est bien entendu mise sous l'égide du *CLG*: "Avec F. de Saussure [cf. *CLG*, p. 185] nous employons le terme de *grammaire* dans son sens le plus général. La grammaire est pour nous tout ce qui concerne l'organisation de la langue, sons, lexique, syntaxe" (Sechehaye 1926a: 4).

4.3. La langue comme auxiliaire de la parole

Je ne saurais quitter la question du rapport entre la langue et la parole sans mentionner que, pour Sechehaye, la langue est comme une émanation régulatrice de la parole, issue de la parole. La première manifestation de cette idée se trouve dans *Programme et méthodes*: "La vie se manifeste en faisant servir à ses fins les propriétés physiques ou chimiques de la matière. [...] Exactement de même, la grammaire ne naît et n'existe qu'en vertu des phénomènes prégrammaticaux qu'elle a su s'asservir; *elle est comme une déformation particulière du langage prégrammatical*" (1908a: 71). Plus de vingt ans plus tard, cette idée se précise: "La langue n'est qu'une règle selon laquelle nous organisons notre parole pour nous faire mieux comprendre, et la parole, qui comporte l'utilisation personnelle de la langue, comporte aussi des facteurs d'expression qui lui sont propres, c'est-à-dire des procédés naturels du langage spontané. Sans ces procédés qui s'adressent uniquement à l'intuition, la langue elle-même serait impuissante" (1930: 353–354). "Dans le parler animé de la vie courante [...] le caractère auxiliaire de l'organisation grammaticale éclate avec évidence et les mots ne disent eux-mêmes qu'une partie restreinte de ce que la situation ou le geste permettent de comprendre" (p. 354).

Dans cette interprétation, "la langue [...] marque plutôt le chemin, comme le feraient une série de poteaux indicateurs placés aux points les plus nécessaires" (ibid.). Quelques années plus tard, une image tout à fait semblable vient illustrer la même thèse: "Dans la parole courante [...] le signe conventionnel n'est jamais qu'un appoint du langage naturel et les mots ne disent par eux-mêmes qu'une partie de ce que la phrase est destinée à transmettre. Ce sont comme des jalons sur une route: une même route peut être jalonnée de diverses façons. [...] L'expression [...] peut donc représenter la même idée de bien des façons différentes. [...] Ces énoncés, tels qu'ils sont, avec leur diversité, sont suffisamment clairs par eux-mêmes en fonction de la situation où ils sont employés" (1933: 71).

L'importance du contexte est telle, pour Sechehaye, qu'elle lui inspire une hypothèse cognitive, à l'occasion d'une petite digression sociolinguistique: "Ce qui sépare les hommes parlant des langues différentes, ou même parlant la même langue, ce n'est pas leur langage: ce sont les différences de développement intellectuel, d'habitudes, de culture, d'expérience, d'éducation. Voilà la barrière infranchissable souvent qui empêche une réelle intercommunication, parce que l'intuition, travaillant avec des données entièrement diverses, ne saurait aboutir à des résultats concordants. Ce n'est pas l'adoption par les divers parleurs d'une langue commune, même admirablement organisée pour le service d'une pensée logique et claire, qui les rapprochera. Donnez-leur le temps plutôt de se connaître [...]" (p. 72).

En 1940, enfin, la thèse en question se présente comme directement opposée à l'enseignement de Saussure; se référant au passage du *CLG* qui affirme l'"interdépendance de la langue et de la parole" (p. 37), Sechehaye y voit l'effet de "ce goût pour les formules paradoxales qui, en d'autres occasions, l'a admirablement servi" (1940: 6); ici pourtant, "le maître s'est [...] laissé induire en erreur" (ibid.): "En réalité la parole est une chose qui logiquement, et souvent aussi pratiquement, précède la langue et le phénomène linguistique dans le sens saussurien du terme" (p. 8). Précisément: "Si la langue est née de la parole, à aucun moment la parole ne naît de la langue; il n'y a pas de réciprocité. La parole s'organise seulement plus ou moins selon les règles de la langue qu'elle a elle-même créées afin de devenir plus claire et plus efficace" (ibid.). La boucle est bouclée; nous retrouvons ici la thèse même que Sechehaye avait soutenue en 1926 (citée ci-dessus, § 4.1, fin).

4.4. Le système et sa nature

La notion de système, si nettement articulée au niveau théorique quand il s'agit des rapports mutuels entre les sciences du langage, n'a pas la même fermeté quand il s'agit des rapports mutuels entre les entités de la langue. Sechehaye mentionne, outre le "système grammatical" (1914: 347), le "système abstrait du langage" (1908a: 40); en vertu de l'équivalence entre la *langue* saussurienne et la *grammaire* de Sechehaye, c'est bien du système linguistique qu'il s'agit quand ce dernier, après avoir dit, à propos de l'évolution des langues, que "la grammaire est moins logique dans ses transformations que dans ses systèmes", admet que "l'histoire du passé [...] éclaire d'une lumière spéciale le système grammatical d'aujourd'hui [...] mais elle n'explique pas le système ni l'état actuel des règles dans ce système" (1914: 344). Or non seulement toutes les régularités relèvent bien sûr du système en vertu de "l'analogie générale de la langue" (p. 350), mais aussi les "anomalies et exceptions, en tant qu'elles font partie d'un *système synchronique d'expression*, doivent être sinon expliquées, du moins démontrées admissibles à l'intérieur de ce système par le jeu du système lui-même" (301–302).

Comment Sechehaye conçoit-il la constitution du système linguistique? Avant les leçons du *CLG*, on trouve bien peu de chose; la valeur, par exemple, n'est encore que la contre-partie sémantique des sons. Ainsi, après que la science s'est livrée à l'étude exclusive "des sons et des formes déterminées par leur qualité matérielle", "un courant assez puissant porte les linguistes du côté des études de sémantique et de syntaxe": "On comprend que la grammaire comparée [...] a besoin d'être doublée d'une science des valeurs" (1908a: 18).

Les oppositions sont un peu mieux représentées. Ainsi, dans la version intégrale en français de sa thèse sur "L'imparfait du subjonctif et ses concurrents dans les hypothétiques normales en français" (1905[1902]), la notion même de concurrent suppose déjà l'opposition et la définition relative des éléments linguistiques concernés. Sechehaye, tout à son intention de mener une étude historique, a découvert chemin faisant l'importance du phénomène en question: "C'est en faisant ce travail [...] que nous nous sommes rendu compte de l'énorme importance qu'avait pour la connaissance et la compréhension des destinées d'un élément de syntaxe la connaissance de ses relations avec ses concurrents" (1905 [1902]: 322). Faute de témoignage plus précis, il est impossible de déterminer la source de ce qui pourrait apparaître comme une influence privée des leçons de Saussure que Sechehaye avait suivies une dizaine d'années auparavant.

Le système phonologique est sans doute la partie du phénomène linguistique qui, chez Saussure lui-même, a été le plus tôt reconnue dans ses propriétés sémiologiques propres (cette reconnaissance remonte au moins au *Mémoire* de 1878). Sechehaye lui accorde aussi, dès 1908, des qualités — notamment la nature non matérielle — qui rappellent Saussure: "Chaque langue suppose un *système phonologique*, c'est-à-dire une collection d'idées ou si l'on aime mieux, de représentations de sons. Ce système phonologique fait partie de sa grammaire; il correspond à une disposition physiologique acquise" (p. 151). Plus loin il affirme: "Le phonème n'existe réellement qu'à titre d'idée ou de représentation. C'est un type moyen auquel on assimile tout ce que l'on entend, et auquel on se conforme plus ou moins exactement dans l'articulation réelle. Les sons varient donc [...]. Leur qualité, leur tonalité, leur quantité subissent des modifications dont l'importance n'est limitée que par les exigences du langage. Il faut qu'il reste intelligible, il faut donc que les phonèmes gardent suffisamment leurs caractères différentiels pour que les symboles qu'ils composent soient reconnaissables" (1908a: 201–202, avec renvoi à la p. 155).

La préfiguration de la dualité langue abstraite (comme *type*) — parole concrète (comme *token*) est clairement identifiable dans ce dernier texte; elle se présente pour les phonèmes tout comme pour le fonctionnement général de l'activité langagière: "Chaque phonème est dans la parole vivante, comme cette parole elle-même, une résultante. A côté de sa qualité grammaticale, il a une qualité extragrammaticale d'ordre affectif" (1908a: 202). Peut-on attribuer ce passage à l'influence privée de Saussure? A cause de la terminologie, la réponse est difficile.

En revanche, cette influence me semble nettement plus probable dans le texte suivant, qui concerne le "système phonologique" lui-même: "Il constitue lui aussi une 'forme' dans le sens où nous avons entendu ce terme, car on peut concevoir le système phonologique sous son aspect algébrique et remplacer les trente, cinquante ou cent éléments qui le composent dans une langue donnée, par autant de symboles généraux qui fixent leur individualité, mais non pas leur caractère matériel" (1908a: 151). On songe immédiatement à la phrase du *CLG* selon laquelle "la langue est pour ainsi dire une algèbre qui n'aurait que des termes complexes" (*CLG*, p. 168).

La même conception élémentaire de concurrence entre termes significatifs, telle qu'elle était brièvement signalée en 1905 apparaît encore en 1914, le phénomène étant alors différencié en "concurrence respectueuse" (p. 341) — par exemple entre l'indicatif imparfait et l'indicatif passé défini (passé simple) en français, qui s'opposent vraiment l'un à l'autre — et "rivalité" (p. 342) — par exemple entre le passé défini et le passé indéfini (passé composé), quasi-synonymes dont le second a éliminé le premier dans la langue parlée. C'est dans ce cadre que Sechehaye introduit explicitement le terme d'opposition; signalant que "l'absence d'article" est l'un des "concurrents respectueux" de l'article, il se justifie par ces mots: "Car l'absence de symbole est aussi un symbole par opposition" (341–342). Mais la terminologie n'est évidemment pas fixée; dans la même page, c'est 'contraste' qui apparaît à la place d'opposition: "La valeur d'un mot est faite en bonne partie des contrastes qu'elle offre avec les mots voisins. Tous les dictionnaires de synonymes en font foi" (p. 342). Rien de tout cela ne semble typiquement saussurien.

Ce même texte proclame hautement l'unité de la valeur; dans toute description, "il faut partir de ce postulat que tout symbole a une signification. *Une* signification, disons-nous, et non pas plusieurs. Ce principe, si souvent violé [...], n'en est pas moins l'âme de la grammaire" (1914: 294). Par ailleurs, les emplois possibles d'un élément linguistique y sont décrits comme des solidarités que l'évolution peut défaire: "Quand un symbole est utilisé en dehors de sa définition, il faut pour que cet emploi soit consacré d'une façon durable par l'usage [...] qu'il choisisse entre deux alternatives: ou bien il doit se désolidariser complètement du cas normal, devenir un symbole homonyme mais distinct [...]; ou bien il faut qu'il garde un contact de solidarité avec le symbole pris selon sa définition, qu'il paraisse en être une variante, [...] et qu'en vertu de cette solidarité il devienne à son tour un élément de la définition générale" (p. 300). Cette même conception du regroupement de sens multiples en une valeur unique "se constate facilement avec les mots, dont les significations évoluent et se fraction-nent de la même façon [que celles des éléments syntaxiques] dans le temps, tout en ayant la même tendance à se grouper à chaque moment dans le système en un ou plusieurs faisceaux solidaires" (ibid.).

Quand Sechehaye parle, en 1908, des associations, il ne s'agit probablement que du phénomène psychologique; décrivant l'activité des "psychologues de l'école nouvelle", il écrit en effet: "On étudia par exemple les phénomènes qui accompagnaient l'aperception des mots sous leur forme auditive ou graphique, et les associations complexes qui constituent ou accompagnent ces éléments de nos phrases" (1908a: 19), texte où il serait peut-être admissible néanmoins d'interpréter "constituent ou accompagnent" comme une allusion vague à ce qui allait être pour le *CLG* les rapports associatifs (qui 'constituent' les mots) et syntagmatiques (qui, définis *in praesentia*, 'accompagnent', si l'on veut, les mots dans le discours) — mais c'est là une hypothèse bien fragile tout de même.

4.5. La théorie du signe

La théorie du signe linguistique, elle non plus, ne présente pas grand-chose de saussurien avant le travail sur le *CLG* — ni même durablement après 1916. On a vu à plusieurs reprises déjà le terme aristotélicien de symbole. Pour Sechehaye, le sujet parlant peut soit créer son signe, c'est-à-dire un moyen d'expression affectif non grammatical, soit se servir d'un signe reçu intellectuel et grammatical, qui est le symbole (1908a: 80). Le symbole a deux faces, le 'signe' et sa 'valeur', tous deux de nature idéale; une fois cette unité bifaciale constituée, "à la place d'un signe nous avons un *symbole*, c'est-à-dire *l'idée d'un signe associée à une idée de valeur*, ce que l'on pourrait représenter par la formule:

$$\text{idée } a = \text{signe } b.$$

Voilà l'acte primordial dont toute grammaire découle" (p. 81; comme on le voit, 'signe' a une polysémie extraordinaire).

L'auteur a soin d'insister sur le caractère indissociable des deux faces du symbole; il y a là une conception qui peut certes venir de la lecture de Humboldt (cf. Humboldt 1963 [1836]: 426), mais qui traduit plus probablement une influence saussurienne privée: "On ne peut pas dans l'analyse de la parole séparer le contenant, c'est-à-dire la forme, le procédé, du contenu, c'est-à-dire la valeur. Il y a solidarité entre ces deux aspects du phénomène. Le parallélisme psychophysiologique demeure un principe absolu et nous présente une seule chose dont nous voyons les deux faces. La pensée sans sa forme et la forme sans sa pensée n'intéressent plus la linguistique. Ce qui resterait après cette opération d'analyse ne serait rien pour elle; l'objet même de son étude serait détruit" (1908a: 110).

On croirait lire une paraphrase anticipatrice du *CLG*: "Abstraction faite de son expression par les mots, notre pensée n'est qu'une masse amorphe et indistincte. […] La substance phonique n'est pas plus fixe ni plus rigide" (*CLG*, p. 155); "dans la langue, on ne saurait isoler ni le son de la pensée, ni la pensée du son; on n'y arriverait que par une abstraction dont le résultat serait de faire de la psychologie pure ou de la phonologie [c.à.d. de la phonétique, au sens moderne] pure" (*CLG*, p. 157).

Pourtant, ce n'est pas comme rapport entre le contenu et l'expression que Sechehaye comprend le rapport entre la pensée (ou valeur) et la forme: "Mais si la forme et la valeur sont inséparables et ne constituent aux yeux du linguiste qu'une seule et même chose, on peut opposer cette chose à un autre élément de langage dont la nature et le rôle sont entièrement différents: nous voulons parler des sons, des éléments articulatoires, de la matière en un mot dans laquelle cette forme se réalise" (1908a: 110). On voit qu'il s'agit, certes, d'une distinction entre entité abstraite et réalisation concrète, mais — par une asymétrie dont il va encore être question — d'une distinction entre le caractère abstrait du contenu et le caractère concret de l'expression: "Ce monde des idées qui est le substitut du monde extérieur, ne saurait exister dans l'intelligence sans un lexique correspondant, comprenant des mots d'une qualité matérielle quelconque mais suffisamment différenciés entre eux. En théorie cependant, on peut concevoir cette forme de la pensée qui est en même temps une forme de la grammaire, en dehors du lexique particulier dans lequel elle se réalise. […] Au lieu de *cheval* rien n'empêche d'imaginer une autre combinaison de signes articulatoires, ou même de n'en imaginer aucune et de penser seulement un symbole algébrique, un *a* ou un *x* qui serait le substitut abstrait et général du signe quelconque dans lequel cette idée se réalise" (111–112).

Cette conception me semble constituer une forme subtile de nomenclaturisme, qui, en conséquence de l'asymétrie dont j'ai parlé, entraîne la dissociation des deux faces du signe. Je m'explique. Pour Saussure, c'est "l'accouplement de la pensée avec la matière phonique" qui "produit une forme, non une substance" (*CLG*, pp. 156, 157); c'est donc le signe tout entier, signifiant et signifié, qui est forme abstraite dans la langue, et c'est cette forme qui se réalise tout entière, sur le double plan de l'expression et du contenu, dans la

$$\frac{\text{signifié}}{\text{signifiant}} \rightarrow \frac{\text{sens concrets}}{\text{sons concrets}}$$

Saussure

La preuve que cette interprétation est correcte se tire du passage suivant: "Nous admettons donc qu'il y a une forme abstraite du langage organisé qui est la forme même de la pensée, et qu'il y a des sons conventionnels par lesquels cette forme abstraite se réalise, comme une forme géométrique se réalise dans une matière quelconque" (1908a: 122).

Il se peut même que ce soit justement cette asymétrie qui ait gêné Saussure: "Plus l'auteur prend de peine à abattre ce qui lui semble une barrière illégitime entre la forme pensée [*sic*; lire 'linguistique'?] et la pensée, plus il nous semble s'éloigner de son propre but, qui serait de fixer le champ de l'expression, et d'en concevoir les lois [...] dans ce qu'elles ont [...] de spécifique, et d'absolument unique, dans le phénomène de la langue" (N 21 = *CLG/E* II, p. 43b, n° 3330,6).

A cause même de cette asymétrie, la place de l'arbitraire – au sens traditionnel du mot – se trouve évidemment limitée à la seule face expressive de la langue; Sechehaye est péremptoire: "*Il n'y a en grammaire* [c. à. d. dans la langue] *convention, c'est-à-dire choix arbitraire, que là où il s'agit de déterminer la qualité matérielle des mots* [= sémantèmes] *et des signes* [= morphèmes] *qui sont nécessaires au lexique et au mécanisme grammatical*" (1908a: 120–121).

De cette manière, l'auteur en arrive à concevoir deux études séparées, concernant ce qui pour Saussure constitue les deux faces inséparables du signe, et qu'il appelle la "morphologie générale", autrement dit l'étude de la forme au sens défini ci-dessus (réservée à ce titre au contenu), et la "science des sons" (1908a: 122). Ces deux disciplines sont en principe organisées de la même manière: "Ce que la morphologie statique fait pour la forme du langage, la phonologie doit le faire pour ses éléments matériels, pour sa convention, afin que le langage

parole, comme sens et comme sons concrets. Mais pour Sechehaye, la forme ne concerne que le contenu, l'expression étant considérée comme la matière indifférente correspondante. A ce qui peut être conçu chez Saussure comme une relation horizontale entre les faces du signe abstrait et leurs réalisations concrètes, Sechehaye substitue une relation verticale entre les deux faces du symbole:

"forme abstraite" (forme)
↓
"signes articulatoires" (matière)

Sechehaye

concret tout entier soit rationnellement expliqué" (p. 150); mais elles sont sans rapport l'une avec l'autre: "C'est donc une science [la morphologie statique] de la forme qui existe en dehors de la qualité des sons, et qui en est entièrement indépendante" (p. 172). On ne saurait être moins saussurien.

Autre conséquence de la disymétrie signalée: la dualité du symbole que Sechehaye envisage est celle de la forme de la pensée mise en regard de la forme grammaticale, et non pas la dualité du signifié mis en regard du signifiant (cela explique peut-être pourquoi Sechehaye n'utilise sauf erreur jamais après 1916 le couple signifié – signifiant); elle se place sur le seul plan du contenu: "Le problème que doit résoudre la morphologie statique semble pouvoir se formuler en ces termes: *comment peut-on, par des symboles de l'ordre articulatoire [...], construire quelque chose dont la suite et la forme correspondent à la suite et à la forme de la pensée?*" (1908a: 142). "Cette science [...] construit avec des symboles des équivalents de pensée, et c'est là essentiellement *un problème de logique*. Mais il s'agit, bien entendu, d'une logique pratique [...] et qui dépend des formes et des conditions de la vie psychologique tout entière" (p. 144); bref! "le principe d'explication rationnelle que cette science fournit pour l'intelligence du phénomène linguistique, est la conformité de la grammaire aux dispositions psychologiques du sujet parlant. L'homme ne peut créer ou adopter en fait de grammaire que ce qui répond aux tendances constantes de son activité psychique" (p. 148), de sorte que "la grammaire est une logique pratique et appliquée" (p. 104).

Dix-huit ans plus tard, dix ans après la publication du *CLG*, Sechehaye formule comme il suit la même bipartition, en se référant explicitement à *Programme et méthodes*:

"Quant à la nécessité de séparer en général et spécialement en grammaire statique l'étude des valeurs de celle des formes et de mettre les valeurs en première ligne comme étant logiquement déterminantes, nous avons essayé d'établir ce point dans notre ouvrage précédent" (1926a: 223). Et il s'agit bien de séparer les deux constituants de la dualité. En effet, à l'*Essai sur la structure logique de la phrase*, qui forme le premier volet de la discipline, devait faire suite un ouvrage sur la 'morphologie statique'; Sechehaye présente du reste l'*Essai* en ces termes: "Nous venons nous acquitter ici d'une promesse faite il y a longtemps. Encore ne tenons-nous qu'une partie de notre engagement, car nous n'abordons que les questions concernant les idées, c'est-à-dire la logique et la psychologie de la phrase, en laissant de côté l'aspect formel du problème grammatical" (1926a: 3).

4.6. La grammaire syntagmatique

Toujours dans l'*Essai*, on voit apparaître les termes saussuriens d'associatif et de syntagmatique, mais employés dans des acceptions très particulières. Pour les comprendre, il faut d'abord examiner comment Sechehaye considère les faits syntaxiques et leur rapport aux faits systémiques. Avant d'avoir pris connaissance de la critique de 'symbole' (cf. *CLG*, p. 101 et Sechehaye 1926a: 220), Sechehaye appelait 'symbolique' la théorie du signe simple; pour commencer, il l'opposait, à l'intérieur de la morphologie statique, aux "procédés d'expression" ou aux "mécanismes grammaticaux" du "symbole articulé" (1908a: 143, 144), qu'il désigne aussi comme le "mécanisme syntactique d'une langue" (pp. 30, 114). C'est seulement en 1914 qu'il introduit le terme de syntaxe en ce sens: "La Syntaxe, c'est pour nous *l'ensemble des faits qui concernent l'expression de la pensée par des combinaisons conventionnelles de signes arbitraires ou symboles*" (1914: 289), la syntaxe étant emboîtée dans la symbolique et constituant avec elle la grammaire, toujours au sens de langue (cf. p. 290). Après 1916, il a dû changer de terminologie; pour désigner l'étude des signes simples, comme *sémantique*, *sémasiologie* ou *sémiologie* étaient déjà réservés, il s'est emparé de la distinction entre syntagmes et associations: la symbolique devient la "grammaire associative", et la syntaxe, la "grammaire syntagmatique" (1926a: 220–221).

Ici encore, j'ai peur que, sous les termes saussuriens, ne se trouve une conception propre à l'auteur. En effet, pour lui, la grammaire associative concerne les sémantèmes, et la grammaire syntagmatique, les morphèmes. L'objet de la grammaire syntagmatique, "ce ne sont pas tous les syntagmes (toutes les successions de signes), mais tous les signes qui n'existent que par et pour les syntagmes" (1926a: 221). Au nombre des exemples, il mentionne "les termes de liaison et de combinaison: verbe copule, prépositions, conjonctions, suffixes, indices divers", ainsi que "des signes qui sont constitués par la seule position réciproque des termes; ce sont les règles d'ordonnance et de construction" (ibid.).

Cette conception, qui répartit curieusement des éléments de la chaîne du discours dans les deux domaines de l'associatif et du syntagmatique, débouche nécessairement sur la confusion des deux domaines: "Il ne faudrait pas croire que la distinction entre ce qui est associatif et ce qui est syntagmatique soit toujours aisée à faire" (1926a: 221–222). Ce n'est pas que Sechehaye ait tort de considérer que les 'unités concrètes' (pour parler comme Saussure) se catégorisent diversement dans la langue; la difficulté naît du fait que, s'il a sans doute compris la différence entre la théorie du signe en général et les spécificités du signe linguistique articulé, il a cru pouvoir interpréter cette différence de points de vue (sémiologique et proprement linguistique) en fonction de la dualité associations ~ syntagmes, qui relève du proprement linguistique.

Je dois bien reconnaître que, quatre ans plus tard, la conception est peut-être plus régulièrement saussurienne. "*La phrase ne se constitue pas uniquement par les rapports de succession qu'elle établit entre des unités expressives* (rapports syntagmatiques), *mais elle fait appel aussi à d'autres rapports qui existent uniquement dans la pensée* (rapports associatifs)" (Sechehaye 1930: 346). Néanmoins, "dire qu'un signe [il s'agit des sémantèmes] est purement différentiel, c'est dire qu'il fonctionne en vertu des rapports associatifs seuls à l'exclusion des autres" (p. 347): la même répartition des sémantèmes et des morphèmes que dans l'*Essai* reprend le dessus, Sechehaye réservant toujours la considération des deux sortes de rapports aux seuls outils grammaticaux: "Tous ces éléments de la grammaire qui ne fonctionnent jamais d'une façon autonome et qui sont parasites des éléments auxquels ils sont joints [les sémantèmes] ne deviennent agissants que par un jeu d'oppositions avec d'autres syntagmes où ils entrent également ou bien dans lesquels ils alternent avec d'autres formatifs [morphèmes]" (ibid.).

Tout cela illustre bien à quel point on doit être attentif à ne pas se laisser tromper, chez Sechehaye, par l'usage des termes saussuriens; presque toujours, il les emploie dans des acceptions qui lui sont propres. D'ailleurs, il désigne aussi les deux sortes de rapports par des termes qui rappellent ceux que Frei avait employés l'année précédente dans la *Grammaire des fautes* (cf. Frei [1929: 33] "rapports discursifs" et "rapports mémoriels"); en passant, Sechehaye mentionne, en effet, les "rapports associatifs ou mnémiques" (1930: 346) et "l'aspect discursif et syntagmatique du fait grammatical" (p. 347).

4.7. Rôles des sujets parlants

L'activité langagière implique en principe un émetteur et un récepteur. On se rappelle que Bally avait signalé, en 1921, que "les sujets parlants et les sujets entendants n'ont pas la même attitude dans l'exercice de la parole" (cité ci-dessus § 3.4, début). Sechehaye est revenu plusieurs fois sur la différence qu'il y a entre les interlocuteurs. Sans reprendre l'ensemble du dossier (cf. Amacker 1988), je cite seulement le passage le plus caractéristique de *Programme et méthodes*: "Pour attribuer à un signe une valeur grammaticale, pour y voir un symbole, il n'est pas nécessaire que ce symbole existe déjà dans ma grammaire à moi. Je le crée en attribuant à celui que j'entends la grammaire dont je crois reconnaître les éléments dans sa parole: c'est un phénomène d'intuition, et cette grammaire, qui au fond est de mon invention, je l'adopte pour moi-même en me basant sur l'autorité de la personne à laquelle je l'ai gratuitement attribuée" (1908a: 165).

C'est le processus même de l'invention du symbole: "Comment le symbole apparaît-il pour la première fois? Evidemment en vertu d'une création inconsciente semblable à celles qui se trouvent à l'origine de toutes les évolutions morphologiques. C'est en s'appliquant à comprendre le langage des autres, et en interprétant les signes naturels prégrammaticaux dont ils se servent, que l'individu en est venu pour la première fois à voir dans certains sons ou dans certains gestes le correspondant objectif et constant de certaines idées. Le signe se transforme en symbole; la grammaire naît" (1908a: 217).

Cette grammaire embryonnaire est d'abord tout individuelle. Ce n'est qu'en second lieu qu'elle se généralise "dans la concurrence qui naît au sein du parler commun entre toutes les grammaires individuelles. La grammaire collective est à la fois une résultante et une moyenne" (1908a: 218). Mais la grammaire collective, qui fixe la langue, est instable: "En effet cette fixation du symbole n'est jamais que relative et n'est à aucun moment quelque chose d'acquis définitivement" (ibid.). De sa création à sa disparition, "le symbole est constamment resté dans la circulation. Ceux qui en ont fait usage l'ont reçu du dehors et proposé à d'autres dans une succession de phénomènes [...] analogues à ceux qui avaient présidé à sa naissance" (ibid.).

L'intervention particulière du sujet entendant est ici essentielle: "Chaque fois que ce symbole a été employé et qu'il a dû être admis par un autre, il a pu se produire un de ces actes de création inconsciente qui fait que le symbole tel qu'il a été compris et adopté, n'est pas tout à fait identique au symbole dont le sujet parlant s'était servi; et chacune de ces modifications individuelles lancée dans la circulation a été proposée à la collectivité qui l'a repoussée ou admise, comme elle repousse ou admet un symbole naissant" (Sechehaye 1908a: 218−219).

La circulation des symboles − c'est-à-dire des signes − rappelle le "circuit de la parole" de Saussure (*CLG*, pp. 27−28), mais avec une différence importante. Pour Saussure, en effet, les deux interlocuteurs sont parfaitement symétriques, tandis que pour Sechehaye, l'asymétrie entre eux est un principe constamment répété. Le rôle créateur de l'interprète, qui repose sur l'intuition d'autrui, fait toutefois écho, chez lui, à une idée analogue exprimée fugitivement par Saussure des années plus tôt, dans une de ses notes *Item*: "En me promenant, je fais sans rien dire une encoche sur un arbre, comme par plaisir. La personne qui m'accompagne garde l'idée de cette encoche, et il est incontestable qu'elle associe deux ou trois idées à cette encoche dès ce moment, alors que je n'avais moi-même d'autre idée que de la mystifier ou de m'amuser. − Toute chose matérielle est déjà pour nous *signe*: c'est-à-dire impression que nous associons à d'autres, mais la chose matérielle paraît indispensable" (N 15, *Item* 15.4 = *CLG/E* II, p. 40a, n° 3320.4).

4.8. Linguistique de la parole

Dans "le système des disciplines linguistiques" qu'il schématise en 1926 (voir plus haut), Sechehaye accorde une place centrale à "la science de la parole comme lien nécessaire entre la connaissance des états de langue et celle des évolutions" (1926a: 221–222). Bally et lui-même l'avaient signalé en 1916, dans leur préface au *CLG*: "L'absence d'une 'linguistique de la parole' est plus sensible. Promise aux auditeurs du troisième cours, cette étude aurait eu sans doute une place d'honneur dans les suivants" (*CLG*, p. 10). Il faut attendre 1940 pour voir Sechehaye réunir ses idées à ce propos, en les opposant, sous le titre de "linguistique de la parole organisée ou du fonctionnement de la langue" (1940: 17), à la "linguistique synchronique ou des états de langue" (p. 11), d'une part, et à la "linguistique diachronique ou des évolutions de la langue" (p. 30), d'autre part, comme la science du concret entre deux sciences de l'abstrait. Là encore, malgré le saussurisme proclamé, la pensée de l'auteur reste attachée à ses conceptions originales; imaginer la langue comme un ensemble de généralités abstraites par approximation du concret de la parole, notamment, n'est pas du tout conforme aux thèses essentielles du *CLG* telles que nous les comprenons aujourd'hui. Or Sechehaye dit justement: "L'objet propre de la linguistique de la parole organisée est d'une tout autre nature que l'objet de la linguistique statique. Tandis que cette dernière travaille nécessairement sur des généralités extraites par abstraction et par approximation du concret, la linguistique de la parole s'intéresse au contraire aux phénomènes concrets, aux actes dans lesquels la langue est mise au service de la pensée, avec tout ce qui fait de chacun d'eux un phénomène occasionnel différent de n'importe quel autre phénomène" (1940: 17).

La définition même de la parole, en revanche, est partiellement saussurienne, notamment en sa qualité d'exécution: "Chacun de ces actes surgit [...] dans un lieu et un temps déterminé, entre des interlocuteurs ayant chacun sa personnalité et dans un ensemble de circonstances spéciales qui le déterminent" (ibid.). Comme Sechehaye l'avait déjà exprimé plusieurs fois, "la parole se manifeste comme une puissance créatrice" (1940: 17), que ce soit positivement, à la suite d'un "effort intelligent pour adapter les moyens disponibles aux exigences d'une pensée personnelle", ou négativement, par l'action des "facteurs négatifs de l'ignorance, de l'incompréhension et de la négligence": "Quel que soit l'acte accompli par le sujet parlant, il est recueilli tel quel par l'entendeur qui le soumet à son analyse et l'interprète pour le comprendre" (ibid.). Nous retrouvons ici le rôle particulier et essentiel dévolu au récepteur: "L'interprétation, comme la parole active, peut être banale, constructive ou destructive" (17–18).

Du côté de l'entendeur, à l'interprétation s'ajoute le classement; ce sont là deux "opérations [...] simultanées et solidaires" (1940: 18–19). Le classement "touche d'abord au problème de l'identification (je reconnais ou je ne reconnais pas tel mot, tel suffixe, etc.), et il comporte ensuite une constante utilisation et révision du jeu des associations mentales des éléments significatifs entre eux ainsi que des éléments significatifs avec les choses, bref tout ce qui représente en nous le système même de la langue" (p. 19). Sans le terme de valeur, il s'agit bien des deux aspects, oppositionnel et échangeable, de cette dernière.

Mais la 'constante révision' entraîne, par réinterprétation continue, le changement linguistique, la diachronie. En ce sens, 'la science de la parole organisée' est bien au coeur du dispositif sémiologique. C'est ce qu'a bien vu et bien décrit Sechehaye, dont la contribution essentielle au débat saussurien est justement dans sa tentative de dessiner, dans ses grandes lignes, la linguistique de la parole, que Saussure n'a pas eu le temps d'aborder dans ses cours.

4.9. La diachronie

A propos de la diachronie, l'apport de Sechehaye consiste à distinguer entre "évolution organique et évolution contingentielle". La question générale qu'il pose s'exprime en ces termes: "Il s'agit de savoir si la langue évolue selon une impulsion interne qui lui est inhérente et qui participe à sa propre nature, ou si, au contraire, elle subit du dehors, par l'intermédiaire des sujets parlants, des impulsions et des contraintes avec lesquelles elle doit s'accommoder tant bien que mal" (Sechehaye 1939: 23). Tant qu'on prétend défendre une thèse au détriment de l'autre, on ne sort pas de l'"antinomie" (p. 21). La solution de Sechehaye consiste à admettre simultanément les deux points de vue. Se fondant sur la croix du *CLG* (p. 115), où l'état de langue figure comme la branche horizontale AB et le temps comme la branche verticale orientée CD, il dit: "Alors que ce qui pourrait détruire ou mettre en danger l'existence d'un système d'expression se déroule sur CD — dans le temps — c'est sur AB, dans la synchronie (et tout spécialement au point de croisement en O [introduit par Sechehaye], c'est-à-dire *dans la parole*), qu'il faut chercher les forces qui constituent la langue, qui assurent la pérennité de son efficience" (1939: 25). Et de conclure: "Voilà la véritable signification de la doctrine saussurienne sur la séparation de la diachronie et de la synchronie" (ibid.).

Si les forces réparatrices, 'organiques', sont pour l'essentiel fondées sur l'analogie, les forces destructrices sont, non seulement les changements phonétiques, mais aussi toutes les vicissitudes auxquelles sont soumis les sujets parlants. En détournant un peu le sens que l'auteur donne à sa phrase, on peut résumer cette position de la manière suivante: "La grammaire, attaquée par une force aveugle et qui lui paraît étrangère, est de ce fait forcée de procéder constamment à des opérations de sauvetage et de replâtrage pour lesquelles elle a recours à l'analogie, c'est-à-dire à des interventions actives, quoique subconscientes, de la pensée organisatrice" (1939: 24). Autrement dit: "Ce n'est que lorsque le fonctionnement du système expressif se trouve plus ou moins compromis qu'une réaction, d'ailleurs très inconsciente, se fait sentir et que les forces organiques entrent en jeu. Procédant par interprétation et utilisation du donné, elles opèrent tant bien que mal les réparations nécessaires. Ce que la parole, influencée contingentiellement [...], a compromis, la parole, influencée organiquement, le restaure" (p. 28). Sans que Sechehaye la mentionne, il faut signaler ici la contribution d'Henri Frei (1929) à cette question: toute la *Grammaire des fautes* montre comment la langue réagit aux déficits linguistiques.

L'évolution organique est finaliste, la contingentielle, comme son nom l'indique, ne l'est pas. La solution de compromis préconisée par Sechehaye tient compte de cet aspect du problème: "Si les innovations sont [...] des éléments de trouble pour le système grammatical et si les réactions qu'elles provoquent se font en utilisant au mieux [c.à.d. organiquement] les moyens appropriés que la parole trouve *fortuitement* à sa disposition, il en résulte logiquement qu'on pourra bien constater une finalité dans chacune de ces opérations réparatrices [...] mais que toute succession prolongée de faits diachroniques s'enchaînant les uns aux autres sera nécessairement dépourvue de finalité et n'aura aucun développement logique nécessaire" (Sechehaye 1939: 28−29).

Je ne saurais mieux résumer la position de Sechehaye qu'il ne l'a fait lui-même: "On voit que si, contrairement à l'orthodoxie saussurienne, nous réintroduisons sur l'axe du temps, avec les facteurs contingentiels, toute la psychologie de la parole et, avec les facteurs organiques, toutes les forces synchroniques, nous ne supprimons pas pour cela les oppositions auxquelles Saussure tenait tant et qui font la valeur de sa doctrine; nous faisons seulement de cet axe le lieu où entrent en lutte deux forces antagonistes, celle qui conserve le système grammatical et sa tradition fondée sur le consentement collectif et sur sa cohérence, et celle qui l'entraîne au contraire dans de perpétuelles innovations et réadaptations. Nous ne croyons pas trahir notre maître en proposant cette vue, qui n'est que le développement logique de sa pensée dépouillée, à la faveur du temps et de la réflexion, de certains partis pris outranciers que les conditions dans lesquelles le *CLG* a été rédigé expliquent pleinement" (Sechehaye 1940: 30).

4.10. La méthode constructive

Sechehaye s'est peu occupé de description concrète; outre sa thèse (1905 [1902]), il ne s'est placé qu'une fois (sans résultat probant, à mon sens) "devant un problème de grammaire descriptive" (1914: 293), celui de "l'article défini en français moderne" (ibid.). En revanche, Sechehaye a présenté en 1916 la méthode qu'il considérait comme la meilleure, scientifiquement et pédagogiquement: la "méthode constructive", dont il emprunte le principe au Père Grégoire Girard (1765−1850), auteur de l'*Enseignement régulier de la langue maternelle* (1844) et du *Cours éducatif de langue maternelle* (1845−1848), qui faisaient suite à un abrégé de sa méthode publié en 1821 sous le titre de *Grammaire des campagnes* (cf. Sechehaye 1916: 48, n.).

Le problème de Sechehaye, c'est de définir "une méthode qui [...] à l'égard de la langue [...] en respecte scrupuleusement le mécanisme" (1916: 48). Présentant brièvement diverses tentatives, l'auteur conclut: "En se faisant constructive la syntaxe obéit à une véritable nécessité qui sera toujours plus sentie" (p. 50). Voici un échantillon de la démarche (cf. Chevalier 1999: 74−76): "La première pierre de notre édifice syntaxique, ce sera la construction grammaticale à la fois minimale et complète nécessaire pour énoncer un fait: un *sujet* et un *prédicat verbal*, la proposition du type: *l'enfant parle*" (ibid.); "de même que la pensée s'analyse toujours en deux idées au moins, notre proposition est faite du rapprochement de deux termes. Il nous faut les séparer provisoirement et commencer par l'examen du premier, le *substantif sujet* qui est le support logique du second" (p. 52), etc.

Inutile de poursuivre, le lecteur aura compris comment se présente la méthode constructive, que Sechehaye applique encore, quoique à un point de vue différent, dix ans plus tard dans l'*Essai sur la structure logique de la phrase*, ouvrage dans lequel il déclare suivre, autant que faire se peut, "un ordre systématique qui conduit des constructions grammaticales les plus simples aux constructions les plus complexes" (Sechehaye 1926a: 6−7). Quatre ans plus tard, malgré sa propre tentative pédagogique exposée dans l'*Abrégé de grammaire française* (1926b; cf. Chevalier 1999: 76−80), il reconnaît que "l'on attend toujours la grammaire constructive qui examinera dans un ordre progressif les divers types de syntagme et donnera pour chacun les séries associatives qui sont à la base de leur fonctionnement" (1930: 348).

5. Conclusion

Charles Bally et Albert Sechehaye sont les seuls membres importants de l'École genevoise de linguistique qui aient connu personnellement Saussure. Ayant eu bien souvent l'occasion de s'entretenir avec lui, comme ils en témoignent eux-mêmes, ils ont pu mesurer ce que les leçons de linguistique générale avaient de nouveau, relativement à ce qu'il leur avait appris dans ses cours de grammaire comparée et à ce qu'ils avaient retenu de leurs conversations avec lui. Mais chacun d'eux avait forgé sa personnalité scientifique avant que Saussure ait eu l'occasion d'enseigner la linguistique générale, et bien entendu avant que la formule d'École genevoise ait pris, avec la publication du *CLG*, un sens qu'elle n'avait pas quand Bréal s'en est servi pour la première fois en 1894 pour désigner le foyer de grammaire comparée qui s'était créé tout récemment dans la cité de Calvin (la nomination de Saussure à la chaire d'histoire et de comparaison des langues indo-européennes remontait à 1891).

Leur jugement à l'égard des idées saussuriennes en matière de linguistique générale se caractérise donc à la fois par une indéniable familiarité (que seuls les collègues et les élèves parisiens de Saussure partageaient) − qu'on a désignée ici comme la source de l'influence privée que Saussure a sans doute exercée sur eux − et par une distance qui ajoutait, à la difficulté objective de ces idées au moment où elles ont vu le jour, leur souci légitime de poursuivre selon leur tempérament l'œuvre scientifique qu'ils avaient déjà entreprise: "La nécessité de s'assimiler la pensée saussurienne dans toute sa profondeur et dans toute son exactitude leur a donné une occasion magnifique de se former des idées personnelles et fermement assises concernant les principes essentiels de cette science. Ces idées, fondées sur les doctrines de leur maître mais marquées aussi d'un sceau individuel, ils les ont développées, chacun de son côté, et en ont cherché l'application dans des directions variées" (Sechehaye 1927: 4).

On a tenté, dans ces pages, de montrer les effets ou l'absence d'effet, sur leur œuvre, de cette familiarité et de cette distance. Il me semble, à la lumière du réexamen auquel m'a contraint cette synthèse, que l'importance de Sechehaye comme théoricien a été trop longtemps éclipsée par le prestige des interprétations postérieures du *CLG*; depuis les *Sources manuscrites* de Godel (1957), en effet, et la publication de l'édition critique du *CLG* de Rudolf Engler (dès 1968), notre vision du premier demi-siècle de discussion sur les thèses saussuriennes s'est trouvée partiellement faussée par la projection rétrospective de ces interprétations sur celles des commentateurs précédents.

On ne peut certes guère douter que Bally a plutôt poursuivi sans relâche ses ambitions initiales − caractériser le français et analyser les aspects affectifs de la communication linguistique − que vraiment tenté d'y intégrer les idées de Saussure. Un dernier exemple. En 1939, Bally étudie la différence qu'il y a entre les types de signaux que sont le signe délibéré et l'indice naturel. S'il cède à l'usage courant pour abdiquer consciemment l'interprétation saussurienne de signe (cf. Bally 1939: 165, n.), il croit être fidèle au *CLG* à propos de l'arbitraire, alors même qu'il le réduit à la convention pure et simple: "Nous constatons en outre que la notion d'arbitraire recouvre celle de conventionnel (au sens strict). L'emploi d'un signe arbitraire repose, au point de vue statique, sur une convention, une sorte de contrat tacite passé entre les usagers du signe" (p. 169). Près d'un quart de siècle après le *CLG*, le saussurisme de Bally semble bien n'être que de façade.

Il en va tout autrement de Sechehaye. On l'a vu abandonner 'symbole' pour 'signe' afin de se conformer à la doctrine du *CLG*; on l'a vu critiquer telle ou telle thèse de Saussure (notamment sur la place de la parole relativement à la langue) au nom de la rigueur de sa propre construction théorique. Or ce même Sechehaye qui envisage dès 1917 "de prolonger et de compléter la pensée qui n'est qu'en germe dans le *Cours de linguistique*" (p. 29), qui affirme en 1930: "*La langue n'exprime pas des idées pures; les idées qu'elle exprime, la logique à laquelle elle est soumise sont des modalités de la vie*. C'est là une vérité que la doctrine saussurienne n'a peut-être pas proclamée de façon particulièrement insistante" (p. 349), qui reconnaît en 1940, concernant les "rapports de la diachronie et de la synchronie" (p. 5): "Nous avons usé évidemment de beaucoup de liberté à l'égard du texte du maître, mais nous croyons, en procédant à une révision de ses principes, avoir continué et précisé sa pensée, retenue et déformée par certaines préoccupations qui dominaient la linguistique de l'époque" (p. 6), ce même Sechehaye a eu le courage intellectuel de repenser, sur le tard, certaines de ses idées en développant et en poussant à leur extrême conséquence les thèses du *CLG*.

Ainsi, en 1942, il se fonde sur la phonologie pragoise et sur les passages du *CLG* qui définissent la valeur comme purement oppositive (pp. 116, 151, 160) pour en tirer une interprétation neuve au milieu du siècle; la définition différentielle, non psychologique, du phonème entraîne, en effet, "une série de conséquences qui retentissent assez loin" (Sechehaye 1942: 45). Il poursuit: "Si le phonème ne saurait se définir psychologiquement, […] il y a de multiples raisons pour en dire autant de toute entité de langue, de quelque ordre qu'elle soit. Par voie de conséquence ou d'analogie, ce qui est vrai du phonème paraît être vrai également de tout autre élément fonctionnel du système linguistique" (45–46), notamment les signifiants et les signifiés. A propos du signifié, Sechehaye a su retenir de Saussure l'essentiel: "Ce signifié, en effet, n'est ni un sens, ni une signification, il ne correspond ni à une idée précise, ni à un objet particulier, mais il est une *valeur*, c'est-à-dire une somme de virtualités expressives résultant des rapports que le signe entretient avec tous les autres signes de la langue qui se partagent arbitrairement entre eux la totalité de la matière mentale à exprimer [cf. la note *Item* de Saussure, N 15.9.3 = *CLG/E* I, p. 37a, n° 3314.3]. De toute manière, il faut donc refuser à ces valeurs − c'est-à-dire aux signifiés en général − la possibilité d'être définies psychologiquement, d'être saisies en elles-mêmes par un acte de conscience" (p. 47).

Le contraste entre Bally et Sechehaye ne saurait mieux ressortir qu'à la lecture des deux articles que j'ai cités pour finir. Après quinze ans, après des revirements théoriques considérables, il appert que Sechehaye avait vu juste en 1927, quand il avait considéré que son point de vue et celui de Bally étaient complémentaires: "On n'enserre le domaine total de la langue qu'en la considérant à la fois dans la réalité vivante qui la nourrit [c'est la position de Bally] et dans l'idéal logique qui l'attire sans cesse et la maintient dans un état d'organisation relative [c'est la position de Sechehaye, qu'il attribue aussi à Saussure (p. 18)], et il est légitime de se placer successivement à deux points de vue pour étudier les phénomènes de la grammaire" (Sechehaye 1927: 19).

Il n'en reste pas moins que, pour la postérité, l'influence la plus durable des principaux représentants de l'École genevoise de linguistique a consisté dans la mise au point du *Cours de linguistique générale*. On n'insistera jamais assez sur le fait que cette publication, avec la première interprétation des idées saussuriennes qu'elle soumettait au public, a été l'un des événements culturels les plus marquants du siècle qui s'achève.

6. Bibliographie

Amacker, René. 1988. "La creatività del ricevente secondo Albert Sechehaye". *Dalla parte del ricevente: Percezione, comprensione, interpretazione. Atti del XIX Congresso Internazionale (Roma, 8–10 novembre 1985)* a cura di Tullio De Mauro, Stefano Gensini & M. E. Piemontese, 61–71. Roma: Bulzoni.

−. 1992. "Le combat de Bally". *Cahiers Ferdinand de Saussure* 46.57–71.

−. 2000. "Le développement des idées saussuriennes chez Bally et Sechehaye". *Historiographia Linguistica* XXVII: 3.205–264.

Bally, Charles. 1905. *Précis de stylistique: Esquisse d'une méthode fondée sur l'étude du français moderne*. Genève: Eggimann.

−. 1909. *Traité de stylistique française*. 2 vols. Heidelberg: Winter; Paris: Klincksieck. [Je cite le vol. I, sauf mention expresse du vol. II.]

−. 1913a. *Le langage et la vie*. Genève: Atar. [Reprod. avec quelques modifications au début du recueil homonyme, 13–93. Paris: Payot, 1926.]

—. 1913b. *Ferdinand de Saussure et l'état actuel des études linguistiques. Leçon d'ouverture du cours de linguistique générale, lue le 23 octobre 1913*. Genève: Atar.

—. 1921. "Langage naturel et langage artificiel". *Journal de psychologie normale et pathologique* 17.625–643. [Cité d'après la reprod. dans le recueil *Le langage et la vie*, 2e éd., 183–211, sous le titre "Langage transmis et langage acquis". Paris: Payot, 1926.]

—. 1932. *Linguistique générale et linguistique française*. Berne: Francke. [Cité d'après la 4e éd., posthume, Berne: Francke, 1965.]

—. 1937. "Synchronie et diachronie". *Vox Romanica* 2.345–352.

—. 1939: "Qu'est-ce qu'un signe?". *Journal de psychologie normale et pathologique* 36.161–174.

—. 1941. "Intonation et syntaxe". *Cahiers Ferdinand de Saussure* 1.33–42.

Chevalier, Jean-Claude. 1999. "Albert Sechehaye, pédagogue et théoricien". *Cahiers Ferdinand de Saussure* 52.69–81.

CLG. Voir Saussure 1916.

CLG/E. Voir Saussure 1968 et 1974.

De Mauro, Tullio. 1972. "Introduction", "Notes biographiques et critiques" et "Notes". Ferdinand de Saussure, *Cours de linguistique générale*. Édition préparée par T. De Mauro. Paris: Payot. [Traduction française de Louis-Jean Calvet de l'appareil interprétatif et critique paru dans Ferdinand de Saussure, *Corso di linguistica generale*. Introduzione, traduzione e commento di Tullio De Mauro. Bari: Laterza, 1967.]

Ducrot, Oswald. 1986. "Charles Bally et la pragmatique". *Cahiers Ferdinand de Saussure* 40.13–37.

Durrer, Sylvie. 1998. *Introduction à la linguistique de Charles Bally*. Lausanne & Paris: Delachaux et Niestlé.

Engler, Rudolf. 1968 et 1974. Voir Saussure 1968 et 1974.

Frei, Henri. 1929. *La grammaire des fautes*. Paris: Geuthner; Genève: Kundig; Leipzig: Harrassowitz.

Fryba-Reber, Anne-Marguerite. 1994. *Albert Sechehaye et la syntaxe imaginative: Contribution à l'histoire de la linguistique saussurienne*. Genève: Droz.

Girard, Grégoire. 1821. *Grammaire des campagnes à l'usage des écoles rurales du canton de Fribourg*. Fribourg: Impr. Piller.

—. 1844. *De l'enseignement régulier de la langue maternelle dans les écoles et les familles*. Paris: Dezobry, Magdeleine & Cie.

—. 1845–1848. *Cours éducatif de langue maternelle à l'usage des écoles et des familles*. 9 parties en 6 volumes. Paris: Dezobry, Magdeleine & Cie.

Godel, Robert. 1957. *Les sources manuscrites du Cours de linguistique générale de F. de Saussure*. Genève: Droz.

Humboldt, Wilhelm von. 1836. *Ueber die Verschiedenheit des menschlichen Sprachbaues und ihren Einfluss auf die geistige Entwicklung des Menschengeschlechts*. Berlin: Dümmler. [Cité d'après l'édition d'Andreas Flitner et Klaus Giel, Wilhelm von Humboldt, *Werke in fünf Bänden*, vol.III: *Schriften zur Sprachphilosophie*. Darmstadt: Wissenschaftliche Buchgesellschaft, 1963.]

Meinong, Alexius. 1894. *Psychologisch-ethische Untersuchungen zur Werth-Theorie*. Graz: Leuscher & Lubensky.

Mélanges de linguistique offerts à M. Ferdinand de Saussure. 1908. Paris: Honoré Champion.

Saussure, Ferdinand de. 1879. *Mémoire sur le système primitif des voyelles dans les langues indo-européennes*. Leipsick: Teubner. [Paru en décembre 1878.]

—. 1916. *Cours de linguistique générale*. Lausanne & Paris: Payot. [Cité comme *CLG*, d'après la seconde édition, Paris: Payot, 1922.]

—. 1968. *Cours de linguistique générale*. Édition critique par Rudolf Engler, tome I. Wiesbaden: Harrassowitz. [Cité comme *CLG/E*, avec le numéro de l'unité Engler, sans autre précision.]

—. 1974. *Cours de linguistique générale*. Édition critique par Rudolf Engler, fasc. 4: *Notes de F. de Saussure sur la linguistique générale*. Wiesbaden: Harrassowitz. [Cité comme *CLG/E* II, avec identification de la note, pagination et numéro Engler.]

Sechehaye, Albert. 1905. "L'imparfait du subjonctif et ses concurrents dans les hypothétiques normales en français. Esquisse de syntaxe historique", *Romanische Forschungen* 19.321–406. [Version française complète de sa thèse de doctorat, rédigée en allemand en 1902 (Sechehaye lui-même renvoie toujours au texte français de 1905).]

—. 1908a. *Programme et méthodes de la linguistique théorique: Psychologie du langage*. Paris: Champion; Leipzig: Harrassowitz; Genève: Eggimann.

—. 1908b. "La stylistique et la linguistique théorique". *Mélanges de linguistique offerts à M. Ferdinand de Saussure*, 155–187. Paris: Champion.

—. 1914. "Les règles de la grammaire et la vie du langage". *Germanisch-romanische Monatsschrift* 5. 288–303 et 341–351.

—. 1916. "La méthode constructive en syntaxe". *Revue des langues romanes* 59: 1/2.44–76.

—. 1917. "Les problèmes de la langue à la lumière d'une théorie nouvelle". *Revue philosophique de la France et de l'étranger* 42: 10.1–30.

—. 1926a. *Essai sur le structure logique de la phrase*. Paris: Champion.

—. 1926b. *Abrégé de grammaire française sur un plan constructif suivi d'un Tableau systématique des conjugaisons*. Zürich: Verlag der Sekundarlehrerkonferenz des Kantons Zürich.

—. 1927. "L'école genevoise de linguistique générale". *Indogermanische Forschungen* 44.217–241.

—. 1930. "Les mirages linguistiques". *Journal de Psychologie normale et pathologique* 27.337—366.

—. 1933. "La pensées et la langue". *Journal de psychologie normale et pathologique* 30.57—81.

—. 1939. "Évolution organique et évolution contingentielle". *Mélanges de linguistique offerts à Charles Bally sous les auspices de la Faculté des lettres de l'Université de Genève par des collègues des confrères des disciples reconnaissants*, 19—29. Genève: Georg.

—. 1940. "Les trois linguistiques saussuriennes". *Vox Romanica* 5.1—48.

—. 1942. "De la définition du phonème à la définition de l'entité de langue". *Cahiers Ferdinand de Saussure* 2.45—55.

René Amacker, Genève (Suisse)

201. The development of functionalism from the Prague school to the present

1. Functional and structural linguistics
2. The Prague school and the Functionalist School
3. The Prague school
4. The Functionalist school
5. Dynamic synchrony
6. Diachrony
7. Axiomatic functionalism
8. Conclusion
9. Bibliography

1. Functional and structural linguistics

The teaching of Ferdinand de Saussure (1857—1913) (→ Art. 198—200) has led to the emergence of a type of linguistics which is generically known as 'structural linguistics'. It can be said that structural linguistics fundamentally operates with the belief that any language is conceivable as a kind of structure (or system) consisting of its interlinked sub-structures (sub-systems). Instead of 'structure', one can talk about 'system', which term Saussure (1879) uses at an early date in connection with what would now be known as a 'phonological system' in the title itself (as well as the contents) of his work in question. According to Mounin (1966: 24—25), 1968: 61—62), Saussure (1916) uses the term 'system' 138 times but avoids the term 'structure' (which Saussure uses with a different specific meaning) as a synonym of 'system', though 'mechanism' (13 times) and 'organism' (11 times) are used as synonyms of 'system'. It is common knowledge that Antoine Meillet (1866—1936), a well-known disciple and friend of Saussure, propagated the dictum "Chaque langue forme un système où tout se tient". Structural linguistics is not monolithic and falls into different types in that structuralist linguists adopt different theoretical concepts and methodologies of analysis of languages whilst all agree about language being a structure (system). Consequently it is appropriate, from that point of view, to talk about structural schools (in the plural) in reference to the separate groups of structural linguists. The point can easily be seen by comparing the Geneva School (→ Art. 200), the Prague School, the Functionalist School, the Glossematic School (→ Art. 202), the Descriptive or Bloomfieldian School (→ Art. 212), the Firthian School which has subsequently been elaborated into what may be called the Systemic School (→ Art. 203), to mention a few.

'Functional structural linguistics' is one of the types of structural linguistics and differs radically from the other types in that it is primordially concerned with investigating the diverse *functions* that are fulfilled by languages, as a language is conceived as a system endowed with functions ("système fonctionnel"; cf. *TCLP* 1: 7). This overwhelming attention to functions is hardly shared by other types of structural linguistics, the Glossematic School and the Bloomfieldian School in particular, though the major concern with functions in the Systemic School must be noted; Lepschy (1968, chap. VI) treats the Prague School, the Functionalist School and the Systemic School under the single heading "La linguistique fonctionnelle"). It is by dint of this primary concern with functions in languages that functional structural linguistics is frequently and appropriately referred to as 'functional linguistics' for short, the term first used by Vilém Mathesius (1882—1945), the originator of the Prague School. This is why it is proper for us to talk about 'functionalism' (short for 'linguistic functionalism') in this chapter.

2. The Prague School and the Functionalist School

What specifically characterizes both the Prague School and the Functionalist School is therefore functionalism. Members of these Schools investigate various functions that are attributable to languages. Linguistic functions, hereafter functions for short, have nothing to do with the concept of function as employed in, or derived from, mathematics, such as encountered in Glossematics. Chronologically speaking, the genesis of the Prague School precedes that of the Functionalist School. The two Schools started independently of each other, and it would therefore be inappropriate to understand that the Functionalist School is a mere continuation, or still less an inheritor, of the Prague School. Both the Prague School and the Functionalist School have been in existence as separate, though related, entities to this day. In the following pages the Prague School is treated first and the Functionalist School next. The identity of the Functionalist School, for those readers who are little acquainted with it, will be clarified in 4.1.

3. The Prague School

3.1. A brief history of the Prague School

The Prague School came into existence both in a negative reaction to the still then reigning Neogrammarian doctrine and in a positive reaction to Saussure's teaching. One can find excellent accounts of the historical aspects of the Prague School (if not for the entire period of the School) in, *inter alia*, Mathesius (1936) and Vachek (1966: 3–14). We limit ourselves here to mention just a few main facts of the history of the Prague School.

The now well-known designation "École de Prague" (later translated as "the Prague School", "die Prager Schule", "la Scuola di Praga", etc.) was created by the organizers of the First International Congress of Linguists (The Hague) in 1928 to refer to members of the pre-existing Prague Linguistic Circle (Pražský lingvistický kroužek, in Czech), a group of linguists of various nationalities who had already been actively engaged in linguistic research and discussions in Prague. The designation was therefore not the Circle's own making. The first meeting of the Prague Linguistic Circle took place on 6 October 1926. The initiator and founder of the Circle was Vilém Mathesius (1882–1945), with Nikolaj Sergeevič Trubetzkoy (1890–1938) and Roman Jakobson (1986–1982) as co-founders. The regular monthly – later fortnightly – meetings of the Circle continued even into the years during which the Circle's activity was seriously, but not completely, hampered by World War II itself and the aftermath confusion (till December 1948), as can be testified by the list of the lectures delivered at the meetings (cf. Matejka 1976a: 607–622). The period of the Prague School activity is generally divided into two, i.e., the so-called 'classical' (or interwar) period, i.e., 1926 to 1939 (or rather to 1948), and the so-called postwar period (1964 onward). For some time during the postwar period, the Prague Linguistic Circle was not quite "resurrected" as such, though it continued to exist within the newly created two linguistic organizations (cf. Vachek 1966: 13). The official revival of the Prague Linguistic Circle was announced fairly recently, with the resumption of its full and independent activity starting on 15 February 1990. The current leader of the Circle is Josef Vachek (1909–1996), a member of the original Circle.

The Prague Linguistic Circle of the classical period brought out eight volumes of *Travaux du Cercle Linguistique de Prague* (abbreviated *TLCP*), the first two volumes being dated 1929 and the seventh volume being the well-known Trubetzkoy (1939) and the eight the commemorative volume posthumously dedicated to Trubetzkoy. *TCLP* should not be confused with *Travaux Linguistiques de Prague* (abbreviated *TLP*) which belongs to the postwar period and which was first published jointly by the afore-mentioned newly created two linguistic organizations – the first volume came out in 1964, the second in 1966 and the third in 1968. *Slovo a slovesnost*, founded in 1935, was a journal of the Prague Linguistic Circle for some time. Vachek et al. (1983) collects, all in English, some major papers from the classical and postwar periods of the School.

3.2. Some characteristics of the Prague School

The members of the Prague School were/are structuralists, i.e., they believe/d that an element of a language can only be evaluated when considered in its relation to the other elements of the language. In this sense, structuralism, as relating to the Prague School, is closely linked to functionalism. They are/were functionalists, i.e., their primary belief was/is that any element of a language exists because it has a function(s) to fulfil. Indeed one of the earliest proclamations of the Prague School runs as follows: "... *la langue est un système de moyens d'expression appropriés à un but* [the original italics]" [... a language is a system of means of expression adapted to an end] ("Thèses" in *Travaux du Cercle Linguistique de Prague* 1: 7).

Functionalism in connection with the Prague School can be understood as being largely teleological. As Vachek (1966: 7) puts in plainly: In the Prague sense the terms [i.e., function, functionalist] simply point out the fact that any item of language (sentence, word, morpheme, phoneme, etc.) exists solely because it serves some purpose, because it has some function (mostly that of communication) to fulfil. The teleological nature of functionalism with the Prague School is of vital importance since it is not shared by the Functionalist School. Teleology is manifest in diachronic studies (including those on language change) as well as synchronic studies conducted by most members of the Prague School but, let it be noted, some members differed by not operating with teleology (cf. 3.17.).

3.3. The principle of relevance

The principle of 'relevance' was mentioned by Karl Bühler (1879–1963) in Bühler (1931: 38), his own designation being "Prinzip der abstraktiven Relevanz" (the principle of abstractive relevance), where abstraktiv is taken in the sense of "abstracting away from" (i.e., "omitting from consideration"). This principle enables the distinction between 'relevant' and 'irrelevant'. What is relevant is retained while what is irrelevant is omitted. Bühler emphasized thereby – he dealt with the distinction between phonetics and phonology in his writing in question – what to retain as relevant and omit as irrelevant in the phonic substance present in phenomena in the linguist's analysis of them. The Prague School phonologists were the first to operate with the principle of relevance, which thereby rendered them functionalists. A small number of specific functions were identified by Bühler in certain of his writings, then accepted and operated with by other members of the Prague School.

3.4. Bühler's three functions

Several functions have been mentioned by the Prague School. Three functions, expatiated on by Bühler in, e.g., Bühler (1920, 1934), are widely and particularly well known. They are, as Bühler himself called them, 'Darstellungsfunktion', 'Kundgabefunktion' (re-designated later by Bühler himself as 'Ausdrucksfunktion'), and 'Auslösungsfunktion' (later re-designated by Bühler as 'Appellfunktion'). These have been translated as, in English for example, 'function of representation', 'referential function'), 'function pf expression' ('expressive function'), and 'function of appeal' ('appellative function'), respectively. Bühler presents these three functions schematically in what he calls "Organon-Modell der Sprache" (Bühler 1934: 28).

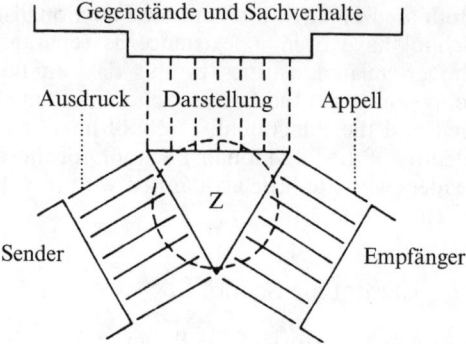

Fig. 201.1: The organon model of language after Bühler (1934: 28).

The triangle Z in the 'Organon-Modell' is said by Bühler to stand for the "konkrete Schallphänomen" (concrete speech phenomenon), i.e. an utterance, and "Gegenstände und Sachverhalte" indicate the objects and facts about which the speech activity takes place. "Sender" is the speaker, and "Empfänger" the hearer/listener. 'Darstellungsfunktion' is the function whereby Z identifies the linguistic message that the speaker wishes to transmit (hence, to communicate) to the hearer/listener. The term 'representation' or 'representative' or 'referential' in part of the English translations of 'Darstellungsfunktion' is to be understood in this specific sense. Perhaps a yet alternative English term for this function may be 'informative function' or, even better, 'communicative function' (cf. Garvin 1963: 502). 'Ausdrucksfunktion' is the function whereby indices about the speaker are provided, i.e., the speaker's sex, provenance (geographical, social, etc.), age, and so on. It is for this reason that the English translation of 'Ausdrucksfunktion' using the terms like 'expression' and 'expressive' may not be altogether free from potential misunderstanding, and an alternative translation like 'indexical function' might be preferable (cf. Akamatsu 1992a: 17−19). 'Appellfunktion' is the function whereby the speaker, via Z, emotively influences the hearer/listener, either positively or negatively, as s/he wishes. This function is alternatively called 'conative function' (cf. in the English translation in Isačenko (1948); the term *conative* (< *conati(on)* + *ive*), first used in 1680−90, means, as a psychological term, "pertaining to or of the nature of conation", and as a grammatical term, "expressing endeavour or effort". In linguistic communication achieved through speech activity it is 'Darstellungsfunktion' that operates indispensably and ineluctably, while one or the other, or both, of the two other functions may be absent, in individual instantiations of linguistic communication. However, the three functions are, in principle, not mutually exclusive. It is possible that, in some instantiations of linguistic communication, 'Appellfunktion' or 'Ausdrucksfunktion' is predominant (e. g., in highly lyrical poetry, or military commands, respectively), though never to the exclusion of 'Darstellungsfunktion'. The three Bühlerian functions may perhaps be expediently summarized in the phrase "Who speaks how about what?".

Other additional functions were/are studied by the Prague School; they include the metalingual function, the poetic function, the phatic function and the emotive function (Jakobson 1960, esp. 353−359).

3.5. Language and society

The Prague School's functional approach to language was/is directed not only to the system of languages itself but also to the function of language in society. Thus, the Prague School was/is interested in the question of standard language, national language, language planning, language teaching, and so on. Such interest on the part of the Prague School is also reflected in their extensive research into written language and poetic language.

3.6. Functional Sentence Perspective

Functional Sentence Perspective is characteristically associated with the Prague School and deserves special mention. The Prague School's belief that 'Darstellungsfunktion', or the communicative function as some members of the School put it, is predominantly important has led to the establishment of a conceptual framework known as 'Funkční perspektiva větná" in Czech ("functional sentence perspective", frequently abbreviated as FSP, in English) which aims at identifying different devices in a given language whereby two types of information, i. e., old information (or 'theme') and new information (or 'rheme'), are imparted in a particular linguistic message (be it spoken or written), given a certain syntactic structure. For instance, in English, an indefinite article *a* or *an*, in cases where it is not employed generically as in *a dog is a faithful animal* or *an elephant is strong* serves to introduce new information (as in *a dog is running*) whereas the definite article *the* serves to impart old information (as in *the dog is running* or *the elephant is drinking*). What is centrally important concerns the distinction and relation between theme and rheme, rather like 'topic' and 'comment', or 'thème' and 'propos', employed by linguists not belonging to the Prague School. FSP has a long history, being carried out for the whole period of the School's activity by Mathesius and his followers. Note in this connection Mathesius (1939), a pioneering work on FSP but employing the earlier Czech designation "aktuální členění větná [modern sentence analysis]". The present-day Czech scholar who is particularly well known for his copius and concentrated research on FSP is Jan Firbas (b. 1921) whose substantial writings (in Czech, Russian, German, English) on FSP can be consulted in journals mostly originating from the former Czechoslovakia. Note, however, the recent publication of Firbas (1992) which is a global exposition of FSP by Firbas and is written in English. One important concept that Firbas operates with (in fact, also a number of his Czech collaborators) is 'communicative dynamism' with regard to which he says that "by a degree of communicative dynamism I understand the relative extent to which a linguistic element contributes towards the further development of the communication" (Firbas 1992: 7−8). See also Firbas et al. (1975) for a bibliography on FSP for the period 1900−1972.

FSP can be said to emanate ultimately in its fundamental principles from research into functional syntax (i. e., functional analysis of utterances) carried out by Mathesius in particular, who delved into the study of linguistic 'characterology' of English, Czech, German, etc. Note in this connection Mathesius (1928), perhaps one of the best known of his works. Mathesius (1975 [1961]), posthumously published, gives a synthesis of his work on linguistic characterology. The object of linguistic characterology itself covers wider fields than just syntax. The study of 'contrastive (or confrontational) linguistics' practised in our days outside the Prague School may be said to follow the spirit and principles of the study of linguistic characterology.

3.7. Phonetics and phonology

The Prague School (i. e., the during the classical period) is probably best known for its contribution to phonology in particular and deserves our major attention. The Prague School's stand on the delimitation between phonetics and phonology is based on the criterion of function. Phonetics has to do with 'phonic substance' when conceived of and studied *irrespective of the functions* it fulfils in given languages, the phonic substance being in this case an object of natural sciences, while, on the other hand, phonology has to do with the same phonic substance studied *with respect to the functions* it fulfils in given languages ("Projet ..." 1931: 309; Trubetzkoy 1939: 7). Phonology is part of linguistics while phonetics is, at best, an auxiliary part of it. The said delimitation is made by the criterion of function and has nothing to do with separation of, or division between, objects of study. This is the basic application of functionalism to the study of phonic substance in the theory and practice of the Prague School. Incidentally, according to Jakobson & Halle (1956: 7), the term phonology was "launched in 1923 and based on the suggestions of the Geneva school"; they refer to Jakobson (1923: 21 ff.).

3.8. Phonology and Bühler's three functions

Functions attributable to the phonic substance of given languags are varied and unequal in their importance in terms of the contribution these functions bring to linguistic communication. It is especially in the domain of phonology that the Prague School's *functional* approach to language is particularly well confirmed.

In establishing and practising phonology, it is to the phonic substance of languages that the Prague School applied the aforementioned three Bühlerian functions, i. e., 'Darstellungsfunktion', 'Ausdrucksfunktion' and 'Appellfunktion'. The Prague School believed that Bühler's 'Organon-Modell' applies to the phonic substance of a language (Trubetzkoy 1939: 18). It is, as might be expected, 'Darstellungsfunktion', the function that is indispensable and of pre-eminent importance to linguistic communication, that formed the principal basis of most of the phonological theory and practice of the Prague School. In what follows, we shall therefore be concerned mainly with 'Darstellungsphonologie' (cf. Trubetzkoy 1939: 27 et passim) as distinct from 'Kundgabephonologie' and 'Appellphonologie'. The two latter types of phonology together constitute 'Phonostilistik' (phonostylistics). It should not be misunderstood that the Prague School disregarded 'Kundgabephonologie' and 'Appellphonologie' in exclusive favour of 'Darstellungsphonologie'. Their concentration on 'Darstellungsphonologie' is ascribable to the fact that according to the Prague School, (1) the communicative function is to be considered hierarchically more important than the two other functions, and (2) there is simply far more to be said about 'Darstellungsphonologie' than about 'Kundgabephonologie' and 'Appellphonologie'.

3.9. Phonology and Trubetzkoy's three functions

Phonology as established by the Prague School is comprehensively represented in Trubetzkoy's writings on this discipline, in particular in Trubetzkoy (1939), his last writing, which actually incorporates a good number of his previous writings on phonology as he progressively developed it.

In 'Darstellungsphonologie', Trubetzkoy proposes three functions, i. e., 'distinktive (bedeutungsunterscheidende) Funktion', 'kulminative (gipfelbildende) Funktion', and 'delimitative (abgrenzende) Funktion'. His proposal of these functions is of course based on the criterion of function. Of these, the first-mentioned is the most important, in fact, the indispensable, function, while the two others are not. Here again, there is a hierarchy among the three functions in terms of their relative degrees of contribution to speech communication. Trubetzkoy (1939) is devoted almost exclusively to his treatment of 'distinktive Funktion', though 'kulminative Funktion' is also dealt with in a small measure. 'Distinktive Funktion' serves, as its designation clearly indicates, to differentiate between such linguistic entities (morphemes, words, phrases, sentences) as are endowed with mutually different semantic contents (or meaning). Meaning here is what Trubetzkoy (1939: 33 et passim) refers to as "Intellektuelle Bedeutung" (intellectual meaning), as distinct from meaning associated with 'Kundgabefunktion' or 'Appellfunktion'. ('Intellectual' here should not be understood in the sense of 'lexical' or/and 'grammatical'.) In what follows, we shall concentrate on the distinctive function.

3.10. The concept of opposition

The distinctive function is based on the concept of opposition ("Opposition", "Gegensatz", "Gegenüberstellung") which necessarily and directly implies the concept of 'paradigmatic relation'. Opposition and the distinctive function are central to a number of phonological concepts typically ascribable to the Prague School such as the phonological opposition (to begin with), the phoneme, and the distinctive or relevant features (and others which will be mentioned later). According to Trubetzkoy (1939: 17), the phonologist's first task is to identify the phonological oppositions, note, not the phonemes, of a given language.

The concept of 'opposition' is strictly distinguished from that of 'contrast' (which is associated with the concept of syntagmatic relation) by the Prague School, as is by the Functionalist School (cf. 4.6.), unlike by non-functionalists to whom the single term 'contrast' generally covers both concepts.

3.11. The concept of the phoneme

The concept of the phoneme follows from, and is dependent on, that of opposition, or more precisely, phonological opposition. As Trubetzkoy (1939: 60) clearly puts it, "Man darf ja nie vergessen, daß in der Phonologie die Hauptrolle nicht den Phoneme, sondern den distinktiven Oppositionen zukommt." Phonemes are conceivable and identifiable because they are the terms of a phonological opposition. That the phoneme is a functional entity (not a physical or psychological entity) and is only definable with regard to its function is essential, as is repeatedly emphasized by Trubetzkoy (1939: 42, 43 et passim). Yet, during the formative period of the Prague School activity, when it was still heavily influenced by the teaching of Baudouin de Courtenay (1845–1929) who entertained the idea of the phoneme as 'Lautvorstellung' (the mental image of a sound), the Prague School considered phonemes as "des images acoustico-motrices les plus simples et significatives dans une langue donnée" (cf. "Thèses" in TLCP 1.10–11). The psychological concept of the phoneme was to be progressively eliminated in the Prague School phonology. The psychological characterization of the phoneme was absent a few years later, in 1931, in "Projet ..." (p. 311). However, this point leads to a question on another aspect in the definition of the phoneme.

The definition of the phoneme in "Projet ..." has it that a phoneme is "Unité phonologique non susceptible d'être dissociée en unités phonologiques plus petites et plus simples" (p. 311). This effectively characterizes the phoneme as a *global* phonological unit. A phonological opposition would, then, be between phonemes conceived as global units. Incidentally, it should be mentioned that "Projet ..." was largely drafted by Jakobson for general discussion at the International Phonological Conference that took place in Prague in 1930. (TCLP 4, published in 1931, constitutes the proceedings of this Conference). The two abovementioned definitions of the phoneme are given, on separate pages, in Trubetzkoy (1939: 34, 35).

Subsequently another definition (hence, characterization) of the phoneme was developed in the Prague School. Jakobson's redefinition appeared, in Czech, in Jakobson (1932: 608) according to which, as translated in English in Jakobson (1962b: 231), "the PHONEME ... [is] a set of those concurrent sound properties which are used in a given language to distinguish words of unlike meaning." This definition characterizes a phoneme as a bundle of distinctive phonic properties which are to be known later as 'distinctive features'. It is of course this definition of the phoneme that is functionally more satisfactory.

3.12. Identifying the phonemes of a given language

Trubetzkoy, who was naturally aware of Jakobson's definition of the phoneme as a bundle of 'distinctive features', had no time left, on account of his premature death, to elaborate on not only the concept of the relevant feature (cf. Martinet 1955: 67n.8, 1957a: 75 = 1965: 127) but also the analytical method whereby the phonemes of a given language are to be identified. One reads in Trubetzkoy (1939: 50–55) merely an expansion of what one reads in "Projet ..." (1931: 311–312) as

"Principes de délimination d'un phonème" and reiterated in Trubetzkoy (1935: 7–10) which in no way involves the concept of relevant features but does, rather, the question of a phoneme and its variants. A proper functionalist analytical method (i. e., 'commutation test') whereby to establish the phonemes of a given language was still absent when the classical period of the Prague School activity came to a virtual halt due to the outbreak of World War II.

3.13. Jakobson's distinctive features

Jakobson's first public presentation of his theory of distinctive features occurred in a paper in Czech (Jakobson 1938). No technical term corresponding to 'distinctive feature' was actually employed in either this paper or its French version (Jakobson 1939) in which he spoke of 'qualité différentielle'. Jakobson's 'qualités différentielles' were conceived as binary and universal characteristics. Trubetzkoy never saw fit to agree with Jakobson about this nature of Jakobson's concept of distinctive features right up to their last private conversation in February 1938. As is well known, Jakobson's concept of distinctive features was further developed and elaborated in the United States, in collaboration with Morris Halle (b. 1923) and Gunnar Fant (b. 1919) during the late 1940s (cf. Jakobson, Fant & Halle 1952). (Jakobsonian distinctive features have come to be utilized in a nonfunctional type of phonology known under the name of 'generative phonology' which has abandoned the concept and use of the phoneme, and therefore they represent a departure from functionalism that characterized the classical period of the Prague School.)

As we shall see in 4.10., relevant features or distinctive features that Trubetzkoy might have developed have subsequently been elaborated by the Functionalist School.

3.14. Neutralization and the archiphoneme

Of especial significance in respect of the Prague School phonology are the concepts of 'neutralization' and the 'archiphoneme' because of their functionalist character. Actually, the two concepts have had, within the Prague School phonology, a somewhat complicated history. Despite the widespread belief held to this day by many linguists that these concepts are among the typically Praguian ones in phonology, they have in fact been abandoned (the archiphoneme explicitly and neutralization implicitly) by the Prague School itself for more than half a century now, since about 1939 (cf. Vachek 1959: 110; 1960: 18; 1966: 62). For the theoretical consequence of the abandonment of the concept of the archiphoneme, see Akamatsu (1992b).

Of the two concepts, that of the archiphoneme was the first to be introduced by Jakobson (1929: 8–9) whose definition of the archiphoneme had, however, nothing to do with what present-day linguists associate with the concept of the archiphoneme in, e. g., Trubetzkoy (1939). Note specifically that Jakobson's archiphoneme was presented independently of the concept of neutralization which was not mentioned anyway. (For a discussion of Jakobson's archiphoneme of 1929, see Akamatsu 1988: 224 ff.) At a subsequent date, "Projet ..." (1931: 315) provides a definition of the 'archiphoneme', with no mention of 'archiphoneme'. It should be recalled (cf. 3.11.) that the phoneme is not defined in "Projet ..." (1931: 311) as a bundle of distinctive or relevant features. As for the concept of 'neutralization', this was first presented by Trubetzkoy (1929: 120 ff.) but without employing any term corresponding to it, and independently of the concept of the 'archiphoneme', though Trubetzkoy (1929: 133 n. 2) knew that the term and a certain concept designated by it had been introduced by Jakobson (1929: 8–9). Be it as it may, the concepts of the 'archiphoneme' and 'neutralization' were conceived of psychological nature. It was Mathesius (1929: 81) who, though without actually employing the terms, presented the two concepts in phonological, not psychological, terms. However, it is not clear from his presentation whether the phonological entity corresponding to the archiphoneme was, in Mathesius' mind, a bundle of distinctive or relevant features, probably not since Mathesius did not analyze a phoneme into distinctive or relevant features (cf. Trnka 1966: 484).

The interdependent and phonological (not psychological) relation between 'neutralization' and the 'archiphoneme' is, as is well known, evident in Trubetzkoy (1939). In fact it was evident already in his earlier writings, notably Trubetzkoy (1936b) but also, albeit briefly, in Trubetzkoy (1935 §§ 20–22). According to Trubetzkoy, then, when undergoes neutralization (*Aufhebung* in German) is a phonological opposition whose (two, as Trubetzkoy specifies) terms are phonemes, and the archiphoneme is a product of neutralization. Besides, the archiphoneme is, in Trubetzkoy's (1939: 71) well-known definition, "die Gesamtheit der distinktiven Eigenschaften [...] die zwei Phonemen gemeinsam sind", though the link between the archiphoneme and neutralization is definitionally inexplicit. This is the definition which occurs already at an earlier date, if not quite verbatim, in Trubetzkoy (1936b: 32) and in French in Trubetzkoy (1936a: 13). At any rate, the Prague School now had, at least in Trubetzkoy's phonological theory, the properly *phonological* concepts of 'neutralization' and 'archiphoneme' linked together, the archiphoneme being a bundle of distinctive or relevant features. It would seem that the two concepts were now unmistakably functionalist. What overshadows this ideal conception is Trubetzkoy's provision of an entity he calls "Archiphonemvertreter" (archiphoneme representative) in Trubetzkoy (1939: 71–75 et passim) and some of his earlier writings, according to which the archiphoneme is 'represented' by one of the two terms of the neutralizable opposition; the term in question is what Trubetzkoy characterizes as the 'unmarked member of an opposition ("merkmalloses Oppositionsglied"). Neutralization is said to occur with the loss of the phonological value ("phonologische Geltung") of the mark ("Merkmal") of the marked term ("merkmaltragendes Oppositionsglied"). The question that arises is whether the archiphoneme representative is a phoneme or a realization (of the archiphoneme). Trubetzkoy's illustration of the archiphoneme representative is sufficiently vague to suggest both interpretations. (Trubetzkoy 1939, with the exception of a single occasion, consistently talks about *Realisation* — the German term — in connection with a phoneme, but never in connection with an archiphoneme.) This is a matter of considerable importance for functionalism since, if the archiphoneme representative is a phoneme, the concept of neutralization itself collapses in favour of 'defective distribution' (the question is discussed in detail in Akamatsu 1988: 367–398). The theory of neutralization and the archiphoneme in the Prague School phonology reached its peak as we find it in Trubetzkoy (1939); actually, it would be more correct to think of the date of 1938, the year in which Trubetzkoy met with his untimely death.

The year 1938 was also, as mentioned in 3.13. that in which the concept of the distinctive feature was publicly for the first time presented by Jakobson (cf. Jakobson 1938, 1939). The concept of the 'distinctive feature' having been pushed to the foreground and having assumed all importance, the concept of the 'phoneme' crucially diminished in its significance. What had formerly been considered as a unitary entity (consisting in a bundle of distinctive or relevant features) called a phoneme, was now simply a bundle of distinctive features but without the concept of the unitary entity which the phoneme would be. Consequently, the archiphoneme itself lost its significance and was abandoned around 1939. At a much later date, Jakobson & Waugh (1979: 28) speak of "incomplete phoneme" instead of "archiphoneme" and besides do not mention neutralization at all. Neutralization itself could now be fully interpreted without involving the concept of phonological opposition or that of the archiphoneme and analyzed in terms of the cancellation of the opposition between two opposite values of a single distinctive feature. The concept of phonological opposition between phonemes was no longer either necessary or viable. At any rate, all phonological oppositions were now conceived as being of the type corresponding to 'privative opposition' as presented by Trubetzkoy (cf. Trubetzkoy 1936a: 14; 1939: 67) or what, at a later date, generative phonologists refer to as 'binary opposition'. The abandonement of the archiphoneme by the Prague School signifies simultaneously that of neutralization itself, though the Prague School itself asserts even at present its continued acceptance of neutralization (cf. Vachek 1990: 103).

Lastly, it should be mentioned that the relation between 'phoneme' and 'archiphoneme' presents an interesting poblem. Vachek (1966: 62) considered the archiphoneme as being subphonemic, but Vachek (1990: 103) renounces his earlier view by considering the archiphoneme as being "hyperphonemic" (his word). Be that as it may, with the abandonment of the archiphoneme from 1939 onward, the present point will most probably be a non-issue so far as the Prague School of the post-war period is concerned.

3.15. Trubetzkoy's classification of phonological oppositions

For quite some time the Prague School operated with the simple dichotomy between 'correlative oppositions' and 'disjunct oppositions'. This is clearly seen in, e. g., Jakobson (1929) and "Projet ..." (1931: 313–315) as well as in other writings of the day. The fundamental condition of a 'correlative opposition' is its being characterized by "Korrelationseigenschaft" (feature of correlation), hence possession of "Korrelationsmerkmal" (mark of correlation) by one of the phonemes (i. e., the marked phoneme) and non-possession of it by the other phoneme (the unmarked phoneme). Trubetzkoy (1936a) replaced the said dichotomy by his proposed reclassification of phonological oppositions, which reclassification recurs in Trubetzkoy (1939). Of the various types of phonological opposition (established by different criteria) proposed by Trubetzkoy, the two which are particularly significant from the point of view of function, hence functionalism, are the 'constant opposition' and the 'neutralizable opposition' precisely because these two types of phonological opposition are directly concerned with the functional typology of phonological oppositions.

Since the Prague School resumed its activity after World War II, phonology has ceased to occupy the central place that it held during the classical period. The School's attention has generally shifted to other domains of language such as morphology, syntax, and semantics.

Let it be added at this point that accounts of the development of phonology, within the Prague School as viewed by Jakobson can be found in Jakobson (1962c) and Jakobson et al. (1979).

3.16. Synchrony and diachrony

In agreement with Saussure's stand which has generally been seen to give priority to synchrony over and above diachrony, the Prague School attached major importance to synchronic studies of different domains of languages. We find the following words in the "Thèses" of 1929:

"La meilleure façon de connaître l'essence et le caractère d'une langue, c'est l'analyse synchronique des faits actuels." (*TCLP* 1: 7)

This is easy to understand and is not surprising since a structuralist view of language is optimally congruent with synchrony and, moreover, the evaluation and identification of the function(s) of elements of a given language are best achieved by investigating them in a synchronic state in the first place.

Diachrony was/is not neglected, however. A good number of works on diachrony exist throughout the period of the Prague School activity, as can be easily confirmed by taking a look at any bibliography of the Prague School works on diachrony (see, e. g., Vachek 1966: 175—176). Particularly substantial contributions were made by Jakobson. Among them, Jakobson (1929, 1931) are especially well known.

Note the absence, in the Prague School, of an antinomy between synchrony and diachrony which the *Cours* manifested. The Prague School saw/sees diachronic phenomena in terms of the replacement of a synchronic state by another over time (cf. *TCLP* 1: 8). It also sees elements of diachronic nature in a synchronic state which are latent and may lead to eventual language change. Thus, diachrony and synchrony are not mutually exclusive.

3.17. Language change and teleology

The Prague School largely views language change from the standpoint of teleology, that is to say, language change is of therapeutic nature in that it takes place in order to put right elements of deficiency in languages, redress the balance and regain the harmony and stability which have been lost in given domains of the language system. In other words, language change is thought to have a purpose, a goal. A teleological view of language change is evident from an early stage of the activity of the Prague School onward (cf., e. g., Jakobson 1929, 1962a). This particular characteristic of the Prague School is one of the important features of the School throughout down to the present. However, some members, including Mathesius, of the Prague School did not resort to teleology. Thus, Trnka et al. (1958) say as follows, as reproduced in Vachek (1966: 477):

Other members of the CLP (V. Mathesius and others), however, emphasized the functional role of language as a system serving to satisfy the communicative and expressive needs of the community and liable to change in order to meet new needs.

Since the major and significant contribution from the functional point of view made by the Prague School during the classical period of its activity is acknowledgedly in the domain of phonology, we have concentrated on this domain in the foregoing lines. For a general account of the Prague School, see *inter alia* Faye et al. (1969), Vachek (1972), Fried (1972), Fontaine (1974) and Matejka (1976b) and also parts of Matejka (1976a). Tobin (1988) collects contributions from Praguians and non-Praguians in homage to the Prague School.

For a succinct but sufficiently wide-ranging account of the Prague School's contemporary contribution in the field of syntax and semantics in which recourse is had to logic, mathematics and generativism, one may consult inter alia Hajičová (1992, 1994), Sgall (1985) and Partee et al. (1996). See also *Prague Studies in Mathematical Linguistics* in successive volumes. For a number of individual members' works on various aspects of language in a relatively recent period − 1940s to the present − of the Prague School, see *inter alia* Luelsdorff (1994) and Luelsdorff et al. (1994). The journal *Philologica Pragensia* (Prague) continues at present as *Linguistica Pragensia* (Prague) and *Litteraria Pragensia* (Prague). *Prague Linguistic Circle Papers* − intended to be revived series of *TCLP* − contains papers by contemporary members of the Prague School. Praguian functional approach is discussed in Novák et al. (1968). For Praguian functionalism and its exentions, see Luelsdorff (1983), and for the role of functionalism in linguistics as seen by the Prague (and also non-Prague) School, see Dirven et al. (1987).

It is worth noting that one finds an assessment of the Prague School's contributions in general as given by a leading member of the Functionalist School in Martinet (1992). It is now time to move on to the other school of functional structural linguistics mentioned at the beginning of this chapter.

4. The Functionalist School

4.1. A brief history of the Functionalist School

By Functionalist School is meant a group of functionalist-structuralist linguists led by and associated with André Martinet (1908−1999). This group of linguists, who are multinational and geographically widespread have formed, for closer organization and collaborative research, the Association Internationale de Linguistique Fonctionelle (abbreviated SILF) − in 1976 − with its headquarters in Paris. SILF publishes its official journal, *La Linguistique* (Paris), twice a year. Actually, this journal started in 1965, i.e., well before the formation of SILF, and became its official journal in 1977. SILF holds annual colloquia in different localities of the globe − the first colloquium took place in 1974 − and the transactions are published following each colloquium. SILF had a joint colloquium with LACUS (the Linguistic Association of Canada and the United States) in 1983, and with the revived Prague Linguistic Circle in 1991. An extensive overview of functional linguistics as practised by the Functionalist School is found in Martinet (1989: 7−64).

The origin of the Functionalist School goes back beyond what may have been suggested in the preceding paragraph. It can be situated at whatever point in time when Martinet started engaging in functional structural linguistics. Seeing that his first published work is dated 1933 (Martinet 1933), it seems reasonable to see the source of the Functionalist School at least round about that time and most probably before. A bird's-eye view of his linguistics activity and thoughts from the beginning to this day can be found in Martinet (1993). It is worth pointing out here that Martinet has never been a member of the Prague Linguistic Circle nor has he ever presented a paper at a meeting of the Prague Linguistic Circle (cf. Martinet 1992: 33), though he published two articles in *Slovo a slovesnost* (Martinet 1936a, 1938) and as many in *TCLP* (Martinet 1936b, 1939). Martinet arrived at his type of functional structural linguistics independently of the Prague School.

Just as the Prague School cannot be simplistically said to be equal to the limited number of well-known members like Mathesius, Trubetzkoy, Jakobson, Bühler, Trnka, Vachek and Firbas − the list could easily be lengthened − whom I happen to have mentioned above, so the Functional School cannot be said to be equal to Martinet alone but is relevant to a large number of linguists clustered round Martinet.

It is also true to say that the Functionalist School is not monolithic any more than the Prague School was/is. It is, however, true to say that any divergence among members of the Functionalist School is insignificant compared with the divergence between the two Schools.

General statement about the principles, nature and scope of the research conducted by the Functionalist School may be found in Martinet (1973b, 1977a, 1989, 1994, esp. secs. 1−2). A few basic works which constitute an introduction to functional linguistics associated with the Functionalist School, as distinct from the Prague School, are Martinet (1962, 1965, 1991).

It seems best to give an account of functionalism with regard to the Functionalist School by comparing and contrasting, i.e., by looking at the differences as well as similarities between, this School and the Prague School, as this course of action will best characterize the Functionalist School.

4.2. The principle of relevance

Just as the Prague School does, so the Functionalist School operates with the principle of relevance (see 3.3. above where Bühler's "Prinzip der abstraktiven Relevanz" was explained). As Martinet (1994: 1323) puts it:

"[...] this principle is to the effect that any scientific approach chooses a viewpoint that determines what observable facts shall be retained and what shall be disregarded as irrelevant for a given research. The principle of relevance determines what it is among multifarious phenomena of phonic substance observed in linguistic communication that the linguist, as distinct from e. g. the musician, the philosopher, the logician, the elocutionist, etc. needs to identify for his research. With regard to the Functionalist School, the principle of relevance may alternatively be known as the principle of communicative relevance. The various functions identified by dint of the principle of communicative relevance will be considered in terms of a hierarchy according to the relative degree of contribution each function brings to the functioning of a language."

In many functionalists' writings including Martinet's, the term *relevant* (in English and Germnan, for instance) appears to be equivalent to *distinctive* (cf. "relevant feature" = "distinctive feature") because of the synonymous use of the two terms. After all it is the German term *relevant* in the sense of "distinctive (phonic features)" for which Martinet elected to allot the French term *pertinent* as the equivalent (cf. Martinet 1973a: 19) in the first place, and the distinctive function is of the utmost importance. However, it is possible that the term *relevant* is to be taken more broadly. Marouzeau (1943: 173; 1951: 173) defines the term *pertinent* [F]/*relevant* [G]/*rilevante* [I] as: "Se dit d'un élément linguistique doué d'une fonction dans un système déterminé [said of a linguistic element endowed with a function in a given system]", which suggests a broad interpretation according to which the term *relevant* is not exclusively 'distinctive'. Buyssens' (1972) plea for the use of the term *relevant* in a broad sense is in the spirit congruent with Marouzeau's above definition, though Buyssens does not mention Marouzeau. I myself have suggested that the term *relevant feature* could be broadly employed so that it is "to designate any feature (phonological or otherwise) that is *linguistically functional*" (Akamatsu 1988: 89). This is indeed what one understands in Martinet (1991 [1960] §§ 2.5−2.6) and when Martinet (1973a: 25) employs such expressions as "la pertinence distinctive" and 'une pertinence démarcative" and further, when Martinet (1989: 150) writes:

La pertinence est le principe d'abstraction qu'on va choisir de telle façon que ne soient retenus que les aspects de la réalité perceptible qui assument *une fonction déterminée* ... [emphasis added] [Relevance is the principle of abstraction whereby one so chooses as to retain only those aspects of observed reality that assume a given function ...].

4.3. Definition of a language according to the Functionalist School

The characteristics of the Functionalist School's research on languages are fundamentally linked to the definitional characterization of languages as (1) an instrument of communication, (2) being doubly articulated and (3) being of vocal character; see, e. g., Martinet (1956: §§ 1.1−1.3; 1991 [1960] § 1.14; 1962: 26; 1965: 1−35; 1989: 12). With the exception of the first-mentioned defining characteristic, the Functionalist School sets itself apart from the Prague School. The characterization of a language as an instrument of communication relates directly to the primordial importance of "Darstellungsfunktion" (Bühler) and "distinktive Funktion" (Trubetzkoy). Functionalism is unmistakably manifest. (I return to 'distinctive function' in 4.5−4.10 in connection with phonology.)

To return to the definition of a language, the two other defining characteristics of a language deserve ample attention. The second-mentioned defining characteristic is known as 'double articulation' in the Functionalist School. (This should not be confused with Hockett's "duality principle" [1958: 574 ff.]). The third-mentioned defining characteristic is 'vocal character'.

The definition of a language in terms of *all* three above-mentioned characteristics enables the functionalists to identify the object of their research as either a language or a non-language. It is thanks to the criterion of double articulation that a language is distinguished as such from other semiotic systems (e. g., semaphore, traffic signals).

4.3.1. The Theory of 'double articulation'

It is the principle of relevance that has led to the criterion of double articulation in Martinet's definition of a language. Martinet (1949a) first emitted in writing his theory of 'double articulation'. An enlarged and better formulated version of the theory is found in Martinet (1965: 1–35). The theory of 'double articulation' is shared by no other school of structural linguistics, not even by the Prague School, or the Systemic School for that matter. In sum, a human experience to be communicated by means of a language is 'articulated' (1) first into a series of monemes (which are basically sequential but can be fused or discontinuous) – a moneme consists in an association between a signifier (i.e., 'signifiant', a vocal expression) and a signified (i.e., 'signifié', a semantic content) – and (2) then the signifier (but not the signified) of a moneme is 'articulated' into a necessarily sequential series of distinctive units called phonemes. The minimum unit of the first articulation is the moneme while that of the second articulation is the phoneme. Each moneme or phoneme corresponds to a choice on the part of the speaker/listener. Both the phoneme and the moneme are discrete units.

While the phoneme fulfils the distinctive function, the moneme is endowed with the significant function, the function whereby different linguistic messages are differentiated from each other. To give just one example, the difference in the content of the messages *I see a room* and *Tom loves a dog* is ascribable to the difference between the sets of different monemes *I* and *Tom*, *see* and *loves*, and *room* and *dog*.

The justification of not recognizing as a third articulation such that a phoneme is analyzable into a (concomitant) sum of relevant (phonological) features of the signified or a moneme into (a concomitant) sum of relevant (semantic) features is that the distinction of primordial importance is to be drawn between distinctive (but non-significant) units on the one hand and significant (but non-distinctive) units on the other (cf. Martinet 1994: 1324). Furtermore, unlike the phoneme or the moneme, the phonologically or axiologically relevant feature (for axiology, see 4.13.) do not correspond to choices on the part of the speaker/listener in language communication.

The criterion of double articulation neither ignores nor rejects the fact that certain linguistic devices which elude the framework of double articulation do occur in their own right in a number of languages. One case in point is tone – a tone language has two or more tones – which is endowed with the distinctive function like the phoneme but eludes the framework of double articulation. Another case in point is a descending melodic curve or an ascending melodic curve occurring at the end of an utterance, signifying varying degrees of definiteness or non-definiteness of the message contained in the utterance. Furthermore, unlike the phoneme or the moneme, the melodic curves of the sort mentioned above are non-discrete units (Martinet 1991 [1960] § 1.16) and, for this reason too, elude the framework of double articulation.

The framework of double articulation has a further implication in that the expressive function, one of the three functions with which the Functionalist School operates (cf. 4.5.), is identifiable and definable as such not only because of the nature of its functional role but because of its eluding the framework of double articulation.

Thanks to the framework of 'double articulation', a language achieves economy at the level of both phonemes and monemes. The signifiers of monemes, instead of being each globally different from all the others, consist in combinations of phonemes in different number arranged in different sequences. Besides, the same phonemes can be used in the make-up of different monemes. Thus it is possible for a language to have a relatively small number of phonemes. This represents economy at the level of phonemes. Also, huge numbers of human experiences to be communicated can be dealt with by a finite number of different monemes into which the experiences are analyzed. Such would not be the case if each human experience corresponded to a global linguistic sign whose signifier is not analyzable into a sequence of phonemes. This represents economy at the level of monemes. Furthermore, the possibility of combining different monemes, and in some cases in different sequences, achieves a high degree of specificity without augmenting the number of monemes necessary for and compatible with the huge numbers of human experiences to be communicated. Without the framework of double articulation, no language can possibly be manageable enough to function.

Double articulation is achieved differently in different languages, that is to say, the same human experience to be communicated will be, depending on individual languages, differently articulated into different monemes in different numbers which are possibly arranged in mutually non-corresponding orders (cf., e. g., *j'ai mal à la tête* in French and *Me duele la cabeza* in Spanish and *I have a headache* in English). Besides, the phonemes, which go into the make-up of the signifiers of monemes of a given language, will be of a different number and entertain a different relation among them from those in another language.

4.3.2. The vocal character of a language

Despite differences of opinion held by linguists the world over concerning the relation between spoken language and written language (or, perhaps more precisely, the spoken medium and the written medium of a language, in cases where the latter medium exists in one but in another language), the view adhered to by the Functionalist School is that a language is definitionally characterized by the vocal character and that spoken language enjoys primacy over written language. This does not mean that the Functionalist School disregards written language. On the whole, however, the School's interest in and contribution to the subject of written language is much less substantial than those ascribable to the Prague School (e. g., Vachek 1973).

The vocal character of a language entails the linearity which characterizes any language, its spoken form to begin with and, where applicable, its written form as a reflection of the spoken form. The vocal character of a language, and its linearity, also entail the fact that the order in which the phonemes of a language occur in the signifiers of monemes and the order in which the monemes occur is linguistically relevant.

The importance that the Functionalist School attaches to *differences* among individual languages leads to the view that "*rien n'est proprement linguistique qui ne puisse différer d'une langue à une autre* [Nothing that cannot differ from language to language is, properly speaking, linguistic]" (Martinet 1991 [1960] §.1.14; emphasis in the original).

4.4. Phonetics and phonology

The Functionalist School's view on the distinction between phonetics and phonology is unequivocally identical with the Prague School's (cf. 3.7.). This is not surprising because both Schools arrive at this view by the criterion of the function which they espouse vigorously. The Prague School and the Functionalist School are the only two types of structural lingiustics, indeed the only two of all types of linguistics, to maintain in both theory and practice the distinction between phonetics and phonology. Phonology, a study of the phonic substance of a given language with respect to its function in this language is, for the Functionalist School, equivalent to what one may otherwise designate as functional phonetics (cf. the very title of Martinet 1949b).

4.5. Phonology and Martinet's three functions

In the realm of phonology, Martinet operates with three functions in particular (cf. Martinet 1991 [1960] § 3.1), two of which correspond to Trubetzkoy's 'distinktive Funktion' and 'kulminative Funktion', designated as 'fonction distinctive' or 'fonction oppositive' and 'fonction contrastive', respectively, while a third function designated as "fonction expressive" (expressive function) does not correspond to none of Trubetzkoy's functions but corresponds, if not quite definitionally, to Jakobson's (1960: 354–355) "emotive function". Martinet's distinctive function calls for no explanation as they are self-explanatory. What Martinet calls the 'expressive function' has nothing to do with Bühler's "Kundgabefunktion" or "Ausdrucksfunktion" which are traditionally translated as "function of expression" or "expressive function" but for which "indexical function" would be more appropriate (cf. 3.4.). The contrastive function, despite its terminological difference, is identical with Trubetzkoy's 'kulminative Funktion', except that the choice of the term *contrastive* makes it quite clear that this function is associated with syntagmatic (and not paradigmatic) phenomena. Just as Trubetzkoy provides "deliminative Funktion" (1939: 29), Martinet does the same, for the corresponding function, with the term 'fonction démarcative' (demarcative function). It goes without saying that the demarcative function is a derivative of the contrastive function, just as 'deliminative Funktion' is a derivative of 'kulminative Funktion'. The expressive function as operated with by Martinet is the function whereby the state of the mind, be it real or feigned, is expressed without recourse being had to the framework of double articulation. A classic example is the lengthened and reinforced consonant in French in an utterance like "*cet enfant est impossible!* [this child is impossible!]" pronounced with [p] prolonged and with reinforced articulation whereby irritation, real or feigned, may be indicated (Martinet 1991 [1960] § 3.1).

4.6. The concept of 'opposition'

For all functionalists (i.e., both the Prague School and the Functionalist School) the concepts and terms of 'opposition' and 'contrast' must be rigorously differentiated from each other. 'Opposition' relates to 'paradigmatic relation', and 'contrast' to 'syntagmatic relation'. In the Functionalist School, the concept of opposition is essential not only in phonology but in other domains of language (e. g., synthematics, axiology) where the paradigmatic relation between the elements of a linguistic system is brought into play. Unlike in the Prague School, an oppposition consists of two or more terms (hence no binarism); thus a phonological opposition consists of two or more phonemes and/or archiphoneme(s), or of two or more tones and/or architone(s). With regard to the types of phonological opposition, the Functionalist School does not resort to Trubetzkoy's types of opposition except for 'neutralizable opposition' and 'constant opposition', since most, if not all, of the rest (such as "bilateral", "multilateral", "privative") are binaristic. 'Correlative opposition' (= 'bilateral privative proportional opposition') is resorted to as this is a useful concept when considering the phonological system of a language, both synchronic and diachronic (cf. e. g., Martinet 1939, 1955). The types of phonological opposition that are accepted and resorted to by the Functionalist School (but never in the Prague School) are 'exclusive opposition' and 'non-exclusive opposition' (cf. Akamatsu 1988: 58–63 et passim; 1992: 53–55) which never correspond, either conceptually or terminologically, to 'bilateral opposition' and 'multilateral opposition', respectively, of Trubetzkoy, in spite of widespread misapprehension. By definition, an exclusive opposition is a phonological opposition whose two or more terms are in an 'exclusive relation' (Akamatsu 1988: 58). The concept and term of 'exclusive opposition' owe fundamentally to those of 'exclusive relation' which pre-existed (cf. Martinet 1945a § 2.7; 1949b: 7; 1956 § 3.17).

4.7. The concept of the phoneme

Unlike in the case of the Prague School, the phoneme has always been conceived of as a sum of relevant features in the Functionalist School (cf. Martinet 1945a § 2.3; 1956 § 3.13; 1991 [1960] § 3.18). The concept and nature of the relevant feature have never been either influenced by, or taken the direction of, distinctive features (binary and universal) that Jakobson developed.

4.8. Identifying the phonemes and their relevant features

As was remarked in 3.12., Trubetzkoy died too soon to develop and elaborate a functionalist analytical procedure whereby to identify the phenomes of a given language; this task was left for the Functionalist School to accomplish. The analytical procedure in question is what has come to be known as 'commutation test'; historically speaking, the term 'commutation' itself originated in Glossematics. The principles of the commutation test in phonology were briefly explained in Martinet (1945a § 2.4; 1956 § 3.14), in some detail in Martinet (1947: 41–45, 1957a, 1991 [1960] §§ 3.12 ff.). At a subsequent date, a detailed account of the principle and practice of the commutation test was given in Akamatsu (1992a: 60–80). The commutation test is functionally the only justifiable and correct operation whereby to identify the phonemes of a given language and their relevant features. That the relevant features are identified is important, something that was neither envisaged nor possible in Trubetzkoy's method of identifying the phonemes of a given language via the relation between a phoneme and its variants. The identification of the relevant features coincides with the identification of the phonemes themselves (cf. Martinet 1947: 44; 1965: 66), since a phoneme is a sum of relevant features.

Note that the 'commutation test' will have been resorted to whereby to elicit the *monemes* of a given language before eliciting the phonemes and their relevant features.

4.9. Neutralization and the archiphoneme

The interest in and acceptance of the concepts of neutralization and the archiphoneme have been evident since an early stage of the activity of the Functionalist School. One can refer as some relevant writings on this subject to inter alia Martinet (1936b, 1957b, 1968a) and Akamatsu (1988, 1992a, 1992b).

The commutation test achieves identifying not only the phonemes and its relevant features (cf. 4.8.) but also instances of neutralization (where they occur) and the neutralizable oppositions themselves and, moreover, the archiphonemes associated the neutralizations in terms of their relevant features. Since the commutation test serves to identify the distinctive units of a given language, be they compatible with the framework of 'double articulation' or not, both the phonemes and the archiphonemes are identified (cf. Martinet 1991 [1960] § 3.22) and, in the case of a tone language, both the tones and the architones in addition (in such tone languages as have the architones as well). Invoking the concept of 'exclusive opposition' during the commutation test makes it possible to not only identify instances of neutralizations but also to distinguish them from cases of defective distribution (of phonemes or tones), for neutralizable oppositions are obligatorily exclusive oppositions while exclusive are not necessarily neutralizable oppositions.

Unlike the Prague School, the Functionalist School attaches the utmost importance to the possibility that a phonological opposition, valid in the context of relevance, is invalid in the context of neutralization. How an archiphoneme is phonetically realized is of secondary importance, as Martinet (1968a: 5) writes: "*Fonctionnellement*, la façon dont se réalise la neutralisation n'importe pas".

Quite unlike the Prague School, the Functionalist School has always adhered to both the concepts of 'neutralization' and the 'archiphoneme'. The only brief exception to this happened in Martinet (1947: 48–49) when non-recourse to (but not discardment of) the archiphoneme and the exclusive relation was temporarily proposed (cf. Akamatsu 1988: 310–314). Full recourse to both these concepts was quickly reaffirmed subsequently. The Functionalist School's adherence to the two concepts is linked ultimately to the School's adherence to the concept of opposition and to the principle that there is no necessary correspondence between physical reality and linguistic function. The said principle can be illustrated by such examples as [ɛ] in Danish being a variant of either /e/ (as in *ret* "correct") or /ɛ/ (as in *net* "pretty"), [o] in French being a variant of either /o/ (as in *paume* "palm") or the archiphoneme /o-ɔ/ (as in *sot* "silly"), or a high-rise melodic curve in Mandarin Chinese being either a variant of the so-called 2nd tone (as in ma^2 "hemp") or a variant of the architone /2–3/ (as in $shou^{2-3}biao^3$ "wrist-watch", where *shou* is actually pronounced with the same melodic curve as generally associated with the 2nd tone). The Functionalist School's adherence to the concept of the archiphoneme – while the Prague School has abandoned it since about 1939 – leaves the concept of neutralization intact instead of transforming it into that of 'defective distribution' (of phonemes or tones). The Functionalist School distinguishes between neutralization and defective distribution and operates with both, as and when necessary, which are two distinct phonological phenomena.

A few specific types of archiphoneme have been proposed by some functionalists without much importance given to them; they are "potential archiphoneme" (Tcheu 1967: 89–90), "logical archiphoneme" (Tcheu 1967: 93n.15), "archi-archiphoneme" (ibid., p. 93), and "archiphoneme as a pure abstraction" (Martinet 1936b: 55; 1945a § 2.9; 1949b: 7; 1956 § 3.19).

The concepts of neutralization and the archiphoneme entertained by the Functionalist School are bound to differ from those entertained during the classical period of the Prague School if only because the Functionalist School does not operate with Trubetzkoy's bilateral opposition or multilateral opposition which is binaristic (instead of which some functionalists employ 'exclusive opposition' and 'non-exclusive opposition', neither being binaristic). The archiphoneme continues to be adhered to, and the concept of the relevant feature (in terms of which the archiphoneme is defined) is different from that of the distinctive feature associated with the Prague School, be it Trubetzkoyan or Jakobsonian.

4.10. The relevant feature

The concept of 'relevant feature' with which the Functionalist School operates has nothing to do with the concept of the distinctive feature which is originally attributable to Jakobson and which has remained conceptually the same even though the generativists have modified it in different ways on a number of occasions. Unlike the Jakobsonian distinctive features, the relevant features with which the Functionalist School operates are not binaristic (e.g., "aspirated" and "unaspirated" which are two relevant features, but not [+ aspiration] and [− aspiration] which is a single distinctive feature with two different values) and are totally founded on the concept of opposition (this is why, e.g., /m/ in French is not characterized as 'voiced' or 'voiceless', unlike, e.g., /m/ in Burmese which is characterizable as 'voiced' in opposition to /m̥/ characterizable as 'voiceless'). They are not universal and applicable to all languages, and are therefore alien to a set of distinctive features from among which each language is supposed to choose. The identity of a relevant feature is determined by and determines the identity or identities of the other relevant feature or features to which it is opposed so that, for example, 'apical' in English is different from 'apical' in Spanish). Furthermore, it is a non-issue whether the relevant features are associated with auditory features or articulatory features or perceptual features or acoustic features.

4.11. Synthematics

One significant development attributable to the Functionalist School is found in the field of what the School designates as *synthématique* (synthematics). The term 'synthématique' derives from *synthème* which was inspired by the term *monème*, on the one hand, and the term *syn* "with, together" on the other, and came into existence in its French form around 1964–65. The concept itself, if not yet the term, of *synthème* (translated as "syntheme" in English) existed at an earlier date, in connection with combinations of monemes which *function syntactically* as if they were single monemes. A few examples of synthemes from English may be *into, television, handrail, richer, widowhood, neighbourliness, decomposition, fahter-in-law, will-o'-the-wisp, stick-in-the-mud, (to) kick the bucket* (when meaning "(to) die"). Martinet (1979: 233) writes:

> Un synthème est une unité significative, formellement et sémantiquement analysable en deux ou plus de deux monèmes, mais qui, syntaxiquement, entretient les mêmes relations avec les autres éléments de l'énoncé que les monèmes avec lesquels elle alterne."

Three defining characteristics of a syntheme are: (1) total syntactic compatibility between a syntheme and a given class of monemes which commutes with it; (2) commutability of the *whole* syntheme by a single moneme; and (3) unmodifiability ('non-détermination' in French) of any *individual* constituent moneme of a syntheme. To illustrate these characteristics with the example of *father-in-law*, (1) this syntheme is syntactically compatible with, e. g., *desk*, in that both *father-in-law* and *desk* can be modified by articles, adjectives, and entertain the same syntactic relation to verbs, etc., (2) it is *father-in-law* as a whole, not *father* or *in* or *law*, that is commutable with, e. g., *desk*, and (3) for example, the adjective *my* in *my father-in-law* modifies the syntheme as a whole and not *father* or *in* or *law*. Note specifically in connection with (2) and (3) that a syntheme corresponds to a single choice on the part of the speaker just as does a moneme. It would for this reason be erroneous to say that *father* in *father-in-law* is commutable with, e. g., *son* (cf. *son-in-law*), since *father-in-law* corresponds to a single choice (not three successive choices), just as *belle-fille* or *bru* in French, both meaning "daughter-in-law", corresponds to a single choice. There is some helpful literature on the subject of synthemes and synthematics (cf., e. g., Martinet 1967 = 1975a: 182–195; 1968b = 1975a: 196–204; 1979: 231–268; 1985: 33–42; 1989: 139–148; 1991: 131–134).

It is crucially important that synthemes should not be confused with syntagms. It is indeed fundamentally in order to distinguish from syntagms that synthemes were conceived. For example, *father-in-law* (a syntheme) corresponds to a single choice on the part of the speaker while *my father came* correspond to three choices which, besides, are successively made. The constituents of a syntheme (e. g., *father-in-law*) are joint monemes ("monèmes conjoints"), while those of a syntagm (e. g., *my father came*) are free monemes ("monèmes libres"). These types of moneme have nothing to do, either terminologically or, more importantly, conceptually, with bound forms (or bound morphemes) or free forms (or free morphemes) employed in other schools. Quite apart from this reason, the term *morpheme* is not employed in the Functionalist School, even if it was in the past, which was proven unjustified in retrospect. Nor is the concept and term 'word' employed (cf., e. g., Martinet 1989).

The critical point of departure for the concept of syntheme is syntactic (i. e., the syntactic behaviour of a syntheme) but since the constituent monemes of synthemes are identifiable, there is no reason why synthematics is not also concerned with the classification of the types of constituent moneme and types of their combination within synthemes (cf. composition, affixation, confixation, 'figement').

One might easily misunderstand that synthematics being practised in the Functionalist School is an equivalent of what has been practised elsewhere (including in the Prague School) under the heading of morphology, i. e., the study of how words are formed out of morphemes. Synthematics is a subject matter treated in close association with syntax. The fact that synthematics involves composition and derivation among other types which contribute to the formation of synthemes does not make synthematics an equivalent of morphology of other school.

As the Functionalist School defines it, morphology is the study of variants of the signifier, i. e., the formal variants of monemes (cf. Martinet 1969; esp. 89—90; 1980; 1991 § 4.6). For example, the formal variation involving /va/, /vɛ/, /al/, /i/, /aj/ of the moneme *aller* "(to) go", is described in morphology. Actually, morphology studies formal variants of not ony monemes but of synthemes as well that result from composition or derivation (cf. Martinet 1969: 89). The School's contribution in the field of what it calls morphology has no association with the Prague School's, or other schools', contribution to what has been generally known as morphology.

4.12. Syntax

Functional syntax is strictly conceived as the study and presentation of the ways whereby the hearer can reconstruct the unity of the message broken down by the necessity of articulating the experience for its linguistic communication" (Martinet 1977a: 12; cf. also Martinet 1994: 1326). This concept of syntax is reflected in the functional classification of monemes and identification of their syntactic function such that the functionalists operate with, for example, 'nucleus' vs. 'satellite', 'predicate' (distinct from 'predicatoid'), "modality" or 'modifier', 'relator' (or 'functional'). Thus, in *his sister studies linguistics*, *studies* is the nucleus (while the rest are satellites) and is at the same time the predicate (always a verb). *His* and *-es* are modalities (or modifiers) which are unmodifiable modifiers and always require nuclei, which are *sister* and *studi-* in the example, and which always function as satellites never as nuclei. The occurrence of *his* is dependent on that of *sister* and therefore *his* is said to be 'subordinated' to *sister*. In *black and white*, both *black* and *white* are 'coordinated' with each other. In *I know that his sister studies linguistics*, *studies* is the predicatoid, occurring as it does in the subordinate clause while *know* is the predicate, occurring as it does in the principal clause. A relator connects two monemes or groups of monemes (either coordinating or subordinating) so that, e. g., *and* in *Tom and Jerry* and *at* in *Harry at the post office* are relators. Types of monemes found in synthemes which, as we have seen in 4.11., are characterized as free monemes or joint monemes are based on their syntactic function for their classification.

Care should be taken not to see a moneme where none exists. In the French phase *la perte*, the feminine gender which is automatically chosen with the choice of the moneme *perte* and which is manifested in *-a* of *la* (*le perte) — this is a matter of concord — should not be considered a moneme, while *-esse* of *poétesse* "female poet" is a moneme as *-esse* corresponds to a choice. In contrast, in *la livre* "pound sterling" as opposed to *le livre* "the book", *la* involves the moneme signifying feminine gender. There is an instantiation of concord in, e. g., *les beaux animaux* "the beautiful animals", in which the moneme signifying plural number is manifested discontinuously at three points [le boz animo] and is characterized as 'discontinuous moneme'. Lastly mention must be made of 'amalgam' in which two or more monemes are amalgamated, fused, into a global unanalyzed form, e. g., *au* in French which is an amalgam of two monemes, *à* "to, at" and *le* the definite article (sing. masc.). The sketchy and partial mini-presentation of functional syntax above must be complemented by reference to excellent works on functional syntax including Martinet (1962: 39—65; 1979, 1985, 1991, chap. 4; 1994).

4.13. Axiology

Application of the concept of function to semantic substance in the Functionalist School has resulted in the emergence of what it calls 'axiology'. Axiology is to semantics what phonology is to phonetics. This means that the blank (indicated with an interrogative mark) which was found inside the square in the diagram in Martinet (1965: 25) has now been filled with the designation 'axiology', while the blank (indicated also with an interrogative mark) outside the square in the same diagram can now be filled with the designation 'semantics' but with the understanding that this is not equivalent to semantics as traditionally understood and operated with in the other schools. Semantics (as distinct from axiology) studies meanings in general relevant to linguistic communication but unrelated to any given language (cf. the relation between phonetics and phonology, as regards phonic substance). Axiology studies the values of meanings within a given language. For example, the value of the meaning of 'singular' in, e. g., English (where 'singular' is opposed to 'plural' only) is different from the value of 'single' in, e. g., Fijian (where 'singular' is opposed to 'dual', 'paucal', and 'plural'). The concept of opposition is of prime importance in axiology just as it is in phonology. All the implications resulting from the establishment of axiology are clearly stated by Martinet (1975b, 1977b, 1991 [1980]: 210). On the question of semantics and axiology, the reading of a group of articles in Mahmoudian (1989: 3—144) is recommended.

4.14. Language change

Unlike the Prague School, language change is not regarded to be a teleological phenomenon in the Functionalist School, as "[...] il n'y a pas de téléologie dans le fonctionnement de la langue" (Martinet 1975c: 68), neither in synchrony nor in diachrony. For one thing, the Functionalist School believes that "La langue change parce qu'elle fonctionne" (Martinet 1975c: 12). A language changes so that it can best adapt itself over time to communicative needs on the part of members of the speech community, as these communicative needs constantly undergo changes due to internal or external causes, and are therefore never immutable (see in this connection Martinet 1975c, chap. 2). For general expositions on linguistic evolution, see, e.g., Martinet (1955, 1962: 134—160; 1968c, 1991 [1960], chap. 6). There are two concepts in particular to be mentioned in connection with language change, which we shall see immediately in 4.14.1. and 4.14.2.

4.14.1. Antinomy between communicative needs and inertia

There always exists an equilibrium between the necessity of communicating human experiences through language as effectively as possible, on the one hand, and human tendency to expend just enough, but not more, energy, both mentally and physically (i.e., articulatorily), compatible with ensuring effective language communication. There is permanent antinomy between them. However, as mental and physical inertia are an immutable factor while communicative needs are a variable factor and as the equilibrium between the two factors varies over time, there results language change. It is therefore the permanent antinomy between the two factors that governs and causes linguistic evolution over time (cf. Martinet 1952: 26; 1955 §§ 4.1— 4.4, 1991 [1960] § 6.5; 1989 § 1.4).

The above-mentioned antinomy between communicative needs and inertia leads to 'economy (of a language)' in two different manners, i.e., syntagmatic economy (associated with linguistic units of greater specificity) and paradigmatic economy (associated with linguistic units of lesser specificity). Either type of economy works against the other type of economy, and a satisfactory equilibrium must be maintained. Thus, for example, the use of monemes of great specificity will enlarge the lexis but results in syntagmatic economy in utterances, while the use of monemes of little specificity will result in syntagmatic expansion in utterances.

4.14.2. Economy

If the term 'economy' mentioned in connection with 'double articulation' in 4.3.1. can be taken in the sense of 'parsimony', it is in addition, and more importantly, also to be understood in the sense of "aménagement" (or "organisation des divers éléments d'un ensemble") in French. As Martinet (1955: 97) puts it:

"Economie recouvre tout: réduction des distinctions inutiles, apparitions de nouvelles distinctions, maintient du statu quo. L'économie linguistique, c'est une synthèse des forces en présence."

It is 'economy' in the sense of "aménagement" that language change is explicated in the Functionalist School (cf. the very title of Martinet 1955 which treats of diachronic phonology). The above-mentioned *aménagement* corresponds to the maintenance of a satisfactory equilibrium between communicative needs and inertia and is achieved in the process of the functioning of a language. This brings about language change as a result, hence the above-mentioned formulation "La langue change parce qu'elle fonctionne" (cf. 4.14.).

5. Dynamic synchrony

Since 'language change because it functions', and since a language functions every time it is used, any language at any given time is never static but is, on the contrary, always dynamic. Language variations of either recessive or progressive nature, which are potential seeds of language change, are present in any synchronic state of the language in that speakers of different generations — speakers of different age brackets — will use their language differently. Synchrony is therefore not static but dynamic in this sense, hence the term 'dynamic synchrony' which is employed by the Functionalist School. The term itself also occurs in the writings of the Prague School when rejecting the Saussurean synchrony/diachrony antinomy (cf. Jakobson & Waugh 1979: 76, 168, 234) but the concept and reference are not identical with those of this term as used in the Functionalist School. 'Dynamic synchrony' is a concept of synchrony in the practice of the Functionalist School, not a concept as operated with by the Prague School whereby language change is seen as the replacement of a synchronic state by another over time for teleological and therapeutic purposes. The Functionalist School does not discard the distinction synchrony/diachrony in the sense that one and the same linguistic reality may be viewed in terms of a synchronic formulation or a diachronic formulation (cf. /ɛ/-/œ̃/ in French). The crucial distinction is between diachrony and dynamic synchrony. Diachrony is then a comparison between successive dynamic synchronies of the same language. Some of the useful literature on the subject of dynamic synchrony is found in Houdebine (1985); Martinet (1945a, b; 1975c: 5−10; 1989 [1984]; 1990, 1991 § 2.2); Walter (1979, 1988).

6. Diachrony

Language change, and dynamic synchrony mentioned above in connection with it, naturally leads to the subject of diachrony. Diachrony is to be understood in the sense of "comparison between successive dynamic synchronies of a given language" (cf. Martinet 1991: 29), which will show the direction and rhythm of the evolution of the language. The Functionalist School has made significant contribution in the field of diachrony, particularly in diachronic phonology. Martinet (1955; 1975c, chap. 4−14) and Hagège & Handricourt (1978) deserve special mention. A number of contributions in the fields of Indo-European should also be noted (cf., e. g., Martinet 1986).

7. Axiomatic functionalism

There exists a minority functionalists (clustered at St. Andrews University, Scotland) whose approach is logical and much less realistic (Martinet is a realist) and who pursues what they call "axiomatic functionalism". Martinet (1991 [1980]: 211) briefly refers to axiomatic functionalism and mentions inter alia Mulder (1968) and Hervey (1979). There is a wide gap in many respects between the functionalists led by Martinet and those led by Mulder. (For a succinct account of axiomatic functionalism, see Hervey 1994.)

8. Conclusion

It will have been seen from the foregoing that the history of functionalism in linguistics in modern times involves two principal schools, i. e., the Prague School and the Functionalist School, which share structuralism and functionalism as their essential characteristics. The type of linguistics the Schools practise is known as 'functional structural linguistics', rightly so as it is above all functionalism that sets these Schools apart from the other structuralist schools. The two Schools' adherence to structuralism and functionalism has not led to identity between the two Schools, however. On the contrary, there is now a substantial gap between the two, as will have been shown above. Collaboration between the two Schools at present is minimal. One would be realistic to recognize the existence of two separate well-characterizable schools.

9. Bibliography

Akamatsu, Tsutomu. 1988. *The Theory of Neutralization and the Archiphoneme in Functional Phonology.* Amsterdam & Philadelphia: Benjamins.

−. 1992a. *Essentials of Functional Phonology.* Louvain-la-Neuve: Peeters.

−. 1992b. 'Whither the Archiphoneme?". *Revue roumaine de linguistique* 37.5−6, 389−394. Bucharest: Editura Academiei Române.

Asher, Ronald E. & J. M. Y. Simpson, eds. 1994. *The Encyclopedia of Language and Linguistics.* Vol. III. Oxford & New York: Pergamon Press.

Bühler, Karl. 1920. "Kritische Musterung der neuren Theorien des Satzes". *Indogermanisches Jahrbuch* 6.1−20. Berlin.

−. 1931. "Phonetik und Phonologie". *TCLP* 4.22−53.

−. 1934. *Sprachtheorie: Die Darstellungsfunktion der Sprache.* Jena: Gustav Fischer. (2nd ed., Stuttgart: Gustav Fischer, 1965.) [Translated into English by Donald Fraser Goodwin as *Theory of Language: The representational function of language*, Amsterdam & Philadelphia: Benjamins, 1990.]

Buyssens, Eric. 1972. "Elargissement de la notion de pertinence". *Proceedings of the 7th International Congress of Phonetic Sciences* ed. by André Rigault & René Charbonneau, 1095−1098. The Hague: Mouton.

Dirven, René & Vilém Fried, eds. 1987. *Functionalism in Linguistics.* Amsterdam & Philadelphia: Benjamins.

Faye, Jean Pierre & Léon Robel, presenters. 1969. *Le Cercle de Prague. Change* 3. Paris: Seuil.

Firbas, Jan. 1992. *Functional Sentence Perspective in Written and Spoken Communication.* Cambridge: Cambridge Univ. Press.

– & Eva Golková. 1975. *An Analytical Bibliography of Czechoslovak Studies in Functional Sentence Perspective, 1900–1972.* Brno: Masaryk University.

Fontaine, Jacqueline. 1974. *Le Cercle linguistique de Prague.* Paris: Maison Mame.

Fried, Vilém, ed. 1972. *The Prague School of Linguistics and Language Teaching.* London: Oxford Univ. Press.

Garvin, Paul. 1963. "Czechoslovakia". *Current Trends in Linguistics* ed. by Thomas A. Sebeok, vol. I: *Soviet and East European Linguistics,* 499–522. The Hague: Mouton.

Hagège, Claude & André Haudricourt. 1978. *La Phonologie panchronique.* Paris: PUF.

Hajičová, Eva. 1992. "Praguian Functionalism as the Basis of a Formal Linguistic Theory: Functional generative description". *Actes XVIIIe Colloque International de Linguistique Fonctionnelle* (Prague, Tchécoslovaquie, 12–17 Juillet 1991), 53–56 Prague. Société Internationale de Linguistique Fonctionnelle.

–. 1994. "Prague School Syntax and Semantics". Asher et al. 1994.3285–3293.

Hervey, Sándor. 1979. *Axiomatic Semantics.* Edinburgh: Scottish Academic Press.

–. 1994. "Functionalism, axiomatic". Asher et al. 1994.1338–1340.

Hockett, Charles F. 1958. *A Course in Modern Linguistics.* New York: Macmillan.

Houdebine, Anne-Marie. 1985. "Pour une linguistique synchronique dynamique". *La Linguistique* 21.7–36.

Isačenko, Alexander V. 1948. "O prizyvnoj funkcii jazyka [The function of appeal in language]". *Recueil Linguistique de Bratislava* 1.45–58. Transl. by A. V. Isačenko in Vachek 1964: 88–97 as "On the Conative Function of Language" and published in Yachele 1969.88–97.

Jakobson, Roman. 1923. *O češskom stixe preimuščestvenno v sopostavlenii s russkim.* Berlin & Moscow: OPOJAZ-MLK. (Translated into German as *Ueber den tschechischen Vers: Unter besonderer Berücksichtigung des russischen Verses.* Bremen: Konstanzer Hus-Gesellschaft, 1974.)

–. 1929. *Remarques sur l'évolution phonologique du russe comparée avec celle des autres langues slaves.* (= *TCLP* 2.) Prague: (Repr. in Jakobson 1962d. 7–116.)

–. 1931. "Prinzipien der historischen Phonologie". *TCLP* 4.247–267. (Repr., with a number of revisions by Jakobson), in French translation by Jean Cantineau as "Principes de phonologie historique", as an appendix to Trubetzkoy 1949.315–336, and repr. subsequently in Jakobson 1962d.202–220.)

–. 1932. "Fonéma". *Ottův slovník naučný nové.* 2nd supplementary volume. Prague. (Repr. as "Phoneme and Phonology" in Jakobson 1962d.231–233.)

–. 1938. "O souhláskách [On consonants]", delivered at the 21 March 1938 meeting of the Prague Linguistic Circle. (The résumé appeared in *Slovo a slovesnost* 4.192. Prague, 1938.)

–. 1939. "Observations sur le classement phonologique des consonnes". *Proceedings of the 3rd International Congress of Phonetic Sciences,* 34–41. Ghent: The Phonetics Laboratory of the Univ. (Repr. in Jakobson 1962d.272–279, and also in Makkai 1972.305–309.)

–. 1960. "Closing Statement: Linguistics and poetics". Sebeok 1960.350–377.

–. 1962a [1920]. "The Concept of the Sound Laws and the Teleological Criterion". Jakobson 1962d. 1–2.

–. 1962b [1932]. "Phoneme and Phonology". Jakobson 1962d.231–233.

–. 1962c. "Retrospect". Jakobson 1962d.629–658.

–. 1962d. *Selected Writings I: Phonological studies.* The Hague: Mouton. (2nd, expanded ed., 1971.)

–, C. Gunnar M. Fant & Morris Halle. 1952. *Preliminaries to Speech Analysis: The distinctive features and their correlates.* Cambridge, Mass.: MIT Press. (Rev. ed., 1962.)

– & Morris Halle. 1956. *Fundamentals of Language.* The Hague: Mouton.

– & Linda Waugh. 1979. *Sound Shapes of Language.* Assisted by Martha Taylor. Brighton: Harvester Press.

Lepschy, Giulio, C. 1968. *La linguistique structurale.* Paris: Payot.

Luelsdorff, Philipp A. 1983. "On Praguian Functionalism and Some Extensions". Vachek et al. 1983. xi–xxxi.

–, ed. 1994. *Prague School of Structural and Functional Linguistics.* Amsterdam & Philadelphia: Benjamins.

–, Jarmila Panevová & Petr Sgall, eds. 1994. *Praguiana 1945–1900.* Amsterdam & Philadelphia: Benjamins.

Mahmoudian, Morteza, presenter. 1979. *Linguistique fonctionnelle: Débats et perspectives. Pour André Martinet.* Paris: PUF.

–, ed. 1989. "Sens et signification". (= *La Linguistique,* 25.) Paris: PUF.

Makkai, Valerie Becker, ed. 1972. *Phonological Theory: Evolution and current practice.* New York: Holt, Rinehart & Winston.

Malmberg, Bertil, ed. 1968. *Manual of Phonetics.* Amsterdam & London: North-Holland.

Marouzeau, Jules. 1943 [^{1}1933]. *Lexique de la terminologie linguistique.* 2nd ed. Paris: Paul Geuthner. (3rd ed., 1951.)

Martinet, André. 1933. "Remarques sur le système phonologique du français". *BSL* 34.191−202.

−. 1936a. "Česká práce o vlivu pravopisu na Francouskou výslovnost". *Slovo a slovesnost* 2.54−56.

−. 1936b. "Neutralisation et archiphonème". *TCLP* 6.46−57.

−. 1938. "Fonologie Francouzštiny". *Slovo a slovesnost* 4.11−113.

−. 1939. "Rôle de la corrélation dans la phonologie diachronique". *TCLP* 8.273−288.

−. 1945a. "Description du français du parler franco-provençal d'Hauteville (Savoie)". *Revue de linguistique romane* 15.1−86. (1945 for 1939).

−. 1945b. *La Prononciation du français contemporain: Témoignages recueillis en 1941 dans un camp d'officiers prisonniers.* Paris: Droz. (Revised as Martinet 1956.)

−. 1947. "Où en est la phonologie?". *Lingua* 1.34−58.

−. 1949a. "La double articulation linguistique". *TCLC* 5.30−37. (Repr., with some modification, as "Le critère de l'articulation" in Martinet 1965. 11−21.)

−. 1949b. *Phonology as Functional Phonetics.* Oxford: Blackwell.

−. 1952. "Function, Structure and Sound Change". *Word* 8.1−32.

−. 1955. *Economie des changements phonétiques: Traité de phonologique diachronique.* Berne: Francke.

−. 1956 [1945]. *La Description phonologique avec application au parler franco-provençal d'Hauteville (Savoie).* Genève: Droz; Paris: Minard.

−. 1957a. "Substance phonique et traits distinctifs". *BSL* 53.72−85. (Repr. in Martinet 1965. 124−140.)

−. 1957b. *La notion de neutralisation dans la morphologie et le lexique.* (= Travaux de l'Institut de linguistique 2.) Paris: Klincksieck.

−. 1960. *Élements de linguistique générale.* Paris: Armand Colin (3rd ed., 1991.)

−. 1962. *A Functional View of Language.* Oxford: Oxford Univ. Press.

−. 1965. *La Linguistique synchronique: Études et recherches.* Paris: PUF.

−. 1967. "Syntagme et synthème". *La Linguistique* 4:2.1−14. (Repr. in Martinet 1975a.182−195.)

−. 1968a. "Neutralisation et syncrétisme". *La Linguistique* 4:1.1−20.

−. 1968b. "Mot et synthème". *Lingua* 21.294−302.

−. 1968c. "Phonetics and Linguistic Evolution". Malmberg 1968.464−487.

−. 1969. "Qu'est-ce que la morphologie?". *Cahiers Ferdinand de Saussure* 26.85−90.

−. 1973a. "La pertinence". *Journal de psychologie normale et pathologique* 70:1/2. 19−30.

−. 1973b. "Pour une linguistique des langues". *Foundations of Language* 10.339−364.

−. 1975a. *Studies in Functional Syntax/Études de syntaxe fonctionnelle.* München: Fink.

−. 1975b. "Sémantique et axiologie". *Revue roumaine de linguistique* 20.539−542.

− 1975c. *Evolution des langues et reconstruction.* Paris: PUF.

−. 1977a. "Some Basic Principles of Functional Linguistics". *La Linguistique* 13:1.7−14.

−. 1977b. "L'axiologie, étude des valeurs signifiées". *Estudios ofrecidos a Emilio Alacros Llorach*, vol. I, 157−163. Oviedo. Univ. d'Oviedo.

−. 1979. *Grammaire fonctionnelle du français.* Paris: Didier (Crédif).

−. 1984. "De la synchronie dynamique à la diachronie". *Diachronica* 1.53−64. (Repr. in Martinet 1989.47−52.)

−. 1985. *Syntaxe générale.* Paris: Colin.

−. 1986. *Des steppes aux océans: L'indo-européen et les "Indo-Européens".* Paris: Payot.

−. 1989. *Fonction et dynamique des langues.* Paris: Colin.

−. 1990. "La synchronie dynamique". *La Linguistique* 26:2.13−23.

−. 1991 [^{1}1960; ^{2}1980]. *Éléments de linguistique générale.* 3rd ed. Paris: Colin.

−. 1992. "Histoire et rayonnement de l'École de Prague". *Actes XVIIIe Colloque International de Linguistique Fonctionnelle* (Prague, Tchécoslovaquie, 12−17 Juillet 1991), 33−41. Prague: Société Internationale de Linguistique Fonctionnelle.

−. 1993. *Mémoires d'un linguiste: Vivre les langues.* Entretiens avec Georges Kassai et avec la collaboration de Jeanne Martinet. Paris: Quai Voltaire.

−. 1994. "Functional Grammar: Martinet's Model". Asher et al. 1994.1323−1327.

Matejka, Ladislav, ed. 1976a. *Sound, Sign and Meaning: Quinquagenary of the Prague Linguistic Circle.* Ann Arbor: Dept. of Slavic Languages & Literatures, Univ. of Michigan.

−. 1976b. "Preface". Matejka 1976a.ix−xxxiv.

Mathesius, Vilém. 1928. "On Linguistic Characterology of Modern English". *Actes du Premier Congrès International de Linguistes*, 56−63. La Haye. (Repr. in Vachek 1964.59−67.)

−. 1929. "La structure phonologique du lexique du tchèque moderne". *TCLP* 1.67−84. (Repr. in Vachek 1964.156−176.)

−. 1936. "Deset let Pražského lingvistického kroužku [Ten years of the Prague Linguistic Circle]". *Slovo a slovesnost* 2.137−145. Prague. (English translation with slight abridgement in Vachek 1966.137−151.)

−. 1939. "O tak zvaném aktuálním členění věty [On the so-called information-bearing structure of the sentence]". *Slovo a slovesnost* 5.171. Prague.

—. 1975 [1961]. *A Functional Analysis of Present Day English on a General Linguistic Basis.* Translated by Libuše Dušková, ed. by Josef Vachek. The Hague: Mouton; Prague: Academia.

Mounin, Georges. 1966. "La notion de système chez Antoine Meillet". *La Linguistique* 2:1.17–29.

—. 1968. *Ferdinand de Saussure ou le structuraliste sans le savoir.* Paris: Seghers.

Mulder, Jan. 1968. *Sets and Relations in Phonology.* Oxford: Oxford Univ. Press.

Novák, Pavel & Petr Scall. 1968. "On the Prague Functional Approach". *TLP* 3.291–299. Prague: Academia.

Partee, Barbara & Petr Sgall, eds. 1996. *Discourse and Meaning: Papers in honor of Eva Hajičová.* Amsterdam & Philadelphia: Benjamins.

Prague Linguistic Circle Papers. Vol. I (1995), vol. II (1996). Amsterdam & Philadelphia: Benjamins.

Prague Studies in Mathematical Linguistics. Vols. VII–X (1981–1990). Amsterdam & Philadelphia: Benjamins.

"Projet de terminologie phonologique standardisée". 1931. *TCLP* 4.309–326.

"Proposition". 1928. *Actes du Premier Congrès International de Linguistes,* 5–7, 33–36. Leiden: A. W. Sijthoff.

Saussure, Ferdinand de. 1979 [1878]. *Mémoire sur le système primitif des voyelles dans les langues indoeuropéenes.* Leipzig: Teubner.

—. 1916. *Cours de linguistique générale.* Paris & Lausanne: Payot. (2nd ed., 1922.)

Sebeok, Thomas Albert, ed. 1960. *Style in Language.* Cambridge, Mass.: M. I. T. Press.

—, ed. 1966. *Portraits of Linguists: A biographical source book for the history of western linguists, 1746–1963.* Vol. II: *From Eduard Sievers to Benjamin Lee Whorf.* Bloomington & London: Indiana Univ. Press.

Sgall, Petr, ed. 1985. *Contributions to Functional Syntax, Semantics and Language Comprehension.* Amsterdam & Philadelphia: Benjamins.

Tcheu, Soc-Kiou. 1967. "La neutralisation et le consonantisme en coréen". *La Linguistique* 3:2.85–97.

"Thèses". 1929. *TCLP* 1.1–29. (Repr. in Vachek 1964.33–58, and in Faye et al. 1969.23–49.)

Tobin, Yishai, ed. 1988. *The Prague School and Its Legacy.* Amsterdam & Philadelphia: Benjamins.

Travaux du Cercle Linguistique de Prague [TCLP]. Vol. 1 (1929), Vol. 2 (1929), Vol. 3 (1930), Vol. 4 (1931), Vol. 5 (1934), Vol. 6 (1936), Vol. 7 (1939), Vol. 8 (1939). Prague: Jednota československých Matematiků a Fysiků.

Travaux linguistiques de Prague. Vol. 1 (1964), Vol. 2 (1966), Vol. 3 (1967). Prague: Academia.

Trnka, Bohumil. "Vilém Mathesius (1882–1946 [sic!])". Sebeok (1966: 474–489) in English translation by Vladimir Honsa. (Originally in *Časopis pro moderní filologii* 29 (1946), 3–13.)

— et al. 1958. "Prague Structural Linguistics". *Philologica Pragensia* 1.33–40. (Repr. in Vachek 1964.468–480.)

Trubetzkoy, N[ikolaj] S[ergeevič]. 1929. *Polabische Studien.* (= *Sitzungsberichte der Akademie der Wissenschaften in Wien*; Philosophisch-historische Klasse, 211: 4.) Wien & Leipzig: Hölder-Pichler-Tempsky.

—. 1935. *Anleitung zu phonologischen Beschreibungen.* Brno: Édition du Cercle Linguistique de Prague.

—. 1936a. "Essai d'une théorie des oppositions phonologiques". *Journal de psychologie normale et pathologique* 33.5–18. Paris.

—. 1936b. "Die Aufhebung der phonologischen Gegensätze". *TCLP* 6.29–45. (Repr. in Vachek 1964.187–205.)

—. 1939. *Grundzüge der Phonologie.* (= *TCLP* 7). Prague: Jednota československých Matematiků a Fysiků. (Repr., Göttingen: Vandenhoeck & Ruprecht, 1958.)

—. 1949 [1939]. *Principes de phonologie.* French transl. by Jean Cantineau. Paris: Klincksieck.

Vachek, Josef. 1959. "The London Group of Linguists". *Sborník prací filosofické fakulty brněské university* 7:8.106–113. Brno.

— (avec collaboration de Josef Dubsky). 1960. *Dictionnaire de linguistique de l'École de Prague.* Utrecht & Anvers: Spectrum. (2nd ed., 1966.)

—, comp. 1964. *A Prague School Reader in Linguistics.* Bloomington & London: Indiana University Press.

—. 1966. *The Linguistic School of Prague.* Bloomington & London: Indiana Univ. Press.

—. 1972. "The Linguistic Theory of the Prague School". Fried 1972.11–28.

—. 1973. *Written Language: General problems and problems of English.* The Hague: Mouton.

—. 1990. A Review of Akamatsu (1988). *Philologica Pragensia* 33.102–105.

— & Libuše Dušková, eds. 1983. *Praguiana: Some basic and less known aspects of the Prague Linguistic School.* Prague: Academia; Amsterdam: Benjamins.

Walter, Henriette. 1979. "Diachronie, synchronie et dynamique en phonologie". Mahmoudian 1979. 121–128.

—. 1988. "Dynamique et diversité des usages en phonologie". *Folia Linguistica* 23:3/4.281–291.

Tsutomu Akamatsu, Leeds (Great Britain)

202. The Cercle linguistique de Copenhague and Glossematics

1. Introduction
2. The Cercle linguistique de Copenhague in Hjelmslev's time
3. The development and propagation of glossematic theory
4. Some basic characteristics of glossematic theory
5. Danish structural linguistics: Professed glossematicians and putative glossematicians
6. The CLC and Danish linguistics after Hjelmslev
7. Bibliography

1. Introduction

The intellectual climate in Europe between the two world wars was favourable for the emergence of structuralist schools. The particular development of structural linguistics in Denmark was most profoundly influenced by Saussure's *Cours*, but was also inspired by the work of more contemporary scholars in a variety of fields, especially those interested in the nature of the linguistic sign, in meaning, and in the formal aspects of language. Since the 1930s, Danish linguists were in close contact with structural linguists especially of the Prague School, but the scholarly impact of these academic friendships was diminishing ever since the mid-1930s, when glossematics established for itself a high degree of autonomy as a theory of language.

As for early American structuralism, the founders of Danish structuralism did not seem to find much in the Bloomfield School that was of relevance to their own groundbreaking work. The indisputable leader of Danish theoretical linguistics, Louis Hjelmslev, thought much more highly of Sapir, who probed into fundamental questions about the nature of language and the typology of language structures, than of Bloomfield, whose theoretical contribution was strongly description-oriented. There was, in fact, a certain congeniality between Sapir and Hjelmslev, although they worked in independence of each other. Hjelmslev's close associate, Hans-Jørgen Uldall, on the other hand, eventually became involved with descriptive work in USA; this helped to create a path of some late American influence on Danish theoretical linguistics shortly after World War II.

The structuralist trend in Denmark, as elsewhere, was encouraged by the fact that there were scholars working on more or less related issues in fields outside linguistics proper, including philosophers such as Cassirer, Husserl, Russell, and eventually also Tarski, the psychologist Bühler with his work on the communicative aspect of language, and the phonometrist Eberhard Zwirner (1899–1984) with his emphasis on a linguistic approach to the statistical analysis of speech sounds.

The work in these various fields put into focus the most basic and most general issue: what is language? Hjelmslev's and Uldall's enterprise, which after the middle of the 1930s was named 'glossematics' (from Greek *glossa* "language"), was directed towards the goal of establishing nothing less than *the* theory of language. In the recent history of linguistics, this high ambition to create a stringent, comprehensive and self-contained theory is probably matched only by Noam Chomsky's enterprise in the late 1950s and early 1960s. In spite of deep-rooted differences between these two programs, which were separated by roughly two decades, there are in fact certain (real or apparent) affinities between them. Although the glossematic approach to language description included certain procedural techniques, it was never the intent of glossematics to arrive at methods with practical applications. Rather, the goal was to establish linguistics on a theoretical basis as an autonomous science. In this respect, glossematics fitted into the dominant trend in continental Europe in the 1920s and 1930s, and distinguished itself from the structuralist trend in America which focussed more on techniques which could be practically applied to the discovery and subsequent description of the phonological systems and grammars of hitherto undescribed languages.

2. The Cercle linguistique de Copenhague in Hjelmslev's time

The Cerle linguistique de Copenhague (henceforth: CLC), was founded in 1931 as a sister organization of the Cercle linguistique de Prague. It has been associated first and foremost with the name of the most influential Danish linguist of this century, Louis Hjelmslev's (1899–1965), who was also one of the founders of the CLC. Altogether, Danish linguistics is traditionally associated with the glossematic theory.

When Holger Pedersen (1867–1953) retired, Hjelmslev became professor of comparative linguistics in Copenhagen in 1937 and in the immediately following years he published several papers developing and explaining his glossematic theories. Especially after World War II (during which *Omkring Sprogteoriens Grundlæggelse* had appeared) there was a lively debate on glossematic issues, and for several years there was a special group within the CLC which met frequently and took up such issues: "Det glossematiske udvalg" ("The Glossematic Committee"). Its most active members included prominent Danish linguists such as Paul Diderichsen, Eli Fischer-Jørgensen, and Knud Togeby. One important name is missing from this list: Hans-Jørgen Uldall (1907–1957), who spent most of his academic career in Africa and the United States and thus was influential mainly through his written work. (Recent publications dealing with the CLC include Fischer-Jørgensen 1997, Canger & Gregersen 2001.)

It must be emphasized that the CLC itself was not meant as a forum for exclusively glossematic debate. A wide variety of linguistic and philological topics were taken up, many of which had nothing to do with glossematics as such. Several contributors disagreed explicitly with Hjelmslev's linguistic approach; especially in the 1930s many were more in line with the approach of the Prague Circle, which was a direct source of inspiration, via the personality of Roman Jakobson, when the Copenhagen Circle was founded.

Although glossematics was by far the most influential trend within the CLC, it deserves special mention that there have been two other trends in Danish theoretical linguistics in the first half of this century. One was almost epitomized by Viggo Brøndal (1887–1943), professor of Romance linguistics in Copenhagen. He was much closer to the basic thinking of the Prague School than was Louis Hjelmslev. Brøndal studied both the structure of vowel systems and (particularly) the abstract semantic properties of word classes. He was a highly original thinker and was hailed as a great *débatteur* who contributed very much to the fruitful intellectual climate of the CLC before World War II (on Brøndal and his influence in Danish linguistics see Gregersen 1991 *passim* and Brandt 1994). Brøndal and Hjelmslev together founded the journal "Acta Linguistica" (later revived as "Acta Linguistica Hafniensia") in 1939, but there was in fact no fruitful scholarly cooperation between these two scholars, who were – each in his own way – highly original and influential within European linguistics of the pre-war period.

The other trend was represented by Otto Jespersen (1860–1943) and by Paul Diderichsen (1905–1964), trained in Nordic philology. Jespersen, who looms large in a whole gamut of linguistic disciplines, is interesting in this context for his work on theoretical syntax, one aspect of which became particularly significant in Danish linguistics, viz. the study of types of relations between grammatical constituents. Syntactic constituency became a major field of interest for Diderichsen, who specialized in early medieval Danish syntax. He devised a scheme for parsing sentences in terms of sequentially ordered fields and slots, and later applied the same type of scheme to modern Danish grammar, on which he became the authority of his time. His so-called 'field scheme' was applied also to the study of Norwegian and Swedish syntax. Although it has received fairly little attention elsewhere, it is interesting that certain components of his descriptive model anticipate much later notions in transformational grammar, whereas others anticipate certain properties of information-structural models. It was Diderichsen's idea that the kernel of Danish sentences comprises two successive major parts or 'fields'. One, the so-called nexus field, contains *inter alia* the finite verb and the subject noun phrase. The other, the so-called content field, contains infinite verb forms and object noun phrases for example. Within each field there is a fixed constituent order defined in terms of the three slots: a verb slot, a noun phrase slot, and an adverbial phrase slot. The true highlight of the model was the introduction of an initial field (preceding the nexus field), the so-called fundament field, to which material of various kinds can be moved from the two other fields. The idea is that in most types of sentences the initial field is obligatorily filled; by default it is occupied by the sentence subject unless something else is moved to the front of the sentence for information-structural reasons. This notion of an initial place to which virtually all kinds of syntactic material can be moved, clearly anticipates the notion of root transformation. (Actually, transformations played a role already in Otto Jespersen's view of syntax, and Diderichsen was considerably influenced by Jespersen.)

Diderichsen's analytical scheme may be referred to as a sentence-topological model since it serves to show the 'spatial' arrangement of the constituents, as it were. With its strict adherence to linear order, the sentence scheme does not in itself suffice to specify the syntactic functions of the sentence constituents and the semantic relations among these. It is important to point out that this whole conception of sentence structure as a sequential arrangement was entirely at variance with glossematics. Although Diderichsen was a great admirer of Hjelmslev's and attempted to work with some of this ideas, there was an unsurmontable gap between their approaches to syntax.

In Hjelmslev's theoretical framework, syntax should be studied as content-form, just like the patterns of morphemes in derived and inflected words and just like the meanings of lexemes. This is true, although all of these phenomena of content-form can be approached only via their reflections in linguistic expression. Such a view of syntax entails that phenomena associated with linearity (e. g., word order) have no well-defined place in glossematic grammar.

As a result, the CLC can be said to have comprised a number of mutually almost independent trends, although the glossematic program was the most conspicuous one. This was not felt to be a weakness of the Circle. Hjelmslev himself once observed that it is a tradition in Danish scholarship to be untraditional.

As long as Hjelmslev was around, he had an enormous influence on the debate because of his extraordinary skills in the art of scholarly discourse. This was not supposed to lead to a dominance of glossematic viewpoints. However, there often was a considerable degree of sharing of assumptions which sometimes made it difficult for interesting ideas from other schools to be taken seriously enough.

3. The development and propagation of glossematic theory

It is a major problem with glossematics that there does not exist a fully comprehensive presentation of the theory by its creators. Hjelmslev himself wrote a famous prolegomena to the theory: *Omkring Sprogteoriens Grundlæggelse* (1943, English version: *Prolegomena to a Theory of Language*, 1953, [2]1961), which still stands as the most inspiring and the best-known presentation of his ideas. About the same time he wrote a semipopular book *Sproget* ("Language"), which was published only much later but then eventually appeared in translations into several languages. In 1957, Uldall published the first part of *Outline of Glossematics*, the work which was supposed to be their joint presentation of the theory itself, and which had been announced already in 1937. During and after Word War II, however, the two scholars had been geographically separated for many years and had drifted apart in their views. After the volume authored by Uldall nothing more appeared. For decades a higly condensed account of the theory, the *Resumé*, had been known to members of the CLC in manuscript form. This account of glossematics, which is extremely hard to read because it is largely a collection of definitory statements and lacks exemplification of how to apply the theory, was finally published in 1975 in English translation by Francis J. Whitfield (1916 – 1996), ten years after Hjelmslev's death.

As other important primary sources to glossematic theory and descriptive practice one may point to (1) the Journal *Acta Linguistica*, (2) the *Bulletins* of the CLC, some of which were published separately, others together with the journal, and with the Bulletin for 1941 – 1965 (published 1970) as a particularly rich source, and (3) the *Travaux du Cercle linguistique de Copenhague*, especially the two anthologies of Hjelmslev's own writings: *Essai I* (1959) mostly consisting of papers about content analysis and *Essais II* (1973) with more emphasis on expression analysis. The *Rapport* for 1931 – 1951 (published 1951) is informative in showing what kinds of papers were given before the CLC, and who were the active contributors during the crucial first two decades of its existence.

The somewhat sparse documentation of several details of glossematic theory has invited more or less elucidating comments and interpretations by subsequent generations of linguists both in Denmark and abroad. Probably the most well-known secondary source is Siertsema's book (1955). A more condensed and highly informative survey of the basic ideas (with special emphasis on the expression analysis) can be found in Fischer-Jørgensen's Phonology monograph (1975: 114 – 143), also her important paper on "Form and substance in glossematics" (1966) and her contribution to *The Linguistics Ency-*

clopaedia (Fischer-Jørgensen 1991) must be specially mentioned here. Semiotic and other aspects of Hjelmslev's theory are approached for instance in a variety of papers in Caputo & Galassi (1985). The most extensive and detailed studies have been published in Danish, viz. Gregersen (1991), vol. I, 171−364, vol. II, 1−228), and Rasmussen (1992). These authors both give penetrating analyses of Hjelmslev's linguistic program but from very different perspectives. Gregersen wants to understand the development as triggered by the more or less harmonious personal relationships between the Danish linguists of the structuralist era and provides a wealth of historiographical information; Rasmussen given an in-depth interpretation of glossematics as a linguistic theory, covering much more ground than any previous presentation of glossematics. Both works contain very extensive bibliographies.

In spite of the fragmentary nature of the primary glossematic literature, it is clear from the existing sources that Hjelmslev and Uldall had the ambitious goal of providing a fully formalized version of the theory of language. This was to be achived by working deductively and by attaining formal explicitness and methodological consistency (cf. Fudge 1995).

With its analytical rigor, glossematics was one of the trends in structural linguistics which inspired other disciplines within the humanities to adopt structuralist views in some form, although the various disciplines rarely share much more than the most general notions of semiotic function, dependency relations, and taxonomic classification.

It has sometimes been claimed by linguists of other schools that glossematics was too abstract and too far removed from empirical facts. No doubt formal analysis in glossematics is abstract in relation to sound or meaning but that does not mean that the theory leaves no place for descriptions of phonic or graphic patterns within the expression analysis or of semantic patterns within the content analysis. Such information is descriptively subordinate to abstract, formal statements, however. As for the issue of empirical foundation, Hjelmslev formulated three principles (cf. Siertsema 1965: 37) according to which a description should be (1) free from contradiction (self-consistent), (2) exhaustive, and (3) as simple as possible. Of these, principles (1) takes precedence over (2), and (2) over (3). The Simplicity principle, Hjelmslev repeatedly emphasized, not only applies to formal statements but to overall descriptions. Thus it also applies to the greater or lesser simplicity with which the relationship between form and substance is stated.

Glossematic theory, as presented programmatically but with only fragmentary elucidation in Hjelmslev's writings, is more specifically characterized by certain basic claims about the nature of linguistic structure. From the perspective of a spectator, these claims can be divided up into at least six separate issues, as done in the subsections below.

4. Some basic characteristics of glossematic theory

In this section, an attempt is made to give a brief account of some of the most important features characterizing glossematic theory and descriptive practice. It is not the goal here to give a rigid and consistent exposition of glossematic theory as such. For one thing, that would require extensive presentations of theory-specific terminology and of essential parts of the complex definitory apparatus. Rather, the attempt is made to characterize glossematics from the perspective of an outsider by discussing in very general terms some of the properties of the theory which made glossematics a special trend in structural linguistics, and which either promoted or impeded its acceptance as a descriptive paradigm. This selectivity and subjectivity in the presentation is a feature not only of the choice and formulation of the issues but also of the more or less detailed commentaries offered in what follows.

4.1. Content and expression, form and substance

Some of the most basic glossematic innovations were within the theory of the linguistic sign. According to Saussurean theory, the language sign has content ('signifié') and expression ('signifiant'). Now, this relation between a content and an expression is not necessarily confined to the sign function of ordinary language; it is possible to envisage sign systems of higher order (metasemiotics) in which either content or expression is in itself a sign system. Hjelmslev extended sign theory in this way and pointed out, among other things, that with the artistic use of language (e. g., poetic style) we have a situation where the expression plane is in itself a semiotic (the use of stylistic features has a semiotic function). In the case of a linguistic statement, it is the content plane that is in itself a semiotic (the statement is about something with content and expression). Viewed in this way, the study of ordinary language, i.e., linguistics, acquires a key role in the study of verbal art and, even more importantly, linguistics becomes the central scientific discipline. Although Hjelmslev never elaborated his sign theory in much detail on these points, his programmatic statements had a strong impact on European scholars of the structuralist era.

Another innovation which is even more basic to the glossematic conception of language, is that glossematic theory recognized not just one linguistic form mediating between meaning and expression but two different forms: 'content-form' and 'expression-form'. This is different from both Saussure and indeed quite different from the traditional grammatical term 'form' (as in 'word form', and so on) which was continued in American structural linguistics. In glossematics, the concept of 'form' is associated with invariance and linguistic function, and it applies separately to content and to expression. One would traditionally say that the English plural form *cat* + *s* exhibits an ending which is a formative with the meaning 'plural' and the expression *s*, but according to glossematic theory it is these content and expression entities taken separately, rather than the synthesis of them into an ending *-s*, that reflect linguistic form.

The rationale for distinguishing between content-form and expression-form is that the linguistic sign is arbitrary. In the words *boy* and *girl*, *bull* and *cow*, we can observe a content difference of 'male' vs. 'female'; the word expressions are also different but there is no match between content and expression differences. The Latin ending *-us* of *dominus* can be analysed into content elements by confronting it with other endings of the same paradigm, and it can be analysed into expression elements, but there is no match. Altogether, then, there is an arbitrary relation between content and expression. Language is a semiotic having this particular property.

Only in specific cases such as degrees of emphasis can one observe a fixed coupling ('solidarity') between differences within content and expression: the more one enhances the acoustic signal, the more content emphasis is conveyed. If this were the situation all through language, the analysis of content and of expression would lead to the same abstract pattern: language would have only one form and its lexicon would consist of symbols rather than bilateral signs.

The arbitrariness of the sign relation is what gives languages its creative potential. The language system itself comprises an abstract system of content elements and an abstract system of expression elements, the structural units in each plane *per se* being established by relations within that particular plane. Language becomes a semiotic by the sign function relating content and expression to each other, but the possible inventory of signs (e.g., lexemes, sentences, paragraphs) is in principle unlimited. That is, a linguistic system is not defined by the associated lexicon but by the structural categories of content and expression. On the other hand, it is the sign function which permits the linguist to arrive at an analysis of monoplanar linguistic structure by looking at the interplay (including the mismatch) between content and expression.

From a broad perspective, sign theory is the aspect of glossematic theory which has had the most lasting influence, not only on linguistics but on semiotics in general and on the philosophy of science. This is witnessed also by a current interest in Hjelmslevian sign theory in Italy and Japan for instance.

The next question is what exactly is meant by the dichotomy of 'form' versus 'substance' in glossematics.

Saussure's *Cours*, as it became known to Hjelmslev's generation of structuralists, contains a statement to the effect that language is form not substance. In glossematics, both form and substance are recognized as components of the design of language. The realm of linguistic form, no matter whether one is dealing with content or with expression, may be said to comprise (i) categories and (ii) 'functions' between or within these (i.e., 'syntagmatic functions' or 'relations' as well as 'paradigmatic functions' or 'correlations'; see further 4.4. below). To be more precise, however, one must observe that the categories themselves are established via their function as the end-points (terms) of functions.

'Substance', like form, has a status in content as well as expression: in the English example above, the meaning of 'plural' and the letter *s* or the sound [s] are entities of linguistic substance; by analytical operations they may be found (and are indeed found) to reflect entities on a higher level of abstraction: content form and expression form.

4.1.1. Expression-form

The formal system emerging from a glossematic expression analysis is of course relatable to language data manifested in some substance, be it phonic or graphic or other. It is essential to note, however, that the entities of glossematic form are not to be understood as classes of material tokens nor as types defined over such tokens. The expression *figura* |s| found in the expression form of spoken English is not a sound type, nor is the figura |s| of written English a letter type; what the formal analysis is supposed to retrieve in both cases is a perfectly abstract entity which should be defined independently of its reflection in a particular substance.

It became one of the most conspicuous claims of glossematics that linguistic substance presupposes linguistic form: form may exist independently of substance but not vice versa. In principle, one can imagine a language which exists as a formal structure without being spoken or, as a transitional phenomenon, without being manifested in any expression-substance at all. One argument in favour of the independence of form from substance was that we observe in actual languages how the same linguistic form can be manifested in different media, e. g., both phonetically and graphically. (This line of argumentation, of course, only implies that form is not tied to a specific substance since a spoken and a written language *may* have the same expression-form; it does not follow that this is always or even typically the case. We all know that, on the contrary, it is the exception rather than the rule that there is conformity between spoken and written language. If there is conformity, it is likely not to be complete, not even in languages with newly created orthographies.)

Eli Fischer-Jørgensen (b. 1911) repeatedly took issue with this claim about the independence of form vis-à-vis substance. She has pointed out that it is substance that is immediately accessible to observation: form cannot be addressed without being manifested in at least *some* substance. If we take spoken language, the identification of variants in different positions as members of the same invariants, e. g., initial *p-* with final *-p*, initial *t-* with final *-t*, etc. (an operation called 'reduction' in glossematic terms) involves consideration of substance. There is, however, no necessary conflict here since the reduction of sets of variants to categories of invariants can be performed so as to give the best fit with substance simply in order for the overall description to be as simple as possible.

Fischer-Jørgensen also pointed out that the very distinction between invariants by means of the 'commutation test' (or the minimal pairs test) crucially involves substance. This is obviously true: if two vowels [i] and [e] are found to be minimally contrastive, as in English *pin*, *pen*, then they are manifestations of different invariants, otherwise they are variants. Hjelmslev eventually conceded that it *is* substance that is immediately observable in the study of commutation. This means that the commutation test is an operation by which the analyst retrieves abstract form behind substance data.

In early glossematics, substance was understood as amorphous matter onto which structure was projected by the abstract linguistic form. In phonic expression-substance there is a continuum of, say, front vowels of different degrees of openness but in expression-form there is a language-specific and limited inventory of invariants, e. g., a set of two: *i, a* or a set of four: *i, e, æ, a*, which in each case divide the vowel space of phonic substance among them, as it were.

It is interesting to consider how glossematic expression-form and expression-substance compare with the descriptive levels that were recognized in other structuralist schools, especially those of the American mould. Hjelmslev's expression-form was established on the basis of criteria enabling him to reduce the inventory of invariants as much as possible. This reduction proceeded along two very different lines. On the one hand, the inventory was reduced by purely distributional operations, as when Danish aspirated stops were reduced to combinations of |h| with |b d g|. Such reductionism is well-known also from American structuralist phonemics. On the other hand, and much more interestingly, Hjelmslev wanted to reduce variation in the representation of linguistic sign expressions to a minimum (a desideratum which he formulated already in 1928 in his *Principes de grammaire générale*, before the development of glossematics proper). This means that German *Rad* "wheel" must be set up with final |d| on the basis of such forms as dative [ra:də] although there is overlapping between |t| and |d| in final position, as in Nom. Sg. [ra:t]. This is in accordance with Prague phonology in which overlapping was recognized as belonging to phonology proper under the name of neutralization. However, expression-form went further than that. In a glossematic analysis, the expression-form of the lexeme *tout* in French indisputably ends in a final consonant although it varies over [tu] in the (uninflected) masculine and [tut] in the (inflected) feminine. In both the German and the French example the variation can be accounted for by rule so that it can be eliminated from the ideal formal notation.

We see that Hjelmslev's expression-form was in fact quite close to a morphophonemic representation in the post-Bloomfieldian sense (cf. Z. S. Harris' morphophonemes) and to an underlying representation in the later framework of orthodox generative phonology. If glossematic expression-analysis was sometimes criticized for 'mixing levels', this seems to reflect an erroneous identification of glossematic expression-form as a kind of phonemics. From the glossematic perspective, the subject-matter of both Praguean *Phonologie* and American mainstream phonemics was the structure of substance rather than linguistic form in the glossematic sense.

The affinity between levels of representation in glossematic expression analysis and in generative phonology goes even further in that Hjelmslev distinguished between so-called 'ideal' notation and so-called 'actualized' notation. In ideal notion, all variation and overlapping predictable by rules was eliminated: *Rad* and *Rat* "council" were given different representations |ra:d| and |ra:t| although they sounded alike. In actualized notation, however, invariants occurring with overlapping, as |t| and |d| in German *Rad* and *Rat*, were represented accordingly, both lexemes having the same actualized form |ra:t/d|. This distinction of levels is reminiscent of what has been referred to in much more recent *phonology* as *lexical* versus *post-lexical*. The fundamental difference between glossematic expression analysis and transformational-generative approaches to phonology is that a glossematic statement is a strictly static description of relationships obtaining within a structural whole: it is not the case that something is derived as the output of rules operating on an input. On this particular point, glossematics is more akin to the configuration-oriented approaches to non-linear phonology that came in vogue since the mid-1970s.

4.1.2. Content-form

According to glossematics, meaning is linguistically structured in a way which is basically analogous to the linguistic structuring of phonic (or graphic) expression. Just as we can see a vowel continuum as divided by expression form into language-specific sets of distinct vowel ranges, so the semantic field of colours is organized language-specifically, as documented by colour names. The pattern constituted by content-form throws a grid over the colour continuum, according to Hjelmslev's metaphor, and thereby structures substance into language-specific colour ranges: green, blue, etc., where both the number of colours that are distinguished and the semantic boundaries between them may vary from one language to another.

The very observation that contrastive meanings entail differences in content-form does not, however, guarantee the feasibility of an exhaustive content analysis although the analysis of both content and expression along analogous lines was programmatically put on the agenda by the founders of glossematics. It was a fundamental tenet that meaning can be interpreted as a reflection of intrinsic content-structure composed of content *figurae* just like phonic or graphic substance can be interpreted as reflections of expression-structure. As for lexical meanings, however, Hjelmslev and other glossematicians only managed to demonstrate this in cases such as *boy* versus *girl* etc. where it is simple to demonstrate and perhaps even trivial that one can extract elementary meanings ('male', 'female') and interpret these as content figurae. It remains a postulate that it is possible to make an exhaustive content analysis. What is more, it has been pointed out that the content figurae posited by Hjelmslev in these examples are such that can be encoded as separate lexemes in the language. This does not invalidate the analysis but raises the question of how to perform *exhaustive* analyses of simplex lexemes into figurae in a non-arbitrary fashion. This would seem to require that the analyst has access to a representation of content-substance (a semantic representation) whose inventory of elementary meanings can be tested for contrast ('commutation'), just as vowel or consonant sounds can be tested for contrast on the expression plane. How else would it be possible to arrive at an inventory of invariants on the content plane?

This leads over to the other crucial issue: the analysis of syntax as content-structure. We here face much the same problem, and in fact, Hjelmslev argued against a separation of syntax and morphology: from the point of view of meaning, it all belongs to content-structure. The question is: can we state a syntactic pattern without reference to the chain formed by concatenated linguistic signs: words, lexemes, affixes, etc.? It is hard to see how. It remains to be demonstrated that there is a non-arbitrary way of specifying intrinsic syntax as something which is autonomous in relation to sign-based syntax. (A very similar problem arose some decades later with the development of Generative Semantics from sign-based Chomskyan syntax.)

The definition of syntax as content form certainly did not preclude the occupation with morphological phenomena in glossematic analysis. In dealing with syntactic issues, which Hjelmslev did in some of his most brilliant work such as the 1948 paper "Le verbe et la phrase nominale', he actually speaks of categories such as Nouns and Verbs and indeed Words. Thus he posits a general, structural definition of a verb: "Est *verbe* un mot conjugué (ou conjugable)": a verb is a word which is conjugated or can be conjugated. What did not emerge with complete clarity was how statements about morphology were to be fitted into the ultimate language description.

One of the fundamental characteristics of a syntax which is *not* sign-based is that sequential order is not a structural property within syntax proper. This is very much in line with Hjelmslev's whole approach to linearity: in the specification of linguistic form he wanted to speak of sequential order not as a primary feature of linguistic form but as the reflex of formal dependency relations (more adequately 'presupposition' relations, see 4.4. below) among the various parts of the linguistic chain. This is a fruitful view of a content-based syntax, but when it comes to the expression side, it is hard to see how one can get rid of sequential ordering in the description of linguistic structure. For instance, how can selectional relations specify that both *ask* and *aks* are possible syllables/words in Danish?

The most interesting feature of Hjelmslev's attempt to approach syntax as intrinsic structure is his handling of inflectional material, in particular verb conjugation. The content elements of verb conjugation are, according to him, immediate constituents of the whole clause (in this case so-called 'extense exponents', see 4.3. below) if considered in relation to intrinsic syntactic structure. In many languages we can observe that such content elements belong to material which is put at the end of verbs, but such observations are made with reference to formatives and words qua linguistic signs (cf. Hjelmslev's definition of verbs referred to above) not with reference to content proper.

4.1.3. Stratification

The 2 × 2 language scheme: content vs. expression and form vs. substance, as defined in glossematics, underwent a significant change with Hjelmslev's 1954 paper "La stratification du langage". When Hjelmslev presented the newly published paper at a meeting of the CLC, he reported that the editor of *Word*, André Martinet, had asked him to write an easily understandable paper about glossematics, but what came out of the exercise was something new and challenging. Hjelmslev now spoke of the language scheme as composed of four strata, viz. two central ones: content-form and expression-form, and two marginal ones: content-substance and expression-substance. Both here and in Uldall's subsequent contribution to the general exposition of glossematic theory (Uldall 1957) substance not only became recognized as belonging to language design proper but was regarded as formed matter in its own right. What this implies is that substance and form may be non-conformous. For example, a feature of phonic substance may extend over a whole word whereas from the perspective of linguistic form the distinctive element in question is localized in a specific consonant or vowel (the standard example is nasalization). Expression substance thus exhibits two kinds of structuring: its intrinsic phonic or graphic structure and the structure projected onto substance by expression-form. That is why form and substance came to be recognized as separate linguistic strata.

According to the Stratification model there is a similar duality when it comes to the relationship between content-form and expression-form. Within each of these Hjelmslev (1954) posited both *intrinsic units* and *extrinsic units*, the former being such that are inherent to the stratum and the latter such that are projected onto it from another stratum. The interplay between content and expression produces extrinsic units (e.g., words) which reflect the sign function.

The distinction between intrinsic and extrinsic units is rather obvious if we look at the expression-form stratum: syllable boundaries are intrinsic, word boundaries are extrinsic. This is roughly what André Martinet dubbed 'double articulation', i.e., the simultaneous and often conflicting segmentation of a linguistic string into entities such as words and morphemes, on the one hand, and syllables and phonemes, on the other. The interesting issue, of course, is what role the two kinds of units play in the analysis of the expression-form. Hjelmslev makes some very lucid statements in the 1954 paper to the effect that intrinsic formal units (*figurae*) are retrievable only by the analysis of intrinsic units. This may have been inspired by Uldall who was familiar with the American structuralist approach with its rigid separation of levels. (In several writings on glossematics Fischer-Jørgensen has emphasized the influence of Uldall's viewpoints on Hjelmslev's in the 1950s.) Hjelmslev's descriptive practice, however, e. g., in his analysis of the Danish expression system of 1949 (Hjelmslev [1973: 247 – 266]), seems to be characterized by much more integration of intrinsic and extrinsic units.

It is much more difficult to see exactly what it implies to distinguish between intrinsic and extrinsic units with respect to the content-form of language, especially since neither Hjelmslev nor Uldall ever went into detail with this issue. The structure which is constituted by such units as lexemes, grammatical formatives and words was never posited as a separate form level in glossematics. This is in perfect agreement with the glossematic conception of content-form also before the introduction of the Stratification model: unlike the traditional notion of 'syntactic structure' which has been used and elaborated in the American tradition from Bloomfield to Chomsky, the glossematic approach to syntactic phenomena was totally integrated into content-analysis.

The stratificational viewpoint did not get elaborated further in glossematics, nor were its viewpoints explicitly modified later, as Uldall died shortly after the publication of his *Outline of Glossematics* in 1957, and Hjelmslev's scholarly work was soon more or less discontinued. The *Resumé* of glossematic theory, which the two left unpublished, does not speak of strata, although it had been updated to some extent over the years.

4.2. Hierarchical structure

The organization of linguistic structure is strictly hierarchical, both in content and in expression. By *analysis* (= a stepwise top-down analysis) one can recognize constituents of different degrees (different hierarchical ranks) and define these with reference to the units they are derived from by the hierarchical analysis. There is no particular upper limit to this hierarchy (such as 'the sentence' in Chomskyan linguistics): linguistic analysis means analysis of a text, and a 'text' may be anything from a short linguistic string to a mass of text (including the complete works of an author, for example). The limitation is that in order to be accessible to linguistic analysis, a text must form an entity with both content and expression.

However, on can observe that below a certain level (roughly: that of the sentence) the content and expression planes become increasingly different in structure, i. e., non-conformous; the specific linguistic form categories are established by dependency relations operating below that level, within one plane or the other.

After the constituents of textual material have been established by analysis, it is possible to perform *synthesis* of units from elements, e. g., units consisting of vowels flanked by consonants, and whole syllables composed of such vowel-consonant aggregations plus syllable accents. This dichotomy of analysis/synthesis means that units of a certain size have dual definitions: an analytical one and a synthetic one. Units defined in these different ways are given different labels, e. g., 'syllabeme' versus 'syllable'.

4.3. Isomorphism of content and expression: Themes and exponents

The two planes of content and expression exhibit a significant isomorphism in the way units on different levels are made up of themes and exponents. As an example of a theme in the expression plane, one may mention the aggregation of consonants and vowel(s) which makes up the segmental part of a syllable, the vowels forming the 'centre' and the consonants forming the 'margin' of the theme. If we switch to the content plane, the content of a lexeme is the isomorphic counterpart of the theme of a syllable. The content elements involved likewise constitute a theme, and if the word is derived, there is a distinction between central and marginal parts of its content theme which is structurally analogous to the distinction between vowels and consonants within the syllable.

Such themes, within content or expression, may in turn be carriers of one or several *exponents* which contract dependency relations with exponents of other themes. An example from the expression is the dependency relation in stress accent languages between the accent manifested as weak stress and the accent manifested as strong stress: the former presupposes the latter, and this relation establishes a syntagmatic whole (of the size of a word or a phrase) consisting of two or several syllables. Similarly, vowel harmony establishes a syntagmatic whole, which may be coextensive with the traditional, morphosyntactic 'word'. On the content plane, the relations traditionally treated as 'rection' (e. g., between a preposition and a case) and 'concord' (e. g., case agreement) are likewise relations between exponents and establish syntagmatic wholes (viz. prepositional phrases and noun phrases, in theory-neutral terminology) which contain aggregations of themes characterized by dependency-related exponents.

The theory of exponents, as presented in Hjelmslev's papers from the late 1930s such as "Accent, intonation, quantité" (Hjelmslev [1973: 181−222]) and "Essai d'une théorie des morphèmes" (Hjelmslev [1970: 152−164]) and followed up in later papers (also reprinted in the 1970 and 1973 volumes), is perhaps the most substantial contribution of glossematics to the modelling of linguistic structure. By the 1930s, the theory of exponential phenomena such as accentual systems had not by far reached the same degree of sophistication in Prague phonology, Firthian prosodics, or American phonemics, and the structural analogy between prosodemes and inflectional material was specific to glossematics.

Expression exponents are *prosodemes*, e. g., the (stress) accents which establish syntagmatic relations between stressed and unstressed syllables in languages having this category of 'expression exponents'. Content exponents are *morphemes* (typically but not necessarily expressed by inflectional material) which establish syntagmatic relations, e. g., of concord or rection = government. There is a crucial distinction between *extense* and *intense* exponents, i. e., exponents which contract syntagmatic relations over a wider versus a more restricted domain (the terms 'extense' and 'intense' are not to be confused with 'extensive' and 'intensive', which in glossematics refer to overlapping elements with different ranges of manifestation, cf. 4.4. below). On the expression plane, intonations (in glossematic terminology: *modulations*) are 'extense', accents are 'intense'. On the content plane there is a distinction between 'extense' verbal morpheme categories and 'intense' nominal morpheme categories: the categories of mood and tense contract distant relations (across clause boundaries) whereas number and case, for example, contract local relations (within a noun syntagm or a clause).

4.4. Functional criteria and analytical operations

The theory of functions is, along with the sign theory, the most distinctive feature of glossematics. Functions may be paradigmatic, i. e., they operate within sets of interchangeable entities, or syntagmatic, i. e., they operate on parts of strings.

From the point of view of language analysis, the paradigmatic function par excellence is 'commutation', i. e., roughly what is called contrast or contrastiveness in other schools. Commutation involves both planes at the same time and thus permits analyses of both content-form and expression-form depending on the perspective of the analyst. In English, one may exchange *a* and *e* on the expression side and observe that this brings about differences in content, cf. the different meanings of *man* and *men*, *pan* and *pen*, *sat* and *set*, etc. The interesting fact is that the criterion works both ways. We may choose instead to exchange 'singular' and 'plural' on the content side and we then observe that in English this brings about differences in expression, cf. *man* vs. *men*, *cow* vs. *cows*, *child* vs. *children*. It is crucial to observe that differences on the two planes do *not* match each other since the sign function is characterized by arbitrariness (cf. 4.1. above). This non-conformity between the planes enables the analyst to categorize commutable entities as discrete entities: although the manifestations of two entities may form a continuum, there is nothing gradual about their formal distinctness as established by the commutation test; this contention is warranted by the non-gradual nature of the differences triggered on the other plane.

Commutation is the most basic analytical criterion in glossematic analysis: no matter whether one is studying content or expression, two entities are to be assigned different formal representations only if the exchange of one for the other is accompanied by differences on the other plane.

The most interesting paradigmatic phenomenon beside communication is the suspension of contrast: 'syncretism', which is manifested as overlapping between two invariants. On the expression plane, syncretism is closely related to the phonological notion of 'neutralization' (the differences in applicability need not concern us here), the example from German mentioned in 4.1.1. above exemplifies syncretism between |t| and |d|. On the content plane, Hjelmslev's use of the term is much more reminiscent of grammatical tradition: whereas there is commutation between dative and ablative in the singular in Latin, there is syncretism beween the two cases in the plural. The suspension of commutation must be statable with reference to a category by which it is 'dominated', e. g., final position in the German example of t/d, plural in the Latin example of dative/ablative. The reflexes of syncretized entities, such as the occurrence of [t] rather than [d] for final t/d in German, are used as a criterion in the ultimate reduction of form entities into irreducible elements: 'glossemes'. Since these are suppsed to be perfectly abstract (unlike distinctive features, which by their anchoring in phonetics belong to the realm of substance), the analysis of German |t| and |d| into glossemes becomes structurally much more interesting the moment we can establish a asymmetry between the two. The skewed manifestation allows us to state that |t| and |d| (and similarly other analogous consonant pairs) are distinguished by a correlation between an 'extensive' term, viz. the one represented by |t|, and an 'intensive' term, viz. the one represented by |d|. Hjelmslev spoke of 'vicariation' or 'participation' in instances where one member of a pair, the 'extensive' member, subsumes the other, 'intensive' member (as when in some languages a masculine personal pronoun can cover both 'masculine' and 'feminine' in appropriate contexts; in his lectures, Hjelmslev used a traditional wedding ritual as an amusing example). There is some reason to believe that the glossematic notion of 'participation' deserves more exploitation; this is certainly true if it is applied to the phonologies of languages not streamlined by an orthography. (The glossematic handling of 'paradigmatic function' is otherwise technically quite complex and will not be dealt with here.)

The basic set of syntagmatic functions between entities comprises (1) unilateral dependency, (2) bilateral dependency, and (3) mutual non-presupposition. In the sometimes rather idiosyncratic glossematic terminology these three relations are called respectively 'selection', 'solidarity' and 'combination', with selection and solidarity subsumed under the term 'presupposition' (which is not to be used in a pragmatic sense in glossematics). It is crucial to discover instances of selection in order to recognize functional categories in a language. This is true for both expression and content. Categories such as vowels and consonants are defined in terms of selection, consonants presupposing vowels. In derived words, the derivational content elements presuppose the radical content elements.

If there is a solidarity, e. g., in a language in which all syllables are of a CV type, one may still recognize different paradigmatic classes, but in the glossematic framework these are not typologically on a par with vowels and consonants in languages in which syllables can consist entirely of vowels.

Ironically enough, the most basic relation in language, namely, that between the content and expression planes is one of solidarity. This means, Hjelmslev pointed out, that one cannot determine which plane to label 'content' and which plane to label 'expression' except by taking the different reflections of form in substance into consideration.

It is characteristic of glossematic analysis that it involves such rigidly defined operations as the use of the commutation test and the application of criteria for dependency relations. This, however, does not mean that linguistic analysis is to be understood as a practical discovery procedure; rather, the operations constitute a formal procedure which identifies the members of the various linguistic categories in accordance with the definitory apparatus of the theory.

4.5. General linguistics as structural typology

It is the goal of a structural approach to language to provide a general framework such that all possible structures can in principle be predicted by means of a general calculus. This further means that structuralism makes possible a rational language typology which is not based on random and subjective criteria but on the application of one and the same set of formal criteria to all languages under consideration.

At least for Hjelmslev himself, the structuralist program as developed in glossematics, led toward an ultimate goal: a general language typology. As for genetic classification of languages, Hjelmslev fully recognized the success of the comparative paradigm developed in the 19th century. The task ahead was to provide for a well-founded typological classification of languages. This, in his view, presupposed a general framework with rigid criteria for the establishment of linguistic categories in order for descriptions of different languages to be comparable on the formal level. The glossematic vision was not a substance-based characterization of languages, let alone a search for substantive universals à la Jakobson's distinctive features, but on the contrary a typology referring to purely formal properties of languages. Much of the excessive formalism in Hjelmslevian linguistics makes sense if seen from this perspective.

From the viewpoint of communication across linguistic traditions, however, one may question the appropriateness of definitions which not only introduce novel terminology but also give some generally used terms a much more specific meaning. An example is the definition of 'verb' referred to in 4.1.2. above. As Hjelmslev says explicitly himself, it implies that a language without conjugation has no verbs (Hjelmslev 1970: 168). Hjelmslev emphasizes that this definition is a *general*, structural definition, not a universal, semantic one. He does not exclude the usefulness of a definition of the latter kind but says that the definitions 'operate on different levels' ("opèrent à des niveaux différents" [ibid. p. 169]).

The same problem arises, e.g., with the structural definitions of 'vowel' and 'consonant' put forward by Hjelmslev in various papers (published in Hjelmslev 1970, 1973). He defines these two categories by the relationship of unilateral dependency (in glossematic terminology: 'selection'), the category of vowels being presupposed ('selected') by the category of consonants. This means, first of all, that only a language in which expression units with no consonants are possible, can be said to exhibit vowels in strict accordance with the definition; in languages whose syllables all contain both vowels and consonants, these two classes are interdependent (in glossematic terminology there is 'solidarity') and are thus not vowels and consonants in the formal sense. Secondly, there must be a domain within which the dependency relation is contracted: this is the syllable, but the syllable in turn must be defined by some formal property in order to serve as the domain of a formal relation. This formal property, according to Hjelmslev, is the commutable accent (as in 'import vs. im'port). The ultimate consequence of this approach is that a glossematic typology will highlight the difference between languages with and without an accent category. The latter type of languages, comprising languages such as French, will be found not only to lack the accent category but also to lack formally defined categories of syllable, vowel, and consonant.

Languages with vowel harmony, such as Turkish, would differ in another way, according to Hjelmslev, since vowel harmony is a dependency relation contracted between parts of syllables, and more specifically between certain components of vowels (e.g., those manifested by front vs. back lingual articulation and rounded vs. unrounded lips). According to glossematic criteria, these harmonizing components do not formally belong to the vowels. Instead, the harmonizing components should be considered as syllable exponents, i.e., prosodic entities. It is only the residue of the vowel segment that forms part of the syllable nucleus. This means that languages with vowel harmony are likewise profoundly different from other languages in terms of vowel typology.

A rather similar view of vowel harmony was put forward but developed in much more detail within the Firthian prosodic school. Altogether, Hjelmslev's approach to prosodic categories is in some ways reminiscent of that of his contemporary J. R. Firth (1890–1960), but since the glossematicians never published any detailed discussions of these aspects of language typology, this affinity between the two schools tends to be overlooked in the historiographical literature.

The extreme formalism which characterizes much of glossematics, apparently at the expense of useful applications to language description and typology, has been a hindrance to a more general acceptance of the theory and the incorporation of glossematic ideas into other frameworks. French and other languages without contrastive accent have indeed got syllables, vowels, and consonants in some descriptive sense. If it were not possible to speak of such segmental categories in accentless languages, there would be no way of making interesting typological comparisons between vowel or consonant patterns across languages with and without distinctive accent. This must be the reason why Hjelmslev introduced the notions of 'pseudo-syllable', 'pseudo-vowel' and 'pseudo-consonant', all of which must be defined on a distributional basis.

Distributional criteria played a much more general role in the version of glossematic analysis which was outlined by Uldall in his portion of the general presentation of the theory (Uldall 1957). During his several years in the United States, Uldall, being an outstanding practical phonetician and general linguist, contributed significantly to the documentation of American Indian languages; in fact, he may now be best known for his work on Maidu. Uldall's approach to linguistic analysis may perhaps be viewed as a synthesis of the glossematic theory of uni- and bilateral dependency relations with certain components of post-Bloomfieldian distributionalism and descriptive realism. This affinity to distributionalism never became the general trend in glossematics, however. Hjelmslev's most influential writings, such as his outline of the Danish expression system (1951 [English translation 1973]), emphasized the hierarchical nature of language design and the descriptive priority of a top-down approach to the definition of structural categories.

5. Danish structural linguistics: Professed and putative glossematicians

As stated in section 2. above, two of the most prominent figures of Copenhagen structuralism, Viggo Brøndal and Paul Diderichsen, belonged outside glossematics, although Diderichsen somewhat unsuccessfully attempted to incorporate glossematic ideas in his work. Both Diderichsen and other Danish and foreign scholars were so inspired and impressed by Hjelmslevs theoretical creativity that their contributions to the Hjelmslev Festschrift in 1949 (*Recherches structurales*) conveys the impression of more unity in Danish linguistics of the period than was actually the case.

It is a somewhat paradoxical fact that the real stronghold of glossematics since the 1940s was among Danish dialectologists. The structuralist trend in Danish dialectology, which was not matched by anything similar in Norway and Sweden, was inaugurated by Anders Bjerrum (1903−1984), who had a background in traditional Nordic philology and eventually got a chair in onomastics at the University of Copenhagen. Bjerrum became convinced of the fruitfulness of a functional approach to expression analysis when he struggled to retrieve the sound system of an extinct Danish dialect (spoken in what is now part of Germany) by comparing a variety of impressionistic data taken down, in the pre-structural period, by various Danish field-workers including himself. Although Bjerrum first associated himself with Prague phonology, he soon declared himself a fullfledged adherent of the stringent, formal approach found in glossematics (e. g., Bjerrum 1944). In this vein, he worked out a grammar of early medieval Danish, based on the manuscript version of a provincial law (ms. B74 of Skånske Lov), in which he carried out a strictly graphemic analysis of the expression side, his whole approach being deliberately in stark contrast with the well-established philological approach of retrieving a more or less hypothetical spoken language behind the written data. This grammar was eagerly studied by students of Danish and Nordic philology since the mid-1950s although it was available only in mimeographed form.

For decades after World War II, Danish dialectology was dominated by a strictly synchronic structuralist approach to analysis and description of sound systems. It was terminologically most indebted to glossematics although the formal framework was rather a compromise between theoretical rigor and the constraints on formalism imposed by the practical task of documenting the lexicon of Danish dialects. There has always been a certain affinity to Prague phonology. It is conspicuous that Danish dialectologists never produced content grammars along glossematic lines.

The leading dialectologist of the 1950s, Poul Andersen (1901−1985), strongly advocated the use of rather abstract notations in the glossematic trend in a large dictionary project comprising all Danish insular dialects which was then in a preparatory phase. Each individual dialect was to be approached as an autonomous synchronic state, and as a result, much of the output from Danish dialectological work consisted in sample analyses of the expression systems of highly localized dialects or even idiolects, each with extensive word lists in structural notation documenting the contrastiveness and the combinatory possibilities of the individual vowels and consonants established for the dialect. A considerable number of publications appeared in the monograph series of the Danish dialect society ("Udvalg for danske folkemål") as a result of this descriptive program, the most important being a series of dialect monographs by Ella Jensen, Børge Andersen, Poul Andersen, Bent Juul Nielsen, and not least by Inger Ejskjær (b. 1926), Poul Andersen's successor as professor of Danish dialectology. Perhaps the methodologically most original work in this series was her description of the Jutland dialect of Brøndum (Ejskær 1954).

As a corollary of the programmatic autonomy of the Danish dialect descriptions, the diachronic aspect was either absent or given marginal attention in most of them, and there was also a tendency to tone down the variational aspect. The influence from Hjelmslev thus had the consequence, for quite a long time, to give Danish dialectology a profile as a descriptive structuralist program which tended to loosen its ties not only with historical linguistics but even with dialect geography and with the eventually emerging sociolinguistics. In return, Danish dialectology had an obvious advance in its analytical rigor and consistent documentation by which it surpassed most of the work done elsewhere within Scandinavian and Germanic dialectology.

In addition to the dialectologists, Hjelmslev and Uldall also had a few other, devout followers in Denmark, notably the Indo-Europeanist Jens Holt (1904–1973), although the most persistent representative of glossematics was the Norwegian Romanist Leiv Flydal (1904–1983); compare Flydal (1954).

Two of the most prominent names which came to be associated with glossematics (by scholars outside Denmark) where those of Knud Togeby (1918–1974) and Eli Fischer-Jørgensen. Their status in relation to glossematics is different, however. Knud Togeby's doctoral dissertation *Structure immanente de la langue française* (1951) was a keen attempt to apply explicit structural approaches to a description of modern French. He was much influenced by Hjelmslev in his rather abstract approach to phonology but he deviated from glossematics in various ways, particularly by establing entities such as sentence intonations ('modulations') as a special category of 'morphophonèmes' having both content and expression (for Hjelmslev, prosody belonged to expression proper).

Eli Fischer-Jørgensen (b. 1911) has always been very influential in the debates of the Cercle linguistique de Copenhague. In the Glossematic Committee, she contributed much to the discussions of syntactic issues, although she eventually concentrated on phonetics and phonology. She published various comments on Hjelmslev's notion of how to analyse linguistic expression; as mentioned earlier, she convincingly pointed out that substance must be taken into account even in the analysis of abstract expression-form. Accordingly, scholars from other camps accorded her the role of a glossematic critic. In actual fact, Eli Fischer-Jørgensen's main field since the 1930s has been phonetics, and her conception of phonology is in many ways closer to that of the Prague phonologists N. S. Trubetzkoy and R. Jakobson. Being extremely broadly oriented within the field, however, she has written the standard survey of phonological theories (Fischer-Jørgensen 1975), which by the way devotes less than one tenth of its space to glossematic expression analysis.

In Norway and Sweden, Hjelmslev's *Prolegomena* inspired several linguists, but glossematics did not become a standard descriptive paradigm. Hjelmslev's main influence was that of inspiring and stimulating linguists to approach language as a self-contained system rather than to work strictly within a particular descriptive framework. He had a close contact (and friendship) with Alf Sommerfelt (1892–1965), but they differed considerably in their emphasis on different aspects of language study: Hjelmslev concentrated on the task of describing pure linguistic form, although his view of language comprised much wider perspectives; Sommerfelt put much more emphasis on the social aspect of language.

6. The CLC and Danish linguistics after Hjelmslev

Toward the end of his career, Hjelmslev's intellectual powers declined, and because of his enormous influence and prestige, there resulted a certain stagnation in Danish linguistics in the 1950s and 1960s. In the late 1950s some of his students formed an informal underground discussion group, the 'Cercle vicieux de Copenhague'. Its agenda were almost totally defined by Hjelmslev's doctrines, however, and since there was at that time little or no momentum within glossematics, the participants eventually felt frustrated, and the once fertile ground of these activities dried up.

Hjelmslev's death in 1965, and no less the death of several other outstanding Danish linguists in the years to follow, left a conspicuous vacuum in Danish linguistics. In spite of Hjelmslev's enormous influence on linguistic thinking in Denmark, glossematics never developed into a 'Neo-Hjelmslevian' trend the way 'Neo-Bloomfieldian' linguistics had established itself two decades before. On the other hand, unlike the situation in Sweden and Norway, where transformational grammar eventually became very influential, the linguistic tradition in Denmark came to function as a barrier against hasty acceptance of new doctrines, especially among linguists who had been part of the intellectual milieu of the CLC back in the 1950s.

It was somewhat different with the next generation. Around 1970 the descriptive potentials of Chomskyan generative grammar caught the interest of a number of younger linguists and linguistics students, and there soon arose an even more widespread interest in such offsprings of Chomsky's theory as generative semantics and (later) relational grammar. The Danish linguistic debate was never dominated by the promotion of generative linguistic theories, however, and in fact, many of those who embraced the 'generative paradigm' in one form or another eventually switched to other approaches or even to other fields. One reason was a strong scepticism toward Chomsky's mentalistic claims, most of which were quickly dismissed. This reaction reflects the structuralist tradition in Denmark and may well be seen as part of the Hjelmslevian heritage since Hjelmslev always stressed the autonomy of linguistics in relation to other fields such as psychology. Another reason why there was never any broad across-the-board acceptance of either transformational grammar or its continuation as 'Government and Binding' (most recently as 'Minimalist' grammar) in Denmark was the clash between Chomsky's version of 'universal grammar' and the notion of 'general grammar' which was part and parcel of the linguistic upbringing in Denmark since Hjelmslev. It is alien to general grammar in the latter sense to promote reductionism by claiming universality of, e.g., a particular structural configuration (such as S = NP + VP). It was never the purpose of structural analysis to reduce languages to a common formula; glossematics is universal in another sense: it defines hierarchies of categories and relations ('functions') from which all possible language structures can be generated.

As for expression analysis, the descriptive affinities between glossematic expression analysis and orthodox generative phonology might have promoted the latter by the late 1960s as the all-dominant approach to phonological description also in Denmark, but among Hjelmslev's students the interest in abstract approaches had dwindled in favour of more 'realistic' or psychologically plausible approaches. There has been a more fruitful interaction with proponents of more recent phonological theories.

In the decade after Hjelmslev's death, the combination of the various factors mentioned above caused most of the Danish linguistic establishment to gradually drift away from formal grammar. Some linguists of the generations born in the inter-war period or later went into pragmatics (e.g., Jacob Mey), and some went into sociolinguistics (e.g., Frans Gregersen), at a time when sociolinguistics had already come of age in the United States. Others went into other types of descriptive linguistics, e.g., documentary and comparative work on almost-extinct languages. Finally, several Danish linguists went into applied linguistics of various kinds, including contrastive language studies for didactic purposes.

Theoretical syntax was, however, revived. Up through the 1960s and 1970s computational linguistics became a fruitful milieu for the study of formal grammars such Head-Driven Phrase Structure Grammar. Even later, Simon Dik's version of functional grammar became very influentiel in Denmark, as a trend within which young Danish linguistics have come to contribute most enthusiastically and in significant ways. Within that very functional trend, however, the spiritual influence of the Hjelmslevian heritage is felt very clearly in the contemporary effort of a post-war generation of Danish scholars to integrate semantics and pragmatics with syntax into a study of linguistic 'content'. This trend is epitomized in Engberg-Pedersen et al. (1996), the introduction of which contains passages such as (p. vii):

"A functionalist approach implies a conception of language as a matching of content that can be communicated with the expressive means of the language. That is, instead of seeing language metaphorically as horizontal levels, one put on top of the other, we return to the basic Saussurean notion that languages have two planes, an expression plane and a content plane."

There is, however, an important difference from Hjelmslev in their approach to syntactic structure. As stated earlier, Hjelmslevian syntax is content-form. To the Copenhagen functionalists, syntax is both content and expression. There are syntactic relations or relationships which are clearly of a semantic nature, and configurations which are clearly expression, but these are all aspects of syntactic structure by virtue of the interplay between content and expression. This view of syntax makes it possible to formulate interesting observations explicitly with reference to the mediating role of syntax between meaning and sound (or writing).

What is left of the Hjelmslevian heritage, then, is Hjelmslev's elaboration and further development of the Saussurean conception of language as a semiotic. In the 1940s, descriptive linguistic work in Denmark, from dialect descriptions to grammars of foreign languages, was much occupied with the search for a rather abstract linguistic 'form' behind the observable data. If we look at recent linguistic thinking in Denmark, however, the most distictive feature is the emphasis on the dichotomy of structurally organized 'content' versus structurally organized 'expression'. Except for the emphasis on both of these organizational 'planes' of language, the glossematic theory and its descriptive apparatus had little prospect of survival in Denmark after Hjelmslev's contemporaries left the scholarly scene.

The CLC is very much alive, however, and its journal and monograph series have been appearing with only minor breaks since Hjelmslev's death. A new generation of linguists is now eagerly participating in the linguistic debate; there is a high degree of openness toward new trends, and it is felt by many as a healthy state of affairs that no single theoretical doctrine has taken absolute control so as to dominate the activities of the Cercle.

Post script

It is no easy task to give a non-technical overview of the glossematic approach without misstating and overly simplifying the notions involved. Rather than giving a collection of citations from Hjelmslev or Uldall, and rather than repeating statements from the extensive literature on glossematics by insiders and outsiders, a non-technical and at the same time rather personal appraisal of the subject-matter has been chosen. This is done on the basis of both primary and secondary literature, of course, but certainly also on the basis of first-hand familiarity with the theoretical debates and descriptive practices of the glossematic milieu, as experienced by a student of Hjelmslev's and a long-time member of the CLC. For more rigorous formal statements and more detailed analyses the reader is referred to the short bibliography below. – Special thanks should be extended to the Grand Old Lady of Danish linguistics, Eli Fischer-Jørgensen, for her critical comments to an earlier version of this article.

7. Bibliography

Acta Linguistica. Copenhagen, 1939–, vol. 1– (continued since 1965 as *Acta Linguistica Hafniensia*.)

Bjerrum, Anders. 1944. *Fjoldemålets lydsystem*. Copenhagen: Munksgaard.

Bulletins du Cercle linguistique de Copenhague. Copenhagen: Munksgaard.

Brandt, Per Åge, ed. 1994. *Papers from the Brøndal Symposium, Copenhagen, 1993*. (= TCLC, 20.)

Canger, Una & Frans Gregersen. 2001. "Honoris causa: Tribute to Eli". *To Honour Eli Fischer-Jørgensen* ed. by Nina Grønnum & Jørgen Rischel (= *TCLC*, 31), 23–53. Copenhagen.

Caputo, Cosimo & Romeo Galassi, eds. 1985. *Louis Hjelmslev: Linguistica, semiotica, epistemologica*. (= *Il Protagora*, anno XXV.) Lecce: Il Protagora.

Ejskjær, Inger. 1954. *Brøndum-målet: Lydsystemet i en Sallingdialekt*. Copenhagen: Schultz.

Engberg-Pedersen, Elisabeth, Michael Fortescue, Peter Harder, Lars Heltoft & Lisbeth Falster Jakobsen, eds. 1996. *Content, Expression and Structure: Studies in Danish functional grammar*. Amsterdam & Philadelphia: Benjamins.

Fischer-Jørgensen, Eli. 1966. "Form and Substance in Glossematics". *Acta Linguistica Hafniensia* 10.1–33.

–. 1967. "Introduction". Uldall 1967 [1957], i–xxii.

–. 1975. *Trends in Phonological Theory*. Copenhagen: Akademisk Forlag.

–. 1991. "Glossematics". *The Linguistics Encyclopaedia* ed. by Kirsten Malmkjaer, 181–189. London & New York: Routledge.

–. 1997. "Hjelmslev et le Cercle Linguistique de Copenhague". *Hjelmslev aujourd' hui* (= *Semiotic and Cognitive Studies*, 5), 27–36. Turnhout: Brepols.

Flydal, Leiv. 1954. *En språklig analyse av norske boktitler 1952: Morfemene i reklamens tjeneste*. Bergen: John Grieg.

Fudge, Eric C. 1995. "The Glossematic School of Linguistics". *Concise History of the Language Sciences* ed. by E. F. K. Koerner & R. E. Asher, 262–268. Oxford & New York: Pergamon.

Gregersen, Frans. 1991. *Sociolingvistikkens (u)mulighed*. 2 vols. Copenhagen: Tiderne skifter.

Hjelmslev, Louis. 1928. *Principes de grammaire générale*. Copenhagen: A. F. Høst & Søn.

–. 1943. *Omkring Sprogteoriens Grundlæggelse*. Copenhagen: Munksgaard. (Cf. Hjelmslev 1961 [1953]).

–. 1970 [1948]. "Le verbe et la phrase nominale". Hjelmslev 1970.165–191.

–. 1951. "Grundtræk af det danske udtrykssystem med særligt henblik på stødet". *Selskab for nordisk filologi, Årsberetning for 1948–1949–1950*, 12–24.

(English transl., "Outline of the Danish Expression System with Special Reference to the *stød*". Hjelmslev 1973.247–266.)

—. 1961 [1953]. *Prolegomena to a Theory of Language*. English translation by Francis J. Whitfield. 2nd rev. ed. Madison: Univ. of Wisconsin Press.

—. 1954. "La stratification du langage". *Word* 10.163–188. (Repr. in Hjelmslev 1970.36–68.)

—. 1970 [1959]. *Essais linguistiques [I]*. (= *TLC*, 12.)

—. 1973. *Essais linguistiques II*. (= *TCLC*, 14.)

Rapport sur l'activité du Cercle linguistique de Copenhague, 1931–1951. 1951. Copenhagen: Munksgaard.

Rasmussen, Michael. 1992. *Hjelmslevs sprogteori: Glossematikken i videnskabshistorisk, videnskabsteoretisk og erkendelsesteoretisk perspektiv*. Odense: Odense Univ. Press.

Siertsema, Berthe. 1965 [1955]. *A Study of Glossematics*. 2nd ed. The Hague: Martinus Nijhoff.

Togeby, Knud. 1951. *Structure immanente de la langue française*. (= *TCLC*, 6.)

Travaux du Cercle linguistique de Copenhague (= *TCLC*). Vol. I–. Copenhagen: [subsequent publishers]: Munksgaard, Nordisk Sprog- og Kulturforlag, C. A. Reitzel.

Uldall, H. J. 1957. *Outline of Glossematics I: General Theory*. (= *TCLC*, 10.) (2nd ed., 1967.)

Jørgen Rischel, Copenhagen (Denmark)

203. Firth, Halliday and the development of systemic functional theory

1. Introduction
2. Linguistics as statements of meaning
3. Languages and 'patterns of life'
4. Malinowski and language as action
5. Tool power and the 'ad hoc' principle
6. Firth and European linguistics
7. Firth's arguments against mentalism
8. Halliday and the elaboration of a functional linguistics
9. Choice and system
10. Networks as a form of argument
11. Firth, Halliday and meaning
12. Meaning, society and grammar
13. From semantics to semantic variation
14. Stratification
15. Probabilistic grammar and cartography
16. A Protean theory
17. Bibliography

1. Introduction

Systemic Functional Linguistics challenges the main articles of theory in the American traditions which have emerged from, and along with, the work of Noam Chomsky. This is not what Systematic Functional theory sets out to do, of course. Rather the contrast is the direct consequence of ideas developed in Britain from before World War II, particularly through the School of Oriental and African Studies in London. These ideas became an orientation, a way of doing linguistics in its own right – an approach so distinct from American structuralism both in its Bloomfieldian and Chomskyan versions, that it has been often misconstrued and inaccurately evaluated. For example, American linguistics has constructed itself according to differing pictures of what can, and what cannot, count as scientific. The earlier Bloomfieldian approach emphasised the separation of descriptions on different strata – phonology, morphology, syntax and so on. Similarly strong boundaries were drawn in the deductivism of Chomsky (with syntax being autonomous from the rest). These kinds of insulations between descriptive processes were never accepted as possible in principle, let alone useful or 'objective', in the British school. Since such assumptions about what constitutes scientific rigour were not shared across the Atlantic, it is not surprising that misunderstanding resulted. In the post-war years, with the influence of the model of Americam universities, and with the prospect of a psycholinguistic El Dorado (i.e., Universal Grammar) capturing the imaginations of many, it was difficult for non-generative linguists to be heard at all.

In particular, the leading ideas of John Rupert Firth (1890–1960), the first Chair of General Linguistics in Great Britain, ran counter to the conceptions of linguistic science which prevailed in his lifetime: rather than adopt isolating procedures for each stratum of language, he sought complementaries between levels of description; he eschewed established conventions about linguistic units, extolling an ad hoc principle in conducting any linguistic investigation; not only did he include 'meaning' as the central motivation for linguistic statements (in contrast to both Bloomfield and Chomsky), he also sought the principled inclusion of sociological parameters from the context of situation; and while the United States' academic culture was moving towards inferred, specific mental organs for a universal 'lingua mentalis' (including the extravagant reliance on intuition, or intention as in Searle's semantics), Firth's legacy was to hold off the introduction of mentalistic language so that the 'serial contextualisations' of data could relate systems of values, from phonetics to patterns of life, free of dichotomies like mind-body, form-content (which contribute no clarification of the experiental matrix (see section 2. below). In Firth's view of science, the object of study is ultimately tractable (or 'effable') while the categories of description, drawn themselves from different meaning systems, must always remain technically 'ineffable'. This follows from the fact that 'turning language back on itself' produces two layers of relativity — the values of terms in the systems of language and the values of the terms which the analyst applies to describing the systems of the language. Furthermore, Firth set the object of study at the level of 'functional varieties' of text, not at a natural language like English or Japanese (which he again saw as unhelpful fictions, obscuring the actual variation in linguistic behaviour).

While Firth, and his tradition of linguists, may have had trouble being heard as scientific linguists against the Bloomfieldian and Chomskyan backgrounds, what counts as science today leans very much more in their favour. Since it is relational and instrumental, with a minimum of formalising terms in the network description, Systemic Functional Linguistics (henceforth S.F.L.) now seems congruent with developments in biology and philosophy, and may have anticipated more recent approaches in artificial intelligence and connectionism. So, too, it has maintained its direct relation with some aspects of European semiotics (from Saussure through to Prague functionalism) and has proven highly adaptive for the systematic analysis of a broader range of sign systems (e. g., plastic arts, film, music, aspects of theatre, and the spatial axis of the sign language of the deaf). And while Firth emphasised 'renewal of connection' of linguistic analysis, first of all with the datum of the text, and then ultimately with its 'pattern of life', in S.F.L. this emphasis has led to rich opportunities for sociocultural analysis — opportunities for linguists to turn the process of their analysis towards interventions in debates on gender, educational equality, and the critique of administrative, scientific and technical ideologies across their communities.

The most distinctive principle of Firthian linguistics was the role of meaning. From this point of view it is paradoxical that while there have been a number of scholarly introductions to the work of Firth (e. g., Robins 1970; Monaghan 1979), many other aspects of linguistic investigation have been typical entry points for interpreting and criticising Firth's work, for example, his approach to phonology. Firth's approach to meaning has generally produced reactions of bewilderment and rejection, for instance in commentators such as Lyons (1966), Langendoen (1968), Sampson (1980), and Butler (1985). These reactions are all the more remarkable when it is appreciated that the role of meaning was absolutely central to Firth himself; and, furthermore, that the criticisms of Firth's approach to meaning, or more accurately to Firth's view of linguistics as 'statements of meaning', have often come from linguists who are variously associated with the British school, of which Firth is properly considered the founder.

The view taken here is that, by clarifying how Firth uses meaning and why it was so crucial to his way of seeing linguistcs, we can better understand the tradition he has created and the reasons why this tradition has been so often misconstrued by outsiders and insiders alike. My own exposition departs from previous treatments in that my central aim is to bring out the coherence and consistency of Firth's view of meaning — the internal consistency of his theory and its applications to different problems. I will argue that Firth's meaning provides the organising principle for a way of conducting linguistics which is only now, in the 1990s, reasserting itself after a long period of misunderstanding and ideological exclusion by those groups (inside and outside linguistics) who have been most committed to psychologism and universalism in the study of linguistic behaviour. Sections 8 to 16 of the discussion will set out the systematic ways in which Halliday has taken up the principles and specifics of Firth's projects. I will go on to discuss certain recent developments in S.F.L., particularly as those developments reveal the longer term consistencies of the approach to linguistics through Firth and Halliday. These recent developments will draw us into brief discussions of the work of a number of Halliday's colleagues — work that has not been encompassed in earlier accounts of this approach to linguistics.

In my use of quotations I have probably erred on the side of including too many from Firth and too few from Halliday. One aim is to dispel the misapprehension that Firth was in any way unclear himself about what he was doing. A further reason is to display how Firth's methods encompassed a series of contextualizations, not mereley a distinctive phonology with remarks on context. My focus on semantic and grammatical strata will, I hope, assist in broadening the interest in current Systemic Functional theory which was already committed to meaning and text at a time when the profession of linguists was experiencing an era of invented sentences. More crucially, the entry through meaning can best display the logic in the methods and careers of the two linguists.

2. Linguistics as statements of meaning

It is not difficult to establish how Firth regarded 'meaning' – most of his articles, often the text of addresses he gave to specific societies of scholars, translators, etc., give accounts of his view of meaning, each with differing orientations or points of departure. By reviewing a corpus of these we can achieve two important steps of clarification: first, we can adopt something of Firth's own method, which eschews definitions and demands that we inspect the way a term is actually used; and second, we can tease out the crucial theoretical terms which all depend on meaning for their own roles in Firthian linguistics. The whole complex of interdependent theoretical ideas can then be clearest seen for its consistency, as a whole approach to linguistics, and its strong motivation, term by term. This strategy is in accordance with Firth's emphasis on the interrelations of systems in an actual text – in particular, with respect to the technical language of linguistics: "they [the terms of linguistics] are, so to speak, defined operatively, that is to say, instead of being equated with other words, they find part of their meaning in collocation in the text. In operational terms, 'they mean what they do'" (1968b: 33). (In the following quotes, Firth's emphasis is in italic and my emphasis is in bold.)

"My own approach in general linguistics and especially in the study of meaning in purely linguistics terms dates back to about 1930 when the linguistic movement in philosophy was also arousing interest. My main concern is to make statements of meaning in purely linguistic terms, that is to say, such statements are made in terms of structures and systems at a number of levels of analysis: for example, in phonology, grammar, stylistics, situation, attested and established texts. I do not attempt statements about a speaker's or writer's thoughts and intentions, ideas and concepts – these are for other disciplines." (1968e [1956]: 97)

"In the most general terms we study language as part of the social process, and what we may call the systematics of phonetics and phonology, of grammatical categories or of semantics, are ordered schematic constructs, frames of reference, a sort of scaffolding for the handling of events. The study of the social process and of single human beings is simultaneous and of equal validity, and for both, structural hypotheses are proved by their own social functioning in the scientific process of dealing with events. Our schematic constructs must be judged with reference to their **combined tool power** in our dealings with linguistic events in the social process. Such constructs have no ontological status and we do not project them as having being or existence. They are neither immanent nor transcendent, but just **language turned back on itself**. By means of linguistics we hope to state facts systematically, and especially to make **statements of meaning**." (1957 [1950]: 181)

"I have suggested that language is systemic. Most grammars and dictionaries are systematic statements of fact – but quite a number are not. Even when they are systematic, they can sometimes fail to represent the language systems, in the sense in which I have used the expression *systemic*. We may assume that any social person speaking in his own personality will behave systematically, since experienced language is universally systemic. Therefore, we may study his speech and ask the question, 'What is systemic?' We must not expect to find one closed system. But we may apply systematic categories to the statement of the facts. We must separate from the mush of general goings-on those features of repeated events which appear to be parts of the patterned process, and handle them systematically by stating them by the spectrum of linguistic techniques. The systemic **statements of meaning** produced by such techniques need not to be given existent status." (1957 [1950]: 187)

"Linguistic analysis must first state the *structures* it finds both in the text and in the context. Statements in structural terms then contribute to the **statements of meaning** in various modes." (1968a [c. 1952]: 17)

"The contextual theory of meaning employs abstractions which enable us to handle language in the interrelated processes of personal and social life in the flux of events. As I emphasised in my little book, published over twenty years ago, 'In common conversation about people and things present to the senses, the most important 'modifiers' and 'qualifiers' of the speech sounds made and heard, are not words at all, but **the perceived context of situation**. In other words, 'meaning' is a property of the mutually relevant people, things, events in the situation. Some of the events are the noises made by the speakers." (Ibid. p. 14)

"The process may be compared, metaphorically speaking, to the dispersion of white light into a spectrum by means of a prism. The prism in our case is descriptive linguistics and the spectrum is the multiple **statements of meaning** at various levels of analysis." (1968e [1956]: 108)

"*Processes* and *patterns* of life in the environment can be generalised in *contexts of situation*, in which the *text* is the main concern of the linguist. *Order* and *structures* are seen in these, and after examining *distribution* in *collocations*, '*pieces*', *words* and *morphemes* may be arranged in ordered series, resulting in *systems* and *sets of systems*, the *terms* of which are functions of one another and of the systems. On a previous study [Firth 1957 [1935]: 17] I have outlined linguistic analysis as a study of meaning in the following terms:

'I propose to split up meaning or function into a series of component functions. Each function will be defined as the use of some language form or element in relation to some context. Meaning, that is to say, is to be regarded as a complex of contextual relations, and phonetics, grammar, lexicography and semantics each handles its own components of the complex in its appropriate context.'

The *abstractions* or *schematic constructs* set up are made at a series of distinct mutually complementary *levels. Renewal of connection* with the *processes and patterns of life* in the *instances* of experience is the final justification of abstract linguistics." (1968a [c.1952]: 24)

Reviewing such extracts produces an inventory of terms and issues, most of which have been cited as key concepts in Firthian linguistics (by students and colleagues such as Catford 1969, Halliday 1978, Henderson 1987, Mitchell 1979, Palmer 1968, Robins 1970). As mentioned already, my emphasis will be to bring out, ultimately, the interdependence, coherence, and motivated character of the ideas as a methodology, but not as a 'procedure', a concept in American linguistics which Firth was reacting strongly against. To achieve this emphasis, I will need to focus upon some aspects of Firth's work that typically receive only marginal treatment. While Firth's use of 'level' is consistently discussed, for instance, the importance of the 'ad hoc' principle, and of the 'ineffability' of linguistic terms, are not so widely appreciated or discussed (however, for the former, see Henderson 1987; and for the latter, see Halliday 1984b).

Almost all of the passages indicate that central to the study of meaning is the notion of *statement*, or of the making of linguistic 'statements'. *Facts* are not, in themselves, given by the 'general mush of goings-on'; rather, facts take on their form or value only as a result of their function or role within statements. Such statements cannot be all of one kind or made in one step; hence there is a dispersion of responsibiliy across different *levels*. Furthermore, the crucial aim of the linguist is to bring the statements of the different levels into a *congruent* relationship. Consequently, the facts need to be *contextualised* as part of a series of statements involving the *systems* and *structures* at all levels. This process of *serial contextualisation* is essentially a means of capturing the relevant *patterns* and interrelationships of linguistic form or behaviour as instantiated in the actual observable text (that is, not in a concocted, hypothetical example). In this way, even *instance* "is brought forward as a technical term" (Firth 1968a: 24). The cline between 'instance' and the 'potential', the latter stated in terms of systems of systems at different levels, becomes an organising principle of Halliday's approach. Of particular relevance is Halliday's metaphor of the weather (the instance) relating to the climate: that system of probabilities against which the instance can be evaluated and which, in turn, will be itself determined by the accumulating variable instances. The theorizing of instance allows linguistic theory to escape that cul-de-sac in philosophical semantics by which no progress can be made on the description of language games beyond, that is, recognizing and enumerating their diversity and individuation. (See also Ellis 1966, for an early account of context with the cline of instantiation.)

3. Languages and 'patterns of life'

All of the statements produced are part of the larger project of linguistics, namely to become clearer about the *creative processes* of human membership in society, the formation and continuity of *personality*, and the wider *patterns of life*. In the clarification of patterns (both wider and more specific), linguistics assists in the activation of one's membership of various, significant *speech fellowships*. As one becomes more able to explain why and how the patterns of a language create a ground of potential against the figure of the text, it is easier to appreciate the ways in which language creates realities rather than reflects them. Firth's defence of the poet Edith Sitwell and *her Emily coloured primulas* must be among the most succinct demonstrations of how symbolic construction works (Firth 1968a: 15–16). These speech fellowships can extend from the individuated semantics of a poet's version of the world, in which the process of reality construction still utilizes the '*larger contexts* in which the words are embedded' (1968a: 18), to the membership of the British Empire (in Firth's time), for which knowledge of patterns at different levels might assist in the teaching of English as a second language. So too, linguistics would have a crucial role in the development of a critical consciousness that could defend us against the Newspeak which is itself an aspect of the constructive power of language.

Firthian linguistics, despite the references to English and Empire in his popular books, did not use English as a Procrustean bed into which the meanings of all cultures must fit, a position that is arguably implicit in claims concerning universal grammar; for example, consider the role of Pro-Drop in earlier Generative Theory. Firth's own experience as an historian and linguist in India should be mentioned in relation to this issue. His own students typically began in a linguistic tradition quite distinct from those of Western Europe (naturally, in the School of Oriental and African Studies). It is fair to claim then that his students tended to see English by 'looking back' from work based on languages other than English and, in many cases, other than Indo-European in historical origin. This can be seen from Halliday's use of perspectives from Chinese linguistics (1993c) as well as, say, in Palmer's recent account of *Grammatical Roles and Relations* (1994). The influence of Malinowski on Firth's thinking, and Firth's own strongly held position on linguistic variation, are both further factors which help to interpret the approach of Firth, and the direction he gave to British linguistics: "To deal with the theory of language, the Western scholar must de-Europeanize himself as the Englishman must 'de-Anglicize himself'" (1968e [1956]: 96).

By reflecting on Firth's determination not to fix the study of meaning in one putative language (or in particular text patterns/relations!), we can better understand why Firth's accounts of his own methods do not settle on definitive versions of his own theory. For example, commentators up to De Beaugrande (1991: 204) have been alarmed that they could not settle on the number of levels in Firth's approach. So too, Firth's use of 'traditional' notions in linguistics while at the same time disavowing the 'nonsense' of past and current (to him) practices, has seemed paradoxical (see Langendoen [1968: 69], for example, on noun and verb). However, the Firthian articulation is rigorously consistent and extends from another position often misconstrued by readers, yet clearly declared in Palmer's editorial remarks on the *Selected Papers* (Firth 1968). Despite Firth's numerous differences with Saussure, which will be brought out below in relation to Hjelmslev, certain of Firth's strictures on what can count as contextualisation and as systemic could be taken from the *Cours* itself. Perhaps strangely, Saussure's *valeur* may be the only absolute in the scaffolding of Firthian principles, a scaffolding carefully crafted to declare its own provisional or heuristic status. Terms in a text being described have the meaning they do because of their place vis-à-vis all the other terms in the relevant environment. This determination of value through serial contextualisations − interrelating of systems across different environments − differs from Saussure's *valeur* in its emphases rather than in its operational role in analysis. The values which Firth emphasises begin at, and return to, the sociological component, the personality, and the patterns of life. Nothing changes the meaning of a word more dramatically than a change in the qualifying dimensions of the context of situation: namely, relevant participants, objects, and the effect of verbal action.

4. Malinowski and language as action

As Professor of Anthropology at the University of London, Bronislaw Malinowski (1884–1942) emphasised the importance, particularly to his translation work, of regarding language as a mode of action, not as a counter-sign to thought. This view, which anticipates much of the later arguments of Wittgenstein (1974 [1953]), was congruent with Firth's own desire to pursue the experiential matrix which supported language rather than mentalistic notions to which words might correspond. Malinowski is widely credited with an influence on Firth. Since the topic has had scholarly treatment from Firth himself (1968f), by Robins (1970) and by Hasan (1985), I will not elaborate beyond drawing attention to those aspects of the relationship which bear on my focus on meaning and on the ways in which Firth's work may have anticipated the social sciences as we now debate them. Levinson (1983: xii) presents Malinowski and Firth as proto-pragmaticists along with the general observation that pragmatics was a remedial discipline – restoring balance to the "starkly limited scope of Chomskyan linguistics". This judgement naturally cannot be applied either to Malinowski or to Firth: they were not so much remedying as they were defining their own orientation to the study of language.

Malinowski led Firth to a linguistics in which language and culture needed to be studied together in a principled way. Firth did not accept Malinowski's over-generalizing of grammatical categories and he also refined Malinowski's concepts of context of situation and context of culture. It was not only that such concepts were necessary levels in the dispersion of specialised statements, the notion of context (as brought out carefully by recent work by Hasan 1998, in particular) had to be moved away from the material situational setting to a fully semiotic concept: namely, one in which the categories are rather of the same abstract nature as grammatical categories and based on the routines of initiated persons in the society under description (Firth 1950: 182). Firth suggests a schematic structure of relevant aspects of the participants including verbal and non-verbal action, the relevant objects; and the effect of verbal action. A critical point here is the mutual delimitation of the linguistic and extra linguistic orders of experience; both are semiotic or meaning bearing, and both are mutually delimiting so that the pre-existence of one side of the relation is not to be assumed. This reciprocation is, I would claim cautiously, much like the *signifié-signifiant* complementarity within Saussure's sign. But Firth has, unlike Saussure, shown how human experience of the material order needs to be part of the relational matrix of linguistic description, just as the material order needs to be recognised for its already meaning bearing (or semiotic) configurations. It is an indication of both the importance to Firth of Malinowski, and the importance of grounding linguistics in the extra-linguistic (but cultural and semiotic), that Firth used Malinowski's terms for the unifying thread linking together the levels of analysis (Robins 1970: 19). For Firth, meaning at all levels was *function in context*. So context becomes the guiding metaphor for the making of linguistic statements; in such a way context neutralizes the dangers of idealism and formalism, which Firth saw in the extrapolations of Saussureanism, most particularly in Hjelmslev's axiomatic treatment of semiology.

5. Tool power and the 'ad hoc' principle

The provisional or heuristic status of linguistic methods, the combined 'tool power', provides the key to the internal coherence and consistency of Firth's overall approach. In Firth's theory, 'ad hoc' is not a negative characterisation of the way a description which is developed. Quite the opposite: any method which is not ad hoc is in danger of imposing an extrinsic system on the data, rather than drawing the systems of possible relations/ alternatives from the text. Firth urges that the categories of linguistics cannot be drawn from outside the relations of the linguistic behaviour/text itself. There is no seeking after ontological bases for linguistic tools, nor for starting points in other disciplines. The schematic constructs of linguistics are just "a sort of scaffolding for the handling of language events" (1957 [1950]: 181) and must be judged on their tool power in relation to "our dealings with linguistic events in the social process" (ibid.). I take this to be a clear instance of the Pragmatism associated with James and Peirce – the criterion of progress is the power to solve a problem, not the mirroring of truth (Griffin et al. 1993; Rorty 1979): facts are merely the myths we believe and live with (Firth 1968 f [1957]: 156). In this Firth appears to be extolling the use of heuristic fictions as explained in Hans Vaihinger's (1852–1933) *Philosophy of As-If* (1925 [1911]).

An important difference appears to emerge then in Firth's theorising. The object of study is quite simply an authentic text, that is, one that has a place in social processes; and, the tools of study are described plainly as "just language turned back on itself" (1957 [1951]: 190). Firth was at great pains, then, to demystify the actifities of the linguist and, as well, to ensure that the interferences that result, inevitably, from the tools of analysis can be removed or minimised (as the scaffolding/ tool and myth metaphors suggest).

But, at the same time as the linguist must work to make the objects of study and the linguistic tools more and more tractable, the ground against which the figure of the text can be discerned is becoming increasingly evanescent. This is to say that the ideas of the linguistic tradition, the backdrop of reference points for the linguist, are problematised by Firth's strictures:

> I do not propose an *a priori* system of general categories by means of which the facts of all languages may be stated. [...]. Science should not impose systems on languages, it should look for systems in speech activity, and, having found them, state the facts in a suitable language." (1957 [1948]: 144)

Given that the linguist must work out the categories of description in an ad hoc way, on the basis of the emerging picture of salient relations, and given that no language provides anything more than one reference point for the value of terms like tense, aspect, subject, finite, as well as noun and verb, etc., the categories of linguistics are 'ineffable': as Firth put it, "elements of structure are mutually inter-related abstract categories set up by the linguist, and are timeless and 'ineffable'" (1968c: 39). This description is a technical one in Firth's theory; it is a declaration that there is, in principle, no resolution to the relative values of the categories linguists employ. Firth is in this way truly the contemporary of Bohr's complementarity, Gödel's incompleteness theorem, Heisenberg's uncertainty principle, and the fundamental consequences of relativity theory. The main points in relation to such modernist theories are that (i) there is no privileged point-of-view; and (ii) there is no scientific language that is ever more than a language (Rorty 1979, chap. 4).

Firthian linguistics is thus a scientific approach which genuinely accommodates the indeterminacies and provisional character of undertaking science in the shadows of these enormous developments, the implications of which are usefully elaborated in Heisenberg's *Physics and Philosophy* (1962). I am not claiming that Firth drew direct inspiration from these particular scientists, but he did take on more of the relativity and relational thinking through his interest in the work of Alfred North Whitehead (1861–1947), who is increasingly quoted in Firth's writings. With regard to Whitehead, see for instance the first 6 footnotes of "Linguistic Analysis as the Study of Meaning", originally prepared 1952–1953; and the title of Firth's "Modes of Meaning" appears to echo Whitehead's *Modes of Thought* (1938). Whitehead was, of all the theorists in the 20th century, the one most engaged in an attack on 'misplaced concreteness' (what Firth attacked as 'hypostatisation' of the abstract categories). Just as crucial as Whitehead's process philosophy, with its uncompromising commitment to "occasions of experience" (Whitehead 1967 [1933]: 179) rather than things, there is also the influence of Whitehead's organic view of the cosmos and the human role in it. Both Firth and Whitehead emphasise the role of speech as the enactment of the past and the future in the present moment, as a 'binder of time', as an event in which there is no seam between nature and nurture, between habit and creativity, between custom and uniqueness:

> "Language, like personality, is a *binder of* time, of the past and future in 'the present'. On the one hand there is habit, custom, tradition, and on the other innovation, creation. Every time you speak you create anew, and what you create is a function of your language and of your personality. From that activity you may make abstraction of the constituents of the context, and consider them in their mutual relations. In the process of speaking there is pattern and structure actively maintained by the body which is itself an organised structure maintaining the pattern of life." (1957 [1948]: 142)

> "The linguistic sciences will find a sure semantic basis in alliance with concepts such as these on the biological side, and the development of proper semantic relationships with the other sciences of man is now vital. Linguists and sociologists have to deal with *systems*, but systems very different from physical systems. Personal systems and social systems are actively maintained (with adaptation and change) in the bodily behaviour of men. Most of the older definitions (and de Saussure's must fall in this category) need overhauling in the light of contemporary science. [...] Language and personality are built into the body, which is constantly taking part in activities directed to the conservation of the pattern of life. We must expect therefore that linguistic science will also find it necessary to postulate the maintenance of linguistic patterns and systems (including adaptation and change) within which there is order, structure, and function." (1957 [1948]: 143)

One aspect of Saussure's theory that does not require an overhaul, however, is the concept of *valeur*. The relevance to the ineffability of linguistic categories again demonstrates how much Firth uses this central clarification of the *Cours*. While at different points Firth argues against the idealising separations of Saussurean theory (especially *langue/parole*), against the emphasis on the 'collectivity' of consciousness of Saussure (who, in Firth's opinion, followed Durkheim), against the totalising, monosystemic approach (by contrast with his polysystemic approach), and against the predominantly conceptual characterisation of the sign, the notion of value provides a key to many of Firth's principles. In fact, the ineffability issue can be formulated as *va*-

leur applied to the metalanguage, although, as we might appreciate, the term metalanguage is out of keeping with a theory of 'language turned back on itself'. If all units (words, for the sake of this explanation) have a value by virtue of the place they hold in the environments in which they can possibly be used, the same conditions pertain to units/ words which are used in the language for describing language. Just as a word is difficult to translate due to the differences of distribution and contrastiveness between two languages, so much more will it be that metaunits in two distinct systems cannot be plausibly (or usefully!) equated.

6. Firth and European linguistics

The return to Saussure provides an opportunity to set out the complexity of Firth's attitude to European linguistics, in particular the legacy of Saussure and its development by Hjelmslev. While it is conventional wisdom that Firth was opposed to their approaches, the situation is not so univocal. Firth's positive views on the concept of value have been stressed above. They need to be stressed yet again in relation to Firth's fundamental organising idea, that of system, or, more accurately, the polysystemic character of language. Firth's use of differential values in a paradigmatic system maintains the link with Saussure despite his misgivings about the dangers of Saussureanism. Against the reification of the language as total system, in which *tout se tient*, Firth appears to be sympathetic to the Russian and Marxist critiques of the Saussurean tendencies to abstract too far away from actual behaviour and to bestow too much autonomy on the system as distinct from the social relations which motivate the linguistic behaviour. In this, Firth is aligned with Valentin Nikola'evič Vološinov (1895–1936) in his *Marxism and the Philosophy of Language* (1973 [1929]) rather than Meillet (see Firth 1957 [1949]: 169; 1957 [1950]: 180–181).

Firth appears to have benefited from, and enjoyed, a strong collegial relationship with his alter-ego in theory, Louis Hjelmslev (1899–1965). In the earlier *Papers, 1934– 1951*, Firth expends more space explaining Hjelmslev's projects than he apparently felt was needed for the work of his more congruent guide and colleague, Malinowski (over eight pages as to six pages, respectively). He appreciates Hjelmslev's effort to establish a technical language for linguistics, a kind of calculus that might serve semiotic enterprise "the way mathematics has served the physical sciences" (1957 [1948]: 140).

Firth approached language as a complex social phenomenon rather than as a mental code. Like his contemporary, Wittgenstein, Firth emphasised the character of language events – actualised, instantiated in behaviour, and contingent upon such varieties of human purpose (different language games) that it was misleading to idealise away from the instance to generalised or global categories. In fact, Firth's views were so strong in this regard that he found the idea of a language (English, Japanese, Chinese, Hindi) quite unhelpful for linguistic purposes, requiring rather that the focus be set upon the study of a register (for him: a restricted language).

Quite unlike the parallel academic projects in Russian criticism, however, and in ways never undertaken by Wittgenstein, Firth tried to elucidate the techniques by which we could see the details of the socio-physical events of language. This is to say, he made proposals about mapping the relations so that the complexity of language could be displayed in a series of statements. As pointed out by Davis, Firthian linguistics is totally taken up with the "hierarchy of techniques for the statement of pattern" and not with a 'theory of language' as such. In this regard Davis (1973: 272) quotes Firth, and then comments himself:

" 'it is not the task of linguistics to say what "language" is' (Firth 1957: 177). The function of a theory is to provide a tool for stating what the linguist sees as patterns without rendering those patterns themselves as part of theory."

So while there were other approaches which kept close to the actual instantiation of meaning in social processes, these tended to use linguistic data either to disparage linguistic enterprises, as Vološinov did in his approach to reported speech (1973 [1929]), or as did Pavel Nikola'evič Medvedev (1891– 1938) on Russian Formalism (1985 [1928]); or they highlighted incongruities between linguistic and philosophical distinctions, as Wittgenstein did with regard to 'seeing' and 'seeing as'. By contrast, Firth took up the enterprise of setting out "the interrelations of the terms of the actual observable context itself" (1957 [1935]). In this way, Firth seeks to state the relevant 'order in the mush of general goings-on':

"From my own point of view, first stated in 1930, maintained and developed since, the whole of our linguistic behaviour is best understood if it is seen as a network of relations between people, things and events, showing structures and systems, just as we notice in all our experience. The body itself is a set of structures and systems and the world in which we maintain life is also structural and systematic. This network of structures and systems we must abstract from the mush of general goings-on which, at first sight, may appear to be a chaos or flux."

"Such an approach requires *no dichotomy of mind and body, thought and its expression, form and content.* It does, however, recognize the distinction between the language texts which are the linguist's main concern and the matrix of experience in which they are set. Meaning is, therefore, a property of all systems and structures of language. At the highest level of abstraction, it may be possible to maintain that the meaning of language may be stated in two sets of relations, the interior relations within the language and the exterior relations between structures and systems in the language, and structures and systems in the situations in which language functions." (1968d [1956]: 90; emphasis added: DGB)

There are many points to observe in this extract and its accompanying paragraphs. Taken together, they exhibit, like so many of the pieces one can take from Firth's writings, the distinctive approach of the linguist. For instance, the interior/exterior relations indicate the emphasis Firth gave to the sociological frame in which a set of contrasts find their values: "As I have so often said, the most important modifiers of words are things and events" (ibid.).

7. Firth's arguments against mentalism

Just as characteristic is the anti-Cartesian position: the "disastrous separation of body and mind fixed on European thought by Descartes is responsible for much blindness in certain sciences and especially in linguistics" (1968d: 90). In this context, it should also be noted that Firth articulates his position with a fastidiousness that I will try to show is characteristic of his exposition. Such a claim by me, I should add, runs counter to the widely stated view that Firth was an unsatisfactory expositor of his own approach (e.g., Palmer in Firth 1968: 2).

When Firth writes that "[t]he notion of pure thought in abstraction from its expression is not one of the most useful figments of the learned world" (1968d: 90), his wording draws attention to the evaluation of ideas by utility rather than by truth. From the term figments, we can see again, from another aspect, the instrumentalist's concern with useful fictions, scaffolding, and heuristics (see Vaihinger, section 5 above) that need to be kicked aside when their practical role has run out (that is, so that they cannot be drawn into the existence postulates of a discipline). Part, then, of his monistic view of meaning can be seen in the continuous exorcism of any approach that will lead to reification – when tool or category becomes 'hypostatised'; or in any approach which implies that there can be no continuum between the human body and the rest of the universe.

In this regard, Firth might seem exposed not only as anti-Saussurean but also as an anti-philosophical behaviourist. A more reliable sense of Firth's position can be achieved, however, by some commitment to the intertextuality of his essays, and by adopting the view that Firth's ideas were constantly and consistently reiterated, albeit from slightly different contexts of utterance and hence distinct perspectives depending, as his own theory urges, on the motivations which underlie each particular occasion of address (e.g., conference of translators; congress for semantics; society of lexicographers). So it is important to consider his words against dichotomies in the light of the numerous other references to the same issue:

"To make statements of meaning in terms of linguistics, we may accept the language event as a whole and then deal with it at various levels, sometimes in a descending order, beginning with social context and proceeding through syntax and vocabulary to phonology and even phonetics, and at other times in the opposite order, which will be adopted here since the main purpose is the exposition of linguistics as a discipline and technique for the statement of meanings without reference to such dualisms and dichotomies as word and idea, overt expressions and covert concepts, language and thought, subject and object. In doing this I must not be taken to exclude the concept of mind, or to imply an embracing of materialism to avoid a foolish bogey of mentalism." (1957 [1951]: 192)

By 1951, Firth feels the need to declare that his position against dichotomies is not a position which excludes the concept of the mind. The *idées fixes* of American linguistics clearly interfered with Firth's being heard in his own time and being read in ours. In "Modes of Meaning" (1957 [1951]), he takes the most direct route explaining our present topic: namely, how he makes use of the term meaning. First, he clarifies the issue in terms available to linguistics and non-linguistics alike: "The use of the word 'meaning' is subject to the general rule that each word when used in a new context is a new word" (1957

[1951]: 190). He then positions his work with respect to 'general linguistics' and with the qualification that linguistics does not have to set out from the theories and existents of other disciplines:

"The constructs or schemata of linguistics enable us to handle isolates that may be called language events. These systematic constructs are neither immanent nor transcendent, but just language turned back on itself [...]. Indeed the main concern of descriptive linguistics is to make statements of meaning." (Ibid.)

This is a genuinely minimalist position. The linguist's tools and practice are to assist in the making of statements concerning regularities or patterns.

The tools themselves are not to take on a status of their own, not to be hypostatised and turned into the targets of ontological enquiry (as in 'evidence for the existence of'). Linguistics is not yet a 'meta'-language but merely 'language turned back on itself'. By the use of this last expression, Firth points his audience away from the all too easy assumption that a metalanguage can be employed as if free of the relativities (of multiple contextualisations) which characterise a natural language.

Firth's strategy, as in a great proportion of his publications, appears to be, on the one hand, a progressive naturalisation of what the linguist undertakes, and on the other, a warning that the complexities of *valeurs* which pertain to a natural language also operate in the terms of the constructs of linguistics. Terms that do service both in the linguistic theory and in the language being described will undergo a relativisation of their already relative values — the problems of *valeur* and contextualisation go up in power, if you like. The whole tone and formulation of Firth's notions, even at the outset of his discussion, are the polar opposite of the myriad of proposals in componential semantics of the 1960s and 1970s in which readers were asked to accept English words, like Animate, Male etc. in square brackets (e.g., [+ Animate]) and regard them as standing in for pre-cultural, pre-semantic, cognitive atoms (with the further prospect of increasingly florid claims of innateness). It seems likely to me that Firth's attitude to such uses of brackets and 'figments' of 'pure thought' would have been just that it was *not* a scientific proposal: namely, such proposals should not be seen as having an ontological base. It is worthwhile reminding ourselves about the kinds of proposals that counted as linguistic sense when it was being written that Firth's approach to meaning was eccentric and unworkable. Given that conventional wisdom in linguistics has changed, it is also appropriate to re-evaluate the judgements concerning Firth's use of 'meaning'.

Many contemporary readers of Firth may find the dismissals of dualisms (mind-body, subject-object, thought-word) overstated, and interpret them as a reflection of the behaviourism of the period. A number of discriminations need to be made in relation to such simplification of Firth's intellectual position. First of all, the 'behaviourism' of the period 1930–1960 was not a monolithic enterprise; nor is it helpful to use Bloomfield in linguistics and B. F. Skinner (1904–1990) in psychology as the measure of how behaviourism was motivated, articulated and argued. Indeed, it is even debatable whether or not Bloomfield's dicta on stimulus-response (S. r. → s. R.), and against the possibility of a scientific study of meaning did justice to Bloomfield's own descriptive work (Bloomfield 1933, chap. 9). Certainly the bundling together of work by experimental psychologists with the subtle position defended by the philosopher Gilbert Ryle (1963 [1949]) is a travesty (such simplification is, unfortunately, a standard line in linguistics, as in Arthur Koestler's (1905–1983) popular polemic of 1967, *The Ghost in the Machine*). This generalising omits, for instance, Continental theory, forms of interactionism, and the degree to which terms like 'habit' were part of a methodology developed to test the limits of our statements on the matrix of experience.

With the influence in America of Chomsky's attack on Skinner, and with the hyperbole of the philosophical framing of his own work in syntax, Chomsky's success short-circuited a network of research projects which encompassed so much more than stimulus-response and operant conditioning. Something of what we lost, and what is now being reconstructed, can be understood from Rorty's account of what he calls the 'Ryle-Dennett' approach (thereby linking the 1940s and the 1980s). Rorty's paper, delivered at the Nobel Symposium (1982a), can be usefully compared with Dennett's own sustained account of the distorting effects of Cartesianism (1991) and with Halliday's grammatical insights on the evolution of consciousness (Halliday 1995), presented to the Nobel Symposium in 1994. Vygotsky's and Luria's own 'anti-Cartesian experiments' (Luria 1976, 1979) offer another, parallel stream of the science of mind in which Cartesianism and specific mental organs were not inevitable inferences in an account of human skills, problem solving, or behaviour. Firth's own formulations, against the usefulness of the intellectual figments of Cartesianism, could serve now as foreword to a plethora of research projects. The similarities between the position of Rorty and that of Firth, and the subtle corrections required in the debate, suggest to me that sustained quotation is again the most direct form of argument on the topic. The central points and the direction of the following passages from Rorty (1995: xvi) could have been taken from Firth's work 40 to 50 years before:

"Lately I have been trying to mark out a position that does not take sides between subject and object, mind and world, but that instead tries to erase the contrast between them. I have, so to speak, been trying to lose *both* us and the world. Whereas Farrell reads me as trying to glorify us at the expense of the world, and hopes to rectify the balance with a 'modest realism', I want to stop using the us-world contrast, and thus to get rid of the realism-antirealism issue."

And earlier Rorty (1982a: 62):

"It is that the distinction between the mental and the physical, or between mind and body, is a very bad distinction. The question 'What is the place of man in nature?' is a good one if it is construed to mean something like: 'What self-image should we humans have of ourselves?' For then it is shorthand for Kant's classic questions 'What do we know? What should we do? What may we hope?' Darwin and Huxley gave us reason to think that Kant, and the philosophical tradition generally, might have given bad answers to these questions. But the idea that we could refocus these questions, make them susceptible to more precise answers, by zeroing in on the notion of 'the mind' turned out to be a mistake. The more one zeroes in, the less there is to discuss. The reason there is nothing there is that the distinction between mind and body is entirely parasitical upon two other distinctions: the distinction between knowers and non-knowers, and the distinction between the morally relevant and the morally irrelevant. It is important for our self-image to think of ourselves as knowers – distinguished from the brute creation in being intelligent, in acting from knowledge rather than from habit or instinct, in being able to contemplate things far away in space and time. It is also important for our self-image to see our species, and perhaps those species close enough to us to share some special faculty (e.g. being conscious, or feeling pain) as part of a *moral* universe – as things which have either obligations or rights or both. The notion of 'mind' looks like a way of bringing these two notions – that of knower and that of a moral agent of subject – together, of subsuming them under a single, clearer, concept. But it is not. The supposedly clearer concept is just a blur – the sort of thing you get when you lay tracings of two delicate and complicated designs down on top of each other." (Rorty 1982a: 62)

"I said earlier that the central claim of the Ryle-Dennett tradition was that we had no intuitions, no 'initial facts' which all theorising must always respect, about the mind. It should now be clear that I mean this not as a remark about the mind but as a remark about intuitions – *it is a methodological strategy rather than an introspective report.*" (Ibid., p. 84; emphasis added: DGB)

Firth suggested that "during the next 50 years general linguistics may supplant a great deal of philosophy; the process has begun" (1957 [1949]: 168). Unfortunately for the study of language, the linguistic turn in 20th century thought has not followed up concerns with the actual linguistic relations on the different levels of language. Many linguistic enterprises in education, literary analysis, social theory and even computation, have turned away from linguistics in order to embrace linguistic notions in other forms or guises, while at the same time casting linguistics as a dangerous, even regressive structuralism. Ironically, the pattern of such contemporary criticisms of linguistics reveals how far Firth had adsorbed, anticipated, and resolved the deepest issues of European structuralism – in particular, he had addressed the lacunae of Saussurean theory: namely, how to connect the relational structure to the social contexts of actual speakers; the role of an individual or person in linguistic theory and description; the problems of variation, functional and historical; the role of the human body as a fusion of cultural and organic histories; and the indeterminacy of categories. Yet the pattern of recent critiques of linguistics has been to overlook the degree to which linguists – Firth, in particular – had come to terms with issues of variation and idealisation of structures. Rather, for example, volumes on literary theory often set out from introductory chapters criticising a caricatured Saussure and then move to Bakhtin or Foucault for a sociological alternative (Eagleton 1983: 96–97, 127–128). Derrida is applauded for what could be plainly seen as the ineffability of categories. Concepts from Foucault, Bourdieu, and Wittgenstein are widely cited while linguistic notions with a direct relevance to such concepts are made relatively invisible by the attitude to linguistics from those outside the subject, or by tendentious surveys by those within (as in the case of Langendoen 1968). So 'restricted language' or 'register' comes back as 'discourse formation' or 'language game'; the contextual provenance of a cultural element can be discussed as 'habitus' but not so comfortably as Bernstein's code or Hasan's semantic variation; and Firth's 'serial contextualisation' is overlooked for a conventionalised but unhelpful division between linguistics and pragmatics.

The naïve abandonment of structure statements in areas of the humanities and social sciences has been in part the result of the face which institutional linguistics most often turned to such themes — Chomskyan linguistics continued to pursue its promisory note of universal grammaticality, and Saussure's *Cours* was simplified and misrepresented by linguists themselves. So too, the very success of linguistics institutionally during the 1960s and 1970s meant that linguists could no longer appropriate the role of the iconoclastic young Turks of academia — they had become the technological oligarchy! Or, at least, that is how they could be positioned in the discourses of post-structuralism.

Linguistics gave language over to such discourses, discourses which were marked, on the one hand, by self-dramatising, playful obscurity, and on the other, by grand revisions/denunciations of structuralism, in particular, denunciations of the Saussurean, linguistic legacy. For example, Derrida's trace appears to be the indeterminacy which follows from the *un*chosen, unactualised relations in a meaning system. Such values are, naturally, in any psycho-social system, also the resource for change in that meaning system. Saussure discussed this issue, especially with respect to associative (paradigmatic) relations, which are clearly determining the value of the chosen when they are *in absentia* (Saussure 1974: 123, 117). In the semiotic theory of Charles Sanders Peirce (1839–1914), the interpretant appears to play a similar role — sign processes are always to be deferred to other sign relations and to other sign relations, i. e., without a final determination (see Hookway 1985: 121; Peirce 1955, chap. 7). With Firth's application of function in context to all the levels of patterning in language, and with the serial contextualization of each level, opening out to situationally and culturally relevant participants, behaviour, objects, Firth could hardly have been surprised at fashionable claims about the ultimate undecidability of the sign.

Firth's radically relativistic approaches (especially to intralevel relations) were balanced, or literally earthed, by the sociocultural levels, by the focus on restricted languages and by the focus upon small speech fellowships, rather than abstract global collectives. Consequently, many of the criticisms made of Saussurean linguistics (e. g., the early work of Vološinov, Bakhtin and their group) do not apply to Firth's approach. The ideas put forward by Medvedev and Bakhtin (1985 [1928]) against the formal method in literary analysis actually sound less radical than Firth's techniques. For instance, Medvedev admits (p. 85) the reality of basic linguistic units but emphasises that linguistics can never have anything to say about qualities like economy, tact or truthfulness in language (p. 93). I take Firth's position to be closer to the inverse — that the units that linguists propose are just useful scaffolding, but that the linguist should try to clarify the basis of all judgements and stylistic/evaluative categories. Which approach, one may ask, is the more radical? And which the post-structuralist?

If Firth's work involved a particular failure, it was not, I believe, a failure of clarity in expressing his position, nor even of demonstrating his techniques — at least, there are few problems in finding examples in his work of how to begin from context to phonology. The problem lies with his rhetorical approach — while there is little difficulty in distilling what Firth thought, he spends very little effort to argue other theorists away from their theoretical positions. A consequence of this is that outsiders could not see how different their own practices were. Langendoen's voice, in his 1968 study of the London School, is one of frustration at why Firth could turn his back on the self-evident. I refer, for instance, to his comments on noun and verb and turning one's back on 2,000 years of grammar — an irony coming from one of the children of the 1957 Revolution! While he may have noted the importance of context (as pointed out by Henderson 1987), Langendoen presents it as a truism which, therefore, has no real bearing on the agenda of linguistics (1968: 37, 45–48). By contrast to Firth's pithy, even perfunctory, allusions to other theoretical positions, Chomskyan linguistics, and Chomsky's own publications are a case in point, have expended much space and rhetorical energy on turning linguists away from other theories and heresies. While this has produced caricatures of linguists like Firth, and articles of faith, such as mothers not teaching or correcting children's language, it has also meant that proponents of the generative school had ready-made rhetorical formulations for why they believed what they do.

Another difficulty might be called 'cartographic', and relates to the nature of Firth's theory. A theory which is set to restricted language, emphatically relational, and with ad hoc categories, does not lend itself to being laid out in a single map. Without such a map, statements can seem to come to the reader in a paratactic rhetorical structure − an aggregate of fresh starts without a global picture of how the vital, separate questions (of child language development; of personality studies; of stylistics; of speech fellowship) all bear upon his form of research into language. For this reason, and because of Firth's own commitment to phonetics, it seems to me no surprise that the majority of the best, earliest demonstrations of Firthian linguistics came out of phonological description. (See Sampson's [1980: 258] emphatic appreciation of this aspect of Firth's work, as well as the commments by him and others that current phonology was 'discovering' Firthian principles under other names, e. g., autosegmental phonology).

The required overarching map of linguistic research has been developed by Firth's student M. A. K. Halliday (b. 1925). As with other students of Firth, Halliday's early work exemplified Firth's concepts: Firth himself cites Halliday's study of the Chinese version of the *Secret History of the Mongols* (1959b) as an instance of a restricted language (Firth 1968b: 29). But Halliday also went on to elaborate the dependencies between the different questions of descriptive, theoretical, and applied linguistics from a Firthian perspective. Such an elaboration has involved the development of new tools, like the network representation of relations, and of new concepts, like 'metafunctions'.

8. Halliday and the elaboration of a functional linguistics

What is central to Firth becomes central to interpreting Halliday's career: linguistics is quite simply the study of meaning. Statements of meaning are, then, the activity around which all linguistic ideas and techniques and modes of representation are organised. But what Firth has set out in his programmatic papers, Halliday has taken up and elaborated in his diverse linguistic projects, projects which work through the implications of functional linguistics for grammar, discourse and prosodic analysis, child language development, linguistic variation and stylistics, corpus linguistics and systemic probabilities, Chinese linguistics, language in education, second language learning, and language in relation to the evolutionary processes of culture and human consciousness. Over his extended debate with all areas of linguistics, Halliday has taken up the major questions of the subject and sought integrating proposals, a unifying theory which equips both linguistics and language consumers for resolving the problems that they experience at their different levels of specialisation. Halliday's approach is reminiscent, I believe, of Darwin's methodology: each area relevant to the theory is ultimately brought into the discourse of his career with deep reflections on how the implications of his proposals can be reconciled internally, each with the others, and out to the relevant, developing literature of data and counterproposals. Given the intense volatility and controversy which have swept across interpretations of language and linguistics, it is not an error of scale or relevance to pursue that Darwinian analogy. Perhaps again, like Darwin, Halliday has not, personally, invested a great deal of energy in the quasi-political quarrels between schools of thought. Rather, he has pursued the elaboration of his ways of doing and viewing linguistics. The effect of this personal consistency has been to draw from others in the field one particularly silly accusation, and also an unfair load of incomprehension and acrimony. The accusation is that Halliday's theory is not concerned with rigorous argumentation in the way that other theories purport to be. I will return to this claim and show how it must be rejected when I discuss the role of networks (viz: networks *are* arguments, see section 10 below). The incomprehension derives in part from the prejudgments that professionals bring to an alternative idea, and in part from the effect those assumptions have on interpretations when the 'new' reader can only take in one aspect of the architecture of the total theory and its *motivations*. The acrimony has been, in my estimation, much associated with Halliday's non-acceptance of the nativist articles of faith in American linguistics of the 1960s. The hubris of psycho-linguistics in that period has been formative in the training of linguists, psychologists and cognitive scientists. Any theory which did not share in the same abundance of feeling for a future of narrowly specified mental organs was regarded as regressive or, at best, marginal, that is, merely classifying an assortment of performance factors.

Halliday's response to this situation was characteristic of the way he has worked throughout his career. In 1975 he published *Learning How to Mean*, a study which demonstrates that there is an internal logic to the way a child develops a mother tongue. A central issue here is that the motivations from context to context, and through stages (from prelanguage to protolanguage to transition and mother tongue) suggest that the researcher is *not* forced into imputing a highly specific, syntactically (or even linguistically) based, innate structure to the human brain. Nor is it reasonable to assume that the child receives inadequate data about language from experience: when we got out from mother, to family, to institutions beyond the home, the child is internalising the structure of the wider culture through the particular mediation of meaning-making behaviours. The relevant issues are semantic and are a function of the social order. The work of Bruner (1983), to cite one important example, shows how far we are now (mercifully!) from the zealotry of the 1960s, as does the notable wave of interest in the work of Vygotsky during the 1980s. Nevertheless, the earlier positioning of Halliday as somewhat eccentric has persisted wherever American theories have set the agenda. The unwillingness in Halliday to invest in Chomsky's version of a Cartesian tradition should not be surprising when the description of behaviour can be taken further, both in terms of systematicity and delicacy. This unwillingness is just one of the deep affinities between Firth and Halliday: theoretical proposals should emerge from improving the study of the accessible/available/actual, pushing up to broader statements of the *probable* and the *potential*, rather than imputing ideal or mental entities. The current pressures in cognitive science and artificial intelligence have confirmed the significance and soundness of motivation of the Firth-Halliday approach. We will find also that Halliday's use of networks, since the late 1960s, has been an interesting anticipation of connectionism (see also Lamb 1984, 1999).

9. Choice and system

In a linguistics based on meaning, and on a broader semiological perspective of how meaning is constructed, the first issue to be addressed is the form of meta-representation. Halliday's linguistics has developed a number of tools relevant to stating the meaningful choices in a paradigmatic system, as these choices function to construct text and the social order. By organising his linguistic statements around systems of choice and around the semantic consequences of those choices (viz. Firth's function in context), Halliday has developed a systemic functional linguistics which sets out an alternative to the stratal fixations of changing fashions in linguistics — consider the gradual climb from methods of isolated phonology and morphemics, against which Firth railed, to the autonomous syntax of the Chomsky era, the begrudging acceptance of semantics as a sub-discipline in linguistics, and then the more audacious inclusion of a further sub-discipline from the dispersed questions of pragmatics (with its early strong remedial role: Levinson 1983: xii). Against this theory of techniques addressing separate strata, Halliday's systemic approach stands out, in particular, for the way the metaphors of choice and system provide a way of representing the patterns of language right across the strata.

Choice is the metaphor which replaces the rules of other conceptions of language (one can think of contrasts with both Chomsky and Searle in this regard). Choice can be represented by networks, virtually diagrams of paradigms, with particular entry conditions relevant to a given 'environment', and with specifiable realisations. Choice as a metaphor changes the linguistic approach with the same dramatic switch that the eye experiences in a figure-ground reversal: no longer are we looking for ill-formed strings, or felicity conditions; rather, from the child's world on to the contexts of professional exchanges, the accumulating choices reveal how speakers increase their cultural repertoire, register by register by register. Linguistic description is a kind of cartography, a mapping of the 'meaning potential' in the dynamic, open-ended spiral of community and personal experience.

The clearest statement of this inter-organism mapping may be found in the work of the early 1970s: in Halliday's *Towards a Sociological Semantics* (1973) and in an interview with Parret (1974). The relation between language events (as the shapes of the social order) and the meaning potential of the grammar can be understood in terms of networks of choice on different strata, as elaborated below, with special regard to network as a cross-stratal form of representation. At this point, it is helpful to obtain an overview of Halliday's progressive use of description from culture to clause. In order to appreciate the ideas involved, it is also useful to build up his diagram (1973: 101) element by element.

The linguist has access to innumerable language events. These are as numerous and as accessible as there are interactants to observe and describe. But as an amorphous spread of actual instances, they do not have any typological or predictive function for the linguist.

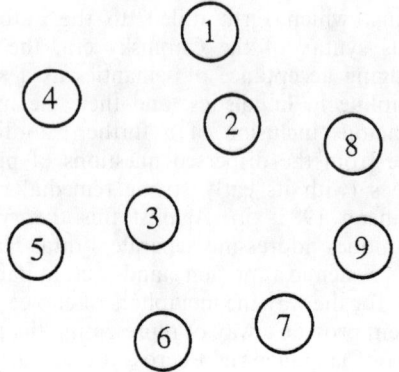

Fig. 203.1: Ungrouped instances of language

These need to be brought into a theory of types of situations (or, more commonly, registers or genres).

tail (1984a; Halliday & Hasan 1985) the probabilities of particular semantic components can be organised into nuclear and non-nuclear, and represented both as choices in paradigms, and as an unfolding structure − a syntagmatic statement of 'generic structure potential'. From the point of view of social context, a variety can be characterised by field, tenor and mode: by the activity structures and purposes (field); by the human dimensions of who is and who can, or cannot, be involved in this kind of context (tenor); and by the pressures of linguistic organisation and channel of delivery which shape the enunciation of the message (mode).

The paradox of rendering complex, variable behaviour from the interlocking networks of basic alternatives should not only be recognisable to readers of Firth. The same approach has been developed over the last 30 years by Sydney M. Lamb (b. 1929), in 'stratificational linguistics'; and relatively recently, the connectionist proposals in artificial intelligence have been impressive both (i) because they can account for complexity from very basic terms and (ii) because the networks can encompass more even than their 'intended' input, including forms of self-correction.

For Halliday, then, sign-making, or semiotic, orders include the 'context of situation'. Meaning is grounded in the configurations of relevant relations in the culture, in the partic-

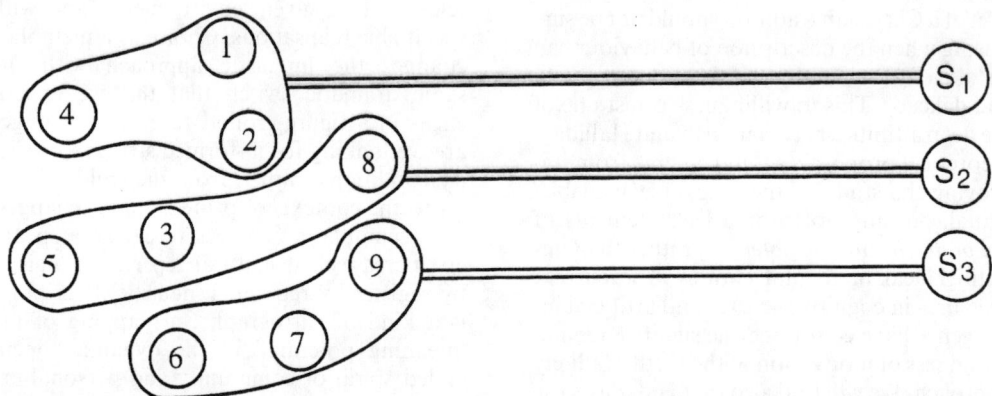

Fig. 203.2: Instances collected as situation types S1, S2 and S3

These situation types are constituted by the consistencies of meaning choices which they in turn reflect. Consistency is, it should be stressed, never total identity. Nevertheless, it is possible to argue for such functional varieties on the basis of meanings that each context demands. As Hasan has shown in de-

ular social context. This is to say: the variables within the *field* of activity, in the *tenor* of human-to-human 'politics', and in the many ways that a spoken or written *mode* can be adopted, all need to be included in order to account for the meaning. While Firth's account of linguistic levels does appear to make 'context of situation' do the work of both semantics and pragmatics (according to conventional theorising in linguistics), Halliday utilizes 5 separate levels or orders in his semiotic model: context of culture, context of situation, semantics, lexicogrammar, and expression in phonology/phonetics.

In order to display both the concepts of 'realisation' and 'metaredundancy', Halliday now sets out this arrangement in circles rather than parallel strata. The strata and the 'circle' version of his model of language can be derived from *Towards a Sociological Semantics* (1973).

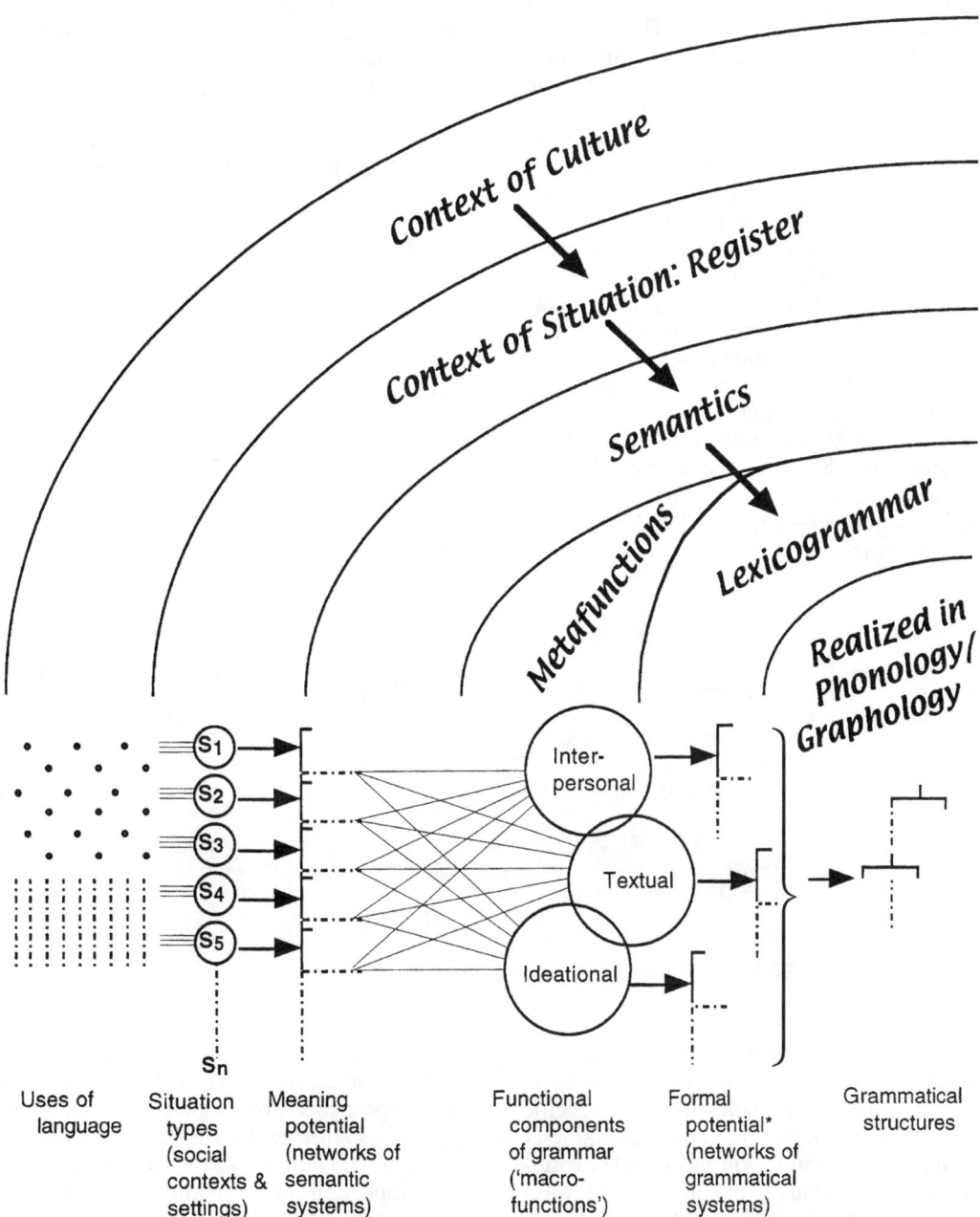

* i.e. meaning potential at the grammatical level, in the system-structure definition of 'meaning'.

Fig. 203.3: Strata of semiotic organisation (modification of Halliday 1973: 101)

The crucial point here is that meaning potential can be addressed as one form of behaviour potential. As a result, the various dimensions of the Firthian project in an autonomous linguistics are integrated: first of all, the making of statements of meaning is based on system, the paradigm of choices relevant to a given environment; and second, the relevant environment extends from the social order to the phonetic expression. The organisation of his linguistics around paradigmatic choices, as systems, actually emerged first in Halliday's work on the grammar of English (1976 [1964]: 101), not, as may seem given the order of my explanation, from a single context type out to the system. Both the systemic character of grammar and its metafunctional organisation were factors that emerged from mapping the interdependent choices in the clause (see section 10 below and Halliday 1976: 14). Halliday demonstrates lucidly the socio-semiotic orientation of his approach by taking the situation of a mother disapproving of her child's behaviour. He first shows that a sample of sixteen expressions (ranging from "I told you I didn't want you to do that" to "You can go there when you're bigger") can all be usefully represented and coded by three simple paradigms:

and pursued to the delicacy that the project demands in order to distinguish the speakers or social groups involved, for instance, the different semantic styles of mothers. In fact, Hasan has elaborated just such networks of choice and the class variants in the patterns of mothers' control and typical rhetorical styles (see below section 13). This form of network representation has the instrumental and ad hoc character that Firth required of the linguistic schema. Furthermore it begins in extremely simple terms (or primitives) which do not themselves bring a high order of interference from the analytic apparatus. Essentially, the network begins from

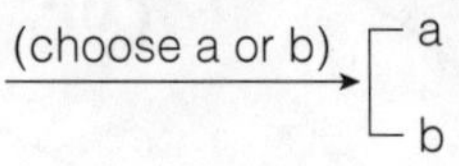

$$(\text{choose a or b}) \longrightarrow \begin{bmatrix} a \\ b \end{bmatrix}$$

Fig. 203.5: Or

and

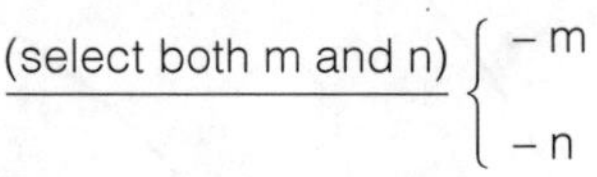

$$(\text{select both m and n}) \begin{cases} -m \\ -n \end{cases}$$

Fig. 203.6: And

$$\begin{cases} (a) \longrightarrow \begin{bmatrix} \text{explanation } (a_1) \\ \text{rule } (a_2) \end{bmatrix} \\ (b) \longrightarrow \begin{bmatrix} \text{general } (b_1) \\ \text{specific } (b_2) \end{bmatrix} \\ (c) \longrightarrow \begin{bmatrix} \text{object-oriented } (c_1) \\ \text{person-oriented} \end{bmatrix} \xrightarrow{(d)} \begin{bmatrix} \text{child} \xrightarrow{(e)} \begin{bmatrix} \text{as individual } (e_1) \\ \text{as status } (e_2) \end{bmatrix} \\ \text{parent } (d_2) \end{bmatrix} \end{cases}$$

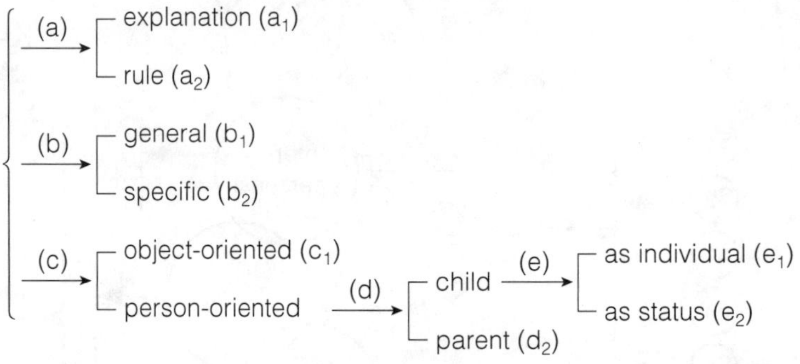

Fig. 203.4: A first network of mother's disapproval

Important to note here are the practical, instrumental motivations for the represention and its ability to be tailored to the specific goals of the analyst. The semantic character of the different choices in the sample expressions can be brought out in different ways and elaborated to different degrees of *delicacy*. The systems a, b and c are relevant to one (minimal) step in semantic clarification; but any dimesion of meaning may be built in

From these terms an involved interconnection can be developed which accounts for the interdependencies of language, including the *valeurs* established by the choices within a given system and the *valeurs* that result from the allocation of semantic responsibilities across the polysystemic architecture of human behaviour, an architecture which must bring out both the regularity and the open-endedness. The basic terms can give greater tool power by being used left to right and right to left. Hence:

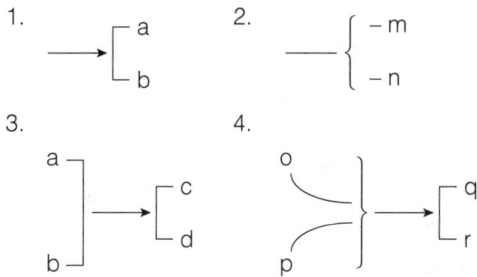

Fig. 203.7: Different combinations of 'or' and 'and' networks

1. Select a or b
2. Select both m and n
3. When either a or b is selected, then either c or d must be selected
4. Only when (if?) o and p are both selected can you then select between q and r

The networks also allow for the description of recursive choices:

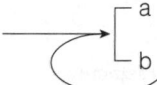

Fig. 203.8: Recursive Choice

5. If option b is selected, return to a previous entry condition and make further selections.

These are the five basic terms by which the description can be constructed. The 'delicacy' of the description can go as far as the analyst's power to discriminate a difference of meaning, or as far as is demanded by the issue which motivated the description. Halliday develops the picture of mother's control to enhance the opposition between threat and warning, as well as the delicacy of distinction concerning agency (child as 'doer'):

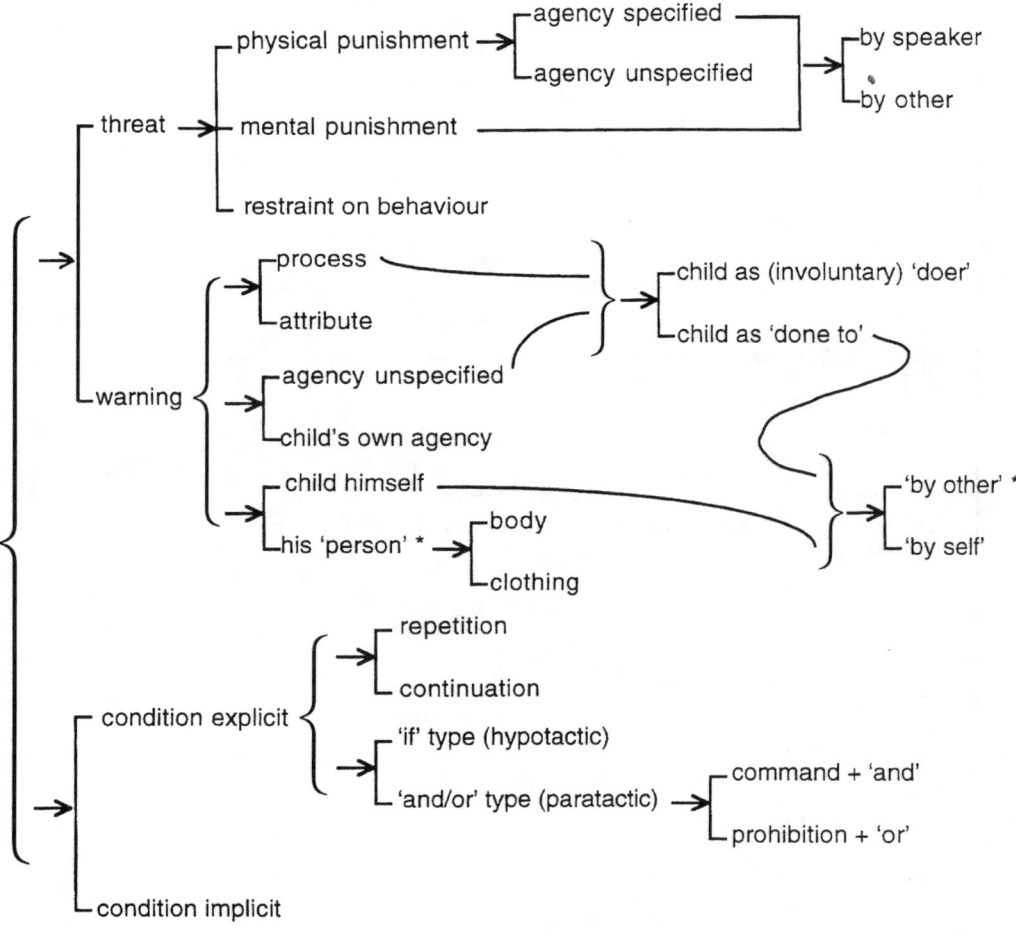

Fig. 203.9: Revised network of mother's disapproval (Halliday 1973: 89)

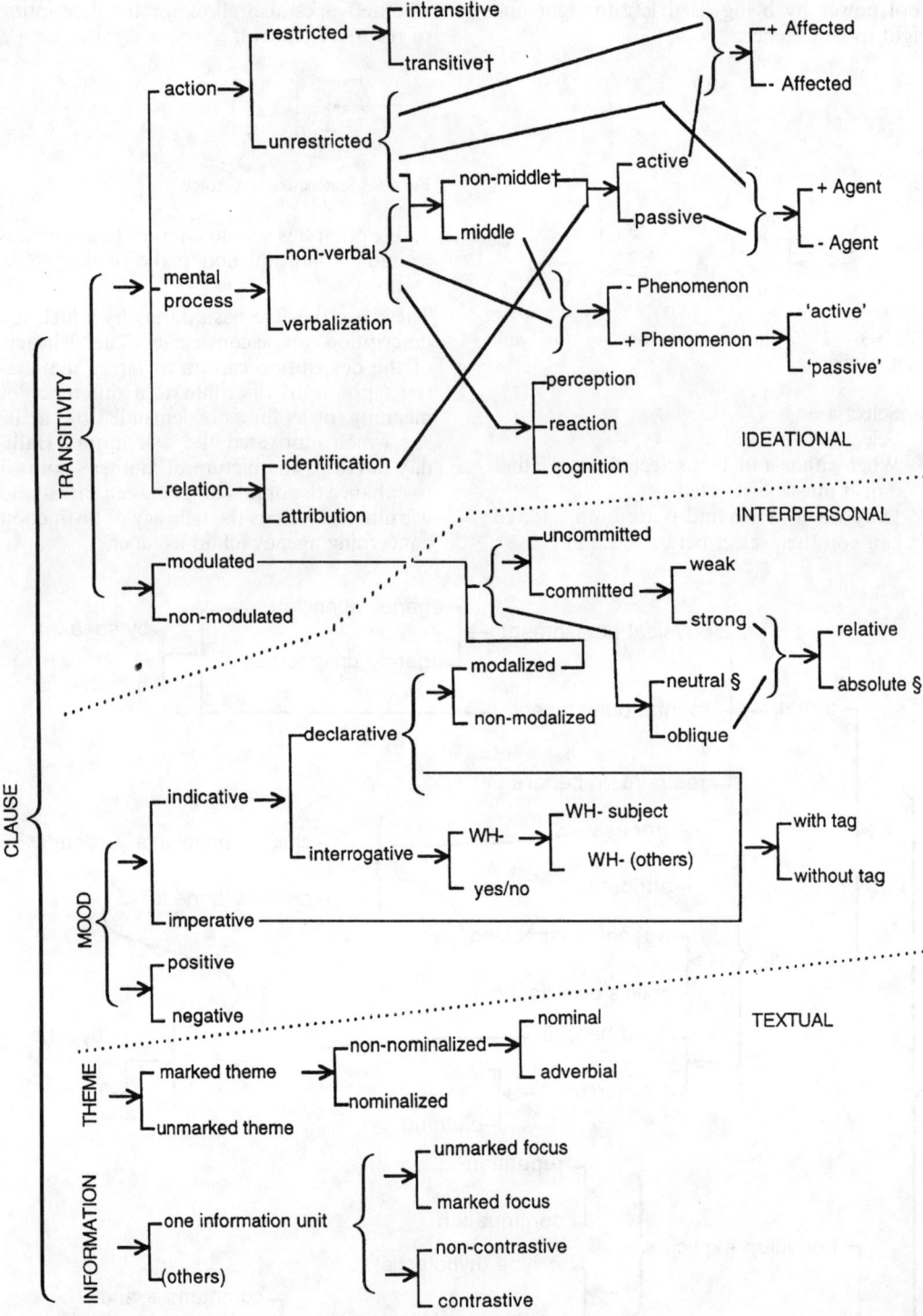

Fig. 203.10: Emergence of the metafunctions from dependency between grammatical systems (Halliday in Kress 1976: 14)

The conventions discussed here as the basis of semantic networks are, then, the Hallidayan method for accounting for the meaning potential of speakers in specific contexts of situation. As mentioned above, unlike other linguistic models (except stratificational theory, which has an isomorphic network theory) systemic functional linguistics utilises the same conventions for all strata. The statements of linguistic meaning are then congruent; at least, they are consistently organised around the principles of *choice/system* or *paradigm*. It must be conceded that these terms of metadescription necessarily take on a somewhat different value on each stratum: for example, 'choice' may not have precisely the same value in the meta-theory at the levels of context, say, and at the level of expression in the phonology. But, nevertheless, the patterns of different strata can still be accommodated by the polysystemic approach, namely, the number of alternatives in the specific envinronment, and the environment in its environment and so on in Firth's serial contextualisation.

10. Networks as a form of argument

The role of the network itself needs to be discussed, since the emphasis on argumentation in comteporary linguistics has been used as a distinguishing mark of the scientific approach and apparently as a reason for self-congratulation. *Networks are, in themselves, a form of argument*. They are a consistent means of checking what is the better motivated proposal in linguistic description. The network either accounts for the linguistic variation and its consequences, choice by choice, *or it does not*. It is straightforward to check and redraw, so it maintains adequacy through a transparent *accountability*, and *modifiability*. One system of choices and its consequences in realisation statements can be wired in with parallel systems so that the relevant patterns of a unit, like the clause in lexicogrammar, can be described in blocks of simultaneous and dependent options. For example, if one looks over an early version of clause systems, the dotted lines mark out the separate domains of simultaneous meaning making: transitivity, mood, and theme. These three systems are like three separate boards of wiring which fall out into three metafunctions. From this perspective, it is easier to see how the metafunctions are a proposal motivated by the organisation of dependent choices in the language: the metafunctions are required by the interdependency of particular options and systems of options. Ideational, interpersonal and textual are, then, a response to order in the grammar, not ideas that have been introduced extrinsically, i.e., from outside semiotics (see Fig. 203.10).

The minimalism of a network is part of its tool power. A network is essentially an iconic version of a central element in the Saussurean-Hjelmsevian theory: this is to say, one *draws out* the differences. The network only represents contrast, systems of contrast and the relational environment of differences. Consequently, we are building, through networks, a totally relational picture of a language without introducing anything more than a minimal interference from the metadescriptive activity. This is quite different then from the formalisations of many other theories in which the metaphor of rule can create a miasma of legislation and arbitrary proposals on technical matters.

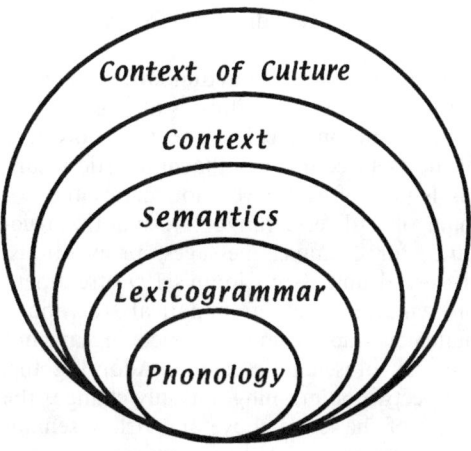

Fig. 203.11: Circular schema: metaredundancy

11. Firth, Halliday and meaning

At this point, by returning to the notion of levels of language, the relationship between Firth and Halliday can be made more clear, in particular in relation to the use of meaning. The circular schema makes it easier to see that a level is not only encoding the level directly 'above' but, rather, the whole overlay of patterning that is expressed (or, in some sense, declared) by the ultimate choices of the smallest circle, phonology or graphology.

This is not a claim that all the meanings of the culture are expressible through, for instance, the sound patterning; what it does draw attention to however is that all strata are interdependent with consequences from above being articulated all down the spectrum (recall Firth's analogy of white light and the prism). There is a second notable difference between realisation relations across different stratal boundaries. While Saussure's line of arbitrariness is most closely matched by the relation between lexicogrammar and phonology/graphology, the relation between semantics and lexicogrammar appears to be of another kind (both content-to-content and content-to-expression). More dramatic differences apply to the connection between context of culture and context of situation. The language of a particular context of situation is characterisable as a *register* (see Firth's restricted language). As mentioned above, the contextual variables are crucial in establishing the language that is relevant to the cultural process. But the notions of unit and structure and system have to undergo considerable reconceptualisation (see Hasan 1998, and Martin, discussed below, section 14).

The issue of metaredundancy between levels of realisation addresses a longstanding issue in an economical way — it is a corollary of the metaredundancy that linguistic meaning is part of each level, not merely the domain of a diverse range of semantic structures, for example, messages, propositions, rhetorical units (see Cloran's 1994 treatment of semantic and grammatical relations). Statements about linguistic meaning are not the task of semantics alone. Adopting this perspective on meaning not only changes the status of the levels above and below semantics — it also makes the instrumental role of the semantics more obvious (and hence, the instrumental/tool power of the linguistic model overall is more transparent). *Semantics is what semantics does in the theory* (cf. Firth's idea that technical terms "mean what they do" [1968b: 33]). And first and foremost, semantics has to make a bridge between the language events in the social order — their regularities of shape and direction — and the meaning as lexicogrammar, as patterns of wording. The statements of choice at the level of context of situation have to be systematically related to the systems of grammar and lexis. Whatever proposal the linguist adopts in this connection, whether formal or informal, paraphrase, feature based or rhetorically based, whether utilising a rank scale or not — that proposal takes on the role and status of semantics.

Hence it is a misunderstanding of the approach by Halliday, I believe, when some earlier contributors to systemic theory suggested that Halliday was unclear about what, for instance, is semantic, and what is grammatical. A strong boundary in this matter would be an error in terms of the whole direction of Firthian and Hallidayan linguistics. For example, the point raised (by both Fawcett 1982 and Butler 1985) is that the categories of transitivity in Halliday's functional grammar (viz. Actor, Process, Goal, Senser, Sayer, Carrier, Attribute etc.) have to be allocated to one stratum, that is, the lexicogrammar. Yet it is clear that the need to label immediately invokes a semantics of the grammar (even if we used nothing more than number labels). And to label, with a characterisation based on *meaning* (which is the central motivation for functional grammar) one has to utilise words/lexis which already have a domain in the lexicogrammar, before they are used again in what Halliday, partly for the clarification of this kind of problem, prefers to call the grammatics (i.e., the theoretical description of grammar).

As stressed by Firth, it is not possible, in principle, to seal off one level of patterning from another. Yet some such self-deluding procedure has often been proposed as the hallmark of rigour in the argumentation and method of linguistic science. By and large, such rigour often comes with granting existent status to the categories of theory. In Firthian terms this would be the error of hypostatisation — namely, giving the scaffolding an ontological status (Firth [1968c: 47]) following Martinet, called this 'rigor mortis').

Halliday's work has in fact ranged over all the subdisciplines of linguistics, motivated (as I have claimed) by the steady elaboration of the Firthian practices and programs. Child language development shows that language is learnt in a complex interaction with cultural knowledge — one semiotic system (the language) is required to construe the culture in the same process that one needs a knowledge of the culture to develop language. Furthermore, children's language is regarded, in Halliday's work, as an extended apprenticeship from neonate to adult (with particular emphasis on schooling). This approach throws crucial illumination on the grammatical system (e. g., of English) in that apprenticeships in different registers involve different meaning-making resources. Around the age of 12 to 13 years, as the child enters secondary school, the technical explanations of English scientific prose put particular pressures of comprehension on the learner. 'Grammatical metaphor' takes an indirect or incongruent route in encoding experience. Technical nominalisations like *the glass crack growth rate* (Halliday & Martin 1993: 79) bundle up experience in order to focus on the abstract and, in the form of a nominal group, give the speaker the best chance to choose in moving the complex term in and out of opening or Theme position in a clause. In an equative (a relational process) the terms can be set up felicitously to express an exact quantity or definition or new symbolic relation, with the noteworthy feature of reversible grammatical roles (Subject to Complement, Theme to Rheme). Token and Value are terms which express the change of symbolic address that is the major contribution to discourse of this identifying structure (namely, the Identified can be viewed in terms of its overt manifestation: Token — how do I recognise 'it'? Or in terms of its role in the scheme of things: Value — what part does it play?). The following example is taken from a teacher's explanation, in junior high school, of topographic maps. The formulation, part of a four-part rhetorical gambit or explanatory trope, brings two clauses into an identifying relationship: the matrix clause is gathering aspects of the previous discourse into a revaluation. The clause is a semiotic resource for working on the symbolic order itself.

A typical pattern emerges in Halliday's approach to linguistics: wherever one sets out from, or to, the various activities of linguistics inform each other, both as the stimulus for new questions, and as the check on the claims of theory (viz. Are we, in fact, forced to infer a mental organ of language? Are the data children hear 'degenerate' with respect to their syntactic behaviour?). The registral significance of grammatical metaphor becomes a source of clarification for the stages of the human's long apprenticeship, in particular from primary to secondary education. The total exposition of learning the mother tongue becomes part of linguistic, or language based, proposals about knowledge and the external evolution of higher mental functions (Halliday 1995c). Language, as the mental tool which provides the mental tools for cultural evolution, has to be accounted for as a fourth stratum of Darwinian evolution — a semiotic level of reality which has itself emerged from the underlying orders of material, biological and sociological reality. Both biological 'information', and the new contexts of electronic 'information', albeit in quite different ways, point to the usefulness of a semiotic model in dealing with complex systems more broadly. In this regard, plastic arts, visual semiotics, and cultural artefacts (from toys to sports) lend themselves to metafunctional and polysystemic interpretation. So language is not the only source of metaphor (see section 16 below). So too is the language for describing language (Halliday 1998; Kress & van Leeuwen 1996; O'Toole 1994).

Other areas offer parallels in this characteristic cycle of clarification: empirical research, serial contextualisation of data, and

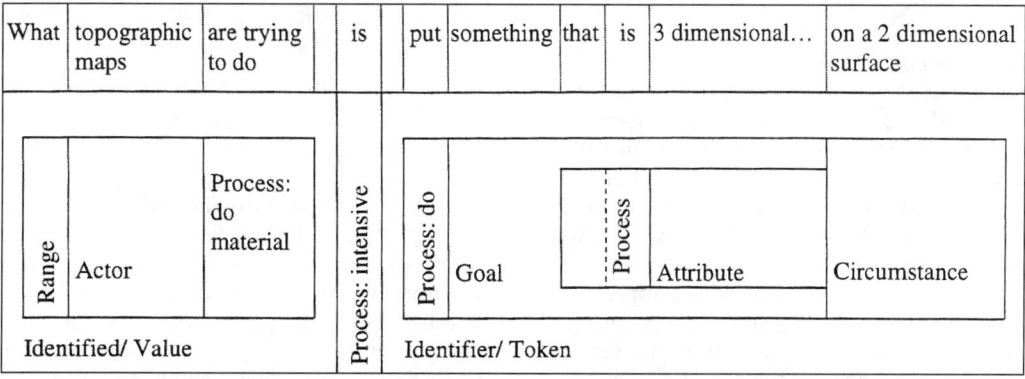

Fig. 203.12: Token-Value structure

integration with the overall functional picture of language. Investigations of corpora of English words and grammar (in particular, with John Sinclair's Cobuild Bank of English, currently a 311 million word corpus organised around written and spoken registers) have provided evidence for conceptualising the choices of grammar on a probabilistic basis. The paradigmatic modelling has also been turned to a renewed computational modelling. Along with the important work by Winograd (1972, 1983), developments by Mann & Matthiessen (1983) have produced an extensive array of resources for natural language processing, including recent interlingual work between texts of English, Chinese, Japanese, French and German.

12. Meaning, society and grammar

It would be just as feasible to set out from other linguistic problems (and other functional varieties of text) in trying to represent Halliday's linguistics and its elaboration across the wider field of contributors in systemic functional theory. What one cannot lose sight of in such an account, however, are the compass points of meaning, society and grammar. Meaning has already been noted. Society is a complex term which I will treat below. And grammar is crucial as both the core of meaning-making resources in a language, and as the most useful of metaphors for interpreting and penetrating other complex semiotic phenomena — the dynamic, open system of a natural language may be a powerful heuristic device for investigating the 'value' systems of society and the informational systems of the brain following the organisational principles suggested by Edelmann (1992), for example. This analogic power in the study of grammar is, of course, a reciprocating relationship, and Halliday himself has found useful analogies from physics, biology and systems theory. One case is the 'complementarity' which can be seen, for example, in systems of transitive/ergative, tense/aspect (Halliday 1987). Furthermore he suggests that there may be more of a homology between the characteristic structures of spoken discourse and the flexible, process-oriented modelling which appears to be a requirement of any metaphor in current physics (so clausal intricacy and the overlaid texturing of Theme/Rheme and Given/New have some affinity with those conjectures of the physicist, David Bohm (1917–1992), on 'rheomodes' see Butt 1989). The American semiotician, Jay Lemke (b. 1950), has been particularly influential in bringing insights from systems theory and natural sciences to Systemic-Functional (S. F.) theory. For example, the concepts of metaredundancy, typology/topology, and open, dynamic system have all been used in the construction of the metalanguage of systemics (Lemke 1995).

The Hallidayan project of elaborating Firthian linguistics has, as can be seen from the foregoing, taken on its own character and directions, its own idiom, and a range of problems that could not have been envisaged even by the historically prescient Firth. This diversification of linguistic projects has been assisted, in particular, by work in computational linguistics by Robin P. Fawcett (b. 1937), in the development of textual theory by the American linguist Peter H. Fries (b. 1937), by the coordination of perspectives from European structuralism in the projects of Michael O'Toole (b. 1934), and by the general theoretical discussions of Margaret Berry (1975, 1977). Along with the continuing elaborations of a Firthian perspective by Michael Gregory (e. g., 1980), these figures turned the systemic work out to developments in others models and other linguistic cultures, from the generativeness of a description, to the relation to cognate ideas coming out of Stratificational linguistics and the Birmingham School. But in trying to present a brief account from Firth to Halliday and S. F. linguistics, I will sketch the work that ties in most directly with my theme: 'How linguists make statements of meaning?' In pursuing this issue, I need to bring out developments in semantic variation (through the work of Hasan, see section 13), in stratification (as argued by Martin, see section 14), and in linguistic cartography (as demonstrated by Matthiessen, see section 15).

13. From semantics to semantic variation

From her earliest work in stylistics, in the 1960s, Ruqiaya Hasan (b. 1931) has organised her approach to linguistics around meaning and the semantic stratum. She first pointed out how approaching verbal art through grammatically rather than, say, sensicality, has been a narrowing, unrewarding approach to the aesthetic function in texts

(Hasan 1971, 1975); and her own theory takes up the earlier work of Jan Mukařovský (1891–1973) in emphasising the consistencies of organisation and selection which constitute the distinctive articulatory strategy or strategies of a work. The approach, through semantic organisation, can encompass any kind of textual design – not merely the overtly signalled forms of rule-breaking that distorted the project (and the public profile) of linguistic stylistics in the generative tradition. In all linguistic problems, her technique has been fundamentally Firthian in that she has been developing and applying the tools for statements of meaning.

The semantic motivation of Hasan's work is also clear in "The grammarians dream: Lexis as most delicate grammar" (1987d), in which her mapping out of meaning contrasts, again in networks or paradigms of systems, demonstrates how one can proceed from a grammatical unit as entry point (viz. the clause) and proceed to a set of choices on which each choice produces only one lexical item. Other early work on Urdu (the verb *hona* "be") re-emerges in work presented in the mid-1970s as "Ways of Saying: Ways of Meaning" (1984c). She presents an extended comparison of implicit devices in her form of Urdu and the English of middle class speakers in England. This comparison includes the implications of Subjectness and forms of Reference in typical contexts – what, for example, is the characteristic threshold in each system for maintaining/requiring explicit coding. Put as a corollary: what degree of 'exophora' (pointing to the context) is the unmarked case in the two systems? Given the differences she finds, between the higher order of implicitness in the unmarked coding pattern of Urdu and the higher explicitness of English (for example the tendency for Subject in the unmarked clause; and the rare appearance of restricted exophoric reference), Hasan argues that the motivations for the differences are a function of the social structure, in particular, the greater reliability of shared views of particular contexts, typical roles, and likely participants in such roles.

In all then, Hasan's approach shows that there is not a distinct boundary between linguistic and social patterning, and that, in the trade off between the coding and the contextual probabilities, one can see the reciprocal delimitation of language and society, a mutual definition which is often dismissed by cognitivists as an uninvestigable truism.

Reading Hasan's explication, it is easier to understand Halliday's observation (in Parret 1974: 81) that, for those coming from the same tradition, linguistics had no need for a separate subdivision of *socio*linguistics. So too, Hasan's exemplification makes clearer her (and Halliday's) wariness about the linguist presenting a social theory which has not emerged from the linguistic facts themselves including, of course, who speaks to whom in the making of what kind of activity. As with the sociosemantic investigations of Bernstein's theory, the social relations are co-determining and co-determined relative to the language. Neither is prior, just as it is illegitimate to regard thought (the content plane) to exist prior to an expression plane which demarcates the contrasts of signification and value (in the Saussurean scheme). Consequently the claim that S. F. linguistics privileges the code over the social structure can be despatched along the following lines: since linguistics can only clarify the complexities of social relations by producing a more plausible account of meaning making practices, it is of little relevance to any kind of progress if the linguist is hectored into some alignment with a 'social' theory as a means of establishing his/her academic bona fide. The idea then that linguistics is, in general, in need of a social theory turns out to be a new fashioned version of the old fashioned fallacy that the form and the content, the linguistic code and the context, are separable. If 'reality' is constructed through symbolic-discursive practices, it is equally contradictory to invoke either the textual or the contextual as the self-evident base of theory. The wording or textual will always be an expression of a social observance of distinction (Saussurean contrast) and the contextual does not correspond to the material situation setting as such, but rather to the semiotically relevant ordering of the material setting. These lines of argument have been presented vigorously in recent papers, which draw on her projects in child language development.

While it may seem paradoxical that a linguistic theory has to defend its preoccupation with meaning, any review of the most influential texts of the discipline in the 20th century (which must include Bloomfield 1933; Chomsky 1957, 1965) makes it immediately clear why it is necessary to foreground, and in a contrastive way, the adherence to meaning in the work of those in the Firthian tradition. Linguistics is, in the Systemic-Functional framework, part of a general account of processes of meaning. A further paradox cannot be so directly explained, however: given the current emphasis, amongst linguists and educationists, on the variability of language behaviour (variation of accent and dialect, for example), why is it that the issue of semantic variation has been so difficult to discuss in professional circles, as well as across the community. The problem of semantic variation has become an organising theme in Hasan's own investigations of meaning — the issue motivated her research with Basil Bernstein's (1924—2000) unit at London University in the 1960s; and it formed the motivation of more than 10 years of research into socialisation at home and school, conducted before her retirement at Macquarie University in Australia. I will allocate space to explain 'semantic variation' in Hasan's work, albeit from my angle, because the topic puts most of the issues of Firthian and Hallidayan linguistics on trial, both in terms of the consistencies of concerns and the problems of their reception and evaluation in the wider fields of linguistics and applied linguistics.

Semantic variation explores the ways in which people habitually mean in different, crucial socializing contexts. In this, it is not a theory of what speakers can and cannot do, but rather what they tend towards in construing their role in a particular situation. Hasan's long-term, multivariate statistical study of over 20,000 messages between mothers and young children in the home shows that these tendencies to mean do not vary in random or unsystematic ways. Class and gender are the fundamental factors in accounting for the variation (Hasan 1989, 1991).

At this point it is crucial to bring contextual theory to bear. At one degree of delicacy, we can compare households by extralinguistic criteria: mealtime, dressing for preschool, taking a bath, etc. All the mother-child dyads will involve such 'situations'. Hasan's data is drawn from three: mother giving care to child; mother doing a chore, with child about; and mother and child in co-operative task. If, on the other hand, we set out from the meaning making practices which each dyad tends to produce in these environments, — for instance, the ways questions are posed, taken up or not; the ways in which praise or threats, speculations, and informational interludes are, or are not, part of the typical-actual; the way opinion, uncertainty and projections are apportioned to the permissable range of topics — then we might wish to argue that the dyads may be constructing and living through quite different contexts of situation, and ultimately, through quite distinct 'climates' of culture.

The extra-linguistic and the linguistic configure each other. And in this co-determination one can see the theoretical space which demands an account, at least from any linguistics concerned with 'patterns of life'. Hasan has demonstrated, from this extensive corpus of checkable data, and from analysis which encompasses a large number of variables for each message, that the Australian urban experience involves unequivocal consistencies of meaning making. These consistencies are along class and gender lines. Given the possibility that Australian society is 'flatter' in its class structure than either Britain or parts of the United States, there is every reason to believe similar investigations elsewhere will find the same or even more marked differences. But while the variations related to gender are received with enthusiasm, those motivated by class are received querulously.

This account of semantic variation brings a new force and confirmation to Firth's emphasis on a linguistics of the sociological component, and a linguistics set at the speech fellowship and its restricted language. It shows that the variability, the 'non-unity', and poly-systemic character of language behaviour, which Firth urged, for instance against Saussure, needs to be recognised even at the core of social experience, often just where social theorists, educators and linguists might have assumed homogeneity (for example, an 'Anglo' Australian school group may still be most varied in this way). Furthermore, semantic variation offers linguistic evidence for the insights and theories of the sociologist Basil Bernstein. Bernstein's code theory explains this *variability* of contextual construal, and the *invariability* of cultural reproduction, but by setting out from the general role of communication in the social structure. Only with such concepts — code and semantic variation — can we conceptualise Firth's "notions of personality and language as vectors of the continuity of repetitions in the social process" (1957 [1950]: 183). And only with such vectors of semantic consistency can linguistics navigate between the Scylla of the intuitive, Chomskyan individual, and the Charybdis of the Saussurean collective.

14. Stratification

Firthian notions of meaning have also been adapted to models with greater stratification than suggested by either Firth or Halliday. James R. Martin (b. 1950), working at Sydney University, has led the way in the development of stratification in relation to context (namely all that is above the semantics). Of particular note is his use of Hjelmslev's notion of a connotative semiotic, a semiotic system which uses another semiotic system as its realization or plane for expression. Martin's most influential proposal in this regard came out his work, with educationists, to describe the text types demanded of schooling, and the kinds of school writing activities that most often discriminated against children in Disadvantaged Schools. In trying to account for the forms of the texts valued in the education process (which are usually only taught implicitly through English Studies), Martin & Rothery (1980; Martin 1998) suggested that S. F. theory needed a level of genre above register, a categorization of staged, goal directed activities that would constitute social formations which may undergo quite different realizations in actual registral forms. Martin's important volume of discourse proposals (1992) also included a stratum of ideology. This was motivated by the observation, clear from the work of Bernstein, Hasan and others, that meaning potential was not equally available to all members of a community or similarly deployed. Martin's disappointment at the lack of dialogue around this extension (Martin 1997: 7) has brought him to a modification which is based on the dynamic of time, and so returns to Halliday's three histories of the text — logogenesis (the unfolding of the text); ontogenesis (its relation to the development in the individual); and phylogenesis (the relation to change and development across the semiotic history of the community).

Conscious of the charge of reification in the architecture of his strata (1997: 10), Martin has also reviewed his expressions of genre staging, "moving away from simple constituency representations" (p. 16). In this direction he has been a leader in conceptualising different types of structure for both genre phasing as well as with respect to the grammar. In fact, it is arguable that across the many publications of his multi-faceted contribution to S. F. linguistics, the most Firthian may be his grammatical work: "Metalinguistic diversity: The case of case" (Martin 1996). In this tour de force he sets out from the rhetorical question of why linguistic diversity is so applauded, yet metalinguistic diversity so abhorred amongst linguists. This article, like Halliday's "On Grammar and Grammatics" (1996), extends Firth's discourse on the ineffability and heuristic status of the categories of grammar.

15. Probabilistic grammar and cartography

The manipulation of corpora by computers, and the power to build probabilities into networks of choice and into register analysis, have produced a revolution in how linguistics can model change, diversity/variation, and the permeability of boundaries between text types. The climate is propitious for Firthian indeterminacy and complementarities. There is, I believe, less reason for linguists to settle on particular versions of a genre or any textual pattern. The critical element is the meaning-making power of the lexico-grammar — a text can be characterised by the accumulating selections when these selections are interpreted as syndromes, motifs, or 'motivated' by a form of trigonometric 'logic', that is, an argument between three strata: context, semantics and lexicogrammar.

Still, the possibilities in these directions depend on consciously exploiting the various dimensions of the meaning space that the grammar provides: Christian Matthiessen (b. 1956) working closely with Halliday, has done more than anyone to map that meaning space and to demonstrate how the separate dimensions provide a basis for a systematic typology of languages. Matthiessen's 1,000 page *Lexicogrammatical Cartography: English Systems* (1995) offers the best account of the S. F. description of English based on Halliday's work. Unlike Halliday's *Introduction to Functional Grammar* (1985, ^{2}1994), Matthiessen lays out the networks for the polysystemic approach. There is also a careful explication of the place of the grammar in the overall S. F. model along with individual subsections explaining the status in the theory of concepts like grammatical metaphor, rank shift, and semogenesis (i.e., concepts which often need clarification for insiders and outsiders alike). As sustained as Matthiessen's text is, it remains for him a 'sketch' of the potential in English and S. F. theory. His research team use this mapping of the grammatical space for natural language processing across and between English, Chinese, Japanese, German and French. Combined with Firthian perspectives on translation being developed by Steiner & Yallop (2001), the Natural Language Processing work (e. g., Matthiessen 1991) shows how current S. F. theory integrates the computational potential of contemporary linguistics with the earliest, ethnographic motivations of Malinowski and Firth.

Again working with Halliday, Matthiessen has set out a construal of cognition and mind based on processes of meaning and grammar: how can we construe the human mind if we use human linguistic experience and do not invoke pre-linguistic mental fictions? (Halliday & Matthiessen 1999). The relevance to Firth's views is clear and direct. What needs to be added is the observation that Halliday's discussions of meaning are not only an inter-organism perspective (Parret 1974: 81). In the construal of the mind, in the interpretation of day by day experiences like pain (through the grammar by which we categorize such experience: Halliday 1998), and through the explication of how the potential to mean is multiplied (semogenesis), we can see that Halliday's linguistics has come to encompass topics of intellectual debate which were once thought to be the domains of the antithetical work of generative linguistics, or of the congruent theory of stratificational linguistics.

16. A Protean theory

Halliday's work has maintained a consistent and explicitly declared relationship with the approaches initiated by Firth. The current form of Systemic-Functional theory, as developed by Halliday, reconciles Firth's requirements of paradigmatic explicitness and 'renewal of connection' with Halliday's own evolving conceptions of a science of semiotics and of problem solving in linguistics. The result is a highly abstract theory which is carefully motivated by the actual circumstances of human lives:

"Systemic theory might be characterized as comprehensive, extravagant, indeterminate, non-autonomous and variable. (1) It is not dedicated to any specific branch of language study; every particular investigation is read and evaluated as part of a general interpretation of language. (This does not mean that it is an all-purpose theory; there are tasks to which it is not well suited, e. g., those requirung a dedicated and easily formalized minigrammar.) (2) It is not constrained by a requirement of simplicity; there are always more theoretical resources available than are necessary for any one given task. (Three reasons may be cited for this: no arguments are derived from the simplicity of linguistic descriptions, e. g., in relation to the structure of the human brain; there are no convincing measures of simplicity which could take account of all components of a description; and what is locally simpler often turns out to be globally more complex.) (3) It treats indeterminacy in language as the norm, rather than as an aberrant feature to be removed by idealization surgery. (4) It locates itself within a general theory of semiotic systems-&-processes, as well as with reference to theory and practice in other areas involving (but not defined by) the study of language; e. g., artificial intelligence, literacy education. (5) It accommodates considerable variation within itself, without any notion of doctrine: e. g., different modellings of register and genre, of the relation between meaning and wording (semantics and lexicogrammar), of the structure of dialogue (exchange structure) and so on. In all these respects, systemic theory stands as a metaphor for language itself: language is comprehensive (it models all human experience, enacts all human relations), extravagant (it is redundant at every level; but also, it is always offering alternative interpretations, e. g., transitive and ergative as construal of processes), indeterminate (if is full of ambiguities, borderline cases and blends), non-autonomous (it is shaped in the course of evolution in tension with other human institutions) and variable ("a language" is a space defined by dialectal and registerial variation). And since language is itself metaphorical, this metaphorical relation of linguistic theory to language becomes a further metaphor — a metametaphor; systemic theory, in that sense, is metametaphorical to language." (Halliday, p. c., 1992)

17. Bibliography

Bazell, C. E., J. C. Catford, M. A. K. Halliday & R. H. Robins, eds. 1966. *In Memory of J. R. Firth.* London: Longmans.

Berry, Margaret. 1975–77. *Introduction to Systemic Linguistics.* 2 vols. London: Batsford.

—. 1981. "Systemic Linguistics and Discourse Analysis: A multi-layered approach to exchange structure". *Studies in Discourse Analysis* ed. by Malcolm Coulthard & Martin Montgomery, 120–145. London: Routledge & Kegan Paul.

Bloomfield, Leonard. 1933. *Language.* New York: Holt, Rinehart & Winston.

Bruner, Jerome S. 1983. *Child's Talk: Learning to use language.* New York: Norton.

Butler, Christopher S. 1985. *Systemic Linguistics: Theory and applications.* London: Batsford.

Butt, David G. 1989. "Randomness, Order and the Latent Patterning of Text". *The Functions of Style* ed. by D. Birch & L. M. O'Toole, 74–97. London: Pinter.

Catford, J. C. 1969. "J. R. Firth and British Linguistics". *Linguistics Today* ed. by Archibald A. Hill, 218–228. New York & London: Basic Books.

Chomsky, Noam. 1957. *Syntactic Structures.* The Hague: Mouton.

—. 1965. *Aspects of the Theory of Syntax.* Cambridge, Mass.: MIT Press.

Cloran, Carmel. 1994. *Rhetorical Units and Decontextualisation: An enquiry into some relations of context, meaning and grammar.* (= Monographs in Systemic Linguistics, 6.) Nottingham: Department of English Studies, Univ. of Nottingham.

Culler, Jonathan. 1976. *Saussure.* Glasgow: Fontana/Collins.

Davis, Philip W. 1973. *Modern Theories of Language.* Englewood Cliffs, N. J.: Prentice-Hall.

De Beaugrande, Robert. 1991. *Linguistic Theory: The discourse of fundamental works.* London & New York: Longman.

Dennett, Daniel C. 1991. *Consciousness Explained.* Boston: Little, Brown & Co.

—. 1996. *Kinds of Minds.* London: Weidenfels & Nicholson.

Eagleton, Terry. 1983. *Literary Theory: An introduction.* Oxford: Blackwell.

Edelman, Gerald M. 1992. *Bright Air, Brilliant Fire: On the matter of the mind.* London: Penguin.

Ellis, Jeffrey. 1966. "On Contextual Meaning". Bazell et al. 1966. 79–95.

Ellis, John M. 1993. *Language, Thought and Logic.* Evanston, Ill.: Northwestern Univ. Press.

Fawcett, Robin P. 1973. "Generating a Sentence in Systemic Functional Grammar". *Readings in Systemic Linguistics* ed. by M. A. K. Halliday & James R. Martin, 146–184. London: Batsford.

—. 1980. *Cognitive Linguistics and Social Interaction.* Exeter: Univ. of Exeter; Heidelberg: Groos.

Firth, J[ohn] R. 1948. "The Semantics of Linguistic Science". *Lingua* 1:4.393–404. (Repr. in Firth 1957.139–147.)

—. 1949. "Atlantic Linguistics". *Archivum Linguisticum* 1:2.95–116. (Repr. in Firth 1957.156–172.)

—. 1950. "Personality and Language in Society". *The Sociological Review: Journal of the Institute of Sociology* 42:2.37–52. (Repr. in Firth 1957.177–189.)

—. 1951. "Modes of Meaning". *Essays and Studies of the English Association*, n.s. 4.123–149. (Repr. in Firth 1957.190–215.)

—. 1957. *Papers in Linguistics 1934–1951.* London: Oxford Univ. Press.

—. 1968. *Selected Papers of J. R. Firth 1952–59.* Ed. by F. R. Palmer. London: Longmans.

—. 1968a. "Linguistic Analysis as a Study of Meaning". Firth 1968.12–26.

—. 1968b. "The Languages of Linguistics". Firth 1968.27–34.

—. 1968c. "Structural Linguistics". Firth 1968.35–52.

—. 1968d. "Linguistics and Translation". Firth 1968.74–83.

—. 1968e. "Descriptive Linguistics and the Study of English". Firth 1968.96–113.

—. 1968f. "Ethnographic Analysis and Language with Reference to Malinowski's Views". Firth 1968.137–167.

—. 1968g. "A Synopsis of Linguistic Theory, 1930–55". Firth 1968.168–205.

Fries, Peter H. 1981. "On the Status of Theme in English: Arguments from discourse". *Forum Linguisticum* 6.1–38.

—. 1992. "The Structuring of Information in Written English Texts". *Language Sciences* 14.461–489.

—. 1994. "On Theme, Rheme and Discourse Goals". *Advances in Written Text Analysis* ed. by Malcolm Coulthard. London: Routledge & Kegan Paul.

—. 1995. "A Personal View of Theme". *Thematic Development in English Texts* ed. by Mohsen Ghadessey. London: Pinter.

Gregory, Michael. 1980. "What Can Linguistics Learn from Translation?". *Perspectives on Translation from the Firthian Tradition* (= Meta, 25), 455–466. Montreal.

Griffin, David R., J. B. Cobb, M. P. Ford, P. A. Y. Gunter & P. Ochs. 1993. *Founders of Constructive Postmodern Philosophy: Peirce, James, Bergson, Whitehead and Hartshorne.* Albany, N. Y.: State University of New York Press.

Halliday, Michael A. K. 1956. "Grammatical Categories in Modern Chinese". *Transactions of the Philological Society* 1956.177–224.

—. 1957. "Some Aspects of Systematic Description and Comparison in Grammatical Analysis". *Studies in Linguistic Analysis*, 54–67. Oxford: Blackwell.

—. 1959a. "Phonological (Prosodic) Analysis of the New Chinese Syllable (Modern Pekingese)". Halliday 1959b.

—. 1959b. *The Language of the Chinese "Secret History of the Mongols".* Oxford: Blackwell.

—. 1961. "Categories of the Theory of Grammar". *Word* 17.242–292.

—. 1963. "Intonation in English Grammar". *Transactions of the Philological Society* 1963.143–169.

—. 1964. "Syntax and the Consumer". *Report of the Fifteenth Annual (First International) Round Table Meeting on Linguistics and Language* ed. by C. I. J. M. Stuart. Washington D. C.: Georgetown Univ. Press.

—. 1966a. "Some Notes on 'Deep' Grammar". *Journal of Linguistics* 2:1.57–67.

—. 1966b. "Lexis as a Linguistic Level". Bazell et.al. 1966.148–162.

—. 1967a. *Intonation and Grammar in British English*. Mouton: The Hague.

—. 1967b. "Linguistics and the Teaching of English". *Talking and Writing: A handbook for English teachers* ed. by J. N. Britton. London: Methuen.

—. 1967–68. "Notes on Transitivity and Theme in English (Parts 1–3)". *Journal of Linguistics* 3:1.37–81, 3:2.199–244, 4:2.179–215.

—. 1969. "Options and Functions in the English Clause". *Brno Studies in English* 8.81–88.

—. 1970a. "Functional Diversity in Language; as seen from a consideration of modality and mood in English". *Foundations of Language* 6.322–361.

—. 1970b. *A Course in Spoken English: Intonation*. London: Oxford Univ. Press.

—. 1970c. "Language Structure and Language Function". *New Horizons in Linguistics* ed. by John Lyons. Harmondsworth: Penguin.

—. 1970d. "Phonological (Prosodic) Analysis of the New Chinese syllable (Modern Pekingese)". *Prosodic Analysis* ed. by F. R. Palmer. London: Oxford Univ. Press.

—. 1971. "Linguistic Function and Literary Style: An enquiry into the language of William Golding's 'The Inheritors'". *Literary Style: A symposium* ed, by Seymour Chatman. New York: Oxford Univ. Press.

—. 1973. "Towards a Sociological Semantics". *Explorations in the Functions of Language*. London: Arnold.

—. 1974a. "Discussion with M. A. K. Halliday". *Discussing Language* ed. by Herman Parret. The Hague: Mouton.

—. 1974b. "The Place of 'Functional Sentence Perspective' in the System of Linguistic Description". *Papers on Functional Sentence Perspective* ed. by F. Daneš. Prague: Academia.

—. 1975. *Learning How to Mean: Explorations in the development of language*. London: Arnold.

—. 1976. *System and Function in Language*. Edited by Gunter Kress. London: Oxford Univ. Press.

—. 1978. *Language as Social Semiotic: The social interpretation of language and meaning*. London: Arnold; Baltimore, Md.: Univ. Park Press.

—. 1979a. "Modes of Meaning and Modes of Expression: Types of grammatical structure and their determination by different semantic functions". *Function and Context in Linguistic Analysis* ed. by D. J. Allerton et al. Cambridge: Cambridge Univ. Press.

—. 1979b. "One Child's Protolanguage". *Before Speech: The beginnings of interpersonal communication* ed. by Margaret Bullowa. Cambridge: Cambridge Univ. Press.

—. 1980. "On Being Teaching". *Studies in English Linguistics for Randolph Quirk* ed. by Sydney Greenbaum et al. London: Longman.

—. 1982a. "How Is a Text Like a Clause". *Text Processing* ed. by Sture Allén. Stockholm: Almqvist & Wiksell.

—. 1982b. "The De-Automatization of Grammar: From Priestley's 'An Inspector Calls'". *Language Form and Linguistic Variation: Papers dedicated to Angus McIntosh* ed. by John M. Anderson. Amsterdam: Benjamins.

—. 1984a. "Language as Code and Language as Behaviour: A systemic-functional interpretation of the nature and ontogenesis of dialogue". *The Semiotics of Language and Culture* ed. by M. A. K. Halliday, Robin P. Fawcett, Sydney M. Lamb & Adam Makkai. London: Pinter.

—. 1984b. "On the Ineffability of Grammatical Categories". *Tenth LACUS Forum* ed. by Alan Manning. Columbia, S. C.: Hornbeam.

—. 1985a. "English Intonation as a Resource for Discourse". *Beiträge zur Phonetik und Linguistik: Festschrift in honour of Arthur Delbridge*, 111–117. Hamburg: Buske.

—. 1985b. *An Introduction to Functional Grammar*. London: Arnold.

—. 1985c. "Dimensions of Discourse Analysis: Grammar". *Handbook of Discourse Analysis* ed. by Teun A. van Dijk. New York: Academic Press.

—. 1985d. *Spoken and Written Language*. Geelong, Victoria: Deakin Univ. Press.

—. 1987. "Language and the Order of Nature". *The Linguistics of Writing* ed. by A. Durant, Derek Attridge, Nigel Fabb & C. MacCabe. Manchester: Manchester Univ. Press.

—. 1988a. "On the Language of Physical Science". *Registers of Written English: Situational factors and linguistic features* ed. by Mohsen Ghadessy. London & New York: Pinter.

—. 1988b. "Poetry as Scientific Discourse: The nuclear sections of Tennyson's 'In Memoriam'". *Functions of Style* ed. by David Birch & L. Michael O'Toole. London: Pinter.

—. 1991. "Corpus Linguistics and Probabilistic Grammar". *English Corpus Linguistics: Studies in honour of Jan Svartvik* ed. by K. Aijme & B. Altenberg. London: Longman.

—. 1992a. "Language as System and Language as Instance: The corpus as a theoretical construct". *Directions in Corpus Linguistics: Proceedings of Nobel Symposium, 82, Stockholm, 4–8 August 1991* ed. by Jan Svartvik. Berlin: Mouton de Gruyter.

—. 1992b. "The Notion of 'Context' in Language Education". *Interaction and Development: Proceedings of the international conference, Vietnam, 30 March – 1 April 1992* ed. by T. Le & M. McCausland. Launceston: Language Education, Univ. of Tasmania.

—. 1993a. "Language as Cultural Dynamic". *Cultural Dynamics* 6:1−2.1−10.

—. 1993b. "Towards a Language-Based Theory of Learning". *Linguistics and Education* 5:2.93−116.

—. 1993c. "A Systemic Interpretation of Peking Syllable Finals". *Studies in Systemic Phonology* ed. by Paul Tench. London: Pinter.

—. 1993d. "Quantitative Studies and Probabilities in Grammar". *Description, Data, Discourse: Papers on the English language in honour of John McH. Sinclair* ed. by M. Hoey. London: HarperCollins.

—. 1993e. "The Analysis of Scientific Discourse in English and Chinese". *Proceedings of the International Conference on Texts and Language Research* ed. by Herman Bluhme & Renzhi Li Keqi Hao. Xi'an: Xi'an Jiaotong Univ. Press.

—. 1994a. "A Language Development Approach to Education". *Language and Learning* ed. by Norman Bird. Hong Kong: Institute of Language in Education.

—. 1994b. *An Introduction to Functional Grammar*. 2nd ed. London: Arnold.

—. 1994c. "Language and the Theory of Codes". *Knowledge and Pedagogy: The sociology of Basil Bernstein* ed. by A. Sadovnik. Norwood, N. J.: Ablex.

—. 1994d. "So You Say 'pass' ... thank you three muchly". *What's Going on Here: Complementary studies of professional talk* ed. by A. D. Grimshaw. Norwood, N. J.: Ablex.

—. 1994e. "Systemic Theory". *The Encyclopedia of Language and Linguistics* ed. by R. E. Asher. Oxford: Pergamon.

—. 1995a. "A Recent View of 'Missteps' in Linguistic Theory (Review article of John M. Ellis, *Language, Thought and Logic*)". *Functions of Language* 2:2.249−267.

—. 1995b. "Fuzzy Grammatics: A systemic functional approach to fuzziness in natural language". *FUZZ-IEEE/IFES '95 (International Joint Conference of the Fourth IEEE International Conference on Fuzzy Systems and the Second International Fuzzy Engineering Symposium, Yokohama, 20−24 March 1995)*. Yokohama.

—. 1995c. "On Language in Relation to the Evolution of Human Consciousness". *Of Thoughts and Words: Proceedings of Nobel Symposium 92 "The relation between language and mind", Stockholm, 8−12 August 1994* ed. by Sture Allén. Singapore, River Edge, N. J. & London: Imperial College Press.

—. 1996. "On Grammar and Grammatics". *Functional Descriptions: Theory into practice* ed. by Ruqaiya Hasan, Carmel Cloran & David Butt. Amsterdam & Philadelphia: Benjamins.

—. 1997. "Things and Relations: Regrammaticizing experience as technical knowledge". *Reading Science: Critical and functional perspectives on discourses of science* ed. by J. R. Martin & R. Veel. London: Routledge.

—. Forthcoming. "Computing Meanings: Some reflections on past experience and present prospects (In English, with parallel translations in Chinese and Japanese). Macquarie Univ.

—. in press. "Linguistics as Metaphor". *Functional Morphosyntax* ed. by Kristin Davidse et al. Amsterdam & Philadelphia: Benjamins.

—. & Ruqaiya Hasan. 1976. *Cohesion in English*. London: Longman.

—. & —. 1985. *Language, Context and Text: A social semiotic perspective*. Geelong, Victoria: Deakin Univ. Press.

Halliday, M. A. K & Z. L. James. 1993. "A Quantitative Study of Polarity and Primary Tense in the English Finite Clause". *Techniques of Description: Spoken and written discourse (A Festschrift for Malcolm Coulthard)* ed. by M. Hoey, J. M. Sinclair & G. Fox. London & New York: Routledge.

Halliday, M. A. K. & J. R. Martin, eds. 1981. *Readings in Systemic Linguistics*. London: Batsford.

—. & —. 1993. *Writing Science: Literacy and discursive power*. London: The Falmer Press.

Halliday, M. A. K. & C. M. I. M. Matthiessen. 1999. *Construing Experience through Meaning: A language-based approach to cognition*. London: Cassell.

Hasan, Ruqaiya. 1971. "Rime and Reason in Literature". *Literary Style: A symposium* ed. by Seymour Chatman. New York: Oxford Univ. Press.

—. 1972. "The Verb 'Be' in Urdu". *The Verb "Be" and its Synonyms* ed. by J. W. M. Verhaar, Part 5. Dordrecht: Reidel.

—. 1973. "Code, Register and Social Dialect". *Class, Codes and Control: Applied studies towards a sociology of language* ed. by Bernard Bernstein. London: Routledge & Kegan Paul.

—. 1975. "The Place of Stylistics in the Study of Verbal Art". *Style and Text* ed. by H. Ringbom. Amsterdam: Skriptor.

—. 1978. "Text in the Systemic-Functional Model". *Current Trends in Text Linguistics* ed. by Wolfgang Dressler. Berlin: de Gruyter.

—. 1979. "On the Notion of Text". *Text versus Sentence: Basic questions of text linguistics* ed. by János Petöfi. Hamburg: Buske.

—. 1984a. "The Nursery Tale as a Genre". *Nottingham Linguistic Circular* 13.

—. 1984b. "Coherence and Cohesive Harmony". *Understanding Reading Comprehension* ed. by John Flood. Newark: International Reading Association.

—. 1984c. "Ways of Saying; Ways of Meaning". *Semiotics of Culture and Language* ed. by R. P. Fawcett et al. London: Pinter.

—. 1985a. *Linguistics, Language and Verbal Art*. Geelong, Victoria: Deakin Univ. Press.

—. 1985b. "Meaning, Context and Text: Fifty years after Malinowski". *Systemic Perspectives on Discourse* ed. by James D. Benson & W. S. Greaves. Norwood: N. J.: Ablex.

—. 1986a. "The Implication of Semantic Distance for Language in Education". *Studies in Bilingualism* ed. by A. Abbi. New Delhi: Bahri Publications.

—. 1986b. "The Ontogenesis of Ideology: An interpretation of mother-child talk". *Semiotics — Language — Ideology* ed. by Terry Threadgold. Sydney: Sydney Association for Studies in Society and Culture.

—. 1987a. "Directions from Structuralism". *The Linguistics of Writing: Arguments between language and literature* ed. by D. Attridge, N. Fabb, A. Durant & C. MacCabe. Manchester: Manchester Univ. Press.

—. 1987b. "Reading Picture Reading: Invisible instruction at home and in school". *The 13th Conference of the Australian Reading Association, Sydney, July 1987.* Sydney.

—. 1987d. "The Grammarian's Dream: Lexis as most delicate grammar". *New Developments in Systemic Linguistics: Theory and description* ed. by M. A. K. Halliday & R. P. Fawcett. London: Pinter.

—. 1989. "Semantic Variation and Sociolinguistics". *Australian Journal of Linguistics* 9.221—275.

—. 1991. "Questions as a Mode of Learning in Everyday Talk". *Language Education: Interaction and development* ed. by T. Le & M. McCausland. Launceston: Univ. of Tasmania.

—. 1992a. "Speech Genre, Semiotic Mediation and the Development of Higher Mental Functions". *Language Sciences* 14:4.489—528.

—. 1992b. "Meaning in Sociolinguistics Theory". *Sociolinguistics Today: International perspectives* ed. by Kingsley Bolton & Helen Kwok. London & New York: Routledge.

—. 1992c. "Rationality in Everyday Talk: From process to system". *Directions in Corpus Linguistics* ed. by Jan Svartvik. Berlin: de Gruyter.

—. 1995a. "On Social Conditions for Semiotic Mediation: The genesis of mind in society". *Knowledge and Pedagogy: The sociology of Basil Bernstein* ed. by A. Sadovnik. Norwood, N. J.: Ablex.

—. 1995b. "The Conception of Context in Text". *Discourse in Society: Systemic functional perspectives* ed. by Peter H. Fries & Michael Gregory. Norwood, N. J.: Ablex.

—. 1996a. "Literacy, Everyday Talk and Society". *Literacy in Society* ed. by R. Hasan & G. Williams. London: Longman.

—. 1996b. "On Teaching Literature across Cultural Distances". *The Language — Culture Connection* ed. by J. E. James. Singapore: RELC.

—. 1996c. *Ways of Saying; Ways of Meaning.* London: Cassell.

—. 1999. "Speaking with Reference to Context". *Text and Context in Functional Linguistics: Systemic perspectives* ed. by Mohsen Ghadessy. Amsterdam & Philadelphia: Benjamins.

—. & Carmel Cloran. 1990. "A sociolinguistic interpretation of everyday talk between mothers and children". *Learning, Keeping and Using Language: Selected papers from the 8th World Congress of Applied Linguistics, Sydney, 16—21 August 1987* ed. by M. A. K. Halliday et al. Amsterdam & Philadelphia: Benjamins.

—, — & David Butt, eds. 1996. *Functional Descriptions: Language form and linguistic theory.* Amsterdam & Philadelphia: Benjamins.

Hasan, Ruqaiya & Peter H. Fries, eds. 1995. *On Subject and Theme: A discourse functional perspective.* Amsterdam & Philadelphia: Benjamins.

Hasan, Ruqaiya & J. R. Martin, eds. 1989. *Language Development: Learning language, learning culture. Meaning and choice in language.* Norwood, N. J.: Ablex.

Hasan, Ruqaiya & Geoffrey Williams, eds. 1996. *Literacy in Society.* London: Longman.

Henderson, Eugenie J. A. 1987. "J. R. Firth in Retrospect: A view from the eighties". *Language Topics: Essays in Honour of Michael Halliday* ed. by Ross Steele & Terrry Threadgold, vol. I. Amsterdam & Philadelphia: Benjamins.

Heisenberg, Werner. 1962. *Physics and Philosophy.* New York: Harper & Row.

Hookway, Christopher. 1985. *Peirce.* London: Routledge & Kegan Paul.

Koestler, Arthur. 1967. *The Ghost in the Machine.* London: Pan Books.

Kress, Gunter, ed. 1976. *Halliday: System and Function. Selected papers.* London: Oxford Univ. Press.

—. & T. van Leeuwen. 1996. *Reading Images: The grammar of visual design.* London & New York: Routledge.

Lamb, Sydney M. 1984. "Semiotics of Language and Culture: A relational approach". *Semiotics of Culture and Language* ed. by R. P. Fawcett, Vol 2. London: Pinter.

—. 1999. *Pathways of the Brain.* Amsterdam & Philadelphia: Benjamins.

Langendoen, D. Terence. 1968. *The London School of Linguistics.* Cambridge, Mass: MIT Press.

Leech, Geoffrey. 1981[1974]. *Semantics.* 2nd ed. Harmondsworth: Penguin.

Lemke, Jay. 1995. *Textual Politics: Discourse and social dynamics.* London: Taylor & Francis.

Levinson, Stephen. 1983. *Pragmatics.* Cambridge: Cambridge Univ. Press.

Luria, Alexander R. 1976. *Cognitive Development: Its cultural and social foundations.* Ed. by M. Cole. Cambridge, Mass.: Harvard Univ. Press.

—. 1979. *The Making of Mind: A personal account of Soviet psychology.* Ed. by M. & S. Cole. Cambridge, Mass.: Harvard Univ. Press.

Lyons, John. 1966. "Firth's Theory of Meaning". Bazell et al. 1966.288–302.

—. 1968. *An Introduction to Theoretical Linguistics*. Cambridge: Cambridge Univ. Press.

—. 1977. *Semantics*. 2 vols. Cambridge: Cambridge Univ. Press.

Mann, William C. & C. M. I. M. Matthiessen. 1983. *Nigel: A systemic grammar for text generation*. Marina del Rey, Cal.: Information Sciences Institute, Univ. of Southern California.

Martin, James R. 1981. "Conjunction and Continuity in Tagalog". *Readings in Systemic Linguistics* ed. by M. A. K. Halliday & J. R. Martin. London: Batsford.

—. 1983a. "Participant Identification in English, Tagalog and Kate". *Australian Journal of Linguistics* 3.5–74.

—. 1983b. "Conjunction: The logic of English text". *Micro and Macro Connexity of Discourse* ed. by Janos S. Petöfi & E. Sözer, 1–72. Hamburg: Buske.

—. 1984. "Language, Register and Genre". *Children Writing: Reader* ed. by F. Christie. Geelong, Victoria: Deakin Univ. Press.

—. 1985a. *Factual Writing: Exploring and challenging social reality*. Ibid.

—. 1985b. "Process and Text: Two aspects of human semiosis". *Systemic Perspectives on Discourse* ed. by J. D. Benson & W. S. Greaves. Norwood, N. J.: Ablex.

—. 1987. "The Meaning of Features in Systemic Linguistics". *New Developments in Systemic Linguistics* ed. by M. A. K. Halliday & R. P. Fawcett. London: Pinter.

—. 1992. *English Text: System and structure*. Amsterdam & Philadelphia: Benjamins.

—. 1996. "Metalinguistic Diversity: The case from case". *Functional Descriptions: Theory into practice* ed. by Ruqaiya Hasan, Carmel Cloran & David Butt. Amsterdam & Philadelphia: Benjamins.

—. 1997. "Analysing Genre: Functional parameters". *Genre and Institutions: Social processes in the workplace and school* ed. by F. Christie & J. R. Martin. London: Cassell.

—. 1999. "Modelling Context: A crooked path of progress in contextual linguistics". *Text and Context in Functional Linguistics: Systemic perspectives* ed. by Mohsen Gadessey. Amsterdam & Philadelphia: Benjamins.

—. C. M. I. M. Matthiessen & Clare Painter. 1997. *Working with Functional Grammar*. London: Arnold.

Martin, James R. & J. Rothery. 1980. *Writing Project Report No. 1*. Sydney: Linguistics Department, Sydney Univ.

Martin, James R. & R. Veel, eds. 1997. *Reading Science: Critical and functional perspectives on discourses of science*. London: Routledge.

Matthiessen, Christian M. I. M. 1985. "The Systemic Framework in Text Generation: Nigel". *Systemic Perspectives on Discourse* ed. by J. D. Benson & W. S. Greaves. Norwood, N. J.: Ablex.

—. 1991. "Lexico(grammatical) Choice in Text-Generation". *Natural Language Generation in Artificial Intelligence and Computational Linguistics* ed. by W. Swartout et al. Boston: Kluwer.

—. 1992. "Interpreting the Textual Metafunction". *Advances in Systemic Linguistics: Recent theory and practice* ed. by M. Davies & L. Ravelli. London: Pinter.

—. 1993. "Register in the Round: Diversity in a unified theory of register analysis". *Register Analysis: Theory and practice* ed. by Mohsen Ghadessy. London: Pinter.

—. 1995a. "Fuzziness Construed in Language: A linguistic perspective". *Proceedings of FUZZ/IEEE, Yokohama, March 1995*. Yokohama.

—. 1995b. *Lexicogrammatical Cartography: English systems*. Tokyo: International Language Sciences Publishers.

—. 1995. "THEME as an Enabling Resource in Ideational 'Knowledge' Construction". *Thematic Developments in English Texts* ed. by Mohsen Ghadessy, 20–55. London & New York: Pinter.

—. 1996. "Tense in English Seen through Systemic-Functional Theory". *Meaning and Form: Systemic functional interpretations* ed. by C. Butler et al. Norwood N. J.: Ablex.

—. 1997. "Construing Processes of Consciousness: From the commonsense model to the uncommonsense model of cognitive science". *Reading Science: Critical and functional perspectives on discourses of science* ed. by J. R. Martin & R. Veel. London: Routledge.

—. I. Kobayashi & L. Zeng. 1995. *Generating Multimodal Presentations: Resources and processes*. (= *Artificial Intelligence in Defence Workshop, Eighth Australian Joint Conference of Artificial Intelligence (AI '95), Canberra, November 13–14, 1995*.) Canberra, ACT.

Matthiessen, Christian M. I. M & Chrisopher Nesbitt. 1996. "On the Idea of Theory-Neutral Descriptions". *Functional Descriptions: Theory into practice* ed. by Ruqaiya Hasan, Carmel Cloran & David Butt. Amsterdam & Philadelphia: Benjamins.

Medvedev, Pavel N. 1985[1928]. *The Formal Method in Literary Scholarship: A critical introduction to sociological poetics*. Cambridge, Mass: Harvard Univ. Press.

Mitchell, T. F. 1975. *Principles of Neo-Firthian Linguistics*. London: Longmans.

Monaghan, James. 1979. *The Neo-Firthian Tradition and its Contribution to General Linguistics*. Tübingen: Niemeyer.

O'Toole, L. Michael. 1982. *Structure, Style and Interpretation in the Russian Short Story*. New Haven & London: Yale Univ. Press.

—. 1994. *The Language of Displayed Art*. Leicester: Leicester Univ. Press.

Palmer, Frank R. 1994. *Grammatical Roles and Relations*. Cambridge: Cambridge Univ. Press.

Robins, Robert H. 1970. *Diversions of Bloomsbury: Selected writings on linguistics*. London: North-Holland.

Rorty, Richard. 1979. *Philosophy and the Mirror of Nature*. Princeton: Princeton Univ. Press.

—. 1982a. "Mind as Ineffable". *Mind in Nature* ed. by R. Q. Elvee. San Francisco: Harper & Row.

—. 1982b. *Consequences of Pragmatism*. Sussex: Harvester Press.

—. 1995. *Rorty and Pragmatism: The philosopher responds to his critics*. Edited by H. J. Saatkamp Jr. Nashville: Vanderbilt Univ. Press.

Ryle, Gilbert. 1990[1949]. *The Concept of Mind*. London: Penguin.

Sampson, Geoffrey. 1980. *Schools of Linguistics*. Stanford: Stanford Univ. Press.

Saussure, Ferdinand de. 1974[1916]. *Course in General Linguistics*. Glasgow: Fontana/Collins.

Steiner, Erich & C. L. Yallop. 2001. *Exploring Translation and Multilingual Text Production: Beyond Content*. Berlin/New York: Mouton de Gruyter.

Vaihinger, Hans. 1991[1925]. *The Philosophy of As-If*. New York: Harcourt, Brace & Co.

Voloshinov, Valentin N. 1973. *Marxism and the Philosophy of Language*. New York: Seminar Press.

Whitehead, Alfred N. 1967[1933]. *Adventures in Ideas*. London: The Free Press; New York: Macmillan.

—. 1938. *Modes of Thought*. New York: Macmillan.

—. 1978. *Process and Reality*. Corrected ed., edited by D. R. Griffin & D. W. Sherburne. New York: The Free Press.

Winograd, Terry. 1972. *Understanding Natural Language*. New York: Academic Press.

—. 1983. *Language as a Cognitive Process, Volume 1: Syntax*. Reading, Mass.: Addision Wesley.

Wittengstein, Ludwig. 1974[1953]. *Philosophical Investigations*. Oxford: Blackwell.

David G. Butt, Sydney (Australia)

204. The emphasis on syntax in the early phase of European structuralism: Ries, Jespersen, Mathesius, Guillaume, Tesnière

1. Introduction
2. 'What is syntax?'
3. 'What is a sentence?'
4. Subject and predicate
5. Word-groups
6. Bibliography

1. Introduction

Contrary to 20th century mythology, syntactic research had not been neglected in the 19th century: the works, e.g., by Steinthal (1855; 1860a, b), Gabelentz (1869; 1874—75), Henri Weil (1879 [1844]), to mention only some scholars active in the field, give evidence of it (for more details, cf. Graffi 2001). Also the most distinguished historical-comparative linguists did not neglect syntactic arguments: the first name which comes to mind is Delbrück (1893—1900), but syntactic topics are also dealt with, for example, in Paul's *Prinzipien* (Paul ⁵1920 [1880]), whose chapter VI is significantly entitled "Die syntaktischen Grundverhältnisse". Another unavoidable reference is Wackernagel (1892). However, scholars like Steinthal or Gabelentz, not to speak of Weil, were undoubtedly extraneous to 'mainstream' 19th-century linguistics; and Delbrück's monumental work is, in fact, more concerned with morphosyntax than with syntax proper, i.e., with the discussion of the structure of the sentence and of the word groups. It must be added that this syntactic work, both on the part of general linguists like Steinthal and of mainly historically-oriented linguists like Paul, was characterized by a 'psychologistic' approach which was felt to be more and more unsatisfactory. Therefore, it is not surprising that at the end of the last century some scholars stressed the need of building a new system of syntax: its task was to deal with the typical questions of the field, and so to trace its boundaries with respect to morphology and semantics. It had also to be built *juxta propria principia*, that is to say not on extra-linguistic categories. Just as syntax had 'divorced' itself from logic with the rise of historical grammar, so it had then to divorce itself from psychology, which had replaced logic in its role of 'basic science' from about the middle of the 19th century. This was also the age in which structuralism was beginning to emerge: many statements of the linguistics we will treat (especially Guillaume and Tesnière) are explicitly connected with Saussurean concepts. However, these concepts seem to have exerted their influence only in the direction of a general search of a systematic point of view, and not on the specific domain of syntax. In fact, we may recall Bloomfield's (1923) review of Saussure's *Cours*, where the American linguist critized the Swiss for basing his analysis on the word, and not on the sentence.

In what follows, we will sketch the main lines of this new approach to syntactic studies. We will take into account the leading figures of this age, whose beginning is probably best marked by the first edition (1894) of the monograph on syntax by the German scholar John Ries (Ries ²1927). We will also present the work of other outstanding European scholars, especially the Dane Otto Jespersen, the Czech Vilém Mathesius, the French Gustave Guillaume and Lucien Tesnière. (The most significant works of these two last linguists were published after their death: therefore, even if their publication years lie between the late 1950 and the late 1980, they were actually written between the 1940 and the early 1950s, respectively.) Occasionally, other scholars will be referred to as well. We will not proceed, however, by presenting one scholar after the other, but we will organize our treatment according to the several topics of inquiry. In discussing each of them we will present the system worked out by the different linguists. All these share, anyway, the common features we hinted at before: the aim of determining exactly the role of syntax and the (partial or total) abandonment of psychologism.

2. 'What is syntax?'

2.1. Syntax vs morphology; syntax vs semantics

2.1.1. John Ries (1857–1933): The role of syntax

The title of this main section is taken from Ries (1927). In fact, this book was characterized by the demand of a definite role for syntax. First of all, Ries was concerned to specify what syntax should *not* be. Syntax should not be 'mixed syntax' (*Mischsyntax*), nor 'syntax à la Miklosich' (the great Slavic philologist, whose work Ries criticizes, tacitly assuming that it is especially representative of the attitude towards syntax held by historical-comparative linguists). A typical feature of *Mischsyntax* is, according to Ries (1927: 147 n. 11), the treatment under the same head of essentially different problems: e. g., the theory of 'parts of speech' and the theory of 'sentence'. This attitude is an old one (Ries traces it back to Apollonius Dyscolus). The followers of *Mischsyntax* are not, therefore, a unitary group: "besteht doch ihre Gemeinsamkeit nur in dem negativen Merkmal ihrer Systemlosigkeit [what they share lies only in the negative feature of their lack of system]" (Ries 1927: 15). One of the pitfalls of *Mischsyntax* is the role given to (allegedly) 'logical' arguments: e. g., the 'main' and the 'subordinate' clause are not defined in grammatical terms, but in logical ones. But this kind of definition has nothing to do with what the real syntactic approach should be. Miklosich's approach to syntax is caused by the need of rejecting the one of *Mischsyntax*. Miklosich, however, considers syntax as the part of grammar dealing with the meaning of word-classes and word-forms (cf. Miklosich 1883: 122). According to Miklosich, therefore, syntax means what we would today call 'morphosyntax' and has no interest in the theory of sentence.

Ries reacts againts a 'nihilistic' view such as the one of Miklosich, and stresses the absolute necessity of a theory of sentence; he also maintains, however, that syntax is not to be identified with it. Actually, syntax is *"die Lehre vom Satze und den übrigen Wortgefügen* [the theory of sentence and of the other word arrangements]" (Ries 1927: 61; original emphasis). The kind of syntax Ries wants to build up is strictly *grammatical* one: logical as well as psychological considerations are extraneous to it (cf. Ries 1931: 33). In a nutshell, we could say that the type of syntax advocated by Ries is in a certain sense an upsetting of the traditional, logical approach to syntax. Like logical syntax, grammatical syntax has to build on a theory of sentence, and, in general, of word arrangements: this theory, however, cannot treat syntactic structures as an expression of independently given thoughts, but it has to find the laws proper to their organization. According to Ries, the fundamental misunderstanding of logical syntax lies in the identification of syntax with *Bedeutungslehre*, while the oppositions are twofold, crossing each other; syntax vs *Wortlehre* on the one hand, and *Formenlehre* vs. *Bedeutungslehre* on the other. So, just as we have a theory both of the forms and the meanings of words, we should have a theory both of the forms and of the meanings of the word arrangements. This theory is syntax according to Ries.

2.1.2. Jespersen (1860–1943): 'Form', 'function' and 'notion'

Jespersen sets syntactic categories against 'formal' categories on the one side and against 'notional' categories on the other. Formal categories are morpho-phonological categories, in our current terminology; notional categories could be identified with semantic categories, or, perhaps more exactly, with logico-ontological ones. "Syntactic categories thus, Janus-like, face both ways, towards form and towards notion. They stand midway and form the connecting link between the world of sounds and the world of ideas" (Jespersen 1924: 56–57). Jespersen illustrates his conception by showing how a single syntactic category (the English preterit) is expressed through different forms and gives expression to different notions. Actually, the English preterit can be formed through very different means: adjoining a suffix -*ed* (e. g., *handed*), or a suffix -*t* (e. g., *fixed*), or a suffix -*d* (e. g., *showed*); the adjunction of a suffix can combine with an inner change, like in *left*; the kernel may remain unchanged (e. g., *put*), or it can show an inner change (e. g., *drank*), or even it can be a different kernel (like in *was*). Nevertheless, all these forms belong to the same syntactic category, and they can all mean several different notions, like the following: past time; unreality in present time ("if we *knew*; I wish we *knew*"); future time ("it is time you *went* to bed"); shifted present time ("how did you know I *was* a Dane?"); all times ("men *were* deceivers ever"); cf. Jespersen (1924: 56).

2.1.3. Mathesius (1882–1945): Syntax vs onomatology

According to Mathesius, the main boundary has to be traced between 'functional onomatology' and 'functional syntax' (cf. Mathesius 1964a [1936]; 1964b [1939]). Functional onomatology deals with the system of names and its application in the concrete speech act (names are to be intended in "the broadest sense of the word", i. e., for any categories of full words; cf. Mathesius 1964a [1936]: 309). Functional syntax has to do with "the ways and means of organizing these names as applied to an actual situation, in sentences" (Mathesius, p. 308). Morphology cuts across this distinction, since it can serve both onomatological and syntactical functions. For example, it can distinguish subclasses of nouns (masculine vs feminine, in the languages which make such a distinction); and it can also express the syntactic phenomenon of concord.

2.1.4. 'Connection' in Tesnière (1893–1954)

In Tesnière's theory of syntax, the key notion is one of 'connection'. It is, in fact, a primitive term of this theory. Syntax exists only by virtue of 'connection'. Connection has never an explicit, morphological expression: Tesnière's work is pervaded by a continual polemic against an approach which subordinates syntax to morphology, and which, according to him, was typical of 19-century linguistics. Connections are 'seen by the mind' (cf. Tesnière 1966 [1959]: 11). So, for example, a sentence like *Alfred parle* is not composed by two elements, but by three: *Alfred*, *parle* and the connection which binds them; without this connection there would be no sentence at all (cf. Tesnière 1966: 11–12).

Connection is an intrinsically hierarchic fact: a relationship of dependency holds between the connected elements. In the simplest case, when the elements are only two, one of them is the 'governing' element, the other one the 'subordinate'. An important achievement of Tesnière's is to have devised a graphic representation of the syntactic connection. So the connective hierarchy of a sentence like *Alfred parle* will have the following representation (cf. Tesnière 1966: 14):

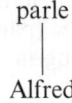

Fig. 204.1

The higher element is the governing, the lower one is the subordinate. The governing element and all elements subordinate to it form what Tesnière calls a 'node'. Every subordinate element can govern other elements in its turn; the several nodes will appear according to a hierarchy which reflects the hierarchy of the connections.

Graphs like Fig. 204.1 express the 'structural order' of the sentence, which must be kept distinct from its 'linear order'. There is an antinomy between those two orders: while structural order allows several lower connections (every node can dominate other nodes), linear order allows only two connections (to the right or to the left). This antinomy is 'the squaring of the circle' in language (cf. Tesnière 1966: 21).

Tesnière sharply opposes syntax not only to morphology but also to semantics. The 'structure' of the sentence is to be kept distinct from its 'sense'. Syntax is independent of both logic and psychology (cf. Tesnière 1966: 40–41). Grammatical categories and logico-psychological categories often correspond with each other, but they nevertheless are essentially different. So grammatical categories can considerably vary from one language to another: for example gender, which in French opposes masculine and feminine, in German masculine, feminine and neuter, in Slavic animate and inanimate, in Swedish common and neuter, etc. (cf. Tesnière 1966: 48).

2.1.5. Guillaume (1883–1960): 'langue' and 'discours'

Guillaume too traces a fundamental opposition between what is a formal expression in language and what is expressed by it. The first one of these two levels is called by him 'psycho-semiotics', the second 'psycho-systematics'. Actually, according to Guillaume, only what has a morphophonological representation of its own can be called semiotic. For example, he maintains that in French 'the same grammatical forms' can play the role both of 'suppletive pronouns' and of 'completive pronouns'. Pronouns of the first type (the standard 'personal pronouns') cannot be followed by a noun; pronouns of the second type (the standard 'determiners') must be. In French, a word like *le* is the same word from the semiotic point of view, but it represents two different pronouns from the psychic one: it is a suppletive pronoun in *Je le connais*, and a completive pronoun in *J'ai lu le livre*. One may remark that, in contrast to Jespersen, Guillaume doesn't appear to make any clear distinction between syntactic categories, on the one hand, and notional categories, on the other. This is also shown by his studies on the verb (cf., e.g., Guillaume 1929). Guillaume doesn't oppose the category of *tense* to the one of *time*, whereas Jespersen say that tense is a syntactic category, and time a notional one. The preterit tense can express, according to the context, several different chronological times (cf. 2.1.2.).

Guillaume, developing and revising Saussurean concepts, opposes 'language' (*langue*) and 'speech' (*discours*). Morphology is typicalla a fact of language, whereas syntax is a fact of speech (cf. *LdeL* III, pp. 24–25). As a consequence, the word is the unit of language; the sentence, the unit of speech (cf. *LdeL* III, p. 13). Many other entities are to be distinguished, according to their belonging to either language or to speech. So, we have 'nouns of language' (*homme, maison, enfant, rivière*, etc.) and 'nouns of speech' (*Que j'ai lu ce livre*); cf. *LdeL* III, p. 169. We also have 'verbs of language' and 'verbs of speech' (the latter are instantiated by the English prepositional verbs; cf. *LdeL* II, pp. 167–169); and a 'predicate of language' and a 'predicate of speech' as well. The first kind of predicate is the verb alone; the second one the verb together with its possible complements (cf. *LdeL* II, pp. 196–198).

2.2. The analysis of the syntactic system

2.2.1. Jespersen's doctrine of the 'three ranks'

During the period under investigation some new systematic approaches to syntax are developed. Their common feature is the aim of providing a set of notions applicable to any type of syntactic construction, that is both to sentences and to word-groups.

The core of Jespersen's system in the so-called doctrine of the three ranks. It owes its name to the fact that it ranks words "according to their mutual relations as defined or defining" (Jespersen 1924: 96). Take, e.g., the combination *extremely hot weather*: *weather* is called the 'primary', *hot*, which defines *weather*, 'secondary', and *extremely*, 'tertiary'. According to Jespersen, there is no need to add further ranks. The three-ranks analysis can be applied to different kinds of syntactic combinations. Let's compare, following Jespersen (p. 97), the two combinations *a furiously barking dog* and *the dog barks furiously*. The word ranking is identical in both cases: *dog* is the primary, the inflected form of *bark* is the secondary and *furiously* is the tertiary. Of course, Jespersen notes that there is a fundamental difference between the two kind of combinations: he calls the first one 'junction' and the second one 'nexus' (for more on this opposition see 3.4. and 5.1.).

Jespersen's system of the three ranks is logically independent from the system of the parts of speech and also had a logical priority over it. Actually, the same part of speech can play the role of primary, secondary, or tertiary: e. g., substantives can be also secondaries (*the* butcher's *shop*; *urbs* Romae) and even tertiaries (*emotions*, part *religious, but* part *human*); see Jespersen (1927: 98–101). It must also be stressed that the ranking applies not only to single words, but also to word-groups and clauses. For instance, the same word-group can alternatively be a primary (Sunday afternoon *was fine*), a secondary (*a* Sunday afternoon *concert*) or a tertiary (*he slept* all Sunday afternoon); cf. Jespersen (1924: 102–103). Clauses which Jespersen classifies as primaries are, in the terminology of Quirk et al. (1985, chap. 15), which I adopt here for convenience: subject *that*-clauses (That he will come *is certain*), direct object *that*-clauses (*I espect* (that) he will arrive at six), *wh*-interrogative clauses (*I don't know* where I was born), nominal relative clauses (Who steals my purse *steals trash*). Clauses classified are secondaries as relative clauses. Clauses classified as tertiaries are adverbial clauses. On the whole matter, see further Jespersen (1924: 103–106).

2.2.2. Tesnière: The notion of 'valency'

The first basic notion of Tesnière's syntax is that of 'valency'. This is a metaphor explicitly borrowed from the technical language of chemistry. Actually, Tesnière (1966: 238) compares the verb to 'a kind of hooked atom' which can exert its power of attraction on a smaller or bigger number of 'participant-roles' (*actants*, in Tesnière's terms; I am here adopting the English terminology introduced by Lyons 1977: 497). These participant-roles indicate the actors of the 'little drama', that is to say of the process expressed by the verb. Furthermore, the sentence may contain also some 'circumstantial roles' (*circonstants*), which express the conditions of place, time, manner, etc., in which the process takes place. Participant roles are always substantives or equivalents of substantives, circumstantial roles are always adverbs or equivalent of adverbs (on the whole subject see Tesnière 1966: 102–103). Participant roles are obligatory; circumstantial roles are optional (cf. Tesnière 1966: 128). The number of participant roles varies according to the verb-class to which the verb belongs: so we have several verb-classes according to their 'valency-sets'. Verbs with no participant roles are called '0-valency verbs' (the traditional 'impersonals'; cf. Tesnière, p. 239); verbs with only one role '1-valency verbs' (the traditional 'intransitives'; cf. Tesnière 1966: 240–241); verbs with two roles '2-valency verbs' (the standard 'transitives'); verbs with three roles '3-valency verbs' (typically, the verbs of 'telling' and of 'giving'; cf. Tesnière 1966, chap. 106).

The other basic notion in Tesnière's system of syntax is 'transference' (as he suggests to render the French word *translation*; cf. Tesnière 1966: 367). It indicates the transformation of words of one kind into words of another kind (cf. Tesnière, p. 364). Actually, the operation of transference reduces any category to one of the four classes of 'full' words, i. e., Nouns, Adjectives, Verbs and Adverbs (on the distinction between 'full' and 'empty' words, cf. Tesnière 1966: 53–58). Also subordination is a result of transference: a verbal node (see 3.3. and 5.1.) is reduced to a noun, or to an adjective, or to an adverb. The transference to a noun yields 'participant' subordinate clauses (cf. Tesnière 1966: 547); the transference to an adjective 'adjectival' subordinate clauses (cf. Tesnière, p. 557); the transference to an adverb 'circumstantial' subordinate clauses (cf. p. 582). As one can easily see, in this way subordinate clauses are fittet into the general scheme of valency and of its properties. We may also remark that, contrary to what happened with Jespersen, in Tesnière's framework the system of the parts of speech has a logical priority over the system of dependencies. In fact, dependent clauses are not defined in terms of their kind of relation with the main clause, but according to the part of speech whose function they eventually take. Transferences inside word-groups are treated identically: for example, a noun in the genitive or governed by a preposition like English *of* is defined as 'a noun transferred to an adjective' (cf. p. 409). This last case of transference is dubbed by Tesnière 'transference of the first degree'; it takes place inside the simple sentence. The other case of transference, involving subordinate clauses, is called 'transference of the second degree' (cf. Tesnière 1966: 385–386).

2.2.3. 'Incidence' in Guillaume

In Guillaume's system, the syntactic dependencies are a consequence of what he calls the 'mechanism of incidence'. 'Incidence' indicates the way of contributing to the formation of meaning from the different parts of speech (cf. *LdeL* II, pp. 137 ff.). The incidence can pertain to language or to speech (cf. 2.1.5.): in the first case, incidence is 'internal', in the second 'external' (cf. *LdeL* II, p. 150). The incidence of nouns is mainly internal; the incidence of adjectives, verbs and adverbs is mainly external. External incidence can be either of the first degree (like the one between adjective and noun in *un homme beau*) or of the second degree (like the one between *fort* and *homme beau* in *un homme fort beau*); cf. *LdeL* II (p. 153). While nouns, adjectives, verbs and adverbs lie inside the mechanism of incidence, the task of prepositions is to establish such a mechanism where it collapses. For example, in *Pierre parle à Paul*, there is no feeling of incidence between *Paul* and *Pierre*, nor between *Paul* and the incidence of *parle* to *Pierre*. The role of the preposition *à* is then "d'intégrer Paul à la phrase construite [to integrate Paul to the constructed sentence]" (*LdeL* II, p. 154).

3. 'What is a sentence?'

3.1. Ries' definition

The title of this section too is borrowed from a book by Ries (1931). In this book, we find the following definition of sentence: *"Ein Satz ist eine grammatisch geformte kleinste Redeeinheit, die ihren Inhalt im Hinblick auf sein Verhältnis zur Wirklichkeit zum Ausdruck bringt* [A sentence is a grammatically formed minimal unit of discourse, which brings to expression its content with respect to the relation of this to the reality]" (Ries 1931: 99; original emphasis). Ries means by 'discourse' language in its actual working, as a tool of communication. 'Minimal unit' is a connected whole which cannot be further analyzed into units of the same kind. A structure is 'grammatically formed' if it is not just any string of words, but it is organized according to a principle of formation of its own. The 'content' of a sentence is the meaning of the words and of the word-groups which make it up, together with the meanings induced by their arrangements. Finally, 'reality' is the extra-mental reality of the intended meanings: it can be conceived by the speaker as given, or as whished, ordered, put into doubt, etc. In the first case, the sentence is declarative; in the order cases, the sentence is optative, imperative, interrogative, etc. (cf. Ries 1931: 99 – 101).

With this definition, Ries aims at distinguishing sharply the sentence from other linguistic units which could mistakenly be identified with it: discourse, word-groups, interjections and/or vocatives. The sentence is distinguished from the discourse by being its minimal unit. What distinguishes the sentence from the words and the word-groups is its capacity of expressing its content with relation to reality: reality can be asserted, questioned, etc., only by means of a sentence, not of a word or a word-group. Finally, interjections or other similar entities can express a relation to reality, but they are not 'grammatically formed'. 'Sentences of the various languages have different forms, but common to all is *form*, form *as such*' (Ries 1931: 97). In practice, Ries identifies this grammatical form peculiar to sentences (as far as Indo-European languages are concerned) with the presence of a finite verb, or at least with the possibility of inserting it, if it were overtly unexpressed. This definition of the sentence was accepted in its essence by many linguists (cf., e. g., *LdeL* III, p. 211), but it was rejected by many others (e. g., Bloomfield 1931, Meillet 1932). Bloomfield rejects Ries' 'mentalistic' approach and explicitly adopts the definition of sentence proposed by Meillet, which is a purely distributional one: sentence is "une forme qui ne fait partie d'aucune autre forme [a form which is part of no other form]" (Bloomfield 1931: 209).

3.2. Mathesius' definition

Mathesius shares with Ries the view of the sentence as an entity conditioned by the grammatical system of the language to which it belongs. Actually, he distinguishes between sentence as 'abstract pattern' and sentence as 'concrete utterance'. He then criticizes views such as the one held by Gardiner (1932), which assigns sentence only to the sphere of speech. However, while Ries saw the relationship between sentence and reality as a direct one, according to Mathesius this relationship is due to the speaker's intervention. Mathesius' definition then runs as follows: "the sentence is an elementary speech utterance, through which the speaker (or writer) reacts to some reality, concrete or abstract, and which in its formal character appears to realize grammatical possibilities of the respective language and to be subjectively, that is, from the point of view of the speaker (or writer), complete" (Mathesius 1964a [1936]: 319n.7; this definition is explicitly borrowed from Mathesius 1924).

3.3. Tesnière: Every node can be a sentence

Tesnière too defines the sentence in a way quite different from Ries' and also from

Mathesius'. The feature of completeness doesn't play any role in it, nor must the sentence show any peculiar grammatical form. Actually, he defines the sentence as an organized set whose constituent elements are words (cf. Tesnière 1966: 11). As can be seen, this definition cannot distinguish sentence from word-group; and so Tesnière is led to conclude that we have as many types of sentences as we have nodes, viz. four: verbal sentence, substantival sentence, adjectival sentence, and adverbial sentence. As examples of the last three kinds of sentences Tesnière often brings forward book titles: *Le stupide XXe siècle* (substantival sentence); *ouvert la nuit* (adjectival sentence); *à la recherche du temps perdu* (adverbial sentence; cf. Tesnière 1966: 100−101). However, if a simple sentence contains a verb, the verbal node is always the central node of that sentence (cf. Tesnière, p. 103).

3.4. Jespersen: Sentence vs 'nexus'

Ries' definition aimed at simultaneously accounting for two different properties of the sentence: its grammatical form and its communicative-semantic value. For Ries, they were bound to each other: only a structure with a peculiar grammatical form (i. e., where a finite verb occurs or may occur) can express a relationship to reality. Both sides of this definition have been severely critized. The result was a kind of skepticism about the possibility of finding some feature that could be considered characteristic of sentence. The purely negative, distributional definition proposed by Bloomfield following Meillet and the huge extension given to the concept of sentence by Tesnière testify of this skepticism. We have to add, anyway, that all these different approaches share one feature: they always consider, in a more or less explicit way, the sentence as a self-contained whole. This can be clearly seen also in their treatment of the subordinate clauses, which are always said not to be real sentences. Ries (1931: 52) says that main clause and subordinate clause are not two coordinate species of the genus 'sentence'; subordinate clauses are structures intermediate between sentence and word-group. Tesnière analyzes subordinate clauses as 'transference' phenomena and so equates them with nouns, adjectives or adverbs (cf. 2.2.2.). Analogously, Guillaume (*LdeL* III, p. 145) defines them as 'many-word nouns'.

The path followed by Jespersen is different. His definition of sentence only takes into account its ability to act as a self-contained whole: "A sentence is a (relatively) complete and independent human utterance − the completeness and independence being shown by its standing alone or its capability of standing alone, i. e. of being uttered by itself" (Jespersen 1924: 307). Jespersen (p. 308) notes that this definition doesn't apply to dependent sentences for which he prefers the more traditional name of 'clauses', restricting 'sentence' only to the independent sentence. Nevertheless, both sentences and clauses share a fundamental property: they are both predicative structures, that is, in Jespersen terminology, both from a *nexus*. Jespersen then sharply distinguishes two notions generally identified in the grammatical tradition (to which also Ries belongs in this regard): that of sentence and that of predicative connection. These two notions are completely independent from each other: "many sentences cannot be analyzed as containing a nexus" (Jespersen 1937: 89). On the contrary, "only an *independent* nexus forms a sentence" (Jespersen 1924: 306). The existence of a nexus doesn't imply the presence of a finite verb. There exist, for example, 'infinitival nexuses', like "*I heard* her sing", "*I made* her sing". A nexus can exist also with no verb at all: the most typical case is that of verbless sentences, but 'object complement constructions' (as they are called in Quirk et al. 1985) are also nexuses [*I found* the cage empty; cf. Jespersen 1924: 122).

4. Subject and predicate

4.1. Subject, predicate and the 'Functional Sentence Perspective'

The traditional notions of subject and predicate were seriously questioned in the last decades of the 19th century (see Graffi 2001: 84−109). For example, Georg von der Gabelentz (1840−1893) proposed to distinguish 'psychological subject' from 'grammatical subject' and 'psychological predicate' from 'grammatical predicate'. Gabelentz defined psychological subject as 'what I want the addressee to think of' and psychological predicate as 'what the addressee has to think concerning the subject' (cf. Gabelentz 1869: 378).

This analysis of the sentence in two communicative parts, different from the grammatical ones, is also the starting point of Mathesius (1939). He, however, prefers to call the psychological subject 'theme' (or 'starting point of the utterance') and the psychological predicate 'rheme' (or 'nucleus of the utterance'), in order more clearly to mark the difference between the 'formal partition' and the 'actual partition' of the sentence (also known in English-speaking world as 'Functional Sentence Perspective'). A good deal of the syntactic research by Mathesius is devoted to the analysis of the relationship between these two different partitions of the sentence. This analysis is developed chiefly on the basis of a comparison between English and Czech. While in English word order is determined mainly by the 'principle of grammatical value', which puts the grammatical subject before the grammatical predicate, and by the 'principle of likeness of elements', which forbids the insertion of extraneous material into the word-group, in Czech these principles have a much more limited impact. The 'actual partition of the sentence' plays the fundamental role in Czech: and so the grammatical predicate, when it is the theme of the sentence, can freely precede the grammatical subject (cf. Mathesius 1941–42). English, much more than Czech, aims at establishing a parallelism between formal and actual partition; as a result, it tends to identify grammatical subject and theme. This tendency explains the development of psychological verb constructions from Middle English to Modern English: *me liketh* became *I like*. This development is unknown to most Indo-European languages, which normally don't have unagentive subjects with verbs in the active form. This is the case of Czech, where the fundamental function of word order is to express the actual articulation of the sentence and hence there is no particular tendency to 'thematize' the subject.

4.2. Subject as a grammatical term

Mathesius, then, doesn't deny the scientific legitimacy of the grammatical notions of subject and predicate. On this topic his views differ from several linguists more or less contemporary to him, like Svedelius (1897), Noreen (1923), Kalepky (1928) or Tesnière (1966): they all maintain that the category of subject is illegitimate, from a linguistic point of view. Furthermore, he doesn't seem particularly interested in giving a satisfactory definition of subject and predicate: but it was just the difficulty of giving such a definition which led many scholars to distrust these notions. Tesnière (1966: 103), in particular, maintains that the analysis of the sentence into subject and predicate derives from an unwarranted transferring of logical categories to grammar. Subject and object, actually, are participant-roles (see 2.2.2.) on the same plane: this is shown by the fact that they can interchange with each other when the sentence becomes passive (see Tesnière 1966: 105). The definitions of subject and object given by Tesnière (p. 108) run as follows: subject is the participant role 'performing the action'; object is the one 'undergoing the action'.

On the contrary, finding a satisfactory definition for subject and predicate is one of the major concerns of Jespersen's. After a detailed examination of several usages of the terms 'psychological', 'logical' and 'grammatical' subject and of the arguments given against the notion of subject itself, Jespersen (1924: 150) states that "it is much better [...] to use subject and predicate exclusively in the sense of grammatical subject and predicate". The grammatical definition of subject varies across the different works of Jespersen. However, the definition given in Jespersen (1909–1949 III, 11.1.5.) seems to have been the most satisfactory to him, since the reproduces it in his last theoretical treatise (Jespersen 1937: 136): "The subject is the primary which is most intimately connected with the verb (predicate)". E. g., *Tom* is the subject in a sentence like *Tom beats John*, but in the sentence *John is beaten by Tom* the subject is *John*. Subject and predicate are then defined in relation to each other; the 'most intimate connection' which realizes this relationship is expressed, according to Jespersen, through the agreement. Therefore, the subject is the noun which agrees with the verb and the predicate is the verb plus its possible complements (cf. Jespersen 1924: 150n.1.).

Guillaume's analysis is rather close to Jespersen's, but his terminology is different: he calls the subject both of an active and of a passive construction 'logical subject' (cf. *LdeL* II, p. 203) and ascribes it to the categories of speech (cf. 2.1.5.).

5. Word-groups

5.1. The structure of word-groups

The notion of 'word-group' seems well established in each of the linguists we are dealing with, but it is especially deepened by Ries, Jespersen, and Tesnière. To Ries in particular we owe the first systematic treatise on the matter (Ries 1928).

First of all, Ries distinguishes between 'word-arrangements' and 'word-groups': the first term refers to all syntactic structures, the second term only to the non-sentential ones. In this way, the analysis of word-groups obtains its complete autonomy from the theory of sentence. The constituency and the kind of a word-group are totally independent from its syntactic function: e. g., the subject of a sentence can be expressed by a single word or by a word-group, and the same word-group can sometimes act as subject, and sometimes as object (cf. Ries 1928: 8).

According to their internal structure, Ries distinguishes three kinds of word-groups: 'loose', 'half-narrow' and 'narrow'. The loose groups show a coordination structure; the half-narrow ones are formed by a noun plus an apposition; the narrow ones are the word-groups known as noun group, adjective group and adverb group. Each group is characterized by a 'leader', which, in the case of narrow groups, is called by Ries 'nucleus': so the noun is the nucleus of the noun group, the verb of the verb group, etc.

Ries' narrow word-groups correspond to the four kinds of nodes identified by Tesnière: substantival, adjectival, verbal, and adverbial node. In Tesnière's terminology (cf. 2.1.4.), these nodes are distinguished according to their governing element: viz., the noun, the adjective, the verb, and the adverb. Tesnière, however, doesn't explicitly distinguish groups according to their degree of narrowness, and so we find, e. g., appositive groups treated together with narrow groups under the same heading of 'substantival' node (cf. Tesnière 1966: 163—164).

The analysis of word-groups by Jespersen is based on his doctrine of the 'three ranks' (see 2.2.1.), which is, however, not a theory of word-groups, but of syntactic dependencies in general. This leads him to see a strict analogy between what is actually a word-group (the junction) and what most probably isn't (the nexus). One of the consequences of this approach is that the finite verb can never function as a primary or as a tertiary, but only as a secondary ('adnex'): this sharply contrasts with the behavior of other parts of speech. The origin of this difficulty lies in the fact that Jespersen doesn't clearly distinguish between the function of the finite verb in the nexus (i. e., as a predicate) and in the verb group (i. e. as its 'primary'): and, in fact, the verb group has no room within the model of sentence analysis proposed by Jespersen. So Jespersen would arrive at the same result of Tesnière (cf. 3.3.): nexus and verb group would coincide. Accepting this result, however, Jespersen would have to give up his analysis of nexus as necessarily formed by a subject and a predicate (cf. 3.4.): this sounds rather paradoxical. Perhaps it is not accidental, then, that Jespersen (1937) doesn't stress the structural equivalence between junction and nexus. In fact, the whole chapter devoted to the concept of 'rank' (Jespersen 1937: 119—127) treats almost exclusively junction phenomena.

5.2. Word order inside the word-groups

In 4.1. we spoke about word-order phenomena inside the sentence when referring to Mathesius' work. In general, no particular attention is given to word-order phenomena inside the word-groups by the linguists we are presently discussing. The only notable exception is Tesnière (1966: 22—25).

According to Tesnière, typological classification of languages is possible according to the way they convert structural order into linear order (cf. 2.2.2.). There are two types of linear order: 'descending' (or 'centrifugal') and 'ascending' (or 'centripetal'). In the centrifugal order, the structurally governing element precedes the subordinate one (French *cheval blanc*); in the centripetal order, the governing element follows the subordinate one (English *white horse*). A language can show these orders in a 'strict' (*accusé*) or in a 'lax' (*mitigé*) way: for example, French is lax, because it shows both ascending and descending order. Languages are therefore classified by Tesnière in centrifugal and centripetal, and each of these two groups is in its turn subdivided into strict and lax languages. Let us supply an example for each combinations. (1) Strict centrifugal languages: Hebrew; (2) lax centrifugal languages: French; (3) lax centripetal languages: German (4) strict centripetal languages: Japanese. This classification clearly anticipates much of what we read in Greenberg (1966): this essay, however, never quotes Tesnière.

6. Bibliography

Bloomfield, Leonard. 1923. Review of *Cours de linguistique générale* by Ferdinand de Saussure (2nd ed., Paris: Payot, 1922). *Modern Language Journal* 8.317—319.

—. 1931. Review of Ries (1931). *Language* 7.204—209.

Delbrück, Berthold. 1893−1900. *Vergleichende Syntax der indogermanischen Sprachen*. 3 vols. Strassburg: Karl J. Trübner.

Gabelentz, Georg von der. 1869. "Ideen zu einer vergleichenden Syntax". *Zeitschrift für Völkerpsychologie und Sprachwissenschaft* 6.376−384.

−. 1874−75. "Weiteres zur vergleichendes Syntax: Wort- und Satzstellung". *Zeitschrift für Völkerpsychologie und Sprachwissenschaft* 8.129−165, 300−338.

Gardiner, Alan H. 1932. *The Theory of Speech and Language*. Oxford: Clarendon Press.

Graffi, Giorgio. 2001. *200 Years of Syntax: A critical survey*. Amsterdam & Philadelphia: Benjamins.

Greenberg, Joseph H. 1966. "Some Universals of Grammar with Particular Reference to the Order of Meaningful Elements". *Universals of Language* ed. by J. H. Greenberg, 2nd ed., 73−113. Cambridge, Mass.: MIT Press.

Guillaume, Gustave. 1929. *Temps et verbe*. Paris: H. Champion.

−. 1971−1990. *Leçons de linguistique*. Paris: Klincksieck; Québec: Presses de l'Université Laval [vols 1−4]. Québec: Presses the l'Universite Laval; Lille: Presses Universitaires [vols. 5−10]. (Cited as *LdeL* followed by volume and page(s).)

Jespersen, Otto. 1909−1949. *A Modern English Grammar*. 7 vols. Heidelberg: Winter; London: Allen & Unwin.

−. 1924. *The Philosophy of Grammar*. London: Allen & Unwin. (Repr., with an introduction by James D. McCawley, Chicago: Univ. of Chicago Press, 1992.)

−. 1937. *Analytic Syntax*. Copenhagen: Ejnar Munskgaard. (New ed., with an introduction by James D. McCawley, Chicago: Univ. of Chicago Press, 1984.)

Kalepky, Theodor. 1928. *Neuaufbau der Grammatik*. Leipzig & Berlin: Teubner.

LdeL. See Guillaume 1971−1990.

Lyons, John. 1977. *Semantics*. 2 vols. Cambridge: Cambridge Univ. Press.

Mathesius, Vilém. 1924. "Několik slov o podstatě věty [Some words on the essence of the sentence]". *Časopis pro moderní filologii* 10.1−6.

−. 1939. "O takzvaném aktuálním členění větném [On the so-called actual partition of the sentence]". *Slovo a slovesnost* 5.171−174.

−. 1941−42. "Ze srovnávacích studií slovosledných [From comparative studies of word order]". *Časopis pro moderní filologii* 28.181−190; 302−307.

−. 1964a [1936]. "On Some Problems of the Systematic Analysis of Grammar". Vachek 1964. 306−319. (Originally published in *Travaux du Cercle Linguistique de Prague* 6.95−107, 1936.)

−. 1964b [1939]. "Verstärkung und Emphase". Vachek 1964. 426−432. (Originally published in *Mélanges de linguistique offerts à Charles Bally*, 407−413. Genève: Georg & Cie., 1939.)

Meillet, Antoine. 1932. Review of Ries (1931). *BSL* 32.17−20.

Miklosich, Franz. 1883 [1874]. *Vergleichende Grammatik der slavischen Sprachen*. Bd. IV. *Syntax*. 2nd ed. Wien: Wilhelm Braumüller.

Noreen, Adolf. 1923. *Einführung in die wissenschaftliche Betrachtung der Sprache*. Halle/S.: Niemeyer.

Paul, Hermann. 1920 [1880]: *Prinzipien der Sprachgeschichte*. 5th ed. Halle/S.: Niemeyer.

Quirk, Randolph, Sidney Greenbaum, Geoffrey Leech & Jan Svartvik. 1985. *A Comprehensive Grammar of the English Language*. London: Longman.

Ries, John. 1927 [1894]. *Was ist Syntax? Ein kritischer Versuch*. 2nd ed. Prague: Taussig & Taussig.

−. 1928. *Zur Wortgruppenlehre*. Prague: Taussig & Taussig.

−. 1931. *Was ist ein Satz?* Prague: Taussig & Taussig.

Steinthal, Heymann. 1855. *Grammatik, Logik und Psychologie*. Berlin: F. Dümmler. (Repr. Hildesheim: G. Olms, 1968.)

−. 1860a. "Assimilation and Attraktion, psychologisch beleuchtet". *Zeitschrift für Völkerpsychologie und Sprachwissenschaft* 1.93−179.

−. 1860b. "Carl Philipp Moritz über die unpersönlichen Zeitwörter". *Zeitschrift für Völkerpsychologie und Sprachwissenschaft* 1.73−89.

Svedelius, Carl. 1897. *L'analyse du langage appliquée à la langue française*. Uppsala: Almquist & Wiksell.

Tesnière, Lucien. 1966 [1959]. *Éléments de syntaxe structurale*. 2nd ed. Paris: Klincksieck.

Vachek, Josef. 1964. *A Prague School Reader in Linguistics*. Bloomington & London: Indiana Univ. Press.

Wackernagel, Jakob. 1892. "Über ein Gesetz der indogermanischen Wortstellung". *Indogermanische Forschungen* 1.333−436.

Weil, Henri. 1879 [1844] *De l'ordre des mots dans les langues anciennes comparées aux langues modernes*. 3rd ed. Paris: Hachette. (Repr., with a preface by Simone Delesalle, Paris: Didier, 1991. Engl. transl. by C. W. Super. Boston: Ginn & Co., 1887. New ed., with an introduction by Aldo Scaglione, Amsterdam: Benjamins, 1978.)

Giorgio Graffi, Verona (Italy)

205. Die Entwicklung der Dependenzgrammatik und verwandter Theorien in der 2. Hälfte des 20. Jahrhunderts

1. Zur Dependenzgrammatik
2. Chronologischer Abriß zur Geschichte der Dependenzgrammatik
3. Ausblick
4. Bibliographie

1. Zur Dependenzgrammatik

Die Dependenzgrammatik (im folgenden: DG) ist einer der grundlegenden Grammatik-Typen, der die grammatische Grundrelation der 'Dependenz' in den Mittelpunkt der Strukturbeschreibung stellt. Die DG bezieht sich — wie andere strukturale Grammatik-Typen auch — weniger auf Morphologie und Stellungsverhalten des Einzelworts, sondern versteht sich primär als Satz-Syntax, wobei in der DG eine enge Verbindung zur Semantik angenommen wird. 'Dependenz' umfaßt einen verallgemeinerten Begriff von 'Rektion' und 'gerichteter Konkomitanz': 'A regiert B' oder 'das Vorkommen von B setzt das Vorkommen von A voraus'; Linearisierung und morphologische Ausgestaltung der Einzelelemente können dabei unberücksichtigt bleiben. Ein wichtiger Unterschied zu anderen, auch verwandten, Grammatik-Typen liegt darin, daß die zugrundeliegenden Kategorien sich direkt auf Einzelelemente (Wörter bzw. Wortäquivalente) beziehen oder explizit durch diese ersetzt werden. Nicht vorgesehen sind in der Regel Kategorien höherer Stufe (wie NP, VP oder PP in der Phrasenstrukturgrammatik), also nichtlexikalische Größen; ebenso wird auf lexikalisch leere Kategorien verzichtet. Dependenzgrammatiken werden deshalb unter die Lexikalisierten Grammatiken gerechnet oder — wegen der tragenden Rolle des Verbs in der Strukturbeschreibung — unter die Verbgrammatiken.

1.1. Dependenz — Valenz

'Dependenz' wird auch 'Valenz' gegenübergestellt: Valenz als (semantisches, syntaktisches) Kombinationspotential von Wörtern und Dependenz (Abhängigkeit) als dessen konkrete Realisierung (Kunze 1982: 17). Zugrunde liegt Tesnières These, daß das Verb das Zentrum des Satzes sei, weil seine Valenz die Strukturmöglichkeiten des Satzes organisiert. Es gibt allerdings keinen zwingenden Grund, DG und Valenz zusammenzubringen; eine Dependenzgrammatik verlangt nicht unbedingt die Berücksichtigung der 'Valenz', und 'Valenz' spielt auch in anderen Grammatikmodellen eine Rolle (z. B. als 'Subkategorisierung' in der Head-Driven Phrase Structure Grammar oder als 'Selektion' in der Transformationell-Generativen Grammatik). Ungeachtet dieser Überlegungen kann ein geschichtlicher Abriß nicht an der Tatsache vorbei, daß sich Valenz- und Dependenzforschung immer in engem Kontakt befunden haben. Entwicklungen der Valenzforschung werden deshalb hier mitbehandelt, soweit sich direkte Verbindungen zur Dependenzgrammatik aufzeigen lassen.

1.2. Lucien Tesnière

Als Begründer der modernen Fassung der Dependenzgrammatik oder (nach Heringer 1993a: 298) des 'klassischen' Modells gilt Lucien Tesnière (1893—1954); die Ursprünge der DG lassen sich jedoch bis in die Zeit um 1300 und später (bei den sogenannten Modisten) zurückverfolgen. In neuerer Zeit hat der Sprachtheoretiker Karl Bühler (1879—1963) die Idee der 'Dependenz' und der 'Valenz' als "Wahlverwandtschaften" zwischen Wortarten umschrieben: "das Adverb sucht sein Verbum" und "daß die Wörter einer bestimmten Wortklasse eine oder mehrere Leerstellen um sich eröffnen, die durch Wörter bestimmter anderer Wortklassen ausgefüllt werden müssen" (1965 [1934]: 173). Kurze Zeit vor der Veröffentlichung von Tesnières *Esquisse* (1953) haben S. D. Kacnel'son (1948) und A. W. de Groot (1949: 113—143) unabhängig voneinander den Begriff 'syntaktische Valenz' verwendet (zitiert nach Engelen 1975: 38—44 und Vater 1996: 175). Erben sprach analog von "Wertigkeit" (1958: 231—238). Engel bemerkt in seiner Tesnière-Übersetzung (1980: 20), daß in der Zeit des Erscheinens der *Éléments* "der Gedanke der durch Valenz geregelten Satzstruktur in der Luft zu liegen" schien.

Lucien Tesnière lehrte von 1924—1937 an der Universität Straßburg, ab 1937 als Professor für Allgemeine Sprachwissenschaft an der Universität Montpellier. Seit dieser Zeit arbeitete er an einem Vorlesungsskript "Cours élémentaire de syntaxe structurale" (1938), später an einem Skript zu den "Éléments de syntaxe structurale", das im Lauf der Jahre mehrfach überarbeitet wurde. Widrige Umstände bewirkten, daß es bis zur Publikation dieses Werks noch fast zwanzig Jahre dauerte. 1947 erkrankte Tesnière und erholte sich nicht mehr. 1953 erschien *Esquisse d'une syntaxe structurale*, eine Kurzfassung seines *Cours* von 1938, die positive aber auch recht negative Kritiken erhielt (Garey 1954). 1954 starb Tesnière. Seiner Frau und einigen seiner Schüler ist es zu verdanken, daß die *Éléments* 1959 doch noch erscheinen konnten. Jean Fourquet (1996: 4) berichtete später, daß Tesnières Ideen noch nach seinem Tod vom akademischen Umfeld als zu neu (häretisch) empfunden wurden, was die Publikation wiederum verzögerte. Als das Buch 1959 schließlich erscheinen konnte, zu einer Zeit, als so gut wie alle Welt von den *Syntactic Structures* Chomskys und der Phrasenstruktur-Grammatik (kurz: PSG) fasziniert war, wurden die Ideen zwar angenommen, kamen aber entscheidende Jahre zu spät. Zumindest entsprachen sie nicht den Erwartungen der Hauptströmungen in den einschlägigen sprachwissenschaftlichen Teildisziplinen. Mögliche Gründe lagen wohl in der Entstehungsgeschichte des Werks selbst – es war lange Zeit von der breiten wissenschaftlichen Öffentlichkeit isoliert – aber auch in seiner Vielschichtigkeit: Fragen der Morphologie, der Satzstruktur, der Wort-Etymologie, der Sprachtypologie, der Wissenschaftsgeschichte, grundsätzliche Fragen der Methodik und Detailprobleme in Darstellungsfragen sind in Tesnières Werk eng miteinander verwoben. Zu einigen Problemen liegen kein einheitlicher Beschreibungsrahmen und keine verbindliche Darstellungsform vor. Pierre Guiraud (1971: 1) bezeichnete Tesnière als "pioneer in the New Linguistics"; (er kam) "too early and in the wrong place, when his ideas could have no appeal against the current trends of the time". Allerdings erscheint diese Einschätzung in der Rückschau als zu pessimistisch. Dazu später mehr.

1.3. Grundprinzipien der Dependenzgrammatik Tesnières

1.3.1. Innere Form des Satzes, ordre structural, Konnexion, Nucleus, Wortarten

Die wichtigsten Prinzipien der DG lassen sich in folgenden Punkten zusammenfassen:

1) Gegenstand der strukturalen Syntax ist die 'innere Form' des Satzes, d. h. die zugrundeliegenden strukturalen und semantischen Ordnungsprinzipien. Die äußere Form des Satzes wird zur Morphologie gerechnet.

2) Im Satz wirken zwei Ordnungsprinzipien: 'ordre structural' und 'ordre linéaire'.

3) Aufgabe der Syntax ist es, die strukturale Ordnung (ordre structural) im Satz darzustellen. Die Beschreibung stellt den Satz dar als Netz von Relationen zwischen den einzelnen Elementen – unabhängig von der linearen Abfolge der Elemente in der 'chaîne parlée'.

4) Die Grundrelation, die zwischen den Elementen eines Satzes vorliegen kann, ist die Konnexion (oder Dependenz); sie hat eine syntaktische und eine semantische Komponente. Syntaktische und semantische Konnexion laufen in der Regel parallel zueinander; d. h. ohne semantische Konnexion existiert keine syntaktische Konnexion – und umgekehrt.

5) Die Schnittpunkte für semantisch-syntaktische Konnexionen in einer Satzstrukturbeschreibung bezeichnet Tesnière als 'Knoten' (nucléus). In der Regel entsprechen ihnen die 'Wörter'; Nuclei können aber auch komplex sein und aus mehreren Wörtern bestehen (im Falle eines 'nucléus dissocié' oder eines Mehrwort-Lexems). Nuclei sind also gemischt syntaktisch-semantische Entitäten. Leere Nuclei sind nicht vorgesehen.

6) Die Wörter werden in zwei große Gruppen unterteilt, in Voll-Wörter (mots pleins) und Leer-Wörter (mots vides). Voll-Wörter drücken Vorstellungen aus, haben semantische und syntaktische Funktionen, bilden Nuclei (z. B. *Pascal, Lied, singt, trauriges, gern*) oder – zusammen mit anderen abhängigen Nuclei – eine Nucleus-Konfiguration (noeud, auch: Nexus). Leer-Wörter allein drücken keine Vorstellungen aus, werden nicht als Nuclei dargestellt (Beispiele: *und, von, daß*).

7) Voll-Wörter werden in vier Klassen eingeteilt: Verb (*singt*), Substantiv (*Pascal, Lied*), Adjektiv/Epitheton (*trauriges*), Adverb (*gern, sehr*). Innerhalb der DG Tesnières gibt es keine höheren Einheiten als diese Klassen.

8) Leer-Wörter sind unterschieden in Indizes (*eine, ich*), 'jonctifs' (Junktoren: *und, oder*), 'translatifs' (Translatoren: *weil, daß*), und – als Sonderfall – Anaphernwörter. Diesen Leerwortarten entsprechen die grammatischen Relationstypen

Indizierung, Junktion, Translation und Anapher. Indizes sind Nuclei konnexionslos zugeordnet, Junktoren sind internuklear, Translatoren dagegen intranuklear, weil sie ihre Funktion innerhalb von komplexen Nuclei ausüben; Anaphernwörter (die semantisch Leer-Wörter, syntaktisch aber Voll-Wörter sind) können Nuclei bilden.
9) Eine Konnexion benötigt mindestens zwei Nuclei: einen übergeordneten (Regens) und einen abhängigen (Dependens). Von einem Regens können mehrere Dependentien abhängen, einem Dependens darf nur **ein** Regens übergeordnet sein. Die Verbindungen zwischen den einzelnen Nuclei sind im Satz in spezifischer Weise gerichtet, asymmetrisch. Dies ist nicht naturgegeben sondern festgelegt; ebenso die Entscheidung, daß von einem Nucleus-Typ alle anderen abhängen.
10) Die Nuclei, denen normalerweise der höchste Rang zukommt, sind die finiten Verben. Von ihnen direkt abhängig sind Substantive oder Adverbien. Es ergeben sich folgende Dependenz-Relationen: Verb regiert Substantiv und/oder Adverb; Substantiv regiert Epitheton/Adjektiv; Adjektiv regiert Adverb; Adverb regiert Adverb.
11) Es gibt noch Spezialfälle der Konnexion; dazu gehört einmal die Apposition, bei der es sich nicht um direkte Abhängigkeit, sondern um eine (horizontale) Zuordnung von Nuclei handelt;
12) zum andern die Anapher: Hier liegt keine Parallelität von syntaktischer und semantischer Konnexion vor; es besteht nur eine semantische Konnexion ohne syntaktische Entsprechung. Anaphern werden im Stemma durch eine unterbrochene Linie dargestellt, die Anaphernwort und Antezedens aufeinander bezieht.

1.3.2. Darstellung der Satzstruktur: Das Stemma

Als Darstellungsmittel für den Bau der Sätze wählt Tesnière das Stemma. Elemente des Stemmas sind Nuclei, die die Vollwörter eines Satzes repräsentieren, und gerichtete Kanten für die Dependenzbeziehungen zwischen den Nuclei. Dargestellt wird die Konnexion als durchgezogene nichthorizontale Linie. Dabei muß sich die Darstellung im Stemma strikt auf die tatsächlich im Satz vorkommenden lexikalischen Einheiten beschränken. Nuclei, die allein logisch motiviert sind, denen also keine Wörter oder Wortäquivalente im Satz zuzuordnen sind, werden nicht erlaubt. Tesnière wendet das Stemma sowohl zur Beschreibung eines aktuellen Satzes an, als auch zur generalisierenden Darstellung von Dependenzbeziehungen. Dabei werden Wörter durch ihre Wortarten-Symbole vertreten; es handelt sich dann um ein symbolisches oder virtuelles Stemma.

1.3.3. Valenz: 'Aktanten' und 'Circumstanten'

Als obersten Nucleus im Satz setzt Tesnière das (finite) Verb fest. Die vom Verbknoten direkt anhängigen Nuclei sind unterteilt in 'actants' (Aktanten) und 'circonstants' (Circumstanten). Aktanten (auch: Mitspieler) sind in konstitutiver Hinsicht an der durch ein Verb ausgedrückten Handlung beteiligt. Eine Handlung, einen Zustand oder ein Ereignis zu benennen heißt, über Leerstellen die Zahl und Art der Aktanten zu bestimmen. Tesnière läßt drei Arten zu: den 1. Aktant (konventionell als 'Subjekt' bezeichnet), den 2. Aktant ('Akkusativ-Objekt') und den 3. Aktant ('Genitiv-', 'Dativ-Objekt'). Circumstanten sind vom Verb direkt abhängig, aber nicht semantisch-syntaktisch konstitutiv für eine Handlung. Sie sind nicht als vom Verb eröffnete Leerstellen aufzufassen, sie bezeichnen die Umstände einer Handlung, eines Zustandes oder Ereignisses: Ort, Art und Weise, Zeit; ihre Zahl ist − unter syntaktischen Aspekten − nicht zu begrenzen. Im Stemma sind Circumstanten mit 'c' abgekürzt und in der Regel rechts von den Aktanten notiert. Diese Vorschrift kann jedoch übergangen werden, wenn die Anordnung der Nuclei im Stemma ihrer linearen Abfolge entsprechen soll. Die Fähigkeit der Verben, Aktanten an sich zu binden, bezeichnet Tesnière als 'Valenz'; sie manifestiert sich unterschiedlich: Die avalenten Verben weisen keine Leerstelle für Mitspieler auf, monovalente Verben) haben nur eine Leerstelle, di- und trivalente zwei bzw. drei. Verben mit höherer Valenz bleiben unberücksichtigt. Präpositionalgruppen läßt Tesnière nicht als Aktanten zu, was innerhalb der Valenz-Forschung zu Kontroversen führen wird. Auch wenn die Abhängigkeit zwischen dem Verb und seinen Aktanten bzw. Circumstanten intuitiv einleuchtend erscheint (zumindest in der eigenen Sprache), ist die Valenz des Verb-Nucleus primär als festgesetzt und nicht als experimentell ermittelt anzusehen. Gerade mit diesem Punkt wird man sich später lange beschäftigen und damit zusammenhängend mit der Unterscheidung von Aktanten und Circumstanten. Erschwerend kommt hinzu, daß im Falle unvollständiger Satz-Konstruktionen Aktanten als Besetzung einer Valenzstelle beim Zentral-Nucleus fehlen können. Das gilt z. B. für Imperativ- oder bestimmte Passivsätze, in denen der 1. Aktant nicht auftritt; auch kontextbedigte Auslassungen sind häufig.

1.3.4. Junktion, Junktoren und Junktionstypen

Der Relationstyp 'Junktion' bezeichnet die Nebenordnung zweier oder mehrerer gleichartiger Nuclei oder Nucleus-Konfigurationen (noeuds) − unabhängig von der Valenz der Wörter. Jungierte Nuclei werden durch die (internuklearen) Junktoren horizontal verbunden. Konnexion unter Beteiligung von jungierten Nuclei wird im Stemma als Junktionsdreieck dargestellt, um anzuzeigen, daß von zwei jungierten Nuclei nur jeweils eine Konnexion nach oben oder unten ausgeht. So wird vermieden, daß etwa im Beispiel 'alte Männer und Frauen' der Nucleus 'alte' von zwei Nuclei 'Männer', 'Frauen' regiert wird. Als Junktionstypen werden vollständige Junktion und unvollständige Junktion unterschieden. Vollständige Junktion ist charakterisiert durch Junktion von Einzelknoten, unvollständige Junktion bezieht sich auf Nucleus-Konfigurationen und damit einhergehende Auslassung.

1.3.5. Translation und Translationstypen

Nun zum dritten Relationstyp der DG, der 'Translation'. Für Tesnière sind Konstruktionen, wie *das Buch von Peter* und *rotes Buch*, vergleichbar. Denn *von Peter* modifiziert *Buch* in gleicher Weise wie *rotes*; *von Peter* funktioniert wie ein Adjektiv zu *Buch*, obwohl das Vollwort *Peter* im Rahmen der Konnexion als Substantiv anzusehen ist. Konsequenz dieser Umfunktionierung von Wortarten: Zwischen Wort und Wortart besteht keine feste Zuordnung; lexikalische Eigenschaften und kontextuell bedingte syntaktische Funktionen sind miteinander verbunden. Die Translation folgt also aus der Einschränkung auf vier Grundkategorien für die Vollwortarten und ihre möglichen Relationen: Neben die kategorielle Einordnung muß eine strukturelle, funktionale Spezifikation gestellt werden. Anders als die Junktion, die die horizontale Erweiterbarkeit betrifft, ermöglicht die Translation den vertikalen Ausbau der Satzstruktur. Dabei handelt es sich jedoch nicht um einen simplen Wortarten-Wechsel mit der Ersetzung eines Konnexionspotentials durch ein neues, sondern um die Anreicherung eines Nucleus mit dem Konnexionspotential der Zielwortart in Richtung auf mögliche regierende Knoten; das nach unten auf abhängige Knoten gerichtete Konnexionspotential der Ausgangswortart bleibt erhalten. Damit wird ein Nucleus für einen neuen Strukturzusammenhang kompatibel gemacht. Gegenüber den Konnexionen und der Valenz, die als weitgehend konstante Elemente der Satzstrukturbeschreibung anzusehen sind, bildet die Translation ein rekursives Element, das die Satzstruktur offenhält. Tesnière unterscheidet zwei wichtige Typen: Die Translation ersten und die Translation zweiten Grades. Die Translation ersten Grades betrifft Einzel-Nuclei und wird dargestellt durch '>': Adjektiv > Substantiv ist demnach zu lesen als 'Translation (1. Grades) von Adjektiv nach Substantiv'. Die Translation zweiten Grades betrifft den Übergang von Verb-Nucleus-Konfigurationen in abhängige Sätze. Sie wird dargestellt durch '≫'; Verb ≫ Substantiv ist zu lesen als 'Translation (2. Grades) von Verb nach Substantiv'. Beide Typen werden unterteilt in einfache und komplexe Translation. Komplexe Translation liegt vor, wenn das Translat einer Translation ebenfalls Transferend einer anderen Translation ist. Es stecken dann mehrere Translationen in einem Nucleus.

2. Chronologischer Abriß zur Geschichte der Dependenzgrammatik

Die Resonanz auf Tesnières Ideen in den ersten 10 Jahren seit Erscheinen der *Éléments* (1959) läßt sich heute aus einer Vielzahl von Publikationen aus unterschiedlichen Bereichen der Sprachwissenschaft ablesen. Das Erscheinen der Dependenzgrammatik hatte zwar bei weitem nicht die durchschlagende Wirkung wie die Phrasenstrukturgrammatik, die Wirkung in der Breite war aber doch beachtlich. Die oben erwähnte Einschätzung Girauds des "appeals" von Tesnières Ideen galt für die 'mainstream'-Linguistik, aber keineswegs für die gesamte Sprachwissenschaft. Die Publikationen zu 'Dependenz' und 'Valenz' aus der Zeitspanne von 1959−1970 wiesen bereits den größten Teil des Spektrums an Forschungen und Anwendungen auf, die in der Zeit danach weiterverfolgt wurden. Viele Fragen, die heute noch aktuell sind, wurden damals schon gestellt, viele Ansätze, die damals grundgelegt wurden, werden heute noch weiterverfolgt. Dazu gehören:

- Beziehungen der DG zu anderen (formalisierten, implementierten) Grammatik-Typen, insbesondere zur PSG (z. B. Konstituenz vs. Dependenz);
- der Einsatz der DG in Systemen zur maschinellen Sprachverarbeitung (kurz: NLP für 'natural language processing');
- Dependenz und Valenz in einzelsprachlichen deskriptiven Grammatiken;
- Valenzkonzeptionen und ihre Anwendung in Lexikographie und Sprachdidaktik.

Später werden noch einige Betätigungsfelder hinzukommen:

- historische Lexikographie und Syntax,
- sprachvergleichende Arbeiten und
- Valenz in satzübergreifenden Einheiten und im Text.

Der nun folgende Abriß zur Entwicklung der DG und – soweit darauf bezogen – der Valenztheorie orientiert sich im wesentlichen an diesen Themenbereichen, und zwar in chronologischer Abfolge. Systematische Darstellungen für die Anfänge und die ersten 15 Jahre nach Tesnière liegen bereits seit längerer Zeit vor (Maas 1974, Baum 1976, Korhonen 1977); über neuere Entwicklungen und Tendenzen informieren Heringer (1993a, b) und Hudson (1993).

Die Darstellung ist in vier Abschnitte unterteilt, die sich auf jeweils etwa 10 Jahre der Entwicklung beziehen. Dieser Zehnjahres-Takt ist zwar willkürlich gesetzt, läßt sich aber auch aus der Geschichte anderer Modellierungen herleiten, die für die Entwicklung der DG von Bedeutung waren. PSG-Forschung und anfangs auch die Kasustheorie haben fast alle 10 Jahre mit einer Erweiterung, einer Revision oder mit einer Neuentwicklung neue Maßstäbe gesetzt, beginnend mit den *Syntactic Structures* (Chomsky 1957), dem *Aspects*-Modell (Chomsky 1965) bzw. der Kasusgrammatik (Fillmore 1968), der *Scenes-and-Frames*-Semantik (Fillmore 1977), der *Lexical Functional Grammar* (Kaplan & Bresnan 1982) und der *Generalized Phrase Structure Grammar* (Gazdar et al. 1985) – bis zur *Head-Driven Phrase Structure Grammar* (Pollard & Sag 1994).

2.1. Die Zeit nach Tesnière (1959–1970)

2.1.1. Konstituenz – Dependenz

Eine unmittelbare Resonanz fand die Dependenzgrammatik in der Heimat der Phrasenstrukturgrammatik, den Vereinigten Staaten (Hays 1960, Gaifmann 1961). Grund für dieses frühe Interesse war, daß man sich in einigen US-Projekten zur Maschinellen Übersetzung (MÜ) von der vorwiegend morphologisch basierten Wort-für-Wort-Übersetzung ab- und sich der Syntax im Rahmen formalisierbarer Grammatikmodelle zuwandte. Dabei spielte die Frage der Vergleichbarkeit der DG zur frühen PSG eine wesentliche Rolle. Ein Vergleich – von Gaifman (1961) freilich ohne direkte Bezugnahme auf Tesnières Publikationen durchgeführt – wurde im wesentlichen mit Vorgaben angestellt, die aus Chomsky (1956) und (1957) stammten (Unique PSG, nur Kategorien erster Stufe). Salopp formuliert, hatte die DG in diesem Kontext kein Heimspiel, denn syntaktische präterminale Kategorien einer PSG sind nicht deckungsgleich mit Nuclei einer DG nach Tesnière. So kann man das Resultat des Vergleichs – schwache Äquivalenz der beiden Typen (beide Grammatiken erzeugen die gleiche Menge von Sätzen) und eingeschränkte starke Äquivalenz (zu jeder DG läßt sich eine kategorial äquivalente PSG konstruieren, aber nicht umgekehrt) oder wie es Baumgärtner später (1970: 60) umschrieb: "eine Dependenzgrammatik ist eine, lediglich beschränkte, Phrasenstrukturgrammatik" – für die DG als Achtungserfolg auffassen.

Erste linguistisch orientierte Überblicksdarstellungen zur Dependenzgrammatik (nach Hays 1960, Gaifman 1961 und Lecerf 1961) gaben Bierwisch (1966: 20–22) mit einer Kritik der Auffassungen Tesnières zur 'Dependenz' und zur Vernachlässigung der Wortfolge sowie Baumgärtner (1965), dem ein weiterer (1967 geschrieben, 1970 erschienen) nachfolgte. Hier findet sich die Formel zur Integration beider Prinzipien, in der für syntaktische Strukturbeschreibungen (mit Berücksichtigung der Linearität) die PSG favorisiert wird, während semantisch fundierte Beschreibungen als Stärke der DG herausgestellt werden. Als Möglichkeit der Weiterentwicklung von formalisierten Grammatiken schlug Robinson 1968 eine hybride Grammatik vor, die sich aus Elementen der Konstituenz- und der Dependenz-Beschreibung zusammensetzt. Motiviert waren derartige Studien aus einem Ungenügen an der PSG (z. B.

an der Konzeption des 'head' einer Konstituente oder der unkontrollierbaren Einführung neuer nonterminaler Kategorien).

2.1.2. Dependenz in frühen NLP-Systemen

Auch in der maschinellen Sprachverarbeitung blieb die dominierende Stellung der PSG unangefochten. DG-Beschreibungen wurden dann eingesetzt, wenn die Möglichkeit der direkten Einbindung lexikalischer Informationen in die Strukturbeschreibungen höher bewertet wurde. Dies war bei frühen MÜ-Projekten in der Sowjetunion (Mel'čuk 1963) und der Deutschen Demokratischen Republik (Agricola et al. 1963) der Fall. Kunze betonte in der Projektbeschreibung, einer der ersten deutschsprachigen Studien zur Dependenzsyntax, ausdrücklich die Vorzüge einer Strukturdarstellung nach Tesnière oder Mel'čuk: "Es erweist sich als sprachlich akzeptabel und formal als sehr günstig, jedes Wort nur **einem** anderen unterzuordnen" (in Agricola et al. 1963: 62). Diese veröffentlichte Wertschätzung Tesnières war jedoch für die damalige Zeit nicht die Regel, insbesondere nicht in der MÜ-Forschung und Computerlinguistik. Es kam nicht selten vor, daß zwar von Tesnières Ideen zur Dependenz, Valenz und seiner Darstellung von Satzstrukturen Gebrauch gemacht wurde, aber die Quelle der Inspiration ungenannt blieb (so beispielsweise bei Gladkij & Mel'čuk 1969: 1; Vauquois et al. 1969: 13, 15, 19). Auch wenn Tesnières Name explizit in Zusammenhang mit Begriffen wie 'dépendence', 'valence', 'actant' im Text erwähnt wurde, konnten die betreffenden Publikationen im Literaturverzeichnis fehlen (z. B. bei Dugas et al. 1969: 13, 20). Über Gründe für dieses Zitierverhalten soll hier nicht spekuliert werden. Es hat jedenfalls mit dazu beigetragen, daß die Isolation um Tesnières Werk in einem wichtigen linguistischen Betätigungsfeld noch länger andauerte.

In MÜ-Projekten war Arbeitsteilung zwischen PSG und DG nicht selten. Dabei wurden PSG-Beschreibungen für syntaktische Oberflächenstrukturen und DG-Beschreibungen für die semantische Zwischenebene ('interlingua', 'langage pivot') aufeinander bezogen. Einige dieser Systeme (für Montréal: Dugas et al. 1969; für Grenoble, CETA: Vauquois et al. 1969) waren inspiriert von Mel'čuk/Zolkovskij (1970) und ihrem System SMYSL ↔ TEKST, einem Mehrebenen-System, über das 'Inhalt/Sinn' und 'Text' einander zugeordnet wurden. Die Aufteilung in fünf Hauptebenen (mit Unterteilungen in Tiefen- und Oberflächen-Ebene) zeigte Analogien zur Unterteilung in Oberflächen- und Tiefenstruktur im *Aspects*-Modell (Chomsky 1965) — in dieser Zeit ein Gütesiegel auch für ein maschinelles NLP-System. Der Anteil der dependentiellen Beschreibung bestand darin, daß die Strukturen auf den einzelnen Ebenen im wesentlichen als Dependenzbäume dargestellt wurden. Übergänge von einer zu anderen Ebene wurden vollzogen durch Operationen auf diesen Baumstrukturen. Knoten waren semantische Einheiten für Prädikate und Argumente (semantische Ebene), abstrakte Lexeme (tiefensyntaktische Ebene), lexikalische Einheiten (oberflächensyntaktische Ebene); die übrigen Einheiten für die tiefenmorphologische, oberflächenmorphologische, phonologische und phonetisch/graphische Ebene sind hier nicht von Belang (außer unter dem Aspekt der Linearisierung).

2.1.3. Valenz und Dependenz in Sprachdidaktik, Lexikographie, Grammatik

Auch in Sprachdidaktik und Lexikographie stießen die Ideen Tesnières, insbesondere zur Valenz, bald nach ihrer Veröffentlichung vor allem im osteuropäischen, deutschsprachigen und skandinavischen Raum auf große Aufnahmebereitschaft, was zahlreiche Veröffentlichungen aus dieser Zeit bezeugen (vgl. Helbig 1971: 105−108). Die Rezeption Tesnières wurde in den deutschsprachigen Ländern auch durch das große Interesse an der Aufarbeitung ausländischer Forschungsbeiträge befördert. Erste Versuche, die Valenzkonzeption für den Fremdsprachenunterricht nutzbar zu machen, wurden von Helbig (1965, 1966) und Engel (1967) unternommen. Auch für die Grammatik-Lehrbücher war an vielen deutschen Schulen "die Zeit der unbefragten Traditionen" (Stötzel 1970: 29) vorbei. Diskutiert wurden verschiedene Ansätze zu Verb- und Satzklassifikationen. Wertigkeits- und Valenzkonzeptionen von Erben (1958) und Tesnière (1959) wurden kritisch miteinander verglichen. Die Anwendung der Dependenzgrammatik und der Valenzkonzeption im muttersprachlichen Grammatikunterricht versuchte Heringer (1970a) auf neue Grundlagen zu stellen. Anhand von Beispielen wurden Satzbeschreibungen nach Chomskys *Aspects* und Tesnières Valenzkonzeption vorgeführt; Ziel des Grammatikunterrichts der Unterstufe sollte sein: "den Schülern die Fähigkeit zu geben, Satzstrukturen in Satzbäumen darzustellen" (Heringer 1970a: 28).

Strukturalistische Grammatiken stimmen darin überein, daß sich sämtliche Sätze einer Sprache auf eine begrenzte Anzahl von Grundstrukturen zurückführen lassen. Als Grundstrukturen in der Syntax galten 'Satzbaupläne', auch mit verwandten Konzeptionen, wie 'Fügungspotenz' (Admoni 1960: 211) und 'Wertigkeit' (Erben 1958) war man vertraut. Diese ließen sich in Zusammenhang mit Tesnières Ideen in einen neuen Rahmen stellen und konnten auch zur Klärung der 'Valenz'-Konzeption herangezogen werden. So beschrieb Engel (1969) die Valenz eines Verbs nicht nur nach der Zahl der Aktanten, sondern auch nach ihrer Ausgestaltung. Von den Wortklassen stand unbestritten das Verb mit seiner Rolle im Satzzusammenhang und Fragen zur Ermittlung seiner Valenz im Mittelpunkt (Heringer 1967). Eine systematische Darstellung für deutsche Verben lieferte das Valenz-Wörterbuch von Helbig & Schenkel (1969). Es beschränkte sich auf die 'syntaktische' Valenz, die — inspiriert von Chomskys strikter und selektionaler Subkategorisierung — noch spezifiziert wurde. Ebenfalls von der PSG beeinflußt war die Grammatik von Heringer (1970b), die ein Konstitutionssystem für syntaktische Strukturen und Lexikonregeln für terminale Elemente mit Angaben zur Wertigkeit von Prädikaten verband. Ungeachtet der Nähe zu PSG-Modellen führte dies zu einer höheren Wertschätzung des Lexikons, denn eine Valenzbeschreibung als geregelte Vorwegnahme eines wesentlichen Teils der syntaktischen Strukturen stand nicht in Einklang mit der Konzeption vom 'Lexikon' als 'Menge der (syntaktischen) Irregularitäten', wie sie den *Aspects* zugrundelag.

2.1.4. Kontroversen

Die Valenzkonzeption stieß nicht nur auf Zustimmung. Es gab verschiedene Kritikansätze, die fundamental dagegen standen. Strittig war insbesondere der Statusverlust des Subjekts in der Satzstrukturbeschreibung; die Einordnung unter das Verb als eine von mehreren abhängigen Größen (als Nominativ-Ergänzung) stand in Gegensatz zur prominenten Rolle in der traditionellen Schulgrammatik und der PSG. Auch Schwierigkeiten bei der verbindlichen Ermittlung der Wertigkeit eines Valenzträgers und damit bei der Abgrenzung von Ergänzungen (actants, compléments) und Angaben (circonstants, adjuncts) gaben Anlaß zu Kontroversen — auch innerhalb der Valenzforschung. Statt einer verbindlichen Festsetzung des 'Valenzrahmens' (untermauert durch Tests) plädierten andere für weniger strenge Unterscheidungen mit der Möglichkeit variabler Valenzen (Rosengren 1970). Auch die Frage, ob 'Valenz' eine spezifisch einzelsprachliche, lexikalische oder eine übereinzelsprachliche, begriffliche Konzeption sei, stand zur Debatte (Heger 1966, 1970; Bondzio 1969). Auseinandersetzungen wie diese zeigten Ähnlichkeiten mit den Problemen, denen später die Tiefenkasus-Theorie von Fillmore (1968) gegenüberstand. Auch hier wurde der linguistische Status der Kasusrollen nicht einheitlich bewertet, Art und Anzahl der Kasusrollen insgesamt oder im aktuellen Kasusrahmen wurden unterschiedlich festgelegt.

2.1.5. Konzeptuelle Dependenz, Tiefenkasus

Mit der lexikalischen Fundierung von Satzstrukturen und der zentralen Stellung des Prädikats, wie sie in der Dependenz- und Valenztheorie charakteristisch ist, rückten semantische Modellierungen stärker in den Vordergrund. Dazu gehörte neben der Kasustheorie die *Conceptual Dependency* (Schank 1969). Als Gemeinsamkeit zwischen Dependenzgrammatik und *Conceptual Dependency* zeigte sich die Konzeption der Dependenz: Einheiten wurden als abhängig von anderen beschrieben, wenn ihr eigenes Vorkommen das Vorkommen der übergeordneten Einheiten zur Voraussetzung hat. Weiteres gemeinsames Kennzeichen mit der DG war der explizite Verzicht auf Darstellung der Linearität (Schank 1969). Auch Schanks Beschreibungsarsenal enthielt — wie bei Tesnière — vier Vollwortarten: Das Verb (ACT), davon abhängig wurden Leerstellen eingeführt, die mit sogenannten 'picture producers' (den 'Substantiven') und 'action aiders' ('Adverbien') sowie mit circumstantiellen Größen wie Zeit (T) und Ort (LOC) besetzt werden konnten. Von 'picture producers' hingen wiederum 'picture aiders' ('Adjektive') ab. Anders als in einem Dependenz-Stemma bestand keine Trennung zwischen vorkommenden (terminalen) und inferierten (lexikalisch leeren) Einheiten. Atypisch war außerdem, daß Prädikate in mehrere Aktionskonzepte zerlegt werden konnten, die ihrerseits wieder charakteristische Rollenkonfigurationen forderten.

Die Kasusgrammatik Fillmores zielte auf eine universelle Tiefenstruktur-Beschreibung des Satzes ab. Im Zentrum des Propositionskomplexes stand das Prädikat, das verschiedene etikettierte Leerstellen (Kasus) eröffnete: Kasus-Rollen wie AGENTIV, OBJEKTIV, IN-

STRUMENTAL, LOKATIV etc., die mit Tesnièreschen Aktanten- und Circumstantentypen vergleichbar waren. Prädikatsteil und Kasusteil wurden als PSG-Komplexe weiterspezifiziert. Insgesamt handelte es sich um eine hybride Beschreibung, in der die Konzeptionen der Verb-Valenz und der Konstituentenstruktur des Satzes verbunden waren.

Beide Modellierungen wurden Ende der 60-er Jahre erstmals publiziert. Fillmore (1968) verwies verschiedentlich auf Tesnières Valenztheorie und die Darstellung durch Stemmata, Schank (1969) bezog seine Konzeption von Dependenz auf diejenige von Hays (1964). Die Begründungen für ihre Modellierung entsprangen bei Fillmore und Schank jedoch in erster Linie aus Gegenpositionen zur damals vorherrschenden Transformationsgrammatik. Die Kasusgrammatik war als Revision von Chomskys Standardtheorie bei Wahrung des Primats der Syntax gedacht; die *Conceptual Dependency* wendete sich vor allem gegen die Syntaxdominanz, die Vernachlässigung von Performanzerscheinungen und einen zu engen Begriff von sprachlicher Kompetenz.

2.1.6. Vorläufiges Resümee

Der Überblick über das erste Jahrzehnt nach Tesnière zeigt die Vielfalt der sprachwissenschaftlichen Ansätze, mit Valenz bzw. Dependenz zu operieren. Zu den Wissenschaftlern, die bereits damals mit richtungsweisenden Arbeiten hervorgetreten sind und die sich bis in die heutige Zeit in diesem Arbeitsgebiet betätigen bzw. betätigt haben, gehören Ulrich Engel (*1928), Klaus Heger (1927–1993), Gerhard Helbig (*1929), Hans Jürgen Heringer (*1939), Jürgen Kunze (*1937), Igor A. Mel'čuk (*1932). Dagegen wurden die Konzeptionen von Dependenz und Valenz in den USA, Großbritannien und erstaunlicherweise in Frankreich anfangs kaum beachtet (oder − wie erwähnt − nur stillschweigend berücksichtigt).

2.2. Weiterentwicklung (1971–1980)

In diesem Zeitabschnitt erschienen mehrere umfassend angelegte Überblicksdarstellungen zu Dependenz und Valenz (Maas 1974, Baum 1976, Korhonen 1977, Hudson 1980); 1980 legte Engel eine Übersetzung von Tesnières Hauptwerk ins Deutsche vor.

2.2.1. Dependenzgrammatiken: Formalisiert, implementiert, deskriptiv

Klein (1971) gab im Rahmen eines Formalisierungsversuchs von DG und PSG eine detaillierte Darstellung der DG nach Tesnière; auch die Translation wurde ausführlich behandelt. Im Anschluß an Robinson (1968) fanden sich weitere Versuche, DG und PSG aufeinander zu beziehen: Vater (1973) und O. Werner (1973) oder Rothkegels Valenzgrammatik (1976), ein hybrider Grammatikentwurf, der Valenzrahmen in PSG-Strukturbeschreibung eingebettet als Zwischenstruktur für maschinelle Übersetzung vorsah. Die Abhängigkeitsgrammatik von Kunze erschien 1975. Sie war strikt am Oberflächenwort orientiert, ging also hinter Tesnières Nucleus-Konzeption zurück. Bemerkenswert war die Einbeziehung des Satzendezeichens in die DG-Darstellung, die das von Robinson (1968) in die Dependenzbeschreibung als obersten Knoten eingeführte Element 'T' für 'Satztyp', das auch von Vater (1973) und O. Werner (1973) aufgegriffen wurde, in die Praxis umsetzte, allerdings ohne eine explizite Satztyp-Indizierung vorzunehmen. Hellwig (1980) bezog die Satzendezeichen als Illokutionsindikatoren in die dependentielle Satzbeschreibung ein: '.' für 'Aussage', '?' für 'Frage' und '!' für 'Befehl'. Kennzeichnend für Dependenzgrammatiken dieser Zeit, insbesondere im Kontext maschineller Sprachverarbeitungssysteme (Kunze 1975, Hellwig 1980, McCord 1980), war die Integration von weiteren PSG-Elementen, wie die Anreicherung der Beschreibung durch meist morphosyntaktische Annotationen zur Darstellung von Kongruenzen. Auch die Wortstellung wurde in die Beschreibung einbezogen − bei Hellwig (1980) über abstrakte Positionsangaben für abhängige Größen; Diskontinuitäten wurden über den Parser bearbeitet.

Neben vertiefenden Arbeiten zur dependentiellen Syntax aus Mittel-, Nord- und Osteuropa (Engel 1972, Goralciková 1973) erschienen nun auch mehrere deskriptive Dependenzgrammatiken fürs Französische (Gréciano 1972, Garde 1977), fürs Deutsche (Engel 1977) und Englische (Emons 1978, Mel'čuk 1979 und Hudson 1976). Dabei legte Hudson (1976) einen Entwurf für eine Erzeugungsgrammatik vor, der − in der Nachfolge von Robinson (1968), Heringer (1970b), Vater (1973) und O. Werner (1973) − auf die Unterscheidung in Tiefen- und Oberflächenstruktur und damit auf eine Transformationskomponente verzichtete und Elemente der DG und der PSG miteinander verbinden wollte. Das Modell reicherte die Dependenzbeschreibung mit PSG-typischen Kategorien höherer Stufe an, um Beziehungen zwischen

Subjekt und Verb oder die Wortstellung angemessener darzustellen. Hudson bezeichnete seinen Entwurf als 'Daughter-Dependency-Grammar', um das Abgehen von der reinen DG hervorzuheben, die nur Beziehungen zwischen Entitäten der gleichen Ebene zuläßt und die Hudson als 'Sister-Dependency' charakterisierte.

2.2.2. Valenz: Syntaktisch – semantisch

In der Valenztheorie ließ die intensivere Bearbeitung Widersprüche und Lücken in den Dependenz- und Valenzansätzen offen zutage treten (Zifonun 1972); man bemühte sich um verbindliche Unterscheidungsmethoden zur Trennung von Ergänzung und Angabe (Andresen 1973). Analog zur präziseren Beschreibung der syntaktischen Valenz über die Ausgestaltung der Leerstellen wurde die Einbeziehung semantischer Elemente erörtert (Bondzio 1971, Ballweg 1974, Wotjak 1975). Fast gleichlaufende Richtungsdiskussionen in der Kasustheorie hatten Aufspaltungen in verschiedene Spielarten zur Folge (Anderson 1971, Starosta 1973).

2.2.3. Valenzlexikographie, Sprachdidaktik

Die Produktivität der Lexikographen blieb davon unberührt: Es erschienen Valenzwörterbücher für englische (Emons 1974), deutsche (Engel & Schumacher 1976) und französische Verben (Busse & Dubost 1977). Das Valenzwörterbuch für deutsche Adjektive (Sommerfeldt & Schreiber 1974) wurde fertiggestellt, 1977 auch das Wörterbuch der Substantive. Teuberts Studie zur Substantiv-Valenz folgte (1979). Das Valenzwörterbuch von Helbig & Schenkel erschien 1971 in zweiter Auflage mit der Unterscheidung von Tiefen- und Oberflächenstruktur-Valenz: die kompletten Valenz-Rahmen wurden der Tiefenstruktur zugewiesen, Auslassungen von Ergänzungen als Oberflächenphänomene erklärt. Damit deutete sich eine Schwerpunktverlagerung an von der syntaktischen hin zur semantischen Valenz.

Im muttersprachlichen Grammatikunterricht allerdings verloren 'systemlinguistische' Ansätze wie PSG, DG und Valenztheorie an Schwung; die Prioritäten in vielen Lehrplänen hatten sich geändert: Die regelgeleitete Analyse syntaktischer Strukturen wurde zurückgestellt zugunsten von Kommunikations- und Handlungsaspekten. Dagegen wurde die wichtige Stellung der Valenztheorie in der Fremdsprachendidaktik weiter ausgebaut: 1972 erschien die *Deutsche Grammatik* von Helbig & Buscha für den Sprachunterricht, ebenfalls für Deutsch als Fremdsprache (Rall et al. 1977), fürs Französische (Happ 1978), auch für den Unterricht in den klassischen Sprachen (Happ 1976, 1977; Dönnges & Happ 1977) wurden didaktisch motivierte Valenzbeschreibungen erstellt.

2.2.4. Neue Anwendungsgebiete

Hinzu kamen zwei neue Anwendungsgebiete der Valenzbeschreibung: historische und kontrastive Grammatik und Lexikographie. Die Valenzforschung für klassische Sprachen und ältere Sprachzustände konnte zur Feststellung der Verbvalenzen nicht auf die in der Valenzsyntax und -lexikographie praktizierten Tests und Methoden zurückgreifen, da die linguistische Kompetenz lebender Individuen als Entscheidungsinstanz ausfallen mußte (Greule 1973, Korhonen 1978). Als Kompensation boten sich die Methoden des klassischen Strukturalismus aus der Zeit vor Chomskys Verdikt an: Korpusinterne Vergleiche, Segmentation und Klassifikation, Frequenzzählungen. Die Ergebnisse zur Valenzbeschreibung von Verben und zur valenzgestützten Lesartenfindung konnten dann über Vergleiche mit Ergebnissen aus anderen Korpora abgesichert werden.

Als weiteres Betätigungsfeld kam die kontrastive Valenzbeschreibung hinzu. Erste Arbeiten erschienen hauptsächlich in Nordeuropa – für Deutsch und Schwedisch (Nikula 1976) und für Deutsch-Dänisch (Fabricius-Hansen 1979).

2.2.5. Frames, Scenes, Scripts

Einen wichtigen Impuls für die semantisch orientierte Valenz- und Kasusforschung gab die durch Minsky (1975) bekannt gewordene Konzeption des 'frame' als Grundeinheit der Organisation von Wissen, auf die sich Valenz- oder Kasusrahmen als spezifische Formate für sprachliches Wissen ohne weiteres beziehen ließen. Auch diese waren angelegt als zusammenhängendes Ganzes mit Leerstellen, die über auslösende Elemente aktiviert und in die Teile von Äußerungen eingepaßt werden können. Die 'frame'-Konzeption beeinflußte Fillmore, der mit der 'scenes-and-frames'-Semantik (1977) wiederum in die Valenzforschung hineinwirkte. 'Szene' war eine Metapher für ein "coherent segment [...] of human beliefs, actions, experiences, or imaginings" (Fillmore 1977: 63). Kasusrahmen bezogen sich auf "any system of linguistic choices [...] that can get associated with prototypical instances of scenes" (ebda.), stellten einen perspektivischen, orientierenden sprachlichen Ausschnitt aus einer umfassenderen kognitiven Szene dar. Damit rückten andere Grenzziehungen in den Vordergrund; die Unterschiede zwischen syntaktischer oder semantischer Valenz wurde von der Unterscheidung zwischen spezifisch sprachlichem und allgemein außersprachlichem Wissen überlagert. Auch die Mitte der 70-er Jahre von Schank eingeführten 'scripts' beeinflußten die semantische Kasus- und Valenzforschung. Als 'script' wurde ein spezieller Typ von 'frame' verstanden — eine vorfabrizierte Struktur, die eine stilisierte Alltagssituation oder Ereignissequenz in einem Kontext beschreibt (Schank & Abelson 1975). Frames, Scripts und Szenen führten mit textlinguistischen Fragestellungen zusammen zur Ausweitung der Valenz- und Kasus-Beschreibungen auf Satzzusammenhänge und Texte (Falster Jakobson & Olsen 1978). Lexikalisch fundierte kohäsionsstiftende Elemente wurden auch im Rahmen satzübergreifender maschineller Analysen eingesetzt. Vor allem die Möglichkeit, ausgelassene Größen über Valenzrahmen zu erschließen, ließ sich zur lexikalischen Disambiguierung ausnutzen (Weber 1980).

2.3. Konsolidierung (1981—1990)

An Überblicksdarstellungen zur Dependenz und Valenz sind für diesen Zeitabschnitt Tarvainen (1981a), Nikula (1986a), Mel'čuk (1988), Welke (1988) und Lobin (1989) zu nennen. Kennzeichnend für die Zeit bis 1990 war die Konsolidierung der ab Mitte der 70-er eingeführten Forschungsfelder und Projekte.

2.3.1. Dependenzgrammatiken und fortgeschrittene NLP-Systeme

Neue Dependenzgrammatiken oder DG-nahe Modelle vor allem aus dem angelsächsischen Raum erschienen. DG-Elemente fanden verstärkt Eingang in Systeme zur maschinellen Sprachverarbeitung. Als charakteristisch für DG-Modelle dieses Zeitabschnitts können gelten: Funktionale Etikettierung der Kanten in Strukturbäumen, Dekoration der Knoten mit komplexen Merkmalstrukturen, verstärkte Bemühungen um Wortstellungsregeln. Als indirekte Bestätigung dependenzgrammatischer Grundlagen ließen sich einige Züge neuentwickelter PSG-Grammatiken auslegen, so das Abgehen von der 'Tiefenstruktur' und die strikte Trennung von Struktur- und Wortstellungsbeschreibung in der *Generalized Phrase-Structure Grammar* (Gazdar et al. 1985). Auch die *Lexical Functional Grammar* (Kaplan & Bresnan 1982) mit der Trennung von PSG-syntaktischer c-Struktur und der f-Struktur, die über Relationen wie Subjekt, Objekt eine Spezifikation der 'Valenz' von Prädikaten enthält, realisierte einen Ansatz, der sich schon seit Mitte der 60-er Jahre mit der Verbindung von Konstituenz und Dependenz bzw. Valenz abgezeichnet hatte. 1984 erschien Hudsons *Word Grammar*, ein darauf bezogener Parser von Fraser 1989. Die *Word Grammar* war eine Revision der *Daughter-Dependency-Grammar*, angelegt als generative, monostratale, strikt wortbasierte Dependenzbeschreibung mit etikettierten Kanten für syntaktische Funktionen, die für ein Wort ggf. mehrere Regentien zuließ. Die *Slot-Grammar* (McCord 1980, 1990) war ein in Prolog geschriebenes Analysesystem, das die Dependenzbeschreibung nach dem 'slot'-'filler'-Prinzip vornahm: Slots wurden von lexikalischen Regentien eingebracht. Über eigene ordering-Regeln wurden die Abfolge von regierenden und abhängigen Elementen bestimmt. Diskontinuität und Koordination regelten Parser-Prozeduren. Die *Slot Grammar* war als MÜ-Grammatik ausgelegt aufs Englische, Dänische, Deutsche. Ein weiteres DG-nahes Modell war Starostas 'Lexicase' (1988). Es lieferte eine Strukturbeschreibung, die auf Spezifikation binärer Relationen zwischen Wörtern beruhte. Wörter wurden durch nicht-kontextuelle (z. B. Kasusrelationen für die Argumente eines Verbs) und kontextuelle Attribute (für abhängige Elemente) spezifiziert. Kontextuelle Merkmalmengen konnten Positionsangaben enthalten und inhärente Merkmale für Kasusrollenbesetzungen. Die Positionsangaben beschränkten sich auf benachbarte Wortpaare. Kunze (1982) und Klimonov (1982) präzisierten die Abhängigkeitsgrammatik mit detaillierten Darstellungen der Unterordnungsrelationen zur Etikettierung der Kanten in Strukturbäumen. Hellwig (1986) aktualisierte das bestehende DG-Modell (Hellwig 1980) in Anlehnung an formalisierte Grammatik-Modelle (LFG, GPSG): Über Unifikation komplexer Merkmalstrukturen (lexematische, morphosyntaktische und funktionale) wurde eine Strukturbeschreibung erstellt, die eine oberflächenstrukturelle und eine funktionale Repräsentation umfaßte. Wortstellungsangaben — ausgenommen Diskontinuitäten — waren als positionale Parameter in den Merkmalkonfigurationen enthalten.

In der maschinellen Sprachverarbeitung hatten sich Dependenz, Valenz und Kasus gegenüber konkurrierenden PSG-Modellen gut behauptet. Insbesondere die Analysekomponenten in neueren Systemen zur maschinellen Übersetzung arbeiteten überwiegend auf dependentieller Grundlage (SUSY, EUROTRA, NEC, DLT; dazu Somers 1987, Nagao et al. 1986, Schubert 1986). Dies galt vornehmlich für Quellsprachen wie z. B. Deutsch, Japanisch, Russisch oder Finnisch, in denen relativ freie Wortstellung vorherrscht. In diesen Sprachen unterliegt (anders als im Englischen etwa) allein das Verb verläßlichen Stellungsbeschränkungen und trägt die Hauptinformationen zur Strukturierung des Satzes. Japanische MÜ-Systeme bevorzugten eine mit Kasuslabels angereicherte Dependenzbeschreibung, um Auslassungen zu kompensieren, vor allem bei unvollständiger semantischer Analyse (Shimazu et al. 1983; Nagao et al. 1986). Als weitere Vorteile im Hinblick auf Übersetzung galten die lexikalische Fundierung der Strukturbeschreibungen zur Quellsprache, die eine lexikalischen Zuordnung auf seiten der Zielsprache erleichtert, die Möglichkeit der Lesartentrennung im Lexikon für Verben mithilfe der Valenzspezifikationen und die Disambiguierung von Verben und Leerstellenbesetzungen im Satzkontext (Weisgerber 1983).

In Zusammenhang mit Fragen der maschinellen Übersetzung wurden auch Tesnières Überlegungen zur 'métataxe' (Tesnière 1959: 283–319) wieder aktuell, die sich mit der Gegenüberstellung von semantisch äquivalenten, strukturell differierenden Dependenz-Beschreibungen in verschiedenen Sprachen befaßten (Schubert 1987).

2.3.2. Valenzlinguistik: Grammatisch, lexikographisch, didaktisch, kontrastiv

Auch die deskriptiven Grammatiken setzten sich weiter mit Tesnières DG-Modell auseinander. 1985 schlug Eroms verschiedene Teiländerungen vor: Satzadverbien sollten als oberste Knoten in die Strukturbeschreibung einbezogen werden; der Artikel sollte das Nomen regieren und nicht wie ein Attribut vom Nomen abhängig sein (Eroms 1988). Die bislang umfassendste Dependenzgrammatik fürs Deutsche legte Engel (1988) vor.

Die Valenz-Lexikographie blieb weiter produktiv: Hier sind Beschreibungen zum englischen Verb (Allerton 1982) und das Großprojekt 'Verben in Feldern' (Schumacher 1986) zu nennen.

In der historischen Valenzforschung wurden die syntaktischen Untersuchungen zum Evangelienbuch Otfrids von Weißenburg fortgeführt (Greule 1982) und der Aufbau einer dependentiellen althochdeutschen Syntax in Angriff genommen (Greule 1983).

In der Fremdsprachendidaktik wurde die wichtige Stellung der Valenztheorie – zumindest fürs Deutsche – durch kontrastiven Arbeiten gestützt (Tarvainen 1981b); die Grammatik von Helbig & Buscha (1972) erschien 1986 in der 9. Auflage; mit dem Ziel einer sprachübergreifenden Definition der Valenz setzte sich Schubert (1988) auseinander.

2.3.3. Texte und Tiefenstrukturen

Über textlinguistische Orientierungen wurde eine Anpassung der valenzsemantischen Beschreibung an typisierte semantische Kontexte und Fachtexte angestrebt (Weber 1985, Nikula 1986b). Versuche dieser Art waren inspiriert von Schanks 'scripts' und Fillmores 'scenes-and-frames'. Die Rezeption der 'scenes-and-frames'-Semantik und die Aufgabe der Tiefenstruktur-Konzeption stellte vor allem die syntaktisch orientierte Valenzforschung in einen anderen Rahmen, erweiterte den Blick für semantische und pragmatische Zusammenhänge (Heringer 1984, Wotjak 1988) und beförderte die Auflösung der Liaison mit der TG Chomskys. Das Aufgeben der Tiefenstruktur-Konzeption wurde nicht durchgängig nachvollzogen. Die Mehrebenensysteme aus dem Umkreis von Mel'čuk und der Prager Funktionalen Satzperspektive hielten weiter am Dualismus von 'Tiefen-' und 'Oberflächenstruktur'-Beschreibungen fest. Mel'čuk & Pertsov veröffentlichten 1987 die *Surface Syntax of English* im Rahmen des SMYSL ↔ TEKST-Modells. Auch sie war in die fünf Ebenen gegliedert und enthielt eine Beschreibung der linearen Abfolge über globale Anordnungsregeln, die ungeordnete Dependenzstrukturen der oberflächensyntaktischen Ebene auf annotierte Lexemfolgen der tiefenmorphologischen Ebene abbildeten. Vorschläge zur Formalisierung dieser Regeln werden sich später in Rambow & Joshi (1994) finden. Im Rahmen der Prager Functional Generative Description waren Dependenzbeschreibungen auf einer tieferen (tektogrammatischen) Ebene in den Zusammenhang der FGD eingebettet (Plátek & Sgall 1984, Sgall et al. 1986); zur Einbeziehung von Fillmores Semantik in die Funktionale Satzperspektive: Hajičová (1988).

2.4. Neuorientierung (1991–1998)

Die besorgte Frage von Agel (1993): "Ist die Dependenzgrammatik wirklich am Ende?" mag für frühere Zeiten begründet gewesen sein; sie gilt nicht für die 90-er Jahre. Noch nie zuvor gab es zum Thema 'Dependenz' so viele Kongresse, Symposien, Rückblicke und Überblicke wie in dieser Zeitspanne – Zeichen eines verstärkten Interesses: der deutsche Romanistentag widmete sich diesem Thema (vgl. dazu Koch & Krefeld 1991), Tagungen fanden statt 1992 in Passau (Eichinger & Eroms 1995) und Rouen, zum 100. Geburtstag von Lucien Tesnière 1993 in Straßburg (Gréciano & Schumacher 1996); Studienbücher zur DG erschienen (Weber 1992, 1997) und mehrere Überblicke (Heringer 1993a, b; Hudson 1993, Allerton 1995, Fraser 1995, Helbig 1996). Die Grammatik von Engel (1988) wurde 1994 zum drittenmal aufgelegt; Heringer (1996) veröffentlichte eine deutsche Syntax für Studierende und Lehrende, 'rein dependentiell', d. h. ohne PSG-Regeln, konzipiert.

2.4.1. Inspirationsquelle Klassisches Modell

Daß die Möglichkeiten des klassischen Modells noch nicht ausgeschöpft waren, zeigten neuere Vorschläge zur Erweiterung, die sich zum Teil mit Tesnière in Übereinstimmung befinden dürften. Dazu zählt der Vorschlag Agels (1991), Aktanten, die unterhalb der Wortebene realisiert sind (z. B. als gebundene Flexive), in die Valenzbeschreibung einzubeziehen. Auf den Umstand, daß in lateinischen oder ungarischen Verbformen Aktanten inkorporiert sein können, hatte auch Tesnière (1959: 139–142) schon hingewiesen. Eine weitere Überlegung, die nicht in Widerspruch zu Tesnières Entwurf stehen dürfte, betraf mit virtuellen und aktuellen Nuclei gemischte Stemmata: Bei deverbalen Translationen ließen sich bestimmte strukturelle Ambiguitäten angemessener darstellen, wenn in einem aktuellen Stemma auch virtuelle Aktanten-Nuclei zugelassen wären – unter der Bedingung, daß diese aus der Valenz vorkommender nicht-leerer Knoten ableitbar sind (Weber 1996: 258–260). Auch diese Möglichkeit wurde von Tesnière in Verbindung mit der Darstellung des nicht realisierten 1. Aktanten im Imperativsatz bereits erwogen (1959: 168–171). Lobin (1995) argumentierte gegen DG-Beschreibungen, die sich strikt aufs Einzelwort beziehen (wie Kunze 1975, Hudson 1984, Schubert 1987, Mel'čuk 1988, Starosta 1988) und befürwortete komplexere Einheiten, wobei die Binnenstruktur eines Nucleus für Relationen zu anderen Nuclei ohne Belang wäre. Auch diese Überlegungen könnten sich auf Positionen Tesnières stützen. In dieser Hinsicht dürften Hinweise von Engel (1996) auf häufige Mißverständnisse zur Dependenzgrammatik Tesnières hilfreich sein.

Ein Revision von Tesnières Modell stellt dagegen die Einbeziehung der Wortstellung dar. Tesnières Entwurf bedachte sie allenfalls nebenbei – bei der Anordnung der Aktanten und Circumstanten und bei der Position der Translatoren im Stemma. Vennemann (1977: 271–274) wies auf den Behelfscharakter solcher Konventionen hin. Die Vernachlässigung der Wortstellung im Kernbereich der Syntax findet jedoch auch Zustimmung: Thümmel argumentierte gegen eine integrierte Beschreibung von Wortfolgephänomenen in Satzgrammatiken, bezeichnete sie als "historische Bürde des sogenannten amerikanischen Strukturalismus", als "Quasi-Physikalisierung" (1991: 220). Trotzdem versuchen vor allem formalisierte und implementierte DG-Systeme – auch bei der Beschreibung der Koordination – in diesem Bereich Anschluß an PSG-nahe Modellierungen zu finden (Lobin 1993).

2.4.2. Gemischte Modelle

An formalen DG-Darstellungen hoben sich Covington (1992), Jung (1995) und Schneider (1998) ab, mit Gegenüberstellungen verschiedener Versionen der DG (Tesnière 1959, Hellwig 1986, Mel'čuk 1988, Engel 1988, der Prager Schule, der *Word Grammar* u. a.) zu prominenten PSG-Typen (HPSG, LFG, X-Bar-Syntax, GB) und ihren Grundlagen. Es ergaben sich eine Reihe von Analogien und Berührungspunkten zwischen DG- und PSG-Modellen, die insbesondere über die Konzeption des 'head' herausgearbeitet wurden (dazu Jung 1995: 33–83; Schneider 1998: 38–53). Es scheint, daß sich DG und PSG in wichtigen Teilen aufeinander zu entwickeln und die reinen Grammatik-Modellierungen an Anziehungskraft verlieren. Damit würden die bereits sehr früh formulierten Zweifel an der Angemessenheit eines einzigen Grammatik-Typs stärker beachtet, die Robinson (1968) zu einer hybriden Modellierung veranlaßten. Auch Joshi, der in dieser Zeit die formalen Eigenschaften unterschiedlicher Grammatik-Typen gegeneinander abwog, befürwortete damals "a study of formal grammars of mixed types in order to take advantage of different styles" (Joshi 1969: 1). Daß sich die

Stärke von Modellierungen auch an ihrer Integrationsfähigkeit ersehen läßt, zeigen mehrere PSG-Beispiele, als jüngstes die 'Head-Driven Phrase Structure Grammar' (Pollard & Sag 1994) mit der Integration der 'Valenz' als 'Subkategorisierung'.

2.4.3. Neue NLP-Anwendungen; DG im WWW

Sprachverarbeitende Systeme waren schon früh Exerzierfelder für Dependenz- und Valenzkonzeptionen. Mit Hinzukommen weiterer Zielsetzungen dürften dependentielle Ansätze an Bedeutung gewinnen. Vor allem beim 'Text-Tagging' und 'partiellen Parsing' haben Dependenz-Ansätze Vorteile: So ist die Ermittlung binärer Dependenzrelationen über Verträglichkeiten nur zwischen Einheiten, die als 'Head' und 'Modifier' in Frage kommen, einfacher und sicherer – weil lokal zu erreichen – als eine PSG-basierte Analyse, die erst mit vollständiger Identifikation einer Phrasen-Konstruktion die Identifikation der einzelnen Konstituenten ratifizieren kann. Auf der Grundlage satzsyntaktischer Dependenzbeschreibungen sind auch semantische Interpretationen in Hinblick auf konzeptuelle Darstellungen (in Anlehnung an Schank 1969 etwa) direkter zu bewerkstelligen, da zwischen beiden Repräsentationsformaten Analogien bestehen können (detailliert dazu Hahn & Romacker 1998: 68–70). Das zunehmende Interesse an der DG zeigt sich auch an einer Vielzahl von Online-Publikationen, verschiedenen DG-Websites (z. B. der Karlsuniversität Prag) und Online-Parsern (Tapanainen & Järvinen 1998).

2.4.4. Valenz: Kontinuität und Neuorientierung

In der Valenzforschung wurden begonnene Projekte fortgeführt: In der historischen Valenzforschung die Arbeiten zum Frühneuhochdeutschen, zu Luther und zum Grimmschen Wörterbuch (Korhonen 1995); ebenso ein DFG-Projekt 'Althochdeutsches syntaktisches Verbwörterbuch' (Greule 1995). 1992 erschien die *Deutsche Grammatik* von Helbig & Buscha (1972) in der 14. Auflage. Für die theoretische Valenz- und Kasusforschung faßte Helbig (1996) die verschiedenen Standpunkte zu Fragen der Beschreibungsebenen (syntaktische, semantische oder pragmatische) zusammen, aus denen sich unterschiedliche Konsequenzen für die Einordnung von 'Valenz' und 'Kasus' ergeben – beispielhaft in der Frage der Unterscheidung von Aktanten und Circumstanten, die immer noch das wichtigste subklassen-bildende Kriterium für Valenzträger darstellt. Traditionelle Positionen zur semantischen bzw. syntaktischen Valenz befürworteten eine Beibehaltung der valenz-konstitutiven Unterscheidung zwischen valenzgebundenen (actants) und freien Gliedern (circonstants); eine Festlegung des Valenzrahmens ggf. mit abgestuftem Übergang statt der häufig getroffenen entweder-oder-Entscheidung. Unterscheidungskriterien wären von der Beschreibung der Valenzträger abzuleiten (Askedal 1996, Heger 1996). Die Gegenposition betonte das Interesse an der Valenzvariation, bei deren Beschreibung die Einbeziehung von perspektivischen Kriterien, semantischen Kontexten und Textsortenspezifika gefordert wurde (Gansel 1996: 121). Ein wesentliches Ziel der Valenz-Forschung würde sich damit erweitern von einer unter dem Aspekt der grammatischen Wohlgeformtheit vorgenommenen, auf Vollständigkeit abzielenden (lexikographischen) Kodifizierung hin zu einer Beschreibung von 'offener' Valenz im Text, die auch unter Beachtung der kommunikativen Angemessenheit zu erstellen wäre.

3. Ausblick

Anders als die Valenztheorie, die sich schon früh ein weites sprachwissenschaftliches Betätigungsfeld erschließen konnte, das von der Fremdsprachendidaktik bis zur historischen Lexikographie reichte, befand sich die Dependenzgrammatik lange abseits der linguistischen Hauptströmungen. Sie hatte zu keiner Zeit eine mit der Phrasenstrukturgrammatik vergleichbare Reputation. Die PSG hat immer davon profitiert, daß sie in wichtigen Teilen in kurzen Zeitabschnitten aktualisiert, revidiert oder revitalisiert wurde und daß dabei eine (oder mehrere) Stifterfigur(en) für bestimmte Spielarten oder Spezialgebiete als oberste Instanz akzeptiert wurde(n). Trotz häufiger Modellwechsel blieb so der Eindruck von Homogenität und Kontinuität gewahrt. Die 'DG-Szene' war stets vielfältiger und offener, gruppierte sich nie um ein Zentrum. Einzelne DG-Versionen führten ein – im Vergleich zur Breitenwirkung von Phrasenstrukturgrammatiken – introvertiertes, zurückgezogenes Eigenleben, wie vom Schicksal ihres Gründers Tesnière geprägt. Die Situation hat sich in den letzten Jahren jedoch zugunsten der DG gewandelt, viele Anzeichen sprechen dafür. Es scheint, daß ein weiterer Zug des Gründers Tesnière, die Beharrlichkeit im Verfolgen eines Weges, sich auch für die Dependenzgrammatik auszuwirken beginnt. DG und Valenztheorie stehen auf breiter Basis — etablierte Anwendungsbereiche sind weitgehend gesichert: maschinelle Sprachverarbeitung, deskriptive Grammatiken, Sprachdidaktik, Lexikographie. Die Tendenzen für neue Entwicklungen der Dependenzgrammatik und Valenztheorie zeigen jedoch in unterschiedliche Richtungen. Für formalisierte und implementierte DGen bieten sich Chancen, vor allem in syntaktischen Kernbereichen, der Linearisierung, der Koordination und der Parsingeffizienz Defizite aufzuarbeiten. Die Valenztheorie dagegen orientiert sich — auch bei grundlegenden Fragen wie der Abgrenzung von Ergänzungen und Angaben — nicht mehr allein an der Satzsyntax, sondern an umfassenderen Beschreibungskontexten, die textuelle und kommunikative Aspekte einbeziehen, strebt jedenfalls über eine Satzstruktur-Beschreibung hinaus.

4. Bibliographie

Admoni, Wladimir. 1960. *Der deutsche Sprachbau.* Moskau & Leningrad. (2. erweiterte Aufl., 1966.)

Agel, Vilmos. 1991. "Lexikalische Ellipsen. Fragen und Vorschläge". *Zeitschrift für germanistische Linguistik* 19: 1.24—48.

—. 1993. "Ist die Dependenzgrammatik wirklich am Ende?". *Zeitschrift für germanistische Linguistik* 21.20—70.

Agricola, Erhard, Jürgen Kunze, Stefan Nündel, Josef Stadelmann & Ingrid Starke. 1963. *Automatische Sprachübersetzung Englisch-Deutsch.* Bericht vom 16. Mai 1963. Berlin: Deutsche Akademie der Wissenschaften (DDR).

Allerton, David J. 1982. *Valency and the English Verb.* London.

—. 1995. "Valency and Valency Grammar". Koerner & Asher 1995.

Anderson, John M. 1971. *The Grammar of Case: Towards a localistic theory.* Cambridge: Univ. Press.

Andresen, Helga. 1973. "Ein methodischer Vorschlag zur Unterscheidung von Ergänzung und Angabe im Rahmen der Valenztheorie". *Deutsche Sprache* 1.49—63.

Askedal, John Ole. 1995. "Valenz und Grammatikalisierung". Eichinger & Eroms 1995. 11—35.

Ballweg, Joachim. 1974. "Einige Bemerkungen zu einem Valenzmodell mit semantischer Basis". *Kopenhagener Beiträge zur germanistischen Linguistik* 4. 83—113.

Baum, Richard. 1976. *Dependenzgrammatik. Tesnières Modell der Sprachbeschreibung in wissenschaftlicher und kritischer Sicht.* Tübingen: Niemeyer.

Baumgärtner, Klaus. 1965. "Spracherklärung mit den Mitteln der Abhängigkeitsstruktur". *Beiträge zur Linguistik und Informationsverarbeitung* 5. 31—53.

—. 1970. "Konstituenz und Dependenz. Zur Integration der beiden grammatischen Prinzipien". *Vorschläge für eine strukturale Grammatik des Deutschen* hg. von Hugo Steger, 52—77. Darmstadt: Wissenschaftliche Buchgesellschaft.

Bierwisch, Manfred. 1970 [1966]. "Aufgaben und Form der Grammatik". *Vorschläge für eine strukturale Grammatik des Deutschen* hg. von Hugo Steger, 1—51. Darmstadt: Wissenschaftliche Buchgesellschaft.

Bondzio, Wilhelm. 1969. "Das Wesen der Valenz und ihre Stellung im Rahmen der Satzstruktur". *Wiss. Zeitschrift der Humboldt-Universität zu Berlin. Gesellschafts- und sprachwissenschaftliche Reihe* 18.233—240.

—. 1971. "Valenz, Bedeutung und Satzmodelle". *Beiträge zur Valenztheorie* hg. von Gerhard Helbig, 85—103. The Hague: Mouton.

Bühler, Karl. 1934. *Sprachtheorie. Die Darstellungsfunktion der Sprache.* Jena: Fischer. (2. unveränderte Auflage, Stuttgart: Fischer, 1965.)

Busse, Winfried & Jean-Pierre Dubost. 1977. *Französisches Verblexikon. Die Konstruktion der Verben im Französischen.* Stuttgart: Klett-Cotta.

Chomsky, Noam. 1956. "Three Models of Description of Language". *IRE Transactions on Information Theory* IT-2.113—124. Cambridge, Mass.: MIT.

—. 1957. *Syntactic Structures.* The Hague: Mouton.

—. 1965. *Aspects of the Theory of Syntax.* Cambridge, Mass.: MIT.

COLING. International Conference on Computational Linguistics. Association for Computational Linguistics.

Covington, Michael. 1992. "GB Theory as Dependency Grammar". Research Report AI1992—03. Athens, Ga: University of Georgia.

DG-Website. 1998. Karlsuniversität Prag. http://ufal.mff.cuni.cz/dg.html.

Dönnges, Ulrich & Heinz Happ. 1977. *Dependenz-Grammatik und Latein-Unterricht.* Göttingen: Vandenhoeck & Ruprecht.

Dugas, André, Myrna Gopnik, Brian Harris & Jean-Pierre Paillet. 1969. "Le projet de traduction automatique à l'Université de Montréal". *COLING-69 Stockholm.* Preprint No.55.

Eichinger, Ludwig M. & Hans-Werner Eroms, Hg. 1995. *Dependenz und Valenz*. Hamburg: Buske.

Emons, Rudolf. 1974. *Valenzen englischer Prädikatsverben*. Tübingen: Niemeyer.

—. 1978. *Valenzgrammatik für das Englische. Eine Einführung*. Tübingen: Niemeyer.

Engel, Ulrich. 1967. "Grundstrukturen der deutschen Sprache". *Deutschunterricht für Ausländer* 17.95–106.

—. 1969. "Zur Beschreibung der Struktur deutscher Sätze". *Neue Beiträge zur deutschen Grammatik. Hugo Moser zum 60. Geburtstag*, 35–52. Mannheim, Wien & Zürich: Bibliographisches Institut.

—. 1972. "Bemerkungen zur Dependenzgrammatik". *Neue Grammatiktheorien und ihre Anwendung auf das heutige Deutsch. Jahrbuch 1971 des IdS*. 111–155. Düsseldorf: Schwann.

—. 1977. *Syntax der deutschen Gegenwartssprache*. Berlin: Schmidt.

—. 1980. Lucien Tesnière. *Grundzüge der strukturalen Syntax*. Herausgegeben und übersetzt von Ulrich Engel. Stuttgart: Klett.

—. 1988. *Deutsche Grammatik*. Heidelberg: Groos.

—. 1996. "Tesnière mißverstanden". Gréciano & Schumacher 1996. 53–61.

—. & Helmut Schumacher. 1976. *Kleines Valenzlexikon deutscher Verben*. Tübingen: Narr.

Engelen, Bernhard. 1975. *Untersuchungen zu Satzbauplan und Wortfeld in der geschriebenen deutschen Sprache der Gegenwart*. 2 Bde. München: Hueber.

Erben, Johannes. 1958. *Abriß der deutschen Grammatik*. Berlin: Akademie-Verlag.

Eroms, Hans-Werner. 1985. "Eine reine Dependenzgrammatik für das Deutsche". *Deutsche Sprache* 13.306–326.

—. 1988. "Der Artikel im Deutschen und seine dependenzgrammatische Darstellung". *Sprachwissenschaft* 13.257–308.

Fabricius-Hansen, Catherine. 1979. "Valenztheorie und Kontrastive Grammatik (Dänisch-Deutsch)". *Gedenkschrift für Trygve Sagen, 1924–1977 (= Osloer Beiträge zur Germanistik*, 3), 40–55.

Falster Jakobson, Lisbeth & Jörgen Olsen. 1978. "Textkohärenz und Involvierungen". *Deutsche Sprache* 6.1–20.

Fillmore, Charles J. 1968. "The Case for Case". *Universals in Linguistic Theory*. hg. von Emmon Bach & Robert T. Harms, 1–88. London & New York: Holt, Rinehart & Winston.

—. 1977. "Scenes-and-Frames Semantics". *Linguistic Structures Processing* hg. von Antonio Zampolli, 55–81. Amsterdam: North-Holland.

Fourquet, Jean. 1996. "Ce que je dois à Lucien Tesnière". Gréciano & Schumacher 1996. 1–5.

Fraser, Norman. 1989. "Parsing and Dependency Grammar". *Working Papers in Linguistics*, 296–319. London: University College.

—. 1994. "Dependency Grammar". *Encyclopedia of Language and Linguistics* ed. by R. E. Asher, vol. II, 860–864. Oxford & New York: Pergamon.

Gaifman, Haim. 1961. "Dependency Systems and Phrase-Structure Systems". The RAND Corporation P-2315. Santa Monica. (Veröffentlicht 1965 in *Information and Control* 8: 3.304–337.)

Gansel, Christina. 1996. "Valenz als Resultat mentaler Operationen". Gréciano & Schumacher 1996. 117–127.

Garde, Paul. 1977. "Ordre linéaire et dépendance syntaxique: contribution à une typologie". *Bulletin de la Société de Linguistique de Paris* 72: 1.1–19.

Garey, Howard B. 1954. Rezension von Tesnière (1953). *Language* 30.512–513.

Gazdar, Gerald, Evan Klein, Geoffrey Pullum & Ivan Sag. 1985. *Generalized Phrase Structure Grammar*. Cambridge, Mass.: Harvard Univ. Press.

Gladkij, A. V. & Igor A. Mel'čuk. 1969. "Tree Grammars". *COLING-69 Stockholm*. Preprint No.1.

Goralčiková, Alla. 1973. "On One Type of Dependency Grammar". *Prager Autorengruppe, Functional Generative Grammar in Prague*. 64–81. Kronberg/Taunus: Skriptor.

Gréciano, Gertrud. 1972. *Les applications de la grammaire de dépendence au domaine allemand*. Diss. Paris-Sorbonne (masch.)

—. & Helmut Schumacher, Hg. 1996. *Lucien Tesnière: Syntaxe structurale et opérations mentales*. Tübingen: Niemeyer.

Greule, Albrecht. 1973. "Valenz und historische Grammatik". *Zeitschrift für Germanistische Linguistik* 1.284–294.

—. 1982. *Valenz, Satz und Text. Syntaktische Untersuchungen zum Evangelienbuch Otfrids von Weißenburg auf der Grundlage des Codex Vindobonensis*. München: Fink.

—. 1983. "Zum Aufbau einer dependenziellen althochdeutschen Syntax. Ein Werkstattbericht". *Sprachwissenschaft* 8.81–98.

—. 1995. "Valenz im historischen Korpus". Eichinger & Eroms 1995. 357–363.

Groot, Albert W. 1949. *Structurele syntaxis*. (Ongewijzigde herdruk met voorwoord en inleiding van Dr. G. F. Bos & Dr. H. Roose.) Den Haag.

Guiraud, Pierre. 1971. "Lucien Tesnière and Transformational Grammar". *Language Sciences* 15.1–6.

Hahn, Udo & Martin Romacker. 1998. "Automatische Erzeugung von medizinischen Wissensbasen durch partielles Textverstehen: Befundanalyse im MEDSYNDIKATE-System". *Künstliche Intelligenz* 1998: 2.65–72.

Hajičová, Eva. 1988. "Remarks on Valency and Order in the Underlying Structure". Helbig 1988. 63–73.

Happ, Heinz. 1976. *Grundfragen einer Dependenzgrammatik des Griechischen.* Göttingen: Vandenhoeck & Ruprecht.

—. 1977. "Syntaxe latine et théorie de la valence". *Les Études Classiques* 45.337–366.

—. 1978. "Théorie de la valence et l'enseignement du francais". *Le Francais Moderne* 46: 2.97–134.

Hays, David G. 1960. "Grouping and Dependency Theory". The RAND Corporation. Research Memorandum RM-2646. Santa Monica. (Veröffentlicht in *Proceedings of the National Symposium on Machine Translation: University of California, Los Angeles* hg. von H. P. Edmundson, 258–266. Englewood Cliffs, N. J.: Prentice-Hall, 1961.)

—. 1964. "Dependency Theory: A formalism and some observations". *Language* 40: 4.511–525.

Heger, Klaus. 1966. "Valenz, Diathese und Kasus". *Zeitschrift für Romanische Philologie* 82.138–170

—. 1970. *Monem, Wort und Satz.* Tübingen: Niemeyer.

—. 1996. "Zum Problem der Gegenüberstellung von 'actants' und 'circonstants'". Gréciano & Schumacher 1996. 203–209.

Helbig, Gerhard. 1965. "Der Begriff der Valenz als Mittel der strukturellen Sprachbeschreibung und des Fremdsprachenunterrichts". *Deutsch als Fremdsprache* (Leipzig) 1.10–22.

—. 1966. "Untersuchungen zur Valenz und Distribution deutscher Verben". *Deutsch als Fremdsprache* (Leipzig) 3.1–11 und 4.12–19.

—. 1971. "Zur Entwicklung der strukturellen Linguistik in der Sowjetunion". *Probleme der Sprachwissenschaft: Beiträge zur Linguistik,* 96–123. The Hague: Mouton.

—. Hg. 1988. *Valenz, semantische Kasus und/oder 'Szenen'.* Berlin: Zentralinstitut für Sprachwissenschaft. Akademie der Wissenschaften der DDR.

—. 1996. "Zur Rezeption und Weiterentwicklung des Tesnièreschen Valenzkonzepts". Gréciano & Schumacher 1996. 41–51.

—. & Wolfgang Schenkel. 1969. *Wörterbuch zur Valenz und Distribution deutscher Verben.* Leipzig: VEB Bibliographisches Institut.

—. & Joachim Buscha. 1972. *Deutsche Grammatik. Ein Handbuch für den Ausländerunterricht.* Leipzig: VEB Bibliographisches Institut.

Hellwig, Peter. 1980. "PLAIN: Eine Valenzsyntax und wozu sie gut ist". *Dialogsysteme und Textverarbeitung* hg. von Dieter Krallmann, 17–41. Essen: LDV Fittings.

—. 1986. "Dependency Unification Grammar". *COLING-86 Bonn.* Proceedings, 195–198.

Heringer, Hans-Jürgen. 1967. "Wertigkeiten und nullwertige Verben im Deutschen". *Zeitschrift für deutsche Sprache* 23.13–34.

—. 1970a. "Zur Analyse von Sätzen des Deutschen auf der Unterstufe". *Linguistik und Didaktik* 1.1–28.

—. 1970b. *Theorie der deutschen Syntax.* München: Hueber.

—. 1984. "Neues von der Verbszene". *Pragmatik in der Grammatik. Jahrbuch 1983 des IdS* hg. von Gerhard Stickel, 34–64. Düsseldorf: Schwann.

—. 1993a. "Dependency Syntax. Basis ideas and the classical model". Jacobs et al. 1993. 298–316.

—. 1993b. "Dependency Syntax. Formalized models". Jacobs et al. 1993. 316–328.

—. 1996 *Syntax: Dependentiell.* Tübingen: Stauffenburg.

Hudson, Richard A. 1976. *Arguments for a Nontransformational Grammar.* Chicago & London: Univ. of Chicago Press.

—. 1980. "Constituency and Dependency". *Linguistics* 18:3, 4.179–198.

—. 1984. *Word Grammar.* Oxford: Blackwell.

—. 1993. "Dependency Syntax: Recent developments in dependency theory". Jacobs et al. 1993. 329–338.

Jacobs, Joachim, Arnim von Stechow, Wolfgang Sternefeld & Theo Vennemann, hg. 1993. *Syntax: Ein Internationales Handbuch zeitgenössischer Forschung,* 1. Halbband. Berlin & New York: de Gruyter.

Joshi, Aravind K. 1969. "Properties of Formal Grammars with Mixed Type of Rules and Their Linguistic Relevance". *COLING-69 Stockholm.* Preprint No.47.

Jung, Wha-Young. 1995. *Syntaktische Relationen im Rahmen der Dependenzgrammatik.* Hamburg: Buske.

Kacnel'son, Solomon Davidovič. 1948. "O grammatičeskoy kategorii". *Vestnik Leningradskogo Universiteta: Serija istorii, jazyka i literatury* 2. Leningrad.

Kaplan, Ronald & Joan Bresnan. 1982. "Lexical-Functional Grammar: A formal system for grammatical representation". *The Mental Representation of Grammatical Relations* hg. von Joan Bresnan, 173–281. Cambridge, Mass: MIT.

Klein, Wolfgang. 1971. *Parsing: Studien zur maschinellen Satzanalyse mit Abhängigkeitsgrammatiken und Transformationsgrammatiken.* Frankfurt: Athenäum.

Klimonov, Gerda. 1982. "Zum System der Unterordnungsrelationen im Deutschen". *Automatische Analyse des Deutschen* hg. von Jürgen Kunze, 65–174. Berlin: Akademie-Verlag.

Koch, Peter & Thomas Krefeld, Hg. 1991. *Connexiones Romanicae. Dependenz und Valenz in romanischen Sprachen.* Tübingen: Niemeyer.

—. 1993. "Gibt es Translationen?". *Zeitschrift für Romanische Philologie* 109.148–166.

Koerner, E. F. Konrad & R. E. Asher, Hg. 1995. *Concise History of the Language Sciences: From the Sumerians to the Cognitivists.* Oxford & New York: Pergamon Press.

Korhonen, Jarmo. 1977. *Studien zur Dependenz, Valenz und Satzmodell,* Teil I: Theorie und Praxis der Beschreibung der deutschen Gegenwartssprache. Dokumentation, kritische Besprechung, Vorschläge. Bern, Frankfurt, etc.: Lang.

—. 1978. *Studien zur Dependenz, Valenz und Satzmodell.* Teil II: *Untersuchung anhand eines Luther-Textes.* Bern, Frankfurt, etc.: Lang.

—. 1995. "Zum Wesen der Polyvalenz in der deutschen Sprachgeschichte". Eichinger & Eroms 1995. 365–382.

Kunze, Jürgen. 1975. *Abhängigkeitsgrammatik.* Berlin: Akademie-Verlag.

—. 1982. "Einführung". *Automatische Analyse des Deutschen* hg. von Jürgen Kunze, 17–34. Berlin: Akademie-Verlag.

Lambertz, Thomas. 1991. "Kritische Anmerkungen zu Tesnières Translationstheorie". Koch & Krefeld 1991. 53–79.

Lecerf, Yves. 1961. "Une représentation algébraïque de la structure des phrases dans diverses langues naturelles". *Comptes Rendues de l'Académie des Sciences de Paris* 252: 2.232–234.

Lobin, Henning. 1989. "A Dependency Syntax of German". *Metataxis in Practice. Dependency syntax for multilingual machine translation* hg. von Dan Maxwell & Klaus Schubert, 17–38. Dordrecht: Foris.

—. 1993. *Koordinationssyntax als prozedurales Phänomen.* Tübingen: Narr.

—. 1995. "Komplexe Elemente – Indizien aus Nominalphrase und Verbalkomplex". Eichinger & Eroms 1995. 117–133.

Maas, Utz. 1974. "Dependenztheorie". *Grundzüge der Literatur- und Sprachwissenschaft,* Bd. 2: *Sprachwissenschaft,* 257–275. München: dtv.

McCord, Michael C. 1980. "Slot Grammars". *Computational Linguistics* 6.31–43.

—. 1990. "Slot Grammar: A system for simpler construction of practical Natural Language Grammars". *Natural Language and Logic.* Hrg. von R. Studer, 118–145. Berlin & Heidelberg: Springer.

Mel'čuk, Igor A. 1963. "Avtomatičeskij analiz tekstov (na materiale russkogo jazyka) [Automatische Text-Analyse (auf der Basis des Russischen)]". *Slavjanskoe jazykoznanie,* 477–509. Moskau: Nauka.

—. 1979. *Studies in Dependency Syntax.* Ann Arbor: Karoma.

—. 1988. *Dependency Syntax: Theory and practice.* Albany: State Univ. Press of New York.

—. & A. K. Zolkovskij. 1970. "Towards a Functioning 'Meaning'<–>'Text' Model of Language". *Linguistics* 57.10–47.

—. & Niklaj V. Pertsov. 1987. *Surface Syntax of English. A formal model within the meaning-text framework.* Amsterdam & Philadelphia: Benjamins.

Minsky, Marvin. 1975. "A Framework for Representing Knowledge". *The Psychology of Computer Vision* hg. von Peter Winston, 211–277. New York: McGraw-Hill.

Nagao, Makoto, Toyoaki Nishida & Jun-ichi Tsujii. 1986. "Dealing with Incompleteness of Linguistic Knowledge in Language Translation. Transfer and generation stage of MU machine translation project". *COLING-86 Bonn.* Proceedings, 420–427.

Nikula, Henrik. 1976. *Verbvalenz. Untersuchungen am Beispiel des deutschen Verbs mit einer kontrastiven Analyse Deutsch – Schwedisch.* Stockholm: Almqvist & Wiksell.

—. 1986a. *Dependensgrammatik.* Malmö: Liber.

—. 1986b. "Valenz und Text". *Deutsch als Fremdsprache* 23.263–268.

Plátek, M. J. & Petr Sgall. 1984. "A Dependency Base for a Linguistic Description". *Contributions to Functional Syntax, Semantics and Language Comprehension* hg. von Petr Sgall, 63–98. Amsterdam: Benjamins.

Pollard, Carl J. & Ivan Sag. 1994. *Head-Driven Phrase Structure Grammar.* Chicago: Univ. of Chicago Press.

Processing of Dependency-based Grammars. ACL-Workshop, *COLING-98 Montréal.*

Rall, Marlene, Ulrich Engel & Dietrich Rall. 1977. *DVG für DaF. Dependenz-Verb-Grammatik für Deutsch als Fremdsprache.* Heidelberg: Groos.

Rambow, Owen & Aravind Joshi. 1994. "A Formal Look at Dependency Grammars and Phrase-Structure Grammars, with Special Consideration of Word-Order Phenomena". *Current Issues in Meaning-Text Theory* hg. von Leo Wanner. London: Pinter.

Robinson, Jane. 1968. "Dependency Structures and Transformational Rules". IBM Research Laboratory, Scientific Report 3. Yorktown Heights, N. Y.

Rosengren, Inger. 1970. "Zur Valenz des deutschen Verbs". *Moderna Språk* 64.45–58.

Rothkegel, Annely. 1976. "Valenzgrammatik". *Linguistische Arbeiten Saarbrücken* 19. Saarbrücken: SFB 100, Universität des Saarlandes.

Schank, Roger C. 1969. *A Conceptual Dependency Representation for a Computer-Oriented Semantics.* Ph.D. Dissertation, University of Texas, Austin. (Auch: Stanford AI Memo 83.)

Schank, Roger C. & Robert P. Abelson. 1975. "Scripts, Plans, and Knowledge". 4th International Joint Conference on Artificial Intelligence 1975, Tbilisi, USSR. Proceedings, 151–157.

Schneider, Gerold. 1998. *A Linguistic Comparison of Constituency, Dependency and Link Grammar.* Dipl. Arbeit, Universität Zürich.

Schubert, Klaus. 1986. *Syntactic Tree Structures in DLT.* Utrecht: BSO Research.

—. 1987. *Metataxis: Contrastive Dependency Syntax for Machine Translation.* Dordrecht: Foris.

—. 1988. "Zu einer sprachübergreifenden Definition der Valenz". Helbig 1988. 55—62.

Schumacher, Helmut, Hg. 1986. *Verben in Feldern: Valenzwörterbuch zur Syntax und Semantik deutscher Verben.* Berlin: de Gruyter.

Sgall, Petr, Eva Hajičová & Jarmilla Panevová. 1986. *The Meaning of the Sentence in Its Semantic and Pragmatic Aspects.* Dordrecht: Reidel.

Sommerfeldt, Karl-Ernst & Herbert Schreiber. 1974. *Wörterbuch zur Valenz und Distribution deutscher Adjektive.* Leipzig: VEB Bibliographisches Institut. (2. Aufl., 1977.)

—. 1977. *Wörterbuch zur Valenz und Distribution der Substantive.* Leipzig: VEB Bibliographisches Institut.

Somers, Harold L. 1987. "Some Thoughts on Interface Structure(s)". *Maschinelle Übersetzung — Methoden und Werkzeuge* hg. von Wolfram Wilss & Klaus-Dirk Schmitz, 81—99. Tübingen: Niemeyer.

Starosta, Stanley. 1973. "The Faces of Case". *Language Sciences* 25. Bloomington: Indiana University.

—. 1988. *The Case for Lexicase.* London & New York: Pinter.

—. 1992. "Lexicase Revisited". Department of Linguistics, University of Hawaii at Manoa.

Stötzel, Georg. 1970. "Über die Grundlagen der deutschen Sprachlehrbücher". *Linguistik und Didaktik* 1.29—39

Storrer, Angelika. 1992. *Verbvalenz: Theoretische und methodische Grundlagen ihrer Beschreibung in Grammatikographie und Lexikographie.* Tübingen: Niemeyer.

Tapanainen, Pasi & Timo Järvinen. 1998. *Functional Dependency Parser.* http://www.ling.helsinki.fi/~tapanain/dg/index.html.

Tarvainen, Kalevi. 1981a. *Einführung in die Dependenzgrammatik.* Tübingen: Niemeyer.

—. 1981b. "Zur Eignung der Dependenzgrammatik für Deutsch als Fremdsprache aus kontrastiver Sicht". *Jahrbuch Deutsch als Fremdsprache* 9. 105—118. München: Fink.

Tesnière, Lucien. 1953. *Esquisse d'une syntaxe structurale.* Paris: Klincksieck.

—. 1959. *Éléments de syntaxe structurale.* Édités par Jean Fourquet. Paris: Klincksieck. (2. Aufl., 1965.)

Teubert, Wolfgang. 1979. *Valenz des Substantivs: Attributive Ergänzungen und Angaben.* Düsseldorf: Schwann.

Thümmel, Wolf. 1991. "Syntaktische Struktur und die Hypothese der Projektivität". *Zeitschrift für Sprachwissenschaft* 10: 2.220—283.

Vater, Heinz. 1973. *Toward a Generative Dependency Grammar.* Trier: L. A. U. T.

—. 1996. "VP-Struktur und Verbvalenz im Deutschen". Gréciano & Schumacher 1996. 169—181.

Vauquois, Bernard, G. Veillon, N. Nedobejkine & C. Bourgignon. 1969. "Une notation des textes hors des constraintes morphologiques et syntaxiques de l'expression". *COLING-69 Stockholm.* Preprint No.17.

Vennemann, Theo. 1977. "Konstituenz und Dependenz in einigen neueren Grammatiktheorien". *Sprachwissenschaft* 2, 3.259—301.

Weber, Heinz J. 1980. "Satzübergreifende Analyse von Valenzstrukturen". *Maschinelle Übersetzung, Lexikographie und Analyse* (= *Linguistische Arbeiten Saarbrücken* NF3) hg. von Hans Eggers, 151—157. Saarbrücken: SFB 100, Universität des Saarlandes.

—. 1985. "Coherence-oriented Lexicon Structures and Text-based Semantic Representation of Lexemes. An Outline of COAT". *Meaning and the Lexicon,* hg. von G. A. J. Hoppenbrouwes, P. A. M. Seuren & A. J. M. M. Weijters, 317—325. Dordrecht: Foris.

—. 1992. *Dependenzgrammatik. Ein Arbeitsbuch.* Tübingen: Narr. (2. Aufl., *Dependenzgrammatik: Ein interaktives Arbeitsbuch,* auch als Bildschirm-Fassung in ToolBook 1997.)

—. 1996. "Translation, Rekursivität und Valenz bei Lucien Tesnière". Gréciano & Schumacher 1996. 249—261.

Weisgerber, Monika. 1983. *Valenz und Kongruenzbeziehungen. Ein Modell zur Vereindeutigung von Verben in der maschinellen Analyse und Übersetzung.* Frankfurt, Bern, etc.: Lang.

Welke, Klaus. 1988. *Einführung in die Valenz- und Kasustheorie.* Leipzig: Bibliographisches Institut.

Werner, Edeltraut. 1993. *Translationstheorie und Dependenzmodell. Kritik und Reinterpretation des Ansatzes von Lucien Tesnière.* Tübingen & Basel: Francke.

Werner, Otmar. 1973. "Von Chomskys 'Aspects'-Modell zu einer linearen Dependenzgrammatik". *Folia Linguistica* 6.62—88.

Wotjak, Gerd. 1975. "Valenzmodelle und semantische Merkmalanalyse". *Linguistische Arbeitsberichte* 11.19—39

—. 1988. "Verbbedeutung, Szenenwissen und Verbvalenz". Helbig 1988. 135—154.

Zifonun, Gisela. 1972. "Über die Unverträglichkeit verschiedener Valenzbegriffe und ihre Verwertbarkeit in semantischen Beschreibungen". *Zeitschrift für Dialektologie und Linguistik* 39.171—205.

Heinz J. Weber, Trier (Deutschland)

206. Linguistische Ansätze in der Stilistik des zwanzigsten Jahrhunderts

1. Die Stilistik − eine linguistische Disziplin?
2. Die Frühgeschichte der Stilistik
3. Stilistik als System von Ausdrucksmitteln
4. Frühpragmatische und funktionale Ansätze in der linguistischen Stilistik
5. Strukturalistische Ansätze in der linguistischen Stilistik
6. Textlinguistik und Stilistik
7. Sprachpragmatische Stilistik
8. Bibliographie

1. Die Stilistik − eine linguistische Disziplin?

Dem ungenauen Blick erscheint die Stilistik weithin als eine Domäne der Literaturwissenschaft. Dieser Eindruck beruht zum einen auf dem lange unhinterfragten Postulat, nur das literarische Kunstwerk besitze Stil, und zum andern auf der Tatsache, daß bis in die jüngere Vergangenheit wenn auch nicht ausschließlich so doch vor allen Dingen literarische Texte Gegenstand der Beschäftigung mit Stil gewesen sind. Die Bemühungen, die Stilistik als eine linguistische Disziplin zu etablieren, haben deshalb immer eine doppelte Stoßrichtung gehabt: Sie zielten auf eine Abgrenzung von der literaturwissenschaftlichen Beschäftigung mit Stil, und sie zielten darauf, die Stilistik als eine eigenständige Disziplin neben anderen sprachwissenschaftlichen Teildisziplinen wie Lexikologie, Wortbildungslehre oder Syntax zu etablieren (vgl. Peukert 1977.)

Gerade diesen Bemühungen scheinen jedoch Grenzen gesetzt zu sein, wofür allein schon die Beobachtung spricht, daß viele Fragestellungen, denen sich die Stilistik widmet oder widmen könnte, offensichtlich auch oder vor allem in anderen sprachwissenschaftlichen Disziplinen behandelt werden. So gibt es eine Fülle von Arbeiten beispielsweise zur gesprochenen Sprache, zur Soziolinguistik, Texttheorie/Textlinguistik, Gesprächs-, Konversations- oder Diskursanalyse, die alle glänzend ohne die Kategorie 'Stil' auskommen, von denen der Stiltheoretiker umgekehrt aber ohne Schwierigkeiten sagen könnte, es seien Beiträge zur Stilistik oder es würden in ihnen zumindest genuin stilistische Fragestellungen mitbehandelt. Dieser Sachverhalt hat Bennison Gray zu der provokanten und extremen Position geführt, die Stilistik mitsamt dem Stilbegriff sei abzuschaffen, da sich die entsprechenden Phänomene mit Hilfe anderer linguistischer Kategorien besser erfassen ließen (Gray 1969). Generell lässt sich eine distanzierte Haltung der Sprachwissenschaft zur Stilistik beobachten, die Jürgen Trabant zu der Einschätzung führt, die Sprachwissenschaft liebe die Stilistik nicht (Trabant 1986: 170). Dennoch gibt es für die Sprachwissenschaft gute Gründe am Stilbegriff festzuhalten, da das Konzept des Sprachstils für die Möglichkeit steht, unterschiedlichste und häufig disparat erscheinende sprachliche Erscheinungen in einen Zusammenhang miteinander zu bringen. Das Stilkonzept besitzt integrative Kraft, oder wie neuerdings formuliert wird: Stil besitzt einen ganzheitlichen oder holistischen Charakter (Sandig 1990; Selting & Hinnenkamp 1989: 7; Fix 1992; Holly 1992). Weiterhin erlaubt die Zusammenschau von Verschiedenartigem auch, die Pluralität von Sprachwirklichkeiten zu thematisieren, die sich in der Vielfalt der Sprachgebräuche manifestiert. Diese Eigenschaft macht den Begriff des Stils für kulturwissenschaftliche Disziplinen auch jenseits von Sprach- und Literaturwissenschaft interessant (vgl. Gumbrecht & Pfeiffer 1986).

Mit dem Konzept des Sprachstils verbindet sich also ein spezifisches Frageinteresse, das in seiner allgemeinsten Form auf den Sprachgebrauch und seine Wirkungen gerichtet ist. In der theoretischen Reflexion dieses Frageinteresses wird die Stilistik etabliert, deren Gegenstandsbereich sich danach bestimmt, was in dem jeweiligen theoretischen Rahmen als stilistisch relevant erachtet wird. Da die linguistische Stilistik in einem starken Maße davon bestimmt wird, was zu den Gegenständen der Sprachwissenschaft zählt, fällt die explizite oder auch nur implizite Bestimmung ihres Objektbereichs recht unterschiedlich aus. Sie reicht von der Beschränkung auf Wortwahl und Satzbau bis hin zur Berücksichtigung aller für das Textverstehen und -interpretieren wichtigen Aspekte, eine Ausweitung, die beispielsweise für Georg Michel "zu einer Hypertrophie sprachstilistischer Fragestellungen" führt (Michel 1988: 551).

Es wäre allerdings irreführend, aus diesem offensichtlichen Einfluss der linguistischen Theorie auf den Objektbereich der Stilistik den Schluß zu ziehen, der Zusammenhang zwischen sprachtheoretischen Ansätzen und stiltheoretischen Konzeptionen ergebe ein einheitliches und übersichtliches Bild. Das Gegenteil ist der Fall, was vor allem daraus resultiert, dass sich aktuelle linguistische Ansätze zwar implizit auf die stiltheoretische Diskussion auswirken oder auch explizit von ihr aufgenommen werden, dass aber − von Ausnahmen abgesehen − die sprachtheoretischen Positionen nicht konsequent als Basis für eine Bestimmung des Stilistischen genutzt, sondern mit überkommenen Anschauungen vermengt werden. Häufig wird dabei theoretisch nicht reflektiert, in wieweit die miteinander verknüpften Positionen kompatibel sind. Trotz dieser eher skeptischen Einschätzung der linguistisch beeinflussten Theoriebildung in der Stilistik bleibt festzuhalten, dass zumindest einzelne linguistische Ansätze auf die Stilistik befruchtend und weiterführend gewirkt haben. Zugleich muss jedoch betont werden, dass der literaturwissenschaftliche Einfluss auch auf die linguistisch ausgerichtete Stilistik in einem kaum zu unterschätzenden Ausmaß als Ferment gewirkt hat.

2. Die Frühgeschichte der Stilistik

2.1. Die Etablierung einer eigenständigen Stilistik

Die Geschichte der Stilistik beginnt in Deutschland in der zweiten Hälfte des 18. Jhs. Zwar hat man sich mit dem Phänomen des Stils seit den Anfängen der antiken Rhetorik beschäftigt, aber die Stilistik als eine eigenständige Fragestellung etabliert sich erst mit der Herauslösung der Elocutio- und Genus-Lehre aus dem rhetorischen System. So fasst Johann Christoph Adelung (1732−1806) Stilistik als die "Lehre von dem Style oder der Schreibart", die die Form der Rede im Hinblick auf den "zweckmäßigen, schönen Ausdruck" betrifft (Adelung 1785: 25), während er die Aufgabe der Rhetorik auf die Erfindung sowie zweckmäßige und wirksame Anordnung der Gedanken beschränkt (ebda.). Adelung vertritt eine normativ-präskriptive Regelstilistik, die ganz in der Tradition von Rhetorik und Regelpoetik Anweisung zur angemessenen Bewältigung von Schreibaufgaben bieten will. Diese Regelstilistik Adelung'scher Prägung entfaltet ihre Wirkung in Deutschland bis weit ins 19. Jh. und zeigt noch heute in Form der 'Praktischen Stilistik', die Anleitung zum 'guten Schreiben' geben will, ihre Auswirkungen. Neben der Regelstilistik findet sich im augehenden 18. Jh. eine weitere Auffassung, nach der sich Stil nicht im Konventionell-Regelhaften manifestiert, sondern in den Eigentümlichkeiten, das heißt den individuellen Eigenschaften des Sprachgebrauchs. Für diese Richtung kann Karl Philipp Moritz (1756−1793) stehen, für den Stil nicht aus der Befolgung von vorgegebenen Regeln resultiert, sondern sich in der 'Schreibart' manifestiert. Diese veränderte Sichtweise auf den Stil ist die Folge der veränderten Auffassung vom Künstler als Genie und der Individualität des künstlerischen Werkes. Wer jetzt etwas über den Stil sagen möchte, muß empirisch vorgehen, denn er ist auf die Analyse der Texte angewiesen, was Moritz in der These fasst: "Die Regeln in Ansehung des Styls müssen auf Beobachtung zurückgeführt werden" (Moritz 1800 [1793]: 3). Damit ist die Abwendung von der normativ-präskriptiven Regelstilistik und die Hinwendung zu einer deskriptiven Stilistik markiert. Die empirisch-deskriptive Sichtweise verstärkt sich im Laufe des 19. Jhs. immer mehr, zum einen gestützt durch die Wissenschaftsvorstellungen der historisch-vergleichenden Sprachwissenschaft (vgl. Linn 1963: 55, 59), zum andern durch die sich etablierende Literaturwissenschaft mit ihrer Auffassung von der Individualität des Kunstwerks, in der sich die Individualität seines Schöpfers ausdrückt. Zwar hat vor allem die positivistische Literaturwissenschaft, für die Literatur als erklärt gilt, wenn alle außerliterarischen Faktoren genannt sind, die das Werk determinieren, kaum etwas zur Stildiskussion beigetragen, aber mit der idealistischen "Wendung nach innen" (Pollmann 1973: 107) wird nach Hans Robert Jauß ein neues Paradigma der Literaturwissenschaft markiert, das "im Heraufkommen und im Siegeszug der Stilistik" zu sehen ist (Jauß 1969: 49). Umreißen lässt sich dieses Paradigma mit den Namen des Philologen Leo Spitzer als Vertreter der idealistischen Philologie und des Literaturwissenschaftlers Oskar Walzel (1864−1944) als Vertreter einer 'werkimmanenten Betrachtung'; es greift dann aber noch weiter aus bis hin zum russischen Formalismus und seinen Spätwirkungen in Westeuropa und den U.S.A und endet mit der Krise der 'werkimmanenten Stilistik' in den sechziger Jahren. Mit dieser Sichtweise auf den Sprachstil ist im Prinzip der Anspruch verbunden erklären zu wollen, was einen Text zum literarischen Text oder Kunstwerk macht. Wenn auch mit anderen Worten hat Emil Gamillscheg (1887−1971) für die Sprachwissenschaft schon 1929 eine dem Jauß'schen Diktum vergleichbare Feststellung getroffen: "Mit der Abkehr weiter Kreise von der historischen Forschung auf dem Gebiet der Sprachwissenschaft geht Hand in Hand eine üppig wuchernde Produktion an Stiluntersuchungen" (Gamillscheg 1929: 89).

2.2. Die Anfänge der linguistischen Stilistik

Obwohl in der historisch-vergleichenden Sprachwissenschaft (und damit auch in der Sprachgermanistik) des 19. Jhs. ein "stilistisches Vakuum" herrschte (Linn 1963: 51), hat diese einen starken Einfluss auf die Eingrenzung des Objektbereichs der Stilistik ausgeübt. Denn diejenigen, die sich mit Stilfragen beschäftigten, orientierten sich eng am grammatischen System, so dass sich die als stilistisch relevant betrachteten Bereiche formelhaft in die Trias von Laut, Wort und Satz fassen lassen. Theoretisch angedeutet wird dieser Objektbereich in dem Postulat von Hermann Paul (1846–1921), es sei "erforderlich, dass man ohne Rücksicht auf praktische Zwecke, wie sie die ältere Stilistik verfolgt, das wirkliche Vorkommende von allen Seiten her sammelt und zweckmäßig gruppiert" (Paul 1901 [1896]: 236). Zweckmäßige Gruppierung meint hier so viel wie die Orientierung an den Kategorien, mit denen die Junggrammatiker vorzüglich arbeiten. Den ersten Versuch, die Stilistik eng an die Gliederung der Sprache anzuschließen, lieferte schon sehr viel früher Karl Ferdinand Becker (1775–1849) (Becker 1848); später will dann beispielsweise Ernst Elster (1860–1940) "ein System, d. h. eine organisch gegliederte Gesamtdarstellung der Stilistik" (Elster 1911: 2) in Form einer 'stilistischen Grammatik' geben. Diese Vorstellungen wirken in der linguistisch orientierten Stilistik weiter bis in die jüngere Vergangenheit. So hat etwa Charles Bally in *Le langage et la vie* von 1913 das Feld des Stilistischen ausdrücklich in die drei Bereiche 'phonologie', 'vocabulaire' und 'syntaxe' eingeteilt (Bally 1965 [1913]: 62–68). Ernsthaft ist diese Beschränkung erst in den textlinguistisch beeinflussten Ansätzen seit den sechziger Jahren überwunden worden (vgl. Abschnitt 6.).

Von dem Wunsch nach 'zweckmäßiger Gruppierung' der Stilmittel, so dass sie zum Zwecke der Analyse, aber auch der Unterweisung nachschlagbar sind, zeugen auch Stilwörterbücher (Becker 1966, Duden 1970 [1938]) und Stilgrammatiken (z. B. Strohmeyer 1910, Aronstein 1924, Deutschbein 1932, Schneider 1969 [1959], Heringer 1989). Doch nicht nur in Spezialwörterbüchern und -grammatiken werden stilistische Informationen präsentiert, sondern auch in allgemeinen einsprachigen Wörterbüchern (vgl. dazu Corbin 1989, Püschel 1989) sowie in allgemeinen Grammatiken. Für letztere kann exemplarisch die Grammatiken des Englischen von Quirk et al. (1972) genannt werden, hinter der die Idee steht, sprachliche Variation systematisch zu erfassen (s. Abschnitt 4.). Ursprünglich ist mit diesen Inventarisierungsbemühungen das Ziel verbunden, die stilistischen Eigenschaften einer Einzelsprache zu erfassen: "Während die Grammatik die ganze Fülle der Sprachmittel, vom einfachen Laut bis zum vollen Satz, nach ihrer Verwandtschaft geordnet einzeln behandelt, versucht die Stilistik, vor allem die subjektive, auf Grund genau desselben Materials, nach anderen Gesichtspunkten geordnet, ein Charakterbild der Sprache zu entwerfen" (Strohmeyer 1910: v). Es soll also nicht nur erfasst werden, welche stilistischen Möglichkeiten in einer Sprache angelegt sind, darüber hinaus soll auch deutlich werden, welche Eigenschaften einer Einzelsprache – es ist auch von deren seelischen Werten die Rede – im Unterschied zu anderen Einzelsprachen zukommen. Doch spätestens seit dem Ende des 2. Weltkriegs steht bei der Kodifizierung lexikalischer wie grammatischer Stilmittel der praktische Nutzwerk des Nachschlagens im Vordergrund.

2.3. Stilistik zwischen Sprach- und Literaturwissenschaft

Wie die bisherige Darstellung ausweist, ist die linguistische Annäherung an die Stilistik von Anfang an in einem hohen Maß 'code-zentriert' (Plett 1979: 269). Daneben findet sich aber auch schon sehr früh ein 'werk-zentrierter' Zugriff, der sich interpretativer Verfahren bedient. Schon Wilhelm Scherer (1841–1886) plädierte für eine umfassende Beschäftigung mit der "dichterischen Hervorbringung", also dem Text:

"es muss die ganze folge vom stoff bis zur inneren und äusseren form, von dem rohen stoff, der überhaupt in den gesichtskreis des dichters fällt, von der auswahl aus diesem stoffe, von der besonderen auffassung bis zur besonderen einkleidung, zur wahl der dichtungsgattung, zu den sprachlichen und metrischen mitteln, mit einem Worte: der gesammte dichterische process, durchlaufen und überall die eigenart aufgesucht und nachgewiesen werden." (Scherer 1884: 308)

Ganz im Sinne des Positivmus gilt es, die Fakten in ihrer ganzen Fülle "mit der kühlen

Beobachtung, Analyse und Classifikation des Naturforschers" (Scherer 1888: 43) zu beschreiben. Doch zumindest tentativ löst sich Scherer von einer rein positivistischen Position, wenn er bekennt:

"Aber ich bin sehr tief davon durchdrungen, daß es zum Verständnis des 'Werther' nicht nothwendig ist, eine Silbe von Goethes Liebe zu Lotte und von dem Selbstmord des jungen Jerusalem zu wissen. Es wäre ein schlechtes Zeugnis für ein Kunstwerk, wenn es nicht den Schlüssel seines Verständnisses in sich selbst trüge, wenn es einer von außen her geholten Weisheit bedürfte, um in das Innere einzudringen [...]" (Zitiert nach Weimar 1989: 472).

Auch wenn es Wilhelm Scherer nicht so formuliert, vertritt er hier eine hermeneutische Position. Zugleich bewegt er sich als Philologe zwischen Sprach- und Literaturwissenschaft, jedoch noch nicht im Sinne eines Brückenschlags. Unter dem Einfluss von Karl Voßler (1872–1949) versucht diesen Brückenschlag dann Leo Spitzer (1887–1960), wenn er ausdrücklich die Stilistik als Bindeglied zwischen diesen beiden Disziplinen etablieren will (vgl. Aschenberg 1984: 89–90). Den Ausgangspunkt bildet für Spitzer ein Konzept, demzufolge Stil "im gebräuchlichen Sinn der bewußten Verwendung sprachlicher Mittel zu irgendwelchen Ausdruckszielen verwandt [wird]" (Spitzer 1928a: ix). Das Ziel ist für ihn als "kunstbeflissenem Linguisten" (Spitzer 1928b: 4), "die Sprache der Dichter in ihren Kunstabsichten zu erfassen, zu charakterisieren und auf das Seelische, das die Dichter sprachlich ausdrücken, zurückzuführen [...]" (ebda.). Der Weg zum Ziel besteht in einem sinnverstehenden Verfahren, von dem Spitzer gesteht: "Lesen, gründliches Lesen ist sozusagen mein einziger Handwerkskniff" (Spitzer 1928b: 526). Spitzer reklamiert in genuin hermeneutischer Weise die Intution als Vehikel der Erkenntnis, er weiß zudem, dass es sich dabei um eine subjektive Erkenntnisform handelt, deren Wahrheitsmodus die Evidenz ist (Aschenbach 1984: 85). Doch Spitzer bleibt nicht beim intuitiven Erfassen, bei einer nachschöpfenden Beschreibung des Textverständnisses stehen, sondern versucht seine Untermauerung mit Hilfe sprachwissenschaftlicher Kategorien:

"Entscheidende Züge der Wortkunst lassen sich erkennen, wenn in die Schule der Wissenschaft gegangen wird, die sich bisher am intensivsten mit dem Wort beschäftigt und seine Wege am genauesten beobachtet hat. Es ist die Sprachlehre." (Spitzer 1928b: 83)

Eine wesentliche Eigenschaft der Spitzer'schen Stilistik bildet ihre strikt empirische Orientierung. Wenn Spitzer etwas aus der positivistischen Sprachwissenschaft übernommen hat, dann die philologische "Andacht zum Text" und die Hochschätzung des "Handwerklich-Technischen am Philologen", weshalb er auch von sich sagen kann, dass er einen "positiven Idealismus oder idealistischen Positivismus" verfechte (Spitzer 1928a: xi). Diese explizite Verknüpfung von Hermeneutik und empirischem Vorgehen findet sich in der linguistischen Stilistik erst wieder in den sprachpragmatisch fundierten Ansätzen der siebziger und achtziger Jahre (s. Abschnitt 6.).

3. Stilistik als System von Ausdrucksmitteln

Beim Versuch, die stilistischen Mittel einer Sprache systematisch darzustellen, erhebt sich die Frage, worin der postulierte Stilwert besteht, so dass sich die stilistische Darstellung von der grammatischen Beschreibung unterscheidet. Ein Resümee der Diskussionen zu dieser Frage zieht Ernst Otto (1877–1959), wenn er feststellt, "daß die Stilistik insofern über die Grammatik hinausgeht, als sie die sprachlichen Erscheinungen unter größeren Gesichtspunkten sieht und dazu den Geist der Sprache tiefer zu ergründen sucht" (Otto 1943: 43). Eine zentrale Rolle spielt hierbei der Gefühlswert, eine Kategorie, die schon Ernst Elster 1897 ins Spiel bringt und die sich auch bei Oskar Weise (1851–1933) 1905 findet. Im Zusammenhang mit Stil fällt ebenfalls bei Karl Otto Erdmann (1858–1932), dessen Studie *Die Bedeutung des Wortes* 1900 erschienen ist, das Stichwort 'Gefühlswert' (Erdmann 1966 [1900]: 119). Weiter geführt wird diese Auffassung vom Stilistischen von Emil Winkler (1891–1942) in seiner *Grundlegung* (1929) und Wilhelm Schneider (1885–1959) in seiner Stilkunde (1968 [1931]), die *Gefühlswert* durch *Ausdruckswert* ablösen, und sie findet ihre Fortsetzung noch bei Herbert Seidler (1905–1965) (1963 [1953]). Allerdings bleibt es fraglich, ob sich eine klare Verbindungslinie von Elster über Winkler und Schneider zu Seidler ziehen lässt (Linn 1963: 65). Vielmehr ist mit dem Einfluss der Arbeiten von Charles Bally (1865–1947) zu rechnen, der in seinem *Traité de stylistique française* von 1909 an allen Manifestationen der Sprache zwei Seiten unterscheidet, den 'côté intellectuel' und den 'côté affectif'. Die erste Aufgabe der Stilistik besteht nun in der Untersuchung der Einstellungen und Gefühle, die der affektiven Seite zugeordnet sind: "elle étudie la valeur affective des faits du langage organisé, et l'action réciproque des faits expressifs qui concourent à former le système des moyens d'expression d'une langue" (Bally 1970 [1909]: 1). Konsequent zeichentheoretisch gefaßt hat diese Verhältnisse Louis Hjelmslev (1899–1965) in seiner *Prolegomena zu einer Sprachtheorie*, die zuerst 1943 unter dem Titel *Omkring sprogteoriens grundlæggelse* erschienen ist. Hjelmslev unterscheidet zwischen Denotations- und Konnotationssprache, wobei die Ausdrucksebene der Konnotationssprache durch die Denotationssprache – bestehend aus Einheiten wie Wort, Satz und Text (vgl. Rossipal 1973: 13) – gebildet wird. Die Inhaltsebene besteht aus Konnotatoren (Hjelmslev 1974 [1943]: 13), die den Stil in seiner ganzen Vielfalt betreffen, so dass die Einheiten der Konnotationssprache auch als 'stilistische Zeichen' betrachtet werden können.

Anstelle der Bezeichnungen *Gefühlwert* und *Ausdruckswert* hat sich nach dem 2. Weltkrieg die Bezeichnung *Konnotation* eingebürgert, die allerdings eine "linguistische Rumpelkammer" darstellt (Dieckmann 1981: 111), da sie sowohl zur Beschreibung von Bedeutungsanteilen lexikalischer Einheiten herangezogen wird als auch eine Rolle bei der Beschreibung von Stilwerten spielt. Versucht man für die 'Konnotations-Stilistik' ein generelles Prinzip zu formulieren, so lässt sich sagen, dass der stilistische Wert der sprachlichen Einheiten auf der Heterogenität von Sprache basiert. Heterogenität bedeutet, dass es für die Wörter unterschiedliche Gebrauchsbereiche oder Gebrauchsrestriktionen gibt. Die stilistischen Wirkungen resultieren dann vor allem aus der Vermischung der Gebrauchsbereiche, sind also ein Phänomen der Parole. Deshalb spricht Stephen Ullmann (1914–1976) im Anschluß an Ballys Ausführungen zu "Les milieux et les effets par évocation" (Bally 1970 [1909]: 217–249) vom "Evokationsvermögen" der Wörter (Ullmann 1967 [1957]: 94) oder ihrer Ausdruckskraft/ expressiveness (Ullmann 1972 [1964]: 113–114). Daneben finden sich jedoch auch Formen der Konnotation, die explizit mit dem Label 'stilistisch' versehen sind und die als der Langue zugehörig betrachtet werden. Dies sind in der germanistischen Tradition zum einen die Stilschicht und zum andern die Stilfärbung, beides Kategorien, die in den allgemeinsprachlichen Wörterbüchern in Form stilistischer Markierungen eine wichtige Rolle spielen (vgl. Corbin 1989, Püschel 1989, Lipka 1990). Die Angaben zur Stilschicht betreffen den Gebrauchsbereich – ganz analog zu denen der arealen Distribution und der Fachsprachenzugehörigkeit. Die Stilfärbung bezieht sich dagegen nicht auf Gebrauchsrestriktionen ganzer Wortschatzteile, sondern sie bietet Hinweise darauf, wie mit einem Einzelwort auf konventionelle Weise Einstellungen zu Personen oder Sachen ausgedrückt werden können (z. B. mit Wörtern, die als 'spöttisch', 'scherzhaft' oder 'vertraulich' gekennzeichnet sind) und wie mit dem Gebrauch eines Wortes weitere Handlungen ausgeführt werden können (z. B. mit einem Schimpfwort jemanden beschimpfen oder mit einem euphemistischen Ausdruck etwas Unangenehmes verhüllen).

4. Frühpragmatische und funktionale Ansätze in der linguistischen Stilistik

Ebenfalls auf der Erscheinung sprachlicher Heterogenität beruht die Prager Theorie der Schriftsprache oder die Theorie der funktionalen Stile, die in ihren Anfängen bis in die zwanziger Jahre zurückreicht. In diesem Ansatz wird zum ersten Mal konsequent der Tatsache Rechnung getragen, dass nicht nur der künstlerische Sprachgebrauch Stil hat, sondern diese Eigenschaft jeder Form des Sprachgebrauchs zukommt. Es handelt sich bei der Prager Theorie – wie wir aus heutiger Perspektive sagen können – um einen frühpragmatischen Ansatz, der von seinen Vertretern selbst als 'funktionale Linguistik' bezeichnet wurde. Mit Vilém Mathesius (1882–1945), einen ihrer Begründer, formuliert, geht die funktionale Sprachbetrachtung von den Ausdrucksbedürfnissen der Sprachbenutzer aus und fragt danach, welche sprachlichen Mittel diese Bedürfnisse erfüllen (Mathesius 1971 [1929]: 3). Die funktionalstilistische Gliederung der Standardvarietät, wie sie vor allem Bohuslav Havránek (1893–1978) 1932 entwickelt hat (s. Havránek 1976), beruht auf unterschiedlichen kommunikativen Bedürfnissen, die zu drei funktionalen Sprachen oder Stilen führen: Der einfach mitteilenden Funktion entspricht der Alltags-, Gesprächs- oder Konversationsstil, der Funktion der praktisch-fachlichen Mitteilung der Sach- oder Arbeitsstil und der theoretisch-fachlichen Funktion der Wissenschaftsstil. Als vierter Bereich kommt noch die ästhetische Funktion oder "die komplexen Funktion der Sprache der Wortkunst" (Havránek 1971 [1969]: 29) hinzu, die die Dichtersprache charakterisiert. Die Dichtersprache unterscheidet sich grundsätzlich von den übrigen Stilen, da sie durch Aktualisierung/foregrounding bestimmt ist, während die anderen Stile durch Automatisierung gekennzeichnet sind. Die Vorstellung von den besonderen ästhetischen Funktion der Dichtersprache hat ihre Wurzeln im russischen Formalismus (Doležel 1968), der beispielsweise durch Roman Jakobson (1896–1982) nach Prag vermittelt (Holenstein 1975: 18) und von Jan Mukařovský (1891–1975) seit den zwanziger Jahren weiter entwickelt wurde (vgl. z. B. Mukařovský 1967 [1948], 1970 [1966]).

Eine starke Auswirkung hatte die Prager Theorie der Schriftsprache, wenn auch in modifizierter Form, auf die Stilistik in der Sowjetunion. Bekannt sind vor allem die Arbeiten von Elise Riesel (1907–1988) zum Stil der deutschen Alltagsrede (Riesel 1964) oder von I. R. Gal'perin (1905–1975?) zum Englischen (Gal'perin 1971). Auch in der Stilistik der DDR hat die Kategorie 'Funktionalstil' oder 'funktionaler Stil' eine zentrale Rolle gespielt. Im Unterschied zur Prager Theorie der Schriftsprache betrachtet man die Stile jedoch nicht als durch kommunikative Bedürfnisse konstituiert, sondern durch außersprachliche Faktoren wie Tätigkeitsbereich, Kommunikationssituation und gesellschaftliche Aufgaben determiniert (Fix 1994: 95–96). Schon Havránek (1976 [1932]: 127–128) bietet allgemein gehaltene Charakterisierungen der Funktionalstile, die die Bedeutungsebene, die Lexik, die Expliziertheit der Formulierungen sowie die Verständlichkeit und Bestimmtheit des Ausdrucks betreffen. Verstärkt empirisch ausgearbeitet finden sich die Charakteristika der Funktionalstile dann in der sowjetischen Funktionalstilistik. Eine zentrale Rolle spielt dabei die Kategorie des Stilzugs, den Elise Riesel unter Berufung auf V. V. Vinogradov (1963) als stilbildendes und stilregelndes Ordnungsprinzip bestimmt (Riesel 1964: 58; vgl. auch Heinemann 1974, Lerchner 1976). Funktionale Stile sind konventionelle Stile, weshalb die Dichtersprache in ihrer Unkonventionalität und auf Grund ihrer ästhetischen Funktion eigentlich nicht dazuzurechnen ist (so schon Havránek 1976 [1932]: 128).

Wenn auch in einer völlig anderen Tradition stehend ist die Theorie der funktionalen Stile dennoch vergleichbar mit der Theorie der sprachlichen Register, die im britischen Kontextualismus entwickelt worden ist (ausführlich Lux 1981). Auch hier geht es um konventionelle Sprachgebräuche, die mit Situationstypen korrelieren. So heißt es bei M. A. K. Halliday, Angus McIntosh und Peter Strevens (1968 [1964]: 149–150):

"The category of 'register' is needed when we want to account for what people do with their language. When we observe language activity in the various contexts in which it takes place, we find differences in the type of language selected as appropriate to different types of situation."

Bestimmt wird ein Register durch das Zusammenspiel dreier Dimensionen: 'field of discourse' oder Gegenstand/Thema, 'mode of discourse' oder die Art der Realisierung, 'style of discourse' oder die Beziehungen zwischen den Kommunikationspartnern. Doch wie schon Hess-Lüttich (1974: 276) und erneut Esser (1993: 43) festgestellt haben, fehlt es an der empirischen Füllung des Register-Konzeptes.

5. Strukturalistische Ansätze in der linguistischen Stilistik

Obwohl sich im 20. Jh. wohl kaum ein Ansatz in der linguistischen Stilistik findet, der von strukturalistischem Denken nicht zumindest beeinflusst ist, erscheint es dennoch als sinnvoll, eine Reihe von stiltheoretischen Konzepten ausdrücklich als strukturalistisch begründet zu betrachten. Es handelt sich dabei um alle diejenigen Ansätze, in denen auf die systematische Unterscheidung von Paradigma und Syntagma aufgebaut wird. Außerdem wirken sich mehr oder weniger direkt Vorstellungen des taxonomischen Strukturalismus aus. Dessen analytische Grundoperationen – Segmentierung und Klassifizierung – werden in ihrer Umkehrung als Selektion und Kombination für die Stilistik nutzbar gemacht. Das Schlagwort für diese Betrachtungsweise lautet 'Stil als Wahl'. Nach Nils Erik Enkvist besitzt jedoch nicht alles, was als Resultat einer Wahl beschrieben werden kann, auch stilistischen Wert. So kennt Enkvist neben der stilistischen Wahl noch eine grammatische, die sich an den Strukturen einer Sprache und damit an der Sprachrichtigkeit bemisst, und eine nicht-stilistische, die sich an außersprachlichen Gegebenheiten und damit an der Wahrheit von Aussagen orientiert (1978 [1964]: 16–27). Auf diese Weise begrenzt Enkvist die stilistische Wahl auf die Fälle, in denen zwischen sprachlichen Mitteln gewählt wird "that mean roughly the same" (ebda., S. 19). Damit wird die Synonymie oder Fast-Synonymie von Äußerungen grundlegend für das Konzept von Stil als

Wahl – eine Bedingung, die beispielsweise auch Charles F. Hockett (1916–2000) formuliert hat:

"Roughly speaking, two utterances in the same language which convey approximately the same information, but which are different in their linguistic structure, can be said to differ in style." (1958: 536)

Ganz konsequent fasst dann Elise Riesel die Stilistik als "die Lehre von den synonymischen Ausdrucksmöglichkeiten im schriftlichen und mündlichen Verkehr einer Nation [...]" (Riesel 1959: 38). Mit dem Kriterium der Synonymie hat sich die strukturalistische Stilistik ein Problem eingehandelt, das die meisten ihrer Vertreter dadurch zu umgehen suchen, dass sie unter Synonymie nicht strikte, sondern nur annäherungsweise Bedeutungsgleichheit verstehen. Nicht umsonst ist in den Zitaten von Enkvist und Hockett in Bezug auf die Äußerungsbedeutung von *roughly* beziehungsweise *approximately the same* die Rede.

Neben der Unterscheidung von Paradigma und Syntagma spielt in der strukturalistischen Stilistik auch de Saussures Unterscheidung von 'langue' und 'parole' eine wichtige Rolle. Wenn Stil auf der Auswahl der sprachlichen Mittel aus einem Inventar von Ausdrucksmöglichkeiten beruht und auf deren Kombination in der chaîne parlée, dann stellt sich die Frage, ob die stilistischen Eigenschaften eines Textes in der Langue angelegt sind oder erst aus der spezifischen Kombination der sprachlichen Mittel resultieren, also eine Erscheinung der Parole sind. Der ersten Position lassen sich diejenigen zurechnen, die in 'code-zentrierter' Orientierung die stilistischen Mittel einer Sprache kodifizieren wollen. Ein radikaler Vertreter der zweiten Position ist Bernd Spillner, der für die Langue-orientierte Stilistik dekretiert:

"Die stilistischen Effekte sprachlicher Einheiten sind innerhalb einer Beschreibung des Sprachsystems überhaupt nicht vorhersagar." (Spillner 1974: 17)

So wie eine Langue-Stilistik offenbar Probleme aufwirft, ist umgekehrt an eine Parole-Stilistik ebenfalls eine Reihe von Problemen geknüpft, wie Enkvist (1973: 37–38) ausführt. Zu diesen Problemen gehört, dass sich mit dem Blick alleine auf die Parole allenfalls singuläre, individuelle Stile, jedoch keine konventionellen Stile erklären lassen. Allerdings bedeutet das für alle diejenigen keinen Nachteil, die genau auf das Singuläre und Individuelle zielen wie etwa Roman Jakobson.

Ihm geht es um den Kunstcharakter des konkreten Textes, der sich aus der formalen Organisation, seiner Struktur ableiten lässt. Das von Jakobson zugrunde gelegte Prinzip – von Holenstein (1975) als 'Zweiachsentheorie' apostrophiert – ist sehr einfacher Natur, da Jakobson die Textstruktur durch Äquivalenzen auf den verschieden sprachlichen Ebenen bestimmt sieht:

"The poetic function projects the principle of equivalence from the axis of selection to the axis of combination" (Jakobson 1960: 358)

Das Analyseverfahren besteht dann in der Herausarbeitung aller Äquivalenzen, an die sich eine Synthese der Einzelergebnisse anzuschließen hat (kritisch dazu Posner 1969). Auch für Michael Riffaterre basiert das Stilistische auf Struktureigenschaften des Textes und ist damit eine Erscheinung der 'parole'. Doch diese Eigenschaften konstituieren sich nicht aus dem Zusammenspiel von Äquivalenzbeziehungen im Text, sondern aus den Überraschungen, die der Leser im Fortgang seiner Lektüre erlebt. Diese Überraschungen werden dadurch vorbereitet, dass im linearen Fortgang des Textes beim Leser eine Erwartungshaltung aufgebaut wird im Hinblick auf die verwendeten sprachlichen Mittel und dann ein unerwartetes Sprachelement eingefügt wird, das im Kontrast zum vorausgegangenen Kontext steht:

"Since stylistic intensification results from the insertion of an unexpected element into a pattern, it supposes an effect of rupture which modifies the context. [...] The stylistic context is a linguistic pattern suddenly broken by an element which was unpredictable." (Riffaterre 1959: 170–171)

Gerade das Riffaterre'sche Konzept bedeutet für Spillner eine wohltuende Abwendung von den Versuchen der 'deskriptiven Stilistik', den sprachlichen Einheiten bereits auf der Ebene der 'langue' einen 'Stilwert' zuzuordnen (vgl. Spillner 1974: 51). Er verweist zugleich darauf, dass mit 'Stil als Kontrast im Text' vor allen Dingen literarische Texte linguistisch schlüssig zu beschreiben seien.

Während für Jakobson und Riffaterre der Stil aus der Weise resultiert, wie die sprachlichen Mittel miteinander verwendet werden, bildet eine weitere Lösung, die Stilkonstitution der 'parole' zuzuweisen, der Vorschlag, die Dichotomie von 'langue' und 'parole' um eine weitere Ebene zu erweitern. Zu nennen ist hier Eugenio Coseriu, der zwischen die 'parole' als konkrete Verwirklichung und die 'langue' als funktionelles System die Norm als intermediäre, den Sprachgebrauch und damit den Stil regelnde Größe stellt (Coseriu 1970 [1969]). Während bei Coseriu die intermediäre Norm als eine innersprachliche Kategorie konzipiert ist, wird sie bei Michel et al. (1968) als außersprachlich betrachtet. Nach dieser Vorstellung kennt die 'langue' keine stilistischen Differenzierungen, sondern nur freie Varianten, die erst in der 'parole' als 'gebunden' oder stilistisch gelten können. Bewirkt wird dieser Übergang von der freien zur gebundenen Variante durch die Vermittlungsinstanz der 'gesellschaftlichen Anwendungsnormen':

"Redestil ist demzufolge die Gesamtheit der an bestimmte gesellschaftliche Anwendungsnormen gebundenen fakultativen Varianten der Rede innerhalb einer Reihe synonymischer Möglichkeiten zur sprachlichen Darstellung eines Sachverhalts." (Michel et al. 1968: 34−35)

Der Übergang von der Freiheit der 'langue' zur Gebundenheit der 'parole' vollzieht sich im Prozeß der "Kodierung unter dem Einfluß sprachexterner Bedingungen", die sich zu "gesellschaftlichen Normen" verfestigt haben (Michel et al. 1968: 34) und deren Status folgendermaßen bestimmt wird:

"Die Bedingungen der Auswahl sind die Faktoren, die den Stilelementen kausal zugrunde liegen, sie gehören nur mittelbar zur linguistischen Stiluntersuchung, zur Textanalyse." (Michel et al. 1968: 40)

Ein Teil der Stiltheoretiker, die sich auf die Unterscheidung von Langue und Parole beziehen, versuchen jedoch, beide Ebenen zu berücksichtigen, wobei sie deren Verhältnis zueinander auf verschiedenartige Weise modellieren. Nach Enkvist (1973: 38) besteht eine Lösung darin, den Gruppenstil der 'langue' und den individuellen Stil der 'parole' zuzuweisen, wie es Lubomír Doležel (1960) vorgeschlagen hat. Weiter verbreitet ist jedoch die Annahme eines Sowohl als Auch. Folgt man V. V. Vinogradov (1895−1969), so kann man von zwei Quellen des Stils ausgehen. Zum einen beruht er auf den stilistischen Eigenschaften, die den sprachlichen Mitteln auf der Systemebene zukommen, zum andern resultiert es aus den spezifischen Kombinationen der sprachlichen Mittel auf der Ebene der Realisierung (Vinogradov 1963). Allerdings muß geklärt werden, auf welche Weise sich aus den spezifischen Kombinationen stilistische Eigenschaften ergeben können. So geht beispielsweise Willy Sanders (1977: 34) davon aus, dass das Wesen des Stils nicht allein "über die Analyse der sprach-stilistischen Grundgegebenheiten" erklärbar ist, sondern "auch die außersprachliche Motiviertheit und Fundierung des Stils" zu berücksichtigen ist. Diese außersprachliche Motiviertheit bündelt Sanders in fünf Faktoren: die psychisch-individuellen, sozioökonomischen und -kulturellen, situativen, funktionalen und textsortenspezifischen (Sanders 1977: 34).

Die Bedingungen der Auswahl im Sinne von Michel et al. oder die Sanders'schen Faktoren stehen in einem größeren theoretischen Zusammenhang, in dem Linguistik als "descriptive study of a part of human social behaviour" (Gregory & Spencer 1978: 64) verstanden wird. Besonders ausgeprägt findet sich diese Position im englischen Kontextualismus, demzufolge die Sprachwissenschaft − in den Worten von John R. Firth (1890−1960) − "the physiology of a whole living mass in his habitat or *Lebensraum*" zum Gegenstand haben soll (Firth 1934: 19). Einen zentralen Punkt bildet die Heterogenität von Sprache und die daraus resultierende Variation im Sprachgebrauch, die es systematisch zu erfassen gilt − eine Aufgabe, die seit dem Ausgang der fünfziger Jahre in Angriff genommen worden ist. Dabei wurde vielfach die systematische Erarbeitung der Varietäten einer Sprache explizit mit der stilistischen Fragestellung verknüpft, wie der Titel *Investigating English Style* von David Crystal und Derek Davy (1969) ausweist. In anderen Darstellungen − wie zum Beispiel Quirk (1962), Quirk et al. (1972), Gregory & Carroll (1978) − spielt der Stilbegriff dagegen keine oder nur eine marginale Rolle. Das gleiche Bild ergibt sich für die amerikanischen soziolinguistischen Arbeiten (u. a. von Dell Hymes, John Gumperz und William Labov), die spätestens in den siebziger Jahren in der englischen Varietätenlinguistik rezipiert werden. Dennoch können diese Untersuchungen als Beiträge zur Stilistik verstanden werden. Mit den Dimensionen der sprachlichen Variation werden zwar "eindimensionale Varietäten" erfaßt (Esser 1993: 10−11), die jeweils durch einen der Faktoren *time, region, social group, intelligibility, individuality, interference, medium, participation in discourse, explicitness, attitude, field of discourse, intention, appropriateness of form to pupose* bestimmt sind. Im Text wirken sich aber nicht einzelne dieser Faktoren aus, sondern sie wirken zusammen und konstituieren auf diese Weise den Stil (Esser 1993: 11). Diese Betrachtungsweise zeugt von dem holistischen Charakter von Stil und der integrativen Kraft des Stilbegriffs (s. Abschnitt 1.).

Auch die Weiterentwicklung des taxonomischen Strukturalismus zur generativen

Transformationsgrammatik hat ihre — wenn auch eher geringen — Spuren in der Stildiskussion hinterlassen. Wie andere strukturalistisch beeinflusste Stiltheorien ist auch dieser Ansatz dem Konzept von Stil als Wahl verpflichtet. Den Ausgangspunkt der stilistischen Wahl bildet die in ihrer Struktur und Bedeutung als invariant betrachtete Tiefenstruktur, über der alternative Transformationen operieren. Je nach gewählter Transformation ergibt sich eine stilistisch andere Oberflächenstruktur mit einer je spezifischen Oberflächenbedeutung (Jacobs & Rosenbaum 1973: 52, 54). Untersuchungen, die sich im Rahmen dieses Grammatikmodells bewegen, können zu höchst subtilen Beobachtungen an der Struktur von Sätzen führen (so zuerst Ohmann 1964). Unter Verzicht auf allen theoretischen Ballast hat dies Judith Macheiner (1991) in ihrem "Grammatischen Varieté oder Die Kunst und das Vergnügen deutsche Sätze zu bilden" vorgeführt. Der 'generativen Stilistik' kommt das Verdienst zu, Ohmanns Vermutung konkretisiert zu haben, dass "syntax seems to be a central determinant of style" (Ohmann 1964: 438). Allerdings — und auch darauf hat schon Ohmann (ebda.) hingewiesen — kann sie nur einen Ausschnitt aus dem Feld des Stilistischen erfassen, da mit ihr Fragen der Wortwahl oder des metaphorischen Sprachgebrauchs ausgeklammert bleiben.

Neben der Beschränktheit des als stilistisch relevant Erfassten wird bei dem generativen Ansatz noch ein weiteres Problem in zugespitzter Weise deutlich, das jedoch bei allen strukturalistischen Konzepten von Stil als Wahl anzutreffen ist, sofern sie überhaupt Bedeutungsfragen mit in die stilistische Betrachtung einbeziehen: Es wird von einer konstanten Größe ausgegangen, die selber nicht stilistischer Natur ist, dafür aber das tertium comparationis abgibt für die Wahl sprachlicher Mittel, die zur stilistischen Äußerungsgestalt führt. Dabei wird angenommen, dass die Bedeutung einer Sprachhandlung oder das Was konstant sei und nur die Art der Realisierung oder das Wie variiere. Die Kurzformel für diese Vorstellung lautet, es gebe verschiedene Arten, denselben Inhalt auszudrücken (van Dijk 1980: 99) oder man könne dieselbe Handlung mit unterschiedlichen sprachlichen Äußerungen vollziehen (Sandig 1978: 6).

Obwohl die Auffassung, es sei zwischen einem konstanten Bedeutungsanteil und einem zusätzlichen, variierenden Bedeutungsanteil zu unterscheiden, in der Stildiskussion immer wieder anzutreffen ist, findet sich selten eine explizite Begründung dafür. Zu den Ausnahmen zählt Teun van Dijk (1980). Für ihn manifestiert sich Stil in charakteristischen Unterschieden im Sprachgebrauch, die sich aber nur im Hinblick auf etwas definieren lassen, dass "konstant oder äquivalent" gehalten wird, und zwar "z. B. die Bedeutung, pragmatische Funktion (Sprechakt) oder bestimmte Kategorien, Regeln oder Konventionen, *in bezug auf welche* ein charakteristischer Stil definiert werden kann" (van Dijk 1980: 103). Daneben finden sich aber auch skeptische Stimmen, die am Postulat eines tertium comparationis vor allem dann Anstoß nehmen, wenn es auf der Synomymie der Ausdrücke basieren soll. So stellt beispielsweise Sanders speziell für die lexikalische Ebene fest:

"Letzten Endes bleibt die 'Synonymie' ein zwar vordergründig plausibles, aber bis heute noch nicht voll operationalisierbares wichtiges Phänomen im lexikalischen Bereich" (Sanders 1977: 27)

Diese Skepsis gegenüber dem Synonymiebegriff reicht bis in die Synonymendiskussion des 18. Jhs. zurück, in der schon die Position vertreten wurde, das gleichbedeutende Wörter nur bedeutungsähnlich seien. Konsequenterweise bezeichnete Johann August Eberhard (1739—1809) nicht die Abwechslung des Ausdrucks als Leistung des Variationsstils, sondern die Abwechslung der 'Ideen', die mit den wechselnden Ausdrücken verbunden seien (Püschel 1986: 245—246). Wollte man im Übrigen an der Existenz strikter Synonymie festhalten, würde dies die stilistische Wahl gerade ausschließen. Deshalb bemüht sich E. D. Hirsch (1974/75: 568—569) so sehr darum zu zeigen, dass beim gemeinsamen Auftreten von *bachelor* und *unmarried man* in einem Text allenfalls Sprach- und Literaturwissenschaftler, aber keine 'normalen' *native speakers* einen stilistischen Unterschied und damit eine Bedeutungsdifferenz erkennen würden.

6. Textlinguistik und Stilistik

Bis weit in die sechziger Jahre hinein galt das stiltheoretische Interesse der Frage, wie das Konzept von Stil als Wahl zu modellieren ist. Dabei bewegte man sich innerhalb der Satzgrenze. Zwar waren vor allem in literaturwissenschaftlichen Überlegungen satzübergreifende und den Text betreffende Strukturen wiederholt als zur Stilistik gehörig in den Blick genommen worden, auf die linguistische Stilistik hatte dies jedoch wenig Auswirkung. Wird aber aus linguistischer Perspektive über die Satzgrenze hinausgeblickt, so muss das keineswegs zu einer Erweiterung des Objektbereichs der Stilistik führen, sondern kann in seine Verschiebung münden, wie dies bei Archibald A. Hill (1902−1992) der Fall ist:

"Stylistics concerns all those relationships among linguistic entities which are statable, or may be statable, in terms of wider spans than those which fall within the limits of the sentence." (Hill 1958: 406)

Die Beschränkung auf die Trias von Laut, Wort und Satz wurde in der linguistisch orientierten Stilistik erst in den siebziger Jahren des 20. Jhs. ernstlich aufgegeben, auch wenn Richard M. Meyer (1860−1914) schon früh den Bogen zum Text geschlagen hat, indem er einen extensiven Satzbegriff einführt:

"Auch das größte Stück menschlicher Rede, auch das umfangreichste Buch ist schließlich, wenn es nur einheitlich ist, nichts anderes als ein unendlich ausgedehnter Satz." (Meyer 1913 [1906]: 166)

Jedoch erst unter dem Einfluss der sich entfaltenden Textlinguistik begann sich auch die linguistische Stilistik ernsthaft mit Erscheinungen zu beschäftigen, die den Text betreffen. Nicht mehr der Satz, sondern der Text wird als das primäre sprachliche Zeichen betrachtet, dessen Konstitution auch unter stilistischem Vorzeichen zu untersuchen ist. Am ehesten ausgearbeitet finden sich solche Konzepte in Arbeiten, die im Sinne der Textgrammatik Beziehungen zwischen Sätzen untersuchen (vgl. Hendriks 1967). Dabei wird zum einen die in dem Zitat von Hill angesprochene Linie fortgesetzt, derzufolge Stil Erscheinungen jenseits der Satzgrenze betrifft — eine Position, die beispielsweise Roland Harweg vertritt, der "Stil als die Art und Weise der Konstitution von Texten" bestimmt (Harweg 1972: 70). Zum andern wird die transphrastische Betrachtungsweise als Ergänzung und Erweiterung des Objektbereichs der Stilistik betrachtet wie beispielsweise von Tamara Silman (1974: 10−11) oder von Bernhard Sowinski (1984: 23), der sich wiederum auf Elise Riesel und Eugenie I. Schendels beruft. Riesel & Schendels (1975) unterscheiden eine Mikrostilistik, die sich mit den "sprachstilistischen Teilsystemen" beschäftigt, und eine Makrostilistik, die sich "der Untersuchung mehr oder weniger geschlossener Textstrukturen unterschiedlicher Arten" widmet (Riesel & Schendels 1975: 3). Im textlinguistischen Kontext, der durch Arbeiten wie die von Dressler (1972), Halliday & Hasan (1976), Quirk et al. (1985) abgesteckt ist, werden die beziehungsstiftenden Mittel in pragmatisch-semantische, lexikalische und grammatische eingeteilt, wozu noch Prosodie und Zeichensetzung kommen (vgl. den Überblick bei Esser 1993: 22−129). Insgesamt ist hier eine Wechselwirkung zu beobachten, da einerseits die Textlinguistik die Stilistik zu ihren Vorläufern zählt (Beaugrande & Dressler 1981: 16−17) und andererseits die Stilistikdiskussion von der Textlinguistik befruchtet wird.

Der textgrammatische Zugriff erlaubt es, ausgehend vom lokalen stilistischen Detail 'bottom-up' zu größeren Zusammenhängen fortzuschreiten. Mit der Übernahme des Textsorten-Konzeptes, das in der Textlinguistik seit dem Beginn der siebziger Jahre eine zunehmende Rolle spielt, bietet sich der Stilistik zusätzlich ein Rahmen, globale, den ganzen Text betreffende stilistische Eigenschaften zu erfassen und zudem 'top-down' zu den stilistischen Details zu gelangen. Auch zwischen der Textsorten-Theorie und der Stilistik ist eine wechselseitige Beeinflussung zu beobachten, was sich dann besonders deutlich zeigt, wenn Textsorten- und Stilprobleme im Zusammenhang behandelt werden. Dies gilt beispielsweise für die Arbeiten von Barbara Sandig (u. a. Sandig 1972a, 1972b, 1978, 1986: explizit auch Püschel 1982). Es zeigt sich weiterhin exemplarisch in den Beiträgen der provokativ mit *Textlinguistik contra Stilistik?* überschriebenen Sektion auf dem VII. Internationalen Germanisten-Kongress in Göttingen 1985 (Schöne 1986). Textsorten als konventionelle komplexe Regeln oder Muster für das sprachliche Handeln weisen konventionelle Stile auf, die mehr oder weniger rigide bzw. flexibel sind. Mittlerweile verstehen sich Analysen einzelner Textsorten vielfach ausdrücklich als Beiträge zur Stilistik (z. B. Sandig 1972a zu Kochrezept und Wetterbericht; Sandig 1978 zu Kleinanzeige und Horoskop; Antos 1986 zum Grußwort). Ebenso wie die Beschäftigung mit Textsorten hat sich auch die linguistische Gesprächsanalyse/ Konversationsanalyse auf die Stilistik ausgewirkt. Davon zeugt die Beschäftigung mit Gesprächsstilen, aber auch mit der Leistung des Stilistischen für die Gesprächsorganisation oder die Beziehungsgestaltung (Sandig 1983, Selting 1983, Tannen 1984, Auer 1986; Hickey 1989, Hinnenkamp & Selting 1989). Auch wenn sich die text- und gesprächslinguistisch orientierte Stilistik in der Hauptsache mit nichtliterarischem Sprachgebrauch beschäftigt, werden ihre Verfahren mittlerweile auch auf literarische Texte angewendet (Noguchi 1978, Püschel 1993, Faber 1994). Damit ordnet sich die linguistische Stilistik in eine vor allem seit den sechziger Jahren zu beobachtende Tendenz ein, erneut eine Brücke zwischen Linguistik und Literaturwissenschaft zu schlagen (vgl. zum Beispiel Sebeok 1960, Ihwe 1971−72).

Im Rahmen der Textsorten-Diskussion werden auch den Text konstituierende globale Strukturen berücksichtigt, die als Superstrukturen (van Dijk 1980), als Kommunikationsschemata der Sachverhaltsdarstellung (Kallmeyer & Schütze 1977) oder als Grundmuster der thematischen Entfaltung (Brinker 1985) bezeichnet werden. Hier wirken sich die linguistische Erzählforschung (z. B. Labov & Waletzky 1967) und die Argumentationstheorie (z. B. Toulmin 1958) aus. Dementsprechend hat man sich in der Hauptsache mit dem Erzählen und Erörtern/Argumentieren befasst, daneben aber auch mit Berichten, Beschreiben und Erklären. Stilistisch relevant sind diese Superstrukturen insofern, als sie vielfältige Realisationsmöglichkeiten aufweisen, die weithin textsortenspezifisch gebunden sind. Globale Textstrukturen lassen sich auch mit Wissensrahmen oder Frames erfassen, die besonders Sandig (1986: 198) zur stilistischen Textanalyse heranzieht (sie beruft sich dabei unter anderem auf van Dijk 1977, Fillmore 1977 und Tannen 1979).

7. Sprachpragmatische Stilistik

Hinter jeder Art von Beschäftigung mit Stil steht in letzter Konsequenz die Frage, wie wir mittels Sprache kommunizieren. Selbst in der strukturalistisch beeinflussten linguistischen Stilistik ist dieser Gesichtspunkt nie ganz verloren gegangen, auch wenn in ihr das System stilistischer Mittel und vor allem das stilistisch geformte Produkt im Fokus des Interesses stehen; schließlich impliziert die Rede von Stil als Wahl, dass jemand wählt und seine Entscheidungen an seinen kommunikativen Zielen ausrichtet. Wieder konsequent in den Vordergrund gerückt wird der kommunikative Aspekt in den sprachpragmatisch und sprachhandlungstheoretisch beeinflussten Stilistikkonzeptionen, die seit den frühen siebziger Jahren entwickelt wurden. Einen starken Einfluss hat hier die Sprechakttheorie ausgeübt, die nach John R. Searle auf der Hypothese aufbaut, "eine Sprache sprechen [sei] eine regelgeleitete Form des Verhaltens" (Searle 1971: 38). Weiterhin spielt die Gebrauchstheorie der Bedeutung, bei der unter anderem auf Ludwig Wittgensteins (1889−1951) Begriff des Sprachspiels zurückgegriffen wurde, eine wichtige Rolle. Die Vorstellung, daß das sprachliche Handeln regelgeleitet ist oder auf Mustern beruht, ist auf den Stil übertragen worden dergestalt, dass das Stilistische an einem Text oder einer Sprachhandlung als nach Stilregeln oder -mustern gemacht verstanden wird. Dabei wird von einem allgemeinen Stilmuster ausgegangen, das Barbara Sandig als 'Durchführen' bezeichnet:

"Die Durchführung der Handlung besteht unter stilistischem Gesichtspunkt darin: Aus den zur Verfügung gestellten Inventaren [...] werden im Äußern (des Satzes, Textes ...) einzelne Elemente verwendet: anderen Möglichkeiten, die die Sprache auch zur Verfügung stellen würde, vorgezogen." (Sandig 1986: 43)

Daneben wird aber auch 'Gestalten' zur Bezeichnung des allgemeinsten Stilmusters benutzt (Fix 1996). Mit dem Prädikat *gestalten* wird der Aspekt des Hervorbringens unterstrichen, das heißt, dass jeder Sprachhandelnde seinem Text oder seiner sprachlichen Handlung eine bestimmte Gestalt verleiht. Das Resultat von Gestaltungshandlungen manifestiert sich demnach in Texteigenschaften.

Mit der Feststellung, dass mit Handlungen nach Stilmustern auf Texteigenschaften gezielt wird, ist aber erst ein Teil dessen erfasst, was mit stilistischen Mitteln erreicht werden soll. Denn an die Gestalt des Textes sind weitergehende Bewirkungsversuche geknüpft, die auf die Adressaten zielen. Damit wird der vor allem in der strukturalistisch beeinflussten Stildiskussion latenten Auffassung widersprochen, das Stilistische sei hinreichend beschrieben, wenn die Machart eines Textes analysiert worden ist. Weiterhin wird, damit der Bogen zurückgeschlagen zur rhetorisch gerahmten Regelstilistik des ausgehenden 18. Jhs., für die die Frage nach den Stilwirkungen auf die Adressaten selbstverständlich war.

Unauflöslich verknüpft mit den sprachpragmatischen Ansätzen ist die Frage nach den Bedeutungen sprachlicher Handlungen. Dementsprechend wird in der sprachpragmatisch-handlungstheoretisch orientierten Stilistik konsequent danach gefragt, welcher Sinn sich mit den stilistischen Erscheinungen verbindet. Exemplarisch verdeutlicht wird diese Position, wenn in einer Einführung in die Stilistik der deutschen Sprache die "erste Umgrenzung des Gegenstandsbereichs" charakterisiert wird mit *Typen stilistischen Sinns und deren Grundfunktionen* (Sandig 1986: 20) oder wenn ein Aufsatztitel *Sprachpragmatische Stilanalyse* spezifiziert ist mit *Überlegungen zur interpretativen Stilistik* (Püschel 1991). Ungeachtet tief greifender Unterschiede in den theoretischen Prämissen läßt sich auch hier ein Bogen zurückschlagen zu Leo Spitzers hermeneutischer Position (s. Abschnitt 2.3.) und zur 'werkimmanenten Betrachtung' in ihren verschiedensten Spielarten (s. Abschnitt 2.1.).

8. Bibliographie

Adelung, Johann Christoph. 1785. *Ueber den Deutschen Styl.* Berlin: Christian Friedrich Voß.

Antos, Gerd. 1986. "Zur Stilistik von Grußworten". *Zeitschrift für Germanistische Linguistik* 14.50−81.

Aronstein, Philipp. 1924. *Englische Stilistik.* Leipzig: Teubner.

Aschenberg, Heidi. 1984. *Idealistische Philologie und Textanalyse: Zur Stilistik Leo Spitzers.* Tübingen: Narr.

Auer, Peter. 1986. "Konversationelle Standard/Dialekt-Kontinua (Code-shifting)". *Deutsche Sprache* 14.97−124.

Bally, Charles. 1970 [1909]. *Traité de stylistique française.* Volume I. 5e éd. Genève: Georg & Cie.

−. 1965 [1913]. *Le langage et la vie.* 3e éd. augmentée. Genève: Droz.

Beaugrande, Robert-Alain de & Wolfgang Ulrich Dressler. 1981. *Einführung in die Textlinguistik.* Tübingen: Niemeyer.

Brinker, Klaus. 1985. *Linguistische Textanalyse: Eine Einführung in die Grundbegriffe und Methoden.* Berlin: Erich Schmidt.

Becker, Henrik. 1966. *Stilwörterbuch.* 2 Bde. Leipzig: Bibliographisches Institut.

Becker, Karl Ferdinand. 1848. *Der deutsche Stil.* Frankfurt/M.: G. F. Kettembeil.

Corbin, Pierre. 1989. "Les marques stylistiques/diastratiques dans le dictionnaire monolingue". *Wörterbücher: Ein internationales Handbuch zur Lexikographie* hg. von Franz Josef Hausmann et al., Bd. I, 673−679. Berlin & New York: de Gruyter.

Coseriu, Eugenio. 1970 [1969]. "System, Norm und Rede". *Sprache: Strukturen und Funktionen* hg. von E. Coseriu, 193−212. Tübingen: Tübinger Beiträge zur Linguistik.

Crystal, David & Derek Davy. 1969. *Investigating English Style.* London: Longman.

Deutschbein, Max. 1932. *Neuenglische Stilistik.* Leipzig. Quelle & Meyer.

Dieckmann, Walther. 1981. "K. O. Erdmann und die Gebrauchsweisen des Ausdrucks 'Konnotation' in der linguistischen Literatur". *Politische Sprache, politische Kommunikation: Vorträge. Aufsätze. Entwürfe* hg. von Walther Dieckmann, 76−158. Heidelberg: Winter.

Van Dijk, Teun A. 1977. *Text and Context: Explorations in the semantics and pragmatics of discourse.* London: Longman.

−. 1980. *Textwissenschaft: Eine interdisziplinäre Einführung.* München: dtv.

Doležel, Lubomír. 1960. *O stylu moderní české prózy.* Praha: Československa Akademia Věd.

−. 1968. "Russian and Prague School Functional Stylistics". *Style* 2.143−152.

Dressler, Wolfgang. 1972. *Einführung in die Textlinguistik.* Tübingen: Niemeyer.

Duden 1988[1938] = *Duden. Stilwörterbuch der deutschen Sprache: Die Verwendung der Wörter im Satz.* 7., völlig neu bearb. und erw. Aufl. von Günter Drosdowski. Mannheim, Wien & Zürich: Duden Verlag.

Elster, Ernst. 1911. *Prinzipien der Literaturwissenschaft.* 2. Bd. Halle/S.: Niemeyer.

Erdmann, Karl Otto. 1966 [1900]. *Die Bedeutung des Wortes: Aufsätze aus dem Grenzgebiet der Sprachpsychologie und Logik.* Darmstadt: Wissenschaftliche Buchgesellschaft. (Nachdruck der 4. Aufl. Leipzig, 1925.)

Enkvist, Nils Erik. 1973. *Linguistic Stylistics.* The Hague: Mouton.

−. 1978 [1964]. "On Defining Style: An essay in applied linguistics". *Linguistics and Style* hg. von John Spencer, 1−56. Oxford: Oxford Univ. Press.

Esser, Jürgen. 1993. *English Linguistic Stylistics.* Tübingen: Niemeyer.

Faber, Marlene. 1994. *Stilisierung und Collage: Sprachpragmatische Untersuchung zum dramatischen Werk von Botho Strauß.* Frankfurt/M.: Lang.

Fillmore, Charles J. 1977 "Scenes- and Frames-Semantics". *Linguistic Structures Processing* hg. von Antonio Zampolli, 55−81. Amsterdam: North-Holland.

Firth, John Rupert. 1934. "Linguistics and the Functional Point of View". *English Studies* 16.18−24.

Fix, Ulla. 1992. "Stil als komplexes Zeichen im Wandel: Überlegungen zu einem erweiterten Stilbegriff". *Zeitschrift für germanistische Linguistik* 20.193−209.

−. 1994. "Stilforschung und Stillehre in der DDR". *Jahrbuch für Internationale Grammatik* 26:1.88−102.

—. 1996. "Gestalt und Gestalten: Von der Notwendigkeit der Gestaltkategorie für eine das Ästhetische berücksichtigende pragmatische Stilistik". *Zeitschrift für Germanistik* N. F. 2. 308–323.

Gal'perin, I. R. 1971. *Stylistics.* Moscow: Higher School Publishing House.

Gamillscheg, Emil. 1929. "Grammatik und Stilistik". *Die neueren Sprachen* 37:89–109.

Gray, Bennison (Pseud. für Barbara Bennison u. Michael Gray). 1969. *Style: The problem and its solution.* The Hague: Mouton.

Gregory, Michael J. & John Spencer. 1978 [1964]. "An Approach to the Study of Style". *Linguistics and Style* hg. von John Spencer, 57–109. Oxford: Oxford Univ. Press.

Gregory, Michael & Susanne Carroll. 1978. *Language and Situation: Language varieties and their social context.* London & Boston: Routledge & Kegan Paul.

Gumbrecht, Hans Ulrich & K. Ludwig Pfeiffer, Hg. 1986. *Stil: Geschichte und Funktion eines kulturwissenschaftlichen Diskurselements.* Frankfurt/M.: Suhrkamp.

Halliday, M[ichael] A. K. & Ruqaiya Hasan. 1976. *Cohesion in English.* London: Longman.

Halliday, M. A. K., Angus McIntosh & Peter Strevens. 1968 [1964]. "The Users and Uses of Language". *Readings in the Sociology of Language* hg. von Joshua Fishman, 139–169. The Hague: Mouton.

Harweg, Roland. 1972. "Stilistik und Textgrammatik". *Zeitschrift für Literaturwissenschaft und Linguistik* 2:5.71–81.

Havránek, Bohuslav. 1971 [1969]. "Die Theorie der Schriftsprache". *Stilistik und Soziolinguistik: Beiträge der Prager Schule zur strukturellen Sprachbetrachtung und Spracherziehung* hg. von Eduard Beneš & Josef Vachek, 19–37. Berlin: List.

—. 1976 [1932]. "Die Aufgaben der Literatursprache und der Sprachkultur". *Grundlagen der Sprachkultur: Beiträge der Prager Linguistik zur Sprachtheorie und Sprachpflege* hg. von Jürgen Scharnhorst & Erika Ising, Teil I, 102–141. Berlin: Akademie-Verlag.

Heinemann, Wolfgang. 1974. "Zur Klassifizierung von Stilzügen". *Linguistische Arbeitsberichte der Universität Leipzig* 10.57–61.

Hendricks, William O. 1967. "On the Notion 'Beyond the Sentence'". *Linguistics* 37.21–51.

Heringer, Hans Jürgen. 1989. *Grammatik und Stil: Praktische Grammatik des Deutschen.* Frankfurt: Cornelsen.

Hess-Lüttich, Ernest W. B. 1974. "Das sprachliche Register: Der Register-Begriff in der britischen Linguistik und seine Relevanz für die Angewandte Sprachwissenschaft". *Deutsche Sprache* 2.269–286.

Hickey, Leo, Hg. 1989. *The Pragmatics of Style.* London & New York: Routledge.

Hill, Archibald A. 1958. *Introduction to Linguistic Structures: From sound to sentence in English.* New York: Harcourt, Brace & World.

Hinnenkamp, Volker & Margret Selting, Hg. 1989. *Stil und Stilisierung. Arbeiten zur interpretativen Soziolinguistik.* Tübingen: Niemeyer.

Hirsch, E. D., Jr. 1974/75. "Stylistics and Synonymity". *Critical Inquiry* 1.559–579.

Hjelmslev, Louis. 1974 [1943]. *Prolegomena zu einer Sprachtheorie.* Übers. von Rudi Keller, Ursula Scharf & Georg Stötzel. München: Hueber.

Hockett, Charles F. 1958. *A Course in Modern Linguistics.* New York: Macmillan.

Holenstein, Elmar. 1975. *Roman Jakobsons phänomenologischer Strukturalismus.* Frankfurt: Suhrkamp.

Holly, Werner. 1992. "Holistische Dialoganalyse: Anmerkungen zur 'Methode' pragmatischer Textanalyse". *Methoden der Dialoganalyse* hg. von Sorin Stati & Edda Weigand, 15–40. Tübingen: Niemeyer.

Ihwe, Jens, Hg. 1971–72. *Literaturwissenschaft und Linguistik: Ergebnisse und Perspektiven.* Bd. I: *Grundlagen und Voraussetzungen.* Bd. 2/1 und 2/2: *Zur linguistischen Basis der Literaturwissenschaft 1.* Bd. 3: *Zur linguistischen Basis der Literaturwissenschaft 2.* Frankfurt/M.: Athenäum.

Jacobs, Roderick A. & Peter S. Rosenbaum. 1973 [1971]. *Transformationen, Stil und Bedeutung.* Frankfurt: Athenäum.

Jakobson, Roman. 1960. "Closing Statement: Linguistics and poetics". Sebeok 1960.350–377.

Jauß, Hans Robert. 1969. "Paradigmawechsel in der Literaturwissenschaft". *Linguistische Berichte* 3.44–56.

Kallmeyer, Werner & Fritz Schütze. 1977. "Zur Konstitution von Kommunikationsschemata der Sachverhaltsdarstellung". *Gesprächsanalysen* hg. von Dirk Wegner, 159–274. Hamburg: Buske.

Labov, William & Joshua Waletzky. 1967. "Narrative Analysis: Oral versions of personal experience". *Essays on the Verbal and Visual Arts* hg. von June Helm, 12–44. Seattle: Univ. of Washington Press.

Lerchner, Gotthard. 1976. "Stilzüge unter semasiologischem Aspekt". *Deutsch als Fremdsprache* 13. 257–262.

Linn, Marie-Luise. 1963. *Studien zur deutschen Rhetorik und Stilistik im 19. Jh.* Marburg: Elwert.

Lipka, Leonhard. 1990. *An Outline of English Lexicology: Lexical structure, word semantics, and word-formation.* Tübingen: Niemeyer.

Lux, Friedemann. 1981. *Text, Situation, Textsorte: Probleme der Texsortenanalyse, dargestellt am Beispiel der britischen Registerlinguistik.* Tübingen: Narr.

Macheiner, Judith. 1991. *Das grammatische Varieté oder Die Kunst und das Vergnügen deutsche Sätze zu bilden.* Frankfurt: Eichborn.

Mathesius, Vilém. 1971 [1929]. "Die funktionale Linguistik". *Stilistik und Soziolinguistik: Beiträge der Prager Schule zur strukturellen Sprachbetrachtung und Spracherziehung* hg. von Eduard Beneš & Josef Vachek, 1−18. Berlin: List.

Meyer, Richard M. 1913 [1906]. *Deutsche Stilistik* 2., verb. und verm. Aufl. München: Beck.

Michel, Georg. 1988. "Zum stilistischen Aspekt von Texten". *Neuphilologische Mitteilungen* 89.547−558.

− & Autorenkollektiv. 1968. *Einführung in die Methodik der Stiluntersuchung: Ein Lehr- und Übungsbuch für Studierende.* Berlin: Volk und Wissen. (Zitiert als Michel et al. 1968.)

Moritz, Karl Philipp. 1800 [1793]. *Vorlesungen über den Styl oder praktische Anweisung zu einer guten Schreibart in Beispielen aus den vorzüglichsten Schriftstellern.* Erster Theil. Neue Aufl. Braunschweig: Friedrich Vieweg.

Mukařovský, Jan. 1967 [1948]. *Kapitel aus der Poetik.* Frankfurt: Suhrkamp.

−. 1970 [1966]. *Kapitel aus der Ästhetik.* Frankfurt: Suhrkamp.

Noguchi, Rei R. 1978. *Stylistic and Conversation: An approach to the analysis of 'talk' in drama.* Doctoral dissertation, Indiana University, Bloomington, Ind. (Printed, Ann Arbor, Mich.: University Microfilms International, 1978.)

Ohmann, Richard. 1964. "Generative Grammars and the Concept of Literary Style". *Word* 20.432−439.

Otto, Ernst. 1943. *Sprache und Sprachbetrachtung: Eine Satzlehre unter Berücksichtigung der Wortart.* Prag: Verlag der deutschen Akademie der Wissenschaften.

Paul, Hermann. 1901 [1896]. *Grundriss der Germanischen Philologie.* 1. Bd. 2., verb. und verm. Aufl. Strassburg: Trübner.

Peukert, Herbert. 1977. *Positionen einer Linguostilistik.* Berlin: Akademie-Verlag.

Plett, Heinrich F. 1979. "Concepts of Style: A classification and a critical approach". *Language and Style* 12.268−281.

Pollmann, Leo. 1973. *Literaturwissenschaft und Methode.* 2., verb. Aufl. Frankfurt: Athenäum-Fischer.

Posner, Roland. 1969. "Strukturalismus in der Gedichtinterpretation: Textdeskription und Rezeptionsanalyse am Beispiel von Baudelaires 'Les Chats'. *Sprache im technischen Zeitalter* 29.27−58.

Püschel, Ulrich. 1982. "Die Bedeutung von Textsortenstilen". *Zeitschrift für Germanistische Linguistik* 10.28−37.

−. 1986. "Joh. August Eberhards Synonymik − bloß historisches Dokument oder auch Vorbild für heute?". *Akten des VII. Internationalen Germanisten-Kongresses Göttingen 1985* hg. von Albrecht Schöne, Bd. III, 243−247. Tübingen: Niemeyer.

−. 1989. "Evaluative Markierungen im allgemeinen einsprachigen Wörterbuch". *Wörterbücher: Ein internationales Handbuch zur Lexikographie* hg. von Franz Josef Hausmann et al., Bd. 1, 693−699. Berlin & New York: de Gruyter.

−. 1991. "Sprachpragmatische Stilanalyse: Überlegungen zur interpretativen Stilistik". *Deutschunterricht* 43:3.21−32.

−. 1993. "Stilanalyse als interpretatives Verfahren: Stifters Ur- und Studienmappe als Beispiel". *Wirkendes Wort* 43.68−81.

Quirk, Randolph. 1962. *The Use of English.* New York: St. Martin's Press.

−. Sidney Greenbaum, Geoffrey Leech & Jan Svartvik. 1972. *Grammar of Contemporary English.* London: Longman.

−−. 1985. *A Comprehensive Grammar of the English Language.* London: Longman.

Riesel, Elise. 1959. *Stilistik der deutschen Sprache.* Moskau: Verlag für fremdsprachige Literatur.

−. 1964. *Der Stil der deutschen Alltagsrede.* Moskau: Verlag Hochschule.

− & Eugenie I. Schendels. 1975. *Deutsche Stilistik.* Moskau: Verlag Hochschule.

Riffaterre, Michael. 1959. "Criteria for Style Analysis". *Word* 15.154−174.

Rossipal, Hans. 1973. "Konnotationsbereiche, Stiloppositionen und die sogenannten 'Sprachen' in der Sprache". *Germanistische Linguistik* 4.1−87.

Sanders, Willy. 1977. *Linguistische Stilistik.* Göttingen: Vandenhoeck & Ruprecht.

Sandig, Barbara. 1972a. "Zur Differenzierung gebrauchssprachlicher Textsorten im Deutschen". *Textsorten: Differenzierungskriterien aus linguistischer Sicht* hg. von Elisabeth Gülich & Wolfgang Raible, 113−124. Frankfurt: Athenäum.

−. 1972b. "Bildzeitungstexte: Zur sprachlichen Gestaltung". *Sprache und Gesellschaft* hg. von Annamaria Rucktäschel, 69−80. München: Fink.

−. 1978. *Stilistik: Sprachpragmatische Grundlegung der Stilbeschreibung.* Berlin & New York: de Gruyter.

−, Hg. 1983. *Stilistik.* Bd. II: *Gesprächsstile.* Hildesheim: Olms.

−. 1986. *Stilistik der deutschen Sprache.* Berlin & New York: de Gruyter.

−. 1990. "Holistic Linguistics as a Perspective for the Nineties". *Text* 10.91−95.

Scherer, Wilhelm. 1884. "'Rezension zu Wilmanns Walther [von der Vogelweide]-Ausgabe". *Anzeiger für deutsches Alterthum und deutsche Litteratur* 10.305−312.

−. 1888. *Poetik.* Berlin: Weidemann.

Schneider, Wilhelm. 1968 [1931]. *Ausdruckswerte der deutschen Sprache: Eine Stilkunde.* Darmstadt: Wissenschaftliche Buchgesellschaft.

—. 1969 [1959]. *Stilistische deutsche Grammatik: Die Stilwerte der Wortarten, der Wortstellung und des Satzes.* 5., unveränderte Aufl. Freiburg: Herder.

Schöne, Albrecht, Hg. 1986. *Kontroversen, alte und neue: Akten des VII. Internationalen Germanisten-Kongresses Göttingen 1985.* Bd. 3. Tübingen: Niemeyer.

Searle, John R. 1971 [1969]. *Sprechakte: Ein sprachphilosophischer Essay.* Frankfurt: Suhrkamp.

Sebeok, Thomas A., Hg. 1960. *Style in Language.* Cambridge, Mass.: M.I.T. Press.

Seidler, Herbert. 1963 [1953]. *Allgemeine Stilistik.* 2., neubearb. Aufl. Göttingen: Vandenhoeck & Ruprecht.

Selting, Margret. 1983. "Institutionelle Kommunikation: Stilwechsel als Mittel strategischer Interaktion". *Linguistische Berichte* 86.29–48.

— & Volker Hinnenkamp. 1989. "Einleitung: Stil- und Stilisierung in der interpretativen Soziolinguistik". *Stil und Stilisierung: Arbeiten zur interpretativen Soziolinguistik* hg. von Volker Hinnenkamp & Margret Selting, 1–23. Tübingen: Niemeyer.

Silman, Tamara. 1974. *Probleme der Textlinguistik: Einführung und exemplarische Analyse.* Heidelberg: Quelle & Meyer.

Sowinski, Bernhard. 1984. "Makrostilistische und mikrostilistische Textanalyse: Thomas Manns 'Luischen' als Beispiel". *Methoden der Stilanalyse* hg. von Bern Spillner, 21–47. Tübingen: Narr.

Spillner, Bernd. 1974. *Linguistik und Literaturwissenschaft: Stilforschung, Rhetorik, Textlinguistik.* Stuttgart: Kohlhammer.

Spitzer, Leo. 1928a. *Stilstudien.* 1. Teil: *Sprachstile.* München: Hueber.

—. 1928b. *Stilstudien.* 2. Teil: *Stilsprachen.* München: Hueber.

Strohmeyer, Fritz. 1910. *Der Stil der französischen Sprache.* Berlin: Weidmann.

Tannen, Deborah. 1979. "What's in a Frame? Surface evidence for understanding expectations". *New Directions in Discourse Processing* hg. von Roy O. Freedle, 137–181. Norwood, N. J.: Ablex.

—. 1984. *Conversational Style: Analyzing talk among friends.* Norwood, N. J.: Ablex.

Toulmin, Stephen E. 1958. *The Uses of Argument.* London: Cambridge Univ. Press.

Trabant, Jürgen. 1986. "Der Totaleindruck: Stil der Texte und Charakter der Sprache". *Stil: Geschichte und Funktion eines kulturwissenschaftlichen Diskurselements* hg. von Hans Ulrich Gumbrecht & K. Ludwig Pfeiffer, 169–188. Frankfurt/M.: Suhrkamp.

Ullmann, Stephen. 1967 [1957]. *Grundzüge der Semantik. Die Bedeutung in sprachwissenschaftlicher Sicht.* Berlin: de Gruyter.

—. 1972 [1964]. *Sprache und Stil: Aufsätze zur Semantik und Stilistik.* Tübingen: Niemeyer.

Vinogradov, V[iktor] V. 1963. Stilistika – teorija poetičenskoječi – poètika. Moskva: Izdatel'stvo Akademii Nauk SSSR.

Weimar, Klaus. 1989. *Geschichte der deutschen Literaturwissenschaft bis zum Ende des 19. Jahrhunderts.* München: Fink.

Weise, Oskar. 1905. *Ästhetik der deutschen Sprache.* 2., verb. Aufl. Leipzig & Berlin: Teubner.

Winkler, Emil. 1929. *Grundlegung der Stilistik.* Bielefeld & Leipzig: Velhagen & Klasing.

Ulrich Püschel, Trier (Deutschland)

207. The exportation of structuralist ideas from linguistics to other fields: An overview

1. Introduction
2. Origins of structuralism
3. From Jakobson to Lévi-Strauss
4. 1950s–1960s Paris
5. Structuralism and its aftermath in America and Britain
6. Further extensions and current reactions
7. Bibliography

1. Introduction

The rise to prominence of a generalized 'structuralism' in mid 20th century thought, traced to the influence of the posthumous *Cours de linguistique générale* of Ferdinand de Saussure, thrust linguistics onto centre stage in the human sciences to a degree unparalleled in modern times. The period of dominance of structuralist linguistics as 'master science' varied by field and country, but in general extended from the mid 1950s through the mid 1980s, reaching its worldwide peak in the 1960s and 1970s. The exportation of structuralist ideas out of linguistics was not a one-way traffic. Structuralism as a term and a concept originated in psychology more than twenty years before its first appearance in linguistics, and its early development in linguistics was closely bound up with, and in some cases propelled from, studies of literature and art.

An account of these developments, unless highly idealized (as many have in fact been), is bound to be intricate and complex because the many structuralist 'schools' which arose across various fields, and even within the same field, did not necessarily share a view of what structuralism meant. Although certain common features link particular individuals and groups, there is no single defining factor uniting them all. More than a few 'structuralists' never called themselves that, and as was noted by the structuralist critic Roland Barthes (on whom see 4.2.), "most of the authors ordinarily labeled with this word are unaware of being united by any solidarity of doctrine or commitment" (1972 [1964a]: 148). In a case like that of the Marxist theoretician Louis Althusser, even steadfast attempts to dissociate himself from structuralism could not prevent his work from being tagged with the label (see 4.3.). One of the first widely circulated anthologies of 'structuralist' writings, De George & De George (1972), opens with selections from Marx and Freud, who together with Saussure are seen by the editors as "clearly precursors of present-day structuralism" (p. vii). They thus establish a superb intellectual pedigree for the movement by expanding it to the point that it loses all coherence.

This is not to deny the intriguing connections structuralism has with Freud, Marx, Darwin and a host of other thinkers prior to and contemporaneous with it, or the legitimacy of the De Georges' concern about structuralism being "too frequently presented as if it were a spontaneous phenomenon of 1960s, owing no debt to the past" (ibid.). But its claim to the status of a universal framework of knowledge uniting the humanities and the sciences brought a temptation to include the whole universe within it, as if to suggest that here at last was the grand synthesis of human understanding toward which the entire history of philosophical and scientific endeavour had been aiming. In hindsight such ambitions seem overweening, perhaps naïve and certainly self-serving, and may account in part for the scathing reactions against structuralism seen for example in Scruton's (1998) reference to "philosophers who faked it all along", under which he would include "pseudo-philosophy (Derrida), pseudo-historiography (Foucault), pseudo-criticism (Barthes), pseudo-musicology (Nattiez) and pseudo-political science (Althusser)", along with Lacan's pseudo-psychology and Kristeva's pseudo-everything. Although our survey will not approach this level of critical severity, one must be cautions in dealing with the myths of origin, extension and unity which some structuralists created for themselves.

If the beginnings of structuralism are hard to pin down, the ending point, if there has been one, is even more elusive. Within linguistics, the position of Noam Chomsky is ambiguous: starting in the late 1950s he brings the structuralist phase of linguistics to either its close or its apex, depending on what definition of structuralism one is using (see 5.2.). Outside linguistics, post-structuralism came onto the intellectual scene even as structuralism itself was entering into general cultural awareness, and recognition of its 'post'-ness was a delayed reaction. The result is a significant disjunction between, on the one hand, what the documentary record establishes as the periods in which structuralism was founded (the first third of the century), extended outward from linguistics (the 1940s and 1950s), and 'overthrown' by post-structuralism (1967–1968); and on the other hand, the periods in which large-scale awareness and institutional force came to structuralism (the late 1950s to mid 1980s) and post-structuralism (the late 1970s to mid 1990s). In some cases one finds the same work by the same individual, for example the late Michel Foucault (see 4.3.) or the still very active sociologist Pierre Bourdieu (b. 1930), classified as structuralist or post-structuralist with roughly equal frequency.

A history of structuralism written in structuralist terms would relegate authors to the background. A search might be conducted, à la Claude Lévi-Strauss (see 3.4.), for binomial oppositions that have been operative throughout the history of all intellectual movements, followed by a consideration of what particular values obtained for them in the structuralist period. Or, following the later methods of Foucault or Bourdieu, one might examine how the words *structure* and *structural(ist/ism)*, then *post-structural(ist/ism)*, acquired the power to sell books and periodicals and get papers accepted, grants funded and academics hired and promoted. (This produced some unwitting beneficiaries: in the Introduction to the 1968 paperback edition of his book *The Structure of Social*

Action, first published in 1937, the American sociologist Talcott Parsons (1902–1979) boasts that 'just under 1200 hard cover copies were sold in the year 1966, some eigthy per cent of the number in the original McGraw-Hill edition, which was exhausted only after approximately 10 years".) Interestingly, and tellingly, most accounts of structuralism eschew any such approach, concentrating instead on the thought and work of individual subjects, just what structuralism denies the significance of.

Nor is this the only irony. A key Saussurean tenet is that everything in the structural system functions purely through difference. The label *structuralist* served as an identity marker for scholars and other intellectuals by making clear what they did *not* believe in at least as much as what they did. Structuralism has stood for the rejection of historicism, atomism, existentialism, humanism, political activism, phenomenology, positivism and anti-positivism, capitalism and Marxism, along with many others more localized isms. At times it has signified little more than a generational or individual declaration of intellectual independence, sometimes for opportunistic ends. "To call oneself a structuralist was always a polemical gesture, a way of attracting attention and associating oneself with others whose work was of moment" (Culler 1975: 3). To call oneself *not* a structuralist could serve the same functions.

This article will not then be dealing with the simple transference of a methodology, but with overlapping sets of methodologies (developed to varying degrees of completeness), terminologies, ideologies and, by no means least, mythologies. While linguistics contributed something to nearly all of these, in the end it may have been in the areas of terminology and mythology that its effects were strongest.

2. Origins of structuralism

2.1. Before Saussure

As noted above, many structuralists were eager to legitimate their enterprise by tying it to the great intellectual achievements of the 19th century and earlier. Seung (1982: 4) extends the term 'structural analysis' to cover the work of Euclid, Plato and Aristotle, as well as Descartes. Vico is frequently cited as a precursor of structuralism, as are the 17th century corpuscularean sceptics (see Garber 1982). Among potential predecessors who actually made apposite use of the term *structural* – which in the 19th century probably still felt metaphorical when extended to living creatures and their activities – the earliest in English would appear to be Herbert Spencer (1820–1903), who from the 1850s divided his sociology into 'structural' and 'functional' domains (cf. Leach 1987: 55). The further extension to *structuralist/ism* would come more than forty years later in the context of an attempt to introduce American psychologists to an approach being developed in Germany, notably by Wilhelm Wundt (1832–1920). An 1898 article by the Wundt-trained Anglo-American psychologist Edward Bradford Titchener (1867–1927) entitled "The Postulates of a Structural Psychology" sets out the case for the structural approach as a necessary corrective to the then-dominant functionalism which Titchener associates with Brentano, Dewey and William James. This initial 'structuralism', as James R. Angell (1869–1949) would first call it in a 1907 article which also contains the first attestation in English of 'structuralist', aimed at the discovery of the elemental units which make up the mind. It would become embroiled in a controversy over the use of introspective data, and would finally be definitively rejected as the Gestalt movement of the 1920s turned the tide against elementalism and toward analysing the mind and its functions in a holistic way. Beyond the terminological overlaps, it is Gestalt psychology, rather than the 'structuralism' it finished off, that has affiliations with the much better-knowm structuralism which would emerge from linguistics some three decades after Titchener's 1898 article. The latter nevertheless has a claim to historical priority, and it is not impossible that this first structuralism pre-empted further use of the term until enough time had elapsed for it to sink into oblivion.

2.2. Saussure

Certainly there is no evidence to suggest that Ferdinand de Saussure (1857–1913) was aware of any of these developments, though he was cultivated beyond the norm even for aristocratic professors in turn of the century Europe. In any case neither the term *structure* nor any of its derivatives were part of his vocabulary; *system* was the term he usually employed to denote that conception of a language as a self-contained entity upon which structuralism would come to be founded. A study of Saussure's sources and influences (the definitive survey being Koerner 1973; see also Koerner 1975) is striking on two counts. The first is how many elements of his thinking have precedents in the work of either the Neogrammarians by whom he was trained, other linguists of the last quarter of the 19th century (and, arguably, scholars working in neighbouring disciplines), or earlier theorists of language from Aristotle and the Stoics through Étienne Bonnet de Mably de Condillac (1714–1780) and Wilhelm von Humboldt (1767–1835). (To note these echoes is not to assert that Saussure was necessarily directly influenced by any of those named — a vexed problem given that he did not always indicate his sources.) Yet no less striking than Saussure's drawing together of so many already existing strands of linguistic thought is the utter originality with which he weaved them into a synthesis that is stunningly modern, and all his own. Thorough surveys of Saussure's approach to language can be found elsewhere in this Handbook (→ Art. 199; also Joseph 1999); our discussion will be limited to nine aspects of his approach were to prove particularly important for later structuralism:

- *The justification of synchronic analysis.* Over the course of the 19th century the academic study of language had come to be strongly dominated by the historical-comparative approach, in which one looked for the oldest existing text in a particular language family and tried to reconstruct backwards into its prehistory. The study of languages in anything other than a historical mode was considered by many to be a branch not of linguistics, but of psychology, and one of the most important non-historical books on language of the beginning of the century is by the psychologist Wundt (1900), mentioned in 1. Saussure argued that, on the contrary, the synchronic study of language must be no less central to linguistics than the 'diachronic' study, a term he coined in 1894, meaning in effect 'historical', but history conducted on the basis of strict comparison of synchronic systems as they existed at different points in time. This meant that the synchronic approach must, if anything, take precedence.
- *Language as a system of signs.* In the face of the historical linguists' approach to languages as being first and foremost collections of vowels and consonants and their combinations, Saussure resuscitated an ancient and medieval tradition of 'semiotic' study of languages as systems of signs. He called for the creation of a science of 'semiology' which would study all sign systems, and within which linguistics would function as the 'pilot' discipline. There is no evidence Saussure was aware of the American Charles Sanders Peirce's (1839–1914) slightly earlier attempts to establish a 'semeiotic' with somewhat comparable aims.
- *Signs as the conjunction of signifier and signified.* Perhaps the single most original, radical and controversial aspect of Saussure's analysis of language is his definition of the linguistic sign as the conjunction of a *signifiant* "signifier" (a sound pattern) and a *signifié* "signified" (a concept), with no further connection to anything outside the sign itself. In other words, the sign *tree* in English is the union of a sound pattern (which can be symbolized as /t r i/) and a concept — not an object existing in the world, but a concept existing in the mind. This concept, the signified, is as much a part of the language as is the sound pattern which signifies it. Hence the sign *arbre* in French cannot have the same signfied as does English *tree*; it cannot, in other words, mean the same thing, even though the two words are generally reckoned as equivalents for purposes of translation. Saussure's radical refusal to tie the meaning of *tree* and *arbre* to particular objects in the world captures a belief expressed in the 19th century by Humboldt and others that each language analyses the world in a unique way.
- *The arbitrary connection of signifier and signified.* In stating that it is generally accepted that the bond between signifier and signified is a purely arbitrary and conventional one, Saussure places himself in a long tradition extending from Aristotle to the American linguist William Dwight Whitney (1827–1894). Nevertheless, through a quirk of historical memory, combined with the strong way in which the internal arbitrariness of signs is asserted at a crucial point in the *Cours*, many in the 20th century would assume that this doctrine originated with Saussure. A later section on 'relative arbitrari-

ness', limiting most of those strong assertions, would attract relatively little attention. Adding to the confusion, Saussure's remarks on arbitrariness, which pertain strictly to the bond between signifier and signified, would also get frequently confounded with his assertion described above about the linguistic sign not being bound to any reality outside itself.
- *Meaning as internally generated value.* If language is a self-contained system of self-contained signs, then meaning is internal to language. What a word means is not a thing or state of affairs 'out there'. Rather, it is a conceptual space defined and limited by the other words in the same language. The same is true, *mutatis mutandis*, of other units of language, from individual sounds through propositions. Saussure thus reconceives meaning as the *value* of a sign, which is generated by its sheer *difference* from the other signs within the system. He gives the example of English *sheep* and French *mouton*, which although they might be used in a particular instance to designate the same animal, nevertheless cannot 'mean' the same thing in the sense that their value is not the same: the conceptual space of *sheep* is limited by the fact that it exists within a system which also includes the word *mutton*, while French *mouton* covers both the concepts of the whole animal and its meat.
- *The negative character of linguistic value; language as form, not substance.* The fact that value is generated by difference means that the identity of the linguistic sign lies not in its positive content, but is purely negative in character. The meaning of the signified derives from the place it occupies within the total system of signifieds, and from nothing outside it. Thus the real existence of a sign is located in the space created by what all other signs are not — i.e., in pure difference. A language is a form and not a substance. Thus Saussure locates the reality of language not in what can be heard or seen but at an extraordinarily high level of conceptual abstractness.
- *Language as a system in which 'tout se tient'.* Everything hangs together. Every element in the language system is connected to and dependent upon every other element. A change in any one element therefore means a change to the entire system — in effect, a new language.
- *Language as psychological, unconscious and socially shared.* As noted above, both signifier and signified are *mental* pattern of sound and concept respectively. Thus the sign, like the entire system of signs which constitutes the language, has a purely psychological existence within the individual. It is essentially unconscious, though certain linguistic operations can involve semi-conscious and conscious processes. Crucially, the language system exists in identical form in the brains of all the individuals who constitute a given speech community.
- *The distinction between* langue *and* parole. Apparent differences in how people speak the same language proceed not from a difference in the system itself (*langue*, language), but in how it is used (*parole*, speech). The central work of linguistics is to discover the unconscious system of negative relations which give value to the signs shared by the speakers of a language.

There is, however, considerable ambiguity in what is meant by *a language* at the end of the last sentence Saussure, who was not writing his course for publication but lecturing mainly to beginners, was never clear about what he took the boundaries of *la langue* to be. It is unclear at what point syntax ceases to belong to *langue* and becomes an effect of *parole*, or whether two *langues* or one are constituted by American and British English on the one hand, 18th and 19th century French on the other, and so on *ad infinitum*. It is not even clear whether, in many of his most significant statements about *langue*, he meant to suggest that linguists should focus their attention on individual languages (French, Chinese, etc.) or on 'language' as a general phenomenon, or both. Certainly his comments about the role of linguistics as the 'pilot science' of a general semiology that would cover all uses of signs suggest that he would not have rejected the wider interpretation. In any case, the later development of structuralism would depend crucially on an understanding of Saussure's *langue* as a kind of *universal* schema underlying all the actually existing languages in the world.

The doctrine of language as a system where *tout se tient* (a phrase which does not occur in Saussure's *Cours* or any of his extant writings but is traditionally associated with him) brings a sense of *holism* to structuralism. It means in effect that any study a structuralist undertakes, however trivial it may seem, is not actually trivial. Whereas in physical systems some bits are essential, like brains, and others not, like toenails, the structuralist system is egalitarian. Everything is essential in equal measure, if a change to any part produces a new whole. Whether one is studying a particular phoneme or the entire morphological structure of a language, a contribution of fundamental significance is being made. Each individual structuralist, by virtue of this faith, is a high priest in direct communication with the invisible structure, that mystical whole of which lay people are unaware, and into the knowledge of which only the select few will be initiated. At the turn of the 20th century one of the great philosophical debates was over the holistic versus analytic nature of the universe (with the followers of Hegel on the former side) and whether any real knowledge could be gained by working through philosophical problems on by one. The importance of Bertrand Russell's (1872–1970) establishment of 'analytic' philosophy was precisely its success in beating back this holistic view, to which Russell himself had subscribed not so long before. In this regard, structuralism was a way of eating one's cake and having it too. Like Russell's logical atomism, it takes the whole to be made up of isolable yet inseparable parts from which the whole itself is projected. There is, then, no choice to be made between the whole and its parts. The whole is not even the sum of its parts; each part *is* the whole.

2.3. From the Geneva School to Russian Formalism

After Saussure's death two colleagues who were early students and associates of his, Charles Bally (1865–1947) and Albert Sechehaye (1870–1946), gathered together surviving manuscripts and especially carefully executed students' notes, and collated them into the published *Cours de linguistique générale* (1916). From 1908 the group around Saussure began calling themselves the 'Geneva school' (on which see Amacker 1995), and they and their successors have always claimed a role as guardians of Saussurean structuralism, sometimes in opposition to later, less conservative transdisciplinary developments. However, one scholar frequently counted among the members of the Geneva school may have played a key role in transmitting Saussure's teaching to those who would get these developments started. The Russian linguist Sergej Karcevskij (1884–1955) attended Saussure's courses from 1905 onward (two years before Saussure began lecturing on general linguistics). He returned to Moscow in 1917, and found an appreciative audience for his transmission of Saussure's ideas among members of the two-year-old Moscow Linguistic Circle, particularly its founder, Roman Jakobson (1896–1982), on whom see further Joseph et al. (2001, chap. 2).

Saussure's impact on the young Jakobson, whose boundless interests were centred on historical and synchronic linguistics, literature and folklore, would become apparent in his work beginning a few years later. Jakobson stood at the centre of a general 'formalist' movement (as its critics dubbed it) encompassing the creation of poetry, art and music as well as their analysis. From the beginning Jakobson appears ambivalent about Saussure, resenting the fact that certain ideas for which the Swiss linguist was given credit had been anticipated by Russian scholars ignored in the West, and objecting to points of doctrine large and small where he believed Saussure did not go far enough or simply got it wrong. But throughout his long life Jakobson would make clear that even if he was far from being an orthodox Saussurean, it was from Saussure that he had acquired the basic vision of language and the framework for analysing it that would underlie his work thereafter.

Over the course of the 1920s Jakobson's evolving proto-structuralist framework, derived from Saussure, interacted so thoroughly with his more general formalist interests that the direction of influences becomes impossible to determine. What we can say with certainty is that during these formative years linguistic structuralism informed approaches to literature, art and folklore and absorbed influences in return. The classic study of the interrelation of formalism and early structuralism is Jameson (1972); see also Erlich (1965). Probably the most famous work of Russian formalist cirticism of the period, *Morphology of the Folktale* by Vladimir Propp (1895–1970), published in Russian in 1928, was widely received as if part of the structuralist canon upon its publication in English (edited by one of Jakobson's wives) in 1958. Propp examines 100 folktales, and analyses their plots into 31 constituent structural units which he calls *functions*, defining the function as

"an act of dramatis personae, which is defined from the point of view of its significance for the course of action of the tale as a whole [...]. Functions serve as stable, constant elements in folktales, independent of who performs them [...]. They constitute the components of a folktale. The number of functions known in the fairy tale is limited [...]. The sequence of functions is always identical". (Propp 1958 [1928]: 20)

Symbolizing the functions with letters and superscripts and charting their combinations as schemes, a procedure which he notes had been undertaken 35 years earlier by the French philologist Joseph Bédier (1864–1938), Propp reduces the folktales to algebraic formulae, for example (93–94):

"If we add up, one after another, all schemes which include struggle–victory and also all instances in which we have a simple killing of the enemy without a fight, we will end up with the following scheme:
ABC↑DEFGHIJK↓Pr Rs° LQ Ex TUW*."

The totality of these units and schemes can be seen as making up a dimension of the human unconscious on a par with Saussure's *langue* (though Propp, who never mentions Saussure, does not claim this). Although Propp's approach would come in for strenuous criticism from reigning structuralists like Lévi-Strauss and Greimas after its 1958 revival (in Lévi-Strauss's case actually before it – see Lévi-Strauss 1955a), its pioneering status would be universally acknowledged and it would prove deeply influential. Another writer of this period, Mikhail Bakhtin (1895–1975), would emerge from decades of obscurity starting in the late 1960s with the publication of English translations of Bakhtin (1940) and Bakhtin & Medvedev (1928), and peaking with the publication in the same year of Bakhtin (1981) in America and Todorov (1981) in France. His views on translinguistics, intertextuality and heteroglossia, which throw into question the autonomous, self-contained nature of the Saussurean system, would be seen as foreshadowing *post*-structuralist thought (see 4.4.–5.), and Bakhtin would be absorbed into the post-structuralist canon much as Propp was into the structuralist one.

3. From Jakobson to Lévi-Strauss

3.1. Jakobson's and Trubetzkoy's 'substantive' structuralism

Jakobson left Moscow for Prague in 1920, then in 1933 took up a chair at Brno. Living in Czechoslovakia meant that Jakobson was physically close to the linguist who would be his most important collaborator during the 1920s and 1930s, Prince Nikolaj Trubetzkoy (1890–1938), who fled Russia at the time of the Revolution and took up a chair at Vienna in 1922. In 1926 the Prague Linguistic Circle was established by the Professor of English at Charles University, Vilém Mathesius (1882–1945), with Jakobson as a founding member and a prime intellectual force. A series of programmatic manifestos written or co-written by Jakobson and published in the years 1928–1929 mark a key moment in the bringing of structuralism to attention beyond his immediate circle.

In October 1927 Jakobson wrote a reply to one of a series of questions sent to participants by the organizing committee of the First International Congress of Linguists, to be held at The Hague in April 1928. This reply, constituting a combined résumé and manifesto for a method of synchronic analysis starting from Saussure and basing itself on binomial oppositions, was countersigned by Karcevskij and Trubetzkoy and published in the proceedings of the congress (Jakobson 1962 [1928]). Also in 1928 Jakobson and Jurij Tynianov (1894–1943) published a brief set of eight theses on 'problems in the study of language and literature' which sketched out a program for the extension of structural principles beyond linguistics, focusing on Saussure's dichotomies of synchrony–diachrony and *langue–parole*, and articulating the need for the study of literature to be put on a scientific footing:

"The immediate problems facing Russian literary and linguistic science demand a clear theoretical base. They must be decisively dissociated from the increasingly frequent practice of pasting together a new methodology with old, outmoded methods, and of surreptitiously introducing naïve psychologism and other methodological relies under cover of a new terminology.
Academic eclecticism and a scholastic 'formalism' which replaces analysis with terminology and with a cataloguing of phenomena must be avoided, as must the repeated transformation of the study of literature and language, which is a systematic science, into episodic and anecdotal genres". (Tynianov & Jakobson 1972 [1928]: 81)

The second paragraph above is notable for its decisive break from earlier Russian 'formalism' as well as for the attack on entrenched academic methods as based on mere taxonomy, the same charge which Chomsky would level against the 'American structuralism' of

Bloomfield and his followers in the early 1960s (see 5.1.).

In 1929 Jakobson led the writing of a set of theses for presentation to the First Congress of Slavists in Prague. This document, like the other two, evinces the distinctive characteristics of Saussurean structuralism, with still greater breadth, including as it does programs for the study of poetic language and applications to language teaching, and the concern with 'functionalism' which would become associated with the Prague Circle.

The International Congress of Linguists of 1928 gave Jakobson a platform for presenting the developing structuralist program, which had a wide appeal both among Europeans who had been prepared for it by their reading of Saussure, and Americans who appreciated the features it shared with their own synchronic descriptive approach. Centres of structuralist linguistics soon developed in Copenhagen, around Viggo Brøndal (1887–1942) and Louis Hjelmslev (1899–1965) – against some resistance from the grand old man of Danish linguistics, Otto Jespersen (1860–1943) – and in Paris around some of the students of Saussure's associate Antoine Meillet (1866–1936), including Émile Benveniste (1902–1976) and André Martinet (1908–1999), and his own distinctive direction, Gustave Guillaume (1883–1960). None of them toed the Praguean line, but all took cues and insights from Prague and to a certain extent looked toward Prague for validation.

In the 1930s Jakobson and Trubetzkoy led structuralism in the radically new direction of what is now called 'markedness' theory, which holds that certain elements in the linguistic system have an interrelation that is neither arbitrary nor purely formal, but defined by the fact that one element is distinguished from the other through the addition of an extra feature, a 'mark'. When the distinction is neutralized it is always the simple, 'unmarked' member of the opposition that appears. For instance, in German there is a 'correlation' between pairs of voiceless and voiced consonants like /t/ and /d/, where the opposition between them is neutralized at the end of the word. Thus the minimal contrast between the genitive nouns *Rates* "council's" and *Rades* "wheel's" is neutralized in the nominative, where both *Rat* "council" and *Rad* "wheel" are pronounced with a final /t/ – the unmarked member of the pair. The 'mark' in this case is the vibration of the vocal cords which differentiates /d/ from /t/, making /d/ the more 'complex' of the two. Because simplicity as here understood includes the physical elements of articulation and sound, markedness undoes the key Saussurean tenet that language is form, not substance. It first occurred to Trubetzkoy in the course of phonological studies he was pursuing in 1930, and he wrote to Jakobson almost casually mentioning the idea, Jakobson immediately saw its full implications, and his reply foresees developments that would not transpire for another three decades:

"I am increasingly convinced that your notion of correlation always being a relation of a marked and an unmarked series is one of your most remarkable and productive ideas. I think that it will become important not only for linguistics, but also for ethnology and the history of culture [...]". (Jakobson to Trubetzkoy, Nov. 1930, transl. in Jakobson and Pomorska 1983 [1980]: 95)

Over the following years Jakobson and Trubetzkoy each developed this 'substantive' structuralism in his own way. Trubetzkoy devoted himself to the search for a universal schema for the analysis of the vowel systems of all known languages (see Trubetzkoy 1939). Jakobson, leaving the vowels to Trubetzkoy, focused on the analysis of consonants while attempting to extend the insight about the mark to morphology. In the second half of the 1930s he moved toward another major rewriting of Saussurean theory as he became convinced that phonemes were not the ultimate units of phonological analysis, but that they should be further broken down into 'distinctive features'. The full impact of this idea would not be felt in linguistics until decades later; but what Jakobson saw at once was that it undid another of Saussure's fundamental principles, the linearity of the signifier. If Jakobson was right that distinctive features signify, they do not occur in linear order, but are realized simultaneously in bundles, like musical chords.

One further aspect of Jakobson's structuralism that emerged during this period and would have far-reaching consequences was its binarism. Jakobson analysed distinctive features according to a grid, where each phoneme received for each future a value of + or − (or in somes cases ±), unless the feature failed to apply at all, in which case no value was entered. This provided a very clear form of analysis that was easy to produce, and it would figure prominently in structuralist analyses from Lévi-Strauss onward (see 3.4.) as well as in the generative phonology of the 1960s and after (see Chomsky & Halle 1968).

Jakobson was not the only structuralist critiquing key Saussurean concepts at this time. The principle of the arbitrariness of the sign was problematized by Hjelmslev, Benveniste and numerous others in a series of attacks on and defenses of the Saussurean view (often poorly represented) appearing from 1939 to about 1947. Of these the most influential would be Benveniste's (1939) argument that the doctrine of arbitrariness is misguided, because it relates only to the historical origin of the signifier-signified link. For the individual speaker with a strictly synchronic perspective, the bond between signifier and signified appears not arbitrary at all, but necessary, and in Benveniste's view this synchronic necessity outweighs any question of arbitrariness.

3.2. The Prague Linguistic Circle

In the 1930s Czech members of the Prague Linguistic Circle initiated the first sustained wave of exportation of structuralist ideas from linguistics to other fields, namely literary theory and general 'aesthetics'. Jan Mukařovský (1891–1975) developed an approach to aesthetics which departs from the Russian Formalist view to explore a 'functionalist' perspective characteristic of Praguean work, with a Saussurean-derived focus on the work of art as "a *sign*, and hence at bottom [...] a social fact" (1970 [1936a]: 83; see also 1936b). Bradford (1994: 145) discusses the interplay between Jakobson's and Mukařovský's views on Saussure's synchrony and diachrony distinction at the end of the 1930s (see Jakobson 1962 [1939], Mukařovský 1940). Mukařovský would get the critical mainstream through the intermediary of the Viennese born René Wellek (1903–1999), who studied at Prague before emigrating to America, where he co-authored what would become the most widely used American textbook of literary studies (Wellek & Warren 1948), in which Mukařovský figures prominently, as does Jakobson.

Other writers who contributed significant work to the early volumes of the Prague Linguistic Circle's journal *Slovo a Slovesnost* (founded 1935) include Bogatyrev (1938) and Veltruský (1940, 1941) on the theatre as sign system, Mathesius (1939) and Trnka (1941) on style, and Wollman (1935) on the structuralist approach to literature. In 1932 Bohuslav Havránek (1893–1978) and Mukařovský published significant papers on the relationship of standard and literary language. In 1942 they co-edited a volume on language and poetry, and in 1947 the two of them, together with Felix Vodička (1909–1974), wrote and published five popular radio lectures on the language of literature. For a section of Prague School writings in these areas see Garvin (1964), and for an overview, Wellek (1969).

An important linking figure for the Prague Circle was the German philosopher and psychologist Karl Bühler (1879–1963), a colleague of Trubetzkoy's at the University of Vienna, whose 1934 book *Sprachtheorie*, outlining a functional analysis of language, had a significant impact on the Prague linguists as well as giving them common intellectual ground with the Vienna Circle of logical positivists. Bühler's Saussurean heritage is evident in remarks such as the following: "[...] words of a particular word-class open up around them one or several 'empty places', which have to be filled by words of certain other word-classes" (1934: 173, transl. by Allerton 1995: 281). Insofar as structuralist ideas were 'exported' to philosophy and psychology in 1920s and 1930s Vienna, Bühler was the key figure, though in fact the relationship here is more complex than the metaphor of exportation captures.

The work of the Prague Linguistic Circle was not widely read except by linguists in this period, and Prague would never fully recover its status as an intellectual centre after the Nazi invasion in 1938. Nevertheless, the Circle continued producing work of substance through the 1940s, including brilliant and daring extensions of structuralism that would go largely ignored for another 15 or 20 years, until they were resurrected in the heyday of worldwide structuralism. Even though its own heyday was over by 1950, the Prague structuralist tradition has continued to the present day, both in Prague and amongst emigrants abroad.

3.3. Jakobson in America; Cassirer

Jakobson and his wife fled Prague in anticipation of the Nazi invasion, traveling first to Denmark, where he was received by the structuralists there; then when it became clear that Denmark would fall under Nazi control, to Sweden. Finally in May 1941 they set sail for America, and according to Jangfeldt (1997) Jakobson spent the two weeks of the crossing in excited conversation with another refugee, the philosopher Ernst Cassirer (1874–1945), himself very well versed in the history of linguistics and keenly interested in the role of language in the philosophical system.

At the start of 1942 Jakobson began lecturing at the 'École Libre des Hautes Études' organized in New York by fellow refugees, most of whom, like Jakobson, had arrived to find no immediate prospect of academic employment. The audience included linguists of several nationalities as well as some of Jakobson's fellow teachers in the École, one of whom was Lévi-Strauss. During the first term Jakobson gave two courses, one consisting of six lectures on sound and meaning (1976 [1942a]) and another on Saussure (1984 [1942b]). The latter course was in fact a thoroughgoing critique of Saussure, and the former too included the challenge to Saussure's doctrine of linearity (see 3.1. and Joseph 1989). Both reflect the new turn introduced into Jakobson's thinking by his analysis of the phoneme into distinctive features. Nevertheless, the lectures were presented to an audience including some not previously acquainted with Saussure and others who knew him only superficially (see Lévi-Strauss's preface to Jakobson 1976 [1942a]), so that in spite of their critical nature they had the effect of drawing attention to the *Cours* and securing its place at the head of the structuralist canon.

Undoubtedly as a result of his shipboard friendship with Jakobson, Cassirer would read a paper a few days before his death in February 1945 on "Structuralism in modern linguistics" to the Linguistic Circle of New York, a group Jakobson co-founded. The paper, published as Cassirer (1945) in the Linguistic Circle's newly established journal *Word*, is important as the first wide-ranging philosophical discussion of structuralism, its aims, methods and meaning. Cassirer situates structuralist linguistics within the history of philosophy and science, comparing it explicitly with various developments across the centuries in which mere superficial empiricism was rejected in favour of the search for underlying organizing principles which operate with perfect regularity: "structuralism is no isolated phenomenon; it is, rather, the expression of a general tendency of thought that, in these last decades, has become more and more prominent in almost all fields of scientific research" (Cassirer 1945: 120). Cuvier's principles of biology are cited as a particularly close example, along with Gestalt psychology. Cassirer also affirms that Humboldt anticipated a central tenet of structuralism with his declaration that language is not an *ergon*, a product, but an *energeia*, a potential (a distinction partly recapitulated in Saussure's *parole* and *langue*). For Cassirer, this amounts to saying that language is organic, "in the sense that it does not consist of detached, isolated, segregated facts. It forms a coherent whole in which all parts are interdependent upon each other" (p. 110). He then goes further (ibid.):

"In this sense we may even speak of a poem, of a work of art, of a philosophic system as 'organic'. Dante's *Divina Commedia*, a tragedy of Aeschylus, Kant's *Critique of Pure Reason* are 'organic'. What we find here are not 'disjecta membra', scattered limbs of a poet, an artist, or a thinker. Everything hangs together: nothing is accidental or superfluous. In a tragedy of Shakespeare or in a lyric poem of Goethe we can hardly remove one word without destroying the character and the beauty of the whole."

Cassirer cannot have been terribly well informed about the textual history and status of Shakespeare's works. Nevertheless, here for the first time the basis of general structuralism was proclaimed by an eminent philosopher who was an outsider to Jakobson's Moscow or Prague entourages, before an unusually multidisciplinary audience brought together by the circumstance of being in exile from Nazi-dominated Europe. The vision of a universal science which even Jakobson had hardly dared put forward outside an isolated letter to Trubetzkoy of 15 years before received its validation in Cassirer's valediction.

Jakobson would go on to become the doyen of Slavic studies in America, even though his influence on linguistics was held in check by the Bloomfieldians, some of whom bitterly resented his intrusion into their domain. After the war Jakobson taught for a few years at Columbia University, then moved in 1949 to Harvard, where he would direct the doctoral thesis of Morris Halle (b. 1923) and would have frequent discussions with Halle's friend Chomsky, who was completing his own Ph. D. under the Bloomfieldian Zellig Harris (1909–1992). From 1957 onward Jakobson would also be affiliated with Chomsky's and Halle's institution, the Massachusetts Institute of Technology.

3.4. Lévi-Strauss's structuralist ethnography

Claude Lévi-Strauss (b. 1908) is one of those figures who blurs any attempt to separate European and American structuralism, and not only because of his wartime exile or later transatlantic renown. Although educated in French philosophy of a rather traditional sort, he identifies the German émigré to America Franz Boas (1858–1942) and the Americans Alfred Kroeber (1876–1960) and Robert H. Lowie (1883–1957), both students of Boas, as his central influences in anthropology (1973 [1955b]: 59). Still, the fact of his having read Boas, the single most important forerunner of 'American structuralism' (see 5.1.), did not prevent Jakobson's lectures on Saussure from striking him as a revelation.

Lévi-Strauss's first foray into structuralism came in a 1944 paper (published as Lévi-Strauss 1945) to the Linguistic Circle of New York, on "structural analysis in linguistics and anthropology". The paper establishes a pattern of discourse that would become extremely familiar over the next two decades, and not just in the writings of Lévi-Strauss. "Linguistics is not just one social science among others", it begins "but the one which, by far, has accomplished the greatest progress; the only one, without a doubt, which can lay claim to the name of science and which has succeeded in formulating a positive method and in understanding the nature of the facts submitted to its analysis" (p. 33, my translation: JEJ). All the other social sciences, beginning with anthropology, should try to imitate it – just as, Lévi-Strauss notes, Marcel Mauss (1872–1950) had already suggested that sociology should do twenty years before. Today, with so many of their core concerns long since consigned to the dustbin of forgotten science, it seems remarkable that linguists at mid-century should have had such sustained optimism about the unparalleled progress of their field. And it is no less remarkable that an anthropologist should want to place his field in 'servitude' to another, just when anthropology and ethnology were enjoying unparalleled prominence in the Anglo-American world thanks to stars like Alfred R. Radcliffe-Brown (1881–1955), in whose work of as early as 1922 the term 'structure' features prominently. But then, within this servitude, it turned out to be Lévi-Strauss who was the master.

It took another decade for that to happen, and the immediate occasion for it was a remarkable book entitled *Tristes tropiques* (Lévi-Strauss 1955b), which became a bestseller in France and later abroad. Subtitled "an anthropological study of primitive societies in Brazil", it is also the story of Lévi-Strauss himself, his background, his education, his experience of teaching at the newly-founded University of São Paulo from 1935–1939 and making various expeditions into Central Brazil during that time, and his dramatic escape from Vichy France. He encountered the cultures of Brazil as they were losing their (perhaps mythical) primeval innocence. It is an irresistible work by an author endowed with extraordinary capacities for observation, analysis and story-telling, who keeps his structuralism well below the surface. The autobiographical portion ends with Lévi-Strauss having arrived in Puerto Rico via Martinique, and getting FBI clearance to enter the United States. Roman Jakobson does not appear, and Saussure's *Cours* gets but a passing mention.

Yet the success of *Tristes tropiques* may well have been the single most important event in the exportation of structuralism from linguistics to other fields. As early as 1946–1947 Lévi-Strauss's friend Maurice Merleau-Ponty (1908–1961), whose previous work was on the phenomenology of perception, had given a course at the École Normale Supérieure in Paris on 'Language and Communication' (published posthumously as Merleau-Ponty 1964) which paid serious attention to Saussure, particularly his theory of the sign, and it might have been he in 1952 rather than Lévi-Strauss in 1955 who brought structuralism to general attention were it not for circumstances to be related in 4.1. In the event, *Tristes tropiques* established Lévi-Strauss as a major intellectual force in France, and since the French look to their intellectual figures as experts on all subjects, it gave him a wide platform for proclaiming structuralism as his slogan. The publication of a collection of his papers in 1958, entitled *Structural Anthropology*, with his 1945 paper discussed above appearing as the first chapter, provided the first widely-read, thoroughly fleshed-out program for structuralist analysis outside linguistics.

For Lévi-Strauss, linguistics provides a template of the structure of the human unconscious which is applicable to the study of myths or indeed any other aspect of culture in any society, from the least to the most civilized. His method of analysis begins by breaking down a myth (for example) into the shortest possible sentences. Each of these sentences will show "that a certain function is, at a given time, predicated to a given subject" (1972 [1958]: 175). Each such relation constitutes a 'gross constituent unit'. The fact that these relations transcend the specific content of any sentence which fulfills them reflects the Saussurean conception of *langue* as 'substance, not form'. The influence of Jakobson can be detected in the assertion that "the true constituent units of a myth are not the isolated relations but *bundles of such relations* and it is only as bundles that these relations can be put to use and combined so as to produce a meaning" (ibid.; emphasis in the original).

Lévi-Strauss's method is to chart the structure of relations in a myth or across two or more functionally comparable myths, often in the form of binomial oppositions such as *raw−cooked*. He often locates 'groups' of myths across cultures which share the same fundamental binomial oppositions but select different values for them. Thus, for example, he finds that the Indo-European Cinderella myth and the North American Ash-Boy cycle are "symmetrical but inverted in every detail", in other words structurally identical at the level of form even though exactly opposition at the level of substance (ibid., p. 190):

	EUROPE	AMERICA
Sex	female	male
Family status	double family	no family
Appearance	pretty girl	ugly boy
Sentimental status	nobody likes her	in hopeless love with girl
Transformation	luxuriously clothed with super-natural help	stripped of ugliness with super-natural help
etc.		

Lévi-Strauss may be said to out-Propp Propp when he states (p. 192):

"[...] it seems that every myth (considered as the collection of all its variants) corresponds to a formula of the following type:

$f(a) : f(b) \cong f(b) : f - 1(y)$

where, two terms being given as well as two functions of these terms, it is stated that a relation of equivalence still exists between two situations when terms and relations are inverted, under two conditions: 1. that one term be replaced by its contrary; 2. that an inversion be made between the *function* and the *term* value of two elements.

This formula becomes highly significant when we recall that Freud considered that *two traumas* (and not one as it is so commonly said) are necessary in order to give birth to this individual myth in which a neurosis consists".

The ability to reconcile conclusions from the study of folktales and myths with Freudian psychoanalysis, using a terminological apparatus carrying the scientific prestige of the linguistics from which it was derived, proved no less heady in 1950s Paris than it had promised to do in Moscow decades earlier. It lent the work of Lévi-Strauss an aura of immense explanatory power. When, a few years later, that work became the target of sustained attacks, they would be largely on the grounds that it was *too* powerful − that the principles which underlay Lévi-Strauss's classifications of elements and functions were not sufficiently rigorous and objective, so that the method could be used to assign virtually anything to any category and to create equivalences wherever and whenever the analyst wished.

Nevertheless, with its constant direct references to and reliance on the work of structural linguists from Saussure onward, and riding on the wave of universal popularity that began with *Tristes tropiques*, Lévi-Strauss's structuralist ethnography opened the way as never before to the spread of structuralist ideas from linguistics to other disciplines. Since Lévi-Strauss never limited himself to any narrow definition of anthropology but took every area of culture as being within his purview, the spread to literature, psychology, philosophy, historiography and what would come to be known as 'cultural studies' was already achieved, in embryo if not fully, in his work. Yet except for anthropology (narrowly defined), younger figures would come to be seen as the structuralist 'founders' for each of these more local areas of interest.

4. 1950s−1960s Paris

4.1. The politics of structuralism

Lévi-Strauss's timing in publishing *Tristes tropiques* was impeccable. As Kurzweil (1980) writes in the insightful introduction to her survey of structuralist thinkers, during the war and its aftermath the overwhelming divide in French intellectual life was Vichy. According to Jean-Paul Sartre (1905−1980), "the strongest bond among the existentialists had been their common hatred of the Nazis" (quoted by Kurzweil 1980: 4). The defeat of fascism and the revelations of the full horrors of Hitler's regime gave a certain moral force to Marxism, Nazism's ideological opposite, and from the liberation onward

"Marxism preoccupied the thinking of French intellectuals. Then, in a climate of growing disillusionment with the Soviet Union and communism, Sartre's existentialist humanism promised to allow for individual fulfillment in modern society. But when Sartre, especially between 1952 and 1956, professed his humanism while continuing to support the Communists (ignoring repression in the Soviet Union), his theories became suspect." (Kurzweil, p. 2)

For many, the Soviet invasion of Hungary in October 1956 was the *coup de grâce*. Part of Sartre's impact lay in his having convinced French intellectuals to reject any notion of scholarly neutrality and objectivity and to recognize the necessity of being *engagé* in political life, whatever their discipline. The immediate appeal of this view, together with the literary expression given to it by Sartre and those associated with him, gave Sartrean thought a kind of excitement that seemed to put it beyond the reach of alternatives, including the intriguing synthesis of phenomenology and structuralism being developed by Merleau-Ponty (see 3.4.). This particular contest was never quite brought to the test, however. Sartre (1947) enunciated a theory of literature oriented toward the act of communicating the freedom of a writer to the freedom of a reader, and to this Merleau-Ponty prepared a response which "was to have been completed in 1952. However, Merleau-Ponty was elected to the Collège de France that year and his research took him in other directions" (Silverman 1994: 396). His book, *The Prose of the World*, would eventually be published in 1969, eight years after his death, by which time his argument that "there are many aspects of language and expression that are simply not direct, that do not give an algorithmic reading of experience" (ibid.) would no longer seem strikingly new.

By the mid 1950s, with existentialism's inherent intellectual weaknesses apparent and its leading exponents disunited, the circumstances were ripe for an alternative — especially a politically neutral alternative — to free academics from Sartrean existentialism and *engagement*.

"The advent of structuralism [...] seemed to supply an honourable intellectual escape from confronting the limitations of both Marxism and existentialism [...]. Those who drifted into the structuralist debates found a means to deradicalize themselves without abandoning their humanist convictions." (Kurzweil, p. 4)

To call oneself a structuralist in 1950s Paris, then, was a way of doing what French society in general was silently conspiring to do — to put the war and its divisions behind them, forgetting about who had collaborated and who had resisted, and displacing the debate over the pros and cons of Marxism from the centre of everything. It is perhaps no accident that the opening chapters of *Tristes tropiques* only incidentally mention primitive societies in Brazil and focus on the author's experience as a Jewish refugee from Vichy France with Marx as one of his three intellectual 'mistresses' (along with Freud and geology, proving the adage that politics makes strange bedfellows). This made the 'front man' for structuralism personally immune from the customary attacks of reactionism and implicit collaborationism which the existentialists had got used to launching automatically at those who declined to play the game their way.

Structuralism seems also to have benefitted in this initial period by the fact that it appeared abstruse and slightly mystical. To quote Kurzweil (1980: 4) again:

"The very complexities of structuralist methods obscured the fact that structuralism would become the new conservatism of the Left. This political bias was not apparent when Lévi-Strauss began to elaborate the methodology that was to explain consciousness by life, as Marx has done [...]"

Paradoxically, the effect of structuralism was largely to replace a militant, engaged Marxism with a quieter, more purely conceptual one. The 'cover' for this replacement had been provided by none other than Stalin himself, when, in 1950, he declared language to be superstructural and therefore ideologically neutral. In late 1950s Paris, in the thick of contradictory attempts to line structuralism up against and for Marxisms of various sorts, this confusion, like the complexities of method alluded to by Kurzweil, probably only increased the chances of structuralism being taken up by people more concerned about what they were escaping from than to.

4.2. Literary criticism and semiology

4.2.1. Barthes

For Culler, surveying 'structuralist poetics' in 1975, there was no doubt that its chief figure was Roland Barthes (1915–1980). A quarter-century on, Barthes's impact on literary studies is not what it was, but he is certainly celebrated for his pioneering role in expanding the realm of critical inquiry from a narrowly defined canon of literature to embrace 'cultural studies', on the grounds that all of culture is a kind of text, and that "literature is not separate from everyday life and its power flows" (During 1993: 44). For although in the study of how ideology shapes culture Barthes would come to be overshadowed by Foucault, it is Barthes's 1957 book *Mythologies* that "begins to examine, concretely, how ideology works. It is the founding text of practical ideology-critique" (ibid.).

Where the exportation of structuralist ideas is concerned, Barthes's most important contribution was probably his 1964 *Elements of Semiology*, at once a synthesis and codification, and to a certain extent a simplification, of the essence of generalized structuralist principles and methodology. With Saussure providing the bulk of its organizational divisions, the short book nevertheless weaves in a surprising number of the developments associated with Hjelmslev, Martinet, Jakobson, Trubetzkoy, Peirce, and others. Insofar as French structuralism of the 1960s and after had a textbook, this was it, and one could hardly have asked for a more effective combination of brevity and richness. Through Barthes, the Saussurean view that language is one among many systems of signs which are instituted in society, and that a general science of signs should develop taking linguistics as its pilot discipline, became common currency and a distinctive characteristic of the broader French structuralism that developed in the wake of Lévi-Strauss.

If Barthes' assertion that the texts of everyday life merit study quite as much as canonical literature was not controversial enough, his attempts at structural analysis of literary sacred cows proved even more so. It was one thing for him to apply the *nouvelle critique* to the *nouveau roman*, a genre he was credited with having identified and brought to popular attention. But when in 1963 he brought structuralist principles to bear on his analysis of the classical playwright Jean Racine, being "no longer willing to make the [author as] individual subject the source of the structures he discovers in the works", but instead "[r]eading individual tragedies as moments of a system" and with an interest in "the common structures that may be derived from them and that serve as the functional oppositions and the rules of combination of the system" (Culler 1975: 98), he unleashed a firestorm of attacks from more traditionalist critics (notably Picard 1965), many of whom misunderstood and misrepresented his analysis in their wrath at what they saw as an attempt to dehumanize some of humanity's most splendid monuments.

Of course the attacks were aimed more widely than on Barthes alone. Their effect was to institutionalize the new division between ancients and moderns and, ironically, to strengthen the academic authority of French structuralism. Barthes's own status as a senior scholar and Director of Studies in the prestigious École Pratique des Hautes Études was unaffected, and when a schism erupted within structuralism, it was he more than anyone else who kept a foot in both camps and maintained some semblance of common purpose amid the strife. As co-founder of the important journals *Communications* in 1962 and *Langages* in 1966, he was a major figure on the rule-based structuralist side (see 4.2.2.) and helped open the way for a younger generation of critics working to carry the methods of linguistics more or less directly over into the analysis of literature. Yet his own critical work evolved steadily in the direction of the opposing camp, the journal *Tel Quel*, whose writers argued for a kind of aporistic structuralism in which linguistics would not offer a strong methodological model. By the end of the decade this development would pave the way to 'post-structuralism', as will be discussed in 4.4.–5.

4.2.2. Structural analysis as applied linguistics

Perhaps the most 'pure', and certainly the most extreme version of structuralist literary analysis was launched in the French journal *L'Homme* by Lévi-Strauss & Jakobson (1962) and pursued by Jakobson in a number of studies thereafter, focusing, as the first one did, on poetry. The method is an extremely close reading of the poem at numerous levels, including syntax, morphology and phonology, looking for hidden structural patterns which subliminally work to abet, or hinder, what the words of the poem are saying on the semantic level. The subject of Lévi-Strauss & Jakobson (1962) is Baudelaire's 1847 sonnet *Les chats*. To take one part of the analysis as an example of the method, the authors contrast the sixth line of the sonnet, which says of cats: *Ils cherchent le silence et l'horreur des ténèbres* ("They seek out the silence and horror of shadows"), with the closing tercet:

"Leurs reins féconds sont pleins d'étincelles magiques,
Et des parcelles d'or, ainsi qu'un sable fin,
Étoilent vaguement leurs prunelles mystiques."
["Their fecund loins are filled with magic sparks,
And particles of gold, as well as a fine sand,
Vaguely veil their mystic pupils"].

The authors assert (Jakobson & Lévi-Strauss 1972 [1962]: 140):

"The last tercet rhymes its suffixes in order to emphasize the narrow semantic relation between the *étin*CELLES, *par*CELLES d'or and *prun*ELLES of the cat-sphinxes on one hand, and on the other hand, between the sparks *Mag*IQUES emanating from the animal and his pupils *Myst*IQUES shining from an inner light, and opened to a hidden meaning [...]. *L'horreur des ténèbres* vanishes before this double luminance. This light is reflected on the phonic level by the predominance of the phonemes of light timbre (acute tonality) among nasal vowels in the final stanza (6 front *versus* 3 back vowels), whereas in the preceding stanzas, the nasal vowels of grave tonality manifest a great numeric superiority (9 *versus* 0 in the first quatrain, 2 *versus* 1 in the second, and 10 *versus* 3 in the first tercet)".

Within the literary world, this approach elicited stronger reactions even than the work of Barthes, which blends in more of a traditional critical sensibility with the structural principles. Lévi-Strauss and Jakobson appeared, on the contrary, to think that merely by counting phonemes they could arrive at the deep meaning of a poem, and this infuriated the more conservative among traditional teachers and critics of literature. Others, however, were impressed with the fresh insights which the method was, in the best cases, able to bring to well-studied material.

By the mid 1960s structuralism enjoyed the privileged position of institutionalized *avant garde* in Paris, with the individuals who emerged as its new leading figures sharing some sort of connection to Barthes. The Bulgarian immigrant Tzvetan Todorov (b. 1939), for example, wrote his doctoral thesis under Barthes (Todorov 1967). A collection of texts by Russian formalists which Todorov assembled and translated made their work available to a non-specialist French audience for the first time (Todorov 1965) and another collection entitled 'What is Structuralism?' (Wahl 1968), featuring an essay on poetics by Todorov, would prove very influential as a summation of 'late' structuralist thought just as post-structuralism was dawning. This essay (Todorov 1968) is a calm and mature position piece for structural poetics that looks past the hubbub over Barthes to establish continuity with literary criticism of the most traditional sort. Tacitly synthesizing principles which underlay work from Russian formalism to structuralism proper, it begins by declaring that a structural poetics will not take the literary work as an end in itself, but will instead attempt to decipher or translate the work into another, 'fundamental' discourse of abstract structures, the nature of which may be philosophical, psychological, sociological, etc. Using Proppian schemata he formalizes the 'narrative syntax' of a number of simple stories, leading to 'concretization' in a threefold process of syntactic specification, semantic interpretation and verbal representation. Echoing Chomsky, he introduced the notion of 'transformations'. But for all his extraordinarily close adherence to the categories of analysis taken over from linguistics, Todorov does not venture far beyond the explorations of Propp, Lévi-Strauss and Barthes. If anything he pulls back, consolidates and synthesizes their gains. Without striving for novelty, his work is nonetheless original in the thorough and direct knowledge it manifests of Slavic sources, as well as for its fresh, non-French perspective on classic works of French literature. Still, it is with reference to Todorov that Culler is led to remark on "how little supposedly structuralist criticism may differ from more familiar modes" (1975: 103).

In 1970 Todorov co-founded the journal *Poétique* along with the critic and novelist Hélène Cixous (b. 1937) and another key figure in the structuralist poetics of the 1960s and 1970s, Gérard Genette (b. 1930), whose work is marked by an attempt to reconcile classical theories of rhetoric with modern structuralist approaches to literature. Like Todorov, Genette followed his linguistic models closely, combining close readings with rigorous organizational schemata. Also working in this vein was Algirdas-Julien Greimas (1917–1992), who had spent several years with Barthes teaching in Alexandria in the late 1940s and early 1950s. His 1966 'structural semantics' attempted a kind of algebra of linguistic meaning, developed to a high level of detail. Although literary analysis was brought in, it was much less central a concern than in other work discussed in this section. Greimas (1966) approached semantics, the science of meaning, as a semiotics, a science of signifying. An extraordinarily ambitious book, it earned its author an entire chapter of Culler's *Structuralist Poetics* (1975), which finally pronounces Greimas's work a failure because it assumes that linguistic meaning is determinate and resides within the text itself:

"Both Jakobson and Greimas start from the assumption that linguistic analysis provides a method for discovering the patterns or meanings of literary texts, and though the problems they encounter are different the lessons which their examples offer are substantially the same: that the direct application of techniques for linguistic description may be a useful approach if it begins with literary effects and attempts to account for them, but that it does not in itself serve as a model of literary analysis. The reason is simply that both author and reader bring to the text more than a knowledge of language and this additional experience [...] is what guides one in the perception and construction of relevant patterns." (Culler 1975: 95)

As a criticism of Jakobson or Greimas it is not clear that this is entirely fair, since neither claims to be discovering determinate meaning but rather the mechanisms by which meanings are constructed. Nevertheless, this is how the goal of structuralism would come to be widely understood, both by its critics and by many of those who took it up. It appeared to use the magical key of linguistic science to solve the problem of multiple interpretations of texts. Structuralism, at last, could tell us what works of literature *really meant*. This was at once its greatest appeal and its greatest vulnerability, opening it to attacks like Culler's and others to be discussed in 4.4.–5.

4.2.3. Semiology

Barthes (1964), discussed in 4.2.1., was by no means the first attempt to develop Saussure's programmatic comments regarding an eventual science of signs. In 1943 both Hjelmslev in Denmark and Eric Buyssens (b. 1900) in Belgium published books devoted to exploring the nature of signs in a Saussurean semiological perspective. In France, similar steps would be undertaken by the end of the 1950s in early work by Georges Mounin (1910–1993) as well as Merleau-Ponty (see e. g., Mounin 1959, Merleau-Ponty 1960). Mounin would become one of the most widely read authors on structuralism generally and semiology in particular, through accessible books like Mounin (1970).

Starting in 1964, writing on the semiology of film by Christian Metz (b. 1931) attracted international attention and did much to help popularize structuralism in France and abroad. In Britain, a semiotics of film largely inspired by Metz would find its organ in 1971 in the film journal *Screen* (see Easthope 1988: 34–70). Music too would become an object of semiological analysis in work by the linguist Nicolas Ruwet (b. 1932) and later, the Canadian Jean-Jacques Nattiez (b. 1945) (see Ruwet 1967, 1972; Nattiez 1975).

By the mid 1960s structural semiology was being taken up elsewhere in Europe, for example in Germany by Bense (1965, 1968) and in Italy by Eco (1968). In 1966 the first international conference on semiotics was held in Poland, at last bringing the European semiological tradition face-to-face with its Anglo-American semiotic counterpart (on which see 5.4.). The French delegation was led by Greimas, leader of the newly established Section de Sémio-linguistique of the Laboratoire d'Anthropologie sociale of the Collège de France, while the American delegation included Jakobson (Sebeok 1974: 229).

4.3. Psychology and philosophy

Along with Lévi-Strauss and Barthes, the other most important first-generation structuralist in 1950s–1960s Paris was the psychoanalyst Jacques Lacan (1901–1981). According to Silverman (1994: 395),

"Louis Marin (1931–92) used to comment that when he was a young man in the early 1950s, he and his wife Françoise were invited to the apartment of M. and Mme Maurice Merleau-Ponty for what was then described as a 'dîner intime'. When he and his wife arrived, he discovered that it was indeed a small dinner party: M. and Mme Merleau-Ponty, M. and Mme Lévi-Strauss, and M. and Mme Lacan. That these three were all friends indicates a certain collaboration and dialogue that was highly charged in the early period in which structuralism was gaining hold".

The core of Lacan's project is a reading of Freud through the prism of Saussurean sign theory, with his operating principle being that *the unconscious is structured like a language*. In a sense this principle is implicit in all of generalized structuralism from Jakobson and Lévi-Strauss forward, where the universal social structures or literary competence or whatever other language-like structures were being sought must themselves be part of the unconscious. But Lacan was the first to approach the whole of the Freudian unconscious directly in this way. In so doing he "generalizes and deepens the anti-individualistic implications of Freudian psychoanalysis" (Harland 1987: 42). Making considerable use of Jakobson and Benveniste as well as Saussure, Lacan reinterpreted such classic Freudian concepts as the Oedipal phenomenon in structuralist terms. He identifies the Phallus as "an abstract signifier" having "a signification which is evoked only by the paternal metaphor" (Lemaire 1977 [1970]: 86), and formulates this metaphor as follows (ibid., p. 86—87):

"In general, metaphor is realized through the substitution, in the signifier-signifed relationship, of one signifier for another, S', the first signifier falling to the level of the signified, as in the formula:

$$\frac{S'}{S} \cdot \frac{S}{s} \rightarrow S\left(\frac{1}{s}\right)$$

When applied by Lacan to the paternal metaphor, this formula is transformed into:

$$\frac{\text{Name-of-the-Father}}{\text{Desire of the Mother}} \cdot \frac{\text{Desire of the Mother}}{\text{Signified for subject}} \rightarrow \text{Name-of-the-Father}\left(\frac{0}{\text{Phallus}}\right)$$

In Lacan's view,

"The phallus is the privileged signifier of that mark in which the role of the logos is joined with the advent of desire. (But) it can only play its role when masked, that is to say, as itself a sign of the latency with which any signifiable is struck, when it is raised to the function of signifier." (Lacan 1966, cited by Lemaire 1977 [1970]: 88)

This of course is no more than one element, albeit a central one, of Lacan's intricate work as it developed over nearly thirty years of weekly or bimonthly seminars. But it perhaps suffices to give a sense of how Lacan's structuralism differs from that of his contemporaries. The inherent mysticism of 'hidden structures' is greatly amplified in its encounter with the still deeper mysticism of the Freudian unconscious and Freud's appropriations of Greek myth. Little wonder, then, that Lacan would become a lightning rod for later attacks on the whole structuralist enterprise as being counterrational. The charge becomes less convincing the deeper one delves into Lacan's thought, but at a superficial level it would be much harder to make against, say, Lévi-Strauss, who as we saw in 3.4. tapped into Freudian mysticism to a far less extreme degree.

In 1. was mentioned the case of Louis Althusser (1918—1990), still one of the first names likely to be raised in a discussion of French structuralism despite his active attempts to dissociate himself from the movement. Althusser's reading of Marx, and of the 18th and 19th century discourses within which Marx wrote, focused on depersonalized ideological structures (see, e.g., Althusser 1965); and what is more, the most direct target of Althusser's writings and political activities were the Sartrean Marxists. All this made his alignment with the structuralist camp seem obvious. Yet the fact is that in Althusser's writings, notions and methods taken over from linguistics play a far less central role than for the other thinkers discussed up to this point. Althusser rejected what he called the 'ideology' of structuralism, which gives experience a central grounding in language. His importance for the structuralist movement is thus quite distinct from the topic of the present survey.

With Michel Foucault (1926—1984), the structuralist ideology itself becomes an object of investigation, and the belief that a truth can be discovered which consists of a matching of ideas to things, and of things to words — a belief central to the structuralist enterprise — is treated as part of one particular 'discursive practice', a historical product (see e.g., Foucault 1966). Like Althusser, Foucault does not directly borrow ideas or tools from structural linguistics, but his attitude toward structuralism is not so much a rejection from without as a critique from within. Foucault pursues the logic of structuralism to its ultimate end, which is that structures themselves do not have any transcendent or natural existence any more than the human subject does. They too are historical products. This makes the attempt to understand human history or culture in terms of supposedly universal categories appear paradoxical, because the categories themselves will always open up as objects of historical and cultural enquiry in a never-ending cycle.

Unlike Derrida, the subject of 4.5., Foucault did not seek out a stylistic break with 'classical' structuralism, and the organization of his analyses follows the patterns of traditional post-Enlightenment scholarship. As a result, the dividing line is often drawn between Foucault as the last structuralist and Derrida as the first post-structuralist. It is by no means clear that this is justified. If Derrida had not come onto the scene, structuralism would still have reached its endpoint and been surpassed with Foucault, less spectacularly, but no less definitively.

4.4. The aporistic structuralism of *Tel Quel*

As noted at the end of 4.2.1., the issue (or perhaps pseudo-issue) of the determinate nature of meaning led to a schism within French structuralism. The journal *Tel Quel* had been launched in 1960 amid the heady atmosphere of the *nouveau roman* and New Wave cinema in France, when structuralism was above all else the rejection of Marxist-existentialist dogmatic certainties. As structuralism itself crystallized into a mainstream methodology with certainties of its own, the '*Tel Quel* group', including the journal's co-founder Philippe Sollers (b. 1936) and, in a significant shift from his earlier positions, Barthes, came to resist these no less strongly. The *Tel Quel* position in the late 1960s and early 1970s was that structuralism as the search for some kind of universal 'literary competence' comparable to Chomsky's linguistic competence was misguided. Instead the writing and reading of literature were understood to be culture-specific and ideologically driven (see Culler 1975: 241 ff.). As Barthes saw it in 1971 (p. 44),

"each text is in some sort its own model [and] must be treated in its difference [... T]he text is ceaselessly and through and through traversed by codes, but it is not the accomplishment of a code (of, for example, the narrative code), it is not the *parole* of a narrative *langue*."

A key member of the *Tel Quel* group, Julia Kristeva (b. 1941) wrote widely on topics in linguistics, semiotics, literature, psychology, feminism and social problems (see Kristeva 1986). Her work in semiotics (e. g. Kristeva 1969) argued for its aporistic nature, contending that semiotics must always develop as a *critique* of semiotics, operating always in a methodological circle. This she offered not in order to reduce semiotics to absurdity but as a positive statement of its essential nature. With statements such as these, the whole structuralist undertaking – which had always relied on a compelling combination of analytical rigour and the mystique of a search to uncover hidden structures – began to move away from charts and formulae and other apparent tools of rational analysis toward a more discursive and mystical dimension, where it was assumed that searches would end not with clear answers but ever more intricate paradoxes.

The first woman to establish a place for herself in the structuralist pantheon, Kristeva contributed significantly to a feminist critique of structuralism which would help give impetus to post-structuralism (see 5.5.). Her early work has recently become one of the prime targets of the 'exposé' of pseudo-science in writings of the period (see 6.2.). But lest it be thought that her being a woman contributed directly to her becoming a target of charges of intellectual nihilism she would be outstripped in this regard by another member of the *Tel Quel* group of this period, Jacques Derrida (b. 1930).

4.5. Deconstruction and the politics of 1968

Derrida exploded onto the scene in 1967 with three books propounding an approach to philosophy, or a philosophical strategy, called 'deconstruction', the goal of which is to locate the conceptual oppositions upon which philosophical, literary and other kinds of works are based, and invert them:

"In a traditional philosophical opposition we have not a peaceful coexistence of facing terms but a violent hierarchy. One of the terms dominates the other (axiologically, logically, etc.), occupies the commanding position. To deconstruct the opposition is above all, at a particular moment, to reverse the hierarchy." (Derrida 1981 [1972]: 41)

One of the central targets of this strategy in Derrida (1967a) is Saussure's *Cours* – which meant that, from the first, deconstruction was seen as standing in opposition to the very foundation stone of structuralist thought. A summary of Derrida's wide-ranging critique of Saussure may be found in Joseph et al. (2001, chap. 13). Lévi-Strauss is likewise subjected to deconstruction in Derrida (1967a, b). Yet deconstruction is by no means to be equated with rejection, and Derrida draws his key semiotic concept of *différance* (differing and defering) from the Saussurean notion of the essentially oppositional, negative character of the linguistic sign. Still, *différance* is Saussure with a difference, being understood in a post-deconstructional way, and it is never the case that Derrida simply applies concepts from linguistics without having first reprocessed them through the deconstructive machinery.

Derrida's timing was nearly as good as Lévi-Strauss's had been just thirteen years before. The student revolts in Paris in May 1968 were a complex phenomenon, but in part represented the coming of age of the generation for whom Vichy was no longer the defining experience. As shown in 4.1., structuralism had risen to prominence within the post-Vichy context, offering as it did an 'honorable retreat' from the political polarization of Christian-conservative-collaborationism vs. Sartrean-Marxist-resistance. By 1968 its success had been such that for the young intellectuals of Paris it was as much an 'establishment' mode of thought as was existentialism or Gallism. Foucault's arguments had made it seem that each of these was a historically and ideologically produced discursive practice serving the interest of some élite, and therefore to be resisted and, if possible, dismantled.

In this supercharged atmosphere the end of structuralism was (perhaps prematurely) declared. Virtually overnight, Jakobson, Lévi-Strauss and all they stood for changed from the *avant garde* to the old guard of the Parisian intellectual scene. The stunning novelty and intellectual power of Derrida's books, together with their slaying of the structuralist fathers, made them well suited to set the tone for a new 'post-structuralist' era. Yet this was at a moment when structuralism was just beginning to attract significant attention beyond Paris, other than for a small number of academic specialists.

5. Structuralism and its aftermath in America and Britain

5.1. How structuralist was 'American structuralism'?

Insofar as linguistics was the birthplace of structuralism, it was also the first area in which an avowed generational challenge to structuralist dominance was successfully mounted. Starting in 1957 and with rapidly accelerating force from about 1960–1962 onward, the 'transformational-generative linguistics' of Noam Chomsky (b. 1928) set out to undo the underpinnings of American 'structuralist' linguistics. Structuralism became the *vieux jeu* of the older 'establishment' generation, swept aside by the transformational generativism of the young rebels. This version of events is accepted for example by Culler (1975: 7), who writes that "generative grammar play no role in the development of structuralism", though Jean Piaget (1896–1980), whose particular motives will be explored in 6.1., makes 'transformations' one of his three defining features of structuralism

and thereby incorporates Chomsky into the very centre of the movement (Piaget 1970 [1968]: 81–92). With another 25 years' hindsight, Piaget's view is all the more convincing. American linguistics before Chomsky shared several features with European structuralism that differentiated them both from the earlier historically-dominated linguistics, but on a number of essential doctrinal points the gulf between them was as wide as the Atlantic. Many of these doctrinal points were the very ones Chomsky overturned, and in so doing he narrowed the gulf considerably. From the European perspective, looking beneath the overt terms of the debate, it was Chomsky who brought fully-blown structuralism to American linguistics for the first time by undoing a decades-long resistance to it.

Here again the story is complex, because the development of linguistics in America and Europe can never be fully separated or integrated. Of the two most prominent American linguists of the first half of the century, Leonard Bloomfield (1887–1949) was German-trained and began his career as a follower of Wundt, while the German-born Edward Sapir (1884–1939) was trained by Boas, a German émigré who became one of the most celebrated anthropologists in America (see 3.4.). Boas is widely credited with establishing the basis of what would become the 'distributional' method for the analysis of languages that is at the heart of what is usually identified as 'American structuralism' (notably by Hymes & Fought 1981). Back in Europe, Lévi-Strauss's debt to Boas has been noted in 3.4., while in America, Bloomfield, in a 1945 letter, responds testily to criticisms of his 1933 book for supposedly ignoring Saussure, saying that in fact Saussure's influence is evident "on every page". Yet as shown in Joseph (1990: 58–63), Bloomfield (1927) read Saussure as a behaviourist *manqué*, a feat he accomplished by 'dropping' the concepts of signified and signifier in favour of 'actual object' and 'speech utterance' respectively, as if in so doing he simply clarified what Saussure was trying to say. Clearly Bloomfield's desire for European-American linguistic integration outweighed any concern to present a faithful and cogent reading of Saussure.

From the early 1930s there were regular, if sporadic, contacts between American linguists and their counterparts in Prague and Paris, London and Copenhagen. The cross-fertilization can be seen most clearly in work on the common core of their interests, the 'phoneme', the minimal meaningful unit of sound in a language (until Jakobson reanalysed it as a bundle of distinctive features). But the differences are no less salient. Even within America, Bloomfield and his followers understood the phoneme as a category for the description of behaviour, while Sapir gave greater weight to its psychological force. In Europe, where behaviourism had not exerted such an impact, there was little problem in accepting the Saussurean view of the language system as being simultaneously a mental and a social reality. Despite this rather fundamental difference, a common faith in the existence of the abstract category of the phoneme sufficed to make transcontinental dialogue possible, with occasional static.

After Sapir's death in 1939, Bloomfield's approach began to take over in America, and its position was definitively solidified when it became the basis for the highly successful preparation of language teaching materials during the War. With its steadfast rejection of anything 'mentalistic' as being inherently metaphysical and therefore not amenable to scientific study, American linguistics under the Bloomfieldian aegis had considerably less in common with structuralism of the European variety than in the 1930s when the bridging figure of Sapir was dominant. If we ask what was 'structuralist' about Bloomfieldian linguistics from a European perspective, looking back to the aspects of Saussurean thought outlined in 2.2. as a grounding, we do find points in common: synchronicity, arbitrariness, the social nature of language, the idea that in language *tout se tient*, distinct syntagmatic and paradigmatic axes. But Saussure's semiology has been reinterpreted as stimulus and response; and perhaps the greatest difference is that meaning no longer exists within language but in all those stimuli out in the world. For Bloomfield there can be no signified because the mind, even if we accept its existence as a matter of commonsense experience, is not objectively observable, and therefore is out of bounds for scientific purposes. Hence there can be no such thing as 'value' in the Saussurean sense – a concept so central to Saussure's thought that it means even the seeming convergences named above are only partial. Nor can the existence of the language system be in any way psychological, or worse, unconscious. Most Bloomfieldian linguists denied the distinction between *langue* and *parole* in the very significant sense that they defined a language as a set of observable utterances, not an unobservable system which, given their refusal to have recourse to the mind, they would have been hard pressed to locate physically, as their methodology demanded. Finally, they were with few exceptions extremely sceptical about any 'universals' of language beyond the basic behavioural schema of stimulus and response. In view of these divergences it is misleading indeed to identify the Bloomfield-dominated linguistics of the 1940s and 1950s as 'American structuralism'.

5.2. Chomsky's structuralism and its impact on psychology

This was the linguistics against which Chomsky would come to position himself. His revolution lay partly in convincing American linguists that the behaviourist rejection of the mind was misguided, and that commonsense intuitions about the mental were not necessarily unscientific. He insisted on a distinction between 'competence' and 'performance' which in early work he likened specifically to the *langue* and *parole* of Saussure (although they were not exactly the same; see Joseph 1990), and maintained that linguistic competence was a discrete, unconscious component of the mind having a fundamentally universal structure, much as European structuralists had interpreted Saussure's *langue*. No less importantly, he introduced a distinction between 'deep' and 'surface' structure in language which was quickly latched onto by people outside linguistics and interpreted in ways far removed from Chomky's original intention, but reshaped by them according to their deep-seated sense that words do not mean what they purport to mean. This sense has been at the root of many 'functionalist' developments in 20th century linguistics, particularly within European structuralism, where the notion of separate conscious and unconscious minds is taken for granted. Hence European structuralists had comparatively little difficulty reconciling Chomsky's basic views with their own, even if the reconciliation was based upon a misinterpretation from Chomsky's point of view. At the same time, his notion of *transformational rules* by which one gets from deep to surface structure, which had no obvious precedent within European structuralism, was absorbed into it as Chomsky's original contribution, revolutionary because it released the structuralist system from the static inertia Saussure had saddled it with. But while injecting structuralism with a new dynamism, it soon became apparent that transformations made the system too 'powerful' in the sense that one could explain anything with no effort, simply by introducing an *ad hoc* transformation.

Although Chomsky maintains a self-propagation myth according to which he was never influenced by any of the teachers whose influence he acknowledged profusely in his early publications, he does not deny his contacts from the 1950s onward with Jakobson, to whom Chomsky & Halle (1968) is dedicated. It was Jakobson who presented him to the (largely European) audience of the 9th International Congress of Linguists in Cambridge, Massachusetts, in 1962 that is generally seen as marking the start of his international prominence. Moreover, the principal intellectual debts Chomsky has acknowledged apart from Saussure and Jakobson, including the linguists of 17th century France (see Chomsky 1966), Humboldt and Jespersen, have been European rather than American. In view of the fact that he set American linguistics on a path significantly less at odds with the Saussurean framework while undoing none of the common points between Bloomfield and Saussure (except perhaps the amount of lip service paid to the social nature of language, which Chomsky did not deny but simply excluded from his realm of interest by defining that realm as the competence of an idealized native speaker–hearer in a homogeneous speech community), it is reasonable to argue that Chomsky introduced structuralism into American linguistics, more fully than any of his predecessors. His new, transformational structuralism, which in Piaget's (1968) perspective looks as if it were an inevitable development in structuralist thought, briefly defined a minor generational gap among French structuralists; and may, through its excessive power, have helped hasten the pace of the reductions to absurdity by which structuralism would ultimately come to be rejected.

For a long period from the 1960s through the 1980s, Chomsky's conception of the mind was very influential in psychology, and moderately so in the more conservative discipline of philosophy. Psycholinguistic studies of language learning continue to be heavily influenced by Chomsky's views. His notion of the 'modular mind' with its genetically determined structural underpinnings was the basis of much early work in cognitive science, and came to form the target in opposition to which new conceptions were aimed. The fact that Piaget blatantly jumped onto the structuralist bandwagon (Piaget 1968) shortly before attacking Chomsky's assertion that language operates as an autonomous module within the mind (rather than, as Piaget believed, interactively with other facets of perception and cognition) only reinforced the widespread notion that the Chomskyan view is the opposite of the structuralist one. If however we are correct in evaluating Chomsky as a structuralist for the reasons outlined above, then the exportation to psychology of the conception of language and mind for which he is primarily responsible figures as a very significant structuralist legacy.

5.3. From structural stylistics to critical linguistics

Nearly all the developments of structuralism surveyed up to 5. were continental, even though some very crucial ones took place within a circle of wartime immigrants on American soil. 5.1. has shown how American linguistics developed its own version of what would come to be labeled as a 'structuralism', sharing some essential features with the European version but in others ways unique. On the whole, the structural linguistics of Europe and America had more in common than either had with British linguistics, particularly as it came to be dominated by John Rupert Firth (1890–1960), who explicitly rejected certain key tenets of Saussure, while extending others, notably the syntagmatic-paradigmatic distinction which he paralleled by that between 'system' and 'structure' (see Firth 1957). Moreover, the presence of Jakobson in the United States and his activity in trying to build bridges between the European and American approaches helped in some degree to lessen the gap. American linguists were not unreceptive to Jakobson's message that exporting structuralist ideas beyond linguistics would increase their visibility and academic clout. A symposium on language and style at Bloomington, Indiana, in 1958 brought together Jakobson and other linguists, mainly European immigrants to America, with prominent literary critics, and the resulting volume (Sebeok 1960) attracted considerable attention, in the wake of which 'stylistics' became fashionable, though in fact it represented for the most part a rather traditional grammatical-philological approach to literary texts recast in the structuralist vocabulary. Efforts in this direction had already been underway for some years in various parts of Europe, including with Saussure's associate Bally (1905, 1908). The wartime immigration to the US of scholars like Leo Spitzer (1887–1960) had given them an American presence as well (see, e. g., Spitzer 1948).

Stylistics had even more of an impact in Britain than the US, possibly because the gulf between linguistic and literary studies had never grown quite so large as in America. 1964 was a watershed year, with the publication of books by Enkvist, Spencer & Gregory as well as the Oxford Professor Stephen Ullmann (1914–1976), and two important papers by Michael A. K. Halliday (b. 1925), a disciple of Firth. Important papers and books in the next two years included Sinclair (1965), Thorne (1965), Fowler (1966), and Macintosh & Halliday (1966). Work in this vein would proliferate in the late 1960s and through the 1970s, by which time French post-structuralism had begun making inroads.

By the 1980s structural stylistics was coming under simultaneous attack from traditional literary critics for being anti-humanistic (though see 6.2.) and from post-structuralists on the sort of grounds described in 4.4. and at the end of 4.2.2. (Culler's critique). Nevertheless, work on textual analysis by Halliday and his wife Ruqaiya Hasan (b. 1931) (e. g. Halliday & Hasan 1976, Halliday 1978) would give rise to a brand of 'critical linguistics' practised mainly in Britain and Australia, which shares concerns about rhetoric and power with Foucault and certain post-structuralists (see, e. g., Kress & Hodge 1979, Fairclough 1989).

5.4. Semiotics and tagmemics

As noted in 2.2. under the rubric 'Language as a system of signs', a distinct Anglo-American tradition of semiotic studies stretched from Peirce's 'semeiotic', to Lady Victoria Welby's (1837–1912) 'significs', to an interaction with the concerns of analytic philosophy in Ogden & Richards (1923), Morris (1938, 1946) and Dewey (1946). American linguists for the most part kept their distance from these matters, a situation Jakobson attempted to rectify by taking every occasion in his work to draw attention to Peirce. Jakobson's protégé Thomas A. Sebeok (b. 1920) would become the leading figure in institutionalizing within American academics a field of semiotics that draws together the Saussurean and Anglo-American strands (cf. 4.2.3.), beginning with the first American congress of semiotics he organized in 1962 (see Sebeok, Hayes & Bateson 1964). The result has been a significant exportation of structuralist ideas beyond linguistics to fields as diverse as law and medicine.

Within the Bloomfieldian school one prominent though extraordinary member, Kenneth Lee Pike (1912–2000), produced his own extended version of structuralism called 'tagmemics', described as "a theory of language primarily, but also of all human behavior, both verbal and nonverbal" (Jones 1995: 314). The fact that Pike was a religious missionary led to a certain marginalization of him among the students of Bloomfield. Yet his position as leader of the Summer Institute of Linguistics, which has trained thousands in linguistic analysis for purposes of recording previously unrecorded languages, ultimately for the purpose of translating the Bible into them, has given Pike a massive non-academic base for his theories and methods. His *magnum opus*, published in three parts between 1954 and 1960, extends his principles of 'etic' (the outsider's perspective) and 'emic' (the native's perspective) analysis (derived from 'phon*etic*' and 'phon*emic*' respectively) following part-whole hierarchies to account for, among another things, the entirety of the behaviour of all those present at an American football game. According to Jones (1995: 319), "The social study of ethnic groups has been studied using tagmemic principles. The field of ethnomusicology [...] has relied heavily on some of the tagmemic principles, again especially the emic–etic distinction. Even more remote fields, such as theology, have been touched by tagmemic studies".

However, tagmemics has not enjoyed the influence inside or outside linguistics one might have expected given the prominence accorded, sometimes grudgingly, to Pike. This is no doubt in part because secular academics tend to steer clear of anything too closely connected to religion, but also because the methodology itself and the theory behind it is somewhat simplistic, making it more useful for the quick training of novice fieldworkers than for providing deep insights into language, let alone anything beyond it.

5.5. Post-structuralism in America and Britain

The first incursion of French structuralism and incipient post-structuralism into Anglo-

American academics came at a 1966 conference at Johns Hopkins University in Baltimore, Maryland, featuring, among others, Barthes, Derrida, Lacan and Todorov (see Macksey & Donato 1970). Their thinking would thenceforth have an impact particularly in American departments of French and comparative literature. Indeed, the extensions of Derrida's method by certain critics at Yale, one of several American universities where Derrida regularly served as visiting professor, led Norris (1982: 92) to refer to their work as "deconstruction 'on the wild side'", as it refused to acknowledge any distinction between, for example, primary works and criticism, following upon Derrida's famous (and untranslatable) assertion that *Il n'y a pas de hors-texte*. American deconstruction became notorious for exploiting Derridean techniques like etymological wordplay, but without the same depth of philosophical insight, leading all too easily to self-indulgent fantasias on impressionistic themes, facilely sceptical or nihilistic in tone.

The British academic establishment was more resistant. But bit by bit younger scholars interested in post-structuralism came to form a critical mass, and in Thatcher's Britain, as in postwar France a quarter-century earlier, the political divide between right and left was decisive. In the wake of Althusser, however, the whole French structuralist—post-structuralist enterprise came to Britain with good Marxist credentials, and fed exclusively into the work of the academic left. As a result, it has come under sustained attack from the academic right of the sort seen in 1. in the comments of Scruton, to be taken up again in 6.2.

In the second half of the 1990s, 'post-structuralism' ceased to be a fashionable word, and the writings of Barthes, Foucault, Derrida & Co. have been folded into a larger category called simply 'theory', which is not limited to structuralists and those who came in their direct aftermath.

6. Further influences and current reactions

6.1. Structuralism in science

The opening section noted the tendency among some structuralists to want to absorb into the movement many different streams of earlier and contemporary thought spanning the arts and sciences, in order to validate their grandiose claims for the universal explanatory capacity of structuralism. In 3.1. we saw how this vast vision was already anticipated by Jakobson in 1930, and over the next half century no one would do more than he to spread the structuralist gospel across disciplines far and wide. How well he succeeded is apparent from the enthusiasm of some of those he converted, such as Jean Piaget (see 5.2.), whose widely-read 1968 introduction to structuralism took a very catholic view indeed of what scholars and scientists it included. It defines structuralism based on the three properties of wholeness, transformation and self-regulation. The focus is on mathematics and the physical and social sciences, with philosophy not entering until the last chapter, so that Jakobson and Lacan appear only in passing, and Barthes and Greimas not at all. The aim is to bring into the structuralist picture as many well-known people as possible whom no one, including themselves, might think to associate with structuralism. These range from relatively easy to accept cases like the Gestalt psychologists (whose importance for the Moscow Linguistic Circle is affirmed by Jakobson & Pomorska (1983 [1980]: 11), the legal theorist Hans Kelsen (1881–1973) and the philosopher of science Thomas S. Kuhn (1922–1996), to more far-flung ones like the biologists Ludwig van Bertalanffy (1901–1971, already cited in the context of structuralism by Cassirer 1945), C. H. Waddington (1905–1975), and the group of mathematicians who published under the collective pseudonym Nicolas Bourbaki. An obvious motive for linking structuralism to the 'hard' sciences in this way was the increasing prestige of the sciences relative to the arts from WW II onward and especially following the start of the 'space race' in the late 1950s. For their part, the scientists were no doubt flattered by the notion that their findings could inform thinking outside their own disciplines.

The opening section noted that the 'end' of the structuralist period is difficult to pinpoint in part because of the uncertain status of particular authors as structuralists or post-structuralists, and in part because intellectual movements do not cease at all once, but can have a long afterlife extending far beyond their abandonment by the *avant garde* that spawned them. As it happens, a 'structuralist program in the philosophy of sciences' emerged in the 1980s and is exemplified by recent work such as that collected in Balzer &

Moulines (1996). According to Moulines (1996: 1), the label 'structuralism' "was first introduced" for this theory of science "by Wolfgang Stegmüller in the late seventies, following a suggestion by Y. Bar-Hillel (see Stegmüller 1979). Yehoshua Bar-Hillel (1915–1975) published work in mathematical linguistics in the 1950s and 1960s that had some influence on the young Chomsky. This structuralism is aware of its counterparts "in the social sciences (psychology, linguistics, ethnology), in (French) philosophy, and in the foundations of mathematics (mainly the Bourbaki program)", but affirms that "Only of the latter can we say that it has a substantial connection with 'our' structuralism. With respect to the other uses of the term, the relationships are quite remote, if present at all" (Moulines, ibid.). This view, which would cast doubt on the link between the Bourbaki program and linguistic structuralism propounded for example by Piaget (1968), is probably realistic.

6.2. Current (over)reactions

Certainly the transdisciplinarity that underlay structuralism was less profound than it was made to appear. Sokal and Bricmont (1997) have made a sobering review of the ignorance and pretentiousness with which some leading French structuralists deployed scientific terminology. The very incomprehensibility of the deployment lent their work an air of mystical learnedness that was quite illusory, and the revelations of its true nature stands to put paid to the whole structuralist and post-structuralist period, other than in linguistics and in those recent areas of extension mentioned in 6.1. which do not necessarily recognize a link with 'classical' structuralism.

Some of the strengths of structuralism became weaknesses when the time came for the transition which marks the maturity of any academic methodology: its bequeathal from the great minds who invented it to the rank and file who wanted to apply it. What structuralism had offered to Jakobson and Lévi-Strauss was a release from enslavement to the historical, into a welcome disciplinary regimen that allowed them to concentrate their thinking and writing and, not eliminate, but harness their tendencies toward the metaphysical. Followers who applied their brand of structuralism produced commentaries and interpretations of value in proportion to their native capacity for insight and ingenuity, so that a Barthes or Todorov or Kristeva might produce solid and original work in the structuralist vein while what others cranked out might be of stupefying banality, because they had, as it were, inherited the dam without the river. At the same time, structuralism was transformed by other first-rank figures – Lacan and Derrida above all – into a method not for controlling speculation, but for launching it in as many directions as possible. When *this* brand of (post-)structuralism came to be imitated by second-raters, the results were arguably even worse than for followers of Jakobson and Lévi-Strauss, with puerile wordplay and unbridled metaphysical extravagances offered as scholarly enquiry. The name of Foucault would frequently be invoked in order to halt any attempt at asserting standards of scholarly enquiry on the grounds that at bottom they amounted to mere power politics. Little wonder that it took only a few years before no first-rank academics anywhere in the world wanted their names linked with (post-)structuralism; and the second rank, as usual, followed along soon after.

The current negative reaction comes in a political and intellectual climate in which safe pieties are preferred to any sort of idealism or search for vast horizons, and where strongly felt but logically shallow demolition tactics can pass as serious criticism. The arch-conservative Scruton, for example, blames the structuralists and their followers for wanting to subvert the great humanistic tradition in order to overthrow the bourgeois values that underlay it, and to substitute for it unfettered relativism masquerading as science:

"Innocent readers may draw the conclusion that studies must be either scientific or whimsical – that there is no room for the humanities, as objective fields of enquiry [...]. By conscripting the humanities to the cause of 'liberation', these pseudo-thinkers cancelled the most important branch of human knowledge – the branch which we know as 'culture' [...]. Under the benign rule of the old curriculum, philosophy, history and criticism were treated as serious disciplines, with the knowledge and judgment of human life as their purpose." (Scruton 1998)

But the innocent reader of Lévi-Strauss's *Tristes tropiques*, Barthes's *Mythologies*, or Foucault's *Discipline and Punish* may be hard pressed to see in these anything other than the deep-seated humanism of authors who love culture enough to want to extend and deepen it. Is this not what all our greatest cultural figures have done, often precisely in the name of liberation, and by means of dissent and subversion, the very crime for which Socrates was put to death? How ironic that critics like Scruton or Ferry & Renaut (1985) do not appreciate the extent to which structuralists (who tend to get lumped together with post-structuralist in their attacks) were reasserting traditional values of humanistic enquiry in the face of a Sartrean 'engagement' that required academic work to be politically motivated, or the condemnations they would endure on that account.

A modicum of tolerance for the structuralist perspective might help these critics see that authors do not control the uses to which their works are put (a sort of *langue—parole* distinction) and that the history of institutions, including academic ones, is never determined entirely by the writers of books. To a large extent, the books that become celebrated and influential do so because they respond to a need within the institution. The social changes affecting education in the 1960s and 1970s were such that academic culture could not have remained unchanged, even if Lévi-Strauss had never met Jakobson. A structuralist analysis might go even further and assert that the reason the whole idea of 'structure' was so intuitively attractive and therefore successful was that it filled, temporarily, the void left by the death of God, in a more tacit, less self-consciously absurd way than did the 'secular religion' of the existentialists. Obviously, to blame structuralism for killing God would not be rational. Yet one does encounter critics who ultimately trace all the woes of the modern world to Saussure's disconnecting of the linguistic signified from its real-world counterpart, as if Nietzsche (to cite just one name among many) had never existed.

Whatever the ideological and stylistic excesses and terminological abuses to which they would give rise, the very best work of Lévi-Strauss, Barthes, Foucault, and Derrida, and to a lesser extent Jakobson, Lacan, Merleau-Ponty, Todorov, and a handful of others, have few peers in this century. If they did not accomplish what they set out to do, they failed magnificently, still managing to change the way of conceiving the world of people who have no idea of having been affected by them.

Structuralism was not aimed at de-humanizing the humanities or cancelling culture. It was an attempt to found an understanding of culture in terms of its most distinctively human element, language. For centuries humanism had been opposed on the grounds that a study not founded in God could never find certainties. The structuralists believed that humanism without relativism was possible, and sought to ground it in the universal structures they believed must exist in all languages, minds and cultures by virtue of the very fact that they are *human*. The reason this attempt was bound to fail had already been laid out 2500 years before by Plato in his dialogue *Cratylus*, which concludes that we can never get to absolute knowledge through the study of language, for the simple reason that we can never know what in language is really universal and what is just the residue of history — understood here in resolutely non-structuralist terms as the sum total of the actions of wilful human subjects — and chance. One of Jakobson's favourite sayings, borrowed from Joseph de Maistre (1753—1821), could serve as motto, and epitaph, for structuralism generally: *Let us never speak of chance ...*

7. Bibliography

Allerton, David J. 1995. "Valency Grammar". Koerner & Asher 1995.280—289.

Althusser, Louis. 1965. *Pour Marx*. Paris: Maspero. (Engl. transl., *For Marx* by Ben Brewster. London: New Left Books, 1969.)

Amacker, René. 1995. "Geneva School, after Saussure". Koerner & Asher 1995.239—243.

Angell, James Rowland. 1907. "The Province of Functional Psychology". *Psychological Review* 14. 61—91.

Bakhtin, Mikhail. 1968 [1940]. *Rabelais and his World.* Cambridge, Mass.: Harvard Univ. Press.

—. 1981. *The Dialogic Imagination: Four essays.* Ed. by Michael Holquist, transl. by Caryl Emerson & Michael Holquist. Austin: Univ. of Texas Press.

— & P. N. Medvedev. 1978 [1928]. *The Formal Method in Literary Scholarship.* Baltimore: Johns Hopkins Univ. Press.

Bally, Charles. 1905. *Précis de stylistique.* Geneva: Eggimann.

—. 1907. *Traité de stylistique française.* 2 vols. Heidelberg: Winter.

Balzer, Wolfgang & C. Ulises Moulines, eds. 1996. *Structuralist Theory of Science: Focal issues, new results.* Berlin & New York: de Gruyter.

Barthes, Roland. 1957. *Mythologies.* Paris: Seuil. (Engl. transl. of selected chaps. by Annette Lavers. London: Cape, 1972.)

—. 1963. *Sur Racine.* Ibid. (Engl. transl., *On Racine* by Richard Howard. New York: Hill & Wang, 1964.)

—. 1964a. *Essais critiques.* Ibid. (Excerpt, "The Structuralist Activity", transl. by Richard Howard. De George & De George 1972.148–154.)

—. 1964b. *Éléments de sémiologie.* Ibid. (Engl. transl., *Elements of Semiology* by Annette Lavers & Colin Smith. London: Cape, 1967.)

—. 1971. "A Conversation with Roland Barthes". *Signs of the Times: Introductory readings in textual semiotics,* 41–55. Cambridge: Granta; The Hague: Mouton.

Bédier, Joseph. 1893. *Les Fabliaux: Études de littérature populaire et d'histoire littéraire du moyen âge.* Paris: Champion.

Bense, Max. 1965. "Semiotik und Linguistik". *Grundlagenstudien aus Kybernetik und Geisteswissenschaften* 6.97–108.

—. 1967. *Semiotik: Allgemeine Theorie der Zeichen.* Baden-Baden: Agis-Verlag.

Benveniste, Émile. 1939. "Nature du signe linguistique". *Acta Linguistica* 1:1.23–29.

—. 1966. *Problèmes de linguistique générale.* Paris: Gallimard. (Engl. transl., *Problems in General Linguistics* by Mary Elizabeth Meek. Coral Gables, Fla.: Univ. of Miami Press, 1971.)

Bloomfield, Leonard. 1927. "On Recent Work in General Linguistics" *Modern Philology* 25.211–230. (Repr. in *A Leonard Bloomfield Anthology* ed. by Charles A. Hockett, 173–190. Bloomington: Indiana Univ. Press, 1970.)

—. 1933. *Language.* New York: Holt, Rinehart & Winston.

Bogatyrev, Petr. 1938. "Znaky divadelní". *Slovo a Slovesnost* 4.138–149. (Engl. transl., "Semiotics in the Folk Theater". Matejka & Titunik 1976.33–50.)

Bradford, Richard. 1994. *Roman Jakobson: Life, language, art.* London & New York: Routledge.

Brøndal, Viggo. 1943. *Essais de linguistique générale.* Copenhagen: Munksgaard.

Bühler, Karl. 1934. *Sprachtheorie: Die Darstellungsfunktion der Sprache.* Jena: Fischer. (Engl. transl., *Theory of Language: The representational function of language* by Donald Fraser Goodwin. Amsterdam: Benjamins, 1990.)

Buyssens, Eric. 1943. *Les langages et le discours: Essai de linguistique fonctionnelle dans le cadre de la sémiologie.* Brussels: Office de Publicité.

Cassirer, Ernst. 1945. "Structuralism in Modern Linguistics". *Word* 1.97–120.

Chomsky, Noam. 1957. *Syntactic Structures.* The Hague: Mouton.

—. 1966. *Cartesian Linguistics: A chapter in the history of rationalist thought.* New York: Harper & Row.

— & Morris Halle. 1968. *The Sound Pattern of English.* Ibid.

Culler, Jonathan. 1975. *Structuralist Poetics: Structuralism, linguistics, and the study of literature.* Ithaca, N. Y.: Cornell Univ. Press.

De George, Richard & Fernande De George, eds. 1972. *The Structuralist: From Marx to Lévi-Strauss.* New York: Anchor Books.

Derrida, Jacques. 1967a. *De la grammatologie.* Paris: Minuit. (Engl. transl., *Of Grammatology* by Gayatri Chakravorty Spivak. Baltimore: Johns Hopkins Univ. Press, 1976.)

—. 1967b. *L'écriture et la différence.* Paris: Seuil. (Engl. transl., *Writing and Difference* by Alan Bass. Chicago: Univ. of Chicago Press, 1978.)

—. 1967c. *La voix et le phénomène.* Paris: Presses Universitaires de France. (Engl. transl., *Speech and Phenomena* by D. B. Allison. Evanston, Ill.: Northwestern Univ. Press, 1973.)

—. 1972. *Positions.* Paris: Minuit. (Engl. transl. by Alan Bass, Chicago: Univ. of Chicago Press, 1981.)

Dewey, John. 1946. "Peirce's Theory of Linguistic Signs, Thought, and Meaning". *Journal of Philosophy* 42.225–247.

During, Simon, ed. 1993. *The Cultural Studies Reader.* London & New York: Routledge.

Easthope, Antony. 1988. *British Post-Structuralism since 1968.* London & New York: Routledge.

Eco, Umberto. 1968. *La struttura assente: Introduzione alla ricerca semiologica.* Milan: Bompiani.

Enkvist, Nils Erik, John Spencer & Michael Gregory. 1964. *Linguistics and Style.* Oxford: Oxford Univ. Press.

Erlich, Victor. 1965. *Russian Formalism.* 2nd ed. The Hague: Mouton.

Fairclough, Norman. 1989. *Language and Power.* London: Longman.

Ferry, Luc & Alain Renaut. 1985. *La pensée 68: Essai sur l'anti-humanisme contemporain.* Paris: Gallimard. (Engl. transl., *French Philosophy of the Sixties: An essay on antihumanism* by Mary H. S. Cattani. Amherst: Univ. of Massachusetts Press, 1990.)

Firth, J. R. 1957. *Papers in Linguistics, 1934–1956.* London: Oxford Univ. Press.

Foucault, Michel. 1966. *Les mots et les choses: Une archéologie des sciences humaines.* Paris: Gallimard. (Engl. transl., *The Order of Things: An archaeology of the human sciences.* London: Tavistock, 1970.)

Fowler, Roger. 1966. *Essays on Style and Language.* London: Routledge & Kegan Paul.

Garber, Daniel. 1982. "Locke, Berkeley and Corpuscular Scepticism". *Berkeley: Critical and interpretative essays* ed. by C. M. Turbayne, 174–195. Minneapolis: Univ. of Minnesota Press.

Garvin, Paul. 1964. *A Prague School Reader on Esthetics, Literary Structure and Style.* Washington, D. C.: Georgetown Univ. Press.

Genette, Gérard. 1966. *Figures*. Paris: Seuil. (*Figures II*, 1969; *Figures III*, 1972. Engl. transl., *Figures of Literary Discourse* by Alan Sheridan. Oxford: Blackwell, 1982.)

Greimas, A.-J. 1966. *Sémantique structurale Recherche de méthode*. Paris: Larousse. (Engl. transl., *Structurale Semantics: An attempt at a method* by Daniele McDowell, Ronald Schleifer & Alan Velie. Lincoln: Univ. of Nebraska Press, 1983.)

Halliday, M. A. K. 1964a. "The Linguistic Study of Literary Texts". *Proceedings of the Ninth International Congress of Linguists* ed. by Horace Lunt, 302–307. The Hague: Mouton.

–. 1964b. "Descriptive Linguistics in Literary Studies". *English Studies Today: Third series* ed. by George Ian Duthie, 25–39. Edinburgh: Edinburgh Univ. Press.

–. 1978. *Language as Social Semiotic: The social interpretation of language and meaning*. London: Edward Arnold.

– & Ruqaiya Hasan. 1978. *Cohesion in English*. London: Longman.

Harland, Richard 1987. *Superstructuralism: The philosophy of structuralism and post-structuralism*. London & New York: Routledge.

Havránek, Bohuslav. 1932. "Úkoly spisovného jazyka a jeho kultura". *Spisovná čeština a jazyková kultura* [Standard Czech and the cultivation of good language] ed. by Bohuslav Havránek & Miloš Weingart, 32–84. Prague: Prague Linguistic Circle. (Engl. transl. of most of pp. 41–70, "The Functional Differentiation of the Standard Language". Garvin 1964.3–16.)

– & Jan Mukařovský, eds. 1942. *Čtení o jazyce a poesii* [Readings on language and poetry.] Prague.

–, – & Felix Vodička. 1947. *O básnickém jazyce* [On poetic lanuage.] Prague.

Hjelmslev, Louis. 1943. *Omkring sprogteoriens grundlæggelse*. Copenhagen: Munksgaard. (Engl. transl., *Prolegomena to a Theory of Language* by F. J. Whitfield, [= *International Journal of American Linguistics*, supplement, vol. 19, 1.] Baltimore: Waverly, 1953.)

Hymes, Dell & John Fought. 1981. *American Structuralism*. The Hague: Mouton.

Jakobson, Roman. 1962 [1928]. "Proposition au Premier Congrès International de Linguistes: Quelles sont les méthodes les mieux appropriées à un exposé complet et pratique de la phonologie d'une langue quelconque?". Jakobson 1962.3–6.

–. 1962 [1939]. "Zur Struktur des Phonems". Jakobson 1962.280–310.

–. 1976 [1942a]. *Six leçons sur le son et le sens*. Préface de Claude Lévi-Strauss. Paris: Minuit. (Engl. transl., *Six Lectures on Sound and Meaning* by John Mepham. Cambridge, Mass.: MIT Press, 1978.)

–. 1984 [1942b]. "La théorie saussurienne en rétrospection". Ed. by Linda Waugh. *Linguistics* 22. 161–196.

–. 1962. *Selected Writings, I: Phonological studies*. The Hague: Mouton. (2nd, expanded ed., 1971.)

– & Claude Lévi-Strauss. 1962. "'Les Chats' de Charles Baudelaire". *L'Homme* 2 (jan.–avr.), 5–21. (Engl. transl., "Charles Baudelaire's 'Les Chats'". De George & De George 1972.124–146.)

– & Krystyna Pomorska. 1980. *Dialogues*. Paris: Flammarion. (Engl. transl. by Christian Hubert. Cambridge, Mass.: MIT Press, 1983.)

Jameson, Frederic. 1972. *The Prison-House of Language: A critical account of structuralism and Russian formalism*. Princeton: Princeton Univ. Press.

Jangfeldt, Bengt. 1997. "Roman Jakobson in Sweden, 1940–41". *Jakobson entre l'Est et l'Ouest, 1915–1939: Un épisode de l'histoire de la culture européenne* ed. by Françoise Gadet & Patrick Sériot, 149–157. Lausanne: Institut de Linguistique et des Sciences du Langage, Univ. de Lausanne.

Jones, Linda K. 1995. "Tagmemics". Koerner & Asher 1995.314–319.

Joseph, John E. 1989. "The Genesis of Jakobson's 'Six Lectures on Sound and Meaning'". *Historiographia Linguistica* 16.415–420.

–. 1990. "Ideologizing Saussure: Bloomfield's and Chomsky's Readings of the *Cours de linguistique générale*". *Ideologies of Language* ed. by John E. Joseph & Talbot J. Taylor, 51–78. London & New York: Routledge.

–. 1999. "Structural Linguistics: Saussure". *Edinburgh Encyclopedia of Continental Philosophy* ed. by Simon Glendinning, 515–527. Edinburgh: Edinburgh Univ. Press.

–, Nigel Love & Talbot J. Taylor. 2001. *Landmarks in Linguistic Thought 2: The Western tradition in the twentieth century*. London & New York: Routledge.

Koerner, E. F. K. 1973. *Ferdinand de Saussure: Origin and development of his linguistic thought in Western studies of language: A contribution to the history and theory of linguistics*. Braunschweig: Vieweg.

–. 1975. "European Structuralism – Early beginnings". *Current Trends in Linguistics* ed. by Thomas A. Sebeok, vol. 13: *Historiography of linguistics*, 717–827. The Hague: Mouton.

– & R. E. Asher, eds. 1995. *Concise History of the Language Sciences: From the Sumerians through the Cognitivists*. Oxford: Pergamon.

Kress, Gunther & Robert Hodge. 1979. *Language as Ideology*. London: Routledge & Kegan Paul.

Kristeva, Julia. 1969. *Semeiotikè: Recherches pour une sémanalyse*. Paris: Seuil.

–. 1986. *The Kristeva Reader*. Ed. by Toril Moi. New York: Columbia Univ. Press.

Kurzweil, Edith. 1980. *The Age of Structuralism: Lévi-Strauss to Foucault*. New York: Columbia Univ. Press.

Lacan, Jacques. 1966. *Écrits*. Paris: Seuil. (Engl. transl. of selected chaps. by Alan Sheridan. London: Tavistock, 1977.)

Leach, Edmund. 1987. "Structuralism". *The Encyclopedia of Religion* ed. by Mircea Eliade, vol. XIV, 54–64. New York: Macmillan; London: Collier.

Lemaire, Anika. 1970. *Jacques Lacan*. Brussels: Denart. (Engl. transl. by David Macey. London & New York: Routledge & Kegan Paul, 1977.)

Lévi-Strauss, Claude. 1945. "L'analyse structurale en linguistique et en anthropologie". *Word* 1.33–53. (Repr. as Chap. 1 of Lévi-Strauss 1958.)

–. 1955a. "Structural Study of Myth". *Journal of American Folklore* 68.428–443. (French version, "La structure des mythes", publ. as Chap. 9 of Lévi-Strauss 1958.)

–. 1955b. *Tristes tropiques*. Paris: Plon. (Engl. transl. [four chapters omitted] by John Russell. London: Hutchinson, 1961; full Engl. transl. by John & Doreen Weightman. London: Cape, 1973.)

–. 1958, 1973. *Anthropologie structurale*. 2 vols. Paris: Plon. (Engl. transl., *Structural Anthropology*, vol. 1 by Claire Jacobson & Brooke Grundfest Schoepf. New York: Basic, 1963; vol. 2 by Monique Layton. London: Allen Lane, 1977. Partial Engl. transl. De George & De George 1972: xx.)

Macksey, Richard & Eugenio Donato, eds. 1970. *The Structuralist Controversy: The languages of criticism and the sciences of man*. 2nd ed. Baltimore: Johns Hopkins Univ. Press.

Matejka, Ladislav & Irwin R. Titunik, eds. 1976. *Semiotics of Art: Prague School contributions*. Cambridge: Mass.: MIT Press.

Mathesius, Vilém. 1939. "O tak zvaném aktuálním členění věty [The so-called information-bearing structure of the sentence]". *Slovo a Slovesnost* 5.171–174.

McIntosh, Angus & M. A. K. Halliday. 1966. *Patterns of Language*. London: Longman.

Merleau-Ponty, Maurice. 1960. *Signes*. Paris: Gallimard. (Engl. transl., *Signs* by R. C. McCleary. Evanston, Ill.: Northwestern Univ. Press, 1964.)

–. 1964. "La conscience et l'acquisition du langage". *Bulletin de psychologie* no. 236, XVIII 3–6. 226–259. (Engl. transl., *Consciousness and the Acquisition of Language* by Hugh J. Silverman. Evanston, Ill.: Northwestern Univ. Press, 1973.)

–. 1969. *La prose du monde*. Paris: Gallimard. (Engl. transl., *The Prose of the World* by John O'Neill. Evanston, Ill.: Northwestern Univ. Press, 1973.)

Metz, Christian. 1964. "Le cinéma, langue ou langage?". *Communications* 4.52–90.

–. 1968, 1972. *Essai sur la signification au cinéma*. 2 vols. Paris: Klincksieck. (Engl. transl. of vol. 1, *Film Language: A semiotics of the cinema* by Michael Taylor. New York: Oxford Univ. Press, 1974.)

–. 1971. *Langage et cinéma*. Paris: Larousse. (Engl. transl., *The Language of Film* by Donna Jean Umiker-Sebeok. The Hague: Mouton, 1974.)

Morris, Charles W. 1938. *Foundations of the Theory of Signs*. Chicago: Univ. of Chicago Press.

–. 1946. *Signs, Language and Behavior*. New York: Prentice-Hall.

Mounin, Georges. 1959. "Les systèmes de communication non-linguistiques et leur place dans la vie du XXe siècle". *Bulletin de la Société de Linguistique de Paris* 54.176–200.

–. 1970. *Introduction à la sémiologie*. Paris: Minuit.

Mukařovský, Jan. 1932. "Jazyk spisovný a jazyk básnický". *Spisovná čeština a jazyková kultura* ed. by Bohuslav Havránek & Miloš Weingart, 123–156. Prague: Prague Linguistic Circle. (Engl. transl. of most of pp. 123–149, "Standard Language and Poetic Language". Garvin 1964.17–30.)

–. 1936a. *Estetická funkce, norma a hodnota jako sociální fakty*. Prague. (Engl. transl., *Aesthetic Function, Norm and Value as Social Facts* by Mark E. Suino. Ann Arbor: Dept. of Slavic Languages & Literatures, Univ. of Michigan, 1970.)

–. 1936b. "L'art comme fait sémiologique". *Actes du 8ème congrès international de philosophie*, 1065–1072. Prague. (Engl. transl., "Art as Semiotic Fact" by I. R. Titunik. Matejka & Titunik 1976.3–9.)

–. 1948 [1940]. "O jazyce básnickém [Poetic language]". *Kapitoly z české poetiky* 1.78–128. Prague.

Nattiez, Jean-Jacques. 1975. *Fondements d'une sémiologie de la musique*. Paris: 10–18.

Norris, Christopher. 1982. *Deconstruction: Theory and practice*. London & New York: Methuen.

Ogden, C. K. & I. A. Richards. 1923. *The Meaning of Meaning: A study of the influence of language upon thought and of the science of symbolism*. London: Kegan Paul, Trench, Trubner & Co.

Parsons, Talcott. 1937. *The Structure of Social Action: A study in social theory with special reference to a group of recent European writers*. 2 vols. New York: McGraw-Hill. (2nd ed., New York & London: Macmillan, 1949; repr., New York: Free Press, London: Collier-Macmillan, 1968.)

Peirce, Charles Sanders. 1931–1935. *Collected Papers*. 6 vols. Cambridge, Mass.: Harvard Univ. Press.

Piaget, Jean. 1968. *Le structuralisme*. Paris: Presses Universitaires de France. (Engl. transl., *Structuralism* by Chaninah Maschler. New York: Harper & Row, 1970.)

Picard, Raymond. 1965. *Nouvelle critique, ou, nouvelle imposture*. Paris: Pauvert.

Pike, Kenneth Lee. 1954–60. *Language in Relation to a Unified Theory of the Structure of Human Behavior*. 3 vols. Glendale, Calif.: Summer Institute of Linguistics. (2nd rev. ed., The Hague: Mouton, 1967.)

Propp, Vladimir Jakovlevic. 1928. *Morfologiia skazki*. Leningrad: Academia. (Engl. transl., *Morphology of the Folktale* by L. Scott; ed. and with an intro. by S. Pirková-Jakobson. Bloomington: Indiana Univ. Research Center in Anthropology, Folklore & Linguistics, 1958.)

Radcliffe-Brown, A. R. 1922. *The Andaman Islanders*. Chicago: The Free Press.

Ruwet, Nicolas. 1967. "Musicologie et linguistique". *Revue Internationale des Sciences Sociales* 19,1.85–93.

—. 1972. *Langage, musique, poésie*. Paris: Seuil.

Sartre, Jean-Paul. 1947. *Qu'est-ce que la littérature?* Paris: Gallimard. (Engl. transl., *What Is Literature?* by Bernard Frechtman. New York: Philosophical Library, 1949.)

Saussure, Ferdinand de. 1916. *Cours de linguistique générale*. Ed. by Charles Bally & Albert Sechehaye with the assistance of Albert Reidlinger. Lausanne & Paris: Payot. (Engl. transl., *Course in General Linguistics* by Roy Harris. London: Duckworth, 1983.)

Scruton, Roger. 1998. "Philosophers Who Faked It All Along". Rev. of Sokal & Bricmont, 1997. *The Times*, 16 July 1998, p. 39.

Sebeok, Thomas A., ed. 1960. *Style in Language*. Cambridge, Mass.: MIT Press.

—. 1974. "Semiotics: A survey of the state of the art". *Current Trends in Linguistics* ed. by Thomas A. Sebeok, vol. 12: *Linguistics and adjacent arts & sciences*, 211–264. The Hague: Mouton.

—, A. S. Hayes & M. C. Bateson, eds. 1964. *Approaches to Semiotics*. Ibid.

Seung, T. K. 1982. *Structuralism and Hermeneutics*. New York: Columbia Univ. Press.

Silverman, Hugh J. 1994. "French Structuralism and After: De Saussure, Lévi-Strauss, Barthes, Lacan, Foucault". *Twentieth-Century Continental Philosophy* ed. by Richard Kearney, 390–408. London & New York: Routledge.

Sinclair, John McH. 1965. "Linguistic Meaning in a Literary Text". Paper read to the Philological Society, Cambridge, March 1965.

Sokal, Alan & Jean Bricmont. 1997. *Impostures intellectuelles*. Paris: Jacob. (Engl. transl., *Intellectual Impostures*. London: Profile, 1998.)

Spitzer, Leo. 1948. *Linguistics and Literary History*. Princeton: Princeton Univ. Press.

Stalin, Joseph V. 1951 [1950]. *Marxism and Problems of Linguistics*. New York: International. (Originally publ. in *Pravda*, 20 June 1950.)

Stegmüller, Wolfgang. 1979. *The Structuralist View of Theories: A possible analogue of the Bourbaki programme in physical science*. Berlin, Heidelberg & New York: Springer.

Thorne, James Peter. 1965. "Stylistics and Generative Grammars". *Journal of Linguistics* 1.49–59.

Titchener, E. B. 1898. "The Postulates of a Structural Psychology". *The Philosophical Review* 7.449–465.

Todorov, Tzvetan, ed. 1965. *Théorie de la littérature*. Paris: Seuil.

—. 1967. *Littérature et signification*. Paris: Larousse.

—. 1968. "Poétique". Wahl 1968.99–166. (Engl. transl., *Introduction to Poetics* by Richard Howard. Minneapolis: Univ. of Minnesota Press, 1981.)

—. 1981. *Mikhaïl Bakhtine: le principe dialogique suivi de Écrits du Cercle de Bakhtine*. Paris: Seuil. (Engl. transl., *Mikhail Bakhtin: The dialogical principle* by Wlad Godzich. Minneapolis: Univ. of Minnesota Press, 1984.)

Trnka, Bohumil. 1941. "K otázce stylu [On the question of style]". *Slovo a Slovesnost* 7.61–72.

Trubetzkoy, N. S. 1939. *Grundzüge der Phonologie*. (= *Travaux du Cercle Linguistique de Prague*, 7.) Prague. (Engl. transl., *Principles of Phonology* by C. A. M. Baltaxe. Berkeley: Univ. of California Press, 1969.)

Tynianov, Jurij & Roman Jakobson. 1928. "Problemy izucenija literatury i jazyka". *Novyi Lef* 12.36–37. (Engl. transl., "Problems in the Study of Language and Literature" by R. T. De George. De George & De George 1972.80–83.)

Ullmann, Stephen. 1964. *Language and Style*. Oxford: Blackwell.

Veltruský, Jiří. 1940. "Člověk a předmět v divadle". *Slovo a Slovesnost* 6.153–159. (Engl. transl., "Man and Object in the Theater". Garvin 1964.83–91.)

—. 1941. "Dramatický text jako součást divadla". *Slovo a Slovesnost* 7.132–144. (Engl. transl., "Dramatic Text as a Component of Theater" by Jiří Veltruský. Matejka & Titunik 1976.94–117.)

Wahl, François, ed. 1968. *Qu'est-ce que le structuralisme?* Paris: Seuil.

Welby, Victoria, Lady. 1911. *Significs and Language: The articulate form of our expressive and interpretative resources*. London: Macmillan. (Repr. Amsterdam: Benjamins, 1985.)

Wellek, René. 1969. *The Literary Theory and Aesthetics of the Prague School*. Ann Arbor: Dept. of Slavic Languages & Literatures, Univ. of Michigan.

— & Austin Warren. 1948. *Theory of Literature*. New York: Harcourt, Brace & World.

Wollman, Frank. 1935. "Věda o slovesnosti: Její vývoj a poměr k sousedním vědám [The science of literature, its development and relation to other sciences]". *Slovo a Slovesnost* 1.193–202.

Wundt, Wilhelm. 1900. *Völkerpsychologie*. Vol. I: *Die Sprache*. 2 vols. Leipzig: Engelmann.

John E. Joseph, Edinburgh (United Kingdom)

XXXII. Traditions of Descriptive Linguistics in America
Der amerikanische Deskriptivismus
La linguistique descriptive aux États-Unis

208. The ethnoluistic tradition in 19th-century America: From the earliest beginnings to Boas

1. Early descriptions
2. Thomas Jefferson
3. American Philosophical Society Americanists of the early 19th century
4. Albert Gallatin, Henry Schoolcraft, and the American Ethnological Society
5. Daniel G. Brinton
6. Major Powell and the Bureau of American Ethnology
7. William Dwight Whitney
8. Boasian organizing and criticizing
9. Describing California's Linguistic diversity
10. Legacies of early American recordings of language
11. Bibliography

1. Early descriptions

From the beginning of European settlement of the Americas, missionaries sought mastery of Native American languages. "The earliest known description of a North American language was a grammar of Guale written by the Spanish Jesuit missionary Domingo Augustín Váez after 1565", according to Goddard (1996a: 17). In 1643 Roger Williams (c. 1603–1683), the founder of the colony of Rhode Island, published *A Key into the Language of America*, a Narragansett phrase and vocabulary collection arranged topically.

Proselytizing in native languages and translating the Christian Bible into them was an early and persisting commitment. For example, Congregationalist missionary John Eliot (1604–1690) translated it into Massachusett, an Algonquian language, and also wrote *The Indian Grammar Begun: An essay to bring the Indian language into rules* in 1663, which in 1666 became "the first published account of an 'exotic' language that can be rightfully be called scientific" in the view of Miner (1974: 170). Like many subsequent writers during the following two centuries, Williams and Eliot thought that there was a single American language with various dialects.

Many Christians were interested in scrutinizing the native people to see if they were some 'lost tribe of Israel'. Rationalists during the 18th century also sought information about the native inhabitants of the Western hemisphere to build and assess models of 'the state of nature'. Catherine the Great (1729–1796), a sometimes patron of the *philosophes*, promoted systematic collection and publication of lists of basic vocabulary from around the world, including Northwestern America, where Russian fur traders dealt with native suppliers. "Some of the results were published in Adelung and Vater's *Mithridates* [1806–1817]. In the New World somewhat similar efforts were being made by Benjamin Smith Barton (1797) who hoped in this way to be able to show that the languages of the American Indian were related to the languages of Asia" (Haas 1978: 112).

2. Thomas Jefferson

Jefferson (1743–1826) — an American rationalist with wide-ranging interests, who was the primary author of the American Declaration of Independence in 1776, the first Secretary of State and, later, the third President of the United States (1801–1809) — was very fascinated by Native American languages and culture. Prior to his election as President, he worked on problems of Native American philology. As president, he promoted the collection of information on native peoples, especially through the (Meriwether) Lewis and (William) Clark Expedition to the Pacific coast (1804–1806). Jefferson himself prepared a research memorandum for them, and stressed the need to record languages. In his *Notes on the State of Virginia* of 1787, he had written of the need for comparative lexical and grammatical data for determining prehistoric relations. Elsewhere in the same volume, Jefferson set forth his own speculations about the ancestry of the American Indian(s), tabulated historical, descriptive, and statistical data on tribal groups, and reported on his own excavation of burial mounds. In contact with leading European and American intellectuals of his time, he "and others of his circle set an example by accumulating new knowledge regarding *Homo Americanus*" (Hallowell 1960: 16).

Since Jefferson vastly extended the frontiers of the United States, he had some less-than-disinterested motivation for learning about the indigenous peoples. Although he viewed their cultures as deserving respect, others viewed Native People as savages in the way of what was claimed to be 'manifest destiny' to supplant them. Once the new American government commited itself to the principle of recognizing native title to western lands, it became of "great practical importance for the government to have reliable knowledge about the Western tribes" (Hallowell, p. 18). Jefferson's own curiosity certainly extended beyond the practical needs of presiding over territorial expansion, but his wider humanistic motivations for inquiry were not necessarily shared by his successors. Jefferson institutionalized a connection between anthropological/linguistic inquiry territorial expansion, and a responsibility for managing Native People within that encroachment.

3. American Philosophical Society Americanists of the early 19th century

The American Philosophical Society (APS), was founded by polymath Benjamin Franklin in 1769 and presided over by him until his death in 1790. Its model was the British Royal Society rather than the French Academy. Franklin himself did not record Native American languages.

Continuing early documentations of Alonquian languages, Moravian missionaries David Zeisberger (1721–1808) and John Heckewelder (1743–1823) both worked among the Delaware. Zeisberger's grammar and most of his Huron lexicon were lost, but his assistant Heckewelder's 1819 book set up to "satisfy the world that the languages of the Indians are not so poor, so devoid of variety of expression, so inadequate to the communication even of abstract ideas, or in a word so barbarous, as has been generally imagined" (p. 125, quoted by Andresen 1990: 95). Adumbrating Boas (1889), Heckewelder attacked the purported inconsistency and difficulty of the sounds of Algonquian languages. The difficulty was not that of the speakers of 'primitive languages', but of the alien observers, specifically, "the numerous errors committed by those who attempt to write down the words of the Indian languages, and who either in their own have not alphabetic signs adequate to the true expression of the sounds, or want an Indian ear to distinguish them" (Heckewelder 1819: 374; Andresen 1990: 95).

A correspondent of Heckewelder's who had broader interests in linguistics than American Native languages was Peter Stephen (originally: Pierre Étienne) Duponceau (1760–1844). Duponceau accompanied Baron Friedrich Wilhelm von Steuben to help the American rebellion against British rule in 1777. After the war he worked briefly in the new nation's departments of state and war, then became a Philadelphia attorney. Elected to the APS in 1791, he was its president from 1827 until his death, and also president of the Historical Society of Pennsylvania from 1837. He sought to obtain manuscript material on American Native languages for the APS library and for publication in its *Transactions*.

Duponceau's (1838) major Americanist writing, which won the Volney prize, included appendices with a comparative vocabulary of the Alonquian language Delaware and the Iroquian language Onondaga, and with a comparative vocabulary of 45 basic terms in 30 Algonquian languages (Haas 1978: 133).

Along with Heckewelder, Duponceau (1818) challenged the characterization of American Native language(s) as 'barbarous'. He saw the need for inductive phonology, historical comparison, and analysis of grammar "showing all the different combinations of ideas that human language can achieve". Specifically in opposition to Turgot, Duponceau defended the view of a language as a plan of ideas. Duponceau seems to have been more interested in what he called 'ideology of language' than in phonology or philology' – at least his borrowing (from crystallography) of the term 'polysynthetic' to characterize American Native languages is the part of his work on language most recognized by later scholars (Duponceau 1838). Although some, notably Mary Haas (1978), have viewed Duponceau as the champion of grammatical form in the history of a 'grammar vs. lexicon' opposition in historical reconstruction, as Andresen (1990: 104) notes. "Duponceau's thought was consistent with the ahistoricism of French ideology' and not without roots in earlier French conceptions of a universal grammar. Indeed, Duponceau and his younger friend John Pickering (1777–1846)

"shared much in their friendship, beginning with their professions: they were both lawyers. [...] They were both "gentlemen scholars," like Jefferson, unlike [Noah] Webster. Again, like Jefferson, they shared a leisurely, wide-ranging interest in language studies. [...] They were both involved with the study and elaboration of writing systems. They both corresponded with the leading European linguistic lights of the day, both in France and in Germany." (Andresen 1990: 105)

Duponceau (1818) considered American languages as a single (polysynthetic) type, continuing what Haas (1978) shows was a formulaic invocation of comprehensive grammatical forms prevailing with little variation among the aboriginal native of America from Greenland to Cape Horn. Like Duponceau, Pickering focused more on grammar and morphology than on the lexicon. Andresen (1990: 110) rightly sees Pickering's entry on "Indian languages of America" in the *Encyclopedia Americana* (1831) as "a kind of *grammaire générale* for the American languages, a last expression in the American nineteenth century of the French eighteenth century."

Maintaining Duponceau's view that American Native languages comprised a single 'genus', Pickering (1831: 584) challenged Jefferson's belief that the Americas contained numerous linguistic families, because this would be "in contradiction of the received opinion of the Christian world as to the age of the earth." Pickering also criticized Wilhelm von Humboldt (1767–1835), with whom he was in sustained correspondence about North American and Polynesian languages. His brother, the explorer Alexander von Humboldt (1769–1859) had met with Jefferson, Duponceau, and Gallatin on a visit to the United States in 1804) for failing to treat American Native languages as having "genuine grammatical forms (*echte formen*)" (p. 582).

With ties to Humboldt, Franz Bopp, Karl Lepsius, and others, Pickering was well aware of the major trends in German scholarships, and was elected a Corresponding Member of the Philosophical and Historical Class of the Prussian Royal Academy of Sciences in 1840. As Guice (1987: 16) characterized their role, Duponceau and Pickering were "middlemen between fieldworkers and [armchair] linguists in Europe". Pickering "worked on Cherokee with the help of a young Cherokee boy who was attending school in Worcester [... and] prepared a grammar of Cherokee (1830)" (Haas 1978: 113). Pickering was quite advanced in this work when Sequoyah (1760–1843) developed the Cherokee alphabet [syllabry] and Pickering abandoned his work after 48 pages of the Grammar had already been printed" (Guice 1987: 15).

Pickering also drew up the instructions for the philologist of the U. S. South Seas Exploring Expedition, which was to tour the Pacific from 1838 to 1842, gathering all kinds of information and laying claim to islands that would be valuable to the whaling industry, and recommended for the position a recent alumnus from his alma mater (Harvard), Horatio Hale (1817–1896), who had done fieldwork on a Micmac language as an undergraduate and would go on to do considerable language data gathering in Oregon, California, and Ontario. After a successful career as a lawyer, Hale worked primarily on Iroquoian languages (including identifying Cherokee as one), and also helped organize research and researchers (including Franz Boas) in British Columbia (Gruber 1967).

4. Albert Gallatin, Henry Rowe Schoolcraft, and the American Ethnological Society

Together with Thomas Jefferson, whose Secretary of the Treasury and advisor on Indian affairs he was, Albert Gallatin (1761–1849) was one of the leading American Enlightenment figures. However, like Pickering, Gallatin "did not undertake serious ethnological studies until the 1820s, a time when Enlightenment assumptions about man were under attack" and German romanticism was increasingly influential (Bieder 1986: 17).

Gallatin was raised in Geneva, immigrating to the US at the age of 18. In 1823, Gallatin supplied Alexander von Humboldt with a classification of 32 North American Indian language families. This number did not seem excessive nor 'inconsistent with mosaic chronology', because (echoing Duponceau),

"amidst the great diversity of American languages, considered only in reference to their vocabularies, the similarity of their structure and grammatical forms has been observed and pointed out. [...] The natives of American from the Arctic Ocean to Cape Horn, have, as far as they have been investigated, a distinct character common to all." (Gallatin 1836: 5−6)

Given the lack of grammars available to Gallatin, and the considerably narrower than Arctic-to-Antarctic geographical range of word lists, this can hardly be taken as an inductive generalization. In the years between supplying information to Wilhelm von Humboldt (who died in 1835) and publishing his own (1836 and 1848) classifications, he supplemented printed material with considerable manuscript material, especially Duponceau's collection, and got Commissioner of Indian Affairs Thomas McKenney to send his agents "a printed questionnaire containing a vocabulary of 600 words, selected sentences and grammatical queries" (Hallowell 1960: 29).

Gallatin shifted from grammatical to lexical data, partly in the belief that grammar changes more slowly than lexicon, partly in the belief in a single New World grammatical system, and partly in replacing the ahistorical concern with typology with a concern with history − or at least evolution (see Haas 1978: 136−139; Andresen 1990: 110−112). By 1848, Gallatin stressed that the families were ascertained "by their vocabularies alone. [...] without any reference to their grammar or structure" (p. cxix, quoted by Haas 1978: 139).

Gallatin participated in the cultural, intellectual, and social institutions of the New York elite in the first half of 19th century. John Russell Bartlett (1805−1886), a fellow officer in the New York Historical Society, proposed to him "a new society, the attention of which should be devoted to Geography, Archeology, Philology and inquiries generally connected with the human race" (quoted by Bieder & Tax 1976: 12). Gallatin was elected president of the new American Ethnological Society (AES) in 1842. Its dinner meetings were held in his home until his death in 1849.

"The active members tended to the gentlemen of some social standing in the New York community who knew each other well, and while they had some intellectual pretensions, they were not "ethnological experts". Nearly all professional men. [...] Very few of the members, even in the early and more fruitful years of the AES had any ethnological experience." (Bieder & Tax 1974: 16)

Through most of the 19th century, "descriptions were often interpreted by gentlemen and philosophers who themselves had not had contact with native peoples" (Darnell 1976: 70−71). Rather than develop (evolve) towards professionalism, the AES foundered (if not degenerated). Its sponsor died, leaving only dilettantes behind. Also,

"philosophical disagreements had an adverse effect on the Society's fortunes. Many members quarreled about what was pertinent and legitimate for discussion. The crux of the matter lay in the fundamental division between the atheistic polygenists [...] and the clerics. [...] The polygenist approach to physical anthropology disturbed both the clergy and other monogenist members, many of whom were mainly interested in Near Eastern antiquities and insisted on a literal interpretation of the Bible." (Bieder & Tax 1976: 17)."

That is, the AES was split by 'paradigm conflict' despite its 'pre-scientific' status. The Bible served as a paradigm for the monogenists who explained diversity as stemming from degeneration (due to the lapsing of divine law) from the original unity of descendants of Adam and Eve. Those who believed in multiple origins of humanity, language, and cultures necessarily challenged the sufficiency of *Genesis* as a description/explanation (see Hodgen 1964: 225−294).

Even within the monogenist paradigm, Gallatin had to contend with the belief that American Indians had degenerated in the adverse environment of the Americas. He argued that Indian languages were primitive against those who saw 'polysynthetic' languages as residues of a higher ancestral civilization (usually assumed to be that of a 'lost tribe of Israel'). Mayan, Aztec, and Inca civilizations, which Gallatin insisted were indigenous, demonstrated the racial capacity to advance to urban, agriculture- and state-based civilization.

Henry Schoolcraft (1793−1864), now better remembered as the white discoverer and namer (Lake Itasca, compounded from *veritas caput*) of the source of Mississippi River than as an expert on North American native peoples, was a geologist on an 1820 government expedition to Lake Superior and the Mississippi River led by General Lewis Cass (1782−1866). In 1822 Schoolcraft was appointed Indian agent at Sault Sainte Marie, Michigan. There, he married Jane Johnson, an Ojibwa woman of mixed descent, whose family's help made his *Algic Researches* (Schoolcraft 1839) and 'expertise' possible.

Schoolcraft was less optimistic about Native American's racial capacity than Gallatin had been, often considering them 'Oriental' − which to him meant impervious to change

– though he also believed that the young could be Christianized and educated.

As governor of the Territory of Michigan Cass circulated questionnaires gathering information on Native American cultures and languages that included a phonetic alphabet (reproduced in Goddard 1996a: 27). A patron of Schoolcraft and of others studying Native Americans, Cass (1826) thought that Gallatin, Heckewelder, Duponceau, and others of their contemporaries romantically overestimated the capacities of American Indians.

Schoolcraft found – to his chagrin – that a 'primitive language' was not as simple to master as Cass's theory of limited mental capacity of Indians predicted. He rationalized that Ojibwa (then called 'Chippewa') was inefficient. Despite the deficiencies of his command of the language. Schoolcraft did identify Ojibwa as an Algonquian language, confirming their oral tradition of an earlier westward movement. He also continued the rationale for focusing on the languages of Native Americans. In contrast to Gallatin's belief that languages do not change, Schoolcraft believes they change slowly, and, therefore,

"conceptions of the world expressed in grammatical patterns also must change slowly. 'I am inclined to think', Schoolcraft later [1851] recorded, 'that more true light is destined to be thrown on the history of the Indians by a study of their languages than on their traditions, or any other feature' of their culture." (Bieder 1986: 156)

However, frustrated by the difficult of linguistic analysis, specifically with demonstrating the connections that he believed had to exist between Ojibwa and Hebrew, and by personal circumstances, Schoolcraft sought another, easier 'royal road' to native American history in folkloristics (Bieder 1986: 158–173; Hallowell 1960: 43). He published sentimentalized versions of Native American folktales in English, while making few descriptive and no theoretical contributions to the study of American languages (Hallowell 1960: 28). Against the increasing dominance of polygenism, which made inroads even in the AES (of which he had been a founding member), Schoolcraft (1851–1857) maintained the '*Genesis* paradigm'.

In stressing 'grammatical categories' in understanding native cosmologies and inferring native (pre-contact) history, Schoolcraft adumbrated Boas, Sapir and Whorf. Although he did extensive (if not intensive) fieldwork with a particular people ('tribe') and collated published reports and questionnaires sent to those familiar with different North American peoples, Schoolcraft continued to treat American Indians as a single people at the stage of 'barbarism' in the evolutionary rise from 'savagism' to 'barbarism' to 'civilization' (see Morgan 1877; Hodgen 1964), defending monogenesis against an increasingly dominant polygenism in which American Indians were considered a distinct species doomed to extinction in competition for territory with the 'Anglo-Saxon race'.

5. Daniel G. Brinton

A firm believer in the psychic unity of mankind, Daniel Garrison Brinton (1837–1899), was a Philadelphia physician and publisher active in many local intellectual societies, including the American Philosophical Society, of which he was president in 1869, and in the *Proceedings* of which he published many anthropological papers. He was also president of the (more truly national) American Association for the Advancement of Science in 1882.

Brinton followed Gallatin in believing that beneath surface (lexical) diversity was a substratum of uniquely American syntax in native languages from Alaska to Cape Horn. Brinton (1885 most explicitly) championed the Humboldt tradition (maintained during Brinton's maturity to Heymann Steinthal [1823–1891]). Brinton's collection of folklore and publication of native texts was premised on there being an 'inner form' of all languages, including those spoken by 'primitive' peoples, and "a fixed relation between the idiom and the ideas of a people" (Brinton 1894: 33). His linguistic classification of the Americas relied on grammatical rather than lexical evidence, in direct and emphatic contrast to the Bureau of American Ethnology classification (cf. Brinton 1891 vs. Powell 1891). "Indeed", Brinton (1902: 166) wrote, "the highest aim of linguistic science, of the philosophy of language is to estimate the influence of the various forms of speech not merely on the expression but on the formation of ideas."

Brinton was "technically the first university professor of anthropology in North America", appointed at the University of Pennsylvania in 1884. However, the appointment was honorary one without salary. Moreover, Brinton did not actually teach classes or have students at the university (Darnell 1970: 82, 85). Although "committed to the development of an academic framework for anthropology" (p. 83), he was at odds with the local patrons of the university and museum, who were primarily interested in classical and Near Eastern antiquities. Like Sapir half a century later, Brinton recognized the need for institutions of instruction in order to improve the data available to armchair theorists and the need to publish texts in native languages for scholarly examination. (Both of them devoted considerable time and energy to failed attempts at organizing research: see Darnell 1988; Murray 1994: 95–108.) Although Brinton did practically no direct elicitation from native speakers, he had the means to publish native texts, understood their import for independent analyses of native languages and cultures, and published a series of them.

Brinton also had a history of conflict with the Bureau of American Ethnology (BAE), especially focused on the classification of Native American language. Brinton proposed a classification of families within what he conceived as a single original American language that had 13 North American units. "Brinton adopted Gallatin's work for the eastern United States virtually without change" (Darnell 1988: 117). In the Duponceau tradition, Brinton (1890: 390) thought that apparent linguistic diversity rested on "some curious identities of internal forms, traits almost or entirely peculiar to American languages, and never quite absent from any of them" and quite distinct from Asian languages (Darnell 1988: 112–114).

Brinton's proposal of a Uto-Aztecan stock is of special interest, both because Major Powell's major fieldwork was with what Brinton characterized as the "wretched root-digging Utes", and because the range in social organization between the Utes and the Aztec empire challenged the equation of language and 'level' (size political units and development of technology) widely assumed at the time (Darnell 1988: 118).

Although Uto-Aztecan has stood as a genetic-group, a single 'Pueblo language' and a single 'Northwest Coast/California' family seem to have been based on cultural similarities (or geography) more than on linguistic data. Neither Brinton's classification of the native language stocks of the Americas nor his typology of basic organizing principles (isolation, agglutination, inflection, incorporation, analysis) has any current significance, although both were taken quite seriously at the end of the 19th century. Brinton's work had little posthumous influence (Kroeber 1960: 4), except as the unnamed object of some of Boas's polemics between 1896 and 1911.

6. Major Powell and the Bureau of American Ethnology

Although John Wesley Powell (1834–1902) began his explorations of the Grand Canyon of the Colorado River as a professor of geology on a scientific expedition funded in part by his university, his early work fits the amateur pattern, and the fruit of that first expedition was more journalistic adventure story than contribution to scientific knowledge (Stegner 1954: 123). Powell was not primarily an anthropologist, and still less a linguist. He was a Western explorer, 'Washington scientific lion' (Scott 1976: 27), head of the Geological Survey of the Smithsonian Institution and, within it, of the Bureau of American Ethnology, which he organized in 1879. He was also president for the first nine terms of its existence of the Anthropological Society of Washington, which was later to become the American Anthropological Association.

As one of his successors recalled, of the collaborators he recruited to the BAE, "there's not one of them [that] had training in anthropology, because there was no place they could train. […] When I first went into the field, there wasn't a trained anthropologist in the whole lot. […] Personal knowledge and interest gained them information" (Hodge 1955: 80, 197). Although Powell lacked professional scientific training, built a staff of likewise self-taught scientists even in fields in which people with professional training were available, and was a major figure in amateur scientific circles in Washington, D. C., he was very interested in establishing an overall framework. In his view, necessary observation could be made by almost anyone. Amateur findings then were synthesized by scientists such as himself.

The self-made ethnologists Powell gathered around himself shared an evolutionary perspective. Powell was especially influenced by Lewis Henry Morgan's (1877) *Ancient Society* and his view of unilineal evolution. While Social Darwinism was immensely popular in late 19th-century America (Hofstader 1944), Powell did not become a Social Darwinist. He preferred the progressivist-guided evolutionary doctrine of his protégé Lester Frank Ward (1841–1913). While many of their contemporaries regarded the era of the robber barons as the inevitable pinnacle of human achievement, Powell and Ward stressed the role of intelligence and planning in human evolution, and were, therefore, implacable critics of Herbert Spencer and his view of mindless social forces (Hinsley 1981: 125–144).

In contrast to all the other 19th-century scholars considered here, Bureau ethnologists did not follow intellectual developments in Europe closely and were largely unaware of contemporary German historical or descriptive linguistic research and theorizing: "The subjects at home were so vast that it took all the time and research, the American Indians" (Hodge 1955: 201).

The central problematic for BAE ethnologists was the observed 'analogies and homologies' between human groups, particularly in North America. Since mankind was "distributed throughout the habitable earth in some *geological period* anterior to the present" one – and also "anterior to the development of organized speech" – what was common had to be accounted for by identical evolution (polygenesis) through fixed stages: "The individuals of one species, though inhabiting diverse communities, have progressed in a broad way by *the same stages*, have had the same arts, customs, institutions, and traditions *in the same order*" (Powell 1881: 80; emphases added: SOM). As a methodological principle, Powell asserted, "all sound anthropological investigation in the lower states of culture exhibited by tribes of men, as distinguished from nations, must have a firm foundation in language" (Powell 1881: xii).

Powell and his subordinates were preoccupied with ordering the cosmos, and cannot be accused of gathering unconnected facts. Orderly classification of phenomena from the American 'Wild West', such as Powell pressed for in geology, geography, hydrography, and ethnology, was useful to the government in Washington. Powell pioneered government science, and tied it to a valiant attempt to plan development of the West based on understanding its aridity. Powell combated the ideological claims of powerful vested interests and popular fantasies. Because Western land speculation was based on such fantasies, Powell's science clashed with powerful popular views (Stegner 1954). Similarly, he opposed the view that Native Peoples were destined to be exterminated. The BAE was small, and somewhat autonomous. It was more removed from congressional scrutiny than the Geological Survey, and, therefore, was the refuge to which Powell retreated when the political storms attendant to his opposition to unplanned Western development broke. Even there, appropriations could be – and were – cut. Nonetheless, it bears stressing that delineating Native Peoples was an administrative need of the U.S. government, responsible for their custody after the final expropriation of their lands. Language was the obvious basis for groupings, so adminstrative needs and theoretical interests dovetailed.

The BAE classification of North American Native languages bears Powell's name, and Powell (1891: 218) claimed 'full responsibility' for it. The work of ordering the data on the premise that grammar relates to the stage of evolutionary development of the speakers of a language, and that "the grammatic structure or plan of a language is forever changing" (Powell 1891: 88), was done by Henry W. Henshaw (1850–1930), an ornithologist: "He was responsible to Major Powell. The Major kept his eye on the work as it went along, but he was the Director of the Geological Survey: he didn't have time to devote to such a subordinate piece of work" (Hodge 1955: 80).

"It was Henshaw who proposed and followed the biological method of linguistic stock precedence and nomenclature, and while he, with the aid of others (notably [Alfred] Gatschet, J[ames] O[wen] Dorsey, and [James] Mooney), conducted the research incident to the classification, Powell was the moving spirit, and the final result, expedited by the approaching appearance of Brinton's *The American Race*, was published in 1891, under Powell's authorship." (Darnell 1971: 83–84; see also Hodge 1931; Kroeber 1960)

A privately-printed 1885 version of the classification listed Mooney and Henshaw as authors, and the published version differs little from it (Darnell 1971: 79). Everyone in the Bureau worked on it some, with the bulk of the fieldwork being done by Gatschet and Dorsey (Hodge 1955: 86). Kroeber (1960: 2–4) asserted that Henshaw was given the task of classification "when Powell found that he could never get his philologist-linguists like Gatschet, [John N.] Hewitt, and [James C.] Pilling to come through with the commitment of a classification", adding that "a natural history taxonomist with experience and an unassuming ego evidently was the needed link – perhaps even arbitrator at times"

Powell created the BAE and organized the research to be done by others whom he recruited, also arranged for the dissemination of findings. The Anthropological Society of Washington, which he had confounded, began publishing the *American Anthropologist* in 1888. He was "a genius at organization, [who] not only conceived a constructive program of research [...] but assembled the able men to carry it out", found positions for them, published and/or synthesized the resulting research, and "established a tradition which gave high priority to linguistic studies" (Hallowell 1960: 93, 33; also see Hinsley 1981). Powell designated what research was valuable and tied together to theoretical implications of the work done by subordinates into theoretically-driven classifications.

The group that developed was not large. Although most of the major late-19th-century researchers on Native Americans (e. g., Jeremiah Curtin, Frank Cushing, James Dorsey, Alice Fletcher and Francis LaFlesche, Washington Mathews, and James Mooney) all did research sponsored by the BAE and elicited some data on one or more Native American language, the number of full-time linguists and ethnolists in Powell's scientific empire was few, arguably none. Those involved in gathering linguistic texts and vocabularies were recruited in their maturity, rather than trained by Powell. Celebrating their own lack of professional training as a virtue, Powell and his followers made no provisions to train successors. Despite successful institutionalization − in government and in a(n incipient) 'professional' society − the failure to train a new generation of workers made easier the eventual eclipse of the Powell group and its paradigm by a university-based group led by Franz Boas: Powell's "theoretical influence did not extend beyond the lifetimes of the men he brought to the Bureau in the 1880's", as Stocking (1968: 278) concluded.

7. William Dwight Whitney

As an Americanist, which he was not in any serious sense, the internationally renowned American philologist William Dwight Whitney (1827−1894; → art. 209) was an orthodox follower of the Duponceau tradition, echoing Duponceau's view of an Arctic to Cape Horn "tedious and time-wasting polysyllabism" (1867: 348) and the late 19th-century view of Native Americans as a stage (barbarism) of evolution, though he rejected the widespread Social Darwinist conflation of language with race, and extolled "study[ing] each dialect, group, branch, and family by itself, before we venture to examine and pronounce upon more distant ["Asiatic"] connections. What we have to do at present, then, is simply to learn all that we possibly can of the Indian languages themselves; to settle their internal relations, elicit their laws of growth, reconstruct their older forms, and ascend toward their original condition." (1867: 351)

Whitney did no fieldwork. He advised the BAE on orthography (though, as Golla [1992: 10] wrote, the orthography he proposed "was strongly biased toward European and Asiatic languages and neglected or omitted many of the common features of American Indian phonetics − such as voiceless unaspirated stops, lateral fricatives, the profusions of affricates, the glottal stop and glottalization; Darnell [1969: 65−66] describes the consternation with which it was received). Even his passing and unused attention somewhat legitimated Americanist work, however.

8. Boasian organizing and criticizing

Franz Boas (1858−1942) was trained in mathematics and physics, "thouroughly grounded in the tradition of atomistic analysis of elements and of mechanistic causal determinism" (Stocking 1974b: 11). His 1881 doctoral dissertation at Kiel was entitled "Contributions to the Understanding of the Color of Water". Problems with objective perception of water led him to psychophysics. Legend has it that his observation of Eskimos in Baffinland (during 1883−1884) freed Boas of geographical determinism, and that fieldwork forever cured him of mixing *Naturwissenschaften* with *Geisteswissenschaften*. Stocking (1968: 133−160; 1974b: 8−15) convincingly argues that there was a more gradual shift and with direct influence from Dilthey after the Baffinland field work, while Boas was in Berlin. (On Boas's reimporting of parts of the German romantic tradition that was already familiar to Duponceau, Pickering, Brinton, and others, see Bunzl 1996 and Koerner 1995: 205−214).

Boas does not appear to have done linguistic fieldwork among the Eskimos: "On his first field trips he had the services of another investigator, Hinrich Rink (1819−1893), a Dane who had lived among the Eskimos for a number of years and who was in fact responsible for nearly all the linguistics analysis of Eskimo material collected" (Anderson 1985: 198). Nor did he engage in anything characterizable as 'participant observation' there.

Boas had no formal training in recording or analyzing languages, so did not learn what was known in Europe about recording the sounds of unwritten languages or about comparing correspondances of sounds. Just like Powell's assistants, in their own view, Boas and his students developed whatever methods their questions seemed to demand.

Boas emphasized the great diversity of American Indian languages in marked contrast to the general tendency after Jefferson to lump them all together as 'primitive' and typical of some lower stage of development than, say, German or English. He gleefully challenged any generalization of his predecessors. Reacting against hasty generalizations and facile guesses about history by his American predecessors. Boas was skeptical of all generalizations and of all hypothesized genetic reconstructions. He assumed any similarities between languages must be due to loans (areal diffusion). Although overcoming his early geographic determinism, Boas retained a geographic rather than an historical perspective on cultural data, even if he gave frequent lip service to 'historical study'.

He strenuously opposed his own students' attempts in the 1910s and '20s to attempt to suggest genetic connections between languages. An irony is that the Powell classification — constructed by means Boas did not approve of, and analyzed by non-professionals — took on a sort of sacred not-to-be-questioned character (see Darnell 1969; Goddard 1996b).

Boas's fundamental linguistic 'discovery', discussed in his 1889 paper "On Alternating Sounds" showed that the variation he and earlier observers found in how the same word was said by informants, and then took as evidence for the disorder of 'primitive language', stemmed from different contrast sets in the observed language and the observer's. 'Untrained observers' (a recurrent target in Boas's campaign for control of the study of Native Americans, despite his own lack of formal training) simply do not perceive differences and similarities because of the unconscious habits of attending to some differences of sound that are important in their native language in determining meaning, and not attending to other differences equally great (in measurable, physical terms) that are used in the language observed but not in the observer's language. Fifty and more years later, "On alternating sounds", could be read as recognizing phonemic contrasts. From later vantage points, one can read too much into statements such as:

"The number of sounds that may be produced [...] is unlimited. In our language we select only a limited number of all possible sounds. Every single language has a definite and limited group of sounds, and the number of those never excessively large. [...] Limited phonetic resources are necessary for easy communication." (1911: 11–12)

Boas does not appear to have grasped the full import of these statements. Edward Sapir (→ art. 211), Leonard Bloomfield (→ art. 212), and Roman Jakobson (1896–1982), for all of whom Boas had great respect, did. Not grasping the structure of oppositions between the "definite and limited group of sounds" in each language (Boas 1911: 16), Boas insisted on elaborate phonetic orthography. As late as 1939, Boas explained that his "objection to phonemic writing of text or material [is that] it is always a falsification of record according to theory. [...] The phonemic analysis is a matter that ought to be discussed connectedly on the basis of the phonetic material represented as objectively as possible" (letter quoted by Amelia Schulz 1977: 57). He vehemently rejected the seemingly-logical 'Boasian' structuring of particular languages by significant (obligatory-for-understanding) differences in sound perception, instead mantaning an elaborate, a priori, physicalist/mechanist orthography and (in effect) preserving the very confusion of recorders' 'alternating perception' with 'vacillation' in 'primitive language' his 1889 paper combatted.

Boas's ostensible aim was to inscribe "the inner form of each language [...] as though an intelligent Indian was going to develop the forms of his own thought by an analysis of his own form of speech" (1911: 77). Sapir took the psychologically real (phonemic and morphophonemic) distinctions of a native speaker as revealing the unconscious patterning of sounds. In quite un-'Boasian' contrast, Boas (1910: v) took "tales written under my direction" by George Hunt (1854–1933) and revised them phonetically. As Anderson (1985: 207) noted, "Phonetic literalness not only dominates the linguists' analysis, but even overrules the native speaker's intuitions in determining the proper way to represent the sound structure of utterances. [...] Boas corrected 'the defect[s] of [Hunt's] writing', in effect so as to make it more phonetically accurate by restoring noncontrastive differences eliminated by Hunt."

In his own practice Boas imposed his own distinctions ('alternating sounds') on the languages being recorded rather than modeling the contrasts that were significantly different for the 'native' (which in the case of Boas's prime informant was a more than usually vexed case in that Hunt had a Tingit mother and an English father, and grew up in the Hudson's Bay Company post at Fort Rupert [Cannizzo 1983: 53]). Although Boas (1889: 48) adumbrated phonemic theory in writing that "sounds are not perceived by the hearer in the way in which they are pronounced by the speaker" so that perception of sound (or of color of seawater) is not determined by physical differences, Boas himself never understood how this insight was fundamental to description or analysis of languages.

He similarly failed to grasp the analogy to analysis of the small number of obligatory grammatical categories in diverse languages. For Boas, the varying necessary choice of grammatical form in each particular language and different necessitities of other languages provided insight into how users of each language think and into differences between the cognitive universes of peoples speaking different languages. In the Herderian tradition, Boas was interested in showing the particular 'genius' of each particular people, as their thought processes are revealed in their language's 'inner form', that is, in mapping the world through differing obligatory and optional grammatical features such as gender, number, animateness, definiteness, tense, or aspect. Boas reasoned that "since the total range of personal experience which language serves to express is infinitely varied, and its whole scope must be expressed by a limited number of phonetic groups, it is obvious that an extended classification of experience must underlie all articulate speech", and in "various languages, different fundamental categories will be found" (Boas 1911: 20, 39). A language channels thought and expression by compelling some of these to be made explicit in utterances. Different languages make different distinctions. What must be noted in one language is optional in another. For Boas (1911: 77), it was the task of the analyst to discover the obligatory − but largely unconscious − categories and patterns of actual languages. Analytical groupings (of grammar, phonology, and lexicon) "depend entirely upon the inner form of each language" and the analyst's goal for Boas was to describe the forms of thought in a language by an analysis of the forms of speech of native speakers, without preconceptions about the important analytical categories organizing the language. In particular, Boas, and those influenced by him who described North American languages, rejected forcing these languages into the 'parts of speech' categories of Latin (or, more properly, Aristotelian) grammar (Boas 1911: 31, 38, 77).

As a critic of simplistic 19th-century schemes of human nature and of human evolution, Boas emphasized the differences between the focuses and the means of different languages, especially those of Pacific Coast North American native peoples, rather than seeking to identify universal grammatical features. Despite the considerable variation which he documented, Boas accepted some grammatical relations as probably universal, specifically, a distinction between a subject and a predicate, and between predication and attribution. In the grammatical section (pp. 14−24) of the one description of a language (Pochutla Mexicano [Nahuatl] from the southern Mexican state of Oaxaca) that Boas himself provided in the first volume of *The International Journal of American Linguistics* (which he founded in 1917), the categories are quite traditional: plural; possessive, composition (mostly diminutives directly parallel to Mexican Spanish); pronouns; preterite, present, imperfect, and imperative verb forms; along with the grammatical processes of reduplication, and composition (Boas 1917: 14−24). Those papers by others in the first two volumes of *IJAL* (between 1917 and 1923) which are not texts lexicons, proposed historical reconstructions, or phonological analyses, deal with verb stems, prefixes, and reduplication. None analyzes sentences, despite Boas's identification of the sentence as the 'natural unit of expression' (1911: 27).

Just as Boas opposed wrenching artifacts out of their cultural context for museum display (see Stocking 1968: 135−136), he suspected the collection and analysis of word lists. He emphasized the collection of texts, i. e., "traditional material from the individual Indian informants recorded in their native tongues [... since] the points that seem important to him are emphasized, and the almost unavoidable distortion contained in the descriptions given by the causal visitor and student is eliminated" (Boas 1909: 30). Texts were also essential because they could be studied later by philologists in the way surviving texts of, say, Sanskrit are. Boas was generating written documents, which is to say, producing objects worthy of study (see Darnell (1990).

The extent to which Boas's master-plan conflicted with the work of the previous evolutionist generation and with what Boas regarded as their premature classifications was muted until Powell's death in 1902. The *Handbook of American Indian Languages* was prepared for and published by the Bureau, although work on it was totally under Boas's personal control. Although his official title was only 'honory philologist' there, he not only decided who could contribute to the *Handbook*, he even decided who could have access to the linguistic holdings of the BAE, and was able to block missionaries trying to contribute to the description of Native American languages. So successful was he in restricting opportunities to do linguistic work to those who were professionally trained – which is to say his own students – that he was able to exclude old-line Bureau members and missionaries from linguistic publications, even those sponsored by the Bureau, and even Albert Gatschet, the BAE ethnographer who had studied linguistics (as Boas had not) and who, as Hinsely (1981: 177) put it 'dispersed his energies at Powell's request over more than a hundred languages [but] kept trying to return to his favorite, the Klamath Indians of Oregon."

Boas always claimed that descriptions were preliminary to historical conclusions, but somehow he never got around to making comparison no matter how much raw material he accumuated. Boas's followers were less committed to amassing data as an end in itself. Interested in theory, they often found themselves in conflict with their mentor. For the most part, they heeded his demand to gather empirical evidence and to describe each language as not merely legitimate, but well-nigh unique. Comparison was kept out of the 'discovery procedures' – and out of the analysis as well. Presentations, although standard, were not made in always to faciliate comparison. The languages described in the first volume of the *Handbook* originally had been chosen "to faciliate comparison of differing psychological types in a single broad geographical region" (Stocking 1974a: 475). But the time for comparison had not arrived by 1911 (or by 1943) and "the *Handbook* is on the whole notably lacking in any sort of systematic comparison of one language to another" (Stocking, p. 475).

Generally, Boas presented massive amounts of 'native' texts with little or no analysis, especially not syntactic analysis. The descriptions of languages in the *Handbook*, neglect analyses of sentences in favor of cataloging kinds of particles and affixes. For instance, there is less than a page on sentence structure in Leo Frachtenberg's (1883–1930) description of Siuslawan, in contrast to 46 pages in grammatical processes and 13 on phonology. There are forty pages on phonology, 202 on morphology, and none on snytax in Vladimir Bogoras's (1865–1936) description of Chukchi (as recast by Boas for the second volume of the *Handbook*). (It might be argued that phonological sketches take less space just because their structures were better understood by Americanists in the first third of the twentieth century, so that more economical means could account for the phenomena. It is impossible to believe that anyone considered sentence formation so transparent that the brief mentions in the 'grammars' accounted for the range of syntactical phenomena in any language, and permitted a similar economy of means, however.)

Boas was predominantly anti-theoretical, eager to attack any generalizations about human cultures and human languages (especially evolutionary ones) without suggesting better hypotheses than those he castigated. In common with many contemporary linguists, Boas was not interested in statistical generalizations or sampling. It was all or nothing for Boas. If he could find one counter-example to a generalization, he was satisfied that no universal had been discovered. A generalization that covered only ninety-five percent of the known cases was of no interest to him. And the representativeness of his 'sample' (often of one speaker) was of no concern. Anyone long immersed in a culture (not even necessarily someone native to it) would do for generating texts that provided direct access to the 'genius' of the people (see Cannizzo 1983).

At Columbia University in New York City, Boas was central to the academic institutionalization of anthropology as a science consisting of interlinked descriptions of language, archaeology, anatomy, and culture, and in the early 20th century became the man gatekeeper of descriptions of Native American languages, editing the BAE handbook, founding the *International Journal of American Linguistics (IJAL)* in 1917 and editing it until 1939. Although his 1889 article and 1911 introduction were read as foreshadowing and justifying the kind of work that linguistic anthropologists did between the world wars, Boas's own practive was to amass texts and to castigate the comparativist and phonemicizing work of his own students, especially the greatest linguist among them, Edward Sapir (→ art. 211).

9. Describing California's linguistic diversity

Boas's first Ph. D. student (finished in 1901) was Alfred Louis Kroeber (1876–1960) who was sent to San Francisco for work funded by Phoebe Hearst, under the nominal supervision of Boas's champion at Harvard, Frederick Ward Putnam (see Murray 1994: 38–39). Kroeber took advantage of opportunities to institutionalize an academic department at the University of California by commencing instruction, and also organized a concerted, desperate program of field research (including that on Yana of Edward Sapir) as the original Hearst endowment ran out in 1907–1908. Collecting and classifying linguistic data were part of his version of what needed to be done in salvaging records of Native California and assessing the prehistoric connections among its many and overlapping speech communities.

Kroeber was interested in patterning – in languages and in other cultural domains – and in using linguistic similarities to infer prehistorical population movements. He did descriptive work on 33 Native American languages (Hymes 1964 [1961]: 691). His historical work included the first combination of Powell language families into larger entities (Dixon & Kroeber 1903) and he was an inaugurator of statistical work on language history (Chrétien & Kroeber 1937). The amount of Kroeber's linguistic work would suffice as a distinguished career for someone else, yet, quite, early, Kroeber's attention was drawn away from the linguistic aspects of culture. He did little linguistic fieldwork after the first decade of the century, when he lost hearing in one ear. Kroeber was quite willing to cede work on the prehistory of California (and other) Native American languages to Sapir's greater competence. Between the world wars, both at Berkeley and in helping Boas (and Sapir) co-ordinate ACLS funding for research on Native American language, he encouraged linguistic research on California languages. After the Second World War and his retirement, he encouraged the systematic work of the California survey run by Sapir's students Mary Haas (1910–1996) and Murray Emeneau (b. 1904), encouraged a still younger generation of ethnologuists, and gave extended attention to lexicostatistics as it was developed by another of Sapir's students, Morris Swadesh (see Murray 1994: 208–12).

The collector who did the most elicitation was the secretive compulsive-obsessive John Peabody Harrington (1884–1961; see Laird's exceptional 1975 memoir). He was little interested in theory (rather than being anti-theoretical like Boas), but he was as eager as some other of his contemporaries to posit genetic connections (especially Hokan ones), although he invested little time in any kind of comparative work.

Stimulated partly by Kroeber, Harrington began Chumash, Yuma, and Mojave fieldwork while a high school teacher. From 1909–1915 he was employed by the School of American Archeology, and from 1915–1954 by BAE. He accumulated vast amounts of recordings and transcriptions of California and Southwestern languages, especially Chumash, Karok, and Yokuts, and a great deal on Chumash ethnobotany, ethnoastronomy, and other cosmological domains. His records from the last speakers of a number of extinct languages are being actively mined and some peoples are using them to re-establish languages with no native speakers.

Another ardent descriptivist working in California in the early 20th century, was Pliny Earle Goddard (1869–1928). He was a missionary among the Hupa (1897–1900) and became interested in Athapaskan languages and cultures. At the University of California he was a protégé in the study of Indo-European philology of President Benjamin Ide Wheeler and a colleague of Kroeber. He became an instructor in the department of anthropology in 1901, completed a dissertation on the grammar of Hupa in 1904, and became an assistant professor in 1906. After moving to the American Museum of Natural History in New York in 1909, Goddard became an ally with Boas in combating 'radical' notions about linking language or proposals by various of Boas's former students. He extended his Athapaskan fieldwork to several languages in Canada and to Navajo in the Arizona. A founding co-editor with Boas of *IJAL* (1917–1928), Goddard also edited the *American Anthropologist* for some time (1915–1920).

10. Legacies of early American recordings of languages

Although many American linguists have abandoned description of language in favor of 'theory' based on their intuitions about their own languages and descriptive linguistics done by Americans has extended beyond the languages that were indigenous to North America before European contact, describing, preserving and reviving Americanist languages is a concern of more people now than when the men discussed in this chapter were salvaging irreplaceable records of the languages of peoples doomed in their view to extinction. What earlier scholars recorded (mostly wrote down, though unwieldly sound recording equipment began to be used in the 20th century) is still being analyzed — and not just by anthropologists and linguists, but by descendants of those whose speech was recorded.

The tradition of making conjectures about history from world lists of highly variable orthography has been continued by Morris Swadesh (1909–1967) and Joseph Greenberg (b. 1915).

The technology of recording speech and even multi-party interaction has permitted examination of records of naturally-occurring speech, supplementing the products of careful, slowed-down diction written down syllable by syllable (see Murray 1983) and prompted interest in trying to recover the prosody and performative contexts of what was inscribed by earlier researchers (see Hymes 1981; Silverstein & Urban 1996). American academic anthropology itself is a major legacy of Franz Boas, and American anthropology has been distinguished from anthropology elsewhere (even in Germany) by especially generating, venerating, and analyzing native-language texts and focusing on category schemata of Native American and other languages (see Darnell 1990). Elicited texts and working with native experts to explicate cultural categories are hallmarks of contemporary American Americanist scholarship, and have influenced American work on other cultures, as well.

11. Bibliography

Adelung, Johann Christoph (1732–1806). 1816. *Mithridates oder allgemeine Sprachenkunde mit dem Vater Unser als Sprachprobe in bey nahe fünf hundert Sprachen und Mundarten.* Ed. by Johann Severin Vater (1772–1826). Part III, Section 3. Berlin: Voss. ("Nord-Amerika" (pp. 172–468).)

Anderson, Stephen R. 1985. *Phonology in the Twentieth Century: Theories of rules and theories of representations.* Chicago: Univ. of Chicago Press.

Andresen, Julie Tetel. 1990. *Linguistics in America, 1769–1924.* New York: Routledge.

Barton, Benjamin Smith. 1797. *New Views of the Origin of the Tribes and Nations of America.* Philadelphia: John Bioren.

Bieder, Robert E. 1986. *Science Encounters the Indian, 1820–1880: The early years of American ethnology.* Norman: Univ. of Oklahoma Press.

– & Thomas G. Tax. 1974. "From Ethnologists to Anthropologists: A brief history of the American Ethnological Society". *American Anthropology: The early years* ed. by John Murra, 11–21. New York: American Ethnological Society.

Boas, Franz. 1889. "On Alternating Sounds". *American Anthropologist* 2.47–53.

–. 1909. *The Kwakiutl of Vancouver Island.* New York: Stechert.

–. 1910. *Kwakiutl Tales.* (= *Columbia University Contributions to Anthropology*, 2.) New York.

–. 1911. "Introduction" to *Handbook of American Indian Languages.* Vol. I (= *Bureau of American Ethnology Bulletin* 40), 1–83. Washington, D. C.: Government Printing Office. (Cited from repr., Lincoln: Univ. of Nebraska Press, 1966.)

–. 1938. *The Mind of Primitive Man.* New York: Macmillan.

Brinton, Daniel Garrison. 1885. "The Philosophic Grammar of American Language, as set forth by Wilhelm von Humboldt with the Translation of an Unpublished Memoir by Him on the American Verb". *Proceedings of the American Philosophical Society* 22.306–354. Philadelphia.

–. 1890. *Essays of an Americanist.* Philadelphia: Porter & Coates.

–. 1891. *The American Race: A linguistic classification and ethnographic description of the native tribes of North and South America.* New York: Hodges; Philadelphia: David McKay.

–. 1902. *The Basis of Social Relations: A study in ethnic psychology.* New York: Putnam's Sons.

Bunzl, Matti. 1996. "Franz Boas and the Humboldtian Tradition". *Volksgeist as Method and Ethic: Essays on Boasian ethnography and the German anthropological tradition* ed. by George W. Stocking, Jr. (= *History of Anthropology*, 8), 17–18. Madison: Univ. of Wisconsin Press.

Cannizzo, Jeanne. 1983. "George Hunt and the Invention of Kwakiutl Culture". *Canadian Review of Sociology and Anthropology* 20.44–58.

Cass, Lewis. 1826. "Indians of North America". *North American Review* 22.53–93.

Chrétien, C. Douglas & Alfred L. Kroeber. 1937. "Quantitative Classification of Indo-European Languages". *Language* 13.183–203.

Darnell, Regna D. 1969. *The Development of American Anthropology, 1880–1920.* Ph. D. diss., Univ. of Pennsylvania. (Rev. version, *And Along Came Boas: Continuity and revolution in Americanist anthropology.* Amsterdam & Phildalphia: Benjamins, 1998.)

–. 1971. "The Powell Classification of American Indian languages". *Papers in Linguistics* 4.70–110.

–. 1988. *Daniel Garrison Brinton: The fearless critic of Philadelphia.* Philadelphia: Department of Anthropology, Univ. of Pennsylvania.

–. 1990. "Franz Boas, Edward Sapir, and the Americanist Text Tradition". *Historiographia Linguistica* 17.129–144.

Dixon, Roland B. & Alfred L. Kroeber. 1903. "The Native Languages of California". *American Anthropologist* 22.367–376.

Dorsey, James Owen. 1885. "On the Comparative Philology of Four Siouan Languages". *Smithsonian Institution Annual Report for 1883*, 919–929. Washington, D. C.

Duponceau, Peter Stephen. 1838. *Mémoire sure le système grammatical des langues de quelques nations indiennes de l'Amérique du Nord.* Paris: Pihan de la Forest.

Eliot, John. 1666. *The Indian Grammar Begun; or, an Essay to bring the Indian language into rules.* Cambridge, Mass.: Printed by Marmaduke Johnson. (New ed., with an introd. by John Pickering [pp. 223–242] and comments by Peter S. DuPonceau [243–246], in *Massachusetts Historical Society Collections*, 2nd series, vol. 9.247–312. Boston, 1822.)

Gallatin, Albert. 1836. "A Synopsis of the Indians within the United States East of the Rocky Mountains and in the British and Russian Possessions in North America". *Archaelogica Americana* (= *Transactions and Collections of the American Antiquarian Society*), vol. II: *Inquiries respecting the History, Traditions, Languages within the United States*) ed. by Lewis Cass, 1–422. Cambridge, Mass.

–. 1848. '[Horatio] Hale's Indians of North-West America, and Vocabularies of North America. With an Introduction". *Transactions of the American Ethnological Society* 2.xxiii–clxxxviii, 1–130. New York.

Gatschet, Albert S. 1879. "Classifications into Seven Linguistic Stocks of Western Indian Dialects Contained in Forty Vocabularies". *Report Upon United States Geographical Surveys* 7.403–485.

–. 1890. *The Klamath Tribe and Language of Oregon.* (= *Contributions to North American Ethnology*, 2.) Washington: Bureau of American Ethnology.

Goddard, Ives. 1996a. "The Description of the Native Languages of North America before Boas". *Handbook of North American Indians*, vol. XVII: *Languages* ed. by Ives Goddard, 17–72. Washington, D. C.: Smithsonian Institution.

–. 1996b. "The Classification of the Native Languages of North America". *Ibid.*, 290–323.

Golla, Victor. 1992. "A Bit of History". *The Society for the Study of the Indigenous Languages of the Americas Newsletter* 11:2.10.

Gruber, Jacob W. 1967. "Horatio Hale and the Development of American Anthropology." *Proceedings of the American Philosophical Society* 111. 5–37.

Guice, Stephen A. 1987. "A Chapter in the Early History of American Linguistics". Paper presented at the Linguistic Society of American annual meeting in San Francisco, December 1987.

Haas, Mary R. 1978. *Language, Culture and History.* Stanford, Calif.: Stanford Univ. Press.

Hale, Horatio. 1846. *Ethnography and Philology.* Philadelphia: Lea & Blanchard.

–. 1883. "Indian Migrations, as Evidenced by Language, Part I: The Huron-Cherokee stock". *American Antiquarian and Oriental Journal* 5.18–28.

Hallowell, A. Irving. 1960. "The Beginnings of Anthropology in America". *Selected Papers from the American Anthropologist, 1888–1920* ed. by Frederica de Laguna, 1–104. Washington: American Anthropological Association.

Heckewelder, John. 1881 [1819]. *An Account of the History, Manners, and Customs of the Indian Nations Who Once Inhabited Pennsylvania and the Neighbouring States.* Philadelphia: Abraham Small.

Hinsley, Curtis M., Jr. 1981. *Savages and Scientists: The Smithsonian Institution and the development of American anthropology 1846–1910.* Washington: Smithsonian Institution Press.

Hodge, Frederick W. 1931. "Henry Wetherbee Henshaw". *American Anthropologist* 33.98–103.

–. 1955. "Frederick William Hodge Ethnologist". MS interview, Bancroft Library, Univ. of California, Berkeley.

Hodgen, Margaret T. 1964. *Early Anthropology in the 16th and 17th Century.* Philadelphia: Univ. of Pennsylvania Press.

Hofstader, Richard. 1944. *Social Darwinism in American Thought.* Philadelphia: Univ. of Pennsylvania Press.

Hymes, Dell. 1961. "Alfred Louis Kroeber". *Language* 37.1–28. (Quoted from Hymes, *Language in Culture and Society.* New York: Harper & Row, 1964.)

–. 1981. *"In Vain I Tried to Tell You": Essays in Native American ethnopoetics.* Philadelphia: Univ. of Pennsylvania Press.

Jefferson, Thomas. 1787. *Notes on the State of Virginia.* London: J. Stockdale.

Koerner, Konrad. 1995. *Professing Linguistic Historiography.* Amsterdam & Philadelphia: Benjamins.

Kroeber, Alfred Louis. 1960. "Powell and Henshaw: An episode in the history of ethnolinguistics". *Anthropolical Linguistics* 2:3.1–5.

Laird, Carobeth. 1975. *Encounter with an Angry God: Recollections of my life with John Peabody Harrington.* Banning, Calif.: Malki Museum Press.

Miner, Kenneth L. 1974. "John Eliot of Massachusetts and the Beginnings of American Linguistics". *Historiographica Linguistica* 1.169–183.

Morgan, Lewis Henry. 1877. *Ancient Society.* New York: H. Holt.

Murray, Stephen O. 1983. "The Creation of Linguistic Structure". *American Anhropologist* 85.356–362.

–. 1994. *Theory Groups and the Study of Language in North America: A social history.* Amsterdam: Benjamins.

Pickering, John. 1830. *Grammar of the Cherokee Language.* Boston: Mission Press.

Powell, John Wesley. 1877. *Introduction to the Study of Indian Languages with Words, Phrases, and Sentences to be Collected.* Washinton: Bureau of Ethnology.

–. 1881. *First Annual Report of the Bureau of Ethnology.* Washington: U. S. Government Printing Office.

–. 1891. "Indian Linguistic Families of America North of Mexico". *Bureau of American Ethnology, Seventh Annual Report*, 1–142. Washington, D. C.: Government Printing Office. (Repr. in *American Indian Languages* ed. by Preston Holder, 82–218. Lincoln, Nebr.: Univ. of Nebraska Press, 1966.)

Schoolcraft, Henry Rowe. 1839. *Algic Researches; comprising inquiries respecting the mental characteristics of the North American Indians.* 2 vols. New York: Harper & Brothers.

–. 1851–57. *Historical and Statistical Information Respecting the History, Condition and Prospects of the Indians Tribers of the United States.* 6 vols. Philadelphia: Lippincott & Grambo.

Schultz, Amelia Sussmann. 1977. "Boas on Phonemics and Dissertations". *IJAL* 43.56–57.

Silverstein, Michael & Greg Urban. 1996. *Natural History of Discourse.* Chicago: Univ. of Chicago Press.

Stegner, Wallace E. 1954. *Beyond the 100th Meridian: John Wesley Powell and the second opening of the West.* Boston: Houghton-Mifflin.

Stocking, George W., Jr. 1968. *Race, Culture, and Evolution: Essays in the history of anthropology.* New York: The Free Press.

–. 1974a. "The Boas Plan for the Study of American Indian Languages". *Studies in the History of Linguistics* ed. by Dell Hymes, 454–484. Bloomington: Indiana Univ. Press.

–. 1974b. *The Shaping of American Anthropology, 1883–1911: A Franz Boas reader.* New York: Basic Books.

Whitney, William Dwight. 1867. *Language and the Study of Language.* New York: Scribner, Armstrong & Co.

Williams, Roger. 1643. *A Key into the Language of America.* London: Gregory Dexter.

Zeisberger, David (ed. and transl. by Peter Stephen Duponceau). 1830 [1816]. "A Grammar of the Language of the Lenni Lenape or Delaware Indians". *Transactions of the American Philosophical Society*, N. S. 3.65–250.

Stephen O. Murray, San Francisco (U.S.A.)

209. The linguistic legacy of William Dwight Whitney

1. Biographical overview
2. General linguistic theory
3. Issues in comparative linguistics
4. Relation to the Neogrammarian School
5. Relation to Saussurian structuralism
6. Whitney's successors
7. Relation to American structuralism
8. Limitations on Whitney's legacy
9. Bibliography

1. Biographical overview

The Sanskritist William Dwight Whitney (1827–1894) was America's first truly professional linguistic scholar and a leading 19-century language theorist. Whitney grew up in Northampton, Massachusetts, where he took an early interest in natural science, chiefly ornithology, botany, and geology. This last was due to the influence of an older brother, Josiah Dwight Whitney, Jr. (1819–1896), who served on several U.S. state geological surveys and later taught geology at Harvard University. W. D. Whitney attended Williams College in Williamstown, Massachusetts (class of 1845), then kept books for three years in his father's bank. During the latter period, he took up the study of various Indo-European languages, including Sanskrit. After a year's preparation at Yale College, in New Haven, Connecticut, under Edward Elbridge Salisbury (1814–1901), Whitney spent nearly three years (1850–1853) studying 'Oriental' languages in Germany: he trained in Berlin under Albrecht Weber (1825–1901) and Richard Lepsius (1810–1884), and in Tübingen under Rudolf von Roth (1821–1895). At this time, Whitney began his long collaboration with Roth in producing an edited text, commentary, and translation of the *Atharva Veda*, one of the four earliest collections of sacred Hindu verse. Much of Whitney's subsequent work focused on the *Atharva Veda* and its attendant literature; Whitney also contributed material to the Sanskrit *Wörterbuch* sponsored by the Russian Academy of Sciences at St. Petersburg. His *magnum opus* was his *Sanskrit Grammar* (1879), a work reprinted as late as 1970. Beginning in 1854, Whitney began his teaching career at Yale in "Sanskrit Language and Literature and Comparative Philology". He remained in this post for the rest of his life (barring several extended visits to Europe), declining an offer in 1869 to assume a professorship at Harvard. To supplement his income, Whitney also taught modern German and French, and eventually produced a number of school grammars and dictionaries in these languages as well as in English.

The central event in Whitney's career as a linguistic theorist was his 1864 lecture series on "The Principles of Linguistic Science", given at the Smithsonian Institution, Washington, D. C. (Whitney 1864), and, in an expanded version, at Boston's Lowell Institute. These became the basis for *Language and Study of Language* (1867), a number of the pieces re-published in *Oriental and Linguistic Studies* vol. 1 (1873), *The Life and Growth of Language* (1875), and many related articles, including one on "Philology" for the *Encyclopedia Britannica* (Whitney 1885d). The first of these works appeared simultaneously in New York and London, and was later translated into German, French, Italian, Dutch, and Swedish. His 1875 volume was more successful in terms of the attention it received abroad and the relative quickness with which it was translated into the major European languages.

Whitney was a pillar of the American Oriental Society (established 1842), which he served for over thirty years either officially or *de facto* as editor of publications. He was President of the AOS from 1884 to 1890, and was also a founder and the first president of the American Philological Association (established 1869). Broader public recognition came from his editorial oversight of the first edition of the *Century Dictionary* (1889–91), the outstanding achievement of 19th-century American lexicography. Whitney received many scholarly honors during his lifetime, including the Bopp Prize for Indological research (1871) and the Foreign Knighthood of the Prussian order 'pour le mérite' for Arts and Sciences, awarded for his *Sanskrit Grammar*. Whitney died of heart failure in June of 1894, at the age of sixty-seven (cf. Lanman 1905).

2. General linguistic theory

Despite the title of his Yale professorship, Whitney was not a 'comparative philologist'. He distinguished between the empirical findings produced by comparative-historical linguistics and the theoretical generalizations produced by 'linguistic science'. He held these two fields to be mutually interdependent yet separate: it was not at all unusual, he charged, for those adept in comparativist research to hold wrongheaded theoretical views (Whitney 1875: 315–319). Whitney deplored especially the romanticist and 'organicist' themes that laced even the most methodologically-rigorous comparative linguistics of his day, and that was being popularized in mid-19th-century England and America as an antidote to scientific and evolutionary materialism. Indeed he set himself against all idealistic views of language. He called, rather, for a 'common-sense' linguistics, and implicitly reasserted the core linguistic Commonsense philosophy. Whitney regarded language as an 'institution', an instrument developed for the practical purpose of expressing thought in a social-communicative context. He also taught that language was made up of "arbitrary and conventional signs", such that there was no necessary tie between a word and the idea it represented. These themes had appeared in Book III, "On the Study of Words", of John Locke's *Essay concerning Human Understanding* (1690) and in the works of most thinkers who followed Locke's lead (e. g., Blair 1783: 98). Accordingly, this was the view of language encountered by most American college students of Whitney's day, in textbooks on 'mental philosophy' and rhetoric by Hugh Blair, George Campbell, and Dugald Stewart. Whitney's distinction lay in using the terms *arbitrary* and *conventional* more precisely than did his predecessors, thereby conveying their nearly opposite meanings: *arbitrary* suggested that one word-symbol was theoretically as good as any other for a particular purpose; *conventional* suggested that the tie that did exist between signifier and signified was given by social attribution, entailing mutual consent (Whitney 1867: 18−19). Again, arbitrariness implied subjectivity and potential anarchy while conventionality suggested the implicit social compact by which arbitrariness was overcome.

Whitney extended these principles to produce the single most innovative facet of his linguistic theory, what we may call *synchronicity*. Although he joined his peers in stressing a diachronic approach to linguistic analysis, he also taught that, in ordinary usage, words were unaffected by their past development. That is, even though each element of language gained its meaning through an historical process, an awareness of this had no bearing on one's subjective understanding of a word; such understanding emerged purely from convention, from direct social interaction. Whitney thus combined two antithetical estimates of etymological inquiry: while it constituted the very foundation of historical linguistic study, it was also a matter of mere "learned curiosity" (Whitney 1875a: 717; 1867: 128). Whitney's textbooks on modern languages displayed consistent application of these general linguistic principles: his *Essentials of English Grammar* (1877), for instance, articulated a relatively *laissez-faire* policy, favoring analysis over the laying down of rules and acquiescing to dominant social usage as the only linguistic 'norm' (Whitney 1877c).

Whitney's linguistic theory dovetailed with his professionalizing campaign. Wanting to give linguistics status as a full-fledged 'science', he taught that the study of language constituted a 'moral' or 'historical' discipline, language being shaped by the free action of its users. To account for linguistic innovation, he formulated an individual-centered, voluntaristic, and interactionist sociology of language: changes arose from an interplay between 'centrifugal' and 'centripetal' forces, a dialectic between idiosyncrasy and social cohesion. An individual's unique speech pattern formed the centrifugal or diversifying force in language, albeit constrained by the tendency to imitate and the need to promote mutual comprehension (cf. Nerlich 1990: 28, Nerlich 1992: 225−330). With this focus on interactive behavior, Whitney foreshadowed the 20th-century 'American' school of sociology. In addition, he explicitly allied linguistics with British evolutionist anthropology, especially that of Edward B. Tylor (1832−1917). Anthropology appealed to Whitney by supplying universal and uniform categories for the analysis of human 'culture': it stressed humanity's 'psychic unity' and taught the uniformity of human nature across time (Whitney 1871b: 281; 1880). Anthropology also appealed due to its emphasis on the gradual elaboration of cultural products and the practical adaptation of means to ends: Whitney likened the on-going development of a language to the development of tools or other cultural implements from primitive beginnings. Another parallel with the emerging human sciences was Whitney's suggestion that linguistics could be given its greatest precision in the form of statistical regularities. This idea showed itself even in his quantitative Indological research: Whitney culled lexical and grammatical frequency data from ancient Hindu texts, according to the positivistic philological principles emerging in Germany at that time (Whitney 1874b; 1877b; Staal 1972: 138−140).

Whitney engaged in polemics against Friedrich Max Müller (1823−1900) and August Schleicher (1821−1868): both of these figures denied the role of human agency in generating linguistic innovation and argued that linguistics therefore constituted a kind of natural science. Max Müller (1823−1901), of Oxford University, was also Europe's most eloquent contemporary exponent of the view that language conditions human thought and that speech first originated because it was inherent in humanity's mental structure. Whitney, however, regarded the origin speech as having taken place via the imitative activity often found in the modern-day creation of neologisms. He based this argument not merely on 18th-century linguistic tradition but on the scientific uniformitarianism popularized in Charles Lyell's *Principles of Geology* (1830−1832), the assumption that the forces of change acting in the past must have been like those observed at present. This origin-of-language debate with Max Müller led to Whitney's brief contact with Charles Darwin and to Darwin's citation of Whitney's views in the revised edition of *The Descent of Man* (C. Darwin 1874: 102 n. 53; G. Darwin

1874). Whitney's quarrel with Max Müller was spread over many years, and is best summed up in his final work on the subject (Whitney 1892). Of more consequence was his polemic against A. Schleicher's 'organic' view of language, a criticism that exerted an important influence on the Neogrammarian school of linguistics (cf. 3. and 4.).

3. Issues in comparative linguistics

Whitney held mostly conservative views with regard to 'comparative philology' (Rocher 1979). Although he paid lip-service to the idea that linguistics encompasses the study of all the world's languages, he shared the myopia that affected most of his peers, regarding the Indo-European family as the chief basis for inductive generalization. Even so, he was outspoken in calling for increased study of the American Indian languages (Whitney 1867: 352; 1870: 5). Whitney held tenaciously to Franz Bopp's agglutination theory of inflective morphology, declaring that 'all building-up of grammatical structure in language, all productions of forms [affixes], or of words having a radical part and a formative part, is carried on by the joint means of combination and adaptation" (Whitney 1885a: 111). He also held to the corresponding theory that monosyllabic roots characterized the lexical inventory of each linguistic family's *Muttersprache*. Whitney regarded genealogical classification as the goal of comparative-historical linguistics, and argued that classification based on morphological type was useful only as a supplement. He subscribed especially to Schleicher's *Stammbaum* theory of the Indo-European languages and affirmed the underlying ethnological cleavages it implied. He rejected the alternative posed by Johannes Schmidt's (1843–1901) 'wave theory', first propounded in 1872 (Whitney 1873a). Accordingly, Whitney also rejected the emerging notion of areal linguistics, which sought to explain similarities between geographically contiguous yet genetically unrelated languages. He did anticipate, however, as we will see in section 4, the related concepts of lexical diffusion and dialect geography. That is, he perceived those 'areal' aspects of linguistic change internal to single speech communities but not those obtaining between mutually unintelligible languages.

Whitney made one crucial break with comparative-linguistic tradition: he revised the Boppian notion of agglutination by construing this process as a timeless mechanism in accordance with the uniformitarian principle. He thereby detached agglutination from Schleicher's two-stage theory of linguistic development, in which linguistic 'growth' was followed by an era of 'decay'. In stressing a steady historical development, Whitney gave new prominence to the concept of analogical leveling, the extension of some grammatical patterns by analogy so as to promote regularity of inflection. The traditional view was that analogies had been introduced mainly in the more recent (decay) stage, to off-set the gradual loss of grammatical distinctions. Whitney, however, 'normalized' the analogy mechanism by arguing that it had operated constantly, even in the earliest phase of linguistic development (Whitney 1875a: 75, 74). He did not anticipate the way his argument would be applied by a new generation of German linguists.

4. Relation to the Neogrammarian School

Whitney was both a forerunner and a severe critic of the Leipzig *Junggrammatiker*, the most important European linguistic school during the latter part of the 19th century. He influenced the Neogrammarian movement (Sievers 1911: 431; Koerner 1988) but was not, as some have argued, a thorough-going sympathizer (Jankowsky 1972: 169). Whitney's influence arose from his stress on grammatical analogy and the individual as the initiator of linguistic change. The Neogrammarians found both of these ideas expressed in Whitney's 1872 critique of Schleicher's 'organic' linguistics as well as in his *Life and Growth of Language* (1875), translated into German in 1876 by August Leskien (1840–1916). Wilhelm Scherer (1841–1886) and Leskien himself set forth views at this time that were similar to Whitney's, and became even more direct sources of inspiration for the Neogrammarians. This was especially so of Leskien, who stressed the regularizing influence of analogy in cases where his predecessors had seen phonetic changes of a sporadic character. He thus used analogic analysis in a new way, to account for the apparent exception in patterns of phonetic shift. Leskien in effect proposed a more rigorous approach comparative-historical linguistics, one that led to the Neogrammarians' central and best-known methodological principle: the absolute regularity or 'exceptionlessness' of the phonetic 'laws', the patterns of sound shift associated with the names of Grimm, Grassmann, Verner, etc. Whitney had not suggested applying the analogy principle in this particular way.

Whitney's stress on the individual as innovator helped open the way for the Neogrammarians' interest not only in 'language itself' but also in the psychology of the speaking person. Bertholdt Delbrück (1842–1922) and Hermann Paul (1846–1921) especially emphasized idiolect variety in their discussions of phonetic law (cf. Paul 1889: 3–8, 26–27, 50–53, 59–64). Yet they carried the ideolect principle to an extreme, virtually destroying the possibility that a language could possess a unified identity. This thesis, coupled with the emphasis on 'mechanical' sound shifts, led Whitney to judge Neogrammarian theory as ultimately incoherent.

Whitney faulted Neogrammarian doctrine on several points, most of them anticipating the better-known critiques made by Hugo Schuchardt (1842–1927; cf. Wilbur 1972). Whitney held the old-school view that phonetic shifts were not universal or absolutely uniform and exceptionless (Whitney 1874c: 312): "To set up the necessity and invariability of phonetic change as a fundamental rule", he said, "seems equivalent to putting a *dictum*, a *machtspruch*, in the place of a demonstrated principle" (Whitney 1886: xxxv). He also criticized the Neogrammarians' application of scientific law to human utterance, arguing that the concept of law should be reserved for truly universal and permanent phenomena (Whitney 1882). He found "economy of effort" to be the one true linguistic covering law (Whitney 1878). Patterns of phonetic shift, on the other hand, which varied according to linguistic community, Whitney regarded as subject to the "recondite" influence of irreducible "national traits". Hence he described the system of sound shifts known as 'Grimm's Law' as "that greatest of phonetic mysteries" (Whitney 1867: 95, 152; 1877a: 28).

Whitney also took the Neogrammarians to task for inconsistently mixing their stress on the individual as the source of phonetic change with strictly mechanical, physiological factors; the latter, he argued, could not be agents of change. Changes in group speech habits emerged, rather, through concerted personal interaction: these occurred not by fiat but by a process of diffusion that brought only approximate unanimity (Whitney 1886: xxxv). Whitney pursued the issue of lexical diffusion in the last article he wrote: this appeared, ironically, in a leading Neogrammarian journal. Here Whitney set forth examples of "sporadic and partial phonetic change" in New England dialects, some of which still used a short vowel-sound in pronouncing *stone*, while using a long vowel in phonetically similar words like *bone*. This discrepancy, Whitney argued, showed that phonetic change did not always emerge in completeness, but could be only partial at any given point in time (Whitney 1894). Whitney also made his case against the Neogrammarians through surrogates (Easton 1884; Tarbell 1886). Over the long term, these polemics helped moderate the Neogrammarians' theoretical formulations: they forced the Neogrammarians to admit the influence of lexical diffusion in slowing the process of phonetic shift, and drove them toward defending the exceptionlessness principle on practical rather than theoretical grounds. Yet Whitney's critique had scarce effect on the Neogrammarian research program, the confident search for regularities behind the apparent exceptions to the known sound laws.

5. Relation to Saussurian structuralism

The question of the relationship between Whitney's linguistic thought and that of Ferdinand de Saussure (1857–1913) is raised by their obvious similarities and by remarks in praise of Whitney appearing in the *Cours de linguistique générale* (Saussure 1916). For example: "In order to emphasize that a language is nothing other than a social institution, Whitney quite rightly insisted upon the arbitrary character of linguistic signs. In so doing, he pointed linguistics in the right direction". Saussure added a qualification, however, charging that Whitney "did not go far enough. For he failed to see that this arbitrary character fundamentally distinguishes language from all other institutions" (Saussure 1986 [1916]: 5, 76). This qualified praise epitomized the way, in his unpublished notebooks, Saussure defined his structuralist theory partly in opposition to Whitney's views: though the two positions shared a synchronic theory of conventional meaning, Whitney's was atomistic and community-attributed while Saussure's was structuralist and internally-generated. This tension was crucial, moreover, for the emergence of linguistic structuralism: Saussure's colleagues sought additional guidance from these notes on Whitney, dating back to 1894, when they edited Saussure's lectures on general linguistics based on detailed students' notes. In this way, they created the published *Cours* after Saussure's death. Saussure's notes on Whitney appear in excerpts in Godel (1957: 43−46, 51) and scattered throughout Engler (1967−74); this material plus additional portions of Saussure's notes on Whitney are reproduced, translated, and explicated in Jakobson (1971).

Although Whitney may have anticipated certain Saussurean themes, he never transcended a common-sense framework in his own linguistics. Saussure, by contrast, declared language to be sui generis, characterized by a unique degree of arbitrariness. He thereby rejected Whitney's analogy between language and other products of human contrivance, such as tools or weapons. He even found language distinct from semiotic devices such as graphic symbols or performed rituals, for language had "no manner of connection with the thing designated" (Jakobson 1971: xxxi, xxxv, xxxvi). Saussure also rejected Whitney's teaching that language comprises a set of nomenclatures (Whitney 1875a: 135, 139; Andresen 1990: 157−158, 161), and so affirmed the 'double' arbitrariness of the linguistic sign (Godel 1957: 43−44; Jakobson 1971: xxxvi; Holdcroft 1991: 10−13). From before Locke's time until Whitney, the Anglo-American concept of a linguistic 'sign' had stood in simple contrast to the signified object or idea. Saussure was more radical: he made the sign embrace both signifier and signified, and considered their relationship arbitrary. Whitney's linguistic theory, moreover, did not imply the concept of linguistic structure, for it represented language as composed of independent words rather than an interdependent system. Whitney found it sufficient to ground the word-by-word assignment of meanings in the external community; he did not anticipate Saussure's insight into the internally-generated matrix of semantic differentials. Once given this constraint, Koerner (1973: 90−91) and Bailey (1980: 74) are right to point out Whitney's probable influence on Saussure's concept of semantic 'opposition' *per se*. Whitney set up an opposition between what he called "material" and "formal" word elements, the first approximating simple root words and the second expressing grammatical elaboration, as in *man*: *men* and *brook*: *brooks*. Whitney held that the semantic distinction between *brook* and *brooks* was generated by 'contrast': even the primary term, *brook*, received its ability to express singleness of number "not by a [positive] sign, but by the absence of an otherwise necessary sign to the contrary" (Whitney 1873b: 90).

6. Whitney's successors

Whitney left no identifiable school yet exerted strong influence on the generation of American linguists that arose after his death. This is clear from works by Hanns Oertel (1902) (Whitney's successor at Yale), Leonard Bloomfield (1914), and Edgar H. Sturtevant (1917). Tributes abounded: in the Preface to his *Introduction to the Study of Language* (1914), for instance, Bloomfield referred to "the greatest of English-speaking linguistic scholars, the American William Dwight Whitney", and praised the "remarkable clearness of truth and comprehensiveness" that Whitney applied to the "historic phase" of linguistics. Whitney's books, moreover, contained "little to which we cannot today subscribe" (Bloomfield 1914: vi, 308n, 312). More importantly, Whitney's substantive views on linguistic conventionalism and language as a social institution entered the early-20th-century mainstream. Also widely-held was Whitney's teaching that no two individuals speak alike and that this fact lay at the root of all linguistic innovation. Accordingly, Whitney's immediate successors adopted his sociology of language, including its picture of an interplay between 'centrifugal' and 'centripetal' forces (Oertel 1902: 150−188; Bloomfield 1914: 17, 260, 273; Sturtevant 1917: 37−56). Yet they incorporated Neogrammarian teaching as well by stressing the regularity of sound change, even while citing Whitney's thesis that innovations were diffused only gradually. The early-20th-century American linguists took inspiration, moreover, from Wilhelm Wundt's (1832−1920) associationist psychology, using this to explain the mental mechanism that sets off trains of phonetic shifts and analogic levelings. Wundt's influence was reinforced by the growing attention to direct observation of linguistic behavior. Bloomfield (1914) thereby departed from the 19th century's exclusive emphasis on the 'historical phase' of linguistic study, the kind at which Whitney excelled. Bloomfield treated language mainly in terms of the individual's 'assimilative habits'. Others still shared with Whitney a propensity to link linguistic change to the influence of 'custom' and 'imitation' as found in all departments of culture (cf. Sturtevant 1917: 25–29). So while Whitney's successors rejected the link to the natural sciences, they still allied linguistics to the social and human sciences as a whole.

7. Relation to American structuralism

The rise of a distinctly American school of structuralist linguistics brought the eclipse of the Whitneyan tradition. This structuralist turn was foreshadowed by Franz Boas (1858–1942) and then codified by his student Edward Sapir (1884–1939) and by Leonard Bloomfield during the 1920s and 1930s. Sapir and Bloomfield offered contrasting formulations of structuralism, one relativist and the other positivist, yet each broke with the common-sense orientation seen in Whitney's definition of language as "the means of expression of human thought" (Whitney 1875: 1). Whitney acknowledged that each language develops the mental powers of its speakers in certain distinctive ways, yet he did not conclude, as did Sapir, that linguistic differences amount to differing constructions of 'social reality'. Equally a departure from Whitney's viewpoint was Bloomfield's neo-positivism. During the 1920s, Bloomfield turned his back on the Wundtian psychology of his 1914 *Introduction* and embraced a behaviorist or 'physicalist' theory of language. He rejected all 'animistic' explanations of human action, those relying on categories of the mind, will, expression, or representation. In a sense, Bloomfield and Sapir both held that language creates humankind's perceptual or symbolic universe. Yet Bloomfield, like the contemporary Vienna Circle philosophers, saw such power in language as a source of prejudice and illusion: it was therefore outside the scope of 'scientific' linguistics (Lepschy 1970: 74–79).

Sapir and Bloomfield stood opposed to Whitney most directly in their use of the phonemic principle. True, Bloomfield ignored the epistemological implications of phonemic relativity, and regarded phonemes as objective entities, while Sapir stressed the 'psychological reality' of the phonemic system (Bloomfield 1933: 85, 129, 78–85, 137–38; Sapir 1949 [1933]). Yet both versions were inherently structuralist and so implicitly counter to Whitney's historical atomism. Finally, unlike Whitney and his immediate successors, as well as the Neogrammarians, Bloomfield asserted the full autonomy of linguistic science soon after he read Saussure's *Cours* in 1923: not only physiological and acoustic description, but also 'mentalist' psychology and social dynamics were irrelevant to linguistic study (Bloomfield 1926: 154). He thus declared the discipline independent even of the social sciences (Bloomfield 1933: 33, 145; cf. Andresen 1990: 235–241). The continued praise of Whitney's linguistic volumes ("incomplete but scarcely antiquated") found in Bloomfield's *Language* should be interpreted in light of his reorientation of the discipline (Bloomfield 1933: 16).

8. Limitations on Whitney's legacy

Whitney's long-term influence was limited by his theoretical assumptions, which were historically grounded but not historicist, conventionalist but not relativistic. These distinctions can be understood best in terms of the shift in anthropological thought from British cultural evolutionism to Boasian cultural relativism. In the evolutionary view of culture, which Whitney saw as an ally, human variety was arranged in a unilinear temporal sequence which was the same everywhere, only manifesting different levels of development at a given time and place (Burrow 1966: 65, 98, 102). Evolutionism thereby imposed a Eurocentric and 'positivist' restraint on historical, cultural, and epistemological relativism in Whitney's linguistic thought. For example, in discussing the different color classifications employed by different languages, Whitney mainly contrasted the refined color distinctions made by European languages with the "less elaborate and complete" systems of other tongues: the latter, he said, "give the eye and mind a very inferior training in distinguishing colors". In this respect, he regarded languages as more or less developed rather than different in terms of their entire systems (Whitney 1875a: 19–20). It is not surprising that Whitney had no ties to or strong positive influence on the various turn-of-the-century revolts against old-style scientific positivism, Common-sense epistemology, and socio-cultural evolutionism. These were the intellectual movements associated with the names of Freud, Durkheim, Boas, and Saussure, which introduced the importance of the unconscious and of 'social facts', and re-emphasized the Herderian ideas of cultural pluralism and the socio-linguistic construction of reality. All of these movements were directed in some sense against the kind of epistemological and historico-cultural assumptions one finds at the base of W. D. Whitney's linguistics. Whitney's mental and social theory precluded his having an enduring legacy in linguistics except in certain limited areas.

9. Bibliography

Abbreviations

TAPA: Transactions of the American Philological Association [numbered by year only].
PAPA: Proceedings of the American Philological Association.
PAOS: Proceedings of the American Oriental Society.

9.1. Works by William Dwight Whitney

(For a full bibliography, see Lanman 1897.)

1864. "Brief Abstract of a Series of Six Lectures on the Principles of Linguistic Science". *Annual Report*, 95–116. Washington, D. C.: Smithsonian Institution.

1867. *Language and the Study of Language.* New York: Scribner & Co.

1870. "Presidential Address". *PAPA* 1.4–6.

1871a. "Sanscrit". *New American Cyclopedia.* Vol. XIV, 334–339. New York: D. Appleton & Co.

1871b. "Present State of the Question as to the Origin of Language". *TAPA*, 84–94. (Repr. in 1873c: 279–291.)

1872. "Strictures on the Views of August Schleicher respecting the Nature of Language and Kindred Subjects". *TAPA*. 35–64. (Repr. in 1873c: 298–331.)

1873a. "On Johannes Schmidt's New Theory of the Relationship of Indo-European Languages". *PAOS* 10.lxxvii–lxxviii.

1873b. "On Material and Form in Language". *TAPA*, 77–96.

1873c. *Oriental and Linguistic Studies.* Vol. I: *The Veda; the Avesta; the Science of Language.* New York: Charles Scribner.

1874a. "On Darwinism and Language". *North American Review* 119.61–88.

1874b. "The Proportional Elements of English Utterance". *TAPA*, 14–17.

1874c. "On Peile's Greek and Latin Etymology". *Transactions of the Philological Society of London*, Part iii, 299–327.

1875a. *The Life and Growth of Language.* New York: D. Appleton & Co.; London: Henry S. King.

1875b. "Are Languages Institutions?". *Contemporary Review* 25.713–732.

1877a. "On Cockneyisms". *TAPA*, 26–28.

1877b. "Comparative Frequency of the Occurence of the Alphabetic Elements in Sanskrit". *PAOS* 10.cl–clii.

1877c. *Essentials of English Grammar: For the use of schools.* Boston: Ginn & Co.

1878. "On the Relation of Surd and Sonant and the Principle of Economy as a Phonetic Force". *TAPA*, 41–57.

1879. *A Sanskrit Grammar.* Leipzig: Breitkopf & Härtel. (2nd rev. ed., 1889.)

1880. "Logical Consistency in Views of Language". *American Journal of Philology* 1.327–343.

1882. "Further Word as to Surds and Sonants, and the Law of Economy as a Phonetic Force". *PAPA* 13.xiii–xiv.

1883. "The Sovereign Reason for Spelling Reform". *The New York Evening Post* (19 May 1883).

1884a. Review of *Über Herkunft und Sprache der transgangentischen Völker* [Origin and language of the transgangetic peoples] by Ernst Kuhn (München: Im Verlage der Königl.-bayr. Akademie, 1883). *American Journal of Philology* 5.88–93.

1884b. "The Study of Hindu Grammar and the Study of Sanskrit". *American Journal of Philology* 5.279–297.

1885a. "On Combination and Adaptation as Illustrated by the Exchanges of Primary and Secondary Suffixes". *TAPA*, 111–123.

1885b. "Remarks" [on Francis Andrew March (1825–1911), "On the Neo-grammarians". *PAPA* 16.xix–xx]. *PAPA* 16.xxi.

1885c. "The Roots of the Sanskrit Language". *TAPA*, xxvii–xxix.

1885d. "Philology". *Encyclopdia Britannica.* 9th ed., vol. XVIII.778–794. (American reprint, Philadelphia: J. M. Stoddart, 1891.)

1886. "The Method of Phonetic Change in Language". *PAPA* 18.xxxiii–xxxv.

1892. *Max Müller and the Science of Language.* New York: Appleton & Co.

1893a. "Simplified Spelling: A symposium". *American Anthropologist* 6.190–193.

1893b. "The Native Commentary to the Atharva-Veda". *Festgruss an Roth*, 89–96. Stuttgart: Kohlhammer.

1894. "Examples of Sporadic and Partial Phonetic Change in English". *Indogermanische Forschungen* 4.32–36.

9.2. Secondary sources

Andresen, Julie Tetel. 1990. *Linguistics in America, 1769–1924: A critical history.* New York: Routledge.

Bailey, Richard W. 1980. "William Dwight Whitney and the Origins of Semiotics". *The Sign: Semiotics around the world* ed. by R. W. Bailey, Ladislav Matejka & Peter Steiner, 68–80. Ann Arbor: Michigan Slavic Publications.

Blair, Hugh. 1783. *Lectures on Rhetoric and Belles Lettres.* London: W. Strahan & T. Cadell. (Ed. and repr., with introd. by Harold F. Harding, Carbondale: Southern Illinois Univ. Press, 1965.)

Bloomfield, Leonard. 1914. *Introduction to the Study of Language.* New York: Holt (Repr., with an introd. by Joseph F. Kess, Amsterdam & Philadelphia: Benjamins, 1983.)

—. 1926. "A Set of Postulates for the Science of Language". *Language* 2.153–164.

—. 1933. *Language.* New York: Holt.

Bloomfield, Maurice. 1884. "On the Probability of the Existence of Phonetic Laws". *AJP* 5:18.178–185.

Burrow, John W. 1966. *Evolution and Society: A study in Victorian social theory.* Cambridge: Cambridge Univ. Press.

Christy, Craig. 1983. *Uniformitarianism in Linguistics.* Amsterdam & Philadelphia: Benjamins.

Darwin, Charles. 1871. *The Descent of Man and Selection in Relation to Sex.* London: J. Murray. (Rev. ed., 1874.)

Darwin, George H. 1874. "Professor Whitney on the Origin of Language". *Contemporary Review* 24.894–905.

Delbrück, Berthold. 1882. *Introduction to the Study of Language.* Transl. by Eva Channing. Leipzig: Breitkopf & Härtel. (Repr., with a foreword by Konrad Koerner, Amsterdam & Philadelphia: Benjamins, 1974; 2nd printing, 1989.)

Easton, Morton W. 1884. "Analogy and Uniformity". *American Journal of Philology* 5.164–177.

Engler, Rudolf, ed. 1967–74. *Cours de linguistique générale.* Édition critique. 2 vols. Wiesbaden: Harrassowitz.

Godel, Robert. 1957. *Les sources manuscrites du Cours de linguistique générale de F. de Saussure.* Genève: Droz.

Holdcroft, David. 1991. *Saussure: Signs, system and arbitrariness.* Cambridge: Cambridge Univ. Press.

Jakobson, Roman. 1971. "The World Response to Whitney's Principles of Linguistic Science". *Whitney on Language* ed. by Michael Silverstein, xxv–xlv. Cambridge, Mass.: MIT Press.

Jankowski, Kurt R. 1972. *The Neogrammarians: A re-evaluation of their place in the development of linguistic science.* The Hague: Mouton.

Koerner, Konrad. 1973. *Ferdinand de Saussure: The Origin and Development of his Linguistic Thought in Western Studies of Language.* Braunschweig: Vieweg.

—. 1988. "L'Importance de William Dwight Whitney pour les jeunes linguistes de Leipzig et pour Ferdinand de Saussure". *Saussurean Studies/Études Saussuriennes* by K. Koerner, 1–16. Geneva: Éditions Slatkine.

Lanman, Charles R. 1897. "Memorial Address"; "Bibliography of the Works of William Dwight Whitney". *Whitney Memorial Meeting*, 7–28, 121–150. Boston: Ginn & Co.

—. 1905. "Preface"; "Brief Sketch of Whitney's Life". *Atharva-Veda Samhita.* Vol. I, xxxvii–xlii, xliii–xlvi. Cambridge, Mass.: Harvard Univ. Press.

Lepschy, Giulio C. 1970. *A Survey of Structuralist Linguistics.* London: Faber & Faber.

Nerlich, Brigitte. 1990. *Change in Language: Whitney, Bréal, and Wegener.* New York: Routledge.

—. 1992. *Semantic Theories in Europe, 1830–1930.* Amsterdam & Philadelphia: Benjamins.

Norman, William M. 1972. "The Neogrammarians and Comparative Linguistics". Ph. D. diss., Princeton Univ.

Oertel, Hanns. 1902. *Lectures on the Study of Language.* New York: Charles Scribner's Sons.

Paul, Hermann. 1889 [1880]. *Principles of the History of Language.* Transl. by Herbert A. Strong. New York: Macmillan.

Rocher, Rosane. 1979. "The Past up to the Introduction of Neogrammarian Thought: Whitney and Europe". *The European Background of American Linguistics* ed. by Henry M. Hoenigswald, 5–22. Dordrecht: Foris.

Sapir, Edward. 1949 [1933]. "The Psychological Reality of Phonemes". *Selected Writings* ed. by David G. Mandelbaum, 46–60. Berkeley & Los Angeles: Univ. of California Press.

Saussure, Ferdinand de. 1986 [1916]. *Course in General Linguistics.* Transl. by Roy Harris. LaSalle, Ill.: Open Court.

Sievers, Eduard. 1911. "Philology". *Encyclopaedia Britannica*, 11th ed., 430–435. London.

Staal, J. F., ed. 1972. *A Reader of the Sanskrit Grammarians.* Cambridge, Mass.: MIT Press.

Sturtevant, Edgar H. 1917. *Linguistic Change.* Chicago: Univ. of Chicago Press. (Repr., 1962.)

Tarbell, Frank B. 1886. "Phonetic Law". *TAPA* 17.5–16.

Wilbur, Terence H. 1972. "Hugo Schuchardt and the Neogrammarians". *Schuchardt, the Neogrammarians, and the Transformational Theory of Phonological Change* ed. by Theo Vennemann & T. H. Wilbur, 75–113. Frankfurt/M.: Athenäum.

Stephen G. Alter, Wenham, Mass. (U.S.A.)

210. Attempts at professionalization of American linguistics: The role of the Linguistic Society of America

1. Introduction
2. The Linguistic Institutes
3. The linguistic craft
4. The Intensive Language Program
5. The official LSA journal
6. Slowth growth and incipient professionalism
7. Bibliography

1. Introduction

Before linguistics departments were organized within North American universities, two professors at Ohio State University with impeccable philological credentials, George Melville Bolling (1871–1963), who specialized on Homeric Greek, and Leonard Bloomfield (1887–1949), a Germanicist who had recorded and analyzed an unwritten Austronesian language (Tagalog) during the mid-1910s, organised a national association of scholars interested more in general linguistics than in the study of the particular languages which they taught. While the organizers of the Linguistic Society of America (LSA) mostly accepted neogrammarian principles for historical analysis, they broke with their elders by focusing on speech rather than literature in teaching languages, concentrated on synchronic analysis, and rejected a priori (especially Latin) grammatical categories in analysis. The prime mover in academic institutionalization of anthropology in North America, Franz Boas (1859–1942), his student Edward Sapir (1884–1939), Bloomfield, and others regarded much linguistic analysis before them as suspect. Generally, they considered it better to start over with data collected by 'scientifically-trained' observers than to try to make sense of data collected by those they regarded as 'unscientific' – especially Christian missionaries.

With their open contempt for how languages were studied at the time, their rejection of received categories and presuppositions, their regard of fieldwork as the only reliable method of gathering data, and their tendency to disregard any previous scholarly work, the founders of the LSA look like scientific revolutionaries. From relatively marginal locations, they openly rejected the verities of academic language study and proposed a new paradigm of structural description, phonemics, in the new LSA journal, *Language*.

In 1924, Bloomfield approached 27 scholars, six of whom were Americanists, to sign the call he had drafted for a society. The first issue of *Language* opened with the text of the Call and an elaboration, also written by Bloomfield (1925), "Why a Linguistic Society?". The immediate answer was to enhance "the possibility of meeting and knowing each other" (p. 1). The promotion of the discipline as a legitimate scientific enterprise was important along with creating bonds and facilitating communication, and applying linguistic knowledge to teaching languages, an abiding concern of his. He also called attention to local objects of study: the need for description of dialects of American English and of "the American Indian languages which are disappearing forever, more rapidly than they can be recorded" (p. 5).

Of the 204 members of the LSA whose memberships in other professional societies was known (from a total of 214 paid members) on 13 March 1925, 17 also belonged to the American Anthropological Association, 61 to the American Oriental Society, 77 to the American Philosophical Asociation, and 88 to the Modern Language Association (Joos 1986: 11).

2. The Linguistic Institutes

Probably the most important institution of all in creating a continent-wide community was the Linguistic Institute (LI). Initially, it was quite tenuously institutionalized and not focused on training at all. The primary purpose of the Institute was to provide "the stimulus of discussion with scholars of similar interest", according to LSA Vice President Edgar Sturtevant (1875–1952), who organized institutes at Yale in the summers of 1928 and 1929. After two LIs at the City College of New York, with no financial support, LIs were suspended. Charles Fries (1887–1967) revived the institution at the University of Michigan in 1936. The Michigan LIs brought together the students who were to become 'neo-Bloomfieldians' at Sapir's 1937 and Bloomfield's and 1938 courses. By drawing together persons normally dispersed among different institution, summer training shortens the time necessary for ideas to diffuse and for students to be trained. (For elaboration, see Hill 1964; Murray 1994: 139−142.)

3. The linguistic craft

Bloomfield believed that there was a teachable craft of linguistic knowledge. His 1933 book *Language* laid out this craft and was used to train students for three decades (Murray 1994: 239; sales figures show that the highest sales of the book in any years was 1966, and that more copies of the book were sold during the 1960s than in previous decades). Bloomfield also sought to guide first- and second-language teaching through a melding of accurate ('scientific') description of language and behaviorist pedagogical principles. With junior colleagues who also became involved in analyzing and teaching languages during World War II, Bloomfield was moving toward professionalization of linguistics, beyond the establishment of university departments focused on theorizing about language.

4. The Intensive Language Program

After US entry into war at the end of 1941, the Intensive Language Program (ILP) integrated 'scientific' analyses of languages by LSA members with the production of teaching materials and actual language instruction in at least 37 languages. First pocket guides and phrase books were prepared, then a

"series of complete, self-teaching, general purpose (i.e., non-military) language courses in 30 languages, each accompanied by four hours of recordings geared intimately to the texts [...] were published by the ILP and the first editions went to the United States Armed Forces Institute [...] copyrighted in the name of LSA." (Cowan 1991 [1975]: 77)

The program − at least funds for participation in it − grew far more rapidly than did the supply of linguists: a massive program was funded one year and terminated the next without any systematic evaluation of success.

As the war ended and civilian life resumed, most linguists returned to academia, although some joined in the U.S. State Department's Foreign Service Institute or in the Armed Forces Institutes, whether in foreign language instruction or in the preparation of materials for teaching English as a second language. J Milton Cowan (1907−1993), who had been the civilian co-ordinator of the ILP, remained LSA Secretary until 1950, and went to Cornell University to organize and run the Division of Modern Languages there along the lines of applied linguistics of the ILP. In general, linguists of the generation termed 'neo-Bloomfieldian' 'applied' linguistics, teaching languages rather than linguistics, and trained relatively few students as linguists (distinct from teachers of specific language). The number of member of the LSA increased only gradually in the immediate postwar years. (For elaboration, see Murray 1994: 144−151.)

5. The official LSA journal

From 1940 until his death, Bernard Bloch (1907−1965) edited *Language*. Within a year, Bloch established his absolute personal authority as editor. Some linguistis felt that Bloch had an animus for diachronic analysis, and no interest in social/cultural factors of language. Bloch (1950: 16) himself claimed that "neither Bolling nor I have ever favored one field of linguistics at the expense of another: each article has been accepted or declined on its own merits alone, without reference to the supply of other articles in the same field." Bloomfield (1946: 2, n. 2) opined:

"*Language* is not the organ of any one school of linguistic theory, but of the Linguistic Society as a whole. It may publish controversial views, and occasionally it may seem to give more space to one side of a controversy than to another, if supporters of that side happen to send in more material."

Patterns of submission were, in their view, happenstance. (For elaboration, see Murray 1994: 160−164.)

6. Slow growth and incipient professionalization

The students of the founders of the LSA did not have an easy time of expanding academic opportunities during the international economic depression of the 1930s. Those who identified themselves as linguists survived in tenuous and temporary niches through the Depression and war years.

In 1950 in the United States, as in 1925, there were scholars committed to a science of linguistics, but they did not constitute a distinct profession with control over any niche, except a few local ones (language programs at Cornell University, the University of Michigan and the Foreign Service Institute). In contrast to the ideal type 'profession' based on those established in the 19th century (i.e., attorneys and physicians), American linguists generally have not been self-employed. Indeed, hardly any of them were employed as linguists, and before the 1960s, most did not have graduate degrees in linguistics. Their professional training had to meet standards set by language professors who were not 'linguists', and few had positions in which they were paid to work fulltime as 'linguists'.

In common with those in many other primarily academic disciplines, linguists' knowledge and/or practical competence were not licensed by any level of government, and 'scientific' linguists were unable to obtain monopolistic control over the production even of those who called themselves 'linguists', let alone everyone claiming to be 'professionally involved' with language. In particular, they were unable to prevent acceptance of foreign credentials and to eliminate competition from an influx of (mostly multilingual) European refugees. Nor does the professional association exercise any effective control over the subsequent conduct of those either calling themselves 'linguists' or marketing their services as 'experts' on or teachers of languages. The LSA continues to lack a written code of professional ethics. (In contrast, an ethics code was established in 1847 with the foundation of the American Medical Association; see Abbott 1991: 378). Similarly, no organization of linguists has persuaded any level of government to establish licensing examinations (in contrast to professions including accountants, social workers, air-traffic controllers, real-estate brokers, and speech therapists) and thereby to restrict the 'practice of language' to state-certified professionals. As Freidson (1986: 33—34) and Abbott (1991: 357) note, the history of professions in Europe more frequently involved affiliation with the state (as 'officials' in bureaucratic sinecures) than in the United States, where professional monopolies sought state protection for selling services outside state institutions.

In 1955, as in 1925, the predominant source of income for those who considered themselves linguists was language teaching. 'Scientific linguists' did not have a monopoly over the practice of language teaching, but had some success in convincing those funding language teaching of the superiority of their practice, and in persuading government and foundation officials that there was a need for more and better language teaching (including in students' first language).

The perceived efficiency of descriptive linguistics for learning languages, developing teaching materials, and translating Christian scriptures provided another niche for linguists within some American missionary institutions, particularly the Summer Institute of Linguistics/Wycliffe Bible Translators. A third niche was teaching linguistic analysis as an anthropological fieldwork tool. Military interest in machine translation and cybernetic models of information transmission would soon support the development of a linguistic profession autonomous not just from language teaching, but from empirical description of distinct human languages. It was these 'professionals' with little or no interest in the differences among natural languages or in language teaching who staffed separate linguistic departments as these appeared and grew during the 1960s and 1970s in American universities, focused on abstractions from American English.

In the contested niches of language departments of universities occupied by LSA members for the first three and a half decades of its existence, reproduction of linguists was slow. Since the mid-1960s, within universities, departments independent of the enterprise of language-teaching have become common and those with degrees in linguistics make decisions about staffing linguistic departments, while having no control and very little influence on language teaching or any other application of whatever theory/ies linguistic students are taught. The founders of LSA were concerned both with general ideas and with application of their knowledge. Bloomfield, in particular, along with some 'neo-Bloomfieldians' aspired to direct technocrats as well as to engage those intellectually interested in developing ideas about language. Ambitions to become technocrats and to control institutions outside universities have been less visible in subsequent generations.

In North America there is not a protected, self-regulated market outside academic institutions for linguists comparable to generally recognized 'professions' such as law or medicine. Insofar as linguists are 'professionals' in a comparative sense, their 'profession' is almost exclusively university teaching (and other activities associated with that occupational niche "insulated from systematic observation and control even by peers", including some outside consulting and unpaid refereeing of journal articles), not providing services (for fees) to governments or to other clients (cf. Freidson 1986: 15—16, 161). Lacking the agreed-upon standards to establish a training school and licensing exams, or a codification of practices to distinguish 'malpractice' and/or 'unethical' conduct from ethical, competent exercise of its craft, or even any concerted effort to persuade legislators (or others) of having a 'service orientation', North American linguistics lacks criterial features of established professions, and does not appear to be moving toward full professionalization (on that process see Freidson 1986; Abbott 1991).

7. Bibliography

Abbott, Andrew. 1991. "The Order of Professionalization: An empirical analysis". *Work and Occupations* 18.35–384.

Bloch, Bernard. 1950. "Publications Committee Report". *LSA Bulletin* 23.12–17.

Bloomfield, Leonard. 1925. "Why a Linguistic Society?". *Language* 1.1–5.

—. 1933. *Language.* New York: Holt.

—. 1944. "Secondary and Tertiary Responses to Language". *Language* 20.45–55.

—. 1946. "Twenty-One Years of the Linguistic Society". *Language* 22.1–3.

Cowan, J Milton. 1991 [1975]. "Americam Linguistics in Peace and War". *First Person Singular II: Autobiographies by North American scholars in the language sciences* ed. by Konrad Koerner, 67–82. Amsterdam & Philadelphia: Benjamins.

Freidson, Eliot. 1986. *Professional Powers: A study of the institutionalization of formal knowledge.* Chicago: Univ. of Chicago Press.

Hill, Archibald A. 1964. "History of the Linguistics Institute". *American Council of Learned Societies Newsletter* 15.311–312.

—. 1991. "The Linguistic Society of America and North American Linguistics, 1950–1968". *Historiographia Linguistica* 18.49–152.

Joos, Martin. 1986 [1976]. *Notes on the Development of the Linguistic Society of America, 1924–1950.* Ithaca, N. Y.: Linguistica.

Murray, Stephen O. 1994. *Theory Groups and the Study of Language in North America: A social history.* Amsterdam & Philadelphia: Benjamins.

Stephen O. Murray, San Francisco (U.S.A.)

211. The Sapirian approach to language

1. Sapir's linguistics
2. Sapir, Whorf, and the Linguistic Relativity Hypothesis
3. Sapir's legacy
4. Bibliography

1. Sapir's linguistics

Edward Sapir (1884–1939) was, beyond a doubt, the most influential American linguist of the first third of the 20th century, and his influence continues to be felt in many sectors of linguistics, both in North America and beyond. But this influence has been diffuse rather than focused on a particular institution, doctrine, or group of students. Only in the study of North American Indian languages did Sapir's work become the defining paradigm, and there largely through far-reaching typological and historical hypotheses that, although bold and stimulating, were not central to his linguistic thought. In most areas of synchronic linguistics Sapir's contributions have either been absorbed into the mainstream, or remain on the innovative periphery. Today, his name is most frequently cited in connection with his student, Benjamin Lee Whorf (1897–1941), as the co-author of the so-called Linguistic Relativity Hypothesis, but Sapir's actual contribution to this 'Hypothesis' (particularly as it was formulated in the 1940s and 1950s, after the deaths of both men) was not as important as it has been made out to be.

Sapir is best seen as the transitional figure in American linguistics between the Boasian concern with languages as ethnographic objects and the structuralist concern with systems of symbolic relationship. Sapir was among the earliest – and in some ways the most thoroughgoing – of American Structuralists, at the same time that he devoted most of his career to extensive, detailed documentation of specific American Indian languages in their ethnographic and historical contexts. It can be argued that a Sapirian tradition still persists, particularly among linguists who work with American Indian languages, in which a productive balance of scholarly commitment between the delineation of overall patterns and the documentation of specific facts remains the ideal.

1.1. Sapir as a Boasian anthropologist

Franz Boas (1858–1942) is rightly credited both with establishing the academic discipline of anthropology in the United States and with fostering the professionalization of linguistics (Darnell 1998). Although his formal training as a student in Germany was in the physical sciences and 'psychophysics' (a combination of physical and cultural geography), and not in philology, he had a deep interest in languages. It was his encounter with the linguistic codification of Baffin Island Eskimo culture that led him, during his first professional field trip in 1883–1884, to refocus his career on a comparative study of the symbolic aspects of human adaptations and to define the objects of study as largely language-defined 'cultures'. After settling in the United States in 1887, he connected this emerging research agenda with the descriptive and historical study of American Indians, and in particular of American Indian languages, that had played so important a role in the development of a pre-professional North American anthropology since the 18th century. Institutional links with John Wesley Powell's (1843–1902) Bureau of American Ethnology, and personal ties with older American scholars, in particular with Horatio Hale (1817–1897), evolved within a decade into a distinctive 'Boasian' anthropology that emphasized the rigorous training of a cadre of professional researchers in university museums and academic departments, and the commitment of these researchers to long-term studies of specific societies, cultural traditions, and languages.

The effective beginning of this paradigm was Boas's appointment to a graduate-level teaching position at Columbia University 1897, when he was nearly 40. Beginning with Alfred L. Kroeber (1876–1960) in 1901, most of the anthropologists (and nearly all of the anthropological linguists) trained in North America were recipients of a doctorate under Boas at Columbia. The details of Boas's training and the rapid fanning-out of these men (and later women) to take up positions of influence in academic anthropology in the United States and Canada, have been described in the previous article (→ Art. 231). By 1920, Boas's students controlled the majority of anthropological institutions in North America, and dominated the research agenda that would define American anthropology for decades to come.

Sapir was among the first generation of Boas's students, and the first to have a primarily linguistic focus. He turned to anthropology only after completing a Master's degree in Germanic Philology with a thesis on Herder's theories of the origin of language (Sapir 1907a). At the end of his first year of graduate study under Boas, in the summer of 1905, Sapir was assigned to work with the upriver Chinookan tribes, the Wishram and Wasco, on the Columbia Plateau of Eastern Oregon and Washington (Boas himself had worked on Lower Chinook). Despite his youth and inexperience, Sapir proved to have a considerable native talent for fieldwork, and the product of this initial foray was an impressively thorough and accurate record of the Wishram-Wasco language (one of the most phonologically and morphologically complex languages of the Northwest Coast) and of associated cultural traditions. In this work, and in Sapir's immediate and later organization and publication of the materials (Sapir 1907b, 1909b), Sapir was punctilious in his application of the principles of documentation that Boas had laid down for his students. Linguistic data was collected largely through the medium of narrative texts, mostly folkloric in nature, directly eliciting vocabulary and paradigms only to supplement the transcription and translation of the texts. He built up a theory of Chinookan grammar as he worked, and also collected extensive ethnographic data (again, largely supplementary to the texts).

Sapir followed this documentation strategy in all of his subsequent fieldwork, refining and fitting it to the specific situation but never departing from it in spirit. The thorough field documentation of specific languages in their ethnographic setting remained Sapir's major scholarly commitment for most of he rest of his life, and included studies of Takelma (1906), Yana (1907–1908, 1915), Ute and Southern Paiute (1909–1910), Nootka (1910–1914), Sarcee (1922), Kutchin (1923), Hupa (1927), and Navajo (1928–1929). The major products of this work included collections of narrative texts (Sapir 1909a, b; 1910b, 1930b, 1942; Sapir & Swadesh 1939, 1955); dictionaries and extensive lexical lists (Sapir 1909a: 201–263, 1931b; Sapir & Swadesh 1960); and grammars (1930a) and grammatical sketches (Sapir 1914, 1922a, 1922b; Sapir & Swadesh 1939: 235–334).

Sapir also made significant contributions to general ethnography (cf. Sapir 1915b, c; Sapir & Spier 1943), although this work was always ancillary to his linguistic studies. Most of it was undertaken during his fifteen-year tenure as Chief of the Division of Anthropology of the National Museum of Canada in Ottawa (1910–1925). Of special interest are his pioneering studies of song (Sapir 1910a; Roberts & Swadesh 1955) and the linguistic indexing of social status (Sapir 1915a, 1929b, c).

Between 1913 and 1921 Sapir maintained an especially close intellectual relationship with Alfred Kroeber (Golla 1984) that spanned a number of areas of mutual interest. Some of these interests lay beyond the Boasian paradigm (Freudian psychology, art, the fundamental nature of cultural patterning) and adumbrated some of the themes of Sapir's later thinking. Much of their correspondence, however, focused on the historical and comparative aspects of Boasian anthropology, in particular the use of linguistic evidence for reconstructing the culture history of prehistoric North America. At Kroeber's urging, Sapir prepared a comprehensive statement of the methods by which 'time perspective' could be gained in North American anthropology, from archaeology and physical anthropology to comparative folklore and the distribution of culture traits (Sapir 1916). The largest part of this monograph, however, was given over to the evidence of language, and especially to the formal comparative methods of historical linguistics.

Sapir believed that application of the methods of Indo-European comparative linguistics to unwritten languages in the Americas could result in major insights into prehistoric connections. His first – and perhaps most effective – use of these methods to elucidate North American prehistory was to show that Wiyot and Yurok, two isolated languages of the northern California coast, were distant outliers of Algonquian (Sapir 1913). Following this, he worked closely with Kroeber to establish the Penutian and Hokan language families, and by 1920 had constructed a general classification of all North American languages which reduced the number of language families to only six (Golla 1986). By this time, however, Sapir had begun to rely on other criteria for genetic relatedness – particularly deep structural patterns – that seemed to most Boasian anthropologists to lie beyond the scope of the discipline (Boas 1920, 1929; Goddard 1920; see also a later assessment of Kroeber's [1940: 463–470]).

1.2. Sapir as a grammarian

Even at his most Boasian, Sapir stood apart from his fellow American anthropologists – even from those who had a strong interest in language, such as Kroeber, Paul Radin (1883–1959), and most especially Boas himself – in the breadth of his linguistic expertise and interests. He was professionally trained in Germanic and Indo-European philology and kept abreast of British and European work in phonetics, lexicography, semantics, and general linguistic theory. In later years he acquired considerable expertise in Tibetan and Chinese, as well as a Talmudic scholar's knowledge of Hebrew (Siskin 1986). It is only to be expected, then, that his descriptive and historical work on American Indian languages rose to a much higher level of linguistic sophistication than that of any other Americanist of his time.

1.2.1. Descriptive model

Grammatical descriptions of American Indian languages began to be written shortly after the European discovery of America, and by the late 19th century an extensive linguistic literature existed on some of the more widely spoken languages of the continent (Goddard 1996). However, when Boas began his anthropological work in the 1880s, he chose to minimize the usefulness of previous descriptive studies of American Indian languages and, in accordance with his ethnographic mode of research, emphasized the need for direct field investigation and the collection of connected discourse in narrative texts (Darnell 1990a; Berman 1996). Looking at language as a comparative psychologist as well as a grammarian, Boas organized his analysis of the formal patterns of grammar in terms of the meanings they represented. In Boas's view, a linguistic description should not be modeled on the grammars of English, Latin, or only any other language (including languages from the same cultural area). Instead, languages should be approached as geographically and historically rooted aspect of the cultures they express; the 'psychological groupings' of meaningful elements should "depend entirely upon the inner form of each language". The grammar of an American Indian language should thus be described "as though an intelligent Indian was going to develop the forms of his own thoughts by an analysis of his own form of speech" (Boas 1911: 81; see also Voegelin 1952). In practice, however Boas' grammatical sketches and those of most of his students (for example, those in Boas 1911, 1922) were at best partially successful. It was Sapir, with his thorough grounding in the European philological tradition, who brought this model to fruition.

What Sapir did in his two full grammars (Sapir 1912, 1930a) and his other grammatical work was adapt the prevailing form of Classical and Indo-European grammars — Whitney's (1889) grammar of Sanskrit was perhaps the exemplary model — to American practice, moulding each description to what he perceived to be the formal patterning of the individual language. The mode of explanation of most European grammars was historical, and patterns were explained in terms of their 'development' from earlier forms, either directly attested or recovered through the comparative method. In transferring this model to American Indian languages, where history was by and large unknown, Sapir made use of the conventions of historical process (e. g., 'basic' forms give rise to 'derived' forms), in part as a mere descriptive device (as in Takelma, a language with — at the time — no known congeners), in part as a tentative hypothesis about actual historical developments (as in Southern Paiute, a Uto-Aztecan language).

Sapir's creative fusion of Boas's culture-specific approach with the historical and comparative approach of the philological tradition gave him a remarkably supple instrument for exploring linguistic structures, synchronically, diachronically, and (ultimately) empirically discovered universal properties and types. Although Sapir first developed this method in his Takelma grammar (Sapir 1912), originally written as his dissertation in 1907 – 1908, at least two decades before the first major wave of structuralist theory in American linguistics, it proved to be a powerful vehicle for the exploration of linguistic structures in later more formal statements (cf. especially Newman 1944). Supplanted by a Bloomfieldian 'taxonomic' approach in the 1940s and 1950s, there are clear connections between Sapir's 'process' grammars and Chomsky's generative grammar.

1.2.2. Structuralism and patterning

Sapir (and most linguists who followed him) can be rather sharply distinguished from their predecessors — in Sapir's case this meant most especially Boas — by his understanding of the role of unconscious formal structures in language. It was mainly through Sapir and his students that the structuralism of Saussure and the Prague Circle entered American linguistic discussion, first in the idea of the phoneme and then — in Sapir's case, very quickly — in a general acceptance of the pervasiveness of structure and patterning throughout all of language, and to some extent in all of cultural life.

Sapir's paper, "Sound Patterns in Language" (Sapir 1925a), was the first major structuralist statement in American linguistics. Although the significance of this paper is usually seen in retrospect to be its introduction of the idea of the phoneme, Sapir made it clear that this was an across-the-board shift in language thinking. Phonological structure units are only "a special illustration of the necessity of getting behind the sense data of any type of expression in order to grasp the intuitively felt and communicated forms which alone give significance to such expression" (Sapir 1925a: 51).

The structuralist turn in linguistics was, of course, part of the general intellectual trend we now call Modernism. The idea of an abstract system of relationships underlying and explaining the observable facts swept the sciences from physics to economics, and was accompanied by developments in art, music, and literature. Sapir grasped the essential fact of patterning earlier and more clearly than most linguists, and many of his writings were seminal, but a distinction needs to be drawn between Sapir's role as a teacher and conduit for structuralist ideas — the sense in which he is (to some extent rightly) seen as a bridge between the Boasian and 'Bloomfieldian' eras in American linguistics — and his own theory of language. As the wording of the quotation above shows, Sapir remained concerned with individual psychological patterning in specific cultural contexts. This essentially Boasian position (Silverstein 1986) distinguished him early on from the emerging view — most forcefully articulated by Durkheim (1895) and his school and expressed in linguistics first by Saussure — that linguistic, cultural, and social structures could be meaningfully apprehended as systems of formal oppositions detached from individual thought and action (Sapir 1917). Sapir believed, instead, that the most meaningful exploration of linguistic and cultural patterning needed to be based in social psychology and psychiatry. The patterning of the individual personality was the primary fact to be studied.

In the last decade of his life he became a close friend and associate of the psychiatrist Harry Stack Sullivan (1892 – 1949; cf. Perry

1982: 242–250, 357–360) and devoted significant amounts of his teaching and research at Yale after 1931 to "the psychology of culture" (Sapir 1993). Sapir's specifically linguistic work during this period focused largely on Boasian descriptive and culture-historical projects (the structure of Navajo, comparative Athabaskan), and on a return to Indo-European questions, rather than on developing formal models of structural linguistic analysis (Silverstein 1986: 73–74). The structural linguistics that arose in the United States during the 1930s — largely the creation of Sapir's students at Yale and others directly or indirectly influenced by him — is thus not unfairly credited to Leonard Bloomfield, rather than to Sapir himself, since it was Bloomfield's book *Language* (1933), rather than any specific work of Sapir's, that spoke to the rising generation of American structuralists as the charter of their belief.

1.3. Sapir as a typologist

The Boasian mode of linguistic description led naturally to an interest in functional typology, i.e., which meanings or kinds of meanings are expressed by which kinds of structural elements in a given language. Typological comparison of this sort was, of course, not new in the European linguistic tradition, but the variety of linguistic structures for which Sapir and other Boasian linguists had accurate and detailed knowledge was considerably greater than that available to earlier scholars. While Boas himself expressed an interest in discovering "fundamental morphological traits" common to certain groups of languages (1911: 56–58), he did not pursue such an investigation, apparently finding it difficult to make generalizations about linguistic structure. However, two of Boas's students, Alfred L. Kroeber and Roland B. Dixon (1875–1934), early along in their California linguistic work proposed a typological classification of the native languages of California, using four basic criteria: 'pronominal incorporation', case marking, locative/instrumental markers, and degree of phonetic complexity (Dixon & Kroeber 1903). A subsequent paper of Kroeber's on the 'trait' of 'incorporation' (Kroeber 1911) stimulated Sapir's first major statement on typological questions (Sapir 1911), arguing that incorporation of a nominal object must be treated as a special case of noun-verb compounding.

During the next few years Sapir worked out a comprehensive classification of form-meaning correlations in language, which he published as a chapter in ("Types of Linguistic Structure") in his general book *Language* (1921b: 120–146). Every language, Sapir maintained, has "a basic plan, a certain cut, [...] a structural 'genius'" that is "much more fundamental, much more pervasive, than any single feature of it that we can mention". Although "it is impossible to set up a limited number of types that would do full justice to the peculiarities of the thousands of languages and dialects spoken on the surface of the earth", nonetheless "languages, traveling along different roads, have tended to converge toward similar forms". Rejecting earlier, Eurocentric classifications, which "generalize from a small number of select languages", "crave [...] a simple formula", and make unfounded evolutionary implications, Sapir proposed a classification by 'conceptual type' based on the degree of 'fusion' used in the expression of derivational and relational concepts. Languages can be divided into 'pure-relational' (in which the basic syntactic categories are directly expressed) and 'mixed-relational' (in which these categories are usually expressed only by techniques that link them with more concrete ideas), and then further into 'simple' (in which roots cannot be modified by derivational techniques) and 'complex' (in which they can). A second, purely structural criterion of 'synthesis' (the extent to which words are morphologically elaborated: Analytic, Synthetic, and Polysynthetic) can be added to refine the typology further. In this scheme, Chinese (Analytic) is 'simple pure-relational', Polynesian (Analytic) and Yana (Polysynthetic) are 'complex pure-relational', Bantu (Synthetic) and French (Analytic) are 'simple mixed-relational', and the more conservative Indo-European languages (Synthetic), English (Analytic), and Algonquian (Polysynthetic) are 'complex mixed-relational'.

Although he hinted that he would return to the subject ("a separate volume would be needed to breathe life into the scheme" [1921b: 146, n. 28]), Sapir did not elaborate this classification in later work. However, he regularly used it in his teaching, requiring his students to write a 'thumbnail sketch' that characterized a language or language family in terms of this classification, and echoes of this are found in some of their published work (cf. especially Haas (1946: 345–346; Whorf 1946a: 158).

1.3.1. Language type and historical relationship

Sapir concluded his 1921 chapter on typology by noting that, divergent as they may be otherwise, languages belonging to widespread families such as Indo-European or Austronesian often conform to the same general type (Austronesian languages are complex pure-relational; Penutian languages complex mixed-relational, etc.). It is evident that such correlations were of great importance to Sapir's thinking.

During the same period he was writing *Language* (1920–1921) Sapir proposed, as was noted above, a classification of North American languages that reduced the number of families from the fifty-eight defined by Powell (1891) to a mere six 'superstocks' (Sapir 1921a, 1929a). It is certainly no accident that Sapir based these six groups — and to a great extent based his classification — on general form-meaning configurations rather than on lexical and grammatical correspondences. Thus the Eskimo-Aleut languages "make a fundamental distinction between the transitive and intransitive verb, to which corresponds the nominal case distinction of agentive-genitive and absolutive (or objective)" (1949 [1929a]: 174) — i.e., what we now call 'ergative' case marking; the Algonkin-Wakashan languages "have a weak development of case, and illustrate to a marked degree of process of building up noun and verb themes by suffixing to stems local, instrumental, adverbial, and concretely verbalizing elements"; the Na-Dene languages have verbal roots which are "probably always nominal in force"; the Penutian languages "make use of suffixes of formal, rather than concrete, significance"; the Hokan-Siouan languages "distinguish active and stative verbs"; and the Aztec-Tanoan languages "make a sharp formal distinction between noun and verb" (ibid.). Although some have assumed that Sapir did not intend his North American 'superstocks' as historical hypotheses but simply as a structural classification (cf. for example Harris 1951: 293–294), it is clear from his correspondence that he believed evaluation of 'fundamental' typological features could uncover old historical relationships, perhaps even hemisphere-wide connections among all American languages (Golla 1984: 347–351).

Shortly after announcing his six-stock classification of North American languages Sapir began seriously investigating the possibility that one of these stocks, Na-Dene, was historically connected to the Sino-Tibetan languages. Although he made only one brief public announcement of this hypothesis (Sapir 1925b) he shared it with several colleagues (Golla 1991: 133–139), and it is clear that similarities in 'conceptual type' were his principal evidence:

"The most typical representative of the earlier stage [of Sino-Tibetan] is Tibetan — which is startlingly Na-Dene-like [...] the transitive verb is really passive, as in Tlingit [...]. In both [Sino-Tibetan and Na-Dene] postpositions are of extreme importance [...]. Indeed, reading Tibetan text gives you precisely the same feeling as reading Haida text [...]. In both groups the fundamental element is really a noun, the verb a kind of denominative structure. In brief, I should say that the similarity in feeling between Tibetan and Nadene is at least as close as between Latin and English, probably closer. Thus the theoretical road to synthesis is clear." (Quoted in Golla 1991: 134)

It is a measure of Sapir's faith in the value of typological evidence in language history that he shaped much of the remainder of his research career around this tenuous hypothesis. The inadequate documentation of Na-Dene (Athabaskan, Tlingit, Haida) prompted Sapir to devote nearly all of his remaining fieldwork to Athabaskan languages — Sarcee, Kutchin, Hupa, and Navajo. It also led him to take up the serious study of Chinese and Tibetan; he originally planned to spend his sabbatical year, 1937–1938, in China (Darnell 1990b: 408–409).

1.3.2. Language type and thought

Scattered through Sapir's writings are various iterations of the conventional warning — one of the leitmotifs of Boasian linguistics — that no linkage can be made between cultural or environmental variables and the structural form a language takes. For example: "There is no general correlation between cultural type and linguistic structure [...]. Linguistic organization, largely because it is unconscious, tends to maintain itself indefinitely and does not allow its fundamental formal categories to be seriously influenced by cultural needs" (Sapir 1949 [1933]: 26–27). But Sapir considered it possible nonetheless that subtle cognitive and behavioral patterns were ultimately responsible for deep-seated configurations of form and meaning. "Back of the face of history there are powerful drifts that move language, like other social products, to balanced patterns", he wrote in *Language*. "Perhaps the psychologists of the future will be able to give us the ultimate reasons" (1921b: 122).

As many have pointed out (cf. Greenberg 1954, for an early statement), this view is ultimately rooted in Enlightenment notions of 'ethnic psychology' and 'national character' that go back to J. G. Herder, with whose work Sapir was thoroughly familiar (Sapir 1907a), and Wilhelm von Humboldt, and which were transmitted to Boas through Heymann Steinthal — Humboldt's most articulate and influential disciple in mid-19th century Germany (Bunzl 1996: 63–71). Boas limited himself to noting that a language "may be arbitrary in its classifications" (Boas 1911: 26) and that these generally reflect the interests of a people (cf. also Mackert 1993). But Sapir, unlike Boas, saw the problem through the lens of structuralism. His strongest statements about the relationship between linguistic form and 'thought' tend also to be strong claims about the pervasiveness of behavior based on unconsciously perceived cultural patterns:

"Language is heuristic, not merely in the simple sense [...] but in the much more far-reaching sense that its forms predetermine for us certain modes of observation and interpretation." (Sapir 1949 [1933]: 10)

"The cultural significance of linguistic form [...] lies on a much more submerged level than on the overt one of definite cultural pattern [...]." (Sapir 1949 [1933]: 26)

Sapir's structuralism, however, as was noted above, was informed by an almost psychiatric concern for the individual personality. In Sapir's view, the only cultural 'patterns' that exist, including linguistic ones, are those expressed in individual behavior, of which the individual is mostly unconscious: "The true locus of culture is in the interactions of specific individuals [... each individual's] system of ideas [is] a more or less distinct cultural entity" (Sapir 1949 [1932a]: 515, 520).

The key idea in the interconnection of language and behavior is what Sapir often called *drift* (cf. Malkiel 1981):

"[...] the very slow but powerful unconcsious changes in certain directions which seem to be implicit in the phonemic systems and morphologies of the languages themselves. These 'drifts' are powerfully conditioned by unconscious formal feelings and are made necessary by the inability of human beings to actualize ideal patterns in a permanently set fashion." (1949 [1933]: 23)

Zellig S. Harris (1909–1992) captured the essence of Sapir's perspective perhaps better than anyone else:

"The cultural patterns that are available to people at any particular time and place favor particular kinds of patterned behavior: the obedient conformists will all be doing much the same thing; those who tend more toward personal variation and expression will be using essentially the same underlying patterns as a base upon which to vary or express [...]. Changes which are attempted [...] will therefore be intimately connected with the [existing] cultural patterns [...] and will lead to patterns which differ in certain directions rather than others." (Harris 1951: 328 = 1984: 109)

1.4. Sapir as a reformer

Particularly during the last decade of his life (which coincided with the Great Depression), but earlier as well, there was a decidedly reformist and utopian strain in Sapir's thinking, both about society in general and about language. Zellig Harris was one of the few commentators to place emphasis on this aspect of Sapir's work:

"His critique of our society and of its effects upon personality comes as groundwork for considering how a society and culture could be more satisfactorily structured, just as his critique of the form-meaning relation in existing languages was offered as groundwork for considering how a more satisfactory language could be constructed." (Harris 1951: 330 = 1984: 111)

It is interesting to contrast this assessment with Kroeber's, who — speaking perhaps for the majority of scholars during the first two postwar decades — found Sapir's later writings on personality and culture to be the "expression of wish-fullfillment against the backdrop of a partly regretted career" (Kroeber 1984 [1959]: 137). In fact, there seems little doubt that the biting irony and trenchant social criticism of such papers as "Why Social Anthropology Needs the Psychiatrist" (Sapir 1938) expressed a long-standing dissatisfaction on Sapir's part with the inequalities of 20th-century 'business civilization' and its superficial culture (cf. Sapir 1924). One often-overlooked aspect of this attitude was Sapir's long-standing interest in an international auxiliary language.

In several late papers Sapir expresses considerable annoyance with the defective linguistic tools available to Western civilization. Perphaps his most trenchant statement is this:

"It is precisely the apparent simplicity of structure which is suggested by the formal simplicity of many languages [such as English and French] which is responsible for much slovenliness in thought, and even for the creation of imaginary problems in philosophy. [This] equally applies to regularity and logic [...]. No important national language, at least in the Occidental world, has complete regularity of grammatical structure, nor is there a single logical category which is adequately and consistently handled in terms of linguistic symbolism [...]. Many categories which are of great logical and psychological importance are so haltingly expressed that it takes a good deal of effort to prove to the average man that they exist at all." (Sapir 1949 [1931a]: 117)

John E. Joseph has made a convincing case that Sapir's critique of 'Standard Average European' (as Whorf later dubbed it) reflected the influence of Ogden & Richard's *The Meaning of Meaning* (1923), and ultimately the analytical philosophy of Peirce, Frege, Russell, and Wittgenstein which viewed 'ordinary language' as a source of obstacles to logical thought (Joseph 1996). Although this may have been the original impetus, Sapir's concern with language reform led him into original empirical research on the semantics of natural languages, which he reported on in two substantial monographs, one on 'totality' (Sapir 1930s) and the other on the 'ending-point relation' (Sapir & Swadesh 1932); the draft of a third paper, on 'grading', was published posthumously (Sapir 1944). Work on these studies was sponsored by the International Auxiliary Language Society, and they were intended to form part of a more general project, in two parts, "Foundations of Language, Logical and Psychological, an Approach to the International Language Problem" and "Comparative Studies in Selected National and International Languages" (Sapir & Swadesh 1932: 3).

These explorations of "the sadly neglected field of the congruities and non-congruities of logical and psychological meaning with linguistic form" (Sapir 1949 [1944]: 49) were undertaken jointly with two of Sapir's students, Morris Swadesh (1909–1967) and (later) Stanley S. Newman (1905–1984). In 1934, with the same collaborators, Sapir inaugurated an even more ambitious project, a descriptive grammar of English, with the aim (in part) of "establishing, on the basis of completely objective criteria, a system of grammatical types which really provides for a complete and satisfactory accounting of all English words" (Sapir 1935: 127).

2. Sapir, Whorf, and the Linguistic Relativity Hypothesis

2.1. Benjamin Lee Whorf

One of Sapir's students at Yale, Benjamin Lee Whorf (1897–1941), has achieved considerable posthumous fame for his writings on the relationship between linguistic and cognitive structures, and his claim that these vary with culture.

Whorf was one of the great autodidacts of linguistics. He was trained as a chemical engineer, and from the age of twenty-two until his death was employed by the Hartford Fire Insurance Company in positions of increasing responsibility. From an early age he showed an interest in Mesoamerican cultures, but after his discovery in 1924 of the quasi-Cabbalistic writings of Antoine Fabre d'Olivet (1768–1825) he became fascinated with the analysis of language, and in the late 1920s fused these interests in intensive avocational study of Nahuatl and in attempts to decipher the Mayan hierogoglyphic script (cf. Whorf 1933). By 1930 his work had begun to gain recognition among Mesoamerican scholars, and he was awarded a research fellowship for fieldwork in Mexico on a dialect of Nahuatl.

It was only when Sapir came to Yale in 1931 that Whorf began the formal study of linguistics. He enrolled as a graduate student and soon became one of Sapir's circle. Although he never took a doctorate, his work earned him wide professional respect, and during the academic year 1937–1938, while Sapir was incapacitated by a heart attack, he filled Sapir's position at Yale as a Lecturer in Anthropology.

Sapir treated Whorf — despite his somewhat irregular status — as he did all of his students. His primary insistence was that they undertake the general and detailed study of a particular language (in nearly every case an American Indian language) through field work of a largely Boasian nature. In Whorf's case allowance was made for his continuing employment in Hartford, and, building on his previous experience with Nahuatl, arrangements were made for him to continue in the Uto-Aztecan field by working with a Hopi speaker who lived in New York City. Sapir's guidance as a teacher came largely in analytic methods and general linguistic theory, and most of Whorf's writing during the period he was at Yale was of a technical nature. These included several descriptive studies of Hopi (Whorf 1936, 1938, 1946a), as well as a grammatical sketch based on the Milpa Alta Nahuatl material he had collected in 1930 (Whorf 1946b) and work on comparative Uto-Aztecan (most significantly Whorf 1935).

Whorf's work on language, cognition, and culture — his 'metalinguistic' writings, as they were dubbed after his death by Trager

(Whorf 1949) – were mostly based on his descriptive work with Hopi, and are foreshadowed in the concluding paragraph of Whorf (1936), which begins: "All this has a wider interest than the mere illustration of an aspect-form. It is an illustration of how language produces an organization of experience". Most of Whorf's more philosophical papers-including a general paper on 'grammatical categories' (Whorf 1945), written in 1937 at Franz Boas's request – were only published after Sapir's death in 1939, and many of them only after Whorf's own death in 1941. Probably the most influential of these was his contribution to the Sapir Memorial Volume (Whorf 1941b), the epigraph of which is a quotation from Sapir, expressing, in Whorf's words, "interconnections which Sapir saw between language, culture and psychology".

Whorf poses two questions: (1) "Are our own concepts of 'time', 'space', and 'matter' given in substantially the same form by experience to all men, or are they in part conditioned by the structure of particular languages?" (2) "Are there traceable affinities between (a) cultural and behavioral norms and (b) large-scale linguistic patterns?" (1941b: 78). His answers are that concepts of time, space, and matter "depend upon the nature of the language or languages through the use of which they have been developed"; and that there are "connections but not correlations or correspondences between cultural norms and linguistic patterns". These connections are not to be found "by focusing attention on the typical rubrics of linguistic, ethnographic, or sociological description" but by "examining the culture and the language [...] as a whole". It is not specific grammatical systems, such as tense or aspect or gender, that must be examined, but "the ways of analyzing and reporting experience which have become fixed in the language as integrated 'fashions of speaking' and which cut across the typical grammatical classifications". Similarly, it is not whether a society is 'agricultural' or 'hunting' that is significant, but rather general patterns of behavior, attitude, or artistic expression (1941b: 92–93).

In both spirit and style, Whorf captures in this paper much of Sapir's general attitude toward the subtle and complex interconnectedness of language and social life. It was his tribute to the teacher he had eulogized: "We are almost like a group of disciples, whose master has indeed left them, but part of whose spirit lives in them" (Darnell 1990b: 417).

Undoubtedly, however, the most 'Sapirian' of Whorf's writing was his 1937 paper on grammatical categories (Whorf 1945). Using examples from a wide variety of languages, Whorf proposes a model for linguistic analysis that distinguishes 'overt' from 'covert' categories (or marked 'phenotypes' and unmarked 'cryptotypes'), and 'selective' (basically lexemic) from 'modular' (basically derivational or relational) categories. Applying this scheme to languages as diverse as Nitinat, Hebrew, and Latin, Whorf notes wide variation on what concepts are expressed in particular types of categories, including in the metalanguage of grammar itself: 'specific' categories, present and functioning in individual languages, must be distinguished from 'generic' categories, which depend "on both the insight and predilections of the systemizer or grammarian" and lead ultimately to "the concepts of a general science of grammar" (Whorf 1956 [1945]: 100).

2.2. Whorfian relativism

Whorf died tragically early, in 1941, at the age of forty-four, only two years after Sapir. By that time, however, he had written an extraordinary series of semi-popular articles for *Technology Review*, published by the Massachusetts Institute of Technology and distributed widely among scientists, engineers, and the technological elite (Whorf 1940a–b, 1941a). These articles, written in Whorf's most engaging and lucid style, explicitly introduced the concept of linguistic 'relativity' (Whorf 1956 [1940a]: 207), and called, in almost Humboldtian terms, for mental evolution through the direct experience of linguistic diversity:

"I believe that those who envision a world speaking only one tongue, whether English, German, or Russian, or any other, hold a misguided ideal and would do the evolution of the human mind the greatest disservice. Western culture has made, through language, a provisional analysis of reality and, without correctives, holds resolutely to that analysis as final. The only correctives lie in all those other tongues which by aeons of independent evolution have arrived at different, but equally logical, provisional analyses". (Whorf 1956 [1941a]: 244)

Although abundantly supported by data drawn from his own Hopi research, and from other languages whose structures he was familiar with through Sapir and others (most notably Shawnee, Eskimo, and Nootka), his examples were necessarily simplified and his arguments broadly painted. These articles, however, were quite influential, particularly after they were reprinted in 1949, together with his paper for the Sapir Memorial, as *Four Articles on Metalinguistics* (more widely distributed in a second edition, 1950). This reprinting was sponsored by George L. Trager (1906−1992), who also edited and published two other previously unpublished papers of a similar nature (Whorf 1950, 1953).

In 1956 John B. Carroll (b. 1916), published a nearly complete collection of all of Whorf's published and unpublished writings on linguistic relativity, Nahuatl, and Mayan. By that time, Whorf had come to be regarded by the majority of American linguists and anthropologists, and by a widening public, as the primary exponent of a somewhat romantic linguistic determinism of a distinctly Humboldtian flavor, although it appears that Whorf had never read Herder, Humboldt, or other sources of this German tradition (Penn 1972). Whorf's distinctive blend of relativism and frequently brilliant linguistic analysis was largely of his own making, and was also tinged with a uniquely American religiosity (cf. particularly Whorf 1942). His writings were extremely influential in the decades following his death, and continue to attract readers. In part this is owing to his lucid and persuasive style, but it can also be attributed to his skillful use of data from the American Indian languages he worked on, most notably Hopi, under Sapir's tutelage.

2.3. The 'Sapir-Whorf Hypothesis'

Two scholars loom large in the development of a strong relativistic philosophy in American linguistics in the years immediately following World War II − George L. Trager and Harry Hoijer (1904−1976). Both had been associated with Sapir, but neither was in his closest circle of students at Yale.

Trager had received a doctorate in Romance Linguistics from Columbia University in 1932, but after teaching for several years in Colorado became interested in the Indian languages of the Pueblos, and, in 1936, went to Yale on a post-doctoral fellowship to study with Sapir. There he met Whorf and the two soon became good friends through a common interest in the languages of the Southwest. They jointly published an important paper on the relationship of Uto-Aztecan to Tanoan (Trager & Whorf 1937), the first serious exploration of 'deep' genetic relationship among North American languages since Sapir's work in the 1920s.

Hoijer had been one of Sapir's earlier students at Chicago, and stayed on there as a junior faculty member after Sapir left for Yale. He devoted much of his research time during the 1930s to field studies of the Apachean languages in loose collaboration with Sapir, and after Sapir's death became the heir of his extensive Athabaskan materials, many of which he saw into publication.

Both Trager and Hoijer, however, were as much influenced by Bloomfield as by Sapir. Trager, together with Bernard Bloch (1909−1965), was at the center of the group of structural linguists who constellated around Bloomfield at Yale in the years following Sapir's death − the 'Second Yale School'. Hoijer, for his part, developed a strongly Bloomfieldian approach to Athabaskan linguistics, and largely confined himself to technically precise statements of phonology and morphology. Neither man evinced much interest, during Sapir's lifetime, in Sapir's explorations of the psychology of culture, but both were greatly attracted by Whorf's later writings on linguistic relativism. As Director of the innovative language research project of the U.S. Foreign Service Institute in the immediate Postwar years, Trager, as noted above, was instrumental in disseminating Whorf's 'metalinguistic' papers, while Hoijer in 1953 joined with the Chicago anthropologist Robert Redfield (1897−1958) to convene a conference on "Language in Culture" to discuss ways in which the interrelations of language, culture, and cognition might be explored.

Hoijer's own contribution to this conference (Hoijer 1954) − basically an attempt to clarify Whorf's ideas and to illustrate them with data from Navajo − was entitled "The Sapir-Whorf Hypothesis". This paper appears to be the source of that term and with it the misleading implication that Sapir and Whorf had collaborated on a theory of linguistic relativity. Whorf undoubtedly took inspiration from Sapir's writing on unconscious patterning, as well as from Sapir's reformist attitude toward 'Standard Average European' (Joseph 1996: 383 ff.), but there is little evidence that Sapir took any active role in the development of Whorf's philosophy.

It also became fashionable in the early 1950s to treat Whorf's view (or by extension Sapir's) on the relationship between linguistic structures and cultural patterns as a testable 'hypothesis'. It is unlikely that Whorf would have been comfortable with this formulation, and it is certainly the case that the more 'testable' the idea of linguistic relativity was made, the more restricted it became. Penny Lee (1996) has recently attempted to disentangle the linguistic relativity hypothesis from what she calls Whorf's more general 'theory complex'.

The further intellectual history of the 'Sapir-Whorf Hypothesis' is beyond our scope here. It has been the subject of considerable debate, much of it centered on its definition and scope (Kay & Kempton [1984] provide a well-balanced analysis of 'strong' and 'weak' varieties of the hypothesis). Some researchers have found it more fruitful to search for universal patterns in the linguistic coding of semantic features, such as universal patterns in the linguistic coding of color (Berlin & Kay 1969) or of botanical and zoological taxonomies (Berlin, Breedlove & Raven 1973). Koerner (1995) has compiled a nearly exhaustive bibliography of the debate.

3. Sapir's legacy

Sapir was far ahead of his time in the breadth and integration of his thinking, which transcended such labels as 'anthropologist', 'linguist', 'psychologist', or 'structuralist' (Harry Stack Sullivan ended his short obituary of his friend and colleague by calling Sapir "a genius largely wasted on a world not yet awake to the value of the very great" [Sullivan 1939]). Most of his students and colleagues saw only part of the whole, and his one general book (Sapir 1921b) was too short and too limited by its largely pre-structural framework to convey his mature vision in a systematic way. As Sapir's widow told an interviewer, "Edward died with the feeling that he had an important point to make that he hadn't managed to get across" (Darnell 1990b: 416).

During the last decade of Sapir's life the science of linguistics that he had done so much to create and legitimize began to be defined in ways that excluded much of Sapir's own vision. Stanley Newman, who, like most of Sapir's closest students, felt the loss keenly, wrote that "at the time that Sapir was seeking to expand the horizons of language study beyond the linguist's traditional universe of discourse, history played a cruel trick on him by directing linguistics into contrary channels". Taking their cue from Bloomfield, "American linguists in the 1930s turned to [...] sharpening methodological tools and rigorously defining the proper limits of their science". The discipline was well on its way to becoming "a microlinguistics" whose analytic efficiency was bought at the price of intellectual parochialism (Newman 1951: 185 = 1984: 64).

Even at the height of Bloomfieldian structuralism, however, many elements of Sapir's intellectual agenda remained of interest in American academic linguistics, although largely in areas peripheral to the mainstream. Zellig S. Harris (1909–1992), who was briefly quite close to Sapir in the late 1930s, seemed for a while in the 1940s to maintain a broad Sapirian focus, combining interests in historical linguistics, cultural processes, semantics, and formal linguistic methods with a strong commitment to social and political reform (the assessment of Sapir's work in Harris 1951 is highly sympathetic; cf. also Nevin 1993). For reasons that are not clear, however, Harris largely severed his connection with Sapirian positions after about 1952.

The most vigorous continuation of a Sapirian agenda was in the descriptive and comparative study American Indian languages. Two of Sapir's students, Mary Haas (1910–1996) at the University of California at Berkeley, and Charles F. Voegelin (1906–1986) at Indiana University, developed training and research programs emphasizing the descriptive study of individual American Indian languages. Several other students, most notably Morris Swadesh (in Mexico from the mid-1950s), Stanley S. Newman (at the University of New Mexico), and Harry Hoijer (at UCLA), had significant careers as Americanists. All of these scholars shared a deep commitment to holistic linguistic description, emphasizing full grammatical studies, lexicography, and even such Boasian tasks as the collection and analysis of long narrative texts. Haas and the Berkeley School in particular kept alive an emphasis on inductive fieldwork that is quintessentially Sapirian (Golla et al. 1996).

A late student of Sapir's, Kenneth L. Pike (1912–2000), took a very influential role in post-1945 American linguistics as one of the founders of the Summer Institute of Linguistics (SIL) and the Wycliffe Bible Translators. Pike created a training program for Christian missionaries emphasizing the use of descriptive linguistic tools for translating the Scriptures into indigenous languages and developing literacy among converts. Himself an Americanist, Pike undertook the descriptive study of a wide range of American Indian languages, and missionary-linguists trained under SIL auspices to some extent shared the

Sapirian orientation of Americanist linguists during the postwar period. However, although Pike expounded a somewhat Sapirian linguistic philosophy in a monograph dedicated to Sapir (Pike 1967), he and other SIL linguists developed a largely Bloomfieldian model for descriptive grammar, which they called Tagmemics (Pike 1966; → Art. 213).

While Sapir's direct influence may be said to have lasted only through the generation of his students (i.e., until about 1970), many elements of Sapirian linguistics survived for one further academic generation in the person of a single scholar, Dell H. Hymes (b. 1927). As a graduate student in the 1950s Hymes sought out two of the most prominent Sapirians, Voegelin and Hoijer, and studied with them both, taking his doctorate at Indiana under Voegelin with a dissertation on Chinook. In 1959 he joined the anthropology faculty at the University of California, Berkeley, which brought him into association with Mary Haas as well as with the legacy of A. L. Kroeber, but left Berkeley in 1965 for the University of Pennsylvania. In an annotated anthology, *Language in Culture and Society* (1964), Hymes defined an agenda of research for a reinvorated 'linguistic anthropology' that would consolidate and build on Sapir's legacy. He later established an influential framework for the analysis of discourse in social context ('the ethnography of speaking'; cf. Bauman & Sherzer 1974), and became a critical historian of American linguistics, with particular interest in Sapir and his legacy (cf. Hymes & Fought 1981; Hymes 1983).

Sapir's direct influence is perhaps most strongly felt in typology and classification. Several of his students continued to pursue Sapir's attempts to reduce the number of language families in the Americas, most notably Morris Swadesh, who after about 1950 devoted almost the whole of his research to creating wide-ranging hypotheses of genetic relationship, at first for the Americas and later for the entire world (Swadesh 1971, Hymes 1971). Swadesh pioneered the use of statistical methods in measuring relatedness among languages, but his claims that 'glottochronology' could be used as a reliable dating technique, or that it could actually uncover previously unsuspected relationships, were widely rejected and, after Swadesh's death in 1967, most speculation about deep genetic relationships fell into disrepute. Interest in such relationships has been revived during the past decade, owing in large part to the work of Joseph Greenberg (b. 1915). Greenberg has taken pains to emphasize his debt to Sapir, both in his earlier work on language typology and universals (Greenberg, ed. 1978) and, more recently, in his explorations of deep historical connections among the languages of the New World and beyond (Greenberg 1987). Although Greenberg's rather unsophisticated 'multilateral comparison' of poorly analyzed lexical material has more in common with Swadesh than with Sapir (Campbell 1988), his proposals have stimulated a revival of interest in Sapir's deep historical and typological work. Particularly Sapirian in its breadth and spirit is the work of Johanna Nichols, who has attempted to identify typologically, historically, and areally stable features in the world's languages and to sort these out by using a mixture of genetic, geographical, and universal determinants (Nichols 1992).

A certain strain of Sapirian linguistics continues to be influential via Whorf, independently — or nearly so — of the Linguistic Relativity Hypothesis. Whorf's more linguistically grounded writings (especially Whorf 1945) have stimulated a number of linguists to continue the empirical exploration of semantic-structural correlations across a variety of languages. Probably the most 'Sapirian' of these has been Leonard Talmy, who analyzed and compared the semantic structures of English and Atsugewi (a Hokan language of northeastern California) in terms of 'situation-types' involving the relationship of objects or events (Talmy 1972). More recently, Stephen Levinson and a team of researchers at the Max Planck Institute of Psycholinguistics in Nijmegen, The Netherlands, have attempted, with some success, to establish a paradigm for cross-cultural research on possible correlations between language-specific coding and the conceptual representations involved in performing non-verbal tasks in a specific domain, the organization of space, such as 'directions' and 'orientation' (cf. the papers in Gumperz & Levinson 1996).

It is likely that Sapir's influence on linguistic theory and practice will continue to be felt in multiple ways for decades to come. Some words spoken by a distinguished formal grammarian in a recent Presidential Address before the Linguistic Society of America could very well have been Sapir's own:

"We should not assume without argument that systems of categories are the same in different languages [...] We need to cherish and study linguistic diversity for reasons that are as important scientifically as they are politically and ethically. It is not a bad idea to let a language unfold itself to you on its own terms for a good long while before you jump to fitting it into your theory or testing your theories against it." (Bach 1996)

4. Bibliography

Bach, Emmon. 1996. "The Politics of Universal Grammar". Presidential Address, Linguistic Society of America, San Diego, California, 6 Januar 1996.

Bauman, Richard & Joel F. Sherzer, eds. 1974. *Explorations in the Ethnography of Speaking.* Cambridge: Cambridge Univ. Press.

Berlin, Brent, Dennis E. Breedlove & Peter H. Raven. 1973. "General Principles of Classification and Nomenclature in Folk Biology". *American Anthropologist* 75.214–242.

– & Paul Kay. 1969. *Basic Color Terms: Their universality and evolution.* Berkeley & Los Angeles: Univ. of California Press.

Berman, Judith. 1996. "'The Culture as It Appears to the Indian Himself': Boas, George Hunt, and the methods of ethnography". Stocking 1996.215–256.

Bloomfield, Leonard. 1933. *Language.* New York: Holt.

Boas, Franz, ed. 1911. *Handbook of American Indian Languages.* Part 1. With an Introduction by F. Boas. (= Bureau of American Ethnology, *Bulletin* 40: 1) Washington: Government Printing Office.

–. 1920. "The Classification of American Languages". *American Anthropologist* 22.367–376.

–, ed. 1922. *Handbook of American Indian Languages.* Part 2 (= Bureau of American Ethnology, *Bulletin* 40: 2.) Washington: Government Printing Office.

–. 1929. "Classification of American Indian Languages". *Language* 5.1–7.

Bunzl, Matti. 1996. "Franz Boas and the Humboldtian Tradition: From *Volksgeist* and *Nationalcharakter* to an anthropological concept of culture". Stocking 1996.17–78.

Campbell, Lyle. 1988. Review of Greenberg (1987). *Language* 64.591–615.

Cowan, William, Michael K. Foster & Konrad Koerner, eds. 1986. *New Perspectives in Language, Culture, and Personality.* Proceedings of the Edward Sapir Centenary Conference, Ottawa, 1–3 October, 1984. Amsterdam & Philadelphia: Benjamins.

Darnell, Regna. 1990a. "Franz Boas, Edward Sapir, and the Americanist Text Tradition". *Historiographia Linguistica* 17.129–144.

–. 1990b. *Edward Sapir: Linguist, anthropologist, humanist.* Berkeley: Univ. of California Press.

–. 1998. *And Along Came Boas: Continuity and revolution in Americanist anthropology.* Amsterdam & Philadelphia: Benjamins.

Dixon, Roland B. & Alfred L. Kroeber. 1903. "The Native Languages of California". *American Anthropologist* 5.1–26.

Durkheim, Emile. 1964 [1895]. *The Rules of Sociological Method.* Transl. by Sarah A. Solovay & John H. Mueller ed. by George E. G. Catlin. Glencoe, Ill.: Free Press.

Goddard, Ives. 1986. "Sapir's Comparative Method". Cowan et al. 1986.191–210.

–. 1996. "The Description of the Native Languages of North America Before Boas". *Handbook of North American Indians*, vol. 17: *Languages* ed. by Ives Goddard, 17–42. Washington, D. C.: Smithsonian Institution Press.

Goddard, Pliny Earle. 1920. "Has Tlingit a Genetic Relationship to Athabascan?". *International Journal of American Linguistics* 1.266–279.

Golla, Victor, ed. 1984. *The Sapir-Kroeber Correspondence: Letters between Edward Sapir and A. L. Kroeber, 1905–1925.* (= Survey of California and Other Indian Languages, Report 6.) Berkeley: Department of Linguistics, Univ. of California.

–. 1986. "Sapir, Kroeber, and North America Indian Linguistic Classification". Cowan et al. 1986. 17–38.

–, ed. 1991. *The Collected Works of Edward Sapir*, vol. VI: *American Indian Languages.* Part 2. Berlin & New York: Mouton de Gruyter.

–, James A. Matisoff & Pamela Munro. 1997. "Mary R. Haas". *Language* 73.826–837.

Greenberg, Joseph H. 1954. "Concerning Inferences from Linguistic to Nonlinguistic Data". Hoijer 1954.3–19.

–, ed. 1978. *Universals of Human Language.* Stanford, Calif.: Stanford Univ. Press.

–. 1987. *Language in the Americas.* Stanford, Calif.: Stanford Univ. Press.

Gumperz, John J. & Stephen C. Levinson, eds. 1996. *Rethinking Linguistic Relativity.* Cambridge: Cambridge Univ. Press.

Haas, Mary R. 1946. "A Grammatical Sketch of Tunica". Hoijer et al. 1946.337–366.

Harris, Zellig. 1951. Review of Sapir (1949). *Language* 27.288–333. (Repr. in Koerner 1984.69–114.)

Hoijer, Harry. 1954. "The Sapir-Whorf Hypothesis". Hoijer 1954.92–105.

–, ed. 1954. *Language in Culture: Proceedings of a conference on the interrelations of language and other aspects of culture.* Menasha, Wis.: American Anthropological Association: Chicago: Univ. of Chicago Press.

– et al. 1946. *Linguistic Structures of Native America.* (= Viking Fund Publications in Anthropology, 6.) New York: Wenner-Gren Foundation.

Hymes, Dell H. 1964. *Language in Culture and Society.* New York: Harper & Row.

–. 1971. "Morris Swadesh: From the first Yale School to world prehistory". Swadesh 1971.228–270.

—. 1983. *Essays in the History of Linguistic Anthropology.* Amsterdam: Benjamins.

— & John Fought. 1981. *American Structuralism.* The Hague: Mouton.

Joseph, John E. 1996. "The Immediate Sources of the 'Sapir-Whorf-Hypothesis'". *Historiographia Linguistica* 23.365–404.

Kay, Paul & Willett Kempton. 1984. "What is the Sapir-Whorf-Hypothesis?" *American Anthropologist* 86.65–79.

Koerner, Konrad, ed. 1984. *Edward Sapir: Appraisals of his life and work.* Amsterdam & Philadelphia: Benjamins.

—. 1995. "The 'Sapir-Whorf-Hypothesis' An historico-bibliographical essay". *Professing Linguistic Historiography* by K. Koerner, 203–240. Amsterdam & Philadelphia: Benjamins.

Kroeber, Alfred L. 1911. "Incorporation as a Linguistic Process". *American Anthropologist* 13.577–584.

—. 1940. "Conclusions: The present status of Americanistic problems". *The Maya and their Neighbors* ed. by Clarence L. Hay et al., 460–487. New York: no publisher.

—. 1984 [1956]. "Reflections on Edward Sapir, Scholar and Man". Koerner 1984.131–139. [Oral presentation given in Berkeley, 11 May 1959, transcribed by Richard J. Preston.]

Lee, Penny. 1996. *The Whorf Theory Complex: A critical reconstruction.* Amsterdam & Philadelphia: Benjamins.

Mackert, Michael. 1993. "The Roots of Franz Boas' View of Linguistic Categories as a Window to the Human Mind". *Historiographia Linguistica* 20.331–351.

Malkiel, Yakov. 1981. "Drift, Slope, and Slant: Background of, and variations upon, a Sapirian theme". *Language* 67.535–570.

Nevin, Bruce E. 1993. "A Minimalist Program for Linguistics: The work of Zellig Harris on meaning and information". *Historiographia Linguistica* 20.355–398.

Newman, Stanley S. 1944. *Yokuts Language of California.* (= *Viking Fund Publications in Anthropology*, 2.) New York: Wenner-Gren Foundation.

—. 1951. Review of Sapir (1949). *International Journal of American Linguistics* 17.180–186. (Repr. in Koerner 1984.59–65.)

Nichols, Johanna 1992. *Linguistic Diversity in Time and Space.* Chicago: Univ. of Chicago Press.

Ogden, C[harles] K. & I[vor] A. Richards. 1923. *The Meaning of Meaning: A study of the influence of language upon thought and of the science of symbolism.* London: Methuen.

Penn, Julia. 1972. *Linguistic Relativity versus Innate Ideas: The origins of the Sapir-Whorf hypothesis in German thought.* The Hague: Mouton.

Perry, Helen Swick. 1982. *Psychiatrist of America: The life of Harry Stack Sullivan.* Cambridge, Mass. & London: The Belknap Press of Harvard Univ. Press.

Pike, Kenneth L. 1966. "A Guide to Publications Related to Tagmemic Theory". *Current Trends in Linguistics* ed. by Thomas A. Sebeok, vol. III: *Theoretical Foundations*, 365–394. The Hague: Mouton.

—. 1967. *Language in Relation to a Unified Theory of the Structure of Human Behavior.* The Hague: Mouton. [Revised from a version first issued by the Summer Institute of Linguistics in three parts, 1954, 1955, 1960.]

Powell, John Wesley. 1891. "Indian Linguistic Families of America North of Mexico". *Seventh Annual Report of the Bureau of American Ethnology for 1885–1886*, 1–142. Washington, D. C.: Government Printing Office.

Roberts, Helen H. & Morris Swadesh. 1955. *Songs of the Nootka Indians of Western Vancouver Island.* Based on phonographic records, linguistic and other field notes made by Edward Sapir. Philadelphia: American Philosophical Society.

Sapir, Edward. 1907a. "Herder's *Ursprung der Sprache*:" *Modern Philology* 5.109–142. (Repr., with a preface by Konrad Koerner, in *Historiographia Linguistica* 11:3.349, 355–388 [1984].)

—. 1907b. "Preliminary Report on the Language and Mythology of the Upper Chinook". *American Anthropologist* 9.533–544.

—. 1909a. *Takelma Texts.* (= *Anthropological Publications* 2: 1), 1–263. Philadelphia: Univ. of Pennsylvania.

—. 1909b. *Wishram Texts, together with Wasco Tales and Myths collected by Jeremiah Curtin and edited by Edward Sapir.* (= *American Ethnological Society Publications*, 2.) Leiden: E. J. Brill.

—. 1910a. "Song Recitative in Paiute Mythology". *Journal of American Folk-Lore* 23:455–472. (Repr. in part in Sapir 1949.463–467.)

—. 1910b. *Yana Texts.* Together with *Yana Myths* collected by Roland B. Dixon. *University of California Publications in American Archaeology and Ethnology* 9.1–235.

—. 1911. "The Problem of Noun Incorporation in American Languages". *American Anthropologist* 13.250–282.

—. 1913. "Wiyot and Yurok, Algonkin Languages of California". *American Anthropologist* 15.617–646.

—. 1914. 'Notes on Chasta Costa Phonology and Morphology". *University of Pennsylvania Anthropological Publications* 2:2.271–340. Philadelphia.

—. 1915a. *Abnormal Types of Speech in Nootka.* (= Canada, Department of Mines, Geological Survey, Memoir 62, *Anthropological Series*, 5.) Ottawa: Government Printing Bureau. (Repr. in Sapir 1949.179–196.)

—. 1915b. *A Sketch of the Social Organization of the Nass River Indians.* (= Canada, Department of Mines, Geological Survey, Museum Bulletin 19, *Anthropological Series*, 7.) Ottawa: Government Printing Bureau.

—. 1915c. "The Social Organization of the West Coast Tribes". *Transactions, Royal Society of Canada*, 2nd series, 9.355–374. Ottawa (Repr. in Sapir 1949.468–487.)

—.1916. *Time Perspective in Aboriginal American Culture: A study in method.* (= Canada, Department of Mines, Geological Survey, Memoir 90, *Anthropological Series*, 13.) Ottawa: Government Printing Bureau. (Repr. in Sapir 1949.389–462.)

—. 1917. "Do We Need a 'Superorganic'?". *American Anthropologist* 19.441–447.

—. 1921a. "A Bird's-eye View of American Languages North of Mexico". *Science* 54.408. (Repr. in Koerner 1984.140.)

—. 1921b. *Language: An introduction to the study of speech.* New York: Harcourt, Brace & Co.

—. 1922 [1912]. "The Takelma Language of Southwestern Oregon". Boas 1922.1–296.

—. 1922. "The Fundamental Elements of Northern Yana". *University of California Publications in American Archaeology and Ethnology* 13.215–234.

—. 1924. "Culture, Genuine and Spurious". *American Journal of Sociology* 29.401–429. (Repr. in Sapir 1949.308–331.)

—. 1925a. "Sound Patterns in Language". *Language* 1.37–51. (Repr. in Sapir 1949.33–45.)

—. 1925b. "The Similarity of Chinese and Indian Languages". *Science* 62, no. 1607, supplement of 16 Oct. 1925, p. xxi. [Unsigned report of an interview.]

—. 1929a. "Central and North American Languages". *Encyclopaedia Britannica*, 14th ed., vol. V, 138–141. Chicago; Univ. of Chicago Press. (Repr. in Sapir 1949.169–178.)

—. 1929b. "Male and Female Forms of Speech in Yana". *Donum Natalicium Schrijnen* ed. by St. W. J. Teeuwen, 79–85. Nijmegen: Dekker; Utrecht: Van de Vegt. (Repr. in Sapir 1949.206–212.)

—. 1929c. "Nootka Baby Words". *International Journal of American Linguistics* 5.118–119.

—. 1930a. "Southern Paiute, a Shoshonean Language". *Proceedings of the American Academy of Arts and Sciences* 65: 1.1–296. (= *The Southern Paiute Language*, Part 1.)

—. 1930b. "Texts of the Kaibab Paiutes and Uintah Utes". *Proceedings of the American Academy of Arts and Sciences* 65: 2.297–536. (= *The Southern Paiute Language*, Part 2.)

—. 1930c. *Totality.* (= *Language Monographs*, 6.) Baltimore: Linguistic Society of America.

—. 1931a. "The Function of an International Auxiliary Language". *Psyche* 11.4–15. (Repr. in Sapir 1949.110–121.)

—. 1931b. "Southern Paiute Dictionary". *Proceedings of the American Academy of Arts and Sciences* 65:3.537–730. (= *The Southern Paiute Language*, Part 3.)

—. 1933. "Language". *Encyclopedia of the Social Sciences* 9.155–169. New York: Macmillan. (Repr. in Sapir 1949.7–32.)

—. 1935. "A Descriptive Grammar of English: Report of progress, 1934". *American Council of Learned Societies Bulletin* 23 (June 1935), 125–127.

—. 1938. "Why Cultural Anthropology Needs the Psychiatrist". *Psychiatry* 1.7–12. (Repr. in Sapir 1949.569–577.)

—. 1942. *Navaho Texts.* Ed. with supplementary texts by Harry Hoijer. Phildalphia: Linguistic Society of America.

—. 1944. "Grading, a Study in Semantics". *Philosophy of Science* 11.93–116. (Repr. in Sapir 1949.122–149.)

—. 1949. *Selected Writings of Edward Sapir in Language, Culture and Personality.* Ed. by David G. Mandelbaum. Berkeley & Los Angeles: Univ. of California Press.

—. 1993. *The Psychology of Culture: A course of lectures.* Reconstructed and ed. by Judith T. Irvine. Berlin & New York: Mouton de Gruyter.

— & Leslie Spier. 1943. "Notes on the Culture of the Yana". *University of California Publications: Anthropological Records* No. 3.239–298. Berkeley.

— & Morris Swadesh. 1932. *The Expression of the Ending-Point Relation in English, French and German.* Ed. by Alice V. Morris. Baltimore: Linguistic Society of America.

—, —. 1939. *Nootka Texts: Tales and ethnological narratives with grammatical notes and lexical materials.* Philadelphia: Linguistic Society of America.

—, —. 1955. *Native Accounts of Nootka Ethnography.* Bloomington: Indiana University Research Center in Anthropology, Folklore, and Linguistics.

—, —. 1960. *Yana Dictionary.* Ed. by Mary R. Haas. (= *University of California Publications in Linguistics*, 22.) Berkeley & Los Angeles.

Silverstein, Michael. 1986. "The Diachrony of Sapir's Synchronic Linguistic Description; or, Sapir's 'Cosmographical' Linguistics". Cowan et al. 1986.67–106.

Siskin, Edgar. 1986. "Reminiscences about Edward Sapir". Cowan et al. 1986.371–403.

Spier, Leslie, ed. 1941. *Language, Culture, and Personality.* Menasha, Wis.: Sapir Memorial Publication Fund.

Stocking, George, Jr., ed. 1996. *Volksgeist as Method and Ethic: Essays on Boasian ethnography and the German anthropological tradition.* Madison: Univ. of Wisconsin Press.

Sullivan, Harry Stack. 1939. "Edward Sapir, Ph. D., Sc. D., 1884–1939". *Psychiatry* 2.159.

Swadesh, Morris. 1971. *The Origin and Diversification of Language.* Edited by Joel F. Sherzer. Chicago: Aldine.

Talmy, Leonard. 1972. *Semantic Structures in English and Atsugewi.* Ph. D. dissertation, Univ. of California, Berkeley.

Trager, George L. & Benjamin L. Whorf. 1937. "The Relationship of Uto-Aztecan and Tanoan". *American Anthropologist* 39.609–624.

Voegelin, Charles F. 1952. "The Boas Plan for the Presentation of American Indian Languages", *Proceedings of the American Philosophical Society* 96:4.439–451.

Whitney, William Dwight. 1889 [1879]. *Sanskrit Grammar.* 2nd rev. ed. Leipzig: Breitkopf & Härtel; Boston: Ginn und Co.

Whorf, Benjamin Lee 1933. "The Phonetic Value of Certain Characters in Maya Writing". With an introduction by Alfred M. Tozzer. *Papers of the Peabody Museum* 13: 2.

–. 1935. "The Comparative Linguistics of Uto-Aztecan". *American Anthropologist* 37.600–608.

–. 1936. "The Punctual and Segmentatative Aspects of Verbs in Hopi". *Language* 12.127–131.

–. 1938. "Some Verbal Categories of Hopi". *Language* 14.275–286. (Repr. in Whorf 1956.112–124.)

–. 1940a. "Science and Linguistics". *The Technology Review (MIT)* 42.229–231, 247–248. (Repr. in Whorf 1956.207–219.)

–. 1940b. "Linguistics as an Exact Science". *Ibid.* 43.61–63, 80–83. (Repr. in Whorf 1956.220–232.)

–. 1941a. "Languages and Logic". *Ibid.* 43.250–252, 266, 268, 272. (Repr. in Whorf 1956.233–245.)

–. 1941b. "The Relation of Habitual Thought and Behavior to Language". Spier 1941.75–93. (Repr. in Whorf 1956.134–159.)

–. 1942. "Language, Mind, and Reality". *The Theosophist* (Madras, India) 63:1.281–291; 63:2.25–37. (Repr. in Whorf 1956.246–270.)

–. 1945. "Grammatical Categories". *Language* 21.1–11. (Repr. in Whorf 1956.87–101.)

–. 1946a. "The Hopi Language, Toreva Dialect". Hoijer et al. 1946.158–183.

–. 1946b. "The Milpa Alta Dialect of Aztec, with Notes on the Classical and Tepoztlán Dialects". Hoijer et al. 1946.367–397.

–. 1949. *Four Papers on Metalinguistics.* Washington, D. C.: Foreign Service Institute, Department of State. (Repr. of Whorf 1940a, 1940b, 1941a, 1941b, with a prefatory note by George L. Trager. 2nd ed., 1950; 3rd ed. 1952, with Whorf 1950 added, under the new title *Collected Papers on Metalinguistics.*)

–. 1950. "An American Indian Model of the Universe". *International Journal of American Linguistics* 16.67–72. (Repr. in Whorf 1956.57–64.)

–. 1953. "Linguistic Factors in the Terminilogy of Hopi Architecture". *International Journal of American Linguistics* 19.141–145. (Repr. in Whorf 1956.199–206.)

–. 1956. *Language, Thought, and Reality: Selected writings of Benjamin Lee Whorf.* Ed. with an Introduction by John B. Carroll. Foreword by Stuart Chase. Cambridge, Mass.: The Technologist [later on: MIT] Press. (18th printing, 1988.)

Victor Golla, Arcata, Calif. (U.S.A.)

212. The 'Bloomfield School' and descriptive linguistics

1. Leonard Bloomfield (1887–1949): Linguist and figurehead
2. Bloomfield's neogrammarian background
3. Revisions of Bloomfield's system
4. Problems of specifying and localizing meaning
5. Distributionalism
6. Conclusion
7. Bibliography

1. Leonard Bloomfield (1887–1949): Linguist and figurehead

In considering the relationship between Bloomfield and subsequent developments in descriptive linguistics in North America, it is important to distinguish between Bloomfield's own linguistic work and the largely symbolic role he played for the next generation of scholars and their students. Leonard Bloomfield was not head of a 'school' of linguistics in the way such a role is commonly understood nowadays. First-hand reminiscences of Bloomfield agree that unless in the company of his immediate family and close friends, he was extraordinarily diffident (Despres 1987, Sayers 1987). Through most of his career he taught classes in modern German, the older Germanic languages, and comparative Germanic and Indo-European. He supervised very few doctoral dissertations. In advising students, he frequently tried to discourage them from pursuing a career in linguistics. Apart from a few summer courses at Linguistic Institutes, he seldom taught descriptive linguistics. Bloomfield addressed his colleagues almost entirely through his publications. Most of these did not deal directly with linguistic theory nor even with general topics in linguistics, but rather with details of Germanic or Algonquian languages and their historical relationships. Of his two general linguistic books, the first (1914) was apparently well received but not particularly influential. Only the second, *Language* (1933), was regarded from its first appearance as a disciplinary milestone. Like Sapir's *Language* (1921), however, it was intended by its author as not as an advanced theoretical statement in an emerging field but as a work for the interested public and the beginning student. In sum, there is little in his professional biography to suggest that he sought a position of leadership, though he probably enjoyed his prestige. Bloch's obituary (1949) makes many of these points as well. For example, the contrast between his decades of largely solitary scholarship and the unremitting and successful disciplinary politics of his older Franz Boas (1858–1942) could hardly be more complete.

Leonard Bloomfield was born in Illinois to a family of Austrian origin; in his boyhood the family moved to Wisconsin. He attended local public schools, not very happily, and went to Harvard at 16, graduating in 1906 after three years of study. He first encountered linguistics when he sought an assistantship in German at the University of Wisconsin that summer. He was introduced to it by Eduard Prokosch (1876–1938), who became his mentor (see Bloomfield 1938). After two years of graduate work and German teaching in Madison, he completed his doctorate at the University of Chicago in 1909, writing his dissertation on 'a semasiologic differentiation in Germanic secondary ablaut' under the direction of Francis A. Wood (1858–1948). The subject of this work was the development after Proto-Germanic, that is, within the daughter languages, of sets of forms related by root-vowel patterns like the original ablaut relationships, as in *sing, sang, sung*. Their 'semasiological differentiation' was the appearance and spread of patterned meaning differences associated with the vowel differences, as in *flip, flap, snip, snap*. This, with its ramifications, was a topic to which he would return many times.

After completing his doctorate, he obtained a position at the University of Cincinnati as an instructor of German. A year later he went to the University of Illinois at the same rank. His academic duties in this period were almost exclusively the teaching of introductory German. In 1913–1914 he studied with Brugmann, Leskien (see p. 9) and Hermann Oldenberg (1859–1920) at the Universities of Leipzig and Göttingen, and then returned to Illinois as an assistant professor, remaining there at that rank until 1921. His teaching assignments were divided between German language instruction and, in step with his advances in rank, courses in Germanic philology and comparative Indo-European.

His publication record suggests continuing interest in three areas: historical, descriptive, and pedagogical applications of linguistic analysis. *Language* is divided almost equally between descriptive and historical chapters. Moreover, he wrote about as much on language pedagogy as on descriptive linguistics, counting his *First German Book* (1923, 2nd ed. 1928), a manuscript English reading primer (© 1940), and a number of articles on language teaching.

Bloch's (1949) obituary notes that besides Germanic, Bloomfield had a specialist's knowledge of Indic, Slavic, and Greek. Moulton (1970) wrote of the depth of learning and the pleasure in textual study displayed by Bloomfield as they read Otfrid together (at Bloomfield's invitation) in 1942, a time when Bloomfield was also deeply and productively involved in writing materials for wartime language pedagogy. Although his work outside Germanic and Indo-European began early, during his stay at Illinios (*Tagalog Texts with Grammatical Analysis*, 1917), he was by training and in his classroom career an elite Germanist and Indo-Europeanist in the Neogrammarian tradition.

The outline of Bloomfield's professional life as it is often summarized by his admirers and critics does not emphasize the philological and pedagogical aspects of his career. Instead, more attention is given to his years at Ohio State University, where he moved in 1921 as a full professor. While there, he came in contact with the psychologist Albert Paul Weiss (1879–1931). They became close friends, and Bloomfield was strongly influenced by Weiss's approach to his science, adopting some of the idiom of behavioral psychology. There also he took part, with

George Melville Bolling (1871–1963), in founding the Linguistic Society of America in 1925. In 1927 he moved to Chicago, where he and Edward Sapir (1884–1939) were briefly and rather distantly colleagues, and where he seems to have enjoyed his most pleasant and productive years. In 1940 Bloomfield went to Yale, as Sterling Professor, replacing Prokosch and to some degree also Sapir. He remained there until his death in 1949, three years after a stroke had ended his working life.

2. Bloomfield's neogrammarian background

Bloomfield's formation as a linguist was guided by professors who belonged to the second generation of the Neogrammarian movement, leaders in Germanic and Indo-European philology in Germany and the United States. This body of theory and historical linguistic scholarship was seen by its leaders as *scientific*, both in its own methods and in the sense of providing an explanation for the phenomena it studied, connecting linguistics with other branches of science, especially phonetics, psychology, and psychophysics, a discipline featuring then as now the experimental exploration of the thresholds and functioning of human perception. Bloomfield's many references to linguistic science should probably be understood within his frame of reference, rather than merely as shibboleths of behaviorism.

The handling of language data in the historical and comparative study of the Indo-European languages had deep roots in the study of classical texts from the Renaissance onwards, when the procedures and logic of textual reconstruction were first made explicit by humanist scholars. The tools of classical philology – contrastive comparison of linguistic forms, textual concordance, the logic of textual variants and the creation of stemmata based on shared innovations leading from surviving corrupted later texts to a reconstructed original text – were the antecedents of the analytical techniques and concepts of the classical comparative method of the Neogrammarians. For Bloomfield as for his mentor Prokosch, and for Brugmann, Leskien, and the other leaders of that movement before them, these were also the basic tools of descriptive and pedagogical applications of linguistic science. Bloomfield wrote with the deepest respect of Prokosch's elementary German teaching materials and method [1970 [1938]: 349]: "Every form, lexical or grammatical, which he uttered before the class, was registered in a card index, with provisions for its recurrence. He used, of course, the direct method [...]" Bloomfield's *Outline Guide for the Practical Study of Foreign Languages*, actually a guide to linguistic field methods of the time before portable sound recording equipment, lays out a very similar procedural toolkit and explains its use. This pamphlet gives a precious glimpse of Bloomfield at work, masterfully playing the parts of both teacher and student. It is written so well that his pedagogical craftsmanship may be overshadowed. After explaining how one's notebooks should be studied, reviewed, recopied, and annotated, with each layer of information carefully distinguished and dated, he goes on as follows (1942: 13):

"The most important of the secondary notations is the card index. People who can affort it use standard library or business office equipment; the present writer has always used slips of ordinary paper cut to one-and-half by five inches and filed in shoe boxes cut down to the proper height. One copies every form on a slip, with its meaning, and files them alphabetically. By comparing and rearranging these slips in every possible way, such as alphabetizing backward from the end of the forms as well as forward from the beginning, one not only gets great help towards memorizing the forms, but also one discovers the similarities between different forms. For instance, if in French one had recorded *ilaləlivr* 'he has a book', *tyamaplym* 'thou hast my pen' *marilavy* 'Mary has seen it', one may finally peel out the form (in nearly every respect it deserves to be called a word) *a* corresponding fairly well to the meaning of the English *has*. In Ojibwa, recordings like *nissônak* "three canoes full", *nî'ônak* "four canoes full", *panônakisse* "he misses his passage (on a boat or train)" finally lead one to peel out the suffix *-ônak* 'canoe'. One classes this as a suffix, because, apart from various other things one learns about the structure of these words, one finds that the independent word for 'canoe' or 'boat' is *cîmân*."

We can see how to make and use a lexical or concordance file from these few lines. We can see Bloomfield's patient siege methods, by which language after language was made to reveal its structure. Two well-chosen examples not only illustrate the use of the card index, but startle the reader, first with the notion that French *a* may not be a word, and then with the analysis of a form that means 'canoe' as a suffix. Thus he sets up the next paragraph, which cautions us against asking or heeding the informants' views on the target language. "Whether our forms are words or affixes and what range of meaning they may cover, are questions for us to determine from our data; the informant cannot tell us." We are not just admonished to avoid preconceptions here; we are also shown what it is like to work without them.

The next section deals with the collection and use of connected text. Here in a few pages is the method of textual scholarship, adapted to the needs of the language learner, whether of French or Ojibwa, by showing the learner how to gather and annotate the texts. The methods are strikingly similar to the recommendations for management of the learner's notebooks advocated above, in which the annotations needed to reconstruct the history of the text are added by the learner-author as the documents are constructed, in a mirror image of the usual process of textual reconstruction. More examples of practical textual analysis follow, showing both familiar and unfamiliar data arranged to teach the recognition and use of morphological and syntactic paradigms, and especially, a way to follow the similarities and differences among the forms of each language to establish the grammatical categories they manifest. At the end of the section on grammar, covering less than a page and a half, he uses a Tagalog example, 35 years after his *Tagalog Texts and Grammatical Analysis* (1917). In it he introduced a set of grammatical terms and categories tailored to fit and define the content of the overt formal distinctions of the language; it did not include *noun* or *verb*. Here he stands by it: "Clearly, a word like *sumûsúlat* is neither verb, adjective, nor noun; such a classification, appropriate to English, is entiry irrelevant to a description of Tagalog" (Bloomfield 1942: 15).

His theoretical tenet of following the forms wherever they lead, though fully in keeping with the use of linguistic tools in tracing the history of forms and categories through the development of a language family, was not often followed by younger descriptivists, who with few exceptions had not been exposed to the details of comparative Indo-European linguistics, but rather came directly to descriptive linguistics from other fields. Bloomfield also complained (in the 1919 letter to Michelson noted below) that many Indo-Europeanists did not regard the category system they used as contingent on the forms of their target languages.

For Bloomfield, then, there was one fundamental procedure of linguistic analysis, which could be put to use in language description, in historical and comparative linguistics, and in language study or teaching. Based on the notion of the linguistic sign, it calls for comparing linguistic forms (signs) that are partly alike and partly different, so as to reach an understanding of just how they are alike and how they are different one from another. Bloomfield alluded to this procedure near the beginning and again near the end of his career. In a letter Truman Michelson written in 1919, he described his method in these words: "My models are Panini and the kind of work done in I.-E by my teacher, Professor Wackernagel of Basle. No preconceptions; find out which sound variations are distinctive (as to meaning) and then analyze morphology and syntax by putting together everything that is alike" (Hockett 1987: 41). Much later, in his response to Trager's account of French verb morphology (Bloomfield 1945: 8), he wrote "Systematic description [...] tries to assemble all forms that have any common feature and to unite them under a single statement."

The reference above to Jacob Wackernagel (1853–1938) as Bloomfield's "teacher" is interesting. Although Wackernagel, an eminent scholar of Greek and Sanskrit, began and ended his career at Basle, he taught at Göttingen from 1902 to 1914. It is likely that Bloomfield met him there during his year of study in Germany, though he apparently did not study formally with him. The same letter refers to correspondence from him in which Wackernagel recommended that Bloomfield get a copy of Saussure's *Cours*. The teaching in question may have involved assimilating Wackernagel's method of careful philological analysis of original text as a source of data for comparative linguistics.

The method of contrastive comparison of forms provides a warrant for analysis without determining how far the analysis should go. In Bloomfield's *Introduction* (1914: 131–135), he discussed several sets of English words forming what he called phonetic-semantic classes. The interesting sets of forms include *flame, flare, flash, flimmer, flicker* and *glimmer, shimmer, flimmer, simmer* as well as *flash, clash, crash, dash, gash, gnash, hash,* etc. Other sets of forms listed just after these are *thirteen*, *fourteen*, *fifteen*, etc., and *thirteen*, *thirty*, *third*, and *three*. As objects of description the two groups of intersecting classes are comparable, but on the former, of whose *fl-* words he noted that "all of them express phenomena of fire with especial reference to its peculiar moving light" he added (Bloomfield 1914: 133):

"This class is of interest in the present connection, because it illustrates the emotional rather than perceptual value and the ill-defined rather than clearcut extent of many of these classes. For there can be no doubt that, in the feeling of many speakers, *flicker* again associates itself with such words as *flutter*, *fly*, and even, further, with *flit*, *flip*, *flop*, *flap*, and so on. All these words share the initial *fl-* and are more or less vaguely related in meaning; indeed the feeling for the semantic connection may vary in the same speaker under different circumstances. In short, the extent or the existence of a phonetic-semantic word class may be very doubtful, and could be determined with accuracy only for a given person at a given time, and here only if a full insight into his associative disposition at the moment were attainable."

Elements like the *fl-* have usually been treated as phonesthemes. The basis for segmenting the *fl-* as a morpheme has generally been perceived as inadequate or totally absent, but the root and affix elements of the number words are segmented (cf. Matthews 1992: 127). In the *Introduction*, Bloomfield treated the sets of *fl-* and number words alike, leaving all of the forms unsegmented in both, viewing what he called their *formative elements* only as anchors for phonetic-semantic associations. In *Language* (1933: 244–245), he again treated both types alike, but this time as made up of separate, bound morphemes, noting there are "clearly-marked phonetic-semantic resemblances between elements which we view as different roots." Bloomfield's use of contrastive comparison had not changed between 1914 and 1933, but his analytical criteria had. In classroom discussions of morphology led by other teachers in later descriptivist courses, the *fl-* forms were often presented very briefly, as illustrating a group of open but unimportant problems, or as representing the dangers awaiting those who rely on meaning tests in place of distribution. Wells & Keyser's monograph (1961), coming when distributionalist descriptive linguistics was on the wane, dealt with them neutrally and at unusual length, examining many of these forms, and others like them, and placing the associated problems in a more general analytical context, using them to expound their notion of an analytical screen whose mesh can be made coarser or finer with differing consequences. Among the consequences of adopting a fine-grained analysis, they note the reduced scope of grammatical operability of each of the resulting more numerous shorter elements, each with necessarily more restricted freedom of occurrence, as the familiar larger roots are segmented. Bloomfield was apparently able to look at familiar material without preconceptions about the outcome of analysis, just as he taught his readers to do.

3. Revisions of Bloomfield's system

The legacy of Bloomfield's system of linguistics was accepted only in part by the next generation of American linguists. They and their students soon began to transmute the elements adopted from his work into several approaches differing in important ways from each other and from Bloomfield's own principles as they were manifested in his descriptive works. Yet, throughout this process, over a period of 25 years of increasing activity, American descriptivists continued to attribute their guiding principles to Bloomfield above all others. The prestige of Bloomfield's reputation and the importance of *Language* were constantly reaffirmed by virtually every scholar in the field.

Rulon Wells (b. 1919) offered a tentative and retrospective characteriziation of descriptive linguistics (1963) which dated its period of florescence between 1933 and 1957. He presents it as a system of prescriptions about good language descriptions. The requisite traits for a description are, first, that it be purely descriptive (not intepretative, historical, explanatory, or normative). A description should also be idioglottal, asemic, static and nonfictive, agglutinatively oriented, procedural, economical, and grammar-reducing. The idioglottal ideal calls for the description of each language in its own terms. Wells does not ascribe this injunction to any particular linguist; instead, he raises two very pertinent questions (1963: 39): "At the first level, what are the best categories for describing language X? And at the second level, in what ways can we find out what are the best categories?" This is closely related to the procedural trait, which calls for a description to present evidence that it is best by virtue of resulting from the best procedures. Most of the other traits have to do with characterizing these best procedures. In explaining the asemic ideal, that the "description of the grammar should make no appeal to meaning" (p. 40), he discusses Bloomfield's advocacy of a weaker policy, which he describes as "Make appeal to meaning as little as possible." The static and nonfictive trait has to do with using the 'item and arrangement' rather than the 'item and process' model, as Charles F. Hockett's (1916–2000) very influential article of 1954 characterized them. Agglutination as a preferred language model, economy, and the reduction of grammar also bear on procedure. Besides Bloomfield (noted as a dissenter), only Hockett and Zellig Harris (1909–1992) are mentioned in this part of the paper. Their characterization of the descriptivist movement is perceptive but chronologically bounded. It characterizes is the distributionalist descriptive linguistics of the period from about 1942.

Whether accompanied or not by open acknowledgement of their disagreements with his views, the wealth of honorific references to Bloomfield, like the similar ones to Chomsky and his works since the 1960s, did not prevent the development of tendencies not only different from but antithetical to the principles expounded by the figurehead. Bloomfield's descriptive theory, an extension of Neogrammarian principles and practice adapted to the study of unfamiliar and undocumented languages, differed in important ways from the distributionalism that came later. In particular, in Bloomfield's system as expounded in 1926 and 1933, lexical forms (*morphemes* whose meanings were *sememes* and which were composed of *phonemes*) were paralleled by complex grammatical forms and relations built from them, *tagmemes*, composed of individually meaningless elements called *taxemes*, and paired with meanings called *episememes*. Taxemes were of several types and widely varying content, and there were quite diverse structures built from them. This complex system was quickly reduced in distributionalist morphology to a single type of element, the morpheme, occurring for the most part in a single type of arrangement, linear sequence. At the same time, the focus of analytical attention shifted from linguistic forms (in later terms, allo- morphs with actual phonological shapes) to patterns of distribution of the new morphemes, counting together those forms with phonological substance like the older lexical morphemes and other forms called morphemes but with partly or wholly abstract or 'grammatical' instantiations as points in the patterns. Descriptions of French verb morphology by Trager (1942, 1944, 1955), Bloomfield (1945), and Hall (1947, 1948) will be offered as evidence of this shift, in agreement with Wells (1963) and with Matthews' more detailed treatments (1992, 1993).

4. Problems of specifying and localizing meaning

Bloomfield and his immediate followers discussed problems of meaning and appropriate solutions to them within descriptive linguistics. A brief consideration here of some of these theoretical matters, involving complex grammatical and semantic considerations in description, may also help in gaining an understanding of later linguists' retrospective views of these same points.

In his *Postulates* (1926: 157), Bloomfield offered a frequently cited version of his reasons for rejecting the study of meaning by linguistic methods:

"The morphemes of a language can thus be analyzed into a small number of meaningless phonemes. The sememes, on the other hand, which stand in one-to-one correspondence with the morphemes, cannot be further analyzed by linguistic methods. This is no doubt why linguists, confronted with the parallelism of form and meaning, choose form as the basis of classification."

In Bloomfield's mature theoretical system, however, a hierarchy of semantic elements matching the form elements was established, to hold meanings when they were someday worked out. Since the number of the semantic container elements was equal to the form elements they matched, the 'size' or capacity of each was also vaguely determined by the forms, to the extent that it was determined at all.

This position, as expressed above, is probably ascribed both to Bloomfield and the distributionalists more widely than any other. However, in view of the attendant frequent claims that Bloomfield 'ignored' or 'rejected' meaning in linguistic analysis in some global or total sense, which also remains a prominent theme in account of descriptive linguistics then and since, it is worth displaying an example of his actual handling of meaning as an aspect of the analysis of forms. His arrangement of examples brings the semantic relations to the very surface of the text, as here in his discussion of derivation, dealing with forms like *duke : duchess and master : mistress* (Bloomfield 1933: 238):

"Once we have established a construction of this kind, we may be able to set up a typical meaning and then, as in the case of inflection, to look for parallels. Our suffix *-ess* for instance, has a definable linguistic meaning, not only because of the parallel character of all the sets like *count : countess, lion : lioness*, but also because English grammar, by the distinction of *he : she* recognizes the meaning of the *-ess* derivatives. Accordingly, we are able to decide, much as we are in the case of inflection, whether a given pair of forms, such as *man : woman*, does or does not show the same relation. This enables us to draw up supplementary statements, resembling our descriptions of paradigms, which show the various formal aspects of some grammatically determined semantic unit. Thus, we find the sememe 'female of such-and-such male' expressed not only by the suffix *-ess*, but also by composition, as in *elephant-cow, she-elephant, nanny-goat*, and by suppletion, as in *ram : ewe, boar : sow*; some such pairs show inverse derivation, the male derived from the female, as *goose : gander, duck : drake*."

Not even an additional analytic step would have been needed to demonstrate by means of these data the propriety of an analysis of meaning comparable to the analysis of sound and of form, and guided by the same principle of relevance in distinguishing between linguistic signs. In a passage in the chapter on meaning he articulated that principle in almost exactly the form it took in structural semantics decades later (1933: 140—141):

"In a favorable case, such as that of the word *apple*, all the members of the speech-community have been trained, from childhood, to use the speech-form whenever the situation (in this case, the object) presents certain relatively definable characteristics. Even in cases like this, our usage is never quite uniform, and most speech-forms have less clear-cut meanings. Nevertheless, it is clear that we must discriminate between *non-distinctive* features of the situation, such as the size, shape, color, and so on of any one particular apple, and the *distinctive*, or *linguistic meaning* (the *semantic* features) which are common to all the situations that call forth the utterance of the linguistic form, such as the features which are common to all the objects of which English-speaking people use the word *apple*."

His own assertions that meaning is beyond analysis by linguistic methods, one version of which is quoted above, became a dogma of later descriptive linguistics. It is nevertheless contradicted by these passages, and by his uncommonly perceptive handling of both descriptive and differential meaning in practical descriptions. What remained unaccountably missing from his work, however, was a recognition of the opportunity suggested by this parallelism between the criteria for recognizing significant features of form and significant features of meaning.

For the distributionalists who followed him, backed by Bloomfield's great prestige, his doctrine was converted into a sweeping warrant for suspending the structural analysis of meaning that remained in force for 25 years before semantic structure, was shown to be approachable again along the very lines indicated in Bloomfield's works. It was reintroduced into American structural linguistics by linguistic anthropologists (Conklin 1955, Goodenough 1956, Lounsbury 1956, 1964a, b; Bendix 1966, Wallace & Atkins 1960), and on a broader front by Weinreich (1966). The decline of linguistics within anthropology and the eclipse of descriptive morphology by Chomskyan syntax beginning at that time surely helped to reduce the impact of this cluster of articles. In any event, Bloomfield's teaching passed on a morpheme that was a unit of form whose phonolotical side was analyzed into distinctive units and grammatically relevant category membership but whose semantic side was a unitary and fixed but barely specified meaning. These properties were accepted as a package by the distributionalists, and indeed are still very much with us. The grammatical units glimpsed in his descriptive works, with occasional displays of parallel forms and semantic analysis, disappeared for decades, reappeared briefly in the componential semantics of the late 1950s, and then faded away again.

5. Distributionalism

The decade following 1933 was marked by a number of important papers on phonology by American structuralists (e.g., Swadesh 1934, Twaddell 1935, Swadesh & Voegelin 1939, Bloch 1941, Hockett 1942, Harris 1944). In these and other papers, they consolidated a descriptive approach based on the phoneme as established through the distribution of sound segments in opposition or complementation. For such phonological analyses, positive characterization of the meanings of linguistic forms was set aside.

The starting point of distributionalist morphology was the application of this type of analysis to the canonical morpheme of Bloomfield (1926, 1933), a unit with either a single, constant phonological shape in all environments, or a set of phonemically similar alternants whose members are in complementary distribution with each other, and whose phonemic differences conform to and are conditioned by the combinatory pattern of the phonology of the language. Morphemes defined in this way were structurally similar to phonemes of the type then being used in descriptive linguistics.

Other groupings of morpheme alternants were established on the model of these uncontroversial morphological elements, with similar meanings and morphologically (rather than automatic, phonologically) conditioned alternations in shape. These descriptive procedures are distributionalist, to be sure, in the sense that a commonly occurring structural pattern is selected as a model for others, and other elements are identified and grouped in such a fashion as to conform to the model.

The scope of these adjustments as advocated and practiced in Bloomfield's work, however, is quite restrained in comparison with what came later. Concern with explicit demonstrations that grouping and distributional standards had been met in a particular descriptive work, or that the standards advocated in a theoretical work would result in acceptable descriptions, was not a prominent feature of Bloomfield's writings. His descriptive works were extremely concise, made up mostly of listings of lexical and grammatical elements arranged in form classes. Forms, including grammatical forms, were kept in the foreground throughout. Bloomfield's account of French morphology (1945), though only meant as a sketch offered in somewhat exasperated response to Trager (1944), is typical of this style: it is only 6 pages in length, compared with 12 for Trager's first paper and the 29 pages of Trager (1955) on the same topic. It was rather in the morphological writings of younger linguists using the distributionalist version of the 'item and arrangement' style of morphological description that segmentation, grouping, and distributional concerns came to the fore.

This second major phase of development began with Harris (1942), in which the first step was taken in relaxing the substantive constraints of Bloomfield's morphology. Harris introduced the criterion of complementary distribution among alternants with the same meaning as a basis for establishing morpheme units whose morpheme alternants were in complementary distribution. Harris understood Bloomfield's system well. He stipulated a range restriction on the newly defined alternating morpheme: alternants could only be grouped if the resulting unit had a combined distribution equal to that of some morpheme with a single shape. He also provided for an expanded notion of 'phoneme sequence' (now characterizing his morpheme alternant) to include not only the normal, additive sequences of phonemes but also zero sequence ("the addition of no phoneme"), negative sequence ("the dropping of a phoneme"), and phonemic component sequence ("the addition of a physiological feature of phonemes"). In this way, the taxemes Bloomfield used were translated into a single arrangement type stipulated to be sequential order. Harris' relatively modest revision, really little more than an explication in distributionalist terms of Bloomfield's position, was offered deferentially:

"A morpheme unit is thus a group of one or more alternants which have the same meaning and complementary distribution. To make these units more similar to our present morphemes, and more serviceable for grammatical structure, we now add a further condition: In units consisting of more than one alternant, the total distribution of all the alternants (i.e. the combined range of environments in which each of them occurs) must equal the range of environments in which some unit with but a single alternant occurs." (Harris 1942: 171).

The subsequent development of distributionalist morphology, in a series of papers over the next decade, took the form of proposals for further relaxing the use of these uncontroversial single-alternant morphemes and their distributions as models for the rest, thereby extending the allowable limits of variation in phonological form as a by-product of the relaxation of distributional limits. More consequentially, this relaxation also permitted the mutual adjustment of distributional patterns overall. Aggressive, repeated use of the criterion of complementary distribution could and eventually did radically extend the notion of the morpheme. Combining this with the use of zero forms as representatives of grammatical categories, the distributionalists enjoyed almost complete freedom in arranging higher levels of linguistic structure. Usually their proposals offered some particular descriptive results viewed as desirable but unattainable under older rules. These papers defined a variety of structuralism in which the morpheme was the foundation of grammar, and distributional criteria played a central part in describing them, in ways deliberately modeled on phonemics: Harris (1942, 1946, 1948), Bloch (1947), Hockett (1947, 1954). Nida (1948) and Lounsbury (1953) were thoughtful critical surveys of this scene. Their advice, if heeded, would have checked the use of zero or portmanteau elements in morphology for well considered reasons.

As the basis for grouping morpheme alternants changed during this period of development, decisions in morphology came to be made based on identity or similarity in meaning rather than phonological form. Because of the settled opinion shared by these scholars and Bloomfield that determinations of sameness or difference of meaning were too imprecise to be scientifically reliable, these grouping decisions were generally stated in distributional terms.

A key link in the chain of reasoning that led to distributionalism was the *denial of synonymy*. Bloch, Hockett, Harris, and a number of others accepted Bloomfield's proposition (1933: 145) that "there are no actual synonyms" – that two distinct forms with exactly the same meaning would necessarily have exactly the same distribution: they would be mutually substitutable in all environments and actually distributed in this way in a suitable large corpus. They contended that there were no such forms. This proposition, and the contention that no such forms occur, form half of the foundation of distributionalism (Fought 1999). It is the most significant trait shared by the systems of Bloomfield and by the later distributionalists. But for them, more than for him, it was used as a justification for paying little attention to the semantic content of either lexical or grammatical form. If differences in the phonological shape of forms always correlate with differences in their meanings, and therefore in their distributions, then differences in the distribution of forms imply differences in their meanings, and tests of distribution may be substituted for considerations of meaning in analysis.

The other half of the foundation of distributionalism is its notion of *patterning*. In this also, both Bloomfield and the distributionalists agreed on a principle, but in this they differed more in their descriptive theory and practices. The distributions of two main types of elements are crucially involved. One is the distribution of overt morphological elements; the other is the distribution of grammatical forms and form classes, viewed as covert morphological elements. In describing the distribution of elements, reference may be made to the absolute distribution of a form, that is, to the sum of the environments where it occurs. This is what Bloomfield meant by the *selection* of a form. Element distribution is however most often discussed in terms of the relative distribution of two or more forms. Complementary distribution owes its central role in the development of American linguistics to the warrant it provides for combining elements so distributed as alternants of a unit on a higher level: they can be combined because they are by definition not directly accessible to contrastive comparison. In descriptive linguistics as in dialectology or comparative linguistics from the beginning, complementary distribution of overt elements (phonological or morphological) was never used as the sole criterion for such grouping decisions, however. There was always a check on it, an additional requirement of similarity or identity of substance (phonetic similarity in phonology, and phonemic similarity in morphology) or of some other identity criterion, such as meaning or formal parallelism, for the distributionalists. With covert morphological elements, unequivocal evidence of identity to use in checks on distributional statements is hard to find. Thus, the way was opened for statements using a predetermined grid of positions in which grammatical elements could be said to occur, and among which a combination of overt forms and putative zero elements could be said to manifest them. It is this freedom from the constraints of actual, audible forms as the substance of grammatical form that was given up, quite willingly, in the 1940s, by the distributionalists most often and misleadingly called Bloomfieldians, such as Bernard Bloch, Zellig Harris, Charles Hockett, George Trager, Robert Hall, and many others.

Parallelism in the distributions of elements or classes of elements is in effect a second layer, a more abstract pattern of the absolute distributions of classes of elements. In an obvious way, this parallelism or pattern, such as it may be, arises naturally and directly from the combination of the absolute distributions of the elements established, assigned to classes, and otherwise described in the grammar. Viewed in this way, a linguistic element, established by other criteria such as similarity of form and meaning, simply *has* a distribution, and any parallelisms with the distributions of other forms are a consequence of the body of analytical decisions made. Because of the strictness of Bloomfield's requirement of formal morphophonemic identity, this is close to his view of distribution in morphology — that the distribution of an element is a consequence, not a criterion, of analysis. There is a fringe of elements around these clearly identifiable cases which could reasonably be decided one way or another; it is these, and these only, which Bloomfield recommended deciding by appealing to parallelism with other, unambiguous cases.

Distributionalism, on the other hand, seeks to maximize (or conceivably, to minimize) such parallelism by making analytical decisions with reference to these secondary or higher levels of distributional patterning. Bloomfield's grouping standard for morpheme alternants as taken up by Harris, using the distribution of members of a form class having but a single alternant as a model for the ranged allowed for groups of anternants, is a conservative example of the critical uses of patterning. What sets distributionalism apart from other descriptive approaches before it is the scope not only allowed but advocated in adjusting the identifications and distributions of elements so as to maximize the parallelism and regularity of the abstract distributional pattern, and the methods used to reach this goal. It should be noted in passing that distributionalists differed considerably among themselves in their choice of means and in how far they would go in pursuing their goals. But all had certain practices in common, revealed by the choices of exemplary problems in their writings, and the solutions they arrived at.

The issues involved can be considered from the perspective of morphological segmentation or from the perspective of grouping morphological alternants. Lounsbury (1957 [1953]: 380) organized the issues in the background of morphological segmentation into four policy options, stated according to the mapping of phonemes or morphemes within a descriptive model applicable to any language, and whose morphemes have phonemic strings as alternants. In this connecgion, the principle of *total accountability*, as Hockett (1947: 332) called it, was generally accepted. It stipulates that all phonemic material in the data must be accounted for in relation to the morphological elements in the same data. Using Lounsbury's labels, and following his wording closely, these policies are as follows:

(α) every phoneme belongs to an allomorph of one and only one morpheme;
(β) every phoneme belongs to an allomorph of at least one morpheme;
(γ) every phoneme belongs to an allomorph of not more than one morpheme;
(δ) every phoneme belongs to an allomorph of zero or one or more than one morpheme.

All four options allow for segmenting the morphological elements of any given language into sequential agglutinative morphs, or into some kinds of interdigitating morphs. The second option (but not the first) also allows for coincident, including, or overlapping morphs, that is, for the sharing of particular phonemes by two or more adjoining allomorphs, as in the often proposed analysis of French *au* /o/ as {à} + {le}. The third option (but not the first or second) allows for what were variously called *empty morphs*, *links*, or *morphemically irrelevant material*. We will see examples of these in the discussion of French. The last mapping option combines all of the possibilities of the other three.

Lounsbury (1957 [1953]: 380) presents as a feature of the first policy the option of using zero elements: "Segmentation is carried as far as possible, and such morphemes (present in meaning) as have not been accounted for in the resulting segments are said to be represented by **zero allomorphs**." Note the parenthesis: the motivation for a zero allomorph is that the morpheme it represents is present *only in meaning*. There is, in other words, something about the meaning of the construction or utterance, but nothing about the form of it, that suggests the presence of a particular morpheme. Accordingly, the morpheme is identified, and a zero representative is duly assigned to some position within the string of allomorphs. Since allomorphs themselves are strings of phonemes, one possible interpretation of this passage is that there is a zero token of a morpheme in the relevant position. Another interpretation is that there is a zero token (an allophone without phonetic features) of some nonzero phoneme. In Lounsbury's model, these are the only possibilities.

Morphemes whose identifying and defining characteristic is the occurrence, in some sense, of an inflectional category, such as first person singular or present indicative, must however be mapped somehow onto the string of phonemes which manifest an utterance. Solutions differed in important ways. Bloomfield (1945: 10), not a distributionalist, treated the French form /don/ (*je donne*) as being present (not indicative!) or subjunctive (not present subjunctive). Its number-person ending, marked grammatically as first person singular, or S1, is morphologically zero, that is, the absence of an 'expected' form, the presence of nothing at all, not even /0/ or {0}. His analysis is parsimonious, built directly on the overt forms, and includes no abstract elements except those represented somewhere in the system by overt forms. His use of zero is apparently the classic use found in Sanskrit grammar, namely removal of something, replacement by nothing, rather than the distributionalist version, in which a 'zero element' is present. The second person plural (P2) form, /done/, does have a suffix; it is segmented as /don-e/.

For Hockett (1947: 338), however, the Spanish S1 form was *am-o* and the /o/ was what he called a *portmanteau morph*, which belonged to two morphemes at once, {present indicative} and {first person singular}, in parallel to such other forms as /amas/, in which his segmentation was /am-a-s/, with the two suffixes {present indicative} and {second person singular}. Infinitive forms, represented in this set by /amar/, do not seem to have this structure, since the infinitive is neither a tense nor a mode in traditional grammar. Hockett treats the form as /am-a-r/, with the -/r/ as the infinitive morpheme and the -/a/ sufix defined as an empty morph. In Hockett's analysis, there is a single sequence of morphological elements in every Spanish form: "This treatment, combined with the empty-morph interpretation of conjugation vowels, reduces all finite Spanish verb forms to a uniform structure: stem + tense-mode morpheme + person-number morpheme." Although Nida (1948: 417–418) was sympathetic to the leveling of distribution thus achieved, he was concerned about other aspects of the solution:

"In handling inflexional endings like the -*o* in Spanish *amo* 'I love', Hockett [1947: 338] says that this is a morph which belongs to two morphemes: a tense-mode morpheme and a person-number morpheme. In this instance, however, he does not provide any overt form for the separate morphemes. Only the morph has overt form; the morphemes are merely structural parallelisms as indicated by such related paradigmatic forms as *amábamos* 'we loved' and *amaréis* 'you (pl.) will love', in which the tense-mode morpheme precedes the person-number morpheme. In the instance of French *au* 'to the' occurring in place of the analogically demonstrable but non-occurring *à le*, there is more basis for speaking of a single morph belonging to two morphemes, since these morphemes may be identified as occurring elsewhere in the language. But in this case of Spanish -*o*, Hockett's morphemes are only statements of sequence evidenced at other points in the paradigmatic series; there are no overt forms to which this particular morph may be referred."

The outcome of a number of such distributional levelings was of course a more regular pattern of distribution, in both senses of regularity: more widespread and more homogeneous distributions of forms. Parallelism in the distribution of morphemes in the same form class was an important desideratum for all of the structuralists. It was a key component of the notion of pattern, of structure itself. For Harris, indeed, the regularization of distributions was an explicit goal with a high priority. In Harris' view, grammar in general could profitably be regarded as a set of restrictions on distribution, of prohibitions of co-occurrence, a mirror image of the more common view of grammar as a set of statements of allowable combinations. To reduce the number and scope of these distributional prohibitions (by homogenizing and broadening the distribution of a consequently smaller number of distinct elements) was to simplify grammar (Wells 1963: 43). For similar reasons, the display of co-occurrence information about phonemes and phoneme classes is a prominent feature of distributionalist descriptions of phonology. Trager (1944), though fairly brief, devotes a page to statements of phoneme occurrence in initial, medial, and final positions in syllable and word environments, and to some consonant clustering properties. Similar but more elaborate examples of this sort of tabulation are found in later distributionalist phonemic descriptions as well. Einar Haugen (1906–1992), in his article on modern Icelandic (1958), an exemplary description of the type using segmental phonemes and their allophones as elements, gives detailed co-occurrence statements of this kind.

Since portmanteau and zero solutions of these pattern-related morphological problems are equivalent, some explanation is needed for the overwhelming preference for zero solutions displayed in the period. Wells (1963: 41) was undoubtedly right to associate this preference with the preference for concatenative or sequential order (instead of simultaneous, subtractive, and other possibilities still offered in Harris 1942). In Lounsbury's apt phrase, they created a fictitious agglutinating analog of the actual linguistic forms, and analyzed that.

Trager's first published description of French verb morphology (1944) displays some characteristics found in a number of his later works. Among the familiar touches in his approach to phonology are the special interest he showed in differences of vowel length and a propensity to factor certain simultaneous combinations of phonological properties into sequences of phonemes. Most striking, however, is the use of a variety of French with an archaizing type of diction as the foundation of his morphological analysis, for which it provides the appearance of abundant phonetic substance as manifestations of his morphological elements. Though Bloomfield, in his reply to this paper (1945: 8), used a variety with a "maximum number of vowel distinctions", it is nevertheless both simpler and more realistic as a representation of modern spoken French than Trager's data. In Robert Hall's treatment of 'colloquial' French, he also remarks on this difference from Trager, through not from Bloomfield (1947: 39).

Of these archaizing features, the most obtrusive is the use of 'mute e', /ə/, as a 'weak vowel', defined in such a way as to place token 'vowels' to the benefit of distributional statements in the phonology and morphology: "The weak vowel /ə/ is the phonemic synthesis of the phonetic entities described as voiceless aspirated release after a voiceless consonant, voiced neutral-timbred release after a voiced consonant, and the vowel [ə^w] between certain consonant sequences and sometimes in final position" (Trager 1944: 132). Bloomfield's forms have only /ə/ where [ə], its only allophone, is found. There are no occurrences of final [ə] in his data; moreover, though Trager places an /ə/ before the /r/ in such forms as *jouerai*, Bloomfield does not, unless a three-consonant cluster would otherwise occur.

Trager treats the phonetically homogeneous nasalized vowels as a sequence /Vn/, parallel to the later handling of the American mid-central R-colored vowel as /ər/ in Trager & Smith (1951). Bloomfield uses a superscript *n* symbol, as in [ɛ^n], apparently as a diacritic rather than as a separate segment.

It is not clear to what extent Bloomfield would have used the system of inflectional categories found in Trager's paper if he had started from scratch rather than recasting someone else's solution for the sake of analytical comparison. Both used the terminology of singular and plural number, and first, second, and third persons (abbreviated S1, P3, etc); Bloomfield uses the traditional terms for French tense-mood categories, whereas Trager uses a few newly coined terms but the same fundamental categories. Bloomfield's use of the terms is innovative in one telling respect, however. His 'present' is not 'indicative'; his 'subjunctive' is not 'present'. That is, he does not specify both a tense and a mood category for each finite form. Here is a comparison of the terms for the finite and nonfinite stem forms for their treatments of French:

Trager (1944)	Bloomfield (1945)
Infinitive	Infinitive
Present Participle	Present Participle (adjective)
Past Participle	Past Participle (adjective)
Imperative	Imperative
Present Independent	Present
Past Independent	Imperfect
Present Subordinate	Subjunctive
Present Future	Future
Past Future	Conditional

Trager's article uses both phonemic and morphophonemic notations, placing both within solidi, but distinguishing them by means of the special morphophonemic symbols in the latter. These include /†/, morphophonemic zero, "the absence of any phoneme where an inflectional morpheme is expected", /./, a marker of morphological boundaries, and /^{z}, ^{t}, ^{r}/ the 'liaison' consonants. The last of these, involving the pronunciation of the final *r* of infinitives ending in *er* before a following vowel, is an especially archaic pronunciation feature.

From this point in the descriptive exposition, Trager's goal of tactical simplicity through distributional regularization becomes more evident. He assigns the inflectional endings to positional categories as *prefinals*, *finals*, and one *postfinal*. The prefinals are tense-mood markers; the finals are person-number markers. Each form has both, though many are quite insubstantial. In the present forms, two of the six tense-mood markers are zero, and the other four are /ə/, which is usually a mere consonant release. He divides the verbs into the traditional three conjugations based on the infinitive forms, calling them Class 1, 2, and 3. A representative subset of the analysis is shown below, adapted from his table (Trager 1944: 135). In each cell of the table, the element before the first hyphen is the prefinal tense-mood marker, and the next element is the final, the person-number marker. Note that all of these are either liaison consonants or zero. In the infinitive inflection of class three, the prefinal is either the zero element as shown, or a form /ua/; the last of the three elements in the Class 3 infinitive is the one and only postfinal.

		Class 1	Class 2	Class 3
Infinitive:		/e-r/ -er	/i-r/ -ir	/†-r-ə/ re
Present	S:	/ə-†, ə-ᶻ, ə-ᵗ/	/†-ᶻ, †-ᶻ, †-ᵗ/	=2
	P:	/†-onᶻ, †-eᶻ, ə-ᵗ/	=1	=1
Past	S:	/e-ᶻ, e-ᶻ, e-ᵗ/	=1	=1
	P:	/i-onᶻ, i-eᶻ, e-ᵗ/	=1	=1
Past Future	S:	/əre-ᶻ, əre-ᶻ, əre-ᵗ/	/r/ + =1	=2
	P:	/əri-onᶻ, əri-eᶻ, əre-ᵗ/	/r/ + =1	=2

The analysis clearly shows the distributionalist habit of establishing a grid of positions and filling it either with phonemic material or zero elements (represented here by the daggers). Moreover, it is evident that Trager's use of the /ə/ phoneme, most tokens of which would have no phonetic substance in environments like these, is actually a second type of zero element within the inflectional morphology. Removing it from the description would sharply reduce the number of distinct inflectional endings, making the separation into the three traditional verb classes more questionable. At this relatively early date in the evolution from the more concrete Bloomfieldian style of description toward more abstract distributionalism, however, and given the decision to distinguish the traditional form classes, it may have been reassuring to give to most morphological markers at least the appearance of phonemic substance. In Trager (1955) and Hall (1947, 1948), this need seems to have faded. Hall's treatment of the French verb gives an explicit formulation of the patterning approach to inflectional morphology in his justification of the use of zero elements (1947: 42n):

"It is necessary to set up zero forms as alternants of the elements following the verb root, in order to provide an over-all classification that will cover the longest verb forms, and a set of elements into which forms may be analyzed. Thus, the two verb forms in ʒədɔn *I give* and nusãtirjõzãkɔr *we should still feel* may be analyzed:

Root	Thematic Vowel	Stem Suffix	Tense Sign	Personal Ending	Liaison Suffix
dɔn	0	0	0	0	0
sãt	i	r	j	õ	z

It goes without saying that the zero elements are listed as such simply by virtue of their contrast with forms in which positive elements occur; zero, in this connection, is a convenient analytical device, just as in bookkeeping and other forms of tabulation, and it is by no means implied that it has any linguistic reality in itself (cf. the remarks of H. Kurath, *American Journal of Philology*, LXVI [1945], 210)."

The paragraph before the examples and the paragraph following do not go together well. Hall clearly states that the zeros are morpheme alternants, and therefore, allomorphs bearing meaning, in this case, grammatical meaning. An element can scarcely be both necessary for analysis and at the same time merely a convenient fiction. The motivation for the zero elements is revealed by the distributionalist credo in the first paragraph, in the form of the assumption that a single overall classification of forms is needed that fits both the longest and the shortest overt forms with the same number of grammatical elements.

Hall's description of French uses a more complex classification of forms than Trager (1944). Each stem type is given a complex label according to a fixed formula. The verb root (the stem of the imperfect form) forms three stems, A (present), B (future), and C (preterite) with suffixation of a thematic vowel and a stem suffix. All verbs have thematic vowel zero in stem A; the thematic vowels of the B and C stems are the basis for identifying the conjugation classes (I, II, IIIa, IIIb, and IIIc). The number of zeros in the inflectional system is impressive, especially in the regular verbs, where zeros are used as placeholders for the material in corresponding slots in the irregular forms.

Trager (1955) was scarcely influenced by Bloomfield's critique of his earlier description, but adopted a number of features similar to Hall's, in particular the apparatus of stem classes. The labelling scheme is comparable in its complexity and abstractness. A more complete morphophonemic notation is provided, along with a numerical indexing system which displays the relative order of each element in the many sequences constructed. Incongruously, both Hall and Trager transplant Bloomfield's two markers, D and L, and Hall also uses the replacement operator > in their thoroughly distributionalist descriptions, though each gives the markers different symbols and neither notes their source.

Bloomfield's treatment of the French verb is organized and presented very differently from Trager's or Hall's. Most noticeably, he does not distinguish three verb conjugation classes. There is one type of regular verb (the traditional first or -er conjugation); the others are all more or less irregular. The regular inflectional endings are presented in less than half a page: infinitive [-é], present participle [-a^{n}t], past participle [-é], P1 [-o^n], P2 [-é]. Of these last, he remarks "Before these two endings, imperfect, subjunctive, and conditional have [-i-]." There is no attempt to assign this vowel to a morpheme; moreover, the liaison vowels are treated similarly: "Wherever liaison is made, 1 and 2 have [-z] and 3 has [-t]." In Bloomfield's system of 1933, taxemes are meaningless elements of form; tagmemes are meaningful arrangements of taxemes, with episememes as their meanings. The French inflectional categories here are apperently being handled as tagmemes, and the co-occurrence of the linking vowels and liaison consonants with various morphemes is a part of the formal structure bearing the grammatical meaning. It is also possible, though probably anachronistic, to construe these items as morphemically irrelevant phonetic material, an "empty morph" (Hockett 1947: 333). Bloomfield specifies three sets of endings for S1, 2, 3, and P3: zero in present and subjunctive, [-è] in imperfect and conditional, and S1 [-é], S2, 3 [a], P3 [-o^n], in the future. The imperative is like the present; future and conditional have a sign [-er-] before the endings. Here are the same forms shown above arranged in the same way to show Bloomfield's formulation:

Infinitive:		[-é]
Present	S:	[, ,]
	P:	[-o^n, -é]
Past	S:	[-è, -è, -è]
	P:	[-i-o^n, -i-é, è]
Conditional	S:	[-er-è, -er-è, -er-è]
	P:	[-er-i-o^n, -er-i-é, -er-è]

Bloomfield's use of zero is best understood as the absence of an expected element; accordingly, in the examples shown, nothing is there. Some forms have a single ending element; others have two or three. Most irregularities in this analysis affect only the finite stems, the infinitives, and the participial formations.

He uses two *markers* of the type found in classical Indian grammar: D and L. They are placed between stem and ending in certain cases, and act as 'morphophonemic operators', as Robert Austerlitz has termed them. Marker L occasions loss of the last consonant of the stem. Bloomfield uses the stem of the imperfect as the base form; thus, the stem of *lire* "read" is [liz]. The infinitive is [liz] − L − [r], that is, [lir]. The stem and infinitive of *finir* are handled in the same way, as [finis] and [finis] − L − [r], but *partir* is just [part] − [ir]. this L marker is also used in deriving masculine substantive forms from their longer feminine stems: *donnante* [dona^{n}t] plus L yields the masculine adjective *donnant* [dona^n]. Marker D is called 'stem loss', meaning "loss of the last vowel and all following sounds of the stem". It comes into play, for example, in deriving the future of *être*, which is *ser-*, an irregular form, from the stem [ét] (in Bloomfield's deliberately near-orthographic notation), in two steps. First, it is stipulated that [ét] > [s] before D; then the stem can be derived by [ét] − D − [er]. The irregular past participle of *avoir*, namely *eu*, is given by the derivation [av] − D − [u], where the D operator removes the whole stem. These operators, which seem rather tame in the light of generative phonology, were of course considered by descriptivists to be vestiges of an older and unacceptable process type of formulation of inflectional morphology. Nevertheless, they were so convenient for French that they were adopted without attribution in Hall (1947, 1948) and Trager (1955).

Bloomfield did not establish a system of verb classes as Trager and Hall did. Instead, he made verbs like *donner* implicitly the regular verbs, showing how they are inflected and then treating all other types as more or less irregular. Sets of irregular verbs are grouped together if their inflectional patterns parallel each other. Thus, "[bat], etc." stands for *battre, fendre, perdre,* etc., and "[bouy], etc." stands for *bouillir, dormir, partir,* etc. The class "[luiz], etc." includes *luire, haïr,* and also *finir, punir.* There are just nine such sets. Smaller sets of only two verbs are listed as, e. g., "[fal, val]" for *falloir, valoir.* Verbs falling generally into one of these irregular classes, but displaying still other irregularities within the pattern, are handled by appending references to one or more the numbered sections, 58 in all, where the particular irregularity is discussed. The first 12 of these 58 items deal with "general irregularities", mostly morphophonemic alternations of stressed syllabic: Items 4 states "[buv] has [u] > [oua]; this is one of a subset (items 2−5) dealing with irregularities "before consonant or zero of a suffix".

The relative ordering of irregularities within such a description is unfamiliar to us nowadays. Item 1 reads as follows: "In all inflections not listed below (29, 33, 40, 53), [asoua] has optionally [oua] > [è]: [je me asouayè, je me asèyè] *je m'assoyais, je m'asseyais.*" After the general section, numbered irregular alternations are grouped by the type of environment in which they occur: Present Participle and Subjunctive (items 13−19); Present and Imperative (items 20−30); Infinitive, Future, and Conditional (items 31−45); and Past Participle (items 46−58).

It is difficult at first to understand and appreciate the merits and drawbacks of this style of presentation, but time spent in studying the original text is well repaid. One shortcoming of his presentation in this article is only incidental: in Bloomfield's incomplete account there is no single place where the reader can find all the information pertinent to a given verb. This section, an alphabetical index, was omitted from the article to save space.

6. Conclusion

Bloomfield's injunction to base classification and analysis on overt from rather than on more abstract foundations was not often accepted, even in his own time. Instead, the traditional terminology of European grammatical categories was often adopted unchanged or slightly adapted to label the grammatical forms of both familiar and exotic languages, or more precisely, traditional labels were used as if there were grammatical forms corresponding to them. In place of Bloomfield's careful working out of category distinctions by following explicit cues in the forms and their distinctive functions, one finds instead the familiar category names of Indo-European grammar applied to a combination of overt forms and zero elements to fill in the 'gaps' among them. Lexical meaning was left for informal specification as a working expedient, and grammatical meaning was left in these traditional terms and categories. Most descriptivists used the tool of contrastive analysis to fashion grammars into relatively familiar shapes.

Bloomfield worked throughout his career against teleological argument in linguistics. It can be argued that there is a teleological element in the appeal to patterning implicit in Trager's or Hall's descriptions of the French verb, and in other morphological solutions featuring numerous zero elements: when so many morphological elements are insubstantial, represented only or usually by nothing audible, it may be because at least some of the categories they are said to manifest have been predetermined by the linguist. Furthermore, it can be argued that to believe these 'morphemes' are really present is to venture beyond firm evidence. Nida (1948) and Lounsbury (1953) warned against such uses of zero in morphology. On this, as on many other key points in linguistics, Bloomfield's own expressed position was strict but not rigid. When, as in French verbs, most forms in the commonest types of paradigms have a phonologically patent morpheme manifesting a particular grammatical feature, Bloomfield used and advocated the use of zeros in a very few positions within the paradigm in order to fill out the pattern defined by the overt forms. But his reliance on concrete linguistic forms as a guide to analysis ruled out the spread of zero elements through whole paradigms and distributional ranges, as they can be found in the descriptions of French by

Trager and Hall, and in many other distributionalist works on other languages.

Finally, it can be argued that the transition from Bloomfield's form-based structuralism to the pattern-based distributionalism that largely replaced it was a crucial step for the discipline at the beginning of a period of rapid growth in numbers, in that it prepared for the adoption of the still more abstract basis of Chomkyan transformational grammar. In giving up Bloomfield's reliance on surface form as an explicit guide in contrastive analysis, in favor of increasingly regularized patterns whose relationship to surface forms became correspondingly more and more complex, the field was prepared for the shift of attention from performance to competence, and from surface to deep structure, led by Zellig Harris' pupil Noam Chomsky.

If this is so, there is tragic irony in the conclusion of the deeply felt eulogy of Bloomfield written by Bernard Bloch, himself a linguist of uncommon thoroughness and seriousness of purpose (1970 [1949]: 530):

"It is not too much to say that every significant refinement of analytic method produced in this country since 1933 has come as a direct result of the impetus given to linguistic research by Bloomfield's book. If today our methods in descriptive analysis are in some ways better than his, if we see more clearly than he did himself certain aspects of the structure that he first revealed to us, it is because we stand upon his shoulders."

7. Bibliography

Bendix, Edward. 1966. *Componential Analysis of General Vocabulary: The semantic structure of a set of verbs in English, Hindi, and Japanese.* (= *Publications of the research center in anthropology, folklore, and linguistics*, 41.) Bloomington, Ind.: Indiana Univ.

Bloch, Bernard. 1941. "Phonemic Overlapping". *American Speech* 16.278–284. (Repr. in Joos 1957. 93–96.)

—. 1947. "English Verb Inflection". *Language* 23.399–418. (Repr. in Joos 1957.243–254.)

—. 1949. "Leonard Bloomfield". *Language* 25.87–98.

Bloomfield, Leonard. 1914. *Introduction to the Study of Language.* New York: Holt & Co. (New ed., with an introd. by Joseph F. Kess. Amsterdam & Philadelphia: Benjamins, 1983.)

—. 1917. *Tagalog Texts with Grammatical Analysis.* (= *University of Illinois studies in language and literature*, 3, No. 204.) Chicago: Univ. of Illinois.

—. 1912. Letter to Michelson. Hockett 1987.41.

—. 1923. *First German Book.* Columbus, Ohio: R. G. Adams & Co. (2nd ed. New York: The Century Co., 1928.)

—. 1926. "A Set of Postulates for the Science of Language". *Language* 2.153–164. (Repr. in Joos 1957.26–31.)

—. 1933. *Language.* New York: Holt, Rinehart & Winston.

—. 1938. "Eduard Prokosch, 1876–1938." *Language* 14.310–313.

—. 1942. *Outline Guide for the Practical Study of Foreigns Languages.* Special Publication of the Linguistic Society of America. Baltimore, Md.: Waverly.

—. 1943. "Franz Boas". *Language* 19.198.

—. 1945. 'On Describing Inflection". *Festschrift für M. Blakemore Evans* (=*Monatshefte für deutschen Unterricht* 37:4/5), 8–13.

Conklin, Harold. 1955. "Hanunoo Color Categories". *South Western Journalof Anthropology* 11.339–344.

Despres, Leon M. 1987. "My Recollections of Leonard Bloomfield". Hall 1987.3–13.

Ferguson, Charles. 1962. Review of Morris Halle, *The Sound Pattern of Russian* (The Hague: Mouton, 1959). *Language* 38.284–298.

Fought, John G. 1999. "Leonard Bloomfield's Linguistic Legacy: Later uses of some technical features". *Historiographia Linguistica* 26:3.313–332.

Goodenough, Ward. 1956. "Componential Analysis and the Study of Meaning". *Language* 32. 195–216.

Hall, Robert A. Jr. 1947. "Colloquial French Verb Inflection". *Romance Philology* 1.39–50.

—. 1948. *French.* (= *Language Monograph*, 24) Baltimore: Linguistic Society of America.

— (with the collaboration of Konrad Koerner), ed. 1987. *Leonard Bloomfield: Essays on his life and work.* Amsterdam & Philadelphia: Benjamins.

Harris, Zellig. 1942. "Morpheme Alternants in Linguistic Analysis". *Language* 18.169–180. (Repr. in Joos 1957.109–115.)

—. 1944. "Simultaneous Components in Phonology". *Language* 20.181–205. (Repr. in Joos 1957. 124–138.)

—. 1946. "From Morpheme to Utterance". *Language* 22.161–183.

—. 1948. "Componential Analysis of a Hebrew Paradigm". *Language* 24.87–91.

Haugen, Einar. 1958. "The Phonemics of Modern Icelandic". *Language* 34.55–88.

Hockett, Charles F. 1942. "A System of Descriptive Phonology". *Language* 18.3–21. (Repr. in Joos 1957.97–108.)

—. 1947. "Problems of Morphemic Analysis". *Language* 23.321–34. (Repr. in Joos 1957.229–242.)

—. 1954. "Two Models of Grammatical Description". *Word* 10.210–233. (Repr. in Joos 1957. 386–399.)

—, ed. 1970. *A Leonard Bloomfield Anthology.* Bloomington, Ind.: Indiana Univ. Press.

—. 1987. "Letters from Bloomfield to Michelson and Sapir". Hall 1987.39−60.

Joos, Martin, ed. 1957. *Readings in Linguistics.* Washington, D. C.: American Council of Learned Societies.

Lounsbury, Floyd. 1953. "The Method of Descriptive Morphology". *Oneida Verb Morphology.* Yale University Dissertation, pp. 11−24. (Page references to reprint in Joos 1957.379−385.)

—. 1956. "A Semantic Analysis of Pawnee Kinship Usage". *Language* 32.158−164.

—. 1964a. "A Formal Account of the Crow- and Omaha-type Kinship Terminologies". *Explorations in Cultural Anthropology* ed. by Ward Goodenough, New York: McGraw-Hill.

—. 1964b. "The Structural Analysis of Kinship Semantics". *Proceedings of the Ninth International Congress of Linguists, Cambridge Mass, 1962* ed. by Horace G. Lunt, 1073−1090. The Hague: Mouton.

Matthews, Peter. 1992. "Bloomfield's Morphology and Its Successors". *Transactions of the Philological Society* 90.121−186.

—. 1993. *Grammatical Theory in the United States from Bloomfield to Chomsky.* Cambridge: Cambridge Univ. Press.

Moulton, William G. 1970. "Leonard Bloomfield as a Germanist". Hockett 1970.512−523.

Nida, Eugene. 1948. "The Identification of Morphemes". *Language* 24.414−441. (Repr. in Joos 1957.255−271.)

Sapir, Edward. 1921. *Language.* New York: Harcourt, Brace & Co.

Sayers, Frances C. 1987. "The Small Mythologies of Leonard Bloomfield". Hall 1987.15−21.

Swadesh, Morris. 1934. "The Phonemic Principle". *Language* 10.117−129.

— & Carl Voegelin. 1939. "A Problem in Phonological Alternation". *Language* 15.1−10. (Repr. in Joos 1957.88−92.)

Trager, George L. 1944. "The Verb Morphology of Spoken French". *Language* 20.131−141.

—. 1955. "French Morphology: Verb inflection". *Language* 31.511−529.

— & Henry Lee Smith, Jr. 1963 [1951]. *Outline of English Structure.* (= *Studies in Linguistics Occasional Papers*, 3.) Washington, D. C.: American Council of Learned Societies.

Twaddell, W. Freeman. 1935. *On Defining the Phoneme.* (= *Language Monograph*, 16.) Baltimore: Linguistic Society of America.

Wallace, Anthony & John Atkins. 1960. "The Meaning of Kinship Terms". *American Anthropologist* 62.458−464.

Weinreich, Uriel. 1966. "Explorations in Semantic Theory". *Current Trends in Linguistics*, vol. III: *Theoretical foundations* ed. by Thomas A. Sebeok, 395−478. The Hague: Mouton.

Wells, Rulon. 1963. "Some Neglected Opportunities in Descriptive Linguistics". *Anthropological Linguistics* 5:1.38−49.

— & Jay Keyser. 1961. *The Common Feature Method.* (= *Technical Report*, 12.) New Haven, Ct.: Interaction Laboratory, Sociology Department, Yale Univ.

John G. Fought, Diamond Bar, Calif. (U.S.A.)

213. Tagmemics and the analysis of non-verbal behavior: Pike and his school

1. Introduction
2. The Tagmeme defined
3. The evolution of Tagmemics
4. A brief comparison of the representation of syntactic structure in Tagmemics and Generative Grammar
5. A brief contrast of comparative tagmemic reconstruction and the reconstruction of word order typology
6. Concluding observations: Contributions of Tagmemics to 20th century linguistics

1. Introduction

As a theory of language in general, and syntax in particular, tagmemics goes beyond language in recognizing that language is a part of human behavior, and must be viewed in that context. Tagmemics is based largely upon structuralist principles, but with some important exceptions. The fundamental linguistic unit in this approach is the tagmeme, which functions as a constituent of a construction called a syntagmeme. In the following, a comprehensive definition of the tagmeme as a linguistic unit within the theoretical framework of structuralism will be presented; crucial to this definition are the notions contrast, emic, etic, complementary distribution, free variation, constituent, construction, set, member of a set, and structural hierarchy (Section 2). Next, it shall be explained how, considering the state of linguistics from the late 1930s to the early 1950s, tagmemics may be viewed as a natural development in the evolution of the field, especially from the point of view of syntax. However, it shall also be pointed out how tagmemics, reflecting the thinking of Kenneth Lee Pike (1912–2000) and several of his contemporaries in those years, also differs significantly from what many of the leading structuralists of the time maintained concerning the study of language, particularly with respect to the treatment of meaning. Moreover, it shall be demonstrated how ideas which originated in the early years of the 20th century in the field of theoretical physics, had a profound effect on how linguistic units like the phoneme, morpheme, and tagmeme, came to be defined within tagmemics. Additionally, the mutually beneficial effect which the Summer Institute of Linguistics and tagmemics have had upon the growth and development of one another shall be touched upon, with respect to non-verbal as well as verbal behavior (Section 3). A brief characterization of tagmemics will follow, via a comparison of one aspect of it, the representation of syntactic structure, with a representation in an alternative synchronic approach to syntax, generative grammar (Section 4), and via a comparison of its goals in syntactic reconstruction with an alternative diachronic approach, the reconstruction of word order typology (Section 5). Finally, the main contributions of tagmemics to 20th-century linguistics shall be presented, considering its theoretical accomplishments as well as its practical applications, from synchronic and diachronic points of view (Section 6).

2. The Tagmeme defined

2.1. The Tagmeme as a linguistic unit of the syntactic level of structural hierarchy

A crucial criterion of a linguistic unit is that it must demonstrably contrast with other linguistic units on the same level of structure. Thus, as linguistic units on the level of syntax, tagmemes contrast with one another as phonemes contrast on the phonological level, and morphemes on the morphological level. Just as the contrastive nature of morphemes may be tested and demonstrated by substituting one candidate for another in an identical morphemic environment, and asking an informant whether the contents of the two resulting stretches are identical or not, so one may also test and demonstrate the contrastive property of tagmemes. For example, with respect to morphemes, the two morphs *red* and *green* may be demonstrated to be contrastive, and hence morphemes, by asking a native informant of English whether the stretches *stop at the* _____ *light*, containing first *red* and then *green* in the slot between *the* and *light*, are repetitions of one another with respect to lexical meaning. In like fashion, the two tagmas represented by the words *here* and *clever* may be demonstrated to be contrastive, and hence representing different tagmemes, by asking an informant whether the stretches *the student was* _____ #, containing first *here* and then *clever* in the slot between *was* and #, are repetitions of one another, with respect to syntactic functions. From a functional point of view, the two stretches are not synonymous, since the function of the tagmeme manifested by *here* is adverbial, and that of the tagmeme manifested by *clever*, adjectival. Such contrast is a characteristic of phonemic, morphemic, and tagmemic (or, stated more generally, emic) units.

A common property of a linguistic unit is that it exhibits (etic) variants which are distributed such that their relationship to one another is not that they are in contrast, but rather in either complementary distribution, or free variation. For example, in American English, on the phonological level, the linguistic unit called the phoneme k (written /k/) exhibits several phonetic (or, stated more generally, etic) variants, called allophones. Two of these, aspirate k (written [k']) and non-aspirate k (written [k⁼]) exist in a relationship of complementary distribution with respect to certain phonological environments: [k'] appears in word-initial position, whereas [k⁼] appears when following the sound s. On the other hand, in some varieties of American English, either [k'] or [k⁼] may occur word-finally when that word is followed by silence; their relationship in this environment is free variation. On the morphological level, the linguistic unit called the morpheme also exhibits etic variants, called allomorphs; e.g., in English, the suffix marking the past tense of regular verbs, most frequently written *-ed*, exhibits several variants. Two of these, /d/ and /t/, exist in a relationship of complementary distribution with respect to certain environments: /d/ occurs after roots which end in a voiced sound (except /d/), and /t/ occurs after roots which end in a voiceless sound (except /t/). In Classical Sanskrit, on the other hand, the allomorphs of the feminine dative singular, *-e* and *-ai*, are in free variation in certain declensions, e. g., root words in *i:* and root words in *u:*. On the syntactic level, the linguistic unit called the tagmeme also may exhibit several etic variants, called allotagmas. For example, the tagmeme having the function *adverbial* exhibits several manifesting variants, called allotagmas, including the adverb and the prepositional phrase. With respect to certain environments, these may exist in a relationship of complementary distribution: only an adverb, such as *well*, may occur in the adverbial slot in a sentence like *the book was _____ written*, whereas only a prepositional phrase may occur in the adverbial slot of a passive sentence like *the book was written _____*, when it is the passive counterpart of *the man wrote the book*. On the other hand, both an adverb and a prepositional phrase may occur in the adverbial slot in a sentence like *Willy wrote _____*, e. g. *Willy wrote well* and *Willy wrote with enthusiasm*; with respect to this and similar environments, the allotagmas exist in a relationship of free variation.

What the tagmeme and morpheme share as linguistic units, in contrast to the phoneme, is that each is a meaningful linguistic unit; put somewhat differently, each is a linguistic unit whose meaning is manifested by form. As is well known, the meaning conveyed by a morpheme may be classified according to the function of the morpheme within a lexical item or word, typically root, derivational affix, or inflectional affix. The meaning conveyed by a tagmeme, however, is the syntactic function of that unit as a constituent within a construction (i. e., a syntagmeme), and as was indicated above, it is important to bear in mind that a single syntactic function may be manifested in one or several ways. For example, noun phrases, infinitive phrases, or clauses may manifest the tagmeme whose syntactic function is 'subject' in the environment [clause _____ + PREDICATE]clause.

What the morpheme and the tagmeme also have in common, then, is that each may be thought of as a set of manifesting forms, where the criterion for set membership in a morpheme is that each form, or morph, manifest the same meaning on the morphological level, and the criterion for set membership in a tagmeme is that each form, or tagma, manifest the same syntactic function on the syntactic level. In morphemic notation, one may indicate a morpheme in a variety of ways, depending upon one's purpose: {cat} or {kæt} may indicate the morpheme *cat* (emphasizing form in a root morpheme), {NOUN PLURAL} may indicate the noun plural morpheme (emphasizing meaning in an inflectional morpheme), and the abstract symbol {-D} may indicate the past tense morpheme (emphasizing form in an inflectional morpheme). Typically, allomorphs are represented via phonemic notation, e. g., the phonologically conditioned allomorphs for the morpheme {-D} are /-t/, /-d/, and /-ɪd/. In tagmemic notation, on the other hand, one must always indicate function and form(s) of a tagmeme simultaneously, in order to give expression to the notion that neither exists independently of the other, e. g., Subject: Noun Phase/Infinitive Phrase/transitive clause, or, in more abbreviated notation, S: NP/Inf/trans.cl. The function is often referred to as the *slot*, and the manifesting form(s), the *filler(s)*. A single allotagma of a tagmeme is often indicated via the slot and just one filler, e. g., S: NP. Clearly, the efforts of scholars like Charles C. Fries, Leonard Bloomfield, Charles F. Hockett, Bernhard Bloch, George L. Trager, and Zellig S. Harris, to carry out linguistic investigation with little or no reference to meaning (→ Art. 212, for details), are not only rejected, but would be impossible, as tagmemics has been conceived.

2.2. The Tagmeme as a constituent of a construction

Every approach to syntax, whether analytic or generative, recognizes that syntax is characterized by a hierarchical structure: constituents make up a construction (called a 'phrase' in some frameworks), which in turn, together with other constructions at the same level, join together and function as constituents of a construction at the next higher level, and so on. As stated above, in tagmemics, the constituents are called *tagmemes*, and the constructions are called *syntagmemes*. To illustrate the hierarchical structure of syntax from a tagmemic point of view, let us consider the following tagmemes (where not all possible fillers are represented):

(1) Determiner slot: definite article/indefinite article (Det: def. art/indef. art.)
(2) Noun Modifier slot: adjective (NM: adj)
(3) Head of a Noun Phrase slot: noun (NPH: n)
(4) Auxiliary Verb slot: auxiliary verb (Aux: aux)
(5) Head of a Verb Phrase slot: verb (VPH: v)
(6) Clause slot: transitive clause (Clause: trans. cl.)

The tagmemes in (1), (2), and (3) may function as the constituents of a construction called a noun phrase: NP [± Det: def. art/ indef. art. ± NM: adj + NPH: n], where "±" indicates that the following tagmeme is optional, and "+" indicates that the following tagmeme is obligatory. The tagmemes in (4) and (5) may function as the constituents of a construction called a verb phrase: VP [± Aux: aux + VPH: v]. The tagmeme in (6) may function as the constituent or one of the constituents of a construction, i.e., a sentence (Sent). Now noun phrases may manifest the syntactic function *subject* (S) as well as *direct object* (O) (and other syntactic functions as well), and verb phrases may manifest the syntactic function *predicate* (Pred); these tagmemes in turn join together as constituents of the constructions at the next higher level, the (transitive) clause. Such a construction, either alone, or together with other such constructions, may function as a constituent or constituents of a construction at the next higher level, the simple, compound, or complex sentence. Thus, the hierarchical structure of the sentence

(7) The advanced student was writing an essay.

may be represented as

(8) Sent [+ Clause: trans cl. [+ S: NP [+ Det: def. art. + NM: adj + NPH: n] + Pred: VP [+ Aux: aux + VPH: v] + O: NP [+ Det: indef. art. + NPH: n]]]

3. The evolution of Tagmemics

3.1. The linguistic setting

As Pike (1976: 94) himself has written, "I date the start of tagmemics, as a general theory, to the period from February 1948 to June 1949." In order better to understand the development of tagmemics, one should be aware of ideas which were prevalent in the linguistic climate of the 1930s and 1940s (and some extent, characteristic of the 1920s and the early 1950s in the United States). Perhaps most fundamental of all at that time was the idea that in order best to understand language one should examine spoken as opposed to written samples of it. This was definitely reflected in *The Structure of English*, published by Charles C. Fries (1887–1967) in 1952, which was a grammar of English based upon a corpus consisting of 50 hours of telephone conversations involving some 300 inhabitants of Ann Arbor, Michigan, amounting to over 250,000 running words, collected between 1946 and 1948 (cf. Fries 1952: viii, 3–5, 7–8).

Another fundamental view of this period was that language was to be investigated by analysis; one need think only of the discussion of phonology, morphology, and syntax in Bloomfield's *Language* (1933), as well as the very title of the influential work of Bloch & Trager, *Outline of Linguistic Analysis* (1942). It was not until the second half of the 1950s that an old claim of Humboldt's, namely that language exhibits an infinite number of outputs from a finite number of rules, once again became audible (albeit without specific reference to Humboldt until several years later):

"We define a *language* to be a set (in general, infinite) of strings in a finite alphabet, each string being of finite length. We define a *grammar* of the language L as a finite device which generates all and only the strings of L in a determinate way." (Chomsky 1975 [1956]: 71)

Those giving priority to this view would come to argue for generative rather than analytic grammars.

Yet another view harking back to earlier decades, but clearly characterizing the 1940s in the United States, was the notion that one could and should carry out linguistic investigation without recourse to meaning. Thus, as early as 1925, in an article entitled "The Periphrastic Future with *shall* and *will* in Modern English", in attempting to carry out an investigation which would be as objective as possible, Fries studied the distribution of these auxiliaries "without imposing upon the words any specific meanings or rules as a basis for interpretation". His strategy would be essentially the same in his *The Structure of English*, published over twenty-five years later. And in 1933, Bloomfield wrote (p. 75), "The study of language can be conducted without special assumptions only so long as we pay no attention to the meaning of what is spoken."

Equally dogmatic were Bloch & Trager, who wrote (1942: 68),

"... all our classifications must be based exclusively on FORM — on differences and similarities in the phonemic structure of bases and affixes, or on the occurrence of words in particular type phrases and sentences. In making our classifications there must be no appeal to meaning, to abstract logic, or to philosophy."

Of the same period, Joseph Greenberg (1994: 21) later wrote:

"A major intellectual influence on me at the time [1941–1942] was that of logical positivism, then in its heyday [...] Structural linguistics and the logical positivist approach did indeed seem to be solidary. Parallel to the positivist attempt to do without mind was the attempt to do without meaning in linguistics. American structuralism at this time was basically a method of segmenting speech, isolating its fundamental units at various levels without, at least theoretically, any recourse to the imprecise concept of meaning."

Nevertheless, after presenting an Immediate Constituent analysis in syntax and morphology in his *Language*, Bloomfield (1933: 161) also wrote, "Only in this way will a proper analysis (that is, one which takes account of the meanings) lead to the ultimately constituent morphemes".

And even Bloch & Trager (1942: 53) had to concede that

"Some considerations of meaning must enter, it is true, even into phonemics; thus we know that [p'] and [p⁼] belong to the same phoneme [in English] because [rɪp'] means the same as [rɪp⁼], whereas [p'] and [b] belong to different phonemes because the meanings of [rɪp'] and [rɪb] are different."

Thus to say that structuralists believed that one could totally dispense with meaning is inaccurate; nevertheless numerous younger linguists of the period, like Greenberg and Pike, found even the structuralists' concessions to meaning too confining, particularly with respect to syntax, and while the younger generation never went quite so far as Jespersen (1931: 291), who stated flatly, "in syntax meaning is everything", they certainly insisted that meaning was inextricably bound to form, and vice versa, and that an attempt to investigate one without the other was bound to fail.

Yet another characteristic of the period was the insistence upon the step-by-step application of procedures, first to the phonology, then to morphology, each one carried out with virtually no reference to the other. A mere five years after the appearance of Bloch & Trager's book, Harris published his *Methods in Structural Linguistics* (1951), the purpose of which was, according to reviewer Paul L. Garvin (1919–1994), "to organize the whole field of descriptive linguistics into a single body of theory and practice, presenting a unitary approach to linguistic analysis." As Harris (1909–1992) himself wrote,

"The whole schedule of *procedures* outlined in the following chapters, which is designed to begin with the raw data of speech, and end with a statement of grammatical structure, is essentially a twice-made *application* of two major *steps*: the setting up of elements, and the statement of the distribution of these elements relative to each other. First, the distinct phonological elements are determined [...] and the relation among them investigated [...]. Then the distinct morphologic elements are determined [...] and the relations among them investigated [...]". (1951: 60; italics added: JRC)

Indeed, the division of the two steps had been drawn even more explicitly by Hockett (1942: 20–21), who in his article "A System of Descriptive Phonology" wrote, "No grammatical fact of any kind is used in making phonological analysis [...] There must be no circularity; phonological analysis is assumed for grammatical analysis, and so must not assume any part of the latter. The line of demarcation between the two must be sharp."

While the preceding is, of course, far from an exhaustive description of the notions prevailing roughly from 1933–1955, it does nevertheless characterize the dominant thinking of the period. This is important, since the significance of the development of tagmemics would fade considerably if not viewed in light of this background. Aside from the structuralists' views on the use of meaning in linguistic analysis, their seeming preoccupation with methods, procedures, and steps was strongly suggestive to some young scholars of the time that with the application of additional effort and rigor, one might well come upon mechanical discovery procedures of grammatical analysis, merely waiting to be introduced to the rest of the linguistic community with a joyful *heureka*!

Yet a number of young linguistis of this period were having serious problems with the prevailing thinking of established scholars, especially when their attempts to achieve what appeared to be reasonable goals turned out to be unsuccessful. This is evident when we look not only at some of their publications in the 1940s, but also at descriptions of those years as they have contemplated the period more recently, with the hindsight of several decades. For example, in 1976, Pike recalled that "In 1942 I had attempted a mechanical discovery procedure for studying allophonic distribution, and had given it up" (cf. Pike 1976: 95–96). In addition, the constraints requiring that analysis in phonology and morphology be carried out separately became problematic for young scholars like Kenneth Pike. In 1947, he published an article, "Grammatical Prerequisites to Phonemic Analysis", where he wrote (1947: 155):

> To eliminate the fact of grammatical relationship and structure from the analysis and presentation of phonological structure is frequently undesirable because many of the phonological facts are inextricably interwoven with grammatical facts and structural relationships; avoiding the portrayal of this relationship means omitting completely or at least temporarily, an important part of the total structure of the language."

Not surprisingly, the article was rejected for publication in *Language* by Bernhard Bloch; André Martinet and Morris Swadesh thought otherwise, and published the article in *Word*. Nor was Pike alone; while definitely not the first to express his misgivings in print, Greenberg was early on clearly uncomfortable with the strict procedures and constraints advocated by Bloch, Trager, Hockett, and their associates, and around the beginning of the 1950s was beginning to argue against them in his classes. As Greenberg later wrote (cf. Greenberg 1994: 23), in the summer of 1953, he "had most clearly strayed far from the orthodox American structuralism in asserting that semantics belonged fully within linguistics. It was not adequate to merely use *difference* of meaning to discover significant contrasts" (italics added: JRC).

To be sure, immediate constituent analysis had already been discussed by Bloomfield in 1933 in his *Language*, but there the method was applied mainly in the context of morphology, and rather thinly, at that. In 1947, however, Rulon Wells (b. 1919) had published his "Immediate Constituents", dedicated primarily to syntax, and thus it is not surprising that Pike, who, as mentioned above, had already attempted to formulate a mechanical discovery procedure for studying allophonic distribution, but who began to devote himself to grammar in 1948, would attempt to establish a mechanical discovery procedure for determining immediate constituents in the same year. As Pike later wrote, however, the attempt failed. The positive outcome of this became apparent in 1949, when Pike began to look at syntax "in a new and different way". In 1974 he wrote (p. 95):

> "I focused on a slightly different question: Would it be possible to find a useful bit of grammar which could be treated in a fashion analogous to the phoneme? If so, would it have descriptive properties related to the phoneme? […] I called this not-yet-discovered unit a 'grameme' (later changed to 'tagmeme' […])."

Pike (1967: 5) viewed this 'search' for a linguistic unit of grammar, actually syntax, as analogous to that of the phoneme:

> "I reasoned that as the phoneme was reflected in practical orthographic work for millenia before being 'found' by scientists […] so some unit of grammar might be present in the work and thought of practical language teachers which was not adequately reflected in current theory of linguistic structure."

Thus a sea change had occurred in Pike's investigations. Instead of searching for mechanical discovery procedures, the task was to be that

> "one searched rather for the relation of the element to something higher in the grammatical hierarchy. This required that hierarchy be an explicit component of theory, and that one not attempt to analyze any unit strictly in terms of its internal structure, but rather that one must also look at a unit's relation to its including structures (i.e. its larger structural environment)." (Pike 1974: 96)

Thus, within the context of linguistics, tagmemics is at least in part a reaction to the excesses of structuralism. The extent to which it otherwise has made it possible to achieve advances in linguistics, realized or potential, can be touched upon only most briefly below.

3.2. The extralinguistic setting

The two most significant extralinguistic influences on the development of tagmemics come ultimately from the field of physics. The first, the so-called unified theory, when viewed as an intellectual goal, has had a profound effect on tagmemics. The second, the simultaneous viewing of light as wave, particle, and field, has, in a general sense, enabled tagmemics to unify several seemingly disparate phenomena; taken in its specifics, however, it has proven to be problematic, as has been recognized by Pike and others.

3.2.1. The unified theory

The influence which movements, theories, and discoveries in fields like literature, philosophy, and especially the natural sciences, have had on linguistics for well over a century has been profound, and the number of such instances is quite high. Early in the 19th century it was Romanticism, with its quest for origins, that influenced the directions that historical linguistics was to take. One may also recall the distortion that marred the achievements of Schleicher, otherwise outstanding in the context of the state of knowledge in the second half of the 19th century, because of the significance that he, enamored of Hegel's theory of the dialectic, saw in groups of three (cf. Pedersen 1931: 271; Costello 1995: 9–10). More recently, the impetus that carbon-14 dating had on lexicostatistics in general, and glottochronology in particular, comes to mind. Additional examples abound. Thus it is not surprising that momentous developments in theoretical physics in the first half of the 20th century should have had an effect on the thinking of at least a few linguists. Broadly considered, theoretical physics, at least with respect to its views on relativity and light, has had a noticeable impact on the development of tagmemics, and other areas in which Pike was worked, as well (see section 3.2.2. below.)

What is often overlooked by commentators on the theory of relativity is that it was Henri Poincaré (1854–1912), and not Albert Einstein (1879–1955), who first formulated the principle of relativity. In particular, in an address presented in St. Louis at the International Congress of Arts and Science on 24 September 1904, Poincaré stated that in view of the results of certain experiments conducted in the last quarter of the 19th century, new laws of dynamics had to be recognized, incorporating the knowledge that the highest velocity is that of light. Building upon this, in 1905, Einstein published a paper entitled "Zur Elektrodynamik bewegter Körper [The electrodynamics of moving bodies]", in which he presented a *special* theory of relativity, i. e., the relativity of time. As is well known, the implications of the theory of relativity for 20th-century physics, and other fields as well, cannot be overemphasized. In 1915 came the announcement that Einstein had worked out a general theory of relativity, based upon his special theory. The goal of the general theory was to account for all of the laws of physics by means of equations that had mathematically identical forms. However, the general theory and its equations did not cover electromagnetism. This led Einstein to attempt to construct a unified theory, one which would account for the forces of electromagnetism as well as gravity. Although Einstein did not achieve this goal, what is significant for the history of intellectual development is the concept of the unified theory itself, and the desire to complete it; see the *International Encyclopedia of Unified Science* founded in 1938, edited by Otto Neurath (1882–1945), Rudolf Carnap (1891–1970), and others.

Turning to linguistics as a social science, parallels with modern physics may be viewed only with the most general references. It is important to stress that in no sense here does this mean that the philosophical or physical notions of space and time that have been reinterpreted by the theory of relativity have been incorporated into, and altered, linguistics, from a tagmemic point of view. Rather the goal of achieving a unified theory to account for all physical phenomena inspired the wish on the part of social scientists to construct a unified theory to account not only for the structure of language, but for the structure of human behavior, of which language is only a part. This, in fact, was the inspiration of Pike's 1967 publication (first edition, 1954–1960), *Language in Relation to a Unified Theory of the Structure of Human Behavior.* As interpreted by Algeo (1974: 2),

"Pike's aim in the study of behavior is analogous to Einstein's in physics. His linguistic theory is not specifically a theory of language, but is rather a special case of a general, unified theory that accounts for all cultural behavior, of which language is itself a special case [...] Pike's concern is to affirm that language cannot be adequately investigated apart from the rest of human behavior."

In general, what the theory proposes is to recognize (1) the hierarchical structure of behavior; (2) the inextricable combination of function with behavior; and (3) behavior which is significantly different from other behavior ('emic'), and behavior which is not ('etic'). For this purpose, a unit of behavior, called 'behavioreme', is posited. Athough further discussion of these intriguing notions goes beyond the scope of this paper, it may be stated that the explicit demand for the incorporation of meaning in its specific as well as in its most general senses (including function) into the study of language, and the extension of what was originally a linguistic theory to all of human behavior, are perhaps the most revolutionary aspects of tagmemics when viewed within the context of the time in which it was conceived.

3.2.2. The phenomenon of light viewed as wave, particle, and field

As is well known, in 1900, Max Planck (1858–1947) stated that light was radiated via *particles* of quanta, i. e., packets of energy (which later came to be known as photons). This was in contrast to an earlier model, which viewed light as a *wave*. According to yet another model, one may also view light as having electric and magnetic *fields*. Disparate though these models may be, the results of some experiments indicate that light behaves like a wave, of other experiments, that light behaves like particles, and of yet other experiments, like electrical and magnetic fields. Thus to accept one of these sets of experimental results to the exclusion of the other two is to exclude vital components of a complete picture. In like fashion, linguists dealing with linguistic units like phonemes and morphemes soon realized that these units could be viewed in more than one way, and that although these views were disparate, choosing one to the exclusion of the others was to introduce distortion. To use the phoneme as an example, linguists recognized immediately that typically, a phoneme was uniquely manifested by one or more phonologically conditioned variants (i.e., allophones) that co-existed in one of two relationships, complementary distribution, or free variation. At the same time, linguists maintained that each phoneme was distinguishable from every other phoneme by a unique combination of distinctive features. Furthermore, each phoneme was distinct from every other phoneme within a system of oppositions. Contrary to other areas of linguistic investigation, e.g., comparative phonological reconstruction, where the phoneme as a set of allophones (and their environments) is all important, or generative phonology, where the phoneme as a set of distinctive features is of primary concern, tagmemics recognizes each of the above-mentioned ways of viewing the phoneme as being of equal importance and validity. Moreover, in tagmemic theory, these observations about the phoneme hold true, mutatis mutandis, for the morpheme, tagmeme, and syntagmeme as well, as linguistic units.

Having been influenced, albeit indirectly, by 20th-century physics, Pike attempted to generalize the notions wave, particle, and field to the extent that they would cover linguistic units as well. Roughly, the term 'wave' was used in connection with allo-units (allophones, allomorphs, etc.): when viewed as an allo-unit modified by allo-units around it, with overlapping and the blurring of unit boundaries, a linguistic unit appears to be (part of) a wave. The term particle was used in connection with distinctive features: when viewed as a bundle of distinctive features, a linguistic unit appears to be a particle. The term 'field' was used in connection with systematic oppositions: when viewed as one of many units opposed to one another, a linguistic unit appears to be placed in a field. However, as Pike (1974: 45) himself noted,

"The metaphor [of the perspective of wave, particle, and field] has been troublesome. To a theoretical physicist and mathematician such as Ivan Lowe, for example, the metaphor of field seems displaced. He and Peter Fries have urged me to define the terms 'wave', 'field', and 'particle' in reference to other terms, so that the metaphor could be in principle dropped."

Alternatively then, within tagmemics, it is maintained that a linguistic unit may be viewed according to the three traits that characterize all linguistic units: manifestations (allo-units), distinctive features, and distribution. These concepts are related, but not identical, to the concepts wave, particle, and field, respectively. However, like the latter three terms, the former reaffirm that each of these ways of viewing linguistic units is of equal importance and validity.

3.3. The Summer Institute of Linguistics and the development of Tagmemics

Although the Summer Institute of Linguistics came into existence some fifteen years before Pike was to begin refining his views on syntax which led to tagmemics, the influence of tagmemics on the work of the Institute was to prove to be immense; likewise, the work of the Institute was to have a profound effect on the development of tagmemics, particularly with respect to its applications. This is not surprising, since many of the linguists working within the theoretical framework of tagmemics are or were also members of the Institute, among them, in addition to Pike himself, David H. Bendor-Samuel, John T. Bendor-Samuel, Ruth M. Brend, Desmond Derbyshire, Benjamin F. Elson, Joseph E. Grimes, Sarah C. Gudschinsky, Robert E. Longacre, William R. Merrifield, Velma B. Pickett, Eunice V. Pike, Evelyn G. Pike, Frank E. Robbins, Viola G. Waterhouse, and Mary Ruth Wise.

3.3.1. The Summer Institute of Linguistics

The Summer Institute of Linguistics (SIL) had its beginnings in a tiny school called Camp Wycliffe, founded in 1934 in Sulphur Springs, Arkansas, by Leonard L. Legters (1873–1940) and W. Cameron Townsend (1896–1982). Earlier in his life, Legters had been a missionary to the Comanches when he became convinced of the need for missionaries to be able to communicate in the language of the people with whom they were working. (Unfortunately he himself was never to be able to realize this goal, because the prevailing view during the time that he was a missionary was that the Comanches and other Native Americans would be better off if they were compelled to learn English.) Townsend was of the same mind as Legters, and in fact, he had already translated the New Testament into the language of a group with whom he had worked, the Cakchiquel-speaking people of Guatemala. Thus the curriculum of the new school aimed to prepare students for Bible translation, and included lectures on an American Indian language, Cakchiquel (by Townsend), anthropology, ethnology, general missionary principles (by Legters), and phonetics (by Dr. Elbert L. McCreery); it had two students. In 1935, the school became the Summer Institute of Linguistics (the name and concept of which had already existed in the mind of Townsend before the opening of Camp Wycliffe), with Townsend as the director of the school as well as of its sister organization, Wycliffe Bible Translators (WBT). In that year the school's enrollment increased to five students, one of whom was Kenneth Pike. After the courses were completed, Townsend, accompanied by his wife and four of the students, travelled to Mexico in order to carry out linguistic fieldwork leading to Bible translation. Their arrival at Mexico City, several weeks later, coincided with the Seventh Inter-American Scientific Congress, and it was there that the Mexican counterpart of the SIL, the *Instituto Lingüistico de Verano*, was born (Wallis & Bennett 1978: 64). As Brend (1987: 35) stated, the SIL-WBT "have the main goal of training students in linguistics in order to prepare them for learning, analyzing, and reducing to writing the unwritten languages of the world, and providing for those languages a literature, including the New Testament."

In the summer of 1936, Townsend asked Pike to teach the course in phonetics. One of the sixteen students that year was Eugene A. Nida (b. 1914). By the summer of 1937, Pike was teaching phonetics, and Nida, grammar. By the summer of 1942, the SIL was located at the University of Oklahoma in Norman, with over 120 students; since that time, it has greatly expanded, and has been meeting in numerous locations around the world. (Thus as the SIL grew, the two founders turned over the teaching responsibilities to others whom they recognized as more qualified than they were. Legters then expanded his activities as a fund-raiser and lecturer at Christian conferences, and Townsend continued as an administrator, fund-raiser, and perhaps most importantly as an ambassador between the SIL-WBT and the governments of countries in which the sister organizations were active.)

3.3.2. The development of Tagmemics

Below is a summary of some of the earliest publications in tagmemics, after which will follow brief mention of those areas, linguistic and non-linguistic, in which tagmemics has been applied, along with one or more publications for each area. (The basis for this section was Viola G. Waterhouse's 1974 *The History and Development of Tagmemics*, to which other items were added.)

The first publication to present tagmemics to the linguistic community was Part 1 of Pike's *Language in Relation to a Unified Theory of the Structure of Human Behavior*, which appeared in 1954; Part 2 and 3 appeared in 1955 and 1960, respectively, and the second revised edition of this work appeared in 1967.

The first publication presenting tagmemic analyses of linguistic data was the July 1957 issue of the *International Journal of American Linguistics*, devoted to the analysis of several Amerind languages. The first of many tagmemic grammars of languages appeared in 1958: *The Grammatical Structure of Oaxaca Chontal* by Waterhouse, and Peeke's "Structural Summary of Zaparo" (published in 1962); like most other grammars in a tagmemic framework, especially those prepared by members of the SIL, these dealt with Amerindian languages which had heretofore been studied very little, if at all. The first textbooks introducing tagmemics to students were Pickett's *An Introduction to the Study of Grammatical Structures* (1956) and Elson's *Beginning Morphology-Syntax* (1958); these were followed by Elson & Pickett's *Beginning Morphology-Syntax* (1960), *Laboratory Manual for Morphology and Syntax* (1962) by Merrifield et al., Cook's *Introduction to Tagmemic Analysis* (1969), and still others in the 1970s and 1980s. The first conference devoted to tagmemics was the Georgetown University Round Table in 1967.

Numerous scholars aside from Kenneth and Evelyn Pike have contributed to the refinement of tagmemic theory, among them Longacre with this articles "String Constituent Analysis" (1960), and "Some Fundamental Insights of Tagmemics" (1965), his book *Grammar Discovery Procedures* (1964), and Peter Fries with his article, "On Surface and Underlying Structure, with Special Reference to Phrase, Clause, and Sentence" (1976).

From 1958 onward, very many languages in diverse language families around the world have been investigated within a tagmemic framework; to mention just a few:

1) Afro-Asiatic, with Longacre's "From Tagma to Tagmeme in Biblical Hebrew" (1961), and Kraft's *A Study of Hausa Syntax* (1963);
2) Austro-Asiatic, with Watson's "Personal Pronouns in Pacoh [Vietnam]" (1964);
3) Carib, with Derbyshire's "Hixkaryana Syntax Structure. 1: Word; 2: Phrase, Sentence" (1961);
4) Dravidian, with Zvelebil's *Tamil in 500 A. D.: An interpretation of early inscriptional Tamil* (1964);
5) Indo-European, with representation in the Italic and Germanic branches:
    a. Italic (Romance), with Blansitt's dissertation "The Verb Phrase in Spanish: Classes and Relations" (1963), Brend's *A Tagmemic Analysis of Mexican Spanish Clauses* (1964), Conway's dissertation, "Order Classes of Adjectives in Spanish" (1964), and Roulet's *Syntaxe de la preposition nucléaire du français parlé: étude tagmémique et transformationelle* (1969);
    b. Germanic, with Pike's "Non-Linear Order and Anti-Redundancy in German Morphological Matrices" (1965), Crymes' *Some Systems of Substitution Correlation in Modern English* (1968), Francis' *The English Language: An introduction* (1965), Becker's "Conjoining in a Tagmemic Grammar of English" (1967), Lowe's "An Algebraic Theory of English Pronominal Reference" (1969), and Glissmeyer's dissertation, "A Tagmemic Analysis of Hawaii English Clauses" (1970).
6) Malayo-Polynesian, with Soenjono's dissertation, "Indonesian Syntax" (1967);
7) Mundari, with Cook's dissertation "A Descriptive Analysis of Mundari" (1965);
8) Waorani (still genetically unclassified) with Wilkendorf's "Waorani Clause Formulas [Ecuador]" (1989).

From the earliest days, tagmemic theory has been applied to many areas of linguistic investigation, including

1) bilingualism, with Costello's "Innovations Increasing Syntactic Complexity in the Native Language of Bilingual children from 5–10" (1989);
2) computational linguistics, with Cook's "Computer Assisted Tagmemics" (1986);
3) contrastive grammar, with Flores' dissertation "A Contrastive Analysis of Selected Clause Types in Cebuano and English [Philippines]" (1962), Liem's *A Contrastive Analysis of English and Vietnamese* (1967), Platt's dissertation, "A Comparative Study of German and English Syntax" (1970), and Fichtner's *English and German Syntax* (1979);
4) dialectology, with Brannen's dissertation "The Dialect of Oomisimi [Japanese] in Three Generations: A tagmemic approach" (1966);
5) discourse analysis, with Pike's "Discourse Structure and Tagmeme Matrices" (1964), Grimes' "Some Intersentence Relationships in Huichol" (1966), Longacre's "Narrative Versus Other Discourse Genre" (1972), Ross' "Chronological and Logical Discourse Chains" (1989), Evelyn G. Pike's "Trees for Constituent Analysis from Discourse to Morpheme" (1989), and Wilt's "Prominence of Waves of Space and Time" (1989);
6) ethnolinguistics, with Franklin's "Kewa Ethnolinguistic Concepts of Body Parts" (1963);
7) language learning, with Gudschinsky's *How to Learn an Unwritten Language* (1967) and Eunice Pike's "Language Learning in Relation to Focus" (1969);
8) language teaching, with Belasco's *Manual and Anthology of Applied Linguistics for Use in NDEA Foreign Language Institutes* (1960);
9) linguistic reconstruction, with Pike's *Axioms and Procedures for Reconstruction in Comparative Linguistics* (1957), Pike & Becker's "Progressive Neutralization in Dimensions of Navaho Stem Matrices" (1964), Costello's "The Absolute Construction in Indo-European: A syntagmemic reconstruction" (1982), Costello's *Syntactic Change and Syntactic Reconstruction: A tagmemic approach* (1983), and other works by the same author (Costello 1984, 1986, 1987a, 1993), and Longacre's "A Feature of Proto-Otomanguean Discourse Structure?" (1986);

10) morphology, with Pride's "Numerals in Chatino" (1961), Lipka's "Grammatical Categories, Lexical Items, and Word Formation" (1971), and Holman's "Waorani Verb Affixes" (1989);
11) philology, with Belasco's "The Role of Transformational Grammar and Tagmemics in the Analysis of an Old French Text" (1961), and Reskiewicz's *A Study in Major Syntax* (1962);
12) phonotagmemics, with Crawford's *Totontepec Mixe Phonotagmemics* (1963);
13) pidgins, with Nagara's dissertation "A Bilingual Description of Some Linguistic Features of Pidgin English Used by Japanese Immigrants on the Plantations of Hawaii" (1969);
14) semantics, with Hale's "On the Systematization of Box 4" (1974), Du Bois, Upton, & Pike's "Constraints on Complexity Seen via Fused Vectors of an N-dimensional Semantic Space" (1980), and P. Fries & Pike's "Slot and Referential Hierarchy in Relation to Charles C. Fries' View of Language" (1985);
15) sign language, with Kakumasus's "Urubu [Brazil] Sign Language" (1968);
16) text analysis, with Ellis' "Tagmemic Analysis of a Restricted Cree Text" (1960), Loos' "Capanahu Narrative Structure" (1963), and Pike's & Pike's *Text and Tagmeme* (1983);

and, last but not least,

17) translation theory, with Deibler's "Sememics and Translation" (1969).

Practitioners of tagmemics have always been interested in exploring their theory with respect to other theories in linguistics, and this has led to viewing tagmemics in light of

1) Case Grammar, with J. T. Platt's *Grammatical Form and Grammatical Meaning: A tagmemic view of Fillmore's deep structure case concepts* (1970);
2) Generative Grammar, with Belasco's "Tagmemics and Transformational Grammar in Linguistic Analysis" (1964), Cook's *On Tagmemes and Transforms* (1964), Liem's *English Grammar: A combined tagmemic and transformational approach* (1966), Becker's dissertation "A Generative Description of the English Subject Tagmeme" (1967), and Hale's "The Relationship of Tagmemic Theory to Rules, Derivation, and Transformational Grammar" (1972);
3) Stratificational Grammar, with Biondi's "A Comparative Study of Tagmemic and Stratificational Grammars" (1965), and
4) Universal Grammar, with Blansitt's "Sentence and Clause in Universal Grammar" (1970).

The attention that tagmemic theory has attracted to itself − in this regard, possibly unmatched by any other school of linguistics originating in the latter half of the 20th century − has led to an amazing array of applications in fields not usually associated with theoretical linguistics, among them

1) folklore, with Dundes' "From Etic to Emic Units in the Structural Study of Folktales" (1962), and "Structural Typology in North American Indian Folktales" (1963), and Scott's *A Linguistic Study of Persian and Arabic Riddles: A language centered approach to genre definition* (1965);
2) matrix theory, with Pike's "Dimensions of Grammatical Constructions" (1962), and "Theoretical Permutations of Matrix Formation in Fore [New Guinea]" (1963), and Young & Young's "The Three Dimensional Classification System of Bena-Bena Nouns" (1965);
3) poetry, with Pike's "Language: Where science and poetry meet" (1965);
4) psychotherapy, with Scheflen's "Stream and Structure of Communication Behavior: Content analysis of a psychotherapy session" (1965);
5) reading, with Gudschinsky's "The Relationship of Language and Linguistics to Reading" (1968);
6) rhetoric and composition, with Becker's "Item and Field: A way into complexity" (1964), Young & Becker's "The Role of Lexical and Grammatical Cues in Paragraph Recognition" (1964), English's "Linguistic Theory as an Aid to Invention" (1964), and Pike's "A Linguistic Contribution to the Teaching of Composition" (1964);
7) social structure, with Bock's dissertation *The Social Structures of a Canadian Indian Reserve* (1962), Pike's "The Hierarchical and Social Matrix of Suprasegmentals" (1963), and Bock's "Social Structure and Language Structure" (1964), and
8) stylistics, with Koch's "On the Principles of Stylistics" (1963), Howes' "A Linguistic Analogy in Literary Criticism" (1964), and Holz' "Field Theory and Literature" (1967).

4. A brief comparison of the representation of syntactic structure in Tagmemics and Generative Grammar

One of the most important tasks in syntax is to represent accurately the relationships which exist among constituents of a construction, and among constructions which function as constituents of larger constructions. In tagmemics, such relationships must always be explicitly expressed, since the theory states that function and form are inextricably linked. As early as 1964, however, this aspect of tagmemics was misunderstood by generative grammarians, and the charge was made that "tagmemic characterization thus seems to miss the relational aspect of grammatical features [i.e., functions: JRC] like 'subject', 'object', 'predicate', and confuses them with constituents" (Postal 1964: 37—38). One year later, the same misunderstanding led to a similar charge, and although no specific reference to tagmemics was made, it is fairly clear that tagmemic analysis was the object of the criticism, since there was no other approach to syntax at that time against which this criticism could have been aimed:

(9) This approach is mistaken in two ways. For one thing, it confuses categorial [e.g., NP: JRC] and functional [e.g., Subject-of: JRC] notions by assigning status to both, and thus fails to express the relational character of the functional notions (Chomsky 1965: 69).

However, tagmemic notation itself, e.g., S: NP, O: NP, Pred: VP, clearly shows that 'grammatical features' or 'functional notions' are always distinguished from 'constituents' or 'categorial notions'; hence both of the above criticism are invalid.

The second criticism against tagmemics by generativists was also based on a misunderstanding; this is clear when one examines the version of a tree diagram wrongly attributed to tagmemics, presented along with the criticism. It was maintained that the diagram in Fig. 213.1.

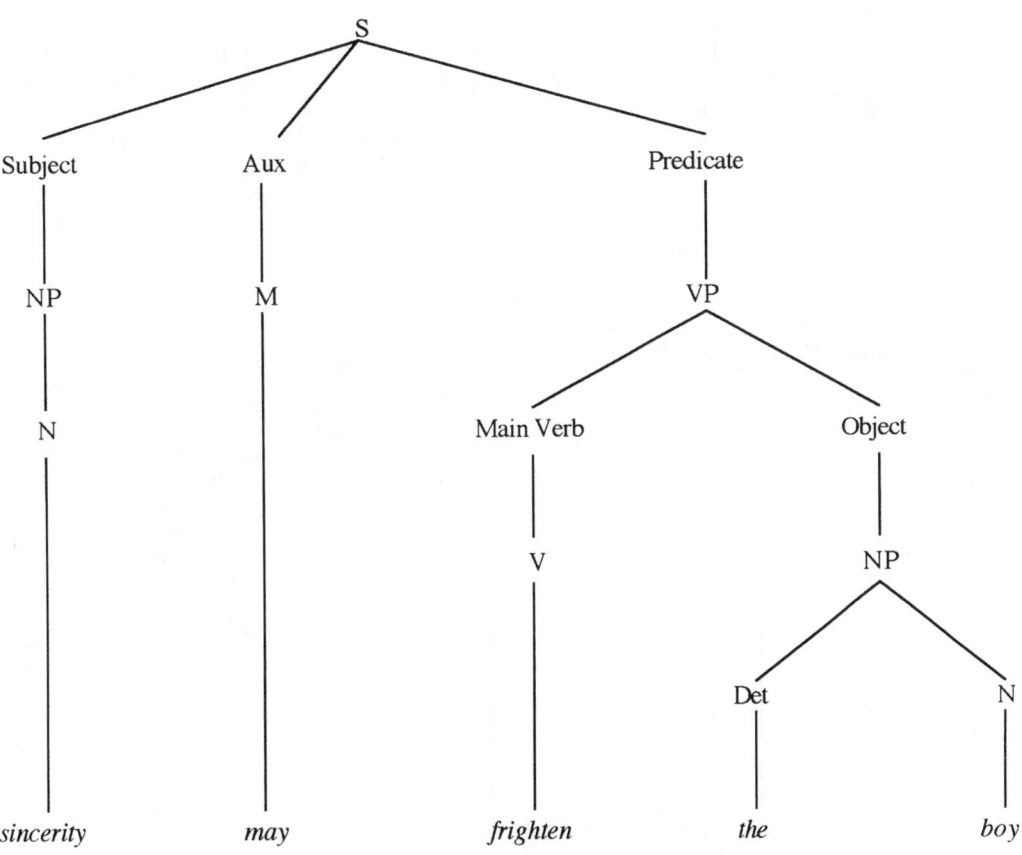

Fig. 213.1

and the grammar (i.e., Phrase Structure Rules) upon which it was supposed to be based, expressed redundancy: syntactic relationships or functions, such as subject, predicate, and direct object, were expressed via labels in the diagram as well as via the configurations in the three diagram itself. It was furthermore maintained that

(10) It is necessary only to make explicit the relational character of these notions by defining 'Subject-of', for English, as the relation holding between the NP of a sentence of the form NP + Aux + VP and the whole sentence, 'Object-of' as the relation between the NP of a VP of the form V + NP and the whole VP, etc. More generally, we can regard any rewriting rule as defining a set of grammatical functions, in this way, only some of which (namely, those that involve the 'higher-level', more abstract grammatical categories) have been provided, traditionally, with explicit names (Chomsky 1965: 69).

This ideal of generative grammar is illustrated via the diagram in Fig. 213.2.

This second criticism errs first and foremost in that as an analytic approach to syntax, tagmemics does not make of phrase structure rules; hence the grammatical relations which are ideally expressed via such rules in a generative approach to syntax, are not so expressed in tagmemics. Rather they are indicated by means of the notations shown above. Thus, true tree diagrams in tagmemics indicate grammatical relations via labels, as may be seen in diagram Fig. 213.3.

And not by the configurations called for in (10).

It is correct that the diagram in Fig. 213.1. is redundant in indicating syntactic functions; however, that diagram is no more of an accurate representative for tagmemics than it is (or was) for a purely generative approach to syntax.

Thus categorial and functional notions are always indicated, and never confused, in tagmemics; yet, when generative grammar is viewed from a tagmemic point of view, it may be seen that the two notions are sometimes confused. Limitations of space prevent a discussion of more instances than the ones which follow. Consider, for example, rules of the form

(11) XP → (Specifier) X'
(12) X' → X (Complement),

exhibiting 'X-bar notation'; these rules appeared in 1967, only two years after the statements in (9) and (10) were expressed (cf. Chomsky 1970: 210; 1972: 200). The tree diagram in 213.4. illustrates these rules.

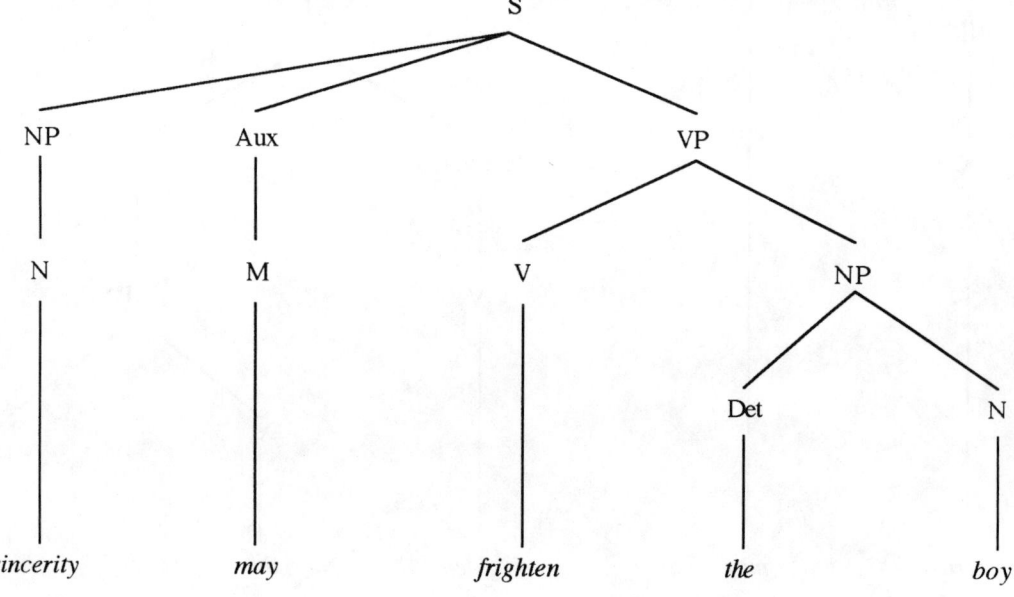

Fig. 213.2

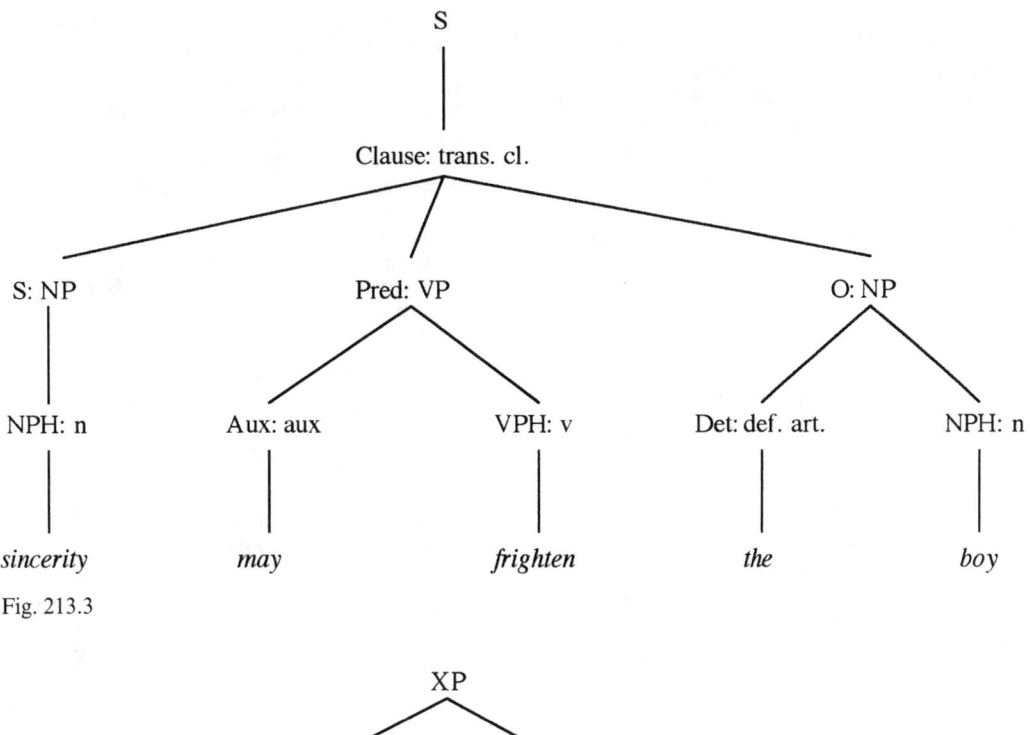

Fig. 213.3

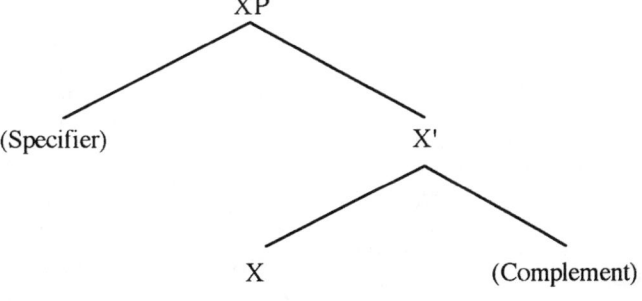

Fig. 213.4

Such generalized rules are intended to reflect the claim that noun phrases (NP), verb phrases (VP), adjective phrases (AP), prepositional phrases (PP) and adverbial phrases (AdvP) each have a three-level structure; viewed in this way, XP is a cover symbol for NP, VP, AP, PP, or AdvP. A discussion of the claim and the accompanying argumentation for a level of structure between XP and X, namely X', goes beyond the scope of this paper. Rather, what concerns us here are the elements *Specifier* and *Complement*. In this approach to syntax, in each of the phrases

(13) *that* theory *about the Doppler Effect* (NP)
(14) *shall* investigate *the case* (VP)
(15) *quite* confident *about the outcome* (AP)
(16) *almost* in *the building* (PP)
(17) *quite* independently *of us* (AdvP)

the initial italicized words are the specifiers, and the final italicized words are the complements. Now according to (10), phrase structure rules of the type (11) and (12) define a set of grammatical functions, holding between, or among, the categorical elements indicated therein. Thus interpreted, *Specifier* should represent a set of categories. Yet if we examine the phrases in (13)–(17), it is clear that *that* (Det) and *shall* (Aux), on one hand, exhibit nothing that would inspire one to include them in the same category, and that there is furthermore nothing that would inspire one to include *quite* (Adv) and *almost* (Adv), on the other hand, in the same category as either *that* or *shall*, and vice versa; thus there is no category *Specifier*. The situation is similar for *Complement*: there is nothing to cause one to unite into one category prepositional phrases like *about the Doppler*

Effect, about the outcome, and *of us* on one had with *the case* (NP) and *the building* (NP), on the other, and vice versa; thus there is no category *Complement*. On the other hand, if one argues that Specifier and Complement each indicate functional notions, rather than categorial notions, then the rules (11) and (12) are subject to the criticism of (9), and violate what is stipulated in (10). Now according to Radford (1988: 229), this is exactly what they are meant to indicate: " 'Specifier' and 'Complement' are not categorial terms, but rather represent grammatical functions or relations; hence they have a similar status to terms such as 'Subject' and 'Object'. Thus the criticism erroneously directed against tagmemics turned out to be valid for the very theoretical framework in which it was conceived.

Though the inclusion of functional notions in phrase structure rules is a violation of (10), one might well wonder whether Specifier and Complement are valid even as functional notions. Specifier would represent a set of functions, each having the same syntactic relationship to XP, according to (11). However, if we examine the phrases in (13)–(17), it is clear that the relationship of *that* (Det) to *theory about the Doppler Effect* is quite different from the relationship of *shall* (Aux) to *investigate the case*, and that these syntactic relationships are also quite different from the relationship of *quite* (Adv) to *confident about the outcome*, of *almost* (Adv) to *in the building*, and of *quite* (Adv) to *quite independently of us*. Moreover, Complement would represent a set of functions, each having the same relationship to X, according to (12). However, in the phrases (13)–(17), it is evident that the relationship of *about the Doppler Effect* to *theory* is quite different from the relationship of *the case* to *investigate*, and that the syntactic relationships differ significantly from the relationship of *about the outcome* to *confident*, of *the building* to *in*, and of *of us* to *independently*. Thus, in the context of (11) and (12), Specifier and Complement are invalid as functional notions.

5. A brief contrast of comparative tagmemic reconstruction and the reconstruction of word order typology

Since the publication of Lehmann's *Proto-Indo-European Syntax* in 1974, the reconstruction of word-order typology was for a long time thereafter the dominant approach to syntactic reconstruction. Lehmann's approach was anticipated by Jakobson who, in his seminal article of 1958, remarked:

"What can typological studies contribute to historical comparative linguistics? In Greenberg's view, the typology of language adds to 'our predictive power since from a given synchronic system, certain developments will be highly likely, others have less probability, and still others may be practically excluded.' […] Schlegel, the anticipator of comparative linguistics and typology, described the historian as a prophet predicting backwards. Our 'predictive power' in reconstruction gains support from typological studies." (Jakobson 1958: 23)

In fact, Lehmann based his method of typological reconstruction on observations found in Greenberg's (1966) article, "Some Universals of Grammar with Particular Reference to the Order of Meaningful Elements". To be sure, in the years following the publication of his *Proto-Indo-European Syntax*, a good number of Lehmann's claims have been disputed, including the basic premise that the fundamental word order of Proto-Indo-European was (Subject-)Object-Verb (i. e., (S)OV)). Nevertheless, most of the disagreements have remained within the framework of typological reconstruction itself, with the major concern being word order. Thus, the dominant issues have been whether the basic word order of Proto-Indo-European was OV or VO, and whether the small number of constructions whose word orders correlated with strictly OV and strictly VO languages did indeed consistently characterize Proto-Indo-European (cf. Andersen 1982).

In 1983 Costello published a monograph entitled *Syntactic Change and Syntactic Reconstruction: A tagmemic approach*. By comparison with the long list of articles and monographs dealing with tagmemics which had appeared up to that time, this work was very nearly unique in that it dealt exclusively with diachronic matters. As a matter of fact, Pike himself had anticipated this approach in a brief, little-known, mimeographed publication entitled *Axioms and Procedures for Reconstructions in Comparative Linguistics* in 1957 (see also Costello 1987b), and Hymes was operating in a very similar vein in his 1955 article "Positional Analysis of Categories" and his 1956 article "Na-Déné and Positional Analysis of Categories". However, the latter two works are not explicitly tagmemic, and the first does little more than hint at the potential of using tagmemics for syntactic reconstruction. *Syntactic Change and Syntactic Reconstruction*, on the other hand, is a full-length treatment, essentially uniting tagmemics with the comparative method as codified in Hoenigswald's (1960) *Language Change and Linguistic Reconstruction*. Thus, in comparative tagmemic reconstruction the chief concern is to reconstruct not word order typology, but rather the tagmemes (and their allotagmas) and the syntagmemes (and their allosyntagmas) for a proto-language. Hoenigswald (1960) demonstrates that phonemes and morphemes undergo parallel patterns of replacement or change: one-to-one replacement, merger, split, obsolescence, and emergence. He demonstrates moreover that when the comparative method is applied to data in descendant languages, these patterns of change may, with some limitations, be reversed, thereby yielding phonological and morphological reconstructions. By analyzing the syntax of genealogically related languages in a tagmemic framework, we observe exactly the same patterns of change for tagmemes and syntagmemes as for phonemes and morphemes, hence, when the comparative method is applied to syntactic data in these languages, the patterns of change may be reversed as they are in phonological and morphological reconstruction, and a syntactic reconstruction is thereby achieved. Word order patterns are revealed in tagmemic reconstructions, but they are not the primary concern; moreover, tagmemic reconstructions indicate that, as in numerous descendent langages, word order patterns in Proto-Indo-European were quite a bit more variable than typological reconstruction claims. Perhaps most importantly of all is that, as presented in Lehmann (1974), and many other publications, typological reconstruction is designed for Indo-European languages (and perhaps other languages claimed to be OV); comparative tagmemic reconstruction, on the other hand, is intended to be applied to all language families, regardless of their typological classifications. Needless to say, in some cases, the two approaches have yielded widely divergent reconstructions, and very different observations concerning the nature of syntactic change; for examples, consult Costello (1982, 1984, 1986, 1987a, and 1993).

6. Concluding observations: Contributions of Tagmemics to twentieth-century linguistics

6.1. The synchronic perspective

6.1.1. Theoretical considerations

Tagmemics is a theory of language which goes far beyond language. It characterizes language neither as mechanistic sequences of stimuli and responses, nor as a set of finite rules capable of producing an infinite number of correct sentences in a language, and no incorrect ones — but rather first and foremost as a part of human behavior. Recognizing that an essential component of the structure of human behavior is the event within its context, tagmemics sees parallels of this reflected in language: linguistic events at the level of discourse, and linguistic units at the level of syntax, morphology, and phonology, can be fully understood only in the contexts in which they occur. As an analytic approach seeking to identify linguistic units and the constructions formed by them at all levels, tagmemics has refined already-existing methods of analysis (notably those developed within the theoretical framework of structuralism), and provided new ones, particularly at the levels of syntax and discourse. Unlike many other theories of language originating in the 20th century, tagmemics maintains that form and meaning are inextricably linked, and that the study of language must be carried out within this context. Differing from linguistic theories that pass over linguistic units at the level of syntax, like Harrisian structuralism, or simply have no place for them, as in generative grammar, tagmemics recognizes and places the utmost importance on a unit of syntax, the tagmeme. Furthermore, tagmemic theory claims that all linguistic units may be viewed in terms of their features, their manifestations, and their distributions. Thus in tagmemics, unlike other theories of language, the units at each level of language are seen to possess parallel characteristics: each unit has a contrastive set of environments as well as one or more sets of characteristic environments; each unit is a set consisting of one or more members; and, the members of each set may exhibit complementary distribution as well as free variation.

6.1.2. Practical applications

Tagmemics has provided methods and procedures for hundreds of linguists to carry out rigorous and extensive (if not exhaustive) field analysis on languages previously studied as well as on languages never before studied. This has led to descriptive grammars, published as articles and monographs, of well over 500 languages from all over the world. Perhaps most importantly, from a humanistic point of view, the analyses and descriptions of tagmemicists have brought literacy in their native language to millions of persons living in remote areas of the world, enabling them, among other things, to document their culture themselves, and thus freeing them from being reliant on outsiders. Literacy has also made formal education available to these individuals, so that they are now able to adapt themselves to change, absolutely crucial for their survival, as contact with outsiders inevitably increases.

6.2. The diachronic perspective

6.2.1. Theoretical considerations

Tagmemics, unique in recognizing the common traits shared by linguistic units at all levels of analysis, has been able to extend the structuralist-based theory that recognizes the five patterns of change that linguistic units may undergo, from phonology and morphology to syntax, thus shedding additional light on our understanding of syntactic change in particular, and language change in general.

6.2.2. Practical applications

Because tagmemics has been able to establish that the units of syntax exhibit characteristics parallel to those of phonology and morphology, it is now possible to apply the comparative method in syntax, thereby providing for the first time an inductive alternative to reconstructing syntax via deduction and appeal to typological tendencies of word order.

All considered, Tagmemics has made unique, significant, and lasting contributions toward out understanding of various aspects of language in the latter half of the 20th century. Its potential is great, and has hardly been tapped.

7. Bibliography

Algeo, John. 1974. "Tagmemics: A brief overview". Brend 1974.1–9.

Andersen, Paul Kent. 1982. "On the Word Order Typology of the *Satapathabrahmana*". *Journal of Indo-European Studies* 10:1/2.37–42.

Becker, Alton L. 1964. "Item and Field: A way into complexity". *On Teaching English to Speakers of Other Languages* ed. by Carol J. Kreidler, 132–138. Washington, D. C.: National Council of Teachers of Education.

–. 1967a. *A Generative Description of the English Subject Tagmeme.* Ph. D. dissertation, Univ. of Michigan, Ann Arbor, Mich.

–. 1967b. "Conjoining in a Tagmemic Grammar of English". *Report of the Eighteenth Annual Round Table on Linguistics and Language Studies* ed. by Edward L. Blansitt, Jr., 109–121. Washington, D. C.: Georgetown Univ. Press.

Belasco, Simon, ed. 1960. *Manual and Anthology of Applied Linguistics for Use in the NDEA Foreign Language Institutes.* Vol. I. Washington D. C.: U.S. Office of Education.

–. 1961. "The Role of Transformational Grammar and Tagmemics in the Analysis of an Old French Text". *Lingua* 10.375–390.

–. 1964. "Tagmemics and Tranformational Grammar in Linguistic Analysis". *Linguistics* 10.5–15.

Biondi, Lawrence H. 1965. *A Comparative Study of Tagmemic and Stratificational Grammars.* M. A. thesis, Georgetown Univ., Washington, D. C.

Blansitt, Edward L., Jr. 1963. *The Verb Phrase in Spanish: Classes and relations.* Ph. D. dissertation, Univ. of Texas, Austin, Tex.

–. 1970. "Sentence and Clause in Universal Grammar". *Anthropological Linguistics* 11:6.167–176.

Bloch, Bernhard & George L. Trager. 1942. *Outline of Linguistic Analysis.* Baltimore: Linguistic Society of America.

Bloomfield, Leonard. 1933. *Language.* New York: Henry Holt & Co.

–. 1939. *Linguistic Aspects of Science.* (= *International Encyclopedia of Unified Science* ed. by Otto Neurath et al., 1: 4.) Chicago: Univ. of Chicago Press.

Bock, Philip K. 1962. *The Social Structure of a Canadian Indian Reserve.* Ph. D. dissertation, Harvard Univ., Cambridge Mass.

–. 1964. "Social Structure and Language Structure". *Southwestern Journal of Anthropology* 20.393–403.

Brannen, Noah S. 1966. *The Dialect of Oomisima in Three Generations: A tagmemic approach.* Ph. D. dissertation, Univ. of Michigan, Ann Arbor, Mich.

Brend, Ruth M. 1964. *A Tagmemic Analysis of Mexican Spanish Clauses.* The Hague: Mouton.

–, ed. 1974. *Advances in Tagmemics.* Amsterdam: North-Holland.

–. 1987. *Kenneth Lee Pike Bibliography.* Bloomington, Ind.: Eurolingua.

– & Kenneth L. Pike, eds. 1976. *Tagmemics.* Vol. II: *Theoretical Discussion.* The Hague: Mouton.

–. 1977. *The Summer Institute of Linguistics: Its works and contributions.* The Hague: Mouton.

Chomsky, Noam. 1956. *The Logical Structure of Linguistic Theory.* Microfilmed. Cambridge, Mass.: Harvard University. (Edited version published New York & London: Plenum Press, 1975.)

–. 1965. *Aspects of the Theory of Syntax.* Cambridge, Mass.: MIT.

–. 1970. "Remarks on Nominalization". *Readings in English Transformational Grammar* ed. by Roderick A. Jacobs & Peter S. Rosenbaum, 184–221. Waltham, Mass.: Ginn & Co.

–. 1972. *Studies on Semantics in Generative Grammar*. The Hague: Mouton.

Conway, Sister M. Ann Charlotte, SNJM. 1964. *Order Classes of Adjectives in Spanish*. Ph. D. dissertation, Univ. of Texas, Austin, Tex.

Cook. Walter, J., S. J. 1964. *On Tagmemes and Transforms*. Washington, D. C.: Georgetown Univ. Press.

–. 1965. *A Descriptive Analysis of Mundari*. Ph. D. dissertation, Georgetown Univ., Washington, D. C.

–. 1969. *Introduction to Tagmemic Analysis*. New York: Holt, Rinehart & Winston.

–. 1986. "Computer Assisted Tagmemics". Elson 1986.69–78.

Costello, John R. 1982. "The Absolute Construction in Indo-European: A syntagmemic reconstruction". *Journal of Indo-European Studies* 10.235–252.

–. 1983. *Syntactic Change and Syntactic Reconstruction: A tagmemic approach*. Dallas: Summer Institute of Linguistics; Arlington: Univ. of Texas at Arlington.

–. 1984. "The Periphrastic Passive Construction in Proto-Indo-European". *Word* 35.125–161.

–. 1986. "Relative Clauses in Proto-Indo-European: A syntagmemic reconstruction". Elson 1986. 233–249.

–. 1987a. "A Comparative Syntactosemantic Reconstruction of the Absolute Construction in Indo-European". *The Eleventh LACUS Forum* ed. by Robert A. Hall, 404–24. Columbia, S. C.: Hornbeam Press.

–. 1987b. "Kenneth Pike and Diachronic Linguistics". Brend 1987.49–50.

–. 1989. "Innovations Increasing Syntactic Complexity in the Native Language of Bilingual Children from 5 to 10: The case for Pennsylvania German". *Studies on the Verbal Behavior of the Pennsylvania Germans* ed. by Werner Enninger, Joachim Raith & Karl-Heinz Wandt, vol. II, 3–16. Stuttgart: Steiner.

–. 1993. "Modal Auxiliaries in Proto-Indo-European". *Comparative Historical Linguistics: Indo-European and Finno-Ugric. Papers in Honor of Oswald Szemerényi III* ed. by Béla Brógyányi & Rainer Lipp, 73–90. Amsterdam & Philadelphia: Benjamins.

–. 1995. "Theory and Data in Phonological Reconstruction: Whence and whither?" *Word* 46:1.9–28.

Crawford, John C. 1963. *Totontepec Mixe Phonotagmemics*. (= Summer Institute of Linguistics Publications in Linguistics and Related Fields, 8.) Norman, Okla: Summer Institute of Linguistics of the Univ. of Oklahoma.

Crymes, Ruth Helen. 1968. *Some Systems of Substitution Correlation in Modern English*. The Hague: Mouton.

Derbyshire, Desmond. 1961. "Hixkaryana (Carib) Syntax Structure. 1: Word; 2: Phrase, Sentence". *International Journal of American Linguistics* 27.125–142, 222–236.

Deibler, Ellis W., Jr. 1969. "Sememics and Translation". *Kivung* 1:3.153–163.

Du Bois, Carl D., John Upton & Kenneth L. Pike. 1980. "Constraints on Complexity Seen via Fused Vectors of an n-Dimensional Semantic Space". *Semiotica* 29:3/4.209–243.

Dundes, Alan. 1962. "From Etic to Emic Units in the Structural Study of Folktales". *Journal of American Folklore* 75.95–105.

–. 1963. "Structural Typology in North American Indian Folktales". *Southwestern Journal of Anthropology* 19.121–131.

Ellis, C. Douglas. 1960. "Tagmemic Analysis of a Restricted Cree Text". *Journal of the Canadian Linguistic Association* 6.35–59.

Elson, Benjamin F. 1958. *Beginning Morphology-Syntax*. Glendale: Summer Institute of Linguistics.

–, ed. 1986. *Language in Global Perspective*. Dallas: Summer Institute of Linguistics.

– & Velma B. Pickett. 1960. *Beginning Morphology-Syntax*. Santa Ana, Calif. Summer Institute of Linguistics.

English, Hubert M. 1964. "Linguistic Theory as an Aid to Invention." *College Composition and Communication* 15.135–140.

Fichtner, Edward G. 1979. *English and German Syntax: A contrastive analysis on generative-tagmemic Principles*. Munich: Fink.

Flores, Frank. 1962. *A Contrastive Analysis of Selected Clause Types in Cebuano and English*. Ph. D. dissertation. Univ. of Michigan, Ann Arbor, Mich.

Francis, W. Nelson. 1965. *The English Language: An introduction*. New York: Norton.

Franklin, Karl J. 1963. "Kewa Ethnolinguistic Concepts of Body Parts". *Southwestern Journal of Anthropology* 19.54–63.

Fries, Charles C. 1925. "The Periphrastic Future with *shall* and *will* in Modern English". *Publications of the Modern Language Association of America* 40.963–1005.

–. 1952. *The Structure of English*. New York: Harcourt, Brace & World.

Fries, Peter H. 1976. "On Surface and Underlying Structure, with Special Reference to Phrase, Clause, and Sentence". Brend & Pike 1976.1–49.

– & Kenneth L. Pike. 1985. "Slot and Referential Hierarchy in Relation to Charles C. Fries' View of Language". *Toward an Understanding of Language: Charles C. Fries in perspective* ed. by Peter H. Fries et al., 105–127. Amsterdam & Philadelphia: Benjamins.

Glissmeyer, Gloria. 1970. *A Tagmemic Analysis of Hawaii English Clauses*. Ph. D. dissertation, Univ. of Hawaii, Honolulu, Hi.

Greenberg, Joseph H. 1966. "Some Universals of Grammar with Particular Reference to the Order of Meaningful Elements". *Universals of Language* ed. by Joseph H. Greenberg, 73–113. Cambridge, Mass.: MIT.

—. 1994. "The Influence of *Word* and the Linguistic Circle of New York on my Intellectual Development". *Word* 45:1.19–26.

Grimes, Joseph E. 1966. "Some Inter-sentence Relationships in Huichol". *Summa Antropologica en Homenaje a Roberto J. Weitlaner* ed. by Antonio Pompa y Poma, 465–470. Mexico City: Instituto Nacional de Antropologia e Historia.

Gudschinsky, Sarah C. 1967. *How to Learn an Unwritten Language*. New York: Holt, Rinehart & Winston.

—. 1968. "The Relationship of Language and Linguistics to Reading". *Kivung* 1.146–152.

Hale, Austin. 1972. "The Relationship of Tagmemic Theory to Rules, Derivation, and Transformational Grammar". Brend & Pike 1976.51–89.

—. 1974. "On the Systematization of Box 4". Brend 1974.55–74.

Harris, Zellig S. 1951 [1947]. *Methods in Structural Linguistics*. Chicago: Univ. of Chicago Press.

Hockett, Charles F. 1942. "A System of Descriptive Phonology". *Language* 18.3–21.

Hoenigswald, Henry M. 1960. *Language Change and Linguistic Reconstruction*. Chicago: Univ. of Chicago Press.

Holman, Thomas W. 1989. "Waorani Verb Affixes". Pike & Saint 1989.57–69.

Holz, William. 1967. "Field Theory and Literature". *The Centennial Review* 11.532–548.

Howes, Alan B. 1964. "A Linguistic Analogy in Literary Criticism". *College Composition and Communication* 15.141–144.

Hymes, Dell H. 1955. "Positional Analysis of Categories: A frame for reconstruction". *Word* 11.10–23.

—. 1956. "Na-Déné and Positional Analysis of Categories". *American Anthropologist* 58.624–638.

Jakobson, Roman. 1958. "Typological Studies and their Contribution to Historical and Comparative Linguistics". *Proceedings of the VIII International Congress of Linguists* ed. by Eva Sivertsen et al., 17–25. Oslo: Oslo Univ. Press.

Jespersen, Otto. 1931. *A Modern English Grammar on Historical Principles*. Vol. IV: *Syntax*. London: Geoge Allen & Unwin.

Kakumasu, Jim. 1968. "Urubu Sign Language". *International Journal of American Linguistics* 34.275–281.

Koch, Walter A. 1963. "On the Principles of Stylistics". *Lingua* 12.411–422.

Kraft, Charles H. 1963. *Study of Hausa Syntax*. Hartford, Conn.: Department of Linguistics, Hartford Seminary Foundation.

Lehmann, Winfred P. 1974. *Proto-Indo-European Syntax*. Austin: Univ. of Texas Press.

Liem, Nguyen Dang. 1966. *English Grammar: A combined tagmemic and transformational approach*. Canberra: Australian National Univ.

—. 1967. *A Contrastive Analysis of English and Vietnamese*. Canberra: Australian National Univ.

Lipka, Leonhard. 1971. "Grammatical Categories, Lexical Items, and Word Formation". *Foundations of Language*, 7.211–238.

Longacre, Robert E. 1960. "String Constituent Analysis". *Language* 36.63–88.

—. 1961. "From Tagma to Tagmeme in Biblical Hebrew". *A William Cameron Townsend en el vigesimoquinto aniversario del Instituto Lingüístico de Verano* ed. by Benjamin F. Elson & Juan Comas, 563–591. Mexico: Instituto Lingüístico de Verano.

—. 1964. *Grammar Discovery Procedures*. The Hague: Mouton.

—. 1965. "Some Fundamental Insights of Tagmemics". *Language* 41.65–76.

—. 1972. "Narrative versus other Discourse Genre". *From Soundstream to Discourse: Papers from the 1971 Mid-America Linguistics Conference* ed. by Daniel G. Hays & Donald M. Lance, 167–185. St. Louis, Mo.: Univ. of Missouri.

—. 1986. "A Feature of Proto-Otomanguean Discourse Structure?". Elson 1986.136–147.

Loos, Eugene E. 1963. "Capanahua Narrative Structure". *Texas Studies in Language and Literature* 4, Supplement, 697–742. Austin, Tex.

Lowe, Ivan. 1969. "An Algebraic Theory of English Pronominal Reference. Part 1". *Semiotica* 1.387–421.

Merrifield, William R., Constance M. Naish, Calvin R. Rensch & Gillian Story. 1962. *Laboratory Manual for Morphology and Syntax*. Santa Ana, Calif.: Summer Institute of Linguistics.

Nagara, Susumu. 1969. *A Bilingual Description of Some Linguistic Features of Pidgin English Used by Japanese Immigrants on the Plantations of Hawaii: A case study in bilingualism*. Ph. D. dissertation, Univ. of Wisconsin, Madison, Wisc.

Neurath, Otto, et al., eds. 1939–70. *International Encyclopedia of Unified Science*. Chicago: Univ. of Chicago Press.

Pedersen, Holger. 1931. *Linguistic Science in the Nineteenth Century*. Transl. by John Webster Spargo. Cambridge, Mass.: Harvard Univ. Press.

Peeke, Catherine. 1962. "Structural Summary of Zaparo". *Studies in Ecuadorian Indian Languages* ed. by Benjamin F. Elson, vol. I, 125–216. Norman, Okla.: Summer Institute of Linguistics of the Univ. of Oklahoma.

Pickett, Velma B. 1956. *An Introduction to the Study of Grammatical Structures*. Glendale, Calif.: Summer Institute of Linguistics.

Pike, Eunice V. 1969. "Language Learning in Relation to Focus". *Language Learning* 19.107–115.

Pike, Evelyn G. 1989. "Trees for Constituent Analysis from Discourse to Morpheme". Pike & Saint 1989.31–46.

– & Rachel Saint, eds. 1989. *Workpapers Concerning Waorani Discourse Features.* Dallas: Summer Institute of Linguistics.

Pike, Kenneth L. 1947. "Grammatical Prerequisites to Phonemic Analysis". *Word* 3.155–172.

–. 1957. *Axioms and Procedures for Reconstructions in Comparative Linguistics.* Glendale, Calif.: Summer Institute of Linguistics.

–. 1962. "Dimensions of Grammatical Constructions". *Language* 38.221–244.

–. 1963a. "The Hierarchical and Social Matrix of Suprasegmentals". *Prace Filologiczne* 18.95–104.

–. 1963b. "Theoretical Implications of Matrix Permutation in Fore". *Anthropological Linguistics* 5.8:1–23.

–. 1964a. "Discourse Structure and Tagmeme Matrices". *Oceanic Linguistics* 3.5–25.

–. 1964b. "A Linguistic Contribution to the Teaching of Composition". *College Composition and Communication* 15.82–88.

–. 1965a. "Language: Where science and poetry meet". *College English* 26.283–292.

–. 1965b. "Non-linear Order and Anti-redundancy in German Morphological Matrices". *Zeitschrift für Mundartforschung* 32.193–221.

–. 1967 [1958–1960]. *Language in Relation to a Unified Theory of the Structure of Human Behavior.* 2nd ed. The Hague: Mouton.

–. 1974. "Crucial Questions in the Development of Tagmemics: The sixties and seventies". Brend 1974.35–54.

–. 1976. "Toward the Development of Tagmemic Postulates". Brend & Pike 1976.91–124.

– & Alton L. Becker. 1964. "Progressive Neutralizations in Dimensions of Navaho Stem Matrices". *International Journal of American Linguistics* 30.144–154.

– & Evelyn G. Pike. 1983. *Text and Tagmeme.* Norwood, N. J.: Ablex.

Platt, Heidi. 1970. *A Comparative Study of German and English Syntax.* Ph. D. dissertation, Monash Univ., Melbourne.

Platt, John T. 1970. *Grammatical Form and Grammatical Meaning: A tagmemic view of Fillmore's deep structure case concepts.* Amsterdam: North-Holland.

Postal, Paul M. 1964. *Constituent Structure: A study of contemporary models of syntactic description.* The Hague: Mouton.

Pride, Kitty. 1961. "Numerals in Chatino". *Anthropological Linguistics* 3:2.1–10.

Radford, Andrew. 1988. *Transformational Grammar.* Cambridge: Cambridge Univ. Press.

Reskiewicz, Alfred. 1962. *Main Sentence Elements in* The Book of Margery Kempe: *A study in major syntax.* Warsaw: Zakład im. Ossolińskich, PAN.

Ross, Deborah. 1989. "Chronological and Logical Discourse Chains". Pike & Saint 1989.9–14.

Roulet, Eddy. 1969. *Syntaxe de la proposition nucléaire du français parlé: Étude tagmémique et transformationnelle.* Brussels: Association Internationale pour la Recherche et la Diffusion des Méthodes Audio-Visuelles et Structuro-Globales.

Scheflen, Albert E. 1965. *Stream and Structure of Communication Behavior: Content analysis of a psychotherapy session.* Philadelphia: Eastern Pennsylvania Psychiatric Institute.

Scott, Charles T. 1965. *A Linguistic Study of Persian and Arabic Riddles: A language-centered approach to genre definition.* Bloomington, Ind.: Indiana Univ.

Soenjono, Dardjowidjodjo. 1967. *Indonesian Syntax.* Ph. D. dissertation, Georgetown Univ., Washington, D. C.

Wallis, Ethel E. & Mary A. Bennett. 1978. *Two Thousand Tongues to Go.* Huntington Beach, Calif.: Wycliffe Bible Translators.

Waterhouse, Viola G. 1958. *The Grammatical Structure of Oaxaca Chontal.* Ph. D. dissertation, Univ. of Michigan, Ann Arbor, Mich.

–. 1974. *The History and Development of Tagmemics.* The Hague: Mouton.

Watson, Saundra K. 1964. "Personal Pronouns in Pacoh". *Mon-Khmer Studies* ed. by David D. Thomas, vol. I, 81–97. Saigon: Linguistic Circle of Saigon & Summer Institute of Linguistics.

Wells, Rulon S. 1947. "Immediate Constituents". *Language* 23.81–117.

Wilkendorf, Patricia. 1989. "Waorani Clause Formulas". Pike & Saint 1989.47–55.

Wilt, Timothy. 1989. "Prominence of Waves of Space and Time". Pike & Saint 1989.99–101.

Young, Richard E. & Alton L. Becker. 1964. "The Role of Lexical and Grammatical Cues in Paragraph Recognition". *Studies in Language and Language Behavior, Progress Report* 2, 1–6. Ann Arbor, Mich.: Center for Research in Language and Language Behavior, Univ. of Michigan.

Young, Robert A. & Rosemary Young. 1965. "The Three-Dimensional Classification System of Bena-Bena Nouns". *Anthropological Linguistics* 7:5.80–3.

Zvelebil, Kamil. 1964. *Tamil in 550 A. D.: An interpretation of early inscriptional Tamil.* Prague: Naklad ČSAV.

John R. Costello, New York, N.Y. (U.S.A.)

214. Distributionalism and immediate constituent analysis

1. Distributionalism
2. Immediate Constituent Analysis and Traditional Syntax
3. Immediate Constituent Syntax in Bloomfield (1914)
4. Syntax in Bloomfield (1926)
5. Pike's Tagmemic Syntax
6. Zellig Harris
7. Rulon Wells
8. Bibliographical References

1. Distributionalism

Distributionalism was a prominent variety of American structuralist descriptive linguistics from the early 1940s through the transition to Chomskyan transformational grammar. Like most other varieties of American structuralism, it incorporated Bloomfield's rejection of exact synonymy, using this as a justification for distributional rather than semantic similarity criteria, and it appealed to patterns of element and element-class distribution as a guide in making analytical decisions. The distinctive trait of distributionalism was its focus on distributional patterns *resulting* from analytical decisions as criteria for making those decisions.

In describing the distribution of elements, reference may be made to absolute distribution, that is, to the sum of the environments where the element occurs. This is what Bloomfield meant by the *selection* of a form. Viewed in this way, a linguistic element, established by other criteria such as similarity of form and meaning, simply *has* a distribution, and any parallelisms with the distributions of other forms are a consequence of the texture of the primary data as manifested through a body of analytical decisions made according to criteria of sameness of substance and function. Because of the strictness of Bloomfield's requirement of morphophonenmic identity of morpheme alternants (1926, 1933), this view of the theoretical role of distribution was very close to his use of distribution in morphology — that the distribution of an element is a consequence, not a criterion, of analysis. But, given the irregularities of natural language, there is a fringe of elements around the clear and simple cases, which could reasonably be decided one way or another. It is in these unclear cases, and these only, where Bloomfield (1926) recommended deciding by appeal to parallelism with the other, unambiguous cases. In Bloomfield's morphology, the exemplars were morphemes with a single alternant.

Parallelism in the distributions of elements or classes of elements is in effect a second layer of distribution, a more abstract pattern formed by the absolute distributions of overt elements and the classes defined by similarities in the absolute distributions of overt elements. In an obvious way, then, this parallelism or pattern, such as it may be, arises naturally and directly from the combination of the absolute distributions of the elements established, assigned to classes, and otherwise described in the grammar.

Distributionalism, however, seeks to maximize such parallelisms by making analytical decisions so as to enhance the regularity or other properties of these secondary or higher levels of distributional patterning. Bloomfield's grouping standard for morpheme alternants, using the distribution of members of a form class having but a single alternant as a model for the range allowed for morphemes having groups of alternants, is a conservative example of the critical uses of patterning. Note that the apparently universal agreement in this period with Bloomfield's rejection of synonymy, which was accepted as a theoretical justification for reliance on differences of distribution rather than differences of meaning in reaching decisions about grouping, does not in itself explain the agressive application of patterning arguments by later distributionalists. Bloomfield's own work, for example, remained quite conservative in this respect, and even includes a rare critical reaction (1945) against Trager (1944), a floridly distributionalist treatment of French verb morphology. What sets distributionalism apart from other descriptive approaches before it is the scope not only allowed but advocated in *adjusting* the identifications and distributions of elements so as to maximize the parallelism and regularity of the abstract distributional pattern, and further, the particular methods used to reach its goal of maximum distributional regularity.

To repeat, the key operation in distributionalist description is this regularizing of item and class-member distributions according to some model. The reasoning, when it is explicit, is very reminiscent of the operation of proportional analogy in language change. A formal irregularity which limits the scope of some regular pattern is replaced by the regular pattern, thus extending its distribution and eliminating an 'exception' to a generalization that would otherwise have to be noted in the description of the pattern. It turns out, of course, that the originally perceived 'irregularity' has not been eliminated, but simply moved, usually to a lower level, where its zero manifestation is masked by the higher level category symbol filling its position in the upper level of the overall pattern. Thus, in describing the phonology of a particular language, the decision to assign onglides and offglides of syllables to the 'vowel' or the 'consonant' class may be based on the *resulting* pattern: if all onglides are called consonants, then perhaps all syllables can be said to begin with a consonant; if they are called vowels or something else altogether, then not all syllables can be so described (cf. Bowen & Stockwell 1955, 1956, and Saporta 1956 on Spanish). Similarly, in the morphology of English, it can be said that all common nouns take a plural suffix, provided that some of them are said to take zero alternants of the suffix. Zellig Harris (1942: 110–111) implicitly uses this reasoning, going so far as to match the range of distribution of the 'plural' morpheme against the exactly corresponding range of the 'singular' morpheme, whose shape is always zero. Charles Hockett (1947: 230 n. 10) discussed the 'dubious status' of this singular morpheme, and offered a further amendment of Bloomfield's and Harris's range restriction, allowing the use of the 'genitive' morpheme as a model, with its alternants roughly matching the distribution and the alternation in shape of the 'plural'. Thus, he used one morpheme with multiple alternants as a model for another, because the resulting distributions were quite similar. In his discussion of the 'tactical equivalence' of submorphemically different distributional analyses, Hockett advocated the use of patterning in choosing among descriptions with equivalent higher-level distributional properties. The mechanism he suggested was the use of *canonical forms*, typical morphophonemic patterns established by clear and uncomplicated cases, expressed in terms of consonant and vowel shapes. If most morphemes in a language have either of two or three canonical forms, perhaps CVC, CVCVC, and -C, then these patterns can be used to help decide the less clear cases. Exactly the same use of canonical syntactic forms as models for deciding the segmentation and classification of syntactic constituents was made, and made deliberately, in IC analysis. The appeal to canonical morphological and syntactic forms also became very prominent within the Summer Institute of Linguistic's tagmemic system of linguistic description.

Since it was believed, with some justification, that syntax was harder to describe than morphology, the achievement of 'tactical simplicity' in syntax by creating regular patterns was considered an acceptable trade-off, even if it came at the expense of complicating the morphology by introducing many zero elements and sparsely realized categories as consequences of the manipulation of the syntactic patterns.

This use of distribution in a criterial role was often called *patterning*. The circularity of patterning arguments did not escape notice. Einar Haugen (1951: 363) referred to distributionalists as 'metalinguists':

"It has been a constant charge brought against the metalinguists that their procedures have seemed circular. They have often appeared to adopt arbitrary and unsupported principles of analysis, more characterized by esthetic than by scientific validity, contributing more to elegance than to learning. Perhaps we may recognize now that this is inherent in the adoption of distributional criteria."

In this same survey paper, Haugen (1951: 362) also called attention to the use of meaning distinctions disguised as distributional differences:

"It is curious to see how those who eliminate meaning have brought it back under the covert guise of distribution. Among the distributions of a form are reckoned its possibilities of combination with other forms. Thus *window* might presumably be distinguished from *door* without reference to any actual situation if we had enough sentences in which they were used. By a technique of replacement we could find out, as in the game of twenty questions, which of various possibilities was intended. But it is important to note that only a native can make such replacements; and by definition a native knows the meanings of the forms he uses."

The distributions of two main types of elements are crucially involved in patterning arguments. One is the distribution of overt elements; the other is the distribution and membership of positional classes having specified distributional properties. In distributionalist structuralism, morphology and syntax can be considered together for these purposes. The overt elements were morphemes with audible phonological shapes, whose actual distributions were the starting point for descriptions. The covert elements were substitutional and positional form classes viewed as covert morphological or syntactic elements. The compelling power of complementary distribution as a descriptive tool, and as a theoretical touchstone, arose from examples of it in manifest relationships among overt elements: among audible and phonetically similar allophones; and later, among audible and phonemically similar allomorphs. Through the use of zero elements; whose establishment is necessarily based on distributionalist criteria of the 'patterning' type, and of 'grammatical' or 'class' meanings assigned either to substitution classes or construction (or sequence) classes, distributionalists built up grammatical structures whose definitions, as patterns of distribution of lower-order units, were relatively regular. The irregularities of co-occurrence were filled in by zero elements. In its mature stage, in the work of Robert Hall (1947) and George Trager (1944, 1955) on French verb morphology, for example, more than half of the inflectional allomorphs in the regular paradigm are phonetic nulls, but each inflected form is endowed with a tense-mood element, a person element, and, for the plural persons, a plural element. Trager was of course aware of the relation between the spoken forms and the morphological pattern he discerned in them (1955: 518):

"The total number of forms is 45. In a verb like *donner* there are only 22 phonemically different forms (spoken in isolation, with maxiumum vowel distinction but no linking); for other kinds of verbs the number will be similar; but of course the morphemic structure can always be ascertained from the part of the paradigmatic frame in which a form occurs."

It is to be understood that each form fills some part of the same paradigmatic frame; zeros are added to do the necessary stretching of phonemically 'shorter' forms. In the forms corresponding to the traditional present indicative, Trager's first person singular and third person plural forms both contain a zero element, indeed, what might be called a total zero: not a morphophoneme with zero phonemic value, nor a phoneme with zero phonetic value, but an allomorphic zero with no morphophonemic or phonemic value at all. But the two zeros are not tokens of the same morpheme: the singular form ends in a zero first person marker, and the plural has a zero plural marker before its liaison consonant.

2. Immediate Constituent Analysis and Traditional Syntax

In principle Immediate Constituent (henceforth: IC) analysis represents the syntactic structure of a sentence as a hierarchy of dichotomies. Much of the discussion of this system of syntax within structuralist descriptive linguistics was cast in procedural form, proposing rules or conditions for segmenting whole sentences into two immediate constituents, and each of these in turn into two, and so on, and also discussing those circumstances under which some non-binary division should be made instead.

It has been widely assumed and often repeated that IC analysis is a continuation of the model of syntax found in traditional grammar (e. g., Chomsky 1957: 26, 1962 [1958]: 124n). W. Keith Percival (1976) conclusively refuted this view of its history, demonstrating that the conception of the sentence and its structure implicit in traditional syntax is fundamentally incompatible with that of IC analysis. Traditional syntax presents the sentence as composed of individual words, not as analyzed by binary divisions into constituents of the kind found in IC analysis. In traditional syntax, it is these individual words that stand in syntactic relations to each other, rather than immediate constituents. Moreover, Percival made it clear in that paper that the transmission of IC analysis into American descriptive linguistics stemmed not from traditional grammar but from the psychology of language propounded by Wilhelm Wundt (1832−1920), by way of the linguistic writings of Leonard Bloomfield (1887−1949).

Basing this presentation of traditional grammar on two standard works (Greenough 1931 on Latin, and Smyth 1916 on Greek), Percival wrote that they identified just two types of traditional grammatical elements consisting of more than a single word. One is complex verb forms: "periphrastic verb forms of the type *amatus est* 'he was loved' are treated as single words for morphological purposes and are listed in paradigms along with forms consisting of single words like *amatur* 'he is loved'" (Percival 1976: 230). The other is the prepositional phrase. Percival noted that in traditional grammar, these are the only phrases recognized, and that they are always adjectival or adverbial in function. A *phrase* in the Latin grammar of Greenough (1931: 166) is defined as "a group of words, without subject or predicate of its own, which may be used as an Adjective or an Adverb." Noun phrases are not recognized in traditional grammar. Percival (1976: 232) added that in this tradition, "a subject is a subject with respect to some finite verb, not with respect to the sentence as a whole. Thus, a student attempting to construe an unfamiliar Latin sentence is told to 'look for the finite verb, and then find *its* subject'. Note that he is not invited to try dividing the sentence in two and to call one portion the subject and the other the predicate."

This convincing account of the differences between the two approaches has failed to gain much ground within what might be called the folk history of linguistics, however. It is therefore rarely asked why such a view of the history of IC analysis has been so persistent, or why this view of syntax was and often still is thought to have been dominant within both American structuralist descriptive linguistics and its eventual successor, early Chomskyan transformational grammar.

It remains to be considered to what extent and in what forms IC analysis was actually used in syntactic theory and in practice by distributionalists and other structuralists. The matter is too complex to be covered in detail here, but some provisional answers will be offered. This article contends that IC analysis and some closely related approaches supplanted traditonal syntax within distributionalist descriptive linguistics for two reasons: first, because of Bloomfield's overall intellectual authority within the emerging discipline; and second, because IC analysis and its relatives were more compatible with distributional analysis than was the older approach. Furthermore, IC analysis may later have come to be the model for phrase-structure grammar in part because its origin myth was by then already widely accepted, so that it was associated by Chomsky and his followers with traditional grammar rather than with distributionalist descriptive linguistics. In particular, the distributionalist whose work Chomsky knew best, Zellig Harris (1946, 1951) had propounded a bottom-up approach to syntax that was not based on ICs, but that offered a formalism by which they could easily be represented. This too may have made IC structure a more attractive model for Chomsky's phrase structure component. However that may be, for many distributionalists, 'IC analysis' came to stand for a range of distributionally based approaches to syntax in which the principle of binary segmentation was accepted strictly, sometimes, or not at all.

3. Immediate Constituent Syntax in Bloomfield (1914)

The syntactic doctrine of IC analysis has two key elements: first, that syntactic analysis proceeds by successive segmentations of a sequence of grammatical forms, resulting in an unbroken hierarchy of constituents; and second, that each segmentation is in principle dichotomous. As they are found in Bloomfield's 1914 *Introduction to the Study of Language*, both of these stipulations are based on Wundt's writings, as Percival (1976: 234–240) and Matthews (1993: 52–55) showed by comparing Bloomfield's presentation with Wundt's original.

Central to both the analytical orientation of IC syntax and its binary principle is the notion of *apperception* as expounded in Wundt's psychology of language. It is by means of apperceptions that we structure experience as "a system of complex recurrent units, a world of objects." (Bloomfield 1914: 56). The theme of recurrent units evokes another important element of Wundt's psychology, one not necessarily associated with any particular view of syntax, namely, its associationism. It would be hard to improve on Bloomfield's brief exposition of this theoretical nexus. In a few pages he sketches how apperception segments experience, and makes the connection between recurrent apperceptions and the association formed between a verbal expression, on the one hand, and the elementary features common to each one of the experiences associated with that expression, on the other. His exposition makes much use of rabbit sightings, then and since apparently primal events for philosophers of language (Bloomfield 1914: 57):

"Like ours, the dog's apperception, – or, as we subjectively say, his attention, – may focus the rabbit as the central object, for the time being, of consciousness. The coherence and unity of such a total experience are due to habits of association formed in earlier related experiences"

Bloomfield sometimes emphasized the complexity and subtlety of meaning in language, placing it outside of linguistics until some future time when much more will be known about the world, allowing complete characterizations. At other times, as in this passage, he distinguished clearly between linguistically significant features of meaning and the merely incidental details of particular events or perceptions (Bloomfield 1914: 57—58):

"We react to countless experiences of a single type (such as 'rabbit') with one and the same utterance, while in fact no two experiences are wholly alike. When we associate the present experience with certain past experiences and utter with it the sound-sequence which we heard and uttered with them, we do so [...] because certain elementary features are common to it and each of them. These elementary features are known as *dominant elements*."

With equal concision, he lays out the Wundtian basis of syntactic analysis as the analysis of a total experience (Bloomfield 1914: 60):

"When we say *white rabbit* we more or less vividly separate the two elements of the total experience. Sometimes we may not attend closely to the analysis, but at others we shall insist on it, as when we say 'No, a *white* rabbit' or 'No, a white *rabbit*'. Such an utterance analyzing an experience into elements we call a *sentence*."

"The relation of the elements of a sentence to each other has a distinctive psychological tone. It is called the *logical* or *discursive* relation. It consists of a transition of the attention from the total experience, which throughout remains in consciousness, to the successive elements, which are one after another focussed by it."

It seems here as if Bloomfield, and Wundt, are asserting that one can only apperceive one thing at a time, and at the same time that the successive elements remain to some degree in focus together. Wundt argued, in his critique of Hermann Paul (1846—1921), that "the principal constituent concepts of sentence are already in consciousness the minute one starts uttering it", and that for the speaker, the sentence "has a twofold character — it is both simultaneous and successive. It is simultaneous in the sense that throughout its production the speaker is conscious of it in its entirety. It is successive in that the state of consciousness ('der Bewusstseinszustand') varies from moment to moment as particular constituent concepts pass into the focus of attention and others pass out" (Percival 1976: 237). Doubtless Wundt ascribed similar capabilities to the hearer, as well. Still, for Wundt and in turn for Bloomfield, the exercise of apperception was the justification for the binary character of immediate constituent analysis, and for the fundamental dichotomies of syntactic categorization (Bloomfield 1914: 60—61):

"The attention of an individual, — that is, apperception, — is a unified process: we can attend to but one thing at a time. Consequently the analysis of a total experience always proceeds by single binary divisions into a part for the time being focused and a remainder. In the primary division of an experience into two parts, the one focused is called the *subject* and the one left for later attention the *predicate*; the relation between them is called *predication*. If after this first division, either subject or predicate or both receive further analysis, the elements in each case first singled out are again called subjects and the elements in relation to them, *attributes*. The subject is always the present thing, the known thing, or the concrete thing, the predicate or attribute, its quality, action, or relation, or the thing to which it is like."

The discussion of syntax in Bloomfield (1914) is carried on in these terms, with scarcely any attention paid to analytical criteria, procedures, or methods. The section is organized around topics (discursive relations, emotional relations, material relations, syntactic categories, cross-reference, government, etc.), each presented in a broadly comparative way, with brief examples from many languages. That is, he presents syntax, like morphology, in just the fashion he came to deplore a decade or so later: as an expression of concepts and relations in the mind of the speaker.

In this treatment of Tagalog (1917), however, though his organization of the treatment of syntax shows many traces of his early view of IC structure, the details reveal that Bloomfield gave first priority, then and later, to the overt linguistic forms and their meanings, lexical or grammatical. As those forms and their distributions are strikingly different from what is found in Indo-European languages, so the resulting arrangement and terminology of the description was different indeed from the familiar model of Indo-European categories. Blake's review (1919) complained especially about this difference. Distant echoes of Bloomfield's Wundtian period are still heard when Malayo-Polynesian 'focus-marking' affixes are discussed, and perhaps also in the terms Wells (1947) chose for the immediate constituents of linguists' apperceptions when viewing a grammatical form as made up of 'focus' and 'environment'.

4. Syntax in Bloomfield (1926)

Bloomfield's "Postulates" (1926), written in emulation of the postulates for psychology of his new colleague and friend Albert Paul Weiss (1925), make no mention of immediate constituents. Instead, the brief section on syntax (VI: Construction, Categories, Parts of Speech) sketches a syntax based on the *order* of elements, whether successive, simultaneous, substitutive, or other. By his definition 23, **constructions**, whether morphological or syntactic, are recurrent sames of order, and the corresponding stimulus-reaction features are **constructional meanings**. It is here, incidentally, that he first adopted Meillet's syntactic definition of the sentence, as a maximum free form, in place of Wundt's conceptual definition, as an analysis of a total experience. The core principles of Bloomfield's new syntactic model are given in items 29–35, quoted here without the accompanying discussion, except for item 34, whose discussion helps to clarify it:

29. DEF. Each of the ordered units in a construction is a **position**.
30. ASSUMPTION 10. Each position in a construction can be filled only by certain forms.
31. DEF. The meaning of a position is a **functional meaning**.
32. DEF. The positions in which a form occurs are its **functions**.
33. DEF. All forms having the same functions constitute a **form-class**.
34. DEF. The functional meanings in which the forms of a form-class appear constitute the **class-meaning**.

Thus, the meanings found in all the functions of the form-class of English object expressions, namely 'actor', 'goal', etc. (§ 32) together constitute the class-meaning of these forms, which may be summed up as 'numbered object' or in the name 'object expression'.

35. DEF. The functional meanings and class-meanings of a language are the **categories** of the language.

This is the framework that is elaborated in *Language* (1933). The skeleton outlined here allows Bloomfield to define 'parts of speech' (in § 38) as the maximum form classes of words in a language. The binary principle is notably absent from this model, perhaps because Bloomfield had not forgotten that its justification had been psychological rather than structural. Notice also the prominence here of 'grammatical meaning', and how it is attached to positions, to classes of positions, and to classes of forms that fit into them, not to morphemes, as it later came to be in distributionalist syntax. Some elements of the 1926 model were continued and elaborated in the 1933 formulation, where the notion of immediate constituents nevertheless reappears, but in a subordinate role, usually in discussions of the internal structure of complex words. A continuation of this 1926–1933 model can also be found in the early development of Kenneth Lee Pike's (1912–2000) view of syntax, where later developments took place within a different theoretical context.

5. Pike's Tagmemic Syntax

Early in his thinking about linguistics, Kenneth Pike rejected the separation of phonological, morphological, and syntactic levels of analysis. He was apparently also unable to contemplate for long a distinction of descriptive levels made by others, even by Bloomfield. In his writings and in published fragments of his correspondence and conversations with Bloomfield, he seems at several points to consider the distinction between the meaningless units constitutive of (meaningful) grammatical form, units thus analogous to the phoneme in morphology, and called *taxemes* by Bloomfield, and the meaningful units of grammatical form, Bloomfield's *tagmemes* (analogous to morphemes in morphology). But he does not maintain this use of terms for long, reverting instead each time to his own view, which does not distinguish these two types of elements. Instead, he calls any element of grammatical form, and the meaning or function of the lexical tokens that might instantiate it in some context, first indifferently by either name, and later, a (Pikean) *tagmeme*. Sometimes the switching between his own pattern of thought and Bloomfield's takes place from one sentence to the next, as it apparently does in this passage, first between the first and second sentences, and more decisively at the paragraph break (Pike 1943: 65):

"Obviously a phoneme means nothing by itself. It is only occasionally that a single phoneme is a morpheme (as in *-s* plural, etc.); the occurrences are, in a sense, mere coincidences.
Taxemes are quite the opposite. A large percentage of taxemes have meanings; where there seems to be no meaning, there frequently is one present, even if it be simply connotative and too ephemeral for ready description."

This passage seems to say quite clearly that what is unusual in morphology, namely, that a single phoneme has meaning, is something quite commonplace in syntax, namely, that a single taxeme has meaning. It suggests that what makes this situation (the meaningfulness of a single phoneme) unusual in morphology is just that most morphemes have longer phonemic shapes. Within Bloomfield's framework, however, with its separate descriptive levels, the phoneme /s/ is a phoneme, not a morpheme, and thus is *never* meaningful, not even when it alone represents a morpheme, or as would later be said, is the phonemic shape of an allomorph. As a phoneme, it is always and by definition a meaningless element, an element that distinguishes meanings but does not *have* them. What does have meaning in this Bloomfieldian example is the plural morpheme, here represented by one of its allomorphs, /s/, and elsewhere by is other allomorphs, such as /z/, etc., according to whatever grouping decisions have been made. Pike had in mind a descriptive model with level mixing; Bloomfield's model had distinct levels. The confusion was in Pike's mind, not Bloomfield's, and it had to do with Pike's apparent belief that when Bloomfield wrote of phonemes, morphemes, taxemes, and tagmemes, he must have meant something very similar to what Pike had in mind. Moreover, he does not seem to realize this, but instead attributes the confusion to Bloomfield (Pike 1958: 274):

"I first attempted to work within his framework, but found many contradictions in which the supposedly-meaningless taxemes of order, modulation, phonetic modification, and selection were treated as meaningful by Bloomfield in various contexts. I pointed out this problem and attempted to salvage the Bloomfieldian tagmeme (1) by an appropriate modification of definitions and (2) by making explicit the necessity of treating all such matters — and linguistics in general — within a hierarchical or pyramidal framework."

A note specifies that he pointed out the problem and this solution in Pike (1943). This paper included ICs as part of its machinery, but, as he later wrote, he was still unable to make it work as he wished. He reports in his 1958 paper that he abandoned these problems for some years, and then, in 1948, began again by asking himself (1958: 274), "whether there might possibly be some structural unit of high relevance to grammatical analysis comparable to the phoneme in the phonological sphere". Meaninglessness is not the relevant trait of the phoneme he has in mind, of course, but rather its status as the smallest element in a hierarchy from which whole utterances can be built by combination. This grammatical counterpart, when he first grasped it, he called a *grammeme*, and later, under pressure of disapproval, changed its name to *tagmeme*. Among other things, this suggests that the tagmeme unit in his 1943 paper is intended to be that of Bloomfield, improved, whereas the tagmeme of his later works is his own. By then, the notion of binary ICs no longer figures in the system, though it remained richly hierarchical, perhaps more so than other varieties of structuralist syntax. In his view, Pike's tagmeme differed from structuralist approaches to syntax based on morpheme classes defined by substitution in frames, such as those of Fries (1952) or Harris (1951), in which (Pike 1958: 276)

"formulas for sentence structures would be couched in terms of symbols for word classes (or morpheme classes, phrase classes, etc.), and would appear to be something like the following: N V N (which is to be read as 'a Noun-Verb-Noun construction')."

He also distinguished it (ibid.) from a 'function view' attributed to Jespersen (1937), in which

"grammatical elements are grammatical-functional-semantic entities, such as subject, object, or other type. The idealized functional unit might normally have — but would not be required to have — a consistent type of class member exercising that function. [...] In work reflecting this view we might expect to find basic formulas something like the following: S O P (which is to be read 'a Subject-Object-Predicate structure')."

He goes on to explain that his tagmeme combines the two other views in one:

"A tagmeme, in my view, always has as one of its basic characteristics a correlation between a functional slot and a morpheme (or morpheme-sequence, etc.) distribution class. Every tagmeme has a function within some larger structure. [...] Each tagmeme, in this view, is manifested by a limited number of morphemes or morpheme sequences. [...] There is a reciprocal relation between a morpheme distribution class on the one hand, and, on the other hand, the functional slot manifested by that class. It is this slot-class correlation which gives a characteristic flavor to our tagmemic approach. Tagmemic formulas are likely to reflect this crucial relationship as follows: SN PV ON (which is to be read as 'a structure containing three tagmemes, of which the first and third contain

Noun as a manifesting class, with the second manifested by the verb class, while the functional tagmemic slots are respectively Subject, Predicate, and Object')."

It is likely that the differences alleged among these three approaches have more to do with what Harris and Jespersen take for granted from their readers. It is more than likely that Pike's model of syntax differs only in its styles of rhetoric and analysis from Bloomfield's (1926) scheme of positional analysis. Pike himself, however, has amply documented his lack of awareness of this parallelism. In what can be seen as yet another example of the symbolic power of Bloomfield's name, Pike returned to the relationship between his syntactic model and Bloomfield's more than 45 years after his first essay, quoting (in Pike 1989: 219) an approving postcard from Bloomfield, dated 28 Jan. 1943, and presumably about Pike 1943: 74–82 (not pages 71–74, as Pike has it), in which Pike had laid out 19 rules of thumb for conducting immediate consitutent analysis. Bloomfield's card is quoted as follows:

"Many thanks for the *Taxeme* article. You have gone a long ways toward straightening out the mess I made of this; your scheme is much better than mine. It is not yet as clear as it should be – I am looking for something one can just put one's thumb on. But I guess that will be a long time coming. Your essay marks a decided step in this direction. Best wishes – as ever LB."

The conflation of formal and functional elements, a fundamental aspect of his thinking throughout most of Pike's career, was the foundation of the distinctive view of syntax within what came to be known as tagmemics, associated first with Pike, and later, in varying forms, also with Robert Longacre and a number of others. It is in some respects still close to its Bloomfieldian origins, but its theoretical foundation stems from Pike's misunderstanding or rejection of Bloomfield's insistence on the separation of lexical and grammatical elements of form in description. The full text of Pike's 1989 "Recollection" makes interesting reading in this connection.

Longacre (1960) develops a view of syntactic structure called string constituent analysis which involves a sequential structure with less layering of constituents than IC analysis. There are many parallels with Zellig Harris's (1962) string analysis approach, and many references to Pike's views: in both string approaches, a typical sentence is seen as containing a sentence as well as additional adjoined material.

6. Zellig S. Harris (1909–1992)

Harris produced several influential statements on distributionalist syntax. The earliest of these was his paper entitled "From Morpheme to Utterance" (1970 [1946]), in which he demonstrated the repeated use of substitution of single morphemes and morpheme sequences within carefully chosen syntactic environments ('frames'). The section dealing with positional analysis based on substitution relations (1946, section 6.1.), corresponding to chapters 15 and 16 in Harris 1951, is a landmark in the field.

In that section, Harris notes that his approach only begins by classing together all morphemes that have similar distributions. By itself, this procedure "would lead to be a relatively large number of different classe." (1970 [1946]: 116). Instead, the analysis is positional, with the crucial foundation for success being the selection of the environments, the syntactic frames, used to define the classes in the most productive way.

"This means that we change over from correlating each morpheme with all its environments, to correlating selected environments (frames) with all the morphemes that enter them. The variables now are the positions, as is shown by the fact that the criterion for class membership is substitution. É. We merely select those positions in which many morphemes occur, and in terms of which we get the most convenient total description." (116–117)

In his bottom-up analysis, Harris first establishes substitution classes of single morphemes. Although there are fewer such substitution classes than there are individual morphemes, Harris wishes to reduce further the number of elements from which syntactic formulas will be constructed. He next establishes sequence classes by examining sequences of morpheme classes and deciding, first, which of these sequence classes are substitutable for a single morpheme substitution class, and only later, which sequences are substitutable for other sequences. The reiteration of this process leads to a system of substitution and sequence classes amounting to a compact and relatively regular set of symbols, formulas and reduction rules (Harris 1951: 274):

"Any utterances can be described as a sequence of these few remaining classes, since any sequence in the utterance can be equated to one or another of these: *These hopeful people want freedom* is *N V* because *these* is *T A*, *hopeful* is *N Na* = *A*, *freedom* is *A An* = *N*, and *T A A N* = *T A N* = *N*, and *V N* = *V* (*see it* for *see* in *I ⎯ now*.)"

Harris also demonstrates how his hierarchical system of classes can be used to represent IC analysis. He first notes that successively more inclusive classes can be compared to reveal what must be added at each level to raise the class to the next higher level of inclusiveness, adding that there will often be a great many possible ways of doing this. Then he outlines IC analysis as another possible application of the class hierarchy. Note that in his equations, more inclusive classes bear higher numbered superscripts (Harris 1951: 278−279):

"We take the utterance and see what equation most simply fits it, i.e. what is the simplest equation such that we can consider our utterance to be a case of it: e.g. *my most recent plays closed down* is a case of N4V4 = utterance. We then take each member of the sequence (on the left side of the equation) and ask for each of these what is the simplest sequence which represents the relevant part of our utterance and for which the member in question is a resultant (on the right hand side): e.g. $TN3 = N4$ (*T* for *my*) would serve for the first part of the utterance, and $V2Vv = V4$ (*Vv* for *-ed*) for the second. This operation is repeated until the members of the sequences represent the individual morphemes of the utterance. Thus *V2* (*close down*) would be analyzed by the equation $V1Pb = V2$, and *N3* (*most recent plays*) would be analyzed first into $N2$ *-s* $= N3$, then into $AN2 = N2$; finally *A* (*most recent*) would be analyzed into $DA = A$. In this analysis, the constituents of our N4V4 utterance were:
 at the first stage, *N4* and *V4*
 at the second stage, *T* and *N3*; *V2* and *Vv*
 at the third stage, *T, N2,* and *-s*; *Vv, V1,* and *Pb*
 at the fourth stage, *T, A* and *N2, -s*; *Vv, V1,* and *Pb*
 at the fifth stage, *T, D, A* and *N2, -s*; *Vv, V1* and *Pb*.

Notice how little is required to convert these formulae into a context-free phase structure grammar fragment. Just begin with an initial symbol, say, and use the appropriate outputs from each line as inputs on the next lines:

N4 V4
N4 T N3
V4 N2 Vv
[...]

In a note on the corresponding section of his earlier paper (1970 [1946]: 125 n. 26), Harris had claimed that his method of substitution and class formation is strictly formal, unlike the form-and-meaning analysis of Otto Jespersen (1860−1943) in *Analytic Syntax* (1937). But his actual analysis, as distinct from his methodology, was distributional in principle only. At that time, and indeed until well into the 1960s, there could be no more than a pretence of selecting one frame instead of another from an actual corpus of adequate size on strictly formal grounds. The same should be said of the alleged differences favoring Harris's 'bottom-up' composition of sentence constituents versus the 'top-down' analysis of whole sentences into immediate constituents, which Harris himself described as a "difficult problem". He adds (1979 [1946]: 117−118) that it "is not clear that there exists any general method" for determining ICs, and that it "would appear that the formation of substitution classes presents fewer theoretical difficulties if we begin with morphemes and work up." Wells (1947: 198) argued that he and Harris used the same methods of analysis (not of presentation), and that they were formally the same whether organized for synthetic or analytic presentation.

Wells also noted that wrong decisions, like right ones, tend to support each other, and that both internal and external criteria must be brought to bear in selecting the best analysis. It is clear that given analytical methods of pragmatic and syntagmatic substitution, there are indeed a very great many alternative analyses of any substantial corpus, that many of these cohere internally in varying degrees, and that no genuine tests of the blind application of strictly distributional criteria to large bodies of data were ever attempted. Nor is it easy to see how the results of such tests, themselves producing huge quantities of alternative classifications, each one a substantial object in itself, could have been evaluated, yielding from among so many alternatives just one as the 'most convenient'. But given the generally very close correspondence between the lexical and grammatical categories in analyses reached 'distributionally' during this period in theoretical and practical treatments, and those already current in the traditional grammars of the same languages, it seems that distributional structures and tests were merely used to prop up these well-known older elements and categories. Later, Chomskyans rightly made much of how greatly the patterns in linguistic data underdetermine analysis. Harris himself saw (1951: 173) that a strictly distributionalist treatment of morphology might yield a different analysis than what would be reached by the use of form-and-meaning criteria.

It may be that the only genuinely distributional analyses of corpora carried out during this period were done as steps toward the breaking of secret codes. Although at least two American linguists of distributionalist inclinations, Martin Joos (1907–1978) and Archibald A. Hill (1902–1992) worked in this field during the war years (Hill 1955), and most American structuralists were involved with the wartime language training program, influence from cryptanalysis would be very difficult to assess, for many reasons. It is arguable also that even the breaking of a code (a system based on substituting arbitrary tokens for lexical items and sometimes for fixed phrases) is after all a less formidable problem than a syntactic analysis, which in principle only begins with a correct segmentation of the corpus.

7. Rulon S. Wells

Matthews (1993: 145) has called attention to the evidence of cooperative communication between Rulon S. Wells (b. 1919) and Zellig Harris (1909–1992) in the period leading up to their respective position papers on the distributional analysis of syntax, as both acknowledged in their publications. Wells built upon the analytical methods of Harris, but covers additional topics in his paper, and addresses the binary principle, without discussing its psychological history. Indeed, the paper makes no reference to the early history of IC analysis.

Wells (1947) is a difficult paper. At each new stage in the exposition, there is a consideration of alternative constituent analyses bearing on it, and often also of alternative methods of analysis. Connections are traced from the constituents identified at a given point in the dissection of the examples to other classes and class hierarchies. As he nearly always did, Wells left indeterminacies identified but indeterminate.

Harris's morpheme-to-utterance procedure is shown to have a generative orientation; Bloomfield's IC analysis is shown to be analytical in orientation. As noted above, Wells's procedures are neutral in this regard, and at times, suggest a cyclial view. Pike is mentioned briefly. Wells gives more concrete illustrations of analytical procedures than Harris, who often resorts to abstract formulae, or Pike, who had offered a collection of rules of thumb for choosing points of segmentation. Wells seek to show the connections between his procedures and the higher and lower levels of syntactic organization they touch on, but he states clearly that there is no single distributional procedure leading to a particular analysis, and that after a certain point, meaning must be brought into play in deciding between alternatives.

Well's goal is clearly stated in the first paragraph (1957 [1947]: 186): "to replace by a unified, systematic theory the heterogeneous and incomplete methods offered for determining *immediate constituents* [...]. The unifying basis is supplied by the famous concept of patterning, applied repeatedly and in divers forms". In its own terms, the paper is successful, in that it gives a clear and self-constitent statement of the methods of substitution and positional analysis. But at the same time, it exposes what Wells saw as the limits of distributional analysis in syntax. In what Matthews (1993: 149–150) identified as the first significant appearance of constructional homonymy as a theoretical issue, Wells argued, in relation to his *old men and women* example, that syntax cannot be adequately analyzed without appeals to meaning. And in his discussion of the binary principle, he sets limits for it too, providing distributional and constructional arguments for deciding on single, multiple, or discontinuous constituents under stated conditions.

What Wells meant by patterning is clearly within the distributionalist tradition. He calls for repeated use of the technique of substitution within frames, beginning with the establishment of morpheme classes, and then of sequence classes, which are sequences of one or more morpheme classes. Within a sequence class, then, each morpheme class is not only a morpheme class in the general sense, but is at the same time occupying a *position* relative to the other morpheme classes in the sequence. He notes that most sequences of morphemes belong to more than one sequence class, because most morphemes belong to more than one (morpheme) substitution class. On this foundation he defines the notion of *expansion*: "sometimes two sequences occur in the same environments even though they have different internal structures. When one of the sequences is at least as long as the other (contains at last as many morphemes) and is structurally diverse from it (does not belong to all the same sequence-classes as the other), we call it an *expansion* of that other sequence [...]"

(1957 [1947]: 1877). He then states that the "general principle of IC analysis is not only to view a sequence, when possible, as an expansion of a shorter sequence, but also to break it up into parts of which some or all are themselves expansions."

Substitution within frames is defined in terms of a focus, where the substitutions occur, and an environment. The class of all sequences substitutable for a given focus in a given environment is the focus class relative to that environment. Wells then notes that some focus classes (those with many sequence classes but few environments, and those with few sequence classes but many environments) are easy to define, but of little importance (1957 [1947]: 190):

"What is difficult, but far more important than either of the easy tasks, is to define focus-classes rich both in the number of environments characterizing them and at the same time in the diversity of sequence-classes that they embrace. Actor and action (or in the older terminology subject and predicate) are such focus classes."

He mentions a number of others, including parts of speech. Finally, after reviewing some more examples of well and ill motivated analyses, he remarks that "right analyses are ultimately supported from without by the method of regarding them as expansions of shorter sequences, whereas wrong analyses lack this ultimate extraneous support." He further characterizes what he means (1957 [1947]: 193):

"One IC analysis involves others; its soundness is not tested until its most far-reaching effects on the system have been explored. Ultimately, what is accepted or rejected is not the analysis of a single sentence but what we may call the IC-*system* of the language, an entire set or system of analyses, complete down to the ultimate constituents, of all the utterances of the language."

In a section on constructions, Wells introduced constructional homonymy as a theoretical problem rather than a curiosity, and as a justification for considering the meaning of constructions as well as the list and sequence of their morphemes.

Wells also addressed the status of the principle that constituent divisions must be binary. In this discussion, Wells draws together references to non-binary analyses in the work of Bloomfield, Bloch & Trager, Nida, and Pike (Wells 1957 [1947]: 198 n. 37). The provisions he made for single, multiple, and discontinuous ICs alongside binary ones amount to a requirement that these be resorted to when binary divisions are arbitrary or otherwise unjustified. Here too, the context is one of direct reliance on tests of constructional or utterance meaning.

What Wells achieved, then, was what he set out to do: to unify and systematize the methods of IC analysis. In doing so, he developed the notion of expansions as a way of capturing the main features of the method. It is noteworthy also that in this paper, immediately and widely recognized as a major statement of the distributionalist approach to syntax, he also recognized limits beyond which distributional analysis could not go, and provided guidelines for suspending the binary principle, which had long since lost its psychological motivation and had been accepted as a matter of economy or convenience in accounting for distributions.

The tagmemic approach to syntax and to the larger study of language retained a large following, and continued to develop under the guidance of Kenneth Pike and its other theorists. Within the academic departments where other varieties of descriptive structuralist linguistics had developed and spread, IC analysis remained the main approach to syntax, and stayed roughly where Wells left it in 1947, taught in courses and in textbooks (Hockett 1958, Gleason 1961, Hill 1958, Francis 1958) until it was replaced in the early 1960s by Phrase Structure Grammar as a foundation for technical linguistic discussions of syntax. However, this replacement taken by itself, as Matthews (1993: 153) explains, was not so radical. In place of pretended distributional analysis of syntax without regard to meaning, what emerged was more open reliance on native-speaker intuitions of meaning and grammaticality.

8. Bibliographical References

Note: Page references to papers are to the reprints in Joos (1957) and Bloomfield (1970).

Blake, Frank R. 1919. Review of Bloomfield (1917). *American Journal of Philology* 40.86–93. (Repr. in Bloomfield 1970.82–89.)

Bloch, Bernard. 1946. "Studies in Colloquial Japanese II: Syntax". *Language* 22.200–248. (Repr. in Joos 1957.154–185.)

Bloomfield, Leonard. 1914. *Introduction to the Study of Language.* New York: Holt. (Repr., with an introduction by Joseph F. Kess, Amsterdam & Philadelphia: Benjamins, 1983.)

—. 1917. *Tagalog Texts with Grammatical Analysis.* University of Illinois Studies in Language and Literature, vol. 3, No. 204. Chicago: Univ. of Illinois.

—. 1926. "A Set of Postulates for the Science of Language." *Language* 2.153–164. (Repr. in Joos 1957.26–31 and Bloomfield 1970.128–138.)

—. 1933. *Language.* New York: Holt & Co.

—. 1945. "On Describing Inflection". *Festschrift für M. Blakemore Evans (= Monatshefte für deutschen Unterricht* 37: 4/5), 8–13.

—. 1970. *A Leonard Bloomfield Anthology.* Ed. by Charles Hockett. Bloomington, Indiana: Indiana Univ. Press.

Bowen, J. Donald & Robert P. Stockwell. 1955. "The Phonemic Interpretation of Spanish Semivowels". *Language* 31.236–240. (Repr. in Joos 1957.400–402.)

—. 1956. "A Further Note on Spanish Semivowels". *Language* 32.290–292. (Repr. in Joos 1957. 405.)

Chomsky, Noam. 1957. *Syntactic Structures.* The Hague: Mouton.

—. 1962 [1958]. "A Transformational Approach to Syntax". *Third Texas Conference on Problems of Linguistic Analysis in English* ed. by Archibald A. Hill, 124–158. Austin Texas: Univ. of Texas.

Francis, W. Nelson. 1958. *The Structure of American English.* New York: Ronald.

Fries, Charles C. 1952. *The Structure of English.* New York: Harcourt Brace & World.

Gleason, Henry A., Jr. 1961. *An Introduction to Descriptive Linguistics.* 2nd ed. New York: Holt, Rinehart & Winston.

Greenough, James B. et al., eds. 1931. *Allen & Greenough's New Latin Grammar for Schools and Colleges, Founded on Comparative Grammar.* Boston: Ginn & Co.

Hall, Robert A., Jr. 1947. "Colloquial French Verb Inflection". *Romance* 1.39–50.

Harris, Zellig S. 1942. "Morpheme Alternants in Linguistic Analysis". *Language* 18.169–180. (Repr. in Joos 1957.109–115.)

—. 1946. "From Morpheme to Utterance". *Language* 22.161–83. (Repr. in Joos 1957.142–153.)

—. 1951. *Methods in Structural Linguistics.* Chicago: University of Chicago Press.

—. 1962. *String Analysis of Sentence Structure.* The Hague: Mouton.

Haugen, Einar. 1951. "Directions in Modern Linguistics". *Language* 27.211–222. (Repr. in Joos 1957.357–363.)

Hill, Archibald A. 1955. "Linguistics Since Bloomfield". *Quarterly Journal of Speech* 41.253–260.

—. 1958. *Introduction to Linguistic Structures: From Sound to Sentence in English.* New York: Harcourt, Brace & World.

Hockett, Charles F. 1947. "Problems of Morphemic Analysis". *Language* 23.321–343. (Repr. in Joos 1957.229–242.)

—. 1958. *A Course in Modern Linguistics.* New York: Macmillan.

Jespersen, Otto. 1937. *Analytic Syntax.* London: Allen & Unwin. (Repr., with an introduction by James D. McCawley, Chicago: Univ. of Chicago Press, 1984.)

Joos, Martin, ed. 1957. *Readings in Linguistics: The development of descriptive linguistics in America since 1925.* Washington, D. C.: American Council of Learned Societies. (4th ed., Chicago: Univ. of Chicago Press, 1966.)

Longacre, Robert. 1960. "String Constituent Analysis". *Language* 36.63–88.

Matthews, Peter. 1992. "Bloomfield's Morphology and its Successors". *Transactions of the Philological Society* 90.121–86.

—. 1993. *Grammatical Theory in the United States from Bloomfield to Chomsky.* Cambridge Studies in Linguistics, No. 63. Cambridge: Cambridge Univ. Press.

Percival, W. Keith. 1976. "On the Historical Source of Immediate Constituent Analysis". *Notes from the Linguistic Underground* ed. by James D. McCawley, 229–242. New York: Academic Press.

Pike, Kenneth L. 1943. "Taxemes and Immediate Constituents". *Language* 19.65–82.

—. 1958. "On Tagmemes ne Grammemes". *IJAL* 24.273–278.

—. 1989. 'Recollections of Bloomfield". *Historiographia Linguistica* 16.217–223.

Saporta, Sol. 1956. "A Note on Spanish Semivowels". *Language* 32.287–290. (Repr. in Joos 1957. 403–404.)

Smyth, Herbert W. 1916. *A Greek Grammar for Schools and Colleges.* New York, Cincinnati, etc.: American Book Co.

Trager, George L. 1944. "The Verb Morphology of Spoken French". *Language* 20.131–141.

—. 1955. "French Morphology: Verb inflection". *Langauge* 31.511–29.

— & Henry Lee Smith, Jr. 1951. *Outline of English Structure.* (= *Studies in Linguistics*; Occasional Papers, 3.)

Weiss, Albert P. 1925. "One Set of Postulates for a Behavioristic Psychology". *Psychological Review* 82.83–87.

Wells, Rulon S. 1947. "Immediate Constituents". *Language* 23.81–117. (Repr. in Joos 1957.186–207.)

John G. Fought, Diamond Bar, Calif.
(U.S.A.)

215. Quantitative methods and lexicostatistics in the 20th Century

1. Definition of the subject
2. Sociolinguistic applications
3. Lexical diffusion
4. Dialectometry
5. Lexicostatistics and glottochronology
6. Swadesh's method
7. Lexical statistics
8. Probabilistic methods
9. Reasons for using quantitative methods
10. Current status
11. Bibliography

1. Definition of the subject

'Quantitative' means different things to different people. Dictionary definitions tend to be either tautological ("having to do with quantity") or not very helpful or representative of actual usage ("capable of being measured"). For many people, especially those with a certain fear of numbers, anything with a number in it is already 'quantitative'. For such people, any method which in any way uses numbers is therefore a 'quantitative method'. Those who would describe themselves as practitioners of quantitative methods, however, mean something far more sophisticated than the mere use of numbers in counting and calculating. By quantitative methods, they mean methods that use some aspect of numerical, computational, or statistical analysis to go beyond simple description of the (empirical) data, to actually wring something further out of the data that simply would not be evident from the mere data alone. Descriptive statistics allows us to summarize complex numerical data, especially in large volumes; these, though, are not in and of themselves quantitative methods, until some further steps – involving some actual analysis and/or inference – are taken. "Statistical tests provide us a way to determine how confident we can be about the generalizations we make" (Davis 1999: x). Inferential statistics and the various quantitative methods built thereon allow us to go even further and make considerable inferences from those data that go well beyond the mere description of those data.

The possibilities for application of quantitative methods in the service of linguistics are virtually endless, limited only by the imagination of the practitioners themselves, and indeed any reader of a moderately wide sample of the linguistic literature will come across novel applications regularly. This can involve either a new application of an "old" statistical technique, or, more rarely, the application of a new statistical technique. In an article such as this, however, only the largest areas of application can be represented; obviously the details of the statistical methods themselves cannot be covered exhaustively either. There are several excellent books on statistics specifically designed for linguists, among them Butler (1985), Rietveld & van Hout (1993), Woods et al. (1986), Brainerd (1974), and for real beginners, the elementary but readable Anshen (1978) and Davis (1990).

2. Sociolinguistic applications

Probably the most widely known quantitative methods, and certainly the only ones to make any widespread appearance in the undergraduate linguistics curriculum, are the applications in sociolinguistics. Appearing under various names (such as variation theory), most of these received their initial impetus from the work of William Labov (b. 1927); a landmark here is Labov (1966), a study involving the Lower East Side in New York City. Here various quantitative techniques (principally regression analysis) are used to discover the underlying structure or regularities in seemingly haphazard distributions of some linguistic phenomenon (sometimes known as "free variation"). Given the quantity of empirical data to be analyzed, along with the number of variables typically involved, the implementation in most cases must be by computer, specific programs have been written to perform this analysis (e.g., VARBRUL, GOLDVARB). In its most basic form, variation theoretical analysis proceeds as follows: Different variants of a linguistic variable (e.g., presence or absence of /r/ in preconsonantal and prepausal position) are found to correlate with various other factors, typically non-linguistic factors, such as style, socio-economic class, age, and gender. The former (linguistic) variables are found to be (at least partially) dependent on the latter (non-linguistic) independent variables. Literally thousands of studies have resulted from this basic insight. Much of the early work involved phonological dependent variables, but later work has involved morphological and syntactic variables as well. The research has covered many different types and sizes of community, in many countries, and involved languages of many different language families. Thus major advances in our knowledge of the genesis and spread of linguistic changes throughout a speech community are due to quantitative methods in sociolinguistics. These results are obviously also of great interest to diachronic linguistics.

3. Lexical diffusion

Interacting with this, but somewhat distinct from it, is the study of how changes spread throughout the lexicon. The Neogrammarian hypothesis from the mid-1870s — that sound change is regular and admits no exceptions — has been challenged by William S.-Y. Wang (b. 1933), later with Mieko Ogura (b. 1956), in a framework known as 'Lexical Diffusion', since the late 1960s; see Wang (1969), Ogura (1990), and Ogura & Wang (1996). Studies on a variety of languages, from a variety of time periods, using large amounts of data, confirm that changes spread gradually throughout the lexicon, from word to word; changes also spread throughout the community, from speaker to speaker. Further, the spread of the changes is initially slow, then speeds up and gathers momentum affecting a large number of words (and speakers) in a relatively short time-span, and then slows down, eventually ceasing; this yields an S-shaped curve when one plots the extent of the change against time. Further work of this nature is likely once again to reinforce the links between sociolinguistics ('horizontal transmission', the study of language in space, wave-like transmission; cf. Ogura 1990) and historical linguistics ('vertical transmission', the study of language in time, tree-like transmission); quantitative approaches enable the researcher to handle simultaneously the great bulk of data required for such work.

4. Dialectometry

More traditional forms of dialectology have perhaps been slower to embrace quantitative methods. The application of quantitative methods in dialectology goes by the cover term dialectometry. Although there are many methods possible, they all begin by establishing a quantitative measure of the distance (D) between all pairs of dialects being investigated, and then applying the principles of numerical taxonomy to the analysis of that data (cf. Schneider 1984: 314); D can be based on any or all of phonetic, phonological, morphological, syntactic, and lexical features. This enables the researcher to use the power of numerical methods to extract information from and recognize patterns in the data that would not be possible without this enhancement (cf. Goebl 1984: iii). This goes well beyond the use of the computer merely as a tool to draw dialect maps (e.g., Rubin 1970) — not to belittle the usefulness of even that in, for example, quickly testing out speculations which would never be attempted by more labour-intensive means. There have been at least seven dialectometrical techniques discussed in the literature; for a brief review, see Embleton (1987, 1995). The best known are those of Jean Séguy (b. 1914) and former students and associates centred in Toulouse, of Hans Goebl (b. 1943) and former students and colleagues centred in Salzburg, of various users of hierarchical cluster analysis (Klemola [e.g., 1990], Linn & Regal [e.g., 1985], Shaw [e.g., 1974]), of dual scaling (Cichocki [e.g., 1989]), and of multidimensional scaling (MDS; see Embleton [e.g., 1993], Embleton & Wheeler [e.g., 1997a, b]). Séguy's [e.g., 1971] is historically the first, mathematically the least sophisticated, and consists simply of writing the value of D, for each pair of locales investigated, somewhere on a line on the map joining the two locales. We then scan the map for larger values of D; where they cluster is the location of an isogloss bundle. Goebl uses the technique of choroplethic mapping. For each locale, a separate map is created, by taking that locale's value of D with all other locales, dividing the total range of D's (from minimum to maximum) into 6 to 8 ranges, and then colouring the tessellated area around each other locale with a colour appropriate to that range. Goebl's earlier work (e.g., 1982) used 6 shades of grey (lightest for the lowest values of D, darkest for the highest values of D), but his later work (e.g., Goebl 1993), availing itself of the ubiquity of colour printing, uses colour for the same effect (red for the lowest values of D, deep blue for the highest values of D). In general, maps corresponding to adjacent locales would be expected to have very similar overall colour-distribution; if there is a radical shift in the overall colour pattern between adjacent maps, this indicates a dialect boundary between those two locales. The mathematical and computational problems involved are non-trivial, but the resulting maps have great visual appeal and give an excellent overall view of the dialect-space. Embleton's (b. 1954) MDS method first constructs a D-matrix, pairwise for each pair of dialects being considered, then reduces this matrix to two dimensions using MDS. This 'linguistic map' of the dialect space can be compared to an actual geographic map of the same dialect space, for discrepancies. If the linguistic distance is greater than the geographic distance between locales, this indicates the existence of isogloss bundles between the two locales; if the linguistic distance is less than the geographic, this indicates some form of rapprochement and increased intercommunication between the two locales. Future productive applications of quantitative methods in both dialectology and sociolinguistics are likely to include factor analysis and principal components analysis, both very commonly applied in other social sciences.

5. Lexicostatistics and glottochronology

Lexicostatistics is another fairly widely known term, even if not a well understood one. Many people confuse lexicostatistics with glottochronology. Since at least the 1930s, linguists have been seriously and practically interested in the development of techniques for assessing the closeness of the relationship between a pair of genetically related languages, using only information from the contemporary languages themselves. This is typically some form of distance measure, and frequently involves measures of lexical similarity. Applied pairwise, this leads to the reconstruction of a family tree for a group of genetically related languages, without the use of any actual historical information about the language family. This has come to be known as lexicostatistics (e. g., Gleason 1959), perhaps somewhat misleadingly, from the fact that it uses numbers (although technically it is usually differential equations, rather than statistics) and usually lexicon (although nothing in the mathematics depends on the distance measures being lexical rather than from any other source). Some work, based on lists of supposedly basic or non-cultural vocabulary (which have come to be known as Swadesh-lists, after their first proponent), has gone further. The meanings on the Swadesh-list are translated into the languages in question, comparison of which leads to a distance measure, as with lexicostatistics. But coupled with a grossly simplifying assumption that such basic vocabulary changes at a universally constant rate (constant over time, but also between languages), it is then possible to calculate a time depth for a reconstructed ancestor language for any pair of languages, based on the proportion of cognates that they share. Such provision of absolute time depths is known as glottochronology.

For a summary of the history of lexicostatics and glottochronology, as well as an overview of various methods in use, see Embleton (1986). The Swadesh method (and variations thereof) clearly dominate the field, both historically and currently. But there is an earlier history of lexicostatistical methods, predating Morris Swadesh's (1909–1967) work. Some see this work as beginning with a principle stated by his former teacher Edward Sapir (1884–1939): "The greater the degree of linguistic differentiation within a stock the greater is the period of time that must be assumed for the development of such differentiation" (1916: 76). Until the basic steps of quantifying both the degree of linguistic differentiation and the rate of change are taken, however, this remains a general statement and not a forerunner of a quantitative method. A more interesting precursor can be found in an early work by Robert Gordon Latham (1812–1888), who states that "the average rate at which languages change is capable of being approximated" and "the maximum difference, at a given period, between two or more languages is also capable of being approximated" (Latham 1850: 565; cited by Gordon Hewes in the discussion included with Hymes 1960: 338). It appears, though, that Latham never followed this up, and thus a quantitative method was not yet born. The first major − and practical − mathematical treatment of the question of genetic proximity of languages was given by Alfred Louis Kroeber (1876–1960) & Charles Douglas Chrétien (1904–1970) in 1937. This had its roots in a method devised by two Polish anthropologists, Jan Czekanowski (1882–1965) and Stanislaw Klimek (1903–1939), and used extensively in physical anthropology and ethnography. For a fixed list of features, for each pair of languages L_1 and L_2 calculate a (the number of features that both languages share), b (the number of features in L_1 but not L_2), c (the number of features in L_2 but not L_1), and d (the number of features in neither language). The quantities a, b, c and d can then be arranged in a 2×2 contingency table, a well-known mathematical concept, and manipulated and analyzed in various standard ways. The concept is relatively simply, but fraught with interpretive dangers: how to construct the feature list, independence of features, how to interpret the resulting correlations (especially if they are negative), how to amalgamate the pairwise results for a larger family, etc. (details may be found in Embleton 1986). The second major statistical treatment of the genetic proximity of languages is by the English philologist Alan S. C. Ross (1907−1980) in a 1950 article; this is a root-retention model, with some important similarities and differences to the Kroeber & Chrétien model (details in Embleton 1986). Perhaps the most interesting point, in light of future developments, was that both models relied for their basis on similarity/distance measures from a standardized feature list. Both models have been virtually abandoned, although elements of them occasionally recur − and the lessons learned from them are important in avoiding certain pitfalls in some current work. Another approach to tree reconstruction has its origins in Gleason's (b. 1917) method of counterindications (1959). In this method, all topologically possible family-trees for the putative language family are reconstructed, and then certain of them discarded based on counter-evidence (e.g., of cognate patterns). This method has also been all but discarded, partly because even with the advent of modern high-speed computing the total number of possible trees in unmanageably large, and partly because such methods are easily confounded by borrowing (which essentially has a smearing effect on a clearly-branching genetic tree). A variant, which relies on hierarchical clustering and also attempts to estimate relative branch lengths (i.e., can be used as a glottochronological method) is presented in Embleton (1986). Warnow et al. (e.g., Warnow, Taylor & Ringe 1995) are developing a character-based (rather than distance-based) method for tree reconstruction. This method grows out of recent advances in both computational methodology and biology (often called cladistics). Although such methods still can have problems handling the amount of borrowing which seems to take place in language evolution, they hold much promise partly because they more nearly simulate the types of thought-processes which go on in the heads of skilled practitioners of traditional techniques, and yet they can handle vast amounts of data simultaneously.

6. Swadesh's method

Swadesh's method is by far the best known; in fact, for many people (who use their terminology more loosely than those specializing in quantitative methods), his method is synonymous with both 'lexicostatistics' and 'glottochronology'. In the early 1950s (Swadesh 1950, 1952), he introduced a model of language change with a vocabulary turnover process fairly closely analogous to radioactive decay (Carbon-14 dating). The claim is that a list of N meanings can be arrived at, which are likely to be found in all cultures and to be particularly resistant to borrowing and other cultural (and inter-cultural) influences; such a list is now known as a 'Swadesh-list'. N has varied from a bit over 200 to a little under 100, mostly as different researchers have found different problems with various meanings on the list over the years. One finds a single gloss for each meaning on the list in each of the languages under investigation. Over time, 'morpheme decay' occurs; in each language, words representing meanings on the list are replaced by other words (for all the usual reasons that languages change), while other words are retained. It is assumed that this rate of morpheme retention, r, is constant over time, and furthermore that it is universal between languages; these assumptions, of course, are not uncontroversial. The 'time depth' t (since a pair of languages separated) is then given by $t = \log c/\log r$ (e.g., Hymes 1960: 4), where c is the fraction of common (supposedly cognate) forms on the test-list. Robert B. Lees (1923−1996) uses this model on 13 pairs of older and newer versions of the same language with written histories so the time-depth is known (e.g., Old English and Modern English) to try to determine the universal rate constant (1953: 118−119). He concludes that r is 81% per millenium for the 200-word Swadesh-list, "for all languages, for all times". Some of the evidence he accumulated even within his own article should have been sufficient to alert him and others to the fact that this constant was far from universal.

This basic equation has been (and continues to be) widely employed; for a representative sample of such applications, see Embleton (1986, Chap. 2). There have also been some attempts to deal with shortcomings of this basic model, all of which of course result in more complicated (sometimes vastly more sophisticated) equations. For example, r can be allowed to vary over time, between languages, and even for different meanings on the test-list; the list itself can be adapted; and, most radically, borrowing can be allowed between languages; details may be found in Embleton (1986).

7. Lexical statistics

Lexicostatistics is quite distinct from lexical statistics ('la statistique lexicale' [Dugast 1980]), quantitative lexicology, and lexicometry which all refer to statistical methods harnessed in the study of the vocabulary present in a discourse and its organization within that discourse (i. e., a subfield of stylistics). A large amount of work has been done in this vein, much centred around Charles Muller (b. 1909) and his former students, colleagues, and other associates (e. g., Dugast 1979, 1980, Thoiron 1980, Thoiron et al. 1988). Stylostatistics and stylometry refer to similar statistical studies of discourse, but not restricted to just lexicon, but utilizing any aspect of language. As but one example, frequency of articles, or the ratio of articles to pronouns, may be an indicator of genre (e. g., Brainerd 1972; 1974, Chap. 6). One practical application of these types of study is authorship identification, for a variety of purposes, from the scholarly ("was this play really written by Shakespeare?") to the forensic; for an excellent introduction to this entire range of problems, see Morton (1978). A more subtle variant involves establishing the chronology of a particular author's work, or in fact of an entire literature (e. g., Fosse 1997, with reference to Sanskrit). A currently active, much newer, school of such work is centred in Trier, under the leadership of Gabriel Altmann (b. 1931) and Reinhard Köhler (b. 1951), entitled on "language synergetics". The basic insights here involve the interrelationships of such factors as frequency, age, and length of linguistic entities; as such, it takes much earlier work by George Kingsley Zipf (1902—1950), e. g., Zipf (1949), and develops it much further, with many possible applications, including to textual analysis.

8. Probabilistic methods

The use of probability theory in casting light on various linguistic problems seems to be increasing recently, after lying more or less dormant since some early suggestions in Ross (1950). Donald Ringe (b. 1954), following in the footsteps of Ross (1950), Oswalt (1970), and Villemin (1983), exploits the fact that the sound-meaning relationship in language is (mostly) arbitrary, and hence that the distribution of sounds within vocabulary lists ought to be random (except for the phonotactic constraints of the language), to explore long-distance relationships (e. g., Ringe 1992). Specifically, if resemblances between word-lists can be shown to be of greater-than-chance frequency, this leads one to hypothesize that the languages involved must be related. The probabilistic problems involved are far from trivial, and although the results obtained can be interesting and probative, they tend to remain unconvincing and merely suggestive to many linguists, as obtaining consensus as to the standard of proof seems impossible. Such work also generally requires so many idealizing and simplifying assumptions — merely in order to render the problem probabilistically tractable — that critics (or those who for various reasons wish to remain unconvinced, so that they can continue to espouse a contrary opinion on the relationship in question) have a fairly easy time legitimizing their reservations by simply demanding a higher standard of proof. Much the same applies to the work of Johanna Nichols, which seeks to integrate typology and diversity in time and space, using probabilistic methods and a 174-language database (e. g., Nichols 1992). These worthwhile probabilistic applications constitute perhaps one of the best demonstrations of how quantitative methods are most usefully viewed as a supplement and complement to 'traditional' methods, rather than a competitor to or replacement for them.

9. Reasons for using quantitative methods

Why do linguists use such methods at all? Especially when so few linguists have a solid understanding of the mathematics and statistics necessary to construct the models, or to use the methods, or to fully appreciate and interpret the results, the conclusions are often greeted with disbelief or controversy, often of a quite emotional and even irrational nature. Without going into details here, much of the research in lexicostatistics (and particularly glottochronology), and more recently in long distance relationships, has been marred by this. Much of the initial impetus in fact came from mathematicians (e. g., Gabriel Altmann, Barron Brainerd [b. 1928], David Sankoff [b. 1942], to name but a few of the most prominent) with an interest in language and linguistics. This can be seen as part of the continual search by mathematicians, particularly applied mathematicians, for new fields of application. There are also the usual attractions of cross-disciplinary or inter-disciplinary research, some of which are rooted in the desire to look at a problem or issue in a holistic way, using the tools and perspective of as many different disciplines as possible. In many cases, quantitative methods promise (and deliver) quick results, especially as initial approximations. They are especially good at handling large volumes of data. But also not to be underestimated is the desire by linguists to be (and be seen to be) more objective and scientific. Statistics and statistical methods have for several decades been widely studied as part of the routine training of social scientists, resulting in a natural exposure of linguists to this type of training, and to colleagues with this type of training, as linguistics began to take on a social science dimension as well as its more traditional humanistic one. Thus it is no coincidence that there was a sudden upsurge of this attraction of linguists to quantitative methods, and hence of new quantitative methods, in the 1950s and 1960s. This era also saw a huge optimism in the power of science and technology — and linguistics was no exception. For example, some people thought that lexicostatistics and glottochronology would render the traditional methods — comparative method and internal reconstruction — completely obsolete. After an initial euphoria, there is typically a counter-reaction, in which the majority impulse is to totally discard the quantitative method. Sober second thought, not just in this case but also in many others, has generally resulted in a sensible outcome, namely that the quantitative method is simply added to the arsenal of techniques at the linguist's disposal, as a supplement and complement to non-quantitative methods. Many applications of quantitative methods were originally thought of (perhaps more accurately, dreamed of) in the 1950s, 1960s, and early 1970s, but only became possible in the later 1970s and 1980s with the advent of high-speed computing (e. g., my own work in lexicostatistics in the 1970s). This time also saw the development of many of the well-known 'black-box' software packages (e. g., SPSS, SAS, BMDP; originally of course on mainframe computers), which have been of enormous use to linguists, both in bringing to their attention techniques of which they might otherwise have been unaware, but also in the convenience of having the latest and best numerical implementations of those techniques in an 'off-the-shelf' format. Further applications, such as many of those in dialectometry, have only been able to blossom with the even higher-speed, larger-capacity computing available in the 1990s.

10. Current status

Quantitative methodology is now firmly established, not only in linguistics, but also in virtually all social science and humanities disciplines. The widespread interest in quantitative method in linguistics is amply demonstrated by the existence (and growing length of) at least two dedicated book series (*Quantitative Linguistics* [formerly Brockmeyer in Bochum and now Wissenschaftlicher Verlag in Trier] and *Travaux de linguistique quantitative* published by Slatkine in Geneva), a journal (*Journal of Quantitative Linguistics*, published by Kluwer in Dordrecht), and a scholarly organization, the International Quantitative Linguistics Association, which also holds triennial international conferences. There is also a forthcoming volume in this HKS-handbook series, to be edited by Gabriel Altmann, Reinhard Köhler, and Rajmund Piotrowski. More importantly, an awareness of quantitative methods and their underpinnings has to some extent percolated and informed the practice of linguists in general — so that questions of sample size, sampling techniques and representativity, precision, objective vs. subjective answers to questions like "is X different from Y" are at least implicitly taken into consideration by those who themselves do not practise quantitative methods. Perhaps this is the truest marker of the maturity of the discipline.

11. Bibliography

Anshen, Frank. 1978. *Statistics for Linguists*. Rowley, Mass.: Newbury House.

Brainerd, Barron. 1972. "An Exploratory Study of Pronouns and Articles as Indices of Genre in English". *Language and Style* 5.239–259.

–. 1974. *Weighing Evidence in Language and Literature: A statistical approach.* Toronto & Buffalo: Univ. of Toronto Press.

–, ed. 1983. *Historical Linguistics.* (= *Quantitative Linguistics*, 18.) Bochum: Brockmeyer.

Butler, Christopher M. 1985. *Statistics in Linguistics.* New York: Blackwell.

Cichocki, Władysław. 1989. "An Application of Dual Scaling in Dialectometry". *Computer Methods in Dialectology* ed. by William A. Kretzschmar, Jr., Edgar W. Schneider & Ellen Johnson (= Special Issue of *Journal of English Linguistics* 22:1), 90–96.

Davis, Lawrence M. 1990. *Statistics in Dialectology.* Tuscaloosa & London: Univ. of Alabama Press.

Dugast, Daniel. 1979. *Vocabulaire et stylistique.* Geneva: Slatkine.

Embleton, Sheila M. 1986. *Statistics in Historical Linguistics.* (= *Quantitative Linguistics*, 30.) Bochum: Brockmeyer.

–. 1987. "Multidimensional Scaling as a Dialectometrical Technique". *Papers from the Eleventh Annual Meeting of the Atlantic Provinces Linguistic Association* ed. by Rose Mary Babitch, 33–49. Shippagan, New Brunswick: Centre universitaire de Shippagan.

–. 1993. "Multidimensional Scaling as a Dialectometrical Technique: Outline of a research project". *Contributions to Quantitative Linguistics* ed. by Reinhard Köhler & Burghard B. Rieger, 267–276. Dordrecht, Boston & London: Kluwer.

–. 1995. "Mathematical Methods in Dialectology". Workshop at the Institute for Research in Cognitive Science, Univ. of Pennsylvania, 17–18 April 1995.

– & Eric Wheeler. 1997a. "Multidimensional Scaling and the SED Data". *The Computer Developed Linguistic Atlas of England* 2 ed. by Wolfgang Viereck & Heinrich Ramisch, 5–11. Tübingen: Niemeyer.

–, –. 1997b. "Finnish Dialect Atlas for Quantitative Studies". *Journal of Quantitative Linguistics* 4.99–102.

Fosse, Lars Martin. 1997. *The Crux of Chronology in Sanskrit Literature. Statistics and Indology: A study of method.* Oslo: Universitetsforlaget.

Gleason, Henry Allen, Jr. 1959. "Counting and Calculating for Historical Reconstruction". *Anthropological Linguistics* 1.22–32.

Goebl, Hans. 1982. *Dialektometrie: Prinzipien und Methoden des Einsatzes der Numerischen Taxonomie im Bereich der Dialektgeographie.* Vienna: Österreichische Akademie der Wissenschaften.

–, ed. 1984. *Dialectology.* (= *Quantitative Linguistics*, 21.) Bochum: Brockmeyer.

–. 1993. "Dialectometry: A short overview of the principles and practice of quantitative classification of linguistic atlas data". *Contributions to Quantitative Linguistics* ed. by Reinhard Köhler & Burghard B. Rieger, 277–315. Dordrecht, Boston & London: Kluwer.

Hymes, Dell H. 1960. "Lexicostatistics So Far". *Current Anthropology* 1.3–44.

Klemola, Juhani. 1990. "Dialect Areas in the South-West of England: An exercise in cluster analysis". Paper presented at the International Congress of Dialectologists, Bamberg, 31 July 1990.

Kroeber, Alfred L. & C. Douglas Chrétien. 1937. "Quantitative Classification of Indo-European Languages". *Language* 13.83–103.

Labov, William. 1966. *The Social Stratification of English in New York City.* Washington, D. C.: Center for Applied Linguistics.

Latham, Robert Gordon. 1850. *The Natural History of the Varieties of Man.* London: Van Voorst.

Lees, Robert B. 1953. "The Basis of Glottochronology". *Language* 29.113–127.

Linn, Michael D. & Ronald R. Regal. 1985. "Numerical Taxonomy as a Tool in Dialect Research". *Papers from the Fifth International Conference on Methods in Dialectology* ed. by Henry Warkentyne, 245–261. Victoria: Dept. of Linguistics, Univ. of Victoria.

Morton, Andrew Q. 1978. *Literary Detection: How to prove authorship and fraud in literature and documents.* New York: Charles Scribner's Sons.

Nichols, Johanna. 1992. *Linguistic Diversity in Space and Time.* Chicago & London: Univ. of Chicago Press.

Ogura, Mieko. 1990. *Dynamic Dialectology: A study of language in time and space.* Tokyo: Kenkynsha.

– & William S.-Y. Wang. 1996. "Snowball Effect in Lexical Diffusion: The development of *-s* in the third person singular present indicative in English". *English Historical Linguistics 1994* ed. by Derek Britton, 119–141. Amsterdam & Philadelphia: Benjamins.

Oswalt, Robert L. 1970. "The Detection of Remote Linguistic Relationships". *Computer Studies in the Humanities and Verbal Behavior* 3.117–129.

Rietveld, Toni & Roeland van Hout. 1993. *Statistical Techniques for the Study of Language and Language Behaviour.* Berlin & New York: Mouton de Gruyter.

Ringe, Donald A., Jr. 1992. *On Calculating the Factor of Chance in Language Comparison.* (= *Transactions of the American Philosophical Society*, 82:1.) Philadelphia: American Philosophical Society.

Ross, Alan S. C. 1950. "Philological Probability Problems". *Journal of the Royal Statistical Society, Series B* 12.19–59.

Rubin, Gerald M. 1970. "Computer-Produced Mapping of Dialectal Variation". *Computers and the Humanities* 4.241–246.

Sapir, Edward. 1916. *Time Perspective in Aboriginal American Culture: A study in method.* (= Memoir 90; Anthropological Series, 13.) Ottawa: Geological Survey of Canada.

Schneider, Edgar W. 1984. "Methodologische Probleme der Dialektometrie". Goebl 1984.314–335.

Séguy, Jean. 1971. "La dialectométrie dans l'atlas linguistique de la Gascogne". *Revue de linguistique romane* 37.1–24.

Shaw, David. 1974. "Statistical Analysis of Dialectal Boundaries". *Computers and the Humanities* 8.173–177.

Swadesh, Morris. 1950. "Salish Internal Relationships". *International Journal of American Linguistics* 16.157–167.

–. 1952. "Lexico-Statistic Dating of Prehistoric Ethnic Contacts". *Proceedings of the American Philosophical Society* 96.452–463.

Thoiron, Philippe. 1980. *Dynamisme du texte et stylostatistique. Élaboration des index et de la concordance pour* Alice's Adventures in Wonderland. *Problèmes, méthodes, analyse statistique de quelques données.* Geneva: Slatkine.

–, Dominique l'Abbé & Daniel Serant, eds. 1988. *Étude sur la richesse et la structure lexicales, Vocabulary Structure and Lexical Richness.* Geneva: Slatkine.

Villemin, François. 1983. "Un essai de détection des origines du japonais à partir de deux méthodes statistiques". Brainerd 1983.116–135.

Wang, William S.-Y. 1969. "Competing Changes as a Cause of Residue". *Language* 49.9–25.

Warnow, Tandy, Ann Taylor & Donald Ringe. 1995. "Character-Based Reconstruction of a Linguistic Cladogram". Paper presented at the Twelfth International Conference on Historical Linguistics. Univ. of Manchester, 14 August 1995.

Woods, Anthony, Paul Fletcher & Arthur Hughes. 1986. *Statistics in Language Studies.* Cambridge: Cambridge Univ. Press.

Zipf, George K. 1949. *Human Behavior and the Principle of Least Effort: An introduction to human ecology.* Cambridge, Mass.: Addison-Wesley.

Sheila Embleton, Toronto (Canada)